Defender of the Realm
1940–1965

Books by William Manchester

Disturber of the Peace (1951)

The City of Anger (1953)

Shadow of the Monsoon (1956)

Beard the Lion (1958)

A Rockefeller Family Portrait (1959)

The Long Gainer (1961)

Portrait of a President (1962)

The Death of a President (1967)

The Arms of Krupp (1968)

The Glory and the Dream (1974)

Controversy (1976)

American Caesar (1978)

Goodbye, Darkness (1980)

The Last Lion: Visions of Glory (1983)

One Brief Shining Moment (1983)

In Our Time (1985)

The Last Lion: Alone (1988)

A World Lit Only by Fire (1992)

The Last Lion: Defender of the Realm (co-author Paul Reid) *(2012)*

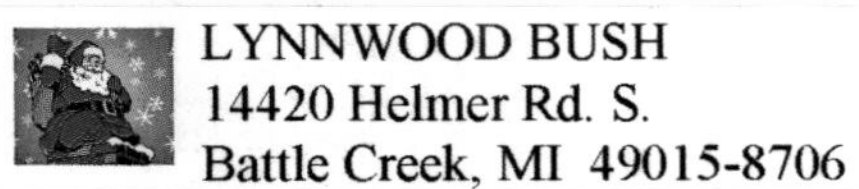
LYNNWOOD BUSH
14420 Helmer Rd. S.
Battle Creek, MI 49015-8706

The Last Lion

Winston Spencer Churchill
Defender of the Realm
1940–1965

William Manchester & Paul Reid

Little, Brown and Company
New York Boston London

Little, Brown and Company
Hachette Book Group
237 Park Avenue, New York, NY 10017
littlebrown.com

First Edition: November 2012

Little, Brown and Company is a division of Hachette Book Group, Inc., and is celebrating its 175th anniversary in 2012. The Little, Brown name and logo are trademarks of Hachette Book Group, Inc.

Photographs appear after pages 436 and 792.

Library of Congress Cataloging-in-Publication Data
(Revised for vol. 3)

Manchester, William Raymond.
The last lion, Winston Spencer Churchill. / William Raymond Manchester and Paul Reid.
Includes index.
Contents: v. 1. Visions of glory, 1874–1932—v. 2. Alone, 1932–1940—v. 3. Defender of the realm, 1940–1965.
1. Churchill, Winston, Sir, 1874–1965. 2. Great Britain—Politics and government—20th Century. 3. Great Britain—Foreign relations—20th century. 4. Prime ministers—Great Britain—Biography. I. Paul Reid. II. Title.
DA566.9.C5M26 1983 941.087'092'4[B] 82-42972
ISBN 978-0-316-54770-3 / Int'l ed. 978-0-316-22409-3

10 9 8 7 6 5 4 3 2 1

RRD-C

Printed in the United States of America

To the memory of

JOHN COLVILLE, C.B., C.V.O.

1915–1987

Etonian, Civil Servant, Fighter, Pilot, Scholar

(William Manchester, August 1994)

FOR BARBARA

(Paul Reid, August 2012)

In freta dum fluvii current, dum montibus umbrae
Lustrabunt convexa, polus dum sidera pascet;
semper honos nomenque tuum laudesque manebunt.

As long as rivers shall run down to the sea,
or shadows touch the mountain slopes,
or stars graze in the vault of heaven,
so long shall your honor, your name,
your praises, endure.

VIRGIL, *AENEID*, 1:607–9

ARRAY

MAPS

AUTHOR'S NOTE

In 1988, William Manchester began writing *The Last Lion: Defender of the Realm,* the third and final volume of his biography of Winston Churchill. Bill's research was complete. He had assembled his notes in fifty-page bound 8½ × 21-inch paper tablets, which he called his long notes, or "clumps." More than forty such tablets were dedicated to the war years 1940–1945, and a few addressed the postwar years 1946–1965.

His notes consisted of photocopied extracts from myriad sources, including Churchill's speeches, wartime memoirs, letters and telegrams Churchill sent and received, diary entries of contemporaries, official documents, newspaper clippings, and numerous secondary sources. They also included excerpts from transcripts of more than fifty interviews Bill conducted in the early 1980s with Churchill's friends, family, and colleagues.

Between 1988 and 1998, Bill, in increasingly poor health, wrote about one hundred pages of *Defender of the Realm,* a first draft covering the German invasion of France and the Low Countries in May 1940, and the beginning of the Battle of Britain in July 1940. Then, in 1998, he suffered two strokes that left his speech slightly slurred and his left leg partially paralyzed. Although the strokes did not steal his memory or his ability to formulate complex thoughts, Bill could no longer connect those thoughts on paper. He could no longer write.

My first encounter with Bill was on the page, when I read his account of the assassination of President Kennedy, *The Death of a President*. By the time I met Bill in person, I had read all of his nonfiction works. Like so many readers, I thought the first two books of *The Last Lion* were magnificent, and like so many, I eagerly awaited the final volume.

In 1996, I covered a reunion in West Palm Beach of Bill's World War Two Marine buddies for the *Palm Beach Post,* where I worked as a reporter. Bill, ill with pneumonia, could not attend. Two years later, in 1998, I accompanied five of those old Marines to Bill's home in Middletown, Connecticut, for a reunion designed to raise his spirits after his strokes and the death earlier in the year of his wife of fifty years, Judy. The Marines had all achieved success in life—an industrialist, a petroleum engineer, an oceanographer and Magellan biographer, and a Baptist minister with a doctorate in divinity—and they were proud of their service as enlisted men. By the end of the weekend, I felt as if all these Marines were my good friends, including Bill.

Our friendship deepened in the years that followed. I visited Bill often, sometimes in the company of the old Marines, who gathered at Bill's house once a year. Bill and I chatted by phone regularly. We talked history, politics, and, always, baseball, specifically the annual autumn demise of our Boston Red Sox. He asked for, and I sent him, copies of my stories. I felt certain that he would never finish *Defender of the Realm,* but when I suggested that he find someone to complete the book, he would shake his head no. He and his publisher, Little, Brown, regularly received calls and letters—even surprise office visits—from fans around the world asking when the book would be finished. In 2001 Bill told the *New York Times* that he could no longer put words to paper. Eventually, he agreed to consider a collaborator, but none proposed worked out. My surprise, therefore, was total when, late one evening in early October 2003, during one of my visits to Middletown, Bill asked me to finish *Defender of the Realm.* "You write," he said, "I'll edit. My red pencils are sharpened and ready."

He sent me home that weekend with about a dozen of his clumps and several books having to do with the Battle of Britain. My mission was to write sixty pages on the Blitz. Based on their impressions of my sample chapter, Bill, Don Congdon, Bill's agent of fifty years, and Little, Brown decided I should proceed. Our collaboration began.

But it would not last long. By early 2004 Bill was very ill. He died on June 1. By then I had realized that his clumps were not intended for literal transcription, but had served Bill as a narrative catalyst. The notes were arranged neither strictly chronologically nor by topic or character. Bill had inked into the margins numerous shorthand reminders and color-coded references to topics and sources only he could decipher. Some he had explained to me, others he had not. The notes had helped guide Bill toward a form—a portrait of Churchill—that he had already envisioned, much as an architect's rough line drawings can conjure in his mind an image of his finished building. The notes contained enormous amounts of information, but they had no outline and no sense of narrative structure. Bill's notes spoke to him in ways they could not speak to me.

Over the course of several months, I assembled much of the original source material Bill had used, including the full transcripts of the interviews he had excerpted in his notes. To this I added a digital edition of *Winston S. Churchill: His Complete Speeches 1897–1963,* edited by Robert Rhodes James, along with new editions of memoirs and diaries of Churchill's contemporaries. I perused official British government documents that had not been released when Bill was assembling his notes. I reread Bill's earlier biographies and histories for insight into his approach to narrative pace and cadence. Only then could I begin to write the book.

Bill spent many years on the Wesleyan University campus as an adjunct professor of history and writer in residence, but he was not an academic. He was a storyteller who made history accessible by masterful use of the dramatist's tools—plot, setting, and character. He and I often discussed his approach, and agreed that the biographer must get out of the way of his subject, who should be placed squarely within his times and be allowed to speak and act for himself. In the case of the greatest Englishman of the twentieth century, the importance of doing this is obvious.

At the start of the project, I spoke at length with the eminent British historian Sir John Keegan, who offered encouragement and guidance. Churchill's namesake grandson, Winston S. Churchill, gave generously of his time, up to his death in 2010, answering yet more questions on the subject of Sir Winston, as did Churchill's daughter, Lady Soames.

I thank the following friends and colleagues who offered wise counsel as the years went by; many read and commented on the manuscript in its various stages: Sanford Kaye, Jim Case, Rich Cooper, Jane Deering, Tess Van Dyke-Gillespie, Bill Gillespie, David Rising, Jeff Baker, Albine Irzryk (Brigadier General, U.S. Army, ret.), John Newton, Craig Horn, Howard Bursen, Dr. Porter Crow, Virginia Creeden, and Alex and Joan Balas. Thanks also to my former editors at the *Palm Beach Post*—Tom O'Hara, Jan Tuckwood, and Melissa Segrest—whose journalistic standards are in the highest and best tradition of American newspapering. Alan White (British Foreign Office, ret.) offered vital insight into the workings of the British government. Journalist John Murawski examined the manuscript with a reporter's eye. Doctors Audrey Tomlinson, Ron Pies, David Armitage, and Michael First brought their vast clinical expertise to bear on matters of Churchill's mental and physical health. My thanks also go to Maggi LeDuc, a recent graduate of American University, who spent many long hours in a successful search for photographs that captured the spirit of Churchill and his times.

Historian Lynne Olson, author of *Citizens of London,* gave sound advice over the years when asked, and I asked often. Roosevelt scholar Warren Kimball provided invaluable guidance on the Churchill-Roosevelt relationship.

Lee Pollock, executive director of the Churchill Centre, put the resources of that organization at my disposal. Those who seek to learn more about the extraordinary life of Sir Winston Churchill are well advised to begin their search by contacting Lee at www.winstonchurchill.org. Richard Langworth, editor of the Churchill Centre quarterly, *Finest Hour,* combed the manuscript for historical accuracy, as he had done for volume two, *Alone.*

Over the past eight years, Little, Brown publisher Michael Pietsch and editorial director Geoff Shandler have given this project their full support. I thank them and assistant editor Liese Mayer, who, with constant good cheer, helped guide the project through its final stages.

I owe my editor, William D. Phillips, an immeasurable debt of gratitude. Six times the manuscript passed between us, and six times Bill wrought improvements. This is his book, too. And after Bill finished his perusals of the work, Pamela Marshall took up her copyediting task, from the first word to the last, twice. It has been a pleasure to work with Bill and Pamela, but foremost, it has been an honor.

I am profoundly grateful to Bob Kopf, Ken Linge, and Jim Miller; Ray Foster, my neighbor from Lynn, North Carolina; my brother, Jim Reid; and my good and true friends Marcello and Diane Fiorentino. Without them, this project could not have come to fruition.

My agent Don Congdon did not live to see the finished manuscript. Don's son and partner, Michael, stepped in and, like so many who had a hand in this project, did so with enthusiasm.

In 2003 Bill Manchester, with one simple declarative sentence, changed my life: "I'd like you to finish the book." Bill died years before he could hold in his hand a complete manuscript of *Defender of the Realm*. But even though he was not here to discuss the project, or to review my pages or help me decipher his cryptic notations, our partnership remained intact. Bill trusted me to tell this story, and for that I thank him.

Five others, who long ago set in motion my role in this story, also did not live to see the completed manuscript: John and Eleanor Reppucci, my childhood neighbors in Winchester, Massachusetts; my sister Kathy; and my parents, Mary and Sam Reid, he a son of South Boston and the United States Naval Academy. They all loved a good tale, and all could spin one. My introduction to Churchill came almost six decades ago. On Saturday mornings I stood next to the stove as my father, attired in his old Annapolis bathrobe and a seaman's cap, flipped pancakes and fried eggs while reciting along to Churchill's wartime speeches, which played on our old RCA Victrola. "Listen to Winston," my father commanded, stabbing the air with the spatula in syncopation with Churchill's words. I listened.

One year my father put the six volumes of Churchill's *The Second World War* under the Christmas tree. Quoting Churchill, he summed up the moral of the story thus: Never give in.

I offer those words to a new generation of readers, including my son, Patrick, who enthusiastically critiqued every permutation of the manuscript, my daughters, Georgia and Mary, and my stepsons, August and Alex. Never Give In.

Paul Reid
August 2012
Tryon, North Carolina

Preamble

The Lion Hunted

On June 21, 1940, the first day of summer, Winston Churchill was the most visible man in England. France accepted Hitler's surrender terms that day and, with virtually all of Europe now under the swastika, with the Soviet Union a Nazi accomplice, and the United States isolationist, Britain and the Dominions confronted the Third Reich alone. Prime minister for only six weeks, Churchill was defending more than his island home. As first minister of the Crown he was also the central figure of the British Empire, then extant, comprising almost one-quarter of Earth's landmass and almost a quarter of its population. The gravity of his role was obvious. Yet though all saw him, all did not see him alike. He was a multifarious individual, including within one man a whole troupe of characters, some of them subversive of one another and none feigned.

At No. 10 Downing Street everyone referred to the newly appointed sixty-five-year-old P.M. as "the Old Man." In many ways he was an alarming master. He worked outrageous hours. He was self-centered and could be shockingly inconsiderate. Because of his lisp, and because he growled so often, his speech was often hard to follow, and aides had to learn what he meant when he referred to "that moon-faced man in the Foreign Office" or "Lord Left-leg-limps." Although he never actually overruled his military advisers, he refused to delegate any of the prime minister's powers to his staff. He wanted to make all decisions because, Sir Ian Jacob recalled, "he was determined to be Number One." Jacob served as military assistant secretary to the War Cabinet during the war, and came to know Churchill's obstinacy well.[1]

Not only did Churchill insist on oversight of strategic matters, he mired himself in the details as well. Because the noise of modern warfare was appalling, he decided soldiers would be issued earplugs. It occurred to him that World War One weapons, taken as trophies, could be made fit for action. A survey was launched. And what would be done, he demanded to know, to safeguard the animals at the zoo if German bombs blew open the cages? Some of his musings on the finer points of warfare were prescient. He asked his liaison to the Chiefs of Staff, Major General Hastings ("Pug") Ismay, to expedite the development of "some projectile which can be fired from a rifle at a tank like a rifle grenade, or from an anti-Tank [*sic*] rifle, like a trench-mortar bomb."

Yet woe unto the underling who brought to Churchill's attention details he considered petty. When King George's minister in Reykjavík suggested that Icelandic civilians be evacuated before the expected German invasion of that country, Churchill shot back, "Surely this is great nonsense." The dangers faced by Icelanders were "trifling" and "anyhow they have a large island and plenty of places to run into." He thoroughly enjoyed his meanderings in the thickets of details. One day that spring, while fiddling with an operational model of a mine intended to be deployed in the Rhine basin, he turned to an aide and said, "This is one of those rare and happy occasions when respectable people like you and me can enjoy pleasures normally reserved to the Irish Republican Army."[2]

This small pleasantry exchanged with a subordinate was not a rare behavior, yet neither was it a regular occurrence. Underlings were more likely to experience his wrath. His pale-blue eyes telegraphed his moods, and when his gaze—"as warm as summer sunshine" when he was pleased—turned ice-cold, his staff knew an eruption was forthcoming. Certainly his roar was awesome—he terrorized his admirals, his generals, and, daily, his staff. "God's teeth, girl, can't you even do it right the second time, I said ripe, ripe, ripe—P P *P*," he bellowed to Elizabeth Layton, a new typist at No. 10 who had the misfortune to interpret a mumbled "ripe" as "right." Yet, as usual after his outbursts, Churchill uttered his version of an apology—he "forgave" Layton—and "was very amiable for the rest of the day." Actually, his nature was informed by humane sympathy for all troubled men, including those Englishmen (he always preferred English and Englishmen to British and Britons) he held responsible for England's present plight. Learning that a mob had stoned Stanley Baldwin's car, he immediately invited the former prime minister to No. 10 for a two-hour lunch (at a time when every minute was precious to him), and when he was told that Neville Chamberlain was dying of cancer—Chamberlain would not survive 1940—Churchill instructed his staff to telephone all good news to the disgraced former prime minister.[3]

Baldwin later told Harold Nicolson* of his lunch with Churchill, adding that he left Downing Street "a happy man" while feeling "a patriotic joy that my country at such a time should have found such a leader." Of Churchill, Baldwin offered, "The furnace of war had smelted out all of the base metals from him." Not all. In private he relished skewering his fallen enemies. He and his wife, Clementine, once recounted for luncheon guests the rumor emanating from Baldwin's household that Baldwin was a

* Harold Nicolson (1886–1968), biographer, historian, diarist, member of Parliament from 1935 to 1945. From May 1940 to June 1941 he served under Duff Cooper as parliamentary secretary in the Ministry of Information. He later moved to the BBC. He was married to the writer Vita Sackville-West. Their sons, Nigel and Ben, served in the British armed forces during the war.

"haunted man." The former P.M. was so disrespected by his family and household staff, so the story went, that when he complained that the wireless was playing too loud, somebody turned it up even *louder.* And when the Baldwin family cupboard went bare, it was Baldwin who was dispatched by his relatives to the grocer to restock the larder. When asked by friends of Baldwin to submit a testimonial for the former prime minister's eightieth birthday tribute, Churchill, through an intermediary (and thinking his remark private), gave them: "I wish Stanley Baldwin no ill, but it would have been much better if he had never lived." And in his most famous cut of Baldwin, he said, "Occasionally he stumbled over the truth, but hastily picked himself up and hurried on as if nothing had happened." As for Chamberlain, Churchill told his new private secretary and a junior member of his staff, Jock Colville, that the former prime minister was "the narrowest, the most ignorant, most ungenerous of men." On one occasion, Churchill managed to denigrate both Chamberlain and Baldwin in one breath, when he offered to his doctor, "Baldwin thought Europe was a bore, and Chamberlain thought it was greater Birmingham." His pettiness was as unfeigned as his generosity, his sentimentality, and his love of England.[4]

Members of the Private Office (private secretaries, orderlies, typists) were expected to be obedient and uncritical; in effect the prime minister said, "Thou shalt have no other god but me." His temper was fearful. When he lost it, he would turn on whoever happened to be nearby, and, like other men of his class and generation, he never apologized or explained, though later he would go out of his way to mollify the injured party by, say, complimenting him on his handwriting, or by murmuring, "You know, I may seem to be very fierce, but I am fierce with only one man, Hitler." On June 27, the week of the French surrender, Clementine wrote him the lone truly personal letter that passed between them that year. She directed his attention to a potentially disastrous state of affairs in immediate need of prime ministerial intervention: his behavior toward his staff. "There is a danger," she wrote, "of your being generally disliked by your colleagues and subordinates because of your rough sarcastic & overbearing manner." No doubt it was the strain, she wrote. Yet, she too had noted deterioration in his manner: "You are not as kind as you used to be." She advised him that he would not get the best results from irascibility and rudeness, which would "only breed either dislike or a slave mentality." She signed the missive, "Please forgive your loving and watchful Clemmie." Beneath her signature she sketched a cat (Winston had called her "Kat" for almost three decades). There is no record of Churchill's response. None would have been necessary. That the letter survived, their daughter Mary later wrote, indicates a temperate reaction.[5]

There would be no long absences from each other in 1940, as there had been in all the previous years of their marriage, when work or war or holidays took one or the other abroad. Proximity, usually in the dank confines of the subterranean No. 10 Annexe, would be the byword in coming months, during which time his ferocity toward his staff diminished not a whit.

All who were with him then agree that the Old Man had more important matters on his mind than the sensitive feelings of subordinates. In any event, in time they came to adore him. Jock Colville later recalled, "Churchill had a natural sympathy for simple people, because he himself took a simple view of what was required; and he hated casuistry. That was no doubt why the man-in-the-street loved him and the intellectuals did not." Churchill, for his part, considered those on the left who anointed themselves the arbiters of right and wrong to be arrogant, "a fault," Colville recalled, Churchill "detested in others, particularly in its intellectual form." For that reason, Churchill "had dislike and contempt, of a kind which transcended politics, of the intellectual wing of the Labour party," which in turn despised Churchill. In 1940 the intellectualism of the left was inimical to Churchill and to Britain's cause, which was simplicity itself: defeat Hitler.[6]

Churchill cared little for obtuse political or social theories; he was a man of action: state the problem, find a solution, and solve the problem. For a man of action, however, he was exceptionally thoughtful and well read. When serving as a young subaltern in India, he amassed a private library that included Aristotle's *Ethics* and *Politics*, Plato's *Republic*, Schopenhauer on pessimism, Malthus on population, and Darwin's *Origin of Species*. Reading, for Churchill, was a form of action. After a lifetime of reading—from the sea-adventuring Hornblower novels to the complete Shakespeare and Macaulay—he possessed the acumen to reduce complex intellectual systems and constructs and theories to their most basic essences. He once brought a wartime dinner conversation on socialism to an abrupt end by recommending that those present read Maurice Maeterlinck's entomological study, *The Life of the White Ant*. "Socialism," Churchill declared, "would make our society comparable to that of the white ant." Case closed. Almost a decade later, when the Labour Party, then in power, nationalized British industries one by one, and when paper, meat, gasoline, and even wood for furniture were still rationed, Churchill commented: "The Socialist dream is no longer Utopia but Queuetopia."[7]

Late in June, Eric Seal, his senior private secretary, remarked upon how much Churchill had "changed since becoming P.M.," how he had "sobered down, become less violent, less wild, less impetuous." That was untrue. It was Seal's view of him that had altered. Churchill himself had not changed at all. His character had been fully formed at the turn of the century, as an officer in Victoria's imperial army, as a war correspondent, and as a young MP under the Old Queen. And he knew it. Listening to recordings of *The Mikado* one evening, he said they brought back his youth and the Victorian era, "eighty years which will rank in our island history with the Age of the Antonines." Upper-class Englishmen who had come of age then, when the empire stood at flood tide, possessed a certitude, an indomitable faith in England, confidence in their own judgment, and an indubitable conviction that they understood the world and were its masters.[8]

In many ways Churchill remained a nineteenth-century man, and by no means a common man. He fit the mold of what Henry James called in *English Hours* "persons for whom the private machinery of ease has been made to work with extraordinary smoothness." His valet warmed his brandy snifter over a neatly trimmed candle; his typists and secretaries kept more candles at the ready in order to light his cigars (Cuban *Romeo y Julieta* were his favorites). He had never ridden a bus. The only time he availed himself of the London Underground was during the general strike in 1926. Clementine dropped him off at South Kensington but Winston did not know how to navigate the system, with the result that "he went round and round not knowing where to get off, and eventually had to be rescued." He never carried cash, except to casinos and the occasional derby, where an aide would take care of the business of procuring chips or placing bets on worthy steeds.[9]

Clementine, ten years Winston's junior and far more versed in domestic economics, kept the household books; she and the staff did the purchasing. Churchill did not (directly) "bestow his custom" upon local merchants. This man who embodied the English spirit never attended a jumble sale or, readying himself for the day's labors, tucked a wrapped pasty into the pocket of his cardigan, or queued in a bakery for a bag of warm, fresh scones. In the years before he became prime minister, even his train tickets were bought for him. As befitted a man of his class and stature, he never prepared a meal in his life. Once, having announced his desire to spend a weekend at his country home, Chartwell, rather than in London, Clementine reminded him that the kitchen staff there was not in residence. "I shall cook for myself," Winston replied. "I can boil an egg. I've seen it done." When he was ready to leave on a trip, he would ask, not whether the chauffeur was behind the wheel but, "Is the coachman on his box?" His bodyguard, Scotland Yard detective inspector Walter Thompson, recalled that on the rare occasions when Churchill drove his own automobile, "he was forever just missing things, or not quite missing them and denting cars, his own and others. People shouldn't be in his way, was his theory."[10]

To drive with Churchill, recalled Thompson, "was to take your life into your hands." On one journey Churchill, then Chancellor of the Exchequer, turned into a narrow lane in Croydon only to encounter a construction project in the road and a long line of backed-up automobiles. A policeman signaled Churchill to stop, but Churchill ignored the constable and instead drove up onto the sidewalk in order to bypass the scene. Many were the occasions when Thompson, to avert disaster, had to reach over and yank the wheel from Churchill's hands. When Churchill actually collided with some hapless Londoner's automobile, he did not believe that any damage could possibly be of his doing, a mind-set he also applied to his frequent collisions with subordinates, parliamentary colleagues, and foreign potentates. Robert Boothby, one of Churchill's most loyal supporters during the Wilderness Years when he was out of office and without influence, recalled that Churchill simply did not much care for what other people thought, and cared not at all about how they might *feel*. "It was this curious absence of interest or affection that may have helped make him a great leader." Churchill "was often callous," Boothby recalled, but then, "he had a war to fight" and little time for social niceties.[11]

Churchill refused to accept changes in geographical names; Istanbul remained Constantinople ("though for stupid people Istanbul may be written in brackets after it"). Ankara remained Angora (he told the Foreign Office he would refuse to call Angora cats by any other name). Peking remained Peiping, Sebastopol, Sevastopol, and Iran, Persia. Likewise, he preferred traditional military terms to the modern—"cannon" for artillery, "muskets" for rifles, and "frigates" for destroyers. When he drafted a cable to Franklin Roosevelt requesting a gift or loan of fifty old frigates, Jock Colville suggested he substitute "destroyers," since the president might not know what the prime minister was referring to. It was in youth and early manhood, especially in the company of the officers of the 4th Hussars, resplendent in their blue and gold, impeccable in manners at the table, that he had acquired his lifelong love of tradition, ceremony, color, gaiety, pageantry, and formality. Protocol was important to him. He told his cabinet: "Gentlemen, we are engaged in a very serious business. We must conduct it in a serious way." In correspondence he expected them to address him as "Dear Prime Minister," and his replies opened "Dear Foreign Secretary," "Dear Chancellor of the Exchequer," "Dear Minister of Aircraft Production," etc. Letters for his signature were not to end with "sincerely" unless he determined that he was, indeed, sincere.[12]

The romantic glow of Victorian militarism, when casualties were few and victories enormous, accounted for his ambivalent view of warfare. He said, "War, which was cruel and glorious, has become cruel and squalid."

But the glory was still there for him. No other British prime minister, not even Wellington, had donned a uniform while in office. Churchill wore the light blue livery of an (honorary) RAF commodore and regretted that British soldiers no longer wore red coats.[13]

Afterward everyone who had been around him in 1940 remembered the Old Man's astonishing, unflagging energy. He was overweight and fifteen years older than Hitler; he never exercised, yet "he was working," Kathleen Hill, one of Churchill's typists, recalled, "all the time, every waking moment." His old friend from the First World War, Edward Spears, who had not seen him in many years before that spring, felt "an astonishment such as I had never felt before at his strength and vitality. I had known he possessed these qualities in lavish measure, but now he exuded power and confidence, radiating them as if he were their very fountain-head." Young Jock Colville marveled at "Winston's ceaseless industry," and wrote that it was "refreshing to work with somebody who refuses to be depressed even by the most formidable danger that has ever threatened this country... he seems to be the man for the occasion. His spirit is indomitable and even if France and England should be lost, I feel he would carry on the crusade himself with a band of privateers."[14]

To the British public he had become the ultimate Englishman, an embodiment of the bulldog breed, with the pugnacious set of his jaw, the challenging tilt of his cigar, his stovepipe hat, his pronouncement that "foreign names were made for Englishmen, not Englishmen for foreign names" (he always sounded the final "s" in Calais), and his fondness for red meat. In a letter to his Minister of Food he wrote, "Almost all the food faddists I have ever known, nut eaters and the like, have died young after a long period of senile decay. The British soldier is far more likely to be right than the scientists. All he cares about is beef.... The way to lose the war is to try to force the British public into a diet of milk, oatmeal, potatoes, etc., washed down, on gala occasions, with a little lime juice."[15]

He himself had always ignored dietary rules and rarely paid a penalty for it, and he drank whatever he wanted, usually alcohol, whenever he wanted it, which was often. Harry Hopkins (Franklin Roosevelt's most trusted adviser and go-to man) entered Churchill's bedroom one morning to find the prime minister in bed, wrapped in his pink robe, "and having of all things a bottle of wine for breakfast." When Hopkins commented on his breakfast beverage, Churchill replied that he despised canned milk, but had no "deep rooted prejudice about wine, and that he had resolved the conflict in favor of the latter." Furthermore, the Old Man told Hopkins, he ignored the advice of doctors because they were usually wrong, that he had lived almost seven decades and was in perfect health, and that "he had no intention of giving up alcoholic drink, mild or strong, now or later."[16]

His normal wartime regimen included a glass of white wine at breakfast (taken as a substitute for tea during the war, when only canned milk was available). Then, a weak scotch and soda, refreshed with soda throughout the morning. At lunch, perhaps a port, always Pol Roger champagne, a brandy or two (likely Hine, and bottled in the previous century), sometimes a beer. After his nap and before dinner he'd nurse another whisky* (Johnnie Walker Red Label was his favorite brand). At dinner, more champagne during the meal, followed often by "several doses of brandy" in the latter stages. He loved his meals as much as the libations that accompanied them. As recalled by his grandson, Winston S. Churchill, his favorite dinner began with *madrilène* (chilled, almost jellied consommé), followed by *goujons* (small filets of North Sea sole), then roast beef, thin-sliced, with Yorkshire pudding and roasted potatoes, followed by his favorite sweet, *bombe glacée* (puffs of ice cream cocooned within ice cream). Before retiring for the evening, his valet (Frank Sawyers, during the war) would pour another port or two, perhaps a final weak whisky while Churchill worked in his study. Another such drinker would recoil from food, but Churchill's appetite was unaffected, and he rarely lost possession of his remarkable faculties.[17]

Clearly he was blessed with a remarkable constitution, one which disposed of alcohol with exceptional efficiency. His detractors and enemies either inferred he was a drunk or, in the case of Hitler and Goebbels, denounced him outright as a "twaddler and a drunkard." Yet Robert E. Sherwood, Franklin Roosevelt's speechwriter and biographer, wrote that although Churchill's "consumption of alcohol . . . continued at quite regular intervals through most of his waking hours," it did so "without visible effect on his health or mental processes. Anyone who suggested he became befuddled with drink obviously never had to become involved in an argument with him on some factual problem late at night. . . ." Churchill's drinking habits, Sherwood wrote, were "unique" and his capacity "Olympian."[18]

Despite his prolonged, consistent, and prodigious consumption of alcohol, Churchill was not a drunk. But neither was he a moderate social drinker, as some of the memoirs and protestations of his close friends and private secretaries maintain. His former staff spin a consistent tale, that Churchill nursed a lone weak whisky and soda all day, replenished and diluted by splashes of soda, which is true but overlooks the daylong augmentation with other spirits. On occasion he would go too far, such as described in Jock Colville's account of taking the Old Man up to bed at around 3:00 A.M. after a brandy-fueled evening. Both Colville and Churchill thought it hilarious when Churchill, attempting to settle into an

* In Britain, Scotch whisky; in the U.S., rye whiskey.

armchair in order to remove his shoes, missed the chair entirely and fell onto the floor in a jumble of legs and arms. "A regular Charlie Chaplin," Churchill offered as he struggled to regain his footing. Later in the war, Field Marshal Sir Alan Brooke, Chief of the Imperial General Staff, was summoned by Churchill in the middle of the day. Brooke, who often noted Churchill's prodigious intake of alcohol, that night told his diary, "I found him very much worse for wear for evidently having consumed several glasses of brandy at lunch." Such slides into outright drunkenness were exceedingly rare for Churchill, but they occurred.[19]

He went nowhere without his supply of whisky close at hand, kept at the ready by his bodyguard or his valet. When he visited the United States during Prohibition, he secreted his whisky (and his Webley service revolver) past U.S. Customs, making him a violator of the Volstead Act, indeed, given his thirst, a habitual violator. When he was struck and severely injured by a car in New York City, he finagled a prescription for alcohol from his attending physician, Otto C. Pickardt. The injury, Pickardt wrote, "necessitates the use of alcoholic spirits, especially at meal times." The quantity was "indefinite" but at a minimum was to be about eight fluid ounces. The British essayist C. P. Snow encapsulated the paradox of Churchill's drinking when he remarked, "Churchill cannot be an alcoholic because no alcoholic could drink that much." It could of course be argued that had he exemplified the ideal of moderation—more exercise, less drink, less reckless behavior, fewer cigars—he might well have lived a full and rich life for many years beyond the ninety he was granted.[20]

Churchill once summed up his relationship with drink thus: "I have taken more out of alcohol than alcohol has taken out of me."[21]

He kept hours that would stagger a young man. Late each evening, at midnight or shortly thereafter, a courier arrived in Downing Street with the first editions of the morning newspapers, eight or nine in all. The Old Man skimmed them before retiring, and sometimes, Kathleen Hill later recalled, he would telephone the *Daily Mail* to inquire about new developments in a running story. On June 18 Colville noted: "Winston was furious because the morning papers, which he likes to see before going to bed, had not arrived. In his emotion he upset his whisky and soda over all his papers."[22]

The prime minister's day began at eight o'clock in the morning, when he woke after five or six hours' sleep and rang a bell summoning his usual breakfast: an egg, bacon or ham or chipped beef (when meat was available), sometimes a piece of sole, all washed down by his glass of white wine, or a pot of tea, a black Indian blend. Then a typewriter arrived, accompanied by a stenographer—usually Mrs. Hill or Miss Watson—to whom he would dictate a stream of memos as she rapidly hammered them out and he worked his way through a large black dispatch box. The typewriters were advertised as "silent." They were not. The Great Man resented every click of the keys, and made his displeasure known to the typists. He hated any noise (including ticking clocks, which he banned from his room) that intruded upon his equilibrium, and his business with the box.[23]

The box, which he had organized, was the absolute center of Britain's war against the Third Reich. Inside were numbered folders containing papers approximately 16″ x 13.″ The first one, the "top of the box," as it was called, dealt with matters considered "really urgent" by his secretaries, according to one of them, John Peck, "not only by objective standards of importance, deadlines, and so on, but in part subjectively by the degree of the Prime Minister's personal interest at the time. So we had to see and understand what was in his mind, and he relied on us to do this." Below the top were folders containing military and foreign office telegrams, reports from the Chiefs of Staff (after screening by Churchill's military liaison Pug Ismay), answers to questions he had raised concerning every aspect of British life—food supplies, crop yields, railroad capacity, coal production. Nothing escaped his attention.[24]

Churchill's private secretaries, John Peck, Eric Seal, John Colville, and John Martin, carried keys to this box. There was another, buff-colored box. Only Churchill had the key to that one. Inside were German military orders—at first from the Luftwaffe, later from the Wehrmacht and the SS, and much later from Admiral Dönitz's U-boats—all decoded and translated for him. In the first days of the war, Polish intelligence officers had captured a German electromagnetic cipher machine; Polish mathematicians subsequently examined the machine and smuggled a replica to the British. The British cryptographers, stationed at Bletchley Park, a Victorian redbrick, white-trimmed, and copper-roofed complex north of London, called the machine "Enigma." Each day the enemy reset the code and each day the men at Bletchley tried to break it, often without complete success. But the Bletchley crowd decrypted enough messages often enough to give Churchill an over-the-shoulder look at German plans (except U-boat plans, for which a slightly different and more complex encoding machine was used). The Bletchley wizards tended to be young and bearded, with long hair, dirty fingernails, and disheveled clothing. When the prime minister first saw them, he remarked to their chief, "Menzies, when I told you to leave no stone unturned, I didn't mean you to take me quite so literally."[25]

At the outset, he told the War Cabinet secretary that "all directions emanating from me are made in writing, or should be immediately afterwards confirmed in writing." Any instruction not in writing was invalid. The edict seems petty at first glance, but it precluded any subordinate from mucking up the works by misinterpreting and passing on down the line a prime ministerial command. The sheer volume of paperwork confirmed the wisdom of Churchill's edict that nothing submitted to him, not even a technical account of changes in the manufacture of tanks, could be longer than a single sheet of paper. During a meeting at Admiralty House, he lifted one that wasn't, and said: "This report, by its very length, defends itself against scrutiny." But Churchill, in turn, contributed to the lengthening paper trail with his river of memos marked "Action This Day" and "Report in 3 Days." Many began, "Pray tell me...," or "Pray explain...," which earned his memos the moniker "Winston's prayers."[26]

When reading and signing his missives at his desk, he often wore special sleeves over the cuffs of his jacket in order to protect them from any graphite or ink that might conspire to besmirch his outerwear. The sleeves, together with the occasional green eyeshade, lent to him the air of a plump typesetter. A perusal of the objects on his desk and side table, however—paperweights fashioned from gold medals, crystal inkstands with sterling lids, numerous bottles of pills and powders, and cut-crystal decanters of whisky—identified the owner as a Victorian gentleman of no small means.[27]

There were snarls, and he was responsible for some of them. Churchill's many gifts did not include the administrative. He had little understanding of organization. When a major issue arose, he gave it his full attention, ignoring his other responsibilities, which, because he had taken personal charge of everything affecting the strategic direction of the war, were many. He procrastinated. In his autobiography, *My Early Life,* he wrote: "I do think unpunctuality is a vile habit, and all my life I have tried to break myself of it." He never succeeded. He was always late for trains, although as P.M. he could demand that the trains wait for him. "Winston is a sporting man," Clementine once told his bodyguard. "He likes to give the train a chance to get away." In crises, he fell hopelessly behind on the box. He avoided dull topics, and boring papers lay unread weekend after weekend, until, gritting his teeth, he waded through them. He would make plans, Jock Colville recalled, but was "inclined to forget to tell any of us and then to forget himself." He once called his military chiefs to No. 10 for a 4:00 P.M. meeting. They arrived at the appointed hour; Churchill did not. Aides were sent off to locate the prime minister. They found him "enjoying a whisky and soda in the smoking room at the House."[28]

Some of his problems emanated from men he himself had selected. His staff believed that he was a poor judge of character and that he sometimes insisted upon unsuitable appointments. Men who had fought valiantly won his uncritical admiration. He wanted to give high office to Admiral Sir Roger Keyes of Zeebrugge, a hero of the First World War, though the admiral's mental powers were clearly failing. Orde Wingate, who would win fame as a daring commander of Burmese guerrillas, also caught his eye, though Wingate, who Churchill's doctor, Charles Wilson (made Lord Moran in 1943), thought was quite possibly insane, proved hopeless when given other responsibilities. Of course, those who had stood with Churchill against Munich always found favor with him. In his eyes Anthony Eden, who had quit the Chamberlain government in protest, could do no wrong. That was not a unanimous feeling; P. J. Grigg, permanent under secretary at the War Office, said of Eden, "The man is complete junk."[29]

Only up to a point did Churchill accept Ben Franklin's maxim that *well done is better than well said*. He liked things well done *and* well said. Perhaps because Churchill himself was so articulate, he sometimes misjudged those who were not. The Middle East commander Lieutenant General Sir Archibald Wavell, though a published poet and fluent in Russian, was shy and unforthcoming—attributes that to Churchill implied Wavell was almost dumb—and he remained tongue-tied when the P.M. tried to elicit his views about the war. His fellow generals thought Wavell a magnificent commander. Thus, the prime minister withdrew his objections to him with great reluctance and later wished he hadn't. He never appreciated the gifts of Air Chief Marshal Sir Hugh Dowding, the greatest RAF hero of the war, because of Dowding's reticence. Ironically, the Old Man's extraordinary fluency in discussion was sometimes a handicap. He could out-argue anyone, even when he was wrong. All who were close to him remember what Sir Ian Jacob (then a colonel, later promoted to lieutenant general) calls his "most devastating method of argument." Jacob recalled how he would "debate, browbeat, badger, and cajole those who were opposed to him, or whose work was under discussion." Churchill did not thrust and parry in such duels; he knew only how to thrust. Only later did it become clear that those who vehemently disagreed with him, and stated their case clearly, were those who won his respect. They survived to fight another day, which given Churchill's temperament was likely the next day. He was hard on those he called on the carpet, but he was harder on himself. "Every night," he told Colville, "I try myself by court martial to see if I have done anything effective during the day. I don't mean just pawing the ground—anyone can go through the motions—but something really effective."[30]

"Idleness was a concept unknown to him," recalled his daughter Mary. Idleness was the handmaiden to boredom, and boredom was an enemy to be vanquished. When Churchill found himself bored, recalled Scotland Yard's Inspector Thompson, he became "a kicker of waste baskets, with an unbelievably ungoverned bundle of bad temper." At such times, Thompson wrote, it is best to stay away from him "and this his family seeks to do." The Old Man's foul mood persisted until—the sooner the better for all concerned—he distanced himself from the agent of boredom. Such was the case one evening later in the war when Churchill, Colville, and several American guests viewed *Citizen Kane*. Colville termed it "a deplorable American film.... The P.M. was so bored that he walked out before the end." He did so again during a White House viewing of *Oliver Twist*, leaving the president and Mrs. Roosevelt sitting alone. Boredom, for the Old Man, was an assault on his equilibrium, inflicted in these cases by movies that failed to engage him but usually by a droning bureaucrat or a dinner guest in whom he had scant interest. He would at first put on an air of civility in such circumstances, his doctor recalled. "Then, as if exhausted by his act of civility, he would make no further attempt at conversation, sitting all hunched up and scowling at his plate." Finally, he would *harrumph* and walk off. Churchill "found it difficult to put on an act of affability even when circumstances positively demanded it," Colville wrote. "He drew a conscious distinction between those with whom it was agreeable to have dinner and those who... were part of the scene."[31]

When boredom struck, he could be depended upon to make a "ruthless break" in pursuit of a more enjoyable source of entertainment. The balm might take the form of dictating a letter, singing off-key renditions of Gilbert and Sullivan, perhaps wielding his trowel to lay bricks in the gardens at Chartwell. (Chartwell was soon closed for the duration of the war, the furniture draped in sheets. Most of the staff of gardeners, kitchen maids, the chauffeur, and housemaids were furloughed. Only a caretaker remained.) He always kept his quiver full of possible activities: read a novel, feed his goldfish, address his black swans, parse the newspapers, declaim on England's glorious past. Painting had long afforded Churchill the happy combination of quietude and a focus for his restless mental energy, but during the war, he would unpack his easel, brushes, and oils only once: at Marrakech after the Casablanca Conference. Gambling had always been another option, but the war had put an end to those pleasures, at least in casinos. He soon was gambling with his armies, tanks, and ships. Whether aboard a train, tucked under his bedclothes with his newspapers strewn about, or presiding at the dinner table, he was "absolutely incapable" of doing nothing, recalled his literary assistant Sir William Deakin: "He could switch off in a marvelously tidy way."

Once years before, recalled Inspector Thompson, during a train journey in North Africa, Churchill (then a cabinet member) decided he wanted a bath. He ordered the train stopped. Then he ordered a tub he had spotted in the baggage car removed and set out in the sands. It was filled to brimming with hot water siphoned from the locomotive's boiler. And there, as the train let off steam, Churchill "bathed with half of Africa agape." It fell to Thompson to shadow Churchill when he made his ruthless breaks. "He will move at a moment's notice. He will move without notice. He is an animal. In war he is particularly feral."[32]

In relief of boredom, almost any action—short of the wicked—would do, with one prerequisite: it had to possess value, and Churchill was the arbiter of the value. There simply was none to be had by sitting through *Citizen Kane* or lingering in reception lines where strangers grabbed for his hand as if they owned it. No value accrued from entertaining humorless dinner guests. In the end, when boredom struck, his most reliable source of relief—the only source of relief he never tired of—was himself. He once told a friend that his idea of a delightful evening was to enjoy fine food in the company of friends, to then discuss the fine food, and then to move on to a good discussion "with myself as chief conversationalist." What could be more stimulating than to listen to the sound of his own voice while declaiming on some topic of abiding interest, such as the Boer War or, in 1940, the need to kill Huns?[33]

He was his own favorite audience. He regularly quoted at great length from Macaulay's *Lays of Ancient Rome,* and Walter Scott's "Marmion," feats of memory Colville found to be "remarkable" yet sometimes "rather boring." Boring for Colville perhaps, but not for Churchill. His old friend Violet Bonham Carter recalled that if a long recitation of Macaulay's verse did not suffice to keep his gears meshed, he would revert to another favorite subject: himself. Lord Moran wrote, "Winston is so taken up with his own ideas he is not interested in what other people think." That was partially true; he was more interested in what other people *did*. Herbert Samuel, Lloyd George's successor as head of the old Liberal Party, believed Churchill was not interested in reasoned arguments, but rather, asked, "Will it work in practice?" One of Moran's observations, however, doesn't pass muster: "He [Churchill] must lose a chunk of his life this way, and must often be lonely, cut off from people." In fact, Churchill found real joy in the company of his friends and family. He loved being with small children; "wollygogs" he called them, and wollygogs were always granted immunity from his growls and snarls. He surrounded himself with people who cared for him, people who hung on his every word. And why should they not; he was Winston Churchill. If he chose not to take an interest in someone, that person remained invisible. Years later, Frank Sinatra, by then the most famous crooner on the planet, rushed up to Churchill, grabbed his hand, and exclaimed, "I've wanted to do that for twenty years." Churchill, not at all happy with being touched by a stranger, turned to a private secretary and demanded, "Who the hell was that?"[34]

* * *

He once complained to Lord Moran of a loss of feeling in his shoulder, apparently caused by a pinched nerve. Should he be concerned about this? Churchill asked. "Sensation doesn't matter," replied the doctor. "No," Churchill shot back, "life is sensation; sensation is life." In this need for stimulation he was one with fellow wit and fellow Tory Dr. Samuel Johnson, who considered *action* the necessary prerequisite for a well-lived life. Churchill needed to complete the circuit between the goings-on in his mind and the external world. Once he generated an idea, he felt compelled to actualize it. When he pledged that RAF bombs would consume Nazi Germany, he did so not simply to hear himself speak—that was a delightful collateral benefit—but because he intended to deliver on his promise. "The only guide to a man is his conscience," he once told the Commons, "the only shield to his memory is the rectitude and sincerity of his actions."[35]

Descartes believed the wellspring of human essence could be expressed thus: *Cogito, ergo sum*. But Churchill was not a man of philosophical bent, and, like most Englishmen, he held continental rationalism in low regard. Empiricism—Locke and Hume—was the English way. Churchill saw things more along the lines of *I act, therefore I am*. Lord Samuel once offered to Lord Moran that Churchill "has never ever taken any interest in speculative thought, in philosophy and religion." That was only partially true. He loved to engage in scientific and technological speculation, intellectual realms where the imagination could soar and where ideas were tested, results obtained, and improvements made in the lives of people. In 1932 he published *Thoughts and Adventures,* a collection of essays in which he predicted the atomic bomb and atomic-powered electrification (and the risks to humanity); bioengineering of crops and animals (and perhaps people); and television (which, when it became a reality, he detested). "Projects undreamed-of by past generations will absorb our immediate descendants," he wrote, "comforts, activities, amenities, pleasures will crowd upon them, but their hearts will ache, and their lives will be barren, if they have not a vision above material things."[36]

On the day France fell, Churchill summoned Dr. R. V. Jones, just twenty-eight and a junior scientist working in RAF Intelligence, to No. 10 to argue his hypothesis (heretical to more senior scientists) that the Germans were using radio beams to target Britain. The raids, infrequent and usually directed at northern ports, had begun the previous October. Churchill expected them to increase in frequency and deadliness now that Hitler had control of the airfields of the Low Countries and France. Backed by Churchill, Jones in the coming months figured out how to jam the German beams and delivered one of the most important victories of the war. Jones later wrote of Churchill: "He understood the essence of supreme decisions: yea or nay, right or left, advance or retreat.... He knew the strengths and weaknesses of experts.... He knew how easy it is for the man at the summit to receive too rosy a picture from his Intelligence advisors.... Alone among politicians he valued science and technology at something approaching their true worth, at least in the military application."[37]

Churchill's embrace of the new did not extend to the art and science of governing. The Oxford philosopher and Latvian Jewish émigré Sir Isaiah Berlin later proposed in his essay *Churchill and Roosevelt* that Churchill remained politically a European man of the nineteenth century, despite his embrace of modern technologies and his belief in their promise, despite his insatiable curiosity and his appetite for new knowledge. Britain's glorious *imperial* past informed Churchill, who presumed it would likewise inform the future. But Franklin Roosevelt, Berlin argues, saw—and Churchill did not—that the past and all of its traditions could be jettisoned in order to produce a new political order from whole cloth. Where Roosevelt was an imaginative though cautious political visionary, Churchill was an imaginative and incautious preservationist. "Churchill... looks within," Berlin wrote, "and his strongest sense is the sense of the past."

After reading Plato and Aristotle as a young man, Churchill declared for agnosticism. Although he embraced the Greek philosophical antecedents of Christianity, he found no intellectual reward in theological exercises. He subscribed to the Christian values of mercy and forgiveness, but his beliefs were not dictated by doctrine, and certainly not by clerics. He had been informed by his experiences as a soldier and journalist, and he rejected the carrot and stick of heaven and hell. The idea of an afterlife was not much more than an afterthought for Churchill, and one he considered equivalent to a belief in ghosts and goblins. He claimed he "did not much believe in personal survival after death, at least not of the memory." The thought of oblivion did not vex him. Where others found only terror in the prospect of the negation of self, Churchill found sanguineness, and fodder for irreverent asides. He did not believe in another world after death, he told his doctor, but "only in 'black velvet'—eternal sleep," which did not stop him from playing whimsically with other possibilities in painterly terms: "When I get to Heaven I mean to spend a considerable portion of my five million years in painting, and so get to the bottom of the subject. But then I shall require a still gayer palette than I get here. There will be a whole range of wonderful new colours which will delight the celestial eye." Churchill's fanciful heaven was also a distinctly pluralistic place where the full spectrum of humanity would mingle forever (although the membership list would never do for Churchill's earthly private dining society, the

Other Club): "Indians and Chinese and people like that. Everyone will have equal rights in Heaven...that will be the real welfare state....Of course, I admit I may be wrong. It is conceivable that I might well be reborn as a Chinese coolie. In such case I should lodge a protest." In a similar impish vein, he once proclaimed a proof for God's existence "is the existence of Lenin and Trotsky, for whom a hell is needed."[38]

As for the act of dying, the transition from consciousness to nothingness or to some manner of *somethingness,* Churchill would have agreed with Dr. Johnson, who said dying "lasts so short a time," and it does a man "no good to whine....It matters not how a man dies, but how he lives."[39]

Such were Churchill's sentiments exactly. In 1915, before departing for the Western Front, he entrusted his lawyer with a letter he wrote to Clementine, to be delivered in the event of his death: "Death is only an incident, & not the most important that happens to us....If there is anywhere else, I shall be on the lookout for you." He believed that were his final moment on earth to arrive via a German bomb, it would be due to chance. To Jock Colville, he quoted the French mathematician Henri Poincaré: "I take refuge beneath the impenetrable arch of probability." Fate, not the Lord, would call Churchill home, although he once told Colville whimsically that were heaven ordered on the model of a constitutional monarchy, "there was always a possibility that the Almighty might have occasion to 'send for him.' "[40]

He detested superstition. A court case being prosecuted by His Majesty's Government caught his attention. He demanded of the home secretary "why the Witchcraft Act, 1735, was used in a modern court of justice?" It was all "obsolete tomfoolery" that inhibited the court's ability to function. He thought much the same of churchgoing. He was at best an infrequent visitor to God's house. His private secretary Anthony Montague Browne recalled that Churchill claimed he "rarely went to church. When approached about this, he [Churchill] said he was not a pillar of the church but a buttress—he supported it from the outside." If he had to sit through a sermon on national days of prayer or state occasions, Jock Colville later wrote, he preferred that the pastor speak to politics or war, "but no Christianity." His visits to church were so rare that Colville was shocked one Sunday late in the war when Churchill attended a service. It was the first time in almost four years that Colville had seen him do so. Only toward the end of the service did Colville grasp Churchill's real motive for attending. After the minister delivered his sermon, the Old Man walked up to the pulpit and delivered one himself. He loved the glory and pageantry of christenings, funerals, and coronations performed within the mossy precincts of Britain's ancient village churches or within the silent grandeur of its great cathedrals, not for any proximity to the divine but because such rituals offered proximity to England's storied past. Churchill was deeply moved by the melodic grace of hymns, by the power of voices uplifted in song. He loved the rolling peal of village church bells calling the faithful to worship, but, writes the British historian Roy Jenkins, there is no record of Churchill ever having left Chartwell in response to the summons. A Bible rests to this day on his bedside table at Chartwell, a sight that moves many visitors to conclude he sought guidance in Scripture. He did not. When Lord Moran, spying the Bible, asked Churchill if he read it, he replied, "Yes, I read it; but only out of curiosity."[41]

Jock Colville thought it the "supreme blasphemy" when, over lunch one day, Churchill said, "Every nation creates god in its own image." Yet history lent credence to that judgment; even Hitler claimed that god was on his side.[42]

He disliked holy men in general: "the old humbug Gandhi," Greek Archbishop Damaskinos ("a pernicious priest"). Church of England prelates did not adorn Churchill's dinner table. He considered the Anglican clergy to be a priggish and hypocritical lot. Why dine with those who would take moral umbrage to his ending an evening singing lustily and dancing about to Viennese waltzes while attired in an outrageous red dressing gown, a warmed snifter of brandy in one hand, and a cigar (or rifle) in the other? The death later in the war of William Temple, the archbishop of Canterbury, "caused the P.M. no sorrow," Colville wrote. "In fact he was quite ribald about it." Temple was a scholar and philosopher, but Churchill "who as far as the English clergy was concerned had a touch of King Henry II about him, disliked Temple's left-wing tendencies and his outspoken political comments." Churchill was a Cavalier, the clergy were Puritans—worse, Puritans with a leftward list. This, for Churchill, made them and their brand of Christianity suspect.

Churchill squeezed the present for all it was worth. He believed meaning is found only in the present, for the past is gone and the future looms indeterminate if it arrives at all. Churchill was an old trooper who, whether at his easel, speaking in the Commons, or dining with his cronies, manifested the soldier's creed: savor the moment, for it may be the last. Yet for Churchill, if there were to be tomorrows, they would arrive on *his* terms. He was an optimist, not a determinist; the world was indeed often cruel, but it need not remain so. He subscribed to a variation of the Nietzschean, monumental view of history that he had arrived at from his youthful reading of Gibbon (*all* of Gibbon) and Winwood Reade's *The Martyrdom of Man*, a must-read for young thinkers in the late nineteenth century. In his book Reade attributed to history a Darwinian, a survival of the fittest, continuum. Churchill, paraphrasing Reade in a letter to his mother, wrote, "If the human race ever reaches a stage of development—when religion will cease to assist and comfort mankind—Christianity will be put aside as a crutch which is no longer needed, and man will stand erect on the firm legs of reason."[43]

He synthesized his Gibbon and Reade and concluded that the greatness and goodness of the past could be recaptured through the exercise of will. God would play no part in the saga, because God, if indeed there was a God, was unwilling or unable to intervene. Yet that paradigm left open the possibility that a force of evil—such as Hitler—might well impose his will on the future. Churchill employed his present moments to plan his—and the world's—better tomorrows through the exercise of *his* will. By doing so he intended to deny Hitler his supposed destiny. Churchill, not God, would safeguard the future of Europe and the British Empire, and he would do so by the vigorous exercise of his imagination and the imposition of his will by the only means he knew—action, action this day, action every day.

He saw communism not as the atheistic negation of Christian ideals (as did Franklin Roosevelt) but as the twisted fulfillment of those ideals. At dinner one evening later in the war he recited to his guests a Soviet creed:

"I love Lenin,
Lenin was poor, and therefore I love poverty,
Lenin was hungry, therefore I can go hungry . . ."

"Communism," Churchill declared when he finished, was "Christianity with a tomahawk."[44]

Traditional religions at least held out the hope of mercy, love, and a forgiving deity. Not so the "non-God" religions that had overtaken Germany and Russia (although Churchill muted his criticism of Bolshevism after his alliance with Stalin). Three years before war came, during the early months of the Spanish Civil War, Churchill warned Britons of the "war between the Nazis and the Communists: the war of the non-God religions, waged with the weapons of the twentieth century. The most striking fact about the new religions is their similarity. They substitute the devil for God and hatred for love. They are at each other's throats wherever they exist all over the world. . . ." Britons, he warned, "must not blind their eyes to the power which these new religions exercise in the modern world. They are equipped with powerful agencies of destruction, and they do not lack their champions, their devotees, and even their martyrs."[45]

Chamberlain—and France—had blinded his eyes to the threat, with the result that Hitler and his apostles brought their gospel first to Poland,

and now to Holland, Belgium, and France. Churchill intended that it not be brought to England.

He believed in Virtue and Right, not as matters of dogma, but as objective realities. Virtue was manifested in action. It took the form of the Aristotelian mean. Courage, the supreme virtue, could be found somewhere between cowardice and foolhardiness. Paraphrasing Samuel Johnson, Churchill wrote in *Great Contemporaries:* "Courage is rightly esteemed the first of human qualities because . . . it is the quality which guarantees all others." Among the others was magnanimity. *In Victory: Magnanimity,* Churchill chimed, never revenge fueled by hatred. This was a virtue first expressed by Aristotle and most recently ignored by Hitler in Poland and, a generation earlier, by the good Christians who drafted the Carthaginian terms (Churchill believed) of surrender imposed upon Germany and Austria after the Great War. The argument put forth then that Germany had behaved like a mad dog since the Franco-Prussian War and deserved to wear the shortest possible leash was, for Churchill, flawed. It violated another of his maxims, *In Peace: Goodwill.* He believed that an economically healthy Germany was necessary for European stability.

Yet here now came the Hun again, waging a war that might soon result in the extermination of England. In fighting his battle to preserve liberty in England and restore it in Europe, there could be no middle path, no mean, and Churchill acknowledged none. Weapons and strategies that showed promise—special operations, assassination, sabotage, bacterial "spore" bombs, atomic fission bombs, aerial obliteration of German cities—were justified by the ends. Any weapon, especially one deployed often, accurately, and ruthlessly, was a fine weapon. His was a distinctly Old Testament approach to rendering justice. As much as he admired the merciful and demanded that generosity follow victory, *In War, Fury** formed his philosophy of battle.[46]

In his youthful readings of Aristotle and Plato he discovered the pre-Christian philosophical antecedents that the Catholic Church later appro-

* For an inscription on a monument to the Great War to be erected at Versailles, Churchill had suggested "In war fury; in defeat defiance, in victory magnanimity, in peace goodwill." The suggestion was rejected (Colville diary, Jan. 24, 1941). Ever willing to rework a phrase with an eye toward future historical considerations, Churchill replaced "fury" with the more temperate "resolution" on the frontispiece of his six-volume war memoir.

priated and folded into its doctrine. He taught himself well and created a code he could live by. He was seduced by the powerful simplicity of Aristotle's mean and Plato's analogy of the charioteer, who in order to successfully navigate his way must keep a tight rein on his brace of winged horses.

Churchill had as much difficulty riding smoothly in double harness as he did in keeping his car on the road, but in the end, he achieved his mean. It was a moral journey of many twists and turns, of chutes and ladders. Images of him in his dressing gown, rifle at his shoulder, marching about late of an evening hardly conjure an image of the Aristotelian mean. He possessed, John Martin recalled, a "zigzag streak of lightning on the brain." The Old Man zigged and zagged in many of his strategic decisions as war leader when, literally and metaphorically, he was all over the map. For every diarist who notes his exuberance, fairness, geniality, or generosity, there is to be found another who alludes to his roughness, his sarcasm, his low moods, and his bellicosity—sometimes the same observer on the same day. Yet Churchill's journey toward the mean could unfold in no other way. "If he hadn't been this sort of bundle of energy that he was," recalled Martin, "he would never have carried the whole machine, civil and military, right through to the end of the war."[47]

Endowed with a prodigious memory, Churchill seemed to remember every poem he had ever read, the lyrics of every song, and the chapter and verse of vast numbers of biblical passages, and he would recite them almost anywhere. Embarrassed once years earlier by not having heard of Keats's "Ode to a Nightingale," he set himself to memorizing all of Keats's odes, and enjoyed reciting them "mercilessly," in the estimation of Violet Bonham Carter. He could endlessly quote Dr. Johnson, and freely appropriated and paraphrased the doctor's witticisms. Byron's *Childe Harold's Pilgrimage* was a Churchill favorite, although he did not share Byron's melancholic view that man's greatest tragedy is his ability to conceive a perfection that he cannot attain. Rather, Churchill told his countrymen in the battle against Hitler, "If we can stand up to him, all Europe may be free and the life of the world may move forward into broad, sunlit uplands." "Invictus," a nineteenth-century ode to willpower by William Ernest Henley, was another Churchill favorite.

It matters not how strait the gate,
How charged with punishments the scroll,
I am the master of my fate:
I am the captain of my soul.[48]

He reserved a special affection for American writers, particularly Twain, Melville, and Emerson. As with the English canon, his knowledge was broad. Once, motoring though Frederick, Maryland, with Franklin and Eleanor Roosevelt and FDR's close adviser Harry Hopkins, Churchill saw a road sign for candy named for Barbara Frietchie, the Union patriot who flew her Stars and Stripes in defiance of Rebel troops marching past her house. Roosevelt, noting the sign, recited two lines of John Greenleaf Whittier's poem about Frietchie:

"Shoot, if you must, this old gray head,
But spare your country's flag, she said."

When Roosevelt allowed that those were the only lines he knew, Churchill weighed in by reciting the entire poem, sixty lines. Then, he began a long monologue on the strategic genius of Stonewall Jackson and Robert E. Lee. He continued on as the miles sped past, oblivious to the effect on his companions. "After a while," he later wrote, "silence and slumber descended upon the company."[49]

Churchill's love of history was abiding and his knowledge profound. Memorizing dates and place-names has always been the bane of schoolchildren. Yet for a few, Churchill assuredly among them, history is more than a time line, more than the sequencing and parsing of collective memory. In those such as Churchill, history, by way of imagination and discipline, becomes part of personal memory, no less so than childhood recollections of the first swim in the ocean or the first day of school. Churchill did not simply observe the historical continuum; he made himself part of it. Classical venues, and Churchill's "memory" of them—from the Pillars of Hercules and on around the Mediterranean to Syracuse, Rome, Sparta, Alexandria, and Carthage—informed his identity in much the same way his memories of his family's ancestral home, Blenheim Palace, did, or his father's London house, where as a boy he charged his toy soldiers across Persian carpets. He may have been born a Victorian, but he had turned himself into a Classical man. He did not live in the past; the past lived on in him. Harry Hopkins, who came to know Churchill well, noted the mystical relationship he had with the past, especially the military past: "He was involved not only in the battles of the current war, but of the whole past from Cannae to Gallipoli." Alexander the Great, Boudicca, Hadrian, King Harold, Prince Hal, Pitt, and of course his luminous ancestor Marlborough had all played their parts in earlier scenes of the same play and upon the same stage that Churchill and his enemies now played their parts.[50]

All who knew him had heard him recite, at one time or another, Macaulay's *Lays of Ancient Rome:*

Then out spake brave Horatius,
The Captain of the gate:
"To every man upon this earth
Death cometh soon or late.
And how can man die better
Than facing fearful odds,
For the ashes of his fathers,
And the temples of his gods."

All who knew him came to know that in Churchill such sentiments were intrinsic.

Churchill's most endearing trait was also his most remarkable. He was probably the most amusing warlord in history. His very appearance could endlessly entertain his family and staff. On June 16, Colville took urgent dispatches to the P.M.'s room and "found him lying in bed, looking just like a rather nice pig, clad in a silk vest." Smoking a long cigar and stroking his cat, Nelson, he prowled the corridors of No. 10 wearing a soldier's steel helmet (called by all a "tin hat"), a crimson dressing gown adorned by a golden dragon, and monogrammed slippers complete with pom-poms. Sometimes he carried on anthropomorphic conversations with Nelson (including an admonition to be more stouthearted after the cat flinched during an air raid). Anticipating the need to move with dispatch during air raids, Churchill designed a one-piece suit with many zippers, permitting him to don it quickly. All members of his staff, including the stenographers, called the suit his "rompers." Churchill called the outfit his "siren suit," because he jumped into it at the first howl of the air-raid sirens. He designed the rompers; Henry Poole & Co. of Savile Row crafted them and delivered them.[51]

Any circumstance might trigger Churchill's humor reflex. Once, after delivering a speech in Parliament on American aid, he rode home to Downing Street in the back of a limousine, belting out "Old Man River." When his doctor once recited lines from John Milton's *Lycidas*—"While the still morn went out with sandals grey..."—Churchill countered, "He was on the wrong side on the Civil War." During a visit to Rome, he was introduced to the leaders of various Italian political factions. Greeting one group, he asked, "What party are you?" "We are the Christian Communists," came the reply. Churchill could not contain himself: "It must be very inspiring to your party, having the Catacombs so handy." One day in the House, he was forced to sit through the delivery of a long and tedious report rife with statistics. He noticed an elderly MP leaning forward with an antique ear trumpet pressed to his ear, struggling to hear the report.

Churchill turned to a colleague and asked, "Who is that idiot denying himself his natural advantages?"[52]

Chequers—the ancient Buckinghamshire country house that had been the country retreat of prime ministers since 1917—was guarded by vigilant sentries and could be approached only by those who knew that day's password. One night during that first week of summer it was "Tofrek," site of an 1855 battle in the Sudan. That evening, excited by the sound of a plane overhead, Churchill ran out, shouting, "Friend! Tofrek! Prime minister!" There, late at night, he would recite lines from *Hamlet,* or Byron, or sing music hall ballads he had not heard since the 1890s. Sometimes, when a recording of *The Blue Danube* was playing, he would waltz around the room alone, his right hand flat against his shirt and his left arm extended as though he were supporting the hand of a partner. Clementine, if present, would likely not join her husband. She understood that he often played and worked simultaneously. While gliding around the room, he very often crafted phrases to deploy in upcoming speeches, and to interrupt him was out of the question. However, on one occasion (years later), two cabinet ministers considered their business more important than Churchill's speech preparation. They bounded up the stairs, headed for his bedroom, where he was dictating his notes. As they waited outside, a secretary announced their presence to the Old Man. "Tell them to go and bugger themselves," came the volcanic response. Then a pause, and, "Tell them there is no need for them to carry out that instruction literally."[53]

The prelude to a speech in the House of Commons was *opéra bouffe*. He would craft it, not in the calm of a study surrounded by reference books but while on the telephone, or prancing around the Great Hall at Chequers, or propped up in bed, or bowed over a map, waging war. He composed every word of every speech; no committee of speechwriters toiled at No. 10. His bath was a favorite venue for speech preparation (he was proud of being able to control the taps with his toes while he dictated). In the midst of other tasks, he would start muttering phrases to himself: "To the gates of India"; "this bloodthirsty guttersnipe"; "this star of England." When a cabinet minister called Germans "sheep," Churchill snarled, "*Carnivorous* sheep." In two words he captured the essence of his foes better than Baldwin or Chamberlain could in two hours of speechifying. When Hitler was the subject, Churchill struck and struck again, each cut more ferocious than the one before: "This wicked man, the repository and embodiment of many forms of soul-destroying hatred, this monstrous product of former wrongs and shame, has now resolved to try to break our famous Island race by a process of indiscriminate slaughter and destruction." He fertilized every phrase with imagery, and weeded them of any word that could choke his message. He tried them out over dinner with colleagues, with different adjectives, different emphasis, to measure their rhythms and to hear how they sounded. He might pause to pluck a pinch of snuff from his gold snuffbox (it had once belonged to Admiral Nelson), pop it into a nostril, and emit a sneeze with robust delight. He sometimes offered a pinch to his young, female typists, who politely declined. The creative process so absorbed him that he often became oblivious to events unfolding in the room, as on the day his cigar ash ignited his bed jacket. One of his private secretaries, noting the rising smoke, offered, "You're on fire, sir. May I put you out?" The P.M., not looking up, responded with nonchalance, "Yes, please do." And kept right at his work.[54]

The climax of his ruminations would come on the day of delivery. Always at least fifteen minutes late, he might still be in bed, dictating the final draft to a typist, or inking in changes, when he should have been on his way to Parliament. Anxious whips would be telephoning from the House, his staff would be begging him to hurry, his valet would be dressing him and flicking cigar ash from his shirt (always a delicate task, for Churchill did not like to be touched). Meanwhile, messengers held the elevator, and his chauffeur, outside, gunned the engine. Finally he would totter out, still dressing, tucking his spectacles and cigar case and loose cigars and his little snuffbox into sundry jacket pockets, checking the numbered pages to be sure they were in the right order.[55]

Moments later, when he rose from the front bench to address the House, he would be greeted by a respectful hush from members and from the galleries, where journalists and foreign ambassadors leaned forward in anticipation. If his words were to be given in secret session, the cue to clear visitors from the Strangers' Gallery would come when he gazed upward and declared, "I espy strangers." Secret sessions of the House therefore posed a small problem for Churchill; his most delightful phrases would be lost to the press and diplomatic pouches, and therefore lost to the outside world. Churchill's solution was simplicity itself; he simply repeated the favored phrases over dinner or in the House smoking room, thus assuring that they would appear in Max Beaverbrook's newspapers the *Daily Express* and the *Evening Standard*. Or, if Churchill wanted the Duke of Alba's daily secret report to Franco to contain a nugget of misinformation from the Old Man himself, he might repeat a phrase to some Foreign Office minion who was known to dine with the Spaniard. Thus, secret session or no, if Churchill wanted to say something, he said it. Only words can live forever, he liked to say; it would simply not do for his words to die on the floor of the House.

Churchill, like Samuel Johnson and Shakespeare, could string together phrases that resonated with Glasgow pub patrons, Welsh coal miners, and Cockney laundresses, as well as with the Harold Nicolsons and Lady Astors. At his dinner table or in the Commons during Questions, he sprayed the room with fusillades of bons mots. But his broadcasts and speeches were strategic assaults, not tactical, and were crafted with infinite care. His broadcasts sound so English, but in fact their structural foundations date to Cicero. Gibbon and Shakespeare, and Churchill's reading of them, had a hand in that. Gibbon, when read aloud, is a slow burn, more fuse than fireworks, yet the prose is perfectly balanced and perfectly ordered; each point meticulously advanced until in the climactic resolution only one inescapable conclusion can be reached. Gibbon's cadence permeates Churchill's speeches, which in structure and delivery were like a trebuchet, its mechanism slowly and steadily wound by Churchill until the maximum tension was reached, at which point he launched his verbal missile. Then, beginning with his next breath, he re-armed his siege engine and prepared for the next shot.

Although Shakespeare's name does not appear in the index of his four-volume *History of the English-Speaking Peoples,* Churchill read and memorized Shakespeare his whole life, and imbued his speeches with metrical tributes to the Bard. He embodied the Shakespearean notion that a man's essence is to be found in his actions, and his words, the authenticity and value of which would be confirmed or debunked by the actions that followed. He did not so much speak to Englishmen (as Franklin Roosevelt did to Americans in his homespun fireside chats), as for them. In doing so he represented their destiny and their role in the current struggle, which could only end in either national survival or national annihilation. Hitler, an opportunist and nihilist romantic, told his people much the same.

Churchill dictated all speeches, memos, and letters to his typists, usually young and female, who typed away while he paced about the room, fetched his thoughts, and put them into words. When he dictated directly to the typewriter, the typists found themselves in peril, for to change flimsies in the middle of a long dictation would produce a "primitive wrath." "Come on, come *on!*" he'd growl. "What are you waiting for!" "Don't fidget so with that paper! *Stop it!*" He was personally insulted by any pause necessitated by the mechanics of the infernal machine. He displayed, wrote his bodyguard, an "appalling, almost childish" unwillingness to learn the mechanics of typing or of typewriters. None of his staff recollect ever seeing Churchill put a finger to a typewriter keyboard. Nor did he ever write his own memos. Other than signing them, recalled William Deakin, Churchill "never wrote a line in his life. I have never seen him put pen to paper." Actually, Churchill had written his early books in longhand, and of course his dispatches from Cuba and the veldt. But once elected to the Commons, and forever after, he indulged his love of dictation.[56]

He disliked the taking of dictation by shorthand, which would have kept the stenographers in the chase and allowed them to type in peace outside his presence. He believed shorthand only added one more step to the process of setting his thoughts down on paper. He allowed an exception to the ban when he was on the move—in a car, onboard a rolling ship, or strutting through the halls of Chequers or Parliament, conditions which even he understood were not conducive to wielding a typewriter. Not a moment was to be wasted by the typists, as young Patrick Kinna, a lance corporal and trained stenographer who had worked for the Duke of Windsor, learned the first time he entered the prime minister's room to take a letter. Without looking up or acknowledging Kinna, Churchill, pacing, intoned, "This is a melancholy story...." Kinna, thinking Churchill was about to tell a tale, set down his pencil and notepad, and said, "Oh dear! How unfortunate." "*Well,*" Churchill grumbled, "*take it down.*" It was a memo to the Admiralty, ruing the paucity of aircraft carriers. Kinna survived the day and served Churchill for the rest of the war as a member of the team.[57]

Woe unto the typist who had to ask the Great Man to repeat a phrase. His staff knew that to guess at what he said was far preferable to asking him to repeat it. The typists had to engage in a fair amount of guessing (as Elizabeth Layton had learned) because Churchill often mumbled and, to make matters worse, often while pacing about far across the room, his back to the typist. When he didn't mumble, he rumbled, strings of phrases all but indecipherable to the struggling scribes. When he dictated while in bed, propped up on his pillows, words were lost as newspapers fluttered to the floor, or the telephone rang, or he summoned his valet to refresh his refreshment. As with the collecting of his thoughts in preparation for a speech, he liked to dictate letters and memos while a gramophone played his favorite recordings of old music hall standbys—"After the Ball," "Goodbye, My Love," perhaps Harry Lauder belting out "Keep Right On Till the End of the Road." The typists had to blot out the background noise in order to parse his phrases, a supremely difficult task when Churchill instructed his valet to turn the volume higher. Finally, when the typist finished, and before she could pull the paper from the typewriter, Churchill would thrust out a hand and utter a curt "*Gimme.*"[58]

Typists earned about two pounds per week, about forty dollars a month, less than the wages of a corporal in the U.S. Army. As well, they were expected to remain at their post even as German bombs fell into nearby courtyards.[59]

Churchill had been a professional writer before he became a statesman; he had supported his family with a tremendous stream of books and articles.

His love of the language was deep and abiding, he had mastered it as few men have, and he was quick to correct anyone who abused it, especially those who tried to camouflage sloppy thinking with the flapdoodle of verbose military jargon or bureaucratese. He believed, with F. G. Fowler, that big words should not be used when small words will do, and that English words were always preferable to foreign words. He said: "Not compressing thought into a reasonable space is sheer laziness." On his orders "Communal Feeding Centres" were renamed "British Restaurants," as "Local Defense Volunteers" had become "Home Guard." And why not "ready-made" rather than "prefabricated"? "Appreciate that" was a red flag for him; he always crossed it out and substituted "recognize that." Another was "intensive" when "intense" was required. Once John Martin, driving along the Embankment with him, described the winding of the Thames as "extraordinary." Churchill corrected him: "Not 'extraordinary.' All rivers wind. Rather, 'remarkable.'" In the margins of official documents, he often quoted *Fowler's Modern English Usage,* a copy of which he sent to Buckingham Palace on his first Christmas as prime minister.[60]

John Martin believed that the P.M.'s "interest in basic English was inspired by politics rather than linguistics: it was a means of promoting 'the English-speaking club.'" Certainly that was one reason. He believed that all countries where English was spoken, including America, should merge. Here lay a profound contrast with the foreign policies of his predecessors at Downing Street. They had focused upon the Continent and the various combinations of the great powers there. Neville Chamberlain had referred to the United States with amusement and contempt, and called Americans "creatures." But Churchill, though a European patriot, looked westward, and not only because he knew Hitler could not be crushed without American troops. British to the bone, he was nevertheless the son of an American mother, and long before the war, he had envisaged a union of the world's English-speaking peoples: the United Kingdom, the United States, Canada, Australia, South Africa, and the far-flung colonies of the British Empire.[61]

In his parliamentary speeches, and particularly in his broadcasts to his besieged island, his genius for the language fused with his idealized image of England and Englishmen, or the "British race," formed in the last quarter of the nineteenth century—a people endowed with fearlessness, gallantry, nobility, a unique sense of honor, and invincibility. He still exulted in the memory of colonial conquests, when the Enfield rifles and Maxim guns of the Queen's armies were challenged only by primitive weapons, imperial flags flew proudly, and British casualties, even in the Indian Mutiny, were always light. The slaughter of the 1914–1918 war had appalled Britons, including Churchill, and had exhausted and disillusioned many, but not Churchill. Now, drawing fire from the terrible red glow across the Channel, he was exhilarated. His first four hundred days in office—from early May 1940 to mid-June 1941, a ghastly time for millions of Europeans—were, for him, the supreme chapter in his life. Later he wrote that it was "the most splendid, as it was the most deadly year in our long British and English story." He believed that 1940 was a time when "it was equally good to live or die." Years after the war, John Martin remarked to him that life was not as exciting as it had been. Churchill replied jovially, "You can't expect to have a war all the time."[62]

Based on his reading of Lord Moran's memoirs, Anthony Storr, the eminent British psychiatrist, believed that the source of Churchill's strength lay in his "inner world of make-believe," the sort of fantasies imaginative men call up from time to time when bored or disappointed. For most of the 1930s, Churchill had been both. After June 1940, Storr believed, that world of imagination "coincided with the facts of external reality in a way that rarely happens to any man." After the fall of France, Churchill became the hero he had always dreamed of being. Storr compares this to passionate love, "when, for a time, the object of a man's desire seems to coincide exactly with the image of a woman he carries within him." In that dark time, Storr argues, what England needed was not a shrewd, composed, balanced leader, but a prophet, a heroic visionary, a man who could dream dreams of victory when all seemed lost—a man who could inspire not only Britons but also Americans. "Had Churchill been a stable and equable man," Storr writes, "he could never have inspired the nation. In 1940, when all the odds were against Britain, a leader of sober judgment might well have concluded that we were finished."[63]

And yet, despite the fact that Churchill was prone to sentimentality, was mercurial, and at times lacked strategic military sense, he had, through intuitive leaps and careful analysis during the 1930s, arrived at an astonishingly accurate forecast of the calamity that had since befallen Europe and England. The events of September 1939 had proven him England's *most* sober statesman, as well as its most prophetic. Other sober and equable men, who lacked his imagination and penetrating vision, had allowed Britain to stumble unprepared into this war.

Storr's Churchill is complex, which Churchill certainly was, and a lifelong depressive, which he likely was not. The widely held belief that Churchill fought depression throughout his adult life stems in large part from Storr's musings and Lord Moran's memoir, in which he recounts his service as Churchill's personal physician. Moran probed Churchill during his last decade with leading questions about his "black dog" of depression and painted the octogenarian statesman in hues of decrepitude and despondency. Based on the writings of Moran and Storr, the idea that Churchill was a lifelong depressive and probably bipolar took hold in mental health circles, and it lingers still in the popular imagination (but not in the minds of Churchill's family, friends, and his official biographer, Sir Martin Gilbert). Yet Churchill likely did not suffer from mental illness. The story of the "black dog" begins in 1911, when, in a letter to Clementine, Winston enthused over a German doctor who was said to be able to cure depression: "I think this man might be useful to me—if my black dog returns." (Samuel Johnson called his bouts with melancholia his "black dog.") Churchill went on to tell Clementine that when the dog departed, "All the colors came back into the picture." His letter describes what modern psychiatrists call a moderate adult depressive episode. The "light faded out of the picture," Churchill wrote. When prompted by Moran in 1944, Churchill recounted the episode, as well as the sensations of vertigo that had long ago troubled him—feeling unease while standing at a ship's railing or on a railroad platform, where he liked to put a pillar between himself and the approaching train. To this, Churchill added a vital conclusion: "And yet I don't want to go out of the world at all in such moments." Despondency or thoughts of self-obliteration never attached to Churchill's low moods. After 1911 he never again wrote of the black dog.[64]

Storr's diagnosis of Churchill has since been supplanted by more exact psychiatric diagnostic protocols. Churchill could indeed be moved to gloom and long silences by events great and small—a crushing naval loss, the death of a much-loved pet, the mention of the name of a long-dead comrade-in-arms. He was easily moved to tears. "I blub an awful lot," he once told a private secretary, and he never apologized for his blubbing. He became quite irritable over unnecessary delays or secretarial foul-ups or generals who proved unwilling or unable to fight. He just as readily could turn off his temper, and his worries. He did not exhibit what are now considered to be the symptoms of major adult depression: prolonged (two weeks or more) and regular (at least yearly) periods of loss of interest in work and family, lack of interest in socializing, difficulty in making decisions, sleep loss, feelings of low self-esteem, and feelings of being unloved or not worthy of being loved, sometimes accompanied by spells of inconsolability. Nor did he show symptoms associated with the mania end of the manic-depressive spectrum: *decreased* need for sleep, rapid speech, racing thoughts, euphoria or extreme optimism, increased sexual drive, spending sprees, and inability to concentrate.[65]

It is true that as an adult Churchill took wildly unnecessary risks at the gaming tables and on the battlefield (which London itself was for much of

1940) and drank heavily—symptoms of depression when accompanied by several others—but he never lost his ability to function. He worried, he fretted, he grew weary at times, but he never despaired. In fact, it is part of the contradictory nature of the man that he manifested various symptoms of depression—risk taking, excessive drinking, mood swings—not intermittently, but regularly, even daily, and for his whole life.

Although psychiatrists caution against trying to prove a negative in the case of Churchill's "black dog," they also caution against any retroactive diagnosis such as Storr's. Jock Colville and one of Churchill's military liaisons, Fitzroy Maclean, recalled rare occasions when Churchill claimed "he had the black dog on his back." He did not mean that he was depressed in a clinical sense, but only that he was having a bad day. Both Colville and Maclean recalled from their own upbringings that English nannies used the term "black dog" to describe the moods and emotional outbursts of young children. Throughout the war, Churchill, knowing that a dark and defeatist exterior inspired no confidence in those he needed by his side in order to win the war, did not indulge gloom but exorcised it. When visitors to Chequers or the underground No. 10 Annexe marveled at Churchill's good cheer, he voiced a variation on a theme he had once voiced to Colville: he took his strength from the "splendid *sangfroid* and morale of the British people." When Pug Ismay, strolling one day with Churchill in the garden at Chequers, offered, "whatever the future held, nothing could rob him of credit for having inspired the country....," Churchill replied, "It was given to me to express what is in the hearts of the British people. If I had said anything else, they would have hurled me from office."[66]

Nothing—not his moods, not Britain's defeats, not the slow strangulation of the U-boat blockade, not his reluctant generals—impeded Churchill's capacity to inspire his countrymen and to fight for their salvation. Nothing diminished his love for his family. Nothing undercut his love of life. If one accepts Freud's dictum that mental health is the ability to love and work, Churchill possessed his full mental health.

If anything, Churchill had attained what the American humanist psychologist Abraham Maslow called "self-actualization," the condition at the top of Maslow's "hierarchy of needs," where is found creativity, morality, spontaneity, and the ability to parse problems, accept facts, and refute prejudices.

Churchill was never modest, yet he bridled at the suggestion that he had transformed Britons. He believed the British race had "the lion heart"; he only supplied the roar. He believed they had always been heroic. Afterward, much as in his response to Pug Ismay, he said: "It fell to me to express the sentiments and resolves of the British nation in that supreme crisis of its life. That to me was an honor far beyond any dreams or ambitions I have ever nursed, and it was one that cannot be taken away." At the time, however, he said, "It is destiny. Destiny has put me here, now, for this purpose." Yet, "destiny" for Churchill meant only that he had arrived at this place and time; destiny did not guarantee the success of his mission. Only his actions, freely taken, could do that. He acknowledged the possibility that human affairs may be watched over and guided, as part of "the Almighty's Great Design into which all our human actions fit if we do our duty." His abiding agnosticism precluded certainty in the matter of divine influence, but not in the matter of doing his duty. Destiny, like fate, is all things to all men. Here it may be seen as that dynamic force within Churchill that, in combination with his will, altered history during the summer of 1940. Europe lay under Hitler's boot, from the Pyrenees to the Arctic Circle, from beyond the Vistula to the English Channel, across which three weeks earlier the British army had fled, leaving French beaches strewn with abandoned tanks, trucks, cannons, kits, rifles, rations, and the bodies of those Tommies who had not made it out. The Führer's victorious generals now paced the French shore and gazed toward England's white-chalk cliffs, just visible across the narrow waters of the Dover Strait.[67]

It would be a mistake to imagine Hitler in 1940 as a deranged Charlie Chaplinesque buffoon given to spewing spittle on the uniforms of dumbfounded Prussian subordinates during purple-faced tirades. The Führer was quite in command of his faculties that spring, at the top of his game. He had served five years with honor in the trenches during the Great War and been awarded the Iron Cross for bravery. He had been wounded three times—twice by shrapnel and once by gas, which temporarily blinded him. He had fought in twelve battles. Hitler anointed himself, the military historian Sir John Keegan wrote, "first soldier of the Reich," yet he had earned that title by virtue of his courage during the Great War. His regiment—the 16th Bavarian Reserve—had suffered more than 100 percent casualties (military statisticians compute casualties based on the ratio of the original number of men in any unit to the number of replacements). Hitler in 1940 knew the inhuman hardships of war better than many of his generals, yet he also found the Great War to be "the greatest of all experiences." Only the final result had proved unsatisfactory, a defeat inflicted as much by Germany's national loss of will as by the Entente armies. Germany, then, had not deserved victory. This time would be different. This time already was different. Hitler was winning.[68]

Adolf Hitler was now the greatest conqueror in German history, his destiny fulfilled, by the exercise of *his* will. The war, such as it was, was just about over. The British must surely sue for peace, and Hitler was prepared to offer generous terms, for he respected the English race. “He liked the Englanders,” recalled one of his SS bodyguards years later, adding, “except for Churchill.” The Führer’s Reich now basked in a splendorous Alpine dawn born of barbarity, deceit, and sheer Teutonic will. Britain stood alone in twilight, awaiting the seemingly inevitable descent of darkness. Were Churchill to prove himself a dangerous fool by rejecting Hitler’s peace terms, one final task would remain before the former corporal, the failed artist—the “housepainter” as Churchill called Hitler—could assume his place as master of his new European order: the severing of the British Empire’s head from its body.[69]

This was the status of Churchill, of London, of Britain and the British Empire, on the longest day of that year.

Hitler and his generals knew that they could crush the remnants of Britain’s army in a matter of days if they could only reach them, there, across the narrows and beyond the cliffs. But the cold Channel waters lapping at the conquerors’ boots only underscored an ancient and elemental truth; they were land warriors. Unlike English general officers, they were not “salt water generals.” They had no plans in place to cross the sea, did not understand the sea, and in fact, they and Hitler feared it. Churchill did not. The Channel was his moat, England his bailey; he intended to fight from his battlements until he could muster the men and arms necessary to strike out, across the Channel and into Europe, and finally someday, however long it took, across the Rhine and into Germany, to Berlin, where he would achieve his stated objective: final and absolute victory over Hitlerism. Were Hitler or destiny to deny him that, he told his cabinet, he fully expected each of them, himself included, to die “choking on his own blood upon the ground.”[70]

THE STORY THUS FAR, SEPTEMBER 1939–MAY 1940

Churchill’s nemesis, Adolf Hitler, was a wicked political genius who rose to power by finding, and then occupying, the dark places in the German mind. The Führer’s gifts were not confined to his Reich, however. Although he spoke no foreign tongues and had never been overseas, he possessed an intuitive gift for exploiting weaknesses in what Germans call *das Ausland,* that revealing Teutonic word that welds together all nations outside the Reich into a single collective noun. Again and again in the 1930s, he had dared the allied governments of Britain and France to stand up to his acts of aggression. Aghast at the prospect of another European war, they had turned away again and again, sacrificing their pride, their honor; even their prospects of national survival. In the meantime, his armed strength multiplied. Finally, at the end of the decade, after six years of preparation, he was ready. At dawn on Friday, September 1, 1939, he sent fifty-six Wehrmacht divisions roaring eastward into Poland. Now London and Paris had no choice. They were bound to Warsaw by military alliances. They had to declare war, and, reluctantly, they did.

In the Berlin suburb of Zossen, headquarters of the Führer's *Oberkommando der Wehrmacht* (Supreme Command of the Armed Forces, OKW), his field commanders were, in their turn, aghast. By turning to the east, ignoring the armies of England and France, he had defied OKW's basic strategic principle, and invited a two-front war. Worse, he had stripped the defenses on the Reich's Western Front, leaving a thin force of twenty-three second-rate divisions to face eighty-five heavily armed enemy divisions. It was a historic opportunity for Généralissime Gustav-Maurice Gamelin of France, who commanded the Allied troops. The German Supreme Command chief, *Generalfeldmarschall* Wilhelm Keitel, later testified that "a French attack would have encountered only a German military screen (*militärischen Schleier*), not a real defense." To win the war, Gamelin had but to issue one command: *"En avant!"* His troops could have marched into the *Ruhrgebeit,* the heartland of German industry, and the war would have been over.

But he didn't do it. Except for a token sortie in the direction of the Saar and its coal mines and steel furnaces—a meaningless gesture meant to encourage the Poles, yet one from which the Nazis fled—Allied troops remained where they were. Then, in five weeks of blitzkrieg, or lightning warfare, the Nazi juggernaut crushed Poland, freeing the Wehrmacht to turn westward. The moment had passed. French and British troops steeled themselves for the shock of a German offensive, but none came. They waited. And waited. By May of 1940 all had remained quiet on the Western Front for eight months. What fighting there was had been largely confined to the open seas, the realm of the Royal Navy, and the barren coast of Norway. On land, the great armies squatted idly opposite one another week after week in an unnatural silence.

Berliners called this extraordinary hush, unique in the history of modern warfare, *der Sitzkrieg.* In Paris it was *la drôle de guerre* (the amusing war), in London the Bore War. Churchill called it the Twilight War; America's Senator William Borah, the Phony War. In England and France, the public, feeling emotionally ruptured after bracing themselves for the worst, returned instead to the pleasures of peace. But as the conflict entered its ninth sterile month, life was about to stir within in it. The greatest of all wars was about to erupt at last in a convulsion of violence, slaughter, and terror.

Afterward everyone remembered the weather. The winter of 1939–1940 had been a white horror, Europe's cruelest since 1895 (and, though neither Paris nor London knew it, the only reason Hitler hadn't attacked), but spring was coming at last, and coming fast. Though March was its usual mottled mess, temperatures were exceptionally mild. Then, across the Continent, primroses were out, fruit trees were budding, crocuses teeming. As early as April 3, Sir Alexander Cadogan, a British diplomat with a green thumb, noted in his diary: "The herbaceous plants seem all alive-oh" and "Meadows are greening up nicely and copses purpling."[71]

Within a fortnight the season had acquired a radiant, crystalline tone. So pure was the air that vision seemed enhanced, objects being perceived with a cameo-like clarity as sharp and well defined as a fine etching. Magnolias, snowdrops, and bright azaleas rioted in Kensington and Whitechapel alike. Mollie Panter-Downes wrote in *The New Yorker* that the floral displays in London parks "have been so magnificent that it's a pity that the garden-loving Britons haven't had more heart to go and see them," adding that the season ahead "looks as though it were going to be the best, as far as weather and growing things go, that England has had in years." Then she noted: "The tulips in the big beds outside Buckingham Palace are exactly the color of blood."[72]

In the Low Countries across the Channel, cultivating garden tulips had been a major Dutch industry since the eighteenth century, selling the world triumph tulips, breeder's tulips, and Darwin, parrot, cottage, and Mendel tulips. These were approaching their peak in late April and would soon to be joined by graceful white tulips, always the loveliest. In tiny Luxembourg, the beauty of the gladioli was unprecedented. Belgium's spring had always been announced by the tall, graceful plane and poplar trees elegantly lining Brussels' wide gray streets, and now they, too, wore veils of pale green.

It was that rarity, a genuine idyll, a blessed time of crystal-clear air, of radiant mornings, of gentle twilights, and of soft, balmy evenings, when a delicate, bluish moisture fell on orchards and gardens. In late April, whipped-cream clouds hung motionless overhead; then the sky cleared. For six weeks not one drop of rain fell. Clothed in sunlight, their spirits soaring, people found pleasure in just lifting their faces to an immaculate heaven that seemed wider and higher and of a deeper blue than any before.

Alec Cadogan was rapturous: "It's a lovely spring with sparkling air and wonderful blossoms and the whole world looking like paradise." The same enraptured theme ran through other diaries, journals, and letters. Anthony Eden noted the "unbroken sunshine." At No. 10 Downing Street, Jock Colville rose early each morning to ride in Richmond Park, rejoicing in the "warm and summery weather." General Sir Edmund Ironside, Chief of His Majesty's Imperial General Staff and thus England's top soldier, wrote of "the most gorgeous weather," and noted a week later that it was "still the most gorgeous weather." In the rue de la Paix in Paris, the Duchess of Windsor, smartly dressed in a *Union des Femmes de France* uniform, supervised a soldiers' canteen, and wrote her Aunt Bessie, "We have never had such a beautiful spring." That spring was, the American war correspondent Vincent Sheean later wrote, "the loveliest Paris had ever known." Then, remembering its climax, he added, "the weather itself formed part of the human drama." In the Reich, some were reminded of August 1914, when German infantrymen in spiked helmets had written home of *Kaiserwetter.* Now their sons called it *Hitlerwetter.* General Heinz Guderian, the Nazi tank commander, was more specific. In his diary he called it *"völlig Panzerwetter."*[73]

Paris, always Europe's most colorful city, had joined the dazzling spectacle with cannas, dahlias, daffodils, and freesias—seen at their best advantage in the gardens of the Tuileries—while along the Seine and the capital's broad boulevards, the trees beloved by Parisians approached the height of their vernal flowering, their blossoms standing like small pink candles, and their dark green lapping leaves so delicately tarnished, in places so exquisite, that *Paris Soir* compared them to Renoir. Clare Boothe, touring Western Europe in that fourth month of 1940, wrote, "Now, in April, chestnuts burst into leaf on the lovely avenues of Paris, sunlight danced off the opalescent gray buildings, and the gold and gray sunsets, glimpsed through the soaring Arc de Triomphe at the end of the long splendid vista of the Champs-Élysées, brought a catch of pain and pleasure in your throat. Paris was Paris in April!"[74]

Paris was *gai*—a gaiety which, in retrospect, seems cruelly ironic. Immediately after the declaration of war, all theaters had closed, but now they reopened and were packed. So were the opera houses, cinemas, restaurants, and nightclubs; the stands at the Auteuil Hippodrome; the flower market at the Madeleine; the spring art exhibition at the Grand Palais; the *Concours d'Élégance* automobile race in the Bois de Boulogne sponsored by Renault and Citroën—even the Left Bank hall where the five academies gathered to hear Paul Valéry deliver his *Pensée de l'art française,* a lecture more widely covered by the Paris dailies that week than the war on all its fronts.

This year French fields had been plowed by troops. It was strange duty for soldiers in wartime, but thus far it had been a strange war; in isolated skirmishes the French arms had suffered only two thousand casualties, a third of the Royal Navy's losses in sea actions. Even so, the *Conseil Supérieur de la Guerre* (Supreme War Council) had bridled at the idea of soldiers manning plows and planting potatoes, arguing that such work was demeaning to their profession. However, the government, at the insistence of deputies with agricultural constituencies, pointed out that although career officers were professional soldiers, their troops were not; the men they commanded were peacetime civilians, many of them farmers, and if someone didn't turn the earth and sow it, France would lose the war by starvation.

Some officers, among them Colonel Charles de Gaulle, were relieved when the generals were forced to back down. France's army had a great reputation, even in Berlin, but idle troops are worrisome. The British Expeditionary Force, or BEF, had dealt with the problem of inactivity during the winter. Although there were still fewer than four hundred thousand British soldiers on the Continent—only 18 percent of the Allied ground forces—their quality was high, in part because officers kept spirits up with programs of vigorous exercise. The French did not. As the war entered its third season, the armies of France were stagnating, even rotting.

Every allowance must be made for the French, and the French soldier of 1940 must be regarded with great compassion. With the exception of Serbia, no nation had suffered so terribly in the Great War. Because their fathers had been bled white, the World War II generation, unlike that of 1914, simply wanted to be left alone.

At the time, this atrophy of spirit was imperfectly understood. In 1938, Churchill had called the French army "the most perfectly trained and faithful mobile force in Europe." In January 1940, to his dismay, he found that the French did not view the war "with uprising spirit or even with much confidence." He blamed the long months of waiting that had followed the collapse of Poland. This hiatus, he believed, had given "time and opportunity" for the "poisons" of communism and fascism to be established. It was certain, he wrote, that the quality of the French army was being "allowed to deteriorate during the winter."[75]

The eight-month lull at the front was seen variously. Vincent Sheean wrote that there was "no possible doubt that a dawn must come, one day or the next, when the gray rivers of the German flood would begin to roll westward over Holland, Belgium and France . . . and yet, in the way people have, I think we only half believed the inevitable until it had taken place."[76]

Since the expected curtain-raiser would have brought vast bloodshed, others were optimistic, including some who should have known better. General André Beaufre saw it as "a giant charade acted out by mutual consent" that would lead to nothing serious "if we play our part right." Alfred Duff Cooper, who had resigned from Chamberlain's cabinet to protest the Munich sellout, fatuously told an American audience in Paris that the Allies had "found a new way to make war, without sacrificing human lives."[77]

Many argued that it must stop, that it couldn't go on this way, that there was no point to it. Prime Minister Neville Chamberlain privately said he had "a hunch" that the war would be over by summer. Others felt otherwise; eminent men in Paris and London were persuaded that the war would continue as it was, with the naval blockade slowly strangling the Führer's Reich. That would take a year or two, of course, but by then the British would have fifty divisions in the field, and doubtless the Americans would sail over with a hundred more to deliver the coup de grâce. (It was the sort of showy thing they liked to do.)

The arguments of the distinguished scholar Alfred Sauvy to the contrary, the French masses had accepted the war, however reluctantly. They believed France would win it. They felt "sure," William L. Shirer, the CBS radio correspondent in Berlin, observed, "that all a democracy had to do to win a war was to declare it, that if a 'free nation' was united in its desire to win, no 'slave-driven force' like Hitler's could defeat it... they talked to you about the gigantic War Effort, and explained to you how, because this was a democracy, the War Effort was certainly greater than in Germany, because it was voluntary." Shirer noted a growing conviction that "in this peculiar war there was no need to suffer, to deprive oneself of the good, easy life. Sacrifice was not this time needed."

The French government encouraged such lullabies. Its deputies had invested Premier Édouard Daladier with dictatorial powers over French industry, including the right to conscript labor, but he had not used them. Factories that could have been converted to munitions manufacture were still turning out civilian goods. The Parisian firms of Lelong, Balenciaga, and Molyneux were exporting silks that Frenchmen would next see in German parachutes. Food was unrationed; so was gasoline, despite the fact that every gallon had to be imported. A subcommittee of *députés* had recommended that ski slopes and the Côte d'Azur resorts be reopened.

De Gaulle, the lonely Cassandra, wrote to Paul Reynaud, then still French Minister of Finance: "Now, as I see it, the enemy will not attack us for some time.... Then, when he thinks we are weary, confused, and dissatisfied with our own inertia, he will finally take the offensive against us, possessing completely different cards in the psychological and material line from those he holds at present." He was right, but when the upstart colonel told Pierre Brisson, editor of *Le Figaro,* that he felt uneasy over the French enemy's passivity, Brisson ridiculed him: "Don't you see that we have already won a bloodless Marne?"[78]

The British, possessing on the whole a better record on European battlefields, ought to have been more realistic. They weren't. Instead, they were complacent. The Isle looked fine; ergo, the Isle *was* fine. In the autumn, the *Times* had proclaimed Britain's "grim determination" to see it all through, but nine months after the outbreak, English life had returned to normal. Idle men dozed on Hyde Park "deck chairs"; the sheep lazed away the days in London's park enclosures, and admiring crowds gathered by the nearby duck ponds. In 1940, the city's skyline was still dominated by St. Paul's, by the steeples of Wren's fifty other baroque churches, by the neo-Gothic Houses of Parliament and Big Ben. Blacked out now, it loomed serenely on moonlit nights, invoking in some memories of the imperial capital before the arrival of electricity. Nightlife was as innocent and diverting as ever; John Gielgud was King Lear; Emlyn Williams's *Light of Heart* played to busy houses; elsewhere in the West End the most popular dance tunes were the American "Deep Purple" and "Somewhere over the Rainbow." Clearly Londoners were less interested in the war than in the rituals of peace. The *Times,* ever the vigilant recorder of multifarious ornithological sightings, reported the return of swallows, cuckoos, and even nightingales.

Churchill tried to wake the nation. Speaking that March on the BBC, HMG's first lord of the Admiralty warned his countrymen that "more than a million German soldiers, including all their active and armored divisions, are drawn up ready to attack, on a few hours' notice, all along the frontiers of Luxembourg, of Belgium and of Holland. At any moment these neutral countries may be subjected to an avalanche of steel and fire, and the decision rests in the hands of a haunted, morbid being who, to their eternal shame, the German people have worshipped as a god." He observed that in Britain "there are thoughtless dilettanti or purblind worldlings who sometimes ask us: 'What is it that Britain and France are fighting for?' To this I answer: 'If we left off fighting you would soon find out.' "[79]

Nevertheless Lord Haw-Haw, a pseudonym for William Joyce, the English traitor who broadcast Nazi propaganda to Britain from Berlin—for which he would later hang—was not yet resented; most Britons considered him merely amusing. At No. 10 Downing Street, the young diarist Jock Colville noted: "The war looks like being an immobile affair on the Western Front." After an evening in town, Colville wrote of seeing "a group of bespectacled intellectuals remain firmly seated while God Save the King was played." He commented: "Everybody looked but nobody did anything, which shows that the war has not yet made us lose our sense of proportion or become noisily jingoistic." He had yet to learn that tolerance is a weakness in a nation at war, and that in wartime, jingoism becomes patriotism. The Germans already knew it. Had Berliners snubbed *"Deutschland Über Alles"* or sat through the *"Horst Wessel Lied,"* they would have been fortunate to lose only their freedom.[80]

The burgeoning spring revealed a minor scandal. The sandbags piled high around entrances to Whitehall government buildings split open and sprouted green weeds, clear evidence that they had been filled, not with sand, as stipulated in contracts, but with cheaper earth. Inevitably a question was raised in the House of Commons, though it was never really answered, largely because no one much cared. Sandbags and the other impedimenta of war—the barrage balloons, the air-raid trenches in the city's parks, the air-raid wardens, and the gas masks, which, as *Punch* pointed out, were carried only by officers and high civil servants—like stories of the evacuated children and jokes about women in uniform—had become banal. Indeed, the war itself had turned into a tiresome commitment to be grudgingly met.

That mood began to shift in the first week of May. The public, misled by the press, which had been misled by the government, had been under the impression that their troops were driving the Germans out of Norway. In fact it was the other way around. The fiasco ended on Thursday, May 2, when Prime Minister Neville Chamberlain rose in the House of Commons to announce that the British troops, having suffered a stunning defeat, were being evacuated. That weekend a Gallup poll revealed the public's disillusionment: fewer than a third now supported Chamberlain.

Parliament debated the Scandinavian losses on the following Tuesday. On Wednesday the Labour Party forced a division—a vote of confidence—and more than one hundred members of Chamberlain's own party deserted him. So stinging a rebuke should have led to the immediate fall of the prime minister's government. Clinging to office, the P.M. spent that evening trying every conceivable political maneuver to stay in office. All failed.

In Berlin that same day—Wednesday, May 8, 1940—William L. Shirer noted "a feeling of tension in the Wilhelmstrasse today." He added, "I hear the Dutch and Belgians are nervous. They ought to be." The Associated Press reported that two German armies, one from Bremen and the other from Düsseldorf, were moving toward the Dutch frontier. That angered the Germans; nevertheless, Shirer wrote that his censors "let me hint very broadly that the next German blow would fall in the west—Holland, Belgium, the Maginot Line, Switzerland."[81]

In Brussels the papal nuncio requested an audience with King Leopold to relay a warning from the Vatican. The pope had learned that a German invasion of Belgium was "imminent." Two coded dispatches to Brussels from the Belgian embassy in Berlin confirmed it. The Hague was alerted by the Dutch military attaché in Berlin.

Hitler was in a state of high excitement. In *Mein Kampf* he had sworn to destroy France in "a final, decisive battle (*Entscheibungskampf*)." Now the hour was at hand. General Jodl noted in his diary: "The Führer does not want to wait any longer.... He is very agitated. Then he consents to postponement until May 10, which he says is against his intuition. But [he will wait] not one day longer."[82]

In the Château de Vincennes, Généralissime Gustav-Maurice Gamelin announced the restoration of normal peacetime leave in the French army. Four days earlier General André-Georges Corap, commander of the French Ninth Army, had told his men: "Nothing will happen until 1941." A Paris headline, welcoming the coming weekend, read: DÉTENTE AU HOLLANDE (Relaxation in Holland).

Because Britannia ruled the waves, the Admiralty in Whitehall determined overall naval policy for the war, but with the 400,000 troops of the British Expeditionary Force outnumbered by over 2,100,000 French, the disposition of troops was fixed by the short, courtly Gamelin. The *généralissime* was confident he could stop the enemy because he believed he knew exactly where they were going to attack. It would be through Belgium, precisely where they had come in August of 1914, when, achieving complete strategic surprise, the gray tide of the Reich's huge right wing, a million strong, had swept down and cut a swath seventy-five miles wide, enveloping France's left flank. That had been among the last imaginative maneuvers on the Western Front in 1914–1918. The French had avoided immediate disaster by falling back and rallying on the Marne. Then the sidestepping had begun as each army tried to outflank the other. Neither could. The result was a stalemate. The Allies found themselves defending for more than four years a snakelike chain of trenches that began on the Swiss border and ended 566 miles away on the English Channel. Breakthroughs were impossible, because whenever a position was in peril it could be swiftly reinforced; troop trains packed with defending troops could rocket to the tottering sector before the attacking infantrymen, plodding ahead at the three-miles-an-hour pace of Napoleonic foot soldiers, could reach their objective.

Gamelin foresaw a precise encore. But this time, he assured his countrymen, the war would not be fought on "the sacred soil" of France. Under his

Plan D, he would send his armies into the great northern plain of eastern Belgium and meet the enemy there on the line of the Dyle River. Where else, he asked, could the Nazis come? It was everyone's opinion that a German invasion through Switzerland was inconceivable, and France's perimeter comprised the Belgian plain (Flanders) on the left, the great Ardennes forest in the center, sprawling across Luxembourg, Belgium, and northern France, and the eighty-seven-mile Franco-German border, where the two hostile powers confronted one another directly.

This last location held no threat. Every inch of it was now defended by the most expensive system of fixed fortifications in history, the mighty steel-and-concrete Maginot Line, manned by forty-one divisions. When Lord Gort, commander of the British Expeditionary Forces, and a group of British generals toured the fortifications, they asked their French guide, René de Chambrun,* how much it had all cost. Fifty-five billion francs, Chambrun replied, over ten years. Then, realizing his English guests were of a seafaring nation and calculated in pounds sterling, Chambrun put the numbers into a nautical perspective: Had France spent the same amount of money building the biggest and fastest of battleships, of which there were about twenty-five in all the navies of the world, the French fleet would now consist of *fifty* such behemoths. Thus, Chambrun explained, the interconnected forts and artillery batteries of Maginot could be thought of as a great line of "land battleships," an analogy the British appeared to grasp. Gort, Chambrun wrote, "could not conceal his astonishment." Chambrun did not disclose to his guests that the cost of the line had precluded investments in tanks and mechanized units. Nor did he and his guests take the naval analogy far enough, for battleships are mobile and can react to changing tactical conditions. Forts—"land battleships"—are not and cannot.

Le Maginot, as the line was known to all Frenchmen, was named for André Maginot, a politician who, like Premier Édouard Daladier, had spent four years suffering in the trenches of the first war and vowed: never again. To be sure, the line ended at the Belgian border. Consideration was given to building it up to the northern French coast but the French believed that would send the wrong signal to Belgium, that their troops wouldn't even bother to fight until the Germans got to the French border. Some members of the *Conseil Supérieur de la Guerre* had urged that the line be extended to the Meuse River, within Belgium, but that was vetoed by

* Chambrun, a descendant of Lafayette, was a lawyer before he was mobilized, and served as a liaison to the British. Following the fall of France, he was a guest of Franklin Roosevelt aboard the presidential yacht *Sequoia,* where he gave the president a briefing on the battle.

Maréchal Henri-Philippe Pétain, the French commander of the army in 1918. To reach the Meuse, the Germans would have to pass through the Ardennes—a thickly wooded Hans Christian Andersen forest, slashed with deep ravines, and fogged with mist rising from peat bogs—"*impénétrable,*" Pétain declared, thus ruling it out as a channel of invasion. By the process of elimination, Gamelin reasoned, that left the Belgian plain as the only possible battlefield.[83]

Although he did not see them, he faced grave problems. Napoleon had warned his commanders against forming a picture—deciding in advance what the enemy was going to do. That is precisely what Gamelin had done. It never occurred to him that the Germans, having watched one great plan fail in 1914, might have formed another. Gamelin had also overlooked an ominous change in Belgium's rulers. In the last war King Albert had been a mighty ally, but in 1936, his son, Leopold III, had astonished Europe by renouncing his country's military alliance with France and Britain. In any new war between Germany and France, he declared, Belgium would be neutral—as though such an absurdity were possible. He had actually gone so far as to fortify his border with France, and had told the French that an extension of *Le Maginot* to the North Sea would be looked upon in Belgium as an unfriendly gesture.[84]

But Gamelin's greatest error was his assumption that warfare had not changed since the Armistice in 1918. His *Conseil Supérieur* took the same view, although there were a few vigorous dissenters, among them Colonel de Gaulle. De Gaulle was making a pest of himself, insisting that the French must study the swift Nazi conquest of Poland with tanks. Tanks, he said, had revolutionized battle; new strategies were needed to turn them back. As early as November 11, 1939, he had sent General Headquarters an aide-mémoire on the lessons of the Polish campaign, chiefly the need for fluidity on the battlefield, specifically the formation of a mechanized shock corps (*armée de métier*), soldiers specially selected and trained to lead an attack. Unless France followed the German example, he predicted, the gasoline engine would demolish French military doctrines even as it demolished fortifications.

But his superiors thought him absurd. One of them asked the others, Suppose the Boche panzers did burst through the lines. Where would they refuel? None of them reflected on the fact that since 1918, thousands of filling stations had appeared in northern France. To them they were irrelevant. After all, these petrol stations—which, like 91 percent of the automobiles in the country, had not existed in 1918—were there to serve civilian automobiles, not German panzers. The fact that both cars and tanks used the same fuel was disregarded.

Some war correspondents, haunted by the spectacle of the Führer's armored columns crushing the gallant Poles, remained troubled, but at Gamelin's *grand quartier général* they were told sharply that a replay of the blitzkrieg here was impossible. General Dufieux, the army's retired commander of tanks, declared that Nazi armored units could not "hurl themselves unsupported against our lines and penetrate deeply without facing complete destruction." Another senior officer chided the foreign press for its doubts: "Ah, my fellows, how naive you are!" A war of movement across the dry Polish plains, yes. But through the Ardennes, through the Dutch floods, through the Belgian defenses, through the Maginot—through the tank-traps and barbed wire and casemates, in the face of our powerful air force—that was absurd."[85]

In adopting the strategic defensive, the French high command was expressing the caution of a France whose World War I wounds were still unhealed. All the great battles had been fought on French or Belgian soil, and 1,315,000 *poilus* ("hairy," "virile") had been killed in action—27 percent of all men between the ages of eighteen and twenty-seven, a figure that does not include the wounded: those left blind, or legless, or armless, or with no limbs at all. The survivors lacked the strength or the will to lift the tricolor again. Unlike generations of Frenchmen gone before them, they understandably felt no craving for grandeur, no desire for Gallic supremacy in Europe. They did not want to lose this war, but neither did they much crave victory. In fact, they did not even *want* victory. France had no war aims. Everything desirable, as they saw it, was already French. They asked for nothing from the Germans but peace.

Thus the decision to leave the initiative to the Nazis was more political than military. *Le Maginot* was as much a state of mind as a fortified line; when Daladier's government fell that March, conduct of the war was entrusted to Paul Reynaud only after he promised to undertake no offensive against the enemy. The idea of attacking Germany was, the deputies agreed, preposterous. After the Polish collapse, the most bellicose had lost heart. In the *Chambre des Députés,* all political parties became defeatist. Even before Hitler could deliver another *Friedensrede,* a peace speech calling on the Western allies to end the war now that he had enslaved another country—he had been posing as a prince of peace for seven years—the Communist delegation in the *Chambre* demanded that the deputies debate the "proposals for peace which are going to be made." Alexis Léger, the secretary-general of the Foreign Office, told the American ambassador William Bullitt: "The game is lost. France stands alone against the three dictatorships. Great Britain is not ready. The United States has not even changed the neutrality act. The democracies are again too late." Alfred

Sauvy concluded simply that the country had "refused the war" (*"on refusait la guerre"*).[86]

But this was not a chess match, where a gambit could be refused. And Hitler would deliver no proposals of peace on the upcoming weekend of May 10. He intended to deliver something else entirely.

The timidity of the French high command had exasperated Churchill ever since the war's outbreak. They had rejected every initiative suggested by him—bombing the Ruhr, for example, or mining the Rhine—on the grounds that it might invite Nazi reprisals. "This idea of not irritating the enemy," he later wrote, "did not commend itself to me.... Good, decent, civilized people, it appeared, must never themselves strike until after they have been struck dead." This Gallic trepidation even ruled out air reconnaissance, which defies understanding because the Luftwaffe was overflying French lines every day. Had Allied planes done the same in early May, they would have been astonished at enemy preparations below. Eight military bridges had been thrown across the Rhine, and three armored columns stretched back from the river for one hundred miles.[87]

In fact, one French pilot did see the buildup on the evening of the eighth of May. He was over the Ruhr, returning from a propaganda mission, dropping leaflets urging the German people to overthrow Hitler and thus bring peace. Above Düsseldorf he looked down and saw a sixty-mile line of tanks and trucks headed for the Ardennes. They were driving with their lights on. He reported his discovery. It was dismissed as not credible.

This was not the first time such intelligence had been dismissed, but it would be the last. Five months earlier, as Europe slept away the winter, a German airplane carrying two staff officers was blown off course and forced to land in Belgium. The officers tried, and failed, to burn the papers they carried, which happened to contain OKW's revised operation orders for the invasion of the Low Countries, including a thrust through the Ardennes. British intelligence perused the captured papers. The high arts of deception and double-cross being well practiced by both the Germans and the British, it was concluded that the papers were a plant, a ruse, and therefore, unbelievable.[88]

On Thursday morning, May 9, the 250th day of the war, Chamberlain faced the bitter truth: he was through. The debacle in Norway had finished him. It had become obvious that Britain needed an all-party national government, and Labour refused to serve under him. Given the huge Tory majority in the House, a legacy of the general election of 1935, the new prime minister would have to be a Conservative. The party's leadership wanted Lord Halifax, the foreign secretary. So did Chamberlain. So did the King. However, Tory backbenchers and Labour MPs leaned toward the first lord of the Admiralty, Winston Churchill. Halifax bowed out. Telephoning London from his battalion, Randolph Churchill asked for news. His father told him: "I think I shall be Prime Minister tomorrow."[89]

At 9:00 P.M. that night Hitler issued the code word "Danzig."

The mightiest army in history was ready, and at 4:19 A.M. on Friday, May 10, 1940, more than two million German soldiers in coalscuttle helmets surged forward. The Wehrmacht was crossing the frontiers of Belgium, Holland, and Luxembourg, attacking on a front extending from the North Sea to the Swiss frontier. Hitler had repeatedly sworn never to violate their neutrality, but he meant to conquer France, and the Low Countries were in his way.[90]

At 5:30 A.M. Belgium asked the Allies for help. Gamelin phoned General Alphonse Georges, his field commander in the northeast.

Georges asked: "Well, General, is it the Dyle operation?"

Gamelin said: "Since the Belgians are calling on us, do you see what else we can do?" (*"Que nous puissons faire autre chose?"*) Georges replied: "Obviously not."

Gamelin sealed it: "We must go into Belgium!" (*"Nous devons entrer en Belgique"*). Five minutes later Georges ordered five French armies and the British Expeditionary Force across the frontier. There was some unpleasantness with the Belgian border guards, who hadn't been told of the decision in Brussels. One official demanded visas from the British 3rd Division—the divisional commander, Major General Bernard Montgomery, put him under arrest—and on several roads Belgian obstacles, erected to block a French invasion, still barred the way. None slowed the Allied troops, now plunging ahead.[91]

The BEF was in high spirits. Tommies blew kisses as they passed smiling women and, wrote Clare Boothe, who was there, "stuck up their thumbs in the new gesture they had, which meant 'O.K., everything's fine.'" They were singing "Roll Out the Barrel," a Czech drinking song that had been popular since Munich, nineteen months earlier, and a ballad based on an Australian folk song:

Run, Adolf, run Adolf, run, run, run!
Here comes a Tommy with his gun, gun, gun!

They also sang songs their fathers had sung a generation ago: "Tipperary," "Keep the Home Fires Burning," and "Pack Up Your Troubles in Your Old Kit Bag." Among older officers there was a remarkable mood of déjà vu. In the *New York Times,* Drew Middleton wrote: "It was almost as if they were retracing steps taken in a dream, they saw again faces of friends long dead and heard the half-remembered names of towns and villages."[92]

By evening the best trained of the Allied troops were deep in both Belgium and Holland. Here, Gamelin assured everyone, was the German *schwerpunkt*—the strategic center of effort as defined by Prussian staff doctrine.

His blunder was fatal.

At Hitler's eyrie at Bad Münstereifel, twenty-five miles southwest of Bonn, the Führer danced with joy. His generals could scarcely believe their luck. General Adolf Heusinger excitedly scrawled in his diary: "They have poured into Belgium and fallen into the trap!"[93]

The upcoming Sabbath was Whitsuntide, traditionally part of a long holiday weekend for Englishmen, and celebrated by Christians as the day the Holy Spirit descended upon Christ's disciples. Londoners were impressed when, on Friday, having learned of the attack upon the Low Countries, their government canceled the bank holiday; it meant, wrote Mollie Panter-Downes for *The New Yorker,* "The government is really getting a move on." No reliable news was coming out of the Low Countries, and that was bad. Yet Britons were calm; no excited crowds took to the streets. Panter-Downes wrote: "It takes a good, stiff dose of adversity to release the formidable strength in what Harold Nicolson called 'the slow grinding will power of the British people.' To that has been added the quickening realization that they are fighting for their lives."[94]

For almost a decade Churchill had drummed warnings to his countrymen that this day would come. Three hundred years earlier, during the English Civil War, both the Royalist and Parliamentary armies introduced drummers into their ranks. They went into battle unarmed and beat out coded orders that could be heard over the crash of muskets and cannon: *form up, face right, left, volley.* The drummers were not meant to inspire or comfort their comrades, or to introduce confusion and fear into enemy ranks, yet within the blinding stinking smoke and bloody mayhem of combat, their relentless, rhythmic, *tap* and *thrum* did just that. Where the drummers of England went, Empire followed. Rudyard Kipling glorified them in "The Drums of the Fore and Aft," in which the courage of two young regimental drummers inspires the regiment, which, on the verge of annihilation at the hands of Afghan tribesmen, regroups, attacks, and at the end of the slaughter claims victory.

Churchill's heroes—Pitt, Marlborough, Nelson—had not only led, they had inspired. Winston Churchill was prepared now to step forward as England's master and commander, and its drummer. But were his King and countrymen ready for him? Would Britons join him when the Hun arrived, and fight alongside him to the end? Were they prepared, each and all, to die in defense of family, home, King, and country? Churchill was. He had readied himself for this moment during every hour of every day for six decades, when he first sent his toy armies charging across the floors of his father's London town house.

The glorious weather held. Lilacs—in English folklore the harbingers of springtime rebirth—bloomed across the land. "Lovely day," Alexander Cadogan noted in his diary hours before Hitler gave his order to attack. "Tulips almost at their best and everything smiling, except human affairs."

Cadogan, a Chamberlain loyalist, by then knew that the Chamberlain government was finished. "But *what,*" he asked his diary, "are we going to put in its place?" Who would lead? "Attlee? Sinclair? Sam Hoare?"

He eliminated one candidate out of hand: "Winston useless."[95]

I

Cyclone

MAY–DECEMBER 1940

Shortly after tea on Friday, May 10, fifteen hours after Hitler drove his steel into the Low Countries, Neville Chamberlain reluctantly returned the seals of his office to King George VI, who received them with equal reluctance: "I accepted his resignation," the sovereign wrote in his diary that evening, "& told him how grossly, unfairly I thought he had been treated." Shortly after six o'clock, the King anointed as prime minister the massive, stooped, sixty-five-year-old first lord of the Admiralty, Winston Leonard Spencer Churchill. Later King George became one of Churchill's most ardent admirers, but his feelings were mixed at the time. In his diary that day Jock Colville wrote that the King "(remembering perhaps the abdication, which Churchill had opposed) is understood not to wish to send for Winston." Nevertheless, an all-party government was essential, and Labour had been adamant: they would not serve under Chamberlain.[1]

Defending Britain and her Empire would be the new prime minister's responsibility for the next five years, or until he was hurled from office by Parliament or Hitler. Yet, as he rode back from Buckingham Palace, neither he nor anyone else in London felt unduly alarmed over the course of the war. Little was known that evening about the day's developments across the Channel. The Luftwaffe had bombed airfields in Belgium and Holland; parachute troops had landed among the Belgians, who were said to be fighting well; Dutch resistance was reportedly "stubborn"; and the Allies were taking up strong positions on the Antwerp-Namur Line, preparing to defend the Albert Kanaal. Everything was going as expected, or so it seemed at that hour.[2]

When the BBC announced Churchill's appointment that night, his daughter Mary, seventeen, listened to the broadcast in the small cottage at Chartwell where her governess lived. When it finished she switched off the wireless and said a prayer for her father.[3]

Churchill was surrounded by his family, whether at No. 10 or in the underground Annexe. Of the older Churchill children, only Sarah, the actress, was still a civilian, living with her husband in a Westminster Gardens flat, and soon she too would be commissioned in the Women's Auxiliary Air Force (WAAF). Sarah's husband, Vic Oliver, Austrian by birth, the son of Baron Viktor Oliver von Samek, had renounced his barony, changed the "k" in Viktor to "c," and was now an American citizen. Churchill, upon first meeting Oliver in 1936, took an immediate dislike to the man, and in a letter to Clementine cut loose. Oliver was "common as dirt," possessed "a horrible mouth," and spoke with "an Austro-Yankee drawl." Yet no mention was made of the one trait which many in the English aristocracy would have found sufficient to dismiss Vic Oliver outright: his family was Jewish. It would not have occurred to Churchill to do so. He measured the man.[4]

Of the other children, Diana and Randolph were already officers, she in the Women's Royal Naval Service (WRNS, or Wrens in naval slang), Randolph in his father's old regiment, the 4th Hussars. Mary worked in a canteen and for the Red Cross and lived with her parents. So did Randolph's twenty-year-old wife, Pamela, who was expecting their first child in October. When the air raids began with June's full moon, Pamela and her father-in-law shared bunk beds in the basement of No. 10. Because she was pregnant, hers was the bottom bunk, and in the early hours of each morning she woke to hear Churchill laboriously climb the short ladder to his. Clementine slept in another basement bedroom.[5]

As prime minister, Churchill was also surrounded by a large official family, "The Secret Circle," as he called them. Always at his elbow were his three private secretaries, John ("Jock") Colville, who remained at No. 10 after Chamberlain's departure, and Eric Seal and John Martin, whom Churchill had brought over from the Admiralty. Also within earshot were his typists, Kathleen Hill, Grace Hamblin, and Edith Watson, who had aided every P.M. since Lloyd George. Pug Ismay served as his liaison with His Majesty's Chiefs of Staff, whose offices were in Richmond Terrace: the chiefs were Admiral Sir Alfred Dudley Pound, General Sir John Dill, and Air Marshal Sir Cyril Newall. Colville told his diary that Churchill considered the three chiefs to be "sound, but old and slow." Air Marshal Sir Charles Portal replaced Newall in October.[6]

A recent arrival at No. 10 was Dr. Charles Wilson, the P.M.'s personal physician, who kept a diary from the day of his appointment. On first meeting the doctor, Churchill treated him as he did all underlings, with a mixture of curtness and impatience. Dr. Wilson had found Churchill in bed, at noon, reading papers, which he continued to peruse as Wilson stood nearby, waiting for some acknowledgment. Finally, from Churchill: "I don't know why they're making such a fuss." Churchill snarled, "There's nothing wrong with me." That was true enough, for the doctor makes no further diary entries for the remainder of the year.[7]

Churchill hadn't wanted a doctor; he claimed that there was nothing wrong with him. Churchill's old friend Max Beaverbrook insisted, however, and no one could insist more strenuously than "the Beaver," as everyone called him. That was why Churchill had named him chief of aircraft production. England had to have planes for the coming air battle. In pursuit of a vital goal, the Beaver was ruthless, unscrupulous, even piratical. He seized factories, broke into warehouses, and imprisoned those who tried to stop him. None of this was against the law. On May 22, Parliament had passed an Emergency Powers (Defence) Act giving His Majesty's Government sweeping prerogatives. One section, 18B, effectively removed the *habeas* from *habeas corpus*. HMG held absolute power over all British citizens, requiring them "to place themselves, their services, and their property at the disposal of His Majesty," specifically of the minister of defence, who happened also to be the prime minister. Churchill could have become a dictator had he so chosen. Instead he became almost obsessive in his belief that the House should be fully informed of all developments.[8]

Among the other newcomers to HMG were three Churchill votaries—"the fearsome triumvirate," Colville called them—whom the civil servants had awaited with dread: Brendan Bracken, MP; Frederick Lindemann ("the Prof"); and Major Desmond Morton, a Westerham neighbor of Churchill who had played a vital role in Churchill's prewar intelligence net, assembling proof of England's military unpreparedness. But Morton lacked access to the most vital intelligence, from Bletchley. Within a year Morton's star began to set, since Churchill, informed by Bletchley, no longer needed his own private secret service, and Morton apparently did not provide enough panache at the dinner table to rate a regular weekend dinner invitation. Churchill's friendships admitted to a certain degree of utilitarian relativity, though for the time being Morton's past loyalty trumped his diminishing utility. Bracken had long been Churchill's most devout supporter in the House of Commons. He was also a very odd young man who, to Clementine's annoyance, had in the 1920s encouraged rumors that he was Churchill's natural son (he ceased doing so at Churchill's request). The Prof was even odder. German born, educated at Berlin University, a bachelor and vegetarian, he believed that all women looked upon him as a sex object. But he was a brilliant physicist and a consummate interpreter of science for laymen. He was to become the strongest advocate for the unrestricted bombing and burning of the cities of his homeland.[9]

Churchill, his family, his colleagues, and his cronies were prepared to meet whatever came their way via Berlin. If Britons were not yet prepared, Churchill intended that they soon would be.

It is impossible to exaggerate the influence of World War I on the opening battles of World War II. Afterward, Churchill wrote that it was "a joke in

Britain to say that the War Office is always preparing for the last war." That was also true of soldiers, and it was equally true of statesmen—even the Führer was preoccupied with the trench fighting of 1914–1918. Churchill was no exception. During the Great War he had learned certain precepts of modern warfare, including one of immense significance: tactical breakthroughs were impossible, because whenever a position was in peril, it could be swiftly reinforced. The continuous front had never broken. And another lesson learned: nothing in that war had happened quickly.[10]

In the current war, *everything* was happening quickly—too quickly—and none of it good. German panzers were smashing all the old strategic and tactical paradigms. Britain's survival depended upon finding the weaknesses in the Nazi strategy, and then exploiting them. This would be Churchill's ultimate problem. His immediate problem was political: Conservative MPs, who held 432 of the 607 seats in the House, dominated Parliament. The source of this problem lay in the country's last general election, five years earlier. Misled by Prime Minister Stanley Baldwin, who had assured Parliament that England's defenses were more than adequate, Britain had elected a House of Commons top-heavy with irreconcilable pacifists and die-hard appeasers. Since then, the country's mood had turned 180 degrees, but in their hearts, the Conservative majority remained loyal to the memory of Baldwin and the disastrous policies of Neville Chamberlain, even though they had led England to this fearful pass.

The new P.M., though a Tory himself, had been their gadfly throughout the 1930s, a vehement opponent of their "Splendid Isolation," which they defined as "a plea for the detachment of Britain from Continental quarrels." Again and again he had warned of the Nazi menace, demanding larger defense budgets. The fact that subsequent events had proven him right and them wrong did not endear him to them. An embittered R. A. ("Rab") Butler (an appeaser and Chamberlain loyalist) called Churchill "a half-breed American" and "the greatest adventurer in modern political history." That Friday, the tenth, Butler denounced "this sudden coup of Winston and his rabble." Another Conservative MP wrote Stanley Baldwin—who had described Churchill as part of "the flotsam and jetsam of political drift thrown up on the beach"—that "the Tories don't trust Winston. After the first clash of war is over it may well be that a sounder Government may emerge." A civil servant noted, "There seems to be some inclination in Whitehall to believe that Winston will be a complete failure and that Neville will return." The pacifist editor Max Plowman wrote: "Perhaps Winston will win the war. Perhaps he won't. How anybody could *expect* him to, I don't know, in view of his unparalleled record in losing everything he puts his hand to."[11]

The permanent secretariat at No. 10 Downing Street, who knew Churchill only as a critic of his predecessors, despaired. For as long as the private secretaries there could remember, Baldwin or Chamberlain had been in power. They were mostly Tories themselves, young gentlemen working in what had been, until then, a comfortable private home, where everything went smoothly and quietly, with messengers summoned at the tinkle of a bell, clean towels and ivory brushes in the cloakroom, and everything, as one of them put it, "reminding the inhabitants that they were working at the very heart of a great empire, in which haste was undignified and any quiver of the upper lip unacceptable." Everything about Churchill's reputation horrified them. Jock Colville wrote in his diary that Churchill's rise "is a terrible risk, and I cannot help feeling that this country may be manoeuvred into the most dangerous position it has ever been in." Later Colville recalled that "in May 1940 the mere thought of Churchill as Prime Minister sends a cold chill down the spines of the staff at No. 10 Downing Street.... Seldom can a Prime Minister have taken office with the Establishment so dubious of the choice & so prepared to have its doubts justified." Quite apart from the fortunes of war, already darkening England's prospects for survival, Churchill's government was being launched in very rough political waters.[12]

They swiftly calmed. "Within a fortnight," Colville wrote, "all was changed." Churchill arrived on the scene like a summer squall at a sailboat regatta. Whitehall was galvanized, and the office at No. 10 was pandemonium. Bells were ringing constantly, telephones of various colors were being installed in every nook at No. 10, and the new prime minister was attaching maroon labels demanding "Action This Day" or green ones saying "Report in Three Days" to an endless stream of directives that were being dictated to typists in the Cabinet Room, the P.M.'s bedroom, and even his bathroom, with replies expected within minutes. Ministers, generals, and senior civil servants appeared and departed within minutes. Working hours began early each morning and ended after midnight. "The pace became frantic," another private secretary, John Martin, recalled. "We realized we were at war."[13]

Chamberlain had been cold and orderly; Churchill, John Martin recalled, was "a human dynamo." In the words of Sir Ian Jacob: "His pugnacious spirit demanded constant action. The enemy must be assailed continuously: the Germans must be made to 'bleed and burn.'" Churchill appointed himself his own minister of defence, thereby assuring that he himself, working through Major General Ismay, would manage the Chiefs of Staff, conducting the war day by day, even hour by hour. Yet Churchill always took care to pass his wishes to the generals through Ismay, whose "loyalty to his seniors and juniors was absolute" such that, in turn, he was never shy about telling Churchill just what the generals and their Joint Planning Staff thought of his suggestions—often, not much, which led Churchill to call the JPS "the whole machinery of negation." Ismay's loyalty to Churchill did not insulate him from prime ministerial outbursts any more than did the allegiance of others on the Old Man's staff. After one contentious meeting with the Chiefs of Staff, he let loose on the "pusillanimity and negative attitude" displayed by the chiefs, "and you are one of the worst," he declared to the indignant Ismay. After another unsatisfactory meeting with his COS and Ismay, Churchill told Colville, "I am obliged to wage modern warfare with ancient weapons."[14]

Sir Ian Jacob recalled that as deferential as Ismay was to his boss and the Chiefs of Staff, Churchill learned quickly that Ismay never allowed the usual feelings of protocol to stand in the way of speed and efficiency of work. "He was without vanity," Jacob later recalled, "and inspired in all those who worked with him the same spirit of loyalty he in such great measure possessed." At about 9:30 each morning (if Churchill hadn't kept Ismay up most of the night), Ismay and Churchill met, the Old Man usually in bed, the early editions of the newspapers strewn hither and yon, the air saturated with the stale aroma of cigars. At these briefings Churchill passed along any memos he had dictated the night before. Most were brief queries or suggestions; some were strongly worded opinions. A memo signed in red ink meant Churchill wanted action. A memo signed in red ink, and affixed with the slip "Action This Day," was the prime ministerial equivalent of a five-alarm fire.[15]

As Ian Jacob later observed, Churchill was "determined to be No. 1 and to use all the political powers of a No. 1 directly." In front of his place at the cabinet table he placed a square of cardboard bearing a quotation from Queen Victoria during the Boer War: "Please understand that we are not interested in the possibilities of defeat. They do not exist."[16]

The impact of all of this on his civil service secretariat was enormous. The journalist Virginia Cowles wrote: "The whole of 10 Downing Street throbbed with an energy it had not seen since the days of Lloyd George."[17]

Parliament was another matter. On his third day in office, Churchill rose in the House of Commons for the first time as prime minister and invited the members to affirm his new government. Harold Nicolson wrote in his diary: "When Chamberlain enters the House he gets a terrific reception, and when Churchill comes in the applause is less." The P.M.'s statement was brief but eloquent; it was then that he said, "I have nothing to offer but blood, toil, tears, and sweat." His peroration was, as usual, a taking of the ramparts by words alone, and, as usual, it was dismissed by his detractors in the Commons and by his enemies in Berlin as typically Churchillian hyperbole, misplaced given unfolding events in France, and perhaps delusional. It was in fact a solemn oath, a statement of literal intent, which admitted to no ambiguity: "You ask, what is our aim? I answer in one word: It is victory, victory at all costs, victory in spite of all terror, victory, however long and hard the road may be, for without victory, there is no survival. Let that be realized; no survival for the British Empire" and all it has stood for, " no survival for the urge and impulse of the ages, that mankind will move forward toward its goal." Labour and Liberal MPs cheered. Many Tories sat silent; they were still fuming over Churchill's ascendancy to No. 10. The historian Laurence Thompson noted: "Conservative anger that the wrong man had been shot over Norway continued for many months."[18]

The campaign for Norway had lasted two months, from early April until early June. By late May, southern and central Norway had been abandoned by British and Norwegian forces, although Narvik, Norway's northernmost ice-free port, had been cleared of Germans by British troops, who, if reinforced, were poised to strike toward the Swedish iron-ore fields so critical to Hitler. Thus to interdict Swedish war shipments had been the objective of the March plan (code-named Wilfred) to lay mines in Norwegian waters. But Wilfred was scotched by Chamberlain and Halifax for fear of offending Norway and Sweden. Narvik (and the million tons of iron ore stored there) had been Churchill's main objective from the start, but by early June, events in France dictated that the cause be abandoned. The evacuation did not go well. On the afternoon of the eighth of June, 1940, the aircraft carrier HMS *Glorious*—fleeing Norway with as many aircraft and men as she could carry—was intercepted in the Norwegian Sea by the German battle cruisers *Gneisenau* and *Scharnhorst*. *Glorious*, and two escorting destroyers, were sunk by gunfire in just over two hours, with the loss of more than 1,500 officers and men of the Royal Navy, Royal Marines, and Royal Air Force. Churchill, first lord of the Admiralty when the Norwegian adventure began, and prime minister when it ended, had already taken responsibility for the disastrous outcome. For much of the remainder of the war, the loss of *Glorious* and the specter of *Gneisenau* and *Scharnhorst* moved Churchill at times to dubious naval strategy. He was still coming to terms with modern naval warfare, and not entirely successfully; the success of the German battle cruisers and the vulnerability of *Glorious* seemed to imply that fast, heavy ships still ruled the waves. In fact, aircraft carriers, if deployed properly, posed a mortal threat to battle cruisers. Hitler, meanwhile, pocketed the Norwegian and Swedish ore, but would pay heavily for those prizes; during the next four years, more than 160,000 of his best troops remained in Norway awaiting the return of the English. Other than shooting Norwegian patriots and chasing down the occasional British commando, more than twelve priceless Wehrmacht divisions would miss the war. Churchill, in turn, became obsessed with returning to Norway, and during the next four years drove his military chiefs to distraction with what Sir Alan Brooke called "his mad Norwegian plans." Hitler, in fact, read Churchill's ambitions exactly.[19]

Because Churchill well understood that criticism of his career centered on his history of questionable strategic judgments and his notoriety for being willing to change sides, his chief political concern was reconciliation with the House, and he made a major effort to do so. He invited Chamberlain into his government both as lord president of the council and leader of the House, and sent him a note: "No one changes houses for a month." Beginning on May 13, his third day in office, he began working at No. 10 afternoons while his predecessor leisurely moved out upstairs, but during those early weeks, he conducted most of HMG's business from Admiralty House, using its drawing room, with its furniture carved with dolphins ("the fish room," he called it), for cabinet meetings. He could scarcely ignore the issues that had divided him and the appeasers for seven years, but his references to them were light, even bantering; introducing one appeaser to his wife, he beamed as he said, "Oh, yes, my dear, he has the Munich medal with bar." He would have been happy to see the last of his foreign secretary and a major appeaser, Lord Halifax, but he kept him in the Foreign Office for the present. This put Churchill in an awkward position with those who had backed him during the lean years and now wanted all "the old crowd" thrown out, but he was adamant. "If we open a quarrel between the past and the present, we shall find that we have lost the future," he said, and, later, "No one had more right than I to pass a sponge across the past. I therefore resisted these disruptive tendencies."[20]

Inevitably politics determined his cabinet choices. He had to form a government with all parties represented, and he hadn't much time. Most senior posts were filled by May 13. Clement Attlee (lord privy seal), Arthur Greenwood (cabinet minister without portfolio), and Ernest Bevin (minister of labour) came from the Labour benches. Bevin's inclusion testified to the true nature of the coalition; he was a former teamster, the son of a domestic servant and unknown father, and most assuredly not one of Churchill's crowd. From the Liberals, Archibald Sinclair, Churchill's longtime friend and second in command of Churchill's battalion in the trenches, went to the Air Ministry. From Churchill's own camp, Sir John

Anderson, a Chamberlain appointee, stayed on as Home Secretary. Leo Amery, Churchill's old friend from Harrow (and sometimes his critic) as well as a pugnacious anti-Chamberlain rebel, was given the India secretariat. Anthony Eden went to the War Office. Only one appointment hit a snag. The problem wasn't political. Churchill wanted Lord Beaverbrook as minister of aircraft production. The King objected. That was understandable: Beaverbrook was a highly controversial figure, objectionable in many ways. However, Churchill was going to need a lot of airplanes soon, and he knew this man had the drive and the ruthlessness to get them one way or another. Beaverbrook, he told Jock Colville, was "twenty-five percent thug, fifteen percent crook and the remainder a combination of genius and real goodness of heart."[21]

The King bowed to his judgment. Churchill did settle one score. Sir John Reith, minister of information and creator of the modern BBC, had barred him from the BBC during the 1930s and, after the war's outbreak, intrigued against him. Churchill fired Reith on May 12 and replaced him with Alfred Duff Cooper, who had quit Chamberlain's government in protest against the Munich Agreement. Churchill soon found new duties for the appeaser Reith, at the Transport Ministry. The War Cabinet—"the only ones," he said, "who had the right to have their heads cut off on Tower Hill if we did not win"—comprised five men: himself, Chamberlain, Attlee, Halifax, and Greenwood.[22]

In the country, where his popularity was soaring, his conciliatory manner toward those who had scorned him was remarked upon and widely praised. Few noticed how he quietly put the greatest possible distance between himself and the most objectionable of them. Sir Samuel Hoare was sent as ambassador to Spain, Lord Harlech to South Africa, Lord Swinton to the African Gold Coast, Malcolm MacDonald to Canada, and, before the year was out, Halifax to the United States. Presently he would use this very effective maneuver to banish the Duke of Windsor, a sometime admirer of the Third Reich, an admiration as narrow and shallow as he was. But Churchill could not banish their abiding doubts of his abilities. On the day Churchill told Halifax he would remain at the Foreign Office, Halifax wrote in his diary, "I have seldom met anyone with stranger gaps of knowledge, or whose mind worked in greater jerks. Will it be possible to make it work in orderly fashion?" Then Halifax answered his own question with such profound understatement as to call into question whether he truly grasped Britain's plight: "On this much depends."[23]

At the outset, Churchill later wrote, "no fresh decision was required from me or my colleagues." Plan D was in operation, British troops had reached the Dyle River, and so, the new prime minister wrote, he did not "in the slightest degree wish to interfere with the military plans"; instead, he merely "awaited with hope the impending shock." The War Cabinet authorized the detention of enemy aliens living in Britain, debated the wisdom and morality of bombing German territory, and approved messages from the P.M. to President Roosevelt and Mussolini. Roosevelt's answer was cordial but disappointing. Churchill had asked for the "loan of 40 or 50 old" U.S. destroyers; the President explained that to honor the request would violate Congress's Neutrality Acts. Il Duce, in reply to Churchill's suggestion to stay out of the fray, was rude. Italy, he bluntly replied, was an ally of Nazi Germany.[24]

The world's eyes were on the Low Countries across the Channel. The British were following this front with special anxiety, aware of the threat to England should the Nazis establish bases that close to Britain. Enemy successes there were spectacular but not really alarming. In the Netherlands 4,000 Nazi parachutists and German infantrymen captured key bridges over the Meuse River and forced a Dutch surrender after the Luftwaffe's terror bombing of Rotterdam, which destroyed 25,000 homes and massacred more than 1,000 (not the 30,000 claimed by the Dutch government, a figure that terrified Britons). Meantime, in Belgium, German airborne troops and specially picked paratroopers had crossed the Albert Kanaal and seized the country's mighty Fort Eben-Emael. Nazi infantry then turned southward to take Liège from the rear.[25]

But the Belgian, French, and British troops were fighting well. Despite furious German assaults, the Dyle Line had not been breached. Two enemy divisions briefly penetrated it in a tangled railroad yard near Louvain, but the Tommies of General Bernard Montgomery's 3rd Division swiftly routed them.

South of Louvain two panzer divisions, supported by waves of Junkers Ju 87s—"Stuka" dive-bombers—mounted an even stronger attack on the grounds of an agricultural school at Gembloux. Instantly General Jean-Georges-Maurice Blanchard ordered a counterattack by the French First Army. These were crack troops, descendants of the poilus whose valor, inspired by the tricolor and their fierce national anthem, had awed Europe in the century and a half since the French Revolution.

They drove the Germans back and back, and Gamelin felt vindicated. This, he said, proved that he had anticipated the German *schwerpunkt;* the Nazis had come where he expected them to come, and the Allied Line was unbroken. The British were less sure. The RAF had not been caught on the ground, but it had been battered in the air. On Sunday, May 12, Air Chief Marshal Sir Cyril Newall reported "undue losses of medium bombers in relation to the results attained," and on Monday, when the Chiefs of Staff committee met in Admiralty House, with Churchill in the chair for the first time as minister of defence, the consensus was that "it was not yet certain" where the enemy's main effort was to be made. General Ironside, Chief of the Imperial Staff, believed the Germans might be consolidating their position on this front before mounting an offense elsewhere, possibly "an intensive air attack in Great Britain." Churchill thought the situation "far from satisfactory." One officer noticed an ominous sign. The Luftwaffe bombers, he pointed out, had achieved air superiority over the northern battlefield, yet they were leaving columns of French reinforcements marching to the front unmolested. Why should the Germans want more Allied troops on this front?[26]

No one, not even Pétain, had declared the Ardennes Forest to be *absolutely* impenetrable, though his error was equally egregious. What he had said was that the Ardennes was "impassable to strong forces." In fact it was good tank country, with many fields and trails. The French should have known that—they had held maneuvers there in 1939. The forest's trees were actually an asset, serving to camouflage armor and troop movements from aerial surveillance.

The German strategy in 1940 could be summed up in the code word by which the Wehrmacht general staff in Zossen anointed the operation: "*Sichelschnitt*," or "scythe cut." Here, as in Poland, the scythe would exploit the Reich's new concept of warfare: deep penetration of enemy territory by mobile armored forces, with infantry following. In planning his drive, Hitler had divided his forces into three army groups. The one that had struck in the Low Countries comprised thirty divisions, including three panzer divisions. A second, tying down the Maginot Line, in the west, was given nineteen divisions. The great blow would be delivered in the center by the third: forty-five divisions, including seven panzer divisions, commanded by Gerd von Rundstedt. This juggernaut would plunge through Luxembourg and the Ardennes, and vault over the Meuse River north and south of Sedan, some 70 miles southwest of Liège, on the east bank of the Meuse and a dozen miles inside France. That would put the main German force at a point roughly 125 miles from Paris and 175 miles from the Channel ports of Calais, Gravelines, and Dunkirk. The German high command knew the Allies were vulnerable in the Sedan sector; the line was thinly held by two French armies of older, poorly trained, and ill-equipped married men.

The French high command had estimated that it would take at least fifteen days for any strong enemy force to negotiate the thickets and deep wooded ravines of the Ardennes. The Germans, who had rehearsed elaborately in the Black Forest, did it in two, sweeping Belgian infantrymen before them. To the horror of the unprepared French defenders in the vicinity of Sedan, on Sunday the twelfth, the mechanized spearhead of Rundstedt's seven panzer divisions—1,800 tanks, 17,000 other vehicles, and 98,000 men—appeared on the east bank of the Meuse. The answer to the question of why the Luftwaffe had allowed French reinforcements to drift northward toward Holland had arrived with terrible certainty: the real *schwerpunkt* was at Sedan.

The Meuse, the Nazis had known, would be their most forbidding obstacle. It was narrow and swift at this point; confronting the attackers on the far bank were well-placed batteries of heavy artillery. That would have sufficed in 1918, but this was a different war. On Monday, Rundstedt silenced every French field piece, every howitzer, by skillful use of tactical air—Stukas and other low-level bombers—which so terrorized the gunners that they abandoned their cannons. Nazi rubber boats reached the opposite shore unmolested; beachheads were established north and south of Sedan; pontoon bridges spanned the Meuse, then heavy bridges, and, finally, on Tuesday morning, lumbering and growling, came the Nazi tanks. By noon on Tuesday, May 14, the Germans had established a formidable pocket on French soil, three miles wide and two miles deep.

It was time, and past time, for a French counterattack. At 5:30 P.M. on the thirteenth, orders were issued, and a strong force of French tanks advanced, backed by the infantry of the 55th Division. History's first great battle of mechanized armor seemed imminent. The French position was far from hopeless. The German flank was exposed to the French tanks, and not all the panzers, artillery, and infantry were across the Meuse and in position. French tanks were well armored; many carried 75mm cannon, heavier than the guns on many German tanks. Unfortunately, the French chose not to mass their tanks for a steel-fisted assault, instead dispersing them along too broad a front. More unfortunately, the *Conseil Supérieur de la Guerre,* having determined that armor was to be used only in support of infantry, had forbidden the installation of radios in their turrets. The French drivers, unable to communicate with one another, could not coordinate an assault. The consequence was disastrous. Within two hours of the battle opening on the fourteenth, the panzers had destroyed fifty French tanks; the rest, a few dozen, fled.

That was the small disaster. The great disaster began sometime between 6:00 and 7:00 P.M., when, according to the French corps commander, "the situation evolved with a disconcerting rapidity toward catastrophe." Bluntly put, the defenders panicked. Men threw down their rifles and ran, crowding the roads, and they did not stop until they had reached Reims, sixty miles away. Few officers tried to discourage them. One who did later recalled their response. "Colonel," they said, "we want to go home, back to our little jobs (*nos petit boulots*). There's no use trying to fight. There's nothing we can do. We're lost! We've been betrayed!"[27]

In a well-disciplined army they would have been shot on the spot. But everyone, officers and men, seemed infected with the fear, which spread. "The roof fell in," wrote William L. Shirer. One regiment after another broke, until the entire Ninth Army—some two hundred thousand men—ceased to exist. A dazed divisional commander wandered into the army's headquarters to report: "Of my division I fear I am the only one left." The Second Army, on the right flank of the Ninth, fell back. Meantime the Germans, who were arriving in great numbers, began to capture them. Charles de Gaulle, moving up to take command of a brigade, was shocked to see "many soldiers who had lost their weapons.... Caught up, as they fled, by the enemy's mechanized detachments, they had been ordered to throw away their arms and make off to the south so as not to clutter up the roads. 'We haven't time,' they had been told, 'to take you prisoners!'"[28]

The French defensive line was now breached by a hole sixty miles wide, and German armor, followed by infantry, was streaming through it. Incredibly, no one in Paris knew what was happening. Field commanders, ashamed to report the truth, played down the debacle, assuring General Georges' headquarters that everything was under control, and hour by hour Georges relayed their optimism to Gamelin in Vincennes. As late as Wednesday, when the Battle of the Meuse was over and the French hopelessly routed, Gamelin's communiqué reported: "To sum up, the day of May 15 seems to show a lessening in the intensity of enemy action.... Our front, which was 'shaken' ('*ébranlé*') between Namur and the region west of Montmédy, is reestablishing itself little by little."

One man knew better. It says much about France's military establishment that the first Parisian to learn the truth was a civilian: Paul Reynaud. The premier had studied the possibilities of tank warfare, and he had spies in the army, informers who sent him word of what was actually happening. At 5:45 P.M. on Tuesday, May 14, the fifth day of the enemy offensive, he wired Churchill: "The situation is indeed very serious. Germany is trying to deal us a fatal blow in the direction of Paris. The German army has broken through our fortified lines south of Sedan.... Between Sedan and Paris there are no defenses comparable with those in the line, which we must restore at almost any cost." He then asked for ten more Royal Air Force squadrons "immediately."[29]

The prime minister told Ironside to check this; the CIGS (Chief of the Imperial General Staff) sent a liaison officer "to find out what the real situation is." Later in the day Ironside told Churchill, "We could get nothing out of" either Gamelin or Georges. Ironside suggested that perhaps Reynaud was being "a little hysterical." But the French premier knew he was right. At seven o'clock the next morning he woke Churchill with an anguished telephone call. "We have been defeated!" he cried in English. "We are beaten! We have lost the battle!" The P.M., his mind still mired in the trenches of 1914–1918, said, "Surely it can't have happened so soon!" As Churchill recalled afterward, Reynaud replied, "The front is broken near Sedan; they are pouring through in great numbers with tanks and armored cars." Churchill told him, "All experience shows that the offensive will come to an end after a while." Within five or six days, he said, the enemy would have to halt for supplies; that would be the moment for a counterattack. But the premier repeated, "We are defeated; we have lost the battle." Churchill said he was willing to come over "and have a talk."[30]

Ringing up Ironside, the prime minister repeated the conversation, commenting that Reynaud had seemed "thoroughly demoralized." Ironside told him that "we have no extra demands from Gamelin or Georges, both of whom are calm, though they both consider the situation serious." The P.M. then called Georges, an old friend. Georges, quite cool, reported that the breach at Sedan was "being plugged." But late that afternoon Reynaud sent another message: "Last week we lost the battle. The way to Paris lies open. Send all the troops and planes you can." Churchill sent four squadrons of fighters, then decided it was "imperative to go to Paris." At 3:00 P.M. on May 16 he took off in an unarmed Flamingo, a civilian passenger plane, accompanied by General Ismay, General Sir John Dill, and Inspector Walter Thompson of Scotland Yard, a fifty-year-old ex-copper who had served as Churchill's bodyguard a decade earlier and had been called out of retirement to again protect the Great Man.

Over the French coast the prime minister peered down, and Thompson saw his face go gray. Churchill was looking, for the first time, at the war's refugees. There were now over seven million of them fleeing from the Germans, swarming down the highways, shuffling, exhausted, aching from the strain of heavy loads on their backs. No one had told them to evacuate the battlefields; they were evacuating themselves. Barns, sheds, and garages had disgorged into throughways an extraordinary collection of vehicles: farm carts, trucks, horse-drawn carts, hay wagons, and ancient automobiles saddled with sagging loads of mattresses, kitchen utensils, family treasures, and bric-a-brac. Cars bombed by the Luftwaffe stood in flames, and here and there among straggling vagabonds lay corpses of children and the very old, who, unable to keep up, had been machine-gunned by Nazi pilots who saw panic as an ally of their comrades in the Wehrmacht.[31]

In their memoirs the generals on both sides would complain about the obstacles these people created, but the refugees looked at it differently, and

Churchill saw it their way. The great tragedy was coming into focus for Churchill. He was also beginning to understand Reynaud's alarm. He later wrote: "Not having had access to official information for so many years, I did not comprehend the revolution effected since the last war by the incursion of a mass of fast-moving heavy armour." This Nazi drive would not have to pause for supplies; as de Gaulle had foreseen, the panzers were filling their tanks at the filling stations of northern France.[32]

The prime minister's Flamingo landed at Le Bourget, and as they alighted, Ismay felt "an unmistakable atmosphere of depression." Events were moving swiftly in Paris. Gamelin foresaw the end. William Bullitt, the American ambassador, had been with Daladier when the *généralissime* called to break the news. He had told them: "It means the destruction of the French army. Between Laon and Paris I do not have a single corps at my disposal." The panic had reached the French capital. Parisians realized that there were an extraordinary number of automobiles with Belgian license plates on the streets "just passing through," the drivers told them; "the Boche is right behind us." Everyone seemed to know that Gamelin had told the highest officials of the republic, "*Je ne répons plus de rien*" ("I am no longer responsible for anything").[33]

At the Quai d'Orsay Reynaud, Daladier, and Gamelin awaited the British in a large room looking out on a garden "which," Ismay wrote, "had appeared so lovely and well-kept on my last visit, but which was now disfigured with clusters of bonfires." The French were burning their official papers. This was Churchill's first meeting as a member of the Allied Supreme War Council, and Ismay was "interested to see how he handled the situation."

He dominated the proceedings from the moment he entered the room. There was no interpreter, and he spoke throughout in French. His idiom was not always correct, and his vocabulary was not equal to translating with exactitude all the words that he required. But no one could have been in any doubt as to his meaning.[34]

He began by telling them that although their plight was grave, this was not the first time they had been in a crisis together; the Ludendorff offensives of early 1918 had nearly destroyed them and their ally, the United States. He was confident that they would survive this one. Then he asked for a briefing. Gamelin gave it. Stepping up to a map on an easel, he talked for five minutes, describing the Germans' breakthrough. He said they were advancing with unprecedented speed. Their intentions were unknown; they could reach the coast or turn on Paris. At the end Churchill slapped him heartily on the shoulder—the general winced—and told him that this would become known as "the Battle of the Bulge." ("Boogle" was the closest he could come to this.) Then he asked him where his strategic reserve was: *"Où est la masse de manoeuvre?"* Gamelin shook his head and replied: *"Aucune."* He had none.

There was a long pause while Churchill, speechless, stared absently at the elderly men carrying wheelbarrows of documents to the fires. *No strategic reserve.* It had never occurred to him that commanders defending five hundred miles of engaged front would have left themselves without reserves; no one could defend with certainty so wide a front, but when the enemy broke the line, the defenders should have a mass of divisions ready to counterattack. He was, he wrote, "dumbfounded."[35]

After the war it was Churchill's recollection, confirmed by Ismay, that he did not argue strategy with Reynaud, Daladier, and Gamelin. "There couldn't have been a disagreement," he said. "We didn't know enough about the situation to disagree." However, the French notes on this point are quite detailed. According to them, Churchill vigorously opposed ordering a general retreat by the Allied troops in Belgium. This, the P.M. said, was a time to "hold fast." He did not believe the panzer breakthrough was "a real invasion." As long as the tanks were "not supported by infantry units," they were merely "little flags stuck on the map," because they would be "unable to support themselves or to refuel." The French records quote him as telling them, "I refuse to see in this spectacular raid of the German tanks a real invasion."[36]

Churchill may not have *argued* strategy that day, but he proposed one—to hold fast—and it was unrealistic. It was characteristic of him that he always approved of attacks, and seldom retreats, even when, as here, failure to withdraw would mean encirclement and annihilation. Reynaud silenced him by pointing out that all the field commanders, including Lord Gort, believed the French should fall back.[37]

Churchill was, however, thoroughly justified in asking Gamelin when and where he proposed to attack the flanks of the German bulge. The *généralissime*'s dismaying, unresponsive reply was "inferiority of numbers, inferiority of equipment, inferiority of method," followed by a hopeless shrug of the shoulders. The *généralissime* saw only one hope of salvation: the commitment of six more RAF squadrons to the battle. It was, he said, the only way to stop the panzers.

Churchill vigorously replied that tanks should be the target of artillery, not of fighter planes; fighters should "cleanse the skies" (*"nett le ciel"*) over the battle. Bombing the Meuse bridges was not a proper job for the RAF; nevertheless they had attempted to do it, at great risk, and had lost thirty-six aircraft. "You can replace bridges," he said, "but not fighters." He had just sent four more squadrons, forty-eight planes, and it was vital that Britain's metropolitan air force be available to command the air over

Britain in order to protect defense factories from the Luftwaffe. Britain had only a limited number of squadrons in England, and, he said, "We must conserve them." He did not think another six squadrons would "make the difference."

Daladier replied, "The French believe the contrary." The discussion became acrimonious. Gamelin had touched a vital nerve. Both sides were, to a degree, disingenuous. What the French really believed was that the British should throw everything they had into the struggle for France, and that if the Allied cause were to lose, both countries should go down together. The British believed that if France went down—and they were beginning to contemplate that possibility—Britain and the Empire should go on alone. That was why Air Chief Marshal Sir Hugh Dowding had put himself on record as "absolutely opposed to parting with a single additional Hurricane."

At the British embassy that evening, the prime minister weighed the French appeal. He should have rejected it, but his sympathy for them outweighed his reason, and he wired the War Cabinet that they should give this "last chance to the French Army to rally its bravery and strength. It would not be good historically if their requests were denied and their ruin resulted." The War Cabinet was apprehensive, but it was difficult to say no to the P.M. They reluctantly agreed, provided the Hurricanes returned to English bases each night. In the interests of security this decision was sent to Ismay, a veteran of the Indian army, in Hindi—*"Han,"* for "yes."[38]

In Paris the embassy staff assumed that the good news would be telephoned to the French. Churchill insisted upon delivering it in person. "This," Ismay comments, "was in character." Churchill reminded him of someone giving children presents and wanting to see the expressions on their faces as they opened their gifts: "He was about to give Reynaud a pearl beyond price, and he wanted to watch his expression as he received it." To the P.M.'s surprise, the premier had left his office—it was midnight—so he sought directions to his home. That was awkward. Reynaud and his mistress, Mme la Comtesse de Portes, were living in a small apartment on the Place du Palais-Bourbon, hiding from his wife. Nevertheless Churchill and Ismay eventually found him there. Receiving them in his bathrobe, he thanked them profusely. Then Churchill insisted that he summon Daladier, with whom the premier was barely on speaking terms. The war minister left *his* mistress, Mme la Marquise de Crussol, to come and wring their hands in silent gratitude.[39]

Back in London, the prime minister found nothing but problems defying solution. Another one hundred thousand Belgians had arrived in Britain, begging for shelter, and every report from the Continent told of a continuing

German advance. The P.M.'s mood was defiant. Roosevelt reaffirmed the impossibility of loaning Britain U.S. destroyers. As well, a strict reading of the Neutrality Act of 1939 forced Roosevelt to deny Churchill's request to send an aircraft carrier to America to pick up some of the more than three hundred Curtiss P-40 fighter planes awaiting shipment. During these months American aircraft purchased by Britain had to be flown to the Canadian border, where, in order to abide by U.S. laws preventing transshipment, they were pushed or towed (often by horse) across the border before continuing on, by ship, to England. The P-40s, Churchill was told, would be ready for delivery in two or three months. After digesting Roosevelt's decisions, he wrote a cordial reply and then growled to Colville: "Here's a telegram for those bloody Yankees. Send it off tonight." It was Trinity Sunday. Clementine attended services at St. Martin-in-the-Fields and returned indignant. The rector had preached a pacifist sermon and Clementine had walked out. Churchill said: "You ought to have cried 'Shame,' desecrating the house of God with lies!"[40]

That evening—May 19—he was to address the nation over the radio. He was driven to Chartwell, soon to be closed for the war's duration. There he could visit his goldfish, sit in the sun, and reflect, but he found no peace there. He wanted to feed his black swans, but to his consternation he found that foxes had eaten all but one. Then Anthony Eden called. The matter was urgent, and would become more so in the days ahead. Lord Gort had just called. The French army south of the BEF had melted away, leaving a vast gap on the British right. He was in a dilemma. He could leave the Belgians to their fate and fight southward to rejoin the French, or he could fall back on the Channel ports and fight it out with his back to the sea. His preference was to withdraw toward Dunkirk. Ironside had told him that "this proposal could not be accepted at all." Churchill, always against retreat, agreed. In Dunkirk, he said, the BEF would be "closely invested in a bomb-trap, and its total loss would be only a matter of time."[41]

After forty years in the House of Commons, Churchill instinctively swung his head from left to right. That would not do on the BBC, so Tyrone Guthrie of the Old Vic stood behind him and held his ears firmly as he spoke at a desk in a small room, his text illuminated by a green lamp. Addressing the country, he began:

> I speak to you for the first time as Prime Minister in a solemn hour for the life of our country, of our Empire, of our Allies, and above all of the cause of Freedom. A tremendous battle is raging in France and Flanders. The Germans, by a remarkable combination of air bombing and heavily armored tanks, have broken through the French defenses north of the Maginot Line, and strong columns of their armored vehi-

> cles are ravaging the open country, which for the first day or two was without defenders.... Side by side, the British and French peoples have advanced to rescue not only Europe but mankind from the foulest and most soul-destroying tyranny which has ever darkened and stained the pages of history. Behind them, behind the Armies and Fleets of Britain and France, gather a group of shattered states and bludgeoned races: the Czechs, the Poles, the Norwegians, the Danes, the Dutch, the Belgians upon all of whom the long night of barbarism will descend, unbroken even by a star of hope, unless we conquer, as conquer we must; as conquer we shall.[42]

"At last the country is awake and working," wrote the diehard Tory Tom Jones.

"The hour has struck," wrote the commander of the Portsmouth Naval Base, Admiral Sir William Milbourne James, "and the man has appeared."[43]

Churchill had spoken of the French "genius for recovery and counterattack, for which they have long been famous," adding, "I have invincible confidence in the French army." He may have believed it. He had always been an arch-Francophile; in 1916, commanding a British battalion in the trenches, he had worn a poilu's helmet to show his confidence in England's ally. Thus far, Fleet Street had supported this view: "One hears," Mollie Panter-Downes reported in *The New Yorker,* "nothing but admiration for the heroic French resistance." But Gamelin was no Foch, and his troops were not the soldiers of 1914–1918. After the men on both sides had laid down their arms, a group of American war correspondents toured the scenes of struggle and concluded, in the words of William L. Shirer, that "France did not fight.... None of us saw evidence of serious fighting. The fields of France are undisturbed. There was no fighting on any sustained line... no attempt to come to a halt on a line and strike back in a well-organized counter-attack."[44]

The Führer's *Panzergruppen* had roared down unmined roads, passed unmolested under overlooking heights unsited with artillery. Strategic bridges had been unblown. French prisoners said they had seen no combat; whenever battle seemed imminent, they were ordered to retreat. The Channel ports, notably Boulogne and Calais, had been defended mostly by the British. Shirer thought the defending armies seemed to have been "paralyzed as soon as the Germans made their first break-through. The French, as though drugged, had no will to fight, even when their soil was invaded by their most hated enemy. It was a complete collapse of French society and of the French soul."[45]

Even Churchill had begun to have doubts about the French. The day before his Sunday broadcast, debating whether to send Britain's 1st Armored Division to Gamelin, he had told Ismay: "One must always be prepared for the fact that the French may be offered very advantageous terms of peace, and the whole weight be thrown on us." Gamelin himself had all but abandoned hope. Saturday evening he had calmly explained "the causes of our defeat" to Reynaud. It was the ninth day of the battle, and the *généralissime* was ready to quit. Even the hopelessly overmatched Poles had held out for three weeks.[46]

On Monday, May 20, the 2nd Panzer Division reached Abbéville, at the mouth of the Somme, and Noyelles on the coast. The Germans had cut France in half, thereby trapping a million Allied soldiers in the north, including the Belgian army, more than half the BEF, and the First and Seventh French Armies—France's best troops. It was a stunning triumph. But it was also the hour of the Nazis' maximum danger. Their tanks had created a corridor almost two hundred miles long and twenty miles wide, from the Ardennes to the Channel, but they had outdistanced the Wehrmacht's foot soldiers, and tanks alone could not hold the German gains against determined counterattacks. They would be vulnerable until their infantry arrived in strength.

Hitler knew it and was frightened. In his aerie he envisaged a second Marne, with the French rallying and striking back with a deadly blow. Jodl noted: "The Führer is terribly nervous. He is worried over his own success, will risk nothing and insists on restraining us.... He rages and screams that we are on the way to ruining the whole operation and that we are in danger of a defeat."

This was, in fact, the critical moment; everything that followed turned upon it. As a disillusioned Churchill told the House of Commons four weeks later:

> The colossal military disaster... occurred when the French High Command failed to withdraw the northern armies from Belgium at the moment when they knew that the French front was decisively broken at Sedan and on the Meuse. This delay entailed the loss of fifteen or sixteen French divisions and threw out of action for the critical period the whole of the British Expeditionary Force, a total of twenty-five divisions of the best-trained and best equipped troops [which] may have turned the scale.[47]

Gamelin finally saw it. On Sunday he drew up "Instruction No. 12," ordering two offensives: the troops in the north were to fight south across the tank corridor while French troops on the Somme drove northward, cutting off the 2nd Panzer Division. But on Monday, before he could issue the orders, Reynaud sacked him and chose seventy-three-year-old General Maxime Weygand as his successor, a short, spruce, fox-faced officer who, as one Englishman said, resembled an "aged jockey." Weygand had never before commanded troops in battle; he had made his reputation as a staff officer. He was a political general, a monarchist, a hero of the militantly conservative Croix de Feu, and an Anglophobe. Despite his age he was exceptionally vigorous, but he had arrived in Paris exhausted, recalled from Syria; immediately after assuming command he went to bed. Before retiring he canceled Gamelin's Instruction No. 12.

The situation in the corridor was fluid. Every hour was critical now. The gap between the German armor and its supporting formations was closing. Yet when the new *généralissime* woke, he announced that he would tour the front before making a decision. By the time he returned and reissued the order, the corridor was thick with defenders. After four strenuous days the enemy had strengthened it by rushing infantry and motorized artillery to beef up both sides of it. The chance had passed.

At 6:30 P.M. Monday, a British officer had wired London that Luftwaffe bombers had severed rail service between Amiens and Abbéville, and that night, panzers at Abbéville cut off the British army's supply bases and the French armies in the south. Ironside, returning from France Tuesday morning, reported that another enemy tank column had been sighted passing Frévent, "probably making for Boulogne." There was "nothing wrong with the French troops themselves," he said, but the commanders seemed "paralyzed." In his diary he wrote, "Personally I think we cannot extricate the B.E.F.... God help the B.E.F., brought to this state by the incompetence of the French command." Dill, who was with Georges, telegraphed that a northward drive by the French was "improbable."[48]

"In London," Ismay wrote, "we felt we were being harshly treated by the French High Command... they had told us nothing, and we were completely in the dark." Aware of the constantly shifting face of the battle, Churchill tried again and again to reach Reynaud by telephone. It was impossible. All lines between Paris and London had been cut. He told Colville, "In all the history of war I have never known such mismanagement." In his diary Colville commented: "I have not seen Winston so depressed." Desperate for information, the prime minister, against the advice of the Chiefs of Staff, decided to fly to Paris the following morning, Wednesday, May 22.[49]

The Flamingo landed at Le Bourget shortly before noon; the P.M. and his party went straight to the *généralissime*'s GHQ in the Château de Vincennes, an old fort suggestive of *Beau Geste*, guarded by Algerian troops dressed in white cloaks and bearing long curved swords. Weygand, greeting them, "was brisk, buoyant, and incisive," Churchill wrote. "He made an excellent impression on us all." Telling them that the panzers "must not be allowed to keep the initiative, he gave them a detailed description of what instantly became known as the Weygand Plan. It was Gamelin's Instruction No. 12, too late, though the British had no way of knowing that then. Churchill put it in writing "to make sure there was no mistake about what was settled." After the *généralissime* and Reynaud approved the text, it was telegraphed to the War Cabinet in London.

Specifically, the plan provided for an attack southward "at the earliest moment, certainly tomorrow," by eight divisions of the BEF and the French First Army. Simultaneously, a "new French Army Group" of between eighteen and twenty divisions, after forming a line upon the Somme, would "strike northward and join hands with the British divisions who are attacking southward in the general direction of Bapaume." The more Churchill thought about it, the better he liked it. That evening, Ironside noted, "Winston came back from Paris about 6:30 P.M. and we had a Cabinet at 7:30 P.M. He was almost in buoyant spirits, having been impressed by Weygand."[50]

The plan was impossible—all of it. The Allied forces in the north could not drive southward; all were heavily engaged with the enemy. And Weygand's own orders to his divisions in the south merely directed them to recapture local objectives. "The Weygand plan," as William L. Shirer later wrote, "existed only in the General's mind." It may not have existed even there. As Shirer noted, "no French troops ever moved up from the Somme."[51]

And Gort received no instructions from Vincennes. Indeed, he had heard nothing from GHQ for four days. Learning of this at 4:50 the following afternoon, Churchill called Reynaud—the lines were open again—to ask why. The voices on the other end were incoherent. At 6:00 P.M. he called again. This time he reached Weygand, who had thrilling news: his new French army in the south had already thrown the Germans back and retaken Amiens, Albert, and Péronne. In Admiralty House, Colville noted that this reversal of fortunes was greeted as "stupendous"; "gloom gave way to elation."[52]

It was a lie. Weygand had known from the beginning that the Allied cause was doomed. His only hope, he had told Georges on May 20, was *"sauver l'honneur des armées françaises"* ("save the honor of the French armies"), whatever that meant. His distrust of England and Englishmen was profound, though not unusual among Frenchmen with his convictions. Reviewing his deception, Colville later concluded that "Weygand was determined...that *we* should go under if *he* did." It is also possible that he was looking for a scapegoat. If so, he found one, and found him quickly. On Tuesday, the day before Churchill's flight to Vincennes, Gort had attempted to break the enemy's encircling line with an attack on the

German flank. He set his sights on Arras and went after it with two British divisions, supported by sixty light French tanks. The enemy commander, then unknown, was Erwin Rommel. The action was unexpected; Rommel reported a "heavy British counterattack with armour." On Wednesday Gort saw that a heavy German force was preparing to move against both his flanks, and he withdrew.[53]

Weygand heard about this Thursday morning. He angrily demanded that Reynaud protest, and the premier sent Churchill—who didn't even know of Gort's attack—two reproachful telegrams, which concluded: "General Weygand's orders must be obeyed." The *généralissime* put his protest in writing, declaring that "as a result of the British retreat" the drive southward had to be abandoned. It was at this point that Churchill assigned Edward Spears* the delicate task of improving relations between the two allies. Spears was half French and completely bilingual, a Conservative MP who had been a friend of Churchill's since the Edwardian era. They had been fellow officers in World War I, in which Spears had been wounded four times. He left a striking description of Churchill at the height of the war's first crisis. Summoned to Admiralty House in the middle of the night he found Churchill:

> ... sitting relaxed and rotund in an arm-chair at his desk. He offered me a cigar, looked at me a moment as if I were a lens through which he was gazing at something beyond, then the kindliest, friendliest expression spread over his face as he focused me, his face puckered in a lovable baby-like grin, then he was grave again. "I have decided," he said, "to send you as my personal representative to Paul Reynaud. You will have the rank of a Major General. See Pug.† He will brief you. The situation is very grave."[54]

It was more than grave. It was catastrophic. Now all France, like ancient Gaul, was divided into three parts:

In the south, below the Somme—where Weygand actually planned to make his stand—lay 90 percent of France, including Paris. It was no longer the serene France of those early spring days, however. Spears reported that the roads were choked with refugees, top-heavy wagons, and

---

* He appears in volume 1 of this work as Edward Spiers. He changed the spelling of his name in 1918.

† Ismay, who looked like one.

"cars with boiling radiators." Over three hundred thousand poilus, members of military formations which no longer existed, were roaming the countryside; some, he reported, had shot their officers and were "robbing passers-by in the forests near Paris." French officers, captured by the Germans but given their parole, had returned to their homes, seemed to be enjoying their families, and weren't even interested in news of the fighting.

In the north, a desperate amalgam of Allied forces—more than half the BEF, the Belgians, and three French armies—was fighting for survival.

Between the two, a broadening, solidifying belt of enemy territory stretched across France from the Sedan, in the east, to Abbéville on the coast. Capturing Paris was every German's dream, and the panzers could have turned that way.

Instead they had wheeled northward and were driving toward the Channel ports, historically England's last line against invasion.

Churchill was aware of the danger. On the Sunday before his flight to Vincennes, Ironside had warned him that the BEF might soon be cut off from the French, in which case they could only be supplied through Boulogne, Calais, and Dunkirk. Now all three had been heavily bombed by the Luftwaffe the previous night. Dunkirk could not be used; ships sunk by the Nazis blocked its entrance. On Tuesday, Boulogne, directly in the path of the panzers, was reinforced by the 20th Guards Brigade and the Irish and Welsh Guards, the last available army units still in England. It was in vain; the German armored columns were irresistible; on Wednesday, while Churchill was being introduced to Weygand, evacuations were under way there. In his diary, Ironside wrote: "4 *p.m.* Boulogne was definitely gone.... So goes all the people in Boulogne, including the two Guards battalions. A rotten ending indeed." He added: "Gort is very nearly surrounded.... I don't see that we have much hope of getting the B.E.F. out." But the following evening he noted: "The German mobile columns have definitely been halted for some reason or other."[55]

Although no one realized it at the time, this was one of the turning points in the war. The "Halt Order" (*Haltordnung*), as it came to be known, has been endlessly debated. Had the panzers continued to advance, evacuation of the BEF would have been impossible. Yet the reasons for the pause seem clear. Rundstedt needed time for the German infantry to catch up with his tanks. Moreover, after fourteen days of offensive action, the men were exhausted and their machines badly in need of repairs.

Hitler lengthened the halt. Two days of downpours had made the Flanders swamps virtually impassable for armored vehicles. General Heinz Guderian, the panzer leader, who had first opposed the halt, conceded that "a tank attack is pointless in the marshy country which has been completely soaked by the rain.... The infantry forces of this army are more suitable than tanks for fighting in this kind of country."[56]

Moreover, the Nazis' chief enemy continued to be France, and they did not believe they had already defeated what was considered the best army in Europe. Their push toward Paris, they believed, would be long and bloody. They needed to refit for that. Finally, they did not know that they had trapped 400,000 French, Belgian, and British men in the north. Afterward, Luftwaffe general Albert Kesselring said: "Even 100,000 would have struck us as greatly exaggerated."[57]

Leaders in both Paris and London continued to debate impractical plans. On Friday, May 24, Weygand bitterly complained that "the British Army has carried out, on its own initiative, a retreat of forty kilometers towards the ports when our troops moving up from the south are gaining ground towards the north, where they were to meet their allies." In another sharp telegram to London, Reynaud commented that the British action "has naturally compelled General Weygand to modify his arrangements" and that he has been forced to abandon "any idea" of uniting the Allied armies. His Majesty's Government was disconcerted. Ironside wrote: "Why Gort has done this I don't know. He has never told us what he was going to do or even when he had done it." In his reply to Reynaud, Churchill said that "no doubt the action was forced on Lord Gort." This was "no time for recriminations," he said, though he conceded that Gort should have kept him informed and that he did not doubt that the French "had grounds for complaint."[58]

They had none. Weygand's troops still weren't advancing, and Gort had not retreated. However, with each passing hour the commander of the BEF realized that he would have to do something, and soon. His army—the only army Britain had—was in mortal danger, nearly encircled, trapped in a pocket seventy miles from the sea and only fifteen to twenty-five miles across. Their lines of communications had been cut. Their only allies were the Belgians and the remnants of the First French Army. The ports through which the BEF's two hundred thousand men were supplied were either bombed out or already in enemy hands. The Tommies were down to a four-day supply of ammunition and rations. Panzers were in Gravelines, barely ten miles from Dunkirk, the BEF's last remaining port of escape. The panzers were closing in, and the Belgians were on the verge of surrender; already their last link with General Alan Brooke's corps, northeast of Menin, had been broken, creating a breach between which the Nazis would pour once they found it.

Of the Channel ports, only Calais and Dunkirk were still free. The army might be cut off from them at any time. In his diary Brooke wrote: "Nothing but a miracle can save the B.E.F. now, and the end cannot be far off." The British had lost all confidence in General G. H. Billotte, the

French commander in the north. Ironside, calling at Billotte's command post on May 20, had been horrified. He wrote of him: "No plan, no thought of a plan. Ready to be slaughtered. Defeated at the head without casualties. *Très fatigué* and nothing doing. I lost my temper and shook Billotte by the button of his tunic. The man is completely beaten."[59]

John Standish, the 6th Viscount Gort of Limerick—"Jack" to his fellow generals—was not greatly admired by them. At best, the French said, he would be a good battalion commander. He lacked intellect, said the British staff officers (Gamelin's intellect had been much admired in London, and even in Berlin). But Gort's courage was extraordinary. As a Guards officer in the last war, he had won the Victoria Cross, three Distinguished Service Orders, and the Military Cross. He was, if anything, an overdisciplined soldier, and now he faced an excruciating decision. He had heard nothing from Weygand for four days. Ironside had brought him orders from the War Cabinet, specifically forbidding a withdrawal to the sea, telling him, instead, to attack southward. But now he knew that only annihilation awaited him there. In Berlin, Germany's foreign minister Ribbentrop had already told the press: "The French army will be destroyed and the English on the Continent will be made prisoners of war." Rommel wrote in his diary: "Now the hunt is up against sixty encircled British, French and Belgian divisions."

During the afternoon of Saturday, May 25, Gort received a distress signal from Brooke: "I am convinced that the Belgian army is closing down and will have stopped fighting by this time tomorrow. This, of course, entirely exposes our left flank." Lieutenant General Sir Ronald Adam, the army's other corps commander, confirmed Brooke. Gort's reserves were gone. The only British soldiers not engaged with the enemy were two divisions, the 5th and the 50th, which were awaiting orders to open the southern attack the next day. In his command post at Prémesques, he spent most of that afternoon staring at wall maps of northern France and the Channel ports. At 6:30 P.M. he canceled the offensive and dispatched the 5th Division to plug the gap on Brooke's flank. Then he wired Eden, telling him what he had done and why he had done it.

The telegram was delayed. At 10:30 that evening, before it could arrive, Churchill independently reached the same conclusion. After consulting Reynaud, he instructed Eden to telegraph Gort: "It is clear…that it will not be possible for French to deliver attack in the south.…You are now authorized to operate towards coast forthwith in conjunction with the French and Belgian armies." The formal evacuation order reached Prémesques the next day, Monday, May 27.

A week earlier, King Leopold had informed the British through Admiral of the Fleet Sir Roger Keyes that should his troops lose contact with the French and British, "capitulation would be inevitable." Leopold also personally warned his fellow monarch George VI of Belgium's "imminent surrender" the same day Brooke wrote to Gort. Still, the shock was great in Paris and London when, on Tuesday afternoon, the twenty-eighth, King Leopold, without informing his allies or consulting his advisers, surrendered the entire 274,000-man Belgian army, opening a twenty-mile gap between Brooke's corps and the coast near Nieuport.[60]

Lord Halifax, HMG's tall, ectomorphic foreign secretary, thought this was an excellent time to negotiate a peace with Hitler. On the twenty-seventh, Halifax—the last of the major appeasers to fall from favor (if not from office)—told the War Cabinet that "it is not so much now a question of imposing a complete defeat upon Germany, but of safeguarding the independence of our own Empire." The Italian ambassador to Britain, he reported, had approached him with "fresh proposals" for a peace conference, and he thought they should seize this opportunity. Churchill replied that, yes, peace could be achieved "under a German domination of Europe," but, no, that was a condition "we could never accept."[61]

Exasperated, Halifax argued that if Il Duce offered terms "which do not postulate the destruction of our independence, we should be foolish if we did not accept them." Provided Britain's independence were not in jeopardy, he held, it would be proper for Britain, confronted with two or three months of air raids, "to accept an offer which would save the country from avoidable disaster." Sir Alexander Cadogan, permanent under secretary in the Foreign Office and a minor appeaser, thought the prime minister's defiant reply "too rambling and romantic and sentimental and temperamental. Old Neville still the best of the lot." To Halifax's horror, Churchill said that if France surrendered, Britain would go it alone. The foreign secretary persisted. The following day he dominated the War Cabinet's afternoon meeting, proposing an Anglo-French approach to Mussolini, suggesting that he "might be persuaded to act as mediator." Attlee replied sharply, pointing out that this would amount to asking Il Duce "to intercede to obtain peace terms for us." Churchill, jaw outthrust, growled that it would "ruin the integrity of our fighting position in this country.... Let us therefore avoid being dragged down the slippery slope with France."[62]

As the meeting broke up, Halifax told Cadogan he was going to resign, saying, "I can't work with Winston any longer." That evening he wrote in his diary: "I thought Winston talked the most frightful rot.... It does drive one to despair when he works himself up into a passion of emotion when he ought to make his brain think and reason." However, the foreign secretary changed his mind after Cadogan, a Foreign Office mandarin of the first order, replied: "Nonsense: his rodomontades probably bore me as much as they do you, but don't do anything silly under the stress of that."[63]

But patriotic ardor was stirring in England. In the 1930s, Churchill had been denounced as a "warmonger." Now his critics were branded "defeatists." A short service of intercession and prayer was held in Westminster Abbey; it was crowded with men who had cheered Munich only twenty months ago. Churchill wrote: "The English are loth [*sic*] to expose their feelings, but in my stall in the choir I could feel the pent-up, passionate emotion, and also the fear of the congregation, not of death or wounds or material loss, but of defeat and the final ruin of Britain."[64]

Now that the war edged closer to their homes and hearths, the British public began to learn the truth. Until the final week of May, Britons had been largely optimistic. The wakening came slowly because they had been told so little. As late as May 24, the *Times* asked, in a headline, ARE WE REALLY AT WAR? Hotels and theaters were crowded, the story reported; idle young men cloistered around amusement parks; holidays were being observed; in London's West End unemployed miners sang for coppers as though Britain and her empire were still at peace.[65]

The press, aided and abetted by military censors, bore much responsibility for this tranquillity. On May 13, a *Times* headline announced, BEF SWEEPS ON. On Tuesday, May 14, the day after Guderian's panzers began pouring across the Meuse, a *Times* analyst told readers: "In general, it may be said that the Germans have not made contact with the bulk of the French and Belgian forces." Other newspapers followed the same line. War news was reaching Englishmen in a promiscuous rush. Vital information was there, if you knew where to look, but it was buried beneath dispatches claiming RAF victories, accounts of French troops forming for a mighty counteroffensive, denials of German communiqués, and such predictions of enemy defeats as "GERMAN MOTORISED UNITS DRIVING INTO FRANCE BELIEVED TO FACE DESTRUCTION." Suddenly on May 22, Britons were told that the Nazis were at Abbéville, 140 miles *behind* the Allied lines in Belgium and heading for the Channel ports. For the next week the papers were full of contradictory stories about fighting in Flanders. Finally, on May 30, the British public were told: "ALLIES TRYING TO FIGHT WAY TO FRENCH COAST IN DIRECTION OF DUNKERQUE." Harold Nicolson wrote Vita Sackville-West, "Oh my dear, my dearest, that we should come to this!" Stanley Baldwin's wife wrote the *Times*, urging churches to fly the Cross of St. George as a sign that England was fighting for Christianity against evil. "It is a daily inspiration to myself," she wrote, "to look out of my window and see that our parish church is bearing the Red Cross of St. George on its tower night and day." The piety of Lady Baldwin was unsurprising. But the crisis brought the war effort some unlikely converts. Bertrand Russell wrote Kingsley Martin that he had renounced pacifism, declaring that if he were young enough to fight, he would enlist. On that desperate Tuesday when the Belgian king surrendered, George Orwell wrote in his diary: "Horrible as it is, I hope the B.E.F. is cut to pieces rather than capitulate."[66]

Gort, having withdrawn his 5th Division from the impossible southern adventure and flung it into the gap left by the Belgians, felt the full fury of the Nazi attack. A vanguard of 85,000 Germans, supported by reserves and, now, by refitted tanks, fell upon famed regiments: the 3rd Grenadiers, the 2nd North Staffordshire, the 2nd Sherwood Foresters, the Royal Inskilling Fusiliers, the Royal Scots Fusiliers, the 6th Seaforth Highlanders, and the Duke of Cornwall's light infantry. They held until the 42nd and 50th Divisions could move up to the line. The battle there, between Warneton and Ypres, raged throughout the withdrawal, with very heavy losses.

The greatest sacrifice was made by the Calais garrison: the 229th Antitank Battery; battalions from the King's Royal Rifle Corps, the Rifle Brigade, the Royal Tank Regiment, and the Queen Victoria's Rifles, supported by a thousand brave French soldiers. British destroyers lay off Calais, ready to save the men. Instead, Churchill decided, they must be abandoned. It was essential, he told Ironside, that they fight to the last man, holding the enemy in check; otherwise, Ironside wrote, "it would have been impossible to have used Dunkirk as a point from which to evacuate the B.E.F. and the 1st French Army," because the vast German divisions would have reached the beach and cut them off. The "grim decision," Ismay called it, was made on the night of May 26. Ironside, Ismay, and Eden were with the prime minister at the time.[67]

It was Eden's lot to telegraph this order to Brigadier C. N. Nicholson, commanding the Rifle Brigade that he must fight to the destruction of his command: "The eyes of the Empire are upon the defence of Calais, and H.M. Government are confident that you and your gallant regiments will perform an exploit worthy of the British name." Shortly before midnight, he again wired him: "Every hour you continue to fight is of greatest help to the B.E.F. . . . Have greatest admiration for your splendid stand." Churchill was uncharacteristically mute during dinner. Later he wrote, "One has to eat and drink in war, but I could not help feeling sick as we afterwards sat silent eating at the table."[68]

Now the two hundred thousand men of the BEF cut off in the north and the remnants of the First French Army, outnumbered three or four to one, fell back down the narrow corridor leading to the sea, fighting by day and retreating at night, with every step contested by the Germans. The 1st Coldstream Guards held the line for thirty hours before disengaging. The 2nd Gloucestershire and the 4th Royal Sussex regiments outflanked a German column. The 2nd Buffs broke the momentum of a German wheeling movement. The 1st Cameroons, reduced to forty survivors, nevertheless counterattacked and drove the enemy back across the Canal de la Lawe. Surrounded, a battalion of the Welch Fusiliers fought their way back to the Lys. Strung out between Ypres and the Warneton-Comines Canal for nine miles, the 6th Black Watch, the 13/18th Hussars, the 3rd Grenadier Guards, the 2nd North Staffordshire, and the 2nd Sherwood Foresters counterattacked, flinging back the claw of a German pincer movement. The 2nd Buffs were reduced to the strength of a weak company but blocked a penetration near Godewaersvelde.

Like all soldiers, they fought best when they had learned to hate, and the enemy they faced, which prided itself on its use of terrorism, gave them strong reasons for rage. After the SS *Totenkopf* division had captured a hundred men of the 2nd Royal Norfolk, many of them wounded, the SS lined their prisoners up against a barn wall and machine-gunned them, shooting or bayoneting those who still showed signs of life. Two Tommies, hidden by the bodies, crawled away to tell the tale. Alan Brooke was deeply shocked. In the first war he had fought Germans, but these were *Nazis*.

Late on May 26, Brooke himself narrowly escaped capture. Sleepless, he was driven from one command post to another, his driver honking his way through demoralized refugees, including the inmates from an insane asylum, who stood by the side of the road wearing inane smiles and waving at the mass of troops and refugees. Brooke commanded by word of mouth—the army's signals communications had broken down—issuing fresh orders to commanders as the situation changed, transferring battalions to other divisions, directing Montgomery to make a dangerous night flank march across the front of the attack. Immediately after he had crossed one bridge over the canal, it blew up behind him. Near Ypres he lay under a cottage fence, having hastily abandoned his car at the approach of thirty-six Luftwaffe bombers. When he tried to take a two-hour nap in a stone hut, he was blown out of bed.[69]

There are a thousand reasons why the withdrawal to the coast shouldn't have worked, but it did. To be sure, the cut-off army paid a dreadful price—68,710 casualties, nearly a third of its strength—but the majority of these were wounded who would fight again. Much of the achievement may be credited to the military traditions of the Empire, which gave Britain skilled professional officers and highly disciplined regular soldiers, the grandsons of Kipling's red-coated Mulvaneys. The very names of their regiments and battalions evoke ghosts of past glory, infantry of the line and cavalry troopers loyal to King and Country, the legacy of imperial armies that had given Britain's soldiers a small island for their birth and the whole world for their grave, regiments in one of which, the 4th Hussars, handsome young Winston Churchill had served as a highly decorated lieutenant.[70]

A week before the Belgian surrender, and after almost two weeks of crushing defeats on the Continent, Churchill asked Chamberlain to study "the problems which would arise if it were necessary to withdraw the BEF from France." On Monday, May 20, staff officers went through the motions of outlining a tentative plan. Assuming that Calais, Boulogne, and Dunkirk would be available, low-level planners believed they could evacuate two thousand men a day. The "hazardous evacuation of very large forces" was briefly mentioned, then relegated to the bottom of the agenda; its possibility seemed very remote. That changed in less than twenty-four hours. Tuesday morning, "the emergency evacuation across the Channel of very large forces" led the agenda, and Churchill ordered steps to "assemble a large number of small vessels in readiness to proceed to ports and inlets on the French coast." Transport officers from Harwich to Weymouth were directed to list all ships up to a thousand tons. The Admiralty appointed Vice-Admiral Bertram Ramsay to command the operation. It was code-named Dynamo. He was immediately given thirty-six ships, most of them cross-Channel ferries. His headquarters, hacked out of Dover's white cliffs, overlooked the troubled waters.

By the twenty-sixth, London was in despair. At seven o'clock that evening the Admiralty, on Churchill's instructions, sent out the message: "Operation Dynamo is to commence." On the twenty-eighth, with the evacuation from Dunkirk under way for almost twenty-four hours, Churchill warned the House of Commons to "prepare itself for hard and heavy tidings." Privately he feared that "the whole root and core and brain of the British army" was "about to perish upon the field or be led into an ignominious and starving captivity." The Chiefs of the Imperial General Staff informed him that, in their view, a full-scale attack on England was "imminent." Yet, each of the three service chiefs—army, navy, and RAF—parsed the data at hand after his own fashion; none was reading the same tea leaves as the others.[71]

The diary of the CIGS reflects Britain's grim mood. On the twenty-third, Ironside had written, "I cannot see that we have much hope of getting any of the B.E.F. out." Two days later he predicted, "We shall have lost all our trained soldiers by the next few days unless a miracle appears to help us." Two days later his entry read: "The news in the morning is bad.... I met Eastwood [the commander of the 4th Division in France] on the steps of the War Office. He had come over last night and described things as very bad. He did not expect any of the B.E.F. to get off at all." The following evening Ismay wrote, "The Prime Minister asked me how I would feel if I were told that a total of 50,000 could be saved. I replied without hesitation that I would be absolutely delighted, and Churchill did not upbraid me for pessimism." As late as May 30, with the Luftwaffe swarming over the Dunkirk beaches, the King was told that they would be lucky to save 17,000. Ironside wrote: "Very little chance of the real B.E.F. coming off. They have now sunk three ships in Dunkirk harbour and so there is very little chance of getting any units off."[72]

Eight months earlier the Poles had lost all hope; the French were losing theirs; but with few exceptions the morale of Englishmen was actually rising. Blessed with that great moat between them and the Continent, they were defiant. On the afternoon of May 28, Churchill assembled the full cabinet—some twenty ministers—in his room in Parliament to tell them everything he knew about the fighting and what lay in the balance. Then he said, "I have thought carefully in these last days whether it was part of my duty to consider entering in negotiations with That Man.* And I am convinced that every man of you would rise up and tear me down from my place if I were for one moment to contemplate parley or surrender. If this long island story of ours is to end at last, let it end only when each of us lies choking in his own blood upon the ground."

To his surprise, several men jumped up, ran to his chair, shouting, and clapped him on the back. Afterward he wrote: "I was sure that every Minister was ready to be killed quite soon, and have all his family and possessions destroyed rather than give in. In this they represented the House of Commons and almost all the people. It fell to me in those coming days and months to express their sentiments on suitable occasions. This I was able to do, because they were mine also."

Hugh Dalton, long his opponent in the House, wrote: "He was quite magnificent. [He is] the man, and the only man we have, for this hour."[73]

In 1940 Dunkirk was an ancient seaport; many of the buildings facing the shore dated from the sixteenth century. Before the war, its ten miles of empty sand had attracted thousands of vacationing French and Englishmen, but when Lord Gort's gaunt, exhausted, unshaven soldiers fell back

* "That Man" to Churchill was always Hitler.

upon it in those last days of May, the Luftwaffe had transformed it into a battered ruin. All the houses had been abandoned. The only sound came from crackling, exploding fires in the city. Buoys had been blasted from the water. Sunken ships blocked entrances to the harbor, which, by all the canons of seamen, had become a shattered, useless port. The wide beaches were within range of Calais-based Krupp artillery, which never let up. Tommies were also vulnerable to shrieking, dive-bombing Stukas and strafing Messerschmitt Bf 109s that were using as their beacon a billowing column of smoke from bombed oil tanks near the west pier. These tanks were to burn throughout the crisis, tainting the air with their foul stench. It was from this cauldron that the Royal Navy, all the available merchant ships, and British yachtsmen in private boats intended to rescue a quarter-million exhausted, bleeding men.

Nor was that all. Apart from the sunken hulks and smashed docks, the harbor confronted mariners with other challenges. Fifteen-foot low tides left a long, shallow foreshore bare for a half mile to seaward, which meant that no vessel could approach closer than that. Neither could Dunkirk be approached directly from the Straits of Dover. Instead, seamen had to navigate an 800-yard-wide deepwater channel that ran parallel to the coast for many miles. The only ameliorating feature of the port, and it was a frail one, was a mole, or breakwater, that sprang in a great curve from an eleventh-century fortress and extended 1,400 yards seaward. This jetty was the East Mole. Most breakwaters are made of stone. This one was a narrow wooden structure barely wide enough to accommodate three men walking abreast. Bringing craft alongside it would be both difficult and, because of the tides, hazardous. Moreover, the East Mole had not been built to survive the stresses of berthing ships alongside it. No one knew whether it could survive the strain.

By the morning of May 26, the navy had assembled a ragtag armada of 860 vessels in Dover. Of Britain's 160 destroyers, almost half were attached to the Home Fleet, and only forty-one were available. These had been augmented by appealing to all yacht clubs along the coast and by commandeering everything afloat in English waters. In addition, French, Belgian, and Dutch skippers had volunteered, bringing the argosy total to 900 boats. On May 26, they were anchored three-deep along the Dover quays: trawlers, river barges, schooners, minesweepers, fireboats, corvettes, hospital ships, fishing sloops, launches, paddle wheelers, smacks, coasters, lifeboats, scows, tugs, the London fire float *Massey Shaw,* the ferries *Brighton Queen* and *Gracie Fields,* Channel packets such as the *Princess Maud,* and every variety of pleasure craft. Tom Sopwith's America's Cup challenger *Endeavour* was there, with him at the helm. So were the launch *Count Dracula;* the yacht *Sundowner,* piloted by Commander Charles H. Lightoller, the senior surviving officer of the *Titanic;* and the Yangtze gunboat *Mosquito*. The Earl of Craven was going to sea as third engineer on a tug. The Honorable Lionel Lambert had armed his yacht and was sailing with his chef. And Captain Sir Richard Pim of the Royal Navy, the commander of the prime minister's map room, was commanding a Dutch *schuit*. Churchill looked around, demanded, "Where's Pim?" and was elated when told.[74]

Just crossing the Channel, forty miles wide at this point, was harrowing for amateurs. The sea was choppy, and since the outbreak of the war, lightships and lighted buoys had been blacked out, and the enemy was continually mining these waters. The navy swept three narrow lanes; vessels that strayed from them, and some did, went down. Lying off the French coast between shoals, awaiting their turn to go in, helmsmen tried desperately, in narrow waters, to take evasive action against the German aircraft, which seemed to be everywhere. Then, when they went in, or as far in as they could get, they saw the long serpentine lines of Tommies stretching over the dunes. To the crews of boats entering after sunset, weaving between the sunken hulks, the beaches seemed to be swarming with fireflies. These were the lighted cigarettes of infantrymen awaiting a ride home. Some men stood waist-deep in water for hours, praying for rescue, but though bombed and machine-gunned, none broke.

During the first day of evacuation—Monday, May 27—small craft dodged in, picked up as many men as they could, and ran them out to the destroyers and Channel ferries, which formed the backbone of the fleet. This continued throughout the nine days and nights of Dunkirk, but only eight thousand soldiers were evacuated that Monday. Clearly the little craft could not do the job alone. The beach master decided to bring the ships in and test the flimsy East Mole. It held. It wasn't the best of moorings; at low tide, men had to jump to decks, and when a rough sea rushed against the pilings, sucking, swirling, and widening the distance to be covered, each leap became a gamble. Some Tommies lost and sank to their death. The Germans bombed the jetty again and again. One morning it took a direct hit from a low-flying bomber. Ships' carpenters patched it. Another bomb hit the hull of the paddle wheel steamer *Fenella* below the waterline just after she had been boarded by six hundred troops. She sank immediately, taking them with her. Nevertheless, the mole did all that could have reasonably been asked of it.

As did the little boats. Repeatedly they ran aground; soldiers would push them off and vault aboard. Sometimes overloaded craft capsized, drowning the heavily laden Tommies. Some crewmen brought collapsible boats; soldiers tried to paddle with their gun butts; it didn't work; they tried their luck elsewhere. Makeshift piers were put together with trucks, wreckage, and driftwood. The skipper of a minesweeper raised his bow as high as possible, came in at twelve knots, and dropped two stern anchors as he beached. Nearly three thousand men used the ship as a bridge to deeper water, where other vessels awaited them. As the Luftwaffe found more victims, oil slicks made rescue filthy work, and flames from burning ships illumined the harbor from sundown to dawn. German bombers also littered the harbor with more sunken hulks. One destroyer was hit while waiting at the mole. She caught fire and drifted out, blocking the harbor entrance until a trawler towed her aside.[75]

Ashore, there was some concern about the French soldiers. Those on the perimeter were fighting magnificently, but idle poilus had become a problem. "French Army now a rabble," Brooke wrote in his diary on May 29, "and complete loss of discipline. Troops dejected and surly, refusing to clear road and panicking every time German planes come over." That, he believed, was one reason the evacuation was slow. Another was an insufficient number of small boats. He asked Gort to pressure the Admiralty. Instead Gort sent two emissaries to the prime minister: Lord Munster, his aide-de-camp, and a junior officer, John Churchill, the prime minister's nephew. Young Churchill arrived at Admiralty House that same evening, "soaking wet," as he later recalled, "and still in full battle kit." Winston and Clementine, both in dressing gowns, greeted him fervently. "Johnny!" his uncle said delightedly. "I see you have come straight from battle!"[76]

Churchill wanted to know why his nephew was so wet: "Have you come straight out of the sea?" Johnny said that he had, and would be returning immediately. Lord Munster, immaculately attired in staff dress and jackboots appropriate to the function, received less attention, though Churchill agreed to prod the Admiralty. All who recall the incident remember not the message but Churchill's enthusiasm for the war. "We felt," recalled General Sir Ian Jacob, "that he would have liked to be fighting on the beaches himself."[77]

Altogether six destroyers were sunk and twenty-six damaged during the ten days of Dunkirk. Another 112 vessels went down, including the *Mosquito* and the *Gracie Fields,* lost on her way home with 300 Tommies. At times men on boats crossing to Dover had to make their way through the floating corpses of their comrades. The progress, or lack of it, was discouraging; by the night of May 28, only about 25,000 soldiers had been evacuated, and on June 2, the heavy air attacks forced suspension of daylight action. Nevertheless, the operation continued, favored by fair weather, and now they had the hang of it. Operation Dynamo, conceived in despair, with faint hope that a small fraction of the army could be saved, was astonishing the world.

On May 28, the number of evacuees was low: 17,800. "All this day of the 28th," Churchill wrote afterward, "the escape of the British army hung in the balance." On May 29, however, the figure was 47,310; on May 30, 53,823; on May 31, 68,014; on June 1, 64,429; and on June 2, 26,256. That was supposed to be the end of it, but Admiral Ramsay made one last perilous attempt to lift off the gallant French rearguard, and he returned with 26,175 polius. Altogether, Dynamo had rescued 338,226 Allied soldiers, 112,000 of them French, although a greater number of French troops turned and went home, to take their chances.

Behind them they had "left their luggage," as Churchill put it: 2,540 artillery pieces, 90,000 rifles, 11,000 machine guns, nearly 700 tanks, 6,400 anti-tank rifles, 20,000 motorcycles, 45,000 trucks and other vehicles, and vast ammunition dumps.[78]

But the great thing, for the English public, was that the men were back. They had heard stories of the heroic rearguard action. "Then," Mollie Panter-Downes told readers of *The New Yorker* on June 2, "it was learned that the first war-stained, exhausted contingent had arrived on British shores, and the relief and enthusiasm were terrific." Churchill never much liked *The New Yorker,* deriding it as *The New Porker* (he had a moniker for everyone), but here came Panter-Downes with journalistic testimony to the heroics in England. He could not have bought more favorable press.[79]

Still, the news added up to disaster. On June 4 Churchill told the House the story of Dunkirk. "Wars," he told them bluntly, "are not won by evacuations" and "what has happened in France and Belgium is a colossal military disaster." Nevertheless, he said, Dunkirk was "a miracle of deliverance, achieved by valor, by perseverance, by perfect discipline, by faultless service, by recourse, by skill, by unconquerable fidelity." Britain would "outlive the menace of tyranny, if necessary, if necessary alone."

> Even though large tracts of Europe and many old and famous states have fallen or may fall into the grip of the Gestapo and all the odious apparatus of Nazi rule, we shall not flag or fail.... We shall go on to the end, we shall fight in France, we shall fight on the seas and oceans, we shall fight with growing confidence and growing strength in the air, we shall defend our island, whatever the cost may be, we shall fight on the beaches, we shall fight on the landing grounds, we shall fight in the fields and in the streets, we shall never surrender.
>
> And even if, which I do not for a moment believe, this island or a large part of it were subjugated and starving, then our empire beyond the seas, armed and guarded by the British Fleet, would carry on the struggle, until, in God's good time, the New World, with all its power and might, steps forward to the rescue and the liberation of the old.[80]

In his diary Jock Colville wrote: "Went down to the House to hear the P.M.'s statement on the evacuation of Dunkirk. It was a magnificent oration which obviously moved the House." Next day the *News Chronicle* called the address "a speech of matchless oratory, uncompromising candour, and indomitable courage." Harold Nicolson wrote his wife, Vita Sackville-West: "This afternoon Winston made the finest speech that I have ever heard." She wrote back: "I wish I had heard Winston make that magnificent speech! Even repeated by the announcer it sent shivers (not of fear) down my spine. I think one of the reasons why one is stirred by his Elizabethan phrases is that one feels the whole massive backing of power and resolve behind them, like a great fortress; they are never words for words' sake." That evening, in a broadcast to the United States, a constituency that Churchill desperately needed to reach, Edward R. Murrow, the CBS man in London, said: "He spoke the language of Shakespeare with a direct urgency which I have never before heard in that House." Later, the historian Brian Gardner wrote of the address that it had "electrified not only his own country, but the world. With it, Churchill won the complete confidence of the British people, which he had never before enjoyed. Whatever was to happen, Churchill's place in the national life was assured; he would never be in the wilderness again."[81]

Churchill also worked a challenge to Hitler into his address: "When Napoleon lay at Boulogne for a year with his flat-bottomed boats and his Grand Army, he was told by someone, 'There are bitter weeds in England.' There are certainly a great many more of them since the British Expeditionary Force returned."[82]

None were more bitter than Churchill.

Charles Corbin, the French ambassador, was alarmed. He called at the Foreign Office to ask what the prime minister had meant by declaring that Britain would, if it came to that, carry on alone. He was told that he had meant "exactly what he had said." That, members of Corbin's staff told diplomatic correspondents, was "not exactly encouraging the French to fight on against fearful odds."[83]

The French were getting nervous. As they saw it, the British army had bolted, leaving them to the enemy's mercies. Of course, the evacuation would have been unnecessary if the French strategy had not been hopelessly wrong or if Weygand had not been a liar. Moreover, the original intent of the operation, as seen by Gort, Churchill, and Ironside, had been to extricate the BEF and then land it in the south, rejoining their allies. The loss of their equipment meant they had to be refitted, but Churchill intended to then send the troops back, and Reynaud, Weygand, and the French high command knew it. Even as Dunkirk wound down, Churchill had landed two fresh British divisions below the Somme. Nevertheless, he had been aware of the uneasiness across the Channel. On May 30, he had decided to convene a meeting of the *Conseil Supérieur de la Guerre* in Paris the following day. With him he would take Clement Attlee, Pug Ismay, and Sir John Dill, the new Chief of the Imperial General Staff, Ironside staying behind as the new commander in chief of Home Forces, to organize English defenses against the invasion threat. Spears would meet them at Villacoublay Airport.[84]

Flying over France had become more hazardous since Churchill's last flight to the theater. Although the Flamingo was escorted by nine Spitfires, north of Paris the sky was swarming with Nazi fighters. Churchill's pilot detoured and they arrived late. Spears saw the hunched but resilient figure of the prime minister emerge, "obviously in grand form. He might not have had a care in the world.... Danger, the evocation of battle, invariably acted as a tonic and a stimulant to Winston Churchill."[85]

The *Conseil* met at 2:00 P.M. on May 31, in a large first-floor room, giving out on a garden, in the Ministry of War in the rue Saint-Dominique, with the conferees sitting at an immense green-baize-covered oval table, the visitors on one side and, facing them, their hosts: Reynaud, Admiral Jean Darlan; Paul Baudouin, a protégé of Reynaud's mistress and an admirer of the defeatist Pétain; Weygand, booted and spurred; and, finally, a newcomer to the war council: eighty-four-year-old Maréchal Henri-Philippe Pétain, in mufti.

Reynaud had appointed Pétain his deputy premier, hoping to increase the public's confidence in the government. In France the old marshal was regarded as a hero of the last war, *le vainqueur de Verdun* (the conqueror of Verdun). The British saw him differently. In 1917 he had suppressed a mutiny in the French army by promising his soldiers that the British and the Americans would do most of the future fighting. He was, moreover, an impassioned Anglophobe who despised democracy; the responsibility for France's present plight, he believed, lay with the leftist Popular Front of 1935. "Now," Ismay thought, Pétain "looked senile, uninspiring, and defeatist."[86]

Churchill opened by suggesting that they consider three questions: the Allied force still in Norway, the fighting in Flanders, and the strong likelihood that Mussolini would soon enter the war at Hitler's side. First, however, he thought the French would be interested in a piece of good news. The Dunkirk evacuation was succeeding beyond all expectations: 165,000 men had been taken off, including 10,000 wounded. It was then that Weygand sounded the first dissonant note. In an aggressive, querulous voice, he interrupted to ask, "But how many French? The French are being left behind?"[87]

The Englishmen present expected a Churchillian outburst. All the signs were there: the light had died out of his face, he was drumming his fingers on the table, and his lower lip jutted out like the prow of a dreadnought. Clearly he was angry, and with reason. Weygand had known of Operation Dynamo for six days, but had neglected to tell his commander in the north and had issued no orders authorizing French participation in the evacuations. Indeed, that was one of the reasons the prime minister had flown over. However, he controlled himself; his expression became sad; he said quietly, "We are companions in misfortune. There is nothing to be gained from recrimination over our common miseries."[88]

Baudouin wrote that there were "tears in his eyes," that he was obviously moved by "the common sufferings of England and France." Spears felt that "a stillness fell over the room." They then proceeded with the agenda, agreeing, first, to reinforce the Allied armies in France by withdrawing their forces from Norway. Briefly they discussed fortifying a redoubt in Brittany, into which they might withdraw if France fell. The RAF would bomb Italian targets if Mussolini entered the war. At that point the French translator, misunderstanding the P.M., said it was understood that British soldiers at Dunkirk would embark before the French. Churchill interrupted him; waving his arms, he roared in his extraordinary accent: "*Non! Partage bras dessous, bras dessous*"—the soldiers from both countries would leave together, arm in arm.[89]

The French wanted more RAF squadrons. Churchill pointed out that His Majesty's Government had already given ten additional squadrons, needed for the defense of Great Britain. If they lost the rest, the Luftwaffe could, with impunity, attack "the most dangerous targets of all, the factories producing new aircraft." It was, he said, "impossible to run further risks" with British aircraft.

What concerned him most was the flagging spirit of all Frenchmen—soldiers, civilians, and, except for Reynaud, members of the government. He could not say that there, of course, but he wanted them to know that England meant to crush Nazi Germany, whatever the cost. "I am absolutely convinced," he said, his voice rolling with oratorical cadences, "that we have only to fight on to conquer. If Germany defeats either ally or both, she will give no mercy. We should be reduced to the status of slaves forever. Even if one of us is struck down, the other must not abandon the struggle. Should one comrade fall in battle, the other must not put down his arms until his wounded friend is on his feet again."[90]

Attlee endorsed every word the prime minister had said, adding: "Every Englishman knows that the very basis of civilization common to both France and Britain is at stake. The Germans kill not only men, but ideas." Reynaud was pleased; that was the line he had been taking with his ministers. They, however, were divided. Spears thought that Baudouin had been swept away by Churchill's fire. Not so; in his diary he wrote that he had been "deeply troubled" by Churchill's vow and asked, "Does he consider that France must continue the struggle, cost what it may, even if it is useless? We must clear that up."

Beaming, Churchill said merrily: *"Fini l'agenda!"*

But he himself was not finished. As they rose from the table, gathering in groups to discuss this or that, Churchill headed for Pétain, followed by Spears. The old man had not said a word. His voice would carry great weight with the people of France, and the P.M. thought he looked "detached and sombre, giving me the feeling that he would face a separate peace." One of the Frenchman said that if events continued on their present course, France might have to reappraise its foreign policy, including ties to Britain, and "modify its position." Pétain nodded. Spears told them in perfect French that such a change would result in a British blockade of French ports. Then, looking directly into Pétain's eyes, Spears said, "That would not only mean blockade but bombardment of all French ports in German hands." Afterward Churchill wrote, "I was glad to have this said. I sang my usual song: we would fight on whatever happened or whoever fell out."[91]

No one had mentioned the Anglo-French *accord* signed by both governments nine weeks earlier—they had solemnly agreed to "neither negotiate nor conclude an armistice or treaty of peace except by mutual agreement." In March, when the pledge was signed, the strength of the opposing forces on the Western Front had been roughly equal, but by May 31, when the *Conseil* was meeting in Paris, the Nazi edge was enormous. The Germans had taken almost 500,000 prisoners at a cost of 60,000 casualties. Unaccountably, Weygand issued no orders to move the seventeen divisions manning the Maginot Line. As a consequence he had to face the coming onslaught with forty-nine divisions. The Germans attacked with 130 infantry and ten panzer divisions—almost three thousand tanks.

On June 5 the Germans launched their offensive against the Somme. The French, fighting desperately, held their line for two days and thwarted a pincer movement toward Creil from Amiens and Péronne, but on June 7, the 7th Panzer Division, led by Erwin Rommel, broke through toward Rouen, and on Sunday, June 9, they were over the Seine. That day they lunged across the Aisne, took Dieppe and Compiègne; then tanks drove through the breach toward Châlons-sur-Marne before turning eastward toward the Swiss frontier, to cut off the huge garrison in *le Maginot*. Rommel drove his tanks so far and so fast that the English called the 7th Panzers the Ghost Division. Nobody—including the German high command—knew where it was until it appeared someplace where it was not expected.

On Monday, June 10, Italy declared war on Britain and France. Franklin Roosevelt declared in a radio broadcast, "The hand that held the dagger has plunged it into the back of its neighbor." Churchill merely muttered, "People who go to Italy to look at ruins won't have to go as far as Naples and Pompeii in the future." He ordered that all male Italian citizens be rounded up and interned. A few hours after Mussolini's declaration of war, mobs smashed the windows of Soho's spaghetti joints, but in London, unlike in Rome, there were no organized demonstrations against the new enemy. Mussolini's dagger was very small. Almost immediately the French hurled back Il Duce's badly led, dreadfully equipped army. Churchill wired Roosevelt: "If we go down Hitler has a very good chance of conquering the world." In that case, small dagger or no, Mussolini would get his share.[92]

That night, as German armies advanced toward Paris, the prime minister decided to fly to Paris once more, hoping to persuade the French to defend their capital. Then a message arrived, telling him the government was leaving it. "What the hell," he growled, fuming until a second telegram told him they could meet at Briare, on the Loire, eighty miles south of Paris. Tuesday morning—the eleventh—he took off with Ismay, Eden, and Spears, escorted by twelve Hawker Hurricanes. He wanted to fly over the battlefields, but the pilot told him that the flight plan made that impossible; he and the Hurricanes were following precise instructions from the Air Ministry.

Briare airfield was deserted. Churchill, massive in black, leaning on his stick, looked around, beaming, as though this airstrip were the place he had sought all his life and finally found. Several cars drove up, the first driven by a sullen colonel "who, from his expression," Spears wrote, "might have been welcoming poor relatives at a funeral procession." The ambiance was equally unpleasant when they arrived at the red-brick Château du Muguet. Spears felt that "our presence was not really desired."

They were shown into a large dining room. There the Frenchmen—with one exception, Charles de Gaulle, whom Reynaud had made a general, serving as the premier's under secretary of state for defense and war—sat with hung heads, staring at the table, like prisoners awaiting sentencing. To Ismay, Pétain seemed "more woebegone than ever," while Weygand appeared "to have abandoned all hope."[93]

Churchill tried to cheer them up by revealing that a Canadian division would be landed in France that night, joining the three British divisions already in the line, and another division would arrive within nine days.

They remained glum. Weygand said that the army's plight was hopeless. The Allies had lost thirty-five divisions—over half a million soldiers. He said: "There is nothing to prevent the enemy reaching Paris. We are fighting on our last line and it has been breached. I am helpless. I cannot intervene, for I have no reserves. It was the break-up of the army ("*C'est la dislocation*").Then he went too far. He was asked what would happen if another breach were made and replied: "No further military action will be possible." Eden noted that Reynaud immediately intervened sharply: "That would be a political decision, Monsieur le Général." Weygand bowed and said, "Certainly," but then he struck again, blaming "those responsible"—the French politicians—"for entering the war with no conception of Nazi power."[94]

Churchill couldn't, or wouldn't, believe that France was in extremis. In the beginning he had hunched over the table, his face flushed, following the *généralissime*'s every word, but at the end he looked away, said nothing, stared at the ceiling, ignoring Weygand but glancing quizzically at de Gaulle several times. He asked to see his old friend General Georges. Georges appeared and confirmed everything Weygand had said. Even as they spoke, he said, the enemy was only sixty miles away. The P.M., though visibly shaken, sought to revive the willpower of the French. His mouth was working; he searched for the words, found them, and spoke warmly and deeply. He wished, he said, to express his admiration for the gallant resistance of the French and Britain's deep sorrow that her contribution had been so slight. "Every Englishman," he told them, "is profoundly grieved that further military help cannot be given to France in this grave hour." Had the BEF not returned from Dunkirk naked, nine divisions of Britons would now be fighting alongside the poilus. As it was, England was sending all she had left, leaving her island virtually defenseless. Then he reminded them of 1918, when the Allies had been so close to defeat, and said that might be true now; all intelligence reports agreed that the Germans were exhausted, at the end of their tether. The cloud might lift in forty-eight hours. Weygand broke in to say they hadn't that much time; they were down to "the last quarter of an hour."[95]

Churchill wouldn't quit. He wanted to set the French afire with the flame of Britain's defiance. His words, Spears wrote, "came in torrents, French and English phrases tumbling over each other like waves rushing for the shore when driven by a storm. No matter what happened, he told them, England would fight—on and on and on, *toujours,* all the time, everywhere, *partout, pas de grâce,* no mercy. *Puis la victoire!*" He offered all the British support he could muster, including troops on their way from Britain's Dominions and colonies, and suggested alternatives to a French defeat, raising again the possibility of a Breton redoubt, into which the troops could withdraw, supplied by the Royal Navy. He wanted Weygand's army to fight in Paris, telling them how a great city, if valiantly defended, could absorb immense enemy armies. He suggested that the French government retreat to North Africa. If all else failed, he proposed guerrilla warfare.[96]

The French were hostile, Weygand scornful, and Pétain, who had sat silent until now, incredulous, mocking, and, finally, angry. The old *maréchal* dismissed the prime minister's vow that the British would fight on alone as absurd: "Since France cannot continue the struggle, wisdom dictates that England should seek peace, for certainly she cannot carry on alone." To make Paris "a city of ruins," he said, would not affect the issue. As for guerrillas, he said: "That would mean the destruction of the country."[97]

The most protracted discussion arose from the French demand that every plane left in the Royal Air Force be committed to the battle now raging. The appeal was unanimous: Pétain, Weygand, Georges, and Reynaud agreed that the RAF was their last hope, and that it could turn back the German tide. If the aircraft were withheld, Reynaud predicted, "Without doubt history will say that the battle of France was lost for lack of planes." "Here," said Weygand, "is the decisive point. Now is the decisive moment. The British ought not to keep a single fighter in England. They should all be sent to France." Ismay, Eden, and Spears were holding their breaths. Air Chief Marshal Dowding, chief of Britain's Fighter Command, had warned the prime minister and the War Cabinet that if any more fighter squadrons were sent to France, he could not guarantee the defense of England, and they were afraid that the prime minister's generosity, his love of France, his impulsiveness, and his innate optimism would prompt him to make a disastrous commitment of further air support.[98]

He didn't. According to Ismay, after a long pause he said very slowly, "This is *not* the decisive point. This is not the decisive moment. The decisive moment will come when Hitler hurls his Luftwaffe against Britain. If we can keep command of the air over our own island—that is all I ask—we will win it all back for you."[99]

Reynaud, Ismay noted, was "obviously moved." The premier asked, "If we capitulate, all the great might of Germany will be concentrated upon invading England. And then what will you do?" Thrusting his jaw forward, the P.M. replied that he hadn't thought about it carefully, but that broadly speaking, he would propose to drown as many of them as possible and then to "*frapper sur la tête*" ("hit on the head") any of them who managed to crawl ashore."[100]

It is odd that none of the Englishmen raised the question of the *French* air force. France had one, commanded by General Joseph Vuillemin, a daring pilot in the last war but now obese and incompetent. Vuillemin had angered the British by commenting that RAF support in the opening days of the German offense had arrived "tardily and in insufficient numbers." In fact, Britain had sent a hundred bombers, all the RAF had then, to bomb the Meuse bridges and had lost forty-five of them. On May 28 Vuillemin had also said the RAF had three hundred planes in England and had sent only thirty to France—this at a time when eight to ten frontline British squadrons—96 to 120 aircraft—were in action every day supporting the French. Indeed, during the fall of France all but ten of the RAF's fifty-three fighter squadrons saw action over France and the Low Countries, and of those ten, three were night fighters, two were in Norway, and one was nonoperational.

During the fall of France the British lost 959 aircraft and nearly 300 pilots.* The French lost 560 planes, 235 of them destroyed on the ground. The performance of the French air force was baffling, even to its leaders and even after the war. At the outset, Vuillemin had more than 3,287 planes. (The Germans had 2,670.) Yet only a third of French aircraft saw action. Furthermore, between May 10 and June 12, French factories delivered 1,131 new airplanes, 688 of them fighters. Indeed, when France dropped out of the war, Vuillemin found that he actually had more first-line aircraft than he had had when the great Nazi offensive began. "What is this mystery about our planes?" General Gamelin asked afterward, testifying before a Parliamentary Investigating Committee. "Why out of 2,000 fighters on hand at the beginning of May 1940 were fewer than 500 used on the Northeast Front? I humbly confess to you that I do not know." Commenting on the confusing figures, he said, "We have a right to be astonished." Certainly it is astonishing that the *généralissime* was astonished.[101]

At 10:00 P.M. the conferees dined. Weygand invited de Gaulle to sit beside him and flushed when the new general chose the chair beside Churchill instead. Already there was an unspoken bond between Churchill and Reynaud's protégé. The formation of that bond was probably the only accomplishment of the Briare meeting. For Churchill the last straw came at bedtime. Before retiring, the prime minister and the premier had coffee and brandy together. Reynaud said Weygand had told him, "In three weeks Britain would have her neck wrung like a chicken." Then Rey-

* Reliable figures are difficult, and often impossible, to find. However, the French official history, *Histoire de l'Aviation Militaire Française* (Paris, 1980), puts the British sacrifice much higher: "The losses suffered by the RAF in France are enough in themselves to demonstrate its effective participation in the battle of May–June 1940. More than 1,500 flyers were killed, wounded, or missing, and more than 1,500 planes of all types were destroyed."

naud revealed that Pétain had told him that "it will be necessary to seek an armistice." Once the *"vainqueur de Verdun"* had been considered the guardian of French honor. Now, the premier said, the marshal "has written a paper on the subject which he wishes me to read. He has not handed it to me yet. He is still ashamed to do it." Churchill, appalled, thought Pétain should have been even more ashamed to have supported, "even tacitly, Weygand's demand for our last twenty-five squadrons of fighters when he has made up his mind that all is lost and that France should give in."[102]

Inspector Thompson, who prepared the prime minister's bath on these trips, had been billeted in another building and was without transportation. Thus Churchill awoke alone the next morning. Two French officers were finishing their café au lait in the conference room, which was the château's dining room, when a big double door burst open, confronting them with what one later described as "an apparition resembling an angry Japanese genie"—an irate, plump Churchill with sparse, mussed hair, dressed in a flowing crimson dressing gown belted with silk, and angrily demanding: *"Uh ay ma bain* [where's my bath]?"[103]

His frustration mounted after a telephone call from a furious air marshal, Sir Arthur Barratt, stationed in Salon. Barratt reported that local authorities, fearful of reprisals, had not permitted RAF bombers to take off for targets in Italy. They had dragged farm carts on the runway, forcing him to cancel the mission. Others in the British party thought that was the last straw. However, the P.M. did not reproach his hosts. Tormented by the martyrdom of the French and by England's niggardly contribution to the Allied cause here, he disregarded the incident.[104]

The next morning, the twelfth, after Churchill had exacted a promise from Admiral Darlan never to surrender the French fleet, the British party left. Near tragedy brushed them on the way home. Unescorted by Hurricanes—an overcast sky had grounded them—they were flying over Le Havre when the sky cleared and the pilot saw two Heinkel bombers below, firing at fishing boats. The unarmed Flamingo dived to a hundred feet above the sea and raced for home. According to Inspector Thompson, one of the Nazi fighters fired a burst at them, but then they were gone, and the prime minister landed safely at Hendon.[105]

In parting, Churchill had told Reynaud that in the event of any "change in the situation," the French premier must let His Majesty's Government know "at once" so that the British could return "at any convenient spot" to discuss the situation before the French took any irrevocable step "which would govern their action in the second phase of the war." Clearly England's allies were at the end of their tether. Late that evening, HMG learned that the British 51st Division had surrendered to the Germans in the fishing port of St-Valéry-en-Caux, a loss of more than 12,000 men. In his diary Jock Colville wrote: "Speaking of the surrender of the 51st Division, W. said it was the most 'brutal disaster' we had yet suffered."[106]

Early on the thirteenth, when Churchill was donning his sleeping smock, Reynaud phoned. The connection was bad. Eventually Colville got through to one of the premier's aides. The message was grim: the premier and his advisers had moved from Briare to Tours; he wanted Churchill to meet him at the Préfecture there that same afternoon. This would be the P.M.'s fifth flight to France in less than four weeks. At 11:00 A.M. he and his party gathered at Hendon—Ismay, Eden, Beaverbrook, Halifax, and Cadogan. Escorted by eight Spitfires, the Flamingo detoured around the Channel Islands and entered French air space over Saint-Malo.

Lashed by a thunderstorm, they landed on an airstrip pitted with bomb craters. The field was deserted. No one was there to meet them. They taxied around the craters, looking for someone, and found a group of French airmen lounging outside a hangar. Churchill disembarked and told them, in his appalling French, that his name was Churchill, that he was the prime minister of Great Britain, and that he would be grateful if they could provide him with "*une voiture*" to carry him and his small staff to the town's Préfecture de Police. The airmen loaned them a small touring car, into which they crammed themselves with great difficulty and much discomfort. Halifax's long legs were a problem; so was the P.M.'s bulk. No one at the Préfecture knew who they were or had time for them. Luckily an officer appeared, recognized them, and led them to a small restaurant, where they lunched on cold chicken, cheese, and Vouvray wine.[107]

It was there that they were found by Paul Baudouin. In what Churchill called "his soft, silky manner," Baudouin lectured them on the hopelessness of French resistance. No one knew when Reynaud would appear, or even where he was. At length the premier arrived, followed by General Spears and Sir Ronald Campbell, the British ambassador. The meeting—destined to be the last of the *Conseil supérieur de la guerre*—was to be held in the *Préfet*'s study, a small, shabby room looking out on an unkempt garden. The study was furnished with a desk, behind which Reynaud presided, and assorted unmatched chairs. Churchill took a leather chair and eyed his French hosts warily. He was confronting France's split personality. Reynaud—still backed by a majority of the Chamber and the Senate—stood for a never-say-die, death-before-dishonor last stand against Nazi barbarism, with which Churchill agreed. Baudouin, Churchill knew, represented the defeatists; in his final report to Whitehall, Campbell would describe Baudouin as a man whose "dominating motives were fear and the desire to stand in well with the conqueror after the inevitable defeat." Even now Churchill had not grasped how eager for peace such men were. U.S. ambassador to France William Bullitt, no admirer of the British, told Washington that "to have as many companions in misery as possible, they hoped England would be rapidly and completely defeated by Germany and [that] the Italians would suffer the same fate." As for their own country, Bullitt reported, they hoped France would become "Hitler's favorite province."[108]

Reynaud told the British that Weygand had declared Paris an open city; panzers were in Reims; Nazi troops were below the Seine and the Marne. It was too late to withdraw into a *rédout Breton*. He himself wanted to "retreat and carry on, but the people would remain; France would cease to exist." Therefore the alternative was "armistice or peace." He asked what the British position would be "should the worst come" and raised the issue of the pledge—made at France's insistence and signed by him—that neither ally would made a separate peace. The French wanted to be left off the hook. They had, he said, "already sacrificed everything in the common cause," had "nothing left," and would be shocked if the English failed to understand that they were "physically incapable of carrying on." Would Britain face the hard facts now confronting France?

Spears quietly pointed out that capitulation was not the only alternative to war. Norway had not surrendered; neither had Holland. In the meantime, Churchill scowled, weighing his words. Britain, he replied at last, knew what France had endured and was still suffering. If the BEF had not been cut off in the north, they would be fighting beside the French now. They could not be there "owing to our having accepted the strategy of the army in the north." The other Englishmen sat up. They had long hoped he would say that. The reason for the present crisis was not a lack of fighter planes. It was GHQ's decision to ignore the Ardennes threat and send the best Allied troops into Belgium. The British had not yet "felt the German lash" but knew its force, the prime minister rasped. "England will fight on. She has not and will not alter her resolve: no terms, no surrender." He hoped France would carry on, fighting south of Paris and, if it came to that, in North Africa. Time was of the essence. It would not be "limitless: a pledge from the United States would make it quite short." A "firm promise from America," he said, "would introduce a tremendous new factor for France."

He was grasping at straws. Churchill knew that Roosevelt's hands were tied by the U.S. Constitution. As well, if Roosevelt announced his intention to seek an unprecedented third term in office, he surely would not do so on an interventionist platform. Indeed, Roosevelt made no announcement that June, telling Americans only that he would abide by the decision of the July Democratic convention. The P.M. also knew that Washington then had no arms to give. So did Reynaud. Although unschooled in American politics, the premier had served as France's *ministre de finance* for the first six months of the war, had bought some arms from the United States, and knew how little matériel was there. Nevertheless he accepted the possibility of American intervention. It was a delusion. Churchill was wrong to have encouraged it, though much of the blame was Ambassador Bullitt's. Alistair Horne points out that "through him [Bullitt] the French government was led to expect far greater aid than could possibly have been forthcoming at that time."[109]

Briefly stirred, the premier agreed to appeal to Roosevelt. Nevertheless he again asked that Britain agree to "a separate peace." The prime minister replied that although Britain would not "waste time in reproaches and recriminations," that was "a very different thing from becoming a consenting party to a peace made in contravention of the agreement so recently concluded." Then he reported that the Royal Navy was fast approaching a tight blockade of the Continent, which could lead to famine, from which an occupied France could not be spared. The French could not withdraw from the war and remain on good terms with the British. Reynaud, disturbed, darkly remarked: "This might result in a new and very grave situation in Europe."[110]

They had reached an impasse. Spears scribbled a note to Churchill suggesting a pause. Churchill told Reynaud he must confer with his colleagues "*dans le jardin* [in the garden]." The Englishmen withdrew to pace around the garden, "a hideous rectangle," in Spears's words, surrounded by a muddy path. After twenty minutes Beaverbrook spoke up: "There is nothing to do but repeat what you have said, Winston. Telegraph to Roosevelt and await the answer." He added: "We are doing no good here"; therefore, "Let's get along home."

And so they did. Everything now depended upon the reply from Washington. Reynaud, who had been joined by Charles de Gaulle, seemed confident that the Americans would save his country. As they prepared to leave, Churchill noted that among the Allied prisoners in France were 400 Luftwaffe pilots. He asked that they be sent to England, and the premier immediately agreed. As the P.M. passed de Gaulle, he said in a low tone, "*L'homme du destin* [the man of destiny]." The general remained impassive, but he understood: The French troops who had escaped from Dunkirk to Britain formed an army in waiting, but were without a leader. Large French forces in Brittany, who might fight on, likewise were in need of leadership. "There is apparently a young French general named de Gaulle," Colville told his diary the day before, "of whom Winston thinks a great deal." He did, and his statement to de Gaulle amounted to both a challenge and a promise of support were de Gaulle to lead a resistance in Brittany. On some level everyone knew that the alliance was finished, and it was in keeping with its last five ragged weeks that it should end in a grotesque scene. Outside the Préfecture, the Comtesse de Portes accosted Churchill, crying: "Mr. Churchill, my country is bleeding to death. I have a story to tell and you *must* hear me. You must hear my side of it. You must!" He ignored her and entered his car. Later he remarked: "She had comfort to give him. I had none."[111]

What Baudouin did was less forgivable. From time to time in the *Préfet*'s study, when Reynaud was speaking, Churchill had nodded or said, "*Je comprends,*" indicating his comprehension of words before they were translated. After Churchill's car had left, de Gaulle called Spears aside to tell him that Baudouin was "putting it about, to all and sundry, notably to the journalists," that Churchill had shown "complete understanding of the French situation and would understand if France concluded an armistice and a separate peace." De Gaulle asked, "Did Churchill really say that?" If he had, it would sway those not prepared to break France's pledge and permit defeatists to argue that there was no point in fighting on when even the English didn't expect it.

Spears replied that Churchill had said no such thing, and decided to race to the bomb-pitted runway before the prime minister's Flamingo took off. He arrived in time and his view was confirmed. Churchill told him, "When I said '*Je comprends,*' that meant I understood. *Comprendre* means understand in French, doesn't it? Well, when for once I use the right word in their own language, it is going rather far to assume that I intended it to mean something quite different. Tell them my French is not so bad as that." Spears did, but few listened, perhaps because Baudouin was telling them what they wanted to hear. The lie found its way into official French records and was even used against Churchill when he tried to remind them of the accord. During the armistice negotiations, Admiral Darlan declared that "the British Prime Minister, informed on June 11 [*sic*] of the necessity in which France found herself of bringing the struggle to an end, said that he understood that necessity and accepted it without withdrawing his sympathy from our country. He is therefore not qualified to speak otherwise."[112]

Reynaud's appeal, cabled to Washington the next morning, June 14, declared that unless the president gave "France in the coming days a positive assurance that the United States will come into the struggle in a short space of time... you will see France go under like a drowning man after having thrown a last look toward the land of liberty from which she was expecting salvation." In Washington, Secretary of State Cordell Hull called the plea "extraordinary, almost hysterical." Nevertheless, the president's reply went further than Hull and his other advisers wished. He assured the premier that Americans were doing everything in their power to send all the matériel they could and were redoubling their efforts because of their "faith and support of" the democratic ideals for which the French were fighting. Roosevelt encouraged the embattled French to fight on even in North Africa.

Although Roosevelt had pointed out that he could not make military commitments on his own authority, Churchill told his War Cabinet that Roosevelt's message came "as near as possible to a declaration of war and probably as much as the President could do without Congress." Beaverbrook thought an American declaration of war was now inevitable, but this was just more straw grasping. Significantly, the president had not made his cable public, and when the prime minister asked for permission to do this, it was denied. On June 14—the day Paris fell and the French government headed for Bordeaux—Colville noted: "It seems that the P.M.'s expectations last night of immediate American help were exaggerated. Roosevelt has got to proceed cautiously, but the plain truth is that America has been caught napping, militarily and industrially. She may be really useful to us in a year; but we are living from hour to hour." That day, the order went out to bring the rest of the BEF home from south of the Seine.[113]

De Gaulle, who had been commuting between London and France as a liaison officer, now proposed a measure born of desperation. On June 16, lunching at the Carleton Club with Churchill and the French ambassador, he argued that "some dramatic move" was essential to keep France in the war. He advanced the idea of a joint Allied declaration. The British and French governments would declare the formation of an Anglo-French Union, the two nations uniting as one. Churchill liked it; so did the War Cabinet, and de Gaulle immediately took off for Bordeaux to submit the proposal. Spears wrote that after reading a draft of the declaration, Reynaud was "transfigured with joy." It came, he said, at the best possible time. The council of ministers was meeting at 5:00 P.M. "to decide whether further resistance is possible," and the premier told Spears that he believed the vision of union would thwart an armistice. However, the premier's mistress Hélène de Portes was with them—she knew every state secret; one vital document, missing for hours, was found in her bed—and she read the draft over a secretary's shoulder. Everything she knew, she shared with Baudouin. Before Reynaud could tell his ministers the news, they already knew it and had been told all the arguments against it.

Meantime Churchill was preparing to cross the Channel once again, this time aboard a warship just after midnight on the seventeenth. At 9:30 P.M. he boarded a special train at Waterloo Station, prepared to leave for Southampton. Clementine had come to see him off. Kathleen Hill, who was also on board, recalled: "We had taken our seats on the train and were waiting. There was a delay. There had been some hitch." Indeed there had. Ambassador Campbell had phoned No. 10 to report that a "ministerial crisis" in Bordeaux made the meeting impossible. Churchill disembarked "with a heavy heart," as he later wrote. He knew what was coming next, and Colville set it down: "Reynaud has resigned, unable to stand the pressure. . . . Pétain has formed a Government of Quislings, including [Pierre] Laval, and France will now certainly ask for an armistice in spite of her pledge to us." Later he added: "The Cabinet met at 11.00 and shortly afterwards we heard that Pétain had ordered the French army to lay down its arms." Churchill growled, "Another bloody country gone west."[114]

Colville wrote: "After the Cabinet the P.M. paced backwards and forwards in the garden, alone, his head bowed, his hands behind his back. He was doubtless considering how best the French fleet, the air force and the colonies could be saved. He, I am sure, will remain undaunted."[115]

De Gaulle was trapped in Bordeaux. The men now forming a new French government believed him to be—as he was—their enemy. They represented one France, he another; if left free, they knew, he would divide the country and offend the Nazis, whose servants they now were. To him their separate peace was shameful. Because he was determined to carry on the war, the British were still his allies. They were also his best hope of escaping from here and forming a new army on free soil, but the British were leaving the new France, which, they knew, did not wish either them or him well.

The issue had already been decided. The French defeatists were preparing to move to Vichy—an appropriate seat for Pétain's new government, the *Times* acidly commented, Vichy being a favorite resort of invalids. They were already drawing up legislation to abolish the republic and set up a dictatorship—the État Français—when General Spears and Ambassador Campbell arrived at Bordeaux's Quartier Général, the premier's temporary office in the rue Vital-Carles. They hoped to persuade him to stay in office. It was a doomed call—he had lost control of his cabinet and had submitted his resignation—which led to unexpected consequences. At 10:00 P.M. they had entered the building's huge, darkened hall. As they were approaching its wide staircase, Spears had noticed a tall figure standing bolt upright behind one of the columns, "shrouded," as he recalled afterward, "by shadow." It was de Gaulle, who had called him in a loud whisper. He said, "I must speak to you. It is extremely urgent." After the general explained that Reynaud awaited them, de Gaulle whispered, "I have very good reason to believe Weygand intends arresting me." Spears told him to stay "exactly where you are," and, after the brief, sad appointment with Reynaud, suggested they meet within the hour at the nearby Grand Hôtel Montré.[116]

De Gaulle explained a plan to encourage a French *Résistance* movement, using London as his base. Spears approved; he phoned Churchill, who agreed. Spears had a plane at the Bordeaux airport. They would fly out at 7:00 A.M. the next morning, the seventeenth. He never knew where de Gaulle spent that night—the hotel was too dangerous—but in the morning the self-appointed leader of the Free French (as those poilus who fled to Britain called themselves) appeared with an aide and an immense amount of baggage. Because there were French authorities at the field—the hunt for de Gaulle had already begun—it was decided that he and his aide-de-camp would behave as though they had come to see Spears off. In Spears's words, "We had begun to move when with hooked hands I hoisted de Gaulle on board"; the aide followed "in a trice." The baggage was tossed on board. De Gaulle arrived at No. 10 Downing Street in time for lunch. Pétain, upon learning what had happened, convened a military court. The expatriated general was found guilty of treason and sentenced to death in absentia. Churchill, of course, took another view. He wrote that de Gaulle had "carried with him, in this small aeroplane, the honour of France."[117]

De Gaulle was one of countless thousands of others escaping Vichy's État Français that week. When the armies ceased fire at 12:40 P.M. on Monday, June 17—Britain's first day alone—French ports and airfields were enveloped in chaos. Escapees from Austria, Czechoslovakia, Poland, and Scandinavia, many of them Jews, had found refuge in France. Their names were on Gestapo lists, they knew it, and they were frantic. RAF fields on French soil were closing down; pilots and ground crews were taking off for home. Forty thousand British fighting men, together with Belgian and Polish soldiers, were being evacuated from Brest, Cherbourg, St-Nazaire, Bordeaux, and Saint-Malo. It was a time of appalling tragedies, unnoted at the time and forgotten in the next five years of struggle for mastery of the Continent. One, which would have shocked the world even in wartime, was the loss of the liner *Lancastria,* just as she was leaving St-Nazaire with five thousand troops and civilian refugees aboard. Nazi bombers sank her, and three thousand drowned. Churchill forbade publication of this, saying, "The newspapers have got quite enough disaster for today, at least." Among the uprooted were Queen Wilhelmina of Holland, a fugitive from her own homeland granted asylum by King George; Somerset Maugham, who had fled his Cannes villa in a boat packed with fellow refugees, in which he spent three weeks without changing clothes; and, most remarkably, the Duke of Windsor, the former King Edward VIII, accompanied by his Baltimore duchess.

On the sixteenth, when de Gaulle was describing his mission to General Spears in a Bordeaux hotel suite, the telephone there had rung. Henry Mack, Ambassador Sir Ronald Campbell's first secretary, answered it and, to his astonishment, found himself talking to the Duke, who was calling from Nice. He and the Duchess were marooned there, he explained. Could a destroyer be sent to pick them up? Mack, shocked, told him there was only one British ship in Bordeaux's harbor, and that was a collier. He suggested that the Windsors drive to Spain. They did. They were staying with Sir Samuel Hoare, Britain's ambassador in Madrid, when the Duke decided to lean on Winston Churchill. After all, they were old friends. Churchill had nearly destroyed his own career trying to keep the Duke, then King, on his throne. Now Windsor wanted to return to England. He also insisted that he be appointed to an official position. And: "In the light of past experience, my wife and myself must not risk finding ourselves once more regarded by the British public as in a different status to other members of my family." All of this he sent Churchill in a telegram. In a separate message, Hoare reported that they wanted to be briefly received by the King and Queen, and that news of the meeting appear in the Court Circular.[118]

Apart from the fact that Churchill was busier than any other prime minister in the history of England, meeting any of these demands was impossible. The Duchess was anathema to the royal family, particularly Mary, the Queen Mother, and their opinion of her husband had plummeted upon learning that he and his wife admired Hitler. The Windsors had since the war's outbreak muted their former openly pro-Nazi rhetoric, but remained vehemently anti-Semitic, and moved comfortably in circles sharing their views. Also, although the Duke may have forgotten it, he was in uniform. At the war's outbreak, he had been commissioned a major general and appointed a liaison officer with the French. After the Germans entered Paris, he had been assigned to the *Armée des Alpes,* then to military headquarters in Nice. Although Ambassador Campbell's private secretary had suggested he go to Spain, no one had authorized him to do so. What to do with him?[119]

King George VI told Churchill: "Keep him out of England *at all costs.*" Churchill wired the Duke, curtly reminding him that he had "taken active military rank," and "refusal to obey orders" would create a grave situation. He added, but then cut: "Already there is a great deal of doubt as to the circumstances in which Your Royal Highness left Paris." The King's private secretary suggested the Duke be appointed to the army staff in Cairo; Churchill vetoed that. By now the Windsors were in Lisbon, where a British agent sent back word that the Duchess's activities were alarming; she was reported to have said that she and her husband could accept the possibility of German victory. The King's private secretary wrote No. 10 that "this is not the first time that this lady has come under suspicion for her anti-British activities, and as long as we never forget the power she can exert over him in her efforts to avenge herself on this country we shall be all right."

It was the King who proposed that his brother be appointed governor and commander in chief of the Bahamas. This was a royal comedown; the Bahamas was down there with the Falkland Islands and Ghana—the Gold Coast—in lack of imperial importance. Nevertheless, Churchill, who had better things to do, offered the Bahamian post to Windsor, adding, "Personally, I feel sure it is the best option in the grievous situation in which we all stand. At any rate, I have done my best." Later that day he asked Beaverbrook, "Max, do you think he'll take it?" According to Colville, who was present, Beaverbrook said, "He'll find it a great relief," and Churchill said, "Not half as much as his brother will."[120]

Windsor accepted it, though noting that he did not "consider my appointment as one of first class importance," and observing that it was "evident that the King and Queen do not wish to put our family differences to an end." But there was more. The prime minister told him there were conditions. His two British servants, being of military age, would have to serve in the army, and neither the Duke nor his Duchess would be permitted to visit the United States. The P.M. further warned that "sharp and unfriendly ears will be picked up to catch any suggestion that your Royal Highness takes a view about the war, or about the Germans, or about Hitlerism, which is different from that adopted by the British nation and Parliament.... Even while you have been staying in Lisbon, conversations have been reported by telegraph through various channels which might have been used to your Royal Highness's disadvantage." Warning Roosevelt that the Duke was on his way, he explained that he had been "causing His Majesty and His Majesty's Government some embarrassment," and that "Nazi intrigue seeks, now that the greater part of the Continent is in enemy hands, to make trouble about him."[121]

Churchill had ended his message to Windsor with "I thought your Royal Highness would not mind these words of caution." Of course the Duke minded, and he flouted them. Interviewed by the American magazine *Liberty,* he encouraged isolationists to leave no stone unturned in their campaign to keep the United States out of the war, this at a time when Churchill was toiling to get the U.S. *into* it. American guests were told by both the Duke and Duchess that their country would be foolish to fight at England's side. It was too late, they said; Britain was finished.[122]

On June 18 the moon was full—a bomber's moon. Colville noted the moon's phase in his diary, adding: "The air raids will now begin. They were bigger last night than hitherto, and Cambridge was hit, a row of houses being destroyed." Colville was correct. The Germans had been sending, intermittently, small forces of bombers in search of industrial and military targets since the previous autumn. Now they began to visit regularly.[123]

The June 22 surrender of the French, beside whom Britons had been prepared to fight to the bitter end, staggered all of Britain. Britons began to realize that the way of life they had known and loved was vanishing. People walked about as though in a daze. Bus conductors punched tickets in silence; Cockney newsboys, usually irrepressibly cheerful, mutely handed out papers. No one could remember when London had been so quiet. "At places where normally there is a noisy bustle of comings and goings," wrote an American observer, there was "the same extraordinary preoccupied silence." Mollie Panter-Downes reported in *The New Yorker* on June 28:

> The French acceptance of the crushing armistice terms came as a profound shock to the public, which had been simple enough to believe Marshal Pétain when he declared that France would make no shameful surrender.... The average uninformed citizen found it difficult to believe that anything could be more shameful than an agreement which handed over weapons of war, airfields, munition works, and industrial areas to be used unconditionally."[124]

It is in this context of anger and bitterness that Churchill's action against the French fleet must be seen. To put it in the best possible light, the behavior of Admiral Jean Louis Xavier François Darlan was duplicitous. As France's naval chief of staff he had given his solemn word to everyone around him that if events led to an armistice with the Nazis, he would order all French warships to take refuge in British ports. To a French general he said that, if necessary, he would place every vessel under the Union Jack. He told a member of the *Chambre des Députés* who was also on his staff: "If an armistice is signed for one day, I shall round off my career with an act of glorious indiscipline; I shall sail with the Fleet." As late as the evening of June 16, with the cease-fire only hours away, he assured Sir Ronald Campbell: "So long as I can issue orders to it [the fleet] you have nothing to fear." Even de Gaulle believed him. "A feudal lord," he said, "does not surrender his fief."[125]

Suddenly Darlan was the most important man in the war. Weygand's army was a shattered hulk, but the French navy—the fourth-largest in the world, after Britain, the United States, and Japan—included some of the fastest, most modern ships afloat: three modern and five older battleships, eighteen heavy cruisers, twenty-seven light cruisers, sixty submarines (twenty-four had been sunk), and more than fifty destroyers. All were important. Were Hitler to grab just one-third of the French navy, he'd almost double the size of the German navy overnight. Britain's army was small and weaponless; her air force was outnumbered by the Luftwaffe. Sea power was vital to the nation's survival, but if the French, German, and Italian navies were combined, the Royal Navy would be overwhelmed. As Churchill saw it, "Admiral Darlan had but to sail one of his ships to any port outside France to become master of all French interests beyond German control"—in short, the entire French colonial empire.[126]

Why did he stay? He appears to have had several motives. His hatred of the British lay deep; he believed that for Frenchmen, there was no difference between England (as the French always called Britain) and Germany; Pétain was offering him power; and he was convinced that the Nazis would win the war. He told Ambassador Bullitt that he was "certain that Great Britain would be conquered by Germany within five weeks unless Great Britain should surrender sooner." When Bullitt remarked that Darlan seemed pleased by that prospect, he smiled and nodded in agreement. As for his promises, he preserved honor, at least in his own eyes, by resigning his commission and taking office as Pétain's minister of marine. It was now his duty to enforce the policies of the new government whether he approved of them or not.[127]

As late as June 22, first sea lord Admiral Dudley Pound told the War Cabinet that Darlan was taking "all possible steps" to prevent his ships from falling into Nazi hands. Churchill believed that they could not rely on one man's word, because the issue was "so vital to the safety of the whole British Empire." Within hours he was vindicated. At 6:50 P.M. they learned the terms of the armistice on June 22. The French had signed it without consulting their ally. Article VIII stipulated that the "French war fleet... will be assembled in ports to be specified and then demobilized and disarmed under German or Italian control."

The British had been betrayed. The ships would be delivered into enemy hands while still fully armed. Hitler declared that Germany did not intend to use them during the war, but as the prime minister rhetorically asked Parliament: "What is the value of that? Ask half a dozen countries, what is the value of such a solemn assurance? Furthermore, the armistice could be voided at any time on any pretext of 'non-observance.'"[128]

The French fleet formed but one part of a much larger story. With the French surrender, the British naval blockade of the Baltic—the closing of the Skagerrak and Kattegat Straits to German ships—was broken. The Germans now held European ports from Norway through Denmark, Holland, Belgium, and France to the Bay of Biscay. The German capture of the Channel ports—Dieppe, Cherbourg, Brest, St-Nazaire, La Rochelle,

Le Havre, and Lorient—had changed the entire dynamic of the war. Operating from these ports the Reich's submariners had to sail for only a day or two in order to reach British shipping lanes. Immediately the British ceased merchant sailings into or out of the Southwest Approaches, the sea-lanes that ran south of Ireland and into the Irish Sea, to Bristol and Liverpool. That left the Northwest Approaches—the sea-lanes between Northern Ireland and Scotland—as the only route into Britain.

Peril also loomed in the Mediterranean, where the French navy had been charged with securing the western part of that sea. The French navy was no longer a factor, unless it fell into the hands of the Germans and Italians, and that, Churchill later wrote, would confront "Great Britain with mortal danger." To fill the void left by the French in the western Mediterranean, the British drew heavily from the Home Fleet—itself preparing against possible invasion—to create Force H at Gibraltar, a powerful fleet of battleships, an aircraft carrier, and numerous cruisers, destroyers, and submarines. The commander of Force H, Vice Admiral James Somerville, was given three objectives: keep the Germans out of the Mediterranean, keep the Italians in, and impose a naval blockade on Vichy France and its northwest African dominions. But how to remove the French fleet from the equation?[129]

Churchill found himself confronted, he later wrote, with "a hateful decision, the most unnatural and painful in which I have ever been concerned." There was no easy solution, although some thought so; on June 25, George Bernard Shaw wrote to him: "Why not declare war on France and capture her fleet (which would gladly strike its colors to us) before A.H. recovers his breath? Surely that is the logic of the situation?" Churchill knew the French fleet would gladly do no such thing, and any use of force to cripple it would enrage Vichy. Yet as the British blockade of Vichy tightened, French hostility would become inevitable anyway. Therefore the War Cabinet, with Churchill the apostle of force majeure, approved an operation that, in his words, would comprise "the simultaneous seizure, control, or effective disablement of all the accessible French fleet." Accessible were ships now in English waters and those anchored at Alexandria, the Algerian city of Oran, and Dakar, in West Africa.[130]

The first phase of the British action was code-named Operation Grasp. In the early hours of July 3, armed boarding parties took over all French vessels in the ports of Portsmouth, Plymouth, Falmouth, Southampton, and Sheerness. There was virtually no resistance; one French and one English sailor were killed when the crew of the French submarine *Surcouf* disputed the issue. Surprise was complete, and the ease with which the French ships were taken demonstrated, as the prime minister pointed out, "how easily the Germans could have taken possession of any French ships lying in ports which they controlled."[131]

The second phase, Operation Catapult, was more difficult. The P.M. called it "the deadly stroke... in the western Mediterranean." In the eastern Mediterranean, at Alexandria, they were lucky. Darlan ordered Vice Admiral René Godfroy to sail his ships to the French-held North African Bizerte; simultaneously, Admiral Sir Andrew Browne Cunningham ("ABC" to his friends), commander in chief of Royal Navy Mediterranean operations, was ordered to stop him. The two admirals, good friends, settled the issue by a gentleman's agreement: Godfroy discharged his fuel oil and placed the breechblocks of his guns and the warheads of his torpedoes in custody of the French consul ashore, with the British consul as co-trustee. All parties signed a formal agreement, thus achieving Cunningham's objective without violating Godfroy's honor.[132]

It was very different at Mers-el-Kébir, the naval base three miles west of Oran. Much of the French Atlantic squadron was anchored here, including two battleships and two modern battle cruisers, the *Dunkerque* and the *Strasbourg,* built by the French to counter the German battle cruisers *Gneisenau* and *Scharnhorst,* which had proven their deadliness when they mauled the British off Norway. *Dunkerque* and *Strasbourg* could not be allowed to fall into German hands. The French commander, Vice Admiral Marcel Gensoul, had been alerted and told to be wary of the British. Admiral Pound said the only way to destroy them would be "in a surprise attack carried out at dawn and without any form of prior notification." But that was impossible. Catapult was asking a lot of Royal Navy officers as it was; just a week earlier the French had been their comrades. They could not be expected to open fire on them without warning. Thus the task given Vice Admiral Somerville was both difficult and delicate.

He arrived off Mers-el-Kébir shortly after 9:00 A.M. on July 3 with the battleships *Valiant* and *Resolution,* the venerable and feared battle cruiser *Hood,* two cruisers, eleven destroyers, and the aircraft carrier *Ark Royal.* Somerville gave Gensoul four choices. He could sail with the Royal Navy against Nazi Germany and Italy; he could sail to a British port; he could sail to a French colonial port or the United States, where the ships would be disarmed for the duration; or he could sink his vessels within the next six hours. Failing these, Somerville's message ended, "I have orders from His Majesty's Government to use whatever force may be necessary to prevent your ships from falling into German or Italian hands."[133]

Eight hours of palaver followed. Gensoul said that under no circumstances would he permit his crafts to be taken intact by the Nazis, who, until now, had been their common enemies. Faced with an ultimatum, however, he would defend himself by force. Somerville radioed London that the French showed no signs of leaving their harbor. Churchill, speaking through the Admiralty, told him to get on with it, to do his duty, distasteful though it was. Somerville gave Gensoul a series of deadlines, telling the Admiralty that the French were awaiting instructions from their government and that he was having problems with French mines. However, as the afternoon waned, he realized that the French admiral was stalling while he gathered steam, putting his vessels in an advanced state of readiness for sea. Then British intelligence intercepted messages to Mers-el-Kébir from the new French government. Darlan was ordering Gensoul to "answer force with force." He had informed the Germans of what was going on, and he told Gensoul that all French ships in the Mediterranean were on their way. The Admiralty radioed Somerville: "Settle the matter quickly or you may have French reinforcements to deal with."[134]

At 5:55 P.M. the British admiral issued the order to open fire. Within ten minutes one French battleship had blown up, and the other was beached. The *Dunkerque* had run aground—torpedo bombers from the *Ark Royal* finished her off—and 1,250 French sailors were dead. Only the *Strasbourg* had escaped, making smoke and fleeing into the gathering darkness.[135]

Mers-el-Kébir was the culmination of nearly eight weeks of increasing disappointment and distrust between the two former allies. Pétain's government was apoplectic. Darlan vowed revenge. Pierre Laval, the new minister of foreign affairs in the Vichy government, whose tarnished star was rising in the Nazi sun over Vichy, called for a declaration of war on England. Baudouin disparaged Britain's war effort and blamed the war on the English. Pétain broke off diplomatic relations with Britain, and the long, sad epic of his État Français's collaboration with the Germans began. Some French warships, including the battleship *Richelieu,* took refuge at Dakar; the rest—three battleships, seven heavy cruisers, sixteen submarines, eighteen destroyers, and a dozen torpedo boats, almost one-third of the prewar French navy—sailed to the naval base at Toulon. There, for the next twenty-nine months, the fleet rode at anchor.

In England the action at Mers-el-Kébir was wildly cheered. Gallup found that confidence in the prime minister rose to 89 percent—at Chamberlain's peak it had been 69 percent. Francophobia had not been so intense since the Napoleonic years. Even as the guns fell silent off Algeria, Britain learned that Vichy had quashed Reynaud's assurance that the 400 Luftwaffe pilots who had become Allied prisoners would be sent to Britain, and were instead on their way back to Germany. In the House of Commons Churchill said: "I leave the judgment of our action, with confidence, to Parliament. I leave it to the nation, and I leave it to the United States. I leave it to the world and history."[136]

Suddenly every MP was on his feet. Jock Colville noted in his diary: "He told the whole story of Oran and the House listened enthralled and amazed. Gasps of surprise were audible, but it was clear the House unanimously approved." Hugh Dalton wrote: "At the end we gave him a much louder and longer ovation than he, or Chamberlain or anyone else, had yet had during this war." Harold Nicolson noted: "The House is at first saddened by this odious attack but is fortified by Winston's speech. The grand finale ends in an ovation, with Winston sitting there with the tears pouring down his cheeks."[137]

Curiously, the most bitter dissent was heard in the Admiralty. All the flag officers who had participated in Catapult agreed with Cunningham that the attack had been "an act of sheer treachery which was as injudicious as it was unnecessary" and was "almost inept in its unwisdom." What they failed to grasp was that Mers-el-Kébir was not just a military action. Churchill's objective, which he reached, was far greater. Later he tried to explain it to Cordell Hull, who thought it a "tragic blunder." As Hull, an anti-imperialist who harbored a smoldering distrust of Churchill's ultimate motives, set it down, Churchill told him that "since many people throughout the world believed that Britain was about to surrender, he had wanted by this action to show that she still meant to fight."

That was the crux. In little more than two years, the Nazis had seized or conquered Austria, Czechoslovakia, Poland, Denmark, Norway, Belgium, Holland, Luxembourg, and France, and they had done it almost effortlessly. To millions, resistance seemed futile, even suicidal. On May 15, America's ambassador, Joseph P. Kennedy, had informed President Roosevelt that Britain was finished, and that the end would come soon; he expected the Germans in London within a month. The British people didn't think so. In May a Gallup poll found that 3 percent of them thought they might lose the war—by the end of July the percentage was so small it was immeasurable. Their King spoke for them when he wrote Queen Mary: "Personally, I feel happier now that we have no allies to be polite to and to pamper." Though abroad his kingdom seemed doomed, at home Mers-el-Kébir ended talk of a British surrender. The prime minister was particularly anxious about the view in Washington. To his great relief Roosevelt approved, believing, he said, that if there was one chance in a hundred that France's warships might fall into German hands, the attack was justified. Seven months later, Harry Hopkins, arriving in London as the President's emissary, told Colville that "it was Oran which convinced President Roosevelt, in spite of opinions to the contrary, that the British would go on fighting, as Churchill had promised, if necessary for years, if necessary alone."[138]

Most, including Hitler, believed Churchill's declaration to fight on alone applied only to the defense of England. But Churchill intended as well to take the fight to Hitler. He told Britons many times in coming months that Hitler must break the Home Island in order to win the war. Actually, Churchill knew there was another way—in another place—for Hitler to win, one that would negate the need for an all-or-nothing invasion of England. It was also the place that afforded Churchill the best chance to take the fight to Hitler's ally and, if Hitler came to his ally's assistance, to Hitler himself. Where all Britons that summer scanned the seas and the skies overhead, Churchill looked far further, to the place he believed the war would be decided: the Mediterranean Sea.

The Mediterranean lay at the center of Churchill's strategic vision, as it had for the ancient Romans, and as it now did for Mussolini. Churchill later called the Mediterranean "the hinge of fate" upon which the outcome of the war turned. Many in the German navy and Luftwaffe high command understood this. Later in the summer the commander in chief of the German navy, *Grossadmiral* Erich Raeder, told Hitler in private that "the British have always considered the Mediterranean the pivot of their world empire." Raeder believed clearing the British from the Mediterranean would sever England from its Empire and force London to come to terms, if the U-boat blockade did not bring Britain to its knees first. Churchill believed likewise. But Churchill not only saw danger in the Mediterranean, he saw opportunity, the *only* opportunity for Britain to go on the offensive, by sea, air, and on land. This, Churchill intended to do. His war strategy can be summed up thus: defend England; defend and attack in the Mediterranean.[139]

Since the time of the Caesars, dominance of the Mediterranean—*mare nostrum*—had been vital to Italian security. The Mediterranean between Sicily and Tripoli, a distance of about 300 miles, was to Rome what the English Channel and the Northwest Approaches were to London. Malta, a British possession since 1814, and home to a Royal Navy fleet, sits directly astride the sea routes from Italy to its North Africa colonies. The main island of Malta, 95 square miles of Tertiary limestone, rises from the sea 100 miles south of Sicily and about 200 miles northeast of Tripoli. The nearest British naval base, in Alexandria, lay almost 1,000 miles to the east, Gibraltar 1,100 miles to the west. When France fell, the entire British air presence on Malta consisted of three obsolete Gloster Gladiator biplanes, dubbed *Faith, Hope,* and *Charity* by their pilots. A fourth Gladiator was stripped for spare parts. Gibraltar and the Suez Canal are the main portals into the Mediterranean, but Malta since the time of Nelson had been the geographical key to free run of the sea. The harbor at Valletta was the only British deepwater port between the anchorages at Gibraltar and Alexandria, and therefore critical to the Royal Navy, almost as vital as Scapa Flow, the Scottish anchorage and main base of the Home Fleet.

But the British, expecting at least an Italian air attack, if not a full-scale naval assault on Malta, moved their warships (but for submarines) from the naval base at Valletta to Alexandria, to help cover the eastern Mediterranean. Mussolini launched his first air raid on Malta on June 11, and never let up; he understood that only when he controlled the sea could his armies secure the perimeter. His navy of six battleships, nineteen cruisers, one hundred smaller vessels, and more than one hundred submarines was larger than the German navy, and larger than the combined British fleets at Gibraltar and Alexandria. Malta was so central to Churchill's war strategy that he told the War Cabinet later in 1940 that if allocations of concrete for use in building coastal defenses had to be adjusted downward, it must not be done at the expense of three "vital" positions: The Home Island, Gibraltar, and Malta. Mussolini and Churchill (and Grand Admiral Raeder) knew that if the British lost Malta, the Mediterranean would become an Italian lake, and Gibraltar and the Suez Canal would become trapdoors to oblivion for the British. Mussolini, in his navy, had the way; whether he and his naval commanders had the will remained to be seen.[140]

Italy, like Britain, was an imperial sea power. Its most prized colonial possessions, Cyrenaica and Tripolitania, were just two days' sail from Sicily. The Italian merchant fleet, protected by the Italian navy, served as the lifeline to those colonies, which in turn fed Italy. On June 10, 1940, the day Mussolini plunged his dagger into France, the Italian merchant fleet, at 3.5 million tons, was the fifth-largest in the world, behind the U.K. (18 million tons), the U.S. (12 million), Japan (5.5 million), and Norway (4.8 million). More than three-quarters of the Norwegian fleet—1,000 ships that were at sea when the Germans struck in April—now sailed in alliance with Britain. Mussolini's rush to climb aboard Hitler's war wagon resulted in one of the least noted but most significant shipping defeats of the entire war. On June 11, the day after Mussolini invaded France, his merchant fleet was reduced by 35 percent when 220 Italian freighters and tankers were seized in neutral ports worldwide. Mussolini had failed to call his merchant fleet home before his betrayal of France. He would never make up the loss. Churchill saw opportunity here. He believed the Italians would strike from Libya toward Cairo, but he also believed that Mussolini, with the loss of so much of his merchant shipping, could no longer support his African adventures. Two days after Dunkirk and four days before Mussolini struck, Churchill sent a memo to the Air Ministry: "It is of the highest importance that we should strike at Italy the moment war breaks out." In the early fall Churchill told the House, "Signor Mussolini has some experiences ahead of him which he had not foreseen at the time when he thought it safe and profitable to stab the stricken and prostrate French Republic in the back."[141]

The possibility of a Nazi onslaught against the Home Island had first been raised at a Defence Committee meeting on May 20, when enemy panzers passed Amiens on their way to Abbéville, cutting off the BEF. After a brief discussion, chiefly about the lack of riflemen and rifle ammunition, eight Bren Guns—light machine guns—were manned in Whitehall, including the entrance to No. 10, and two more were placed above Admiralty Arch. They would have been useful only if Germans swarmed out of Buckingham Palace or Trafalgar Square. Three days later graver news from the Channel ports led to more realistic planning; Churchill alerted the Dominion prime ministers to the possibility of an "early heavy attack" on England and told his Chiefs of Staff that "some means of dealing with the enemy's tanks"—he suggested land mines—might be found. By then the issue was judged to be serious. Martin Gilbert writes, "Invasion was now the dominant concern of those at the center of war policy. By the end of June it excluded virtually every thought in Englishmen's heads." In his diary Ironside wrote: "It is the weakness of waiting for an attack that preys upon people's minds." By then the French had surrendered to Italy, too, and RAF scouts were reporting the assembling of barges, lighters, and ferries in the ports of Belgium and northern France, and Whitehall knew that across the Channel, Nazi troops were singing, "We're sailing against England."[142]

In Parliament Churchill first addressed the question of defense against invasion on June 4, as the Dunkirk evacuation was winding down. Yet, even at that early date, with British fortunes approaching their nadir, offense, not defense, underlay his strategic vision:

> The whole question of home defence against invasion is, of course, powerfully affected by the fact that we have for the time being in this Island incomparably more powerful military forces than we have ever had at any moment in this war or the last. But this will not continue. We shall not be content with a defensive war.... We have to reconstitute and build up the British Expeditionary Force once again.... All this is in train; but in the interval we must put our defenses in this Island into such a high state of organization that the fewest possible numbers will be required to give effective security and that the largest possible potential of offensive effort may be realized. On this we are now engaged.[143]

Three weeks later, in a letter to South African prime minister Jan Smuts, a staunch British ally, Churchill made his offense-minded thoughts perfectly clear: "Obviously we have to repulse any attack on Great Britain by invasion." He predicted that Hitler might turn toward Russia and "he may do so without trying invasion." Then: "Our large army now being created for home defence is being formed on the principle of attack and opportunity, for large scale amphibious operations may come in 1940 and 1941."[144]

But for the time being he could attack Hitler only with words. His most eloquent challenge to the Nazis was delivered the day after the French laid down their arms. He spoke for thirty-six minutes, reading from twenty-three pages of typewritten notes. He foresaw a climax:

> What General Weygand called the Battle of France is over. I expect the Battle of Britain is about to begin. Upon this battle depends the survival of Christian civilization. Upon it depends our own British life, and the long continuity of our institutions and our Empire. The whole fury and might of the enemy must very soon be turned on us. Hitler knows that he will have to break us in this island or lose the war. If we can stand up to him all Europe may be free, and the life of the world may move forward into broad, sunlit uplands.
>
> But if we fail, then the whole world, including the United States, including all we have known and cared for, will sink into the abyss of a new Dark Age, made more sinister, and perhaps more protracted by the lights of perverted science.
>
> Let us therefore brace ourselves to our duties, and so bear ourselves that, if the British Empire and its Commonwealth last for a thousand years, men will still say, "This was their finest hour."[145]

Later, Edward R. Murrow would say of Churchill: "Now, the hour had come for him to mobilize the English language and send it into battle."

It was as though a great bell had tolled, summoning Englishmen to sacrifice everything save honor in defense of their homeland and western civilization. The world beyond, other than the Empire, was deaf to it. Although listeners then and since took from Churchill's words the impression that he was speaking about the bravery of Englishmen to Englishmen, he was not. He had chosen his words with care. He had not said that a thousand years hence, people would say this was England's finest hour, but that it was the *British Empire*'s finest hour. Hitler had declared that his Reich would last one thousand years; Churchill had now claimed the same for his Empire. Each believed only one empire could survive. Neither considered the possibility that both might perish. Britain fought on that summer, alone in Europe—the Dominions and colonies too distant to offer meaningful help, yet with the Empire comprising one-quarter of the earth's population, sturdy in its support of the Home Island. But the Empire—including India and the outliers of South Africa, Australia, and New Zealand—could not respond fast enough or with enough force to thwart Hitler. Only one Canadian division, withdrawn from France, was in Britain.

Americans were sympathetic but pessimistic, and political leaders there and on the Continent were unimpressed by Churchill's inspired words. Franklin Roosevelt, facing reelection in a country opposed to going to war, was not about to say or do anything that might appear to endorse Churchill and the British Empire. "For those who were not Germans," writes Alan Brooke's biographer, "there seemed that summer only one way of safety—instant and unconditional surrender—and for those who delayed only one fate—certain and imminent destruction." Indeed, Hitler believed that the war was over. He had already staged a victory parade, marching conscripts of the 218th Infantry Division through the Brandenburg Gate. Forty of the Wehrmacht's 160 divisions had been demobilized, and the Führer had drafted a peace treaty he was sure the British would sign, knowing that the alternative was annihilation.[146]

Some Englishmen would sign such a treaty. There existed therefore an alternative to Hitler having to "break us in this Island." In a May 20 telegram to Roosevelt, Churchill had raised the possibility of a peace movement sweeping him from office and his successors having to negotiate with Hitler "in utter despair and helplessness." He mentioned that possibility again in a June 15 cable to the president, suggesting that Hitler in effect need only *bend* Britain, bend it to near the breaking point, and the result would be a new government formed to negotiate a terrible peace in hopes of gaining deliverance for "a shattered or a starving nation." The result would leave Britain "a vassal state of the Hitler empire." Such a settlement would deny the warrior Churchill his battle, the political Churchill his office, and England its sovereignty. All were unacceptable. The Vatican indeed proposed a peaceful settlement of the conflict, and on August 1, King Gustav of Sweden, the doyen of European monarchs (and the source for much of Hitler's iron ore), wrote King George VI, proposing a conference "to examine the possibility of making peace." Some Englishmen—they called themselves "sound" and Winston "unsound"—thought this suggestion merited discussion. The men of Munich were still a force, particularly in the Establishment. Halifax, of course, was one. The United Press quoted him as inviting "Chancellor Hitler to make a new and more generous peace offer." R. A. Butler, Halifax's under secretary, was an energetic supporter of Gustav's peace overtures. According to Björn Prytz, then the Swedish minister in London, on June 7, when the prime minister was commuting to France, attempting to stiffen French resolve, Butler told Prytz that Churchill's inflexibility toward the Third Reich was "not decisive." He saw no reason why the war should not end now in a compromise peace, provided German terms were acceptable, and assured the Swede that British policy would be guided "not by bravado but by common sense."[147]

Hearing of this, the P.M. sent the foreign office a blistering memo scoring the "lukewarmness" in Butler—Butler, whining, protested that he had been misunderstood—and restated the government's determination "to fight to the death."

Churchill told the King that "the intrusion of the ignominious King of Sweden as a peace-maker, after his desertion of Finland and Norway, and while he is absolutely in the German grip ... is singularly distasteful." His sovereign agreed. King George had caught the mood of his people; in his diary he wrote: "How can we talk of peace with Germany now after they have overrun and demoralized the peoples of so many countries in Europe? Until Germany is prepared to live peaceably with her neighbors in Europe, she will always be a menace. We have got to get rid of her aggressive spirit, her engines of war & the people who have been taught to use them."[148]

Afterward, Englishmen as skeptical of politicians as Bernard Shaw and Malcolm Muggeridge agreed that had anyone but Churchill been prime minister in the summer of 1940, Britain would have negotiated an armistice with Hitler. In London the tenacious Swedish envoy informed Stockholm that several influential MPs had echoed Butler. Two of His Majesty's ambassadors—Hoare in Madrid, and Lord Lothian in Washington—were seeking contacts with their Nazi counterparts, preparing for diplomatic "conversations."

In Parliament the most prominent defeatist was Lloyd George, England's prime minister in the Great War. Jealous of Churchill, once his colleague, the old Welshman had refused to join his cabinet. Instead he planned to replace him and approach the enemy, asking for terms. "I argue," he told the House in his mellow, persuasive voice, "that the Government should take into consideration any proposals of peace which ... review all the subjects that have been the cause of all the troubles of the last few years." He made his position public. In the July 28 *Sunday Pictorial,* he wrote, "I foresaw the catastrophe impending." Had his advice been followed, he continued, it would have led to "a better understanding between the angry nations and to the rebuilding of the temper of peace.... I wish to point out that conditions were then more favourable for a discussion on equal terms than they are today, or probably will be a few weeks hence."[149]

In Berlin Lloyd George was being seriously considered as a possible leader of a puppet government. German psychologists told the Führer that Lloyd George reflected Britain's mood. He didn't; neither did Butler nor the Swedish ambassador's informants; they were no longer in step with their countrymen. Every literate Londoner, it seemed, was reading *Guilty Men,** a Labour attack written under the pseudonym Cato on the appeasers that indicted fifteen Tories, among them Baldwin, Chamberlain, Halifax, and Hoare, for neglecting England's defenses. It seemed that Englishmen everywhere were scorning any suggestion of negotiations; in the old British army phrase, they were "bloody-minded." Even Tom Jones, a former deputy secretary to the cabinet, wrote from Cliveden, "Everyone is willing to be conscripted for any duty and the main regret is that we cannot all be used."[150]

Not only had the collapse of the French failed to discourage them; it had actually raised their morale.

Churchill's defiant spirit had set the whole kingdom afire. Dunkirk had been a defeat, yet Englishmen had decked it with the laurels of victory. They had always been braced by the thought that their backs were against the wall, that the odds against them were hopeless. Now they recalled the maxim: "England always loses every battle except the last one." They were, they reminded one another, descendants of Englishmen who, Macaulay wrote, had "lit the bonfires from Eddystone to Berwick-bound, from Lynn to Milford Bay, warning of the Spanish Armada's approach undismayed and had watched, unintimidated, the twinkling of Napoleon's bonfires at Boulogne."[151]

Dorothy L. Sayers wrote:

This is the war that England knows,
When no allies are left, no help
To count upon from alien hands,
No waverers remain to woo,
No more advice to listen to,
And only England stands.[152]

On their display boards, news vendors chalked: "We're in the final—to be played on home ground." Somerset Maugham, reaching Liverpool at last, found no discouragement over the French debacle, only men who said confidently, "It doesn't matter; we can lick the Jerries alone" and "Fear of invasion? Not a shadow of it. We'll smash 'em. It'll take time, of course, but that's all right; we can hang on." "It was," Maugham concluded, "a

* Cato was the pseudonym of three journalists, Michael Foot, Frank Owen, and Peter Howard.

very different England from the England I had left a few weeks earlier. It was more determined, more energetic and more angry. Winston Churchill had inspired the nation with his own stern and resolute fortitude."[153]

In *The New Yorker,* Mollie Panter-Downes described the public temper as "grimly sane." On June 22 she wrote: "The individual Englishman seems to be singularly unimpressed by the fact that there is now nothing between him and the undivided attention of a war machine such as the world has never seen before. Possibly it's lack of imagination; possibly again it's the same species of dogged resolution which occasionally produces an epic like Dunkirk." By late summer she herself seemed to have been caught up in the emotional firestorm. "The ordinary individual is magnificent in a moment like this," she wrote, and, two weeks later, "The calm behavior of the average individual continues to be amazing." Like Maugham she finally concluded that the key to the nation's soaring morale was the new prime minister. She quoted the *Times,* which had considered Churchill unsound for ten years, as continuing its suspicions—"Mr. Churchill is still, in some respects, a solitary figure"—and commented: "That solitary figure continues to command the devotion and confidence of all classes which has probably been equaled only by the great William Pitt in 1759, 'the year of victories.' England would seem to have found her man of destiny at a critical juncture, when her well-wishers were beginning to fear that destiny was taking the down, not the up, grade. An extraordinary leader and the determination of an extraordinary people have brought back hope and dignity to a scene that has long and humiliatingly lacked them."[154]

During the summer after France fell, Englishmen awaited, at any moment, the appearance, by sea and by parachute, of the German army. That was the German way. They appeared on the Polish frontier the previous year; they appeared off the coast of Norway that spring; they emerged from the Ardennes in May; they dropped from the sky into Rotterdam. Englishmen, therefore, believed themselves to be in deadly peril, and continued to do so with varying degrees of trepidation until the late summer of 1942, in large part because Churchill told them so. Churchill, in turn, believed the Germans *might* come, and demanded every necessary precaution be taken *should* the Germans come, but he did not believe—that summer or the next—that they *would* come. Soon after the French surrender, he told Colville: "Hitler must invade or fail. If he fails, he is bound to go East [to Russia], and fail he will."[155]

That statement was not the most precise formulation of his beliefs, but it contained the essence: Hitler could try to invade England, and would fail, or Hitler would turn against his partner Joseph Stalin. To that end, Churchill wrote a letter to Stalin in late June in hopes of opening up communications with the Marshal of the sort he had established with Franklin Roosevelt. He entrusted the letter to his new ambassador to Moscow, Sir Stafford Cripps, a socialist whose very appointment as ambassador Churchill intended as a signal to Stalin.

The issue, as Churchill told Stalin (Churchill always pronounced his name *Schtaleen*), was whether Hitler's "bid for hegemony of Europe threatens the interests of the Soviet Union." It certainly threatened England's. Churchill acknowledged that relations between London and Moscow had "been hampered by mutual suspicions" (a marvelous understatement), but said that now only they could contest Hitler's quest for continental hegemony, by virtue of their geographical positions, which were "not in Europe but on her extremities." The idea that Britain was part of Europe but not "in" Europe informed Churchill's political beliefs for his entire life. He would have found nothing parochial or comical in the apocryphal London headline: FOG IN CHANNEL—CONTINENT ISOLATED. Indeed, Hitler had now isolated the Continent. Great Britain's two objectives, Churchill told Stalin, were to "save herself from Nazi domination" and "to free the rest of Europe" from Nazi domination. The message was meant to reassure Stalin. Stalin never replied. Cripps reported that Stalin, after reading the letter, denigrated the possibility of German territorial ambitions and asserted his belief that Germany posed no danger to Russia. After Cripps was dismissed, Stalin ordered his minister of foreign affairs, Vyacheslav Molotov, to pass the minutes of his conversation with Cripps on to Berlin, a gesture intended to remind Hitler of Stalin's abiding friendship.[156]

Churchill had not read Hitler's mind; Hitler had broadcast his intention to crush the Bolshevik Soviet Union in his autobiography, *Mein Kampf*. It was all there. He had written with absolute clarity: "This colossal empire [Russia] in the East is ripe for dissolution. And the end of the Jewish domination of Russia will also be the end of Russia as a state." Hitler, in turn, had no need to try to read Churchill's mind; he was reading his mail. It is not surprising, therefore, that in mid-July, Hitler declared to his military chiefs that "Britain's hope lies in Russia and America." He was correct. He noted that Britain was "back on her feet," sustained in part by their Russian hopes. Therefore, he declared, "if Russia is smashed, Britain's last hope will be shattered.... Decision: In view of these considerations Russia must be liquidated. Spring, 1941."[157]

Churchill arrived at his certainty regarding Germany and Russia through a balance of cold logic and intuition, although some of his colleagues would say it was more of a collision. This was how he approached all problems. Whether parsing geopolitical matters such as continental hegemony, or the Mediterranean theater, or the finer points of the defense of England, Churchill came at every issue with a painter's eye; the whole was larger than the sum of its parts. He saw the beauty and vitality of details, and their effect on larger strategic issues, and demanded that they be scrutinized all the time. The most obvious and simplest of facts portended larger strategic issues. One fact, often neglected in the telling of the tale of that summer, underlay Churchill's planning for a German invasion: A day is divided into daylight hours and nighttime hours. The Battle of Britain is often described as "a battle for air supremacy." In fact, it was a battle for *daytime* air supremacy. Everything changed after dark. Night bombers—British and German—flew without fear of fighters, and with little fear of anti-aircraft fire, but sacrificed targeting accuracy. Fighter planes went aloft at night only when the moon was full, or nearly full, to protect their bombers or search the skies for the enemy's. Armies could maneuver and fight by night or day. But in late June, the German army was in France, while the British army—hobbled but rebuilding—was in England. Churchill of course could not know that the Germans had not yet even contemplated an invasion. But he did know that if the Germans attempted one, they could arrive on English soil in meaningful numbers only by sea. Churchill believed they could not do so. In order to land at dawn, an invasion armada would have to sail at night, but with German fighter planes grounded during darkness, the Royal Navy—its largest ships equipped with radar—owned the night. At night, the Royal Navy could hunt the enemy's invasion barges and ships at will. In a July 7 memo to Ironside, Churchill wrote: "Except in very narrow waters, it would be most hazardous and even suicidal to commit a large army to the accidents of the sea in the teeth of our very numerous armed patrolling forces."[158]

Churchill warned the House that it would be impossible for the Royal Navy "to prevent raids by 5,000 or 10,000 men flung suddenly across and thrown ashore at several points on the coast some dark night or foggy morning." But those raiders would soon find themselves surrounded by units of the British army. If such a force came ashore in northern England or Scotland, it would find itself hundreds of miles from London, and irrelevant. No, the Germans had to come in overwhelming force, and land within one hundred miles of London. Churchill believed that Hitler—if he came—would try to decapitate the British government in London, in order to force a settlement with a new, more malleable government. A military conquest and occupation of all of Britain, from Devon to the Midlands to Scotland, was simply beyond the means of the Wehrmacht, not because the German army lacked the men and tanks, but because Germany lacked the shipping to even *try* to carry such a force to England.[159]

If the Germans tried, Churchill expected to annihilate them. On June 18 he sketched his vision for the House:

> The efficacy of sea power, especially under modern conditions, depends upon the invading force being of large size. It has to be of large size, in view of our military strength, to be of any use. If it is of large size, then the Navy have something they can find and meet and, as it were, bite on. Now, we must remember that even five [German] divisions, however lightly equipped, would require 200 to 250 ships, and with modern air reconnaissance and photography it would not be easy to collect such an armada, marshal it, and conduct it across the sea without any powerful naval forces to escort it; and there would be very great possibilities, to put it mildly, that this armada would be intercepted long before it reached the coast, and all the men drowned in the sea or at the worst blown to pieces with their equipment while they were trying to land.... There should be no difficulty in this, owing to our great superiority at sea.[160]

The previous summer Hitler, unlike Mussolini on June 10, had had the good sense to bring his merchant fleet into the Baltic before striking into Poland. The small size of the German merchant fleet, about 1.2 million tons, was one of four fundamental facts—after the different conditions imposed by daylight and nighttime operations—upon which Churchill based his belief that if the Germans came to England, they would fail. For Churchill, these were the details on which all else turned.

The first: He estimated that to put the first wave of 60,000 to 80,000 German troops ashore would require almost 60 percent of all German merchant shipping. To put a second wave of 160,000 ashore, along with ammunition, tanks, and heavy artillery, would require far more shipping than Germany had at its disposal. As will be seen, those same figures, which boosted Churchill's optimism, dismayed the high command of the German navy.

The second: Germany lacked the specialized landing craft that could put tanks and heavy artillery right on a beach. The Germans would have to capture a port to offload their armor and equipment. If they sailed into a port, they would find the facilities destroyed by the British, the harbor entrance mined behind them such that they could not sail out, and a ring of British artillery pouring fire down on the port.

The third: Churchill later wrote that although the RAF—in both bombers and fighters—was outnumbered by almost 3 to 1, "I rested upon the conclusion that in our own air, in our own country and its waters, we could beat the German air force."

The fourth: Sea power. The Royal Navy was overwhelmingly more powerful than the German navy. Only a "hostile air power could destroy" the almost one thousand British warships deployed around England, Churchill wrote, "and then only by degrees." Gaining the upper hand in only one or two of these categories would gain the Germans nothing; they had to successfully address all four. "These were the foundations of my thoughts about invasion in 1940," Churchill wrote. Still, "the possibility of a cross-Channel invasion, improbable though it was at that time, had to be most closely examined."[161]

On June 30, General Sir Andrew Thorne, who commanded a corps in the southeast, told Churchill he thought the Germans would land up to 80,000 men, probably between Thanet and Pevensey on the Kentish coast, and just sixty miles from London. Churchill, Colville wrote, "is less pessimistic and thinks the navy will have much to say to this." Still, if the Germans evaded the Royal Navy and made it to shore, Churchill wanted defenders on all possible shores in East and West Sussex, Kent, and Surrey. On his instructions, pillboxes and barbed-wire barricades were built there. Touring them, he asked for a chart of tides and moonrises for the next six weeks. He saw that once the enemy had committed himself, the outcome would be determined by mobile brigades stationed inland, and by Royal Navy destroyers mining and shelling the beaches, at night. Colville noted that General Thorne, whose men were expected to take the greatest blow, thought "the German left wing could be held in Ashdown Forest, but he did not see what could keep the right wing from advancing through Canterbury to London." Mobility and imaginative tactics might prevent that. Survival would depend on flexibility, intuition, and imagination, traits (some would say eccentricities) lacking in many of England's generals and certainly in the previous government. But not in Churchill.[162]

Throughout June, Royal Meteorological Office records show, the Channel was calm; skies were clear, with temperatures in the sixties, and the British people—including high-ranking military officials—had no doubts that the invaders would arrive soon. It is all there in their diaries and letters. As early as June 12, Harold Nicolson wrote: "The probability is that France will surrender and that we shall be bombed and invaded." "The weather still remains very fine, worse luck," Ironside wrote early in July. Now that the Germans had "airfields within twenty-five miles of our shores," Ismay noted, "the possibility of invasion of Britain" seemed "highly probable... within a matter of weeks." At Cliveden Thomas Jones noted: "Speculation is rife about the 'invasion.' Wherever one goes one sees pillboxes and road barriers and field obstacles." "Speculation" is the operative word, that week and in the weeks that followed.[163]

Most Britons were scared. Yet, Churchill later wrote: "Certainly those that knew the most were the least scared." Those words were written long after the fact, but they reflect his belief during 1940. His private conversations and his memos to his ministers that summer and fall bear out his confidence.

At night primeval darkness descended upon blacked-out Britain. Drivers crept along at twenty miles an hour. The windows of commuter trains were painted black. London lampposts were ringed with white paint to warn oncoming motorists. Still, collisions were common between bicyclists and automobiles, between pedestrians and lampposts. To baffle invading troops, signposts had been removed from the countryside, baffling the locals as well. Late in June, postmen slipped official pamphlets in the mail telling householders what to do when the invasion began. Nearly everyone had some sort of crude weapon, if only a garden tool. German paratroopers would likely arrive by night. In a speech to the Home Guard the prime minister proclaimed that if Nazi paratroopers arrived, "you will make it clear to them that they have not alighted in the poultry-run, or in the rabbit farm, or even in the sheep fold, but in the lion's den at the Zoo!"[164]

Fleet Street had advice, too. "A hand-grenade dump by each village pump," was the slogan of Beaverbrook's *Daily Express*. The *Express* also distressed many who had grown up in a quieter time by pointing out that any boy capable of pitching a cricket ball could throw a grenade. Civilians, even clergymen in their seventies, were armed with whatever was available, often shotguns. Most lacked firearms of any sort. Awaiting rifles from America, members of the Home Guard drilled with pikes, pick handles, and broomsticks. Wives were told to make homemade Molotov cocktails with kitchen kerosene; elderly men were taught how to disable panzers by pouring sugar into their fuel tanks or thrusting crowbars in their track wheels.

People then still thought of war in personal terms. There is no way a twenty-first-century citizen can oppose fleets of modern missiles, but in 1940 one Briton with a weapon, however primitive, could make a difference in the defense of the island. If the Nazis established a beachhead, King

George was prepared to lead a resistance movement. The King ordered a shooting range built in the gardens of Buckingham Palace, and there the Royal Family and royal equerries practiced daily with small arms, including submachine guns and a carbine given to the King by Churchill. The young royal princesses took their target practice with their parents. Clementine later told her daughter that Elizabeth and Margaret "have the most amusing lives, with lots of dogs (although they are those horrid 'corgies') & poneys [*sic*] & a delightful mother." The delightful mother was a crack shot. On July 10, Harold Nicolson noted that the Queen "told me she is being instructed every day in how to fire a revolver. I expressed surprise. 'Yes,' she said, 'I shall not go down like the others.' I cannot tell you how superb she was.... *We shall win*. I know that. I have no doubts at all."[165]

In the Nazi invasion the number of deaths would be unfathomable. It was a time when, at every parting, husbands and wives, mothers and children, knew they might be looking their last upon one another. Vita Sackville-West wrote, "It must be in both our minds that we may possibly never meet again." Nicolson replied, "I am not in the least afraid of... sudden and honourable death. What I dread is being tortured and humiliated."[166]

Torture would be the certain fate of those who possessed special knowledge of the island's defenses. Anticipating possible capture, many carried on their persons the means for quick suicide. A week after the French collapse, when the government was preparing to evacuate all civilians from Kent and Sussex, Nicolson, now at the Ministry of Information, wrote Vita, "I think you ought to have a 'bare bodkin' [after Hamlet] so you can take your quietus when necessary. But how can we find a bodkin which will give us our quietus quickly and which is easily portable? I shall ask my doctor friends." Ten days later she wrote him that she had her "bare bodkin." Probably it was poison, not a dagger. Churchill had repeatedly vowed that he would never be taken alive; according to Kathleen Hill, his bodkin was cyanide, which he carried in the cap of his fountain pen.[167]

Britons braced themselves, but against exactly what—gas, invasion, aerial bombardment, parachutists, all of the above?—they did not know. They were quite willing to fight and die, but they lacked the means to fight. Wars are fought by soldiers with weapons. In the first four weeks after Dunkirk, Britain had few of either. Ironside, then commanding Home Forces, including the Home Guard, was attempting to organize the defense of the island. He envisioned "arming of the whole population" with the "existence of the Empire" at stake. On June 22, the day the French signed the armistice at Compiègne, Ironside wrote: "Even the stoutest heart begins to wonder whether he [Churchill] can meet all the eventualities he pictures to himself. I felt it myself as I went round the endless coastline of East Anglia yesterday."[168]

No one had foreseen this. For two centuries His Majesty's Government had sent troops to every corner of the globe while the homeland enjoyed peace. The last battle on English soil had been fought on April 16, 1746, when the army of the Duke of Cumberland, son of King George II, routed the forces of the Stuart pretender, Bonnie Prince Charlie. Now in June 1940 the country seemed defenseless. Harold Macmillan recalled, "Having shipped almost everything we had, we now find ourselves not only alone, but unarmed." He was of course referring to the army; the navy was quite well armed. Still, as Churchill had noted, the success of the Dunkirk evacuation obscured the fact that the men had left their guns, artillery, ammunition, and tanks behind. In England, there were only half as many rifles as needed to defend the island. The evacuation was still in progress when the United States agreed to sell Britain—*sell* is the key word—500,000 World War I rifles, 80,000 virtually obsolete machine guns, 900 howitzers, and 13,000,000 rounds of ammunition. Although British factories were toiling around the clock, they wouldn't make up the losses for at least three months, possibly six. Yet, within two weeks, with great difficulty, equipment for two divisions was scraped together. Churchill ordered that the most battle-ready brigade, languishing for weeks in Northern Ireland, be brought home. As for the Home Guard, realists in the military—including A. J. P. Taylor, who served in the Home Guard—concluded that if the militia somehow managed to assemble at their appointed rendezvous points, they would be massacred.[169]

"I have no scruples," Churchill told Colville, "except not to do anything dishonorable." Exactly where he would draw the line if the Germans came was left unspecified. The question of mustard gas was raised. It was thought the Germans would use it. Churchill wanted to use it first. To Ismay he wrote in a memo: "In my view there would be no need for the enemy to adopt such methods. He will certainly adopt them if he thinks they will pay." Stocks of mustard gas were readied, to be dropped from bombers or shot from artillery. He envisioned "drenching" the beaches with gas, leading Colville to tell his diary: "I suppose he does not consider gassing Germans dishonorable."[170]

Some of his ideas were quaint. He recalled that "a fire ship had been used" by Elizabethan Englishmen against the Spanish Armada. Might something similar be contemplated now? He would scorch England's earth if need be. Oil storage tanks, which had fueled the panzers in France, would be destroyed once the fighting began. The Strait of Dover was already mined. Against the possibility that Germans might wear British uniforms, Tommies would wear a strip of cloth dyed a new shade of yellow. White circles were painted atop British tanks, to warn the RAF off. Army intelligence (incorrectly) believed the Luftwaffe could land as many as twenty thousand troops; therefore, to disrupt gliders, four-hundred-yard-long ditches were plowed across large fields, even those seeded for crops. All bridges over all rivers within one hundred miles of London were rigged for demolition.[171]

For the Home Guard, improvisation was the order of the day. Cans of gasoline were stored near important intersections, the idea being that members of the Home Guard, upon spotting the approaching Germans, would pour the fuel in the road, toss a grenade into the puddle, and make good their escape. British anti-tank mines, so complex and overengineered that they could not be produced in sufficient quantities, were replaced by commercial cake pans stuffed with eight pounds of TNT and fitted with a simple compression trigger. Churchill's imagination turned to his beloved gadgets and scientific schemes. The floating of fuel oil on harbor waters to ignite the invasion barges was one such. Another: Could slender gasoline-filled pipelines be readied behind seaside dunes, to spray flaming fuel upon the invaders? Yes, but what if the invaders came ashore elsewhere, or the winds blew those flames and smoke toward the defenders, which is exactly what happened when the system was tested. That was how things stood in late June and the first days of July, a time when *ad hoc* best describes Britain's defenses. None, including Churchill, knew during those weeks that the Germans had not even drawn up an invasion plan.

The Admiralty told Churchill that the likeliest time for hostile seaborne landings was a moonless night, at high tide, near daybreak. Once the onslaught began, all the church bells in England were to start ringing. Speculation about the German timing continued. On July 11 Harold Nicolson wrote in his diary: "They expect an invasion this weekend." But he also wrote: "I am cocky about this war. Cocky. I really and truly believe Hitler is at the end of his success." On July 20 he noted: "I think Hitler will probably invade us within the next few days. He has 6,000 airplanes for the job.... We know we are faced with a terrific invasion.... Yet there is a sort of exhilaration in the air." Actually, the Luftwaffe force assembled across the Channel was composed of about 2,500 bombers, fighter-bombers, and fighters.[172]

The news was blacked out, beaches and military installations off-limits. Ship arrivals and departures were no longer reported in newspapers. Even weather reports were banned; why tell the enemy what the conditions might be in Sussex next week? Nicolson was still expecting the great attack two months later; on September 13 he wrote: "There is a great concentration of shipping and barges in France, and it is evident that the Cabinet expect invasion at any moment." Ironside had thought it was coming on July 9. On July 12 Sir Alan Brooke told his diary: "This was supposed to be the probable day of invasion!" Colville told his diary on July 14: "There is an ominous calm... and it looks like *der Tag* may be imminent." On that day, Colville noted, even Churchill lacked his usual confidence. On July 22, Sir Alan Brooke, who had only the day before replaced Ironside as commander of Home Forces, went "to the War Cabinet Room where I may have to be near the PM if an invasion starts." That night, while dining alone with Churchill at No. 10, Brooke found Churchill to be "full of the most marvelous courage, considering the burden he is bearing." Brooke added an observation, variations of which would find their way into his diary for the next five years: "He [Churchill] is full of offensive thoughts for the future."[173]

Dining with three of his generals on Friday, July 12, Churchill declared that if the Germans came, he wanted "every citizen to fight desperately and they will do so the more if they know that the alternative is massacre." Colville that night noted that Churchill "is sufficiently ruthless to point out that in war quarter is given, not on grounds of compassion but in order to discourage the enemy from fighting to the bitter end." Contrary to the French experience, no panicked streams of civilian refugees (Churchill preferred the term "fugitives") would clog British roads if the Germans arrived, for there was no escape. Churchill offered that the citizens would fight, even if only with "scythes and brickbats." One of the generals declared that the citizenry should be ordered to stay home; Churchill replied that they would not obey such an order. Then, wrote Colville, Churchill arrived at the root of the matter:

> He emphasized that the great invasion scare (which we only ceased to deride six weeks ago) is serving a most useful purpose: it is well on the way to providing us with the finest offensive army we have ever possessed and it is keeping every man and woman tuned to a high pitch of readiness. He does not wish the scare to abate therefore, and although personally he doubts whether invasion is a serious menace he intends to give that impression, and to talk about long and dangerous vigils, etc., when he broadcasts on Sunday.[174]

On Bastille Day, Sunday, July 14, four days after the first large-scale dogfights between the Luftwaffe and the Royal Air Force, Churchill spoke to the nation over the BBC. Britons believed their plight was desperate, and he did not paint it otherwise, as he had promised Colville he would not. Their losses in France and Flanders had been enormous, "including a very large part of our Air Force." Their enemy was the fiercest in history. Nation after nation had fallen beneath the Nazi juggernaut.

> And now it has come to us to stand in the breach, and face the worst that the tyrant can do. Bearing ourselves humbly before God, but conscious that we serve an unfolding purpose, we are ready to defend our native land against the invasion by which it is threatened. We are fighting *by* ourselves alone; but we are not fighting *for* ourselves alone. Here in this strong City of Refuge which enshrines the title deeds of human progress and is of deep consequence to Christian civilization; girt about by the seas and oceans where the Navy reigns; shielded from above by the prowess and devotion of our airmen we await undismayed the impending assault. Perhaps it will come tonight. Perhaps it will come next week.

Then, the caveat, which conveyed his own feelings and offered Britons a speck of hope:

> Perhaps it will never come. We must show ourselves equally capable of meeting a sudden violent shock, or what is perhaps a harder test, a prolonged vigil. But be the ordeal sharp or long, or both, we shall seek no terms, we shall tolerate no parley; we may show mercy. We shall ask for none.[175]

He knew the "monstrous force" of the Nazi war machine. But, he added, Britain now had a million and a half soldiers under arms on her own soil, and more than a million volunteers in the Home Guard, and a thousand armed ships sailing under the white ensign, binding them to the United States, "from whom, as the struggle deepens, increasing aide [*sic*] will come." And the Nazis should know the ferocity of British determination: "Hitler has not yet been withstood by a great nation with a will power the equal of his own."

> Should the invader come to Britain, there will be no placid lying down of the people in submission before him, as we have seen, alas, in other countries. We shall defend every village, every town, and every city. The vast mass of London itself, fought street by street, could easily devour an entire hostile army; and we would rather see London in ruins and ashes than that it would be tamely and abjectly enslaved.

Nevertheless, he told them, that "while we toil through the dark valley we can see the sunlight on the uplands beyond" provided they remembered who they were: "all depends on the whole life strength of the British race . . . doing their utmost night and day, giving all, daring all, enduring the utmost to the end." This was "a war of the Unknown Warriors; but let all strive without failing in faith or in duty, and the dark curse of Hitler will be lifted from our age."[176]

The Führer had assumed that invasion would be unnecessary. After the fall of France he considered the war over. In the East his pact with Stalin assured continuing peace as long as neither side abrogated it, which Hitler intended to do once the English came to terms. When Hitler ordered the demobilizing of forty divisions, he told *Reichsmarschall* Hermann Göring, commander in chief of the Luftwaffe, that all war plans could be scrapped; he would reach an "understanding" (*Übereinkommen*) with the British. Actually, he expected London to take the initiative; he told Dino Alfieri, the Italian ambassador in Berlin, that he "could not conceive of anyone in England still seriously believing in victory." To Lieutenant General Franz Halder, chief of the Army High Command (OKH), he said that "England's situation is hopeless. A reversal of the prospects of success is an impossibility." His generals agreed; on June 30 Jodl, OKW's chief of operations, wrote: "The final German victory over England is now only a question of time. Enemy offensive operations on a large scale are no longer possible."[177]

The Führer preferred a settlement, freeing the Wehrmacht from the need to defend a Western Front when he attacked his mortal enemy, the Soviet Union. Though he despised Churchill, he admired the British Empire; its existence, he believed, was essential to world order. (All SS officers were required to watch the film *Gunga Din;* that, he told them, was the way a superior race should treat its inferiors.) Therefore he was prepared to offer England a generous treaty. Convinced that they must realize the hopelessness of their situation, he dismissed Churchill's defiance as bluff and expected the British to come to him. After four weeks of waiting, on July 19 he made his move in a Reichstag speech. After insulting Churchill—"I feel a deep disgust for this type of unscrupulous politician who wrecks whole nations"—he said of himself, "I am not the vanquished begging favors, but the victor speaking in the name of reason." He promised Britons that absent a settlement, "great suffering will begin." Speaking directly to Churchill, he said, "Believe me when I prophesy that a great Empire will be destroyed—an empire which it was never my intention to destroy or even to harm." Hinting at liberal terms, he concluded dramatically, "I can see no reason why this war must go on."[178]

The answer came within the hour. Churchill did not deign to comment on the offer—"I do not propose to say anything in reply to Herr Hitler's speech," he said, "not being on speaking terms with him"—but a BBC broadcaster, later supported by the foreign office, addressed the Führer directly: "Let me tell you what we here in Britain think of this appeal to what you are pleased to call our reason and common sense. Herr Führer and Reich Chancellor, we hurl it right back into your evil-smelling teeth!"[179]

In Rome the diarist Count Galeazzo Ciano noted that "a sense of ill-concealed disappointment spreads among the Germans." Actually Berlin was astounded, and Hitler nonplussed. The German General Staff had always assumed that Britain could be defeated only by cutting its sea routes. Although all great powers spend peacetime preparing contingency plans for war against other countries, including their closest allies, the German army did not draft preliminary plans for an offensive against England until June 1937, and the Luftwaffe did not follow through with similar memoranda until 1938.[180]

And these were merely paper exercises. As A. J. P. Taylor has pointed out, Hitler had foreign policy ambitions but no war plans at all; he was, in the words of the historian and novelist Len Deighton, "one of the most successful opportunists of the twentieth century," making it up as he went along. Indeed, it is an astonishing fact—the military historian Basil Liddell Hart calls it "one of the most extraordinary features of history"—that neither the Führer nor his General Staff in Zossen had studied or even contemplated the problems arising from Britain's continued belligerency. They hadn't done it when war broke out; it was still undone nine months later, when the French capitulated. They had worked out elaborate strategies for seizing every European country, including Spain, the Balkans, and their Italian ally; they had drawn up orders of battle for Scandinavia and the Soviet Union; they even knew how, if it became necessary, to overwhelm the Vatican. The German naval war staff, knowing the *Kriegsmarine* would be charged with ferrying German troops to England if the orders came down, had studied the problem in desultory fashion since the previous autumn. The army and Luftwaffe had not. On May 27 the naval war staff had drafted a vague *Studie England,* but in all the banks of steel files in Zossen, there was not so much as a single memorandum on the question of how the greatest army the world had ever known could subjugate Great Britain.[181]

To reach England the Wehrmacht had to cross the Channel or the North Sea. Hitler hated the idea. "On land I am a hero but on water I am a coward," he told *Generalfeldmarschall* Gerd von Rundstedt. Since Nazi Germany had no landing craft and no plans to build any, German troops, if they went to England, would do so aboard river barges. The barges were intended for river traffic; flat-bottomed, 90 feet long, 20 feet wide, with a top speed of 7 miles per hour, they were not built for seagoing excursions. Some operated under their own power, many were towed. Not a single unit in the German army had been trained in the skills of amphibious warfare. The Continent and contiguous lands were the only world the *Generalstab* knew. That world ended at its edge, the western coast of France. Paris had been the objective of the Nazis' great spring offensive, to the exclusion of all else, the last step before the invasion of Russia.[182]

In England the Royal Navy was the senior service. The War Office deferred to the Admiralty, the oldest of England's war ministries, founded during the reign of Henry VIII. Officers in the British army were respected and often distinguished, though army commands scattered throughout the empire depended upon the navy for supply and reinforcements. The various far-flung components of the British Empire were tethered together, nurtured, and protected by the Royal Navy. Cruisers and destroyers at Gibraltar protected the western end of the Mediterranean, while the fleet at Alexandria did likewise for the central and eastern Mediterranean. The Home Fleet, from its main anchorage at Scapa Flow, almost five hundred miles north of London, in far northern Scotland, had been charged by the Admiralty with protecting Atlantic merchant shipping and, most important, protecting the Home Island much as escort squadrons protect an aircraft carrier. Destroyers would play a key role in contesting a German invasion. The British began the war with more than eighty destroyers available for deployment in the North Sea and around the Home Island, and a dozen or more for North Atlantic operations. They were fast, could weave and shoot their way through an invasion armada at speeds of thirty-five miles an hour, and were vital to the blockade of Germany and to Britain's survival. But since January, two dozen had been sunk by U-boats, German mines, and the Luftwaffe. The registry of Royal Navy destroyers might have been larger but for the Chamberlain government's decision in 1938 to stop constructing ships, as a means to economize. That was why Churchill sought destroyers from Roosevelt.

By the end of June, the Home Fleet had stationed forty destroyers, several cruisers, and two battle cruisers in ports ranging from Aberdeen and Rosyth in Scotland, to Hull and Yarmouth down the coast, to Dover and Ramsgate in the southeast of England. In the south and southwest, warships were stationed in Portsmouth, Portland, Plymouth, Falmouth, Cardiff, and Swansea. The big ships were supported by more than 900 anti-submarine trawlers, gunboats, minesweepers, motor torpedo boats, minelayers, anti-aircraft ships, and cutters. Almost 200 corvettes—1,000-ton, 200-foot-long gunboats that carried depth charges—were available to escort Atlantic convoys into home waters or, if need be, to help repel an invasion. Three aircraft carriers were available for island defense; the Germans had no carriers. The Royal Navy would charge into the Channel if the Germans came, and do so under the protective fire of 150 six-inch naval guns sited on bluffs along the Channel coast. Except for submarines, the portion of the Home Fleet that *remained* at Scapa Flow—a "fleet in being"—was larger than the entire German navy. Of Hitler's eighty U-boats, the fifty assigned to the blockade of Britain posed a mortal threat, but only if they kept up the hunt for British merchant shipping on the high seas and the Northwest Approaches to Britain's ports. Churchill expected Hitler to throw a dozen or two of his U-boats into the invasion. Even if they were to inflict pain on British warships, the Royal Navy and any surviving RAF fighters and bombers would hunt them to extinction in the narrow Channel. Hence Churchill's confidence in his navy. Britannia still ruled the waves, and Hitler had to ride them to get to England.

Germany had lost its few colonies in 1918, and with them the imperative for a worldwide navy. Except for U-boat commanders—feared and respected by the British, glorified in Germany—German military glory was reserved for German soldiers, and if Göring had his way, German airmen. German naval officers were considered social inferiors in Germany; they lacked the self-assurance essential to military aggression. Thus, when the Führer issued the first reluctant order to "prepare a landing operation against England and if necessary carry it out," and assigned the task of ferrying the Wehrmacht across the Channel to his admirals on the Bendlerstrasse, the response there was neither confident nor ardent, and for sound reasons. Unless the Luftwaffe hobbled the British Home Fleet along with British fighter planes and British bombers, any success in the daytime skies over southern England would be offset when the Royal Navy sailed forth—at night, as the invaders came on—to thwart the seaborne invasion.[183]

Destroying British ships was critical, and the British had a great many ships. The Germans had no large warships outside the Baltic (and had only four inside the Baltic) to counter the overwhelmingly superior numbers of Royal Navy destroyers and larger capital ships (cruisers, battle cruisers, and battleships). The German navy had begun the war with only twenty-one destroyers and had paid dearly for its April success in Norway, where ten destroyers were sunk or scuttled. Thus, when the subject of supporting an invasion of England was raised, the commander in chief of the German navy, *Grossadmiral* Erich Raeder, submitted a confidential report to the Führer listing his objections to an invasion. Raeder concluded: "The C. in C., Navy cannot for his part advocate an invasion of Britain as he did in the case of Norway."[184]

The other German services were also wary. The Luftwaffe high command concluded that "a combined operation with a landing as its object must be rejected," and Zossen curtly sent a memo that the army "is not concerning itself with the question of England. Considers execution impossible... General Staff rejects the operation." Nevertheless, Hitler persisted, as only he could, and in mid-July *Oberkommando des Heeres* (OKH), the army's high command, drew up plans for an operation encoded *Seelöwe,* or Sea Lion. It was an ambitious strategy, envisioning the landing of 90,000 troops in the first wave. By the third day, 160,000 reinforcements would be landed, to be followed by forty-one divisions, six of them panzers and two airborne. Each force had a specific objective; one would block off Devon and Cornwall, for example, while another cut off Wales. OKH opinion, swayed by Hitler's iron will, reversed itself. The generals now expected the operation to last less than a month. In fact, they thought it would be easy.[185]

But the Führer's naval staff was appalled by *Seelöwe,* for many of the same reasons Churchill was encouraged. Just putting the first wave ashore on so wide a front would require 1,722 barges, 1,161 motorboats, 471 tugs, and 155 transports. Raeder protested that this was self-evidently impossible; naval protection for so vast an armada, even if it could be assembled, would expose every warship and merchant ship the Reich possessed to the gunners of the Royal Navy. He proposed a landing on a much narrower front between Folkestone and Eastbourne with fewer troops, thus minimizing the risk to his fleet. The General Staff rejected that. In such an operation, Zossen argued, the German soldiers might be overwhelmed by defenders.

Actually, there was no need to reconcile differences between the Nazi services. Churchill had been right at Briare. The decisive moment—an air assault on England—was yet to come. The enemy could not try to ferry the Channel until his warplanes were absolute masters of the daytime skies over Britain. OKW realized it. In a paper for the Führer, *"Die Weiterführung des Krieges gegen England"* ("The Continuation of the War Against England"), Jodl noted that administering the deathblow, a landing on British shores, could "only be contemplated after Germany has achieved control of the air."[186]

Before Hitler could invade England, he must first destroy the Royal Air Force and hobble the Royal Navy. Hermann Göring declared that the Luftwaffe had changed its mind; they could do it, he said, and do it easily.

In christening what would come to be known as the Battle of Britain, Churchill envisioned a mighty struggle on the beaches between infantrymen, masterminded by admirals and generals and supported by armor and sea power. Scarcely anyone gave thought to the challenges of aerial warfare. Professional airmen were an exception, of course, but all they knew for certain was that the aerial combat of 1914–1918—the duels between

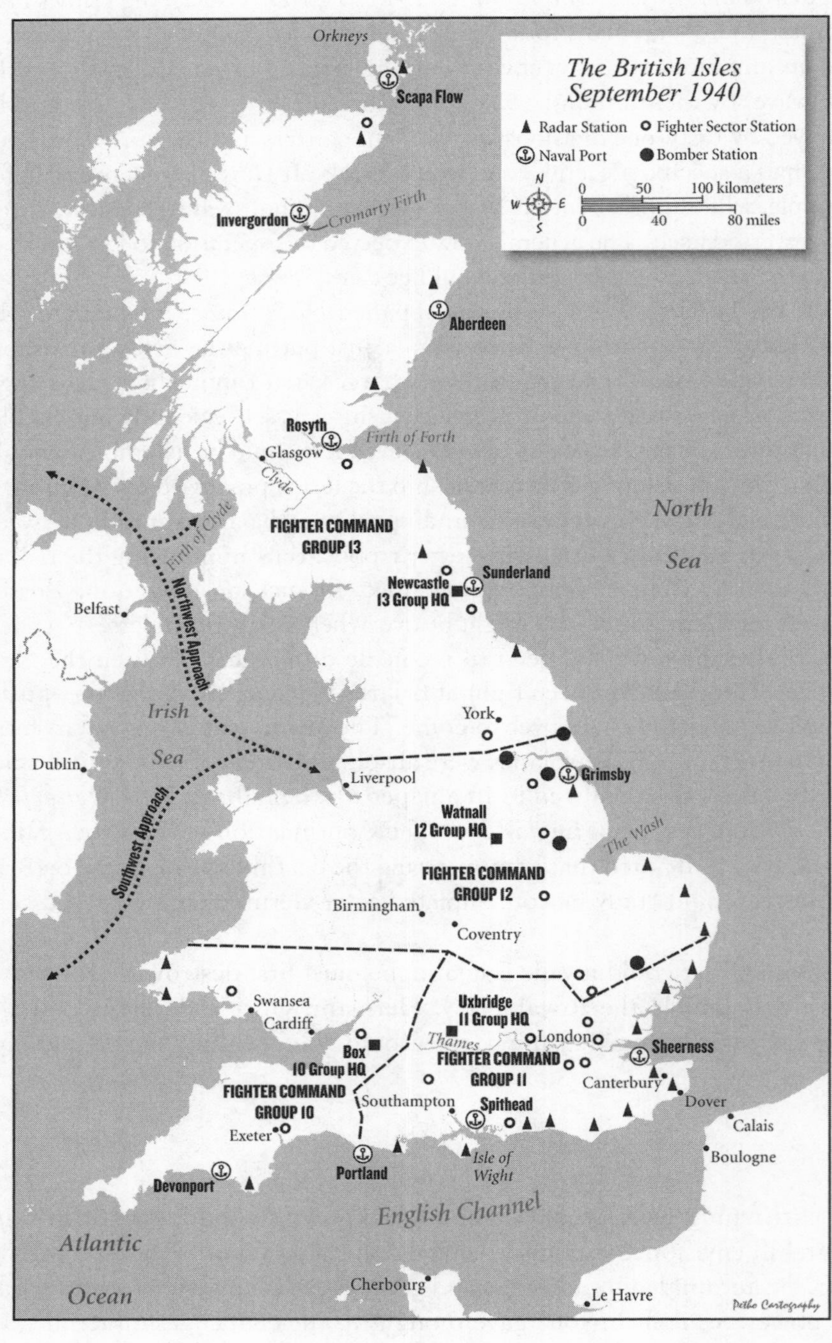
The British Isles
September 1940
Radar Station
Fighter Sector Station
Naval Port
Bomber Station
N
W
E
S
0
50
100 kilometers
0
40
80 miles
Orkneys
Scapa Flow
Invergordon
Cromarty Firth
Aberdeen
Rosyth
Firth of Forth
Glasgow
Clyde
Firth of Clyde
FIGHTER COMMAND
GROUP 13
North
Sea
Newcastle
13 Group HQ
Sunderland
Belfast
Northwest Approach
Irish
Sea
Dublin
Southwest Approach
York
Liverpool
Grimsby
Watnall
12 Group HQ
The Wash
FIGHTER COMMAND
GROUP 12
Birmingham
Coventry
Swansea
Cardiff
Uxbridge
11 Group HQ
London
Thames
Box
10 Group HQ
FIGHTER COMMAND
GROUP 11
Sheerness
FIGHTER COMMAND
GROUP 10
Southampton
Spithead
Canterbury
Dover
Calais
Exeter
Portland
Isle of
Wight
Boulogne
Devonport
English Channel
Atlantic
Ocean
Cherbourg
Le Havre
Pétho Cartography

individuals piloting wood and fabric biplanes while listening to the wind in the wires—had been rendered obsolete by advancing technology. Clearly future combat would be far more complex. However, the most influential of their leaders between the wars—Giulio Douhet in Rome, Lord Trenchard in London, Billy Mitchell in Washington, and Hermann Göring in Berlin—had made the wrong assumption. They believed that victory would belong to the air forces which launched the fastest, most powerful bombing offensives. Thus the Luftwaffe had leveled Spanish cities, the Italians Ethiopian villages, the Japanese Chinese cities. There was, air ministries told their governments, no defense against a knockout bombardment from the sky.

Stanley Baldwin was speaking for them in November 1932 when, endorsing unilateral disarmament, he told Parliament that there was no defense against "the terror of the air." In an uncharacteristically emotional speech, he had warned the House of Commons, and hence the country: "I think it well . . . for the man in the street to realize that there is no power on earth that can prevent him from being bombed. Whatever people tell him, the bomber will always get through. The only defence is offence, which means that you have to kill more women and children more quickly than the enemy if you want to save yourselves."

That dogma still held after the fall of France. Even Churchill believed that victory lay through offensive airpower. On July 8, he told Beaverbrook that the "one sure path" to victory lay in "bombing Germany into submission." It was understood that the targets would be military. Baldwin's terrible thesis of killing women and children aside, the war planners took aim at arms factories, power plants, steel mills, rail yards, and the like, not residential neighborhoods.[187]

Airpower had been crucial in the defeat of Poland, but after the fall of Warsaw, little thought had been given to ways of countering it. During the phony war, RAF strategists, following the dogma Douhet had set forth in his futuristic book, *The War of 19—*, had proposed sending fleets of bombers against industrial targets in the Ruhr. To their chagrin, His Majesty's Government vetoed unprovoked daylight raids. Dropping propaganda leaflets over the Reich that promised destruction to Germans on the ground was approved, but even this went badly; none of the raiders found their targets, and the bombers, unescorted by fighters, suffered such heavy losses that the project was abandoned. On the night of May 16, with General Guderian's panzers beyond Sedan, the British had sent one hundred bombers to pound industrial targets in the Ruhr. The RAF official history acknowledges that the bombardiers "achieved none of their objects." The crews, unable to find a single target, had jettisoned their bomb loads and returned to England having accomplished nothing. That should have given the air marshals pause. It didn't; in the words of A. J. P. Taylor, they continued to believe that "bombing unsupported by land and sea forces could win a war."[188]

Little thought had been given to providing bombers with fighter escorts, and for a valid reason: Both British and German fighter planes lacked the range to escort their bombers on the 1,000-mile round-trip journey to the other's homeland. British and German fighter planes had a maximum range of between 300 and 400 miles—150 miles out, 150 miles home. They could remain in the air for about 90 minutes and could not reach the other side's borders, let alone linger there in support of bombers. Nobody in Bomber Command had considered the possibility that Germany would defeat France and Belgium, capture their airfields—some just 100 miles from London—and park fleets of bombers, dive-bombers, and fighter planes on them. Although the senior ranks of the RAF were convinced in the late 1930s that Bomber Command was the key to victory, and that, by implication, fighter aircraft and other defenses had marginal roles to play, their faith in air offensives was not without heretics. In 1937 a cabinet minister, Sir Thomas Inskip, facing the hard fact that Nazi Germany was winning the bomber race, argued that it really didn't matter. "The object of our Air Force," he said, "is not an early knock-out blow but to prevent the Germans from knocking us out." The RAF, in other words, didn't have to win; it merely had to avoid defeat. For that, the RAF needed fighter planes. The Air Ministry, appalled at this heresy, vehemently disagreed, but HMG accepted Inskip's recommendation, and it was Britain's good luck that the senior member of the Air Council agreed with it.

He was Air Chief Marshal Sir Hugh Dowding. In retrospect, "Stuffy" Dowding—as anointed by his fliers—is seen as the true hero of the Battle of Britain, though his contemporaries were slow to realize it. One reason lay in the nature of the man. He was a difficult man to like. Ever since Trafalgar, Britons had expected their military heroes to be Nelsons, and Dowding was far from that. Tall, frail, and abstemious, he was a bird-watching widower whose career had suffered from tactlessness, unorthodox views, and a remarkable lack of social graces. That he dabbled in spiritualism and was a vegetarian only augmented the perception of his flyboys that he was a strange duck. In the mid-1930s, his seniority—during the first war he had been ten years older than Germany's air ace von Richthofen—entitled him to the RAF's highest post, chief of air staff, but his fellow marshals denied him it. Instead they sidelined him, or so they thought, as head of Fighter Command. If the war was going to be won by aerial bombardment, the only outcome they foresaw, there would be little glory for fighters.[189]

Ignoring them and their strategy, Dowding pursued his own goals with quiet tenacity. In his headquarters in Bentley Priory, an eighteenth-century

Gothic mansion outside London, he organized Britain's anti-aircraft defenses, inspected the balloon barrage that would encircle London when war came, presided over the RAF's change from biplane fighters to metal monoplanes powered by the Rolls-Royce V-12 Merlin engines, pressed for all-weather runways at fighter fields, and took the first, historic steps toward military use of Radio Direction Finding (RDF), or radar, as the Americans later called it.

By July 1940, Dowding had about eight hundred operational Spitfire and Hurricane single-engine fighter planes. He arrayed them in four groups—two frontline and two in reserve. In reserve were No. 10 Group in the southwest of England, and No. 13 in northern England and Scotland. Six hundred Hurricanes and Spitfires went to the frontline groups, No. 12 in the midlands, and No. 11 Group north and south of London, roughly from Ipswich to the Isle of Wright, and most predominantly on the Kent promontory. This was the sector the German invasion barges would most likely target, either north of the Thames estuary, or on the south coast, just west of Dover, or in both places. Therefore, it was the sector Göring targeted. No. 11 Group had to be destroyed before an invasion could be launched, for No. 11 Group served as the shield over southeast England.

But radar was destined to be England's greatest shield in the critical months ahead. Dowding had been one of its champions from the beginning. Before his promotion to Fighter Command, he had commanded RAF research and development, and while there, he had studied the RDF experiments of Robert Watson Watt, a scientist at the National Physical Laboratory. Watson Watt convinced Dowding and those around him that airplanes could reflect radio beams. Yet in his push for radar, conducted with utmost civility and professional aplomb, Dowding had put himself on the wrong side of Churchill's good friend the Prof, Frederick Lindemann. For this, Dowding would later pay. Meanwhile, the Nazis knew something about radar technology but had entrusted development of it to their navy, seeing it as a reconnaissance device, and there it had languished.

Even before the war, Dowding had believed that radar could become a priceless defensive weapon. In 1937 he had ordered work begun along the country's eastern and southern coasts on a chain of coastal RDF stations, a mix of low-level stations, with an effective range of about 50 miles, and high-level, with a range of about 120 miles. By the spring of 1940, Britain possessed a mesh of radio beams comprising, as one Englishmen later called it, an "invisible bastion" against hostile aircraft. Thankfully for the British, Hitler had prohibited spending on any technological research that he believed would not contribute to his objective of a swift victory; radar was one such technology. In July 1940, German technicians were not even sure of the purpose of all those tall towers along the British coast, although many suspected that they were radar towers. Thus, the Luftwaffe began its campaign with an imperfect, at best, understanding of the towers.

Fifty radar stations scanned the skies from northern Scotland on around the Home Island to Wales. Most were located in the east and southeast, facing the North Sea and the English Channel, just twenty-one miles wide at its narrowest point. The outgoing radio signal was sent from wires fixed between two 360-foot towers; the return signal reached twin fixed receivers perched on 240-foot towers. In wooden sheds beneath the towers, technicians studying monitors would phone details on the range, direction, and size of advancing Nazi forces to the central operations room at Bentley Priory, where blue-shirted members of the Women's Auxiliary Air Force (WAAF) plotted their progress on a huge table map, using croupier rakes to move colored counters representing RAF and German aircraft. RAF officers radioed orders to the nine No. 11 Group operations centers—"sector stations"—scattered throughout the southeast and around London. There, orders were radioed to commanders of fighter squadrons, who then led their pilots aloft. German pilots listened in confusion as British pilots received updates by radio, updates that guided them toward the German fighters. How, the Germans wondered, could someone on the ground know where distant German planes were and where they were heading? They did not know that they faced two enemies in the Battle of Britain: RAF airmen in the sky and British radar crews on the ground.[190]

It was now possible for the British to detect enemy aircraft approaching England's shores while they were still as far as 120 miles away—thirty or more miles inside Belgium and France, and more than 70 miles beyond Calais—flying at altitudes of up to 30,000 feet. Although the RAF's long-range radar could peer 30 or so miles into the Low Countries and France, the altitude at which radar could "see" enemy aircraft increased with distance, due to the curvature of the earth. At the extreme range of the radar, that altitude was almost 14,000 feet. Anything flying beneath that altitude, at that range, was "below" the radar. The calculus of time, distance, fighter aircraft climb rate, altitude, and speed became absolutely critical, and would determine the outcome of the air battle over the Channel and the Kent promontory. The controllers at RAF sector stations, once notified by Bentley Priory of a radar fix, needed about five minutes to radio orders to fighter squadrons, during which time the German fighters climbed a further 6,000 to 8,000 feet. A Spitfire needed almost fifteen minutes to reach 20,000 feet. The Germans, therefore, had a head start of around twenty minutes. The "service ceiling" (maximum operational altitude) for both German and British fighter planes was beyond 35,000 feet, for German medium bombers beyond 26,000 feet. Not only could the RDF operators not "see" below certain altitudes, but they were finding that aircraft at tremendous altitudes disappeared from their sight. And all other RAF problems were compounded by the fact that a Luftwaffe squadron could cross the Channel at its narrowest point in five minutes.

Arrayed against the RAF were three German *Luftflotten* (air fleets). *Luftflotte* 3 was stationed in France, *Luftflotte* 2 in Belgium, under the command of Field Marshal Albert Kesselring, and *Luftflotte* 5 in Denmark and Norway. Because of the distances *Luftflotte* 5 had to fly, and the short range of Germany's best fighter, the Messerschmitt Bf 109, the bombers of *Luftflotte* 5 would have to fly without escorts. The burden of carrying out the German attack would therefore fall on *Luftflotten* 2 and 3, with a combined strength of 750 bombers, 250 Stuka dive-bombers, 600 Bf 109 fighters, and 250 twin-engine Bf 110 fighters. Hermann Göring issued his first operational directive for the Battle of Britain on June 30. The first step, code-named *Kanalkampf,* would be a struggle for mastery of the sky over the Channel.

Over the Channel is not where Hugh Dowding thought the fight would take place. He believed the fight, when it came, would take place over southeast England, in No. 11 Group's zone. The Germans kept a fleet of small seaplanes—white and marked with the Red Cross—at the ready, to rescue Luftwaffe pilots shot down over the Channel. British pilots who found themselves in the sea could only hope that a Royal Navy cutter or a local fisherman might happen upon them before they drowned, and many drowned. Göring intended to lure Dowding's Spitfires and Hurricanes out over the Channel by the approach, at high altitude, of his Bf 109s. Then, Stuka dive-bombers, Bf 109s armed with a single 550-pound bomb, and Bf 110s carrying a single 2,200-pound bomb, would scoot far under the fray to attack coastal shipping, Royal Navy warships, and the Channel ports. One million tons of merchant shipping, escorted by the Royal Navy, passed through the Channel each week. Although the Battle of Britain is recalled in the collective consciousness as the first great clash of air forces in history—and it was—the German objective was to attain supremacy over the *seas* by attaining supremacy in the air. This, Göring pledged, was to be accomplished in July, setting the stage for "*Adlerangriff*" ("Eagle Attack"), the weeklong climactic assault on England's military installations, railroad junctions, port facilities, oil depots, and aircraft factories, with the destruction of Fighter Command's coastal airfields the first objective.[191]

Dowding believed England's only hope of survival lay in radar and the RAF's single-engine fighters. He ordered his pilots to avoid direct combat with German fighters whenever possible, diverting them instead to shooting down enemy bombers stripped of their fighter escorts. Thus the RAF would keep its Spitfires and Hurricanes in the sky until the autumn's worsening weather ruled out any possibility of a seaborne Nazi attack across the Channel.

The *Kanalkampf* began on July 10, when twenty Nazi medium bombers, escorted by some two dozen twin-engine Bf 110 fighters and forty Messerschmitt Bf 109s, attacked a convoy off Dover. They were challenged by two squadrons (twenty-four to thirty aircraft) of Hurricanes. That day's dogfights resulted in thirteen German and seven RAF planes going down, a ratio that would hold for the next two months. Heavy fighting—and these first collisions of the RAF and Luftwaffe were deadly—continued for a full month, most of it over the Channel and the southern coast of England. It was a testing time for both air forces, a time of feints, of probes, of changing tactics.

And for the Royal Navy it was a time of terrible losses, from the air, from mines, from U-boats. Early in the month—before the main air battle opened on the tenth—the anti-aircraft ship *Foylebank* was sunk off Portland by a swarm of Stukas, with the loss of one hundred seventy of its three-hundred-man crew. A U-boat sank the destroyer *Whirlwind* south of Ireland, with forty-seven dead. On the eighteenth, two anti-submarine trawlers and a minesweeper were mauled; on the nineteenth and twenty-second, armed patrol trawlers were sunk by the Luftwaffe, with the loss of eleven men. Two British submarines went down off England's shores that month, with the loss of seventy-seven crewmen. On the twenty-sixth, the destroyer *Boreas* was raked by the Luftwaffe, with twenty-one dead. The next day, the destroyer *Wren* was sunk off Dover and the destroyer *Codrington* was sunk off Suffolk, with thirty-six dead. So severe was the air attack on Dover that the Royal Navy pulled its destroyers from the port. This was exactly what Göring had set his sights on. On the twenty-ninth, the destroyer *Delight* was damaged in Portland harbor, with six dead. The remainder of the crew were rescued, but without a ship they were effectively out of action. The Royal Navy had more sailors killed in July than the RAF would lose pilots during the next two months. New sailors could be trained in a matter of weeks, but even the smallest gunboats took several months to build.

Although the Royal Navy was being hit hard, it had no intention of withdrawing from the Strait of Dover without a fight. But Dowding took a hard line against daylight patrols in support of merchantmen and their naval escorts. Grudgingly, the Admiralty barred the strait to destroyers in daylight. The merchantmen were given a choice: either they reached Dover at dusk, in which case they would be escorted, or they entered the Channel naked.

At dawn on August 8, twenty colliers took the risk. As the colliers formed themselves into a convoy off the Isle of Wight—a daily occurrence—*Kriegsmarine* radio operators at Wissant, opposite Folkestone, listened as the colliers and their Royal Navy escorts exchanged messages in preparation for the run through the Channel. A Luftwaffe strike followed. When the RDF station on the Isle of Wight picked up a strong blip, signaling the approach of a heavy raid, more than thirty Spitfires and Hurricanes went aloft to form an umbrella over the convoy. However, General Johannes Fink, after luring the RAF fighters away with decoys, sent in Stukas, which sank five ships and damaged seven others in less than ten minutes. The survivors scattered, tried to reassemble, and were attacked again, this time by a strong force of Stukas escorted by Bf-109s. The RAF lost sixteen planes, the Germans about twice that number.

The attacks on shipping continued throughout August, with the toll of cargo ships, tankers, armed trawlers, and sailors mounting. Late in the month, the destroyer HMS *Esk* hit a mine and went down off the Dutch coast, taking almost 130 tars with her. The coordinated attacks of the Luftwaffe and *Kriegsmarine* were yielding results, but Göring did not pursue his objectives with alacrity. Rather than trade his replaceable planes for irreplaceable British ships, he preferred the glory that devolved upon the Luftwaffe when his pilots engaged the boys of the RAF head-on, high in the sky, where contrails wrote the story of each day's heroics. German planes flying at 26,000 feet did not sink ships. The German army and navy high command, Churchill later wrote, "regretted the lower priority assigned by Göring to the naval targets, and were irked by the delays."[192]

Britain regretted the *Kanalkampf* sinkings but could spare the ships. On Friday evening, August 9, Churchill dined at Chequers with Pound, Ismay, Eden, Dill, and General Sir Archibald Wavell. Even under the threat of invasion Churchill cherished plans for British offensives. After the women had retired to the drawing room, he spoke at length about de Gaulle's plan for an invasion of French North Africa, supported by the Royal Navy, at Dakar. His view of that day's losses in the strait was philosophical; England, he said, would have to continue using her coastal vessels as bait, though he acknowledged that "the surviving bait are getting a bit fed up." Pound, also undiscouraged, said that they "even had a surplus of coasting vessels."[193]

During July, the RAF lost 70 aircraft and the Luftwaffe more than 180, more than half of them bombers. On neither side was the damage mortal. British spirits were high. All Britain was aroused by the RAF's heroism. The young pilots knew that every Englishman's eye was on them; they were, in Liddell Hart's phrase, "the heroes of the nation."[194]

Each day the German raids grew heavier and more frequent. Afterward, those who fought in the sky were haunted less by memories of fear—their engagements rarely lasted more than ten or fifteen minutes—than by the relentless tension and nerve-sapping fatigue. After a third or fourth sortie, men would fall asleep in their cockpits as soon as they had landed. Two or even three more sorties would lie ahead of them, and although they may have brushed death more than once, their weariness was so great that when dusk fell and darkness gathered, they had no immediate recollection of that day's fighting, not even of their kills. They awoke to the BBC's report of the latest score and, thus rejuvenated by the BBC and the miraculous powers of youth, would head for the village pub.[195]

All of England and all of Germany—indeed, the entire world—anxiously awaited each day's scores, upon which the outcome of the battle, and the likelihood of invasion, seemed to hang. No. 10 echoed with hurrahs after the Air Ministry reported, typically: "The final figures for today's fighting are 85 certain, 34 probable, 33 damaged. We lost 37 aircraft. 12 pilots being killed and 14 wounded." After dinner on Saturday, July 13, Colville wrote in his diary: "Winston said the last four days have been the most glorious in the history of the RAF. Those days have been the test: the enemy had come and had lost five to one. We could now be confident of our superiority."[196]

Churchill believed it. He was citing the figures he had been given, and no one had deliberately deceived him. No one was deliberately misleading the Führer either, but the numbers sent to his Luftwaffe commanders were very different. According to them, those days had been among the most glorious days in Luftwaffe history, and therefore clear evidence of *German* superiority. In retrospect it is clear that the communiqués being issued by both sides were quite worthless.

The RAF accepted their pilots' claims of German trophies without question. However, British accounts of their own losses were always correct. That was not true of Luftwaffe reports. Announcing light casualties for the Luftwaffe and severe British losses was a mighty tonic for Reich morale, and Germans concluded that their airmen were winning the battle.

One problem with deception is that the deceivers deceive themselves. That is what happened to the Luftwaffe's high command. "The Germans," as Churchill told Parliament later in the war, had "become victims of their own lies." The Germans had lost control of the battle's vital statistics, which, by the beginning of August, had become simply incredible. At one point William L. Shirer observed dryly: "German figures of British losses have been rising all evening. First (they) announced 73 British planes shot down against 14 German; then 79 to 14; finally at midnight 89 to 17. Actually, when I counted up the German figures as given out from time to time during the afternoon and evening, they totaled 111 for British losses. The Luftwaffe is lying so fast it isn't consistent even by its own account."[197]

At his country estate Göring studied these bogus figures, counted the number of British ships sunk, and declared that the *Kanalkampf* had been a stunning German victory. After the French capitulation, he had been told that the Royal Air Force had been reduced to fewer than two thousand frontline aircraft, of which between five hundred and six hundred were fighters. That was largely true—then. The *Reichsmarschall* had written the number on a pad of paper and pocketed it. In the fighting that followed, he subtracted the day's losses, as reported to him, at the end of each day. In a Luftwaffe intelligence report dated August 16, he read that the British had lost 574 fighters since July, and that since their factories had provided them with no more than 300, they were left with about 430, of which perhaps 300 were serviceable.

As the remainder on Göring's pad approached zero, he was confident that the invasion could soon begin. But German pilots knew that RAF squadrons were still defending Britain's skies. The *Reichsmarschall* was confused. He would have despaired had he been shown the latest figures from Ministry of Aircraft Production in London. In July alone, British workers had produced 496 fighter planes, four times the monthly rate before Dunkirk. By the end of August, Beaverbrook made 1,081 fighters available, with another 500 undergoing repair. Dowding, it seemed, would end the battle in the skies over England with more fighters than he had at the beginning.[198]

Moreover, the wrecks of aircraft downed over Britain could be recovered by Beaverbrook's Civilian Repair Organization. So efficient was the Beaver's CRO that by the end of summer, one-third of Dowding's fighters comprised parts from crashed Hurricanes and Spitfires. Indeed, through CRO ingenuity, crashed German planes flew again as RAF aircraft. On August 10, Colville noted in his diary: "Beaverbrook, he [Churchill] said, has genius, and, what is more, brutal ruthlessness." Never in his life, "at the Ministry of Munitions or anywhere else," had he seen "such startling results as Beaverbrook has produced." After studying the Aircraft Production charts, General Sir Henry Pownell, who was with them, "agreed that there had never been such an achievement." To be sure, it was a backbreaking job, and one from which the temperamental Canadian was forever resigning. Churchill wouldn't allow it. On September 2, at the end of one memorandum to the prime minister, Beaverbrook lamented, "Nobody knows the troubles I've seen." Beneath it Churchill wrote, "I do."[199]

An elated Göring put his statistics before Hitler, declaring that the RAF was helpless. The Reich, he said, had mastered the sky over *Der Bach* (the

German nickname for the Channel). Now, he proposed preparations for the second phase of the battle: *der Adlerangriff,* the Eagle Attack—Germany's all-out air assault in England. Yet Dowding was noting in his journal that he still believed time was on England's side "if we can only hold on." That day his pilots claimed to have destroyed sixty German planes, and though he may have thought that figure suspect, he was impressed by the skill with which the young Englishwomen at his radar stations had interpreted the direction and ranges of the attackers. In the long run, if the RAF were to prevail, the performance of the WAAF would be crucial.[200]

Luftwaffe airmen were as dangerous as ever. Their superiors were not. Officers of higher ranks committed the blunders and mismanagement within the Luftwaffe. The intelligence that Göring was receiving was appalling. The Germans had only a meager understanding of the British defense system; indeed, at the outset they didn't know where key British airfields were. Operational maps did not distinguish between fields used by Fighter and Bomber Commands. The two factories where Rolls-Royce built the Merlin engines that powered Hurricanes and Spitfires were never bombed, though their location was no secret. Vital orders miscarried. Weather reports were unreliable. Staff work was slow and sloppy. Göring summoned his generals and ordered that under no circumstances should he be disturbed by subordinates in search of guidance. Worst of all, he adopted no coherent strategy, no priority of targets. After the war, Adolph Galland, one of his officers, wrote that "constantly changing orders betraying lack of purpose and obvious misjudgment of the situation by the Command and unjustified accusations had a most demoralizing effect on us fighter pilots."[201]

British RDF (radar) baffled the enemy. Picking up its signals, German airmen reported British radio stations with special installations. Nazi intelligence decided it was a communication system linking RAF pilots with ground controllers, and concluded, on August 7, that "as the British fighters are controlled from the ground by radio-telephone, their forces are tied to their respective ground stations and are therefore restricted in mobility," which, had it been true, would have meant that resistance to mass German attacks was limited to local fighters.[202]

The commander of the Luftwaffe Signals Service, who was among the few Germans who understood the role of radar, urged that an attack on the RDF stations be given priority. A limited attempt on them, made on the day before the first major assault on the British mainland, was ineffective. At Dover, the Germans rocked a radar pylon, but the 360-foot-tall lattice masts were almost impossible to hit; returning after an attempt to destroy four of them, the pilots reported total failure. Göring assumed that the British electronic gear and crews were deep underground and hence safe. (In fact they were in flimsy shacks beneath the towers.) He issued the order: "It is doubtful whether there is any point in continuing the attacks on radar sites, in view of the fact that not one of those attacked has so far been put out of action."[203]

Nevertheless, this was still the mighty Luftwaffe, and its huge fleets of superb aircraft outnumbered the defenders by two to one. After the *Kanalkampf*, they completed plans for *Adlertag* (Eagle Day), the launch of *Adlerangriff* (Eagle Attack). The Führer, unaware that Göring's figures were inflated, authorized him to open *Adlerangriff*. Depending on the weather and other imponderables, the *Führerordnung* (*Führer Directive*) decreed, *Adlertag* could fall as early as August 5. British intelligence officers in Bletchley Park relayed the decision to Churchill, and Dowding issued an Order of the Day to his men: "The Battle of Britain is about to begin. Members of the Royal Air Force, the fate of generations lies in your hands."

On August 6, the *Reichsmarschall* set Eagle Day for August 10, a Saturday. The weather forced him to reschedule it for the following Tuesday, when heavy skies were expected to clear. They did, and that morning, 74 twin-engine Dorniers (which could carry 2,200 pounds of bombs) and 50 Bf 109s took off. The clouds returned; Göring issued a recall order. That afternoon, the clouds rolled away and the offensive was officially on, targeting a 150-mile arc of southern England from the Thames estuary to Southampton. Commanding it was Göring's ablest subordinate, *Feldmarschall* Albert Kesselring, commander of *Luftflotte* 2. Kesselring's men called him "Smiling Albert" (he liked to flash his perfect enamels). He had much to smile about. Soon after daybreak every RAF radar tower in the southeast was sending urgent warnings to Dowding's headquarters.[204]

Among those awaiting the onslaught were a dozen American war correspondents on the cliffs of Dover, including H. R. Knickerbocker, Edward Murrow, Helen Kirkpatrick, Quentin Reynolds, Whitelaw Reid, Virginia Cowles, Eric Sevareid, and Vincent Sheean. Their mood was fatalistic. Among them, Sheean wrote, a "sense of inevitable tragedy had grown heavy." Some had been covering the spread of global conflict since the Japanese seizure of Manchuria in 1931. The Reich seemed invincible. They heard the familiar hum of the desynchronized Messerschmitts, Heinkels—the workhorses of the Luftwaffe, with a range of 1,250 miles and a bomb load capacity of 5,500 pounds—and Dorniers, which grew to a roar as the glittering wings of the great Nazi armada emerged from the dazzling sun-drenched mist over the Channel and approached a coast that had not seen an invader in nine centuries. Experience had taught the newsmen to expect another defeat for democracy.[205]

And then, Sheean wrote, from RAF fields inland, they saw twenty-one squadrons—more than 300 aircraft—of challenging Spitfires rising "like larks, glittering against the sun," maneuvering for position and attack.

They heard the "zoom of one fighter diving over another...the rattle of machine-gun fire, the streak of smoke of a plane plummeting to earth, and the long seesaw descent of the wounded fighter falling from the clouds beneath his shining white parachute." Sheean and his companions no doubt saw a great flotilla of RAF fighters, but they could not have all been Spitfires. On any given day, No. 11 and 12 Groups could count only about 250 operational Spitfires, and around 320 Hurricanes.[206]

The scenes were repeated all that day and all week along the southern coast. Sheean wrote: "In every such battle I saw, the English had the best of it, and in every such battle they were greatly outnumbered." Repeatedly "five or six fighters would engage twenty or thirty Germans.... I saw it happen not once but many times." He remembered the Spaniards and the Czechs and wrote: "At Dover the first sharp thrust of hope penetrated our gloom. The battles over the cliffs proved that British could and would fight for their own freedom, if for nothing else, and that they would do so against colossal odds.... The flash of the Spitfire's wing, then, through the misty glare of the summer sky, was the first flash of a sharpened sword; they *would* fight, they *would* hold out."[207]

The battle reached its peak between August 24 and September 6, which became known to Fighter Command as the critical period. In the five weeks of fighting between July 10 and August 13, Luftwaffe tactics had been tested by Dowding's strategy. His orders to his pilots to avoid Messerschmitts, to flee from them if necessary and go after the German bombers, had paid off. Nazi fighters flying escort had been at a disadvantage; enemy bomber losses had continued to be high; and, far more important, the RAF continued to be a force in being, warding off the threat of invasion.

With Eagle Day this pattern changed. Kesselring massed a great concentration of Messerschmitts in the Pas de Calais, in northern France. He meant to wipe out the sector airfields of Sir Keith Park's 11 Group—London's air defenses—leaving the capital naked. During this time Churchill repeatedly visited RAF bases at Stanmar, Uxbridge, Dover, and Ramsgate. These were the castle gates, from which its last defenders sallied forth, behind which all England waited. Colville noted that what Churchill saw at the bases "brought the war home to him." The Germans, in fact, had brought the war to his home.[208]

On Thursday, August 15, the Germans decided to test RAF Fighter Command's strength by attacking it from all sides simultaneously. For the first time, *Luftflotte* 5 (Air Fleet 5), in Norway and Denmark, was assigned a major role, to sweep into northern England near Tyneside and seek out industrial targets near Newcastle and Bomber Command airfields. *Luftflotte* 5 sent one hundred bombers escorted by forty twin-engine Bf 110s. The distance from Denmark precluded the possibility of using single-engine Bf 109s to protect the bombers. The Germans paid dearly for their lack of fighter cover. Days earlier, Dowding had moved eighty Spitfire pilots and their planes north, to give both a needed rest. They rose to meet the attackers. The Germans lost sixteen Heinkels and six JU-88s—one-fifth of their bombers—and seven Bf 110s. There were no British losses. Throughout the Luftwaffe, that day became known as *der schwarze Donnerstag:* Black Thursday.[209]

In the south, however, that day's fighting was very different. Here the airfields of No. 11 Group were the targets. In Essex and Kent, airfields at Martlesham, Eastchurch, and Hawkinge were hit; then the enemy attacked two aircraft factories near Rochester and fighter fields at Portland, Middle Wallop, West Malling, and Croydon. Both sides suffered the highest losses for any single day. Before dusk the Germans had flown an unprecedented 1,786 sorties, and the total losses for both sides—109 aircraft—were the highest for any single day of the battle thus far.

Churchill followed the day's fighting from No. 11 Group headquarters at Uxbridge, and he left clearly affected. Climbing into his limousine with Ismay, he said, "Don't speak to me. I'm too moved." His lips were trembling. They rode in silence for a few minutes. Then Churchill turned to Ismay and said something that "burned into" Ismay's mind, so much so that he went home that night and repeated the words to his wife.[210]

Five days later, when the most difficult and dangerous period in the battle was about to begin, Churchill paused during a long address to the House of Commons on the overall war situation, and delivered his tribute to the RAF:

> The gratitude of every home in our island, in our Empire, and indeed throughout the world, except in the abodes of the guilty, goes out to the British airmen who, undaunted by odds, unwearied in their constant challenge of mortal danger, are turning the tide of the World War by their prowess and their devotion.

Then, he spoke the words that had so moved Ismay: "Never in the field of human conflict was so much owed by so many to so few." Those words have become immortal, yet they were but a prelude to Churchill's main point, the RAF bombing campaign:

> All hearts go out to the fighter pilots, whose brilliant actions we see with our own eyes day after day; but we must never forget that all the

time, night after night, month after month, our bomber squadrons travel far into Germany, find their targets in the darkness by the highest navigational skill, aim their attacks, often under the heaviest fire, often with serious loss, with deliberate careful discrimination, and inflict shattering blows upon the whole of the technical and war-making structure of the Nazi power. On no part of the Royal Air Force does the weight of the war fall more heavily than on the daylight bombers, who will play an invaluable part in the case of invasion and whose unflinching zeal it has been necessary in the meanwhile on numerous occasions to restrain.[211]

Bomber Command had more than six hundred medium and light bombers stationed on airfields north of London. Churchill did not intend to restrain them much longer.

On Friday the sixteenth, Kesselring continued to press the attack. *Luftflotte* 5 was grounded—indeed, for the remainder of the battle—but the Germans put up more than 1,700 sorties, raiding airfields almost at will and bombing the hangars at Brize Norton flight-training school. That Sunday the Germans lost seventy-one aircraft, nearly 10 percent of those committed. Nevertheless, after a day's lull the enemy again arrived in force, undiscouraged by the costs of the offensive.[212]

Göring summoned his three *Luftflotten* commanders to Karinhall and ordered them to go after aircraft factories and steel mills as "bottleneck" targets. Four days later he summoned them again to announce: "We have reached the decisive period of the air war against England." As in past conferences he was astonishingly ill-informed. He grossly underestimated the significance of Dowding's radar chain, thus assuring its continued immunity, and his summation of Luftwaffe accomplishments in the battle was wildly unrealistic.[213]

Nevertheless, Fighter Command's situation was critical. Unlike the enemy, Britain had no bottomless reserve of trained pilots. RAF bomber pilots were being retrained to fly Spitfires and Hurricanes. In a single week Dowding had lost 80 percent of his squadron commanders. One of their replacements had never even flown a Hurricane, yet after just three landings and three takeoffs, he led his men into battle. Often pilots had logged no more than ten hours of flight before sighting an enemy fighter. In August, Fighter Command's operational training period was cut from six months to two weeks. Some new pilots had never fired their guns. Some were boys in their teens.[214]

The RAF pilots pushed the limits of human endurance, sleeping in their cockpits between sorties, "undaunted by odds," in Churchill's words, "unwearied in their constant challenge and mortal danger." On the final day of August, accompanied by Clemmie, Pamela, and Colville, he drove to Uxbridge, the frenzied headquarters of Sir Keith Park's No. 11 Group, controlling all the fighter squadrons in southeastern England. The rest of his party took walks in the countryside, but he wanted to talk to the airmen, look into their faces, and hear their stories. That evening Colville wrote: "The P.M. was deeply moved by what he saw this afternoon at Uxbridge."[215]

Park could replace his pilots but not his airfields. If the Germans knocked them out by bombing and strafing, British fighters could neither take off nor land; the Nazis would then command the air over southeast England, and Hitler's invasion could begin. To protect No. 11 Group's fields, Park told his pilots to engage the enemy as far out as possible, but when the Germans greatly increased the proportion of fighters to bombers, the Spitfires and Hurricanes of No. 12 Group had to stay behind to provide No. 11 Group fields with air cover, and there weren't enough of them. The enemy onslaught was too great. Kesselring was putting up over a thousand sorties a day. Charging in from the sea each morning at an altitude too low for British guns, Bf 109s and 110s would sweep the RAF fields in strafing attacks, wrecking repair shops, destroying hangars, ripping apart grounded planes, leveling operations buildings, and leaving airstrips unfit for landing and taking off. The Bf 110s, armed with 2,200-pound bombs, were especially deadly. Once the RAF was shot out of the sky and its airfields smashed, Göring planned on sending his Bf 110s far inland in search of military and industrial targets.

RAF ground crews worked heroically, but before new craters could be filled in, a second flight of raiders would arrive. By dusk all British communications were paralyzed, and when the operations rooms were reduced to ruins, the whole ground-control system failed. One by one the advanced fighting fields were abandoned. And on the tenth day of the new Nazi offensive, a dozen Ju 88s slipped through Britain's fighter protection and hit the Vickers factory near Weybridge, destroying the works and inflicting heavy casualties. The output of Wellington bombers dropped from ninety a week to four.[216]

Minister of Information Duff Cooper told No. 10 that British morale was "extremely high," but the public did not know what its leaders knew. Fighter Command was in crisis. Under Beaverbrook, British factories were producing 115 or more new fighters each week—twice as many as the Germans—but the Nazis were now shooting down more than that. Dowding's aircraft reserve was shrinking. On the last two days of August, the Nazi attacks reached a crescendo with 2,795 sorties. Their primary targets continued to be No. 11 Group's vital sector stations at Biggin Hill and

Kenley. By September 1 both were destroyed. Hangars, aircraft repair shops, operations buildings, communication grids—all were leveled. Of No. 11 Group's seven major airfields, six had been demolished and the five advanced airfields were hors de combat. Still, Churchill and Park conferred on the first and agreed that the Germans had reached their maximum effectiveness and "could not stand the strain much longer as far as an air offensive is concerned."[217]

Incredibly, the German high command didn't grasp the implications of the Luftwaffe's successes. An exception was *Generalfeldmarschall* Fedor von Bock, one of the Wehrmacht's highest-ranking officers. Bock realized that the tide of battle had shifted; while preparing to move his army-group headquarters from France to Poland, he tried to impress upon his commander in chief, Walther von Brauchitsch, the importance of the shift. Finding von Brauchitsch uncommunicative, Bock insisted that for the first time in the battle, the Luftwaffe was making some real headway.

Every day now the Germans were coming in larger numbers and they were threatening Britain's inner defenses. When, after a visit to Fighter Command headquarters at Stanmore, Churchill dined at Chequers with Dowding, Lindemann, and Gort, the enemy bombed Great Missenden, just four miles away.

By the first week in September, the RAF was in desperate straits. Dowding's pilots were no longer permitted to pursue enemy aircraft out over the Channel. Because he lacked rested and refitted squadrons, he could no longer rotate them. In just two weeks he had lost 230 pilots, killed and wounded—25 percent of his pilots. At that rate, in another week Fighter Command would cease to be a disciplined fighting force. The entire air-defense system of southeast England was in danger of destruction. Already the Luftwaffe could very nearly do what it pleased over the area that Sea Lion had targeted for invasion. "If what Göring wanted was air superiority over southeast England for the invasion," Deighton writes, "then by 1 September it was almost his." Air Marshal Park wrote that "an almost complete disorganization made the control of our fighter squadrons completely difficult.... Had the enemy continued his heavy attacks (against fields and the control system)... the fighter defenses of London would have been in a perilous state." Group captain Peter Townsend believed that "on 6th September victory was in the Luftwaffe's grasp." On September 7, he said, Wehrmacht divisions, panzers, and artillery "could have begun massive landings on British soil."[218]

But the key event determining the outcome of the air battle had taken place on the night of August 23–24. It was a matter of chance. A few of 170 German Heinkels that had been ordered to bomb oil installations at Thames Haven and Rochester became lost. Before turning for home, they jettisoned their bombs. As it happened, the lost raiders were over London. Fleeing homeward, they left behind raging fires in Bethnal Green and East Ham.[219]

This was an error Hitler could not countenance. He had issued a directive to the Luftwaffe: "Attacks against the London area and terror attacks are reserved for the Führer's decision." This was a political rather than a strictly military decree. He was still hoping to bring Churchill to the conference table.[220]

Churchill saw his chance. A month earlier he had sought from the Air Ministry a guarantee that were the Germans to bomb residential areas of London, Bomber Command would be ready "to return the compliment the next day against Berlin." The night following the errant German attack on London—August 25—eighty-one twin-engine Wellingtons and Hampdens carried the war to the heart of the Reich. Berlin was covered with dense cloud; only half the bombers found it. Railroad yards and utilities were the targets. Damage was slight. Ten German men were killed by a bomb that fell near the Görlitzer railroad station, and the Siemens electrical works suffered a temporary loss of production. Unable to locate their targets, many of the British pilots brought their planes home still fully loaded with bombs.[221]

The following morning Churchill sent a memo to the Chiefs of Air Staff: "Now that they have begun to molest the capital, I want you to hit them hard, and Berlin is the place to hit them."[222]

The British had been targeting German military and industrial targets since May—sporadic raids over the Kiel Canal, Rhine River shipping, railroad junctions. But until that Sunday night, no bomb had fallen on the capital of the Reich. William L. Shirer wrote in his diary: "The Berliners are stunned. They did not think it could ever happen. When the war began, Göring had assured them that it couldn't.... They believed him. Their disillusionment today is all the greater. You have to see their faces to believe it.... For the first time the war has been brought home to them."[223]

The club-footed Nazi propaganda minister and former so-called journalist Dr. Paul Joseph Goebbels ordered German newspapers to run the headline EIGER ENGLISCHER AGRIFF (Cowardly British Attack). The bombers came again on August 28 and again the following night, and after the third raid, the headlines in the Nazi press screamed, ENGLISCHE LUFTPIRATEN ÜBER BERLIN! (English Air Pirates over Berlin!)[224]

Bombing cities was still an issue in 1940. Both the Hague and the Geneva Conventions—which the Reich was pledged to support—outlawed indiscriminate assaults on peaceful civilians. In May, when a flight of Heinkels had mistakenly killed nearly a hundred German women and children in the old university city of Freiburg im Breisgau, the Germans had blamed it on the RAF. A Nazi communiqué had reported it as an "enemy attack." Goebbels condemned it as the "*Kindermord in Freiburg*" (the "murder of the innocents in Freiburg"), and the British traitor Lord Haw-Haw had denounced it as a "perfectly substantiated atrocity."[225]

Granting London immunity had never been popular in the Luftwaffe. As the autumn of 1940 approached and with no victory in the skies over England, Göring repeatedly asked Hitler to reconsider. Discontent was particularly keen among German fighter pilots. In his postwar memoirs, Adolph Galland—then a Luftwaffe major and fighter pilot, later a general—described London as a target "of exceptional military importance, as the brain and nerve center of the British High Command, as a port, and as a center for armament and distribution." He wrote, "We fighter pilots, discouraged by a task which was beyond our strength, were looking forward impatiently and excitedly to the start of the bomber attacks."[226]

So was Göring, who, unaware of how much damage he had inflicted on the RAF, argued that a strategic shift from fighters over Dover to bombers over London might bring about the hoped-for peace conference, and preserve the Luftwaffe's reputation in the bargain. Göring, Shirer later wrote, made a mistake "comparable in its consequences to Hitler's calling off the armored attack on Dunkirk on May 24." Admiral Raeder, too, championed terror attacks against London, in part as a means to preserve his navy, which he believed would be destroyed in an invasion attempt. If the Luftwaffe and the threat of invasion could not force Churchill to the conference table, perhaps a panicked London citizenry might do so. On August 31 Hitler approved massed raids—by day and night—against the London docks. They were to begin in a week.[227]

On September 4 Hitler delivered a withering attack on the British leadership in Berlin's *Sportpalast*, a winter sports arena and the largest meeting hall in the capital. Addressing an audience of social workers and nurses, he dismissed Minister of Information Duff Cooper as a "*Krampfhenne*" (a Bavarian word for "a nervous old hen"), and said, "The babbling of Mr. Churchill or Mr. Eden—reverence for old age forbids the mention of Mr. Chamberlain—doesn't mean a thing to the German people. At best, it makes them laugh." He then took up the bombings. "Mr. Churchill," he said, "is demonstrating his new brain child, the night air raid." Hitler said he had believed that such madness would be stopped, but "Herr Churchill took that for a sign of weakness." Now he would learn better: "We will *raze* their cities to the ground!" He shouted, "The hour will come when one of us will break, and it will not be National Socialist Germany!" The women leapt to their feet, joyfully shouting, "Never! *Never!*"

Hitler knew that the British were wondering when his invasion would begin. He said, "In England they're filled with curiosity and keep asking 'Why doesn't he come?' Be calm, he's coming! Be calm, he's coming!"[228]

Yet to those who knew the Führer and his byzantine court, there was an air of uncertainty about the Reich's intentions. After listening to Hitler's speech, Count Ciano was baffled. Something about it was not quite right. He wrote in his diary that Hitler seemed "unaccountably nervous."[229]

He was. He had conquered France in six weeks. Now, almost twelve weeks after the French surrender, the English—their army weak but rebuilding, their navy spread thin, their air force down on one knee—had fought him to a standstill. The strategic shift to massed bombings was his last option. If it worked, he would not need to invade England. But on that account, time was not on his side. Churchill understood that there existed one condition among many necessary, though not sufficient, for a successful invasion of England, a circumstance over which nobody had any control and that defied accurate prediction. To launch an invasion, according to the Joint Intelligence Committee, the Germans were dependent upon "a calm sea and restricted visibility." The Channel weather in autumn, when it deteriorated into "equinoctial gales" (as Churchill called them) could prove England's most steadfast ally. The North Sea in autumn was no place for flat-bottomed river barges made top-heavy by troops, artillery, and tanks. In winter it was even worse, and each day that passed brought winter one day closer. That was reassuring; that it was still only early September was not.[230]

On September 6, the Joint Intelligence Committee pored over a sheaf of reports, Enigma decrypts, and aerial photographs. The evidence before them seemed compelling. Enigma decrypts reported that all German army leave had been stopped; maps of English coastal areas had been issued to German officers in Normandy; the transfer of dive-bombers from Norway to France was complete; aerial photographs showed a "large-scale and disciplined" massing of barges (*Sturmboote*) in the Channel ports. Forty-eight hours after that moon and tide, the reports concluded, conditions would be "particularly favorable" for enemy landings. Warning of the "large-scale and disciplined" movement of troop transports toward forward bases on the Channel, the committee concluded that the last enemy preparations were complete. The next afternoon, the seventh, the director of military intelligence told the Chiefs of Staff that the invasion was imminent. At Bletchley Park the Naval Intelligence Section concluded that the landings might begin the following day. The chiefs therefore ordered all defense forces in the United Kingdom to "stand by at immediate notice." The Air Ministry issued an "Invasion Alert No. 1" to all RAF commands, signaling the expectation that the Germans could be expected within the next twenty-four hours.[231]

Late on the cloudless afternoon of Saturday, September 7, Hermann Göring and Albert Kesselring stood with their staffs on the cliffs of Cap Blanc Nez, opposite the White Cliffs of Dover, and watched their huge formation of *Luftflotten,* one thousand aircraft, a third of them bombers, cross the Channel and head for London. It was an awesome spectacle. The enormous armada seemed to shut out the sun and rose nearly two miles high.[232]

The RAF had no warning that London was the target. At 4:00 P.M. Dowding was at his desk in Bentley Priory when he was told British radar had picked up the huge formations approaching from Calais. During previous Luftwaffe raids, including over the past few days, the raiders had split up upon reaching the coast, where British fighters patrolling at 25,000 feet waited for that moment to pounce. On this day that moment never came. *Valhalla* was German slang for an extraordinarily large formation of aircraft. Wave after wave of Valhallas crossed the east coast of Kent, near Deal, and headed straight for London. Eagle Attack was still under way; the targets were industrial centers along the Thames. The Germans hit Woolwich Arsenal first, then the Victoria and Albert Docks, the West India Dock, the Commercial Dock, and the Surrey Docks. Behind them they left a flaming vision of apocalypse. Ships were sunk, catwalks mangled, cranes toppled, and fires set that covered 250 acres and served as a beacon for a second heavy raid. Many German bombs missed their marks and fell into East End neighborhoods—civilian neighborhoods. At dusk that evening, observers in the West End took note of what appeared to be a spectacular sunset. But the glow came from the east. The observers quickly grasped the horrific truth: this was not the tangerine handiwork of the setting sun; the East End was burning.[233]

In the late spring of 1940 it was decreed that the bells of London's churches, which had pealed morning wake-up and evening curfew and called London's faithful to Sunday service for almost three centuries, would ring now only to announce Cromwell, the code word that would alert all Britain to an imminent invasion. When the Chiefs of Staff ordered all troops in Britain to full readiness, that was enough for the Home Guard. At 7:30 they proclaimed Cromwell. Church bells throughout the kingdom rang out their warning. Men deployed. Civilians readied their homemade weapons. The Royal Engineers blew up key bridges, and in the confusion, several civilians were injured stumbling over hastily laid mines.[234]

It was a false alarm. No Germans arrived by sea, but for Londoners, the terror from the skies had begun. Given the hideous glow churning the clouds high above the East End, it would not have been unreasonable had Londoners concluded that their city was soon to be reduced to cinders and ash.[235]

The next day Home Forces commander Sir Alan Brooke told his diary of the night's heavy bombing and fires, and added, "Went to the office in the morning, where I found further indications of impending invasion." He predicted that the next few weeks would prove "the most eventful weeks in the history of the British Empire." The full moon and tides would align the next week. The Germans had not come during the July moon, or the August. They would have to come in the next ten days, or take their chances in October, when the weather, their ally since June, would become their enemy.[236]

To oppose an invasion, reinvigorate the blockade, and hunt U-boats, Churchill needed more destroyers. Help in that regard—very modest help—was on the way at last, but at a price. Franklin Roosevelt's position on sending destroyers to Churchill had shifted (just slightly) between May and late August, a period of twelve weeks during which Churchill fumed to the cabinet that "although the president is our best friend, no practical help has been forthcoming from the United States as yet. We have not expected them to send military aid [troops or pilots], but they have not even sent any worthy contribution in destroyers or planes." At one point, the kingdom's finances looked so bleak that Chancellor of the Exchequer Kingsley Wood suggested requisitioning the nation's gold wedding rings in order to raise twenty million pounds. Churchill approved the plan but suggested it be implemented at a later date, not to retain the twenty million in gold but "for the purpose of shaming the Americans" if for lack of American help England's fortunes should evaporate.[237]

Churchill followed up his original request to Roosevelt for destroyers with another, and another, and another. His missives to Roosevelt became increasingly desperate, the memos to staff more disdainful of the timeliness and quality of American help. To HMG's ambassador in Washington, Lord Lothian, in June: "We really have had no help worth speaking of from the United States so far." That month had been the low point, symbolized perhaps by Henry Ford's refusal to produce engines for British planes for fear his sales of new cars to Americans might be hurt, to say nothing of getting paid were England to lose, as Ford thought likely. In a late July telegram to Roosevelt, Churchill simply begged: "It has now become most urgent for you to give us the destroyers, motor boats and flying boats for which we have asked.... Mr. President, with great respect I must tell you that in the long history of the world this is a thing to do now."[238]

Churchill lowered his request to forty ships, and then he raised it to sixty. He cautioned Roosevelt that the Italians, by sending some of their submarines into the Atlantic (Mussolini had more than one hundred, more even than Germany), could help the Germans isolate England. He informed the president that ten British destroyers had been sunk in ten days, and almost one-third of the Royal Navy destroyer fleet had been lost since the start of the war. And he linked the destroyers to his strategic plans for the following year: "Our intention is to have a strong army fighting in France for the campaign of 1941." Finally, he told Roosevelt that "time is all important," for it would not be until February that British production of destroyers and anti-submarine craft could fill the shipping gap, which, however, could be filled by the prompt delivery of U.S. destroyers.[239]

By mid-August, more than three months after Churchill's first plea for older destroyers, Roosevelt began to believe that Britain might, just might, hold on. Ignoring both the isolationists and the Neutrality Acts, the president sent Churchill a message through the State Department in which he proposed a two-pronged deal: a guarantee from England that its Home Fleet would sail to Canada were the Home Island to find itself in extremis, and a straight-up swap of several British naval bases for the American ships. The negotiations for the destroyers imparted a certain sticky relativism to the concept of U.S. neutrality. Germany and Italy, with whom America was not at war after all, would receive no such friendly overtures. Regardless of the sovereign right of nations to trade with any combatant not under legal blockade, a transfer of fifty destroyers to Britain was a clear step in the direction toward war, and that pleased Churchill. But the terms Roosevelt proposed did not. Churchill told Colville that Roosevelt wanted to put a "lien" on the British fleet in return for the destroyers. It was not the deal he expected; in fact, he expected a gift, with no strings attached, and told Roosevelt so: "I had not contemplated anything in the nature of a contract, bargain or sale between us" but rather "a separate spontaneous act." Cadogan found Churchill "rather incensed" over Roosevelt's proposed swap. Churchill, Cadogan jotted in his diary, "says he doesn't mind if we don't get destroyers." But of course he did.[240]

Churchill could not abide Roosevelt's linking the destroyers to a guarantee that were England to fall, its Atlantic fleet would run westward to Canada. He complained in a letter to Canadian prime minister William Lyon Mackenzie King that the Americans sought to "get the British fleet and the guardianship of the British Empire, minus Great Britain." In essence, were the United States to lose a friend, it would gain a fleet. It was the same sort of guarantee the British had wanted from the French. Yet the United States was a noncombatant, not an ally fighting alongside the British as the British had fought alongside the French. Churchill, not pleased, sent a cool response to the president on August 31: "You ask, Mr. President, whether my statement in Parliament on June 4th, 1940, about Great

Britain never surrendering or scuttling her Fleet 'represents the settled policy of His Majesty's Government.' It certainly does. I must, however, observe that those hypothetical contingencies seem more likely to concern the German fleet or what is left of it than our own."[241]

These were bold words, yet Churchill had done his naval calculations: Britain had a fleet of capital ships, including aircraft carriers, and more than nine hundred smaller, but very dangerous, craft. The Germans had nothing of the sort. In the end, no direct linkage between U.S. destroyers and a defeated British fleet made its way into the deal. Rather, the down payment for the destroyers took the form of British naval bases in Newfoundland, Bermuda, and the Caribbean, leased to the Americans for ninety-nine years. Roosevelt, in explaining the transaction to Congress, could not resist the urge to gloat over the killing he had just made in the real-estate market: "The right to bases in Newfoundland and Bermuda are gifts—generously given and gladly received. The other bases mentioned have been acquired in exchange for fifty of our over-age destroyers." The first eight of the over-age destroyers sailed to Britain in early September. Churchill took them. At that point he'd take anything.

Despite the ad hoc nature of England's defenses in June and early July, by September a transformation had taken place. All summer the War Office, under Anthony Eden, had worked around the clock, rebuilding the army. By mid-July Britain had 1,500,000 men under arms; five weeks later Churchill told the House of Commons, "More than 2,000,000 determined men have rifles and bayonets in their hands tonight, and three-quarters of them are in regular military formations. We have never had armies like this in our island in time of war. The whole island bristles against invaders, from the sea or from the air." Those numbers included the Home Guard, but they also included rebuilt regular army infantry and armored units, and the Canadian division. Churchill could not, of course, speak publicly of the specifics of the military transformation, but with each passing week, he grew more sanguine about the fate of any Germans who arrived on British soil. By August the regular army fielded seven divisions between the Thames and the Wash, the great estuary one hundred miles north of London, where the chiefs expected the Germans to come. But by then, invasion barges were streaming through the Channel at night toward the French Channel ports. That meant the Germans might come to the south coast, where only five divisions stood ready, with three in reserve. But by September the situation was even further improved. The troop disposition north of London amounted to four divisions and an armored brigade. In the south, nine divisions were deployed, and two armored brigades. One division was stationed near London, where, if the Germans got that far, Churchill intended to fight street by street. And two divisions and six hundred tanks formed a reserve.[242]

As England's defenses improved, Churchill felt confident enough to send to Egypt almost half of the best tanks in Britain, 48 anti-tank guns, 20 Bofors light anti-aircraft guns (desperately needed in London), and 250 anti-tank rifles. He did so to blunt an anticipated Italian attack, which duly took place on September 13.[243]

In August, having secured his gains in Ethiopia, Il Duce had marched his armies into British Somaliland, where they humiliated the British. Churchill fumed to Eden that "the losses sustained are not compatible with resolute resistance." In particular, Churchill's doubts about his Middle East commander, Archibald Wavell, were growing. Yet, given that Somaliland's entire defense budget for the year was less than £900 ($3,600), how much resistance *could* have been forthcoming? Wavell's casualties during the withdrawal from Somaliland had been light, a fact that the MP for Aberdeenshire, Robert Boothby, recalled infuriated the Old Man, who took it as a sign of a lack of fighting spirit, and so informed Wavell. Wavell replied, "Butchery is not the mark of a good tactician." Churchill was wrong, and he knew it. Generally, those who stood up to him were accorded his respect, but Wavell was the exception to the norm.[244]

On September 13, Mussolini plunged his dagger into Wavell's western flank. On that day, General Rodolfo Graziani, in command of the Italian Tenth Army and 80,000 of Italy's finest troops—infantry, motorized, and led by 300 tanks—lunged eastward out of Libya and into Egypt, driving Wavell's surprised and disordered troops before him. Technically, by crossing the Egyptian frontier, Mussolini had invaded a neutral country, not that such diplomatic niceties were of any concern to Il Duce. Egypt had gained its independence from Britain in 1922 and had been ruled since 1936 by King Farouk I. Farouk despised his British protectors, who were in Egypt by virtue of a 1936 treaty that granted Britain de facto sovereignty were the Suez Canal to be endangered, which, theoretically, it was. Farouk rather admired fascism, especially the Italian variety, as did many of the younger officers in the Egyptian army, including a pair of unknowns named Gamal Abdel Nasser and Anwar Sadat. Egypt's politics were so striated by anti-British, pro-Axis, and nationalist factions that a declaration of war against the invading Italians could not be agreed upon. Thus, HMG kept a watchful eye on Farouk while British diplomats and generals ran the country. Graziani's fight was never with the Egyptian people—many welcomed his presence—but with the British. In Graziani, Mussolini had found his hero. To subvert the Italians' progress Churchill ordered Wavell to poison any wells that "we do not need for ourselves." The Italians pressed on for five days and sixty miles, to Sidi Barrani, where they paused to resupply. Then, inexplicably, given their advantage, rather than strike toward Alexandria and the Suez, they made camp, to the great relief of the outnumbered Tommies to the east. In addition to Graziani's 80,000 men, the Italians had 150,000 more in reserve in Libya. Wavell's Cairo command consisted of fewer than 40,000 men, including cooks, chaplains, and orderlies. His isolation was now total, but Churchill intended to reinforce him.[245]

Brooke had been correct when he told his diary that Churchill was offense-minded. To that end, the prime minister ordered 70,000 troops shipped to Egypt, a journey of almost 14,000 miles and fifty days around the Cape of Good Hope, a trip made necessary because the Mediterranean was, by virtue of the Italian fleet, no longer a British lake. The troops would be followed, Churchill hoped, by more than 50,000 before late December. They were sent not merely to defend Egypt against the Italians but because Churchill intended to take the attack to the Italians in Libya. His private secretary, John Martin, later declared that the dispatch of the troops and armor at a time when Britain herself was vulnerable was an act of courage by Churchill, Eden, and the Chiefs of Staff.[246]

It was also necessary. The security of the British Isles, as it had been since the Napoleonic Wars, was bound to the security of the Mediterranean. The Battle of Britain and the Battle for Egypt were two sides of the same coin. Neither would survive if the other fell. The tanks and men had to be sent.

On the day Graziani struck, September 13, Hitler lunched with the army's Halder and von Brauchitsch, the navy's Raeder, and a Luftwaffe *Jagdfliegerführer* (fighter pilot commander) representing Göring. Luftwaffe intelligence continued to be wildly inaccurate; they were told that although "the prerequisites for *Seelöwe* have not been completely realized," in the past five weeks, their airmen had shot down 1,800 British planes, which would have been double Dowding's total fighter strength. (The actual figure was about 500 RAF fighter planes.) However, the Führer mused, destruction of the RAF might be unnecessary; if their capital was subjected to terror bombing, the British might be seized by "mass hysteria," and the invasion could be canceled. The bombing of London, which had begun on September 7, would continue.[247]

In shifting the German *schwerpunkt* (focus point) from specific military and industrial targets to Greater London, Hitler gave permission, Jodl wrote, "for the use of strong air forces in reprisal attacks against London." It was to mean monumental suffering for British civilians. It also meant defeat for Göring's strategy just as it was about to meet with success.[248]

The fighting in the air reached a climax on Sunday, September 15, which later became known as Battle of Britain Day. Churchill witnessed it; because "the weather on this day seemed suitable to the enemy," he wrote, he and Clementine drove to Park's headquarters at Uxbridge. There they were taken to the bombproof operations room fifty feet belowground, which he compared to "a small theater," adding, "We took our seats in the dress circle." A large-scale map table with rows of lightbulbs above made the chaos in the sky overhead comprehensible. The defenders' commitment was total; when his visitor asked about reserves, Park looked grave and replied, "There are none." In Churchill's words, "The odds were great; our margins small; the stakes infinite." Like the Battle of Waterloo, also fought on a Sunday, this was what Wellington had called "a close-run thing." But it, too, ended in a great British triumph. At the end of the afternoon, Churchill was told that 138 German planes had been shot down at a cost of 26 RAF aircraft, and though the figure for German losses later proved to be higher than it actually was, the significance of the day's fighting could not have been greater. That evening, in a message to Dowding meant for enemy consumption, Churchill declared that the British, "using only a small proportion of their total strength," had "cut to tatters separate waves of murderous assault upon the civil population of their native land." Two days later he told Parliament, "Sunday's action was the most brilliant and fruitful of any fought up to that date by the fighters of the Royal Air Force."[249]

The Germans had been badly stung, and they knew it. The German Supreme Command of the Armed Forces (OKW) reported "large air battles and great losses for the German formations due to lack of fighter protection." The day's operations, involving over three hundred German bombers and one thousand German fighter sorties, were called "unusually disadvantageous," with the heaviest losses when the raiders were homeward bound. In addition, the invasion forces could not be kept at the ready, because the RAF, hitting the Channel ports, was taking a mounting toll of German barges and transports. Churchill and his intelligence chiefs could not know, but it was the death of Sea Lion. On September 17, Hitler postponed the invasion indefinitely on the grounds that winter was approaching and the RAF was "by no means defeated." The Führer had turned his attention to maps of Russia. A German staff officer expressed relief at the prospect of "a real war."[250]

The German high command had been induced to make a momentous strategic shift by a handful of young men in their Hurricanes and Spitfires. More than 400 of those airmen came from overseas: Czechs (80), Poles

(140), New Zealanders (120), Canadians (110), a smattering of Americans, Irishmen, Australians, Belgians, South Africans, and a lone Palestinian from the British Protectorate. Churchill felt profound admiration for the pilots. "But, it is terrible," he told Colville, "terrible, that the British Empire should have gambled on this." That Britain survived to designate September 15 Battle of Britain Day was as much due to Hitler's change of strategy—from destroying the RAF to destroying British cities—as it was to British radar, RAF fighter planes, and their pilots. The German air assault, Churchill later wrote, "was a tale of divided counsels, conflicting purposes and never fully realized plans. Three or four times in these months the enemy abandoned a method of attack which was causing us severe stress, and turned to something new." Thus, that phase of the Battle of Britain did not end with either side in retreat or with Germany mounting a final assault. It did not end with the British knowing that by not losing they had won. Rather, the Battle of Britain overlapped and merged with a new battle, the Battle of London, which, though no one knew it on the fifteenth, had actually begun the previous week. In time, Londoners, looking back, gave the battle a starting date: September 7. They soon gave it a name: the Blitz.[251]

In the East End, the fires of September 7 burned into the morning of the eighth. Not for 274 years—to the week—had London burned so. Seven feet below street level in the ancient precincts once bounded by Roman walls, and later by medieval ramparts, a thin layer of ocher earth testifies to the Great Fire of September 2, 1666. A stiff easterly wind fanned that conflagration for five days, during which it consumed St. Paul's Cathedral, 87 parish churches, and more than 13,000 houses. Yet only twenty unfortunate citizens perished. Within fifteen years Christopher Wren had built fifty-two new parish churches, and by the end of the seventeenth century, he had almost completed his new St. Paul's Cathedral, the dome of which, along with the spires of his churches, had since defined the London skyline. The steeple of St. Mary-le-Bow was one of the most fabulous. In time, Londoners born within earshot of the bells of St. Mary's claimed the right to call themselves Cockneys. They were the first to experience the fury of German bombs. Within days the German bombers no longer made an effort to pinpoint the industrial facilities. London, all of London, became the target, and the entire city was soon hit. It was, said Churchill, "an ordeal for the world's largest city, the results of which no one could measure beforehand."[252]

Several feet beneath the strata of gravel that marks the Great Fire of 1666, another layer of clay, rust-red from oxidized iron, records the first-century story of the warrior queen Boudicca, who torched Roman Londinium. She watched as the Romans came to steal her country, and after she had seen enough, she killed and burned the invader. Plague, smallpox, typhus, and cholera had in the centuries since killed tens of thousands of Londoners, and fire was a constant enemy, but not in the nearly nineteen centuries since Boudicca's revolt had any foe slaughtered Londoners wholesale or reduced the city by fire. By air, here now came Hitler, who had promised to raze English cities, London first.

On the morning of September 8, Churchill and Clementine visited the East End. They noted the "pathetic little Union Jacks" flying from the rubble of what until the previous night had been homes. They stopped outside a shelter that had taken a direct hit, and where forty men, women, and children had died. Churchill, visibly moved, dabbed his eyes with a large white handkerchief. For a moment he and the residents commingled in silence. Then someone yelled: "When are you going to bomb Berlin?" He replied, "You leave that to me." General Ismay recalled the crowd storming Churchill with cries of "We thought you'd come" and "We can take it." An old woman said, "You see, he really cares, he's crying." Some in the crowd begged, "You've got to make them stop." More than one million East Enders had returned to their homes after having been evacuated the previous autumn, when a German bombing campaign was expected at any moment. When the air war did not materialize, they drifted back to familiar neighborhoods, which now collapsed and burned around and atop numbed and terrified residents. Churchill told the gathered what they wanted to hear, that he would hit back, yet a profound grasp of the precariousness of their situation underlay his words: Hitler might reduce their homes, their city, but only by reducing their spirit could he inflict defeat. That test of will had begun. No Europeans had thus far withstood the ordeal. The Luftwaffe, two hundred bombers strong, escorted by four hundred fighters, returned while Churchill was still in the East End. As the raid began, he left through narrow streets blocked by houses that had been blown across them. The warehouses near the docks still burned, spewing forth the merchant wealth of Britain—torrents of flaming whisky, molten sugar, textiles, foodstuffs, and ammunition ablaze and exploding.[253]

More than four hundred East Enders died in the first raid. Thousands more were made homeless. Yet the next day, while the East End burned, Churchill asked Admiral Pound for his help in explaining to Roosevelt the need for merchant ships outfitted with prows and side ports, "to enable tanks to be landed from them on the beaches, or into tank landing craft which could take them to the beaches." The tank transports were not due for delivery until 1942. The beaches Churchill had in mind were those of France. Weeks earlier, with his air forces and country in mortal peril, he told Colville he expected "by 1942 we shall have achieved air superiority and shall be ready for the great offensive operations on land against Germany." Only an optimist could make such a statement. Yet during Britain's darkest hours, when its airborne defenses were being subjected to relentless attack, Churchill plotted his offense.[254]

Defense, however, was London's first order of business against the German aerial armadas. But the world's greatest city could muster virtually none. Many of the city's anti-aircraft guns had been moved to protect outlying airfields and aircraft factories. Only ninety-two AA guns remained to safeguard London. Their previously limited use proved they fired with pathetic effect. For three straight nights, from the seventh to the ninth, they did not fire at all. With the anti-aircraft guns quiet, London's defenses were handed off to night fighters from No. 11 Group. They inflicted few kills. Hundreds of searchlights threw long spears of light into the night sky, a comforting sight to Londoners but of no tactical significance; searchlights could not find targets that flew higher than 12,000 feet. German pilots flew far above the light. Radio-controlled coordination between searchlights and anti-aircraft guns held promise, but the technology—code-named Elsie—had entered the testing stage only weeks earlier. Not until early 1941 would the first AA guns (Churchill always called them "cannons") be outfitted with fire-control radar. Barrage balloons (used to support wires or nets as protection against air attacks) kept enemy planes high, making German targeting more difficult and reducing bomb accuracy, but the Germans were more intent on causing terror than achieving accuracy.[255]

Churchill ordered a doubling of the number of anti-aircraft guns, at the expense of Sheffield, Birmingham, and the tidy West Midlands city of Coventry. Still, the guns remained silent. He then ordered a battery placed in Hyde Park, "where people can hear them blast off." Finally, on the tenth, London's AA guns opened up, pouring thousands of shells into the night sky; the trails of tracer rounds and the beams of searchlights converged and intersected and splayed crazily in the blackness. The guns fired blind, in a box barrage rather than at particular targets. The effect on the German bombers was nil. The guns themselves probably suffered more damage, as their barrels had to be retooled after a few hundred rounds were fired. But the cacophony comforted Londoners. The next day, Harold Nicolson wrote in his diary, "The barrage put up by our A.A. guns cheered people enormously, although people in the East End are still frightened and angry."[256]

For Londoners (except those flush few who could escape to their country houses), the second week of September ushered in a terrible new way of life, and death. German bombers returned most mornings and afternoons for the next month, and for seventy-six consecutive nights, except November 2, when the weather grounded anything with wings. At about eight o'clock each evening, Londoners heard the nervous wailing of the air-raid sirens, which they called "Weeping Willies"; Churchill compared them to "a banshee howling."At the alarm, those with shelters headed there. Within minutes the German bombers were overhead, sowing terror into the night. The first Heinkels marked targets by dropping incendiaries. These were nasty little two-pounders with thermite cores that burned at two thousand degrees, igniting wooden rooftops, which, as they blazed high, became signal fires to guide in more waves of planes bearing high-explosive bombs. Now the blinding flashes of explosions illuminated the vast city, followed by the orchestrated sounds and smells of the raid—the odd *crumping* of the discharged bombs, their whistling as they fell, the stench of cordite and, later, the odor of gas escaping in the shattered buildings—and then the buildings burning in the quenchless flames of hell. Hour after hour it continued until, at dawn, the all-clear sounded and people emerged from homes and shelters into the new day's light: "gray disheveled figures," Malcolm Muggeridge wrote, "like a Brueghel painting of resurrection day—predestined souls rising from their graves."[257]

They rose from the terror bombing that Stanley Baldwin had so feared, against which he said there could be no defense and for which he had planned no defense. They emerged each morning into broken streets covered with smoldering rubble, the dead yellow eye of the sun leering down through a sky smudged by the ashes of their homes, the ashes of their neighbors, their families. They emerged to encounter scenes of monstrous destruction. Smashed pipes swung wildly from skeletal buildings, the facades peeled off, to reveal furnished interiors, like the sectional view of a child's dollhouse. They rose to fires still burning, to stinking raw sewage seeping down gutters. They emerged to unexploded bombs buried up to the fins in marl and mud, just waiting for the clumsy jolt that would start the fuse softly buzzing. They stumbled into lanes so strewn with the glass of shattered windows that Churchill feared a "glass famine." And each morning, hundreds who had sought shelter the night before or rode out the storm in their flats—14,000 Londoners by year's end—did not emerge at all.[258]

On some mornings, folks wandering the wreckage espied a beefy apparition: the prime minister, *their* prime minister. They called him "Winnie," the boyhood nickname he hated but now grew to love. He might be bundled in his Royal Air Force overcoat, his gold-topped walking stick employed to smack rubble out of his path, and he'd likely be gripping a substantial cigar. He might be in the company of Ismay, Clementine, his brother, Jack, or MP and longtime friend Brendan Bracken. But most important, he was there, with them.

Bertrand Russell—logician, pacifist, and Churchill's contemporary—predicted in 1936 that an air attack would turn London "into one vast raving bedlam, the hospitals will be stormed, traffic will cease, the homeless will shriek for help, the city will be a pandemonium," and the government itself "will be swept away by an avalanche of terror." British Fascists and Communists—"those filthy communists," Churchill fumed, were more dangerous than the Fascists—had in turn predicted that an air assault on the East End and London's poor would lead inexorably to either revolution or, at the very least, Churchill's ouster, the formation of a new government, and a negotiated peace. Hitler was counting on very much the same. Britain's Communist newspaper, *The Daily Worker,* remained stridently anti-war, and encouraged workers to take to the streets to display their displeasure with the government. London authorities had predicted the need for regular army troops to maintain order at shelters, but the primary focus of officials was not to control mobs but to tend to the wounded and bury the legions of expected dead. For this they were well prepared. London hospitals had readied beds for 150,000 casualties, but that was thought inadequate; the Imperial Defence Committee estimated that a Luftwaffe bombing of London would leave 600,000 dead and over a million wounded. They had bulldozers dig huge pits outside London; these would become mass graves. Thousands of papier-mâché coffins were readied and a million burial forms were printed, but little consideration had been given to sheltering the obstinate unwounded.[259]

This was more than an assault on bricks and mortar; it was an attack on the spirit of London's eight million citizens. Churchill said as much in a defiant BBC broadcast on September 11: "These cruel wanton, indiscriminate bombings of London are, of course, a part of Hitler's invasion plans. He hopes, by killing large numbers of civilians, and women and children, that he will terrorize and cow the people of this mighty imperial city.... Little does he know the spirit of the British nation, and the tough fibre of Londoners."[260]

During that broadcast he again invoked the "invasion scare," in pursuit of his dual objectives—to build up his armies and air forces in 1941 in order to launch large-scale offensive operations on the Continent in 1942. In a BBC broadcast that day, he prepared the British people for the worst. If the invasion was coming, he told them:

> It does not seem that it can be long delayed. The weather may break at any time.... Therefore, we must regard the next week or so as a very important period in our history. It ranks with the days when the

> Spanish Armada was approaching the Channel, and Drake was finishing his game of bowls; or when Nelson stood between us and Napoleon's Grand Army at Boulogne. We have read all about this in the history books; but what is happening now is on a far greater scale and of far more consequence to the life and future of the world and its civilization than these brave old days of the past.[261]

He described the assembly of self-propelled barges at Dunkirk, Brest, and Cherbourg; the "tens of dozens" of merchant ship convoys moving through the Strait of Dover into the Channel; the concentration of shipping in German, Dutch, Belgian, and French harbors; and the troop ships in Norwegian harbors. No one, he warned them, "should blind himself to the fact that a heavy, full-scale invasion of this Island with all the usual German thoroughness and method may be launched now upon England, Scotland, or Ireland, or upon all three." Or, as he believed, an invasion may *not* be launched.[262]

His words blazed. So did London. Churchill fully realized that given enough bombs, London, especially the older buildings, would be reduced to rubble. He knew that the mettle and "tough fibre" of Britons had not yet been fully tested, let alone proven. This would be a battle of attrition of unknown duration, and increasing fury. How long—how many weeks, perhaps months, perhaps years—could the Luftwaffe keep up the punishment? He knew Londoners were looking skyward with fearful certainty that the bombardment was the softening up before the final blow—invasion. And if the invasion did not come that year, it might come the next.

But Londoners, though pummeled, did not crack. Scores of tens of thousands had not been killed, as officials had expected. Their ordeal was terrible, but Londoners were taking it. They might have called the bombing raids "The Great Terror" or "The Burning," or any number of monikers that captured the enormity of their predicament, but the word that stuck was *Blitz*. It conjures *blitzkrieg*, with all its ferocity, yet it also diminishes it, cuts it down to size, and manifests a hint of defiance, of spirit.

Even blacked out, London's geography and layout conspired to make it an ideal aerial target. From 15,000 feet overhead, bathed even in modest moonlight, the entire metropolis stretched before German pilots like a well-marked parchment chart. The Thames estuary guided the Germans westward from the North Sea, past refineries and oil tank farms. The great

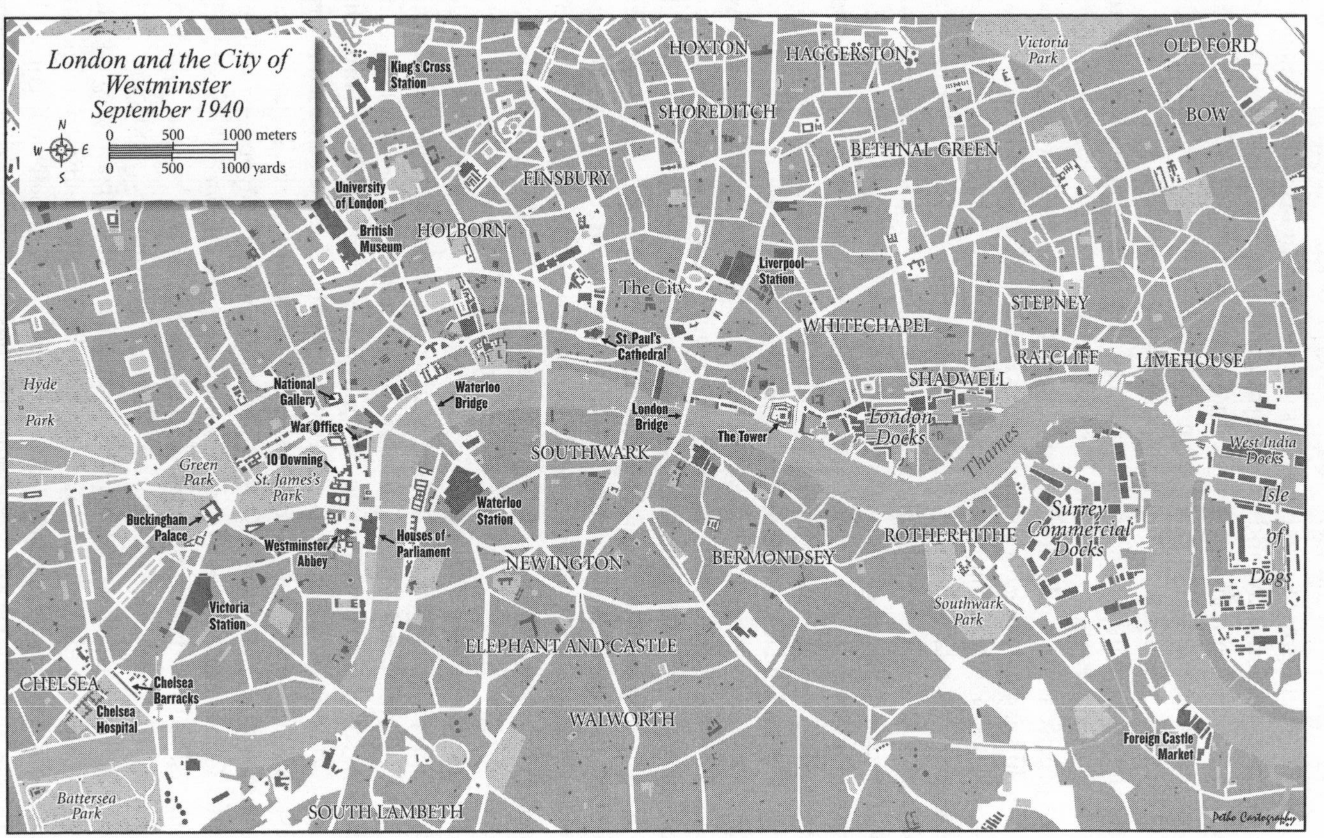
London and the City of Westminster September 1940
N
S
E
W
0
500
1000 meters
0
500
1000 yards
King's Cross Station
HOXTON
HAGGERSTON
Victoria Park
OLD FORD
SHOREDITCH
BOW
BETHNAL GREEN
FINSBURY
University of London
British Museum
HOLBORN
Liverpool Station
The City
STEPNEY
WHITECHAPEL
St. Paul's Cathedral
RATCLIFF
LIMEHOUSE
SHADWELL
Hyde Park
National Gallery
Waterloo Bridge
London Bridge
London Docks
The Tower
War Office
Thames
West India Docks
SOUTHWARK
Green Park
10 Downing
St. James's Park
Isle of Dogs
Waterloo Station
Surrey Commercial Docks
Buckingham Palace
Houses of Parliament
ROTHERHITHE
Westminster Abbey
NEWINGTON
BERMONDSEY
Southwark Park
Victoria Station
ELEPHANT AND CASTLE
CHELSEA
Chelsea Barracks
Chelsea Hospital
WALWORTH
Foreign Castle Market
Battersea Park
SOUTH LAMBETH
Petho Cartography

bend in the river announced the presence below of vast warehouses, the West India Dock and the Victoria and Albert Docks. On clear and moonlit nights, St. Paul's great Latin cross was visible from thousands of feet in the air and from miles away, and marked the center of London as clearly as an "X" on a treasure map. The dark and empty swaths of Hyde Park and St. James's Park served to guide bombardiers to still more targets: Whitehall, Buckingham Palace, and the Houses of Parliament.[263]

In fact, Churchill had known since the first days of summer that the German night bombers were being guided to their targets by something far more precise than landscape features. In late June, the British confirmed long-held suspicions that the Germans were employing a shortwave navigational beam—code-named *Knickebein* ("crooked leg")—to guide their bombers to targets. This was very unwelcome news. Here indeed was an innovation that just might help Hitler make good on his promise to raze English cities. *Knickebein* was based on the Lorenz radio–controlled instrument-flying technology that had been developed in Germany eight years earlier and was used on many U.S. and European commercial flights to guide pilots the final few miles to airfields.

But a Lorenz-like signal was accurate only over short distances; at two hundred miles it could bring an aircraft to within only one or two miles of a target. The Germans had been doing much better than that in night raids, which raised the specter of their having developed a new and very sophisticated radio-beam technology. Bombing accuracy equates to navigational accuracy; if a bomber could be guided at night or in clouds to a precise point over a target, its bombs could accordingly be dropped with precision.

Two of Churchill's science advisers, Sir Henry Tizard and Prof Lindemann, agreed on one generally accepted scientific belief: shortwave radio signals did not bend—that is, follow the curvature of the earth—and therefore could not serve as effective long-range navigational and targeting guides. That attribute of radio waves was why the altitude at which British coastal radar could "see" German aircraft increased as the distance from the transmitter increased. It was to Tizard as much as anyone—including Fighter Command's Hugh Dowding—that the British owed thanks for the Home Island's radar preparedness in 1940. Sir Henry was an old RAF man, chairman of the Aeronautical Defence Committee, and one of the most respected scientists in England. In the late 1930s, Tizard pushed hard to build coastal radar stations and stressed the need for radio coordination between RAF pilots and those radar stations. Tizard believed, correctly, that radar opened a wide window on the position and heading of enemy aircraft. He believed, incorrectly as Dr. R. V. Jones was to demonstrate, that radio waves could not contribute to precision navigation. Tizard was of the old school of RAF celestial navigation by "shooting" the stars. Airmen did so because no better method of navigation had been developed. In Tizard's estimation, the rumored German beam could not improve long-range navigation because it simply would not work due to the earth's curvature.

But in early June, Jones, one of Lindemann's former Oxford students (he was just twenty-eight), demonstrated to Lindemann's satisfaction that the Germans were in fact using long-range radio beams for targeting. A few days later, Jones briefed Tizard. Tizard, who understood radio waves as much as anyone alive (or thought he did), voiced doubts.[264]

Tizard and the Prof had fought an academic feud for almost a decade. They had tangled in 1935 when both served on an Air Defense subcommittee chaired by Tizard. Lindemann's appointment to the committee came via Churchill, who was also a committee member. Tizard had argued for coastal radar, Lindemann for more fighter planes. Both were correct, but Lindemann, frustrated, left the committee. While Tizard continued his work on radar, Lindemann became a Churchill crony and primary science adviser. Tizard retained the respect of the science community, but not of Churchill. The Prof realized that if he and young Dr. Jones solved *Knickebein,* he would not only solidify his position with Churchill but also finally put paid to his old adversary Tizard.

Lindemann prevailed upon Churchill to give young Jones a hearing. Churchill called Tizard, Jones, and Lindemann together on June 21, along with the minister of air, Archie Sinclair, sundry RAF brass, Beaverbrook, and Robert Watson Watt, the father of radar. Dr. Jones held the group spellbound for twenty minutes. He hypothesized that Germans pilots were flying between two radio signals originating at different towers. One beam emitted a series of "dots," the other a series of "dashes." The pilot maneuvered his plane between the beams until the "dots" and "dashes" he received merged into a steady buzz, indicating that he was exactly between the signals and on course. Guided by such a beam, German bombers could put their bombs within an area one mile square, which in 1940 amounted to pinpoint accuracy. Jones asked permission to conduct field tests that he believed would verify his hypothesis. Even Churchill listened without interruption and in awed silence as Jones told the tale, a "chain of circumstantial evidence," Churchill later wrote, "the like of which for its convincing fascination was never surpassed by tales of Sherlock Holmes or Monsieur Lecoq."[265]

When Jones finished, no one spoke. There was in the room, recalled Churchill, "a general air of incredulity." Then Churchill angrily pounded the table and demanded countermeasures to the beams from the Air Ministry, which had up to this point given him only "files, files, files!"[266]

The meeting was finished. So was Tizard. Churchill recalled that "one high authority" in attendance "asked why the Germans should use a beam, assuming that such a thing was possible, when they had at their disposal all the ordinary facilities of navigation." Others at the table, however, "appeared concerned." The insouciant high authority, who clung to the same belief Lindemann had jettisoned just days earlier, went unnamed by Churchill.[267]

It was Tizard. Whether or not Sir Henry had been set up, the result was the same: he had stepped into an open manhole. Having failed to identify the danger of the German beams in his capacity as defender of the air, Tizard offered to resign. Churchill declined, and instead sent Tizard off to the United States—out of sight, out of mind—as head of a small delegation of British scientists. Their mission to explore the exchange of new technologies with the Americans emerged as one of the most critical successes of science and diplomacy during the war. (Yet the mission almost didn't leave home, when Churchill fretted that too much in the way of British technological know-how might be going to the Americans.)

Before he left, Tizard set up a science committee, code-named Maud (for Military Application of Uranium Detonation), to investigate the feasibility of building a nuclear fission bomb using uranium-235. Two expatriate German physicists, Otto Frisch and Rudolf Peierls, thought it could be done; Tizard himself thought the prospects doubtful. Still, Sir Henry appointed six British scientists to the Maud Committee; Frisch and Peierls, by virtue of their alien status, could not serve. With Maud in place, Tizard set off for America. As a direct result of Sir Henry's American mission, Bell Labs began mass-producing for use by the British the cavity magnetron, an English invention and the key to more accurate long-range radar. Tizard's mission resulted, too, in a sense among his American peers that Britain just might survive, or at the least not die just yet. Tizard was astute enough to bring along film footage, shot from Hurricanes and Spitfires, of dogfights and of burning German aircraft spiraling earthward. His contacts in the U.S. military were mightily impressed. Sir Henry converted the unfaithful. Churchill had long warned anyone who listened that science—for good or ill—would win the war, and in the end he was proven correct. But the "Wizard War," as Churchill termed it, was at first fought as desperately between his wizards—Lindemann and Tizard—as between his wizards and those of Hitler's.

Having discovered the German beam (which the RAF code-named Headache), the British needed to defeat it, and soon. Jamming *Knickebein* wouldn't do; the Germans would simply broadcast on another frequency. The British needed a craftier solution to *Knickebein*, and by August had come up with their antidote, which they code-named Aspirin. British transmitters broadcast "dashes" on the same frequency as the German signals, but boosted the power of the decoy "dashes," with the result that German pilots slowly drifted off course while trying to align themselves with the false signal. By late August, Churchill took delight in reports that entire loads of German bombs dropped at night were falling harmlessly into cow pastures, miles from the intended targets. However, those targets were airfields, factories, small ports, and cities, where an error of only a few miles put the enemy over farmland, but no cow pastures dotted the London landscape. A German bomb that missed St. Paul's or the docks by a county mile would detonate not in the countryside but somewhere in Greater London. Still, in his memoir, R. V. Jones claims that "a substantial proportion of bombs went astray" due to the British countermeasures against *Knickebein,* though he does not say how far astray.[268]

Even without the beam, German night bombers could hardly miss London, and German day bombers did not need the beam. Metropolitan London, twenty-eight boroughs comprising more than 750 square miles, and home to almost eight million people, spread outward in all compass points from the center. Yet London's most critical communications centers and supply links were packed together within walking distance of St. Paul's: six railroad stations, the Wood Street Telephone Exchange, General Post Office, London Telephone Exchange, Royal Exchange, and Bank of England. The Guildhall, rebuilt after the 1666 fire, was still the seat of municipal government and the control center for the city's firefighting operations. It would soon burn again. Bombs now dropped into streets of old London lore and nursery rhyme fame, such as Shoe Lane, where Beaverbrook's *Standard* took a direct hit in its rooftop water tower, flooding the building. A David Low cartoon in the next day's edition showed a Cockney lad hawking papers. The headline: BOMB SEVERELY DAMAGED IN SHOE LANE.

Pudding Lane, where the Great Fire had started in a bakery, burned again. Buildings that were standing more than two centuries before Berlin was founded were battered and smashed. Red dust from their ancient bricks drifted through demolished interiors, to settle in old undercrofts, the newest strata in London's soil, someday long hence to tell the story. From the center, narrow and twisting lanes lined with small shops and great nineteenth-century textile warehouses ran east and northeast to the East End, where London's working class lived on narrower streets lined with mean brick tenements, music halls, and old breweries. The workhouses of the East End had come down at the turn of the century, but vast tracts of Dickensian slums remained in some of the poorest areas. These were neighborhoods that still smelled of smoke and sweat, of horses and the effluent from old wood and iron pipes that leeched into the Thames: Silvertown, Poplar, Millwall, Stepney, and West Ham. Neighborhoods whose names rolled musically off Cockney tongues and conjured a locale's medieval origins were blown to dust and burned to ashes: the Minories (after the abbey of the Minoresses [or nuns] of St. Mary), and Elephant and Castle (after a famed eighteenth-century coaching inn), south across the Thames. Clement Attlee was the MP from Limehouse, named for the lime kilns, and as degraded a place in 1940 as it had been in 1919, when D. W. Griffith and Lillian Gish portrayed it in *Broken Blossoms*. And in Wapping, the descendants of Famine Irish, who had fled to London almost a century earlier, lived packed together in vile slums hard by the London docks. And there they died.[269]

The London docks and nearby warehouses accounted for almost one-quarter of the jobs in Metropolitan London, and almost all of the work for East End men. The previous year more than 50,000 ships had tied up to load and unload almost 40 percent of Britain's commerce. By 1942, fewer than 15,000 would steam up the Thames. The docks were the mercantile life of London, and they were dying.

Northwest of central London, the borough of Hampstead was home to 25,000 Jews, and would have been home to far more but for the government's reluctance to allow more Jewish refugees into the country for fear of fostering anti-Semitism. George Orwell thought there was less anti-Semitism abroad in the land than there had been thirty years earlier, but there was still enough dangerous and ugly anti-Jewish sentiment to blind Londoners to Nazi persecutions on the Continent. Orwell told his diary, Jews were "not only conspicuous, but go out of their way to make themselves so," with the result that "you switch off the wireless when the announcer begins talking about the ghettos in Warsaw." Jews monopolized the shelters, so went the canards, and demanded full compensation for bomb-damaged houses, and seemed to be eating pretty well, and never volunteered as fire wardens. These opinions were all lies built on misconceptions and old prejudices. The Home Office conducted a weekly survey of conditions in the shelters and determined that Jews behaved no differently than Gentiles; neither group, they found, "predominates among those who have evacuated themselves voluntarily through fear and hysteria." Jews, along with their Gentile neighbors, were getting by as best they could.[270]

To the north of the city, Islington and Stoke Newington, tidy locales, reached toward the new suburbs growing beyond the metropolitan boundary. Skilled workers, clerks, and factory managers lived there in neat flats, with well-tended gardens in the rear, and room enough among the roses and mums for an air-raid shelter. It was all a long way from the East End, but the bombs came. To the northwest, small factories—aircraft, machine tool, and auto parts—had moved into old textile plants. More than 14,000 such factories were scattered throughout Greater London. One-quarter of Britain's workforce labored there; one-half of all goods produced in England were manufactured within twenty miles of St. Paul's. This was the industrial heart of the empire.[271]

Two miles to the west of St. Paul's, the streets broadened and fed into the West End and the City of Westminster. More than a century earlier, John Nash had widened Regent Street, built the Carlton House terraces, designed St. James's Park, and transformed Piccadilly Circus into a pedestrian mall, thus assuring that the moneyed classes could stroll without care from their grand Regency town houses to their private clubs, to the pastoral precincts of St. James's Park, to the theaters of Piccadilly, and to the shops of New Bond Street.[272]

By mid-September, German bombs had smashed into Regent Street, into a courtyard within Buckingham Palace, and into St. James's Park, Churchill's favorite London venue for a midday stroll, which always included a stop by the lake to feed the ducks, who had by now taken themselves off to safer climes. Members of Parliament doused an incendiary bomb that had dropped into the House of Lords. The West End was hit, but not hard enough for some in the East End. On September 15, about fifty East Enders, outraged by the filthy shelters in their neighborhoods, invaded the West End. The Cockneys, spurred on by their Communist ward bosses and led by six pregnant women with babes in arms, streamed into the Savoy, where management maintained a splendid basement shelter, furnished with bunks, fresh bed linens, and bathing facilities. The constabulary was summoned. Shocked hotel guests and the surly Cockneys faced off in the lobby. In an inspired maneuver, the hotel managing director opened the dining room to the protesters. The staff brewed tea. All ended in calmness. The East Enders departed, without incident.[273]

Every quarter was hit. Chelsea and South Kensington, cityscapes of town houses, their limestone facades blackened by more than a century of London's fuliginous air, marked the far western reaches of Georgian London. Bombs crashed down in Chelsea and onto Victoria Station. South across the Thames and along its banks stretched Southwark, where the Archbishop of Canterbury kept his official residence, Lambeth Palace. When the bombs threatened his cathedral and its treasures, the archbishop expressed his deep concern to Churchill, who assured the prelate that every precaution had been taken to protect it. The archbishop asked what would happen if a bomb were to score a direct hit. Churchill, ever ready with a blasphemous aside, replied, "In that case, my dear Archbishop, you will have to regard it as a divine summons."[274]

Eastward from Southwark, the boroughs of Battersea, Greenwich, and Woolwich spread along the south bank of the Thames. The Woolwich Arsenal, which produced bombs for the RAF, had been the first target hit on September 7.

London's buildings presented stone and brick faces, but their bones were wood—rafters, beams, struts, stairs, flooring, millions of board feet of lumber, old, dry and combustible. The Thames served as London's main source of water for fighting fires. When the moon's phase so conspired, the Thames ran low and narrow. The London Fire Brigade—1,500 spit-and-polish firemen who manned 130 red fire engines and ladder trucks—formed the city's regular fire service. They were backed up by the Auxiliary Fire Service, the mechanical end of which consisted of three thousand small pumpers that had to be towed behind another vehicle, often a black London taxi. Twenty thousand men and five thousand women from all manner of professions—carpenters, cooks, nannies, clerics, and clerks—manned the pumpers, five to a pump. Together, they could clamp 87 miles of hose to the city's 31,439 fire hydrants. A fire's size was measured by how many pumpers were needed to fight it. Prewar, a thirty-pumper was considered a large and dangerous fire. During the Blitz, one-hundred-pumpers were common. December 29 brought the firefighters' most terrible night. They called it the Second Great Fire of London. The regulars and auxiliaries would not so much fight the fire as watch it as it reduced to ash the heart of Wren's London, because the moon was new, and the Thames ran narrow and shallow, and there was scarce water to pump.[275]

On September 17 delayed-action bombs fell into St. James's Park. High explosives dropped near No. 10 and the Foreign Office, which had to be evacuated. Buckingham Palace suffered a hit, and in the ruins of Madame Tussaud's, waxwork arms and legs—including Hitler's—lay scattered about. The Germans, said Nicolson, had "smashed about Bond Street and readjusted the balance." West End, East End, they were all in it together.[276]

It was the night of the harvest moon. By then the Churchill family had been residents of No. 10 for three months, since the week of the French surrender (they had stayed in Admiralty House for the first four weeks of his premiership). No. 10, like the White House, was both a home and the office of the nation's leader. The first floor was all business, dominated by the grand Cabinet Room and the Private Office, as the prime minister's staff and their rooms were known. That was also true of the large state dining room on the second floor, though a white-paneled family dining room adjoined it, and upstairs was all private: large bedrooms with sash windows, cheerful red carpeting, and egg-shell-blue passages. In winter, coal fires glowed in every grate. It was, quite simply, a very pleasant place to live.[277]

Unfortunately it was also combustible and frail. Since June the Churchills had spent more and more time in the basement, either in the air-raid shelter or beside the kitchens, in fortified rooms that had been strengthened with huge beams, and with steel shutters shielding the windows. But the first week of the Blitz brought home the reality that No. 10 Downing Street was a potential death trap. One nearby explosion that Colville described as vast shook the house just as he was entering. He met Churchill, who insisted he had seen, from his bedroom window, a bomb hit Buckingham Palace. A bomb that fell near the Treasury split the east walls of No. 10. Another bomb exploded nearby one evening as Churchill hosted a dinner in the basement dining room. He excused himself and went to the kitchen, located in the rear, on the Treasury side, and ordered the cooks and servers to take shelter. Twenty seconds after they were gone, another large bomb fell between No. 10 and the Treasury. It lifted the entire kitchen floor of No. 10, flattened it against the wall, and crushed everything in between, including the iron cook stoves.[278]

Colville and Bracken agreed that it was "only a matter of days" before No. 10 "fell a victim" to the bombs. Safer quarters were available for the prime minister in Storey's Gate, two blocks away, where a bland stone government building, bearing a dull plaque reading CENTRAL STATISTICAL OFFICE, stood facing St. James's Park. Deep in the earth beneath it lay the Cabinet War Room. The CWR, also known as "The Hole," was actually an underground warren of small rooms, including a bedroom for the prime minister, with a desk, to which was affixed a BBC microphone.[279]

The CWR was for emergencies. For day-to-day living, the building's ground floor had been converted into a concrete-reinforced, steel-shuttered apartment, the No. 10 Annexe. The Annexe was comfortable, though, as Churchill's daughter Mary recalls, his and Clementine's rooms were off a corridor connecting government offices (there were 180 rooms in all, guarded by Royal Marines), "and embarrassed officials would often encounter Winston, robed like a Roman emperor in his bath towel, proceeding dripping across the main highway to his bedroom." Churchill, of course, was never disconcerted. He could appear completely nude without loss of dignity, and sometimes did.[280]

Yet the Annexe, as with No. 10, would be obliterated by a direct hit from a two-thousand-pounder. Churchill's family, friends, and even Chamberlain appealed to him to find more secure sleeping arrangements.

He finally succumbed to the pressure and in mid-October availed himself of the Down Street Underground shelter he called "The Burrow." Located eighty feet below Piccadilly, reinforced by steel and concrete, and closed off to trains, the shelter was the deepest, most secure, and most comfortable haven in London, built as the result of prescient prewar thinking on the part of the directors of the London Transport Executive. The directors had also considered the culinary needs of future shelterees: Caspian Caviar, Perrier-Jouët 1928, and 1865 brandy were always available. The finest cigars were plentiful, thanks to the Cuban consul who, late in the year, delivered five thousand after Churchill's inventory had atrophied. Churchill, when in London, took his rest in Down Street many nights that autumn. Then, for the remainder of the war, he and Clementine resided in the labyrinth of the Annexe (along with almost 270 officials, military planners, and armed soldiers). Clementine hung old pictures on the walls to add a bit of welcoming warmth. Winston protested that the walls should remain bare. She prevailed. He insisted on climbing to the exposed roof to view the raids. Clementine protested. He prevailed.[281]

During the first week of the Blitz, more than 5,000 East Enders, mostly women and children, fled London, some to Greenwich Park, Hampstead Heath, and by railway to points west. The residents of a West Country town compared them to refugees from Bordeaux during the collapse of France. Their possessions and rations fit into kerchiefs and pillowcases. Yet by month's end, fewer than 25,000 residents of the hardest hit neighborhoods had fled. The men stayed behind, to scrape up what work they could find. Many of their women stayed behind to keep an eye on their men. London's middle and upper-middle classes remained at their jobs and in their homes. Unlike Parisians, Londoners did not flee. The general panic and pandemonium predicted by Bertrand Russell was nonexistent. Russell, having renounced his pacifism in May, now safely bicycled between his mistress and his lectures at Harvard University, thousands of miles away in Cambridge, Massachusetts, where the only objects falling from the sky were the crimson maple leaves of autumn.[282]

Discipline, not squads of soldiers, ruled in the London shelters. Eight thousand sheltered each night at a railway goods disposal yard under the Tilbury Arches off the Commercial Road. They segregated themselves: Jews, Irish, Indians, West Indian blacks, Cockneys—each group spent the night in its own enclave, sleeping among horse droppings and standing water on piles of rubbish, folded cartons, and old newsprint. Two buckets served as communal latrines. The prewar planners who had predicted the need for regular army troops to maintain order were wrong. It took only a lone metropolitan policeman to control the long queue that formed each night.[283]

Such was life in the public shelters. The government also produced small, private shelters called Anderson shelters, designed in 1938 by the engineer William Paterson and named for Home Secretary Sir John Anderson. The Anderson shelters had been distributed to 150,000 London residents months earlier. They were flimsy affairs, assembled by bolting together thin sheets of galvanized steel. They lacked floors and were prone to collecting rainwater. They could accommodate six uncomfortably and offered some protection against shrapnel, but not against a direct or nearly direct hit. Their installation called for setting the footings deep in garden soil. Their very design rendered them largely useless for the Cockneys: the East End had been paved over for a century. London's poor held Anderson shelters and their namesake in contempt; if the contraptions had offered any real protection, it's a good bet they would have been called Paterson shelters.[284]

To look at Anderson, humorless and cold, recalled Viscount Antony Head (then a major in War Plans), "You could never possibly conceive that he had ever been a child. He was the opposite of Winston, who retained an awful lot of his childhood with him."[285]

In August 1939 Anderson and Chamberlain crafted the Emergency Powers (Defence) Act, which granted—like similar acts during the Great War—sweeping powers to the executive. But in May of 1940, when the 1939 act came up for renewal, Anderson, in a calculated circumvention of the King's Bench (the division of the English courts system that hears civil and criminal cases), added a new, draconian article (18B, 1A), which allowed for the detainment of people who were suspected of being Nazi sympathizers, thereby stripping Britons of rights they had held close since King John signed Magna Carta. Anderson argued that since detainees under 18B were not charged with a crime but were seized in order to *prevent* a crime, habeas corpus had not been compromised. Sir Oswald Mosley, of impeccable high birth, and for a decade the black-shirted head of England's Fascists, was one of the first detained. That his wife, Diana Mitford Guinness Mosley (one of the Mitford sisters), was also hauled away proved an embarrassment to the Churchill family, as she was Clementine's cousin. By year's end, more than a thousand British citizens (including known Fascists) and hundreds of refugees who had fled Hitler were detained, secretly imprisoned, without arraignment or trial.[286]

Anderson had been one of Chamberlain's most loyal toadies, a Tory's Tory. Churchill kept Anderson on as Home Secretary until October, when he brought him into the War Cabinet as Lord President of the Council. There his duties involved organizing Britain's civilian and economic financial resources, and arresting troublemakers who might impede the war effort. In that capacity Anderson set to work under 18B, rounding up suspected evildoers. Churchill instinctively loathed the idea of keeping "political opponents in prison on *lettres de cachet*," but embracing his emergency powers, he shot off a memo to Anderson: "Let me see a list of prominent persons you have arrested." A few days later he sent along to Anderson a list of "suspected persons" who resided in areas likely to be invaded. He instructed Sir John to "pray let me know in three days what action you find yourself able to take."

Where Churchill was only idly curious about the status of suspected fifth-columnists, he was deeply concerned about the status of London's poor. He ordered Anderson to address the drainage problem in Anderson shelters by instructing residents to place bricks on the edge and cover them with linoleum. The need to introduce some comfort into the shelters soon became moot when steel shortages decreed that England could have ships or shelters but not both. The Andersons were no longer built.[287]

East Enders resented their plight. Harold Nicolson noted the depth of their bitterness in his diary entry of September 17: "It is said even the King and Queen were booed the other day when they visited the destroyed areas. Clem (Davies) says that if only the Germans had the sense not to bomb west of London Bridge there might have been a revolution in the country."[288]

Yet, if fermenting a peasants' revolt was a collateral German hope, that dream died weeks later when a squadron of Stukas targeted Buckingham Palace during a midday raid and put three bombs into the palace courtyards, just one hundred meters from the King and Queen. If not for the good fortune of their windows being swung open at that moment, their majesties would have been cut to pieces by glass shards. The attack indicated, Churchill said, that the Germans "meant business." In terms of assault on hearth and home, it meant the royal family was now one with the East Enders. "I'm glad we've been bombed," the Queen said. "It makes me feel I can look the East End in the face." Churchill was furious when he learned that government censors had ordered news of the palace attack squelched. "Dolts, idiots, fools," he fumed. "Spread the news at once. Let the humble people of London know that they are not alone, and that the King and Queen are sharing their perils with them."[289]

Despite the fact that the Empire stood with them, the people of London, including their King and Queen and prime minister, were all of them indeed alone and virtually defenseless against the air attacks. Communist organizers circulated petitions calling for Churchill to initiate peace talks at once. "One cannot expect," Harold Nicolson confided to his diary, "the population of a great city to sit up all night in shelters week after week without losing their spirit." During September thousands of tons of bombs fell on London; more than six thousand Londoners, mostly East Enders, died in the fires. But the morale of Londoners did not crumble with their houses; the peace petitioners got few takers. By the end of September, Edward R. Murrow sensed that spirit. He broadcast from the roof of the BBC, "I have seen many flags flying from staffs. No one told these people to put out the flag. They simply feel like flying the Union Jack above their roof." And, said Murrow, "No flag up there was white."[290]

German parachute bombs, which were actually 2,200-pound naval mines, brought new terrors. These monsters were made more sinister in that they could not be aimed, a condition that necessarily resulted in indiscriminate slaughter. Built to sink battleships, the mines could demolish old brick-and-timber buildings within a five-hundred-meter radius. Churchill demanded that "we should drop two for every one of theirs." At dinner on September 21, he told Lord Gort and Hugh Dowding that although he was averse in principle to retaliation in kind, every German parachute bomb should be answered by an identical British response over an open German city. Gort agreed: "It's the only thing they understand."[291]

The Chief of the Air Staff informed the War Cabinet on September 23 that he had ordered one hundred heavy bombers to attack Berlin. Fifty more medium and heavy bombers were dispatched to bomb German invasion barges in the Channel ports. That evening Churchill told Colville: "Remember this, never maltreat your enemy by halves. Once the battle is joined, let 'em have it."[292]

Although his stated policy in early October remained one of no retaliation, Churchill was, in fact, targeting German civilians. That this was the case was due in part to the abysmal nighttime targeting accuracy of British bombers, less than two-thirds of which actually located their assigned targets, and of those that did, less than one-third placed their bombs within five miles of the target. In the area of the Ruhr, where industrial haze was constant, the figure was a pathetic one in ten. Targeting was so inaccurate, Churchill told Ismay, "If we could make it half and half we should virtually have doubled our bombing power."[293]

The random spray of British bombs meant that even if the targets were industrial or military, German civilians were being hit. Nonretaliation was a polite fiction. On October 16 the War Cabinet instructed Bomber Command to order its pilots to drop their bombs on the nearest German city, including Berlin, if cloud cover obscured industrial targets. The bombers were not to return home with any unused bombs. If Londoners could not take safely to their beds, neither would Berliners.[294]

The fiction of nonretaliation continued when, on October 17, while sipping a glass of port in the smoking room of the Commons, Churchill fielded questions from members who wanted to know when retaliation would begin. As Robert Cary, a Conservative MP from Eccles, gave a long dissertation on the public demand for unrestricted bombardment, Churchill listened. He took a long sip of his port while gazing over the glass at Cary. "My dear sir," he said, "this is a military and not a civilian war. You and others may desire to kill women and children. We desire, and have succeeded in our desire, to destroy German military objectives. I quite appreciate your point. But my motto is, 'Business before pleasure.'"[295]

Churchill took no pleasure in killing women and children. But three days later, in a secret memo to minister for air Archibald Sinclair, he ordered that retaliation with parachute mines be conducted on an experimental basis and that the "use of the heaviest 1,000 pound and 2,000 pound bombs on Berlin is much desired."[296]

Göring's and Goebbels' claim that Berlin airspace was inviolate took on elements of the absurd on the night of September 24, when Goebbels and his dining companions at the Adlon Hotel had to flee to the basement air-raid shelter as British bombs fell. The next night's raid lasted five hours. "The British ought to do this every night," William L. Shirer wrote, "no matter if not much is destroyed. The damage last night was not great. But the psychological effect was tremendous." The Germans had foolishly believed they could bomb Warsaw, Rotterdam, and England without themselves being bombed. Then again, the Germans had believed the war would be finished by autumn.[297]

The Nazi high command considered the raids mere nuisances, and for the most part they were correct. In raids conducted by seventy, eighty, sometimes ninety RAF bombers, little damage was done, in part because the planes had to trade bomb load for fuel in order to make the 1,200-mile round trip, and in part, as usual, targeting at night was a game of guesses. Yet the Soviet high command began to consider the possibility that England was not quite so down and not yet out. In mid-November, Soviet foreign minister Vyacheslav Molotov and his German counterpart, Joachim von Ribbentrop, met in Berlin to hold meetings intended to burnish their agreement on trade and postwar spoils. Churchill, in his memoir (*The Second World War*), writes that the British "though not invited to join in the discussion did not wish to be entirely left out of the proceedings." The ensuing RAF raid forced Molotov and Ribbentrop into a shelter, where, as Stalin later told Churchill, Ribbentrop continued to insist to the Russian that England was finished. "If that is so," replied Molotov, "why are we in this shelter and whose are these bombs which fall?"[298]

By mid-October almost five hundred thousand London children had been evacuated to the countryside. The city they left behind was falling down.

The rail system was in crisis: of six major London stations, only Paddington and King's Cross were in full operation. The main sewage outfall pipe had been smashed, rendering the Thames an open sewer. Churchill fretted that a mixing of sewage and drinking water would be disastrous—cholera had killed thousands a century earlier; it could do so again. Public shelters remained packed full and filthy, open invitations to outbreaks of diphtheria and influenza. The "glass famine" Churchill feared was far more than a matter of aesthetics; living conditions would be medieval in a windowless London at the onset of winter. Driving past a smashed greenhouse, Churchill commanded that all the glass that was salvageable be carted off and stored for use during the winter. "The power of enduring suffering in the ordinary people of every country, when their spirit is roused," Churchill wrote in his memoirs, "seems to have no bounds."[299]

Humor trumped fear. Golf courses posted new rules. A free drop was allowed when a ball fell into a bomb crater; members would not be penalized for playing out of turn during a raid. Golf had its hazards, including British anti-tank mines planted near seaside links. Churchill one evening told his companions of a golfer who drove his ball onto the shingle. "He took his niblick down to the beach, played the ball, and all that remained afterwards was the ball which returned safely to the green."[300]

As civilian deaths far outstripped army casualties, a joke made the rounds of the East End: Join the army and miss the war. Evelyn Waugh quipped that if the Germans were really intent on destroying British morale, they'd parachute in hundreds of marching brass bands. *Gone with the Wind* was the most popular movie of the year, and it was a good bet that as patrons departed the cinema, a red glow could be seen somewhere over some corner of their city. Taxi drivers complained that the glass in the roads was popping their tires. But they motored onward. Stores without facades hung signs: "We are *wide* open for business." A newspaper hawker defiantly chalked his bulletin board: "Berlin claims 1,000 tons of bombs on London. So what?" Vaudeville and the almost-nude review went on nonstop at the Windmill, just off Piccadilly, and the showgirls high-kicked as usual at the Palladium and Prince of Wales. Hotel doormen proudly told visitors how many air raids had taken place and scoffed at the enemy's poor aim. A charwoman from the East End showed up at work in the City, only to find the office building where she had scrubbed floors for years had vanished the night before. "I guess old Hitler wanted me to have a change," she quipped. H. G. Wells—who had predicted such aerial onslaughts thirty years earlier—was lunching with Somerset Maugham and Lady Diana Cooper when the bombers appeared. Wells refused to leave the table until he had finished his cheese: "I'm enjoying a very good lunch," he said. "Why should I be disturbed by some wretched little barbarian in a machine?" Agatha Christie came upon a farmer in a lane near her home. He was kicking an unexploded bomb: "Dang it all," he said. "Can't even explode properly." Every Briton had a story.[301]

Londoners went to work in the morning and arrived home by curfew, knowing full well that one or the other, home or work, might not be there by the next morning. The landscape changed nightly. If home and work survived the night, the bus route or rail line might not. And there was always the possibility of arriving home to meet an air-raid warden who bore the news of an "incident"—the death of a wife or husband, son or daughter. Still, Londoners made their way around the bomb craters, over the rubble, on foot, by bicycle when the streets were passable. They queued for their food rations, and listened, attuned to rumblings from over the horizon, not knowing if the disquieting basso profundo carried on the east wind was the arrival home of their flyboys or more of Göring's. In the East End, those with neither home nor work took shelter under railway bridges, in brewery basements and warehouses, and in crypts originally built for coal storage.[302]

Churchill sought them out. They were the only Europeans who had not wilted before Hitler. Bundled into a heavy topcoat, his odd little homburg pulled down low, he hurtled through the city streets in an armored car that somebody described as looking like a huge painted thermos. He detested the cumbersomeness of the vehicle, but his bodyguard pleaded with him to use it. As soon as it delivered him to a scene of destruction, out he'd climb to take off on foot. He might poke at the edge of bomb craters with his walking stick, or scramble up a pile of rubble to get a better view of the damage. He left his aides, literally, in the dust. With a careless slouch and his shoulders hunched, he charged down streets, through puddles and over fallen bricks. Always, he sought out the people. He possessed, said Mollie Panter-Downes, a "great gift for making them forget discomfort, danger, and loss and remember that they were living history."[303]

He told the Commons in early October: "In all my life, I have never been treated with so much kindness as by the people who have suffered most.... On every side there is the cry, 'We can take it,' but, with it, there is also the cry, 'Give it 'em back.'" London, he promised, would be rebuilt, more beautiful than before. But before then:

> Long dark months of trials and tribulations lie before us. Not only great danger, but many more misfortunes, many shortcomings, many mistakes, many disappointments will surely be our lot. Death and sorrow will be the companions of our journey; hardship our garment; constancy and valor our only shield.[304]

Before the speech, Churchill had introduced, to much applause, Randolph, who had won a by-election in Preston. Churchill, in his youth, had wished that his father, Lord Randolph, would one day escort him into the Commons, where the son would serve the father "at his side and in his support." That dream was denied by Lord Randolph's calamitous fall from grace and power, scuttled by his mental and physical decay and early death. It would be left to the son, Winston, to escort Lord Randolph's grandson, Randolph, into the chamber. The applause that greeted the pair was for Winston a spontaneous display of support that told him his popularity remained untarnished by the Blitz or by the failure two weeks earlier of his gambit at Dakar, the results of which were just becoming known.[305]

Dakar, before the fall of France, was an obscure French West African port. After France fell, it assumed strategic significance, especially if the Germans were to use it as a base of operations against British convoys sailing for Egypt via the Cape of Good Hope. To scuttle that possibility, Operation Menace was conceived, a straightforward plan that would employ British warships to insert Free French forces led by de Gaulle into Dakar. British intelligence indicated that the Vichy forces at Dakar would not welcome de Gaulle warmly, but this information was ignored. Further, the Free French in London leaked the plans; the scheme might as well have been announced in the *Times*. On September 23 the Free French landed and were met not by a warm welcome but by hot and heavy fire. A British cruiser and battleship were hit by fire from shore batteries and the Vichy battleship *Richelieu*. After two days of desultory firing, Menace was called off. Churchill telegraphed Roosevelt with the unfortunate news. Clementine later called the failure "a classic example of Hope deferred making the Heart sick." Still, after the first sting of regret, Churchill found the positive within the negative: Britain had done *something*. As with Oran, Churchill had shown the world—especially Roosevelt—that Britain was not finished.[306]

Joseph Kennedy thought otherwise. Dakar had been a disaster, he reported to Washington, and Churchill's popularity was falling (it was not). In late October, Kennedy fled to America, the first ambassador to abandon London. Ostensibly, Kennedy departed in order to tender his resignation to Roosevelt in person, but he could have phoned it in while manning his post. His flight earned him the enmity of Londoners and the moniker "Jittery Joe." Once safely home he told the *Boston Globe* in an off-the-record interview that British democracy was finished, that Britain was finished, that Britons were fighting for the preservation of empire rather than for democracy, and that to think otherwise was bunk.[307]

Where Kennedy saw gloom, Churchill saw courage. Of Londoners, he told Colville: "I represent to them something which they wholeheartedly support, the determination to win. For a year or two they will cheer me." In a letter to Chamberlain, who was dying in excruciating pain of bowel cancer, Churchill wrote: "The Germans have made a tremendous mistake in concentrating on London to the relief of our factories, and in trying to intimidate a people whom they have only infuriated." Londoners preferred, he told Colville, "to all be in the front line, taking part in the Battle of London, than to look on helplessly at mass slaughters like Passchendaele."[308]

Throughout October, the War Cabinet pondered the ultimate question: are the Germans coming? All month the Ultra intelligence, the code name for information gleaned from Luftwaffe and Wehrmacht radio traffic, indicated ongoing preparations for the invasion. German logistical units had asked the high command what distance the troops would have to march to reach their port of embarkation. Also: How many "S" days, or Sea Lion days, were to be allotted for vehicle packing and delivery, and how many days for troop embarkation. Aerial intelligence confirmed that the Germans were rehearsing the invasion under cover of synthetic yellow fog. Radio transmissions indicated the invasion date would likely be sometime after October 20. Was it all part of a German disinformation campaign? The Secret Circle had no choice but to carry on its business as if invasion was imminent; to do otherwise would have been a dereliction of duty. The navy patrolled, the RAF patrolled, Bletchley listened. Yet, a sense that the invasion was "off" began to manifest itself more in Churchill's words, private and public. On October 4 he cabled Roosevelt: "The gent has taken off his clothes and put on his bathing suit, but the water is getting colder and there is an autumn nip in the air. We are maintaining the utmost vigilance."[309]

On October 21, while broadcasting to the French, Churchill tossed out a phrase that could only have arisen from his growing optimism: "We are waiting for the long promised invasion. So are the fishes." The words sizzle—defiant, sure to conjure respect from neutral observers. His speeches of June and July had been somber admissions to the probability of invasion and drumbeats to fight on to the end with courage and dignity, and to die likewise. Those speeches had been intended to inspire, but should England fall under the Nazi boot, they were also intended as epitaphs to be read and pondered by future generations. The one-liner built into the October speech was pure Churchillian wit, a wisecrack of the sort he simply could not resist and for which he was so well known. He had not uttered it to cronies in a drawing room over port but broadcast it worldwide and directed it at the most powerful leader and the most awesome military force on the planet. This lone phrase casts Hitler as the fool. It demeans him, tells him, You may yet defeat us, but you will never, not *ever*, beat the spirit out of us.[310]

The address, recorded in French and English, was intended in part to allay French fears that the British had designs on its fleet and West African colonies. "We seek," Churchill said, "to beat the life out of Hitler and Hitlerism. That alone, that all the time, that to the end. We do not covet anything from any nation except their respect." To some Frenchmen, Churchill's claim of not coveting anything rang hollow. The British had tried to sink the French fleet at Oran in July, and had just tried to land a Free French force at Dakar. Churchill added a final pledge:

> Remember we shall never stop, never weary, and never give in, and that our whole people and Empire have vowed themselves to the task of cleansing Europe from the Nazi pestilence and saving the world from the new Dark Ages.... We are on his track, and so are our friends across the Atlantic Ocean, and your friends across the Atlantic Ocean. If he cannot destroy us, we will surely destroy him, and all his gang, and all their works. Therefore, have hope and faith, for all will come right.[311]

Faith that their "friends" across the Atlantic would make their presence known was all Britain and France had. Yet nine days later, Franklin Roosevelt told a Boston audience, "Your boys are not going to be sent into any foreign wars." He did not add his usual qualifier, "except in case of attack." Even had America the will to fight—which it did not—it lacked the way. Churchill ended his address with words that resonated with his own romanticism as well as with the idealized egalitarian spirit of the Republic that Frenchmen so cherished: *"Allons, bonne nuit; dormez bien, reassemblez vos forces pour l'aube* [Good night, then; sleep well to gather strength for the dawn]. For the morning will come. Brightly will it shine on the brave and true, kindly on all who suffer for the cause, glorious upon the tombs of heroes. Thus will shine the dawn. *Vive la France!*"[312]

That night, the painter Paul Maze, who had escaped from Bordeaux in June and was living in Hampshire, wrote Churchill: "Every word you said was like every drop of blood in a transfusion." The inspirational effect of Churchill's words might have been lost had the microphone in the radio studio been turned on when he arrived. Jacques Duchesne (pseudonym of the French actor Michel Saint-Denis), the BBC's French expert and translator, was standing in the room, waiting to perform his duties. "Where is my frog speech?" asked Churchill. Colville, who accompanied Churchill, said Duchesne "looked pained."[313]

Within a week Churchill, thanks to Ultra, became convinced that the invasion was off, or at least postponed until the spring of 1941. On the twenty-eighth, the Combined Intelligence Committee stated that photo reconnaissance indicated a movement of German shipping *eastward*, out of the Channel, a movement that, "if maintained, could reduce the risk of invasion." But the U-boats still posed a mortal threat. And the German bombers were still paying their nightly visits.

More than five hundred RAF fighter pilots had been killed fighting Göring's daylight raids since July, but their sacrifice brought results. By late October, daylight bombings had virtually ceased. Göring ordered them stopped entirely in early November; his daytime losses since July ran almost ten times higher than his night losses. The night skies over Britain promised safety to German aircrew. Göring's switch to night bombing and the dropping of incendiaries randomly throughout London meant the Germans had abandoned any pretense of bombing military targets. The midnight bombs that fell regularly in Berlin meant the British had as well.

By November Chequers had become the regular weekend retreat of the Churchill family. It would be the last autumn of the war that the entire family spent time together. Mary, seventeen, had gone on vacation in July to stay with old family friends, the Montagus, in Norfolk; the Blitz and threatened invasion had prolonged the visit. She wanted to return to London, but her parents were adamant that she not. In September she was packed off to Chequers. Pamela took up residence there in mid-September to await the birth of her first child. Her doctor insisted on accompanying her. He stayed for two weeks, recalled Pamela, to "have some peaceful nights" at the height of the Blitz. Clementine thought the doctor's presence an awkward distraction for Winston, and she expressed her displeasure to Pamela, who replied, "Mama, I can't do anything to make this child appear." Churchill presumed the child would be a boy, to be named Winston, and was therefore not happy when his cousin the Duchess of Marlborough was delivered of a baby boy whom she named Winston just days before Pamela was expected to give birth. Churchill called the duchess and told her, "Pamela and Randolph expect to call their son Winston." The duchess asked, "How do you know it's going to be a boy?" He replied, "If it isn't now, it will be later. I would like to ask you to change the name." The duchess changed the name to Charles. Pamela's son, Winston Spencer Churchill, "Little" Winston, was born in a four-poster bed at Chequers on October 10. Pamela awoke from a chloroform-induced sleep to hear murmurings of "It's a boy, it's a boy." And, she recalled, "Old Winston was right there. It meant a great deal to him."[314]

Randolph, on temporary leave from his army unit and serving in Parliament, took his weekends in the country with Pamela and his parents. Churchill's brother, Jack, a financier six years Winston's junior, always self-effacing and discreet, added his avuncular presence to the scene. His London house bombed out, Jack took to bunking wherever he could, including No. 10 and the Annexe. Jack's wife, Lady Gwendeline "Goonie" Churchill, had long been one of Clementine's most loyal friends, but by late 1940, dying of cancer, Goonie had moved to the country. Her absence on weekends eliminated one of Clementine's connections to social goings-on in the outside world, from which she, too, had of necessity withdrawn. Winston and Clementine's eldest daughter, Diana Sandys, sometimes appeared on weekends to add her own urbanity to the dinner conversation. Her children—Julian, four, and Edwina, two—afforded Churchill the opportunity to behave like a normal grandfather, that is, like a big child, albeit with cigar ashes sprinkled on his vest. He, far more than Clementine, recalled Pamela, knew how to make a child laugh. For Mary, Chequers felt like a great and gloomy house during the week, yet it came alive with the arrival on weekends of her siblings, her parents, and their guests.[315]

Colville, as a private secretary, was often present. He was drawn to Mary's spunk, although he noted that she was often somewhat tense and on occasion peevish. He sometimes arranged to join her and Clementine on their walks about the grounds, strolls that often turned into wild footraces between the two youths. Leaving Clementine behind, Mary and Colville sprinted down forest paths, past the ancient oaks, and dashed to the tops of the low hills. She usually won the race, perhaps because Colville was being gallant, perhaps because he was winded from his cigarette habit. In the presence of her father, Mary's behavior was muted. Such deference to Papa was inculcated early in all the children. Yet during one family luncheon, Mary's spirited nature surfaced. Churchill, expressing surprise and dismay at the speed of the French collapse, announced that the French debacle was so swift it was as if the Germans had simply bypassed France and thrown their full weight against Britain. Mary listened in silence. Then, in a soft and nervous voice, she paraphrased the words her father had spoken months earlier in tribute to the young fighter pilots of the RAF: "Never before has so much been betrayed for so many by so few."[316]

Randolph, not yet thirty, displayed neither his sister's reticence nor her sly humor. He was, recalled Colville, "a most unattractive combination of the bombastic, the cantankerous and the unwise; and yet at times he makes shrewd and penetrating comments and at times can be pleasant. He has none of Winston's reasonableness." He drank heavily, Colville noted, and was not a drinker of good cheer. Randolph, during one dinner, opined at length on how Baldwin had destroyed the fire in politics and deprived the empire of its greatness. World domination, said Randolph, was the greatest ideal and he admired the Germans for desiring it. Randolph's arguments, Colville noted in his diary, "make one shudder." Colville found him to be one of the most "objectionable" people he'd ever met: "Noisy, self-asserting, whining and frankly unpleasant" . . . and "at dinner anything but kind to Winston, who adores him." Randolph's treatment of his father so vexed Clementine that she threatened to ban him from No. 10 lest he give his father a heart attack. Yet Winston's love for Randolph was infinite. At Chequers, Churchill was at his ease with his cronies and his family nearby. And, of course, he loved the food and liquor, spirits of a quality not found in the canteen beneath Storey's Gate. He knew the joys of family life at Chequers might easily be short-lived; the games of croquet on the lawns (he watched), the family strolls and footraces (he avoided all exercise), brandy and reminiscences before the great fireplaces, even Randolph's pathetic tirades. Of Chequers and the Germans, he said: "Probably they don't think I am so foolish as to come here. I stand to lose a lot. Three generations at a swoop."[317]

His family, though in close physical proximity that autumn, was coming apart. Sarah's marriage to the actor and comedian Vic Oliver had dissolved. His music man act had enjoyed a long run of playing the Palladium, the house always packed. But as an Austrian of Jewish ancestry, he had been warned to flee England before it was too late. America seemed the safer place now for an Austrian expatriate and comic actor on the rise. Sarah, if Vic left for the United States, would accompany him out of matrimonial duty, but she harbored no desire to leave England, her parents, and her nascent theatrical career. Vic stayed on in London into 1941, a gesture Sarah found noble given "the sorrow he would have caused me if he asked me to leave Britain at that time." By the following summer the marriage was finished, and Sarah had been commissioned as an RAF section officer. Clementine thoroughly endorsed Sarah's remaining in England because she felt no "Churchill child" should leave the country in its hour of distress. When she learned that one of her nieces was to depart for Canada, she had the child's passport revoked. Churchill disapproved of the entire emigration scheme, calling it a "stampede from the country."[318]

In any case, the program to evacuate children overseas had effectively ended on September 17. That night, the steamship *City of Benares,* bound for Canada, was making poor headway in a gale when it was torpedoed. Seventy-three of ninety children on board perished, as well as more than two hundred of their adult escorts. Many initially made it into the lifeboats. The children began singing *Roll out the Barrel,* but by the time they got to "We'll have a barrel of fun," the ship was gone. The seas then took over, smashing the lifeboats. Four days later Churchill told the Defence Committee that in view of the sinking, the evacuation of children overseas must cease.[319]

Since the days almost two decades earlier when he topped the Irish Republican Army assassination list, Churchill liked to sleep with a gun within reach. He had carried a Colt revolver on his person since the fall of France, but tended to lay it down and forget where, forcing Inspector Thompson to loan him one of his revolvers. Churchill was given to drawing his gun and waving it about while exclaiming, "You see Thompson, they'll never take me alive." In fact, he was a good shot with a rifle and absolutely deadly with his Colt .45. He and Thompson repaired on a regular basis to the outdoor shooting range at Chequers, where Churchill would fire a hundred or so rounds each from his Mannlicher rifle, his .32 Webley & Scott revolver, and his favorite Colt. He was, recalled Thompson, so deadly a shot that anyone who came within range of his gun would stand no chance. Colville recorded one such session: "[Churchill] fired his Mannlicher rifle at targets 100, 200, and 300 yards away. He also fired his revolver, still smoking a cigar, with commendable accuracy. Despite his age, size, and lack of practice, he acquitted himself well.... He always seems to visualize the possibility of having to defend himself against German troops!"[320]

The idea of the prime minister of Great Britain blazing away at the enemy was, with all Britons expecting an invasion, anything but preposterous. Churchill lived daily with the very real possibility of a last stand, a shoot-out between himself and the invaders. Recalled Lord Geoffrey-Lloyd,* "Winston was like an animal in the jungle, his senses attuned to any kind of danger. He had this primitive desire for survival, which was an immense inspiration to the country and the world."[321]

During the ordnance exercise, Churchill opined, "The best way to kill Huns was with snub-nosed bullets." He was referring to hollow-point slugs called dumdums, which pancake upon hitting flesh, crash through internal organs, and leave an exit wound as big as a teapot. They were named after the Dum Dum arsenal near Calcutta, where they were first

* Geoffrey-Lloyd (1902–1984) managed the Petroleum Warfare Department within the War Department. In 1945 he was appointed minister of information.

produced in order to give the British an advantage over mutinous locals. Such bullets, Randolph protested to his father, were illegal in warfare. Indeed they were. Churchill in 1906 had declared his opposition to using the slugs against any "civilized foe." The Nazis had forfeited any claims in that regard. To Randolph, Churchill rumbled that since the Germans would "make short shrift" of him if captured, he saw no reason at all why he should have "any mercy on them."[322]

Goebbels tried to parlay Churchill's shooting sessions into a propaganda coup. He procured a photo of Churchill that had run in British newspapers which displayed the prime minister attired in dark pinstripes, immense cigar firmly set in his mouth, a Thompson .45-caliber submachine gun outfitted with a circular magazine (favored by Chicago mobsters) cradled in his arms. The Germans produced a leaflet from the photo with these words: "WANTED, FOR INCITEMENT TO MURDER. THIS GANGSTER, WHO YOU SEE IN HIS ELEMENT IN THE PICTURE, INCITES YOU BY HIS EXAMPLE TO PARTICIPATE IN A FORM OF WARFARE IN WHICH WOMEN, CHILDREN AND ORDINARY CITIZENS SHALL TAKE LEADING PARTS." Goebbels had thousands of the leaflets dropped over Britain. He ceased the program within two weeks, when he realized the image was only boosting Churchill's popularity among Britons.[323]

Plinking with small arms might conceivably address some practical need for self-protection, but whether he was at No. 10, the Annexe, or Chequers, Churchill's behavior during air raids was another matter entirely. With the swagger of Victorian men, he scorned personal danger. Courage, he believed, was the greatest virtue. In October he was sitting in the Cabinet Room when aides told him that an unexploded two-ton bomb in St. James's Park threatened everyone in Downing Street. Churchill glanced up from his papers and said he hoped none of the park's ducks would be hurt. During one raid he summoned Colville to escort him from No. 10 to the Annexe. Colville recalled: "As we emerged from the India Office arch into King Charles Street, we heard the loud whistles of two descending bombs. I dived back under the arch for shelter, and the bomb exploded in Whitehall. Churchill, meanwhile, was striding along the middle of King George Street, his chin stuck out and propelling himself rapidly with his gold-headed walking stick. I had to run to catch him up.... I am sure that in a shipwreck he would have been the last to step into the lifeboat."[324]

He liked to watch the enemy bombers come in, and thoroughly enjoyed the crash and *crump* of the bombs, and the *crack* of the anti-aircraft guns. He relished the entire spectacle. Four decades earlier he had quipped that nothing in life quite so exhilarates as "being shot at without result." When the sirens sounded, Churchill chose between sitting underground watching dust shake out of the rafters and going forth into the raids. Out he went.[325]

His outings sent Clementine, his cabinet, and his bodyguards into fits of angst. Inspector Thompson believed that Churchill's insistence on putting himself in danger was the Marlborough in him. At the first wail of the sirens Churchill donned his tin hat—he called it his "battle bowler"—and, attired in his mauve siren suit or one of his vivid dressing gowns, sometimes both, would depart the underground Annexe for the roof or, if he was at Chequers, for the gardens, there to watch and wait while the enemy approached, or, as he put it, "to walk in the moonlight and watch the fireworks." He did not at all like the fit of the helmet; when it regularly slipped down over his eyes as he gazed skyward, he'd fling it into the bushes for an aide to later retrieve. He might chew on an unlighted cigar, or light one up, in defiance of all rules against smoking during air raids. He ignored any rule he chose to ignore. His Royal Marine valet, in an attempt to impede his mobility, hid his shoes. Churchill demanded they be returned. "I'll have you know," he proclaimed, "that as a child my nurse maid would never prevent me from taking a walk in the park if I wanted to do so. And as a man, Adolf Hitler certainly won't."[326]

His favorite position from which to take in the fireworks was the flat roof of the Annexe. Sited as it was across from St. James's Park, it afforded a splendid view of London, a foolishly dangerous prospect even with an overhanging roof to guard against stray shell fragments. There, gas mask at his side, armed with a glowing cigar and binoculars, he watched for bomb flashes. He counted the seconds until the crunch of the bomb reached him. Five seconds, one mile. Persuading him to leave the roof proved difficult at best.[327]

If he did depart, it was likely because he demanded that his aides locate the exact area bombed, and that they bring the motorcar around in order that he should tour the scene. On one such outing, the blast from a nearby German bomb lifted Churchill's car up off all four tires. The vehicle returned to the ground and rolled along for several yards on two wheels, before finally righting itself. It regained its stability, said Churchill, due to "my beef." On another evening, Churchill, Minister of Labour Ernest Bevin, Pug Ismay, and Jock Colville packed themselves into the armored car. All were well plied with brandy. Their destination was Raynes Park, where they hoped to watch the anti-aircraft guns in action. On the way, a policeman tried to arrest them for driving with too-bright lights. The dutiful bobby was dismissed with a loud, "Go to Hell, man." The phrasing of the outburst excludes Bevin as a suspect in uttering it. Born in a remote West England village and educated in secondary (public) schools, he dropped his "h's" and "g's" in the west country fashion. Bevin would have said *"G' ta 'ell man."* Thus, someone other than Bevin must have told the constable where to go. Colville was too junior, Pug Ismay too polite. Only one suspect remained.

In any event, the group motored onward to the park, where they found the big guns silent. It was raining, and, with no German aircraft overhead, Churchill stopped by the officers' mess, where he sipped a whisky and soda and awaited the fireworks.[328]

Inspector Thompson could do little during air raids to protect the prime minister from the potential folly of his own reckless behavior. On two occasions Thompson had to heave his charge bodily out of exposed doorways in Whitehall as bombs fell nearby. The blast from one wounded some of Thompson's men. Churchill, infuriated at having been shoved, took no notice of the wounded men. Instead he "swore, shook, and stomped about." He bellowed, "Don't *do* that." Thompson could not quite decipher the rest of the "whole gush of ugly sounds" emanating from Churchill. The curses strung together by a perturbed Churchill, Thompson wrote, were "a sin against the language." Such eruptions were well known to everyone who worked for him, from the Chiefs of Staff to his secretaries. But Thompson gave as good as he got, telling Churchill that his behavior was "selfishly stupid." After the tantrum, Churchill voiced a non-apology, after his fashion, for leading Thompson into danger: "I would not do it, only I know how much *you* like it." Yet he could never quite leave it at that. Invariably a glare of long duration followed such scenes, a signal that he considered the entire affair finished, but only on his terms. As for taking to heart Thompson's professional advice, Churchill, with the next keening of the sirens, flew out the door, rooftop bound. His explanation: "When my time is due, it will come."[329]

One early October evening after a late dinner at No. 10, and knowing that on the following day he would be addressing the Commons as well as sponsoring Randolph's entry into Parliament, Churchill, rather than retire, as would most sixty-five-year-old men burdened with great responsibilities, made straightaway for the action. As recalled by anti-aircraft commander Sir Frederick Pile, they first drove to Richmond, where the big guns were banging away and bombs were falling. As usual, Churchill refused his helmet. At about eleven he was told that a demonstration of the new radar-controlled searchlights had been prepared for him at Biggin Hill. He didn't want to leave. "This exhilarates me," he told Pile. "The sound of these cannon gives me a tremendous feeling." Finally, persuaded to move on, they went off in Pile's car, and immediately became lost. Two hours later, after navigating blocked streets in total darkness, the bombs still falling, they found their intended rendezvous point—"the worst two hours of the war for me," Pile wrote. The night was wet and cold. Churchill asked for a whisky and soda. The commander of the searchlight unit replied that there was as much chance of getting a whisky there as in the Sahara, but that he'd send to his mess, ten miles distant. The radar failed to operate, but the whisky was produced, without the dilution of a splash of soda, which was the Old Man's custom. He took one sip, spluttered, and said, "Good God, I have been poisoned. It is neat whisky."[330]

A display of aerial rocket mines was also scrubbed. The rocket experiments off, the party set out for London, bombs still falling. Upon arrival at No. 10—it was now about 4:30 A.M.—Churchill rapped upon the door with his gold-tipped walking stick and announced "Göring and Goebbels coming to report." He invited Pile in for a snack of sardines and Bovril, a foodstuff resembling liquefied beef with the consistency of molasses and rife with the overriding taste of salt. But a spoonful in a tall glass topped off with boiling water and a dash of sherry served as a traditional antidote to London's chills, and in company with tinned sardines, it became a staple of wartime Britain. Churchill and Pile downed their snack, Pile departing as dawn broke. A few hours later, Churchill, looking no worse for his sleepless night, addressed the Commons.[331]

His doctor, Charles Wilson, was among those made exceedingly uncomfortable by his forays into the exploding night. Wilson recalled that during that summer and autumn he visited Churchill regularly, and was begrudged every moment he sought. As the Blitz hardened, Churchill became a source of worry for Wilson: "I used to watch him as he went to his room," he wrote, "the head thrust forward, scowling at the ground, the somber countenance clouded, the features set and resolute, the jowl clamped down as if he had something clamped between his teeth and did not let it go . . . carrying the weight of the world, and wondered how long he could go on like that and what could be done about it."[332]

His jaunts while the bombs fell seemed to be just the medicine, self-prescribed. Harold Nicolson, in November, noted Churchill's healthy glow: "He seems better in health than he has ever seemed. That pale and globular look about his cheeks is gone. He is more solid about the face, and thinner." His eyes especially moved Nicolson. The lids evidenced no weariness, no pouches or dark lines were to be seen. "But the eyes themselves are glaucous, vigilant, angry, combative, visionary and tragic . . . the eyes of a man much preoccupied." He *was* preoccupied—with Hitler, the Americans, and the nightly bombings. Yet he was determined that all would end on his terms. In spite of the dangers, the defeats, and the grim prospects for national survival, he was content. Unable to pursue his usual enjoyments—writing, painting, and the laying of row upon row of red Kentish bricks in the gardens of Chartwell—he found a new source of joy. The glow Nicolson noted was due to Churchill's new pastime, the fireworks.[333]

His fondness for late-night outings should not be construed as a fondness for war. He hated the carnage of war. In 1898, at Omdurman in the Sudan, he carried a Mauser pistol into the last great cavalry charge in British history. At close range, he shot dead at least three Dervishes during two minutes of bloody chaos. He had sent letters home to his mother from the Sudan condemning the "dirty, shoddy business" of battle. "You can not gild it," he wrote, "the raw comes through." The glorification of war he saw as a fraud. Of war, he wrote in 1930, "we now have entire populations, including even women and children, pitted against one another in brutish mutual extermination, and only a set of blear-eyed clerks left to add up the butcher's bill." War's utility was altogether another matter. He told Colville that those who complain that wars settle nothing were speaking nonsense, because "nothing in history was ever settled except by war." War, in spite of its horror, was the answer when the questions were framed in terms of liberty and the preservation of the West's most humanistic traditions.[334]

Inspector Thompson couldn't keep his charge from climbing rooftops while the bombs fell, but the assassination of Churchill was something Thompson could plan against. Churchill, understanding that the rules of gentlemanly warfare had changed since his youth, said to Colville, "If you are allowed to bomb Heads of State, surely you may shoot them?" Thompson's chief concern centered on two possibilities: an attempt by commandos or a targeted air raid by fighter-bombers. A pinpoint air raid on Chequers might not get Churchill, but Thompson wanted to reduce the chances to nil. To thwart an ambush by suicide parachutists, he posted policemen, some from the local force, some from London, throughout the grounds, on the roofs, in every outbuilding. The army was also deployed. Sentries manned the gates and patrolled the grounds. Passwords were issued and constantly changed. Each sentry maintained an intersecting field of fire with neighboring positions. Each guard was assigned a specific sector of the grounds and each, at random times during the night, flicked on his flashlight to illuminate his area, just for a moment in order to ascertain who, if anybody, might be lurking. Thompson thought the precautions critical. Churchill loathed the entire routine. It brought the war into his gardens. It destroyed charm. It introduced suspicion, and nonsense.[335]

German reconnaissance planes made passes overhead, shooting photographs. Incendiary bombs fell nearby on a regular basis, dropped by Heinkels going to or from London. Coincidence could not explain the many bomb craters that dotted the grounds of Chequers; the house was clearly a target. The German use of beam navigation gave Churchill pause about the vulnerability of Chequers to bombing. He told Colville he did not object to chance but felt it "a mistake to be the victim of design." To preclude the possibility of the prime minister's becoming the victim of design, Thompson told Churchill he'd have to do what he was told from now on, which was to sleep in the air-raid shelter. Churchill replied that he would cooperate the moment he thought it wise to do so. This meant, wrote Thompson, he "would continue to do as he pleased, which was to stay outside and watch." To a Royal Marine who tried to reinforce Thompson's caution Churchill said, "Let me know when they start dropping the bombs."[336]

Chequers was especially vulnerable to attack when the moon was full. To further reduce the chances of Churchill's being consumed by German ordnance, an alternate weekend retreat was proposed, Ditchley Park, the Oxfordshire home of Nancy and Ronnie Tree. Their house stood on forested grounds, thirty miles west of Chequers, away from German glide paths. Both were half American by birth. Ronnie had been brought up in Britain, and Nancy was from Richmond, Virginia, the widow of Henry Field, he of the family of Chicago mercantile fame. As the MP from Leicestershire, Ronnie, though not an intimate friend of the Churchills, had long supported rearmament, and for that he had earned Churchill's respect. Ditchley Park happened to be located just a few miles from Blenheim, a coincidence that appealed to Churchill. His first sojourn to Ditchley took place on Saturday, November 9, as there was a full moon that weekend. Nancy wrote Churchill a short, gracious note in which she bade him to "use the house as your own," whenever convenient and "no matter how short the notice." She may not have realized that Churchill did not travel alone. Ditchley was about to become a full house.[337]

Whether at Ditchley or Chequers, weekends began with the same routine, usually on Friday afternoon, sometimes on Saturday morning. One or two of Churchill's police bodyguards arrived before the rest of the party in order to inspect the house from garret to cellar. The valet and maid then arrived with much luggage. Next, a platoon of thirty-five soldiers arrived by truck, to protect the great man throughout the night. Private secretaries, stenographers, and guests followed, often including the Prof, Bracken, and brother Jack. Finally, in the late afternoon, Clementine and Churchill made their appearance. Churchill's first order of business was a hot bath, to which he might stroll from his dressing room stark naked, to the consternation of newer female typists. On Saturdays and Sundays, he stayed in bed until noon, working and dictating, a supply of Malvern natural spring water at the ready. After dictation came a hearty lunch followed by a short (but certainly not rigorous) walk, then tea, or more likely a whisky. More work until 6:30, at which time he took his nap, always in the company of a hot water bottle. At 8:00, dinner. Although prime cuts of meats were no longer readily available to Britons, some still found their way to Churchill's table. But old favorites such as bushels of fresh oysters, black truffles, or Caspian caviar, even if available, were avoided. All Britons, Churchill included, were on short rations. He kept a somewhat simple table for the duration.

Conversation always flowed at dinner, as did champagne. Pol Roger

(Churchill favored 1928 and 1929) was hauled up from the basements nightly. As always, Churchill dominated at the table. Conversation with him, wrote his doctor, was similar to cricket: he batted and everybody else caught. "Winston talks to amuse himself; he has no thoughts of impressing anybody.... He requires no help, least of all from women."[338] After the meal came brandy, port, cigars, and a movie. The first screenings took place at Ditchley. Among his favorites were *The Great Dictator,* released in December, and *Gone with the Wind*. He displayed a schoolboyish love for Vivien Leigh, who played Scarlett O'Hara. He was "pulverized," he said of the characters in the latter film, "by the strength of their feelings and emotions." The film happened also to be one of Hitler's favorites (along with *It Happened One Night*).[339]

The respite afforded by weekends with family and friends at Chequers and Ditchley fed his optimism. Still, somber thoughts swam beneath the surface. A dinner one evening with Clementine and Pamela was had in silence, each alone with his or her own thoughts. Then, cocking his chin and brandishing his knife like a rapier, Churchill told them he expected them to do their duty and take one or two Huns with them when the time came. "But, Papa," Pamela protested, "I neither own nor know how to fire a gun." He nodded toward the kitchen. "There are butcher knives in there," he growled. "Take one out and use it. You can always take a Hun with you." He later said he considered "You can always take one with you" his slogan if the invasion came.[340]

A vicious array of bombs fell upon London throughout the autumn, wicked little incendiaries and two-ton "land mines" delivered by parachute to destroy all and sundry within five hundred meters, and concussive high-explosive bombs and their sinister kin, time-delay bombs that slept soundly until the moment their internal clock went *tick*. On the moonlit night of October 14–15, the Germans mixed in thousands of incendiary bombs with the usual component of high explosives, with catastrophic results. The Balham tube station, where 650 sought shelter, suffered a direct hit: the entrance collapsed; gas, water, and sewer lines in the street above were demolished; the station flooded. More than 250 Londoners drowned in the deluge of sewage and water or were crushed by debris, including a double-decker bus. Leicester Square was rendered a desert. Pall Mall was badly smashed up, the Carlton Club wrecked, the Travellers Club splintered, its members trapped within. No. 10 sustained more damage when the Treasury was hit yet again.

The incendiaries introduced a new and terrifying element. That night almost 400 German medium bombers dropped more than 70,000 incendiaries onto the kindling that was London, starting 900 fires. "To the basements," the civilian rallying cry during raids, was replaced with "To the roofs," where an agile homeowner with a well-placed bucket of sand could erase the danger, if he moved fast enough. The firebombs forced an immediate change in the fire-spotting system. Throughout Britain, almost 1,400 local fire brigades were consolidated into the National Fire Service. Uniforms—dark blue tunics and trousers—were issued, training standardized. Duty consisted of sitting alone on a roof with only a tin hat for protection. In the early going, London seemed to be falling down all around the firewatchers. Churchill foresaw the possibility of the complete destruction of the city, but his faith in Londoners remained undiminished: "Soon, many of the bombs would only fall upon houses already ruined and only make the rubble jump. Over large areas there would be nothing more to burn or destroy. And yet human beings might make their homes here and there and carry on their work with infinite resource and fortitude."[341]

Fortitude was in great demand. A lone civilian wielding a bucket of sand could dispose of an incendiary, but the far more complex and dangerous disposal of unexploded bombs fell to the Royal Engineers. The tools of their trade were simple: a drill, a wrench, and a spool of string. After gaining access to a bomb's fuse *via* wrench and drill, the engineers attached the string to the primer, then uncoiled the spool to a safe distance before giving a firm but measured tug on the line in order to remove the detonator. In the ordinary course of events, the now-impotent ordnance would be trucked far out of the city, to the Hackney Marshes, to be harmlessly detonated. But the laws of physics conspired to render bomb disposal anything but ordinary. Bombs buried nose-down in deep and muddy craters had to be hauled out by rope and pulley. A slip of the rope could start the timing mechanism. Unexploded bombs by the hundreds fell through buildings and into basements; they fell onto rooftops, hung from church steeples, were ensnared by electrical wires, and dropped onto railway lines. One eight-hundred-pounder landed just in front of the steps of St. Paul's and burrowed deep down among gas and water lines. It was hauled out inch by inch over several hours and taken off to the marshes, where, when detonated, it made a crater one hundred feet wide. One bomb parachuted onto the Hungerford railroad bridge, which spanned the Thames. It didn't explode but became welded to the electric rail. Even unexploded, it crippled railroad traffic. Göring was throttling Britain in ways he had not imagined.[342]

Almost 20 percent of German (and British) bombs were duds, but they still closed long stretches of railway lines, important junctions, roads, and airfields as efficiently as time-delay bombs, and both fell at the rate of three thousand per week. They caused such a bottleneck in the transport of food and military supplies that Churchill commanded the ministers of War and Supply to make disposal of unexploded bombs their highest priority. With his usual attention to detail, he told Anthony Eden that he had learned of an American auger that could dig a trench in a matter of hours that otherwise would take several men two or three days to dig manually. "You should, I think, consider ordering a number of these appliances for the use of the bomb disposal squads. The essence of this business is to reach the bomb and deal with it with the least possible delay."[343]

Yet reaching the unexploded bomb was but the first step in a sequence that often proved deadly. German engineers built even more unpredictability and terror into the bomb disposal process. They employed double fuses, one behind the other, so that the removal of the first triggered the unseen second. They installed fuses sensitive to light, in which the detonation sequence began when a UXB squad opened the bomb, exposing the fuse to sunlight. Of all the detonator types, the time-delay fuse was the most terrifying. Because a mechanical time-delay device would likely be damaged in the crash landing of the bomb, the Germans employed an acid drip that burned through a thin metal plate covering a secondary triggering mechanism. It was, said Churchill, "an especially effective agent in warfare, on account of the prolonged uncertainty which it creates." UXB squads knew that if they put an ear to a bomb casing and heard the soft buzzing of the timer, they had fewer than fifteen seconds to find shelter. The largest bombs precluded any chance of success in such a dash. Churchill later wrote: "In writing about our hard times we are apt to overuse the word 'grim.' It should have been reserved for the U.X.B. Disposal Squads."[344]

Despite Clementine's plea to treat his staff more mercifully, Churchill's behavior toward his subordinates continued to be downright ill-tempered, brusque, and often pedantic regarding insignificant details. One night Colville reported to him two unexploded bombs in the Horse Guards Parade. "Will they do us any damage when they explode?" asked Churchill while lying in bed. Colville replied that they would not. "Is that just your opinion," demanded Churchill, "because if so it's worth nothing. You have never seen an unexploded bomb go off. Go and ask for an official report." Trivialities did not escape his attention. Strolling from No. 10, he noticed the flag atop the Admiralty was in tatters. He messaged the First Lord: "Surely you can run a new Admiralty flag. It grieves me to see the present dingy object every morning." He complained of delays when there were none, changed carefully prepared plans at the last minute, and constantly insisted on personal amenities that his overworked staff could not produce. Sounds of hammering during the reinforcement of No. 10 and the CWR brought outbursts of fury. Broad indeed was the spectrum of noises that set him off. The *clang clang* of cowbells drove him to distraction. His secretaries dreaded the possibility on rural outings that a cow or, worse yet, a herd of bell-wearing cows might appear when the Old Man was collecting his thoughts. Whistling in his presence produced a disturbance so immediate and immense that his aides sometimes made whirling motions at their temples to convey their assessment of the wheels in Churchill's head. He issued an order to the entire government against whistling in the corridors. When he heard whistling while walking in St. James's Park or through Whitehall, anywhere, at any time, he confronted the offender—even young boys—and demanded immediate cessation. His horror of whistling, said Churchill, was the only thing he had in common with Hitler.[345]

When workmen resumed their rush to hammer together protective barriers in Whitehall after Churchill had ordered them to cease, he again ordered the hammering stopped, thereby almost bringing to a halt the safeguarding of the very heart of government. His turbulent behavior, Colville wrote, could be explained by a string of disasters from Norway to Dunkirk, to the shipping losses in the Atlantic, and by the threat of invasion. Yet sometimes, when his staff expected an outburst after a particularly bad piece of intelligence had been gleaned, Churchill surprised all by his nonchalance. Ismay recalled a conference convened in August to discuss the role of the Home Fleet in case of invasion. The commander in chief of the Home Fleet, Admiral Charles Forbes, allowed that, in the event of invasion, his heaviest ships would not operate south of Wales. With the fate of England in the balance, it was expected that such a proposal to save the fleet while losing the war would surely drive Churchill to spontaneous combustion. Ismay, somewhat taken aback by Forbes's statement, waited for the inevitable explosion. It never came. Churchill listened in silence. Then, gazing over his spectacles with an indulgent smile, he declared he never took much notice of what the Royal Navy said before an event, because he knew the navy would, once the action began, undertake the apparently impossible without a moment's hesitation if the situation demanded it, as it surely would were the Germans to come across the Channel.[346]

Where he could dismiss out of hand the advice of his valets and bodyguards, the advice of senior officials had at least to be treated with the appearance of sober reflection, although the end result was usually the same: Churchill got his way. An October conversation with General Alan Brooke turned to the whereabouts of General Percy Cleghorn Stanley Hobart, an erratic tank genius whose services were going unused. "Hobo," as Hobart was known in the ranks, had retired and was serving as a corporal in the Home Guard. As Colville recalled the scene, Brooke believed Hobart too wild to recall to duty, but Churchill, citing General Wolfe brandishing his sword while standing on a chair in front of Prime Minister Pitt, declared. "You cannot expect to have the genius type with the conventional copy-book style." Days later, Churchill met with Hobart and formed a favorable impression. He demanded that General Dill, Chief of the Imperial General Staff, give Hobart a tank division that week, if not *that day*. "Remember," Churchill told Dill, "it is not only the good boys that help to win wars; it is the sneaks and stinkers as well." Dill acceded to the order after protesting that Hobart was "impatient, quick-tempered, hotheaded, intolerant, and inclined to see things as he wished them to be instead of as they were." The description fit Churchill. Hobart got his division, two in fact. Three years later Hobart's "Funnies"—flame-throwing "Crocodile tanks" and mine-clearing "Flail" tanks—would be some of the first armored vehicles to come ashore on the beaches of Normandy. By then, the resurrected Hobart had been knighted for services rendered to the Crown.[347]

By late October, Colville wrote, as the invasion threat ebbed, Churchill had regained a quotient of his engaging, if often infuriating and idiosyncratic, self. He followed outbursts—which still came frequently—not with a direct apology, but with generous praise of some disassociated virtue such that the injured party escaped with dignity intact. He reserved his most ferocious epithets for the enemy. "I never hated the Hun in the last war," he told Ismay earlier in the year, "but now I hate them like . . . well, an earwig." During a luncheon at Chequers, he allowed that, "A Hun alive is a war in prospect." The parachute mines resulted in his "becoming less and less benevolent towards the Germans," noted Colville, "and talks about castrating the whole lot." Still, his loathing of the Hun in general was softened somewhat when it came to the individual soldier, sailor, or airman: When Sir Hugh Dowding advocated shooting at parachuting German pilots, Churchill disagreed, saying that parachuting pilots were "like sailors drowning at sea."[348]

He was easily brought to tears: the sight of an old Londoner poking among the smoking ruins of her home, movies great and silly, the successes—and failures—of his children, a christening, a choir in song. A good politician can harness such sensitivity to effect, and he was a master politician. No other leader on the world's stage then or since dared wring himself dry so often. Churchill could pull it off. Common citizens and peers alike, on the political left as well as on the right, viewed his displays of emotion as proof of Churchill's depth of character, never as weakness.

Partisanship had evaporated under the heat of Hitler's threat; Churchill could do no wrong. His national government, unified and resolute, transcended the politics of the past. His every word, every tear, every scowl that terrible autumn, was seen as pure Churchill to be sure, yet above politics, other than the politics of survival.

Then he accepted the leadership of the Conservative Party. Chamberlain, dying of cancer, resigned from the War Cabinet early in October, leaving the Tories leaderless. Churchill was offered the post. He accepted over the passionate protest of Clementine, who correctly predicted that by taking the leadership, her husband would alienate large numbers of voters who had looked upon him as the "voice of the nation, irrespective of party." Yet his logic in accepting it amounted to: Who else? There was nobody. It was either Churchill or someone of minimum ego, a man of such little substance he could find nourishment in Churchill's wide shadow, because Churchill already *was* the leader—of the party, of Britain, of the Empire. As well, the party chairmanship was an office his father, Lord Randolph, had aspired to but failed to attain. Churchill, by accepting, may have done so more with the vindication of his father in mind than the political consequences. Given his own turbulent relationship with the Tories over the years, accepting the party chairmanship offered him a sweet opportunity for besting his former adversaries. Just a year earlier, in a letter to Clementine, he had lambasted "these dirty Tory hacks who would like to drive me out of the Party" because he had the audacity to oppose the appeasers.[349]

Now, the opportunity presented itself to shepherd the hacks. Mary wrote that her father and mother had "several ding-dong arguments" over the issue. In the end, he took the post. Colville attached no special significance to the decision. He wrote in his diary: "The P.M. went to a meeting of the Conservative Party to accept the leadership." Churchill tried in his acceptance remarks to remove politics from a purely political office, a clever gambit doomed to failure because no outsiders were on hand to appreciate the subtlety of his rhetoric. He accepted the role as leader, he told his fellow Tories, to preserve "the greatness of Britain and her Empire and the historic certainty of our Island life.... The Conservative Party will not allow any party to excel it in the sacrifice of party interests and party feelings." It was his lone domestic political miscalculation that autumn, but it was a whopper, and brought fateful consequences almost five years later.[350]

The North Sea and the English Channel were England's faithful allies. Summer's gentle mists and mild breezes had indeed given way to the "equinoctial gales" that Churchill surmised would, if frequent and ferocious enough, keep the German invasion barges in their French ports. The Old Man was one with British sailors, who for centuries believed that the equinoxes were alone responsible for the particularly powerful seasonal weather they encountered on their worldwide travels. Fortunately for Churchill, the old myths were correct in regard to the Channel weather. But the night skies offered no respite. By late October the nightly toll of London's civilian casualties had fallen somewhat and the incidence of unexploded bombs had dropped considerably. Churchill asked Ismay whether the "easement which we feel is due to the enemy not throwing them, or to our improved methods of handling?" The answer was both. German bombers arrived each night, but the number of sorties was declining. The Luftwaffe was punching itself out. Of Hitler and his air offensive, Churchill declared, "That man's effort is flagging."[351]

London Can Take It, a British propaganda film, gave Americans a visceral look at the courage of Londoners as their city burned. By the end of November the movie had played in 12,000 U.S. theaters. Charles Lindbergh—pro-German, Anglophobe, and isolationist—opined from his Long Island estate that such heroics were no reason to support the British cause, let alone join it. Joe Kennedy was that very month advising Hollywood producers not to make any such films, as they might annoy Hitler. The Luftwaffe in late October and November pounded other British cities—Birmingham, Bristol, Sheffield, Manchester, Coventry three times, Oxford, and Southampton and its port facilities. A November Gallup poll found that only 13 percent of Londoners took shelter when the sirens wailed, although almost 16,000 now lived in the Underground and beneath railroad bridges. Those with homes simply stayed in bed when the alarm sounded, making sure to pull their comforters tight in the event the windows blew in. HMG issued citizens jars of varnish mixed with liquid rubber, with instructions to paint the mixture over windowpanes in order to prevent shards. The stuff was useless.[352]

On October 27 Churchill sent Roosevelt a message that captured Britain's declining fortunes and the growing dangers facing the Empire. It was part boosterism, part desperate appeal. Churchill told the president that the U-boat and air attacks on the Northwest Approaches—"our only remaining lifeline"—could be "repelled only by the strongest concentration of our flotillas." Yet in order to concentrate its destroyers in the approaches, the Home Fleet would have to lessen its presence in the North Sea, or reduce its destroyer presence along the south coast of England, or both. It could not be in all places at once. British food stocks were low and shipping losses were growing very worrisome, for in the last week of October, losses reached almost 160,000 tons, a figure that would have been thought a disastrous *monthly* loss the year before. Churchill told Roosevelt that much in the way of American matériel was needed for Home Island defense, and that the war would probably widen sometime in 1941 to include both Greece and Turkey, further threatening Britain's already precarious position in the eastern Mediterranean. He ended his telegram with: "The world cause is in your hands."[353]

Churchill's prediction regarding Greece proved spot-on, but his timing was off. The next day, October 28, Mussolini—without consulting Hitler—ordered eleven divisions, including the elite Alpini regiment, Italy's finest fighters, across the Albanian border, over the Epirus Mountains and into Greece. The Italians far outnumbered the Greeks, had tanks where the Greeks did not, and fielded superior artillery. But, writes historian John Keegan, Mussolini had window-dressed his army "with expensive new equipment," to the detriment of its fighting integrity. Thus, the Italians were overall weaker in arms, particularly in infantry. Infantry and machine guns made the difference in the mountain passes that tanks could not traverse. Mussolini's troops lacked something else critical to attaining victory, too: motivation. They did not share Il Duce's sense of destiny.[354]

Mussolini's motives were that he didn't much like the Greeks and sought to assert enlightened Italian influence in the Balkans, and that he craved to show Hitler that Germany was not the only great power in Europe. Mussolini's son-in-law Count Ciano had scribbled in his diary the previous November: "For Mussolini, the idea of Hitler waging war, and worse still, winning it, is altogether unbearable." The charge into Greece would show Hitler that he, Il Duce, was no *fantoccini* (puppet). A collateral benefit could be expected to accrue as well from the takeover—the occupation of Greece would provide secure bases in closer proximity to British targets in the eastern Mediterranean. Yet the Italian charge across the doorstep of Egypt had brought Mussolini within reach of the biggest prizes short of London—Alexandria, Cairo, and the Suez. To capture those trophies, he would need to send his navy into full-blown battle against the Royal Navy. With the French fleet neutralized, the Italian and British Mediterranean fleets were fairly evenly matched; the Italians in fact held the edge in submarines and capital ships, the British in aircraft carriers, of which Mussolini had none. But where Mussolini sought to avoid a climactic naval battle, Churchill, in the spirit of Nelson, *invited* a fight. Mussolini's prospects at sea appeared solid. His prospects on land appeared even more solid. In the Western Desert the Italians outnumbered Wavell's forces by almost three to one, with another 180,000 Italian troops bivouacked to the southeast in the Horn of Africa. Even were an attack on Wavell to result in a bloody stalemate, the British would be pushed to the brink.[355]

Yet Mussolini's superior numbers on the ground counted for nothing without control of the sea. The Mediterranean formed the four center squares of Mussolini's chessboard, and Churchill's. By all that was strategically sound, Mussolini should have tried to drive the British out, supported in the air by his own air forces and the Luftwaffe. But in his most disastrous decision of the war (after joining Hitler in the first place), Il Duce chose to safeguard his navy and throw his ground troops into Greece, where the Greeks let the Italians wear themselves out assaulting mountain redoubts. Hitler learned of Mussolini's strike while aboard his armored train en route to meet Il Duce in Florence. Arriving at the station, the Führer stepped from his car onto a red carpet. Mussolini strode forward, saluted, and announced, "Führer, we are on the march! Victorious Italian troops crossed the Greco-Albanian border at dawn today." They repaired to a small room, where Hitler's first words, spoken quietly as they clasped hands, were, "The whole outcome will be a military catastrophe."[356]

Churchill learned of Mussolini's gambit early on the twenty-eighth when Colville interrupted a meeting at the CWR to announce that the Italians were bombing Athens. "Then we must bomb Rome," replied Churchill. Within hours the War Cabinet authorized the bombing, with specific orders to avoid dropping any ordnance on Vatican City. "We must be careful not to bomb the Pope," Churchill told Colville, because "he has a lot of influential friends." Churchill's concern for the safeguarding of His Holiness's person had little to do with the pope's moral presence on the world stage. Churchill's view of the Papacy ran to the traditional Anglican; the pope was largely irrelevant. As British bombers made for Rome, Hugh Dalton, knowing of the woeful inaccuracy of their aim, expressed hope that the pope not be hit. Churchill replied, "I should like to tell the old man to get down into his shelter and stay there for a week." The pope may have had friends in high places, but Churchill was not one of them. Within days the Italian army in Greece learned it had no friends—divine or otherwise. Mussolini threw in reserves that brought his strength up to fifteen divisions, but in just over four weeks, the outnumbered Greeks drove the Italians back through the mountain passes, back into Albania, whence they had come. If Greece were fated to fall to the Axis powers, Germany would have to do the heavy fighting.[357]

The Greeks had a friend: Churchill. And they had a guarantee from Britain: a pledge made by Chamberlain in 1939 to step up with military help if Greek sovereignty was threatened. Given the sorry state of British military affairs, that was now an empty promise. To Churchill, however, a promise was a promise. Greek survival was at stake. That British survival was at stake as well had to be weighed against a very compelling, very English reason for keeping its promise to Greece: honor. Britain had failed the Czechs. It could not fail the Greeks. "We will give you all the help in our power," Churchill told Greek prime minister Ioannis Metaxas, who at first demurred, for fear of invoking Hitler's wrath. Only one military option was available to Churchill to meet his diplomatic obligation, to divide British forces in the Near East and send some to Greece and Crete. The rest would remain in Egypt to face down the Italian armies encamped since September at Sidi Barrani.

It was a solution that defied the most fundamental military maxim: Do not divide forces if the division results in the increased likelihood of the destruction of all forces in detail. To send part of the Egyptian command to Greece was, Eden wrote in his diary, "strategic folly." Eden, in Cairo since mid-October on a mission to assess the offensive possibilities offered there, telegraphed Churchill on November 1: "We cannot from Middle East resources send sufficient air or land reinforcements to have any decisive influence upon course of fighting in Greece." Churchill replied the next day: "Greek situation must be held to dominate other now. We are well aware of our slender resources." All three senior commanders in the Middle East—General Wavell, Admiral Cunningham, and air chief marshal Sir Arthur Longmore—shared Eden's opinion. Churchill did not. Wavell and General Dill expressed their doubts to each other but did not express them forcefully to Churchill, who thought Wavell and Dill pessimistic in any event, and chalked up any hesitancy on their parts to their natural conservatism. Yet their positions called for them to give the boss the bad with the good, regardless of the boss's reaction. They chose—after Churchill made clear his displeasure with their opinions—to hedge their bets.[358]

Churchill retired early on All Hallows Eve, felled by a stomach ailment for which Dr. Wilson prescribed castor oil, but he was out and about on November 1, and in fine fettle. Attired in his RAF uniform, he inspected a Hurricane squadron at Northolt, of which he was honorary commodore. During the ride to the base, he told Colville he was much annoyed at the Italians—several Italian pilots had been captured after being shot down over London—and planned to bomb Rome regularly as soon as he could put Wellingtons on Malta. Colville expressed hope that the Colosseum not be damaged; to which Churchill replied that it wouldn't hurt if the Colosseum had a few more bricks knocked off. He quoted from Byron's *Childe Harold's Pilgrimage:*

> *"While stands the Coliseum Rome shall stand,*
> *When falls the Coliseum Rome shall fall..."*

As they drove on, he continued his harangue against the Italians, "whose impertinence in sending bombers to attack us [Britain]," Colville said, "has much annoyed him." He expressed regret at not having studied Greek, lamented the failure of Eton and Harrow to send fighter pilots to the RAF, and predicted a smashing electoral victory for Roosevelt. He also predicted America would enter the war. He punctuated his monologue with bursts of *"Under the Spreading Chestnut Tree."* He mused on the pleasures of the game chemin de fer and the joy he found at the gaming tables of the Riviera. "I should now like," he said, "to have dinner—at Monte Carlo—and then to go and gamble!"[359]

He would soon enough go and gamble in the Mediterranean, with men and arms in the deserts of Libya, in Greece, and in the air above Malta, on Crete, and at the anchorage in Taranto, where the pride of the Italian fleet rode at anchor. Churchill was about to test his luck on several fronts at once. He should have known that to do so with any hope of success requires virtually limitless resources. His were slender; he knew it, and since May had repeatedly cabled that fact to Roosevelt. He had also rued the state of his resources in a memo that went out the day *before* Mussolini invaded Greece. It took the form of a sharp reply to his old Harrow schoolmate Leo Amery, secretary of state for India, who had proposed sending even more reinforcements to Wavell: "I regret very much," Churchill told Amery, "the use of expressions like 'gamble' when applied to the necessary precautions for the life of this country against far superior air forces." He reminded Amery that more than 70,000 troops had already sailed to Egypt; another 53,000 were due there by year's end. "It is very easy to write in a sweeping manner when one does not have to take account of resources, transport, time and distance."[360]

Yet despite his dismissive missive to Amery, and despite his understanding on a strategic level that Egypt—and only Egypt—was the hand to play, he intended to play both the Greek and Egyptian hands. The advantage to be gained in Egypt by offense was the reason that Eden had been dispatched to the Middle East in the first place—to push Wavell into deploying his reinforced army westward in order to forestall an Italian attack before the Germans wandered mightily onto the scene. Wavell had staked out a sound defensive position, but a defensive posture was, for Churchill, no posture at all. He had not sent 70,000 troops from England merely to sit and wait for the Italians. He had sent them to fight Italians, and on British terms. He did not much respect the Italian fighting man. To Colville he allowed, "The Italians are harder to catch than kill." He knew that the North African desert was the place to deal decisively with the Italians, and he had built up his forces accordingly. Then, all the plans changed—within the day—when Il Duce barged into Greece. Churchill justified the decision to help Greece by citing Britain's prewar pledge to Greece, but the decision was borne in large part by his loathing of Mussolini and the Italian soldier. He believed he could lick Il Duce in any fight, anywhere, anytime, so why not two fights at once? Thus, a few days after Il Duce's thrust, Churchill admonished Dill, "Don't forget—the maximum possible for Greece."[361]

Two days *before* the start of Mussolini's Greek crusade, Churchill, intending to take the fight only to the Italians in the desert, telegraphed concise instructions to Eden, then in Cairo, and about to depart for Khartoum: "Before leaving, you should consider searchingly with your Generals possibilities of forestalling [an Italian] offensive.... I thought their existing plans for repelling an attack by a defensive battle and counterstroke very good, but what happens if the enemy do not venture until the Germans arrive in strength? Do not send any answer to this, but go into it thoroughly and discuss it on return." Churchill, in his memoirs, writes that his memo to Eden of October 26 included the opinion, expressed clearly, "that any forestalling operation on a large scale in the Western Desert would command my keen support." Yet his memoirs fail to note his clear instructions to Eden, also contained within the memo of the twenty-sixth, to keep mum on any big plans until his return to London. Rather, in a nimble rearrangement of the history of those weeks, Churchill writes of Eden: "He was told in extreme secrecy [by Wavell, in Cairo] that a plan was being drawn up to attack the Italians in the Western Desert instead of waiting for them to open their offensive against Mersa Matruh, in Egypt. Neither he nor Wavell imparted these ideas to me or the Chiefs of Staff. General Wavell begged the Secretary of State for War not to send any telegram on this subject, but to tell us verbally about it when he got home. Thus for some weeks we remained without knowledge of the way their minds were working."[362]

Quite so, but the lack of knowledge coming out of Cairo resulted from Churchill's direct orders to Eden, cabled on the twenty-sixth. Churchill, it seems, in writing those pages of his memoirs indulged in what Mark Twain called "stretchers." Then again, he often said that history would be kind to him, because he would write it. In fact, while Eden was in Cairo with Wavell's plan in hand, Churchill, with his political obligations to Greece foremost in mind but lacking the requisite military intelligence to make a fully informed decision, committed critical resources to Greece and Crete. He ordered three squadrons of Blenheim bombers sent to Greece and two battalions of troops to Crete, to be followed by four thousand more as soon as possible in order to free a Greek division on Crete for battle at home against the Italians. Telegrams flew back and forth between London and Cairo. Eden expressed his concerns, as well as those of Wavell,

Cunningham, and Longmore. Cunningham fretted that the lack of anti-submarine protection in Souda Bay made it a dangerous place for his ships to linger. Churchill believed the proper role of warships was to seek out danger. Longmore, for his part, feared that without anti-aircraft protection or revetments, his Blenheims would be exposed while parked on airfields in Greece and Crete. Wavell sought more reinforcements for Egypt (and his planned desert offensive, which Churchill did not yet know of). Ambassador to Egypt Sir Miles Lampson cabled Eden that a diversion of forces to Greece was "completely crazy," a choice of words that brought a rebuke from Churchill. On November 3, Churchill replied to Eden: "Greece, resisting vigorously with reasonable aid from Egypt and England, might check invaders.... Trust you will grasp the situation firmly, abandoning negative and passive policies and seizing opportunity which has come into our hands. 'Safety first' is the road to ruin in war, even if you had the safety, which you have not. Send me your proposals earliest, or say you have." It was then that Eden told his diary, "It seems that Greece is now to dominate the scene. Strategic folly."[363]

Eden, back in London, finally told Churchill of Wavell's plan over dinner of oysters and champagne at the Annexe on November 8. It was an aggressive and quite possibly brilliant plan. In late September, Graziani's Tenth Army, after conducting its virtually unopposed one-week march east out of Libya, stopped at Sidi Barrani. Unmolested by the British, Graziani was unsure of what to do next. Wavell expected him to attempt to press on 75 miles to the vital railhead at Mersa Matruh, and from there the final 145 miles to Alexandria (this was why Wavell balked at sending forces to Crete and Greece). Instead, the Italians set up a line of seven fortified camps that stretched south and slightly southwest for fifty miles from the Mediterranean coast to the great Saharan escarpment. In their camps, Italian officers lived in such comfort that their tactical field guide might as well have been written by Michelin. Orderlies laid out handwoven linen tablecloths and fine porcelain, silk sheets for the officers' nocturnal ease, and cologne to refresh parched skin. Enlisted men were well supplied with canned tomatoes and pasta packaged in cheery blue boxes. Content, they took their ease in their seven forts. Had they reconnoitered the entire line, they would have divined a fifteen-mile-wide gap between their two southernmost camps. They had not. Wavell had. He and General Sir Henry Maitland "Jumbo" Wilson (he was quite a large fellow), Wavell's commander in chief of Egyptian forces, believed that they could insert their troops and tanks unseen between the camps and attack from the rear. Churchill later wrote that he was "delighted" and "purred like six cats" upon hearing the particulars of the plan, code-named Compass. It was due to kick off in early December.[364]

On the night of November 2, but for tethered barrage balloons overhead and searchlight beams stabbing into the blackness, the skies over London were empty. No German bombers came. It was the first quiet night since September 7. Since July 10, 1,300 German aircraft and 2,400 pilots and airmen had been lost over Britain—one highly trained airman lost for every six British civilians killed. These were unacceptable losses for Hitler, not only because the Luftwaffe had not beaten Britain, but because each plane lost over England meant one fewer experienced pilot and crew available for the final, deciding battle he foresaw, a battle not in the west, above London, but in the east. He had made his decision to attack Russia in July; now, on November 4, he told Lieutenant General Halder, "Everything must be done so we are ready for the final showdown." Some in the high command presumed this would be a lunge through the Dardanelles and the Bosporus (the straits) and thence through neutral Turkey to Vichy-controlled Syria, then east to the Iraqi oil fields, or south to the great prize—the Suez, there to join hands with Mussolini, if only he would attack the outnumbered British at his front. Success would eliminate Britain from the Mediterranean and slice the British Empire into isolated halves. It was the strategy demanded if crushing England was Hitler's intent. But he told Halder, "We can only go to the Straits when Russia is defeated."[365]

On the same day as Hitler looked east, Churchill's gaze was fixed westward, on the Atlantic sea-lanes, where the British merchant fleet had lost its five-hundredth ship since the start of the war, bringing shipping losses to more than two million tons, more than 10 percent of the prewar fleet. In November, for the first time in the war, fewer than one million tons of food reached Britain; the Home Office had determined the nation needed to import at least 1.2 million tons of foodstuffs per month to survive. Victory against the Heinkels over London would count for nothing if Britain were starved into submission by the U-boats. Churchill had three months earlier declared in a memo to his military chiefs that the Royal Navy could not win the war, but it could still lose it. Airpower, he had written, could win the war. His two top priorities were to bomb Germany, as heavily and often as possible, while simultaneously securing his sea-lanes. He wanted more bombers dropping more bombs more often on Germany: "The discharge of bombs on Germany is pitifully small," he wrote to Portal and Sinclair. He pulled no punches with Portal: "The first offensive object of the Royal Air Force is the delivery of bombs overseas, and particularly on

Germany. . . . It is deplorable that so few Bombers are available even on good nights." Yet, realities forced Churchill to attach more importance to the Northwest Approaches than to raining revenge upon Berlin. The supply situation was so critical, he told the Defence Committee, that "the use of naval and air bases in Eire would greatly simplify our problems, but it would be unwise to coerce Ireland until the situation was mortal." Irish neutrality, if Britain's situation became "mortal," wouldn't be worth a half-pence.[366]

All of this he contemplated on November 4, the eve of the American presidential election. Colville predicted a close contest. Churchill predicted a big win for FDR. His hunch proved correct. Roosevelt dispatched his Republican opponent, Wendell Willkie, with almost 55 percent of the popular vote and by a margin of 449–82 in the electoral college. Churchill cabled his congratulations: "I did not think it right for me as a foreigner to express my opinion upon American politics while the Election was on, but now I feel you will not mind my saying that I prayed for your success and that I am truly thankful for it." He predicted a "protracted and broadening war," a struggle "that will be remembered as long as the English language is spoken in any quarter of the globe. . . . The people of the United States have once again cast these great burdens upon you, I must avow my sure faith that the lights by which we steer will bring us all safely to anchor."[367]

Roosevelt did not reply. Perhaps Churchill's choice of "we" and "us" was presumptuous; perhaps by not replying Roosevelt sought to remind Churchill of his status as supplicant. Maybe he simply forgot. Almost three weeks later Churchill asked Lord Lothian to "find out most discreetly whether President received my personal telegram congratulating him on re-election." Those weeks spent waiting for a signal—any signal—from America brought a mixed bag of news, the most welcome of which arrived on November 12, when Churchill learned that British naval fliers had overnight smashed a good part of the Italian fleet at Taranto.[368]

The raid on Taranto, like a sucker punch, was so unexpected, so awesome in execution and results, that a reprisal in kind was out of the question. The British had done the impossible: they had torpedoed an enemy fleet in the shallowest of waters. Moreover, it was the first attack in history by carrier-based aircraft on capital ships. A Cockney newsboy captured the essence of the raid as only a street urchin can: *"Eyetalian fleet done in. No more macaroni."* Taranto, tucked into the heel of Italy, was an ideal port from which to sally forth into the central Mediterranean if, in fact, an admiral's inclination was to sally forth to fight. But Admiral Dominico Cavagnari, Italian naval chief of staff, was not so inclined; he preferred to preserve his fleet rather than fight with it. Thus, six battleships and two cruisers were among the Italian ships riding at anchor at Taranto on the night of November 11. Limited British success against Mussolini's submarines and destroyers notwithstanding, up to that night the central Mediterranean belonged to the Italians.[369]

By the morning of November 12, the sea from Gibraltar to Alexandria was once again a British lake. The Royal Navy Air Arm had carried the day with just twenty-one Fairey Swordfish torpedo bombers—steel-ribbed, canvas-skin biplanes that could summon a top speed of only 138 miles an hour. The planes were virtually obsolete but could still inflict damage if the enemy was asleep, and the Italians had been sound asleep. The Swordfish had lifted off from Britain's newest aircraft carrier, HMS *Illustrious,* at a distance of about 170 miles. They came into the anchorage low, just twenty feet above the water, in two squads, their paths marked by flares dropped from the lead planes. When the Swordfish departed, three of Italy's six battleships had settled into the mud, knocked out of commission for six months. Two cruisers were hit. It was a severe blow, and for Churchill, the best news of the autumn. "We've got some sugar for the birds this time," he quipped while on his way to the House, where he announced, "I felt it my duty to bring this glorious episode to the immediate notice of the House." The result of the raid, "while it affects decisively the balance of naval power in the Mediterranean, also carries with it reactions upon the naval situation in every quarter of the globe." Strictly speaking, he was correct. The lessons learned, or not learned, at Taranto would in just over a year affect the balance of naval power worldwide. Takeshi Naito, Japan's assistant naval attaché to Berlin, thought the raid so significant he flew to Taranto to assess the damage.[370]

Ambassador Joseph Kennedy tendered his resignation on November 6; Neville Chamberlain died on November 9, the war having overtaken and smashed the dreams of both. Kennedy was by then in the United States, infuriating Roosevelt with his public diatribes against England, against the wisdom of U.S. intervention, and even against Eleanor Roosevelt. During a weekend visit by Kennedy to Hyde Park, Roosevelt listened for several uncomfortable moments as Kennedy ranted about the injustices he had been subjected to by Washington bureaucrats. When Kennedy finished, Roosevelt asked him to step from the room for a moment. He called Eleanor in and told her: "I never want to see that son of a bitch again as long as I live." Churchill, in his memoirs, does not accord Kennedy's departure a single word.[371]

Chamberlain's departure was another matter. His bowel cancer had been diagnosed just four months earlier. He remained in the cabinet until early October, when he took to his bed after an excruciating and unsuccessful surgery. He died with sure knowledge that Great Britain, brought to this juncture in large part by himself and his government, might yet win under Churchill's defiant leadership. Churchill, with the permission of King George, had been diligent to the end in sending Chamberlain the latest intelligence reports, a generous gesture and astute, for there simply was no longer any political currency to be gained from pummeling the appeasers. Generosity, or the perception thereof, paid better dividends. Besides, the seismic crunch of every German bomb emphatically rebutted the politics of the old gang. By bringing Chamberlain and Lord Halifax into the cabinet, Churchill signaled an end to the recriminations, if not the divisions. He knew, as Lincoln had known during his great national crisis, that it is far preferable to have naysayers on the payroll—where the need to maintain the appearance of national unity precludes any naysaying—than off, and free to make mischief.

Not that any unreconstructed appeasers could any longer make much mischief. The Duke of Windsor had been shanghaied to Bahamian oblivion. Sir John Reith had been maneuvered into the transportation secretariat, where with the irony Churchill may have intended, he went nowhere. Halifax served at the Foreign Office at Churchill's pleasure. And time had run out for Chamberlain who, to his credit, left his appeasement beliefs behind when he left No. 10.

German bombs denied his parliamentary colleagues the chance to praise him a final time in the chamber where he had served for so long—those in the event who would not damn him. The Parliament buildings, prime targets located as they were alongside the Thames, were taking such a beating from the Luftwaffe that the Commons was forced to convene at Church House, the administrative headquarters of the Anglican Church in Westminster. There, on the twelfth, Churchill eulogized Chamberlain in a powerful and for the most part sincere address. Chamberlain, he told the gathered MPs, "loved peace, toiled for peace, pursued peace...even at great peril and certainly to the utter disdain of popularity or clamour." Chamberlain's reputation, Churchill said, once it was brought into resolution by the "flickering lamp" of history, would be shielded by the "rectitude and sincerity of his actions," but at the end he was "to be contradicted by events, to be disappointed in his hopes, and to be deceived and cheated by a wicked man."[372]

Yet Neville Chamberlain shifted forever the popular meaning of "appease" from "pacify" to "give in," to such an extent that to brand someone an appeaser has since been almost as venomous an accusation in British and American politics as traitor. Churchill, in his eulogy, tried to stave off the inevitable damning. It was a noble public gesture. He had earlier, however, shown the address to Clementine, who pronounced it "very good." Winston replied, "Well of course I could have done it the other way round."

The funeral took place on November 14 in the gloomy precincts of Westminster Abbey, its cold stone walls gripped by the pitchy fingers of the ancient buttresses, the entire edifice smeared by the accumulated soot of seven centuries, the color of dried blood. Inside it was frigid, German bombs having shattered numerous of its windows. Churchill and most of the War Cabinet served as pallbearers. Colville, sitting among the ushers, noted that some in attendance wore looks of disdain and boredom. Churchill was seen to cry. The exact location of the funeral had been kept secret and was divulged to Parliament just two days earlier, out of fear that the exactness of the Luftwaffe's "beam navigation" greatly increased the risk of a calamitous hit on the assembled dignitaries.[373]

That week, Churchill and Lord Lothian (who had come over from Washington) worked together on a proposal to Roosevelt for American aid with no strings attached. Churchill approved a cable from Lothian to Roosevelt that made clear Britain's needs, including help in securing three Irish ports* (if the need arose), help in safeguarding Singapore, and of course more food and more weapons. The telegram, Colville observed, "was intended to make R. feel that if we go down, the responsibility will be America's."[374]

Late on the afternoon of the fourteenth, a Thursday, Churchill and John Martin prepared for a weekend in the country at Ditchley, a safer venue than Chequers on moonlit nights. The Thursday departure—rather than Friday—came about because Churchill was to secretly meet Lothian there, to continue their discussions on securing American goods. As

* Churchill, dismayed by Irish intransigence on the use by the British of three Irish naval bases, proposed to the War Cabinet that Britain no longer subsidize Irish agricultural products and no longer risk British ships and sailors to deliver vital food supplies to Ireland. A treaty of 1922, which Churchill helped draft, gave the British the right to use the bases, but the Chamberlain government in 1939, with astounding lack of foresight with war looming, gave control back to the Irish. Churchill telegraphed his tough new stance on Ireland to Roosevelt on December 13. Churchill was ready and willing to take back the Irish ports by force. Britain, he wrote Roosevelt, would no longer help the Irish "while de Valera is quite content to sit happy and see us strangled." (C&R-TCC, 1:112–13)

Churchill was about to depart, Martin was handed a sealed and urgent message for the prime minister, which he passed to Churchill.[375]

The message contained an update on a looming Luftwaffe raid that the War Cabinet had known about for several days based on intelligence gleaned from captured German fliers and verified by Ultra decrypts. The Germans, prone to literalness in their codes, had anointed the operation "*Mondscheinsonate*" ("Moonlight Sonata"). As yet unknown to the British were the exact where and the exact when of the attack, although the interrogations of prisoners seemed to indicate London, Birmingham, or both. The Air Ministry considered the most likely time frame to be sometime between the fifteenth and the twentieth—when the moon was at its most full. The message Martin handed to Churchill contained the latest Air Ministry estimate of the target and date: London, that night.[376]

By then the wizards at the Air Ministry, having solved the problem of the German targeting beam *Knickebein,* had run up against a far more complex German navigation beam, one that ensured a type of night bombing accuracy the RAF could only wish for from its bombers, accuracy that guaranteed more destruction more often for more British cities. The Germans code-named the new beam *X-Gerat* (X-Gadget), another literal encoding, for the system worked by the intersection of radio beacons above the intended target, in the fashion of an "X." Two of *X-Gerat*'s four beams were of such high frequency that two hundred miles from transmission they were just one hundred yards wide. The final genius of *X-Gerat* was its use of two clocks that timed—to the second—the release of the bombs. The entire scheme depended upon the pilot's keeping a precise airspeed. The radioman on board the bomber, upon receiving a radio signal that his plane was ten kilometers from the target, started his clocks. At five kilometers from the target one clock stopped, and the other started backwards. Given a steady airspeed, the time taken to travel the final five kilometers would be identical to the previous five kilometers. When the time expired, the bombs were released automatically. It was accurate, and was the most efficient system yet devised to strike industrial targets. If something were to go slightly amiss and the bombs dropped a mile or so off target, houses, hospitals, schools, churches, and shelters would pay the price. *X-Gerat* therefore could hurt British production when it functioned flawlessly, and British morale when it did not.

Because the complexity and expense of the radio equipment precluded rigging the entire German air fleet with receivers, an elite unit, *Kampfgruppe 100,* was outfitted with *X-Gerat* receiving gear. By dropping flares and incendiaries precisely on targets to guide the squadrons that followed,

K-Grup 100 became the eyes of the Luftwaffe. In 1940, the epiphany that Germany could bomb at night, in almost any weather, moonlight or no, was chilling. British fighter planes flew blind after sunset. The *crack* of anti-aircraft guns brought comfort to the citizens but didn't bring down many Germans—less than 10 percent of Göring's losses to date took place at night. Britain, after dark, mustered no adequate defense. Churchill later recalled that he experienced one of the blackest moments of the war when he grasped the import of the German beam. He called it "an invisible searchlight." He tried years later to denigrate it: "German pilots followed the beam as the German people followed the Führer. They had nothing else to follow." But in 1940, both the beam and Hitler had yet to miss. The light of perverted science shone upon London, upon all England.[377]

Laymen and leaders alike considered navigation beams used for such purpose and to such terrific effect to be futuristic dark forces, ethereal conduits of death, incredible and wicked beyond all imagination. The British governing class was largely made up of Victorian gentlemen who were out of university before Marconi broadcast his first scratchy radio signals across the sea. Churchill was on the threshold of his middle years when the Wright brothers took flight. Britons lived lives where electrification was a relatively new luxury, where central heat was still a dream, and all things flying were a mystery. The wonder of radio resided not in the programming but in the sheer magic of human voices transported through the air. "I am still young enough to be amazed at hearing a voice from Washington as if it were in my own room," Harold Nicolson wrote, after listening to a speech by Roosevelt. The Luftwaffe had replaced wonder with fear.[378]

Mollie Panter-Downes was told by "experts" that the solution to the German night raiders would "be found in the air," with anti-aircraft guns, searchlights, and fighters. One measure proposed by the experts and looked upon with favor by Churchill was to drop sand from above German planes in order to foul their engines. It was never tested. Some in the London press chirped that a solution to the night raiders (top secret, *hush-hush*) had been found. It hadn't. The real solution, when perfected, Panter-Downes wrote, would dispel "the popular dream of some Wellesian or Jules Verneish machine that would intercept and cripple raiders by the pressing of a button."[379]

In fact, the real solution was just that fantastic, was indeed push-button, and became real when radar-controlled aerial interception (AI) was made workable the following year and installed on Beaufighter aircraft. Progress in jamming *X-Gerat* had been made by late autumn. But by November 14, the antidote, designated Bromide, was not yet fully formulated. That night, by the light of the hunter's moon, a British city would pay the price, but it would not be London.[380]

As Churchill neared Hyde Park, he read the message Martin had passed along. Believing the beam was on London, he ordered the car turned around and returned to the CWR. He sent the typists at No. 10 to the deep shelters at Dollis Hill. John Peck and Colville were packed off to the Down Street shelter, where they dined on caviar, old brandy and Havana cigars, and slept soundly. Churchill, pacing the CWR while awaiting the raid, grew impatient. He climbed to the Air Ministry roof, to scan the skies for the raiders.[381]

None appeared. They were on their way to Coventry, where the "Moonlight Sonata" was about to play out. More than four hundred Heinkel bombers made the run to the Midlands, led by thirteen pathfinders of *K-Grup 100*. They came in multiple waves over ten hours to drop more than six hundred tons of high explosives, parachute mines, and incendiaries. Only one German plane was lost, to accident or pilot error, perhaps to a lucky shot by an anti-aircraft battery. Many of Coventry's AA guns had been previously carted off to London. As the German bombers came over Coventry, Fighter Command put one hundred Hurricanes into the air to meet them. They scored not one hit.[382]

Coventry was destroyed by the morning of the fifteenth. The water main had ruptured; firemen stood and watched, helpless, as flames consumed almost one hundred acres in the city center. More than five hundred citizens lay dead in the rubble. Dozens of vital aircraft-component factories had been hit. They had been scattered by Beaverbrook throughout the city and beyond, a wily plan, yet one that failed to account for the new logic of the Luftwaffe, which was to assure a particular target's destruction by destroying everything nearby. The fourteenth-century cathedral was erased, but for its few walls and its spire. Gas, electricity, and water were knocked out. With no water to drink, the stunned survivors quenched their thirst with whisky and beer. Civil authorities surveying the sullen crowds feared a riot and imposed a curfew. Their concern was overwrought; the people of Coventry were too traumatized to riot. When King George arrived, many citizens were too shocked to recognize the tall stranger in their midst.[383]

Berlin declared that Coventry had been knocked out of the war and promised other cities would soon be *"Coventrated."* Yet Coventry's machine-tool production, knocked down by two-thirds, was restored within weeks. In one respect, Churchill got it as wrong as the Germans. He confided to de Gaulle that the carnage of Coventry would surely raise a "wave of indignation" among Americans and bring them nearer to war. In fact, the carnage of Coventry moved Americans to tears, but not to war, or even preparation for war.

Soon after the raid, Air Marshal Sir Philip Joubert felt the need to squelch press accounts that a solution to the German night raiders was nigh, as if the ruins of Coventry had not dissuaded the optimists. Birmingham, Southampton, Oxford, and Canterbury, throughout November and into December, took their turns in the crosshairs of *X-Gerat*. The Luftwaffe pounded the Clyde and the Mersey. Casualties in some of the attacks exceeded those of Coventry, but the government did not publish the figures, for there was no currency in broadcasting the statistics of defeat. Besides, it was not a one-way fight; the British bombed Berlin on the fourteenth and sixteenth, killing more than three hundred civilians. The bombers always got through, as Baldwin had prophesied. Months earlier, Churchill had told Beaverbrook that offensive airpower was the one "sure path to victory." He still believed that. Yet, whatever level of respect was properly due an air offense, few in late 1940 accorded much respect to the current state of *defensive* measures against nighttime raiders. The ease with which vast numbers of German bombers flew unmolested to their targets was due, Churchill said, to the "complete failure of all our methods."[384]

Mollie Panter-Downes saw Coventry as retaliation for the November 8 RAF raid over Munich, strategically not a significant target but dear, so dear, to the Nazis, home as it was of their putsch of November 8, 1923—Hitler's failed attempt to overthrow the government and establish a right-wing government. Colville speculated that the Coventry raid was in retaliation for the November 11 British success at Taranto. Neither was correct. Coventry, Munich, London, Berlin, and Taranto were all part of a murderous slugfest—take a punch, hit back, take another punch.

After Coventry, Churchill told Portal to draw up a plan "for the most destructive possible bombing attack against a selected German town." In early December, Portal outlined his recommendations, which were approved a few days later in a secret session of the War Cabinet, and code-named Abigail. Among the objectives: "We should rely largely on fires, and should choose a closely built-up town, where bomb craters in the streets would impede the firefighter." And: "Since we aimed at affecting the enemy's morale, we should attempt to destroy the greater part of a particular town. The town chosen should therefore not be too large." Mannheim, Frankfurt, and Hamburg were among the cities considered. The War Cabinet minutes end with a recommendation that no announcement be made "that this attack was being carried out by way of reprisal for the German attacks on Coventry... and no special publicity should be given to it afterwards." Hamburg, Germany's second-largest city, was eliminated from consideration as too large. The War Cabinet selected Mannheim as the target. It was hit on December 16. The results were meager, about thirty civilians killed, but Abigail and Churchill were just getting started. His goal for 1941, he told Colville, was "to bomb every Hun corner of Europe."[385]

On the last day of November, Churchill celebrated his sixty-sixth birthday at Chequers in the company of Clementine, the children, Beaverbrook, Bracken, and the American writer Virginia Cowles. It was a working birthday, the Old Man dictating his usual large volume of memos to sundry ministers, admirals, and generals. How, he asked Admiral Pound, with more American destroyers coming into service, did serviceable vessels "go down from 84 to 77"? He demanded an update on cement production, not only because cement was needed for bunkers but because he fancied the idea of huge, floating concrete gun platforms. He queried a minister as to why soldiers had been forbidden to "purchase cheap vegetables in the districts where they were quartered." And he authorized "the ringing of church bells on Christmas Day, as the imminence of invasion has greatly receded," although he counseled that steps be taken to ensure the people knew the bells were ringing for church services, not invasion.[386]

The next day, Sunday, December 1, the family repaired to the dim confines of the Ellesborough Parish Church, nearby Chequers, where "little Winston" was christened. Local parishioners stayed on after Matins to witness the ceremony, and the tears streaming down Churchill's cheeks. "Poor infant," he whispered within earshot of Virginia Cowles, "to be born into such a world as this."[387]

Harold Nicolson, believing at midsummer that he and his wife, Vita, had only three weeks to live, pledged to each other that they would carry a "bare bodkin." Yet he told his diary at the time: "I think it practically certain that the Americans will enter the war in November, and if we can last till then, all is well." Colville, too, looked toward November for salvation: "If we can hold on until November," he jotted in his diary on June 14, "we shall have won the war."[388]

It was December 1. November was safe away. They had made it that far.

Almost 4,600 more civilians had not. The Blitz had now killed more than 18,000 Britons, including 2,000 children. Yet, for all the ongoing loss, "it was plain," Churchill wrote, "that the Island would persevere to the end" for "winter with its storms had closed upon the scene."[389]

War had always been a seasonal affair. Winter, as long as men had fought wars, was the season to dig in and await spring's rains followed by the heat of summer. Then, when the roads dried, armies could resume the march and get on with the business of killing. The German invasion was surely off until spring, but modern aircraft flying above the weather rendered winter obsolete. Modern war, or at least the high-altitude aerial component, was an all-weather affair, a truth strongly suggested by the German bombs that fell from on high—and killed Britons—regardless of the meteorological conditions below. The sailing was always clear at 26,000 feet.

Any succor England and Churchill derived from foul weather was offset by the mounting disaster in the Atlantic. Britain's Northwest Approaches were in danger of being pinched shut by U-boats, which were sinking British merchant ships faster than new keels could be laid. More than 250,000 tons of British shipping went down in September, more than 300,000 tons in October, almost 376,000 tons in November, and 60,000 tons during the first week of December. One eastbound convoy from North America lost twenty-one of thirty ships. U-boat crews called these months "*Die Glückliche Zeit*" ("the happy time"). Since June, the only assistance America offered in the Atlantic battle had arrived in the guise of Roosevelt's old destroyers, which were proving more of a burden than a godsend. During a December dinner with Eden, Churchill announced that the few destroyers that had arrived "aren't much good" and were "badly built." Later in the month, he demanded the Admiralty furnish an accounting of the condition of the destroyers, "showing their many defects and the little use we have been able to make of them so far." The destroyers, dating mostly from the early 1920s, had been rendered obsolete by British improvements in destroyer design even before they were launched. The American ships were called "flush-deckers" because they lacked an elevated foredeck—a forecastle; they could not fire their forward gun in rough seas or at top speed. That did not bode well for convoy escort duty in the wild North Atlantic. They had been designed for coastal defense, Churchill explained to Roosevelt, before the era of dive-bombers. On picket duty in the North Sea, they would make "frightfully vulnerable" targets for Stukas.[390]

In any case, by December the destroyers had not arrived in meaningful numbers; only nine were fully refitted and commissioned by year's end. They dribbled into British ports, their condition deplorable, all of them in need of refitting. One, rechristened HMS *Lewes,* was such a rust bucket that it was still undergoing repairs the following April when a German bomb knocked it out of commission (not out of action, for it had seen none) until 1942. Another was in such sorry shape that it was cannibalized for spare parts. Between May and December 1940, Churchill composed at least thirty-seven memos and letters to his staff and to Roosevelt on the subject of the destroyers and their lamentable condition.[391]

The promised destroyers were not the only American goods not showing up. Modern rifles, B-17 bombers, and ammunition topped Churchill's shopping list. "What is being done," he queried Halifax, "about our 20 motor torpedo-boats, the 5 PBY [patrol bombers], the 150–200 aircraft, and the 250,000 rifles.... I consider we were promised all the above, and more too." Remember, he told Halifax, "Beg while the iron is hot." Sir Alexander Cadogan, on Churchill's orders, rang up Ambassador Lothian with the same question: "What is the status of the 'other desiderata' promised to us?" Lothian told Cadogan that the U.S. attorney general had held up the torpedo boats until at least January 1941, and that only *one* B-17 was ready to wing its way to Britain.[392]

Churchill was fed up. He told Hugh Dalton that he was tempted to simply tell Roosevelt, "If you want to watch us fighting for your liberties, you must pay for the performance." The Prof egged him on: "The fruits of victory which Roosevelt offers seem to be safety for America and virtual starvation for us." Always ready with a statistic, the Prof tossed more fuel onto the fire: "We are putting between 1/3 and one-half of our national effort into fighting Nazidom." The American contribution so far—sold, not given—was "about 1/20 of the annual American national effort." The Americans, Lindemann reminded Churchill, had from an accounting standpoint long ago written off the old destroyers, which were not even carried as assets on the U.S. books. These were hard facts to digest, given that the price England had paid for the fifty rust buckets took the form of British naval bases from Newfoundland to British Guiana, bases that American warships now sailed from in order to protect... America.[393]

Churchill peeled away pieces of the British Empire in exchange for obsolete boats. The Atlantic bases were the first to go, the first installment in the transfer of global supremacy from Britain to America. At the time, nobody, Churchill included, saw it quite that way. Indeed, he tried to frame the deal in terms of British largess when he told Parliament:

> Some months ago we came to the conclusion that the interests of the United States and of the British Empire both required that the United States should have facilities for the naval and air defense of the western hemisphere... [and] had decided spontaneously, and without being asked or offered any inducement... to place such defense facilities at their disposal.... There is of course no question of any transference of sovereignty."[394]

In fact, British sovereignty as measured in pence, shillings, and gold sovereigns was fast disappearing. Since the start of the war, Britain had paid almost $4.5 billion in cash (about $160 billion in modern dollars) for American food and matériel. The United Kingdom's total remaining reserves of gold and dollar-denominated marketable securities was less than $2 billion, a sum accumulated since the start of the war mostly by exporting pottery, Scotch whisky, and South African gold. Yet Britain's immediate needs would cost twice that, a ratio that would not necessarily have proven disastrous in peacetime, but the U.S. terms of sale were cash-and-carry. Britain desperately lacked the cash to buy, and needed more ships in which to carry. "It was a time," Churchill wrote, "marked by an acute stringency in dollars." Lord Lothian summed up the situation when, with decidedly nondiplomatic clarity, he told Washington reporters: "Britain's broke." Roosevelt offered to send a cruiser to Cape Town in order to pick up and deliver to the United States $20 million in British gold bullion as a down payment for services rendered, an offer akin to a noncombatant lifting the boots and pocket watch from a dying trooper.[395]

Churchill's weekend meeting with Lothian in mid-November resulted in the framework of a plan to address the supply and money questions, which Churchill worked into a long letter to Roosevelt. The letter, containing nineteen sections and which Churchill called "one of the most important I ever wrote," went out on December 7. In essence, he told the president, it all came down to two things: control of the seas, a battle Britain was losing; and money, of which Britain had almost none.[396]

Churchill addressed the worldwide strategic situation for 1941 in the first sixteen sections of his letter. Absent is any sign of his previous fawning or pleading; this letter was straightforward and powerful. He was polite, yet firm. On the "mortal danger" of shipping losses, Churchill wrote: "Would this diminution continue at this rate it would be fatal.... In fact we have now only one effective route of entry to the British Isles... against which the enemy is increasingly concentrating." To combat that threat, he asked for "a gift, loan or supply of American vessels of war."[397]

Such was his concern that the Germans might either charm or shoot their way into Irish ports, he dangled before Roosevelt the prospect of a united Ireland. "It is not possible for us to compel the people of Northern Ireland against their will to leave the United Kingdom and join southern Ireland," he wrote, "but I do not doubt that if the Government of Eire would show its solidarity with the democracies of the English-speaking world at this crisis, a Council for the Defense of all Ireland could be set up out of which the unity of the Island could probably in some form or another emerge after the war." Given that a large portion of Roosevelt's voter base consisted of Irish-Americans, this was a rumination that would play well in America, but wreak havoc in Belfast were it revealed. Churchill, more concerned with American sensibilities than those of Ulstermen, sent Minister of Health Malcolm MacDonald to Dublin three times to offer Prime Minister Eamon de Valera a united Ireland, if de Valera joined Britain against Germany. MacDonald, as Chamberlain's Dominions secretary, had negotiated a trade agreement with Ireland in 1938. Churchill despised the treaty but thought MacDonald might be an Englishman the Irish could work with. He was not. Three times de Valera declined MacDonald's approaches, arguing that Churchill could not deliver on the promise even were he so inclined. Later in the year, when MacDonald was made High Commissioner to Canada, the back-channel dialogue ceased.[398]

In his letter to Roosevelt, Churchill moved on to the possibility of Japan's grabbing the oil of the Dutch East Indies. There wasn't much to say on the matter, and he said it quite forthrightly: "We have to-day no forces in the Far East capable of dealing with this situation should it develop." Then, to point number seventeen: money. Churchill let loose. It was clear, he wrote, that the more rapidly the United States fulfilled Britain's needs, the sooner Britain's finances would collapse, until, "we shall no longer be able to pay cash for shipping and other supplies.... It would be wrong in principle...if, at the height of this struggle, Great Britain were divested of all saleable assets, such that after the victory was won with our blood, civilization saved...we should stand stripped to the bone." Reduced to its essence, the letter is more a moral argument than a financial plea. Churchill closed by telling—not asking—Roosevelt to "regard this letter not as an appeal for aid, but as a statement of the minimum action necessary to achieve our common goals."[399]

Roosevelt had a great deal to chew on. He received Churchill's letter while aboard the cruiser *Tuscaloosa* on a two-week vacation in the Caribbean, which included stops at some of America's new (and Britain's former) naval bases. As later related by Churchill, his "great friend" read and re-read the letter, "as he sat alone in his deck chair, and that for two days he did not seem to reach any conclusion. He was plunged in intense thought and brooded silently." The brooding may have been a result of what Churchill made clear in his letter: Britain vanquished would leave the United States alone and unprepared for war, swayed by the isolationists into a mortally dangerous neutrality that could result in a U.S. accommodation with Hitler, a brokered peace both fatal and without honor.[400]

To avoid that outcome, Roosevelt had to find a way to help America's proxy before the proxy went broke, or worse. He had been contemplating a possible solution to the problem for several months, urged on by his interior secretary, Harold Ickes, who had told him in an August letter that it would not reflect well on America if "Britain went down" and America had not sent destroyers to prevent an invasion. Ickes added a homey analogy: "It seems to me that we Americans are like the householder who refuses to lend or sell his fire extinguisher to help out the fire in the home that is next door, although the house is all ablaze and the wind is blowing from that direction." By the time Roosevelt arrived back in Washington from his Caribbean vacation, he thought he had found his legal basis for funneling aid to Britain. It came by way of an obscure federal law that allowed the U.S. military to *lease* property not required for public use. On December 17—without offering any details of what he was pondering—Roosevelt told reporters (for the purpose of publication but without naming the source) of his struggle to find a way to help Britain. He told them, "What I am trying to do is to eliminate the dollar sign." Then he offered a variation on Ickes's parable: "Suppose my neighbor's house is on fire and I have a length of garden hose four or five hundred feet away. If he can take my garden hose and connect it up to his hydrant, I may help him to put out the fire.... I don't say to him...'Neighbor, my garden hose cost me fifteen dollars; you have to pay me fifteen dollars for it.' No!...I want my garden hose back after the fire is over." A reporter asked, "Mr. President, before you loan your hose to your neighbor you have to have the hose." The reporter went on to point out that if British orders for goods could be met only by second and third shifts at American factories, no federal authority was in place to mandate that factories add those shifts. They were fair points; America could not help Britain while running on one shift. Roosevelt avoided mention of the fact that the neighbor in this case needed not only the hose but an army of firemen as well.[401]

On December 12, Lord Lothian, who had been instrumental for more than a year in pleading Britain's case to Americans, died suddenly in Washington. When taken ill, Lothian, a Christian Scientist, refused medical attention. "What a monstrous thing," Churchill exclaimed, "that Lothian should not have allowed a doctor to be called." Lothian's death, coming the very week Roosevelt was pondering Churchill's letter, created a political vacuum in Washington at the worst possible moment. Churchill needed to appoint a new ambassador, and fast. He liked Lloyd George for the job, but only, he told Colville, "if he could trust him." Were Lloyd George to prove disloyal, Churchill added, "he could always sack him." But the ambassadorship would place the former prime minister under Halifax, which Colville argued "would be an obstacle from L.G.'s point of view." On the other hand, if Halifax went to Washington, yet another former appeaser would have been exiled. Churchill drafted Halifax. "His high character was everywhere respected," Churchill later wrote, "yet at the same time his record in the years before the war and the way in which events had moved left him exposed to much disapprobation and even hostility from the Labour side of our National Coalition." Churchill told Colville that if Halifax remained in Britain he "would never live down the reputation for appeasement" and that he "had no future in this country." Without the United States in the war, Churchill told him, the very best

Britain could hope for was an unsatisfactory peace and that he, Halifax, "had a glorious future in America" if he proved successful in getting the United States in.[402]

In the final weeks of the year, while Roosevelt pondered his congressional strategy, Churchill could not do much more than watch as London burned, and ponder two questions: What exactly were the Americans going to do and when? And where was Hitler going to go and when? Spain and Gibraltar had been a source of angst for months. Ultra recently divined a German operation code-named Felix, about which nothing was known beyond the name. Churchill thought Felix might entail a strike into Ireland or Spain. He thought Spain more likely, he told Colville, because that's where he would go if he were Hitler. That is exactly where Hitler sought to go, but Franco, in power largely through the sponsorship of Hitler and Mussolini, demurred. If Gibraltar was to be taken, Franco told Hitler, it would be taken by Spanish troops, not by a coalition of Germans and Spanish.[403]

In fact, the *generalissimo* had no intention of attacking Gibraltar. Spaniards were kept alive by food imports that Britain allowed to arrive only because Spain remained neutral. Franco understood that were he to allow Germans passage to Gibraltar, London would starve Spain by blockade. Thus, despite his debt to Hitler, he thought it best to forestall Hitler's call to arms. In fact, he thought it best to sit this war out. Churchill, in late November, had telegrammed a warning to Roosevelt about the danger of losing Gibraltar and suggested that Roosevelt offer Franco "food month by month so long as they keep out of the war." If Gibraltar were lost, Churchill told Roosevelt, it "would be a grievous addition to our naval strain, already severe."[404]

Gibraltar corked would trap the entire British Mediterranean fleet in the bottle, but only if the Suez Canal was corked as well. Franco, wily and possessed of a sense of global strategy that Hitler lacked, told the Führer that if Germany took the Suez Canal, Spain would then take Gibraltar. The German grand admiral Raeder, who understood very well the centricity of naval power to Britain's status as a world power, had long grasped the importance of the Suez to London, and had tried in September to convince Hitler to pursue the same strategy. Taking Gibraltar *and* the Suez, Raeder argued, would open pathways to the Middle East and make "doubtful whether an advance against Russia from the north will be necessary." Churchill did not know that on the thirteenth of December, Hitler had canceled Felix, or that on December 18, he had signed a directive that began: "The German armed forces must be prepared to crush Soviet Russia in a quick campaign before the end of the war against Britain." Preparations were to be completed by May 15. The operation was code-named Barbarossa.[405]

Churchill later wrote that when the Germans massed on the French and Belgian frontiers in May of 1940, and then cascaded across, he grasped that "we were about to learn what total war means." Indeed, total war had come to France, and was being waged in the Atlantic, and in the skies over England. But in December 1940, the status of life in much of continental Europe—and in Manchuria and the Horn of Africa—was more of a gruesome peace brokered by bayonet than total war.

Stalin, having the previous year partnered with Hitler in the obliteration of Poland, was digesting his Baltic, Finnish, and Romanian territorial takeovers. In December, Stalin's most trusted lieutenant, Soviet foreign minister Molotov, returned from Berlin after negotiations with Ribbentrop over how best to share the spoils, including the carcass of the British Empire. Churchill called Molotov "a man of outstanding ability and cold-blooded ruthlessness" whose very survival within the Bolshevik world of lies, insults, intrigue, and the always present threat of "personal liquidation" fitted him out "to be an agent and instrument" of a leader such as Stalin. Yet in Hitler, Stalin and Molotov encountered a better liar and a more ruthless, more cold-blooded intriguer. Though in December Hitler faced his armies to the west, his vision had already turned to the east.[406]

In the Far East, the Japanese had begun the tenth year of their Manchurian depredations, enslaving the populace in the name of pan-Asian solidarity. "China," Churchill wrote in 1937, "is being eaten by Japan like an artichoke, leaf by leaf." Now, the fourth year of the Sino-Japanese war found a frontline stalemate between Chinese general Chiang Kai-shek's nationalist troops and Japanese general Hideki Tojo's invading armies. Behind the Japanese lines, 400,000 of Mao Zedong's Communist troops were making the emperor pay dearly for Chinese real estate. Japan's moderate prime minister, Prince Fumimaro Konoye, found himself trying to appease Tojo's war party, which believed in purchasing empire by brute force. If Konoye emerged from the political intrigue with more power, the greater Pacific region might yet live in peace. If Tojo proved stronger, a pan-Pacific war was most certainly inevitable, though Churchill stuck to his long-held premise that Japan would think twice before mixing it up with a power as mighty as Great Britain.[407]

Germany, Japan, and Italy had signed the Tripartite Pact in Berlin, on September 27, which pledged support for any signatory who was attacked by a power not already at war with the signatories. By doing so, the Axis arrayed itself against the rest of the world. Churchill later wrote that the agreement "opened wider fields," but the Tripartite Pact posed a conundrum for Churchill concerning the Burma Road. The road wound seven hundred tortuous miles from Lashio, a Burmese railhead four hundred miles north of Rangoon, to Kunming, in Yunnan Province, China, and was absolutely vital to the supply of Chiang Kai-shek's Chinese nationalist army. The British had closed it in August, Alec Cadogan wrote, in an agreement with Japan that "special efforts be made to produce a lasting peace in the Far East." Japan had made no such effort, special or otherwise, because Japan was dealing from strength. The Imperial Japanese army and navy, fueled in large part by the importation of seven million barrels a year of American oil, could go anywhere they pleased in order to make good on their threats. Nearly three months later, in October, the Burma Road was reopened, but the question was, how would Japan react? If Tokyo responded with force, what would Italy and Germany do? Attack England (again)? And what would America do?[408]

With those questions in mind, and with no military means available to dissuade the Japanese from mischief, Churchill cabled Roosevelt and asked for a bit of show-the-flagmanship in the Pacific, a friendly visit by an American naval squadron—"the bigger the better"—to Singapore, to help persuade the Japanese to behave. That such a display of American sea power might provoke the Japanese to a warlike response against the Americans certainly occurred to Churchill, because he understood the true intent of the Tripartite Pact. *Not already at war* was the key concept of the pact, unmasking it as a transparent attempt by the Axis to forestall intervention by the only nation of import not yet at war: the United States. As Churchill saw it, an American fleet cruising menacingly across the Japanese sea routes to Malayan rubber and Indonesian oil might be just the ticket to get the United States into the war. The U.S. fleet made no such foray.[409]

The United States all year had been in no mood for handling any hot potatoes tossed its way by Churchill. Navy chief admiral Harold ("Betty") Stark wanted to keep his ships safe at Pearl Harbor, not send them traipsing about the Singapore Strait in support of Churchill's empire. Even if willing, America wasn't ready. The United States was still struggling out of the Depression, half aware of the coming storm and not half prepared to deal with it. America was willingly isolated in a state of blissful peace, the blush of renewed economic prosperity on the horizon. No mere three-way Axis deal could keep America out of war if that peace was disturbed; nor could Churchill's pleas bring America into it if it was not. America was not entirely oblivious to far-flung events, or at least European events. The most listened-to broadcast of 1940 had been Roosevelt's "dagger in the back" speech. Millions of Italian-Americans still thought Il Duce a stand-up guy. Americans knew old Europe, from where their parents had come, but the

Pacific was another story. Dozens of islands—Guam, Corregidor, Wake, Midway, Guadalcanal—were terra incognita to most Americans. Not until the final weeks of 1941 would they—and most Britons—know just where Pearl Harbor was located.[410]

America was re-arming, after a fashion. With an eye toward strengthening its global presence, the U.S. Navy (at 160,000 officers and men, smaller than both the Italian and German navies) ordered eight new aircraft carriers. Delivery was specified for 1945. The army, an anemic force of 500,000 (if the National Guard was included) field-tested its tough new General Purpose vehicle, GP for short. The GOP's nomination of Wendell Willkie, rather than the isolationist Robert Taft, to run against Roosevelt had sent a subtle message to the world that neither American political party had completely buried its head in the sands of isolation. Roosevelt signed into law America's first peacetime draft bill, a call-up of 800,000 men to serve for one year. Without once using the word "draft" when announcing the law, he termed it the revival of "the three-hundred-year-old American custom of the muster." If his ongoing pledges that American boys would not be fighting in any overseas wars was to be taken at face value, an obvious question arose: Where in the world *would* 800,000 mustered men serve?[411]

Since May, Churchill had wrangled, pestered, and beseeched Roosevelt to join him in his battle for Britain's survival, without success. His missives to Roosevelt were, on the surface, full of facts and figures concerning British air and sea losses, arms production, and finances, yet, with the exception of his long December 7 letter, they are similar in voice to the letters that nine-year-old Winston wrote from St. George's School, seeking the approval of his mother and father. Churchill recalled that, as a boy, his father seemed to him "to own the key to everything or almost everything worth having." Roosevelt held that key in 1940.[412]

Churchill had gained the heights of power only to gaze down upon a nation at its military nadir. He was the defender of a realm that quite possibly would soon prove defenseless. RAF successes against Göring—limited and by no means guaranteed to continue—served up a meager and teasing hope of future victory. These were the months about which Churchill later wrote that it was "equally good to live or die." During those December days, a prediction Churchill made after witnessing the French disaster seemed as likely to be fulfilled as not: in mid-June, on his last flight from France, he had turned to Ismay and asked, "Do you realize we probably have a maximum of three months to live?" Those three months were now coming up on six, but absent an ally, the months gained were simply a stay of execution. Britain's finest hour had given way to its longest nights. The Germans had not arrived by sea, but when the Channel calmed in April and May, when the lilacs announced the coming of spring—and

Hitlerwetter—surely the Germans would come. Yet, as he had since June, Churchill believed that if the Germans came, they would fail.[413]

On December 6, from the North African desert, came news that a British imperial army was on the march, and, unlike the BEF in June, this army was marching forward. Just after midnight, Operation Compass—Wavell's plan to push the Italians out of western Egypt—began when British troops, tanks, and trucks departed Mersa Matruh and headed west, toward the seven Italian camps anchored at Sidi Barrani, seventy-five miles and a two-day march distant. Mersa Matruh, an azure sea to its front, stone cliffs rising around the town on the landward sides, had been an active port and sponge-fishing center since before the Greeks first came to Cyrene (modern Libya) almost twenty-six centuries earlier. It was from here in around 500 BCE that the Persian forces of Cambyses II turned into the desert, in search of the oasis of Siwa, about two hundred miles south, and the first stop on the ancient caravan route to the Sudan. Cambyses and his entire army disappeared somewhere in the desert, perhaps in the great Sand Sea to the southwest, perhaps in the Qattara Depression, an enormous and lifeless bed of salt and sand fifty miles wide, two hundred miles long, and, at more than four hundred feet below sea level, one of the most hellish geographical features on the planet. Alexander the Great, also in search of Siwa, followed the route of Cambyses in 331 BCE. After nearly meeting the Persians' fate, the Macedonian finally made it to the oasis, where the oracle of Zeus Ammon confirmed that the young warrior was indeed of divine ancestry. Alexander departed, sure of his destiny, and conquered the world. Three centuries later, the divine Cleopatra and her lover Anthony favored Mersa Matruh (then named Paraetonium) for frolics in the surf, and elsewhere.

Mersa Matruh was tethered to Alexandria by a small-gauge railroad that snaked 150 miles alongside the same coastal road Alexander had marched on. The British could therefore supply themselves, but the Italian supply lines, though secure, reached back hundreds of miles. That (and the array of their forts) was their weakness. The plan called for the British field commander Lieutenant General Richard O'Connor to move his Western Desert Force—30,000 men supported by six hundred Bren Gun carriers, and scores of light and heavy tanks—undetected from Mersa Matruh to Sidi Barrani. In the tradition of the Saracens, who had learned a millennium earlier the need to live by the desert's rules or die by them, fuel and water had been secreted in cisterns along the route. O'Connor's tanks and men would drink their fill on the two-day journey west. Then, upon reaching the Italian camps, O'Connor's plan called for his armor and troops to insinuate themselves unseen and unheard (not likely in the emptiness of the desert) behind the gap between camp Nibeiwa and camps Sofafi and Rabia. O'Connor then intended to run his tanks and infantry smack into the exposed flanks and rear of the Italians, a most daring maneuver given that O'Connor's forces were outnumbered by almost three to one.

Traditionally, an entrenched defensive force equal in numbers to an attacking force is judged to hold an effective advantage of at least three to one over the attackers. O'Connor's army of 30,000 was, in that sense, at a nine-to-one disadvantage, or would have been had the Italians been facing in the right direction. To the west of Sidi Barrani, almost 150,000 more Italian troops waited in northern Libya. However complete O'Connor's surprise, if a division or two of the Italian forces in Libya drove to the aid of Sidi Barrani, O'Connor's imputed numerical disadvantage could run to nearly twelve to one. He was placing his army in a nutcracker in hopes that the nut would shatter the cracker. With a little overreaching and a bit of bad luck, his army might find a place in military history alongside Custer's 7th Cavalry at Little Bighorn, the Light Brigade at Balaclava, and the Anzacs* at Gallipoli.

Distance was O'Connor's other enemy. Once he motored out of Mersa Matruh, each mile thereafter stretched his supply lines. Were he to find success at Sidi Barrani and thrust westward, he faced nothing but emptiness. Libya spanned one thousand miles of desert except for a narrow strip along the coast where a single road twisted from Bardia in the east to Tripoli in the west. The country was a sea of sand and flaked stone, without roads, devoid of vegetation, bereft of any landscape features that afforded troops protection. The Italians in Libya were linked to Italy by secure seaborne supply lines, and thus the cologne, silk bedsheets, and fine cutlery. O'Connor's force found itself alone in the desert, a true expeditionary unit, fully detached from all that sustained it.

Wavell and O'Connor knew how to fight in the desert, whereas apparently the Italians knew only how to camp there. The British understood that desert warfare was a fluid thing, with mobility the key. Destruction of enemy forces was more important than possession of turf, which could no more be held in the desert than could a patch of water in the open ocean. Wavell's immediate goal was not to sail O'Connor's army across the wide

* Although the Australians and New Zealanders ("Anzacs," for Australian New Zealand Army Corps) were not configured as a corps during World War Two, the term "Anzac" stuck, and was used in reference to units of those nations deployed in any theater or operation.

sand seas of Libya, but simply to smash up the Italians at Sidi Barrani and, if things went well, to raid twenty-five miles farther to the west, to Buq Buq. To pull that off, the British would need stealth, great good luck, total surprise, and an enemy with scant fighting will.

They got all four. During the night of December 8 and early hours of the ninth, O'Connor's infantry and supporting Matilda tanks threaded their way between Nibeiwa and the two southernmost Italian forts. To guide their movement, a British advance force had lit a string of beacons crafted from oil drums with one side peeled away, that side facing east, to be seen by O'Connor's troops but not by the Italians. The British had been spotted by an Italian flier, but when he gave his initial (verbal) report, he was told to put it in writing. If he did so, it was either ignored or not read. By 2:00 A.M. on the ninth, O'Connor's force was in place behind Nibeiwa. It was a true imperial army made up of Englishmen, Hindus, Sikhs, Ulstermen, and Highlanders, with New Zealanders manning the troop transports. Two regiments of Matilda tanks were drawn up, ready to support the infantry. This was what the twenty-six-ton monsters had been built for. Virtual castles on steel treads, their two-pound guns could outshoot Italian light tanks while giving cover to the imperial infantry. After a breakfast of bacon, hot tea, and a shot of rum for the road, O'Connor's men moved out. From the Italian camps the breeze carried the aromas of cooking fires and fresh coffee and hot rolls.[414]

The British interrupted breakfast. The pipers of the Cameron Highlanders sounded the charge, the keening of their pipes reaching Nibeiwa as the first rounds from the Matildas smashed into the Italian lines. The tanks came on in ranks, flanked by Bren Gun carriers, their heavy machine guns raking the Italians. Charging pell-mell behind the tanks came the Highlanders, the morning sun bright upon their helmets and bayonets. The Italians fought furiously with machine guns and grenades; General Pietro Maletti burst from his tent, shooting, and was immediately shot dead. Twenty Italian light tanks were reduced to piles of smoking steel by the Matildas, which rolled on, crushing defenders under their treads. It was over in less than three hours, the camp destroyed, more than two thousand prisoners taken. Ten miles north, two more camps waited. The 1st Royal Fusiliers, kicking a soccer ball, led the charge. White flags went up in the Italian camps. The commander of one stood five hundred of his men at attention when the British entered to accept his surrender.

O'Connor's men and tanks rolled onward for two days, north toward Sidi Barrani. By December 12, the entire line of fortifications was swept away, and Sidi Barrani taken, after being shelled to rubble by Matildas and Royal Navy cruisers. The success was so stunning and unexpected that the British found themselves outnumbered by their 39,000 prisoners. One battalion commander radioed that he had captured "five acres of officers, about 200 acres of other ranks." Churchill, delighting in the early reports, referred to the Greek general battling the Italians when he told Colville, "So, we shan't have to make use of General Papagos after all!" He phoned the King: "My humble congratulations to you, Sir, on a great British victory, a great Imperial victory." It was, wrote Colville, "the first time since the war began that we have really been able to make use of the word victory."[415]

O'Connor thrust farther west to Buq Buq, where the original plan called for the raid to end. Wavell, in Cairo, received a message: "We have arrived at the second B in Buq Buq." O'Connor rolled right through, bagging more prisoners. The Italians were on the run, in full flight to Libya. Mussolini was furious. "Five generals are prisoners and one is dead," he told Ciano. "This is the percentage of Italians who have military characteristics and those who have none."[416]

Before Compass kicked off, Churchill had worried to Dill that Wavell might be "playing small" by not "hurling in his full available forces." Within a week of launching his operation, Wavell—shy, tongue-tied Wavell—considered just months earlier by Churchill to be somewhat "dumb," became his hero of the hour. Churchill learned that Wavell had written two books; knowing neither the titles nor the subject matter, he ordered Colville to locate the volumes. It seems the reticent Wavell was a poet, historian, and biographer as well as a fighter. He had penned *The Palestine Campaigns* in 1928 and had just published his latest work, *Allenby*, in which he recounted how Field Marshal Viscount Allenby accomplished in Palestine during the Great War what no other British general in that war could bring off: the total destruction of the enemy at his front with minimum loss to his own men. Wavell had served under Allenby in the Middle East and shared that field marshal's philosophy of leadership: trust subordinates, give them clear orders, and allow them to fill them. Display courage, moral and physical, where called for, not for love of danger but because hard work is to be done. This was the sort of stuff Churchill admired, admitting as it did to a larger view of things, a certain bon ton that would fit in well at his dinner table, as a foil of course for his even larger view of things.[417]

By December 16, O'Connor was across the Libyan border. Churchill cabled Wavell: "Your first objective now must be to maul the Italian Army and rip them off the African shore to the utmost possible extent." His message to Wavell on the eighteenth dispensed with literalness altogether, reading in its entirety, "St. Matthew, Chapter 7, Verse 7." ("Ask, and it shall be given to you; seek, and ye shall find; knock, and it shall be opened unto you.") Churchill had risked all by sending men and tanks from Britain to Egypt when invasion appeared imminent. He had gambled, and so far had won.[418]

The Blitz grew more murderous as the year went out. On December 8 the House of Commons was hit. The next day, Henry "Chips" Channon* wandered upon the scene as Churchill rambled among the rubble. "Suddenly I came upon Winston Churchill wearing a fur-collared coat, and smoking a cigar.... 'It's horrible,' he remarked... and I saw he was much moved, for he loves Westminster." Channon, surveying the smoking ruins of the ancient building, remarked, "They would hit the best bit." Churchill, chewing on his cigar, grunted, "Where Cromwell signed King Charles's death warrant." That night Channon wrote that he had "sensed the historical significance of the scene—Winston surveying the destruction he had long predicted, of a place he loved."[419]

London had seen more than 450 raids between September and late December; the bombs sometimes fell at the rate of one hundred per minute. On December 29 the capital sustained its worst beating. It was Sunday, the preferred day for bombing commercial areas, when warehouses full of combustible goods were locked tight for the weekend, with no employees on duty to snuff out the incendiaries. The new moon promised relief for the raiders, and in tandem with the recent solstice, it made for a low tide that brought the Thames down to the level of a stream. High cloud cover and a heavy mist favored the raiders. *K-Grup 100* leading the way in specially equipped Heinkels lifted off from the squadron's base in Brittany at about 5:30 P.M. local time, an hour later than London time. Once airborne, they picked up the main *X-Gerat* radio beam, broadcast from Cherbourg. The beam was on St. Paul's. Behind the pathfinders came more than two hundred bombers, from bases all over northern France. The raid lasted only two hours, but the incendiaries did their work. The first flight of *K-Grup 100* missed its target by one thousand yards, putting its incendiaries on the south side of the Thames, near Elephant and Castle. Somehow the remainder of the fleet missed the pathfinders' markers and put their bombs square on the designated target, the City (London's financial district), with the result that fires raged along both banks of the river. In fact, even the river burned.[420]

Edward R. Murrow, on the roof of the BBC, opened his broadcast:

---

* Channon (1897–1958), American by birth, was elected the Conservative MP for Southend in 1935. According to Jock Colville, Sir Henry was "a leading light in London café society," a friend of Lady Cunard's and R. A. Butler's. He wrote with elegance and deployed a sharp wit.

"Tonight the bombers of the German Reich hit London where it hurts the most, in her heart. St. Paul's Cathedral, built by Sir Christopher Wren, her great dome towering over the capital of the Empire, is burning to the ground as I talk to you now." But St. Paul's, wrapped in a cowl of filthy black smoke, was not burning. As Murrow spoke, a few fire wardens scrambling among the ancient joists under the lead roof of the cathedral managed to stay ahead of the firebombs.[421]

Other precincts fared worse. The Germans dropped "Molotov breadbaskets," containers that spit out dozens of incendiaries as they fell. The Guildhall went down, and eight of Wren's churches. Paternoster Row disappeared, the publishers and bookbinders done in—as they had been in the Great Fire of 1666—by their stockpiles of glue and paper. Among the lost and irreplaceable treasures: William the Conqueror's eleventh-century parchment charter granting London its freedom. More than a thousand fires started in the East End, always the recipient of ordnance when the Germans released their bombs thirty seconds too soon. Fire wardens, silhouetted by the whipping flames and the glow of exploding incendiaries, scrambled along smashed rooftops, while firemen below scrambled as walls collapsed. The fires burned for two days. Across the river, in Southwark, firemen ran hoses out hundreds of feet onto the mudflats of the Thames, only to watch them melt. "Poor old" London, Harold Nicolson wrote, "is a char woman among capitals, and when her teeth begin to fall out she looks ill indeed." When Churchill and Clementine toured the wreckage the next day, an old woman approached and asked when the war would end. Churchill turned to her and replied, without a smile: "When we have beaten them."[422]

While London burned into the early hours of December 30, Americans gathered around radios as Franklin Roosevelt chatted from his fireside about the state of the world. He stressed the need to safeguard the Atlantic Ocean by supporting Britain, and the need, ultimately, to help Britain defeat the Nazis. Aware that many voters of Irish and Italian ancestry might find aiding Britain an unpalatable prospect, he predicted that both Ireland and Italy—the former neutral, the latter "forced to become accomplices of the Nazis"—would sooner or later be enslaved by Nazi Germany. In Asia the Chinese were putting up a "great defense" against the Japanese. Then, as if to say "enough said," he added a phrase long since forgotten: "In the Pacific is our fleet." The danger as he saw it lay in Europe, where the British fought alone, and to the British must go material support.

The plan went like this: "As planes and ships and guns and shells are produced, your Government, with its defense experts, can then determine how best to use them to defend this hemisphere.... We must be the great arsenal of democracy.... There will be no 'bottlenecks' in our determination to aid Great Britain.... Their strength is growing. It is the strength of men and women who value their freedom more highly than they value their lives."[423]

The phrase "arsenal of democracy" would long be remembered on both sides of the sea. These were defiant words, reassuring and full of promise, but what did they mean in terms of Britain's inability to pay? "No bottlenecks"? Was not Britain's lack of specie a bottleneck? Roosevelt had also declared his intention to "eliminate the dollar sign" but had offered no specifics on how to do so. On the final day of the year, Churchill telegraphed his appreciation to Roosevelt for "all you said yesterday... especially the outline of your plans giving us the aid without which Hitlerism cannot be extirpated from Europe and Asia." He omitted a line he had written in a draft: "Remember Mr. President, we do not know what you have in mind, or exactly what the United States is going to do, and we are fighting for our lives."[424]

Churchill and Britons had survived to the end of what he called "the most splendid, as it was the most deadly, year in our long English and British story." It was a year, he later wrote, that surpassed the year of the Spanish Armada, Marlborough's campaigns, Nelson's victories against Napoleon, even the entirety of the Great War. During 1940, "this small and ancient Island... had proved itself capable of bearing the whole impact and weight of world destiny." He added, "Alone, but upborne by every generous heartbeat of mankind, we had defied the tyrant at the height of his triumph."[425]

He and his countrymen had indeed, without flinching and without wavering, defied the tyrant. But they had not yet defeated him.

They fought on, into the New Year of 1941. Alone.

2

The Rapids

JANUARY–DECEMBER 1941

Shortly after midnight on January 1, 1941, Churchill telegraphed Franklin Roosevelt: "At this moment when the New Year opens in storm, I feel it is my duty on behalf of the British government, and indeed of the whole British Empire, to tell you, Mr. President, how lively is our sense of gratitude and admiration for the memorable declaration which you made to the American people, and to the lovers of freedom in all the continents on Sunday last." He again resisted the urge to remind the president that he and the British people had no idea whatsoever of just exactly what America was going to do, or how, or when. He had no knowledge of the particulars of the Lend-Lease bill—titled, with no end save symbolism, H. R. 1776—about to be introduced into the U.S. House of Representatives, nor of course could he know the content of the bill when it emerged from the Senate, *if* it emerged from the Senate. When Lend-Lease began its trip through Congress, it would do so on Washington's terms, not Churchill's. If the congressional journey devoured too much time, Britain would go broke, a sorry enough circumstance for the greatest empire in history but now, with the Wehrmacht poised across the Channel, likely fatal as well. It was that close-fought a thing. Still, Jock Colville found Churchill's demeanor "mellow" on the last day of the old year. The telegram to Roosevelt manifested that measured good cheer, taking the form of holiday salutations in which he left unstated an obvious truth, one he could never articulate in public: only if 1940 proved to be America's last year of peace could 1941 prove to be Britain's first year of hope.[1]

Although Churchill claimed he had but one goal, the defeat of Hitler, those who worked for him often had no idea how he proposed to reach it. "His restless mind," wrote Lord Noel Annan, who as a young man in 1941 worked in the War Cabinet office, "bred one military scheme after another." Annan arrived at work each morning "wondering which rabbit had jumped out of the hat during the night." Would it be "Churchill's plan to land at Bordeaux, or at Spitzbergen, or Sardinia, North Africa, the tip of Sumatra? What such expeditions were expected to achieve, and how they would escape annihilation by superior forces, was clear only to Churchill." Maps were blank canvases, the contours of which Churchill filled in and studded with pins and painted with arrows—*his* arrows—pointing hither and yon toward hoped-for glorious victories in some far-distance place. But, wrote Annan, he was "oblivious of mountains or logistics" that the maps might bring to light and in so doing render his arrows pointless.[2]

Vanquished continental statesmen, royals, and the entire Dutch, Belgian, and Polish governments in exile greeted the New Year in the London clubs, hotels, and private houses where they had taken up residence. King Zog, of Albania, lived at the Ritz. King Haakon of Norway dined at Claridge's, where meats, fishes, and fruits not available to most Londoners appeared nightly on the menu. Queen Wilhelmina of the Netherlands lived at Claridge's and asked strangers for the latest news while wandering the corridors in her woolen bathrobe. Czechoslovakia's ousted president, Eduard Beneš, made the best of his hopeless cause in the capital of the empire that two years earlier had betrayed him. When in the autumn King Carol II of Romania, a royal playboy, sought asylum, the Foreign Office denied his request on the grounds that he kept a mistress. Churchill shot off a note to the FO: "It is true he has a mistress... but since when have private morals been a bar to asylum?" Carol was given permission to flee to Bermuda. His teenage son, Michael, grabbed the crown, remained in Romania, and waited for the proper moment to outmaneuver the dictator Ion Antonescu. He would have a long wait. The kings of Greece and Yugoslavia arrived later in the spring after disasters by way of the Wehrmacht befell their kingdoms. King George II of the Hellenes took up residence at Claridge's. Peter, the seventeen-year-old king of Yugoslavia enjoyed viewing American westerns from the balconies of West End cinemas, where he was often seen, his thumb cocked, picking off desperadoes with his forefinger, *bang, bang.*[3]

The Polish prime minister in exile Władysław Sikorski spent much of his time in Scotland, where 20,000 Polish troops trained, and dipped into mostly empty pockets to raise almost £500 to help repair the London Guildhall, which the Luftwaffe had toppled. While the Poles trained in Scotland, the Free French cooled their heels in the south of England. Charles de Gaulle—referred to by many around Whitehall as "that ass de Gaulle"—had been ensconced since June 1940 in his shabby office on the third floor of St. Stephen House, where he fumed as much at Vichy leaders as at Germans. Although he had in October set up a Free French "state" in Brazzaville, French Equatorial Africa (modern Chad), in actuality, the closest he could get to French Dominions in Asia and North Africa were old maps pinned to his office walls. De Gaulle, Wilhelmina, Beneš, Sikorski—all the beaten leaders—dreamed of someday returning to their homelands, victorious. Meanwhile, London, command center of the Free World, would have to do.[4]

The children in British cities, more than 600,000 in all, had been packed off to the countryside, but they were no longer sent abroad. They would stay in England to the end. A copy of Magna Carta had been sent to Washington, DC, but Churchill decreed that Britain's works of art stay. "Bury them in caves and cellars," he declared. "None must go. We are going to beat them." London was now the last redoubt, for the Empire's art, for the continental refugees of high birth and low who had poured into the city for two years, the final stop for the lot of them, Churchill included.[5]

T. S. Eliot, a fire warden at the Faber Building, where he was an editor, crafted a phrase that captured the essence of the nation's ordeal in five words:

"History is now and England." ("Little Gidding")

On January 1, Churchill, fuming over Roosevelt's desire to haul off to America the remaining British gold in South Africa, suggested to Colville that America's love of doing good business might overrule its inclination to become a Good Samaritan, with fatal consequences for Britain. He had inserted into and then deleted such accusatory ruminations from his New Year's Eve telegram: "I will gladly give directions for any gold in Capetown to be put on board any warships you may send.... I feel however that I should not be discharging my responsibilities to the people of the British Empire if, without the slightest indication of how our fate was to be settled in Washington, I were to part with this last reserve, from which alone we might buy a few month's food." This was an opinion best offered in person, between friends. The ongoing traffic between them in telegrams notwithstanding, Roosevelt and Churchill had yet to formalize a partnership, let alone a friendship.[6]

In the final hours of New Year's Day, Churchill climbed to the Foreign Office roof with his new foreign secretary, Anthony Eden. Eden was "vain and occasionally hysterical" in Colville's opinion, and very protective of his political patch. P. J. Grigg, Eden's successor at the War Office, considered him to be "complete junk." Churchill thought otherwise and had big things in mind for Eden, beginning with the Foreign Office. Eden was content to stay at the War Office following the death of Lord Lothian and Halifax's appointment as ambassador to the United States, but he heeded Churchill's summons to higher office. He later recalled that when Churchill first offered him the Foreign Office, Churchill "reiterated that he was now an old man, that he would not make Lloyd George's mistake of carrying on after the war, that the succession must be mine." That would prove a long time passing.[7]

Eden came from the finest English stock. His lineage on his father's side included Robert Eden, the last colonial governor of Maryland. His mother's side included the Calvert family and Lord Baltimore (whose family crest adorns the Maryland state flag) and reached back to the Greys. Eden's first wife could cite Thomas à Becket as a distant relation. Eden had won the Military Cross during the Great War, and at twenty became the youngest brigade major in the English army. At Oxford he had studied Russian, Persian, and several Arabic and Chinese dialects. When Chamberlain in late 1935 made the young war hero and rising Tory his foreign secretary, Churchill opined in a letter to Clementine, "I think you will now see what a light-weight Eden is." But Eden, repulsed by appeasement, resigned in early 1938, thus earning Churchill's respect. Churchill groomed, encouraged, and rewarded the younger man in a generous and protective spirit of a sort he could not possibly have learned from his own father.[8]

Thus it was with his successor-designate that Churchill climbed to the roof of the Foreign Office that night. The air was infused with the aroma of woodsmoke from dozens of still smoldering fires. Broken clouds drifted overhead; a cold, light rain fell. Below spread London, wrapped in darkness blacker even than in Norman times, when the meager light of pitch and tow torches lent to the Thames a zinc hue and cast London Bridge into relief to guide pilgrims home. Gazing skyward, the skies quiet but for sporadic anti-aircraft firing, Churchill and Eden wondered, What would the new year bring? The entire world wondered the same, yet even the mere posing of the question was an act of self-deception, for the answer was inescapable: it would bring a year of storm.

Some in those dark hours heard the knock of opportunity. Newly promoted Lieutenant General Bernard Law Montgomery, fifty-three, a career soldier, Dunkirk evacuee, and son of an Anglican priest, believed his future bright. He commanded V Corps and coastal defense of Britain, having replaced General Claude Auchinleck, a tough Ulsterman who as commander of the Norwegian fiasco asked for and did not receive the tactical air support he needed to press the attack. He came away certain that ill-supported troops cannot give battle. Auchinleck's open disdain for sending men into battle without the tools to finish the job—especially close air support—earned him unjustified enmity in Whitehall and a reputation for undue caution. It also earned him a transfer to India where, early in his career, Auchinleck had studied and become fluent in almost all the dialects of the subcontinent. In his new position of commander in chief, India, it was presumed that Auchinleck's caution would not be exploited by any adversary. Montgomery had never gotten along with Auchinleck and welcomed his departure. "Monty," as Montgomery's troops called him, considered his own chances for promotion splendid, and justifiably so in his estimation, an assessment not shared by some of his superiors who found him pompous and mischievous, a term that, when employed in England, connotes sneakiness, not playfulness. He was four years a widower, his wife having died in his arms of an infection caused by an insect bite. On the day of the funeral, Montgomery appeared late for a staff meeting. "Gentlemen," he told his staff, "I ask you to forgive this display of human weakness." Since then, he had given himself over to the army. Montgomery's "pugnacious attitude" and his willingness to gas the Germans should they arrive impressed Churchill, who kept an eye on the man.[9]

A forty-year-old Royal Navy hero also impressed Churchill. Captain Louis ("Dickie") Mountbatten—great-grandson of Queen Victoria, second cousin of George V, and cousin to the murdered Romanovs—was awarded the Distinguished Service Order for his gallantry in 1940 when he brought his destroyer, HMS *Kelly,* safely to port from the North Sea, where it had been cut almost in half by German torpedoes. Churchill dictated a congratulatory note, and scribbled in the margin of a copy: "I hardly know him." That soon changed, for Churchill had known Mountbatten's father, Prince Louis Battenberg, a naturalized Austrian who in 1914, as first sea lord, worked with Churchill, then at the Admiralty, to bring the British Navy up to a state of war readiness. Battenberg's reward was to be forced into early retirement by the wave of Germanophobia that washed over Britain. Churchill stood by, silent, as Battenberg was banished. Perhaps to atone for his silence then, or because he could not resist a hero, especially one of aristocratic lineage, Churchill took a keen interest in Mountbatten, which much enhanced the captain's prospects of advancement. Mountbatten was charming, fearless, and reckless. And lucky: in just fourteen months Dickie had been torpedoed, bombed, and strafed, had collided with another ship, and had run over a floating mine. At the beginning of the new year, Mountbatten commanded a destroyer squadron in the Mediterranean, where such small warships as *Kelly* were lost with distressing regularity. Mountbatten's command of such a vulnerable ship as well as his wild fighting style much diminished his chances of surviving long enough to gain any further promotion.[10]

The new year found James Joyce in Geneva, dying. F. Scott Fitzgerald soon followed the expatriate Irishman into the night. Virginia Woolf, who had long suffered from depression, followed them both, by her own hand. German bombs had erased her London house. Confiding her thoughts on the war to her diary, Woolf wrote, "I was thinking: we live without a future. That's what's queer, with our noses pressed to a closed door." As she gazed from her window upon the downs and spires and old stone walls of the countryside that she loved, she summoned Walter de la Mare's melancholy words "Look thy last on all things lovely," and in twelve weeks' time filled her pockets with stones and drowned herself in the River Ouse.[11]

Most Britons—Churchill foremost among them—saw a future, and were willing to fight and die for it. That winter, Britons gave way to inexplicable bursts of primitive emotion. "*We want more!*" cried Londoners in defiance as they danced madly though the streets while stomping out incendiaries during one early January raid. Malcolm Muggeridge found himself delighting—disturbingly so—in "the sound, the taste and smell of all this destruction... the faces of bystanders wildly lit in the flames... it seemed as if the Book of Revelations had verily come to pass." Churchill was one with Londoners and Muggeridge. Every night lit by flames was another glorious occasion to either live or die, to stride toward the day when he could deliver unto Germany his version of justice.[12]

For many young American men who wondered if they'd be one of the 800,000 draftees Roosevelt needed for his "muster," revelations arrived via the local draft board as the new year came in. The army got all the draftees; navy and Marine corps recruiting standards were set higher than draft standards, a policy that would leave the bluejackets and leathernecks vastly undermanned should America ever to go to war. All told, almost one million young American men marched off to boot camp, but not yet to war. Those Americans who had already chosen army careers pondered their prospects for advancement. Dwight Eisenhower, a fifty-year-old U.S. Army lieutenant colonel, had until late 1939 served in Manila as chief of staff to Douglas MacArthur, commander of U.S. Army forces in the Philippines. On January 1, Eisenhower served as chief of staff for the 3rd Division. He sought a field command and had told an old friend, George Patton Jr., that he considered himself qualified to command a regiment—perhaps one of Patton's—but that he harbored few hopes of ever attaining higher rank. Eisenhower's name appeared on a list drawn up for General of the Army George Marshall of eighteen career officers who might qualify for division command: Eisenhower was ranked eighteenth.[13]

Although Roosevelt, in 1939, had ordered Army chief of staff George Marshall to build up American armed forces, by early 1941, America fielded only the seventeenth most powerful army in the world, strong enough to lick Canada or Mexico should the situation arise, but no match for the Wehrmacht.

The French in the new year cared little for the latest news from London, or America, or any place in between. The world Frenchmen knew and loved had died the previous June. The Nazi occupiers made sure little news reached Frenchmen in any event. The winter weather was brutal. Gales pushed freezing cold and snow south to the Riviera. Marseille found itself isolated from the rest of southern France by snowdrifts. In Paris, breadlines lengthened, and a shortage of coal for fireplaces spelled doom for the trees of the city's parks. Parisians could only watch as German troops stole food that came by way of America and Morocco and southern France. The French were beaten, and they discerned a future that offered only misery, hunger, and slavery. On New Year's Day, Pétain told his countrymen that for the foreseeable future, "We shall be hungry." The old marshal had to have the coupons clipped from his ration card just like everyone else. He was a beaten man.[14]

Charles de Gaulle, in London, was not. He understood the unbreakable strength of dreams. On New Year's Day, he called on the people of France to remain indoors for an hour, a purely symbolic yet powerful protest that left the streets empty but for the enemy. Most Frenchmen had never heard of de Gaulle until June 18 of the previous year, when, in a BBC address broadcast from London, this minor general declared himself the regent of French honor, its guardian and protector. He told Frenchmen, "Whatever happens, the flame of French resistance must not and shall not die."

He was a Catholic whose politics ran to the right; his oratorical skills were meager, yet they transcended politics. He was not a man of any party; he was a man of France, specifically of the *myth* of France, where given his exile, his presence was, necessarily, a spiritual one. Posters bearing photos of Churchill, Hitler, Mussolini, Stalin, and Roosevelt hung on walls throughout their lands, but Vichy had erased from France all pictorial representations of de Gaulle. Vichy propagandists described him as short, fat, ugly, and a misfit. Frenchmen had no image of the man. Instead, and despite German efforts to jam the BBC, they were guided by only his disembodied voice crackling across the airwaves. By the time Napoleon was de Gaulle's age, his life was nearly finished; the myth surrounding him was complete. De Gaulle was just beginning. Now he called for resistance, and in the dark of night a spark was struck. He wrote in his memoirs: "I felt within myself a life coming to an end.... At the age of forty-nine I was entering upon adventure, like a man thrown by fate outside all terms of reference." Churchill saw the immense importance of imbuing Frenchmen with the will to fight, the *need* to fight. He had done much the same for Britons by leading his listeners back into the mists and myths of English history, where the soul of England resided. There was a critical difference, however: Britons could see and touch their Winnie. Yet, even though Frenchmen could form no image of de Gaulle, he had won over their souls. Churchill recognized this; Franklin Roosevelt did not, with unfortunate results for all concerned.[15]

January 1 arrived in a somber Berlin. The Wehrmacht had months earlier demolished the Maginot Line. Its coal stoves, bunks, and rations enough to feed 250,000 for a year were packed up and shipped off to

German air-raid shelters, where the citizens, based on assurances from their leaders, had presumed the ill-gotten supplies would gather dust from want of use. Instead, dust settled now into Berlin shelters, sifted down from the streets above, where the homes of Berliners burned under RAF bombs.[16]

Berliners crowded shelters on a regular basis, though Jews were forbidden entrance, forbidden in fact to take shelter in any of the basements of Berlin. If they could gain access to a building, Jews were confined to the ground floor; otherwise they took their chances in the streets. Berliners were depressed by the bloody harvest of Hitler's adventures and by their increased awareness that their lives under the Nazis bore no resemblance to the lives they had once lived, or had hoped to live. The Tiergarten was empty, dark, silent, and studded with bomb craters. Such festivities as there were took place behind shuttered windows. In his New Year's Eve address, Hitler excoriated "this criminal" Churchill who for three months has bombed German cities by night "and—as especially the inhabitants of Berlin know—has made special targets of hospitals." The Führer promised he would respond to "the Churchill crimes" and assured Germans that "the war will be waged to the end—until the responsible criminals have been eliminated." He added, "It is the will of the democratic war-inciters and their Jewish-capitalistic wire-pullers that the war must be continued.... We are ready.... The year 1941 will bring completion of the greatest victory in our history." William L. Shirer saw only gloom in Berlin. He had just left Europe after fifteen years on the Continent, leaving behind the "Nazi blight and the hatred and the fraud and the political gangsterism and the murder and the massacre and the incredible intolerance and all the suffering and the starving and the cold and the thud of a bomb blowing the people in a house to pieces, the thud of all the bombs blasting men's hope and decency."[17]

Berliners, as did Londoners, found ways to express their cynicism. The lyrics of the German war song *"Wir fahren, wir fahren, wir fahren gegen Engeland"* ("We are marching, marching, marching against England"), which had played over and over again on state radio the previous summer as the BEF was encircled at Dunkirk, had been revised: *"Wir fahren, wir fahren, wir fahren, schon seit Jahren, mit langen weissen Haaren, gegen Engeland."* ("We are marching, marching, marching; we have for years been marching; with hair turned white by the passage of time we go on marching, against England.") Shirer noted a riddle making the rounds in Berlin: "An airplane carrying Hitler, Goebbels, and Göring crashes; all three are killed. Who is saved? Answer: The German people." Shirer, with insight into the Nazi mind-set that was lacking in Whitehall, predicted that the British blockade of Germany would not succeed in starving Germans, because "Hitler, who is never sentimental about non-Germans, will see to it that every one of the one hundred million people in the occupied lands dies of hunger before one German does. Of that, the world can be sure."[18]

Excepting the myriad peoples who lived within the British Empire, Churchill was not himself overly sentimental about non-Britons and, since their surrender, the French in particular. Pétain, on New Year's Day, told Frenchmen that food shortages in southern France were the result of the British blockade. He did not tell his countrymen that food shipments from the United States to French Morocco, intended for occupied France, were being diverted by the Germans—with Vichy compliance—to Germany. Pétain's obfuscations infuriated Churchill, who in coming months complained bitterly to Roosevelt. When in a few weeks' time the American secretary of state Cordell Hull expressed his opposition to Britain's continued blockade of Vichy, Churchill exploded, telling Halifax, "I cannot believe the United States government would wish us to do simply nothing, and have the war prolonged by having all these cargoes, containing not only food but rubber and other war materials, pass unhindered into Germany." He voiced his cynicism to Roosevelt in typically Churchillian fashion. "For instance, there is a French ship . . . with 3,000 tons of rubber on board which is certainly not all for the teats of babies' bottles." All kinds of munitions and raw materials, he told Roosevelt, "are going straight to Germany or Italy." From Churchill's perspective, if food shipments to France had to be cut off in order to prevent leakage of matériel to Germany, then so be it. The ships needed to supply Britain could not be spared to supply France, he told Roosevelt, especially as he did not want the British people, "who, apart from heavy bombardment likely to be renewed soon, are having to tighten their belts and restrict their few remaining comforts, to feel that I am not doing my best against the enemy." If the British blockade meant that Frenchmen went hungry so that Englishmen might live, such was war.[19]

In Britain, the U-boat blockade had resulted in all goods but the essential disappearing from pantry shelves. Everyone, including the cabinet, was on half rations (everyone except the swells at Claridge's, the Savoy, the Ritz, and any London dining clubs that remained unbombed). City dwellers with friends in the country might come into a few eggs a month; all others would go eggless. Alec Cadogan was thankful after procuring a few chickens; then they stopped laying. Turkeys were in short supply, and expensive. Meat was parceled out at less than one pound per person per week, bone in, half the ration of a year earlier. To a nation of meat eaters who, for centuries, had begun their day with a mutton chop and ended it with roasts, puddings, and kidney pies, this was *carnivoricide.* Not only were meat and eggs disappearing, but so were the cooks, butlers, and scullery maids of the rich and near rich. A domestic servant crisis developed in the kitchens and laundries of the West End and in the country houses of the gentry when cooks and laundresses marched off to work in the armaments factories. Mollie Panter-Downes observed a marked increase in newspaper help-wanted advertisements taken out by "anguished ladies" in search of servants who would find, it was promised, "enormous wages, happy homes, and safe locales, where a bomb is guaranteed to be unknown." Those servants had less to iron and more to mend: clothing rationing took full effect later in the year, limiting purchases to the value of coupons, no cash allowed, regardless of the shopper's cash flow. Women's Sunday-best dresses would have to do until the end of the war. Suede elbow patches on men's jackets now served a purely functional purpose.[20]

East Enders meanwhile, lower on the social ladder than even those in service to the rich, had no need to fret over the paucity of clothing or beef: they could afford neither in any event. The poor supped on "Blitz soup," a viscous canned concoction foisted upon them by the Ministry of Food. The ministry also supplied dried eggs, which Londoners anointed "dregs." The good citizens of Britain were told that tripe was restricted but chickens for the time being were not. Horsemeat—approved for human consumption—appeared in butcher shops. No coupons were required for its purchase, but sales flagged. Britons avoided horsemeat with the same fervor as Muslims avoid pork.[21]

Fresh meat was not the only item absent from the British retail scene. Silk stockings had gone missing from stores; tobacco was priced beyond the means of most; razor blades were scarce; and pipe cleaners were nonexistent, having been appropriated by women for use as hair curlers. A tea crisis occurred when the Pelton gasworks was hit. It took up to an hour to boil water for tea over small fires stoked from sticks and paper. The problem of how to roast the Sunday joint of beef without gas was rendered moot by the absence of joints of beef. A coal shortage loomed if deliveries from the Welsh mines to London did not increase to 410,000 tons per week from the current 250,000 tons, a situation Churchill found difficult to understand given the slackening in the Blitz and the general good repair of the railroads. Other statistics showed that in spite of German bombs, Britons maintained their humanity after a fashion denied those who lived under Hitler: almost 50,000 British dogs and cats had been rescued from bombed houses.[22]

HMG conducted surveys. The divorce rate was down by half. The birthrate had not declined, and "Winston" as a first or middle name for baby boys more than tripled in popularity.* Surprisingly, in light of dietary restrictions and the lack of central heat, cases of pneumonia and diphthe-

* Among those who chose the name were a young, working-class Liverpool couple, "Alf" and Julia Lennon, who honored the Old Man when they named their son—born during an October air raid—John Winston Lennon.

ria were down. The crime rate was also down, curiously, thought Churchill, given the ample opportunities for looting, an "odious" crime in his estimation. Some looting could be excused. He told home secretary Herbert Morrison that a sentence of five years penal servitude given to six auxiliary London firemen caught stealing whisky from a burning pub was "out of proportion when compared with sentences of three or six months for stealing valuables." The firemen, after all, had procured the whisky for "immediate consumption" rather than for personal enrichment. Such bureaucratic blockheadedness riled the Old Man. When a Londoner was fined £100 for disposing of a delayed-action bomb "without authorization," Churchill's fuse ignited. Was this man fined, he asked Morrison, for saving his home? Rather than official opprobrium, he decreed that the heroic citizen should be "awarded the George Medal." And when an obviously "crazy female" was given five years penal servitude for expressing the opinion that "Hitler was a good ruler, a better man than Mr. Churchill," he told Morrison that the sentence was "far too heavy."[23]

On January 2 Harold Nicolson, while strolling through old London—still smoldering from the December 29 raid—noted small groups of sullen civilians standing around in the ruins. He noted their quiet mutterings about the need for revenge, the more revenge the better, and sooner, too. "We are fighting devils," Nicolson wrote that night, "and I don't see why we shouldn't fight like devils in order to let them see what it is like." He noted on his rambles a subtle but definite decline in esprit de corps. When the news of the Taranto raid played across the newspapers in late November—grainy aerial photos of wrecked Italian ships—it was met with skepticism, especially among the lower economic classes, who thought the photos fake. The welcome news that the Greeks were trouncing the Italians in Albania was held up by Cockney newsboys as proof of the sorry state of British arms, for the Italians, trounced by the Greeks, had trounced the English in Somaliland. The string of recent British victories against the Italians in North Africa were seen by East Enders as meaningless. The real enemy, Hitler, still prowled Europe, uncontested and unmolested.[24]

London's poor were skeptical, yet socialist ward bosses in Silvertown, Stepney, and the East End slums had failed to kindle any revolutionary fires among them. East Enders remained faithful to the cause even as their filthy tenements burned and crashed down around them. Most now chose to stay home when the bombs came, and scorned the Anderson shelters, which, carped the ward bosses, "couldn't protect a rooster from rain."

Anderson shelters at least posed no public health menace, unlike the ersatz shelters under railroad overpasses, which were not much more than vectors for disease. A constable visiting one first heard and then smelled it before he saw it: "The first thing I heard was a great hollow hubbub, as if there were animals down there moaning and crying. And then . . . this terrible stench hit me. It was worse than dead bodies, hot and thick and so fetid that I gagged and then vomited. Ahead of me I could see faces peering towards me lit by lanterns and candles. It was like a painting of Hell." The Cockneys were refused even the satisfaction of reading of their plight in the newspapers; the Ministry of Information, under Duff Cooper, forbade any reporting of where bombs fell or the number of casualties. Those workingmen who took their news from the Communist, alarmist, and decidedly adversarial *Daily Worker* could no longer do so after January 21, 1941, the day HMG took the extraordinary step of shutting it down. Still, newspaper obituaries offered clues; bomb victims were said to have died "very suddenly." If the obituaries contained a grouping of "very sudden" deaths in a particular neighborhood, it was a good bet that the neighborhood in question had been hit hard.[25]

That certain squalid sections of the East End and Southwark, of Manchester, Birmingham, and Britain's other industrial areas, had been destroyed brought forth an ironic response from many of the displaced. The Germans were ridding Britain of slums, a job HMG had avoided for forty years. Londoners who lost their homes to bombs waited an average of five months before being placed in livable abodes. Churchill had outlined to Colville a relief plan to reimburse homeowners up to £1,000 (about $55,000 U.S. in 2012) for their losses, but Parliament had yet to make good on the promise. Soon after John Reith took up his new duties as minister of works (after Churchill eased him out of the Ministry of Transportation), he was instructed by Churchill to "press on" in rebuilding bombed neighborhoods. Yet Churchill told Edward Bridges, secretary to the cabinet, that as far as reconstruction of wrecked cities was concerned, "We must be very careful not to allow these remote post-war problems to absorb energy which is required, maybe for several years, for the prosecution of the war." Cockneys—all Britons—would have to wait a decade for new homes, for reliable supplies of electricity, coal, gas, water, and petrol. The wait for clothing, paper goods, and fresh, plentiful food would last well into the next decade. The only commodities delivered to Britons with any regularity in early 1941 were German bombs.[26]

In his memoirs Churchill equated 1940 with "shooting Niagara" and termed early 1941 a "struggle in the rapids." In January 1941 the lifeline of

Lend-Lease lay coiled on the far shore. Churchill and England fought on, *alone,* a fact he made clear when he articulated the "theme" of his memoirs of 1940:

> HOW THE BRITISH PEOPLE
> HELD THE FORT
> ALONE
> TILL THOSE WHO HITHERTO HAD
> BEEN HALF BLIND WERE
> HALF READY.

In the historical memory of many Americans, the year 1941 does not begin until December 7. For Churchill and Britain, the entire year indeed saw a long and terrible struggle in the rapids. It is true that the Home Island fought with the full support of the Dominions, and given the fact that one-quarter of the world's population lived within the British Empire, it might appear facile to suggest that England stood alone. But in large part it did. Canada would ultimately send 90,000 airmen to Britain; they would play a significant role in the bombing of Germany. But the first Royal Canadian Air Force bomber squadron was not commissioned until mid-1941. Three Royal Canadian infantry divisions and two armored divisions were available for the fight but were widely scattered throughout the Empire, including a division in Britain and a battalion in Hong Kong. Australia offered four infantry divisions. Canberra's enthusiasm for the European war decreased throughout the year as the threat of Japanese attack increased. New Zealand sent 50,000 soldiers and 10,000 airmen overseas during the next two years, but only Lieutenant General Bernard Freyberg's North African corps was operational in early 1941. South Africa offered three divisions, but only for deployment in Africa, where Erwin Rommel mauled them as the year wore on. In early 1941, the forces sent by the Dominions, when combined with British forces, were vastly outnumbered by the Axis. After the fall of France, Hitler had *demobilized* forty divisions, far more than all the armed forces of the Dominions combined. Even late in 1941, after it scrambled for months to put men into uniform, the entirety of the British Empire's armies worldwide—ninety-nine divisions—was dwarfed by the Wehrmacht by a ratio greater than two to one. In early 1941, *all* of Hitler's troops were stationed within six hundred miles of London.[27]

British prospects in the Mediterranean and the Balkans, if the Germans appeared on the scene, looked precarious at best. By the first week of January, the Luftwaffe had stationed more than 150 bombers and fighters in Sicily, just one hundred miles and thirty minutes from Malta. Such a force could menace the Mediterranean from the French Riviera to North Africa. To oppose the German air fleet, the British had but fifteen beat-up Hurricanes parked on Malta, the most critical piece of real estate in the central Mediterranean. Malta was under siege, ringed by Italian minefields and submarines, the Luftwaffe and Italian air force overhead. It was England in miniature—isolated and battered—but with two vital differences: the Germans and Italians, not the RAF, controlled the skies over Malta, and the Italian navy, not the Royal Navy, surrounded the island. Aggressive strategy demanded, as it had since the previous summer, that Mussolini send his fleet and Hitler his paratroopers to take the island.

Menacing German forces had been dispatched to the greater Balkan region. By mid-January almost 500,000 German troops—"tourists," Berlin claimed, who happened to bring along their tanks and artillery—took up positions along the Romanian side of the Danube, again as in Roman times the boundary that separated the barbarian from the civilized world. This sojourn by the Wehrmacht was Romania's reward for joining the Axis in November, a decision born more of necessity than choice. Having succumbed in 1940 to Stalin's demand for the provinces of Bessarabia and Northern Bukovina, and to Hitler's demand that northern Transylvania be ceded to Hungary, the Romanian dictator, General Ion Antonescu, could turn only to Hitler for a guarantee that the rump Romania remain intact. It had not occurred to Stalin that 500,000 German troops were about 480,000 more than needed to guarantee Romania's sovereignty. Yugoslavia and Bulgaria lay south across the Danube. The kingdom of the Bulgars was essentially an eighteenth-century, pre-industrial nation. Its leaders and people lived with the sure knowledge that sooner or later, either Stalin or Hitler—with their mechanized might—would no longer tolerate Bulgarian neutrality. Wherever Hitler intended to go—to Greece in aid of Il Duce seemed a logical destination—he first had to push through Bulgaria. Yet, Bulgarian roads were decrepit and its railroads were in no shape to move a modern army. Bulgaria offered a route south and beyond, but not the best route. Not so Yugoslavia, where the old Hapsburg railroad system connected to the rail lines of Greece, Hungary, Romania, and Austria. Hitler wanted Yugoslavia; Churchill needed Yugoslavia. Hitler could take Bulgaria; Churchill could not protect it. He deduced that the German "tourists" were destined for the Balkans, the threshold to the Mediterranean, the "hinge of fate."

The German naval war staff understood Churchill's thinking, and had prepared a paper in the autumn that warned, "The fight for the African area" is "the foremost strategic objective of German warfare as a whole.... It is of decisive importance for the outcome of the war." The Italians, ill led and inefficient, could not win that fight alone, as their humiliation at the hands of the Greeks and their losses at Taranto and against O'Connor in the desert confirmed. The cagey Franco would not do it, at Gibraltar. Raeder predicted that if the Axis did not occupy Vichy northwest Africa (Morocco, Tunisia, and Algeria), Churchill and the Gaullists would do so in due time, supported by American industrial might. Therefore, the German naval planners concluded, Germany must do it. It was Britain's good fortune that Hitler was a land warrior who rarely (other than in the matter of U-boats) embraced the advice of his very capable admirals. Hitler, looking toward Russia, agreed only to the half measure of sending aircraft to Sicily, and troops to Romania, in anticipation of some future foray into the Balkans, most likely to Greece in support of his hapless ally.[28]

Churchill outlined his Mediterranean strategy on January 6 in a long memo to "Pug" Ismay and the Chiefs of Staff Committee. He saw three critical objectives, reverse images of what the German naval staff saw. The British must hold what they had from the Suez to Gibraltar; engage and defeat the Italian navy and drive the Italian army from Africa (which O'Connor, having taken Bardia the day before, was doing); and keep the Germans out of the Mediterranean. Churchill interwove his immediate goals and his operational wish list, the former concise, the latter detailing the hopes of an impatient man. Yet in contrast to Hitler, who issued Führer Directives that were orders pure and simple and allowed for no interpretation, Churchill probed and examined and sought guidance from his military chiefs. His first priority for early 1941, he wrote, was "the speedy destruction of the Italian armed forces in North-East Africa." Tobruk must be established as a base from which to conduct Libyan operations. In East Africa, the Italians must be swept away. That would secure the Suez and the southeast shore of the Mediterranean.

In the western Mediterranean, there was a chance that Franco would deny Hitler transit to Gibraltar, which raised the happy prospect that Hitler might try to force his way to Spain through unoccupied France in violation of the June surrender terms. In that case, Churchill believed that "the Vichy Government . . . may either proceed to North Africa and resume war from there, or authorize General Weygand to do so." To that end Churchill offered Pétain and Weygand Britain's assistance were they to take the fight to Africa. It was a pipe dream. The Vichy leaders were edging closer to, not away from, willing servitude to their German masters. They believed that Germany would win the war; indeed, they *wanted* Germany to win the war. As well, Weygand, in Morocco, loathed de Gaulle, while de Gaulle loathed Weygand and hated with a fury the Fascist-minded Vichy premier, Pierre Laval. The French accorded more importance to their personal grudges than to their national honor. The previous June, Weygand and Pétain had squandered their chance to fight for the honor of France. They had quit, but not before a final act of treachery when they tried to draw in the RAF's last reserves. With each passing month, Churchill's goodwill toward the French had diminished. He allowed to Colville on one occasion and to luncheon guests on another that had Britain "thrown away those planes in France... the war might have been lost."[29]

He would get no help in the western Mediterranean from Vichy France. As Laval's collaboration with the Nazis became ever more apparent, Churchill told Colville he rued the "lamentable lack of Charlotte Cordays."[30]

To secure the eastern Mediterranean he proposed a Balkan bulwark of Yugoslavia, Greece, and Turkey. In essence he hoped to convince the Balkan nations that a bundle of wheat was not as easily broken as individual stalks. With the Italians on the run in Africa, the time had come to divert some of Wavell's desert forces to Greece, not only to support the Greeks but to gird the loins of the Yugoslavs and Turks. "The attitude of Yugoslavia," Churchill wrote, "may well be determined by the support we give to Greece," as would be the attitude of Turkey. He was inviting a showdown with Hitler. But the Greeks understood that the surest way to provoke Hitler was to invite British troops into the fray. As General Alexander Papagos drove the Italians back through mountain passes into Albania, the military situation appeared promising, but Greeks were going hungry. Winter, not the Italian army, was reducing Greek resolve. Mussolini could reinforce his Albanian legions, but Prime Minister Metaxas could not. He desperately needed supplies—tanks, anti-tank guns, rifles, airplanes, ammunition, food, and clothing. He asked the United States for help, but Congress had yet to begin debate on the Lend-Lease bill, and Britain, not Greece, would be the primary beneficiary of any U.S. aid. Metaxas could not crush the Italians without help, yet he continued to decline Churchill's help, a quite reasonable demurral given the half million Germans encamped on the Romanian side of the Danube.[31]

Churchill took a regional view. He predicted that if the Germans came to Il Duce's aid in Greece by way of Romania, Bulgaria, and the Black Sea, "Turkey will come into the war." He followed this hopeful prognostication with a string of first-magnitude "ifs." "If Yugoslavia stands firm and is not molested, if the Greeks take Valona and maintain themselves in Albania, if Turkey becomes an active ally, the attitude of Russia may be affected favorably." That is, Russian fear of an "obnoxious and indeed deadly... German advance to the Black Sea or through Bulgaria to the Aegean" would be lessened by a British presence in the Balkans. Indeed, he wrote, a British presence might persuade Stalin to side with Britain, "but we must not count on this." True. With Hitler's armies poised in Romania, it was highly unlikely that any of Churchill's "ifs" could come to pass. The Yugoslav government was so petrified of provoking Hitler that it refused in March to even meet with Eden, who by then was prowling the region, pleading Churchill's case for solidarity. Metaxas, in Greece, continued to decline with a polite "no" Churchill's offers of military aid right up to his sudden death at the end of January, leaving General Alexander Papagos, the hero of the battle against Italy, to ponder Churchill's proposals, which he finally accepted in early March. The Turks, for their part, wanted nothing whatsoever to do with Churchill's invitation to commit national suicide. They faced Hitler on one side, and their ancient enemy, Russia, on the other. Against these foes, their army contained not a single tank. In fact, Anthony Eden wanted Turkey to remain neutral for the simple reason that Britain could offer no military protection to Ankara if the Turks joined the British cause.[32]

Churchill finished his memo with a confident prediction, which echoed the prediction he had made to Colville and to the House the previous summer: "One cannot doubt that Herr Hitler's need to starve or crush Great Britain is stronger than it has ever been. A great campaign in the East of Europe, the defeat of Russia, the conquest of the Ukraine, and the advance from the Black Sea to the Caspian, would none of them separately or together bring him victorious peace while the British air power grew ever stronger behind him and he had to hold down a whole continent of sullen, starving peoples." But British airpower was not yet strong enough to make a difference, and against a continental enemy it might never prove sufficiently strong. Armies and well-armed allies would make the difference. But Churchill had no armies, and he had no allies. Even if he had, even were he to build his Balkan bulwark, he could not, unlike Hitler, furnish modern weapons to his friends. Churchill, in fact, had no weapons, old or new, to furnish to anyone. Britain, under U-boat blockade, its cash balances evaporating, had but one option, to hold out at home and in the Mediterranean.[33]

Churchill's stream of memos, many dealing with the most mundane of matters, had widened into a river; some of his subordinates would claim a river in flood. The Chief of the Imperial General Staff, Sir John Dill, dining one evening with Sir John Reith, a prewar Chamberlain loyalist, allowed that of Churchill's memos "one...out of ten was perhaps useful—occasionally very good." Important ministers wasted a great amount of time, Dill offered, by having to deal with "silly minutes from the P.M." Some of Churchill's memos indeed treat of subjects not usually associated with Great Men of History, but Churchill would not have been Churchill without his memos. He loved to ponder the finer details of making war, and to then compose the memos that drove Dill to make his intemperate remarks to Reith.[34]

Among Churchill's inquiries, he asked after the progress in developing a four-thousand-pound bomb, for he desired to deliver to the Reich the

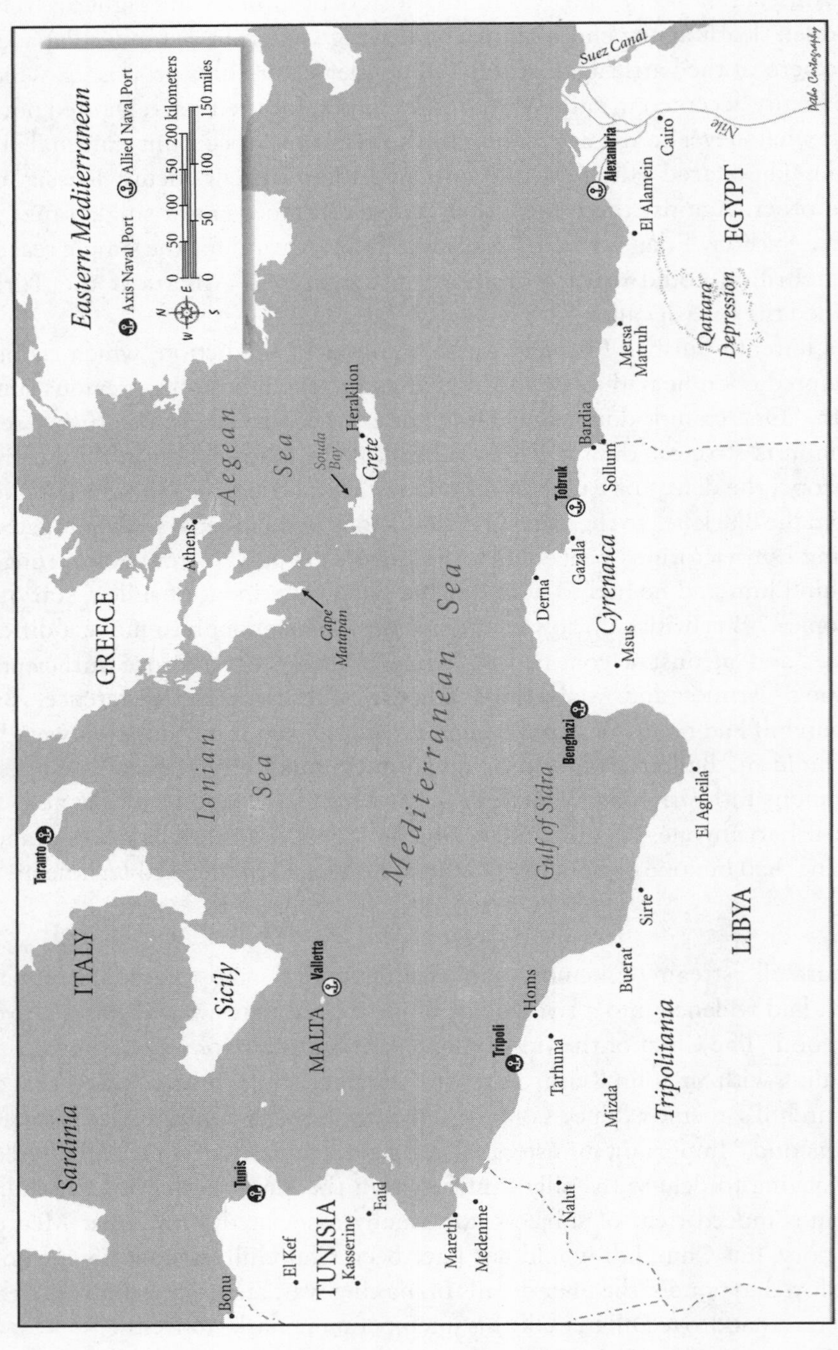

Eastern Mediterranean
Axis Naval Port
Allied Naval Port
0 50 100 150 200 kilometers
0 50 100 150 miles
N
E
S
W
Sardinia
ITALY
Sicily
MALTA
Valletta
Taranto
GREECE
Athens
Ionian Sea
Aegean Sea
Cape Matapan
Souda Bay
Crete
Heraklion
Mediterranean Sea
Gulf of Sidra
TUNISIA
Bonu
El Kef
Kasserine
Faid
Tunis
Mareth
Medenine
Nalut
Mizda
Tarhuna
Tripoli
Homs
Tripolitania
Buerat
Sirte
LIBYA
El Agheila
Benghazi
Msus
Cyrenaica
Derna
Gazala
Tobruk
Sollum
Bardia
Mersa Matruh
Qattara Depression
El Alamein
EGYPT
Alexandria
Cairo
Nile
Suez Canal
Dabo Cartography

deadliest bomb possible, as soon as possible. Enamored of the idea of dropping incendiaries into the Black Forest with the intention of burning every stick of lumber to the ground, he suggested the RAF test its wares on the French forest of Nieppe, where drought had turned the undergrowth into kindling. Operation Razzle, a scheme to burn German crops, held his interest, although much of Germany's farmland was in the east, beyond the reach of the RAF. He pushed Duff Cooper at the Ministry of Information to take a more honest approach with the news so that Britons might actually believe some of what they read in their newspapers and heard on the BBC. He insisted the press not announce civilian casualty numbers, reasoning that such figures depressed the morale of frontline troops, which he considered Britons to be. Food was always an issue. In one memo he lamented the egg crisis, in another he proposed a solution: "Backyard fowls use up a lot of scrap, and so save cereals." He overlooked no beast: "Have you done justice to rabbit production.... They eat mostly grass... so what is the harm in encouraging their multiplication in captivity?" He tagged the rabbit memo "Action This Day." He believed feeding Britons was more important than buying weapons, and he demanded the import of enough food "to maintain the staying power of the people even if this meant a somewhat slower" buildup of the army. On occasion his coolness bled through. Asked by a minister how best to help the thousands of homeless wandering about London, he suggested they be sent to far-flung places where they would no longer be in the way during air raids.[35]

He launched a classic memo after reading an account of a general who ordered every soldier in his division to run regular seven-mile jogs:

> Is it really true that a 7-mile cross-country run is enforced in this Division from Generals to Privates?... A Colonel or a General ought not to exhaust himself in trying to compete with young boys in running across country 7-miles at a time.... Who is the General of this division, and does he run the 7-miles himself? If so, then he may be more useful in football than in war. Could Napoleon have run 7-miles across country at Austerlitz?... In my experience... officers with high athletic qualifications are not usually successful in the higher ranks.[36]

Churchill's memos, Dill told Reith, suggested that he "seemed often unable to appreciate or understand major issues." Actually, both Dill and Reith were unable to appreciate Churchill's grasp of *all* the issues, not only those issues apparent to everybody but also those apparent only to himself. Dill fell silent when Reith asked whether he thought Churchill "did more harm than good—i.e., more nuisance and upset to those running the war." Reith took Dill's silence as a yes. "I am sure," Reith jotted in his diary, "that he [Dill] would have said more harm than good, which is what I feel."[37]

What Dill and Reith failed to recognize was that Churchill saw but one "major issue": victory over Hitlerism. As to his memos having a deleterious effect upon "those running the war," Reith allowed his partisan wrath to unhinge his logic. Churchill was running the war. In doing so he tried to project the image of a ruthless warlord, emitting thunder and lightning, partly in hope of striking fear into the hearts of the Germans—he failed there—but largely to rouse the spirits of his countrymen. There his success was tremendous. Margery Allingham, the mystery novelist, wrote an American friend:

> Mr. Churchill is the unchanging bulldog, the epitome of British aggressiveness and the living incarnation of the true Briton in fighting, not standing any damned nonsense, stoking the boilers with the grand piano and enjoying-it mood. Also he never lets go. He is so designed that he cannot breathe if he does. At the end of the fight he will come crawling in, unrecognizable, covered with blood and delighted, with the enemy's heart between his teeth.

By putting Churchill in the saddle, she wrote, "the British horse gave himself the master whom he knew to be far more ruthless in a British way than anything possible to be produced elsewhere in Europe."[38]

The sailors of the French fleet at Oran had the year before experienced Churchill's "British way" of ruthlessness. Hundreds of thousands of Germans—in Dresden, Hamburg, and Berlin—soon learned the veracity of Allingham's observation. Two years hence, 40,000 Germans would die during three nights of RAF raids on Hamburg—the same number of Britons who had died during the first year of Luftwaffe bombing. Churchill took no pleasure in such methods, but he believed war could be waged only with fury. His upbringing and his worship of the British Constitution guaranteed lifelong deferential relationships with Parliament and the Chiefs of Staff, relationships that precluded, up to a point, any unilateral actions that might smack of the bloodthirsty, the foolhardy, or the dictatorial. Yet as he demonstrated when he pressed ahead with the raid on Oran, at times he behaved like a coalition of one, his options open-ended. He was not a dictator, but even if he had been, in early 1941 he lacked the means to sate any dictatorial inclinations. He expressed to Dill the core truth of the matter: "I feel very doubtful of our ability to fight the Germans anywhere on the mainland of Europe."[39]

Churchill—not knowing with certainty Hitler's planned betrayal of Stalin—could only surmise that the Germans and Soviets had between themselves agreed upon more efficient means for the exchange of critical matériel than had Britain and America. In fact, in the four months since Roosevelt had agreed to send fifty American destroyers, only a few that had arrived were battle ready, and all of them, of course, had been given in exchange for British territory. American matériel was not killing many Germans. And Roosevelt's welcome and inspiring words killed no more Germans than did Churchill's. Britain's financial crisis of the previous summer had not ameliorated; it was worsening, daily. Shipping losses had not been stemmed; they worsened each time a convoy sailed. American factories were now turning out British tank turrets and engines—paid for with Britain's diminishing cash reserves—yet all would be for naught if the cargoes never reached Britain. Just before the new year, Churchill, Eden, Beaverbrook, and Chancellor of the Exchequer Kingsley Wood met to discuss a major problem with supplies—the price demanded by the Americans. Rumor out of the London embassy had it that the Americans were prepared to "wash their hands" unless Britain spent more than $250 million—half of its remaining cash reserves—on "Programme B," arms and munitions enough to outfit ten full divisions, forces not needed until late 1942 at the earliest. The British, on the other hand, sought the matériel proposed in "Programme A"—aircraft engines, tanks, and patrol boats, of which they were in desperate need. The meeting ended with the decision to tell the Americans that if they insisted that "B" must precede "A," the British wanted neither.[40]

Churchill had let loose in a mid-December telegram he drafted to Roosevelt: "If you were to 'wash your hands of us' i.e. give us nothing we cannot pay for... we shall certainly not give in," and though Britain could survive for the time being, it "could not be able to beat the Nazi tyranny and gain you the time you require for your rearmament." Again he held his tongue, and the letter. It was never sent.[41]

Churchill, in the spirit of postwar thankfulness, titled his memoir of 1941 *The Grand Alliance*.* Given the meager, though widening, stream of war matériel arriving from America early that year, a more appropriate title might have been *The Grand Abeyance*. He needed an American in London, a man of high official capacity, a man he could trust, a man who grasped what was truly at stake. Roosevelt needed a fixer in London, someone whose advice he could trust and act upon, a man who could

---

* Churchill's choice of *The Grand Alliance* as the title for the third volume of his war memoirs is pure Winston: he bestows his thanks on the Americans for their wartime help while at the same time, in the fashion of an inside joke, invokes a comparison between his war leadership and that of his glorious ancestor, John Churchill, 1st Duke of Marlborough, whose Grand Alliance defeated the Franco-Bavarian army at Blenheim in 1704 during the War of the Spanish Succession.

debunk or verify Joe Kennedy's claims of poor English morale, a man who could judge if Churchill was a drunk, and if he liked or disliked Roosevelt. Both Churchill and Roosevelt needed a man in London who by virtue of his conductivity would complete the circuit and start the juice flowing between the two leaders. In London, during the first week of January, there was no such American.

But he was on his way. Franklin Roosevelt had dispatched to London a man who appeared about as average an American Joe as ever trod the halls of the White House: Harry Hopkins, son of an Iowa gold prospector and traveling salesman, his mother a schoolteacher. Yet Hopkins was no average guy; he was Roosevelt's most trusted adviser, despised equally by those who hated Roosevelt and those who loved the president but, according to Hopkins's biographer Robert E. Sherwood, considered to be "an Iowan combination of Machiavelli, Svengali and Rasputin." He was due to arrive in Britain via floatplane by way of Lisbon on January 9. His visit was considered so inconsequential by the Foreign Office that its minions failed to pass on to Churchill the telegraph announcing his advent. When Churchill first learned that a certain Harry Hopkins would soon be arriving in London, he asked, "Harry who?" When apprised by Brendan Bracken of Hopkins's special relationship with Roosevelt, Churchill, grasping the importance of the visitor, called for the unrolling of red carpets, if any had survived the Blitz.[42]

While dressing for dinner on January 6, the day he delivered his long memo to Ismay, Churchill delivered to Colville "a discourse on Ladysmith and why he always remembered January 6th." Earlier that day he sent a short note off to General Sir Ian Hamilton, a friend since their India days: "Am thinking of you and Wagon Hill when another January sixth brings news of a feat of arms." In his message to Hamilton he recalled as "one of the most happy memories" the two months spent as a newly recommissioned lieutenant in the South African Light Horse during the British march to lift the Boer siege of Ladysmith. There Hamilton commanded a brigade of mounted infantry that held a vital ridge south of the city, Waggon Hill.* In the early hours of January 6, 1900, the Boers smashed into Hamilton's lines. Inexplicably, he had left his left flank exposed. But Hamilton stood his ground and rallied his troops, and for sixteen hours, until thunderstorms put a finish to things late in the afternoon, defended the hill, which if lost might have spelled a different ending for that war. The

* Boer spelling.

besieged British held on until the South African Light Horse appeared on the scene seven weeks later. Churchill, ever in a hurry, was the first of the Light Horse to ride into the relieved city.[43]

Waggon Hill was fought by nineteenth-century men under nineteenth-century conditions. Earthworks snaked along ridgelines, and targeting balloons drifted high overhead. From gun pits came the flash and rumble of rifled cannon. Messages flashed rearward via heliographs; horses sought purchase on muddy slopes as they strained to haul caissons up to the lines. The weapons on the field and all of the slaughter would have been familiar to veterans of Antietam or Cold Harbor, or Balaclava. Yet Waggon Hill qualifies as one of the first battles of the twentieth century, not only temporally but by virtue of the deployment of water-cooled machine guns, sandbagged gun emplacements, and the lethal steel ribbons of rusted barbed wire, upon which hung the bodies of young Englishmen and Boers. The era in which they had grown to manhood died there with them that day. Four decades on, their battle had long since been forgotten, except by those few still alive who had fought alongside them and those, like Winston Churchill, who wished they had.

The feat of arms that Churchill brought to Hamilton's attention—the capture of Bardia—was a minor affair against the Italians on the Libyan coast, and by no means a victory to compare with Ladysmith. As Churchill spun his tale to Colville, Franklin Roosevelt was preparing to deliver his State of the Union address before the U.S. Congress, giving Churchill a new reason to remember the date of January 6. At 2:03 P.M. eastern standard time, Roosevelt steadied himself behind the podium. Then before the assembled senators and representatives, three network microphones, and his wife, Eleanor, who looked down from the gallery, he sketched the general outline of Lend-Lease. During the next fifteen minutes, in terms sure to encourage Churchill and infuriate Hitler and isolationists alike, he pledged American support for those countries fighting against the Axis, and more:

> I... ask this Congress for authority and for funds sufficient to manufacture additional munitions and war supplies of many kinds, to be turned over to those nations which are now in actual war with aggressor nations.... They do not need man power, but they do need billions of dollars worth of the weapons of defense.
>
> The time is near when they will not be able to pay for them all in ready cash. We cannot, and we will not, tell them that they must surrender, merely because of present inability to pay for the weapons which we know they must have.
>
> I do not recommend that we make them a loan of dollars with which to pay for these weapons.... Let us say to the democracies....

> We Americans are vitally concerned in your defense of freedom. We shall send you, in ever-increasing numbers, ships, planes, tanks, guns. This is our purpose and our pledge.[44]

There it was. No American cruisers would be going to Cape Town to haul away Britain's gold. Roosevelt would stand in as Churchill's second in the great duel. To Greece, China, and Britain foremost would go several billions of dollars' worth of tanks, clothing, food, guns, ammunition, and fuel. With crude oil priced at about $1.15 per barrel, a Colt .45 "tommy gun" at about $200, the newly tested half-ton reconnaissance car—the Jeep—at around $800, and new B-17s rolling off the line at $276,000 apiece, several billions of dollars' worth of matériel would go a long way indeed.[45]

The president's words—*if* they translated into congressional action—eased the most acute of Churchill's financial worries, for an infusion of American matériel with costs deferred would buy time. Yet Roosevelt had spoken to matters far beyond merely buying time for Britain. He spoke to America's future, with profound consequences for Churchill and the British Empire. His address has been known since as the "Four Freedoms" speech, in reference to the four moral precepts he attached to the end, a caboose that evolved into a locomotive. The address was a sublime statement of American generosity and American democratic ideals. It contained no mention of Churchill and, but for two offhand references to the British navy, no reference to the British Empire. To those who might reasonably seek a moral basis for aiding nations arrayed against Japan and Germany, to those who asked why this largess, Roosevelt offered his "Four Freedoms":

> In the future days, which we seek to make secure, we look forward to a world founded upon four essential human freedoms.
>
> The first is freedom of speech and expression—everywhere in the world.
>
> The second is freedom of every person to worship God in his own way—everywhere in the world.
>
> The third is freedom from want...which will secure to every nation a healthy peacetime life for its inhabitants—everywhere in the world.
>
> The fourth is freedom from fear, which, translated into world terms, means a world-wide reduction of armaments to such a point... that no nation will be in a position to commit an act of physical aggression against any neighbor—anywhere in the world....
>
> Freedom means the supremacy of human rights everywhere. Our support goes to those who struggle to gain those rights or keep them....To that high concept there can be no end save victory.

Franklin Roosevelt had pushed open an imposing portal that America would never, could never, close. He did not immediately step through. He and America were not prepared. Yet he had announced his intent to remake the world in America's image. *"Our support goes to those who struggle to gain those rights or keep them"* is an absolute statement that admits to no moral relativism and cannot be applied on a sliding scale. Roosevelt usually favored building coalitions, yet he had just made a case for unilateralism in the propagation of freedom.

He had made plain that dictators would not be tolerated in this new world order. He decreed that the Four Freedoms held everywhere. Yet "the democracies" he pledged to support included Greece, run by a dictator, and China, run by the corrupt Chiang Kai-shek. And what of empires of the democratic, liberal, British variety? Here, Roosevelt was silent. In Churchill's world, "empire" and "freedom" were interchangeable, if the empire in question was the British Empire. Not so in Roosevelt's world, as Churchill would learn to his enormous consternation in the coming months and years. Of democratic rights, Roosevelt had not declared, "Our support goes to those who struggle to keep those rights." Rather, he announced his intent to support those who struggle to *gain* or keep those rights. Yet within the British Empire such rights were granted by His Majesty's Government. Within the British Empire, some who struggled to gain those rights—Louis Botha, Michael Collins, Gandhi—were considered terrorists.

Reaction to the address was predictable. The influential German newspaper *Deutsche Allgemeine Zeitung* dismissed it as "Eccentric Arguments for a Lost Cause." The *Chicago Tribune* took much the same position: Lend-Lease would prove "a bill for the destruction of the American Republic."

Churchill's wait was almost over. He would not see the actual wording of the Lend-Lease bill for four days, but, despite his uncertainty as to its specific content, he had heard enough to express his thanks to Roosevelt in a speech January 9, on the occasion of Lord Halifax's imminent departure to Washington as the Crown's new ambassador: "I therefore hail it as a most fortunate occurrence that in this awe-striking climax in world affairs there should stand at the head of the American Republic a famous statesman . . . in whose heart there burns the fire of resistance to aggression and oppression, and whose sympathies and nature make him the sincere and undoubted champion of justice and freedom, and of the victims of wrongdoing wherever they may dwell."[46]

Halifax's departure was eclipsed by the golden promises from Washington. Still, Churchill found much good to say about the repentant appeaser: "In Edward Halifax we have a man of light and leading, whose company is a treat and whose friendship is an honor to enjoy," a man who has "never swerved from the path of duty as he saw it shining out before him." Halifax did not behold any prospects of luminous paths in his new position. He confided to Alec Cadogan that he felt the prime minister was trying to get rid of him. Cadogan had not the heart to tell Halifax that he was correct, or that he, Cadogan, thought the appointment "a grave mistake." Then there was the matter of Halifax's feelings about Americans. To Stanley Baldwin, Halifax wrote, "I have never liked Americans, except the odd ones. In the mass I have always thought them dreadful!" Yet Halifax embraced his new American duties with alacrity, and conducted them with wisdom and finesse.[47]

Churchill, in his send-off for Halifax, avoided any trip wires. In any case, he wasn't speaking to those millions, nor directly to Roosevelt, but to Roosevelt's good friend and adviser Harry Hopkins, who, just arrived in London, would surely hear of the kind words Churchill had spoken about his boss, sugary words that would no doubt be fresh in Hopkins's mind when he lunched with Churchill the following day. And that was a good thing, for Churchill by now understood that Hopkins was no ordinary visitor.

Before the new partners could get down to the business of financing Britain's war, Churchill had first to win over Hopkins, and Roosevelt had to fight a political battle. Roosevelt knew that no critic could with truth say Lend-Lease committed a single American soldier to the British cause. The president's position, a slippery foothold on the truth, was that Lend-Lease would help guarantee only that Britain get the job done *without* American troops. Roosevelt had talked himself into a Harold Lloyd sort of pickle, out on a ledge with no place to go. He had to nudge America close enough to Churchill's fight to make a difference, yet not so close as to be drawn over the edge. The last war and the sordid peace that followed (both of which looked to many Americans like sops to Old Europe) were fresh in Roosevelt's memory. He was not a European patriot and in fact believed European spheres of influence led inexorably to European wars. If Roosevelt was to join Churchill's cause, he knew that he must articulate new principles—his Four Freedoms—on which to base his proposed policies. Roosevelt truly believed that England defeated meant America threatened, that is, American *interests* threatened. Many in Congress did not. Yet the president and the Congress had plenty of time to work things out. America would not be rushed by anyone.

Churchill was "delighted" by the Lend-Lease bill, Colville told his diary on the eleventh, adding that Churchill considered Lend-Lease to be "a virtual open declaration of war" or "at any rate an open challenge to Germany to declare war if she dares." But the prime minister was well aware, too, of the sentiments of his Chancellor of the Exchequer, Kingsley Wood, who told Colville on the tenth: "In view of this bill [Lend-Lease] it will be more difficult for us to resist the American tendency to strip us of everything we possess as payment for what we are about to receive."[48]

As Lend-Lease was making its way through the U.S. House of Representatives and, if passed there, the U.S. Senate, Churchill knew he must keep his frustrations with American inertia private, and muzzle those of his many colleagues who bitterly protested the lease of the West Indian bases to America as amounting to the same sort of "capitulation" Britain had demanded of Turkey and China in the nineteenth century. Churchill understood that the sorry state of the American destroyers and the injury to national pride over the loss of West Indian bases were ultimately irrelevant. The real significance of Lend-Lease, for which he was effusively grateful, was that it brought America a step closer to war. Lend-Lease took shape not because Churchill had begged so effectively or had outfoxed Franklin Roosevelt—he had not—but because Roosevelt, in spite of tremendous political risk and strong popular dissent, considered it to be in America's interest to aid Britain and, of more immediate political concern, judged his countrymen ready to join him in taking that step.[49]

Roosevelt knew that in defending Lend-Lease he must avoid any statement that bolstered the isolationist case. He had to focus more on the morality of the war than on the weapons Churchill needed, because without a national consensus on the former, the latter would never be manufactured in sufficient quantities to make any difference. In shepherding America to war, or at the least, to preparedness for war, he could not take too long or too heavy a step. He shanghaied Harvard University president James Conant into testifying in support of Lend-Lease before Congress and impressed upon him the need to address only what it authorized, not what it might portend, though failure to pass the bill would, Roosevelt argued, put America at risk of attack should Britain be defeated.

The isolationists did not buy any of it. Although they supported modest aid for Britain, Conant believed they wanted a guarantee that Lend-Lease "would not be a step toward America's involvement in the war." They would get no such guarantee even were Roosevelt in a giving mood, which he told Conant he was not. Yet Roosevelt had preempted the isolationists, who could not afford to appear weak on defense, nor could they criticize the self-evident Four Freedoms. Any attack in that quarter would engender as much support as an attack on motherhood. Still, they knew their countrymen. Vanquishing true and absolute Evil didn't much cut it in 1941 America. Nor among the isolationist America Firsters did the Wilsonian mandate that America "must make the world safe for democracy." America had turned inward during the 1930s, properly so, claimed the isolationists, for danger lurked without.[50]

The isolationist argument was simple, and inflexible. Britain's plight did not much move isolationists, because they saw Britain as everything America strove not to be: imperial, elitist, defined by class distinctions, made wealthy by virtue of taking goods from its colonies rather than by virtue of making goods at home. Could this realm, this distant island, this England, even be properly termed a democracy? Such were the questions Congress would debate. The isolationists prepared massive opposition, much of it centered on Churchill. In the minds of America Firsters, Churchill's pledge to *never* negotiate an end to the war had lured Roosevelt into a cursed web.[51]

For many Americans, and not just the America Firsters, here was Old Europe at it again. Americans had gone over once before and received small thanks, had not even been repaid the money they loaned to defeat the Kaiser. Churchill understood this. He respected Americans enough to stay out of their debate, or at least to not enter it directly. Rather than try to inspire Americans, as he had his countrymen in 1940, he intended to inspire Hopkins.

Churchill knew that his people were willing to take the aerial punishment, but only as long as they believed something greater than aerial revenge upon German cities was forthcoming. Britons craved a real victory in the field against Hitler's armies. A victory of any size would do, obtained in any fashion, and on any front. Still, although he had yet to deliver such a victory, a visit by Churchill to a wrecked neighborhood always brought cheers from the locals. Londoners, when they stuck tattered little Union Jacks into their piles of smashed bricks and snapped timbers, sent a statement of deadly purpose to Churchill. Churchill, in turn, with each appearance, told them that he heard them.

That year he toured every major industrial city and port in England, Scotland, and Wales. He liked to drop into airfields, barracks, AA emplacements, and coastal defenses, and hoist a toast to the defenders, preferably with whisky ("I like my tea cool and *yella*" he told a young officer who offered him a spot of tea during one such visit). If, when he was strolling along St. James's Street on his way to business in Whitehall, a passing workman proffered a hand, he took it. He understood the need to be seen and heard by the people. He grasped the power of photographs to record visits to blasted neighborhoods, such that every citizen who viewed the images felt as if their Winnie had visited their house and theirs alone.[52]

He chose settings with dazzling skill, where the symbolism of the moment could be captured on film, as with his visit later in the spring to the House of Commons after a bomb the night before obliterated the debating chamber. He was seen to have tears in his eyes as he surveyed the wreckage and pledged, in a steady but strained voice, to rebuild the chamber. But when a photographer appeared, his demeanor changed. The resultant photograph captured the scene as choreographed by Churchill. There he stands, in profile, the sharp white northern latitude light diffused by a fine haze of pulverized stone, a scene of utter wreckage, the ancient seat of government smashed. Yet it is Churchill more than the wreckage that the observer notes, his chin thrust forward in defiance, an invitation to Hitler to take another swing. His gaze in such photos is firm, and always directed at a particular shocked or bewildered bomb victim, or skyward, toward some unseen enemy, perhaps toward a higher power, though he put little faith in higher powers. His eyes are never downcast. There is a contemplative quotient to his stare, as if he were regarding a vista he intended to paint. And there is a calmness, too, as if his thoughts were simultaneously with the bomb victim—whether an old Cockney woman or the Commons itself—and in some faraway place. It is the hard, unsettling gaze of a man who has been wronged, and who is intent on righting that wrong.

A visit to a burning street, a few words, a symbolic pose assumed at the instant the photographer triggered his flash, a posture of immutability and imperturbability—this was about all Churchill could offer Britons as the Blitz wore on. He could not of course tell them of naval and troop dispositions; even weather forecasts were censored. He told them he would share with them in the suffering. He told them they must wait for victory. And he told them, "I make no promises and give no guarantees, except that we will do our best." And from them he expected their best. He presumed that not only *could* London take it, but that London *would* take it. Harold Nicolson recorded his appreciation: Churchill "does not try to cheer us up with vain promises." Churchill knew his countrymen. When offered the choice to deliver false good news or the hard truth, he served the bad, for Englishmen, he proclaimed, "seem to like their food cooked that way."[53]

Like Nicolson, so, too, did Churchill hear the murmurings for revenge during his wanderings about town. In Berlin, the Tiergarten, roped off, became increasingly pocked with bomb craters. But British bomb damage, measured by smashed machine tools and fuel depots, was meager, a fact Churchill was acutely aware of. The Germans had dropped far more bombs on Britain since September than the RAF had dropped on Germany, almost four tons of bombs for each ton the British dropped. Even had the British attained tonnage parity, RAF targeting was so terrible that the awful results would not have changed. As well, the price paid in manpower for such inefficiencies could not be maintained. More RAF bomb crews had been killed or captured over Germany than Berliners had been killed on the ground. The most recent testimony to RAF aerial inefficiencies took the form of a message delivered on the last day of 1940 from the British embassy in Budapest. The American naval attaché in Berlin had stated that British air raids on Berlin had done "little damage." Churchill found that intelligence the most troublesome of many such "melancholy reports." The matter of bombing imprecision, he told his staff, "causes me a great deal of anxiety." And yet, although the RAF raids had little effect on German industrial production, they boosted the morale of Englishmen, a trade-off Churchill was forced to accept.[54]

Big four-engine Stirling and Halifax bombers were rolling off assembly lines; they could tote almost seven tons of bombs, nearly triple the capacity of the Luftwaffe's Dorniers and Heinkels. The Avro Lancaster heavy bomber (ready for flight tests) would comprise a horrific weapons system when loaded with a four-thousand-pound bomb (not yet fully developed) and dozens of thirty-pound phosphorous bombs (not yet produced in sufficient quantities) along with hundreds of incendiary bombs. The big bomb was intended to blow away roofs and windows within a wide radius, thus assuring an ample supply of air to fuel the incendiaries and the phosphorous bombs, the former designed to start fires, the latter to melt anything, including people, that came in contact with the phosphorous gel. The Prof believed that German morale would suffer under such an onslaught, a beneficial side effect of the bombing strategy, the primary objective of which was the destruction of Germany's industrial capacity. It was based on the assumption championed by Churchill that even were Hitler to reach the gates of India or the Suez, if Germany itself was destroyed, Hitler must lose his war. Churchill, throughout the year, told his friends and family in the most graphic terms what he planned to do to German cities; in his broadcasts, he told Hitler and the people of Germany. He warned them:

> You do your worst and we will do our best. Perhaps it may be our turn soon; perhaps it may be our turn now. We live in a terrible epoch of the human story, but we believe there is a broad and sure justice running through its theme. It is time that the Germans should be made to suffer in their own homeland and cities something of the torment they have twice in our lifetime let loose upon their neighbours and upon the world.[55]

Few in Germany took him seriously. Hitler derided him as "that noted war correspondent." Churchill was well known for his bluster. Yet he yearned for the day when his Lancasters—hundreds of Lancasters flying in great formations—would show them all, Hitler foremost, that his threats had been anything but bluster. He pressed the Ministry of Production for "the largest supply of aircraft gas containers for immediate retaliation" after learning that the army was well supplied with gas artillery shells, an anomalous state of affairs given that "one would hardly expect the army to be engaged in firing gas shells for the next few months. Only invasion would seem to render this necessary." The very quantity—seven thousand—of aircraft gas bombs indicates he envisioned for them a strategic rather than a tactical role.[56]

Hitler considered Churchill the obstacle to peace, and promised "to drop 100 bombs" for each British bomb until Britain gets rid of "this criminal and his methods." The Führer termed Churchill's speeches to Englishmen "symptomatic of a paralytic disease, or the ravings of a drunkard." Such bellicosity delighted Churchill, who listened on a gramophone to translated versions of Hitler's rants. He instructed the technicians to leave intact on the recordings the background cheers of the Führer's adoring hordes. Churchill liked to march around his study in his dressing gown while repeating the parts where Hitler mentioned him by name. Had Hitler better understood the tenacity of Britons and their Parliament, he would have known that Churchill was here to stay. At the height of the Blitz, by a vote of 341–4 the Commons rejected an Independent Labour Party motion to negotiate an armistice. Given the traditional fractiousness of British politics, this was a remarkable declaration of intent to fight on, and to do so behind Churchill.[57]

Yet many, including Jock Colville (who shuddered at the idea of a Nazi victory), thought the prospects afforded by a compromise peace preferable to the prospect of "western Europe racked by warfare and economic hardship; the legacy of centuries, in art and culture, swept away; the health of the nation dangerously impaired by malnutrition, nervous strain and epidemics; Russia and the U.S. profiting from our exhaustion; and at the end of it all compromise or a Pyrrhic victory." Such a scenario had recently been advanced by the military historian and strategist Basil Liddell Hart, who predicted that Hitler, with Napoleon's fate in mind, as well as his outrage over the punishing Versailles peace terms imposed after the Great War, would be emboldened to fight on even were that to ensure the destruction of Germany and all Europe. Of Liddell Hart's thesis, Churchill declared, "It is out of date and he seems more a candidate for a mental home than for serious action." Curiously, Churchill had long adhered to another of Liddell Hart's theories, to always attack the weaker of two military enemies.[58]

As to the immediacy of any German threat to British soil and the climactic battle he so sought, Churchill concluded after a perusal of early January Ultra decrypts that invasion would not come in the winter and likely not in the spring either. It appeared that German troops in the northern coastal areas of France and Belgium were being shipped to the south, thereby reducing the chances of invasion. This opinion he chose not to share with the Americans, for fear that the U.S. supply effort might wane. Some of his military advisers—who read the same Enigma decrypts—disagreed with him and insisted that invasion was still imminent. He encouraged them to prepare for that eventuality—to seek more tanks, more artillery, more gunboats, more infantry divisions. The greater the buildup of military might, the better, he reasoned, for, as he had since the previous June, Churchill intended to use it elsewhere. As his own minister of defence, he told the War Cabinet he wanted to again reinforce Wavell in the Middle East as he had in the autumn, with even more troops and tanks stripped from Britain. He possessed great persuasive skills but not dictatorial powers; the War Cabinet had to approve the reinforcements, and the army, air force, and naval chiefs sought to keep the troops on the Home Island. Churchill demanded that the fight be taken to the Italians in North Africa. He sought, as well, to bait Hitler into reinforcing Mussolini in Africa. He confided to Colville that he "did not see how invasion [of England] could be successful and he now woke up in the mornings... feeling as if he had a bottle of Champagne inside him and glad that another day had come." As the Germans appeared unwilling to put themselves within his reach by descending onto British beaches, Churchill would satisfy himself with battling Italians until such time as Hitler came to their assistance. Then he could fight Germans.[59]

What he could do on the Continent that winter was limited to a few inaccurate bombs and much bombast lobbed in Hitler's direction. He launched pleas to Roosevelt, scribbled numerous memos, attended War Cabinet meetings, kept the King apprised, and waited for American help and better bombing weather to arrive. That was a meteorological knife that cut both ways. The same storms that grounded German night raiders grounded Bomber Command. The first weeks of the new year administered repeated doses of wretched weather. From Moscow, where temperatures fell to below minus twenty-five degrees Fahrenheit, to the Dover coast, which froze, snow, sleet, and bitter cold swept the Continent. Blizzards hit southern France before whipping northwestward across Brittany, and then across the Channel, across Britain, and out into the Atlantic, where Allied convoys pitched and rolled in the furious gales. Central France suffered its worst snowstorm in fifty years, Hungary its coldest winter in more than one hundred. Spaniards, already starving, now froze. Belgians found themselves down to less than two ounces of meat per person per day. Typhus killed the children of Warsaw; bread in that city was not to be had, because Stalin and Hitler had split between themselves the entire Polish wheat harvest.

Although the Luftwaffe in January proved less a strategic presence than a deadly nuisance, almost 1,600 Britons died that month. At the end of the month, the civilian death toll since the start of the Blitz stood at 30,000, fully half of the total British casualties, military and civilian, since the start of the war. Almost 500,000 apartments and houses had been destroyed. The cost to the Germans since late September had been about 600 planes and crews, less than 2 percent of sorties flown. Yet despite their relatively modest losses, the Germans had little to show. British aircraft production had not in the least been hobbled.

The Blitz in 1941, Churchill later wrote, fell into three phases, the first phase being the January lull. Londoners termed the relatively quiet skies the "Lullablitz." The quiet only heightened the uncertainty of where and when the Luftwaffe would next strike and made these weeks a time, Churchill later wrote, "to peer into the future and attempt to measure our ordeal." He asked his RAF chiefs, Beaverbrook, and the intelligence chiefs to determine if the abeyance in raids was due solely to foul weather or to the depletion of German air capabilities, or, the most troubling scenario, if it was purely voluntary, with more sinister plans being readied for the spring. What, Churchill demanded, were German capacities and limitations when it came to airmen, engines, training, planes, and bombs? As the assessments of German strength arrived from various ministries, the Prof weighed the increasingly conflicting statistics while Churchill kept his distance and allowed everyone to have at it. When he convened his chiefs at Chequers to distill the conclusions, the overriding consensus was that nobody knew what the prime minister needed to know.[60]

One certainty stood out among the uncertainties: if things were to be made right in the air, Max Beaverbrook would do so. The Beaver had the face of a gargoyle, a Canadian maritime accent as heavy as a sodden goose-down comforter, and the absolute loyalty of Churchill. He suffered from asthma and continued to threaten to resign when he felt put out, which was often. Churchill refused to consider any such exit. Beaverbrook's mid-1940 crusade at the Ministry of Aircraft Production to expand fighter production had "played havoc with the war policy of the RAF," lamented air chief marshal Joubert, "but he most certainly produced the aircraft that won the Battle of Britain." By early 1941, the strength of RAF bomber and fighter squadrons had increased by almost half over 1940's total, but Britain's three thousand combat-ready planes remained far outnumbered by the Luftwaffe's fleet. That the gap was closing was due to Max.

All Britons wondered about the quiet skies, and worried, for surely this must be the calm before the storm. Had not a disquieting calm settled over all of Hitler's previous targets in the days and weeks before he struck? Mollie Panter-Downes observed that Londoners appeared "to be taking advantage of what may be the last few weeks of comparative sanity to warn everybody else that complete chaos is approaching." Chemical warfare was expected. But what exactly did *chemical* warfare mean? Would pestilence, plague, and other unimaginable vectors of death be delivered by fantastical weapons? Rumor spread that English women would be compelled by the conquerors to bear German babies and that English males would be sterilized. (The truth was more appalling. SS Reichsführer Heinrich Himmler put forth his plans the previous summer in the *Sonderfahndungsliste GB*, or Special Search List for the invasion of Great Britain, which called for all healthy Englishmen of military age to be shipped to Greater Germany as slaves. Six battalions of *Einsatzgruppen*—the hunter-killers of the SS—would be stationed in a half dozen major British cities to facilitate the roundup.)[61]

The paranoia found its way into official circles. Sir John Anderson, now Lord President of the Council, kept up pressure on refugees from the Continent, including Jews who had fled the Nazis without proper paperwork.* Hundreds were rounded up and made to join thousands of other continentals who had been interred in camps since the summer. Arthur Koestler, the repentant former Communist, arrived in Britain without proper paperwork and was packed off to Pentonville Prison, where he resided behind bars for almost two months, during which time *Darkness at Noon* was published. "It was a terrible time," recalled the actor Paul Henreid. "We jumped at every ring of the doorbell... an apprehensive dread took hold of us. How long before it was our turn?" Yet most detainees—excepting hardcase Fascists such as Oswald Mosley—were released in coming months. Henreid's dread would have deepened had he known that Himmler knew who had fled to England; their names were on the *Sonderfahndungsliste GB*. They were to be found and killed. The dread and paranoia spread to Ireland after Luftwaffe raiders overflew their British targets in early January and dropped their payloads onto Irish farms. A one-ton parachute bomb dropped into Dublin's Jewish quarter and hit the city's

* Two hundred thousand European Jews had been granted immigration status by HMG since 1933, more than twice the per-capita rate of the U.S., which had accepted 160,000. See Peter Clarke, *The Last Thousand Days of the British Empire* (New York: Bloomsbury Press, 2008), 409.

largest synagogue, an incident that Goebbels claimed the British had perpetrated in order to sully the good name of Germany among Irishmen.[62]

For Churchill, Britons' fears begat vigilance, which was good. His most pressing problem early in the year was not keeping the Germans out of England—he did not believe they were coming, other than by air. His critical problem was getting food and munitions in. Since October, U-boats in the Western Approaches had sent more than 150 British ships to the bottom, an average of 70,000 tons per week. January's miserable weather helped moderate the losses, but in early February, with Göring on vacation enjoying his toy trains and pilfered art, Admiral Raeder asked Hitler to augment Admiral Karl Dönitz's U-boats with several dozen of Göring's two hundred or so four-engine Focke-Wulf 200 long-range bombers. The pride of Göring's air fleet, they cruised at 220 miles per hour, could tote a 4,400-pound bombload, and had enough range to take off from Norway, fly around the British Isles, and land in occupied France. The bombers, Raeder argued, could perform reconnaissance duty and hit ships threading their way into ports. Hitler approved the request, and the results were immediate. February saw 320,000 tons of British shipping sunk, including 86,000 tons sent down by German aircraft. So great were British shipping losses and so meager was British air cover over the ports, especially at night, that a suggestion to put cats in the cockpits of fighter planes made the rounds in the RAF. The idea was that RAF pilots (who had been issued extra rations of carrots to augment their night vision) would shoot in the direction in which the cats looked, cats presumably seeing better than humans at night. If anyone had a better idea, now was the time to propose it, for between the losses at sea and the German's smashing up of the ports, Britain found itself more isolated than ever. "This mortal danger to our lifeline gnaws at my bowels," wrote Churchill. "The decision for 1941," he predicted, "lies upon the seas."[63]

He did not know that Dönitz had only twenty-two U-boats in the French Atlantic ports or that he could send only a dozen or so to sea at any one time. These months afforded the German navy its best opportunity to squeeze the life out of Britain, but Dönitz lacked the boats to do so. Still, he appeared near enough to ruling the waves that when an Admiralty report of yet another shipping disaster reached Churchill, he fretted to Colville (who had termed the news "distressing"): "Distressing? It is terrifying. If it goes on it will be the end of us."[64]

Hyperbolic though Churchill's outburst might now seem, at the time it was anything but. In the coming months, the battle in the Atlantic would decide Britain's fate. U-boats hunted British shipping westward to the central Atlantic, far beyond the range of British air patrols. Without enough hulls to carry the food they needed, Churchill faced a terrible choice: food shortages or weapons shortages. Britain could afford neither. Unless Franklin Roosevelt expanded the U.S. patrol zone into the eastern Atlantic, Britain's losses could only worsen. Roosevelt, to Churchill's dismay, declined to expose his navy to any new dangers by doing so.

The steel monsters plying the surface matched the terror of the U-boats. *Bismarck* and *Tirpitz,* undergoing final fitting-out somewhere in the Baltic, loomed as two of the Führer's instruments of springtime destruction. Almost 42,000 tons of displacement each, *Bismarck* and *Tirpitz* were armed with eight fifteen-inch guns, powered by three Blohm & Voss turbines and a dozen Wagner boilers that generated 138,000 horsepower and speed in excess of 31 knots—over thirty-five miles an hour. Their optical equipment for targeting purposes was far superior to anything the British had, and they could outrun and outshoot any British battleship afloat. Yet Churchill, during the first weeks of 1941, did not even know where *Bismarck* was. The very uncertainty as to the two ships' whereabouts was their greatest strength. Churchill later wrote that had Hitler kept "both in full readiness in the Baltic and allow rumors of an impending sortie to leak out from time to time," the Royal Navy "should thus have been compelled to keep concentrated at Scapa Flow...practically every new ship we had," with the result that convoys, already insufficiently guarded, would remain so. Allied (British, Dutch, Norwegian, and Canadian) merchant ships sailed with so little escort and were attacked so regularly that crews kept their lifeboats slung out over the sides for the entire voyage, ready for use.[65]

Such were the generally deplorable conditions upon the seas and in the air during the first two months of 1941. Living conditions on the Continent, from Poland to France, had only worsened since the previous May. Someday, somehow—if Churchill could drag the U.S. into the fight—the final and determining battles would be fought there. Until then, Churchill could only use the occasional broadcast to try to boost the morale of the enslaved Europeans as he had the spirits of Britons in 1940.

It was a hopeless task. Hitler had buried the hopes of all those he had conquered. Hitler held the western half of Europe, Stalin the eastern half. With the release of winter's grip, the dictators planned to tighten theirs. They were partners. Stalin had been a faithful and dependable vendor to the Reich since Hitler struck westward to vanquish the imperialist democracies. He pledged to pour millions more tons of Russian grain and oil into Germany in the coming year. In return, Hitler promised to boost shipments of steel and capital goods to Russia. The target date for the first influx of German steel was mid-1941.

Hitler was most conciliatory regarding Russia in his New Year's greeting to Mussolini: "I do not envision any Russian initiative against us so long as Stalin is alive, and we ourselves are not victims of any serious setbacks.... I should like to add to these general considerations that our present relations with the U.S.S.R. are very good." Those words were a work of pathological obfuscation. German intelligence could detect no hint of any Soviet "initiative" against Germany because none was in any way contemplated. The Soviets sought only increased trade with Germany and increased influence in Eastern Europe, although Soviet foreign minister Vyacheslav Molotov manifested a stubborn greed during his November talks with Ribbentrop. Molotov demanded more leverage in the Balkans. He demanded that German troops leave Finland and that Germany acknowledge Bulgaria to be within the Soviet sphere of influence. As well, he demanded that Hitler divulge any plans he might have pertaining to the Balkans and Greece.[66]

Such impudent requests infuriated Hitler, for he needed free rein in the region, especially in Bulgaria, in order to protect his southern flank from anticipated British adventures in Greece, and for another compelling reason, which he of course did not disclose to Stalin. The previous July he had told his commanders that he intended to attack Russia in the spring. This was why Bulgaria assumed new strategic importance; it not only protected the German southern flank from the British should they land in Greece but also anchored the southern flank of Hitler's line opposite Stalin. In order to deflect Stalin's gaze from central Europe, Hitler dangled the tantalizing prospects of a Russian share in the spoils of the dismembered British Empire were the Soviets to make the Tripartite Pact a four-way deal. So much plunder would there be, and so rich the rewards for the Soviets—in the Far East, the Near East, and in attaining their ancient goal of ready access to the Mediterranean. The idea appealed to Stalin. Yet England fought on, and Hitler could not yet deliver the corpse of the British Empire.

To Stalin, a greater role in the Balkans and Bulgaria appeared the more modest and surer bet and would result in Moscow's geographical buffer edging farther west. In essence, it would result in Germany and Russia sharing hegemony in east-central Europe. Churchill believed Hitler never intended to share power, and he had tried to warn Stalin of that the previous June. Hitler had made clear in *Mein Kampf* that Germany's destiny lay in the east. He had written that modern Germany would pick up where the Teutonic knights had left off six hundred years earlier, in east Prussia. He described the "regents of present-day Russia" as "common blood-stained animals" who belonged to "a nation which combines a rare mixture of bestial horror with an inconceivable gift for lying." Hitler had always believed *Lebensraum* ("living space") lay in the east, that is, in Russia. That was why in mid-1940 he ordered OKW to begin planning for the invasion of Russia, and why, in December, he approved OKW's plan (Barbarossa), which called for the attack to begin in mid-May, with victory expected in five months, before winter.[67]

The logic of a betrayal of Stalin was lost on everybody except Hitler and some—but by no means all—of his inner circle. Churchill, as he had the previous summer, tried to open up a line of communication with Stalin of the sort he had with Roosevelt. He failed. Stalin believed any warnings sent his way by London were ruses, ploys to precipitate trouble between Russia and its good friend Germany. In any case, Churchill had no hard intelligence to confirm his suspicions. Nor, early in the year, did the Americans. The American diplomat George Kennan later wrote that the American legation in Berlin, where Kennan then served, was "slow to recognize that in Hitler's logic the inability to invade Britain would inevitably spell the necessity of invading Russia." William L. Shirer's sources in Berlin hinted at that outcome, but Shirer assumed along with the rest of the world that England must first be conquered. In late 1940, Shirer pondered in his diary the prospects of Hitler going to war with either America or Russia: "I am firmly convinced he does contemplate it and if he wins in Europe and Africa he will in the end launch it unless [because of isolationist appeasement] we are prepared to give up our way of life." Once victorious in Europe, Shirer wrote, Hitler "will attack Russia, probably before he tackles the Americas." Yet, "Hitler's Germany can never dominate the continent of Europe as long as Britain holds out."[68]

Churchill had believed that for a year, too. But he realized that were Hitler to crush the Russians, he could build more sinister heavy bombers at leisure, and perhaps even rocket weapons. He could build ships, U-boats, and modern landing craft. The Führer could then turn his armies westward, toward Britain. Churchill prepared Britons for that eventuality, and prepared his home armies, as well. The next move was Hitler's. If he came to England in the spring, Churchill, his armies growing by the week, would be ready. If Hitler did not come to England, the day would come—perhaps two years hence—when Churchill would go to Europe. That was the plan. But Churchill faced a plethora of unknowns. He sensed the course Hitler would take in the east, but he lacked the counterintuitive instincts and the hard intelligence necessary to parse Hitler's contorted logic. He could only wait.

Other than by air, Churchill could not take the battle directly to Hitler, but he could take it to him indirectly. The previous summer he had approved a proposal to finance and arm those brave enough among the conquered peoples to rise up against their Nazi jailers, to resist by any means and with any weapon. He encouraged those who were too fearful to strike at the enemy; many listened, and in time many fought. During the Battle of Britain he had ordered Ismay to create a force of "specially trained troops of the hunter class" to bring a "reign of terror" to Nazi positions along the European coasts, at first with a strategy of "butcher and bolt," to be followed in time with the storming and reducing of "Hun garrisons" while "leaving a trail of German corpses behind." It was to be a dirty but necessary business.[69]

At the time, Hugh Dalton, minister for economic warfare, which included covert "black" propaganda (lies and misinformation), argued the need "to organize movements in enemy-occupied territory comparable to the Sinn Fein movement in Ireland, to the Chinese Guerillas now operating against Japan...or—one might as well admit it—to the organizations which the Nazis themselves have developed so remarkably in almost every country in the world." A socialist, Dalton called his proposed organization the "democratic international." It would employ tactics such as "industrial and military sabotage, labour agitation and strikes, continuous propaganda, terrorist acts against traitors and German leaders, boycotts and riots." It was clear to Dalton that such an organization must operate "entirely independent" of ordinary departmental or cabinet rules and supervision, including the War Office. In essence, he proposed to Halifax an organizational structure of the sort Americans decades later termed "stand alone and off the shelf." Not only would this special unit function without oversight, but in Dalton's estimation, the success of its future operations depended on "a certain fanatical enthusiasm."[70]

Churchill heartily embraced the scheme. If fanaticism proved necessary in the battle against Hitlerism, then let the mayhem commence. If it did not prove effective, Dalton and his socialist friends could take the blame. In July 1940 Churchill summoned Dalton to join him and the "usual nocturnal visitors"—the Prof and Bracken—to work things up. Over dinner and drinks Churchill asked Dalton to head "a new instrument of war," the Special Operations Executive (SOE). It was exactly the organization Dalton had proposed to Halifax, and it would engage in exactly the sort of murderous raids Churchill had proposed to Ismay. Churchill termed it the "Ministry of Ungentlemanly Warfare." The meeting over, Churchill sent Dalton off with a final command: "And now, set Europe ablaze."[71]

Though that phrase has long been cited as an example of Churchill's determination to smite Hitler, Dalton's biographer, Ben Pimlott, points out the sad irony of the utterance, given the obvious military weakness of Britain at the time. Many within Churchill's circle did not share Dalton's enthusiasm. The Foreign Office was keener on avoiding trouble in Europe than on stirring it up; deceiving friends and neutrals would someday lead to repercussions. And, later in the year, soon after taking over the Ministry of Information, Brendan Bracken, long a political enemy of Dalton, unleashed his own campaign of ungentlemanly rumors directed at the SOE and Dalton. Bracken sought to discredit the SOE in order to merge the "black" propaganda conducted by the SOE into the Ministry of Information, which produced "white" (largely truthful) propaganda. It was a turf war plain and simple. Rumors flourished. Within certain circles the SOE was said to be "infested with crackpots, communists, and homosexuals." T. E. Lawrence, it was whispered around Whitehall, would have given his approval to this "cult of intimate friendship with peasant partisans."[72]

General Auchinleck and Air Marshal Portal had complained to Churchill that the section of SOE that dealt in agitation and subterfuge (versus intelligence) was "a bogus, irresponsible, corrupt show." However unseemly it might appear to refined gentlemen such as Auchinleck and Portal, if assassins could bloody the Nazis, Churchill was all for them. Dalton set up his secret shop in Baker Street.[73]

Whenever they were captured by the Nazis, Dalton's saboteurs and resistance fighters and their families paid a terrible price. Reports of Nazi reprisals against those who defied them arrived daily in Whitehall. When Polish patriots murdered an ethnic German, the Gestapo seized 160 hostages and shot seventeen. Death was the penalty for singing the Polish national anthem. Death was the penalty for two Norwegian trade unionists who had the temerity to speak publicly of fair labor practices. Eighteen Dutch resistance fighters sang their national anthem on the way to their execution. To remind the Dutch that they were not forgotten, British bombers dropped thousands of pounds of tea in two-ounce tea bags with a message: "Greetings from the Free Netherlands Indies. Keep a good heart. Holland will rise again." With the creation of SOE, Churchill came up with something far more lethal than a barrage of tea leaves to help the Dutch—all Europeans—to rise again. To that end, the SOE during the next four years inserted almost five hundred agents, including sixty women (thirteen of whom would be tortured and killed by the Gestapo), behind enemy lines throughout the Continent. If women could spy and if need be kill, Churchill wanted them out there spying and killing. Churchill's SOE agents became—in modern special-forces terminology—force multipliers, sent with his blessing to train the locals, to organize mass mayhem, to spy, and to kill those who needed killing.[74]

HMG could not of course disclose any of this to Britons. Churchill's relationship with Britons was based on the trust he asked them to place in him, and the symbolism he gave in return. During 1941 he had not much else to give but inspiring words, somber poses, and his most inspired gesture of all, the "V" for victory. The "V campaign" began in January when

Victor de Laveleye, a Belgian refugee and head of the BBC Belgian section, made shortwave radio broadcasts from London in which he urged Belgians—who had been scrawling "RAF" on sidewalks and walls—to show their defiance of the Germans by marking the letter "V" in public places. The symbol caught on. In French it stood for *Victorie* (victory); in Flemish (the second major language in Belgium), *Vrijheid* (freedom); in Dutch it stood for *Vryheid* (freedom); in Serbian, *Vitestvo* (heroism); in Czech, *Vitězstoi* (victory). However, with predictable arrogance and astounding stupidity, the Nazis also adopted the symbol. Berlin radio claimed credit for the campaign, noting that the "V"—for *victoria,* the Latin word for "victory"—showed up wherever Germans went in Europe. Indeed it did, but by trying to appropriate the "V" as their own, the Nazis backed themselves into a corner: German soldiers could do nothing but smile and return the salute whenever a Belgian, Dutchman, or Frenchman proffered it. In July, a "Colonel Britton" (the broadcaster Douglas Ritchie) broadcast on the BBC a message from Churchill to occupied Europeans: "It is dark now. Darkness is your chance. Put up your 'V' as a member of this vast army. Do it in the daytime too." They did. In short order, whenever Churchill flashed the "V," flashbulbs popped. The symbol merged with his bulldog snarl into a single defiant entity. For the remainder of his life, he raised it on any occasion of national duress or personal ordeal.[75]

To his staff's amusement and chagrin, Churchill, a cigar gripped between his index and middle fingers, often proffered the "V" with his palm facing inward—the British equivalent of the American raised middle finger—instead of giving the proper, palm-outward salute. Whether the nasty or the patriotic "V," crowds howled with delight, for surely the P.M. was telling Hitler—one way or the other—to bugger off. So powerful was the connection, that had Churchill lost his voice, his two upraised fingers could have done his speaking, without diminution of his message. For the introduction of its nightly overseas programming, the BBC borrowed the first four notes of Beethoven's Fifth Symphony, which corresponded to the Morse code designation for "V"—*dot, dot, dot, dash.* Colonel Britton encouraged the people of occupied Europe to tap the signal on wineglasses and coffee cups whenever Germans entered a room. The Germans were powerless to respond; they claimed to have invented the campaign, after all.[76]

When touring America in 1940, Duff Cooper found that most of the Americans he met held erroneous opinions about Britain. Americans believed the larger Dominions were still colonies of Britain, something like the thirteen American colonies had been. Virtually every American Cooper met had no idea of the bloodshed that HMG believed would likely result in India between Hindu and Muslim were London to abandon that nation, but Americans were steadfast in their opinion that the British were wrong to be there and should get out. Cooper grew to believe that Britain was losing not only the war in Europe but also the propaganda war in America. Churchill believed he knew Americans. He had written, and Americans had read, numerous magazine pieces, collections of essays, and three great works—his biography of Marlborough, his history of World War One, and his eminently readable account of his youth, *My Early Life*. In 1939 he published a collection of essays, *Step by Step,* that explained how during the 1930s Europe marched toward war. But most Americans did not read books by foreign politicians in order to formulate their political opinions or take a man's measure. On his earlier journeys to America in the late twenties, Churchill attained a minor celebrity status, drawing audiences of three to five thousand to his big city lectures, a sizable number, particularly at a time when most Americans cared little about faraway events. (Granted, his speeches then were not designed to unmask the risks to humanity of totalitarianism but to sell his books and articles.)[77]

Churchill's style, wit, and literary abilities had been well documented in the U.S. press for two decades: *Time* magazine in early 1923 put him on the cover of its seventh issue. By the late 1930s Churchill, an exile within his own party, had been much heard in America, and his words were often prescient. In a 1938 *Saturday Evening Post* article he called for a united states of Europe and the jettisoning of European tariffs. And, of course, he predicted the catastrophic violence that had since overtaken Europe. Yet up until December 1941 most Americans, according to Gallup polls, cared neither about the unsavory events in distant lands nor about whether Winston Churchill was correct in his predictions of a new Dark Age. In 1941, Charles Lindbergh filled sports stadiums with tens of thousands who flocked to his isolationist speeches and hissed whenever Lindy mentioned Churchill's name. Americans grasped a simple truth: If America went to war, their sons would fight, and tens of thousands of them would die.

Churchill might have been half American, but he was all English, and an aristocratic Englishman at that. He put on his pants one leg at a time, but his valet held the pants. He wore a large Breguet pocket watch—the "turnip," he called it—on a heavy gold chain pulled across his waistcoat, which imparted to him a Daddy Warbucks look, this during a decade when most Americans could afford neither a waistcoat, a gold watch, nor a gold chain to hang it on.*

---

* Breguet, Paris made since 1775, the timepiece of choice for Washington, Wellington, Napoleon, and most of Europe's royal swells, including Marie Antoinette.

Churchill's political genius did not extend to the mind-set of working-class Americans, yet it was their support he needed. His greatest weakness as he sought American help was his history. Until 1940, Americans knew of only Churchill the loose cannon, impetuous, often witty, sometimes spot-on in his predictions, but in the end unreliable. "He was all snakes and ladders during much of his earlier career," recalled A. J. P. Taylor, "but on the occasions when he climbed the ladder, he'd seem to find a way to snake right back down." Since becoming prime minister, he had inspired Britain, but Britain teetered still on the edge of the abyss. Given his irregular history, he might prove just the man to administer the final push.[78]

Time, in its first issue of January 1941, named the previously unreliable Churchill 1940 Man of the Year. Churchill, the editors declared, shared with Lenin and Hitler a genius for the spoken word. Through their words, these three giants had changed history, two for ill and one, Churchill, for good, but only should he prevail in the current struggle: "He [Churchill] gave his countrymen exactly what he promised them: blood, toil, sweat, tears, and one more thing—untold courage." Some readers wrote the magazine to express surprise. Churchill as Man of the Year? Why not Hitler? Hitler could lay claim to the prize, not because of the enormity of his misdeeds since 1939 but because Hitler, in the opinion of many Americans, had rebuilt Germany. When the first electric lights in Appalachia were just sputtering into incandescence, the *Reichsführer* was building his autobahns, a system of futuristic roadways Americans would not see for another generation. Now he was busting up the old order pretty smartly. A New Jersey letter writer said: "If England wins... the world will have lost the opportunity to be governed by the smartest master since the days of Moses." Though pairing Hitler with the biblical hero who delivered the Jews from tyranny resounds now with terrible irony, many Americans did not consider Hitler—and certainly not the whole of Germany—an enemy. And, Americans wondered, were Britain and Churchill worthy of American aid, or were they imperialists on the brink of defeat, for whom any help would come too late.[79]

To answer those questions Roosevelt had sent Harry Hopkins to London. He arrived in London on January 9, escorted by Brendan Bracken, who had met him at Poole, on the south coast. Hopkins stopped for the latest news at his embassy on Grosvenor Square and then checked into Claridge's. Churchill had sent Bracken to greet Hopkins for good reason. He had been Churchill's friend and fixer for almost two decades. He, like Churchill, was an optimist, but without the pouts and sulks. When the Old Man went into a funk, Bracken could be depended upon to yank him out. He was also a one-man Ministry of Information, full of knowledge across a broad spectrum. Discussions that took place in Bracken's presence, Colville wrote, "required no books of reference." Within hours of Hopkins's arrival, Bracken pronounced Hopkins the "most important visitor to ever arrive on this island." Given his natural enthusiasm, Bracken's hyperbolic assessment of Hopkins's importance seems predictable, yet when Bracken offered an opinion, people listened, Churchill foremost among them.[80]

To Pamela Churchill, Hopkins appeared a "little shriveled creature with a dead cigarette out of the corner of his mouth," huddled against the winter chill wrapped in his great overcoat. His wardrobe looked as if it had never met a flatiron. His dour, crumpled features were usually topped by an equally crumpled fedora, pulled low. "His was a soul," Churchill wrote, "that flamed out of a frail and failing body." He was a welfare expert, four years a widower, and prone to cynicism. He had served as Roosevelt's commerce secretary from December of 1938 until the previous September when, afflicted with intestinal ailments, he resigned. When Roosevelt learned Hopkins was alone and adrift in Washington, he invited him and his young daughter Diana to live in the White House. Diana took a small room on the third floor, Hopkins, the Lincoln study, just down the hall from the Boss.[81]

On the morning of the tenth, Bracken escorted Hopkins to a basement room at No. 10 Downing St. There, while nursing a glass of sherry and waiting for the prime minister, Hopkins took note of the smashed windows, the scrambling repairmen, and the overall decrepitude of the place. Soon, "a rotund-smiling-red-faced gentleman appeared—extended a fat but none the less convincing hand and wished me welcome to England." They adjourned to a small dining room where over lunch they spent more than three hours in private talks. Churchill made plain his desire to meet the president, the sooner the better, a request Hopkins passed along to Roosevelt. Hopkins probed for any ill will toward Americans on Churchill's part by allowing that in some quarters rumor had it that Churchill disliked Roosevelt. Churchill responded with a "bitter though fairly constrained attack" on Joe Kennedy, who Churchill knew (via a tap on Ambassador Kennedy's phone) was virtually an enemy of Great Britain. To prove his warm feelings for Roosevelt, Churchill sent a secretary to fetch a copy of the telegram he had sent on the occasion of Roosevelt's reelection (which Roosevelt had not responded to).[82]

He told Hopkins that Greece was likely lost, and that Britain would gas Germany if Hitler used gas first. Thus began one of Churchill's bloodthirsty performances: "We, too," he told Hopkins, "have the deadliest gasses in the world," and said that they would use them if up against the wall.

On the humanitarian aid front, Churchill declared that he was opposed to feeding the peoples conquered by Hitler, for that would only make Hitler's job of controlling enslaved populations easier. Finally, he told Hopkins that no secrets would be kept from America. That wasn't true, and Churchill knew it; British interagency telegrams marked "Guard" were not to be shared with the Americans. By the time lunch was cleared, the two had connected; Churchill insisted Hopkins join him for a weekend at Ditchley.[83]

They had Ditchley to themselves, Ronnie Tree having gone off to check conditions in his constituency while his wife took her squadron of mobile canteens to Portsmouth, which had caught the full force of the Blitz the previous night. As Ditchley's midday meal was being readied, Colville recalled that "Mr. Hopkins arrived and his quiet charm and dignity held the table," where small talk and champagne put the diners at ease. Hopkins brought news of the Duke of Windsor, who recently had visited Roosevelt on board his yacht off the Bahamas, where Windsor now served as governor general. Apparently the duke "spoke very charmingly of the King" (a fact that touched Winston), but Hopkins allowed "the Duke's recent entourage was very bad." Windsor—forgotten but, alas, not gone—had been keeping company with a stridently pro-Nazi Swede, a fact that would not play well in America were the press to run with it.[84]

The talk turned to Britain's needs. Colville recorded that Hopkins offered that the proposed Lend-Lease program "would arouse loud controversy, but he felt sure it would succeed." Then the discussion turned—or rather, Churchill turned the discussion—to politics. He told Hopkins, forcibly, that socialism was bad, that jingoism was worse, and that the two combined formed "a kind of debased Italian fascism," the worst creed ever designed by man. Churchill may not have been aware that Hopkins's politics ran beyond the liberal to the fringes of socialism. Roosevelt's conservative enemies hated Hopkins even more than they hated the president. In any event, Hopkins was not there to talk political creeds.[85]

Later in the afternoon, dinner guests began to motor up to the front door. The Marquesa de Casa Maury came at teatime, and also Oliver Lyttelton and the Prof. Bracken, who had chatted with Hopkins, reported to Churchill that Hopkins had told him his mission was to see what Britain needed so that the United States might deliver it—even if it meant transferring to Britain armaments the U.S. Army did not want transferred. Roosevelt, Hopkins had told Bracken, was determined to give Britain everything needed for victory. Hopkins did not inform Bracken that Roosevelt's intentions were conditional on his reporting to the president that Britain was worth the investment. Nor did Hopkins relate that Roosevelt, to placate his generals, would see to it that military equipment shipped in the earliest stages of Lend-Lease was likely obsolete or close to it.[86]

For that night's dinner at Ditchley, the large dining room was lit only by candles aloft in a spreading chandelier and in sconces on the walls. The table was set simply with white linen and four gilt candlesticks with tall yellow tapers in the center. The food, Colville noted, "is in keeping with the surroundings, though I notice some attempt to be less lavish since [Minister of Food] Lord Woolton's recent strictures on over-feeding." Woolton's strictures did not extend to Churchill's champagne.[87]

Later, when the ladies departed after dinner, the men got down to business. Hopkins paid a graceful tribute to Churchill's speeches, which had, he said, "produced the most stirring and revolutionary effect on all classes and districts in America. At an American Cabinet meeting the President had had a wireless-set brought in so that all might listen to Churchill." Upon hearing this, Churchill "was touched and gratified." He said that he hardly knew what he said in his speeches last summer, he had just been imbued with the feeling that "it would be better for us to be destroyed than to see the triumph of such an imposter." When, at the time of Dunkirk, he told Hopkins, he had addressed the cabinet, he had realized that there was only one thing the ministers wanted to hear him say: that whatever happened to their army, they should still go on. He had said it.[88]

Churchill then proceeded on to one of his two favorite topics, the future (the past being the other). He claimed that after the war, he could never lead a party government against the opposition leaders who had co-operated so loyally. He hoped a national government would continue for two or three years so that the country might be undivided in its efforts to put into effect certain measures of reconstruction. He offered that the text of the Lend-Lease bill, which he had read that morning, had made him feel that a new world had come into being. Then he described that future, as he visualized it. He began by predicting that were the socialists of the world to unite, the new world would be one of communism and squalor (he later told the House in 1945: "The inherent virtue of Socialism is the equal sharing of miseries"). But if the Germans built the new world, tyranny and brute force would reign. He pledged that Britain sought no territorial gains, but only the restoration of liberty to those robbed of it by the Nazis. He sought only peace for his English yeomanry, who deserved to feel safe each night within their humble cottages. He had made this speech over numerous dinners for the benefit of numerous guests, some of whom, such as Colville, had heard the talk numerous times. Hopkins wasn't any more interested in the future than in political creeds; still, he listened politely.[89]

Churchill asked Hopkins what he thought. Colville recalled the American's reply as "slow, deliberate, halting... a remarkable contrast to the ceaseless flow of eloquence" to which Churchill had treated the room. In Colville's recollection, Hopkins said that there were two kinds of men: those who talked and those who acted. The president, like the prime minister, was one of the latter. Hopkins claimed Roosevelt was intent only upon one end: the destruction of Hitler. Where Colville paraphrased Hopkins's reply to Churchill, another guest, Oliver Lyttelton, recalled Hopkins's exact words: "Harry Hopkins did not reply for the better part of a minute—and how long that seems—and then, exaggerating his [Midwest] American drawl, he said, 'Well Mr. Prime Minister I don't think the president will give a damn for your cottagers.'" Lyttelton thought: "Heavens alive, it's gone wrong."[90]

Hopkins paused again, and then continued: "You see, we're only interested in seeing that goddamn *sonofabitch* Hitler gets licked."[91]

Colville: Churchill, taken aback, "hastily explained that he had been speaking very freely and was simply anxious to let Hopkins realize that we were not all devoid of thoughts of the future. He would be the first to agree that the destruction of 'those foul swine' was the primary and overriding objective."

As for the future, Hopkins recounted that he had heard Roosevelt sketch out an idea very similar to Churchill's, but that Roosevelt refused to listen to those who talked too much of postwar aims. That was a curious aside, for in his State of the Union address the previous week, Roosevelt—a witness to, but not a participant in, the current ordeal—had linked ongoing aid to Britain to a vision (*his* vision) for the postwar world. Roosevelt had, in essence, declared his intention to win both the war *and* the peace, a bit of hubris given that Churchill and England were doing the fighting, alone. Churchill had earned the right to speculate on the future (although he did not say anything of the sort to Hopkins). Following the speechifying, Churchill, Hopkins, and the other guests—brandy and cigars in hand—adjourned to the projection room to watch some German news films, one of which included a scene of the March 1940 Brenner Pass meeting between Hitler and Mussolini, "which with its salutes and its absurdity," Colville noted, "was funnier than anything Charlie Chaplin produced in *The Great Dictator*." Churchill, always the last to retire, went off to bed sometime after 2:00 A.M. Despite Churchill's relentless monologues, Colville concluded that the boss had sold Hopkins on the idea that some members of the British ruling class were indeed men of action, not words.[92]

The salesmanship continued the following day. *Night Train to Munich* was the night's celluloid feature, followed by more drinks and more robust conversation, less formal and more relaxed than the previous evening. Churchill's mood was upbeat; Enigma decrypts that day revealed that the German invasion forces were moving to southern France to take their target practice, a good sign that the invasion was off at least until spring. This secret he chose not to share with Hopkins. With the fate of his South African gold still in doubt, he asked Hopkins what Americans planned to do with all the gold in the world once they accumulated it? Fill teeth? Hopkins replied they'd put their unemployed to work guarding it. Late in the evening, flush with the news of the German pullback, to say nothing of a brandy or two, and knowing full well the Germans were not coming to England anytime soon, Churchill proclaimed to Hopkins that even though it was wrong to say Britain would welcome invasion, that's just how he and the British people felt. Colville thought the evening a success, telling his diary, "I think Hopkins must have been impressed."[93]

He was. The next day, he wrote to Roosevelt, "The people here are amazing from Churchill down, and if courage alone could win the result will be inevitable. But they need our help desperately, and I am sure you will let nothing stand in the way." He continued: "*Churchill* is the gov't in every sense of the word—he controls the grand strategy, and often the details—labour trusts him, the army, navy, air force are behind him to a man . . . I cannot emphasize too strongly that he is the one and only person over here with whom we need to have a full meeting of the minds."[94]

Churchill, seeking more than a meeting of the minds, again asked Hopkins about a parley between the leaders. Hopkins advised Roosevelt that a meeting was "essential—and soon—for the battering continues and Hitler does not wait for Congress." But Roosevelt wanted no meeting until his "problem" of Lend-Lease made its way through Congress. As to the rumors rife in Washington (instigated, Roosevelt believed, by Joe Kennedy) that Churchill harbored a personal dislike for Roosevelt, Hopkins declared, "I cannot believe that it is true Churchill dislikes either you or America, it just doesn't make sense." He added, "This island needs our help now, Mr. President, with everything we can give them."[95]

On the fourteenth, Churchill, Clementine, Hopkins, Dr. Wilson, John Martin, Churchill's naval assistant Commander "Tommy" Thompson, and Lord and Lady Halifax entrained at King's Cross for the five-hundred-mile overnight trip to Thurso, the northern terminus of the British rail system and the northernmost town on the British mainland. From there Halifax would sail for America aboard Britain's newest battleship, *King George V,* the pride of the Royal Navy. Martin recalled that they arrived at dawn to the frozen Scottish landscape, the deserted heath covered with snow and "a blizzard howling at the windows." Churchill, fighting a cold, added a morning whisky to his arsenal of medicines. Their final destination was Scapa Flow, reached from Thurso by an overnight run through maniacal seas on board *King George V.* The next morning Halifax and the battleship continued on to America. Churchill, Hopkins, and the rest of the party made their way back south to Edinburgh and on to Glasgow, where on the seventeenth, Churchill told dockyard workers (and Hopkins), "We do not require in 1941 large armies from overseas. What we require are weapons, ships and aeroplanes." Churchill knew 1942 might prove another story altogether, but why peer too far ahead?[96]

That night, after dinner at the Station Hotel, Hopkins lifted his glass in a toast that was to become one of the best remembered of the twentieth century. "I suppose you wish to know," he began, "what I am going to say to President Roosevelt on my return. Well, I'm going to quote you one verse from that Book of Books . . . 'Wither thou goest, I will go; and where thou lodgeth, I will lodge: thy people shall be my people, and thy God my God.' " Then, he quietly added, "Even to the end." Churchill was in tears. Hopkins's words, Dr. Wilson noted in his diary, "seemed like a rope thrown to a dying man."[97]

The first weeks of 1941 brought Churchill good military news from one quarter only, North Africa. His generally mellow mood noted by Colville at the turn of the year had its genesis in early December with news of the first British victories over the Italians in western Egypt, during Operation Compass. He grew more mellow with each report of a new Italian retreat, first in North Africa, then, within weeks, by the smashup of Mussolini's East Africa empire. By sending men and tanks considered critical to the defense of the Home Island to Africa, he had finally taken the fight to the enemy. In his memoirs Churchill wrote that although Britain's American friends "took a more alarmist view of our position" and considered "the invasion of Britain as probable, we ourselves felt free to send overseas all the troops" the Royal Navy ships could carry in order to "wage offensive war in the Middle East and the Mediterranean. Here was the hinge upon which our ultimate victory turned, and it was in 1941 that the first significant events began."[98]

The events had begun on December 6, 1940, when O'Connor kicked off Operation Compass. By the new year, he had raced fifty miles west from Sidi Barrani and was closing on Bardia, intent on fulfilling Churchill's order "to maul the Italian Army and rip them off the African shore to the utmost possible extent." Bardia, next up on the firing line, was no mere camp in the desert. Sited high above a harbor, it was protected on the landward side by almost twenty miles of trenches and fortifications. Within the lines, General Annibale Bergonzoli, veteran of the Spanish Civil War and a true fighting general, commanded almost 45,000 men. To Mussolini, Bergonzoli radioed: "In Bardia we are, and here we stay." By then, O'Connor's armor had been reduced to just two dozen heavy tanks. He knew that his infantry would have to do the hard work, work that devolved upon the 6th Australian Division, newly arrived from Palestine. On January 3, following an all-night aerial pounding of Bardia and the surrounding trenches, the Sundowners advanced. Waves of them came on, screaming as one, "We're off to see the Wizard, the wonderful wizard of Oz." They went right through the wire and poured into the trenches. Slashing and shooting, they drove a mile-wide wedge to the heart of the city. Three Royal Navy battleships sailed up to the city walls and pummeled the seaside cliff literally into the sea. By dawn on the fourth it was over. Bergonzoli had fled in the night with a few troops, west toward Tobruk. He had, in a manner of speaking, fulfilled his promise to Il Duce. Almost all of his 45,000 troops stayed in Bardia, but as prisoners of the British.[99]

On January 5, following the fall of Bardia, Churchill cabled Wavell: "Hearty congratulations on your second brilliant victory, so profoundly helpful at this turning-point to the whole cause. You knocked and it was opened." He took such delight in the fall of Bardia that he declared January 5 "Bardia Day." Victories of any sort were in such short supply that one would expect such a reaction from such a naturally enthusiastic man as Churchill.[100]

Victory, the word Colville noted had vanished from Britain's vocabulary, had found its way home to Whitehall, to Fleet Street, Chequers, Buckingham Palace, and to the East End. Churchill encouraged Wavell to pursue his foe: "It is at the moment when the victor is most exhausted that the greatest forfeit can be extracted from the vanquished." True enough. This was the same message Lincoln had sent to General George Meade following Meade's victory over Lee at Gettysburg. But Churchill pulled a switch where Lincoln had not. An opportunity had presented itself, as he saw it, of inflicting more damage on the Italians, not in the desert, but in Greece. Churchill's priorities had changed soon after the new year. What he had previously given to Wavell, he now took. He made that clear in a cable on January 11: "Nothing must hamper capture of Tobruk, but thereafter all operations in Libya are subordinated to aiding Greece.... We expect and require prompt and active compliance with our decisions, for which we will bear full responsibility."[101]

The victories over the Italians validated for Churchill his long-held belief that when fighting two enemies it is wise to "consider whether the downfall of your strongest foe cannot be accomplished through the ruin of his weakest ally; and in this connection, a host of political, economic, and geographical advantages may arise and play their part in the argument." In the Great War he applied his strategy to Germany's weakest ally, Turkey, his target the strait between Turkish Asia and Europe—the Dardanelles.

As the Dardanelles campaign took shape, Sir Henry Wilson, former subchief of the General Staff, pronounced *his* philosophy of secondary theaters: "The way to end this war is to kill Germans, not Turks.... All history shows that operations in secondary and ineffectual theater have no bearing on major operations." The veracity of Wilson's maxim was relative to time and place. He was wrong in 1915, because the business of killing Germans had been brought to a bloody standstill by the trench and the machine gun. Churchill's Dardanelles plan offered a strategic alternative to the butchery of Flanders. The strategy made sense, but the execution of it proved wanting and resulted in the debacle of Gallipoli. In fairness to Churchill, the British army's Gallipoli campaign became necessary only when the French and British fleet lost its nerve in the Dardanelles at the very moment the Turks were about to quit their defense of those straits. The fiasco on the peninsula followed.[102]

Now Churchill was again striking the weaker enemy, but killing Italians in Africa inflicted no pain whatsoever on Hitler's Reich. Killing Italians in the desert was not a strategic alternative; it was a sideshow that depleted Churchill's forces against the day when he might have to fight Germans in not one, but two theaters. By his own choice, that day was almost upon him. The strategy of striking the weaker of two enemies contains at least one flaw: the stronger might strike back. Churchill expected Germany to do just that in Greece or North Africa, and he welcomed the prospect.

But on January 10, the blow came in the Mediterranean. On that day, at the height of O'Connor's stunning Libyan push, the aircraft carrier *Illustrious,* escorting a convoy from Alexandria to Malta and steaming about one hundred miles east of that island, scrambled her Fulmar fighters in pursuit of two lurking Italian torpedo bombers. The Italians were decoys. Almost three dozen German Junkers Ju 88 bombers and Stuka dive-bombers based in Sicily swept down upon *Illustrious* and put six bombs through its flight deck. *Illustrious,* afire and unable to land or sortie its planes, limped to Malta, where it was bombed again, in port. The vital aircraft carrier would be lost to the war effort for more than a year. During the attack, the cruiser *Southampton* was crippled, and scuttled the next day. In less than ten minutes, a handful of German fliers wrenched control of the central Mediterranean from Britain. Wavell in Cairo, along with all of his ships, planes, tanks, and men, had, in just minutes, been cut off from London. Reinforcements would have to again arrive via the 14,000-mile Cape route. Churchill received the news at Ditchley, while delivering a discourse on war to Harry Hopkins.[103]

No such calamities were befalling the British in the Libyan desert. Wavell, despite having fourteen Italian divisions at his front and Churchill with his Balkan plans on his back, ordered O'Connor to drive on. Tobruk, sixty miles beyond Bardia, fell on January 21, the Australians again leading the charge, this time donning gas masks as they fought through a vicious sandstorm that gave more fight than did the defenders. So paltry was the Italian opposition that an Aussie who had served in Palestine proclaimed, "The police in Tel Aviv gave us a better fight than this." Large groups of Italians tried to surrender to anybody in uniform, including an Associated Press reporter. One Australian commander told a crowd of prospective prisoners that he was quite busy and could they please come back the next day. After hauling down the Italian flag and hoisting one of their bush hats in its stead, the Australians changed the name of Via Mussolini to Via Ned Kelly. The insult was complete.[104]

Despite Churchill's new Balkan priorities, O'Connor was determined to hunt down the fleeing Italians. Derna, one hundred miles west of Tobruk, fell without a fight on the twenty-ninth. The Italian garrison fled, joined by the Italian farmers who had colonized this green and fertile slice of coast. A joke made the rounds among the Aussies—the Italians were fleeing Cyrenaica with hopes of getting to Rome and the protection of the Vatican Guard. Churchill could not resist taking a shot at Il Duce. This was the story, he mused, "of the decline and fall of the Italian Empire...that will not take a future Gibbon so long to write as the original work."[105]

O'Connor drove farther west, and inland. His 7th Armoured Division took the fort at Mechili, but the Italians got their tanks out and fled for Tripoli along the coast road, which curved to the south between Derna and Benghazi. O'Connor struck out overland in hopes of hooking around and blocking the Italians at Beda Fomm, south of Benghazi. He intended to trap Marshal Graziani, General Bergonzoli, and the whole lot. It took the British thirty hours to navigate the 150 miles of trackless desert. They arrived at Beda Fomm on February 5 with just a half hour to spare before the first Italian columns came into view. Many of O'Connor's tanks never finished the journey; the unforgiving terrain of ravines, jagged boulders, and spindles of volcanic rock murdered tracks and engines. But the Italians operated with a greater handicap. In drafting their armored tactics, they (like the French) allowed for only one in thirty tanks to carry radios. Once the dance began, they could not choreograph any new moves.[106]

A wild shootout ensued, lasting more than a day, and the Italians got the worst of it. The scene turned bizarre when Arab traders wandered upon the battlefield and proceeded to sell fresh eggs to both sides. Italian commanders threw crew after crew into the battle, only to watch them burn in their tanks. Those who survived were captured, and those few who escaped disappeared into the emptiness of the desert. O'Connor, victorious, had taken his army farther than any armored force in the brief history of tank warfare. Churchill had thought his "tremendous swoops and scoops" through Cyrenaica would take most of February, but it was all over by February 7, all of it finished. Almost the entire Italian army in eastern Libya had been captured or killed, ten divisions obliterated, 130,000 prisoners taken, 400 tanks destroyed. The battle for Cyrenaica was over.[107]

To further humiliate Mussolini, O'Connor radioed the news of Bergonzoli's surrender to Wavell on an open frequency: "Fox killed in the open." Graziani escaped westward with the remnants of his Libyan army, reduced now by half, to 125,000 troops and soon to be bottled up in Tripolitania, a threat to nobody, respected by no one, including the Bedouins who with impunity picked over the charred carcasses of tanks in which rested the incinerated corpses of young Italians. Even Eden, not known as a fount of humor, fired an insult Mussolini's way: "Never have so many lost so much to so few." Mussolini—Churchill called him "the crafty cold-blooded black-hearted Italian"—gazed now from Rome upon the ruins of his North African ambitions.[108]

The road to Tripoli and the heart of Italian North Africa lay open. The first of Churchill's strategic priorities—to sweep the Italians from Africa—was nearly fulfilled. O'Connor, intending to keep up the hunt, sent an aide to Cairo to convince Wavell of the need to pursue the Italians. But Wavell, who had for weeks known of Churchill's Balkan strategy, had already begun planning his new spring campaign. The maps on the walls of his headquarters were no longer of Libya, but of Greece. Almost 60,000 of his best troops under the command of Jumbo Wilson packed their kits and readied for the journey across the sea. When Greek prime minister Metaxas died suddenly in late January, his successor, Alexandros Koryzis, accepted Churchill's offers of assistance. O'Connor was soon replaced by Philip Neame and given command of the Army of the Nile.

When Wavell unveiled his African plans the previous autumn, Churchill had purred like six cats, and more. "He was rapturously happy," recalled Ismay, in his memoirs. "Wars are won by superior willpower," Churchill had declared, "and now we will wrest the initiative from the enemy and impose our will on him." Churchill, Ismay wrote, "was always prone to count his chickens before they hatched." But the results Wavell and O'Connor obtained exceeded even Churchill's grandest predictions.[109]

On February 6, Hitler briefed the man he was sending to North Africa to boost the spirits of the beaten Italians: Lieutenant General Erwin Rommel, who the previous May famously drove his 7th Panzer Division to the English Channel. In Africa, Rommel would command only one smallish armored division and a light mechanized division. His eighty new Panzer Mark III and Mark IV tanks were faster and tougher than anything the British had, but they were vastly outnumbered by Wavell's medium and heavy tanks, and would remain so unless Wavell was ordered to do something inexplicable, such as send his tanks off to Greece, Crete, or some other destination. Rommel called his command the *Afrika Korps*. If the convoying across the Mediterranean of the tanks and men of his 15th Panzer Division went as planned, he'd be fully operational by mid-May. His mission until then was something like O'Connor's, but in reverse—to hold the line in Tripolitania, and to probe eastward if possible. A British push to Tripoli was expected; basic military principles called for exploiting success. Rommel's orders were to blunt the expected advance, and to absolutely avoid committing himself to any general engagement in Cyrenaica against the more numerous British. Although he was the sort of general who followed orders to the letter, he also thought it a general's supreme duty to take the fight to the enemy. He considered nothing finer than waging a well-planned, well-executed battle—offensive, not defensive. His standing orders now conflicted with his love for action, yet the truly innovative soldier always finds a way to have his way, to derange events in his favor, as Churchill liked to put it.[110]

On the same day Hitler briefed Rommel, O'Connor received orders to send his remaining tanks east to Cairo, for maintenance. It was the wrong day to order up repairs, one of those seemingly minor events that in war weigh heavy on the future, though no commander on either side could reasonably predict the consequence at the time. The order seemed to make good sense. The British 7th Armoured Division had atrophied to less than brigade strength, just a few dozen tanks. Any tanks not in need of repairs would be by the time they rolled almost five hundred miles east to where their journey had begun, for prewar British planners had not thought of putting tanks on flatbed trucks in order to transport them to and from the battlefield. Libya had no railroad facilities; British tanks in the desert traveled to where they were going, however great the distance, under their own steam. Thus, as Rommel made for North Africa, Wavell's armor made for Cairo. It was altogether the wrong direction. Churchill months later called the decision an "act of improvidence."[111]

In East Africa that week, a force of British and colonial troops was well on its way to securing another of Churchill's objectives—to flush the Italians from the Horn. Abyssinia (modern Ethiopia), where the Duke of Aosta commanded a flimsy and ill-supplied army of occupation, was Churchill's first target. Eden, during his October visit to the region, met in Khartoum with Wavell, Emperor Haile Selassie, and South African prime minister Jan Smuts, who sent more than 30,000 South African troops to the Sahara to fight for London. Selassie, the first world leader to take refuge in London after the fall of his regime, had returned to Khartoum to tell anyone who listened that the time was right for him to become the first leader to reclaim his capital, and could do so if his men were better armed and better led. Eden and Smuts agreed to help, but each for different reasons. Eden, pushed by Churchill, sought a juncture between the Arabian and African sectors of the Muslim world, a unity of political purpose that would offset the growing anti-British Islamic presence in Jerusalem and Baghdad. Smuts needed a victory to overcome opposition from Boer nationalists, who had no love for England. Smuts had fought on the Boer side forty years earlier but grew to appreciate the British worldview. He believed in the British Empire, yet as one of the architects of the League of Nations, he also believed in a world council dedicated to righting wrongs. Deeply religious—he always carried in his kit a copy of the New Testament—he believed nations (white nations, in any event) had a moral obligation to wage war against nations guilty of self-evident ethical abominations, such as Germany under Hitler. In this interventionism he stood foursquare with Churchill, in part because economic benefits tended to follow intervention. It had been Britain and France, after all, who used their League of Nations mandates to open new imperial pathways in the eastern Mediterranean and Middle East. Selassie's cause was just; Smuts was on board.[112]

The command of Selassie's troops went to an experienced desert fighter, Lieutenant Colonel Orde Wingate, who represented the style of irregular soldiering manifested famously by the likes of General Charles George Gordon in the Sudan, and Lawrence of Arabia, the adventurous sort of soldiering that Kipling lauded and Churchill loved, having done more than a bit of it himself. Wingate showed up in Khartoum in early November bearing a suitcase containing one million pounds sterling. Backed by his start-up money and a firm belief that he was the man who would put the Lion of Judah back upon his throne, Wingate assembled a little army. It was a motley crew: eight hundred men from the Sudan Frontier Battalion and about eight hundred Abyssinian troops, the entire group led by about seventy British commandos. Wingate—a Bible scholar, and a bit beyond eccentric—christened his command "Gideon Force."[113]

Overall command of the expedition went to Lieutenant General Alan Cunningham, brother of Admiral Sir Andrew Browne Cunningham, commander in chief of the Royal Navy in the Mediterranean. Cunningham was a fine infantryman and not afraid of a fight. Sir John Keegan called the East Africa campaign "a *Beau Geste* episode" rife with dashing colonials upon prancing camels, long desert treks, upraised scimitars, oasis gunfights, all in all a series of colonial brawls, fought for the most part between colonial troops for colonial advantage. It was nineteenth-century stuff. Churchill loved it, not least of all the public humiliation inflicted upon Il Duce. Yet, given that Italy's per capita economic output in 1941 was akin to that of Britain's a century *earlier,* it was truly nineteenth-century stuff, and a cakewalk for Churchill.[114]

On January 20, Haile Selassie and Wingate had crossed the frontier where the Blue Nile cascades into the Sudan from Ethiopia. Wingate's column, though almost comically weak, drove up the Ethiopian plateau toward the capital of Addis Ababa, three hundred miles distant. Two Indian divisions marched across the frontier north of the Blue Nile on a bearing for Gondar. The following day, the Sudan Defence Force crossed into Ethiopia south of the Blue Nile. On February 11, Cunningham's army of South Africans, the King's African Rifles, and the Royal West African Frontier Force marched out of Kenya and into southern Ethiopia and Italian Somaliland. The Italians fled from the south of Abyssinia so rapidly that Cunningham's forces could not keep up. The Italians were on the run and British prestige was on the rise.[115]

Events in the desert and East Africa, therefore, made for good news to impart to Hopkins, who stayed on until early February, and to Wendell Willkie, who arrived in late January. Willkie, the Republican loser in the November election, was a big six-foot-one, 220-pound Hoosier who pronounced America "Amurica." He strongly opposed what he called Roosevelt's "alphabet soup" social programs and had campaigned against Roosevelt's relief programs on the slogan "You can't beat Santa Claus." His presence in London as Roosevelt's informal ambassador therefore informed the world that *Amurica* was acting as one. The isolationists might yet dispute that, but Roosevelt was in the process of shoving the American Firsters off the stage. Willkie carried with him a handwritten note from Roosevelt:

> Dear Churchill,
>
> Wendell Willkie will give you this. He is truly helping to keep politics out over here. I think this verse applies to you people as it does to us.
>
> *. . . Sail on, O ship of State!*
> *Sail on, O Union strong and great!*
> *Humanity with all its fears,*
> *With all the hopes of future years,*
> *Is hanging breathless on thy fate.*
>
> As ever yours,
> Franklin D. Roosevelt

The Henry Wadsworth Longfellow verse was personal, symbolic, perhaps, but it meant a great deal to Churchill. He had the letter framed and toted it about, frame and all, to show visitors, a material manifestation of true friendship.[116]

John "Gil" Winant, Roosevelt's replacement for Joe Kennedy, also arrived in early February. A former governor of New Hampshire, Winant, though a New Yorker by birth, manifested a dour taciturnity often associated with natives of the Granite State. Harold Nicolson found Winant to be "very shy"; he tended to twist his hands while proffering "coy platitudes." Yet Nicolson concluded that Winant was a man of "superb character" who carried himself with "ungainly charm" and manifested a "real if inarticulate force." Winant's credentials were impeccable: St. Paul's School and Princeton. An early supporter of the New Deal, he was rewarded with a post on the new Social Security Board. Roosevelt confided to Harvard's James Conant that Winant would get along well with the Labour faction in Britain, which, Roosevelt told Conant, would almost certainly "be in power when the war is over."[117]

Winant, tall and lanky, considered dark, somber suits to be the only appropriate attire for a gentleman. Photographs of him are reminiscent of Abe Lincoln at his most weary. The resemblance to Lincoln, when noted, pleased Winant no end. Yet the resemblance in large part stemmed from a deep sadness in his eyes, due in no small measure to his being a most unhappily married man. Within weeks of arriving in London he fell in love with Sarah Churchill, an "innocent" affair according to Colville, but one doomed from the start, innocent or not. It simply would not do for the married American ambassador to take up with a married woman who happened also to be the prime minister's daughter. As she had with Vic Oliver, Sarah had fallen for a much older man, a lifelong habit: "Maybe I was looking for a substitute father [she wrote of her marriage to Oliver]; indeed, I have sometimes thought I was trying to marry my father." Winant was Churchill's junior by a decade, yet his dour countenance made him appear a decade older than the Old Man. Within days of arriving, he reinvigorated the American embassy by returning all operations to No. 1 Grosvenor Square from the country estate to which Joe Kennedy had decamped the year before, when the first bombs fell.[118]

Churchill trusted Winant, enough to allow him to vet those of his speeches that might be interpreted by Americans as meddling in U.S. affairs. As with the other Americans who came to call that winter (William Averell Harriman, Colonel William "Wild Bill" Donovan, Hopkins, and Willkie), Churchill opened his weekend houses to Winant. Rare was the weekend in 1941 when Churchill did not host one or more of the Americans. He grew truly fond of their company, and he valued their forthrightness. As well, he knew he must allow them to witness how he managed the war. R. A. Butler wrote that Winant and the other Americans "react well to exhibitions of resolution." This, of course, was exactly how Churchill wanted them to react, and it perhaps led to a third reason he extended weekend invitations: the visiting Americans became an audience for his frequent declamations on resolve and revenge, on war and on peace.[119]

Harry Hopkins departed England on February 8, sold on Churchill's resolution and on the inevitability of invasion. Churchill had portrayed to Hopkins a grim and desperate scene when the Germans would come ashore, which Hopkins reported to the president: "The most important single observation I have to make is that most of the cabinet and all of the military leaders here believe that invasion is imminent. They believe it may come at any moment, but not later than May 1." Indeed, many in the military and the cabinet believed that, but Churchill did not. He believed the surest way for Hitler to lose the war would be to invade England, which would expose his shipping to annihilation, and likewise any Germans who made it ashore. Hopkins, too, came to believe that, telling Roosevelt "her sun would set" were Germany to invade. Yet, that was a premise—an all-or-nothing premise—Churchill did not want to test. But if the test came, Britons were ready. Two weeks after first meeting Churchill, Hopkins cabled Roosevelt: "The spirit of this people and their determination to resist invasion is beyond praise. No matter how fierce the attack may be you can be sure they will resist it, and effectively. The Germans will have to do more than kill a few hundred thousand people here before they can defeat Britain." In fact, as Hopkins grasped after his exposure to Churchill's late-night sessions, Hitler would have to kill them all.[120]

Lend-Lease passed the U.S. House of Representatives on February 8, by a vote of 260–165, thanks in large part to the efforts of an intensely loyal young Democratic Texas congressman and majority leader on the House Armed Services Committee, Lyndon Baines Johnson. Now the bill would move on to the Senate, where passage was by no means assured. The following night Churchill—his African victories mounting and his meetings with Hopkins and Willkie having concluded with success—addressed Britain and America, his first radio broadcast in five months, and the first since September 1939 in which a British leader could cite any military successes, however modest. He intended to give something of a State of the Empire address. Knowing that America was listening, he served up the good news first, the "series of victories in Libya which have broken irretrievably the Italian military power on the African Continent.... Thus, we have all been entertained, and I trust edified, by the... humiliation of another of what Byron called 'Those Pagod things of saber sway / With fronts of brass and feet of clay.' "

Of Hitler, Churchill asked, "What has that wicked man... been preparing during these winter months? What new devilry is he planning?" Would the coming "phase of greater violence" center on England? "What fresh form of assault will he make upon our Island home and fortress; which let there be no mistake about it is all that stands between him and the dominion of the world?" Churchill then made an astonishing statement, given that he believed through his Ultra decrypts just the opposite of what he now said:

> A Nazi invasion of Great Britain last autumn would have been a more or less improvised affair. Hitler took it for granted that when France gave in we should give in; but we did not give in. And he had to think again. *An invasion now will be supported by a much more carefully prepared tackle and equipment of landing craft and other apparatus, all of which will have been planned and manufactured in the winter months* [italics added]. We must all be prepared to meet gas attacks, parachute attacks, and glider attacks, with constancy, forethought and practiced skill.

He had told his military chiefs since June that the invasion scare begat vigilance on the part of Britons. In his broadcasts and speeches, he chose his words with great care. He never told Britons that Hitler *was* coming, but only that they must be prepared *if* Hitler came. Britons learned little or nothing from their newspapers and the BBC of German troop movements on the Continent or British deployments on the Home Island. They were in the dark. Thus, when they heard their prime minister speak of gas attacks, or the need to fight on the beaches and in the fields, they understandably came away quite concerned, which was Churchill's intent.

Churchill followed the invasion warning with an oft-repeated premise:

> He [Hitler] may carry havoc into the Balkan States; he may tear great provinces out of Russia, he may march to the Caspian; he may march to the gates of India. All this will avail him nothing. It may spread his curse more widely throughout Europe and Asia, but it will not avert his doom.

Here was yet another warning to Stalin, and a signal to Hitler that the British intelligence services were aware of his intentions. Churchill had a message for Bulgarians, as well, advising them not to repeat their mistake of the Great War when they "went in on the losing side." This time around, Churchill said, "I trust the Bulgarians are not going to make the same mistake again." Then he gave voice to his dream of a bulwark in the Balkans: "Of course, if all the Balkan people stood together and acted together, aided by Britain and Turkey, it would be many months before a German army and air force of sufficient strength to overcome them could be assembled." Yet Ultra decrypts had by then shown that the requisite German strength to smash Greece had already been assembled.[121]

Sidestepping his inability to mount any real offense against Germany, he worked in more good news regarding the Italians. At dawn that day Admiral James Somerville had sailed his squadron of three battle cruisers into the harbor at Genoa and proceeded to bombard "in a shattering manner" the naval base there. It appeared Somerville had as easy a go of it with the Italians as Drake had with the basking crocodiles of Cartagena. "It is right," Churchill pronounced, "that the Italian people should be made to feel the sorry plight into which they have been dragged by Dictator Mussolini; and if the cannonade of Genoa, rolling along the coast, reverberating in the mountains, reached the ears of our French comrades in their grief and misery, it might cheer them with the feeling that friends—active friends—are near and that Britannia rules the waves." *Rules the waves?* Britannia, in the Mediterranean and Atlantic, and most distressingly, in the approaches to the Home Island, by no means ruled the waves. Britannia, in fact, for the first time in her history had good reason to fear the sea.[122]

Of Japan, Churchill made no mention. Yet Alec Cadogan had reported to Eden three days earlier that the Foreign Office had listened in on "some very bad-looking Jap telephone conversations from which it appears they have decided to attack us." Such rumors of impending Japanese belligerency abounded throughout the year, but Churchill faced more than enough problems in Europe to preclude his having any meaningful influence in the distant Pacific. Events in the Far East were not only beyond his ability to control by diplomatic carrot, but beyond his means to address with military stick, should the Japanese attack British interests there.[123]

He ended with a reading of the Longfellow verse Roosevelt had sent along with Willkie, which segued into a final slavish expression of thanks to "this great man" Roosevelt. To address the fears of Americans that Lend-Lease would someday result in American boys going abroad, Churchill declared, "We do not need the gallant armies which are forming throughout the American Union. We do not need them this year, nor next year, nor any year that I can foresee." He needed arms, aircraft, and especially shipping, but he did not need armies. This war, he claimed, differed from the Great War, when "America sent two million men across the Atlantic. But this is not a war of vast armies, firing immense masses of shells at one another." "The fate of this war," he declared, "is going to be settled by what happens on the oceans, in the air, and—above all—in this island." And then: "We shall not fail or falter, we shall not weaken or tire. Neither the sudden shock of battle, nor the long-drawn trials of vigilance and exertion will wear us down." The last line of the speech lives on as one of Churchill's best known: "Give us the tools, and we will finish the job."[124]

That statement appears at first pass to be a whopper, given that Germany was a land power, one that only armies could defeat. Yet Churchill—and many of his generals—was informed by his experiences in the Great War, when massed armies faced off for four years along five hundred miles of trenches. Stasis defined the Great War. When the armies did meet—as at the Somme and Passchendaele—unimaginable slaughter resulted. Warfare had since changed, and though Churchill knew intellectually that it had, he did not know it in his gut. Even after the Germans, employing new tactics and new weapons, swept to victory over France in six weeks the previous spring, even as British tanks now swept across Libya, Churchill remained convinced that if great armies met in Europe, the lines would stabilize, and the slaughter commence. This belief would underlie his thinking for the next three years. He believed that if the Germans came to England, they would be obliterated on the seas, on the beaches, and in the fields. Likewise, he believed that if the British returned to Europe too soon and undermanned, they, too, would be obliterated. He therefore sought other means to bring Germany to its knees. He had told his military chiefs the previous summer that airpower was Britain's "one sure path" to victory, but that remained an untested premise, and Britain lacked the aircraft to prove it in any event. Neither the Royal Navy nor the RAF could, alone or together, kill the German army, and killing the German army was the *only* path to British victory. To do so Churchill needed troops, millions more than Britain and the Dominions could muster. Only two nations could supply the manpower: the United States and the Soviet Union, and neither in early 1941 was prepared to do battle with the Wehrmacht. Churchill was correct when he offered that Western Civilization would either be lost or saved in the coming conflagration. Yet he had no strategy in place to meet the challenge.

Jan Smuts, who heard the speech in South Africa, cabled, "Each broadcast is a battle." Everything about Churchill's speeches was extraordinary, not least the speed with which they were scrawled in longhand or dictated straight to the typewriter in odd moments between pressing duties. All his life, critics had called his language florid and overstated. After Dunkirk, overstating England's plight was impossible; after forty years in Parliament, he had finally been provided with a canvas high enough and broad enough to bear his brilliant colors. He gave the lie to Theodore Dreiser's line in *Sister Carrie* "How true it is that words are but vague shadows of the volumes we mean." His words cast their own shadows, and they were long and deep. Certainly he demonstrated that powerful words could alter the course of history. Yet powerful weapons, which Churchill then lacked, and Hitler did not, can alter the course of history more quickly.[125]

One effect of Churchill's warning on invasion was for Dominion ministers worldwide to telegraph their great concern for the fate of the Home Island to Whitehall. Churchill's Dominions minister, Viscount Cranborne, sent Churchill a copy of a telegram he had drafted to the Dominion governments, outlining the pros and cons for German invasion. Churchill responded with vehemence. "What is the point," he asked, "with worrying the Dominions with all this questionable stuff?" He went on to tell Cranborne that if the Germans came, they would be cut off from resupply and communications within a week. RAF bombers would obliterate their landing sites and shipping. Then, "apart from the beaches we have the equivalent of 30 divisions with 1,000 tanks" in reserve, "to be hurled" at the invaders. A million members of the Home Guard stood ready to "deal with sporadic descents of parachutists." All of this information was for Cranborne only; Churchill saw no purpose in it being passed on to the Dominions, where it would likely be leaked. The most telling number in Churchill's reply to Cranborne is the number of divisions under arms in England: thirty. When, in March, Churchill's secretary of state for war, David Margesson, proposed limiting reinforcements to Egypt to two divisions, Churchill shot back: "I do not accept the view that only two divisions can be spared from the immense force now gathered at home. We must not get too 'defense minded.'" Ten months earlier Churchill's regular army in England consisted of the drenched and unarmed survivors of Dunkirk. Now he had an army, a small army relative to Hitler's, but an army.[126]

On February 15, Churchill sent Eden and Dill back to Cairo and Greece. Their mission was not to push Wavell into furthering his Libyan gains, but to push him to prepare for Churchill's planned foray into the Balkans, a strategy Churchill had outlined in a long cable to Wavell. In essence, Churchill wrote, as German intervention in Greece "becomes more certain and imminent," it will be necessary to ship from Egypt to Greece "at least four divisions, including one armoured division." Churchill's hope was that if "Greece, with British aid, can hold up for some months German advance, chances of Turkish intervention will be favoured." If events in Greece didn't work out as planned, "we must, at all costs, keep Crete." It was an ambitious plan, given that Churchill lacked the tools to challenge Hitler not only in Western Europe but anywhere. The prime minister also instructed Wavell to "take all possible precautions for the safety of our two Envoys having regard to nasty habits of Wops and Huns."[127]

Across the Atlantic that month, Franklin Roosevelt was trying to sell Lend-Lease to the U.S. Senate. The isolationists were not buying. Senator Burton Wheeler, a Montana Progressive, crony of Joe Kennedy's, and one of the founders of the America First Committee, proclaimed in a radio address that Roosevelt was going to "plow under every fourth American boy." Roosevelt called the accusation "dastardly." Wheeler, taking his rest at Kennedy's Palm Beach manse, declined to say more. He didn't have to. Dastardly or not, he had a point.

Although the goal of the America Firsters was to create a fortress America immune from foreign attack and insulated from the perils of international intrigue, partisans like Wheeler and Kennedy knew that the most direct route to the hearts of American parents was not to explicate complex geopolitical scenarios but to cite the likelihood of their sons' dying in defense of the old and corrupt imperial order. Wheeler's point was unassailable in its logic: if America was dragged into war, American boys would die. All of them—Churchill, Roosevelt, even the America Firsters—expected the price of Britain's survival to soon be calculated in U.S. dollars. The isolationists, though rankled by that prospect, could, just barely, live with it. But that the price of British survival might soon be calculated in U.S. lives was a calculus the isolationists simply could not abide. Churchill could.

In arguing his case for U.S. assistance, Churchill had to avoid, at all cost, any word or deed that smacked of imperialism, anything that would make Roosevelt's task that much more difficult. To Halifax, he wrote, privately: "It is astonishing how this misleading stuff put out by Kennedy that we should do better with a neutral United States than with her warring at our side should have traveled so far." Publicly, he could voice no such opinion. Hopkins had warned Churchill that Lend-Lease and the isolationists were Roosevelt's battles to fight, that "any move on the part of Great Britain to suggest that the United States would eventually fight on the British side would be fatal" to Lend-Lease and the supplies Churchill so desperately needed.[128]

Churchill told Colville he found it discouraging that Roosevelt was being led by public opinion, but in fact, he understood that Roosevelt was guiding the crowd in a direction of his choosing. This was real leadership, not cheap manipulation, for the herd could only arrive at the desired destination if the shepherd was a masterful shepherd. Churchill could not advise Roosevelt, nor could he interfere in the president's shepherding. Given his personality and the power vested in him in Britain, this frustrated him, and he freely expressed that frustration to the War Cabinet, but never to Roosevelt. Keeping his counsel was not one of Churchill's most dominant traits; the unsent messages to Roosevelt at the turn of the year are cases in point. That those communications remained unsent underscores another of his traits: the wisdom, when occasion demanded, to hold his tongue.[129]

Joe Kennedy and Charles Lindbergh testified against Lend-Lease. Lindbergh declined to draw any moral distinction between Germany and Britain and, in the tradition of Baldwin and Chamberlain, cautioned against provoking Germany. He stated several times he wanted neither Germany nor Britain to win, that "it would be a disaster for Europe" if either side won, a curious line of thought given that one side or the other would have to, someday, win. Of Hitler, he said: "I feel I should maintain a position of absolute neutrality." He favored a negotiated end to the war rather than a British victory, which could only be obtained by invasion of Germany and would result in "prostration, famine, and disease" throughout Europe. America, he said, should not "police the world."[130]

Joe Kennedy, hoping for reinstatement within Roosevelt's inner circle, unleashed a weak and unassertive message that avoided any mention of Hitler and urged America to build up its own defense. Lend-Lease, Kennedy declared, posed some constitutional problems vis-à-vis abdication of congressional oversight in foreign affairs, but all in all, he considered aid to Great Britain a good thing. Then he voiced his true sentiments to newsmen, on background: A certain "anonymous American statesman" (almost certainly Kennedy) told the British writer John de Courcy that many Americans felt "the American people have been bamboozled" and that increased aid to Britain would "lead to inflation and bankruptcy for many of us." The anonymous statesman resented the fact that those Americans who disagreed with Mr. Churchill were tagged as isolationists, "a word that has lost most of its meaning and has become a term of abuse." His congressional appearance and anonymous sniping finished "Jittery Joe" politically.[131]

In early February, James Conant made his interventionist plea before the Senate Foreign Relations Committee, a call against "acquiescing in silence to policies which might lead to the wiping out on this continent of the free way of life." Conant termed the conflict less an imperialistic battle than a "religious war" waged "by picked men fanatically devoted to a philosophy which denies all premises of our American faith." And then Conant, one of Roosevelt's leading science advisers, tossed in a cautionary aside, reminding the nation that the Fascists "are well armed by modern science." Within days of testifying, Conant was on his way to London, sent by Roosevelt to ascertain just how well armed Britain was by modern science.[132]

The *Chicago Tribune* continued to editorialize against Roosevelt and Lend-Lease. Americans listened to the America Firsters, but they began to listen less and were moved by them even less. The isolationists, the writer and political commentator Walter Lippmann wrote, had "forced the United States to make a separate peace and to withdraw from all further association with the other democracies to keep the world safe for democracy." Lend-Lease, he wrote, would ensure that "this country passes from large promises carried out slyly and partially by clever devices to substantial deeds openly and honestly avowed."[133]

Roosevelt had been doing some substantial avowing. His "Arsenal of Democracy" speech had moved America. His "Four Freedoms" speech had moved the world. By late February, Gallup polls showed that 55 percent of Americans thought Britain worth saving and worth supplying. Churchill had sold Roosevelt, and Roosevelt had just about closed his sale with the Congress. Yet, Lend-Lease still lingered in the U.S. Senate, and Gallup polls throughout winter found that almost 80 percent of Americans were against sending an army overseas.

Curiously, in his memoirs Churchill fails to credit an instrumental voice, Edward R. Murrow, in bringing Americans on board his foundering vessel. As much as Churchill and Roosevelt used the new medium of radio to great effect in order to sell their views (it had been just seven years since Roosevelt made his first fireside chat), they knew they could not take to the airwaves too often or try to sell too hard. Fortunately for Churchill, Americans tuned their sets to CBS and Murrow, a newsman who possessed, Eric Sevareid wrote, "a hard core of integrity which the impact of no man however powerful or persuasive ever has chipped." Murrow's reports from London came straight from the heart, and went straight to the heart of the matter, so much so that Ed Murrow was one of the first people Harry Hopkins sought out upon his arrival in London. Murrow spoke of the plight of a people at war. He was, wrote Sevareid, "the greatest broadcaster by far in the English tongue" and "a Boswell-to-a-great-city" in whose broadcasts "one will never find a case of sentiment becoming sentimentality." Murrow's reportage, more so even than Churchill's brilliant rhetoric, served to replace in (some) Americans the image of Britons as appeasers and imperialists with an image of them as courageous lovers of freedom. After a night of bombs, Murrow broadcast that as he "walked home at seven in the morning, the windows in the West End were red with reflected fire, and the raindrops were like blood on the panes." No America Firster could summon such imagery with such power for his cause.[134]

Yet Churchill understood America well enough to know that such imagery, no matter how powerful, was not enough to move America to war. When a luncheon guest at No. 10 suggested that the bombing of Athens by the Germans might prove "a good thing from our point of view as it would shock American opinion," Churchill dismissed the notion. Americans' sentiment, he declared, was not a "classical sentiment" and such raids on ancient and beautiful cities would not horrify Americans any more than other raids on other helpless cities, including London, then the most bombed city in the world. Churchill understood that America would not come in until America itself was the victim of attack.[135]

Much of the intelligence Churchill received (other than Ultra, and some of that was fragmentary) was murky and given to multiple interpretations. Much was rumor. Hints of incomprehensible deeds lurked within the tales. In Romania, rumor had it, Premier General Ion Antonescu—dictator since September and Hitler's ally since November—was "committing sadistic atrocities unsurpassed in horror." In fact, Antonescu was putting down a revolt by his erstwhile allies in the Fascist Iron Guard, still a powerful Romanian force. Colville told his diary that the Iron Guard had rounded up Jews, herded them into slaughterhouses and killed them "according to the Jews' own ritual practices in slaughtering animals." Antonescu's loyalty to Hitler was such that the Führer included a qualified kudos (along with a threat) in his New Year's greeting to Mussolini: "General Antonescu has recognized that the future of his regime, and even of his person, depends on our victory. From this he has drawn clear and direct conclusions which make him go up in my esteem." Churchill drew his own conclusions regarding the Romanian. He instructed Eden to inform Antonescu that "we will hold him and his immediate circle personally responsible in life and limb" were the rumors of mass murder to prove true.[136]

More such stories from occupied nations made the rounds, and more often. Hangings for espionage or treasonous offenses against the Reich were to be expected, as was the hanging of Germans who spied against the British Empire. This was war, after all. The British had hanged two German spies just after the close of the old year. But the Germans were taking retaliation to new and unimaginable heights. Polish priests who had fled

Warsaw told their superiors at the Vatican that they feared the Germans planned to "exterminate" the entire Polish people. Another seemingly preposterous story, this one out of Germany, reached the United States. Doctors in the Reich, so the story went, were transporting tens of thousands of "lunatics and cripples" by buses into the forests and there murdering them. *Time*, under the headline EUTHANASIA? made brief mention of the tale, but prefaced its report with the caveat that the British had admitted to concocting and spreading similar tales during World War One. William L. Shirer stumbled across the same story months earlier and committed it to his diary before departing Berlin. Given German censorship, broadcast of the news was patently impossible. Shirer feared he'd be shot if the Gestapo were to discover his diary.[137]

The world now knows that the rumors which long ago seeped from the Continent augured an unimaginable terror. Between 1935 and 1941, Hitler invited the world to witness as the Reichstag pushed through laws that deprived Jews first of privileges, then of rights, then of citizenship, and then of their status as human beings. But the window went dark in late 1940 and was shuttered tight when many Western journalists departed Berlin in early 1941. Increasingly harsh Nazi excess was expected, but how far into the deepest and blackest regions of human depravity it would go, nobody then knew, or could imagine. Hitler had promised in a January 1939 speech that a new war would mean "the end of the Jews." He repeated the threat in January 1941. Should "the rest of the world be plunged into a general war through Jewry, the whole of Jewry will have played out its role in Europe." He made his intentions clear. But it bears remembering, that even one with so fertile an imagination as Churchill could not imagine at the time the utter evil that the Reich was distilling, and would soon tap.

Churchill tried nonetheless to look beyond the present dangers to the world he envisioned after the war. However wide the range of topics discussed at his dinner table—invasion, the Americans, Charlie Chaplin's latest, the need to bomb every Hun corner of Europe—he often steered the conversation to the postwar world. At Chequers one evening he sketched his concept of a Council of Europe made up of five nations—England, France, Italy, Spain, and Prussia (old Prussia, which had risen a century earlier to unite all the German principalities)—together with four confederations—Northern, Danubian, Mitteleuropean, and Balkan. These nine powers, vested with a supreme judiciary and a supreme economic council to work out currency and trade questions, would manage the affairs of the Continent. There would be no reparations, no war debts, and no demands made on Prussia, although, other than a defensive air arm, Prussia would be limited for one hundred years to fielding only a militia. The English-speaking world would exist apart from the council and yet be connected. And, the English-speaking world would control the seas as a reward for final victory. Russia would somehow (Churchill offered no details) fit into an Eastern reorganization. This was his "Grand Design." Yet he could not make such ideas public, he told Colville, while "every cottager in Europe was calling for German blood and when the English themselves were demanding that all Germans should be massacred or castrated."[138]

Churchill reserved for the dinner table any speculation on the postwar world. In public his only stated goal was victory. Any public discussion of the postwar world would have invited the distractions and divisiveness of partisan politics, of Labourites versus Liberals versus Tories, all touting their respective views on education, "class," jobs, and housing. No good could come of that during wartime. As well, anything short of victory would result in a world not worth living in. When a speech Harold Nicolson gave to the members of a private club on the postwar world was later published, Churchill "absolutely blew up." Nicolson had spoken of a world federation, of the need to grant economic concessions to British colonies, and of the need to offer food to any country that liberated itself. "On what authority," Churchill demanded of Nicolson's boss at the Ministry of Information, "does Mr. Nicolson say we are offering a 'New World government' or a 'Federation'?" That an under secretary should declare his opinions on such matters was improper, Churchill wrote, "especially when I have on several occasions deprecated any attempt to declare [post] war aims." Nicolson feared for his job, but Churchill relented after Nicolson explained that the speech had not been intended for publication. A much-relieved Nicolson scribbled in his diary: "Winston has no capacity for meanness, and that is why we love him so."[139]

Actually, Churchill's penchant for petty and at times outright nasty behavior was quite well known, but Nicolson, having escaped his wrath, can be excused for voicing his relief in such glowing terms. Nicolson made no further speculative public forays into the realm of postwar political affairs. In public, Churchill needed to speak with great care, for many of the words he loved to use had very different connotations across the Atlantic. In America, "class" was a dirty word, and "empire" evoked old men of the old order in the Old World—the very order and world Churchill cherished.[140]

His vision for postwar England was another matter. On that subject, he spoke. During a visit to Harrow late in 1940, he told the young boys of privilege who would someday administer the Empire, "When this war is won, as it surely will be, it must be one of our aims to work to establish a state of society where the advantages and privileges which hitherto have been enjoyed only by the few shall be far more widely shared by the men and the youth of the nation as a whole." He allowed to Colville that since young men of all walks of life were fighting the heroic battles in the air, they should inherit the reins of power at war's end. Churchill knew it could not hurt the cause were those sentiments to reach the American press. Later in 1941, he allowed Eden to speak in public of the postwar world. But Eden sounded more like the vengeful Versailles peacemakers of 1919 than one who might support Churchill's brand of magnanimity in peace. Germany, Eden declared, was the worst master that Europe had ever known: "Five times in the last century she has violated the peace. She must never be in a position to play that role again." Eden's thoughts played well to the vengeful masses, yet Churchill told Colville that he envisioned a "re-united European family in which Germany will have a great place. We must not let our vision be darkened by hatred or obscured by sentiment. A much more fruitful line is to try to separate the Prussians from the south Germans." That line reflects the belief long held by Englishmen that Prussia was the incubator of German militancy. It was true that for almost a century Prussia produced generals, but it was also true that National Socialism was incubated in Bavaria, in the south.[141]

Eden's generalizations on Germany's postwar status—essentially, Germany as POW—were distilled into explicit policy points in an article published by Sir Robert Vansittart, a brilliant thinker and hater of all things German, who as a Conservative MP in the late 1930s had been one of Churchill's allies in the Commons. Vansittart, who served as diplomatic adviser to the foreign secretary, did not differentiate between Germans and Nazis, and desired that after the war, the lot of them be fenced in and left to survive as best they could. "If your policy means anything," Churchill wrote Vansittart, "it means the extermination of 40 or 50 million people." Churchill intended "to talk rather more about the Nazis and rather less about the Germans." When he learned that Vansittart intended to broadcast a speech that presumably would be rife with hatred, Churchill blocked it, that is, until he learned Vansittart intended to speak in French to the French people. This could be allowed, Churchill concluded, because "to the French people... his [Vansittart's] particular views have a real attraction and value."[142]

The French had been crushed. They were too afraid to hate. The resistance leader, Georges Bidault, later wrote that "Paris, in 1941, was paralyzed; it would take a very long time to find men able, or even willing, to risk their lives for the sake of a vague and remote victory." What harm could be done, Churchill decided, if Vansittart stoked Frenchmen's dreams of revenge against Germans? Were the French to replace fear with hatred, they might greet each day sustained by the thought of killing their oppressors.[143]

A luncheon guest at No. 10 wondered aloud how long it would take to sterilize every German. As recalled by another guest, Charles Eade, the editor of *Sunday Dispatch,* "Winston brought the lunch party back to reality by observing that if people like his guests, the product of a very high order of civilization, could be capable of discussing such subjects . . . it must surely give us some idea of what sort of things that the Germans themselves might be ready and willing to do to us if they ever have the chance." The seepage of Vansittart's brand of hatred into the hearts of decent Englishmen would turn them into the soulless murderers they were now fighting. That, for Churchill, was the same as defeat, and unacceptable.[144]

He kept any hatred he harbored in check in public and usually in private. He told Hopkins that he "hated nobody," and didn't feel he had any enemies—"except Hitler, and that was professional." To dining companions on more than one occasion he offered that "anger is a waste of energy. Steam which is used to blow off a safety valve would be better used to drive an engine." Yet in the heat of the moment following some new and diabolical feat of the Luftwaffe performed at the expense of British civilians, Churchill, in private, often poured forth his loathing of Huns in general and Hitler in particular. He would "castrate the lot" or bomb "every Hun corner" of Europe. It could be fairly asked if his rages were fueled by alcohol, yet in Churchill's case this would amount to a rhetorical question. The rages could come anytime, morning to night, and Churchill drank every day, morning to night. And his rage always and swiftly subsided. He understood the difference between ruthlessness born of the necessity of war, and thuggish cruelty born of pathological hatred. He ended many evenings with a final word to a secretary (or whoever remained awake at that late hour) on the need for Europeans, including Germans, to live together in harmony following the war. Hitlerism was his enemy, not the German people.[145]

Whether behind a microphone or with his cronies in private, Churchill was canny enough to know when a calculated quotient of righteous anger was called for. When Clementine, during a March luncheon held in honor of James Conant, offered that the people of a nation such as Britain, where old ladies served tea and cigarettes to downed German pilots, could never grow to hate Germans, Churchill growled that before the war was over the British would be hating their enemies all right. He said that for Conant's benefit, for the Germans had just dropped their latest bomb—a four-thousand-pounder—on Hendron, killing about eighty civilians. Such a monster bomb, unimaginable just two years earlier, shocked the sensibilities of civilized people. To address such dastardly technologies and tactics with an overly generous heart would undermine Churchill's status as warlord in front of an important luncheon guest. He had to appear resolute yet not bloodthirsty.

Another of his luncheon guests that day, Charles Eade, offered that British bombing was probably accurate enough to avoid killing innocent Germans. Knowing that wasn't so and that German civilians were paying a high price, Churchill ducked the topic. Perhaps for this reason he decided not to inform Conant that the British had just readied for deployment their own four-thousand-pound bomb. When the talk came around to the calls by Britons for retaliation, Churchill fell back on the remark he had made in the Commons smoking room the previous autumn: "Duty before pleasure." Eade recalled that Clementine laughed at this, and said, "'You are blood-thirsty,' a remark which the Prime Minister did not quite get, and it had to be repeated several times for his benefit."[146]

In his account of the Conant luncheon, Eade hints at another current of conversation at the table, but understandably failed at the time to grasp its import. When the topic of the German four-thousand-pound bomb came up, he asked if it contained "any new form of explosive," which sparked a lively conversation among the well-lubricated guests. Anything new in weaponry, even the rumor of something new, begot terror. Death rays, magnetic mines that floated to the sea surface to seek out targets, huge new bombs—which were fact and which were fiction? Eade notes that at one point during the conversation, the Prof chose to ruminate on the subject of uranium, saying, "Uranium is continually halving itself. Why is there any uranium left on earth?" At the time, uranium was an element most people in Britain and America had never heard of, the physical properties of which very few even in scientific circles understood.[147]

Conant understood. A chemist by education, he served under Vannevar Bush on the National Defense Research Committee, charged by Roosevelt with the task of funding research in order to bring the latest in science and technology to the American military. The NDRC reported directly to Roosevelt and had funded research on uranium. Just weeks earlier, two University of California (Berkeley) physicists had produced minuscule amounts of the hitherto unknown element 94, which they christened plutonium. Conant was familiar with the enormous power inherent in the uranium-235 isotope, though he considered the possibility of unleashing that power to be more science fiction than scientific fact. The Prof thought otherwise, in part because the Maud Committee, formed by Sir Henry Tizard the previous year to determine the feasibility of building an atomic bomb, had kept Lindemann apprised of its progress. The Maud conclusion to date held that with enough money and in about four years' time, a nuclear bomb equal in power to almost two thousand tons of TNT might, just might, prove possible. Two thousand tons equaled the bombing capacity of three hundred Lancaster bombers. This was a terrible power.

During a private lunch with Conant a few days later, Lindemann again brought up the subject of uranium. Conant had recently dined at Oxford with a French physicist who predicted that nuclear power would someday drive electric power plants and possibly even submarines. Thus, when the Prof mentioned uranium, Conant, recalling the Frenchman, replied that some use for uranium might someday be found but that he and his fellow scientists at the NDRC "thought it unwise . . . to devote the precious time of scientists, with the German threat so critical, to a project which could not affect the outcome of the war."[148]

At that, Lindemann leaned into the table and said portentously, "You have left out of consideration the possibility of the construction of a bomb of enormous power." Lindemann explained that by "arranging for two portions of the element to be brought together suddenly the resulting mass would spontaneously undergo a self-sustaining reaction." This was a startling and provocative statement. Conant had assumed that uranium research in the United States, and most likely in Britain, had as its distant goal a sustained and controlled nuclear reaction, not a catastrophic event. Conant's mission to England consisted largely of setting up a London center where American and British scientists would share secrets, mostly about improvements on proximity fuses, bombsights, and radar. Yet with Lindemann's extraordinary hint at British interest in developing an atomic bomb, Conant realized that he had been made privy to the most secret of information. He knew, too, that proper channels of communication for such information needed to be established, and soon. For his part, Lindemann knew that Conant—directly or through his boss, Vannevar Bush—had the ear of the president, although he did not know, as Conant would learn to his "astonishment," that Roosevelt had little interest in and was rarely briefed on technical matters, including radar and the critical role it had played in the Battle of Britain.[149]

Conant took Lindemann's revelation home to Bush, Roosevelt's point man on atomic research. Within weeks, Bush was made director of a new and top-secret committee, the Office of Scientific Research and Development, in which Conant served as Bush's deputy. In October, the British passed on the Maud report in its entirety to the Americans, and a partnership was soon born.[150]

Lindemann's motive in bringing up the subject went beyond the sharing of science secrets with his American counterpart. The Prof was a truly Strangelovian character, called "Baron Berlin" by those of his many enemies who resented his Teutonic roots. His detractors—including Randolph Churchill—whispered the rumor that he was Jewish, to which Winston Churchill replied that he did not care and could not see why it mattered even if it was true. In fact, Colville wrote, the Prof "looked with contempt on Jews and coloured people" but he reserved his deepest hatred for Germany, not simply Nazis, but all things German. He shared with Churchill the desire to pulverize Germany but did not share Churchill's dream of rebuilding Germany after the war. Lindemann's preferred postwar Germany would be a dead Germany. In uranium he had found an extraordinary means to render it so.[151]

Churchill knew that such a weapon made hatred all the more dangerous and made all the more necessary a vision and plan for the postwar world. However, he also believed that any weapon that could end the war sooner—mustard gas, bacterial warfare, assassinations and sabotage by the SOE, even something as futuristic and dastardly as an atomic fission device—possessed great utility. For the time being, however, conventional bombs would have to suffice. Lindemann, at Churchill's request, commenced work on a scientific and policy paper that addressed how best to deal from the air with German cities. The Prof's conclusions and their implementation by Halifax, Lancaster, and B-17 bombers would within three years go a long way toward fulfilling his dream of destroying Germany.[152]

Churchill tried in his speeches to offer hope to his listeners, whether they were enslaved on the Continent or cowering in British air-raid shelters. As he regularly did for Englishmen, in a spring broadcast he offered the Poles his message:

> All over Europe races and States whose cultures and history made them a part of the general life of Christendom in centuries when the Prussians were no better than a barbarous tribe, and the German empire no more than an agglomeration of pumpernickel principalities, are now prostate under the dark cruel yoke of Hitler and his Nazi gang.
>
> Every week his firing parties are busy in a dozen lands. Monday he shoots Dutchmen: Tuesday Norwegians; Wednesday French or Belgians stand against the wall; Thursday it is the Czechs who must suffer...to fill his repulsive bill of executions. But always, all the days, there are the Poles....A day will dawn, perhaps sooner than we now have a right to hope, when the insane attempt to found a Prussian domination on racial hatred, on the armoured vehicle, on the secret police, on the alien overseer and on still more filthy Quislings, will pass like a monstrous dream.
>
> And in that morning of hope and freedom...all that is noble and fearless in the New World as well as in the Old, will salute the rise of Poland to be a nation again.[153]

His words on this occasion fell short of the mark, for the Poles were suffering depredations not visited upon any of the Western European peoples conquered by Hitler. Poles were starving faster than Himmler could shoot them. Himmler and Hitler as yet ruled no lands farther east on which they could resettle the Polish people, although they had concluded that Siberia would do nicely. Absent a place to send the Poles (and soon enough, to send all Slavs who lived west of the Urals), Reich policy was to put them to work readying the countryside for the millions of German warrior-farmers who would emigrate there to start new lives and make fine German babies. The Poles, at least the Catholics among them, would labor as slaves for the Nazis. But more than three million of Poland's prewar population of thirty-four million were Jews. For them, the most sinister of Himmler's programs had yet to begin, but already Poles, both Christians and Jews, beheld in their future nothing resembling Churchill's "morning of hope and freedom." Rather, they beheld darkness and slavery and unspeakable evil.

No speaker could turn a phrase with Churchill's skill, yet he sometimes turned one too many. Churchill's "real tyrant is the glittering phrase," Australian prime minister Robert Menzies jotted in his diary, "so attractive to his mind that awkward facts have to give way." "Pumpernickel principalities" is just the sort of glittering phrase Churchill could not resist, but perhaps should have on that occasion.[154]

Curiously absent from his broadcast to the Poles was any mention of Stalin, who in partnership with Hitler had chewed off eastern Poland in 1939. Churchill was by now convinced Russia would be Hitler's next victim, and soon. It was inopportune to criticize the Russian Bear for its predations on Poland when at any moment the Bear might himself be mauled, securing for Churchill a new ally and a modicum of respite for Britons. The Poles, for their part, understood with terrible certainty that whether or not Hitler attacked Stalin, their prospects in no way changed for the better. Churchill's words on this occasion were eloquent, the sort that inspired his countrymen, who were further inspired by the sight of captured German airmen, the wreckage of Luftwaffe bombers, searchlight beams stabbing into the night, and the *crack* of AA guns, all of which meant Churchill was giving it back. But Poles could give back nothing. Churchill's words offered them only the modest succor afforded by the knowledge that Winston Churchill was out there, across the miles, and that he had not forgotten them.

Menzies remained in London for much of the year. Though he supported Churchill, he knew that voters back home sought more say in the deployment of Australian troops. His political opposition in Canberra thought him too cozy with London, more British than the British. He pestered Churchill constantly for a greater role within the London government, including a permanent seat in the War Cabinet. Although Menzies, along with Jan Smuts, was frequently invited to sit in on War Cabinet meetings, Churchill was constrained by law—a happy coincidence, given his opposition to the idea—from giving a representative of an autonomous commonwealth nation a permanent seat in the War Cabinet. Still, Churchill found Menzies estimable and entertaining enough to sponsor him for membership in the Other Club, Churchill's private dining society, where a man's company was valued more than his politics. But as the year wore on, Churchill's frustration with Menzies grew. The Australian, recalled Viscount Antony Head (at the time a colonel working in war plans), had taken to "laying down the law to Winston" and telling him where he was wrong on strategy and policy. After a sullen meeting between Churchill and Menzies, held at Chartwell, the Australian made ready to depart. Clementine called out to him, "Oh, Mr. Menzies, you must sign the guest book." Churchill murmured, "Yes, and you know what to write—J. Christ."[155]

The second phase of 1941's Blitz—the "Luftwaffe's tour of the ports"—began in mid-February with four straight nights of raids on Portsmouth, where the quays were smashed and the city center reduced to rubble. The town anointed itself "the smitten city." Then Plymouth came in for it, and the Mayflower stone, which marked the spot from which the Pilgrims had ventured forth to the New World, was blown to smithereens. Göring put Hull, Bristol, Merseyside, Swansea, and Glasgow in his sights, and hit them hard, especially—and worrisomely—just as convoys made port. Göring's uncanny ability to find convoys on the open seas and hit the ports at such opportune times (for Germany) inclined Churchill to believe that a spy had to be forwarding information to the Germans. In fact, the Germans had cracked the British merchantman code years earlier. U-boats and Luftwaffe planners simply followed ships' radio signals. Almost 150,000 tons went to the bottom within sight of land in the last days of February and first days of March, the third worst week of shipping losses since the war began. "The sinkings are bad and the strain is increasing at sea," Churchill cabled Roosevelt.[156]

The president did not reply.

The previous summer, Spitfires and Hurricanes helped keep the Germans out of Britain, but bombers, not fighters, were now Churchill's weapons of choice. Despite Fighter Command's protests, Churchill, in his capacity as minister of defence, demanded more bombers. He understood that British night fighters accounted for few German kills, and would not do so until British airborne radar—the "smeller," he called it—was made far more efficient and lighter. The Germans meanwhile, stung by Fighter Command, had ceased daylight raids the previous October. More RAF fighters, therefore, would not result in more downed German pilots, but more RAF bombers would result in more dead Germans. To accomplish that, Churchill turned to the Aircraft Ministry and Beaverbrook.[157]

Beaverbrook, though not as steadfast a believer as Churchill in bomber warfare, complied. It was the correct decision, made at the correct moment, for by the end of 1940, with growing numbers of RAF bombers lost and in need of repairs (for which there were scarcely any spare parts), Bomber Command was flying only about one-half the sorties flown in the summer. The tonnage of bombs dropped on Germany had fallen to barely a third of the tonnage dropped in September. The RAF was inflicting no pain on the Reich. By January, Beaverbrook's factories began to meet Churchill's demand. The first Lancaster bombers—powered by four Rolls-Royce Merlin engines, and toting up to six tons of bombs—had taken their shakedown flights in mid-January. The Germans had nothing to match the armament, range, and bomb capacity of the Lancasters. These were the instruments of destruction that Churchill needed in order to fulfill his strategic priority, which was, as he stated frequently and with no equivocation, to deliver "an absolutely devastating, exterminating attack by very heavy bombers from this country upon the Nazi homeland."[158]

Beaverbrook took it as his mission to make good on Churchill's oath, and he did so in a manner that pleased no one but the prime minister. The Beaver's staff resented his holding his cards close, and neither the fighter nor bomber wings of the RAF were satisfied with their allotments. But he was not to be denied. He changed production schedules seemingly at random, broke aircraft factories into smaller components, and scattered them in the countryside, where the Luftwaffe could not find them. He unilaterally granted permission to American factories to build Merlin engines under license, and Hurricanes and Spitfires, too, if they desired (the British had to pay cash for the end products). Harold Macmillan thought him "half mad, half genius...who thinks only of his present work, and that all his old fortune, newspapers and women are completely forgotten." Beaverbrook managed by cajoling and by instinct; he operated at full steam ahead, until a crisis arrived, which he would fix before steaming off again at flank speed. Randolph cautioned his wife, Pamela, to avoid at all costs "Beaverbrook's spell, because nothing amuses Beaverbrook more than to have complete control of people's lives, to smash them or put them together as he sees fit." In his dealings with everyone (including Churchill), Beaverbrook was clever to the point of deviousness, yet Churchill, recalled Pamela, "had great respect for Beaverbrook's shrewdness and cunning and ability—tremendous respect." He kept his production schedules and inventory needs on scraps of paper in his pocket and available in case Churchill asked about such matters, which he did often. For this trait alone Churchill respected Beaverbrook, a happy confluence of utility in a friendship of three decades' standing. In Churchill, Beaverbrook found the hero he had sought out since childhood—a great man who appreciated his talents and who welcomed him into his inner circle. In return, Beaverbrook reciprocated with absolute loyalty, although when he and Churchill agreed to disagree—which they did on a regular basis—he was not the sort to back down.[159]

By late February, O'Connor's VIII Corps, now commanded by General Philip Neame, held the Libyan flank, five hundred miles west of Cairo. On the Horn, the Italians still fled before Wingate and Cunningham. All looked well. Harold Nicolson saw the African campaigns as "mere chicken-feed." He told his diary there was no doubt where the real threat lay, "We know that the Great Attack is impending. . . . When the climate improves they may descend upon us with such force as they have never deployed before. Most of our towns will be destroyed." Expecting the worse, Nicolson closed his diary entry with: "Well, if they try, let them try. We shall win in the end."[160]

On March 1, Hitler secured his right of way to Yugoslavia and Greece when Bulgaria ignored Churchill's warning of February 9 and signed on with Hitler. The Bulgarians had no choice. Since the previous autumn, Hitler had pressed Yugoslavia and Bulgaria to join the Tripartite Pact, as had Hungary and Romania, each in its own turn humiliated and cajoled into becoming Nazi cat's-paws. Bulgaria was the latest to succumb. Its king, Boris, ruled a country that was Russia's only real friend in Europe, a good friend of long standing, by mutual agreement. Czar Nicholas II was Boris's godfather; Russia had backed Bulgaria in its exit from the Ottoman Empire sixty years previously. These were cultural bonds of a sort Hitler could not tolerate, for if Boris and Stalin were to strengthen them, Hitler would be denied his most direct transit to Greece. The Führer made Boris the same offer he had made Antonescu the previous autumn, a guarantee of protection. Of course, the refusal of such protection would result in problematic relations with the Reich. Boris faced a choice between two evils: to make way for the Wehrmacht or to be taken out of the way.

Boris, a peaceful man who liked to collect butterflies and tinker with automobile engines, was made of stern enough stuff to say no to Hitler, but his army could not back him up. No army in Europe could back up any leader who said no to Hitler. Had Bulgaria been protected by an oceanic tank ditch, as was Britain, Boris might have bought more time. Furthermore, Boris's ministers were pro-German, his wife pro-Italian, and his people pro-Russian. His safest move was to put himself under Hitler's protection, which he did on March 1. Hitler now held both banks of the Danube down to the Black Sea, and he had plans for the seven hundred German pontoon bridges sitting on the Romanian bank.[161]

On March 6 Lend-Lease began the third month of its journey through Congress; the U.S. Senate had been debating the bill for almost a month. That day, Churchill displayed his displeasure over the lethargic pace of the legislation when he appeared late, tired, and "grumpy" at No. 10 for a luncheon held for James Conant. The guests dined in awkward silence until Conant voiced his "belligerent" interventionist views. At that, Churchill became animated and turned the talk to Lend-Lease: "This bill has to pass," he snarled. Conant recalled the Old Man's "irritation rising as he spoke." Churchill went on: "What a failure he [Roosevelt] would appear if this bill is not passed. What would happen in the United States if the bill was rejected? Would the president resign" and if so, "who would become president, the vice-president?"[162]

Conant was stunned. He asked himself if Churchill might "really have such a profound ignorance of the American constitutional system." The Harvard man—wary of angering Churchill—gently informed him that an American president, unlike a British prime minister, did not resign after major political setbacks, and that America "did not operate under a parliamentary system," as did the British. Emboldened by "gaining the ascendancy for a moment," Conant tossed out the prospects of American armies coming to the rescue. "We don't want your men," Churchill snarled, "just give us the tools and we shall finish the job." Conant realized at that moment what many of Churchill's dinner companions had long known: "Mr. Churchill had this way of quoting from his own speeches even in casual conversation." Churchill plowed on, insisting to Conant that nobody in England had ever in public asked America to enter the war. Conant took Churchill's words at face value but was skeptical and felt that "Mr. Churchill and his associates were not entirely frank" and tended to say one thing "while thinking quite another," although "no responsible statesman is required to be completely candid." Conant concluded that Churchill had "rather let himself go" during the luncheon, "perhaps unconsciously, perhaps consciously for my benefit."

Conant did not yet understand that Churchill put on a show whenever he had an audience. Ambiguity was alien to the man. Churchill, wrote Sir John Keegan, "had no capacity for sustained dissimulation." His outburst produced the intended results. Conant rushed back to his hotel and—"upset at Churchill's troubled eloquence"—fired off letters to his wife and colleagues in which he asked, "Why don't they pass Lend-Lease? Why doesn't FDR appeal to the country in another radio speech?"[163]

Roosevelt had no need to. Conant, overseas for three weeks, was unaware that during those weeks, Roosevelt's victory in the Senate had gone from a possibility to a certainty. Apparently Churchill's Washington embassy was furnishing him with no better intelligence than Conant was deriving from his friends. In any case, Lend-Lease cleared the U.S. Senate by a vote of 60–31 on March 8. Roosevelt signed it on the eleventh. "The bill," Churchill told Winant, "is a draught of life." But it was not as sweet a draught as he thought. The *New York Times* reported that the president had said the first matériel to be sent to the British and Greeks was not very large in dollars and cents, but, whatever the amount, it would be charged against the limitation of $1.3 billion "placed by the lease-lend bill upon the value of materials that may be transferred from the existing facilities of the Army and Navy. Figures before the President did not necessarily mean the billing price inasmuch as much of the material was considered out of date, or surplus, and *not worth the money paid a good many years ago*" (italics added).[164]

Britain's first shipments of arms, therefore, would consist of junk, long since written off America's books. British pilots were training in America, and American pilots, including women, were ferrying bombers to Britain. Fuel and ammunition arrived at British ports weekly. But as with the obsolete destroyers, Roosevelt told Americans they were getting the best of the deal. No doubt Churchill, too, would get a good deal, *if* Congress passed—and passed rapidly—the pending appropriation of $7 billion. That was a lot of money in 1941. Yet even fully funded, Lend-Lease would only partially address Britain's needs. On the day the bill passed, a dozen oil tankers and refrigerator ships were scheduled to sail for England. In peacetime such a fleet could, by way of round-trip relays, fuel and feed a moderate-size city, indefinitely. Yet, at the rate U-boats were sending British hulls to the bottom in early 1941, Britain would have to spend much of its Lend-Lease windfall on new ships, with little left over to fill their holds.[165]

Churchill put a good face on the matter, as he had with the fifty old destroyers. To the House of Commons, he declared that by taking this action, "the Government and people of the United States have in fact written a new Magna Carta, which not only has regards to the rights and laws upon which a healthy and advancing civilization can alone be erected but also proclaims . . . the duty of free men and free nations, wherever they may be, to share the burden and responsibility of enforcing them." Later in the year, as tens of thousands of tons of American matériel sailed to Britain, he told the audience at the annual Lord Mayor's Day luncheon, "Never again let us hear the taunt that money is the ruling thought or power in the hearts of the American democracy. The Lend and Lease Bill must be regarded without question as the most unsordid act in the whole of recorded history." Lend-Lease was a start, but enough of a start for Churchill to conclude that Britain no longer would fight with its back to the Atlantic but henceforth with America at its back. That alone would not ensure a British victory, but it would make British defeat almost impossible—almost but not absolutely, because American industrial capacity had yet to reach a level that could guarantee British survival. Harry Hopkins told Churchill he believed America would reach its stride in eighteen months. Churchill estimated America needed at least two years to attain full war production. Hitler's best estimate, which he imparted to the Japanese foreign minister, was four years.[166]

Two years would prove a year too many if Britain's shipping losses continued at February's pace, when almost 320,000 tons went down. March was shaping up as the worst month yet. Losses in the first week approached 150,000 tons, more than twice the average for any *three* weeks of the war, and were easily on a pace to exceed 400,000 tons for the month. Britain's importing capacity—the gross tonnage of material it could handle with its fleet, its docks, and warehouses—had fallen from almost 43 million tons in 1939 to under 29 million, a level not seen since 1917. The Atlantic Ocean, Churchill had predicted early in the year, would be the major battleground of 1941. He anointed the ordeal the Battle of the Atlantic with the same intent as when the previous summer he anointed the pending battle the Battle of Britain, to focus the attention of the government and the people upon the most immediate threat to their existence. But whereas in 1940, the RAF could put into the skies enough Spitfires and Hurricanes to fight the Luftwaffe to a stalemate, the Royal Navy in March of 1941 had not the ships, nor the weapons, nor the advanced radar needed to stop Dönitz's U-boats. As well, the Focke-Wulf 200 bombers that Raeder had snatched from Göring had taken their toll, until Göring returned from his vacation and demanded their return. British shipping losses due to German aircraft began to fall, and continued to do so throughout the spring and summer. By recalling his bombers, Göring had committed a strategic blunder. Still, by March the German navy and the Luftwaffe had just about severed the sea-lanes into Britain.[167]

The continuing success of the Germans against British shipping and the prospect of greater losses to come was, Churchill wrote in his memoirs, "the only thing that really frightened me during the war." U-boats and German bombers had so far sent 15 percent of Britain's prewar merchant fleet of eighteen million tons to the bottom. One million tons had gone down since the American election. Norway had added a thousand ships and almost three million tons to the Allied merchant marine, but Norwegian ships were being hit as hard as British. Were half of the remaining British shipping to go to the bottom, Britain would starve. National survival depended upon convoys bearing wheat getting through. A halving in wheat imports could, in a few months time, result in a Malthusian halving of the British population. It was just that simple. Churchill pleaded with Roosevelt throughout the first seven months of the year to move the American patrol zone into the far eastern Atlantic, to arm American merchantmen (a violation of the Neutrality Act of 1939), and to show the flag in the vicinity of the Azores (where U-boats resupplied and re-armed with impunity). In Churchill's estimation, if Lend-Lease had put America on the path to war, let the journey continue apace.[168]

Roosevelt, though ready to help, was not ready to fight. Restrained by conflicting and strongly held public opinion, he made his way along his chosen path with the same tortured gait he displayed while thrusting himself through the rejuvenating waters of Warm Springs, in the central Georgia foothills of the Appalachians. There, he took his measured and painful steps, with the utmost care, lest his footing be unsure. Heroic as his progress was—in the medicinal springs of Georgia and in the politics of war—Roosevelt's progress when it came to Hitler was not swift enough for Churchill.

With Lend-Lease on the books, Roosevelt dispatched Averell Harriman as his special envoy to London with the extraordinary mandate, to "recommend everything we can do, short of war, to keep the British Isles afloat." Harriman reported directly to Hopkins and the president, a ploy that kept Secretary of State Cordell Hull (to Hull's increasing annoyance) on the sidelines. Harriman also consulted directly with Churchill, thus bypassing the Foreign Office. Lend-Lease was not strictly speaking a matter of foreign affairs but rather one of American national security and, for Britain, national survival. Roosevelt's choice of Harriman was brilliant.

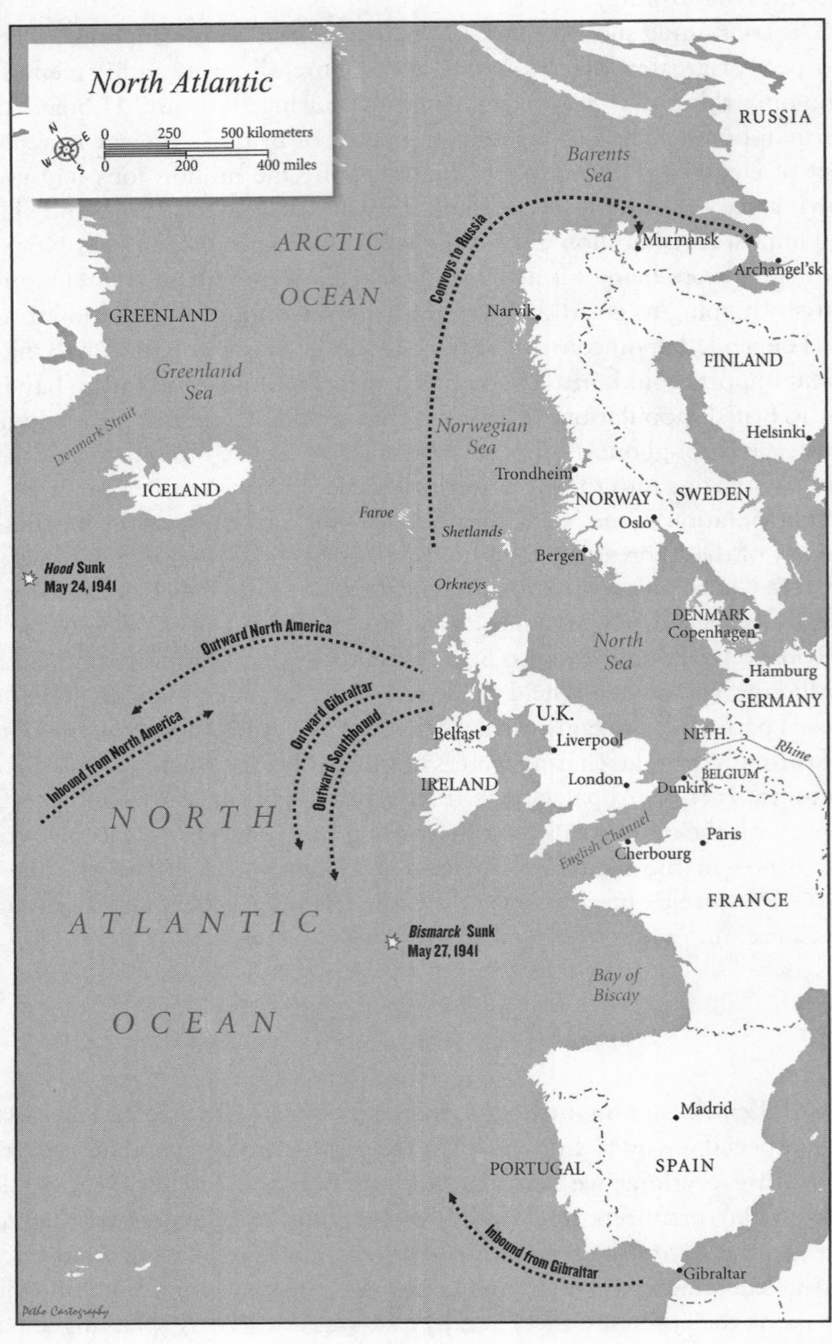
North Atlantic
N E S W
0 250 500 kilometers
0 200 400 miles
RUSSIA
Barents Sea
ARCTIC OCEAN
Convoys to Russia
Murmansk
Archangel'sk
GREENLAND
Narvik
FINLAND
Greenland Sea
Denmark Strait
Norwegian Sea
Helsinki
Trondheim
ICELAND
NORWAY
SWEDEN
Faroe
Oslo
Shetlands
Bergen
Hood Sunk
May 24, 1941
Orkneys
DENMARK
Copenhagen
Outward North America
North Sea
Hamburg
Outward Gibraltar
GERMANY
Outward Southbound
U.K.
Inbound from North America
Belfast
NETH.
Liverpool
Rhine
IRELAND
London
BELGIUM
Dunkirk
NORTH
English Channel
Paris
Cherbourg
FRANCE
ATLANTIC
Bismarck Sunk
May 27, 1941
Bay of Biscay
OCEAN
Madrid
PORTUGAL
SPAIN
Inbound from Gibraltar
Gibraltar
Petho Cartography

He represented America's capitalist class rather than the Democratic Party's ideological class. He was a product of Groton (the motto of which is *cui severe est regnare,* "to serve is to rule") and Yale. His politics was business. The captains of industry Roosevelt needed on his side listened to Harriman. Almost fifty, he had never lacked that which Churchill always had lacked: money, and not simply money, but *capital.* He dressed the part. If Anthony Eden was the most impeccably attired Englishman in the land, Harriman took the honors for visitors, always smartly attired in trim, custom-made dark suits that accentuated his sharp WASP features. Pamela Churchill was certainly taken with him, and within a few weeks, taken by him.[169]

Young Averell had expanded the railroad holdings of his father, E. S. Harriman, and moved into banking, oil field equipment, and shipbuilding. He was board chairman of the Union Pacific Railroad and of his banking firm, W. A. Harriman & Company, which after a merger became Brown Brothers Harriman. His fellow Yale alumnus, Prescott Bush, son-in-law of W. A. Harriman's president, George Herbert Walker, had recently been made a junior partner. Together, Harriman and Bush sustained a modest loss that year when the U.S. government seized the German accounts maintained by Brown Brothers Harriman. Yet those losses, as well as the Depression itself, were but potholes on Easy Street for Harriman. He had two daughters by his first marriage; one, Kathleen, became fast friends with Pamela Churchill, and they soon shared a London flat, Randolph having been posted to Cairo. Harriman's first marriage had ended in divorce. He was now married to Marie Norton Whitney, the former wife of Cornelius ("Sonny") Vanderbilt Whitney, the son of Gertrude Vanderbilt Whitney, she of the Whitney Museum. Harriman's credentials therefore were as solid as those of Churchill's late cousin, John "Sunny" Spencer Churchill, the ninth Duke of Marlborough, himself the former husband of Consuelo Vanderbilt, who dwelled now mostly in Palm Beach, the Nazis having confiscated her French manse. Sunny's son, "Bert," made do at Blenheim, where the roof leaked and a distinct mustiness permeated the old palace. Harriman and Churchill were connected therefore by marriage, however distantly, like members of one big happy Anglo-American family, but for the distinction that one side was well off and living in peace, while the other was nigh broke and being bombed into oblivion.[170]

Harriman set to work with Beaverbrook to ensure that Churchill received the goods he needed. Since the Beaver spent most weekends with Churchill, Harriman, too, became a regular weekend guest at Ditchley and Chequers, the better to sort things out with Beaverbrook, as well as with Hopkins back in Washington. Harriman and Hopkins had been good friends for almost eight years, having met on a train while both were on their way to Washington during the early days of the New Deal. It was an unlikely relationship — the impeccably dressed tycoon and the scruffy liberal social worker — and for Churchill a fortuitous one.[171]

Churchill sold Harriman, as he had sold Hopkins, on the inevitability of invasion. On Harriman's second visit to Chequers, Churchill offered him a somber assessment. The times called for a "holding action," he said, not "bold new strokes." For his part, Harriman told Churchill that the boldest and most necessary stroke would take the form of a U.S. declaration of war, which he fully supported. That was exactly what Churchill wanted to hear.[172]

Rather than bold strokes, Churchill told Harriman, only two strategic imperatives existed, defense of the Home Island and of the Suez Canal. Loss of one would result in the loss of the other, and of the war. (Yet Churchill was at that moment stripping troops from both the Home Island and Egypt in order to make a very bold stroke in the Balkans.) He played the invasion card not only with his American guests but also continually with Britons, if for no other reason than to impress upon Americans that Britons were not complacent. With both Harriman and renewed Luftwaffe bombing arriving in London at the same time, Churchill set to work imparting to Harriman a concise understanding of Britain's predicament. Peaceful and empty beaches belied the invasion threat, so Churchill found other means of inducing fear of the Hun in Harriman. To that end, he allowed Harriman the great privilege of sitting in on secret Battle of the Atlantic War Cabinet meetings, where the news was all bad all the time. And to give Harriman a taste of fire, Churchill, at the howling of the sirens, escorted him to the roof of the Air Ministry, where after witnessing the horrors, Harriman concluded that Hitler might yet starve or burn Britain into submission. This he soon reported to his boss, as Churchill presumed he would.[173]

To Harriman, as he had to Hopkins, Willkie, and Winant, Churchill expressed his strong desire to meet Roosevelt in person. From Roosevelt, as winter turned to spring, there came no reply.

Early in March, Churchill's team in the Balkans, led by Eden, concluded that they had a good fighting chance in Greece, but only if everything fell perfectly into place by way of getting the troops into position. Four months earlier Eden had thought any such adventure in Greece to be "strategic folly." Now he was putting the best face on it, cabling the War Cabinet from Athens that despite the risks, the operation should go forth. Indeed,

Eden reported that General Papagos and the Greeks now appeared stalwart. To fight and perchance to lose, Eden concluded, was preferable to not fighting at all. Eden, Wavell, and Dill were in agreement that if the British arrived in Greece and got into position before the Germans came, "there was a good chance of holding them." They also concluded, "If the Germans arrived first, it should be possible to withdraw the majority of our forces without great loss." But Dill considered the Greek situation "grimmer than we had thought." He did not express those doubts with absolute precision to Churchill. In any case, the War Cabinet approved the Greek operation on March 7. The cabinet minutes noted Churchill's view "that we should go forward with a good heart." Wavell's troops, who were doing the actual going forward, were taking on more and more of a symbolic role, the embodiment of Churchill's lofty decision to do the right and proper thing. Generals such as Wavell are loath to send men into battle to die for political symbolism. Yet Wavell, like Dill, had not made his concerns clear to Churchill. Thus the War Cabinet made its "bleak decision" (as characterized by Eden) to fight in Greece. Then, with the decision made, Eden, in Athens, related to Churchill that General Papagos, who just a week earlier had seemed stalwart, was now "discouraged." Colville, to his diary, expressed his fear that "our troops will find themselves in a dangerous plight." Churchill was now growing wary of the whole business and felt, Colville wrote, that "it was thrust upon us," partly in order to preserve British prestige in the eyes of the Americans, and partly because Eden, Dill, Wavell, and Cunningham—even after warning of the dangers of stretching resources—"recommended it so strongly." In fact, Eden and company, worn down by Churchill, were only delivering the Balkan front that Churchill had insisted upon for months.[174]

Churchill informed Roosevelt of the decision on March 10:

> Although it is no doubt tempting to try to push on from Benghazi to Tripoli...we have felt it our duty to stand with the Greeks, who have declared to us their resolve, even alone, to resist the German invader. Our Generals Wavell and Dill, who accompanied Mr. Eden to Cairo, after heart searching discussions with us, believe we have a good fighting chance.[175]

Any hope for success in Greece rested in large part not with Wavell or Papagos but with Yugoslavia (and, as Eden had pointed out, with whoseever army arrived in Greece first). To Roosevelt, Churchill declared: "No country ever had such a military chance. If they [the Yugoslavs] fall on the Italian rear in Albania, there is no measure of what might happen in a few weeks." Here he was again with his hypothetical reasoning—*If this, then that, then maybe this*. In fact, the Yugoslavs had no real "military chance" because they lacked the military muscle to take advantage of any so-called opportunity that might present itself. The Yugoslav army stood at more than a million men, but it was a late nineteenth-century army. Its entire armored strength consisted of fewer than one hundred World War One–era tanks. Its air force was minuscule. The Yugoslavs in no way thought that several German armored divisions poised on their borders constituted an opportunity. Churchill knew this, and soon enough so did Roosevelt, after Colonel Bill Donovan, who on the spot and surveying the war situation for the president, reported to Roosevelt that although he, Donovan, respected the fighting spirit of the Yugoslavs, they could no more stop Hitler than had any other small European nation. A fuller and more accurate accounting by Churchill would have informed Roosevelt of Admiral Cunningham's fear that without air cover, his fleet sailed naked in Greek waters, and of Longmore's fear of spreading dangerously thin his meager airpower, and of Jumbo Wilson's fear of spreading his lines too thin. A full accounting would have informed Roosevelt of Wavell's distress at the peeling away from Libya of 60,000 of his best desert troops.[176]

The North African situation was thus: at the very moment Erwin Rommel was about to launch his panzers east toward Egypt, Churchill began moving his best and most battle-hardened troops from Libya to Greece, replacing them with green reinforcements.

March had commenced with the Bulgarians sounding their sour note and Churchill declaring that the Battle of the Atlantic, if not soon won, would spell disaster. After the passage of Lend-Lease, the remainder of the month brought forth a steady stream of encouraging news, and went out with a hurrah of military and political good fortune.

In East Africa, British and colonial armies continued to push through Abyssinia toward the port of Massawa on the Red Sea, where several Italian warships and thirty-five cargo ships rode at anchor. Churchill cabled Eden in Cairo that were the Italians to scuttle the ships, "we shall consider ourselves relieved of feeding the Italian population of Eritrea and Abyssinia." Harold Nicolson had been quite correct when he opined that all of this East African business and much of the Libyan success had been a lot of chicken feed. Yet the African adventures—Sir John Keegan calls them "flights of his [Churchill's] strategic imagination"—boosted morale at home and fed Churchill's resolve to fight the war to a successful conclusion.[177]

The real threats lay in the eastern Mediterranean—in Greece, Crete, and Syria, should the Germans advance along those lines—and in the Western Desert, with Erwin Rommel. As March rolled into its final week, those fronts remained quiet but for a probe by Rommel. Then, good fortune came Churchill's way on March 25, when an Italian battle fleet sailed from the heel of Italy to attack British troop transports bound for Greece. Mussolini, pressed by the Germans to intercept and sink British transports, had taken up the challenge.

The Royal Navy knew of the operation in advance; British code breakers had solved the Italian cipher the previous summer. Admiral Cunningham, from his headquarters in Alexandria, ordered four cruisers and nine destroyers to lie in wait for the Italian fleet. Cunningham himself sailed from Alexandria on March 27 with his main battle squadron and the carrier *Formidable*. The two fleets met off Cape Matapan, the southernmost point of mainland Greece, late on the twenty-eighth. The Italian commander, Admiral Angelo Iachino, on board the battleship *Vittorio Veneto,* had divided his force into three squadrons, one of which, Iachino's, the British found and harassed, damaging the *Vittorio Veneto* and stopping the cruiser *Palo* dead in the water. Admiral Iachino, presuming Cunningham's main force was still in Alexandria, sent two cruisers and two destroyers to the aid of *Palo*. The British saw them coming on radar screens, a technology the Italians fatally lacked. A British searchlight stabbed across the water; gunners found their range, and in minutes the entire Italian squadron was sent to the bottom, along with more than 2,400 sailors and officers. The Italians had been caught so completely unawares that their guns were trained in the wrong direction. Churchill, elated by the news, told Colville that with "the tearing up of the Italian paper fleet" the British could now ferry their troops unmolested to Greece.[178]

The final grand news of the month came out of Yugoslavia. With Bulgaria in Hitler's fold and Turkey resolved to stay out of the war, Yugoslavia was Churchill's last best hope for creating his Balkan front. Colville wrote that week: "The diplomatic battle for the soul of Yugoslavia is reaching its height and sways either way with vertiginous speed." Churchill knew that if diplomacy did not deliver Yugoslavia to Hitler, Hitler would use other means. Yugoslavia's regent, Prince Paul, understood the precariousness of his position. Paul, Churchill had told Colville weeks earlier, was like a man in a cage with a tiger, "hoping not to provoke him while steadily dinner time approaches." Prince Paul had tried to stall for time. But time had run out. Harangued by Hitler at a meeting early in the month, and knowing his position was untenable, Paul (whom Churchill derided as "Prince Palsy") overrode his own sentiments and those of his countrymen. He sent his ministers by secret night train to Vienna, where they signed the Tripartite Pact on the twenty-fifth. Cadogan had predicted the outcome days earlier, when he told his diary, "Yugoslavs seem to have sold their souls to the Devil. *All* these Balkan peoples are trash. Poor dears." Learning that they had finally thrown in with Hitler, he scribbled, "Jugs are signing... silly, feeble, mugs." Within hours of the agreement's being signed, Churchill cabled the British ambassador in Belgrade, Ronald Campbell, and urged him to take whatever action he could to ensure that the pro-British factions in the Yugoslav government knew that London was behind them. "Continue to pester, nag, and bite," Churchill told Campbell, but if the present government "have gone beyond recall," then "we may have to resort" to other measures. He meant a coup d'état.[179]

When the signing of the pact was announced in Belgrade, the city exploded into revolt, a rebellion nurtured into being by the resident RAF attaché, who inspired the Yugoslav air forces to action, having prepared the ground with cash and influence peddled by the SOE. "Good news," Cadogan wrote, "of *coup d'état* in Belgrade." Peter, the seventeen-year-old prince, was declared king and put upon his father's throne. Prince Paul fled to Athens. "A great day," Colville wrote on the twenty-seventh. "Revolution in Belgrade, which puts an entirely different complexion on events in the Balkans and turns darkness into dawn. The P.M. is overjoyed." So much so that he cabled Hopkins with all the good news coming out of East Africa and Belgrade: "Yesterday was a grand day."[180]

It was a false dawn. When the reports from Yugoslavia were confirmed, Churchill concluded, "We must expect bad news." He was correct. Hitler would not abide a double-cross and a revolt within the same week. Churchill's practitioners of ungentlemanly warfare in the SOE had produced the coup; but it would be Hitler who set Yugoslavia ablaze. He greeted the news with fury. The time for pseudodiplomacy had passed. He told his generals his decision, dispensing with his usual verbosity: "I have decided to destroy Yugoslavia."[181]

On March 24, Rommel, fully eight weeks or more before he (and Churchill) expected his desert force to reach full strength, probed tentatively toward the British lines at El Agheila, four hundred miles west of Bardia and five hundred miles east of Tripoli, near the border between Cyrenaica and Tripolitania. Churchill had taken at face value Wavell's prediction sent to London three weeks earlier that "no large scale attack was likely to develop [against Wavell] *before the end of the summer*" (italics added). Wavell had misread his opponent. And Rommel had misread his. He presumed he would find the British at El Agheila in great strength, and preparing to continue their westward attack. Instead, he found them ill prepared to receive even a reconnaissance in force. Rommel was not one to let such an opportunity pass without making mayhem. O'Connor may have weeks earlier telegraphed to the world that he'd "killed the fox in the open," but a new fox had crept right up to the coop, and found the door wide open. Rommel stepped right in. He did so against the expressed orders of his commanders in Berlin, and against the wishes of General Garibaldi, under whom Rommel nominally served. Just the previous week, Berlin had ordered Rommel to avoid any general offensive actions until the early May arrival of his 15th Panzer Division. Churchill, too, had concluded that Rommel's diminutive African army would not grow strong enough to pose any threat until mid-May. Therefore, upon learning of Rommel's probe, Churchill cabled Wavell: "I presume you are only waiting for the tortoise to stick his head out far enough before chopping it off." It was the same message he had sent to French commander in chief Georges in May 1940, when the long thrusts by German panzers appeared to have exposed their flanks.[182]

Rommel probed for six days, but on the thirtieth, he launched a two-pronged blitzkrieg attack toward Benghazi, eighty miles up the coast, and overland toward Derna. Churchill had failed to take into account the character of his enemy. General Philip Neame, commanding the Western Army, had failed to study both his enemy and the terrain. Not until the week before Rommel made his move, and too late, did Neame inform Wavell that the escarpment south of Benghazi failed to protect his flank. He had believed the escarpment could be penetrated only at a certain few choke points; in fact it was porous. Had Neame flown over the terrain, he would have seen this.[183]

In East Africa the news was better; by March 30 the British occupied the whole of Eritrea. The war there was about over, in large part due to Wingate's stunning campaign, which earned him no promotion. He was a little too irregular for the old school generals in Cairo and London. As well, he soon had a breakdown and tried to kill himself by slitting his throat. His reward for his role in conquering Ethiopia was virtual banishment, to Burma. But in less than a year, his nonconformist qualities would serve Churchill well in battling a new enemy far more dangerous than the Italians.[184]

Rommel's mischief aside, the run of good fortune—the victories over Aosta in Ethiopia, the battering of the Italian fleet, and the Yugoslavs' "recapture of their soul"—made for "a wonderful weekend," Colville told his diary, "the culmination of a week of victories." They were at Chequers, where Churchill, attired in his dressing gown, "spent much of the weekend pacing—or rather tripping—up and down the Great Hall to the sound of the gramophones (playing martial airs, waltzes and the most vulgar kind of brass-band songs), deep in thought all the while."[185]

He wandered the halls, deep in thought, because Ultra had revealed on March 26 that following the Yugoslav pact with Hitler (hours before the Yugoslav coup), several divisions of German troops and mechanized infantry had been ordered from the Yugoslav border to southern Poland. Most significantly, so had three out of the five panzer divisions bivouacked in Romania. Thus, when Ultra revealed the orders to move out were canceled following the Belgrade revolt, the import of the reversal in German movements became clear. Russia had been Hitler's next target, until the insolent Yugoslavs defied him. A Joint Intelligence Committee report also included the fact that the Germans had lengthened and reinforced runways at several Polish airfields, and they were not doing so, Cadogan concluded, "for the benefit of Lufthansa."[186]

On March 30, Churchill cabled Eden, in Athens with Dill, that as a result of the Yugoslav coup and "sure information recently received" (the Enigma decrypts), it looked as if "Bear will be kept waiting a bit." The orders and counter orders that Ultra revealed made clear to Churchill Germany's "magnitude of design" directed both southeast toward the Balkans and, eventually, east to Russia: "My reading is that the bad man concentrated very large armoured forces…to overawe Yugoslavia….The moment he was sure Yugoslavia was in the Axis he moved three of the five panthers towards the Bear believing what was left would be enough to finish the Greek affair." He noted that "it looks as if heavy [German] forces will be used in the Balkan Peninsula." On the same day, he cabled William Fadden, acting Prime Minister of Australia (Prime Minister Robert Menzies was in London at the time): "German plans have been upset [by the Belgrade coup] and we may cherish renewed hopes of forming a Balkan front with Turkey….Result unknowable, but prize has increased and risks have somewhat lessened." Turkey, in fact, had nothing to gain by coming in on Britain's side, and did not. Actually, were an enraged Hitler to fling his forces into the Balkans, the foremost risk to Britain—a broad front that would overstretch the already thin lines of the Greek and British forces—would become a reality.[187]

Although Colville did not understand the reason at the time, Churchill's belief that the Bear was soon to be baited was why the Old Man had given "a short lecture on the various invaders of Russia, especially Charles XII." Charles XII, king of Sweden, had in 1700 crushed the Russian army in a battle on the banks of the Narva River. Rather than press his advantage against Czar Peter's beaten army, Charles turned toward Poland, a strategic blunder that devoured four years and much of his army, and allowed Peter to reform his incompetent and corrupt military and regroup his forces. When, late in the decade, Charles again tried his hand in Russia, Peter was ready, and in 1709, earned his moniker "The Great" by smashing Charles's army. Colville leaves unrecorded whether in telling the story

Churchill meant to compare the unprepared Stalin, his army purged of its best officers, to the unprepared early Peter, or the later Charles, impetuous and overconfident, to Hitler.[188]

As horrific had been the fighting on the Western Front in May and June 1940, a clash between Germany and Russia would result in a titanic struggle unlike any the world had ever known. On April 3, Churchill took a calculated risk and sent a personal message to Stalin (as he had the previous summer), through the British ambassador to the Soviets, Sir Stafford Cripps. Churchill made no reference to his highly secret source, but with his usual aversion to obliquity, made his point with clarity and honesty:

> I have sure information from a trusted agent that when the Germans thought they had got Yugoslavia in the net, that is to say, after March 20, they began to move three out of the five Panzer Divisions from Romania to Southern Poland. The moment they heard of the Serbian revolution this movement was countermanded. Your Excellency will readily appreciate the significance of these facts.[189]

Cripps duly received the message. And did nothing with it. Cripps was a devout socialist, and may have been more concerned about Stalin's reaction to the message than the import of the message itself. In an address to Londoners before the war, Churchill had said of Cripps, "Then there is Sir Stafford Cripps, who is in a class by himself. He wishes the British people to be conquered by the Nazis in order to urge them into becoming Bolsheviks. It seems a long way round. And not much enlightenment when they get to the end of their journey." Churchill had sent the socialist Cripps to Moscow as a signal to Stalin that Churchill was willing to let bygones be bygones. The signal was either not received or ignored.[190]

Presuming his first message had been delivered or, given the usual time lost by encoding and decoding, was soon to be delivered, Churchill cabled Cripps again the next day. He advised Cripps on how to develop the argument in person and instructed him to stress to the Soviets that the German move back toward the Balkans could buy time for the Russians to "strengthen their own position." Again Cripps did nothing. He then made one of the most inexplicable and stupid decisions made by any diplomat during the war: he sat on the message for almost two weeks. When Churchill learned of Cripps's lapse, he made plain to Eden his incredulity: "I set special importance on the delivery of this message from me to Stalin. I cannot understand why it should be resisted. The Ambassador is not alive to the military significance of the facts. Pray oblige me." Admonished by Eden, Cripps, the recalcitrant obligee, *again* failed to deliver the message. In coming weeks, Eden warned the Soviet ambassador to the Court of St. James's,

Ivan Maisky, of the probable German attack. Despite Cripps's behavior, Stalin was warned by Maisky. By then Churchill's attention had turned back to the Balkans.[191]

When Churchill first tried to warn Stalin, the impending battle in Greece, not the possible turn of events in Russia, was the most immediate question at hand. Had the Yugoslavs not revolted, Churchill's 60,000 troops in northern Greece might have faced a far smaller German force. Then again, absent the Yugoslav coup, large German troop movement through a compliant Yugoslavia would likely have flanked the British in any event. A plethora of Ultra decrypts pointed to only one certainty during the first days of April—that British and Anzac troops arriving in Greece would soon face attack by an overwhelmingly superior force.[192]

There, Jumbo Wilson's eastern flank, the Aliakmo Line, was anchored near Salonika, on the Aegean, and stretched for almost fifty miles northwest toward Monastir. Northeast of the British line, six Greek divisions of the Greek Second Army formed the Metaxas Line, which also ran west from the Aegean, and faced north toward Bulgaria's Struma Valley, the ancient invasion route into Thrace. To the west, the Greek First Army faced the Italians on the Albanian front. The entire front snaked for more than six hundred miles from the Aegean Sea to the Ionian Sea, through high mountain passes and difficult, trackless countryside. It was the exact sort of front Frederick the Great had in mind when he pronounced, "To defend everything is to defend nothing." Worse, the British lines were not entirely dressed; British battalions still drifted into position. Eden captured the problem in an early March cable to the War Cabinet: "Militarily problem is one of time and space." By early April the troops needed more time to make ready their defense.[193]

They would not get it.

As London and the world waited for news of a German thrust into Greece, Yugoslavia, or even Turkey, Rommel's diminutive forces—short on food, gasoline, and bullets—rolled eastward against Wavell in Cyrenaica. The leagues of Libyan desert so gloriously snatched from Mussolini by O'Connor were again a battleground. But this time the Germans had taken the field. "It seems most desirable," Churchill telegraphed to Wavell on April 2, "to stop the German advance against Cyrenaica." Any "rebuff" to the Germans, he added, would have "far-reaching prestige effects." A rebuff was not a victory, but after Norway and Dunkirk, "rebuff" had about it a certain ring. Ground could be given up for the purposes of "tactical manoeuvre," Churchill instructed Wavell, "but any serious withdrawal from Benghazi would appear most melancholy."[194]

On April 2, the day that Churchill sent his telegram, Rommel's tanks overran and busted up Neame's front line. Wavell ordered a brigade from the 7th Australian Division to deploy from Cairo to Libya in order to stanch the bleeding. It would have made no difference whether the outgunned Tommies and Aussies faced the Germans in Greece or in Libya; they would have fared the same in either theater. Churchill had forced Wavell to block two invasion forces, one intent on barging into Egypt, the other into Greece. With his armies intact and arrayed against one or the other of the German forces, Wavell might have stood a chance. But with his armies divided, Wavell stood little chance against either.

Even before he learned of the Australians' redeployment, Churchill saw the implications, military as well as political, of Rommel's advance. He cabled Eden, in Athens: "Far more important than the loss of ground [in North Africa] is the idea that we cannot face the Germans and that their appearance is enough to drive us back many scores of miles. This may react most evilly throughout Balkans.... Sooner or later we shall have to fight the Huns."[195]

They *were* fighting the Huns, in the Libyan desert, and not faring well. Churchill, having correctly guessed that Rommel had overextended himself, tried to encourage Wavell: "I cannot feel that there is at this moment a persistent weight behind the German attack....If this blob, which has come forward against you, could be cut off you might have a prolonged easement." Of course, were Rommel's forces to "succeed in wandering onwards they will gradually destroy the effects of your victories."[196]

Rommel wandered powerfully onward. The seasoned Australian 6th Division had been recalled to Cairo to prepare for deployment to Greece. Its replacement in the desert—the Australian 9th Division—lacked the experience to stop Rommel. On April 3 news reached official London that Wavell had ordered Benghazi evacuated. It was as if a diabolical projectionist were running backward the reel of O'Connor's victories: Mersa Brega, Beda Fomm, now Benghazi, all taken by the British early in the year, all now lost to Rommel in just days. Wavell told Churchill that in view of the situation, withdrawal toward Derna would be necessary.

The withdrawal turned into a rout.

Short on tanks and gasoline, Rommel commanded his supply trucks to stay close behind the few remaining panzers and to raise as much dust as possible, to simulate a much larger force. The trick worked. Tommies and the newly arrived Aussies of the 9th Division, thinking at least two divisions of German and Italian tanks—six hundred in all—were heading their way, fled eastward, pell-mell toward Derna, 150 miles up the coast.

The Australians, never at a loss for gallows humor, dubbed the race to safety the "Benghazi Handicap." To his wife Rommel wrote that "the British are falling over themselves to get away."[197]

British command had broken down; troops lacked orders, whether to stand and fight or retreat. They ran, covered in yellow dust, their shirts soaked with sweat and stiff as sandpaper. Their faces took on a sickly yellow cast. By the platoon, by the battalion, by the regiment, they fled. Neame tried to restore order. He could not. Wavell flew out from Cairo and saw that Neame had lost control. O'Connor was summoned, too late to turn things around. Derna fell on the night of the sixth. The main British units beat such a hasty exit from the city that the Northumberland Fusiliers realized what was happening only when they saw the 9th Australian division roaring past them out of town. O'Connor and Neame were among the last to flee, in darkness, by car to Timimi, about one hundred miles to the east. Alas, the hero of Operation Compass got turned around somewhere in the desert and ended up rambling down a lost highway, directly toward Derna and the Germans. Within a few minutes, O'Connor and Neame found their car surrounded by men shouting in a foreign tongue. Their driver presumed it was Cypriot, for many of the British truck drivers were Cypriot. When German machine pistols were thrust into his face, O'Connor understood that the Cypriot thesis was terribly wrong. He and Neame spent the next three years as prisoners of war in Italy.[198]

London's citizens were not privy to the debacle in the desert. Nor did they know of the troop buildup in Greece. Of Wavell's prospects, Colville wrote on April 3: "The PM is greatly worried." Churchill's worry stemmed not only from Wavell's ongoing struggle against Rommel in Africa, but because he knew that the British people had been fed only rumors about the Greek deployment. "I must return to the need of telling public," Churchill cabled to Wavell, "that we have sent strong forces to Greece." The American press was running with the story, he explained, while the British press had so far honored HMG's plea for restraint. Even Colonel Donovan had spilled the beans, praising the valor of Britain for sending troops from Egypt to Greece. Such sentiments could only cause Britons to ask, *What* troops have been sent from *where,* and *to where?* It was time for Churchill to come clean with his yeomanry.[199]

He had given to Wavell, then taken, and now would give again. On April 4, Churchill cabled Wavell: "I warned the country a week ago that they must not expect continuance of unbroken successes and take the rough with the smooth." Therefore, he added, "be quite sure that we shall back you up in adversity even better than in good fortune." He was true to his word, taking the great risk of running a convoy (code-named Tiger by Churchill) of six ships carrying almost three hundred new tanks straight through the Mediterranean from Gibraltar to Alexandria, under the guns of the Luftwaffe. He called them his "tigercubs." When one of the ships, approaching Malta, hit a mine and went down, Churchill lamented to Colville, "My tiger has lost a claw." Though he harbored great hopes for his remaining cubs, they would not arrive in Alexandria until early May, at which time it was learned that because their gearboxes tended to jam and they lacked the proper filters to keep the desert sand from mucking up the works, the tanks could not be readied for action until late May at the earliest. Until then, Wavell would have to make do with what he had, which, with Rommel stripping away more each hour, was not enough.[200]

With Derna lost, Churchill concluded that Tobruk, one hundred miles to the east, held the key. From that city the British could swing out to meet Rommel's advanced guard and then swing back north and west to pin the overextended Germans between the escarpment and the sea. "Bravo Tobruk!" Churchill cabled Wavell. "We feel it vital that Tobruk be regarded as sally-port, and not, please, as an 'excrescence.'" The plan looked good on paper. Churchill encouraged Wavell: "Tobruk is your best offensive hook.... All our best information shows they are frightfully short of everything. It would be a fine thing to cop the lot."[201]

Rommel, intending to cop Tobruk at his leisure, drove right past the city. By April 10, he had rolled up almost three hundred miles of British turf as if it were a throw rug.

Ten days earlier, on March 31, Churchill had told Colville that he was quite sure Germany would attack Yugoslavia before either Greece or Turkey. He was partially correct. On April 6 Hitler attacked *both* Yugoslavia and Greece.[202]

Belgrade was hit first, as punishment for its insolence. German bombers flying in relays from Romanian airfields cruised overhead all day on the sixth, unopposed but for ineffectual AA. They came on for the next two days, hundreds of bombers unleashing thousands of pounds of bombs, enough to bury more than 17,000 of the city's residents under the rubble. CBS newsman Cecil Brown reported from the scene: "Belgrade one-quarter destroyed and thousands dead in a few hours... refugees streaming from Belgrade far across the fields for as far as the eye can see." The terrorized animals at the Belgrade zoo escaped. A great bear, dazed and uncomprehending, shuffled past burning buildings, through the smoke, and down to the banks of the Danube. With Stalin in mind, Churchill later wrote, "The bear... was not the only bear who did not understand."[203]

On its march from the Hungarian border to Belgrade, the Wehrmacht lost just 151 men killed to the Yugoslav's untold thousands killed, wounded, missing, or captured. CBS's Brown, arrested briefly by the Germans as a spy, saw firsthand "young murderers bent on wiping out the Serbian people." The Nazis shot down Serbs "the way you would not shoot a dog, not even a mad dog." The Yugoslavs fought on; they sent ammunition to the front on carts drawn by steers "moving at four miles an hour against twenty-two-ton Nazi tanks speeding into battle at forty miles an hour." Brown watched in horror and in awe as the Serbians committed national "suicide by defying Hitler and the New Order." It was not a battle, but a massacre.[204]

Once the Germans crushed Yugoslavia and poured through the Vardar Valley, the British, Anzac, and Greek forces arrayed to the south were doomed. Had the Germans attacked only by way of Bulgaria, the Greek and British lines would have been perfectly arrayed. But as the German attack came from both Bulgaria and Yugoslavia, the Allies found themselves cut off, east from west. For eighteen days, outflanked and outnumbered by more than four to one, the British fought a valiant and well-executed rearguard action, covering almost 250 miles from Salonika to Olympus, then to Larissa, to Thermopylae, and on to Thebes and Athens. All the while, German infantry, German tanks, and German planes ripped at their flanks.[205]

The rearguard action at Thermopylae, fought mostly by the Anzacs, was as heroic and futile a feat as the battle fought there in 480 BCE, when King Leonidas and his bodyguard of three hundred Spartans checked ten thousand Persians. The terrain had changed over the centuries, to the detriment of the British defenders. The pass in ancient times was only about a dozen yards wide, a strip of high ground between the mountains and the sea. The Spercheios River delta had since widened the pass by more than a mile in places. The Germans, as had the Persians, approached from the north. The British and Anzacs, as had the Spartans, dug in at the pass and on the slope of the hillside, which by virtue of its soil content and the oblique angle of the sun's first light, glows bloodred at sunrise. The modern coast road to Athens approaches the pass but turns inland and cuts through a small valley before climbing above and skirting the ancient pass. The Germans came on, the rumble of the three armored divisions audible for miles, the seismic pounding of their approach enough to disturb the water in a canteen, or a man's guts. To bring fire down on the modern road necessitated placing artillery and machine guns all the way up the slope above the ancient pass. This the Anzacs did and, once dug in, for a short while checked the Germans. But the British left flank hung in the air. Wavell asked the Greeks if they could cover the naked flank.[206]

They could not. So rapid was the German advance that by the time Churchill fumed to Wavell that Jumbo Wilson was tardy in getting news out of Greece, the battle was over. On April 20, Churchill cabled Eden in Cairo to ask if Thermopylae might be held for three weeks in order to delay the Germans and allow the "Libyan situation to be stabilized." Such a delay, Churchill wrote, would allow reinforcements to be sent from Egypt to Greece. He asked Ismay for a map of the Thermopylae Line.[207]

He needn't have bothered. Thermopylae fell, not in three weeks, but in three days.

George II, king of the Hellenes, offered that it was now Wavell's "duty to take immediate steps for the re-embarkation of such portion of his army as he could." Wavell and Wilson agreed. So, too, on April 21 did Churchill and the War Cabinet. Churchill wanted it "made clear to the Commanders-in-Chief that the main thing was to get the men away, and we should not worry about saving vehicles." The Anzacs, Churchill told the War Cabinet, "had fought with distinction a rear-guard battle against heavy odds in the most depressing form of action for soldiers." They have "added one more glorious page" to their history. They may have fought a glorious rearguard action, but it was for naught. The Spartans had at least delayed the Persians long enough for the Athenian fleet to ready a trap at Salamis, where it defeated the invaders, who fled for home. This time, the defenders fled. As the Tommies boarded their transports, Greek civilians showered them with flowers, as they had when the Tommies arrived. Then the ships set sail with their cargoes of defeated warriors.[208]

Hitler celebrated his fifty-second birthday on April 20, ensconced in his special train *Amerika,* which had pulled onto a siding just outside a tunnel near Mönichkerchin in the Austrian Alps, lest any unfriendly airplanes appear. None did. The skies remained clear and the Führer enjoyed his latest success amid the splendor of an alpine spring and the accolades of a swarm of OKW big shots, parked in their train at the other end of the tunnel. Hitler, in a gesture both curious and rare for him, ordered that when the Greek army surrendered—as it must, as all his foes must—all prisoners were to be freed. This was his way of paying tribute to the inheritors of the hoplite tradition, brave warriors who happened to meet in battle modern Teutonic warriors more brave and more numerous. Hitler had not sought the battle. He believed Greece was a conflict forced upon him by the mad dog Churchill who had had the bullheaded temerity to send his meager armies to interfere with the Führer's plans for the Balkans.[209]

With the British and Greek forces flushed from the eastern flank, General Thrasyvoulos Tsakalotos, commander of the Greek First Army, saw the hopelessness of his position in the western part of the country. Tsakalotos, in parley with the commander of the SS division at his front, requested that he be allowed to surrender to the Germans, and only the Germans, for even though Tsakalotos knew his war was over, he was determined not to surrender to Mussolini's forces who, he felt, had earned nothing. Mussolini, seeing that he was about to be denied a role in the armistice, dispatched an envoy to Berlin, where Hitler once again sated the needs of his inept ally. While Il Duce waited for the Führer's reply, he kept up the attack against Tsakalotos, who inflicted six thousand *more* casualties on the Italians, this while the war in Greece (or at least the German-Greek-British part of it) had concluded days before. But in the end, Il Duce slipped in on German coattails, and the British skulked out, fleeing by ship to Crete, their baggage once again left behind.[210]

Greece surrendered on April 27. The swastika flag flew that night above the Acropolis. In just three weeks Hitler had destroyed the Yugoslavs, the Greeks, and the British Expeditionary Force. Churchill had divided and re-allocated to Greece his Middle East resources, knowing full well—as he had told Hopkins in January—that Greece was likely lost. Historians have since sniped at him for the military folly of his Greek foray. Yet that is a narrow assessment. It was actually a political decision backed up (insufficiently) by military means. Britain had honored its commitments to Greece, as it had not to Czechoslovakia. In doing so Churchill displayed his bullheaded propensity for doing the right thing with the best of intentions but often in the most wrong of places and at the most wrong of times. He possessed—the Achilles in him—a keen intelligence that was sometimes overridden by improbable notions born of passion disguised as contemplation. Greece was a fitting place for Churchill to have failed so tragically.[211]

Rommel, by roaring right past Tobruk and the Australians holed up within, had cut off Tobruk without a fight, as if it were a lone island fortress upon the sea that, when bypassed, became by virtue of its isolation irrelevant. Thus ended Churchill's plan to hook out of Tobruk in order to bring Rommel to bay. In Tobruk the men of two Australian divisions, the 9th and the 7th, surrounded but for sporadic relief delivered by sea, peered from the trenches from which they had so boisterously driven the Italians just three months earlier. And there—joined by a ragtag mix of Indians, both Muslims and Hindus, free Poles, and British regulars, more than 22,000 in all—they would remain, under siege for almost eight months. Lord Haw-Haw anointed the besieged men "The Rats of Tobruk." Trenches and barbed wire and minefields ran for thirty miles around the city. As in the Great War, any man who showed himself by day would not likely live to nightfall. Remembrances of Gallipoli began to resurface half a world away, in Canberra. Australia had sent its three best divisions for deployment to the Middle East, where it now appeared they would be sacrificed to Churchill's desert strategy. Churchill had cited in his February address the "love for us which has flowed from the Dominions." With their best troops holed up in the desert, and the threat of Japanese hostilities on the horizon, Australians had about run out of love for King and Empire and Churchill. Australia wanted its men home.[212]

One piece of good news emerged from the desert in late April. Rommel appeared to have finally lunged a dune too far. Having pushed almost three hundred miles east from Benghazi, Rommel and his Italian helpmates, as Churchill had predicted, found themselves too far removed from their supply depots. Rommel needed Tobruk and its port in order to resupply and keep up the push to Egypt. He had scarcely any reserves left, except of sheer will and determination. Wavell was coming up short in both will and determination; he was tired, and Churchill knew it. Wavell's forces—especially his tanks—were in worse shape than Rommel's. By sending an army to Greece, the British had, in effect, reinforced Rommel, and had paid the price. Churchill had accepted the risks in Greece and North Africa not only because of the pledges made to Greece and because Alexandria, Cairo, and the Suez were Rommel's ultimate objectives, but because British military prowess was under worldwide scrutiny. Churchill had American public opinion in mind when he told Eden that the fight in the desert must go on, if for no other reason than to debunk the notion "that we cannot face the Germans and that their appearance is enough to drive us back many scores of miles." Actually, their appearance in the desert had been enough to drive the British back many *hundreds* of miles. The battle for Cyrenaica was over, again. And Greece was lost.[213]

In America that week, Charles Lindbergh told audiences in St. Louis, New York, and Chicago that American weapons were killing innocent Europeans, that no amount of arms would gain England parity with Germany, that the British had lost not only Greece but any claim of righteousness, and their prestige, and the war.[214]

In late April, Stafford Cripps finally passed along Churchill's warning of the German troop movements to the Soviet foreign minister Molotov, who passed it along to Stalin. Stalin's response was identical to his response to Churchill's friendly overtures of a year earlier: he never replied. Churchill was furious, more with Cripps than with Stalin. Yet Churchill kept Cripps on as ambassador, for during Churchill's Wilderness Years, Cripps had supported Churchill on the Hitler menace and the need to re-arm.

By late April, Yugoslavia and Greece had been crushed, and Hitler's roads east to the Urals stretched away open and dry through measureless fields of spring wheat greening under cobalt skies. The conquest of the Balkans had forced a postponement of Operation Barbarossa from mid-May to mid-June, a justifiable delay in the Führer's estimation given that the defiance of the Yugoslavs could not go unpunished. The punishment took some time to administer, yes, but Hitler presumed he had all the time he needed to deal with Russia. Yet, wrote William L. Shirer, the Führer's decision to "vent his personal spite against a small country that had dared to defy him was probably the single most catastrophic decision of Hitler's career." This was so because, unless Hitler crushed the Russians by late October, Russia's most fearsome ally would appear on the battlefield: winter.[215]

Yet Hitler had not made his decision in a vacuum; he had been provoked by the British-sponsored coup in Belgrade and by the British troops assembling in Greece. It is worth noting that Royal Navy sea power underlay Britain's ability to put an army into Greece, albeit an ally. Sea power had brought the men across the Mediterranean, and sea power took them back again. When Churchill had declared almost a year earlier that the Royal Navy could not win the war but could still lose it, he was speaking in terms of the navy's role in defeating the U-boats. He also had reflected upon the fact that if more than a quarter million men could be gotten off the beaches of Dunkirk by ships, a quarter million men could be put *on* other beaches by ships. Greece had been a crushing defeat for Churchill, but the Royal Navy had demonstrated the vital role of sea power in putting thousands of men on beaches, friendly or unfriendly. If Churchill could put an army into Greece, he could someday put a larger army into France, Italy, or French North Africa.

But in late April 1941, Churchill's foray into Greece appeared the single most catastrophic decision of his career, a greater disaster than even his 1915 Dardanelles gambit. His Balkan strategy had ended in a complete and devastating rout. The British did not need nearly as many transports to ferry their troops from Greece as had carried them there. Jumbo Wilson made his way back to Egypt; General Sir Bernard Freyberg, commander of the New Zealanders in Greece, was ordered to prepare a defense on Crete. More than 40,000 British, New Zealand, and Australian troops were taken off the beaches between April 24 and 30, but at the cost of several hospital ships lost. Stukas sank the transport *Slamat,* putting seven hundred survivors into the sea. They were picked up by two destroyers, which in turn were sunk by German dive-bombers, killing almost all the survivors.

Evacuees included Palestinian Jews, Yugoslavs, Greeks, and Cypriots. With more than two dozen ships lost, Admiral Cunningham's fleet was ill prepared to defend Hitler's next target, Crete. Greece joined Norway and Dunkirk on the list of inglorious British evacuations, the most inglorious to date, in fact, for where 90 percent of the men were gotten off the French and Norwegian beaches, almost 30 percent remained behind in Greece, killed or captured.[216]

The British press, informed by the Ministry of Information of the impending news, reacted with respectful reticence. Some in the American press tried to put things in a cheery light. According to *Time,* "although the campaign had been lost, there were indications that after details of the Battle of Greece became known, the Greek campaign might possibly go down in history as one of the most brilliant tactical operations of British Empire arms." *Time* also offered, "Although Hitler's men have not yet been stopped, this battle showed that if ever Britons confront Germans on anything like equal terms, Britain stands a good chance of winning." Not only was the British army—the entire British, colonial, and Dominion armies throughout the Empire—outnumbered by more than two to one by the Führer's armies, Hitler had yet to engage any enemy on anything like equal terms.[217]

Churchill had some explaining to do. The "bulwark" of Yugoslavia-Greece-Turkey had failed to materialize, and neutral Turkey now found itself facing two potential enemies—Germany and Russia—without the means to defend itself against either. Churchill, in his memoirs, insists that had Wavell only protested the depletions of his North African forces for deployment to Greece, the War Cabinet would have heeded his advice. He alluded to Wavell's veto power when he explained the Greek debacle to the Commons. Indeed, Wavell had cabled Churchill in mid-March that it had been "very fortunate" that Eden and Dill were in Cairo when "difficult and dangerous decisions had to be taken." Wavell added: "I am sure the decisions were the right ones, though they will bring us new hazards and anxieties." Yet Churchill's telegrams to Wavell leave no doubt that he put his Middle East commander in a box. Wavell could either accede to Churchill's wishes or protest them and face the consequences, which usually took the form of a verbal bludgeoning. A favorite Churchill tactic when faced with a field officer who questioned his military judgment was to stress political goals over strictly military, thus placing the recalcitrant commander—who was not after all a political animal—in a hopeless position. Wavell was about as strong a soldier as there was, but Churchill was the stronger politician.[218]

In the end, and too late, Wavell's predictions of new hazards proved spot on. With Greece overrun, the door was now open for Stalin to swing toward the Dardanelles, or for Hitler to do likewise, or for both to move in concert. Churchill had long been "working on the Turks" to bring them in on Britain's side, but he admitted in a cable to Cripps that the Turks "are unresponsive through fear." Indeed, the Turks were justifiably fearful that either Hitler or Stalin, or both, would soon put an end to their sovereignty. Sound military logic demanded it. After crushing Turkey, Hitler could elect to strike into Iraq, or swing through Syria to the Suez Canal, or both. Were he to sate a modicum of Stalin's appetite for greater influence in Bulgaria and Romania (traditional Russian spheres of influence), Hitler would find himself free to pursue his Mediterranean strategy with an ally on his eastern flank. It was the strategy that his naval planners had stressed was necessary in order to defeat Britain. He was poised to eviscerate the greatest empire in history, to succeed where Napoleon had failed. He prepared to take the next step, to the island he deemed vital to his plan: Crete. But the plan that Crete was vital to was Barbarossa. Crete was home to three RAF airfields, from which long-range British bombers could reach the Ploesti oil fields, in Romania. Hitler needed that oil to fuel his march to Moscow. He was going to Crete to fight the British, but first and foremost, he was going in order to secure his flank.[219]

In early April, Mollie Panter-Downes wrote in *The New Yorker:* "For the past fortnight Londoners had been listening to the unnatural silence at nights and wondering what was brewing." By mid-month they knew. The Blitz, in its third incarnation, had returned. The Luftwaffe again had England's biggest cities dead in its sights. On April 16 more than five hundred German bombers pounded London until dawn. During the raid, Colville dashed to the American embassy in Churchill's armored car to ask Winant's advice on a telegram. He found the ambassador on duty, his wife by his side. The bombs, Colville wrote, "came down like hailstones." By the next morning the city looked as devastated as had been predicted in the late thirties, when the appeasers claimed that the bombers would always get through. The Admiralty wore a new gash. St. James's Palace, where Churchill's parents had moved in 1880, was burning. Austin Thompson, the vicar of St. Peter's, Eaton Square, stepped out onto the steps of his church to call people in to shelter; a bomb erased both the vicar and his church from the cityscape. Chelsea Old Church was demolished, Jermyn Street wrecked, Mayfair badly damaged. Pall Mall, Piccadilly, and lower Regent Street were heavily damaged. Mounds of glass shards lined the edges of roads. Of the more than five hundred German bombers that had made the run, only a dozen had been shot down.[220]

Daylight and fair weather brought out the sightseers, including Pamela Churchill in the company of Averell Harriman, the two of them observed by Colville poking about the devastation in the Horse Guards Parade (in fact, they had just begun their love affair). Churchill made his way through the smoldering rubble in time to chair the 11:30 War Cabinet meeting, where he stunned Cadogan by noting that the damage to the Admiralty improved his view of Nelson's Column—which had emerged undamaged—from his place at the table. Much of the capital did not share Nelson's good fortune. By afternoon a steady, cold rain swept through the city, lending an air of desolation to the scene.[221]

The map of Europe in late April looked as if the sinister octopus of newsreel fame had spewed its black ink into almost every corner of the Continent. Switzerland, Portugal, and Sweden survived only at Hitler's pleasure; each offered him a secure diplomatic conduit to the world beyond. Switzerland also afforded safe haven for his stolen gold, Sweden a steady flow of iron ore. Spain sat in his camp philosophically, but fearing an end to his U.S. food shipments—and sure starvation for his people—the wily Franco was still not about to grant the Wehrmacht free passage to Gibraltar, although Hitler could certainly force his way through Spain were he so inclined. But for these few exceptions to Hitler's rule, the entire map of Europe had gone black. All, that is, but the obstinate Island.

On April 27, Churchill sent Eden to take responsibility in the Commons for the Greek debacle. By virtue of the power traditionally vested in him, a British foreign secretary would be expected to face the Commons after such a disastrous overseas gamble, yet Churchill made sure that the Foreign Office under Eden no longer operated with the smug independence it had enjoyed for more than a century, ever since "Pam" Palmerston made the office a virtual co-equal of the Office of Prime Minister. Churchill "had no love of the foreign office" Colville wrote, and "suspected them of pursuing their own policy" and of being "defeatist and prone toward socialism." He "mistrusted their judgment." Eden labored at Churchill's pleasure, and served with absolute loyalty. Despite that loyalty, Churchill allowed Eden to assume the role of archery target for the MPs, as if Eden actually had initiated the unfortunate course of events in the Balkans. Yet, at the end of the day, by a vote of 477–3, the Commons voiced its support for the government.[222]

Several months later, to Colville's astonishment, Churchill proclaimed that he "had instinctively had doubts" about the Greek venture from the beginning. The Greeks, Churchill told Colville, should have been advised to make the best terms they could with Hitler. He claimed blame for the fiasco lay with the War Cabinet and especially with Dill, whom, Colville noted, Churchill "has now got his knife right into." Colville, incredulous at Churchill's claims, wrote of the incident as if he doubted his own powers of recollection, such were Churchill's powers of persuasion. But on April 27, Churchill would have been hard-pressed to blame the government for the Greek tragedy, for everybody knew quite well that the prime minister *was* the government. That evening, in his first radio address since his "Give us the tools" speech of February 9, he took to the airwaves to explain as best he could this latest in the series of damnable events.[223]

The list of troubles was long and growing longer. As in every speech since the previous May, he offered reassurances to a brave people who needed but did not demand reassurance: "I thought it would be a good thing to go and see for myself...some of our great cities and seaports and which have been most heavily bombed...and to some of the places where the poorest people have had it worst." What he saw "reassured and refreshed." It was like "going out of a hothouse onto the bridge of a fighting ship...a tonic which I should recommend any who are suffering fretfulness to take in strong doses when they have need of it." The morale among the poor and the bombed, he proclaimed, was "splendid." It all added up to the "vindication of the civilized and decent way of living" and "proof of the virtues of free institutions." The cause would be "fought out...to the end. This is the grand heroic period of our history, and the light of glory shines on all." He presumed all Englishmen felt the same.

Many did. When Wendell Willkie, conducting an unscientific survey during his visit, asked a laborer if he supported the war and wanted to go through with it, the man replied, "Hitler ain't dead yet, is he?" and turned back to work. The citizens of Hull were proud of the beatings they took, and informed *The New Yorker* columnist A. J. Liebling that Coventry had nothing on them. Hull, regularly hit hard by virtue of its location on the North Sea, and being the British port nearest to Germany, was but one of Britain's major ports and cities that were taking such beatings. During the Blitz not one mayor of any British city ever asked Whitehall for special protection, not that any could have been arranged. Londoners, of course, never hesitated to tell anyone within earshot that they could take it. Yet Churchill's attachment of glory to mass slaughter rang hyperbolic to many in America, where a clear majority of voters still answered no to the question of going to war for Britain. And no lights of glory shone on the Continent. Enslaved Europeans—who now truly lived dangerously—found scant hope in his words. Yet Poles and Dutchmen, Frenchmen and Norwegians, Czechs, Belgians, Slovenes, Croats, Serbs, and now, too, the Greeks all knew that Churchill was the only European leader who remained to carry on the fight against Hitler. They all knew, as well, that he could not fight alone for much longer.[224]

Churchill had taken to the airwaves not only to thank Britons but to explain the failures in the Balkans. Lowering his voice, he moved on to Greece. He told Britons: "Great disasters have occurred in the Balkans. Yugoslavia has been beaten down.... The Greeks have been overwhelmed. The victorious Albanian army has been cut off and forced to surrender." And then to Africa, where the news was as dreadful: "Our forces in Libya have sustained a vexatious and damaging defeat. The Germans advanced sooner and in greater strength than we or our generals expected." Strictly speaking, this was true. Although Churchill had not *expected* Rommel to attack so soon, in early March Ultra had revealed that Rommel would be ready weeks earlier than the British had predicted. Wavell's hesitancy all along had little to do with the speed or strength of the Germans, either in Greece or North Africa. He assumed German advances on any front would be fast and strong; that was the German way. His overriding concern stemmed from dividing *his* forces. Yet Churchill, in his broadcast, without naming Wavell, rebuked the commander for the decision to send his tanks to Cairo for repair when future events—indeterminate when the decision was made—proved they were best left in Libya. Churchill: "The single armoured brigade which had been judged sufficient to hold the frontier till about the middle of May was worsted and its vehicles largely destroyed by a somewhat stronger German armoured force." Without quite declaring so, Churchill had just told his people that the British had been trounced yet again.[225]

Then, growling, he deflected the audience's attention from HMG's defeats onto Mussolini:

> I daresay you may have read in the newspapers that by a special proclamation, the Italian Dictator has congratulated the Italian army in Albania on the glorious laurels they have gained by their victory over the Greeks. Here surely is the world's record in the domain of the ridiculous and the contemptible. This whipped jackal, Mussolini, who to save his own skin has made all Italy a vassal state of Hitler's Empire, comes frisking up to the side of the German tiger with yelpings not only of appetite—that can be understood—but even of triumph.[226]

And then he moved on to the guttersnipe. As for Hitler, Churchill repeated his January message to Ismay: "Hitler cannot find safety from avenging justice in the East, in the Middle East, or in the Far East. In order to win this war he must either conquer this Island by invasion, or he must cut the ocean life-line which joins us to the United States." Churchill believed the arithmetic of the situation precluded either possibility: "There are less than seventy million malignant Huns—some of whom are curable and others killable.... The peoples of the British Empire and the United States number more than 200 million in their homelands and the British Dominions alone." This English-speaking alliance possesses "more wealth, more technical resources, and they make more steel than the rest of the world put together."[227]

Churchill failed to cite a third possible path to victory for Hitler besides invasion and blockade. It was the strategy Admiral Raeder and Franz Halder (Chief of the German Army General Staff) had advocated for ten months, albeit meekly, given Hitler's determination to burn Moscow. Halder proposed to dismember the British Empire before the Americans came in, beginning in the Mediterranean, east from Gibraltar to Egypt. Then he advised a strike across Iraq and Persia while enticing the Japanese into smashing Hong Kong and Singapore. The objective was to drive Britain out of Asia. The United States would then reassess the value of supplying Britain with war matériel for an increasingly futile battle. England finding itself cut off from its Dominions, from its Iraqi and Persian oil, and denied use of the Suez Canal, would be ripe for the kill. This was Churchill's fear exactly.[228]

He chose invective over full disclosure. No one objected to his classification of Mussolini as a jackal, but his reference to malignant Huns, *killable* at that, drew protests from Corder Catchpool, a Great War conscientious objector and pacifist who, in an open letter to Churchill, lamented the prime minister's message as "not in accordance with truth, and that the spirit it breathes is a pagan spirit, the opposite of what Jesus taught as to the Christian attitude toward sinful mankind." Catchpool predicted that "if this spirit predominates" in the British people and their leaders, "then the present generation will pass away without any hope of realizing that new and better world for which men are agonizing now." Churchill made no reply to Catchpool.[229]

Churchill ended his address with the final two stanzas of a poem by the Victorian poet Arthur Hugh Clough, words "appropriate to our fortunes to-night, and I believe they will be so judged wherever the English language is spoken or the flag of freedom flies:

For while the tired waves, vainly breaking,
Seem here no painful inch to gain,
Far back, through creeks and inlets making,
Comes silent, flooding in, the main,
And not by eastern windows only,
When daylight comes, comes in the light,
In front the sun climbs slow, how slowly!
But westward, look, the land is bright.[230]

Westward was America, where vast quantities of Lend-Lease wheat, dried milk, powdered eggs, flour, canned pork, and canned fish were being assembled for shipment to Britain. But the first ship would not arrive for a month. Though Churchill proclaimed in public that setbacks stiffened resolve and would somehow in time transform into stepping-stones to victory, when he received bad news in private, he resorted to a behavior associated with children, artists, and geniuses: he sulked. He termed each new defeat the gloomiest, the most troublesome, the most fearful, the blackest. Yet he was never long gloomy, and never afraid. At dinner, among his cronies and family, he could, with a pout, a quiver of the lip, a growl and a scowl, shut down all conversation. Yet Robert Menzies, the Australian prime minister, noted in his diary Churchill's inevitable progress during conversations from doom to effervescence: "The PM in conversation will steep himself (and you) in gloom on some grim aspect of the war . . . only to proceed to fight himself out while he is pacing the floor with the light of battle in his eyes. In every conversation he reaches a point where he positively enjoys the war: 'Bliss in that age it was to be alive. . . . Why do we regard history as of the past and forget we are making it?' " Churchill could be moody, petulant, rude, and mercurial, but he never subscribed to the patently obvious logic that given enough setbacks, defeat must necessarily follow. Menzies jotted in his diary, "There is no defeat in his heart."[231]

To Wavell, after Rommel pummeled the British in Libya, Churchill cabled, "We seem to have had rather bad luck." Like a cowboy who gambled away his wages, he added: "I expect we should get this back later." He had a way of seeing gold where others saw dirt. Had Britain not sent troops to Greece, Churchill told his cabinet, "Yugoslavia would not now be an open enemy of Germany." It is true that Yugoslav guerrillas tied up several German divisions for the remainder of the war, but the sacrifice in Greece of more than 16,000 of Britain's finest troops killed and captured in order to bring about that result cannot be construed as a design of strategic magnificence. Luck had not abandoned Wavell; Churchill had.[232]

Since the previous June, when Churchill treated of such calamities in public, even as he promised more dangers to come, he did so with the remarkable result that with each phrase he applied another dash of mortar to the foundation of public trust, until his April 27 speech. For almost a year he had told his ministers that he did not want Britons' tension over possible invasion to abate. It had not. The public's tension was so acute, wrote Panter-Downes, the news from Greece and North Africa so bewildering and so bad, that the morning newspapers "became just about as comfortable as a bomb lying on the breakfast table."[233]

Churchill's speech of April 27 had pushed the dinner hour back to almost 10:00, following which, General Sir Alan Brooke recalled, Churchill "was in great form... and kept us up till 3:30 A.M." His great form may have been intended to mask his growing distress, for in the hours following his broadcast, one of his "golden eggs" had hatched. Enigma decrypts confirmed that the Germans were going to Crete, and that they would arrive via parachute and glider, with Crete's three airfields as the objectives. This intelligence was so vital that Churchill suggested to the Chiefs of Staff that the actual texts be secretly flown to General Freyberg, the commander on Crete. Churchill assumed that Freyberg, once assured that the intelligence was valid, would deploy his forces in order to ambush and crush the German airborne units, so that any German seaborne forces that might appear—if the Royal Navy did not first sink them—would find themselves cut off on the beaches. If used to effect, the decrypts could prove a godsend. If not, and were Crete to fall, Egypt had to be the next target, and as things now stood, Egypt's defense could not be guaranteed. The loss of Egypt and the Suez Canal, Churchill told the War Cabinet, "would be a disaster of first magnitude to Great Britain, second only to successful invasion and final conquest" of the Home Island.[234]

Should Rommel reach Cairo, an evacuation from North Africa would have to take place that would make Norway, Dunkirk, and Greece look like training exercises. A War Cabinet directive of April 28, drafted by Churchill, called for plans to be drawn up for an evacuation but stipulated "no whisper of such plans is to be allowed." But before any retreat took place, "no surrenders by officers or men will be considered tolerable unless at least 50 percent casualties are sustained by the Unit or force in question. According to Napoleon's maxim, 'when a man is caught alone and unarmed, a surrender may be made.' But generals and staff officers surprised by the enemy are to use their pistols in self defence. The honor of a wounded man is safe." Churchill was fond of the Napoleonic maxim regarding the surrender of an unarmed man. Had Wavell read Churchill's autobiography, *My Early Life,* he would have known that Churchill once applied the maxim to himself when he found himself unarmed and staring down the barrel of a Boer rifle. In the telling of that tale, Churchill took pains to inform the reader that his pistol remained some distance away; he was thus both surrounded *and* unarmed.[235]

The directive continued: "Anyone who can kill a Hun or even an Italian, has rendered a good service." Then, having already broached the subject of evacuation, Churchill decreed, "It will be utterly impossible to find the shipping for moving a tithe of the immense masses of men and stores which have been gathered in the Nile Valley." All the ships of the Royal Navy could not get them away, and this time there'd be no heroic fleet of yachts, trawlers, and dories sailing to the rescue. Conceivably, the British could flee south, through the Sudan to Kenya and safety. Those who survived would find themselves out of the war. Given the fact there was no real exit, the battle plan called for—as it did on the Home Island—a last stand.[236]

The language in the directive was the sort Dill had in mind when he told Reith that nine out of ten of Churchill's ideas as expressed in memos were less than brilliant. From Wavell's perspective, the directive was a waste of paper. He needed no man to tell him to do his duty. Churchill envied Wavell his opportunity for glory. To Colville, he admitted that he would "lay down his present office—yes and even renounce cigars and alcohol"—for the chance to lead the resistance in Egypt.[237]

Freyberg, meanwhile, on Crete, received and digested the Enigma intelligence, but the Secret Intelligence Service, in accordance with standard procedures, instructed him not to act on any *single* intelligence source without first verifying the information through a second source. Here was a piece of bureaucratic nonsense, for Ultra came straight from the horse's mouth, and was therefore unimpeachable, as well as unverifiable. Freyberg maintained in later years that the real intent of the SIS directive was to scuttle the defense of Crete's three airfields in order to protect the Ultra secret. Were the airfields to prove too well defended, the Germans might have deduced the leak in their security. Still, Freyberg decided he would man the airfields, and reinforce as best he could whichever airfield came under the heaviest attack. His problem was that the westernmost airfield, at Maleme, near the Royal Navy anchorage at Souda Bay, was seventy miles west of the airfield at Rethymnon, which in turn was eighty miles west of the third airfield, at Heraklion. Still, for the first time in the war, a British commander knew in advance exactly what was coming his way, and when. However, his forces had been so torn up in Greece that he lacked the men and internal lines of communications to mount an effective, coordinated defense of Crete, with or without help from Ultra.

Max Beaverbrook resigned from the Ministry of Aircraft Production on April 30. He had made more enemies in the RAF than he had in the Luftwaffe. Beaverbrook's liability now exceeded his utility, in part because he was willing and eager to gainsay Roosevelt, which could only hurt

Churchill. Max believed the Americans were out to grab everything they could from Britain, including its remaining gold and, when the war was won, its overseas markets—the Empire. He proposed to send a mission to the United States to set the American people straight regarding Roosevelt's canniness and the U.S. government's unwillingness to fulfill promises made to Britain, promises that Max's newspapers had endorsed. "The American government... is asking for the moon," he wrote to Churchill, "and appears unwilling to pay six pence."[238]

Max's mission to the United States could only hurt Churchill and the cause. Max had enough enemies in London; it would not do for him to make new ones in America. Churchill, seeking a way to keep Max in the game and the cabinet, resurrected him on May 1 as minister of state. It was an appointment that carried no specific duties, and invited trouble, for Max might poke his nose into the affairs of other departments, which would beget the enmity of the heads of those departments. Yet the lack of duties freed up time for Max to serve Churchill as friend, foil, and incubator of questionable ideas. Britons, not quite understanding the vagaries of the position, greeted the news with cheers, because they presumed Beaverbrook, given his talents for producing goods, would be overseeing war production. Many Britons considered Britain's war production—and Churchill's management of it—to be pathetic. War production wins wars; yet Britain's factory output was, according to Fleet Street, in a state of slumber. Factory managers and workers shut down their plants on Fridays and took their usual holidays in the country; very few third shifts hummed away in the nation's factories. The *Sunday Express:* "Do we even now understand that we are at a death grips in a fight for our lives?" The taking of holidays, chimed the newspaper, was "a scandalous situation." The *Daily Mail:* "When are we going to get down to the job of winning the war? When are we going to run machines, factories, and shipyards to full capacity?" The solution, according to the press, was a shake-up in government, a radical shake-up. Mollie Panter-Downes wrote that Beaverbrook's new job "carries with it a roving commission to kick inefficiency and departmental dawdling hard wherever it is encountered." Though Britons were suspicious of Beaverbrook's "Canadian accent," his "Fleet Street Methods," his Tory loyalties, and even his "street urchin" face, they knew he was just the man to straighten out the bureaucrats who had mucked up the production of everything from tanks to Blitz soup.[239]

The month of May proved anything but merry. Disaster struck from the air, in the Atlantic, and in the eastern Mediterranean. Shipping losses in the Atlantic were still horrific; a chart tracking them looked "like a fever patient's graph," Mollie Panter-Downes wrote. The Blitz of 1941 had entered its third and most terrible phase, with London taking beatings more vicious than those of 1940. Tarpaulins had disappeared, leaving Londoners to root about inside their roofless houses in dampness and filth. Clocks moved ahead another hour, to double daylight savings, affording Londoners another two hours of fitful sleep before the sounding of the morning all clear and two more hours of daylight in the evening to contemplate the destruction all around. The government could offer them scant aid. When a member of Parliament asked Churchill "not to close his mind" to the question of welfare relief for bombed-out citizens, Churchill replied, "I will keep my mind ajar." Still, Londoners did not complain. Rather, wrote Panter-Downes, they would gladly "lose their homes all over again for the pleasure of hearing that Berliners had just caught as big a packet of hell" from the RAF as they had caught from the Luftwaffe. Londoners could still no doubt take it, Panter-Downes wrote, but had begun to wonder if their government could dish it out. The twelve-month toll of dead Britons approached 47,000.[240]

Gibraltar was the last British toehold on the continent. Tobruk was under siege. Crete was clearly Hitler's next target, its defense problematic at best. The Vichy government was powerless to oppose German troop movements through France to Spain, if Berlin so demanded. Vichy was powerless, too, if Berlin insisted on putting troops into Syria as a prelude to going to Iraq, where an advance guard of Germans pilots and troops were preparing in consort with the Iraqi prime minister to grab the Mosul oil fields. Franklin Roosevelt, as usual, did not accede to Churchill's pleas for a more belligerent American role. May came in with the usual question hanging fire: Where next would Hitler or one of his surrogates strike, and when?[241]

The answer arrived at sunrise on May 1. The Iraqis had struck the night before. Alec Cadogan jotted in his diary: "Those dirty Iraqis are attacking us at Habbaniya. We have authorized bombing." Cadogan, the Foreign Office mandarin whose duties as permanent under secretary of state for foreign affairs included the articulation of the legal details and niceties of making war, ran into Churchill as the two were entering Parliament. "So you've got another war on your hands tonight," Churchill offered before disappearing down the hallway. Yet, Iraq was another sideshow. The Iraqis were led by Rashid Ali El Gailani, who after staging a coup in March appointed himself prime minister and drove the pro-British regent into exile. Now he had attacked, in violation of a treaty of long standing that granted the British free transit of Iraq and the airbase at Habbaniya, which Rashid's troops had surrounded. The Iraqi port of Basra was the door to Persia. From Basra came the oil that fueled the Royal Navy worldwide.

Churchill could not allow such Iraqi insolence to stand, not only because of the risk of losing the Mosul oil fields, but because he himself, as colonial secretary, had created Iraq one Sunday afternoon in Cairo twenty years earlier, a day, he fondly remembered, spent in the company of T. E. Lawrence and the Hashemite princes he had chosen to rule the newborn nations of Transjordan and Iraq.[242]

Yet to rid Iraq of Rashid and the German threat he needed to peel away more of Wavell's Middle East forces. Wavell, justifiably wary of further diminutions of his troops, suggested instead a parley with Rashid, in hopes of resolving the issue without a fight. Churchill and the War Cabinet overrode the reluctant general. The battle began with the relief of the RAF garrison under siege at Habbaniya, then moved on to a brief fight at Fallujah, west of Baghdad. Then, after a swift march to the capital by a brigade of the 10th Indian Colonial Division, Rashid was put to flight. The 10th was commanded by the profane and savvy Major General William ("Billy") Slim, of whom Churchill said in jest, "I cannot believe that a man with a name like Slim can be much good." Slim was not only good, he had a knack for moving his forces rapidly and over great distances, a talent that he would put to use in Burma in two years. With the 10th Indian Colonial Division on the offensive, Berlin sent a contingent of officers to bolster Rashid's resolve. The German commander, while on final approach to Baghdad's airport, was killed by shots fired by nervous Iraqi gunners. The few German squadrons that Hitler had sent to Iraq left for home, never to return. The British needed just a month to retake Baghdad, and then just three days to set up a new Iraqi government.[243]

Churchill accorded the Iraq campaign a very few pages in his memoirs, calling Iraq a "swift and complete success." Yet he noted that Hitler missed a grand opportunity. "The Germans had, of course, at their disposal an airborne force which would have given them... Syria, Iraq, and Persia, with their precious oil fields." From Persia, where he was held in high regard by the Shah, Hitler could reach "out very far toward India, and beckon to Japan." But Hitler's gaze was fixed upon Russia. Not even the prospect of gaining Iraqi and Persian oil at small cost, nor even the prospect of flying the swastika flag over the Suez Canal, could move him to alter his focus.[244]

Still, although Hitler gazed intensely eastward, he intended to follow through on his Greek and North African successes. For that reason, in Crete, Churchill was about to find himself with another Mediterranean battle on his hands. His "golden eggs" aside, given the sorry state of Freyberg's forces, a successful defense of Crete would prove dicey at best. Yet when logic went against him, Churchill went against logic. When the Ultra decrypts of late April revealed the German plans to attack Crete, he had cabled Wavell: "It seems clear from our information that a heavy airborne attack by German troops and bombers will soon be made on Crete.... It ought to be a fine opportunity for killing the parachute troops." The island, he told Wavell, "must be stubbornly defended." Yet Churchill soon jettisoned his fantasy of slaying paratroopers and faced the facts. He confided to the War Cabinet—but not to Freyberg—that he thought the defense of Crete impossible in the long run. Crete lost would result in German control of the air in the eastern Mediterranean. That, Churchill told the cabinet, "is the greatest menace we have to face."[245]

A map of the eastern Mediterranean shows why Hitler was going to Crete. As the largest and southernmost of the Greek islands, it is located in the center of the eastern Mediterranean. The aerial radius from Crete extended to Tobruk, to Alexandria, and north to Athens, and to Romania beyond. British bombers could reach the Romanian oil fields at Ploesti from Crete; German bombers could reach Alexandria. The loss of Crete would place British sea-lanes to Alexandria in mortal danger. Tobruk, already under siege by Rommel, would become vulnerable to massed German air raids. The loss of its naval base at Souda Bay would force the Royal Navy to sail the eastern Mediterranean under the guns of the Luftwaffe. Yet the map also showed Crete to be a most difficult piece of real estate to attack, a long and slender mountainous spine that stretches 200 miles west to east, but is no more than 35 miles wide at its widest. Three mountain ranges from five thousand to eight thousand feet in height run laterally along the island and effectively isolate the north coast from the south. A German invasion by sea was problematic at best; the coastline consists of more cliff than beach. Even had gently sloping beaches awaited the invaders, the Germans had no shallow-draft landing craft in the Mediterranean capable of putting an army on the shore quickly. That left the air, and an air operation of this scope had yet to be attempted in that brief span of warfare since men had first parachuted from aircraft.

General Kurt Student proposed exactly that. Student commanded the Luftwaffe's elite airborne unit, XI Corps. During the 1940 invasion of the Low Countries, Student's first parachute division, 7 *Flieger,* proved the utility of dropping support troops behind enemy lines, to harass and create diversions. On Crete, Student envisioned his men in the lead role. Their targets as Ultra had revealed were the three RAF airfields, which were the keys to Crete. Göring, having been humbled in the air over Britain, embraced Student's plan as a means to recoup his prestige as well as steal yet more territory for Hitler.[246]

Churchill had all winter believed that Crete could be successfully defended from conventional attack, but until the Ultra transcripts, he knew nothing of Student's bold plan. He did know, however, that the loss of Crete would mean the virtual isolation of the Suez Canal and of Wavell's command, a prospect so dangerous to British survival that he cabled Roosevelt: "I feel Hitler may quite easily gain vast advantage very cheaply, and we are so fully engaged that we can do little—nothing to stop him spreading himself."[247]

His gloom would have deepened had Hitler chosen a far more important target. Malta, not Crete, was the correct target to hit first if Hitler's objectives were to secure his North African position and to isolate the British in the eastern Mediterranean and then to kill them via the stepping-stones that led to Cairo: Crete, Syria, and the Libyan desert. Churchill and Mussolini had long known that whoever held Malta would hold hostage the east-west sea-lanes critical to British resupply of Cairo, as well as the north-south Axis supply routes to North Africa. Hitler understood this, too. When Mussolini invaded Albania the previous year, Hitler fumed that Malta and Crete were better targets if Il Duce was intent on securing the Mediterranean. Hitler's closest military advisers at OKW—to a man—pleaded the case for sending Student's force to Malta. When Keitel and Jodl brought Student the plan, he refused on the grounds that Malta was too heavily defended. It was not, but Hitler and Student lacked the intelligence data that might have told them otherwise.[248]

As critical as Malta was to the British, by May 1941, the RAF air fleet on the island—a few squadrons of Hurricanes—had not grown much in a year. The Italian navy had been bitten hard at Taranto and Cape Matapan, but it was still larger than the British fleets at Gibraltar and Alexandria. Mussolini had more submarines in the sea than the British had ships of all classes. But Mussolini's admirals, who operated virtually independent of Il Duce, did not want their ships to fight the decisive battle for the Mediterranean. In effect, they did not want to lose their ships even if by doing so they might win the war. Thus, the Führer chose to let the Luftwaffe pummel Malta, as it had London. Between January 1941 and July 1942, the Luftwaffe and Italian air forces dropped more tons of bombs per person on the island's 270,000 residents than on any other target in Europe. Malta became the most heavily bombed target in the history of warfare. During one stretch, the bombs fell for 179 of 180 days. The Maltese learned to live in caves carved deep into the limestone. Churchill urged the Commons to adopt a relief plan for Malta, similar to the reimbursement scheme he sought for Britons whose homes had been destroyed. In an astounding affront to the people of Malta, the House of Commons did not even respond. Had British civilian casualties during the Blitz been proportional to those on Malta, almost 800,000 Britons would have perished. Yet the Maltese hung on, even as they died under German bombs.

The far western Mediterranean looked poised for disaster as well. On

April 24 Churchill had cabled Roosevelt: "The capacity of Spain and Portugal to resist the increasing German pressure may at any time collapse, and the anchorage at Gibraltar be rendered unusable. To effect this the Germans would not need to move a large army through Spain but merely to get hold of the batteries which molest the anchorage, for which a few thousand artillerists and technicians might be sufficient." Were Gibraltar to be abandoned, the effect on Royal Navy operations in the Mediterranean would be immediate and disastrous, as would the effect in the eastern Atlantic. The Portuguese Azores, 950 miles off the Iberian coast, and the Cape Verde Islands, 350 miles off the western coast of Africa, were perfect staging areas for U-boats. The islands assumed the same strategic significance in the Atlantic as did Malta in the Mediterranean. If Germany controlled the Atlantic islands, her U-boats could patrol far into the South Atlantic, to the west, and, most worrisome for Churchill, station themselves astride his convoy routes around the Cape of Good Hope. For months German submariners had been secretly putting into the islands' coves for minor repairs. Churchill pleaded with Roosevelt to order carrier-based reconnaissance flights to safeguard British convoys in the vicinity of the Azores and Cape Verde Islands.[249]

Time, as always, was not on Churchill's side. He told Roosevelt that a British force was ready to take the Atlantic islands should Hitler take Spain or Portugal but that the force needed more than a week to deploy. He asked the president to "send an American squadron for a friendly cruise in these regions." Harriman, in complete agreement with Churchill as to the immediacy of the danger, had days earlier sent his own desperate cable to Roosevelt: "England's strength is bleeding. In our own interest, I trust that your Navy can be directly employed before it is too late."[250]

Roosevelt declined a show of naval force in the vicinity of the Azores, declined to order reconnaissance flights into the fray, declined all of Churchill's pleas and suggestions. The president's refusal, Colville observed, made Churchill "gravely depressed." On May 3, Churchill—"in worse gloom than I have ever seen him"—dictated to Colville another telegram to the president, this one "drawing a somber picture of what a collapse in the Middle East would entail." Iraq could fall, and Turkey, and the eastern flank of Egypt—Palestine—would be threatened. The Mideast command would collapse. The telegram complete, he indulged in his habit of divining the future. In this instant, the gloom bled through. He sketched for Colville, Ismay, and Harriman—as he had in the cable to Roosevelt—a picture of the world controlled by Hitler, with the United States and Britain isolated and forced to accept a terrible, and in time, fatal peace.[251]

Churchill was just desperate enough to add a remarkable request to his cable apprising Roosevelt of the situation: "Therefore, if you can not take more advanced positions now [in the Atlantic], or very soon, the vast balances may be tilted heavily to our disadvantage. Mr. President . . . the one decisive counterweight I can see to balance the growing pessimism . . . *would be if the United States were immediately to arrange herself with us as a belligerent Power*" (italics added). It had come to this: the British prime minister was asking—*begging*—America to declare war.[252]

He had asked Roosevelt much the same question the previous year as France was falling but had framed that request in terms of the "moral effect" an American declaration might have on the French. His new plea was based on a far more fundamental need: survival. Roosevelt, again, declined. He lacked the support to give Churchill what he needed, with the result that Churchill found himself, as usual, desperately short on time and desperately lacking in matériel.

On the moonlit night of May 10, the Luftwaffe smashed London and continued pounding it with high explosives and incendiaries until dawn on the eleventh. The Anglo-Irish poet Louis MacNeice had arranged to spend the night in the dome of St. Paul's Cathedral. He wrote that soon after the raiders appeared, "great tawny clouds of smoke, rolling in sumptuous Baroque exuberance, had hidden the river completely and there we were on the dome, a Classical island in a more than Romantic Inferno. It was far and away the most astonishing spectacle I have ever seen."

Churchill was safe at Ditchley that night, watching a Marx Brothers movie and making inquiries about the damage to London when word came in that the Duke of Hamilton, an old friend of his, had telephoned and sought most urgently to speak to Churchill. Churchill asked Brendan Bracken to take a message from the duke. A few minutes later Bracken returned and informed the P.M.: "Hess has arrived in Scotland." Churchill thought it a joke and told Brendan to inform the duke to "kindly tell that to the Marx Brothers." But a flood of new messages soon confirmed the story. Rudolf Hess, deputy Führer, third in command of the Third Reich, member of Hitler's secret cabinet council, leader of the Nazi Party, Hitler's friend—perhaps his only true friend—for more than a dozen years, had parachuted into Scotland. Either through luck or skill, Hess had actually landed quite near the duke's manor. Thus began an episode of sheer lunacy.[253]

Nobody knew what to make of the news. Pamela Churchill, who was at Ditchley that weekend, recalled that the secretaries, who were vital in connecting Churchill to "whatever was happening" in the outside world, could garner no intelligence on Hess's adventure. Everybody who was present—Pamela, the secretaries, Churchill—"had no idea what was happening" and could only speculate and wonder if "it might be the biggest thing in the whole war" or if perhaps "Germany was breaking up." History anointed Hess a sideshow, but when news of his advent first arrived "it was a very thrilling moment."[254]

Hess's immediate objective was to reach the Duke of Hamilton, who had met Hess but once, at the 1936 Olympic Games, but who Hess presumed to be a fan of Hitler. Hess's delusional and singularly unilateral mission was to bring the war to a peaceful conclusion. Knowing of Hitler's hatred for the Russians (but not being privy to the invasion plans), Hess believed (in part on being told so by his astrologer) that he and Hamilton could arrange peace through the large anti-war faction Hess believed existed in Britain. In interviews with doctors and cabinet officials, Hess stressed that Hitler was pained deeply over the need to sink British ships and bomb British cities. The Führer, Hess claimed, found it most difficult to give the orders necessary to fight such a ruthless war with Britain. Hess, in what Churchill termed his "keynote," claimed he "thought that if England once knew of this fact it might be possible that England on her part would be ready for agreement." In other words, once England realized how kind and considerate a fellow Hitler really was, England would meet the Führer's wishes.[255]

Churchill in his memoirs writes that he attached no special significance to Hess's arrival, though in the first hours after learning of Hess's mission, Churchill was as much in a tizzy as everyone else. In short order it became clear that Hess was crazy. In fact, Hess's arrant mental condition was so evident that Churchill considered his subsequent sentence of life in prison to be unjust. Hess may have once stood close to Hitler, Churchill wrote, but he "had, in my view, atoned for this by his completely devoted and frantic deed of lunatic benevolence." He was, wrote Churchill, "a medical and not a criminal case, and should be so regarded."[256]

The weirdness of the entire episode captured imaginations worldwide, just as it had captured Churchill's. Days after Hess's arrival, Roosevelt, dining with Sumner Wells, Harry Hopkins, and Robert E. Sherwood, asked Wells if he had ever met Hess. Wells had, and described Hess as fanatically loyal to Hitler and somewhat brutishly stupid. The men discussed Hess's flight. Roosevelt fell silent for a moment. Then he posed the question everybody was asking: "I wonder what is *really* behind this story?" Stalin (who never trusted the British) asked both Beaverbrook and Churchill the same question months later. The whole thing was just too strange, and the obvious explanation—that Hess was crazy—seemed too pat. Churchill, or Hitler, or both, *had* to be up to something.[257]

Hess's misadventure handed Churchill a grand opportunity to make mischief at Hitler's expense. With Hess under wraps in the Tower of London and Hitler unsure of just what his protégé was saying to the British, Churchill told Roosevelt that "we think it best to let the press have a good run of it for a bit and keep the Germans guessing." Hitler was not only guessing but sweating, from the moment he was apprised of Hess's errand by two of Hess's adjutants, who had the misfortune to deliver to Hitler a letter of explanation from Hess along with the news that Hess had already departed. They were immediately arrested. Hitler expressed to his personal architect, Albert Speer, his worry that Churchill might use the incident to pretend to Germany's allies that the Reich had extended peace feelers toward Britain. "Who will believe me," the Führer lamented to Speer, "that Hess did not fly there in my name, that the whole thing is not some sort of intrigue behind the backs of my allies?" Japan might change its policy. People would snicker. Hitler regained his buoyancy with the thought that Hess might drop into the North Sea and drown. After the news of Hess's safe landing arrived, Hitler devised his official explanation: he declared that his old friend had gone mad. He also consulted his astrologer, who always divined happy portents from the tea leaves.[258]

Churchill, aware of Hitler's use of astrologers, once summoned one himself. In a what-the-hell moment, he asked the surprised fortune-teller to tell him what *Hitler's* fortune-teller was telling Hitler. Churchill told his friend Kay Halle the story years later with the caveat that "this is just between us."[259]

Hess himself, cursed with good health, given his fate, lived on for another forty-six years, locked away in prison every day and hour and minute of them. His wife sued for divorce in 1944 on the grounds of "desertion and insanity."[260]

Hess's flight was one of two stories from overseas that year—until December 7—that held young American boys spellbound. The other was the hunt for the great German battleship *Bismarck*. The essayist and sportswriter Robert W. Creamer devotes almost as much ink to these two events as he does to Joe DiMaggio's hitting streak in his memoir of that memorable baseball season, *Baseball and Other Matters in 1941*. "Hess and the *Bismarck* served in my innocent mind, and in the minds of other half-thinking Americans," wrote Creamer, "to counterbalance the Nazi victories in the Balkans and North Africa."

The morning after Hess landed, a fine Sunday morning of sun and blue skies, fires still burned in London from the previous evening's air raid. Almost three thousand Londoners lay dead in the rubble, the deadliest one-night toll since the Blitz began nine months earlier. Services were canceled at Westminster Abbey. St. Mary-le-Bow was destroyed, its bells crashing down into the debris. The William Rufus roof of Westminster Hall was gone, the hall itself now a smoldering wreck. Colville watched from Westminster Bridge as fires burned all along the Embankment. Big Ben had been struck, but still tolled out the hours. The debating chamber in the Commons, at the northern end of the Palace of Westminster, had taken a direct hit and, to Churchill's profound sorrow, "was blown to smithereens." (The Lords' chamber was undamaged; the House met there and at Church House for the remainder of the war.) In a letter to Randolph, Churchill mourned the loss of the chamber where he had served for almost forty years. He had once, during the Great War, called it the "the shrine of the world's liberties." Since September, MPs had prowled the darkened halls of Parliament by the light of hurricane lamps; the windows overlooking the Thames had long since been blown out and boarded up; the tapestries had been removed for safe-keeping. Even the smoking room closed early so the attendants could get home to their families before the bombs came. The House chamber was destroyed, but Parliament, Churchill told his son, continued to function "undaunted amid the storms." Days earlier he had ended an address in the old chamber with, "I feel sure we have no need to fear the tempest. Let it roar, and let it rage. We shall come through." They were the last words he spoke there. A decade would pass before the Commons was rebuilt.[261]

As that Sunday evening came on, Colville noted yellow, smoldering bits of burnt paper from some wrecked Fleet Street publishing house raining down like leaves on a breezy autumn day. Hess was by then on his way to the Tower. Londoners waited in homes as dark as Hess's prison cell for the expected nightly onslaught. It appeared obvious that Hitler was softening up Britain for the final attack. They imagined the worst was yet to come.[262]

Within days of Hess's arrival, more critical events overtook Churchill. He had been partially correct when he told Wavell that he thought the invasion of Crete would afford a good opportunity to kill parachutists. When dropped behind, or directly onto, British positions, the German air-borne troops would find themselves outnumbered and cut off from sup-port. If the Royal Navy—protected by Air Marshal Longmore's too-few aircraft—could keep the coast clear of German reinforcements, the para-chutists would be doomed.

That hope was stillborn. Having left so many men and so much equip-ment behind in Greece, the British on Crete found they lacked the troops, anti-aircraft guns, and requisite radio communications between units to stop the Germans. The 30,000 Commonwealth and 10,000 Greek troops on Crete, though outnumbering the expected Germans by more than two to one, were at a disadvantage by having to cover all the airfields and ports along the length of the north shore, whereas the Germans could concentrate their forces at will, and with surprise. The British would have to react, and when they did, they'd face bad terrain and long distances along the single coast road. In essence, at any particular point, the Commonwealth forces would find themselves, as usual, outgunned. The situation in the air was even grimmer. Longmore's air force on Crete consisted of fewer than a dozen Hurricanes and two dozen older planes. The air chief as well did not grasp the need to integrate air support with ground operations, a concept superbly practiced for two years by the Germans. Longmore's few planes therefore did not coordinate with Freyberg's infantry, rendering the former irrelevant and the latter exposed, as was the Royal Navy, which sailed without air protection. Churchill suggested that a dozen Hurricanes be sent from Malta. Such a pittance would have made no difference. The German air fleet assembling in southern Greece, fewer than 150 miles from Crete, was made up of more than 250 bombers, 150 Stuka dive-bombers, 200 fighters, 500 tri-motor Junkers Ju 52 transport planes carrying paratroopers, and 80 gliders carrying 750 airborne troops.[263]

The battle opened on May 19, with Stuka dive-bombers striking at British ships in Souda Bay; then the German fighters destroyed most of the meager British air fleet. Early the next morning, German paratroopers—almost four thousand strong—descended upon the Maleme airfield and the heights above Souda Bay. Sir John Keegan called it "the first great parachute operation in history." Three battalions of New Zealanders, veterans of the desert and Greek campaigns, guarded the Maleme airfield. A New Zealand lieutenant recorded his thoughts as Germans drifted down: "Seen against the blue of the early morning Cretan sky, through a frame of grey-green olive branches, they looked like little jerking dolls" and "those beautiful kicking dolls meant the repetition of all the horror we had known so recently in Greece." An Australian brigade guarded the Rethymnon airfield, seventy miles to the east and a little less than halfway to Heraklion, where just a few British battalions prepared to defend that airfield.[264]

By late afternoon on the twentieth, another wave of almost four thousand paratroopers landed in the vicinity of the Rethymnom and Heraklion airfields. Within hours Churchill telegraphed Roosevelt: "Battle for Crete has opened well." The battle had opened well, but that situation lasted for only a few hours. The Germans, dispersed and confused at first, rallied throughout the night. A New Zealand battalion inexplicably withdrew from a vital hill above Maleme. The Maleme airfield fell to the Germans on the twenty-first. Ju 52 transports began ferrying in the five thousand troops of the 5th Mountain Division, but at great cost: More than half of the Ju 52s sent to Crete never returned. British anti-aircraft guns accounted for only a few of the planes; most were lost while trying to land on beaches, on wrecked airfields, and in plowed fields in order to disgorge their cargoes of troops. The RAF was in far worse shape. By late on the twenty-first, the RAF had no planes on Crete. Freyberg's ground forces were dispersed and unable to coordinate movements. On the night of the twenty-first, the Royal Navy turned away German transports—mostly commandeered Greek fishing boats and small coastal steamers—carrying seven thousand troops. But daylight on the twenty-second brought the Stukas. "A lot of ships lost," noted Colville, "including [cruisers] *Gloucester* and *Fiji*." More than seven hundred of *Gloucester*'s eight hundred crew members went down with the ship. In reply to Colville's expression of grief at the naval losses, Churchill growled, "What do you suppose we build ships for?" The Royal Navy's deflection of the German transports was welcome news, but those losses were not enough to keep the Germans off the island, because the Germans were coming by air. Less than thirty-six hours after telling Roosevelt the battle had opened well, Churchill was forced to inform the president: "Battle in Crete is severe." "Severe" did not do justice to the circumstances. Another last stand was shaping up.[265]

The Germans fought as if Crete were a sacred Teutonic site, pressing the battle, Colville wrote, "with blind courage." They fought with such fury because there would be no escape were they to fail. The British could always evacuate by sea in the event of defeat, and had in fact developed a talent for doing just that. The German paratroopers, on the other hand, were there to stay, one way or another. Their brethren in the Luftwaffe controlled the air, and the parachutists grabbed the airfields. The British had blasted the airstrips to rubble, but the Germans held and repaired the fields. Supplies and reinforcements were flown in during the next seven days, while Stukas riddled any British or Greek troops who tried any heroics. Once in possession of the airfields, the Germans were, in effect, in possession of Crete. But the cost of victory for Student's paratroopers was extraordinary; five thousand out of nine thousand had been killed. Hitler told Student the cost was too high to justify ever staging another operation of that magnitude. The loss of so many of the Ju 52s—the workhorse of supply for the Wehrmacht—was also disturbing. Hitler would need all he could get to feed and arm his armies as they struck deep into Russia.[266]

As of the twenty-eighth, the port of Sphakia, on the island's south side, was still held by the British, but in the end, it would serve as this battle's Dunkirk and Narvik. That day Freyberg's army began the trek over the mountains to Sphakia, with the German mountain troops in pursuit. By battle's end, three days later, the army had lost more than 1,700 killed and 2,000 wounded. Almost 12,000 British and Anzac troops stayed behind as prisoners of the Reich. Just ten days after Churchill told Roosevelt that the battle was "severe," Crete was lost, and the British again were forced to flee the scene of a disastrous defeat by sea. Mountbatten's destroyer HMS *Kelly* was among the Luftwaffe's victims. Captain Dickie survived, but more than half of the crew were lost when *Kelly* capsized and sank while plowing ahead at full speed. Between May 21 and June 2, the Royal Navy, pummeled from the air, lost three cruisers sunk and four damaged, six destroyers sunk and eight damaged, and more than 2,000 officers and seamen killed. The battleships *Warspite* and *Valiant* were damaged, as was the aircraft carrier *Formidable*. It was the Royal Navy's most costly naval battle of the war. German aircraft—in daylight operations—had accounted for all the British ships. Göring had achieved over Crete what he had failed to achieve over Britain: air superiority. He had redeemed himself.[267]

On May 21, the second full day of the battle for Crete, other ominous news arrived at No. 10. It appeared *Bismarck* was preparing to make its run for the high seas. Surface raiders such as *Bismarck* and her sister ship, *Tirpitz,* if free to roam the Atlantic, were as equal a threat to shipping as, or greater than, U-boats. German submarines engendered a primal fear in the crews and passengers aboard their targets; they were the monsters under the bed, lurking unseen beneath the sea, their presence announced by a thunderous eruption of flame from the bowels of some unfortunate merchantman. *Bismarck* was a monster plain and simple. A tanker or freighter captain who espied *Bismarck* setting a course across his bow knew his ship was doomed. Convoy escorts (destroyers and corvettes) proved adequate at hunting and killing submarines, but their small guns and depth charges were useless against capital ships. *Bismarck* amok, undetected by RAF reconnaissance planes, which lacked the range to patrol to the vast reaches of the central Atlantic, could run down any convoy, immune to the minuscule fire of the escorts. *Bismarck,* if she chose, could *ram* her way through a convoy; a thin-skinned five-thousand-ton freighter would perish beneath her bows like a rowboat.

The January German sortie of *Scharnhorst* and *Gneisenau* resulted in the mauling of one convoy—ten ships were sunk in one day—and the loss of more than 115,000 tons of shipping. As a result, the British gained a great deal of respect for the lethality of the *Kriegsmarine*'s surface ships and now had a double-edged problem. Locating the German battleships was difficult enough, but what to do when they were located? Churchill faced two bad choices if Hitler let loose his surface ships. He could chase the Germans and expose the British coast or leave the Germans unmolested and expose the convoys. He lacked the warships to do both. It was an old predicament for the British, which, when Napoleon grasped its significance, led him to contemplate a naval feint in 1804. By sending a French fleet to the British West Indies, he hoped to lure the British Home Fleet into a wild goose chase, thereby allowing his main fleet to land an invasion force on British soil. Had Hitler studied Napoleon's seafaring tactics or only his Russian escapades? Churchill also feared that the mere appearance of German capital ships on the high seas would dissuade America from risking its merchantmen to convoy supplies to Britain, let alone risk its outdated Atlantic fleet to protect those ships. He later wrote that a concentration of surface raiders "in the great spaces of the Atlantic Ocean would subject our naval strength to a trial of the first magnitude." *Scharnhorst* and *Gneisenau* had in January given the trial's opening arguments. *Bismarck* presumed to close the case.[268]

On the evening of May 21, *Bismarck* and the heavy cruiser *Prinz Eugen,* escorted by six destroyers, slipped out of Bergen fjord in Norway under the command of Admiral Günther Lütjens, a stern, humorless veteran of the Great War's coastal gunboat battles, in which his willingness to attack superior forces and his skill at coming away victorious earned him a reputation as a brilliant and courageous tactician. He was Grand Admiral Raeder's first choice to command *Bismarck* on this, her maiden operation, code-named *Rheinübung* (Rhine Exercise). Lütjens, prone to fatalistic premonitions, told fellow officers that *Rheinübung* was to be his "death voyage." The admiral had secured his place on this mission by his superb command of the heavy cruisers *Scharnhorst* and *Gneisenau* during their murderous January spree. The original plan for *Rheinübung* called for these two ships to sail with *Bismarck,* but the British had driven them into French ports, where they were undergoing repairs. *Bismarck* and *Prinz Eugen* (named for Eugene of Savoy, Marlborough's ally at the Battle of Blenheim) would conduct *Rheinübung* alone. Riding at anchor in Bergen fjord, the two ships made tempting targets for the RAF, as dusk lingers in late spring at those latitudes. Were the RAF to appear overhead, Lütjens stood a fair chance of seeing his fatal premonition fulfilled before he even weighed anchor. But high clouds and clinging fog afforded the Germans a perfect opportunity to escape into the North Sea. Not willing to risk an improvement in the weather, Lütjens made his dash for the open sea. In his haste to depart Bergen, he failed to top off *Bismarck*'s fuel tanks.[269]

The British, expecting just such a rapid departure, hoped to shadow the

German ships. If *Bismarck* and *Prinz Eugen* reached the North Sea undetected, the Royal Navy could then only guess which of four routes they would take to break out into the Atlantic. Two of the routes took the ships within British air-patrol range north of the Orkney Islands; the third ran between the Faroe Islands and Iceland, within range of British spotter planes stationed there. Lütjens's fourth choice was the longest—to loop to the north of Iceland and run down the chute of the Denmark Strait, the ice-choked channel between Greenland and Iceland. This was the route he had taken in January. He chose to take it again. Everything was going his way. When the clouds broke over Bergen on May 22, a lone Spitfire, rigged for photo reconnaissance, roared up the fjord just a few feet above the waves and into the teeth of enemy fire. The pilot took a fast look around, turned hard for home, and radioed his message: *Bismarck* is gone.

This news troubled Churchill. Eleven convoys were at that moment on the open seas or preparing to depart British ports. One of them, escorted by two cruisers, both of which *Bismarck* could easily dispatch, was sailing south of Britain, destined for the Middle East with 20,000 reinforcements for Wavell. Were *Bismarck* and the troop transports to cross paths, Churchill's war in Africa would be over. *Bismarck* had to be located, and sunk.

Early on the twenty-second, the escort destroyers dropped away from the far swifter *Bismarck* and *Prinz Eugen*. Alone now, Lütjens steamed north until the early afternoon, when he turned northwest in readiness for the run down the Denmark Strait, fog-bound at this time of year and full of newly calved icebergs. Just before midnight, the German ships turned into the strait. If his luck held, Lütjens would break out into the Atlantic in about thirty hours. This was the most dangerous part of the venture; the navigable part of the channel was at most only thirty miles wide at this time of year, narrow enough that if the British were lucky, their naval radar—limited in range to about twelve miles, and unreliable—could pick up the German ships, that is, if the British had vessels on station. They did. Two cruisers, *Norfolk* and *Suffolk,* positioned themselves in the lower part of the strait. Neither was a match for *Bismarck* or *Prinz Eugen.* Their job was to spot the Germans and shadow them until the battle cruiser *Hood* and Britain's newest battleship, *Prince of Wales,* appeared on the scene. *Prince of Wales* carried ten 14-inch guns and was built to hunt and kill almost anything afloat. *Hood*—the *Mighty Hood* to Britons—was twenty-two years old, armed with eight 15-inch guns, and the pride of Great Britain, feared even by German sailors. When Churchill learned that it was to be *Hood* that would give battle to *Bismarck,* he retired to bed content.[270]

Hood and *Prince of Wales* departed Scapa Flow a few minutes after midnight on the twenty-second, dispatched by Admiral Sir John Cronyn Tovey, commander in chief of the Home Fleet. They made for the Denmark Strait on a course that would take them across the other three exit points into the Atlantic. Had Lütjens elected to make his run through one of them, *Hood* would cross his path. If not, the Germans and British would likely meet and fight at the southern end of the Denmark Strait. When he received the baleful report from the lone spitfire, Tovey put his flag aboard the new battleship *King George V* and sallied out of Scapa Flow with the aircraft carrier *Victorious,* four cruisers, and seven destroyers. Tovey intended to straddle the three exit routes east of Iceland. Somebody was bound to run into the Germans. Such was the plan.

If *Bismarck* avoided the net, Churchill would need help from Roosevelt. Accordingly, he cabled the president: "Should we not catch them going out, your Navy should surely be able to mark them down for us" and "Give us the news and we will finish the job." That request, to act as Britain's eyes in the Atlantic, created a diplomatic problem for the Americans, for Grand Admiral Raeder had made clear his intentions to shoot any American warship he thought "committed an act of war" by reporting to the British the position of German ships on the high seas. Raeder had a point. International law demanded that neutrals on the high seas mind their own business. But in early April, Roosevelt—in yet another tentative step toward hostilities—declared that American warships would henceforth patrol to twenty-six degrees west longitude, roughly from between Iceland and Greenland south to Brazil. He also declared that if American ships spotted German warships, they would broadcast their location on an open frequency, fully realizing that doing so might trigger an act of war on Germany's part, which presumably (Churchill hoped) would trigger a declaration of war by America. Yet Roosevelt knew that America was not yet prepared in either martial spirit or armaments to carry through on such a declaration. His initiative had been largely bluff, though it had elated Churchill. Colville and Harriman were at Chequers when the news arrived. When Colville asked Harriman if this might mean war, Harriman replied: "That's what I hope."[271]

Churchill would have welcomed a crisis on the seas, and, in fact, he soon tried to engineer just such an incident. Roosevelt's declaration meant that American warships patrolled east almost to the Azores and north to Greenland but not into the hottest battle zones, within one thousand miles of Britain, thereby lessening the chances of running into Germans. Roosevelt had struck a deal with the Danish government in exile to build airbases on Greenland. Had the bases been operational by late May, they might have benefited Churchill in his search for *Bismarck;* but they were not. In any case, the Denmark Strait went unobserved by the U.S. Navy as

Bismarck slipped through. Churchill's ships would have to find *Bismarck* on their own.

Suffolk did just that. She spotted the two German ships in the early evening of May 23 and signaled the contact before running for cover in a fogbank. *Norfolk,* also hiding in the fog, picked up *Suffolk*'s report. Admiral W. F. Wake-Walker, directing the action of both ships from *Norfolk,* and eager to make visual contact, ordered *Norfolk* to the edge of the fogbank, directly under *Bismarck*'s fine optical sights. *Bismarck* loosed its first ever shots in anger, which straddled *Norfolk*. Walker fled back into the fog. It would fall to *Hood,* guided by *Suffolk* and *Norfolk,* to sink the *Bismarck*.

Vice Admiral Lancelot Holland, second in command of the Home Fleet, was on board *Hood,* about three hundred miles away and closing at such high speed that his escort destroyers gave up the chase and dropped back. At about 8:00 P.M. *Hood*'s captain, Ralph Kerr, told his crew that the Germans had been sighted in the strait. All hands were ordered to ready their battle gear—life jackets, flashlights, helmets—and were reminded to change into clean underwear, to prevent infection from shrapnel wounds. The ship was darkened, battle flags run up the masts. Shortly after midnight—it was now the twenty-fourth—the crews of *Hood* and *Prince of Wales* manned their battle stations. *Bismarck* was now about 180 miles to the north, her bottleneck into the Atlantic corked.

Churchill, dining at Chequers, demanded that all news be immediately brought to his attention. The evening's dinner was, as usual, an "entirely male party," Colville noted, consisting of Churchill's brother, Jack, Colville, Harriman, and Ismay. Although the awful news from Crete weighed on Churchill and his guests, the conversation at the table, recalled Ismay, "was confined almost exclusively to the impending clash at sea." They sat up until after 3:00 A.M., late even for Churchill, with hopes of getting some further news from the Admiralty. None arrived. Churchill recalled, "There was nothing for me to do and I went to bed...so well tired with other work that I slept soundly. I had complete confidence in The First Sea Lord, Admiral Pound, and liked the way he was playing the hand. I awoke in peaceful Chequers about 9 A.M. with all that strange thrill which one feels at the beginning of a day in which great news is expected, good or bad."[272]

While Churchill slept, the last great duel of battleships in the Atlantic Ocean began. It was over in less than eight minutes. Just before 6:00 A.M., *Prince of Wales* and *Hood* maneuvered to bring themselves east and south of *Bismarck* and *Prinz Eugen,* such that the rising sun brought the approaching German ships into sharp relief. *Prinz Eugen* came along first in line, which confused the British, for *Bismarck,* the logical leader, was trailing behind and appeared to be the smaller of the two ships. *Prince of Wales,* much of its crew green, and *Hood,* plagued by ineffectual range-finding radar, opened fire on *Prinz Eugen,* to no effect. *Bismarck,* meanwhile, took leisurely aim at *Hood*. One of *Prinz Eugen*'s eight-inch shells scored a hit amidships on *Hood,* igniting a fire that popped off ammunition kept at the ready. Captain Kerr ordered his crew to let the fire burn itself out and to take shelter near the superstructure. Kerr, realizing he had shot at the wrong target, ordered a turn to port, in order to reduce *Hood*'s profile and to bring its four 15-inch bow guns to bear on *Bismarck*. The turn came too late.

Bismarck's first salvos had straddled *Hood*. Now *Bismarck* had *Hood*'s range. She fired another salvo. An officer on *Prinz Eugen* saw the shell splashes and thought that this salvo, too, had missed. But at least one shell had found its mark, possibly beneath the waterline. Within a second or two, a great shaft of flame shot straight up from *Hood*'s midsection, high into the morning sky, followed a few seconds later by a catastrophic explosion. *Hood* disappeared for a few moments in the smoke, but large pieces of the ship were seen lofted high into the air. Within a few minutes, the smoke drifted off. *Hood* was gone. Three of her crew of 1,412 bobbed alive in the water. They called out until they found each other amid the oil and debris and dozens of inflatable life rafts, all of which were empty. *Hood,* its stern blown off, its bow broken off, took Admiral Holland and Captain Kerr and every other crewman down with her. Churchill awoke at Chequers to this worst possible news: *Hood* was lost and *Bismarck* was on the loose. He wandered into Harriman's bedroom. Harriman bolted awake to behold an apparition dressed in a yellow sweater over a short nightshirt, his pink legs exposed. "Hell of a battle going on," Churchill mumbled. "The *Hood* is sunk, hell of a battle."[273]

Gloom descended upon Chequers that morning, but Churchill shed no tears at the news of *Hood*. His tears flowed when sentimentality was in the air—a christening, the prospect of casualties among the creatures confined in the London zoo, the recounting over brandy of long-past heroic deeds. The sight of bombed-out civilians brought tears to his eyes; they were innocents. News of the death of soldiers or sailors in battle moved him to resolve, often to anger, sometimes to impetuous decisions, but not to tears. Upon learning of *Hood*'s demise, he came downstairs to find Clementine, Sarah, and Vic Oliver in a parlor, Vic at the piano, tapping out on the ivories a few measures of Beethoven, which Churchill took to be a funeral march. "Nobody plays the Dead March in my house," Churchill growled. All in the room but Churchill laughed—a mistake, followed by another. "It's not the Dead March," said Oliver. "It's the Appassionata Sonata." Churchill glowered. "You can say what you like, I know it's the Funeral March." Vic then made a final error, by playing a few more chords from the Appassionata. Churchill erupted. "Stop it! Stop it! I want no

Dead March, I tell you!" Only when Sarah rushed to the piano and advised Vic to play another piece did the moment pass. Vic at least had had the good sense not to whistle the tune.[274]

Churchill learned later that morning that *Prince of Wales* had taken several hits. One shell from *Prinz Eugen* passed without exploding clear through the gunnery plotting station in the superstructure, killing most of the plotters and knocking Captain Leach senseless. Still, *Prince of Wales* let loose four more salvos before withdrawing. Churchill fumed to Colville that the retreat was "the worst thing since Troubridge turned away from *Goeben* in 1914." Churchill berated the Admiralty, the first sea lord, and, when his criticism of the Atlantic action waned, berated Cunningham in the Mediterranean for not risking his ships to block the invasion of Crete. Churchill demanded risk, not caution, from his naval commanders. Yet Cunningham *had* risked his ships, and he had scattered the German invasion fleet. Cunningham had put thousands of British troops on Crete, and by the twenty-fourth, with his ships under constant attack, he was preparing to get them off. His losses were horrific. Cunningham's place in Royal Navy history was secure. Churchill, in his memoirs, finally gave him his due, and he included an anecdote that captures the spirit of the admiral. When an officer protested the risk to the fleet in getting the survivors off Crete, Cunningham responded, "It takes the Navy three years to build a ship; it will take three hundred years to build a new tradition."[275]

It was May 24, Empire Day,* when millions of schoolchildren throughout the Empire were granted a school holiday to celebrate their monarch, salute the Union Jack, and sing patriotic songs. A generation of children had heard inspirational speeches and listened to tales of heroic deeds from the imperial past, tales of Clive of India, Wolfe of Québec, and "Chinese Gordon" of Khartoum, Marlborough, and Nelson. Empire Day 1941 passed without celebration. Churchill would have to impart the news of *Hood* to the Commons the following week, but first a new diversion was to be unveiled that night at Chequers. The Old Man had recently insisted the great house be outfitted with a movie projector. His mood improved somewhat that evening as Marlene Dietrich, starring in *Seven Sinners,* made her Chequers premier.

But he continued to spread his anger between Cunningham and the admirals pursuing *Bismarck*. "The loss of half the Mediterranean fleet," he snapped to Colville, "would be worthwhile to save Crete." In fact, with

---

* In the next decade it would be rechristened Commonwealth Day, and the date moved first to June 10, Queen Elizabeth's birthday, then to the second Monday of March. By the time Churchill celebrated his ninetieth birthday, its original meaning was fast fading from the collective memory.

Cunningham's mounting losses off Crete, about half the Mediterranean fleet *had* been lost since the start of the year. Churchill was incorrect in ascribing hesitancy—cowardice by any other name—to Cunningham, and he was wrong about Admiral Wake-Walker on board *Norfolk* and Captain Leach on board *Prince of Wales*. Leach was correct in withdrawing *Prince of Wales,* damaged, outgunned, her range-finding radar useless. Wake-Walker and Leach ran, not for lack of fighting spirit, but to live to fight another day. It was the correct decision.[276]

Churchill did not at all see things that way. Livid, he wanted to welcome the two commanders home with courts-martial, but Admirals Pound and Tovey insisted the officers on the spot had acted correctly. Years later, his wrath softened by the passage of time, Churchill wrote in his memoirs that Wake-Walker had been "indisputably right" in his decision.

Prince of Wales had put at least three 14-inch shells into *Bismarck,* and as a result the German ship suffered a serious fuel leak and loss of rudder control. The Admiralty did not yet know this. But Lütjens now knew his decision to not refuel at Bergen was fatal. *Bismarck,* wounded and lacking the fuel to make a run for home, had to run for a port in occupied France. *Prinz Eugen,* undamaged, ran for Brest. *Rheinübung* was finished. It remained to be seen whether *Bismarck* was as well. That night, Churchill was told that the Royal Navy would give battle the following morning, but in the early hours of the twenty-fifth, *Bismarck* vanished from *Suffolk*'s radar. Colville recalled that this dashing of Churchill's hopes caused the entirety of the twenty-fifth to be passed as "a day of fearful gloom." Over the next two days and across 1,200 nautical miles, a truly epic naval chase took place on the high seas. Churchill dearly would have loved to be in on the chase and particularly the kill, but he had to satisfy himself with observing from the Admiralty War Room, where he meddled. The "former naval person" had never heard a naval gun fired in battle. His had been an administrative naval career consisting in large part of sticking pins into his wall maps at the Admiralty. On this day, he made a nuisance of himself.[277]

On the morning of Monday, May 26, having vanished for more than thirty hours, *Bismarck*'s position and heading were at last confirmed by an RAF Catalina flying boat, piloted by an American. Tovey, on board *King George V,* gave chase, with *Bismarck* now 130 miles ahead of him. The older battleship *Rodney* joined the hunt. Churchill, ensconced in the Admiralty War Room, oversaw a riotous scene of charts spread across old oak tables, pins marking known positions, admirals demanding information from subordinates, and Churchill needling them all. He pressured Pound to order Tovey to keep up the chase even if it meant *King George V* had to be towed to port for lack of fuel. Pound needed no encouragement; he was an old seadog who believed a captain's place was on the bridge.[278]

The Royal Navy found the *Bismarck* late on the twenty-sixth. Early on the twenty-seventh, as Tovey ran in for the kill, he flashed a message to his ships that lives on in Royal Navy lore: *"Get closer. Get closer." Bismarck,* its rudder jammed and unable to steer, was doomed, but she could still shoot, her final salvos straddling both *Rodney* and *King George V.* Lütjens radioed the homeland with a last message: "Ship out of control. Will fight to the last shell. Long live the Führer." The British poured hundreds of shells into the wounded ship, its guns now silent. It burned furiously, the hellish glow of the fires belowdecks visible to British gunners. Slowly, it began to settle by the bows. But it would not go down. Its crew attempted to scuttle her; still the great ship remained afloat. The battle, if it could be called that, had lasted for more than six hours. At around 10:30 A.M. the British cruiser *Dorsetshire,* already having fired 250 shells at a range of just three miles—point blank in naval terms—ran close in and finished *Bismarck* with two torpedoes. Lütjens, his premonition fulfilled, died along with 2,100 of the 2,200 men on board. The sinking of *Bismarck,* ironically, bolstered the old timers' case that battleships still ruled the seas. It had taken a task force of carriers, battleships, destroyers, cruisers, submarines, aircraft, bombs, shells, and innumerable torpedoes to sink the great ship, even as it limped along, crippled.[279]

British destroyers conducted a brief search for survivors, but fearful of lurking U-boats they soon departed, leaving hundreds of Germans behind in the water. Or so went the official explanation. Word had already arrived from Crete that the Luftwaffe had bombed and strafed defenseless British sailors whose ships had been sunk from under them; Dickie Mountbatten soon confirmed the rumors to Churchill. Both sides, it appeared, had jettisoned any pretense to gentlemanly rules of engagement. Late in the day a Spanish cruiser came upon *Bismarck*'s final position and found only hundreds of bodies bobbing on the greasy gray swells.[280]

There would be no sugar for the birds when Churchill addressed Parliament that day. Crete was on the brink; Cairo and the Suez Canal lay exposed. The Vichy government in Syria was thought to be welcoming German military advisers. Rommel appeared unstoppable. The ports and London had taken fierce hits since March. Leslie Hore-Belisha, a Liberal and former member of the Chamberlain government who fancied himself better qualified than Churchill to run the war, had made unflattering comments to the press concerning the "tempo of our war effort." The old Marxist Harold Laski had lauded Churchill as a "war leader." But

Laski—whose bushy eyebrows, plush mustache, long nose, and horn-rimmed eyeglasses qualified him as a double Marxist—cited production bottlenecks and lack of adequate evacuation plans in case of invasion as evidence of Churchill's failings as prime minister and chief administrator. The *Daily Mail* put it bluntly: "When are we going to see an end of masterly retreats? Something is wrong. Britain needs new ideas. She certainly needs a radical shake-up on the home front." Churchill needed a victory, and the sinking of *Bismarck* had given him one, or so he thought.[281]

At noon that day, the twenty-seventh, as he addressed the Commons, Bracken handed him a note. Churchill glanced at it, then told the House, "I have just received news that the *Bismarck* is sunk." He paused to read the mood in the chamber. "They seemed content," he later wrote.[282]

They were anything but. The Germans had lost a battleship; Churchill was losing Crete. Another evacuation—more flight than retreat—was under way. The British press did not, as it had with Greece, extend the benefit of the doubt. Opposition MPs, as they had throughout the month of May, expressed in the strongest possible terms their growing belief that Churchill and his coalition government lacked the ability to win the war. Defeat after defeat testified to Churchill's shortcomings as a strategic war leader. His status as the beloved and brilliant orator who had roused Englishmen was secure, but his reputation as warrior was not. He "is undergoing a slump in his popularity," Chips Channon noted in his diary, "and many of his enemies, long silenced by his personal popularity, are once more vocal."[283]

The leading critic was Leslie Hore-Belisha, who shortly after Churchill announced *Bismarck*'s demise, moved the discussion to the subject of Crete, telling the House that the debacle on Crete was due in large part to the virtual absence of anti-aircrafts guns on the island. He made a fair point. The defense preparation on Crete had been a sorry affair. Churchill, forewarned that Hore-Belisha intended to go after the anti-aircraft guns, was ready with his retort. It took the form of one of his favorite tactics, the bait and switch. Not for nothing had Churchill's dearest friend, F. E. Smith (the late Lord Birkenhead), once said that Churchill spent his entire life rehearsing his *impromptu* remarks. Churchill deflected Hore-Belisha's criticism by declaring that Hore-Belisha, in charge of the armed forces for almost three years under Chamberlain, had left them in "lamentable" shape. Hore-Belisha protested Churchill's slapping him with the appeasement label; he had in fact advised Chamberlain to modernize the army and introduce a draft. Churchill responded with bare knuckles. "I am not throwing all the blame for this on my right honourable Friend at all—certainly not—but I think it is only fair when he... sets himself up as arbiter and judge, and speaks so scornfully of the efforts of some others who have inherited his dismal legacy.... I think when he speaks this way... it is only fair to point out to him that he is one of the last people in this country to take this line." Among the mumbles and murmurs an MP raised his voice: "No recriminations."[284]

Churchill had not finished. "The honourable Gentleman said something about no recriminations, but extremely violent and hostile speeches have been spread about, doing a great deal of harm." He cut to the heart of the matter, as he saw it: "The question arises as to what would happen if you allowed the enemy to advance and overrun, without cost to himself, the most precious and valuable strategic points? Suppose we had never gone to Greece, and had never attempted to defend Crete? Where would the Germans be now? Might they not... already be masters of Syria and Iraq, and preparing themselves for an advance into Persia?... There is... this vitally important principle of stubborn resistance to the will of the enemy." The doctrine implied by some members that battles be chosen "only with a certainty of winning" and that without such certainty "you must clear out" flies against the "whole history of war" and "shows the fatal absurdity of such a doctrine." It was masterful. With an angry rush of rhetorical questions and brass asides, Churchill had transferred the egg from his face to the face of Hore-Belisha, who had played no part whatsoever in the debacle unfolding on Crete. Meanwhile, Churchill avoided the vital questions of why British factories limped along far below capacity. He never got around to explaining why the AA defense on Crete had been so weak, although the answer was self-evident—very few anti-aircraft batteries were available.[285]

Although correct in his admonition to Hore-Belisha that in battle there is no certainty of winning, Churchill, having for more than a year applied his own doctrine of giving aggressive battle when possible, had so far produced defeats. He had lamented to Colville the previous August that in his first three months as prime minister, "everything had gone wrong and he had nothing but disasters to announce." The disasters had only grown in the ensuing ten months. Nothing had worked against the Germans, or against the Americans for that matter. The effort to bring America in proved an ongoing chore and so far as fruitless as the military escapades. Churchill's moods began to take greater swings than usual, and more often. He expressed to Colville his dismay that the rearguard on Crete of 1,200 Royal Marines had been left behind. It was a shameful episode, he told Colville, the responsibility for which rested with all branches of the Middle East command. He began to suspect that his generals, even his cabinet, lacked a fighting spirit. He held them all responsible for the misfortunes.[286]

He was worn out. Three days after *Bismarck* went down, Clementine convinced him to take a few days' holiday at Chartwell. The house had been closed, the staff furloughed. It would be a spartan holiday. After dinner on the first night, Churchill lifted himself up from the table, took a step or two, lay down, and stretched out on the floor next to the table. There, while Clementine and Colville played backgammon, he proceeded to doze, unperturbed by the rattle of dice. The holiday was intended as a much-needed respite for Clementine as well as for Churchill. But the weather was cold, wet, and deplorable and Churchill was, in Colville's words, "restless," "brooding," and "perturbed." He left for London the next day. Always irritable around his staff, his peevishness even extended one morning to Clementine. He became, Colville wrote, "morose at lunch when he discovered Mrs. C had used some of his favorite honey, imported from Queensland, to sweeten the rhubarb." Churchill, who had always mumbled to his ginger cat, goldfish, and ducks, now mumbled to himself. His health was taking the same turn as his moods. The head cold of early March had hung on, come and gone and come again, and at one point had festered into bronchitis, in part because he treated it with snuff,* which only made matters worse.[287]

He displayed no generosity toward his colleagues, especially Eden, who, after months of diplomacy in the Balkans conducted at Churchill's behest, was now soundly criticized by the press and Parliament. Churchill mounted no defense of Eden. Wavell, too, became a favorite Churchillian target, as did the press, the Royal Navy, and the "highly strung and quarrelsome" de Gaulle. The anger extended to Roosevelt's habit (according to Churchill) of following American public opinion rather than leading it. Desperate for America to get in, and frustrated by its inertia, Churchill told Roosevelt, "I hope you forgive me if I say there is anxiety here.... What ever happens you may be sure we will fight on and I am sure we can at least save ourselves. But what good is that?"[288]

With his defeats mounting, he took to interfering in matters best left to others. "John Peck and I agree that the P.M. does not help the government machine to run smoothly," Colville noted in his diary. "He supplies drive and initiative, but he often meddles where he would better leave things alone and the operational side might profit if he gave it a respite." The Admiralty, after the *Bismarck* episode, would have agreed, as would have Wavell. Yet how could Churchill give respite to his subordinates when Hitler gave none to Britain? The Blitz from April into early May had been as bloody as the previous autumn, with Clydeside, Liverpool, Belfast, and London hit. Was the renewed bombing campaign a softening up before

---

* Sixty members of the Other Club had the previous autumn each contributed one pound sterling to buy Winston a solid gold snuffbox known to have been owned by Lord Nelson, one of Churchill's heroes. A dip into the gold box would, for a romantic, invoke an almost spiritual experience. Winston dipped often.

invasion? With their Mediterranean positions tottering, with Hitler still at peace with Stalin, and with the beneficent spring weather upon the Channel, Britons could only wait for the answer.[289]

As if to confirm their worst fears, during the final weeks of May, no bombs fell on London. A hush of suspense—as Churchill had termed the uneasy quiet before September 1939—again spread throughout the land. Other than the occasional German reconnaissance plane droning high overhead, the skies remained empty. The silence was unsettling. Beaverbrook told his fellow press magnate Lord Camrose that the Germans "would launch a very full attack against us... in the next few days." He emphasized "in the next few days" and added, "In my opinion invasion is imminent," and although some people thought otherwise, "I know I am right."[290]

The Luftwaffe did not return to London in late May, nor in early June, nor again in any massed formations for almost three years. Sporadic night raids took place in retaliation for Churchill's ongoing devastation of German cities, but the Luftwaffe was moving east, toward its jump-off points for a far greater, far more dangerous enterprise. Unknown to all the Englishmen who waited each night for the German raiders, the Blitz, part one, had ended on the terrible night of May 10.

On May 28, after pondering for weeks the benefits to Britain of a violent German-American incident on the high seas, Churchill pushed the Admiralty to make such an incident happen. With *Bismarck* sunk but *Prinz Eugen* still on the loose, Churchill informed the first sea lord in a "Most Secret" memo of just how he'd like the cards played. The search for *Prinz Eugen* "raises questions of the highest importance. It is most desirable that the United States play a part in this. It would be far better, for instance, that she [*Prinz Eugen*] should be located by a United States ship, as this might tempt her to fire upon that ship, thus providing the incident for which the United States Government would be so thankful." By orchestrating "a situation where *Prinz Eugen* is being shadowed by an American vessel, we have gone a long way to solve this largest problem."[291]

Although Roosevelt would not have been at all thankful for such an incident, the previous day he had taken a significant step in the direction of war. Moved by the distressing news of *Bismarck*'s raid, he went on the radio to declare an "emergency" in the Atlantic. He ordered the U.S. Navy Atlantic patrol zone pushed as far eastward as the security of American shipping demanded, even if that meant into the hottest war zones near Britain. Since Hitler's U-boats did not operate in the western Atlantic, Roosevelt, by pushing his patrol zones eastward, appeared to be inviting a fight. More than eighty-five million Americans heard their president, at that time the largest radio audience in U.S. history. The speech interrupted the Dodgers game at Ebbets Field, the only instance before or since when an American major league ball game was preempted by a live presidential announcement. "Ladies and gentlemen," intoned the Ebbets announcer, "the president of the United States." Something big was up. Roosevelt was savvy enough to know that the mere interruption of regular broadcasting, more than his actual message, would powerfully convey his point, which was that America was almost but not quite at war: "It is unmistakably apparent to all of us that, unless the advance of Hitlerism is forcibly checked now, the Western Hemisphere will be within range of the Nazi weapons of destruction." He had not volunteered America to do the forceful checking—England was doing that—but he made clear that Hitler must be checked. This was significant. He had moved America a step closer to the battle.[292]

On previous occasions Roosevelt, knowing the effect on Americans of the terrifying newsreels depicting London aflame, tried to instill a sense of urgency in his countrymen by claiming that German bombers had the range to bomb the American east coast. That was a stretch on Roosevelt's part; other than Focke-Wulf 200s, German bombers lacked the range to reach much beyond the halfway point over the Atlantic. Roosevelt knew that no "weapons of destruction" would anytime soon arrive by air. After proffering his terrifying but impossible aerial scenario, Roosevelt turned to the Atlantic. The goal of the Axis powers was world domination, Roosevelt proclaimed; to attain it they must take control of the seas, and to take control of the seas they must defeat Britain. "They could then have the power to dictate to the Western Hemisphere. No spurious argument, no appeal to sentiment, no false pledges like those given by Hitler at Munich, can deceive the American people into believing that he and his Axis partners would not, with Britain defeated, close in relentlessly on this hemisphere of ours." His words packed punch. "Yes, even our right of worship would be threatened. The Nazi world does not recognize any God except Hitler; for the Nazis are as ruthless as the Communists in the denial of God." Roosevelt was prepared to start shooting in defense of international law. The mere threat of attack within the expanded patrol zone would henceforth be considered an attack upon America.[293]

Roosevelt had spoken like a belligerent neutral, and Churchill read too much into the president's words. The problem for Roosevelt was not how to provoke an incident, but how to avoid one. In any case, *Prinz Eugen* sailed home unmolested by the Royal Navy and undetected by the Americans. Churchill would have to wait for another incident to push America into war.

As the troops who had fled Crete regrouped in Egypt, it became clear to Wavell that the entire Middle East command—navy, army, and air force—was so wounded that there really were no further offensive strategic gambles to take. It was time to dig in and await the Germans, from Syria to Tobruk, where the Australians already were dug in—dug in and cut off.[294]

Churchill thought otherwise, and told Wavell "everything must be centered on destroying the German forces in the Western Desert." The attack, code-named Battleaxe, was on for mid-June. Yet by the first of June not a single fully operational unit larger than a battalion remained of the 60,000 men—the best in his army—whom Wavell had ferried to Greece in March. Two entire divisions had vanished. More than 4,000 British and Anzac men had been killed, 8,000 wounded, and 21,000 captured in Greece and Crete, including the Royal Marines left behind on the beaches. Churchill later wrote that North Africa and the Balkans were but two theaters that formed part of a larger theater—the Mediterranean—which in turn was part of the European theater, with the Atlantic theater on one side and the Russian, after June 1941, on the other. Churchill stressed to the Commons that operations undertaken with the best of intentions within limited theaters (Norway, Greece, Crete, North Africa) that resulted in disasters did not necessarily spell the inevitability of defeat in the overall conflict. Yet as he had told Britons a year earlier, victory does not accrue from defeats and evacuations. Since Narvik, Britain had known nothing but defeats and evacuations.[295]

Early June brought one small victory, but at the expense of further denuding Wavell's army. Reports had arrived in Whitehall for weeks that the Vichy government in Syria was allowing Germans transit to Iraq. When in May, Vichy armed forces in Syria disputed the presence of Free French and British troops in Palestine and Transjordan, Churchill suggested to Wavell that he conduct a surprise attack on Vichy warships moored in Syrian ports, "killing without hesitation all who withstand us." In early June, to forestall a large and dangerous German presence in Syria, made all the more easy by the fall of Crete, Wavell's colonial and Free French troops wrenched Syria from Vichy France. Vichy and Free French forces fought their own little civil war for a week, but in the end, the British occupied Damascus. In a letter to Randolph, Churchill chimed that Syria was no longer "in the hands of the Frogs." De Gaulle protested that Churchill had in effect stolen Syria. Churchill ignored de Gaulle; in fact, he told Colville he was "sick to death" of the Frenchman. This was a sentiment he expressed with increasing regularity over the next four years.[296]

As the events of early June moved inexorably toward a climax in North Africa, both Rommel and Raeder saw that the supreme opportunity was at hand to crush the British in the eastern Mediterranean. Raeder drew up a naval plan to attack Alexandria and the Suez in consort with Rommel, who would push east from the Western Desert. Conceding to OKW the need to go ahead with Barbarossa—they could not persuade Hitler to postpone the Russian gambit, and knew it—they argued that a diversion to Egypt of less than one-quarter of the forces intended for the Soviet front would deal a fatal blow to the British in the Middle East. Churchill had been expecting just such a coordinated attack for more than a month, warning both Roosevelt and the War Cabinet that the loss of Egypt would be tantamount to the loss of the Home Island. It was a concern he voiced regularly, as his fortunes turned upon his "hinge of fate"—the Mediterranean.

On June 6, Hitler told his Wehrmacht commanders that during the coming battle in Russia, the commissars of the Soviet Union must all be killed. He added, "Any German soldier who breaks international law will be pardoned. Russia did not take part in the Hague convention and therefore has no rights under it." Hitler's hatred had overruled sound military strategy. At the very moment when he could kill the British in the Mediterranean, he rejected Rommel's and Raeder's plan to do so. He believed more important business needed to be conducted—the opening up of the *Ostland* to German soldier-farmers, and the business of securing that precious farmland by killing the racially impure, the vermin, who stood in his way—killing if need be all of the Slavs, Bolsheviks, commissars, judges, doctors, teachers, and especially, and first, all the Jews of Eastern Europe.[297]

Summer was approaching, and shipping losses now far outstripped Britain's capacity to replace them. That Churchill's War Plans staff and their American counterparts had been meeting and planning in Washington, in secret, since February was comforting, but it didn't save a single merchant ship. The Americans sent three battleships and the carrier *Yorktown* from their Pacific fleet to the Atlantic, which boded well for Churchill's Atlantic convoys. Unfortunately, Admiral Stark, who opposed these moves, kept these warships near America's east coast, which rendered them useless to the British. To the east, were Hitler to attack Russia, as Churchill believed he would, Britain might find itself better off overnight, but it would be short-lived if Hitler defeated Stalin quickly and decisively—which many in London and Washington thought a good bet. In that case, the Americans might rethink the wisdom of supporting Churchill, and Hitler at that point would have won his war, but for a final stroke against Britain. Always the possibility existed that some unexpected event, somewhere, might alter the American outlook, either to the betterment or detriment of Churchill's European strategy.

Meanwhile, Churchill needed a victory against the Germans, a strategic victory, something bigger than the colonial scuffles of Iraq, Syria, and East Africa. Although always eager to make mischief in Norway—where Hitler now kept seven divisions—Churchill saw his best opportunity in the same theater as Rommel saw his, North Africa. Churchill had shipped new tanks to Egypt at great risk in order that they could fight, and by all that was holy, Wavell had better fight with them. He did, though he knew that the British tanks carried puny cannons and tended to break down. Wavell, his forces depleted by the misadventures in Greece and Crete, launched his counterattack, Battleaxe, on June 15. Rommel, his forces arrayed before Tobruk, expected the attack, and was ready. The attack sputtered from the start. On the morning of June 17, according to Churchill, "everything went wrong." By that evening Battleaxe was seen for what it was, a total failure. The end came near the Halfaya pass, where German 88mm guns, secreted in the brush, held their fire until the British tanks came within spitting range. The tanks advanced no further; all but one were destroyed. The survivors dubbed the place Hellfire Pass. Again the British had to run. They fled eastward, *away* from their objective, Tobruk, sixty miles to the west and still surrounded. Wavell, flying to the front from Cairo, found his army in full retreat. Rommel had by then cut the British forces in two. Wavell had no choice but to concur with his commanders' advice to withdraw. Almost one thousand British troops were left behind, dead and captured. The horizon was speckled with thick black plumes of smoke from more than two hundred British tanks burning like tiny oil refineries. The door to Egypt was open, and Rommel stood astride the threshold.[298]

It was the end for Wavell. As the Army of the Nile fled for home, Churchill saw to it that it did so without Wavell. On June 21 he sent a cable to Wavell in which he lauded the general's "command and conduct of these armies, both in success and adversity," but said, "I feel however after the long strain you have borne, a new eye and a new hand are required in the most seriously menaced theater." Churchill needed a savior of the Nile, a Nelson who, as Nelson had promised his King, would hunt down and annihilate the enemy.[299]

Just six months earlier, Churchill had told his ministers, "In Wavell we have got a winner." Now Churchill needed a new winner, a leader who would take the fight to Rommel. His choice was General Sir Claude Auchinleck, commander in chief in India. He had been criticized by some for his conduct of the Norwegian campaign, but Norway had been an almost impromptu gambit, lacking in air and sea coordination. Churchill was now intent on giving his new commander everything he needed to wage war in the desert. Wavell, in turn, would relieve Auchinleck in India. Colville thought Wavell might go into a sulk and refuse the India posting. Churchill pondered that while they strolled that evening in the gardens. Merely firing Wavell, Churchill allowed, "would excite much comment and criticism." He did not want Wavell "hanging about in London living at his club." Happily, India was about as far from London as any place on the globe. When Dill predicted that Wavell would "use his pen" to write up his side of the story after the war, Churchill replied that "he could use his too, and would bet he sold more copies." Where Dill saw Wavell as the victim of Churchill's strategic folly, Churchill told Colville that he "never really had much confidence" in Wavell, who he had thought played slow for many of the same reasons Lincoln had said of General George McClellan, "He suffers from the slows." Both Lincoln and Churchill harbored grand hopes of victories that never came. Yet where Lincoln generously supplied McClellan (who essentially sat on his hands), Churchill, after reinforcing Wavell in 1940, had since stripped him of his forces.[300]

Dill disapproved of Wavell's dismissal, but he disapproved more of the appointment of Auchinleck. Wavell, he told Colville on the twenty-first, "has got twice Auchinleck's brain." Auchinleck's first significant—and most fateful—decision was to appoint Lieutenant General Alan Cunningham, brother of the admiral, to command the newly renamed and soon-to-be strengthened Eighth Army. Cunningham had led the armies that had swept the Italians from Somaliland. He was a fine infantryman, but he did not know tank warfare. The Chiefs of Staff wrought a final change to the Middle East command when they relieved Air Marshal Longmore and put his deputy, Arthur Tedder, in command. This proved to be one of the more fortuitous promotions of the entire war. Tedder believed in using his aircraft in close ground support of infantry and tanks, a view shared by Dickie Mountbatten who, on June 21, told Churchill, "No naval or military operation should be undertaken without strong air cover." Tedder had developed the tactic—"Tedder's carpet"—of laying down bombs in front of advancing troops. Armies supported by air moved faster and farther, as Rommel had shown at Longmore's expense. Tedder, in fact, allowed the army to direct his planes in tactical operations, something Longmore never countenanced. Still, Tedder shared one burden with Longmore: he did not have enough planes to make a difference, regardless of tactics.[301]

Churchill told Auchinleck that he expected him to attack, and in the next two months at that. Auchinleck replied that his forces would not be ready until the autumn, at the earliest. Churchill fumed but backed off. He had no choice. His Middle East forces were denuded to such an extent that the question was not when to attack, but how best to defend. Such were Churchill's contradictions. Stand up to the Old Man, as Auchinleck did, and he might back down; failure to stand up to him (Wavell) engendered his disrespect. He liked fighters.

The unfortunate business of Wavell having been addressed, a large gathering sat down to dinner at Chequers on the twenty-first: Clementine, Mary, Ambassador Gil Winant and his wife, Constance, Colville, Commander Tommy Thompson, and the Edens. Churchill took the floor—he rarely relinquished it—and mused upon Russia. Days earlier, Stafford Cripps had warned Eden that Russia was weak and could "not hold out against Germany for more than three or four weeks." Dill thought six or seven. Churchill, having perused his Enigma decrypts, announced at dinner "an attack on Russia is certain and Russia will surely be defeated." Still, he claimed he was prepared to go all out to help Stalin. Days earlier he had told his military chiefs that he expected the Germans to very soon bring the war to Russia, with the Baku oil fields and Ukrainian wheat as objectives, and that Britain should "take every advantage which such a conflict offered." The greatest advantage would be gained by giving the Russians the help they needed. Winant agreed, and told Churchill that the United States, too, would send Stalin everything it could. When Colville suggested that support for the Soviets might prove problematic given Churchill's longstanding loathing of all things Bolshevik, Churchill replied that if "Hitler invaded Hell he would at least make favorable reference to the Devil."[302]

After dinner Eden and Colville joined Churchill on his nocturnal prowls in the garden. Colville had noted in his journal a few days earlier the arrival of hot and sunny weather; rhododendrons in full bloom, the heat "tropical and heavy with the scent of flowers." Eden, holding forth on some topic, took a step backward and tumbled "head over heels into the deep ha-ha* and barbed wire fence at the edge of the lawn." The three of them guffawed and traipsed though the moonlit woodlands, on the solstice, like the ancients, and fortified no doubt like the ancients by strong spirits. It was a fine time to be alive, Churchill told Colville, adding, "You will live through many wars but will never have such an interesting time as you are having

---

* Ha-ha: a deep garden trench, one side vertical, the other gently sloping, designed to keep livestock out of gardens. Popular since the seventeenth century, the ha-ha allowed for views uncluttered by walls or fences.

now." The Old Man, who lately had lectured Colville on the various invasions of Russia throughout history, somehow failed to note that this week marked the anniversary of Napoleon's 1812 invasion of Russia.* The men did not retire until well into the earliest morning hours, Churchill not to be seen again until at least 8:00 A.M., for his instructions were clear: he was not to be awakened before eight for any reason other than the invasion of Britain.[303]

The skies were silent, empty of German aircraft, as they had been for the better part of a month. The ports slept unmolested, London untroubled.

One thousand miles to the east, the engines of more than 3,600 German panzers growled to life. Gunners eased high-explosive shells into the breeches of more than 7,200 pieces of artillery; officers stood ready, lanyards in hand. More than 600,000 mechanized vehicles, their engines idling, spewed exhaust that drifted low through fields and woodlands along a front that stretched almost nine hundred miles, from the Baltic, through occupied Poland, and south to the Black Sea. The weather held, pleasant and breezy. The German army of the east, the *Ostheer,* 153 divisions strong, was ready. More than three million assault pioneers and infantrymen (including fourteen divisions of reluctant Romanian infantry) crouched behind railway grades and in shallow ditches. Men checked their Mauser rifles and gave final nervous tugs to chin straps. They smoked a last ersatz cigarette or gulped down a final mouthful of ersatz coffee, for real tobacco and coffee had gone missing from their rations months earlier. If the ordeal before them went as planned, they would enjoy both again by Christmas, at home with their families, the war over, victory complete.[304]

A few miles to their rear, nearly a million pack horses—almost five thousand per division—grazed on the infinite sea of grass. They were harnessed to wagons full of rations, shells, tents, and clothing. The metallic ring of bits and buckles carried on the breeze, a familiar morning song to young country boys and old infantrymen. Farther still to the rear, companies of *Einsatzgruppen,* SS killers, waited near their trucks for the word to go forth, to carry out their orders and their glorious destiny as codified by

* Goebbels, in his diary, cites June 21 as the anniversary. Hitler, to avoid the obvious comparison, later held June 23 to be the anniversary. Historian Will Durant places Napoleon at the Russian frontier—the Niemen River—on June 23. It was at the Niemen that Napoleon and Czar Alexander five years earlier had pledged their friendship for life.

Jodl on Hitler's order: to kill commissars, Jews, intellectuals, Bolsheviks of any age, and nationalists of any persuasion. Farthest to the rear, in the Reich Chancellery, Adolf Hitler paced, and waited.[305]

Seven hundred miles behind the Soviet lines, Joseph Stalin took his rest at the Kremlin. So sanguine was Stalin concerning his relations with Hitler that he had weeks earlier ordered Soviet forces to leave their concrete-reinforced and entrenched defensive positions to take up new positions farther to the east. He did so in order to reassure Hitler that Soviet troop deployments were not meant to be provocative and to show that he trusted Hitler. During those weeks more than eighty German reconnaissance flights took place over Soviet territory. They were dismissed by Berlin as a British ruse intended to create tensions between Germany and its friend Russia. Stalin bought the explanation.

Throughout the spring Stalin had received detailed intelligence reports about Germany's planned treachery from numerous sources, including the Americans in early June and his own chief of intelligence, who months before the invasion proffered the prescient scenario of a German three-pronged attack upon Russia almost exactly like the one that was about to unfold. Nothing if not consistent, Stalin ignored the warnings as he had Churchill's warnings of April and early June. When on June 15, Stalin's best spy in Tokyo, Richard Sorge, informed the Kremlin of the exact date of Barbarossa, Stalin, distrustful of spies, dismissed the intelligence. As for his trade agreements with Germany, the head of the German War Ministry later wrote: "The Russians executed their deliveries up to the eve of the attack." The Soviets had deployed more than thirty-five new divisions near the border during the spring, but again, in order to not provoke Hitler, they were not put on alert. Just after midnight on the twenty-second, a German deserter told his Soviet captors that the invasion was to be launched at 4:00 A.M. The report made its way to the Kremlin, where it was dismissed out of hand. Two hours before dawn, after phone lines were cut, Soviet commanders were finally allowed to place their troops on full alert. Just before 4:00 A.M. more than 2,600 German Messerschmitts, Stukas, and Junkers medium bombers lifted off from airfields in Poland, East Prussia, and Romania, their departures timed such that they would overfly the infantry and artillery exactly at dawn. In the Wilhelmstrasse in Berlin, Ribbentrop was curtly informing Soviet ambassador Vladimir Dekanozov that German troops in Poland and on the Soviet border were at that instant taking "military countermeasures."[306]

Minutes later, as the German aircraft screamed overhead, German artillery opened the greatest cannonade in all history. Along the entire line, almost three million German troops lunged forward. The eruption and flashes of the great guns would have been visible from space, but mankind was twenty years distant from gaining any such heavenly perspective. In those few seconds and within the choking clouds of cordite, the Nazi-Soviet friendship pact disappeared.

The Germans were arrayed in three Army Groups—North, Center, and South—commanded by field marshals Wilhelm Ritter von Leeb, Bock, and Rundstedt, under the overall command of Field Marshal Walther von Brauchitsch. Each group sat astride a historic invasion route into European Russia. Army Group North would ply the Baltic coast, with Leningrad as its ultimate objective. Army Group Center would follow Napoleon's path to Minsk and onward to Moscow. The southern group would strike toward the breadbasket of Russia, the Ukraine; its route demarcated to the north by the impassable Pripet Marshes—about the size of Indiana or Portugal—and to the south by the ridge of the Carpathian Mountains.

Arrayed against the Germans were almost three million Russians, 120 Soviet divisions out of a total national force of 230. The Soviet infantry was backed up by the world's largest, though mostly untested, air force—10,000 fighter aircraft—and almost 24,000 tanks of mixed quality, although the new, fast, and deadly T-34 was scheduled to roll off Russian assembly lines at the rate of 1,700 per month—*if* the factories survived the German onslaught. Sir John Keegan wrote that from the standpoint of matériel, "Stalin the warlord stood on equal, perhaps superior footing to Hitler." Yet almost five hundred of Stalin's generals had been promoted to that rank only the year before in an attempt to replenish the ranks thinned by Stalin's murderous purges. The new generals were all untested. Worse, they and the millions of troops they led were peacefully asleep at their posts when the attack came. Churchill, too, was fast asleep, as was Stalin. Stalin's lack of preparedness, and the immensity of the surprise that overtook him, indicates he had been in hibernation for quite some time. The Bear's somnolence, Churchill later wrote, was astounding, given the intelligence available to him: "So far as strategy, policy, foresight, and competence are arbiters, Stalin and his commissars showed themselves at this moment the most completely outwitted bunglers of the Second World War." Almost ten million Russian soldiers and at least fifteen million Russian civilians would pay with their lives in the next four years for Stalin's bungling.[307]

It was a "marvelous morning," Harold Nicolson told his diary on the twenty-second, "with the smell of roses, hay, and syringa in the air." If the day proved quiet, Jock Colville planned to steal some time to traipse the countryside. It was not to be. Just after dawn, a phone call from the

Foreign Office awoke Colville with the news. Heeding Churchill's standing order, he waited until just past 8:00 to notify the prime minister of the attack. Churchill greeted the news with a grim smile and instructed Colville to "tell the B.B.C. I will broadcast at 9 to-night." So great was his initial joy at the news that he dispatched his valet to Eden's bedroom, bearing a large cigar on a silver platter, and a message: "The Prime Minister's compliments and the German armies have invaded Russia."[308]

Harold Nicolson, upon hearing the news, told his diary that he was "not so optimistic.... And if, as is likely, Hitler defeats Russia in three weeks, then the road to the oil is open, as also the road to Persia and India." Gil Winant at first thought the news was a "put-up job between Hitler and Stalin," an opinion Churchill and his secretaries (out of the ambassador's earshot) "laughed... to scorn." The laughter was born more of pure relief than real scorn.[309]

Days earlier, burdened by defeats, his sensitivities scuffed by the increasing backbiting of backbenchers, Churchill ruminated over the fate of Tobruk's garrison and the possible fate of Egypt while moping about his Chartwell gardens in the company of his yellow cat. He apologized to the cat during lunch for the absence of cream, the cat being seated in the chair to Churchill's right. That week he told Eden that he now "wore the medals" of the Dardanelles, Narvik, Dunkirk, Greece, and Crete. On the automobile journey to Chartwell, Churchill stopped along the coast to steal a glimpse of France, but as if to underscore Britain's isolation, haze hid the Continent.[310]

Everything changed with Hitler's betrayal of Stalin. A year to the day after the French signed their armistice, Churchill looked eastward and, haze or no, beheld salvation, *if,* that is, the Russians could avoid defeat. The logic of the situation was compelling. Russia defeated would likely lead to Britain defeated. But Russia supported by Britain might buy enough time for the feet-dragging Americans to produce the tools Churchill needed to keep up the fight. Were America to extend Lend-Lease to Stalin, so much the better. Russia victorious was altogether another matter. The ideological enemy of twenty years would not likely change its stripes after the war, but Hitler's gambit had rendered that question, for the time being, moot. Thus, without a War Cabinet policy in place to address the morning's turn of events—let alone a strategy to implement such a policy—and after only a moment's thought, and no hesitation, Churchill made his decision. He would embrace his new fighting partner.

"Ally" seemed an inappropriate moniker given Stalin's brutal history of pogroms and mass murder. The man, in fact, was a monster. His collectivization of Ukrainian farms in the early 1930s resulted in the death by starvation of at least five million peasants, and the execution of thousands more for the crime of hoarding state property—seed for the next year's grain crop. His Siberian gulags were packed with almost two million prisoners, mostly political, who were worked to death building dams, railroads, and canals. Mass graves lay scattered around Moscow, full of murdered Russian Orthodox priests, university professors, doctors, lawyers, Trotskyites, and other enemies of the state. Churchill, for more than a decade after the Russian Revolution, had considered the Soviet Union to be "the moral foe of civilized freedom"—until Hitler came along. Yet where Hitler was all talk during the mid-1930s, Stalin was all action. By the time he invaded eastern Poland in 1939, he had, in his own provinces and among his own people, established his bona fides as the butcher of the century, perhaps of all time. Churchill, since 1917, had striven to destroy Communist Russia, to "strangle at its birth" this "sullen, sinister state." Now the Soviets and British, Stalin and Churchill, battled a common enemy. Churchill that evening would try to convince Britain—and himself—that old differences must be put aside. The effort would tax even his oratorical skills, for in the eyes of fully half his countrymen, the godless Joseph Stalin was more fundamentally evil than Adolf Hitler.[311]

Stafford Cripps came for lunch that day, June 22, during which Churchill baited the ambassador by calling the Russians "barbarians" and offering that "not even the slightest thread connected communists to the very basest type of humanity." Colville recalled that Cripps took it "in good part and was amused." Churchill was roused. Reversing his prediction of the previous day, that Russia would soon lose, he offered five-hundred-to-one odds that Russia would still be fighting, indeed, "fighting victoriously," two years hence. He adjourned to his study to prepare his speech and remained there for the rest of the afternoon and into the early evening. It was a lengthy speech, an address at once lyrical, poetic, and powerful, promising the free world redemption and Hitler destruction. It was an address that no modern committee of speechwriters could produce, for Churchill painted with his words, creating images that, like all great art, become more real than the scenes depicted, and more evocative than the sum of his grammatical strokes and rhetorical shadings. Colville recalled that, as with his paintings, Churchill made revisions and added final touches to the speech, right up to nine o'clock, the hour of delivery. And as with his paintings, his intent was to challenge his listeners' imaginations and not merely their intellect.[312]

His pace was measured. The invasion of Russia, he declared, was one of the "climacterics of the war," wherein all of Hitler's "usual formalities of perfidy were observed with scrupulous technique." He tagged Hitler "a monster of wickedness, insatiable in his lust for blood and plunder" and "a bloodthirsty guttersnipe" who found satisfaction "grinding up human lives and trampling down the homes and rights of millions of men." The Führer's bloodlust, moreover, "must be fed, not only with flesh but with oil," an oblique way of saying that were Hitler to steal enough Soviet oil, just imagine the places he would go. And although he did not employ the phrase "unconditional surrender," he set out his terms of war, and of peace, which could only be termed unequivocal and unconditional: "We are resolved to destroy Hitler and every vestige of the Nazi regime." And: "We will never parley, we will never negotiate with Hitler or any of his gang." Britain would take the fight to Hitler on the land, in the air, and on the sea until "we have rid the earth of his shadow and liberated its peoples from his yoke." He took a few moments to remind his listeners that "no one has been a more consistent opponent of communism than I have for the last twenty-five years," but said that "all this fades away before the spectacle that is unfolding." Without naming Stalin, he declared that the past "with its crimes, its follies, and its tragedies flashes away." And then he treated of the struggle in the style of a perfectly scored symphony, where the spaces between the notes carry as much weight as the notes themselves:

> I see the ten thousand villages of Russia, where the means of existence was wrung so hardly from the soil, but where there are still primordial human joys, where maidens laugh and children play. I see advancing upon all this in hideous onslaught the Nazi war machine, with its clanking, heel-clicking, dandified Prussian officers....I see also the dull, drilled, docile, brutish masses of the Hun soldiery plodding on like a swarm of crawling locusts....Behind all this glare, behind all this storm, I see that small group of villainous men [who launched] this cataract of horrors upon mankind.

This was not a class war, he offered, but a war to rescue mankind from tyranny, fought "without distinction of race, creed, or party." And lest after such a performance Britons might still hesitate to fight and die for Stalin and his creedless Communists, he brought the Soviet battle home to Britons by declaring it "no more than a prelude to an attempted invasion of the British Isles." He closed with a message to both Britons and Americans: "The Russian danger is therefore our danger, and the danger of the United States."[313]

He had more than put in a kind word for the devil; he had rehabilitated him and outfitted him with wings and a halo. An old Balkan proverb (one of Roosevelt's favorites) proclaimed that it is permissible to walk hand in hand with Satan when crossing a bridge over a chasm. Churchill had just made the transit.[314]

Harold Nicolson thought the address "a masterpiece." Although

Churchill conveyed the sense that Russia might fall—and China, Europe, and India—"he somehow leaves us with the impression that we are going to win this war." Yet Nicolson believed the Russians, "incompetent and selfish... will be bowled over in a touch."[315]

Churchill again had displayed his genius for inspirational rhetoric, but a transformation of sorts was taking place. Sir John Keegan pegs the invasion of Russia as the moment when Churchill's "campaign of bold words" began to give way "to a battle of brute facts." The real killing—in numbers even Stalin could not yet imagine—had begun.[316]

Hitler's astounding betrayal of his partnership with the Russians paralyzed Stalin and many of his senior commanders. Soon after the attack began, a field officer used his radio to inform his superiors that his unit was under fire. He asked, "What shall we do?" He was told, "You must be insane," and reprimanded for making the call on an open frequency. Not until the Germans had advanced twenty miles did Stalin begin to grasp the situation, and not until late in the evening did the Soviet government inform its citizens that Germany had invaded the Motherland. Molotov, not Stalin, made the announcement. No official reaction to Churchill's speech came out of Moscow. Stalin remained in his dacha for a week, stunned, as Hitler's three army groups struck two hundred miles into Soviet territory. When Molotov encouraged him to return to the Kremlin, Stalin replied, "Lenin left us a great legacy, and we, his heirs, have fucked it all up."[317]

Such was his shock that Stalin did not broadcast any message to his nation until July 3. When he spoke, listeners heard the tremulousness in his voice and the clinking of a glass as he refreshed his throat. By then Finland had joined the German ranks and the front extended a further six hundred miles, from the Baltic to Petsamo on the Arctic Ocean. The Finns attacked the northern flank as the Romanians did at the southern, while the Germans mauled the center.

With the Führer's turn eastward, the threat to Britain of invasion vanished—for the time being. In his memoirs Churchill captured his joy at hearing of Hitler's foray with two words: "Eastward ho!" Yet on the morning of the invasion, his grin had been one of grim determination, for he understood that unless the Russians became the first Europeans to keep up the fight against the Wehrmacht, the consequences for Britain would, in the end, prove fatal. The Russians did not have to defeat the Germans (they could not), but they *had* to keep up the fight. As events developed on the Russian front over the next several months, Churchill stood firm on that premise. At an August meeting of the War Cabinet, he offered that were "Germany to beat Russia to a standstill and the United States had made no further advance toward entry into the war, there was a danger that the war might turn against us." "Standstill" meant stasis, which next to an outright Russian defeat was what Churchill most feared. "Standstill" meant breathing room for Hitler, but not for England. Weeks later Churchill telegrammed Roosevelt to share his concern that "as soon as Hitler stabilizes the Russian front, he will begin to gather perhaps fifty or sixty divisions in the west for the invasion of the British Isles." Indeed, Hitler had strong forces in the west, although the Luftwaffe had gone east, and the French ports contained few invasion barges. But that could change.[318]

Churchill, therefore, told his ministers that Britain must remain prepared to repel an invasion. He did so in part because the collateral benefit of preparation was the creation of forces that he could deploy elsewhere. Two memos that Churchill sent to his ministers days after Hitler's betrayal of Stalin capture the workings of his mind. The first reduces his invasion strategy to its essence. In it he told Dill and Ismay that September 1 would be a good date to announce that anti-invasion defenses had been brought to the highest efficiency. He added, "It would be necessary to make it clear...that meanwhile no vigilance is to be relaxed. On the contrary, a note of invasion alarm should be struck, and everybody set to work with redoubled energy." Then, to the real root of the matter: "This however, must not prevent the dispatch of necessary reinforcements to the Middle-East."[319]

The second memo captures the collision of logic, intuition, and imagination that made Churchill who he was (and regularly confused his generals, and was beginning to confuse his American friends). In it, he told Dill and secretary of state for war David Margesson that the success of German parachutists on Crete raised a new and disturbing specter: "We have to contemplate the descent from the air of perhaps a quarter of a million parachutists, glider-borne or crash-landed airplane troops." This was the aeronautical equivalent of his outrageous claim the previous autumn that 500,000 German troops could be carried to England by ship, in a single sailing. Churchill did not know the exact numbers of German parachutists killed on Crete, but he knew that of a force of around nine thousand, about half had been killed; of the five hundred Ju 52s that carried them, about half had been destroyed. This, to capture three airfields. The Ju 52, when configured for civilian duties, carried seventeen passengers. Lufthansa, the German airline, flew Ju 52s; Hitler's private plane had been one, until he switched to a Focke-Wulf 200. Configured for military use, the Ju 52 could carry about a dozen parachutists. Thus, at least 21,000 Ju 52s would be required in order to land 250,000 parachutists on England's scores of airfields in a single drop. Germany had built only about 3,000 of the aircraft since its introduction in 1931. But Churchill could not rest on the assumption that Hitler lacked such a massive air fleet; perhaps the Führer had been building airplanes in some huge, secret underground factory. Churchill's solution was to order that every one of the RAF's 500,000 support personnel, "without exception," should be armed "with a rifle, a tommy gun, a pistol, a pike or a mace" in order to greet the enemy when he came. If the enemy did *not* come, Churchill would be in possession of 500,000 weapons—made in America—that he could someday issue to his armies, when the day came that they ventured back into Europe.[320]

That day, he told Roosevelt in July, would come in 1943, after subjecting Germany and Italy to naval blockade and "ceaseless and ever growing air bombardment. These measures may themselves produce an internal convulsion or collapse." That statement captures the essence of Churchill's war strategy, and his faith in airpower. But plans should be made, Churchill added, to land "armies of liberation when opportunity is ripe." Those landings, in turn, would be spearheaded by thousands of tanks off-loaded from the special tank ships Churchill was asking Roosevelt to build. In coming weeks Churchill made clear where he envisioned those landings would someday take place: in Norway and French North Africa. In the meantime, Churchill told Roosevelt, he intended to bring his tanks to Cyrenaica, to battle Germans and Italians. Churchill's telegrams to Roosevelt in the weeks after the Russian invasion foreshadow a disagreement over strategic priorities that would bedevil the Anglo-American partnership for the next three years. George Marshall and his military advisers did not contest Churchill's call for tanks, especially as Churchill was fighting Hitler, where the Americans were not. "The tools" were Churchill's to use as he saw fit. Marshall and his planning staff had for months been forming a strategy in the event that America's civilian leadership sent the U.S. army into war. Marshall's preferred strategy was simplicity itself: Carry American armies to England, and from there take them to Europe by the shortest and straightest line, across the Channel and into France. This was the direct approach, versus Churchill's indirect approach, which was coming now into focus.[321]

But the invasion of Russia had changed the calculus of tanks and their deployment. Stalin needed tanks, now. For that reason, Churchill demanded that Britain must do for Russia what Roosevelt was doing for Britain—supply the tools, not only because to do so was the best way to help Russia, but because it was the best way to keep the wolf away from Britain. He knew just the man to produce the tools. Within the week, Beaverbrook took over the Ministry of Supply, which together with the ministries of Aircraft Production and Labour formed a three-legged beast that addressed the matériel needs of the armed forces. Immediately the Beaver ordered more factories built, more night shifts, and instilled in the department a sense of urgency he found lacking. The ministry dealt mostly with the army. When Churchill wanted bombers in January, the Beaver had delivered. Now Churchill wanted tanks, for Stalin, who Beaverbrook believed could survive if reinforced rapidly and heavily enough. Beaverbrook produced the tanks and in coming months persuaded the Americans to produce more, thousands more. "Some people take drugs," Churchill told Colville. "I take Max."[322]

By mid-July Stalin had recovered enough of his composure to request that Churchill establish "a front against Hitler in the West [France] and in the North [the Arctic]." By such maneuvers, he argued, "the military situation of the Soviet Union, as well as Great Britain, would be considerably improved." Then, either because he was still in shock or simply ignorant of British public opinion, Stalin proclaimed that such a front "would be popular with the British Army as well as the whole population of southern England."[323]

Thus began Stalin's crusade for a second front. Within weeks he enlarged upon his request by asking Churchill "to create in the present year a second front somewhere in the Balkans or France, capable of drawing away from the Eastern front thirty to forty [German] divisions." Stalin asked for 400 aircraft and 500 tanks *per month,* twice the quantities Britain had available, along with the delivery within three weeks of 30,000 tons of aluminum, enough to build more than 10,000 fighter planes. Then, Stalin offered, "It seems to me that Great Britain could without risk land in Archangel twenty-five to thirty divisions" in order to establish "military collaboration" between the Soviets and British on Russian soil. Churchill not only lacked the transports to dispatch thirty divisions—more than 450,000 men—to Russia, he lacked the divisions. Thanks to Churchill's "invasion scare" re-armament program, thirty just happened to be the number of combat-ready divisions Churchill had in England that summer. Stalin wanted them all.

Stalin's request, Churchill later wrote, was "almost incredible," and indicated "a man thinking in terms of utter unreality." Cripps, always eager to help the Soviets, suggested that Churchill display his solidarity by sending just a few British divisions to fight alongside the Russians. Churchill attached much irony to the pleas of Cripps and Stalin, because just the previous year there had *been* a second front, in France. And just three months before Hitler smashed into Russia, Churchill had pushed into *another* front, the Balkans, thereby buying Stalin several more weeks to take defensive steps. But Stalin, secure in his pact with Hitler, chose to sit on the fence as events played out in France and in the Balkans. Now, he had no fence to sit on; the Wehrmacht had obliterated it. Churchill told Cripps as much after Cripps called for a "super-human effort" to help the Russians: "It is not our fault that Hitler was enabled to destroy Poland before turning his forces against France, and to destroy France before turning them against Russia." As for any "super-human effort" "rising superior to space, time, and geography, unfortunately these attributes are denied us."[324]

When Cripps implied that the Soviets justly distrusted the British given Churchill's refusal to send men to Russia or invade France, Churchill—still fuming over Cripps's failure to deliver his April warning to Stalin—sent a scathing reply: "We have acted with absolute honesty. We have done our very best to help them at the cost of...exposing ourselves...when the spring invasion season comes." To send two or three divisions to Russia "would be silly" and result in those troops being "cut to pieces as a symbolic sacrifice." The Soviets, he told Cripps, had "brought their own fate upon themselves when...they let Hitler loose on Poland, and so started the war." That the Russian government would "accuse us of trying to gain advantage...at their expense...leaves me quite cold. If they harbor suspicions it is only because of the guilt and self-reproach in their own hearts."[325]

There would be no second front anytime soon. Churchill could not comply with Stalin's wishes, and the Chiefs of Staff would not, even had Churchill been so inclined. It was simply unthinkable, Churchill informed Cripps, to contemplate a return to France, where "the bloody repulse... that would be sustained" would result in "the loss of the Battle of the Atlantic and the starvation and ruin of the British Isles." The British Expeditionary Force had been swept from France in 1940 and again just weeks earlier from Greece and Crete. Churchill could do no more. Hitler, Churchill informed both Cripps and Stalin, had "forty divisions in France alone." As well, "the whole coast has been fortified with German diligence...and bristles with cannon, wire, pill-boxes, and beach mines." Any British invasion "would only lead to fiascos" and "would be over without them [the Germans] having to move or before they could move a single unit from your [Russian] front." As for a new Balkan front, it had taken seven *weeks* to land just two unopposed divisions in Greece. The best he could do, he told Stalin, was to send submarines to patrol the Arctic, and dispatch a few fighter squadrons to Murmansk, the vital and northernmost ice-free port in the Soviet Union.[326]

To the Chiefs of Staff he advocated less traditional means of helping the Russians. He told them to "make Hell while the sun shines." Thus Churchill sent his beloved commandos out to ignite Norwegian warehouses and blow up Italian bridges. The results were so paltry—one or two Germans captured for three or four British casualties—that Churchill demanded the cabinet keep all news of commando results away from the press. If the Continent was ablaze, it was at the bidding of Hitler, not Churchill. And Stalin was on his own, alone with his hopes, as had been Churchill while England burned.[327]

By September, Harriman, Beaverbrook, and Hopkins had made their way to Moscow to coordinate a rescue effort. Lend-Lease was Moscow bound. "You can trust him [Hopkins] absolutely," Churchill cabled Stalin. "He is your friend and our friend." Churchill, though disinclined to sacrifice British troops in France, nonetheless was eager to prove himself Stalin's friend. When the service chiefs objected that "not a rowing boat, rifle, or Tiger Moth could be spared [for Stalin] without . . . grave risk" to England, he told them he expected all branches to give equally, and generously. For the remainder of the year, he made up the middle link in a three-man bucket brigade. He snatched from Roosevelt the munitions he sorely needed, dipped into his own stocks of tanks and guns, and passed everything along to Stalin via Arctic convoys and Iranian railroads. To further encourage Stalin, he promised that a "terrible winter of bombing lies before Germany. No one has yet had what they are going to get."[328]

Stalin was unmoved. He had twice, while pleading for a second front, reminded Churchill that Hitler had already dealt Russian soldiers and civilians more terrible blows than Churchill proposed to inflict on Germany a few months hence. The Red Army, not Churchill's promise of a "terrible winter," was all that stood between Hitler and Moscow. To encourage his armies to fight, Stalin proclaimed his policy regarding surrender. Up to a point, his words echo Churchill's when Egypt appeared threatened: "Those falling into encirclement are to fight to the last and try to reach their own lines." Yet where Churchill declared that to surrender if not surrounded and unarmed would result in dishonor, Stalin declared, "Those who prefer to surrender are to be destroyed by any means, while their families are to be deprived of all state allowances and assistance." Lest anyone doubt him, when Army Group Center overran Minsk just six days into the invasion, Stalin recalled to Moscow the general in charge of the city's defense, Dmitry Pavlov. Pavlov and his top generals dutifully reported to the Kremlin, where they were tried, found guilty of incompetence, and summarily shot. Under Stalin, harshness in defense of the homeland took on new and unimaginable meaning. When he heard that the Germans were using tens of thousands of old men, women, and children as human shields, pushed along in front of the Wehrmacht as it approached Leningrad, and that the Bolshevik defenders of Leningrad held their fire for fear of injuring the civilians, he announced, "I think that if there are such people among the Bolsheviks, then they should be destroyed first, because they're more dangerous than the German Fascists."

The citizens of Minsk might have disagreed; the Germans massacred thousands when the city surrendered in early July. From the Baltic to the Black Sea a war of annihilation had overtaken the dairy farms, granaries, small factories, and mills of Mother Russia. The peoples of White Russia, the Ukraine, and the Baltic states now found themselves crushed between two unforgiving armies—the largest in history—commanded by two unforgiving warlords.

Churchill could not publicly excoriate Stalin for his myopia. He focused his anger on another blunder, one quite minor in the greater scheme of things. He just could not let go of Cripps's bungling of the April telegram in which he had warned Stalin. Cripps's delay roiled the Old Man well into the autumn, when far bigger fish were in need of frying. It was simply too much when he learned in the fall that Stalin had told Beaverbrook that he could not recall "when he was warned." A half year had passed since Cripps's error, and the Germans were by then hurtling toward the outskirts of Leningrad and Moscow. Stalin's lack of concern when given credible warning was frustrating enough, but Cripps's effrontery in sitting on his warning had infuriated Churchill for months. He told Eden, then in Moscow, that Cripps must bear "a great responsibility for his obstinate, obstructive handling of this matter." Had Cripps "obeyed his instructions, it is more than possible that some kind of relationship would have been constructed between me and Stalin."[329]

That was unlikely. Stalin's ongoing suspicion of Britain, not Cripps's blunder, stood in the way of a relationship. In July 1940, Cripps had conveyed to Stalin Churchill's warning of German designs in the East, which Stalin ignored and, incredibly, had actually passed on to Berlin in order to demonstrate his loyalty to Hitler. Cripps's tenure as ambassador was marked by a measured and perceptive approach to the Soviet regime, which he rather admired. This was not a surprise, given his political persuasions, too far left even for his Labour Party. Cripps was a lawyer, considered by many the best in Britain. But Churchill cared little for the man's legal talents; Cripps lacked the conviviality that Churchill desired in his companions. The ambassador came across as austere if not gloomy. He was both deeply religious and a vegetarian, a combination that had earned him around Whitehall the monikers of "Christ and Carrots" and "Stifford Crapps." Years later, espying Cripps walking past (just out of earshot), Churchill offered, "There but for the grace of God goes God." Yet many in Churchill's circle considered Cripps's talents wasted in Moscow and believed he could better serve the government in a post where his great intellect could be brought to bear. Churchill dismissed that notion, calling Cripps "a lunatic in a country of lunatics and it would be a pity to move him."[330]

The war had shifted east on June 22, and in so doing lowered the price

Britons would pay in coming months to preserve their homeland. The price Russians would pay was incalculable, but Stalin let it be known that price was no object. Churchill believed that Stalin intended to fight to the end. To read of his demands on his people, and his threats to those who did not embrace the sacrifice required, is to shudder, in part because his show trials, his pogroms, and his gulags were all manifestations of who he was—a stone-cold killer. He had murdered to gain power, and murdered to keep it. No colleague ever wrote of Uncle Joe, as Churchill's colleagues wrote of him, that he was all bluff and bluster. Stalin possessed none of Churchill's eloquence, nor anything that could be called nobility of character. He saw no need to inspire his people, no need to ask his people to give their blood, toil, sweat, and tears. Yet, whatever their myriad differences in personality, politics, and spirituality, and they were profound, in Stalin Churchill had found an ally who, like himself, was willing to kill as many Germans as it took to defeat Hitler. Over the next three years, many in Washington and London came to believe that Stalin, like the Bolsheviks in the Great War, would quit if he could find a satisfactory way out. Churchill never believed that.

Time magazine had just days before Hitler smashed into Russia noted under the headline of UNMURDEROUS WAR, the "most extraordinary thing about World War Two is not its speed, not its extent, not its tactical scope—but its relative unmurderousness." This proved a colossal mischaracterization when, within four weeks, more soldiers and civilians perished by fire and steel in Russia than had been killed by any manner of weapons in all the previous twenty-two months of war in all of the European, Mediterranean, and African theaters. And it was only the beginning.[331]

Stalin needed British and American help to make up his losses in matériel. Given that during the first seven weeks after the German invasion, only five American bombers were delivered to Russia, his prospects appeared bleak. Yet American bombers did not hold the key to Stalin's survival. Millions of Soviet foot soldiers, armed and clothed and fed by America and Britain, and backed up by thousands of tanks, held the key. Stalin understood attrition. His war would be fought hand to hand and street by street for as long as Soviet soldiers stood. If they could buy enough time, Churchill and Stalin had between them the makings of a lethal one-two punch. Churchill would one day possess enough airpower—supplied by American industrial muscle—to destroy German cities and every person within. "We will make Germany a desert," he had told Colville, "yes, a desert." Stalin, meanwhile, had the manpower to kill German soldiers indefinitely, if, that is, he and Churchill could buy enough time. America seemed to be edging closer to the conflict, yet Churchill had warned Harry Hopkins early in the year that in spite of re-armament plans, America was at least eighteen months—more likely two years—away from full production. That would put America in fighting trim by mid-1942 at the earliest, a half year too late were Hitler to finish off Stalin by Christmas 1941.[332]

On July 20 a dinner was held at Chequers in honor of Harry Hopkins, who had arrived a few days earlier by way of a B-17 bomber. Hopkins brought smoked hams, cigars, and pledges of support from his boss, but carried no invitation for the meeting with Roosevelt that Churchill so craved. That alone would have been enough to put the P.M. in a funk, yet as frustrated as he was with Roosevelt's inertia regarding a face-to-face meeting, he knew he could voice no such thoughts in front of Harry. He could, however, safely rail at the usual subjects—Mussolini and Hitler—and the need for revenge, and he did just that. He and Hopkins sat up chatting until almost 3:00 A.M. on the twenty-first, Churchill as usual doing most of the talking. Colville recalled, "When Winston started on what he was going to do to the Nazi leaders after the war—and the Nazi cities during it—Hopkins said that he—Winston—only read the bits of the Bible that suited him and they were drawn from the Old Testament."[333]

On July 24, Churchill received the invitation he had sought for so long. "Harry Hopkins came into the garden of Downing Street and we sat together in the sunshine. Presently he said that the president would like very much to have a meeting with me in some lonely bay or other." Hopkins telephoned the president. Churchill was so enthused that when he got on the line, he mentioned "a certain rendezvous" before realizing that the line was not secure. He was mortified, Colville wrote. Mortified, but elated.[334]

The time and place of the meeting—code-named Riviera—were agreed upon: sometime around August 9 or 10, at Argentia, Newfoundland, a small fishing village on Placentia Bay. By August 5 newspapers on both sides of the Atlantic, having noted the disappearance of both Churchill and Roosevelt from their capitals, concluded a secret meeting was about to take place, somewhere in the northwest Atlantic. The United Press called it a "sea tryst." Although Churchill's and Roosevelt's staffs maintained absolute secrecy, the boys of the press knew better, or thought they did. American reporters believed they saw their president on the deck of *Potomac* on the fifth when the presidential yacht steamed through Buzzards Bay, under the Boston & Maine railroad trestle, and north through the Cape Cod Canal. But the man wrapped in a shawl and waving from his deck chair was a Secret Service agent. Before dawn that morning, off

Nantucket, Roosevelt had transferred from *Potomac* to the cruiser *Augusta,* which was now pounding north through the Bay of Maine.[335]

Churchill entrained for Scapa Flow on August 3 in the company of Hopkins (just "returned dead-beat from Russia"), Harriman, Cadogan from the Foreign Office, and a bevy of private secretaries (but no female typists, for it was thought the journey too arduous for women). The Prof was on board; elevated to a barony, he had taken the title of Lord Cherwell of Oxford—a two-fingered poke in the eyes of his enemies among Oxford dons—as the River Cherwell runs through Oxford on its way to join the Thames. Inspector Thompson was making the trip, toting his trusty Colt. Churchill left his valet behind; the Old Man's wardrobe and laundry duties—which were prodigious—fell to the gumshoe. The military was duly represented: Dill, Dudley Pound, and sundry colonels and group captains from the Defence Ministry, including Lieutenant Colonel Ian Jacob, who accompanied Churchill on most of his wartime journeys. It was a retinue, Colville recorded, that "Cardinal Wolsey might have envied." Lunch on board the train consisted of sirloin steak followed by fresh raspberry and currant tart. Churchill took his with champagne. Jacob recalled Cherwell calculating on his slide rule (at Churchill's request) the amount of champagne the Old Man had consumed in his lifetime, given that he claimed, "I have drunk fine Champagne with every dinner for the past twenty-years." Cherwell's answer—slightly less champagne than the volume of the railroad car—was a source of mild disappointment for Churchill. He was in fine fettle.[336]

Late on the afternoon of August 4, the entourage departed Scapa Flow aboard *Prince of Wales,* its scars inflicted by *Bismarck* erased by new bulkheads and a fresh layer of gray paint. Captain Leach—the object of Churchill's wrath after the *Bismarck* chase—was in command. The ship ran fast, blacked out, and in complete radio silence. Were Churchill to need any medical attention while on board he would have to see the ship's doctor. Clementine had pleaded with him to take along his physician, Dr. Wilson, but Winston declined, averse as he was to the possibility that the American president might catch sight of a stethoscope following the British prime minister around. Brendan Bracken, newly named head of the Ministry of Information, had suggested Churchill take along cameramen and ministry scribes to record the important, though largely symbolic meeting. Churchill heartily embraced that idea. This being a sea journey, and his every move being filmed, he chose a naval theme from his ample wardrobe, including a dark blue Royal Navy sea coat—the mess dress of the Royal Yacht Squadron—nicely set off by a seaman's cap. Thus attired, he chugged up and down ladders and along the lower decks of *Prince of Wales* (rising seas having rendered the quarterdeck unsafe), looking like a busy little tugboat captain. After dinner on the fifth, the party viewed *Pimpernel Smith,* with Leslie Howard, before turning in around midnight. The seas grew heavier and the great ship heaved. Churchill, finding the voyage a respite from the confines of London, retired to his cabin near the bridge with a C. S. Forester novel, *Captain Hornblower R.N.*[337]

As the ship lurched westward, Churchill brooded over his prospects in the Western Desert, where his tanks had taken a beating at the hands of Rommel. He dictated a memo to the Chiefs of Staff admonishing them to "find a way to restore artillery to its prime importance upon the battlefield, from which it has been ousted by heavily armoured tanks." The father of the tank was harboring doubts about his offspring, yet he should have known after the lessons of France and the Western Desert that the skillful deployment of massed tanks counted for far more than the thickness of their skin. Sheer volumes of tanks, supported by fighter aircraft, could overrun almost any position. The agenda for the coming meeting included tanks, thousands more tanks, made in America. But how many would go to Britain, to be deployed by Churchill where he saw fit, and how many to Russia, where they were most needed?[338]

He therefore decided en route that he needed Beaverbrook at the meeting. The Beaver, asthmatic and claustrophobic, hated the freezing confines of bombers as much as he loathed being stuffed belowdecks on a ship. Still, he made his way to Newfoundland by airplane, arriving after a twelve-hour journey. The plane following, which carried Arthur Purvis, head of the British Supply Council, crashed into a hill shortly after takeoff, killing Purvis and his entire staff. The loss of Purvis (who had overseen British munitions purchases from America during the Great War) was "grievous," Churchill later wrote. When the news broke, Beaverbrook "made no comment. It was wartime." Beaverbrook, exhausted and not as well liked by the Americans as Purvis, would have to bear the burden of resupply alone, a burden made heavier by Churchill's long shopping list, the pages of which he separated with a little red leather strip on which were engraved the words "Ask, and it shall be given. Seek and ye shall find." Inspector Thompson, catching sight of the strip, remarked that the words were a good omen. Churchill agreed: "Yes, Thompson, I hope it is a good omen, for I have much to ask for."[339]

His sought far more than supplies. He planned to ask Roosevelt to take the necessary diplomatic steps—and military, if need be—to garrison U.S. troops, aircraft, and ships in the Azores and Cape Verde Islands. To do so would violate Portuguese sovereignty, but Churchill could no longer afford to abide by diplomatic niceties. And, given Britain's weak position in Asia, he intended to ask Roosevelt to issue an extraordinary warning to Japan: Cease immediately all further territorial expansion or the United

States would go to war. Churchill's motive was transparent. Any explosion in Asia that brought the Americans in against Japan could only strengthen Britain's precarious position in the Far East. He considered the present about as fine a time as any to force Japan's hand. To guarantee that neither Roosevelt nor the State Department diluted the intended message, he set about drafting the threat himself.[340]

On August 6, Roosevelt and Churchill sped toward their rendezvous, their actual whereabouts still unknown to the press. That day the editors of one of America's most widely read newspapers, the *Brooklyn Eagle,* concluded, for no other reason than "the inability of American and British officials to deny" the rumors, that a meeting was indeed about to take place. Two nights later, Churchill took in *That Hamilton Woman,* which crudely plumbed the parallel between Britain's struggles with Napoleon and Hitler. It starred Laurence Olivier as Nelson, grimacing behind his blind eye, and Vivian Leigh (Olivier's wife of one year). Miss Leigh's "dramatic progress," a U.S. critic mused, "has left her only a gender's distance from Mickey Rooney." The film, a romantic hash Churchill much enjoyed (he penned a congratulatory note to the producer, Alexander Korda), treated of Nelson's affair with Emma Hamilton, wife of the British ambassador to the Kingdom of Naples. The movie gave Churchill all of his victories that year; five times he viewed the movie, and five times Nelson emerged victorious. Churchill, Cadogan recalled, was "moved to tears" at the film's climax, when the mortally wounded Admiral Nelson is told the battle is won. When the lights went up, Churchill addressed some of the ship's crew who lingered in the wardroom: "Gentlemen, I thought this film would interest you, showing great events similar to those in which you have been taking part." Cadogan retired for the evening, leaving Churchill and Hopkins at backgammon. Churchill's luck was running strong; he took the American for the equivalent of almost two hundred dollars.[341]

Harry's boss, from whom Churchill sought billions, was known to display more talent as a horse trader than a gambler. Roosevelt was at that hour riding at anchor off Argentia, which as a result of the destroyers-for-territory deal had been transformed in just months from Crown property into one of the U.S. Navy's largest bases. Roosevelt had taken title in fair trade.

As *Prince of Wales* dropped anchor in Placentia Bay at dawn on August 9, Inspector Thompson offered to Churchill that the impending meeting with Roosevelt would surely make history. "Yes," replied Churchill, "and more so if I get what I want from him." Then he made ready to board a launch for the short trip across the water to *Augusta,* where Roosevelt waited. Bracken's insistence on filming the occasion paid off. Footage of the ensuing meeting, released weeks later, had the effect of erasing from the public consciousness the sort of suspicions such secret assignations often engender. Had the sound not failed on the movie camera at the moment of truth, Churchill's and Roosevelt's greetings to each other would have been recorded for posterity.[342]

There stands Roosevelt, near the gangway, his legs made stiff by the steel braces underneath his trousers. He grasps the arm of his son, Elliott, who is attired in his army service uniform. The president wears a lightweight summer business suit. He is smiling broadly, but the cigarette holder is missing; the absence of that jaunty prop means he's all business. And there comes Churchill, scrambling up the ship's gangway, resplendent in his nautical getup. A dark sailor cap is pulled low over his brow. He clutches a pair of gloves in his left hand, which precludes his doffing the cap, which in turn precludes the possibility of any photo being snapped of Churchill arriving hat in hand. He stoops somewhat, and manages an almost subservient slouch as he offers his right hand to the president, who stands almost a head taller than Churchill. Churchill, Colville noted, was keenly aware of the constitutional differences in the roles of prime minister and president: the British prime minister was the King's first minister but was not, unlike the U.S. president, the head of state, or commander in chief. Churchill, therefore, always gave precedence to Roosevelt. In this case, he also gave the president an official letter of introduction from George VI. Unofficially, Churchill and Roosevelt should have needed no introduction because they had met at a dinner at Gray's Inn in 1918, when Roosevelt served as assistant secretary of the navy. Unfortunately, Churchill had forgotten the meeting, a slight to the patrician American and just the type of minor itch that might have festered in a lesser man. But Roosevelt let the oversight go, and over lunch the two men got down to the business of Churchill's wish list.[343]

Roosevelt, however, had also arrived with a wish. He attached no specific conditions to it, yet his intent was implicit in the asking. If Churchill wanted to take home from Argentia news of American guarantees for massive amounts of aid, Roosevelt sought to take home something as significant, if less tangible—a joint statement of postwar aims. Both had for months avoided any public elucidation of their postwar aims, yet within hours of shaking Roosevelt's hand, Churchill set to work on a joint statement, in part to negate "all the tales of my reactionary, Old World outlook, and the pain this is said to have caused the president." Churchill, in his memoirs, took pride in having "cast in my own words" the "substance and spirit of what came to be called the " 'Atlantic Charter.' "[344]

On August 10—Sunday—the two leaders allowed photographers to shoot some pictures for the folks back home. Roosevelt, his staff, and several hundred American sailors crossed over to *Prince of Wales,* where

Churchill had personally choreographed a worship service for his guests, down to the details of seating, the hymns to be sung, and the order in which they would be given voice. He was seen to dab away tears as he and Roosevelt joined the ships' crews in singing, "O God, Our Help in Ages Past." "It was a great hour to live," he wrote in his memoirs, adding, "Nearly half of those who sang were soon to die."[345]

After the ceremonies, Churchill, Harriman, Inspector Thompson, and Alec Cadogan climbed into a whaleboat for a sojourn to the flinty and rain-swept beach, where Thompson observed a change in Churchill's demeanor "as soon as we were on shore." For the first time after "more than a year of some of the most crushing disappointments and reverses ever sustained by a single individual," Churchill seemed to allow all his troubles to "sink into the deep ocean we had traversed." He talked and talked and puffed on his cigar and pointed out sights to the group, and when the rain grew harder, he simply "cupped his hand over his cigar and went on talking and pointing and puffing." Here was a good measure of his buoyant mood, for Thompson knew that when in Churchill's presence "You don't talk if he doesn't." He was talking, and at a clip. Cadogan recalled the party spending several hours wandering along the coastal crags, Churchill "like a schoolboy, taking great pleasure out of rolling boulders down a cliff." He was animated; the meeting with Roosevelt was going quite well. Yet after two lunches, a dinner, and Sunday service with the president, Churchill was waiting for some sign, some confirmation of that which he sought most of all from this meeting: Roosevelt's approval. He soon got it. Later that afternoon Churchill learned from Lieutenant (junior grade) Franklin Roosevelt, USN, that the young man's father "said quite plainly and without reservation that you are the greatest statesman the world has ever known." With that, the granting of Roosevelt's wish for a joint statement became a sure thing.[346]

In its final form, the Atlantic Charter contained eight points, including the pledge that the United States and Great Britain would seek no territorial gains "after the final destruction of the Nazi tyranny." That phrase delighted Churchill, for it meant that America, a neutral power, had made what he called an "astonishing" and "war-like" statement of intent. Point Four had to do with free trade; specifically, it guaranteed that raw materials and trade would be enjoyed by all states "on equal terms." Given America's long history of protectionism versus Britain's history of free trade, Churchill winced at the implication that Britain needed reminding on the subject and gave Under Secretary of State Sumner Wells an earful. Throughout the 1920s and early 1930s, the Americans saw tariffs and protectionism as the best defense against trading blocks, of which the British Empire (with its policy of imperial preference) was the world's largest.

Now, to mollify Churchill and the Dominions, which traded with London on special terms, the president and Wells agreed to modify Point Four by adding the words "with due respect for their existing obligations." The negotiations over the fourth point offered insight into Roosevelt's postwar economic aims. U.S. economic security could only, necessarily, come at the expense of Britain and its special relations.

Point Eight as initially phrased also troubled Churchill. It called for world peace following the war, but recommended no means to keep that peace. He sought inclusion of a declaration of intent to form a world organization—a sort of League of Nations with muscle—led by the English-speaking world in order to guarantee the peace. Many in America wanted nothing whatsoever to do with any such international coalition, given the abject failure of the League. Still, Roosevelt granted Churchill his point (the establishment of a wider and permanent system of general security), which greatly pleased the Old Man because it amounted to "a plain and bold intimation that after the war the United States would join with us in policing the world."[347]

Point Three vexed Churchill most of all, for it contained the seed most likely to grow into bitter fruit. It guaranteed "the right of all peoples to choose the form of government under which they will live" as well as the restoration of "sovereign rights and self-government to those who have been forcibly deprived of them." Churchill saw this as being directed to those nations conquered by the Nazis; but over the course of the next year he began to grasp that the charter lent itself to a "wider interpretation" than he and Roosevelt had intended, or wider than he, at least, intended. The Atlantic Charter, he later warned Roosevelt, could just as easily be interpreted by Arabs as a mandate "to expel the Jews from Palestine." This Churchill could not abide, given that he was, he said, "strongly wedded to the Zionist policy, of which I was one of the authors." Most troubling to Churchill was the prospect that the Atlantic Charter might be cited by rebellious British colonial elements in Africa and India as justification for breaking away from the Empire to gain rights denied them by London. That is exactly how Roosevelt, from the start, intended it to be construed. Yet for the King, the cabinet, and the Foreign Office, that simply would not do. In any event, at Argentia, Churchill, construing the words in a manner to his satisfaction (*restoration* of rights, not the *granting* of), approved the inclusion of Point Three. Oliver Harvey, Anthony Eden's senior private secretary, called the result a "terribly woolly document." Eden, Harvey confided to his diary, felt Roosevelt had "bowled the PM a very quick one." Yet Churchill considered the Atlantic Charter as symbolic and nothing more than a gesture by the two leaders, a nonbinding piece of paper, ratified neither by Congress nor Parliament. "It is silly," he told L. S.

Amery, "to make such heavy weather about these broad affirmations of principle."[348]

Cadogan had attended to the nuances of diplomatic verbiage within the Atlantic Charter, fabulously so in Churchill's estimation. "Thank God I brought you with me," he told Cadogan, who jotted in his diary, "The simplicity of the seven word tribute and his manner of saying it were proof of its sincerity, I was deeply moved and puffed up with great pride." Such sentiments did not come easily to the austere Cadogan, who Inspector Thompson found to be "the coldest" Englishman he knew, and who had "a look that can wither croupiers." It had been fifteen months since Cadogan told his diary on the eve of Churchill's taking the premiership what he thought of Churchill's leadership qualities: "Winston useless. . . . I am not at *all* sure of W.S.C." He was sure now.[349]

Churchill left for home with what he had come for: the promise of far more food, oil, and weapons. Roosevelt also pledged to replace the British forces in Iceland with American troops and to take over air and sea patrols west of Iceland, thus freeing up fifty British warships for patrol of the Northwest Approaches. As well, Roosevelt had agreed to voice Churchill's ultimatum to the Japanese. Churchill, in memos to the cabinet and to acting prime minister Clement Attlee, took delight in pointing out that *he* had drafted the warning. In return, Churchill gave Roosevelt the Atlantic Charter, Point Three and all. The charter was duly announced to the people of both nations, and the world, on August 14.[350]

Prince of Wales was on that day making for home, the seas still rough. The notables spent that evening playing backgammon (Churchill played rashly, but won) and watching a Laurel and Hardy movie and Donald Duck cartoons. When a convoy of more than seventy ships was spotted, *Prince of Wales* threaded its way among the freighters and tankers while Churchill, sweeping his binoculars over the ships, their decks crammed with airplanes and "cannons," declared the sight "delectable." After a stopover in Iceland followed by two more days at sea, Churchill reached Scapa Flow on August 18. The last British prime minister to venture abroad to meet a foreign leader had come home waving a worthless piece of paper. Churchill returned from overseas with something that would prove as valuable as Roosevelt's promise of untold supplies of weapons — a growing fondness for, and trust in, the American president. A friendship had germinated, and would grow, although, as in any friendship, there would be rough spots, in time, very rough. Churchill arrived home content, rested, and enthusiastic, and it showed. Cadogan recalled that on the train journey from Scotland, the Old Man "did himself well, finishing up with a Benedictine, ten minutes later he called for a brandy. The attendant reminded him he had had Benedictine. He [Churchill] said, 'I know, I want some brandy to clean it up.' "[351]

He arrived back at the Annexe on the nineteenth, "smiling broadly," Colville observed, "and still dressed in his nautical clothes." An ebullient Churchill told the cabinet that Argentia "symbolizes . . . the marshalling of the good forces of the world against the evil forces." He added, "The American Naval Officers had not concealed their keenness to enter the war." Lieutenant Colonel Ian Jacob, who had recorded the sessions between the American and British military chiefs—Churchill did not attend—reached the opposite conclusion. To his diary Jacob confided that "not a single American officer had shown the slightest keenness to be in the war on our side." Rather, the Americans "seem to think that the war can be won by our simply not losing it at sea." Yet Churchill and Roosevelt had hatched a plan for changing the course of the sea war, perhaps the entire war. Roosevelt, Churchill told the cabinet, was all for provoking an "incident" on the high seas and was prepared "to wage war without declaring it." That pledge sustained Churchill throughout the autumn, but in fact, the only thing Churchill had in writing from the president was the Atlantic Charter, which was, if nothing else, an eight-barbed hook on which Roosevelt could reel in empires, evil or benign.[352]

Almost immediately upon his return to London, Churchill learned that Roosevelt had reneged on the promised threat to Japan. Roosevelt's roar of the lion at Argentia, wrote his biographer James MacGregor Burns, "had become a lamb's bleat." Roosevelt instead tried to buy time by keeping up the talks with the Japanese, a process Hugh Dalton called "rather a humbugging negotiation." Several attendees of the Argentia conference told Dalton that "there had been a slide-back in U.S. opinion since May or June" and that Roosevelt's chance to bring America in had gone out with that tide. As for the promise of limitless supplies finding their way from America to Britain, the latest U.S. production figures showed a *decrease* in factory output since the first quarter of 1941, while only two billion of the seven-billion-dollar Lend-Lease program was actually under contract, not enough to make a difference if Russia fell.[353]

Meanwhile, the news from Russia only grew worse. Ultra revealed that the Nazis had engaged in "mass shootings of [almost 40,000] victims described variously by Berlin as 'Jews,' 'Jewish plunderers' [and] 'Jewish Bolsheviks.'" Hitler's armies, seemingly omnipotent, were hell-bent for Leningrad and Moscow. The Führer ordered that Leningrad "be wiped off the face of the earth." He soon decreed that Moscow be likewise erased. The situation in Russia was so dire that Churchill considered asking Stalin to destroy his own oil fields if defeat appeared imminent. He went so far as to advise the War Cabinet that "we must be ready to bomb the fields ourselves if the Russians did not destroy them."[354]

"We have not yet declared or taken a direct part in a shooting war," declared a September 2 *New York Times* editorial. "But we have taken a position which must force us ultimately to take such a direct part if our present policy does not prove sufficient to defeat Hitler. It is a position from which we cannot now retreat... a position from which the overwhelming majority of Americans have no wish to retreat." No one seriously thought that the "present policy" of avoiding conflict with Germany while supplying Britain food and weapons would bring down Hitler. In essence, the *New York Times* had proclaimed: We have taken a position that at some point will lead to war, and we will stick by that position.[355]

That line of thought held that America was a ship drifting toward war, and that wasn't good enough for Churchill. To persuade Roosevelt to steer America into the war remained Churchill's priority for the remainder of the year. When persuasion failed, the utility of chicanery presented itself. When his pleas to Roosevelt for more American naval action in the eastern Atlantic went unheeded, he cooked up schemes. One night earlier in the year, Churchill, Winant, and Harriman chatted over drinks about the benefit to Britain of an "incident" on the high seas involving a German attack on an American ship. The U.S. government—at least Congress—would have been shocked, and anything but thankful, had it learned that Winston Churchill was engaged in a ploy to precipitate a widening of the war, at America's expense. His request that American ships locate and track *Bismarck* had been an attempt to drag the Yanks in. As were his pleas for American naval patrols in the Azores. Throughout the spring and summer, Roosevelt refused Churchill's bait, and for good reason. The president had no solution to the problems that would arise from a U.S. warship running into the wrong German ship in the wrong place and with disastrous results. Roosevelt could only hope that nothing unfortunate took place on the high seas until such time as the U.S. Navy and the American people were prepared, militarily and emotionally, for war.[356]

Then, at Argentia Roosevelt himself brought up the value of "an incident" on the high seas, and told Churchill that the United States planned to put at least one U.S. merchantman, flying the U.S. flag, in every convoy under escort by U.S. warships. The challenge to Hitler was obvious; were he to shoot at an American merchant ship guarded by American warships, he would face the consequences. Again, it seemed as if Roosevelt had given Churchill what he sought.

The incident duly occurred on September 4, when the destroyer USS *Greer,* while making a mail run to Iceland, made sonar contact with a U-boat. *Greer* notified the British of the position and waited for British destroyers to show up. None appeared. *Greer,* meanwhile, dodged two torpedoes fired from the lurking U-boat, while the German sub dodged nineteen depth charges loosed by *Greer.* This potentially incendiary business on the seas ended with *Greer* and its crew steaming unscathed into port. Roosevelt seized the occasion on September 11 to deliver another of his fireside chats, one in which he brought America nearer to outright involvement in the European war. Declaring that Germany was guilty of an "act of piracy" in attacking *Greer,* he unleashed American ships and planes for offensive action. In waters "which we deem necessary for our defense," he declared, "American naval vessels and American planes will no longer wait until Axis submarines lurking under the water, or Axis raiders on the surface of the sea, strike their deadly blow first." They would shoot on sight. By moving the American defense zone even farther east, Roosevelt had, in effect, declared "undeclared war" in the mid-Atlantic. He then proclaimed—as he had to Churchill at Argentia—the right of U.S. ships to escort any nation's ships, anywhere. Still, as he had in late April, he kept his warships out of the hottest battle zones—the Northwest Approaches, the Azores, and along the West African coast—where the dangers to British convoys bound from Britain around the Cape to the Middle East were greatest.[357]

"There has now come a time," Roosevelt told his countrymen, "when you and I must see the cold inexorable necessity of saying to these inhuman, unrestrained seekers of world conquest and permanent world domination by the sword: 'You seek to throw our children and our children's children into your form of terrorism and slavery. You have now attacked our own safety. You shall go no further.'" The United States sought "no shooting war with Hitler," he declared, "but neither do we want peace so much that we are willing to pay for it by permitting him to attack...our ships while they are on legitimate business." To that end, he asked Congress to amend the Neutrality Acts such that merchantmen could be armed (cargo ships were at the time allowed to carry only a handgun and harpoons). He wanted those ships, once armed, to sail under the escort of U.S. warships. Congress acceded to Roosevelt's wishes, in essence claiming sovereignty of the seas in America's name, another virtual declaration of war. Such measures as Roosevelt proposed were costly, but America now spent willingly. The production decline of the first two quarters was reversed. By September, the U.S. government, not even at war, was plowing

$1.8 billion per week into war production, more than was spent at the height of the Great War. With each new motion to Congress, with each new address to Americans, with each new contract let out for planes and tanks, Roosevelt edged closer to war, too close for the America Firsters, yet still not close enough for Churchill.[358]

On October 17 a second and far more serious incident than the *Greer* episode took place. That day, the destroyer USS *Kearny*, escorting a North Atlantic convoy, took a German torpedo in the side; eleven sailors belowdecks were killed. American blood had been spilled, but still Congress remained silent, and America remained at peace.

Then, on October 31, the old four-stack destroyer USS *Reuben James*, escorting a convoy south of Iceland, steamed into the crosshairs of a U-boat, which with two torpedoes sent *Reuben James* and 115 of its crew of 159 to the bottom. Here was the sort of incident that started wars. Churchill telegraphed Roosevelt his regrets: "I am grieved with loss of life you have suffered with *Reuben James*. I salute the land of unending challenge." But the *Reuben James* was not to prove the *Lusitania* of World War Two. Churchill understood now that only an incident far greater than the sinking of a small warship—which had been sailing, after all, in harm's way—would bring America into the war. He admitted as much when he told the War Cabinet the next day that Roosevelt faced "difficulties... as a result of the slow development of American opinion and the peculiarities of the American Constitution. Nobody but Congress could *declare* war. It was however in the president's power to make war without declaring it."[359]

Churchill knew after the *Reuben James* went down that this was a war America would declare on its own terms in its own time for its own reasons, or not declare at all. He thus advised his War Cabinet that "in the last twelve months American opinion had moved under his [Roosevelt's] leadership to an extent nobody could have anticipated." As well, he told the cabinet, the American "Navy was escorting the Atlantic convoys; and finally they were taking a firm line with the Japanese"—though a far less firm line than Roosevelt had promised at Argentia. Churchill said that it would "be a grave error on his part to press President Roosevelt to act in advance of American opinion." Not only would it be a grave error to press Roosevelt, it would be futile. Americans and their president were not to be pressed. On several occasions Churchill voiced his preference to trade six months' worth of supplies for an immediate declaration of war. He'd have to satisfy himself with the supplies, for he'd get no war from America, declared or undeclared, until America was willing.[360]

Roosevelt had injected for effect into his September 11 address a phrase that resonated with beer-and-a-shot Americans: "When you see a rattlesnake poised to strike, you do not wait until he has struck before you crush him." It was just the sort of turn of phrase, brash and dashing, that Churchill relished. Yet by November 1 the rattlesnake had struck repeatedly: USS *Greer, Kearny, Reuben James*. American sailors had drowned. Roosevelt's threat had been cold and clear, but while his actions, in relation to his words, appeared to be ambiguous, they were not: America had been attacked and America had done nothing.[361]

Back in May, a few days after *Bismarck* went down, Churchill cabled his thanks to Roosevelt for declaring a state of emergency in the Atlantic and for his promise of shipping more matériel, on American ships, to the Middle East. Churchill concluded the cable with the arithmetic of battleships in the Atlantic: Britain and Germany had traded great ships, but Germany could not afford the trade. Elated over *Bismarck*'s demise, Churchill ended the telegram with a prediction: "The effect upon the Japanese will be highly beneficial. I expect they're doing all their sums again." In fact, the Japanese had been doing just that for quite some time.[362]

The previous year, Churchill (after the Americans declined his request to rattle their saber on his behalf in the Pacific) planned to send *Hood* and a squadron of cruisers and destroyers to Singapore in order to show the flag and give the Japanese something to think about. That option was now off the table; *Hood* was gone. In late October, to discourage any Japanese incursions westward toward Singapore or India, Churchill dispatched *Prince of Wales* to join the battle cruiser *Repulse,* already on station near Singapore. He informed Roosevelt of *Prince of Wales*'s mission, and outlined his Pacific strategy, such as it was: "This [*Prince of Wales*] ought to serve as a deterrent on Japan. There is nothing like having something that can catch and kill anything."[363]

Churchill's love of the Royal Navy betrayed his judgment. A 35,000-ton fast battleship couldn't catch an airplane, and only with great shooting skill and good luck could it kill an airplane. Even after the British victory at Taranto, even after the disastrous attacks on *Southampton* and *Illustrious,* after the carnage inflicted by the Luftwaffe upon Cunningham's fleet at Crete, Churchill could not concede that an airplane armed with just one torpedo or a single five-hundred-pound bomb might be able to kill his fast battleships. That an Asian race might accomplish such a feat did not square with his belief in the stature of Englishmen and their warships, and the importance of both in the orderly conduct of world affairs. Churchill "attributed to battleships," recalled Ian Jacob, "a power . . . that they no longer retained."[364]

Churchill was one in his thinking with the old admirals in the navies of the Western world—including the British Admiralty—for whom it was accepted fact that successfully dropping a bomb from several thousand feet onto the deck of a moving battleship was a matter of chance. As for torpedoes, an aerial torpedo attack might prove dangerous on the open ocean, but in the navies of the world and among naval aviators it was accepted fact that in the shallow waters of anchorages, torpedo attacks were not possible. Torpedoes dropped from airplanes hit the water and descended more than one hundred feet before rising to running depth; when dropped into shallow harbors they simply buried themselves in the mud and posed no threat. Yet the British at Taranto the previous November had carried off just such an operation. In Japan, Admiral Isoroku Yamamoto and his naval aviation planners were duly impressed by the raid, and took note especially of the depth of the waters the British torpedoes had run in, just forty feet in places, shallower even than the waters of Pearl Harbor, home of the U.S. Pacific fleet. Some within the U.S. government grasped the turn taken by naval aviation at Taranto. Admiral Harold Stark, chief of naval operations, suggested to Admiral James Richardson, commander in chief of the U.S. fleet in Hawaii, that torpedo nets be strung at Pearl Harbor. Richardson, believing the nets would only get in the way of his ships, did not deploy them.[365]

Churchill, although he hadn't learned the larger strategic lesson of Taranto, remained mindful of remote strategic possibilities—however remote in time, miles, or probability. He had asked Eden early in the year what was planned regarding the 22,000 Japanese-Canadians in British Columbia were Japan to attack the Empire. "The matter is of course for the Canadian government," Churchill wrote, "but it would be interesting to know if adequate forces are available in that part of the Dominion. About thirty years ago, when there were anti-Japanese riots, the Japanese showed themselves so strong and so well organized as to be able to take complete control." The sons and daughters of those immigrants had since grown to be loyal Canadian citizens; a young couple in Victoria, Mr. and Mrs. Hayashi, that very year named their newborn son Winston Churchill Hayashi. In asking what measures were in store for Canada's Japanese, Churchill was a full ten months ahead of Roosevelt, who waited until late November to request from the U.S. Census Bureau the names and addresses of more than 125,000 Japanese-Americans—"Hitler's little yellow friends," *Time* called them—who lived on the American west coast.[366]

In Churchill's estimation, no flank should remain unguarded. Yet when Ismay suggested reinforcing the garrison at Hong Kong, Churchill shot him down: "This is all wrong! If Japan goes to war with us, there is not the slightest chance of holding Hong Kong or relieving it." Any imperial losses in the Pacific would be "dealt with at the Peace Conference after the war," presumably won by Britain. When it came to planning for contingencies in the Pacific, Churchill tended to shoot wide of the mark. Weeks after his inquiry into the Canadian flank, he ordered Ismay to "report on the efficiency of the gunners and personnel managing the 15-inch gun batteries and searchlights at Singapore. Are they fitted with RDF [radar]?" The question implies that he assumed the Japanese would arrive by sea. Some tactical situations demand a creative, counterintuitive approach; this was one. Churchill should have followed up his question about the fifteen-inch guns by asking whether Japanese infantry could negotiate the supposed impenetrable jungle of the Malay Peninsula in order to attack Singapore from the *landward* side. In fact, the new commander in Singapore, Lieutenant General Arthur Ernest Percival, had ordered a study to ascertain whether Singapore could be "burgled by the back door" and concluded that the entire Malay Peninsula, almost three hundred miles in length, needed more airbases, more planes, more tanks, and more men. He was ignored by London; there were no resources to spare in any event. London settled upon a scorched-earth policy for Malaya; if the Japanese came by land, they would find it ravaged. Even were such a policy successfully implemented, the Malay Peninsula stretched like a welcoming gangplank, right up to the gunwales of Singapore island.[367]

On occasion Churchill's strategic vision was distorted by his racial bias. When Harry Hopkins predicted in January that the incident that could spark U.S. involvement would be with Japan, Churchill replied that Tokyo must have been deterred by the demise at Taranto of the Italian fleet, which had appeared so strong on paper. "Fate holds terrible forfeits," he told Hopkins, "for those who gamble on certainties." Churchill believed, correctly, that the highest ranks of the Italian navy preferred to safeguard their fleets rather than fight with them. The Italians had paid for their caution when Churchill's English sailors and fliers struck with the "bold strokes" he championed. He simply could not conceive of the Japanese employing similar bold strokes against American or British fleets. Yet the Japanese had indeed learned a lesson from Taranto, and they intended to apply it. As for the likelihood that Japan would unleash its forces on British interests, Churchill had told Ismay, "Japan will think long before declaring war on the British Empire."[368]

In April, Japanese Foreign Minister Yosuke Matsuoka visited Moscow with hopes of codifying a Russo-Japanese neutrality pact, which by virtue of both Matsuoka's and Stalin's total ignorance of Hitler's looming treachery, it would be Matsuoka's (and Stalin's) good fortune to secure. Weeks earlier, Matsuoka had met with Hitler, who, along with Ribbentrop, planted broad hints that a Japanese adventure against Singapore might pay dividends to both Germany and Japan by virtue of dividing British forces and discouraging the Americans from coming in against either Germany or Japan. Ribbentrop dropped even heavier hints regarding the Führer's designs on Russia, implying that if Japan tied down Stalin's troops in far distant Asia, Germany could dispatch Russia, the traditional enemy of both Germany and modern Japan. But the Reich's foreign minister, a plainspoken thug, failed to articulate his message in terms that a sophisticated diplomat might understand, thus sending Matsuoka to Moscow firm in the mistaken belief that Germany, Japan, and the Soviet Union would for many years to come live together in peace, each pursuing empire after its own fashion.

On July 21, the Vichy government accepted Japanese demands for air and naval bases in the southern part of French Indochina. Four days later, Roosevelt announced an oil embargo against Japan to take effect August 1, together with a freeze of all bank transfers between the United States and Japan. An embargo on American scrap steel sales to Japan had gone into effect months earlier, too late for the Chinese killed over the last decade by Japanese shells and tanks that might as well have been stamped "Made in the USA" (the scrap steel also helped build Japan's new navy). Great Britain followed America with similar measures the next day, and on July 26 the Dutch government in exile in London joined the embargo. Japan, if denied Dutch East Indian oil—some of it so pure it needed no refining—could not exploit its conquests or defend its empire. On Monday, July 28, Dutch authorities in Batavia (modern Jakarta) ordered a cessation of all trade with and payments to Japan. Two Japanese tankers that had just finished taking on oil at Tarakan Island were allowed to leave. An American diplomat offered that the oil gauge and the clock now stood side by side; each drop in the level of Japanese oil brought nearer the hour of decision.[369]

In November 1940, secret and informal talks among the British, Australian, and Dutch had begun in Singapore with the intent of drawing up plans for a response to German raiders in the Pacific or to a Japanese attack. Previous contacts among the parties treated of the usual humdrum issues pertinent to powers in close proximity to one another, mostly how to stay out of one another's way. A second meeting had taken place in Batavia and was followed by a third in Singapore in February 1941, in which U.S. military personnel were present as "observers." At the next conference, in April, the Americans became full participants. Yet by mid-November 1941—after a full year of parleys—the talks had failed utterly to produce any plan to respond to Japanese aggression. The conferees did agree on one point: the need for reconnaissance flights in order to track Japanese naval movements in the South China Sea. The flights yielded nothing. No plan was ever produced to act in unison in the event of a Japanese attack, whether surprise or otherwise.

Dutch East Indian oil, Burmese rice, and Malayan tin and rubber were Japan's ultimate objectives, but to gain them, they had to locate and destroy the American and British Pacific fleets. The location of the former was easy to ascertain; in late November the American fleet rode peacefully at anchor at Pearl Harbor. Locating the British fleet was easy as well, because there was no British fleet to speak of. With ongoing losses in the Mediterranean, the British could not maintain in Asia any concentration of sea power that could fairly be called a fleet.

When it came to the prospect of war in the Pacific, Churchill's thinking throughout 1941, except for the final three weeks of the year, was sometimes contradictory and often naive. He admitted as much in his memoirs when he wrote, "I do not pretend to have studied Japan, ancient or modern, except as presented to me by newspapers and a few books." Yet he was one with Bismarck, who admonished statesmen to imagine themselves in the position of their enemy, "The Other Man." To be effective, such an imaginative leap into the mind and motives of an opponent requires knowledge. Churchill never lacked imagination, but when it came to Japan, he lacked knowledge. As well, as a Victorian gentleman, he thought little of the brown races, the black, and the yellow.[370]

He knew just enough to know that he didn't want a fight with Japan. A year earlier he had told Roosevelt that were the Japanese to thrust toward Singapore or the Dutch East Indies, "We have today no forces in the Far East capable of dealing with this situation should it develop." Months earlier he had told the cabinet that a Japanese attack on the Dutch colonies "would mean war with us." He did not believe they stood a good chance of beating the Japanese, and he told Ismay so. But, as with Greece, they might have to fight over a point of honor. To not contest a Japanese takeover of Dutch possessions would amount to "allowing ourselves to be cut off from Australia and New Zealand, and they would regard our acquiescence as desertion." Yet he didn't see the Japanese precipitating such a crisis. He had told Hopkins early in the year that if faced with the prospects of armed Anglo-American resistance, the Japanese would not come in. He clung to that opinion, despite the fact that Hopkins told him quite clearly that America would very likely *not* go to war with Japan over Dutch interests, or British. During an April War Cabinet meeting, Churchill expressed doubt that Japan would enter the war unless Hitler successfully invaded Britain. In cabinet memos to the Chiefs of Staff and Eden, Churchill claimed the Japanese would be "most unlikely to come in if they thought that by doing so they would bring in the United States." In July he reiterated his April assessment: "I must repeat my conviction that Japan will not declare war upon us at the present juncture, nor if the United States enters the war on our side." And, if Japan acted upon Hitler's suggestions and attacked British Asian possessions, Churchill "felt sure the United States would declare war."[371]

But why? No treaty obligated the United States to do so. And declare war on whom? Japan, *possibly* but not necessarily, and certainly not on Germany, where Churchill most needed America. Although Churchill pledged to Roosevelt in late October to declare war on Japan "within the hour" if Japan mixed it up with the Americans, Roosevelt had made no corresponding pledge should Japanese armies pour into Singapore or Hong Kong. A Japanese move against the Americans—which Churchill all year made clear he did not expect—would not necessarily bring America into Churchill's war against Hitler. Only two events could bring that about, the first being an act of war by Hitler against America; yet he had already attacked the U.S. Navy three times without triggering a declaration of war. The second scenario would find Hitler declaring war on the United States in support of his Asian ally were Japan to attack America. The latter possibility, an invitation to ultimate German and Japanese obliteration, was almost too preposterous even for Churchill to contemplate, for only a fool or a madman would declare war on America where no state of war existed. And yet, Churchill long held to another maxim regarding the human condition and warfare: "Madness is however an affliction which in war carries with it the advantage of surprise."[372]

Thanks to the Bletchley crowd, Churchill had known since August that Josef ("Sepp") Dietrich, a general in the Waffen-SS and one of Hitler's oldest favorite cronies, had assured the Japanese ambassador in Berlin—in Hitler's name—that "Germany would at once declare hostilities in the event of a collision between Japan and the United States." Hitler would prove himself a madman later in the war, but in 1941 he was on top of his game. Given his craftiness and pathological willingness to lie, his message to the Japanese, relayed through Dietrich, meant everything, and nothing. The Führer might join the Japanese if they attacked British or American interests; then again, he might not.[373]

Churchill told the War Cabinet in November that he did not want to be boxed in by "an automatic declaration of war" against Japan that would "give the anti-British party [American isolationists] cause for saying that the United States were again being dragged into a British colonial war." By then he understood that America had to go in first, and that nothing short of an attack against America could bring that about.[374]

Throughout most of 1941, Churchill ascribed to Japan sober enough judgment to not willingly and with forethought provoke the Americans into war, an opinion shared by the American isolationists. Robert McCormick's *Tribune* declared in late October that Japan "cannot attack us" and that

Pearl Harbor "is beyond the effective striking power of her fleet." Yet Churchill also understood that Roosevelt's ban on oil sales to Japan had been a virtual act of war, one that Japan's war minister, Hedeki Tojo, could not abide, for reasons of both national pride and national survival. Tojo's elevation to prime minister (he remained war minister, as well) in mid-October should have served to close the debate on Japan's immediate inclinations; the war faction in Tokyo had swept away all of the moderates. For Tojo, if the stakes were Japan's survival, which they now were, any distance and any objective, including Pearl Harbor, four thousand miles from Tokyo, must be overcome. McCormick, his head in the sand, can be forgiven his limited vision. But Churchill should have seen Tojo coming. American oil had propelled the Japanese navy for years, until just five months earlier. Only the Dutch East Indies could now supply that oil. And in order to take the Dutch refineries, the Japanese would first have to take Singapore.[375]

Yet Churchill considered the Japanese to be an obedient and compliant race, which, once warned against aggression, as he had done, would heed the warnings. Hugh Dalton, who thought Churchill's demeaning public references to the Japanese "rude," captured the essence of the Old Man's rationale: "The PM does not think the Japs will go to war with us," because he had given the Japanese "very serious warnings" against further aggression in the Pacific.[376]

That Churchill spoke of the Japanese as he might of little children, and to further presume that continued Japanese pursuit of an Asian empire could be forestalled by his "very serious warnings," and to still further presume that Japan's strategic plan was somehow conditional on Hitler's successful invasion of Britain, betrays a dangerous Anglocentric naïveté. Britain was Churchill's Home Island; the British Empire, including the autonomous commonwealths, spanned the globe, which made Britain, in that sense, the world's only global power. Although England's geographical position, within sight of the French coast, was strategically critical to Hitler, it was not to Tojo. Singapore held far more significance than London for the Japanese.

Singapore's six-year-old naval base—twenty-six square miles of protected anchorage, and built to send a clear message to Japan—straddled the sea-lanes to and from the resources Japan most needed, Dutch East Indies oil and Malaya rubber. It had been Hitler's strategic misfortune to knock his head against the unyielding wall of fortress Britain for more than a year. Singapore, for the Japanese, was another matter entirely. It was many things—symbolic of British imperial might, one of the world's great harbors—but given its defenses, it was no fortress. Churchill considered Singapore his Far Eastern jewel. Tojo considered it as nothing more than a target of opportunity.

Throughout November, in a furious flow of telegraphic traffic, Churchill and Roosevelt discussed, and pondered, Japan. The British, having been given access to the American Magic intelligence (which decrypted Japanese diplomatic messages, but not Japanese military communications), could read the tea leaves as well as the Americans could. The Magic decrypts hinted that Japan might take extreme but unspecified measures were its demands—including Japanese hegemony in China—not met. Still, the Americans and Japanese held talks in Washington, with Roosevelt keeping Churchill apprised of the progress or lack thereof. Japanese ambassador Numura and special envoy Saburu Kurusu presented U.S. secretary of state Cordell Hull a modus vivendi that "might give the Japanese government opportunity to develop public sentiment in Japan in support of a... comprehensive program of peace." Roosevelt considered the proposals inadequate and "not in harmony" with America's "fundamental principles" and demands. " I am not very hopeful," he cabled Churchill on November 24, "and we must all be prepared for real trouble, possibly soon."[377]

On Sunday, November 30, Churchill turned sixty-seven. He was now just three years shy of the Bible's allotted three score and ten years, and by any measure, biblical or actuarial, he was indeed an old man. He looked it. His face was deeply creased; his fair skin, which had always exuded a healthy glow, seemed pinched and parched. His stoop was more pronounced. He wore his scowl in public and in the Commons, for the benefit of the press photographers, who that year rarely captured him with any other expression. Before he retired to bed in the early hours of his birthday he cabled Roosevelt—his junior by almost eight years—and again, as he had in May, with full knowledge of Roosevelt's "constitutional difficulties" asked the president—in a roundabout way—to declare war, this time against Japan. The plan, as Churchill outlined it, would have Roosevelt tell the Japanese that any further aggression, anywhere and against anyone, would result in Roosevelt placing "the gravest issues before Congress, or words to that effect." Churchill, as he had in May, apologized to Roosevelt for the temerity of his suggestion, which given the very real constitutional restraints Roosevelt indeed labored under was impossible to execute. "Forgive me, my dear friend," he wrote, "for presuming to press such a course upon you, but I am convinced that it might make all the difference and prevent a melancholy extension of the war."[378]

Birthday salutations arrived from around the world. The King and Queen sent along greetings in a message that would have been a firing offense for a

Hallmark copywriter: "Many happy returns on the day from us both." Churchill dutifully thanked Their Majesties for the "charming message which I received and read with great pleasure." Beaverbrook dispatched a rather more emotional message: "This letter carries Birthday greetings of a difficult colleague & devoted follower. . . . For those who have served you it will be sufficient glory to be known as Churchill's man." And from Harry Hopkins: "Dear Winston. Happy birthday. How old are you anyway?"[379]

Dill sent greetings, a gentlemanly gesture given that Churchill had just two weeks earlier approved the general's promotion to field marshal and then sacked him. Their relationship had long been unsatisfactory, with Dill unwilling to stand up to Churchill, who was unwilling to appreciate Dill's caution in the face of overwhelming German military superiority in Russia, where Dill foresaw likely defeat for Stalin. That Dill was sixty, the mandatory retirement age for regular army officers, offered Churchill a convenient means of easing him out.* He chose not to consult Eden in the matter. When Eden, who thought Churchill underrated Dill (the P.M. called him "Dilly-Dally"), expressed his chagrin for sacking the CIGS without consulting the Foreign Office, the Old Man replied that he had done so because "I know you will not agree." That was how he conducted his business. When a subordinate objected to a scheme, Churchill badgered the protester. When a subordinate gave in without a fight, Churchill doubted the man's fighting spirit. Colville had noted two months earlier that Churchill's dagger was in Dill's back; in late November he gave it the final twist.[380]

Dill's replacement as CIGS was the commander in chief of Home Forces, General Sir Alan Brooke, a slim fifty-seven-year-old Ulsterman and soon to be the most famous of the Brookes of Colebrooke, a family long known for its military service to the Crown. Twenty-six members of his Ulster clan had fought in the Great War, twenty-seven were fighting in World War Two. The Brookes embodied the spirit of Cuchulain, the mythical Ulster warrior hero; they lived to fight.

Knighted for his heroics at Dunkirk, Sir Alan Brooke was an outdoorsman and avid bird-watcher. In the opinion of Bernard Montgomery, he proved himself "the greatest soldier—soldier, sailor, airman—produced by any country" during the war. Brooke told his diary that he was wary of

---

* Churchill planned to promote Dill to field marshal and ship him to Bombay, a consolation prize for the old soldier, but after Argentia, where Dill displayed an easy ability to get along with the Americans, especially Marshall, Churchill took the new field marshal with him to Washington in late December, there to leave him as liaison to the American chiefs. Dill became, in the estimation of George Marshall and Roosevelt, one of the primary talents of the war, instrumental in creating a genuine working relationship between the Americans and British.

Churchill's "impetuous nature, his gambler's spirit, and his determination to follow his own selected path at all costs." Brooke ("Brookie" to his friends) was not a churchgoing man, but upon Churchill's elevating him to CIGS, the new chief's "first impulse was to kneel down and pray to God for guidance and support" in working with Churchill. His new boss had his own reservations about Brooke: "I know these Brookes," Churchill told Ismay, "stiff necked Ulstermen, and there's no one worse to deal with than that." Actually, Brooke's older brother Victor had been Churchill's best friend in India, and Alan Brooke had commanded II Corps in France with honor and distinction. Like Churchill, he did not countenance woolly thinking. His usual rejoinder in a debate was brutally straightforward—"I flatly disagree," often accompanied by the snapping of a pencil. His nickname in the War Office was Colonel Shrapnel. He combined prudence and rigor; he was both feared and liked by his men. He disliked flamboyance, and therefore disliked Churchill's cronies, especially Beaverbrook. Brooke found himself "revolted" one evening at Chequers as Beaverbrook poured "himself one strong whiskey after another.... The more I saw of him throughout the war, the more I disliked and distrusted him." For Brooke, self-control was a duty, for Churchill, an impediment to life's joys. Both men tended to demean lesser minds, and both, having experienced the slaughter of the Great War (Brooke at the Somme), resisted any strategic initiatives that might result in static lines and a repetition of that slaughter. Both were stubborn. In the years to come when Brooke went up against Churchill, he always gave as good as he got. Brooke, too, sent along birthday greetings.[381]

Jock Colville had not sent a birthday message, busy as he was earning two shillings a day as a pilot trainee in the RAF. Churchill, over the objections of Eden, had in September finally given his blessings to Colville's aviation ambitions, telling the young secretary that his patriotism was "gallant." When they said their good-byes in the Cabinet Room, Churchill offered his hand and parting words: "I have the greatest affection for you; we all have, Clemmie and I especially. Goodbye and God bless you." Colville departed with "a lump in my throat such that I had not had for many years." Within several weeks, somebody with great influence prevailed upon the Treasury to raise Colville's pay to the £400 per year he had earned while on Churchill's staff.[382]

L. S. Amery, in a birthday tribute voiced during a BBC broadcast, called Churchill "the spirit of old England incarnate, with its unshakeable self-confidence, its grim gaiety, its unfailing sense of humour... its unflinching tenacity. Against that inner unity of spirit between leader and nation the ill-cemented fabric of Hitler's perversion of the German soul must be shattered in the end."[383]

Tojo's ongoing perversion of the Japanese soul was manifested by his threats that week to cut the Burma Road in order to inflict new terrors upon the Yunnan province of China. Chiang Kai-shek appealed to Churchill for help, specifically to fill the Burma Road with trucks bearing arms. Churchill had to inform Chiang that no help would be forthcoming. As he explained to Roosevelt, Britain was "tied up elsewhere." Tied down, tied up, it was all the same—he lacked the means to further his own cause, let alone Chiang's. Ever optimistic, Churchill was pleased that Emperor Hirohito appeared to be "exercising restraint" even though the Anglo-American embargo was "forcing Japan to decisions of peace and war." He was correct, but Tojo, not the poetically inclined Hirohito, would make the final decision. Churchill, clinging to his belief that the Japanese would pursue a sane course in the Pacific, ended his message to Roosevelt with a prediction: "I think myself that Japan is more likely to drift into war than to plunge in."[384]

On his birthday he told the War Office that war with Japan would "prejudice our chances of defeating Germany." Above all, he advised, "Our policy must... be avoidance of war with Japan." But that choice—war or peace in the Pacific—rested entirely with Japan.[385]

Churchill had much to be grateful for; he was in good health, Clementine and the children likewise. Mary, just eighteen, had enlisted in the Auxiliary Territorial Service and was posted to an AA battery near Enfield. Randolph was back behind the lines in Cairo after seeing action in the Western Desert. He had been promoted to major and made a press liaison, a safe posting that afforded him nightly opportunities to drink, gamble (without success), and chase women. To his father Randolph conveyed his "love and deepest admiration." Diana, prone as was her mother to severe bouts of nervous tension, did her duty as an air-raid warden, an unlikely sight, Sarah recalled, dressed in trousers and high heels. She also had been keeping vigil for months at the bedside of her husband, Duncan Sandys, as he recovered after suffering crushed legs in an auto accident. Sandys, wounded in the abortive Norway operation, had harbored hopes of returning to the field, until the car crash. He had since resumed work on his radar and anti-aircraft projects, including rockets, for which he had developed an affinity. Churchill sought to appoint Sandys under secretary for foreign affairs, a critical position, and one for which Sandys possessed no qualifications. Eden objected. Churchill dropped the scheme but brought Sandys into the War Office, an act of such flagrant nepotism that John Peck offered Colville five pounds if he suggested to the Old Man that Vic Oliver be made head of the Ministry of Information.[386]

Vic Oliver sent birthday greetings but had months earlier gone his own way when he and Sarah parted company for good. Clementine had grown fond of Vic, but Churchill had never bothered to get to know him. Sarah, commissioned in the Woman's Auxiliary Air Force, applied herself to learning the skills of photographic interpretation. Her acting career, such as it was, would have to remain on ice for the duration, but she had never possessed either great talent or a great following, and would never do so. She did possess and heavily indulged an affinity for fine wine and good liquor, but unlike her father did not possess the requisite metabolic talent to both drink freely and function flawlessly. She was stubborn, like her father, and Churchill had long ago given her the nickname, "The Mule." It stuck. Churchill expressed his pride at The Mule's secret work, but other than an occasional dinner at Chequers, Sarah—in fact, all of the children—had seen little of their father that year. For that matter, Clementine did not see all that much of her husband.[387]

She found succor in her relief work. She was the driving force behind the Aid to Russia Fund, which by war's end raised more than £8 million for Russian relief, mostly from factory workers, although several well-heeled Tories wrote checks for more than £200,000. Mary found her mother to be "desperately tired, both physically and mentally" from the "strain of her social and domestic life." The reference to the strain of Clemmie's domestic life was Mary's delicate way of implying that her mother suffered from nervous tension and that her parents' relationship bore little resemblance to anything recognizably normal. So "totally preoccupied with events of national importance" was Churchill that year that he left all matters of the children for Clementine to grapple with, including Mary's precipitous (and short-lived) engagement to her young beau, an event Churchill was not even aware of. He had little time for family affairs, and little inclination to find the time. Clementine dressed for dinner every night; most nights her husband did not appear.[388]

His most welcome birthday gift arrived by way of North Africa. Auchinleck had shown Rommel during the preceding week that some British generals could fight. The operation, code-named Crusader, was the largest desert offensive yet undertaken by the British. Under the command of General Alan Cunningham, the hero of Ethiopia, its mission was to swing south around Rommel's lines, which ran fifty miles from his headquarters in Bardia to Sidi Omar. Then, Cunningham planned to swing part of his force northwest in order to draw Rommel into a set-piece battle that, when successfully concluded, would lead to the relief of Tobruk and drive Rommel westward and out of Cyrenaica. Each army fielded about 115,000 men, but Cunningham's seven hundred tanks outnumbered Rommel's by more than two to one, and the British general had surprise on his side. Steady rains had kept German air reconnaissance on the ground; Rommel had no idea the British were about to attack. In fact, Rommel was about to attack Tobruk at the very moment the British emerged from the desert mists on November 17. So complete was the surprise that Rommel's forces were facing the wrong way.

Cunningham made the mistake of thinking Rommel would behave in accordance with his plan and wander into his trap. Rommel did not, because for almost two days he did not believe a British attack was actually taking place, so intent was he on taking Tobruk. When Rommel failed to respond as predicted, Cunningham blundered by spreading his tanks across the desert in a series of isolated columns. Rommel, finally realizing the extent of the British attack, quickly massed his tanks, turned them around, and on November 23, in the largest tank battle thus far fought in the desert, smashed into and through the British lines. The British, in isolated batches and without coordinated command, turned eastward, and fled for home. The Germans also raced east, all the way to the Egyptian border, and then fifteen miles beyond. So confused were the British that entire units of Tommies mingled with Germans, all rushing pell-mell and hell-bent for the Egyptian border. Were Cunningham an aggressive optimist, he might have concluded that he had the Germans surrounded, and that Rommel was ripe for the kill. But he concluded the exact opposite and lost control of the battle.[389]

Auchinleck regained it. On November 25, he relieved Cunningham and ordered the Eighth Army to regroup and attack, presuming, correctly, that Rommel had outrun his supply lines. Within four days Auchinleck drove a corridor through to Tobruk. By the following week, Cunningham was hospitalized in Cairo; the official explanation was that he suffered from "exhaustion." Rommel withdrew into the desert. But then, the best fighters can take a punch or two without sustaining any real damage. Rommel would surely re-arm, and return. On the day before Churchill's birthday, soon after the Eighth Army made contact with the besieged troops in Tobruk, Auchinleck wired the prime minister: "birthday message to you is, Corridor to Tobruk clear and secure. Tobruk is as relieved as I am."[390]

The Home Island was now a fortress. More than a thousand tanks—the equivalent of three fully equipped armored divisions—were deployed within one hundred miles of London, ready to swarm the beaches and strategic ports should the Germans come ashore the following spring. Two days after his birthday Churchill told the Commons:

> We have several million men who will fight to the death if this country is invaded, but for whom we have not been able to manufacture

> the necessary number of rifles, although our rifles are now numbered by a good many millions. Therefore we supplement them with machine-guns, tommy-guns, pistols, grenades and bombs, and, when other things fail, we do not hesitate to place in the citizen's hands a pike or a mace, pending further developments. After all, a man thus armed may easily acquire a rifle for himself.[391]

But Churchill envisioned another use for his ever-growing forces. Believing since June of 1940 that the Germans would not come, he had built up his armies in anticipation of the day they would drive Rommel into the sea, the day they would go to French North Africa, and the day they would cross the Channel to fight on the Continent. Royal Navy engineers had been at work all year designing Churchill's artificial harbors—named "Mulberries" by Churchill. New corvettes and destroyers were sliding down shipyard ways. Tank transport ships had been designed. Lancaster heavy bombers rolled off assembly lines. Europe was Churchill's ultimate objective. When the time was right, he would go there in overwhelming numbers of ships and tanks and men and airplanes, and he'd bring his ports with him.

The Commons and King stood foursquare behind him, although the British army had yet to win a real victory against Hitler. In fact, against the Germans in 1941 Churchill could show nothing but defeats and a few diversions by his commandos and saboteurs. True, *Bismarck* had been dealt with, but that action was more symbolic than strategic as the registry of shipping losses from U-boats confirmed. True, Auchinleck had put Crusader back on track, but Rommel was by no means beaten. Harold Nicolson cringed when Churchill exulted in the House at Auchinleck's good fortune. Libya was a sideshow, Nicolson recorded. "Moscow may fall, Japan may come in against us. France may join the Axis. We may be beaten in Libya." Were any of these eventualities to come to pass, he lamented, "I feel [it] will react very badly on Winston's prestige."[392]

His prestige did not suffer, even as fresh vegetables, sugar, coal, and new clothing grew as scarce as victories. Britons, pummeled since 1940, stood by their Winnie, who, wrote Nicolson, "is the embodiment of the nation's will." Yet his political enemies were of a mind that one or two more disasters on the magnitude of Greece or Crete would spell the end of him. "Christ and Carrots" Cripps, in fact, was aiming to take his rightful place, as he saw it, in the cabinet, perhaps even at the head of a new government, should Churchill lose another battle.[393]

Kathleen Hill compiled a list of more than 120 well-wishers who had sent birthday greetings from around the world—kings, queens, and displaced continental potentates, from the entire ship's company of HMS

Churchill, as well as from all the boys of Harrow. Dominion officials high and low sent messages. Winant jotted a note, Wavell, from India, paid his respects, as did "that ass" de Gaulle. Eden, Attlee, and most of the cabinet sent their regards, as did the maharaja of Nepal. Even Stalin sent a note. No birthday salutations arrived from Franklin Roosevelt.[394]

Churchill lacked only that which he desired most of all, his American cousins fighting at his side. America stood behind him, but not beside him. With just four weeks remaining in 1941, he had no good reason to believe that America would be fighting when 1942 arrived. After almost two years of pleading, cajoling, flattering, prodding, and warning Roosevelt, he had come up short. As with others who brought their cases to Roosevelt, Churchill heard magical words but came away with no answers to his questions. Though the relationship he had with Roosevelt was just ambiguous and promising enough to sustain Churchill's hopes of salvation, it lacked a real strategy. It lacked singleness of purpose. Roosevelt still saw it in terms of "all help short of war." To Churchill, that meant ultimate stalemate, or worse. He sought a relationship with Roosevelt built on his premise "victory or death." The word for such a relationship is "alliance."[395]

During the first days of December, Stalin's most dependable and merciless ally, winter, caught the Germans unprepared. The first snow had fallen on October 6, early even for Moscow, and a harbinger of a winter that would long be remembered for its ferocity. Still, the Germans pressed on. By December 2, a German reconnaissance battalion worked its way through Khimki, a suburb of Moscow. On December 4, the temperature fell to minus thirty-two degrees Fahrenheit; wind-whipped snow slashed at men's skin and eyes like jagged steel filings. The next day, the temperature fell to minus thirty-seven, turning rubber brittle and gasoline into jelly. When their gearboxes froze solid, tanks went nowhere. German soldiers froze to death in their summer uniforms, within sight of Moscow, because Hitler's military chief of staff, General Alfred Jodl, had decreed that the issuance of winter uniforms would cast doubt on the Reich's promise of victory before winter. The Red Army counterattacked on December 5, smashing its way through the German lines in front of Moscow. This was a real counterattack, even though it rolled the Germans back only a few dozen miles. The Germans dug in. For thousands of Germans, clad in their summer gray, their foxholes became their graves. In the first week of December, almost two thousand German soldiers had had frostbitten limbs amputated. The Wehrmacht's ordeal was only beginning.[396]

During the first week of December, Churchill regularly telephoned Bletchley to ask about the disposition of the Japanese Combined Fleet (*Kido Butai*). The Imperial Japanese battle fleet, flying the flag of Vice Admiral Chūichi Nagumo, had disappeared into the vastness of the north Pacific. Another Japanese fleet was rumored to be making for the South China Sea, with designs upon Siam, Malaya, or Java; nobody knew. Each time Churchill asked, the Bletchley reply remained the same: No intelligence was forthcoming. The Japanese navy had vanished.

3

Vortex

DECEMBER 1941–NOVEMBER 1942

By the first days of December 1941, Churchill knew that events in the Far East were moving far ahead of his knowledge of them. Was it to be Peace or War? He had no say in the matter and could do nothing but wait, a state of inactivity he loathed, which demanded a trait he lacked, patience.

These were the longest nights, when the omnipresent bleakness of an English winter seeped into the ancient oak timbers and cold stone floors of Chequers. Churchill's bodyguard, Walter Thompson, recalled that when the winter rains arrived, the ancient house took on a "preternatural and malign" aura. The household staff tried to invest the home with as much Yule warmth as was allowed by the strictures imposed by war and the lack of effective central heat. Churchill spent his weeknights in London, deep within the Annexe, his small room there outfitted with one modest stuffed chair, a small desk, an electric feet warmer, and a twin-size dormitory bed. Naked incandescent bulbs hung on long wires that coiled downward from the concrete ceiling, buttressed by walls of heavy timber, yellowed by eighteen months of cigar smoke. Against the confines of that dank place, Chequers offered succor. The domestic staff bustled about placing sprays of pine boughs and holly branches throughout the great house. Old English country houses display a singular knack for generating more raw cold during winter months than the great outdoors. Chequers being no exception, housemaids piled Welsh coal into the grates, except in the great hall and Churchill's bedchamber, where as was his wont at Chartwell, he demanded log fires, which he liked to prod with an iron poker, in silence and for long periods of time.[1]

Churchill's favorite weeks of the year, the Christmas holidays, were approaching, their start marked at Chequers by servants maneuvering the tall Christmas fir into the great hall, where they adorned it with baked cookies, glass ornaments, and wax candles. Lest the tree ignite, housekeepers tied large sponges onto broomsticks and soaked them in buckets nearby—Churchill's favorite bath sponges, in fact, purloined from the Old Man, who was given to rumbling downstairs, barefoot in a damp silk dressing gown, and demanding his bathing accoutrements of the first servant he encountered.[2]

The wine cellar at Chequers, always well stocked thanks to the generosity of friends, contributed much to a spirit of holiday good cheer. Pol Roger Champagne flowed at each meal. Friends had donated enough Napoleon brandy to pickle a ship's company of would-be Nelsons, "enough to last twenty years of war," Pamela recalled. Churchill's valet, Frank Sawyers, kept a little spirit lamp on hand in order to warm the Old Man's brandy glass, a ritual repeated two or three times each evening. Numerous boxes of cigars arrived, gifts from all over the world. The Cuban government had been generous in that regard, having honored Churchill with a lovely old Queen Anne dresser, the drawers of which were stuffed with hundreds of the finest Havanas. The Exchequer assessed a hefty excise tax on the cigars; Churchill fumed but paid it. The Prof—Lord Cherwell—insisted Churchill forsake the cigars because he feared German agents lurking in Havana might have poisoned the filler. The task of testing the gifts of food and cigars for sinister ingredients fell to young Victor Rothschild, the 3rd Baron Rothschild, a chemist at MI5, and an expert in solving booby-trapped devices. Rothschild concluded that the goods were safe. Still, the Prof cautioned Churchill not to smoke his Romeo y Julietas. He smoked them anyway, whisky in hand, as he wandered the halls of his armed fortress. He had everything he needed to face the dangers beyond the walls—safety for his family, ample food, strong drink, and good company.[3]

The weekend following his birthday, Churchill invited Averell Harriman and his daughter Kathleen to Chequers. Kathleen, a correspondent for *Newsweek*, was a close friend of Pamela's, and as the American woman's twenty-fourth birthday was in a few days, the Churchills proposed a birthday celebration in the country, with Gil Winant and many of the usual gang in attendance, a little something that promised modest respite from the strains of war. Churchill inscribed for Kathleen a copy of his memoir of the Sudan campaign, *The River War*. Though her birthday fell on Sunday, the party was held on Saturday, December 6, the feast of St. Nicholas, the patron saint of sailors (and merchants, archers, and children), celebrated throughout Britain with gifts for the children and with much ceremony in Canterbury Cathedral and in the hundreds of small churches erected in Nicholas's name along the coast, from where Englishmen had sailed to build the Empire and from where they now sailed to defend it. With the gales of winter in mind, British sailors called Nicholas "the saint of cold December," and in chapels ashore and on board ships sought his protection:

One there is whom once our fathers
Took their own, their saint, to be
Since his prayers had helped the children

And the sailors on the sea;
Lord, who dost thine angels send,
Make Saint Nicholas our friend.

On the night of the sixth, Clementine, with a cold coming on, retired early, as did the rest of the household but for Churchill. He drafted several memos addressing the food situation—excepting the armed forces, the average Briton's diet had fallen below the minimum level to sustain good health or the strength to work a full shift in an armaments factory. As Churchill worked away, Brooke telephoned with the news that a Japanese fleet of transports and warships *might* be heading into the Gulf of Siam toward either the Kra Peninsula or Bangkok. Or it might be a bluff, no one knew. Britain lacked the means to stop such a force in any event. Before donning his silk smock, Churchill checked in a final time with the Bletchley analysts, in hopes that they might lay a golden egg with regard to the whereabouts of the Japanese battle fleet.[4]

They could not. The Japanese fleet remained invisible.

Since his birthday Churchill had contemplated more than the location of the Japanese navy. Stalin that week had finessed Britain into declaring war on Finland, Hungary, and Romania. The two latter states had tried and failed to avoid war by appeasing both Germany and Russia. Finland, invaded by Stalin in late 1939 and not surprisingly seeking revenge—and its pre-1939 borders—had joined the Axis days after Hitler strode into Russia. Though Churchill thought Finland's choice of partners "obnoxious" and loathed Romania's Antonescu, he told the War Cabinet that he wanted it to be "on record that in his view this declaration of war on Finland (and also on Hungary and Romania) would not assist either our cause or that of the Russians. The sole justification for it was that it was necessary in order to satisfy the Russian Government." Churchill threw Stalin a bone—three bones—because he could not deliver fast enough the airplanes and tanks Stalin sought. Most important, he could not deliver a second front in Europe. Instead, that week he ordered Eden to Moscow to mollify Stalin.[5]

He continued to ponder the diplomatic conundrum he and Roosevelt might soon face in Asia. Were the Japanese to attack British or Dutch interests but not American, Britain would find itself fighting a new war. But would America come in under such circumstances? For almost six months Churchill had asked Roosevelt for a direct answer. The president had not given one. Accordingly, Churchill informed Harriman that in the event of a Japanese attack, Britain would *not* declare war "within the hour" as he had earlier promised, but would wait until Roosevelt took "such action as, under the circumstances, he considers best." Then, and only then, would Britain—"within the minute"—declare war on Japan.[6]

The two leaders had agreed that week to proceed as partners in an extraordinary venture, the building of an atomic bomb. When American physicists weeks earlier endorsed the Maud Committee's conclusion that a nuclear fission bomb was feasible, Roosevelt diverted several millions of discretionary (and off the books) funds to Vannevar Bush and his atomic scientists. Bush and his cohorts so successfully wrapped a curtain of secrecy around themselves and their work that within months, the American press reported that exploration of the atom at universities had come to a stop, except for the pursuit of "artificial radioactive materials for medical research." Bush, at Roosevelt's request, told Churchill of the American decision to build the bomb, and suggested the joint Anglo-American project be code-named Mayson, in case Maud had been compromised. Churchill replied: "I need not assure you of our readiness to collaborate with the United States Administration in this matter." He appointed Sir John Anderson—"the man without mercy"—as chief administrator on the British side, and put Lord Cherwell in charge of the scientific end of the operation. The atomic project offered Cherwell an opportunity to spite his enemies in academia. It also held promise as a means to annihilate his most hated enemy, Germany.[7]

On the morning of December 7, spurred by the report of Japanese naval forces in the Gulf of Siam, Churchill drafted a proposed threat to Japan, and sent it off to Roosevelt. He sought Roosevelt's approval to inform Tokyo that the British and Dutch would construe any incursion by Japanese forces from Indochina into Thailand as an attack on their interests and "should hostilities unfortunately result the responsibility will rest with Japan." Two days earlier, Halifax had cabled the news that Roosevelt finally agreed to join Britain in such a warning, though no such assurance had yet arrived from the president. Given Britain's state of readiness in the Far East, Churchill's note to the Japanese amounted to his brandishing an empty scabbard.[8]

At Argentia, in August, Roosevelt had told Churchill that he, Roosevelt, could fight a war without declaring war. Such words of defiance (defiance of the U.S. Congress at any rate) offered hope to Churchill, but Roosevelt could not defy Congress, and Churchill knew it. Roosevelt had challenged Hitler by putting American troops into Iceland; he had embargoed the Japanese, and he had overseen the virtual nullification of the Neutrality Acts. The president had irritated many within his military by sending to Churchill America's newest tanks, on the grounds that Britain was fighting a war while America was not. Roosevelt's carefully trod path to war led him even to defy the American labor movement, the very heart of his constituency. Congress in the autumn had threatened to scuttle his quest to arm merchant ships unless he told John L. Lewis and his United Mine

Workers that a contemplated coal strike would be considered virtually treasonous, for without coal, there could be no steel, and without steel, no tanks for Britain, or Buicks and Fords for Americans. Roosevelt strongly advised Lewis to back off; he did. Roosevelt had talked a big game for months, but of America, Field Marshal Dill wrote, "Never have I seen a country so utterly unprepared for war and so soft."[9]

Churchill's luncheon guests on the seventh were Lady Alexandra Mary Cadogan, Duchess of Marlborough, and her teenage son, John George Vanderbilt Henry Spencer Churchill, Marquess of Blandford, grandson of Consuelo Vanderbilt, and the future 11th Duke of Marlborough. Young Lord Blandford was one-quarter American (Churchill, of course, one-half), yet the Vanderbilts and Spencer-Churchills embodied moneyed aristocracy of the sort America Firsters railed against. Fortunately for Britain, the fourth lunch guest, Gil Winant, believed with Churchill that the war was about liberty, not privilege. While making his way to the dining room, Winant encountered Churchill, pacing the hall. He asked Winant if he thought there was going to be war with Japan. "Yes," Winant replied. Then, "with unusual vehemence" Churchill asked if America would declare war on Japan if Japan declared war on Britain. Winant explained that only the American Congress could declare war. Churchill remained silent for a moment, and Winant in that instant grasped the source of his bleak demeanor. If Japan attacked British interests but not American, Churchill might find himself fighting a second war, alone. The fate of Britain, Winant realized, "might be hanging on one turn of pitch and toss."[10]

The evening of December 7 found a somber Churchill taking his dinner at Chequers in the company of Winant and Harriman. Churchill's naval assistant Tommy Thompson and his senior private secretary, John Martin, were also present at the table.* To Harriman, Churchill appeared tired and depressed. "The hunt for the Japanese fleets had turned up nothing. He sat for long moments with his head in his hands." Harriman had learned what the Churchill family long knew: depending on the events of the day—a favorite swan consumed by a badger, news of an old friend's ill

---

* A private secretary almost always dined with Churchill in order to receive, assess, and pass along to him communications deemed vital. The principals at such dinners—Winston, Harriman, Dill, Hopkins, etc.—often neglect to note in their memoirs any lesser aide who might also have attended, referred to as a dogsbody by the British, because they were always around and underfoot, as it were.

health—Churchill at the start of the evening meal regularly sat in curmudgeonly silence while his family sat and waited until the somber moment passed, as it inevitably did, often after the first or second glass of champagne, when Churchill began quoting Macaulay or recalled some glorious deed performed by himself long ago and painted the scene in words for those around the table.[11]

This night proved a singular occasion. Shortly after nine, he rose and switched on a small flip-top wireless. A spate of headlines narrated by the BBC's Alvar Liddell rolled in on the static. Something was said of a Japanese attack on British ships in the Dutch East Indies, and on American ships at some other location. Churchill and his guests, having missed the first words of the broadcast, sat in confused silence. The butler appeared from the kitchen and announced, "The Japanese have attacked the Americans." Commander Thompson chimed in, claiming he thought he had heard the announcer say the Americans had been attacked "at Pearl River." That would have put the Japanese at the mouth of China's third-largest river, about 150 miles from Hong Kong. Yet what manner of American shipping would be navigating in those waters? Liddell then repeated his leading headline: American shipping in Hawaii had been attacked. Yet what sort of shipping? And how large an attack? Churchill and his dining companions sat for a moment in silence.[12]

Churchill then leapt to his feet and started for the hall, announcing his intent to make good his pledge to declare war on Japan within the hour if Japan attacked the United States. "Good God," Winant exclaimed, "you can't declare war on a radio announcement." Churchill stopped, looked at Winant quizzically, and asked, "What shall I do?" Churchill then turned to John Martin and barked, "Get me the president on the phone at once." Winant spoke first to Roosevelt, who confirmed the attack but omitted any details as to the extent of the damage, not only because he didn't know the extent, but because the phone line was a regular, unsecured wire, a source of constant worry to Martin because Churchill used it often. Churchill took the phone. "Mr. President, what's this about Japan?" "It's quite true," replied Roosevelt, "They have attacked us at Pearl Harbor. We are all in the same boat now."[13]

Though Churchill did not know exactly where in the broad expanse of the Pacific the Japanese main battle fleet was, he now knew with terrible certainty where it had been hours earlier. He had not yet learned that the Japanese had bombed Hong Kong. And Singapore. And had landed troops near Hong Kong and, an hour before attacking Pearl Harbor, that Lieutenant General Tomoyuki Yamashita had put troops ashore at Kota Bharu, four hundred miles north of Singapore. Japanese bombers were at that moment winging their way from Formosa to Manila. In Washington, with the catastrophic news of hundreds, perhaps thousands, of deaths in Hawaii, with the apparent loss of most—perhaps all—of his Pacific battleships, Franklin Roosevelt's need for political subtlety came to an end, and so, too, did his, and America's, long and dreamlike journey to war. The isolationist cause died on the spot. And with the death of almost 2,500 young American sailors, Marines, and soldiers—their war had lasted about as long as it takes to smoke a Lucky Strike or kiss a pretty girl goodbye—Winston Churchill had finally gained his Western ally. Yet only against a new enemy, and in a new war.

Churchill, in his memoirs, titles the chapter devoted to December 1941 "Pearl Harbor!" His use of an exclamation point is not meant to underscore the shock to America of the devastating Japanese attack on its naval base, but to underscore his profound relief. He wrote that late on the seventh, a thought took shape: "So we had won after all." Indeed, he took to his bed happy that night, and "slept the sleep of the saved and thankful." Brooke's diary entry of the seventh stands as a clear measure of the differences between him—a dedicated staff officer—and Churchill, a statesman whose perspective included events and their consequences over the entire globe: "All our work of last 48 hours wasted! The Japs themselves have now assured that the USA are now in the war."[14]

Such was Churchill's joy over the news from Pearl Harbor that he, curiously, chose to share it first with Eamon de Valera. During the early hours of the eighth, Churchill composed a telegram to the Irish prime minister, an odd choice of correspondent, given the twenty-year history of antipathy, if not outright loathing, between the two. To the Irish prime minister, Churchill wrote, "Now is your chance. Now or never. 'A nation once again.' Am very ready to meet you at any time." Yet there was method in Churchill's apparent madness. He had told Roosevelt the previous year that he was prepared to consider a united Ireland if de Valera granted use of three Irish ports to the Royal Navy or, better yet, came in on the Allied side. "A Nation Once Again" happened to be the marching song of Irish republicans two decades earlier. Churchill was offering de Valera a roadmap to Irish unity.[15]

Churchill had long considered Ireland to be the wayward daughter of the Empire for whom a candle always burned in his window. De Valera did not share Churchill's enthusiasm for a family reunion; he never responded to the overture. Rather, he invited both the Japanese consul and German minister to maintain their staffs and embassies in Dublin. Churchill got the message. Though he dispatched subordinates to woo the Irish government into the Allied ranks (without success), and regularly mulled over the option of taking the three Irish ports by force, he made scant official reference to de Valera for almost three years, until late in 1944, when he cabled

Roosevelt concerning the need "to do something for Poland" and the necessity "to do something to de Valera." Many sons of Ireland volunteered for the RAF, Royal Navy, and British army, but the Irish daughter never returned home. Yet, as Churchill sifted the implications of the news from Oahu—victory had in an instant become only a question of time, unheard-of sums of money, and unfathomable casualties—he looked beyond the war and beheld there an opportunity to preserve and strengthen the entire British Empire, even those parts, like Ireland, long lost to London.

By the morning of December 8, events in Asia overshadowed Churchill's quixotic Irish initiative. He had gone to bed with a clear view of the far horizon but failed to see the chasm immediately in front of him. North of Hong Kong, 25,000 Japanese troops had overnight crossed the Sham Chum River into the British leased territories, where fewer than 2,000 Indian and Scottish troops were strung out along lines that were too lengthy and too weak. Forced to retreat four miles to the island of Hong Kong, they joined three battalions of Indians and two of Canadians, the Winnipeg Grenadiers and the Royal Rifles, sent in late October to reinforce the garrison despite Churchill's warning months earlier that Hong Kong would fall, reinforced or not. The Canadians in Hong Kong knew that the Japanese encamped on the mainland were not there to lay siege to the city but to take it, a result now ordained, for no reinforcements could be gotten to the outnumbered defenders.

On the Malay Peninsula, the Japanese force under Lieutenant General Yamashita that had landed to stiff but futile opposition far north of Singapore had by the time Churchill awoke blasted the small RAF contingent and secured a foothold. Within a day, Japanese infantry and light tanks crossed the forty-mile-wide Kra Isthmus and reached the Andaman Sea—that is, the Japanese had reached the Bay of Bengal and the Indian Ocean. British forces on the isthmus consisted mostly of two undersize divisions of Indian troops, supported by fewer than 160 older planes, and no tanks. They were all that stood between the Japanese army and an easy march down the peninsula to Singapore. Seaward, a few destroyers plus *Prince of Wales* and the battle cruiser *Repulse,* recently arrived on station in the Strait of Johore, were all that stood between the Japanese navy and Singapore, where Duff Cooper, newly appointed resident minister, was awakened by sirens and AA guns and exploding Japanese bombs. He could do nothing but try to compose himself to sleep again.[16]

Yet another Japanese force made its presence known in the Philippines when, about four hours after the raid on Pearl Harbor, carrier-based Japanese fighters and bombers struck Mindanao, six hundred miles south of Manila. From that attack it could be deduced with certainty that further air attacks, and landings, were likely on the Philippines' most vital island, Luzon. General Douglas MacArthur, asleep in his penthouse apartment at the Manila Hotel, was awakened and apprised of the Oahu attack moments after it took place. Events over the next few hours showed that MacArthur, though forewarned by the attack on Pearl Harbor and with full knowledge that the Philippines—the strategic gateway to Malaya—were the real Japanese objective, had been caught napping, disastrously and inexcusably so.[17]

A complete breakdown had occurred between MacArthur, his chief of staff Richard K. Sutherland, and his chief of air operations Lewis Brereton, with the result that virtually the entire U.S. air arm in the Far East was sitting on the ground at Clark Field when more than nine hours after Pearl Harbor, two hundred Japanese bombers and fighters based on Formosa swept in and within the hour destroyed the airfield and everything on it—planes, fuel, and hangars. The *New York Times* reported later in the week that MacArthur claimed little damage had been done. In fact, MacArthur had lost his aerial umbrella. The next day, Japanese bombers obliterated the Cavite Navy Yard, eight miles from Manila. Five hundred American and Filipino men were killed. Admiral Tommy Hart, commander of the anemic U.S. Asiatic Fleet, watched from Manila as his anchorage disappeared under hellish clouds of black smoke. He decided on the spot to take what remained of his little navy, less his submarines, to the Dutch East Indies. On December 10, the Japanese made their first landings on Luzon. MacArthur could oppose them neither by sea nor air. MacArthur's army of 30,000 Americans and three times as many ill-trained Filipinos was effectively surrounded and cut off from reinforcement.[18]

A few days after the attacks on Pearl Harbor and Manila, U.S. Army chief of staff General George Marshall summoned Dwight Eisenhower, recently promoted to brevet brigadier general, to Washington. Eisenhower's first assignment was to come up with a plan to solve MacArthur's supply problem. The new deputy, who displayed a knack for logistics, pondered the challenge for about an hour before concluding that his mission was hopeless. The army had nothing to send MacArthur, and the navy lacked both the ships and the fighting spirit to ferry men or supplies to the Philippines. Eisenhower could do nothing other than recommend that bases be put in Australia from which future forays might originate. No reinforcements would reach MacArthur's stranded army, ever.[19]

On the morning of the eighth, Roosevelt followed up his conversation with Churchill with a cable in which he again offered that they were now in the same boat, adding, "it is a ship which will not and can not be sunk," an ironic choice of words given that the Japanese visitations to Honolulu and Manila had left neither the British nor the Americans enough in the way of ships to harass, let alone destroy, the Japanese navy. Hours later, when Congress declared war by a vote of 382–1, it did so only upon Japan. When Roosevelt spoke to the Congress, he made no mention of Churchill, or Hitler. Japan had plunged America into war but not against Hitler.[20]

Churchill made his way to the House early in the afternoon on the eighth, wielding a rolled-up mass of the morning papers as a battering ram to clear a path through the crowd gathered outside for himself, Clementine, and Pamela. Nicolson, to his diary: "Winston enters the chamber with bowed shoulders and an expression of grim determination on his face." The prime minister told MPs that the War Cabinet had met earlier and had declared war on Japan. He spoke of facing new dangers, pledging, "When we think of the insane ambition and insatiable appetite which have caused this vast and melancholy extension of the war, we can only feel that Hitler's madness has infected the Japanese mind, and that the root of the evil and its branch must be extirpated together." He reminded the House that "some of the finest ships in the Royal Navy have reached their stations in the Far East at a very convenient moment." That was meant for American ears, for with the loss of the fleet at Pearl Harbor, *Prince of Wales* and *Repulse* now formed the Allied naval presence in the western Pacific, perhaps the entire Pacific. The ships signaled to Washington Churchill's intent to contribute to the Far East war. In Tokyo the ships were seen for what they were—targets.[21]

That morning, Churchill sent a personal letter to the Japanese ambassador in which, very politely, he announced that a state of war existed between their two countries. Some of his colleagues thought the note too proper. "But after all," Churchill later wrote, "when you have to kill a man it costs nothing to be polite." He told King George later in the day that he hoped to leave for Washington "without delay, provided such a course is agreeable to President Roosevelt, as I have no doubt it will be," and added that he would defer proposing a visit until the situation with Germany and Italy (neither had yet declared war on America) became "more clear." Then, too impatient to defer, he cabled Washington with a request to meet with Roosevelt in order to "review the whole war plan." Roosevelt did not reply directly; instead, he told Halifax that perhaps sometime around January 7 might work for everybody. For Churchill, that would simply not do. But it would have to. The next move was Roosevelt's alone to make.[22]

Eden, about to depart Scapa Flow for Moscow, thought it unwise that both he and Churchill should leave the country at such a critical time. He also believed that Stalin, who trusted no one, would conclude that Churchill and Roosevelt were up to something. He telephoned his concerns to John Winant, who replied that as far as he knew, no meeting had been arranged. Eden's parliamentary secretary Oliver Harvey told his diary: "Really, the PM is a lunatic; he gets in such a state of excitement that the wildest schemes seem reasonable." Eden set sail later in the day somewhat secure in the belief that the King, Winant, and the War Cabinet would prevail upon Churchill to stay at home. Churchill intended otherwise. Yet, still no invitation had arrived from Roosevelt. And, still, Hitler remained silent.[23]

It was time for Churchill to roll out long-ignored charts of Pacific islands and archipelagos, many of which were unfamiliar even to high-ranking British leaders, including the prime minister. Churchill loved maps, as much for their utility as for their ability to stoke his imagination. Maps and naval charts lifted him away to far-off places and conjured images of heroic adventures long past. This caused problems when he—regularly—meddled with his military planners. Antony Head, a decorated Dunkirk survivor and a junior staff officer in War Plans, recalled Churchill stabbing a finger at a chart of the Philippines while offering that a particular island—which Churchill claimed was actually part of the Dutch East Indies—was "inhabited by dragons." Clementine had supplied much of his knowledge (or lack thereof) of the region in her letters home during a four-month cruise to the East Indies seven years earlier.

Virtually every stop on her tour, from Rangoon to Singapore to Borneo, had now been or soon would be attacked by the Japanese. From Singapore Clementine had suggested to Winston that he procure from the Admiralty a map of the new British naval base, located between Singapore Island and the mainland. Had he done so he would have learned that no fixed defenses were planned for the Malay mainland, an oversight Wavell brought to his attention only weeks before the final battle for Singapore. Clementine had also visited Komodo, where indeed she took part in a "dragon" hunt. Distances across the Pacific and Indian oceans defied imagination, including Churchill's—14,000 miles and fifty-five days sailing from London to Calcutta via Cape Town, 8,000 miles and three weeks from San Francisco to Bombay. Churchill simply referred to "vast expanses" without quite understanding just how vast the expanses were in that watery part of the world. The entire European and North African theaters and much of the eastern

Atlantic war zone fell within a 1,300-mile radius extending from Berlin, within which the newest British and German bombers could depart a base at sunset, cruise halfway across the theater, and arrive home again in time for breakfast. Railroads, which had shuttled troops to the trenches in 1914, could now carry entire armies across the Continent. Modern technology had made Europe a smaller place, but not so the Pacific. All of Europe, the Mediterranean, the Near East, and the entirety of North Africa could disappear into the Pacific Ocean several times over.[24]

In this vastness Churchill expected *Prince of Wales* and *Repulse* to impart to the Japanese a lesson in sea power as practiced by the world's greatest sea power, perfected long before Captain A. T. Mahan, U.S.N., set about putting his thoughts on that subject to paper.* The Japanese understood, as did the British, Mahan's maxim that in distant seas—where colonial fortresses and naval bases were separated by hundreds or even thousands of miles—the destruction of an enemy's fleet must precede any attempt to take a fortress or anchorage. This was in essence a waterborne version of Prussian military philosopher Karl von Clausewitz's dictum that the destruction of enemy armies, not the capture of real estate, should be a commander's first objective. Mahan believed that the destruction of an enemy fleet virtually guaranteed the success of any land-based assault that followed. Churchill wrote of that very circumstance in *History of the English-Speaking Peoples,* where he attributed Cornwallis's surrender at Yorktown to the inability of the Royal Navy to prevent the French fleet from getting between Cornwallis and his seaborne reinforcements: "Sea-power had once more decided the issue, and but for the French blockade the British war of attrition might well have succeeded." The rebel American army in the meantime had marched overland four hundred miles to trap Cornwallis, who, encamped and besieged at Yorktown, at the foot of the Virginia Peninsula, realized that he was at the end of his rope. Singapore was now in an identical position. The Japanese forces that had landed four hundred miles to the north were moving smartly down the Malay Peninsula. Unless *Prince of Wales* found and killed the enemy's warships, Yamashita could reinforce at will.[25]

For almost two centuries the security of the British Empire had been guaranteed by great ships, wooden before the late nineteenth century, weighing in at several hundred tons, driven by wind, armed with smoothbore cannons capable of splintering enemy ships, and with a range of a mile or so inland, just far enough to dissuade native troublemakers from harassing British coastal trading posts. In the mid–nineteenth century, James

* A. T. Mahan, *The Influences of Sea Power upon History* (Boston: Little, Brown and Co., 1890).

Brooke, a Lord Jim sort of fellow and the self-made Rajah of Sarawak on the northern coast of Borneo, wrote to London that with "a frigate...a slight military force and the English Union Jack," he could "control all the neighboring evildoers." He was correct. Nineteenth-century warships carried all the power necessary to dissuade competing colonial powers and unfriendly natives from harassing the British in their territorial waters.

By 1942 a pair of battleships displaced almost as many tons as Nelson's entire main battle fleet at Trafalgar. Twentieth-century British war wagons were encased by more than a foot of steel, and by 1942 they were equipped with radar and driven by huge motors that could generate enough electricity to light a small city. Most sailed armed with fourteen- and fifteen-inch guns that could loft 1,500-pound projectiles more than twenty miles. *Nelson* and *Rodney* were armed with sixteen-inch guns. These great ships, *Prince of Wales* foremost among them, were the steel needles and iron threads that stitched together the quilt of the Empire, and secured the sea lanes that bound the Empire to London. When Churchill contemplated the Pacific and Indian oceans, he did so only in terms of the sea routes from London to India and, to a lesser extent, British Malaya, Australia, and New Zealand. Churchill and the Admiralty had for two decades paid scant attention to the outlying archipelagos snatched from Germany after World War One—New Britain, northeastern New Guinea, the Bismarck Archipelago, Buka and Bougainville in the Solomon Islands. The remainder of the Solomon Islands, a British protectorate since 1893, had for decades gone largely ignored by London.

But not by Tokyo. The Solomons stretched away into the South Pacific like a fleet of derelict ghost ships, forgotten and undefended. Other than machete-wielding natives and a few remaining British coconut planters, all other Britons had been evacuated to Australia. Other western Pacific archipelagos—the Marshall Islands and the Mariana Islands—had been German territories until they were handed to Japan (then an ally) following the Great War. Japan also ruled the Caroline Islands, which together with the Marshalls and Marianas, formed a buffer midway between Tokyo and New Guinea. These island chains offered jump-off points for further advances in the Pacific. The Japanese had long understood the importance of the Solomons. Their capture would isolate Australia, a scenario now grasped with fear in Canberra but not yet fully appreciated in London. One of these long-ignored Crown possessions, a mostly uncharted mountainous jumble of rivers, malarial swamps, and thick jungle, was virtually unknown to Londoners—Guadalcanal, located at the southern end of the Solomons. Churchill took note of these far-flung places, not because the entire southern Pacific might soon become a furnace in which the antipodal Dominions could perish, but because the sea routes from those regions were vital to transporting reinforcements to the theater of war he most cared about: North Africa. "I wouldn't have thought the Pacific was something which had much troubled Churchill," recalled Mark Bonham Carter, the son of Churchill's old friend Violet Bonham Carter: "He thought in rather continental terms."[26]

That is why Churchill took umbrage at increasing Australian resistance to his demand for more Australian troops. If Londoners had not complained while being slaughtered, he asked his doctor, why should Australians, who had yet to see a single enemy bomb fall? Yet Australia, with just three army divisions stationed at home, feared now for its safety, its survival even. Churchill reassured Australia's new prime minister, John Curtin, that *Prince of Wales* would keep Australia safe from Japanese depredations.

When he first proposed sending *Prince of Wales* to Singapore, the Admiralty, fearing *Tirpitz* might emerge in the Atlantic, "expressed their dissent." Churchill thought likewise, but in reverse, recalled Sir Ian Jacob: "He was thinking in terms of the annoyance caused us by the *Bismarck*, and thought *Prince of Wales* would cause the Japanese a great deal of trouble." Yet "the parallel was not a good one because the Japanese hadn't a vital lifeline, as we had across the Atlantic, which could be threatened and which required constant protection." Churchill was so sure of *Prince of Wales*'s deterrent threat, so enthused at the prospect of his great battleship mixing it up with the Japanese navy, and so positive of the outcome that he instructed the ship's arrival at Cape Town to be "reported to the enemy" *via* radio broadcast. The Japanese duly noted the news. *Repulse* was by then on station at Singapore. With no destroyers available for escort, *Prince of Wales* made the journey to Singapore alone. Too late, having insisted the venture proceed, Churchill told the Admiralty that he regretted the lack of a destroyer escort. "This is a case where I am for 'Safety First.'" The mission itself belied that claim. Churchill discussed the mission in several telegrams, including a message reassuring Curtin, and another to Stalin, which employed the same phrase he had used when he told Roosevelt of *Prince of Wales*'s departure: "It is grand to have something that can catch and kill any Japanese ship."[27]

Admiral Tom S. V. Phillips, in command of *Prince of Wales,* agreed with Churchill's assessment of his battleship's prowess, with one caveat. The Japanese fleet, Phillips told the War Cabinet, consisted of a mix of newer and older ships, as did the British fleet, but Britain's newest and best ships, such as *Prince of Wales,* operating near British Asian possessions "*under cover of shore based aircraft*," would prove more than a match for the Japanese (italics added). No such land-based air cover was available anywhere near Singapore on December 8. Months earlier Churchill had dissuaded his military chiefs from sending "very great diversions" of aircraft to the Far East. "The political situation in the Far East does not seem to require," he told the chiefs, "and the strength of our Air Force by no means warrants, the maintenance of such large forces in the Far East at this time." Churchill's Far East strategy, recalled Ian Jacob, was based on the premise that "if the Japanese came into the war, it will bring in the Americans and we shall win the war and then, anything we lose we shall get back; that was his simple view of the matter, yet in many ways it was a sensible view." Thus, as the political situation in the Far East wobbled and then collapsed, Churchill chose to keep his aircraft close to home. Had he kept rigidly to his strategy of not reinforcing the Far East with men, planes, or ships, *Prince of Wales* would not have sailed. But he had sent the ship, and now it sailed without air cover. Churchill had suggested to the Admiralty that an aircraft carrier accompany *Prince of Wales* to the Far East. Yet when it became clear that no carrier could be spared, Churchill and the Admiralty sent the battleship anyway, alone.[28]

Foretold by Britain of its coming, the Japanese were waiting for *Prince of Wales* somewhere in the South China Sea, waiting not only with ships, which the powerful British man-of-war might catch and kill, but with airplanes. Late on December 8, *Prince of Wales, Repulse,* and four old destroyers ventured together from Singapore and down the Strait of Johore in search of the Japanese transports that had landed troops far up the Malay Peninsula. Absent air cover, Phillips was sailing into a deluge without an umbrella. He knew this, and although the Admiralty had not *ordered* him to depart Singapore, implicit in the orders that sent him there was the understanding that he behave like an English admiral, that is, that he fight.

Max Beaverbrook and his lieutenant, George Malcolm Thomson,* considered the mission of *Prince of Wales* to be "pure rubbish." The Beaver had begun to think a great many of Churchill's schemes—Greece, Crete, and now the sojourn of the battleships—were rubbish, and had begun to fancy himself a suitable replacement as prime minister should Churchill not survive a vote of confidence or an errant German bomb. Beaverbrook differed with Churchill on North Africa, where Max would abandon the shifty sands in order to establish a second front on the Continent. He differed with just about every Allied military man on the prospects for Russia when he claimed soon after Barbarossa began that with prodigious British and American help, Stalin could last far longer than several weeks, maybe

---

* George Malcolm Thomson, a Scottish-born journalist, served during the war as a deputy to Lord Beaverbrook. By the 1970s, Thomson had earned a reputation as a talented historian and novelist.

even win. By November, Beaverbrook had helped deliver the first installments of that aid to Moscow. But Max harbored doubts about Churchill. He "had not so much respect for Winston's intelligence" and strategic acumen, recalled Thomson, but respected Churchill "as the godsend leader that we had to have." Churchill's dispatch of *Prince of Wales* to the Pacific only reinforced Beaverbrook's uncertainty. Sir Ian Jacob agreed: "Churchill was much too ardent and active a man. He thought something should be going on all the time" and "was so desperately keen for us to have the biggest part in whatever was going on." He was "not at all a theoretical strategist" who "considered the best thing to do and then made quite certain nothing detracted from it, and that the proper forces were concentrated in the proper place."[29]

Admiral Tom Phillips *was* a theoretical strategist, and that was the problem. He was a desk admiral, vice chief of the Admiralty staff, a thinker who was considered by many to be the brains of the Admiralty. He shared four traits with Churchill: he was prone to anger; he was given to meddling in operational plans; he thought Britain's seagoing admirals lacked aggressiveness; and he worshipped battleships. The Far East venture was to be his first fleet command, and although the previous year he had objected when Churchill divided Wavell's Middle Eastern forces between Greece and Egypt, he embraced the Singapore adventure with alacrity. Knowing of the absence of air cover in Malaya, Phillips might have better served Churchill (and improved his own chances for survival) by pointing out the potential folly in the Singapore gambit. But here was Phillips's chance for glory. Physically, the admiral was a wee man—he had to stand on a box to see from his bridge—who possessed an oversize ego; Admiral James Somerville called him "the Pocket Napoleon." Phillips was well aware of the damage inflicted on capital ships at Taranto and Pearl Harbor, yet those ships had been riding at anchor; *Prince of Wales,* under his command, could zig and zag at speeds of almost thirty-five miles per hour, all the while shredding the sky and everything in it with its vast array of armaments. Yet, any gardener who has ever fled a swarm of wasps knows that size and maneuverability do not always carry the day.[30]

The Japanese, like Churchill and Phillips, were not burdened with any doubts whatsoever of their military talents. They had demonstrated at Pearl Harbor the means to deal with the battleships of the world's most powerful navies. When it came to airborne torpedo and bomb attacks against great warships, the Japanese understood what the blasé British and Americans still, incredibly, did not: the Taranto raid and the sinking by aircraft of *Southampton* (a cruiser) had marked late afternoon in the era of battleships. December 7 marked the end of that era.[31]

On the ninth, Churchill outlined to the cabinet his plan for the *Prince of*

Wales and *Repulse,* already at sea, to "vanish into the ocean wastes and exercise a vague menace" akin to the behavior of "rogue elephants." By then, the *Prince of Wales,* flying Phillips's flag, and captained by John Leach (whom Churchill had wanted to court-martial the previous May), was steaming up the Malay coast escorted by the four old destroyers and the HMS *Repulse. Repulse*'s captain, William Tennant, offered to Cecil Brown, an American reporter who was on board: "We are off to look for trouble. I expect we'll find it."[32]

Near Saigon, more than four hundred miles away, Japanese ground crews were arming two dozen long-range Mitsubishi "Nell" bombers and several dozen "Betty" torpedo-bombers. Churchill and the Admiralty knew that the Japanese were reinforcing the Indochina airfields, but, Churchill later wrote, "sound reasons"—the distance, four hundred miles—implied that *Prince of Wales* "would be outside the effective range of enemy, shore-based torpedo bombers." Here was an astounding case of errant reasoning, given that two days earlier, Japanese airmen had flown almost three hundred miles to Pearl Harbor from aircraft carriers. What was another hundred miles to the best fliers in the world? Churchill—who had once denigrated the Japanese as "the Wops of the Pacific"—later wrote that "the efficiency of the Japanese in air warfare was at this time greatly underestimated both by ourselves and by the Americans."[33]

Tars aboard the two British battlewagons certainly underestimated the Japanese. When late on the ninth word came down to Cecil Brown that a Japanese battleship, three cruisers, and at least four destroyers were thought to be somewhere close ahead, Brown joked that he'd like to get a taxi back to Singapore. "Oh, but they are Japanese," an officer replied, "there's nothing to worry about." Another officer chimed in: "Those Japs can't fly," he said, "they can't see at night, and they're not well trained." Churchill happened to feel the same way: he had told luncheon guests months earlier that as far as Japanese airplanes were concerned, "We are of the opinion that they are not very good." On board the *Repulse,* yet another officer claimed that the Japanese "have rather good ships but they can't shoot straight." The Japanese had in fact been shooting pretty smartly all over the Pacific, while the men on board *Repulse* had yet to fire a single shot in anger during the first twenty-seven months of war.[34]

The next morning, the tenth, at 11:07 in Malaya—3:07 A.M. in London—Brown jotted in his notebook: "Enemy aircraft approaching... action stations." At 11:14 he spied nine Japanese planes at an altitude of around 12,000 feet. "And here they come," he wrote. A wave of torpedo bombers came in low. The *Repulse* dodged nineteen torpedoes "thanks to Providence," the captain signaled to Admiral Phillips. The very next torpedo hit *Repulse* near midships, throwing Brown to the deck. Immediately the ship heeled sharply to one side. Within a minute, from the loudspeakers came the captain's final order: "Prepare to abandon ship." A pause: "God be with you."[35]

A half mile ahead, the *Prince of Wales,* the victim of two torpedo hits, rode low in the water, its steering smashed. Fires burned along its length. On the *Repulse,* Brown slumped to the deck and watched as a dozen Royal Marines dove overboard; all were swept into the still-churning propellers. A sailor leapt from the radio tower and straight down the smokestack. Three dozen tars climbed from belowdecks up the inside of the decoy funnel only to find themselves fatally trapped by a steel grate at the top, locked from the outside. Brown watched, stunned, as hundreds of men scrambled over the sides and into the sea, yet he could not bring himself to join them. Finally, he took a last look at his watch—smashed at 12:35—and jumped. He landed in a mess of debris and heavy oil discharged from the ship, in which he and Captain Tennant and hundreds of sailors struggled to get themselves away from *Repulse* before it went down. Bloodied and soaked by the thick oil, they watched in silence minutes later as the ship, its bow stabbing "straight into the air like a church steeple," heeled over and plunged under the swells with more than half the crew of 1,300 still on board. But the *Repulse* wanted a larger ship's company on its final journey, and Brown, who felt his legs were being pulled from his hips, watched in horror as several nearby sailors were sucked back aboard as the ship went under. *Prince of Wales* followed an hour or so later, with Admiral Phillips and Captain Leach still on the bridge. They were last seen bidding God bless to the crew, of whom more than five hundred joined them at the bottom of the South China Sea. British destroyers arrived later in the day to pluck Brown and the other survivors from the water.[36]

Later, Averell Harriman said of Churchill, "He sent those two battleships to Singapore in order to help. He was very anxious to do his share in the Pacific. He knew it would be mostly the United States, but he wanted Great Britain to do its share." Churchill had tried, and failed.[37]

Before sunrise on December 10, Churchill sent a message to Anthony Eden informing him that the government expected a declaration of war by Hitler within two days. He also told Eden that news had arrived overnight from North Africa by way of Auchinleck that Rommel was "in full retreat" westward. And in Russia, "magnificent Russian successes" had put the Germans on the "defensive and retreat." Still ebullient over the U.S. entry into the Pacific war and its likely entry into the European war, he signed off with, "We are having a jolly time here." The jollifications ended when Churchill, in bed opening his boxes of intelligence briefs, picked up the ringing telephone at his bedside. "It was the First Sea Lord," he recalled. "His voice sounded odd. He gave a sort of cough and gulp, and at first I did not hear quite clearly. 'Prime Minister, I have to report to you that the *Prince of Wales* and the *Repulse* have been sunk by the Japanese—we think by aircraft. Tom Phillips is drowned.'" In all the war, Churchill wrote, "I had never received a more direct shock." As he lay in bed, speechless, he realized that in all of the Indian and Pacific oceans, there were no British or American capital ships, other than the survivors of Pearl Harbor, which he had been told were "hastening back to California." He had no need to consult a map to grasp his position in the Pacific: "Over this vast expanse of water, Japan was supreme, and we everywhere were weak and naked."[38]

Within that expanse the Japanese were rampaging faster and more furiously than any warrior nation in history. Japanese fliers had needed only a few hours on the seventh and eighth to rattle the foundations of three centuries of British, Dutch, and American imperialism. Within days the foundations cracked. Churchill, after the loss of the *Prince of Wales*, told Britons that with the American fleet based at Singapore, the city and naval base could hold out for six months, until offensive Allied operations could be undertaken. But there was no American fleet. Other than a few destroyers and the cruiser *Houston,* no American naval force existed in the western Pacific. Churchill did not grasp that Singapore's fate—in large part due to London's having underestimated the enemy—would likely be determined within weeks. Hong Kong's tenure as a British possession could likely be measured in days. "The Japanese rising sun," wrote Mollie Panter-Downes, was "sending ever more trenchant beams over that empire on which a benign British sun was supposed never to set.[39]

Inspector Thompson kept his counsel as Churchill "moped about, wept, and sat staring off to nowhere for two days after *Prince of Wales* and *Repulse* went down." Thompson had "never seen him take a war shock so hard." Churchill had suffered the sort of devastating loss experienced by Caesar Augustus who, after the slaughter of his finest legions in the Teutoburg Forest, allowed his beard and hair to grow out for months and took to wandering about his palace calling out, "Quinctilius Varas, give me back my legions." Churchill, like the Roman, had sent the pride of his Empire to do battle with an enemy he little understood and vastly underrated, and had paid the price. Thompson recalled Churchill sitting for long moments while mumbling repeatedly to himself, "I don't understand what happened. I don't understand it."[40]

For more than a year he had been shuffling his army and naval forces about, much as he had once so long ago deployed with enthusiastic abandon his army of 1,500 toy soldiers across the Arabian rugs of his father's London town house. He recalled in his autobiography, *My Early Life,* that his decision to embark on a military career was "entirely due" to sending "infantry divisions with cavalry brigades" into battle as a child. Those mock campaigns allowed him to study "the noble profession of arms" (although the young Winston stacked the deck against his "enemy," brother Jack, whose army, at Winston's insistence, consisted only of "coloured" troops, and lacked artillery). The toy soldiers, Churchill later reminisced, "turned the current of my entire life." Those lead and tin legions (and every man jack of them a British soldier, no colonials or foreigners in Churchill's ranks) were hand-cast and painted in Germany by Heyde and in Paris by C. B. G. Mignot. They would today be valuable to collectors for their craftsmanship and priceless for their association with the young Winston Churchill, but they are long lost. Churchill's daughter, Lady Soames, attributes the paucity of early Churchill memorabilia to his parents seeing no reason to preserve for posterity anything of Winston's. "In those days his [Churchill's] hopes were so unpromising...they wouldn't have had any idea he was a child prodigy." A military career, at the time, was the only choice available to an aristocratic lad of meager talent. Had Lord Randolph lived to witness the Greek and Crete fiascoes, the siege of Tobruk, the loss of *Prince of Wales,* the looming threats to Hong Kong, Singapore, Burma, and the very essence of the Empire, India, he would have judged the decision to discard his son's toy lancers and fusiliers self-evidently correct. The adult Winston had juggled his armies and fleets like an inept prestidigitator; he slipped his peas under shells, shuffled them about, and Hitler and Tojo made them all vanish.[41]

Upon learning of the fate of his two warships, Churchill hastened to the Commons to deliver a brief statement. He returned the following day to summarize in a long address the news from various fronts and to explain more precisely the circumstances surrounding the loss of the *Prince of Wales*. "The House is depressed," Nicolson jotted in his diary, and the loss of *Prince of Wales* "has numbed us." The House expected Churchill to explain how the ships were lost; instead, he gave them: "These ships had reached the right point at the right moment and were in every respect suited to the task assigned to them." Both ships were sunk, Churchill told the House, by continuous waves of airborne bomb and torpedo attack "delivered with skill and determination." Seven Japanese planes were destroyed, but Churchill did not explain whether by anti-aircraft guns or by British fighter planes. Following Churchill's remarks, Admiral of the Fleet Sir Roger Keyes—old, frail, but still sharp—rose and asked Churchill to assure the Commons that, "erroneous deductions" to the

Churchill inspects bomb damage during the Blitz. More than 800,000 Londoners lost their homes during the bombing raids. (*Getty*)

Between May 26 and June 3, 1940, a flotilla of almost 1,000 British ships, large and small, evacuated more than 330,000 British and French troops from Dunkirk. (*NARA*)

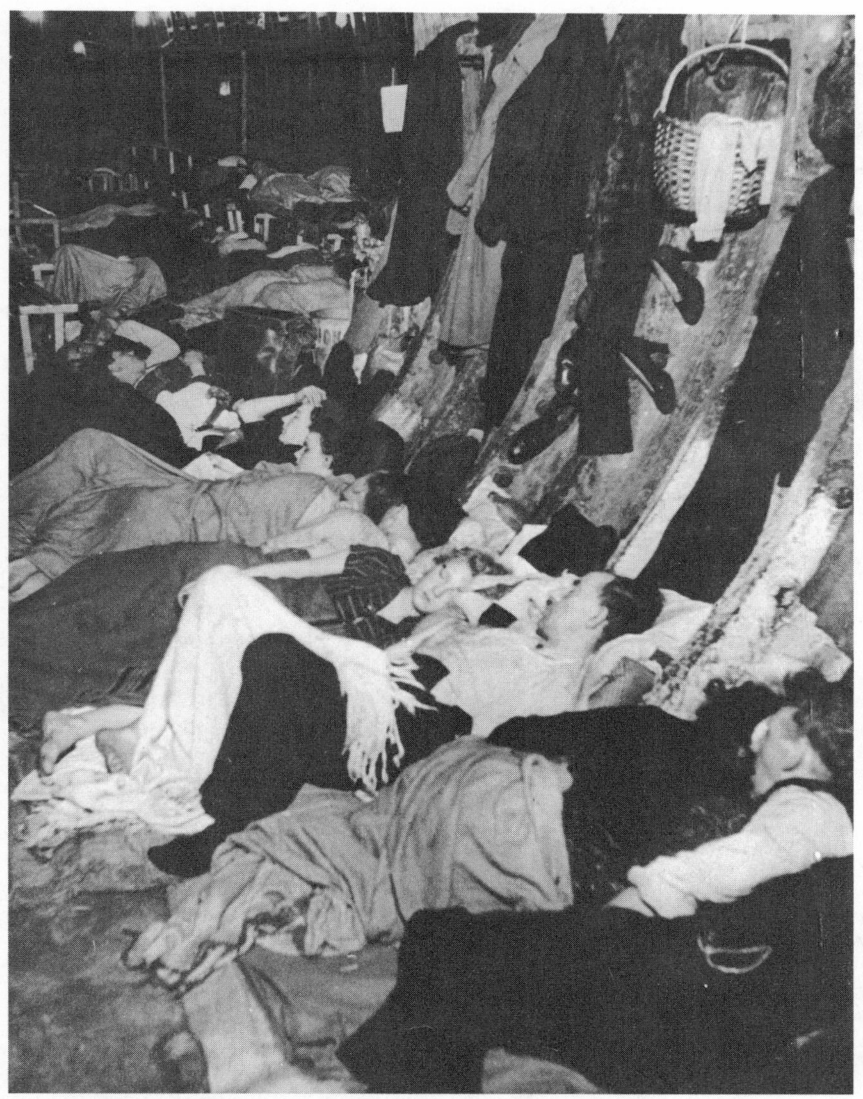

At the height of the Blitz in the autumn of 1940, more than 150,000 Londoners took shelter in the Underground nightly. By war's end, 60,000 British civilians had been killed by German bombs and rockets. (*Getty*)

London, during the Blitz, autumn 1940. St. Paul's Cathedral is wrapped in a cowl of smoke as London burns. (*Associated Newspapers/Rex USA*)

Churchill, Brendan Bracken (middle), and Harry Hopkins, 1941. Bracken had been Churchill's "fixer" for two decades; Hopkins served Franklin Roosevelt in the same capacity. (*Getty*)

RAF
WHISK
NOTRE GLORIEUSE RAF. A PROUVÉ SA PUISSANCE A L'ALLEMAGNE, EN BOMBARDANT ET MITRAILLANT LE TERRITOIRE FRANCAIS...
QUANT A NOS BATEAUX !... LES MERS EN SONT PLEINES..!!

A Vichy cartoon takes a jab at Churchill's bombing policy. (*Kenneth Rendell*)

Max Beaverbrook. As minister of aircraft production, he gave Churchill the fighter planes he needed in order to defend England, and the heavy bombers to take the fight to Germany. (*Getty*)

John ("Jock") Colville. But for a stint in the RAF, 1942–1943, Colville served as private secretary to Churchill throughout the war and again during Churchill's premiership from 1951 to 1955. (*Getty*)

Below: Frederick A. Lindemann, Lord Cherwell ("Prof"). Called "Baron Berlin" by his enemies, Cherwell served as Churchill's science adviser for more than three decades. (*Getty*)

Above: Charles Wilson, Lord Moran. Moran served as Churchill's personal physician from 1910 until Churchill's death, in 1965. (*Getty*)

Churchill on board HMS *Prince of Wales,* Argentia, 1941. At his first conference with Roosevelt, Churchill arrived with a long list of needs, aircraft and tanks at the top. (*Getty*)

Churchill with Franklin Roosevelt, escorted by his son Captain Elliott Roosevelt, aboard HMS *Prince of Wales* during the Argentia conference, 1941. (*Imperial War Museum, London*)

"Chip off the Old Block" little Winston struts along a London street with his mother, Pamela Churchill, June 1942. (*NARA*)

Clementine greets Winston on the tarmac at an RAF airfield outside London in August 1942 upon his return from Cairo and Moscow. The journey was the first of several he made aboard the B-24 Liberator *Commando*. (*University of South Carolina*)

Churchill and daughter Mary, a sergeant in the Auxiliary Territorial Service, wait for a demonstration of artillery to begin. (*AP*)

Bernard Montgomery, the hero of El Alamein. His victory there, in November 1942, after three years of British defeats and retreats, marked a turning point in the war. (*George Rodger/Life*)

Churchill, Joseph Stalin (center), and Averell Harriman in Moscow, August 1942. (*NARA*)

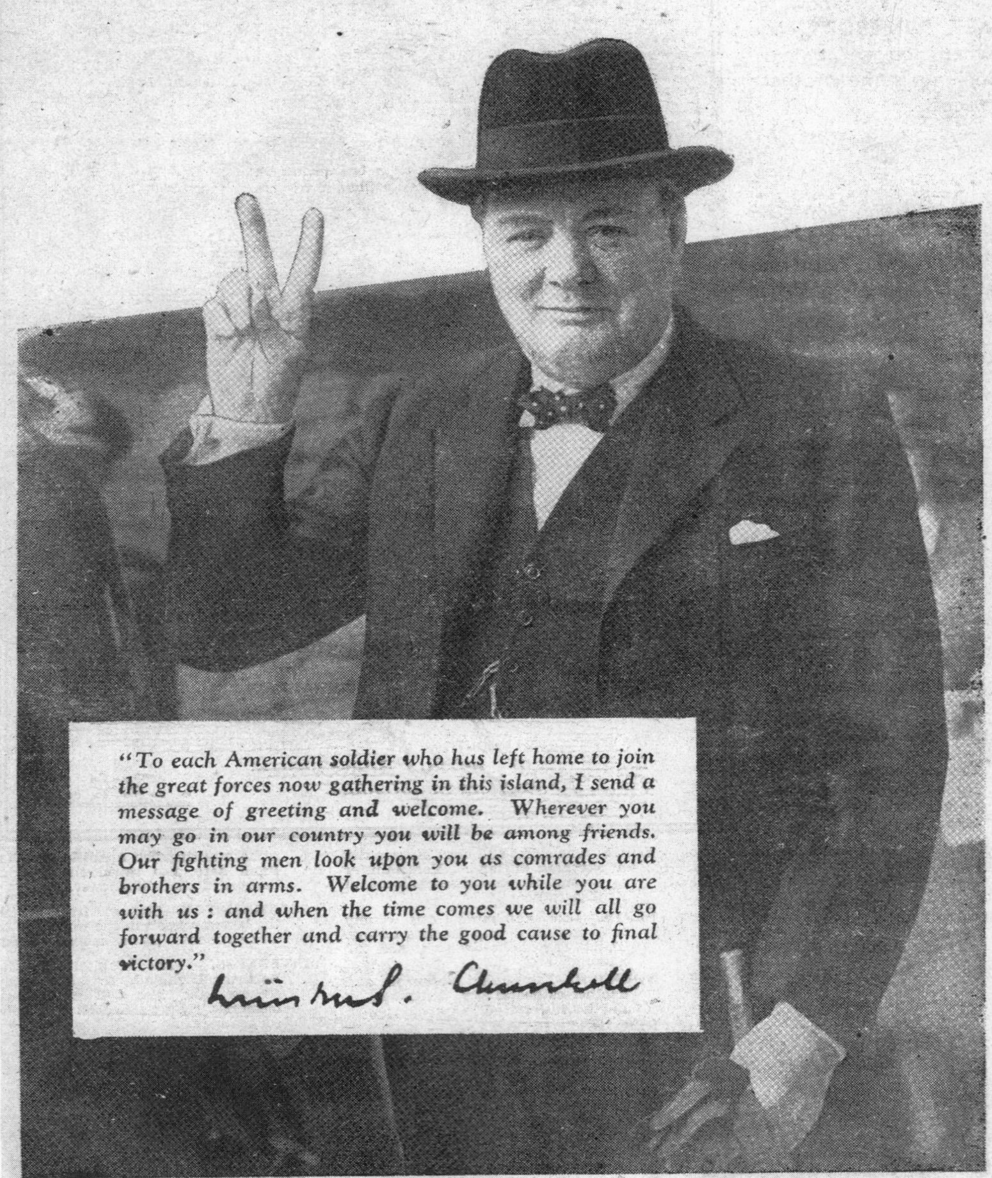

WELCOME!
"To each American soldier who has left home to join the great forces now gathering in this island, I send a message of greeting and welcome. Wherever you may go in our country you will be among friends. Our fighting men look upon you as comrades and brothers in arms. Welcome to you while you are with us : and when the time comes we will all go forward together and carry the good cause to final victory."
Winston S. Churchill

A 1942 poster greets arriving American troops deployed to Great Britain. By late 1943, more than 300,000 had arrived. (*Kenneth Rendell*)

With victory in North Africa in hand, Churchill in Algiers plans his Mediterranean strategy, June 1943. Seated from left: Anthony Eden, Alan Brooke, Churchill, General Marshall, and General Eisenhower; standing (behind seated men) from left: Air Chief Marshal Tedder, Admiral Sir Andrew Cunningham, General Alexander, and General Montgomery. (*NARA*)

Churchill and Roosevelt at the Casablanca Conference, January 1943. It was here that Roosevelt announced the Allied terms of surrender to Germany, Italy, and Japan: "Unconditional Surrender." (*NARA*)

Churchill arrives at the first Quebec Conference, August 1943. Beside him is Canadian prime minister William Lyon Mackenzie King. Riding shotgun is Churchill's bodyguard, Scotland Yard's Walter Thompson. (*NARA*)

First Lady Eleanor Roosevelt (left) and Clementine Churchill prepare to make an address over the Canadian Broadcasting Company, September 13, 1943. (*AP*)

Churchill addresses the U.S. Congress, 1943. (*NARA*)

Churchill inspects British paratroopers before D-day, June 1944. (*NARA*)

From left: Dwight Eisenhower, Churchill, and General Omar Bradley put new carbines through their paces before D-day, 1944. (*NARA*)

contrary, "the battleship is still the foundation of sea power and that . . . the *Prince of Wales* was as well protected against under-water and air attack as the *Bismarck*." The old admiral appeared to have learned nothing from Pearl Harbor. But the latter part of his statement held the key to his query. He asked again, Were the two ships "acting without the support of land-based or seaborne fighters?" The Speaker of the House deemed Keyes's statement inappropriate.[42]

Keyes persisted. Churchill at first ducked, then deflected, the question by asking Keyes if he meant to imply that Admiral Phillips had "acted otherwise than on sound naval grounds." Certainly not, replied Keyes. Another MP asked directly how the seven Japanese planes had been shot down, by British AA or British airplanes? Churchill finally responded: "They were destroyed by anti-aircraft fire." Britain "had only a certain amount of aircraft" to meet its needs, Churchill explained, but had nonetheless sent "as many reinforcement as we could many months ago" to Singapore. In fact, not enough aircraft had been sent to protect the battleships. The fault for that did not reside with the late Admiral Phillips, but with those who had ordered him into hostile waters without air support. That would be the prime minister, with the consent of the War Cabinet and the Admiralty.[43]

Churchill claimed in his memoirs that "chance played so fatal a part" in the tragic loss of the ships. Yet chance was aided and abetted by Churchill adhering too long to his notions of battlewagons and their mythic prowess. The loss of his beloved ships moved him to at last grasp the strategic significance of sending airplanes, whether from airfields or carriers, against heavy ships, though he by no means abandoned his reverence for battle-wagons—"gigantic castles of steel" he called them in 1923 (volume 1 of *The World Crisis*). A battleship took five years to build, but an aircraft carrier could be rigged out of a hull in months. Overnight, in keeping with his oft-voiced motto of K.B.O. (keep buggering on), he embraced carriers with enthusiasm. Days after the loss of *Prince of Wales,* he displayed his lifelong ability to learn fast when, on December 13, he approved Admiral Pound's recommendation to send a task force of up to four aircraft carriers to the Indian Ocean, under the command of Admiral James Somerville. "I agree that Admiral Somerville should come home," Churchill told Pound, "to organize this form of warfare." Those words are telling for, although Somerville had been running carriers through the Mediterranean for two years to deliver fighter planes to Malta and Alexandria, large-scale, coordinated carrier operations—*"this form of warfare"*—were new and mysterious to Churchill and the Admiralty. The British proved quick studies, but the Japanese had developed carrier tactics years before, and in the previous week had demonstrated their skill at this form of warfare.[44]

Throughout his life, Churchill's critics—wanting it both ways—claimed on the one hand that he stuck to outdated positions for too long, and on the other hand that he was an opportunist, ever ready to switch positions. He did and he was, and he liked to say, "I would rather be right than consistent." Margot Asquith in 1908 called him a man of "transitory convictions."* But his old colleague Rab Butler attributed Churchill's tendency to switch sides to "the independence of his ideas" and to his "ever testing, courting, and encouraging new ideas." He was as contradictory as the criticisms leveled against him. He had been adjudged a mental case by the military establishment when during the Great War he championed a new and heretical weapon, the tank, which he called his "land ship." Yet in those years, the military establishment had demonstrated—if not mental illness—gross stupidity. The cartoonist David Low chose the army as Colonel Blimp's profession after reading a serving British colonel's letter to *The Evening Standard* that protested the mechanization of the cavalry but insisted that if tanks were to be brought into service, tank crews must be made to wear spurs.[45]

Churchill's vision extended well beyond the known horizon, yet the same man who could envision as revolutionary a change in warfare as the tank, could not, in the face of overwhelming evidence, concede that battleships were dinosaurs. Days after the *Prince of Wales* went down, the old-school Churchill proposed to the War Cabinet the formation of a combined British and American battle fleet consisting of four new, sixteen-inch-gun battleships, along with older American ships in "numbers sufficient to enable a fleet action." He simply did not grasp that fleet actions of that sort were now a thing of the past. Although he could never bring himself to entirely give up the old, when the facts demanded, he embraced the new, in the case of sending carrier task forces to the Indian Ocean, almost literally overnight.[46]

There would be no *Time* Man of the Year honors for Churchill that year. Stalin was in the running for the 1941 prize but failed to take it on the grounds of "grave disqualifications, one moral, the other empiric." Stalin, by virtue of his 1939 pact with Hitler, had opened the floodgates for the Führer; now that coup "had proved a grim joke at the expense of Joseph Stalin." The Indian Confederation of America did, however, vote Stalin "1941's outstanding warrior," and sent him a war bonnet. *Time* named Franklin Roosevelt Man of the Year "because the country he leads stands

* She was the wife of Herbert Henry Asquith, who served as prime minister from 1908 to 1916, and the mother of Violet Bonham Carter.

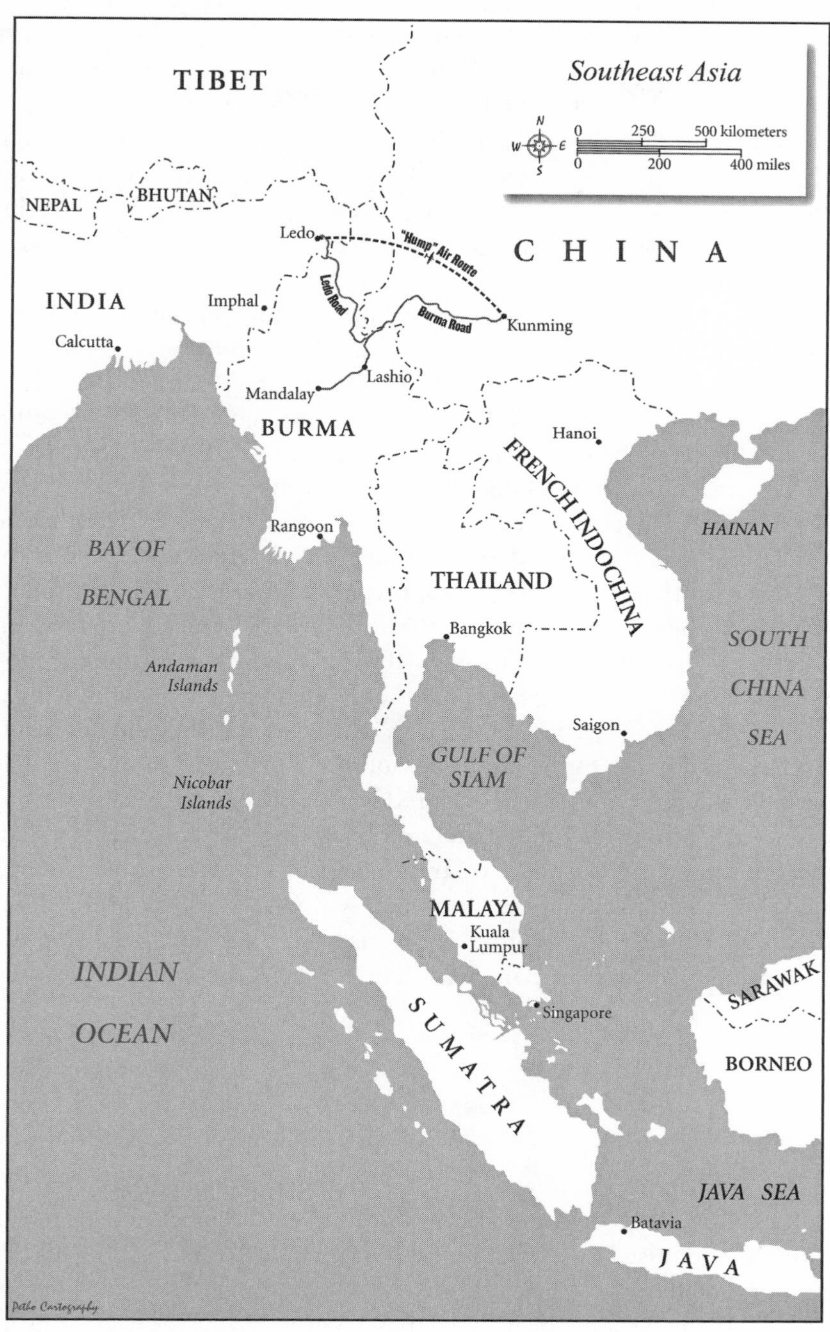
Southeast Asia
N
W
E
S
0
250
500 kilometers
0
200
400 miles
TIBET
NEPAL
BHUTAN
CHINA
INDIA
Ledo
"Hump" Air Route
Ledo Road
Burma Road
Imphal
Kunming
Calcutta
Lashio
Mandalay
BURMA
Hanoi
FRENCH INDOCHINA
HAINAN
Rangoon
BAY OF BENGAL
THAILAND
Bangkok
SOUTH CHINA SEA
Andaman Islands
Saigon
GULF OF SIAM
Nicobar Islands
MALAYA
Kuala Lumpur
INDIAN OCEAN
SARAWAK
SUMATRA
Singapore
BORNEO
JAVA SEA
Batavia
JAVA
Pethe Cartography

for the hopes of the world." Roosevelt, who "in his own right and on his own record . . . stood out as a figure for the year and for the age," had led America in mastering its "creeping paralysis" and "had guided the U.S." to its "rendezvous with destiny." He had forced America to grasp "what it can be and therefore will be." Churchill, *Time* recorded, had had "no great moment in 1941." True, Churchill had twice taken Cyrenaica—but only because he "lost it between times." He had "met disaster" in Greece and Crete. British armies "were still losing campaigns" under his leadership. Yet *Time* dabbed salve on the wound: Churchill "was a man of the year, of the decade, and, if his cause is won, of all time."[47]

The news from the Far East did not bode well for his cause. The news from America, specifically from Franklin Roosevelt, was disquieting. There was none. By the early hours of December 11, Churchill still had received no reply from Roosevelt to his request for a meeting. Hitler settled the issue that day when he declared war on the United States. Benito Mussolini goose-stepped right along. From the balcony above the Piazza Venezia in Rome, Il Duce anointed Roosevelt a "supreme fraud" who had led America into war through "diabolical obstinacy." Mussolini pledged that the "powers of the pact of steel" were prepared to inflict more "formidable blows" upon their enemies. "Italians!" he bellowed. "Once more arise and be worthy in this historical hour. We will win!" His lackeys scattered among the crowd cheered. But thousands of other Romans assembled in the piazza below listened in silence. This was a war, and an enemy, they did not want.[48]

And there it was. Hitler and Mussolini with complete disregard for American industrial might had declared war on the United States of America. The U.S. Congress immediately returned the favor. America was in. Roosevelt signed the German declaration at 3:05 P.M. One minute later, he signed the Italian declaration. Only then was Churchill's Grand Alliance finally realized. Harold Nicolson wrote his wife, "We can't be beaten with America in," yet "not an American flag flying in the whole of London. How odd we are."[49]

The previous June, on the eve of the German invasion of Russia, Churchill told Jock Colville that the Russians would likely be quickly defeated. By autumn he had raised his expectations. In late October, after asking his chief of military intelligence to give odds for Moscow falling by winter, Churchill offered his own, "I should be inclined to put it even." Now the Red Army had gone over to the attack. On December 11 Churchill told the Commons that winter's onslaught had not only brought the Germans to a standstill outside

Moscow but had "inflicted upon the German armies and the German nation, a bloody blow, almost unequaled in the history of war." And December, he added, marked "not the end of the winter... but the beginning." Where Russians were "habituated to the severity of their native climate," the German invaders could only scratch meager shelter from the frozen ground, there to conclude, Churchill told the House, that Hitler's Russian gambit was proving to be "one of the outstanding blunders of history."[50]

With Hitler's declaration of war Churchill concluded that it was vital to meet with Roosevelt, immediately. Yet he had *already* asked and been rebuffed. He dispatched another cable to Roosevelt: "Am most anxious" to discuss the Vichy situation in North Africa. Actually, as he had been since the eighth, he was most anxious to discuss everything. This time Roosevelt gave him what he wanted. "Delighted to have you here at the White House," he cabled back.[51]

Overnight, Roosevelt found himself at war in two oceans, and overnight, Churchill's gingerly approach to the Americans changed. When Lord Woolton, minister of food, proposed to increase food rationing, Churchill told him that with the Americans in, "our position is immeasurably improved," and therefore, "we have no longer any need to strike attitudes to win the United States sympathy, we are all in it together, and they are eating better meals than we are." When one of his military chiefs advised a continuation of the careful attitude toward America, Churchill replied, with a leer, "Oh that is the way we talked to her when we were wooing her, now that she's in the harem we talk to her quite differently."[52]

Within twenty-four hours of receiving Roosevelt's invitation, Churchill, Beaverbrook, Harriman, First Sea Lord Dudley Pound, and Air Marshal Charles Portal were rolling north on board the prime minister's private train, bound for the River Clyde, where the battleship *Duke of York*—sister ship of the *Prince of Wales*—waited to carry them to America. Also on board were the newly retired Field Marshal Dill (Alan Brooke stayed behind to man his new headquarters) and Churchill's doctor, Charles Wilson (Clementine insisted Winston take the doctor along). Eighty ancillary staff and two dozen cryptographers also went; all of Churchill's outgoing cables had first to be encoded before being sent to the intended recipient, as did the incoming traffic for the prime minister. His daughter Mary accompanied her Pa-*pa* on the train but would not be making the Atlantic crossing. Late morning on December 13, after bidding "Good-bye, darling" to Mary—who was last off the ship—Churchill and the *Duke of York* made for the Atlantic.[53]

Soon after clearing the Clyde, the ship ran into the worst weather the North Atlantic could throw its way. The escort destroyers, tossed about like rowboats, fell behind. The seas were so roiled that *Duke of York* spent most of the voyage battened down. Dr. Wilson possessed no medicines to combat the nausea and lassitude that overcame almost everyone on board, including the prime minister. Churchill, in his longest letter to Clementine since a forlorn missive sent during a 1936 trip to Marrakech, rued the confinement but allowed that an extra dose of Mothersill's Travel Remedy had staved off any serious bouts of seasickness. The seas were so violent, he wrote, that two of the party suffered broken legs and arms. Paraphrasing Samuel Johnson, he wrote, "Being in a ship in such weather as this is like being in a prison, with the extra chance of being drowned."[54]

He never enjoyed the confinement of long sea voyages; this was the worst ever. Yet aboard the ship he found pleasure in the usual places: his cronies, good food, strong drink, and bad movies. Beaverbrook's lieutenant, George Malcolm Thomson, recalled "there was one movie one night, *The Sea Hawk,* in which there was an attack on a British naval ship by pirates as I remember it. A great deal of countless stuff going on the deck of this sailing ship and I remember Churchill, who was always in his dressing gown. He had dined rather well I think, as usual. I can remember him getting up and shouting 'We're winning, we're winning!' "[55]

Actually, wherever they were fighting, on sea and on land, but for a thin slice of North Africa, they were losing. And so, too, were the Americans. A *New York Times* headline that week screamed: U.S. FLIERS SCORE: BOMBS SEND BATTLESHIP, CRUISER AND DESTROYER TO THE BOTTOM. The *Times* did not say exactly where in the Pacific these alleged heroics took place. In fact, U.S. fliers had not only not hit a Japanese ship, they had not yet even located a Japanese ship.[56]

Still, one item of good news emanated from *Duke of York*'s radio shack: Auchinleck in Libya had accomplished as much in thirty days as Wavell and O'Connor had in sixty the previous year. Axis troops in Bardia, where Rommel had set up his headquarters in anticipation of taking Tobruk, found themselves surrounded. Rommel, outnumbered in tanks by four to one, had fled west with his remaining armor, toward Benghazi, which Auchinleck would claim on Christmas Eve. Days later, Rommel drew up his lines at El Agheila, four hundred miles west of Tobruk. It was an orderly retreat, but it was a retreat, Rommel's first. The Western Desert had changed hands again. Yet this time, the enemy retreating across Cyrenaica was not Italian but German. Given the back-and-forth nature of the battle, and the resourcefulness of Rommel, Churchill resisted any temptation he may have harbored to proclaim in the name of the King, as he had a year earlier, another "Bardia Day."[57]

While aboard ship, Churchill learned from Eden, in Moscow, that Stalin still maintained a healthy appetite for real estate, in spite of having lost much of western Russia to the Wehrmacht. Churchill told Eden that although Britain had declared war on "the cats-paws" of Hungary, Romania, and Finland, the War Cabinet would refuse to satisfy Stalin on this new matter of postwar boundaries. Although Stalin's defeat in the coming summer seemed as likely as, if not more likely than, eventual victory, he had his maps out, and he wanted assurances that Russia's postwar western boundaries would preserve his territorial gains in eastern Poland, Romania, and Finland. As for the three Baltic states, Latvia, Lithuania, and Estonia, which had all bolted the czar's collapsing empire in 1918, Stalin wanted them back. To Attlee, Churchill cabled: "Stalin's demand about Finland, Baltic States, and Roumania [*sic*] are directly contrary to the first, second, and third articles of the Atlantic Charter, to which Stalin has subscribed. There can be no question whatever of our making such an agreement, secret or public, direct or implied without prior agreement with the United States." He told Eden that to "approach President Roosevelt with his [Stalin's] proposals would be to court a blank refusal and might experience lasting trouble on both sides."[58]

He had often during Britain's bleakest hours privately shared with friends and close associates his visions for the postwar world. "After the War" was a phrase heard in popular songs and a turn of phrase used often at the Churchill dinner table, in telegrams to Roosevelt, and in his addresses. It was shorthand for subjects not to be formally considered until Hitler was dead and Europe had reached the "broad, sunlit uplands" of liberty. He had earned the right to muse on the subject of "After the War," yet not once in his first fifteen months as prime minister had he done so in public. Then, curiously given his public reticence on the matter, within a few hours of sitting down with Roosevelt at Argentia, he had set to work drafting the Atlantic Charter, which amounted to a bilateral declaration on international civil rights and the Anglo-American blueprint for the postwar peace (as well as a moral imperative that Americans might fight for). After the two leaders agreed on the text (without consulting Stalin), they announced the Atlantic Charter to the world.[59]

If Churchill and Roosevelt felt it their duty to state their vision of the postwar world, why should not Stalin? Stalin, whose borders after all had been violated, and whose capital was now under siege, believed his claims on the Baltic states to be self-evidently proper. Churchill downplayed Stalin's maneuvers: "No one can foresee where the balance of power will lie... at the end of the war," he cabled Eden, yet most probably it would lie with the *bloc* of America and Britain, which would emerge from the war far less "exhausted" than Stalin, who would need Anglo-American help to rebuild more than the Americans and British would need Stalin. Still, Churchill heard enough in Stalin's demands to make him wary, though like a denizen of Plato's cave, he could divine only shadows of things beyond his immediate vision, which was entirely focused on crushing

Hitler. He could not make out exactly what was coming by way of Moscow, or its size, or its speed, but he didn't much care for it. Always remember, he had cautioned Eden, that Bolsheviks are "crocodiles" who understand only force. Years later he told his grandson, Winston Spencer Churchill, that he *knew*—at the first mention by Stalin of postwar boundaries—exactly where the seeds for the next European conflict would germinate, adding that from early 1942 on, he put every strategic decision in the war against Hitler under two lenses: "How will it shorten the war, and how will it prevent the Bear from stealing the peace."[60]

Those may well have been the sentiments of an old man who wanted to reposition himself more favorably in the historical story line. Yet, given the Faustian pact Churchill and Roosevelt made with Stalin, it seems improbable that Stalin's demands suddenly awakened in Churchill the prospect of postwar trouble. This was Joseph Stalin, after all, Hitler's former partner, a gunman who in his youth robbed banks for the Marxist cause and later—also for the cause, his own—resorted to mass murder. Why did Churchill and Roosevelt during the next three years fail, utterly, to hatch any plans between themselves that addressed the possible—probable, even—*consequences* to Europe of their alliance with the Soviet dictator? Both spoke in the starkest terms of the consequences to the world were Hitler to win. From a moral perspective, Stalin was simply the lesser of two evils; he killed his political opponents because they opposed him, not because of their bloodlines. Hitler, victorious, would kill everybody. The death of Hitlerism was therefore the main objective of the Anglo-American-Soviet alliance, but each of the three Allied leaders had a different political agenda, and each envisioned a postwar world different in structure from that envisioned by the other two. Stalin's political objectives were patently at odds with both the Atlantic Charter and Churchill's hopes for democratic European spheres of influence, which he intended first and foremost would serve to keep Prussia (but not all of Germany) down on the farm, quite literally.

The wonder is not that in late 1941 Churchill foresaw future problems with Stalin, but why he ever could have thought otherwise. Churchill was well versed in the history of Russia's relationship with Europe. He had lectured Colville the previous June on the Swedish invasion of 1700 and of Napoleon's 1812 gambit. Now, twice within a generation, the Germans had turned on Russia. Russia was an Asian nation with a foot in Europe, and Western Europeans had regularly stomped on that foot. Protection of Russia's western frontiers had driven Russian foreign policy for two centuries, Czarist, Leninist, and Stalinist. Moscow had always sought a security belt between itself and the West. The West, meanwhile, maintained a cordon sanitaire between itself and the Muscovites. The Poles had historically paid the price for their geographical position in relation to Russia's security needs, and had done so again when Hitler and Stalin signed their 1939 pact. By signing the pact, Stalin believed (incorrectly as he had learned in June) that he had widened his security belt. His war aims were to reclaim it, and to destroy the German threat once and for all. He articulated those aims often during the next three years. He linked all of his war decisions with Russian territorial interests and the German threat to those interests. He never disguised his aim, and held to it, wrote James MacGregor Burns, "with steel-like tenacity." For Stalin, defeating Germany and reclaiming Russian security were two sides of the same coin. Churchill's was a one-sided coin: defeat Hitler. His and Stalin's objectives, therefore, were similar but not identical.[61]

It was a vital distinction. Stalin believed that were Hitler to be assassinated or overthrown, possibly by the Prussian officers whom Hitler despised, the West might reach an agreement with the new Hitler-less Germany and then turn—with Germany—against Russia. It was a paranoid belief, but one strongly held nonetheless. Churchill indeed considered Hitler an interim enemy; he held Germany to be part of the European family, destined to again take its place at the table after Hitler was dealt with. Stalin, however, saw Germany as Russia's perpetual enemy, now more than ever deserving of annihilation. Once Hitler was vanquished, as Stalin saw it, the West would once again consider Moscow and communism to be its supreme enemies, a status cemented with the revolution of 1917. For the duration of the war, Stalin's relationship with his allies was informed by his certainty that Churchill and Roosevelt were not and never would be true friends of Russia.

For their part, Churchill and Roosevelt never entirely trusted Stalin. For the next three years they weighed every decision against the possibility that Russia might quit the war, as the Bolsheviks had done in 1917. They withheld the Ultra secret from Stalin (although they passed along Ultra decrypts as information gained from reliable "agents"), and of course they did not bring Stalin into the atomic bomb project. Yet, where Churchill's trust in Stalin was qualified, his *loyalty* to Stalin was not, and never diminished throughout the war. In Churchill's moral paradigm, loyalty was an absolute, where trust admitted to degrees. Even as Stalin made the extent of his territorial ambitions known in 1943 and 1944, Churchill remained loyal, cabling Roosevelt in April 1944, "I have a feeling that the [Soviet] bark is worse than its bite." Even as victory became certain and Stalin's demands for territory—at the expense of liberty within those territories—hardened, Churchill remained the steadfast partner. After Yalta, in early 1945, Churchill told the Commons that Stalin's "word was [his] bond.... I know of no Government which stands to its obligations... more solidly than the Russian Soviet Government."[62]

Given their distrust of Stalin, why did two such brilliant politicians as Churchill and Roosevelt remain so loyal to an ideological enemy who for almost twenty years had terrorized his own people while declaring capitalism to be his mortal foe? Because, Churchill wrote in his memoirs, they had no decent alternative. "Neither Roosevelt nor Churchill was blind to the continuance of terror and tyranny in the Soviet Union," Harriman later wrote. But they needed Stalin and the millions upon millions of Russian men he could feed into the teeth of Hitler's war machine. Stalin, supported by the West, could buy the time America needed to arm. For England, each day the Russians fought diminished the prospects of a German invasion of the Home Island. As well, Roosevelt and Churchill truly believed that a man's word was his bond; they were gentlemen, after all. As the war progressed, they became quite confident that they could handle Uncle Joe (they often called him "UJ" in their private communications) much as they handled each other—with tenacity (Churchill) and charm (Roosevelt). Yet they never appreciated the fullness of the man. "Let no one think Stalin is a thug... or roughneck," the journalist and author John Gunther wrote three years earlier. Stalin was a reader of Plato, a student of the American Civil War, a man of brains as well as prescient political instinct. He once dismissed a group of Bolshevik writers by telling them to "read Shakespeare, Goethe and other classics, as I do." He had a sense of humor, which Hitler did not. He was perhaps the most politically adroit of all the principals, Allied and Axis. Yet Churchill and Roosevelt believed he was malleable, reachable, and teachable.[63]

Harriman later recalled that Churchill's and Roosevelt's certainty that "they knew how to get along with Stalin" infected the judgment of "lesser lights," including, Harriman admitted, himself. He confessed in his memoirs that he "was not entirely immune to that infectious idea" of getting along with Stalin given the "tough talks" he had held with the marshal in "tough sessions." Beaverbrook tried to prove his loyalty to Stalin by shipping to the Soviets the Lend-Lease matériel Stalin demanded, matériel that Britain desperately needed. Churchill feared Beaverbrook's generosity would result in Britain being "bled white." All of the players, American and British, thought they could handle UJ. In fact, Uncle Joe had never been a man to be handled. Rather, he had proven himself the consummate manhandler.[64]

Eden that month took a pragmatic approach to Stalin's demands, telling the War Cabinet that the Soviets would inevitably, one way or another, get the Baltic states, the implication being now was as good a time as any. For Churchill, this would not do. The time for drawing boundaries, he told Eden, was not yet at hand, and such questions "can only be resolved at the Peace Conference when we have won the war." He then went easy on Eden, whose journey to Moscow was the most important of his career to date.

The Old Man expressed his overall satisfaction with the mission and advised his emissary to "not be rough with Stalin." A discussion of boundaries, however, was out of the question. Such was Churchill's political, and moral, position in regard to Eastern Europe, a position that events and Stalin in time undermined.[65]

Confined by the weather to his cabin aboard the *Duke of York*, Churchill dictated three long memos in which he outlined to the War Cabinet and the COS his plans for Europe and Asia in 1942, and his worldwide plans for 1943, which included the "advantage in declaring now our intention of sending armies of liberation into Europe in 1943." Those words were intended not only for the British chiefs but for Roosevelt and his advisers. Nowhere in the three memos did Churchill refer to the possibility of sending large Allied armies into Europe in 1942; he knew it could not be done. Yet the Americans were already thinking of doing just that—opening a second European front by autumn. Stalin had demanded one since July. Churchill, within months, would find himself under fire from the Americans, Stalin, and British leftists, accused by all of opposing a second front, when in fact, on the advice of his military chiefs, he opposed only a premature second front, a distinction he tried without success to impress upon his allies that year, and upon his critics for the rest of his life.[66]

While Churchill was at sea, Adolf Hitler sated the curiosity of all who had wondered for several days just who would replace Field Marshal Walther von Brauchitsch as commander in chief of the German army and head of *Oberkommando des Heeres* (OKH), the army's high command. Given that Germany was a land-based power, OKH had been, traditionally, the primary military voice within the Wehrmacht, until 1938, when Hitler configured his personal military mouthpiece, *Oberkommando des Wehrmacht* (OKW), which directed all branches of the German military. From then on, the professional staff officers of OKH, loathed by Hitler for their Prussian and aristocratic lineage, exercised less influence. In reality, OKW, sprinkled throughout with Hitler's lackeys, planned and directed operations in all theaters except Russia, where OKH had been left to manage the eastern army (*Ostheer*) under the eye of and at the pleasure of OKW, a relationship that played nicely into Hitler's strategy of pitting his military services against one another. Von Brauchitsch, his heart failing and lacking the stomach to argue with Hitler—who had been outraged by Brauchitsch's strategy of taking Moscow before the Caucasus oil fields—resigned.

It was clear to Hitler that only one German possessed the requisite military genius to replace Brauchitsch, who, he later told Goebbels, was "a coward and a nincompoop." And so on December 19, the Führer appointed himself commander in chief of Germany's army. He was of course already supreme commander of all German armed forces, but C in C was a hands-on job of tactical—not only strategic—decisions. A purge of the ranks had begun; Rundstedt, Guderian, and Erich Hoepner, considered panzer geniuses just a year earlier, were pushed out, and Bock was retired. Field Marshal Wilhelm Keitel stayed on as chief of staff of the supreme command of the German armed forces, an imposing title that belied his status as a rubber stamp for Hitler. Franz Halder stayed on as chief of staff at OKH with hopes of serving as a counterweight to Hitler's increasingly baneful influence over the army. Halder was just the sort of professional soldier Hitler distrusted. The disfavor was returned; more loyal to his army and to Germany than to Hitler, Halder loathed the Führer, yet duty demanded he serve him to his best ability. Colorless and professorial, Halder protected the army's traditions and was one of the very few in the highest ranks who felt it his duty (and was man enough) to apprise Hitler of the Führer's strategic weaknesses. Still, Halder later told a historian that he carried his pistol to staff meetings in the Reich Chancellery with the intent of ridding Germany of the poisonous Austrian, but "as a human being and a Christian" could not bring himself to do so. Yet had he done so, the porcine Göring would have taken Hitler's place, and were Göring to be toppled, Hitler's number three man (and Rudolf Hess's successor), the thuggish yet clever and ambitious Martin Bormann, would assume the leadership, that is, if the more thuggish and more ambitious Heinrich Himmler did not dispute the issue. No lone assassin could dismantle the Nazi apparatus.[67]

Hitler's decision was equivalent to Roosevelt taking over day-to-day operations from Marshall, or Churchill supplanting Brooke. But whereas a peevish Hitler squelched dissent, Churchill (himself often peevish) fostered an often-fractious give-and-take between himself and his generals, with the result that decisions taken were made stronger by having been annealed in the furnace of debate. Hitler's takeover of the army apparatus not only banked the fires of debate, but further fractured his chain of command and set up fiefdoms within the German armed forces, each reporting to Hitler but not to the others, such that Hitler and Hitler alone was privy to *all* information. He thus deprived himself of the unified and coherent counsel of the experts who could best counsel him. But Hitler, suspicious of the lot of them, felt he served his own cause more efficiently by forcing his generals to toil in partial darkness. It later proved a disastrous decision, but at the time it appeared inspired, for as Mollie Panter-Downes wrote that week, "The idea of Hitler as a crazy, Chaplinesque commander who would quickly blunder toward disaster isn't so popular as it was before some of those supposedly crazy notions of his proved pretty sound after all." If anyone was blundering to disaster that week, it was Churchill and Roosevelt, in the Far East.[68]

Late in the afternoon of December 22, after almost ten terrible days at sea, the *Duke of York* sounded Hampton Roads, at the mouth of Chesapeake Bay. The plan had been to cruise right up the Potomac, but Churchill had had enough. He took a military plane to Washington, accompanied by a few of his aides. As the aircraft made its final approach along the Potomac, the group gazed out the windows and "transfixed with delight" took in a sight none had seen in more than two years: "the amazing spectacle of a city all lighted up." When Churchill touched down at the Anacostia naval air station, he saw Franklin Roosevelt sitting in the backseat of a large black sedan that had pulled onto the tarmac. The president had come across the river to welcome his guest in person. It was the sort of generous, seemingly offhand gesture that Roosevelt was master of. Nobody, especially Churchill, was immune to such charm. From Roosevelt's perspective, the arrival by air of a foreign leader was an event not to be missed; no American president had ever flown on an airplane while in office, let alone learned to fly one, as had Churchill more than two decades earlier. Roosevelt watched from his limousine as the prime minister of Great Britain emerged from the aluminum skin of a flying machine into the Washington night as if to proclaim, change is in the air.[69]

Churchill was put up in a suite just down the hall from the president's private rooms and across the hall from the Lincoln study, where Hopkins resided. Rarely was a foreign dignitary accorded such treatment. Late that night the two leaders met in Roosevelt's second-floor study, where Churchill passed on to Roosevelt drafts of the three strategic papers he had composed during his journey. Taken as a whole, the papers were prescient: Churchill saw a maritime war against Japan while Allied ground forces retook islands in a stepping-stone march to Tokyo. He envisioned hitting Germany on the periphery until such time as Russian and Anglo-American armies could squeeze Berlin from the east and west. He saw the need to control the Atlantic as a prerequisite for any European forays. And he saw the strategic value in clearing North Africa and claiming the Mediterranean—knocking Italy out of the war in the bargain—before undertaking an invasion of Europe. Roosevelt was familiar with the gist of Churchill's thoughts, Churchill having worked them into a long letter to the president in late October, to which Roosevelt had made no reply. As well, during the secret meetings of a year earlier between American, British, and Canadian military chiefs (ABC-1 talks), an overall war policy had been worked out in the event of America coming in against both Germany and Japan. The plan called for the defeat of Germany first, beginning with aerial bombing and naval blockade, accomplished in part by shifting some of America's Pacific fleet to the Atlantic. That gentleman's agreement, Churchill hoped, would be codified during the next few days, because with Japan having set America to raging, he feared the American military chiefs might shift to a Japan-first strategy, with disastrous results for Britain if Hitler dispatched the Russians before the Yanks showed up.[70]

Code names for hoped-for operations abounded in Churchill's plans, many chosen by himself. Acrobat was to be the assault that would leave Auchinleck "in possession of Tripoli" within weeks, with his tanks poised "on the French frontier of Tunis." Churchill had no desire to chase Rommel across North Africa; he meant to crush the German's armored forces and then kill Rommel's infantry, pinned down as it would be on the coastal plain. Yet with each passing day it appeared that Auchinleck—low on supplies, his troops exhausted—might come up short. That would imperil Churchill's hopes of getting the Americans into the desert war. When Auchinleck kicked off Crusader, Churchill (taking a naval analogy too far) told the Commons that the outcome of desert battles, like sea battles, could be determined in a matter of hours. The battle had now lasted more than a month, and although Rommel had retreated to the Tripolitania frontier, Auchinleck's Eighth Army, under the command of General Neil M. Ritchie, lacked the tanks to finish him off. Acrobat, therefore, looked to be finished before it started. Still, "the Auk" cabled Churchill with just the news he needed to get Roosevelt on board: the Germans were "hard-pressed," he reported, and he advised that Churchill "press forward with Acrobat." He believed he'd be ready to go on the attack by mid-February.[71]

Auchinleck's optimism also bade well for Whipcord, the most optimistic of Churchill's plans, which was based on the belief that after taking all of Tripoli, the British could jump right to Sicily "while the shock of battle still reigns" in North Africa. With Sicily in the bag, any remaining Germans and Italians in the desert would presumably find themselves isolated, and doomed. That, in turn, would set the stage for Gymnast, the pacification of all of French North Africa, with or without the consent of Vichy, accomplished by landing British—and, hopefully, American—forces commanded by the hero of Dunkirk, Harold Alexander, near Dakar and Casablanca. To bolster Auchinleck, Churchill ordered that several transports carrying the 18th British Division, along with squadrons of fighter planes, anti-tank guns, and one hundred new American tanks, be sent to Cairo via the Cape of Good Hope. Days earlier he had told the Defence

Committee that its "guiding principle" should be that "no resources" required for North African operations "should be diverted elsewhere."[72]

His strategic musings were one with his grand strategies of a year earlier, hopes within hopes. He always saw the European theater in terms of forging a ring around Germany, by naval blockade in the North Sea and eastern Atlantic, and on land from French North Africa, east to Cairo and north through Baghdad to the Caucasus, the eastern perimeter of the ring delineated by the 1,800-mile Soviet front. Churchill meant to probe and test the ring by sea, by air, and on land until he found weaknesses, and then exploit them. He wanted to take the fight everywhere at once, a strategy that frustrated his military advisers (and would frustrate his American allies for the next three years). "Churchill is the greatest military genius in history," Ismay told Averell Harriman. "He can use one division on three fronts at the same time." The editor of Brooke's diaries, Arthur Bryant, writes that "until the end of 1941 Britain had no real strategy for winning the war," and sought only to avoid losing the war by swinging "wildly with all she had, whenever and where ever she was able, and contain her European enemies in a ring of salt water and sand." Yet unlike the previous year, Churchill now had an ally capable of supplying limitless numbers of men and weapons. The Christmas conference where all this would be parsed was code-named Arcadia, an appropriate moniker given Arcadia's literary association with refuge and calm, as well as being home to the temple of Zeus. In Washington, Churchill would find refuge, and in Roosevelt, Zeus, for there was no longer any doubt about who would craft the lightning bolts that would destroy Hitler. The question foremost in Churchill's mind was who would decide where and when to loose them.[73]

Max Beaverbrook considered Churchill's myriad operations to be diversions from the real war, in Russia, where he believed British tanks and troops would serve a greater purpose than in North Africa. General George Marshall also considered Africa a sideshow; he wanted to go ashore in France that year. Dwight Eisenhower, Marshall's deputy for all of a week, held a similar view, though with an eye toward a different theater of war: "I've been insisting that the Far East is critical," he noted in his diary, "and no sideshows should be undertaken until air and ground there is in satisfactory shape. Instead, we are taking on Magnet, Gymnast, etc." Eisenhower, unhappy with his desk job, confided to his diary that he'd "give anything to be back in the field." Averell Harriman, however, agreed with Churchill's ring strategy, and saw the strategic significance of Turkey and the Middle East, where others, especially Beaverbrook, did not.[74]

General Sir Alan Brooke, on the job as CIGS for only three weeks, agreed with Churchill that clearing North Africa and the Mediterranean held the key, but only if overwhelming force could be brought to bear there, an impossibility given the shifting of resources from the Middle East to the Far East, and the ongoing shipping losses in the Atlantic. British generals had for two centuries been trained to think in terms of the naval strategy necessary to sustain land forces in any given theater. Unlike the continental powers, Britain did not have to maintain a standing army of four or five million men to protect its borders; the North Sea and Channel did that. The British army was, by virtue of England's island geography, always an expeditionary force dependent on the Royal Navy. Brooke was such a "salt water" general. He understood that the most significant benefit to be gained by Allied control of the Mediterranean would be an immediate, effective increase in merchant tonnage of one million tons—the equivalent of 200 cargo ships—as a result of cutting the Middle Eastern supply route from almost 14,000 miles around the Cape to less than 4,000 directly through the Mediterranean. Such "new" shipping could then be used to carry more arms and food to Britain, and American troops to Britain or the Far East. Unless and until the Mediterranean was cleared, Allied shipping would descend further into crisis. Another factor contributed to Brooke's enthusiasm for Mediterranean operations. He had come off the beaches at Dunkirk and harbored no desire to return to France until he could do so in overwhelming force.[75]

This brought him into line with Churchill's belief in the need to return to France as well as with Churchill's Mediterranean thinking, but for different, and ultimately conflicting, reasons. As for Churchill's desire to fight in Norway, the Far East, and Africa simultaneously, Brooke knew that Britain—the entire Empire—lacked the men and matériel, especially the shipping, to attempt most, let alone all, of Churchill's multiple and far-flung operations. But Brooke was in London; Churchill was in Washington, where he had the full attention of the president and his military chiefs. Roosevelt, within days of Churchill's arrival, deferred to his advice on the matters of Acrobat, Gymnast, and Magnet, the plan to replace British troops stationed in Northern Ireland by four or more American divisions in order to free up British troops for deployment to North Africa. The details were to be sorted out by the newly created Combined Chiefs of Staff Committee—made up of the American and British army, navy, and air chiefs and their delegates in each capital. The first meetings stunned Dill, who telegraphed to Brooke that the Americans came with no agenda and recorded no minutes. Dill concluded that "at present [the United States] has not—repeat, not—the slightest conception of what the war means, and their armed forces are more unready for war than it is possible to imagine."[76]

To further complicate matters, where Churchill saw opportunities in North Africa, Roosevelt saw them in China. Chiang Kai-shek was dependent on the Burma Road, China's only link to the outside world, over which went fuel and ammunition for Chiang's armies. Were the Japanese to cut the road, Chiang would likely be finished. The entire Allied air defense along the Burma Road consisted of a few squadrons of RAF fighters in Burma and about seventy American mercenaries of the American Volunteer Group, whose few squadrons of fighter planes were divided between Kunming and Burma. The AVG irregulars were paid five hundred dollars for each confirmed Japanese kill. The Americans painted a shark's toothy snout on the noses of their Curtiss-Wright P-40B Tomahawks, and added an evil eye near the radiator intake in hopes of spooking Japanese pilots. They called themselves the Flying Tigers, and they served under a master tactician, Claire Chennault, a retired American army air corps captain who now held the rank of brigadier in Chiang's Chinese air force. Madame Chiang Kai-shek called the Americans her "flying angels." They were few in numbers and lacked spare parts and bullets, but they were the only Allied force since Pearl Harbor to have inflicted any pain whatsoever on the Japanese.[77]

Within days of Churchill's arrival in Washington, Archie Wavell, at Roosevelt's urging, was appointed supreme allied commander in the Far East. His mandate was to hold Malaya, and to coordinate with Chiang in defense of the Burma Road. The latter directive appealed to nobody except the Americans—the Burmese hated the Chinese as much or more than they hated the British. Wavell thought Chiang's forces not up to the task; and Churchill considered all of China a sideshow. Although his father had brought Burma into the Empire in the mid-1880s, Churchill saw value in defending the place in terms of shielding India rather than in saving Burma or defending Chiang and his supply route. Wavell's ABDA (American-British-Dutch-Australian) command was to set up shop in Batavia as soon as possible.

Lacking meaningful air and naval support, his lines of supply already in jeopardy, Wavell was in effect being asked to take one for the home team. Neither Churchill nor his chiefs liked the idea, yet, Churchill later wrote, "it was evident we must meet the American view." With that, he avoided the first spat in the partnership he had sought for so long. Churchill and Roosevelt understood they must accommodate each other much like partners in a three-legged race, where individual mobility and strengths are subordinated to the common cause. Disparate strategic goals, political and military, must not be allowed to undermine the common cause. They understood that for the duration they could not exploit each other's weaknesses, as they might in a friendly rivalry over tariffs. They knew they had to act as one and speak as one, because both their foe in Berlin and their new friend in Moscow were absolute masters of exploiting weakness. The avoidance of a spat in the early days of the alliance did not mean that there would be none down the road, but it meant that the two leaders trusted each other enough to handle the spats as they came along. There would be many.[78]

Shortly after 5:00 P.M. on Christmas Eve, Roosevelt and Churchill made their way to the south portico of the White House. There, the president flipped an electrical switch to illuminate the national Christmas tree, a thirty-foot-tall live Oriental spruce planted far down on the South Lawn and draped with red, white, and blue lights. Roosevelt had ordered the gates opened, and a crowd had gathered behind ropes on the lawn. Following a brief statement by Roosevelt, Churchill delivered a few remarks of his own, which were broadcast back to London by the BBC. As Churchill spoke, soft golden light spilled from the mansion's windows, a sight that would appear strange to most Britons and virtually every European, even the victorious Germans, whose leader had ordered that Germany be blacked out. Churchill, in his Christmas message, simply noted that for at least one night every home "throughout the English-speaking world should be a brightly-lighted island of happiness and peace. Let the children have their night of fun and laughter. Let the gifts of Father Christmas delight their play." And then it was off to drinks, dinner, and a late-to-bed, to prepare the address he would make to Congress in two days. So this was Christmas 1941, another year gone, and a new war just begun. America would not light its national Christmas tree again until 1945.[79]

Adolf Hitler, in Berlin, had forbidden the singing of all Christmas carols except "O Tannenbaum." Fir trees represented the towering strength of the Aryan race. The swastika, not an angel or cross, topped Berliners' Christmas trees, what few there were. Those *Volk* fortunate enough to procure trees likely used them for fuel. Winter had arrived, but coal had not. Food grew scarce, even as it was stolen from the Belgians, French, Poles, and Dutch, who by late 1941 had taken to boiling tulip bulbs for sustenance. Berliners greeted each other with *"Ach, das leben ist shwer"* ("Life is hard"). For German troops in Russia, life was hard, brutish, and short. Soviet propagandists smuggled thousands of Christmas cards into Germany, entitled "Living Space in the East." They depicted "a frozen vista of rows of wooden crosses topped with German helmets."[80]

Soon after Churchill addressed America's children, three hundred Free French sailors descended upon the islands of St-Pierre and Miquelon, France's oldest and smallest colony, located just off the Newfoundland coast. The islands were Vichy property, and Roosevelt, who hoped to lure Vichy into the Western fold through kindness, wanted them to stay that way. But the Vichy government had set up a radio transmitter on St-Pierre for purposes, wrote Churchill, "of spreading Vichy lies and poison" and quite possibly to "signal U-boats now hunting United States ships." Secretary of State Cordell Hull pressured Canada to shut down the station, but Ottawa, not wanting to offend Pétain, declined. De Gaulle, however, saw an opportunity for a symbolic victory over the Vichy lackeys, and before Churchill left for America, he informed him of his plans to capture the islands. Churchill at first approved but then objected after Hull voiced his vigorous disapproval. De Gaulle went ahead anyway. His forces arrived in gunboats and captured the islands without a fight. The victors raised their flag, emblazoned with the Cross of Lorraine. The British were elated. The Canadians were relieved to be off the hook. The Americans were aghast, as was Vichy France. Hull, infuriated (for here was a bald violation of the Monroe Doctrine), referred to de Gaulle and his followers as the "so-called Free French," thus assuring enmity between America and Frenchmen of all political persuasions at the exact moment Churchill saw the looming necessity to court the Vichy in North Africa. For if the Allies were ever to take the fight all the way from Egypt to Morocco, Tunisia, and Algeria, a compliant—better yet, a cooperative—Vichy regime would be far more vital to success than a brigade or two of de Gaulle's troublemakers.[81]

De Gaulle, therefore, had just mucked up the works. Yet he and his cohorts appeared to be the only Frenchmen willing to die in the fight against Hitler, and for that he had earned Churchill's respect and (guarded) support. Cordell Hull, on the other hand, treated de Gaulle with aloofness bordering on contempt. As punishment for his insolence, Hull—the "so-called Secretary of State" according to many in the American press—insisted the Free French be excluded from the roster of Allied countries that were to sign a pledge of allegiance to one another on New Year's Day. Churchill argued for the inclusion of the Free French, but Hull, backed by Roosevelt, carried the day. Churchill sidestepped another spat, and France, free or otherwise, did not officially exist within the alliance, known around Washington as the Associated Powers.

For a century Hong Kong had manifested handsomely the imperial British way of life. It was built on the profits of opium and piracy, ruled in fact from the offices of the towering Hongkong and Shanghai Banking Corporation, and fueled by gin slings and afternoon handicaps at the Happy Valley Racecourse. Hong Kong had been the free-wheeling, free-trade heart of Britain's Far East empire, open for business to any sea captain of any nationality willing and able to journey there, including Franklin Roosevelt's maternal grandfather, Warren Delano Jr., who made and lost several fortunes in the Clipper trade. Delano's daughter Sara, having actually sailed to that city during the American Civil War, inculcated in her son, Franklin, a romantic concept of Hong Kong and China and their roles in the world. Hong Kong was about to assume a new role. Since December 8, fewer than 8,000 Scots, Englishmen, Indians, Canadians, and some local Chinese had been surrounded by more than 30,000 Japanese troops. When the Japanese crossed from the mainland and cut off the water supply, the fight was all but over. Hong Kong's defenders understood that London considered the city a tactical position, to be held as long as possible in order to delay the Japanese and gain time to reinforce the more vital city of Singapore.

Despite Churchill's order to the defenders of Hong Kong to fight "from house to house" if necessary, and his exhortation "to resist to the end," Hong Kong's governor Sir Mark Young, surrounded and outgunned, surrendered on Christmas Day. It was the first colonial possession the British lost in the Pacific, ever. The victors took prisoner thirty Maryknoll missionaries and forced the captive proselytizers to bear witness as Japanese infantrymen bayoneted dozens of hog-tied British and Canadian prisoners. Prisoners spared the sword were beaten with rubber hoses and had water forced "down their throats until they nearly drowned." The rape of Hong Kong's Eurasian, Chinese, and white women began immediately. Three British nurses were raped, then bayoneted, and then burned. Three days later, Japanese troops—*Time* dubbed them "the dwarf-like men"—strutted through the city in triumphal review. By then, their brothers in Yamashita's Twenty-fifth Army had negotiated one-third of the Malay Peninsula, their target, Singapore. That fortress, Churchill told Wavell, "was to be held at all costs."[82]

On the day after Christmas, Churchill addressed the U.S. Congress. Listeners in Britain, where the BBC aired programs without corporate sponsorship, were surprised to learn that their prime minister's message was brought to them by a toothpaste company. Although such cultural divergences between the two nations lent credence to Bernard Shaw's observation that they were two countries separated by the same language, Churchill considered that language the uniting factor and, intending to demonstrate to Americans his mastery of it, had spent more than twelve hours crafting his words. Relieved to be among friends and cousins now (he could trace his American ancestry back five generations, to an officer who served under Washington), he began on a light note and surged ahead without regard to whether the moment was proper for glib pleasantries: "I cannot help reflecting that if my father had been an American, and my mother British, rather than the other way around, I might have got here on my own." With their applause and cheers, the assembled gave him what he came for: approval. Warming to his topic—retribution—he saw no need to inspire the Americans; Japan had done that. He saw no reason to gird Americans against the prospect of firestorms in their cities, of four-thousand-pound bombs obliterating their Parliaments and cathedrals and families, since other than the possibility of nuisance attacks on each coast, massed assaults were far beyond the technological reach of Germany and Japan. Lloyd's of London, in fact, was offering odds of ninety-nine to one against the chance of any property damage occurring on the Atlantic coast.[83]

Churchill worked in this bit of I-told-you-so, which engendered absolute silence from the gallery: "If we had kept together after the last war, if we had taken common measures for our safety, this renewal of the curse need never have fallen upon us. Do we not owe it to ourselves, to our children, to tormented mankind, to make sure that these catastrophes do not engulf us for the third time?" He excoriated the usual suspects with his usual delicious words and phrases: the "wicked men" who spread their "pestilences" and will "stop at nothing that violence and treachery can suggest." Churchill went after the "filthy Quislings" and "the boastful Mussolini... a lackey and serf, the merest utensil of his master's will." Then he gripped his lapels, slowly rocked forward, and delivered the line that brought Congress to its feet, including the isolationists. Of the Japanese he asked, "What kind of a people do they think we are? Is it possible they do not realize that we will never cease to persevere against them until they have been taught a lesson which they and the world will never forget?"[84]

The *New York Times* (under the headline CHURCHILL PREDICTS HUGE ALLIED DRIVE IN 1943) called the speech, which ran for more than thirty minutes, "typical" Churchill, "full of bubbling humor, biting denunciation of totalitarian enemies, stern courage, and hard facts." Yet some of Churchill's so-called hard facts were flabby. Citing Auchinleck's "victory in the Libyan campaign," Churchill declaimed, "Had we diverted and dispersed our gradually growing resources between Libya and Malaya, we would have been found wanting in both places." That was, at best, a lawyerly way of putting things. In spite of his autumn admonition to the British Chiefs of Staff that no diversions detract from Auchinleck's offensive capabilities, Churchill days earlier had ordered the 18th Division, then en route to the Suez, diverted to Singapore. Then, on the day *before* he addressed Congress, he ordered Auchinleck "to spare at once" for Singapore's defense heavy artillery, AA guns, trucks, one hundred new American tanks, and four squadrons (about forty-eight aircraft) of fighter planes, all of which Auchinleck was in need of, soon desperately so. Brooke lamented to his diary that Auchinleck was "struggling along with the forces at his disposal...little knowing his activities must be shortly curtailed" by Churchill's transfer of men and matériel to the Far East. Churchill didn't see things that way. The diminution of his forces, he told Auchinleck, could be accomplished "without compromising Acrobat," the push through Tripoli to Tunisia. And Gymnast, Churchill told his general, was still in good shape because America was now in. He added: "All our success in the West would be nullified by the fall of Singapore." That was true.[85]

That night he was awakened by "oppressive" heat in his bedroom, which was likely caused by a radiator valve stuck in the open position, a familiar nuisance to Americans who lived with central heat but a mystery to Britons, who for the most part did not. He attempted to remedy the situation by lifting a window, which stuck fast. He heaved, and felt a pain in his left arm and chest. In his memoirs he wrote, "I strained my heart slightly." Actually, as Dr. Wilson ascertained the next morning, Churchill had suffered a mild heart attack. Although Moran's memoirs* were considered by Churchill's friends and family to be self-serving and often inaccurate, the doctor's medical sense was sound. In this case he correctly diagnosed Churchill's heart problem, with the result that Churchill found a new detail to dwell on: his pulse. He demanded at all hours that Wilson check his heart rate, yet he also told the doctor not to impart any unsettling news. On several occasions over the next few days, Wilson observed Churchill making quick and furtive checks of his pulse. The doctor told him to ignore his heart rate, which is akin to telling someone not to conjure an image of a polar bear. When his self-diagnosis continued, Wilson took a calculated risk; he persuaded Churchill to slow down a bit but did not tell him what had actually happened, or that what he really needed was several weeks of bed rest. Such a prescription would have terrified Churchill and, more important, Wilson believed, the Americans and Britons.[86]

Two days after his heart episode, Churchill boarded a special train and chugged north to Ottawa in order to thank Prime Minister Mackenzie King and the Canadian people for their support. It seemed to Dr. Wilson that Churchill expected nothing less from the Dominions, and in fact took the Canadians for granted, especially the prudent and plodding Mackenzie King, who was prone to such banal observations as "the great thing in politics is to avoid mistakes."[87]

Canada had paid for its loyalty. Most of its merchant and cruise fleets had been placed at HMG's disposal; many Canadian ships had been lost. The Canadians in Hong Kong were now prisoners, or dead. Churchill was most grateful for Canadian support vis à vis Vichy France. Although Canada, like

---

* First published in Britain as *Churchill: The Struggle for Survival, 1940–1965* (Constable and Company, 1966). Published in the United States as *Churchill: Taken from the Diaries of Lord Moran* (Houghton Mifflin Company, 1966). Knighted in 1942, Sir Charles was made the first Lord Moran in January 1943. The book is part diary and part after-the-fact recollection presented as diary entries. Moran was not present in many of the scenes he paints himself into, and in which he quotes Churchill. Churchill's postwar secretary, Anthony Montague Browne, later declared (author interview, Nov. 15, 1980) that Churchill would no more hold substantive conversations with Moran about politics "than he would discuss the state of his bowels with his chiefs of staff." Browne held suspect much of the "debating, conversations and quotes he [Moran] put into people's mouths."

America, officially recognized Vichy, the vast majority of Canadians shared Churchill's contempt for the puppet government. When he addressed the Canadian Parliament on December 30, with full knowledge that such sentiments would further agitate Cordell Hull, he praised the fighting spirit of Charles de Gaulle. Then he reminded his audience of the prediction made by Weygand before the fall of France: "In three weeks England will have her neck wrung like a chicken." He paused, and directed a hard stare toward the assembly. Then: "Some chicken! Some neck!" That brought every man in the chamber to his feet. It was his most buoyant speech in eighteen months; the Canadians loved it, and Churchill knew it. Before departing Parliament, Churchill posed in the Speaker's Chambers for the photographer Yousuf Karsh. Seeking to capture Churchill at his most leonine, Karsh, without warning and just before he triggered his camera, snatched Churchill's cigar from his mouth. Karsh got the result he sought, a highly perturbed Churchill, looking more the pugilist than the statesman. The artist called his iconic photograph "The Roaring Lion." Moments later, after the storm had passed, Karsh made another photo, this of a benign Churchill, a smile creasing his almost cherubic face. Clementine called it the "happy" picture.[88]

Having regaled and thanked his obligors (though promising many more "dark and weary months of defeat" before victory was theirs), Churchill left Ottawa by train on New Year's Eve. The outside temperature had dropped to minus fifteen degrees Fahrenheit. The mood in the cars was somber. At the stroke of midnight, as the train highballed through the Hudson River Valley, Churchill stepped into the press carriage, a glass of champagne in hand. He raised it: "Here's to 1942. Here's to a year of toil—a year of struggle and peril, and a long step forward towards victory. May we all come through safe and with honor."[89]

One hundred miles to the south, the biggest and gayest crowd in memory gathered in Times Square. Only the military police standing in pairs on street corners and a huge white sign that asked "Remember Pearl Harbor" served notice that this celebration was unique. Just before midnight, as the glowing ball atop the New York Times Building began its descent, Lucy Monroe, the official soloist of the American Legion, began singing "The Star-Spangled Banner." The crowd listened at first in silence, but soon joined in. Radio networks beamed the anthem across the nation. In Washington, the mood was not gay. Troopers of the 3rd Cavalry Regiment, searching for saboteurs, spent New Year's Eve crawling along the aqueduct that carried drinking water to the capital from western Maryland. Infantrymen with fixed bayonets and live ammunition patrolled the Potomac bridges, while others put a cordon around the White House. Not since Confederate general Jubal Early knocked on the city's defenses in the summer of 1864 had so many soldiers swarmed the streets of Washington.[90]

In blacked-out London, a crowd that was gathered around St. Paul's Cathedral sang "Auld Lang Syne" when the clock struck midnight. The bells of London's churches remained silent, as they had for more than a year and a half. Then, inexplicably, the crowd broke into a chorus of "She'll Be Coming 'Round the Mountain," before dispersing and breaking up into ever smaller groups, each to wander home through the dark streets, with the occasional nervous glance jerked skyward. Harold Nicolson had not ventured out, but he listened to his wireless as Big Ben struck midnight. In his diary, Nicolson wrote, "And 1941 is finished.... It has been a sad and horrible year." No fires burned, but London could have served as a model for *Destruction*, the fourth painting in Thomas Cole's five-picture series, *The Course of Empire*. With America in, the odds had improved that London might never resemble Cole's final canvas: *Desolation*.[91]

General Sir Alan Brooke, looking back on the old year, asked for God's help in dealing with the "difficult times with the P.M. I see clearly ahead of me." As for the status of the Dominions, Brooke concluded, "We're not doing too bad. We've only lost about a quarter of the empire." Measured in square miles, his dour estimate was exaggerated. Measured in public confidence, especially among those of the Empire's citizens who dwelled in the Far East, it was not. Given the speed with which the Japanese were building their new empire on the ruins of Britain's old empire, Brooke's calculation seemed destined for fulfillment, and soon. His prediction of the looming difficulties inherent in working with Churchill was of course self-evidently correct.[92]

Churchill now operated in two worlds, one London, where "Action This Day" brought immediate results, the other a new world of action (and inaction) by committees seeking consensus. Churchill, Roosevelt, and Stalin were in overall agreement on the broadest objective, victory, but when they set about drawing up a declaration of solidarity, the devil began insinuating himself into the details. When the Soviet ambassador to the United States, Maxim Maximovich Litvinov, objected, at Stalin's insistence, to the inclusion of the phrase "religious freedom" in the draft declaration of the Associated Powers, Roosevelt (a truly religious man) lectured the ambassador "about his soul and the dangers of hell-fire." Roosevelt then reminded Litvinov that "freedom of religion" can be also construed to mean freedom *from* religion. Stalin approved the insertion of the clause. The alliance between a Christian republic, a parliamentary democracy, and a murderous Godless dictator could hardly have begun otherwise.[93]

Stalin wanted the declaration to reflect another position dear to him. The first article of the pact called for each signatory to employ all military and economic resources "against those members of the Tripartite Pact and its adherents with which such government is at war." As the Soviet Union was not at war with Japan, the final seven words of article 1 gave Stalin an out should anyone suggest down the road that he declare war on Japan. Roosevelt, meanwhile, happy with the entire document but not happy with the moniker "Associated Powers," came up with a more vivid name: the United Nations. Intent on sharing his suggestion with Churchill, the president wheeled himself down the hallway and into Churchill's room, where the prime minister, preparing for his bath, was wandering about stark naked. Taking no notice of Churchill's nakedness, Roosevelt suggested his proposed name change. Churchill replied, "Good," and added that Byron employed the same choice of words in *Childe Harold's Pilgrimage*. Churchill later told King George that he was the first British prime minister in history to greet a head of state naked. He later wrote he thought Roosevelt's "United Nations" "a great improvement" over the "Associated Powers."[94]

On December 12, the *New York Times* had run a list of the twenty-five* allied combatants. India—whose troops had so far fought in North Africa, Malaya, Iraq, and Persia—was absent from the *Times* roll call. India's exclusion made sense to Churchill; India was, after all, part of the British Empire, its foreign policy dictated by London. Churchill had for months made clear that any change in India's colonial status could only take place after the war, and that he could not, by law, dictate terms to a postwar Parliament in which he and his coalition government might play no role. But Roosevelt sought India's inclusion in the pact, and he instructed Hull to prod the British on the matter, an assignment Hull embraced with alacrity as a staunch anti-imperialist and still fuming over the St-Pierre incident (which he suspected Churchill of encouraging). The War Cabinet objected to India's inclusion, rightly so in Churchill's opinion. Halifax, keen to avoid trouble with the Americans, suggested to Churchill that India's participation in drafting the Versailles Treaty two decades earlier might serve as a precedent for its inclusion in the allied pact, and thus mollify Roosevelt. A compromise was reached: India would be included in the roll call of allies, but without any notation that implied sovereignty. With India, as with the exclusion of the Free French, Churchill deferred to Roosevelt.[95]

He did so again when Roosevelt demanded that the United States be the first signatory to the pact, followed by the other three powers: Great Britain, the Soviet Union, and China. China's emotional importance to Roosevelt was bolstered by strategic considerations. Here was a nation of

* The U.S., U.K., U.S.S.R., China; Australia, Belgium, Canada, Costa Rica, Cuba, Czechoslovakia, the Dominican Republic, El Salvador, Greece, Guatemala, Haiti, Honduras, India, Luxembourg, the Netherlands, New Zealand, Nicaragua, Norway, Panama, Poland, South Africa, and Yugoslavia.

almost five hundred million people, he told Churchill, which would emerge from the war armed and eager to fill the vacuum created by the defeat of Japan. Better to court the Chinese now than to have to face them later. China, for Churchill, was an ally, but "not a world power equal to Britain, the United States, or Russia." Yet so firm was Roosevelt regarding China's status that Churchill cabled Wavell: "If I can epitomize in one word the lesson I learned in the United States, it was 'China.'" China took fourth billing.

On one point of language the president failed to prevail; he disliked the designation favored by the press, "World War Two," and called for suggestions for a more poetic name. H. L. Mencken compiled a list of the many proposals that flowed into the White House, including the "War for Survival," the "Necessary War," the "Crazy War," the "War Against Tyrants," the "Devil's War," and "Hell." Any and all of those names applied to the conflict, but the press stuck with World War Two. Churchill, too, offered Roosevelt a name for the war; it summed up in three words the entire legacy of the appeasers and isolationists: "The Unnecessary War."[96]

On January 5, after almost two weeks of discussions, not wanting to further tax Roosevelt's hospitality yet not ready to return home (the American and British military chiefs were just getting down to business), Churchill accepted the offer of Lend-Lease administrator Edward Stettinius to spend a few days at Stettinius's Pompano Beach, Florida, seaside manse. The Old Man needed a break, and Roosevelt and Hopkins needed a break—from Churchill. Eleanor Roosevelt later recalled, "I was solicitous for [Churchill's] comfort, but I was always glad when he departed, for I knew that my husband would need a rest, since he had carried his usual hours of work in addition to the unusual ones Mr. Churchill preferred." The meetings had so drained Harry Hopkins he checked into the Washington Naval Hospital for a week of bed rest.[97]

Churchill and a dozen or so of his party along with a Secret Service detail flew down to the small airfield in West Palm Beach aboard Marshall's plane. From there they motored an hour south to Pompano, where the locals were told that the activity out at the Stettinius house was due to the arrival of an English invalid by the name of Mr. Lobb. Mr. Lobb, upon arrival, headed straightaway for the beach, where he reveled in the warm ocean waters, and swam about, naked, until somebody spotted a large shark. "They said it was only a 'ground shark,'" Churchill later wrote, "but it is as bad to be eaten by a ground shark as any other." Inspector Thompson ordered him out of the water, but Churchill stayed put, pawing happily about. The shark, after describing a long, slow circle, swam off. "My bulk," Churchill shouted to those on shore, "has frightened him into deeper water." Still, from then on he kept to the shallows, where he basked "half submerged in the water, like a hippopotamus in a swamp." Thompson thought Churchill, sunbathing, nude, "looked like a huge, well adjusted, and slightly over-bottled baby boy."

Roosevelt sent along his personal chef and a favorite recipe for clam chowder, but Churchill preferred Bovril washed down with champagne. He smoked his cigars and drank and frolicked in the surf in sunny and isolated South Florida, about as far from the war as he could get. It was his first holiday in three years. Although in early January Americans had no real idea of just what troubles were heading their way, Churchill, bobbing in the Florida surf, knew "without doubt" what lay before them all—"a time of tribulation" and "disappointments and unpleasant surprises." He had told Britons as much for almost two years, and had told Americans the same just days earlier. He knew that upon his arrival in London—"it was to no sunlit prospect that I must return"—he would again have to inform the King, the Parliament, and Britons that the worst was yet to come. After five days of whisky, hot baths, and warm Florida, Churchill telephoned Roosevelt to inform the president that he was about to depart for Washington. Mindful of John Martin's pleas to exercise *some* caution when speaking over nonsecure phone lines, he whispered, "I can't tell you how we are coming, but we are coming by puff-puff, got it? *Puff-puff*."[98]

Mrs. Roosevelt invited a special guest to dinner on Churchill's penultimate evening in the White House: Louis Adamic. Slovenian by birth, Adamic by 1942 had become one of the most popular and controversial ethnic American writers. His progressive ideas had found favorable conditions in which to sprout at the traditionally anti-imperialist State Department, which had developed on certain desks a list to the left. Having read and enjoyed Adamic's latest book, *Two-Way Passage*, the First Lady must have known Churchill would find no comfort in the author's company. Adamic argued the case for America to take the lead in postwar European political reconstruction by sending "qualified" liberal expatriate thinkers such as himself back to the Old World to inculcate in its citizens a less chauvinistic outlook, such that undesirable elements could not influence events. Chief among these undesirable elements was the "Eagle of Yugoslavia" Draja Mihailovich and his 150,000 mostly Serbian Chetnik guerrillas who had for seven months been fighting a vicious war against Hitler's occupying forces, tying down ten German and Bulgarian divisions in the process. For this Mihailovich was hailed as a hero in the West, and by Churchill.

Adamic, however, supported the partisans led by Josip Broz, a Croat by birth, Socialist by choice, and virtually unknown in America. His followers called him Tito (Churchill, per his habit of getting names wrong, called him Toty). As for other European elements, Adamic saw the Soviets as posing no threat to anyone after the war. Britain was another matter; Britain followed Mihailovich on Adamic's list of undesirable scallywags to be excluded from postwar influence, especially in the Balkans. The Roosevelts, husband and wife, much impressed with Adamic, passed his book along to Churchill. He hated it.[99]

In his memoir of that evening, *Dinner at the White House,* Adamic described Roosevelt as "vivid and agile," the picture of charm. Even Fala, Roosevelt's little Scottie dog, who roamed the room sniffing shoes and performing tricks, came in for Adamic's praise. Adamic portrays Churchill as "a great leader and... also evil" and noted that he was "mostly stomach" with a fat cigar plugged into his "large, round mug." His mouth and eyes "were shrewd, ruthless, unscrupulous." When Adamic asked him how he liked *Two-Way Passage,* Churchill snarled, "I'm r-reading your book and I-I find it—int'r-resting." Adamic's sentence construction seems to ascribe a stutter to Churchill; yet although he experienced difficulty with the sibilant "s" (he had a very slight lisp), he did not stutter. In any case, Adamic correctly concluded before dessert that Churchill would never accept his utopian scheme, or anything like it. His demeanor, Adamic wrote, "was one of complex annoyance.... I was a bloody nuisance dragged in by F.D.R. and he had had to put up with me. This was implicit in his manner, integral with his whole personality.... He muttered something I did not understand. His half-closed eyes squinted up at me, and he stuck the cigar into his face and pressed his back against the wall." That sounds like Churchill, when perturbed, bored, and, as Adamic implies, running on 80 proof. It was a safe bet that Churchill would not be sponsoring Adamic for membership in the Other Club.[100]

It should be remembered that Churchill during those early weeks of the alliance could not predict with any certainty who among the men he met were destined to go down in history as giants, and who (like Adamic) were destined for the dustbin. George Marshall was still army chief of staff, but if responsibility for Pearl Harbor was to be assigned at the highest link of the command chain, Marshall might be sacked. Churchill would have sacked his top commanders after such a debacle. How much credence, therefore, to give Marshall's opinions? The navy's top man, Admiral Harold ("Betty") Stark, though not officially accused of allowing Pearl Harbor to happen on his watch, was in fact within months kicked upstairs, as commander of the U.S. European Fleet (of which there was none) and naval liaison to London, where, like Field Marshal Dill in Washington, he acquitted himself well. Churchill had yet to hear the names Eisenhower, Patton, or Bradley. He knew of Douglas MacArthur's reputation, yet it appeared during those weeks that MacArthur—the prime candidate to lead American forces, either in Europe or in Asia—was more likely to die a hero's death in the Philippines, and soon. Admiral Ernest King, promoted to chief of naval operations (at Stark's expense, as King saw it), resented Marshall and itched to bring the fight to Japan. Could King—hot-tempered, tough, and no admirer of the British Empire—be made to see the merits of Germany first? Churchill would just have to wait and see. Although Adamic in time faded from the scene, his presence at Roosevelt's table could not be ignored.

Nor could Churchill ignore Mrs. Roosevelt, who "was allowed to sit in at such White House after-dinner conversations." This, recalled one of his secretaries, "so distressed Winston," for in England, following dinner, the women left the men to themselves. Churchill's Chartwell dining table was round (at his insistence, in order to erase any implied hierarchy among guests), but after dinner it rarely included women. Churchill, Colville recalled, "did not in general find the company of women particularly stimulating."[101]

To that rule there existed certain exceptions: Lady Diana Cooper was one, Violet Bonham Carter, the daughter of Prime Minister Asquith another. And above all, there was Clementine. Yet Clementine, for her part, would never think of joining the men for a snifter of old Napoleon, not so much because she considered her place to be elsewhere, or because Churchill forbade her presence—he would not—but because her politics ran just far enough to the left of his that a forceful expression of her opinions in the presence of her husband's circle of cronies would likely result in awkward silence. (Though Churchill was a liberal Tory in the manner of his father, Clementine was at heart an Edwardian Liberal, more comfortable with the traditional Liberal Party.) As well, she did not much care for two of his most favored pals—the Irishman Bracken and the Canadian Beaverbrook, whose aircraft production she respected but who had always annoyed her. So she chose not to participate in the after-dinner sessions, or in politics in general. When she hosted a luncheon or dinner, Clementine, reading her husband's mood, steered the conversation away from any topic that might roil or bore him. If the talk turned to politics, Mrs. Churchill kept her counsel. As for Eleanor Roosevelt's eagerness to socialize with guests such as Adamic and to participate in manly conversations, Churchill was astute enough to grasp that the First Lady was not merely performing wifely social duties, but was a political force, one heard and respected by her husband. Churchill, therefore, as a guest in the president's house, and more beholden to Roosevelt with each tank and plane that rolled off American assembly lines, was willing, if not happy, to put up with the political pronouncements of Adamic and Mrs. Roosevelt.[102]

* * *

Franklin Roosevelt, over the course of Arcadia, served up to Churchill everything he sought, and more. Roosevelt's deference to Britain on military matters was understandable given that Britain had been fighting a war for more than two years, while the Americans had been losing one for two weeks. There were disagreements: Marshall wanted the Allied effort to begin with a landing on the French coast, in 1942, while Churchill had his sights on Gymnast, the landing in North Africa. To Churchill's surprise and immense relief, as Auchinleck seemed about to stall in the desert, Roosevelt came up with Operation Super-Gymnast—the occupation at the earliest opportune moment of French North Africa by at least 100,000 American and British troops. If Eisenhower thought little of Gymnast, the man tapped by Marshall to lead American troops ashore—Major General Joseph Stilwell—thought even less. Stilwell—"Vinegar Joe" to his men—was chosen after his name topped a list prepared for Marshall of America's most talented generals. Stilwell's diary entries regarding Gymnast illuminate both the validity of his nickname and his loathing of the British. "Gymnast," he wrote, had the potential to become "a rathole," hard to supply and harder to keep. It was "a crazy gamble.... The whole goddamned thing is cockeyed." Roosevelt, "a rank amateur in military matters, given to whims, fancies and childish notions," had been "sucked in... by the Limeys."[103]

The lack of shipping and landing craft to undertake Gymnast ensured that it could not be carried out for several months, at best. In fact, within two weeks, with Auchinleck stalled in the desert, the prospects for Gymnast, super or otherwise, evaporated. Stilwell was told to forget about North Africa and was instead ordered to China, where Chiang—who Stilwell thought "a crazy little bastard"—waited for the help promised by Roosevelt. Yet, other than Stilwell, not much more help was forthcoming for Chiang. As for war matériel, the Americans pegged production of Grant and Sherman tanks at 45,000 for 1942, compared with just 4,200 since May 1940. Roosevelt proposed to build twice as many warplanes in 1942—45,000—than the United States and Britain had built in the previous two years. It was a staggering goal, four times the rate of German and Japanese production combined. Goebbels derided the projections as "insane figures."[104]

When during the meetings the Americans offered that at most they could convert 15 percent of U.S. auto plants to military production, Beaverbrook replied that 100 percent of British automobile factories had been converted, and encouraged Roosevelt to aim higher. He did, and on January 1 he ordered U.S. auto production halted by late February. Within weeks the dearth of new cars became moot when rubber, 90 percent of which came from Malaya and Indonesia, was rationed. The U.S. had no synthetic rubber factories to make up the shortfall. Americans soon learned what Britons had long known; without a spare tire or three stashed in the garage, the family car had a very limited range. Passage by rail—where for fifty years the Pullmans had been Americans' preferred means of conveyance—was soon limited to troops and businessmen on official war business. And then the airlines—their routes and the national fleet of 434 aircraft—were commandeered. By spring, gasoline rationing, as a means to preserve rubber more than oil, dribbled onto the Eastern Seaboard and in the following year spread nationwide, guaranteeing that Americans in the heartland could no longer take their vacations at east or west coast beaches even if their bald tires could carry them there. That proved okay with most because by summer, oil and bilge tar and decomposing bodies—the U-boats' harvest—regularly washed up onto America's eastern beaches.[105]

Roosevelt had agreed to truly power up the American dynamo, yet early in the new year, the steady, relentless hum of infinite American industrial power could only be imagined. America, humiliated in Guam, Wake Island, Pearl Harbor, and Manila, was itching for a fight but was not in the least ready for one. More worrisome from Churchill's standpoint was that Americans including Anglophobes like Admiral Ernest King and Stilwell—and the thousands of volunteers who lined up outside recruiting offices—wanted to take the fight to the Japanese, and the sooner the better.

The damage inflicted at Pearl Harbor precluded any such action. So devastating was the Japanese attack that a small aircraft carrier task force sent to relieve the five hundred U.S. Marines stranded on Wake Island ran for home when its commander, Rear Admiral Frank ("Jack") Fletcher, decided that his need for fuel overrode his mission to relieve the Marines on Wake. When Secretary of the Navy Frank Knox asked Churchill what he would do with such a cautious admiral, Churchill held his tongue in deference to his new allies. Before surrendering, the doomed leathernecks on Wake inflicted the only damage thus far upon the Japanese navy, by damaging a cruiser and sinking a destroyer—with field artillery. So acute was the American navy's embarrassment over the month's events that one of King's first actions as the new navy chief was to change CINCUS—the abbreviation for commander in chief, U.S. Navy—to COMINCH, because CINCUS was pronounced as it looked. Meanwhile, MacArthur and his army were in danger of going the way of Jim Bowie and his Texans at the Alamo. This Americans could not abide, especially if they detected a willingness in Washington to bolster the British Empire at the cost of sacrificing MacArthur. To Secretary of War Henry Stimson, Churchill made clear his fear that an American preoccupation with the Pacific in general and the Philippines in particular would hobble the Europe-first strategy that had been in the works for months, with the result that the war might be lost in both theaters before America entered either. Stimson happened to loathe Admiral King and believed in Europe-first. It was said that Stimson, trying to reassure Churchill, said of MacArthur's army, "There are times when men have to die." So it would be Europe first, after all.[106]

Yet even such a seemingly unambiguous pronouncement as "Europe first" meant different things to different men. The decisions as to where and when and how to attack Germany would have to be hammered out by the newly configured Combined Joint Chiefs of Staff Committee, its first members being George Marshall, U.S. Army chief of staff; Admiral Harold Stark, U.S. Naval Forces Europe; Admiral Ernest J. King, chief of U.S. Naval Operations; and Lieutenant General Henry H. ("Hap") Arnold, U.S. Army Air Forces. For Britain: the aging first sea lord, Sir Dudley Pound; Sir Charles Portal at the RAF; and General Sir Alan Brooke as Chief of the Imperial General Staff. The "imperial" in Brooke's title grated on the political sensibilities of Marshall and King, this before they even met the man. The Combined Joint Chiefs was not formally inaugurated until February, and the principals would not meet until spring, by which time they were in near total disagreement over exactly what "Germany first" or "Europe first" meant. By summer those differences would grow into the first real test of the alliance.

On his final night in Washington, Churchill dined alone with Roosevelt and Hopkins before departing late in the evening for Norfolk, Virginia. The next morning he climbed aboard a Boeing Clipper for a three-hour flight to Bermuda, where the *Duke of York* awaited his arrival. Churchill found the flight much to his liking. The weather was fair, the food and drink plentiful. The big plane cruised at eight thousand feet at a steady 145 miles per hour. Churchill even took the controls for a spell. Recalling the unpleasant shipboard trip westward, he prevailed upon the plane's captain, Kelly Rogers, to take him and a few of his staff all the way to England. The rest of the party followed by ship. The air journey almost proved disastrous when at dawn the next day, after an eighteen-hour flight, Rogers brought his plane out of low clouds, only to realize that he was off course. Where all aboard should have seen the coast of England, they beheld nothing but gray seas. They flew on, and on. Churchill recalled in his memoirs that after several minutes of disconcerting silence, Rogers announced he was turning sharply northward. It was a snap judgment, and a good one, for had they kept on their original course for another few minutes, they would have drifted over Brest, and the hundreds of German AA guns protecting the pride of Germany's surface fleet—the battle cruisers *Prinz Eugen, Scharnhorst,* and *Gneisenau*—moored in the harbor. The turn, however, appeared to RAF radar operators as the track of a lone German bomber heading for England from Brest. Six Hurricanes were scrambled, with orders to shoot down the interloper. Thankfully, Fighter Command's aces failed to locate their target. After five weeks and more than nine thousand miles, Churchill arrived safely home, the first leader of any nation to undertake a transoceanic flight.[107]

Churchill enjoyed travel destinations—Marrakech and the Riviera especially, almost any place warmer than England—far more than he enjoyed the journey, especially if undertaken by way of warship or small plane, where the accoutrements of fine dining and plump mattresses were sadly lacking. When he was confined in a steel or aluminum shell, his restlessness and imagination overtook him. Of his air journey, he later wrote, "I must admit I felt rather frightened," when contemplating the endless ocean spaces below and the distance, more than a thousand miles, from land. "I had always regarded an Atlantic flight with awe." As well he should have. Just two years earlier it was considered sheer folly to attempt an aerial crossing of the North Atlantic in winter, when the weather was at its most unpredictable. The fact that American bomber crews now hopscotched to Britain via Newfoundland and Iceland was due more to their need to refuel rather than to any improvements in weather forecasting or navigation, both of which were still primitive. At night, if the skies were clear, pilots charted their course by the stars. High cloud cover could prove lethal. A plane that lost its way most likely ended up downed, with little chance of rescue for those on board. So perilous was the crossing that the preferred means of getting bombers to Europe was by ship, a means of conveyance Churchill on that occasion found to be unacceptably slow. He was now an old man in a hurry.[108]

Soon after he arrived back in London, the news of his heart problems became known, in large part because he could not keep quiet. He told Eden that he felt "his heart a bit" and had some breathing problems when he tried to dance. Eden passed that news along to his parliamentary secretary, Oliver Harvey, who noted in his diary, "The doctors have told him [Churchill] his heart is not too good and he needs rest." Harvey also told Eden that he had best be ready to assume power if Churchill's health worsened. Harvey also noted that in sickness and in health, Churchill's enjoyment of his Edwardian luncheons was never diminished: "He had beer, three ports, and three brandies for lunch today, and has done it for years." Yet Churchill was down. Hong Kong was gone, Singapore soon to be threatened. And Rommel that day had emerged yet again, viperlike, from under his rock. After drinks with the Old Man, Eden jotted in his diary,

"Winston was tired and depressed, for him.... He is inclined to be fatalistic about the House [of Commons], maintained that the bulk of the Tories hated him...and would be only too happy to yield to another." Yet any thoughts of promotion Eden might have entertained were premature (by more than thirteen years, as events turned out). Churchill, his gloomy musings to Eden aside, had no intention of quitting.[109]

On his first day home, while reading the papers on the train to London, he turned to Dr. Wilson and, in a tired voice, said, "There seems to be plenty of snarling." There was. Attlee had warned him by cable that his reception in London would be something less than a triumph. Much mumbling and interruption had occurred in the Commons, Attlee reported, when the first lord of the Admiralty, A. V. Alexander, attempted to give members more details of the circumstances in which the *Prince of Wales* had been caught. The House seemed "fractious," Attlee wrote, and the public and press were "rather disturbed" about the overall situation in the Far East, for which they blamed the government's lack of preparedness. Of more concern to Attlee, the House—and the *Evening Standard* and *Daily Mail*—was "a good deal apprehensive" about India, specifically about the political situation there. Murmurs emanated from the Antipodes as well; the tone in Australia, Attlee reported, was "very negative." Churchill—the entire world—was well aware of that fact. Australian prime minister John Curtin, fearful of a Japanese invasion, had declared in a signed article in the *Melbourne Herald* his nation's intent, taken "free of pangs as to our traditional links with the United Kingdom," to align its foreign policy with and seek the protection of the United States. In effect, Australia had bolted the Empire, an action codified ten months later when the Australian parliament ratified the Statute of Westminster,* retroactive to September 3, 1939, the day London declared war. It was a slight Churchill never forgot. Despite his oft-expressed appreciation for the wartime sacrifice of the Dominions and despite his love of warm, beachy destinations, Churchill would never visit Australia, even when the jet age rendered such a journey no more arduous than a long nap in a garden chair.[110]

A great many MPs of all political stripes and many in the press, Tory and Labour alike, were calling for a cabinet shake-up. Some questioned whether Churchill, as prime minister, could still lead the country; more had concluded that as minister of defence he could no longer lead the war effort. The Commons seemed primed for revolt. Churchill attributed the criticism to the "vast, measureless array of disasters" approaching by way

* The Statute of Westminster, passed by Parliament in 1931 over Churchill's violent opposition, granted autonomy to certain Dominions—Canada, Newfoundland, Australia, New Zealand, subject to ratification by their respective parliaments.

of Japan, as well as the belief held by many Britons that the new alliance with America meant that the survival of the Home Island "was no longer at stake." The relief engendered by that conviction allowed "every critic, whether friendly or malevolent, to point out the many errors that had been made." Chief among those errors, according to his critics, was Churchill's creation of the office of minister of defence and appointment of himself the first chief of that department, where he had nothing to show but a plethora of defeats. They wanted him out of that job. Yet a defense "establishment" of the sort the Americans were about to house in their new Pentagon Building did not exist in Britain. Churchill's Ministry of Defence consisted mainly of himself. If replaced, he would be denied his channels of communication with the Chiefs of Staff, and that was unacceptable. His critics acknowledged that he had inspired the nation and procured his Grand Alliance, but at the cost of alienating the Australians, who feared for their lives, and further alienating Indian nationalists who, along with many Americans, including Roosevelt, considered Churchill to be an old school imperialist. He came home to "unhappy, baffled public opinion, albeit superficial, swelling, and mounting about me on every side." He decided to meet the criticism head-on, first by warning the nation that more defeats were on their way, and then by demanding a vote of confidence in the House. It was an astute maneuver, one his critics should have anticipated given Churchill's philosophy in matters both military and political: when attacked, counterattack.[111]

On January 20, as Churchill prepared to address his countrymen, Adolf Hitler spoke to his. By then Goebbels had seen to it that any mention of Churchill in German newsreels or newspapers carried with it some reference to his being a strategic nincompoop, a pawn of the Jews, or a drunkard. Hitler outdid Goebbels:

> That twaddler, that drunkard Churchill, what has he achieved in all his lifetime? That mendacious creature, that sluggard of the first order. Had this war not come, future centuries would have spoken of our age, of all of us and also of myself, as the creators of great works of peace. But had this war not come, who would speak of Churchill? . . . one of the most abominable characters in world history, incapable of a single creative action, capable only of destruction.

Hitler then repeated a boast made in 1940. Given the fate of the Third Reich, his choice of words have now an oracular and ironic ring to them: "True, one day they will speak of him as the destroyer of an empire he, not we, have ruined."[112]

Also on that day, January 20, Reinhard Heydrich, Himmler's second in command of the SS, and the ruthless acting protector of Bohemia, convened a conference in the Berlin suburb of Grosser-Wannsee. Göring had months earlier demanded from the SS a "final solution of the Jewish question." The fifteen Nazi bureaucrats and members of the SS who met at Wannsee intended to coordinate nothing less than the extermination of the eleven million Jews who dwelled in Europe and the Soviet Union. "Europe would be combed of Jews from east to west," Heydrich declared. SS lieutenant colonel Adolf Eichmann, a thirty-six-year-old technocrat, served as conference secretary. He kept concise minutes, which were subsequently edited by Heydrich, who inserted coded language of the sort Nazis employed when referring to lethal actions taken against Jews, partisans, and Communists. "Eliminated by natural causes" referred to death by a combination of hard labor and starvation. "Transported to the east" referred to the mass deportations of Jews to ghettos in occupied Poland, and then on to the gas chambers planned for Belzec, Treblinka, Sobibor, and Auschwitz. "Special actions" and "treated accordingly" served as Nazi code words for summary execution by firing squad or death by gassing in the specially rigged trucks of the *Einsatzgruppen,* as had been taking place in the East since Barbarossa began. Tens upon tens of thousands of Ukrainian Jews had already been shot, their bodies dumped into mass graves that are still being discovered seventy years later. So confident were the attendees at the Wannsee conference of ultimate success that the nation-by-nation list they compiled of Jewish populations included Ireland (4,000) and England (330,000). So efficient was the Nazi killing machine that Estonia, it was duly noted, was already "free of Jews."

Three weeks before Heydrich convened his conference—Churchill was just arriving in Ottawa—two Czech commandos were parachuted from a British Halifax bomber into the Czechoslovakian countryside. They made for Prague, where Heydrich—hated by all Czechs—had his headquarters. The two Czechs had been trained by Hugh Dalton's Special Operations Executive. Their mission, sanctioned by the Czech government in exile, was to shadow Heydrich until such time as the opportunity presented itself to assassinate him.[113]

Sir Stafford "Christ and Carrots" Cripps, having been granted his wish to leave Moscow, arrived home to London on January 23. He was not yet ready for a retirement dinner and a return to the law courts. The political left had anointed him as the best successor to Churchill were the prime minister to be shoved from office, a shake-up that even some on the right thought overdue. Goebbels, too, thought Cripps was destined for No. 10, from where it was assumed in Berlin that he would Bolshevize England, a feeling shared by many Tories. Cripps was a dour man and an uninspired orator whose only enjoyment seemed to be an occasional cigar, but early in the war he declared he'd given up cigars as a symbolic sacrifice. It was said that Churchill's reaction to that gesture was to mumble, "Too bad, it was his last contact with humanity." Two days after Cripps's return, the prime minister offered him a place in the cabinet as minister of supply, where he would in effect serve under Beaverbrook if Churchill could persuade the Beaver to take the post of minister of production. This would put Cripps in the cabinet but outside the War Cabinet and, worse, under Beaverbrook, whom Cripps despised. Cripps, cautious and adroit politician that he was, deferred his decision on the matter until after the vote of confidence about to take place in the Commons.[114]

Cripps was the most viable of three possible contenders for the premiership in early 1942. Eden and Minister of Labour Ernest Bevin were the others. But Eden and Bevin were Churchill loyalists of high magnitude; their betraying him and the coalition government was out of the question. Attlee, head of the Labour Party and Churchill's natural opponent, had also placed his loyalty to the government above his ambitions. But Cripps was interested, though he was unwilling to make his move until he was sure his support ran deep.

Beaverbrook also saw himself as a possible contender. He had his admirers, himself chief among them. Averell Harriman recalled that Beaverbrook "in the winter of '42 when things were going very badly . . . thought that Churchill was going to be consumed by the power and he [Beaverbrook] would have a chance at that time to become prime minister." Undoubtedly Beaverbrook possessed some of the qualities of a war leader, foremost his ability to marshal production. But his abrasive personality bled through in public and guaranteed that he could never marshal, as had Churchill, the spirit of Englishmen. This Beaverbrook understood at some level, and he admitted as much in a letter in which he berated Churchill for his North African policy: "On the rock bound coast of New Brunswick the waves beat incessantly. Every now and then comes a particularly dangerous wave that breaks viciously on the rocks. It's called the 'rage.' That's me." His best side, wrote his biographer Kenneth Young, emerged in his service as Churchill's lieutenant and friend, where his agile brain appealed to Churchill, and which the Old Man used "as a whetstone on which to sharpen his own remarkable wits." The Beaver's worst side would be exposed by any shifty attempt to promote himself to captain. In the end, the friendship of three decades trumped ambition; Beaverbrook publicly dismissed the notion of seeking high office and soon after, in a letter to

Churchill, professed his devotion to "the leader of the nation, the savior of our people." Still, he soon began quietly telling Labourites that Churchill was on his way out. He did so behind Churchill's back, knowing full well that such talk could only hurt his old friend. Churchill was not blind to the Beaver's shenanigans. Ernest Bevin said of Churchill's relationship with Beaverbrook, "He's like a man who's married a whore; he knows she's a whore but loves her just the same."[115]

No pretender had earned, as Churchill had since 1940, the wide public respect and popularity needed to assume command in wartime. With criticism coming at him from the Commons and the press, Churchill "resolved to yield nothing to any quarter." He had three unassailable advantages, and he knew it. In 1940 and 1941 he had shown himself the guardian of the national will; unlike Chamberlain, he loved the House of Commons and held sacred that body's place in English life; and though he had critics, he had no rival who could best him in the hearts of Englishmen. Years later, Brian Gardner, Fleet Street veteran and historian, wrote, "Most Britons were prepared to go on waging war with the man they knew, whom many loved, in the siren suit, with the cigar, the V-sign, and the grin. His removal would have been resented. The House of Commons knew this, and most members acted accordingly."[116]

The attack against Churchill was led by the Labour MP Aneurin ("Nye") Bevan, a forty-four-year-old hard-drinking product of the North Wales coalfields, and a speaker whose oratory was as tempestuous and cutting as the gales that raced down the Snowdon Massif. He managed *The Tribune*, a left-wing sheet begun by Stafford Cripps five years earlier, which, on the twenty-third, went after Churchill, and went to the nub of the problem as Bevan saw it: "The question is beginning to arise in the minds of many: is he [Churchill] as good a war maker as he is a speech maker?"[117]

Beaverbrook, who pollinated his newspapers with young, up-and-coming left-wing intellectuals, had mentored Bevan in the 1930s. But for Bevan's lack of ruthlessness, Beaverbrook believed he might have emerged as the Lenin of England, although Beaverbrook also claimed Bevan had become enthralled "with the pleasure of high living," which diverted him from a more pure-Leninist path. Yet, along with Cripps, Bevan had opposed appeasement in the late 1930s and at the time reluctantly saw Churchill as the only alternative (as had Cripps), yet not so much to save the British Empire as to help safeguard the Soviet socialist experiment. This was not patriotism, as Churchill saw it, but the opportunistic championing by the left wing of foreign causes and complex philosophical/political systems of a sort only an intellectual could love. When Colville later wrote that Churchill "hated casuistry," he had Bevan in mind. While Churchill "considered parliamentary opposition to be the lifeblood of British politics, the form in which Aneurin Bevan applied it seemed to contribute nothing toward our principal objective, which was to win." Yet Churchill thought personal animus a waste of time, once telling colleagues in the House, "Such hatred as I have left—and it isn't much—I would rather reserve for the future than the past." He called that "a judicious and thrifty disposal of bile." Churchill enjoyed the company of many of those with whom he disagreed, but he drew the line at Bevan, not because of Bevan's views but because Churchill doubted his patriotism.* That, for Churchill, was an unforgivable sin.[118]

Bevan was the MP for Tredegar, a coal town in the Sirhowy Valley of western Gwent, a place where the local surgeons were kept busy setting the smashed bones of miners and quarrymen, and where the leading causes of death for males were tuberculosis (the Cough) and pneumoconiosis (Black Lung), the disease that killed Bevan's father. Bevan's grandfather had forged the iron fences around a cemetery built far outside town in the mid-nineteenth century, a burial ground where every headstone bears the date 1849, for that was the year cholera swept the valley. The North Wales of Bevan's youth was a place where few over forty had their teeth, where fresh water was so scarce that baths were a rare luxury, and where "cobwebs were used to stop bleeding." There, the cure for coal dust in the eyes was "a comrade's lick." There, in the Ebbw Vale, Bevan early on pledged himself to enlist the government to bring modern medicine to his people. When he spoke to what was in his heart, he did not summon images of distant gathering storms or promise sunlit uplands; he explicated the here and now in words and phrases that crashed down upon listeners like wind-driven hail. Bevan (like Roosevelt and unlike Churchill) spoke to his audiences, not at them. Churchill's listeners basked in his phrases as if at a great distance from some cosmic power source, but Bevan pummeled his audiences with his words. His thick black hair was usually mussed; he was a tad jowly; and his dark eyes telegraphed anger, determination, and inflexibility. Churchill years later called Bevan "as great a curse to this country in time of peace, as he was a squalid nuisance in time of war." Yet Bevan had earned the respect of many of his enemies, for there wasn't a false bone in the man. When he wore a scowl, which he habitually donned in Churchill's presence, he bore a resemblance to John L. Lewis, a grandson of Wales and himself a product of the coal mines of America. Churchill, when peering at Bevan across the House chamber, saw in the Welshman's eyes "the fires of implacable hatred." Indeed, Bevan's goal, for the rest of his life, was nothing less than the extermination of the Conservative Party.[119]

Churchill never asked why Bevan—and Bevan's constituency—so hated

* When, in 1960, Churchill was told of Bevan's death, he mumbled a few words of moderate respect, then paused for effect before asking, "Are you *sure* he's dead?"

him and his fellow Tories. "He [Churchill] has no gift for getting into other people's minds," his doctor later wrote, "sometimes he does not even appear to be interested." Churchill had promised Britons only victory over Hitler, nothing more. But now they wanted more; they wanted some sort of explanation from Churchill of Tory peace aims, Churchill's war aims being well known to all. Britons had deduced that with America in, victory was someday assured, and therefore there was no time like the present to begin a discussion of postwar housing and health and Social Security insurance. Churchill, as he had since 1940, considered any public discussion of the postwar world to be ill conceived, as it could only degenerate into a partisan affair. His stance would prove a costly misjudgment in three years, for although Britons loved their warrior Churchill, he refused to tell them which Churchill they'd get in peace, the old Tory or the old Liberal.[120]

It was the old warrior who showed up in the Commons for three days of debate. The doubters spoke their piece, including John Wardlaw-Milne, Herbert Williams, and Earl Winterton, all Conservatives, and Emanuel ("Manny") Shinwell, an old Glasgow radical and Red Clydesider, a tough, blunt-spoken patriot who shared at least one trait with Churchill, a loathing of pompous intellectualism. On this day, however, Shinwell shared nothing with Churchill. Harold Nicolson thought Shinwell's attack on Churchill "vicious." Randolph, on leave from Cairo, leapt to his father's defense and attacked "most cruelly" those who had abused his father. Nicolson found Randolph to be "amusing and brave," yet along with Bob Boothby, Nicolson "harbored a dreadful feeling that Randolph may go too far." Pamela, in the gallery, "was squirming" as her husband let fly. Yet here was Randolph's chance to do for his father what was denied Winston by his father's early death—mount a display of dynastic solidarity. The result, however, was pure Randolph, pure bombast, and gave new meaning to the concept of bully pulpit. Nicolson noted that Churchill himself looked "embarrassed."

In the end, the father came to the defense of the son after Archibald Southby interrupted Randolph and implied that by virtue of Randolph's being in London rather than in the Western Desert, he was not a fighting soldier. Churchill afterward chased Southby down in the lobby and, shaking his fist in the MP's face, shouted, "You called my son a coward. You are my enemy. Do not speak to me." Randolph, Colville later wrote, was a talented journalist, "a natural orator, an original wit." He made friends easily but lost them more easily. He was "imaginative and original in his ideas," but he became "excessively addicted to drink" and regularly turned "inexcusably abusive." He "squabbled with his father," but remained devoted to him, as the father did to the son. Southby's mistake was not only to attack Randolph but to imply that he was not a brave soldier. Randolph was a brave soldier. His experience in the House that day, the jeers of his peers, and the awakening realization that he would always walk in his father's shadow, moved him within months to volunteer for the newly formed Special Air Service and still later to volunteer for an extremely dangerous mission—to parachute into the mountains of Yugoslavia in order to fight alongside Tito's partisans. Randolph, as did his father before him, chose to earn his country's respect on the battlefield, or die trying.[121]

The following day Churchill wound up the debate with what Nicolson thought a "very genial and self-confident" address wherein he congratulated his opponents on their adroit speechifying. But the engaging and conciliatory Churchill gave way in his peroration to the emphatic: "I make no apologies. I offer no excuses. I make no promises. In no way have I mitigated the... impending misfortunes that hang over us." He ended with an avowal of his certainty in final victory. With that, he said he was finished. Nicolson had already concluded two days earlier that "it is clear there really is no opposition at all." The Old Man insisted on a division—a vote. The bells were rung summoning members into the voting lobbies. The final tally: 423–1 in support of the government, with James Maxton, another old Red Clydesider, the lone dissenter. Bevan abstained. Dozens more could not vote; they were overseas, in uniform.[122]

Though badly misjudging the mood of both the public and the House, Bevan increased his attacks. *The Tribune* let loose on January 30: "It would be an excellent thing for Mr. Churchill to make certain changes in his team, but it would be a profound mistake to suppose that from this alone any fundamental improvement would result.... This is no National Government and Churchill is no National Leader. He struts in that guise but in fact he insists that the war shall be conducted in accordance with the principles of the Tory Party. The British Empire is finished. Nothing can save it. Who wants to? Not the millions who suffered under it. They rejoice to see it go.... We shall need a different spirit than the one which breathed through the speech of the last Imperial spokesman—Winston Spencer Churchill."[123]

As Harold Nicolson exited the vote of confidence debate on the twenty-ninth, he stopped at the electronic ticker in the lobby, where he learned from the uncoiling stream of paper that "the Germans claim to have entered Benghazi." Randolph Churchill was there and told Nicolson that only half of Rommel's reinforcements had reached Africa, a spot of good news among all the bad, had it been true. In fact, all of Rommel's supplies had gotten through, including sixty new panzers.[124]

It had been just over a week since Rommel—his forces newly christened Panzer Army Africa—probed outward from his lines at El Agheila, near the Tripolitania frontier. That Rommel could even contemplate an offensive was due to Churchill's Asian strategy. When Churchill stripped away Auchinleck's men and matériel in hopes of saving Malaya, he dashed all prospects of the Eighth Army crushing Rommel. Of greater significance, in combination with the ongoing ravishing of the Royal Navy in the Mediterranean, the attrition of Auchinleck's forces threw into question his ability to defend against Rommel. In fact, Auchinleck's Operation Crusader had been destined to stall before it began, by events that took place ten weeks earlier, at sea. On November 12 the aircraft carrier HMS *Ark Royal*, returning home from ferrying planes to Malta, was torpedoed twenty-five miles from Gibraltar. Only one crewman perished and more than 1,500 survived, a ready-made crew for another carrier, but no new carriers were on hand. Two weeks later, the battleship HMS *Barham* was torpedoed off Tripoli. *Barham* and more than 800 men of the crew went down so quickly that the U-boat commander who had shot her assumed the battleship had escaped when just moments later he raised his periscope to survey the scene and beheld an empty sea.

Within days, with no jubilant announcement of the sinking coming out of Berlin, the British realized the Germans did not know *Barham* was gone. Churchill of course knew, but he sat on the news until after the vote of confidence. Then, on December 19, Churchill learned that six Italian frogmen riding atop miniature submersibles (he called them "human torpedoes") had penetrated the Royal Navy anchorage at Alexandria and affixed mines to the battleships *Queen Elizabeth* (with Admiral Andrew Cunningham on board) and *Valiant*. The frogmen were captured, but not before the two largest ships in the eastern Mediterranean, their keels ripped apart, settled into the mud, useless hulks. The news was kept from the British people for six months. Churchill and the press had for more than a year denigrated Italian seamanship. *Time* ran a photo taken from astern of several Italian destroyers with the caption: "The British usually see them this way." Yet the Italians, with much help from Stukas based in Sicily, had by late December reduced the entire British eastern Mediterranean fleet to a few destroyers and light cruisers.[125]

In late December, Hitler sent Rommel ten ships bearing gasoline and rations along with an entire air corps transferred from the Russian front. At the time, both Churchill and Hitler considered Rommel to be in "mortal peril." Then, in the last days of the old year, a British task force of three cruisers and four destroyers searching for Rommel's supply ships sailed into a minefield. Within minutes all three cruisers were damaged; one of the destroyers was crippled, while another blew up and sank with the loss of all but one of the ship's company. Thus, a lucky U-boat captain, six Italian swimmers, and an uncharted minefield succeeded in destroying virtually the whole of Britain's eastern Mediterranean battle fleet. The Royal Navy no longer needed the largest anchorage in the eastern Mediterranean to shelter its ships. A cove would have sufficed. And Churchill possessed not nearly enough sea power in the eastern Mediterranean to interdict Rommel's supplies.[126]

By mid-January the supplies Rommel needed had arrived in Tripolitania, as had Rommel, having made good his retreat. Contrary to Randolph's optimistic assessment, not a single German vessel had been lost. On the British side of the equation, Malta was cut off and under constant air attack; its dwindling fleet of aircraft could neither protect the island nor stop Rommel's reinforcements. He had retreated before Auchinleck, but more to the point, he had *escaped* and re-armed. The peril had shifted to the Auk, although the danger was belied by the quietude that had settled over the desert, where the armies dug in and faced each other just beyond field artillery range.

Nights were cool. Intermittent rain showers brought forth blooms to stunted shrubs. Small desert flowers scrabbled from beneath the cracked stones as sunshine as weak as chamomile tea threw indeterminate shadows across the sands. At nine each night both armies tuned their radios to the German news beamed from Belgrade, not for edification but to listen to the melancholy love song played at the end of every broadcast, a tune called *Lili Marlene*. Based on a little-known Great War poem called "The Song of a Young Soldier on Watch," and later set to music and recorded by the Berlin cabaret singer Lale Anderson as "The Girl Under the Lantern," with an understated *omp-pah* rhythm of a march, it told the tale of a young soldier who sought to meet his sweetheart under the lamppost beyond his barracks. Rommel loved the tune, Goebbels loathed it, and Frau Göring crooned it at parties to Nazi big shots. British Tommies, not understanding the German lyrics, made up their own words. The song, once heard, became hard to shake, a haunting presence in the mind. Churchill hated it, given its German genesis.[127]

On January 21, Rommel probed the British lines with a reconnaissance in force, just as he had almost a year earlier. Within hours, the first British troops that Rommel's panzers encountered crumbled before the Germans, just as they had a year earlier. It was now the turn of the British Eighth Army to retreat, again, this time under the command of General Ritchie. A good man and former staff officer under Alan Brooke, Ritchie had never commanded a corps, let alone an army in the field. Auchinleck, meanwhile, had replaced his experienced 7th Armoured Division at Rommel's front with the newly arrived and green 1st Armoured Division, which was now falling back with heavy losses before the oncoming Germans. The Auk, as well, could no longer use the port of Benghazi in order to supply his troops; Rommel had leveled the place on his way out of town in December.

By January 29, as Nicolson learned from the news ticker, Rommel was back. Recalling Churchill's warnings to the House, uttered two days earlier, Nicolson that night jotted in his diary, "Grave disasters indeed." By February 5 the Germans had raced two hundred miles from Benghazi to near Gazala, where they halted. The British dug in behind a defensive line running about forty miles southeast from Gazala before hooking east and partway around Bir Hacheim. Rommel was now approximately forty miles from Tobruk, which Auchinleck told London he intended to abandon if Rommel attacked. There would be no siege this time. Churchill did not object to the plan, but in the days that followed—based in part on incorrect Ultra decrypts—he pushed Auchinleck to execute a counterstroke within weeks. When Churchill learned that Auchinleck's army would not be ready for any such undertaking until June, he termed the situation "intolerable," adding that it would be "judged so by Roosevelt, Stalin, and everybody else."[128]

Auchinleck could fall back in semi-orderly fashion before Rommel, but no such option existed for Arthur Percival, the military commander of Singapore. He was trapped. Percival's enemy, Lieutenant General Tomoyuki Yamashita, had since early December proved his mettle on the Malay Peninsula. Now came Percival's turn to prove his. Yamashita considered his Twenty-fifth Army—charged with capturing Singapore—to be so well prepared for jungle combat in Malaya that it could accomplish its mission with only three of its five divisions. He had fought Chinese guerrillas for three years and noted their tactics of stealth and fast movement, which he trained his troops to emulate. He had spent six months in Germany the previous year, where he became familiar with the genius of blitzkrieg tactics—tanks in the spearhead, close air support, and bold strokes. Hitler had been so impressed with Yamashita that he'd promised him he would stipulate in his will that Germans "bind themselves eternally to the Japanese spirit."[129]

Yamashita had opened his campaign on December 8, when Japanese bombs from a dozen aircraft crashed down outside the Raffles Hotel in Singapore. That morning his troops made two landings four hundred miles north of Singapore, at Singora and Patini, on each side of the Thai-Malay border. The British had long anticipated such a stroke, but their immediate problem was diplomatic. When a British force arrived at the Thai border, Thai border guards refused it entry. Not knowing of the unfolding events at Pearl Harbor, and not wanting to precipitate a political crisis (the Americans would look very much askance at such an incursion), the British turned around and headed south. Yamashita had also made a diversionary landing farther south near Kota Bharu and the nearby airfield with the object of drawing the RAF to the airfield's defense and away from his transports and main forces to the north. Within hours he took the airfield. By afternoon the few squadrons of RAF fighters in the region had been halved in numbers, leaving only mostly inexperienced Indian troops standing between Yamashita and an easy march to Singapore. Light tanks from Yamashita's 5th Division smashed through the Indians, some of whom had never before seen a tank. Implicit in that fact is that the British had no tanks deployed to defend northeast Malaya. The capture of the Kota Bharu airfield rendered the few remaining British aircraft in northern Malaya orphans. Those losses and the loss of the *Prince of Wales* left Singapore hanging like low fruit, and Yamashita was keen to pluck it.[130]

The British Plan B for Malaya had called for a scorched-earth policy similar to the ruin Churchill advised Stalin to inflict on Russian foodstuffs and, especially, Russian oil fields. Rubber and tin were Malaya's most abundant natural resources. More than 40 percent of Britain's rubber came from Malaya; more than half of the world's tin came out of the mountainous spine of the peninsula. It was impossible to chop down the rubber trees, but all equipment having to do with mining and smelting tin should have been destroyed. It was not. The first elements of Yamashita's 5th Division who rode into Kota Bharu not only found ample stocks of rice and gasoline but also discovered that, such was the haste of the British exit, the power plant had not even been turned off, let alone destroyed. Within a week the Japanese crossed the Kra Peninsula to smash the British airfield at Point Victoria, the southernmost point of Burma. With that stroke Yamashita cut off Singapore from airborne reinforcement by way of Europe and India.

Throughout December, Yamashita's 5th and 18th Divisions—the former moving down the eastern shore while the latter scoured the western—found rubber plantations and tin refineries abandoned but intact. They found British lorries topped off with petrol and ready to bring tin and rubber to ports, where docks that should have been demolished were ready to receive Japanese cargo ships. When the Japanese flushed the British from Penang, on the west coast of the peninsula, they found a small fleet of coastal gunboats in perfect running order, which they used to mount raids on British coastal positions. They came upon stores of rice and $250,000 in cash left behind in the British treasury. And they found a radio station, with the microphones on and the generator running, from which on Christmas

Day they broadcast "Merry Christmas and an *Unhappy* New Year" to the residents of Singapore, who did not grasp their terrible position because British censors withheld all information regarding the whereabouts of the Japanese. On the day Penang fell, the British press office told reporters, "There is nothing to report." In fact, all Europeans in Penang had been evacuated, leaving the natives to fend for themselves. The conquerors, wrote Cecil Brown, were "reverting to type... that is to say, they are looting food shops and... raping the native women." Within a week the Japanese outflanked Kuala Lumpur, the capital of the Malay federation and the railroad center of the country. The railway was intact. In retreat, the British performed exceptionally well—as quartermasters to the Japanese. By New Year's, Yamashita had raced halfway to Singapore.[131]

There, Lieutenant General Arthur Ernest Percival and almost 90,000 men—including 17,000 Australian, 33,000 British, and 40,000 Indian—prepared to destroy the city and naval base if need be, and to fight amid the rubble to the last man, per Churchill's orders. Yet Churchill's initial hope that Singapore might hold out for six months under Percival's command faded overnight when, upon his return to London from Washington, he was "staggered" to learn from Wavell that Singapore's largest, fifteen-inch naval guns faced out to sea. The landward side of the city, which gave out to a gorge, was without heavy defenses. To Ismay, Churchill wrote, "I must confess.... It never occurred to me for a moment... that the gorge of the fortress was not entirely fortified against an attack from the northward." Why, he asked, had he never been informed? Why, when he had for two years so stressed the defense of Singapore over the Kra Isthmus fallback strategy, had no defenses been erected? "I warn you," he continued, "this will be one of the greatest scandals that could possibly be exposed." In fact, Singapore was no "fortress" in the manner of Gibraltar; it was an island of gentle hills and ridges, twenty-seven miles long by thirteen miles wide. Churchill had formed images of the terrain and of the "fortress," and they were incorrect. The only way to keep the Japanese off the island would have been to bring them to decisive battle on the peninsula; instead, the British fell back, toward the presumed safety of the fortress that wasn't. As for the big guns facing the wrong way, Wavell had sent Churchill incorrect intelligence; several of Singapore's fifteen-inch Vickers guns indeed covered the straits, but they had been supplied with armor-piercing ammunition intended for use against ships. Against men they were useless.[132]

The fault for that lay with Arthur Percival. Percival was a thinker, a planner, and he had displayed great intellect while serving under Dill as a staff officer in the 1930s. Yet, like Admiral Tom Phillips, he lacked field experience. Staff officers fight their battles in map rooms. In ordering Percival to Singapore, Dill broke ranks with those in the British military—and there were many—who traditionally gave more credence to a general's character than his intellect, often with disastrous results. British generals, wrote T. E. Lawrence, "often gave away in stupidity what they had gained in ignorance." But here was an instance where character and courage would have trumped a superior, methodical mind. Following the Great War, Percival served as the intelligence officer for the Essex Regiment in Ireland, where his penchant for torturing suspected Irish rebels resulted in the partisans putting a price on his head. The Irish Republican Army had put prices on a great many heads, including Churchill's, but Percival's case was different; it was personal. The man was despised not only because he had tortured Irish rebels but also because he had enjoyed it. The defense of Singapore would require planning, which Percival had done, and character, of which Percival had none.

But for the British colonial buildings, Englishmen's clubs and polo fields, and Raffles Hotel, Singapore was no paradigm of orderliness or cleanliness. The British called it the city of "Chinks, drinks, and stinks." Most of its 750,000 Malay and Chinese citizens lived in nineteenth-century squalor. Monkeys roasted in open-air markets, where the blood of pig carcasses hanging from meat hooks flowed slowly into shallow gutters. With a blackout on since mid-December, the sounds of the city after sunset consisted in large part of the creaking of oxcarts hauling night soil out of town and the occasional blind firing of anti-aircraft batteries. Yet Singapore's citizens, especially the Chinese among them, got along secure in the knowledge that the British would at the very least protect them. In fact, by mid-January most British officials had left, including Duff Cooper, who Churchill had appointed resident minister after the early December attacks. With the city's fate in the hands of the army, Cooper and his wife, Diana, left for London on January 13. Lady Diana had a final gin sling before leaving for the airport, which helped fortify her when Japanese bombers appeared overhead just as they arrived. Chinese friends hustled the Coopers into the air-raid shelter. It was made entirely of glass. "It seemed a suitable end," Cooper later wrote, "to our mission to Singapore."[133]

By February 1 the Japanese were within twelve miles of the city, but the citizens of Singapore did not know this due to British censorship. For a week the British fought a holding action, but by late on the seventh, the last British troops fled the mainland across the causeway, blowing it up just after they reached the island. The demolition was no more effective than the scorched-earth policy; it took only a few hours for the Japanese to repair the causeway. Soon thereafter, the first of Yamashita's troops, skinny apparitions in tattered uniforms and helmets covered in twigs and banana leaves, crossed over to Singapore. Churchill, trying to inspire the defenders, cabled Wavell in Batavia: "The 18th Division has a chance to make its name in history" (that would be the 18th Division originally destined for Egypt and rerouted by Churchill). He tried to shame the defenders: "The honour of the British Empire and of the British Army is at stake." Attempting, too late, to plan a coherent defense, Churchill drew up for the Combined Chiefs a ten-point plan to convert Singapore into a "citadel," which included the conscription of all able-bodied males to dig anti-tank ditches and build barricades and gun emplacements. He directed again that the city was to be defended to the death and no surrender entertained. "Commanders, Staffs, and principal officers are expected to perish at their posts." The chiefs sent these orders to Wavell—less the order that everyone perish at his post. Not to be denied, Churchill got his message through in a private telegram: "The fight should continue to the bitter end in the ruins of Singapore. Commanders and senior officers should die with their troops."[134]

Then, too late, Churchill and the chiefs ordered as many troops as possible evacuated to Rangoon. But by then Percival and his army (he outnumbered the Japanese by three to one) were fully engaged with the enemy. Percival's air cover had dwindled to just two dozen old fighter planes; the Japanese had more than five hundred modern aircraft available. The 18th Division landed at Singapore just in time to be captured. The Japanese sealed the city's fate when they captured the outlying reservoirs and cut off drinking water. Yet Japanese supply lines were stretched to breaking. An all-out assault by Percival of the sort Churchill demanded might have turned the tide, but Percival, his communications in total disarray, declined the fight. The British still possessed enough anti-tank guns and ammunition to kill every Japanese tank twice over, but the top commanders lacked the resolve to carry the fight to the Japanese. Some of Percival's men—including the war artist Philip Meninsky—wanted to continue the fight but were dismayed to find that the maps they had been issued were of the Isle of Wight. The 8th Australian Division, its four brigades strung along the northern part of the island, briefly pushed the enemy back into the sea, until, that is, the Australians' communication broke down and their commanding general elected to not perish at his post but to flee homeward in a small boat, leaving his troops stranded, and doomed.

Singapore fell on February 15. It was a death foretold—too few defenses, a weak commanding general, a demoralized garrison, and too savvy an enemy. Churchill had known since early January that defeat was inevitable, though he thought the inevitable would arrive in a matter of months, not weeks. Percival and a contingent of six officers met Yamashita at the Ford Motor factory late in the morning. The Japanese general, by then hailed in Tokyo as "The Tiger of Malaya," demanded unconditional surrender by 8:30 that night. It was a bluff; Yamashita knew that *his* forces were outgunned and in the minority. Yet Percival, with no fight in his belly, decided he had no choice; not only had the commander of the Australian 8th Division fled, but the Indian and Malay troops were deserting and the city was almost out of potable water. Thus, for the defenders of Singapore, it was hands up, guns down.

A Japanese newsman reported watching a group of Scottish Highlanders marching off to a POW camp while their bagpipers piped. To the reporter's amazement, the Scots displayed no sadness and, given their surrender, no shame. Such behavior was beyond understanding to the Yamoto people. For a short while after the surrender, Union Jacks still fluttered above Singapore's municipal buildings like artifacts from the distant past. Then the Japanese yanked them down. Intending no irony, the victors renamed the city Shonan—Light of the South. Night fell on a chaotic scene. Two nights earlier, the conquerors had massacred scores of doctors, nurses, and patients in a hospital just outside the city. Now the victors set to massacring Chinese residents, more than five thousand in all, whose severed heads soon adorned pikes throughout the island. Apprised of the debacle, Brooke jotted in his diary: "If the army cannot fight better than it is doing at present we shall deserve to lose our Empire!" Churchill had no need to resort to hyperbole when days later he informed Roosevelt that the fall of Singapore was "the greatest disaster in our history."[135]

So confident were the Japanese that they would keep the city in perpetuity that they rigged the big Vickers naval guns for transport to other Pacific conquests. They already knew the mechanics of the guns; the British and Vickers—the Krupp Works of England—had supplied the Japanese navy with fourteen-inch guns since 1910. Japan had built its latest naval weapons on the Vickers design, and rightly so, for Vickers produced the finest naval gun of the era. The fast and deadly Japanese battle cruiser *Kongo*, which had covered the December landings north of Singapore, was armed with Vickers guns. The British had built *Kongo* for Japan in 1913. The Royal Navy had instructed a generation of Japanese officers in the art of gunnery. "Uncle Sam and Britannia were the godparents of the new Japan," Churchill later wrote, adding that in fewer than two generations the Japanese had gone from the samurai sword to the battleship. The British had taught the Japanese well, as Tommies and tars were now learning from Java to Singapore.[136]

Singapore, which the British over the previous 123 years had nurtured from fishing village to trading post to financial capital of South Asia, had been lost in just seven days. The British and Australian prisoners were soon marched and transported north, to the banks of the River Kwai, in Thailand, where as slave laborers, they began building a 250-mile railroad to Thanbyuzayat, in Burma. More than 13,000 died during the next three years by Japanese bullet and bayonet, as well as from malnutrition and a host of hideous tropical diseases. The survivors dubbed their works project the Death Railroad. Most of the Indian troops, on the other hand, did not share that fate. More than 30,000 mostly Hindu prisoners—they called themselves the Indian National Army—declared their allegiance to the mesmeric Hindu nationalist and Fascist Subhash Chandra Bose, and to Tokyo, which bankrolled Bose. They took up arms against London, and joined the Japanese on the march to the next objective: Burma. Percival survived his captivity. When he returned home after the war, he became a "nonperson," excluded from all victory celebrations and shunned, wrote Sir John Keegan, "for his catastrophic mismanagement of the Malay campaign." Churchill never forgave him.[137]

The Japanese were making Hell while the sun shone, which propelled Joseph Goebbels to flights of celebratory fancy. "If I were an Englishman," he declared to his diary, "I would tremble for the fate of the Empire.... There was a time we considered the existence of the British world empire a necessity for the welfare of Europe. This time is past.... Churchill gambled away the chance we gave England. England will have to pay dearly for this statesman." As for Churchill's political future, both Goebbels and Hitler agreed that "his fall may possibly be expected."[138]

Many in London agreed. Most believed that any further defeats of such magnitude would spell the end for Churchill. Then again, there weren't that many more pieces of the Empire to lose.

Churchill had known since his outward passage to America that Singapore was in serious trouble. The Japanese, he told his Canadian hosts in December, had inflicted upon the British a "cataract of ruin." He had warned of more pain to come, and come it had. Churchill announced the loss of Singapore on February 15 in a broadcast carried around the world. Harold Nicolson wrote that Churchill appealed "for national unity and not criticism, in a manner which recalls Neville Chamberlain." Britons, "too nervous and irritable to be fobbed off with fine phrases," found the speech wanting. Yet, Nicolson asked, "What else could he have said?" Two days later, Churchill took his case to the House and promptly closed it with the announcement that there would be no official investigation into the fall of Singapore (such as had been convened for most of the military disasters since 1939) lest "we were drawn into agitated or excited recriminations at a time when all our minds are oppressed with a sense of tragedy and with the sorrow of so lamentable a misfortune." No such official inquiry ever took place. Recriminations were indeed making the rounds, in the streets and in pubs, and in the Commons, where Churchill that day, in response to questions of the how and why of Singapore, "became irritable and rather reckless." Harold Nicolson feared "a slump in public opinion which will deprive Winston of his legend."[139]

Britons, wrote Mollie Panter-Downes, though openly criticizing Churchill—unthinkable a year earlier—"don't intend to lose Mr. Churchill, but they don't intend to lose the war, either." Britons were fed up with the BBC and the newspapers for having touted successes in the Western Desert and Singapore, when only failures came to pass. They were fed up with increased rationing—two pints of milk per adult per week, strict limitations on cereals and dried fruits. They had been shocked that week when the German battle cruisers *Scharnhorst* and *Gneisenau,* along with *Prinz Eugen,* slipped out of Brest and made a successful daylight dash right up the mine-choked English Channel, past British radar (the Germans had jammed it), and past the big coastal guns (they could not aim in the gathering mist). All three of the ships suffered minor damage from mines, but not enough to keep them from reaching Germany's North Sea ports that afternoon. Torpedo bombers that might have stopped the ships had been sent to Alexandria to prevent further Italian frogman depredations. Six Fairey Swordfish torpedo bombers sent aloft to halt the ships were all lost, along with four Hampden medium bombers. Contrary to rumor, the Admiralty had not been caught entirely flat-footed but had long suspected the German ships might make a break for it. Churchill said he pointed this out to the Commons in order to reassure Britons "that our affairs are not conducted entirely by simpletons and dunderheads." Yet the escape of the German ships and the fall of Singapore led Britons to conclude that a fresh start was needed by way of a cabinet shake-up that, to be effective, must include Sir Stafford Cripps, whose "straight talking," Panter-Downes wrote, was of the sort "people have long and in vain hoped to hear from the Prime Minister."[140]

Cripps had been biding his time for a month, waiting for just such a popular summons, but he was still wary of serving under Beaverbrook.

The January vote of support for Churchill's government may have appeared overwhelming, but the military disasters of February and rising tensions in political circles moved Churchill by mid-February to restructure the cabinet and the War Cabinet. In so doing he reduced the War Cabinet from the supreme nine to the supreme eight, thus further consolidating his power. Secretary of State for War David Margesson was among the first to go. Churchill's treatment of this loyal Tory was less than laudatory, recalled Lord Geoffrey Lloyd: "I must tell you that I could never quite forgive Churchill the way in which he dismissed my old friend Lord Margesson, who was a great friend of his." In fact, Margesson was loyal to

Churchill but no great friend. Margesson, as Chamberlain's imperious chief whip before the war, had been ruthless in suppressing Tory dissent over Chamberlain's appeasement policy, and was instrumental in keeping Churchill out of the government and more or less in exiled opposition. Yet, though Margesson had been a dedicated Chamberlain enforcer, he helped ease both Tory and Labour fears during the transition from Chamberlain to Churchill. He had since served Churchill loyally, and since early 1941, as secretary of state for war, a position he neither sought nor desired but could not refuse when Churchill offered it. The War Office—the name notwithstanding—was administrative, less about strategy and more about updating regulations and keeping records of the whereabouts of men and matériel. With Churchill acting as his own minister of defence, Margesson's job was almost symbolic and consisted more in catching javelins than throwing them, and often Churchill's javelins, as many of his curt, often dismissive memos to Margesson suggest. In one of his last memos to Margesson, written as Singapore tottered, Churchill bemoaned the willingness of British officers in that city to openly discuss—aye, confess to—the collapse of resistance: "They seem to be giving everything away about themselves in the blandest manner," he wrote. "After all, they are defending a fortress and not conducting a Buchmanite* revival."[141]

That was a clever (and petty) way of putting things. Margesson's skills had never been administrative; under Chamberlain he had excelled as a whip in keeping the party in line. For more than a year now he had served Churchill loyally, only to be sacked, Lord Lloyd recalled, when Churchill "needed a scapegoat for all the disasters in the western deserts, but he couldn't face up to doing it personally." Churchill, in his memoirs, simply states that Margesson "ceased to be Secretary of State for War." In fact, Margesson first learned his fate from his own permanent under secretary, Percy James Grigg, who had served as Churchill's private secretary when Churchill was at the Exchequer. Churchill asked Grigg to take Margesson's job, but the career civil servant was hesitant to do so, for the jump from civil service to Crown minister meant a loss of all accrued pension benefits. Churchill pushed. Grigg took the job "as an act of patriotism," recalled Malcolm Muggeridge, even though Grigg suspected that "Winston wanted a Secretary of War who would be a pure stooge." Grigg proved anything but. Brooke later wrote, "Providence was indeed kind to me dur-

* A reference to Dr. Frank Buchman, an American evangelical who relocated to England and formed the Oxford Group to preach his creed of reaching God through the practice of frequent and robust confession—"sin and tell," *Time* called it (Jan. 18, 1943). By the late 1930s Buchman's theology formed the underlying creed of Alcoholics Anonymous.

ing the war to have placed P.J. [Grigg] at the helm of the W.O." Grigg served until the war's end. When Grigg retired, recalled Muggeridge, his finances were "wiped out... finished," and Churchill "never again communicated with him in any way."[142]

As Churchill shuffled his cabinet, he waited for Beaverbrook's decision on the Ministry of Production post, which, when it arrived in mid-February was, to his delight, in the affirmative. But less than two weeks later, Beaverbrook again offered his resignation. He was an ill man. He had long suffered from asthma; now it had worsened to the point where he contemplated ordering an RAF plane to fly him around at high altitude to clear his lungs and allow him some sleep. His breathing became so labored that Churchill, during a meeting, mistook the wheezing for a cat's meow and ordered, "someone stop that cat mewing." Beaverbrook was on the cusp of what Churchill later rather unnecessarily termed "a nervous breakdown." Clementine took the occasion to advise her husband by letter: "My darling—Try ridding yourself of this microbe which some people fear is in your blood—Exorcise this bottle imp & see if the air is not clearer & purer—you will miss his drive & genius, but in Cripps you may have new accessions of strength." Churchill accepted her advice, and Beaverbrook's resignation. And with that, Cripps was in, lord privy seal and leader of the House of Commons.[143]

Yet what appeared to be a political defeat for Churchill can be seen as his snookering Cripps, whose talents were not in massaging the House but in coolly arguing legal issues, attributes that serve little purpose in that raucous chamber of partisan free-thinkers. Churchill soon dispatched Cripps to India on a mission to convince Gandhi to pledge his loyalty to the British in return for a guarantee of Dominion status after the war. Gandhi and the National Congress had rejected a similar offer a decade earlier. Now, with Gandhi preaching that Indians not fight for Britain but rather prostrate themselves peacefully before the Japanese invader, Cripps's mission could only end in failure. Thus Cripps, argues historian and parliamentarian Roy Jenkins, found himself in a nominally high position that was, in fact, "more shell than kernel." Before departing for India, Cripps, seduced by his romantic vision of Stalinist Russia, predicted—without the slightest supporting evidence—that the war would be (successfully) concluded in a year. Britons kept tallies on the predictions of their politicians; the public man who offered up a promise had better keep it.[144]

Churchill, too, had made promises—that Crete would be defended to the death, Singapore held, the Germans and Italians swept from North Africa. Churchill, for almost two years, had been telling his family, his secretaries, little schoolboys at Harrow, that "these are... the greatest days our country has ever lived." The times were great for Churchill not because his

England was winning—it most decidedly was not—but because England was fighting Germany, and now Japan, to the death. Yet, Mollie Panter-Downes wrote that month, that although Britons trusted Churchill in the past because he had always told them the truth, "there's an uneasy suspicion that fine oratory may carry away the orator as well as the audience." By February Churchill understood that, which is why he now promised only more sacrifice, more defeats, and more hard times, promises he delivered on."[145]

The honorable fight for British survival made the war great for Churchill. His faith in the rightness of his cause and the valor of ordinary Englishmen was unbounded. Calling upon reserves of patriotism that should have been exhausted, he had won the allegiance of almost fifty million Britons gathered around wireless sets in homes and pubs, in West End clubs, and East End warehouses. Even as Singapore tottered, and as Rommel again drove toward Egypt, and despite his unkept promises, polls showed that 79 percent of Britons supported Churchill. These were people who, believing that peace was worth any price, had rejoiced in Britain's betrayal of Czechoslovakia just four years earlier. His words then had failed to move them. Had they listened then, they would not have had to listen now as he told them of one disaster after another, and reminded them that he expected that they all go down fighting in defense of their country.

Now they listened, and Churchill persuaded them that the fate of mankind hung in the balance, and he roused their ardor, stitching the fabric of their resolution with gleaming threads of eloquence and optimism. Thus, from June of 1940 to early 1942, at a time when defeat and enslavement of the Home Island seemed, at first inevitable, then probable, and finally still quite possible, Churchill's star continued to rise, to challenge the dark star of Hitler, whose oratory, though in a different language with contrary rhythms, and to very different ends, had spawned a murderous dystopia. The Führer and Tojo were a pair of Genghis Khans bent upon the destruction of all that civilized men cherished. Churchill was determined to preserve it, and preserve it while wearing a smile and flashing his "V" sign. "It is surprising how he maintains a lighthearted exterior in spite of the vast burdens he is bearing," Alan Brooke observed, himself bearing a heavy burden as Chief of the Imperial General Staff, and charged by Churchill with plotting the strategies to fight their way to final victory.[146]

In a broadcast beamed the previous year to the University of Rochester—located in the upstate New York city where his grandfather Leonard Jerome had practiced law before hitting it big in the New York stock market—Churchill wondered how Hitler had done it, how "nations were pulled down one by one while the others gaped and chattered" until they, too, fell into slavery and darkness. Now "the old lion with her cubs at her side stands alone against hunters who are armed with deadly weapons and are propelled by desperate and destructive rage." Will the lion now fall, the final victim? "Ah no!" declared Churchill, "the stars in their courses proclaim the deliverance of mankind. Not so easily will the onward progress of the peoples be barred. Not so easily will the lights of freedom die."[147]

To the Commons, on the day after Pearl Harbor, he had invoked the same imagery: "In the past we have had a light which flickered, in the present we have a light which flames, and in the future there will be a light which shines over all the land and sea." No matter that Hitler had extinguished the lamps across all of Europe, Churchill generated his own illumination.[148]

Whether it would be enough to light the path to victory grew more doubtful with each mile of desert Rommel stole, with each ship killed by U-boats, and with each new Japanese depredation. On February 12, Alec Cadogan wrote in his diary: "The blackest day, yet, of the war.... We are nothing but failure and inefficiency everywhere and the Japs are murdering our men and raping our women in Hong Kong." The weather was horrid, food in short supply, his chickens had stopped laying. He wrote, "I am running out of whisky and can get no more to drink of any kind. But if things go on as they're going, that won't matter." Cadogan wrote that pessimistic assessment three days *before* Singapore fell.[149]

On February 19, Admiral Chūichi Nagumo's carrier strike force bombed Port Darwin, Australia, inflicting enough damage to force the abandonment of the port as a supply depot. The admiral had sailed his five aircraft carriers unmolested thousands of miles from the northern Pacific to Australia. The raid served to finish off any residual Australian sanguinity. Prime Minister Curtin wanted his troops home, now. The troops in question were the war-hardened 7th Division, then en route by ship to Australia from the Middle East. By that date the Japanese had advanced from Thailand into Burma, with Rangoon the obvious target. Churchill was far less concerned with Australian paranoia than he was with Burma, the final frontier between the Japanese and India. On the nineteenth, Churchill asked Curtin to allow the 7th Division to be diverted to the defense of Burma. Curtin refused, firm in his belief that with Singapore now lost, the 7th Division was needed for the defense of Australia. Both Roosevelt and Churchill had concluded otherwise; they believed that the Japanese would not risk sending tens of thousands of troops four thousand miles by sea from Java to Australia. But for Curtin, the bombardment of Darwin confirmed his worst fears. Roosevelt sent two messages to Curtin in which he stressed the strategic importance of Burma and the need for Australians to help defend it. Curtin stood his ground. The next day Churchill, after repeating his request and before an answer arrived from Curtin, ordered the convoy to Burma. Two days later he informed Curtin, and in so doing verified for Curtin the very arrogance he had ascribed to the war planners in London. Curtin, furious, insisted the convoy turn away from Burma and make for Australia. Churchill backed down. No Australians would defend Rangoon. Instead, the 7th Division went home to join the almost 90,000 American troops Roosevelt had sent to Curtin, an army that by summer would make Australia one of the most secure places on the planet.[150]

By February 24, Wavell had been recalled to Bombay from the Dutch East Indies. Brereton's minuscule air fleet, by then a mere two dozen planes, joined the exodus. A Dutch admiral, C. E. L. Helfrich, replaced Tommy Hart, "a good skipper in a bad storm," not because Hart had failed—he lacked the ships to succeed—but because the Dutch intended to make a last stand off the coast of Java. Helfrich's fleet consisted of five cruisers, including the USS *Houston* (aboard which Roosevelt once enjoyed taking his seafaring holidays), HMS *Exeter,* and ten destroyers. Under certain circumstances it might have proven a formidable force, but with supplies running low at Surabaya, Indonesia, and against the overwhelming Japanese force headed its way, the Allied fleet was sailing on hope, sailing alone, and, like *Prince of Wales,* sailing without air cover.[151]

The torrent of disasters was taking its toll on Churchill. On February 27, Mary Churchill told her diary: "Papa is at a very low ebb. He is not too well physically—and is worn down by the continuous crushing pressure of events." That day, in the Java Sea, events were about to take yet another turn against Britain and her allies. In preparation for the invasion of Java, two Japanese naval task forces, each guarding about fifty troop transports, and each more powerful than the entire Allied fleet, closed on the north Java coast. Admiral Helfrich's little navy, commanded at sea by a fighting Dutchman, Rear Admiral Karel Doorman, was about to refuel at Surabaya when Doorman received word of the Japanese presence. Flying his flag from the light cruiser *HMNS De Ruyter,* Doorman went looking for the Japanese transports in hopes of inflicting some damage before the more numerous and heavily armed Japanese warships of Rear Admiral Take Takagi found the Dutch. Just after 4:00 P.M., the two forces sighted each other and began shooting at a range of about six miles. Churchill was correct when he said that naval battles could be settled in minutes, but this one turned into an eight-hour slugfest. An American newsweekly tallied up the amazing results: "The Jap paid...Japanese heavy cruiser sank. Another Jap cruiser, the *Mogami*...retired in flames. Hits crippled a third

8-inch gun cruiser. Three Jap destroyers blazed up, appeared to be sinking.... Allied bombers reported hits on two more Jap cruisers. At least 17 Jap transports were bombed."[152]

Jolly good news, were any of it true. In fact, not a single Japanese warship was sunk; only one sustained any damage whatsoever. Admiral Doorman drowned inside his doomed ship, followed before midnight by half his fleet. A few nights after the battle, HMS *Perth* and USS *Houston* charged into Banten Bay, near Sunda Strait, and in desperation attacked an overwhelmingly superior Japanese force. Both cruisers were destroyed. Later the same day, HMS *Exeter* (the hero of the December 1939 Battle of the River Plate, where the *Graf Spee* was scuttled) and two destroyers tried to flee Java. All three were sunk. The Japanese had taken the Java Sea without losing a single warship. The annihilation of the Allied fleet was a catastrophic defeat, especially for the Dutch, who had been a major power in the East Indies for three hundred years. The British were on the run, to Burma and India, where they hoped to regroup. But the Japanese were outrunning them. On February 28, Japanese forces landed on Java. Eight days later the island was theirs, as were more than 90,000 Dutch, and thousands of British, Australian, and American prisoners. With the surrender of Java, Wavell's ABDA command simply disappeared.[153]

In Rangoon all order had disappeared a month earlier. The evacuation of Rangoon, ongoing since the Christmas raids, had grown desperate with the first concerted bombings of early February. By February 20, refugees and vehicles of all sorts packed the road north. Thousands took to the Irrawaddy River in small boats. Professional thieves—*dacoits*—fell upon the fleeing citizens, British and Burmese alike, and killed them for what they carried. The fire brigade fled, as did the police and the entire British diplomatic contingent. A British official wrote that city streets were empty except for "criminals, criminal lunatics, and lepers." Somehow, five thousand felons had been released from prison. After sundown they made Rangoon "a city of the damned." Lepers, wild dogs, and lunatics fought over scraps of rotting food at garbage dumps and in back alleys. Business owners and the few remaining Burmese soldiers implemented a scorched-earth policy, burning factories, stores of medicines, and supply depots. The few remaining Flying Tigers—the last defenders of the city—departed the deranged scene that night for Magwe, to the north, where the remnants of the RAF and the main British force, such as it was, had already dug in.[154]

Churchill, in late February, dispatched to Rangoon general Harold Alexander, who had served in France under Brooke and was the last senior officer to get off the beach at Dunkirk. "If we could not send an army," Churchill later wrote, "we could at any rate send a man." "Alex" was an aristocrat, an Ulsterman, a fighter and a man of honor, but two decades earlier, two of his instructors at the staff college, Alan Brooke and Bernard Montgomery, had concluded that he was "an empty vessel." Perhaps Monty and Brooke did not see that Alexander's lack of enthusiasm for planning was due to his greater love of fighting. In France in 1940 he had displayed a knack for which British generals had "always shown a special aptitude ... the art of retreat and evacuation." That talent helped save the British army. He also displayed a flair for interservice diplomacy, a trait that would well serve Churchill and the Allied cause. In Burma Churchill needed both a man and an army. In Alexander he had the man, but he lacked an army. British colonial forces in Burma did not number enough to properly be called a corps, let alone an army. An Indian division stationed on the far side of the Sittang River, to the east of Rangoon, had been mauled by the oncoming Japanese Fifteenth Army, itself a force of only two small divisions, about sixteen thousand men. The only Burmese division in the vicinity was suffering attrition through desertion, fueled not by cowardice but by Burmese hatred for the British. A lone British armored brigade held Rangoon. Such was Alexander's "army." He arrived in Rangoon on March 5, just in time to preside over the loss of the city and lead the chaotic breakout from the capital northward to Prome. Rangoon, aflame and abandoned, fell on March 8.[155]

The Japanese used the port to bring in 20,000 more men, and the reinforced Fifteenth Army soon spread outward from Rangoon into the Irrawaddy delta, the most fertile and productive estuary in the British Empire and the source of surplus grains and rice critical to the sustenance of Bengal. The delta had for five decades supplied Bengal enough rice to stave off want; no major famine had occurred in India for more than fifty years, in part because of the relationship between the Burmese rice surpluses and Bengal's needs. The Japanese broke that connection, stealing the Irrawaddy's bounty for Tokyo's consumption and destroying what they couldn't steal. The delta's loss, along with unprecedented cyclones in Bengal later in the year and a worsening drought on the upper Subcontinent, guaranteed rising prices and grain and rice shortages in Bengal, whether or not Japanese troops arrived there anytime soon. The Japanese objective was nothing less than to drive the British out of Burma, starting at Rangoon, six hundred miles south of the Assam frontier. Alexander promptly put Lieutenant General William ("Billy") Slim in charge of the newly formed Burma Corps (Burcorps) in hopes of repelling the invader. Slim was a real fighter, who had subdued the Iraqi and Iranian revolts the previous year. Yet Burcorps was an army on paper only. The British receded before the Japanese tide, Alexander withdrawing north toward Prome while Vinegar Joe Stilwell, commanding six undersize and unenthused Chinese divisions, covered his eastern flank.[156]

The presence of the hated Chinese on Burmese soil—reluctantly agreed to by Wavell—served only to bring more Burmese deserters into the Japanese ranks. A week after the fall of Rangoon, Alexander and Stilwell met for the first time in a pretty little hillside colonial town near Mandalay, a village the British had named May Town—Maymyo. The two generals did not exactly hit it off. Stilwell, with a good ear for upper-class English speech, later declared, "*Extrawdinery!*" Alexander, with a condescending gaze, "looked me over as if I had just crawled from under a rock."* Yet if a joint command was what it took to fight the Japanese, Stilwell was glad to be on board. He wanted not only to hold the city of Toungoo but to attack. But Chiang, to Stilwell's fury, delayed his decision to order Chinese forces south from Mandalay until it was too late, with the result that by the end of the month, the Japanese overran Toungoo. Stilwell and Alexander now had but one decision to make, whether to run to China or to India. Stilwell sent half his Chinese forces back up the Burma Road, the other half north toward Myitkyina, near the Indian frontier, and the only navigable track from India to China. The Japanese commenced chasing Stilwell's troops up the Burma Road and Alexander's emaciated force up the west bank of the Irrawaddy. Burma was doomed.[157]

It took the entire month of April for the Japanese to finish the job, during which time Alexander and Slim skulked off toward Assam, while most of Stilwell's Chinese troops fled to Chungking, joined by hundreds of Burmese deserters. Stilwell, offered a ride out for himself and his immediate staff on an Army Air Force plane, chose instead to walk out with 114 men to Assam, a miserable journey of over two hundred miles along the Irrawaddy and through high mountain passes. His men no longer looked up when an airplane passed over; the Allies had none in the skies. The trek took almost three weeks. As they slogged toward the Assam frontier, Alexander, Slim, and Stilwell raced the Japanese and the coming monsoon rains. When on May 17 Alexander arrived in Kalewa, a border town at the confluence of the Chindwin and Myittha rivers, he had with him just two dozen field guns and as many trucks. It was the longest retreat in British military history. Almost one-third of his original force of thirty thousand stayed behind as casualties and deserters. Stilwell did not lose a man, but his little band arrived in Assam half starved, with the Japanese at their

---

* Churchill wrote of the Englishmen of his generation who either would not or could not pronounce the letter "r." In *My Early Life*, he described an attempt by the commanding officer of the 4th Hussars, Colonel John Brabazon, to catch a train: After waiting for some time on the station platform, Brabazon turned to the stationmaster and asked, "Where is my *twain?*" Told that his train had already gone, the colonel responded, "Gone? *Bwing* me another."

back. The monsoon rains arrived three days later. The Burma Road was lost, along with Burma, Lord Randolph Churchill's imperial legacy, presented by him to Queen Victoria as a New Year's present in 1886.[158]

Blame for Burma's loss and the failure of the first joint Chinese-American-British operation was apportioned along nationalist lines. Chiang, in a letter to Churchill, wrote bitterly, "In all my life of long military experience, I have seen nothing to compare with the deplorable, unprepared state, confusion, and degradation of the war area in Burma." Such words did not endear the generalissimo to Churchill. Stilwell told Washington that he thought the British would rather lose Burma than be indebted to the Chinese for saving it. While Burma tottered, the United States suffered a humiliation of its own when Douglas MacArthur fled Manila for Australia on March 11. Allied thoughts concerning Operation Gymnast (the invasion of French North Africa) went up in the smoke of Rangoon, leading Roosevelt and Churchill to agree that "Gymnast cannot be undertaken." Roosevelt also noted the irony that Stilwell and Alexander, the commanders designate of Gymnast, met instead in Burma, where the Japanese drove them out. Alexander, stranded in Assam and knowing a cul de sac when he saw one, put Billy Slim in charge of the remnants of Burcorps and returned to London. Roosevelt, who never really had a dog in the fight, offered jaunty condolences to Churchill: "I have never liked Burma or the Burmese.... I wish you could put the whole bunch of them in a frying pan... and let them stew in their own juices." Churchill, in a note to Roosevelt, offered that the wisest course for the Japanese to now take would be to drive right up the Burma Road to China, and "make a job of that."[159]

This the Japanese did, for a short while, chasing Chiang's tattered army into Yunnan province. Then the Japanese stopped. They had neither orders from Tokyo nor a strategic plan to carry though on their stupendous victories.

Weeks earlier, in early March, Eden and Alec Cadogan suspected the fight might have gone out of Churchill. His most loyal friend, Brendan Bracken, and his most omnipresent political critic, Stafford Cripps, agreed that Eden should be made deputy defence minister. Cadogan and Eden also noted that for several weeks "there has been no direction of the war. War Cabinet doesn't function.... There's no hand on the wheel (probably due to P.M.'s health)." In fact, the alliance itself was drifting, rudderless.

Throughout March and April and into May, Churchill and Roosevelt exchanged telegrams and letters that, taken in the aggregate, underscore Eden's pessimism and show that the two leaders had differing objectives, militarily and politically, and lacked the means to achieve any of them, alone or together. The alliance was looking all hat and no cattle.[160]

These were the weeks when Japanese armies rolled up Burma and Java and the Philippines, where the 75,000 American and Filipino troops trapped on Bataan surrendered on April 9, and marched off to a captivity that would kill almost half of them. Fortress Corregidor fell a month later. In Java, the Japanese had advanced from island to island, up and down the East Indies, until, on March 23, less than a month after landing, they took the Andaman Islands, located three hundred miles off the Thai and Burmese coasts in the Bay of Bengal. Nothing but open ocean separated the islands from Ceylon.

Stalin, meanwhile, began expressing interest in a treaty with his allies that would secure the Soviet Union's prewar borders, a concept entirely unacceptable to Roosevelt and Churchill, both of whom had long believed such matters should be addressed only at the postwar peace conference. Yet Churchill now began to see the practical merit in moderating that stance given that America and Britain had made no plans whatsoever to do anything anytime soon to ease Stalin's burden, other than send small Arctic convoys, which U-boats regularly mauled. Roosevelt considered himself capable of mollifying Stalin, and so notified Churchill. "I think you will not mind me being brutally frank when I tell you that I think I can personally handle Stalin better than either your Foreign Office or my State Department. Stalin hates the guts of all your top people. He thinks he likes me better, and I hope he will continue to do so."[161]

Throughout March, the most pressing question at the Admiralty was, where is Admiral Nagumo's carrier strike force? Churchill thought it only a matter of time, and likely not a great deal of time, before Nagumo launched air and amphibious attacks on Ceylon to gain complete control of the Indian Ocean. That would put the Japanese athwart the sea-lanes to the Persian Gulf and from the Suez to India, and threaten the supply of Stalin by way of Basra as well as the supply of the British in India and Chiang Kai-shek in China. One of Churchill's deepest fears—the loss of access to Persian and Iraqi oil—appeared a distinct possibility. Those two nations, lightly garrisoned by British colonial troops, now lay exposed between the forces of Tojo and Hitler, who was certain to make a spring push into the Caucasus, which, if successful, would bring him that much closer to the Middle East. Rommel, too, appeared poised to strike toward Cairo. Were he to get there, the roads to Baghdad would lie open. The troops Churchill had hoped to array on the Levant-Caspian front were now headed to India. The defense of the northern route into the Mosul oil fields, Churchill cabled Roosevelt, "now depends on the success of the Russian armies." He had summed up the problem to Colville months earlier: "With Hitler in control of Iraqi oil and Ukrainian wheat... not all the staunchness of our Plymouth brethren would shorten the ordeal." The Middle East was the only theater of war exposed to both Germany and Japan, and its defense fell exclusively to the British, who lacked the manpower to repel Rommel and the sea power to repel the Japanese. As March lurched toward April, the question remained, where was Nagumo?[162]

Four months earlier. Louis "Dickey" Mountbatten, a mere captain, and an unlucky one at that—he had lost his ship at Crete—had been promoted to the rank of commander and shortly thereafter replaced Admiral Keyes as director of Combined Operations. Churchill charged Mountbatten and his small staff with planning raids on the Continent, and coordinating those raids with the Royal Navy, Royal Marines, Army, and RAF. Churchill told him to think of only offense, never defense, and to begin drawing up the matériel and personnel requirements—specialized landing crafts, close air support, waterproof tanks, beach spotters, aerial photography—required for a full-fledged invasion of France. Churchill promoted him over far more senior and experienced Royal Navy officers to vice admiral and sat him down on the Combined Chiefs of Staff Committee, where, Brooke later wrote, Dickie "frequently wasted his own time and ours." Then Churchill—reasoning that the interservice nature of Combined Operations required a grand gesture—insisted that Mountbatten be promoted to the rank of lieutenant general in the army *and* air marshal in the RAF, thus earning Mountbatten the enmity of dozens of more senior offices in those branches of the military. From Churchill he earned the moniker of "triphibian," a word Churchill coined for the occasion, and which soon found its way into *Webster's*.[163]

March closed with Mountbatten's first significant foray as director of Combined Operations, a commando raid on the French port of St-Nazaire, located five miles upstream from the mouth of the Loire. The dry dock at St-Nazaire, built for the French passenger liner *Normandie* (which had burned at its Hudson River pier the previous month), was one of the largest in the world and the only one on the Atlantic coast that offered *Bismarck*'s surviving sister ship, *Tirpitz*, space enough for repairs. *Tirpitz* had for two months been riding at anchor in a fjord at Trondheim, safe from British aircraft. Yet for Germany, the battle cruiser's safety came at a price. *Tirpitz*, at anchor, posed no threat to British convoys. Churchill and Mountbatten were of a mind that the destruction of the St-Nazaire dry dock, which would leave *Tirpitz* no place to run to if damaged, would make a sortie from Trondheim into the Atlantic too dangerous to risk. The British plan was audacious. Escorted by destroyers, gunboats, and 250 commandos, one of the fifty old American destroyers—*Campbeltown*—its bow packed with three tons of TNT, would sail right up the Loire estuary in the dead of night and crash through the gates of the drydock. The plan called for the crew to scuttle the ship while commandos destroyed the port facilities. Then the small gunboats would pick up the sailors and commandos, and everybody would get the hell out of town. Soon thereafter, if all went as planned, the explosives hidden on *Campbeltown*—set on a timer to allow the crew to escape—would blast the drydock to smithereens.

Campbeltown crashed the dock at 1:34 A.M., remarkably just four minutes behind schedule. Everything had gone as planned, with the exception of the most vital component of all—the fuse that triggered the explosives. After *Campbeltown* crashed the gates, nothing. There she sat, a fish out of water. By the time those commandos not killed or captured got away down the Loire or into the countryside, Germans had swarmed aboard *Campbeltown.* A few dozen German technicians, precise as usual, began a methodical inspection of the ship. They worked through the morning while several hundred officers and men toured the vessel and took snapshots for their girls back home. More than four hundred Germans were aboard when, just before noon, the fuse elected to function. The explosion killed them all. For two days, teams of Germans collected bits and pieces of human remains scattered near the wrecked dock. The raid had its intended effect. Hitler treasured *Tirpitz* so much that he allowed it to make only two brief North Sea excursions that year in pursuit of Allied convoys. He thereafter refused to send it into the Atlantic proper. Instead, *Tirpitz* waited for two years in Norwegian fjords for the British invasion that never came. Finally, in November 1944, RAF Lancaster bombers destroyed the ship with six-ton bombs.

The St-Nazaire raid made little strategic difference in the Battle of the Atlantic, other than to keep *Tirpitz* out of the Atlantic, but like the hunt for *Bismarck,* it captured the imaginations of Americans and Britons alike. Churchill, with a nod to the florid, picturesque narrative style of Thomas Macaulay, termed the raid "brilliant and heroic" and "a deed of glory." The commandos, he wrote, had "been eager to enter the fray," and did so "in the teeth of a close and murderous fire." It was the sort of small, sparkling victory he so relished.[164]

In North Africa and Asia, Churchill was getting nothing of the sort. Rommel sat in front of Ritchie's Eighth Army just forty miles west of

Tobruk. The German was reinforcing almost at leisure. That he meant to attack was certain; the only question was when. In Asia and the Pacific the Japanese had conquered everything in their path. In Russia the German spring offensive would surely come, when panzers would pour down Ukraine roads that wound east and south toward Stalingrad, and all the way to the Caucasus, and Iraq and Persia beyond. Almost three months had elapsed since Churchill warned the Commons that multiple disasters would strike; they indeed had. And now, with different motives and different goals, Stalin and Roosevelt prodded Churchill to action. Stalin not only sought to cement his 1939 borders, he insisted upon the opening of a second front. Roosevelt desired a decision on where and when American troops would fight, for it had been four months since Pearl Harbor and American voters were starting to wonder if it might be six more before American fighting men actually went on the attack. Franklin Roosevelt did not want the November midterm elections to come and go without American boys fighting Germans *somewhere*.

As if to deride British arms, on the night when Mountbatten's commandos steamed up the Loire, Admiral Nagumo and his force of five modern aircraft carriers, four battleships, and a bevy of cruisers and destroyers sallied into the Bay of Bengal, steaming for Ceylon. The Admiralty no longer need wonder where the Japanese admiral was. Against Nagumo the Royal Navy arrayed a far less powerful fleet made up of four older battleships, three smaller aircraft carriers, a few cruisers, several destroyers, and a great many inexperienced seamen. Its commander, Admiral James Somerville, a veteran of Mediterranean operations, based his ships in a secret anchorage (code-named Port T) at Addu Atoll rather than in Colombo and Trincomalee, where Nagumo expected to find and destroy the British fleet. Fortunately for Somerville, after four days of cruising south of Ceylon in search of Nagumo, he took most of his fleet back to Port T to refuel. When Nagumo appeared off Ceylon on Easter Sunday, April 5, he didn't find Somerville, but over the next few days he did find 100,000 tons of British merchant shipping, an aircraft carrier, two cruisers, and a destroyer, all of which he sent to the bottom. The British and Japanese traded aircraft casualties, about fifty each, but the net loss for the British was far more severe. Churchill could count only fourteen heavy bombers in all of India. Nagumo, in turn, still had almost nine hundred of his original one thousand pilots and aircraft, more than enough to destroy either the British or the American fleet, whichever he found first. Admiral Somerville, overwhelmingly outgunned, was forced to flee the Indian Ocean and seek refuge on the east coast of Africa, leaving the Bay of Bengal—and India—completely unprotected.[165]

* * *

Great Britain had been driven from the Indian Ocean. And yet, incredibly, it appeared that Nagumo had departed as well. Contact was again lost with the admiral. Churchill was sure Nagumo would soon return to finish the job. On April 7, Churchill (who inexplicably presumed that American naval strength was now "decidedly superior to the enemy forces in the Pacific") asked Roosevelt to use those naval forces in order to lure the Japanese back into the Pacific Ocean. Churchill's calculations are difficult to explain unless Roosevelt had failed to apprise him of the facts, which were that the Japanese outnumbered the Americans in battleships eleven to zero, and in aircraft carriers ten to four. A fifth carrier, *Wasp,* and America's newest battleship, *Washington,* which Admiral King wanted to station in the Pacific, had been sent to Britain in order to ferry Spitfires to Malta, a task the depleted Royal Navy could no longer undertake. Symbolic of the plight of the Allied navies, the American admiral who commanded the *Wasp* task force was washed overboard in the mid-Atlantic and lost. And when Admiral Cunningham tried to run a relief convoy from Alexandria to Malta—the island was almost out of oil and food—*every* ship was lost. Brooke confided to his diary, "These are black days."[166]

The Allied naval situation was desperate in all oceans. Churchill's tone reflected that truth when, on April 15, he warned Roosevelt that the British position was "grave" and that unless Admiral Yamamoto's fleets were brought to battle and defeated, there was "no reason why the Japanese should not become the dominating factor in the Western Indian Ocean. This would result in the collapse of our whole position in the Middle East." On April 17 he upped the ante when he cabled Roosevelt: "It is essential that we should prevent a junction of the Japanese and the Germans." The junction Churchill had in mind was one between Rommel and the Japanese, the most likely scenario being a Japanese fleet pounding the port of Basra while Rommel slashed his way to Baghdad. Yet only half a junction could prove as fatal as an actual Axis hookup. Japanese control of the Persian Gulf would as effectively deny Britain oil as an actual Axis junction in the Middle East. A Japanese reduction of Basra and the nearby Iranian port of Abadan—home to the world's largest oil refinery—would guarantee that Abadan oil could not be gotten out of Iran, supplies to Russia could not be gotten in, and, as Churchill warned Roosevelt, the British would be unable to "maintain our position either at sea or on land." Brooke later wrote that from a strategic standpoint, Abadan was more important than Egypt, in that the loss of Egypt did not necessarily mean the loss of Abadan, but the loss of Abadan meant the loss of Egypt. Yet, as Averell Harriman learned later in the year, the British were so stretched worldwide that the only defense Churchill could throw up around Abadan consisted of six obsolete biplanes and a few antiaircraft guns. If Hitler punched through from North Africa or from the

Caucasus (once he took that region, which he intended to do by late summer), Abadan and all of Persia would be his for the taking.[167]

Roosevelt, in reply to Churchill's pessimistic musings, stated that *his* situation in the Pacific was "very grave" and pointed out that the American navy was supplying and protecting Australia and New Zealand. Left unsaid was the obvious: America was doing so because London could not. Roosevelt also deprecated the possibility of an Axis hookup, calling it a "remote prospect." Yet that conclusion was no more based on fact than was Churchill's presumption that the American navy had been fully reconstituted in the Pacific.[168]

Churchill (and Brooke) had believed since December that any junction between Germany and Japan would either prolong the war for years or lead to a negotiated settlement, and at the least would mean the end of Churchill's government, if not the British Empire. This was the ordeal as Churchill had outlined it to Jock Colville on several occasions.[169]

Yet, as events turned out, Admiral Nagumo himself shortened Churchill's Asian ordeal. Nagumo was one with all Japanese commanders in his absolute belief that imperial orders must be followed to the letter. Creativity in the face of changing battlefield conditions was not a Japanese trait. The Japanese navy liked to divide its forces, which led to highly scripted and complex operations that demanded perfect coordination. The Japanese also favored diversionary tactics intended to lure the enemy into traps or to disrupt the enemy's plans, but tactical inflexibility prevented them from reacting with vigor when their own plans were disrupted. Changes in plans are, necessarily, unscripted, and were therefore studiously avoided by Japanese commanders. The failure of Nagumo's airmen to return a third time to Pearl Harbor on December 7 to destroy the fuel depots and repair shops is the best-known example of a Japanese opportunity lost in rigid adherence to the master plan. Such an attack had been hoped for but not planned to the letter and, more important, not *ordered*.[170]

Admiral Yamamoto planned to dispatch in late April a carrier force to the Coral Sea to cover the planned invasions of Tulagi, in the Solomon Islands, and Port Moresby, on the southeast coast of Papua New Guinea. A Japanese victory in New Guinea would isolate Australia and mark a significant milestone on the road to Yamamoto's main strategic war aim: the erection of an impenetrable ring of air and naval bases around the entire perimeter of the Co-Prosperity Sphere—the bloc of Asian nations led by the Japanese and free of Western powers—before the Americans could re-arm to dispute the issue. With the South Pacific in hand, Yamamoto planned to then take an outer Aleutian island or two in the North Pacific, and to take Midway Island, the outermost link in the Hawaiian chain, 1,100 miles west-northwest of Pearl Harbor. That would close his ring. It was an audacious goal.

The fifty-eight-year-old admiral had studied English at Harvard two decades earlier and had served as naval attaché in Washington in the late 1920s. During his time in Cambridge and Washington, he had grown to respect Americans, and had also learned to play a ruthless game of poker. He was not a gambler, but he knew how to play a hand. Once he took Port Moresby and Tulagi, he intended to shut the door on American designs in the South Pacific by building an airfield on the small British protectorate of Guadalcanal. In support of those objectives, his Port Moresby task forces were to seek out and destroy the meager American fleet that would surely steam into the Coral Sea to dispute the matter. The American response would have to be meager; two of its four aircraft carriers in the Pacific stood off the Hawaiian Islands, which left only two available for duty in the Coral Sea. The odds lay heavily with the Japanese, whose strength and experienced airmen far exceeded the Americans' and Britons' combined. Yamamoto held the cards, a hand made sweeter by virtue of his having dealt it himself.[171]

Then, Franklin Roosevelt launched an audacious—though largely symbolic—strike of his own. In early April, Roosevelt dispatched two of his four carriers to within five hundred miles of Japan in order to carry out a bombing raid on Tokyo. From one of the carriers, USS *Hornet,* sixteen American twin-engine B-25 medium bombers commanded by Colonel Jimmy Doolittle set off for Japan. The damage Doolittle's raiders inflicted was minimal, but Yamamoto, shocked at the affront to his emperor, decided that the time had come for "the annihilation" of the American Pacific fleet. He ordered that the Midway and Coral Sea ventures be carried out virtually simultaneously. Doolittle's raid was just the sort of diversion Churchill had pressed Roosevelt to undertake, and it had had the desired effect on the Japanese. Roosevelt, ebullient over Doolittle's success, telegraphed Churchill, "We have had a good crack at Japan," and added that he hoped it would lead to Japan pulling its "big ships" from the Indian Ocean. This was why the president had played down Churchill's concern over an Axis juncture in the Middle East as a "remote prospect." Yet the prospect would prove to be remote only if the Japanese navy committed an inexplicable error.[172]

This Admiral Nagumo did when, after pummeling the British in the Indian Ocean, he sent three of his aircraft carriers back to Japan for refitting. In trading planes with the British in the Indian Ocean—about fifty each—Nagumo had come out the winner by virtue of the fact that the British were just about out of aircraft, while Nagumo still had almost all of his. Nagumo's fleet emerged, as usual, unscathed. By mid-April, the Royal Navy had virtually nothing left, and what little it had was steaming for East Africa. The Americans had not much more. Churchill's desperation during those weeks was entirely justified. Yet, rather than finish the job, Nagumo, evidencing early symptoms of what the Japanese later called Victory Disease, chose to go home and perform a cosmetic refitting on his ships. Churchill often complained that his generals preferred certainty to hazard. In this case, Nagumo certainly did.

His decision proved disastrous when in early May a diminished Japanese carrier force met the Americans in the Battle of the Coral Sea. It was the first aircraft-carrier battle in history and the first naval battle where combatants could not see the opposing fleet. The Americans lost one carrier sunk and one damaged. The Japanese lost one light carrier sunk—the first such Japanese casualty of the war—and two heavy carriers damaged. The American navy's losses, relative to its overall strength, were far more egregious than the Japanese losses. But Yamamoto folded his hand. By doing so he lost an opportunity and the battle. Churchill later wrote that had the Japanese sailed into the Coral Sea with two or three more carriers, the Americans might well have never sailed out. Yamamoto had long maintained that in order to force a settlement with America, Japan had to destroy the U.S. Pacific fleet within six months of the start of war, or face the consequences of a re-armed United States. Although the Coral Sea affair was an opportunity lost for Yamamoto to do just that, another soon presented itself. He scheduled his decisive battle for dawn on June 6—one day shy of six months after Pearl Harbor. The place would be Midway Island.[173]

In their exchange of telegrams that winter and spring, Churchill and Roosevelt weighed almost every issue in terms of shipping tonnage, to the point where they became experts on the calculus of hulls and cargo and "man-lift," the capacity needed to carry men from one place to another. When Churchill asked for the use of American ships to move 40,000 troops to India, Roosevelt agreed, but he told Churchill that such a shuffling of resources would result in a cascade of disrupted plans: the end of Gymnast; the gutting of the effort to send American troops to Britain for a 1942 invasion of Europe; a halt to shipping munitions to China; and a further reduction in the amount of goods reaching the Russians, who, Roosevelt offered, "are killing more Germans... than you and I put together." He further declared that America's 1942 man-lift capacity was only 90,000 men, a figure he hoped to double in 1943. This shocked Churchill, who in reply proposed that Roosevelt could solve the problem by "giving orders now to double or treble the American man-lift by 1943," as if Roosevelt could somehow conjure ships. Churchill offered that if no improvement could be made to those figures, "there may well be no question of restoring the situation [in Europe] until 1944," which obviously meant that all the inter-Allied talk about a large-scale invasion in 1942 or 1943 was just that, talk. In that case, he wrote, the Allies would reap the "many dangers that would follow from such a prolongation of the war." Shipping was now a zero-sum game. Roosevelt replied with a remarkably detailed calculation of future American "man-lift" that ended with: "Thus, neglecting losses, the total troop-carrying capacity of U.S. vessels by June, 1944, will be 400,000 men." Since these figures were known to the two leaders and their most trusted lieutenants only, the press on both sides of the Atlantic—and Stalin—continued to beat their drums for an immediate second European front, unaware that shipping constraints and the lack of American preparedness, not Churchill, to whom the press ascribed a hesitancy in the matter, were the reasons that there could be none in 1942, and most likely not in 1943 either.[174]

Roosevelt had not pulled his estimate of 400,000 men from a hat; it was the minimum initial number of American combat troops the Combined Chiefs agreed were needed for a successful invasion of Europe. Roosevelt's prediction of when these troops would be ready—June 1944—proved remarkably accurate, and it is largely ignored by those, then and since, who blame Churchill for not busting into Europe earlier. Yet, in the spring of 1942, Churchill and Roosevelt knew that they could not simply wait out Germany for two years. They had to fight, in tandem. But where, and when?

Sir Stafford Cripps arrived in Delhi on March 22. For the next three weeks he conducted lengthy discussions with leaders in Gandhi's National Congress, offering them autonomy down the road. The offer was based on the War Cabinet's promise of postwar Dominion status for India in exchange for absolute loyalty in the war against Japan. Dominion status amounted to de facto independence. The talks went nowhere. If politics is the art of compromise in furtherance of a cause, Gandhi, by not giving an inch, hurt his cause. He persisted in his belief that the British presence in India was bait for the Japanese, who were more likely to invade India if the British did not depart. He demanded either immediate independence or, at the least, a national government. Chiang had just weeks earlier tried to impress upon Gandhi the need to fight the Japanese, for the Japanese despised peacemakers more than war givers, and gave no quarter to either, as the recent slaughters in Singapore and the Nanking massacre in 1937 attested to. The Japanese would spare no one, Chiang warned, whether the British stayed or left. Gandhi listened politely; the generalissimo went home rebuffed. Gandhi understood, George Orwell later wrote, that "if you are not prepared to take life, you must often be prepared for lives to be lost in some other way." Gandhi accepted that a nonviolent opposition to a Japanese invasion might cost millions of lives. Cripps argued the same case as had Chiang, and got no further. Churchill expected as much. He later wrote, "In the intensity of the struggle for life from day to day, and with four hundred million helpless people to defend from the horrors of Japanese conquest, I was able to bear this news, which I had thought probable from the beginning, with philosophy. I knew how bitterly Stafford Cripps would feel the failure of his Mission, and I sought to comfort him." Churchill may have been feeling unusually expansive when writing those words, for upon his return to London, Cripps, not Churchill, found his name associated with the mission and its failure.[175]

It was over India and empire that Churchill and Roosevelt had their first serious political argument. Roosevelt presumed he could speak frankly to Churchill on most matters, including—and mistakenly—India. Churchill, out of politeness, kept Roosevelt abreast of Cripps's progress, or lack thereof. When the talks broke down, Roosevelt blamed Churchill, in the most frank terms. The two men had very different long-term objectives. Beyond the defeat of Hitler, Churchill wanted above all to preserve the British Empire, including of course India, a goal that was anathema to Roosevelt, a devout anti-imperialist. "Preserve," for Churchill, meant "protect." For Roosevelt it meant "keep." On April 11, Roosevelt sent a private letter to Churchill, by way of Harry Hopkins, in which he outlined his position on India in terms of the thirteen colonies and George III. Roosevelt suggested Churchill consider that India might be ripe for the same transformation as the American states had experienced—from colonies to loose federation and finally to nationhood. Churchill in his memoirs offered a benign take on Roosevelt's musings: "The President's mind was back in the American War of Independence.... I, on the other hand, was responsible for preserving the peace and safety of the Indian continent, sheltering nearly a fifth of the population of the globe. Our resources were slender and strained to the full." Had Roosevelt not offered one final incendiary opinion in his missive, the matter might have remained benign. But he added this: "The feeling is almost universally held here that the deadlock has been caused by the unwillingness of the British government to concede to the Indians the right of self-government. I feel I must place this issue before you very frankly, and I know you will understand my reasons for so doing."[176]

Churchill not only did not understand but was enraged by what he saw as Roosevelt's meddling. He had thought that his reaction in December to Roosevelt's verbal lecture had set things straight regarding India, but here was Roosevelt again, and in writing, no less. The note reached Chequers at 3:00 A.M. on Sunday and found Hopkins and Churchill still up and chatting. Upon reading the message Churchill unleashed a barrage of curses that echoed throughout the great house. After regaining (some) of his composure, he voiced his long-held belief that any imposition of political will by the Hindus upon one hundred million Indian Muslims would result in a total breakdown of order, and large-scale bloodshed, and this at the very moment the Japanese were waiting in the wings, with Gandhi and his "Quit India" cohorts ready to accept the enemy peacefully, thereby easing a Japanese passage to the Middle East. Meanwhile, the Muslim League was demanding the creation of a separate Muslim state, Pakistan. To accede to Gandhi's demands would necessitate acceding to the Muslim League. With the war on, Churchill was unwilling to do either. India's defense against Japan required military action, not political. India was poor and life was hard—the average Indian earned less than $15 per year and could expect to live just twenty-seven years. Yet, without its tether to London it would be a far poorer place, and were the Japanese to arrive, Churchill believed it would become a desolate place.[177]

At the end of his tutorial, he told Hopkins that if his resignation would advance the alliance and American opinion, he was willing to do so, but even in that case he was sure the cabinet would continue with its present Indian policy. It was an idle threat, but credible in that the free world looked upon Churchill as the hero of the war. Roosevelt could ill afford to be seen as the man who drove Winston Churchill into political exile. Roosevelt, Harriman later recalled, "was for breaking up the British empire, and Churchill had no intention of doing so.... India was a known subject, but not one to discuss with Churchill." Hopkins concluded likewise after Churchill's harangue, and cabled Roosevelt accordingly.[178]

Churchill drafted a sober reply to Roosevelt in which he told the president that a serious disagreement between them "would break my heart, and would surely deeply injure both our countries at the height of this terrible struggle." He also allowed that Roosevelt's letter would remain private, a backhanded yet clear way of telling Roosevelt that the cabinet would erupt if it got wind of his preachifying. Yet, Churchill appears not to have grasped a nuanced element of Roosevelt's thinking: Roosevelt was willing to fight for the survival of Britain, but not for the survival of British *interests*, that is, the British Empire. "The winds of change had begun to blow," Christopher Soames, later Churchill's son-in-law, recalled, "but Churchill had yet to see them."[179]

Within months, Gandhi and the Indian National Congress called for strikes. The "Quit India" movement took to the streets. Ten battalions of British and Indian troops who should have been killing Japanese soldiers became tied down fighting Indian nationalists; more than one thousand Indians were killed. When it was over, the British placed Gandhi under house arrest at a small palace at Poona, and jailed his deputy Jawaharlal Nehru and thousands of "Quit India" partisans for the duration of the war. Gandhi had distanced himself from reality when he advised not only Indians but also Czechs and European Jews to accept their fate: "I can conceive [of] the necessity of the immolation of hundreds, if not thousands, to appease the hunger of the dictators." That proved to be an ironic choice of words given that Hitler's final butcher's bill exceeded six million Jews, and several hundred thousands of Czechs and Dutchmen and Frenchmen, and at least twenty million Polish and Russian civilians. On April 19, Joseph Goebbels dropped an entry into his diary that Churchill himself could have written: "Gandhi gave an interview in which he once again urged non-resistance. He is a fool whose politics seem merely calculated to drag India further and further into misfortune."[180]

Writing years later, Churchill minced no words: The "people of Hindustan...were carried through the struggle on the shoulders of our small island." By 1942 the cost to Britain of defending India was running at almost one million pounds per day, an amount fixed by contracts drawn up in India at exorbitant rates and at the inflated prewar rate of exchange. In essence, the viceroy and India were billing London for India's defense. Churchill informed the viceroy, Lord Linlithgow, that HMG reserved the right to file counterclaims after the war. Yet for Churchill, the fact that more than a million Hindu and Muslim men "*volunteered* to serve" (italics Churchill) in the defense of India, trumped all criticisms of HMG's imperial policy, whether by Roosevelt or Gandhi or anyone else. Loyalty, not British imperial might, kept India bound to London. In return, Churchill wrote, London "effectively protected" India from "the horrors and perils of World War."[181]

In their ongoing correspondence, both Roosevelt and Churchill displayed a knack for knowing when a personal touch was called for—a best wishes to a spouse, or a few generous words about the other fellow's predicaments. Shortly after the India episode, Roosevelt gave Churchill a stamp that had been canceled at Argentia the previous August. This gesture was pure Roosevelt, simple, understated, and symbolic, much like his fireside chats. Churchill reciprocated with a typically Churchillian flourish; he sent Roosevelt specially bound volumes of the complete works of Winston Leonard Spencer Churchill.[182]

Churchill's most cutting response to Roosevelt's position came when, in his memoirs, he took a mighty swipe at his old friend. Of the president's suggestion that the British simply walk away from India, he wrote: "I was thankful that events [the war against Japan] made such an act of madness impossible." Idealism was all well and good, Churchill continued, but not "idealism at other people's expense and without regard to the consequences of ruin and slaughter which fall upon millions of humble homes." Such ruin and slaughter in fact descended upon India in 1946, and led in 1947 to its partition into Pakistan and India, after the murder of thousands of Hindus and Muslims, and the forced migration of millions more.[183]

Hopkins had come to London not to discuss India but to accompany General George Marshall, who was there to brief Churchill and the British chiefs on the proposed American strategy in Europe. Marshall's plan, drawn up by Eisenhower, was straightforward. Operation Sledgehammer would relieve pressure on the Russians—who Eisenhower expected to soon be in dire straits—by putting several divisions ashore in France in the vicinity of Cherbourg on the Cotentin Peninsula. The plan, Roosevelt cabled Churchill, "has my heart and mind in it." It didn't have Churchill's. He told Roosevelt that Sledgehammer should not be undertaken if Russia was losing, but only if Russia was *winning*, for if Russia "is in dire straits, it will not help her or us to come a nasty cropper on our own."[184]

This was Marshall's first introduction to Churchill's late hours and long monologues, in this case on the American Civil War and World War One. Brooke observed that Marshall "was evidently not used to being kept out of his bed till the small hours of the morning, and not enjoying it much!" Marshall told Brooke that he usually left the office at around 6:00 for a short ride on his horse and an early dinner at home, and that he might meet with Roosevelt once every month or six weeks. Brooke replied that he'd be lucky if he did not see Churchill for six hours. Despite the long hours and Churchill's digressions, the talks moved along, the British appearing to agree to an entry into Europe that year. In any case, the lack of shipping and landing craft settled the issue; the Americans could spare only enough ships to transport fewer than three U.S. divisions to Britain. That meant that British troops would be in the van of any invasion, and that meant that the British held veto power over any such proposal. As well, although Royal Navy engineers were designing artificial harbors to supply the troops on the beaches, construction was at least a year off. In addition, no effort had been made to build the specialty tanks that could clear minefields or double as massive flamethrowers. What most disturbed Brooke was that all the landing craft then in Britain could deliver only four thousand men to the beaches in the first wave, a force so paltry that it invited annihilation.

This was the hardest fact that Marshall had not addressed, leaving Brooke to jot in his diary that although Marshall displayed "a great charm and dignity... he did not impress me with his brain." When Brooke expressed his surprise to Marshall that he had given no thought to what the Allies might do after landing—go east, go south, go north—Marshall had no answer, and in fact shocked Brooke by saying that he "had not even studied any of the strategic implications." Still, Marshall left for Washington believing that the British had accepted his proposal to put men ashore that year. In fact, Churchill had agreed only to study the proposal.[185]

Churchill had done to Marshall what Brooke and the British chiefs regularly did to him when he proposed a scheme not to their liking: voiced enthusiasm and then studied the proposal to death. Ismay, seeing through Churchill's maneuver, told the chiefs, "Our American friends went happily homeward under the mistaken impression we had committed ourselves to both Roundup [the larger invasion of France] and Sledgehammer.... I think we should have come clean, much cleaner than we did" by reminding the Americans of the horrors of the last war and the debacle of 1940, as well as by telling Marshall that an invasion could be undertaken only when there was "a cast iron certainty" of success.[186]

George Marshall harbored a soldier's natural distrust of politicians. His April meetings with Churchill allayed that distrust; in Churchill, Marshall believed he had found a true statesman, a man he could trust. And in Marshall, Churchill had found a man he could respect, a man who told the truth, whatever the political costs. Thus, Churchill felt regret when Marshall, a few weeks after departing, realized the British had no intention of landing in France, in force, in 1942. The statesman had snookered the soldier. Yet Churchill claimed in his memoirs that he hadn't intended to mislead Marshall, only to bolster his morale and voice British support for their shared, ultimate goal, a second European front. But Marshall, a man who expected to be told the truth, believed what the British had told him. Henceforth, he would prove himself not so easy a mark.[187]

On April 17, the day Marshall and Hopkins left London, Operation Gymnast, the invasion of French North Africa, out of sight and mind for two months, again made its presence known, like a mole in the arcade game. The trigger this time lay with the Vichy government, which that week was hijacked by Pierre Laval, personally despised as much by Hitler as by Roosevelt and Churchill. But Laval was as pro-German a Frenchman as the Führer could wish for. Pétain, old and infirm, had recalled Laval to the government as vice premier, but within days Laval showed who was in charge when he began cooperating with the Gestapo in its quest to round up and ship east those Jews who had fled central Europe for the safety of France—both occupied and unoccupied France. With Laval in, American policy toward the Vichy regime became obsolete overnight. The American ambassador to Vichy, Admiral William Leahy, was recalled; within weeks Roosevelt made Leahy his chief of staff.[188]

A neutral if not welcoming reception by French North Africans to any Anglo-American invasion had always been of primary importance to Roosevelt. For two years he had resisted the urgings of his liberal colleagues and continued to do business with Vichy. His motive was sound. Knowing that American boys would sooner or later be landing on French soil, or French colonial soil, Roosevelt had hoped to have Vichy as an ally when that day came. Counseled by Leahy, the president believed that French North Africa might not obey Laval's orders and that Pétain, now a figurehead, might fly to Algiers to rally patriotic Frenchmen. The wild card was Admiral Jean Darlan, who remained in the Vichy government as commander of all French armed forces. He had long hated the English, even more so since Churchill had obliterated his beloved ships and hundreds of his sailors at Oran, where Darlan had sent them in order to stay out of German hands. Darlan was also despised by Washington. The Vichy French had at least behaved with consistent poltroonery. Churchill called Darlan a "naval crook," yet even after Oran, Darlan pledged to never allow the French fleet to fall into German hands, a pledge he had so far kept. Still, Churchill considered the admiral's word to be worthless, which is somewhat ironic given that it had been Churchill who had struck Darlan at Oran. From a military standpoint, Darlan, more than Laval, was the riddle in need of a solution. Would the admiral send his fleet to fight the Americans and British if they sailed to Vichy North Africa? From Brooke's standpoint, the whole affair was a mess, a political minefield of the sort military men are keen to sidestep. The CIGS thought nothing would come of the regime change in Paris, by way of any new opportunities in North Africa. And nothing did. With Gymnast again in play (possibly), Churchill made plans to send Dickie Mountbatten to Washington to whisper its merits in Roosevelt's ear in hopes that Roosevelt—despite the opposition of Marshall and King—would embrace the North African plan a second time.[189]

On May 27, Churchill cabled Roosevelt: "Dickie will explain to you the difficulties of 1942... and outline plans for a landing in the north of Norway." Churchill added that he welcomed Rommel's attack and that South African premier Jan Smuts, on the scene with Auchinleck, "expresses high confidence in the result." He closed with, "We must never let Gymnast pass from our minds." This was not what Roosevelt wanted to hear. Marshall—who had been dragooning as many ships as he could to build up forces in Britain—understood with clarity that Churchill and Brooke had misled him. Now here Churchill came, suggesting a gross diversion from their agreed-upon goal of a landing in France. Churchill's cable was at least straightforward; Mountbatten's mission was to impress upon Roosevelt the "practical difficulties," as Churchill saw it, entailed by Sledgehammer.[190]

The choice of Dickie was inspired. He was staunchly pro-American and, like Roosevelt, charming and high born. Mountbatten was a naval hero, and Roosevelt, a naval animal, greatly admired naval heroes. Within a week, to the great distress of Marshall and King, Mountbatten had almost persuaded the president of the perils of Sledgehammer and had praised the wisdom of Churchill's beloved Jupiter, the proposed invasion of northern Norway, which Brooke had been trying to kill for weeks. Even Churchill by then, with reluctance, sensed that any invasion of Norway was a long shot for that year. Yet Jupiter might well serve as a bargaining chip, to be dropped in favor of something more practical such as Gymnast. By the first week of June, Mountbatten had just about sold Roosevelt, whose choices had been whittled down (as Churchill intended) to Gymnast or nothing. Marshall and King did not see things at all that way; the Pacific, after all, was also a theater of war. They pressed Roosevelt for moves in that direction. Although Marshall and King suspected otherwise, no guile underlay Churchill's dealings with Roosevelt. Unless three criteria were met for Operation Roundup—sufficient troops, sufficient landing craft, and artificial harbor facilities—an invasion of France in 1942, or 1943 for that matter, could only end in disaster. Roosevelt understood this; after all, he had done the calculations as to man-lift. He simply needed a push in the proper direction; Churchill and Dickie gave it.

Hopkins and Marshall's route home from London in April had taken them over the North Atlantic, where fifty-nine American cargo ships destined for Murmansk were idled in Scottish and Icelandic ports. The reasons for the logjam were many and complex—lack of escorts, overburdened port facilities, the long wait to form convoys—but the most obvious explanation was simple: Admiral Dönitz's U-boats were winning the Battle of the Atlantic. Since January, much of the battle had been fought within sight of the American east coast. Dönitz's U-boat strength was up to 250 with more than 90 boats on patrol on any given day—50 or more in the Atlantic, 20 in the Mediterranean, and a dozen or more hunting Russia-bound convoys in the Arctic. On January 12, Dönitz, with American coastal shipping in his sights, had launched Operation *Paukenschlag* (Drumroll) off the east coast of America. U-boat commanders called the next several months their "second happy time," referring to the easy pickings offered by unescorted American ships, which sailed—inexplicably—with running lights ablaze along the well-illuminated east coast of the United States. Resorts from New Jersey to Miami, desperate for business, had kept their seaside lights burning for fear that dousing them would spoil the tourist season, but vacationers, denied planes and trains, could not get there in any event.

The U-boats found their targets starkly silhouetted by the luminous shoreline, a state of affairs that Admiral Samuel Eliot Morison (the official U.S. Navy historian of the war) called "one of the most reprehensible failures" of local governments and the American military during the war. Not until mid-April were the lights ordered turned off. American naval and Coast Guard ships and airborne patrols had begun, but the American navy, failing to grasp the hard-earned lessons of the Royal Navy, had yet to establish coastal convoys to protect ships heading from the Gulf of Mexico to Nova Scotia, where Atlantic convoys began and ended. Getting to Halifax was the responsibility of individual captains. U-boats simply lay in wait for them from New Orleans to the Canadian Maritimes coast. Thirty merchantmen were lost in the Maritimes alone in January, and almost twice as many in February. Churchill had since Pearl Harbor made clear to his subordinates that the war would be won *if* the Allies did not bungle the job. Off their coast, the Americans were bungling it, with the result, Churchill believed, that the U-boats threatened to bring about "the disaster of an indefinite prolongation of the war."[191]

At the Argentia conference, the Americans had pledged to increase annual merchant shipping production by almost sevenfold, to eight million tons. They would need every ton, as residents from Long Island to Florida's east coast who regularly beheld the glow of exploding oil tankers out at sea knew. The flames continued unabated during a seven-month attack that Churchill called a "terrible massacre of shipping along the American coast." The U.S. Navy was so unprepared to meet the challenge that Britain sent some of the fifty formerly American destroyers back across the Atlantic. Not until mid-April did the Americans destroy a U-boat by surface ship. By May the amount of fuel oil reaching New England from the Gulf of Mexico had plummeted by 90 percent. But where New Englanders could don an extra sweater, Russian troops needed guns, munitions, and trucks. Churchill tried to oblige. Stalin was desperate for spare parts to repair the Hurricanes that Britain had sent. Churchill ordered the RAF to dismantle several Hurricanes and ship the needed parts to Russia, a gesture that impressed Harriman, who noted that the American air force would never contemplate such a sacrifice. Stalin needed more than gestures. If the U-boats ravaged the Arctic convoys as they were shipping off the American coast, the Red Army would begin its summer campaigns lacking both a second front in France and the means to hold its own front. Between mid-April and mid-June, twenty-three out of eighty-four ships that left U.S. ports destined for Murmansk were sunk. Seventeen had to take shelter in Scotland, which prompted Stalin to accuse the British of "stealing" goods meant for the Red Army.[192]

And then the situation got worse. When twenty-two of thirty-four ships in one late June convoy went down, Churchill was forced to cancel the Arctic convoys for two months. This infuriated Stalin, embarrassed Churchill, and further fueled the "Second Front Now" crowd in Britain, where the heroic deeds of the Red Army so enthralled the populace that a London publisher used his meager ration of paper to reprint Tolstoy's *War and Peace*, which sold out within days.[193]

The devastation on the seas underscored the importance of the Wizard War. Britain's shipping losses had ameliorated somewhat during the last half of 1941, due to small improvements in radar, the protection offered by Icelandic and Greenland-based air patrols, the American presence across most of the Atlantic, and a decrease in German air attacks on coastal shipping following the invasion of Russia. Still, total losses of British, Allied, and neutral shipping exceeded four million tons in 1941. The losses would have been far greater but for the fortuitous capture on May 9, 1941, of an Enigma machine and code books from U-110 in the North Atlantic. The U-boat's captain, F. J. Lemp, had just lost a running battle with the British escort destroyer HMS *Bulldog*. Lemp, presuming his boat was doomed, ordered it abandoned. But U-110 did not go down. As its crew bobbed in the seas, a boarding party from *Bulldog* stripped her of everything they could carry, including her codes and Enigma machine. The submarine was taken under tow, but soon sank. The *Kriegsmarine* believed her crew and secrets had gone down with her. The British now had in their possession a German naval Enigma machine, not a model but the real deal. Churchill waited more than seven months to tell Roosevelt the good news. By early 1942, already wary of too many "coincidental" interceptions of U-boats—best explained by the British having cracked the German codes, which the army and Luftwaffe dismissed as an impossibility—*Kriegsmarine* cryptologists added a fourth wheel to their Enigma machines, boosting the number of possible letter permutations from the billions into the trillions. The army and Luftwaffe elected to stick with their older, three-wheel models. It was the wrong decision, for Alan Turing and the Bletchley crowd were just now beginning to make calculating machines that possessed the single most critical attribute necessary for breaking a code: computational speed. There are, after all, only so many letters in the alphabet.[194]

The addition of the fourth wheel to Enigma, however, gave the *Kriegsmarine* a hefty advantage in the Atlantic. Compounding that advantage, the German radio intercept and monitoring service (*Beobachtungsdienst*) had broken the British merchant code, allowing the *Kriegsmarine* to listen in on Allied intra-convoy conversations, including Royal Navy situation reports, which tracked the location of U-boats. The accuracy of the British reports greatly distressed Dönitz, but the advantage was his. He knew what the British knew, but the British did not know that he knew. Adding the fourth wheel to the naval Enigma machines resulted in a renewed slaughter of Allied shipping. Between January and June of 1942, U-boats sent six hundred ships, eight thousand crewmen, and three million tons of shipping to the bottom, about one-third of the total tonnage lost since 1939. British, Allied, and neutral losses during the first three months of 1942 increased at a "murderous" rate, Alexander Cadogan told his diary, from 420,000 tons in January to 835,000 in March. The holds of a 7,000-ton freighter such as the American-built Liberty Ships held enough cargo to fill almost one hundred railroad freight cars. Each ship lost, therefore, was the equivalent of a mile-long freight train falling into the sea, taking with it enough supplies to feed, clothe, and fuel a small city or an army division for three weeks. Although American shipyards would launch 2,710 Liberty Ships by 1945, in mid-1942, the Germans were sinking them far faster than they could be launched.[195]

Yet, Hitler, ever fearful of a British invasion of Norway and the disruption of his supply of Swedish iron ore, played small with his U-boats. The Führer "sacrificed the glittering chances in the Atlantic," Churchill later wrote, "and positioned every available surface ship and many a precious U-boat in northern Norwegian waters," the area Hitler considered to be "the zone of destiny" in the war. He also stationed four new infantry divisions in Norway, bringing the total to eleven, more than 120,000 men. There they sat, and waited for the Englishmen who never came. Even though he used it as a bargaining tool, northern Norway truly topped Churchill's list of invasion targets, a fact that Brooke knew only too well. But the three British military chiefs, unlike their German counterparts, could step back from their own interservice rivalries and unite in opposition to their leader's latest questionable scheme. Germany's best chance to secure its perimeter lay in an all-out assault in the Atlantic, but Hitler ignored Dönitz and shepherded his resources, not only in Norway but in the vicinity of the Canary Islands, off the northwest coast of Africa, in hopes of sinking an invasion fleet, which also never came. Had he not done so, had he thrown his boats all in, Allied losses would have been far more horrific. As it was, Churchill termed the U-boat menace "our worst evil." By summer, with Russia in desperate need of supplies, it became Stalin's worst evil as well.[196]

Despite the shipping losses, one statistic above all others offered comfort to Churchill: American oil-refining capacity was twenty times that of Germany. America had more oil underground than it could pump. The war would someday come down to who could afford to bleed the most oil. America's enormous industrial productive capacity came powerfully into play, but only as a function of America's ability to pump—and *deliver*—oil. British factories ceased production without American oil. Tanks went nowhere without gasoline. The United States had enough capacity to pump oil and build factories, tanks, and airplanes far into the future. But with oil, as with food and weapons, delivery was hobbled by the lack of ships to get the oil to Britain and Russia. In May, during the "second happy time," just six U-boats operating in the Gulf of Mexico sank sixty-six ships, of which more than half were oil tankers. The Allies could not afford to lose oil-toting vessels at that rate and expect—or hope—to relieve Russia. Ships, Hopkins now believed, were more important than their cargoes. A few weeks after the Gulf of Mexico massacre, U-boats sent four hundred thousand tons of Allied shipping to the bottom in just seven days, a rate, Churchill informed Roosevelt, "unexampled in either this war or the last, and if maintained evidently beyond all existing replacement plans."[197]

If the Allies could solve the U-boat menace, their oil problem would solve itself. Not so, Hitler's fuel problems. He had to now steal more than Polish and Ukraine wheat in order to move his armies. He needed a great deal more oil. The Ploesti oil fields—Churchill called Romanian oil the taproot of German might—located north of Bucharest supplied as much as 60 percent of Germany's crude oil, enough to sustain a peacetime German economy, but not enough to power the Wehrmacht as well. Because the gasoline consumed by his mechanized forces taxed Germany's modest refining capacity, the solution to Hitler's oil problem lay farther east, in the Caucasus, or even in the Middle East. Each of the almost four thousand Wehrmacht tanks in Soviet territory quaffed enormous quantities of fuel simply standing still—more than twenty-two tons every eight weeks. Hitler's tanks alone would need several hundred thousand tons of fuel to reach and hold the Caucasus. The vast spaces of the Ukraine and the Don Basin contained no petrol stations such as those in Belgium from which German tankers had helped themselves. The panzers were only the first drawdown on Hitler's fuel supplies; his mechanized units, more than six hundred thousand vehicles in all, required thousands of times as much fuel as his tanks.

On Hitler's orders Luftwaffe fighter planes had been designed to fly on synthetic gasoline, which was refined from coal at two large plants in Leipzig and Stettin. But Hitler lacked the capacity to refine the gasoline he needed to move his armies. The Russian Baku oil fields—*if* he conquered them—would contribute to his mobility, but only in two years' time, when new *autobahns* and railroads of the proper gauge were built in order to connect the Caucasus to Greater Germany. The northern Iraqi oil fields located near Mosul offered the same benefit as the Romanian and Caucasus oil fields, but following Rashid's failed 1941 coup, Hitler had abandoned any thought of forcing his way into Mosul. Likewise, in Iran, the British had barred the door in August 1941 when British and Indian forces invaded Iran from Basra, while the Soviets poured in from the north. That war, if it could be called that, lasted six days, one day longer than a cricket test match. The British lost twenty-two killed. When Reza Shah fled the country, Churchill propped the Shah's twenty-two-year-old son, Mohammad Reza Pahlavi, on the Peacock throne.

But in early 1942, with British and Soviet forces spread so thin, the doors to Iraq and Iran were virtually unguarded. If Hitler smashed through Baku in the north or the Suez in the south, the oil riches of the Middle East would be his for the taking. But he had no plans to do so, and for reasons that appeared to him to be strategically sound. In order to get to Iraq and Iran from the north, he would have to drive through Baku, that is, he would have to *take* Baku. Taking Baku would sate his oil needs and negate the need to proceed farther. But in February, with Rommel cruising toward Cairo, and the Japanese steaming into the Indian Ocean, Admiral Raeder convinced Hitler that the real strategic significance of the Middle East was not its potential source of oil for Germany but its importance to Britain: It was where the British got *their* oil, and where they were most vulnerable. Raeder, in a memo to Hitler, anticipated Churchill's and Brooke's concerns exactly: "Suez and Basra are the western pillars of the British position in the East. Should these positions collapse under the weight of concerted Axis pressure the consequences for the British Empire would be disastrous."[198]

Raeder and Rommel had long proffered a southern plan (*Plan Sud*), wherein Germany and Japan would link up in Basra or Tehran. Britain depended upon Persian* oil to fight its war and Persian railroads to supply Russia. If the Axis took Persia, Britain would lose its primary source of oil. Early in the year Churchill told Ismay, "The oil stringency, which is already serious in Germany and German conquered countries, makes the seizure

---

* Persia had taken the name Iran in 1935. To avoid possible confusion with Iraq in official communications, Churchill ordered that "Persia" be used rather than "Iran" in all wartime memos regarding Iran.

of the Baku and Persian oil fields of vital consequences to Germany, second only to the need of successfully invading the British Isles." Brooke seconded that motion when he told his diary, "All the motive [British] power at sea, on land, and throughout the Middle East was entirely dependent on the oil from Abadan.... If we lost the Persian oil, we inevitably lost Egypt." Egypt lost meant Empire lost, and the war.[199]

Hitler finally grasped that fact in early 1942 and, executing an about-face, approved of Raeder's *Plan Sud,* including that part of the plan that called for securing the Mediterranean flank by either capturing or destroying Malta. To that end, during March and April, the Germans dropped twice the tonnage of bombs on Malta than they had on London during the 1940 Blitz. Bombs formed only part of the peril faced by the Maltese. With London unable to supply the island, the threat of starvation was real, and imminent. "Above all, there was Malta," Ismay later wrote. "To lose her would be almost as painful as to lose part of England itself."[200]

If Malta fell, Rommel could resupply at will and punch past Cairo and into Iraq. But unless Rommel got to Basra, Hitler's oil options came down to Russian oil, or none. Stalin would have to fight the battle for his oil alone. Churchill had no say in the outcome. Yet he pondered a horrific means to deny Hitler the oil: Stalin might be persuaded (if the battle went against him) to destroy his own oil wells. The Baku fields were so saturated with petroleum that Churchill predicted that their destruction would result in "a conflagration on a scale not hitherto witnessed in the world." Rumor in Berlin had it that British commandos were already on the ground, awaiting final orders to blow the Russian oil wells, a prospect that shocked Goebbels, who scribbled in his diary, "That's exactly like them! They [the English] have proven themselves throughout the world as great destroyers of other people's property." Churchill quickly shelved the idea, not because of the insult Stalin might attach to the scheme, but because he and Roosevelt lacked the ships needed to make up the shortfall. In any case, Stalin had no intention of destroying his oil fields. The dictator summoned Nikolai K. Baibakov, deputy to the oil commissar. Cocking his thumb, Stalin pointed two fingers at Baibakov's head and said, "If you fail to stop the Germans getting our oil, you will be shot. And when we have thrown the invader out, if we cannot restart production, we will shoot you again."[201]

Stalin understood that Russia's only hope for salvation lay in the attrition of German men, machines, and fuel. Attrition formed the backbone of Churchill's strategic vision as well. He intended to do his part in constructing a ring of steel around the Reich, a ring he could slowly tighten until nothing remained within it but Hitler's bombed-out Chancellery—preferably with the Führer dead inside. Germany, vulnerable to naval blockade, its navy too small to break out into distant waters to procure needed resources, had to grow geographically in order to sustain itself, a process that in time, if Russia held on, would collapse upon itself. Churchill summed up his philosophy in a memo to the Chiefs of Staff that treated of RAF losses, but his words also applied to tanks, artillery, and men (especially if the men were Russian): "Indeed, like General Grant in his last campaign, we can almost afford to lose two for one, having regard to the immense supplies now coming forward in the future." Churchill had read Ulysses S. Grant's Civil War memoirs when he was thirteen; the utility of attrition as practiced by Grant had been lodged in Churchill's psyche for more than fifty years. Yet Grant at Petersburg had been fighting his last campaign, and he was on the verge of victory; Churchill and Roosevelt had yet to fight their first campaign together as allies. The question that vexed Churchill throughout 1942 was, would American industrial output hit its stride before German armies arrived in the Caucasus?[202]

Yet if Ismay, Dill, and many of the American planners were proven correct in their predictions of a German victory over the Soviets, Hitler's fuel and food problems would solve themselves. The loss of Baku oil would cripple Russian industry and agriculture; further resistance would be futile. Famine, widespread and horrific, would follow. Hitler, victorious, would then turn westward, toward England.

Churchill once told Colville that May was his least favorite month. But at least it ushered in good fighting weather, especially on the Continent, where in 1942 only two options for offensive action presented themselves, "butcher and bolt" raids and RAF bombing. Whenever he summoned Brooke late at night, the CIGS presumed the Old Man had just cooked up another strategic initiative of likely dubious value to Brooke's way of thinking, impossible to pull off, and costly in the execution. This was especially so on weekends when Churchill was at Chequers, recalled Sir Ian Jacob, because the hours and company Churchill kept at Chequers always caused a distressing sense of "anticipation" among the staff officers, especially if Dickie Mountbatten arrived bearing schemes. The staff called these sessions "the midnight follies." During such weekends Churchill put forth ideas like a masting oak spews acorns, some to root but most destined to decay. The invasion of Norway—Operation Jupiter—had been of abiding interest to Churchill, for no other reason Brooke could discern than that Churchill once told him that "Hitler had unrolled the map of Europe starting with Norway, and that he [Churchill] would start rolling it up again from Norway." Archie Wavell, a victim in North Africa of Churchill's strategic misfires, believed

"Winston is always expecting rabbits to come out of empty hats." Churchill now looked to Madagascar, where, were the Japanese to secure a foothold, the entire Indian Ocean would be lost. As well, Madagascar was a French colony, intensely loyal to Vichy ever since Churchill had bombed the French fleet at Oran in July 1940. Here was a grand opportunity to block further Japanese adventures (not that Japan planned to go there) and pluck some real estate from the Vichy portfolio.[203]

This the British did, in a May 5 raid, executed by the 5th Commando at Diego Suarez, on Madagascar's northern tip. It was carried off with total surprise. Vichy forces on the island, however, incited by Admiral Darlan, who told them to never forget Oran, turned the affair into a guerrilla war and fought the British for months. The flash-bang success of the St-Nazaire and Madagascar raids—as they saw them—emboldened both Churchill and Mountbatten who, as chief of Combined Operations, cooked up plans some distance removed from the watchful gaze of the military chiefs, but close enough to Churchill to whet his appetite for action.

By May the Russians had been dug in for six months within artillery range of the German army. The Red Army had the benefit of short supply lines, along which rolled the new and innovative T-34 tanks, steel behemoths armed with 76mm cannons and, most important, built with sloping armored surfaces. No other tank in the world was so designed. The sloped profile effectively doubled the protection offered by the T-34's steel armor; German anti-tank shells simply bounced off. The T-34 tank kept the Russians in the game that year, as did the Soviet conscripts who marched down frozen roads in seemingly infinite numbers, for, as the Germans had learned throughout the autumn, when the Red Army lost an entire division, even an entire army, another appeared almost at once. In late February, with all of Europe clenched in winter's grip, Hitler had told Goebbels that "snow had become physically repulsive to him." By March, Goebbels asked his diary, "Will this winter never end? Is a new glacial age in the offing?" Hitler now grasped that the plight of German troops was "a catastrophe" of the very sort that had befallen Napoleon. Yielding to reality for a change, Goebbels called upon German citizens to donate warm clothing for the troops.[204]

The Führer waited for the "majestic coming of spring," when he intended to preside over a thaw that would flow with fresh blood. He had promised as much when he made his declaration of war upon America: "The beginning of winter only will now check [our] movement; at the beginning of summer it will again no longer be possible to stop the movement." It was a boast typical of Hitler, to be sure, but one taken seriously in Moscow, London, and

Washington. By the late spring of 1942, Roosevelt, Marshall, Ismay, and the man in charge of U.S. war plans, Dwight Eisenhower, all thought it a fair bet that Russia would either be defeated or sue for peace by autumn, as the new Soviet government had done in early 1918. Brooke and Churchill thought otherwise, for a simple yet overriding reason: after almost a year of carnage that left more than a million troops on each side killed or wounded, neither Stalin nor Hitler could call a stop to the battle without risking a loss of prestige in the eyes of their own people, and possible political extinction at the hands of their disillusioned cohorts. No, the business would be settled with finality one day, either in Moscow or Berlin.[205]

Spring brought no relief to Russian civilians, who had so far had the worst of it, especially in Leningrad, where, under siege since late August and lacking coal, food, and oil, more than two hundred thousand perished by early May. Hitler had ordered the complete destruction of the city and its nine million inhabitants, including six million refugees who had fled the countryside for the supposed safety of Leningrad. The Wehrmacht was ordered not to accept a surrender if one was offered. The composer Dmitri Shostakovich managed to escape with his family and a suitcase that contained his almost completed Seventh Symphony, *Leningrad*. He was one of the very few.

The city was surrounded by German armies and three Finnish corps, except for Lake Ladoga to the east, where in winter a rail line had been thrown across the ice in order to keep Leningrad from dying. Still, the people of Leningrad were starving to death at a rate of more than two thousand per day, and would do so for another nine months, until the Soviets punched through a narrow land corridor. With water and sewer lines smashed, epidemics raged. German heavy artillery and bombers pummeled the city day and night. By the time the siege was finally lifted in January 1944, more than a million bodies filled communal graves, more fatalities than British and America casualties, military and civilian, combined, for the entire war. Even Dr. Goebbels flinched at the carnage and the stories of cannibalism, confessing to his diary that a Russian deserter's report that "a great part of the population was feeding on so-called human flesh jelly... is so revolting that it makes one's stomach turn to read it." In their dietary need for fat during the horrific winter of 1942, hundreds of thousands of Russians, from Leningrad to the Black Sea, added a touch of axle grease or crankcase oil to whatever rotten food scraps and bones found their way into cook pots. Even if not one more Russian died as a result of Hitler's eastern designs—and almost twenty million would—Leningrad, by the spring of 1942, served up to Joseph Stalin the requisite justification to smash and burn Germany back into the distant hunter-gatherer past whence it came.[206]

Yet he lacked the means to do so. Churchill could promise Stalin only three convoys every two months made up of twenty-five or thirty-five ships each. And even that promise soon proved impossible to keep. With the Arctic days lengthening to more than twenty hours, German air and sea forces based in Norway simply waited near the Arctic Circle for fat targets to heave into view, with the result, Brooke lamented to his diary, that tanks and munitions Britain desperately needed in North Africa ended up at the bottom of the Arctic Ocean. A bitter Stalin reiterated his demands that Churchill and Roosevelt make good on their promise to draw off German troops from the Russian front by an attack in France. But Churchill and Roosevelt lacked the ships even to carry American troops to Britain. Each ship that sailed for Russia reduced by one the number available for Operation Bolero, the buildup of U.S. forces in Britain in preparation for a cross-Channel foray. Each ship that sailed from America to Britain meant one fewer ship to transport to Cairo the troops and tanks that Churchill needed to build a reserve against Rommel, or for deployment to the rest of the Middle East, or India, should the need arise. The final battles of the European war would someday take place on land. Yet, as Churchill had told Molotov during a tutorial on naval power, the war would be won or lost on the oceans. "Everything," Churchill told Roosevelt, "turns upon shipping."[207]

Hitler's generals had advised him the previous year not to fight a two-front war, the classic nightmare of Prussian military strategists. Yet his gamble had so far paid off handsomely. In fact, his war was a one-front war, the Eastern Front. He had to keep a weather eye on Norway, North Africa, the Atlantic, and the Mediterranean and that obstinate rock, Malta. But in the east he had no enemy at his back. Since December, he had faced two enemies at his front—winter, the destroyer of armies, and the Red Army. Neither, by May, had destroyed the Wehrmacht. The early spring *rasputitsa,* the twice-annual Russian wet season, had halted movement as effectively as the cold of winter, yet warm and dry weather was now spreading northward from the Black Sea in ever widening circles. In early May, the German line in northern Russia was anchored just outside Leningrad, where the swamps were still frozen and snow continued to fall. In the center, the line lunged eastward from Smolensk to encompass Rzhev and Vyazma in a huge salient—a bulge. The roads there remained muddy but would dry within the month. Hitler's Führer Directive No. 41 of April 5 stipulated that the line in central Russia—the Moscow front—be held, while in the north, Leningrad be taken. Farther south, the Ukraine front ran from just east of Orel, Kursk, and Kharkov—where the Red Army had forged its own salient—south to the Sea of Azov. In this sector, General Fedor von Bock (who had been called out of retirement) commanded Hitler's Army Group South, which consisted of six German armies, three of them armored, and two satellite armies. This organization was so massive that within weeks it was divided into two army groups, A and B, each with a different objective. Here in the Ukraine, as famously described by Igor Stravinsky, "the violent Russian spring that seemed to begin in an hour and was like the whole earth cracking" had arrived with all its promise. White birch and oak forests wore thin veils of green, and mushrooms pushed through the still damp soil. Ukraine's rivers and streams ran high from the winter snowmelt and spring rains.[208]

To the south, in the Black Sea sector, three German armies under Erich von Manstein controlled most of the Crimea. The *Ostheer* had yet to take Rostov, the Kerch Peninsula, or Sevastopol. This Manstein intended to do. But the main German thrust would begin in the Ukraine sector, where Army Group South (including Friedrich Paulus's Sixth Army and Fourth Panzer Army) was to smash east into the Donets Basin and make for Voronezh, located on the far side of the Don (and which city Bock was ordered to bypass). The Fourth Panzer Army was then to wheel south, keeping the Don on its left flank until it reached the great bend in the Don, just sixty miles from Stalingrad and the Volga—Stalin's last great natural barrier. Hitler decreed, "We must try to reach Stalingrad," and if they could not take it, smash it with artillery and air attacks until it became useless as an industrial base. Army Group South's final objective, after destroying Stalingrad, was to punch south between the Volga and the Don and drive into the north Caucasus hills. Part of this German force, arrayed in the Black Sea sector, was to wheel sharply south, take Rostov-on-Don, and make for the Baku oil fields and the Caucasus Mountains beyond. Vital to the success of the entire enterprise was that once across the Don, these two massive forces move toward the Caucasus shoulder to shoulder, with the Volga on one flank and the Black Sea on the other, across an eight-hundred-mile-wide front. Once the Caucasus were taken, the war in the east would be over. The result, Hitler told Goebbels, would be that Russia "will then be to us what India is to the British."[209]

Hitler named his offensive Operation Blue. Stalin, as he had a year earlier, had gained reliable intelligence as to Hitler's plans, and, as he had a year earlier, he ignored the information. He presumed any action in the Ukraine sector was meant to be a feint, while the real attack would come against Moscow. As he had been a year earlier, Stalin was soon proven wrong. The preliminaries to Operation Blue opened in the Crimea on May 8 with a German dash down the Kerch Peninsula. It was all over within the week. The Germans captured 170,000 Soviet troops, who had dutifully obeyed Stalin's orders to stand firm. Only Sevastopol, surrounded, remained under Soviet control. Then, on May 12, in a bold stroke that took everyone but the Germans by surprise, the Red Army struck at the Kharkov salient with almost 650,000 men, 1,000 airplanes, 13,000 guns, and 1,200 tanks. The counterstroke, approved by Stalin, was the brainchild of the theater commander Semyon Timoshenko, and the political boss of the Ukraine, Nikita Khrushchev. For three days the Soviets drove the Germans westward, but by doing so they exposed their flanks. Although Hitler's worried generals called for a frontal defense of Kharkov, the Führer termed the Soviet attack "a minor blemish" and refused to change his master plan. He was soon proven correct when Paulus and Erwin von Kleist wheeled their armies into the Soviet flanks and within the week encircled the Soviet army. Stalin had no reserves to throw in. By May 22, the Soviet defeat was total, with almost 240,000 Soviet prisoners taken, and most of the guns and all the tanks lost. Khrushchev, summoned to Moscow by Stalin to explain how it had all gone wrong, presumed he'd be shot. That Khrushchev survived his inquisition was not due to mercy on Stalin's part—the concept was alien to the man—but because Stalin believed in the motivational power of terror.[210]

The Kharhov and Kerch battles had cost Stalin more than 410,000 killed and captured even before the curtain went up on Operation Blue. Given that few of the Red Army prisoners would survive the German slave labor camps, Russian losses that May measured twice the combined Union and Confederate battlefield deaths during the American Civil War, and almost half of British and Dominion battlefield deaths during the four years of the Great War. Hitler, a serious student of Clausewitz, was holding to the Prussian's dictum to annihilate enemy armies rather than try to capture cities. By the end of May, all roads east and south lay open to the Germans.[211]

Months earlier Churchill made a grim prediction to King George, who recorded it in his diary: "If by the spring, Russia was down and out, and Germany was renewing its blitzkrieg here, all our hopes of victory and help from USA would be dashed if America had not by then sent us masses of planes etc." The King seems to have confused "blitzkrieg" and "blitz," but no matter, Hitler would launch both against Britain were Stalin to go down before America tooled up.[212]

On May 31 Roosevelt cabled Churchill: "I have a very strong feeling that the Russian position is precarious, and may grow steadily worse during the coming weeks."[213]

Roosevelt's pessimism stemmed in part from two days of talks with Soviet foreign minister Molotov, who had arrived in Washington from

London on May 29 with demands for an immediate second European front and a doubling in Lend-Lease aid, without both of which the Soviet position loomed dire at best. Regarding the latter demand, Roosevelt explained that each ship that went to Russia meant one fewer ship to build up forces in Britain for the very second front Molotov sought. To placate Molotov on that point, Roosevelt agreed to release an official announcement (which had been dictated by Molotov) after Molotov returned to Moscow: "In the course of the conversations full understanding was reached with regard to the urgent tasks of creating a Second Front in Europe in 1942." Here was Roosevelt at his most politically astute, for he knew that Churchill considered such a front in 1942 a strategic impossibility. The president had served the ball into Churchill's court. Yet, Harriman later wrote, Roosevelt felt that raising Soviet expectations for a second front could only bolster Soviet morale, an end in itself. Soviet morale was about the only thing Roosevelt could boost because, as he told Molotov, the U-boats prevented the boosting of Soviet matériel. Harriman acknowledged that Roosevelt's statement "provided employment for a whole generation of... historians who solemnly argued its merits" in myriad books and journals. Yet the measure of an event has to be taken in the immediate context of the times, and at the time, Roosevelt's pledge helped preserve the alliance, even if it amounted to a Potemkin village of a promise.[214]

Molotov had spent the week before his Washington visit in London, where he and Eden had negotiated a twenty-year treaty of peace in which the Soviets agreed to address the issue of borders only after the war was won. Churchill had been prepared to jettison his long-standing position on that subject and accede to Stalin's demands regarding prewar borders and the Baltic states. Churchill later wrote: "My opinions about the Baltic states were, and are, unaltered, but I felt I could not carry them farther forward at that time." Cordell Hull furiously disagreed, and in a cable to Winant, approved by Roosevelt, threatened to disavow the entire business if Britain appeased Stalin. For Hull, at stake were the tenets of the Atlantic Charter. As well, he insisted that all border issues were to be settled after the war by a new world organization (which he championed mightily). An open break loomed for the alliance. Then Roosevelt suggested to the British that a verbal *promise* of a second front "should take the heat off Russia's diplomatic demands upon England" regarding postwar borders. Eden made the pitch, and to his surprise and relief Molotov went for it. It was a masterful bit of negotiation, one that kept both the Russians and Americans happy, and the alliance intact.[215]

With Roosevelt's promise in hand Molotov returned to London for the formal signing of the friendship treaty. But he arrived bearing a new demand: that the British put *in writing* their own guarantee of a second front. Churchill tried to impress upon Molotov that Britain in Western Europe and North Africa was tying up almost one-half of Luftwaffe fighter strength and one-third of its bombers. Thirty-three Axis divisions sat idle in Western Europe, and eleven more, including two armored divisions, fought on in North Africa. That Britain and America had not launched a second front of the exact sort Stalin sought did not mean they were not forcing Hitler to spread his forces thin. The Allies might not be killing many Germans in the west, Churchill argued, but neither were those Germans killing any Russians. Molotov listened politely, but he still wanted his guarantee. And so to placate both the Americans and the Soviets, Churchill drafted a communiqué for Molotov to take home. It was similar to Roosevelt's promise, and stated "full understanding was reached with regard to the urgent task of creating a second front in Europe in 1942." With that "understanding" in hand, it appeared to Molotov that *both* the Americans and the British had given him what he wanted. In fact, they had given him nothing. Understanding the need to open a second front and doing something about it was not the same thing. To further clarify his (somewhat disingenuous) promise, Churchill composed an aide-mémoire to Stalin in which he reiterated his belief in the need for a second front: "We are making preparations for a landing on the Continent in August or September, 1942." Then Churchill added the caveat that all was conditional and nothing was guaranteed: "We can therefore give no promise to the matter." Molotov left London for Moscow on June 10, and dutifully passed Churchill's letter and his logic on to Stalin, who didn't buy any of it.[216]

Molotov's party had stayed at Chequers during the earlier treaty negotiations, at which time burly Russian bodyguards and two (also burly) Russian chambermaids attended to the needs of Molotov and his two aides. The bodyguards swept the bedrooms for listening devices—"infernal machines"—Churchill called them. Revolvers were dutifully placed on Molotov's bedside table and under the diplomats' pillows. Their beds were made up to leave an opening in the middle of the bedcovers "out of which the occupant could spring" were assassins to appear on the scene. The maids sat without a word on chairs outside their bosses' doors day and night. The entire scene struck Churchill as peculiar. But Churchill, in turn, treated the Russians to an unforgettable experience. They witnessed him at rest, which was a relative concept. Churchill's visits to Chequers afforded him a chance to unwind, and to do so in company of his choosing (although the Russians were an exception to that rule).[217]

The diary entries and letters of visitors to Chequers cast light on a consistent Churchillian pattern of behavior: nobody got as wound up unwinding as Churchill did. The heavier his previous week's burdens, the greater his need for an Alice in Wonderland weekend, as Brooke called them.

Thus, the sense of "anticipation" within the ranks noted by Ian Jacob whenever Churchill appeared at Chequers. Brooke later wrote that he took away no "happy memories" from these long and liquid weekends, each evening "extending well into the morning hours." The Old Man relaxed with a fury, and always with a quotient of wit and good cheer in inverse proportion to what might fairly be expected from a man who had just suffered a terrible week, and most of the weeks since May 1940 had brought terrible news of one sort or another.[218]

The week of Molotov's first visit was no exception. While Eden and the Russian worked out the details of the treaty, Erwin Rommel sent the British Eighth Army packing. On May 26 Rommel swung around General Ritchie's Gazala Line south of Bir Hacheim. Ritchie was not ready. Worse, although he outnumbered Rommel in tanks 700 to 560, he had not massed his tanks in order to strike Rommel's vanguard. Rommel, as usual, *had* massed his tanks. He expected to break Ritchie's lines in a day, but he ran up against General William ("Strafer") Gott and his XIII Corps along with a brigade of Free French. Gott and the French gave Rommel more of a fight than he had yet experienced in North Africa. It took the Desert Fox ten days to clear out the truculent French, who then took to calling themselves the Fighting French. But by then, Ritchie had lost control of the battle.[219]

Once again, the desert winds had turned against Churchill, who often appears in his colleagues' diaries at his most animated after having taken just such a hard military hit. Talking (at length) was Churchill's way, recalled John Martin, "of clearing his head." He talked at the table and he talked on the march. His staff had been delighted when he insisted on the installation of a movie projector at Chequers: "We thought if we had a nice film in the evening he would go to bed," John Martin recalled. "But far from it; he started all over again after the films."[220]

During his weekends of rest he displayed the uncanny ability to work, relax, and rage simultaneously. After telling dinner guests one evening that he hoped victory would bring "an end to bloodshed," he followed with "I must confess I would like to see Mussolini, that bogus mimic of ancient Rome, strangled like Vercingetorix in old Roman fashion." Hitler he would exile to some remote island, "though he would not so desecrate St. Helena." He soon took a harder stand on Hitler's fate, telling the cabinet, "This man is the mainspring of evil. Instrument—electric chair for gangsters no doubt available through Lend Lease." He liked to pepper his dinner-table asides and speeches with the sort of clichés favored by Moscow propagandists in attacks on the bourgeois West (until the alliance): "hyena," "lackey," "dupe," "flunky," "jackal." When used by *Pravda,* such phrases conjured up in Englishmen images of raving Reds, but they worked for Churchill. His often preposterous asides were easily misconstrued as the mirthful musings of a merry old man. They were anything but. Hopkins was more correct than he knew when he quipped that Churchill must have read only the Old Testament.[221]

Along with Molotov, spring had arrived in Britain—the traditional invasion season. Travel by British civilians to the south coastal regions was restricted, as in the previous two years. The word in the pubs was that the Allies were building up armies down on the coast and getting ready to jump a big one across the Channel. The Allies were doing nothing of the sort. In fact, Churchill told Molotov, defenses were fully manned with the expectation that the Germans would arrive if Moscow capitulated. He offered that pessimistic assessment only after Molotov had asked, what will England do if the Red Army collapses? Out came the maps, and Churchill commenced a lesson on the difference between land powers and sea powers. It had become clear to him that neither Stalin nor Molotov understood a fundamental truth: the Allies could not win on land until the seas were cleared of Germans. He told Molotov that he was confident that, backed by American industrial might, the Allies would win, but he stressed, as he had to the King, that if the Red Army collapsed, Hitler would turn toward England.[222]

In that case, he expected Britons to offer themselves up by the scores of thousands. "It would be better," he told Colville the previous July, "to make this island a sea of blood than to surrender." Those were Stalin's sentiments exactly regarding Russians, dictated to his terrorized subordinates from the dacha where he took his weekend rest. His orders to stand firm were dutifully executed by Russians as the mounting slaughter in his country bore out. At Hitler's Berchtesgaden retreat, the *Berghof,* the topic of defending the homeland had not arisen during weekend retreats. The Führer and his cronies consumed tea and pastries while Hitler delivered monologues on the Roman Empire, Jews, and Christianity (and how its "mendacity and hypocrisy" had sapped Nordic development). In the evenings the Führer strolled mountain paths while he opined at length in the company of his Alsatian bitch, Blondi, and his cohorts—Goebbels, Himmler, Bormann, and Göring. They never discussed defeat. And for good reason: they were winning.[223]

On the night of May 30–31—the day Roosevelt cabled to Churchill his deep concern about the Russian front—the RAF threw everything it had against Germany, a demonstration of power and destruction that Churchill hoped would underscore the validity of his claim that the aerial front was indeed a real second front. That night, more than 1,100 British heavy bombers plastered Cologne, ushering in a short-lived era of thousand-bomber raids. The chief of the RAF's Bomber Command, Arthur ("Bomber") Harris, faced with American opposition to the shipment of even more B-17s to Britain (the planes were accumulating on airfields), conceived the idea of massive nighttime raids in order to show the Americans the efficiency of the British strategic air offensive. Harris had to put crews still undergoing training into his bombers in order to assemble a fleet large enough to carry out his plans. He had waited almost two years for the opportunity to punish Germany with such force. In the autumn of 1940, while surveying the destruction the Luftwaffe had inflicted on London, he offered a bit of Old Testament wisdom to his superior, Air Marshal Charles Portal: "Well, they are sowing the wind." Harris now intended that they would reap the whirlwind. Portal believed the RAF could bring Germany to its knees—and the war to an end—sometime in late 1943. Churchill was far less sure. His oft-stated wish to make Germans bleed and burn aside, on the strategic efficacy of bombing Germany, Churchill had offered to Portal, "I have my own opinion about that, namely, that it is not decisive, but is better than doing nothing." In Churchill's estimation, the immediate value of RAF bombing lay in showing the Russians that Britain was doing something. Intending to do much more, Churchill proclaimed the raid "a herald of what Germany will receive city by city from now on."[224]

It had been more than fifteen months since he had asked Lord Cherwell to devise a punishing, retaliatory bombing strategy. It had been less than five months since Bomber Harris was promoted to air marshal and brought to Bomber Command his strategic bombing philosophy, that volume trumps accuracy. It was a strategy born of necessity, since the accuracy of British night raiders was still pathetic; fewer than one-quarter of RAF bombs fell near their targets. Harris would have preferred a scalpel, but he was handed a cudgel. Among the RAF's unintended targets that spring was the ancestral home of Thomas Mann. Better known as the Buddenbrookhaus, the house had stood in the Baltic port city of Lübeck for two hundred years. In fact, 80 percent of the old city of Lübeck was destroyed in what Goebbels called "the British craze for destruction." Mann, safely ensconced in a California bungalow, broadcast a message back to Germany: "I remember Coventry and realize that everything must be paid back." Such were Bomber Harris's sentiments exactly.[225]

Within days of the Cologne raid, the Ministry of Information sent to Russia thousands of propaganda posters: "We lost 44 planes on that [Cologne] raid, but we are prepared to give our lives to destroy Fascism, as you are giving yours. The Fascists will not be able to stand the hell we shall give them together." But from Stalin's perspective, faced as he was with almost two million Germans rolling toward Leningrad, Moscow, Stalingrad, and the Caucasus oil fields, the British were neither giving enough hell nor sacrificing enough men.

Two nights after Harris's heavies smashed Cologne, more than 950 bombers hit Essen, selected as a target specifically because its ancient wood houses and warehouses would fall easy prey to incendiary bombs. A month later, 1,000 of Harris's fleet visited Breman. The bombers flew in new "streaming" formations, a parade of death that stretched from the target almost all the way back to the North Sea. RAF bombing accuracy, though still dismal, had been improved somewhat by the development of the "shaker" system, whereby planes equipped with the latest electronic navigation systems flew ahead and marked targets with flares and then a next wave of aircraft deposited loads of incendiary bombs on the target, thus providing a concentrated area of fire where the bombers of the main force could drop their high-explosive bombs. The results were devastating. Harris enthused to the press, "Give me a thousand bombers over Germany every night, and I will end the war by October. Give me 20,000 and I will stop it in a single night." The RAF's massed raids impressed the Americans, as Harris intended. Deliveries of B-17s and the American pilots and crews to man them spiked upward. German civilians got the message as well; while Russian and British soldiers as yet posed no threat to Germans, British bombers could get through to burn German cities. Yet Harris took away new and distressing knowledge: his nightly losses, more than 5 percent, were too high, and his resources were too meager to sustain such losses. He needed the Americans to get up to speed, but the American Eighth Air Force had yet to fly a mission.[226]

The Cologne raid was seen by many in Britain and the United States as retaliation for the Luftwaffe's Baedeker raids of April, so named because Göring had targeted several British national treasures that had earned honorifics in the *Baedeker Guide,* including Bath, Canterbury Cathedral, Bury St. Edmunds, and Ipswich. Britons joked that German pilots flew with a copy of *Baedeker* propped next to the bomb sight. It was a time, wrote Mollie Panter-Downes, when owning "a house next door to Anne Hathaway's cottage is...an uncomfortable liability...not a picturesque asset." RAF response to the Baedeker raids was swift. In America, the *New Republic* parsed the question of whether it was retaliatory as well, and concluded that although Cologne had not been an act of revenge, the Allies should continually weigh both sides of the question in order to avoid any action that could "stain our record in the war or drag us down to the Nazi level."[227]

* * *

Americans and Britons had not yet fully grasped just how low the Nazi level in fact was. Within days of the Cologne raid, Berlin demonstrated the real nature of cold-blooded retaliation, and it was not about Cologne. Goebbels and his Führer had been mulling over for some time the best and most efficient manner to confiscate the property of those convicted—and executed—for treasonous actions or speech, or for simply being born racially impure. When Goebbels suggested that the confiscation of "terrorists'" bicycles would send a message to would-be troublemakers, Hitler "regarded this proposal as wonderful" and ordered its implementation. For almost three years, far more disproportionate Nazi retaliation against civilians (such as one hundred hostages shot for each German killed) for wrongs against the Reich had been well documented in the West—photos of hanging bodies, firing squads, pushcarts in Warsaw full of emaciated corpses. German vengeance was so swift and terrifying that some of Churchill's advisers in Special Operations cautioned against taking isolated direct action (assassinations and large-scale sabotage) on the Continent until an Allied invasion was imminent, in order to protect civilians from German retribution. Yet Churchill had urged Special Operations to "set Europe ablaze." As usual with implementing any such edict, timing is critical.[228]

That lesson was learned in London after Reinhard ("the Hangman") Heydrich, genius behind the Final Solution and deputy chief of the Gestapo, was assassinated in Prague by the British-trained Czech resistance fighters whom the RAF had parachuted into the country five months earlier. The assassins struck on May 27, lobbing a bomb into Heydrich's Mercedes coupe, shattering the Hangman's spine. He lingered for a week before dying a ghastly death from blood poisoning and infections caused by festering tufts of upholstery that had blown into his gut. Germany's minister of justice—Hitler—moved swiftly to punish the evildoers. More than 1,300 Czechs were immediately executed. More than 100 Czechs—including the assassins—took refuge in a Prague church, where they were all killed. But that was only the beginning. More than 3,000 Jews were transported from the "privileged" concentration camp of Theresienstadt to their deaths in the east. Goebbels, on the day Heydrich was attacked, had 500 of the few remaining Jews in Berlin rounded up; more than 150 were shot the night Heydrich died.[229]

Then the Reich took the blood-letting to levels not anticipated by anyone, including Churchill. On the morning of June 9, a battalion of German security police surrounded the fourteenth-century Czech village of Lidice. Nobody was allowed to leave. The next day the men and boys over age sixteen of the village, 172 in all, were taken behind a barn in groups of ten and shot. Several women were shot, too, and the rest—almost 200—were sent to slave labor camps in Germany. At the local hospital, the Germans found four women who had just given birth. The newborns were murdered, the mothers shipped off to labor camps. The village children, about 90 in all, were sent to Germany, where, if medical professionals established their Aryan purity, they were placed with good Nazi families. Before departing Lidice, the Security Police burned the village, dynamited the ruins, and bulldozed the rubble into a flat, dead landscape, including the cemetery, where the interred had been dug up and bulldozed back into the soil. Berlin ordered the entire operation be photographed. Goebbels called the result his *Gemäldegalerie* (picture gallery). Then, Goebbels announced the details of the Lidice operation to the world, lest anyone else have the temerity to murder another one of Hitler's favorites. It was a tale even Bracken's disinformation wizards could not have conjured in their most macabre moments.[230]

Lidice, Goebbels proclaimed, was justice administered, not retaliation for Cologne. However, he added, if the Allies did not cease the mass bombing of German cities, "he would exterminate Germany's Jews." In fact, he had confessed to his diary almost three months earlier that at least 60 percent of the Jews transported to the east were to be "liquidated," the remaining 40 percent were to become slave laborers, and worked to death. In this regard, the little doctor proved himself a man of his word.[231]

The full extent of the British role in Heydrich's assassination was not revealed for over fifty years. Hugh Dalton, head of SOE and considered a "blabber" who might promise Churchill something he couldn't deliver, was kept in the dark by his subordinates in the Czech section. There is no record of Churchill approving the operation, but SOE had been created as a standalone entity, the better to facilitate plausible deniability. Churchill mentions neither the assassination nor Heydrich in his memoir of the war.[232]

In a broadcast ten months before the Lidice massacre, Churchill proclaimed that "scores of thousands—literally scores of thousands" of Russians had been executed by the Germans. He couched his words in terms of reports from visiting British generals, but his real source was impeccable. German commanders, with their penchant for precise bookkeeping, radioed the death tallies directly to Berlin, and therefore to Bletchley. Thousands of victims were described as "Jewish plunderers" and "Jewish bolshevists." This Churchill chose not to share with the public. He cautioned that the slaughter was "but the beginning" and went on to predict that "famine and pestilence" would "follow in the bloody ruts of Hitler's tanks." The Führer, he declared, was outkilling even his Teutonic ancestors. And not since the Mongols came in the thirteenth century had Europe seen such "methodical, merciless butchery" on such a monstrous scale. "We are in the presence," he concluded, "of a crime without a name." From the Ukraine to the Baltic states, from the Jewish ghetto in Warsaw where four hundred thousand souls existed on rotten flour and foul water, to Holland

and to occupied France and Belgium, the crime grew more monstrous by the day. The previous October, the prison camp for political prisoners at Auschwitz, about forty miles west of Krakow, was enlarged in order to accommodate tens of thousands of prisoners, mostly Jewish. The new camp, Birkenau, was built not as a forced labor camp but as an extermination facility. In late 1941, the SS conducted tests of the gas Zyklon B on Jewish and Russian prisoners in the camp basements. Satisfied with the deadly results, the SS set to work building industrial gas chambers and crematoria that could process two thousand bodies at a time. By mid-1942, a few—very few—escapees from Auschwitz had brought news of the genocide to the West. At the time, the tales could not be verified. The crime Churchill cited still had no name. But Goebbels' *Gemäldegalerie* had given it a face.[233]

By June 12 Churchill felt that a meeting between himself and Roosevelt was past due. They needed to unravel the tangled mess created during Marshall's April visit, to settle on an objective for their armies, and to discuss "Tube Alloys," the atomic bomb project. On that topic, there was not a great deal to discuss; unbeknownst to Churchill, the Americans were about to contract for *all* of Canada's uranium. (It would be almost a year before Churchill learned the extent of America's uranium dealings.) In any case, Britain had no money in its Exchequer to build an atomic bomb, even if it could procure the uranium to do so. The Americans would have to carry the ball on atomic research, and carry it quickly. It was well known in both Washington and London that the Germans were trying to use "heavy water"—available in large quantities as a by-product of ammonia production at a Norwegian hydroelectric plant—to serve as a moderating solution in the creation of element 94 (plutonium) from uranium. Goebbels months earlier had scribbled in his diary one of his more prescient thoughts: "Research in the realm of atomic destruction has now proceeded to a point where its results may possibly be made use of in this war.... Tremendous destruction can be wrought.... It is essential that we be ahead of everybody, for whoever introduces a revolutionary novelty into this war has the greater chance of winning it."[234]

But it was not only the future of atomic research or the timing of the second European front that spurred Churchill's request for a meeting with Roosevelt, but also a naval battle that began in the Pacific on June 4. Churchill had predicted in January that the Americans would regain fleet superiority in the Pacific by May or June, a wildly optimistic assessment based on no empirical evidence. He simply ignored the fact that Admiral

Yamamoto had proven himself the most daring and successful naval strategist of the century, if not of all time. A more realistic line of thought would hold that if the Americans built more capital ships, Yamamoto would sink them.

Yet Churchill's hunch paid off on the morning of June 4 near Midway Island. Yamamoto intended to take Midway that day, and to annihilate the American fleet, which he expected to come in search of his own forces. As usual, his plan was complex, and it depended upon the Americans doing exactly what he expected. Five Japanese naval task forces participated; in aggregate strength at that point, the Japanese force was greater than the Royal Navy's Atlantic and Home fleets combined, and it dwarfed anything the Americans could send to meet it. One Japanese force made for the Aleutian Islands, where it shelled the airbase at Dutch Harbor and occupied the islands of Attu and Kiska, at the western end of the chain. Four Japanese task forces made for Midway, consisting of an advance guard of sixteen submarines and an occupation force of five thousand men in twelve transports protected by two battleships and a bevy of cruisers and destroyers. Then came the big guns: Nagumo's Pearl Harbor Strike Force of four heavy aircraft carriers, well screened by cruisers, and shadowed by seven battleships, on one of which Yamamoto put his flag. In all, more than 160 Japanese warships and support craft were involved. The strike at the Aleutians, intended to draw away Admiral Chester Nimitz's forces, began at sunrise on June 3. By nightfall on the third, with his plan unfolding flawlessly, Yamamoto prepared to execute the final two phases: the occupation of Midway while the Americans presumably sailed north on a wild goose chase, and then the deployment of his fleet to hunt down and annihilate Nimitz's navy. But Nimitz's code breakers had parsed a strand of the Japanese naval code, which told them exactly where Yamamoto and his main force were headed: Midway.[235]

As Yamamoto steamed for Midway, Nimitz prepared an ambush northeast of the island, in an empty swath of the sea that flanked Yamamoto's expected course. Nimitz threw in his lot—the aircraft carriers *Hornet, Yorktown,* and *Enterprise,* along with as many cruisers and destroyers as he could afford. He put in no battleships because he had no battleships. At first things went exceedingly well for the Japanese. Just after daybreak on June 4, they bombed Midway, and then they massacred forty-three misnamed Devastator torpedo bombers from Nimitz's carriers that had the misfortune of locating the Japanese fleet. Sixty American dive-bombers dispatched from Midway along with more planes from U.S. carriers failed to even locate Yamamoto's ships. Shortly after 10:00 A.M., and for about two minutes, Yamamoto thought he had won the battle, and the war. He ordered his bombers re-armed and refueled for another run at

Midway. But the slaughter of the low-flying American torpedo planes had left Yamamoto's shield of Zero Fighters buzzing around his ships almost at sea level when they should have been hovering protectively high overhead. No commander on any Japanese bridge took note of this. Then, a few seconds before 10:26 A.M., three dozen Dauntless dive-bombers from *Enterprise* cruising at 14,000 feet beheld below four Japanese aircraft carriers, the fattest of targets, and the pride of Yamamoto's fleet. The carriers' decks were crammed with refueling aircraft, gasoline lines, bombs, and torpedoes. The U.S. Navy pilots rolled their planes and nosed down. Within six minutes the tide of war in the Pacific was reversed in a maelstrom of exploding fuel and bombs on the blazing flight decks of three of Yamamoto's crippled carriers, including *Akagi,* which had led the attacks on Pearl Harbor, Darwin, Colombo, and Rabaul, the New Britain port that since its capture in January served as the Japanese base of operations in the South Pacific.[236]

Six minutes. Here indeed was a small agate point of the sort Churchill relished and upon which fortunes turned.

Churchill cabled his "heartiest congratulations" to Roosevelt. The battle, he wrote, had "very decidedly altered the balance of the Naval war." Here he fell into characteristic hyperbole, except in this case he was absolutely correct. The balance in the Pacific had shifted so dramatically that he now worried that Admiral King—with the American people fully behind him—might persuade Roosevelt to finish off Japan before taking on Germany. King, who in fact was thinking along those lines, elicited the support of Marshall (still disgruntled over his April mishandling by Churchill), and the two began plotting just such a Pacific-first policy. Roosevelt quashed it. Still, Marshall planned to ship five times as many troops to MacArthur as to Britain, and was already shipping scores of B-17s to the Pacific that had been destined for Britain. The American chiefs appeared ready to abandon Europe-first. This disquieting prospect—in conjunction with Rommel's latest misdeeds—led Churchill, in the same telegram, to call for a meeting with Roosevelt: "I feel it is my duty to come and see you."[237]

Prospects in Africa were troubling. Rommel had paused for a week in early June after bending back Ritchie's southern flank and throwing the Eighth Army into disarray. Initially outnumbered, by mid-June the Germans held a two-to-one edge in tanks. Tobruk, and the 35,000 mostly South African, mostly green troops holed up there, lay exposed just thirty miles to Ritchie's rear. The Tobruk garrison had been told by headquarters that if circumstances developed as they appeared to be developing, the plan called for an evacuation, not a defense. Yet Ritchie failed to order either an evacuation or a buildup of the city's defenses. He had lost control of events, and of the battle. Auchinleck presumed Ritchie would stick to the fall-back-and-evacuate plan; Churchill presumed Auchinleck would hold the city. Auchinleck had infuriated Churchill three months earlier when he claimed he would not be ready to attack until mid-June. When Rommel first struck in late May, the question became, would Auchinleck be ready to *defend* by mid-June? When Rommel lunged out of his positions on June 13 to send Ritchie's army reeling even farther east, the answer became self-evident.[238]

Thus, with American fortunes on the rise in the Pacific while British fortunes again evaporated in the desert, Churchill fretted over a disruption in the Europe-first strategy. Although Roosevelt was firmly disabusing his military men of their Pacific inclinations, no plans existed for a European thrust. Roosevelt wanted something done about that. Years later Marshall told Admiral Samuel Eliot Morison that "the one great lesson he learned in 1942 was that the political leaders must 'do something'; they could not afford the impression of fighting another 'phony war' that year." The U-boat war wasn't phony in the least, and the Allies were losing it. Rommel appeared unstoppable. Russia, again, stood unsteadily at the precipice, and Hitler, again, seemed poised to push the Soviets off. Three days after congratulating Roosevelt on his victory at Midway, Churchill made ready to return to Washington.[239]

The two leaders had to work out the business of where to attack the Germans, of where best to *do something*. Their desperate ally in Moscow wanted to know not only where but when, and more specifically how soon. On June 16, before departing London for Washington, Churchill wrote a letter to King George asking the King's "gracious permission" to propose that the King appoint Eden—"an outstanding minister"—to form a new government should Churchill be killed en route. Then Churchill and his entourage, minuscule compared with his January host, departed the capital. Dr. Wilson, with his supply of sleeping pills, came along, as did Pug Ismay, John Martin, stenographer Patrick Kinna, Frank Sawyers, the valet with Churchill's whisky, and Inspector Thompson with his revolver. Commander Tommy Thompson, Churchill's naval aide, and Brigadier D. G. Stewart, the director of War Plans, also made the trip. Shortly after arriving in Strannraer, Scotland, late on the seventeenth, the group boarded a Boeing flying boat captained by the self-same Captain Kelly Rogers who had flown Churchill home from Bermuda. Churchill, wielding a gold-topped Malacca walking stick and dressed in a siren suit topped off with a black Homburg, was quite animated. But remembering that long and dangerous flight home in January, he was heard by Brooke humming a favorite tune of Tommies during the Great War, "We're here because we're here, because we're here."[240]

They cruised at five thousand feet, high enough to see the red smear of the solstice twilight on the northern horizon. Brooke was entirely enthralled by his first trans-Atlantic flight. Unfamiliar with the jargon of airmen, he noted in his diary that he slept well "after paying a visit to the pilot in his driving compartment on top bridge." All aboard were bemused by the fact that their watches, as they crossed time zones, no longer kept time with the sun. Brooke consulted his watch to determine when in "real time" he might take breakfast. Churchill consulted neither the sun nor his watch but his stomach. For the duration of the war on such journeys Churchill took his meals on "stomach-time" regardless of what his timepiece or the sun told him. Tommy Thompson recalled that on that voyage, as the flying boat neared the American coast, the passengers discussed "the advisability of having lunch or high tea before arrival." The question was put to Churchill, who "settled it with a flat statement that it was time for 'high whisky.'" Sawyers produced the beverages. Captain Rogers took the party over fog-bound Nantucket Shoals and began the run down to Washington. Churchill took his usual seat in the co-pilot's chair. Three hours later, as Rogers ran low up the Potomac, Churchill, spotting the Washington Monument and ever alert to navigational dangers, warned Rogers "that it would be particularly unfortunate if we brought our story to an end by hitting this of all other objects in the world." After almost twenty-seven hours, the big plane skimmed up the Potomac and floated to a stop. On board, it was "stomach-time." The evening meal was served as the party bobbed on the river in the fetid, still air of a Washington summer evening, in the sort of close heat that had driven every president since John Adams to seek relief elsewhere, which is exactly what Roosevelt had done, having decamped to his nine-hundred-acre Hyde Park estate, where cool breezes fanned his forested haven high above the Hudson River.[241]

Churchill and his party spent the night of the eighteenth at the British embassy. Rommel spent that night directing his engineers—"sappers" to the British—toward the British minefields in front of Tobruk. Earlier in the day, his panzers had broken Ritchie's lines, which meandered from Tobruk about thirty miles to the south, where they gave out in a naked flank. Ritchie had chosen to stand firm there when his Gazala Line broke two weeks earlier. A better choice would have been to clear out of Tobruk and fall back nearer to the Egyptian frontier. With his lines broken, that is exactly what Ritchie now attempted. But the day's battle lurched eastward so quickly that Tobruk and its garrison were bypassed. By nightfall the city was surrounded, retreat and resupply impossible. Churchill had told Auchinleck three days earlier that he expected Tobruk to be held. Rommel intended otherwise. On the nineteenth, as Churchill made for Hyde Park, Rommel, his path through the minefields cleared, made straight for Tobruk.[242]

Churchill brought to Hyde Park a memorandum that he had composed for Roosevelt in which he argued that any attempt to invade France that year had no "chance of success unless the Germans became utterly demoralized, of which there is no likelihood." What then to do, he asked Roosevelt, in a manner that answered his own questions: "Have the American staffs a plan? At what points would they strike?" And what of shipping and landing craft? Roosevelt had no answers. Operation Bolero, the buildup of forces in Britain, should continue, Churchill offered, but with an eye to striking somewhere other than France. As Churchill saw things, that left northern Norway (Operation Jupiter) or North Africa (Operation Gymnast) as the only alternatives. During two days of relaxed talks above the Hudson, Roosevelt pondered Churchill's memo but made no commitments. He did agree verbally and informally to exchange information on the atomic bomb project. More important, Roosevelt pledged to fund the entire project. Yet, as Churchill would learn within months, the Americans, for security reasons (or for political reasons couched as security concerns), intended to exchange only information that Britain could use to construct weapons on British soil. Since Britain could in no way build the facilities in which to construct an atomic bomb, the Americans began withholding information.[243]

Churchill and Roosevelt returned to Washington early on the twenty-first. Later that morning, as Roosevelt, Churchill, and Pug Ismay chatted in the president's study, an aide entered and handed Roosevelt a telegram. He glanced at the contents and passed it to Churchill. It read: "Tobruk has surrendered with twenty-five thousand men taken prisoner." Churchill, thinking it must be a mistake, sent Ismay off to get the facts. Presently Ismay returned to not only confirm the fall of Tobruk but advise Churchill that much of the remaining British fleet at Alexandria had been sent south of the Suez Canal to avoid exposure to the Luftwaffe attacks that were expected any minute. Churchill, for a change, was speechless. He later wrote that the shock of the loss was great, but even more shocking was the performance of the army. Singapore, and now Tobruk, had destroyed the reputation of the British army. "Defeat is one thing," he wrote, "disgrace is another." After a moment of respectful silence, Roosevelt leaned forward and asked, "What can we do to help?" Churchill asked the president to ship at once as many new Sherman tanks as he could spare. Roosevelt summoned Marshall, who reported that a few hundred brand-new Shermans were on their way to American armored divisions. He added that it would be a shame to take them away from his men, but if Britain needed them, they'd be on their way. Within days, three hundred new tanks, many so new they lacked engines, were loaded onto five cargo ships. A sixth ship carried the engines. When it was sunk by U-boats, Roosevelt dispatched another. Roosevelt also tossed in one hundred self-propelled 105mm guns. It was a gesture Churchill never forgot. But at the time, given Rommel's genius for tank warfare, and given the decimation of the British desert army in terms of men, machines, and morale, it remained to be seen whether the American tanks would arrive in time to save Cairo.[244]

Over the next four days, Rommel struck deep into Egypt; on June 25 he took Mersa Matruh, just 140 miles from Alexandria. That evening Auchinleck flew out to the front, relieved Ritchie of command, and took personal command of the Eighth Army. The citizens of Cairo and Alexandria were now as distressed as the disintegrating Eighth Army. Panicked Alexandrians caused a run on Barclays Bank. Merchants in Cairo sold out their inventories of luggage within hours. A steady drizzle of ashes fell onto Cairo's streets, the result of the British high command's burning of secret papers. Rommel was expected, and soon. Auchinleck, meanwhile, took his ragged army seventy miles east, to a defensible neck of sand that ran forty miles from El Alamein on the sea to the edge of the great Qattara Depression, a natural obstacle that even Rommel dared not challenge. Rommel paused, too. He intended to wait and hit the British head-on as soon as he was reinforced. Until then, he would bide his time west of El Alamein—just 60 miles west of Alexandria and 140 miles northwest of Cairo—with just a dozen tanks fit for battle.[245]

It was then that Benito Mussolini decided his presence was called for upon the field of battle. Mussolini's motto was *"Il Duce ha sempre ragione"* ("Mussolini is always right"). By the last days of June, he was convinced that Rommel, now poised before El Alamein, would push the final miles to Alexandria, and then to Cairo. The marshal of the Empire—the highest rank in the Italian military, created by Mussolini for himself—journeyed to Derna, where a magnificent pure-white stallion groomed for his triumphant entrance into Cairo waited in its stall for its magnificent rider. Resplendent in his pure-white uniform, Mussolini inspected the troops in Bardia, more than two hundred miles from the action. There he awaited Rommel's invitation. But Rommel had stopped replying to Mussolini's communiqués. Mussolini ended his adventure at Bardia. Rommel, his lines drawn tight at El Alamein, awaited the infusion of tanks and gasoline and men that he had been promised, and that he needed in order to drive to Alexandria and east to Iraq. But RAF cryptologists were reading messages between Berlin and Rommel, with the result that when Berlin radioed the departure date of German supply ships sailing from Italy to Tobruk, RAF pilots started their engines. There was hope yet for the Desert Rats.[246]

Shortly after Churchill learned of the disaster at Tobruk, Harry Hopkins suggested he meet two American generals whom the president and Marshall held in high regard, major generals Mark Clark and Dwight D. Eisenhower. Just two years earlier both had held the rank of lieutenant colonel. Both had since risen high in the ranks due in large part to having earned Marshall's complete loyalty. Eisenhower, fifty-one and Clark's senior by five years, had never held an active field command. He had been promoted to brigadier general less than a year earlier; within days he would arrive in London a major general and gain a third and fourth star within a year. His only field experience was administrative—as chief of staff of the 3rd Division during the Louisiana maneuvers the previous summer, where the audacious tactics of George Patton's 2nd Armored Division had much impressed Eisenhower. Yet Eisenhower had shown Marshall his stuff soon after Pearl Harbor, when given the task of getting relief to his old boss, Douglas MacArthur. Eisenhower failed, but not for want of effort; there simply was no relief to give at the time. He had since labored for Marshall as deputy chief of staff in the War Plans division, or had until the previous week, when Eisenhower—his friends called him Ike—finally got his field command, the biggest of them all: commander of the U.S. Expeditionary Force assembling in Britain. Clark would go along as Eisenhower's deputy.

Churchill, prostrate by the news from Tobruk and the oppressive Washington heat, met the two generals in his "air-cooled room," the same rooms he had occupied in January, just across the hall from Hopkins's suite. It was Hopkins's command center, from where he did the president's bidding. It was no accident that important White House guests were billeted across the hall from Hopkins—Harry could more easily choreograph events, as he did on this day with Churchill and the generals.[247]

Churchill listened as Clark and Eisenhower chatted up the prospects of a cross-Channel invasion in 1943. The two generals had just left their first meeting with Roosevelt, where Operation Roundup, the full-scale invasion of France set for 1943, had been the primary topic of conversation. Churchill let the Americans do most of the talking. The disaster at Tobruk had put North Africa in the forefront of his thoughts, and Laval's coup had brought Gymnast back into the mix. With Eisenhower about to leave for London, it had become clear to all concerned that the American Chiefs of Staff should also depart for Britain for further talks with their British counterparts. The agreement reached by the Combined Chiefs of Staff in Washington amounted to nothing more than an agreement to meet again in London.

Churchill, too, planned to sit in on those meetings—if not guide them—and made ready to depart Washington on the twenty-fifth. As in January, he knew his homecoming would not be a celebratory affair. U.S. newspaper headlines gave him fair warning: ANGER IN ENGLAND; TOBRUK FALL MAY BRING CHANGE OF GOVERNMENT; CHURCHILL TO BE CENSURED.[248]

Rather than make straightaway for London to face the crisis, Churchill, along with Ismay, Marshall, and the dutiful Sawyers, journeyed by train to Fort Jackson, South Carolina, where they watched a newly formed American infantry division conduct a live-fire exercise. As the recruits strutted their stuff, Churchill asked Ismay what he thought of the exercise. Ismay replied, "To put these troops against continental troops would be murder." "You're wrong," Churchill replied. "They are wonderful material and will learn very quickly."[249]

Late on June 25, Churchill and his party, joined by Averell Harriman (who toted some kerchiefs and a Virginia ham for Clementine), boarded a flying boat at Baltimore. At breakfast time the next morning (according to their watches), they landed at Botwood, Newfoundland, for fuel and a sturdy morning meal that most Britons could only dream of: "excellent lobster washed down with Scotch whisky." That week, to placate the vast majority of Londoners who could not afford to pay two or three pounds ($10 to $15) for a meal out, the government placed a cap of five shillings (about one U.S. dollar) on restaurant meals. The plan didn't work; proprietors simply added overhead costs to the bill and trebled the price of wine, on which there was no price limit. Worse, whisky, long rationed at one bottle per month per customer, was in such short supply (alcohol was needed to manufacture smokeless gunpowder) that even regulars could no longer procure their allotted bottle from local merchants. Nobody was starving in Britain, yet very few Britons washed down lobsters with aged Scotch whisky.[250]

Almost seven hundred thousand British homes had been destroyed since 1940. Six million Britons lived without operating sewage systems. In London, more than three hundred thousand houses, one in eight, had been wrecked. Water lines remained smashed. Basements of ruined buildings had been converted (after the bodies of the drowned and burned had been removed) to rainwater catch basins. When the British offered the arriving Americans the use of a barracks for their general headquarters, a Yank who reconnoitered the place learned to his dismay that sewage flowed openly and, given that the newest building was built in 1860, there was no heat. Tens of millions of continental Europeans (and several thousand

Britons who lived in the Underground) would have happily taken up residence in such a place. The American officer wondered how his staff could work there during the winter.[251]

He needn't have asked. A nationwide coal shortage meant cold hearths throughout the land. As Churchill winged his way home, Parliament debated the rationing of coal, which would mean even less coal to heat homes and coal gas to power factories. More than 30,000 coal miners, meanwhile, were in uniform, yet the same citizenry that demanded a second front were demanding that those miners return home to dig the coal. The people demanded their coal; they demanded a second front; they demanded a victory *somewhere*. And they demanded their fish. Fresh salmon and cod had disappeared from fish markets. Britons found themselves chilled in their houses, with no fish in their pots, a ration of two eggs and two thin chops per week, and with little whisky in the cupboard. Starved for sugar, they queued up at candy counters for a penny's worth of gumdrops, "as though," wrote Mollie Panter-Downes, "it was biblical manna." Yet, these were strictures the British could live with, *if* their leaders delivered a victory. "Bewilderment has been the outstanding national emotion," Panter-Downes wrote, ever since Rommel took Tobruk "with the seeming ease of shattering a child's toy." Newspapers told Britons that "everything was going well." It was not. Yet, Panter-Downes noted, Britons remained true to form, "grousing about their leaders in the corner pub while remaining fully determined to fight behind those leaders to the last ditch."[252]

Some in Parliament did not share in that determination. Churchill arrived home to find a motion had been placed in the Commons by a Conservative MP, Sir John Wardlaw-Milne: "That this House, while paying tribute to the heroism and endurance of the Armed Forces of the Crown in circumstances of exceptional difficulty, has no confidence in the central direction of the war." Admiral of the Fleet Sir Roger Keyes, supported by Leslie Hore-Belisha, seconded the motion. By the time Churchill arrived at the Cabinet Room on the twenty-seventh to plan his parliamentary defense, Aneurin Bevan was hard at work honing his parliamentary attack. The mood among conservatives, Churchill noted, was "fairly glum."[253]

He had occupied No. 10 for almost twenty-six months, during which time he had presided over nothing but defeats. He fully expected to survive the vote of censure, telling a Roosevelt aide he thought at most twenty MPs would abandon him. That outcome might under different circumstances be enough to bring down a partisan government but not a national coalition. Yet Churchill understood there could be no more defeats. "Only a few more marches," he later wrote, "one more success, and Mussolini and Rommel would enter Cairo, or its ruins, together. All hung in the balance, and . . . who would predict how the scales would turn?"[254]

The debate took place during the first two days of July. Churchill remained silent on the first day, but straightaway it became clear to everyone that the opposition was steering toward the rocks. The first rebel, Wardlaw-Milne, a Scottish Conservative, stated his case well enough. The problem, he said, was Churchill serving as both P.M. and minister of defence. The solution was to strip him of the latter office and pass on the leadership of the war to a qualified and dominating commander in chief. Churchill had often told his cronies that he would resign within the hour if any such degradation of his powers took place. Milne had set up the pitch; he then proceeded to throw the ball away. The "dominating" figure he recommended was the Duke of Gloucester, the corpulent and somewhat dim-witted brother of the King, and as unqualified a nominee as could be found in the Isle. As Wardlaw-Milne spoke, mumbles of "why, the man must be an ass" percolated through the House. Harold Nicolson noted in his diary that Wardlaw-Milne had begun well enough, but his mention of the Duke resulted in "a wave of panic-embarrassment" passing through the House. Wardlaw-Milne, Nicolson wrote, "is in fact rather an ass." Mollie Panter-Downes compared Wardlaw-Milne's proposal to the Duke of York of the old nursery rhyme:* "Judging by the reception of the house . . . a nursery rhyme is just now the most likely place for such martial royal excursions." Churchill could not have asked Wardlaw-Milne to do more for his cause.[255]

Churchill's old friend Admiral Keyes—though a dotard now in Churchill's opinion—followed Milne. The old admiral made clear that he objected to the handling of the war effort by the Chiefs of Staff, yet, curiously, not by Churchill, whose loss to Britain were he to be forced out of office, Keyes declared, would be a "deplorable disaster." A member noted that the admiral appeared to be claiming that Churchill both interfered in the war and at the same time didn't interfere enough. Since the entire showdown was, supposedly, about Churchill's performance, Keyes's peroration, by its illogic, served only to bolster Churchill while undermining the opposition.[256]

The next day, Aneurin Bevan demonstrated why he was almost Churchill's equal in parliamentary close combat (Churchill cites the speech in the fourth volume of his war memoirs but fails to name the speaker;

---

* Oh, the grand old Duke of York,
He had ten thousand men;
He marched them up to the top of the hill,
And he marched them down again.

And when they were up, they were up,
And when they were down, they were down,
And when they were only halfway up,
They were neither up nor down.

such was his antipathy toward Bevan). He began well enough. Of Churchill, he proclaimed: "The Prime Minister wins debate after debate and loses battle after battle." Then, after a pause for effect, he delivered his most memorable criticism of Churchill: "The country is beginning to say that he fights debates like a war and the war like a debate." Unfortunately for the opposition, Bevan, as had Milne, proposed a questionable solution to the lack of military zeal. Bevan's was to put British troops under the command of the many French, Polish, and Czech generals who had fled their homelands to London. This absurd suggestion self-evidently did not lend itself to further scrutiny by the House. Bevan then worked some class-warfare rhetoric into his address, claiming that had Rommel been born British, he would likely not have risen above the rank of sergeant, a preposterous assertion given Rommel's upper-middle-class lineage and his long Imperial Army career, which began as an officer candidate and included a stint at the War College in Danzig. Still, Bevan had adroitly exposed the rot in the British class structure, a truth Churchill had acknowledged to Colville almost two years earlier when he declared that the boys from the secondary schools (public schools in America) who had won the Battle of Britain (they made up more than 70 percent of Fighter Command) deserved to run the country after the war. Churchill, an old reformer, was sincere in his sentiments, but by failing to express in public what he felt in private, he allowed Bevan to claim the issue as his own.[257]

Hore-Belisha spoke last, but the old Liberal had learned nothing from his attack of the year before when, attempting to blame Churchill for the fall of Crete, he instead called attention to his own lackluster tenure under Chamberlain as secretary of state for war. Churchill turned that history against Hore-Belisha then, and did so again on this day. Twice within thirteen months, Hore-Belisha opened the door for Churchill, and twice Churchill burst through. When Hore-Belisha asked about the many mechanical and armament problems of the Churchill tank (designed and produced by the Chamberlain government), Churchill turned the tables by noting that only when the tank's defects became known was it christened the Churchill. These defects had been overcome, he added, laughter now percolating through the chamber, and the tank could be expected to give long, strong, and massive service in the war effort. Churchill's address, Harold Nicolson told his diary, amounted to an explication of the concept of attrition. Britain would soon have more guns and men and tanks in the desert than the Germans, and although Rommel had not yet been brought to bay, numerical superiority must, in time, spell the difference. Toward the end of his address, knowing that the opposition had inflicted fatal wounds upon itself, Churchill sounded "quite fresh and gay."[258]

When the House divided for the vote, the tally was 475 for the government, 25 against. Churchill had survived the strongest parliamentary assault of the war, and by a margin extraordinarily close to the prediction he had made in Washington. Twenty-five votes had been the maximum figure mustered against Pitt the Younger in 1799 when Napoleon appeared poised to rule both the waves and the Continent. Pitt had declared himself the only man in England capable of defeating the little Corsican, and Parliament gave him its vote of confidence. Yet for Churchill, the July vote was more a warning than a victory.

Within days of arriving in Britain, Dwight Eisenhower learned that most Americans in London believed the European war would be lost within weeks unless Stalin parried Hitler's lunges toward the Russian oil fields and the Don. Pug Ismay thought as much, and he told Harriman the Red Army would be finished "in three weeks," although Harriman noted that Ismay had been saying as much for twelve months. This time, however, events seemed to validate Ismay's dismal predictions. By early July, Eisenhower thought the Russian position so desperate that he proposed another look at Operation Sledgehammer, the plan for the cross-Channel invasion of Europe. "Even an unsuccessful attack" in France, he told his public relations aide, Lieutenant Commander Harry Butcher, would be "worthwhile" if it brought relief to the Russians. Churchill and his military chiefs wanted no part of Sledgehammer for the self-evident reason that it was bound to fail and would *not* result in any succor for the Russians. Butcher predicted to his diary: "If Germany rolls up Russia's armies and gains the rich oil fields that seem to be easily in her grasp, will the United States then concentrate on licking Japan first and leaving Germany until later? How much later it is impossible to tell." This was Churchill's fear exactly. But if not Sledgehammer, then what?[259]

Harold Nicolson saw the political implications this way: "If the Russians collapse, they and their friends here will say it was due to Churchill's refusal of a second front. I very much fear that Churchill's own position will not survive a Russian defeat."[260]

Marshall and King arrived in London in mid-July to address the question of a second front. They carried a memorandum from Roosevelt that outlined his priorities and conclusions. The events unfolding in Russia and in the North Atlantic made it perfectly clear to Roosevelt that it was past time to do something. Yet the question of what to do remained, as it had for almost seven months, what exactly? Roosevelt, although seeing the possible merits of Gymnast, still sided with Marshall and Stimson on the need to get into Europe, preferably before the American elections. "Roosevelt was always afraid the American public would get very Pacific minded," recalled Averell Harriman, "and force him to change his Europe first policy." Yet, if Europe proved beyond reach, North Africa—which Marshall considered a sideshow—presented a suitable political alternative. It would remove some of the moral high ground from beneath Stalin. The president made it clear to Marshall that he wanted American boys fighting somewhere before November 3, Election Day. Further, he made clear that if no action was taken by the Allies in 1942, the effect on morale at home and in Great Britain would be disastrous. The Middle East must be held, Roosevelt wrote, in order to prevent a "joining hands between Germany and Japan, and the probable loss of the Indian Ocean" as well as the loss of Egypt, Syria, the Suez, and Iraqi oil. Sledgehammer should be studied, he advised, but if it could not be executed, they should pick another target. One method of protecting the Middle East, he suggested, would be to consider a joint Allied operation "in Morocco and Algiers intended to drive in against the back door of Rommel's armies." And there it was, Gymnast reborn. Secretary of War Stimson called Gymnast Roosevelt's "secret war baby." Churchill, with his barrage of telegrams and personal visits, had brought Roosevelt around. But Churchill had not yet sold Marshall, and Roosevelt, despite his directives to Marshall, left the final decision in the hands of his top general.[261]

As the Combined Chiefs in London prepared to choose a target in order to take pressure off Stalin, the Soviet leader's position only worsened. The previous summer, the Germans had bypassed and cut off Sevastopol, the largest Soviet naval fortress on the Black Sea. During the Crimean War almost a century earlier, Sevastopol withstood a British and French siege for 329 days, time enough for Leo Tolstoy, then a young Russian lieutenant of artillery who happened to be marooned in the city, to write three "sketches" of life under siege. They are fairly short pieces, the first an almost lyrical celebration of the heroics of the brave and patriotic defenders. Yet in the final sketch, written after Sevastopol fell, a deepening despair and intense loathing for the brutality of war permeates the narrative. Tolstoy and much of the czar's army escaped the city. Hitler, when he finally moved fourteen divisions against Sevastopol in early June, took the city in twenty-three days. Boris Voyetekhov, a correspondent for *Pravda*, wrote the epitaph this time—of Soviet naval destroyers unloading shells and leaving port with their decks and holds full of women and children, of the city in flames, and of the last defenders, out of ammunition, swimming out to sea, to certain death. Few in the garrison escaped alive; almost 90,000 were killed and captured. Hitler now owned the Black Sea coast, from Yalta to Kerch, along a two-hundred-mile front. Farther to the north, his armies poured into the Donets Corridor.

By July 7, Army Group B had reached the Don, opposite Voronezh. Hitler's April directive had called for this force to now begin wheeling south down the west bank of the river toward the great bend, where only sixty miles separate the Don and the Volga, and Stalingrad. But Army Group B's commander, Fedor von Bock, feeling a soldier's natural unease at leaving a strategic rail hub such as Voronezh unmolested on his flank, threw his Fourth Panzer Army across the Don and into Voronezh. The operation, he told Hitler, would take only a few days. Paulus's Sixth Army, meanwhile, began its push down the west bank of the Don, alone, and with every mile that much more removed from its panzer screen.

To the British press, Stalin's situation looked dire, at best. Not privy to all the facts, and careless with the few it had, it was full of calls for a second front, sooner rather than later; in fact, a second front now. *The Daily Worker* was again free to join the chorus when HMG lifted the January 1941 ban on its publication, a sop to Stalin. The slogan "Second Front Now" was being scrawled on walls throughout Britain, the handiwork of labor agitators who, in Churchill's estimation, were nothing more than "fools or knaves." Dissatisfaction with Churchill had spread from the Parliament into factories and the armed services. Scottish and Welsh Communists were now one with certain London intellectual elites in believing that Churchill was as much a disaster as the disasters he presided over. Beaverbrook's newspapers, while still supporting Churchill, now framed the moral essence of the fight in terms of helping Russia, as did the British people, who, Mollie Panter-Downes noted, "can't or won't recognize the existence of any substitute for a genuine, slap-up opening of a land offensive on the Continent." Spring was the season, Panter-Downes wrote, when an "Englishman's fancy lightly turns to thoughts of invasion." This summer, however, the question Britons asked was not when the Germans would come to England, but when Englishmen would cross to the Continent. What Britons expected, Panter-Downes wrote, was a demonstration of "the old national talent for the brilliant impromptu, the type of piratical, sea-borne foray which has often studded and sometimes made English history."[262]

Mountbatten had been planning just such a foray for months, the target Dieppe, the strategic port in northwest France. Yet Churchill had also understood for months that a strategically meaningful landing in Europe that summer was out of the question, although throughout the year he harbored hopes for 1943. Yet by July, even 1943 began to look problematic.

Eisenhower, in his memoirs, wrote: "It became increasingly doubtful... that a full-out frontal attack could be launched in the early spring of 1943, and because it would be extremely hazardous to begin a major operation across the English Channel in the fall of the year, we began to realize that a large-scale invasion might not be possible before the spring of 1944." Eisenhower reluctantly concluded, as had Roosevelt, that the spring of 1944 might be the earliest the Allies could put an army into France, far too late to help the Russians. Whether a landing in North Africa—or anywhere, for that matter—would do anything to improve the Soviet situation was now the question du jour among the military planners. Eisenhower's aide Harry Butcher believed that German and Japanese "industrialized strength," along with the rubber and oil of Malaya, the Dutch East Indies, and Burma, would spell the end of the "British Empire, as we have known it" and leave the United States in "a defensive position, virtually alone in the world." *Time* reduced the implications to a stark reality: "Hitler is winning in Russia." If the Red Army does no better than it has so far, "Russia will be defeated. Germany will win the present phases of World War II in Europe.... The allies will then have lost their best chance to defeat Germany and win World War II."[263]

The time had come for the Anglo-Americans to fight; to not fight was to lose the war in Europe. With that appalling scenario in mind, in early July Roosevelt instructed King and Marshall to remember three "cardinal principles" when they sat down in London with the British Chiefs of Staff: "speed of decision on plans; unity of plans; attack combined with defense but not defense alone." So eager to get to work were the American and British staffs that they held informal meetings on July 19 in Churchill's absence. That was a mistake. Churchill, as minister of defence and per the authority vested in him, had intended to preside at the first meeting. The chiefs' violation of protocol resulted in a Churchillian detonation at Chequers, where, in front of Hopkins, he paraded up and down the great hall reading from a book of British war laws. As he finished each page, he ripped it from the book and threw it down. The chiefs got the message. Then, within two days of sitting down with the British on the nineteenth, the Americans reluctantly agreed that Europe was beyond reach in 1942. Three days later they agreed upon North Africa as the target. On July 24, Operation Gymnast was rechristened Operation Torch, and a jumping-off date of late October was settled upon. Torch meant that Roosevelt would have his men on the beaches before the election; for Churchill and Brooke, it meant taking the first step in their push to clear the Mediterranean. But Eisenhower—who within a few weeks would be promoted to three-star rank and named commander in chief of Torch—saw things differently from both Roosevelt and Churchill. Like Marshall, Eisenhower looked upon Torch primarily as a sideshow to Roundup, its only merit being that it possibly would "contain" the Germans after the Wehrmacht defeated the Red Army, a defeat that, as the last days of July arrived, Eisenhower believed was imminent. Torch for Ike was a colossal mistake. Its approval by Roosevelt, he told an aide, "is the blackest day in history."[264]

On July 27 Roosevelt cabled Churchill: "I cannot help feeling that the past week represented a turning point in the whole war and that now we are on our way shoulder to shoulder." Actually, they were about to start bumping shoulders. The British and American principals, military and political, had agreed on a target, but for different and possibly conflicting reasons. It became apparent in coming weeks that neither the specific objectives in North Africa nor a follow-through strategy had been addressed. Even the makeup of the invasion force was in doubt. Roosevelt wanted the entire land portion of the venture to be an American operation, based in part on his political need to put American boys into action and in part on his belief that the French North Africans hated the English and would welcome the Americans. He proposed to Churchill that if the British desired to attack Algiers, they do so a week after the Americans landed on the Atlantic coast of Morocco. The British role in Torch, Roosevelt insisted, must be limited to air and sea support. This stunned Churchill. Knowing that Roosevelt heeded the advice of his generals, Churchill tried to persuade Eisenhower to persuade the president to approve a real joint Anglo-American venture. He succeeded a few weeks later, but his influence over Roosevelt was lessening. Churchill understood, Harriman told the president, "that he is to play second fiddle in all scores and then only as you direct."[265]

As for Charles de Gaulle and any role he might play in the invasion, Roosevelt looked upon the Frenchman as a mere soldier and one who manifested Bonapartist ambitions, although nothing in de Gaulle's deeds or words had ever indicated an ambition to become a military dictator. Eisenhower grasped what Roosevelt did not: de Gaulle was hated by the Vichy because he had not surrendered while they had, and because he was everything Vichy loyalists were not—patriotic and courageous. Roosevelt simply did not understand that, with the result that Eisenhower was told by Washington that "under no circumstances" was the Frenchman to be told of the decision on Torch. Churchill, too, had more than his share of problems with de Gaulle, but they came about as a consequence of trying to work with the obstinate Frenchman, not against him.[266]

As Churchill saw it, the major flaw with the original plan for Torch resulted from Marshall's fear that to venture too far into the Mediterranean—specifically to Algiers—might result in his army being cut off. The news of American resistance to attacking Algiers came as a "bombshell," Churchill told the president, and he asked that a British contingency be added in order to strike Algiers, and that American troops be transferred from the Moroccan part of the invasion in order to facilitate a drive east from Algiers, with Tunis the ultimate objective. Roosevelt took his time pondering the concept, but he found Eisenhower in fundamental agreement with Churchill. By mid-September Roosevelt agreed to transfer ten thousand men to the eastern operation, which would now take place simultaneously with the Moroccan landings. This opened up opportunities that Brooke and Churchill had sought all along. For Brooke, a continental second front could not be contemplated as long as Malta lay under siege and Tunis was held by the Axis. Churchill, with his eye on flushing Italy from the war before thrusting northward into Germany's southern flank, strongly believed that if Torch did not include a push from Algiers into Tunisia, with the capture of Tunis as the ultimate objective, it risked becoming a dead end. Churchill prevailed on the matter of Algiers, but the Americans and British continued to debate the details and objectives of Torch into late September, prompting Eisenhower's aide Commander Butcher to complain to his diary, "Trying to follow the evolution of Torch is like trying to follow the pea in a three-shell game."[267]

During the July meetings, the British and American military chiefs had begun to take the measure of one another, and the results were decidedly mixed, and not strictly along national lines: Dudley Pound, the first sea lord, was in Brooke's estimation "an old dodderer" and "beyond retirement." Pound, who was almost sixty-five, was so given to falling asleep at staff meetings that he was replaced by Brooke as chairman of the Chiefs of Staff Committee: "He [Pound] is asleep 90% of the time," Brooke told his diary, "and the remaining 10% is none too sure what he is arguing about." Brooke had no way of knowing that Pound's drowsiness was due to an undetected brain tumor. The CIGS considered Pound's American counterpart, Admiral Ernest King, to be "a shrewd and somewhat swollen headed individual" who was "biased entirely in favor of the Pacific." King (so tough, blue jackets claimed, that he shaved with a blowtorch) had long been known for his hair-trigger temper and heavy drinking. He had sworn off whisky for the duration, but not, as Brooke was to note, champagne or wine, which on more than one occasion resulted in King's becoming quite "nicely lit up" and combative. King joined Eisenhower and Churchill in Brooke's pantheon of those who lacked strategic vision. Marshall, too, in

Brooke's estimation "has got no strategic vision, his thoughts revolve around the creation of forces and not on their employment." Yet Marshall shared Brooke's steadfast belief in "Europe First," although they disagreed on where and when to strike. They both had to keep an eye on Admiral King. As for the strengths of the other major American players, Brooke found Eisenhower "quite incapable of understanding real strategy." The Army Air Force's Hap Arnold "limits his outlook to the air," and General Mark Clark was "very ambitious and unscrupulous." Yet as a group, Brooke later chirped, the Americans were "friendliness itself."[268]

Churchill, for his part, did not think much of his own Chiefs of Staff or high-ranking officers in general. Referring to the COS during a luncheon, he told his guests, "I am obliged to wage modern warfare with ancient weapons."[269]

For their part, the American military chiefs thought as little of their boss's strategic acumen as the British chiefs thought of Churchill's. Marshall was especially wary of politicians. He had pledged to himself never to laugh at Roosevelt's jokes, and he upheld the pledge. Churchill, in April, had displayed his political side to Marshall, who, though completely loyal to Roosevelt and respectful of Churchill as a statesman, remained loyal first and foremost to his troops. He saw no glory in death. He hated to see men die under any circumstances, most of all the transparently political, and that is how he looked upon Torch.[270]

Although Brooke (and Churchill) had sent Marshall home in April with the false impression that they had agreed to a 1942 invasion of France, the two generals got along well professionally, recalled Sir Ian Jacob. This was despite Brooke's "hard, distant, lofty" demeanor, which was manifested by his speaking rapidly and, according to Jacob, with an overbearing air of self-assurance. Brooke also, recalled Jacob, tended to allow his tongue to dart out of his mouth and flit around his lips, lizardlike, an unfortunate quirk that distracted listeners from the merit of his words. If Brooke possessed a sense of humor, it was well concealed.[271]

Compared to Brooke, the dour George Marshall was a cutup. He was also—blessedly for the alliance—unaware of Brooke's contemptuous diary jottings in which he pilloried his American counterpart. Brooke called Marshall a "great man, a great gentleman, a great organizer, but definitely not a strategist." In fact, Brooke termed Marshall's strategic abilities "the poorest." Marshall, in turn, thought much the same of Brooke, and told Hopkins that although Brooke "might be a good fighting man, he lacked Dill's brains." Brooke, though critical to a fault, harbored no ambition other than to win the war. Years later, when he prepared his diaries for publication, he took pains to add italicized explanations for many of his biting pronouncements. Marshall by then was a dying old man whose stature in American and European history could in no way be diminished by Brooke's long-ago scribbling. And Eisenhower by then was president, a shock to Brooke, who wrote: "He certainly made no great impression on me at our first meeting... and if I had been told then of the future that lay in front of him I should refuse to believe it."[272]

Brooke was egalitarian; he criticized everybody, American and British, Mountbatten and Churchill most of all. Churchill, Brooke concluded, "never had the slightest doubt that he had inherited all the military genius of his great ancestor Marlborough!" Yet he could not "understand a large strategic concept and must get down to detail!" As with all who dealt with Churchill, Brooke learned that he was "quite impossible to argue with" and if he did concede a point, tended to later "repudiate everything he had agreed to."[273]

Brooke's worst invective was directed toward Dickie Mountbatten, who the CIGS found to be "the most crashing bore," prone to "always fiddling about with unimportant matters and wasting other people's time." Mountbatten "suffers from the most desperate illogical brain," he told his diary, "always producing red herrings."[274]

The paths of Eisenhower and Bernard Montgomery also crossed during the early summer. Several weeks before the July meetings, Eisenhower paid a courtesy call on Montgomery, who commanded the 3rd Division in southeast Britain. Ike made the mistake of lighting one of his daily ration of eighty Chesterfields while waiting for Monty to wind up a staff briefing. The ascetic Montgomery (a devout nonsmoker and nondrinker) detected the aroma of tobacco smoke in the air and barked out that whosoever was the offender should snuff out the fag, immediately. Eisenhower complied, and so learned his first lesson about the diminutive and combative Englishman: Monty liked things his way and only his way. This was true also on the battlefield, where he preferred a set-piece style of combat in which events unfolded in strict accordance with his well-laid plans. Churchill, on the other hand, liked to quote Napoleon's maxim, to wit, that forming a "picture" of a battle was foolish, for conditions could easily be deranged by Providence. Churchill had run up against Montgomery's asceticism the previous year, when after a day of inspecting Montgomery's troops near Brighton, he repaired with Monty to the Royal Albion Hotel, where Churchill anticipated a good whisky and a cigar. Monty declined the libations, declaring that he neither drank nor smoked, and furthermore was 100 percent fit. Churchill rejoined that he both drank and smoked and was 200 percent fit.[275]

The teetotaler Montgomery, with his rumpled corduroy trousers and nonregulation turtleneck sweater, was not the sort who would normally grace Churchill's dinner table, but Montgomery had acquitted himself well in France and at Dunkirk. He was egotistical and brusque, but most of all he was a fighter, and this Churchill respected. In late July, it appeared unlikely, however, that Eisenhower, Montgomery, and Churchill, each possessed of a wildly differing temperament, would anytime soon be conducting vital military business in close proximity with one another, each dependent on the others for common success. The final week of July found Churchill, troubled by events in the Middle East and by personalities in the Kremlin, intent on visiting both venues. Eisenhower had begun planning the North African campaign. Monty, meanwhile, cooled his heels in southeast Britain, awaiting an improbable German invasion or an even more improbable promotion to an active field command in an actual war zone.

By July 14, Hitler's eastern army (*Ostheer*) had established its bridgehead across the Don at Voronezh, but it had taken Army Group B's Fourth Panzer Division a week to take the city. The delay would prove costly as the seasons changed. Meanwhile, Paulus's Sixth Army had kept to the original plan and wheeled south along the Don's west bank. The *Ostheer* had now driven 140 miles farther than in the previous summer, yet the dawdling of the Fourth Panzer Army in Voronezh while Paulus raced south meant that Army Group B was being stretched thin. Stalin by then had rescinded his "stand firm" orders and was now allowing the Red Army to retreat before the *Ostheer*, which lessened the chances of entire Soviet armies being encircled and captured. As a result, although the Germans had captured more than 90,000 Soviet troops within the Donets Corridor since their victory at Kharkov, five times that many Russians had backtracked to fight another day. Still, by the first days of August, the *Ostheer* had driven another 150 miles. Rostov-on-Don, gateway to the Caucasus, fell, and with it the last direct Soviet rail links with the Baku fields. For Stalin, this was a personal affront; in 1908 he had robbed the Rostov–Moscow train in order to help the revolutionary cause. For the same cause he had robbed the Tiflis bank in his native Georgia, leaving three dead at the scene. Rostov and Georgia had been his stomping grounds. They were now Hitler's.

Farther south, elements of Army Group A's First Panzer Army reached Stavropol on August 5, one hundred miles from the foothills of the Caucasus. On the ninth, after racing across the Kuban Steppe, German panzers cruised to within sight of the oil derricks at Maikop. Far to the east-northeast, Army Group B, less Bock, whom Hitler sacked for dawdling at Voronezh, had resumed its offensive and had shot across the Don north of the great bend. Paulus's Sixth Army was now heading full bore for the Volga, and Stalingrad. The question being asked in Moscow, London, and Washington was, would the Germans bypass Stalingrad or try to take it? In fact, on July 23, Hitler had issued Führer Directive No. 45, an order Sir John

Keegan described as the "most disastrous of all issued over his signature." The Führer decreed that while Army Group A made for the Caucasus, Army Group B would take and hold Stalingrad. The city was of high strategic value to the Soviets, which is why Hitler had ordered it smashed in his April directive. Yet destroying a position is not the same as holding it. Stalingrad carried symbolic weight for Hitler, named as it was for his Bolshevik nemesis. In deciding to inflict a symbolic defeat on Stalin, the Führer had forsaken his Clausewitz.[276]

Stalin had allowed his troops to fall back since the Germans crossed the Don, but five days after Hitler issued his directive to take Stalingrad, Stalin issued one of his own; all available forces would be thrown into Stalingrad, and "not a step back" would be tolerated. "Die, but do not retreat" became the Order of the Day on the banks of the Volga.[277]

Western dailies dutifully updated their maps of the Russian front as the German advance pushed ever eastward. A great deal of black ink was required to mark German-held terrain. Yet the maps failed to tell the true story. Army Group A, stretched as it was along a five-hundred-mile front, was rolling though territory, but not holding territory. Panzer spearheads far outran the infantry, which could only slog along at ten or fifteen miles a day. Even farther to the rear, supply trains struggled along roads not made for modern vehicular traffic. The result, wrote Sir John Keegan, was a front so broad that in some places just a few hundred Germans "held" dozen of miles of ground. Western readers who took their news seriously were dismayed at what they read of the Soviet plight. Stalin's generals, however, saw an opportunity.[278]

With the vote of censure behind him and the decision made in favor of Torch, Churchill's attention turned to Egypt, and Stalin. Based on Ultra decrypts, he had prodded Auchinleck for weeks to take the offensive against Rommel, unfairly in Brooke's estimation. Ultra allowed Churchill to peer over his generals' shoulders as if he were with them in the field poring over intelligence reports. Yet Ultra was sometimes wrong. Churchill took Rommel's (decrypted) pleas for reinforcements at face value, while some at Bletchley cautioned that Rommel might be exaggerating his needs in order to force action in Berlin. On one occasion Churchill goaded Auchinleck by citing a decrypted Luftwaffe signal that appeared to reveal the Germans had only half as many tanks in Africa as Auchinleck believed based on his field intelligence. But Bletchley was incorrect; the deciphered message referred only to the German tanks at Auchinleck's immediate front. Rommel, after taking several necessarily desultory and ultimately futile cracks at Auchinleck's El Alamein positions during the first weeks of July, settled into a defensive mode and awaited his promised reinforcements. For his June victory over Ritchie, he was awarded by Hitler a field marshal's baton. He would later say he would have preferred to be given a division. With Rommel dug in before El Alamein and with the fight possibly gone from Auchinleck, Churchill concluded that the situation in the desert called for his presence.[279]

His getting to Egypt involved doing so without contracting any of numerous diseases he would be exposed to along the way. In order for the aircraft to avoid Germans, the outbound leg of the journey would take at least five flying days, going south from Gibraltar to Takoradi, in the Gold Coast, followed by a three-day, three-flight hopscotch across central Africa. This sojourn through "tropical and malarious regions," as Churchill put it, would require a series of inoculations, some of which required ten days to take effect. Dr. Wilson and the War Cabinet sought to put an end to the idea. Just that week, news of a great medical discovery had sifted through the ranks. Two American doctors visiting London from Johns Hopkins University had told Harry Butcher over a few bottles of port of a new drug "called penicillin and derived from bread mold. Takes eleven acres of mold to cure the scorched face of one flyer." Such a drug would have made Churchill's trip safer, but it had yet to be mass-produced. Given the risks posed by African insects and German fighter planes, it appeared that Churchill would not be straying far from London.[280]

Then an American pilot, Captain William Vanderkloot, twenty-six years old and a veteran of ferrying Lend-Lease bombers to Britain, suggested a daring approach: depart England for Gibraltar late in the evening by a four-engine B-24 bomber and refuel in Gibraltar the following morning; then, after departing the Rock at dusk, overfly Spanish Morocco, dodge far south over the desert during the night, and then swing east almost 1,900 miles to the Nile, south of Cairo. A fully gassed-up Liberator could cruise slightly more than seventeen hours at an average speed of 240 miles per hour. It had what it took to make such a journey in two legs.

Churchill liked the spirit of the idea, and he liked the means of transportation—Vanderkloot's modified B-24 Liberator, named *Commando*. The bomb racks had been removed, and eight seats had been bolted down amidships. Toward the rear of the plane, wood slats had been rigged into two berths for the comfort of the highest-ranking passengers, but comfort was a relative concept. The plane was neither heated nor pressurized, necessitating at high altitude the use of oxygen masks, another source of worry to Churchill's doctor, who feared the consequences to his heart of freezing temperatures and thin air. Churchill, not sharing Wilson's concern, asked the RAF ground crew to customize his oxygen mask in order to allow him to smoke his cigars. The request was dutifully carried out. Vanderkloot's proposed route to Cairo could be covered in twenty-three hours compared with five days spent amid "Central African bugs." If they could reach Cairo, there was no reason they could not reach Moscow; Churchill had not yet met Stalin and he felt a face-to-face meeting was the best way to establish a relationship and clear the air. There was much air to clear. Churchill made an executive decision: he would journey to Cairo. When Stalin invited Churchill to Moscow on the thirty-first, the itinerary was expanded to include the Kremlin. The entire journey would prove a daunting undertaking, even for young pilots, and an exhausting slog for an overweight old man with a quirky ticker and seemingly perpetual chest colds that he unwisely chose to treat with snuff and whisky, a generous supply of which Sawyers secreted into *Commando*'s bomb bay.[281]

Brooke left Britain for Cairo by air early on the morning of August 1, intending to swing through Malta on his way. The journey was too dangerous to risk having both Brooke and Churchill on the same airplane. The previous year, Eden and Dill had overshot Malta on their way to Greece and almost flew into the sea. German and Italian fighter planes sought out lone British bombers accompanied by Spitfires on the sound premise that a big shot might be aboard. Brooke arrived at Malta to find scenes of "incomprehensible" destruction, food and gasoline shortages, a harbor full of wrecks, and a population on the brink of starvation. The roads were so full of rubble, and petrol was in such short supply, that Malta's military commander, Field Marshal Gort, had to ride his bicycle around the island. Gort appeared "depressed," as he and his little garrison waited in this "backwater" for the final German assault, which good strategy dictated must be imminent. In fact, a joint German and Italian invasion had been approved in April. But days before Brooke's arrival—and unbeknownst to the British—Hitler, with the cost of the Crete invasion still fresh in his memory, postponed the invasion of Malta because it appeared Rommel might get to Cairo on his own.[282]

Churchill departed London just after midnight on August 1. As he waited on the tarmac, a cable reached him from Dill, in Washington, which concluded: "In the American mind, Roundup in 1943 is excluded by acceptance of Torch." This was not at all what Churchill wanted to hear, given that after Cairo he was going to Moscow to inform Stalin that no second front would materialize in Europe in 1942, a chore he compared to "carrying a large lump of ice to the North Pole." He was not prepared to add 1943 to the equation. The cable, however, served one useful purpose: it would show Stalin that decisions on the second front had not been made by Churchill unilaterally, but had resulted from American and British solidarity. To bolster that argument, Roosevelt, at Churchill's request, instructed Averell Harriman to meet Churchill in Cairo and to continue on with him to Moscow.[283]

With Dill's message in hand, Churchill boarded *Commando*. Box lunches had been stowed in the bomb bay; there was no space for anything resembling a galley, and no meals could be prepared. A little propane camp stove was rigged to heat water for tea or Churchill's hot-water bottle. Tommy Thompson and Churchill's doctor made the trip, along with Inspector Thompson, Sawyers, Ian Jacob, two secretaries, and Alexander Cadogan, who represented the Foreign Office. Eden remained in London to run the store in Churchill's absence. Clementine motored out to the airfield and watched as the "monster bomber, throbbing, roaring & flashing blue lights," lifted off into the night sky. Once aloft, *Commando* swung low over blacked-out southern England, past Land's End and out over the Atlantic, where it climbed to 15,000 feet and ran the 1,500 miles to Gibraltar. Lest any Axis spies prowling that citadel spot him, Churchill told Brooke he intended to disguise his identity with a gray beard. He spent August 2 on the Rock, and lifted off again at dusk. Conversation on board was impossible; the plane had not been soundproofed. Just before sunrise, Churchill climbed from the bomb bay and into the copilot's seat, from where he beheld "in the pale, glimmering dawn the endless winding silver ribbon of the Nile."[284]

He had first seen the river from horseback more than forty years earlier, and although at the time he had yet to dab a canvas with oils, he described it in painterly tones as "a thread of blue silk drawn across an enormous brown drugget; and even the blue thread is brown for half the year... the picture painted in burnt sienna is relieved by a grateful patch of green." Now the whitewashed concrete sprawl of Cairo spilled out of the patch of green, the western edges of the city thrusting toward al Jizah and the pyramids. Rommel, after again testing Auchinleck's lines during the preceding week, sat just 140 miles to the northwest. And here came Churchill, exhilarated to find himself "the man on the spot."[285]

He came not to praise Auchinleck, but neither had he yet decided to bury him. Of two things Churchill was certain: the Eighth Army needed a new commander (Auchinleck had taken over from Ritchie), and Auchinleck should return to Cairo from the front in order to tend to the business of his entire Middle East command, which stretched from Tehran to El Alamein. Brooke arrived firm in his belief that Auchinleck had lost the confidence of the Eighth Army, was a poor judge of character, and should be replaced. Churchill, not yet sure, had invited the general he most respected, Jan Smuts, to Cairo for consultation. Wavell also arrived, from India, in order to brief Churchill and Brooke on events in that theater. It became clear to Churchill that Wavell and especially Auchinleck were so preoccupied with the immediate threats to their fronts that all of Iraq and Iran were essentially without central command, and this with the Germans driving toward Baku and the Caucasus. Churchill proposed setting up a new command in Baghdad, to be called the Middle East command. Brooke had been advocating just such a change for weeks. Auchinleck's old command would be renamed the Near East command, a change Churchill had long championed the self-evident reason, as he later wrote, that Egypt and the Levant "was the Near East... India, Burma, and Malaya, the East... and China and Japan, the Far East." The name changes were fine and well, the sort of housekeeping details Churchill relished, but the obvious and as yet unasked questions were, who would command, and where.[286]

Auchinleck sealed his fate by nominating Lieutenant General Thomas Corbett as the new commander of the Eighth Army. Corbett, in Brooke's estimation, was a "small man" and clearly "totally unsuited" for that command, further proof that Auchinleck could not pick a leader. The Eighth Army was tired. The troops, Churchill told the War Cabinet, were poised to retreat to the Nile delta if an attack came. Late on the third, Churchill kept Brooke up until all hours, lecturing the CIGS on the need for Auchinleck to return to Cairo in order to tend to the business of the Middle East command while someone new took command of the Eighth Army, which led Brooke to exclaim to his diary: "Exactly what I have always told him from the start!" Churchill offered the command to Brooke, a proposal that sorely tempted the CIGS, who in France had "tasted the thrill of commanding a formation in war." Yet he knew he was the wrong man for the job, having no experience in desert warfare, and so told the Old Man.[287]

On August 6, after visiting the front with Auchinleck and meeting Corbett, who Churchill found to be agreeable but without personality, Churchill made the decision to ease the Auk out of Cairo and into the new command in Baghdad. Then the plans collapsed. Churchill offered Auchinleck's job to Brooke, who, like Marshall, was greedy for just such a theater command but was also honest enough to acknowledge (again, as he had three days earlier when offered the Eighth Army) his lack of desert warfare experience. More important, Brooke was selfless enough to not wish the job of working with Churchill on anyone else. The CIGS concluded (but did not inform Churchill in so many words) that the best service he could render England was to stick with Churchill, for better or for worse. Churchill cabled the War Cabinet that Harold Alexander, an obvious choice, be sent at once to replace Auchinleck. Yet Alexander had just been appointed to lead the British forces in Torch, and he had already begun planning that mission with Eisenhower. As for the Eighth Army, Brooke favored Montgomery, whose career he had nurtured for years. Churchill was inclined toward William ("Strafer") Gott, the man who, along with the Fighting French, had in May delayed Rommel for a week, thus saving Ritchie's army, and perhaps Cairo. Brooke thought Gott tired and in need of rest rather than a new command. Churchill, having spent part of the day with Gott, thought otherwise. The P.M. prevailed. The command of the Eighth Army went to Strafer Gott. Bernard Montgomery was chosen to replace Alexander in Torch, and Eisenhower was duly notified of the changes by London.[288]

By lunchtime the next day, Gott was dead, his flying boat shot out of the sky by a rogue German fighter as the general flew from the front to Cairo for a hot bath and few days of rest. Churchill and Brooke, stunned by Gott's loss, shuffled their dwindling deck and produced Bernard Montgomery. Lest Eisenhower conclude that his British allies could not make up their minds, Churchill sent a cable to London asking that Eisenhower not be informed of Montgomery's promotion. But Montgomery had already reported for duty at Eisenhower's headquarters. It fell to Ismay to inform Eisenhower that Montgomery, too, was being posted to Egypt, and that yet a third British general would be assigned to Torch. Eisenhower, taking in the news, told Ismay, "You seem to have a lot of Wellingtons in your army. Tell me, frankly, are the British serious about Torch?"[289]

Churchill was serious. On August 8 he relieved Auchinleck of command, offering the general the consolation prize of the new Middle East command at Baghdad. It was a posting, Churchill admitted, that would be much smaller than Cairo, given that HMG could spare few troops in Iraq and Persia, but a theater nonetheless that "may in a few months become the scene of decisive operations." Given his and Brooke's lack of confidence in Auchinleck in combination with their fears of Hitler punching through to Iraq from the Caucasus, it is ironic that Churchill offered Auchinleck the Iraq command. But after pondering the offer for a few days, the Auk declined. Brooke thought Auchinleck behaved "like an offended film star" rather than putting duty first and taking the command, where he might "restore his reputation as active operations are more than probable." But as Brooke well knew, the Tenth Army in Iraq was woefully unprepared to rebut a German attack, and, with Britain's armed forces stretched to the limit, no reserves could be spared to boost its fighting strength. Were Hitler to break through to Iraq, the Tenth Army would not so much assume a role as suffer a fate. Knowing this, Auchinleck instead departed for India and retirement. Churchill, relieved at having made his decision, took himself off to the beach, where, as he later related to Harold Nicolson, "I then took off all of my clothes and rolled in the surf. Never have I had such a bathing."[290]

In a letter to Clementine informing her of the command changes, Churchill credited Smuts, who "fortified me where I am inclined to be tender hearted, namely in using severe measure against people I like." He used much the same language three months later when he told Harold Nicolson that sacking Auchinleck was "a terrible thing to have to do. He took it like a gentleman." Churchill may have truly liked Auchinleck, but he had conducted this unfortunate piece of business with the general not in person, but by letter.[291]

"That was how he did it," recalled Bob Boothby, "in writing, 'You are dismissed,' signed in red ink, WSC typed in red ink under the signature. When he sacked somebody he never thanked them. I don't remember any occasion when he thanked anyone for doing anything." Around Whitehall, a sacking by Churchill was known as "the awarding of the Order of the Boot." Boothby is partially correct, his recollection colored by his own exit from HMG. Early in 1941, he was accused of extorting commissions from Czech citizens who sought his help in reclaiming Czech assets seized by HMG after Munich. Boothby, who in the early 1930s had been touted as a possible future prime minister, had made many Tory enemies for his role as an anti-Chamberlain rebel. In 1941, with the Czech banking irregularities offered as their raison d'être, those enemies maneuvered to bring Boothby down. Boothby defended himself admirably in the House against the kickback charges, and sought Churchill's help on the matter. Returning from the House that day, Churchill told Colville that "if there was one thing in the world he found odious, it was a man-hunt." Yet he let Boothby go it alone, with the result that although Boothby managed to keep his seat in the Commons, he lost his position at the Ministry of Food. "I never forgave Churchill for that," Boothby later recalled. "He ruined my wartime career."[292]

Yet there is an element in Boothby's tale that is common to the recollections of many who ran afoul of Churchill. Boothby never forgave Churchill for that incident, but he understood that Churchill's "ruthlessness and aloofness may have helped to make him a great leader." Churchill had his own awkward way of thanking those who served him. After the war he arranged for Boothby, an ardent European unionist, to go as one of the first five British delegates to the Council of Europe in Strasbourg. Later, Churchill sponsored Boothby for knighthood. The two dined together on occasion for the remainder of Churchill's life.

Auchinleck had joined Boothby, Margesson, Wavell, Dill, Dowding, General Alan Cunningham, Dr. Tizard, and Admiral Dudley North on Churchill's roll call of those he found wanting. Churchill believed that most of his admirals and many of his generals lacked spirit, and he succeeded in sacking several, vested as he was with great powers and an unforgiving temperament when he sensed a lack of aggressiveness. The Royal Navy's admirals, Churchill once told Pound, "seem quite incapable of action." Worse, some—including, Churchill believed, Andrew Cunningham at Crete—displayed a tendency to fear "severe losses" rather than to throw themselves and their ships into the teeth of the enemy. They "shirked" their tasks,

Churchill told Colville. Churchill was said to be so autocratic that Hitler told his own generals that they were fortunate to work for such a reasonable leader as himself rather than for the mercurial Churchill.[293]

Bob Boothby believed that Churchill's ruthlessness toward subordinates was prompted not by any latent, mean-spirited inclination, but solely by the need to defeat Hitler. Churchill himself saw things that way; in his letter to Clementine recounting Auchinleck's downfall, he offered that the changes made in Cairo "were necessary to victory." As for Bernard Montgomery, who by August 10 was hastening to his new command in Egypt, Churchill told Clementine: "In Montgomery... we have a competent daring and energetic soldier" who "if he is disagreeable to those about him he is also disagreeable to the enemy."[294]

While Churchill wrapped up his business with Auchinleck, great events transpired on a South Pacific island that few in London or Washington had heard of. Early on August 7, almost ten thousand U.S. Marines from the 1st and 5th regiments, First Marine Division, slogged ashore on the stinking, hot island of Guadalcanal, where the Japanese had almost completed an airfield from which they intended to sever the American shipping lanes that sustained Australia. Most of the leathernecks carried World War One Springfield bolt-action rifles and wore World War One–era leggings. They secured the beachhead with ease, and the next day they took the airfield. Much of their equipment and almost all of their rations failed to follow them ashore when on August 8, Admiral Frank ("Jack") Fletcher, who had already had two aircraft carriers sunk from under him, turned his ships for home with the meager excuse that he needed to refuel (just as he had when he steamed away from the relief of Wake Island in December), thus earning him the everlasting antipathy of Marines and the moniker Frank "Always Fueling" Fletcher. Still, the Marines meant to hold their ground. America had taken the first step in the journey to Tokyo. For Churchill, the American action on Guadalcanal again raised the concern that had dogged him since January: Would the Americans proceed on that journey at the expense of the European front?[295]

Late on the tenth, Churchill departed Cairo for Tehran, the first leg of his journey to Moscow and "his visit to the Ogre in his den," as Clementine had put it in a letter earlier that week. He later noted the irony of the pilgrimage to "this sullen, sinister, Bolshevik state I had once tried so hard to strangle at birth." Had Hitler kept his bond with Stalin, the Soviets "would have watched us being swept out of existence with indifference and gleefully divided with Hitler our Empire in the East." What, Churchill wondered, did he owe the Soviets? Wavell gave the answer in a poem of many verses, the last line of each being: "No second front in nineteen forty-two." Brooke offered his opinions about Moscow to his diary, and they were not conciliatory: "Personally I feel our policy with the Russians has been wrong from the very start, and as begun by Beaverbrook. We have bowed and scraped to them" without ever asking in return for information on Soviet "production, strength, dispositions, etc. As a result they despise us and have no use for us except what they can get out of us."[296]

Three B-24 Liberators were needed to ferry the entire party to Moscow, including Brooke, Air Marshal Tedder, Cadogan from the Foreign Office, and Archie Wavell, who spoke Russian. It was an unnecessarily large party, Brooke wrote, made so because Churchill felt such a retinue of generals, admirals, and air marshals "increased his dignity."[297]

Harriman had arrived in Tehran two days before Churchill, and he used the time to inspect the British-run Iranian railroad system, which he found to be "the worst mess I have ever seen." He would know; railroading was in his blood. When Churchill arrived on the eleventh, Harriman proposed that the U.S. Army take over the railroad in order to expedite the delivery of Lend-Lease goods to Stalin. Churchill, dubious, agreed to discuss the matter in the autumn. Harriman then joined Churchill on *Commando* for the run to Moscow. The plane was routed east of the Caspian in order to avoid any stray German fighters. The din in the aircraft was such that the two men passed written notes between themselves whenever they had something to say.[298]

Brooke and his party followed in his B-24, but when one of the engines flared out, they had to return to Tehran for the night. The next day the Brooke contingent climbed into an American DC-3, a Lend-Lease offering that the Russians had lavishly outfitted with thick seats and Persian carpets. They flew north by west to Baku to refuel. To Brooke's delight, the plane scared up thousands of water birds as it came in low over the Volga delta. From there they flew north along the Caspian coast, with the Caucasus just twenty miles to the west. The plain below, between the sea and the mountains, was the main line of advance from Russia into Iran. With the Germans driving from the north, Brooke expected to see trenches and anti-tank traps and concrete fortifications in numbers to match the Volga birds. He saw none. "The back door seemed to be wide open for the Germans to walk through for an attack on the Russian southern supply route," he wrote, "and more important still, the vital Middle East Oil supplies of Persia and Iraq!"[299]

On his way to Moscow, Churchill learned that an eleven-ship relief convoy bound from Gibraltar to Malta had lost eight ships and an escorting aircraft carrier to German submarines and aircraft. The three remaining ships brought 12,000 tons of food and petrol to Malta, relief, but at a terrible price. Churchill was not pleased, not only because of the losses, but because he knew that Stalin would demand a resumption of the Arctic convoys, and there were just not enough ships.[300]

After a ten-hour flight from Tehran, Churchill arrived in Moscow late in the afternoon of August 12. Greeted by Molotov, he climbed into a bulletproof car and set off at high speed for a dacha about a dozen miles outside Moscow. There, after availing himself of a hot bath, Churchill found that everything in the guesthouse had been "prepared with totalitarian lavishness." Three hours later he was escorted into the blacked-out Kremlin. Stalin was attired in a gray rough-cloth peasant's blouse and trousers of the same material, tucked into high boots. A handsome handworked leather belt was cinched around his blouse. His eyes had a yellow cast, his face was pocked, his teeth discolored, and his mustache scrawny and streaked. Harriman thought he looked noticeably older and grayer than he had the year before. The marshal and Churchill were close to the same height, around five foot seven, with Churchill an inch or so taller. Where Churchill was given to looking directly into the eyes of his conversation partners, Stalin gazed away into the distance as if he were not listening. But he was. Harriman described the three meetings that took place over the next three days as running "hot and cold"—very hot, and very cold.[301]

The first, which lasted three hours, began on a somber note when Churchill, getting right to the point, announced that there would be no second front in France that year. Any attempt to do so would be so paltry as to offer no help to Russia, and would likely result in the annihilation of the forces on the beaches. But in 1943, Churchill offered, the Allies were prepared to throw twenty-seven divisions ashore, half of them armored.

Stalin, Harriman reported to Roosevelt, "took issue at every point with bluntness." He first lectured Churchill on the need to take risks in order to win wars, and then proclaimed, "You must not be so afraid of the Germans." Churchill, keeping his cool, replied that the British air offensive against Germany was a success, and with American participation would visit ruin on Germany. Here, Stalin expressed some enthusiasm, suggesting that houses as well as factories be targeted. Churchill backed away, saying that any damage inflicted upon "working men's houses" was a by-product of bombs missing industrial targets. He then steered the talk to Torch, which he declared was in fact a second front. Here, he sketched a crocodile and, poking his pen at the crocodile's belly, offered that it was just as sound to strike here, in its soft underbelly, as it was—he now tapped the crocodile's nose—to attack "its snout." At that, Stalin seemed to take interest, asking a great many questions about the operation before pronouncing Torch militarily sound. He added, "May God help this enterprise to succeed," a strange utterance from the leader of an atheist dictatorship (he had been a seminarian before devoting himself to revolution and murder). After more questions from Stalin about the African campaign (including the need to bring de Gaulle in), the meeting adjourned. All in all, it had been a productive start.[302]

The next day's meeting was scheduled for late in the evening to allow Brooke, Tedder, and Cadogan to reach Moscow first. After an eleven-hour flight from Baku they arrived in time for dinner at Churchill's dacha. All recorded similar impressions of the extravagant accoutrements in the villa, including marble walls, wood paneling, rooms too numerous to count, a large aquarium full of tropical fish (which Churchill wanted to feed), and patches of ripe raspberries in the walled gardens. Most of all, they were struck by the food, in variety and abundance unlike anything they had seen in three years. Cadogan thought it all "really rather vulgar." Before dinner Churchill sat down with Tedder to recount the previous day's meeting with Stalin, whom he called "a peasant" and one he could handle at that. Tedder was mortified; all except Churchill knew that the walls likely contained microphones. Tedder scribbled a note and shoved it across the table; it read, "*Méfiez-vous*" ("Beware"). The Kremlin, too, Tedder assured Churchill, was bugged. At this, Churchill turned and addressed the walls: "The Russians, I have been told, are not human beings at all. They are lower in the scale of nature than the orang-outang [*sic*]. Now, then, let them take that down and translate it into Russian."[303]

Shortly after ten on the thirteenth, Churchill left for the Kremlin and his second meeting with Stalin. It proved a disaster. Harriman saw it coming. The previous year when he and Beaverbrook brought Lend-Lease to Moscow, their first meeting with Stalin had gone well, but he had arrived at the second in full offensive mode, blunt and insulting. He did so again this day, when he began by reading from a memorandum that Harriman described as "bristling with recriminations," all directed toward Churchill and his "refusal" to open a second front in 1942. He demanded that the front be opened that year. Churchill, shrewdly, promised to respond in writing, thus delaying further recriminations. Stalin came at him verbally, demanding greater sacrifices by the Western powers. Ten thousand* Russians were sacrificed daily, he declared. What were the British doing? Churchill touted the RAF bombing campaign and promised to "shatter

* This was not an exaggeration, if both civilians and soldiers are included. Every three months, more Russians died than did Americans in all the wars in American history.

almost every dwelling in every German city" as the war went on. Stalin smiled at that, but claimed a "reluctance" to fight on the part of the British. It was fear, in fact. He accused the British of stealing Lend-Lease material, and snarled that they should try fighting for a change, like the Russians, to which Churchill replied, "I pardon that remark only on account of the bravery of the Russian troops." Harriman, recalling his experience of the previous year, slipped Churchill a note telling him not to take Stalin too seriously. But Churchill hit back, speaking so rapidly that his interpreter fell behind. "Did you tell him this?" Churchill asked his interpreter, and again, "Did you tell him this?" He wanted Stalin to hear each and every point. The British and Americans were *not* cowards, and they would demonstrate that soon. He and Roosevelt were willing to sacrifice 150,000 men in France if they thought it would help Russia, but a foolish enterprise would serve no one. *"Did you tell him this?"* again he asked after each rejoinder. Harriman thought it was Churchill's "most brilliant" performance, during which he not once reminded Stalin of his pact with Hitler. Stalin finally leaned in to the table, and said, "Your words are of no importance, what is important is your spirit." With that, the tension eased. Stalin invited Churchill and Harriman to dine with him the next evening. When the meeting ended at midnight, Churchill, enraged, banged down the corridors of the Kremlin, "looking neither left nor right. He struck a match on the Kremlin wall and without breaking stride lighted a cigar."[304]

He kept Harriman up into the wee hours analyzing Stalin's change in demeanor. Their best guess was that other commissars on the Politburo, holding more power than the West believed, insisted that Stalin take a harder line. Harriman predicted a return to affability at the next meeting.

The next night—later that day, in fact—Stalin hosted a dinner for forty in Catherine the Great's state rooms. Harriman thought the affair more subdued than the feasts he and Beaverbrook had been treated to the previous year. Churchill later wrote, "Silly tales have been told of how these Soviet dinners became drinking bouts. There is no truth whatever in this." Actually there was a great deal of truth. Brooke called the banquet "a complete orgy" of nineteen courses and vodka toast after vodka toast raised by all around the table, a dozen or more in the first hour. The table "groaned" under the weight of hors d'oeuvres and fish and chickens and a suckling pig with a black truffle eye and orange peel mouth. Stalin's aide General Kliment Voroshilov almost drank himself under the table, which he had in fact done at a dinner for Eden in December. When Voroshilov held up his glass to click Stalin's, Brooke was sure the general must have been seeing a half dozen glasses. But the toast came off, as did the banquet. The verbal jousts were friendly, but still pointed. Stalin recounted Lady Astor's comment made during her prewar visit to Moscow: "*Oh,* Churchill, he's finished." The marshal told Churchill he had disagreed. "If a great crisis comes," he recalled saying, "the English people might turn to the old war horse." That pleased Churchill, who asked if Stalin had forgiven him for trying to crush the Bolshevik revolution after the Great War. "All that is in the past," Stalin replied. "It is not for me to forgive. It is for God to forgive." The leg-pulling and toasts went on for four hours. Upon leaving the Kremlin after 1:00 A.M., and still smarting from the talks of the previous day, Churchill told Cadogan he did not really know what he was doing here and he planned to return to London without seeing Stalin again. "He was," Cadogan told Dr. Wilson, "like a bull in the ring maddened by the pricks of the picadors."[305]

But when he again met with Stalin, all went well, as Harriman had predicted. They gathered at seven that evening in Stalin's private rooms in the Kremlin. Bottles were uncorked, food prepared, and the leg-pulling began again, but with good humor. Churchill could not resist chiding Stalin on his pact with Hitler; Stalin, in turn, asked why the British had tried to bomb Molotov when he was in Berlin in 1940. Churchill replied, "In war no advantages can ever be neglected." Stalin, still smarting from the cancelation of Arctic convoys, asked, "Has the British Navy no sense of glory?" Churchill replied that he knew a great deal about navies. Stalin shot back, "Meaning that I know nothing." Churchill then delivered a monologue on the differences between sea powers and land powers, as he had with Molotov in May. The meeting pushed past ten o'clock. Churchill, remembering that he had plans to dine with the Polish general Wyadłsław Anders, who was in Russia searching for thousands of missing Polish army officers, sent off a note canceling their engagement. Stalin and Churchill talked—and drank—past midnight, trading tales and information. Churchill told Stalin that a major British raid would soon take place on the French coast, at Dieppe; Stalin offered to share with the British the blueprints for a new type of rocket (he never did). At 1:00 A.M., a suckling pig was produced, which Stalin fell upon. Churchill finally departed after three with a "splitting headache" (his only reference to the effects of alcohol in his memoirs). By dawn he was bound for Tehran.[306]

He arrived back in Cairo on August 17, having concluded, as he later told the House, that Stalin was "a man of massive outstanding personality...a man of inexhaustible courage and will-power, and a man direct and even blunt in speech....Above all, he is a man with that saving sense of humour which is of high importance to all men and all nations, but particularly to great men and great nations....I believe I made him feel that we were good and faithful comrades in this war but that, after all, is a matter which deeds, not words, will prove."[307]

Early in the morning of August 19, Louis Mountbatten launched his largest military venture of 1942, a triphibious raid on Dieppe by air, sea, and land of five thousand mostly Canadian infantry supported by thirty Churchill tanks. This was the operation Churchill had played up to Stalin. In Cairo, Churchill waited for reports on the results. The results were disastrous—almost one thousand killed and two thousand captured. Churchill and the Chiefs of Staff, who had approved the Dieppe raid, shared responsibility for the horrific results of Mountbatten's misjudgment.

The first post-battle report from Mountbatten that reached Churchill proclaimed that the "morale of returning troops is excellent.... All I have seen are in great form." He could not have seen very many, given the numbers of dead and captured. Based in part on that faulty intelligence, Churchill cabled the War Cabinet, "The results fully justified the heavy costs." Only weeks later, as the real casualties were tallied, did Churchill see the folly of the scheme. Yet, the raid served a tangential political purpose, arguing against any further continental excursions for 1942. Even if the Allies possessed the right type and sufficient quantities of landing craft to mount an invasion, and they did not, the results at Dieppe spoke directly to the need for much heavier firepower in such landings, more tanks, specialized tanks for clearing mines, and paratroop disruption behind enemy lines. It verified Brooke's (and Eisenhower's) thesis that a beachhead could only be held if supported by massed aerial bombing of German positions and transportation links leading to the beaches. It verified the need for overwhelming fire support from the navy right up to the moment when troops hit the beach, and after, by way of long-distance barrages laid down by battleships, not pot shots by gunboats. Given that the American Eighth Air Force was just getting off the ground and that the scores of warships needed to support any large-scale landing were dispersed across the Atlantic on convoy escort duty, only one conclusion could be drawn from Dieppe as it pertained to a second European front: no further landings could be contemplated for at least a year. Any reasonable man could understand that, but, as Churchill had learned days earlier, Stalin was not that kind of man.[308]

Churchill liked to proclaim that he judged the results, not the man. The slaughter of Dieppe should have cost Mountbatten his career, and it would have had he not been a Churchill favorite. Churchill was ruthless in purging those who displeased him, but his treatment of Mountbatten was an altogether different matter. By the late summer, Mountbatten's staff at

Command Operations numbered more than 350, including dozens of Americans. Combined Operations had grown from a minuscule unit to Dickie's fiefdom. Although on paper Vice Admiral Lieutenant General Air Marshal Mountbatten answered to the Chiefs of Staff, he in fact had been granted a unique measure of power that he exercised almost unilaterally. Brooke didn't think much of his command qualifications, and he thought even less of many of his schemes. Yet Dickie charmed many, including Franklin Roosevelt, who, as a former naval person himself and the scion of seafarers, liked the cut of Dickie's jib. Lady Emerald Cunard, the queen of London's hostesses, did not, and offered to Jock Colville that Mountbatten "was one of the most tedious men she knew; he thought a mask of superficial charm could compensate for never having read a book." In fact, in the coming months, Churchill was to give Dickie far more significant commands, in Burma, and later in India. He had earned Churchill's confidence and, most important, his absolute loyalty. That's all he needed.[309]

Churchill later wrote that valuable lessons were learned at Dieppe, that the Canadians had not died in vain. But the British chiefs should not have needed a debacle like Dieppe to learn the lessons; they were paid to plan, not to experiment. The maxims of fire support and overwhelming force that Mountbatten violated were well known, including by Churchill, who in this case did not pay his usual attention to the smallest of details. The raid was a complete failure, and the many lives sacrificed in attempting it were lost with no tangible result. Yet Brooke had discussed the plan during at least two staff meetings and had voiced no dissenting opinion at the time. Only when the butcher's bill was tallied did Brooke confide to his diary that "for such an enterprise" the total casualties—three thousand out of five thousand men—were "far too heavy." Usually quick to denigrate Mountbatten, Brooke did not. Nor did Churchill, whose first concern was that his new Eighth Army commander, Bernard Montgomery, might have had a hand in planning the debacle before departing England for Cairo. He had not. In fact, the raid was originally scheduled for early July, but foul weather and German aircraft attacks had forced its postponement. Montgomery, at the time, advised that it be permanently scrubbed. Montgomery bore no responsibility for Dieppe, and Mountbatten escaped taking any. But Beaverbrook took the slaughter of his fellow Canadians hard, and for the remainder of his life loathed Dickie Mountbatten.[310]

After almost thirty-six months of war, the only general Churchill could bring himself to pay tribute to was not British, but Erwin Rommel, who he anointed "a great general" in front of a very surprised House of Commons. The British government that summer conducted a survey in order to gauge the public's opinion of the army, which, Mollie Panter-Downes wrote, had never been accorded the kudos bestowed upon the Royal Navy and Royal Air Force. In one of the questions, homeowners were asked to name the war's "outstanding general." The government presumed respondents would offer the name of a British general. A distressingly high percentage of those surveyed answered "Rommel." England and Churchill liked a "first-class performer." Yet Churchill's respect for Rommel went only so far. Before departing Cairo, he issued orders to Alexander and Montgomery. They were to "take or destroy at the earliest opportunity the German-Italian army commanded by Field Marshal Rommel."[311]

Late on August 23, Churchill, Dr. Wilson, and Harriman boarded *Commando* in Cairo for the run to Gibraltar, with Brooke and his staff following fifteen minutes later in a B-24 Liberator. The fourteen-hour flight took Churchill over the desert and French North Africa and out to sea, where under low clouds they ran just thirty feet above the Mediterranean. According to the captain's reckoning, Gibraltar should have heaved into view, but a heavy mist hung low over the water. The Rock was invisible. Churchill, as was his habit on final approaches, climbed into the cockpit. After a glance out the window, he voiced his fear that they were going to crash into Gibraltar. Vanderkloot, busy at the controls, muttered a few words of encouragement, and flew on. After several anxious minutes, Churchill recalled, the plane "flew into clear air, and up towered the great precipice of Gibraltar." Vanderkloot's reckoning was spot on. Once they were all on dry land, Churchill's military bodyguards, fearing an assassination attempt, confined him to Governor's House. He would have none of it, and proposed disguising himself as an Egyptian demimondain or an American tourist with a toothache (presumably with a knotted bandage around his head) in order to tour the fortress. But in Governor's House he stayed, where over lunch he made clear that he would rather be in Egypt, on the front lines, especially were Rommel to attack within days, which according to Ultra he would do. But he was the prime minister, not a field marshal, and his place was in London, not on the line. Late in the afternoon, angry at having to fly from, not toward, the pending battle, he boarded his plane.[312]

Rommel attacked on August 31. "What I now needed," Montgomery later wrote, "was a battle which would be fought in accordance with my ideas." He got exactly that. Rommel's plans called for turning the Eighth Army's southern flank, above the Qattara Depression, much as he had turned Ritchie's flank on the Gazala Line three months before. Montgomery, anticipating that tactic, fortified the Alam-el Halfa ridge to his rear with an entire infantry division along with dug-in artillery. Then he massed four hundred tanks in front of the ridge, intending to let Rommel flail against his protected left flank. Rommel expected Montgomery to counterattack, at which time he planned to swing past Montgomery's flank and drive through the center of the Eighth Army. When Montgomery refused Rommel's gambit, the German cabled his Mediterranean commander, Field Marshal Albert Kesselring, "The swine will not attack." Actually, Montgomery's command of just two weeks—"brave but baffled" Churchill had called the Eighth Army—was not yet ready to attack, but they were ready to defend their turf. One of Montgomery's first orders to his troops was that if attacked, they would not withdraw. Like the Spartans at Thermopylae, "We would fight on the ground we now held, and if we couldn't stay there alive, we would stay there dead." Rommel learned by September 3 what those who knew Monty had long known: Bernard Montgomery fought battles on his terms and his terms only. By September 4, Rommel had punched himself out against the Alam-el Halfa lines. The two opposing armies settled again into a dusty and belligerent stasis, with two critical differences between this standoff and all the others since 1941. The RAF had established overwhelming air superiority, and the three hundred new Sherman tanks had arrived to add muscle to Montgomery's army. Rommel, in desperate need of the men, gasoline, and tanks that Hitler had promised, would have to make do with what he had.[313]

Churchill, enthused by the Eighth Army's gallant stand, but impatient as always, pestered Brooke for an early *offensive* stroke by Montgomery. Churchill, Brooke told his diary, "started all his worst arguments about generals only thinking about themselves and their reputations and never attacking until matters were a certainty." Monty, not yet prepared to go on the offensive, stood his ground, against both Rommel and Churchill. And so Churchill, too, learned what Rommel had gleaned at Alam-el Halfa.[314]

Early October brought messages from Stalin that worrisomely implied a deteriorating Red Army position. The Luftwaffe had established a two-to-one air superiority in Russia. Stalin requested five hundred fighter planes per month—more than 10 percent of American production—to remedy the situation. Implicit in the Luftwaffe's air superiority was verification of Stalin's argument that RAF bombing of Western Europe had done nothing to take the pressure off Russia. In fact, the Americans had yet to drop a single bomb on Germany, whereas the Luftwaffe by early October had destroyed most of Stalingrad.

Paulus's Sixth Army had been fighting within the city limits for a month and had destroyed the Red October and Tractor factories. All that remained for Hitler to secure his victory was for Paulus to reach the banks of the Volga and hold his ground. The possibility of Stalin negotiating a separate peace with Germany once again dominated Churchill's thoughts. Montgomery, meanwhile, was not yet ready to attack in the desert. The tanks he needed had been sent to Russia, but not enough to placate Stalin, who asked for eight thousand more *per month,* far more than America produced. In the Atlantic, the U-boats were still sending more tonnage to the bottom than the Allies could replace. With the need to deploy all available destroyers out to protect the Torch fleet, which was then readying to sail from America and Britain, no further convoys to Russia could be contemplated. Stalin, in need of 500,000 tons of supplies per month (about seventy shiploads), accused the British again, as he had in the summer, of stealing food, weapons, and matériel that the Red Army needed. As if to validate Stalin's paranoia, the British and Americans canceled the October convoy to Murmansk, this *after* Stalin pleaded for more help. The situation in the Mediterranean was no better. Malta was down to less than two weeks' supply of food, leading Brooke to lament to his diary, "God knows how we shall keep Malta alive." Churchill, meanwhile, prodded Brooke to prod Alexander and Montgomery into launching their attack, well before they were ready, in Brooke's estimation. To his diary, Brooke offered, "It is a regular disease he [Churchill] suffers from, this frightful impatience to get an attack launched."[315]

As Churchill waited for the curtain to go up in Egypt, Eleanor Roosevelt arrived in London for a three-week visit. Like Harriman, she came bearing a Virginia ham. During her stay she and Clementine conducted exhaustive (and exhausting) tours of wrecked neighborhoods, RAF bases, and air-raid shelters. When she met with a contingent of black American troops, she "liked it when their officer, white, insisted that his men were the best in the army." The First Lady, a political activist, was the sort of woman men of Churchill's generation usually beheld from afar, other than when the suffragettes had pushed their way into manly venues where they did not belong. Churchill understood Mrs. Roosevelt to be politically significant, and not merely because she was the wife of the president. A Gallup poll had found that for every two Americans who thought the First Lady talked too much, three "approved of her courage and ability to speak out." Eleanor Roosevelt regularly and with passion advised her husband on matters of policy, including the matter of blacks serving alongside whites in the U.S. military. Her prodding in that regard had brought results. George Marshall pledged to Roosevelt that blacks would make up 10 percent of the troops sent to Britain.[316]

That ratio engendered resentment among many of the 90 percent of American troops who served alongside blacks. Eden tried to persuade Eisenhower to cease the influx of black soldiers, not because HMG or Britons harbored racist beliefs but because white Americans were regularly beating the hell out of black Americans on the streets of London. And the need to find separate quarters for black and white Americans placed a further burden on the atrophied stocks of housing. Eisenhower was only obeying a directive from the Adjutant General's Office that ordered "wherever possible separate sleeping accommodations be provided for Negro soldiers" but in all other regards they be treated as the equals of white soldiers. In fact, they were not. American dining facilities were segregated; black American women were brought over to staff the roving Red Cross canteens that served blacks. The British people, for the most part, accepted blacks in their midst more readily than did the Americans, especially American officers, all of whom were white and many of whom refused to dine in restaurants that served blacks. British villagers were especially welcoming of the blacks. One pub owner, disgusted by the behavior of white Americans, placed a sign in his window: "For the use of the British and coloured Americans only." But in London, to placate white Yanks (who were flush with dollars), many restaurants banned black Americans, and by doing so inadvertently closed the doors on British citizens. When a black official from the Colonial Office was refused service at his favorite restaurant after American officers complained to the proprietor, the repercussions reached all the way to the cabinet, where, after pondering the incident, Churchill commented, "That's all right, if he brings a banjo they'll think he's one of the band."[317]

Something other than precise analysis affected Churchill's opinions of all peoples other than English-speaking. He shared with the Western press and much of the English-speaking world a condescending attitude toward people who were of other than Anglo-Saxon ancestry. Churchill's memos, his dinner-table asides, even his public addresses, are rife with references to Japs, Wops, Frogs, and Huns, often modified with such choice adjectives as "foul," "filthy," "wretched," and "nasty." His friends, family, and colleagues expressed themselves likewise: Sir Alexander Cadogan's diary entries are xenophobic romps, peppered with demeaning references to just about everybody of any nationality other than English—this from the permanent secretary of the Foreign Office, responsible during the war for vetting the legal niceties of Britain's foreign affairs, including the wording of the Atlantic Charter, parent document to the United Nations. Cadogan considered the Slavs to be "poor dears," the Iraqis "filthy," and the Japanese "monkeys." The usually polite and progressive Harold Nicolson referred to "the Japanese" when he contemplated Japan in his diary, until, that is, Japan began trouncing the British in Asia, after which Nicolson wrote of the "monkey men." Lord Cherwell despised Jews. Even Clementine could demean with the best of them. In a late 1941 letter to Winston, who at the time was America-bound on board the *Duke of York*, Clementine wrote words of encouragement: "Well my beloved Winston—May God keep you and inspire you to make good plans with the president. It's a horrible World at present, Europe over-run by the Nazi hogs, & the Far East by yellow Japanese lice.... Tender Love & thoughts, Clemmie." Such were the times.[318]

Churchill called peoples of African ancestry "blackamoors," and he didn't much like them. Once, late in life, he asked his physician, Lord Moran, what happened when blacks got measles; could the rash be spotted? When Moran replied that blacks suffered a high mortality rate from measles, Churchill offered, "Well there are plenty left. They've got a high rate of production." When, during his second premiership, his cabinet debated the adoption of new laws limiting West Indian immigration, Churchill proposed his suggestion for a national motto: "Keep England White."[319]

The First Lady therefore arrived in England during a difficult period for race relations. Normally, she would have spoken her mind. But to the relief of Secretary of War Stimson, her behavior in Britain was "very temperate." She was there to improve morale, not to reform the armed forces. Speaking her mind to Churchill was another matter. When, during a dinner at No. 10, the First Lady took him to task for first backing Franco and then, after Franco showed his Fascist stripes, not backing the Loyalists during the Spanish Civil War, Churchill growled that had the Loyalists won, the first heads to roll would belong to people such as herself and her husband. Mrs. Roosevelt responded by saying she didn't care whether she lost her head. "Well," Churchill snarled, "I don't want to lose mine." Clementine did not help matters when she offered that Mrs. Roosevelt was correct. As Churchill fumed, Clementine separated the combatants, announcing that it was time for the ladies to adjourn to the sitting room and leave the men alone with their brandies and cigars. Of her dining experiences with Churchill, Mrs. Roosevelt later wrote, "I found the P.M. not easy to talk to."[320]

Churchill's behavior could be forgiven given the events unfolding in the Atlantic and in the desert, although in truth he had treated Mrs. Roosevelt no differently than any guest. Of dining with Churchill, Harold Nicolson wrote, "Winston is bad at putting people at ease.... There is a mask of boredom and another mask or film of obstinacy, as if he were saying, 'These people bore me and I shall refuse to be polite.'" Yet, suddenly Churchill would "cease thinking of something else, and the film will part and the sun comes out." The First Lady saw the sun come out at Chequers, when she was treated to the spectacle of Churchill playing with his two-year-old grandson, little Winston. "They sat on the floor," she later wrote, "and played a game and the resemblance was ridiculous." The scene reminded her of the story of the lady who, catching sight of Churchill and little Winston, remarked to Churchill on the resemblance. Churchill looked up and replied, "You are quite wrong, I resemble every baby." He also showed the First Lady a room that he intended to have redecorated in order to accommodate the special needs of her husband, who, Churchill hoped, would soon visit England.[321]

Late on the moonlit night of October 23, almost a thousand pieces of British heavy artillery commenced firing along the El Alamein front. The barrage, which continued into the early hours of the twenty-fourth, served notice to Erwin Rommel that Bernard Montgomery was on his way. At first light, the Highlanders screamed their ancient battle cry, *Caberfeidh,** as the skirl of their bagpipes rent the silence. They attacked through the blowing grit of a dry desert dawn. By daylight, the Eighth Army—190,000 men, 1,400 anti-tank guns, and almost 1,000 tanks—smashed into Rommel's lines across a six-mile front. The tanks soon stopped while sappers cleared narrow paths—just wide enough to accommodate tank treads—through the half million landmines Rommel had buried at his front. It soon became apparent that the British possessed too few sappers and too few mine detectors. But overall, numbers were with the British. On the northern, coastal end of the German lines (Montgomery's real objective), the XV Panzer Corps was outnumbered at least six to one, in both tanks and men. Panzer Army Africa, more than half of which was made up of Italians, was outmanned and outgunned by almost two to one. To make matters worse for the Germans, Rommel had taken a sick leave weeks earlier and was at that moment resting in a hospital bed in Semmering, a lovely town perched on the pine-forested slopes of the southern Austrian Alps, as far removed from the war as any hamlet in Europe. At about noon, Hitler telephoned Rommel personally with the news from North Africa. "The situation looks very black," the Führer offered. "Would you be willing to go back?"[322]

Rommel's replacement in the field, General Georg Stumme, had assumed the British would attack the southern end of his lines, thirty miles from the sea, in part because the terrain was more favorable and in part

* "The antlers of the deer."

because Montgomery had positioned three dummy regiments in the south and had begun construction of a dummy waterline to the dummy forces. Stumme, in turn, lacked the gasoline to move his tanks about at will, north to south and back. He would have to stand and fight where he was. By late morning, under the onslaught of RAF fighters and Montgomery's massed artillery, Stumme found himself completely cut off from almost all of his forces and commanders, north and south. By day's end, Stumme was dead, felled by a massive coronary. Montgomery's field guns raked the German panzer deployments, to horrific effect. Artillery, as Churchill had urged a year earlier, had finally found its place on the desert battlefield. Rommel, returning on October 25 to find a rout in progress, stanched his ruptured lines enough to blunt Montgomery's initial thrusts. Rommel placed his Italian infantry between German mechanized units, in part to protect the Italians, in part to ensure that they remained on the battlefield. Yet unless he was resupplied, his diminishing numbers of men, tanks, aircraft, and artillery could only add up to retreat. He needed gasoline most of all. He radioed his status to Hitler—a message that the Bletchley crowd soon deciphered and Montgomery soon read.[323]

In London, Churchill, desperate for the latest news, badgered his generals without respite. For the first two days, Churchill simply asked Brooke how Montgomery was doing. When Montgomery's progress stalled, Churchill's tone changed. He prepared a stinging telegram for Alexander in which he sought answers to the apparent collapse of the offensive—a conclusion he reached after chatting with Eden over whisky rather than consulting with his military advisers over maps. Brooke recalled the unpleasantness in his memoirs: "What, he [Churchill] asked, is *my* Monty doing now, allowing the battle to peter out. (Monty was always *my* Monty when he was out of favor.)" Why, asked Churchill, had Montgomery "told us he would be through in seven days if all he intended to do was fight a half-hearted battle?" For Churchill, more than a line in the desert was at stake. A by-election weeks earlier had gone against the government by a margin of 66 to 34 percent, a stunning yet symbolic rebuke. Churchill had convinced Cripps, who was threatening resignation, to stay on as Speaker until the battle in the desert was finished, win or lose. A defeat in the desert would very likely result in Churchill being known henceforth as the former prime minister.[324]

For seven days Monty fought, and for seven days he had nothing to show but almost eight thousand wounded and two thousand killed, including the son of Churchill's first true love of almost five decades earlier, Pamela Plowden. The Eighth Army could not punch through the minefield, which had become a no-man's-land. Montgomery threw British and Australian tanks into the minefield with results that evoked the slaughter of the Great

War. His divisional commanders advised he quit the battle and regroup. Having none of it, he threatened to sack those who lacked the appropriate aggressive spirit and replace them with fighters. He understood that if he could not win by fast and bold strokes, he would win though attrition. He could afford to trade tank for tank and man for man until he carried the day. And so he continued to feed his men and tanks into the maw. The next few days would mark a turning point, one way or another, for Churchill, for Britain, for the future conduct of the war.

If Montgomery failed, Torch could not succeed, at least according to plan, not with the British Eighth Army tied down in Egypt, 1,600 miles from the Allied invasion force. In that case, Hitler, on his Russian front, would gain invaluable weeks, if not months, to drive farther into the Caucasus and to pour forces into Stalingrad with no need to watch his back. If Montgomery failed or if Stalingrad fell, Europe-first might become Europe-maybe for the Americans. Stalemate or defeat at El Alamein would exact a heavy political as well as a military price. Churchill informed Brooke that the office of prime minister would go to somebody else if Rommel held his desert position. In that case, Sir Stafford Cripps—who in private regularly deprecated Churchill's war record, but as leader of the House was forced to explain the defeats to Parliament—might start serving vegetarian dinners in a new residence, No. 10 Downing Street. All depended upon Montgomery. Churchill was "finding the suspense almost unbearable," Bracken told Dr. Wilson as the world waited for news from the desert.[325]

On October 30, thanks to Ultra decrypts and on the advice of his lieutenants, Montgomery shifted his main thrust from the coast about ten miles to the south. It was the sort of improvisation Montgomery disliked, but it worked. Rommel, by shifting his armor to the far north, to counter Montgomery's initial strike, had weakened his southern sector. By then, the Desert Fox had fewer than four dozen tanks remaining fit for battle, and they were almost out of fuel. Two ships carrying gasoline to Rommel were sunk as they approached Tobruk, again thanks to Ultra. Montgomery pressed on. His New Zealanders broke Rommel's lines on November 2. Rommel counterattacked in a furious two-hour tank assault, but realizing he was waging a battle of attrition he could only lose, he called off the attack. Early the next day, he left behind a rearguard and turned west. Hopes ran high, Churchill later wrote, that the moment had arrived for the "annihilation" of Rommel's army. Rommel, too, expected as much, as he raced for Tripoli. But the late autumn rains had arrived. Rather than compete with foul weather and washed-out desert tracks, Monty, after a desultory twenty-hour chase, called for a one-day halt. British fighter pilots who were tracking the Germans and calling in the enemy's positions were dumbfounded. Where was the final, fatal strike? Where was the Eighth Army?[326]

Just after he began his retreat, Rommel received a direct order from Hitler: "Stand fast, yield not a yard of room." Sheer will could prevail, the Führer believed, and not for the first time in history, and "as to your troops, you can show them no other road than to victory or death [*Sieg oder Tod*]." Mussolini, completely misreading the situation, sent a telegraph congratulating Rommel on "the successful counter-attack." Rommel's lieutenant, General Ritter von Thoma, called Hitler's directive "a piece of unparalleled madness." Rommel paused for twenty hours in order to adhere to the spirit if not the letter of the order. Then the Desert Fox and his few dozen tanks—soon to be pursued by ten times as many—ran for Libya. Left behind in the flinty scrabble were almost six thousand dead Germans and Italians, their corpses already blackening in the desert heat. British intelligence officers wandered among the bodies and yanked from pockets postcards and love letters from home, written in German and Italian, to sons and lovers and husbands: "We are so glad you are now in beautiful Egypt"; "May Saint Dominic protect you." As night fell the discarded letters scudded across the desert on the breezes, as if following the survivors to sanctuary.[327]

Churchill, elated by the news from Egypt (and a handwritten congratulatory note from the King), told luncheon companions on November 6 that Rommel's army had been cut from its positions, like a limpet is cut from a rock. Slashing the air, as if with a knife, Churchill asked, "And what happens to a limpet when it is cut from its rock. It dies a miserable death." But not for nothing was Rommel called the Desert Fox. He had escaped and would live to fight another day, giving the lie to Machiavelli's maxim that the fox cannot outrun the wolves. The Italian infantry were not as fortunate as their mechanized German brethren. To evacuate their own, the Germans commandeered what little transportation the Italians had. "The Italians," Churchill told the Commons on November 10, "were left to perish in the waterless desert or surrender as they are doing." The Battle of Egypt was won.[328]

On the final day of October, U-559 was depth-charged by the Royal Navy and forced to the surface off Port Said. Its crew was taken aboard British cutters while three tars boarded the submarine and made for the radio room. The scene played out almost exactly as it had aboard U-110 the previous year. U-559 foundered and went down, taking two of the British sailors with her. But the third managed to escape with the boat's codebooks and Enigma machine, complete with the fourth wheel that had stymied

Bletchley for almost a year. The British now held the key to unlocking Dönitz's naval communications. With that month's U-boat codes in hand, Bletchley began reading German radio traffic even as the Torch armada lingered off North Africa. But the advantage vanished when Berlin changed the codes later in the month. Bletchley's wizards found themselves once again stymied. The captured Enigma machine ensured a breakthrough, sooner or later, but later would not do. Dönitz now had more than two hundred U-boats available for duty in the North Atlantic. He sent one hundred or more on patrol during each of the next six months, more than twice as many as at the start of the year. British losses alone pushed over 710,000 tons in November, the worst of any month of the war; 117 ships went down that month, far more than could be made up by new construction.[329]

On the political front, Cripps, having had his fill as leader of the House, resigned and finally agreed to take the job Churchill had offered early in the year—minister of aircraft production. Cripps's flame had flared in February; El Alamein had snuffed it out, along with any hopes he harbored of leading the nation after the war. Cripps, an American newsweekly offered, had proven himself "politically inept," and had been adroitly kicked by Churchill onto the sidelines. Eden took over the leadership of the House, while keeping the Foreign Office. Beaverbrook, meanwhile, under whom Cripps had refused to serve, returned to London after spending the summer in America, where he had adroitly pushed for a second front while simultaneously defending Churchill against criticism that he wasn't pursuing a second front fast enough. The Beaver was back, and a regular dinner guest at No. 10.[330]

On November 6, as Churchill conjured up images of limpets over lunch, the Torch invasion fleet—more than 650 transports, tankers, hospital ships, and 172 warships, carrying 90,000 men—made for the African coast. It had been at sea for more than two weeks. The ships had sailed from Canada, Hampton Roads, and Britain, and had arranged themselves into three task forces. The Western would land Patton's 34,000 men on the Atlantic coast of Morocco. On the fifth, the Center and Eastern task forces had run past Gibraltar on their way to Oran and Algiers. The armada expected a hot welcome from U-boats, but as the hours passed, not an enemy periscope was seen. The Germans, as the British learned from Ultra decrypts, did not know the fleet was on its way. Bletchley also passed on the astounding (and welcome) news that the Germans had no plan in effect

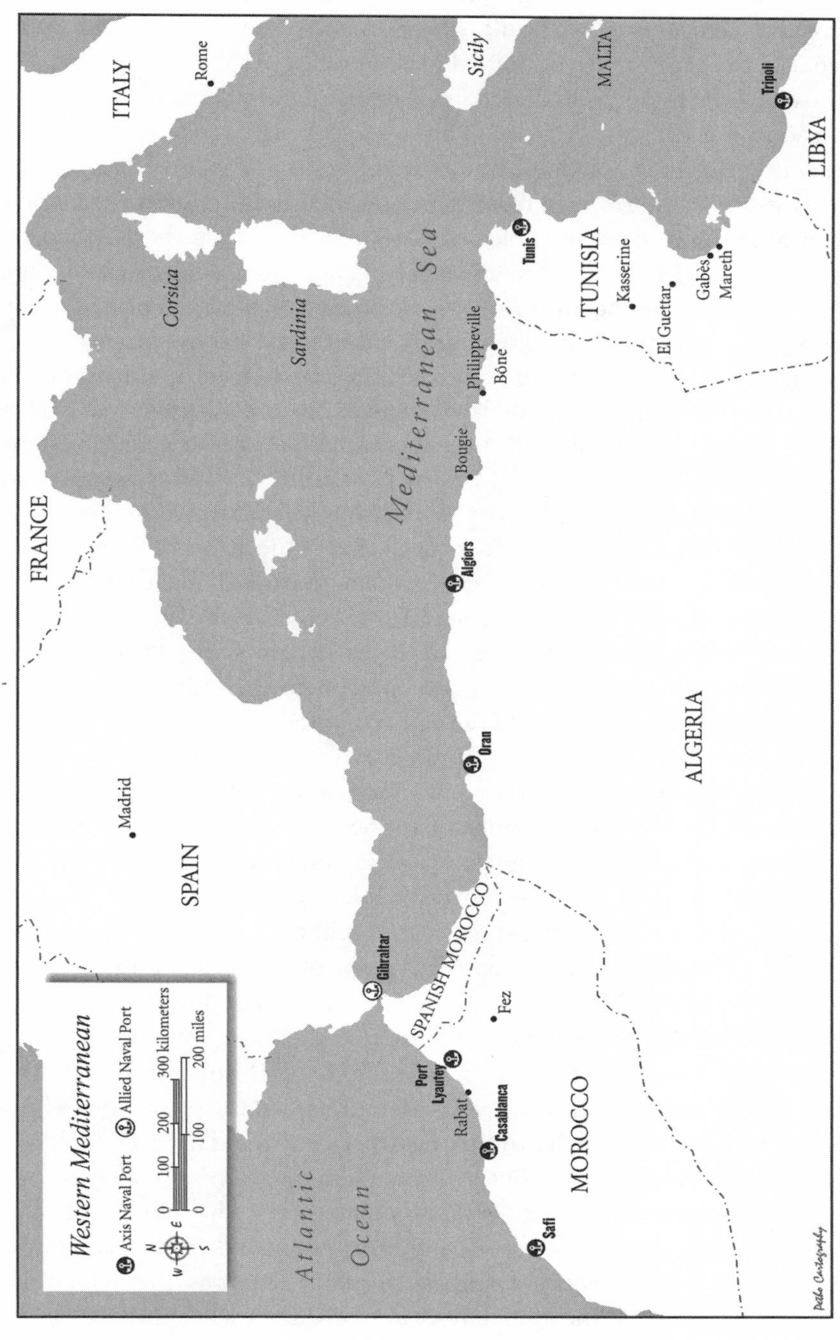
Western Mediterranean
Axis Naval Port
Allied Naval Port
N
W
E
S
0 100 200 300 kilometers
0 100 200 miles
FRANCE
ITALY
Rome
Corsica
Sardinia
Sicily
MALTA
Tripoli
LIBYA
TUNISIA
Tunis
Kasserine
El Guettar
Gabès
Mareth
Philippeville
Bône
Bougie
Mediterranean Sea
Algiers
Oran
ALGERIA
SPAIN
Madrid
Gibraltar
SPANISH MOROCCO
Fez
Port Lyautey
Rabat
Casablanca
MOROCCO
Safi
Atlantic Ocean

to either destroy or blockade Gibraltar—the key to the entire enterprise, as the Allies needed to run the straits in order to first land and then reinforce the Central and Eastern task forces. But, as Churchill had learned earlier in the year in Egypt, Bletchley was not always correct.

Eisenhower wrote in his memoirs: "British Gibraltar made possible the invasion of northwest Africa." This was so because in early November 1942, the Allies occupied not one other piece of real estate in Europe and the western Mediterranean from which an invasion of North Africa might be launched. The Rock was blessed with a deep harbor where Allied warships could refuel and re-arm, and also was home to a small airfield, which in the weeks before the invasion was crammed full of fighter planes—fourteen fighter squadrons of sixteen craft each—and drums of gasoline. To Eisenhower's dismay, the airstrip was separated from Spain by nothing more substantial than a barbed-wire fence, against which "almost physically...leaned any number of Axis agents." The Spanish government was leaning, as well, toward Hitler. In order to put troops ashore at Oran and Algiers, Allied ships would have to sail through the thirty-mile-long gauntlet between Spain and Spanish Morocco that is the Strait of Gibraltar, less than ten miles wide in places. Were Spanish guns sited on either side of the straits to take those ships under fire, Torch would be doused. Eisenhower could only hope that the Spanish and the French in North Africa remained aloof from the fray and that the Axis presumed the buildup in Gibraltar was a prelude to the relief of Malta (as in fact they did). Regardless, sound strategy called for the Axis to bomb the Rock. Each night, Eisenhower waited for bombings that never came. Each night, Allied soldiers found fitful sleep in the twenty-five miles of tunnels cut deep within the Jurassic limestone, and each morning, they awoke "puzzled, even astonished," to find that no German planes had drubbed the Rock.[331]

During the early planning stages for Torch, the bottleneck of the straits was considered so dangerous by the Americans that they refused to send their ships into the Mediterranean lest they be trapped in that inland sea. Safety first had never been one of Churchill's dictates. Secrecy, not danger, was the first concern of the British. Churchill and Brooke believed that the Americans, inexperienced in such operations, might prove loose-lipped enough to jeopardize the entire plan. American trepidation and ability to keep a secret were but two concerns among many. Churchill also expected the Italians to send out their fleet, still dangerous with six battleships and dozens of supporting warships. Eisenhower—mistakenly—thought the Germans had two aircraft carriers with which to harass the Allied invasion fleet. Darlan and the French fleet were always a wild card.[332]

A vexing question remained up to the eve of the invasion: Did the Germans and Italians have any idea of where the Allies were going, and when?

Brooke, for his part, considered Eisenhower's headquarters to be "conspicuously leaky as regards information and secrets." The unexpected could always be depended upon to happen. In late September, British intelligence had learned that the body of a British officer killed in an airplane crash off the coast of Spain had washed up on a Spanish beach. The dead man carried letters in his tunic that contained enough veiled references to the invasion to clarify for the Germans where the invasion was to take place—if, that is, the Spanish allowed the Germans access to the body. But the Spanish handed the body over to the British, who deduced from beach sand still wedged between the tunic's buttons and buttonholes that the letters had most likely not been extracted from the tunic. The episode troubled London, but it also served to stimulate furtive imaginations within Combined Operations, where the idea took hold of misleading the Germans by planting a body carrying false information on a European beach. The following year the British would do just that with a ploy aptly named Operation Mincemeat.[333]

Eisenhower's main problem as his army neared the African coasts was not compromised intelligence or strictly military, but political. He later wrote that Torch was "a most peculiar venture of armed forces into the field of international politics; we were invading a neutral country to create a friend." Such an action has not, traditionally, been a recipe for friendship. The Americans had known for weeks that the chances for a successful invasion would be greatly increased by having a Frenchman of great stature on their side and on the ground in North Africa when the landings took place, someone who could rally both pro- and anti-Vichy elements and, most important, 230,000 Vichy troops and their officers. But the Allies had done little in the way of addressing the question of who that would be. Pétain or some other authority within the Vichy government would not do; the Americans, having pulled their ambassador in April, no longer recognized Vichy as a legitimate government. America's formerly cozy relationship with Vichy was resented by many in France, and viscerally by the Fighting French, yet de Gaulle, around whom Frenchmen now rallied, was loathed by the Americans and had not even been told of Torch. Representatives of Admiral Jean Darlan had sent messages to the senior American diplomat in Algiers, Robert Murphy, to the effect that the Germans suspected something might soon occur on the Moroccan coast and when it did, they, the Germans, intended to occupy French North Africa. Murphy and Eisenhower concluded that Darlan might be willing to "play ball" and bring the French fleet over to the Allies. Yet Washington and London distrusted Darlan more than all other Frenchmen but Laval. Then, almost on the eve of the invasion, the Americans discovered General Henri Giraud, a brave and decent man. Captured during the fall of France,

Giraud had escaped a German fortress to Vichy France, where he was allowed to live under house arrest only after he promised loyalty to Vichy. He was senior to de Gaulle in rank and beloved by Frenchmen. He looked every inch the gallant soldier—tall, stiff, plainspoken. He was also vain and stupid.[334]

Eisenhower secreted Giraud to Gibraltar by submarine and flying boat on November 7, and that evening as the invasion fleets neared the beaches, he made his pitch to the Frenchman to accompany the Allied forces to North Africa, and there to join the Allies in the first step on the road to the liberation of France. Giraud eagerly embraced the concept, but with two caveats. Honor demanded that he must assume overall command of the entire enterprise, including American and British troops; and the supporting invasion must be launched directly into France. Eisenhower, taken aback, thanked the general for his support but told him his conditions were quite impossible to meet. Giraud was adamant; he must command. They talked well into the evening, but Eisenhower simply could not bring Giraud around to the fact that a Frenchman could not command the Allied armies, in which not a single Frenchman served. The discussion, Eisenhower later wrote, was "one of my most distressing interviews of the war."[335]

That evening in London, the Soviet ambassador to the European governments in exile gave a reception. There, a Czech diplomat took one of de Gaulle's colleagues aside and whispered, "It's for tonight." A telephone call was placed to de Gaulle, who was awakened at home and took the call in his pajamas. Thus, de Gaulle learned that Anglo-American armies were about to land on French soil. His reaction was typical, if understandable: "I hope the Vichy people throw them into the sea! You don't go into France like a pack of burglars."[336]

Churchill was at Chequers that night. Since early October, Ultra decrypts had told him that Field Marshal "Smiling Albert" Kesselring—whose *Luftflotte* 2 had almost brought Fighter Command to bay in 1940—knew that the British were up to something big, but he didn't know when or where and so could not deploy his aircraft to best effect. Many in the German high command were convinced that the Allied destination was northern Norway, which it might have been had Churchill gotten his way with Operation Jupiter. Admiral Raeder, in 1940, had predicted Churchill would strike French North Africa, but he had been ignored by Hitler and the army sycophants at OKW. Most in Berlin thought the attack zone would be the Mediterranean, but not the southern shore. Why land there if the objective was to fight the German army in Europe? Armies fought at close quarters, on land, not from across seas. That had been George Marshall's argument exactly, until Brooke and Churchill—two saltwater strategists—wore him down with relentless argument.

Thus, while the Germans and Italians scanned the sea approaches to Sardinia, Sicily, and Malta, more than three hundred Allied transports and warships, having run the straits, turned southward on their true course. They divided into two streams, the Center force, carrying the American 1st Infantry and 1st Armored Division, on a heading for Oran; and the Eastern, Anglo-American force, bound for Algiers with 23,000 British and 10,000 American troops. Part of the Algerian force—not much greater in size than a division, and wistfully designated British First Army—was ordered to wheel east from Algiers after landing and strike 450 miles to Bizerte and Tunis. Its commander, Lieutenant General Kenneth Anderson, was a blunt, abrasive, and dour Scot given to skepticism that bordered on pessimism. A man of few words, he was nicknamed "Sunshine" by his men. Expecting to be reinforced as he moved east (after all, fully 90 percent of the Torch forces were at his rear), he concluded that he might well reach Tunis in two weeks, before the Germans could reinforce the city and dispute the issue. The first hours of the invasion certainly justified his unusual spate of optimism. Only a single American transport suffered any damage, after being torpedoed far out to sea by a stray U-boat. Undeterred, the battalion of soldiers on board climbed into their landing crafts and headed for shore, a hundred-mile journey. Despite the inexperience of the landing-craft crews, the Algerian landings came off the next morning better than any of the planners had hoped for.[337]

Sarah Churchill, commissioned in the Women's Auxiliary Air Force, was assigned to photographic interpretation and intelligence duties at Medmenham, near enough to Chequers for her to hitchhike there to spend weekends with her parents. She arrived at the house late on November 7, to find her father toweling off in his dressing room as Sawyers assembled his evening attire. As Churchill wielded a pair of ivory hairbrushes to part the few remaining hairs on his dome, he turned to Sarah and said, "Do you know, that at this moment six hundred forty-two ships are approaching the coast of North Africa?" "Six hundred forty-*three,*" replied Sarah. "How do you know?" he asked. "I've only been working on it for three months," answered Sarah. "Why didn't you tell me?" Churchill asked, his feelings slightly bruised. "I believe there is such a thing as security," Sarah answered. He chuckled, and retold the story at dinner. Some hours later, as father and daughter sat together before the hearth, the clock in the great hall struck one o'clock. At that moment British troops, including Randolph, began to go ashore on the Algiers beaches.[338]

They met virtually no resistance. This was what the planners had hoped for. Torch was a bold plan, and it was extremely risky. No American involved had ever participated in such an operation, and very few had even seen combat. No such "ship-to-shore" invasion had ever before crossed an ocean to reach the target. Except for the Guadalcanal invasion in August, Torch was the first large-scale amphibious operation conducted by American forces in forty-five years. At Algiers all went well, although two British destroyers were sunk in the harbor while trying to put American Rangers ashore. The fighting was finished by late morning, and the city surrendered early that evening. "Well, here we are," Randolph wrote in a letter to his father, "safe and sound." The trump card in the African deck was in the Allies' hands. It had been secured by Churchill's and Brooke's insistence on attacking Algiers.[339]

Then a message from Algiers reached Eisenhower though Admiral Cunningham: "Darlan wants to negotiate." By a stroke of supreme good luck, Admiral Jean Darlan, commander of all Vichy armed forces, was in Algiers, visiting his son, who had contracted poliomyelitis. Just before Eisenhower left London the previous week, Churchill had told him, "If I could meet Darlan, much as I hate him, I would cheerfully crawl a mile on my hands if by doing so I could get him to bring that fleet of his into the circle of Allied forces." To Cunningham, Churchill made his point more bluntly: "Kiss Darlan's stern if you have to, but get the French Navy."[340]

Vichy loyalists contested the assault at Oran, where the naval forces were British and the landing parties American. Two British cutters trying to land American troops at the harbor docks were raked by ferocious fire from French shore batteries. The docks remained in Vichy hands. The fighting continued throughout that day and the next. The defenders awaited orders; they had not heard from Pétain. In effect, America had gone to war against a people who had been allies since Lafayette helped George Washington secure his Great Republic. Herr Dr. Goebbels believed that the entire North African campaign was a "fight between the City and Wall Street for French colonies." Edward R. Murrow and many of his fellow correspondents in North Africa harbored similar suspicions. American policy, Murrow wrote to a friend, "looks like a sort of amateur imperialism, which aims at making the continent safe for the National City Bank."[341]

The Cross of Lorraine had long suspected as much. During lunch on the eighth, Churchill informed de Gaulle of the landings (about which de Gaulle already knew). Yet Churchill, true to his May pledge to hold Madagascar in trust for the French, also turned over the administration of that island to the Free French, in effect a recognition of de Gaulle's claim to constitutional authority. The Americans, meanwhile, to the chagrin of Churchill—and especially Eden—continued to ignore de Gaulle. In fact, having discovered Darlan in Algiers, they were about to actively court him. Early on November 9, Eisenhower put Mark Clark and General Giraud aboard separate planes bound for Algiers in hopes that Clark could bring Darlan and his fleet into

Allied hands while Giraud persuaded the Vichy forces there to lay down their arms. Darlan could not ignore Clark when the American appeared at his villa. But the Vichy commanders in Oran ignored Giraud; they had taken an oath of loyalty to Pétain. With de Gaulle consigned to irrelevancy by the Americans and hated by Vichy, only Darlan remained as a possible peacemaker. He was the worst of all possible choices.[342]

On the ninth, the Germans volunteered to Pétain to put men and planes into Tunisia in order to "help" Vichy defend its sovereign territory. Pétain had no choice but to agree to this "favor." The first Germans arrived in Tunis by air that evening, followed by squadrons of Stukas and Messerschmitts. Then, by ship, came Mark IV tanks, the twenty-five-ton workhorses of the German army, armed with 75mm cannons, deadlier than any American or British tank and manned by experienced crews who had learned their trade on the Russian front. And by ship came heavy artillery, German 88s, the deadliest field guns ever built.[343]

On the Moroccan coast, where Patton's troops had come ashore at three points—the port of Safi, Fedala, and Mehdia—the weather and landing crafts proved as troublesome and deadly as the enemy. The seas, roiled for a week by storms, calmed somewhat in the last hours before the landings but not enough. The first lesson learned, before a boot hit the beach, was that American landing craft of the era—Higgins Boats—were obsolete. They were made of plywood and without bow ramps, and the troops on board disembarked by jumping over the sides. Dozens of Americans drowned when they jumped into the turbulent waters; Patton himself pulled at least one body from the surf. Tanks and trucks were swept off the flimsy, flat-bottomed barges that carried them. After avoiding the enemy and without the loss of a single ship across the thousands of miles of ocean, Patton's command lost more tanks and trucks in the landings than it did during the day's combat with the defenders.[344]

Patton's troops had the benefit of five hours of darkness to cover their drive to the beaches. The American naval historian Samuel Eliot Morison, who served as an officer aboard one of the covering cruisers, described the night as quiet, with not a light to be seen, the African shore "veiled in clouds and hushed in silence." An offshore breeze carried "the smell of charcoal fires and parched dry grass" out to the ships. An hour passed, and another. Then a beam from a French searchlight shot seaward. Within minutes a dozen French warships—destroyers, a cruiser, and submarines—sailed to engage the Allied fleet. The American admiral Kent Hewitt issued his prearranged signal for a general engagement: "Play ball." And then came the bursts of machine guns, "blinding gun flashes," and the "crash of heavy ordnance." For the next several hours, the new French battleship *Jean Bart,* not yet entirely fitted out and incapable of sailing but able to use its fifteen-inch guns, waged a furious gun battle with USS *Massachusetts.* By the end of the day, *Jean Bart* was a burned-out wreck, and seven French warships along with three French submarines and a thousand French sailors lay at the bottom of the Atlantic. George Patton watched the battle unfold from the deck of USS *Augusta;* the landing craft that was to have taken Patton ashore was blown into splinters by the concussion from *Augusta*'s guns. Eisenhower, meanwhile, was unaware of any of the goings-on in Morocco. He had lost all radio contact with both Patton and the navy when the shock waves from *Augusta*'s heavy guns knocked out all of his radio equipment as well.[345]

Once ashore, Patton's 34,000 men received a hot reception from Vichy forces, a resistance spurred in part by Roosevelt's decision to broadcast a message of peace to the Vichy French in Morocco hours *before* Patton came ashore, thereby giving the defenders time to prepare. In Rabat, the resident governor general, Auguste Paul Noguès, his honor at stake, ordered an attack against the invaders. Noguès commanded at least 60,000 men in the protectorate, including several hundred fighter pilots. Fortunately for Patton's men, the French pilots who arrived over the Fedala beaches were not the cream of the Vichy air force and missed the beach entirely on their strafing runs. On the other hand, the American navy had put many of Patton's troops on the wrong beaches, where U.S. Navy planes proceeded to bomb them, as did some elements of Patton's artillery. The scene was utter chaos. While curious Arabs wandered among the wreckage, green American troops fired at shadows or, having lost their weapons in the surf, crouched behind trees. Some of the troops carried a new weapon. Alan Brooke called it a "rocket-gun" after watching a demonstration in June; the Yanks called it a bazooka. Indicative of the confusion on the beaches, the first bazooka fired in anger at a French tank missed its target and slew a nearby tree. Patton's tanks could not communicate; their radio batteries had drained during the sea voyage. His signal corps was in total disarray. The plan called for Patton to take Casablanca with the consent of the citizens, not to have to conquer it, for the simple reason that he might not be able to take the city should the Vichy put up enough of a fight against the untested Americans. With that in mind, Churchill had warned Roosevelt, "The first victory we have to win is to avoid a battle." But by noon on the eighth, Patton was in the thick of a bloody battle, and it was not going his way.[346]

The next day, Eisenhower, desperately trying to bring Darlan around to the Allied side, discovered a fact of French military life long known to Churchill: "the traditional French demand for a cloak of legality over any action they might take." French generals, Eisenhower later wrote, had cast their surrender in 1940 as "merely the act of loyal soldiers obeying the legal orders of their civil superiors." Honor was thus preserved. Churchill, in explaining the Darlan negotiations to the House, offered a less subtle explanation: "The almighty in His infinite wisdom did not see fit to create Frenchmen in the image of Englishmen." The French need for legal justification—"this peculiar form of French mentality"—stemmed from a belief that "an unbroken chain of lawful command" insulates those in the chain from any recriminations, moral or legal. Pétain resided at the top of the chain. So dominant among Frenchmen was this legalistic mind-set, Churchill told the House, that "if Admiral Darlan had to shoot Marshal Pétain he would no doubt do it in Marshal Pétain's name."[347]

On November 10, before Patton took the battle into the streets of Casablanca, Admiral Darlan ordered a cease-fire throughout the theater. As he was senior military commander on the scene, the order was within his authority. Pétain, exercising *his* authority, immediately rescinded the order and dismissed Darlan.[348]

The next day, in violation of the armistice signed in 1940, Hitler invaded unoccupied France. This freed Darlan entirely from the restraints imposed by law and Gallic honor. With Pétain now virtually a German prisoner, Darlan's orders carried the legal weight to deliver both North Africa and the French navy to the Allies. That morning, the commander of Vichy troops in Casablanca approached Patton's lines carrying a white flag. It was a flag not of surrender or capitulation but only of cease-fire. But it ended the hostilities. Thanks to Darlan, Patton, who had promised Roosevelt and Marshall that he would leave the beach "either a conqueror or a corpse," was ashore to stay. Yet, with Darlan, Eisenhower had on his hands a political poison pill. The Frenchman was universally reviled in Washington and London. Although Darlan had issued the orders that secured Casablanca and Oran, he had yet to give the most critical order of all, the order that the French fleets in Toulon and Dakar make for North Africa.

On the night of November 8, the high holy anniversary of his 1923 Beer Hall Putsch, Adolf Hitler made his yearly address to his brown-shirted cronies in Munich. The Führer spoke at the more elegant *Löwenbräukeller,* the old *Bügerbräukeller* having been bombed in a bungled 1939 assassination attempt on his life. Hitler informed his audience that Stalingrad, but for a few pockets of resistance, "was firmly in German hands." The job of erasing the city from the banks of the Volga, he promised, would soon be finished, but to avoid another Verdun, it would be done methodically. After all, he announced, time was now of no consequence. This was an exaggeration but not an outright lie. After losing twenty divisions during five weeks of murderous fighting in metropolitan Stalingrad, Paulus's Sixth Army had reached the Volga in the northern part of the city two days earlier. The Fourth Panzer Army was just two miles away from the south bank, which, when secured, would complete the encirclement of the inner city. The first reports from North Africa, meanwhile, were positive—fierce resistance by the French on all the beaches, German reinforcements about to depart for Tunis. Hitler did not disclose that Operation Anton, the occupation of Vichy France, was set to begin in thirty-six hours. From all appearances, the tide was still rising under the Third Reich. In fact, during the very hours Hitler spoke, and while his train got up steam for the journey to his East Prussian headquarters, and while his loyal brown shirts strutted and swayed under a thick haze of cigarette smoke on the beer-drenched floors of the *Löwenbräukeller,* the Third Reich reached flood tide.[349]

A freezing blue haze drifted low over the Volga that night and the next morning, a harbinger of the hard freezes that very soon would render the river a land bridge to Stalingrad. Fifty miles to the north and south of Stalingrad, the number two man in the Red Army after Stalin, Marshal Georgy Konstantinovich Zhukov, had assembled two gigantic forces made up of eight infantry and four tank armies. Now Zhukov waited. In a sense, Hitler had spoken the truth to his Munich cronies when he offered that time was of no consequence. Zhukov had it all on his side, while for the Germans in Stalingrad, it was running out.

When the Germans broke into unoccupied France on November 11, they drove straight for Toulon, where French naval commanders awaited orders to scuttle the fleet—two battleships, several heavy cruisers, sixteen submarines, eighteen destroyers—and therefore deny the Nazis a naval force that might have won them the Mediterranean. Only Darlan could give the order. He had promised in 1940 that he would never allow the French fleet to fall into German hands; on that day he made good on his promise. He ordered the French fleet to bolt Toulon and make for Africa, to join the Allies. The French naval commanders in Toulon, still loyal to Pétain, chose to stay in Toulon. By then, the Germans had surrounded the port. Even were the French captains inclined to obey Darlan, any attempt to do so would result in the Germans commandeering the fleet, which they were in fact drawing up plans to do. For almost two weeks, the French warships rode at anchor and in their slips. On November 27 Hitler struck. It took less than an hour for German tanks and troops to smash into the naval base and make for the dockyard, but that was more than enough time for the French commanders, sure now that they had been betrayed, to issue the orders to scuttle. Almost the entire fleet was sent to the bottom. Darlan, whatever his other faults, had kept his promise.

Reaction to the courtship of Darlan and the marriage of convenience came fast and furiously in Britain, and in America, where Roosevelt liberals, Churchill later wrote, were "agog . . . at what seemed to them a base and squalid deal with one of our most bitter enemies." Millions of Britons, Mollie Panter-Downes wrote, "are convinced that appeasement of a man of Vichy or a man of Munich smells just about the same, no matter what fancy name you want to call it." Churchill, for his part, thought the military gains achieved by Darlan's cease-fire orders outweighed the political risk. Yet, in a cable to Roosevelt he expressed his conviction that the Darlan deal "can only be a temporary expedient." Roosevelt issued a public defense of Eisenhower; Churchill did not. He spoke to Parliament in Secret Session, where he described Pétain—whose name he pronounced as "Peatayne"—"as an antique defeatist." Roosevelt had not consulted HMG on the Darlan matter, Churchill told the House. Yet, from the standpoint of reaching military objectives and saving the lives of his troops, "General Eisenhower was right" to court Darlan. But in public he accorded Eisenhower no such endorsement. Since the Americans, after all, had insisted that Torch was to be an all-American affair, they could stew in their own juices. Stalin, ever pragmatic, offered his thoughts on the subject to both Churchill and Roosevelt. The value of military diplomacy justified not only the relationship with Darlan, Stalin wrote, "but with the Devil himself and his grandma." Stalin also tossed out a phrase that was being much heard around London: the tide has turned.[350]

The Darlan expedient indeed proved temporary when on Christmas Eve, Darlan, who had managed that year to earn the enmity of de Gaulle, Vichy France, Churchill, Eisenhower, and Hitler, was shot dead by a young French royalist named Ferdinand Bonnier de la Chapelle. Although trained by the SOE, Chapelle was not acting under orders from London. He was tried, convicted, and shot, all in less than two days. The mystery around the murder deepened when it was revealed that MI6 chief Stewart Menzies, having left England for the first time during the war, was dining just a few hundred yards away from Darlan's house. Darlan's last words were said to have been "the British have finally done for me." Whether or not the English had a hand in the murder, Darlan's exit freed the Allies from having to further explain their association with the disreputable admiral. Churchill, in his memoirs, acknowledged that Darlan—a Fascist and Anglophobe who had made wrongheaded decisions for two years—had in the end made a decision that allowed the Allies to gain their foothold in North Africa. Had he ordered resistance against the Allies, Torch might have failed. Whether or not Darlan at the time fostered ambitions of ruling over French North African under Allied protection became moot with his death. He had deservedly earned the reputation of an arrogant, conniving turncoat, but his last turn of coat had finally put him on the right side. "Let him rest in peace," Churchill wrote of Darlan, "and let us all be thankful we have never had to face the trials under which he broke."[351]

Darlan's exit left Giraud as head of the French military in North Africa, but it also left a vacuum in French civil affairs. The way was now open for de Gaulle and the Fighting French to assume a place at the table—at the head of the table if de Gaulle was to realize his ambitions. He was loathed in Washington, where Cordell Hull called the Free French "polecats." Roosevelt, in a sarcastic handwritten addition to a cable to Churchill asked, "Why doesn't de Gaulle go to war? Why doesn't he start North by West half West from Brazenville? It would take him a long time to get to the Oasis of Somewhere." The reference was to Brazzaville, located on the Congo River, and the capital of French Equatorial Africa. Yet despite the Frenchman's arrogance, de Gaulle remained for Churchill and Britons the symbol of French valor, the hero who had wanted to fight Germans for three years and deserved the opportunity to do so. Two weeks before Darlan's assassination, Eden had asked de Gaulle whether, if Darlan were to disappear from the scene, de Gaulle could reach some sort of agreement with French North African authorities. De Gaulle answered yes. Darlan had indeed disappeared. In order that the British (and therefore de Gaulle, to whom the British had made commitments) not be excluded from North African politics, Churchill appointed Harold Macmillan (with Roosevelt's approval) as resident minister to Allied Headquarters, where, Churchill hoped, he would serve as a counterweight to Roosevelt's man in Morocco, Robert Murphy. Macmillan, Churchill informed Roosevelt, "is animated by the friendliest feelings towards the United States, and his mother hails from Kentucky." Actually, his mother was a Hoosier, and although Macmillan, like Churchill, was half American, he was British to the bone, and a Tory. Churchill had just dealt himself into the political game in North Africa. Given the stubbornness of Charles de Gaulle, it was to prove a risky and frustrating game of chance.[352]

On November 10, 1942, Churchill delivered two of his most memorable lines while addressing the traditional Lord Mayor's dinner at Mansion House (the Guildhall having been destroyed during the Blitz). Referring to Montgomery's desert victory, Churchill cautioned, "Now this is not the end. It is not even the beginning of the end. But it is, perhaps, the end of the beginning." Then, after calling himself Franklin Roosevelt's "active and ardent lieutenant" in the "mighty undertaking" taking place in French North Africa, Churchill sought to dispel any notion that he had just admitted to a subordinated role within the alliance. "Let me, however, make this clear.... We mean to hold our own. I have not become the King's First Minister in order to preside over the liquidation of the British Empire." In uttering those words Churchill appeared to have confirmed for critics, then and since, his status as an outdated imperialist who either could not see or could not abide a simple truth—the age of European colonialism was just about over, its expiration aided and abetted by Franklin Roosevelt. Yet Churchill's next line, infrequently noted, completed his thought: "For that task, if it were prescribed, someone else would have to be found, and under democracy, I suppose this nation would have to be consulted." Churchill had been asked to form a government for one reason only, to win the war. He was determined that at war's end Britain would regain territories lost to the Axis, much as America expected to recover Guam and Wake Island. If future events demanded a restructuring of the British Empire, the British people would decide the issue. Churchill ended his address with words that encapsulated his belief in both England and the Empire: "Here we are, and here we stand, a veritable rock of stability in this drifting world."[353]

For Churchill, the British Empire was a variation on German philosopher Gottfried Liebniz's best of all possible worlds. Yet that sentiment formed only a part of his worldview. He was a great European patriot as well as a British patriot, and his willingness to stand alone against Hitler was both an expression of that patriotism and the defense of a truth as Churchill saw it: Europe was the birthplace of Western political and aesthetic traditions, the defense of which, since the fall of France, had fallen to Britain. During his Wilderness Years, he had warned of the danger Hitler posed to Europe and by extension to Britain and the Empire. Even after war came, sober men such as Baldwin and Halifax believed they could preserve the Empire by reaching an agreement with—by again appeasing—Hitler. Churchill did not. Britain had gone to war to restore liberty to Europe. Yet he knew that if Britain emerged from the war victorious, it would possibly emerge broken as well.

Churchill, peering backward though history, grasped the ultimate mortality of empires, all save the British Empire, which functioned as a parliamentary democracy, a fact that for Churchill justified—demanded—its continuance. He once told Colville that the one great lesson he had learned from his father was that "the British alone had managed to combine Empire and Liberty." There were inequalities, to be sure, and he wanted them rectified. He told Attlee that the old order was changing and the "pomp and vanity must go." He told Eden that in Egypt "too many fat, insolent and party interests had grown up under our protection" and that in time the rich pashas and landowners would have to pay taxes at the rates paid by the wealthy in Britain, which rates Churchill intended to keep high in order that the financial burden of the war did not fall unfairly on Britain's working class. He pondered as a slogan for postwar reconstruction: "Food, house, and work for everyone." Yet his cousins across the Atlantic considered "empire" and "liberty" to be antonyms. Of Churchill, Eleanor Roosevelt wrote, "He's very human and I like him, tho' I don't want him to control the peace." Churchill understood, wrote Colville, that "republicanism and anti-colonialism were shibboleths in Washington and that no American paused to consider the implications of either."[354]

Churchill believed that the diaspora of English-speaking peoples that had taken place since the sixteenth century had resulted in an empire unique in history, an empire, he wrote, "based on Government by consent and the voluntary association of autonomous states under the Crown." He was one with Aristotle: rule shows the man—to which could be added, rule shows the nation. His was an empire of shared democratic ideals, shared risks, and shared rewards. It was a nation, the mightiest oak in the forest of nations, yet it cast a beneficent shadow in which less civilized peoples might find shelter and grow. On accepting the Tory chairmanship in 1940, he repeated his father's words that he had shared with Colville, that Britain "alone among the nations of the world...found the means to combine Empire and liberty. Alone among the peoples we have reconciled democracy and tradition." He considered the Empire synonymous with democracy, and worthy of long life—even perpetual life—whatever the sacrifice required of himself, of Britons, and of the King's colonial armies.[355]

A year before his Mansion House speech, Churchill addressed the boys of Harrow. He told them: "Never give in. Never give in. *Never, never, never, never*—in nothing, great or small, large or petty—never give in, except to convictions of honour and good sense. Never yield to force. Never yield to the apparently overwhelming might of the enemy."[356]

He had not yielded in 1942, when defeat had been the order of the day.

Even with America in (and for eleven months Clementine regularly reminded Churchill that America was in, yet not *really* in), he lacked the requisite military might to kill his enemies. What remained for Churchill but optimism? The dark days of the previous two years did not justify it, yet he always found the sunny side. He was no man of sorrow. Gloom regularly overtook him after the military disasters that had occurred with depressing regularity, yet it did not linger. It never, his daughter Mary recalls, "un-manned him."[357]

An air of inevitable Allied victory is attached to America's entry into the war; yet 1942 had passed with Britain still on the knife edge. Only in hindsight do we know that El Alamein and Midway Island were turning points; that Hitler erred in his U-boat deployment; and that he erred in not erasing Malta from the map. As 1942 drew to a close, Churchill remained true to his conviction that the rings of steel and concrete that Germany and Japan had thrown up around their respective conquests should be relentlessly probed until weak spots were exposed, and then exploited. By air the RAF had penetrated the German ring, and now, by land, in North Africa, the Allies were testing the tensile strength of the ring, as was Stalin in his namesake city. On Guadalcanal the Americans refused to relinquish their tenuous grip on the southernmost radius of the Japanese ring.

Shortly before Montgomery attacked at El Alamein, Churchill replied to a request by Anthony Eden for his opinion on the "Four Power Paper," a Foreign Office summary of the postwar organization of the Four Great Powers—Britain, China, the Soviet Union, and the United States. Churchill cautioned Eden against jumping to conclusions as to just who would be included in the so-called four great powers. "We cannot, however, tell what sort of a Russia and what kind of Russian demands we shall have to face." He added, "It would be a measureless disaster if Russian barbarism overlaid the culture and independence of the ancient states of Europe." As for China, "I cannot regard the Chungking Government as representing a great world power. Certainly [China] would be a faggot-vote on the side of the United States in any attempt to liquidate the British Empire." In general, Churchill told Eden, he favored a "United States of Europe capable of defending itself against all threats.* Yet, he advised, as enjoyable as it was to

* Although he frequently spoke of a "United States of Europe," Churchill did not specify whether that entity would be a loose confederation or a federal system, with member states bound together by a constitution. He continued to speak only in broad and imprecise terms even while championing a "united" Europe after the war.

ponder such questions, "the war has prior claims on your attention and mine." He closed with a piece of homegrown wisdom: "I hope these speculative studies will be entrusted mainly to those on whose hands time hangs heavy, and that we shall not overlook Mrs. Glasse's Cookery Book recipe for the jugged hare—'First catch your hare.'"[358]

In celebration of Montgomery's glorious deeds (and before the Allies landed in North Africa), Churchill ordered that the church bells be rung throughout the land on the following Sunday, November 8. Brooke, Clementine, and daughter Mary were aghast at the suggestion. Clementine became "violent" in her opposition ("quite rightly," thought Mary); Brooke "implored" Churchill to wait until the Torch forces had gained undisputed control of the beaches. Since 1939, too much had gone too wrong too often to risk ringing out false hope. Churchill heeded their advice, but only for a few days. By November 12, the Anglo-American army was safely ashore in North Africa, its eastern elements already pushing toward Tunisia. Montgomery by then had sent Rommel packing and had captured six divisions' worth of Italians.[359]

The church bells rang on Sunday, November 15. After three years of hope, there finally had arrived from El Alamein a dash of glory. Exhilaration was in the air, wrote Mollie Panter-Downes, "a wave of emotion . . . that makes this moment something like those moments in the summer of 1940. There's a big difference, however. Those were grim days in 1940. Today, though sensible Britons think there's certain to be plenty of grimness ahead, for the first time they believe sober reasons for hope are at last in sight."[360]

In an essay he wrote earlier that year, George Orwell observed that Englishmen always remember the military disasters—Mons, Ypres, Gallipoli, Passchendaele. These were the battles "engraved" upon common memory. The battles of the Great War that finally broke the Germans were simply unknown to the general public. "The most stirring battle poem in English," Orwell wrote, "is about a brigade of cavalry which charged in the wrong direction."[361]

El Alamein not only engraved itself upon the common memory, it erased the old memories. Churchill had found his Wellington in Montgomery, a general as ruthless in pursuit of victory as himself. In 1940, Mollie Panter-Downes compared Churchill and his influence on British morale to Pitt's leadership in 1759. In 1942, Churchill lost all of his battles before finally winning in the desert. As the year went out, nobody compared El Alamein and 1942 with Waterloo and 1815, still less with 1759, "the year of victories," of Pitt, and Wolfe at Quebec, of the Royal Navy smashing French fleets at Quiberon Bay and Cape Lagos, and of Minden, where English and Prussian foot soldiers and artillery ended French dreams of continental hegemony. "Our bells are worn threadbare with ringing for victories," Horace Walpole bragged to a friend that year. This was the Empire in ascendancy. In the summer of 1759, the keel of a 3,500-ton man-of-war was laid at the Chatham Dockyard, and the next year, in commemoration of Britain's *"annus mirabilis"* the ship was christened HMS *Victory*. At the end of 1759, David Garrick composed "Heart of Oak," his paean to the ships and men of the Royal Navy. As 1942 neared its end, the last stanza of Garrick's poem applied to all branches of HMG's military:

Through oceans and deserts,
For freedom they came,
And dying, bequeathed us
Their freedom and fame.

Early in 1942, Churchill promised Britons more grave disappointments and disasters. As the months sloughed off the calendar, he certainly made good on that pledge, in Singapore, Burma, and the North African desert. The year had been anything but a year of victories, but it had been a year *with* victories. And that was enough.

Churchill alone among the Big Three had journeyed overseas that year—twice to Washington, once to Moscow—in order to prod the alliance into strategic agreement and in order to preserve the alliance. "The Big Three" was a phrase that might conjure an image of a mighty war wagon pulled by three noble steeds; yet, while Churchill and Roosevelt and the Combined Joint Chiefs of Staff made every awkward effort to ride together in harness, Stalin rode alone. In fact, for most of 1942, the so-called Big Three were more a Big Two plus One. The Allied war effort, George Kennan later wrote, was less one of common, coordinated strategy than of simultaneous action, the Americans and the British in the west, Stalin in the east.[362]

Stalin's military chiefs did not consult the British and Americans; they consulted Stalin. Stalin, in turn, was relentless in pressing his demands upon his two allies—for more matériel and a second front—which

Roosevelt and Churchill tried in good faith to meet. The Russian front exerted an almost gravitational effect on decisions made by Roosevelt and Churchill, like the moon on the tides. In fact, the Russian front might as well have been on the moon for the lack of intelligence that Stalin allowed to seep out. Roosevelt, sure that he could handle Uncle Joe, had yet to meet the man; Stalin, for his part, refused to leave Russia to meet his allies and did not trust the British. That month, the British ambassador to Moscow, Clark Kerr, reported to Churchill that Stalin not only did not believe the Americans and British would keep their promises to open a second front, but "feared we were building up a vast army which might one day turn around and compound with Germany against Russia." Though sustained by Churchill's letters and telegrams to Roosevelt and Stalin, the "Big Three" largely remained an impersonal linguistic contrivance until Churchill made his pilgrimages to Washington and Moscow. Then, and only then, did the Trinity become personal. The journeys he undertook that year were so hazardous that General Douglas MacArthur proposed Churchill be awarded the Victoria Cross: "No one of those who wear it deserves it more than he," MacArthur told a British officer, if for no other reason than such journeys "through foreign and hostile lands may be the duty of young pilots, but for a Statesman burdened by the world's cares, it is an act of inspiring gallantry and valor."[363]

Churchill had found the path to glory during the year he fought alone after the French surrender, the Last Man Standing. "God knows where we would be without him," Brooke had written in his diary at the close of 1941, "but God knows where we shall go with him." In 1942 Churchill cemented his alliance, though like the foundation of an old country house, it was in need of constant repointing. With his alliance gained, he had found the path to victory. *That* was where they were going.

He liked to "pester, nag, and bite." Speaking in the House shortly after the Torch landings, he anointed himself a "prod." "My difficulties," he admitted, "rather lie in finding the patience and self-restraint to wait through many anxious weeks for the results to be achieved." Actually he pursued neither patience nor self-restraint with any real effort; he was too impatient. He told a member of his Defence Secretariat that action and results were all that mattered: "It was all very well to say that everything had been thought of. The crux of the matter was—has anything been done?" In the Western Desert, something had.[364]

"And now at last," Brooke told his diary, "the tide has begun to turn."[365]

4

Crosscurrents

NOVEMBER 1942–DECEMBER 1943

Within days of the North African landings, Churchill concluded that Torch might wrap up by Christmas. Alan Brooke, too, was confident, telling his diary that Ultra decrypts, if correct, indicated a good chance of "pushing him [the enemy] into the sea before long." Churchill, enthused, began work on a "most secret" memo for the British Chiefs of Staff. His objectives included the "completion of Torch by Christmas"; "bringing Turkey into the war" by March; the buildup of the Anglo-American force in Britain by June; the assembly of landing craft and completion of "preparations for Roundup" by July. Finally, in August or September, "Action." Such was the plan.[1]

On November 12, British paratroopers dropped into Bône, two hundred miles east of Algiers and halfway to Tunis, into which German reinforcements were now pouring. British commandos in small motor launches leap-frogged along the Tunisian coast ahead of General Anderson's diminutive First British Army, which had begun its race to Tunis the day before. Anderson made good progress for a few days, but a lack of locomotives and rolling stock held up his tanks and supplies. The transport situation worsened when the late autumn rains arrived, turning roads into slurries. Anderson, balancing his need for speed against the need to protect his flanks, divided the First Army into three prongs, with the result that he found himself trying to crack a coconut with a fork rather than a bayonet.

Field Marshal Albert Kesselring, commander of German operations in the Mediterranean, had already sent his vanguard to Tunis, and by the end of the month he had put 20,000 Germans there, along with Stukas, panzers, and artillery, forces equal in size to Anderson's and far more experienced. The rest of Eisenhower's troops sat static in Oran and Morocco, the result of a lingering American fear that Hitler would strike into the American rear through Spain with the Luftwaffe and paratroops. Colonel Ian Jacob recorded in his diary that the American chiefs "regarded the Mediterranean as a kind of dark hole, into which one entered at one's peril." Marshall told Roosevelt that week that of three possible Axis options—invading Spain, driving through the Caucasus, and attacking Britain—the invasion of Spain seemed most probable. Accordingly, safety first was Eisenhower's order of the day. On November 23 Brooke complained to his diary of "the very slow rate of progress in North Africa," which he blamed on Eisenhower's inability "to handle the military situation confronting him." By then, the Allies, with 250,000 troops ashore, had doubled the original landing force. Yet only Anderson was making headway, and not much at that. Churchill, unable to prod Eisenhower, unloaded on Brooke. Torch, he told the CIGS, "must be a springboard and not a sofa."[2]

Success in Tunisia depended on two factors—bold initiative (lacking, other than Anderson's drive toward Tunis) and the continued commitment of American resources. Any large-scale diversion of American men, planes, or ships to the Pacific could snuff out Torch. In fact, America that year had sent more troops—460,000 soldiers and Marines—to the Pacific than to Britain and North Africa, where a total of 380,000 Americans served, the vast majority far in the rear. Getting anything, men or machines, to Britain was the problem. U-boats in the Atlantic harvested more than 100 ships and 720,000 tons of Allied shipping that month, the greatest monthly loss of the war to date. Trying to explain the realities of the German naval blockade to Stalin, Churchill wrote, "You who have so much land may find it hard to realize that we [Britain] can only live and fight in proportions to our sea communications." The U-boat successes, Churchill told Stalin, were the "limiting factor" in Anglo-American planning. And every American warship sent to the Pacific made the deadly work of the U-boats that much easier. Then, just days after Torch began, a naval battle in the Pacific whetted the appetites of Americans for more action against Japan, naval action, and this at a time when, as Churchill told Stalin, the Allies lacked the warships to protect both the Torch landings and the Arctic convoys upon which Stalin depended.[3]

On November 12, two days after Churchill's Mansion House address, American and Imperial Japanese naval forces met again in "Ironbottom Sound," hard by the coast of Guadalcanal. Since August, the Japanese had run troops and fast warships—the "Tokyo Express"—from Rabaul to Guadalcanal, four hundred miles down "the Slot," and since August, the American navy had contested the Tokyo Express. In mid-October Tokyo had decided the time had come to obliterate the Americans on Guadalcanal. The Japanese plan called for a task force to shell the Marine airfield into oblivion in support of an invasion force, which would land during daylight sometime on or about November 13. The Americans, meanwhile, were running in their own reinforcements. Forewarned by coast watchers of the Japanese fleet headed their way, the Americans were ready when, at dusk on November 12, the Japanese made for Guadalcanal. The American naval historian Samuel Eliot Morison later wrote that the ensuing battle (two, actually, separated by a day of uneasy quiet) "recalled the Anglo-Dutch battles of the seventeenth century, when each side slugged the other until all but one went down." No quarter was given. By the time it was over, the Americans had taken an awful beating, and had in fact suffered a tactical defeat. But the Japanese admirals, fearing that even larger U.S. forces might be on their way, failed to press on with the destruction of the airfield. Instead, they turned for home and in so doing handed the Americans a strategic victory. The cost to the U.S. Navy was terrible: a battleship, several cruisers and destroyers damaged, two cruisers and six destroyers sunk, and more than sixteen hundred bluejackets killed. It was a price Washington could bear.[4]

Days later, Churchill cabled congratulations on the victory to Roosevelt. Shortly thereafter, Roosevelt announced, "It would seem that the turning-point in this war has at last been reached." Churchill preferred for the time being to stick with his hedged bet of "the end of the beginning." After the war a captured contemporary Imperial Japanese Navy document validated Roosevelt's enthusiasm: "It must be said that the success or failure in recapturing Guadalcanal... is the fork in the road which leads to victory for them or us."[5]

The Americans had taken the most advantageous fork. But Alan Brooke and Air Marshal Portal feared that if the Americans chose now to strike hell-bent down the road to Tokyo, they would do so at the expense of the European theater. Portal argued that because the Americans considered North Africa an exercise in containment rather than a springboard to the Continent, they saw no contradiction in shifting resources from Britain to the Pacific. For Churchill, this would not do. He had promised Stalin a second front in 1943, and the initial success of Torch had, in his estimation, made that promise a practical possibility.[6]

In Russia later that November week, the Wehrmacht and Red Army reached another fork in another road. At dawn on November 19, Marshal Zhukov threw his armies north of Stalingrad against the German flank. The following day, his armies south of the city struck. Both armies then shot toward the great bend of the Don, thirty miles west of Stalingrad. Zhukov saw the German position around Stalingrad for what it was, more of a "fragile shell" than a steel ring. Supported by an artillery barrage of more than two thousand guns, their movements obscured by a ferocious blizzard, the Soviets—a million strong—smashed through the ill-equipped and none-too-enthusiastic Romanian, Hungarian, and Italian forces guarding Paulus's flanks, killing and capturing more than three hundred thousand of Hitler's allies. By the twenty-first, Paulus and the remainder of his Sixth Army—almost a quarter of a million men—found themselves within the Soviet pincers, which were closing fast. Two days later, the Soviets linked arms at Kalach, on the Don. The Fourth German Panzer Army was forced to flee westward, leaving Paulus's Sixth Army trapped in the ruins of Stalingrad. Paulus's options were reduced to either standing and fighting or attempting a breakout westward from the city to the Don, there to join Field Marshal Erich von Manstein's Army Group Don. But the genius of Zhukov's plan was that it called for a broad encirclement of the Germans rather than a narrow pinch from which Paulus might escape. When Manstein, Germany's greatest strategist, tried to break through to relieve Paulus, he got to within thirty-five miles of Stalingrad before he was stopped. In mid-December, Hitler, who a month earlier had broadcast to the world that the Sixth Army would never leave Stalingrad, reiterated his orders. Paulus, his escape now blocked by Zhukov, obeyed. He had no other choice.[7]

Stalin, as usual, failed to disclose to Churchill or Roosevelt the exact disposition or strength of the Red Army (a habit Churchill and Brooke found infuriating given Stalin's regular belittling of Britain's effort). Only the combatants amid the ruins of Stalingrad knew how the battle was going, and they didn't know much. Their horizons could be measured in yards and feet. Soviet loudspeakers informed Paulus's troops that a German soldier was dying every seven seconds. The most titanic battle in history raged within lines so compact that there were more troops than in all of Tunisia battling each other among a few square miles of rubble, a zone of death not much greater in size than Lower Manhattan or Kensington. The rotting viscera of the dead and the bodily wastes of the living bred typhus and dysentery that killed men as surely—but not as mercifully—as the storm of bombs and bullets. Stalingrad had become like a collapsing star, pulling all in its orbit toward its ever more compressed core, a fiery hell from which nothing escaped. The city was "a vast furnace," a German survivor wrote, a world of "burning, blinding smoke . . . lit by the reflection of the flames." At night—"scorching, howling, bleeding nights"—terrified dogs plunged into the Volga and paddled madly for the Russian side. Those in London and Washington who waited for news from Stalingrad would have to bide their time until broadcasts announcing the outcome issued forth from Berlin and Moscow. The loser would no doubt accompany an announcement with a somber dirge, the victor with a celebratory march.[8]

During the last week of November, Dwight Eisenhower transferred his headquarters from Gibraltar to Algiers, where he and his second-in-command, Mark Clark, and their retinue took over the St. George Hotel and two villas. That put Eisenhower about three hundred miles west of the Allied front lines, which hooked south from the Mediterranean about fifty miles west of the port of Bizerte to a terminus high in a mountain pass called Kasserine, located in the Western Dorsal of the Atlas Mountains, seventy miles southwest of Tunis. There, drifts of daisies and red poppies spilled over the flinty, wind-swept landscape; the ground was impermeable to entrenching tools, and the terrain offered little defilade.

Near the northern end of the line, Anderson's forward elements had advanced to within just a dozen miles of Tunis. From the heights west of the city, British scouts looked across the plains that had once fed ancient Rome. In the far distance the minarets of Tunis stabbed up into the Mediterranean haze. Beyond Tunis, the ruins of Carthage overlooked the sea. The Romans had come 2,100 years earlier, intent on utterly destroying Carthage, and did so, but only after a long naval siege and house-to-house combat. If Anderson's little army drove into Tunis, this battle could only end in like fashion. The race for Tunis was tightening, but Churchill, still confident that Anderson would take the city by Christmas and that Montgomery would soon run Rommel to ground, began in earnest his campaign for the next Allied effort: Operation Roundup—the invasion of France. Indeed, Montgomery that week pushed Rommel to El Agheila, halfway to Tripoli. Twice before, in 1941 and 1942, Rommel had turned from here and sent the British scrambling back toward Cairo. Short of tanks and gasoline, he could not do so again. After a brief standoff, the Desert Fox fled west, stalked by Montgomery, who now had struck into Tripolitania, the garden of Mussolini's African empire. On December 2, Churchill, enthused by Monty's exploits, told Roosevelt "the chances for Roundup may be greatly improved" by the successes in North Africa and Russian resistance at Stalingrad.[9]

George Marshall, too, was optimistic. He told Roosevelt that Tunis could be occupied within two or three weeks "provided that [Anderson's] two divisions were sufficient to accomplish the task" and the Axis did not do something unexpected. Implicit in that astoundingly qualified assessment are two obvious questions. What plans were in place in the event Anderson's little force proved *insufficient* to take Tunis and, what if the Axis *did* do something unexpected? There was no answer to either question. Meanwhile, more than one hundred thousand American troops served as reserves far in the rear of Anderson, out of action and on guard for an Axis strike through Spain.[10]

Churchill's newfound enthusiasm for Roundup brought him into agreement with Marshall, and into disagreement with Alan Brooke. Churchill had made clear to Brooke that Torch must be a springboard, but a springboard to where? Western France? Southern France? Sardinia, Sicily, Italy, or the Balkans? Both Churchill and Brooke saw opportunities in Sicily and Sardinia to secure air supremacy over the Mediterranean and southernmost

Europe, possibly to bomb Mussolini out of the war. And always in Brooke's calculations was the immediate benefit to Allied shipping gained by opening the Mediterranean, thereby reducing round-trip journeys to Egypt by thousands of miles and effectively adding scores of ships to the fleet. But Churchill had a far more aggressive strategy in mind—he had rediscovered Roundup *and* he wanted to proceed in the Mediterranean. And Operation Jupiter, the invasion of northern Norway, had crept back into his calculations as a means to help safeguard the Arctic convoys and aid Stalin. As for Sicily and Sardinia, Churchill told Brooke, "You must not think you can get off with your 'sardines.'...No, we must establish a western front." In Brooke's judgment any talk of a continental second front was premature. Britain had the troops but lacked the means to feed and fuel them once ashore, and in fact lacked the landing craft to put them ashore. America was not yet prepared to carry the load, not in the air, not at sea, and most assuredly not on the ground in France. Operation Bolero, the buildup of American forces in Britain, had actually slowed, as Churchill knew full well, as did Roosevelt, having been reminded by Churchill that without Bolero, there could be no Roundup.

In wanting to attack everywhere, Churchill manifested two abiding traits: impatience and flexibility in the face of changing fortunes. His belief in an opportunistic strategic approach—attack the weaker of two enemies if the stronger could not be engaged—had not diminished since the 1941 Greek debacle, nor since 1915 and the Dardanelles, for that matter. Now Italy was weak and getting weaker. Once driven from Africa, it would be ripe for the kill. As usual, Churchill was consistent in combining the political and the military in his strategic thinking. In this, he was one with Clausewitz, but increasingly at odds with the Americans, who adhered to other Clausewitz maxims: avoid turning flanks and take the fight directly to the enemy if an opportunity presents itself, and *if*—a critical Clausewitzian caveat—your armies are equal to or greater in strength than the enemy's. Those conditions had clearly not yet presented themselves on the Continent.

But Sicily held promise. The military and political repercussions for Mussolini would be far greater were the Allies to take Sicily rather than Sardinia. Yet from a strictly military standpoint (which the Americans adhered to), Sardinia had much to offer. It was half again closer to southern France and northern Italy than was Sicily. Allied bombers based there would be that much closer to European targets, and an invasion of Tuscany from there would have the effect of cutting off Rome and most of the boot of Italy from Germany, eliminating the need for a three-hundred-mile slog from the toe of Italy to Rome. But Churchill called Sardinia "that piddling option." Only Sicily ("the glittering prize") was worth going after.

On the subject of Sicily, Brooke and Churchill were not far apart. For Brooke, taking Sicily was necessary in order for the British to retake the Mediterranean; Sardinia would not accomplish that. For Churchill, Sicily offered the first step of a campaign north toward Vienna by way of Italy (which would be crushed in the bargain), the Balkans, and the Ljubljana Gap through the Julian Alps and into Austria, but—and this was critical—*only* if Turkey entered the war on the Allied side in order to protect the Balkan flank. Churchill's plan was simplicity itself, to drive Italy from the war in order to induce Turkey to enter it.[11]

Roosevelt, too, grasped the strategic benefits of striking at Germany from the south, and told Churchill so in a November 11 telegram in which the president suggested that he and Churchill and their military chiefs begin planning a follow-up to Torch to include "forward movements directed against Sardinia, Sicily, Italy, Greece and other Balkan areas and including the possibility of obtaining Turkish support for an attack through the Black Sea against Germany's flank." Churchill responded with enthusiasm. He proposed to Roosevelt that after consolidating their North African positions, they "strike at the under-belly of the Axis in effective strength and in the shortest time." Here, exactly, was the strategy he had outlined to Stalin in August. And here came Franklin Roosevelt offering encouragement in the matter.[12]

Churchill needed no convincing. His generals and their American counterparts, however, did. Other than the Italian lack of will to fight (as Churchill believed), there was nothing soft about Europe's underbelly. The Apennine Mountains thrust north through Italy to the Alps, where from France to Slovenia the terrain favored defensive and guerrilla tactics, as several German and Bulgarian divisions were learning in Yugoslavia, and as Mussolini had learned in Greece. Of the Ljubljana Gap, Eisenhower later told his naval aid that he would be damned if he'd put his army into "that gap whose name I can't even pronounce." Admiral King saw the Mediterranean as a dead end, a place where American ships would go to die. The soft underbelly, wrote Samuel Eliot Morison, was "boned with the Apennines, plated with the hard scales of Kesselring's armor, and shadowed by the wings of the Luftwaffe."[13]

Marshall had always advocated a straight-line approach from Britain across the Channel, not only because it was the shortest distance between two points, but because the countryside of northern France and the Low Countries was indeed "soft" and conducive to large-scale armor movement, as the Germans had shown in 1940. Marshall intended to take that straight line in 1943. Yet he lacked the men to do so; Torch had been undertaken at the expense of Bolero, the buildup of American troops in England. Roosevelt backed Marshall, nominally, although just months earlier, the president had concluded with reluctance that the shipping shortage and the final decision on Torch precluded any such venture in France until 1944. Days before he sent his cable to Churchill, Roosevelt assured Marshall that the cross-Channel strategy still had his full support; it did, but Roosevelt had no timetable in mind. His biographer James MacGregor Burns writes that "tactical developments had outrun his [Roosevelt's] strategic decision making" and that Roosevelt "had no definite battle plan." Yet, in his November cable to Churchill, Roosevelt clearly indicated that the underbelly option appeared to be the most promising answer to the question of where next after North Africa.[14]

Thus, Roosevelt proposed a favorite Churchillian scheme to Churchill while Churchill proposed Marshall's favored strategy to Brooke, who was appalled at the prospect of a premature landing *anywhere* on the Continent. Of course, Churchill's newfound enthusiasm for Roundup (even if it had been incubated in the need to placate Stalin) did not in the least diminish his desire to go to Italy. They could do both. Northern Norway, too, was never far from Churchill's thoughts, nor was the Aegean. They could do it all.

Robert Sherwood later wrote that those who accuse Churchill of hesitancy if not outright cowardice in regard to the invasion of France (as had Stalin, quite bluntly, during Churchill's Moscow visit) take a too linear and simplistic approach. Three months before Torch kicked off, Churchill told Roosevelt that the British would willingly accept Marshall as supreme commander of Roundup. Churchill did this knowing full well that Marshall had one and only one strategy in mind, to strike straight into France. Sherwood: "This nomination of the most vehement proponent of the Second Front would hardly indicate that Churchill was attempting to relegate it [Roundup] to the Files of Forgotten Things." He was not trying to do that, yet he had also begun to proclaim a truth as he saw it, that a disastrous defeat on the coast of France "was the only way in which we could lose this war." That conclusion was self-evidently correct. A defeat on the coast of France would lead, if not to immediate defeat, to Marshall and King's shifting the entire American effort to the Pacific. Harry Hopkins, at the time, told an audience at Madison Square Garden that there would be a second front, "and if necessary a third and a fourth front, to pen the German army in a ring of our offensive steel." These were Churchill's sentiments exactly. Roundup was to be one of *several* operations. His multifront thinking was a constant source of worry to Brooke, who wrote in his diary, "He is now swinging away from those [Sardinia and Sicily] for a possible invasion of France in 1943!" Eisenhower, meanwhile, was swinging *toward* Sardinia, where three German divisions were dug in. But to Brooke's astonishment, Eisenhower's "very bad plan . . . never went beyond the landing on the beaches."[15]

On the day Roosevelt sent his underbelly telegram (November 11), Churchill told the Commons that the Allies would in the coming year bring strong force to bear against Hitler in Western Europe. He did not promise a timetable for an actual invasion, nor did he define just what "strong" meant. The invasion, he said, would take place only when "in due course" Germany became demoralized (presumably by the pounding inflicted by the Russians and the RAF). He said, "Moreover, you have first to get sufficient ascendancy even to prepare to strike such a blow." He stressed that planning and preparation for such operations may look like inertia, but were in fact critical. The *New York Times* ran with that story the next day, under the headline: INVASION ACROSS CHANNEL IS PLEDGED BY CHURCHILL. In fact, he had made no such pledge, but the horse was out of the barn. Ever since, the Allied failure to cross the Channel in 1943 has been attributed to Churchill's reluctance, beginning with a pledge he never made, an irony given that by late November 1942, Churchill (next to Marshall) was Roundup's biggest booster.[16]

The American military suspected Churchill liked to engage in "eccentric operations" that depended on bravado, surprise, and speed for success. He did, but that was in part because the British army could not engage the Wehrmacht on anything like equal terms, and the American army had yet to prove its battle worthiness. Cordell Hull and the U.S. military chiefs (and the Free French) also suspected Churchill of harboring imperial designs in the eastern Mediterranean; he did not. He had attacked Vichy "intriguers" in Syria and Madagascar in order to safeguard the Suez Canal and Middle East oil supplies, upon which the British war effort depended. Marshall also suspected, correctly, that Churchill wanted to first clear the entire Mediterranean as a prelude to any contemplated landing in France, thereby, in Marshall's estimation, further delaying his straight-line strategy. And now here was Marshall's boss, the commander in chief, encouraging Churchill on his underbelly strategy. Yet Roosevelt was only approaching the business of war in the same way he approached politics; he liked to allow events to proceed until a choice of action became self-evident. By December no single strategy had become self-evident. Clearly, it was time for Churchill, Roosevelt, and the Combined Chiefs of Staff to sit down and work one out.[17]

The news from North Africa only added to the urgency to do so. On December 1, Kesselring's reinforced troops skirmished with Anderson's forward units and drove the British back. Tanks would occupy a central place in the battle for Tunis, and Anderson's tanks, the American M3 Lee and its modified cousin, the M3 Grant, were obsolete—the main gun was not fitted to a traversing turret, rivets used in construction became lethal projectiles when the tank was hit, and its high profile made it an easy target. They were no match for the German Panzer Mark IV tank and its

75mm gun. A week later, General Dieter von Arnim took command of the Fifth Panzer Army at Tunis, now 25,000 strong, with almost a quarter million Italians and Germans soon to arrive by way of Europe and Rommel's approaching army. The previous year at Kiev, Arnim's masterful tank deployments led to the encirclement of an entire Russian army. He intended, after joining forces with Rommel, to annihilate the Americans and British in Tunisia. Within a week of arriving in Tunisia, he went on the offensive.[18]

To the relief of Churchill and Brooke, Kesselring could not bring himself to undertake the one operation that would most benefit the Germans in North Africa, which was to rub Malta from the map. A convoy of four British ships reached Malta in late November, leading Brooke to exclaim to his diary, "Thank god. This puts the island safe for a bit." It put Torch safe for a bit, too, because holding Malta—from where RAF aircraft and Royal Navy submarines could hunt German troop and supply ships—was critical to the success of Torch. Many of the troops Kesselring was shoving into Tunis had been training for the invasion of Malta. Had Kesselring thought like an admiral rather than a Luftwaffe *Generalfeldmarschall,* and had those troops been dropped into Malta, a swastika would likely have been flying over Valletta, and Rommel, freely resupplied, would have been driving toward Baghdad rather than away from Benghazi. But Kesselring, like Göring during the Battle of Britain (and now at Stalingrad), had placed his hopes in his pilots and bombers. Crete had claimed many of them, and the Russian front called for more. The leaders of the Reich never truly grasped the significance of Malta: "We should frankly tell the German people that we aren't interested in conquering Malta," Goebbels wrote months earlier. "And that's the truth too." Now, as the year neared its end, Goebbels confessed to his diary: "Those in the know see quite clearly that Rommel cannot do anything if he doesn't have gasoline. That is decisive." The British had understood that for two years; it was why they sent convoy after convoy and dozens of warships on suicidal missions to Malta. Now submarines based at Malta ravaged Rommel's supply ships, with the result that, Goebbels lamented, "our supplies are, for the most part, lost" and "the situation in French Africa is not exactly rosy."[19]

Nor was it rosy in Russia, where, Goebbels observed with rare understatement, "we are having some trouble about Stalingrad." He also expressed his feelings on the upcoming Christmas season: "I'll be glad when this whole Christmas racket is over. One can then devote oneself quietly again to real tasks." It would not do, he wrote, for the people to "fall too much for the sentimental magic of these festival days." High on Goebbels' list of real tasks was the "wiping out of the Jewish race in Europe, and possibly in the entire world." The Jewish race, Goebbels wrote, "has prepared this war; it is the spiritual originator of the whole misfortune that has overtaken humanity. Jewry must pay for its crime."[20]

In mid-December, in response to claims by the Polish government in exile that two million Polish Jews had been shipped east to their deaths, Anthony Eden addressed the Commons, where he read from an Allied proclamation that condemned "this bestial policy of cold-blooded extermination" and made a "solemn resolution to ensure that those responsible for these crimes shall not escape retribution." After Eden spoke, a rare moment of silence was observed in the House, in memory of European Jews. "Bestial," a word little used in temperate twenty-first-century political speech, appears to reduce the Nazi barbarities to their most elemental and evil. Yet George Orwell later observed that "bestial" was one of the clichés that by overuse in the 1930s and early 1940s had reduced political discourse to blather. Eden's message went largely unheard outside Britain. The *New York Times* ran a brief story inside the paper (over the course of the war, the *New York Times* ran no page-one lead story on the plight of Polish Jews). In Britain, Sikorski's Free Poles kept the story alive in the British press, which, though having seen its newsprint cut by 20 percent, always made room for the news from Warsaw. Goebbels also recorded his impressions of Eden and the moment of silence: "The English are the Jews among the Aryans" and the Commons "is really a sort of Jewish exchange." As for Eden: "The perfumed British Foreign Minister... cuts a good figure among those characters from the synagogue.... His entire bearing can be characterized as thoroughly Jewish."[21]

Thirty plays were running in London's West End in December, twice as many as the year before. Londoners' infatuation with all things Russian was evidenced by the production of Turgenev's *A Month in the Country* at the St. James Theatre, where a second box office had to be opened to accommodate the crowds. A Soviet flag flew above Selfridges; inside, the department store's nearly empty shelves gave the place the feel of Moscow's *Gosudarstvenny Universalny Magazin* (GUM). Such was London's love affair with Russia that the Soviet ambassador, Ivan Maisky, was made an honorary member of the Athenaeum, while at the Windmill Theatre, the nude dancers wore Cossack fur hats and red stars in their navels while performing their special ode to Russia, *Moscow Nights*.

British patriotism found expression in Noël Coward's cinematic directorial debut, *In Which We Serve*. Based on Dickie Mountbatten's exploits in command of HMS *Kelly*, which was sunk from under Mountbatten the previous year, the movie, which Coward also produced and starred in, became an instant hit with Britons, although some wits in the Royal Navy dubbed it *In Which We Sink*. Beaverbrook loathed it, because in an early scene, a copy of his *Daily Express* with a 1939 headline proclaiming No War This Year floats on the waves among the wreckage of a doomed ship and the bodies of dead tars. *Time* called the movie "the first really great picture of World War II." Coward was also a presence in the West End, where his latest play, *Blithe Spirit,* a comedic ghost story, had been pulling crowds into the Savoy Theater for a year and a half, and would keep Londoners laughing for the remainder of the war. Coward, along with his old friends King George VI and Winston Churchill, was one of few Britons as popular in the West End as in the East End, though nobody's popularity topped Churchill's.[22]

On the eve of his birthday, Churchill made his first radio address since May, when he told Britons that conditions would worsen before they got better. Now, with the Allies marching toward Tunis, he used the airwaves to tell Mussolini that Italy would be next to feel Allied wrath: "The fair land of Italy," he promised, would soon suffer "prolonged, scientific and shattering air attack." In fact, the previous night, the RAF had bludgeoned Turin's industrial areas with two-ton bombs. Churchill derided Mussolini as "the hyena" who "broke all bounds of decency" and advised Italians to depose Il Duce (whom Churchill also called "a serf" and "a utensil") if they wanted to save their "fair land" from further withering attacks. He promised to clear Africa of the enemy "before long." Of the future course of the war, he offered, "I promise nothing... I know of nothing which justifies the hope that the war will not be long or that bitter, bloody years do not lie ahead." Britain would fight on, he said, "with a bold heart and a good conscience." He quoted his favorite Kipling:

If you can dream—and not make dreams your master;
If you can think—and not make thoughts your aim;
If you can meet with Triumph and disaster
And treat those two imposters just the same.[23]

He gave Britons fair warning. El Alamein was a battle won, but not a war won.

With Christmas coming, the official view held that only the children should receive presents. Yet, Mollie Panter-Downes wrote in *The New Yorker,* "even the children won't come off so handsomely this Christmas, for toys are scarce, poorly made, and appallingly expensive." The personal columns of newspapers were full of notices from desperate parents in search of secondhand toys and tricycles and doll carriages. None could any longer be bought new. Those Londoners who planned to gift-wrap a bit of their tea or sugar rations for friends or family found themselves on the wrong side of the law when the Food Ministry announced that it was illegal to give away rations, a decision Churchill lamented as "contrary to logic and good sense" and a blow against "neighborliness and friendship." The Board of Trade was set to lower Britons' allotments of clothing coupons from sixty-one to forty per year, which, at about thirteen coupons for a simple dress or man's suit jacket, limited options in the clothing department. To save material, only three-button single-breasted jackets could be made, with no buttons on the sleeves. Waistcoats were limited to two pockets. Still, the news from the desert made up for food, clothing, and toy shortages. Britons were optimistic, although, wrote Mollie Panter-Downes, "several official utterances lately have warned the people that the ramparts they watch are still the White Cliffs of Dover and that an attempt upon them is quite in the cards at some moment when Hitler may believe that popular attention has been diverted elsewhere."[24]

The attention of children playing football in the streets of London's poorer neighborhoods was focused on the automobiles that regularly appeared, not because the car might break up the game, but because automobiles could be used only for official business, and most East End residents neither owned a car nor had any official business to conduct. When a car turned onto an East End street—or the meaner streets of Manchester, York, Glasgow, Liverpool, or Birmingham—it could mean but one thing. The children stopped their games and watched to see whose house received a visit from uniformed officers bearing terrible tidings from North Africa. Bernard Montgomery's victory had resulted in a marked increase in such visitations. The official cars cruised the streets of Mayfair, Chelsea, and Knightsbridge, where the upper classes had embraced their duty. "Britain is class ridden," Pamela Churchill Harriman told a visitor years later, "but it is not class conscious." The gentry had come in for it along with everyone else; their sons had fought and died in the desert beside East Enders.[25]

Pamela remembered that holiday season as being if not the gayest, the least gloomy of the war, in part, she recalled, because of the sense of peace she had attained with the knowledge that her marriage to Randolph was over and, Averell Harriman making a cuckold of Randolph notwithstanding, its end was not her fault, nor was it entirely Randolph's. "I began gradually to realize that there was a deep difficulty between Clemmie and Randolph, and that in fact Churchill worshipped his son and was trying by every possible means to give him any help or advantage he could." Churchill lived for his son—"like all Englishmen, the son, or eldest son, is everything"—while Clemmie lived for Churchill, with the result that soon after her marriage, Pamela "sensed this tremendous antagonism . . . a deep difficulty between Clemmie and Randolph." Randolph once told her that his mother hated him, and that he had known as much since Clementine went down to Eton and slapped his face in front of the other boys. Pamela, having "come from a normal English family," thought that claim to be "exaggerated and ridiculous." Yet, "gradually through the months and years I began to realize there was a certain truth to what he was saying... that this thing of the eldest son was terribly important to Winston and that the only thing that ever came between Winston and Clemmie was Randolph." Winston, over Clementine's opposition, would call Randolph's commanding officers and say, "I would like my son for three days," and pull Randolph from his military postings in order to accompany Churchill to France, to Cairo, to Tehran. Randolph's absences from his post resulted in him "catching the flak" from his superiors and Churchill catching it from Clementine, whose only concern was that criticism might be directed at her husband.

"It's awfully difficult explaining Clemmie," Pamela recalled, "because I was really fond of her. She was wonderful to me, but she was a very strange woman. She lived totally for Winston." As did Randolph, with the result that Pamela, just twenty-one, found herself a spectator to a battle between Randolph and Clementine for Churchill's love, an unnecessary battle in Pamela's estimation, because his love for his wife and son was unconditional and total, as it was for Pamela and her small son. "I remember going to the Cabinet Room and telling Winston that we wanted to get a divorce. He was wonderful about it. He said, 'Never forget, not only are we devoted to you but you are the mother of my grandson.'" That was "Little Winston," with whom Churchill liked to roll on the floors of Chequers: "Winston was much better with small children than Clemmie was," Pamela recalled. "Clemmie was not good with her grandchildren...she really didn't have any affinity for the young."[26]

In mid-December, with Rommel retreating toward Tunisia, and the Allied drive for Tunis opposed now by a combination of battle-hardened Germans, desert rains, mud, and high mountain passes, Churchill and Roosevelt began planning for what was supposed to be the first meeting of the Big Three. The time had come to make a final decision on the strategic goals for 1943. Topping the agenda, a means had to be found to defeat the U-boats and take command of the Atlantic. The sea war had to be won before any continental European excursions could be contemplated. And how much naval power to assign to the Pacific war? And what to do with

Giraud and de Gaulle? And the vital question, where to go next after clearing North Africa of the Axis.

Churchill suggested that Iceland or North Africa might prove suitable venues for a conference, but Roosevelt vetoed Iceland on account of "the vile climate" and the likelihood of ice forming on aircraft wings (he had last flown before his first election and did not like to fly in any weather, especially in bad weather). The two leaders settled on North Africa. They invited Stalin, who demurred, claiming quite honestly that his focus was entirely on Stalingrad. Stalin, who was also terrified of flying, replied that he need only be apprised of any decisions taken by Churchill and Roosevelt, wherever they chose to meet. He also advised his allies that they take care to ensure that "no time is being wasted" in fulfilling their promise of opening a second front in Europe in 1943.[27]

They settled on Casablanca in the newly liberated French protectorate of Morocco as the conference site, and on Symbol as the code name for the meeting. As it would be a parley to mull over military strategy, Roosevelt told Harriman to inform Churchill that the president wanted "no ringers" at the conference. That is, he wanted to exclude his secretary of state, Cordell Hull. This put Harriman in a delicate spot, for Churchill worked in harness with Anthony Eden. Harriman had to persuade Churchill to exclude Eden, not because Eden had nothing to add, but because Roosevelt sought to distance himself from Hull, who was "forceful, stubborn, and difficult to handle" and would likely prove "a nuisance at the conference." Churchill reluctantly agreed to the decision. Hull, offended, complained to Harriman that the president was not keeping him informed. That was true; Franklin Roosevelt served as his own secretary of state. Yet the exclusion of Eden did not diminish Churchill's enthusiasm for the meeting. He proposed to Roosevelt that they travel under the aliases Don Quixote and Sancho Panza, but British officials thought the aliases were an invitation to the more cynical members of the press to term the venture quixotic. Churchill agreed, and cabled Roosevelt that in order to confuse the enemy, they should travel *incognito* "as Admiral Q and Mr. P.... We must mind our P's and Q's." Although he agreed to leave Eden behind, he informed Harriman that he was bringing along "a couple of private secretaries," his map room staff, and "one or two of the Joint Staff Secretariat."[28]

On Christmas Eve Eisenhower notified Roosevelt and Churchill that the winter rains had forced a shutdown of Tunisian operations for two months. The Germans had driven the British forward elements from the aptly named Longstop Hill, within sight of Tunis. Kesselring and Arnim had won the race. Brooke told his diary: "I am afraid that Eisenhower as a general is hopeless. He submerges himself in politics and neglects his military duties, partly, I am afraid, because he knows little about military matters." The words echo Brooke's sentiments regarding Churchill, of whom he wrote, "Perhaps his most remarkable failing is that he can never see the whole strategical problem at once. His gaze always settles on some definite part of the canvas and the rest of the picture is lost." Yet Brooke, as coolly logical as Stafford Cripps, failed as did Cripps to grasp the essential Churchill. Churchill had not learned his debating skills at an army staff college, where officers are trained to remove the emotional from strategic planning; nor had he learned his skills as a barrister at the bar. His education took place in the House of Commons, where knife fights were fought with words and the objective was to gut an opponent's policy by gutting the opponent. After four decades of honing his skills in the House, Churchill could approach Brooke in no other manner but to cajole, belittle, and berate. In fact, Churchill, more intuitive than logical, possessed the painter's gift for seeing myriad vistas, far and near. He scanned the entire canvas and when he came upon a scene of interest, he paused and pondered before moving on, never fast enough for Brooke. Thankfully for Brooke, Churchill manifested another trait. After arguing his case as if compromise were evil incarnate and the chiefs were too foolish to understand the perfect wisdom of his position, he acceded to their viewpoint if, that is, he had failed to bring them around to his. Brooke did not grasp that when it came to strategic thinking, Churchill could weigh the value of and consequences of several strategic solutions at once, military and political. It fell to Brooke to nudge him toward the most practical.[29]

And that is what Brooke did in the days before the Casablanca parley. He outargued the master arguer, with the result that soon after the new year, the British, in reaching a strategic consensus, accomplished what the Americans did not. Roosevelt warned his generals that the British would arrive at Casablanca with a plan, "and stick to it." They did, but only after Brooke persuaded Churchill to abandon his newfound enthusiasm for Roundup. When Churchill, arguing his case, informed Brooke that "we had promised Stalin we would do so when in Moscow," Brooke replied, "No *we* did not promise!" Brooke, after much difficulty, convinced Churchill that 1943 would afford opportunity in one theater only, the Mediterranean. And that was the case the British prepared to argue at Casablanca. In fact, Churchill prepared so well for the conference that he needed a cruise ship, HMS *Bulolo,* to carry his support staffs, secretaries, and cryptologists to Africa. He had told Harriman he'd be bringing some people along; in fact, he was bringing practically everybody.[30]

Before Churchill made for Casablanca, a messy political affair intruded into the war-making machinery. Late in the year, his old friend Noël Coward, who had worked undercover for Bracken's Ministry of Information, was nominated for knighthood, a reward Coward's good friend King George thought appropriate but that Coward's friend Winston Churchill considered ill advised. Churchill argued against the knighthood based on Coward's having been fined £200 by HMG as a result of spending more than £11,000 during trips to America, which was in violation of the Exchequer's currency laws. This was an extraordinary amount of money, and more than the average British family earned in ten years.[31]

Almost seven decades later, Churchill's resistance to the knighthood was ascribed by some in the press to his "homophobic" mind-set, a charge not supported by any of Churchill's inner circle, who dutifully recorded in their diaries his regular and often acerbic criticisms of men and women, great and small. Did Churchill know who in his circle was a homosexual and who was not? "I wouldn't think he cared," recalled Jock Colville. Churchill was well aware of the homosexual proclivities of certain of the West End theater crowd, sundry university dons, as well as myriad luminaries in HMG and the military, such as his former secretary Eddie Marsh and his bisexual friend Bob Boothby, and T. E. Lawrence, to whom Churchill remained loyal long after Lawrence's death. Winston and Clementine lunched on occasion with W. Somerset Maugham ("Willy" to his friends), who late in life found "great pleasure" in Churchill's presence at his dining table. Evelyn Waugh (who had had a few homosexual affairs at Oxford) was always welcome in the Churchill house, Churchill grateful to Waugh for watching out for Randolph when they served together in Yugoslavia. Churchill, a presiding member of the louche aristocracy (as characterized by the British historian Roy Jenkins) that ruled England, lived a life of valets, gardeners, chauffeurs, champagne, perfumed handkerchiefs, and pink silk underclothes, all the while surrounded by a coterie of the most eccentric Englishmen and -women—including his mother, father, and son—who enjoyed flirtations with debauchery. Homosexuality, illegal in Britain, was considered dangerous but not immoral by Churchill's crowd, and only for the political scandal that might attach to public disclosure. Homosexuals might be a security risk, Churchill once told one of his private secretaries, not only because of the danger of blackmail but because they might feel alien in the mainstream of their own society, "like a black in a white country, or a white in a black one."[32]

Though he cared little about a person's sexual preference, Churchill was often quick with clever barbs about homosexuals. Of the notorious Tom Driberg—Beaverbrook protégé, Labour MP, and serial seducer of young men—Churchill remarked, "That's the man who brought sodomy into disrepute." When he learned from MPs in the smoking room that Driberg had married a somewhat plain woman, Churchill announced, "Buggers can't be choosers." Yet when it came to something as serious as a knighthood for Coward, Churchill stuck to the facts.

Churchill opposed the knighthood because he took HMG's currency laws seriously. He complained about (and paid) heavy excise taxes on the Cuban cigars that found their way to his humidor. He was not a diligent manager of his own money, but he was diligent in paying his taxes (and in taking advantage of any tax loopholes that presented themselves). Despite Coward's secret intelligence work, which could not be divulged in any event during wartime, it simply would not do for news to escape in the midst of fiscal drought, coal shortages, and food rationing that Noël Coward, having been fined for burning through the equivalent of ten years of middle-class wages in a few months while sating his voluptuary appetites in America, had been rewarded with a knighthood.*[33]

Churchill's personal physician, Sir Charles Wilson (who had been knighted the previous year), was another case altogether. Although Churchill never called Wilson a friend, as he did Coward, the doctor had committed no transgressions that might reflect poorly on Churchill or England. On New Year's Day, Doctor Wilson was made a peer, and became the First Baron Moran.

Churchill had intended to depart London for Casablanca on January 11, but when foul weather pushed his departure back a day, he used the time to fire off a memo to Sir Henry Tizard, who had recommended the RAF follow the lead of the Americans and resort to daytime bombing raids, with the objective of gaining more accuracy. Churchill replied that "since a great proportion of our losses are due to flak, which is more accurate by day than by night, the day bombers will have to fly at a very great height," which would further reduce their accuracy. This was the great tactical conundrum. The Americans, with faith in the protective firepower of their Flying Fortress's eleven .50-caliber machine guns, had embraced the tactic of daylight raids. Yet while conducting a very few such raids over France and the Netherlands, and not one over Germany, they had suffered terrible casualties among their bomber crews. Six months earlier, on July 4, six American bombers—in a statement of American independence—took part in a daylight raid on German airfields in Holland; the planes missed

* Coward was finally knighted in 1969.

their targets and two of the six never returned. Churchill believed the best—and safest—way to reduce Germany was by night bombing. Five hundred American bombers were parked in East Anglia, and he wanted them in the air over Germany, at night, even though such a tactical shift would require the retraining of every American airman. Churchill intended to voice his opposition to daytime bombing to the Americans at the upcoming Casablanca meeting. He also meant to ask the Americans just when they might begin dropping bombs on Germany.[34]

The ongoing dispute between Prof Lindemann—Lord Cherwell—and Tizard only served to further muck up the works, and ill serve Churchill. Sir Henry sought to bury the hatchet with Cherwell, but Prof saw no reason to extract it from between Tizard's shoulder blades.* Churchill told Tizard that his bombing suggestion was "all a matter of numbers" and instructed him to prepare a report for his return. But Cherwell, not Tizard, accompanied Churchill to Casablanca, and nobody could assemble numbers like the Prof. Cherwell's objective was to destroy German morale, ergo German houses, which usually contained residents. He and Churchill of course hoped to destroy German industry as well, but poor bombing accuracy—day or night—proscribed inflicting a mortal wound on German industry. But Cherwell knew that as long as bombs fell somewhere within a city, they destroyed houses, and therefore morale. He had advocated that strategy almost a year earlier, in a study that came to be known as the "Dehousing Paper." He had Churchill's full support. Thus, there could be no doubt that Tizard's numbers would never stack up to Cherwell's, or that Sir Henry's suggestion would ever fly.[35]

By this date, after almost forty months of war, the British had poured 70,000 tons of bombs into Germany, the equivalent of 6,000 sorties by Lancaster heavy bombers and more than four times the tonnage the Luftwaffe dropped on Britain during the height of the 1940 Blitz. Within six months, Bomber Command would double that tonnage. But the American Eighth Air Force had yet to get off the ground in any meaningful way. It was headquartered near Bomber Command at the Wycombe Abbey, a girls' school in a former country house tucked into the lovely meadows and crofts of Buckinghamshire. In the months since the school's students and teachers were sent packing, the Eighth had done little more than unpack its charts, sextants, and slide rules. The Eighth Air Force's commander, Major General Carl Spaatz (whose name Churchill mispronounced as "spots"), and much of the Eighth had been siphoned off to North Africa,

* In September 1959, Lord Cherwell offered to a colleague that he had finally "buried the hatchet with Tizard.... But," the Prof added, "I know where to find the handle." Tizard died the next month (Moran, p. 813).

with the result that the Americans, in a few night raids, dropped fewer tons of bombs on Germany during the final months of 1942 than the Luftwaffe had dropped on London on the first *night* of the Blitz. This was unacceptable to Churchill, who intended to say as much in Casablanca to the overall U.S. air commander, General Ira Eaker, himself a believer in the invincibility of airpower. "The Americans had been in the war for more than a year," Churchill later wrote, "but so far had never thrown a single bomb on Germany by daylight methods."[36]

He never ceased to express to the Chiefs of Staff both his keen desire to bomb Germany and his suspicion that the effects on German industry were neither "decisive" nor up to the "hypothetical and indefinite" objectives cited by Air Marshal Portal and Bomber Harris. "It is very disputable," he wrote in a memo to Portal, "whether bombing by itself will be a decisive factor in the present war." Yet Churchill had also tried to sell Stalin on the idea that the air war was not only a de facto second front but also an effective second front, a claim that Stalin dismissed (but Eisenhower agreed with, as did Goebbels when the bombs took an increasingly greater toll). At the core of Churchill's fluctuating beliefs regarding airpower was the unsettling prospect that if airpower did not reduce Germany to ruin, large Anglo-American armies would have to do so. He had long known that armies would have to go ashore someday, but airpower, as seductively portrayed by Portal and Harris, held up the possibility of sparing the troops (although at terrible cost to the air crews). In one of Churchill's disputatious memos to Portal he argued that even if "all the towns in Germany were rendered largely uninhabitable it does not follow that the military control would be weakened or even that Germany's war industry could not be carried on." In fact, Churchill feared Hitler would scatter war production throughout Eastern Europe such that it became independent of events in the Reich, and untouchable.

In the end, his doubts proved justified. German production of tanks, planes, artillery, and submarines increased during each year of the war, and fell off only during the final twelve weeks (although the rate of increase was assuredly slowed by bombing). Churchill saw the inherent contradictions in the arguments put forth by the strategic bombing advocates. On the one hand, pinpoint accuracy (which was unattainable) was not necessary for a reduction in German morale, but it was absolutely necessary if German industry was to be destroyed. He had no choice but to continue the bombing. It *might* erode morale; it *might* smash industrial targets. Whatever the results, British morale would be boosted. Britons were not to be denied their revenge. By war's end the effort cost Britain almost 11,000 aircraft and 55,000 killed, the Americans more than 8,000 planes and 26,000 killed. As for Spaatz, who later commanded all U.S. air forces in Europe and believed those forces could alone defeat Hitler in 1944, Churchill offered to

Harris that the American was "a man of limited intelligence." Harris's reply to Churchill is ironic, given his bomber mania and the slaughter within his RAF ranks: "You pay him too high a compliment."[37]

Neutral nations also thwarted the destruction of German industry. Sweden, Switzerland, Portugal, and Spain all carried on robust and profitable trade with Germany, to the ongoing frustration of the Allies. Almost 100 percent of Europe's wolframite, a tungsten ore critical to the manufacture of armored steel plate, came from the Iberian Peninsula. Half of Portugal's wolframite went to Germany, a trade policy that resulted in dead Britons. That was one reason Churchill for two years had considered the possibility of taking the Azores by force if Portugal's dictator, Dr. António Salazar, did not agree to grant Allied ships and aircraft refueling rights in those islands. Were Allied aircraft allowed use of the Azores, the air cover over convoys would effectively double. Salazar continued to play both ends against the middle until late 1943, when—after Churchill threatened to take the islands by force—he finally granted refueling and landing rights to the Allies. When Salazar objected to American troops being stationed in the Azores, Churchill again threatened direct action, cabling Eden, "There is no need for us to be apologetic in dealing with any of these neutrals who hope to get out of Armageddon with no trouble and a good profit."[38]

The neutrals profited handsomely from their relations with Berlin. The Swedes supplied the Reich iron ore, canned fish, and ball bearings. The Swiss sold Hitler arms and ammunition, and industrial diamonds used in cutting tools and bomb fuses. Pressed in early 1943 by the British and Americans to curtail their arms trade with Germany, the Swiss promised to look at their trade practices, and then went on that year to increase shipments to Germany by over 50 percent. The Swedes were stubborn when pressed to limit trade with Germany, wrote Dean Acheson, then an assistant secretary in the State Department, but "the Swiss were the cube of stubbornness." The neutrals argued that self-preservation drove their trade policies; it did not pay to say no to Germany. Even Franco, a Fascist and hostile neutral who flirted with outright union with the Axis, had to watch his back. To keep him on the fence the Allies continued to send Franco food to feed his people. There were consequences. The American press attacked Churchill as an appeaser after word leaked out of the State Department that he was pondering an offer to Franco to increase food and oil shipments in return for Spain's making small concessions to Britain, including a reduction in Spain's sale of wolframite to Germany. Lord Cherwell proposed turning the behavior of neutrals against the Germans. He developed a plan to clandestinely introduce botulin into the canned fish Sweden sold to Germany. "A small amount of it [botulin] would be enough to destroy all mankind," he later told one of Churchill's secretaries.[39]

An irony attached itself to dealings with neutral nations. The Allies considered German-occupied countries to be legitimate targets of economic and military warfare. The citizens of those nations were therefore doubly victimized—by the Nazis and by RAF bombs, which were no more accurate when dropped on Holland or Norway or France than when dropped on Germany. But neutrals such as Ireland, Portugal, Sweden, and Spain were immune from RAF bombs, immune from the bloodiest consequences of the war. Neutrals might be persuaded by diplomacy to adopt policies acceptable to the Allies, but they could not be cudgeled into good behavior. Meanwhile, they supplied skilled workers, raw materials, machine tools, and bullets that killed American and British soldiers, and banked the profits. Eamon de Valera (whose term for the war was "the Emergency") was an adroit fence-sitter, dutifully interning both German and British pilots who were forced to land in Ireland (and Americans, too, until an arrangement was made later in the year).

The Swiss allowed Britain to manufacture their deadly efficient Oerlikon 20mm cannon under license but also sold the cannon and ammunition to Berlin. Both Tokyo and Berlin had reached an agreement years earlier with Switzerland to manufacture versions of the gun. Thus, when a Messerschmitt Bf 110 armed with Oerlikon cannons attacked a British frigate, also armed with the anti-aircraft version of the gun, each side found itself shooting at the other with the same Swiss weapon. Only Turkey among the largest neutrals displayed a modicum of moral fortitude, when it risked incurring Hitler's wrath by suspending shipments of chrome to Germany; but it did so only in mid-1944, when Hitler was on a sure path to destruction and only after a threat of economic blockade by the Allies. Neutral nations could not be persuaded to act reasonably by B-17 bombers; nor could they be punished by B-17s when they did not. If Allied bombers blew one of Hitler's munitions factories to smithereens, he could bank on the Swiss making up his loss, and the Swedes for the iron to smelt into new cannons. The ring of steel Churchill envisioned around Germany always admitted to a degree of porosity.[40]

On January 11, the same day that Churchill mulled over Tizard's bombing projections, the *Sunday Dispatch* announced the possibility of "one little bomb that would destroy the whole of Berlin... a bomb that would blast a hole twenty-five miles in diameter and wreck every structure within a hundred miles.... The explosive in this bomb would be the energy contained in the uranium atom." HMG saw no need to comment on such a ludicrous example of sensationalist journalism.[41]

Churchill also used the delay on the eleventh to take a first and perfunctory look at a three-hundred-page paper on postwar domestic policy titled "Social Insurance and Allied Services," produced by Sir William Beveridge, released to Parliament in November and published by the government as a white paper in early December.* The British and American press had been parsing Beveridge's plan for weeks. Churchill had not; the sheer length of the report argued against his reading it.

Beveridge was Britain's leading authority on unemployment insurance, master of University College, Oxford, and an old colleague of Churchill's from his days as a Liberal, when he and Lloyd George had asked Beveridge to prepare the nation's first comprehensive plan for national insurance. The 1942 paper—the Beveridge Report, as it came to be known—amounted to a manifesto of social reform, which the *Manchester Guardian* called "a great and fine thing." It outlined a compulsory, flat-rate national program that would address wage loss, maternity care, pensions, disability insurance, housing, education, widows' benefits, health insurance, funeral expenses—every financial need encountered by Britons from birth to funerary interment. Churchill didn't like what little he read, not because he opposed the idea of HMG restructuring Britain's social security apparatus, but because, as he told the War Cabinet, he did not wish to deceive the people "by false hopes and airy visions of Utopia and El Dorado." Besides, he offered, Britain would be nearly broke after the war, the United States would be a formidable competitor, and Britons would "get very angry if they felt they had been gulled or cheated" by promises made, and then unmade. Yet Beveridge, anticipating Conservative opposition, argued that in a postwar world of reduced tariffs and free markets, a shift of pension and health insurance costs from corporations to the government would make British industry more competitive in world markets.[42]

Beveridge convinced some Conservatives but by no means all. Harold Nicolson thought Beveridge took delight in "upsetting governments and wrecking constitutions" with his radical agenda. "He is a vain man," Nicolson wrote. The usual Conservative strategy in such cases, Nicolson told his diary, would be "to welcome the Report in principle, and then whittle it away with criticism." Many Tory MPs had already concluded that Beveridge's plan was "an incentive to idleness." Nicolson's wife, Vita

---

* In Britain, the publishing of a report such as Beveridge's as a "white paper" signifies HMG's overall intent (without necessarily announcing a time frame) to analyze, debate the merits of, and possibly act upon some or all of the recommendations made.

Sackville-West, expressed her opinion on the matter in tones that would not have surprised anyone who claimed the British upper class lacked empathy for the common man: "I am all for educating the people into being less awful, less limited, less silly, and for spending lots of money on (1) extended education; (2) better paid teachers, but *not* for giving them everything for nothing, which they don't appreciate any how" (italics Sackville-West).[43]

Churchill had so far kept to his self-imposed prohibition of any public rumination on postwar policies. Yet he had known since Pearl Harbor that the war would someday be won. He had told his countrymen in November that the end of the beginning was at hand; now Britons sought some sense of where their government intended to go once victory was attained. They especially sought some sense of where the Conservatives were going, for according to Labour, the party of Baldwin, Chamberlain, and Churchill had brought Britain economic depression, the shame of appeasement, and, finally, war. That Labour could make such a claim with a straight face, having done its best to retard re-armament and having voted against even limited conscription just four months before Hitler invaded Poland, did not among Britons diminish doubts about the Tories.

For more than two years, Britons had merrily sung "The Lambeth Walk" (which Berlin radio called "Jewish mischief and animalistic hopping") as they scrambled down into the Underground when the sirens wailed. Six thousand Londoners scuttled into the shelters every night, a decrease of 10,000 from the previous year and 150,000 from the height of the Blitz. Yet a census of the shelters found that almost 6,000 lived there permanently. Two-year-old children who had never seen the inside of a real house had spent their entire lives beneath the streets. Britons had taken everything the Luftwaffe had thrown their way. They loved Churchill and would recoil against any partisan attempt to change horses in midstream, but someday they would be across the river. They wanted to know what they'd find on the other side, other than Churchill's sunlit uplands. Churchill, after returning from Casablanca, and after a more careful examination of the Beveridge Report, told the War Cabinet that the plan "constitutes an essential part of any postwar scheme of national betterment." This was the old Liberal voicing his belief that government could and should rearrange the social structure, and could do so without degrading into doctrinaire socialism, which he loathed.[44]

Yet, by not telling the British people as much, he missed an opportunity to claim as his cause the postwar rebuilding of Britain. He considered parts of the Beveridge Report worthy, but also a nuisance that interfered with the war effort. Attlee and the Labourites, meanwhile, saw the Beveridge Report as a blueprint for their political future. Many Britons approaching the age of thirty had never voted in a national election, had never had the opportunity to choose their leaders. Their patience was not infinite.

The nation's food supply, as always, occupied Churchill's thoughts as he prepared to leave for Casablanca. Hunger was not killing Britons, but it was diminishing their ability to work, in fields and factories. Churchill dictated a memo on January 12 that reflected the major consequence of the shipping crisis: the food crisis. To the Ministry of Agriculture and Fisheries he wrote, "Please make me a plan to have more eggs." Of the millions of tons of barley and oats grown and imported, he asked, could not some be diverted to "garden hens" in order to increase the egg yield? The memo was similar to many he had sent regularly for almost three years, a combination of desperation and a call for clear thinking. After a visit to Britain months earlier, the Lend-Lease administrator Edward Stettinius reported that forests had been chopped down to harvest the lumber and to make room for farms. Golf courses and parks had been plowed up and converted to crop cultivation. Marshes had been drained. And still, rationing was tightened, and tightened again. Stettinius asked Americans in radio addresses and newspaper interviews to try to imagine that one-third of them lived in New England, rather than one-sixteenth, and that they depended for survival on shipments from thousands of miles away through U-boat-infested waters. Before leaving for Britain, Stettinius asked a colleague what an appropriate gift might be for his hosts.* The answer was "food."[45]

After dispensing his thoughts on eggs, Churchill departed No. 10, pausing for a moment to hug his cat, Smokey, and to instruct Elizabeth Layton to make sure that the feline did not suffer from loneliness in his master's absence. He then set off for an RAF airfield near Oxford, where *Commando,* the B-24 that had ferried him to Cairo and Moscow in August, was being fueled for the nine-hour flight to Casablanca. The trip was of course top secret, but Churchill's exit belied the fact. Harriman and Ismay, who were also making the trip, were already at the blacked-out airfield

* As with many of the Americans who visited the Churchills, Stettinius brought them a Virginia ham, from his own farm. When he learned that the maximum weight he could bring on board the Pan American Clipper out of New York was forty pounds, he trimmed the fat off the ham. In London, a colleague told him, "Ed, you should have left your shoes at home if necessary, but not the fat off that ham." Churchill, thanking Stettinius for the diminutive ham, peered into the bag, smiled, and told him *never* again to trim the fat.

when they saw "in the distance a convoy of limousines led by one car with the brightest headlights" in spite of the blackout. The convoy roared up to the aircraft with sirens screaming and lights flashing. Churchill—code-named Air Commodore Frankland—stepped from his car "thinly disguised in the uniform of an air commodore." The real air commodore exclaimed, "Good God, the only mistake they made was they didn't put it in the local newspapers." Churchill's bodyguard tried to hustle him aboard the B-24, but he lingered on the runway and at his leisure reduced his cigar to a stub. Air Commodore Frankland would board when he was ready and not before.[46]

A few minutes later *Commando*'s four big Pratt & Whitney engines growled to life and the plane with its precious cargo lifted into the night. The captain took it up to seven thousand feet. It was midwinter, and frigid inside the metal shell. The aircraft had since August been updated with a heating system of sorts—a kerosene-powered contraption rigged up near the cots. The device almost made an Icarus of Churchill. He awoke in the night with a sharp pain in his foot, caused by the heating element glowing red hot upon his toes. Kerosene fumes permeated the cabin. Afraid the heater would ignite his blankets or the fumes, Churchill jostled Portal awake. The air marshal assessed the situation and reached the same conclusion. They disabled the heater and flew on, chilled and sleepless. All aboard bundled up with their extra layers of clothing, all but Churchill, who wore nothing but his silk nightshirt. "On his hands and knees," recalled Lord Moran, "he cut a quaint figure with his big, bare, white bottom." Before departing for Casablanca, the passengers had been issued parachute harnesses, extra clothing, and currency from all the countries they would overfly, as well as notes written in Arabic promising a reward to whosoever gave the bearer safe passage.[47]

In the early morning, they descended out of high clouds over the Moroccan coast, just west of Casablanca. Below, feluccas drifted on fair seas, and in the harbor dozens of stranded yachts rode at anchor, unable to repatriate to Italy, Greece, or France. Landward, verdant smudges of ancient date palm, orange, and olive groves sketched the outer reaches of the city, in which the minarets of dozens of mosques stabbed skyward and the red-tile roofs of whitewashed limestone houses looked as if a sack of pomegranates had burst and scattered its contents across the landscape. Far to the southeast, the snowcaps of the Atlas Mountains, gilded by morning light, cast their ragged shadows seaward. On the far side of the mountains, Bernard Montgomery was driving Erwin Rommel west, through Tripolitania and toward Tunisia. After landing at the Medouina Airfield, Churchill, to the dismay of his bodyguards, chose to light a cigar and wait on the tarmac for the arrival of Ismay's B-24. The secrecy of the entire mission was going up in smoke. When Ismay stepped from his plane, he was horrified to see Churchill standing in the open, attired in his light blue airman's livery. "Any fool can see," Ismay exclaimed, "that is an air commodore disguised as the Prime Minister."[48]

Casablanca promised an oasis of gay colors after the dead gray of a London winter, a painter's delight. Expecting as much, Churchill had instructed Sawyers to bring along brushes, paints, and palette. The weather, Churchill wrote to Clementine, proved to be very un-English and much to his liking, "bright with occasional showers and like a nice day in May for temperature."[49]

It had been a year since he departed the warmth of south Florida, a year that closed without a second front in Europe. The errant Dieppe raid of August had only underscored his doubts in that regard and had demonstrated to the satisfaction of most of the Combined Chiefs (but not to George Marshall) the futility of trying to establish that front in 1942. Stalin, however, expected that Churchill and Roosevelt would use their time together to deliver that front in 1943. Yet, by the time Churchill landed in Casablanca, he had been convinced by Brooke's arguments and Kesselring's reinforcement of Tunis that Roundup was effectively scotched for 1943. He arrived prepared to argue the case for further action in the Mediterranean. It was the only strategy within reach. However, he was always open to suggestion if the suggestion had to do with taking the fight to Germany. He counseled his military chiefs that if the lessons of Dieppe and the vicissitudes of weather and logistics led the Allies to require a guarantee of success before considering taking offensive action, they would find themselves unable and unwilling to take *any* action. "The maxim 'Nothing avails like perfection,'" he warned, "may be spelt shorter, 'paralysis.'"[50]

Dwight Eisenhower had commandeered the Anfa Hotel and eighteen surrounding villas a few miles outside Casablanca and near enough to the beach that the rumble of the surf carried up to the compound. Churchill enjoyed strolling along the beach and dipping into the surf when the seas allowed. When they did not, noting the fifteen-foot breakers, he came to understand how so many landing craft had foundered during the landings. One villa was reserved for de Gaulle, if he showed up. The *New York Times* later reported, "Many acres of the resort were enclosed in two lines of barbed wire, on which tin cans were hung. If any one had been foolhardy enough to approach these lines he would have been riddled by bullets from machine guns or bayoneted by some of the hundreds of American infantrymen who stood helmeted atop roofs or patrolled the shady walks around the area." Actually, one overweight sixty-eight-year-old former trooper was foolhardy enough to do just that. Returning one evening from a stroll along the beach, Churchill and his bodyguard, Walter Thompson, were dropped off by their driver on the wrong side of the compound, and outside the wire. Unwilling to walk the long perimeter, Churchill, eyeing the wire, saw a solution. "We can climb that, Thompson," he declared, and began to swing a leg over the wire. Thompson heard the *click* of a round being snapped into a rifle, followed by shouts of "Halt!" Four soldiers leveled their rifles at the intruders. "It's *Churchill,*" Thompson yelled. The soldiers lowered their weapons, cursing at having almost shot the prime minister, and cursing the prime minister for almost forcing their hand.[51]

Field Marshal John Dill and Roosevelt's military chiefs arrived on January 13. Dill, more than any other Briton, had so far earned Marshall's respect, so much so that Brooke's roster of conference attendees had Dill listed in the American contingent. Yet Dill, in the preceding weeks, had passed on to Brooke the general's strategic goals and plans, gleaned by Dill's close friendship with Marshall. Thus, Brooke went into the meetings doubly armed, with his plans and with Marshall's. That evening, Brooke met with Churchill and stressed that although the Americans and certain members of the British Joint Planning Committee favored an invasion of Sardinia over Sicily, he did not, and intended to make his case to the Americans accordingly. He sought Churchill's assurance that the British delegation would speak with one voice. Churchill concurred.

In all of North Africa, from Cairo to Casablanca, the British had more troops on the ground than the Americans did and more planes in the air, and they were alone in patrolling the Mediterranean Sea, where the Americans feared to go. It rankled within HMG that Franklin Roosevelt did not acknowledge these facts in his addresses to his countrymen. Eden later wrote that he was "concerned about the fact" that Roosevelt's declarations "contained not a single word about the British share in the operations," due in large part to the "legend" that the British "were most unpopular in North Africa." Eisenhower's deputy, Mark Clark—in Brooke's estimation a "very ambitious and unscrupulous" man—was intent on promulgating that legend. He infuriated Brooke by spreading the rumor that the French in North Africa would not fight alongside the British. But Brooke's respect for Eisenhower increased when Eisenhower eased Clark out as his deputy and put him in command of the reserves. Still, Clark's and Roosevelt's political shenanigans aside, until such time as the Americans put more men in the field in the fight against Hitler and conducted that fight with better results than Eisenhower had so far obtained, Churchill possessed leverage. He intended to use it at Casablanca—next target, Sicily, followed by Italy. The proposed Sicilian campaign already had a code name: Husky.[52]

The president arrived late in the afternoon on January 14 after a five-day journey by Boeing flying boat with stops at Miami, Trinidad, and Brazil, and an eighteen-hour flight across the Atlantic to Bathurst, a squalid outpost at the mouth of the Gambia River in West Africa. From there he flew in an army C-54 to Casablanca. His doctor, Admiral Ross McIntire, was as concerned about his patient's health as was Moran for Churchill's. McIntire, worried about Roosevelt's heart, kept digitalis on hand lest the cruising altitude of eight thousand feet trigger an angina episode. Flying was a dangerous business. The American press was not apprised for ten days of the daring journey. When told, the scribblers were agog: "Franklin Roosevelt, with his great sense of historical drama, had again created history with a dramatist's breath-taking stroke. No President of the U.S. since Abraham Lincoln had ever visited a battle theater. No President had ever left the U.S. in wartime. None had ever been to Africa. None had ever traveled in an airplane." Now, *Time* reported weeks later, came Franklin Roosevelt, thirty-second president of the United States, "to shatter all four precedents at once." All true, as was the fact that Roosevelt and his men arrived in Casablanca unprepared for Churchill.[53]

That much became clear during preliminary discussions and at an informal dinner on the fourteenth. Marshall and King stated their desire to wage "all out" war in the Pacific rather than holding actions against Japan. King proposed—to Brooke's amazement—that 70 percent of the war effort be directed toward the Pacific, 30 percent toward Europe. Brooke pointed out that "this was hardly a scientific way of approaching war strategy."

Brooke knew he had a fight on his hands regarding Sicily but presumed he had the full backing of all the British chiefs. Yet some within the British planning staff and one among the contingent had gone off the reservation: Dickie Mountbatten. Mountbatten considered Sardinia the best target, and he crossed the aisle to argue to Harry Hopkins in private the merits of Sardinia. This schism in the British command might have proved problematic had not Mountbatten also argued the case to Hopkins for two other of his favorite schemes—battleships made of ice, and a Rube Goldberg–style weapon Hopkins described as "fantastic." According to Mountbatten, a new type of explosive could be crammed into an old submarine and run right up to the base of a fifty-foot bluff somewhere on the coast of France. The subsequent explosion, Mountbatten proclaimed, would "blow a road right into France." Then, rather than invasion forces having to assault an enfiladed port (as at Dieppe), they could proceed directly through the newly created pass. Mountbatten may not have studied the results of a similar scheme, when Union forces burrowed a huge mine under Confederate lines during the siege of Petersburg in 1864. The mine indeed created an opening, a crater into which Union troops poured—and into which

Confederates poured deadly fire, annihilating the attackers. Hopkins listened, politely, to Dickie's proposal, and judged Mountbatten to be a "courageous, resourceful man" whom the British chiefs "push around." Only time would tell what might become of Mountbatten's indestructible frozen dreadnoughts and exploding submarines.[54]

At dinner that night, King, who had sworn off hard liquor for the duration, consumed enough wine to become "nicely lit up," as recalled by Brooke. Churchill, not realizing King's condition, tried to rebut the admiral each time King—"with a thick voice and many gesticulations"—advised Roosevelt on how best to dismember the French empire and how to fight the war in general, and in the Pacific in particular. The discussion continued well into the early morning hours, the scene lit by candles after an air-raid alert forced the dousing of the electric lights. It was a remarkable scene, the military and political leaders of the English-speaking world chatting by candlelight high on a Moroccan bluff while great armies bivouacked and battled five hundred miles away across the sands.[55]

Over the next week, the Combined Chiefs of Staff met fifteen times to work out a strategy for the coming year. Roosevelt and Churchill dined together daily and spent many hours in private meetings, during one of which Churchill reminded Roosevelt that contrary to their gentleman's agreement of the previous summer on the matter of "Tube Alloys," the British had in fact been excluded from the atomic bomb program. Harry Hopkins assured Churchill that this situation would be "put right" immediately upon Roosevelt's return to Washington. Each evening, the Combined Joint Chiefs briefed the two leaders on the day's discussions, which had not gotten off to a heady start. Brooke called the first few days of discussions "desperate" at one point, concluding, "The USA Joint Planners did not agree with Germany being the primary enemy and were wishing to defeat Japan first!!!" They disagreed, too, on Burma; the Americans wanted a concentrated British and American effort there in order to reopen the Burma Road in support of Chiang, while the British wanted to bide their time until they had the men and matériel to take a solid shot. The air war presented another opportunity for dispute; Churchill conveyed to General Ira Eaker his displeasure over the American Eighth Air Force and its lack of punch, but after spending an hour hearing Eaker out, he withdrew his opposition to daylight raids, in the main because Eaker sold him on the idea of round-the-clock air attacks, Americans by day and the RAF by night. Churchill liked that, later telling a group of American reporters, "There is nothing like a 24-hours service."[56]

Eisenhower flew over from Algiers to outline his plan for taking Tunis. He proposed a strike eastward to the sea with Major General Lloyd Fredendall's II Corps to drive a wedge between Arnim's and Rommel's armies.

Brooke destroyed the idea, pointing out its most obvious defect: with Montgomery and the Eighth Army still five hundred miles to the east, a thrust by II Corps would result in its being trapped *between* Arnim and Rommel. The most likely result would be the defeat in detail of Fredendall's force in the south and Anderson's forces in the north. The idea went nowhere, and Eisenhower flew back to Algiers. Yet with the need to coordinate the British First and Eighth Armies, as well as the French and American forces, it was obvious that a Supreme Commander had to be chosen. It was Eisenhower. He "had neither the tactical nor strategical experience" for such a task, Brooke later wrote, but by "being pushed up into the... rarified atmosphere of a Supreme Commander," he could attend to "his political problems." Brooke believed the appointment, while flattering the Americans, would allow British commanders to fight the battles and restore "the necessary drive and co-ordination which has been so seriously lacking." Eisenhower, with just three stars on his shoulders, was outranked by his trio of British lieutenants—Alexander, Tedder, and Cunningham. Marshall, not impressed with Eisenhower's results in Tunisia, told Roosevelt that he "would not promote Eisenhower [to four stars] until there was some damn good reason for doing it." He meant a good military reason. Roosevelt had in mind a good political reason; Eisenhower's promotion would tell the American people that they were taking charge of the war. Two weeks later, Roosevelt submitted Eisenhower's name to the U.S. Senate, and Ike got his fourth star on February 11.[57]

Although Roosevelt remained committed to Marshall's cross-Channel strategy, he was opportunistic enough to see the merit of Churchill's Sicily initiative. After five days of debate, the Combined Chiefs of Staff reached the same conclusion. They also agreed on eight overall strategic priorities. Brooke later wrote that Dill was instrumental in forging the agreement; the alternative, Dill had warned Brooke and Marshall, was to allow Roosevelt and Churchill to make the final decisions, and "what a mess they would make of it!" The final agreement codified the need to defeat Germany first, with wresting control of the Atlantic taking top billing. Second, and closely tied to the first, was the need to get all aid possible to Russia. The plan to take Sicily was third, followed by the continued buildup of American forces in Britain, with the goal of running a small-scale version of Roundup on the Cotentin Peninsula that August. This was a sop to Marshall. Fifth, the British agreed on the need to retake southern Burma (Operation Anakim, scheduled for later in the year) in order to open a supply route to Chiang and to draw the Japanese from MacArthur's flank as he moved northward. This was a sop to Roosevelt and King; Churchill believed China would play no role of any importance in defeating Japan. In any event, the British lacked the requisite forces to retake Burma that year even if they believed it would result in an earlier defeat of Japan. The sixth term of the agreement called for a study of Axis oil needs and industrial capacity, for purposes of planning the "heaviest possible air offensive" to destroy German industrial capacity (which both Spaatz and Harris believed might end the war in 1943). Next came the need to establish naval and air control over North Africa and the Mediterranean. The final article stipulated that all matters connected with Turkey would be handled by the British. The entire eight-point plan was "a strategic menu they [the Allies] could not digest," Samuel Eliot Morison later wrote, a case of planners who "had eyes bigger than their stomachs."[58]

Churchill was so eager to get Turkey and its forty-five (underarmed) divisions into the war that he notified the War Cabinet that immediately following the conference he intended to first visit Cairo, to consult with Alexander, who would soon be setting off for Tunisia. Then Churchill intended to set off for Turkey and a meeting with President İsmet İnönü. The War Cabinet objected; the journey was long and dangerous, and Churchill was needed in London. Churchill replied that he was going anyway, and he instructed Eden to arrange with the Turks for an invitation to be sent to Cairo, where Churchill expected to receive and accept it.

Churchill and Roosevelt had one final piece of business to conduct. It centered on Generals Giraud and de Gaulle. Churchill had included in his birthday eve broadcast the battle cry "France will rise again!" Whether de Gaulle would rise with it was the question. Roosevelt's feelings on the subject were well known to Churchill, to wit, the Frenchman was an obdurate obstacle to the advancement of American policy, which held no promise of any meaningful war role (or postwar role for that matter) for France and the French Empire, de Gaulle or no de Gaulle. Roosevelt had for months artfully avoided any official recognition of de Gaulle by arguing that the sovereignty of France rested solely with its people.

But the French, prisoners of Germany, could make no such choice. In contrast to Sikorski and Beneš, who were leaders of governments in exile, de Gaulle was only the leader of certain military units in exile. Churchill had tolerated and supported de Gaulle in that role for thirty months, but on December 10, in secret session, he told the House, "We must not be led to believe that General de Gaulle is an unfaltering friend of Britain." Quite the contrary, de Gaulle possessed the "traditional antagonism engrained in French hearts" toward the English, and had left "a trail of Anglophobia behind him" wherever he went. Churchill's strategy was clear: by sketching de Gaulle in dark shades, he prepared the House for his removal from the political scene were the Americans to demand it. The scathing attack on de Gaulle was symptomatic of Churchill's evolving relationship with Roosevelt and the subtle lessening of Britain's influence over inter-alliance political affairs. Once Darlan was removed from the picture, Roosevelt's man in North Africa, Robert Murphy, lost no time in propping Giraud up as the civil and military leader there. De Gaulle knew the Americans foresaw no role for him, Eden later wrote, and "began to suspect that the British and United States governments were going to make an agreement with Giraud over his head." Eden rode to the Frenchman's rescue when he drew from de Gaulle a promise to meet with Giraud, but Giraud refused on the flimsy pretext that Darlan's assassination created "an unfavorable atmosphere" for such a meeting. The strain imposed by the totality of the political situation in North Africa—Darlan, Giraud, Mark Clark, and Murphy, and their sundry intrigues—led Eden to later observe, "I was not alone in feeling the physical and mental burden. As the months passed we were all to show it, even the Prime Minister."[59]

De Gaulle proved himself the most tiresome Frenchman of the lot. Roosevelt and Churchill had brought Giraud around; he agreed to meet de Gaulle in Casablanca in order to work out a civil and military partnership. But de Gaulle refused, telling Eden that he would agree to meet Giraud alone, perhaps in Chad, but not in Casablanca, where such a meeting could only amplify the subordinated stature of the French. Gallic honor was at stake. Eden tried a different tack; the president, he told de Gaulle, would like to meet with him in Casablanca. De Gaulle again refused, telling Eden that if Roosevelt wanted to meet, they could do so in America. Eden reported de Gaulle's recalcitrance to Churchill, who responded with a warning that de Gaulle's failure to appear would result in his forfeiting any chance of assuming *any* role in Algiers, even the subordinate role envisioned by the Americans. The message was, show up or HMG will be done with you. Roosevelt, who had prevailed upon Giraud to come to terms with de Gaulle, cabled Eden: "I have got the bridegroom, where is the bride?"[60]

After a weeklong sulk, de Gaulle finally agreed to go, arriving in Morocco on January 22. That night, he met with Churchill. "I was pretty rough with him," Churchill told Lord Moran after the meeting, as the two watched de Gaulle make his way down the hill from the residence. Yet, Churchill added, "France without an army is not France. De Gaulle is the spirit of that army...the last survivor of a warrior race." Moran asked Churchill if he had heard Roosevelt's quip that de Gaulle fancied himself a descendant of Joan of Arc. Churchill had and "was not amused." De Gaulle was defiant and arrogant, Churchill told the doctor, but he offered that, with tears now in his eyes, "England's grievous offense in de Gaulle's eyes is that she has helped France. He cannot bear that she needed help." The tears appear to be plausibly Churchillian, yet so do the sentiments he expressed in a letter to Clementine two days later, when he wrote that de Gaulle brought "comic relief" to the conference. "He thinks he is Clemenceau (having dropped Joan of Arc for the time being)." Of French leaders, including de Gaulle, Churchill told Clemmie, "They hate each other far more than they do the Germans" and they "care more for power and place than for the liberation of their country."[61]

De Gaulle met with Giraud on January 23 and afterward issued a typically enigmatic announcement: "We have met. We have talked." Roosevelt also met with the two Frenchmen, separately. Giraud and the president chatted with no bodyguards in attendance, but when de Gaulle arrived at Roosevelt's villa, the Secret Service detail—many of the agents armed with tommy guns—took up concealed positions behind shrubs and draperies. The union of sorts between the reluctant Frenchmen appeared to be a fait accompli, although the governing body that was struggling into existence was so ill defined as to be nonexistent, and was not recognized by London or Washington as having any official role elsewhere within the French empire, or in France, where de Gaulle was considered a national hero.[62]

Just after noon on Sunday the twenty-fourth, a fiercely sunny and hot day, de Gaulle and Giraud's union—a "shotgun wedding," Eden and Roosevelt called it—was consummated with a ceremonial handshake on the lawn of Roosevelt's villa, with Roosevelt (hatless) and Churchill (under a gray homburg) looking on. Fifty shocked reporters were also present; they had been brought over from Algiers not knowing whom they'd be meeting. One photographer in the group was Sammy Schulman, a short, mustachioed, and brassy shooter whom Roosevelt had known for a decade. A month later, Roosevelt regaled Washington reporters with the story of what happened next: "I worked it out beforehand with Sammy. After the pictures of the four of us were taken, Sammy Schulman in the front row said, 'Oh, Mr. President, can we have a picture of the two Generals shaking hands?' So I translated Sammy to Giraud, and Giraud said, '*Mais, oui,*' and he got right up and held out his hand. It took Churchill and myself five minutes to persuade de Gaulle to get on his feet to shake hands. And we got them to do it. And I think you have all got that picture. If you run into a copy of the picture, look at the expression on de Gaulle's face!"[63]

The expression of feline contentment Churchill wears betrays the fate of the canary. Sammy's shots of the four leaders and of de Gaulle and Giraud are some of the most iconic images of the war. Yet they capture a false image; de Gaulle, in fact, had agreed to nothing more substantive than a handshake with Giraud. As much as Roosevelt derided de Gaulle, the Frenchman had had the last laugh at Casablanca. His Fighting French forces numbered 50,000, just one-fifth the number of former Vichy troops serving under Giraud, yet de Gaulle and his men supplied the spirit of the French army in North Africa. De Gaulle's army had been formed in reaction to established authority; in a legal sense they were mutineers, first against the defeated Third Republic, then against Vichy, where they were considered freebooters. Charles Maurass, a septuagenarian royalist, Vichy mouthpiece, poet, polemicist, and Pétain counselor, pronounced, "De Gaulle is a traitor who leads the scum of the earth." This the Gaullists took as a compliment. The Fighting French would never serve willingly under former Vichy loyalists, and although Giraud was brave and decent, many in his officer corps were not. Giraud himself served at the pleasure of the Americans, an insult to Gallic pride, and he had so far failed to repeal anti-Jewish Vichy laws or free Gaullist prisoners. The handshake altered nothing, and meant nothing. The marriage lent credence to an old saying in the French cavalry: "Beware of women when they are in front of you, beware of horses when they are behind you, and beware of your leaders wherever they were."[64]

Moments after Sammy snapped his photos, Roosevelt uttered one of the most iconic phrases of the war. Speaking from notes, he outlined in general and necessarily imprecise terms the decisions taken over the previous ten days. Then he nonchalantly added an incendiary line: the Allies demanded "unconditional surrender" from the Axis. Hopkins later recalled the president telling him that the phrase had simply "popped into his mind" as he compared the difficulty of getting Giraud and de Gaulle together to that of arranging a meeting between Robert E. Lee and Ulysses S. "Unconditional Surrender" Grant. "And the next thing I knew," Roosevelt told Hopkins, "I had said it." Roosevelt the multilateralist had just seemingly issued one of the most unilateral declarations in American history, but it was not spur of the moment. In fact, Churchill days earlier advised his War Cabinet that he and Roosevelt had discussed the matter and decided upon terms of "unconditional surrender" for Germany and Japan. The War Cabinet insisted Italy should be included. Churchill understood the matter was to be kept secret. But Roosevelt let it slip. Churchill, in his memoirs, took a mild swipe at Roosevelt when he wrote of Roosevelt's explanation of how he came to utter the words: "I do not feel this frank statement is in any way weakened by the fact that the phrase occurs in the notes from which he spoke."[65]

"Churchill was indignant" at dinner that night, recalled Averell

Harriman, angered not so much by the policy of unconditional surrender but the "unfortunate way Roosevelt announced it." The words "unconditional surrender" sent several messages to several quarters. To the British and American people it signified that there would be no "Darlan deal" with Hitler, Tojo, or Mussolini. It meant that no mere armistice would leave Germany free to refit for purposes of future misdeeds. It meant that no Wilsonian-style Fourteen Points—imprecise, and open to infinite interpretation—would infect the negotiations. In fact, there would be no negotiations. "Unconditional surrender" told Stalin that the Americans and British were in it for the duration. Yet it also told Stalin that his allies expected him to go the distance. The prospect of Stalin making a separate peace with Hitler had worried the Anglo-Americans for more than a year.[66]

Churchill's memory proved fallible when in 1948 he told Roosevelt biographer Robert Sherwood that he had "heard the words 'Unconditional Surrender' for the first time from the president's lips at the conference." Ernest Bevin's memory, too, proved faulty when in 1949, as a cabinet member in Clement Attlee's Labour government, he excoriated Churchill and "unconditional surrender" for the crippling costs associated with rebuilding Germany. Churchill replied to Bevin as he had to Sherwood, that he had heard the words for the first time from the president's lips at Casablanca. Only later did Churchill recall the telegram to the War Cabinet of January 1943. Such errant recollections have muddled the issue ever since.[67]

Criticism and controversy attended the expression from the moment Roosevelt uttered it. Eisenhower didn't like it because it did not define "unconditional," and when the time came for cease-fires and surrenders, Eisenhower would be the man on the spot. "Around headquarters," wrote Eisenhower's press aide, Harry Butcher, such troubles were "attributed to the hard-boiled" insistence of Churchill and Roosevelt on "unconditional surrender.... No surrender has ever been made without some conditions." Eisenhower would later ask his superiors to precisely define the term; they would not. Stalin had said he need not be consulted but only be apprised of decisions taken at Casablanca, and so he was. He did not make a public statement on "unconditional surrender" until his annual May Day speech, where he turned the tables on his two allies by implying that unless they kept their promise to open a second European front that summer, any talk of unconditional surrender was just that, talk. Later in the year, Stalin told Harriman that Roosevelt's remark "was an unfortunate statement." Two years hence, Goebbels employed it as a propaganda tool, extolling Germans on the need to fight to the death because the enemy had left open no other option. "It was a godsend to Goebbels," Harriman later recalled. By the end of the year, Churchill, too, harbored doubts, and told Stalin as much. That conversation remained private until after the war. In public, Churchill never wavered on "unconditional surrender."[68]

Following the news conference, Churchill persuaded Roosevelt to delay his departure to the United States for one day in order to accompany him to Marrakech, "the most lovely spot in the whole world." It is "the Paris of the Sahara," he told the president, where for centuries caravans had arrived from central Africa and where the traders were swindled in the markets and entertained in "the most elaborately organized brothels in the African continent." The two leaders—Macmillan called them the Emperors of the West and the East—sent most of their troop on ahead by air. A small motorcade carried the president, Churchill, and a few aides on the 150-mile trip. The road was lined on both sides by American sentries positioned a few dozen yards apart, an entire division of Patton's infantry, which might better have served the cause by fighting in Tunisia than by performing guard duty in Morocco. In Marrakech the party bivouacked in the Villa Taylor, an oasis of orange and olive groves surrounded by high walls, and home to the American vice consul Kenneth Pendar. A narrow three-story tower rose skyward from the house. Churchill ordered Roosevelt and his wheelchair carried up in order that the president might take in the Atlas Mountains at sundown when, as the sun fell into the Atlantic, the distant snow-covered peaks slowly faded from white to rose to blood red. The two partners enjoyed a "jolly" dinner that night after composing a joint telegram to Stalin in which they congratulated him for his leadership at Stalingrad. The cable also outlined the decisions made during the conference, only one of which held any interest for Stalin, the pledge to put men into France that year.[69]

When Roosevelt left for home the next morning, Churchill accompanied him to the airfield, dressed in velvet slippers and his green-and-red-and-gold-dragon dressing gown. He was thus attired a few hours later, supine in bed under the cover of a light-blue silk bedspread with a six-inch-wide entredeux, the scene lit by numerous candles, when he summoned Brooke and announced that they would "be off" at 6:00 P.M. that evening. Brooke had come to expect that a summons from Churchill might well find him in bed, or emerging from his bath, toweling off his round, white Humpty-Dumpty self, climbing into his silk underclothes, all the while declaiming on some new scheme that he had hatched. On this occasion, Brooke pleaded that he had presumed they'd be staying for two days and that he hoped to get a day of needed rest and do some bird-watching in the foothills. Churchill did not budge. Brooke tried to turn the tables, arguing that a day of painting would be a welcome respite for the P.M. This, too, failed to move the Old Man. "We are off at six," he replied, a cigar plugged into his face. "To where?" asked Brooke. "I have not decided yet," Churchill answered. To either London or Cairo, he added, pending an answer from the Turks.[70]

It was to be Cairo. Churchill spent a few hours before his departure up in the villa's tower, where he painted his only picture of the war, a landscape scene he later gave to Roosevelt. At dusk, *Commando* and an accompanying B-24 carrying Brooke and staff officers lifted off from Marrakech, eastbound for the overnight flight to the Nile. As they climbed to more than 14,000 feet to clear the mountains, the temperature inside the planes fell to below freezing and the clatter of the engines blotted out all conversation. Churchill's craft had been outfitted with windows and a salon with armchairs, such that he at least could peer out in order to track his progress. Brooke and those on board the other Liberator could do nothing but count rivets on the plane's cold aluminum skin. Churchill's party reached Cairo at dawn after an eleven-hour flight. Shortly thereafter they arrived at the home of the British ambassador, Miles Lampson, and his wife, Jacqueline, who asked if they might like breakfast. Brooke suggested they wash up first, but Churchill proclaimed, "No! We shall have breakfast now!" Mrs. Lampson escorted the party into the dining room and asked if the prime minister would like a cup of tea. "I have already had two whiskies and soda and two cigars this morning," Churchill replied, and then asked for a glass of white wine, which, when produced, he emptied in one long gulp. He was in fine fettle and ready for business.[71]

On the morning of Saturday, January 30, Churchill and his party, joined now by Alexander Cadogan from the Foreign Office, boarded their Liberators for the flight to Turkey, their destination, Adana, near the coast just over the Syrian border. Adana had been selected because Ankara was considered too dangerous and too ripe a target for the Luftwaffe, the very situation that underlay Turkish fears of joining the Allies. As Churchill and Brooke flew north along the Mediterranean coast, Hitler promoted General von Paulus to field marshal on the premise that no German field marshal had ever been captured. It was Hitler's way of telling Paulus that he was to fight to the end in Stalingrad, or use his pistol to take his leave with honor. With more than 100,000 of his men killed that month, and with his remaining forces cut in two, Paulus had no army and no fight left. He surrendered his headquarters that night, but the remnants of his army fought on. Churchill by then had boarded a train at Adana and traveled the few miles to where President İnönü waited aboard a train of his own on a rain-drenched plain that had become a sea of mud. The downpour was so

Eastern Europe and the Middle East
0 200 400 kilometers
0 150 300 miles
N
S
E
W
Murmansk
Archangel
Luleå
FINLAND
Helsinki
Leningrad
ESTONIA
Riga
LATVIA
LITHUANIA
Volga
Gorki
Oka
Moscow
SOVIET
UNION
Smolensk
Minsk
Warsaw
POLAND
Kursk
Farthest Extent of German Advance
Don
Stalingrad
Kharkov
Kiev
Dnieper
Donets
Lvov
Astrakhan
Rostov
Bessarabia
Odessa
Kerch
ROMANIA
Grozny
Caspian Sea
Sevastopol
Bucharest
Black Sea
Batum
Baku
BULGARIA
Sofia
Istanbul
Ankara
Tehran
TURKEY
Aegean Sea
GREECE
Athens
Adana
PERSIA
IRAQ
Iranian Oil Fields
Baghdad
SYRIA
Ahvaz
Cyprus
Damascus
Basra
Crete
Mediterranean Sea
PALESTINE
KUWAIT
TRANS-JORDAN
Alexandria
Suez Canal
SAUDI ARABIA
EGYPT
Cairo
Petho Cartography

relentless that Turkish sentries assigned to protect Churchill took cover beneath blankets, a dereliction of duty that disgusted Brooke. After the two trains "docked," the friendly but reluctant neutral and the confident warlord got down to business, a state of affairs remarkably similar to the meeting between Hitler and Franco at Hendaye in October 1940. The results proved similar as well, although Brooke took some satisfaction in the fact that Turkey appeared to assume "a more biased nature in favor of the Allies."[72]

The Turks feared two possible consequences of an alliance with the Allies: an attack by Germany in retaliation; and behavior of an imperialistic sort by the Soviets once the war was won. The czars had, after all, coveted the Dardanelles and egress from the Black Sea into the Mediterranean for two centuries (İnönü had fought the British at Gallipoli in 1916). Churchill expressed his belief that the Soviets might indeed "become imperialistic," but he argued that Turkey's best protection in that case would be a pact with Britain and America. As well, Churchill offered that a postwar world council would possess sufficient military power—unlike the League of Nations—to reel in states that went astray. He made his case in French (or French as only he spoke it, as noted by Cadogan), "with English words pronounced as French" as he waved his arms about for effect. The argument expressed in English, Cadogan wrote, was excellent, but in French, "I have no idea!" Churchill, wisely, did not pressure the Turks, who, Cadogan wrote, "were resolutely disinclined to be drawn into a war." The Germans knew all of this by virtue of reading Turkish signals traffic. Brooke termed the meeting "a great success."[73]

It was not, other than in the narrow sense that Brooke's Mediterranean strategy could only fare better with Turkey friendly than with Turkey unfriendly. Yet neither was the meeting a complete failure. The Turks accepted a British offer to help modernize their army and allowed vast stores of British war matériel to be stockpiled in southeast Turkey, in case it was needed in Syria, Iraq, or Turkey, should Hitler violate Turkish neutrality. Still, one of the eight priorities decided upon at Casablanca could now be checked off, as unfulfilled.

On February 2, Churchill—back in Cairo—learned that the rest of Paulus's army in Stalingrad had surrendered that day, including twenty-three generals and more than 90,000 troops, who marched off to Soviet prison camps. Only 5,000 of them survived their captivity, the sole living remnants of Paulus's original army of 450,000. The bells of the Kremlin rang the next day. In Berlin, radio programming was interrupted by the roll of muffled drums, followed by the announcement that the Sixth Army had been "overcome by the superiority of the enemy and by unfavorable circumstances confronting our forces." The second movement of Beethoven's Fifth Symphony followed the reading of the communiqué. Regular programming did not resume for three days. Hitler's generals soon witnessed a marked change in the Führer. "His left hand trembled," wrote General Heinz Guderian, "his back was bent, his gaze was fixed, his cheeks were flecked with red. He was more excitable, easily lost his composure, and was prone to angry outbursts and ill-considered decisions." Hitler later told one of his doctors that his sleepless nights were filled with visions of maps marked with the final positions of his armies before they were destroyed.[74]

Stalingrad was the single greatest military defeat in German history and only one of several disasters that had befallen the *Ostheer* since the beginning of the new year. On the Baltic, the Red Army brought relief to Leningrad in mid-January. After 515 days of siege and a yearlong rain of steel from six thousand German guns, the Russians opened a narrow land bridge into the city. In the Caucasus, Hitler's Army Group A, reduced now to just a single army, had been driven back two hundred miles to Rostov, which the Red Army took in mid-February, thereby cutting off the Germans on the southern shore of the Sea of Azov. Two hundred miles to the north, Field Marshal Erich von Manstein's armies had been driven west from the Don and out of Kharkov and Kursk. Since their November lunge across the Volga, the Russians had raced 250 miles across the Don and the Donets rivers. They were now only fifty miles east of the Dnieper. Marshal Zhukov had asked for much from Stalin in the way of men, weapons, tanks, and planes, and Stalin had delivered the goods. Now Zhukov had delivered the results. Stalin—like Churchill, a student of the American Civil War—began telling Western visitors to the Kremlin that Zhukov was his George McClellan except that Zhukov had never lost a battle. (General McClellan had likewise asked President Lincoln for much support, and received it, but he was meek in his approach to the Confederates, and delivered no victories.)[75]

The news from Russia put Churchill in top form. He dined on February 2 at the British embassy, where he watched a film of British troops entering Tripoli and held forth until almost midnight on one of his favorite topics, the 1898 Omdurman campaign in the Sudan. Randolph, on leave, joined the party. Alexander Cadogan, who sat between Randolph and Churchill, found Randolph to be "a dreadful young man. He has been an incubus on our party since Casablanca." The father and son snapped and growled at each other throughout the evening. Had Cadogan been a frequent visitor to Chartwell, he would have known this was how dinner went when father and son shared the table. Accompanying Randolph (and keeping an eye on him) was Churchill's prewar literary assistant, Bill Deakin, now Captain Deakin of the Special Operations Executive. Churchill had just learned from Deakin that while Serbian forces under Mihailovich were keeping Axis troops occupied in Serbia, farther north in Croatia and Slovenia, the peasants, schoolteachers, and intellectuals under Tito were doing likewise, but with no support from the Americans or British. After asking for a report on the matter, which Deakin produced in two days, Churchill shifted British policy in a manner nobody had foreseen.[76]

Tito was a Communist, but he was killing Germans and their Croat Ustasha puppets, and was therefore worthy of assistance. That he was also killing Mihailovich's Chetniks and King Peter's supporters was troublesome, as London backed the return of the king. This was how matters tended to play out in the Balkans, where murderous ethnic feuds had been fought for centuries and where myriad peoples, Churchill once said, produced more history than they could consume. Still, within days of reading Deakin's proposal, Churchill asked Eisenhower for long-range B-24 bombers capable of reaching northern Yugoslavia in order to drop supplies to Tito's partisans. In April, Captain Deakin parachuted into German-occupied Croatia in order to establish relations with Britain's newest and most unlikely ally, Josip Broz—Tito.[77]

On February 3, Churchill prepared for the flight to Tripoli in order to congratulate the general who, like Zhukov, had asked for much, and had delivered: Bernard Montgomery. Late that day Montgomery's forward elements crossed the Tunisian frontier. Tripolitania, the richest Italian colony in Africa, had fallen. A generation of Sicilian and Italian émigrés had paved roads and planted vineyards and olive groves there; they had built irrigation systems worthy of the ancient Roman aqueducts in order to nourish their holdings. It was the last of Italy's African possessions. Il Duce, once emperor of more than 1.2 million square miles in Africa, had lost it all. Now, an American weekly reported, "Italians had only the sands blown across the Mediterranean by the sirocco to remind them" of their lost empire.[78]

Per the agreements made at Casablanca, Alexander and the British now served under Eisenhower. Henry Maitland ("Jumbo") Wilson replaced Alexander as commander in chief, Middle East. Alexander, when he reached Tunisia in two weeks' time, would command all Allied land forces in that theater, a fortuitous circumstance in the estimation of Churchill, because Alex could do no wrong, while Eisenhower had so far done little right. Eisenhower's performance had been so lackluster that George Marshall later expressed to Churchill his surprise that at Casablanca the British had not demanded the lead role in the North African operations. In his memoirs Churchill wrote that the idea never occurred to him. Indeed, Churchill had grown to truly like and admire Eisenhower. Yet with Cunningham directing the efforts at sea, Tedder in the air, and Alexander on the ground, and with the agreement for the invasion of Sicily in hand, Churchill had gained everything he sought while giving Roosevelt what he wanted, an American commander. Harold Macmillan captured the essence of the relationship when he later wrote that the British would run the American show in North Africa like "the Greek slaves ran the operations of the emperor Claudius." Eisenhower, whom Brooke denigrated for never having commanded even a battalion in the field, brought one supremely valuable trait to the task—he brokered no chicanery among and between the Allies. "Everyone is entitled to his own opinion," Eisenhower warned his staff. You can call a fellow officer a son of a bitch, he told them, "but the instant I hear any American officer refer to a brother officer as that *British* son of a bitch, out he goes." He would need every bit of the goodwill engendered by his equable command instincts, for American troops in Tunisia were about to display their complete lack of readiness to fight Germans.[79]

Churchill arrived in Tripoli on the fourth, and after a tour of the harbor by motor launch, he watched as the first British supply ship steamed into the port. With the harbor in British hands, the supply lines for the Eighth Army were reduced by 1,200 miles. Later that day, Brooke and Churchill reviewed the 51st Division, the reincarnation of the old 51st, which had surrendered in France almost three years before. The men of the 51st, who had come to Africa "pink and white" and inexperienced, were now "bronzed warriors of many battles and of a victorious advance." Churchill, standing high on a reviewing stand, watched as the troops paraded past, pipers leading the way. Brooke, a tear running down his cheek, turned to Churchill, who shed tears as well. "One could sense the fathomless depth of relief," Brooke later wrote, "caused by a realization that victory had now become a practical proposition."[80]

The next day, the party was off to Algiers, for what was scheduled to be a brief layover in the company of Eisenhower and Admiral Andrew ("ABC") Cunningham before heading home to London late that night. Cadogan, having now experienced the travails of long-distance travel in an unheated bomber, pledged to his diary never to be "dragged around the world again in these conditions, which are filthy. I don't think P.M. has ever looked into our plane or realizes how beastly it is."[81]

Eisenhower knew from experience exactly what Churchill's visit would entail. Before he left London to command Torch, he and Churchill had instituted regular Tuesday luncheons and frequently took their business to Chequers on weekends, where, given Churchill's work habits and absurdly late hours, Eisenhower often found himself having to stay overnight. Ike knew to expect late nights and long dinners upon Churchill's arrival, and dreaded it. Compounding Eisenhower's discomfort, a rumor had it that German—or Vichy, or Arab—assassins planned on ridding the world of the "Big Cigar Man," whose presence in Algiers could bring nothing but headache to Eisenhower. Ike wanted Churchill out of town as soon as possible. "Safe in London," wrote Eisenhower's aide, Commander Butcher, Churchill "was worth an army, in Algiers he was a target and therefore a heavy responsibility."[82]

But Churchill had come to rest and dine, and this he did, over a long lunch hosted by Eisenhower and attended by Giraud and the resident general of Morocco, Paul Noguès, the former Vichy loyalist who three months earlier had tried to drive Patton's army back into the sea. Cunningham hosted the evening meal at his villa, just across the compound from Eisenhower's. Around the villa Churchill was known as "the man who came to dinner." In fact, he told Brooke his intent was to be the man who came for a day or two, or more. But arrangements were already in place for a midnight departure, which would get Churchill to London without braving the daytime skies. Late in the evening Churchill and his party departed for the Maison Blanche airfield, where, after exchanging farewells with their hosts on the runway, they climbed aboard their two Liberators. Lord Moran swallowed his sleeping pills and took himself off to bed. Brooke donned his pajamas, over which he tugged a fur-lined flight suit and boots. Maps, charts, and beverages were stowed.[83]

But the passengers went nowhere. One of the magnetos had failed on the number one engine of Churchill's Liberator. After a fruitless two-hour attempt to start the engine, the pilot called it a night. The passengers disembarked, and the aircraft was locked down. Moran, by now fast asleep, was left behind. At about 2:00 A.M., residents of the two headquarter villas awakened to knocking upon the doors. Winston was back. Commander Butcher and the Americans believed that Churchill had planned the whole caper in order to grab an extra day in the sun, perchance a dip in the sea. In any event, the man who came to dinner finally left for home late on February 6.[84]

Clemmie had cabled Winston before he arrived in Algiers: "I am following your movements with intense interest.... The door is open and it is hoped that soon Mr. Bullfinch will fly home." Churchill replied, "Keep the cage open for Saturday or Sunday, much love." He returned to the nest on Sunday the seventh.[85]

He had been away from King, wife, and country for twenty-six days. It was to be his last flight on *Commando*. The aircraft, with a different crew, later disappeared with all hands. Cadogan was correct in describing the beastly discomforts and dangers of flight, but he was wrong about Churchill. Churchill had known full well ever since his first flights to Cairo and Moscow six months earlier exactly how beastly such journeys were, and how necessary.

In Burma that week, Brigadier Orde Wingate took his brigade of jungle fighters—he called them his Chindits, the Burmese word for "lion"—across the Chindwin River and proceeded to harass the Japanese behind their lines. The need to reopen the Burma Road had been agreed upon at Casablanca, but Wingate lacked the men, and the RAF lacked the aircraft, to make good on that agreement. General Joe Stilwell, cooling his heels in northern India, the victim of Washington's decision to reinforce MacArthur at his expense, lacked an army. And Churchill lacked the will. China, in his estimation, was not worth the effort. That week, the American press reported that large numbers of Japanese ships were sailing for Guadalcanal, most likely to reinforce the garrison there. But this report soon proved false; the Japanese were sailing to "the Canal" in order to *evacuate* their remaining troops. On February 9 a headline in the *New York Times* declared, FOE QUITS ISLAND. New Guinea was the next Allied target; the Australians would lead the charge. The march to Tokyo had begun.[86]

For thirteen months the Americans, having no real choice in the matter given their lack of preparedness, had deferred to Churchill's strategic judgment. They did so again at Casablanca. It would be the last time. The military tide had turned against Hitler at Stalingrad; now the political tide was turning against Churchill. His vision of the postwar world was drifting into crisper focus, and he was testing the words and phrases he intended to use to articulate that vision when the time was right. Yet, as the months went by, the shapes and forms that the new world would assume increasingly became a matter for Roosevelt and Stalin to determine. Churchill's future, and that of his Empire, was now tied inexorably to the political wishes of his two allies who, Sir John Keegan wrote, "were now supplanting him in importance." The decline in Churchill's influence would be gradual; indeed, in early 1943 Churchill had yet to sense it, but it had begun.[87]

On February 2, a *New York Times* story explicating the decisions made at Casablanca was headlined PRESIDENT IMPLIES 1943 INVASION PLAN. Actually, that decision had not been made in Casablanca. It was more hope than goal, and with each passing week an atrophying hope at that. On February 11, tired and with a head cold coming on, Churchill addressed the Commons. He did not promise a great invasion of Europe but promised that Britain's enemies would "burn and bleed" (a favorite phrase) and that stern justice would be delivered to "the wicked and the guilty." He had sent Roosevelt a draft of the speech for comments. Firm in his belief that the French hated the British and respected Americans, Roosevelt replied that "cooperation by French forces will be best if the American Supreme Command in North Africa is stressed." Churchill duly edited his working notes and placed Eisenhower at the forefront. Within a week he found himself supremely relieved to have done so.[88]

In the days following his address, he could not shake the fatigue and head cold he had brought home from Africa. On the evening of February 16, his temperature shot up. Lord Moran, after listening to his chest, concluded his patient had "a patch" on his left lung. "What do you mean by a patch?" Churchill grumbled. "Have I got pneumonia?" An X-ray taken the next day and a second opinion by Dr. Geoffrey Marshall confirmed Moran's suspicion: Churchill had contracted pneumonia. But given his age, it was the strain on his heart, not his lungs, that worried Moran. The patient took to his bed, with a copy of *Moll Flanders*. He ordered his paperwork reduced to a minimum and jotted notes to Roosevelt, himself taken ill by some African bug, and to Hopkins. To both he lamented his "heavy and long" condition. They responded with get-well notes. Churchill was not a difficult patient, Moran wrote, and did what he was told, "provided, of course, that he is given a good reason." Dr. Marshall did not help matters when he referred to pneumonia as "the old man's friend." "Pray explain," asked Churchill. "Oh, because it takes them off so quickly," Marshall replied. Churchill was thus already in his sickbed when news arrived from the North Atlantic, from Russia, from India, and from Tunisia that might have put him there anyway.[89]

By mid-February, Rommel had barred the back door to Tunisia with his positions along the Mareth Line, a decade-old French defensive network that ran from the Gulf of Gabès inland to a great salt marsh. To Rommel's northwest, on the far slopes of the Eastern Dorsal of the Atlas Mountains, the Allied flank was held against several of Arnim's panzer divisions at Sidi Bouzid and along an eighty-mile front by the green American troops of the II Corps, under the command of Major General Lloyd Fredendall. His job was to keep Arnim in place and to watch and wait for Rommel, who sooner or later, with Montgomery in pursuit, would try to join Arnim. North of

Fredendall, poorly equipped brigades of formerly Vichy French held the ground. In the far north, Anderson's First Army had been stalled for eight weeks on its drive to Bizerte and Tunis, where Kesselring had reinforced Arnim's positions faster than the Allies could harass them. The Eastern Dorsal, thinly held by the Americans and French, defined the German left flank from Gafsa to just west of Tunis.

Eisenhower presumed correctly that Rommel would strike north toward Tunis, but the American was unsure of exactly which route Rommel would choose—the coastal plains or a swing through Gafsa followed by a sharp turn north. And would Arnim attempt a strike in the Faid Pass in the Eastern Dorsal, which would put Sidi Bouzid in his sights and threaten the Allied rear? Allied intelligence thought that scenario unlikely based on the belief that the mountain passes were not conducive to tank warfare. Also, Ultra decrypts gave no indication that Arnim was hatching such a plan. But after visiting Fredendall's Sidi Bouzid deployments on February 13, Eisenhower concluded that the defenses were inadequate, and that this was where the Germans would strike. Eisenhower returned to Fredendall's headquarters at Tebessa (ill placed and more than seventy miles west of Sidi Bouzid), intent on drawing up new plans.

He was too late. Arnim and Rommel attacked the next morning. By nightfall Rommel was through Gafsa, and Arnim's tanks had plowed through the American positions at Sidi Bouzid. Both German panzer forces then made for the Kasserine Pass, in the Western Dorsal, which they overran on February 19 and 20, after overrunning two American battalions that had chosen poor defensive positions. Rommel's panzers then poured north out of Kasserine on the twenty-first, his target Tebessa, where the Allies had stockpiled millions of pounds of food, fuel, and ammunition. Another panzer force swung north toward Thala, which if taken would put the Germans behind Anderson's lines. With Arnim's northern flank anchored at Tunis, Anderson and the French would find themselves in a vise. Alexander arrived from Tripoli on February 20 and, shocked at what he saw, immediately assumed command of all ground forces. He found the Americans at Kasserine totally unprepared for Rommel's push, "too defensive" and too "shell and bomb conscious." They had suffered the consequences of poor command, poor intelligence, and a hardened enemy. When Eisenhower (just that week promoted to four stars) ordered B-17s to bomb Kasserine, the planes became lost and bombed a friendly Arab village within the Allied lines and more than one hundred miles from the intended target. The Americans' first major engagement with Germans ended as it had begun, in complete confusion. Alexander now found himself, as at Dunkirk and in Burma, presiding over a disaster.[90]

Within a week of crashing through Kasserine, Rommel, outrunning his supplies and unable to exploit his success, fell back through the pass to the Mareth Line. So stunning was Rommel's stroke that King George wrote a three-page letter to Churchill stating his dismay over both the political and military situations in North Africa. Churchill dutifully replied that his support of Eisenhower for supreme command had been proven "providential." Had a British general overseen the defeat, he told the King, Britain's enemies in America would have been served up a fine opportunity "to blaspheme." Churchill reminded King George that the Eighth Army, 160,000 strong and "perhaps the best troops in the world," was about to play a key role in Tunisia. Moreover, the great General Alexander would henceforth be in charge of strategy on the ground. This was not meant to disparage the Americans, Churchill offered, for they were brave, "but not seasoned."[91]

Eisenhower sacked Fredendall on March 1 and replaced him with George Patton, who, Ike liked to say, "hates the Hun like the devil hates holy water." The debacle at Kasserine Pass underscored Brooke's doubts about conducting a large-scale invasion of France in 1943, even were the landing craft available. Although the American planners left Casablanca believing that they had been snookered by Brooke and Churchill, the rout at Kasserine proved the British correct. The Americans had to first learn how to conduct a modest campaign before contemplating an invasion of fortress Europe. Tommies in Anderson's army soon came up with a line that captured the essence of Kasserine: *How Green Was My Ally*.[92]

While Rommel undertook his audacious strike, Mohandas Gandhi, half a world away, conducted one of his own. Before Churchill left for North Africa, the War Cabinet endorsed the arrest of Gandhi and hundreds of India National Congress members. On February 9, Gandhi, seventy-two, frail, and under house arrest at Poona, announced that he would fast for three weeks. British and Indian doctors monitored his condition. Churchill, suspecting Indian doctors were slipping glucose into Gandhi's drinking water, informed King George that "the old humbug Gandhi" had remained so healthy "one wonders whether his fast is bona fide." On the sixteenth day of the fast, with somber reports emanating from Gandhi's doctors (which Churchill did not believe), Churchill telegraphed Jan Smuts: "What fools we should have been to flinch before all this bluff and sob-stuff." On the following day, he cabled the viceroy, the Marquess of Linlithgow: "It now seems almost certain that the old rascal will emerge all the better from his so-called fast." Lord Linlithgow replied that he believed that Gandhi ("the world's most successful humbug") was not in dire straits and that his doctors had "cooked" their bulletins to produce the desired effect, all as part of a "wicked system of blackmail." The American press championed the Mahatma's cause; the British press for the most part derided Gandhi's gesture as a ploy, as did Churchill, with sly nonchalance, when he later wrote in his memoirs that Gandhi's taking glucose while on the hunger strike in conjunction with his "intense vitality and lifelong austerity" allowed him to safely ride out the dietary crisis. In fact, Churchill had learned during Gandhi's fast that Indian doctors were not giving him glucose. He did not quite equate Gandhi with the wily main character in Kafka's "A Hunger Artist," but he came close. As for Gandhi's stature in India, he wrote, "Mr. Gandhi's death could have produced a profound impression throughout India, where his saintly qualities commanded intense admiration." In arresting Gandhi, he wrote, the British "had judged the situation rightly."[93]

Roosevelt's special envoy to India, William Phillips, in Delhi since January, asked permission of the viceroy to visit Gandhi and Nehru. Lord Linlithgow refused, and instead invited Phillips on a tiger hunt. Phillips could hardly make a complete report to Roosevelt without seeing Gandhi, but he'd have to try, for Churchill had put Gandhi off-limits. Leo Amery, secretary of state for India and Burma, advised Churchill, "I do hope you will make it quite clear to the president that his people must keep off the grass." Churchill's explosion in front of Hopkins the previous April and the treatment accorded Phillips were clear signals to Roosevelt to stay out of British affairs. The president kept his counsel, despite the pro-Gandhi editorializing of the American press. Roosevelt and Churchill never saw eye to eye on India. In fact, Harriman recalled, "They couldn't see *at all* on India" (italics Harriman).[94]

Gandhi ended his fast on March 3. In newsreels he appeared to be in good health. Churchill, still recuperating from his illness, was not.

By early March, Bernard Montgomery, in position in the town of Medenine, about twenty miles southeast of the Mareth Line, knew with certainty that Rommel would attempt a spoiling attack by hooking out from his Mareth defenses toward Medenine. Air reconnaissance and Ultra decrypts gave Montgomery an advantage he intended to exploit. He prepared for Rommel's attack by massing and concealing his anti-tank artillery. Ultra had been so precise that Montgomery knew which brigades of panzers Rommel intended to deploy, and where he intended to deploy them. On March 6, Rommel struck. Thanks to Ultra, he stood no chance. Montgomery, his anti-tank guns in position, destroyed fifty-two of the oncoming panzers. The Germans and Italians stopped, turned, and retreated to their Mareth defenses. The importance of the British victory at Medenine cannot be overstated; had Rommel sent the Eighth Army sprawling eastward, the Allied timetable in North Africa would have been set back indefinitely. A British defeat would have scotched the invasion of Sicily in 1943, and Italy as well. Stalin, already doubting the ability of his allies to kill Germans, would have had no choice but to at least contemplate a separate peace. But Montgomery held. On March 9, Rommel, hobbled by malaria and festering skin lesions, handed over command of his army to General Giovanni Messe, who now served under Arnim in the newly created Army Group Africa. That night, Rommel departed North Africa for Berlin, never to return.[95]

On the Eastern Front, the victories at Stalingrad and Rostov reinvigorated the Red Army, which struck west throughout January and into February. Yet, as it had the previous spring, it advanced too far and too fast, with the result that its lines thinned. Once across the Donets River, the Russians discovered the Germans had changed the gauge on the railroads, forcing the Red Army to send tens of thousands of trucks and horse carts down muddy and rutted roads. Manstein, sure that Stalin's army had overextended itself again, waited for his moment. He struck in the third week of February with fourteen tank and infantry divisions, and within a fortnight he retook Kharkov, driving the Russians back eighty miles along a two-hundred-mile front. Stalin blamed Churchill and Roosevelt for the setback, claiming the German success "involved a lessening of the German forces in France" due to the lack of Anglo-American aggressiveness. Hence, "renewed Russian complaints about bearing the whole weight of the war." In fact, Stalin *was* bearing almost the entire weight of the war, and Churchill and Roosevelt, to their consternation, were not yet prepared to relieve Stalin of some of that weight. This the Germans knew, and were thankful for. On March 2, Hermann Göring told Goebbels that he was "somewhat worried about our having pretty much stripped the West in order to bring things to a standstill in the East. One dreads to think," Goebbels confessed to his diary, "what would happen if the English and Americans were suddenly to attempt a landing."[96]

The English and the Americans were making no such plans. In fact, during the bleak days of mid-February, when everything everywhere appeared to be unraveling, Eisenhower recommended pushing Operation Husky back from June until July. Churchill received the news in bed, his pneumonia coming on hard. A month's delay would be disastrous, he cabled Eisenhower, and to Harry Hopkins he predicted that if during May and June "not a single American or British soldier" was killing any Germans or Italians "while the Russians are chasing 165 divisions around," the result would be "grievous reproach at the hands of the Russians." Britain, he told his military chiefs, "would become a laughingstock." In fact, the original statement of intent drawn up by the Combined Chiefs at Casablanca called for Husky to begin with "the favorable July moon," those nights of the month when the crescent moon before setting gave paratroopers just enough light to find their targets in advance of the amphibious troops. At Casablanca, Churchill and Roosevelt pushed hard for the June moon, and the Combined Chiefs had since asked Eisenhower to reconsider, but General Ike held firm to his timetable. Nonetheless, Eisenhower only further fueled Churchill's doubts about his aggressiveness when in early April he warned that the presence of two German divisions in Sicily cast doubt on the Allied ability to invade the island. Churchill erupted. How, he asked the Chiefs of Staff Committee, could they reconcile "the confidence the General showed about invading the continent across the Channel" with his discomfort at the prospect of sending one million men now in North Africa to face two German divisions in Sicily? "I don't think we can be content with such doctrines." He added, "What Stalin would think of this when he has 185 German divisions on his front, I cannot imagine."[97]

Actually, he knew exactly what Stalin would think. He had twice promised Stalin a second front in 1943, most recently when he predicted that Tunisia would be cleared by April "if not earlier." By early April, with Eisenhower's armies stuck for three months in the mud and mountains of Tunisia, Churchill's promises to Stalin were self-evidently worthless. Even had Eisenhower taken Tunis by then, the omnipresent shipping shortages guaranteed that no second front could materialize in France that year. Churchill tried to placate Stalin, telling him that Husky was forthcoming, that the RAF was preparing to pummel the industrial heart of Germany, the Ruhr Valley, with heavy raids, including a planned operation to destroy the dams and hydroelectric plants that powered German armaments factories. Dönitz's submarine pens were being bombed; the American Eighth Air Force, with more than six hundred bombers, was now up and flying. Churchill indicated his willingness to embrace more sinister tactics. Told of the German successes in Russia, he instructed Ismay to inform the military chiefs that if Hitler used poison gas in Russia, "we shall retaliate by drenching the German cities with gas on the largest possible scale." That was bluster, but by no means was it bluff. Stalin needed help, and Churchill intended to give what he could. Stalin's armies faced twenty times as many Germans as the Anglo-Americans faced in Tunisia. In only one military classification did the Western allies exceed the Russians in manpower: chaplains.[98]

At Casablanca Roosevelt and Churchill made "control of the seas" their first priority. They meant the Atlantic. In the three months since, as measured by men and ships, they not only failed to control the seas, but had lost control.

On January 30, Karl Dönitz was promoted to *Grossadmiral* and replaced Erich Raeder as commander in chief of the navy (*Oberbefehlshaber der Kriegsmarine*). The appointment of the submariner Dönitz could only mean that the submarine war would intensify. It did, with horrific results for the Allies. Churchill warned Roosevelt that they must assume that Dönitz would be "ready to play a game in which the cards are in [his] hands." Dönitz was as firm a believer in the lethality of his U-boats as Göring was of his airplanes, with the difference that Dönitz's U-boats had hobbled Britain, and might yet cripple her. Britain's convoy escort ships were, Churchill informed Roosevelt, "quite inadequate to deal with the German forces."[99]

The U-boats cruised safely that winter, aided by the worst weather in North Atlantic history. The gales kept escort ships in harbors and Allied long-range bombers battened down on airfields. Such was the fury of the North Atlantic between November and March that ninety-two ships were lost at sea to waves and wind. The U-boats rode out the storms beneath the waves and took their harvest. In March, two convoys bound from New York and sailing on parallel courses with eighty-eight merchant ships were attacked over three nights by fifty U-boats. Twenty-two Allied ships and almost four hundred seamen went to the bottom. German sailors called it the "greatest convoy battle of all time." That massacre brought to almost 21,000 the number of British merchant seamen killed since the start of the war, more than one-fifth of Britain's civilian sailors and, relative to the other services, the highest casualty rate of the war. Ships could be replaced; experienced crews could not.[100]

In mid-March, as the losses mounted, Stewart Menzies informed Churchill that Bletchley had finally broken the German naval code. The Bletchley wizards had also deduced from charting Allied convoy and U-boat positions that the British merchant marine code must have been long compromised, with catastrophic results. Bletchley reworked the British convoy code such that the Germans could no longer listen in on ship-to-ship transmissions and Dönitz could no longer pinpoint convoy locations. Despite that progress, Allied losses in March totaled 108 ships and 627,000 tons, more than half the total British shipping lost during the *ten months* of March to December 1941, when Churchill had given the battle its name.

The British would exploit the Bletchley breakthrough in coming months, but March's horrific losses certainly did not auger a change of Allied fortune, given that they came against the sinking of just fifteen of the more than one hundred U-boats operating in the North Atlantic. The U-boats were so numerous that the Allies could no longer resort to evasive routing for convoys, with the result that the entire convoy program began to disintegrate. March's losses, Churchill cabled Roosevelt, brought Britain near to a "hand-to-mouth" subsistence level. Dönitz had reduced Britain's annual food, fertilizer, and fuel imports from 50 million tons prewar to under 23 million, a figure considered by Churchill to be below the minimum needed to sustain the island. Roosevelt, against the wishes of his military advisers, finally came down on the side of Harriman, who advised that feeding Britain, even at the cost of fighting Germans, was the most pressing issue. Food would go to Britain at the expense of the American armed services, whose demands, Roosevelt believed, were inflated and whose ability in utilizing available ships to meet those demands was notoriously lacking. Churchill, to make more hulls available for transatlantic shipments, reduced sailings to India by half, a measure that, in combination with the Japanese occupation of Burma and an ongoing drought, brought Bengal to the verge of famine.[101]

The Atlantic convoys sailed with little protection, and paid a dear price. Escort ships normally assigned to convoy duty were needed for the run-up to Husky. In mid-March, with losses rising, and on the advice of the Admiralty, Churchill and Roosevelt agreed to cancel that month's convoy to Russia, and to not run any more until September. Roosevelt suggested they not break the news to Stalin for "three or four weeks." He volunteered Churchill for the duty, and asked to see a copy of his message before it was sent. He also offered to send "a supporting message" in tandem with Churchill's, in order to present a unified front. Churchill expressed his thanks for the gesture. On March 30 Churchill cabled the bad news to Stalin. Roosevelt never sent the supporting message.[102]

Stalin's reply was curt, the final line worrisome: "You realize of course that the circumstances cannot fail to affect the position of Soviet troops." What, exactly, did he mean by that? It was well known that German diplomats in Stockholm had expressed interest in a German-Soviet prisoner exchange, brokered by the Swedes. Stalin refused the offer; he tended to prefer that repatriated prisoners be shot or imprisoned in case their experiences in the West had resulted in their embrace of anti-Bolshevik blasphemies. But the mere mention of talks between Germans and Russians could only lead to the worrisome question of what else they might be discussing.

Fear of a separate peace had been omnipresent in the Foreign Office and the State Department for almost two years.[103]

Churchill believed that Stalin would never negotiate with Hitler, but the surest way of discouraging such thoughts on Stalin's part was to win the Battle of the Atlantic. However, the slaughter of March implied that the Allies were not doing so. The Germans had improved U-boat propulsion and radar detection. The *Kriegsmarine* deployed sonar decoys, small radio canisters launched while submerged to confuse listening posts on British escorts. They also deployed buoyant anti-radar decoys that when launched from U-boats mimicked the radar profile of a U-boat on the surface, with the result that Allied bombers took to chasing nonexistent targets. Each *Kriegsmarine* measure and countermeasure was soon countered by British improvements in sonar and especially radar, which was being made more powerful and small enough to fit into the nose of a Sunderland flying boat. It was all part of the naval quotient of Churchill's Wizard War.

The Germans, far ahead in submarine design, had drawn blueprints for bigger, faster boats with six forward torpedo tubes, and that were capable of deep dives to greater than seven hundred feet at high speed. But Dönitz couldn't build them fast enough due to the relentless Allied air attacks on German shipyards. He outfitted his boats with *schnorchels*—telescopic breathing tubes that allowed the U-boats to cruise just beneath the waves on diesel power rather than on batteries. But all the German innovations would prove for naught, for the most effective weapon in the Allied arsenal was the American shipyard, where workers were just beginning to build cargo ships and escort destroyers faster than Dönitz could sink them. And, although Dönitz suspected that Bletchley was now reading *Kriegsmarine* radio traffic, he could not bring himself to accept it as fact. Still, his successes against Allied shipping in March convinced him that more U-boats, better radar, and the most advanced torpedoes could finish the job. Samuel Eliot Morison later wrote: "No enemy ever came so near to disrupting Atlantic communications as Dönitz did that month."[104]

Goebbels, since Casablanca, had been preaching the evils of "unconditional surrender" to the German people. The Hun-hating Lord Vansittart played into Goebbels' hand when he told the House of Lords in March that all Germans were accomplices to Hitler and that Germany should be destroyed "utterly and forever as a military power." It fell to the government's advocate, Lord Chancellor Viscount John Simon, to rebut Vansittart by declaring that the British government (and Premier Stalin) held that, although Nazism must be destroyed, "the whole German people is not, as Dr. Goebbels has been trying to persuade them, thereby doomed to destruction." The *London News Chronicle* welcomed Simon's statement: "It shows that the Government is making a rational and a constructive approach to the problem of Germany's future."[105]

Stalin had made public his thoughts on the subject on February 23 in his Order of the Day, celebrating the twenty-fifth anniversary of the founding of the Red Army. The Red Army, the marshal declared, "was not created for the purpose of conquering" other nations. It was now prepared to drive the Wehrmacht from its borders, Stalin added, and would do so that year, but its strength must be preserved to guarantee the peace. These words raised more questions in London and Washington than they answered. Did Stalin mean to assuage German fears of annihilation as proffered by Goebbels? Did he really intend to stop at his borders after expelling the Nazis? How, if the defeat of Hitler was the first priority of the Allies, could Hitler be beaten if the Red Army halted at its borders after driving out the Germans? Or might Stalin, after driving out the Germans, stop inside Poland's old eastern border, to reclaim the lands he and Hitler had taken in 1939? That would create—at far less cost in Russian lives—a buffer between Russia and a subdued but not yet vanquished Germany. The message within the message was clear, and disturbing. If the Western Allies were not fighting on the Continent by the time the Red Army restored its borders, the Red Army might stop its westward march. Stalin added his favorite gibe: "In view of the absence of a second front in Europe, the Red Army alone is bearing the whole weight of the war."[106]

That was true. Only an Anglo-American victory over Germans would provide an effective response to Stalin. Bernard Montgomery intended to deliver such a victory. He struck on March 20, when 25,000 New Zealanders under General Freyberg, after a long and difficult trek far around the Mareth Lines, delivered a left hook to the enemy flank. Gaullist forces operating just north of Freyberg lent a hand when the New Zealanders encountered Germans dug in on mountain ridges. "Can you clear the Germans?" Freyberg asked a French officer, a viscount whose name was Jacques Philippe de Hautecloque, but who went by the nom de guerre Leclerc. "But of course," Leclerc answered. The French soon began killing Germans and collecting large numbers of prisoners, a modest victory, but their first since June of 1940. To the northwest, George Patton's II Corps had been hammering the German flank at El Guettar since March 16, with the objective of slashing its way east to the Bay of Gabès. It was a battle of American artillery and the 1st Infantry Division—known to its men as the Big Red One—versus German tanks. Patton would not win it, but his troops proved their mettle while drawing two German armored divisions away from Montgomery's immediate front, thereby making Monty's job a great deal more manageable.[107]

Montgomery's main force consisted of Englishmen, Poles, Czechs, Australians, Gurkhas, with their wicked curved kukris, which could take an arm off at the shoulder, and Highlanders, who would happily chase the devil himself—Auld Clootie to a Highlander—straight through Hell if so ordered. At 10:00 P.M. sharp on March 21, they attacked the Mareth fortifications. Eisenhower called the Eighth Army "the most cosmopolitan army to fight in North Africa since Hannibal." It was indeed an imperial army, recalled Sir William Deakin, and the fact that a British *imperial* presence was being brought to bear on the European conflict was a source of abiding pride for Churchill. If the Eighth Army was to be the last truly imperial army, Deakin recalled, Churchill wanted it to play "a decisive part." Montgomery was intent on its doing just that. His tactic of delivering a hook and a jab in tandem, of hitting the Germans in places they didn't anticipate and in ways that disrupted their order of battle, had served him well at El Alamein, and it served him well on the twenty-first.[108]

On the night the Eighth Army threw its left hook—March 20—Churchill broadcast to his countrymen and the world. The topic, for the first time during his premiership, was the postwar world. He outlined in broad strokes his plans for Britons at home, and Britain abroad. He cautioned that 1943 would not see an end to the war, nor perhaps would 1944, but in the end, the Allies would beat "Hitler and his powers of evil unto death, dust, and ashes." And then they would do the same to Japan; it would take time, but victory in the East would be attained. After victory, the three great powers—Britain, America, and Soviet Russia—would form the backbone of a "world organization" that would serve as "safeguard against future war." Within this organization, there would be smaller "councils" in Europe, where the last two great wars had begun. Lesser states could then express themselves through these councils. In Europe, he predicted that the "largest common measure of integrated life" could be achieved without destroying the ancient and individual characteristics of its myriad peoples. Russia must be one of the guarantors of that life; "thus and thus only will the glory of Europe rise again." He had obviously not consulted Roosevelt on the speech. Other than references to China's "long torment" and its need of "rescue," he did not include China as one of the great postwar powers. At best, if Churchill had a say in the matter, China would take its rightful place as a lesser state with friends in high places. Anthony Eden, in Washington that week for talks with Roosevelt (who believed in a *four*-power postwar structure), was told in no uncertain terms by Cordell Hull that "Churchill had made a serious mistake in his speech . . . by not mentioning China."[109]

After sketching his vision of postwar Europe, Churchill moved on to the

Beveridge Report and postwar social changes in Britain. The policies he championed that evening would have appeared radical even to a New Dealer. "You must rank me and my colleagues as strong partisans of national compulsory insurance for all classes, for all purposes, from cradle to grave." On health: "We must establish on broad and solid foundations a national health service." On education: "I hope our education will become broader and more liberal." No one who aspired to higher education would be denied the opportunity, including factory workers, for whom some sort of "part time release" from work must be found. Housing: Entire cities and towns had to be rebuilt, "an immense opportunity not only for improving our housing, but for employment." The taxes to pay for all this would be heavier than before the war, but not so heavy as to "destroy initiative and enterprise." Yet, caveats: "First of all we must beware of attempts to over-persuade or even to coerce His Majesty's Government to bind themselves or their unknown successors, in conditions which no one can foresee and which may be years ahead, to impose great new expenditure on the State without any relation to the circumstances which might prevail at that time.... I am not in any need to go about making promises in order to win political support or to be allowed to continue in office." And, "I tell you around your firesides to-night that I am resolved to not... make all kinds of promises and tell all kinds of fairy tales to you who have trusted me and gone with me so far, and marched through the valley of the shadow, till we have reached the upland regions on which we now stand with firmly planted feet."[110]

It was masterful; he had declared himself for reform and against fairy tales, leaving unanswered the question, was Beveridge's report reform or fairy tale? That question was partially answered by a Tory public relations campaign that began within days of Churchill's call for individual initiative and enterprise. Posters appeared on buildings throughout the land reminding Britons of "Our National Heritage." The centerpiece of each poster was a picture of a national hero—Drake, Elizabeth, Marlborough, Pitt, Nelson, Wellington. Churchill's photo assumed a lesser place on each poster. The message was clear: heroes and individual initiative underlay Britain's greatness. Partisan politics had been dormant for almost three years in the comforting shade of the flag of truce that flew over the coalition government. Churchill wanted things to stay that way, although he looked the other way as Tory posters with his portrait sprouted across Britain. Labour rank and file, meanwhile, feared a loss of their political identity if they continued to serve in a national government that proscribed partisan rhetoric. For weeks many Labourites had advised Attlee and his cabinet cohorts to bolt the coalition, the idea being that Labour would declare absolute loyalty to Churchill on the war effort but simultaneously reclaim its identity and the freedom to oppose the Tories on the domestic front. Harold Nicolson believed such a split was certain to take place within four months.[111]

Nicolson rued the fact that Conservatives were forcing Labour's hand by not coming at the Beveridge Report more honestly, by arguing against the improbable parts while trying to find a way to make the more practical elements work. When the report was brought up for debate in the House, the government paraded out a coalition of cabinet ministers—Tories Sir John Anderson and Kingsley Wood, and Labourite Herbert Morrison—to argue the government's case, which amounted to, as Nicolson feared it would, a transparent attempt to sweep it under the rug. That the dour Anderson did much of the sweeping only hurt the Tory cause. Labour argued for the immediate creation of a Ministry of Social Security; Tories insisted that such decisions await the end of the war. The leftist *Manchester Guardian* called the Tory performance "a lamentable exhibition of how not to handle political dynamite." The *Times* warned Parliament, "The public is in earnest in its determination to secure a new and firmer social foundation . . . after the war." Still, in a vote that came in at 338 for the government, including 23 Labourites, versus 121 against, the House endorsed the Tory strategy, which was to accept the plan in principle but not in detail. The Conservatives had employed the same strategy of obfuscation that Churchill had himself four decades earlier called "terminological inexactitude"; that is, the Tory response to Beveridge did not exactly add up to lies, but neither did it add up to anything comprehensible.[112]

Churchill believed that the best way to outflank Beveridge without threatening the national government was to stress the absolute necessity of maintaining the coalition, such that when the war ended, Britons would remember who had insisted on solidarity and brought them through the ordeal. To stem the rising tide of Labour unrest and to preserve his status as war leader, Churchill told the Commons that per the agreement made in 1940, a general election would not be permitted. Labour MPs asked why, if the Americans can hold interim elections without harming the war effort, could not Britons? Churchill held firm; there would be no contested elections. Those intent on "seeing the war through to a victorious conclusion," he warned the House, should "avail themselves of every occasion to mark their disapproval of truce breakers." This was less a renewed call for national unity than an adroit maneuver by Churchill, who in effect had just equated parliamentary dissent with disloyalty. Yet beyond the walls of Parliament, Churchill's Tory functionaries felt free to declaim at will on the evils of socialism, because such exhortations were neither disruptive to the war effort nor disloyal to the war leader. Oliver Lyttelton, intent on explicating the perils of Labour collectivism versus Churchill's theme of heroic individualism, told a Conservative meeting: "The great periods in our history were nearly always associated with an outstanding individual and not with a political system.... Nothing could be more ghastly than a uniform cow-like public opinion, which is left willing to browse on artificially fertilized fields, and chew the cud of common pasture."[113]

"Mr. Churchill's historic broadcast dominated the minds and the talk of a majority of Britons last week," Mollie Panter-Downes wrote on March 28. Yet "the general exhilaration was overshadowed by the almost simultaneous setback" in Tunisia when, on the twenty-second, German panzers counterattacked Montgomery's Mareth forces. The German strike kept the Eighth Army off balance and in place for two days. Britons steeled themselves for more bad news, for since 1940, British setbacks had displayed a disconcerting tendency to grow into British defeats. Montgomery responded to the Axis stroke by shifting his main thrust to Freyberg on the left, who, reinforced by the British 1st Armoured Division, and supported by hundreds of RAF fighter and bomber sorties, smashed through the Tebega Gap on March 27. The Germans and Italians directly in front of Montgomery, fearing encirclement, fled north. The next day, Montgomery telegraphed Churchill: "My troops are in possession of whole Mareth defences." An otherwise bleak month—in the North Atlantic, in North Africa, on the Russian steppes—was going out with a victory, and not just a British victory but, with Patton's reinvigorated forces in the thick of it, an Allied victory.[114]

Anthony Eden had been in Washington since mid-March for talks with Roosevelt and Secretary of State Cordell Hull on the makeup and security of postwar Europe and the world. This was the Four Power Plan as Roosevelt saw it, with China as one of the powers, and France excluded. The War Cabinet had approved the plan in principle in November, but the Foreign Office was well aware of Churchill's position on China. Hull held a similar position on France: it was irrelevant. Eden professed a fondness for Hull, but he noted a vindictive streak directed especially toward France and Germany, a mind-set Eden attributed to Hull's having been raised in the hills of Tennessee, where feuds among the hill folk lasted for generations or until everybody was killed off. Hull, over tea with Eden and Roosevelt, suggested the Allies avoid trials after the war by simply shooting Hitler and his cohorts, as the Germans no doubt would shoot the Allied leaders if given the chance. Indeed, Hull had taken Hitler's measure, but such a brutal (yet pragmatic) approach to settling scores offended Eden's gentlemanly sensibilities. He later wrote that he was familiar with the hit song, "The Martins and the Coys," adding, "I felt he [Hull] too could pursue a vendetta to the end."[115]

So could Roosevelt. When it came to France and Germany, he thought little of the French and less of Germans, especially Prussians. During their talks, Roosevelt reiterated to Eden his position on unconditional surrender: Germany would have no rights and East Prussia would disappear within the new Poland. Germany, too, would disappear, dismembered into harmless rump Germanys. Developing his idea a few months later, Roosevelt told Averell Harriman that postwar Germany would be denied airplanes, and German citizens would be forbidden to learn to fly. Germany, Roosevelt proclaimed, would be broken up "into three, four, or five states." Churchill harbored doubts about the wisdom of reducing Germany to an amalgam of impotent agrarian states. His vision for the postwar world included his councils and federations of European nations, with Germany as a participant, but not Prussia. On Prussia he aligned himself with Roosevelt. George Kennan later wrote that both Roosevelt and Churchill failed to see "the true lower-class basis of the Nazi movement; how sure they both were it was still the Prussian Junkers they were fighting." In fact, Hitler and his thugs despised the conservative Prussian class, a hatred that resulted in the degradation first of Prussia, and finally of all of Germany. In Prussia, Kennan wrote, lived courageous and idealistic sons and daughters of the conservative class who despised Hitler for the lower-class criminal he was. Here was a potential source of opposition to Hitler that neither Roosevelt nor Churchill cultivated. Instead, they intended to turn Prussia into a large meadow.[116]

For Churchill (but not Roosevelt) the rest of Germany was another matter entirely. He had told Jock Colville two years earlier that he always included Germany as a member of the "European family." Germany existed before the Gestapo, he told Colville, and it would exist after the Gestapo. "When we abolish Germany, we will certainly establish Poland—and make them a permanent thing in Europe." But what exactly did "abolish" mean? And the Free Poles in London wondered exactly what "establish" meant when it came to Poland. And Stalin had long suspected that Churchill meant to revitalize Germany, which to the Russians amounted to an existential threat. Churchill had not defined his terms. Yet certain beliefs underlay his postwar plans. The future security of Western Europe depended on the strength and cooperation of the nations of Western Europe, and not on the good graces of Russia, or America, for that matter, which indeed had no treaty obligations with Poland or France. Churchill saw the need for an economically healthy Germany as a trading partner for Britain, but first and foremost, he tied Britain's postwar military security to a vibrant France.[117]

Yet for Roosevelt, France occupied the same place in his worldview that China held for Churchill; to wit, no place at all. Over dinner one evening, the president outlined to Eden his concept for postwar power sharing in Europe. It did not include France but rather would be based on the military might of the great powers—Britain, the United States, and the Soviets. The rest of Europe, Roosevelt told a stunned Eden, would be disarmed but for rifles. And France would be partially dismembered, portions of Alsace-Lorraine and northern France lopped off to join a chunk of Belgium in a new state, Wallonia. The president's "ignorance of France was profound," wrote the British historian John Grigg, "yet no impediment to his holding obstinate views on the subject." Noting an unsettling consistency to the president's thinking, Eden asked if France and Germany were to be dismembered, why not the British Empire as well? Roosevelt replied by suggesting that Britain contemplate giving Hong Kong back to China as a "good will" gesture. Eden, amused (and alarmed), asked Roosevelt what territories *he* intended to give up. Roosevelt made no reply. Eden also voiced his opinion that Chiang's regime—corrupt and hated by legions of his countrymen, especially Mao Zedong—did not embody China and that a revolution of some sort would have to take place before China could assume a place among the great powers. Eden found the president's musings to be "alarming in their cheerful fecklessness." Roosevelt made his points with grace, he noted, but "it was too like a conjuror, juggling balls of dynamite, whose nature he failed to understand."[118]

All agreed that the military alliance known as the United Nations should emerge after the war as a world council of some sort. Stalin, in due time, would have to be brought into the discussions. Churchill, Hull, Eden, and Roosevelt each articulated different notions of how the postwar world should be configured, and in particular the Russian role in that world. But together, they lacked a vision of where they were going and how they would get there. Yet as regarded Russia, Roosevelt believed one thing with absolute certainty: if he were only given the chance to sit down alone with Stalin, all would be put right. This belief, George Kennan wrote, was born of F.D.R.'s assumption that although Stalin "was a somewhat difficult customer," he could be brought around "if only he could be exposed to the persuasive charms of someone like F.D.R. himself.... For these assumptions, there were no grounds whatsoever; and they were of a puerility that was unworthy of a statesman of F.D.R.'s stature." Churchill (and Eden) hoped for some sort of postwar continuation of the partnership with Russia, but ever since Stalin made known his postwar territorial ambitions, both Churchill and Eden had grown increasingly wary of his intentions. Thus, for London, France represented an insurance policy should Uncle Joe abrogate his agreements. In the coming months, Churchill reminded dinner companions of a truism that formed the heart of Britain's desire to ally itself after the war with a strong France: if nothing stood between Moscow and the English Channel, then the Russians might someday stand on the Channel coast opposite the White Cliffs of Dover.[119]

Roosevelt spoke in general terms of a continued American role in safeguarding the peace, but later in the year he told Harriman that he "had no intention of stationing large American forces in Europe after the war, whether to help keep the peace or occupy Germany." Even were Roosevelt to change his mind, a different president a few years hence might negate the policy and turn America inward, as had happened after the Great War. Eden suspected the U.S. Senate would never ratify any treaty that handcuffed America to the military fortunes of postwar Europe. How then to safeguard the peace? Churchill, on the one hand, sought to tie Britain's postwar security to a special relationship with America. On the other hand, his responsibilities to his King and country demanded that he strive for a final settlement in Europe that did not depend entirely on an active American presence, or on the good graces of Stalin. In late March (over a dinner, Brooke recalled, of "plover's [*sic*] eggs, chicken broth, chicken pie, chocolate soufflé and with it a bottle of champagne...port and brandy!"), Churchill expressed "his disapproval of Roosevelt's plan to build up China while neglecting France." Vital to Churchill's plan for postwar Europe was a French state that emerged as a power, not a pauper.[120]

With Stalin voicing his disappointment in, if not outright distrust of, the Americans and British, Vice President Henry Wallace publicly framed the postwar stakes in stark terms. "We shall decide sometime in 1943 or 1944," he told reporters, "whether to plant the seeds of World War III." That war will become a certainty, Wallace said, "if we allow Germany to rearm militarily or psychologically." That war will be "probable if we double-cross Russia....Unless the Western democracies and Russia come to a satisfactory understanding before the war ends, I very much fear that World War III will be inevitable." Wallace's remarks were a clear indication that America had reached no clear understanding with Stalin on postwar policies in Europe, specifically, the fate of Germany. The British press—which with Wallace accorded the Red Army heroic status—praised Wallace. The *Manchester Guardian* declared: "There is one-hundred times more anti-Russian feeling in the United States than there is in this country." The paper also noted that in the United States "there is much more tolerance for fascist systems of government." The *Times* stressed the point in an editorial: "To suppose that Britain and the U.S. with the aid of some lesser European powers could maintain permanent security in Europe through a policy which alienated Russia and induced her to disinterest herself in Continental affairs would be sheer madness." Yet the problem, as

Churchill and Eden increasingly saw it (and as Churchill had told the Turks in January), was that the Soviet Union might prove *too* interested in continental affairs following the war. How far west into postwar Europe Soviet influence extended would depend in large part on how far east Anglo-American armies were when someday they shook hands with the Red Army.[121]

Trust and loyalty do not necessarily march together in lockstep. Churchill saw no need to abridge his loyalty to Stalin even as he sensed trouble over the far horizon. In fact, each of the major Western political players—Churchill, Roosevelt, Harriman, Hopkins, Beaverbrook, Hull, and Eden—was intent on proving that his deep and abiding loyalty to Stalin was equal to if not greater than that of the others. The Anglo-American political theme for 1943 was not really Europe First, but Uncle Joe First. Opening the second front was the *only* action that would demonstrate to Stalin's satisfaction the loyalty of his allies. Within the highest Allied councils Beaverbrook became Stalin's most vocal supporter, so much so that Harriman wrote, "Beaverbrook is for the appeasement policy toward Russia...and doesn't give a hoot in hell about small nations. He would turn over Eastern Europe to Russia without regard to future consequences, the Atlantic Charter, etc." For his part, Harriman favored a high-minded relationship with the Soviets that "must be friendly and frank but firm when they behave in a manner which is incompatible with our ideals." Those lofty sentiments presumed that Stalin's endorsement of the Atlantic Charter was sincere and that he actually gave a hoot in hell about Western ideals of democracy.[122]

As he had shown with the Baltic states two years earlier, and with eastern Poland in 1939, Stalin first asked for what he wanted, and if his wishes were not granted, he took it. Roosevelt and Churchill believed that the opening of the second front would give them the leverage they needed to demand that Stalin cease all talk of borders and reconfigured European states until the peace conference following victory. This is what they insisted upon with their lesser allies, the Free Poles and Free French. They also believed they owed Stalin a second front, given the burden he was carrying and their fear that he would "lay this burden down" were they not to open that front. George Kennan ascribes a certain naïveté to this reasoning, given Stalin's history. Would Stalin really contemplate laying his burden down in order to reach another agreement with Hitler, another "pact" that was only as good as Hitler's word, which was no good at all, as Stalin had learned in 1941? Yet, how much, if any, leverage Churchill and Roosevelt gained by opening a second front could only be determined after they opened that front and, after opening that front, how far east they pushed it. Those questions were moot for the remainder of 1943.

The Blitz had ceased in May 1941, but during the first months of 1943, German raids conducted by small groups of Focke-Wulf fighter-bombers took place with frightening irregularity, just often enough and just deadly enough to keep Britons on edge. The Germans flew in beneath the radar to bomb roadways, buses, trains, and. with sinister regularity, schools. A January raid saw a lone Focke-Wulf strafe a school in Woolrich before flying on to the Sandhurst Road School in Catford, Lewisham, where it dropped a 1,100-pound bomb, killing thirty-eight students and four teachers. FIENDISH ONSLAUGHT OF A MURDEROUS FOE read the next day's headline of the *Kentish Mercury.* British rage only grew when the commander of the raid, a Captain Schuman, told reporters in Paris, "The bombs fell just where we wanted them to."[123]

The most deadly incident that year involved no bombs falling at all. It took place in London at the Bethnal Green tube station in the early evening of March 3. Thousands of pedestrians were making their way toward the station when the sirens sounded, followed immediately by the murderous cacophony from anti-aircraft rockets being launched in nearby Victoria Park. The rockets, though developed six years earlier, were newly deployed. What was terrifying about the "rocket guns," the war correspondent Ernie Pyle wrote, was not their actual report, but that "a rocket going up sounds like a bomb coming down." When the rockets went up that evening, the crowd panicked and raced for the entrance to the Underground. A young writer for *Stars and Stripes* named Andy Rooney was among the throng. "I almost turned toward the shelter," Rooney recalled, "but I wasn't that far from my rooms and decided to keep going. I didn't learn what happened until the next day, and then I realized, that's where I almost went down into the station." Rooney made the right decision; almost two hundred Londoners did not. A young woman carrying either a baby or a bundle tripped partway down the steep stairs, causing the people in front of her to fall and the crowd behind her to collapse into one deadly mass. Within fifteen seconds, the shelter had been converted into a charnel house, where 178 men, women, and children were suffocated and crushed. The Ministry of Information kept the details of the tragedy under wraps, with the result that Londoners, not knowing exactly what had happened, concocted their own explanations. One rumor had it that a German agent on the sidewalk had screamed that petroleum bombs were being dropped, thus panicking the crowd. Another, more popular explanation was that it was all the fault of the Jews, who were again accused, as during the Blitz, of losing self-control and rushing the shelter. A poll showed that while 29 percent of Londoners thought favorably of Jews, since the Blitz, those who thought unfavorably had doubled to 26 percent. There was talk in Parliament of proposing a law that forbade anti-Semitism. "A law against hating Jews," Goebbels wrote in his diary, "is usually the beginning of the end for Jews."[124]

Churchill had moved to Chequers the night before the Bethnal Green incident in order to continue his convalescence. Brooke, too, had gone down for two weeks with influenza. The CIGS was so ill that he could not even summon the energy to jot in his diary or undertake his birding. He and Churchill could do nothing but observe from their sickbeds as the situation in the Atlantic worsened, as the alliance drifted toward new shoals, and as Generals Alexander and Montgomery waited for the weather to clear in Tunisia.

In March, Iran declared war on Germany and thus joined the United Nations. Averell Harriman, upon his return to Washington from Tehran the previous August, relayed to Roosevelt the young shah's respect for Churchill and his belief (based on a personal promise from Churchill) that Iran had nothing to fear from the British. But, the shah had told Harriman, "Russia may be difficult!" The shah feared the postwar Soviet government might prove "aggressive" and expressed his desire for stronger ties to Washington. Harriman, the old railroad man, saw an opportunity. The Iranian railroad was in deplorable shape, an opinion he had offered to Churchill the previous summer along with an offer to rebuild and operate the railroad, which Churchill politely declined at the time. Now Harriman prevailed upon friends at the Union Pacific to send surveyors, rolling stock, and modern diesel locomotives to Iran in order to double the capacity of the Iranian railroads, which would double the supplies reaching Stalin and help offset the loss of the Arctic convoys. The British had been running just four or five trains a day from Basra north to Russia, with a capacity of three thousand tons. By late March, teams of American technical advisers, doctors (typhus was rampant; seven of ten Iranian children died before age nine), and railroad men had drifted into Tehran, including the former head of the New Jersey State Police, Colonel H. Norman Schwarzkopf, the man who had hunted the Lindbergh kidnapper and whose new duty involved instilling discipline in the ranks of the Iranian police.[125]

The takeover of the railroad meant that responsibility for the transport of British troops and matériel into Persia, and of British oil out, now rested with the Americans. It was the very erosion of autonomy that had troubled Churchill and Brooke the previous summer. Yet for the sake of their Soviet ally, they had no choice other than to agree. Harriman's management skills paid off; by late 1943, capacity on the Iranian railroad had increased to over six thousand tons per day. Harriman knew railroads, and he knew oil. In 1925 he had been a partner in a consortium to modernize the newly nationalized Soviet Baku oilfields, until the U.S. government barred American companies from doing business with the Reds. By 1943 they were all friends, by virtue of treaties—the Reds, the British, the Americans. The Americans in Iran had come only to help the Allied cause, although Harriman, consummate businessman that he was, had his eye on the future as well. The war would not last forever, but Iranian oil would.

Churchill had tried since Casablanca to keep Stalin abreast of the progress (or lack thereof) in building up sufficient armies in Britain to seriously contemplate a second front on the scale Stalin demanded. The Old Man touted the eight objectives agreed upon at Casablanca, all of which remained unfulfilled by April. He touted British airpower and Montgomery's success at Mareth; Stalin was not impressed. In March (before canceling the Arctic convoys), Churchill informed Stalin that of the twenty-seven divisions America had pledged to send to the United Kingdom to prepare for the invasion of France, seven had gone to Torch, and three more were set to go to Husky. In Britain there is "only one, in addition to the strong air force.... The reason why these performances have fallen so far short... is not that the troops do not exist, but the shipping at our disposal and the means of escorting it do not exist."[126]

This was Churchill's elongated way of telling Stalin that in the spring of 1943, there was one fewer American division in England than when Churchill had visited Stalin the previous August. Despite the pledge made at Casablanca to carry twenty-seven divisions and 938,000 American troops to Britain by December 31, 1943, the Americans had so far come up twenty-six short, although they still had eight months to fulfill their promise. Churchill told Stalin he did not mean to denigrate the American effort, although in effect that was what he was doing. He pointed out that in order to sustain operations in North Africa, the Pacific, and India, and to supply Russia, Britain had to cut its own imports "to the bone." This was true; yet here Churchill in deference to Roosevelt failed to point out the obvious. Had the Americans not dedicated so much shipping to supplying Douglas MacArthur, more would have been available for the "Europe First" strategy. Finally, Churchill told Stalin that were Germany to weaken, Britain would contemplate an assault on the Continent, but if Germany did not weaken, "a premature attack with inferior and insufficient forces would merely lead to a bloody repulse... and a great triumph for the enemy."[127]

Yet any weakening on Germany's part could only be induced by the Red Army. Roosevelt had implied as much in his own message to Stalin: "We hope that the success of your heroic army, which is an inspiration to all of us, will continue." Stalin was not in the least satisfied with the logic of Roosevelt or Churchill. In a telegram on March 15, he repeated his demand that the "blow from the West should... be struck in the spring or early summer." Anglo-American "uncertainty" and delay of cross-Channel operations, he told them, "arouses grave anxiety in me, about which I feel I cannot be silent."[128]

By mid-April, four weeks after Stalin expressed his anxiety, the threat in the North Atlantic appeared to have abated, as had the threat of an Axis counterstoke in Tunisia. Yet everyone from King George to Britain's bakers and candlestick makers had long since learned to put little stock in appearances. The weather in Britain by mid-April showed signs of improvement, but clear skies were always a worrisome invitation to the Luftwaffe. The few unbombed flower beds in parks put on subdued shows, while American soldiers commandeered rugby pitches in Hyde Park, where they played pickup games of baseball (and sometimes faced down British troops who sought to take over the pitch for its intended purpose). The sheep in Hyde Park took to grazing along nearby streets, the iron fences of the park having been torn out and melted down to build tanks and bombs. One Hyde Park battery of AA guns was commanded by Auxiliary Territorial Service sergeant Mary Churchill (who once intervened between two groups of Brits and Yanks about to come to blows over the use of a rugby pitch). Spring, indeed, was nigh. But with HMG still forbidding weather forecasts, Britons never knew what was coming their way.[129]

As always, this included German aircraft. "The London public fears that the German air *blitzkrieg* will suddenly break out again overnight," wrote Goebbels. "Would to God that we were in a position to do it!" Now the RAF regularly bombed the Ruhr Valley and Berlin in increasingly heavy assaults. Churchill kept Stalin apprised throughout April of the massed attacks on Berlin and Hamburg, of tonnage thrown in excess of 700 tons a night, then 800, and then, "the best Berlin has got yet," 1,050 tons. Some Church of England clerics took exception to "the frankly jubilant way in which the press whoops about the tonnage of bombs dropped on German cities." But the average Briton, Mollie Panter-Downes wrote, saw the RAF bombing as "a bad job which has got to be done." Britons, who had "got hell" during the Blitz, allotted little sympathy to German citizens. German propaganda called the raids "terror bombings." They were. And they were necessary; Churchill could give Stalin little else.[130]

In mid-April, the War Cabinet decreed that Britain's church bells could once again call worshippers to Sunday service, beginning on Easter Sunday. And after a superbly nonsensical debate in the Commons, it was agreed that church bells would no longer be reserved for use as a warning in the event of invasion. When an MP asked Churchill what warning system would replace the bells, he replied, "For myself, I cannot help thinking that anything like a serious invasion would be bound to leak out." Austin Hopkinson objected: "How can news possibly leak out," he asked, "when it is an offense to spread alarm and despondency?" "Factual statements," Churchill replied, "especially well intentioned, would fall into that category." That week, St. Paul's regained its voice and Londoners heard the Stedman Cinques flawlessly rendered by Alfred Peck and his thirteen assistants, who had been practicing for three years with muffled clappers. In Coventry, only the cathedral's spire remained, and from it came a bronze tolling. The peal of bells rolling over greening meadows and newly plowed fields augured a return to the splendid isolation from (most) continental calamities that Britons had enjoyed for almost nine hundred years, until the Luftwaffe arrived overhead in 1940. The bells need never have been silenced in the first place; Britons would have known the enemy invasion was at hand by simply turning on their wireless, or by opening their front door and looking up. Yet the bells connected Churchill's yeomanry—and Churchill—to England's past. That they were allowed to ring again only reinforced that connection. All was well.[131]

Then, over the course of the next few days, Churchill was apprised of three developments that raised new and serious questions about the security of Britain, inter-Allied politics and the second front, and the possibility of a new Blitz carried out by new and terrifying weapons. The first shock came on April 13, when Churchill was told for the first time that the Chiefs of Staff had agreed that all available landing craft be sent from Britain to North Africa in order to meet the needs of Husky. Furthermore, the craft were to be kept at the ready in order to exploit any favorable opportunities that developed, presumably by way of a venture onto the Italian mainland. Churchill was a strong backer of exploiting opportunities, but he had not been made aware until this meeting that the paucity of landing craft forced an either/or choice: exploit Sicilian gains, or meet the needs of Sledgehammer, the small-scale strike into France. The shock was more emotional than intellectual; everyone had concluded almost a year earlier that Torch effectively moved Roundup (the large-scale invasion) into mid-1944. In spite of that certainty, Churchill (and Roosevelt) had made promises to Stalin that they could not deliver on. The latest news on the landing craft amounted to the final knell. Over dinner with Brooke that evening—"started being stormy, then improved"—Churchill agreed to the proposal. He informed the War Cabinet that Sledgehammer (and, necessarily, Roundup) were off the table for that year, but he did not inform Stalin.[132]

The second piece of unsettling news arrived two days later, on April 15, when Churchill was informed that RAF intelligence indicated that the Germans were building rockets near Peenemünde, on the Baltic Sea coast. These rockets were not just an advanced version of the small but deadly *Nebelwerfer* rockets shot from tubes mounted on trucks, or the three- and five-inch solid fuel missiles deployed on ships and in anti-aircraft batteries. The German rockets were large, unmanned, and wingless craft propelled by exploding gases and guided by gyroscopes and navigation technology of a sort the British had yet to imagine.

It was the stuff of science fiction. The British had known for four years that the Germans were designing rockets, but nobody in British intelligence knew exactly how far along in the testing and production process German scientists and technicians might be. Nothing was known of propellant, range, guidance system, or payload. At the suggestion of Pug Ismay, Churchill's son-in-law Duncan Sandys was assigned the task of finding out what the Germans were up to, and how to best develop countermeasures. This was nepotism straight up, but Sandys had been involved in the development of anti-aircraft technologies until his 1941 car accident put him out of the air defense planning hierarchy. He saw a future for rockets in warfare, not just for the short-range projectiles fired from tubes, but for futuristic vehicles like the Germans were apparently building, and might soon be testing. Sandys set up a committee code-named Crossbow to recommend countermeasures. Yet Crossbow had first to ascertain just what the Germans were doing. Nobody knew. Days after learning of the German rocket work, Churchill and Brooke motored to the Hatfield Aerodrome to witness a display of the latest British advances in fighter aircraft, described by Brooke as "without propellers, driven by air sucked in in front and squirted out the back! Apparently likely to be the fighter of the future." It had been on the drawing board for more than a decade, and the first British turbo-jet engines had been tested in 1941. But the Exchequer lacked the specie to go into full production. Thus, the jet age arrived along with the rocket age, although neither had yet been christened. Hitler would do that.[133]

The third piece of news that reached Churchill was in some ways the most unsettling of all. That April week, Hitler told the Hungarian regent, Admiral Miklós Horthy, that Jews were "pure parasites" which "like tuberculosis bacilli" infected healthy bodies. "Nations which did not rid themselves of Jews," Hitler told Horthy, "perished." Hungary, a German ally, had not been forced by Berlin to deport its Jewish citizens, and to his credit Horthy did not start now, although he had no objection to forcing Hungary's Jews into slave labor. Other leaders in other capitals had no such choice and no compunction about sending Jews east. Over the next few days, trains carrying more than 2,400 Belgian and French Jews left Brussels and Paris for Auschwitz. On April 19, German authorities in Warsaw decreed that the Jewish ghetto there be combed for Jews to be transported to the death camp at Treblinka. Since early 1940, more than 300,000 Warsaw Jews had died or been sent east. When German trucks and soldiers arrived to collect their cargoes, they encountered something entirely unexpected. More than 1,200 Jews armed with just a few dozen rifles, hand grenades, and homemade bombs fought off 2,100 German troops for almost three weeks, killing 300. The Germans blocked and then flooded underground tunnels and sewers through which Jews tried to flee. They brought in heavy artillery and shelled the ghetto for ten days, and then set the ruins ablaze to smoke out survivors. When they finally retook the ghetto, they shot 7,000 Jews and sent another 7,000 to Treblinka. Several thousand more, who had fled to the Christian part of the city, were hunted down or betrayed. News of the massacres seeped from the Reich and was given much play in the Free Polish and London press. By then, fewer than 50,000 Jews remained alive in Warsaw.[134]

Goebbels and Hitler ignored Allied condemnations of such alleged atrocities. Instead, they hatched a diversion. It took the form of a postwar plan of their own in response to the nebulous federations and world councils being discussed in Washington and London. This was a new "European Charter" that made no mention of *Herrenvolk* (the master race) or *Lebensraum* ("living space," the plan to resettle Germans on conquered lands in the East). Instead, it pledged Germany's intent, as a sort of European attorney, to guarantee the freedoms of every citizen under its care, a pledge the British could not make, said one German newspaper, because Britain lacked a National Socialist Party capable "of guiding the fate of European countries." Goebbels intended to sell Europeans on the wisdom of "European cooperation," a phrase he believed might prove effective in furthering his aims, which had nothing to do with European cooperation but rather with driving a wedge between the Soviets and their Western allies, especially Poland.[135]

The London Poles had in the previous weeks given Goebbels an opening and Churchill a headache. In contravention to Allied policy that discussion of postwar boundaries take place only following the defeat of Hitler, the London Poles published their intent to restore to Poland those portions of the Polish Ukraine grabbed by Stalin in 1939 (and earlier grabbed by Poland after the Russian Revolution). Stalin, for his part, suggested in imprecise terms that the Poles should think of looking to East Prussia for satisfaction. What did that mean? Was Stalin intent on moving his zone of protection against future German aggression farther westward into Polish territory? Complicating matters was the fact that Poland had grabbed the Teschen portion of Czechoslovakia during the Munich crisis, thereby forfeiting some of the moral high ground when it came to talk of restoring boundaries. Eduard Beneš, whose country had been betrayed by the British at Munich, looked now to Moscow for help in restoring the Teschen region to Czechoslovakia. Britain had gone to war over Poland, but which Poland—the Poland that had been violated by Hitler, the Poland that had been violated by Stalin, or the Poland that had, in Churchill's words, "jumped on the back of Czechoslovakia" in 1938? At best, the diplomatic situation was now all bollixed up. Goebbels, gleeful, saw his opportunity, but how best to exploit the suspicions that swam beneath the surface of Allied relations, how best to portray Stalin and the Bolsheviks as the true villains of Europe? For a decade, when the Nazis faced such a challenge, the most reliable arrow in their quiver was also the most crooked: the lie.[136]

On the morning of April 13, Berlin radio triumphantly announced that German troops operating in the Katyn forest, west of Smolensk, discovered mass graves that contained the bodies of more than 8,500 Polish army officers and men, their hands bound behind their backs. It appeared the victims had been shot in the back of the head at close range. Young conifers had been planted over the graves in an apparent attempt to disguise the atrocities. According to Berlin, the Russians had captured the men in 1939 (when Stalin in partnership with Hitler, chewed off his piece of Poland). The Soviets moved the prisoners east to three camps and, Berlin claimed, subsequently marched them out of those camps and murdered them. That the alleged execution methods matched exactly those of Hitler's *Einsatzgruppen* did not perturb Dr. Goebbels, and for good reason. He knew the Russians had indeed murdered the Polish officers (who deserved it, he told his diary, since the Poles "were the real instigators of this war"). He even managed to express his shock over the news to his diary: "Gruesome aberrations of the human soul were thus revealed."[137]

Thus the third troublesome development to come Churchill's way that week. General Anders, who had gone to Moscow the previous year in search of missing Poles, had finally found them. The London Poles, already wary of Britain's resoluteness in restoring Polish borders, now demanded resoluteness in pursuing the truth about Katyn. Two days after the radio bulletin, over lunch at No. 10, Churchill cautioned Władysław Sikorski, who intended to call for a Red Cross investigation, not to pursue the matter. Cadogan was present, and he recorded Churchill as saying, "Alas, the German revelations are probably true. The Bolsheviks can be very cruel."

He advised Sikorski to look to the future, not the past. He was referring to the immediate urgency to preserve the alliance in order to defeat Hitler; only then could Poland emerge as a free member of the European community. As for the Polish officers, Churchill told Sikorski, "If they are dead, nothing you can do will bring them back." But Sikorski, against Churchill's advice, called for the Red Cross investigation. A few days later, Berlin also invited a Red Cross investigation. Goebbels enthused to his diary of the propaganda possibilities. Given that the disputes and hairline fractures within the Anglo-American-Soviet alliance were common knowledge, he saw a chance to help bring about an outright schism, and possibly a negotiated peace. "Our propaganda is suspected everywhere of having blown up the Katyn incident to enable us to make a separate peace either with the English or the Soviets." Although this was not his intention, "such a possibility would naturally be very pleasing."[138]

The Russians had a saying: Poles never learn, and they never forget. Poles, in turn, said of Russians: they are Slavs, but Slavs without hearts. Stalin's reaction to the Polish accusations was swift and final. Within days he broke off relations with Sikorski's government in London, of whom Stalin declared, "They think themselves clever tacticians, but God has given them no brains." Churchill and Roosevelt each advised Stalin to suspend rather than break relations with the London Poles. He would not do so, the Poles having so clearly displayed their "treachery" with their "hideous charges." Roosevelt warned Stalin that the break would have negative repercussions in the American Polish community. Stalin didn't care in the least about Poles living in Buffalo or Chicago. Churchill warned Stalin that Goebbels would make much of the schism, at Allied expense. He assured Stalin that the London Poles were honorable and not "in collusion with the Germans" and added that he was convinced that "German propaganda has produced this story to make a rift" in Allied ranks (the imprecise word "produced" might be taken as either "concocted" or "disclosed"). Stalin did not bend. Churchill contemplated shutting down those Polish newspapers that criticized the Soviets, and told Stalin so. Stalin held firm. In fact, he announced that he would sponsor a new Polish government in exile, in Moscow. When the London Poles pressed the issue, Churchill warned that their "charges of an insulting character against the Soviet Government" would "seem to countenance the atrocious German propaganda." On that front, Goebbels was winning. On April 28, Churchill cabled Roosevelt: "So far this business has been Goebbels' greatest triumph."[139]

In the appendix to *Closing the Ring,* the fifth volume of his war memoirs, Churchill printed part of a January 1944 memo to Eden that implies he was still trying to get to the bottom of the Katyn matter. But he left off the final line: "we should none of us ever speak a word about it." The memo was written at about the time in late autumn when the Soviets gave Kathleen Harriman and American correspondents a tour of Katyn. The correspondents noted many contradictions; if the Germans killed the prisoners in the summer of 1941, why were some wearing winter uniforms? And why were letters written in 1940 but never mailed found in some of the dead men's pockets? On the return trip to Moscow, Kathleen Harriman and her fellow correspondents drank and sang to dull the images of the day. Despite the contradictory evidence, the correspondents came down on the side of the Soviets (considered heroes by most Americans). Cabled *Time* correspondent Richard Lauterbach: "As far as most of us were concerned, the Germans had slaughtered the Poles." Four decades later, Averell Harriman, in defense of his daughter's judgment, said, "She was not a historian, and it wasn't her job to decide whether what she saw was right or wrong."[140]

In fact, within six weeks of Berlin's April announcement, Churchill and Eden knew what had happened at Katyn. Eden had asked for and on May 31 received a report by Sir Owen O'Malley, the Foreign Office liaison with the London Poles. O'Malley was clear in his opinion: "Most of us are convinced that a large number of Polish officers were indeed murdered by the Russian authorities." In his detailed report, seen only by Churchill, the War Cabinet, and King George, O'Malley concluded, "We have, in fact, perforce used the good name of England like the murderers used the little conifers to cover up a massacre; and in view of the immense importance of an appearance of Allied unity and of the heroic resistance of Russia to Germany, few will think that any other course would have been wise or right." O'Malley then plumbed an ethical implication that was not strictly within his diplomatic purview: "What in the international sphere is morally indefensible generally turns out to be in the long run to have been politically inept." London's support of Moscow had come at the expense of the Poles, O'Malley wrote, who have been portrayed as reckless and tactless and who "have been restrained from putting their own case before the public." HMG "have been obliged... to distort the normal and healthy operations of our intellectual and moral judgments." Churchill ordered that O'Malley's report be kept in a locked box and passed only by hand among members of the War Cabinet. Churchill, however, sent Roosevelt a copy in August. They were partners, after all. The report, Churchill told the president, "is grim, a well written story, perhaps too well written."[141]

This was realpolitik in the most Germanic sense of the word. Those who like to debate just when the Cold War began—during the Anglo-Russo struggle for power in Persia and Afghanistan (the Great Game) in the nineteenth century, in Moscow in November 1917, with the 1939 Nazi-Soviet pact—could do worse than look to the Katyn incident, not necessarily at the actual murders, but at the Allied response in the months that followed as Stalin proclaimed his outrage (but never specifically his innocence). Churchill later wrote of the compromises that had to be entertained in the war against Hitler: "terrible and even humbling submissions must at times be made to the general aim." He spoke those words while addressing a tragic affair that took place in 1944, during the Warsaw uprising, when Stalin refused British bombers the right to overfly Poland and land in Soviet territory. Yet his words applied to Katyn as well.[142]

Nancy Astor, during a visit to Moscow in 1931, had with her usual forthrightness asked Stalin when the mass murder of western Slavs would end. "When it is no longer necessary," Stalin replied. Apparently, it was still necessary.[143]

Throughout April, relations between the Allies deteriorated—not only relations between Russia and Poland, but between the Anglo-Americans and Moscow. The need for Roosevelt and Churchill to meet became evident, if only to do (or say) whatever was needed to placate Stalin, and to decide where to go after Sicily, although that decision rested by default with George Marshall, who had yet to make any decision. Yet Brooke, by sending all available landing craft from Britain to North Africa, had effectively settled the question for that year in favor of his Mediterranean strategy. Brooke made his decision, in part, in reaction to Admiral King's sending *his* landing craft to the Pacific, where MacArthur and Admiral Nimitz were preparing to begin their island-hopping march to Tokyo. This was yet another blow against "Europe first" as Brooke saw it. Yet Brooke's shift of the landing craft did not play well at the newly built Pentagon, and underscored the need for Churchill and Roosevelt to meet again relatively soon. Churchill later wrote, "I was conscious of serious divergencies beneath the surface which, if not adjusted, would lead to grave difficulties and feeble action during the rest of the year."[144]

That was a roundabout way of saying the British and the Americans had no strategy in place to fight the war in Europe after the war in Africa was finished. On that front, Allied fortunes had improved. Since busting through the Mareth Line in late March, Montgomery had pushed north, while Patton had punched away at mountain passes and squeezed eastward on the Axis left flank. On April 7, forward units of the Eighth Army and Patton's II Corps awoke to find the enemy had vanished from their front. That morning a British reconnaissance patrol stumbled across a similar patrol from Patton's II Corps. "This is certainly a pleasant surprise," offered Sergeant Bill Brown, from Devon. "Well, it's good to see somebody besides a Nazi," replied Private Perry Pearce of Kentucky. During just six critical weeks—from about the time Rommel went home sick in early March to mid-April—the advantage had shifted in Tunisia from the Germans to the Allies, in the air, on the sea, and on land. By April 20, Montgomery, General Anderson, the French, and George Patton had put Arnim's army in a vise.[145]

The battle for Tunis had entered its most critical phase, a time of "scrunch and punch," Churchill told Harold Nicolson and Duff Cooper on the twentieth over port in the House smoking room.* That night Nicolson wrote of Churchill: "As usual he is very gay." At times during the worst setbacks of the previous three years, his gaiety had been feigned, but Churchill, always determined, was now confident as well. When Nicolson asked about the status of the bey of Tunis, Muhammad VII al-Munsif, whom the Free French accused of being a Vichy sympathizer and German puppet, Churchill replied, "He will have to call himself *Obey* in future." He told Nicolson of a virtual RAF massacre of German transport planes returning to Sicily after landing reinforcements for Arnim. And he revealed that the Vatican had just released a list of prisoners that included Violet Bonham Carter's son Mark. "I only pray," he told Nicolson, that the German planes "were not carrying our prisoners."[146]

No British prisoners had been shot down, but Churchill was correct about the scrunch and punch. By April 22, Arnim had only seventy-six tanks in running order and was so short of gasoline that his men distilled local wines for fuel. The Allies had pushed the Germans into a pocket behind a 130-mile front that looped in a lazy half circle from just south of Cape Bon, where the Eighth Army was dug in, west and northward to Anderson's First Army, hard by the Mediterranean coast about forty miles west of Bizerte. More Axis troops than were captured at Stalingrad were dug in behind the line; every ridge held artillery, every wadi and every road and track was covered by German machine guns and anti-tank guns. Alexander had originally tapped the American II Corps, which held the line between Anderson and the Fighting French, for a supporting role in the final push. Then politics intruded from Washington. Eisenhower, under pressure from home, explained to Alexander that if the American people believed their men "have not played a substantial part they will be even more intent upon prosecuting the war against the Japs" and commensurately less inclined to fight Hitler. To that end, Ike asked Alexander to assign the II Corps a greater role in the end game. Alexander acquiesced,

* Cooper had been a minister without portfolio since the fall of Singapore, where he had been resident cabinet minister.

and ordered the II Corps shifted to the north of Anderson's First Army, where it would now form part of the van in the final battle. Patton would not be on hand to lead the charge; he had left for Rabat to plan the Sicilian campaign, where he was to lead the American effort. Eisenhower put his deputy, Major General Omar Bradley, in command of the II Corps. The French held the line between Anderson and Montgomery, at Cape Bon. All was in place. Churchill had Arnim in a vise, and it was closing.[147]

After Bletchley broke the U-boat code in March, convoys were routed away from known wolf pack hunting grounds, with the result that the Allies lost almost two-thirds less tonnage in April (250,000 tons) than in March—a significant improvement, but still terrible, and not worthy of a declaration of victory. And if Dönitz's objective was to fight the battle to a stalemate, thereby preventing an Allied landing on the Continent, he was succeeding. In fact, the American press declared he was winning, period. *Time* wrote that "the hard and hopeful fact—for the Germans" is that "Germany [is] still winning the Battle of the Atlantic.... Churchill and Roosevelt both had indicated that the Allies could not hope to launch a major offensive before that margin was beaten in." By early May, the margin had not been. Admiral Ernest King, blunt and incapable of obfuscation, declared, "The submarine menace is being dealt with.... We expect to bring it under control in four to six months." That meant October, the close of the invasion season. Here was the first (and inadvertent) public acknowledgment on the part of the Anglo-Americans that no large-scale invasion of fortress Europe could possibly be undertaken until favorable weather again descended upon the English Channel. And that would be in May or June of 1944, at the earliest.[148]

Patrons of Washington bars and London pubs asked, what will one million American and British soldiers in England and Africa do for a year? Churchill pondered the same question. Secure now in the results soon to be obtained in Tunisia, and quite positive as to how best to exploit them, he proposed to Roosevelt on April 29 that they meet in order to decide where to go after the coming victory and the planned assault on Sicily. Italy appeared to Churchill to be the self-evident target. Another matter had to be addressed. The Americans had failed to exchange information on the atomic bomb, as agreed upon the previous year. Harry Hopkins had promised Churchill at Casablanca that the situation would be "put right." It had not been. The Americans, Lord Cherwell told Churchill, had completely cut off the flow of information. Churchill, furious, asked how soon British scientists could start work on a unilateral basis. Perhaps six to nine months, Cherwell replied, if given the highest priority, and that at the expense of all other war programs. Other issues needed to be discussed as well: the Poles, the Free French, Arctic convoys, the Pacific theater. When Roosevelt did not respond in a timely fashion to the proposal that they meet, Churchill took his case to Hopkins, adding that, as his doctors forbade his flying due to fears of reinvigorating his pneumonia, he could travel by ship in order to arrive in Washington by May 11. Finally, on May 2, as if inviting an old Harvard roommate down for a weekend of bridge, Roosevelt replied, "I am really delighted you are coming.... I want you of course to stay here [at the White House] with me."[149]

The meeting, code-named Trident, was on. Stalin would not be there; his presence was required in Moscow for the start of Hitler's summer offensive. In Russia, from Leningrad to Rostov, the spring *rasputitsa* had turned forest floors to marshes, marshes to lakes, and roads to quagmires. A *New York Times* correspondent wrote that along the entire front, "rusting cannon and broken tanks marked the course of old battles." The relative strength of the two opposing armies was about equal. That raised the specter of stalemate. Yet near Kursk, Hitler had assembled the largest tank army in history, and it now awaited orders to attack. With Arctic convoys halted and the Iranian railroad unable to make up the loss, the Red Army would face the Wehrmacht, and soon, with only the men, weapons, and tanks on hand. Stalin's factories and farms contributed 95 percent of the matériel and food his armies needed, but the 5 percent Lend-Lease contributed had proven critical. He needed that boost now, but it was not forthcoming. There was no doubt that the coming battle would be horrific, and quite possibly deciding. In London and Washington, there was growing doubt as to whether Stalin and the Red Army could sustain the effort much longer.[150]

The Soviet leader, as he had for sixteen months, sought from his partners only one answer to only one question: the date of the opening of the second front. Settling that question was high on the Trident agenda. With relations with Stalin at their lowest point since Pearl Harbor, Roosevelt considered his need to meet with Stalin clear and compelling, and to meet without Churchill. As Churchill prepared to sail for Washington, Roosevelt drafted a letter to Stalin wherein he proposed they choose an acceptable place to meet, perhaps Siberia or Alaska, but not Africa—too hot—and not an Atlantic venue such as Iceland, where Churchill, uninvited, might feel excluded. The letter, carried by the former ambassador to the Soviet Union Joseph Davies, was to be hand delivered, and Churchill was under no circumstances to be made aware of its existence. Churchill's claim on Roosevelt's time and attention was lessening in proportion to (as the president saw things) Roosevelt's growing stature within the alliance, a role cemented by virtue of American factory output, and armed forces that now numbered six million strong, and Roosevelt's conviction that he could make things right with Stalin if only they could sit down for an intimate chat.[151]

Early on May 11, RMS *Queen Mary* glided through the Verrazano Narrows and dropped anchor off Staten Island. The grand ship had spent half of the seven years since her maiden voyage in war service, as a troop transport. She was known around the fleet as the "Gray Ghost." Her prewar red-and-black smokestacks had been slathered with gray paint, as well as her black hull and pearl-white superstructure. Anti-aircraft guns rather than deck chairs now spread across the upper decks. Her interior finery—paneled walls, overstuffed settees, China services, acres of carpets, and the world map in the main dining room—had been carted off to New York warehouses at the start of the war, to be stored alongside the innards of *Queen Elizabeth* and *Normandie*. She could carry 16,000 troops, and had ferried almost that many to Australia shortly after the Japanese attacked Pearl Harbor. Her speed—almost thirty knots—made her uncatchable. No U-boat possessed the speed to plot a shot at her unless it found itself fortuitously positioned close abeam as she lunged past.

British and American cruisers had escorted the ship westward while Sunderland flying boats cruised overhead. Aboard the *Queen Mary* for this crossing were more than five thousand Italian and German prisoners of war captured in Tunisia, and destined for a not unpleasant internment in sunny midsouth locales. The prisoners were pleased with their fate; when taunted by Italian-speaking Americans in North Africa, they rejoined, "All right, laugh. But we're going to America. You're going to Italy." The highest-ranking German officers fared the best; they would be billeted at the Greenbrier Hotel in White Sulphur Springs, West Virginia, where they could buy from the Sears catalogue, where vegetable gardens were encouraged and coffee and tobacco were plentiful. Yet the Atlantic passage had not been pleasant for the prisoners, six days locked belowdecks, egress to the upper decks blocked by barbed wire and sandbagged machine gun emplacements manned by Royal Marines. The ship was infested with lice, the result of a previous cargo of kit bags that had been stored in a Cairo warehouse. The prisoners (or any German spies who scouted the ship in Scotland) might have concluded from numerous newly printed signs in Dutch hung throughout the vessel that somebody important—perhaps Queen Wilhelmena—was on board. Ramps that could accommodate a wheelchair had been conspicuously built in certain sections of the ship, as if in preparation for Franklin Roosevelt on the return voyage. That was exactly what British intelligence hoped the Germans would conclude.[152]

The prisoners would be marched off the ship under guard at a Hudson River pier. Another group of passengers would leave the ship here, at anchor in the outer harbor. Among them was Sir William Beveridge, on his way to an international food conference at Hot Springs, Virginia. Beveridge and his wife were not part of the official delegation—anointed "the holy of holies" by Ismay—and therefore had not been quartered in the part of the ship that had been hurriedly deloused for the comfort of the holies. As a result, by the time the *Queen Mary* reached New York, Sir William and Lady Beveridge "bore unmistakable signs of ravage." Max Beaverbrook and Averell Harriman were also on board, as well as Lord Cherwell and Lord Moran. The Chiefs of Staff and Archie Wavell were accompanied by a troop of almost one hundred staff officers. One passenger among the group traveled with a great many crates, boxes, and trunks packed with an odd assortment of habiliments. He was attended to by a platoon of private secretaries and Royal Marine bodyguards. *Queen Mary* had been chosen for the mission to ensure his safe passage. On deck, Air Commodore Spencer, attired incongruously in a navy blue yachting squadron jacket and cap, lit a cigar and gazed toward Manhattan, mostly hidden behind a steady mist and low fog. It had been almost forty-eight years since Winston Churchill first sailed into New York Harbor aboard the Cunard steamship *Etruria;* Victoria was queen and the sun never set on the Union Jack. Now Americans were singing a popular new tune, a syrupy hillbilly number composed by Paul Roberts and Shelby Darnell, "There's a Star-Spangled Banner Waving Somewhere."[153]

For the passengers on the two upper decks, the voyage had had about it a holiday atmosphere, made jollier with each new telegram from Alexander. On May 7, he cabled that the 1st United States Armored Division had entered Bizerte while the British had poured into Tunis. On the eighth, as Germans and Italians tried to flee Tunis by ship, Admiral Cunningham issued the order: "Sink, burn, and destroy. Let nothing pass." On the tenth, Churchill suggested to Attlee and Eden, in London, that England's church bells be rung that night. The date happened to be the third anniversary of his premiership. The bells were rung.[154]

Goebbels found the celebrations in London distasteful: "The capture of Tunis and Biserte is . . . blown up by the English as a sensational event. . . . All London is drunk with victory." Yet, Goebbels confessed, "We are indeed experiencing a sort of second Stalingrad."[155]

On board the *Queen Mary,* each day's news had been celebrated over long luncheons and longer evening meals followed by hands of bezique and poker. (Beaverbrook and Harriman agreed beforehand that they would not take advantage of Churchill's limited poker skills.) The African victory instilled in the pilgrims a sentiment absent from Allied ranks since Pearl Harbor: confidence.[156]

The principals talked their way across the Atlantic; or rather, they listened as Churchill spoke. Reverting to his opposition to the American Air Force daylight strategy and its paltry destruction of German industrial targets achieved at great cost to the fliers, he told Harriman he intended to voice his displeasure to Roosevelt. Harriman warned that the surest way to provoke the American Joint Chiefs to pack off their B-17s to the Pacific was for Churchill to denigrate the American effort in Europe. Churchill deferred to Harriman on the matter. During one of his shipboard monologues, Churchill put his hand on Beaverbrook's knee and said softly, "You don't talk anymore." Nobody could talk, Beaverbrook later told Harriman, "because the P.M. talks all the time." Yet the Beaver managed to produce "a tirade against the Poles" when informed by Churchill of a telegram from Stalin that excoriated HMG for allowing the London Poles to conduct their "anti-Soviet smear campaign." Beaverbrook—who Harriman considered naive about Stalin—threw his support to Stalin. Churchill threw his support to both Stalin and the Poles, a dual loyalty that could not end well. The subject changed to Burma. Churchill was displeased with Wavell's progress there, yet he and Wavell agreed that Burma was a malarial swamp unsuited for modern warfare. The British spring push in the western Burmese province of Arakan had ended in failure, and would have ended in utter disaster but for the inspired retreat brought off by General William ("Billy") Slim. Churchill held Wavell accountable. Wavell, in turn, fed up with Churchill's long-standing lack of faith in his abilities, threatened to resign. He did not, but only after Brooke told him that if he, Brooke, resigned every time Churchill took an unfair swipe at him, he'd have to do so "at least once a day." Brooke, for his part, told his diary that the upcoming Washington meetings "will entail hours of argument and hard work trying to convince [the Americans] that Germany must be defeated first...they will pretend to understand...and will continue as at present to devote the bulk of their strength to try and defeat Japan!!" Of the pending meetings, Brooke wrote, "I hate the thought of them."[157]

During a lifeboat drill five days out from New York, Churchill disclosed to Harriman that he had ordered a .50 caliber machine gun mounted on the lifeboat which was to carry the highest-ranking personages. "I won't be captured," he told Harriman. "The finest way to die is in the excitement of fighting the enemy." Harriman, distressed at the thought they might actually have to take to the lifeboats, reminded Churchill of his guarantee that a German torpedo could not sink the *Queen Mary*. "Ah," Churchill replied, "but they might put two into us." Here was the bluster of the old warrior who loved a good fight. Of the more than six thousand soldiers on board, Allied and Axis, very few had actually killed an enemy. Churchill had; several, in fact. He loved a fight, but he hated unnecessary fights that cost men their lives. So, too, did Marshall and Roosevelt. But the Americans' sensibilities were informed by politics, decency, reason, and the lessons of Scripture, to which as good Christians they subscribed. Churchill's sensibilities were informed from having witnessed slaughter firsthand on battlefields, in the Sudan and India in the previous century, in Belgium in 1916, and in London in 1940. More so than the American military chiefs, he could see the slaughter that would take place if an inadequate or ill-prepared Allied army landed on French beaches. In coming months, the conflict between his fertile imagination and his fervent desire to kill Germans took its toll on him, and on the alliance.[158]

Churchill loved a parade as much as a good fight. He proposed to Harriman, at Beaverbrook's prodding, to disembark the *Queen Mary* off Battery Park in order to make an unannounced progress by motorcar up Manhattan's avenues, no doubt to great and spontaneous popular acclaim in light of the news from North Africa. Harriman impressed upon the P.M. the dangers inherent in such a venture, the possibility of lurking Italian and Irish radicals, to say nothing of German operatives. With regret, Churchill withdrew his proposal and instead disembarked on Staten Island, where the presidential train, with Roosevelt's private car *Ferdinand Magellan* bringing up the rear, waited on a dockside spur. Harry Hopkins was on board, ready to greet his friend.[159]

Lunch was served during the run down to Washington, "small steak" being one of the menu choices. The entire British contingent went for the "small steak," which turned out to be so generous that none finished his portion. "It resembled a whole week's meat ration," Pug Ismay later wrote. "We were out of practice." By late afternoon on May 11, Churchill and Roosevelt were drinking cocktails in Roosevelt's oval study upstairs at the White House. The following day, Sir John Anderson learned that the supplies of Canadian uranium and heavy water Britain needed in order to produce an atomic bomb had been purchased by the United States—the entire Canadian production capacity. The Americans had frozen Britain out of the Manhattan Project. Indeed, there was much to discuss with the president.[160]

On May 13, Churchill received a message from Alexander: "Sir, it is my duty to report that the Tunisian campaign is over.... We are masters of the

North African shores." Arnim had been captured by the British on Cap Bon along with 150,000 prisoners who included twelve generals and 110,000 Germans. All of this since Churchill set sail. The *New York Times* reported that when a German general approached Bernard Freyberg somewhere north of Enfidaville and asked for peace terms, the New Zealand commander replied: "Unconditional surrender." British tanks, with infantry hanging on their sides, were taking joy rides along the coastal roads of Cap Bon. Every time a tank swung its gun, groups of Germans and Italians rose from the scrub and poppies, hands raised. It was like a grouse shoot; everybody among the Allies took their bag. The French, defeated in 1940, captured 25,000 Axis troops, the Americans almost 38,000, of whom almost 34,000 were Germans. That brought to 400,000 the total of Axis prisoners taken in North Africa since November, at a cost to the British Eighth and First Armies of 35,000 killed, wounded, and missing. The Americans lost about 18,000 killed, wounded, and missing.[161]

The war in North Africa was over. The genesis of the victory, Averell Harriman believed, lay in Churchill's "desperate gamble" in late 1940 to send England's tanks to Egypt at the moment of the Home Island's and the Empire's greatest peril.[162]

A few days after arriving in Washington, Churchill told the U.S. Congress that "the proud German Army has once again proved the truth of the saying, 'The Hun is always either at your throat or at your feet'; and that is a point which may have its bearing upon the future. But for us, arrived at this milestone in the war, we can say 'One Continent redeemed.' "[163]

On the day of the North African surrender, Mussolini took himself off to Rocca delle Caminate, his summer palace near Forlì, where he spent several days clipping articles from newspapers and underlining stories about the African campaign with red and blue crayons. The strut had left his step. His aides noticed that where once his desk was a paradigm of order, it was now cluttered, "like a junk-stall with half opened books, Fascist badges and medals, sheaves of wheat bound in tricolour ribbon." He was embittered, and believed Italians had lost their will to fight, due in part to dozens of Allied air raids on Genoa, Turin, and Naples. The raids had had the effect Churchill intended. Rome's turn came on May 16. The RAF had been hitting Italy in spot raids for almost three years; now hundreds of American B-17s appeared over Rome. Il Duce concluded the bombing was a prologue to the invasion of Sicily (not Corsica or Sardinia, or southern France, or Greece, as was thought in Berlin). And after Sicily, Mussolini believed, the Italian mainland would be the Allies' next target.[164]

Il Duce's instincts were sound, but he no longer had the power to inspire his people to heroic resistance, or to convince Berlin that Sicily was the next target. As he was prone to wild pronouncements, and evidencing the onset of either failing nerves or senility, his opinion was ignored in Berlin.

A *New York Times* headline that week read: INDIA STAFF HERE: WAVELL'S PRESENCE SEEN AS HINT OF EARLY ACTION AGAINST JAPANESE. The *Times* of London ran a similar story, prompting Clementine to write to her husband, "I'm worried at the importance given by the Press...to the presence of Wavell...in your party. I'm so afraid the Americans will think that a Pacific slant is to be given to the next phase of the war.... *Surely* the liberation *must* come first." She had perfectly captured Brooke's fear, and Churchill's, and England's.[165]

To a degree, Wavell's presence at the conference was about taking the war to Japan, but not by way of Burma, where the weak British winter push toward Akyab had been mauled by the troops of Major General Masakazu Kawabe. Churchill and Brooke had decided on their way to Washington to tell Roosevelt that Operation Anakim, the planned invasion of southern Burma, was off the table until 1944. The manpower and resources simply did not exist. Still, two strategies for taking the fight to Japan by way of China were debated in Washington, and Burma played a role in each. Joe Stilwell favored an overland strategy from India, through northern Burma and into China. Yet MacArthur was siphoning off the American troops that had been allotted to Stilwell, and Stilwell's Chinese troops showed no fight. Claire Chennault, who sought to configure his Fourteenth Air Force on Chinese soil as soon as possible, championed an aerial strategy conducted against Japan from bases in China. Wavell saw the obvious flaw in Chennault's plan: China had no gasoline refineries and no means of fueling bomber groups or fighter squadrons. In fact, Allied DC-4 transports flying over the eastern Himalayas—"the Hump"—to deliver fuel and ammunition to China had to make room in their cargo bays for the gasoline needed for the return trip to India. The lack of available troops (especially American troops), tanks, and trucks argued against Stilwell, who concluded that his theater of war was neglected because "Churchill has Roosevelt in his pocket.... The Limeys are not interested in the war in the Pacific, and with the president hypnotized they are sitting pretty." Stilwell, fluent in Mandarin Chinese, respected the Chinese people but thought Chiang corrupt and inept. Although Churchill thought little of Stilwell's plan, he was in complete agreement with Vinegar Joe's assessment of Chiang. Neither Stilwell nor Chennault could put forth any plan to help Chiang that could be seriously considered until Burma was retaken, and for this endeavor there was no plan, only a name. When it came to capturing Burma, Churchill told Brooke, "You might as well eat a porcupine one quill at a time."[166]

Churchill soon shifted his animal analogy from porcupine to shark: "Going into the jungles to fight the Japanese is like going into the water to fight a shark." Instead, he believed the Allies should "set a trap or capture him on a hook." The best place to set such a trap, he concluded, was the northern tip of Sumatra, from where the Royal Navy could harass Japanese supply lines between Tokyo and Singapore. This strategy soon exercised a hold over him, much the same as had Jupiter, the invasion of northern Norway.[167]

Contrary to the *New York Times* headline, Wavell's presence in Washington had more to do with India than with taking the fight to Japan. Churchill thought it time to shuffle the entire command structure in India and Burma, by way of appointing a new viceroy and new commander for Indian military affairs, and creating the position of supreme commander, Southeast Asia. The latter position would not be going to Wavell, about whose aggressiveness Churchill still voiced doubts. No, he had his eye on Wavell for viceroy of India. Eden had politely refused the offer for fear it would end his career; traditionally the viceroy was made a lord, and lords were traditionally denied the premiership. Churchill's choice of Wavell as viceroy, therefore, would signal to Roosevelt that HMG thought that the situation in India demanded a strong military hand rather than a deft political touch.

Churchill favored Auchinleck for commander in chief, India. He liked Air Vice Marshal Sholto Douglas, formerly of Fighter Command, now RAF chief in the Middle East, for the head of the new Southeast Asia Command, or SEAC. Churchill thought the appointment was inspired, in part because Douglas, as an airman, would better appreciate the logistics of supplying Chiang's forces by air. The Americans objected to Douglas. He was as vocal a critic of America as Stilwell was of Britain, and his transparent ambition, as well as his part in the downfall of the hero of the Battle of Britain, Hugh Dowding (who had been kicked upstairs to Washington), were well known on the Potomac. For their part, the Americans began to refer to SEAC as See England Acquire Colonies, so firm was their belief that Churchill wanted to regain his lost Asian domains and had no intention of helping Chiang.[168]

During the two weeks of Trident, Roosevelt gave Churchill what he sought on the atomic bomb project: full cooperation and a promise to share the finished product, which Roosevelt thought might be ready for use in the current war, which he believed might last into 1946 or even 1947. Churchill informed the War Cabinet that a formal agreement would follow. The president also finally acted on Harriman's March suggestion and directed the War Shipping Administration to transfer more ships to the British flag—fifteen to twenty hulls per month. Yet Roosevelt had been singing that tune for months; this latest promise, too, would go unfulfilled. Admiral King and MacArthur needed those hulls. The shadow of King and his Pacific strategy darkened every meeting, from the British standpoint. "The swing toward the Pacific is stronger than ever," Brooke complained to his diary, "and before long they will be urging that we defeat Japan first!"[169]

Brooke believed the Americans felt they had been "led down the garden path" by Torch and Husky, "and now they are not going to be led astray again." France and only France formed the core of George Marshall's strategic plan. Yet there existed one simple and sublime way to satisfy Marshall as well as avoid a full American tilt toward the Pacific, and that was for the British to wait until the Americans insisted upon a date for the invasion of France, which they did, and then agree to it, which the British chiefs did. In doing so, Churchill and Brooke gave Roosevelt and Marshall what they had all along demanded. Acceding to the cross-Channel strategy ensured that the president's and Marshall's attention would be focused at least as much on the European front as on the Pacific. The date agreed upon was May 1, 1944. But whether this was to be the small-scale landing, Sledgehammer, or the larger investment, Roundup, was not decided. So much confusion attached to just what exactly these code names meant that at the State Department and around Eisenhower's headquarters, the newly proposed operation was referred to as Roundhammer. Whatever they chose to call it, it meant that yet another pledge made at Casablanca, and the most important to Stalin—to put men somewhere into France by August 1943—would go begging for another year.[170]

Churchill did, however, have in mind a supreme commander for the invasion, Alan Brooke. That a British general should assume command seemed self-evidently correct to Churchill. After all, Britain had far more men, planes, tanks (albeit many were American built), and ships within the European and North African theaters than did the Americans. As well, at the time of Eisenhower's appointment as commander of Torch, there had been an implied understanding (as Churchill saw it) between himself and Roosevelt that a Briton would command the invasion of France. A committee had been set up to plan that invasion (soon code-named Overlord), headed by an Englishman, Lieutenant General Frederick E. Morgan, whose title was COSSAC—Chief of Staff to the Supreme Allied Commander (designate). Morgan shared with Marshall the belief in a straight-line approach to Germany. He took his assignment seriously and was in no way inclined to put on a show of championing the merits of Overlord simply to placate (or deceive) the Americans.

Churchill and Brooke, too, were believers in Overlord, but only if the operation was undertaken when Germany was on the ropes, put there by the Red Army in the east, the RAF in the west, and Allied armies in Italy and the Balkans (if Churchill had his way). Although they believed it self-evidently true that to go into France prematurely invited calamity, they had agreed to the May 1, 1944, date without proposing the invasion be conditional upon certain objectives having first been met. This lapse in communication invited trouble with Marshall and Roosevelt, which duly arrived in coming months. Meanwhile, from Churchill's perspective, if these conditions were met by the agreed-upon invasion date of May 1, 1944, Brooke should command Overlord. One of Brooke's friends, upon return from Algiers, reported to him that Eisenhower had been quite firm in his belief that only two men were qualified to lead the invasion: George Marshall and Sir Alan Brooke. Brooke was therefore thrilled when, two weeks after Trident, Churchill told him of his likely promotion to supreme commander. The CIGS felt the appointment would be "the perfect climax to all my struggles to guide the strategy of the war" in order to make such an invasion of France possible. Sworn to secrecy by Churchill, Brooke did not tell even his wife.[171]

While the Combined Chiefs of Staff clawed their way toward a consensus on strategy, the president and Churchill shadowboxed over postwar politics. As he had with Eden, Roosevelt outlined to Churchill his vision of postwar Europe, including a diminished France and an utterly destroyed Germany. This was the postwar Germany envisioned by Prof Lindemann and the American secretary of the treasury, Henry Morgenthau Jr., an old Roosevelt friend and fellow gentleman farmer above the Hudson River. Morgenthau, a dour fellow whom Roosevelt called Mr. Morgue, did not hate Germans, but he hated evil, and he especially hated Nazis. His Treasury Department would help determine the fate of Germany, for Lend-Lease was a program with immense foreign policy implications, but at its core it was a banking construct, controlled by the Treasury Department. Treasury, therefore, not State, would take the lead in determining how best to make Germany pay—literally and figuratively—for its transgressions. Morgenthau intended to extract a crushingly heavy price. Such were Morgenthau's sentiments. More significantly, Roosevelt shared them.

Churchill sought something else. During Trident he proposed to Roosevelt a plan for postwar security that consisted of a world council and three regional councils, Asian, North and South American, and European, within which blocs and federated associations would form bulwarks against aggression. The greatest bloc of all would take the form of a "fraternal association" between America and Britain, including a continuation of the Combined Chiefs of Staff. It was all very similar to the ideas he unveiled in his March broadcast, and that Eden conveyed to Roosevelt and Hull during his visit to Washington. Churchill also proposed a "Danubian federation," with Vienna the seat of government, a democratic federation of states, including Bavaria, that would fill the void left by the disappearance of the old Austrian-Hungarian Empire. This new state, in loose alliance with Great Britain (ideally, in partnership with America) and a rejuvenated France, could defend itself against incursions by other powers, including a reinvigorated Germany and the Soviet Union, should Stalin manifest postwar expansionist proclivities. If Stalin proved true to his word and adhered to the twenty-year friendship treaty, France would assume its old role of containing Germany in the west while the Soviets contained it in the east. Germany (demilitarized), however, would emerge as a contributing partner to the economic rejuvenation of Europe. Even Stalin would need German steel after the war. Eden's policy, taking shape at the Foreign Office, was based on three goals: to contain Germany, to resurrect France, and to be prepared to contain the Soviets. "These arrangements," Eden wrote in a memorandum, "will be indispensable for our security whether or not the United States collaborate in the maintenance of peace on this side of the Atlantic." To American ears, all of this had the ring of "spheres of influence" and "alliances," both military and economic, the very structures that had led not only to the current war but to every European conflict since the early Middle Ages.[172]

Where Roosevelt and the State Department saw the greatest threat to postwar Anglo-American relations in Churchill's old order, Churchill increasingly saw it in Stalin's new order. How far west Stalin's influence spread in Europe would initially be determined by where the Soviet and Anglo-American armies met at the end of the war. That was why postwar Anglo-French solidarity meant so much to London despite de Gaulle and his inability to get along with anyone. It meant little to Washington. Roosevelt believed he did not need Frenchmen (especially de Gaulle) to win the war, but Churchill needed a resurgent France to win the peace in Europe. As much as he disliked de Gaulle, he understood that the people of occupied France saw de Gaulle as their savior. Reports circulating in London claimed 80 percent of Frenchmen considered Charles de Gaulle their "symbol of resistance." Roosevelt in turn, and based on Robert Murphy's facile reports from Africa, considered such sentiments nothing more than Gaullist propaganda. He made his thoughts on the subject sneeringly clear in a memorandum he prepared for Churchill during Trident: "He [de Gaulle] may be an honest fellow but he has the Messianic complex." The people of France were behind the Free French movement, Roosevelt believed, but not behind de Gaulle, whose "conduct continues to be more and more aggravated." It was clear to Roosevelt that "when we get into France itself we will have to regard it as a military occupation." He proposed to dump de Gaulle and his French National Committee and oversee the formation of "an entirely new French Committee and subject its membership to the approval of you and me." Churchill later recalled that "not a day went by" in Washington without Roosevelt expressing his "stern" feelings about de Gaulle.[173]

Harangued by Roosevelt, Churchill cabled London on May 21 and advised that HMG break off relations with de Gaulle. Eden replied immediately with a strong dissenting opinion. Giraud and de Gaulle had agreed to meet in Algiers the next week to consummate their marriage by way of creating a new French National Committee. Would it not be wiser, Eden asked, to await the results of that meeting before making such a profound decision? Churchill agreed. A final decision could wait until after Giraud and de Gaulle met. In this decision, Churchill displayed a consistency he held to throughout the war. He deferred (often with great reluctance) to his Chiefs of Staff in military matters, and he deferred (again, often with reluctance) to the War Cabinet in strictly political matters. As a believer in the "Parl" he could not do otherwise. Eden later kidded him about his back-and-forth on de Gaulle, attributing the duality of his opinions to his being half American. But both knew the real reason Churchill inclined to bow to Roosevelt lay with the increasing leverage the Americans had over the British. Here, Eden served the P.M. well, as did Brooke on military affairs, by steering Churchill away from his more incendiary and quixotic inclinations, political or military. In turn, he led them forward, relentless in his quest for their common objective: victory.[174]

Yet, how to fight the war, not how to manage the French or the postwar world, was why Trident had been convened. Left unresolved as the talks neared their end was the strategic question Churchill considered the most critical: where to go after Sicily. What would become of twenty battle-hardened divisions, of Tedder's four thousand aircraft and Cunningham's navy? The momentum of the African victory and the pending Sicily campaign must be maintained. Churchill for his part had Italy and Mussolini in his sights. Only one obstacle stood in his way: George Marshall. Late on May 25, Marshall stopped by Roosevelt's office to say his good-byes to Churchill. He found the two leaders putting the finishing touches on a communiqué to Stalin before setting off to bed. Roosevelt had told Churchill that if he wanted to argue the case for invading Italy, he'd have to stay in Washington for another week. That would not do. Churchill had been gone from London for almost four weeks. He would be off just after sunrise, to visit Alexander and Eisenhower in Algiers. Marshall, having paid his respects, was about to leave, when Roosevelt said, "Why don't you go with Winston?" Coming from the commander in chief, this was more an order than a suggestion. It was now past 2:00 A.M. Churchill was due to depart in six hours. The dutiful Marshall had so little time to pack for the trip that he left his dress slacks behind. But he made the flight.[175]

Churchill and Marshall departed Washington aboard the Boeing Clipper *Bristol,* bound for Newfoundland, the first leg of the journey to Algiers. Accompanying Churchill, along with Marshall, were Ismay and Brooke, as well as Churchill's doctor, Lord Moran, himself the victim of a stomach virus that would force him to leave off at Gibraltar and return to London. Churchill's stenographer Patrick Kinna, was on board, having become in his twenty-two months of service a trusted member of the team. Scotland Yard's Thompson and another detective were also on hand, as was Captain Richard Pim, the caretaker of the maps, all of which were rolled and stowed. Sawyers the valet served, as usual, in his capacity as quartermaster of Churchill's beverages, his Quadrinox sleeping pills, and his hot-water bottle.[176]

The journey much impressed Brooke, who for every leg of every trip that year kept a log of the miles covered and time spent in the air (almost nine hours and 1,300 miles on the leg to Newfoundland). All on board signed one another's "short snorters." These were banknotes carried by those who had made a transatlantic flight, signed by others who had done the same. The "sect," as Brooke called it, was the idea of the first Americans who had undertaken the crossing. Anyone who failed to produce his short snorter upon demand forfeited a dollar or bought a short snort of whisky. In time, as such journeys became more frequent, the participants taped new banknotes to the old in order to accommodate the growing numbers of signatures. Churchill gamely signed his short snorters as the flying boat made its way north through steady mist. After a four-hour stopover at Botwood for dinner, and with foul weather dropping fast upon the coast, *Bristol* lifted off at dusk for the seventeen-hour flight to Gibraltar. The outside temperature was zero, inside not much warmer. Sometime during the night lightning struck the plane, twice. After spending a moonlit night seven thousand feet above the Atlantic, the group reached Gibraltar late in the afternoon of May 27, and stayed the night at the governor's residence. The next afternoon, they climbed into their new Avro York aircraft, a converted Lancaster fitted out with five berths, drawing room, lavatory, and eight windows to take in the views. By nightfall they were drawing warm baths in Algiers, at the villas of Cunningham and Eisenhower.[177]

On the day Churchill and Marshall departed Washington, a British convoy steamed into Alexandria after an uneventful two-thousand-mile run from Gibraltar through waters free of Axis mines and Axis ships. The Mediterranean was open for the first time since 1941. Brooke, always calculating shipping tonnage, concluded that an effective gain of one million tons of shipping was realized by cutting forty-five days and ten thousand miles from the London-to-Egypt voyage via the Cape of Good Hope.[178]

Allied shipping losses in May fell to 200,000 tons—about forty ships. But Dönitz paid with forty U-boats to attain those meager results, twice his losses for March and April when he had sent almost one million tons to the bottom. By June he had pulled his fleets back to the far eastern Atlantic. For the month of June, his U-boats claimed just six ships and 27,000 tons of Allied shipping, a 95 percent reduction from March. British aircraft equipped with microwave radar could now detect surfaced U-boats at night or in fog; coordinates were relayed to surface ships, which then closed in on the targeted submarines. Thirty-eight U-boats were lost to such tactics in the Bay of Biscay during May (called "Black May" in the *Kriegsmarine*) and early June, three fewer than the number of Allied merchantmen sunk in the Atlantic and Arctic oceans, and twelve more than the number of U-boats launched during those weeks. Even as he abandoned the western Atlantic, Dönitz's losses mounted. Since early 1943, British and American merchant ships had been launched faster than the U-boats could sink them, while increased Allied air patrols and the improvements in radar ensured that U-boats were being sunk in far greater numbers than Hitler could replace them. By July American ship construction outpaced losses from all sources—U-boats, mines, surface ships, and aircraft. America had finally hit its stride, building half again as much shipping that year (more than 12 million tons) than Britain produced during the entire war.

Churchill no longer fretted over either the strangulation or the invasion of Britain. Yet final victory was by no means imminent. The American armies had to mature and American shipbuilding had to reach even greater levels, levels that could sustain Britain, Russia, MacArthur, and a second European front all at the same time. "Henceforth," Churchill later wrote, "the danger was not destruction but stalemate."[179]

Beaverbrook agreed. "There seems a real danger," he wrote to Harry Hopkins, "that we shall go on indefinitely sewing the last button on the last gaiter." If the Allies were not prepared to assume the risks and suffer the casualties of a second front, "then let us concentrate at once exclusively on the production of heavy bombers and think in terms of 1950." Churchill had told the U.S. Congress much the same when on May 19 he cautioned, "No one can tell what new complications and perils might arise in four or five more years of war. And it is in the dragging-out of the war at enormous expense, until the democracies are tired or bored or split, that the main hopes of Germany and Japan must now reside. We must destroy this hope."[180]

Every North African port from Alexandria to Casablanca was full of warships, troop transports, landing craft, and cargo ships. Of the one million men holding the North African shore, 160,000 of them would be going to Sicily. Like Lincoln in the months after Grant drove his men across the Rapidan toward Richmond, Churchill now knew his army—British, colonial, French, and American—had gained confidence and strength in the killing fields of North Africa. This army must not be brought to a halt. It had to push on. Such a force had to be led to greater triumphs, to the end.

Churchill told Marshall and Eisenhower that this monstrous machine, once set in motion, could be recalled only with great difficulty. To take this army only as far as Sicily would be to defy momentum, and to defy the strategic maxim to always exploit gains. "Keep on until you get Italy," he told Eisenhower, again and again. Within forty-eight hours of arriving in Algiers, Churchill brought Marshall and Eisenhower around to fundamental agreement. By air and sea the Allies would pound Italy. The rail yards of Rome, just five miles from the Vatican, were the first target. (Churchill, while in Washington, had assured New York archbishop Francis Spellman that precautions had been taken to avoid destroying the Eternal City itself.) Airpower alone might drive Italy out of the war. If it did not, the army could. The final decision to land it on the Italian mainland would rest with Eisenhower. Where on the boot of the mainland the Allies might strike after Sicily would depend on how many Germans poured into Italy, and where they set up their defense. If the Germans drew their line north of the Po River, an Allied thrust toward Tuscany would cut off any Axis forces to the south and avoid a four-hundred-mile slog up the boot. Another strategy entailed stabbing into Naples, followed by a quick run north to Rome. Churchill was so sure that Italy was ripe for the kill that he told Eisenhower that British civilians would gladly halve their rations for a month if it helped flush Italy from the war, an outcome that might, he proposed, come in time for the two of them—himself and Eisenhower—to meet in Rome for Christmas dinner.[181]

Marshall endorsed the Italian gambit, but like Churchill in Washington (who neglected to stipulate the conditions necessary for Overlord to proceed), Marshall failed to articulate a belief that he held to be self-evident: operations in Italy, whatever form they took, would in no way interfere with the planning and execution of Overlord. This oversight, like Churchill's, would lead to trouble within the Anglo-American ranks before the year was out.

Marshall went home and Eisenhower put his staff to work to determine where in Italy to strike. Churchill's demeanor accordingly grew gay. "I have no more pleasant memories of the war than the eight days in Algiers and Tunis," he later wrote. On one morning, an Eisenhower aide found Churchill breakfasting in bed on "one bottle of white wine, one bottle of soda, and a bucket of ice." He was in fine fettle. He had prevailed. On June 1, the party flew to Tunis and motored on to Carthage, where Churchill addressed the troops in the Roman amphitheater. The acoustics were so perfect that no loudspeakers were needed. That night at dinner Churchill offered, "Yes, I was speaking where the cries of Christian virgins rent the air whilst roaring lions devoured them, and yet I am no lion and am certainly not a virgin." At another dinner, the table had been set for thirteen, but "in deference to British superstition," Eisenhower's aide, Harry Butcher, was invited to make it fourteen. When the talk turned to diaries, Churchill proclaimed the practice was foolish because a diary reflected only the daily intuitions and emotions of the writer, which events might later prove incorrect or unsound, thereby making the diarist appear the fool. For his part, Churchill said he'd prefer to wait until the war was over to write his impression, such that "if necessary he could correct or bury his mistakes." All in all, Brooke concluded, Churchill was "in remarkable form." He was, but for de Gaulle.[182]

De Gaulle's presence in Algiers unsettled him. To Clemmie he wrote, "Everyone here expects he [de Gaulle] will do his utmost to make a row and assert his personal ambition." To counter that prospect, the British had secreted out of France General Alphonse Georges (whom Brooke had last seen during the doomed defense of Brittany). It was hoped that the new French Committee would be sufficiently packed with anti-Gaullists such as Georges to keep the tall Frenchman in line. After lunching with Giraud and Georges, Churchill wrote Clementine, "In their company I recaptured some of my vanished illusions about France and her Army." Within two days, the gathered Frenchmen defied Churchill's low expectations and agreed to form the French Committee of National Liberation. It appeared that de Gaulle's influence would be diluted by the presence of Giraud and Georges. Roosevelt believed the agreement would be short-lived and told Churchill that whatever the French agreed to among themselves, they still operated under Anglo-American martial law. “The bride [de Gaulle] evidently forgets there is still a war in progress,” Roosevelt wrote. “Good luck in getting rid of our mutual headache.” But getting rid of the Frenchman was not that simple. Within weeks, at de Gaulle’s insistence, the new French Committee demanded official recognition as the government in exile of France. Roosevelt refused, demanding, as he had during Churchill’s visit to Washington, that France when freed was to be “occupied” by Anglo-American forces until such time Frenchmen chose their own government. He offered to “accept” the French Committee but not to recognize it.[183]

And so, on the afternoon of June 4, with no movement on the French question, Churchill boarded his Avro York for the flight to Gibraltar, having brought the Fighting French as close to solidarity as he could, and having brought Marshall around. At the last minute he asked Alexander to accompany him to London to settle some matters known only to himself. Alexander—in the thick of planning the Sicily campaign—could only acquiesce. This meant the York now had one passenger too many. Churchill, in a snap judgment, told Pug Ismay that he must depart the aircraft because “he was very heavy and would overload the airplane.” Ismay grabbed his suitcase and hitched a ride on a transport, which subsequently experienced an engine fire on the way to Gibraltar. Neither Alexander nor Ismay “felt in the least aggrieved” by Churchill’s “deliciously ingenuous lack of consideration” for their personal safety and convenience because “we knew he would treat himself in exactly the same way—and worse—if he thought it would help the war.” Churchill had planned to transfer at Gibraltar to a Boeing flying boat for the final leg of the trip, but hideous weather forced him instead to go by B-24 Liberator. He arrived home the next morning. He had been out of the country for a month.[184]

That day, a German spy at the Lisbon airport reported to his superiors that a thickset man smoking a cigar had been seen boarding a commercial flight, another flying boat, destination London. Phone calls were made, German fighter aircraft scrambled. The hapless aircraft was shot down over the sea, killing all fourteen passengers, including the popular screen actor Leslie Howard. The brutality of the Germans, Churchill later wrote, “was only matched by the stupidity of their agents.” Yet, he wrote, his safe arrival home was another example of the “inscrutable workings of fate.”[185]

The incident unsettled Britons. The prime minister was out there somewhere in the air, and Britons felt ill at ease about his absence. Upon his safe return, Panter-Downes wrote: “It’s not only the conventional clucking old ladies who are hoping to goodness that the Prime Minister won’t find it necessary to make any more long and dangerous trips for quite a while.” It was the week of the favorable June moon. No invasion forces sailed for Sicily, but they were ready, and waiting, as was Churchill. The lunar cycle put July 9 in the middle of the three most favorable nights for action.[186]

Churchill had long voiced hopes that Stalin would emerge from the war as a guarantor rather than a disturber of the peace. He envisioned Poland and Czechoslovakia—along with Britain and America—standing "together in friendly relations with Russia." Yet in June, Poland's formal relations with Stalin, already suspended, ceased altogether, while Anglo-American relations with Russia reached, in Harriman's estimation, the "low point in the history of the alliance." When apprised of the decisions made during Trident, Stalin scorned them. He briefly pondered Roosevelt's request for a private meeting but declined as soon as he learned of the postponement of a second front until 1944. There was no point in meeting and nothing to discuss. He spit out identical and bitter messages to Roosevelt and Churchill wherein he listed their previous promises for a second front in 1943 and warned that the Soviet government "cannot align itself with this decision, which... may gravely affect the subsequent course of the war." He told them, "Your decision creates exceptional difficulties for the Soviet Union... and leaves the Soviet Army... to do the job alone." Churchill tried to mollify him: "I quite understand your disappointment but" the best way to help Russia would be by "winning battles and not by losing them" and certainly not by throwing away 100,000 men in a false start on French beaches. That produced even greater bitterness: "You say you 'quite understand' my disappointment," Stalin replied, pointing out that Churchill could not understand, because he was not in Moscow to witness the fact that "the preservation of Soviet confidence in its Allies... is being subjected to severe stress."[187]

Harriman arrived in London late in the month, sent by Roosevelt on another difficult mission: to inform Churchill that Roosevelt had asked for a one-on-one meeting with Stalin, was rebuked, and was now asking again. Harriman told Churchill over a dinner that lasted into the early morning. After all, Harriman argued, you and Brooke went to Moscow in August to make the relationship personal. Why should the president not do likewise? Churchill voiced disappointment, yet he appeared to understand Roosevelt's rationale. But overnight, as the disappointment turned to hurt and then anguish, he changed his mind. The following morning he shot off a cable to Washington in which he argued that his journey to Moscow the previous year was intended to get the relationship going, whereas if Roosevelt met with Stalin at this juncture, it would appear to Britons—and the world—to be a slight to Britain. He was correct, yet his opposition was unnecessary. Stalin had no intention of meeting Roosevelt. He ignored a request from Roosevelt to allow American bombers to land in Russia after attacking the Romanian Ploesti oil fields (54 of 178 American bombers were lost on the mission). He had recalled Maisky from London and Litvinov from Washington. There was an atmosphere now "alarmingly reminiscent" of the tensions that preceded the Molotov-Ribbentrop pact of 1939. That is, the question of Stalin making a separate peace, never far below the surface for months, had again bobbed into view. "It was fortunate," Robert Sherwood later wrote, "that Hitler did not know how bad relations were between the Allies at that moment, how close they were to a disruption which was his only hope of survival." Churchill grew so tired of Stalin's diplomatic obduracy that he stopped communicating with him for weeks. There was no more to say.[188]

Late on July 9, the largest armada in history hove to thirty miles off the coast of Sicily, 2,600 troop transports, tankers, and ammunition ships, landing craft, and warships, divided about equally between American and British. The British contingent, carrying Montgomery's Eighth Army, lay off the southeast coast, between Cape Passero and Syracuse. The American ships carrying Patton's Seventh Army aligned themselves roughly between landfalls near Ragusa and Licata, in the west. They had sailed from every North African port, as well as from Canada, Britain, and the United States, from where an entire infantry division was dispatched with all its rations, Jeeps, field guns, trucks, fuel, and ammunition. The men on board the troop ships knew that almost 200,000 Italians and 35,000 Germans waited on shore, although some relief was found in reports that three or four Italian and one German division were deployed in the far northwest corner of the island, having been taken in by false radio messages and an Allied naval feint in that direction. Still, the men knew that the Hermann Göring Division was dug in behind the American beaches. Though torn up in Tunisia, the men and panzers of the Hermann Göring Division were still ready for whatever came their way.

The Allies had no doubts as to Kesselring's willingness to fight. Success depended in large part upon the Italians displaying the same lack of warrior spirit they had shown before the surrender of Pantelleria, an island fortress midway between Tunis and Sicily. Pantelleria—called the Italian Gibraltar—was crisscrossed by tunnels and redoubts and protected by dozens of artillery batteries and squadrons of fighter planes. Mussolini had long pledged that the garrison would fight to the last man. In early July, an Allied fleet began shelling the island. After a week of naval and aerial shelling, and as Allied landing craft circled off the coast, awaiting final orders to make for Pantelleria's lone beach, the garrison's commander signaled that he was out of water and ran up the white flag. He had received permission to do so directly from Mussolini, who was now certain that he alone was the last Italian willing to fight. Mussolini's doctor had for a long time been dosing his patient with ever increasing amounts of Bellafolina and Alucol for the stomach cramps that afflicted Il Duce in times of stress, especially stress brought on by military defeats. The regimen was now administered on almost a daily basis. The patient, in fact, was as broken as his people.[189]

Churchill, who thought that three thousand Italians at most garrisoned Pantelleria, had made a wager with Eisenhower: five centimes (one-twentieth of a cent) for each Italian captured beyond the three thousand Churchill predicted. Eleven thousand surrendered. Eisenhower chose not to collect his four dollars from Churchill.[190]

Now, on July 9, as his fleets battled the seas, Eisenhower pondered whether the Italians on Sicily would put up more of a fight when the Allied armies went ashore at dawn. The weather was already proving itself a formidable enemy, a gale out of the west worsened as the flotilla approached Sicily. On Malta, Eisenhower pondered maps and weather reports in his headquarters, deep inside a tunnel in the Lascaris Bastion, built by the Knights of Malta and used since the start of the war as a communications center by the Royal Navy. Admiral Andrew ("ABC") Cunningham's meteorologists had given Eisenhower hourly updates as the day progressed, and a tutorial on the Beaufort scale—a measure of wind and waves on a scale of one to twelve. Each hourly report was worse than the previous. Air Marshal Tedder, at Eisenhower's side in the tunnels, noted the audacity of an attempt to invade Italy by sea: "Fancy invading Italy from the south. Even Hannibal had the sense to come in with his elephants over the Alps." All day, vast fleets of aircraft passed overhead as even more departed from Malta's newly reconditioned airfields, all on their way to bomb Sicilian beaches and two dozen Axis airfields. Late in the evening Eisenhower stepped outside to watch paratroopers from the American 82nd Airborne Division and the British 1st Air Landing Brigade sail overhead toward their drop zones. The British troops were in towed gliders, many of which, cut loose too soon, lost their way in the winds and the darkness and dropped into the sea with the loss of all aboard.[191]

As Eisenhower watched the aerial flotilla drift by, a cable arrived from Marshall: "Is the attack on or off?" Eisenhower had no answer and did not reply. But the hour was fast approaching when the landings could not be aborted. Montgomery's forces, on the east side of Sicily, found themselves in the lee of the wind, Patton's troops, with no protection from the prevailing winds, had a rough ride. If all went well, the three American and four British and Canadian divisions would stake a claim to more than one hundred miles of Sicily by dinnertime on the tenth. As the troop ships marked time, the cruisers, destroyers, and battleships of the fleet ran in along the coast and raked the beaches with high-explosive shells. But orders to go ashore had yet to come down. Then, toward midnight, the winds abated. Eisenhower had already decided that the invasion would go on, storms or no. The word went down to the men on the ships.[192]

That evening, Churchill and Clementine, with "customary instinct for the proper gesture," attended a showing of *Watch on the Rhine*. After the show Clementine, not feeling well, sent one of her handwritten notes to Pamela, requesting that she keep Churchill company as he parsed the news from Eisenhower's headquarters. The two passed the hours playing bezique, the game interrupted regularly by secretaries reporting the delays and deteriorating weather off the Sicilian coast. "I remember thinking," Pamela later recalled, "that if there is anything I can do for the war at least I have to stay awake to keep him company."[193]

Londoners went to bed that night, wrote Mollie Panter-Downes, with a sense of unease, not because of the pending battle in Sicily, about which they knew nothing, but because of the battle on the Russian front. It was clearly the most titanic struggle between armies in the history of the world, and it could go either way.[194]

It was developing along a 190-mile bulge in the lines—a salient—that looped around Kursk, a vital Soviet rail hub located between Orel and Kharkov about five hundred miles southwest of Moscow. Hitler had told his generals to "light a bonfire" there. Stalin, by virtue of Ultra decrypts (couched as the reports of "secret" agents) shared by the British, knew where and when Hitler would attack. The Germans struck on July 5, with 700,000 men, 2,400 tanks and assault guns, and 1,800 aircraft, hitting the salient from the north, west, and south. Opposing them were more than one million Soviet troops, 3,400 tanks and assault guns, and 2,100 planes. Another quarter million Soviet troops were held in reserve, near Kursk, about forty miles within the bulge. Thus, as just seven Anglo-American divisions and six hundred tanks went ashore in Sicily, two million Soviet and German men and almost six thousand tanks were fighting the greatest tank battle of all time. For the next week the world focused its undivided attention on Kursk.

Meanwhile, the aptly named Fighting French were at it again. De Gaulle, unable to fight Germans in Sicily because his North African army (actually

Giraud's army, as he was commander in chief) had been left in Tunisia, picked a fight with the British government over HMG's suppression of the Free French newspaper, *La Marseillaise*. It had been put out of business by the Ministry of Information, which cited war needs as the reason to withhold its newsprint. This was a clever tactic on the part of Brendan Bracken, and one that Londoners readily saw through, especially as anti-Russian Polish newspapers were again free to print as many copies as they liked. De Gaulle regularly was his own worst enemy, yet Londoners remembered that he had been the only Frenchman to back England in June 1940 when it appeared that London would follow Paris into the Nazi maw. For this he had garnered the respect of Britons. Churchill believed with Roosevelt that France was greater than de Gaulle, but he reluctantly disagreed with Roosevelt and Hull, who considered the Cross of Lorraine not worth bearing.

For Roosevelt, the French Empire stood behind only the British Empire on his list of entities he sought to dissolve after the war. "Governing authorities in Washington," Eden wrote in a Foreign Office memo, "have little belief in France's future and indeed do not wish to see France again restored as a great imperial power." If Roosevelt could abet that outcome by ignoring the Fighting French and de Gaulle, so much the better.[195]

"American hatred of him [de Gaulle] is keen," Eden wrote in a memorandum that July week. And now it had come to a head. Roosevelt again, as he had in May, wanted Churchill to break with de Gaulle, leaving Giraud (who, against the advice of the Foreign Office, was visiting Roosevelt that week) in sole control of the French Committee of National Liberation. Churchill was so fed up with de Gaulle that he told Eden the Foreign Office's support of de Gaulle might precipitate a break between Eden and himself. The message to Eden was clear: only one of them would survive such a fissure, and it would not be Anthony. Eden stood fast, based on his belief that "American policies toward France would jeopardize their relations and ours with that country for years to come." Churchill relented on July 20. Eden found him to be "in good form" at dinner that evening, although his mood was darkened somewhat by the death of his black cat, Munich Mouser, who had taken himself off from No. 10 to the Foreign Office to expire. The cat, Churchill told Eden, "died of remorse and chose his death-bed accordingly." The two major obstacles to Roosevelt ridding himself of the troublesome Frenchman lay with Eden's persistence in aligning Churchill with the Foreign Office, and on French public opinion, which Roosevelt ignored. Weeks earlier the Resistance leader Jean Moulin had informed London that the National Council of the Resistance had met and called for the creation of a provisional government in Algiers presided over by de Gaulle, "the sole chief of French Resistance."[196]

De Gaulle's latest stunt over French newspapers played directly into

Roosevelt's hand, and distracted Churchill from the far more pressing events in Sicily and Kursk. Churchill feared that continued financing of the Fighting French (actually American financing, Britain being broke) would lead to a strain in Anglo-American relations, an outcome "that no one would like better than de Gaulle." Brooke told his diary: "A long tirade of abuse of de Gaulle from Winston which I heartily agreed with. Unfortunately his dislike for de Gaulle has come rather late, he should have been cast overboard a year ago." Yet Brooke the military man did not see the politics at the core of Eden's support of de Gaulle. Churchill, sustained by Eden's argument, grudgingly backed de Gaulle because he understood what Roosevelt did not: the Allies needed de Gaulle, and Britain would someday need France.[197]

Like de Gaulle, the Polish prime minister Władysław Sikorski had also brought his defeated soldiers to London when all was lost in the homeland. Unlike de Gaulle, Sikorski was respected *and* revered by Britons. But earlier in the week, as if to foreshadow the troubles that lay ahead for Poland, Sikorski, his daughter Zofia, and several aides were killed when their B-24 spun into the sea just seconds after taking off from Gibraltar. Sikorski's loss disrupted not only the Allied war effort but the postwar world and Poland's place in it. Since 1940 Sikorski had gotten along well with the Russians, who, as much as they now resented the "smear campaign" conducted by the London Poles over Katyn, respected Sikorski. If anyone could have navigated his way to a successful solution of the Polish-Soviet political crisis, it was Sikorski.[198]

The political subtleties and de Gaulle's behavior being parsed by Londoners during the first half of July were shunted to the rear when at midmonth it became clear that the German attack at Kursk was going nowhere. That week the Soviets mounted a counterattack toward Orel, north of the salient; within days the Germans were retreating westward across a three-hundred-mile front. A Soviet attack toward Belgorod, south of the salient, stalled, but Field Marshal Manstein informed Hitler that Army Group South lacked the reserves to hold back the Red Army much longer. The same could be said of Dönitz's ability to hold back Allied shipping in the Atlantic, where Germany was losing one U-boat per day on average. Churchill (who called U-boats "canaries") cabled Roosevelt, "My cat likes canaries... we have altogether 18 canaries this month."[199]

The news from Sicily and the Mediterranean was also welcome. After the men had gotten safely ashore on July 10, the Italians had receded from the beaches, and by the fifteenth, it appeared that Sicily might go into the bag within two or three weeks, despite ferocious German resistance. Reports from the Balkans indicated a precipitous fall in the morale of the twenty-four Italian divisions scattered from the Aegean islands to northern Yugoslavia. They would rather surrender to Anglo-American forces than be massacred by the Greeks, or by Tito's partisans. And in Italy, British intelligence concluded that the Italian forces south of Naples would surrender after putting up a token resistance if the Allies landed, but they would not surrender beforehand. The time to strike Italy proper was almost at hand.

By the third week of July, Montgomery's army, halfway to Messina, was meeting heavy resistance from the Hermann Göring Division at Catania, south of Mount Etna. The Eighth Army had the Germans to its front and several rivers and malarial wetlands on its flanks. Malaria began to fell more of Monty's men than did German bullets. But within the week, Montgomery's army resumed its slog toward Messina along the coastal plains. Patton, after a rough start on the beaches—also at the hands of the Hermann Göring Division—had detached a corps, which was now racing toward Palermo. The battle for Sicily was going well.

In June, Eisenhower had told Churchill that a decision on whether or not to invade Italy would depend upon how the Sicily operation turned out. But Eisenhower had made no decision about where in Italy the Allies would go after Sicily, or when. He rejected Naples as too far north. The toe of Italy, just across from Messina and 350 miles south of Rome, appeared as far as Eisenhower was willing to go. He did tell Jan Smuts, then in Algiers, that Rome should be the ultimate target. Eisenhower's German counterpart, Albert Kesselring, was already planning the escape of his forces from Messina, across the narrow straits to the mainland. He could contemplate such a withdrawal only because the Allies had not seen fit to cut off his escape route by invading the toe of Italy when they first went ashore in Sicily, an error Eisenhower grasped weeks later. Meanwhile, on July 19, seven hundred Allied heavy bombers hit the rail yards of Rome. John Martin assured Churchill that "the Pope has a good shelter." By the twenty-second, Patton's detached corps had taken Palermo, cutting Sicily in two.[200]

A visit to London by Secretary of War Henry Stimson during these days threw Churchill's plans for furthering his Italian gains into utter confusion. Stimson, seventy-five, a tough old trooper, had served as secretary of war under William Howard Taft and as a colonel of artillery in France during the Great War. He hated the Hun and was in agreement with Marshall in favor of the cross-Channel strategy. While in London he was told by one of the planners of the French invasion that any prolonged activity in the Mediterranean might threaten the timetable for operations in France.

This deeply troubled Stimson, who saw no future in Italy or the Balkans. When Churchill pointed out to him that Marshall had agreed to a push into Italy proper, Stimson rejoined that Marshall envisioned only temporary action there, perhaps to capture Italian airfields in order to take the bombing to southern Germany. This discussion took place while the Germans at Catania had stopped Montgomery in his tracks.

Churchill used that setback to paint a horrific picture for Stimson of the fate that would befall 50,000 Allied troops on the beaches of France were the Germans to show up in force, which they surely would. The Allies would be driven back into the sea, leaving "the Channel full of corpses" and the entire Western Front in disarray. Churchill added that were he C in C, he would not support Roundhammer (as Stimson mistakenly called the cross-Channel strike), but as prime minister he had pledged his support to whatever the Combined Chiefs decided upon. Stimson pronounced the entire episode a colossal double cross, "like hitting us in the eye." Arriving in Algiers, he told Eisenhower that Churchill "was obsessed with the idea of proving to history" that a Balkan strategy was wise "and would repair the damage history now records for [his] misfortunes at the Dardanelles in the last war." Eisenhower, in turn, feared that if he did not follow up the impending victory in Sicily, he'd be accused of "missing the boat." His aide, Harry Butcher, recorded the frustration at headquarters: "Yet our own government seems to want to slam on the brakes just when the going gets good." These were Churchill's feelings exactly.[201]

Stimson's intuitive reading of Churchill was correct. The secretary's suspicions would have been confirmed had he known that Churchill in mid-July had told the British Chiefs of Staff that the twenty-seven divisions allotted to the cross-Channel thrust "will not be equal to the task of landing and maintaining themselves on land." Instead, he again argued that Jupiter, the invasion of northern Norway, be brought back into play, and that Mountbatten's proposed aircraft carriers made of ice be used there in a supporting role. Stimson might have become unhinged had he been privy to Churchill's line of thought regarding Roundup. That operation, Churchill told the chiefs, should be relegated to the status of a feint. He proposed a similar strategy in Italy, in which he advocated luring German reinforcements into the toe of Italy: "we could contain them there with our right hand and hit out at Naples with our left."[202]

Stimson took himself home to Washington, intent on warning Roosevelt and Marshall of Churchill's wavering before Churchill appeared on the scene to ambush them all. That Churchill was coming to North America had been agreed upon midmonth when he and Roosevelt decided that their need to meet was acute and growing more so. Roosevelt had suggested September 1, but Churchill pushed for mid-August, as he believed events in

Sicily were fast outpacing plans. "I must say," Eden's parliamentary secretary Oliver Harvey told his diary, "the PM doesn't let the grass grow under his feet." The leaders settled upon Quebec City, mid-August, at the Citadel, where in 1759—the year of victories—on the Plains of Abraham, Wolfe and the English snatched Canada from Montcalm and the French. Churchill and Roosevelt invited Stalin, who withheld his response for almost two weeks before declining, although he did acknowledge the need to meet, and suggested a winter rendezvous. Churchill selected the code name for the Quebec meeting, Quadrant, and he put Italy at the top of the agenda. Smuts had sent him a report from Algiers in which he argued, "Rome may mean virtually Italy and its possession may mean this year a transition of transforming the whole war situation and next year finishing it." This was the position Churchill intended to stake out at Quadrant, for he respected Smuts's military judgment above all others', including, on rare occasion, his own. Yet wires had already been crossed; Eisenhower had agreed with Smuts on the need to take Rome at some point, but he had not agreed with Smuts on the timetable to attack Rome. General Ike had his sights set much lower down the leg of Italy.[203]

Churchill, enthused over Smuts's rosy predictions, sent Roosevelt a copy of Smuts's letter. Roosevelt replied, "I like General Smuts's idea and I hope something of that kind can be undertaken." That response would have mortified Stimson, but for Churchill, the president's message was as tasty as one of those Virginia hams the Americans so generously carried to London.[204]

Brooke, too, had reason in late July to allow a smile to crease his usually dour visage; Churchill for the third time in as many months told the CIGS that he was the man to lead the invasion of France, a mere feint was Churchill to have his way, but a vital command none the less. The occasion was a sherry party at No. 10, at which Churchill asked Brooke's wife, Benita, what she thought of her husband becoming the supreme commander of the invasion of France. She was stunned. Brooke had still not told his wife.[205]

On the hideously hot Sunday afternoon of July 25, King Victor Emmanuel III summoned Mussolini to the Villa Ada, where more than four hundred acres of gardens and forest scrubbed Rome's air of grime and heat. Mussolini, like Churchill, lunched with his king each week, on Mondays in Il Duce's case. The Sunday summons was anomalous but not necessarily troubling. Il Duce was well aware of the machinations of many within his Grand Council, including his son-in-law Count Ciano. The previous day, the council passed a motion that gave the King added powers, which amounted to a vote of no confidence in Il Duce. Yet, although his minions had mutinied, Mussolini had no doubts as to who would emerge triumphant; he had fought these political wars for more than two decades. This was, after all, *Anno XXI* of his rule.

The King, wearing a gray marshal's uniform and trousers seamed with red stripes, was at the villa's main door to greet his minister. They moved to a ground-floor salon. Mussolini stood as the King spoke. Things were not going well in Italy, the King offered. Even the Alpine Brigade—one of Italy's more storied units—was rumored to be on the verge of mutiny, and, most insultingly, the troops were singing a nasty little ditty about Il Duce. The council's vote, the King added, accurately reflected the country's feelings toward him. In that case, Mussolini replied, I should tender my resignation. He presumed the King would reject that idea. But Emmanuel did not. "I have to tell you," he replied, "that I unconditionally accept it." Mussolini slumped into a chaise. The King informed his former premier that he intended to appoint the old warrior and head of Mussolini's armies, Marshal Pietro Badoglio, as premier. He then offered to take Mussolini under his personal protection, since he, the King, was his only remaining friend in Italy. A car was waiting outside; it happened to be surrounded by several carabiniera. Il Duce understood: he was under arrest. Emmanuel had undone two decades of fascism in just twenty minutes.[206]

The German ambassador to Rome had the day before reported to Berlin that "Mussolini's position has never been stronger." The ambassador was soon recalled to Berlin. Goebbels lamented Il Duce's downfall to his diary: "It is simply shocking to think that in this manner a revolutionary movement that has been in power for twenty-one years could be liquidated."[207]

Badoglio, Ciano, and the Grand Council presumed that Fascist rule would be preserved, simply without Il Duce. But by nightfall, King Emmanuel, now an absolute monarch, dissolved the Italian Fascist Party. Badoglio, who was to be in charge of only civil authority, took to calling himself the King's executive assistant. The Italian people assumed that Emmanuel would secure peace with honor within days. Nobody in Rome seemed to consider how the Germans might react. The Italian people's renewed faith in royalty was to be short-lived. The new government signaled Berlin that it would continue the fight, but Goebbels and Hitler considered the message nothing more than a delaying tactic to afford Badoglio time to make a separate peace with the Allies. Indeed, within days, Italian diplomats in neutral capitals began to quietly extend peace feelers in the Allied direction.

Churchill learned of Il Duce's downfall at Chequers while watching a movie, *Sous les Toits de Paris,* in the company of Clementine, daughters Mary and Sarah, Alan Brooke, Lord Moran, and John Martin. The projector was stopped, the lights went up, and everyone clapped. London learned of the news during the BBC midnight broadcast, when the Roman decree announcing Mussolini's "resignation" was read. Harold Nicolson noted that the decree did not bear the date of *Anno XXI*. Violet Bonham Carter telephoned Nicolson, overjoyed because this meant the release of her son, Mark, who had been captured in Tunisia. Churchill addressed the Commons on July 27. Peace should be made quickly with Italy, he advised. He condemned the sordid treatment in the British and American press of Italy and its King; the House of Savoy always claimed a special little corner of his heart. He went on: until matters were settled, however, "Italy can stew in its own juice." Nicolson found this phrase to be vulgar, and worse, it defied translation into Italian for BBC rebroadcast to Italy. Nicolson settled on *"L'Italia fara il suo proprio minestrone"* (loosely: "Italy must boil in its mixed-up soup").[208]

"A memorable moment," wrote Brooke of Mussolini's end, "and at least a change from 'the end of the beginning' to 'the beginning of the end.'" As for Churchill's speech, Goebbels recorded, "This old rogue [*dieser alte Gauner*]" was "riding triumphantly on his high horse."[209]

The Mediterranean hinge had turned. Yet Sicily lay more than 1,200 air miles from Berlin, almost four times the distance from Normandy to the Rhine, and with the Alps blocking the way. Allied troops and tanks would not be traversing the Apennines and Julian Alps anytime soon, and if they someday set out on that course, they would find the going far more difficult than a race across the Low Countries. The Americans knew geography and they knew arithmetic. Measured in miles and the difficulty of terrain, attacking Germany from southern Italy was like attacking Washington, DC, from Houston by way of the Appalachian Mountains. Attacking Germany from Normandy, on the other hand, was like going to Washington from the North Carolina coast by way of farmlands, plains, and forests. As Churchill and Brooke prepared for the voyage to Canada, their main concern was that Roosevelt, goaded by Stimson, would scotch any further initiatives in Italy. "Marshall absolutely fails to realize what strategic treasures lie at our feet in the Mediterranean," Brooke complained to his diary, "and always hankers after cross-Channel operations."[210]

Churchill, who hungered for any and all operations that promised success, as Italy surely did, meant to settle the issue once and for all during Quadrant.

Shortly after midnight on August 5, Churchill, accompanied by Clementine, Mary, and a court of 250, departed London by train bound for

Glasgow, and then by launch for the short run to Greenock, where the *Queen Mary,* riding at anchor in the Firth of Clyde, awaited his arrival.[211]

That Mrs. Churchill was among the company was surprising. Her husband's love for her was absolute. He respected her opinions, which she stated with force. But he rarely sought her advice on policy matters. Clementine traveled only as the Great Man's wife, and in that regard, given the immense responsibilities he faced, he tended to ignore her. He had business to conduct on board ship, and did so over lunches and dinners. She was shy and found no joy in sharing her table with eight or ten strangers who sought only her husband's time and energy. She did not manifest a natural or carefree demeanor in such surroundings, her daughter Mary later wrote, and "thus, in a life full of people, she knew much loneliness." She was prone to tension and anxiety. This, Churchill did not understand, given his lack of interest in any "illness which was rooted in nervous or psychological origins." (He once told his doctor he liked neither psychiatrists nor their "queer ideas about what is in people's heads.") The "nervous strain" under which Clementine had lived for four years was "extracting its price," Mary later wrote, and by the time she departed for Quebec, "she was in a state of profound physical and nervous exhaustion." She had no outlets whereby she might find some private joy, did not paint, write books, garden, or gamble. In fact, she hated gambling. Her father had lost much of her legacy at the tables. Churchill did not fare very well himself on the green baize, where, until the war came, he loved to spend an evening while she took to her bed to worry over the probable damage to the family finances. It was hoped the sea voyage might alleviate her stress, yet a voyage such as this, cooped up with strangers, was sure to put her in bed, ill, and soon did.[212]

Averell Harriman, accompanied by his daughter, Kathleen, joined the party. They were heading to their Arden, New York, home for their first vacation in two years. Brigadier Orde Wingate also made the trip, having arrived in London from Burma less than twelve hours earlier, in time to dine with Churchill. Wingate's "brilliant exploits" leading his Chindits in Burma so impressed the Old Man that he decreed the general must go to Quebec. Such was the haste to get Wingate on the train that "Clive of Burma" did not even have time to change out of his rumpled field uniform. Lord Moran was along, as usual. Within minutes of meeting Wingate, about whom he had heard so much from Churchill, Moran concluded that the jungle warrior "is only a gifted eccentric. He is not another Lawrence." After further chats with Wingate, Moran decided that the hero of Burma was "hardly sane—in medical jargon, a borderline case."[213]

Late on the afternoon of August 5, the *Queen Mary,* with the P.M. and his party safe on board, slipped down the Firth of Clyde and past the headlands of Arran. The weather, Brooke noted, was "dirty" and blowing hard. The great ship rolled slightly as it made its way into the North Channel of the Irish Sea and then into the Atlantic proper. She had been repainted and partially refurbished and, like England, appeared fresh, powerful, and confident. Yet Brooke believed the ship was heading for troubled waters. "The nearer I get to this conference the less I like it. I know we shall have hard fighting with our American friends."[214]

The previous November, Churchill had proclaimed the end of the beginning for Hitler's Reich. August of 1943 marked the beginning of the end. Each day at sea, news arrived to bolster that conclusion. The Red Army took Belgorod on August 5, and began pushing west. The lower Dnieper River, Kiev, and the Ukraine were its autumn targets. When Field Marshal Manstein told Hitler that Berlin must send twenty divisions' worth of reinforcements or yield the Donets Basin, Hitler replied that he could spare no forces; they were going to Italy. The previous week, General Heinz Guderian, the architect of blitzkrieg, told Goebbels of his "grave concern" over the status of the war, especially in light of the fact that "we can't afford to be active on all fronts." Also galling to Guderian was the futility of pulling armored units away from the Russian front, where they were desperately needed, for service in Italy and the Balkans, where the geography favored infantry and artillery over tanks. Since early May, sixteen German divisions (including four evacuated from Sicily) had been shifted to Italy, where in April there had been none. Eight more had gone to the Balkans and Romania, and thirteen now stood vigil in Norway. Guderian's observations, taken together with Goebbels' admission that the RAF was now administering ever more punishing blows to Germany, amounted to a complete validation of Churchill's strategy of flexibility and opportunism.[215]

On the sixth, Churchill received word from Eden that an Italian diplomat in Tangier had approached his British counterpart with authorization from Badoglio to open negotiations with the Allies. "Don't miss the bus," Churchill replied, adding that although surrender must be unconditional, "we shall be prepared to accord conditions as acts of grace and not as a bargain." He suggested the term "honorable capitulation" be used in the talks, but Eden reminded him that "unconditional surrender" had been announced publicly at Casablanca. This was a problem. Churchill instructed Eden to convey to the Italians that their surrender would have (possibly favorable) conditions attached, conditional upon their surrendering unconditionally. Roosevelt had concurred in this line of reasoning the previous week, when he cabled Churchill: "Eisenhower should be authorized to state conditions when and if the Italian Government asks him for an armistice." Berlin was well aware of the developing situation; a branch of its intelligence service was intercepting phone calls between Churchill and Roosevelt in which they discussed surrender terms for the Italians. One condition Churchill insisted upon was that 70,000 British prisoners in Italy must be repatriated to England, not transported to "the land of the Huns." The Vatican suggested that by declaring Rome an open city, the Allies might entice the new Italian government to the peace table more quickly; Churchill nixed the idea. Rome was to be bombed relentlessly, he told Eden, until the new government surrendered. A few weeks later, Churchill told reporters, "Of this you can be sure, we will continue to operate on the Italian donkey at both ends, with a carrot, and with a stick." The Italian matter was on the Quebec agenda.[216]

The Battle of the Atlantic was not. The Allies were on the verge of victory. There would be many lost ships and lost sailors over the next twelve months and beyond, but the German blockade was broken.

Elsewhere, the air battles over the Ruhr and Hamburg were reaching monstrous climaxes. Churchill had told the U.S. Congress in May what he had in mind for Japanese cities; his words applied to German cities as well: "It is the duty of those who are charged with the direction of the war to... begin the process, so necessary and desirable, of laying the cities and other munitions centres of Japan in ashes, for in ashes they must surely lie before peace comes back to the world." Since May, residents of the Ruhr Valley, who otherwise knew little of the battles in the Atlantic and Russia, were aware from nightly visitations by the RAF that a horrific turn had come in the air war. The RAF had been trimming wicks since 1940; during the early summer of 1943, it set western Germany ablaze. So relentless was the bombing that Churchill, while viewing a British reconnaissance film of the carnage in the Ruhr Valley, turned to his dinner companions and asked, "Are we beasts? Are we taking this too far?" He posed that question in late June over brandy, and it did not mark a philosophical turn on Churchill's part. In the weeks since he posed the question, they had taken it further, and indeed Churchill was intent on taking it much further still. He had his doubts about the effectiveness of the air war, but as he once told the press, "Opinion is divided whether... air power could by itself bring about collapse in Germany. There is no harm in finding out."[217]

Many of Goebbels' diary entries between May and late July treat either of the treachery of Jews (he had reconfirmed his thoughts on Jewish treachery after rereading the anti-Semitic screed *The Protocols of the Elders of Zion*), or the increasingly effective RAF bombing in the Ruhr Valley and on Hamburg. The Krupp Works at Essen was hit, completely halting steel production. Three dams in the Ruhr Valley—the Eder, Sorpe, and Moehne—were damaged or destroyed on May 17 when just nineteen Lancasters from the specially trained 617 Squadron, flying only sixty feet above the water, dropped two-ton, barrel-shaped "bouncing" bombs, which skipped upstream to hit the dams just below the waterline. Eight of the Lancasters and their crews were lost, but explosions breached the Moehne dam with catastrophic effect. The resultant flood drowned several dozen factories, and 1,200 residents downstream. "The attacks," Goebbels wrote, "were very successful."[218]

As Goebbels noted the increasing damage inflicted by the RAF, he took some satisfaction in the numbers of British bombers shot down each night. Now, nightly, came flights of five hundred, seven hundred, nine hundred or more Halifax and Lancaster bombers; by day, the American B-17s arrived, in far smaller numbers. The Anglo-American air forces were now administering vicious round-the-clock punishment to the Reich. This was the "24-hours service" that Churchill had promised the American press. Yet the German fighter defense was especially devastating against the American daylight raiders. As a result, in June the Combined Joint Chiefs amended the Casablanca bombing directive, which called for the destruction of German morale (houses), transportation hubs, oil refineries, and armaments industries. Henceforth the air forces were to destroy Germany's aircraft industry. The new directive was code-named Pointblank. In coming months it would serve less as a blueprint for joint Anglo-American strategy than as a source of dispute between RAF and the American planners. Indeed, Bomber Harris simply continued bombing German cities. If aircraft factories were hit in the bargain, so much the better.

With RAF casualties running disturbingly high, often more than 5 percent, approval was given to employ the secret Window program—strips of aluminum foil dropped from incoming bombers that caused German radar screens to dissolve into meaningless static. Window had been kept quarantined in the year since its development for fear that if it was deployed, the Germans would solve it and turn it against Britain. During that year, 2,200 RAF heavy bombers had been lost and almost 18,000 trained airmen killed or captured, including 4,000 airmen captured or killed during the recent offensive. To stanch the bleeding, the War Cabinet allowed Harris to deploy Window. Goebbels, in his diary entry of July 26, noted an unexplained drop-off in RAF casualties, just twelve aircraft shot down of more than seven hundred. This was Window at work.[219]

Hamburg, Germany's second-largest city and largest port, suffered the consequences that week, during what Brooke described as "a new climax of horror." On July 24, the RAF dropped 2,400 tons of bombs on Hamburg, an amount almost exactly equal to the tonnage of bombs the Luftwaffe had deposited on Britain during the previous *twelve months*. The RAF returned two days later, but low clouds and rain forced most of the raiders to turn back. Clear skies and the RAF returned on the night of the twenty-seventh and again on the twenty-ninth. Again Goebbels rued the ease with which the RAF penetrated German defenses. He also rued the death of Hamburg, "A city of a million inhabitants has been destroyed in a manner unparalleled in history." The British in three raids dropped almost ten thousand tons of high explosives and incendiaries on the city. The result, a German official wrote, was "beyond all human imagination." Almost 800,000 citizens were left homeless; the fire storm consumed oil depots and the port, twelve square miles of the city, and more than 40,000 residents.[220]

In one night and in one city and during one firestorm, the RAF had made up for all of London's casualties during the Blitz. A secret German document recounted the disaster: "Trees three feet thick were broken off or uprooted; human beings were...flung alive into the flames by winds which exceeded 150 miles an hour."* Residents who took shelter underground "were suffocated by carbon-monoxide poisoning and their bodies reduced to ashes as though they had been placed in a crematorium." Churchill took along on the *Queen Mary* stereoscopic slides of the damage, along with a small device to view the images. Desiring that Stalin be apprised of RAF results, shortly after arriving in Quebec, Churchill sent the slides and the viewfinder on to Moscow. The images, Churchill wrote Stalin, "give one a much more vivid impression than anything that can be gained from photographs." On August 9, a *Daily Mirror* headline crowed: 50 GERMAN CITIES WILL BE HAMBURGED. The raids were, as Brooke wrote, a climax of sorts. They also marked the beginning of even more deadly raids. With almost 80 percent of Hamburg erased from the map, Bomber Harris now put Berlin—he called it "The Big City"—in his sights.[221]

The Luftwaffe did not turn Window against Britain that year, in part because with much of the Luftwaffe deployed in the east, attacks against Britain had all but ceased; fewer than 2,400 Britons died by German bombs that year. The Germans did, however, invigorate their nighttime fighter defenses, including locating and targeting British bombers by triangulating RAF electronic emissions, and refining their radar to penetrate Window. The RAF soon began paying its previously high price. On average, six hundred RAF airmen were killed or captured each week during the next year. When the *Economist* opined that the air raids were costing the Allies too much, Goebbels lamented to his diary, "Would to god that

* The destruction, Bomber Harris later wrote, "must have been even more cataclysmic than the bursting of the two atom bombs over Japanese cities." (Sir Arthur Harris, *Bomber Offensive*, p. 179)

were true." By forcing Germany to defend itself, the raids assured that the Luftwaffe could not attain air superiority over the Russians. And in Italy, where the Allies now held a ten-to-one superiority, the Luftwaffe had all but disappeared. The Germans also had to commit massive ground forces in the west, where more than ninety-five divisions—one-third of German troop strength—were arrayed, including thirteen in Norway, forty-five in the Low Countries and France, and twenty-four in Italy and the Balkans. None were fighting Americans or Britons, but neither were they fighting Russians. They were as effectively tied down as if under attack, but Stalin, who was losing ten thousand Russians—soldiers and civilians—per *day*, did not see things that way. Churchill believed this validated his strategy of hitting Germany from all sides, by all methods, at all times. Goebbels agreed, writing, "It is not a soothing thought to imagine the English attacking us at any point they please with relatively small forces."[222]

That was the very strategy that Henry Stimson was urging Roosevelt to repudiate, even as the *Queen Mary* and Churchill closed on Nova Scotia. "None of these methods of pinprick warfare," Stimson wrote to Roosevelt, "can be counted on" to either lead to the defeat of Germany or "to fool Stalin into the belief" that the West had kept to its pledge to open "a real second front." It was time, Stimson urged the president, to demand Churchill make good on that pledge. Further, it was time that an American was appointed commander of the invasion. He told Roosevelt, "We cannot rationally hope to be able to cross the Channel . . . under a British commander" because, although the British "have rendered lip service to the operation their hearts are not in it."[223]

Where Stimson saw ineffectual pinpricks, Churchill saw flexibility, the essence of his opportunistic strategic vision. The Americans tended to underestimate the complexity of a cross-Channel operation, while Churchill and the British Chiefs of Staff tended to exaggerate its potential pitfalls, leaving each side in doubt of the other's strategic vision. Marshall stunned Brooke during the conference when he offered that "20 or 30 divisions" landed in France would suffice to rid Europe of Hitler. Brooke knew that such a paltry force would be slaughtered. Stimson and Marshall, for their part, suspected the British did not consider the North African and Italian ventures to be a means to an end—a softening up of Europe as prelude to Overlord—but intended to delay if not undermine the cross-Channel thrust.[224]

Eisenhower believed so as well, and later wrote, "The doctrine of opportunism, so often applicable in tactics, is a dangerous one to pursue in strategy." The Americans suspected the British sought only to nibble away at the edges of the Reich by sea and air and on land in order to drive Germany to the brink, at which time an invasion of France would result in an almost bloodless march from Normandy to Berlin.

That was not true. Churchill and Brooke sought to punch away at Germany until such time as the march to Berlin—and it would be bloody, not bloodless—would have a strong prospect for success. Churchill later reduced the differences in strategic thinking to a few choice phrases. The Americans, he wrote, "feel that once the foundation has been planned on true and comprehensive lines all other stages will follow naturally and almost inevitably.... The British mind does not work quite in this way. We do not think that logic and clear-cut principles are necessarily the sole keys to what ought to be done in swiftly changing and indefinable situations." These ideas informed Churchill's strategic thinking. Its essence was "to assign a larger importance to opportunism and improvisation, seeking rather to live and conquer in accordance with the unfolding event than to aspire to dominate it often by fundamental decisions. There is room for argument about both views. The difference is one of emphasis, but it is deep rooted." Churchill had, since 1940, endorsed a cross-Channel thrust, but as a means of exploiting a collapse in German morale and firepower, not as a means of evoking the collapse. Ismay, writing after the war, confirmed that philosophy when he wrote, "Mr. Churchill and his advisors always recognized that ultimately the *death blow* to Germany must be delivered across the Channel" (italics added).[225]

Onboard the *Queen Mary,* Churchill was receiving his first briefings on Overlord, the proposed invasion of Normandy. He liked what he saw, up to a point. General Frederick Morgan had been ordered by the Combined Chiefs to produce a plan for a "full scaled assault" on Europe. He had been warned that based on Admiral King's needs in the Pacific, he could expect only 3,300 assault and troop ships to carry out his plan. Thus limited, Morgan's plan called for three seaborne and two parachute divisions to land in the general area of Caen. Two dozen British, Canadian, and American divisions would follow in the first weeks after the initial landings. That, Churchill concluded, would not trigger a German collapse if that was the intent; nor was it enough to exploit a German collapse if one was imminent. Churchill suggested that more troops go ashore along a broader front. Five months would pass before the Americans saw the wisdom of his suggestion.

Satisfied with the overall plan, Churchill, as usual, fretted over the details. Given that twenty-foot tides were common along the Normandy coast, he demanded to be briefed on the progress in building the Mulberry artificial harbors he had championed more than two years earlier. Only by building these harbors could enough men, machines, rations, and ammunition be gotten safely ashore in a timely fashion. The target was 12,000 tons daily; success depended on reaching it. Fuel for the trucks and tanks would come by way of another technological marvel, a pipeline under the ocean (Pluto) from southeast Britain to the Normandy town of Port-en-Bessin. The pipeline's deployment would be made more complex because it would probably take place under Luftwaffe attack. A third marvel was intended to protect the artificial harbors from high seas—an artificial breakwater (called a lilo) that consisted of large inflatable rubber bladders that supported underwater concrete screens. A demonstration took place in Churchill's stateroom bathroom. The Great Man watched, perched upon a stool and dressed in his dragon dressing gown, as an admiral and a brigadier splashed away at the overflowing bathtub in which a miniature lilo calmed the waves. A stranger who witnessed the scene, Ismay wrote, "would have found it hard to believe that this was the British high command studying the most stupendous and spectacular amphibious operation in the history of war."[226]

Churchill sought assurance that progress was being made on another concept he held dear: Mountbatten's floating airfields made of ice and code-named Operation Habakkuk. The idea, Churchill stressed, "deserves very keen examination." He had selected the code name, citing the Old Testament text from Habakkuk, "Behold ye among the heathen... for I will work a work in your days... which ye will not believe." Indeed, many among the planning staff were nonbelievers. The idea, which Mountbatten introduced to Churchill during a Chequers weekend, had taken shape in Canada, not surprisingly given the sometimes frigid temperatures there. But Churchill envisioned deploying these million-ton monsters off the coasts of France and in the Indian Ocean, where they would serve as refueling stations for the RAF. No consideration appears to have been given to one critical design flaw: even outfitted with their planned refrigeration systems, the ice crafts would melt. Brooke disparagingly called Habakkuk "one of Dickie Mountbatten's bright ideas," but promised Mountbatten that he would be given an opportunity to present the idea in Quebec. The CIGS really had no choice but to acquiesce, for Dickie, having Churchill's ear, operated on the principle of why talk to the monkey when you have the organ grinder. Thus, the disdain in Brooke's diary entry upon being told by Churchill that he planned to elevate Mountbatten to the Southeast Asia Command: "He [Mountbatten] will need a very efficient Chief of Staff to pull him through."[227]

The Atlantic voyage passed much like the one of May, with nightly games of bezique played with Harriman, who on the previous voyage had cautioned Churchill against deprecating the American daylight bombing strategy. Harriman now cautioned Churchill, who feared Overlord would derail his plans in Italy, against deprecating Overlord. Roosevelt, Harriman warned, was intent that Overlord take place in May 1944, and that was that. Churchill responded that he hoped only to reach the Po River in northern Italy, hold that line, and strike into the Balkans from the Aegean. Given the difficulties of terrain, supply, and the enemy, on any march to the Po, three hundred miles north of Rome, that was far more easily said than done. Eisenhower believed that any plan to reach the Po would necessitate withholding so many men from Overlord "that the cross-Channel operation could not be undertaken in the spring of 1944." That was unacceptable to the Americans.[228]

Meanwhile, Churchill had decided that an invasion of northern Sumatra, which he had first proposed in May, now offered the greatest strategic opportunity in Southeast Asia. On that score, Brooke lamented to his diary: "He [Churchill] has during the sea voyage in a few idle moments become married to the idea that success against Japan can only be secured through the capture of the north tip of Sumatra!" Churchill, Brooke added, "has become like a peevish child asking for a forbidden toy."[229]

On August 9, *Queen Mary* dropped anchor in Halifax Harbor. Churchill and his party required two Canadian National Railway trains for the trip to Quebec City, which they reached late in the afternoon of the tenth. Churchill left the train just shy of the city in order to complete the journey by car with the Canadian prime minister, Mackenzie King. The principals bunked at the Citadel, on the cliffs above the Old City, while hundreds of staff officers took over the nearby Château Frontenac hotel, whose six hundred rooms had been cleared of guests but for one suite occupied by an elderly woman who was expected to die within days (she, however, lived, and was residing in the same room a year later when the second Quebec conference convened). The Americans were not due for three days.[230]

Prime Minister Mackenzie King and the Canadians found themselves looking in from the outside at their own garden party. Other than being given vague summaries of decisions made by the Combined Chiefs, the Canadians were excluded from the conference. Canada fielded five divisions in Britain and Sicily, including a division under Montgomery. During the Great War, Canada buried 66,000 of her sons, America, 117,000 of hers; adjusted for the difference in populations, America would have needed to plant more than one million crosses in Flanders. Canada had bled for England. Now, again, this nation of just eleven million was suffering several times more casualties on a per capita basis than the United States and almost as many as Britain. When, two weeks earlier, the Canadian commander in chief in London, General Andrew McNaughton, traveled to Malta in expectation of reviewing his troops in Sicily, Montgomery refused. Alexander backed Monty up; Eisenhower did not intercede. It was an appalling slight to Canada, yet since September 3, 1939, HMG's position was that Dominion forces served under British command. The Dominions had neither a permanent seat in the War Cabinet nor any binding say in its deliberations. The logic behind London's arrangement with the Dominions was compelling from a military standpoint. Given that British troops (and British casualties) far outnumbered those of the Dominions, the apogee of the command structure must therefore be British. Franklin Roosevelt also understood that logic and was about to turn it against Churchill.[231]

Within a day of arriving in Quebec, and before Quadrant began, Churchill boarded a train for a journey south to Hyde Park and a private meeting with Roosevelt. He was accompanied by Mary but not by Clementine, brought low by the long sea voyage. Mary had become the darling of the American press as soon as she set foot in North America. Other than being the prime minister's daughter and manning an ack-ack battery in Hyde Park, she lived a normal life, *Time* reported. She did not much frequent London's bare-boned nightclubs, did not smoke cigarettes. She loved to dance. Unlike her sister, Sarah, her father, and her brother, she drank only modestly, although late at night of an evening, she liked to sit before the fire in the company of her father and smoke a cigar. She dated British and U.S. officers. *Time* reported that when one of them, the American cartoonist and creator of G.I. Joe, Sergeant Dave Breger, fifteen years her senior, took her to see prizefights between British and U.S. soldiers, "she saw her first boxing. She asked everyone around her about the rules, cheered, chewed gum." Her nickname was Chip; "she was a member of the jukebox generation" but wise beyond her years and "intelligent without thick lenses.... She has watched too many big minds grapple with too many big problems."[232]

Churchill chose not to take the most direct routes from Quebec to Hyde Park, south through Vermont or along the Hudson. Never one to let the privileges of rank go begging, he instead took his party on a one-day four-hundred-mile detour in order that Mary might behold the majesty of Niagara Falls. While flashing the "V" sign for onlookers at Niagara, Churchill was asked by a reporter what he thought of the falls. He replied that he had been there before, in 1900, and that "the principle seems the same. The water still keeps falling over." Then, after driving across to the American side, he reboarded his train. He loved trains, especially American trains. A decade earlier he had written in *Collier's* of the luxuries of American Pullman cars, the wide and comfortable berths in the deluxe sleepers, the "gargantuan meals" prepared with "skill and delicacy" and served by "the darky attendants with their soft voices and delightful drawl and courteous, docile, agreeable ways" and who were "an unfailing source not only of comfort but of perpetual amusement." Thus ensconced in his favored mode of transportation—and taking delight in flashing his "V" at farmers in their fields as he stood at the window—he made the four-hundred-mile run east on the New York Central main line, past farms and fields alongside the Erie Canal, through the Mohawk Valley, and finally down the Hudson Valley to Hyde Park.[233]

There, the president awaited Churchill with homey meals of hot dogs, hamburgers, and clam chowder (Inspector Thompson thought the hot dogs "abominable"). Roosevelt, jaunty and the picture of civility, was ready to serve up to Churchill a nonnegotiable proposition. Henry Stimson, always wary of Churchill's sway over Roosevelt whenever the two met alone, had delivered his brief to the president. Based on his unsettling conversations with Churchill in London, Stimson advised Roosevelt to repudiate the British "pinprick" strategy and to demand from Churchill a second front in France by May of 1944, and an American commander for that front, George Marshall. During his May visit to Washington, Churchill had told the U.S. Congress: "I was driving the other day not far from the field of Gettysburg, which I know well, like most of your battlefields. It was the decisive battle of the American Civil War. No one after Gettysburg doubted which way the dread balance of war would incline, yet far more blood was shed after the Union victory at Gettysburg than in all the fighting which went before." Now, in mid-August, no one doubted how the war would end, and if the majority of the blood to be shed in France was to be American, Franklin Roosevelt wanted an American in command.[234]

This had not been the case just weeks earlier. Roosevelt and the American military chiefs considered that fair play called for the British to command the French invasion; after all, an American had commanded Torch and Husky. It was now London's turn. Measured by casualties, it certainly seemed only fair that a Briton command Overlord. At the end of operations in North Africa, the U.S. Army and Army Air Force accounted for approximately 18,200 of 70,000 Allied casualties in that theater—2,700 dead, 9,000 wounded, and 6,500 missing. The British and Dominions suffered the vast majority of the remaining 52,000 casualties. By August, more than 100,000 British airmen, soldiers, and sailors had been killed in action since September 1939, along with 45,000 civilians and more than 20,000 merchant seamen. In Sicily, the British army finally surpassed the Home Island civilian casualty count. The final calculations in Sicily showed 13,000 British and Canadians killed, wounded, or missing, along with the equivalent of two infantry divisions laid low by malaria and typhus, versus 10,000 American casualties. Measured by casualties thus far, Churchill had a far stronger case than Roosevelt in the matter of command of Overlord. But Roosevelt's case rested on the assumption that by the time the invasion of France took place, or soon thereafter, American forces would equal the British, and within months would outnumber the British by as many as five to one. Therefore, he concluded, command of Overlord must go to an American.[235]

Shortly arriving at Hyde Park, Churchill acquiesced. Thus, one of the most significant military decisions made at Quadrant wasn't made in Quebec, but on the banks of the Hudson River before the conference even began.

At Quebec, in the days that followed, Churchill and the British chiefs managed to extract four qualifications from the Americans: Overlord would take place only if the invasion forces did not face more than twelve mobile German divisions, including three on the beaches; and only if the Germans could not build up their forces by fifteen divisions within two months. As well, Germany's airpower had to be reduced before the invasion could take place; and artificial harbors had to be operational in order to reinforce and supply the initial force. The British saw these conditions as sound planning, especially as the plan for Overlord called for only three seaborne and two parachute divisions to land on the first day. The Americans saw them as loopholes through which Churchill and the British would try to escape their obligations. Still, Marshall and the Americans signed off, for in spite of the conditions, the Americans had demanded and been granted one of their own: if needed, seven divisions that were now in North Africa and Sicily would be siphoned away for Overlord. Brooke opposed this, telling Marshall that "by giving full priority to the cross-Channel preparation you might well cripple the Italian theater and thus render it unable to contain German forces necessary to render the cross-Channel operation possible." Brooke's logic was sound, but Marshall and the Americans carried the day. In fact, they added a new dimension to the French strategy by proposing an invasion by two divisions on the Mediterranean French coast in support of Overlord. The operation—named Anvil—was intended to draw German troops away from Normandy. Not addressed for the time being was the question of where those two divisions would come from. It soon became clear to Churchill that they would come from the Italian campaign.[236]

Churchill later wrote that his decision to endorse an American commander for Overlord was based on his agreement with Roosevelt's argument that the Americans were likely to put more men on the beaches than the British were; therefore the command should go to an American. Yet

Churchill and the British chiefs also presumed that Eisenhower would replace Marshall, and that Alexander in turn would replace Eisenhower in the Mediterranean. Churchill's logic (and motive) in accepting second billing for Overlord was consistent with his multifaceted strategy. He considered Overlord to be but one of several ventures, critical, to be sure, but not necessarily destined to be more significant than any other. In fact, the success of Overlord, as Churchill saw it, would depend upon the success of all the other operations. Handing over command of Overlord to the Americans placated Washington and opened the way for the British to command most, perhaps all, of Churchill's hoped-for ventures—in the Aegean, the Balkans, Burma, Sumatra, the Middle East, northern Norway, and, most important, Italy, where the Allies had more men in combat than would be going ashore in the early days of Overlord. And, as the Americans already suspected, if the agreed-upon conditions for undertaking the invasion of France were not met, there would be no invasion, leaving the Americans with the command of a nonentity, while Churchill held the rest of the marbles.[237]

But Churchill did not yet grasp that the supreme commander of Overlord would necessarily become de facto supreme commander of all Anglo-American forces in Europe, with veto power over secondary operations and authority to move men and machines throughout the theater in support of Overlord. Churchill thought only in terms of putting men ashore in France, and of holding that position before advancing with caution while other killing strokes were made in Norway, Italy, and the Balkans, and by the Russians in the east and the RAF and American Eighth Air Force over Berlin. Yet, if his Mulberry harbors performed as planned and the port of Cherbourg was captured, tens upon thousands of men and hundreds of thousands of tons of supplies would land in Normandy in the weeks following the invasion. The commander of such a magnificent force—armies within army groups—could only supplant all others. George Marshall understood this. The command of a lifetime within his grasp, he and his wife began quietly sending furniture from their Maryland post to the family home in Leesburg, Virginia, in anticipation of their move to London.[238]

By handing the command over to Marshall, Churchill denied Brooke his dream of a decisive role in the destruction of Hitler's armies (as well as his escape from Churchill's direct influence). On August 15, the CIGS scribbled in his diary: "Winston gave in, in spite of having previously offered me the job!" Churchill explained his reasoning while he and Brooke stood on a terrace of the Citadel high above the Saint Lawrence, and then asked Brooke how he felt about the decision. "Disappointed" was about all Brooke could muster. Years later he wrote, "Not for one moment did he [Churchill] realize what this meant to me. He offered no sympathy, no regrets at having had to change his mind." It took several months for Brooke to recover from this "crashing blow," in part because he suspected Churchill had traded command of Overlord for the appointment of Mountbatten as supreme commander in Southeast Asia. In this, Brooke was partially correct, but Churchill's horse trading with Roosevelt in regard to Asia was more political than military. Roosevelt got on famously with Mountbatten; the American press adored the man. By sending Mountbatten to take charge, Churchill could claim the British were doing their part against Tokyo.[239]

Each night at Quebec, Brooke found a new way to tell his diary what he thought of that day's discussions: "long," "trying," "poisonous," especially as pertained to the Japanese war, and especially as pertained to Churchill's approach to the Pacific theater, which Brooke described as "chasing hares." Where Churchill wanted to nibble at the edges of the Japanese empire, Nimitz and MacArthur wanted to drive from the South Pacific straight to Tokyo, with MacArthur on the left taking aim at the Philippines, and Nimitz on the right island-hopping northward. The Americans therefore demanded more from the British in Burma in support of Chiang, who they believed would prove his worth by holding down Japanese armies in China while the main thrust came from the South Pacific. China, for the Americans, had a vital supporting role in the whole show. But Churchill, Gil Winant reported to Washington, "was quite willing to see China collapse." The Americans suspected the British were fighting in Burma, not for China but for the restoration of British imperial holdings. This, the Americans could not be a party to; the greater the American presence in Southeast Asia, the greater the risk that Roosevelt would be accused of aiding and abetting British imperialism.

Each side was driven by conflicting political strategies, with the result that the strictly military objectives they shared were often made orphans to politics. Wingate's six thousand raiders, Stilwell's Chinese troops in India, and the Fourteenth Army, under General Billy Slim, found themselves the forgotten men in a forgotten theater. Mountbatten's presence would signal a change; Churchill could claim he sent his best man, his "triphibian" warrior, to take up the reins. To placate the Americans, Stilwell would go in as Mountbatten's deputy. Stilwell, caught in the middle and denied a real opportunity to kill his hated Japs, reacted with his usual fury. In a symbolic thumb in the eye to the British, he refused to stand and sing when "God Save the King" was played. After a plea from Marshall, he agreed to stand for the ceremony, but he would not sing. As for his new supreme commander, Stilwell considered Mountbatten to be a "limey mountebank" and "as dumb as that thick-headed cousin of his, the King." Such sentiments lent credence to a saying Churchill liked to toss out over drinks: "There is only one thing worse than fighting with allies, and that is fighting without them."[240]

The same could be said of Brooke's difficulties in fighting a war in harness with Churchill. The meetings of the Combined Chiefs of Staff were contentious, but progress was made. Then, just as Brooke appeared to reach an understanding with the Americans on the need for a general plan for the war against Japan, Churchill insisted again on capturing northern Sumatra, and letting events elsewhere play out on their own. Brooke exploded to his diary, "He [Churchill] refused to accept that any general plan was necessary, recommended a purely opportunistic policy.... I feel cooked and unable to face another day of conferences." Pug Ismay, Churchill's liaison with Brooke, found himself caught in the middle of this clash of supremely different personalities. Churchill, well aware of Brooke's disdain of his strategic talents, once dispatched Ismay to ask Brooke why he so hated the prime minister. Ismay returned with Brooke's reply; he in fact loved the prime minister but could not serve him well without disputing that which he disagreed with. Churchill listened, bowed his head, and whispered, "Dear Brookie."[241]

On August 17, Alexander cabled Churchill the news that the last Germans had been flung out of Sicily. The campaign was over; it had lasted just thirty-eight days. But the victory was incomplete: Kesselring's 60,000 men had escaped to Italy. That day, the new Italian government scrambled to meet surrender terms laid down by Eisenhower. The problem, ironic as Churchill saw it, was that the Italian negotiator in Lisbon, General Giuseppe Castellano, wanted to learn from Eisenhower's lieutenant, Bedell ("Beetle") Smith, how best Italy could take the field against the Germans, whom Castellano, a Sicilian, hated. But Smith replied that he could only discuss unconditional surrender. With the invasion of the toe and heel of Italy now scheduled to take place in two weeks, Churchill worried that a quisling government might take power in Rome, or that the Germans would occupy Rome and take direct control. He wanted Eisenhower to convey to the Italians that if, when the Allies landed, they encountered Italian troops fighting Germans, Italy would be welcomed as a co-belligerent in the war against Hitler. But Castellano wanted assurances; the Italian *forze amate* stood no chance in a fight with the Wehrmacht. And Eisenhower could not deliver any such guarantee until the Italians surrendered, unconditionally. Eisenhower also sought reassurance from Castellano that Mussolini would not reappear in the guise of savior. When asked by Smith where Mussolini was being kept, Castellano replied, "Hitler would like to know, too." In fact, Hitler soon learned that Il Duce was being held at Campo Imperatore Hotel, a mountaintop ski resort in Abruzzo, and put plans into place for the very resurrection Churchill feared.[242]

In late June, an RAF reconnaissance flight over Peenemünde, on the Baltic Sea island of Usedom, had photographed a rocket that the Germans had failed to camouflage. With that, Duncan Sandys and Churchill finally knew what manner of vehicle Hitler was building on the Baltic coast, though they lacked any knowledge of weight, speed, propellant, and explosive capacity. On the night of August 17, more than five hundred British heavy bombers hit Peenemünde. The RAF sought to destroy not only the laboratories and test facilities but also the housing where engineers and technicians and thousands of slave laborers lived. Hitler's armaments minister, Albert Speer, had approved the transfer of slave laborers, mostly Poles and Russians, to work at the site after the director of the rocket program, a boyish-looking thirty-one-year-old aeronautics engineer and rocket enthusiast named Wernher von Braun, argued that if the supply of workers could not be maintained, neither could the rocket program (code-named A-4). The RAF raid killed one scientist and several hundred slave laborers. Speer and von Braun soon scattered A-4 research and production facilities throughout Germany, including far under the Hartz mountains. Engineering tests on the A-4 continued at Peenemünde, and on a simpler flying bomb, essentially a small pilotless jet aircraft. This weapon was code-named *Flakzielgert 76* (Anti-Aircraft Target Device 76) to throw British intelligence off the scent. Once the engineering bugs were worked out, they were to be produced at the Volkswagen factory at Fallersleben, near Hamburg. Hitler was so enthused about his new weapons, and so impressed with young von Braun, that he ordered Speer to find a way to make the young scientist a full professor. Meanwhile, at Peenemünde, the Germans did not clear away the rubble from the RAF raid, presuming that RAF reconnaissance flights would conclude from the damage that Peenemünde had been abandoned. The British did exactly that, and did not return for nine months. By then von Braun's rockets were almost ready for deployment.[243]

As Quadrant wound down, Brooke took delight in recording Mountbatten's most inglorious moment, after Dickie finally persuaded the CIGS to allow a demonstration of Habakkuk, the ice aircraft carriers, for the Combined Chiefs. To illustrate the efficacy of the idea, Mountbatten had two large blocks of ice delivered to a conference room, where an emotional discussion had just taken place between the American and British chiefs. Mountbatten explained to the conferees that one block was ordinary ice and the other was called Pykrete, fabricated by strengthening the ice with a specially treated wood pulp mixture. Then Dickie unholstered his revolver and shot the first block, which, as expected, shattered, as did the composure of the men seated at the table. Then Mountbatten proclaimed, "I shall fire at the [other] block to show you the difference." The difference was that the second block was bulletproof. Mountbatten's shot ricocheted off and around the room, barely missing Portal and Ernest King. Outside, a group of junior officers heard the shots. "Good god," one exclaimed, "they've started shooting now." No ice fleet ever sailed.[244]

As the Combined Chiefs scraped their way through the agenda—it was really mostly about Overlord, with a detour to Burma—Churchill and Roosevelt followed Eisenhower's progress on the Italian surrender. This was the first conference attended by the senior diplomatic players—Eden, Cadogan, and Hull arrived on August 18—and the first one that assumed a duality of purpose, military and political. On the diplomatic front, Roosevelt insisted that Eisenhower conduct all negotiations with the Italians, while Churchill argued that politicians handle political matters. There was a further complication: Roosevelt loathed King Victor Emmanuel and Marshal Badoglio for their long and loyal support of Mussolini. Churchill, however, had told Roosevelt two weeks earlier that he'd do business with "anybody who could deliver the goods." Roosevelt had no love for European constitutional monarchies and preferred, as had Woodrow Wilson, to remake Europe in a republican image. Churchill believed that had the victors in the Great War fished a Hohenzollern or Hapsburg heir out of oblivion and put him back on the German or Austrian throne to lead a constitutional monarchy, there would have been no Hitler. Churchill believed in kings, and Victor Emmanuel was a king. He was also the only player in the game; there simply were no republicans in authority in Rome for Roosevelt to deal with. Along with his antipathy toward royalty, Roosevelt harbored a justified distrust of Badoglio. Churchill, too, distrusted the Italian general and expected a double cross, but a double cross of Hitler, he told Roosevelt, not of the Allies.[245]

As Churchill and Roosevelt mulled over the terms of Italian surrender, neither thought to bring either Stalin or the Free French into the discussions. The two leaders kept Stalin informed of developments but assumed he sought no role in furthering them. The French were simply ignored, not surprisingly given Roosevelt's and Hull's disdain for de Gaulle, but ironic given that Roosevelt's most listened-to broadcast of 1940 had been his "dagger in the back" condemnation of the Italian invasion of France. France had vital territorial issues to settle with Italy. Yet Hull—Alec Cadogan called him an "old lady"—refused to even recognize the French Committee of National Liberation. That week the British chose to recognize the FCNL as a legitimate organization in North Africa but not as the presumed provisional government once France was liberated. It was a start. The Americans chose only to "acknowledge" the Gaullists.[246]

The assumption that Stalin sought only updates on events unfolding in Italy was proven wrong in a telegram that arrived on August 22 in which Stalin protested (with his usual bluntness) Soviet exclusion from the Italian surrender: "To date it has been like this," Stalin wrote, "the U.S.A. and Britain reach agreement between themselves, while the U.S.S.R. is informed of the agreement.... I must say that this situation cannot be tolerated any longer." Churchill thought the message "rude," and fired off a cable to Stalin that, to Eden's horror, included the line "I am entirely unmoved by your statement." The Old Man and Roosevelt, who was "alarmed" at Stalin's tone, summoned Alec Cadogan, who, after reading the telegram, concluded that Stalin had made a fair point, albeit with his usual rudeness. Anthony Eden solved the problem when he advised that bringing Stalin into the picture now might pay dividends down the road when Stalin wielded the same leverage in Eastern Europe that the Anglo-Americans now wielded in Italy. Welcome Stalin into the Italian negotiations, Eden argued, and a precedent would be set that might prove useful when the Red Army struck out beyond Russian borders and into the Baltics, Romania, and Poland. Churchill agreed with Eden's logic but doubted Stalin would abide by any understanding. He predicted "bloody consequences in the future.... Stalin is an unnatural man. There will be grave trouble."[247]

To Harriman, Churchill meant "bloody" in the literal sense. A few weeks later, with such Soviet mischief in mind, Churchill asked the British Chiefs of Staff to draw up a plan to counter a Moscow-backed Communist coup d'état in Greece in the event of a German withdrawal, which Churchill sought to hasten by invading Rhodes and some of the Dodecanese Islands (occupied by Italy since 1912) as soon as Italy surrendered. Churchill saw an impending vacuum in Greece, and he intended to fill it before Moscow nosed onto the scene. His concern stemmed from reports that the two Greek partisan groups—the large and Communist People's National Liberation Army (ELAS), and the small and democratic National Democratic Greek Army (EDES)—were fighting each other with weapons supplied by the Special Operations Executive. Both sides despised King George II of the Hellenes, whom Churchill sought to restore to his throne. Churchill instructed the chiefs to arrange for at least five thousand "troops with armoured cars and Bren guns" to be held ready for a drive into Athens in order to support "the restoration of lawful Greek government." His timing was off by more than a year, but his instinct regarding Stalin's ambitions was prescient. The Soviet leader's bearishness grew with every mile the Red Army gained.[248]

Stalin's inadvertent exclusion from the Italian negotiations drove home the need for the Big Three to meet, not necessarily in Roosevelt's estimation to parse strictly military matters, but to address questions that pertained to the postwar world. Roosevelt, confident that victory against Hitler was not only inevitable but would come within a year (although he thought the Japanese might hold out until 1946 or 1947), had delegated military decisions to his military and turned his attention to winning the peace. Hopkins that month wrote Winant that the Russian offensive, "together with our increased bombing of Germany, is going to make it tough on Hitler and I do not see how he can stand it for more than another eight months." That was the exact amount of time General Carl Spaatz believed it would take for his strategic air forces to put Hitler on the ropes, followed by surrender a few months later. This belief was shared by Bomber Harris. Were Hopkins and Spaatz to be proven correct, the collapse of Germany would take place sometime around May 1944, thereby rendering Overlord unnecessary. An American senator, Sheridan Downey of California, was even more optimistic, predicting that ten big bombing raids per month would finish off Germany by February. Roosevelt and Hopkins hedged their bets in public, but it was time, Roosevelt believed, to find the diplomatic means by which the military alliance known as the United Nations emerged from the war as an international body with muscle, its backbone formed by the Four Powers—America, Britain, China, and Russia. It was time to initiate a dialogue with Stalin on the postwar world, a world that might be only a year distant.[249]

Churchill and Eden believed it premature to bring such an agenda to any meeting with Stalin, but they told Roosevelt that they would bring up the matter of a postwar league with the War Cabinet (including Chinese participation if, Churchill offered over dinner, "they become a nation"). Stalin had only two items on his agenda, Eden argued: "the second front and [Russia's] western frontiers." The question of borders, by implication, also went to the question of Germany's postwar borders, that is, the question of how thoroughly to dismember Germany. Since there would be no second front that year, and since boundaries were not to be addressed until victory was won, a meeting of foreign ministers now, Eden argued, "would almost certainly do more harm than good." Still, the need for the three Big Boys (as anointed by Cadogan) to meet was self-evident, especially as there would be no second front that year. An invitation was dispatched to Moscow. Anchorage, London, and Scapa Flow were suggested as venues for the foreign ministers and, soon thereafter, the Big Three. As Quadrant played out, Stalin agreed to a meeting late in the year, insisting that the foreign ministers meet first in order to set an agenda for the three leaders to follow at their meeting. He suggested the preliminary meeting take place in Moscow, with the Big Three meeting either there or in Tehran. Churchill lobbied for London; he after all had made one trip to Moscow and was now nearing the end of his fourth journey to Washington. The discussion of possible sites dragged on for almost three weeks, until Roosevelt finally agreed to Stalin's proposal of Moscow for the foreign ministers. Churchill, his proposal of London snubbed, could only acquiesce. The diminishment of British influence within the alliance now troubled Eden, who thought Roosevelt was bowling them a fast one: "I am most anxious for good relations with the U.S. but I don't like subservience to them.... We are giving the impression, which they are only too ready by nature to endorse, that militarily all the achievements are theirs."[250]

Eden made that diary entry on September 10, and added, "W., by prolonging his stay in Washington, strengthens [the] assumption" of British subservience. Quadrant had ended on August 24. Most of the staff departed for London and Washington the next day, by train, plane, and ship. The chiefs, Ismay, Eden, Cadogan, Churchill, his secretaries, and his family stayed on for a six-day fishing vacation in the Quebec wilderness. Churchill took his rest on the shores of Lac des Neiges, Eden and his people at Lac Jacques-Cartier, about an hour's drive from Churchill's lodge and three thousand feet up in the Laurentian Mountains. When Eden stopped by Churchill's camp on August 27 to say his good-byes before departing for London, Moran told him the P.M. was tired and unable to shake off troubles known only to himself. Eden found Churchill in his bath, not looking "at all well and was of a bad colour." When Churchill expressed a desire to extend his holiday in the mountains, Eden advised him to do so. Then, splashing about in his bath, Churchill said, "I don't know what I should do if I lost you all. I'd have to cut my throat. It isn't just love, though there is much of that in it, but you are my war machine. Brookie, Portal, you and Dickie, I simply couldn't replace you."[251]

The respite by the lake was just what the doctor ordered, or would have ordered had anyone, including Moran, been able to give orders to Churchill. Log fires burned in the great stone fireplace. Bears and wolves were said to lurk nearby. By day Churchill fished for trout from a canoe, all the while "laying down the law about the fisherman's art" to Moran, who hooked nary a fish. Loons—"divers" to the British—drifted and dunked and cried far out on the lake. Late in the evenings Churchill strolled out to the end of a pier to take in the northern lights. Grilled trout was served up for lunches and dinners; the party accounted for a depletion of the local trout population in excess of three hundred. Clementine, "too overtired for enjoyment," took herself back to Quebec after one day. Her "nervous state," Mary later wrote, resulted in "perplexity and worry" out of all proportion to events. Not so Churchill. The rest worked wonders. By August 29 he was back "in terrific form," Cadogan wrote, "singing Don Leno songs and other favorites of the halls of forty years ago, together with the latest Noel Coward." All the brass but Cadogan, Ismay, and Dudley Pound, who had been troubled by excruciating headaches and was too ill to fly, left by August 29.[252]

Pound, who Brooke for months had criticized in his diary for falling asleep during meetings, in fact was host to an undetected brain tumor and had suffered a minor stroke. His wife of more than three decades had died a month earlier, but he still took himself off to Quebec. When he complained to Churchill of headaches and numbness in his legs, the Old Man insisted he join him aboard *Renown* for the trip to England. On September 1, Churchill, and his now much reduced party, returned to Quebec City. There, joined by Clementine and Mary, he entrained for Washington. His holiday had only just begun. "This quiet life is doing him good," Moran wrote, "but he feels like he is playing truant."[253]

He was. By September 10, Churchill's subordinates agreed with Moran's assessment, including Eden, who told his diary that he found himself depressed and not feeling well, "partly, I think, because of exasperating difficulty of trying to do business with Winston over the Atlantic." Brooke, too, noted Churchill's absence. After attending a cabinet meeting chaired by Attlee, the CIGS wrote that although the meeting was conducted with greater efficiency than Churchill brought to the table, it was a "cabinet without a head." Indeed, Brooke, who was always willing to denigrate Churchill in his diary, took a far softer position during Churchill's long vacation. After delineating Churchill's contradictions and failings—"the most marvelous qualities of superhuman genius mixed with an astonishing lack of vision at times"—Brooke (still smarting from losing command of Overlord) wrote that although Churchill "is quite the most difficult man to work with...I should not have missed the chance of working with him for anything on earth."[254]

Much transpired in the Mediterranean during Churchill's therapeutic truancy. The Italians surrendered (secretly and unconditionally) on

September 3, although thirteen conditions were attached to the "unconditional" surrender, including the transfer of the Italian fleet to the Allies. And that day, two divisions of the Eighth Army crossed the Straits of Messina and landed near Reggio, in Calabria, on the toe of the foot of Italy. It was a tentative foray. Montgomery, denied the landing craft he needed to put more forces on the heel of Italy, or to swing around to the Adriatic coast, could only hold his toehold. Eisenhower hoarded the landing craft for use in Avalanche, the planned seizure of Salerno by the Fifth Army, scheduled for September 8 and 9. In support of that operation, Eisenhower planned to drop the 82nd Airborne Division near Rome to secure the airfields.

This was not the bold strategy of striking into northern Italy favored by Smuts and expressed in his July letter to Churchill. In fact, Mark Clark, in command of the Salerno forces, had argued for a landing north of Naples, but Air Marshal Tedder and Admiral Cunningham were hesitant to send their airships and warships too far afield in support of ground troops, and Eisenhower was loath to send his ground forces beyond his aerial and naval umbrellas. Thus, by caution and default, Salerno became the target. And thus, the Eighth Army, the most seasoned force in the Allied camp, was relegated to a supporting role some two hundred miles south of the main event at Salerno. Montgomery, in his memoirs, wrote with his usual directness of the entire strategy: "If the planning and conduct of the campaign in Sicily were bad, the preparations for the invasion of Italy and the subsequent conduct of the campaign in that country were worse still."[255]

Churchill arrived at the same conclusion the previous week after one of Alexander's staff officers reported that the full complement of twelve Allied divisions would not be ashore in Italy until December 1, and worse, ashore only near Naples. The problem as Churchill saw it was that any delay in getting to Rome would only give Kesselring time to throw in more troops of his own. "The lateness of this forecast," Brooke jotted in his diary, "has sent him [Churchill] quite mad."[256]

The race to Rome was on. But with eight German divisions stationed in northern Italy under Rommel, and eight more to the south under Kesselring, including two near Rome, the Allies stood little chance of grabbing the Eternal City unless they moved with dispatch and landed somewhere near Rome, where five Italian divisions were poised to join the Allies. But Eisenhower's caution gave Kesselring the time he needed to convert south-central Italy into a fortress. Eisenhower now saw his error in not having landed at Calabria in July as part of Operation Husky, thus cutting off Sicily and capturing the troops trapped there. "History would call it [my] mistake," he told Commander Butcher. Had he pursued that strategy, his armies might now be moving north through Italy, but as it was, "a quick collapse of Italy has disappeared into uncertainty." This was due in part, Butcher wrote, to the limitation imposed upon Eisenhower by the insistence of Churchill and Roosevelt on unconditional surrender. Yet, in fairness to the self-critical Eisenhower (who, exhausted, spent three days in the infirmary under his doctor's care), neither the Allied air forces nor navies had wanted anything to do with heavy operations over or within the Messina Straits. All of this came as a great relief to Kesselring, who later wrote, "A secondary attack on Calabria would have enabled the Sicily landing to be developed into an overwhelming Allied victory."[257]

As Eisenhower prepared to hit Salerno (and not with a roundhouse punch), Churchill, still in Washington, proposed to the War Cabinet that the agenda for the agreed-upon tripartite meeting be topped by discussions on the fate of Germany after the war and Russia's role in determining that fate. Russia, and its possible behavior in the future, had become for Churchill a pressing political concern. To Smuts, on September 5, he offered that "Russia will be the greatest land power in the world after this war" and that a continuation of the Anglo-American alliance and its overwhelming airpower would supply the necessary "balance with Russia at least for the period of rebuilding." After that, Churchill wrote, "I cannot see with mortal eye, and I am not yet fully informed about the celestial telescope."[258]

On September 5, President Roosevelt invited Mrs. Ogden Reid to join himself and Churchill for lunch at the White House. She was the publisher of the *New York Herald Tribune* and a strong supporter of Indian independence. She was known for speaking her mind, and Roosevelt had no doubt that she would speak it to Churchill. She did, asking Churchill, "What are you going to do about those wretched Indians?" He replied, "Before we proceed further let us get one thing clear. Are we talking about the brown Indians in India, who have multiplied alarmingly under benevolent British rule? Or are we talking about the Red Indians in America, who, I understand, are almost extinct?" Mrs. Reid was speechless. Roosevelt could not contain his laughter; it was the sort of awkward moment he relished.[259]

The next day Churchill, who had accepted an invitation from Harvard president James Conant to speak there, took himself off by private train for the overnight run to Boston. On September 7, he addressed a standing-room-only crowd of more than 1,300 students and faculty in Harvard College's Sanders Theatre, tucked into Memorial Hall, a redbrick Victorian Gothic edifice as grand as a cathedral and, with the names of Harvard's Civil War dead embossed on twenty-eight white marble tablets affixed to the walls of the transept, as sacred a place as can be found in that fount of secular wisdom. Teddy and Franklin Roosevelt had walked its corridors, as had Cabots, Lawrences, and Lowells; and Admiral Yamamoto, dead now four months at the hands of American fliers. Inspired by Christopher Wren's Sheldonian Theatre at Oxford, Sanders boasted a semicircular lecture hall with perfect acoustics, high vaulted ceilings, and dark hardwood paneling. But for the statue that stood to the right of the lectern—the Revolutionary War agitator James Otis, depicted speaking out against George III and his Writs of Assistance in 1761—Sanders offered as English a venue as Churchill could hope for to unveil his remarkable proposal for the postwar world. There he stood, the chancellor of Bristol University, upon a Harvard stage, attired in the cap and gown of an Oxford don borrowed from Princeton for the occasion. He spoke for about four minutes on the cooperation thus far between Britain and America, then:

> The great Bismarck—for there were once great men in Germany—is said to have observed towards the close of his life that the most potent factor in human society at the end of the nineteenth century was the fact that the British and American peoples spoke the same language. That was a pregnant saying. Certainly it has enabled us to wage war together with an intimacy and harmony never before achieved among allies. The gift of a common tongue is a priceless inheritance and it may well some day become the foundation of a common citizenship. I like to think of British and Americans moving about freely over each other's wide estates with hardly a sense of being foreigners to one another.... All these are great possibilities, and I say: "Let us go into this together. Let us have another Boston Tea Party about it.
>
> Let us go forward as with other matters and other measures similar in aim and effect—let us go forward in malice to none and good will to all. Such plans offer far better prizes than taking away other people's provinces or lands or grinding them down in exploitation. The empires of the futures are the empires of the mind."[260]

Churchill was always diligent in seeking Roosevelt's approval for remarks he intended to make on American soil. His extraordinary proposal of common citizenship had certainly been cleared by Roosevelt, who in fact assured him that America was now so far removed from its isolationist past that the idea of dual citizenship would not "outrage public opinion or provide another Boston Tea Party." Eager to measure public reaction to the speech, Churchill ordered the British embassy to sift American newspapers for opinions. The Oxford political philosopher Isaiah Berlin, a Latvian expatriate and staff member at the embassy, was assigned the task. He reported that because the White House had announced the speech would contain little of political significance, it had not been covered. As well, two horrific train crashes that week occupied the front pages of American newspapers. Churchill's great American moment went largely unnoticed. Still, the *New York Times* declared the speech "has opened a vast and hopeful field of discussion....Down the grim corridors of war light begins to show."[261]

On this day Churchill quite possibly reached the high-water mark of his war leadership. He had nurtured, nagged, and prodded the alliance for almost two years to such a degree that inevitability now attached to the future. First would come victory over Hitler in Italy—I'll soon be meeting Alex in Rome, he told Lord Moran—and then victory over Hitler in Germany. And now here came Roosevelt in apparent agreement on the need to forge a permanent Anglo-American relationship. The potential appeared limitless, including the prospect of the two nations sharing a common military staff system, perhaps even a common currency, the dollar sterling, a Churchillian dream of long standing. Outside Memorial Hall, a battalion of cadets, male and female, stood smartly at attention, while Churchill addressed them briefly from the steps. He had doffed his robes, which had lent him an air of a Cardinal Wolsey, and was attired in a dark blazer, navy bow tie, and light trousers. The cadets listened in respectful silence as Churchill paraphrased his earlier address, punctuating his words by jabbing the granite steps with his walking stick. Then, to cheers, he stepped back and thrust up his "V" for victory. He was ebullient on the return trip to Washington, flashing his "V" to the engineers of passing trains, and darting out to the rear platform of the Pullman in his flowered dressing gown to flash the sign as the train slowed at each station along the way. It was left to Lord Moran to find the poignant irony in Churchill's behavior: "The P.M. stood for some time at the window of his car giving the victory sign to odd workmen in the fields, who could see nothing but a train rushing through the countryside."[262]

That day, September 7, the Italian naval minister promised Albert Kesselring that the Italian fleet was about to sail "from Spezia to seek battle with the British Mediterranean fleet," and "would conquer or perish" in the ensuing showdown. This pleased Kesselring, although doubting the trustworthiness of the entire Italian government, he had crafted a battle plan to occupy Rome were the Italians to evidence any treachery. He had also concluded that the Allies would play small and invade near Salerno rather than farther north.

Late in the afternoon of the eighth, the BBC announced the Italian surrender. The news came as a complete surprise to Victor Emmanuel and Marshal Badoglio who, not having been informed of Allied plans, thought they had more time to deploy Italian troops in order to make the changeover from enemy to co-belligerent. Later that night and into the morning of the next day, 55,000 men of the British X Corps and the U.S. VI Corps, under overall command of Mark Clark and the Fifth Army, went ashore near Salerno, almost 160 miles south of Rome and 35 miles south of Naples. No aerial or seaborne bombardment preceded the landings in order to keep Kesselring guessing right up to the moment the men went ashore.

But it was exactly as Kesselring expected. He had seen the tentativeness of Eisenhower's campaigns in Tunisia and Sicily and foresaw more of the same in Italy. And he got it, first with Montgomery's landings in Calabria, and now at Salerno. Berlin radio had predicted both operations three weeks earlier. Kesselring had deployed five divisions such that they could rapidly respond to landings from Naples to Salerno. Now they responded. John Steinbeck wrote as a war correspondent from the beaches: "The Germans were waiting for us. His 88s were on the surrounding hills and his machine guns in the sand dunes. His mines were in the surf and he sat there and waited for us." Allied caution had again trumped aggression, and the price paid not only by the troops on the beaches, but by Rome—by all of Italy—was dear. Kesselring, his plans to take Rome in place for weeks, hit the city on September 9 and occupied it the next day after the Italian divisions there drifted off to Tivoli without a fight. "Thus the main problems connected with our security in Italy have been solved," Goebbels chimed to his diary. Life changed overnight for Rome's citizens; they had committed "treachery" in Goebbels' estimation, and deserved the fate that awaited them. Romans joined the citizens of Warsaw, Paris, Rotterdam, and Brussels as prisoners of the Reich.[263]

Churchill believed that Italy's collapse, if it could be capitalized upon quickly, opened up opportunities in the Aegean. On September 8, as the troops were going ashore at Salerno, a British officer parachuted into the Italian lines on Rhodes, just off the Turkish southwest Anatolian coast. The island was the linchpin of Churchill's Balkan strategy; its capture would take pressure off the Turks (who claimed sovereignty over the Dodecanese Islands) and, he hoped, persuade them to come into the war on the Allied side. If the Turks came in, the Black Sea would become an Allied lake and the Danubian Basin would be made ripe for Churchill's ultimate Balkan thrust north into the German flank. The mission of the officer was to persuade the commander of the 30,000 Italian troops on Rhodes to attack the 7,000 Germans across the island. The Italians hesitated; the Germans did not. They attacked preemptively and routed the defenders, executing more than one hundred Italian officers in the aftermath.

Churchill's Aegean initiative was off to a most inauspicious start. He ordered his Middle East commander, Maitland ("Jumbo") Wilson, to dispatch a brigade of four thousand infantrymen to Leros, Kos, five other islands of the Dodecanese, and nearby Samos. The brigade, sliced into battalion-size formations, joined commandos already at work, and the now-friendly Italian troops deployed in the Dodecanese. But until Rhodes was taken, any gains in the Dodecanese would be difficult if not impossible to hold. "This is the time to play high," Churchill cabled Wilson. "Improvise and dare." (Churchill later lamented, "He improvose and dore.") On the thirteenth, Churchill sent off more encouragement to Wilson: "This is the time to think of Clive and Peterborough and of Rooke's taking of Gibraltar." Yet the brigade amounted to less than half the force called for by the original plans drawn up after Casablanca, and the Germans, not the RAF, controlled the airfield on Rhodes. Wilson lacked the troops and planes needed to take Rhodes, but Eisenhower had plenty of both. Churchill presumed that once Eisenhower saw the Aegean treasures to be gained at little cost, he would climb on board. He did not.[264]

While events on Rhodes spiraled into mayhem on September 9, Admiral Cunningham sailed his fleet right up to the Taranto quays in order to put ashore the British 1st Airborne Division, six thousand strong, a gallant operation necessitated by the lack of landing craft to carry the men ashore. The troops landed with only five jeeps, no trucks, no tanks, no artillery, and therefore no means to exploit their audacious arrival. The operation was ironically and aptly named "Slapstick." This unfortunate choice came just a month after Churchill demanded that staff planners not use code names that were boastful or lent themselves to ridicule. It would not do, he wrote, for "some widow or mother to say that her son was killed in an operation called BUNNYHUG or BALLYHOO." Whoever came up with Slapstick had either not read or had ignored the message.[265]

On the way into Taranto, Cunningham's ships passed the Italian fleet coming out. Tense moments ensued; Cunningham had no way of knowing if the Italians would abide by the terms of surrender or fight. The Italian minister of marine, whose fleet now sailed quietly past Cunningham headed for Malta and surrender, had not exactly been straightforward with Kesselring. Hitler had hoped the Italians would at least have the decency to deliver their navy to neutral Spain. Göring had thought otherwise, predicting that Italian treachery would extend to surrendering the fleet to the Allies. He was correct and was prepared for this eventuality. Dornier bombers carrying newly designed radio-guided gliding bombs were ordered aloft to punish the retreating Italians. *Roma,* the flagship, hit by two bombs, broke in half and went down with more than 1,300 of its crew. The rest of the fleet was delivered safely into British hands. Kesselring soon turned the new bombs on the British fleet at Salerno; a cruiser was lost and tars fast learned that aerial bombing had taken a great and dangerous leap forward. The guided bombs portended even more sinister weapons. If an engine was strapped to such a device, and if it was outfitted with even a rudimentary guidance system, it could be flung across the Channel into London. Days later, Duncan Sandys delivered a memo to Churchill that predicted exactly that. After reading it, Churchill told John Anderson that some sort of futuristic German rockets would descend on London by the end of the year.[266]

By the evening of September 10, the entire Mediterranean Sea—but not the airspace over its eastern reaches—belonged to the Allies. Yet by the twelfth, it became distressingly clear that Salerno did not. The men there, pinned down by furious German resistance, hadn't gotten off the beaches. Before going ashore, they had been told by their commanders that they'd be in Naples in three days. Instead, they were still fighting so near the beaches that they could watch their supply ships burn under the new bombs of the Luftwaffe and hear the screams of men in the water. By then, Badoglio and Victor Emmanuel had fled Rome to rendezvous with Allied gunboats, which took them off to Malta. "Surprise, violence, and speed," Churchill wrote, "are the essence of all amphibious landings." At Salerno, Albert Kesselring had turned those criteria against the invaders. It was now obvious to Churchill that the rake of war would have to tear over the length of Italy. Churchill, still in Washington, grumbled to his doctor, "These things always seem to happen when I'm with the president."[267]

There was good reason for that. Churchill went abroad when he saw an acute need to prepare for or react to battlefield climacterics, as after Pearl Harbor and Midway and before Torch and Husky. He liked to conduct business face-to-face, which usually resulted in his getting what he wanted. Now he wanted to get into the Balkans. The Americans believed his motive for doing so was to redress the errors of the Great War, and by comparing the ordeal at Salerno to the mishandled invasion at Gallipoli in 1915, Churchill only reinforced the Americans' belief in that regard. In fact, he wanted to get to Vienna before the Russians. Cadogan told his diary that Churchill, at the White House, spent his days "hurling himself violently in and out of bed, bathing at unsuitable moments and rushing up and down corridors in his dressing gown." He also kept Roosevelt up past 2:00 A.M., and during these long parleys pressed him to keep an open mind on the need for flexibility regarding Overlord. In effect, in spite of the agreements just made in Quebec, he was asking Roosevelt to view Overlord as one of many options, including the developing situation on Rhodes. Roosevelt rebuffed him. Then, in need of respite from Churchill and the hours he kept, the president took himself off to Hyde Park. Before leaving he told Churchill to make himself at home in the White House.[268]

Harriman knew from experience that it was always flexibility with Churchill, whether the battleground was military or diplomatic. Churchill's postwar union with America was a case in point; he told Harriman he "liked the idea of a loose association rather than a formal treaty... an association flexible enough to adjust itself to historical developments." Flexibility had defined since early 1942 the meetings between the British and American chiefs. The discussions were always disputatious, yet so far they had always ended with unified statements of intent. If circumstances later deranged the timely realization of those pledges, that was war and all of its vagaries. The critical point was that the strategies agreed upon admitted to flexibility. Churchill and Roosevelt never flinched from trying to impose design upon chance, which so often rules the business of war, but to date neither had demanded rigidity in strategy. The alliance—a real coalition as Churchill saw it—was functioning. After all, he had been handed the keys to the White House by Franklin Roosevelt, from wherein he conducted high-level meetings, a British prime minister chairing sessions of the American Chiefs of Staff. Here was his dream being made real, a British premier presiding over the crafting of collective policy, in the White House, no less. Of course, the courtesy would be reciprocated when Roosevelt journeyed to London, and especially once some sort of "union" between the English-speaking peoples had been agreed upon in the legislatures of both lands. It need not at first be strictly formal, as he told Harriman, for formal relationships often begin as informal understandings, as had this alliance.[269]

On September 12, their thirty-fifth wedding anniversary, Winston and Clementine journeyed to Hyde Park, their last American stop before leaving for Halifax and the voyage home. The president toasted their health at dinner and tried to dazzle Clementine with "the magnetic quality of his charm" but failed. Clementine, her daughter Mary later wrote, "got along well" with Roosevelt but quickly concluded, "his personal vanity was inordinate." It did not help when Roosevelt called Clementine "Clemmie," a breach of etiquette in Mrs. Churchill's estimation, as she regarded the use of Christian names a "privilege marking close friendship or long association," neither of which described her relationship with Roosevelt.[270]

After dinner that night, Churchill and Roosevelt agreed that an infusion of several divisions of Polish infantry in aid of Tito's partisans might be just the ticket for the Balkans, where Italian troops were already joining the Allied cause. "Any opportunity" that presented itself in the Balkans, Roosevelt told Churchill, should be taken advantage of. This understandably struck Churchill as a validation of his Balkan strategy, although Roosevelt, when announcing the third war bond drive earlier that week, had made no mention of the Balkans, or Tito, or Poles. Roosevelt told Americans that their troops—*your* boys, *our* boys—were on their way to Berlin and Tokyo. Indeed, in the Pacific, the Americans held Port Moresby; their bombers were pounding Rabaul, and a carrier task force was about to strike Wake Island. The invasion of Tarawa Atoll in the Gilbert Islands was planned for November. The advance to Tokyo had begun. Given that the Chinese were incompetent, the Russians were not at war with Japan, and the British were incapable of driving from India to Tokyo, it would be Americans and only the Americans who someday entered Tokyo.

On the European front, it began to look like the Russians and only the Russians would someday reach Berlin. If the Red Army kept rolling west at its current pace, Anglo-American forces would someday enter Berlin only by invitation of Stalin. Churchill had argued for two years that unless agreement was reached with the Soviets to discuss borders only after final victory, whoever in the meantime took territory ruled that territory, which brought the question around, as always, to Poland. What would be the fate of Poland—and Czechoslovakia, the Baltic states, and Austria, Hungary, Bulgaria, and Romania—after the Red Army swept through on its way to Berlin? Roosevelt's suggestion of a move into the Balkans, therefore, helped assuage Churchill's growing uncertainties in regard to Russia.[271]

Happy to have Roosevelt in his court on the Balkans, Churchill returned the favor on the matter of the atomic bomb. The two leaders concluded what amounted to a private treaty. It bypassed both the (written) U.S. Constitution and the (unwritten) British in that neither Congress nor Parliament (nor the full cabinet in either country) knew that an atomic bomb was being produced. They agreed privately that all atomic secrets would be shared, that neither party would ever use the bomb against the other, and that each party would inform the other of intended use against a third party. The fourth clause held that postwar Britain would not pursue commercial use of atomic energy based on knowledge gained in the development of the bomb. This caveat stemmed from American fears that Britain might try to reap commercial rewards from America's wartime financial sacrifice. Churchill's acceptance of the condition shocked R. V. Jones, who had solved the question of how to jam the German targeting beams and now headed the scientific intelligence branch of the Air Staff. Churchill, Jones later wrote, "had signed away our birthright in the postwar development of nuclear energy." Yet Jones understood two truths—the Americans had leverage, and it was typical of Churchill to make such a "magnificent gesture" in order to allay American fears. Churchill had conducted such business throughout Quadrant over dinners with Roosevelt and Hopkins, where men of honor transacted such business. Cadogan's diary entries testified to the good fellowship. Churchill: "This water tastes funny"; Hopkins: "Because there's no whisky in it. Fancy you a judge of water!" And Harry to "Mr. P.M." as Churchill paced the room delivering another monologue: "Your pants is coming down." Yet Churchill, in presuming that the bonhomie he found at the president's table carried weight, failed to grasp a basic tenet of American politics: good cheer is nonbinding. Only the U.S. Congress can bind, and Churchill did not understand just how binding the U.S. Congress can be. Unlike Clementine, Churchill was quite dazzled by Roosevelt's charm.[272]

On September 12, Churchill learned early in the day that Waffen SS parachute commandos had plucked Benito Mussolini from his mountaintop confinement. As Churchill feared, a quisling government was about to be formed in northern Italy, but he had not foreseen that Mussolini, imprisoned for six weeks, would be at its helm. "Italy," Churchill later wrote, "was now to pass through the most tragic time in her history." Goebbels' Italian labor force was growing exponentially. Tens of thousands of Italians were fleeing the developing battles in the south of Italy. Of the flood of "fugitives," Goebbels confided to his diary, "Gigantic columns of Italian prisoners are on their way into the Reich. They are very welcome here as skilled workers." "Slaves" would have been a more accurate description.[273]

That week, German military propaganda celebrated the good news coming out of Italy, especially the drubbing inflicted on Mark Clark at Salerno, which the propagandists compared to Dunkirk and Gallipoli. But Salerno was not yet a battle won, which Goebbels knew well. He had warned the military propagandists to show caution; they had not. He summed up the situation to his diary with a line that happened also to be one of Churchill's favorites: "I have always held . . . that the skin of the bear must not be distributed until the bear has been killed."[274]

By the time Churchill boarded HMS *Renown* on September 14, the U-boats had all but disappeared from the central and southern Atlantic but for irregular sniping along the South American and African coasts. Since late May, sixty-two convoys comprising 3,246 merchant ships sailed between America and Britain on the northern route; not a single ship was lost. In the southern and mid-Atlantic and Indian Ocean (where Dönitz had sent several U-boats), September's losses from all causes came to about 208,000 tons, not much more than a week's losses earlier in the year. October's losses would come in under 100,000 tons, at a cost to Dönitz of twenty-three U-boats; earlier in the year the British had budgeted a loss of 550,000 tons for October. The Allies were on track to lose less than half the tonnage in 1943 than they had lost in 1942. And Dönitz's losses began to increase exponentially. As summer prepared to give way to autumn, Dönitz pulled his fleet even farther east.[275]

Still, in the Arctic, the threats from U-boats, from *Scharnhorst* and *Tirpitz,* and from long-range German bombers conspired against restarting the Russian convoys. Hitler placed his faith in technological advances, in the air and under the sea. Goebbels enthused to his diary over a new German torpedo (called Gnat by the Allies) that "listened" for and homed in on cavitation noise of around 24.5 kHz, which was equivalent to the "noise" made by propellers on a destroyer cruising at moderate speed. Nine Allied destroyers (and more than a thousand sailors) were lost in September to the new torpedo, but with Dönitz's U-boats leaving the battlefield, the torpedo's deadly efficiencies could not be exploited. With the sea-lanes to Britain secure, the buildup of troops and tanks in Britain in preparation for Overlord proceeded at will. Hitler had long held that control of the Atlantic Ocean was his best defense against the West. His defense had disappeared.[276]

By November, American transports were arriving at British ports after ten-day journeys during which the green troops stuffed belowdecks played poker, wrote letters, and ate hot navy chow. Some of the ships' captains allowed army personnel to set up shipboard radio stations that played records over the PA system for the listening ease of the men below. One recording, however, was often banned: Bing Crosby's new hit, "I'll Be Home for Christmas."[277]

Renown brought Churchill safely into the Clyde on September 19. The voyage had been uneventful but for Mary almost being washed overboard when she accepted a young officer's invitation to stroll the quarterdeck at the moment the ship made a sharp turn in high seas. Had she not snagged herself on a stanchion, she would have been swept away, the event witnessed by Ismay from the bridge but not by Churchill. "We had visions of plunging overboard," Ismay later wrote, "rather than face the Prime Minister."

Churchill received daily briefing on the Salerno landings during the five-day voyage, and the news was worrisome. Little progress was being made, which is to say the men remained trapped on the beaches. For months Hopkins and Stimson had deprecated Churchill's fears of French beaches running red with blood; yet the situation at Salerno was developing in exactly that way. Very worrisome was the fact that more men had gone ashore at Salerno in the first three days than were called for in the Overlord plan for France. Churchill continued to proclaim that the landing was beginning to look like the landings at Suvla Bay during the Gallipoli campaign. Each day of delay at Salerno brought ever increasing concentrations of Germans on the beach perimeter, and increased the chances of the Allies being thrown back into the sea. Churchill proposed to fly there himself to take charge, but Alexander, anticipating such an offer, had already left for the front. Not until Churchill was back on British soil did he receive the news he had been waiting for: "I can say with full confidence," Alexander wrote, "that the whole situation has changed in our favor, and that the initiative has passed to us." Yet it had taken Alexander almost three weeks to establish his armies in the toe and ankle of Italy, and he still had 150 miles to go before reaching Rome.[278]

Shortly after Churchill arrived home, Admiral Dudley Pound submitted his resignation. His brain tumor killed him a month later, on October 21, Trafalgar Day. He was "the smartest sailor in the Royal Navy," Churchill told Jock Colville, "but cautious." Yet Pound's conservative deployment of HMG's fleets had kept England in the chase for four years. Pound lived to see victory in the Atlantic, and the victory was his. Old British sailors will argue that the British Home Fleet at Scapa Flow, by virtue of being a "fleet in being," played as critical a role as the boys in their Hurricanes and Spitfires in keeping Hitler out of England. Hitler tested Fighter Command but could not bring himself to test the Home Fleet. Myth attached to "the few," but the sailors had done their duty, Pound foremost. Andrew ("ABC") Cunningham, hero of the Mediterranean, replaced Pound as first sea lord.

Harry Hopkins checked himself into the hospital in a state of exhaustion as soon as Churchill departed for London. Eisenhower was also worn out and under a doctor's care. Dill, too, was being ground down; he had injured himself while hunting boar in India the previous year and would not live out the next. And Chancellor of the Exchequer Sir Kingsley Wood, whose stewardship of the British purse had kept the Island afloat financially, died suddenly two days after Churchill's return to London. A shake-up in the ranks was taking place of a sort and magnitude no one had foreseen.

The same could be said of the shake-ups Britons experienced at home and at work. On September 23, Churchill addressed six thousand women from all walks of British life in Albert Hall. As with all of his speeches, he had composed it himself. He told the women:

> We are engaged in a struggle for life.... This war effort could not have been achieved if the women had not marched forward in millions and undertaken all kinds of tasks and work for which any other generation but our own unless you go back to the Stone Age would have considered them unfitted.... Nothing has been grudged, and the bounds of women's activities have been definitely, vastly, and permanently enlarged.... It may seem strange that a great advance in the position of women in the world in industry, in controls of all kinds, should be made in time of war and not in time of peace. One would have thought that in the days of peace the progress of women to an ever larger share in the life and work and guidance of the community would have grown, and that, under the violences of war, it would be cast back. The reverse is true. War is the teacher, a hard, stern, efficient teacher. War has taught us to make these vast strides forward towards a far more complete equalisation of the parts to be played by men and women in society.

He had come a long way in the three decades since declaring of the suffragettes, "What a ridiculous tragedy it will be if this strong Government and party which has made its mark in history were to go down on petticoat politics."[279]

Churchill, the Chiefs of Staff, and the cabinet were in need of rest, but none was forthcoming. John Anderson moved over to the Exchequer, Attlee took over as lord president. Max Beaverbrook, who for health reasons had taken himself away from the pressures of producing goods, rejoined the government as lord privy seal. This was an ill-defined position that admitted to elasticity, perfect for Beaverbrook, whose real role in the new command structure was to serve as Churchill's crony, booster, and foil. South Africa's Jan Smuts now sat in on the War Cabinet meetings (informally, at Churchill's invitation) and brought with him a growing distaste for Overlord, which he imparted not only to Churchill, who had his own doubts, but also to King George. The migration of ministers from post to post struck Churchill as both worrisome and comical; when the reorganization was complete, he took a partisan swipe at his Labour colleagues when he told Eden, "Except for me and you, this is the worst government England has ever had."[280]

British troops entered Naples on October 1 to find that the Germans had very efficiently destroyed the port and its facilities before departing. Since coming ashore at Salerno, the Fifth Army had advanced on average just over a mile per day. Still, Churchill cabled Alexander that he looked forward to meeting him in Rome in a month or so. But at Alexander's rate of advance, his armies would not reach Rome, 120 miles to the north, until sometime in February 1944. Churchill's hopes for the swift capture of Rome and a drive to northern Italy had been wrecked on the road to Naples. Albert Kesselring later said of the weakness inherent in the Allied strategy: "An air landing on Rome and sea landing nearby, instead of at Salerno, would have automatically caused us to evacuate all the southern half of Italy." Now the Allies would have to pay in blood for every mile of ground between Naples and Rome, ground they could have purchased at little cost. By early October, the Eighth Army had moved up the Adriatic coast to take the port of Bari and the airfields at Foggia, and had connected with the Fifth Army in a continuous 120-mile line across the Italian peninsula from Naples on the Tyrrhenian Sea to Termoli on the Adriatic. Montgomery's army formed the right flank of the Italian campaign, but in Churchill's mind it also formed the left flank of the Balkan front. A million Allied troops stood idle throughout Eisenhower's command in the western Mediterranean; landing ships and craft were plentiful (although Eisenhower was about to transfer 85 percent of them to Britain). Churchill wanted to put a small percentage of those men and landing craft into the Aegean, where with the capture of Rhodes, the Balkan right flank would be turned, leaving the underbelly of the Balkans exposed. Tito waited with 200,000 well-armed partisans; the Chetniks fielded another 150,000. The Turks, beneficiaries of one hundred million dollars in British and American aide, fielded forty-five divisions, albeit poorly trained, poorly armed, and lacking armored support. Tito held strips of the Dalmatian coast, where supplies could be put ashore. Turkish airfields would allow the RAF to lend air support. The Allied forces Churchill sought would be needed only to prime the pump. Brooke years later wrote that it might have all been accomplished "without committing a single man in the Balkans." Tito, Mihailovic, and the Turks (if they came in) could do most of the rest. Thus began Churchill's newest Aegean adventure.[281]

He climbed onto his new hobbyhorse, Rhodes, which took its place in the stable alongside Norway and Sumatra. On October 3, German troops attacked the Dodecanese island of Kos just three miles off the Turkish coast. British control of the airfield there was vital if the RAF hoped to cover the Royal Navy as it advanced toward the Greek mainland. Holding Kos would also demonstrate British resolve to the Turks. Yet with the airfield and the island virtually undefended, the Germans took Kos in four days, along with more than 1,300 British soldiers and airmen. Now the Germans were within shouting distance of the Turkish mainland. The

Turks, not sanguine and for good reason, decided the time was not yet right to join the Allies.

"Another day of Rhodes madness," Brooke wrote on October 7 after a particularly nasty "battle with the P.M." over the wisdom of the Rhodes strategy. Churchill announced that he was leaving for Algiers in order to bring Eisenhower around. Brooke was beside himself: "This is all to decide whether we should try and take Rhodes.... He [the P.M.] is in a very dangerous condition, most unbalanced, and God knows how we shall finish this war if it goes on."[282]

Churchill cabled Roosevelt with a request to send Marshall to Tunisia in order to settle the Aegean strategy. Roosevelt's reply was "cold," Brooke wrote, a flat refusal that left no room for interpretation. The president refused to force any decision on Eisenhower even if he agreed with Churchill's strategy, which he did not. "It is my opinion," Roosevelt wrote, "that no diversion of forces or equipment should prejudice Overlord as planned." Churchill replied the next day, telling Roosevelt that the Aegean plan required only a few weeks' use of nine landing ships, which would not be needed for Overlord for at least six months. He asked for "some elasticity and a reasonable latitude in the handling of our joint affairs." The Mediterranean, he pleaded, was being "stripped bare at a moment when great prizes could be cheaply won." Roosevelt stood firm. "If we get the Aegean Islands," he replied, "I ask myself where do we go from there, and vice versa where would the Germans go if... they retain possession of the islands?" But Churchill didn't care where the Germans might go. He cared about British influence in the eastern Mediterranean. He wanted the Royal Navy there, on station, to send a message to not only Hitler but also Stalin that the Balkans were within the British sphere. It was not to be. The German capture of Kos meant that the British troops on Leros could be neither reinforced nor evacuated. Hitler had no intention of going anywhere after taking the Dodecanese; his goal was to keep the British from grabbing these plums and going someplace themselves, such as the Dardanelles and the Balkans. He succeeded in doing just that. And with Germans now camped just off the Turkish coast, the prospect of Turkey joining the Allies all but disappeared. Churchill instructed Eden "to coerce the Turks into the war." Asked by Brooke how Eden should go about doing that, Churchill replied, "Remind the Turkey that Xmas is coming."[283]

Although Brooke regularly savaged Churchill's strategic priorities, the two were actually in agreement on the Aegean. Yet events had bypassed the Aegean strategy, a fact that Churchill simply could not grasp. Brooke understood what Churchill did not: Rhodes was the correct play, but the timing had gone wrong. Churchill's push for Rhodes could only result in increased American suspicion of his (imperial) motives and a decrease in

American support of operations in Italy, a double disaster. It was a tragedy in Brooke's judgment, the blame for which he put down to his own lack of "sufficient force of character to swing those American Chiefs of Staff and make them see the daylight." Brooke later wrote that he was on the verge of a nervous breakdown that October, not because of Churchill's "Rhodes madness," but because the Americans were stripping the Mediterranean of resources "for a nebulous 2nd front." On November 1, he told his diary what might have been: "We should have been in a position to force the Dardanelles by the capture of Crete and Rhodes, we should have the whole Balkans ablaze by now, and the war might have been finished in 1943." These were Churchill's sentiments exactly. But the Combined Chiefs had agreed at Quebec to strip the Mediterranean of at least six divisions in order to feed Overlord. "It is heartbreaking," Brooke wrote.[284]

Caution, Churchill told one of his stenographers, Marian Holmes, had again prevailed over aggression. Miss Holmes found the P.M. "distressed" by the refusal of Roosevelt to see things his way. Churchill told her he felt "almost like chucking it in" and "the difficulty is not in winning the war; it is in persuading people to let you win it—persuading fools." A few weeks later, on his way to Cairo and Tehran, Churchill offered to HMG's new resident minister to Allied Mediterranean headquarters, Harold Macmillan: "Such caution leads to weak and faltering decisions—or rather, indecisions. Why, you may take the most gallant sailor, the most intrepid airman, or the most audacious soldier, put them at a table together—what do you get? The sum of their fears." Churchill, bitter, never forgave Eisenhower for making the decision. "I was grieved," Churchill wrote in his memoirs, "that my small requests" resulted in Ike's "obdurate" resistance to and ultimate rejection of the Rhodes venture.[285]

Yet it was Eisenhower's decision, not Eisenhower the man, that fueled Churchill's bitterness. In a typically Churchillian display of generosity, the very week Eisenhower scuttled the Rhodes gambit, Churchill received permission from King George to commission a special North African campaign ribbon for Eisenhower and Alexander. The ribbons were embossed with the numerals "1" and "8" in reference to the two Allied armies. Churchill, on his way to Cairo, personally pinned the awards on Ike and Alex. Brooke, for his part, lacked Churchill's ability to maintain numerous (and often conflicting) opinions about a man, with the result that Brooke's criticism of his colleagues' professional judgments, including Churchill's, often took the form of ad hominem assaults. The CIGS blamed Eisenhower and Marshall for the inertia in the Mediterranean, the former for being seduced by Overlord due to its "being easier to understand" than the complexities of the Mediterranean theater, the latter due to the "limitations of Marshall's brain" and his inability to "ever, ever see the end of his nose."[286]

On Overlord there could be no turning back, but not for want of trying on Field Marshal Jan Smuts's part, with the support of King George. Even before Churchill arrived home from Quebec, Smuts whispered the folly of Overlord to the King. Smuts and the King dined together on October 13 and ratified their anti-Overlord alliance. The next day in a letter to Churchill, the King made known his doubts about the cross-Channel plan and expressed his belief that the "underbelly" strategy was correct. He advised Churchill to take the matter up with Roosevelt and Stalin when they met in late November. Churchill swiftly disabused the King of any notion of backing out, writing in return, "There is no question of our going back on what is agreed." Yet there *was* a question, and Churchill raised it at the Chiefs of Staff meeting on the nineteenth when he requested a swing around to the Mediterranean even at the expense of Overlord. "I am in many ways entirely with him," Brooke wrote that night, "but God knows where that may lead us to as regards clashes with Americans." The next week Churchill and Smuts argued to the COS that the Mediterranean theater had more merit than a French landing and that since Britain controlled her own destinies, Britain could choose to fight where she chose. Even Max Beaverbrook, who was in attendance, came around. The Beaver had backed the cross-Channel strategy loudest and longest but, after pondering Churchill's arguments, announced that since they had committed to the Mediterranean, they "should make a job of it." Yet they couldn't go it alone, and they knew it.[287]

On November 1, Churchill wrote a memo to the chiefs in which he lamented Britain's lack of available manpower for expanding operations: "We cannot add to the total; on the contrary, it is already dwindling." All able-bodied men sixteen to sixty-five had been mustered for the services and armaments work, as had all able-bodied women aged eighteen to fifty. The manpower pool had evaporated. Still, Churchill found comfort in the fact that when Marshall took over command of Overlord, and Eisenhower replaced Marshall in Washington, a British commander in the Mediterranean, unfettered by American constraints, could then fulfill British destinies. Yet many in the American press argued that Overlord amounted to a demotion for Marshall and were calling for a bigger role, that of supreme Allied commander in the European theater. In mid-October, Churchill had asked Roosevelt for clarification on the matter, only to receive an indeterminate answer two weeks later. A week later, Churchill instructed Dill, in Washington, to make clear to Hopkins and Admiral Leahy that the British would never accede to a single European supreme commander; to do so would in effect deprive the British Chiefs of Staff of their sovereign authority. Churchill also expressed his doubts about Overlord to Roosevelt, but with not quite the conviction he had displayed to the British chiefs. "I do not doubt our ability . . . to get ashore and deploy," he told the president. "I am, however, deeply concerned with the build-up and with the situation that may arise between the 30th and 60th days." Getting ashore would be easy; staying ashore was what worried Churchill. A repulse, he told Roosevelt, could only "give Hitler the chance of a startling comeback."[288]

There was clearly much to thrash out before they met Stalin, and at Roosevelt's suggestion, Churchill agreed to a bilateral conference, code-named Sextant, in Cairo before moving on to meet Stalin, presumably in Tehran, although there were growing doubts both in Moscow and Washington about meeting in such an out-of-the-way place. Roosevelt also suggested that Chiang Kai-shek join the party in Cairo in order that Pacific strategies could be addressed. This should have sounded alarms, but Churchill agreed and, with the Chinese legend of the celestial dragon that protects the holiest places in mind, chose Celestes as Chiang's secret identity.

During the eight weeks between the Allied landing at Salerno and early November, the Red Army struck along a five-hundred-mile front. By October 1 it had taken Smolensk and Katyn, three hundred miles north of Kiev. Stalin intended to fight on through the winter. His factories beyond the Urals were turning out almost 2,000 tanks per month; German factories struggled to produce 350 panzers per month. The Luftwaffe, having been peeled away from the Eastern Front to protect the Reich from the RAF, had lost air superiority. The Iranian rail line was pumping six thousand tons per day of matériel into Russia. The weather was worsening, but winter was not the enemy of the Russian soldier; thirteen million pairs of fleece-lined boots stamped *Made in the USA* ensured that the Red Army marched in relative comfort. One hundred thousand American-made Studebaker trucks assured that the troops' supplies would follow close behind. The Americans offered to ship thousands of armored cars, but Stalin declined; he considered them to be death traps.

The Soviet attack was fashioned on Marshal Foch's broad-front strategy of 1918, whereby gains were exploited until the advancing troops needed replenishment, at which time other strikes were launched elsewhere on the front. As conducted by the Red Army, the strategy resulted in the Germans having to hurry reinforcements to points under attack while simultaneously restricting their ability to reinforce points that might be struck next. It was a strategy, Liddell Hart wrote, that "paralyzed [German] freedom of action." The Red Army command "might be likened to a pianist running his hands up and down the keyboard." On November 6 it took Kiev (just 120 miles from the Polish border) and crossed the Dnieper at several points south of Kiev. The crossing of the Dnieper was a crippling blow to Hitler, for the high west bank of the river offered him the best natural barrier in southern Russia and was expected to form the backbone of the eastern wall, which Hitler had just ordered built. The fortification—the easternmost bulwark of Hitler's empire—was to run from the Sea of Azov north along the Dnieper to Kiev, and from Kiev north to the Baltic at Narva. But the eastern wall was to remain only a line on paper.[289]

"The more furious the storm," Goebbels told his diary in late September as the southern Russian front deteriorated, "the more determined is the Führer to meet it." Still, he added, "It gives one the creeps to look at the map and compare what we had under our dominion ... last year with how far we have now been thrown back." Later that month Goebbels wrote, "We must achieve success somewhere. A kingdom for a victory." Dimly grasping the possibility of national obliteration, he broached the subject of a negotiated peace to Hitler. Their thinking on the matter was in turns precise and delusional. Negotiations with either Britain or Russia would prove problematic, Hitler offered, for "England is not yet groggy enough nor sufficiently tired of war." Any attempt at negotiation would only be seen by London "as a sign of weakness." But in time, "the English would come to their senses." In the east, "Stalin has the advantage," and any peace feelers would only be seen in the Kremlin as dealing from weakness. Thus, in the east, "the present moment is quite unfavorable" for negotiations. That was because the Germans were losing in the east. So they pondered England again. "The Führer believes it would be easier to make a deal with the English than with the Soviets.... Churchill is absolutely anti-Bolshevik." But the problem with the English *was* Churchill. Goebbels believed Stalin the safer bet as he was a "practical politician," whereas "Churchill is a romantic adventurer, with whom one can't talk sensibly.... The Führer does not believe that negotiations with Churchill would lead to any result as he is too deeply wedded to his hostile views, and besides, is guided by hatred and not by reason." In order to better understand his English enemies, Goebbels that month read *How Green Was My Valley*. He concluded the English would never "become Bolshevized." This might prove valuable from a negotiation standpoint; the Reich and England shared a common enemy, after all. Both Hitler and Goebbels seemed to have forgotten that Stalin had once been *their* ally.[290]

On September 23 Goebbels displayed a modicum of sense on the matter while dining with Hitler at the Wolf's Lair (*Wolfsschanze*), the Führer's East Prussian headquarters near Rastenburg. "We must come to an arrangement," Goebbels advised, "with one side or the other. The Reich has never yet won a two-front war." England seemed the better choice because "one can always make a better deal with a democratic state." Yet here was Churchill indulging "in orgies of hatred against the Reich" while promising Britons (and Germans) that "the Reich is to face total destruction." Falling under a momentary spell of rationality, Goebbels concluded that "it is quite doubtful whether we can choose between Russia and England." Yet an approach must be made to one or the other. The German people, Goebbels told Hitler, are "yearning for peace." Hitler allowed that he, too, yearned for peace. "The Führer stressed this," Goebbels wrote. "He said he would be happy to have contact with artistic circles again, to go to the theater in the evening and visit the Artist's Club." He had plans for grand art museums in his hometown, Linz, but at the same time was intent on pushing "Vienna back artistically." In the meantime, Hitler told Goebbels, "our big rocket...fourteen tons...is a murderous tool" that would set the English straight. This delighted Goebbels: "I believe that when the first of these missiles descends upon London, a sort of panic will break out among the English people." That night the RAF smashed Hanover.[291]

The Reich's leaders saw their salvation in the planned "great reprisal campaign by rockets" set for February, target: London. Churchill was privy to just enough intelligence to form an incomplete yet increasingly worrisome picture of just what German rocket scientists were up to. He advised Roosevelt, "The Germans are preparing an attack on England, particularly London, by means of very long range rockets which may conceivably weigh 60 tons and carry an explosive charge of 10 to 20 tons." England had no defense against such a weapon. Yet Churchill's most trusted science adviser, Lord Cherwell, was offering "5 to 1 odds against" the Germans developing a rocket. Alexander Cadogan agreed with Cherwell, but confessed his lack of certainty to his diary: "They're preparing *something* there's no doubt" (italics Cadogan).[292]

On October 3 Harriman departed Washington for his new assignment as American ambassador to the Kremlin. He stopped in London for a few days, but only to take his leave. Roosevelt had been pressing him to take the job for months. Since March the Russians had ignored the current ambassador, Admiral William H. Standley, after Standley disagreed publicly with Stalin's declaration that the Red Army alone was bearing the full brunt of the war. Standley, whose remarks had not been cleared by Hull, urged *Izvestia* to publish full and honest accountings of Lend-Lease aid, including 85,000 trucks, 6,100 aircraft, and 8,600 tanks shipped to Russia. The Russian press soon made mention of Lend-Lease, but within weeks came the Katyn incident, the abandonment of Roundup, and the Anglo-American exclusion of Russia from the Italian negotiations. The Moscow post needed new blood; with reluctance Harriman took it. It meant goodbye to London and to Churchill, whose company Harriman thoroughly enjoyed, and to Pamela, whose bed he enjoyed (the lovers' hiatus lasted almost three decades, until 1971, when Pamela Beryl Digby Churchill Hayward became the third Mrs. Harriman). Soon after Harriman left for Moscow, Ed Murrow and his wife, Janet, began frequenting Pamela's salon where, not yet twenty-four, she led England's best and the brightest in discussions that parsed the political mysteries of their age. She spoke French fluently, had dazzling blue eyes, a fabulous figure, and met Henry James's ideal of the English beauty: a complexion "as bright as a sunbeam after rain." She exerted a strong gravitational pull on men, including Murrow. Soon, Murrow and Pamela were conducting their own private salon. Murrow's boss at CBS, William S. Paley, who also fell under Pamela's spell, later called her the greatest courtesan of the twentieth century. It was meant as a compliment. Whatever Churchill knew of all this he kept to himself, for he cared deeply for Pamela, who, by delivering to Winston a fair-haired blue-eyed grandson, could do no wrong in his estimation.[293]

Harriman, accompanied by his daughter Kathleen, arrived in Moscow on the eighteenth. His first duty was to open up the ambassador's residence, Spaso House, to Eden, Molotov, and Hull, who were about to convene the first meeting of the Allied foreign ministers. The talks were intended as a prelude to the first meeting of the Big Three the following month in Tehran, although Stalin still held out for Moscow because, as Molotov explained to Eden, the marshal was "indispensable" to the Red Army's fight. Roosevelt, fearing Tehran would find him so far afield that he'd be unable to meet his constitutional obligations to remain in contact with his government, requested that they meet in Ankara or Basra, but Stalin held firm. Eden, at first skeptical of Molotov's assessment, soon witnessed Stalin in action and concluded that Molotov was not exaggerating. Stalin was in regular contact with his generals on the front lines, and was deeply involved with the planning of an operation in Crimea. Where Roosevelt happily delegated military strategy to his lieutenants and Churchill unhappily did likewise, Stalin was a hands-on commander in chief. Urged by Eden, he finally committed to go as far as Tehran, but no farther. Stalin was not in a giving mood. He wanted guarantees on the second front, and he demanded the Arctic convoys be resumed.[294]

In the spring the Admiralty had proposed, and Churchill accepted, a cessation of Arctic convoys, infuriating Stalin in the process. Now in the autumn, with *Tirpitz* crippled weeks earlier by an audacious attack by three British mini-submarines, and the U-boats having all but disappeared from the Arctic routes, Churchill pushed a reluctant Admiralty to send four large convoys to Murmansk, one per month until February. Presuming that Stalin would welcome the news, Churchill sent a message along to Moscow. Stalin, in a blunt response, claimed Britain had "an obligation" to send the four convoys and virtually demanded they make the run to Murmansk immediately. The Foreign Office found the telegram "outrageous." Churchill refused even to respond, handing it back to the new Soviet ambassador, Feodor Gousev. But to Eden, in Moscow, Churchill cabled that he thought the Soviet "machine," not Stalin, was behind the tone of the cable, in part because it took twelve days to prepare. "The Soviet machine is quite convinced it can get everything by bullying, and I am sure it is a matter of some importance to show that this is not necessarily always true." Stalin shrugged off Churchill's refusal, telling Eden, "I understand Mr. Churchill does not want to correspond with me. Well, let it be so." Then Stalin came at Eden over the only matter that really mattered: the second front. It was exactly as Eden had predicted at Quebec. Unless Stalin got his assurances, and until he believed that the Anglo-Americans were fighting the same war on the same Continent, he was content to let the West stew over the two questions that would not go away: Would the Red Army stop at its borders after expelling the Germans, and would Moscow seek a separate peace with Hitler?[295]

To placate Stalin, Churchill instructed Eden to reassure the marshal that three British divisions had been pulled from the Mediterranean for deployment in Overlord, in accordance with the Quebec agreement. Yet he also informed Eden (but not Stalin) that he objected to this depletion of his forces and that he was gathering four more divisions to "repair the loss." "This is what happens when battles are governed by lawyers' agreements, and persisted in without regard to the ever-changing fortunes of war." It fell to Eden to convince Stalin that Overlord had the full support of the prime minister, when in fact, that very week, Churchill told the Chiefs of Staff he wished to delay Overlord if doing so meant that the battle in Italy (and the Balkans, if he only could get there) would be "nourished and fought until it is won." "We will do our very best for Overlord," he told Eden, but "it is of no use planning defeat in the field in order to give temporary political satisfaction." Three days later, he told Eden, as he had Smuts and the King, "There is of course no question of abandoning Overlord, which will remain our principal operation for 1944." Yet delay amounted to abandonment. Overlord might safely be pushed back to June, or even early July 1944, but any further delay would take it into the spring of 1945. That, Stalin could not abide.[296]

The Anglo-American commitment to Overlord gave Stalin leverage. He used it to effect on Eden and Hull. Eden came to Moscow with hopes of parsing Stalin's intentions as to Russia's postwar borders, but he was hobbled by the refusal of the London Poles and their new leader, Stanisław Mikołajczyk (who had not been invited to Moscow), to allow him to even discuss the matter. Eden acceded to their wishes, yet it was clear that Stalin, too, saw no need to discuss anything. He had already made up his mind. As divulged by *Izvestia,* he intended to preserve his territorial gains of 1939 and to exercise great influence in the "security belt" of the Balkans. *Izvestia* claimed that when the second front was launched, and only then, "will it be easier to decide all other necessary questions." For five hundred years, Western Europe had maintained a cordon sanitaire of small client states as a buffer between itself and the Russians, who Europeans considered an Asiatic race. Stalin intended to turn the tables; the new cordon, under his control, would serve as a buffer against the West, especially Germany. Indeed, a few weeks later Czechoslovak president Eduard Beneš, justifiably wary of France and England, signed a twenty-year treaty of mutual assistance with Stalin.[297]

Together, Hull and Eden might have brought some political will to bear on the question of borders, but to Eden's amazement, Hull dismissed the boundary questions as "a Pandora's box of infinite trouble" and refused to discuss the matter. Harriman offered Eden his full support if he pressed the issue with Stalin, but Eden, respecting the decision of Mikołajczyk, chose not to. Hull proceeded to spend his political capital—all of it—by demanding that Stalin acknowledge China as the fourth power in the nebulous four-power postwar league under discussion. Stalin was only too happy to oblige. He was not at war with Japan. If by signing a four-party declaration of solidarity in fighting "respective enemies" and pledging to participate in a postwar international peacekeeping body he could make the boundary issues disappear, he'd sign, and did. Hull was quite pleased that Stalin had not even raised the question of frontiers, but, Harriman later wrote, Hull failed to grasp the essential truth: Stalin considered the issue settled. The Moscow Accord, though celebrated in Washington and London, was symbolic at best. Stalin might as well have signed it with disappearing ink. But the table had been set for Tehran. An agenda had been worked out for the Big Three to work through. Roosevelt had gained acceptance of his nascent international organization, or at least gained Stalin's willingness to talk about it. Stalin had gained a pledge by the Anglo-Americans to open the second front in the spring of 1944. England and Churchill had gained nothing, and the Polish question had simply been postponed.[298]

By early November both the Italian campaign and the air campaign over Germany were flagging. This was not news Churchill wanted to deliver to Stalin in a few weeks' time. In mid-October, Ultra decrypts had revealed Hitler's decision to strengthen and hold his positions in Italy rather than stage a gradual, fighting retreat. Hitler ordered Kesselring's strength increased from sixteen to twenty-three divisions. That bit of intelligence guaranteed that Eisenhower would not fight in both the Aegean and Italy. News mid-month that Erwin Rommel had been sent to Yugoslavia to command German forces there only reinforced Eisenhower's decision to avoid Rhodes and the Balkans. He considered the mission in Italy fulfilled by the capture of Naples and the Foggia airfields, and the establishment of the 120-mile line that ran from the Tyrrhenian Sea to the Aegean. Eisenhower and Marshall had always seen a secondary and diversionary role for Italian operations—more Germans sent to Italy meant fewer Germans to oppose Overlord. Hitler's decision to reinforce Kesselring, Eisenhower later wrote, "was a great advantage to the Allies elsewhere." He believed that although the Italian campaign was "a distinctly subsidiary operation...the results it attained in the actual defeat of Germany were momentous, almost incalculable." Churchill, too, endorsed the idea of drawing Germans away from France and into Italy, telling Roosevelt so in a telegram on October 26: "The fact that the enemy have diverted such powerful forces to this theater vindicates our strategy." Yet Churchill, seeking to fight far more than a holding action, also told Roosevelt, "At all costs we must win Rome and the airfields north of it." Roosevelt, committed only to Overlord, did not reply. Eisenhower did not have a strategy (or orders) to get to Rome, and the Fifth Army lacked the means. Since taking Naples on October 1, the left flank of the Fifth Army had managed to slog northward about thirty miles; it had maintained its mile-a-day pace for almost two months.[299]

As October went out, Mark Clark's army straddled Highways 6 and 7, about twelve miles south of the town of Cassino and the routes north to Rome. At Cassino, Highway 6 turned north through the Liri Valley. And there, Monte Cassino, a Benedictine monastery called the abbey of abbeys by Benedictines, sat atop the mountain. Its oldest parts dated from the sixth century, when Benedict of Nursia and twelve disciples set to work building their refuge. Clark had to take the monastery in order to get on the road to Rome. But before he could take Cassino, he had to take other hills and towns along Highway 6—Monte Camino, Monte Lungo, Monte Sammucro, and the villages of San Pietro Infine and San Vittore. Although Clark had almost 250,000 men under his command, by late October, ferocious German resistance, freezing rains, and mud had stopped his army. On November 11, Clark called a two-week halt.[300]

The air war over Germany brought its own disappointments. Operation Pointblank, the June decision to target German aircraft factories, was proving more costly than anyone, especially the Americans, had foreseen. American casualties were kept low as long as their B-17s flew missions protected by their P47C Thunderbolt fighters, which when fitted with a reserve fuel tank had an operational radius of five hundred miles, to beyond the Ruhr Valley and back. But when the Thunderbolts peeled away for home, the B-17s suffered horrific losses. During the second week of October, 148 went down with their ten-man crews, including 60 of 291 sent to destroy the ball-bearing factory at Schweinfurt. Pointblank was proving deadly and ineffectual. Bomber Harris continued his night raids against German cities. But his losses also mounted. The efficacy of massed attacks against German cities was in doubt. Churchill, knowing that Stalin approved of the raids, encouraged Harris to pursue his strategy. It was the only help Britain could give Stalin. Harris sent his air fleets to Kassel, where three thousand died and fires burned for a week; four thousand died in Würzburg; six thousand in Darmstadt; nine thousand in Weser; twelve thousand in Magdeburg. In November, Harris threw his bombers at Berlin, which the RAF visited sixteen times between November and March. The aircrews paid dearly. It was a price Churchill accepted because throughout 1943, the RAF, alone among Anglo-American forces, had inflicted pain on the German heartland. Anglo-American soldiers and sailors were fighting, but not well enough or near enough to Germany to satisfy Stalin, with whom Churchill had an appointment in Tehran.[301]

On November 12, Churchill and his usual troupe departed Plymouth aboard HMS *Renown,* final destination Alexandria, with ports of call at Gibraltar, Algiers, and Malta. Sarah accompanied her father as his ADC, and Gil Winant came along, since the agenda in Tehran would treat of both political and military issues. Winant therefore would find himself for several weeks in close proximity to Sarah, and the romantic affections they shared would have to remain unrequited in public. If Churchill learned of the affair, he never mentioned it. After calling on Gibraltar, *Renown* made for Algiers, where during his short layover Churchill did not see fit to meet with de Gaulle, who was in residence. De Gaulle was outraged, doubly so because Churchill *had* thought to invite General Joseph Georges for a chat. De Gaulle considered Georges, unfairly, to be one of the architects of France's defeat in 1940. Duff Cooper, who had just been named minister to the French Committee of National Liberation, later wrote that de Gaulle, "ever on the lookout for an insult," had found one in Churchill's breach of etiquette.[302]

Renown made Malta late in the afternoon of the seventeenth. It is fitting that Churchill spent the next two nights on the little island that had taken such a long and savage beating at the hands of the Luftwaffe, for the next day, the RAF conducted its largest raid yet over Germany. Mannheim, Ludwigshafen, and Berlin came in for it. Two weeks earlier Bomber Harris had briefed Churchill on cumulative RAF and Luftwaffe bomb damage to German and British cities. Whereas Coventry had lost 5 percent of the city center to German bombs, Hamburg had been 75 percent destroyed. As had Malta; its houses, quays, and roads—all constructed of brittle Maltese limestone—had for the most part been blasted back into the fossil particulates whence they came. But the fact that Churchill could take his rest on the island meant that the Maltese had come through the worst of it.[303]

German cities were now getting the worst of it. The next raid over Berlin erased the homes of Goebbels' mother and mother-in-law, blew the windows out of the Goebbels house, and reduced Hitler's favorite hotel, the Kaiserhof, to rubble. Goebbels, the *Gauleiter* (a local political leader) of Berlin, bemoaned to his diary this "time of universal misfortune which has now fallen upon this city of four and a half million.... Hell itself seems to have broken loose over us." A November 24 *New York Times* headline crowed: ZOO ANIMALS ROAM BERLIN STREETS; HEAT OF FIRES FELLS PEDESTRIANS. In fact, in regard to fires, Berliners could count themselves fortunate. The cool autumn weather and Berlin's wide avenues and modern buildings kept firestorms of the Hamburg sort from breeding. Bomber Harris's response to Berlin's structural integrity was to send more bombers from England more often. And from Foggia, from where the Allied air forces could reach targets in southern Germany and Romania, came even more bombers.[304]

The Old Man arrived on Malta with a bit of a sore throat, which within a day had festered into a nasty cold that kept him in bed for most of his short visit. He stayed in the Governor's Palace as the guest of Lord Gort, and as the palace could offer no hot water for his bath, his mood worsened in lockstep with the worsening head cold. His room overlooked a busy promenade up from which drifted the sounds of Maltese making their way through the rubble. It was too much for Churchill, who flung off his bedclothes, threw open the windows, and bawled to the crowd below: "Go away, will you? Please go away and do not make so much noise."[305]

His funk worsened when he learned that Leros had fallen that day; the battle had been a Crete in miniature. The Germans arrived by sea and air; the RAF and Royal Navy did not dispute the issue; British troops on the ground were poorly led. The Royal Navy's lack of aggression grated on Churchill, who christened the new naval commander of the Mediterranean, Admiral Sir John Cunningham (no relation to Andrew), "'Dismal Jimmy'—and not without cause," in Harold Macmillan's estimation. The upcoming meeting of the military chiefs in Cairo also riled Churchill. He and the Americans still held opposing and irreconcilable views. He supported Overlord, but not at the expense of Rhodes, and especially Italy, the only theater where Anglo-American troops were taking pressure off the Russians. He intended to force a showdown. This troubled Brooke, who told his diary: "He [Churchill] is inclined to say to the Americans, all right, you won't play with us in the Mediterranean we won't play with you in the English Channel. And they will say all right then we shall direct our main effort in the Pacific." To Clementine, Churchill cabled: "It is terrible fighting with both hands tied behind one's back."[306]

Alexander and Eisenhower arrived on Malta in order to receive their special North African campaign ribbons. Both men lamented the stasis in Italy but for different reasons. Alexander, as the commander on the spot, had to report that the campaign had stalled. "All roads lead to Rome," he told Lord Moran, "and they are all paved with mines." The entire Mediterranean command believed that an amphibious flanking operation—preferably two, one on each coast—was the best way to get around Kesselring's lines. Earlier in the month, Eisenhower's staff began drawing up plans for such an operation. Code-named Shingle, it called for landing a reinforced division at Anzio, birthplace of Nero and Caligula and since Roman times a holiday resort. Anzio, and its sister city, Nettuno, sat on the Tyrrhenian coast about fifty miles north of, and behind, Kesselring's lines. The towns, about a mile apart, faced narrow beaches. They were built in a basin ringed by woodlands and the Pontine Marshes. Several miles beyond the marshes high hills rose to the west and north. Alexander had sought at least five divisions for the venture, but neither the troops nor the transports were available; they were going to England, for Overlord.

By the time Churchill arrived on Malta, the plan languished in the file of improbable operations. Eisenhower, by the time he arrived on Malta, and presuming he was headed to Washington to replace Marshall as chief of staff, was preparing his exit from the Mediterranean. He considered any new Italian venture a drawdown to the buildup for Overlord. Churchill gave Eisenhower an earful, on both the need to grab Rome and the risks inherent in Overlord. "How often I heard him say," Eisenhower later wrote, "in speaking of Overlord's prospects, 'We must take care that the tides do not run red with the blood of American and British youth, or the beaches be choked with their bodies.' " Eisenhower, like Brooke, departed Malta believing Churchill would press the matters of Italy and Rhodes in Cairo and Tehran. Churchill meant to untie his hands.[307]

During the two-day sail to Alexandria, he drew up a strategic plan. It amounted to Rome first, then Rhodes, by January. Churchill presumed the Sextant talks would be all about settling the Mediterranean issues, with the Pacific theater relegated to a lower slot on the agenda. But Roosevelt had invited Chiang Kai-shek and Madame Chiang to Cairo with the intention of turning the agenda on its head. Brooke made the trip by air, aboard Churchill's Avro York. Upon reaching Cairo, he told his diary: "I wish our conference was over."[308]

It had not even begun. When it did, Churchill saw at once that Roosevelt meant to deny him his showdown. During the first plenary session on November 23, held at Roosevelt's villa a few miles outside Cairo, the president announced that he wanted to talk about the Pacific. Furthermore, Roosevelt pledged to Chiang that large-scale naval operations would soon start in the Bay of Bengal in support of an amphibious operation (codenamed Buccaneer) in Burma, all intended not so much to knock Japan back but to get support through to Chiang's forces, whose role in the Pacific war Roosevelt still saw as vital. Thus, Churchill wrote in his memoirs, the Combined Chiefs of Staff "were sadly distracted by the Chinese story, which was lengthy, complicated, and minor... with the result that Chinese business occupied first instead of last place at Cairo." Yet, that week, General Sir Billy Slim (he had been knighted earlier in the year) drove from Assam into central Burma, with one of his corps heading for the Chindwin River, which it crossed on December 3. The Japanese at Slim's front, confused by a British deception campaign, did not even know where Slim was headed. Though Slim was forging opportunities ripe for exploitation, he and Burma were at the bottom of Churchill's agenda.[309]

Roosevelt told Churchill that he had put the Pacific war ahead of the European on the agenda because he did not want Stalin to think they "had ganged up on him on military action." He believed that if they made Japan the primary focus of Sextant, Stalin's suspicions would be allayed. Yet the decision also ensured that the Anglo-American bloc would arrive in Tehran without having reached solid agreement on the second front. Churchill, in his memoirs, could not resist taking a swipe at Roosevelt and Chiang. In spite of vast American aide to China (several millions of dollars of which was stolen by Madame Chiang's family), Chiang "had been beaten by the communists in his own country, which is a bad thing." Brooke, in his memoirs, was more blunt: "Why the Americans attached such significance to Chiang I have never discovered. All he did was lead them down a garden path to communist

China!" As for Stilwell and Chennault, who were feuding over whether Lend-Lease matériel should go to Stilwell's soldiers or Chennault's Chinese air forces, Brooke wrote that Stilwell was "nothing more than a crank," while Chennault, though "a gallant airman" had "a limited brain." During the meetings, Madame Chiang, who spoke perfect English, translated for her husband, leaving Brooke with the impression that Madame "was the leading spirit of the two, and I would not trust her very far.... The more I see of her the less I like her." Not so the other staff officers, whose collective breathing almost stopped when Madame's "closely clinging dress of black satin with yellow chrysanthemums displayed a slit which extended to her hip bone and exposed one of the most shapely of legs."[310]

Churchill warmed to Madame Chiang, telling Clementine by letter that he withdrew "all the unfavourable remarks which I may have made about her." (Madame had voiced strong criticism of British imperial policies during a visit to India the previous year, inciting Churchill to "breathing fire and slaughter against her" to the Foreign Office.) The Chiangs had come out of the shadows to light up the Cairo conference, Madame Chiang by her very presence, but they did so at the expense of Anglo-American cohesion. The meetings with Chiang, Brooke told Marshall, were "a ghastly waste of time," to which Marshall replied, "You're telling me." Still, Roosevelt brought Churchill around on the need for action in Burma, but Churchill's initial support for Buccaneer evaporated when he realized that the landing craft needed for Burmese operations would come from the Mediterranean. Within ten days, as a result of Churchill's counterarguments, Roosevelt overrode his military chiefs and conceded that Buccaneer was dead. Not until April 1945, with American Marines and U.S. soldiers fighting on Okinawa, just 325 miles from the Japanese homeland, would Allied troops finally reopen the India-China road links in northern Burma and retake Rangoon in the south, too late to make a difference in the war against Japan.[311]

After the disagreeable first meetings with Chiang, the conference only went further downhill. The Americans stunned the British by again arguing for an American supreme commander in Europe, an issue Churchill considered settled. The British flatly rejected the proposal. Lest the Americans pursue the question, Churchill pointed out that because of the long-held understanding between the Allies that theater commanders came from the partner with the most forces in the theater, a supreme commander for all of Europe would have to be British because Britain had more men, planes, and ships in Europe than the Americans did. Roosevelt dropped the issue, but he stuck to his Burma plans, which Brooke coldly and methodically dismantled during a meeting of the military chiefs. Admiral Ernie King, enraged by Brooke's demeanor, rose from the table as if to settle the issue with fists. Stilwell, who witnessed the scene, wished King "had socked" Brooke. Pug Ismay thought King's ongoing animosity threatened the cohesion of the Combined Chiefs, and told King so. King replied, "Look here, General, when there's a war they send for the sons of bitches, and that's me." Churchill, meanwhile, argued for his Aegean plans, cautioning Roosevelt that Overlord must not be spelled T-Y-R-A-N-T, a display of rhetoric Brooke thought "masterly." Even the irascible King showed signs of supporting Churchill, but only because if the British navy stayed in the Mediterranean, it couldn't get in his way in the Pacific. Churchill pushed his Aegean strategy with flights of oratory: "His Majesty's government cannot have its troops standing idle; muskets must flame," and Rhodes was the place they must flame. That display led Marshall to smack the table with his fist and exclaim, "Not one American soldier is going to die on that goddamned beach." Marshall's outburst quieted the room, including Churchill, who did not again mention Rhodes in Cairo. But the issue had not been resolved; Churchill carried his Aegean hopes to Tehran.[312]

The British had taken over the grand Mena House hotel in Giza, where Churchill and T. E. Lawrence had stayed two decades earlier when they created new states in the Middle East. The hotel's grandiosity had moved Lawrence to remark that it made him a Bolshevik. Churchill loved it. There, he and Brooke hosted evening dinners as jovial as the afternoon meetings were disputatious. "King was as nice as could be and quite transformed from his afternoon attitude," wrote Brooke after one such meal. Roosevelt's dinner companions included Harry Hopkins and Hopkins's son, Robert, a U.S. Army war photographer who had seen action in Italy. General Edwin M. ("Pa") Watson, Roosevelt's old friend and political adviser, was on hand, as was Roosevelt's son-in-law, Major John Boettiger. Colonel Elliott Roosevelt joined the party, a case of nepotism, but only fair as Alexander Cadogan remarked to his diary, "I suppose we can't talk if we trail Randolph around with us." As always, Roosevelt's squad of Filipino mess men were on hand to produce his meals, including a turkey on Thanksgiving Day, which Roosevelt carved "with masterly, indefatigable skill." A small dance followed, the music supplied by gramophone. All the young men danced with Sarah; Churchill danced with Pa Watson. The gathered sang *Home on the Range*. It was a jolly evening, although tears were visible on his cheeks when Churchill toasted the president. Churchill's cold had abated; the bright Egyptian skies invigorated him, and his spirits brightened, as evidenced the next night when his small party dined and chatted until 1:30 in the morning. "P.M. talked to the whole table from 8:30 . . . to 1:35," recorded Cadogan, "then expressed surprise at having a sore throat." Dickie Mountbatten fell asleep during Churchill's oration, and even Sarah had trouble keeping her eyes open.[313]

The congeniality reached a high point when Churchill and Sarah suggested to Roosevelt that they all take a drive out to the pyramids, which the president had never seen. The idea so enthused Roosevelt, recalled Sarah, that "he leaned forward on the arms of his chair and seemed about to rise," but of course could not, "and sank back again." While the president readied himself, Churchill and Sarah waited outside, where Sarah noted that her father's eyes "were bright with tears." He turned to her and said, "I love that man." Such was Sarah's recollection two decades later. At the time she failed to mention the tears or the affection in a letter to her mother, but she did write, "It really is wonderful how they both get on—they really like and understand each other. The outing, like the evening festivities, had been a smashing success."[314]

The staff meetings were not. Roosevelt, Churchill offered to Anthony Eden, who had arrived on the fourth day of talks, "was a charming country gentleman" but deficient in "business methods." The conference had been planned on short notice, and it showed. Eisenhower had flown in for the second plenary session and confounded Marshall (while pleasing Churchill) by suggesting that the greatest support Alexander's Italian army could give to the European campaign would be to successfully sweep into the Po Valley. Then, as Eisenhower saw it, Alexander could either strike toward southeast France, or turn northeast toward Trieste and Vienna. Given the conditions in Italy, Eisenhower thought one of these thrusts could be undertaken—and accomplished—by the summer of 1944. Inadvertently, Ike had given new life to Churchill's Mediterranean strategy, which Marshall all week had been trying to knock down. After five days of talks, the British and Americans had reached no final agreement on any of their respective strategies, in Europe or the Pacific. That they had agreed upon goals in the Pacific, but not on the means for reaching them, was evidenced by the wording of the Cairo Declaration, issued by the three leaders at the end of the conference. It called for Japan's unconditional surrender and its expulsion from the Asian mainland. It called for an independent Korea and mandated that all Japanese conquests in China, including Taiwan, be restored to China. But the declaration made no mention of how any of this would come to pass.[315]

Just after sunrise on November 27, Roosevelt boarded his Douglas C-54, which Admiral Leahy had anointed *The Sacred Cow*. Churchill climbed into his Avro York. They were heading, unprepared and in fundamental disagreement, to Tehran and the most important meeting to date in the life of the alliance. But Stalin was prepared for them. Harry Hopkins told Moran that if Churchill proved obdurate in Tehran in regard to the second front, Roosevelt would back the Russians. "I am not looking forward to the next few days," Brooke told his diary.[316]

Alec Cadogan thought the weather in Tehran lovely. The skies were Persian blue, the sunshine golden. Tehran, however, came in for a dose of his cynicism: "a squalid town of bad taste.... Bazaars quite good—as a sight. Nothing in them." Churchill found Persian security sadly lacking for the advent of three such prestigious personages. A column of mounted Iranian cavalrymen lined the streets, which only showed "any evil people that somebody of consequences was coming, and which way." The cavalry would prove useless if "two or three determined men with pistols or a bomb" attempted to rush the automobiles that carried the distinguished guests. Still, to Inspector Thompson's chagrin, Churchill, who had been warned his life might be threatened, "was very excited, even pleased." As the crowds pressed up against the car, "he looked into everyone's face with the happiest sort of suspicion." Thompson had been told by his army contacts that British agents had rounded up several German evildoers who had parachuted in for the occasion. Meanwhile, the Soviets, who claimed to have uncovered the plot, suggested it might prove beneficial to Roosevelt's health for him to stay at the fortified Soviet legation, next door to the British, rather than at the American legation, two miles removed from the city. Roosevelt made the move on November 28. Ismay thought the Soviet story "a trick" and believed the Soviets had already planted microphones in the walls of Roosevelt's apartments.[317]

Churchill considered it vital that he and the president confer before they met with Stalin. Roosevelt did not think likewise. He was determined that Uncle Joe not feel ganged up on, and equally determined not to be pinned down by Churchill over his Rhodes scheme. Roosevelt meant to see Stalin first, and to see him alone. Shortly after 3:00 P.M. on the twenty-eighth, Stalin paid the president a brief private visit. Forewarned by Ismay that Churchill's exclusion had caused "storm signals" to be run up among the British delegation, Harriman strolled over to "calm the waters." He found Churchill "in a grumbling but whimsical mood." The Old Man told Harriman he would "obey orders" but that he had a right to chair the upcoming meeting because he was the most senior leader, because his name came first alphabetically, and because of the historic importance of the "British Empire, which he represented." He insisted that if nothing else, he host a dinner on the thirtieth, his sixty-ninth birthday, where "he would get thoroughly drunk... and leave the next day."[318]

Stalin and Roosevelt meanwhile were getting along famously. The president announced that Russia deserved a warm-water port at the end of the

South Manchurian railroad, and that some of the British and American merchant fleets should be transferred to Russia after the war. "That would be a fine thing," Stalin replied. Roosevelt had not consulted Churchill on either matter. The subjects of France and de Gaulle came up; both leaders agreed that de Gaulle was out of touch "with the real France." The real France, Stalin offered, was busy helping the Germans and would have to be punished after the war. Roosevelt agreed, and added that no Frenchman over the age of forty should be allowed to participate in postwar French affairs. They moved on to Southeast Asia and India, where almost one billion people—Roosevelt often called them "brown people," "of short stature," and "not warlike"—lived under British and French subjugation. Roosevelt proposed that the Allies hold French Indochina in trust after the war, as America had held the Philippines. India, Malaya, and Burma, Roosevelt proclaimed, should be "educated in the arts of self government." He suggested "reform from the bottom" in India "somewhat on the Soviet line." Stalin replied that reform from the bottom would result in revolution. India, he told the president, was "a complicated society." Harriman thought Stalin "showed rather more sophistication than the president." The two leaders agreed that the subject of India should not be brought up with Churchill. Roosevelt's clearest signal to Stalin had to do with Poland. The president made no mention of Poland.[319]

Harriman had earlier in the day offered an impromptu lecture to Eden and Cadogan on the art and science of properly conducting an international conference, leading Cadogan to proclaim to his diary, "I've forgotten a great deal more about that than he [Harriman] ever knew." The waters were anything but calm, and the conference had yet to begin.[320]

As the Big Two broke the ice, Churchill took himself to his villa's garden to shuffle through official papers, including memos to Home Secretary Herbert Morrison. The previous week Morrison had ordered that the Blackshirts Oswald and Diane (Mitford) Mosley be released from prison and placed under house arrest, a decision Morrison made for humanitarian and health reasons. The Mosleys had been held without trial for three years under the special powers granted HMG by section 18B of the legal code. The response to Morrison's decision among workingmen was immediate; ten thousand marched through London's streets to protest what they saw as favoritism. The Commons erupted as well. To Clementine, Churchill wrote, "If I were at home I'd blast the whole [18B] blasted thing out of existence." He offered that Morrison could "sweep it [18B] away" if he followed the "overwhelming arguments I have mentioned to him." Indeed, Churchill made clear to Morrison the constitutional peril of 18B, his loathing of the law, and his desire that 18B be abolished. Yet, he also advised Morrison to argue that although the special powers were deplorable, "the time has not yet come when it [18B] can be fully dispensed with, but we can look forward to that day." In fact, the day *had* come; the peril of invasion had long passed, but Churchill was not yet willing to give up this extraordinary power; 18B stayed on the books. The British electorate took note.[321]

Brooke stopped by the garden to propose that Churchill offer the Americans the Andaman operation in exchange for American guarantees in the Mediterranean. Churchill vetoed the idea, telling Brooke, correctly, that any such promise would prove impossible to keep. Once the large landing ships left the Mediterranean for the Pacific venture, they would never return. By now Churchill's cold had worsened and his voice had almost abandoned him. "He is not fit," Brooke concluded, "and consequently not in the best of moods." That was because his friend Franklin Roosevelt was meeting privately with Uncle Joe. When word reached the British concerning the substance of Roosevelt's meeting with Stalin, Brooke told Moran, "This conference is over when it has only begun. Stalin has got the President in his pocket."[322]

The first plenary session was convened at four o'clock in a large room in the yellow-brick Soviet legation. The principals gathered around a grand round table covered in green baize. Heavy draperies blocked the Persian sunshine. Admiral King and Harry Hopkins were there, but Generals Marshall and Arnold had somehow gotten their wires crossed and were off sightseeing in Tehran, thus leaving Roosevelt to his own devices. Churchill had his full complement of chiefs in attendance. Stalin was accompanied by only an interpreter and Marshal Kliment Voroshilov, a sixty-two-year-old career officer and Stalin toady who had led the (unsuccessful) assault against the Finns in 1939 and had been replaced by Zhukov at Leningrad in 1941 after allowing the Germans to surround that city. Voroshilov, Brooke wrote, would supply Stalin "nothing in the shape of strategic vision." But then, in Brooke's opinion, Stalin had no need of advice: "He [Stalin] had a military brain of the highest caliber," Brooke recalled, and could grasp "all the implications of a situation with a quick and unerring eye.... In this respect he stood out when compared to his two colleagues."[323]

Roosevelt, as the only head of state, was nominated by Stalin to serve as chairman. After the president delivered a long summary of the Pacific war ("a lot of *blah-flum*" according to Brooke), Stalin announced that as soon as Germany was defeated, the Soviet Union would multiply its forces in Siberia and join in the war against Japan. This unexpected turn had the effect Stalin intended. He knew that his Siberian airfields and troops could help the U.S. bring Japan to bay much faster than the Chinese nationalists, who in the seven years since the rape of Nanking had yet to defeat a Japanese army or bomb a Japanese city. And although Churchill had always pledged to throw all of Britain's resources into the war against Japan upon the defeat of Germany, Britain was running out of resources. Both Roosevelt and Churchill believed—and continued to believe throughout 1944—that the Pacific war would go on for at least eighteen months, perhaps two years, after Germany was defeated. Stalin's announcement was therefore most welcome, but it was clearly conditional upon Anglo-American armies going to France in May 1944 in order to shoulder their share of the burden. Then, and only then, would the Red Army march with them to Tokyo. Left unsaid was the possibility, always present in the back of Anglo-American minds, that a failure to get into France by May would place the Soviet Union in untenable military straits, that is, would foster an atmosphere conducive to a negotiated peace. Stalin had leveraged that fear for two years, and did so again, in masterly fashion, over the next three days.[324]

He spoke quietly, as he had done the year before in his first sessions with Churchill. He doodled on a notepad and smoked hand-rolled cigarettes, which he kept loose in his breast pocket. His brown eyes gave away nothing. He had changed his wardrobe since they last met, discarding his comrade ensemble of "grey-brown cloth tunic buttoned to the chin and the trousers of the same material, tucked into knee-boots." He had "blossomed out into a multi-coloured uniform" designed, it seemed to Moran, by a tailor who "has put a shelf on each shoulder. And on it has dumped a lot of gold with white stars." A fat red stripe ran down the marshal's creased trousers. When he spoke, he gazed into the distance and looked no one directly in the eye. "Stalin would have made a fine poker player," Ismay later wrote. "His expression was as inscrutable as the Sphinx."[325]

He listened as Roosevelt proposed that once Italy was wrapped up, the Anglo-American armies might swing into the Balkans, link up with Tito's forces, and drive northeast toward Romania and a conjunction with the Red Army as it drove west. This suggestion surprised and disturbed Hopkins, who scribbled a message to Admiral King, asking, "Who's promoting this Balkan business?" King replied that it seemed to be Roosevelt's idea. But Roosevelt and Churchill had previously discussed this idea, or at least had discussed Churchill's idea of a thrust through Slovenia toward Vienna. Churchill followed the president's remarks with a synopsis of his case for driving from Rhodes through the Dardanelles, if Turkey came in on the Allied side. If Churchill thought that some version of his Balkan strategy was on the verge of validation, Stalin quickly disabused him of the notion. Turkey "was beyond hope" and would not come in, the marshal declared, and the Dardanelles were not worth the effort. Stalin then proposed that southern France, not the Balkans, should be the next Anglo-American objective, the better to coordinate with the Normandy invasion. Churchill expressed support for the southern France venture but stressed that it must not come at the expense of Italian operations.[326]

Stalin then suggested that it might be best to cease operations in Italy before April, whether or not Rome had been taken, and to then shift six divisions from Italy to the southern France gambit rather than toward some hoped-for conjunction with the Red Army. He proposed that the southern France operation take place on April 1, a month before Overlord. Roosevelt, to Brooke's chagrin, voiced his approval. Operation Anvil, as the southern France plan was then code-named, called for two divisions, with four more to follow. As Brooke saw it, to strip six divisions out of line in Italy, where they were successfully engaging Germans, and throw them ashore in France would allow the Germans to shift their forces to the beachhead, where the defender would have a great advantage. Brooke predicted the "annihilation of these six divisions" if they were thrown into southern France. After dispensing with the Anvil threat, the Germans would then at their leisure shift forces against Overlord. This was the exact scenario Churchill most feared.[327]

Brooke saw that Stalin was pushing a political strategy couched as military strategy. Militarily, any conjunction of Allied armies on the Eastern Front would lead to profound questions of command and control. Who would lead this combined force west to Berlin? Stalin was a unilateralist in military matters. Besides, the tensions within the Anglo-American arm of the alliance testified to the difficulties of joint commands. Stalin's military logic was sound, and Brooke now grasped the politics behind it. The marshal was determined to keep the Anglo-Americans out of any territories he considered to be within his "security belt," which was to say, the Balkans, and perhaps Hungary, Austria, and Czechoslovakia. Stalin did not want the Dardanelles opened; that, too, would bring the British and Americans onto his left flank, in the Black Sea. Thus, as for a thrust through the Balkans, Roosevelt proposed and Stalin disposed. Churchill hadn't even been able to fully develop his argument for Rhodes. Brooke saw the ramifications: "His [Stalin's] political and military requirements could now be best met by the greatest squandering of British and American lives in France." Churchill began to see it as well. After the meeting, Moran found him so dispirited he asked if something had gone wrong. "A bloody lot has gone wrong," Churchill replied. Roosevelt had given Stalin an opening, and the marshal had marched right through.[328]

The dinner that night, hosted by Roosevelt, came to an early end when the president, stricken by a gastrointestinal bug, went green in the face and was wheeled off to his quarters, but not before he and Stalin took turns and delight in excoriating the French and German peoples. The Germans, Stalin proclaimed, understood only authority, and he intended to give them authority, by keeping them firmly underfoot for at least a generation. He also voiced concern about unconditional surrender; the president, Stalin said, should clarify his terms. Otherwise, the resolve of the German people would only be strengthened, and the Red Army would be the primary victim of any such resolve. Harriman agreed with the marshal, but Roosevelt stood firm; he would not make the same mistake Woodrow Wilson made when he announced his Fourteen Points (imprecise and open to wide interpretation). Regarding France, Stalin insisted that the entire French people were helping the Nazis and should be punished accordingly after the war. French colonial possessions should be stripped away and held in trust, as per Roosevelt's suggestion earlier in the day. The demeaning of France continued until Churchill, who had remained silent, protested that he could not envision a civilized world without a strong and vibrant France. Stalin's reply, Harriman recalled, "was contemptuous." France was a charming place, Stalin offered, but it would have no role in postwar international affairs. And no real importance should be attached to de Gaulle, who had little real influence in any affairs. Roosevelt voiced hearty agreement. Churchill was finding himself more the odd man out with each passing hour.[329]

After Roosevelt was wheeled away, Churchill, finding himself alone with Stalin, escorted the marshal to a sofa. There, joined by Eden and Molotov and two interpreters, Churchill and Stalin, in a bilateral conference of their own, settled down to discuss the fate of Poland. But Stalin had not finished his treatise on Germany and Germans. He recounted that when German prisoners of war from the laboring classes (the Communist Party) protested that they were only following orders, he ordered them shot. He was convinced that Germany would re-arm within fifteen or twenty years. Churchill, keen to display his solidarity, replied that Germany had to be kept under wraps for at least fifty years, all the while denied civil and military aviation and an army high command capable of plotting new depredations. Anything less, Churchill offered, would be a betrayal "of our soldiers." When he advised that the three Allies must be willing to take and maintain control over Germany, Stalin answered, "There was control after the last war, but it failed."[330]

Then Churchill wavered on his long-held belief that Germany should emerge after the war a member of the European family—albeit militarily impotent but economically strong. Instead, he threw his lot in with Roosevelt, Morgenthau, Lord Cherwell, and Stalin, all of whom favored a dismemberment of Germany into, as Churchill told Stalin, "a broad, peaceful, cow-like confederation." (Several months later he told Lord Moran, "If the

Ruhr were grassed over our trade would benefit.") This was an about-face from his stance in August 1941, when in announcing the Atlantic Charter, he proclaimed: "Instead of trying to ruin German trade by all kinds of additional trade barriers and hindrances as was the mood of 1917, we have definitely adopted the view that it is not in the interests of the world and of our two countries that any large nation should be unprosperous or shut out from the means of making a decent living for itself and its people by its industry and enterprise."[331]

The Germany of the future that Churchill described to Stalin bore a close resemblance to Roosevelt's postwar Germany, a Carthaginian future, in fact, which is to say, no future. Then Stalin—who had spoken at dinner of punishing Germany—spoke of an economically strong Germany, but denazified and demilitarized, broken into several zones occupied by the victors, but not quite the impoverished pasture envisioned by Roosevelt. Stalin would need German steel and machine tools after the war, but he told Churchill he did not want to wake up one day to find German watchmakers producing rifles and German carmakers building tanks. Only active Allied control applied well into the future would keep Germany in line. Churchill proposed isolating Prussia and folding portions of Bavaria into the Danubian Federation that he had long envisioned. "We are the trustees for the peace of the world," Churchill offered. "If we fail there will be perhaps one hundred years of chaos." So wedded was he to the idea of his Danubian Federation that Churchill seems to have forgotten that the previous "Danubian federation"—the Austro-Hungarian Empire—had been torn asunder by the nationalist tendencies of its component parts, a cascading series of events that led to the Great War.[332]

Then, like two hungry guests at an inn where the kitchen had only one veal chop remaining, they fell upon Poland, specifically its postwar borders. Had Cordell Hull been in the room, he would have argued that any such questions be discussed only at the postwar peace conference, a policy that stemmed in part from Hull's distrust of the British, whom he presumed would try to reclaim all of the Empire's losses, if not more. Every military strategy the British proposed was parsed by Hull and the U.S. State Department (and many in the U.S. military) in terms of, what are the British really up to? Robert Sherwood later wrote, "The State Department was traditionally on the alert against any of its Foreign Service officers who displayed the slightest tendency to become pro-British." But Hull was in Washington. So complete was Hull's isolation that he did not see any transcripts of the Tehran discussions for more than nine months, when Anthony Eden, as a courtesy, briefed him. If Churchill was going to broach the subject of Polish borders with Stalin, now was the moment, with Roosevelt ill in bed and Hull in limbo.[333]

Churchill began by reminding Stalin that Britain had gone to war for Poland. But, he added, Britain was now fighting alongside Russia, and "nothing was more important than the security of the Russian western frontier." Churchill was a pragmatist; the subject had to be addressed before Russian troops overran Poland. Earlier in the day, Hopkins had told Eden that Americans were "terrified of the subject" of Polish borders, which Hopkins called "political dynamite." Large blocs of American voters of Polish, German, Lithuanian, and Ukrainian descent would be voting the following November, and any talk of Polish borders would unsettle them all. Eden stressed to Hopkins that if the matter wasn't addressed now, it would be worse in six months, with Russian armies in Poland and the American elections that much nearer. Those were Churchill's sentiments, but for the part about the American elections. He believed that Poland was "an instrument needed in the orchestra of Europe." It was not a card to be played in American elections.

So, with Stalin, over cigars and coffee, Churchill opened the door: "Are we to try," he asked, "to draw frontier lines?" Stalin replied, "Yes," and asked if it was to be done without Polish participation. "Yes," Churchill replied. Then, using wooden matches, Churchill demonstrated his idea of moving Poland westward, "like soldiers taking two steps 'left close.' If Poland trod on some German toes, that could not be helped." This pleased Stalin.[334]

Churchill was executing a nimble sidestep. Henceforth, the European war would be fought to restore freedoms, but not necessarily borders. The Atlantic Charter stipulated that "sovereign rights and self-government be restored to those who have forcibly been deprived of them" and "all the men in all the lands live out their lives in freedom from want and fear." The charter also contained the fuzzy pledge that after "the final destruction of Nazi tyranny" the subsequent peace must "afford to all nations the means of dwelling in safety within their own boundaries." But boundaries did not draw themselves, nor did they result from elections along strict ethnographic lines; otherwise, Eire would swallow Ulster, and Scotland might opt out of the United Kingdom. Boundaries were drawn by the strong, ideally with due consideration given to ethnographic and geographic realities. Indeed, the eastern Poles were far outnumbered by their Ukraine and Belarus neighbors. That entire swath of Poland, pried from Soviet Russia in the early 1920s, had been part of czarist Russia. Why would the Poles want to maintain dominion over the vast Pripet Marshes and the peoples there when German farmland and industry could be had with the stroke of a pen? Churchill told Stalin that if Germans in the western reaches of the new Poland chose to flee westward into the new Germany, so be it. The Poles could have it all, territory and liberty.

Churchill was setting a new course among numerous shoals. Poland was an ally; two Polish divisions were readying for deployment to Italy. Polish pilots had defended London. Poland was dying, its citizens butchered, its crops plundered to feed the Reich. Yet the Polish government in exile, in London, had not been elected, so, in fact, there was no real Polish government in exile, only Polish democrats biding their time before returning to Poland. Churchill would fight henceforth to restore their freedoms, but not their borders. As allies, the London Poles would of course be consulted in the matter, but they would not be allowed to unilaterally determine the borders of the Poland they might someday return to. German borders would be determined by the victors in order to protect Europe, and especially Poland, from Germany. And in deference to Stalin, Polish borders would be drawn to protect Russia's western frontier, necessarily at the expense of Poland. Before bidding Stalin good night, Churchill suggested that the three leaders—himself, Stalin, and Roosevelt—"form some sort of policy which we could recommend to the Poles, and advise them to accept."[335]

Before adjourning, Churchill offered his most favored caveat: "I have no power from Parliament...to define any border lines." Indeed, Churchill was reverential of his King, his cabinet, and Parliament, but this out afforded him safety and deniability. He knew that the last British prime minister to sit down with a European dictator to draw frontiers had helped precipitate this war.[336]

The next morning, when Churchill again suggested to Roosevelt that they meet for lunch before the plenary session, Roosevelt again refused. The second snub by Roosevelt fully alerted Churchill to the course change Roosevelt was steering in their relations. "The change came about," Sir Ian Jacob later wrote, "when the Americans felt they had developed enough power to conduct their own line of policy."

> It showed the President in a new light. He [Roosevelt] was determined to break free from entanglement with Churchill and the British, and to meet Stalin without any prior consultation or agreement on a common line beforehand. Churchill was greatly disturbed by this development....That the president should deal with Churchill and Stalin as if they were people of equal standing in American eyes shocked Churchill profoundly, and seemed to nullify all the patient work that he had done during the previous three years.

Roosevelt's execution of his strategy could generously be described as petty, mean-spirited, and conducted at his friend's expense. Roosevelt's behavior "shocked Churchill," but underlying his actions, Jacob wrote, was "a superficial" and "dangerous" understanding of Russia's "age-long goals in Eastern Europe."[337]

The image many Americans had of Russia was formed in part by the fawning praise of Russia spewed by Henry Luce and all but the most rabid anti-Roosevelt newspapers. *Time* had named Stalin its 1942 Man of the Year. Luce's saccharine salute to Stalin was purged of any reference to Stalin's purges. No mention was made of the *Holodomor,* the famine that resulted in the slow death by starvation of several million Ukrainians in the early 1930s. Rather, Stalin faced "immense disorderliness" and "the problems of providing enough food for the people," which he solved by "collectivizing the farms" and the introduction of "20th century industrial methods" to his "superstitious, illiterate people." Stalin and the Russians were heroes, and "have fought the best fight so far" against Hitler. No mention was made of England fighting alone for two years while Stalin was in league with Hitler. *Life* displayed acute myopia when it reported that Russians are "one hell of a people" who "think like Americans." The murderous secret police organization NKVD was described as "a national police force similar to the FBI." Americans who didn't read newspapers and magazines could take the measure of Mother Russia in one of the year's most popular films, *Mission to Moscow,* based on the memoirs of Joseph E. Davies, the former American ambassador to the Kremlin. One reviewer wrote that the film's "Russians look like fur-coated Americans, and the Soviet Union is pictured as a land of magnificent food and drink, as it probably was in the circles in which the Davieses moved.... Despite its Hollywood flourishes, *Mission to Moscow* has power.... But Franklin Roosevelt and Joe Davies are the ones mainly glorified. Of President Roosevelt, even the Russians speak in hushed, reverent tones." The movie might have had power, but it was Hollywood fantasy power, though it at least made a passing reference to Stalin's purges.[338]

Roosevelt had arrived in Tehran firm in his belief that his powers of charm and persuasion would carry the day, although his knowledge of European politics was thin and his knowledge of Russia thinner still. Sir Ian Jacob, describing Roosevelt, used almost the same phrases as did Averell Harriman and George Kennan: "He [Roosevelt] had no idea.... He seemed to imagine that he could handle Stalin." That he could not became apparent to Churchill as the three leaders worked their way through three more meetings and two dinners, which Cadogan called "woolly and bibulous." As for Roosevelt's performance, Cadogan wrote, "[The] President, in his amateurish way, has said a lot of indiscreet and awkward things."[339]

During their second private meeting, Roosevelt outlined to Stalin his concept of a postwar international organization that would be charged with keeping global peace. It would consist of a General Assembly composed of members of the alliance. Overseeing this assembly would be an executive committee consisting of the Soviet Union, the United States, the United Kingdom, and China. This committee would deal with nonmilitary matters such as food and health. Stalin (like Churchill) thought China a curious choice as the world's fourth "great" power, but he did not press the issue. Of the executive committee, Stalin asked, would its decisions be binding? Likely not, Roosevelt replied, as the U.S. Congress would never permit America to be bound by decisions made by such a body. The third branch of the organization would take the form of "The Four Policemen"—Russia, the United States, the United Kingdom, and China—and would be charged with keeping the peace, if necessary by bombing and invading aggressor nations. Stalin listened politely, then steered the discussion to the treatment of Germany. As he had told Churchill the previous evening, Germany, once defeated, must be forcibly kept from reinventing itself as a military power. Yet from what he had heard so far, Roosevelt's proposed international organization could not supply the safeguards that he, Stalin, thought necessary.[340]

No discussion took place about the possibility that one of the Four Policemen might be the aggressor of the future. As with all the talks at all the conferences, the press (never in attendance) were given only broad summaries after the fact. Roosevelt did not publicly unveil his blueprint for a world organization until late May of 1944.

After Roosevelt and Stalin finished their chat and before the start of the second formal session, Churchill, with anthems playing and honor guards standing at attention, presented Stalin with the Sword of Stalingrad, a gold and jewel-encrusted dagger offered as a gift from King George VI, "in token of the homage of the British people... to the steel-hearted citizens of Stalingrad." Stalin accepted the sword, and passed it on to Voroshilov, who proceeded to drop it out of its scabbard and onto his great toe. Despite Voroshilov's gaffe and the obvious discomfort of all present, Churchill later wrote that as the sword was carried out of the room by an honor guard, he spied Roosevelt sitting off to one side, "obviously stirred by the ceremony." In fact, Roosevelt found such displays of pompous imperial symbolism to be distasteful contrivances. The show meant much to Churchill, little to Roosevelt, and still less to Stalin. British historian Roy Jenkins later noted that Joseph Stalin was not about to accept a jeweled bauble as any sort of substitute for an assault on France.[341]

Stalin, with characteristic bluntness, said as much a few minutes later at the start of the second plenary session, when he came right at Roosevelt much as he had come right at Churchill during their second session in Moscow the previous year. "Who will command Overlord?" the marshal demanded. Roosevelt replied that the decision had not been made. Stalin replied that he could hardly take Overlord seriously until it had a commander, and by the same logic, until it had a commander, it would appear the Anglo-Americans were not taking it seriously. He insisted the commander be named within the week. A brief, uncomfortable silence followed. Roosevelt had no answer ready. Churchill then made a gallant attempt to defend the merits of action in Rhodes and Turkey. As for Overlord, he again stressed the conditions that had to be met in order to undertake the invasion, including that of the Germans having no more than twelve divisions in reserve in France on the day of the invasion. Where Churchill saw sound planning and contingencies, Stalin saw equivocation. He interrupted: "I wish to pose a very discreet question to the Prime Minister about Overlord.... Do the Prime Minister and the British Chiefs really believe in Overlord?" Certainly, replied Churchill, given that the conditions as outlined were met. "When the time comes it will be our stern duty to hurl across the channel at the Germans every sinew of our strength." Given that Stalin and Roosevelt had already agreed upon the date, May 1, Churchill had no choice but to accept the inevitable. Hopkins had warned him that Roosevelt would come down on the side of Stalin, and he had.[342]

Brooke was livid. "After listening to the arguments put forward for the last two days," he told his diary, "I feel more like entering a lunatic asylum... than continuing with my present job." And as for the way his boss and Roosevelt had comported themselves in the meeting, "Winston was not good, and Roosevelt even worse." Stalin, alone but for Voroshilov at the table, and surrounded by twenty-six American and British luminaries, including Franklin Roosevelt and Winston Churchill, had taken control of the conference. In what John Keegan called "one of the most brutal contrivances of public embarrassment recorded in diplomatic history," Stalin had shamed Churchill into conceding his total commitment to Overlord, as well as the need to appoint a commander, and soon.[343]

Stalin hosted that night's dinner, due to start in just an hour. Churchill, while changing into his evening dress, had Sawyers summon Moran to treat his sore throat, which had lingered now for more than two weeks. Asked by Moran how the day's business had turned out, Churchill growled, "Nothing more can be done here." But he held out hope that something could be done with President İnönü and the Turks, whom he planned to meet in Cairo in a few days. With Turkey in, he told Moran, he could more reasonably argue the case for his Balkan strategy and perhaps a delay in Overlord. He would have developed the thought further, but Stalin awaited his arrival. Sawyers interposed, "You are late, sir." "Bloody," Churchill growled, and stomped out.[344]

Only the principals and their closest aides attended that night's feast—Hopkins, Molotov, Eden, Harriman, and Ambassador Clark Kerr. Sarah had not been invited, nor had Elliott Roosevelt. But he successfully crashed the affair by lingering just outside the door until Stalin waved him in. Stalin's banquets, as Churchill had learned in Moscow, were fueled by prodigious quantities of vodka and wine, and humor of Stalin's crude variety. The marshal needled Churchill relentlessly throughout the evening, Harriman recalled, and several times implied that Churchill, "nursing some secret affection for the Germans, wanted a soft peace." Roosevelt listened, smiled, but did not rise to Churchill's defense. Rather, the president delighted in Churchill's unease. Roosevelt "always enjoyed other people's discomfort," Harriman recalled. "It never bothered him much when other people were unhappy."[345]

Churchill did not rise to the bait until Stalin proposed to shoot at least 50,000 German officers after the surrender in order to ensure Germany's docility well into the future. "I would rather," Churchill replied, "be taken out to the garden here and now and be shot myself rather than sully my own and my country's honour by such infamy." Roosevelt then chimed in with a compromise; he suggested that only 49,000 officers be shot. Eden, meanwhile, was making desperate gestures in Churchill's direction intended to peg the whole scene as a joke. It might have ended there had not Elliott Roosevelt, by then drunk, wobbled to his feet and endorsed Stalin's plan, adding that he was sure the U.S. Army would support it.

At that Churchill walked out. He found himself alone in a semidarkened room. A few minutes passed; then he felt hands clasping his shoulders from behind. He turned to find Stalin and Molotov, each smiling broadly. They had "been playing," they assured Churchill, adding that "nothing of a serious kind had entered their heads." Stalin had a very captivating way about him when he chose, Churchill recalled, and this was his most captivating moment of all. Still, Churchill later wrote that he "was not then and am not now fully convinced that all was chaff and there was no serious intent lurking behind." He wrote those words long before the official documents regarding the Katyn massacre were released by HMG. The law forbade him to write what he knew, which was that Stalin and the Politburo were guilty of ordering the NKVD to murder the Polish officers in the Katyn forest. The obtuse reference to "no serious intent lurking" in Stalin's remarks was as close as he could get to the root of the matter. And of course, the law kept him from telling the world that Roosevelt, too, knew that Stalin had murdered the Poles. Churchill had sent Roosevelt the very precise and damning Foreign Office report on the matter. Stalin's joke, if he was joking, was crude but in character. Roosevelt's participation, given his knowledge of Katyn, was disgraceful.[346]

In Cairo, Roosevelt had taken to delivering seemingly good-natured jabs at Churchill during the cocktail hour or at dinner. "Winston," the president declared one evening, "you have four hundred years of acquisitive instinct in your English blood, and just don't understand why a country might not want to acquire land somewhere if they can get it." At Tehran, the ribbing took the form of bullying gibes uttered with forethought solely for the pleasure of Stalin, who joined with Roosevelt in the "teasing," as Roosevelt biographer Robert Sherwood termed it. It was a shabby display, perhaps to be expected from the coarse Stalin, but not from Churchill's genteel friend Franklin Roosevelt. As he had after demeaning de Gaulle at Casablanca, Roosevelt took delight in recounting to his cronies back home, including America's first female cabinet secretary, Secretary of Labor Frances Perkins, the humiliations he inflicted upon Churchill. "As soon as I sat down at the conference table, I began to tease Churchill about his Britishness, about John Bull, about his cigars, about his habits. It began to register with Stalin," who smiled, and then laughed aloud, as Roosevelt pressed on. Roosevelt said he had felt enough at ease to call Stalin Uncle Joe, which brought forth another guffaw from the marshal. "The ice was broken," Roosevelt told his cabinet, "and we talked like men and brothers." Alan Brooke termed Roosevelt's display a "betrayal." Years later, Lady Mary Soames offered, "The president's behavior hurt my father," but as with all tribulations that came Churchill's way, "it did not unman him."[347]

The next day, November 30, was Churchill's sixty-ninth birthday. Lord Moran expected to find his patient in "poor fettle" that morning, after the previous evening's sordid events, but Churchill had already dismissed the episode as if it were "only a bad dream." After breakfast he met privately with Stalin, where he argued the case for further actions in the Mediterranean before Overlord. Stalin did not buy it. Instead, he warned that if by May Anglo-American forces had not landed in France, "bad feeling" and an erosion in Russian resolve would result, for Russians were "war weary." Here again was Stalin playing his negotiated peace card.

During the third plenary session, as friendly as the previous night's dinner had not been, Roosevelt and Churchill pledged their absolute allegiance to Overlord. And they pledged their support of a warm-water port for the Soviet Union. The military decision on Overlord having been taken, Churchill could only promise to support and nurture the operation, although he reminded Stalin that landing craft, not British reluctance, would determine the issue. Having gotten what he came for, Stalin stressed secrecy and deception in planning the invasion; were the Germans to learn even the meanest of details, the Allied invasion forces and the Red Army would find themselves in extreme peril. The Germans had proven themselves quite adept at such subterfuge, Stalin admitted, at the expense of the Red Army. Churchill and Stalin agreed on the need for false radio messages, dummy tanks and planes and airfields, and covert cover plans. They stressed the need for covert radio traffic intended to confuse the Germans as to when the Anglo-American invasion and the Soviet summer offensive would be launched—simultaneously or sequentially—thus denying the Germans the option of shifting troops from one front to the other. And of course, disguising the "where" of both Allied offenses was paramount. "The truth is so precious," Churchill told Stalin, "that she should always be protected by a bodyguard of lies."[348]

The formal session adjourned on that note, and the principals and military chiefs wandered off to their lodgings to dress for dinner, which was to take place in the British legation, at Churchill's insistence. The children were invited, Elliott, Randolph, and Sarah, as were the leading diplomats. It was to be quite the affair, and why not, it was his birthday, after all, Churchill later wrote. As well, he was the oldest of the leaders. And in a barely disguised jab at his allies, he wrote, "We were by centuries the longest established of the three Governments; I might have added, but did not, that we had been the longest in the war."[349]

As the dinner hour approached, Stalin made his appearance, escorted by fifty Russian policemen who took up positions at the doors and windows. Roosevelt's Secret Service men shadowed the Russians. Inspector Thompson supplied Churchill's security. Thompson, when among Russians, liked to carry two guns under his jacket. Roosevelt brought along a birthday gift, a lovely Kashan bowl Harriman had purchased from a museum curator earlier that day after Roosevelt, realizing he had not thought to procure a gift for Churchill, had dispatched his ambassador to find something appropriate.[350]

The banqueting room in the British legation was done up in county house elegance—white linens, bone china, numerous candelabra casting a golden light over the scene. Portraits of British royals hung on the walls, which were inlayed with glass mosaics. Thick red draperies covered the windows. Persian waiters in red-and-blue livery and wearing white gloves tended to the needs of the assembled. Brooke noted that the waiters' gloves seemed too large, which resulted in the fingertips flapping when they handled the plates. A cake with sixty-nine candles sat in the middle of the table.[351]

Churchill announced that the meal would be conducted in the Russian style, with toasts encouraged, but with champagne instead of vodka. One of the first salutes raised was to Sarah, by Roosevelt. Churchill then proclaimed that the whole political world was now a matter of tints, and England's was getting pinker. Stalin replied, to much laughter, "A sign of good health." Roosevelt returned to the tint theme later in the evening when he announced that the effect of the war would be to "blend all those multitudinous tints, shades, and colors into one rainbow where their individuality would be lost in the whole." Brooke thought that a "fine idea." He had had a fine day, prevailing upon the Americans that the window for Overlord should be expanded to June 1 to allow for changes in circumstances, which had a habit of changing. By doing so, Brooke bought more time in the Mediterranean. The CIGS that night was, for a change, in a festive mood, a good thing, because the festivities continued into the new day. Churchill raised a glass to "Stalin the Great" and another to Roosevelt, in tribute to the president's "devotion to the cause of the weak and the helpless." And when Stalin raised a toast to Brooke, which in effect accused him of not liking Russians, Brooke responded by referring to Churchill's remarks earlier in the day regarding lies and deception. Then he raised his glass to Stalin, and asked, might "one's outward appearance deceive one's friends?" In fact, Brooke added, he felt only "friendship and comradeship" toward Stalin and the Red Army. Stalin liked that, and told Brooke that "some of the best friendships of this world were founded on misunderstandings."[352]

Toast followed toast; Churchill drank to the proletarian masses, Stalin to the Conservative Party. Then the marshal turned to Roosevelt and lifted his glass to America, without whose production of tanks and planes "the war may have been lost." This facile salute ignored the fact that for almost two deadly years, while America prepared for war and Stalin avoided war, Churchill and Britain alone had fought the war. Still, Churchill later wrote that he "went to bed tired but content, feeling sure that nothing but good had been done. It certainly was a happy birthday for me."[353]

The next afternoon, when Churchill and Stalin sat down to discuss Polish borders, they did so without Roosevelt's direct participation. The president explained at length to Stalin his domestic political difficulties, and announced that he could not take part in any such discussion for at least a year; nor could he be publicly associated with any arrangement arrived at. "This," Eden later wrote, with great understatement, "was hardly calculated to restrain the Russians." When Stalin sensed weakness, he struck.

Pressed by Churchill to outline his frontier demands, Stalin responded with anything but restraint. He "asked for the Curzon Line, with Lvov to go to the Soviet Union." The Curzon Line, proposed as Poland's eastern border by British foreign minister George Curzon in 1919, ran from the Baltic to the Czech border. But when Polish borders were finally established in the early 1920s, the frontier fell 150 miles east of the Curzon Line, in territory that had been part of czarist Russia. Stalin wanted that territory back. In many places the Curzon Line almost exactly overlay the Ribbentrop-Molotov Line of 1939, a happy coincidence for Stalin, who pointed out that the frontiers of 1939 were the most ethnographically correct. Eden and Churchill saw immediately where Stalin was going and asked if he was proposing the Ribbentrop-Molotov Line. "Call it what you will," replied Stalin.[354]

He indeed was proposing that the British in effect ratify the Ribbentrop-Molotov pact, but he couched his argument in terms of the British accepting a Polish frontier of their own invention. Churchill ordered a map produced, and pointed out differences between the two lines in the Baltic north and in the south, where Lvov fell on the Polish side. Stalin waved off the differences. He wanted the Polish border moved such that Lvov would end up on the Russian side. Churchill later wrote, "I was not prepared to make a great squawk about Lvov." In the north, Stalin sought Königsberg, which Churchill had no objection to. Königsberg going to the Russians would solve the problem of a year-round Baltic port. Churchill then suggested the new western Polish border follow the Oder River, which Stalin did not object to. However, the Oder flows from two tributaries, the Western Neisse and the Eastern Neisse. No one in the room thought to clarify which branch of the Neisse would define the new Polish border. Churchill concluded by telling Stalin, "The Poles would be wise to take our advice." But Eden began to doubt they would ever reach a settlement that the Poles would agree to. And he joined Churchill, Brooke, Ismay, and Cadogan in feelings of dismay and perplexity with the "American unwillingness to make ready with us for the conference in advance." "Above all," Eden later wrote, "I began to fear greatly for the Poles."[355]

The final piece of political business conducted in Tehran was an agreement in principle by the Big Three to the Curzon Line and the need to reward Poland with German territory. Roosevelt had sat in on but had not contributed to the discussion, but he joined his partners in endorsing the solution. He did not tell Cordell Hull of this, and indeed told the London Poles months later that he had not agreed to any such arrangement. But whether through a translator's indiscretion or Roosevelt's unwillingness to articulate his position for fear of domestic political repercussions, Stalin believed Roosevelt had agreed. Consequences accrued a year later.[356]

Stalin had come to Tehran seeking assurances on only two matters: Overlord and his western borders. He left Tehran with both. Roosevelt had arrived believing Stalin to be, in his own term, "getatable." The president left believing he had got at Stalin, although he told reporters that Stalin proved "tougher than he had expected." Robert Sherwood called the end of the Tehran Conference the "supreme peak of Roosevelt's career." Perhaps, but Roosevelt had paved his chosen path to Stalin's good graces over his friendship with Churchill. Alec Cadogan concluded that Churchill's lack of guile was as vital to the alliance as was Roosevelt's wit and homespun charm. Churchill was as he appeared; Franklin Roosevelt was not. Cadogan believed Churchill "has very few reticences; U.J. is shrewd enough to spot that, and must, I think, have satisfied himself that he was reading an open book, that there was no concealment or duplicity, and he could have faith."[357]

Stalin indeed thought he was reading an open book, but the conclusions he took from it were not at all those Cadogan had in mind. Four months later, Stalin regaled Milovan Djilas, Tito's third in command, with stories of the Tehran Conference. Djilas, in Moscow as head of a Yugoslavian diplomatic mission, arrived at the Kremlin at about the same time Randolph Churchill and his mission arrived at Tito's headquarters. "Perhaps you think," Stalin told Djilas, "that just because we are allies of the English we have forgotten who they are, and who Churchill is. They find nothing sweeter than to trick their allies.... And Churchill? Churchill is the kind who, if you don't watch him, will slip a kopeck out of your pocket. Yes, a kopeck out of your pocket. By God.... And Roosevelt? Roosevelt is not like that. He dips in his hands only for bigger coins. But Churchill? Churchill—even for a kopeck." At a later meeting, even the wooden Molotov displayed a stunted sense of humor when he recounted a toast Stalin had made to Churchill, a salute to the importance of secrecy in the coming invasion. But the toast, Molotov allowed, was actually a backhanded slap at Churchill's 1915 gambit in the Dardanelles, where the "failure occurred because the British lacked sufficient information." The irony escaped Churchill who, Molotov said, had been "in his cups." Djilas concluded that "Churchill had left a deep impression on the Soviet leaders as a farsighted and dangerous 'bourgeois statesman'—though they did not like him." Nor did they have faith in him. Cadogan had it backwards.[358]

Of Tehran Churchill later wrote: "On my right sat the President of the United States, on my left the master of Russia. Together we controlled practically all the naval and three-quarters of all the air forces in the world, and could direct armies of nearly twenty million men, engaged in the most terrible of wars that had yet occurred in human history." Yet Churchill understood that the United States and the U.S.S.R. accounted for the vast majority of that awesome power. With an American soon to command the largest of the Western armies and Stalin in command of the Eastern, Churchill's influence over the management of the war could only diminish. Churchill had arrived in Persia secure in his nineteenth-century belief in England's imperial destiny; he left having learned a cold lesson. He now had no choice but to regard the status of his small island nation from a mid-twentieth-century vantage point, and it was one of declining geopolitical might. He had always been good at adapting to changing conditions, political or military, but this was different: the sun was setting on an entire era.[359]

The magnitude of the shift in power taking place was captured in an offhand remark made to reporters a few weeks after Tehran by Harold L. Ickes, the American secretary of the interior. It had nothing to do with Polish borders or the autonomy of Greece or France, or the fate of Germany, or the restoration of continental monarchs. It had to do with the resource that powered the great powers, a commodity Britain had monopolized and taken for granted for almost a quarter century. "Tell me the sort of agreement that the United Nations will reach with respect to the world's petroleum reserves when the war is over," Ickes proclaimed, "and I will undertake to analyze the durability of the peace that is to come." This cautionary note stemmed from the fact that America, which produced 95 percent of Allied aviation gas (from its domestic oil supply), was, according to Ickes, "on the verge of becoming a net importer of oil." Of the current oil production in the Middle East, America controlled about 15 percent, Britain 85 percent. That, America could not abide. The war was being fought in Europe and the Pacific, but the spoils would be found in the Middle East. Of the future, *Time* reported, "the oil-conscious British are fearful."[360]

Churchill later told his old friend Violet Bonham Carter, "I realized at Tehran for the first time, what a small nation we are. There I sat with the great Russian bear on one side of me, with paws outstretched, and on the other side the great American buffalo, and between the two sat the poor little English donkey who was the only one, the only one of the three, who knew the right way home."[361]

Despite a growing awareness of his diminishing role within the alliance, Churchill departed Tehran fully intending to find the right way home. As always, the path led through the Mediterranean.

5

Pilot

DECEMBER 1943–JUNE 1944

On December 1, the day they departed Tehran, Churchill, Stalin, and Roosevelt put their signatures to a statement of intent. Issued to the world on December 6, it became known as the Tehran Declaration. In it the three leaders pledged: "No power on earth can prevent our destroying the German armies by land, their U-boats by sea, and their war plants from the air. Our attack will be relentless and increasing." Reuters called it a "death sentence for the Axis." No mention was made of dividing Germany into four, five, six or more demilitarized duchies, or of reparations; no call was made for Germans to throw off their Nazi leaders to avoid annihilation. The Big Three pledged their "determination that our nations shall work together in war and in the peace that will follow." The declaration included the remarkable line, "We look with confidence to the day when all peoples of the world may live free lives, untouched by tyranny.... We leave here, friends in fact, in spirit and in purpose." Harriman later wrote that the declaration "was an astonishing statement for Stalin to have signed....His ideas of tyranny were quite different from ours. Tyranny, for him, did not exist in the Soviet Union." Rather, tyranny for Stalin "was capitalism exploiting the downtrodden." Churchill, in his memoirs, explained that he and Roosevelt could see no decent alternative: "It would not have been right at Tehran for the Western democracies to found their plans upon suspicions of the Russian attitude in the hour of triumph and when all her dangers were removed."[1]

That is a generous enough sentiment, but after Tehran—and for the duration of the war—Churchill pondered ways to check the Soviets in the event Stalin abrogated agreements made in good faith. Roosevelt, meanwhile, began to voice his intent to avoid postwar European entanglements. Indeed, in an early February telegram, the president told Churchill what he had told Harriman in mid-1943: other than maintaining a zone of occupation in Germany, American troops would be coming home after victory. "I am absolutely unwilling to police France and possibly Italy and the Balkans as well," Roosevelt wrote, adding, "after all France is your baby and will take a lot of nursing in order to bring it to the point of walking alone."[2]

Even before the secret talks in Tehran had finished, Stalin made public his demand that several million German laborers and all German industry be shipped to Russia after victory in lieu of 1.6 billion gold marks in reparations, demands that led Goebbels to snort to his diary, "We would rather defend the last remnants of our walls than to accede to such a demand." The English, wrote the little doctor, "would like to use this occasion to sell out the entire German future." Actually, it was Roosevelt and Stalin who led the charge to do so, although Churchill's post-dinner comments to Stalin certainly indicate that he now endorsed the harshest possible treatment of Germany.[3]

Then Goebbels expressed a prescient thought: "Nobody in England seems to recognize that once the Soviet Union is in Europe, it will be a much more dangerous opponent of the British Empire." Churchill's proposal to cede eastern Germany to the Poles in exchange for Stalin getting eastern Poland had been leaked to and reported by the yellow press in London. "I can hardly imagine that the leading English statesmen are so stupid and shortsighted," wrote Goebbels, "as to put that sort of an estimate on Bolshevism. Stalin won't think of fulfilling obligations entered upon with England and America." At least one old Englishman was not so stupid and shortsighted.

While the Big Three had been laying plans in Tehran, Jan Smuts delivered a speech in London that Goebbels thought "sensational." Smuts predicted that following the erasure of the Reich from the map ("nothing new," wrote Goebbels), the "Russian colossus would dominate the entire European Continent. England would come out of this war with honor and glory but poor as a beggar. The United States would in large measure be the heir to the British Empire." Why, Goebbels asked himself, would the British pursue such a ruinous policy? He was truly befuddled. Every Allied bomb that fell on Berlin reminded Goebbels and Hitler—indeed, all Germans—that their English and American cousins considered the sins of the Reich to be far more egregious than the sins of Stalin and his Asian Bolshevik hordes. Goebbels and Hitler could not understand how this could be and (until their final moments on earth) remained hopeful that England and America would see the light.[4]

On December 2, two tired old men along with their military chiefs and aides arrived back in Cairo to resume their talks. Three days later Roosevelt and Churchill signed a statement of purpose. Foremost, nothing would be allowed to interfere with Overlord. Churchill offered that he was committed to the operation "up to the hilt." Likewise, nothing would be allowed to interfere with Anvil, the curtain-raiser for Overlord in southern France. Yet in Tehran, Brooke and Churchill had gained the vital endorsement that they should reassess Anvil in the spring, based on the availability of landing craft. Anvil, as Churchill saw it, was not written in stone. During their talks, to Churchill's great relief, Roosevelt agreed to kill Buccaneer, the operation in Burma that Roosevelt had promised Chiang. It died in part because Mountbatten had demanded 50,000 troops for the task when Churchill expected a request for 15,000. As well, and as usual, no landing craft could be spared for the adventure. Mountbatten would have to make do with what he had for the foreseeable future. Finally, Churchill and Roosevelt agreed that nothing would interfere with operations in the eastern Mediterranean, *if* Turkey entered the war. In pursuit of that objective, President İnönü and the Turks arrived for three days of talks, during which neither Roosevelt nor Churchill could move them into the Allied camp. İnönü "pleaded his country's unpreparedness" but "expressed his readiness 'in principle' to come into the war." The most the Turks would accede to was use of their airfields by Allied airmen. General Marshall was well satisfied with that; he feared Turkey's entry on the Allied side would "burn up our logistics right down the line." Weeks later Jock Colville found Churchill smoking a Turkish cigarette, the first time Colville had seen the P.M. indulge that habit. Churchill, holding the cigarette aloft, declared, "They were the only thing [I] ever got out of the Turks."[5]

Churchill also took up the problems of Yugoslavia and Greece. In each country a civil war was being fought between Communist and non-Communist partisans. All sides in each conflict were being armed by Britain. In both countries the Communists fielded the more powerful force, Tito in Yugoslavia, and the ELAS in Greece. In late November Tito set up a provisional government in Bosnia; one of its first acts was to forbid King Peter to return to Yugoslavia. Churchill and Eden, concluding that Tito's partisans would rule Yugoslavia once the Germans were expelled, believed King Peter's only hope for a role in future Yugoslavian affairs was to repudiate Draja Mihailovic and his Serbian Chetniks, who were colluding with the Germans in the fight against Tito. But the Chetniks were also working closely with the Americans and harbored dozens of American airmen—hundreds by summer—shot down during raids on Romanian oil fields. It was a dicey situation. Churchill, with his man in Yugoslavia, Bill Deakin, acting as intermediary, began negotiations with Tito. In coming weeks the Old Man offered significant military assistance in return for Tito's keeping an open mind on the subject of a working accommodation between himself and King Peter. Churchill was offering a great deal with no guarantees in return.[6]

The situation in Greece, Cadogan wrote, "bore unpleasant similarities to that of Yugoslavia." All the Greek partisans despised King George of the Hellenes. Here, in obverse of their treatment of Tito, Churchill and Eden decided to cease aiding and arming the Greek Communists. That alone would not help King George, because the non-Communist EDES loathed him as much as did the ELAS. The solution, Churchill concluded, was to persuade the king to agree to not return to Greece until and unless asked to do so by the electoral choice of the Greek people. As with King Peter, compromise was King George's only hope; his best chance for seeing a royal government installed under Prime Minister Georgios Papandreou was to stay out of Greece and above the fray. Eden brought the reluctant king around during two days of long talks. Then to Eden's disbelief, Franklin Roosevelt wandered onto the scene and told King George to stick to his guns and to not make any declaration. The president's intervention, Eden later wrote, was "irresponsible," more so because Eden had briefed Winant and Hopkins on the British policy. But they had failed, in turn, to brief Roosevelt. King George, convinced that "the British now wanted to get rid of him," took Roosevelt's advice to heart and refused to give the public pledges Churchill had demanded. The Greek civil war continued until an uncertain cease-fire was patched up in February.[7]

Jock Colville later wrote, "It would be hard to find two worse advertisements for hereditary monarchy than George of Greece and Peter of Yugoslavia."[8]

On December 4, Roosevelt, in one of the most difficult and most momentous decisions of his presidency, chose Dwight Eisenhower to command Overlord. Roosevelt informed Churchill, who told Brooke over dinner, but Marshall did not learn of the decision until the next day, when Roosevelt summoned his Army Chief of Staff and told him, "I feel like I could not sleep with you out of the country." Marshall, disappointed but as always dutiful, immediately sent a radiogram to Eisenhower, but the wording in the cable was so garbled that Eisenhower "was unable to deduce his [Marshall's] meaning with certainty." Eisenhower knew only that the president would be arriving in Tunis late on the seventh or early on the eighth. In his memoirs he wrote, "There can be little doubt that the President felt that the command only of 'Overlord' was not sufficient to justify General Marshall's departure from Washington." Churchill saw the appointment of Eisenhower as validation of his belief that Overlord was to be but one operation among many, and not necessarily the biggest or most critical. Overlord, so far, was just a name on a piece of paper. In fact, during December, both Churchill and Eisenhower directed their efforts toward Italy, where a real battle with real consequences was being fought.[9]

On December 5, Roosevelt drafted and Churchill initialed a memorandum to Chiang outlining the decisions made in Tehran. There was no mention of Stalin's promise to join the Pacific campaign once Germany was defeated (it was thought security at Chiang's headquarters was far too lax for such news to be divulged). One line in the memo underscores Roosevelt's state of mind: "Conference with Stalin involves us in combined operations on European continent in late spring giving fair prospect of *ter-*

minating war with Germany by the late summer of 1944" (italics added). Throughout the coming year, such optimism infected the thinking of many Allied military and political leaders. Churchill harbored no such illusions.

General Spaatz and Bomber Harris were two of the leading optimists. They believed that if enough bombers were sent often enough, Germany would be reduced to rubble, its people rendered incapable of resistance. They believed that Germany might crack by March, certainly by midyear, because the RAF and Eighth Air Force were erasing German cities and their inhabitants from the landscape. In late November, the *Daily Mirror* crowed: RAF WENT OUT AGAIN; KNOCKOUT ASSAULT STARTS. In December, the *Daily Express* proclaimed that airpower meant "no more Passchendaeles."[10]

The optimism was also fed by the Russian winter offensive, which began the first week of December when the Red Army struck westward in the Kiev sector along a front that stretched from the Pripet Marshes south to the Black Sea. In the southern Ukraine, the Germans fell back toward the Bug River. Just 150 miles beyond lay the Prut River and Bessarabia, a former czarist dominion in eastern Romania. Within weeks an entire German army in the Crimea found itself bypassed by the Russians, and cut off. In mid-January, the Red Army struck in the Leningrad sector, relieving that city on January 27 after almost three years under siege. The Soviets then turned west, and drove the Germans back to the Estonian frontier. The overall length of the Russian front remained the same, close to 1,200 miles, but as German manpower shrank, defense of the front became more difficult. The Russian strategy, wrote Liddell Hart, "provided the clearest possible demonstration of the decisive importance of the ratio between space and force." The Russians "could live where any Western army would have starved." The Red Army "rolled on like a flood, or a nomadic horde." A German officer wrote, "The advance of a Red Army is something Westerners can't imagine. Behind the tank spearheads rolls a vast horde, largely mounted on horses. The soldier carries a sack on his back, with dry crusts of bread and raw vegetables collected on the march.... The Russians are accustomed to carry on for as long as three weeks in this primitive way, when advancing." But in German troops "weakness and wide spaces produced a feeling of helplessness." Stalin intended to exploit those feelings until he reached Berlin.[11]

The Russian army was not the only Allied force on the march in early December. On the second, Mark Clark and the Fifth Army struck out toward Monte Camino, with Monte Cassino its final objective. Clark was on his way to Rome. Some at Eisenhower's headquarters thought he'd be there by New Year's. All, including Eisenhower, were bucked up by Clark's near-term prospects. Two days after Roosevelt told him that his appointment as supreme commander would become effective January 1, the president asked Eisenhower if he'd prefer the official announcement be delayed "until Rome is captured." Eisenhower's press aide, Commander Butcher, thought that a fine idea because "since [Ike's new command] isn't effective until January 1, we might get Rome by then, which would make the transition perfect." But between December 8 and Christmas Day, German reinforcements and terrible weather stalled Clark's advance. He did not get to Rome by January 1. By then, Eisenhower was on his way to a two-week leave in the United States, and the Fifth Army was stalled in mud and freezing rain, within sight of its objective, Monte Cassino. By then, Churchill was plotting a new way of getting to Rome.[12]

A few weeks before the Cairo Conference, Eisenhower and Montgomery had made a five-pound bet (even odds) on whether Germany would fall by Christmas 1944. Ike bet yes, Monty no (Montgomery recorded his bets in a ledger). General Freyberg bet Monty ten pounds that the war against Germany would be over by October 31, 1944. Admiral Bertram Ramsay, who had planned the naval operations for Torch and Husky, bet an even fiver that the war would be over by January 1, 1945. Over dinner in Cairo on December 7—Roosevelt had flown that day to Tunis—Churchill polled Smuts, Eden, and most of the military chiefs as to their opinions of when the war with Germany would end. Admiral King—"consumed more than a bottle of champagne... and was showing wear"—predicted sometime between March and November 1944. Marshall agreed. Brooke gave six-to-four odds on March. Dill gave even odds. All the military men—Portal, Cunningham, Hap Arnold, Major Leslie Hollis—put their money on sometime between March and November. Churchill, Eden, and Smuts were not so sanguine. Churchill later wrote that he "was struck by the optimism. The idea was rooted that Hitler would not be strong enough to face the spring campaign, and might collapse even before Overlord was launched."[13]

Eisenhower, in his memoir *Crusade in Europe*, wrote that Churchill and the British hoped the Italian campaign "might lead to an unexpected [German] break that would make the Channel operation either unnecessary or nothing more than a mopping-up affair" to be conducted only when "the Allies could go in easily and safely." Yet the votes of the American chiefs at the dinner indicate that it was *they* who thought that way. Churchill had pledged in Tehran that Overlord would take place in May; he knew it would be both a difficult and bloody affair. After seeing the initial plans for the invasion the previous August, he advised that more men go ashore. Otherwise, he feared a repulse on the beach. He never saw it as a mopping-up affair. Eisenhower by December had taken only a cursory look at the plans for Overlord. On his way to Washington, he told reporters, "We will win the European war in 1944."[14]

Other prognosticators had already seen their predictions go belly-up.

Admiral William ("Bull") Halsey, commander in chief of U.S. Navy South Pacific forces, had stated with confidence months earlier that 1943 would bring "complete, absolute defeat for the Axis." Halsey no longer engaged in such speculation, telling reporters, "I refuse to gaze into the crystal ball anymore.... Only God knows."[15]

By December 9, unable to shake the sore throat and cold that had dogged him since he left London, Churchill felt he was on the cusp of a physical breakdown. Smuts thought the Old Man had "exhausted himself, and then had to rely on drink to stimulate [himself] again." The South African began to doubt whether Churchill could stay the course. At lunch that day, Churchill admitted to Brooke that he felt tired, flat, "and had pains in his loins." His degree of fatigue was evidenced by the fact the he had lost his appetite and hardly spoke. Between small spoonfuls of soup he swatted flies with a fly whisk and counted the corpses. He could summon only enough energy to pronounce the soup "*dee*-licious" while sending more flies to the mortuary. Brooke wondered how near Churchill was "to a crash." Churchill wondered the same. He later wrote that he found himself so tired that he no longer dried himself after his bath, but lay on the bed wrapped in a towel.[16]

Shortly after midnight on December 11, Churchill and his party left Cairo in their Avro York, bound for Tunis to pay a courtesy call on Eisenhower. Churchill intended to fly on to Italy from there, to buck up Alexander, whose armies were being ground down by the enemy, by the terrain, by the worst winter weather in years, and by an outbreak of typhus. Lice and malaria were the common enemy for both armies.

At daybreak Churchill's plane landed at an airfield outside Tunis. The place appeared abandoned. No guards were in evidence; no cars waited. Churchill's pilot had brought them down to the wrong field. The prime minister hauled himself and his official boxes out of the York and sat down on the edge of the runway. There he waited, recalled Brooke, "in a very cold morning wind like nothing on earth." A steel-cold mist blew out of the north. Moran pressed Churchill to get himself back inside the heated plane. He refused. He remained perched upon his boxes, a very long way from home. He wore a scowl on his face, which shone now with perspiration. "He seemed to be going from bad to worse," Moran wrote. When the mix-up was sorted out, the party reboarded the York and made for the right airfield. By then Churchill had gone gray in the face, to Moran's professional discomfort. After arriving finally at Eisenhower's headquarters near Carthage, Churchill slumped into a chair, where he remained for the rest of the day, too weak even to read his telegrams.[17]

Moran by then was sick with worry. His patient spiked a temperature of 102; he was exhausted, mentally and physically. His lungs were seriously congested. Here was a combination of blows even the Old Man might not survive. He was indeed an elderly man, having just begun the final year of his biblical three score years and ten. Moran believed with medical certainty that Churchill would probably not make it to the next year. The prime minister needed the best that medicine offered, but other than sulfa drugs and serums, mid-twentieth-century medicine did not offer much hope for an elderly man. Moran lacked the equipment and facilities to make a proper diagnosis. Of particular concern was the possibility that Churchill had contracted a virulent strain of influenza that was making its way around the world. In Germany it was called *Kellergrippe* (cellar flu), and it killed 2,000 Berliners that week. Britain reported 1,148 deaths for the week. When Goebbels learned that King George had taken ill, he gushed to his diary, "How wonderful if the epidemic were to prove fatal!"[18]

Moran had a very sick man on his hands. A standing joke among Churchill's private secretaries held that if the Old Man became suddenly ill, the secretary on duty was to summon Lord Moran, who would then summon a real doctor. Moran proceeded to do just that, requesting that a pathologist, Dr. Robert Pulvertaft, and two nurses be flown out from Cairo, and that an X-ray technician and his machine be sent from Algiers, along with a supply of digitalis, lest Churchill's heart act up. A heart specialist, Dr. D. E. Bedford, was also summoned from Cairo. During the afternoon of December 13, the X-ray was duly taken. It showed a shadow on Churchill's lung. "Do you mean I've got pneumonia again?" he demanded of Moran. Moran prescribed treatment with M&B (so called after the British company that made it, May and Baker), a sulfonamide early antibiotic. The next day, Moran found Churchill "breathless and anxious looking." His pulse was racing and irregular; he was suffering from cardiac fibrillation. "My heart is doing something funny," Churchill said. When it worsened, he pleaded, "Can't you do anything to stop this?" Moran gave him a dose of digitalis and promised it would soon take effect. It did, but not for four hours, during which time Moran, holding Churchill's hand and monitoring his pulse, realized "that we were at last right up against things."[19]

"No signs of improvement yet," Moran wrote in his diary on December 15. That day, Pilot Officer John Colville received an urgent summons to report to No. 10 Downing Street in uniform. There he was told that the prime minister was "seriously, perhaps fatally, ill with pneumonia at Carthage." Colville's orders were to escort Mrs. Churchill to Tunis at once in order for her to be at her husband's bedside. A twin-engine Dakota was waiting for them at Lyneham airfield, but Beaverbrook insisted the party wait until he could procure a four-engine B-24 Liberator. Twenty hours later, Clementine, Colville, and Grace Hamblin, serving as Mrs. Churchill's secretary and orderly, boarded an unheated, blacked-out Liberator, and were soon Africa bound. The overnight flight to Gibraltar lasted nine hours, and from there, after a brief stopover, they continued on to Tunis, another six hours in the air, during which time they were cut off from any news. They could only speculate on the Old Man's condition, and from Clementine's somber demeanor, that was just what she was doing. Colville and Grace passed the hours sipping coffee and quietly chatting, in order to keep an eye on Mrs. Churchill, who "could not sleep and was rather alarmed."[20]

Hustled from the airfield at first light by Eisenhower's staff, the party arrived outside Churchill's villa, where inside Churchill lay in bed, barely stirring and somewhat disoriented, having realized Sarah was absent from the chair where she had been keeping a vigil. A moment later, Sarah escorted Clementine into the room; Churchill had not been told of her arrival and could have been excused if he thought he was delirious at the sight of an apparition. Colville entered a few minutes later, expecting to find a "recumbent invalid." Instead he beheld "a cheerful figure with large cigar and a whisky and soda in his hand." The crisis had passed.[21]

Colville rejoined Churchill's staff that week, and but for a brief interlude that summer when he was granted leave for RAF duty, he remained in the private secretariat until the end of the war.

Eisenhower's appointment as commander of Overlord (not yet made public) resulted in a shake-up of commands throughout Allied ranks. Air Chief Marshal Tedder would serve as Ike's deputy, with authority over all air forces, strategic and tactical. Admiral Bertram Ramsay was given command of Overlord naval operations, including the landings, code-named Neptune. Churchill wanted Eisenhower's chief of staff Bedell ("Beetle") Smith, who got along well with the British, to remain in the Mediterranean, but Ike took Smith to London. Within weeks, Eisenhower insisted upon and was granted complete control of all Allied air forces, tactical and strategic. Air Chief Marshal Trafford Leigh-Mallory, of Fighter Command, went in as Eisenhower's air commander in chief, with control of all tactical air forces. Bernard Montgomery was to leave the Eighth Army at the end of the month to command Twenty-first Army Group, the designation for the Allied troops in Britain dedicated to Overlord. In that capacity Montgomery would command all Overlord ground forces during the initial stage of the invasion. Churchill (and Eisenhower) preferred Alexander in that role, but the War Cabinet insisted upon the hero of El Alamein. Churchill acceded peacefully, in the belief that Alexander would emerge as the hero of Italy, where glory would accrue with the capture of Rome and the pursuit of the enemy all the way to Vienna. Henry Maitland ("Jumbo") Wilson, Middle East commander in chief, was raised to supreme commander Mediterranean. Brooke remained as CIGS and with Churchill's sponsorship was promoted to field marshal. Portal was elevated to air chief marshal. By Christmas, many of the appointees were on their way to London to take up their new posts. Jumbo Wilson, not yet familiar with the central and western Mediterranean, could not immediately bring anything to bear in that theater, where the command shake-up had created a power vacuum. Churchill, alone at Tunis with time on his hands and frustrated by the stasis in Italy, decided to fill it himself.

On Christmas Eve, Franklin Roosevelt announced in a radio broadcast the appointment of Dwight Eisenhower as supreme commander Allied Expeditionary Force. Henceforth, wherever General Ike put his headquarters would be known as SHAEF, Supreme Headquarters Allied Expeditionary Force. The president also asked Americans to pray for Churchill, ill in North Africa. Roosevelt and Eisenhower were religious men. The president told Harriman after Tehran that he believed the Russians "as deeply religious people were bound to stand up against the atheist ideology of Soviet communism and its repressions," a naive sentiment that presumed that whoever stood up against Stalin would not be scythed down. In the spring, Roosevelt would write a prayer for the soldiers going ashore in Normandy; it ran on the front page of the *New York Times* on June 7. Churchill didn't write prayers, and he didn't say prayers. Eisenhower, who believed the God of Justice was on the Allied side, once told Lord Moran, "Freedom itself means nothing unless there is faith." Bernard Montgomery claimed his chaplains were more important than his artillery. General Alexander, too, was a man of abiding faith, as was Jan Smuts, who kept his Greek Testament close at hand and examined every decision under the lens of Christian doctrine. Over dinner one night, Smuts admonished Churchill, "Gandhi... is a man of god. You and I are mundane people. Gandhi has appealed to religious motives. You never have. That is where you have failed."[22]

In fact, Churchill believed that was where he had succeeded. On Christmas Day, the Coldstream Guards hosted a church service in an old corrugated-steel warehouse that the army was using to store ammunition. Although feeling well enough to attend the service, Churchill, per his habit, chose not to. Instead, he prepared to discuss the Italian campaign with Eisenhower, who was due to arrive before noon. Clementine attended the service, along with Sarah, Colville, General Alexander, and Moran. As the padre intoned the Gloria in Excelsis, the bells of a nearby church rang out, and a white dove, which had been roosting in the rafters of the warehouse, "fluttered down in front of the congregation." After the service, when Clementine told Winston of the dove, he dismissed the episode as a conjuring by the minister who, he said, most likely released the bird from under his surplice. When Alexander, who believed the mysteries of this life would be revealed in the next, told Churchill of the message from above delivered on the wings of a dove, Churchill huffed, "There is nothing in such stuff."[23]

The remark surprised no one. He regularly reminded those around him that he had declared for agnosticism early in manhood. He had so informed his mother, Jennie, in letters home from India. He informed the world at large in his autobiography, *My Early Life,* where he wrote that while in India he passed through "a violent and aggressive anti-religious phase," which in turn led to an embrace of good old-fashioned British empiricism. He soon realized under fire in combat that a dash of faith offered some comfort. The result was typical Churchill: "I therefore adapted quite early in life a system of believing whatever I wanted to believe." His meager relationship with God was neither reverential nor deferential, but one that reflected Stanley Baldwin's political philosophy: "Never complain and never explain." He did not begin his speeches with pleas to the Almighty for guidance, nor did he end them with supplications for divine blessing. He did not ask Providence for the strength or wisdom to win the war. He told Britons, "As long as we have faith in our cause and unconquerable will power, salvation will not be denied us."

Late one evening in Tehran, he told Stalin, "I believe God is on our side. At least I have done my best to make Him a faithful ally." Stalin grinned, and replied, "And the devil is on my side. Because, of course, everyone knows the devil is a Communist and God, no doubt, is a good Conservative." That was Churchill playing the straight man to Stalin. He did so again when (as told by Jan Smuts) he suggested the pope might play some role in securing the peace. "The Pope," Stalin replied thoughtfully, "the Pope. How many divisions has he?" Stalin, Churchill noted with irony, seemed to bring up God quite frequently in conversation.[24]

Churchill did not.

Churchill's scant theological leanings tended to incline toward Spinoza's hands-off deity: God helps those who help themselves. Providence may have put him—and Cromwell, Marlborough, Pitt, and Nelson—on earth, but Providence disclosed no plan for success, and offered no guidance or revelation. Churchill guided himself.

Thus, while his wife and daughter and colleagues beheld the white Christmas dove and were moved to quiet contemplation and wonder, Churchill, in bed with his dispatch boxes, cigars, and whisky, found guidance in his maps and plotted the course of his armies. The agreed-upon date for Overlord was just four months away. Eisenhower was due to arrive at any moment to discuss operations in Italy, including putting an invasion force ashore south of Rome, at Anzio, a gambit that Churchill believed would open the road to Rome.

Churchill had awaked from his fever one day at Carthage to find Sarah sitting at the bedside. She had been reading *Pride and Prejudice* aloud to him, even as he slept. "Don't worry," he told her. "It doesn't matter if I die now, the plans of victory have been laid, it is only a matter of time."[25]

Yet by Christmas Day, it had become obvious to Churchill that not enough plans had been laid. The Fifth Army, slogging toward the Liri Valley, had gained less than ten miles in almost three weeks. It would certainly not be in Rome by New Year's. The recollections of Eisenhower and Churchill part company at this point. Eisenhower fails to mention in his memoir the optimism at his headquarters in early December, when he thought a delay until January 1 of the announcement of his elevation to supreme commander was a grand idea, since by then the Allies might be in Rome. Churchill, in his history of the war, writes that the deadlock in Italy "led General Eisenhower to yearn for an amphibious flanking attack." Strictly speaking, if to hope is to yearn, Eisenhower yearned for such an operation. But by Christmas he considered it beyond reach and believed that to attempt it would be overreaching, with possible catastrophic consequences. A plan for such an operation, code-named Shingle, had been on the books for two months. By Christmas, Churchill considered it absolutely critical to Allied success.[26]

Eisenhower described Shingle as an "end run" around Kesselring's flanks. Churchill, unfamiliar with the American football term, asked what the expression meant. In English parlance it was a "cat-claw." In boxing terms, it was a left hook delivered in conjunction with an uppercut by the Fifth Army at the Rapido River near its confluence with the Liri. Then, if all went well, Fifth Army would take Monte Cassino and strike up the Liri Valley to join hands within the week with the Shingle force. Then, with Kesselring's forces presumably in disarray, the Fifth Army would march the final thirty-five miles to Rome, while the Eighth Army, on the Adriatic side of the Apennines, executed a sweeping left turn in the same direction. Eisenhower saw great risk in the Anzio operation, and he warned Churchill. He voiced his fear of "the hazard of annihilation to the landing force if Fifth Army should be unable to reach it by land." He further feared that without resupply by the landing ships soon departing the Mediterranean for Britain and Overlord, the Anzio beachhead would remain exposed. It was one thing, in Eisenhower's estimation, to draw German troops away from France to Italy. It was another matter entirely if the Germans sent enough troops to Italy to defeat the Allied armies there. The force Eisenhower considered large enough to hold and exploit the Anzio landings simply was not available. These concerns he expressed to Churchill on Christmas Day, and again during their final meeting a week later, before Eisenhower left for Washington and London. But Shingle would not come on Eisenhower's Mediterranean watch; he had no dog in that fight.[27]

Eisenhower expressed his doubts about Anzio in almost the same terms Churchill used to express his concerns about Overlord. Churchill was not the only commander who feared that an undersize force thrown onto a beach faced "annihilation." The Christmas meeting was attended by most of the military brass in the theater—Eisenhower, Air Marshal Tedder, Jumbo Wilson, and Alexander. Brooke, who never backed down when he disagreed with Churchill, had already left for London. Another man whose opinion might have carried weight, Mark Clark, had not been invited to the meeting. His Fifth Army would supply the men for Shingle. The assembled agreed that the operation should be enlarged to two reinforced divisions, and should go forward. But it could not. With the exodus of landing ships from the Mediterranean to England, the planners came up fifty-six ships short.

Only Roosevelt could approve a change of plans regarding landing craft. Churchill sent a cable to the president: "The landing at Anzio . . . should decide the battle of Rome." Yet, he told the president, eighty-eight landing ships were required, and that number could only be reached by delaying the scheduled transfer of the fifty-six ships to England for Overlord. It would "seem irrational" not to do so, Churchill wrote. To send the ships to England would result in "stagnation" or worse on the Italian front. He was angry, and he was frustrated. Between them, the Americans and British had pledged to build 1,500 ships and landing craft of all types per *month,* and yet in the only European theater where Anglo-American forces were fighting Germans, the fate of the Allied campaign rested with just fifty-six landing craft. Two days later, Roosevelt approved the use of the landing craft. Operation Shingle was on, and Churchill himself was planning the details, including an increase in the force from 20,000 to more than 70,000.[28]

Splendid news from the polar region arrived on Boxing Day. The Royal Navy had brought the *Scharnhorst* to bay off the Norwegian coast. (This was especially welcome news, as *Scharnhorst*'s escape from Brest in February 1942 had nearly brought down Churchill's government.) When the German battle cruiser had in the previous days attacked a convoy bound for Russia, Admiral Sir Bruce Fraser, aboard the *Duke of York*, gave chase. *Scharnhorst* made for the safety of Norway, but by Christmas night, Fraser and his heavy ships had closed in on the German ship. On the twenty-sixth, surrounded, nearly out of ammunition, aflame, and crippled by torpedoes and shells, the *Scharnhorst* finally went under, taking all but thirty-six of her crew of two thousand to the bottom. *Tirpitz*, wounded in late September by Royal Navy midget submarines, still lived, but the German navy, having already lost the submarine war, now had to face a reality that Churchill had seen in early autumn: the Battle of the Atlantic was over. There had been a time when the mere threat of sorties by the German surface fleet terrorized Allied shipping and kept the Home Fleet near home. Now the German threat—its surface fleet, and much of its U-boat fleet—had vanished. Hitler ordered newer, faster, more heavily armed submarines built, but they were not due for deployment until mid-1945. As 1944 came on, the buildup for Overlord proceeded apace. With the arrival of each fresh American division, Britain was being transformed into the largest military staging area in history.

On December 27, Churchill, under doctor's orders, left Carthage for a two-week convalescence at Marrakech, during which time he took de facto command of the Mediterranean theater. He hinted at his intentions in a medical bulletin he wrote, which was issued from No. 10 Downing that week: "I feel a good deal better than at any time since leaving England, though of course a few weeks in the sunshine are needed to restore my physical strength.... The M and B, which I may also call Moran and Bedford, did the work most effectively.... I have not at any time had to relinquish my part in the direction of affairs, and there has been not the slightest delay in giving the decisions which were required from me. I am now able to transact business fully.... I shall not be idle." In fact, with the British chiefs and War Cabinet in London, Churchill found himself free to plan his own war.[29]

At Marrakech, as after Casablanca, he again took over the Villa Taylor, surrounding himself with a diminished troop of family and friends—Beaverbrook was summoned for companionship—and a skeletal staff of typists, private secretaries, and military advisers. Randolph and Sarah joined their father, the son, as usual, tending toward bellicosity and drunkenness, which inevitably led to "a bickering match" between himself and Winston. Randolph was especially poisonous toward de Gaulle, whom he advised his father to dump, in part because de Gaulle had just arrested five former Vichy leaders for treason. Three of the five had aided the Allies during Torch, and their safety had been spoken for by Roosevelt and Churchill. Henri Giraud opposed the arrests, but de Gaulle was forcing him out as co-president of the FCNL. De Gaulle was now the state, such as it was. To Harold Macmillan's chagrin, Churchill listened to his son, who was feeding Winston numerous reports on de Gaulle that were "mostly invented." "Randolph was the cause of the trouble," Macmillan told his diary. "It is really too bad for the boy to worry his father. But Winston is pathetically devoted to him." After witnessing several such scenes, Colville wrote, "Randolph is causing considerable strife in the family," and when Randolph again went off on de Gaulle, Colville noted, "Winston almost had apoplexy and Lord Moran was seriously perturbed." Randolph's commanding officer, Fitzroy Maclean, assured Colville that Randolph's behavior would change once they joined Tito in Yugoslavia, "owing to the absence of whisky and a diet of cabbage soup." Years later, Evelyn Waugh, who served with Randolph in Yugoslavia, was told that Randolph, a heavy smoker, had undergone a biopsy for a suspected cancerous growth in his lung. To everyone's surprise, including Randolph's, the biopsy came back negative. "A typical triumph of modern science," Waugh offered, "to find the only part of Randolph that was not malignant and remove it."[30]

Yet Randolph, in his own insufferable manner, brought into clearer focus the trouble that was brewing with de Gaulle. De Gaulle, not Randolph, was the real source of the difficulty. To address it, Churchill sent his York aircraft to Algiers in order to retrieve his old friends Alfred Duff Cooper and his wife, Lady Diana Cooper. He was in his new position of HMG's minister to the French Committee of National Liberation, and Lady Diana was a notable in her own right, at fifty-one still one of England's great beauties. Her portrait had graced a *Time* magazine cover in 1926; she was a respected actress and one of England's best-known hostesses. Over men, including Churchill, she exerted a certain power, as Lord Moran witnessed at dinner one evening in Marrakech. "There," Moran whispered to Colville, "you have the historic spectacle of a professional siren vamping an elder statesman." Duff Cooper, who loved France and the French, could only hope that he could exert such sway over de Gaulle. Cooper's new assignment—to make peace with de Gaulle, or at least to avoid more trouble—proved difficult from the start.[31]

When Roosevelt telegraphed orders directly to Eisenhower to not allow the Gaullists to prosecute three of the arrested Vichy luminaries, Macmillan—now resident minister for the entire Mediterranean—feared a complete collapse of relations between the French and the British and Americans. Roosevelt added a handwritten postscript to his cable: "It seems to me that this is the proper time effectively to eliminate the Jeanne d'Arc complex and return to realism." Upon learning of the cable, Macmillan told his diary, "The president hates de Gaulle and the French National Committee.... He would seize on any excuse to overthrow them and restore Giraud." De Gaulle delayed a showdown when he announced that the three Vichy leaders would not be tried until a French government was in place. Still, Roosevelt wanted de Gaulle out, and Churchill was leaning that way.[32]

The antics of Randolph and de Gaulle were distractions for Churchill, who wanted to focus his attention on only Italy. He summoned Captain Pim and his entire map room staff to Marrakech in order to better plot his Anzio campaign. Montgomery, on his way to London to assume his new command, flew in for New Year's. Eisenhower, about to leave for a two-week vacation in the States before reporting for duty in London, was summoned by Churchill to discuss Anzio; again Eisenhower expressed his fears about the gambit—too small a force thrown against too powerful an enemy. On New Year's Eve, Churchill asked Montgomery to look over the plans for the Normandy campaign. Montgomery at first protested that since the Combined Chiefs of Staff had approved the plans, it was not his place to second-guess them. Churchill insisted. Montgomery (never a man for celebrations anyway) cut short his New Year's Eve dinner with Churchill and Clementine to take up the task. In deference to Monty, the rest of the party celebrated the New Year before the midnight hour. Punch was served, and orderlies and typists wandered into the room to partake of the festivities. After a brief speech by Churchill, everyone linked arms and formed a circle to sing "Auld Lang Syne."[33]

Montgomery wrote fondly of the evening in his memoirs, noting that it marked the beginning of a friendship between himself and Churchill and Clementine that only deepened over the next two decades. That was true; Montgomery signed the guest book at Chartwell forty-six times, second only to the Prof's eighty-six. Yet the friendship almost sputtered at the start when Clementine invited Monty's aide-de-camp, Noel Chavasse, to the New Year's Eve dinner. "My ADC's don't dine with the Prime Minister," Montgomery replied tartly. "In my house, General Montgomery," said Clementine, "I invite who I wish and I don't require your advice." Chavasse dined.[34]

The next morning, New Year's Day 1944, Churchill marched into Clementine's room and announced, "I am so happy. I feel so much better." Later in the day, the Old Man and his party, including Montgomery, motored to an olive grove in the countryside for a picnic, one of many during his days of recuperation. There, Monty delivered to Churchill his first, unfavorable, impressions of the Overlord plan. "This will not do," Monty declared. "I must have more in the initial punch." He had earlier offered his opinion to Eisenhower, who told him to recommend any and all changes he thought appropriate when they next met in London. But Eisenhower had Italy, not Normandy, on his mind. He departed Marrakech that morning with the unsettling feeling that "the insistence of the P.M. indicated he had practically taken tactical command of the Mediterranean." He had. Eisenhower's staff began referring to Shingle as "the P.M.'s pet project." It was. Marrakech picnics were "sacrificed to stern duty," Moran wrote. "Councils of war" were held in the gardens of the Villa Taylor. When Moran pointed out to Churchill that Hitler not only made war policy but even planned the details, Churchill replied, "Yes, that's just what I do." With all the brass having departed, he found himself alone in Marrakech, happily so, prompting Lord Moran to tell his diary, "As the P.M. grows in strength his appetite for war comes back."[35]

In early January 1944, RAF and American bomber crews sailed off on a series of secret missions over France that their superiors were closemouthed about. Normally, the flyers' commanders briefed flight crews on intended targets—a particular factory, for example, or rail yard in a particular city. But now the flight crews were given only coordinates, and told not to miss. The airmen were not privy to the fact that throughout the late autumn, British reconnaissance flights had snapped photos of dozens of strange-looking wooden and concrete structures scattered from Normandy to the Pas de Calais. The structures looked like Alpine ski jumps—narrow and about five hundred feet long. Some sat upon concrete foundations. Heavy electrical cables and winches implied that the structures might serve as some sort of catapult. When analysts marked the sites on maps, they reached an unsettling conclusion: each was positioned such that its axis pointed toward London. It was left to one sharp-eyed WAAF (Woman's Auxiliary Air Force) analyst to spot a propellerless aircraft near one of the sites. Another analyst recalled similar buildings being photographed at Peenemünde the previous May. The analysts could only conclude that they were looking at German launch sites. Exactly what manner of device was to be launched remained unknown. RAF and American bomb crews now flew in the service of Crossbow, Duncan Sandys's operation to destroy the mysterious sites. But accuracy, as usual, left much to be desired. "The bombing of the launching emplacements," Brooke confided to his diary on January 11, "is not going well." The bombing, in fact, continued to not go well for seven more months.[36]

Not so Churchill's Moroccan holiday. He worked mornings, picnicked in the afternoons, and dined splendidly by candlelight each night. Late in the evening, dressed in his dragon robe, he sang along to Gilbert and Sullivan recordings sent to him for Christmas by Mary, "the best present I ever gave him." Eduard Beneš, on his way home from Moscow, where he had signed a friendship treaty with Stalin, stopped by for dinner, during which Beneš expressed his belief that "we must be ready for a German collapse any day after May 1." Again, as he had in Cairo, Churchill polled his dinner companions as to whether they believed Hitler would still be in power on September 3, 1944. Answering no were Sarah, Commander Tommy Thompson, John Martin, Beneš, and Major General Leslie Hollis. Hollis's pronouncement carried weight; he was Ismay's deputy and attended many of the overseas conferences and most of the military planning sessions throughout the war. Churchill and Beaverbrook answered yes.[37]

On January 12, Charles de Gaulle, after a month of what Duff Cooper termed "boorish" refusals to meet with Churchill, agreed to dine with the prime minister. Still offended by Churchill's not seeing him while en route to Tehran, and furious over Roosevelt's intervention in his plan to try the three Vichy loyalists, the general arrived in Marrakech in a "difficult and unhelpful" mood. Churchill, too, was in a low mood, having been shocked that day to learn that Count Ciano and the other conspirators who had ousted Mussolini had been shot. As Churchill waited for de Gaulle, Duff Cooper later wrote, he pondered ridding the alliance of the Frenchman once and for all, not only because Roosevelt sought to but because, as Churchill told Cooper, "You like the man, I don't." As the hour of the meeting approached, Cooper and Clementine advised Churchill to act with civility toward de Gaulle. "I hope there will be no explosions," Clementine wrote in a letter to Mary. There were not. After a cool start (de Gaulle "talked as if he were Stalin and Roosevelt combined") the two leaders "parted friends" two hours later. Churchill even agreed to attend a review of French troops the following day. The review, where Churchill and de Gaulle stood side by side, "was a great success," Cooper wrote, and Churchill was "much moved by the cries of '*Vive Churchill,*' which predominated over the cries of '*Vive de Gaulle*' as the Spahis and Zouaves marched past." Years later Cooper wrote of Churchill, "After spending more than a half century in the de-humanising profession of politics, Winston Churchill remains as human as a school-boy." The words were written in appreciation of Churchill's willingness to stick with de Gaulle—despite de Gaulle's misdeeds—for the greater good of France and Europe.[38]

A picnic in the mountains (without de Gaulle) followed the review of troops. Such outings were not simple affairs to bring off. American troops guarded the surrounding area, which included a deep gorge through which a river ran. Churchill's orderlies laid out long trestle tables, white tablecloths, folding chairs, Berber carpets, and large wicker baskets containing oranges, olives, grilled lamb, and chilled liquid refreshments, "the whole caboodle," recalled Lady Diana Cooper. So luscious were the oranges that Montgomery, who was leaving for London later in the day, ordered that an aircraft be procured, loaded with oranges, and sent ahead to England. As with any meal with Churchill, the picnic began on an uncertain note. Lady Cooper, a friend of three decades, had long known how to best approach Churchill at the dinner table. "He was always grumpy before dinner," she recalled, "then after a couple of drinks, became funny and more witty." After his first glass of brandy Churchill leaned in toward Lady Diana and whispered, "Lord Moran says I am to have another glass of brandy." Yet Moran had said no such thing. "Well," Lady Diana recalled, "three times he had another glass of brandy with the result that I saw it coming." What she saw coming was an excursion by Churchill and several aides down to the river in the gorge, where he scrambled about on the boulders in the streambed. When it came time to ascend from the ravine, the Old Man found he lacked the mobility. Lady Diana lowered a long white tablecloth, into which Churchill was wrapped like a baby in a bundle. With two aides pulling, two pushing, and another carrying the Old Man's cigar, they regained the high ground.[39]

Churchill's long absence from London had been noted at the highest levels. Brooke told his diary on January 7, "Winston, sitting in Marrakech, is now full of beans and trying to win the war from there.... I wish to god he would come home and get under control." He was coming home soon, but with no intention of getting himself under control. Yet he was not fully fit, was prone to bouts of exhaustion, and experienced occasional trouble on his feet, as borne out by the expedition into the ravine. One evening in Marrakech, Clementine confided to Lady Cooper, "I never think of after the war. You see, I think Winston will die when it's over.... You see... we're putting everything we have into this war, and it will take all we have."[40]

It was taking all Roosevelt and Harry Hopkins had. In a New Year's Eve cable to Churchill, the president made casual reference to spending a few days in bed "with a mild case of the 'flu.'" Five days later, Roosevelt told Churchill that Harry Hopkins, too, had come down with the flu and would be spending a few days in the Naval Hospital. The illness wasn't severe, Roosevelt offered, but "it makes you feel like an Italian soldier looks." In fact, Roosevelt was a sick man, experiencing abdominal pains, fluid in his lungs, and heart palpitations. Hopkins was an even sicker man. He did not in fact spend a few days in hospital, but the better part of seven months, during which time he underwent surgery for his stomach ailments, all of which, he would learn within a year, his doctors had misdiagnosed. Hopkins, in great pain, was shuffled between the Mayo Clinic and the Naval Hospital before undertaking a long convalescence at White Sulphur Springs. So sudden and total was his disappearance that Churchill concluded he had had a falling out with the president. In February, Churchill dispatched one of the few letters he sent to Hopkins that year. It was a scroll, actually, hand-lettered with five lines from the final scene of *Macbeth*. It began: "*Your son, my lord, has paid a soldier's debt....*" Stephen Hopkins, Marine Private First Class, eighteen, had been killed in the Marshall Islands. For three years Churchill had found a friend and ready ear in Hopkins, who had championed England's cause more strongly and more effectively than did the president's chief of staff, Admiral Leahy, and his secretary of state, Cordell Hull. Hopkins, not Roosevelt, had been Churchill's best friend in the White House. He had completed the circuit between his boss and Churchill. That connection was now fraying.[41]

By January 3, the Russians had driven one hundred miles beyond the 1939 Polish frontier; that is, the Red Army had struck into Poland for the second time in four years. Churchill saw the political implications of the Red Army's success and telegraphed his concerns to Anthony Eden. The questions of the Baltic States and Bessarabia, Churchill wrote, "have largely settled themselves through the victories of the Russian armies." Churchill reminded Eden that when at Tehran they offered Königsberg in East Prussia to Stalin, they made no mention of the Baltic States, "which clearly would be compromised" by a Russian march through them to East Prussia." In fact, Churchill wrote, once the Russians take "physical possession of these territories...it is absolutely certain that we shall never be able to turn them out."[42]

The implication for Poland was clear. Then Eden cabled with the news that the London Poles insisted "Poland, as a reward for Polish suffering and fighting," must "emerge from this war with...her eastern provinces intact and her western provinces increased." That would not do; Churchill had already proposed to Stalin the ceding of a large swath of eastern Poland to Russia. Were the Poles to refuse the offer, Churchill told Eden, he would consider England's obligations to Poland fully discharged: "I would certainly not take any further responsibility for what will happen in the future." The London Poles, Eden reported, feared that in Poland's war-weakened state, chewing off of large portions of Germany would prove difficult "in digesting." As well, Eden offered, in light of the heroic victo-

Churchill in his siren suit with Eisenhower, May 1944. (*NARA*)

Churchill and Brooke on their way to Normandy aboard a Royal Navy destroyer, June 12, 1944. (*NARA*)

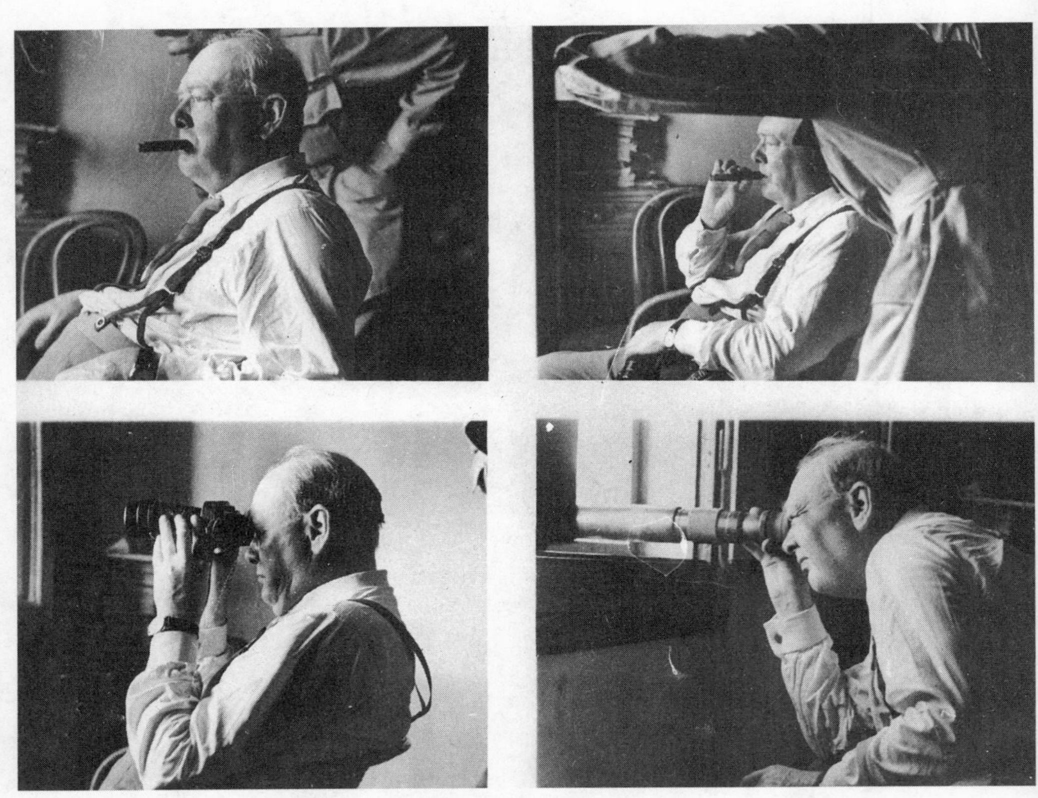

Churchill watches an artillery barrage, Italy, August 1944. (*NARA*)

Churchill receives a bouquet of flowers from a little girl in Italy, August 1944. (*NARA*)

Churchill and de Gaulle lay a wreath at the Tomb of the Unknown Soldier, Paris, November 11, 1944. (*NARA*)

Left to right: Brooke, Churchill, Montgomery, and General William Simpson crossing the Rhine, winter 1945. (*NARA*)

Churchill scribbles a message to Hitler on a British artillery shell at the Rhine, winter 1945. (*NARA*)

Churchill climbs the wreckage of a Rhine bridge, March 1945. He had fulfilled his longstanding promise to make Germany "burn and bleed." (*NARA*)

Churchill exits Hitler's bunker, Berlin, July 1945. (*NARA*)

Churchill prepares to give his radio address announcing the German surrender, May 8, 1945. (*NARA*)

Churchill joins the royal family, from left, Princess Elizabeth, Queen Elizabeth, and King George VI, on the balcony of Buckingham Palace on VE-day, May 8, 1945. (*AP*)

Churchill, with Clementine, campaigns in the general election, June 1945. A victory would give him the electoral mandate he lacked when he formed his 1940 government. (*NARA*)

Churchill, in his rompers, and Clementine, taking a few days' rest before the Potsdam Conference, pose for a photographer on a French beach, July 1945. (*NARA*)

Churchill, Truman, and Stalin at the Potsdam Conference, July 1945. (*AP*)

Churchill, with Harry Truman, arrives at Westminster College, Fulton, Missouri, March 1946, to deliver what became known as the Iron Curtain speech. (*National Churchill Museum, Westminster College, Fulton, Mo.*)

Churchill sits for a portrait by Douglas Chandor, 1946. (*NARA*)

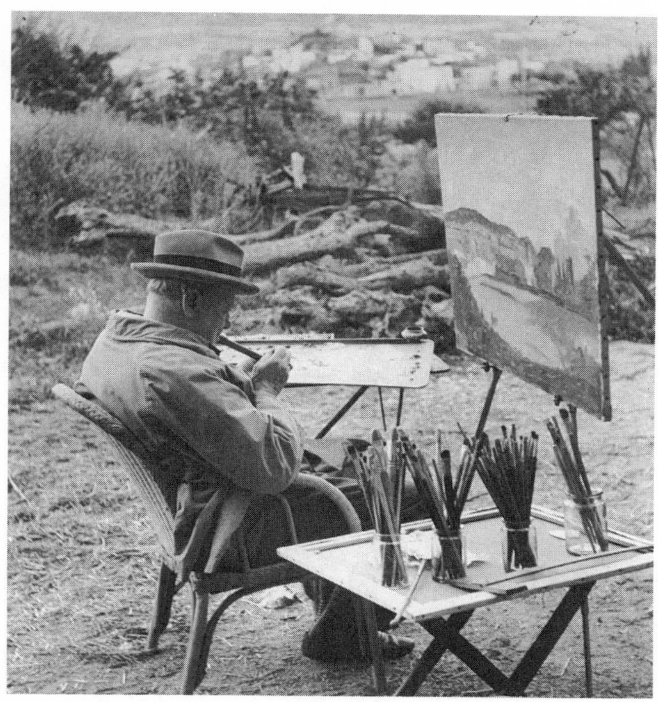

Churchill lights a cigar as he paints a landscape on a hilltop outside Château de Lourmarin, near Aix-en-Provence, 1948. Wherever Churchill went in retirement, his brushes and paints went, too. (*Getty*)

Out of office, Churchill with new friends, Miami, 1946. (*History Miami*)

Churchill in his Order of the Garter regalia with his son, Randolph, and grandson, Winston S., 1953. (*Library of Congress*)

Clementine (left) looks on as Churchill greets Queen Elizabeth II on his last night as prime minister, April 1955. (*Getty*)

Diana and Randolph, holding his ever-present cigarette, on a London street, 1960. (*Corbis*)

Sarah Churchill under arrest for public drunkenness, Southern California, 1958. (*George Lack Estate*)

Sir Winston and daughter Sarah, nicknamed "the mule" in childhood. (*Corbis*)

Sir Winston Churchill greets New York from his chair on the deck of the yacht *Christina*, as she arrives in the Hudson River, April 12, 1961. The owner of the yacht, Aristotle Onassis, stands behind Churchill, glass in hand. (Others unidentified.) (*AP*)

Churchill's casket, draped by a Union Jack, is carried from St. Paul's Cathedral by members of the Queen's Royal Irish Hussars, January 30, 1965. (*Getty*)

ries of the Red Army, "there is public impatience with the Poles." Britain may have gone to war for Poland, but Britons, like their American cousins, had put the Russians on a pedestal. Still, Eden was optimistic. But that faith was shaken by a telegram from Stalin to Churchill on January 7 wherein the marshal stated that the declarations of the London Poles left him to conclude that "there is no foundation for reckoning on the possibility of bringing these circles to reason. These people are incorrigible." The London Poles, pressed by Eden, finally agreed to discuss "all outstanding questions" with the Russians, including the Curzon Line. But they would not accept the Curzon Line before any such discussions. Moscow rejected the offer. The London Poles, Stalin informed the British, "did not want neighborly relations with the Soviet Union." That news, Eden later wrote, came "like a blow to the face." With the Red Army now one hundred miles beyond Poland's 1939 border, Churchill grasped the inevitable. To Eden he cabled: "Considering that Russia has lost perhaps thirty millions of citizens . . . they have the right as well as the power to have their western frontiers secured."[43]

Churchill departed Marrakech on January 14, intent on being in London when the troops went ashore at Anzio. He went by air to Gibraltar, and then by *King George V* to Plymouth, and finally by train to Paddington Station, where late in the morning of the eighteenth he was met by the entire cabinet and Chiefs of Staff. He had been away for sixty-seven days, an extraordinary amount of time for any leader to be absent from his capital, and doubly so for a leader during wartime. He took himself straightaway to the House, which had just reconvened after the Christmas recess. Harold Nicolson recorded Churchill's entrance: "We were dawdling through questions . . . when I saw (*saw* is the word) a gasp of astonishment pass over the faces of the Labour Party opposite. Suddenly they jumped to their feet and started shouting. . . . We also jumped up and the whole House broke into cheer after cheer while Winston, very pink, rather shy, beaming with mischief, crept along the front bench and flung himself into his accustomed seat." He rose to take questions, and although Nicolson applauded his effort, he also noted that he "looked pale when the first flush of pleasure had subsided, and his voice was not quite so vigorous as it had been." Concerns about Churchill's health now regularly found their way into the diaries of the Old Man's colleagues.[44]

Following Questions, Churchill chaired a cabinet meeting during which he disabused Brooke of any hopes that he would return to London under control. The P.M. "rambled on till 1:30 P.M.," Brooke told his diary that night. "He was looking well, but I did not like the functioning of his brain much! Too much unconnected rambling from one subject to another." Indeed, at the following day's Chiefs of Staff meeting, Churchill launched into his plans for operations "after Anzio is over." This was three days before Anzio even began. He foresaw putting several thousand commandos supported by tanks on islands off the Dalmatian coast. For Churchill, the Aegean still held its place as a theater of destiny. That night, Brooke unloaded to his diary: "The P.M. is starting off in his usual style!! I don't think I can stand much more of it.... His method is entirely opportunistic, gathering one flower here, another there! My God how tired I am of working for him. I had not fully realized how awful it is until I suddenly found myself thrown into it again after a rest."[45]

Churchill was back.

Eisenhower had arrived in London on January 16, assured by Roosevelt and Marshall that they would not second-guess his decisions, would never try to force commanders on him, and would back him completely. The president had put the "supreme" in supreme commander. Eisenhower had told the president that he intended to deploy his forces in pursuit of one military objective—the destruction of Hitler's armies. All decisions would be taken with that objective in mind. "Geographical points," he later wrote, "were considered only in their relationship" to killing German armies. And politics was not to be considered at all. He made clear to Churchill in coming weeks that were his superiors—Roosevelt and Marshall—to order him to undertake operations based on political priorities, he would of course obey those orders. But he would not otherwise bend his military strategy to politics. Eisenhower noted Churchill's "concern as a political leader for the future of the Balkans...but as a soldier I was particularly careful to exclude such considerations from my own recommendations." Churchill also harbored a deep concern for Poland; in fact, with the Red Army driving west, he increasingly harbored concerns for all of Europe. This divergence in philosophies between Eisenhower the warrior and Churchill the warrior-politician would in coming months have profound consequences.[46]

The Yanks had arrived in Britain, almost one million strong. Another million were due by June, and yet another million by year's end. Dwight Eisenhower's Irish driver (and alleged mistress), Kay Summersby, later wrote that London, "like a discreet matron carried away by one too many cocktails," had become "a playgirl of a city." Since the Battle of Britain, RAF pilots on weekend leave had hastened to London for forty-eight hours of whiskey and women. The GIs' arrival "really blew the lid off." The Americans spent their dollars in any number of stores and pubs and clubs; the locals had little money to spend and, with everything from sweets to eggs to clothes rationed, little to spend it on. Summersby declared her pride at watching the poorest of Londoners slide right past American PXs while casting "not a glance at the American boys emerging with cigarettes and sweets and other treasures." Britons, meanwhile, saw their milk ration reduced to two pints per week. Irving Berlin's all-soldier musical *This Is the Army,* starring its New York cast, was entering its third month of playing to standing room only crowds at the Palladium; every shilling of the proceeds went to the British armed forces.[47]

One evening months earlier, after he had viewed photos of destroyed German cities, Harold Nicolson's thoughts turned to London, which was largely unvisited by the Luftwaffe in 1943. Whereas almost three years earlier, Nicolson and all Londoners had feared for their lives, they now felt free to complain about their sacrifices. Nicolson was pleased that one of his favorite restaurants "retained all its old atmosphere," but "the Travellers, on the other hand, has become a battered *caravanserai,* in which the scum of the lower London clubs are served inadequately by scared Lithuanian waitresses." And when Nicolson came across boozy American troops frolicking in the Underground with their "East End Jewish girls," he went home and told his diary, "I hate it."[48]

England, wrote Mollie Panter-Downes, resembled "a vast combination of an aircraft carrier, a dock jammed with men, and a warehouse stacked to the ceiling with material labeled 'Europe.' "[49]

The legions of soldiers had time on their hands, if not on their side. Arriving GIs joined the uniformed Welshmen, Scotsmen, Norwegians, Poles, Dutch, Indians, Czechs, Belgians, Canadians, Newfoundlanders (until 1949, Newfoundland was a self-governing Dominion), Aussies, and New Zealanders who had turned Piccadilly Circus into the Times Square of England. It was the sort of chaotic commingling that had occurred on the island with regularity since prehistoric times and of which Daniel Defoe wrote:

From this amphibious ill-borne mob began
That vain, ill-natured thing, an Englishman.

At night battalions of tarts strutted down the blacked-out streets, as they had at the height of the Blitz (Ed Murrow had called them "London's bravest"). Now they solicited clients with whispers of "*tovarisch*" ("comrade"). Darkened doorways became love nests and from alleys drifted the sounds of fistfights and catcalls and blasphemies in a babel of languages.

The whores carried small flashlights that they played on their faces for a few seconds when a soldier nodded interest, the narrow beams dancing in the deep shadows with a flickering, strobe effect. Old air-raid wardens in tin hats barked orders to cut the torches. They were ignored. When low-pressure atmospherics wrapped the city in a vile mix of acrid chimney effusions and impenetrable Channel fog, the nighttime became downright bizarre. Automobiles—the top half of their headlights painted black—crept along like purblind beasts of burden, led by passengers or Good Samaritans who placed one hand on the front fender while reaching out with the other in hopes of feeling their way to the proper destination. After much tribulation, many stumbles, and a bit of good luck, the autos and their caretakers might actually find their way home. London, after almost five years under blackout conditions, was still wrapped, Jock Colville wrote, "in Stygian blackness."[50]

On January 21, Eisenhower's senior Overlord staff met for the first time, at Norfolk House, a neo-Georgian building just off St. James's Park, which had been put off limits to civilians in part to mask the comings and goings at the former mansion. Montgomery presented his findings on the initial plans for Overlord. As he had told Churchill, he now told his colleagues, "The initial landing is on too narrow a front and confined to too small an area." As well, the landings—code-named Neptune—called for too few men, just three divisions, which invited congestion on the beaches and possible disaster were the Germans to concentrate their tanks and send in their planes. Monty supported the concept of the Mulberry artificial harbors but stressed the need to capture the port of Cherbourg. That objective necessitated the widening of the landing zone to include a beach on the Cotentin Peninsula, which was separated from the main landing beaches by the four-mile-wide double estuary of the Vire and Douve rivers. To resolve that problem, Montgomery proposed dropping two divisions of American paratroops ten miles inland from the beach and west of the Douve. Finally, he insisted "the air battle must be won before the operation is launched." Eisenhower, who had taken only a cursory look at the plans before he left North Africa, found himself in general agreement with Monty's suggestions, but for one. Montgomery proposed scrapping Anvil, the two-division invasion of southern France, in order to free up the troops and landing craft needed to expand Overlord. Eisenhower acknowledged that Anvil could not now precede Overlord as planned, but he declared that it must follow soon after. He would consider an outright cancellation only as a last resort. All agreed that the time needed to assemble the appropriate force for Overlord—and to destroy German airpower and disrupt French rail lines—would delay the invasion for a month. That was exactly the flexibility Churchill and Brooke had sought, and believed they had gained, in Tehran.[51]

Given the need to make the Normandy landings under a nearly full moon, and on a rising tide within sixty minutes after dawn, the delay effectively pushed Overlord into the first week of June. Secrecy being as critical as logistics to Overlord's success, Operation Bodyguard was soon born, a multifaceted campaign of radio intercepts, double agents, and false intelligence. Its stepchild, Operation Fortitude, entailed the creation of phony armies from Scotland to southeast England. The phantom armies broadcast phony radio messages that the Germans were welcome to intercept and interpret at their own risk. The ranks of the nonexistent units consisted of brigades of inflatable rubber tanks and squadrons of plywood planes, which when photographed from the air by German reconnaissance flights indicated massive troop buildups.

New Allied weapons also contributed to the cause. Major General Percy ("Hobo") Hobart, the erratic tank genius whom Churchill had brought back into service in 1940 (over Brooke's objections), was put in command of building specialty tanks—"swimming" tanks that could come ashore under their own power; tanks that "flailed" minefields with wildly spinning chains; and flame-throwing tanks capable of incinerating large buildings. Montgomery and Eisenhower added dimensions to Overlord not imagined by the original planners. Three days later, Eisenhower briefed the Combined Chiefs of Staff on his new plan. Even though events were now going the way Brooke had argued for, he could not bring himself to write a complimentary word about Eisenhower: "I certainly agree with his [Eisenhower's] proposal, but it is certainly not his idea, and is one of Monty's. Eisenhower has got absolutely no strategical outlook and is totally unfit for the post he holds."[52]

Days after Montgomery argued for the cancellation of Anvil (and Eisenhower agreed to postpone it), Churchill came up with another means to reinforce Overlord. It took the form of landing three armored divisions in Bordeaux a few weeks after the start of the Normandy venture, which, according to plan, by twenty days after D-day would find Allied troops well inland. He code-named the operation Caliph, and proposed that the three divisions be moved from the Mediterranean to Morocco before being shipped around the Iberian Peninsula and into the port of Bordeaux. In Caliph, Churchill beheld a solution to a problem he anticipated: Anvil must necessarily draw down Alexander's landing ships and troops and thereby force a halt in the springtime Italian campaign. In Churchill's estimation, a shift from Anvil to Caliph would both support the Normandy invasion (Eisenhower's first priority) and improve prospects in Italy (Churchill's theater of destiny). It would establish two distinct theaters—France and Italy/Mediterranean—under two supreme commanders (Eisenhower and Jumbo Wilson). This was an alternative far superior to the god-awful muddle that would result from two simultaneous and mutually dependent operations within close proximity, one in southern France and the other in northern Italy, where Churchill presumed Alexander would be by May. Brooke dismissed Caliph as a "wild venture." After the British Chiefs of Staff and Churchill discussed the matter, Brooke wrote, "I think we have ridden him of this for the present." They had, but only for the present.[53]

More than 25,000 Allied troops, British and American, went ashore at Anzio and Nettuno on January 22. Surprise was total. The beaches were undefended; the men came ashore with ease and by noon reached the first day's objective of driving three miles inland. This put the invasion force about forty miles north of Kesselring's rear, and sixty miles north of the Fifth Army. That morning, Brooke enthused to his diary over bagging 172 pheasants on a one-day shooting holiday and, in reference to the surprise attained at Anzio, added, "This was a wonderful relief."

That was the last positive diary entry Brooke would make in regard to Anzio for several months. By the next day, 15,000 more troops came ashore, along with almost four thousand vehicles (far too many, Churchill believed, and he told Alexander to make sure he landed enough men to fill his thousands of trucks). Then, instead of striking inland, the men sat static on the Anzio beaches for two days. And that was the problem. With their backs to the sea and six divisions' worth of German reinforcements rushing from northern Italy to their front, the Allies found themselves ripe targets for the German 88s hastily dug into hillsides above and around the beach. By January 28, Churchill knew the invasion had failed. He famously described the situation a few weeks later when he told Colville and Brooke, "I thought we should fling wildcat ashore and all we got was an old stranded whale on the beach." Churchill liked to repeat his favorite phrases for effect; this one was accurate and it captured exactly the stasis on the beaches. Even the code name, Shingle, took on a terrible irony, for it was on the seashore shingle that the army remained. The fault for that, as Churchill saw it, lay with the American commander, General John P. Lucas. He came, he saw, he consulted, and as a result, his men died. Kesselring, in contrast, deployed his forces with precision. Yet Sir John Keegan sided with Lucas in a critical regard: "Had Lucas risked rushing at Rome the first day, his spearheads would probably have arrived, though they would have soon been crushed."[54]

The idea of Italy having any sort of soft underbelly was being refuted daily sixty miles south of Anzio. The coordinating blow by Mark Clark's Fifth Army in support of the Anzio landings had begun on January 17 when British forces attacked across the lower Garigliano River. On January 20, six thousand Americans from the 36th Texas Division tried to attack across the Rapido, swollen by winter rains, its currents deadly. The surrounding terrain was a quagmire; no roads led in or out of the area. For three days the Texans tried, and for three days they failed to take the far banks, with more than one thousand killed. It was a gruesome defeat for the Texans, the Fifth Army, and Churchill. In order to get to Anzio and the great prize—Rome—the Fifth Army had to get across the Rapido and take Monte Cassino, where the German 1st Parachute Division was now dug in on the slopes. On January 24, Clark threw the American 34th Division onto the mountain; on February 12, after almost three weeks of close combat, the Germans threw it off. The road to Rome had not been shortened by as much as a foot.[55]

The most formidable obstacle the Allies faced in Italy was Albert Kesselring's Gustav Line, which began just north of the mouth of the Garigliano River on the Tyrrhenian coast. Built by the quasi-military German construction company Organization Todt, which was also rushing to complete Hitler's Atlantic Wall, the Gustav Line—a man-made bifurcation of the Italian peninsula that was as formidable as a mountain range—was an extraordinary feat of engineering, a coast-to-coast concrete fortress with interlocking artillery sites, barbed wire, machine guns, and mines, behind which Kesselring deployed the thirteen divisions of his Tenth Army. In the west, the line was anchored by Monte Cassino, which overlooked Highway 6, the road to Rome. From there the line ran east over the spine of the Apennines to the mouth of the Sangro River on the Adriatic coast, where the Eighth Army was engaged in its bloodiest action of the war. Unlike the Maginot Line, the Gustav Line could not be easily outflanked, as the battle for the Liri Valley proved, hourly.

Yet, in a critical regard, Hitler's decision to dig in and stand fast rather than to have his army slowly pull back into northern Italy played into Churchill's hands. Hitler's Italian forces were tied down and therefore not available to reinforce the Atlantic Wall. This result had been the goal of Churchill and Brooke from the start. They had always seen Italy as both an end in itself and a means to restrict Hitler's ability to deploy his forces on his terms only. But Churchill had never sought stalemate; he wanted to lure Hitler's armies to their doom. That strategy was only half fulfilled. Hitler's divisions in Italy would not be going to Normandy, but unless and until Alexander got his armies off the beach at Anzio and around the German flank at Cassino, the Allies would not be going to Rome. Rome was not only a great political prize but a vital military objective, for without control of the airfields near Rome, there could be no Anvil; nor of course could there be a swing by Alexander northwest to France or northeast toward the Balkans and Austria. Thus all roads led to Rome. In early February, Brooke and the British Chiefs of Staff wired Washington with the opinion that "the only thing to do is to go on fighting the war in Italy and give up any idea of a weak landing in southern France." This was just what Churchill had anticipated two weeks earlier when he proposed Caliph, a plan Brooke considered "a wild venture." Yet unless the Combined Chiefs came up with a better way to reinforce Overlord, Anvil would have to go forward sometime after the Normandy invasion, at the probable expense of Italian operations.[56]

In mid-February, Kesselring unleashed an all-out attack upon the Anzio beachhead. Had it not been for the Ultra decrypts that warned the Allies of Kesselring's plans, Lucas and his little army would have been thrown into the sea. Alexander sacked Lucas on February 23. The men on the beachhead moved into underground warrens of muddy trenches, foxholes, and basements—and not just the infantry but the support troops, too, including mechanics, weathermen, medics, and cooks. There was no rear to move back to. Lice infested uniforms and bedrolls; malarial mosquitoes swarmed out of the marshes, which Mussolini had drained years before but the Germans had now flooded. Allied ranks were swelled by hundreds of Italian orphans who, their parents dead and their homes destroyed, wandered into the lines, as did hundreds of stray dogs and cats, which the troops adopted. German artillery and Stukas raked the beach, daily, hourly, constantly. A German bomb fell so close to the stone house where newspaperman Ernie Pyle was sleeping that the concussion tossed him out of bed and blew his cigarettes out of the pack. He gathered them up and smoked them all by lunchtime. Nearly 4,500 Allied troops never made it off the beach alive.[57]

As February went out, Hitler, who had promised retaliation for months, turned the Luftwaffe loose upon London. The Blitz was back and with a fury. The raids came like hammer strokes; smaller fleets of Heinkels came in fast and dropped more powerful bombs than in 1940. They no longer came during the "bomber's moon" but on the darkest of nights, guided by their navigation beams. The raiders knew not to linger over London, due to the improvements the British had made in radio-controlled anti-aircraft targeting. Bell Laboratories manufactured an electronic gun director that measured the speed, course, and altitude of aircraft, along with wind direction and muzzle velocity of the anti-aircraft shells. The final calculation determined the altitude at which the proximity fuses of the anti-aircraft shells were set to burst. All of these calculations, and the automatic aiming and firing of the guns, were performed by a component of the system that Bell called the "computer."[58]

The Germans, in turn, befuddled British radar by turning Window—tinfoil streamers—against Britain, as the British had done over Hamburg. London's children called the foil streamers "flutterers" and danced around trees laden with them, like Maypoles, wrote Mollie Panter-Downes. But other than the children, no one enjoyed the onslaught (with the exception perhaps of one old man, his tin hat always at the ready). When the sirens wailed, Churchill once again took himself off, as he had during the 1940 Blitz, to Hyde Park now, where Mary's AA battery produced the music of the night. Once again Londoners had to shovel glass from gutters; once again crowds lined up at shelters before sundown. The windows were again blown out of No. 10. Londoners demeaned the attacks as the "Baby Blitz." But the bombers were getting through. "The glow of fires in the sky shows the damage was widespread," Colville wrote after one raid. "London seems disturbed by the raids, and less ebullient than in 1940–41."[59]

By mid-February the battle for the Gustav Line was faring no better than that for Anzio. A second attack on Monte Cassino, by the New Zealanders, was planned for February 16. The ferocity of the battle for the town of Cassino and the monastery above it led some in the English clergy to express fears that Rome, too, would be subject to destruction, a worry Mollie Panter-Downes downplayed in a February 13 column in *The New Yorker,* in which she wrote of "anxious concern over the fate of Rome—concern which, judging by the extreme solicitude the Allies were showing for the Monte Cassino Monastery, seemed hardly necessary." The solicitude ended on the night of February 15–16 when the Americans, believing that Germans had taken up positions in the monastery, dropped 1,400 tons of bombs onto it, almost twice the tonnage the Luftwaffe dropped on London during the first night of the 1940 Blitz. The bombing left the monastery in ruins, although its walls remained somewhat intact. The New Zealanders attacked the next morning and were repulsed. The

Germans had not, in fact, been inside the monastery, but they soon occupied the ruins, which afforded them almost perfect protection.[60]

That the Allies could send almost an entire air force to bomb a single church testified to the awesome power of their air fleets. But thousands of planes meant thousands of casualties. On February 19, Colville noted that nine hundred bombers had been sent out to Germany the previous night, and that 5 percent did not return. Actually, as Churchill told the House on February 22, a thousand bombers had been sent to four German cities, nine thousand tons of bombs were loosed, and seventy-nine aircraft—8 percent—did not return. RAF losses were staggering, and mounting. But Churchill remained committed to the bombing campaign. He spoke to the House that day for one hour and eighteen minutes, his first major address in five months. He directed most of his remarks at Germans, telling them that unconditional surrender did not mean they would become slaves.

He also promised Germans that he intended to bomb Germany into ruins. He told MPs (and reminded Americans), "Turning to the air, the honour of bombing Berlin has fallen almost entirely to us. Up to the present we have delivered the main attack upon Germany." Then he spoke of the cost: "Excluding Dominion and Allied squadrons working with the Royal Air Force, the British islands have lost 38,300 pilots and air crews killed and 10,400 missing, and over 10,000 aircraft since the beginning of the war and they have made nearly 900,000 sorties into the North European theatre." But there would be no respite, for air crews or Germans: "Scales and degrees of attack will be reached far beyond the dimensions of anything which has yet been employed or, indeed, imagined." He advised German citizens to flee their cities and take refuge in the countryside. He predicted German retaliation for the air campaign, and not the usual sort of raids that had been taking place. He disclosed for the first time in public what form the retaliation would take: "There is no doubt that the Germans are preparing on the French shore new means of assault on this country, either by pilotless aircraft, or possibly rockets, or both, on a considerable scale."[61]

Mollie Panter-Downes noted that Londoners did not much comment on Churchill's warnings of impending attack "by pilotless planes and rocket shells." Most people, she wrote, "had enough to worry about right now with planes that did have pilots." But she had misheard Churchill. He had not warned of "rocket shells" of the sort batteries in Hyde Park shot skyward in search of German planes. Rather, he had warned of *rockets*.[62]

In his address, Churchill covered every world battlefront, and every political nuance on the international scene and at home. He cautioned that the war in Europe would probably not end in 1944. He gave details of his pledge to Stalin made at Tehran that Soviet borders would be protected and that Polish borders would be moved. He declared the Curzon Line as

HMG's policy, and declared his faith in Stalin's promise that he sought "a strong integral independent Poland as one of the leading Powers in Europe." He added, "He [Stalin] has several times repeated these declarations in public, and I am convinced that they represent the settled policy of the Soviet Union." Then he took a swing at naysayers in Britain and America who denigrated the Grand Alliance:

> My hope is that generous instincts of unity will not depart from us in these times of tremendous exertions and grievous sacrifices, and that we shall not fall apart, abroad or at home, so as to become the prey of the little folk who exist in every country and who frolic alongside the Juggernaut car of war, to see what fun or notoriety they can extract from the proceedings. There is one thing that we agreed at Tehran, above all others, to which we are all bound in solemn compact, and that is to fall upon and smite the Hun by land, sea and air with all the strength that is in us during the coming Spring and Summer.[63]

When earlier that week the former Archbishop of Canterbury decried the bombing of German cities and the prospect of Rome being bombed wholesale, the House of Lords responded with an official declaration that the bombing of German cities must and would go on.

March 1, and the invasion of France, was just three months distant. Churchill insisted it be called a "liberation" and that "invasion" be used only in reference to crossing the enemy—German—frontier. The Combined Chiefs of Staff obeyed the directive, and even Roosevelt agreed to do so. Invasion or liberation, Overlord would be the most critical step yet taken by the Anglo-Americans toward the destruction of Hitler. The Russians could not do it alone; nor, it appeared, could Bomber Command. Brendan Bracken saw Overlord as "the most desperate military venture in history." Alec Cadogan, the permanent under secretary for Foreign Affairs, called it "the most hazardous enterprise ever undertaken." It was that (at least from the Anglo-American standpoint), yet it was just one operation among many, one element on the military landscape.[64]

There were other landscapes—economic, political, social—over which the players had to make their way. For the next three months, Dwight Eisenhower's horizon justifiably extended to Normandy, and not much further. Charles de Gaulle, in Algiers, had his sights set on getting to Paris, the London Poles on getting to Warsaw, Beneš on getting to Prague. The

Allied military chiefs parsed vistas worldwide—in Italy, in the vastness of the Pacific, in Burma. Likewise in the political sphere, Harriman, Halifax, Hull, and Eden shared many problems, and many solutions, but certainly not all. British diplomats around the world tussled with local leaders over local problems; in Bengal the famine was worsening. At home, British authorities clashed with disgruntled Britons over wages, ration cards, food shortages, and a beer shortage. Each participant in the drama operated in a limited sphere, but Churchill's responsibilities encompassed all things military, political, and economic—internationally and in the Home Island. And it was all in flux. His duties were kaleidoscopic in their haphazard variety. Poland and Overlord certainly dominated his thoughts, but there were numerous other worries as well.

It was obvious that Romania, which had been extending peace feelers in Stockholm since late 1943, would soon be overrun by the Red Army. Churchill knew that once the Soviets gained Bucharest, the matter of a separate peace with Romania would become moot. The Hungarians and Bulgarians, too, were getting jittery as the Red Army rolled toward the Carpathians. In mid-March, after Hitler learned that the Hungarians had sent out peace feelers to the West, he sent in the Wehrmacht to occupy the country and installed a pro-Nazi puppet government. The new government soon ordered the deportation of 450,000 Hungarian Jews and Romas to the death camps. The Finns, too, saw the writing on the wall. With Leningrad freed, the Finns knew that the Red Army would soon come their way. It did, in an early June surprise attack. Finland's Marshal Carl Mannerheim concluded a separate peace with the Soviets in August.

Greece was in a state of civil war. When Greek troops in Egypt mutinied in April, Churchill told General Bernard Paget, in Cairo, that HMG was "prepared to use the utmost force if necessary, but let us avoid slaughter, if possible." Paget put down the revolt with the loss of one British officer and no Greeks. Yugoslavia, too, was in a state of civil war; by April Churchill threw his full support to Tito and cut all ties with the Chetniks. Churchill finessed King Peter, a Serb, into sacking his cabinet and appointing Dr. Ivan Šubašić—a Croat, pro-Tito and acceptable to Stalin—as prime minister. Tito did not ask for a seat in the government and agreed to defer a plebiscite on King Peter until after the war.[65]

Italian politics came into play in March, when Roosevelt, citing American "public opinion" (it was an election year), pushed Churchill to sack King Emmanuel and Badoglio, who was, after all, a Fascist holdover. Churchill, preferring the strong hand of Badoglio to the fractious Italian politics that would surely result from his sacking, thought the idea foolish. "Why break the handle of the coffee pot," he told Brooke, "... and burn your fingers trying to hold it, why not wait to get to Rome and let it cool off?"[66]

Roosevelt sifted all questions of Italy, Poland, and Ireland in terms of election year politics—Italian, Irish, and Polish Americans formed the backbone of his constituency. On the one hand, he did not want to lose the Polish bloc; on the other, he did not want Stalin doubting the sincerity of the agreements made at Tehran with regard to Poland. For his part, Churchill examined Poland strictly in terms of Britain's commitment to the Free Poles. He considered other European countries—Romania, Yugoslavia, Greece, Italy, Bulgaria—largely in terms of their susceptibility to Communist takeover. Upon Ireland, where he expected mischief, he kept a wary eye. Indeed, late in the year de Valera proclaimed Ireland's duty and right as a neutral to offer sanctuary to Germans accused of war crimes. Where Roosevelt weighed issues regarding Europe in terms of American politics, Churchill weighed them in terms of Europe, its future, and Britain's role in that future. Stalin, likewise, weighed matters in terms of Russia's role in postwar Europe. His armies were now inside Poland, or as Roosevelt pointed out to Polish Americans throughout the year, inside one of the many configurations of Poland that had come and gone for over a century. He asked, which was the real Poland? His point was, Poland defied geographical definition, which even the American Polish community admitted was true. Yet American Poles and especially the London Poles were repulsed by the idea of ceding even one inch of prewar Poland to the Bolsheviks. Still, ever politically agile, Roosevelt managed to keep the Polish voting bloc in his pocket, as well as Stalin, or so he thought.[67]

In the forgotten war in Burma, the Americans and Chinese under Vinegar Joe Stilwell could only slog though the northern Burmese jungle in their mission to build the Ledo Road from northern India to China, their flanks protected by the guerrilla warfare genius Orde Wingate and his Chindits. Brooke thought the stress of battle "had sent Wingate off his head," but before any consideration was given to relieving him, Wingate, the "Clive of Burma," was killed in an airplane crash in March, thus removing the unique fighter from the scene. General Sir Billy Slim and the Fourteenth Army had captured a major Japanese supply base sixty miles south of Mandalay but had outrun their own supply lines. Further operations were canceled until after the monsoons. Malaria, as it had in Italy, felled more troops than the enemy. But the Allies had a new and secret scientific weapon in the war against mosquitoes and lice. Later in the year the British and American governments lifted censorship from "one of the great scientific discoveries of World War II." It was a discovery, proclaimed *Time,* that would "be to preventive medicine what Lister's discovery of antiseptics was to surgery." Churchill told the Commons, "It is an insecticide called D.D.T. We have discovered many defences against tropical disease, and, above all, against the onslaught of insects of all kinds, from lice to mosquitoes and back again. The excellent D.D.T. powder, which has been fully experimented with and found to yield astonishing results, will hence-forward be used on a great scale by the British forces in Burma and by American and Australian forces in the Pacific and, indeed, in all theatres."[68]

Worldwide, disparate commanders demanded from the planners in Washington and London more men, more ammo, more medicines, and more 120-octane aircraft fuel. There was Overlord, to be sure, but there were also Burma, Norway, the Aegean, Anzio, the Philippines, the Marshall and Gilbert islands, and always, for Churchill, Sumatra. In mid-March he again proposed to his Chiefs of Staff a strike into Sumatra as a stepping-stone to Rangoon, an idea Brooke called "impossible" and "full of false deductions and defective strategy." It was never carried out.[69]

Problems demanding solutions abounded. Palestine presented a singular one, not of any immediate military nature, but one with significant long-term implications. In 1939 the Foreign Office produced a white paper that called for an end to Jewish immigration to Palestine in 1944 and the establishment of a single Palestinian state in which the Arabs, by virtue of holding veto power on any further Jewish immigration, would outnumber Jews three to one. The white paper, produced as a gambit should war come, was intended to placate Arabs throughout the Middle East. Chamberlain believed that if war came, the Arab world would be a far stronger ally against Hitler than five hundred thousand Palestinian Jews. Parliament was to take up the white paper in May 1944. The British military chiefs advocated adoption. Churchill did not, and considered the white paper to be a betrayal of the Balfour Declaration* and a betrayal of Jews. He had opposed the policy in 1939 and still did, because the Arab majority within a single Palestinian state would never allow the Jewish minority to execute a partition into two separate states. If trouble arose over partition, Churchill told Ismay, it will come from the Arabs and that "left to themselves, the Jews would beat the Arabs." He used parliamentary procedures to keep the bill from coming to a vote, thus delaying the debate until after the war. His support for Zionism never flagged, even when later in the year, two young Zionist terrorists assassinated Lord Moyne (Walter Guinness), resident minister in the Middle East. Moyne was an old Churchill family friend and had hosted Clementine onboard his yacht *Rosaura* during their pacific journey a decade earlier. He had long opposed Zionism,

* Promulgated in 1917 by Foreign Minister Arthur Balfour, which called for HMG to support "the establishment of a national home for the Jewish people" in Palestine with the guarantee that "nothing shall be done which may prejudice the civil and religious rights of existing non-Jewish communities in Palestine."

but he had moderated his opinions somewhat since his posting to Palestine. When Churchill learned that Zionists worldwide protested the death sentence imposed on Moyne's assassins, he advised Cairo officials, where the murder took place, to hang the killers, and hang them quickly. The sentence was carried out.[70]

Churchill, like many in senior army and Foreign Office positions, was sympathetic to Arab nationalism—the Arabs had helped Britain drive the Turks out of the Levant. As well, Muslims were at least monotheistic, unlike Gandhi and his troublesome Hindus with their grotesque pantheon of hydra-headed gods and multi-appendage goddesses. Yet unlike many of the Arabists in the military and Foreign Office, Churchill never courted Arabs at the expense of Jews. Relations between Anglican and Jewish Englishmen were often based on complete ignorance. At the end of the war and soon after the Nazi atrocities against Jews became known, Harold Nicolson, upon learning that the *Daily Mirror* (which he thought was owned and run by Jews) was encouraging service members to vote Labour in the upcoming election, confessed to his diary, "Although I loathe anti-Semitism, I do dislike Jews."[71]

Churchill was no anti-Semite, although his words had smacked of anti-Semitism in 1920 when he opposed giving economic aid to Soviet Russia, citing "the gravest objections to giving all this help to the tyrannic Government of these Jew commissars." He was at first wary, too, of the Balfour Declaration. Its call for a Jewish "national home" did not necessarily mean "autonomous state," but the door was opened and Chaim Weizmann led his Zionist followers through. When it came to Palestinian Jews, although many of his generals were mostly pro-Arab if not anti-Semitic, Churchill pushed hard for the creation of a Jewish state in Palestine, Arab opposition or no. During a cabinet meeting the previous July, he had reiterated his support: "I'm committed to the creation of a Jewish national home in Palestine... and at the end of the war we shall have plenty of force with which to compel the Arabs to acquiesce in our designs."[72]

The French always demanded Churchill's time. In Algiers the French were at each other's throats, again, which only reinforced Roosevelt's belief that de Gaulle should have no role whatsoever in Overlord or the civil administration of liberated France. In early March, the Gaullists in Algiers put former Vichy minister of the interior Pierre Pucheu on trial for conspiring with the Germans in the executions of hundreds of French citizens. Harold Macmillan considered Pucheu to be a traitor and "a black criminal," but he feared repercussions for de Gaulle if Pucheu were shot. The trial itself damaged de Gaulle's reputation. The prosecutor, General Pierre Weiss, was "an object of universal contempt," Macmillan wrote, not least because he was "an open and known pederast, surrounded by 'pansy' officers." Although Macmillan thought Pucheu put up a strong defense, he predicted "rough justice will be done." It was. Pucheu was found guilty and shot, an act, Churchill told Colville, that did de Gaulle and the French "very great harm" in London and "above all in the United States." Still, Churchill insisted that the Leclerc Division, heroes of the Tunisian campaign, be brought from North Africa to Yorkshire in order to train for their as yet undefined role in the Battle of France. Duff Cooper would later write that he admired de Gaulle for his "superb intransigence" and admired Churchill for sticking with de Gaulle despite his own misgivings and despite Franklin Roosevelt, whom Cooper called "the stumbling block" to restoring France to its proper place in the European family.[73]

In late March, de Gaulle took his intransigence to new levels when his French Committee of National Liberation declared itself the provisional government of metropolitan France—all unoccupied French territories worldwide. Macmillan saw the decree as a direct rejoinder by de Gaulle to Roosevelt over the president's refusal to recognize the authority of the FCNL. Henri Giraud opposed the gambit, but Giraud no longer cast a shadow in French politics. His greatest sin, in de Gaulle's eyes, had been his willingness to act as America's protégé. Giraud had been America's man in Algiers; de Gaulle considered himself France's man. "Giraud has been an unconscionable time dying," Macmillan wrote an underling in Algiers, adding, "Let him die." Churchill, counseled by Macmillan and Duff Cooper, accepted the fact that de Gaulle—now sole president of the FCNL—was destined to return to France as that nation's leader. He advised Roosevelt to invite de Gaulle to Washington in order that the Frenchman might bask in symbolic recognition. It would have to be symbolic because the Americans still refused to recognize the FCNL.[74]

Anthony Eden violently disagreed with Roosevelt on the matter of de Gaulle, telling his diary, "President's absurd and petty dislike of de Gaulle blinds him. It would be folly for us to follow him in this." Roosevelt made his disdain for de Gaulle clear in a late April telegram in which he told Churchill, "I do not have any information which leads me to believe that de Gaulle and his Committee of National Liberation have as yet given any helpful assistance to our allied war effort." Still, Roosevelt, urged on by Churchill, agreed to meet de Gaulle in Washington at some point down the road, but only if de Gaulle requested the meeting. "I will not ever have it said," Roosevelt told Churchill, "that I invited him to visit me in Washington."[75]

The men of the two Moroccan-French divisions that had suffered 2,500 killed and wounded on the Gustav Line had just cause to dispute Roosevelt's denigration of French help in the war effort. As did the men of Leclerc's 2nd Armored Division. As did the more than one hundred thousand members of the French resistance armed by the Special Operations Executive. Dozens of independent French resistance groups had taken up dozens of disparate duties. Some printed clandestine newspapers—*La Voix du Nord, Libération (sud), Défense de la France*. Some helped downed Allied flyers escape over the Pyrenees into Spain and Portugal. The resistance was populated by Communists, Gaullists, monarchists, Jews, Catholics, Protestants, republicans, socialists. More than 90,000 were killed during the war, and the Germans, in reprisal for resistance activities, murdered several thousand more Frenchmen—including women and children. In the final weeks before D-day, French railroad workers (*cheminots*) sabotaged their own rail lines; other resistance cells blew up German communications centers and electric power stations. They operated even as Allied bombers intent on disrupting German communication and rail hubs dropped ordnance right on top of them.

Forty thousand Maquis (the Corsican name for the brushwood in which fighters took cover), poorly armed and lacking ammunition, were prepared to do their part. They were young men who had fled to the Massif Central and Savoy Alps to avoid slave labor in Germany. By the spring, German soldiers and Vichy police were battling the Maquis in their mountain redoubts. The Maquis, like the rest of the resistance, waited for more guns, bombs, and ammunition. They listened for the secret phrases inserted into BBC broadcasts that warned them and guided them—"The dice are on the table." ... "It is hot in Suez." ... "The tomatoes should be picked." They especially waited to hear two lines from Paul Verlaine's poem *"Chanson d'automne"* ("Autumn Song"). The first, *"Les sanglots longs des violons de l'automne"* ("The long sobs of the violins of autumn"), was to be broadcast on the first two nights of the invasion month. The second, *"Blessent mon coeur d'une langueur monotone"* ("Pierce my heart with a dull languor"), would signify that the invasion was imminent. The French underground awaited those words, and awaited the return to France of the man all of France considered their leader: Charles de Gaulle.[76]

The Anglo-American alliance had from the beginning lumbered along despite political and military differences of opinion over de Gaulle, the Aegean, India, the timing of Overlord (and now Anvil). With victory assured if not yet in sight, differences in American and British postwar economic goals began to seep into the relationship like sand into a well-oiled gearbox. Late in 1943, five senators, including Republican Henry Cabot Lodge Jr. of Massachusetts and Democrat Russell Long of Georgia, proclaimed that America had become a "global sucker." They called for American aid to be used as a lever—the British saw it as a cudgel—to obtain postwar economic and political advantages. Churchill had had the five in mind when he excoriated "naysayers" in his February speech. By early 1944, Roosevelt was troubled enough by the trade picture (and by congressional pressure) to drop from Lend-Lease all British purchases of discretionary goods that did not directly contribute to the war effort. The cost to Britain to buy these goods stood at about $400 million, or roughly one-third of its $1.5 billion in gold and dollar balances (a balance Roosevelt had kept hidden from the U.S. Congress).

The new policy could only add more debt to the British balance sheet and undercut Britain's ability to compete in world markets after the war, especially against the United States. Treasury Secretary Henry Morgenthau Jr. was then working up the financial and banking parts of that policy in detail. From a strictly financial standpoint, such machinations were journal entries, a way to manage accounts. It was only business. Morgenthau, an abiding friend to Britain during his decade at Treasury, was in fundamental agreement with the demand for Britain to spend down its balances, but he advised taking no action until later in the war to avoid disrupting—possibly obliterating—postwar Anglo-American relations. But the five senators, the press, and the Congress had forced the issue.

There were other issues. Roosevelt asked Churchill—demanded, really—that British and American trade officials sit down in Washington (the meeting to be chaired by Roosevelt) to work out a postwar oil policy. Churchill didn't like that idea at all, and in late February he told Roosevelt that many in Britain saw such a meeting as the first step "to deprive us of our oil assets in the Middle East." Roosevelt replied with a curt rebuff; the talks must proceed, in Washington. "I cannot change my position in this regard." As for British worries over Middle East oil, Roosevelt replied, "I am disturbed by the rumors the British wish to horn in on Saudi Arabian oil reserves." In late February Roosevelt sent two telegrams to London in which the president cited the "manifest need" for all of the United Nations to address the issues of postwar trade and monetary policy, oil, tariffs, commodities, and cartels. Believing the telegrams had been ghostwritten by Roosevelt underlings (as usual, he could not bring himself to denigrate his "friend") and signed by the exhausted president, Churchill sent a memo to Eden and advised they simply ignore the communications: "All this frantic dancing to the American tune is silly.... My recommendation is to let it all rip for a bit."[77]

Britain exported virtually nothing to offset Lend-Lease imports; the ratio in dollar imports and pound exports was near one hundred to one. That would appear to set up an economic disaster in the making, yet the eminent British historian Peter Clarke points out in *The Last Thousand Days of the British Empire* that Britain's problems were more financial than economic. Clarke pegs the spring of 1944 as the start of those one thousand days. The country was running at full employment, with factories humming along on three shifts, but they were producing weapons and munitions, not exportable goods. The question, addressed later in 1944 by 1,200 international bankers at the Bretton Woods Conference in New Hampshire, was how could Britain trade its way out of the financial hole it would find itself in at war's end? The short answer was: on terms set by America. After Bretton Woods, the U.S. dollar served as the world's reserve currency; artificial exchange rates were banished; nations paid their debts at the new—and ultimately burdensome to Britain—rates of exchange. The World Bank was created on the principle that nations could not draw down from their "paper" account surpluses without first making real deposits, at exchange rates set by the markets, with the result that by the end of the war, the British pound—and Britain—was relegated to secondary status. Churchill did not deem Bretton Woods worthy of mention in his memoirs of the war.[78]

Roosevelt convened his preliminary oil summit in the spring, at which time the British had no choice but to abandon their policy of restricting production at their Middle East concessions in order to maintain profit margins. Yet, concluded *Time,* the "big problem" with oil "in the postwar world will not be scarcity but surplus [and price collapse]."[79]

In early March, Churchill received a short letter from Roosevelt that contained an extraordinary proposal in the form of a memorandum on the future of Iran prepared for the president by Major General Patrick Hurley, an Oklahoma oilman, former secretary of war under Herbert Hoover, and now Roosevelt's man in Tehran. In his note, Roosevelt offered that it would take "thirty or forty years to eliminate the graft" in Iran and to properly prepare the people for democracy. In the interim, the country would "need trustees"; Roosevelt nominated America, Russia, and Britain for that role. The trustees' mandate would be the "care and education" of Iranians. For comic relief he tossed in, "From your and my personal observation I think we could add something about cleanliness as well." One line offered a direct challenge to Churchill and the British Empire: "I do not want the United States to acquire a 'zone of influence'—or any other nation for that matter."[80]

Hurley's report had to do with Iran, but his vision went far beyond the Middle East. "This plan," he wrote, "may become the criterion for the relations of the United States toward all the nations which are now suffering from the evils of greedy minorities, monopolies, aggression, and imperialism." Although Hurley included Germany in his pantheon of evil imperialists, Great Britain was his real target. France, Holland, and Belgium would no doubt emerge from the war too hobbled to maintain their empires. Italy had already lost hers. Germany would lose all. That left Britain, which to be maintained (by America) as a power in the new order "must accept the principles of liberty and democracy and discard the principles of oppressive imperialism." Hurley did not mince a word: "I must say that if imperialism is dead, it seems very reluctant to lie down." He expressed his belief that "the ultimate destiny of the English speaking peoples is a single destiny," yet "British imperialism is being defended today by the blood of the soldiers of the most democratic nation on earth." That relationship had to change. America was "approaching the irrepressible conflict between world-wide imperialism and world-wide democracy" and had to assert its values, specifically the Four Freedoms. Hurley called his policy "nation building." Roosevelt did not inform Churchill that Hurley held a stake in the Sinclair Oil Company, which was then in negotiations with Iran for oil concessions.[81]

Roosevelt sent Hurley's proposal to the State Department for comment. Dean Acheson, then an assistant secretary of state, thought Hurley "vain and reckless," and characterized his plan as "messianic globaloney." Upon hearing that, Hurley charged Acheson with being "for monopoly and imperialism and against democracy." Roosevelt, by pitting his minions against each other, avoided direct involvement in the entire unseemly affair. Although Hurley left government work in 1945 and Acheson later rose to secretary of state, the philosophical underpinnings of Hurley's "nation building" intrigued many in Washington, then and since. Likewise, the question of whether Roosevelt's economic agenda was simply imperialism of a different stripe has been pondered ever since. Churchill's war was indeed imperial, in the sense he fought to *preserve* the British Empire by deploying—with the advice and consent of the Dominions—its imperial troops worldwide. He sought no financial gain; Roosevelt did. Churchill sought no territorial gain; Stalin did.[82]

Much was in need of discussion. Churchill proposed meeting Roosevelt in Bermuda at the end of March. Roosevelt, having never fully recovered from Tehran and in increasingly ill health, declined. The president, in fact, spent the entire month of April fishing and reading and relaxing at financier Bernard Baruch's 23,000-acre South Carolina plantation, during which time no one outside of his cabinet knew his whereabouts.[83]

Churchill did not reply to Roosevelt's "nation building" letter for almost three months. When he did, he told Roosevelt that Hurley's pronouncements "make me rub my eyes." He added, "I make bold, however, to suggest that British imperialism has spread and is spreading democracy more widely than any other system of government since the beginning of time." Churchill thought in terms of postwar nation *rebuilding,* but Roosevelt had in mind something else entirely.[84]

The question of Polish borders above all other political issues commanded Churchill's attention. The Poles were proving themselves as stubborn as Stalin. Colville feared that the effort to persuade the Poles to cede territory would be compared to the betrayal of the Czechs at Munich. Owen O'Malley in the Foreign Office believed so, and he repeated to Colville a line from his report on the Katyn murders: "What is morally indefensible is always politically inept." The Poles, for their part, refused to entertain any notion of ceding territory, this despite pledges by Stalin that Poland would remain free and independent. Then Stalin announced he could no longer communicate with Churchill on the matter because their correspondence was regularly leaked to the press by the British. In fact, the Soviet embassy was the source of the leaks. Stalin further mucked up the works when he permitted *Pravda* to run a story that claimed the British were in secret peace negotiations with Berlin, a charge that prompted Churchill to proclaim to Brooke, "Trying to maintain good relations with a communist is like wooing a crocodile.... When it opens its mouth you cannot tell whether it is trying to smile, or preparing to eat you up." By mid-March, Churchill concluded that his efforts to forge a Polish-Soviet agreement had failed and that he soon would have to "make a cold announcement to Parliament" on the matter. "It all seems to augur ill," Colville told his diary on March 18, "for the future of relations between this country and the U.S.S.R."

The Old Man began telling friends that he would not be around to witness those relations, because he had not long to live. One evening in March he informed the gathered—while "*La Marseillaise*" played on the gramophone—that although he had not much time left, he had a political testament for after the war: "Far more important than India or the Colonies or solvency is *the Air.* We live in a world of wolves—and *bears*" (italics Colville). Three nights later the Old Man lamented to Colville that "this world ('this dusty and lamentable ball') is now too beastly to live in. People act so revoltingly they just don't deserve to live." Yet, as always, he remained cautiously optimistic. On April 1 he wrote to Roosevelt of Stalin's belligerency, "I have a feeling the bark may be worse than its bite."[85]

By then, more than two months after the first assaults on the Gustav

Line and the Anzio landings, no progress whatsoever had been made at either place. The New Zealanders again tried to storm Monte Cassino on March 15, with the same bloody results as in February. On the twenty-fifth they called it off. Clark's army had gained but a few miles in two months. The troops under siege at Anzio had gained nothing.[86]

Events on the Home Island vexed Churchill as well. Three by-elections did not go well for the coalition government and especially for the Tories. In the first one, in January, a hitherto unknown Common Wealth Party (a Socialist party formed in 1942) candidate beat both the Tory and Labour candidates. This was a rebuke to the coalition and foreshadowed events to come. The Tories barely won the second election, held in a traditional Conservative constituency. This was a rebuke to Churchill, who had taken a strong stand against the Independent candidate. The third election proved even more of a disaster. For all but five of the previous 210 years, a member of the Cavendish family, one of England's wealthiest, had represented West Derbyshire. When an Independent challenged the sitting Cavendish MP, twenty-six-year-old William John Robert Cavendish, Marquess of Hartington, Churchill weighed in, calling the election a mandate on the government and telling electors "their votes can prove the heroic temper of our island in these tremendous days." Voters gave Cavendish the boot.[87]

The elections, like the Polish affair, did nothing for Churchill's peace of mind. Colville found him in the Annexe one night, "sitting in his chair," looking "old, tired, and very depressed." He was muttering that any more such defeats might force a general election. "Now," Churchill said, "with great events pending, when national unity was essential: the question of annihilating great states had to be faced." Yet, he added, it was beginning "to look as if democracy had not the persistence to go through with it."[88]

Even his beloved Parliament briefly rebuked him, or so he believed when in late March an amendment was inserted into a groundbreaking education-reform bill, which passed the House by one vote. The amendment, sponsored by Thelma Cazalet, a former suffragette and the Conservative MP from Islington East, called for equal pay for women teachers. The problem, as Churchill saw it, was not with giving women equal pay (this would come to pass in his next premiership) but that the government bill had not included any such clause. The vote, therefore, amounted to a vote of no confidence. Churchill—who championed the reforms—demanded that the offending clause be removed and that the House pass the original government bill in a vote of confidence. Harold Nicolson blamed the episode on "the idiocy of the House" and hoped that Churchill might back down. He did not, telling one MP, "I am not going to tumble around my cage like a wounded canary. You knocked me off my perch. You have now got to put me back on my perch. Otherwise I won't sing."

Cazalet withdrew her amendment. The House put Churchill back on his perch by a vote of 425–23. Roosevelt, who had just had his veto of a tax bill (which he said served the greedy, not the needy) overridden by Congress, thought Churchill's battle with the Commons "splendid," and cabled his congratulations, adding, "Results here would be almost as good if we operated under your system." Colville thought Churchill's forcing the issue was like "cracking a nut with a sledgehammer."[89]

That the House and prime minister had drifted into conflict was due in part to the fact that Anthony Eden was both Leader of the House and foreign secretary. No man could possibly do both jobs, and by late March, Eden was doing neither very well. Eden feared himself on the verge of a breakdown. He broached the subject of quitting the Foreign Office to Churchill, who rejected the notion: "You will have to go on as you are for a few months longer." Then, in early April, with Eden clearly an ill man, Churchill offered some words of sympathy—"You are my right arm; we must take care of you"—and packed Eden off for three weeks of rest. In Eden's absence Churchill took over the Foreign Office.[90]

Thus, in the run-up to the great gambit in Normandy, Churchill served as prime minister, defence minister, and foreign minister. In his multiple roles, he chaired cabinet meetings, and War Cabinet meetings, and Chiefs of Staff meetings, and took his weekly lunches with the King and Eisenhower. Alec Cadogan, at the Foreign Office, now serving temporarily under Churchill, began to pepper his diary entries with many of the same impressions Brooke and Colville confessed to their journals. On April 12, Colville told his diary: "Struck by how very tired and worn out the P.M. looks now." The same day, Cadogan wrote: "[P.M.] kept me from my work for three hours today on matters that shouldn't have taken twenty minutes. How does he get through his work?" Cadogan on April 19, after a late afternoon cabinet meeting: "An awful day.... P.M., I fear, is breaking down.... I am fussed about the P.M. He is *not* the man he was 12 months ago, and I really don't know if he can carry on." Brooke, the same day, after a Chiefs of Staff meeting that ran to 1:30 A.M.: "P.M. tired, listless, and lacking decision."[91]

The Old Man was tired—from setting a pace others had difficulty keeping up with. He promised Colville he would make his bedtime 1:30, but he regularly stayed up past three o'clock. He had a bed installed in his room adjacent to the House so that he could take short naps between sessions. He carried the greatest burden, and he not once considered laying it down. While Cadogan took himself home to dine at 8:00 P.M. after the "awful" cabinet meeting of the nineteenth, Churchill prepared for the Chiefs of Staff meeting that Brooke found so unproductive. Eden was, of course, on sick leave. "Everyone's exhausted," Alec Cadogan told his diary, "but I suppose we've got to plug along." Even the young, strapping Jock Colville allowed a quotient of pessimism to penetrate his natural optimism. Everyone is "gloomy," he wrote on April 14. "Now in the shadow of an impending struggle which may be history's most fatal, a restless and dissatisfied mood possesses many people in all circles and walks of life. And over everything hangs the uncertainty of Russia's future policy towards Europe and the world."[92]

"Public opinion at the moment is not good," Harold Nicolson told his diary. "They are exhausted by five years of war." Factory workers were sending HMG a message by voting with their feet throughout the land. More than two hundred thousand coal miners had gone out on strike in Wales and Yorkshire. Textile workers went out in Scotland. More than four times as many working days were lost to strikes that year as in 1940. Britons had not gone to the polls in a general election since 1935. They were impatient and exhausted. Brendan Bracken, foreseeing more unrest over the horizon, predicted to Jock Colville (much as Roosevelt had predicted to Harriman in 1941) "a crushing defeat for the Conservative Party at the next election and its possible collapse like the Liberals after the last war." Nicolson, upon stepping into the lavatory at the Blackheath Railway Station, beheld a scrawl on the wall: "Winston Churchill is a bastard." Nicolson, furious at the insult, feared that "Winston has become an electoral liability now rather than an asset. This makes me sick with human nature. Once the open sea is reached, we forget how we clung to the pilot in the storm."[93]

The pilot, as usual, was scrutinizing the seas all around, near and far, with the result that he failed to set a steady course. He became mired in details and his dispatch boxes backed up. He had learned that the Americans were no longer painting their aircraft, which lessened their weight and added twenty miles an hour to their speed; "Pray let me know," he asked the Aircraft Ministry, if the RAF was considering doing likewise. When he noticed an "untidy sack with holes in it and sand leaking out" in St. James's Park, he demanded it be removed. The park had been closed to civilians, and other than military men on their way to secret meetings and a scaup duck that Brooke liked to observe, St. James's Park was empty and neglected. Other details had political overtones. Churchill objected to a proposal by the Home Secretary to hold a national day of prayer for the success of Overlord. Such an event would be a "grave mistake," Churchill wrote. "In my view there is no need for a national day of prayer or thanksgiving at this time." Mollie Panter-Downes noted that Montgomery was making a show of touring the land inviting "God to scatter the Allies' enemies and the public to scatter its cash in war bonds." Churchill took note of and shut down Montgomery's public relations and prayer tour. The prayers being said by Britons that spring were not only for the safety of their sons, but for rain; a severe drought was killing winter crops and did not bode well for the summer harvest. Rural wells ran dry, forcing villagers into long lines to procure buckets of water. Panter-Downes wrote that with millions of troops moving about the country, England was in the position of the hostess of a modest house whose "influx of guests has run the cistern dry."[94]

Churchill's relations with his military chiefs were as arid as the countryside. On the heels of Operation Caliph, his plan to support Overlord by sending three divisions into Bordeaux, came proposals to liberate Norway, and to drive into the Aegean "in the event of Overlord not being successful" or German troops there being "beyond our power to tackle." He saw these ventures as "flanking movements." But the time for flanking movements had passed. He and Britain were committed to Overlord. Yet Churchill was not trying to evade that commitment; he was performing due diligence in the event that the Germans sent enough panzers to France to trigger a cancellation of the invasion, as agreed upon in Tehran. Eisenhower pondered the same question. His son and biographer later wrote that Eisenhower was in constant contact with Marshall during February and early March regarding the problem of what to do "should German moves in the next several weeks rule out Overlord as impractical." As Eisenhower saw it, Anvil, the south of France operation, presented the only possible alternative. Churchill and Eisenhower understood that perfect certainty about Overlord could never be achieved, and that "an irrevocable commitment to Overlord was not possible until the troops were ashore in France." And they could not go ashore until the Combined Chiefs of Staff delegated to Eisenhower the absolute authority to do whatever needed to be done in order to not only carry out Overlord but also sustain it. This they did in February when they formally designated him supreme allied commander, giving him authority over all Allied land, sea, and air forces. Churchill could probe and prod Eisenhower, but he could make no demands.[95]

This did not apply to Churchill's British chiefs, from whom he demanded much. Brooke's diary references to Churchill grew more furious. After one particularly difficult February meeting (and most were now difficult), Brooke wrote, "I often doubt whether I am going mad or he is really sane." After another he wrote, "I can not stick any more meetings like this." During a March meeting, Churchill claimed to have discovered a new island off the coast of Sumatra, and proposed sending a fleet there. Admiral Cunningham replied that with the Japanese fleet in Singapore, such a move would be "courting disaster." Of the meeting Brooke wrote, "I began to wonder whether I was in Alice in Wonderland, or whether I was really fit for a lunatic asylum." And of Churchill: "I... am honestly getting very doubtful about his balance of mind.... I don't know where we are or where we are going as regards our strategy.... It is a ghastly situation." And on March 23, "I feel like a man chained to the chariot of a lunatic!!" To Dill, in Washington, Brooke wrote: "I am just about at the end of my tether." Brooke was not alone in fighting ongoing battles with Churchill. Admiral Sir Andrew Cunningham's autobiography, *A Sailor's Odyssey,* conveys the same frustration. Air Chief Marshal Portal also expressed his doubts about Churchill, who, Portal felt, did not appreciate the proper role of airpower. Yet Portal grossly overrated the effectiveness of strategic bombing. He shocked Brooke that spring when he claimed that he could have won the war by early 1944 if not for "the handicap of the other two services!!" Brooke usually reserved his double exclamation marks for prime-ministerial quotations.[96]

Brooke's diary entries, when cherry-picked, portray a meddlesome and infuriating prime minister, the strangler fig in Brooke's neatly tilled garden of military strategy. Yet Brooke's diaries—and those of the other journal keepers—are informative only when taken as a whole. After a particularly disputatious afternoon meeting, Brooke was summoned to dinner by Churchill. The CIGS expected to be sacked. "On the contrary," he wrote, "we had a *tête-à-tête* dinner at which he [Churchill] was quite charming, as if he meant to make up for some of the rough passages of the day." They discussed their children and Churchill's difficulty in controlling Randolph. They discussed "the President's unpleasant attitude lately." They mused on Italy, and the latest German air raids. Concerned for Brooke's health, Churchill told him to take some time off so as not to wear himself out. Later that night, after a post-dinner meeting of the Chiefs of Staff where Brooke found Churchill to be "much more reasonable," the CIGS told his diary, "He has astonishing sides to his character." Equally astonishing is that it had taken Brooke almost three years of working side by side with Churchill to reach that conclusion. When thirteen years later Brooke—by then Lord Alanbrooke—sent a personally inscribed copy of his published (and abridged) diaries to Churchill, he wrote that his criticisms were his way of unwinding each night, mere "momentary daily impressions." He added, "I look upon the privilege of having served you in war as the greatest honour destiny has bestowed on me."[97]

Despite the tumultuousness of the staff meetings, to say nothing of the tumultuous goings-on in Churchill's mind, the chiefs and Churchill complemented each other. Churchill brought illumination, which his chiefs brought into focus. Churchill never seriously considered sacking any of them, and none of them ever seriously considered resigning. In his capacity as minister of defence he never overrode their policies. Anthony Eden wrote that attending a meeting with Churchill was "a splendid and unique experience. It might be a monologue. It was never a dictatorship." Colville noted the criticisms leveled at Churchill by the Chiefs of Staff, who, in Colville's opinion, lacked Churchill's "imagination and resolution" and could not see that it was Churchill who provided them "guidance and purpose." The chiefs and Churchill worked together in harness, the black steed of Churchill's passion and the white steeds of the coolly logical Brooke, Cunningham, and Portal.[98]

Clementine Churchill later said of Brooke, "We might have won the war without Alanbrooke; I don't think we would have won it without Winston."[99]

The diarists noted Churchill being in "top form" as regularly as they noted his fatigue or inattention to his boxes or tendency to ramble on. A narrow sampling of "P.M. tired" diary entries yields as incomplete and distorted an image of Churchill as a narrow sampling of "P.M. in top form" entries. He had to be taken whole in order to form an accurate image of the man. Not for nothing did John Martin later say that Churchill had about him "a zigzag streak of lightning on the brain."[100]

When he addressed his countrymen on March 26 the lightning was missing. The subject was the postwar world. He promised Britons that national health insurance would follow victory, along with a complete overhaul of housing, including "a clean sweep of all those areas of which our civilization should be ashamed." The slums would go, but nothing would be done that would interfere with the war effort. Change would come, but only after victory. He proclaimed that "the greatest scheme of improved education that has ever been attempted by a responsible Government... will soon be on the Statute-book." Britons were not impressed. "They feel like they have asked for bread," Mollie Panter-Downes wrote, "but have been given, if not a stone, simply a promise of thousands upon thousands of prefabricated houses, at modest rent." Steel shares rose immediately on the promise of the prefabricated future, "but peoples' spirits noticeably did not." Harold Nicolson was pained by the comments of colleagues who thought Churchill had sounded like "a worn and petulant old man.... The upper classes feel that all this sacrifice and suffering will only mean that the proletariat will deprive them of all their comforts and influence, and then proceed to render this country and Empire a third class state."[101]

On his way to bed in the early hours of April 5, Churchill allowed to Colville that although the prospect of the second front worried him, "I am hardening to it." By "hardening" he meant that his support for Overlord was growing. He had used the same term a month earlier in a cable to Marshall, which he referenced in a March 18 telegram to Roosevelt, where he repeated, "I am hardening for Overlord as the time gets nearer." On April 1, he again cabled Roosevelt, "As you know, I harden for it the nearer I get to it. Eisenhower is a very large man." On April 7, Good Friday, Montgomery unveiled to the Chiefs of Staff and Churchill the final plans for Overlord. Brooke was duly impressed, calling it "a wonderful day." According to Brooke, Churchill—"in a very weepy condition" and lacking "vitality"—addressed barely a few remarks to the assembled.[102]

In fact, Montgomery's presentation had lessened Churchill's anxiety over the invasion, for since the first meetings of January, Montgomery had put meat on the bones of Overlord. Six divisions would now go ashore in the first wave, supported on the flanks by three airborne divisions. By D-day plus two days, a further six divisions would be ashore. Montgomery laid out the particulars. Four natural phenomena had to fall into alignment like plums in a slot machine for the invasion to have any chance for success. Three could be predetermined: the tides, the phase of the moon, and the length of time between morning nautical twilight—dawn—and sunrise. The tides had to be near ebb but rising, such that combat engineers could clear exposed German mines and obstacles from the beaches. Then, three hours of rising tides would serve to carry the men farther up onto the beaches. The moon had to be a bomber's moon—full or near full, in order that the paratroopers could operate in the lunar beam. Finally, the optimum length of time between dawn and sunrise had been calculated to be about sixty minutes, enough time for the navy and air forces to rake the beaches with shell fire but not so long as to allow the Germans to recover and coordinate their defense and counterattack. Three mornings in June fell into nearly perfect alignment on all three counts, the fifth, sixth, and seventh. Montgomery picked June 5 as the most favorable. The fourth natural element was entirely unpredictable: the weather. Ideally, Eisenhower told his press aide, the morning of D-day should be clear, with a light offshore breeze blowing the dust and smoke of battle inland, to confuse and blind the Germans.[103]

A few days after the April 7 meeting, Churchill telegraphed Roosevelt with a brief summary. Again he stressed his support for the enterprise. "I am becoming very hard set on Overlord." He told Roosevelt that he had expressed to Eisenhower and Montgomery his "strong confidence...in this extraordinary but magnificent operation." And he expressed his disagreement with "loose talk" on both sides of the Atlantic that predicted horrific Allied casualties. It would be the Germans who suffered, he told Roosevelt. To Eisenhower, Churchill offered that if by the coming winter, the Allies had taken the Channel ports, Cherbourg, and Paris, he would "assert the victory to be the greatest of modern times." Eisenhower replied that the Overlord timetable called for Allied armies to be on the German borders by winter. Churchill late in the month told Colville that on D-day he intended to be onboard a Royal Navy warship just offshore the beaches, and to be "one of the first on the bridgehead, if he possibly could—and what fun to get there before Monty."[104]

On the day after Montgomery's briefing, the debate over Anvil assumed new and troublesome dimensions. Ten days earlier, George Marshall proposed a halt in Italian operations once the Anzio beachhead was united with Alexander's army, in order that ten divisions could be siphoned away from Italy in support of Anvil, which Marshall insisted must follow Overlord by July 10. The Americans' rigidity on Anvil led Brooke to exclaim to his diary that it was "impossible to accept" Marshall's plan to "go on the defensive in Italy. They fail to realize the forces available do not admit to two fronts in the Mediterranean." Eisenhower told his naval aide, Commander Butcher, that he was "delighted" by Marshall's decision "to forget Rome."[105]

Eisenhower and the British Chiefs of Staff debated the matter, Eisenhower arguing that the German army, not a psychological prize such as Rome, should be the target. Brooke and the British counterargued that Rome was a military target and had to be taken in order for the Allies to continue northward into France or toward Trieste. By April 8, the Anvil question had become an unholy mess. Brooke, seeing Anvil's negative consequences to the Italian campaign, joined Churchill in trying to introduce some flexibility into the debate. Roosevelt and Marshall, for their part, remained inflexible; they had promised Anvil to Stalin at Tehran, and that was that. Ironically, it was the continuing stalemate on the Italian front that had brought the wisdom of Anvil into question. "There was no use in landing in France," Churchill later wrote, "unless we did so at the right time.... All turned on the capture of Rome." Churchill fired off a telegram to Marshall protesting the abandonment of Rome, and was coolly rebuffed. Jumbo Wilson advised scrubbing Anvil altogether because there were simply not enough landing craft in the Mediterranean to undertake the operation. The Americans offered to bring landing craft from the Pacific to the Mediterranean, but only for use in Anvil, thus thwarting any British plans for amphibious operations in the Aegean. Then they withdrew the offer.[106]

Admiral King once again, as he had in 1942, began grumbling about the need to shift the war effort to the Pacific. Eisenhower played that card by reminding Brooke that U.S. Republicans wanted to draft Douglas MacArthur for a presidential run. MacArthur, in correspondence with Nebraska congressman Albert Miller, had disparaged the New Deal and offered that he believed the European war was just about over. The letters, which Miller leaked to the press, gave Britons pause. The implication of Eisenhower's gambit was that as president, MacArthur would shift everything to the Pacific. But Brooke held firm: Italy must be reinforced, and certainly not stripped. Marshall saw Italy as a stalemate and a diversion from striking into Germany through France. Churchill saw Italy as a substitute for Anvil. Eisenhower, whose first and most critical duty was to make Overlord a success, was caught between his American superiors and the British. Finally, on April 19, after General Alexander announced his plan to begin his Italian offensive in mid-May with a hoped-for junction with the Anzio forces by early June, the Americans conceded that Anvil could not take place in July. Eisenhower and Brooke hammered out an "appreciation" for the Combined Chiefs that did not mention Anvil and called for Rome to be Alexander's springtime objective. The Anvil debate, full of twists and turns, lay dormant until mid-June, when it metastasized into crisis.[107]

In the east, Hitler had staked his hopes on the Wehrmacht's resolve and the inability of the Red Army to fight on during a terrible winter, but the Red Army had ignored the winter. In February the Russians encircled 50,000 Germans on the lower Dnieper front. In March, the Red Army swept past Odessa, crossed the Dneister River on a three-hundred-mile front, and closed on Czernowitz, in Bukovina. The Russians bypassed the Crimea, leaving a German army trapped there. The Russian winter offensive had been so powerful that many in London and Washington believed the war would be over before summer. But even the Russians could not ignore the spring rain and mud season—the *rasputitsa*. In April the battle lines began to stabilize from the Baltic to the southern Ukraine.

The stabilization of the Eastern Front, John Eisenhower later wrote, "dashed lingering hopes on both sides of the Atlantic that Germany would be defeated before summer." This is a vital observation, and it relates to several other unsettling lines of thought that percolated through the ranks and led to "a climate of doubt that persisted at all levels." Most obvious, Eisenhower writes, was the realization that if the war did not end before summer, Overlord would have to take place. That truth, in turn, led to doubts over the ability of green American recruits to stand up to the Wehrmacht; the debacle at Kasserine had taken place only a year earlier, and at Anzio—"part of the Kasserine legacy"—the men were still on the beaches. Those doubts commingled with growing doubts about Soviet intentions. Would the Red Army attack as agreed upon or stand by while the Anglo-Americans and Germans punched themselves out in the west? This was a fear Brooke had expressed to his diary at Tehran. On April 8, Eisenhower cabled the Normandy invasion date to Moscow. The Kremlin did not respond for two weeks, during which time the doubts only grew.[108]

The question of unconditional surrender weighed on everyone. Eisenhower sought permission from Roosevelt to "clarify" the terms of surrender in order that he could drop propaganda leaflets over Germany assuring Germans that fundamental rights—religion, assembly, trade unions—would be restored. From Eisenhower's soldierly perspective, Germans willing to surrender were far more desirable than an entire nation fighting to the last man standing. Roosevelt flatly refused, telling his Chiefs of Staff, "I am not willing at this time to say that we do not intend to destroy the German nation." Any "clarification" of surrender terms would be read by Moscow as backtracking on the annihilation of Germany agreed upon in Tehran. Stalin was quite willing to expend millions of Russian lives to gain that end. Churchill, like Eisenhower, saw in unconditional surrender the potential for horrific loss in Allied lives, but he thought better of bringing the subject up with Roosevelt. Churchill's frustration over his diminished role in all matters political and military was evidenced by a remark he made in mid-April to Cadogan: "This battle [Overlord] has been forced upon us by the Russians and by the United States military authorities." That was true, as was the fact that he had "hardened" to the plan.[109]

During April, as the invasion forces conducted field exercises on English beaches and in the countryside, the Allied air forces fully implemented Eisenhower's pre-invasion air strategy known as the Transportation Plan, the object of which was to bomb every French rail hub, bridge, and tunnel that led to Normandy in order to isolate German forces and deny them mobility. Almost one hundred individual targets were marked for destruction, as well as dozens in Calais, to put the Germans off the scent. More than 120 German radar sites were added to the list. Eisenhower later wrote that Churchill feared that up to 80,000 Frenchmen would die in the bombings. Churchill was indeed worried, and told Roosevelt in an April telegram that he and the entire War Cabinet feared the "French slaughters" would result in 80,000 casualties, including 20,000 dead, an estimate that ultimately proved correct. It would be another Oran, a slaughter of Allies by friendly fire, Churchill argued, on a far bloodier scale. It was a strategy that would make enemies of the French. Churchill's fear of French resentment did not in the end prove justified.

The French themselves were divided on the issue, with several resistance leaders telling HMG that the bombings would be resented in France, while

Major General Pierre Koenig, commander of French forces in Britain, told Eisenhower that the French people would accept twice the casualties if the sacrifice helped rid France of the reviled Boche. The War Cabinet asked Eisenhower to restrict targets to those that would yield no more than one hundred French casualties. Eisenhower refused, on the grounds that such restraint would "emasculate" the strategy. He assured Churchill that thousands of warning leaflets were dropped into the French countryside before the bombers came on. Not satisfied, Churchill went over Eisenhower's head, to Roosevelt, and asked the president to overrule his general. Roosevelt flatly refused, telling Churchill, "However regrettable" the loss of French lives, "I am not prepared to impose from this great distance any restrictions on military action by the responsible commanders that in their opinion might mitigate against the success of Overlord or cause more Allied casualties." The president's reply hinted at a fundamental change in their relationship. Although Churchill was the man on the spot, in London and at the center of the planning and the action, his advice no longer carried the weight with Roosevelt that it once had. Roosevelt henceforth and from his great distance would be the final arbitrator in all such matters.[110]

A German radio transmission intercepted in May vindicated Eisenhower's air strategy: "The raids carried out in recent weeks have caused systematic breakdown of all main line; the coastal defences have been cut off from the supply bases of the interior."[111]

May came in, and brought with it the most beautiful weather in years. Alec Cadogan, spending a few days at his Northiam cottage, effused to his diary, "The daffodils are over, except the very late white ones. And the narcissi are still out, and the spiraea arguta, like little snowmen. And the wallflowers a warm cloth of gold and bronze. The old pear tree in full bloom.... Lilac coming out.... Another gorgeous summer day." It was all "heavenly." He also noted the need for rain. Churchill, however, ushered in the new month with "gloomy forebodings" about the future behavior of Russia. "I have always not liked the month of May," he offered to Jock Colville, who recalled that one of the first remarks Churchill had made to him four years earlier was, "If I were the first of May, I should be ashamed of myself." But May 1944 began to prove itself praiseworthy.[112]

On May 11, Alexander made his move against the Gustav Line. In light of Anvil's being postponed, it was hoped that this thrust would draw Germans away from Normandy. It did; twenty-five German divisions were now in Italy, and more had been sent to the Balkans in anticipation of an

Allied thrust north toward Vienna. On May 15, after four days of preparatory strikes, a Canadian corps was thrown into the battle for Monte Cassino. On the seventeenth, two Polish divisions led the final assault on the monastery. Along the Gustav Line twenty Allied divisions faced seven divisions of the German Tenth Army. The preponderance of Allied men, artillery, and aircraft began to bend the German lines. Kesselring ordered that reinforcements be rushed south from Anzio to defend his line.

It was too late. The end for the Germans at Monte Cassino came on May 18 when, after a point-blank artillery barrage and an assault by the Polish II Corps, the heights were taken. On that beautiful spring morning, Polish troops—less four thousand killed and wounded—entered the ruins of the monastery. The Germans had fled overnight. The Allied army pursuing them was one of the most cosmopolitan in history. In the Imperial Army: Britons, Canadians, New Zealanders, South Africans, Newfoundlanders, Indians, Ceylonese, Swazi, Mauritians, and Caribbeans. In the American: a black division and a Japanese American regiment. Among the Allies: Italians, French, Poles, Moroccans, Algerians, Tunisians, and Senegalese. By May 18, more than 32,000 men—including Germans—lay dead and buried within sight of St. Benedict's mountain sanctuary. But Highway 6, the road to Rome, was open. With Kesselring's withdrawal of troops from Anzio, the time was ripe for an Allied breakout there, which if successful would cut off the German Tenth Army, now fleeing north from the Gustav Line. On May 23, the Allies finally broke out from the beachhead, where they had lived under fire for four months. Three days later they linked up with Clark's Fifth Army. Then they turned toward Rome.[113]

As the Italian campaign came to life, a meeting was held in London that would have far more repercussions in coming years than the bloody battle for Monte Cassino. The previous November the London press had reported that the Nobel Prize–winning Danish physicist Niels Bohr had escaped to London from German-occupied Denmark by way of Stockholm. In fact, the RAF secreted him out in the cramped bomb bay of the aptly named Mosquito bomber, where he passed out for lack of oxygen. In London the scientist spoke with various luminaries, including Alec Cadogan, who gushed to his diary: "Bohr. What a man! He talked...for ¾ hour, about what I haven't the least idea." Soon thereafter Bohr disappeared. In fact, he had been taken to the United States, to Los Alamos, as an official British consultant to the Tube Alloys project; that is, he was working on the Manhattan Project. He brought with him German drawings for the design of a uranium heavy-water pile, which if built, would behave more like a reactor than a bomb, with resultant explosive forces not much more powerful than conventional bombs.[114]

This should have told the Americans that the Germans were heading in the wrong direction if building an atomic bomb was their goal. But General Leslie Groves, head of the Manhattan Project, believing that the drawings had been allowed to fall into Bohr's hands in order to put the Allies off the scent, dismissed that intelligence. Bohr also believed that the results obtained at Los Alamos might prove to be either the biggest disaster to befall mankind—if the bomb was built and deployed down the road by nations now left out of the program—or the biggest boon, if it made war unthinkable. This was a new and unique way of looking at things, a concept Roosevelt and Churchill had not yet considered. An atomic bomb, for Churchill, was simply a bomb bigger than all others, a weapon to be used in pursuit of strategic objectives. That was the purpose of weapons, after all. Bohr saw more transcendent implications.[115]

Such was Bohr's renown that he was invited to meet with Franklin Roosevelt, to whom Bohr advised a policy of sharing atomic research with the Russians in order to maintain the trust between the Allies that had been nurtured for almost three years. The alternative—keeping the Russians out of the picture—would lead, Bohr believed, to a breakdown of trust, possibly of the alliance, and would have potentially disastrous postwar consequences, the most likely being a nuclear arms race, with the Russians making their own bomb sooner or later. Here was the scientist grasping immense political implications while so far the politicians grasped only the immediate military implications. Roosevelt sent Bohr back to London in March after telling him that any such proposal to expand the nuclear family would have to be approved by Churchill per the Quebec agreement of the previous year. This Bohr attempted to do. Sir John Anderson sent Churchill a memo that outlined Bohr's thoughts and proposed a meeting be arranged. On it, Churchill scribbled, "collaborate" and "on no account." Weeks went by. On May 16, after R. V. Jones impressed upon Lord Cherwell, Churchill's science adviser, the importance of the meeting, Bohr was finally summoned to No. 10. Cherwell accompanied him.[116]

The meeting did not go well. Bohr, who often told R. V. Jones that clarity and accuracy of statement are mutually exclusive, elected to err on the side of accuracy, thus delivering such a long and complex monologue that Churchill thought him "a muddled thinker" who wanted to give away British secrets to the Russians. "Indeed," R. V. Jones later wrote, "Churchill did wonder if he was a Russian agent." Churchill reiterated his belief that the atomic bomb was simply a bigger bomb than all others and that he and his friend Franklin Roosevelt had everything under control. Then he dismissed Bohr. R. V. Jones bumped into Bohr after the meeting and asked how it went. "It was terrible!" replied the great scientist. "He scolded us like two schoolboys!"[117]

That week, Cherwell briefed the Chiefs of Staff on N spores—anthrax and bacteriological weapons. This was not the mustard gas of the Great War but something far more deadly. Churchill informed Ismay: "As you know, great progress had been made in bacteriological warfare and we have ordered a half million bombs from America for use should this mode of warfare be employed against us." Cherwell explained in detail the effectiveness of the bacterial agents; victims died suddenly and peacefully a week after exposure. Just six bombers could drop enough "gas" to kill everyone within a square mile. Churchill intended his threat as a "deterrent" lest Hitler gas the troops on the Normandy beaches. The invasion forces would carry no gas masks. Were they gassed, Churchill intended to unleash every poison he had on the population of Germany. He had on many occasions since May 1940 pledged to his nation, to his family, and to the world that Britain would never be the first to use poison gas, but now, with the liberation of the Continent imminent, he pushed the chiefs for a plan to gas Germany if by doing so the war would end sooner. This shocked the Foreign Office, recalled Antony Head, who drafted a planning memo in response to Churchill's query. "A Foreign Office chap wanted to include a paragraph," recalled Head, "saying that such a policy would forfeit moral principle. In other words, it's a bit of a shit streak to use gas, which we were all aware of. We put the paragraph in because he [Churchill] wanted it in such a hurry." As for the Foreign Office scribe who authored the paragraph that raised objections to the use of poison gas, Churchill scribbled on the memo: "Pray tell, who are the uniform psalm-singing defeatists who have written this paper?"[118]

By mid-May every soul in Britain—2.8 million Allied troops and 47 million Britons—knew the big show was close at hand. Almost five hundred American war correspondents reached that conclusion when they were told to sign powers of attorney and wills. The British people knew because Home Guardsmen were posted at just about every crossroads in the country, checking civilians' papers and directing never-ending streams of jeeps and trucks this way and that. Late in the month, civilian travel to Ireland was banned. Military bases were locked down. HMG, at the insistence of Eisenhower, had a month earlier forbidden all diplomatic communications between embassies and their home countries—including those conducted by courier and cipher — except when initiated by the United States, Poland, or the U.S.S.R. No foreign diplomats were allowed to enter or leave the country. A ten-mile-wide coastal strip from the Firth of Forth to Land's End had been made off-limits to civilians. Intra-island commercial shipping was shanghaied in its entirety for the invasion. The ports were jammed with every sort of ship afloat, as well as hundreds of components of the artificial harbors, on which thousands of workers applied final welds, after which the sections were submerged to hide their presence from German reconnaissance flights. Railways had announced that schedules could change without notice and that certain routes and trains would be off-limits to civilians, also without notice. This had now come to pass.

Milk and mail delivery went by the boards because the milkmen and mailmen had been recalled to Home Guard duty. Regular commerce came to a halt; fresh fish disappeared from markets, coal from cellars, and beer from pubs. Mollie Panter-Downes wrote that if the High Command was seeking to confuse the Germans with all the troop movements, they had clearly succeeded in confusing the locals. Residents of villages that were full of Yanks one night awakened to find them gone by dawn, replaced by Canadians, who were in turn replaced by the British. The big London railway stations were full of only soldiers and their wives and girlfriends. "The women who have come to see their men off nearly always walk to the very end of the platform," wrote Panter-Downes, "to wave their elaborately smiling goodbyes as the train pulls out. Sometimes they look to one as if they're standing on the extreme tip of England itself."[120]

And from across the Channel came the regular dull throb of Allied bombs falling in France, similar to the roll of distant thunder, with the unsettling difference that the concussive pulse generated by high explosives moves through bedrock at the speed of sound and can spawn a tremor in a tumbler of water at forty miles, or in a man's belly.

The French knew nothing, but de Gaulle suspected much. On May 15, de Gaulle, in Algiers, unilaterally declared the French Committee of National Liberation the provisional government of France, with himself as president. He proclaimed the Third Republic had not ended but had only been interrupted by the bastard Vichy regime. Roosevelt, driven as Eden saw it "by his absurd and petty dislike of de Gaulle," still wanted to throw de Gaulle overboard. Eden considered that option to be "folly" and advised Churchill in the strongest terms to not do so. Although Churchill heeded Eden's advice, he was one with Roosevelt in telling de Gaulle nothing about Overlord until after it had been launched.[120]

In London on the fifteenth, the very few in the land who knew the exact dates and time of the invasion gathered for a final briefing at Montgomery's headquarters at St. Paul's School. Eisenhower and the SHAEF command attended, as did the entire War Cabinet, King George, the British Chiefs of Staff, dozens of American generals, Jan Smuts, and Winston Churchill. No representative of the Free French attended, even though Eisenhower planned to land the First French Army in Marseilles in the follow-up to Overlord. Churchill again offered a few fighting words after the briefing, as he had on April 7. Butcher called Churchill's address a real "stemwinder," wherein he proclaimed "bravery, ingenuity, and persistence as human qualities of greater value than equipment." One phrase in particular struck Eisenhower: "Gentlemen," Churchill intoned, "I am hardening toward this enterprise." Eisenhower took this to mean that Churchill, who "had long doubted its feasibility and had previously advocated its further postponement in favor of operations elsewhere... had finally, at this late date come to believe with the rest of us" that Overlord was the "true course of action in order to achieve victory." Eisenhower wrote these words just three years after the war, in his memoir *Crusade in Europe*. The passage has dogged Churchill ever since. The British historian Max Hastings cites Eisenhower's recollection when he writes in *Winston's War* that Churchill had all along believed Overlord "represented an option but not an absolute commitment."[121]

In fact, it was both. Churchill had at first considered Overlord a commitment lacking muscle, and he had argued (successfully) that the early, puny version be beefed up. Every plan in war is an option, to be examined, weighed, and adjusted, until it is carried out, or not. Eisenhower later wrote that part of his job was to make alternate plans in case Overlord proved "impractical" to carry off, or if strategic objectives changed in a way that brought that particular option into doubt. In war, several options must be kept open at the same time; if only one option is on the table, it is not an option. By early March, within five weeks of Eisenhower and Montgomery's strengthening of the plan, Churchill began sending his "hardening" telegrams to Marshall and Roosevelt. By May 15 he had long since hardened to the plan, a hardening that had not come about with the speed of quick-set cement, but the end result was the same. On May 8, just a week before the final unveiling of the plan, during a private lunch with Eisenhower, Churchill leaned into the table and announced, with tears in his eyes, "I am in this thing with you to the end." Eisenhower failed to mention the luncheon in his memoir. When John Eisenhower wrote of the May 15 meeting in his 1986 book, *Eisenhower at War,* he did not imbue Churchill with the monolithic resistance to Overlord that his father had in his book. Rather, the younger Eisenhower refers to the evolution over three years of Churchill's position on cross-Channel operations, from Sledgehammer to Roundup and finally to Overlord.[122]

Churchill had not been alone in his concerns about Overlord. Air Chief

Marshal Leigh-Mallory expressed serious doubts to Eisenhower about the wisdom of the American airborne attacks. The terrain was atrocious, unsuitable for both parachutists and gliders. German anti-aircraft batteries would have a field day in targeting the slow-moving transport planes, whose gas tanks were not self-sealing, and were thus flying firetraps. He foresaw a "futile slaughter" of the paratroopers followed by the likely failure of the landing at Utah Beach on the Cotentin Peninsula, which in turn would lead to the ruination of the entire enterprise. Eisenhower heard Leigh-Mallory out before conducting a "soul-racking" examination of the problem, alone. He decided to go ahead with the airborne operations. Yet, Eisenhower instructed Leigh-Mallory to put his concerns in writing, to protect the airman from condemnation in the event his dire predictions came to pass. In that case, Eisenhower expected to bear the responsibility.[123]

Churchill often expressed his concerns through emotion accompanied by tears, thus appearing indeterminate, even weak. Yet all the participants were concerned; they would have been foolish not to be, and they were not foolish men. Montgomery expected the Germans to begin throwing panzer and mechanized infantry divisions at the beachhead within hours of the landings. His logic was simple. The trickery of Bodyguard would expire at H hour, when the troops went ashore, at which time the Germans would finally know the truth and react with force and speed and fury. Eisenhower, concerned that the Germans would mass on the beaches, asked Churchill to extend the ban on diplomatic communications beyond D-day, to lull the Germans into believing the real invasion was yet forthcoming. Again, his logic was simple: if the Germans did not believe D-day was a feint, the invasion was in deep trouble from the start.[124]

Years later, when it was all over, Eisenhower in his memoirs stressed the abominable consequences had Overlord failed. Churchill could have written the words. "The two countries [Britain and the United States] were placing all their hopes, expectations, and assets in one great effort.... Failure... would be almost fatal. Such a catastrophe might mean the complete redeployment" of U.S. forces to the Pacific. The effect on Allied morale would be "so profound that it was beyond calculation." Finally, if Overlord failed, Russia "might consider a separate peace." Churchill had argued that very case ever since he first saw the preliminary—and inadequate—plans for Overlord the previous August.[125]

Since early in the year, Erwin Rommel's command, Army Group B in northwestern France, had been working to batten down the northwest

French coast. Rommel could not know of the delay in Allied plans wrought by Montgomery's proposals of late January, but he knew the Americans and English were coming, if not in May, then in June. His orders were to complete construction of a defensive barrier roughly four hundred miles in length—Hitler called it his Atlantic Wall—from Brittany, east through the Cotentin Peninsula, and on through Normandy, across the Seine estuary to the Pas de Calais. Rommel believed that the Allies were not likely to attempt a landing on the Cotentin, where the Germans would only have to seal the seventy-mile-wide neck of the peninsula to trap the invaders. Brittany, farther south, was also a similar dead end. Even were the Allies to find a way to put men ashore on Brittany's inhospitable beaches, they would find the ports of Brest, Lorient, and St-Nazaire well fortified and bristling with arms. Any landings even farther south would take the Allies beyond the range of their Spitfire fighter support, which was critical to the operation. Brittany would put the Allied armies closer to the Pyrenees than to Paris. The Seine estuary was too irregular; the chalk cliffs of the Pays de Caux were too high; they gave out near Dieppe, which by virtue of the British raid in 1942 had demonstrated the unwisdom of trying to invade a fortified port directly. That left Normandy or Calais.[126]

Rommel's superior in the west, Field Marshal Gerd von Rundstedt, agreed with Rommel's overall assessment but favored the Pas de Calais as the target; it offered the straightest line and shortest distance between England and France. The German Fifteenth Army, nineteen divisions strong, was stationed there, and in Allied headquarters it was assumed that it would be released promptly to deliver a counterstroke in Normandy when the troops came ashore. Hence, the Allied campaign of false radio transmissions. German intelligence was intercepting a great deal of radio traffic between numerous Allied units in the southeast of Britain. The signals were as false as the phony units sending them, all part of Operation Fortitude and intended in part to keep the German Fifteenth Army tied down in Calais. Although in general agreement on the site of the invasion, von Rundstedt and Rommel disagreed on the fundamental question of how best to meet the invader, wherever he arrived. In addition to static defenses manned by artillery and infantry, six panzer divisions were available in northwestern France. Rommel, the apostle of armored war in 1940, was now an apostate. He wanted to dig in on the beaches and fight a defensive battle, yet one that admitted to flexibility and timely deployment of reserves, a battle such as Montgomery successfully fought during Rommel's first assault at El Alamein in 1942.

To that end, Rommel insisted that the six panzer divisions—more than 1,100 tanks and self-propelled guns—be placed under his command in order to bring them to bear on the beaches. Von Rundstedt favored holding the tanks in reserve until he could launch a decisive counterattack once the Allies showed their hand. His logic was simple: the Wehrmacht by brilliant armored maneuver had defeated both the French and the BEF in 1940, and it could do so again. Flexibility underlay von Rundstedt's claim on the panzers. But Rommel wanted the tanks put under his command, because, unlike in 1940, the Allies now controlled the air, as evidenced by the ongoing destruction of the very rail and road routes that von Rundstedt needed to deploy his tanks for counterstrokes. The debate lasted into April.[127]

Thanks to Ultra, the Allies were privy to almost every exchange of views between Rommel, von Rundstedt, and Berlin. Churchill was reading messages soon after they were sent. Hitler, who initially favored Rommel's strategy (and his prediction of Normandy as the target), finally made a decision that effectively hobbled both Rommel and von Rundstedt. Employing the wisdom of Solomon, the Führer divided the panzers between Rommel and OKW—the German army supreme command. Von Rundstedt would have no claim on the tanks. Hitler further ordered that the panzers under OKW could be deployed only on his authority. Only three of the six armored divisions were arrayed south of the Seine, and only one was under Rommel's direct command near the Normandy coast. Hitler's decision served himself, Rommel, and von Rundstedt ill, but it served the Allies well. It was "probably the most important decision of all those affecting the Allies and the Overlord plans," F. W. Winterbotham wrote in *The Ultra Secret*.[128]

Yet Winterbotham failed to note that the British often did not know with certainty if Ultra decrypts were valid or as phony as the Allied Fortitude signals. The intelligence game was a wilderness of mirrors. Almost every SOE agent the British dropped into Belgium and Holland was captured by the Germans and forced to relay false information back to London. Likewise, every German agent dropped or smuggled into Britain during the war was captured, and then offered a choice: become a double agent or hang. Almost all chose to cooperate, and in their roles as part of Bodyguard fed phony intelligence to Berlin, where Hitler upon reading it gradually grew to believe that Calais, not Normandy, would be the target, especially as the Fortitude signals (from phantom Allied units) seemed to verify the intelligence. Or did Hitler falsely appear to favor Calais? Three times in the early spring, the British intercepted messages from Hitler that clearly indicated he favored *Normandy* as the objective. Which was it? The Allies could not know with certainty until after the landings. Then, and only then, would German panzer and troop deployments tell them what Hitler believed.[129]

All spring Rommel pleaded with Berlin for more barbed wire, concrete, and men. Intercepted communications reinforced Churchill's concern that

Rommel would mass his forces on and near the beaches, throwing everything he had against everything the Allies had, in a Great War–style battle. Another Somme or Passchendaele was what Churchill (and Brooke) most feared. Montgomery read the tea leaves differently. He believed Rommel would never simply sit behind his defenses until the opportunity for a "big push" presented itself, but would constantly assault and harass the Allies from the start. Yet if Rommel assembled a powerful enough force in short order, the nature of his counteroffensive would not be "harassment" but "onslaught." When Ultra verified Rommel's plan to gather his panzer reserves and throw them upon the beaches, Churchill's fears seemed confirmed. If Rommel could stall the first three or four waves of invaders long enough for more panzers (and the Fifteenth Army, from Calais) to appear on the scene, he would win the battle. Hitler had sixty divisions in France and the Low Countries; sound strategy called for him to hurl as many as could be spared at the invaders.[130]

Chance would play its usual role in the affair, whether induced by miscommunication, misunderstanding, or the weather. Churchill's strategic musings and regular proclamations on the roles of chance in warfare put him in general agreement with Clausewitz, who wrote, "War is the province of chance," a force constantly present on the battlefield, where it "increases the uncertainty of every circumstance and deranges the course of events." Clausewitz believed fighting a war demanded finding a balance between reason and unreason, where success required both intuition and planning, and where luck always lurked. Most of all, fighting a war demanded political and military leaders who understood this. Clausewitz was no Prussian automaton, but a complex man and complex thinker. Liddell Hart, Britain's premier strategic thinker in the years between the wars, discounted the importance of Clausewitz. Many in the British military establishment—who presumed a Prussian could teach them little—blamed Clausewitz for the murderous turn that warfare took in the trenches of 1915, an ironic assessment that implies that the long-dead Prussian had somehow ordered Britain's often stupid generals to conduct the Great War as they had. British political leaders traditionally had little interest in the actual practice of war and for the most part had left the planning and fighting to the admirals and generals. Not Churchill. As a trained soldier who possessed, Ismay later wrote, "an encyclopedic" knowledge of the history of warfare, Churchill had arrived at many of the same truths Clausewitz held dear—confuse the enemy; add creative and idiosyncratic elements to the conflict; control the deranging of events on the battlefield. When it came to fighting, Ismay recalled, Churchill "venerated tradition, but ridiculed convention."[131]

Clausewitz also advised simple plans and tactics not prone to easy foul-up. He advised that attacks should be made only on important objectives, with overwhelming force, and that goals should not be overly ambitious. Overlord was anything but simple; its ambitions were great. Whether its forces were overwhelming would be determined on the beaches. And now the day of battle—June 5—was almost at hand.[132]

On June 3, a sunny and breezy day, Eisenhower called a meeting of his commanders and meteorologists at Southwick House, the Royal Navy compound where Eisenhower kept his Portsmouth headquarters. His chief meteorologist, Group Captain John Stagg, who the day before had forecast several days of moderate weather, now predicted gale-force winds, high seas, and low cloud cover for June 4 and 5. A series of low-pressure areas in the North Atlantic were lined up and making for England and Normandy. The Allies could take hourly barometric readings as far afield as Iceland and Greenland, and those readings did not bode well for the fifth. The Germans could not gather weather data in the far reaches of the North Atlantic, an intelligence deficit that would soon blindside them. At the 9:30 P.M. meeting that night, the skies still clear, Stagg reaffirmed his prediction. Eisenhower polled his commanders; they were unanimous in agreeing that the invasion should be pushed back a day, pending a review at the 4:30 A.M. meeting on June 4, just eight hours hence. Parts of the great invasion task force were already at sea; ships that had not yet sailed waited in harbors, packed with troops. At the 4:30 A.M. meeting, Eisenhower asked Stagg if he foresaw any change in his forecast. Stagg replied in the negative. Asked when he thought the front would begin to close on the Channel, he replied, in four or five hours. Eisenhower ordered the postponement.

By ten that morning, the winds had risen and the clouds had closed in. By eleven o'clock, gale warnings had been run up for the Channel. The June 4 storm scrubbed the fifth. That left the sixth, possibly the seventh, but only if the weather cleared. By then the men would have been aboard the transports for almost four days. A cancellation until late in the month would disrupt the entire logistics structure, to say nothing of the morale of the men and the leaders in London, Washington, and especially Moscow, where Stalin might conclude that his allies had never been sincere in their promise of a second front. A two- or three-week delay would give Rommel time to further reinforce his positions. Nothing could be gained by a postponement, but much would be lost. Eisenhower ordered that they reassemble at 9:30 that night to review the situation.[133]

Churchill by then was aboard his private train, parked on a siding outside Portsmouth near Eisenhower's tented field headquarters. Brooke, as usual, took a dim view, writing in his diary, "Winston... is touring the Portsmouth area and making a thorough pest of himself." The P.M. designated the train his "advance headquarters," a moniker Eden found to be absurd, given that the train was cramped and there was only one telephone and one bath and "Mr. Churchill seemed to be always in the bath and General Ismay always on the telephone."[134]

The P.M. had entrained on June 2 with the intention of boarding a Royal Navy cruiser at Portsmouth for a front-row seat as the men went ashore in Normandy. He had asked Admiral Ramsay to make the necessary arrangements but had not informed Brooke, knowing full well the CIGS would vehemently oppose such showmanship. Days earlier, Eisenhower had gotten wind of Churchill's plans and insisted that he cancel them. Churchill refused, citing his position as HMG's minister of defence, and the power vested in him by that office to go wherever he pleased in order to conduct HMG's military business. Eisenhower, who thought Churchill's presence in the fleet would be a distraction, and dangerous, took his case to King George, who, over three days and in three letters, pleaded with Churchill to reconsider. Finally, when the King inferred that he, too, would join the battle—he was a former Royal Navy sailor, after all, and veteran of the Battle of Jutland—Churchill relented. He stressed in his memoir that he had deferred to his King, not to Eisenhower.

That squall behind him, Churchill waited aboard his train for another tempest to blow in: Charles de Gaulle. The War Cabinet had insisted the Frenchman be at least informed of the date of the invasion; to not do so would be an insult to France. On June 3, Churchill sent his York to Algiers to retrieve the general, several of his aides, and Duff Cooper. After an overnight flight, they arrived at Northolt Airport just past dawn on the fourth, as the Channel weather deteriorated.[135]

At Portsmouth, Churchill, Ernest Bevin, Jan Smuts, and Ismay waited on the railroad spur for de Gaulle, who soon could be seen walking up the line in the company of Duff Cooper, Anthony Eden, and Pierre Viénot, de Gaulle's ambassador to HMG. Churchill, sensing the historic nature of the proceedings, stepped forward arms outstretched to embrace de Gaulle, who, in his khaki uniform and kepi, two stars on his collar, stood stiffly at attention. Of Churchill's gesture, Eden later wrote, "Unfortunately, de Gaulle did not respond easily to such a mood." The tableau resembled a short man trying to embrace a telephone pole. Smuts was altogether the wrong man to be on hand, having declared in a radio address that France would never regain its former position of authority in Europe, an insult the French could never forgive (although Smuts had also predicted the British

Empire would emerge from the war in extremis). The parley in the railroad car began well enough, with Churchill outlining the particulars of the military plan while de Gaulle, a military man first and foremost, listened intently, posed questions, and seemed to be enjoying himself. Then Churchill strayed to the topic of the civil governance of France, and the need for de Gaulle to ask Roosevelt's permission to conduct civil affairs. With cold finality, de Gaulle cut Churchill off. "Why do you seem to think," he thundered, "I have to submit my candidacy for the government of France to Roosevelt?" The French government existed as a matter of fact, de Gaulle stated, with himself at its head, and that was that. Churchill responded in kind, "I want you to know, General, that every time we must choose between Europe and the open sea we will choose the sea.... Between you and Roosevelt, I will always choose Roosevelt." Bevin objected, telling de Gaulle that not all in the British government felt that way. Eden, too, tried to calm the waters, but to no avail. "The meeting," he later wrote, "was a failure."[136]

Franklin Roosevelt spent the weekend of June 3 and 4 resting at Edwin ("Pa") Watson's Blue Ridge Mountains home. He read his Book of Common Prayer in order to find the proper words for a blessing to be read on the night of the invasion. He intended to make a radio address on the fifth, but of course would make no mention of events in the English Channel. Rather, his purpose was to congratulate Alexander and Mark Clark on the liberation of Rome—"the symbol of Christianity"—which took place on June 4. It was a hollow victory, Sir John Keegan later wrote. Rome had been declared an open city. Clark should have bypassed it in pursuit of the retreating Germans, which the Fifth Army could then have encircled and captured, with General Oliver Leese's Eighth Army driving in from the right flank to close off the German retreat. That was Alexander's plan, drafted in accordance with the Clausewitz maxim that he, Eisenhower, and Churchill held dear: capture armies, not real estate. But Clark, suspicious of British tactics and intent on securing the glory he thought due him, instead took his army directly into Rome, and thus lost his chance to encircle the Germans. Kesselring and his armies began a fighting retreat 150 miles to their Gothic Line in the Apennines—the Allies called it the Pisa-Rimini line—where they successfully thwarted Allied advances into the Balkans until the final weeks of the war. Within eight weeks of the capture of Rome, at the insistence of Roosevelt and Marshall, and against Churchill's earnest disapproval, Jumbo Wilson's Mediterranean forces were reduced by seven divisions, four French and three American, for deployment in Anvil. Clark got his front-page glory, for one day, until events in Normandy on June 6 erased Rome from the collective consciousness of Britons, Canadians, and Americans.[137]

At Eisenhower's Portsmouth headquarters, the rain smacking the windows during the evening meteorological meeting of June 4 testified to Group Captain Stagg's forecasting prowess. Across the Channel the gale was in full blow. An attempt to land on June 5 would have proven disastrous. Prospects for the next day appeared hopeless as well. Then Stagg made what Eisenhower called an "astonishing" forecast: late on June 5 fair weather in the form of a weak high lasting perhaps thirty-six hours would form a break between the low-pressure systems. That sounded promising for the sixth, but opened the unsettling possibility that the first landings might take place under suitable conditions while the follow-up landings would have to be scrubbed as the second storm arrived, leaving the initial forces trapped on the beaches. Eisenhower asked Stagg what exactly the weather would be like in twenty-four hours. "To answer that question," Stagg replied, "would make me a guesser, not a meteorologist." After pondering Stagg's assessment, Eisenhower announced the invasion was on, pending a final review at the 4:00 A.M. meeting on June 5, in seven hours. When they reconvened before dawn on the fifth, Stagg held to his forecast; a break in the weather was imminent. Eisenhower put questions to his commanders: Could the navy gunners spot targets? Could the parachute transports find their drop zones? Could the landing craft reach shore? The answer from each of the commanders was in the affirmative. "Okay," Eisenhower announced, "we'll go."[138]

Later that morning, after paying a visit to British troops who were boarding their landing ships, Eisenhower played a game of checkers with Butcher; the result was a draw. That night, June 5, Dwight Eisenhower wrote by hand a message to be broadcast if the liberators were repulsed. It began: "Our landings... have failed to gain a satisfactory foothold and I have withdrawn the troops."[139]

Churchill, scrubbed from the mission by King George, took his train back to London. As the evening of June 5 came on, Churchill cabled Stalin with the news that the invasion was on for the following morning. Stalin was dining with the Yugoslav writer and Tito's number three man, Milovan Djilas. Handed Churchill's telegram, Stalin turned to Djilas and said, "Yes there will be a landing, if there is no fog. Until now there was always something else that interfered. I suspect tomorrow it will be something else. Maybe they'll meet up with some Germans."[140]

Field Marshal von Rundstedt dined with cronies that night at his headquarters at Château St-Germain. Thanks to the misinformation of Fortitude, he now believed that the invasion in the west would come in the Pas de Calais and in tandem with the Russian summer offensive. Since the Eastern Front showed no signs of activity that week, the west should remain quiet as well. Shortly after nine o'clock he was informed that the second line of the Verlaine couplet—"Pierce my heart with a dull languor"—had just gone out over the BBC. German intelligence had known the meaning of the line for weeks. Von Rundstedt didn't buy it. "Does anyone think the enemy is stupid enough to announce his arrival over the radio?" he exclaimed to a guest. Then, a bit worse for drink, he retired for the evening.[141]

Erwin Rommel had told his superiors that the first day would spell the difference between victory and defeat for the Reich. That day, he said, would be *Der längste Tag* ("the longest day"). The evening of June 5 did not find Rommel in Normandy, because on the morning of the fourth, after studying the latest weather reports, which predicted a continuation of high winds, high seas, and rain, Rommel concluded that the Allied invasion would not come for at least several days. Thus reassured by the gales blowing in the Channel, he took himself off to Bavaria to celebrate his wife's birthday. Because his meteorologists could not peer as far west into the Atlantic as could Eisenhower's, Rommel had no idea that a brief break in the foul weather was on its way.

Brooke that night offered to his diary: "I am very uneasy about the whole operation. At the best it will fall very far short" of expectations, and "at the worst it may well be the most ghastly disaster of the whole war. I wish to God it were safely over."[142]

Churchill dined with Clementine in the Annexe that evening, one of just four dinners alone in each other's company since January. After dinner he made a final trip downstairs to the map room to assess the latest airborne dispositions. Shortly before she went to bed Clementine joined him, a rare foray for her into the domain of the planners and chartists. Churchill told her, "Do you realize that by the time you wake up in the morning twenty thousand men may have been killed?" His calculation did not include Germans. He knew that if his estimate of Allied casualties proved accurate, the invasion had been repulsed on the beach. His declaration—part melodrama, part cold calculation wrapped in sentiment—was in character. And consistent; he had proclaimed for two years that a disastrous defeat on the coast of France "was the only way in which we could lose this war." And now the moment was at hand. He lingered in the map room for a few moments before going to bed at about the time the first of the airborne troops glided and parachuted into the Normandy countryside.[143]

It was shortly after midnight, June 6.

Guided by the near-full moon, Bomber Command spent the first hours of the day dropping more than five thousand tons of bombs on coastal batteries and nearby rail lines, the greatest tonnage of bombs dropped in a single night during the war. To deflect German attention from the goings-on in Normandy, a Montgomery look-alike had days earlier been sent to Gibraltar along with his "staff" with orders to make his presence there known, which would presumably lead the Germans to conclude that with Montgomery (who Berlin knew was to command the invasion) out of the country, no invasion was imminent.* Another deception operation, aerial in nature, took place early on June 6 off the Pas de Calais, where the lead planes in a fleet of British aircraft dropped tinfoil strips just off the English coast, and then turned and took up position in the rear of the little aerial armada. The radar "picture" created by the tinfoil told the Germans that *something* was out there. Then, the next squadron of planes dropped their tinfoil a mile or so in front of the first, before turning for the rear, while the first squadron by then had come around and dropped more tinfoil another mile or so toward Calais—and so on slowly across the Channel, with the effect that the steadily advancing (and confusing) radar "picture" appeared to confirm for the Germans in Calais an oncoming seaborne invasion fleet. Meanwhile, two squadrons of RAF bombers carrying radar-jamming equipment overflew Normandy in order to blind the remaining German radar operators there. By 2:00 A.M. the Germans no longer could "see" what was coming their way.[144]

What was coming their way was an Allied armada divided into two broad streams and subdivided into five lesser streams—one for each target beach. The fleet, under the overall command of Admiral Sir Bertram Ramsay, was made up of almost 7,000 vessels, including 1,200 combat ships (four-fifths of them Royal Navy), 700 tugs and minesweepers, and 800 large transports, many towing sections of the Gooseberry prefabricated breakwaters, which would protect the Mulberry harbors. Ten miles off shore, on board more than 4,200 landing ships and landing craft, more

* The operation almost unraveled when the fake Montgomery was seen "swaggering about half-drunk in Gibraltar, smoking mammoth cigars like a chimney." The real Montgomery—a nonsmoker and teetotaler—took great umbrage with his portrayal. (Butcher, *My Three Years with Eisenhower*, pp. 549, 583)

than 132,000 British, Canadian, and American young men of the Twenty-first Army Group under the command of Bernard Montgomery waited to make their run into the beaches. Shortly before dawn, while the troop transports stood off shore, seven battleships, two dozen cruisers, and one hundred destroyers hammered the beaches with thousands of high-explosive rounds. Four years ago that week, Admiral Ramsay had directed the evacuation of 337,000 British and French troops from Dunkirk, a feat performed over nine days under the guns and bombs of the Luftwaffe. The fleeing army of 1940 had left all of its baggage—tanks, guns, trucks—behind in Dunkirk. On this day, Ramsay intended to put his army ashore in nine hours, and they would be bringing their baggage with them, thousands of trucks, armored cars, field guns, tanks, bulldozers, and jeeps.[145]

The Second British Army under Lieutenant General Miles Dempsey would land one Canadian and two British divisions on Sword, Juno, and Gold beaches, which ran westward for sixty miles from just east of Caen and the Orne River, where the 6th British Airborne Division, eight thousand strong, was assigned the task of taking key bridges. Then there was an eleven-mile break marked by cliffs, beyond which lay the two American beaches, where the three divisions of Omar Bradley's First U.S. Army would land. The first beach, Omaha, ran west for almost twenty miles, from just west of Port-en-Bessin, which in ten weeks' time would serve as the terminus of Pluto, the fuel pipeline under the sea. The port, guarded by gun emplacements and German flak boats, had to be taken intact. Finally, across the Vire and Douve estuaries, Utah Beach curved westward for three miles. It was the beach nearest Cherbourg. The early capture of the port facilities of Cherbourg was so great a priority, Eisenhower later wrote, that "rapid and complete success on Utah Beach was . . . a prerequisite to real success in the whole campaign." Marshes traversed by a few causeways stretched behind Utah Beach to the roads that led to Cherbourg. To secure those causeways and crossroads, 15,000 American paratroopers of the 82nd and 101st Airborne divisions arrived by glider and parachute soon after midnight, the parachutists dropped from 850 C-47 transports into the hedgerows and fields near the villages of Ste-Mère-Église, Ste-Marie-du-Mont, and St-Côme-du-Mont. The towns had to be taken in order to secure the neck of the Cotentin Peninsula. Many of the C-47s overshot the landing zones by miles, and dropped their paratroopers into the sea, or into the marshes, where they disappeared forever into the mud under the weight of their packs.[146]

When shortly after dawn the battleships ceased their bombardment, the destroyers ran in to rake the beaches. It was a risky piece of business because German long guns—155mm and 177mm artillery—that could shoot far out to sea were arrayed in bunkers behind the beaches. The largest naval bombardment in history culminated with a barrage by several tank transports that had been converted into rocket platforms, each capable of unleashing salvos of 1,100 three-inch rockets, each salvo the equivalent of one hundred cruisers firing at once. The brilliant flashes of red and yellow that tore the sky, and the shudder of explosions on the beaches felt even aboard the ships, belied the ineffectiveness of the attack, because for all the flashing and banging and booms, very few Germans were killed, because the Germans had taken shelter in reinforced concrete bunkers deep under and behind the bluffs. As the destroyers finished their run and turned seaward, American B-17s came on a final time to hit the beaches and coastal defenses. But in the faint light and haze, most of the pilots overflew their targets and dropped their bombs inland.

A short while later, the first wave of infantry made for shore, about a platoon to each landing craft. The little boats came on in neat formations, stitching the sea with hundreds of long gray wakes. Behind them more landing craft steered in lazy circles, waiting their turn. Stinking blue-gray plumes of diesel exhaust overlay the seas, which were running to three feet, a combination sure to induce retching in the human cargo. As each soldier embarked, he had been issued writing paper, a carton of cigarettes, and a small packet; its contents included seven sticks of chewing gum, one razor blade, chewing tobacco, insecticide, twelve seasickness pills, and two vomit bags. The seasickness pills had the unfortunate side effect of inducing a drugged lethargy. Sailors who knew that refused to take them; soldiers who took them soon wished they hadn't. But the bags were put to use that morning.[147]

The second wave would bring in combat engineers to deal with remaining mines, spotters to direct air and naval fire, and bulldozers to clear paths through the dunes, but all plans hinged on the first wave holding the beaches while sappers cleared the way for the following waves. As the landing craft of the first wave closed on the beaches, the big guns on the Allied ships fell silent; no fighter planes screamed close overhead, no bombers droned far above. In Britain seven thousand heavy bombers and five thousand Spitfires and P-51B Mustangs awaited further orders and targets. The German Third Air Fleet, stationed on the Normandy coast, consisted that morning of just 169 planes and pilots.[148]

German gunners behind the beaches, not knowing if the Allied bombers would return, risked glances from their pillboxes, earthen bunkers, and fire holes strung along the bluffs. Gazing with incredulity through lifting haze and drifting smoke and the dust of pulverized concrete, they beheld the incoming landing craft, and behind that fleet, an armada that stretched to the horizon in all directions—seaward, eastward up the coast, westward down the coast. Thousands of barrage balloons drifted above the ships. For many Germans, the scene could only unfold in silence—their eardrums had been ripped by the concussions of the naval barrage. Though unprepared for what they saw, Erwin Rommel had prepared them well to defend against it. More than 11 million mines lay buried on the beaches, in the dunes, and in the waters around the anti-tank obstacles. Hundreds of miles of concertina wire curled in front of and on top of seawalls, up gullies in the dunes, and crosswise on the sand, where deep ditches had been dug that could swallow tanks. Even had no Germans waited, the mines and the barbed wire would have taken a terrible toll. But the Germans were there, and now they fingered their triggers and held lanyards slack and awaited the command to fire. The difference in the exact set of the tide along the entire front determined that H hour was slightly different on each beach. On Omaha, H hour was now, 6:30 A.M.[149]

A bloodred sun climbed over Normandy's farms and fields. Apple orchards were in full bloom. For a few lingering moments, all was quiet on the Western Front.

Then, as the landing craft steered for the shingle, the warships opened up again, now lobbing their shells far inland. On Omaha Beach, where the Americans expected to encounter one or two battalions numbering perhaps 1,500 men (Ultra was not perfect), 7,000 men of the veteran 352nd Division raked the oncoming Americans with machine guns, mortars, and 88s pre-sighted onto every square meter of beach. Amphibious tanks swam toward the beaches; of twenty-nine going in to Omaha, twenty-two sank with their crews; five were blown up. Now the combat engineers and infantry were wading and swimming and crawling ashore under murderous German fire. Ernie Pyle took it all in from a ship standing off Omaha Beach. A bureaucratic snafu had kept him from going ashore in the first wave. He could only wait his turn, and did so by playing gin rummy while Bing Crosby crooned "Sweet Leilani" over the ship's PA system. Pyle found the scene incongruous. Men sat reading *Life* magazine as the ship shuddered from nearby misses. They listened to BBC reports that told them "how the war before our eyes was going." The ship was dry, warm, the coffee fresh. "But," wrote Pyle, "it wasn't like that ashore. No, it wasn't like that ashore."[150]

Jock Colville, granted two months' fighting leave from No. 10, had rejoined his 168 Squadron of the Second Tactical Air Force two weeks earlier. He flew a Mustang over the Normandy beaches shortly after the first men went ashore. Low cloud cover kept the fliers under two thousand feet, low enough to identify individual Allied ships and "their huge guns belching flame and smoke" as they kept up the barrage. And low enough to prove dangerous. The vagaries of war were brought home to Colville when, "by a million to one chance," a fifteen-inch shell from HMS *War-*

spite struck one of the planes in Colville's squadron. The plane and its pilot simply disappeared.[151]

Shortly after 6:30 A.M. on June 6, Erwin Rommel received an urgent telephone call from OKW. The Allies were ashore, in Normandy. As at El Alamein, Rommel found himself away from his command at the very hour when his presence was most vital. He immediately asked OKW to send two panzer divisions to the beaches. He was told that only Hitler could make that decision, and that the question could be put to Hitler only when he awoke. The Führer had as usual worked well into the early morning hours and had elected to sleep in. No one dared wake him. Not until two in the afternoon did Hitler convene a staff meeting.[152]

Rommel had based his defense on the tactical principles of the Great War—static positions, bunkers, tunnels, trenches, barbed wire, mines, all defended by concentrated fire. But whereas in the Great War the attacking British could always haul themselves back to their own trenches after a failed gambit, today there was no place to run to. Shortly after waking at eight o'clock, Churchill took himself to the underground map room to follow the plotting of Allied positions. The lines on the charts inched inland as the morning wore on, a hundred yards here, a half mile there. The news from the British and Canadian beaches was good, as it was from the westernmost American beach, Utah, where fewer than 200 men of 21,000 were killed going ashore. Tanks had raced across the causeways and established contact with the airborne units. But on Omaha it was a bloody and close-fought affair. There, as if to confirm Brooke's and Churchill's fears, the battle bore far more resemblance to the Somme and Passchendaele than to any action fought thus far in the Second World War.

At noon, satisfied that the landings had not been repulsed out of hand, Churchill was driven to the House. All there knew that Rome had fallen, and presumed he would be speaking on that subject. He did, and at great length, delivering a history of the Italian campaign from Sicily to Rome. Then he paused. "I have also to announce to the House that during the night and the early hours of this morning, the first of the series of landings in force upon the European Continent has taken place." The House erupted. Churchill continued: "So far the commanders who are engaged report that everything is proceeding according to plan. And what a plan! This vast operation is undoubtedly the most complicated and difficult that has ever taken place." He later in the day telegraphed the same message to Stalin. Thus, within a span of just thirty hours, Rome had been taken and the Atlantic Wall breached. And neither bad luck nor the enemy had so far deranged events on the battlefield. Four years after being thrown out of France, the British were back.[153]

By then, on the beaches and in the heavily wooded bocage, almost 2,500 American and 500 British and Canadian men lay dead, and 6,000 more had been wounded. The vast majority of American casualties took place on Omaha Beach, but by early afternoon the beach was theirs. Even as Churchill spoke, a half million more men in two dozen southern English ports and numerous small harbors and coves prepared to embark for Normandy. Patton's 4th Armored Division was conducting war games on the Salisbury plain, awaiting its turn. More than one hundred tugboats readied to tow across the Channel the two Mulberry artificial harbors—made up of four hundred steel and concrete components weighing 1.5 million tons. Churchill first sketched these technological marvels in a 1917 memo to Lloyd George, and again in 1940. Each artificial harbor could handle more than ten thousand tons of supplies per day, enough to feed and arm twenty-five divisions. The men were ashore, and the means to supply them was on its way. Still, Churchill harbored enough doubts to return to the House later that evening, where he warned that the reports from the beaches gave no "indication of what may be the course of the battle in the next days and weeks, because the enemy will now probably endeavour to concentrate on this area, and in that event heavy fighting will soon begin and will continue without end, as we can push troops in and he can bring other troops up. It is, therefore, a most serious time that we enter upon. Thank God we enter upon it with our great Allies all in good heart and all in good friendship."[154]

For weeks English farmers had been hoping for rain for the sake of their crops. The rain had finally arrived, Mollie Panter-Downes was to write, but the farmers now wished for blue skies "for the sake of their sons, fighting in the skies and on the earth across the Channel." By early evening, trains carrying the first of the wounded began running through an English countryside in full springtime bloom, "festooned with dog roses and honeysuckle." Women who had weeks earlier waved good-bye to their men now stood at railroad crossings, shopping baskets on their arms, and watched as the trains sped past. "They don't know whether to wave or cheer or cry," wrote Panter-Downes. "Sometimes they do all three."[155]

The second front was now an irrevocable reality. Germany had never won a two-front war. Indeed, in Italy Hitler faced a third front. If he deployed his reserves properly, or if he robbed from his eastern front to eliminate the threat in the west, he might soon find himself, again, fighting a one-front war. The Bletchley crowd and Churchill—and the men on the beaches—awaited the Führer's next move.

The Overlord plans called for the Americans to put thirteen divisions ashore in the first few weeks, the British and Canadians twelve. By early August, twenty-one of thirty-seven divisions in France were to be American. The disparity in Anglo-American numbers—and casualties—could only widen, and that begat another irrevocable reality. Not only was the slow but relentless transfer from Britain to America of command of the war nearly complete, so, too, was the transfer of global supremacy from London to Washington. Roosevelt, who on numerous occasions had made clear to Churchill his disdain for spheres of influence, was carving out the world's largest. Indeed, America's sphere of influence was expanding far beyond North and South America (claimed by James Monroe) to encompass the entire Pacific once the Japanese were defeated, which assuredly they would be. Australia, in 1942, had chosen America, not London, as the partner it would march beside into the future. The Philippines, when cleared of Japanese, would remain an American interest. Churchill did not begrudge Roosevelt the spread of American might, and could not stop it in any event. The potential for Soviet hegemony in much of Europe was what worried Churchill.

Triumph over Hitler was now—almost—a certainty, as was the prospect for postwar tragedy in Eastern Europe. Churchill and Britons might yet remain captains of their souls, but they were no longer masters of their fate. The European war would be fought on Eisenhower's and Zhukov's terms, the peace conducted on American and Russian terms, if America intended to make its presence known in postwar Europe, but Churchill had known since receiving Roosevelt's February telegram that the president sought to get out of Europe at the first available opportunity. Churchill did not know that in March, Roosevelt had told the State Department he wanted no part in maintaining order in France, Belgium, and Italy, where he foresaw chaos, and the Balkans, which were already in an advanced state of chaos. Further, to keep American troops as far as possible from trouble, he instructed the State Department to insist that northwest Germany form the American zone of occupation, the better to get his boys home from North Sea ports should trouble occur elsewhere in Europe. In a memo to Edward Stettinius, Roosevelt frankly acknowledged that "political considerations in the United States makes [*sic*] my decision conclusive." In late May, the president telegraphed Churchill with a summation of his directive to the State Department. Then, four days before D-day, Roosevelt reiterated his stance to Churchill. Quoting his February telegram,

Roosevelt said: "I am absolutely unwilling to police France and possibly Italy and the Balkans as well." And, he offered, "The reasons are political, as you well know." It was an election year.[156]

Beyond Europe, the British were no longer masters of the fate of hundreds of millions of subjects throughout the Empire. This was underscored in early June when Churchill received a reply from Roosevelt to his desperate plea for American shipping to relieve the "grievous famine in Bengal." More than seven hundred thousand Bengalis had died since early 1943, in large part because the Japanese controlled Burma and its surplus rice. Churchill informed Roosevelt that although 350,000 tons of surplus Australian wheat was available, the ships to carry it were not. Could the president supply the ships? After waiting more than four weeks, Roosevelt replied in the negative, and with "regret." He cited the effect of such a "diversion" on military operations. Churchill—and King George and London—could do almost nothing for the Bengalis; at least a million more died during the next twelve months.[157]

Edmund Burke wrote that empires die for a number of reasons, including the inability to govern disparate peoples in far-flung lands. Churchill possessed the will to save His Majesty's Empire, and to guarantee the peace in Europe, but he lacked the way. Despite the staggering losses the British had sustained since 1939, despite their sacrifice and their refusal to give in when they fought alone, the peace, when it came, would be Stalin's to violate. With the Americans in their ascendancy, the solution to containing a belligerent Stalin no longer rested with London. For better or worse, it rested with Washington. And Franklin Roosevelt had just made his thoughts clear on that subject.

Sometime in 1944, a new word crept into the lexicon of international politics: "superpower." It was not coined with the British Empire in mind.

6

Anchorage

JUNE 1944–MAY 1945

Few U-boats roamed the Atlantic in early June; their harvest was meager. The sea routes to Britain were secure, the flood of American men and matériel unstoppable. The British, Canadians, and Americans were ashore in Normandy. And with seven thousand American and British heavy bombers based in Britain, with Alexander driving to the Po Valley in northern Italy, and with the Russians poised to strike in the East, Germany had lost the war. But the Allies had yet to win it. Some, including President Roosevelt, believed they all but had.

A week before D-day, Roosevelt dropped a "blockbuster" on Washington reporters. In an almost offhand manner he outlined his "blueprint" for a postwar world organization. This was the first the press heard of the world council Roosevelt had proposed the previous November in Tehran. Roosevelt divulged no particulars, thus leaving both isolationists and internationalists somewhat befuddled. The president did stress that whatever came into being would not impinge on the "integrity" of the U.S. He chose the word carefully. It is synonymous with "sovereignty," *Time* reported, a "wicked, isolationist word" in the minds of internationalists (known then as "one-worlders"), who championed a world government. Yet "sovereignty" formed the essence of isolationism and the national identity as championed by Senator Robert Taft and the anti-one-worlder Republican Party. Roosevelt was sending a message to both the internationalists and Republicans: his world organization would not diminish U.S. autonomy (the Republican fear), but it would move the United States toward a cooperative, multilateral role in world affairs (the one-worlder dream). The "blueprint," Roosevelt told the press, envisioned an organization that would stop aggression, not an organization "which you would have to call on whenever some country wanted to build a bridge over a creek." Roosevelt then permitted "some high authority" to leak more details to the press, including his intent to establish a World Court, and to build his new world council around the Four Powers, with smaller nations sitting in on a rotating basis.[1]

In June, Henry Luce editorialized in *Life* magazine on the coming new world order, and America's role in it: "With the establishment of a firm lodgment on the continent, we are now the most powerful nation on earth." But with that power came responsibilities, wrote Luce, including the moral imperative for America to participate in the postwar recovery of Europe, especially as the Allies' stated military strategy entailed the utter destruction of Germany. Europe would need to be rebuilt, not simply policed. Economic order had to be restored. The military story would end, perhaps soon, but the political story was just beginning. Here came Roosevelt with his vision of a postwar world council, a vision Churchill shared. And here came Luce with his vision for an American role in postwar Europe, which Churchill also shared. But Roosevelt, despite his call for a world organization, had made clear to Churchill that American troops would get out of Europe at the first opportunity. As for rebuilding Germany, Secretary of the Treasury Henry Morgenthau Jr. was working up a plan that amounted to a Carthaginian peace of the very sort St. Augustine decried in his reflections on the obliteration of Carthage by the Romans, a peace that offered no hope to the vanquished, a peace, as St. Augustine saw it, bereft of any moral quotient, a peace that disgraced the victors.[2]

Churchill found this troubling. He envisioned the special relationship between Britain and America as forming the backbone of postwar European stability. Churchill, knowing that postwar Britain would not wield anything like the power of prewar Britain, and knowing that Russia would emerge as the greatest continental power, believed that if America intended to play no role, European salvation lay with the old diplomatic standby: spheres of influence. Roosevelt and Hull loathed any arrangement that smacked of European spheres of influence, believing, as had Woodrow Wilson, that they led ultimately to war. Churchill, with his eye on Greece, had just proposed to Stalin a division of labor in the region: Britain would manage Greek affairs, while Stalin would manage Romanian. It was an understanding between gentlemen. On June 1, Churchill asked Roosevelt for his blessing, and assured the president that Britain and Russia "do not of course wish to carve the Balkans into spheres of influence." Yet that is exactly what Churchill and Stalin were edging toward, on Churchill's part because Greece was an ally, and on Stalin's part because Romania was an enemy. The two leaders indeed had "interests" in the region.[3]

As he had for a decade, and as he would in coming years, Churchill saw Britain as being in Europe, yet not fully "in." It was as he had told Stalin in 1940: Britain lay just off the west coast of Europe (as Asiatic Russia lay just beyond the eastern reaches). As he had for four years, Churchill believed European peace and security could best be guaranteed through regional European councils and federations, including a Danubian federation in central Europe, and a Balkan council in that region. Central to Churchill's vision for Western European security, recalled his son-in-law Lord Soames, was "France taking Germany by the hand and leading her back into the community of nations." But Roosevelt held France, and especially de

Gaulle, in something approaching contempt, while Morgenthau wanted to take Germany by the neck, and wring it.[4]

Later in the summer, delegates from thirty-nine allied nations met at the Dumbarton Oaks conference, held at a Federal-style mansion in Washington, DC, that had once belonged to South Carolina senator John C. Calhoun and since 1940 had housed a Harvard University research center. There Roosevelt's "blueprint" was used to lay the groundwork for the "United Nations Organization," including a General Assembly and Security Council where the Four Powers would sit, joined by three other nations on a rotating basis. The Russians insisted that they be granted sixteen seats in the General Assembly, one for each Soviet republic. The Americans replied that in that case, the United States should have forty-eight seats. The Americans proposed that each permanent member of the Security Council have a veto, but also barred any party with a dispute before the Security Council from voting on it. The Russians objected to the implication that the Security Council might pass judgment on one of its own members. The Americans had no ready reply. The questions were left unresolved. France was excluded from the parley, rightly so, claimed Senator Tom Connally, chairman of the Senate Foreign Relations Committee, because Britain, Russia, China, and the United States had "shed their blood for the rest of the world, while France has played the role of only a minor state in this war." In London the European Advisory Commission had been sitting for over a year, its American, British, and Russian delegates studying questions of how best to deal with a defeated Germany. France—de Gaulle—had been excluded from any role.[5]

The war was not being fought to determine who fielded the strongest armies. Politics—*interests*—underlay the war, in the Clausewitzian sense, as it did all wars. This was why Churchill had reached out to Tito, and why he took in the wayward Romanian king, and insinuated HMG into Greek affairs, and grudgingly tolerated de Gaulle. He was positioning Britain for the future in those areas of Europe that he saw as critical to British interests. Stalin was doing much the same. And that was why Churchill had been trying to draw Roosevelt into a postwar role in Europe. If not America, who? The answer was self-evident: the Soviet Union. The writer and political commentator Walter Lippmann published a slim but important volume that summer, *U.S. War Aims,* in which he foresaw the implications of the power shifts taking place. Spheres of influence were a reality, he argued. After the war, America, splendidly protected by the moats of the Atlantic and Pacific oceans, would need to protect the perimeters of its sphere—in Asia (where the restored European colonies would serve as buffer to China), and especially in the Atlantic. Anticipating NATO by five years, Lippmann argued that the Atlantic now assumed the central role in global politics that the Mediterranean had played for two thousand years. To secure the Atlantic in alliance with Western European democracies would ensure that all of Western Europe formed a cordon sanitaire between the U.S. sphere and the Russian. This, Lippmann argued, would make war between the two powers "a virtual impossibility." This was so, he wrote, because neither side could conceivably put an army into the other's heartland and no other technology existed that might alter the military balance in a war.[6]

Lippmann's "safety-in-distance" reasoning came undone a year later in a sunburst of atomic energy in the New Mexico desert. But his prediction of the Atlantic's centricity in American affairs was prescient. His proposed alliances with Western European nations to safeguard America's interests brought some comfort to Churchill, who sought some form of union with America. Yet Taft Republicans hated the word "alliance" as much as one-worlders hated the word "sovereignty."

Thus, if Hitler was defeated by October, as many in Washington and London believed, no plan whatsoever was in place to safeguard and rebuild Europe. October was just sixteen weeks distant.

Early on June 9, Ultra revealed the unsettling news that Hitler had ordered his Fifteenth Army from the Pas de Calais to Normandy, and also ordered two panzer divisions rushed from Poland to Normandy. This was the hammer blow the Allies most feared. A panzer division and a brigade of SS Hitler Youth were already pounding Montgomery's positions near Caen, with another panzer division on the way. Yet another panzer division was hitting the Americans near Carentan. The arrival of the Fifteenth Army and more panzers could doom the invasion. Then, late on the ninth, Ultra revealed one of the most welcome Führer directives of the war: Hitler, still suspicious that the Pas de Calais might be the real Allied target, rescinded his orders (OKW knew that George Patton and the Third Army were not in Normandy and concluded they might be heading for the Pas de Calais). Dumbfounded by Berlin's change of mind, von Rundstedt and Rommel considered resigning. The next day Montgomery declared the beachhead secure, the eleven-mile gap between the British and American beaches having been closed. For Churchill, Montgomery's assessment amounted to the unofficial opening of the summer travel season. The Old Man called Brooke and proposed they meet Monty at Montgomery's Normandy headquarters on Monday, the twelfth. They were going back to France.[7]

Despite Montgomery's declaration, Churchill feared a "crystallization of a front in France" and the subsequent repetition of the horrors of the

Great War, a concern, recalled Harriman, shared by Roosevelt. In static lines Churchill saw the potential for slaughter. So, too, did Rommel, but the slaughter of the invader, on or near the beaches. A few days after D-day, as the beachhead slowly widened and deepened, General Ian Jacob found Churchill in the map room pondering large charts of Normandy. How soon after all of the Allied divisions are fully ashore, Churchill asked, will the battle lines stabilize? They most likely will not, replied Jacob, until the Allies reach the Rhine. Such large-scale fluidity of entire armies ran counter to the Old Man's Great War experience. He had known all along that many men would die on the beaches, and if not on the beaches, then in the bocage in the following days and weeks. Even if the lines did not stabilize, and the Allies advanced as Jacob predicted, there would be slaughter, and it would only increase as Allied armies neared the German homeland. Churchill knew the veracity of Marlborough's admonition to his cautious Dutch ally during their war against the French: the pursuit of absolute victory without slaughter will, in the long run, result in slaughter without victory.[8]

The maps Churchill gazed at were marked by "phase lines," series of concentric rings running inland from the beaches like ripples on a pond. They marked the timetable for the planned expansion of the beachhead in the days and weeks following D-day. Each line carried a notation of D + and a number. Caen, for example, was to be taken on D-day, and bridgeheads to be thrown east across the Orne River by D + 1. By D + 9, the lodgment was to be more than eighty miles wide and a dozen deep. By D + 17 (June 23), the entire Cotentin Peninsula, including Cherbourg, was to be secure. By then the Allies expected to hold a line stretching from south of Caen near Falaise, west through Vire, and ending at Granville on the Bay of Biscay. At that point, the plan called for a wheeling breakout by D + 20 from the western (American) flank, while the British and Canadians pivoted on the eastern, Caen flank. By D + 40, the Allies hoped to be halfway to the Loire. Somewhere near that date, the Anvil landing would take place, with the objective of driving up the Rhone Valley to Lyon and on to Dijon, there to make contact with the Normandy forces driving east. By D + 90, the British would be across the Seine and facing the Low Countries, with the Americans on the right facing Verdun. Such was the grand plan. Both Eisenhower and Montgomery later wrote that all of the Overlord objectives were met. They were, but the timetable was not. The lines indeed stabilized, slowly and steadily. During the first few days, the delays could be measured in hours, as could be expected for such a supremely complex operation. Yet, as happens to a navigator whose course is off by just a degree, time and distance have a way of turning small variances into very large errors.[9]

Eisenhower knew this. On June 10, meeting with the American Joint

Chiefs, who had arrived the day before, he put to them almost the same question Churchill had asked Jacob, what to do if a "stabilization" of the lines took place? Sixteen Allied divisions—four hundred thousand men—were now ashore. But at least six panzer divisions and the Fifteenth Army (if Hitler again changed his mind) presented a real threat. Eisenhower set his SHAEF planning staff to work to find a solution. George Marshall had come to London not to discuss options, but to demand that Anvil, the Marseilles landing conceived as a complement to the hammer of Overlord, be carried out as soon as possible. But after just two meetings between the British and Americans, Marshall conceded that Anvil could take place only when conditions were right. This was fine with Brooke, but only if Anvil did not come at the expense of Italian operations. To throttle Alexander's momentum, Brooke told his diary later in the month, would be "madness."[10]

The fall of Rome and the D-day landings triggered the need for a final decision on Anvil. That, in turn, triggered a crisis in the Allied ranks. Churchill, Roosevelt, and the Combined Chiefs of Staff all agreed that the only military objective was to defeat Germany as quickly as possible. But they disagreed on how best to meet that objective. Eisenhower's overriding concern was to reinforce and supply Overlord. He was open to alternatives to Anvil, including Caliph, the infusion of troops into the Bordeaux ports. He was willing to consider allowing Alexander to exploit his Italian victories in order to draw more Germans away from France. His was a strictly military objective, and yet he possessed the sharp political skills needed to bring it off, for Churchill and Marshall brought both military and political perspectives—and talents—to the table. Marshall had promised Stalin Anvil at Tehran, in part because of Stalin's transparent political discomfort with his Western allies appearing on his flanks (within his sphere of influence) by driving north through Austria, as Churchill advocated. Churchill's strategy was as political as Stalin's; he wanted to get to middle Europe before the Soviets did. Brooke, like Eisenhower, took a strictly military position, but one at odds with Ike's. Anvil formed Churchill's penultimate great strategic debate of the war; the last debate came in the final weeks of the conflict when Eisenhower refused to strike toward Berlin. To be sure, Eisenhower and Montgomery soon differed over a broad-front or narrow-front strategy as the best way to get across the Rhine and to the Elbe, but that was for the two commanders to debate and resolve in coming months.

"Now," Brooke told his diary on June 11, Marshall finally saw the wisdom of the Italian operations Brooke had championed for a year. He added, "I do not believe he [Marshall] has any strategic vision whatsoever." Eisenhower's support of Anvil was conditional; if the Normandy beachhead did not expand according to the timetable, a Brittany landing would put reinforcements next to Bradley and the First Army. If the Allies

broke out of Normandy, Anvil might be the better choice. Ike, wisely, wanted to wait and see. Marshall, on the other hand, backed Anvil unconditionally. But after five days of talks between June 9 and 13, the Combined Chiefs arrived at a decision satisfactory to all.[11]

It took the form of a directive to Eisenhower and Jumbo Wilson, commander in chief of the Mediterranean theater. The directive held that all Allied forces should be deployed "to assist in the success of Operation Overlord." To that end, three amphibious options in support of Overlord were to be considered, and the best one selected: the choices were Brittany; the south of France; or the head of the Adriatic, with the dual objective there of cutting off Kesselring in Italy and then racing to Vienna. Option three invited trouble, which duly arrived not long after the ink dried. Field Marshal Alexander and Jumbo Wilson endorsed the Adriatic operation, code-named Armpit, no doubt by the Americans. Anvil, meanwhile, was soon rechristened Dragoon, no doubt by the British. Churchill, who believed that too much miscellaneous equipment was going ashore, argued that wherever the Allies went, they should be filling the landing crafts with fighting men and bayonets rather than "dental chairs and Y.M.C.A. institutions."[12]

By the twelfth, when Churchill and Brooke crossed the Channel on board the destroyer HMS *Kelvin,* the Allies were a few days behind schedule, yet not distressingly so. Men and supplies were pouring in through the Mulberries; the Germans had virtually no presence in the air. Still, progress had been so minimal that Churchill had to take his picnic lunch with the sea at his back, just four miles behind the front lines. There, Montgomery displayed his maps and again stressed his strategy, arrived at in January, to draw the Germans to his front in order that the Americans could swing out from their zone. Brooke was taken not only with Montgomery's expert presentation but by the fact that the French countryside looked remarkably undisturbed after five years of German occupation and five weeks of Allied bombardment. Churchill described the situation thus: "We are surrounded by fat cattle lying in luscious pastures with their paws crossed." He reboarded *Kelvin* late in the afternoon, and after a short cruise up and down the beach during which *Kelvin* fired a few salvos toward the German lines for Churchill's benefit, the ship turned for England. The last time he departed France, five years earlier, he told Ismay that they likely had but three months to live.[13]

Just before midnight that night, as Churchill and Brooke neared London aboard Churchill's train, the first pilotless German bombs lifted off from their ramps in Belgium and northern France. They flew at between three thousand and four thousand feet and at speeds around 350 miles per hour.

Each carried a 1,875-pound high-explosive warhead. They were all targeted on Tower Bridge, but only four of the twenty-seven that were launched hit Greater London that night and early on the thirteenth. Some fell into the sea, and others veered off course over the English countryside, a trend that continued for the next month when out of 2,754 flying bombs that hit Britain, only 800 hit Greater London. Most were catapulted from the ramps the RAF had been targeting for months; some were launched from Heinkel 111s, to little effect.

They were devilish devices, propelled by a pulse-jet engine that worked by alternately gulping compressed air and jet fuel, which accounted for the pulsing, throaty *thrump, thrump, thrump, thrump* as they rumbled overhead. Their most sinister feature (aside from the payload) was the terrifying screech they made as they fell to ground. Their targeting was rudimentary. A miniature propeller (a vane anemometer) on the nose of each bomb was preset to spin a certain number of times (based on distance and air speed) between launch and London. When the preset number of revolutions was reached, the propeller tripped the diving controls, putting the bomb into a nosedive. The screech—or buzz—of the falling bomb was a result of the engine stalling during the dive, an unintended design consequence of the weapon. Thus, as Londoners fast learned, as long as you could hear the damnable things passing overhead, you were safe. If you heard the engine stop, you were in trouble. Berlin called the bombs the vengeance weapon, V-1 for short. Londoners anointed them doodlebugs and buzz bombs.[14]

On the third night of the attacks, Duff Cooper dined at the Dorchester with Lady Cunard, who, as she had during the Blitz, refused to leave her apartment. Told by Cooper that the new attacks were being carried out by pilotless planes, she claimed that was impossible and that anyone who believed "such rubbish" was stupid. A hotel servant who overheard the conversation offered that the pilotless planes were a good sign, "as it proved how short of men the Germans were, that they were obliged to send their aeroplanes over empty." During a meeting of the Chiefs of Staff on June 19, Churchill decreed that henceforth the weapons would no longer be called "pilotless planes" but "flying bombs." Brooke found Churchill "in very good form" that night, "quite 10 years younger, all due to the fact that the flying bombs have again put us into the front line!!"[15]

The arrival of the flying bombs marked the start of a new era, soon anointed the "rocket age," a concept made all the more horrifying by virtue of the fact that Hitler—and only Hitler—had all the rockets. During the next four weeks, the 2,754 V-1s that hit Britain killed 2,752 Britons and destroyed more than eight thousand houses. That ratio continued into early August, by which time, Churchill told the House, "5,735 of these robots have been launched upon us, killing 4,735 persons, with 14,000 more or less seriously injured." He told the House that while he was touring a wrecked neighborhood, an old man asked him, "'What are you going to do about it?' I replied, we have never failed yet. He seemed contented with the reply. That is the only promise I can make." The need to bomb the V-1 launch sites in northern France disrupted operations in Normandy, and reduced the number of missions over Germany. Still, where Hitler delivered 4,500 tons of explosives to Britain that summer, the British and Americans dropped 48,000 tons on Germany, but at a terrible cost of more than 14,000 flyers killed or missing. The V-1s did not kill many, but coming as they did hourly, day after day, week after week, they set everyone's nerves on edge. "I am sure of one thing," Churchill told the House, "that London will never be conquered and will never fail, and that her renown, triumphing over every ordeal, will long shine among men." But, as Brooke told his diary, "The danger really lies in the flying rocket with a 5-ton warhead." This was the V-2, which the British high command—but not the British people—knew was coming, and soon.[16]

As the buzz bombs came on, the battle of the beachhead turned into a stalemate, and the alliance itself appeared poised to self-destruct. The core dispute was over Anvil, the secondary invasion of France. After being guided by Eisenhower and Brooke to a wait-and-see attitude toward Anvil, Marshall had journeyed to Italy in mid-June, where he learned from Alexander and Wilson that they were keen on the Adriatic operation. His response, and that of the other American Joint Chiefs, was to harden their stance. Anvil must go forward, sometime in August at the latest. Now what had been a debate turned into a crisis. Alexander and Churchill argued to the British Chiefs of Staff for the Adriatic plan. Brooke dismissed any strike toward Vienna as "wild hopes," not least because such an operation could not start until September and they would then "embark on a campaign through the Alps in winter!" At a June 21 meeting, Churchill, "who had evidently been lunching very well," Brooke wrote, "meandered for ¾ hours producing a lot of disconnected thoughts which had no military value." Over the next few days Churchill and the British chiefs drafted separate but almost identical memos for Roosevelt and his chiefs that called for no diminution in Alexander's forces; that is, they implicitly called for the cancellation of Anvil. On June 27, the importance the British attached to Italy appeared to be validated by an Ultra decrypt that revealed Hitler's intent to defend the northern Apennines, since a breakthrough there would have "incalculable military and political consequences." Churchill argued in his long memo that Overlord could be nourished without stripping Alexander's army. He ended with "Let us not wreck one great campaign for the sake of winning the other." Roosevelt's reply, Brooke wrote, was "a rude one at that." The Americans insisted that Anvil be "carried out at once." And the most unseemly part of Roosevelt's reply in Brooke's estimation was his last paragraph: "Finally for pure political considerations over here I would never survive even a slight setback in Overlord if it were known that fairly large forces had been diverted to the Balkans."[17]

Yet the British had not argued for a diversion but wanted only to press on in Italy. Churchill drafted an angry response, including the line: "The whole campaign in Italy is being ruined, and ruined for what?" For, as he saw it, ten mostly untrained divisions, including seven French made up mostly of black North Africans, to advance "up the Rhone Valley about five months hence." He offered to fly to Washington, Bermuda, Quebec, wherever Roosevelt would meet him, in order to resolve the deadlock. In the end, he did not send the cable. He had no leverage. As Brooke put it to Churchill on June 30, it came down to essentially telling the Americans, "All right, if you insist on being damned fools, sooner than falling out with you, which would be fatal, we should be damned fools with you, and we shall see that we perform the role of damned fools damned well."[18]

By mid-June the war in the east had remained relatively dormant for six weeks. With the Eastern Front stabilized, the Russians faced a strategic dilemma as to how to deal with the three German Army Groups they faced: North, Center, and South. To continue the attack in the southernmost sector held the promise of striking deeper into Romania on a track for Bucharest, Belgrade, and Budapest. Yet by virtue of a huge salient that Army Group Center had forged beyond Minsk, such a course would leave the right flank of the Red Army exposed. Similarly, in the north, if the Red Army struck out westward from Estonia toward Riga with the Baltic on its right, it would find its left threatened by Army Group Center. Neither strategy would result in the Red Army taking a direct bearing on Berlin; the southern strategy would grind to an end in the Balkans, the northern in East Prussia.[19]

Most significant, if Hitler took the strategically correct course and pulled in his northern and southern flanks, as well as the Minsk salient, he could establish a defensive line strong enough to prolong the war indefinitely in both the east and west. If Hitler folded Army Group North three hundred miles back to Königsberg and ran his line due south through Brest-Litovsk to Kovel and the Carpathians, he would cut the length of his front in half and effectively double his strength. He could then contemplate shifting some his 166 divisions in the east to the west, a prospect that troubled Washington and London, and especially Montgomery, who for three weeks after the D-day landings expected a counterattack but did not know when or in what strength. The possible consequences of a German counterattack to the Red Army and the Anglo-American forces were vastly different. Punching holes in the Red Army lines was like digging on a beach; the next wave erases the effort. If Hitler wiped out thirty Soviet divisions, Stalin would replace them. But if he wiped out half of the twenty-five Allied divisions that were in France by late June, he would fling the Allies from the Continent. Sound strategy called for Hitler to do just that, to tighten his eastern line and concentrate his western armies against the invader.

But, like Napoleon, Hitler could not bear to exchange conquered territory for security. To not do so was a faulty strategy, and, as Brooke put it, the Germans "were bound to pay the penalty" for it. The Russian high command had concluded in May that the key to opening the entire Eastern Front was to destroy Army Group Center, which still occupied the most critical sector of historic White Russia and blocked the roads to Warsaw and Berlin. The Russian operation was code-named Bagration, after Pyotr Bagration, a hero of Russia's 1812 repulse of Napoleon. Stalin personally chose the day of attack: June 22, the third anniversary of Hitler's plunge into Russia. To put the Germans off the scent, the Soviets conducted a disinformation campaign consisting of false radio signals that indicated a massive buildup of Soviet artillery and armored units south of the Pripet Marshes, which led the Wehrmacht to conclude that the main attack would come in the southern Ukraine. Then, to further muddle German thinking, on June 11 the Red Army struck out from the Leningrad sector into Finland. This assault was conducted with two objectives in mind: to serve notice to the Finns that their doom was nigh, and to keep Hitler wondering if the Soviets and British might be on the verge of launching dual operations through Finland and Norway for the purposes of cutting off Germany's supply of Swedish iron ore. The Führer now kept seven divisions in Finland and twelve in Norway against that possibility. From the Allied perspective, the more Hitler scattered his forces, the better the chances for success in Normandy and on the Eastern Front.[20]

As the date for Bagration neared, Montgomery found himself in virtually the same place he had been since D-day. He had planned to take Caen on D-day and then drive his armies east, with the Channel on his left and the Americans on his right, destination, the Seine. Failing to do so, he was forced to change his strategy. Rather than strike Caen, he allowed the Germans to punch themselves out at his front. Still, sooner or later (and Churchill was wary of anything that smacked of "later"), Caen would be the hinge upon which the entire plan turned. The American role was to break out from their beaches, take Cherbourg to the west, and swing around south and east to cover Montgomery's right flank. But Rommel and the weather disrupted the plans. On June 19, the worst Channel storm in four decades blew for four days, destroying the Omaha Beach Mulberry harbor and bringing the war in Normandy to a halt. Eisenhower later called the action during June and July "The Battle of the Beachhead." Had the master plan gone as planned, the battle would have been over by the time Churchill made his visit on June 12.

The Channel storm was still raging on June 22, when on the Eastern Front a far more murderous storm broke at dawn as Operation Bagration kicked off. So effective was the Soviet misinformation campaign that only 37 weakly supported German divisions along the five-hundred-mile Minsk salient found themselves facing 166 Red Army divisions supported by 2,700 battle tanks and 1,300 field guns. The results were immediate, and staggering; the Red Army pushed one hundred miles west within days. Three weeks later, on July 11, another entire Soviet army hooked south under the Pripet Marshes on a general heading for Cracow. The Western press proclaimed Germany to be finished but for the formalities. A *Kansas City Star* headline brayed RED SPEED STUNS NAZIS, YANKS STRIKE IN FRANCE. In fact, the Germans had conceded the Cotentin Peninsula to the Americans. The Yanks took Cherbourg on June 25 after the German commander—ordered by Hitler to fight to the last man—asked his American counterpart to fire one artillery round at the main gate in order to preserve German honor. The Americans fired, and honor preserved, the Germans surrendered. Along the rest of the Normandy front the Allies had not advanced much beyond the beaches. Monty finally took Caen on July 9—D + 33—after bombing it almost to powder on July 8. That week George Patton and the first units of his Third Army—whose whereabouts vexed the Germans—landed in Normandy. That night was the last one of favorable moon and tides for an invasion at Calais; given that no Allied army appeared there, the Germans should have concluded that Patton was headed elsewhere, probably to Normandy. They did not.[21]

By then von Rundstedt no longer commanded the armies to Montgomery's front. In late June, with the Cotentin taken, von Rundstedt told his superiors that any counterattack on the British sector was bound to fail. "What should we do?" asked OKW's Keitel. Replied von Rundstedt: "Make peace, you fools, what else can you do?" On July 1, von Rundstedt was forced into an early retirement. His replacement, Field Marshal Hans Günther von Kluge, a hero of the Russian battles and a born fighter, arrived on the scene full of fire in his belly. He castigated Rommel for his lack of initiative, and announced his intention to attack. But after his first visit to the front, he realized how desperate the situation really was. Von Kluge also carried a secret. For almost two years, a group of anti-Hitler conspirators had sought his support in a plot to kill the Führer. It was their understanding that von Kluge had agreed to join the plot, but only after

Hitler was dead. Rommel, too, was aware of the plot. Not reporting that information to authorities was no less treasonous than joining the plot.[22]

The Red Army, in the six weeks between June 22 and the last week of July, smashed more than two hundred miles west—in the center to the east bank of the Vistula and the outskirts of Warsaw, in the north to the borders of East Prussia, and in the south to northern Bukovina and the Hungarian frontier. Operation Bagration occupies little space in the collective memory of the West, where Normandy, the Ardennes Bulge, and Dunkirk have assumed sacred status, yet Bagration, more than any other action that year, served to put Germany down on one knee. Churchill did not even name the battle in the final volume of his war history, where he wrote with stupendous understatement, "The Russian summer offensive brought their armies in late July to the river Vistula." Yet, Churchill was one with many in the West in his inability or unwillingness to grant Bagration its due. During those late June and July weeks when the Red Army swept through an area about the size of Great Britain (north to south and east to west), the Anglo-Americans were still fighting the Battle of the Beachhead on a front only a few miles deep and eighty miles wide, in a swath of Normandy about the size of Cape Cod.[23]

On July 20, Churchill visited Cherbourg and Utah Beach before moving on to visit Montgomery's positions over the next two days. He had notified Montgomery that he'd be coming, which led Monty to ask Eisenhower to keep visitors away at all costs. Montgomery's planned breakout, code-named Cobra—a sweep to the Brittany ports and an envelopment of the Germans at Bradley's front—was set to start within days.

Churchill's reaction to Montgomery's query to Ike was to summon Brooke and fly into "an unholy rage" over Monty's insubordination. "And who is Your Monty that he thinks he can dictate to me? Who does he think he is, trying to stop the Prime Minister from visiting?" It was now D + 44, and the Allied armies were not that much farther away from the beaches than they had been on his first visit of June 12. Churchill, fed up, told Eisenhower that he would support him in any decision having to do with relieving British generals who did not live up to Ike's expectations. Although Eisenhower, too, was losing patience with Monty, he had no intention of relieving Britain's revered hero of Alamein. Still, on July 20, Eisenhower's naval aide, Commander Butcher, told his diary that Ike was "blue as indigo over Monty's slowdown." The problem, as Eisenhower saw it, was that Montgomery's stated strategy of letting Rommel punch himself out against the British and Canadians depended upon Rommel's following the script. He wasn't doing that. "Rommel knew that play by heart," Butcher wrote. He simply kept his panzers out of range of Montgomery's artillery. Butcher did not know that Rommel was no longer in Normandy; he had been injured when an Allied fighter strafed his car on July 17, and he was on his way to a hospital in Germany. In any event, another week of foul weather delayed Montgomery's Operation Cobra. Still, though Eisenhower was not about to relieve Monty, he was so fed up with the general that he asked Churchill "to persuade Monty to get on his bicycle and start moving."[24]

As Churchill toured the American lines on July 20, at Hitler's East Prussian *Wolfsschanze,* Colonel Claus von Stauffenberg, who had lost his left eye, right hand, and two fingers on his left hand during an RAF attack in North Africa, was readying himself to report to the Führer on the state of Germany's homeland defenses. Von Stauffenberg was at the center of a small but dedicated ring of conspirators who believed Germany's only hope of avoiding obliteration lay in the killing of Hitler. Rommel and von Kluge, who had taken over the injured Rommel's command, had agreed to back the mutineers if their plot succeeded.

Von Stauffenberg carried a briefcase, which contained two bombs, into Hitler's East Prussian headquarters. Each had to be armed. When Stauffenberg stepped into a restroom to do so, his damaged hands confounded him. He had armed only one by the time he was called into the conference room. Shortly thereafter he excused himself and left the building. When the subsequent explosion tore through the hut, Stauffenberg, convinced that no one in the room could survive, ordered his driver to take him to a nearby airfield, where he boarded a small plane for Berlin. His assessment of the damage was wrong. Although four people were killed and almost all the survivors were injured, Hitler, shielded from the blast by the heavy, solid-oak conference table, emerged only slightly wounded, his composure and clothes in tatters. Upon his return to Berlin, Stauffenberg urged his co-conspirators to begin the second phase of the coup, the takeover of Nazi offices and radio stations. But after Hitler personally spoke on the state radio, the conspirators realized the coup had failed. They were tracked to their Bendlerstrasse offices and arrested after a brief shoot-out. Stauffenberg was taken outside and shot. Churchill later told the Commons, "When Herr Hitler escaped his bomb on July 20th he described his survival as providential; I think that from a purely military point of view we can all agree with him, for certainly it would be most unfortunate if the Allies were to be deprived, in the closing phases of the struggle, of that form of warlike genius by which Corporal Schicklgruber has so notably contributed to our victory."[25]

Hitler believed Rommel and von Kluge were both involved in the plot, and rather than face the hideous torture Hitler was unleashing on suspects, Kluge bit down on a cyanide capsule on August 18. Rommel, told by Berlin that he could chose between a trial for high treason or suicide, did likewise on October 14.[26]

By July, the stasis in the west and the Soviet advance in the east served to highlight the need for the Big Three to convene. "When are we going to meet, and where?" Churchill cabled Roosevelt on July 16. A week later, when the Red Army took Lublin, Stalin established a Polish Committee of National Liberation there, in effect a puppet government. That made the need to meet critical. Churchill suggested Scotland to Roosevelt and Stalin, but as usual Stalin would not leave Russia, and Roosevelt was not about to travel to Britain during the American election season. He had just been nominated for a fourth term and had eased out Henry Wallace—seen by Democrat party regulars as too pro-Soviet—as vice president and put Missouri senator Harry S. Truman on the ticket. In reply to Churchill, Roosevelt suggested they meet in Bermuda or Quebec. Churchill, as usual, would have to go to Roosevelt. With the Red Army closing on Warsaw—it reached the eastern outskirts days later—Churchill insisted that Stanisław Mikołajczyk, the head of the London Poles, make straightaway for Moscow in order to take part in the formation of a Polish government. Otherwise, the London Poles might find themselves the odd men out when Stalin liberated Warsaw. Seeking a "fusion of some kind" between the Poles backed by Moscow and those backed by America and Britain, Churchill asked the president to send Mikołajczyk and Stalin a message stating his strong support for Mikołajczyk.[27]

Roosevelt's letters to the two, wherein he simply told them he hoped they "could work out the whole matter" between themselves, amounted to the mildest of endorsements of the London Poles, and a signal to Stalin and Mikołajczyk that the United States was not as keen as Britain regarding the fate of Poland.

At the end of July, on orders from the London Poles, 40,000 lightly armed members of the Polish resistance in Warsaw commanded by General Bór Komorowski rose up against their German jailers. The Red Army stood off across the Vistula while for almost six weeks a battle reminiscent of Stalingrad raged in the Polish capital. Komorowski asked Eisenhower to bomb airfields near Warsaw; he declined, explaining honestly that Warsaw was not in his theater. Churchill asked Stalin to send in his troops, but the marshal considered the uprising to be an "adventure" by "a group of criminals" intent on seizing power. Churchill found the Soviet behavior "strange and sinister" but could do nothing to change Stalin's mind. The Soviet refusal to allow Allied planes to land behind Red Army lines after parachuting supplies into the city killed any chance of serious relief. Warsaw was beyond the range of Allied aircraft based in Britain (which would have to overfly the entire Reich in any event) but not beyond the range of Italian-based aircraft. RAF and Polish air force pilots flew almost two hundred relief missions, a round-trip jaunt of 1,400 miles. Stalin held airfields just fifty miles from Warsaw. Roosevelt refused to send American aircraft on any relief missions. Unbeknownst to Churchill, the Americans were negotiating with Stalin for use of Siberian airfields and did not want to upset that applecart by asking to use his Polish fields as well. Stalin changed his mind six weeks later, but by then it was too late. Half the resistance fighters had been killed, and more than two hundred thousand civilians murdered. In early October, after sixty-three days of fighting, Komorowski surrendered his remaining forces to the Germans. The Red Army would not relieve Warsaw until January 1945. "Such was their liberation of Poland...," Churchill later wrote.[28]

Another piece of intelligence found its way out of Poland that July. On July 7, Dr. Chaim Weizmann and the Jewish Agency for Palestine brought the atrocities taking place at Auschwitz to Churchill's attention. Although Weizmann offered no specifics, especially as to the numbers of murders there, Churchill demanded action. The RAF's Portal replied that only pinpoint daylight raids could hit the railroads leading into Auschwitz. That meant the Americans would have to act, because the RAF flew only night missions, which by any measure would likely prove more dangerous to the prisoners at the camp than to the railroad leading to it. Yet for American heavy bombers to reach Auschwitz from Italy or Britain they would have to fly over the heart of the Reich, by day and without fighter support. No raids were undertaken. Three years later, during a debate on setting up a Jewish state in Palestine, Churchill told the House: "I must say that I had no idea, when the war came to an end, of the horrible massacres which had occurred; the millions and millions that have been slaughtered. That dawned on us gradually after the struggle was over." The word "Auschwitz" does not appear in the Churchill-Roosevelt correspondence.[29]

In mid-June Roosevelt, through Eden, had let it be known to de Gaulle that if the Frenchman found himself in Washington in early July, the president would meet him. This was as much of an invitation as de Gaulle would get. He arrived on July 6 on board Roosevelt's personal Skymaster (a four-engine C-54 configured for civilian use), which the president had put at his service. De Gaulle was greeted with a seventeen-gun salute instead of a twenty-one-gun salute, a simple and concise way of telling him that his was not a state visit. When the two leaders met, Roosevelt outlined his four-power plan and indicated that America might station forces around the globe, including in France, in order to safeguard the locals, because other than the Big Four, the rest of the world's nations, including France, would be grouped on a lower tier. De Gaulle came away shocked, he later wrote, that the president—"this artist, this seducer"—by "considering Western Europe as a secondary matter risked endangering the Western World" and civilization itself. "It is the West," de Gaulle told the president, "that must be restored." If the West declined, de Gaulle argued, "barbarism will ultimately sweep everything away." France "above all" must be restored along with its "political vigor" and "self-reliance." Roosevelt claimed he was "open to these considerations," as he felt "a genuine affection for France." The talks ended with de Gaulle concluding that Roosevelt's "idealism...cloaks a will to power." As a parting gift, Roosevelt gave the general a framed photo of himself, signed: "To General de Gaulle, who is my friend."[30]

Meanwhile, in Charlottesville, Virginia, scores of Americans were attending an intensive sixty-day French-language program in preparation for journeying to France to administer civil matters there until Germany was defeated. De Gaulle pledged to not countenance these sixty-day wonders, and in fact did not. Soon after leaving Washington, de Gaulle learned of a letter Roosevelt had written to New York congressman Joseph Clark Baldwin, in which Roosevelt described de Gaulle as "tractable" in regard to future problems, adding, "I suspect he is essentially an egoist." In his memoirs, de Gaulle wrote, "I was never to know if Franklin Roosevelt thought in affairs concerning France whether Charles de Gaulle was an egoist for France or for himself."[31]

In fact, like Churchill, he was an egoist both for his nation and for the West. As disparate as their personalities were and as much as de Gaulle grated on Churchill, they shared the belief that postwar Europe must not be left defenseless and must not depend entirely on the Americans for security. On July 13, de Gaulle, back in Algiers, learned that the American government had issued a statement in which it declared the French Committee of National Liberation "qualified" to oversee the civil administration of France. But "qualified" does not equate with recognition. Two weeks later, de Gaulle, Roosevelt, and Churchill reached agreement on a statement that "only" the provisional government of France could exercise governing authority and issue currency. This statement, too, did not equate with recognition of the FCNL as the provisional government, but it edged closer. Seven French divisions now made ready to land in Marseilles. Leclerc's 2nd Armored Division landed in Normandy on August 1. De Gaulle later wrote, "We returned to France bearing independence, Empire, and a sword." The sword was short, de Gaulle wrote, but it was a sword.[32]

The stasis on the Western Front finally ended on July 25 when, with Montgomery holding the eastern flank, the American First Army, now part of Omar Bradley's Twelfth Army Group, wheeled from its positions around St-Lô. Eisenhower later wrote, "The line we actually held when the breakout began on D + 50 was approximately that planned for D + 5." Five days later, when George Patton and the Third Army poured through the lines, the Germans no longer had need to ponder Patton's whereabouts. The stalemate had actually worked to Allied advantage. Rather than push slowly into France for the previous seven weeks, with the likelihood of horrific casualties and the possibility of decisive German counterattacks on their overextended flanks, the Allies built up their forces almost at leisure until the day arrived—and now it had—when those forces could be unleashed with an awesome fury. Patton's 4th Armored Division entered Avranches on July 29; within the week, Patton was outrunning his communications on his drive toward Le Mans. Von Kluge (not yet unmasked as being sympathetic toward the plot against Hitler) sent off messages to Berlin, decrypted by Bletchley: The front had been "ripped open" and indeed had "collapsed." Churchill was highly enthused; the stalemate he feared, and that had indeed developed, had broken. His enthusiasm was contagious. Ike's naval aide, Harry Butcher, told his diary that Churchill had infected Eisenhower with his optimism. Ike now believed the war would end in 1944. His intelligence chief, Major General K. W. D. Strong, told Butcher that he "thought the war would be over in three months." Butcher told his diary, "I expect we will be home for Christmas."[33]

The breakout should have spelled the absolute end of any further debate over where to go next. Operation Dragoon (formerly Anvil), the south of France gambit, was on for August 15. But Churchill did not go quietly. On August 4, as Brittany was tumbling into Allied hands, he cabled Roosevelt with the suggestion to put troops into the Brittany ports. The next day, during a long lunch with Eisenhower at the supreme commander's forward headquarters at Sharpener Camp near Portsmouth, Churchill pleaded his case—"using phrases that only he can use," Butcher wrote—to shift Anvil/Dragoon to the Brittany ports, in order that Alexander's Italian campaign not be hobbled. "Ike said no," Butcher wrote, "continued saying no all afternoon, and ended up saying no in every form of the English language at his command." At one point Churchill threatened to "lay down the mantle of my high office" if Eisenhower did not come around. Ike said no, again. Butcher found Eisenhower "limp" after the parley and quite sure Churchill would raise the matter again in a few days "and simply regard the issue as unsettled." But it was settled. Two days later, Churchill—with the support of the British Chiefs—went over Eisenhower's head as he had in late June and sent cables off to Hopkins and Roosevelt. Their responses were predictable. Hopkins ventured that the Boss would respond in the negative. He did, telling Churchill that resources for Dragoon could not be diverted for operations in Brittany. On August 8, Churchill replied to Roosevelt, "I pray God that you may be right. We shall, of course, do everything in our power to achieve success."[34]

Earlier that week, Churchill had delivered a long address to the House in which he declared that the future peace in Europe would be guaranteed by four great powers, Britain, Russia, the United States, and France. Churchill's France, unlike Roosevelt's France, would reclaim its glory (and its colonies). "It is one of the main interests of Great Britain that a friendly France shall again be raised," Churchill told the House, "and raise herself, to her rightful place among the great Powers of Europe and of the world." And he acknowledged the leader of that resurgent France: "In these last four years I had many differences with General de Gaulle, but I have never forgotten, and can never forget, that he stood forth as the first eminent Frenchman to face the common foe in what seemed to be the hour of ruin of his country, and possibly, of ours." Duff Cooper, in Algiers, thought the speech marvelous. And with Churchill due to stop in Algiers on the tenth en route to Naples, Cooper believed "an excellent opportunity" was at hand for de Gaulle and Churchill "to make up their quarrel." De Gaulle did not share that belief, and he refused to meet Churchill. He gave no reason, Cooper later wrote. It was simply another example of de Gaulle's "superb intransigence." Churchill, in a letter to Clementine, described de Gaulle's behavior as "insolent."[35]

Denied the chance to meet with de Gaulle, Churchill spent his time in Algiers talking politics with Randolph, who was recuperating at the Duff Coopers' from back and knee injuries he suffered when his aircraft crash-landed in Yugoslavia, killing nine of nineteen on board. Evelyn Waugh had been aboard, and he came away severely burned. Of Randolph, Churchill wrote to Clementine: "He is a lonely figure by no means recovered as far as walking is concerned." He was also a notoriously difficult houseguest, known to fancy the women and the contents of the liquor cabinet, but most of all the telephone, which he'd use for hours at a time to place calls throughout the world, recalled *Country Life* travel writer Graham Norton, who moved in those circles. "And as the phone was infinitely more expensive than liquor they [hostesses] used to say 'unlock your liquor cabinet and disconnect your telephone.'" Norton was using the telephone at Chartwell when he first met Randolph, who strode up to him and uttered the first words Norton heard from the scion of the Churchill family: "Give me my fucking phone." Yet, despite his arrogance, noted by all, Randolph's political instincts were sound. He advised his father to bear with de Gaulle, as he was a man without a country, while Churchill had the Empire behind him.

Family matters were not discussed during the brief stay; to do so was to invite a scene. Randolph's marriage to Pamela was in ruins, and all of London knew it. Harold Nicolson, in a letter to his sons, wrote, "Randolph's marriage is going wonky and Winston is terribly distressed. The old boy is tremendously domestic and adores his family."[36]

For four years the Mediterranean had occupied the center of Churchill's strategic military vision, and rightly so, Harold Macmillan and Jan Smuts believed. Now it occupied the center of his political vision. From Brooke's standpoint, Churchill's vision, both military and political, had often not been acute; now it was failing utterly. "Life has a quiet and peaceful atmosphere about it now that Winston is gone [to Italy]!" he told his diary that week. "Everything gets done twice as quickly." He added: "I feel we have now reached the stage that for the good of the nation and the good of his own reputation it would be a godsend if he [Churchill] could disappear out of public life. He has probably done more for this country than any other human being has ever done," yet "I am filled with apprehension about where he may lead us next." Churchill was tired, and knew it. A few weeks earlier he had told Clementine and Harold Macmillan, "I am an old and weary man. I feel exhausted." Clementine countered with, "But think what Hitler and Mussolini feel like!" Winston replied, "Ah, but at least Mussolini has had the satisfaction of murdering his son-in-law." Macmillan noted that the repartee followed by a short stroll seemed to revive Churchill.[37]

The trip to Italy revived him even more. After arriving in Naples on August 11, Churchill spent the next seventeen days organizing the eastern Mediterranean to his satisfaction. After two days of talks with Tito and Dr. Ivan Šubašić, the Ban of Croatia, he was rewarded with only a vague promise from Tito—who was using half the ammunition supplied by Britain to fight Serbs—to strive for a democratic government following the war. To Clementine, Churchill wrote: "It may well be the case of Tito first, the Ban second, and the king nowhere." Still, Tito was one with Churchill on the need to kill Huns. Churchill was pursuing two strategic goals, one wartime and short-term, the other postwar and long-term. He sought compliant, friendly neutrals in the region postwar, in order that the Mediterranean remain a British lake. Yet to reach that goal he had to arm the very antimonarchist and sometimes pro-Communist partisans who wanted no part of being British stooges in peace. The fires of nationalism—which had torn apart Austria-Hungary—were again burning throughout the region. In Tito's case, the saving grace (for Churchill) was his unwillingness to live under any thumb, be it Moscow's or London's. A well-armed neutral was almost as good as an ally. Greece presented a similar set of problems. Ultra decrypts verified a German withdrawal, which could leave Athens in the hands of the ELAS Communists, and that would surely result in civil war, an outcome that Churchill could not abide. In a cable to Roosevelt, he proposed sending ten thousand British troops to Greece to maintain order until elections took place, and he asked for American logistical support to carry it off. Roosevelt approved.[38]

The readmission of Italy to the regional community of nations also came in for Churchill's scrutiny. He wanted the process to be gradual, and controlled from Washington and London, for the Italians had committed vile deeds. Yet he wanted the process to continue. "He was like a dog on a bone" over the matter, Harold Macmillan told his diary, adding, after listening to a long dissertation on Italy by Churchill, "Winston gave a really remarkable demonstration of his powers." Over dinner with Macmillan he advised, "We should be guided by the precept of Machiavelli that, if one has benefits to confer, they should not be conferred all at once."[39]

It was a working holiday. He took four dips in the sea, including one at the Blue Grotto, and thoroughly enjoyed several outings with Alexander during which he fired a howitzer (missing the target), toured the Cassino battlefields, and witnessed a firefight between German and Allied forces from just five hundred yards away. The firing was "desultory and intermittent," he later wrote, "but this was the nearest I got to the enemy . . . and heard the most bullets in World War Two." He could not let go of his Viennese ambitions, telling dinner guests one evening that the full-scale assault on the Gothic Line that Alexander planned to launch on August 26 might result in a breakthrough that would allow the Allies to "swing to the right, overcome Austria, and so change history." When days earlier Roosevelt informed him that a conference was on for September in Quebec, Churchill had replied that he sought to put the Adriatic amphibious operation on the agenda. It was not to be. The Balkans and Eastern Europe held no promise—other than the promise of trouble—for Roosevelt and America.[40]

Years later, Malcolm Muggeridge, veteran of MI6, editor of *Punch,* and a frequent and sometimes vicious critic of Churchill, sided with the Old Man on the Aegean/Vienna strategy. "If he [Churchill] had had Roosevelt's support that could have altered the whole war." After the collapse of Italy, "there was nothing to stop them [an Allied thrust north], absolutely nothing.... All those populations [in Austria, Romania, Hungary, Bulgaria] wanted someone to come in there before the Russians came. They didn't give a damn as long as it wasn't the Russians." But it was the Russians, and they were coming.[41]

On August 15, Churchill watched the Dragoon landings from the deck of the Royal Navy destroyer *Kimberly.* Three American divisions went ashore in St. Tropez Bay, near Marseilles, and seven French divisions soon followed. Days earlier, during a short boat trip across Naples Bay, Churchill waved to American soldiers on board their landing ships and sailing for France. He later wrote, "They did not know that if I had had my way they would be sailing in a different direction." The glittering prize of Austria was all but lost. Still, Churchill told Alexander that even if the war came to an early end, he should make "ready for a dash with armoured cars" to Vienna.[42]

In France the breakout phase was over; the pursuit phase had begun. Patton's Third Army took Orleans on August 17. On August 23, the resistance in Paris staged a general uprising. On the twenty-fifth, after two days of gun battles in the streets, the Germans withdrew, a maneuver that spared Paris. Leclerc and his 2nd Armored Division liberated the City of Light that day, while de Gaulle, with a thespian's timing, arrived that afternoon at the Ministry of War. Inspecting the premises, he found nothing missing after four years of occupation "except the state. It was my duty to restore it: I installed my staff at once and got down to work."[43]

By the time Churchill returned to London on August 29, Montgomery had pushed the Germans back across the Belgian border and captured almost all of the V-1 launch sites. On August 31, Patton's spearheads crossed the Meuse River at Verdun. Three days later, elements of the American First Army captured Namur, one hundred miles to the north. During the last week of August, Hitler ordered 20,000 slave laborers to reinforce the *Westwall,* which the Allies referred to by its Great War name, the Siegfried Line, consisting of four hundred miles of bunkers and anti-tank ditches that faced the old Maginot Line and ran along the Belgian and Dutch borders all the way to the Rhine.

In early September, the American First Army probed the Siegfried Line in the Eifel, the low range of mountains that spread from east Belgium into western Germany. Patton, by then, had pushed on another thirty-five miles to the Moselle, just thirty miles from the German frontier and the great industrial area of the Saar, and just one hundred miles from the Rhine. But so rapid had been his charge that Patton's main forces had run out of gasoline. His six strong divisions faced five weak German divisions, but he could not take the fight to them. Meanwhile, the British freed Brussels on September 3 and Antwerp the next day (but not the Scheldt Estuary, the gateway to the port), also less than one hundred miles from the Rhine, and the Ruhr, the heart of German industry. On this flank the British faced a gap almost one hundred miles wide; no Germans were available to fill it. "Rarely in any war," Liddell Hart later wrote, "has there been such an opportunity." To Montgomery, promoted to field marshal on September 1, Churchill cabled: "How wonderful it is to see our people leaping out at last after all their hard struggles." On that day, Eisenhower took over direct command of the battle from Monty. Eisenhower's decision to assume the dual role of supreme commander of air, sea, ground, and air forces "is likely," Brooke wrote, "to add 3 to 6 months on to the war!"[44]

In the east, the Red Army remained halted outside Warsaw but had driven into Finland. There Marshal Mannerheim, who had replaced Risto Ryti as president in mid-August, was negotiating a peace treaty with Moscow, which was signed on September 19. In the south, the Red Army had smashed into Romania, where, after King Michael ousted Antonescu in a coup on August 23, the Romanians quit the Axis. At a stroke Hitler had lost—and Stalin gained—twenty Romanian divisions in front of the Red Army, and thirty more in Romania. When the front collapsed, the roads opened to Bulgaria and Yugoslavia, and Hungary beyond.

Bulgaria was next. The economy was in ruins; food prices had risen 700 percent since 1939. Consumer goods were nonexistent. Berlin had forced Bulgaria, an unenthusiastic partner from the start, to convert its industry to armaments production. But the Bulgarians had served Hitler well by embracing their role in the occupation of Yugoslavia and Greece, where they were known to take pleasure in torturing captured partisans. A story made the rounds that they had tied prisoners to the open tops of corrugated barrels and lit fires under them. To the House, Churchill condemned the Bulgarians and the "wickedness for which they have been responsible both in Greece and Yugoslavia. They have suffered nothing themselves. No foot has been set upon their soil.... The conduct of their troops in harrying and trying to hold down, at Hitler's orders, their two sorely pressed small neighbours, Greece and Yugoslavia, is a shameful page for which full atonement must be exacted." Since April, Moscow had been pressuring the Bulgarians to quit the Axis, but they could not as long as Hitler's armies were closer at hand than the Red Army. On September 8, with the Red Army almost at the border, Bulgaria's new prime minister, Konstantin Muraviev, declared for the

Allies. The Red Army crossed the border the next day and within a week had rolled across the country, putting Stalin's armies just two hundred miles from the Adriatic. By late September, Stalin's bulwark against any future threat from the West was taking shape. Churchill was likewise trying to build his bulwark against Russia on the northern Mediterranean littoral. And Hitler, but for his fanatical Austrian Nazis, was now virtually alone.[45]

On the homeward-bound flight from Naples to Britain, Churchill spiked a temperature of 103 degrees. A large party that included Clementine, Jock Colville, and the Chiefs of Staff awaited his arrival at Northolt airfield. But upon landing, Moran bundled up his charge and rushed him from the aircraft to a waiting car, which sped off to London. The Old Man's temperature hit 104. An X-ray revealed a spot on his lungs; his pneumonia had returned for a third time. Again Moran paraded out the M&B doses and again Churchill took to his sickbed, this time at the Annexe. His recovery was swift; by September 1 his temperature was normal; Colville noted he had cleaned up his box and was "in tearing form." On September 4, Churchill, infuriated by Stalin's treatment of the Warsaw partisans, sent Roosevelt a copy of a telegram that had gone off to Stalin in which Churchill noted the slaughter in Warsaw (the Germans were now murdering doctors, nurses, and patients in the city's hospital), adding that if the Warsaw Poles were overwhelmed, and it appeared they would be, "the shock to public opinion here will be incalculable." When Stalin made no reply, Churchill proposed cutting off convoys to Russia but was persuaded by Eden that to do so would only further hurt the Poles. Stalin's armies were legitimately in need of refit and resupply; to cease the convoys would only delay that effort. Days earlier Moran had told his diary, "Winston never talks of Hitler these days; he is always harping on the dangers of communism. He dreams of the Red Army spreading like a cancer from one country to another. It has become an obsession, and he seems to think of nothing else." Churchill intended to address those concerns, and more, with Roosevelt at the upcoming conference in Quebec.[46]

The skies over Britain had been empty of V-1 flying bombs for four days by the time Churchill boarded the *Queen Mary* at Greenock on September 5, bound for Quebec. Of slightly more than 10,000 V-1s launched toward Britain, 7,488 had crossed the Channel. Of those, more than 3,900 were shot down; 2,419 reached Greater London, killing more than 6,000 and injuring more than 18,000. On September 7, Duncan Sandys told reporters, "Except for a last few shots, the Battle of London is over."

Sandys's pronouncement was about as wrong as wrong can be. Early the next evening, the first two V-2 rockets fell in Greater London. They measured forty-six feet high, weighed fourteen tons at launch, and flew at more than 3,600 miles an hour, propelled by liquid oxygen and a three-to-one alcohol-to-water mixture. Launched from near The Hague, they covered the two hundred miles to London in just under five minutes. Outrunning their own concussive sound, they descended in silence at almost two thousand miles per hour; their roar, like a freight train overhead, arrived only after they detonated. Their 2,200-pound warhead could eradicate a city block. HMG, not wanting to tell the Germans if their targeting was effective, did not announce the assaults and instead told Britons that gas mains had exploded, a story HMG held to for weeks, even as Britons put two and two together when "gas mains" began erupting at the rate of five a day.[47]

By September 8, Churchill and the *Queen Mary,* with four thousand passengers on board, including wounded American soldiers, were more than halfway across the Atlantic. Clementine and Sarah made the trip, as did Jock Colville, Lord Moran, favored science adviser Lord Cherwell, and a vast number of British military representatives. The *Queen* took a southerly route in order to avoid any lurking U-boats, and thus the passengers found themselves sweltering in the Gulf Stream as temperatures reached eighty degrees, which to an Englishman is a heat wave. Churchill, still under the weather as result of his large doses of M&B, passed the time playing bezique and reading *Phineas Finn* and *The Duke's Children.* He did not prepare for the upcoming conference, to Brooke's chagrin. At meals he waxed pessimistic on the postwar world. He would miss none of his Labour colleagues except Bevin—"mediocrities," he called them—if they bolted the coalition. And if he was voted out of office: "What is good enough for the English people is good enough for me." Dark days were ahead, he pronounced over dinner one evening. Peace would find consumer goods in short supply, Britain in dire financial straits. All he wanted to do was get the soldiers home and see to it that they had houses. And, he said, "The idea that you can vote yourself into prosperity is one of the most ludicrous that was ever entertained."[48]

The menu at one dinner included oysters, roast turkey, ice cream, cantaloupe, and Stilton cheese, "all washed down by a remarkable Liebfraumilch, followed by 1870 brandy; all of which," Colville wrote, "made the conversation about the shortage of consumer goods a shade unreal." All noted Churchill's lethargy as the *Queen* drove west. Brooke: "He [Churchill] looked old, unwell, and depressed. Evidently he found it hard to concentrate and kept holding his head between his hands." Lord Moran told Colville he did not give Churchill a long life, and, Colville wrote, "he thinks when he goes it will either be a stroke or the heart trouble" that had first showed itself in the White House in 1941 and then again at Carthage in 1943. "May he at least live to see victory," Colville told his diary, adding, "Perhaps it would be well that he should escape the aftermath."[49]

The Château Frontenac and the Citadel were again taken over by Anglo-American luminaries, both military and civilian. The setting was familiar, but the business at hand was new. The Quebec conference (code-named Octagon) was more about managing the peace than winning the war—how best to keep Germany down once it was defeated, and how best to coordinate Allied forces in the Pacific. It had been nine months since Churchill had said his good-byes to Roosevelt in Cairo, their longest separation since sailing into Placentia Bay three years before. European military strategy was not on the agenda. The European Front was effectively in the hands of Eisenhower, who, although having made clear that he intended to pursue a broad-front strategy, was willing to exploit any German weaknesses, including the apparent gap to Montgomery's immediate front. Churchill, still fixed on the Adriatic, declared to the Chiefs of Staff that "we are coming to Quebec solely to obtain landing ships out of the Americans" to land in Istria and seize Trieste. In the Pacific, the chiefs argued, Britain had to display solidarity with the United States by contributing large Royal Navy forces to the American push in the central Pacific. Churchill disagreed and stuck to his Sumatra and Singapore strategy. All of this led Brooke to tell his diary: "I am feeling *very, very,* depressed at the thought of this meeting, unless Winston changes radically we shall be in hopeless situation."[50]

Brooke's worries did not materialize. Churchill, not wanting to be seen as shirking his duties in the Pacific, agreed to a British naval presence in the central Pacific, where Admiral Nimitz's fleets—and soldiers and Marines—were driving north, with Okinawa their penultimate destination, the Japanese homeland their final objective. MacArthur, meanwhile, was driving toward his objective, the Philippines. Nimitz and Admiral King wanted no part of any plan that included the Royal Navy; in fact, the Americans, so mightily re-armed, believed they had no need of the Royal Navy in order to defeat Japan. As always, they suspected Churchill was only after reclaiming lost British colonies. Churchill did nothing to help matters when he announced at one of the plenary sessions that Vienna and Singapore were the most important objectives in their respective theaters. By doing so, Brooke wrote, "he was not assisting with our discussions with the American Chiefs." Yet, despite Churchill's detours to Austria and Malaya, the military meetings went well, in part because the American Joint Chiefs, flush with victories in the Pacific and confident that the European war could end by Christmas, were in a conciliatory frame of mind.

The Americans agreed to seek no further reductions in Alexander's army. Indeed, Brooke told his diary, "The Americans have shown a wonderful spirit of cooperation." The optimism had spread to many in high office, but not Churchill, who told Colville that "it was even money the Germans would still be fighting at Christmas, and if they did collapse the reasons would be political rather than military."[51]

The Americans proved themselves amenable, as well, on the matter of zones of occupation in a vanquished Germany; they desired to occupy part of western Germany shoulder to shoulder with the British and sought only egress to Essen. Here, guided by Eden, Churchill introduced a new element by proposing that the French, too, be given a zone. This was a wily incremental stroke of the sort Roosevelt was master of. The Americans had yet to recognize de Gaulle's FCNL, which by then was the de facto government of France, if not de jure in the eyes of Roosevelt. By not rejecting outright a French role in postwar Germany, Roosevelt tacitly acknowledged de Gaulle's leadership, for if the time to carve the zones arrived within weeks, as many thought, who else but de Gaulle could accept such a proposal in the name of France? Roosevelt was not on his usual game. Churchill told Colville he feared the president was now "very frail."[52]

On the matter of how to punish postwar Germany, Churchill, who had long proposed an economically reinvigorated but disarmed Germany, displayed his growing subservience to Roosevelt and the Americans. In late July, the Red Army had liberated the Majdanek death camp on the outskirts of Lublin. Unlike the Treblinka and Sobibor camps, which the Germans had destroyed and plowed under before the Red Army arrived, Majdanek was abandoned with such haste that it was functional when the Soviets marched through the gates. Reports reached the West within weeks. A hut lined with asbestos was used to burn inmates alive. Four gas chambers were used to kill up to 250 prisoners at a time, with either carbon monoxide or Zyklon B pellets, which produced cyanide gas when exposed to air. Bodies were carted to a nearby crematorium, where the remains were rendered into ashes; the ashes, in turn, were used to fertilize the cabbage crop. A warehouse contained tens of thousands of shoes. A local woman told a visiting American journalist that when the camp was in operation, loudspeakers continually played Strauss waltzes. " 'The Beautiful Blue Danube,' " she said, "can never be beautiful to us again." Another woman repeated words the Americans had heard many times that day: "I hope you Americans will not be soft with the Germans."[53]

At a dinner on September 13 attended by Churchill, Roosevelt, Lord Moran, Lord Cherwell, and Admiral Leahy, Henry Morgenthau outlined his plan for Germany's future: plowing German industry under, destroying its shipyards and coal mines, and converting the country to a pasture.

Harry Hopkins was not at the table, nor was he even in Quebec, a source of worry for Churchill, who had always counted on Hopkins to explain and champion his thoughts to Roosevelt. Instead, here was Morgenthau, who had attended none of the previous conferences. When Morgenthau finished his presentation, Churchill objected. He was all for disarming Germany, he said, but not for making it a wasteland. "I agree with [Edmund] Burke," he said. "You cannot indict a whole nation." The English people, he warned, will not stand for the enslavement of their fellow working-class Germans. Morgenthau pointed out that destroying the Ruhr could only help British steel exports and Britain's balance of payments. As Stalin had at Tehran, Roosevelt offered that a German factory turning out steel furniture could be easily converted into an armaments plant. Churchill had no counterplan to offer, but he made clear he would not go along with Morgenthau. His reaction had been "instinctive revulsion," Moran noted, adding, "He hates cruelty." But within forty-eight hours Cherwell had brought Churchill around. (It was during these weeks that Churchill told Moran that "if the Ruhr were grassed over it would be good for our trade.") Roosevelt and Churchill signed off on the Morgenthau Plan on September 15.[54]

It was a stillborn concept. Stimson, Hopkins, and Hull thought the plan hideous, and told Roosevelt so. In early October, Hull told Roosevelt it would be inhuman to condemn Germans to starvation, and he read back to the president a transcript from a meeting where Roosevelt had endorsed the severest treatment of Germany: "Looking forward to converting Germany into a country primarily agricultural in character." Roosevelt did not recall the quote, but soon after his talk with Hull he scotched the Morgenthau Plan.

Both Churchill and Roosevelt had come to Quebec, as many of their companions had noted, tired and unfocused. The same could be said of the alliance. Robert Sherwood later wrote, "The Allies were well prepared for war to the death in Europe, but they were ill prepared for the cataclysm of sudden total victory." The meeting in Quebec had really been called in order that the British and Americans could reach agreement on an agenda for the next gathering of the Big Three, which Roosevelt soon proposed to Stalin. It appeared a meeting of the minds had taken place at Quebec, when in fact it had not. Poland—Stalin's first priority, and Churchill's—was not even discussed.[55]

When the conference ended on September 17, Churchill, his family, and a few aides journeyed by train to Hyde Park. There, with the pressures of plenary sessions out of the way, Churchill regained his strength, helped in

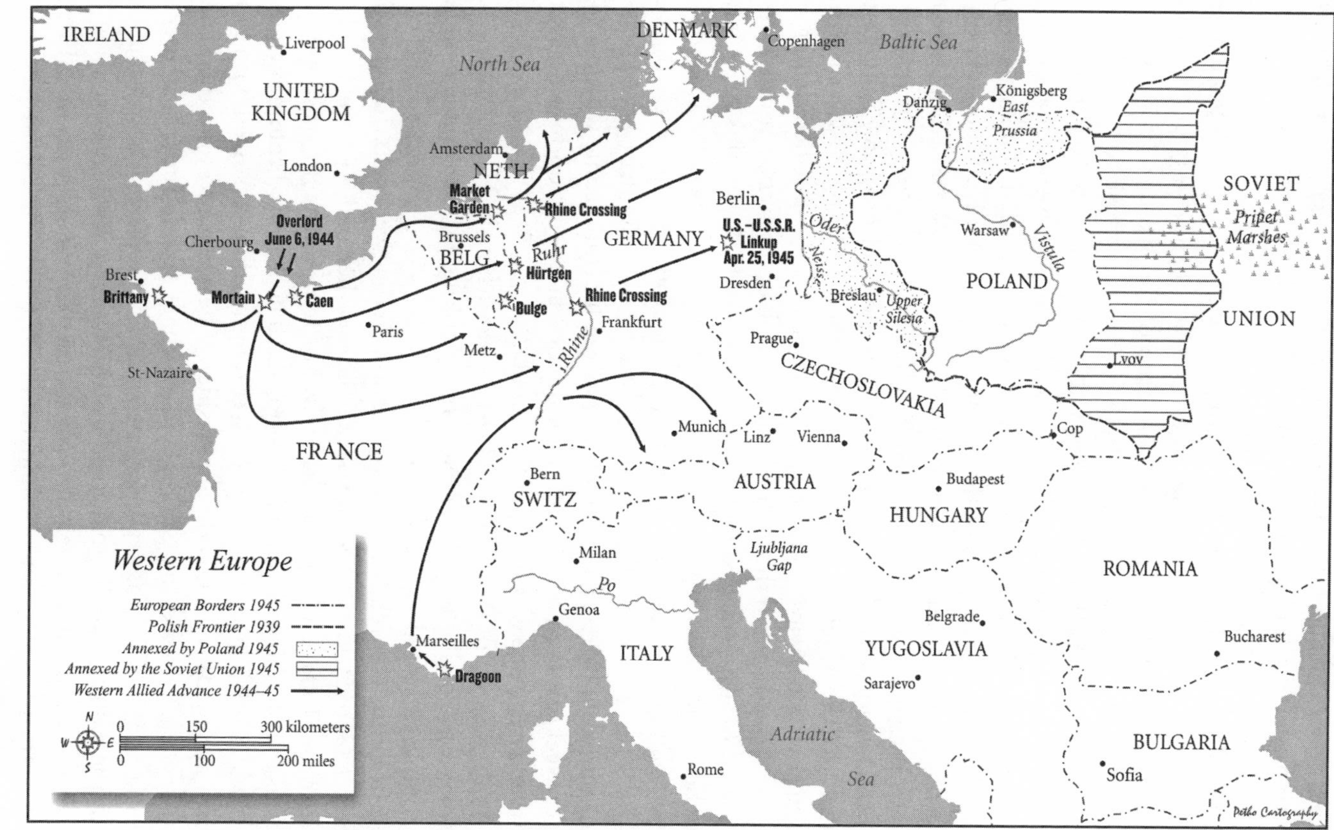
IRELAND
Liverpool
UNITED KINGDOM
London
North Sea
DENMARK
Copenhagen
Baltic Sea
Amsterdam
NETH
Market Garden
Rhine Crossing
Overlord June 6, 1944
Cherbourg
Brest
Brittany
Mortain
Caen
Brussels
BELG
Ruhr
Hürtgen
Bulge
Paris
Metz
St-Nazaire
Rhine Crossing
Frankfurt
Rhine
GERMANY
Berlin
U.S.–U.S.S.R. Linkup Apr. 25, 1945
Dresden
Oder
Neisse
Breslau
Upper Silesia
Danzig
Königsberg
East Prussia
Warsaw
Vistula
POLAND
Lvov
SOVIET UNION
Pripet Marshes
Prague
CZECHOSLOVAKIA
Cop
FRANCE
Munich
Linz
Vienna
AUSTRIA
Budapest
HUNGARY
Bern
SWITZ
Milan
Po
Genoa
Ljubljana Gap
ROMANIA
Bucharest
Belgrade
YUGOSLAVIA
Sarajevo
Marseilles
Dragoon
ITALY
Adriatic Sea
Rome
BULGARIA
Sofia
Western Europe
European Borders 1945
Polish Frontier 1939
Annexed by Poland 1945
Annexed by the Soviet Union 1945
Western Allied Advance 1944–45
N W E S
0 150 300 kilometers
0 100 200 miles
Pethö Cartography

part by a succession of picnics that Clementine described as "rather fun, really," high praise coming from her. Harry Hopkins was on hand, which greatly cheered Churchill, who believed Hopkins's absence in Quebec was due to his having fallen out with Roosevelt. In fact, Hopkins had been ill for most of the year.[56]

The news from Europe was startlingly good, although Colville noted, "From the American papers one would scarcely believe any British troops were fighting." *Time* that week ran a map of the Western Front with the caption "The Yanks are coming." In fact, after stabbing into a slice of German territory at Aachen, the Yanks had stopped to refit. To Patton's fury, his gasoline quota was cut to the bone so that Montgomery could be fueled and armed in order to launch Operation Market Garden. This was to be a strike by the paratroopers of the 1st British Airborne Division, supported by a Polish parachute brigade, on the north bank of the Rhine at Arnhem—the supposed gap at his front. The American 101st and 82nd Airborne Divisions would likewise drop into Holland near the Wilhelmina Canal and the Meuse River, respectively. Once the bridges over these and four other waterways were taken, the plan called for Allied armor and infantry to roar north through Holland to link up with the paratroopers at Arnhem. Monty intended to exploit the gap—which was closing, if it had ever been wide to start with—in front of the Ruhr. It was the British who were coming. Montgomery began his attack on September 17. By then, wrote Robert Sherwood, the highest authorities in the British and American command believed that "German surrender could come within a matter of weeks or even days." Churchill did not share that optimism, but the news from Europe was indisputably good.[57]

As the Churchill party boarded the *Queen Mary* in New York on September 20, Colville found the Old Man "looking far, far better—indeed as John Peck would say, 'in rude health.'"[58]

By the time Churchill arrived in London on the twenty-sixth, Operation Market Garden had failed, terribly. The weather had worsened and the skies over Holland precluded the arrival of reinforcements or supplies, as well as the bombing of German positions. Allied armored columns clogged the two-lane highway that ran north through Holland (sowed with minefields, and with wetlands on either side). The failure to take the Scheldt Estuary had allowed the Germans to evacuate 60,000 men from there to fill the gap Monty was trying to penetrate. The offensive failed utterly, with the result, Colville told his diary, "The First Airborne Division has been wiped out at Arnhem." Nobody on the Western Front—British, Canadian, or American—would be going home for Christmas. Three days later, Churchill cabled Roosevelt: "It seems pretty clear to me Germany is not going to be conquered this year."[59]

Churchill tried to put a good face on the Arnhem disaster when he addressed the House on September 28, but it could not be gilded, even by Churchill. "Full and deeply-moving accounts have already been given to the country and to the world of this glorious and fruitful operation, which will take a lasting place in our military annals, and will, in succeeding generations, inspire our youth with the highest ideals of duty and of daring. 'Not in vain' may be the pride of those who have survived and the epitaph of those who fell." As for the foolhardiness of Hitler's decisions that summer to give up no ground in France and in the east, Churchill offered, "I always hate to compare Napoleon with Hitler, as it seems an insult to the great Emperor and warrior to connect him in any way with a squalid caucus boss and butcher. But there is one respect in which I must draw a parallel. Both these men were temperamentally unable to give up the tiniest scrap of any territory to which the high watermark of their hectic fortunes had carried them."[60]

Since his July 20 visit to Normandy, Churchill had spent more time out of Britain than in. This was a source of worry to deputy prime minister Clement Attlee, who believed the P.M.'s absences were deleterious to getting business done on the home front, including putting into place a plan to rebuild the thousands of houses destroyed since 1940, and by the V-weapons that month. Attlee therefore would have reacted poorly had he known that on the night Churchill arrived back in London, he asked Ismay and Air Chief Marshal Portal to arrange a travel itinerary that would get him to Moscow as soon as possible. With Stalin's armies in Romania and Bulgaria, and poised to strike up the Danube for Belgrade and Budapest, events in and near the Balkans needed to be addressed. As well, with the Red Army standing idle as Warsaw burned, the issue of Polish freedom had to be addressed.

On September 29, Churchill informed Roosevelt of his travel plans, and his agenda in Moscow, which included summing up for Stalin decisions made in Quebec, discussions on the Balkans and Poland, and the Pacific Front. As Roosevelt had already told Churchill that he was about to propose to Stalin another meeting of the Big Three, Churchill framed his visit to Moscow only in terms of laying the groundwork for that meeting. He pledged to keep Roosevelt informed as the talks progressed, asking that Averell Harriman be allowed to sit in on the meetings in order that Stalin would conclude that he was in the presence of both of his allies, not simply his British ally.

Harry Hopkins saw danger—just a little over a month before the presidential election—in the possibility that Stalin and Churchill might make some sort of joint statement that would have the effect of relegating Roosevelt to the sidelines. Roosevelt, persuaded by Hopkins, sent off a message to Stalin in which he made clear that Churchill was not authorized to speak for the United States. Stalin saw that message, Harriman later wrote, as a sign that his allies lacked cohesion and will, especially regarding Poland. Harriman believed Roosevelt erred by not encouraging Churchill to stress the solidarity of America and Britain while pressing questions of Polish borders and the formation of a democratic Polish government. Consequently, Stalin sensed weakness. Before departing for Moscow, Churchill told Colville that he was making the trip in order "to discourage any idea that the U.K. and the U.S.A. are very close to (as exemplified by the Quebec conference) the exclusion of Russia." He intended to show Stalin that he was not being left "in the cold." Yet Roosevelt's message to Stalin had the effect of putting Churchill out in the cold. It allowed Stalin to conclude, Harriman believed, that any decisions he reached with Churchill were nonbinding.[61]

On October 3, Churchill and Clementine attended a performance of Shaw's *Arms and the Man;* the next night they attended a stage production of *Richard III*. It was an astute public relations gambit. As in 1940, Churchill's ventures out in public told Londoners that he was with them, that he, too, accepted the risks. Although Cherwell calculated that the odds were 648,000 to 1 against a rocket falling on Churchill on any given night, it was a time when only optimists bought green bananas.

Late on October 7, Churchill boarded his Avro York for the run to Moscow. Churchill's aircraft was comfortable, but the journey to Moscow was still long and dangerous; Moran, worried about Churchill's heart, wanted assurances that the plane would not fly higher than eight thousand feet. The Old Man tended to become ill on such pilgrimages. He was just eight weeks shy of turning seventy and was not the robust specimen he had been in 1940. The trip took thirty-six hours—twenty-three of them in the air—with stops in Naples and Cairo. Churchill arrived in Moscow on October 9. He was understandably tired; Stalin was not.[62]

Averell Harriman, writing years later, pointed out two errors that Churchill committed when recalling these Moscow days in his war memoirs. The first is insignificant: Churchill wrote that Stalin put him up in a Moscow house, when in fact he stayed in the country again, although a Moscow apartment was made available, and Churchill used it for one night during the next ten days. The second errant recollection was egregious: Churchill wrote that Harriman attended the first session of the talks (code-named Tolstoy). He did not. He thus could not have known (and in fact only learned in bits and pieces over the next three days) of the agreement reached by Stalin and Churchill, a carving up of Eastern Europe into spheres of influence of the very sort Hopkins feared and Roosevelt loathed.

Alone with Stalin, Churchill sketched their agreement on a half sheet of paper. In Romania the Russians would have 90 percent "predominance," while the British would exercise 90 percent influence in Greece. Yugoslavia and Hungary would be managed equally by Russia and Britain, and Bulgaria would be 75 percent Moscow, 25 percent Britain and America (which effectively meant Britain, since the United States wanted no part of any such arrangement, either there or in Greece). Stalin studied the paper briefly, and then with his blue pen checked his agreement. The deed done, Churchill asked Stalin, "Might it not be thought rather cynical if it seemed we have disposed of these issues, so fateful to millions of people, in such an offhand manner? Let us burn the paper?" Stalin replied, "No, you keep it." Before leaving for Moscow, Churchill had told Roosevelt he was glad Harriman would sit in on the meetings, but he had added, "You would not, I am sure, wish this to preclude private *tête-à-têtes* between me and U.J.... as it is often under such circumstance the best progress is made. You can rely on me to keep you constantly informed of everything that affects our joint interests." On October 11, Churchill brought Roosevelt up to speed on the talks, cabling "we have considered the best way of reaching an agreed policy about the Balkan countries." In fact, they had already reached a policy, although in Stalin's estimation, it, and anything else they agreed upon, was nonbinding.[63]

Churchill also told Roosevelt that the next phase of the talks was about to begin—a parley over the Curzon Line among Stalin, Churchill, the London Poles, represented by Stanisław Mikołajczyk (whom Churchill had summoned from London), and Bolesław Bierut, a Communist International veteran and head of the Lublin Poles. Harriman, who on the twelfth sat in as an observer at the first meeting between Churchill, Stalin, and the London Poles, realized within minutes that a serious miscommunication had taken place, the responsibility for which lay with Roosevelt. The president had personally assured Mikołajczyk in June that he had not endorsed the Curzon Line at the Tehran Conference. He had indeed not participated in discussions of the Polish eastern border, but apparently he had told Stalin and Molotov that he endorsed moving the western Polish frontier almost 150 miles west to the vicinity of the Oder, and did so in language that was just imprecise enough to be "warped in translation." To Stalin's ears, that implied a shift westward in Poland's eastern border as well, which is exactly what Churchill had proposed to Stalin over after-dinner drinks at Tehran. But with the American election now less than four weeks away, there was no chance that Roosevelt would clarify those remarks for public consumption.[64]

Churchill had for almost a year accepted the Curzon Line or something very close to it as the best demarcation of a new eastern border for Poland. Stalin demanded it, and Lvov as well. When Lord Curzon proposed the line as Poland's eastern border in 1919, he did so after taking into account the ethnicity of the region's citizens. Poles lived west of the line for the most part, Russians to the east.

With that logic in mind, Churchill set to work on Mikołajczyk for the next five days in order to bring him and the London Poles around. In doing so he deployed the same weapons he used in negotiating with his Chiefs of Staff. First he asked; then he pleaded; then he threatened, harangued, and demeaned. In Stalin's presence he told Mikołajczyk that this would be a poor time for HMG and the London Poles to split. The Old Man held out the prospect of Danzig and East Prussia going to Poland, parts of Silesia and its mineral riches as well, and a 125-mile-wide fertile swath of eastern Germany. Mikołajczyk said he could make no decision, that only the Polish nation could do so. Public opinion, he said, would not allow such a unilateral decision on his part, to which Churchill replied, "What is public opinion? The right to be crushed!" When the Lublin Poles joined the discussions on October 14, it became immediately clear that they were pawns of Moscow. They "seemed creepy" to Eden, who, nodding in the direction of Bierut and another, whispered to Churchill, "the rat and the weasel." Churchill cabled a report of the talks to King George, and with a directness he would not have employed had the Polish leader in exile been a constitutional monarch (and perhaps a cousin of the King), wrote: "The day before yesterday was 'All Poles Day.' Our lot from London are, as Your Majesty knows, decent but feeble." The Lublin Poles, Churchill told the King, appeared to be "purely tools." He held out hope of a settlement, but added, "If not we shall have to hush the matter up and spin it out until after the [American] election." He didn't get the settlement. Mikołajczyk insisted on Lvov remaining in the new Poland. Churchill dismissed him with the threat that England might well consider its obligations to Poland to have been met, and at an end.[65]

When Churchill proposed a fifty-fifty power sharing between the London and Lublin Poles within a new Polish government, Stalin and Molotov refused, demanding instead that 80 percent of power be vested in the Lublin party. And, Lvov was nonnegotiable. Eden, to his diary, confessed, "And so at this time, after endless hours of the stiffest negotiations I have ever known, it looks as though Lvov will wreck all our efforts." Mikołajczyk, who Eden thought showed "a calm courage" throughout the meetings, returned to London, promising Churchill he would do his best to bring his colleagues around. He said he hoped to return with an answer within a few days.[66]

Moscow nights were filled with banquets that stretched into early morning. The luminaries attended a performance at the Bolshoi Theater on October 16. It was Stalin's first appearance at the theater since the start of the war, and for him to attend in the presence of a foreigner was even more remarkable. When Stalin and Churchill stood in their box to acknowledge the crowd, the audience erupted with a "sound like a cloudburst on a tin roof," Eden wrote. Between acts, Churchill and Eden hastened to the restroom, where they discussed at length—or Churchill declaimed at length on—a new strategy to deal with the Poles. Eden reminded the prime minister that the show could not continue until they returned, and reminded him again, and again. When they finally returned to the box, their hosts made no mention of their absence, although at dinner the following night in Stalin's Kremlin apartments, Stalin pointed toward a door and said, "That's where you can wash your hands if you want to, the place where I understand you English like to conduct your political discussions." Churchill found himself warming to Stalin, telling Clementine in a cable from Moscow, "I have had vy nice talks with the Old Bear. I like him the more I see him. *Now* they respect us here."[67]

On October 27, five days after returning to London from Moscow, Churchill told the House: "I am very glad to inform the House that our relations with Soviet Russia were never more close, intimate and cordial than they are at the present time." Yet, he warned, "The future of the world depends upon the united action in the next few years of our three countries [America, Great Britain, and Russia]. Other countries may be associated, but the future depends upon the union of the three most powerful Allies. If that fails, all fails; if that succeeds, a broad future for all nations may be assured." He told the House that the three great powers "are all firmly agreed on the re-creation of a strong, free, independent, sovereign Poland loyal to the Allies and friendly to her great neighbour and liberator, Russia." That Churchill anointed Russia Poland's "liberator" is at best an ironic choice of words given Stalin's eagerness to destroy Poland in 1939. Churchill then went on to scold the London Poles, who, had they taken the advice "we tendered them at the beginning of this year, the additional complication produced by the formation of the Polish National Committee of Liberation [*sic*] at Lublin would not have arisen; and anything like a prolonged delay in the settlement can only have the effect of increasing the division between Poles in Poland, and also of hampering the common action which the Poles, the Russians and the rest of the Allies are taking against Germany." He had not said so in so many words, but in effect he had just told the Poles that they were responsible for whatever came their way.[68]

Mikołajczyk never returned to Moscow in search of an agreement. Instead, unwilling to agree to any settlement before the peace conference (the same stance Churchill had taken early in the war), he resigned from the Polish government in late November, handing over the reins to the moderate voice of Polish socialism, Tomasz Arciszewski. Arciszewski then reconstituted the London Poles, Churchill told the House, "in a form that in some respects I certainly am not able to applaud." Had Mikołajczyk reached a settlement with Stalin, Churchill added, "he would be at this moment at the head of a Polish Government, on Polish soil, recognized by all the United Nations, and awaiting the advance of the Russian Armies moving farther into Poland as the country was delivered from the Germans." He pressed the point—and the rebuke—further: "If the Polish Government had agreed, in the early part of this year, upon the frontier there never would have been any Lublin Committee to which Soviet Russia had committed herself, so I now say that if Mr. Mikolajczyk could swiftly have returned to Moscow early in November... to conclude an agreement on the frontier line, Poland might now have taken her full place in the ranks of the nations contending against Germany, and would have had the full support and friendship of Marshal Stalin and the Soviet Government." Churchill's message was clear: the London Poles had done nothing, and now all of Poland would face the consequences.[69]

Stalin had told Churchill during their meetings that he personally favored recognition of de Gaulle and the FCNL but had not stated so publicly for fear of introducing division into the ranks of the Big Three. Churchill sent a telegram to Roosevelt on October 14 in which he proposed the recognition of de Gaulle's provisional government. France was cleared of Germans, he told the president, and de Gaulle was firmly in charge of civil matters. It had been Eden who brought Churchill along slowly to this day. The foreign secretary later wrote: "No one was wiser than Mr. Churchill in giving weight to arguments which he had resisted at the time if, on later reflection, he judged them sound." Hull had likewise advised Roosevelt that a failure to recognize de Gaulle would reflect badly on the United States if Russia and Britain did so. Roosevelt's turnaround came so fast that when Churchill arrived back in London on October 22, he learned that the Americans had announced their recognition of the FCNL the day before, even before official notification from Roosevelt arrived in London.[70]

This meant that Duff Cooper served now as ambassador to the government of France, not simply as representative to the FCNL. When Churchill visited de Gaulle in Paris on November 10, his host was no longer simply *le général*, but *l'état*. The next day, the twenty-sixth anniversary of the armistice, Churchill and de Gaulle laid a wreath to the Unknown Soldier at the Arc de Triomphe and then, swept along by a crowd of hundreds of thousands of ecstatic Frenchmen, marched side by side down the Champs-Élysées. The crowd, Cadogan recorded in his diary, chanted "Chur-chill, Chur-chill" the entire time, the P.M. grinning and waving wildly all the while. When Churchill laid a bouquet at the foot of Clemenceau's statue, the military band struck up, on de Gaulle's orders, *"Le Père la Victoire"* ("Father Victory"). De Gaulle leaned into Churchill, and said, in English, "For you." "And it was only justice," de Gaulle wrote in his memoirs.[71]

Over dinner at the Hôtel de Ville—the Paris city hall—de Gaulle asked Churchill what had struck him the most during the day's events. Churchill responded, "Your unanimity." Still, despite the amity attached to the occasion, de Gaulle made absolutely clear to Churchill that France sought—and deserved—a role in the occupation of Germany and that although he appreciated an Anglo-American-Soviet invitation to sit on the European Advisory Commission, which would plan Germany's postwar fate, it was only a first step. De Gaulle demanded that France become a "full associate" in managing the peace. Churchill agreed, and told Roosevelt so in a telegram on November 16. Roosevelt's reply was lukewarm at best—Eden called it "snarky to the French, and generally arrogant and aloof." The president proposed putting off any talk of French involvement until the next meeting of the Big Three. He added a familiar refrain that could only disturb Churchill, and did: "You know, of course, that after Germany collapses I must bring American troops home as rapidly as transportation problems permit."[72]

Roosevelt intended to bring the troops home in order to speed them by rail across the country so that they could make ready to embark from the American West Coast for the invasion of Japan, where all within the U.S. military expected American casualties to exceed one million. The president's vision extended to the distant Pacific, to the enemy that drove America into this war. Churchill and Eden gazed across the Channel, as Englishmen had for centuries. They saw that Roosevelt's decision would leave in Europe an undermanned and ill-equipped French army of barely eight divisions, an exhausted British army, and the Red Army.

By late fall, Churchill's attention turned to Greece, where in early December civil war again ignited. Communist ELAS paramilitary forces had taken over half the police stations in Athens and attacked the British embassy; their political arm, the EAM, had walked out of Prime Minister Georgios Papandreou's royal government. At issue, as Eden saw it, was the necessity of bringing the Greeks around to settling their differences "through the ballot box, and not by the bomb." Eden pressed King George of the Hellenes to agree to a regency under the Greek Orthodox archbishop Damaskinos, in order to take the wind out of the EAM sails. Churchill, who knew that the Germans had allowed Damaskinos to perform his duties in the See of Athens, where the late dictator Ioannis Metaxas had not, believed the archbishop was "both a quisling and a Communist." Cadogan quipped that the archbishop was Churchill's "new de Gaulle." Churchill refused to press the Greek king on the matter, telling the cabinet, "I won't install a dictator [Damaskinos]—a dictator of the left." Under no pressure from Churchill to do otherwise, King George persisted in refusing a regency, claiming the appointment of a regent would signal the Greek people that he had abandoned them. At least two dozen civilians were killed when demonstrations erupted in Athens in early December. There, Lieutenant General Ronald Scobie and five thousand British troops found themselves on the verge of going to war against the Greek Communists.[73]

On December 5, Churchill cabled Scobie with orders to open fire if need be to restore order. One sentence in the cable soon brought trouble: "Do not however hesitate to act as if you were in a conquered city where a local rebellion is in progress." "Occupied" would have been a far better word choice, but Churchill was on the warpath, sustained by his belief that the 30,000 British casualties suffered in the defense of Greece in 1941 justified a return to Greece; indeed, he believed that the Greek people had appreciated the British effort then, and desired it now. As well, Churchill had paid a goodly price in Moscow for influence over Greek affairs, and he intended to keep the bargain he had reached with Stalin. He advised Scobie to handle the situation without bloodshed if possible, "but also with bloodshed if necessary." Churchill told Roosevelt that he knew little of Damaskinos, but that British officials in Athens believed the archbishop "might stop a gap or bridge a gully." Had Churchill tended to his boxes—three "hopelessly overcrowded" boxes by then, Colville noted—he would have known that the archbishop was the best choice if the goal was to bring the warring parties in Greece to the conference table. The difficulty with taking a hard—military—stance in Greece, as Eden saw it, lay in the possibility that world opinion would hold that British troops were trying not to restore order, but rather to restore the king at the point of a gun.[74]

American opinion on the matter soon arrived by way of the new U.S. secretary of state, Edward Stettinius, and the American columnist Drew Pearson. Stettinius had taken over on December 1 from a very tired Cordell Hull, who had served in his office for almost twelve years, the longest term of any American secretary of state. Stettinius, upon assuming his post, issued a statement that strongly implied that British actions in Italy and Greece were nothing more than imperial interference in the affairs of allied states. This was insult enough, but someone at either the State Department or the White House leaked to Pearson Churchill's "shoot to kill" cable to Scobie. Pearson ran with it in the *Washington Post,* thus raising again the question of whether American boys were dying for opportunistic British imperialism. Churchill was "incensed," Colville wrote, that his private communication should find its way into the American press. It appears that Pearson came into possession of the cable because a very tired Jock Colville, who composed the telegram to Scobie at 4:00 A.M. on December 5, forgot to mark it "Guard," which would have signified that the cable was not intended for American eyes. Instead, it was routed through American military and diplomatic channels, and finally to Pearson. Colville confessed his omission to the Old Man, who very "kindly" told the young secretary "that it was his [Churchill's] fault for keeping me up so late."[75]

The *Times, New Statesman,* the solidly leftist *Manchester Guardian,* and the Labour Party joined Pearson in fits of indignation, criticism that Cadogan called "swill" and "dishonest and libelous trash." Aneurin Bevan and the more rebellious Labour MPs "see a heaven sent opportunity," Colville wrote. Churchill's intervention in Greece brought on a vote of confidence on December 8. During the House debate, Churchill slashed away at those who faulted his policy, including the U.S. State Department and Franklin Roosevelt. Proclaiming his resolve to proceed in Greece, he announced: "I say we march along an onerous and painful path. Poor old "England! Perhaps I ought to say 'Poor old Britain.' " This was a direct jab at Roosevelt, who insisted—for fear of offending Scots, Welshmen, and the Northern Irish—that U.S. government communications never refer to "England," only "Britain." Churchill pushed on, again with America in mind: "We have to assume the burden of most thankless tasks and in undertaking them to be scoffed at, criticized and opposed from every quarter; but at least we know where we are making for, know the end of the road, know what is our objective." The objective—in Greece, Italy, every place the Nazis had occupied—was democracy. He told the House that British troops in Athens were there not to impose democracy but to safeguard the right of Greeks to make their choice—be it democracy, socialism, constitutional monarchy, even communism—in secret, without fear, at the ballot box. "Democracy," he offered, "is no harlot to be picked up in the street by a man with a tommy gun."[76]

Churchill won the vote of confidence by a margin of 279–30. Two days later, he sent a note to Harry Hopkins in which he wrote, "I hope you can tell our friend" that law and order in Athens is "essential" and a condition for any talks with the warring parties there. Churchill also told Hopkins: "I consider we have a right to the president's support in the policy we are following." He did not get that support, at least not in public. Instead, on December 11, Roosevelt sent a telegram in which he told Churchill, "As anxious as I am to be of the greatest help to you in this trying situation, there are limitations imposed... by the mounting adverse reaction of public opinion in this country."[77]

By mid-December, all armies on the Western Front, German and Allied, were refitting in anticipation of an Allied thrust to the Rhine within weeks. Five mostly green American divisions held the heavily wooded and hilly Ardennes sector of the front, where General Omar Bradley considered any German attack "only a remote possibility." On December 15, Field Marshal Montgomery told reporters that the Germans were incapable of staging "any major offensive operation." The following day, ten panzer divisions and fourteen infantry divisions appeared as if by sleight of hand in front of the Americans in the Ardennes sector. The surprise was complete, the German buildup having been conducted under strict radio silence. The skies were threatening, perfect cover for the Germans, and inhospitable for Allied fliers. Within days, the German salient—the bulge in the lines—extended almost to the Meuse at Dinant. The vital port of Antwerp was the German objective. All in the West followed the battle, anointed the Battle of the Bulge. The German successes of December 16–24 "were enormous shocks to the public," Mollie Panter-Downes wrote, adding that most Britons, who had believed this would be the last Christmas of the war, now believed they were in for "at least another year of fighting." One Englishman did not. Churchill, believing the Germans had made a fatal error by attacking the Ardennes rather than girding their defenses on the Rhine, told the cabinet, "I think this battle is more likely to shorten the war than to prolong it."[78]

By Christmas Eve, secure in the ultimate outcome of the Battle of the Bulge, Churchill turned his attention to Greece. Chequers had been prettified for what should have been a peaceful family Christmas. The great fir was up, sent as a gift by the American public for the second year in a row. Little Winston, now four, anticipated much in the way of sweets and cakes. Mary believed she knew what her papa would bestow on her in the way of a Christmas gift. She loved horses. Each Christmas, she recalled, her father gave her "generous cheques towards my post-war wish for a hunter, usually accompanied by a drawing." Her father "was quite difficult to give presents to from a family point of view, as there was so much competition!" On his birthdays, Mary always gave her father a carnation for his buttonhole. Clementine liked to give him velvet slippers with his monogram, or perhaps an "evening" siren suit in velvet. And to his children Churchill always gave copies of his books upon publication.

On this Christmas Eve, Churchill gave his family something entirely unexpected; after pondering the Greek crisis all day, he ordered his new C-54 (a gift of General Arnold) readied and, after informing—but by no means consulting with—his War Cabinet, left Chequers after dinner in order to take charge of events in Athens. To accompany him on the journey, the Old Man shanghaied Jock Colville, two female typists, his doctor, Lord Moran, and Anthony Eden. "Hell," Eden told his diary before departing, "I was looking forward to a quiet family Christmas." So began Churchill's strangest odyssey of the war.[79]

Brooke committed his thoughts on the matter to his diary: "Winston has done a spectacular rush to Greece, to try and disentangle the mess.... And what are we to get out of it all? As far as I can see, absolutely nothing!" The British would have to withdraw sooner or later, Brooke wrote, and Greece "will become as communistic as her close neighbors consider desirable." Brooke had weeks earlier predicted that Churchill would ultimately shift 80,000 men to Greece. That week, when the remainder of the 49th Division was ordered to Greece, British forces there numbered close to 80,000. They were fighting Greeks, who months earlier had been fighting Germans. Brooke needed those troops in Italy, where the campaign had stalled at the Gothic Line just north of Pisa and Florence, and sixty miles south of the Po River. The Po was Alexander's and Clark's objective. Sixty miles, a distance Hitler's panzers once advanced in a day early in the war, a distance Montgomery advanced in the first two days following his victory at El Alamein. It had been almost fifteen months since Anglo-American forces landed in Salerno. Those forces had needed nine months to advance 150 miles to Rome, and in the six months since, had crawled only another 150 miles. Fifteen months, 450 days, three hundred miles, an average advance of less than three-quarters of a mile per day. And now the prime minister was off to Greece. "Meanwhile," the CIGS told his diary, "the campaign in Italy stagnates."[80]

The overnight flight, with a refueling stop in Naples, brought Churchill into Athens early on Christmas afternoon. Machine-gun fire could be heard throughout the city. British Beaufighters circled overhead, in search of ELAS positions to strafe with cannons and rockets. General Alexander had come in from Italy; Harold Macmillan, HMG's resident minister in the Mediterranean, was also on hand. Churchill and Eden met them on board the aircraft for a two-hour discussion, during which Churchill's position on King George of the Hellenes began to shift under the guidance of Macmillan and Eden, who suggested convening a conference of all Greek parties, chaired not by Papandreou but by Archbishop Damaskinos. It was likely that the ELAS would boycott any other arrangement. The British embassy was without heat and often without electricity; the weather had turned bitterly cold, so from the airport the party traveled down to the harbor in armored cars and boarded HMS *Ajax,* which offered relative safety. Sleep for the weary was not to be had, Colville noted, because gun battles continued on the mainland, and depth charges were detonated at random intervals to discourage any underwater assault on *Ajax*. Shortly after dusk, Papandreou and the archbishop boarded *Ajax* to meet—separately—with Churchill. The visitors were greeted by the ship's company singing a robust version of "The First Noel." Events almost took an unfortunate turn. It is a tradition in the Royal Navy for tars to dress up in silly costumes on Christmas Day and then to spring silly pranks on their crewmates. When crew members spied a tall, bearded man walking up the gangway, dressed in ecclesiastical robes and carrying a long black staff, they presumed he was one of their own and made ready. Fortunately, *Ajax*'s commanding officer intervened, and Damaskinos was escorted to a stateroom without incident.[81]

While Churchill took the measure of Papandreou, the archbishop entertained the lesser lights in Churchill's party. Damaskinos had brought a bottle of ouzo as a gift, which the British partook of heartily, thinking the clear liquid was water. After downing a tall glass of the stuff (mixed with whisky), Colville told his diary, "I have never felt closer to death." He also concluded that Damaskinos cut "a magnificent figure and also has a sense of humor." Churchill thought likewise after meeting with Damaskinos. Thus, the holy man whom Churchill had weeks earlier called a quisling and dictator now found himself in the prime minister's good graces, addressed now by Churchill as "Your Beatitude." Colville noted that "we are now in the curious topsy-turvy position of the Prime Minister feeling strongly pro-Damaskinos (he even thinks he would make a good regent)." That was Churchill's way; nothing substituted for a face-to-face meeting. It was agreed that Damaskinos would indeed chair the meeting of all parties scheduled for the next day. Papandreou—who Macmillan thought "a worthy man, but vain, and therefore shifty"—was being marginalized, and that meant King George of the Hellenes was as well.[82]

The meeting with the Greek factions took place on December 26 at the Ministry of Foreign Affairs. Getting from *Ajax* to the ministry proved a dangerous business. Two artillery shells straddled the ship as Churchill prepared to leave. A burst of machine-gun fire peppered a stone wall above his head. Churchill went by armored car, scolding Colville on the way for not carrying a weapon in such perilous circumstances. To placate the Old Man, Colville borrowed a tommy gun from the driver. "What is *he* going to do" in case of attack? asked Churchill. "He will be busy driving," Colville replied.[83]

They found the ministry blacked out and without electricity or heat. Kerosene lamps burned in the bleak conference room. Damaskinos took his place at the head of the table, a signal to the ELAS that movement toward a settlement was under way. The problem was, the ELAS were not in attendance. Then, after Churchill and the archbishop made their opening remarks, "three shabby desperados, who had been searched and almost stripped before being allowed to enter, came into the dimly-lit conference room." The Communists had arrived, ready to talk rather than shoot. Churchill and the British departed, leaving the Greeks to sort things out among themselves. By the next afternoon they had reached an agreement. The Communists accepted Damaskinos as regent. Papandreou drafted a letter of intent to King George of the Hellenes in that regard, a statement Macmillan believed would prove Papandreou's death warrant. (It did not. He served as prime minister twice again from 1963 to 1965.) At Churchill's request, Damaskinos pledged absolutely and without reservation to guarantee Papandreou's safety. King George promised not to return to Greece until the people had spoken in a plebiscite. By late on December 27, it was done. Churchill had not strictly speaking secured a cease-fire, let alone a signed truce, but he had secured the regency. "Greece's troubles were by no means over," Eden later wrote, "but at the least the Greek people would now have a chance to choose their destiny without fear."[84]

On December 29, the day he returned from Greece, Churchill received a cable from Stalin in which the marshal threatened to recognize the Lublin Poles to the complete exclusion of the London Poles. The interests of the entire Polish people, Stalin wrote, cannot be sacrificed "in favor of a handful of Polish emigrants in London." Roosevelt, when informed, cabled Stalin that he was "disturbed and deeply disappointed" by the message. "I am more than ever convinced," the president wrote, "that when the three of us get together we can reach a solution of the Polish problem." Stalin, in reply, promised a "free and democratic Poland" but also reminded Roosevelt,

"The problem of Poland is inseparable from the security of the Soviet Union." As well, Stalin told Roosevelt, he did not want Polish anti-Soviet partisans operating in the rear of the Red Army as it drove into Germany. In fact, the Soviets and their Lublin puppets had been systematically destroying the Polish resistance movement since August. Churchill joined Roosevelt in asking Stalin to delay any irrevocable decision on the Lublin Poles until the three leaders met at the end of January. Since October, when Roosevelt first proposed a Big Three meeting to coordinate the final assault on Germany and its partition into occupied zones, events had outpaced plans.

The Red Army was now poised to overrun western Poland and strike into Germany. The war in Europe could be over in weeks, yet no agreement had been reached on the structure of the United Nations Organization, which would keep the peace, or on the makeup and role of the European Advisory Commission, which would manage German affairs, or on the fundamental question of Polish borders. The president had proposed to Stalin that they all meet in Scotland; Stalin declined and suggested the Crimean seaside resort city of Yalta as an alternative. Roosevelt, an ill man, protested the vast distances he'd have to travel to the Crimea, and proposed Malta, or Athens, or Cyprus. He had lost twenty pounds during the fall campaign, which had ended in his election to a fourth term. He had been hit that year by influenza, angina, and bronchitis. He was weak and could no longer stand behind a podium, supported by his steel braces, to deliver speeches. His lungs crackled with fluid retention, a symptom of congestive heart failure. He allowed to Stalin that his doctors were worried that a journey to Russia would be dangerous.[85]

Stalin gave no ground. He could not leave Russia, he told Roosevelt, on the advice of *his* doctors. The leaders agreed after much back-and-forth to convene in Yalta. The town was a two-day ride by armored train for Stalin, but for Roosevelt it would require a 4,800-mile, ten-day sea journey to a secure Mediterranean port, and a 1,300-mile flight from there to Yalta. Churchill's journey would not be nearly as arduous, but its long air legs would prove tiring for any traveler. The Crimean climate would do nothing to ameliorate the situation. Conditions in Yalta were so bad, Churchill told Hopkins, "we could not have found a worse place for a meeting than if we had spent ten years on research."[86]

On New Year's Eve, Harold Nicolson and his wife, Vita, crouched in front of the dining room fireplace at their ancient Kentish estate, Sissinghurst, and listened to the "gabbles" of Adolf Hitler as he broadcast to his countrymen. The reception was bad, but they heard enough of Hitler's "horrible... voice" to grasp that he was warning Germans of their fate were they to lose their "moral staunchness." He declaimed "on the strength of the *Führung,* on the need for unanimity, on the order of the *sein oder nicht sein* [to be or not to be] theme." Jock Colville also listened, and thought Hitler "seemed in low spirits." His Ardennes gambit had stalled, but it had made for a bleak Christmas in London.[87]

The New Year arrived in a snowbound Europe—"Sunshine and frost," Colville told his diary on January 1. The skies blued that morning, perfect flying weather, as evidenced just after dawn, when eight hundred Luftwaffe fighter planes screamed over Allied airfields in Holland and Belgium "at zero feet" and destroyed 130 RAF planes caught on the ground, including Montgomery's new American-built C-54. With fields and roads covered in drifting snow and with hard frosts coming daily, the countryside looked like "a fairyland," Colville wrote, and added, "The V-2 rockets are falling like autumnal leaves."[88]

Churchill, icebound at Chequers with the roads to London impassable, spent most of New Year's Day dictating memos in bed, far too many, in Brooke's estimation, and "all of a futile nature... due to faulty reading of documents... or concern with details he should not get himself mixed up with." The meeting with Roosevelt and Stalin at Yalta was on, but getting there was proving problematic. When Roosevelt's doctors objected to the president flying over the Alps in his unpressurized Skymaster, Churchill suggested that he and Roosevelt meet in Malta, and then fly at a more friendly altitude on a southern route over the Black Sea: "We shall be delighted if you come to Malta.... Everything can be arranged to your convenience. No more let us falter! From Malta to Yalta! Let nobody alter!" Churchill also suggested Argonaut—"which has a local but not deducible association"—as the code name for the conference (it was to the Black Sea that Jason sailed in search of the Golden Fleece). His cables implied a jaunty optimism that Churchill did not in fact feel. John Peck thought that the end of the war "and the problems it will bring with it are depressing the P.M." Churchill's mood can be measured by New Year wishes he sent a colleague: Best wishes "for this new disgusting year."[89]

Montgomery and Patton were preparing to hit the Ardennes salient, the former from the north, the latter from the south. Once the salient was sealed, Eisenhower intended to turn his armies toward the Rhine. Churchill cabled Roosevelt with the opinion he had expressed to the cabinet at the height of the Battle of the Bulge, that the German gambit in the Ardennes "is more likely to shorten than to lengthen the war." Yet Eisenhower had not yet decided upon his strategy for exploiting the German defeat in the Ardennes. He had no plan for the endgame, and was weighing the advantages of encircling—and destroying—the Ruhr Valley before continuing east on the north German plains against an attack on a broad front along the upper and lower Rhine. He could make no decision, he told the chiefs, until he knew what the Russians intended to do, and when. To answer that question Air Marshal Tedder had been dispatched to Moscow, but he was held up in Cairo by foul weather. Churchill, with little faith in Tedder's ability to extract any information from Stalin, told Colville that sending Tedder to Moscow "is like sending a man who has learned to ride a bicycle to paint a picture." The Old Man took matters into his own hands and telegraphed Eisenhower's concerns directly to Stalin.[90]

While awaiting Stalin's reply on military matters, Roosevelt and Churchill heard from the marshal on political matters. On January 4, Stalin informed Roosevelt by cable that given the fact that the London Poles were "aiding the Germans," the presidium of the Supreme Soviet of the U.S.S.R. had no choice but to recognize the Lublin Poles. Roosevelt duly informed Churchill, adding that he was not going to reply to Stalin, "but we may discuss the matter at the meeting." Harriman later wrote that Roosevelt "held fast to his belief that he personally could accomplish more in man-to-man talks with Stalin than Churchill, the State Department or the British Foreign Office." Churchill became less sanguine as the month went on: "Make no mistake," he told Colville. "All the Balkans, except Greece, are going to be Bolshevised; and there is nothing I can do to prevent it. There is nothing I can do for poor Poland."[91]

Roosevelt continued to freeze Churchill out, much as he had before Tehran. "Much to my regret," he cabled, the Yalta trip will force the postponement of "my projected visit to the United Kingdom until a later date." The president had long promised to make such a trip, and had told Eden at Quebec that he would visit London after the election, "win or lose." The London press had run with the rumor of a presidential visit for months. Mollie Panter-Downes wrote that were Roosevelt to come to England, "he will get as big a hand here as Churchill got in Paris." But Roosevelt, Harriman later wrote, "with careful regard for Stalin's suspicions," was approaching Yalta exactly as he had approached Tehran; he avoided Churchill in order to placate Uncle Joe. As well, he was concerned that a visit to England so soon on the heels of Churchill's Greek sojourn might appear to Americans as a presidential endorsement of British imperialism in the eastern Mediterranean. Eleanor Roosevelt, fearful of a domestic backlash, advised her husband not to visit London or Paris. When Churchill suggested to Roosevelt that they spend at least a few days on Malta planning for the conference, Roosevelt declined. He told Churchill he'd be heading straight to Yalta within hours of arriving in Malta. Furthermore, he offered the opinion that the Yalta portion of the trip should last no more than "five or six days." Churchill was "disgusted" by Roosevelt's unwillingness to spend more than a few days at the most important meeting of the war, Colville wrote, "and says even the Almighty required seven to settle the world. (An inaccuracy which was quickly pointed out to him. Viz. Genesis I)."[92]

Late on January 8, Field Marshal Brooke, summoned by the P.M., found Churchill working in bed "sipping coffee, drinking brandy and smoking his big cigar." The Old Man was in fine form because he had received directly from Stalin the information Eisenhower most desired and that Tedder, stuck in Cairo, could not procure. To Churchill's delight, Stalin informed him that the Red Army would soon be on the move, not later than midmonth. The message had been personal. Colville had long noted the ease with which Churchill could be charmed, and Stalin, for all his bluntness, could charm with the best of them.[93]

In the east, eight Soviet armies had been reorganized along the eight-hundred-mile battle line from the Baltic to Belgrade. Each Soviet army was given a designation that identified the portion of the front it occupied; any two of the armies were as large as the Anglo-American forces in the west. The Eastern Front, static in the Warsaw/central sector since August, ran south from just east of the East Prussia frontier to within a few miles of Warsaw, and then along the east bank of the upper Vistula. The remnants of Hitler's Army Group North, twenty-six divisions and almost two hundred thousand men, were trapped behind Soviet lines in Latvia. In the far south, Tito and the Soviets had held Belgrade since late October, but the Germans still held the Yugoslav-Hungary border region. The Red Army had surrounded Budapest, where almost two hundred thousand Germans found themselves trapped within the city. The overall length of the Eastern Front had shrunk by four hundred miles since the summer, which benefited both the attackers and the defenders, but Soviet supply lines now stretched rearward more than eight hundred miles. Since August, the Red Army had rebuilt the railroads, and they now brought up millions of tons of supplies by rail and by road, aboard tens of thousands of American-made Studebaker trucks. By January, Soviet armies north of the Carpathians were ready, but until Churchill extracted that fact from Stalin, the Western allies had no idea of just how ready. In fact, Russian complaints about the weather, Russian secrecy in general, and Russian stasis on the front since the Warsaw uprising had led many in Anglo-American circles to doubt Russian intentions, and to underestimate Russian capabilities.[94]

Hitler certainly underestimated the threat in the east. On January 9, he confidently told his generals that the Red Army lacked the threefold superiority in men that an attacker traditionally needed to forge a breakthrough.

When first apprised of the Soviet buildup, Hitler scoffed, "It's the greatest bluff since Genghis Khan! Who's responsible for this rubbish?"[95]

The Führer was correct in regard to the entire length of the front, but incorrect regarding that portion Stalin intended to attack. Marshal Zhukov commanded the First Belorussian Front, which was arrayed just east and south of Warsaw. To Zhukov's left, the armies of the First Ukrainian Front under the command of Marshal Ivan Konev were astride the Vistula about thirty miles east of Cracow. Together, Zhukov and Konev commanded 160 divisions, twice as many as the Allies had arrayed west of the Rhine, and 32,000 pieces of artillery. These two massive Soviet armies alone accounted for almost one-third of the Red Army's total strength, and outnumbered the Germans at their front by six to one in men, eight to one in artillery, six to one in tanks, and eighteen to one in aircraft. The Berlin-Dresden axis lay just over three hundred miles due west.[96]

On January 12, Konev struck. His heavy artillery put down a barrage with a density of more than six hundred shells per mile of front, a display Sir John Keegan called "an earthquake concentration of artillery power." Zhukov followed on January 14. The rest of the Soviet armies north of the Carpathians, but for the northernmost on the Baltic, soon followed. The German front collapsed. On the sixteenth, Hitler transferred his headquarters from Ziegenberg, near Frankfurt, to the Chancellery in Berlin. Warsaw fell to Zhukov on January 17. To the south, Konev was driving for Cracow and Breslau. Upper Silesia, Germany's second-most-important industrial area, lay just beyond. Albert Speer had scattered armament factories throughout the region, which had so far escaped damage at the hands of the RAF and the Eighth Air Force. On January 20, Hitler, to the dismay of his commanders east and west, announced to his captains, "I'm going to attack the Russians where they least expect it. The Sixth SS Panzer Army is off to Budapest!" It was a wild diversion born of delusion.[97]

On January 22, Konev's forces crossed the upper Oder, less than two hundred miles from Berlin. South of there, on January 27, the Red Army entered the Nazi extermination camp at Auschwitz. On Himmler's orders (issued months earlier in anticipation of this day), the Germans had blown up the last of the gas chambers and fled, leaving behind almost eight thousand starving Jews and Polish POWs, along with the pilfered luggage, dentures, and eyeglasses of their victims. The pelf included almost one million women's dresses, and 38,000 pairs of men's shoes. By then, another Soviet army had driven deep into East Prussia, where fleeing SS troops blew up Hitler's *Wolfsschanze* on their way out of Rastenburg. All along the front, SS units herded Allied POWs and slave laborers westward toward concentration camps in Germany. Those who straggled or collapsed from hunger were left to die on the roadside or shot.[98]

Two million East Prussians now fled in a human stampede before the Red Army. "It was as if," Sir John Keegan wrote, "the submerged knowledge of what the Wehrmacht had done in the east" seized Germans "with terror and flung them on the snowbound roads in an agony of urgency." Eight centuries of Germanic settlement was undone in days. "Speed, frenzy and savagery characterized the [Soviet] advance," professor John Erickson wrote. "Villages and small towns burned, while Soviet soldiers raped at will and wreaked an atavistic vengeance" on any home or village that displayed any insignia of Nazism. Soviet T-34 battle tanks chased down and crushed German refugees "in a bloody smear of humans and horses.... Raped German women were nailed by their hands to the farmcarts carrying their families." When Tito's number three man, Milovan Djilas, visiting Stalin in Moscow, voiced his disdain for such atrocities, Stalin answered, "Does Djilas, who is himself a writer, not know what human suffering and the human heart are? Can't he understand it if a soldier who has crossed thousands of kilometers through blood and fire and death has fun with a woman or takes some trifle?" Stalin told Djilas, "You have imagined the Red Army to be ideal, and it is not ideal, nor can it be.... We have opened up our penitentiaries and stuck everybody in the army."[99]

On January 27, Zhukov's forward units crossed the Oder, the last natural obstacle between his armies and Berlin, less than one hundred miles distant. Having again outrun his supplies, he paused.

That day, Hitler moved to his new Berlin headquarters—a concrete-and-steel bunker deep beneath the Chancellery. While chairing the first meeting there, Hitler asked Göring and Jodl, "Do you think the English are enthusiastic about all the Russian developments?" Jodl replied, "They [the English] have always regarded the Russians with suspicion." Göring added, "If this goes on we'll get a telegram [from the English] in a few days." No telegram was forthcoming, but the RAF was, and the American air forces, and the Red Army. Three days later, Albert Speer prepared a report for Hitler that summed up the consequences of losing Silesia. The coal supply would last two more weeks; aircraft were plentiful, but supplies of synthetic fuel were exhausted. The report began: "The war is lost." Hitler read the first line and ordered the report placed in his personal safe. By February 3, Zhukov had established secure bridgeheads across the northern Oder.[100]

Churchill, Sarah, Eden, and the chiefs left by air for Malta on January 29, reaching the island the next morning. Churchill arrived chilled, tired, and with a temperature that spiked to 102 degrees. Sarah thought, "Here we go again." Lord Moran told his diary: "He [Churchill] has a bad habit of running a temperature on these journeys." The Old Man, lacking the strength to leave the plane, spent six hours in restless sleep on the tarmac before being whisked off to a cabin on board HMS *Orion*.[101]

While Churchill recuperated, the British and American Chiefs of Staff sat down for talks on the proper strategy Eisenhower should pursue in order to kill the German armies at his front. Eisenhower had finally submitted his "appreciation" for future actions in which he proposed to attack along the length of the Rhine, and cross it at several points. This broad-front strategy displeased the British, who argued that Germany was, in essence, already defeated and that Eisenhower's plan was too methodical and too cautious. Instead, the British argued, Eisenhower should hurl Montgomery's army into the Ruhr basin with Berlin the ultimate objective while the American armies along the upper Rhine guarded that flank. Eisenhower had already expressed his total opposition to this "pencil line thrust on Berlin." Marshall, at times "brutally frank . . . stood four-square behind Eisenhower," Ismay later wrote, "and the British had no option but to give way." Brooke and Churchill had understood since late summer that through "force of circumstances"—the Allied army "was predominantly American"—they would have to accede to the Americans' wishes. Still, they came away believing that Marshall, although closing the door on any further discussion, did not close it on the prospect of getting as far east into Germany as possible in order to discourage the Russians from pushing west. The British welcomed this prospect, believing it left open the possibility of getting to Berlin, and of denying the Soviets the North Sea and Baltic coasts. But Marshall had not endorsed, let alone championed, a run to Berlin, and he had made it absolutely clear that he would continue to back Eisenhower in his strategy, wherever it took the Allies.[102]

Had Field Marshal Sir John Dill, the British liaison to the American Joint Chiefs, been present, he might have guided Marshall to a more precise statement of intent and mediated Marshall's growing dislike of the supercilious Brooke. But Dill had died in November in Washington. So great was Marshall's respect for Dill that he arranged for the field marshal to be buried in America's Valhalla, Arlington National Cemetery.

With brass bands playing national anthems and with the Stars and Stripes and Union Jacks snapping in the breeze, Roosevelt sailed into Valletta Harbor on February 2 on board the cruiser USS *Quincy*. Wearing a cloth cap, and with a cape hanging off his shoulders, he waved from the bridge as *Quincy* passed alongside *Orion*. All who saw the president were shocked by his gaunt, almost skeletal, appearance. He would ordinarily have emerged refreshed and invigorated after a ten-day sea voyage. Instead, he looked frail and exhausted. After a brief informal meeting with Churchill, Eden, and the Combined Chiefs in the ship's wardroom, Roosevelt kept to his stateroom until the aircraft were readied to ferry the delegation to Yalta late that night. Eden told his diary: "He [Roosevelt] gives me the impression of failing powers."

The president spoke little during the meeting. Again, as before the Tehran Conference, Churchill and Roosevelt failed to forge a united front to present to Stalin. The matter of the framework of the United Nations Organization had been settled in the early autumn at Dumbarton Oaks, but the exact mechanism for Great Power voting had yet to be worked out, and Stalin had stated his belief that any Great Power that was party to a dispute should be able to exercise its veto prerogative; that is, any of the Big Four could effectively override the wishes of the General Assembly. Allied zones of occupation in Germany had been proposed at the second Quebec conference, but the question of whether the French would gain such a zone had not been settled, and nor had the question of German reparations. Stalin had made himself quite clear in that regard; he wanted everything not nailed down in Germany carted off to Russia. Most critically, Roosevelt and Churchill had not agreed on a policy to guarantee Polish borders and Polish liberties. Eden confided to Harry Hopkins that "we were going into a decisive conference and had so far neither agreed what we would discuss nor how to handle matters with a Bear who would certainly know his mind."[103]

Pug Ismay framed the Yalta Conference in Clausewitzian terms: "War is a continuation of policy by other means." Both sides, Ismay later wrote, the potential losers and winners, must give political consideration to the consequences of their military decisions, the loser to preserve what he can from the wreckage, the winner "in order to ensure that the purposes for which he took up arms, will be realized in the post-war." The main German armies had now been compressed to the German frontiers, east and west. They would henceforth fight on German soil for German soil, if not for German honor. The Greater Reich had disappeared. Sixteen Wehrmacht divisions in Norway, and more than twice that many in Croatia and Italy, were effectively cut off from Berlin. German troops in Amsterdam were now trapped behind Allied lines. The end was coming, and it was coming fast. For Poland the end had come; the Red Army now occupied the entire country. While on board *Orion* Churchill wrote a long letter to Clementine, in which he offered: "The misery of the whole world appalls me and I fear increasingly that new struggles may arise out of those we are successfully ending."[104]

At about midnight on February 2, twenty American Skymasters and five British Yorks began lifting off at ten-minute intervals from Luqa airfield on Malta for the seven-hour flight to the Crimea. A sixth York, carrying staff members from the Foreign Office and War Cabinet, had lost its way and crashed in the Mediterranean on the trip to Malta. Most on board were drowned, including aides to Cadogan and Brooke. Seven survivors were picked up, but the plane took vital maps, charts, and papers to the bottom. Churchill had not done much preparation for the Yalta meeting to begin with; now he could not catch up. The loss of the papers, Harold Nicolson wrote, "will cast a gloom over the conference."[105]

The Russians had been told originally that about thirty-five Americans and a like number of British would make up the entourage traveling to Yalta. That figure now stood at close to seven hundred. Yet only two members of it really mattered.[106]

The fate of Poland—of all central and Eastern Europe—rested with a dying man, a tired man, and Joseph Stalin, described by his comrade Milovan Djilas as "an ungainly dwarf of a man" whose "conscience was troubled by nothing, despite the millions who had been destroyed in his name and by his order."[107]

The aerial flotilla arrived at the Laki airfield in the Crimea early on February 3. Yalta was about eighty miles distant, a seven-hour drive on rutted and washed-out coastal roads. Soviet troops, many of them stout women, guarded the entire route. Stalin arranged for Roosevelt and the Americans to take up residence in Yalta itself, at the Livadia Palace, the summer home of Czar Nicholas II, where once a thousand servants tended to the care and feeding of seven royal Romanovs. The plenary sessions would take place there. Churchill and the British were put up at the Vorontsov Palace, about twenty minutes from Yalta. Alec Cadogan found the place to be of "indescribable ugliness," built in 1837 "in what Baedeker so aptly describes as a combination of the Moorish and Gothic styles. You couldn't possibly imagine what it looks like." The furnishings, Cadogan wrote, were "of an almost terrifying hideosity." Sarah Churchill tried her hand at a description: "It looked like a Scottish baronial hall inside, and a cross between a Swiss chalet and a mosque outside." It was perched on a bluff high above the sea. A great stone staircase on the seaward side was set off by three pairs of sculpted lions: one pair slept on their paws, another stared seaward, the third bared their fangs to roar. A pair of stone lions guarded the front gates. Another huge lion sculpture occupied a prominent place in the grounds. This beast had one eye open and one closed. Whether Churchill saw—or Stalin intended—the irony in the menagerie of stone lions remains unrecorded. The British were warned by the Soviets to take care where they strolled; the area had not been fully cleared of land mines.[108]

Stalin arrived on February 4 and took up residence in the Yusupov Palace, more a country estate than a palace, situated between the Churchill and Roosevelt sanctuaries. The Germans had looted all three residences of furniture and fixtures but, remarkably, had not destroyed them on their way out of town. Stalin, in turn, stripped three Moscow hotels of furniture and fixtures, along with cooks, chambermaids, and waiters, which he sent by train to Yalta so that the gathered Allied elites might sleep and dine in relative comfort as they charted the course of the postwar world. Churchill raised a toast in that regard at a small dinner party hosted by Roosevelt the evening of February 4: "The whole world will have its eyes on this conference. If it is successful we will have peace for one hundred years."[109]

Five years later, Churchill wrote in his memoirs, "Poland had indeed been the most urgent reason for the Yalta conference, and was to prove the first of the great causes which led to the breakdown of the Grand Alliance." He had telescoped his memory by the time he wrote those words. Each of the Big Three brought his own most important priority—or two—to Yalta; Churchill's was Poland. Roosevelt came seeking a final determination on the structure of his beloved United Nations Organization. He came, as well, seeking firm commitments from Stalin on the Pacific war. General MacArthur had taken Manila that week, and the war against Japan had entered a new and critical phase. Issues in need of discussion abounded: the Russians, by sending troops into northern Iran, seemed poised to make mischief there. The issue of German reparations had to be addressed, along with the "dismemberment" of Germany (a term Stalin insisted upon) and the organization of Allied zones of occupation in Germany and Austria. Should France have such a zone? Churchill thought it should; Stalin, having months earlier signed a friendship treaty with de Gaulle, thought France should have a role, but limited; Roosevelt, though he loathed de Gaulle, was not about to cast a veto or waste political capital over that issue. A great deal more than Polish borders and the structure of a Polish government was on the Yalta agenda—or, rather, would have been if the Big Three had arrived with an agenda in place. They had not. Instead, during eight days of afternoon meetings and evening feasts, the agenda presented itself as each of the leaders waited for just the right moment to lay claim to the matter that most concerned him.[110]

Stalin certainly held Poland to be a matter of interest, but for reasons different from—and at odds with—Churchill's. Churchill later wrote that Poland was discussed at seven of the eight plenary sessions. Poland indeed was mentioned often, but not until the third session did the Big Three get down to brass tacks on Poland, because, as Averell Harriman later wrote, "the fate of Poland...had been largely decided before Roosevelt and Churchill took up the subject with Stalin at Yalta. Events were in the saddle." The dispute, at its core, came down to this: Was Poland (its borders and future government) a clean slate to be filled in (Churchill and Roosevelt), or was the Communist Lublin government (in place in Warsaw) to form the basis for the evolution of Polish self-government (Stalin)? Churchill reminded Stalin that Britain had gone to war for Poland on a point of honor. Stalin, as he had for three years, reminded Churchill that Poland was not simply a matter of honor for the Soviet Union, but a question of both honor and security—honor because the Russians had been in regular conflict with the Poles for centuries, and security because Poland occupied that swath of Eastern Europe that emptied onto the Russian homeland. He also pointed out to Churchill that he thought it ironic that Churchill wanted to dictate terms to Poland, while he, Stalin, who was called a dictator, simply wanted the Poles (guided by his Lublin puppets) to chart their own course. It was a mess that defied solution.[111]

And although Roosevelt composed a handwritten letter to Stalin during the conference that made clear his concerns about Poland, the president displayed an insouciance that regularly took the form of jokes that served only to undercut the importance of the issue. Eager to end one discussion that was going nowhere, Roosevelt offered, "Poland has been a source of trouble for over five hundred years." Toward the end of another meeting, Roosevelt, while perusing a map of Eastern Europe, asked Molotov how long ago certain areas belonged to Poland. When Molotov replied, "a very long time ago," Roosevelt said, "This might lead the English to ask for a return of the United States to Great Britain." On that note, Roosevelt, exhausted, adjourned the meeting. Of Roosevelt's behavior Eden later wrote, "I do not believe that the president's declining health altered his judgment, though his handling of the conference was less sure than it might have been."[112]

During the plenary sessions of February 9 and 10, the Big Three finally reached an agreement on Poland, or, more accurately, an interim agreement. Despite his insistence that nothing be dictated to the Poles, Stalin prevailed. The Lublin Poles would be recognized as the Polish provisional government; in turn the Lublin government would pledge to hold elections as soon as possible (Stalin thought within a month), but the validity of the elections was to be guaranteed not by representatives of the three Allies on the spot, but rather by the Big Three foreign ministers, who would meet in Moscow. This barely satisfied Churchill's insistence that Poland be "mistress in her own house and captain of her soul." He could return to London and truthfully tell the House that he and Roosevelt had not thrown over the London Poles, had not accepted in toto the Lublin government, but had agreed to a mechanism (free elections) for all Polish factions to take their cases to their countrymen. Yet no Polish leaders of any stripe had been invited to Yalta to air their opinions on the matter. Finally, the Big Three settled the matter of Polish borders, but again, as an interim recommendation to be taken under consideration at the peace conference. The borders east and west would take the general shape discussed a year earlier at Tehran—half of East Prussia to the Poles, half to Russia; the Curzon Line would define the eastern border, and Upper Silesia would go to the Poles, but Lvov to Russia. The new border would shift to the Neisse River in the west, but, as at Tehran, no final decision was made on which branch of the Neisse, the Eastern or Western. In effect, the final decision on Polish borders, like many of the issues discussed at Yalta, had been taken "under consideration." Churchill later wrote, "It was the best I could get."[113]

"For further consideration" became the order of the day. Stalin insisted that German reparations amount to $20 billion and that half go to Russia. Churchill objected. Twenty billion was far more than Germany could pay; it was the oppressive peace of Versailles redux. He insisted that an actual figure not be included in any declaration; Stalin prevailed, though Roosevelt saw the resolution as agreeing to disagree, the matter to be settled later. Likewise, the matter of German "dismemberment" was sidestepped by all agreeing that the first step in that direction must take the form of Allied zones of occupation. There would be four: France was in. On the makeup of the United Nations, the Russians—to Roosevelt's delight—dropped their demand for separate membership for their sixteen republics and said they'd settle for just two. Roosevelt agreed that the offer "deserved sympathetic consideration." Molotov had shot for the stars and was rewarded with the moon. Yet this agreement, too, was only "in principle," to be considered and possibly codified at the first meeting of the United Nations in San Francisco, in April (Belarus and Ukraine were admitted in October). That was Roosevelt's style—move things along but don't press.

On the Pacific front, Roosevelt sought concession from Stalin for airbases on the Asian mainland; Stalin sought the return to Russia of Sakhalin and other territories grabbed by Tokyo in 1905. Manchuria would be a Russian "sphere" (Roosevelt's quest to quell spheres of influence did not extend to Russia). Asia was an area of discussion that Churchill claimed he had no interest in. "To us," he later wrote, "the problem [Pacific deals and agreements] was remote and secondary." Perhaps, but Stalin and Roosevelt had reached agreement on a number of Asian matters in secret and without consulting the British or Chiang. "This [agreement]," Eden wrote, "was, in my judgment, a discreditable by-product of the conference." It also, Eden wrote, undermined the argument of those who attributed Roosevelt's decisions at Yalta to his illness. During a conference that was "strenuous even for a man of Churchill's energy," Roosevelt found time and energy to conduct a parallel conference with Stalin.[114]

It was left to Roosevelt to utter perhaps the most important statement—or at least the statement most full of portent—of the conference. In what Churchill called a "momentous declaration," Roosevelt volunteered during the first plenary session that he did not think American troops would stay on in Europe much longer than two years after Germany's defeat. He had told Harriman much the same two years earlier, and had told Churchill several times in 1944. The statement was meant to diminish Stalin's wariness of the West ganging up on him. It reconfirmed for Churchill his belief in the need for a strong France. To Stalin it also sent a clear message of indecision, if not weakness. It told Stalin that agreements made at Yalta depended on trust for their implementation but might be abrogated through force. To Eden it was another occasion when Roosevelt "mistakenly as I believe, moved out of step with us, influenced by his conviction that he could get better results with Stalin direct than could the three countries negotiating together. This was an illusion."[115]

The illusion was conjured under circumstances that would try the stamina of a young man, let alone three old men. Churchill's day began at midnight, when he took to his bed to read dispatches and newspapers until the early hours. He rose and bathed shortly before noon, and took what he referred to as "brunch," appropriating the American name for the midday meal. Plenary sessions began around 4:30 each afternoon and ran until about nine at night. Each of the Big Three hosted a feast during the conference, Churchill's turn coming on February 10. These liquid affairs were defined by lengthy toasts and "buckets of champagne," as described by Cadogan. "I think we're making some progress," Cadogan told his diary, "but this place is still rather a madhouse." During these affairs, myriad jolly men leapt to their feet to offer, as they thought, toasts of warmth and wisdom. Churchill raised one such to the Soviet army: "The men who have broken the back of the German war machine." They toasted political parties, the King of England, the common man, leaders, women, the alliance, the future. During Stalin's dinner, given at the Yusupov Palace, Cadogan estimated that fifty toasts had been raised; Edward Stettinius pegged the toasts at forty-five and the courses at twenty. Celebrants fell asleep; some slipped beneath the table. Thus, the future of the world was agreed upon. "I have never known the Russians to be so easy and accommodating," Cadogan wrote in a letter to his wife. "In particular, Joe has been very good." He added, "The president in particular is very wooly and wobbly." The president, Churchill confided to his doctor, "is behaving very badly.

He won't take any interest in what we're trying to do." But what were they trying to do? After eight days they had agreed to disagree, agreed to postpone final decisions, and, as Churchill put it, agreed "to consult about a consultation."[116]

On February 11, the Big Three signed their Declaration on Liberated Europe—the Yalta Declaration, as elastic a document as produced during the war. In essence it was a reprise of the Atlantic Charter, that is, not a law but a loose confederation of words upholding the "right of all people to choose the form of government under which they will live" and pledging the "restoration of sovereign rights and self-government to those people who have been forcibly deprived of them by the aggressor nations." Two weeks later, Churchill explained it all to the House. First, he placed blame for the need to even conduct such negotiations squarely at the feet of the London Poles:

> Let me remind the House, and those who have undertaken what I regard as the honourable duty of being very careful that our affairs in Poland are regulated in accordance with the dignity and honour of this country, that there would have been no Lublin Committee or Lublin Provisional Government in Poland if the Polish Government in London had accepted our faithful counsel given to them a year ago.

Then, after posing rhetorical questions on the viability of the Yalta Declaration—will it work, will elections be "free and unfettered"—he gave his answer:

> The impression I brought back from the Crimea, and from all my other contacts, is that Marshal Stalin and the Soviet leaders wish to live in honourable friendship and equality with the Western democracies. I feel also that their word is their bond. I know of no Government which stands to its obligations, even in its own despite, more solidly than the Russian Soviet Government. I decline absolutely to embark here on a discussion about Russian good faith.[117]

Churchill left Yalta early on the evening of February 11. The plan called for him to stay one more night, but upon driving into the grounds of the Vorontsov Palace, he turned to Sarah and said: "Why do we stay here? Why don't we go tonight—I see no reason to stay a minute longer—we're off." He strutted into the private office and announced, "I don't know about you—but I'm off. I leave in fifty minutes." And he did, in ninety minutes, to be exact. The staff packed up everything, including laundry that was still damp, and were off within two hours. Churchill motored forty miles to Sevastopol, where the Cunard liner *Franconia* rode at anchor, his home for the next three nights. Meanwhile, Stalin, Sarah wrote, "like some genie, just disappeared." Roosevelt flew off to Cairo on the morning of the twelfth. On the fourteenth, Churchill boarded his Skymaster at Laki for a flight to Athens, where he checked in on Archbishop Damaskinos, the new regent, and where, although the crowds cheered the old Englishman, the underlying political infections that Churchill had treated seven weeks earlier still festered. From Athens, deeply anxious now about the future, Churchill flew on to Cairo, to say his farewells to Franklin Roosevelt, who was taking his rest on the USS *Quincy* after conducting a parley with King Ibn Saud of Saudi Arabia. The president, Churchill later wrote, seemed "placid and frail. I felt that he had a slender contact with life." They never met again.[118]

Within a few weeks, throughout the European theater, the agreements taken at Yalta strained under their structural flaws and Roosevelt's "momentous statement" that American troops would remain in Europe for only two years after the war. This was an opening Stalin soon seized, and exploited. Churchill and Britain now lacked the political and military means to change the course of events in Poland, Czechoslovakia, and Austria—as well as in Yugoslavia, where Tito was prepared to play the Soviets and Anglo-Americans off against each other. But not in Greece, where Stalin, keeping his word, had not interfered. In Greece, Jock Colville later wrote, Churchill's show of force—to guarantee free elections, not override them, as was Stalin's wont—brought Greeks "twenty or so years of...freedom and democracy." Still, a sense of failure had gripped Churchill for the entire journey. By early spring, Stalin's abjuration of the decisions taken at Yalta would guarantee the veracity of Churchill's intuition. One vital matter was not even addressed by the Big Three in Yalta: just exactly where in Germany would the Allied armies finally stop?[119]

Churchill returned to London on February 19. By then the RAF and American air forces were dropping more bombs on Germany on any given night than the Germans had thrown at Britain during any month of the Blitz. During the first ten months of 1944, 250,000 tons of bombs were dropped on Germany—double the amount that had been dropped during the years between 1939 and 1944. Now, entering the final months of the conflict, the British and American air forces were determined to double that figure; 500,000 tons was the goal. It was reached. Roosevelt and Morgenthau may have backed away from their plan for a desolate Germany, but the Allied air forces were well on their way to producing exactly that result. On January 25, four days before leaving for Yalta, Churchill had asked Arthur ("Bomber") Harris whether Berlin and Dresden, along with Leipzig and Chemnitz, might not be "especially attractive targets" by virtue of their importance to German communication and rail networks. Air Chief Marshal Portal sought to concentrate on German tank factories, which were still rolling out new Tiger tanks. The tanks were no longer intended for massed attacks but for the defense of German towns and cities; just one of them could hold up an infantry company for a day. Harris thought he could hit both the tank factories and the rail centers. The RAF and the Russians believed that such a bombing offensive was critical not only to shortening the war but to winning it. The Red Army could not do it alone. On January 29, the day Churchill had departed for Yalta, Portal agreed to launch attacks on tank factories and on Berlin, Dresden, Leipzig, and Chemnitz.[120]

As long as rail hubs such as Dresden functioned, Hitler could move freely within his interior lines. The Germans had transferred three divisions to the Russian front and were bringing up eight more. Indeed, that prospect so troubled Stalin that he asked Roosevelt and Churchill at Yalta to direct Anglo-American air forces to destroy all such rail hubs, especially Dresden. The Allied air forces did just that over three nights beginning on February 13, when two thousand tons of high explosives and incendiaries were dropped into the center of Dresden. Water fountains boiled away; ancient bricks and stonework exploded into shrapnel. The Elbe burned, ignited by the jelly of incendiaries. At least 20,000 citizens perished, perhaps as many as 30,000; there could be no exact tally, for most of the victims had been reduced to ash. Ten days after the Dresden raid, Churchill took his weekend at Chequers. Colville and the usual retinue, along with Bomber Harris, accompanied the Old Man. While waiting in the great hall for Churchill to appear for dinner, Colville asked Harris what the effect of the Dresden raid had been. Harris replied, "There is no such place as Dresden." Churchill spoke of the raid in rather less sensational terms. In fact, Colville later wrote, Churchill "never mentioned it in my presence, and I am reasonably sure he would have done so if it had been regarded as anything at all special."[121]

Six weeks later, on April 1, Churchill wrote a memo to the Chiefs of Staff: "It seems to me that the moment has come when the question of the so-called area bombing of German cities should be reviewed from the point of view of our own interests." He went on to say that with the war almost won, continued bombing of that magnitude would result only in the Allies inheriting a ruined nation that could supply no matériel for the rebuilding of British houses, let alone German. In a draft of the memo (which he called his "rough" memo) he had used the word "terror" to describe the bombing, and had added, "The destruction of Dresden remains a serious query against the conduct of Allied bombing." He dropped those lines from his final version after the Chiefs of Staff objected. Yet he had made his point: the time had come to cease the airborne onslaught he had championed for four years.[122]

On March 6, on the grounds that they needed stability behind their lines, the Soviets set up a puppet government in Romania. Churchill had ceded to Stalin during their autumn meetings a 90 percent "interest" in Romanian affairs, but he had not intended that to mean the right to unilaterally install new governments. The coup, Colville wrote, "inflamed the P.M. who saw that our honour was at stake.... The P.M. and Eden both fear our willingness to trust our Russian ally may have been vain and they look with despondency to the future." That future was coming fast.[123]

Since June 1941, the premise that Hitler must be defeated was the mortar that bonded together first Churchill and Stalin, and then the alliance, for more than three years, even as cracks appeared in the foundation. With Hitler and Nazi Germany now doomed, that bonding ingredient no longer sustained the Anglo-American-Soviet alliance. The Yalta meeting had been called not to make plans to defeat Hitler but to settle once and for all the matter of the political shape of postwar central and Eastern Europe. Yet whereas the three Allied leaders had fought together for three years with a common aim, each now positioned himself at cross-purposes to the others, even as to how the final act of the war should play out.

On March 7, forward elements of the American First Army made their way across a railroad bridge that crossed the Rhine at Remagen, about a hundred miles south of Montgomery's British and Canadian armies, which faced the Ruhr. The Germans had intended to destroy the Remagen bridge but the Americans secured it with minutes to spare before the explosive charges were set off. By the morning of March 8, the Americans had a foothold on the east bank. A week later, the American Third Army crossed the Moselle, and seven days after that, it crossed the Rhine in force at Oppenheim, south of Mainz and about 150 miles south of Montgomery. It had taken Montgomery a month to slog to his current position; with the Ruhr at stake, von Rundstedt, under orders from Hitler to defend the Ruhr at all costs, had flooded the lowlands at Montgomery's front. Von Rundstedt (called out of retirement months earlier) had slowed the British advance, but by March 21 Montgomery was ready. That night, the first squads of the Black Watch crossed the Rhine. Two nights later, Montgomery began throwing his main forces across, including the American Ninth Army, which was attached to his command. The operation was code-named Plunder, and Winston Churchill had arrived by air in order to see the curtain go up.

Montgomery had asked Brooke to keep Churchill away, but the Old Man was not to be denied. Not since 1813 had British troops fought on German soil. Accompanied by his naval aide, Tommy Thompson, along with Brooke and Jock Colville, Churchill took up residence at Montgomery's forward headquarters. The Old Man was given two caravans (trailers, to a Yank), one for work and one for sleep. Monty had several caravans, Colville noted, of varying nationalities. One had belonged to the Italian general Bergonzoli; another was used for sleeping, a third was filled with caged canaries and served as a map room. Two portraits of Rommel hung on the wall. On the morning of March 24, Colville and some friends repaired to a hillside overlooking the river. They watched and listened as two thousand big guns put down a barrage, and as fighters and bombers streamed overhead. Far overhead, an aerial armada of gliders and paratroop transports drifted past on its way to the drop zone. At one point Colville spied a distant contrail arching high into the sky on a westerly bearing: a V-2 on its way to Antwerp or London. Churchill took all this in from Monty's headquarters. Everyone noted that some of the Allied planes returned in flames, with parachutes popping open high in the sky.[124]

The next day, the prime minister went on a special quest to the river's edge. There, near Wesel, he climbed onto a wrecked bridge to take in the scene. Brooke thought the adventure misguided, especially when German snipers and gunners began pouring fire at British engineers a few hundred yards downstream. With shells falling nearby and raising great columns of mud and spray, Brooke advised Churchill to depart. Instead, Churchill "put both his arms round one of the twisted girders of the bridge and looked over his shoulder... with pouting mouth and angry eyes! Thank heaven he came away quietly, it was a sad wrench for him, he was enjoying himself immensely!" The next day, after driving south to Eisenhower's headquarters, the Old Man asked Montgomery to join him in taking a motor launch across to the German side. "Why not," answered Montgomery. Churchill later wrote: "We landed in brilliant sunshine and perfect peace on the German shore, and walked about for half an hour or so unmolested." Later that day, as recorded by Brooke, Churchill took himself on a long trek down to the river, where "on arrival he solemnly relieved himself in the Rhine." Brooke could only see Churchill's back, but was sure the Old Man wore a "boyish grin of contentment."[125]

Within a week, Montgomery and the American Ninth Army had established a secure beachhead about twenty miles deep and thirty-five miles wide on either side of Wesel. The American Ninth and First Armies encircled a German army in the Ruhr and met at Lippstadt, near Paderborn. By April 4 Montgomery's Second British Army had pushed even farther east to Hamelin, on the Weser River. This put the British and the Americans on their right about 150 miles from Berlin, a straight shot across the northern German plains. The Russian armies on the lower Oder, meanwhile, had been resupplying for eight weeks and had yet to commence their final, fifty-mile drive to Berlin. In fact, the Russians had told Eisenhower that they would likely not begin that assault until mid-May.[126]

In mid-March, Molotov refused entry into Poland to a British diplomatic mission. On the sixteenth Churchill cabled Roosevelt: "At present all entry into Poland is barred to our representatives. An impenetrable veil has been drawn across the scene.... There is no doubt in my mind the Soviets fear very much our seeing what is going on in Poland." Two weeks later, Churchill protested to Stalin "the veil of secrecy" drawn around Poland and warned that if "our efforts to reach an agreement about Poland are doomed to failure, I shall be bound to confess the fact to Parliament." But they *had* reached an agreement on Poland at Yalta, albeit one so imprecisely worded that it was open to wide interpretation. The word "interpretation" appears repeatedly in telegrams between Roosevelt and Churchill during the last weeks of March and the first week of April (by which time most of Roosevelt's communications were written for his signature by Admiral Leahy or the State Department). A less vague and more rigidly legalistic declaration might not have forestalled Stalin's abrogation of it, but it would have at least served as a means to articulate the exact nature of Stalin's abrogation. The vagueness of the declaration underscores Stalin's adroit (and deceitful) negotiating skills. Now, with the Red Army preparing for the final drive down the roads to Berlin and Vienna, Stalin was free to interpret that agreement in terms satisfactory only to himself.[127]

Then, in late March, Eisenhower, without explaining the decision to the satisfaction of the British Chiefs of Staff (and Churchill), swung his main American forces south, on the Leipzig-Dresden axis, and away from Berlin, in an effort to cut Germany in two. To Montgomery's fury, Eisenhower soon detached the American Ninth Army from his command and swung it toward the southeast rather than into the heart of the Ruhr Valley. To the further displeasure of Churchill and the British military chiefs, Eisenhower had cabled his plans directly to Stalin on March 29, thus bypassing his civilian leaders in London and Washington as well as his only military boss, George Marshall. "Eisenhower," Brooke told his diary, "has no business to address Stalin direct...he produced a telegram that was unintelligible, and finally what was implied in it appeared to be entirely adrift and a change in all that had been previously agreed upon." Churchill, Brooke wrote, "was in a hopeless mood." Montgomery, in his memoirs, produced a telegram Eisenhower had sent him six months earlier: "Clearly, Berlin is the main prize. There is no doubt whatsoever, in my mind, that we should concentrate all our resources and energy on a rapid thrust to Berlin." "But now," wrote Montgomery, "he did not agree....It was useless for me to pursue the matter further."[128]

Eisenhower, William L. Shirer wrote, had become "obsessed" by the idea of an Alpine German national redoubt, where, Ike's intelligence chiefs told him, Hitler and the remainder of his armies would take to caves and Alpine passes to fight on for months, perhaps years. Food, weapons, and ammunition had been gathered or manufactured in deep underground chambers, Ike was told. It was a myth; the national redoubt never existed other than in Goebbels' propaganda bleats. "It would seem," Shirer wrote, "that the allied Supreme Commander's intelligence staff had been infiltrated by British and American mystery writers." Eisenhower had long claimed his objective was to kill German armies; now he thought there were German armies where there were none.[129]

Montgomery might not have been willing to pursue the matter of Eisenhower's new strategy, but Churchill was. For Churchill, Berlin had always been both a military objective and a political objective. He believed, he told Roosevelt in an April 1 cable, that "nothing will exert a psychological effect of despair upon all German forces...equal to that of the fall of Berlin." With the probable betrayal of the Poles and the Yalta agreement in mind, he warned Roosevelt: "If they [the Russians] also take Berlin will not their impression that they have been the overwhelming contributor to our common victory be unduly imprinted in their minds....I therefore consider that from a political standpoint we should march as far east into Germany as possible, and that should Berlin be in our grasp we should certainly take it. This also appears sound on military grounds." Roosevelt, having gone down to Warm Springs on March 29 in hopes of regaining some of his waning strength, replied on April 4 in a long and imprecise telegram that said little to address Churchill's concerns but included the line: "I do not get the point." Eisenhower by then was hell-bent for the national redoubt.[130]

As well, unbeknownst to Eisenhower, who had been told by the Soviets in mid-March that their attack from the northern Oder would not begin until mid-May, the Soviets had moved up the date. On April 1 Stalin met in Moscow with his high command, including generals Zhukov and Konev, whose two armies sat near the Oder just fifty miles east of Berlin. Even with Eisenhower's disarmingly honest disclosure of his strategy in hand, Stalin believed the British and Americans were about to launch an operation toward Berlin. It made good military sense for Eisenhower to do so. Therefore, the marshal told Zhukov and Konev to commence a friendly race from the Oder to Berlin as soon as possible. This decision moved up the attack from mid-May to mid-April. Stalin informed the American ambassador of the decision the next day.[131]

At about this time Czechoslovakian president Eduard Beneš made a comment to Churchill over lunch; as paraphrased by Jock Colville, Beneš said that "America might be materially far more powerful than England," but that "England's cultural dominance was supreme and unchallenged." For Churchill, this was no mean consolation, for he agreed mightily with Macaulay that were Englishmen ever to lose their physical empire, they could be justifiably proud of leaving behind "the imperishable empire" of their laws, their morals, their literature, their sense of justice. England, Churchill told Beneš, "was a small lion walking between a huge Russian bear and a great American elephant, but perhaps it would prove to be the lion which knew the way." It was much the same thought he expressed to Violet Bonham Carter, with the Tehran conference in mind. But now, as the war entered its final weeks, it no longer mattered if Churchill knew the way.[132]

The last substantive exchange of views among the Big Three took place during the final days of March and the early days of April. On March 27 Churchill pleaded with Roosevelt to join him in taking a firm stand against Stalin on the Polish question:

> As you know, if we fail altogether to get a satisfactory solution on Poland, and are in fact defrauded by Russia, both Eden and I are pledged to report the fact openly to the House of Commons. There I advised critics of the Yalta settlement to trust Stalin. If I have to make statement of facts to the House, the whole world will draw the deduction that such advice was wrong.... Surely we must not be manoeuvered into becoming parties to imposing on Poland, and on much more of Eastern Europe, the Russian version of democracy?... There seems to be only one possible alternative to confessing our total failure. That alternative is to stand by our interpretation of the Yalta declaration.[133]

In a cable to Stalin on March 29, Roosevelt addressed Stalin's intransigence as well as a threat by Stalin to effectively boycott the San Francisco conference by not sending Molotov:

> I MUST MAKE IT PLAIN TO YOU THAT ANY SOLUTION WHICH WOULD RESULT IN A THINLY DISGUISED CONTINUANCE OF THE PRESENT WARSAW REGIME [THE LUBLIN GOVERNMENT] WOULD BE UNACCEPTABLE AND WOULD CAUSE THE PEOPLE OF THE UNITED STATES TO REGARD THE YALTA AGREEMENT AS HAVING FAILED....[134]

Stalin had also accused Churchill and Roosevelt of encouraging secret negotiations in Bern, Switzerland, between Allen Dulles, the OSS bureau chief in Bern, and SS General Karl Wolff, who served under the theater commander, Albert Kesselring. Bern, like Stockholm, was a hotbed of intrigue, and Dulles had indeed held preliminary talks with Wolff, but he had not, strictly speaking, conducted surrender talks. Wolff, for his part, had no authority to do so and was only putting out feelers—and seeking terms—in hopes of bringing Kesselring and Field Marshal Alexander to the table. Why, Stalin asked Roosevelt, were Soviet representatives excluded from the Bern talks? Roosevelt replied—without answering Stalin's question—that the entire unfortunate episode "has developed an atmosphere of fear and distrust deserving regrets." Stalin's reply to Roosevelt was scathing; the marshal quoted Roosevelt's fear and distrust line, and wrote: "You are absolutely right." Churchill, upon seeing Stalin's note, wrote to Roosevelt: "I am astounded that Stalin should have addressed to you a message so insulting to the honour of the United States and also Great Britain.... All this makes it the more important that we should join hands with the Russian army as far to the east as possible, and if circumstances allow, enter Berlin." But Roosevelt had already rejected that strategy. Churchill added: "If they [the Russians] are ever convinced that we are afraid of them and can be bullied into submission, then indeed I shall despair of our future relations with them, and much more."[135]

On April 5 Churchill followed his cable to Roosevelt with his own reply to Stalin, in which he categorically rejected the charge that military negotiations had taken place in Bern. He added: "Still less did any political-military plot, as alleged in your telegram to the president, enter into our thoughts, which are not as suggested of so dishonourable a character."[136]

On that subject, as on Poland and Eastern Europe, there was little left to say, and nothing left to do. It was done.

Early in the afternoon of April 12, in his Warm Springs parlor, Roosevelt complained of "a terrible headache" before slumping over in his chair. He had suffered a massive cerebral hemorrhage. At 3:35 P.M., doctors declared the president dead. The news did not reach Churchill until almost midnight. He ordered his plane to be made ready for the trip to the United States in order to attend the funeral on April 14. He sent off three cables, to Harry Hopkins, to the new president, Harry Truman, and to Eleanor Roosevelt, whom he told: "I have lost a dear and cherished friendship which was forged in the fire of war. I trust you may find some consolation in the magnitude of his work and the glory of his name." Churchill did not in the end travel to Hyde Park. With the war nearing its finish—perhaps within days—it was clear that he considered London the most advantageous place to be. Clementine was not there to advise him. She had left for Moscow two weeks earlier, to tour Red Cross installations as the guest of Stalin. On the fourteenth, Churchill wrote to her: "At the last moment I decided not to fly to Roosevelt's funeral on account of much that's going on here."[137]

On the seventeenth, Churchill paid tribute to Roosevelt in the House. Harold Nicolson thought the address uninspired, "nothing like as good as when he [Churchill] made the funeral oration on Neville Chamberlain, which was truly Periclean." Yet, Nicolson offered to his diary, Churchill's speech showed that "when one really does mind deeply about a thing, it is more difficult to write or speak about it than when one is just faintly moved by pity or terror." Churchill ended his remarks with the words "For us, it remains only to say that in Franklin Roosevelt there died the greatest American friend we have ever known, and the greatest champion of freedom who has ever brought help and comfort from the new world to the old."[138]

On April 13, three days before Zhukov and Konev launched their final drive to Berlin, Vienna fell to the Red Army. Stalin's troops then began moving up the Danube while Eisenhower's forces moved down, in the general direction of Linz. On April 16, American troops took Nuremberg, the locus of Nazidom's most holy rallies. It was a symbolic victory; Nuremberg lay almost 240 miles south of Berlin. The Americans, committed to their broad-front strategy, were wandering farther and farther away from the battlefield that Churchill considered most important: Berlin.

On April 20 Churchill dined alone with his first true love of almost a half century earlier, Pamela Plowden, now the Countess Lytton. Her son John had been killed at El Alamein. Churchill had first met her at a polo match in Assam, India, where her father was the police chief. She was both handsome and pretty, the belle of any city she chose to grace with her presence. After two years of polite courtship by Churchill, she had sought more ardor from him, and informed him so by letter. His pride wounded, he responded, "Why do you think I am incapable of affection? Perish the thought. I love one above all others. And I shall be constant." He proposed marriage while rowing a punt on the Avon under the ramparts of Warwick Castle. Pamela declined. In a sense, his declaration that he loved one above all others was true, but his love was for politics, and to politics he had remained constant during all the ensuing decades.[139]

The previous day, Eisenhower told Churchill of the horrors uncovered at the newly liberated concentration camp at Buchenwald. Only then did Churchill and the British people begin to realize that the propaganda stories about unspeakable murders on an unimaginable scale had been true all along. With some satisfaction Colville told his diary that after the mayor of Weimar and his wife were escorted to Buchenwald to survey the carnage, they went home and hanged themselves.[140]

As Churchill and the countess dined on April 20, the RAF bombed Berlin for the last time, not in order to give any respite to Berliners, but to avoid hitting Britain's allies, the Red Army, who were now at the gates. It was Hitler's fifty-sixth birthday.

That day in Hamburg, twenty Jewish children who had been brought there for medical experimentation were hanged by the SS in the basement of a former school at Bullenhuser Damm, a part of the Neuengamme concentration camp. Twenty Soviet prisoners were also hanged. British troops were inside the Hamburg city limits, but the Germans held the port, where ten thousand Russian POWs and Jews were made ready to march to the Bay of Lübeck, forty miles distant on the Baltic, from where the Germans intended to ship them up the coast to Kiel. Eden and Churchill believed that Montgomery should push on and take Lübeck. This would bar the door to Denmark, which would not only keep the Germans in, but keep the Red Army out. A Russian occupation of Denmark, Eden wrote, "would cause us much embarrassment." Churchill and Eden also agreed on the wisdom of the Americans getting to Prague before the Soviets.[141]

On April 20, Soviet artillery of the 1st Belorussian Front, positioned just outside Berlin, began to shell the heart of the city. Other Russian artillery units soon joined in, lofting high explosives from the east, northeast, and southeast into the Tiergarten, a dead landscape now, where no May flowers bloomed. The shells raked the zoo, empty now of zoological exhibits but for the three hundred German artillerymen who occupied a massive concrete pillbox from which they fired their 88s toward the Soviet lines. Soviet Katyusha rockets fired from American Studebaker chassis raked the Unter den Linden boulevard until only long rows of shredded, blackened stumps of linden trees remained. Heavy Red Army artillery lobbed ordnance into the Reich Chancellery, and into the shell of the old, burned-out Reichstag at virtual point-blank range. Russian gunners hurled tons of explosives into the immediate neighborhood around the Brandenburg Gate, which somehow survived the onslaught and where Victory, astride her quadriga, still clutched the Iron Cross, which the Nazis had substituted for her olive branch. The Pariser Platz was in ruins, yet somehow the Academy of Arts remained unscathed, although its next patrons would be drunken Soviet troops. Nearby, the Adlon Hotel, partially aflame, did not lack for patrons, of a sort: the basement, where Nazi swells had once sheltered themselves at leisure from errant British bombs, had been converted into a field hospital. Yet, for the wounded, there was little medicine, and no hope.[142]

Hitler's Olympischer Platz, its columns and walls ripped by shrapnel, resembled the ancient ruins of Carthage. The Russian artillery fire persisted for twelve straight days without a moment's pause, an inundation of tons upon thousands of tons of steel. Hundreds of Berliners were driven mad. Thousands now committed suicide rather than face the murderous wrath of the Red Army. Fathers murdered wives and daughters rather than allow them to fall into the hands of rapacious Soviet troops. The city waited for the end. In his *Führerbunker* thirty feet below the Chancellery—under six feet of compacted earth and a sixteen-foot-thick concrete roof—Adolf Hitler waited, waited for his imaginary armies to appear to crush the invaders and save everything he had striven to create. Yet the *crump* of each Soviet shell exploding in the streets above was heard, *felt* by Hitler and his dwindling band of fellow true believers. Hitler's oldest and most trusted Nazi cohorts were on hand to celebrate the Führer's birthday—Goebbels, Himmler, Göring, Bormann, and Ribbentrop. The last of the military chiefs were there—Dönitz, Jodl, and Keitel. Albert Speer arrived with birthday greetings but departed soon after, his orders from Hitler clear: to destroy any industrial and electrical centers that the Allies had not. Nothing was to remain standing or operational; the German people, having failed their Führer, deserved nothing. Speer departed with no intention of obeying the order. After the subdued birthday ceremony, Hitler made the trip up to the courtyard in order to encourage a platoon of *Hitlerjugend*—adolescent boys—to fight to the end. He patted one or two on the head, then sent them off to die. Late in the day, Hitler's generals advised the warlord to leave the city and set up a new command. He made no decision, but sent Dönitz to Flensburg, near the Danish frontier, to take command there. That night, Göring made good his escape in a caravan of automobiles loaded down with the air marshal's stolen loot. Himmler, too, fled. Ribbentrop also prepared to flee. Each was secure in his knowledge that Hitler would soon be dead, and each presumed he would soon take control.[143]

On April 22, both Dönitz and Himmler telephoned the bunker and urged Hitler to leave, but by then the Führer had decided to stay, to die at a time and place of his choosing. That night, he sent Keitel and Jodl south, toward Bavaria, to prepare for a last stand under the command of Göring in the phantom mountain redoubt (Hitler, like Eisenhower, had come to believe Goebbels' propaganda). Jodl protested that Hitler, cut off in Berlin, could not control the battle, and added that the Wehrmacht would not fight under Göring. Hitler shot back: "What do you mean, fight? There's precious little more fighting to be done!" The moment was a small island of clarity in a sea of delusion. Albert Speer called the surreal world in the bunker "the Isle of the Departed."[144]

On April 23, Himmler and Göring made their respective bids to supplant Hitler. Göring, by then in Berchtesgaden, wrote a letter to Hitler that cited a 1941 decree that should Hitler lose control of the government, the *Reichsmarschall* was to take command. Himmler that night met with Count Bernadotte in the Swedish consulate at Lübeck, on the Baltic. Himmler proposed, in writing, an astoundingly naive yet not unsound concept: he would arrange for the surrender of German armies in the west while continuing the fight against the Red Army until such time as Eisenhower and the Allies appeared on the scene to take over the battle against the Bolsheviks. By that night, only Hitler's SS guards, Ribbentrop, and Bormann remained with Hitler. Bormann, like Himmler and Göring, was plotting his own escape and ascendancy to supreme power. Hitler, learning of Himmler's and Göring's gambits, flew into a rage. He declared the fat *Reichsmarschall* a traitor, and ordered that he be found and shot, an order Bormann was only too happy to send out over the airwaves. Albert Speer that day had made the dangerous journey by air from Mecklenburg to Berlin, where he landed his cub aircraft in front of the Brandenburg Gate. He had come to ask Hitler to grant him his leave, and he fully expected to be hauled outside and shot for failing to obey Hitler's scorched-earth directive. Instead, after Speer confessed his disobedience, the two chatted amiably, if clumsily. For a moment, Hitler's "eyes filled with tears." Then he waved off Speer with a curt *auf Wiedersehen*. They parted without a handshake, and for the last time Speer left the Chancellery, now in ruins, which he had designed and built seven years earlier.[145]

By April 25, Berlin was surrounded, although a narrow corridor to the northwest was still open, along which thousands fled in hopes of reaching the refuge of the Anglo-American lines. That day, recalled one of Hitler's bodyguards, SS staff sergeant Rochus Misch, Hitler stunned those within earshot when he declared the war lost. Yet Hitler, like Himmler, still clung to a final delusion. After a junction between the Germans and the Americans, both armies would then turn to fight the Soviets. "Hitler didn't think a people like the Englanders would bind themselves with the communists to crush Germany, and he still believed... something could happen. He liked the Englanders," recalled Misch, "except for Churchill."[146]

That day, Russian and American advance patrols met at Torgau on the Elbe, just seventy-five miles south of Berlin. Germany was cut in half. Churchill and Truman had their first telephone conversation that day, the topic Himmler's offer to surrender German armies in the west. They pondered the proposal for less than a minute and agreed that Himmler was not a man to deal with and that all German armies must surrender simultaneously to the three powers, on all fronts. Churchill cabled Stalin with the decision. Churchill would remain loyal to Stalin to the end, but in fact he was now one with Himmler on the need to keep the Bolsheviks from reaching the western borders of Germany. "My mind," Churchill later wrote, "was oppressed with the new and even greater peril which was swiftly unfolding itself to my gaze." As he contemplated the consequences to Europe if the Russians kept up their westward march (they had reached Paris in 1814 and could do so again now), he pondered a response, a military response.[147]

On Saturday, April 28, the Russians moved into Potsdamer Platz, a mere block from Hitler's bunker. The seismic footfalls grew closer. By early the next morning, Hitler had heard enough. He put Dönitz in charge of the government, such as it was, and then dictated his last will and testament, in which he blamed "the ruling clique in England" and "International Jewry" for the war and its forty million dead. Sometime before dawn on the twenty-ninth, Hitler and his somewhat dim-witted mistress of twelve years, Eva Braun, were married in a civil ceremony witnessed by Bormann and Goebbels. The bride wore a dark-blue silk dress; a small private reception followed. The guests listened as the Führer rambled on about the old days, the good days. Later that afternoon, Hitler received one of the last reports to reach him from the world outside. Mussolini and his mistress, Clara Petacci, had been murdered the previous day by Italian partisans. By the time Hitler learned of the deaths, their bodies had been brought to Milan and strung up by the heels from lampposts. Garbled communications spared Hitler from learning of the other momentous event that took place that day in Italy: General Heinrich von Vietinghoff agreed to surrender his Italian forces on May 2. Above the Chancellery, the Red Army swept down the avenues of Berlin.[148]

As Hitler toasted his bride, Churchill dispatched a long telegram to Stalin in a final attempt to salvage the agreements on Poland made at Yalta. In effect, it was a final attempt to salvage the peace. The plan for Poland agreed upon at Yalta, Churchill wrote, called for "universal suffrage" and truly democratic elections. "None of this has been allowed to move forward." Britain had gone to war for Poland, Churchill reminded Stalin. "The British people can never feel that this war has ended rightly until Poland has a fair deal in the full sense of sovereignty, independence, and freedom on the basis of friendship with Russia." Rumors were now coming out of Poland that indicated Polish patriots were disappearing (indeed, the Soviet secret police, the NKVD, was orchestrating mass liquidations of Polish officers and men). In late March, sixteen Polish republicans had been granted safe passage from Warsaw to Lublin in order to meet with Soviet generals. They had disappeared. Molotov, attending the San Francisco conference of the United Nations, at first refused to divulge to Eden any information on the goings-on in Poland. The Allies had agreed at Yalta that representatives from each government were to have free access to areas controlled by the others. Yet, Churchill declared to Stalin, "neither I nor the Americans are allowed to send anyone into Poland to find out for themselves the true state of affairs." A horrific crisis was in the making, Churchill warned: "There is not much comfort in looking into a future where you and the countries you dominate... are all drawn up on one side, and those who rally to the English-speaking nations and their associates... are on the other. It is quite obvious that their quarrel would tear the world to pieces." Colville thought the telegram a "masterly... final appeal to resolve the Polish crisis."[149]

Stalin, that week, imparted his philosophy of war to Milovan Djilas, a guest at the Kremlin: "This war is not as in the past; whoever occupies a territory also imposes on it his own social system. Everyone imposes his own system as far as his army can reach. It cannot be otherwise.... If now there is not a communist government in Paris, it is because Russia has no army which can reach to Paris in 1945."[150]

Austria's turn to go under the Soviet boot came later, on April 29, when Moscow radio announced the formation of a provisional government in Vienna. American troops occupied the western two-thirds of the country, but in spite of that and in spite of the agreement made at Yalta, the Soviet government refused to allow American or British missions to enter Vienna. In reality, there was not that much left to enter; the Germans had burned St. Stephen's Cathedral and much of the old city on their way out of town.

In Berlin early the next day, Monday, April 30, Hitler was told the city's defenders would run out of ammunition by nightfall. Late that afternoon, after testing the effect of a cyanide capsule on his Alsatian bitch, Blondi, Hitler proffered one to his new wife. Frau Hitler dutifully took the capsule, and bit down. Adolf Hitler had murdered his last German. A moment later, the widower put the barrel of a German pistol into his mouth and pulled the trigger.

The Americans occupied Munich that morning, and in Italy they entered Turin, where Italian partisans had been fighting Germans for three days. The war in Italy was effectively over, although Albert Kesselring, now commanding all German forces in the west and south, sacked von Vietinghoff, who had proposed to surrender. Two days later, Kesselring saw the futility of his situation, and surrendered the Italian armies to Alexander.

On the thirtieth, Eisenhower guaranteed the Soviet deputy chief of staff that the right wing of Patton's Third Army in Austria would not advance farther than "the general area of Linz," the city where Hitler had spent most of his childhood and where he had intended to build his *Führermuseum,* to house his stolen art. His tomb, too, was to be in Linz, to which he presumed Nazi pilgrims would journey for centuries. A model of the museum had been brought down into the bunker; the Führer could not have helped seeing it as the Russians closed in. Two hundred miles north of Linz, the left flank of Patton's Third Army was just sixty miles west of Prague, and under orders from Eisenhower to proceed no farther east. To Truman, Churchill pleaded the case for Patton to continue. The president backed Eisenhower, who had told him that he would not contemplate "any move which I deem militarily unwise." Churchill's concerns, as they had been since before Yalta, were not strictly military. He told Truman: "There is little doubt that the liberation of Prague... by your forces might make the whole difference to the post-war situation in Czechoslovakia and might well influence that in nearby countries." Truman and Eisenhower held firm. Eisenhower, in fact, assured the Russians that when the surrender came, Allied troops would withdraw 140 miles from those areas within the Russian zone agreed upon at Yalta. The Russians took Prague on May 4. "The [American] failure to take Prague," Eden later wrote, "meant the Red Army was able to put its creatures firmly in command." The was not the sort of "mutual assistance" Eduard Beneš had in mind when he signed the twenty-year treaty of friendship with Stalin eighteen months earlier.[151]

Also on the thirtieth, Tito's partisans entered Trieste, and by nightfall they were fighting Italians within the city limits. Churchill ordered New Zealand troops to occupy the city, advising that no violence should occur, except in self-defense. But Tito had won the race for Trieste, and Istrea. "It's hard to see how he can ever be dislodged," Colville told his diary. Yet Tito's claim on northeast Italy, Colville wrote, "may split the Italian Communist party and thus at least save Italy from the Russian imperialist clutches." It did, and Churchill's show of force ended with the Yugoslavs returning home by mid-June. Truman took a strong stand in support of Churchill on the matter, leading Churchill to conclude that the new president would likewise be stern with the Russians if the need arose, which appeared more likely with each passing day. Colville thought the prospect of the Soviets and their Yugoslav proxies dominating Europe "from the North Cape to Trieste" depressing, but for the fact that "the Americans occupy *de facto* great parts of Germany which belong *de jure* to the Russian zone of occupation." He and Churchill were as yet unaware of Eisenhower's pledge to move his armies out of the Russian zone.[152]

It was the night before May 1, *Walpurgisnacht* (a traditional festival in Europe in which witches are said to await the arrival of spring). For centuries on this night, from Romania to the Baltic, peasants lit bonfires intended to keep at bay demons who they believed roamed the landscape. They stoked the flames with hopes of surviving to the morrow, May Day, the ancient pagan day of rebirth. For a dozen years under Adolf Hitler, *Walpurgisnacht* was also a sacred Nazi holiday when good Germans celebrated the fertility of Nazi youth destined to breed glorious Nazi babies. Soon after the Führer had put an end to himself, a small contingent of SS men hauled his corpse and that of Eva Braun into the courtyard of the Chancellery, rolled them into a bomb crater, and with the help of twenty gallons of gasoline, added one more pyre to the inferno that was Berlin. It was twelve years and three months to the day since Hitler became chancellor of Germany. His thousand-year Reich would survive him by a week.[153]

Goebbels survived him by a day. Two years earlier the little doctor had drawn a bittersweet picture of family life in his diary: "In the evening I am able to devote a little time to the children, with whom I'm having much fun.... Once the war is over I shall be able to devote myself more than hitherto to their upbringing. I could not think and wish for any more beautiful task for the coming peace." With the war now over, the peace Goebbels planned for his children would be everlasting. On the evening of May 1, Herr Doktor and Frau Goebbels poisoned their six children. The little bodies were taken aloft to the courtyard, where two SS officers, as ordered by Goebbels, dispatched the doctor and his wife with two shots to the back of the head. Then the Goebbels family was doused with gasoline and set aflame. Not enough gasoline was available to make a decent job of it, and the Red Army soldiers found the smoldering remains the next day.[154]

By the evening of May 1, the abandoned *Führerbunker* had been set ablaze by the Red Army. The Reichstag had been shelled at point-blank range by eighty-nine Red Army field guns, and then taken after a fifteen-hour gunfight between Russians, who occupied the second floor, and a band of Germans, who occupied the third. The civilian population of Berlin took shelter in the city's basements. The streets above contained only

Soviet troops and dead Berliners. The last Nazi holdouts were fighting from the sewers. Bormann and several hundred of Hitler's entourage had taken refuge at the New Chancellery. They attempted a breakout on foot to the River Spree by way of a subway tunnel under the Wilhelmsplatz. Hunched over in their filthy gray greatcoats, they leaned into the walls and crept through the destruction en masse in the dark. Bormann didn't make it, the victim of a shell that crashed into a tank he had hoped would afford him shelter.[155]

Across the Continent, April had brought splendid weather, with temperatures more reminiscent of the dog days of summer than early spring. "Nobody seems to remember such weather in April before," Colville told his diary. "Surely there has never been such a spring.... The cherries are weighed down with blossom, the chestnuts and the lilac are already out, as is the wisteria in Great Court, before the daffodils have faded." Beneath a "China blue sky" tall elms wore their early coats of pale green. In London during the early hours of May 1, after two weeks of such glorious weather, a wet, heavy snow fell. By daybreak, window boxes were encrusted and lilacs bent under the hoary cloak, but their stubborn blooms pushed through the puffs of snow, an odd sight but somehow appropriate for the day of rebirth. Late in the afternoon, as Churchill strolled through the smoking room of the House, he was asked by an MP how the war was going. He replied, "Yes, it is definitely more satisfactory than it was this time five years ago."[156]

That evening Hamburg radio interrupted Hitler's favorite Wagner, *Götterdämmerung,* with the announcement that *"Unser führer, Adolf Hitler, ist... gefallen."* He had died bravely, according to Hamburg, "fighting with his last breath against Bolshevism." Wagner himself wrote the original program note for *Götterdämmerung:* "The will that wanted to shape an entire world according to its wish can finally attain nothing more satisfactory than... annihilation."[157]

Churchill hosted a political dinner in the Annexe that night; no military marshals sat in. It was nigh time to reposition himself as England's best choice as peacetime leader. The Japanese had yet to be vanquished, but the war in Europe—England's war—was over. A general election would have to be called. Beaverbrook (and Eden, from San Francisco) argued for a June vote, when victory would be fresh in the minds of the people, rather than a later date. Joining Churchill at dinner were the Beaver, Oliver Lyttelton, the chief whip James Stuart, and Ralph Assheton, all of them Tory political operatives, the field marshals of their party. Brendan Bracken did not attend. Tory regulars had begun to "look askance at the

Brendan-Beaver combination," Colville later wrote, in part because these two supreme Churchill loyalists violently opposed the liberal Tory stance on national health care, housing, and education, which Churchill (an old Liberal) supported. His support of reform in those three spheres, he believed, would deliver him and the party a victory in the general election. He was thus forced to preserve party unity by relegating one of his two best friends to the sidelines. It was Bracken, soon awarded first lord of the Admiralty for his services and loyalty. He had desired the Exchequer, an office even his old friend Winston Churchill knew he was unqualified for. For the first time in five years, Adolf Hitler was not a subject of dinner conversation, or wasn't until Jock Colville brought Churchill the news of the Führer's death. The Old Man, believing Hitler had died fighting, said, "Well, I must say I think he was perfectly right to die like that."[158]

And with that, the party caucus resumed, and continued on past 3:00 A.M. A plan took shape, which had been fermenting since late March, to ask Attlee and Labour to continue the national government until the defeat of Japan, at which time a general election would be held. That might take the elections well into 1946, when Churchill would presumably still be basking in the light of victory. Attlee and Labour, for their part, sought an election by October at the latest, regardless of the status of the Pacific war. All believed that an invasion of Japan would be necessary, a bloody business in which Churchill fully intended Britain would meet its obligations.

Hitler's cannonade of June of 1941 had announced his intention to liquidate Russia; Zhukov's twelve-day barrage had reduced Berlin to rubble. Russian Katyusha rockets now raked the rubble, which heaved from underground explosions as Soviet sappers used dynamite and flamethrowers to clear subway tunnels where Nazi holdouts fought on, and from where the stench of burnt flesh drifted up to the streets. The Russians outnumbered the three hundred thousand defenders of Berlin by more than five to one, outnumbered them in artillery by fifteen to one, and in tanks by six to one. When the end came, the Soviets had suffered 350,000 casualties, including almost 80,000 killed. Within the city limits, where barricaded defenders could hold off large numbers of Soviet attackers, five times as many Red Army troops as Germans had been killed. More than 125,000 Berliners died, many by suicide, and as many women were raped, although exact counts were impossible to ascertain given the fury of the final days. To this day, bones of the dead are unearthed. Hitler's bones will not be among them. The Soviets scraped together Hitler's remains by the night of May 1 and sent them east, toward Russia. Immediately a rumor took hold across the Continent: Hitler had escaped, to his mountain redoubt, to the west, to places unknown. Churchill suspected the Russians were behind it. They were. Weeks later, Stalin "speculated" that Hitler and his top aides might have escaped to Japan via giant U-boats. It was a clever way of manipulating popular fears, a twist on *Walpurgisnacht* that held out the terrible possibility that Hitler might emerge from hiding to rekindle the ashes of his Reich. In fact, parts of Hitler's jaws and skull made it to Moscow. The rest of him was buried beneath a military parade ground in Magdeburg, Germany, which the Soviets occupied for more than forty years. Sometime in the 1970s, the Führer's remains were exhumed and incinerated for a second time. The ashes were flushed into the city's sewer system, where they suffered the fate of Mary Shelley's monster, *borne away by the waves and lost in darkness and distance.*[159]

By May 1, Eisenhower had shifted his attention to the Pacific theater. He was sending the First Army as soon as possible, and he was likely to send Patton and the Third Army as well. Half the American air forces in Europe would be going. In Germany, those American units that had overshot the agreed-upon Soviet and Anglo-American lines of demarcation were already retiring westward.

On May 2, Eamon de Valera, prime minister of Ireland, motored to the German legation in Dublin to offer his condolences on the occasion of Hitler's death. The "Dev" and Ireland had pulled it off, the only English-speaking country in the world to win the war by missing it. Days later Churchill excoriated de Valera during a worldwide broadcast. Referring to the U-boat menace of 1940 and 1941, Churchill said, "This was indeed a deadly moment in our life, and if it had not been for the loyalty and friendship of Northern Ireland, we should have been forced to come to close quarters with Mr. de Valera or perish forever from the earth. However, with a restraint and poise to which, I say, history will find few parallels, His Majesty's Government never laid a violent hand upon them, though at times it would have been quite easy and quite natural, and we left the de Valera government to frolic with the Germans and later with the Japanese representatives to their heart's content."[160]

In Flensburg on May 2, *Reichspräsident* Dönitz's newly appointed leading minister, Count Schwerin von Krosigk, made a radio broadcast to Germans in which he told them, "In the East the iron curtain behind which, unseen by the eyes of the world, the work of destruction goes on, is moving steadily forward." The London *Times* ran the story the next day.[161]

Montgomery took Lübeck on May 2, just twelve hours before the Russians got there. That put Monty's army astride the neck of the Danish peninsula. The next morning, shortly before noon, four German officers were escorted to Montgomery's trailer under a flag of truce. Monty, like the neighborhood curmudgeon who neither seeks nor welcomes visitors, threw open the door and demanded of his interpreter, "Who are these men? What do they want?" They were representatives of Field Marshal Keitel, and they wanted to surrender to the British three German armies that faced the Russians. They said they feared for civilians caught between the armies, and they feared savage treatment at the hands of the Red Army were they to surrender in that direction. Montgomery told them they should have thought of that before they started the war. The Germans asked how they could be saved. Essentially they were seeking Montgomery's approval to continue the fight against the Russians without British interference in their rear. Montgomery refused. He told them that their situation was hopeless, and that until they surrendered, he would continue killing German soldiers and civilians. Then he directed them to a tent where he suggested they have lunch and think things over. They ate, they pondered; they agreed to return the next day with an answer. Two of the officers went back to Flensburg with Montgomery's ultimatum. After consulting Dönitz, they returned the next day, May 4, and at 6:30 P.M. signed the instrument of surrender Montgomery had prepared. Expecting the Germans to do just that, Montgomery had ordered his troops to cease fire late on the third.[162]

The British war in Europe was over. And in the Far East, British and colonial troops had freed Rangoon the previous day. That afternoon, Churchill called his military chiefs to No. 10, where Brooke found him "evidently seriously affected by the fact that the war was to all intents and purposes over as far as Germany was concerned. He thanked us all very nicely and with tears in his eyes for all we had done in the war.... He then shook hands with all of us."[163]

In San Francisco that day, May 4, Molotov admitted to Eden that the sixteen Poles who had been granted safe passage from Warsaw to Lublin had been arrested. Stalin, calling the Poles "diverginists," admitted likewise in a cable to Churchill. Fifty of the fifty-one Allied nations had sent representatives to San Francisco. The fifty-first, Poland, had in effect ceased to exist. The Soviets proposed a horse trade to the British: they would approve the British and American nomination of Argentina for admittance to the United Nations in return for the admission of—in Cadogan's words—"[the] beastly sham Polish Government." This was a deft ploy on the part of Stalin and Molotov. Argentina, its government quasi-Fascist, had been a pro-Axis neutral for five years until finally seeing the light in late March, when Colonel Juan Perón took over and declared war on Germany. The Lublin Poles, whatever their Bolshevik leanings, had fought against the Nazis since 1939.

If Argentina was to be granted admittance, Molotov argued, why not the new Polish government? Eden refused.[164]

Eisenhower's turn to accept a German surrender came at 2:41 A.M. British Double Summer Time on Monday, May 7, at his headquarters in Reims. General Alfred Jodl, for Dönitz, and Bedell Smith, for SHAEF, signed the instrument of unconditional surrender, with French and Russian officers as witnesses. Hostilities were to cease at midnight, and the German entourage was to proceed to Berlin to sign the Russian ratification on the ninth. Shortly before dawn, Pug Ismay had received a call from Eisenhower. "What's happened?" Ismay asked. Came the reply: "It's all over." But it wasn't over until Stalin said it was over. His troops were still mopping up in Czechoslovakia and along the Baltic. He sought to postpone any official announcement until the formal ratification by all parties in Berlin on the ninth.[165]

A predawn thunderstorm broke over London with "an imitation of the blitz so realistic," Mollie Panter-Downes wrote, "many Londoners started awake and reached for the bedside torch." The V-2s had ceased coming over in late March, but nerves were still raw. The blackout had been lifted a week earlier, after 2,061 consecutive nights of darkness. But when the switch was thrown, London's streetlights failed to flare, and though most Londoners took down their heavy blackout curtains (which they converted to black clothes and funeral coverings), they pulled their old curtains closed out of habit. A five-year-old girl who had lived her entire life behind the blackout curtains said to her mother, "It's lovely to let out the light, but how shall we keep out the dark?"[166]

On the afternoon of May 7, as crowds began to gather in expectation of an official announcement, Churchill hosted a lunch for his military chiefs at No. 10. It was a "disturbed" affair, Brooke wrote, marked by Churchill taking phone calls from Truman and Eisenhower over the matter of the official announcement, which Churchill sought to make that evening and Stalin wanted postponed for a day. "As usual," Ismay later wrote, "he [Stalin] had his way." Churchill agreed to delay the announcement, but for only twenty-four hours. Tuesday, May 8, was to be V-E day in England and America; the Soviets would celebrate victory on May 9. The lunch party adjourned to the garden for photographs. Champagne and glasses sat ready on a side table, put there by Churchill himself. He raised a toast to the chiefs as "the architects of victory," and thanked them for the years of work that had brought them all to this day. Inexplicably, none returned the toast. Ismay could not bring himself to believe the slight was intentional. "I had hoped," he later wrote, "that they would raise their glasses to the chief who had been the master planner; but perhaps they were too moved to trust their voices."[167]

That night, the BBC announced that the prime minister would address the nation from No. 10 at 3:00 P.M. the following day. In New York, Paris, Brussels, Moscow, and London, crowds had already taken to the streets. By dawn on May 8, more than a million Londoners—men, women, and children—pressed toward the gates of Buckingham Palace from Whitehall and Piccadilly and Trafalgar Square, from Hyde Park, Parliament Square, the Strand, and St. James's Park and Green Park. London's bells began ringing at sunrise, and rang throughout the morning, a tolling that carried away into the countryside and rolled down the Thames to the Channel. Children paraded through the streets wrapped in American flags and British and Russian flags. Thousands of Union Jacks flew from windows, joined by the Stars and Stripes and the Hammer and Sickle. Mothers hoisted children onto their hips, and the children in turn waved little Union Jacks fixed on slim sticks. Housewives in long breadlines (there was a loaf shortage) waved little Union Jacks while keeping a hand on their string bags. A group of sailors and girls formed a conga line in Piccadilly. Owners of bulldogs paraded their charges outfitted in Union Jack sweaters. Eight times that day, the masses called for their King and Queen, and eight times the royal couple stepped from their rooms onto a balcony at Buckingham Palace, King George attired in his Royal Navy uniform.

Churchill lunched at the palace with the King, the man who five years earlier had handed the seals of office to him with great reluctance. When the crowd again called for a royal benediction, the King invited Churchill to join him and the Queen and the royal princesses, Margaret and Elizabeth, on the balcony. Always respectful of the monarchy, Churchill stood a discreet foot or so behind King George, his posture that of a five-foot-eight-inch man under a five-foot-six-inch ceiling. In photos of the scene, Churchill wears the impish smile of a little boy who has just been told, *Behave yourself.* When the crowd caught sight of Churchill, Mollie Panter-Downes wrote, "there was a deep, full-throated, almost reverent roar."[168]

King George delivered a brief radio address later that day. "Today we give thanks to Almighty God for a great deliverance," he began, and asked Britons "to join with me in that act of thanksgiving." He ended by noting that "in the hour of danger we humbly committed our cause into the hand of God, and He has been our strength and shield.... Let us thank Him for His mercies in this hour of victory." Across the Atlantic, President Truman, who was celebrating his sixty-first birthday, issued a proclamation that began "The Allies, through sacrifice and devotion and with God's help, have wrung from Germany a final and unconditional surrender." Declaring it "fitting that we as a nation give thanks to Almighty God, who has strengthened us and given us the victory," he appointed "Sunday, May 13, to be day of prayer." Neither the King nor the president made any mention of Winston Churchill.

In Paris, Charles de Gaulle was swept along the Champs-Élysées and under the Arc de Triomphe by a throng of nearly one million Frenchmen. He told his countrymen: "Honor, eternal honor to our armies and their eternal leaders. Honor to our nation, which never faltered. . . . *Vive la France*." Two months later, the provisional French Assembly delivered a vote that serves as a measure of how completely Franklin Roosevelt and the State Department had misread de Gaulle and France. The Assembly, a cantankerous mix of socialists, communists, liberals, conservatives, republicans, and monarchists, offered Charles de Gaulle the presidency of the Council by a unanimous vote. In October, when the United Nations officially opened, France, its soul reclaimed, took its place as the fifth permanent seat on the Security Council. Three months later, in January 1946, de Gaulle, contemptuous of the proposed new constitution that would underlie the Fourth Republic, resigned. He was, one of his ministers once said, "a man equally incapable of monopolizing power and of sharing it." His self-imposed political exile lasted thirteen years, until January 1959, when, after capturing almost 80 percent of the electoral college vote, he was sworn in as president of the Fifth Republic.[169]

In London on May 8, as three o'clock neared, MPs gathered in the palace yard, where loudspeakers had been set up to carry Churchill's speech. "As Big Ben struck three," Harold Nicolson recorded, "there was an extraordinary hush over the assembled multitude. And then came Winston's voice." His statement ran to just over five hundred words, and took only moments to deliver. Clementine listened at the British embassy in Moscow. Mary heard the address while playing bridge in the country with Jock Colville. Randolph was on an airplane over Yugoslavia when he heard his father's words. Diana and Sarah listened in London. Churchill's recitation of the signing of the surrender and the signatories was as droll as a stationmaster announcing departures and arrivals, until he intoned, "The evil-doers now lie prostrate before us." At that the crowds gasped. Churchill ended with, "Advance Britannia!" The BBC played a recording of buglers sounding

Last Post and closed with "God Save the King," which Nicolson and the House sang along with, "very loud indeed."[170]

Lord Moran listened to Churchill's speech in an overflowing House of Lords (where the Commons had met since the bombing of May 10, 1941). When Churchill finished, a peer turned to Moran and expressed his surprise that the prime minister had made no allusion to God. Moran turned to poet laureate John Masefield and asked what he thought. Masefield replied, "I'd rather have the honest utterance of Winston than the false rhetoric of a lesser man." Abraham Lincoln, Moran offered, "would have struck a deeper note." True, replied Masefield, but "he [Lincoln] was a man of deep piety."[171]

After delivering his statement, Churchill made ready to go to the House of Lords in order to read it to the MPs. On any other day, he could have made the short trip from No. 10 to Parliament in minutes to take Questions, which automatically closed at 3:15, but on this day, his car had to thread its way through the raucous crowds. MPs therefore made supplementary questions until Churchill arrived, which he did at 3:23, Harold Nicolson noted, looking "coy and cheerful." "The House rose as a man," Nicolson wrote, "and yelled and yelled and waved their Order Papers." Churchill responded with a jerk of the head and a wide grin. He read his statement, and added two lines. The first was an expression of thanks to the House for its "noble support" throughout the war. Then, recalling the House's response when, on November 11, 1918, it learned of the Armistice, he moved that "this House do now attend at the Church of St. Margaret's, Westminster, to give humble and reverential thanks to Almighty God for our deliverance from the threat of German domination." He added, "This is the identical Motion which was moved in former times." The motion carried, and the sergeant at arms took up the mace (which, with the House cat, Minny, had survived the Blitz), and the MPs all streamed out, through the lobby, though St. Stephen's Chapel, and into the sunshine of Parliament Square, where mounted policemen tried to forge a path through the gathered tens of thousands.[172]

When Churchill appeared, the gathered erupted in a chorus of "*Winnie, Winnie.*" "The crowd," Mollie Panter-Downes wrote, "had ears, eyes, and throats for no one but Churchill." Mothers held up babies who would later be told they had seen the Great Man. A Cockney cried out, "*That's 'im. That's 'is little old lovely bald 'ead!*" After the service, Churchill departed in an open car, a fat cigar and the "V" for victory prominently displayed. Later in the afternoon, he stepped out onto a Whitehall balcony and told the crowd gathered, "This is your victory."

The crowd roared back, "*No,* it is yours."[173]

It was a day, Brooke told his diary, "disorganized by Victory! A form of disorganization that I can put up with." He was pleased when Lady Grigg told him that she had seen him get into his car in Whitehall "with a crowd looking at you, and none of them realizing that beside them was the man who had probably done most to win the war against Germany." "It was all wrong," she said, adding, "tell Lady Brookie from me." Brooke could not resist some parting shots at Churchill, including, "The P.M. has never once in all his speeches referred to the Chiefs of Staff" or how the chiefs conducted the war "at the highest level." Churchill, during a broadcast five days later, paused in the middle of delivering what was in essence a history of the war, and said:

> And here is the moment when I pay my personal tribute to the British Chiefs of the Staff, with whom I worked in the closest intimacy throughout these heavy, stormy years.... In Field-Marshal Brooke, in Admiral Pound, succeeded after his death by Admiral Andrew Cunningham, and in Marshal of the Air Portal, a team was formed who deserved the highest honour in the direction of the whole British war strategy and in its relations with that of our Allies.

The irascible Brooke waxed philosophic in his V-E day diary entry, citing God—as Churchill had not—as the source of his strength (in having to deal with Churchill) and his belief that victory was "ordained" by "a God all powerful looking after the destiny of the world." "And yet," Brooke wrote, despite his troubles with Churchill "of almost unbearable proportions....I would not have missed the last three and one-half years of struggle and endeavor for anything on earth."[174]

Churchill returned to the Annexe as evening came on, and as hundreds of searchlights that had chased German planes and rockets for five years threw their beams upon London's public buildings and the remaining spires of Wren's churches. Buckingham Palace and the Houses of Parliament were bathed in white light; the face of Big Ben, Mollie Panter-Downes wrote, "loomed like a kind moon." A searchlight picked out Nelson's column. From Fleet Street, Harold Nicolson looked toward St. Paul's and beheld "a concentration of lights upon the huge golden cross." He could hear the sound of cheering in the parks, and found the crowds to be happy "but quite sober." As he made his way home, he noted the smell of distant bonfires in the air. "So I went to bed," he wrote. "That was my victory day."[175]

Churchill dined that evening at the Annexe with Sarah, Diana and Duncan Sandys, and Lord Camrose, publisher of the *Daily Telegraph*. Camrose had long financed Churchill's literary efforts, having paid £5,000 for the serial rights to *Marlborough* (the biography of his luminous ancestor) more than a decade earlier. His presence at the table augured a resurrection of his and Churchill's publishing and financial arrangements.

At about 10:30 P.M. Churchill was told the crowd in Whitehall was still calling for him. Wearing his siren suit now, he returned to the balcony where he had spoken in the afternoon. He told the assembled:

> My dear friends, this is your hour.... There we stood, alone. Did anyone want to give in? [The crowd shouted "No."] Were we downhearted? ["No!"] The lights went out and the bombs came down. But every man, woman and child in the country had no thought of quitting the struggle. London can take it. So we came back after long months from the jaws of death, out of the mouth of hell, while all the world wondered. When shall the reputation and faith of this generation of English men and women fail? I say that in the long years to come not only will the people of this island but of the world, wherever the bird of freedom chirps in human hearts, look back to what we've done and they will say 'do not despair, do not yield to violence and tyranny, march straight forward and die if need be—unconquered.'

He told them that Germany "awaits our justice and our mercy." He told them that Japan, "stained with cruelty and greed," would likewise be vanquished. And he told them that Britain would fight the battle "hand in hand" with America.[176]

That night, bonfires burned the length and breadth of the Home Island, on Beacon Hill in Hampshire and on other similarly named hills in Wales and the Lake District. They burned in town squares from Cornwall to Cambridge, from Oxford to Liverpool. They burned in Coventry and Manchester and Bath and Bristol, and from the Scottish Highlands to the windswept northernmost reaches of mainland Scotland. They burned on Guernsey and Jersey, freed that day, and they burned seven hundred miles to the north on the Orkney Islands. The fires glowed on the Isle of Man and the Isle of Arran, from north to south and east to west, from the Scillies to the Shetlands. Englishmen and Welshmen and Scotsmen and Ulstermen young and old, male and female, danced in the withering firelight, their faces glowing with sweat and dusted by soot and creased by wild grins. Since 1939, as in ancient times, they had proven that they were the warrior races. It was a scene that would have been familiar to Iron Age Britons, to Picts, Scots, and Celts, to the Romans, the Angles and Saxons and Danes, to King Harold, Thomas à Becket, and Eleanor of Aquitaine, to Elizabeth I and Raleigh, to Cromwell. And to Marlborough.

Late in the evening a telegram arrived at the Annexe from Clementine in Moscow: "All my thoughts are with you on this supreme day my darling. It could not have happened without you." Eden expressed similar sentiments from San Francisco: "It is you who have led, uplifted and inspired us through the worst days. Without you this day could not have been." As was his wont, Churchill worked past midnight and well into the early hours of May 9. Hundreds of telegrams had to be answered; the box was in dire need of attention. As he worked on, London officials doused the searchlights in hopes of encouraging the crowds to disperse. In the streets, Churchill's Englishmen, victorious, made for their homes.[177]

It was five years to the day since Hitler had ordered his armies into the Low Countries. In those black days, Churchill told Englishmen that to give in was to sink into the abyss of a new Dark Age. But, he told them, if they never gave in—and they had not—they would someday reach the broad sunlit uplands.

At that latitude and at that time of year dawn comes early, a faint blush on the far horizon. Night defeated, retreats. And light is born again.[178]

7
Ebb Tide

1945–1955

After almost six years of total war, Europeans had reached the upland regions. But from Warsaw to Paris, Berlin to Prague, they found themselves not in Winston Churchill's sunlit pastoral, but in a mutilated, desolate, and blood-drenched landscape. The war had left Europe literally a shambles—a slaughterhouse. In triumph, the victors took measure of the appalling tragedy that had overtaken the Continent since 1939. At least 40 million Europeans had been killed, about equally divided between civilians and armed forces. Poland had paid the highest relative price. More than six million Poles, almost 20 percent of Poland's prewar population, were dead, including three million Polish Jews. This is a number that defies comprehension. A modern reader might form some idea of the enormity of the Polish slaughter if he imagined picking up the morning newspaper every day for five years and reading that three thousand of his fellow citizens had perished the previous day in a terrorist attack. In Warsaw alone, seven hundred thousand had died, more than worldwide British, Commonwealth, and American battlefield deaths combined. Almost half of Poland's doctors, dentists, lawyers, and university professors were among the dead. Weeks after the German surrender, Churchill, still furious over the failure of the London Poles to reach some sort of agreement with Stalin in 1944, told the House, "There are few virtues that the Poles do not possess, and there are few mistakes they have ever avoided." Yet Poland's biggest mistake was the accident of geography that had placed it between the Wolf and the Bear, and the Bear had prevailed. The Lublin Poles accounted for thirteen of the twenty ministers in the new Warsaw government. The sixteen Polish democrats arrested in late March were found guilty of crimes against the state and packed off to prison. Poland had, in effect, become the seventeenth Soviet republic.[1]

Meticulous Nazi records soon accounted for another three million murdered Jews, gassed or shot, along with at least one million other "enemies of the state": Communists, gypsies, and homosexuals. Vichy France had been most accommodating in arresting and handing over to the Germans such undesirables. At least 70,000 of France's prewar Jewish population of 350,000 (of whom about one-half were naturalized citizens or refugees) were sent to their deaths in the east. Three-quarters of Holland's 140,000

Jews were likewise trundled east to their deaths. Italy could count almost 350,000 war dead, split about evenly between soldiers and civilians. The French had lost 200,000 men in 1940, but by 1945, the number of civilians who had perished in bombing raids and concentration camps was 400,000. Ongoing civil and guerrilla wars in Greece and Yugoslavia had so far left 150,000 and 1.5 million dead, respectively. Partisans in both countries were still killing each other, a state of affairs that led Churchill, with Tito in mind, to tell Brooke, "When the eagles are silent the parrots begin to jabber."[2]

Meanwhile, Communist movements grabbed their share of power in Italy and France; the Red Army was or soon would be placing Communists in power in Poland, Bulgaria, Hungary, and Romania. Eduard Beneš returned to Czechoslovakia, where he was confirmed as president by a coalition of Democrats and Communists in the National Assembly. The three Baltic states had disappeared within the Soviet empire. Stalin felt that Russia, given its horrific and heroic sacrifice, had earned the right to take what it pleased. Almost eleven million Red Army soldiers were dead or missing; Soviet civilian casualties have never been calculated with exactness; perhaps fifteen million, perhaps as many as twenty million, were killed by bullet, noose, fire, and starvation, fully half of the Continent's casualties. And still Europeans were dying. Millions of German land mines, from the Oder River to Brittany and Normandy (where six million were buried), were killing civilians at a rate of several hundred a week. Churchill proposed to Brooke that "the Germans find all the mines they have buried, and dig them up. Why should they not? Pigs are used to find olives." Brooke shared the prime minister's sentiments but could not resist pointing out to Churchill that pigs were used to find truffles.[3]

On May 11, the third day of European peace, Churchill cabled President Truman with a request that they jointly invite Stalin to a tripartite meeting at "some unshattered town in Germany" not within the Russian zone of occupation, and that Truman first stop off in London in a display of unity. Churchill pointed out that twice the Americans and British had met Stalin on or near his territory, Churchill four times in all. He further stressed his belief that it was critical that "the American front will not recede from the now agreed upon tactical lines." Truman's response was immediate, unsatisfactory, and reminiscent of Roosevelt's wartime hesitancy. Truman proposed that their respective ambassadors try to persuade Stalin to call for a meeting, and that he and Churchill travel to it separately in order to avoid the appearance of "ganging up" on Stalin. Churchill sent off another cable the next day, telling Truman, as he had Roosevelt, that he was "profoundly concerned about the European situation." American armies were "melting" away, the French were virtually defenseless, and the Russians had two to three hundred divisions on active duty. "An iron curtain is drawn down upon their [the Russian] front." Behind it, Poland was isolated, and controlled by Stalin's Lublin puppets. It would be easy for the Russians, Churchill warned, to drive all the way "to the waters of the North Sea and the Atlantic." He again proposed a meeting of the Big Three at the earliest possible opportunity in order to forge "a settlement with Russia before our strength has gone."[4]

To Eden, in San Francisco for the opening of the United Nations, he cabled similar sentiments:

> TODAY THERE ARE ANNOUNCEMENTS IN THE NEWSPAPERS OF THE LARGE WITHDRAWALS OF AMERICAN TROOPS NOW TO BEGIN MONTH BY MONTH. WHAT ARE WE TO DO? GREAT PRESSURE WILL SOON BE PUT ON US [AT HOME] TO DEMOBILIZE PARTIALLY. IN A VERY SHORT TIME OUR ARMIES WILL HAVE MELTED, BUT THE RUSSIANS MAY REMAIN WITH HUNDREDS OF DIVISIONS IN POSSESSION OF EUROPE FROM LUBECK TO TRIESTE, AND TO THE GREEK FRONTIER ON THE ADRIATIC.... ALL THESE THINGS ARE FAR MORE VITAL THAN THE AMENDMENTS TO A WORLD CONSTITUTION [THE UNITED NATIONS] WHICH MAY NEVER WELL COME INTO BEING TILL IT IS SUPERSEDED AFTER A PERIOD OF APPEASEMENT BY A THIRD WORLD WAR.[5]

By the end of the month, Stalin and Truman set a tentative date of July 15 for the meeting. Churchill considered that to be a month too late, and he proposed mid-June or early July at the latest. A delay of a month or more, Churchill believed, would allow the Red Army and the Lublin Poles time enough to effectively settle the matter of new Polish borders without Anglo-American input or oversight. But Truman held firm. As well, he sent word to Churchill through former U.S. ambassador to Moscow Joe Davies that he [Truman] wanted to meet with Stalin before the Big Three met. Churchill warned Truman that any such bilateral meeting would be "regrettable" and would raise issues "wounding" to Britain, the Commonwealth, and the British Empire. Truman backed off but held to the mid-July date. The place would be Potsdam, a suburb of Berlin and the Versailles of Prussian princes. The town was heavily damaged but not utterly destroyed.[6]

Throughout Germany, there was little left "unshattered." Every major city and most of the larger towns had been completely destroyed—Berlin, Hamburg, Dresden, and Stuttgart in the south, Breslau in the east. The RAF and American Eighth Air Force had paid a heavy price for these results: 26,000 American and 55,000 British airmen died over Europe. But the air campaign had wiped out twenty-eight major towns of the Ruhr. On the ground, German soldiers paid a far heavier price. More than five million German soldiers, sailors, and airmen had been killed since 1939 in service to Hitler's vision. Almost two million German citizens had died, as many as six hundred thousand under Allied bombs. The end of the war marked only the beginning of more pain for Germans. Near Berlin—a dead city—squads of German civilians overseen by Allied soldiers dug one hundred thousand graves in anticipation of filling them during the coming winter with the bodies of the frozen and the starved and no doubt thousands more suicides. At least half the German civilian war dead had perished at the hands of the Red Army while fleeing westward early in the year. Within twelve months, most of the Germanic population east of the Elbe—in East Prussia, Poland, the Czech Sudetenland—would be forcibly relocated into the Allied occupation zones, some fourteen million in all as a result of the Yalta agreement to redraw German and Polish borders, and Stalin's demands at Potsdam that no Germans remain within the new Poland. At least one million died of starvation in the process.

The Germanic population of the former Greater Reich fell to under three million from more than seventeen million before the war. The survivors had to be fed, along with eight million displaced persons within Germany—former slave laborers, of which four million lived in the Soviet zone. Hundreds of thousands of Dutch, French, and Polish displaced persons had to be sent home. And Stalin demanded that tens of thousands of Russian POWs be sent east, along with thousands of White Russians and Cossacks who had made the fatal error of joining the German side. The Western Allies dutifully delivered these Russians later that summer—some with families brought from the Ukraine—to Red Army checkpoints. Many were gunned down before even boarding the trains east; others committed suicide rather than return to face the noose. In his memoirs, Dwight Eisenhower makes mention of these "persecutees" and the "terror" they felt, and the suicides, but no mention of their nationality.[7]

One million Germans had fled before the Russians and into Montgomery's zone of occupation, where another million wounded Germans wasted away, with little medicine, little food, and little hope. Montgomery also had to tend to the upkeep of almost two million German soldiers who were now his prisoners and feared falling into Russian hands. In his memoirs, Montgomery wrote: "From their behavior it soon became clear that the Russians, though a fine fighting race, were in fact barbarous Asiatics who had never enjoyed a civilization comparable to the rest of Europe." He told his diary, "Out of the impact of the Asiatics on the European culture, a new Europe has been born." Two immediate problems had to be tackled, the feeding of Germans and the containment of the Russians, were they to wander farther westward. Britain could do neither alone. Weeks later, Churchill told the House that it "would be in vain for us in our small Island, which still needs to import half its food, to imagine that we can make any further appreciable contribution in that respect [trying to feed Germans]." And on the mass expulsion of Germans from newly configured Poland, he predicted, "It is not impossible that tragedy on a prodigious scale is unfolding itself behind the Iron Curtain which at the moment divides Europe in twain."[8]

On May 13 Churchill took to the airwaves, warning Britons:

> I wish I could tell you tonight that all our toils and troubles were over. Then indeed I could end my five years' service happily, and if you thought that you had had enough of me and that I ought to be put out to grass, I tell you I would take it with the best of grace.... There would be little use in punishing the Hitlerites for their crimes if law and justice did not rule, and if totalitarian or police governments were to take the place of the German invaders.... I told you hard things at the beginning of these last five years; you did not shrink, and I should be unworthy of your confidence and generosity if I did not still cry: Forward, unflinching, unswerving, indomitable, till the whole task is done and the whole world is safe and clean.

He also warned of the coming battle with Japan, and repeated his pledge of five years: "We seek nothing."[9]

He did not disclose in his broadcast his belief that the Russians were now intent on making Europe unsafe and unclean. Nor could he disclose his favored solution to the Russian threat. That day, May 13, Brooke wrote of Churchill: "He gives me the feeling of already longing for another war! Even if it entailed fighting Russia!" He was. One of the wagers Montgomery recorded in his ledger in 1943 was a £100 bet between himself and George Patton, who gave even odds that "the armed forces of Great Britain will become involved in another war in Europe within ten years of the cessation of hostilities in the current war." Patton's bet was looking pretty good even before London streets were swept clean of streamers and rosettes from the V-E day festivities. Churchill now asked the British joint planners to study the feasibility of war with the Russians, code-named Operation Unthinkable. In fact, eight months earlier, the British chiefs had composed a paper for the Foreign Office on the possibility of Russia's becoming a future adversary. At the time, Brooke wrote, the Foreign Office "could not admit that Russia may one day become unfriendly" and "considered it very remiss" for the chiefs to contemplate war with Britain's current ally. Yet planning for future military contingencies is the responsibility of military planners. Eden accepted the paper. Still, Brooke told his diary later in May, after revisiting Operation Unthinkable, "The idea is of course fantastic, and the chances for success quite impossible. There is no doubt from now onwards Russia is all powerful in Europe."[10]

Of these weeks Churchill later wrote, "I could only feel the vast manifestation of Soviet and Russian imperialism rolling forward over helpless lands." Almost a decade later, while addressing his Woodford constituency, he let slip that soon after V-E day, he had directed Montgomery "to be careful in collecting the German arms, to stack them so they could easily be issued again to the German soldiers whom we should have to work with if the Soviet advance continued." No such telegram has been found in official records, but Montgomery, in his memoir, wrote that he protested to London an order that "these [German] weapons should be kept intact." He does not name the official who issued the order.[11]

A message Churchill sent to Eisenhower on May 9, however, contains the same sentiment:

> I have heard with some concern that the Germans are to destroy all their aircraft in situ. I hope that this policy will not be adopted in regard to weapons and other forms of equipment. We may have great need of these some day. And even now they might be of use, both in France and especially in Italy. I think we ought to keep everything worth keeping. The heavy cannon I preserved from the last war fired constantly from the heights of Dover in this war.[12]

Neither telegram (if the Montgomery message ever existed) makes clear whether Churchill intended German troops to bear those surrendered weapons.

Churchill, while contemplating a response to the Red Army, hoped for a diplomatic solution, but he planned for war. His fears were well founded, but he failed as he had a decade earlier to correctly read the mood of the British public. For four years, while the Red Army fought valiantly, the British and American people gave it its due. Indeed, the people of both nations had elevated the Red Army and Russians to heroic stature. Churchill had, too, for a year or so after June 1941.

But circumstances had changed, dramatically and dangerously. The Red Army now occupied Warsaw, Budapest, Bucharest, Vienna, Prague, and Berlin. In March 1936 Churchill had told the House:

> For four hundred years the foreign policy of England has been to oppose the strongest, most aggressive, most dominating Power on the Continent, and particularly to prevent the Low Countries falling into the hands of such a Power.... Observe that the policy of England takes no account of which nation it is that seeks the overlordship of Europe.... It has nothing to do with rulers or nations; it is concerned solely with whoever is the strongest or the potentially dominating tyrant.

That policy had never changed. As he had a decade earlier, Churchill identified an existential threat to Europe. And, as he had in the mid-1930s, he arrived at the right conclusion at the wrong time. And the British military, as it had been a decade earlier, was in no state to deter the Soviet threat. The final butcher's bill would include 244,000 British soldiers, airmen, and sailors. Commonwealth nations and other imperial comrades-in-arms suffered another 100,000 dead—Australia, 23,000; Canada, 37,000; India, 24,000; New Zealand, 10,000, and South Africa, 6,000. Militarily, Britain and the Empire were in no shape to fight a new war.[13]

Yet this time Churchill's worries were shared, not dismissed, by Tories and Labour alike. All within HMG knew him to be correct regarding the Russian threat. In any case, Britain in 1945 lacked not only the will to force the issue with the Soviets, it lacked the way: Britain was broke. When in 1940 Lord Lothian told American reporters that Britain was broke, he meant only that London lacked the cash and gold reserves to buy American arms and food. Now, having emerged victorious, London owed $4.3 billion to America and $1.2 billion to Canada. Britain had little to export and faced American tariffs in any event, and, as Churchill repeatedly told his countrymen, half the food consumed on the Home Island had to be imported.

When Foreign Minister Anthony Eden asked Labourite Ernest Bevin what cabinet position he might seek if Bevin's Labour Party won a general election, Bevin replied that he hoped for the Exchequer. Eden was stunned: "Whatever for?" he asked. "There'll be nothing to do there except to account for the money we have not got." Meat was rationed (horsemeat, not rationed, had lost its stigma), as were cheese, eggs, butter, soap, flour, clothing, and paper. Even a decade later, British high school students performed their math lessons on the backs of old grocery receipts. Petrol, coal, oil—all rationed. Whisky was in short supply, fresh fish, too. The Germans had destroyed or heavily damaged more than 750,000 houses. Public services were paralyzed. London's lights would not fully function for three more months. Transportation was in disarray, delivery of water and electricity unreliable. On May 11, President Truman summarily cut back Lend-Lease shipments to France, Russia, and Britain. Weeks later, he ceased shipments of American coal to Britain—five hundred thousand tons per month and every ounce desperately needed. The message was clear: Britain would soon be on its own. In this want, the Labour Party saw opportunity. Aneurin Bevan famously observed, "This island is almost made of coal and surrounded by fish. Only an organizing genius could produce a shortage of coal and fish in Great Britain at the same time." He assigned responsibility for this state of affairs to the Conservatives, to whose complete extermination as a political party he dedicated his political life.[14]

In mid-May, while planning his unthinkable war against Russia, Churchill proposed to Clement Attlee a continuation of the coalition government until Japan was defeated. Attlee agreed, on the condition that Churchill pledge in writing that the interim government would actively pursue reforms in housing, education, and social security. Churchill made the pledge, believing that Attlee would present the document to the annual Labour Party conference under way in Blackpool, where he would carry the day. Instead, the old socialist Harold Laski, that year's chairman of the conference, opposed Churchill's plan, and was joined by Ernest Bevin, Hugh Dalton, and Home Secretary Herbert Morrison. Attlee, always more conciliator than leader (Eden thought him timid), had no choice but to reject Churchill's offer. The coalition was dead. Just nine months earlier, Laski had proposed to Churchill the setting up of a "Churchill Fund" to support the Royal Society and the British Museum. "As I look at the Europe Hitler has devastated," Laski wrote at the time, "I know very intimately that, as an Englishman of Jewish origin, I owe you the gift of life itself." Churchill expressed his gratitude to Laski but affirmed that he'd prefer a park or playground to be built in his name on the south side of the Thames, "where all the houses have been blown down." That included Limehouse, Clement Attlee's constituency. But now, with Hitler dead, Laski and his Labour cohorts had their sights set on nothing less than the remaking of British government and British life. Five years earlier, Labour support had made it possible for Churchill to become prime minister and create the coalition government. Now Labour walked out.[15]

On May 23, Churchill motored to Buckingham Palace to tender his resignation to King George, who asked Churchill to form a caretaker government until elections could be held and the soldiers' vote from overseas tallied. The elections were scheduled for July 5, the final results to be announced some three weeks later. Churchill had kept to his pledge of nonpartisanship for five years. Now he would assume his partisan demeanor, and few in England could be as partisan as Churchill when he set his mind to it. He had gained the office of prime minister twice, in 1940 and again that day, but neither time through the ballot box. He intended to return to office for a third time, with a mandate from the people.

He had forewarned Britons of his keenness to wage a verbal war against Labour when in March he told the annual Tory conference, "We have all abstained from doing or saying anything which would be likely to impair the unity of the British people.... In doing this we have endured patiently and almost silently many provocations from that happily limited class of Left Wing politicians to whom party strife is the breath of their nostrils, and their only means of obtaining influence or notoriety." He pledged to "maintain this patriotic restraint as long as the National Coalition... continues to work together in loyal comrade-ship." That partnership was no more. He had told Britons: "Our Socialist friends have officially committed themselves—much to the disgust of some of their leaders—to a programme for nationalizing all the means of production, distribution, and exchange." Labour's "sweeping proposals," he warned, "imply not only the destruction of the whole of our existing system of society, and of life, and of labour, but the creation and enforcement of another system or other systems borrowed from foreign lands and alien minds." He asked:

> Will the warrior return, will the family be reunited, will the shattered houses be restored...? They do not regard themselves as a slum-bred serf population chased into battle from a land of misery and want. They love their country and the scenes of their youth and manhood, and they have shown themselves ready to die not only in defence of its material satisfactions but for its honour.... Let there be no mistake about it; it is no easy, cheap-jack Utopia of airy phrases that lies before us.... This is no time for windy platitudes and glittering advertisements.... This is no time for humbug and blandishments, but for grim, stark facts and figures, and for action to meet immediate needs."[16]

In reply some months later, the novelist, playwright, and Labour's literary spokesman J. B. Priestley wrote a thirty-four-page pamphlet titled *Letter to a Returning Serviceman*, in which he warned ex-Tommies to beware "the charmed cozy circle" of home life promised by Churchill. Priestley's BBC broadcasts throughout the war were as patriotic as Churchill's, and almost as well known. His audience consisted of those Britons whom Churchill liked to call his yeomanry. They listened to Priestley, and they paid heed when he told them, "Modern man is essentially a communal and cooperating man.... I do not believe in economic liberty.... Economic life is necessarily a communal life."[17]

"After the war" had for almost six years been a teasing dream. Churchill had used the phrase in speeches for more than a decade, during the 1930s in collating the mistakes of HMG after the Great War, and since 1940 in reminding Britons that numerous questions—jobs, housing, education—could be addressed only "after the war." A generation earlier, the soldiers had returned from the Great War to find no plans in place for the peace. They were expected to take up their plows and tools after a four-year absence as if the whole bloody business—where one *million* men of the Empire had died—had not even taken place. Normalcy had been the byword then, on both sides of the Atlantic. In 1943 Churchill told England:

> War cuts down...on forward planning, and everything is subordinated to the struggle for national existence. Thus, when peace came suddenly, as it did last time [1918], there were no long carefully prepared plans for the future.... We must not be caught again that way. It is therefore necessary to make sure that we have projects for the future employment of the people and...that private enterprise and State enterprise are both able to play their parts to the utmost.[18]

Now, after six years of living in a tightly controlled society, necessary in order to defeat Hitler, the returning soldiers and indeed many Britons saw the need for more sacrifice and planning in order to defeat poverty, remove slums, and improve education and services. Planning (at Churchill's behest) had since 1941 led to improvements in the high schools, this while under severe wartime stringencies. A Tory, R. A. ("Rab") Butler, had been the driving force behind the 1944 Education Act, which guaranteed free education for all children through high school. Sarah tried to persuade her father that rationing—on which the prime minister himself had written numerous memos concerning chickens, eggs, and rabbits—had been so well planned that it had resulted in better-fed and better-educated children. Wartime controls had led to a more just sharing of the burdens, and therefore a more just society. Why not continue the planning and shared sacrifice in peace, she asked, in order to build houses, schools, and a better society? Churchill saw things entirely differently, and had said so in March, when he told the Tory conference, "If we are to recover from the measureless exertions of the war, it can only be by a large release from the necessary bonds and controls which war conditions have imposed upon us. No restriction upon well-established British liberties that is not proved indispensable to the prosecution of the war and the transition from war to peace can be tolerated." He touted the Tories' Four-Year Plan, a variation of the Beveridge Report, and built on voluntary cooperation between the government and private enterprise. The plan, he claimed, was an undertaking so liberal that even Gladstone and Lloyd George might shrink from it.[19]

For Churchill, state domination of planning and the attendant control the state needed to implement its plans were two sides of the same coin, a coin minted by socialists for socialists. This he made clear in his first campaign broadcast, delivered from Chequers on Monday, June 4—with disastrous results. He had spent the weekend preparing the speech, and had shown a draft to Jock Colville, who called it "fighting and provocative," and to Clementine, who objected vehemently to one phrase in particular that he intended to deploy. He ignored her protests. The BBC allotted him thirty minutes, too little time in Churchill's estimation. Speaking against the clock for the first time since 1940, he rushed his delivery. After telling listeners that he and the Tories and "many of my Labour colleagues would have been glad to carry on [the coalition]... the Socialist Party as a whole had been for some time eager to set out upon the political warpath, and when large numbers of people feel like that it is not good for their health to deny them the fight they want. We will therefore give it to them to the best of our ability." So far, so good—Englishmen expected nothing less than his best from their Winston.[20]

Churchill went on, paraphrasing the economist Friedrich Hayek from *The Road to Serfdom*. "My friends, I must tell you that a Socialist policy is abhorrent to the British ideas of freedom."

> Socialism is inseparably interwoven with Totalitarianism and the abject worship of the State.... Look how even today they [Socialists] hunger for controls of every kind, as if these were delectable foods instead of war-time inflictions and monstrosities. There is to be one State to which all are to be obedient in every act of their lives. This State is to be the arch-employer, the arch-planner, the arch-administrator and ruler, and the arch-caucus-boss.... Socialism is, in its essence, an attack not only upon British enterprise, but upon the right of the ordinary man or woman to breathe freely without having a harsh, clumsy, tyrannical hand clapped across their mouths and nostrils.

He laced into Labour's Herbert Morrison, who had outlined "his plans to curtail Parliamentary procedure and pass laws simply by resolutions of broad principle in the House of Commons." And he excoriated Sir Stafford Cripps for advocating what amounted to a rubber-stamp role for Parliament in the new socialist state. Then he arrived at the passage Clementine thought hideous:

> I declare to you, from the bottom of my heart, that no Socialist system can be established without a political police.... They would have to fall back on some form of Gestapo, no doubt very humanely directed in the first instance. And this would nip opinion in the bud; it would stop criticism as it reared its head, and it would gather all the power to the supreme party and the party leaders, rising like stately pinnacles above their vast bureaucracies of Civil servants, no longer servants and no longer civil.[21]

Churchill thundered and roared, confident that Clement Attlee lacked the oratorical skills to respond in kind. Ed Murrow of CBS believed so, offering that Attlee approached a subject "as if elucidating some obscure, unimportant passage in a Latin translation." The night following Churchill's Gestapo speech, Attlee—whom Colville described as having "no shred of either conceit or vanity"—took to the airwaves and delivered a devastating reply. Churchill's object, Attlee declared, was to make "electors understand how great was the difference between Winston Churchill, the great leader in war of a united nation, and Mr. Churchill, the party Leader of the Conservatives.... The voice we heard last night was that of Mr. Churchill, but the mind was that of Lord Beaverbrook." The timid, balding, sometimes fussy Attlee had made himself overnight into a campaign leader. As for Beaverbrook's role in crafting Churchill's speech, he had "no hand" in the matter, Colville wrote. Beaverbrook and his newspapers had been "firing vast salvos" of late, which mostly, Colville believed, "miss their mark." Churchill, trying to cast Attlee as a bogeyman, had also missed his mark, but Attlee, casting Beaverbrook *and* Churchill likewise, had not.[22]

The Beaver put on a relentless, shrill, and clumsy demonstration of loyalty to Churchill in the pages of his *Express*, but Beaverbrook had never really understood Englishmen and, critically, Englishwomen. The tabloid *Daily Mirror*, Britain's largest-selling paper, did. The only large newspaper not controlled by Camrose, Beaverbrook, or Bracken, the *Mirror* went after the service *wives*, telling the women of Britain on the eve of the election, "Vote for them!" [the servicemen] who "for five long years... from Berlin to Burma... have fought and are still fighting for YOU.... You know which way your men would march. Vote for them!" Even Churchill loyalists began to doubt their man; Vita Sackville-West wrote to her husband, Harold Nicolson: "You know I have an admiration for Winston amounting to idolatry, so I am dreadfully distressed by the badness of his broadcast election speeches.... If I were a wobbler they would tip me over to the other side." Nicolson's friend the literary critic Raymond Mortimer also jotted a note to Nicolson, in which he wrote, "I think that Churchill more than anyone else was responsible for the squalid lies in these elections. He started the rot with his talk of Mr. Attlee's Gestapo."[23]

Churchill's "favorability rating" as measured by Gallup polls had exceeded 90 percent since El Alamein, but for a brief drop during his January 1944 recuperation in Marrakech and his Christmas 1944 foray to Greece. After V-E day, his favorability numbers dipped into the 80 percent range, a mere bag of shells, for he was the most popular leader in living history, the savior of England. Yet, Gallup's newfangled computations were inexact. Asked if they had an "overall" favorable impression of Churchill,

Britons responded, politely, yes. Thus, as Churchill campaigned up and down and across the land by private train and open auto, delivering ten speeches and broadcasts in the process, he was deeply moved, Eden wrote, by the goodwill and cheering crowds he found along all his routes. Yet, Eden later wrote, "He [Churchill] could not be expected to sense that there was also something valedictory in their message. He would not have been Winston Churchill if he had."[24]

Colville was not optimistic about the election, telling his diary, "Without Winston's personal prestige the Tories would not have a chance. Even with him I am not sanguine of their prospects, though most of their leaders are confident of a good majority." That was true; Churchill, Eden, and Beaverbrook all believed they would take the House with a majority of perhaps eighty seats, maybe even as many as one hundred. Even Attlee believed the Tories would win, later telling Colville that "there might, with luck, be a Conservative majority of only some forty seats." Much would depend on the soldiers' vote, four million strong, and almost 20 percent of the total electorate. Over lunch, Churchill asked General Billy Slim, the hero of Burma, how he thought his troops would vote. "Ninety percent Labour," Slim replied. Churchill grunted. "What about the other ten percent?" Slim said, "They won't vote at all."[25]

On July 3, Churchill delivered his final campaign speech at Walthamstow Stadium, a greyhound racing track in East London. After a band warmed up the crowd of 20,000 with "Deep in the Heart of Texas" and "Umbrella Man," Churchill, accompanied by Clementine, took the stage to tremendous cheers. He had no sooner begun speaking when several thousand Labour rowdies scattered throughout the stadium let him have it. "*We want Attlee,*" they shouted over his words. When he tried to engage them on the topic of free speech—"In a free country like ours..."—they shouted him down with a chorus of boos. "Surely that is not a party question," said Churchill. He went on: "I want to congratulate London... upon her wonderful record in the war.... Would you like to boo that?" He went after the socialists and their "absurd utopias," proclaiming that there must be "improvement of human hearts and human heads before we can achieve the glorious Utopia that the Socialist woolgatherers place before us. Now where is the boo party? I shall call them henceforward in my speech the booing party. Everyone have a good boo." Some in the audience jeered at that. He closed with an election prediction: "I give my entire forgiveness to the booers. They have this to take away with them—I am sure they are going to get a thrashing such as their party has never received since it was born."[26]

That day Churchill instructed the cabinet to prepare legislation for a national insurance plan and a national health service. This was not cynical posturing; Churchill had supported both programs since he put Sir

William Beveridge on the case more than three decades earlier. As for the fate of the coal mines, since the General Strike of 1926 he had been much more sympathetic to the miners than to the mine owners. Churchill did not hate Labour programs; he hated the intellectual arrogance of the left—of Bevan, Cripps, and Laski. Churchill, Colville later wrote, was "never anything but hostile to Socialist theory." He had certainly made that clear during the campaign. In any case, voters were unaware of Churchill's instructions to the cabinet when they went to the polls on July 5.[27]

On July 7, Churchill, Mary, Clemmie, Lord Moran, and Colville made for the Basque coast of France near St-Jean-de-Luz for a one-week vacation before Churchill undertook the next order of business: the Big Three conference due to open in Potsdam on the sixteenth. Churchill himself had code-named the conference Terminal, a curious choice given that the final phase of the war against Japan had yet to begin and the atomic bomb, which might hasten the end of the Pacific war, had yet to be tested. Many military men, including Franklin Roosevelt's chief of staff, Admiral Leahy, who gave odds and took bets, believed it would not work.

Churchill's valet, Sawyers, made the journey to France, as keeper of the Old Man's brushes and palettes and paints. It was intended as a beach and painting vacation, and the absence of paperwork and urgent telephone calls ensured an air of quietude. The Old Man spent his mornings swimming about "like a benevolent hippo" off a sandy beach while a squad of French gendarmes dog-paddled around the Great Man to provide a cordon sanitaire between the P.M. and curious locals. So complete was Churchill's rest and relaxation that he utterly failed to prepare for the Potsdam Conference. To make matters worse, neither had Anthony Eden, who had returned from San Francisco with a duodenal ulcer and, under Lord Moran's orders, had spent much of June in bed resting. Churchill—with the election always intruding on his thoughts—had no heart for the upcoming Potsdam parley, telling his doctor, "Nothing will be decided at the conference...I shall only be half a man until the result of the poll. I shall keep in the background at the conference." A report from Max Beaverbrook arrived that lifted Churchill's spirits; the Beaver now predicted a Conservative majority of one hundred. And although Churchill now believed that he might have lost the service vote, he told Clementine he was quite sure the servicewomen were for him. When Clemmie reminded him that early in his career he had opposed giving women the vote, he replied, "Quite true."[28]

On July 15, Churchill, Sawyers, Mary, and Moran flew on to Berlin, while Colville and Clementine returned to London. Attlee and Ernest Bevin also journeyed to Potsdam; it was Churchill's wish that the British present a unified front to the Americans and especially to Stalin. When Churchill told the House of his desire to bring Attlee to Berlin, a Labour MP called out, "Is the right honourable Gentleman going to take the Gestapo with him?" The Old Man thus arrived at his lodgings in Babelsberg, about six miles from Potsdam, with a hostile House waiting in London, a hostile Stalin waiting in Potsdam, and without any guarantee from President Truman that the Americans were prepared to play hardball with Stalin on the matter of free Polish elections.[29]

Truman also arrived in Babelsberg on the fifteenth, and took up residence in a grand town house two blocks from Churchill's residence. Elements of the British, American, and Red armies—out in force—guarded both houses. The next day at dawn—early afternoon in Berlin—the Americans successfully detonated an atomic bomb in the New Mexico desert. On the seventeenth, before the first plenary session with Stalin, Henry Stimson shoved a piece of paper across a table to Churchill. On it Stimson had scribbled, "Babies satisfactorily born." Churchill did not understand, until Stimson made clear just what had taken place in New Mexico. Of this news, Churchill later wrote, "Here then was a speedy end to the Second World War, and perhaps to much else besides." In that moment, Churchill saw no further need to seek Russian help against Japan, and he saw a possible solution to the Soviet tide rolling westward in Europe. The Prof—Lord Cherwell—beheld a way to make this horrific new weapon even more terrible. Knowing that the initial burst of such a bomb would blind anyone who happened to be looking skyward at the moment it detonated, Cherwell advised that preliminary pyrotechnics be set off as the bomb made its descent in order that the optimum number of Japanese were looking skyward at the moment of truth.[30]

Churchill had anticipated the fate of Japan more than three years earlier. Weeks before the fall of Singapore, with the British Empire reeling from the Japanese blows in the Far East but fully appreciating that the home islands of Japan were the key to the Pacific theater, as much as England was to the European, Churchill communicated to the Chiefs of Staff his strategy: "The burning of Japanese cities by incendiary bombs will bring home in a most effective way to the people of Japan the dangers of the course to which they have committed themselves." The word "incendiary" jumps from the memo. He does not propose the use of parachute bombs or four-thousand-pound high explosives. He does not envision bringing Japan to bay with commandos, sabotage, or trickery. He goes straight to the most efficient solution. He would set Japan ablaze, literally, for Japanese cities were built of paper and wood. That strategy now fell to Truman to implement.

The first plenary session opened late on July 17 at the Cecilienhof Palace in Potsdam, originally built for Crown Prince Wilhelm ("Little Willie"). Eden and Alec Cadogan both found Truman to be "quick and business-like." And both thought Churchill's performance was a disaster. Eden: "W. was very bad. He had read no brief & was confused & wooly & verbose." Cadogan: "Every mention of a topic started Winston off on a wild rampage.... So it was a pretty useless meeting, but these conferences always have their infantile complaints."[31]

Several issues were on the Potsdam agenda—a warm-water port for Russia, Russian participation in the Pacific war, the withdrawal of Russian troops from northern Iran, the fate of the German fleet—but only two items were of abiding concern to Churchill: free elections in Poland, and the western Polish border. On the former, Stalin, as he had at Yalta, simply promised free elections—a lie—and Churchill chose to believe him. On the latter, Stalin (and the Lublin Poles) would not budge; the occupation of eastern Germany was a fait accompli, and Stalin was of no mind to withdraw from any part of this fertile swath of conquered territory. Churchill had believed since Tehran that the new Polish frontier should be delineated by the Eastern Neisse River where it fed into the Oder, in compensation for the Poles agreeing to the Curzon Line. Stalin claimed the Western Neisse. More than one million Germans lived between the two rivers, and Stalin and the Lublin Poles demanded they be packed off to Germany, to make room for Polish settlers. Had Churchill and Stalin scrutinized a map at Tehran when they first proposed shifting Poland westward toward the Oder (and checked off their acceptance as they had with the "naughty" memo in October 1944, when they divided the Balkans into spheres of influence), they might have avoided the current predicament. And had Roosevelt displayed resolve at Yalta rather than, as described by Eden, "playing it by ear," a more concise accord might have been reached. And, had Harry Hopkins been on hand in his role as presidential fixer, he might have guided Truman to more resolve. But Hopkins was an ill man, and he had severed his connection with the U.S. government early in the month. In any case, the Lublin Poles in essence had become the fifth occupier of Germany.

Churchill believed his tête-à-têtes with Stalin would yield results. Eden did not. After Churchill enjoyed a five-hour dinner with Stalin, Eden told his diary: "He [Churchill] is again under Stalin's spell. He kept repeating 'I like that man.' I am full of admiration of Stalin's handling of him." Full of foreboding for Poland, Eden wrote a long memo to Churchill, ending it with: "I am deeply concerned at the pattern of Russian policy, which becomes more clear as they become more brazen every day."[32]

During the conference, Churchill attended nine plenary sessions, with detours to the usual nightly banquets and to dispiriting one-on-one talks with the Lublin Poles ("Communist creatures," Eden called them). The Old Man also spent an afternoon in Berlin, where hungry Berliners cheered when he alighted from his automobile in front of Hitler's Chancellery. Churchill strolled into the crowd. "My hate had died with their surrender," he later wrote. "I was much moved... by their haggard looks and threadbare clothes." After a brief tour of Hitler's bunker and the pit where the bodies of Hitler and Eva Braun were disposed of, Churchill looked about and declared, "Hitler must have come up here to get some air, and heard the guns getting nearer and nearer." He also spoke at the opening of the Winston Club, a nightclub and cabaret opened for British servicemen. There he received a cool reception from the gathered troops, who had voted weeks prior in early balloting.[33]

On the matter of the atomic bomb, Churchill enthusiastically endorsed Truman's decision to use it. Churchill and Roosevelt had agreed in 1943 that both the U.S. and Britain must approve the bomb's use. Yet, although a Royal Navy carrier task force was then attached to Admiral Halsey's Third Fleet, and Churchill was determined to do his part in Japan, the decision to drop the bomb was Truman's alone to make, by virtue of the overwhelming role America would play in the planned invasion of Japan. When Churchill suggested that the Japanese be forewarned that their country would be as utterly destroyed as Germany and that their only chance to preserve lives and honor would be to surrender now, Truman replied that the Japanese had had lost any claim to honor at Pearl Harbor. Still, the Allies sent an ultimatum—the Potsdam Declaration—to Tokyo in which they guaranteed the Japanese rights of free speech and religious assembly, and promised that they had no intention of enslaving the Japanese or destroying Japan as a nation. The declaration ended with: "We call upon the government of Japan to proclaim now the unconditional surrender of all Japanese armed forces, and to provide proper and adequate assurances of their good faith in such action. The alternative for Japan is prompt and utter destruction." Tokyo ignored the statement.[34]

Eden later recalled that he and Churchill had discussed the delicate matter of telling Stalin of the atomic bomb, and the more delicate matter of refusing Stalin the "know how" of the bomb's technology if he asked for it. They advised Truman to inform Stalin before the bomb was dropped on

Japan. Truman, in his memoir, *Year of Decisions,* recalls that on July 24 he "casually mentioned to Stalin that we had a new weapon of unusual destructive force. The Russian premier showed no special interest." Truman did not tell Stalin of the "atomic" nature of the new weapon. Churchill and Eden stood a few feet away as Truman spoke with Stalin. As recalled by Churchill, in his memoirs, "I was sure that he [Stalin] had no idea of the significance of what he was being told. Evidently in his immense toils and stresses the atomic bomb had played no part. If he had the slightest idea of the revolution in world affairs which was in progress his reactions would have been obvious.... But his face remained gay and genial and the talk between these two potentates soon came to an end." But as recalled by Marshal Zhukov in his memoirs, "Stalin did not betray his feelings and pretended that he saw nothing special in what Truman had imparted to him. Both Churchill and many other Anglo-American authors subsequently assumed that Stalin had really failed to fathom the significance of what he had heard. In actual fact, on returning to his quarters after this meeting Stalin, in my presence, told Molotov about his conversation with Truman. The latter reacted almost immediately. 'Let them. We'll have to talk it over with Kurchatov and get him to speed things up.' I realized that they were talking about research on the atomic bomb."[35]

Churchill, meanwhile, told Brooke that the new bomb made it "no longer necessary for the Russians to come into the Japanese war, the new explosive alone was sufficient to settle the matter." Churchill, Brooke told his diary, "was completely carried away" by the news from New Mexico and believed the bomb could "redress the balance with the Russians!" Churchill, "pushing his chin out and scowling," declared that "now we could say [to Stalin] if you insist on doing this or that, well we can just blot out Moscow, then Stalingrad, then Kiev, then Kuibyshev ... Sevastopol etc. etc. And now where are the Russians!!!" Brooke tried to "crush his [Churchill's] over-optimism" and to "dispel his dreams" based on "the half-baked results of one experiment," but Churchill stood firm. Yet Britain did not have an atomic bomb, and Truman would have been as shocked as Brooke if Churchill had proposed dropping one on the ally that had made the largest sacrifice in the war against Hitlerism.[36]

One other matter occupied Churchill at Potsdam—Lend-Lease. He stressed to Truman the British desire—and need—for a continuation of the program; food was in short supply, and London needed assurance that it could parcel out Lend-Lease matériel to European countries on an as-needed basis. "The president said he would do his utmost," Churchill wrote in his memoirs, "but of course I knew the difficulties he might have in his own country." A month later Truman told his closest advisers that "he was dead set against the U.S. adding to its reputation as a Santa Claus;

he wanted Lend-Lease cut to a minimum now, liquidated as soon as possible."[37]

Churchill left Potsdam without an agreement on Poland. The Red Army was in control of central Europe. Not since 1814, when Russian troops entered Paris, had a Russian army thrust so far west into Europe. With SHAEF decommissioned that week, with Truman sending his armies home and his air forces to the Pacific, and with British troops outnumbered by the Red Army by more than three to one, the fate of not only Eastern Europe but Western Europe rested with Joseph Stalin. It was this state of affairs that led Churchill eight years later to title the sixth and final volume of his war memoirs *Triumph and Tragedy*.

Churchill returned to London with Mary late on July 25 in order to learn his electoral fate. If Beaverbrook's optimistic predictions proved correct, Churchill would be going back to Potsdam in a few days. Father, daughter, son, and Clementine dined together that evening in the Storey's Gate Annexe. Churchill's brother, Jack, joined the party; Beaverbrook and Bracken dropped by. Churchill retired early (for him), shortly after 1:00 A.M., sanguine in his belief that he would receive his electoral mandate. He later wrote that he awoke just before dawn "with a sharp stab of almost physical pain. A hitherto subconscious conviction that we were beaten broke forth and entered my mind.... The power to shape the future would be denied me. The knowledge and experience I had gathered, the authority and goodwill I had gained in so many countries would vanish." He slept until nine, late for Churchill, and was in his bath when, shortly after ten, Captain Pim requested he make for the map room, where charts of battlefronts had been replaced by lists of constituencies. Colville, Bracken, and Beaverbrook joined Churchill there. The P.M., attired in his siren suit, sprawled in his chair, cigar in hand, as had been his habit in 1940 while he waited for the howl of the air-raid alarm to announce the fireworks.[38]

The first results were unfavorable, and the numbers only worsened as the morning wore on. Early reports showed forty-four Labour gains to just one for the Conservatives. Alexander Hancock, a farmer and unknown Independent crackpot who advocated a one-hour workday, had opposed Churchill in Woodford, a new district carved out of Churchill's old Epping district. The new Epping seat went to a Labourite, and Hancock took 35 percent of the vote in Woodford. Churchill kept his seat, as did Eden. But Bracken lost his, as did Duncan Sandys, Harold Macmillan, and Randolph. The only satisfying news to come over the transom was that Sir

William Beveridge and Leslie Hore-Belisha, both Liberals, had lost. Labour took 393 seats in the new Parliament, the Conservatives 213 (down from 585 in 1935). Had not the Liberals, who ran more than three hundred candidates, siphoned away Labour votes, the Tories would have fared even worse. The Liberals in the end won just twelve seats and were reduced to distant third-party irrelevancy. The *New York Times* declared the Tory defeat "one of the most stunning electoral surprises in the history of democracy." The London *Times* held Churchill accountable for his own political demise: "Mr. Churchill himself introduced and insisted upon emphasizing the narrower animosities of the party fight." The *Daily Telegraph* attributed the results to "a revulsion of feeling against the government rather than to an excess of support to the Socialist policy."[39]

Lunch at the Annexe that day, Mary told her diary, took place "in Stygian gloom." Sarah "looked beautiful and distressed." All in the room "looked stunned & miserable." "Papa struggled to accept this terrible blow—this unforeseen landslide." At some point, Clementine said of the defeat, "It may well be a blessing in disguise." To which Churchill replied, "Well, at the moment it's certainly very well disguised." Neither his sense of humor nor his dignity deserted him. When Lord Moran wandered onto the scene, Churchill asked, "Well, you know what has happened?" Moran replied that he knew, and added something about the ingratitude of the people. "Oh, no," Churchill answered, "I wouldn't call it that. They have had a very hard time." Moran had been so sure that Churchill would be given his mandate and that they'd return to Berlin that he had left his luggage there.[40]

At 6:00 P.M. Churchill ordered drinks and cigars to be brought in for the map room staff. Then he departed the Cabinet War Room—never to return—for Buckingham Palace. At 7:00 P.M. King George accepted Churchill's resignation, telling his former first minister that "the people were very ungrateful after the way they had been led in the war." After a brief audience, Churchill left for No. 10, while King George summoned Clement Attlee to form the new government. No crowds gathered outside Buckingham Palace, and the streets of London were as quiet as a country village. A cold light rain fell. The *New York Times:* "Tonight there were fewer persons at Buckingham Palace for the changing of the Government then there usually are for the changing of the guard."[41]

Before the election, a London *Times* editor informed Churchill that the newspaper was about to advocate two points—that Churchill should campaign as a nonpartisan world statesman and then ease himself into retirement sooner rather than later. "Mr. Editor," Churchill said to the first point, "I fight for my corner." And, to the second: "Mr. Editor, I leave when the pub closes."[42]

The pub had just closed.

Dinner at No. 10 that evening was a somewhat muted affair, Mary later wrote, but less gloomy than lunch. Uncle Jack was on hand, and Diana and Sarah, and Sarah's friend Robert Maugham (Somerset's nephew). Bracken attended, as did Anthony Eden, a remarkable gesture of fealty on his part given that he had learned just five days earlier that his son Pilot Officer Simon Eden, RAF, had been killed in Burma. Clementine took herself off to bed before dinner. The others tried "to say and do the right thing" for Churchill's sake, with some success. Maugham told Harold Nicolson a few days later that Churchill had accepted his defeat with good grace. When someone at the dinner table said to Churchill, "But you have won the race, sir," he replied, "Yes, and in consequence I've been warned off the turf."[43]

Sometime earlier that afternoon, Churchill composed a concession statement, which he sent to the BBC to be read during the nine o'clock news. Brian Gardner, writing in *Churchill in Power,* called the statement "perhaps the most gracious acceptance of democratic defeat in the English language." Churchill:

> The decision of the British people has been recorded in the votes counted today. I have therefore laid down the charge which was placed upon me in darker times. I regret that I have not been permitted to finish the work against Japan.... It only remains for me to express to the British people, for whom I have acted in these perilous years, my profound gratitude for the unflinching, unswerving support which they have given me during my task, and for the many expressions of kindness which they have shown towards their servant."[44]

Friday, July 27, was a day for farewells at No. 10. As Churchill took his leave from the Chiefs of Staff, Alan Brooke found himself "unable to say very much for fear of breaking down. He [Churchill] was standing the blow wonderfully well." A decade later, when Brooke—by then the 1st Viscount Alanbrooke—edited his diaries for publication, he inserted a line that stands in sharp contrast to his wartime rants against Churchill: "On reading these diaries I have repeatedly felt ashamed of the abuse I had poured on him [Churchill], especially during the latter years." Then, as if he could not let go, Lord Alanbrooke felt compelled to remind readers that during the latter part of the war "Winston had been a very sick man... with repeated attacks of pneumonia.... This physical condition together with his mental fatigue accounted for many of the difficulties in dealing with him.... I shall always look back on the years I worked with him as some of the most difficult and trying in my life." Only after enunciating his caveats did the viscount finally add the now oft-quoted tribute to Churchill: "For all that I thank God I was given an opportunity of working alongside such a man, and having my eyes opened to the fact that occasionally such supermen exist on this earth."[45]

Eden thought the entire afternoon a "pretty grim affair." He was the last to leave, having been called into the Cabinet Room by Churchill for a final chat. That night, Eden wrote in his diary: "He [Churchill] was pretty wretched, poor old boy.... He couldn't help feeling his treatment had been pretty scurvy." Before Eden left, Churchill looked about and said, "Thirty years of my life have been passed in this room. I shall never sit in it again. You will, but I shall not."

Eden assured Churchill that "his place in history could have gained nothing" by a return to No. 10 in the postwar years, adding, "That place was secure anyway." Churchill accepted that, and the two men parted. As Eden left he reflected upon the six war years he had spent in that room, writing that night: "I cannot believe I can ever know anything like it again."[46]

Churchill departed No. 10 for Chequers, which the new prime minister had put at his disposal for the weekend. Chartwell was not yet reopened and staffed, and although the Churchills were interested in purchasing a London town house at 28 Hyde Park Gate, they had not yet finalized the transaction. Under other circumstances, Mary later wrote, the weekend would "have been a very cozy jolly party" but "we were all still rather stunned by the events of the previous week." Ambassador John Winant was on hand, as was Sarah, who had decided to end their long love affair. It had always been more courtly than torrid, but it was doomed in any event by the fact that Winant was a married man and Sarah—aptly nicknamed the Mule—was a very independent woman. She later wrote that it had been an affair "which my father suspected but about which we did not speak."[47]

Colville—who now served Attlee—was on hand that weekend in order to help Churchill gather his personal effects. The Prof—Lord Cherwell—had motored out, as had Brendan Bracken. Churchill's former bodyguards and private secretaries had gone off to Berlin with the new prime minister. No motorcycle dispatch riders roared up the drive; the phones did not ring; the Chiefs of Staff did not report in. Most noticeably, the secret boxes and Ultra decrypts did not appear. "Now there was nothing," Mary wrote. "We saw with near desperation a cloud of black gloom descend." To dispel the cloud, they played records on the gramophone—American and French marches, Gilbert and Sullivan, and the Noel Gay tune "Run Rabbit Run." They ran movies, too—*The Wizard of Oz* was a favorite. They played cards and staged a croquet match, which Churchill watched from the sidelines. The cloud lingered. On Sunday, the twenty-ninth, the clan of fifteen sat down to dinner at the great round table, where they drank a Rehoboam of champagne in a futile attempt to make merry. At some point during dinner, Churchill said "it was fatal to give way to self-pity, that the Government had a mandate" and that "it was the duty of everyone to support them." Before retiring, they all signed the Chequers guestbook, Churchill last. Underneath his signature he wrote: *Finis*.[48]

Churchill and Clementine took up residence at Claridge's the next day. Two weeks later, on August 14, Churchill hosted a dinner in his Claridge's suite for Eden and a few Conservative colleagues. Late in the evening, they learned that the Japanese had surrendered. The Americans had dropped atomic bombs on Hiroshima and Nagasaki on the August 6 and 9. Tokyo had been silent in the days since, but now, as Eden put it, "the six years of ordeal was over." The dinner companions adjourned to another room, where a wireless was set up. There, they listened as Clement Attlee "barked out a few short sentences, then gave the terms.... The war was over."

"There was a silence," Eden wrote. "Mr. Churchill had not been asked to say any word to the nation. We went home. Journey's end."

Churchill had by all rights at age seventy reached the sixth and penultimate of Shakespeare's seven stages of life. The fields and orchards and rose gardens at Chartwell, wild and overgrown after five years of neglect, were in need of his attention, as were the fish ponds, and the fish, and the house itself. Little Winston and the other "wollygogs" needed him, as did Sarah, Mary, Diana, Randolph, and Clementine. Yet he had no intention of becoming Shakespeare's "slipper'd pantaloon." He considered his journey by no means over. He was the leader of the opposition, in which role he enthusiastically took his seat in the front row of the opposition bench in the Commons and proceeded to oppose. On his return to the House (still meeting in the Lords' chamber while the bombed-out Commons was being rebuilt), Conservative MPs leapt to their feet and sang "For He's a Jolly Good Fellow." Labourites countered with "The Red Flag."

Though England's greatest leader led the opposition, Churchill could not reverse the Labour mandate, and knew it. Labour had pledged to nationalize the Bank of England, the coal and utility industries, railroads, and the steel industry. As Labour in coming months and years created government control boards to manage each industry, bureaucracy became Britain's fastest-growing industry. Two years after V-E day, Churchill told the House: "A mighty army of 450,000 additional civil servants has been taken from production and added, at a prodigious cost and waste, to the oppressive machinery of government and control. Instead of helping national recovery this is a positive hindrance." That was one of his gentler rebukes of the socialist experiment. Labour's showcase priority was the creation of the National Health Service (which came to pass in 1948, with Aneurin Bevan installed as its first administrator). Labour proposed free health care, free false teeth, free eyeglasses. Just four months after the election, Churchill told the House:

> The queues are longer, the shelves are barer, the shops are emptier. The interference of Government Departments with daily life is more severe and more galling. More forms have to be filled up, more officials have to be consulted. Whole spheres of potential activity are frozen, rigid and numb, because this Government has to prove its Socialistic sincerity instead of showing how they can get the country alive and on the move again.

Sir Stafford Cripps, Churchill declared, "is a great advocate of Strength through Misery."[49]

Churchill, sure that the Labour tide would someday ebb, looked beyond England. He intended, with two broad objectives in mind, to transcend British politics and reinvent himself as an international statesman. He sought a special relationship (that he as yet had not explicitly defined) among the English-speaking peoples, including the Americans, and a similar but more crisply defined relationship among Western European countries—his old idea of a United States of Europe. He was, and had always been, a European patriot. Britons had sacked him, but Europeans loved him. This was political capital he began to invest. On November 16, he told an audience in Brussels that in order to prevent another "Unnecessary War" (caused in part, he said, by America's unwillingness to join the League of Nations and confront German re-armament), "we have to revive the prosperity of Europe: and European civilisation must rise again from the chaos and carnage into which it has been plunged: and at the same time we have to devise those measures of world security which will prevent disaster descending upon us again." He proposed a "United States of Europe, which will unify this Continent in a manner never known since the fall of the Roman Empire, and within which all its peoples may dwell together in prosperity, in justice, and in peace."[50]

Not all in the Tory leadership shared his visions for the future of Britain, of Europe, and even of the Tory party. The voters having thrown out the Conservatives, many in the Tory hierarchy felt it was time for Churchill to step down from the party leadership, to take "a long rest," as Lord Moran framed it. Churchill should write a history of the war, as only he could. He should paint, travel, and enjoy life. "Prefaced by elaborate protestations of admiration and respect," some of Churchill's colleagues began to advance the theme of retirement to Moran. They no longer would tolerate Churchill's grudging, sometimes cruel, and usually overbearing style of leadership. "In short," Moran wrote, "with the war behind them the Tory leaders were no longer prepared to stomach [Churchill's] summary methods." Churchill had no intention of abdicating the Tory leadership. "A short time ago I was ready to retire and die gracefully," he told Moran in 1946. Of the new Labour government, Churchill offered to Moran: "Now I'm going to stay and have them out. I'll tear their bleeding entrails out of them. I'm in pretty good fettle." It was "the Jerome blood," Winston said.[51]

During the first week of January 1946, foreign secretaries and diplomats from around the globe convened in London for the opening session of the United Nations General Assembly. Churchill was not among the luminaries. On January 9 he, Clementine, and Sarah boarded the *Queen Elizabeth,* bound for New York and a two-month vacation in Florida, Cuba, and the eastern United States. Not having yet decided to write his memoir of the war, he worked on his unfinished *History of the English-Speaking Peoples* during the voyage. But soon after he arrived in Miami, he read recently published essays by Eisenhower's aide, Captain Harry Butcher, which Butcher had based on his diary entries. Butcher's tales of Churchill's late nights and liquid lunches were incomplete, trivial, and not at all flattering to the Old Man, who, not about to take such "history" lying down, summoned his prewar European literary agent, Emery Reves. Butcher (and Elliott Roosevelt, with *As He Saw It*) helped force the decision; Churchill would write his version of the war.

On January 22, Harry Hopkins, who been hospitalized for more than two months, wrote a short letter to Churchill, in which he signed off with, "Do give my love to Clemmie and Sarah . . . all of whom I shall hope to see before you go back." Hopkins's doctors had been treating him for cirrhosis of the liver, but their diagnosis was wrong. The terrible pain he had suffered for almost a decade was due to hemochromatosis—a metabolic disorder of the digestive tract. His letter to Churchill was the last he wrote.

He died a week later. He took to the grave two firm political beliefs. The first was that Britain was the best friend America had and any attempt by America to horn in on British trade would only injure that relationship. His second was that Russia in coming years would become more nationalistic and less inclined to spread communism around the globe. But, regardless of Moscow's intentions, Hopkins believed America's "relations with the Soviet Union are going to be seriously handicapped" by differences over "fundamental notions of human liberty—freedom of speech, freedom of the press, and freedom of worship."[52]

In early February, while Churchill took his ease in the sun, Stalin addressed his party congress and, as recollected by Under Secretary of State Dean Acheson, "with brutal clarity outlined the Soviet Union's postwar policy." Russia would re-arm, Stalin declared, at the expense of producing consumer goods, because "capitalist-imperialist" monopolies guaranteed that "no peaceful international order was possible." George Kennan, then chargé d'affaires in Moscow, wrote an eight-thousand-word policy paper for the Truman administration that later became known as the "Long Telegram." In it Kennan predicted that Stalin's "neurotic view of world affairs" and a tyrant's fear of political insecurity would result in a Soviet foreign policy that would use "every means possible to infiltrate, divide and weaken the West."[53]

Kennan advised a policy of stiff resolve in the face of Soviet belligerence, in part because he believed Russians respected strength, and in part because Russia was exhausted from the war and in no position—yet—to assume a more sinister role on the world stage, other than through proxies (as in Greece and Yugoslavia). Kennan later wrote that had he sent his telegram six months earlier, it would have "raised eyebrows," and had he sent it six months later, it would have "sounded redundant." Fundamental to his diplomatic strategy was his belief—held since before Yalta—that Stalin would never grant to the peoples of Soviet-occupied countries such as Poland and Bulgaria democratic rights that were denied Russians. For the West to think otherwise was naive. To "act chummy" with Moscow, or "make fatuous gestures of goodwill" in hopes that Moscow would grant those rights, would gain nothing, partly because "no-one in Moscow believes the Western world" would "stand firm" against Soviet threats. Yet, Kennan also believed the military requirements needed to advance Moscow's cause were "beyond the Russian capacity to meet. Moscow has no naval or air forces capable of challenging the sea or air lanes of the world." Kennan's strategy later became known as "containment" and for more than four decades, it underlay U.S. policy toward the Soviet Union.[54]

Kennan's dismissal of Soviet air and naval capabilities put him in Walter Lippmann's corner in that regard, but neither one saw (as Churchill did soon after the Dresden raid) the coming reality of long-range bombers and rockets. Bernard Montgomery also believed that the Russians were down and out militarily, noting that when "1,700 American and British aircraft" gave "an impressive display of airpower" during a post–V-E day celebration in Frankfurt, the message "was not lost on the Russians" in attendance. Months later, after a visit to Moscow, Montgomery came away believing that "the Russians were worn out" and "quite unfit to take part in a world war against a strong combination of allied nations." But Churchill was concerned by Moscow's threat to *Europe,* not to the entire planet. And although Russia was not a worldwide naval power, neither anymore was Great Britain. Indeed, a naval vacuum existed in the Mediterranean, a vacuum easily filled by Russia if it decided to finally throttle its enemy of two hundred years, Turkey, or extort from Ankara free passage through the Dardanelles. Most worrisome to Churchill was the fact that there was no Western alliance in place to meet a Russian threat. The war was over; America was building new Packards and Chevys and Philco televisions and General Electric washing machines. "Alliance" was still a troublesome if not dirty word to many Americans, especially the Taft Republicans in Washington.[55]

Three months before Churchill's Florida vacation, he received an invitation from the president of Westminster College, in Fulton, Missouri, to deliver a series of lectures at that school. Churchill received many such invitations, but the postscript on this letter was handwritten—by President Truman. In it, Truman reminded Churchill that Missouri was his home state, and he offered to introduce Churchill at the lectures. Truman asked Churchill—whom the president considered to be "the first citizen of the world"—if he'd like to stop off in Washington first and travel to Missouri from there with Truman aboard the presidential train. Churchill accepted the offer with enthusiasm, suggesting one lecture might be more appropriate, as a series would quite tax his speech-writing skills. He had for months sought to articulate his worldview in a speech that would reach the largest possible audience, and here now came the president of the United States with an invitation that, Churchill told Truman, was "a very important act of state." At noon on March 4, after breakfasting with Truman at the White House, Churchill and Truman made for Union Station. A few White House aides went along on the trip, including Admiral Leahy, press secretary Charlie Ross, and General Harry Vaughan, a beefy, profane, a hard-drinking, cigar-smoking political operative and a Truman crony since the Great War. Truman's newly appointed special counsel Clark Clifford, thirty-nine and a product of Missouri's Washington University Law School, also boarded the presidential train for the eighteen-hour run to St. Louis. Drinks were served as soon as the train left the station—scotch for Churchill, which he took with water, telling his hosts that adding ice to liquor was a "barbaric" American custom, as was the American habit of not drinking whisky during meals.[56]

The meetings between Churchill and Truman in Potsdam the previous July had been brief and formal. Churchill, in fact, came away from Potsdam harboring "deep reservations about Truman," Clifford later wrote. Churchill himself years later claimed he "loathed the idea of [Truman] taking the place of Franklin Roosevelt." Yet at Potsdam, Churchill had been preoccupied with the coming election and the Russians. Since then, the Attlee government, not Churchill, had worked with Truman. The president, as Churchill learned during the train journey, was what Americans call a regular guy. He was blunt, honest, and not given in the least to the wily, often facile machinations that Franklin Roosevelt brought to the table. (Some months later, Lord Moran told Churchill he had learned that Roosevelt told his cabinet that if Churchill had one hundred ideas a day, four might be any good. Churchill responded, "It [was] impertinent for Roosevelt to say this. It comes badly from a man who hadn't had any ideas at all.") Truman, like Eisenhower and Hopkins, came from simple Midwestern stock. What you saw was what you got. With Hopkins now gone, Churchill could not have asked for a better American friend than Harry Truman. At Potsdam, Admiral King had leaned over to Lord Moran, and said, "Watch the President. This is all new to him, but he can take it. He is a more typical American than Roosevelt, and he will do a good job, not only for the United States, but for the whole world."[57]

The rail journey offered the two men a chance to get to know each other. Truman insisted Churchill call him Harry; Churchill agreed with delight, insisting that the president call him Winston. Truman at first demurred, telling Churchill that given his importance to England, America, and the world, "I just don't know if I can do that." Churchill: "Yes, you can. You must, or else I will not be able to call you Harry." Truman replied, "Well, if you put it that way, Winston, I *will* call you Winston." Truman told Churchill that he intended to send the battleship USS *Missouri* accompanied by a naval task force to Turkey, ostensibly to return the body of the Turkish ambassador, Münir Ertegün, who had died in 1944. The president's real intent, however, was to signal the Soviets that America was prepared to play a significant role in the eastern Mediterranean, a role Britain could no longer undertake alone. The U.S. Sixth Fleet, though not yet identified as such (and a presence in the Mediterranean ever since), was born on the trip to Westminster College. Yet, although Truman was growing increasingly wary of the Soviets, he had by no means settled on an adversarial policy toward them. He had been briefed on Kennan's long telegram, but he still harbored hopes of working with Stalin. America, its duty done, her boys coming home, was at peace. The Depression was long past. A new era had dawned, later anointed "The Good Times" by journalist Russell Baker. America, with over 400,000 of her boys buried overseas and at home, was in no mood to hear the rattle of sabers.[58]

As the presidential train rolled past a cyclorama of sleeping towns and darkened farms, Churchill excused himself to work on his speech. He had shown a draft to Secretary of State James Byrnes, who expressed no reservations to Truman, who in turn told Churchill he did not intend to read the final text so that he could tell reporters as much if they asked, which they surely would. But when Churchill emerged from his salon with the finished product, Truman could not resist. After reading it, he called it a "brilliant and admirable statement." As the president handed it back to Churchill, he predicted it would "create quite a stir."

During dinner Churchill asked if it was true that Truman enjoyed playing poker. "That's correct, Winston," the president replied. Churchill offered that he had first played poker during the Boer War, and suggested the cards be brought out for an evening game. Truman said that he and his colleagues would be delighted to set up the game. Green baize and chips were produced; drinks poured. When Churchill excused himself for a moment, Truman warned his companions that Churchill had played poker for more than forty years, was "cagey," loved cards, "and is probably an excellent player." The reputation of American poker was at stake, the president said, adding that he expected "every man to do his duty." Soon after the first cards were dealt, it became apparent to the Americans that their distinguished guest was not a poker player of distinction; in fact, Clifford pegged him as "a lamb among wolves." Within an hour Churchill was down almost $300 (£75, more than $3,500 in current dollars), a great deal of money in 1946, more so for an Englishman whose finances, like his country's, were in a regrettable state. When Churchill again excused himself for a few moments, Truman laid down the law to his four colleagues: They were not to exploit their guest's obvious lack of poker skills. "But boss," Harry Vaughan replied, "*this guy's a pigeon!*" Thus, during the early morning hours of the day on which he delivered one of the most memorable speeches of the twentieth century, Churchill tried his best to beat his hosts at their own game. He did not fare well.

Spring had come early to Fulton; the day was warm, the windows thrown open in the college gymnasium, where a small stage had been set up. Churchill was to be awarded an honorary doctor of laws degree, and he had dressed for the occasion in his crimson Oxford robes. A television camera was to have been brought in to broadcast the event, but Churchill, fearing that the bright lights would be a distraction, nixed that idea. Instead, a lone Paramount movie camera was set up. Churchill began his address with broad brushstrokes: the United States with its nuclear monopoly now stood at "the pinnacle of power," and with "an awe-inspiring accountability to the future." He advised that the nascent United Nations be endowed with an international air force. He believed all men should live in their "myriad cottages" free and without fear. "To give security to these countless homes, they must be shielded from the two giant marauders, war and tyranny." He spoke in conciliatory terms of the Soviet Union:

> A shadow has fallen upon the scenes so lately lighted by the Allied victory. Nobody knows what Soviet Russia and its Communist international organization intends to do in the immediate future, or what are the limits, if any, to their expansive and proselytising tendencies. I have a strong admiration and regard for the valiant Russian people and for my wartime comrade, Marshal Stalin.... We welcome Russia to her rightful place among the leading nations of the world. We welcome her flag upon the seas.... It is my duty however, for I am sure you would wish me to state the facts as I see them to you, to place before you certain facts about the present position in Europe.

Then:

> From Stettin in the Baltic to Trieste in the Adriatic, an iron curtain has descended across the Continent. Behind that line lie all the capitals of the ancient states of Central and Eastern Europe. Warsaw. Berlin. Prague, Vienna, Budapest, Belgrade, Bucharest and Sofia, all these famous cities and the populations around them lie in what I must call the Soviet sphere, and all are subject in one form or another, not only to Soviet influence but to a very high and, in many cases, increasing measure of control from Moscow.

He could not resist telling the audience that although a terrible war had been fought to a successful conclusion, that war need not ever have happened because "no one would listen and one by one we were all sucked into the awful whirlpool." Although he did not believe the Russians wanted another war, he did believe they sought "the fruits of war and the indefinite expansion of their powers and doctrines." Then he arrived at his central message:

> If the population of the English-speaking Commonwealths be added to that of the United States with all that such co-operation implies in the air, on the sea, all over the globe and in science and in industry, and in moral force, there will be no quivering, precarious balance of power to offer its temptation to ambition or adventure. On the contrary, there will be an overwhelming assurance of security. If we adhere faithfully to the Charter of the United Nations and walk forward in sedate and sober strength seeking no one's land or treasure, seeking to lay no arbitrary control upon the thoughts of men; if all British moral and material forces and convictions are joined with your own in fraternal association, the high-roads of the future will be clear, not only for us but for all, not only for our time, but for a century to come.[59]

To safeguard the West's liberties, he proposed a fraternal association of America and Britain, calling that idea "the crux of what I traveled here to say." He offered specifics, including "the continuance of the present facilities for mutual security by the joint use of all Naval and Air Force bases in the possession of either country all over the world."[60]

He had titled his speech "The Sinews of Peace." Many heard more of a war chant. The reaction was immediate, and not favorable. *The Nation,* a small, sober, left-wing magazine, said that Churchill had "added a sizeable measure of poison to the already deteriorating relations between Russia and the Western powers," and added that Truman had been "remarkably inept" by giving Churchill the platform from which to administer his poison. The *Wall Street Journal,* echoing the isolationist mantra of earlier in the decade, rejected Churchill's call for an English-speaking alliance, saying that "the United States wants no alliance or anything that resembles an alliance with any other nation." The *New York Times* noted that the speech was "received with marked applause in the passages where it dealt with the responsibility of this country to see that another World War was avoided, but the proposal for 'fraternal association' brought only moderate handclapping." In fact, the Paramount movie camera set up to capture the scene caught Harry Truman applauding with vigor during Churchill's more controversial passages: Churchill had declared himself an Atlanticist, in the Walter Lippmann mode, and Truman liked it.[61]

Stalin did not, and his reaction was also immediate. He granted an "interview" to *Pravda,* wherein he took the shrewd position that Churchill, by calling for an English-speaking union, was no less a racist than Hitler, and no less a "war monger." By arranging the Anglo world against the rest of the world, Stalin claimed, "Mr. Churchill... [is] presenting those nations who do not speak English with a kind of ultimatum—recognize

[Anglo-American] superiority over you, voluntarily, and all will be well—otherwise war is inevitable." The marshal had a point, and one not lost on the French, who had been seeking an understanding with Moscow for two years (de Gaulle had long predicted France and Russia would emerge as the two great postwar European powers). Truman's response to Churchill's address was muted. When asked by reporters in Fulton if he had read the speech beforehand, Truman declared he had not. "Much to our relief," Clifford later wrote, "Churchill... did not contradict" the president. Still, to placate the peanut gallery, Truman forbade Under Secretary of State Dean Acheson to attend a New York reception for Churchill. Yet the arrival of Kennan's "Long Telegram" just two weeks earlier had set the stage for a reevaluation of U.S. foreign policy, a process Dean Acheson believed necessary although slow in coming about. Churchill had spoken with emotion in contrast to Kennan's lawyerly white paper, but their messages were similar. In those weeks a new era came into being.[62]

The Cold War, as it soon came to be known, had had its start before World War Two ended, but soon enough—from Moscow to London to Washington and on around the globe—all agreed that it had been declared on March 5, 1946, by the Citizen of the World Without Portfolio, in Fulton, Missouri. That month, Truman sent Averell Harriman—who just weeks earlier had resigned his Moscow post in hopes of leaving government—to London as ambassador to the Court of St. James's. Stalin had not withdrawn Soviet troops from Azerbaijan, in northern Iran, as promised, a circumstance, Truman believed, that "may lead to war." "I want," Truman told Harriman, "a man in London I can trust." Stalin pulled his troops from Iran weeks later, but within the year the Russians shot down a British aircraft that had strayed from one of the three Western air corridors leading to Berlin. The fires of war remained banked, but a banked fire, in English folklore, holds the most heat. From the day Churchill delivered his Fulton speech until more than four decades later, all knew the Cold War could turn hot at any time, through weakness of will, geopolitical overreach, or a cascading series of diabolically unfortunate events. Churchill left Fulton secure in his belief that peace would be guaranteed as long as America maintained its monopoly on nuclear weapons. It could not be guaranteed by a nuclear-armed Britain because the U.S. Congress that year passed the McMahon Act, which dissolved the gentleman's agreement Churchill and Roosevelt had reached on atomic bombs. Henceforth Washington would share no atomic secrets with London. Harriman thought the law "shameful" given that during the war Britain "had given us everything they had.... Now the Congress of the United States had made it illegal even to exchange information with the British."[63]

On September 19, 1946, seven weeks after Truman signed the McMahon Act, Churchill told a Zurich audience, "The atomic bomb is still only in the hands of a State and nation which we know will never use it except in the cause of right and freedom. But it may well be that in a few years this awful agency of destruction will be widespread and the catastrophe following from its use by several warring nations will not only bring to an end all that we call civilization, but may possibly disintegrate the globe itself."[64]

He had gone to Zurich not to expressly wax melancholic about the possible doom of Europe in the atomic age, but rather to propose a defense. He told the Zurich audience that the recent war had been fought to prevent a return of "the Dark Ages" and "all their cruelty and squalor," though he warned, "They may still return." Then:

> Yet all the while there is a remedy which, if it were generally and spontaneously adopted, would as if by a miracle transform the whole scene, and would in a few years make all Europe, or the greater part of it, as free and as happy as Switzerland is today. What is this sovereign remedy?... I am now going to say something that will astonish you. The first step in the re-creation of the European family must be a partnership between France and Germany.... There can be no revival of Europe without a spiritually great France and a spiritually great Germany.... We must build a kind of United States of Europe.[65]

His Fulton speech had marked the postwar renewal of his long-held vision of a special Anglo-American relationship. The 1946 Zurich address marked the start of his active campaign for a united Europe, one that would include Germany but would not necessarily include Britain. Historians ever since have plumbed the seeming paradox of Churchill's desire for Britain to be in, but not really *in,* a united Europe. Jock Colville had listened to Churchill's pronouncements on a united Europe throughout the war and had come to understand the root of the matter: in essence, the Old Man sought European stability such that the Royal Navy (which he presumed would assume its former role in global politics after the war) might roam over the high seas without having to fret potential troubles back home. United Europe, for Churchill, meant global opportunity for England. He had called for a "Council of Europe" in a March 1943 broadcast, and had made mention of a "United States of Europe" in a November 1945

Brussels speech. He sought such an arrangement not only to create a Franco-German bulwark against Soviet transgressions but also to align the interests of Germany and France such that they would never again have reason to go to war against each other. That would benefit both Europe and England. Churchill believed that a robust France living in harmony with a rebuilt Germany would, someday—if time and the Russians did not derail events—form such a buffer. In late 1946, neither nation, alone or together, was in any shape to form a buffer between Russia and Britain. Germany had been conquered, partitioned, and reduced in size, and the rump occupied. In France the Fourth Republic, just wobbling into existence, was conducting a pogrom against all things Vichy, while overseas it was fighting a war in Indochina against Ho Chi Minh and the Viet Minh, who had declared a breakaway republic in the north of Vietnam the year before. Rapprochement with Germany was not high on the French agenda.

The reaction to Churchill's Zurich address was, as with his Fulton speech, muted at best. Attlee and Labour thought the objectives of European security "would be better achieved through the United Nations." Chancellor of the Exchequer Hugh Dalton believed any such movement should be driven by Europe's Socialists and for Europe's socialists, an attitude Churchill later derided as "squalid" and "a declaration that if Europe is to unite and Britain is to play any part in such a union, it can only be on a one-party basis—and that party the Socialists." Ironically, Attlee, on the very day he belittled Churchill's grand idea, also gave Churchill "Top Secret" reports that showed the Red Army maintained 116 divisions in occupied Europe, enough force, one Ministry of Defence official concluded, to make "a Russian conquest of western Europe" a "practical possibility." When Churchill sent his son-in-law and champion of the united Europe movement, Duncan Sandys, to France to measure the French reaction to his Zurich speech, Sandys had to tell the Old Man that the French people "were violently opposed" to reconstituting a unified German Reich, although de Gaulle (out of office) "believed firmly in the project." Yet de Gaulle's endorsement came with a caveat: although he sought a unity of purpose between Britain and France with a possible role for Germany, the precise part Germany would play in any such arrangement had first to be determined. De Gaulle was not in the least prepared to endorse a resurgent and re-armed Reich.[66]

Over the next eighteen months, the European unity movement gained momentum, with Churchill pushing from the sidelines. In May 1948 he addressed Europeanists at The Hague:

> Since I spoke on this subject at Zurich in 1946, and since our British United Europe Movement was launched in January 1947, events have

> carried our affairs beyond our expectations.... Great governments have banded themselves together with all their executive power.... Sixteen European States are now associated for economic purposes; five have entered into close economic and military relationship.... Mutual aid in the economic field and joint military defence must inevitably be accompanied step by step with a parallel policy of closer political unity.

He moved on to a vital part of his vision, one not shared by many on both sides of the Atlantic—the inclusion of Germany in this new Europe:

> Some time ago I stated that it was the proud mission of the victor nations to take the Germans by the hand and lead them back into the European family, and I rejoice that some of the most eminent and powerful Frenchmen have spoken in this sense. To rebuild Europe from its ruins and make its light shine forth again upon the world, we must first of all conquer ourselves.

On May 5, 1949, ten nations signed the Treaty of London, which brought into being the Council of Europe. That August, after having invested much of his political capital on the issue, Churchill was rewarded with an invitation to Strasbourg and the first session of the Council of Europe Assembly. This was a true, though nascent, European parliament, a congress not of parties but of principles—of the rule of law, free speech, and international cooperation. The Germans were not in attendance, but by the following year, they would be.[67]

Full vindication for Fulton duly arrived a year later when on March 12, 1947, President Truman, with Greece and Turkey in mind, declared to a joint session of the U.S. Congress that henceforth it would be "the policy of the United States to support free peoples who are resisting attempted subjugation by armed minorities or by outside pressures." Greece, where a civil war was being fought, and Turkey, Truman argued, needed aid, hundreds of millions of dollars in aid, to prevent their slipping beneath the Communist wave. He did not propose military action, but the threat of force was implicit in his words. The *New York Times*'s James Reston declared the speech as important as the Monroe Doctrine. The tectonic shift in American foreign policy may have taken Truman only twenty-one minutes to announce, but the ground had been shifting for five years, the final jolt arriving on Friday, February 22, when Lord Inverchapel, the British ambassador, tried to deliver a note to George Marshall, secretary of state for all of thirty days. Marshall had already left Foggy Bottom for the weekend, but his deputy, Dean Acheson, persuaded Inverchapel to leave a carbon copy of the message. The British note was blunt and to the point: having "already strained their resources to the utmost," the British wished to inform Marshall that all aid to Greece and Turkey would end on March 31. Britain was broke and could no longer maintain any force—or influence—in the eastern Mediterranean.[68]

The new policy became known as the Truman Doctrine, a bold declaration of America's intent to guarantee not only the sovereignty of Greece and Turkey, but of nations throughout the world. George Marshall at first thought it unwise. He had learned firsthand doing battle with Churchill during the war that the Balkans were a dangerous place. He had undercut Churchill's ambitions then; now his own president had picked up Churchill's mantle. Marshall was not at all convinced that the Russians were the sinister threat their enemies made them out to be, and he was not certain that Moscow posed any threat to Greece or Turkey.

Marshall that week was in Moscow for talks with Molotov on the occupation of Germany and Austria, and the rebuilding of industrial capacity in those conquered states. The war had ended almost two years earlier, yet peace terms regarding the old Reich had yet to be agreed upon between the U.S. and the U.S.S.R. Marshall had left Washington in an optimistic mood, but by the time he returned home in April, his hopes had evaporated. The Russians, who had stripped Germany and Austria of factories and machines, told Marshall that more would be squeezed from them, the horrific plight of their peoples be damned.

That winter was particularly ferocious, and millions of refugees still roamed central Europe. Each morning in cities and towns throughout Germany and Austria, the frozen bodies of the starved were picked up from streets and alleys by their starving fellow citizens and carted off to communal graves. Stalin, his own country in ruins (as Marshall saw firsthand), would not give an inch, and in fact argued for a delay in the reconstruction of Germany. The German pasture that Stalin (and Henry Morgenthau) had envisioned had come to pass, but far too many millions of people lived there to be sustained. Starvation was the only certainty for millions of Germans. And that was fine with Stalin. The Moscow talks ended in utter disagreement. The Americans and Russians would not meet again for fifteen years. Truman and Marshall did not voice in public the concerns they now harbored about Stalin's intentions—the Red Army was still considered heroic in America. But the Truman Doctrine served notice of a course correction. It amounted to the Atlantic Charter with muscle, and vindication as well of Churchill's 1944 Christmas journey to Athens. A week after Truman's address, Dean Acheson declared: "A Communist dominated Government in Greece would be considered dangerous to United States security." Although Churchill was not one to say "I told you so," Lord Moran wrote, "[Churchill's Mediterranean policy] had been taken over lock, stock, and barrel by the United States."[69]

Marshall understood that only the United States possessed the economic might to lift Europe out of the morass. Yet the British and Americans had not helped matters since 1945 by embargoing sales of raw materials to Germany. Without factories, with its steel industry dead, and without raw materials to build new machine tools to outfit new factories, Germany could only descend deeper into ruin. This Marshall now understood. A European economy without a German presence was something akin to an American economy without New York finances and Pennsylvania coal and steel. Yet the British economy, too, was foundering. This deeply troubled Dean Acheson, for Britain was one of just two European countries where citizens believed in their government, where order was maintained, and where old ethnic and wartime scores were not being settled by gun and bomb. The other was Russia, and that, for Acheson, was the problem. It had been a year since Stalin declared his antipathy toward the West; even those Americans who had put Stalin and the Russians on a pedestal now saw the danger. Acheson and a very few others in the State Department believed America had to help Europe, and especially Britain, not only because it was the right thing to do for the nation that had fought alone for almost two years against Hitler, but because a strong Britain and a reinvigorated Europe could only make for a stronger America in the new world order.[70]

Shortly after Marshall returned from Moscow, Acheson persuaded him to take to the airwaves in order to tell Americans of "the suffering of the people of Europe, who are crying for help, for coal, for food, and for the necessities of life." Marshall did, warning Americans that "the patient is sinking while the doctors deliberate." On June 5, while giving the Harvard commencement address, he announced his plan for European recovery, known since as the Marshall Plan. "The initiative," he stressed, "must come from Europe," but the dollars would come from America. At a press conference on June 12—three years to the day since he and Churchill had visited the D-day beaches—Marshall cited Churchill's 1946 Zurich speech calling for a united Europe as one of the influences underlying his belief that Europe would emerge from the ruins a better place. Stalin, always suspecting the Americans of seeking "control" in any transaction, opted out of receiving aid. Soviet satellites, too, opted out on orders from Moscow, including Hungary, where Moscow had engineered a Communist coup in late May. But sixteen nations of free Europe opted in.

Churchill called the Marshall Plan "a turning point in the history of the world." Almost $13 billion—about 5 percent of yearly U.S. gross domestic product, and 16 percent of the federal budget—would find its way to Europe over the next four years, including more than $1 billion a year to Britain. It was the embodiment of Churchill's fourth moral principle, *In Peace: Goodwill*. Churchill had been advocating European solidarity for two years. Marshall's plan addressed the economic way; now it fell to Europeans to find the necessary political will.[71]

By 1947 Churchill's financial status had improved measurably. His daughter Mary later wrote that for the first time in his life, and through the good graces of friends and publishers, "Winston was rich." Churchill's revenue stream flowed from two sources. Late in 1945, his friend Lord Camrose hatched what Churchill called a "princely plan" to make Chartwell a national possession. Camrose formed a trust to which he contributed £15,000 and by August 1946 had raised another £80,000 through sixteen other subscribers, enough to purchase Chartwell for almost £45,000 and make a gift of it to the National Trust with an endowment of £35,000. Churchill was granted a life tenancy at £350 per year. Upon his death Chartwell—and the documents, paintings, furniture, and mementos Churchill promised to leave there—was to be opened to the public.[72]

By late 1946, with the Chartwell transaction complete, Churchill directed his attention and money toward purchasing nearby farms and remodeling his London house at 28 Hyde Park Gate (and the adjoining No. 27, also purchased). A prize Jersey cow arrived at Chartwell, and Landrace pigs, and in 1948 a Land Rover to tour the estates, which during 1947 had grown to almost five hundred acres. German prisoners of war—Churchill called them all "Fritzy"—supplied much of the labor. One of the Germans fell in love with the countryside and a country girl, and chose to marry and make a new life among the Englanders. The prisoners cleared fields and planted legumes; the walled gardens were home to lettuces; the hothouses hosted cucumbers. Peach and nectarine trees were groomed, grapevines trimmed. The apple and pear trees, which Churchill had planted two decades earlier, were tended to. Roses and wisteria were likewise pruned; the pathways through the rose gardens—laid out by Clementine in the 1920s—cleared. The Chartwell tennis court was converted to a croquet lawn; the mistress of the manor no longer had the stamina for tennis, but she enjoyed long croquet matches with visiting friends, including Field Marshal Montgomery, who Colville in coming years described as having become a "mellow, lovable exhibitionist, tamed but lonely and pathetic." Monty and Clementine had gotten off to a rocky start during Churchill's recuperation in Marrakech in 1943, when Montgomery presumed to dictate the guest list for dinner to Clementine. It got even rockier when Montgomery, who then served as Chief of the Imperial Staff under Attlee, declared that soldiering was a more honorable profession than politics, at which point Clementine shot back, "How dare you have the ill-bred impudence to say such a thing in my house." He was soon forgiven. For the next decade, Monty and Clementine passed many afternoons doing battle on the croquet field. The master of the manor did not compete, though he sometimes watched the games.[73]

Churchill stocked the three fishponds with giant goldfish, which he fed by hand with maggots delivered in tins from London. He attempted to protect his fish from marauding birds by means of a device of his own invention—a floating "pinwheel" of sorts cobbled together from a bicycle wheel outfitted with a series of small mirrors. He explained the mechanics of the contraption to the American journalist Stewart Alsop as they strolled the grounds: as the wheel turned in the breeze, the mirrors, catching the sun's rays, would emit bright flashes, which presumably would frighten off the birds. "Unfortunately," Churchill told Alsop, "on this small island the sun hardly ever shines."[74]

Chartwell's fauna continued to multiply. The Australian government sent two red-beaked black swans as a gift; they were joined by three more, the lot of them furiously ill-tempered. The swans coexisted on the lower lake with a pair of Canada Geese (called Lord and Lady Beaverbrook) and two white swans, a female, Mr. Juno, and a male, Mrs. Jupiter, so named, Churchill explained to Lady Diana Cooper, because the sexes were misidentified to begin with. Sundry ducks and "five foolish geese" also made their home on the lower lakes.

Late each morning, Churchill would summon his Scotland Yard protector and announce, "Sergeant, I'm ready for my walk now." He might ask a typist with a stenographer's pad to accompany him, in case a thought in need of recording burst forth. Then, as recalled by one of the new typists, Cecily ("Chips") Gemmell, "he would stomp out wearing this terrible old battered hat with swan feathers sticking out of it" to feed his "poor little birds" from a basket of stale bread that he carried hooked over an arm. By the lakeside "he'd bark, *arf, arf, arf,* and the swans came running." He used wads of bread as ammunition with the aim of inciting the birds to battle among themselves, the foolish geese versus the ferocious swans. He was more conciliatory toward defenseless winged creatures. Fearing a decline in native butterflies, he oversaw the creation of a butterfly garden and the conversion of a garden shed to a butterfly farm. At one point he contemplated nourishing the butterflies with fountains that would flow with honey and water, but he thought better of the idea. More Jersey dairy cows arrived, along with ponies. The purchase of one neighboring farm brought in a herd of Shorthorn cattle. And in 1947, a poodle named Rufus II arrived, replacing Rufus I, killed by an automobile. Rufus took his dinner with the family in the Chartwell dining room, from a bowl placed upon a special cloth on the Persian carpet, and next to his master's chair. The butler always served Rufus before serving their first course to the guests at table.[75]

In February 1947, Mary married Christopher Soames, a captain in the Coldstream Guards, and assistant military attaché in Paris. The newlyweds took up residence on one of the Chartwell farms, while Churchill began work on his war memoirs there and at 27–28 Hyde Park Gate. By then, Mary later wrote, "Winston now had, if not a veritable kingdom, at least a principality." Two years later, when Christopher Soames prevailed on his father-in-law to purchase a French-bred Grey, Churchill took up the sport of kings. The horse—Colonist II—proved a champion, winning the Salisbury and Lime Tree stakes in 1949 under Churchill's colors (his father Randolph's colors, pink and gray), and six more prestigious races by 1951, when he was put out to stud. Clementine, in a letter to their friend journalist Ronnie Tree, expressed her wonderment at "this queer new facet in Winston's variegated life. Before he bought the horse (I can't think why) he had hardly been on a race course in his life. I must say I don't find it madly amusing."[76]

That Churchill could indulge in such extravagances stemmed from the second and ultimately far more powerful financial stream that irrigated his fortunes: the Chartwell Trust, created with Lord Camrose's help to hold title to Churchill's personal papers and to shield him from the punishing taxes of the times. Clementine, Lord Cherwell (Prof Lindemann), and Brendan Bracken would serve as trustees, and would be charged with two paramount duties: to sell Churchill's wartime memoirs, and to make Churchill's earlier papers available to Randolph when the time came for him to write his father's official biography, "but not until five or ten years after his death." The trust, far more than selling Chartwell, made Churchill a rich man. The British film director and producer Alexander Korda (who also donated a full-fledged cinema to Chartwell) paid £50,000 ($200,000) for the film rights to *History of the English-Speaking Peoples,* a four-volume work that would not be published for another decade. The American publisher Henry Luce paid Churchill £12,000 ($50,000) for the American book rights to his wartime secret-sessions speeches to the House of Commons. Odhams Press ponied up £25,000 ($100,000) for the residual value of his pre-1940 book copyrights. *The Second World War,* Churchill's war memoir and history, proved to be a most powerful generator of wealth. Houghton Mifflin agreed to a $250,000 advance for the American book rights; Henry Luce's *Life* magazine agreed to pay $1.15 million for the American serial rights. These were princely sums, the equivalent of a modern $12 million. The memoir was to run to six volumes.[77]

Churchill's intent was not to write a history of the war but to explore the wartime Anglo-American relationship, and to refute the "rubbish" being written about him by Captain Butcher, Elliott Roosevelt, and left-leaning London newspapers. He oversaw the operation with his usual military precision, with himself as minister of war directing his battalions of literary troopers, who anointed themselves The Syndicate. Captain William Deakin DSO ran the tactical side of the campaign, supported by seven secretaries and typists and a host of current and former Churchill advisers, including Pug Ismay, Field Marshal Alexander, Air Marshal Park, Duncan Sandys, the Wizard Warrior R. V. Jones, Mountbatten's former Chief of Staff General Sir Henry Pownell, and Emery Reves as agent, fixer, and arbiter of editorial content. The Prof checked statistics and translated arcane scientific data into plain English. Denis Kelly, a young barrister, was charged with cataloging Churchill's papers, assisted in that task by Chips Gemmell, just eighteen. The volatile Randolph, who his sister Mary later wrote "could pick a quarrel with a chair," was not part of the team. The key to the entire operation was an extraordinary agreement Churchill struck with the cabinet secretary Edward Bridges. Churchill asked for and Bridges approved that all wartime documents written by Churchill, and replies, be removed to Chartwell for Churchill's use in preparing the memoirs. HMG would have final approval before publication. This arrangement meant that Churchill, with exclusive access, could cull the complete record at his leisure, whereas under British law the papers would be put off-limits to other historians for more than three decades. Kelly had much to catalog.[78]

An early Dictaphone was installed at Chartwell to aid the Great Man in the production process. Churchill gave the machine a test run one day after allowing all the typists the day off. But he failed to press the start button. When it failed to record anything, he banished it. Instead, he dictated his work to the typists, a total of almost one and a half million words over seven years. When critics later demeaned the effort as being carried off more by The Syndicate than by Churchill, Denis Kelly replied with words to the effect that a master chef cannot be expected to prepare each course for a grand banquet. The Syndicate indeed furnished Churchill with official documents, letters, telegrams, and the recollections of some of the principals, but Churchill dictated the narrative and assembled the entire work. The first volume, *The Gathering Storm,* was published in mid-1948, and the final volume, *Triumph and Tragedy,* came out the United States in late 1953, and in Britain in April 1954. Though in places factually incorrect—by commission as well as omission—the memoir "is an invaluable record," wrote parliamentarian and Churchill biographer Roy Jenkins, who also called it "the ultimate literary achievement of the outstanding author-politician of the twentieth century." Churchill's attitude toward the work, as recalled by Deakin, was "This is not history, this is my case."[79]

He prepared his case not only at Chartwell and 27–28 Hyde Park Gate, but on the shores of Lake Léman in Switzerland (August 1946); in Marrakech (New Year's 1947 and winter 1950–51); at the Hôtel de Paris in Monte Carlo (December 1948); at Lake Garda and Lake Carezza for a month; at Beaverbrook's villa, La Capponcina, at Cap d'Ail (summer 1949); at Reid's Hotel in Madeira (January 1950); and in Annecy and Venice (1951). He also took time to slip across to America in 1949 in order to promote his book, visit with Bernard Baruch and Harry Truman, and address the students at MIT. With draconian British currency restrictions in place during these years, Churchill and his party often traveled as the guests of his American publishers (who often paid Churchill's expenses with French francs rather than British pounds) in order to avoid a breach of British currency law.

Churchill's easel and paints always went along on these trips, but Clementine often did not, although she and Lord Moran hastened to Marrakech when Churchill came down with bronchitis during his 1947 visit there. He enjoyed his painting and basking and swimming on these jaunts, although in a letter to Clementine written from Marrakech before the onset of the bronchitis, he wrote of bleak weather and his fear of catching a cold, adding: "England and politics seem very distant here. I continue to be depressed about the future. I really do not see how our poor island is going to earn its living when there are so many difficulties around us." He was back in the wilderness, but with two critical distinctions. He now led the opposition, whereas in the 1930s he had been in opposition to his own party. And he believed he would play a vital role as the future played out, if not in Downing Street, then in his beloved House of Commons. Yet, in response to a 1946 birthday toast raised by Bracken, Churchill, after expressing appreciation at having his friends and family by his side, added: "But we are the past."[80]

The bronchitis crisis of early 1947 passed without effect, but the taps on Churchill's shoulders grew more frequent, more varied, and more serious. His brother, Jack, six years his junior and long afflicted with a bad heart, died in February 1947. "As you get older these things seem less tragic," Churchill told Moran. "In any case there is not much time left." Jack was buried next to his parents in the little churchyard at St. Martin's, in Bladon, just a mile south of Blenheim Palace. Later that year, Churchill underwent a hernia operation, in preparation for which and on the advice of his surgeon, who feared a pulmonary crisis might occur while the Old Man was under anesthesia, he promised to quit cigars. He did not. He then promised the surgeon to reduce his alcohol intake by half. This, too, he failed to do, yet apparently to no ill effect. The surgery went well. By 1948, Moran believed Churchill's arteries were hardening, and the Old Man by then complained regularly of feeling tightness in his shoulders. In August 1949, he lost feeling in his right arm and leg. Moran was summoned from London. He diagnosed a minor stroke, telling Churchill that he had not suffered a hemorrhage but that a "very small clot has blocked a very small artery." A year later, Moran detected a "disturbance of cerebral circulation." If hardening of the arteries is a sign of old age, Moran later wrote, "Winston was an old man before he began writing *The Second World War*." Churchill believed he should not look too far forward; however much of a future he was to have, it could not be long. But he could always look back, to the days of honor. When asked by Moran's wife which year of his life he'd want to live over, he replied, "Nineteen-forty every time. Every time."[81]

As Churchill's financial fortunes improved during the late 1940s, those of Britain continued their descent. "Victory," Churchill told Moran in 1946, "has turned into sack cloth and ashes." When the Attlee government sent John Maynard Keynes to the United States in 1946 to negotiate a $3.75 billion loan to finance reconstruction, the great economist secured his loan, but on hard terms. Interest was pegged at 2 percent over fifty years (with the proviso that London could skip annual payments in times of economic duress, which it did six times in the coming two decades). This was generous on America's part. But Washington also insisted that London leave the gold standard and make the pound fully convertible in accordance with the Bretton Woods agreement.* This proved a calamity when in 1949 the Attlee government—under continuing economic pressure, and despite months of denials that it would do so—devalued the pound by 30 percent, from $4.08 to $2.80.

A devalued currency results in that nation's products becoming cheaper in foreign markets, but Britain had little to export, and very little that Americans wanted. Of Britain's plight, Churchill told the house in 1950:

* The British government paid the final £100 million installment on the loan in December 2006.

"Owing to their [the Attlee government's] follies and wrongful action, a great part of all the loans and gifts we have received from abroad has been spent not upon the re-equipment of our industry, nor upon the import of basic foodstuffs: instead much of this precious aid was lavishly frittered away" on socialist programs. He excoriated Attlee for "[raising] our taxation until it is the highest in the world, and even stands higher today than in the worst years of the war." Between the loans "and the unparalleled sacrifices exacted from the taxpayers" there was no reason why Britain should not have attained "solvency, security and utopian independence. This has been denied us not only by the incompetence and maladministration of the Socialist Government and their wild extravagance, but even more by the spirit of class hatred which they have spread throughout the land, and by the costly and wasteful nationalization of a fifth part of our industries."[82]

That U.S. products were made more expensive in Britain by the pound's devaluation was of little concern in America: Americans were buying American—GM, Studebaker, Ford, Packard, and Chrysler automobiles, and electric clothes dryers, radios, and televisions. American children rode bright-red Schwinn bicycles, sales of which—as with all American products—benefited from tariffs slapped on European imports. Now that Parker Pen could make pens instead of bomb fuses, it rolled out the Parker "51" pen—the latest in writing tools—which sold out at Gimbels in New York. Housewives who had been forced through war rationing to buy the Hormel company's Spam—"the taste tickler"—kept buying it. After all, it was easy to prepare as a suitable and delicious main course for breakfast, lunch, and dinner.[83]

In America, consumption was now a way of life; in Britain, consumption was still a disease that took off old people. Other than shipping their best scotch whisky and linen to America, Britons were not exporting much, not producing much, and not buying much, including British-made Fords or even squat and cheap little Morris Minors. Daimler, Austin, Rolls-Royce, and Humber still produced machines that were virtually handcrafted (Churchill always preferred a Humber), but most Britons could not afford them, and little else for that matter. Ford U.S.A. produced more than 1.1 million motor cars in 1949; Morris Minor produced only 250,000 *between* 1948 and 1953. Londoners did not experience traffic jams because few Londoners owned automobiles, and those who did found petrol to be in short supply and expensive. Britons stayed home and, as they had for decades, found their entertainment via gramophones and little Bakelite wireless sets.

Americans went on a spending spree while Britons banked their sallow coal fires and pulled on another sweater. Most could not even commiserate over the telephone: fewer than 10 percent of British homes contained one.

When Harold Nicolson attended a January 1947 meeting of the Historic Buildings Committee of the National Trust, he did so wrapped in a greatcoat because there was no heat. Lighting, too, was a matter of chance after Attlee's government imposed rolling blackouts between 9:00 P.M. and 12:00 A.M. and 2:00 and 4:00 P.M. That winter was one of the worst in memory. Its "most crushing blows fell on Britain," Dean Acheson later wrote, with blizzards regularly battering the island, with six million out of work, and with rations below wartime levels.[84]

"Gloom reigned in the bomb-devastated streets of London and the provincial cities," Jock Colville later wrote of those winter months. "London was grey; life was grey." By then Colville toiled as private secretary to the Heiress Apparent, Princess Elizabeth, just twenty-one. It was a post he accepted with reluctance, spurred on by Churchill, who told Colville, "It is your duty to accept." Britons depended for sustenance upon millions of food parcels that arrived from the United States and the Commonwealth, including several thousand sent to Buckingham Palace. Princess Elizabeth organized a group of more than one hundred women volunteers who wrapped each parcel and dispatched them to shops and homes throughout the land. Even the royal family carried their clothing ration books that year. Elizabeth had to use her coupons to procure the material for her wedding gown in order to walk down the aisle of Westminster Abbey in November with Philip Mountbatten, her second cousin once removed (and Dickie's nephew). The currency stringency grew so severe that year that the Attlee government slashed the importing of foods and essential commodities, even going so far as to slap a 75 percent import duty on Hollywood films. Hollywood responded by ceasing all shipments of movies to Britain. England found itself now a pale moon eclipsed by the blazing sun of the United States. "My God!" Nicolson proclaimed to his diary in late 1947. "What the poor people of this country have had to suffer in the last seven years." Clothing rationing did not end until 1949. Food rationing had fully seven more years to run. Londoners dwelled now in pea-soup fogs—smog, really, a poisonous, stinking by-product of hundreds of thousands of fireplaces burning soft coal and coal gas. Day was almost as dark as night. Britons called it "austerity," but conditions were not much different from what Americans knew during the Great Depression.[85]

On November 30, 1947, Colville, after dining with the Churchill family in celebration of the Old Man's seventy-third birthday, told his diary: "Winston is in a sombre mood, convinced that this country is going to suffer the most agonising economic distress." The Battle of the Atlantic, Churchill had claimed, was but "a mere pup in comparison." Had Franklin Roosevelt lived just a few years more, he would have witnessed the complete fulfillment of his strategic vision for imperial Britain and its role in the world. The United Kingdom had been reduced to debtor status, and the Empire, with the departure of Burma, Ceylon, and India by 1948, was vastly reduced in geographical scope. King George remained King, but he had to scrub "Emperor" from the royal stationery.

"Never in his [Churchill's] life has he felt such despair," Colville wrote, "and he blamed it on the Government whose 'insatiable lust for power is only equalled by their incurable impotence in exercising it.' " Colville took heart from Churchill's "phrases and epigrams [that] rolled out in the old way, but I missed that indomitable hope and conviction which characterized the Prime Minister of 1940–41." For this misery Churchill held Attlee accountable. Over drinks with Chips Channon one evening at Claridge's, the Old Man said of Attlee: "Anyone can respect him, certainly, but admire—no!"[86]

In the House Churchill registered his displeasure with the Attlee government regularly and with increasing vehemence. He told Britons that it was not the government's management of unfolding events within the diminishing empire, but its *mismanagement*. Of the continuing need of rationing, he said: "What the German U-boats could never do to us has been achieved by our own misguided fellow countrymen through their incompetence, their arrogance, their hordes of officials, their thousands of regulations and their gross mismanagement of our affairs, large and small." On at least seventeen occasions between 1945 and 1950, he delivered addresses wherein he spoke (with a snarl) of "socialism" and "utopia" in the same breath, often tossing in a "feeble," "foolish," "squalid," or "fantasy" for good measure. He just as consistently reminded his listeners that he had been Lloyd George's loyal lieutenant when the great Welshman overhauled British social services earlier in the century. Making his case required a nimble performance; here was Winston Churchill—the leader of the Conservative Party—championing the philosophical underpinnings of Labour's social programs. He was up to the task. It was the heavy-handed implementation of programs, not the programs themselves, he objected to. In July 1946, he told Britons (and three years later told MIT students much the same):

> It is 38 years ago since I introduced the first Unemployment Insurance Scheme, and 22 years ago since, as Conservative Chancellor of the Exchequer, I shaped and carried the Widows' Pensions and reduction of the Old Age Pensions from 70 to 65. We are now moving forward into another vast scheme of national insurance, which arose, even in the stress of war, from a Parliament with a great Conservative majority. It is an essential principle of Conservative, Unionist, and Tory policy—call it what you will—to defend the general public against abuses by monopolies and against restraints on trade and enterprise,

> whether these evils come from private corporations, from the mischievous plans of doctrinaire Governments, or from the incompetence and arbitrariness of departments of State.[87]

Later that year he recycled a line he had used during a March 1945 memorial service for Lloyd George (who had died that month): "We do not seek to pull down improvidently the structures of society, but to erect balustrades upon the stairway of life, which will prevent helpless or foolish people from falling into the abyss. Both the Conservative and Liberal Parties have made notable contributions to secure minimum standards of life and labour. I too have borne my part in this." Indeed, he had done so, when he had "ratted" to the Liberal Party four decades earlier. By the late 1940s—long after "re-ratting" back to the Tories—he was one of very few Conservatives who could honestly say that he had been in favor of social reforms from the beginning, albeit while sitting on the opposing bench at the time.[88]

Winston is happy at Chartwell," Moran told his diary in 1946, "as happy as he can be when the world has gone all wrong." Churchill could only bear witness from the opposition bench between 1946 and late 1951 as Britain's knights and castles—India and Burma, its influence in Egypt and Palestine—were swept from the chessboard.[89]

In early May 1946, Attlee announced his government's intent to remove all British forces from Egypt, including the Suez Canal Zone. This was a policy Churchill could not consent to, telling the House on May 24: "I assert that it is impossible to keep it [the canal] open, unless British personnel are permanently stationed in the Canal Zone. There may be doubts about our ability to keep it open in the air age, even if we have garrisons and fighter aircraft in that zone. But at any rate without that personnel there is no chance of keeping it open whatever." Especially galling to Churchill was the fact that Britain owed Egypt £400 million for services rendered during the war when, as Churchill told the House, Egyptian troops did not fight and "the debt which Egypt owes to us is that in two world convulsions she has been effectively defended by Great Britain and not only by this island. The Australians and New Zealanders and South Africans have shed their blood freely to prevent Cairo and Alexandria being looted and ravished, ground down and subjugated, by Italian and German hordes." To safeguard the Suez, Attlee proposed using one hundred thousand British troops then in Palestine, from where they could respond to a crisis in the Suez. But guarding the canal with troops bivouacked three hundred miles away struck Churchill as ludicrous. As well, British troops in Palestine made easy targets for Zionist terrorists.[90]

In the House of Commons on August 1, with the Suez and Palestine debates ongoing and civil war likely in India, Churchill delivered something of a valedictory for the British Empire:

> Take stock round the world at the present moment; after all we are entitled to survey the whole field. We declare ourselves ready to abandon the mighty Empire and Continent of India with all the work we have done in the last 200 years, territory over which we possess unimpeachable sovereignty. The Government are, apparently, ready to leave the 400 million Indians to fall into all the horrors of sanguinary civil war—civil war compared to which anything that could happen in Palestine would be microscopic; wars of elephants compared with wars of mice. Indeed we place the independence of India in hostile and feeble hands, heedless of the dark carnage and confusion which will follow. We scuttle from Egypt which we twice successfully defended from foreign massacre and pillage. We scuttle from it.[91]

The entire world, Churchill believed, not only the British Empire, was poised on the brink of great and deadly trials. A week after his speech, over lunch with Clementine and Lord Moran, Churchill predicted another war. "You mean in eight or ten years?" Moran asked. "Sooner," Churchill replied. "Seven or eight years. I shan't be here." He thought it would take the form of a final battle between England, Belgium, France, and Scandinavia against the Russians. "We ought not to wait until Russia is ready," Churchill offered. "I believe it will be eight years before she has these [atomic] bombs." He smiled. "America knows that fifty-two percent of Russia's motor industry is in Moscow and could be wiped out by a single bomb." He smiled again. "The Russian government is like the Roman Church; their people do not question authority."[92]

By the autumn of 1946, Attlee chose to keep British troops in the Canal Zone, where Egyptians resented their presence much as Palestinian Arabs (and many Zionists) resented the British presence in Palestine. The debate over Palestine continued into 1947, when in March Churchill told the House: "One hundred thousand Englishmen [are] now kept away from their homes and work, for the sake of a senseless squalid war with the Jews in order to give Palestine to the Arabs, or God knows who. 'Scuttle,' everywhere, is the order of the day—Egypt, India, Burma. One thing at all costs we must preserve: the right to get ourselves world-mocked and world-hated over Palestine."[93]

If the British in Palestine could not or would not force a settlement between Arabs and Jews, Churchill advised Attlee to hand over the British Mandate of Palestine—which was costing London eighty million pounds a year—to the United States, which as the world's greatest power had, in Churchill's view, inherited such responsibilities but had yet to spend a dollar or send a battalion to Palestine. If not to the United States, Churchill advised passing the mandate to the United Nations, which had been created for such purposes. Churchill believed doing so would help Britain keep its promise to help create a national homeland for Jews, a pledge it could no longer make good on by itself. He also proposed transferring troops that were then serving in Palestine to India, where the bloodshed he had long predicted had begun. It made no sense, Churchill told the House in January 1947, that British troops should stay in Palestine because the Labour government believed their exit "would lead to a terrible quarrel between Jews and Arabs." Yet in India, "We are told to leave the Indians to settle their own affairs." Churchill titled his speech "Blood and Shame."[94]

On November 29, 1947, the United Nations, which had taken over the British Mandate in May, voted to partition Palestine into two states, Jewish and Arab. Arabs in Palestine rejected the UN solution.* The Jewish state—Israel—proclaimed its independence on May 14, 1948. The next day, three Arab armies—from Transjordan, Syria, and Egypt—attacked. Churchill believed the Arab coalition would "fall to pieces" as soon as it met Israeli forces. It did. Eight months later, on January 26, 1949, with Britain still not having recognized the new Israeli state, Churchill took to the floor of the House to assault the Attlee government's performance in the Middle East since 1946:

> It took another year after I had urged the Government to quit Palestine, if they had no plan, for them to take the decision to go. They took it a year later when everything was more difficult. Great opportunities were cast away. They took it in such a way as to render themselves unable to bring perfectly legitimate pressure to bear upon the United States to leave the sidelines and come into the arena of helpful, and now that it [Israel] has come into being it is England that refuses to recognize it, and, by our actions, we find ourselves regarded as its most bitter enemies.

Like it or not, Churchill told the House, Israel's statehood marked "an event in world history to be viewed in the perspective, not of a generation

* Since 1921, both Arab and Jewish citizens of Palestine referred to themselves as Palestinian; the concept of an Arab Palestinian people evolved in the 1960s.

or a century, but in the perspective of a thousand, two thousand or even three thousand years." Then he launched a shocking accusation at Foreign Secretary Ernest Bevin, who throughout the war had served Churchill with absolute loyalty:

> All this is due, not only to mental inertia or lack of grip on the part of the Ministers concerned, but also, I am afraid, to the very strong and direct streak of bias and prejudice on the part of the Foreign Secretary. I do not feel any great confidence that he has not got a prejudice against the Jews in Palestine. I am sure that he thought the Arab League was stronger and that it would win if fighting broke out, but I do not suggest for a moment that he wished to provoke war. . . . but the course he took led inevitably and directly to a trial of strength, and the result was opposite to what I believe he expected it to be.[95]

It was a grossly unjust remark. As foreign secretary, Bevin had pursued a foreign policy largely in accordance with Churchill's philosophy of strength through affiliation with America. There had been setbacks in the Middle East, but they were uninvited, and they certainly did not derive from any anti-Semitism on Bevin's part. But Churchill, liberated from the constraints of the coalition, had embraced his role of leader of the opposition with alacrity, and on occasion with venom. Self-restraint had never been Churchill's long suit.

In Egypt and Palestine the British had lost prestige. In Asia they were losing everything. In March 1947, Churchill pressed Attlee to clarify the mandate under which the new (and last) viceroy of India, Lord Louis Mountbatten, was to serve. Mountbatten had been given fourteen months to work with Jawaharlal Nehru's transitional government with the goal of getting Britain out of India, but no one had told him exactly how to do so, or what compromises to make, especially in the matter of splitting Muslim Pakistan from Hindu India. Churchill told the House:

> This [interim] government of Mr. Nehru has been a complete disaster. . . . Thirty or forty thousand people have been slaughtered in the warfare between the two principal religions. . . . I do not think that the fourteen months' time limit gives the new Viceroy a fair chance. We do not know what directives have been given to him. . . . We are told very little. What is the policy and purpose for which he is to be sent

> out, and how is he to employ these fourteen months? Is he to make a new effort to restore the situation, or is it merely Operation Scuttle on which he and other distinguished officers have been despatched?[96]

"Will it not be a terrible disgrace," he asked the House, "to our name and record if, after our fourteen months' time limit, we allow one fifth of the population of the globe, occupying a region nearly as large as Europe, to fall into chaos and into carnage?" On August 15, 1947—a date Nehru called "a tryst with destiny"—India and Pakistan gained their independence. In coming months, more than seven million Hindus fled Pakistan for India, and a like number of Muslims fled India for Pakistan. At least five hundred thousand Hindus and Muslims were slaughtered in the Punjab alone, the responsibility for which, Churchill told the House, rested with the Socialist government. In late October, India and Pakistan went to war over Kashmir. On January 30, 1948, a Hindu extremist murdered Mohandas Gandhi, who shared with Churchill a vision of a united India and the end of the caste system.[97]

Since the war's end, Churchill had also advised Attlee and Bevin to reach an agreement with Burma, before it, too, bolted the Empire, which it duly did on January 4, 1948, when it exited both the Empire and the Commonwealth as an independent republic. Churchill told the House: "In Burma also my solemn warnings have been fulfilled. Burma has been cast away and is now a foreign country. It is already descending rapidly into a welter of murder and anarchy, the outcome of which will probably be a Communist Republic." Matters were no better in Malaya, where the eleven Malayan states were reconfigured as a British protectorate in 1948. There, Churchill told the House, "the long arm of Communism, unchecked by feeble British Administration, has begun a campaign of murdering British planters and their wives as part of the general process of our ejection." Repeatedly Churchill described Attlee's foreign policy as a scuttle from responsibilities—in Egypt, Palestine, India, Malaya, and Burma—with a resultant loss of both honor and innocent lives. "It does not matter where you look in the world," Churchill told the House in June 1948, "you will see how grievously the name and prestige of Britain have suffered since the British Nation fell flat upon its face in the moment of its greatest victory."[98]

By early 1948, the Western allies had ceased dismantling German factories and shipping them to Russia. In late February the Czech Communist Party, on orders from Moscow and protected by the Red Army, seized power. Eduard Beneš resigned three months later rather than protest the takeover and risk civil war. He would have gotten no military assistance from the West, which once again, as in the days of Munich, lacked the political will to influence events in central Europe. On April 17, the new American ambassador to Britain, Lewis "Lew" Douglas, reported to the State Department that Churchill had told him "now is the time, promptly, to tell the Soviets that if they do not retire from Berlin and abandon Eastern Germany, withdrawing to the Polish frontiers, we will raze their cities." A week later, Churchill told the Conservative Women's Conference:[99]

> Their lot [the Czechs] has been indeed hard. No sooner were they freed from the tyranny of Hitler's Gauleiters than, like Poland, they were dragged down into subjugation by the Soviet Quislings.... I hear people say of the Soviet aggressions and intrigues, "Thus far and no farther." That is no doubt a widely-held resolve. But we must not delude ourselves. There will never be a settled peace in Europe while Asiatic Imperialism and Communist domination rule over the whole of Central and Eastern Europe.[100]

But how, other than by force, would "Communist domination" be reversed?

Ten weeks later, on June 24, the Soviets threw a road-and-rail blockade around Berlin. Britain and the United States, in order to feed and fuel their occupation zones, sent thousands of C-54s and C-47s—which had once dropped Allied paratroopers into France—along the air corridors to Berlin. Between June 1948 and May 1949, every meal consumed by Berliners in the Allied sectors, every ounce of coal they burned to heat their homes—a daily requirement of food and fuel of more than 4,500 tons—came by way of the U.S. Air Force and the RAF, which flew more than two hundred thousand flights in all. The decision on whether to go to war rested with the Russians. Were they to shoot down a British or American aircraft flying within the air corridors, even by accident, there would be war. Were the Red Army to march on the Allied sectors of Berlin, there would be war. In a display of resolve, the United States flew squadrons of Flying Fortresses into East Anglia. B-29s followed. They carried atomic weapons. The presence of the aircraft in Britain was not lost on Moscow, which responded by announcing that Soviet air forces would conduct war games over Berlin. "The City is getting panicky," Harold Nicolson told his diary. "It seems to be the final conflict for the mastery of the world." He added: "The Barbarians are at the gate."[101]

In the autumn of 1948, Bertrand Russell shocked liberals on both sides of the Atlantic (including Harold Nicolson) when he stated that "we should make war on Russia while we have the atomic bomb and they do not." The "we" of course was America, since Britain had no atomic bomb. Nicolson believed the Russians were preparing "for the final battle for world mastery," which would result in the "destruction of western Europe" and "a final death struggle with the Americas." Yet he thought the idea of a preemptive attack "evil," even if it resulted in "centuries of Pax Americana—an admirable thing to establish." He believed there might be a frail chance—"not one in ninety"—that "the danger may pass and peace can be secured by peace." That slimmest of chances, Nicolson told his diary, should be taken. "Better to be wiped out by the crime of others...," he wrote, "than to preserve ourselves by committing a deliberate crime of our own."[102]

On the other side of the globe, another country jointly occupied by the Russians and Americans was stumbling toward civil war: Korea, annexed by Japan in 1910 with the compliance of London and Washington. Koreans had spent thirty-five years as virtual slaves of the Japanese. Under a United Nations trusteeship, the Russians occupied the northern part of Korea, the Americans the southern, below the 38th parallel. In 1948 Stalin pulled out his troops. National elections were scheduled to take place, to be supervised by the United States. The North Koreans refused to participate. Instead, in early September 1948, the Communists in the north, with Stalin's blessing, declared the Democratic People's Republic of Korea. Both North and South Korea claimed sovereignty over the entire peninsula.

The Soviet blockade of Berlin—and the danger of war—entered its tenth month in April 1949. On April 4, President Truman signed the North Atlantic Treaty, an outgrowth and expansion of the 1948 Treaty of Brussels, in which Britain, France, Belgium, the Netherlands, and Luxembourg had arrayed themselves as a bulwark against Stalin's Red Army. But without America in, the Brussels treaty was a bulwark in name only. Truman's pen stroke created NATO, and brought America in, along with Canada, Denmark, Norway, Portugal, Iceland, and Italy. The treaty stipulated that an attack against any one of the member nations was an attack against all, and would be met with "all necessary assistance," including the use of military force. Yet it would be two more years before NATO's first supreme commander was named: Dwight Eisenhower, who set to work building a true command structure. When in 1952 Hastings ("Pug") Ismay—the 1st Baron Ismay—was made NATO's first secretary-general, he declared NATO's purpose was "to keep the Russians out, the Americans in, and the Germans down." That statement—given that containing the Reds had become settled policy in America and Britain—made for good politics, but Churchill believed then, and had believed since late in the war, that Germany must be up and armed in order to help Britain and France keep the Red Army out.[103]

In 1949 Russia, not Germany, was the threat. If a war began, Berlin would be the place. In late March, just days before Truman signed the North Atlantic Treaty, Churchill told guests at a New York dinner hosted by Henry Luce: "It is certain in my opinion that Europe would have been communized and London would have been under bombardment some time ago, but for the deterrent of the atomic bomb in the hands of the United States." The best way to deal with the Soviets, Churchill proclaimed, was "by having superior force on your side on the matter in question and they must also be convinced that you will use—you will not hesitate to use—these forces, if necessary, in the most ruthless manner." On April 1, the *New York Herald Tribune* ran the headline CHURCHILL DECLARES ATOM BOMB ALONE DETERS RUSSIA FROM WAR. Actually a credible deterrent could only arise from a promise to *use* the atomic bomb if Russia started a war. Churchill advised Truman to make such a statement. To Churchill's satisfaction, he learned while on his way home on board *Queen Mary* that Truman had done just that, telling reporters that he "would not hesitate" to use atomic weapons if the peace and security of the democracies—anywhere—were at stake.[104]

The nuclear consequences to Moscow of provoking war overrode any inclination—if there was any inclination—within the Politburo to head in that direction. Moscow could blockade Berlin, but it could not take it without suffering annihilation. On May 12, six weeks after Truman brought NATO onto the world stage, Stalin and the Politburo lifted the blockade and climbed down. Jock Colville believed an old saying still applied:

Whatever happens, we have got
The Maxim gun, and they have not.

It did not apply for long. When the Soviet Union exploded its first atomic bomb three months later, on August 29, 1949, the world became a far more dangerous place.[105]

It became even more dangerous in early October when the Communist Party in Russian-occupied eastern Germany—sponsored and sustained by Stalin and the Red Army—declared the formation of the German Democratic Republic, known in the West for the next forty years as East Germany. It was a puppet police state, neither democratic nor a republic.

And in the Far East, the Communist menace gathered strength in inverse proportion to the decline of the French, Dutch, and British empires. When in April 1949 Communist artillery fired on British gunboats in the Yangtze River, even anti-Communists throughout Asia hung photos of the wounded ships on their walls. On October 1, Mao Zedong declared the People's Republic of China after driving Chiang Kai-shek and two million Kuomintang followers literally into the sea, and to Taiwan. The bloodiest civil war in modern history—more than three million military casualties and at least twelve million civilian—had lasted twenty-two years, interrupted only by the Sino-Japanese War and World War Two, which proved even more deadly to Chinese civilians. Earlier in the year, as the Chinese Communists pressed their advantage, Churchill could not resist working a deft criticism of Franklin Roosevelt into a speech he gave in New York City:

> I was very much astonished when I came over here after Pearl Harbor to find the estimate of values which seemed to prevail in high American quarters, even in the highest, about China. Some of them thought that China would make as great a contribution to victory in the war as the whole British Empire together. Well, that astonished me very much. Nothing that I picked up afterwards led me to think that my astonishment was ill founded.[106]

Now the two old allies, China and Russia, were declared enemies of the capitalist West. "Are we winning the Cold War?" Churchill asked the New York audience. He had no answer. He saw danger in Europe, and in the Far East. All was uncertain. Yet for Churchill, at least one certainty remained—his belief that he was the man to lead Britain in these dangerous times, and would sooner or later have the chance to do so.

Churchill saw Britain's security tied to three interlocking geopolitical circles, each separate from but overlapping the others, and each forming an association in which Britain might again flourish. Taken together, they promised safety and an honorable peace, one worthy of the sacrifice of Britons and Europeans in the late war. In June 1950 Churchill told the House: "First, there is the Empire and Commonwealth; secondly, the fraternal association of the English-speaking world; and thirdly, not in rank or status but in order, the revival of united Europe as a vast factor in the preserving of what is left of the civilization and culture of the free world." To address the concerns of many Bevan Labourites—and Anthony Eden—who did not share his sentiments of a unified Europe, Churchill offered, "With our position as the centre of the British Empire and Commonwealth and with our fraternal association with the United States in the English-speaking world, we could not accept full membership of a federal system of Europe." Much later, in the House, he needed only eight words to state his position on continental Europeans and their drift toward unity: "We are with them, but not of them."[107]

To stake out such a seemingly contradictory position took political adroitness: Britain would in some ways (not yet articulated with exactness by Churchill) be in a united Europe, but not *completely* in, which amounted to saying that Britain would in some ways be "out" of a united Europe. Indeed, from that time to this day, British governments have held to that policy. Although Churchill had voiced his belief in a united Europe for years, he had never addressed the details of the form and authority a European parliament might assume. This was a strategy more in line with Franklin Roosevelt's approach to complex issues—offer few details—than Churchill's usual blunt and clearly stated approach to all matters great and small. As Tories and Labourites debated the role of Britain, if any, in a European union, Harold Macmillan told his diary the question came down to "'United Europe' *with Britain,* on a loose basis of cooperation; 'United Europe' *without Britain*" (italics Macmillan). The extent of Britain's participation in a European parliament would depend on whether that entity took the form of a "functional" body, having broad powers within strictly defined areas (coal and steel production, and tariffs, for example), or a federal model, with its authority vested in a European constitution. As Macmillan saw it, the former structure would not necessarily result in an erosion of sovereignty on the part of member nations, but the latter might, depending upon the political, economic, and military authority vested in the central government by the constitution.[108]

For two decades Churchill approached European union much as he had played polo—first, slash and dash and drive the ball up the field to get in range, then let the details take care of themselves. Likewise, although for two decades he had championed a union of some sorts with the United States, he had not offered details of just what form that union would take. Despite the linguistic and historical bonds between London and Washington, despite Churchill's dream of a shared currency (the dollar-sterling), and his hopes for political and economic ties that were more than "agreements," Churchill knew that Britain would never find itself "inside" the United States. But NATO brought the United States "inside" Europe and promised security, although in 1950 its command structure—both political and military—had yet to be determined. Strengthening Britain's relationship with the United States and developing a closer relationship with continental Europe were Churchill's paramount objectives. "The fact that there is a grave Soviet and Communist menace," he told the House in 1950, "only adds to its [European unity's] value and urgency. Here surely we can find agreement on all sides of the House. No one can say with justice that we are acting and feeling in this way in prejudice to the interests of the British Empire and Commonwealth. Everyone knows that that stands first in all our thoughts."[109]

To the security offered by his three interlocking rings could be added the security provided by the United Nations, but, although Churchill claimed for the United Nations a central role in world affairs, he harbored doubts about its efficacy. During a Brussels conference on European unity in 1949 he declared:

> But there are also fundamental defects in the structure of the United Nations Organization which must be corrected if any progress is to be made. I had always felt during the war that the structure of world security could only be founded on regional organizations.... In consequence, the supreme body has been cumbered and confused by a mass of questions, great and small, about which only a babel of harsh voices can be heard.... It is vain to build the dome of the temple of peace without the pillars on which alone it can stand.

For Churchill, Europe—led by Britain, France, and someday Germany—would form the strongest pillar and the greatest regional organization on the planet. Pointing out that numerous Eastern European nations could not send representatives to the conference, Churchill added, "The yoke of the Kremlin oligarchy has descended upon them and they are the victims of a tyranny more subtle and merciless than any hitherto known to history."[110]

Churchill's sole domestic political objective from 1946 well into 1951 was to push, prod, and excoriate the Attlee government on its economic performance. In 1948 he told the House, "We are oppressed by a deadly fallacy. Socialism is the philosophy of failure, the creed of ignorance and the gospel of envy. Unless we free our country while time remains from the perverse doctrines of Socialism, there can be no hope for recovery." He delivered a variation on that theme again and again, in the House, at constituent meetings, and at Conservative rallies. During one such rally at Blenheim Palace he summed up his position on Labour thus: "Since [1939] two disasters have come upon us: the Second World War and the first Socialist Government with a majority. By supreme exertions we surmounted the first disaster. The question which glares upon us today is: 'How shall we free ourselves from the second?'" Labour had "squandered" first the American loan of almost four billion dollars and then the generous allotments of the Marshall Plan, with the result that "we are now dependent upon further American generosity and also eating up from hand to mouth the remaining overseas investments and assets accumulated under the capitalist system of former years." Out of loyalty to King and country, he muted his criticism when he spoke abroad, but at home, he pressed the attack.[111]

He reserved his most scathing and personal criticism for his old political nemesis, Aneurin Bevan. In July 1948, on the occasion of the launch of the National Health Service, Churchill told his Woodford constituents:

> One would have thought that a man who had been only a burden to our war effort in the years of storm and who had received high office in the days of victory would have tried to turn over a new leaf and redeem his past.... We speak of the Minister of Health, but ought we not rather to say the Minister of Disease, for is not morbid hatred a form of mental disease, moral disease, and indeed a highly infectious form? Indeed, I can think of no better step to signalize the inauguration of the National Health Service than that a person who so obviously needs psychiatrical attention should be among the first of its patients. And I have no doubt that the highest exponents of the medical profession would concur that a period of prolonged seclusion and relief from any responsible duties would be an equal benefit to Mr. Bevan and to the National Health Service.[112]

Here was Churchill in top form, and whether he was in gentlemanly form was not of any concern to him. That sort of harangue sold newspapers and would be quoted in pubs throughout the land. In times of austerity, comic relief is a balm. Churchill delivered regular doses of that relief. Attlee's Labour colleagues spoke in bureaucratese. Churchill did not. He spoke to the common man and, more important, could speak *like* the common man when the situation demanded.

Between mid-1945 and early 1950 Churchill delivered more than two hundred speeches, many quite lengthy. He dictated, polished, and delivered every one of the four hundred thousand words of his addresses—enough to fill a thousand-page volume—that he sent into battle against socialism, in defense of the Empire, and for European unity. It is an extraordinary achievement given that during these years, he was also writing his memoirs and fulfilling his duties as the leader of the Shadow Cabinet.

That he could produce so much was due to the remarkable way he structured his waking hours, which allowed him to squeeze almost two days of work into each day. He spent his weekends at Chartwell, arriving on Thursday night and leaving for London Tuesday morning. At Chartwell, if breakfast was the start of his day, it began sometime after nine in the morning, later if he had dictated into the early morning hours, which he regularly did. Then, as he bid them good night—or good morning—the typists collected the day's work and sent it off by taxi to the printers in London in order that galleys could be delivered to the Great Man by midday. He breakfasted alone, in bed. He once told a Chartwell visitor that he and Clementine had "tried two or three times in the last forty years to have breakfast together, but it didn't work." His bath and a tour of Chartwell's grounds followed breakfast. Early afternoon found the typists on the day shift drifting into the library from their rooms in the village and Chartwell's orchard cottage. There they waited while Churchill, attired now in a dark blue suit, waistcoat, and gold watch and chain, perused galleys and ordered his thoughts in his second-floor study. When he was ready to dictate, he depressed a switch on an intercom connected to the library, and announced, "Come."[113]

For the typists, the terror began as soon as they sat down at the—not so silent—silent typewriters. This was the routine of a quarter century, during which the lion had not lost his roar. He dictated three, four, sometimes five drafts of his addresses. Bill Deakin and Denis Kelly fed him statistics, and transcripts of Labour speeches, and budget and banking data, and military dispositions. All was bustle. Misspellings on the part of typists were met with sighs and sharp rebukes. The omnipresent intrusion of the gramophone did not help matters. "You just typed away and handed it in and sometimes it was dreadful and he'd just scowl," recalled Chips Gemmell. Foreign names especially tripped up the typists. Once, upon glancing at Miss Gemmell's handiwork, the Old Man barked: "You have not got one word in *fifty* right." He used a special code, known only to himself, to delineate sections of a speech—P-1 for housing, or H-3 for foreign affairs, for example. At his command, the typists scribbled the codes in at the appropriate places. At the end came "the great moment" when Churchill announced, "Now I am going to clop." The "clop" was his paper punch; he had no use for paper clips. The pages were arranged, numbered, punched, and finally bound by a thin strip of cloth. Jane Portal*—whom Churchill always called "the Portal"—committed a mortal sin one day when she assembled the pages in the wrong order, which Churchill only discovered while delivering the speech. She was

* Later Lady Jane Williams, she was the niece of both R. A. ("Rab") Butler and Air Marshal Sir Charles Portal, later Viscount Portal of Hungerford.

sure she would never again be entrusted with that duty. When a few days later another speech reached the binding-together moment, Miss Portal was duly surprised—and moved almost to tears—when Churchill said, "Let the Portal do it." "You see," she recalled years later, "he was saying 'I've forgiven you, I trust you.' It was a small, personal instant, but it meant a great deal to me. He would do that often with people."[114]

His humor, as with his impatience, was never far beneath the surface. George Christ (rhymes with "whist") joined the team in 1949 and was assigned the duty of procuring official government documents from which Churchill culled salient points for inclusion in his addresses and memoirs. Churchill pronounced Christ's name as one would the Savior's, and delighted in ordering his typists to "get me Christ on the phone" or "get Christ down here at once." Upon such occasions of levity, a pause and a raised eyebrow were Churchill's signals to the typists that they were free to laugh. They were just as free to weep, as he often did while dictating passages that moved him: "I mean I would be weeping and he would be weeping," Jane Portal recalled, "and all the while he was dictating in his marvelous voice and I'd be tap-tapping away, the both of us weeping."[115]

His generosity was as much in evidence as his temper, his humor, and his tears. He ordered that the Chartwell gates remain open as a sign of welcome to any neighbors who might be inclined to stop by. Many did. A supply of old jackets, heavy coats, gloves, and old boots was kept near the front hall during the first bitter winters of victory, to be given to those in need. There were many. He was always willing to pay Randolph's debts, although he would not disclose to his son the exact terms of the Chartwell Trust. He provided for Pamela after her divorce. Lord Moran had never been well off. Churchill insisted on helping him out and executed a seven-year deed of covenant for Moran's wife, which brought her the modern equivalent of $20,000 a year tax free. Chips Gemmell recalled a trip to the races (a typist always accompanied Churchill wherever he went) during which Churchill told her he would not need her services for several hours. He sent her and the driver off with orders to enjoy themselves however they pleased and to meet him at the car after the day's events. When Miss Gemmell climbed into the car late in the day, the Old Man passed her a racing form, on which he had circled various horses. He announced they were winners and that he had wagered one pound on each of them for her. "Well, count up what you won," he ordered. But Chips, confused by the mathematics of odds and payouts, could not. "He was very mad that I couldn't read the numbers," she recalled, "and told me I had won twenty pounds, which was a great deal." It dawned on Miss Gemmell that the Old Man hadn't really placed any bets but had "suddenly thought in the car, poor girl, I'll say I put money on the horses and I'll say to her, work out how much and collect your money; it was a lovely gesture." When his scheme derailed, Churchill pressed a twenty-pound note into her hand.[116]

One Churchillian gesture stood out above all others for Miss Gemmell. "I was the paint lady," she recalled. "On Tuesdays, before returning to London he'd call me upstairs. 'Miss, you'll clean the palettes up and the paintbrushes, and see if I need paints.' And I'd say 'Yes sir.'" She found cleaning the brushes in turpentine a "ghastly business" but attended to her duties, ordered new paints, and tidied up Churchill's studio in preparation for his return. She was thus much moved when one day he called her into the studio and presented her with one of his paintings, "a very flattering portrait." It was a portrait of her.[117]

As he waded ahead on his memoirs and speeches, he faced a daily mountain of letters from persons great and small throughout the world. Replies to such missives did not always flow directly from the Old Man, although his tears often flowed upon reading them. Chips Gemmell was assigned the duty of composing responses on her own, for his signature. One such letter she wrote was to go off to the Massey Ferguson Company, which had sent Churchill an automated bread-making machine. Miss Gemmell composed a long and flowery thank-you note that moved Churchill to observe, "Jesus Christ, Miss, you've really over-egged the omelet this time. It was only a piece of farm machinery." Such moments of silliness were inevitably followed, usually sooner rather than later, by sinister eruptions due to secretarial misfeasance of one sort or another. And so it went each day until early evening, when the staff wandered into the village for dinner and Churchill took his evening meal in the company of any family or friends who happened to be present in the house. Lord Moran was a regular guest. Jane Portal noticed that he used a pencil to scribble notes on his pure-white shirt cuffs, the better to capture the Old Man's wisdom in the book Moran intended to write. Then, sometime after nine or ten, having returned from their meal in the village, the typists reassembled in the library and, as in the morning, awaited the summons from the Great Man: "Come." After he took himself off to bed near midnight, with brandy and a cigar in hand, yet another summons was issued, and the early morning dictation began. Thus, he effectively squeezed almost two working days into each twenty-four hours and left himself time to feed his goldfish and provoke battles between the swans and the geese on the lower lakes.[118]

Churchill turned seventy-five on November 30, 1949. "I am ready to meet my Maker," he told friends that day. "Whether my Maker is prepared for the ordeal of meeting me is another matter." Actually, neither was ready to meet the other. In 1874, the year of Churchill's birth, the great Conservative leader Benjamin Disraeli anointed the great Liberal leader William Gladstone—whom Disraeli had just replaced as prime minister—an "exhausted volcano." But Gladstone, sixty-four at the time, was not exhausted and returned to that high office three more times before resigning at age eighty-four in 1894. Lord Randolph Churchill had derided Gladstone as "an old man in a hurry." But Randolph died young, at forty-five, and therefore did not live long enough to grasp a truism known to old men. As the new decade came in—and with it the second half of the twentieth century—Winston Churchill understood that an old man had best hurry if he is to get someplace in the time remaining to him. *Time,* in early January, named him the *Man of the Half-Century.* The first half of the century had brought Europe and the world a succession of shocks and calamities, the editors wrote, with Churchill offering solutions—and suffering defeats—from within and without the British government. "That a free world survived in 1950, with a hope of more progress and less calamity, was due in large measure to his [Churchill's] exertions." Knowing that a British general election might soon be called, *Time* predicted that "[Churchill] would fight it—as he had fought all his other great battles—on the issue of freedom. Churchill likes freedom."[119]

Not all on the western shores of the Atlantic shared Luce's sentiments. James Reston, one of the premier political reporters at the *New York Times,* later wrote of a dinner party Churchill attended at the *Times* during his 1949 trip to America. "He [Churchill] looked considerably more rounded fore and aft.... There was a curious sort of grayness to his flesh.... He asked for a glass of tomato juice, which I thought was newsworthy, but corrected this impression when the brandy was passed around, and he complained that everybody kept him talking so much that he didn't have time to drink." Reston thought that Churchill "snorted and lisped more than usual, but this may have been induced by sobriety." As Churchill left, "a little shuffly and a little bent, Dr. Howard Rush, the *Times*'s favorite doctor, remarked, 'Jesus, prop him up.' I thought his [Churchill's] political days were over." Reston—Scotty to his friends—had been born in Scotland and grew up with a Scots Presbyterian's natural and ancient distrust of Englishmen. As for Churchill's political days being over, the often-prescient Reston got it wrong this time.[120]

Churchill planned to spend the first few weeks of 1950 at Reid's Hotel in Madeira. Clementine made the trip, as did Diana. Two secretaries and Bill Deakin accompanied Churchill; it was to be a working holiday. But in early January, Attlee called for a general election on February 23. Churchill packed his kit and returned to Chartwell to chart the Conservative campaign. Clementine stayed on in Madeira for a few days before returning to 28 Hyde Park Gate, where on January 19 she received a letter from her husband: "I have not thought of anything since I returned except politics." He and the Tory hierarchy had spent long days at Chartwell planning their manifesto. The problem, he told Clementine, was "not what to *do*" but "what to *say* to our poor and puzzled people." He noted that Gallup polls showed the Tory lead over Labour had fallen from nine to three points, but that four hundred Liberal candidates (running as spoilers and not expected to win many seats) would invariably skewer the final results. "How many seats the Liberal 'splits' will cause us cannot be measured." He thought that "at the outside" the Liberals might win seven seats. He closed with "I am much depressed about the country because for whoever wins there will be nothing but bitterness and strife, like men fighting savagely on a small raft which is breaking up. 'May God save you all' is my prayer."[121]

By the arrival of the new decade, his arteries had further hardened and he was going deaf. His ear, nose, and throat specialist told him he'd soon not be able to hear "the twittering of birds and children's piping voices." Churchill's walking stick no longer served as a fashion statement but served a practical purpose. Before the election campaign even got under way, Churchill summoned his doctor, Lord Moran. Everything had suddenly "gone misty," Churchill told Moran, and he asked, "Am I going to have another stroke?" Moran tried to reassure him by offering that he was likely experiencing "arterial spasms" when very tired. The patient looked up sharply and said, "You mustn't frighten me." It was Moran who was frightened, telling his diary, "This is a grim start to the racket of a General Election."[122]

Roy Jenkins, at the time the youngest MP—the Baby of the House—later wrote that Churchill conducted a more restrained campaign than in 1945. Churchill had the good sense to make no mention of a socialist Gestapo. And although he harangued the Labour Party and its cabal of intellectuals on their nationalization schemes, such topics as coal, steel, and railroads do not lend themselves to flights of oratorical fancy. On the foreign policy front, Churchill was more or less in agreement with Attlee and Bevin, who championed closer ties to the United States, the re-armament of Germany, and a containment policy toward the Soviets. Ignoring his doctor's advice to not stump the country, Churchill delivered eleven campaign speeches in cities and towns throughout the island, including Cardiff, Manchester, Edinburgh, Leeds, and three in his constituency of Woodford. The election was a family affair: Duncan Sandys, Christopher Soames, and Randolph were standing for office as well, and the Old Man campaigned for them. He kept bile out of his message, and instead reverted to humor and metaphor to skewer Labour. It was during this campaign that he coined the term

"Queuetopia." In Cardiff on February 8 he reduced Labour's stultifying jargon to silliness:

> I hope you have all mastered the official Socialist jargon which our masters, as they call themselves, wish us to learn. You must not use the word "poor"; they are described as the "lower income group." When it comes to a question of freezing a workman's wages the Chancellor of the Exchequer speaks of "arresting increases in personal income."... There is a lovely one about houses and homes. They are in future to be called "accommodation units." I don't know how we are to sing our old song "Home Sweet Home." *"Accommodation Unit, Sweet Accommodation Unit, there's no place like our Accommodation Unit."* I hope to live to see the British democracy spit all this rubbish from their lips.[123]

In Edinburgh on February 14, he told the audience that "by one broad heave of the British national shoulders the whole gimcrack structure of Socialist jargon and malice may be cast in splinters to the ground." In his second campaign broadcast, delivered in London on the seventeenth, he again advised his countrymen to free themselves with one heave of their shoulders, and warned that they might not get a second chance to do so. Then he offered the parable of the Spanish prisoner who, after years of bondage, "pushed the door of his cell—and it was open. It had always been open. He walked out free into the broad light of day."[124]

In Leeds he warned:

> Remember also that, as a Socialist Prime Minister working for the establishment of a Socialist State, Mr. Attlee and his party are alone in the English-speaking world. The United States at the head of the world today vehemently repudiate the Socialist doctrine. Canada repudiates it.... Remember also there is no Socialist Government in Europe outside the Iron Curtain and Scandinavia. It seems to me a very perilous path that we are asked to tread, and to tread alone among the free democracies of the West.[125]

It was during the Edinburgh address that Churchill made his most important foreign policy statement of the campaign, and in so doing not only coined the term "summit meeting" but outlined a belief that would underlie his relations with both America and Russia for the remainder of his political life. First came a warning: "The Soviet Communist world has by far the greatest military force, but the United States have the atom bomb; and now, we are told that they have a thousand fold more terrible manifestation of this awful power." Although the United States had lost its monopoly on atomic bombs, it had a great many in its arsenal. "When all is said and done it is my belief that the superiority [in numbers] in the atom bomb...in American hands is the surest guarantee of world peace tonight." Then:

> Still I cannot help coming back to this idea of another talk with Soviet Russia upon the highest level. The idea appeals to me of a supreme effort to bridge the gulf between the two worlds, so that each can live their life, if not in friendship at least without the hatreds of the cold war. You must be careful to mark my words in these matters because I have not always been proved wrong. It is not easy to see how things could be worsened by a parley at the summit, if such a thing were possible. But that I cannot tell.[126]

He repeated the theme a few days later during his London broadcast: "It is only by the agreement of the greatest Powers that security can be given to ordinary folk against an annihilating war with atomic or hydrogen bombs or bacteriological horrors. I cannot find it in my heart and conscience to close the door upon that hope." This was his first mention of "hydrogen bombs." In Edinburgh he had referred only to weapons a "thousand fold" more powerful than atomic bombs. Indeed, the power of thermonuclear weapons (hydrogen bombs, or H-bombs) is reckoned in megatons versus kilotons for atomic bombs, and in this new calculus Churchill beheld the horrifying difference between the two weapons. One could destroy cities, the other civilization. Five years earlier he had seen the A-bomb as merely the biggest bomb in the arsenal. No more. The Americans were yet two years away from exploding an H-bomb, but in early 1950 Churchill saw—the first world leader to do so—that the enormity of that weapon must preclude its use. Churchill's vivid imagination, not cold logic, drove his thinking on the matter. He had seen London burn once; he could now shut his eyes and behold the entire nation in flames, the entire world. The conclusion was obvious: world wars could still be fought, but could no longer be won.[127]

On Election Day, February 23, Churchill told some Tory cronies that he'd drop into the Savoy later that evening to stand a round of drinks if the early returns showed promise. He never appeared, but rather closeted himself at Hyde Park Gate to listen as the BBC reported the early returns from the larger cities. Labour was holding its own. By late in the morning of the twenty-fourth, town and country returns evidenced a shift to the Tories. But it wasn't enough. Labour saw its great majority of 1945 all but erased, a stunning turnaround and a defeat by any other name, but Attlee and his government survived, barely. The final results showed Labour held 315 seats (13,331,000 votes); the Conservatives 298 seats (12,415,000 votes); and the Liberals 9 seats (mostly in Wales, 2,679,000 votes). That gave Labour an overall majority of six. Churchill, Christopher Soames, and Duncan Sandys fared well, but not Randolph, who for the fourth time in four contested elections was rejected by voters. In a sense, Labour had lost the election—certainly it had lost its mandate—but the Conservatives and Churchill had not won it.

Churchill was seventy-five. He complained to his doctor of tightness in his shoulders and he feared another stroke. Time was now the enemy. But in one regard time was also his ally. Turmoil among the leadership of the Labour party, any internal Labour dissent on matters of budgets, banking, or defense, would lead to a vote of no confidence. In America Churchill would have had to wait four years before another shot at the top, but in Britain—especially in Attlee's Britain, that year—another general election might be called within months. Although Anthony Eden, Rab Butler, and Harold Macmillan each aspired to higher status within the party leadership (and ultimately the leadership itself), Churchill's position as leader was secure. Under his command, the Conservatives had retrieved 85 of the seats they had lost in 1945, and Labour had lost 78. Those Tories who had wanted Churchill to take a long rest in 1945 would have to wait their turn. They could not throw over the man who had brought them this far, in war and in peace. Churchill, therefore, though disappointed by the election results, was not shattered. He believed that his day would yet come. He returned to Chartwell to continue work on his memoirs—only two volumes remained. He prepared, too, for the new Parliament and the battles sure to be fought there. Late one night not long after the election, while dictating a section of his memoir, he turned to Jane Portal and announced, "I know I'm going to be Prime Minister again. I know it."[128]

One among the family was not shattered in the least by the election results: Clementine. Chartwell was her safe haven; the guest list included children and grandchildren and old friends. In 1945 she believed Winston should have retired, and she believed so still. Increasingly afflicted with neuritis, streptococcal infections, and by a bout of lumbago later in the year, she was ready for a pacific retirement at Chartwell. It was not to be.

On March 6, the new Parliament opened with the traditional Gracious Speech, the King's message to the Houses of Lords and Commons. The next day, March 7, the first day of debate, Churchill made clear his intent to press his attacks on the socialist experiment: "The basic fact before us is that the electors by a majority of 1,750,000 have voted against the advance to a Socialist State, and, in particular, against the nationalization of steel and other industries which were threatened. The Government, therefore, have no mandate." He moved that a full debate of all issues "be accorded us in the next fortnight or so." Hansard transcripts record the following exchange:

> Mr. H. Morrison [Speaker of the House] indicated dissent.
> Mr. Churchill: It will take more than the oscillation of the Lord President's head in this Parliament necessarily to convince us that our desires must be put aside; I ask for a full Debate.[129]

He pressed his attacks for the next twenty months. Debates (and Questions) in the House of Commons are far livelier affairs than business conducted in either the Senate or House of the United States, where long and often boring statements are read into the Congressional Record by members (often to an empty chamber), and where oral interruptions are considered breaches of decorum. In the British House of Commons "Rubbish" and "Nonsense" are oft-heard rejoinders. Laughter—and its cousin the snicker—is a weapon. Members mumble and rustle papers in shows of displeasure at an opponent's words (or mumble and rustle papers in agreement with their party colleagues). Churchill came to do battle. His political nemesis Aneurin Bevan described Churchill's approach to the House thus: "He had to wheel himself up to battle like an enormous gun." When Churchill fired a salvo, his opponents knew it.[130]

Labour MPs once jeered Churchill as he was leaving the chamber; he turned and blew them kisses. No barb could go unanswered. When Churchill castigated Labour for the fiscal hardships Britons lived with, a Labour MP called out, "Why don't you sell your *horse?*" Churchill looked up, and replied, "I was strongly tempted to sell the horse, but I am doing my best *to fight against the profit motive.*" A nod of dissent, a derisive grunt, were gauntlets thrown down. When a member mumbled, "Rubbish," to one Churchill pronouncement, the Old Man replied, "That may be what the right honourable and learned Gentleman has in his head, but it does not carry conviction." When a member called out, "Rubbish," after Churchill claimed Czechoslovakia had become a pawn of Moscow, the Old Man replied: "The right honourable Gentleman seems to have nothing in his head but rubbish." Interrupted during one debate on Moscow's geopolitical intentions, Churchill shot back, "I think the Communist Members and fellow travelers have a pretty good run in this House." Here was an incendiary claim that even the junior senator from Wisconsin,

Joseph McCarthy, would not make on the U.S. Senate floor. But Churchill could toss out such a retort without causing an uproar, because all knew he was without guile. As well, wrote Tory MP Earl Winterton (who in 1950 was the Father of the House, its longest-serving member), Churchill could read the mood of the House: "Winston Churchill is steeped in its atmosphere and traditions; he is familiar with all its varying moods... he has an instinctive understanding of what it will accept and what it will not accept." The British House of Commons was populated by agile minds and quick wits, and after almost fifty years, Winston Churchill was still one of the most agile and quick-witted. Indeed, at about that time, Winterton called him "the greatest living parliamentarian."[131]

Another colleague, Sir Alan Herbert, the Independent MP for Oxford University, called Churchill "the greatest living British humorist." When giving lectures on the topic of humor, Herbert cited the usual suspects: P. G. Wodehouse, Noël Coward, Nat Gubbins, even Aneurin Bevan. But Herbert's top choice was "Winston Churchill, who, at any time, in any conditions, in any company, on any subject, with never a fault of taste or tact, can make laughter when he wills."[132]

Not all agreed. Roy Jenkins believed Churchill's humor was sometimes "not... wise... or gracious" as a result of "one of Churchill's narrownesses"—his hostility to left-wing intellectuals. Churchill believed incorrectly that Labour's leading lights were all products of Winchester University, which he considered a breeding ground of the casuistry he saw and detested in certain intellectuals. Indeed, Hugh Gaitskell and Stafford Cripps, among several other Labour leaders, had come out of Winchester. As a result, Jenkins wrote, Churchill made "constant not very funny anti-Wykehamical [anti-Winchester] jokes in the House." He did, but one's man's humor is another man's poison. Churchill, responding to a Labour claim: "We suffer from the fallacy, *deus ex machina,* which, for the benefit of any Wykehamists who may be present, is 'A god out of the machine.'" On another occasion: "I do not know whether they learn French at Winchester." And during a June 27, 1950, debate on British participation in a European coal and steel community, Churchill tossed out: "In this Debate we have had the usual jargon about 'the infrastructure of a supra-national authority.' The original authorship is obscure; but it may well be that these words 'infra' and 'supra' have been introduced into our current political parlance by the band of intellectual highbrows who are naturally anxious to impress British labour with the fact that they learned Latin at Winchester." In fact, the word "infrastructure," a perfectly good Latin-derived word, had come out of France, but Churchill never missed a chance to ridicule his political enemies.[133]

The "supranational authority" under discussion was known as the

Schuman Plan, proposed on May 9 by French foreign minister Robert Schuman, who called on European nations to join together in a community dedicated to shedding tariffs and sharing resources—coal and steel, to start with—in order to regain a competitive edge in the international marketplace and, most significant, to eliminate the resource monopolization that inevitably ended in European wars. Schuman called for talks in Paris. The Attlee government refused to participate, a decision Churchill denounced as "a squalid attitude at a time of present stress." He was not advising a blanket acceptance of the Schuman Plan, but merely a willingness to discuss it. He added that if asked, would he "agree to a supranational authority which has the power to tell Great Britain not to cut any more coal or make any more steel, but to grow tomatoes instead?' I should say, without hesitation, the answer is 'No.'" What he opposed, he said, "is State ownership and management—or mismanagement as it has proved so far—of the industry." He pointed out that under Schuman's proposal, private ownership of industry remained unaffected, adding, "We see no reason why the problems of the British steel industry should not be discussed in common with the problems of the other European steel industries."

And he pointed out the ultimate beauty of the plan: it would bring France and Germany together in mutually beneficial enterprises. It would be "an effective step," Churchill told a meeting of Scottish Unionists, "in preventing another war between France and Germany and lay at last to rest that quarrel of 1,000 years between Gaul and Teuton. Now France has taken the initiative in a manner beyond my hopes." He told the House during the debate of June 27 that to reach this day was why Britain had refused to quit in 1940:

> We fought alone against tyranny for a whole year, not purely from national motives.... It was not only our own cause but a world cause for which the Union Jack was kept flying in 1940.... The Conservative and Liberal parties declare that national sovereignty is not inviolable, and that it may be resolutely diminished for the sake of all the men in all the lands finding their way home together.

He predicted the consequences if Attlee refused participation in the talks about the Schuman Plan:

> The absence of Britain deranges the balance of Europe. I am all for a reconciliation between France and Germany, and for receiving Germany back into the European family, but this implies, as I have always insisted, that Britain and France should in the main act together so as

> to be able to deal on even terms with Germany, which is so much stronger than France alone. Without Britain, the coal and steel pool in western Europe must naturally tend to be dominated by Germany, who will be the most powerful member.[134]

Attlee stood firm; he would not send any ministers to Paris.

Schuman held his meetings without the British. Almost a year later, in April 1951, France, Italy, West Germany, Belgium, Luxembourg, and the Netherlands signed the Treaty of Paris and by so doing created the European Coal and Steel Community. The six states pledged to create a "common market" for steel and coal. Here, then, was the first step on the road to the European Economic Community and, ultimately, the European Union. May 9—the date Schuman first read his proposal in the French National Assembly—is now celebrated by European Union member nations as Europe Day. (The Council of Europe, which Churchill championed, is not part of the European Union; its member states do not transfer any national legislative or executive sovereignty to the body, which acts through international legal conventions.) The evolution of Schuman's concept into the European Union is a long and fascinating story, but it is not Churchill's story. Events on the other side of the globe that June week in 1950 changed the trajectory of Churchill's thinking, and the final years of his career.

On June 25, the Cold War turned hot. On that day, 230,000 North Korean soldiers, supported by more than 250 Russian-made T-34 battle tanks (the best tank on the planet) and as many pieces of heavy artillery, drove south across the 38th parallel and into South Korea. South Korean forces were outnumbered by more than two to one in men. They had no tanks. On the twenty-seventh, the day the Commons debated the Schuman Plan, the United Nations passed Security Council Resolution 83, calling on member states to offer military support to South Korea. Moscow did not vote, having boycotted the Security Council for six months. The next day, the South Korean government fled Seoul. Within four weeks, the North Koreans had bottled up the South's army and the American Eighth Army in the southeast corner of the Korean peninsula, near Pusan. Given that the North Koreans were clients—proxies—of Moscow, Churchill and the West had to entertain the very real possibility that with the attention of the United States drawn to Korea, Moscow might strike in Europe. If that came to pass, Europe west of the Iron Curtain was virtually defenseless.

Overnight, Churchill's Europeanism became far more narrowly focused. Coal and steel matters could wait. There was now only one priority: the creation of a unified European defense force. By the same token, Churchill's Atlanticist vision, too, became more narrowly focused: America, which had all but abandoned Europe in 1945, had to be brought back into the European picture, in force.

In June 1950, the NATO treaty of 1949 was backed up by nothing more than the paper it was printed on. In 1945, more than 2.8 million American soldiers and almost 300,000 airmen served in Europe. By 1946, 90 percent of both had gone home. By mid-1950, only 80,000 American troops and 20,000 airmen remained, and many of those were support troops.

In late July, based on figures supplied by the Attlee government, Churchill outlined to the House the situation in Europe. The Russians fielded 40,000 tanks; how many were deployed in Europe was unknown, but Stalin had little reason to deploy tanks east of the Urals. The Americans and British each possessed about 6,000 tanks; America's were sitting in America but for a couple of hundred in Europe. Soviet troop strength stood at least at 175 divisions, including 25 or more armored divisions, versus a total of a dozen French, American, and British divisions, of which only two were armored. The East Germans had been allowed by Moscow to create a defense force of 50,000, even though the Red Army provided more than enough men to defend East Germany. That was the status on the ground.[135]

When it came to the air, nobody in HMG seemed to know how many aircraft the Soviets had, perhaps as many as 19,000. And how many of them were stationed within range of Britain? Again, nobody knew. Churchill hammered away at the Attlee government's decision to sell one hundred jet fighters to Argentina, which claimed sovereignty over the Falkland Islands, and another 110 to Egypt, which was blocking Israeli ship traffic in the Suez Canal. What British air forces were available, he asked, to protect those American bombers in East Anglia? If the Soviets had only fifty atomic bombs, he told the House, and if Moscow dropped some of them on Britain, "It would not be pleasant." The Soviets had captured the German rocket works at Peenemünde, he reminded the House, and had learned enough to launch devastating guided missile attacks (armed with conventional warheads) against Britain. And on the seas—or under them—the Soviet U-boat menace appeared to be "far more severe than was the German U-boat force in 1939 and 1940." The European situation was beginning to look like the mid-1930s again, with an existential threat in the East, and Britain unprepared to defend itself. Churchill began again to sound like the voice from the 1930s wilderness. He warned the

House that if the Soviets threw only half their strength against the West, the West would be outnumbered by at least eight to one. He added: "If the facts that I have stated cannot be contradicted by His Majesty's Government, the preparations of the Western Union to defend itself certainly stand on a far lower level than those of the South Koreans."[136]

Ever since Fulton, Churchill's hopes for world peace had rested with the deterrent of the atomic bomb. The Americans now stationed 180 "atomic bombers" in East Anglia. Moscow was aware of that figure because Attlee had announced it in the Commons. But Churchill sought—demanded—a British atomic deterrent. For four years he had pressed the Attlee government to reveal its progress, if any, in building a British atomic bomb, and for four years Attlee had disclosed nothing. His government was, in fact, hard at work building a bomb, for the same reason Churchill would have pursued the matter: to guarantee British sovereignty. Attlee was as determined as Churchill that British foreign policy and defense not be held hostage to the whims and wishes of the U.S. State Department or White House. Attlee's refusal to discuss his atomic plans was proper; Churchill led the opposition, not HMG. Some in Britain concluded that the fourteen inscrutable men in the Kremlin had no design on Western Europe for the simple reason that Moscow could take it with impunity if it so desired, and since it had not, ergo, it had no desire to do so. This was the sort of convoluted logic—peace through trust—that infuriated Churchill. His position was clear, and he had stated it repeatedly since 1945, including to his New York hosts months earlier: "It is certain in my opinion that Europe would have been communized and London would have been under bombardment some time ago, but for the deterrent of the atomic bomb in the hands of the United States. That is my firm belief and that governs the situation today." As for trusting to the goodwill of Stalin after the experience of trusting Hitler, who had claimed too many times that his appetite for geography was satisfied, Churchill added: "Well, once bit, twice shy."[137]

In July, shortly after the North Koreans invaded the south, and with his stances on the need to re-arm and build a British atomic bomb in mind, he told a Plymouth audience, "The fourteen men in the Kremlin are not drifting with events. They work on calculation and design. They have a policy the aim of which we can see; but the execution and timing of their ambition for Communist world government we cannot predict." He told a London audience: "We have always to be very careful nowadays—we politicians, if we take an interest in military matters, or are held to have accumulated some knowledge and experience about them—lest we should be described for electioneering purposes as warmongers." In fact, Labour and many in the press slapped that label on him now on a regular basis. Yet, if the state of Western arms (other than the atomic bomb) was the measure, he was correct. France, which in 1940 sent 140 divisions against Hitler, now fielded fewer than ten. Britain had difficulty assembling a token force of one brigade to send to Korea in support of the Americans. Harold Macmillan told his diary: "It seems that to scrape together 3000 men and their equipment for Korea will take two months!...What have they done to the war equipment? It would appear that they have thrown it into the seas."[138]

On July 27 Churchill moved that the House go into secret session—"I spy strangers"—in order to address the status of the British atomic bomb. His motion lost by a single vote, 295 to 296. But if Churchill continued to push for divisions—votes—the day would come when Labour would lose one, and then another. The day would arrive when Attlee would have to call a general election. "Mismanagement" was the word Churchill now introduced into almost every critique of the Attlee government: "the mismanagement of the housing problem"; "the mismanagement in civil and domestic affairs"; "the mismanagement of our defence forces." And this, directed at Attlee in the House: "The Prime Minister has appealed to us for national unity on Defence. That does not mean national unity on mismanagement of Defence."[139]

His message—and the phrases he used to deliver it—recalled the previous decade: "We must never despair. We must never give in," he told the House. "Our scientific and technical ability is unsurpassed. We may well have time to reorganize and develop the mighty latent strength of Britain surrounded by her Commonwealth. But I warn the House that we have as great dangers to face in 1950 and 1951 as we had ten years ago." The next day Harold Nicolson told his diary that the "state of public opinion after Winston's grim speech...is one of paralyzed shock....We are in a position of blind and dumb dread."[140]

The next week, in early August, the Consultative Assembly of the Council of Europe met for the second time in Strasbourg. "Consultative" was the operative word: motions passed by the Assembly were nonbinding on the governments of member nations. Schuman was there to present his plan. Paul Reynaud, now France's defense minister, was on hand. The Germans sent two contingents, one of Socialists and one made up of members of the conservative Christian Democratic Union, whose leader, Konrad Adenauer, had been elected in 1949 the first chancellor of the Federal Democratic Republic of Germany—West Germany. British socialists led by Hugh Dalton were in attendance, as were Duncan Sandys, Harold Macmillan, and Winston Churchill for the Conservatives. On August 11, Churchill addressed the Assembly. He welcomed the Germans, and called for "a real defensive front in Europe" formed by a continental army made up of "large forces" of Americans, Britons, the French, Greeks, Italians, the Scandinavian countries, and the Low Countries. He forgot to mention the Germans, but his intent was clear. It would take compromise and sacrifice, he warned, and then he added words that anticipated the inaugural address of a young American president a decade later: "Those who serve supreme causes must not consider what they can get but what they can give." He ended by offering a motion calling for "the immediate creation of a unified European Army subject to proper European democratic control and acting in full co-operation with the United States and Canada."[141]

Macmillan thought the speech masterful, delivered with power and touches of humor that found their mark. "It is really more like a broadcast than a speech," he told his diary. "But then the trouble is that WSC's broadcasts *are* speeches." Churchill staked his reputation on his motion; defeat could end his long crusade for some sort of federal European structure, and certainly would mean the end of the idea of collective European security. He had addressed no details of command and control of such a European army, knowing that offering details might undermine the whole edifice. The French were wary of the Germans. The Germans were afraid of re-arming, believing that any German army would be large enough to provoke the Russians but not strong enough to repel them. The German General Staff had been abolished; Germans who served in a European army would therefore serve under the command of other nationalities. Macmillan, fearing that German volunteers would likely be former Nazis, preferred an army of conscripts—that is, if the Germans agreed to an army of any sort. The members of the Assembly pondered all of this and more before taking their vote. "No one is quite sure what turn the debate will take," Macmillan wrote.

The vote came in at 89 for the motion, 5 against, with 27 abstentions (including most of the British socialists). "It is strange," Macmillan wrote that week, "how, abroad as well as at home, what Churchill puts forward one year as a daring paradox, becomes an accepted truism a year later." Macmillan dined with Churchill the night of the vote, and found the Old Man "to be *very* pleased and *very* excited." Given that the object of the Europeanists was to bring about reconciliation between Germany and France, Churchill had "a right to be pleased. Without his immense personal prestige, which he has thrown quite recklessly into this campaign, it might not have been achieved."[142]

In mid-September two divisions of U.S. forces under the overall command of General Douglas MacArthur staged an amphibious assault at Inchon, in northwest South Korea. The invasion was a stunning success; within two weeks the Inchon forces and the Pusan armies met and then drove the North Koreans back across the 38th parallel. Pyongyang, the North Korean capital, was liberated, "the first Communist capital to be liberated by the forces of the free world," crowed *Time*. By late October, UN forces were chasing the North Korean army up the peninsula toward the Yalu River, the border with China. MacArthur declared that the boys might well be home by Christmas. In mid-November MacArthur informed George Marshall—the new secretary of defense—that he was launching a general offensive by the U.S. Eighth Army northward to the Yalu, to detect how many, if any, Chinese might be in North Korea, and to secure the peninsula once and for all. In defiance of the most basic military doctrine, MacArthur divided the Eighth Army into four separate columns. MacArthur had earlier told President Truman that at most three hundred thousand Chinese might get into the fray but that he did not believe the Chinese would send in any forces. But they did. The Eighth Army had almost reached the Chinese border in northwest North Korea when, on November 25, one million Chinese troops smashed into the American lines, into the flanks, even into the rear of some forces. The Chinese armies, hidden on both sides of the Yalu in deep mountain passes, had gone completely undetected by the Allies. By the end of the year, UN forces—mostly American—had been driven back over the 38th parallel, and in the weeks that followed, driven eighty miles south of Seoul, which again was lost. It was the longest retreat in American history.[143]

On November 30, Churchill's seventy-sixth birthday, President Truman told reporters that the UN would not abandon its mission in Korea. He followed that with a promise to "take whatever steps are necessary" to meet military objectives. A reporter asked if the atomic bomb might be one such step. Truman replied that use of the atomic bomb was under "active consideration." That statement, Dean Acheson later wrote, and a false news report that MacArthur might be given authority to use the bomb, threw the Attlee government into a panic, and resulted in Attlee's "scurrying across the ocean" to meet with Truman. Macmillan saw Truman's remark as a typically "diplomatic" response, "a cliché as a synonym for doing nothing." Attlee saw it as a step toward atomic war. The prime minister, in Macmillan's words, "bolted, like a rabbit, from his hole, and is off to Washington (what a picture and what a contrast to the great Churchill days)."[144]

Macmillan and Churchill did not know—and would not learn for another year—that Attlee had good reason to fret about the American position. The previous year Attlee had agreed to abolish the Anglo-American Combined Chiefs of Staff organization. That body had been critical to

Churchill's plans for continued Anglo-American military cooperation. Attlee shared Churchill's desire for a continuation of the Anglo-American partnership, but whereas Churchill had always badgered the Americans for a real role in that relationship—even in 1944, when Britain was clearly the junior partner—Attlee had willingly assumed the subservient role. He had twice in 1950—in secret—assured Washington that if American air forces commenced bombing operations in China, Britain would commit her air forces to the cause. In doing so, he had written Washington a blank check. Now, with Truman mumbling about the possibility of using the atomic bomb in Korea or China, Attlee had to either stop payment or secure guarantees from Truman that Britain would be consulted if any such measure was taken under consideration. Thus, Attlee went to Washington in early December with hopes of resurrecting the gentleman's agreement on the use of the atomic bomb that Churchill and Roosevelt had forged in 1943, which stipulated that neither country would use the bomb without the approval of the other, but which the McMahon Act of 1946 had effectively quashed. In this, Attlee failed utterly. Truman flatly refused to "consult" with the British, or anyone, on how America would defend itself. Truman offered to keep Attlee "informed" as a courtesy, but there'd be no "consultation."

Dean Acheson, by then secretary of state, let Attlee down gently by explaining that any agreement made between the president and another leader was considered by the U.S. Senate to be a treaty, and therefore subject to Senate approval. As the talks progressed, Acheson realized Attlee had arrived with other items on his agenda, including the need to negotiate with—and mollify—China. More than 60,000 British and Commonwealth troops served in Korea during that war, including legendary regiments such as the Black Watch, the Royal Canadian Regiment, the King's Own Scottish Borderers, and the Royal Irish Fusiliers. But the Americans sent 450,000 men, and the prospects of those now on the ground appeared bleak. Presuming more defeats were imminent, Attlee proposed that Truman offer a cease-fire in order to pull out the troops. Acheson told Attlee that to negotiate with the Chinese after taking "a licking" was the absolute wrong policy. State Department policy was based on George Kennan's belief (shared by Churchill) that to negotiate with Communists from a position of weakness was to invite disaster. "To cut and run," Acheson later wrote, "was not acceptable conduct." Attlee also proposed that the time was right to give the Communist Chinese government a seat in the UN. He was hoping, as Tories saw it, to detach China from Moscow through kindness. Nothing, he told Truman, was more important than relations with China, to which Acheson replied "acidly" that "the security of the United States was more important." Attlee was in an appeasement frame of mind. "Clement Attlee," Acheson later wrote, "was a far abler man than Winston Churchill's description of him as 'a sheep in sheep's clothing' would imply, but persistently depressing."[145]

When the House of Commons adjourned in December for the winter holidays, it did so from its rebuilt chamber, where it first met in late October. It had been almost ten years since a German bomb had obliterated the old chamber. Clement Attlee generously named a surviving stone arch the Churchill Arch. The new chamber was built to hold only two-thirds of the members, a design Churchill had suggested, such that if only half the members showed up, the room would appear almost full. The decision to build the chamber so, Churchill told the House, confused many around the world who "cannot easily be made to understand why we consider that the intensity, passion, intimacy, informality and spontaneity of our Debates constitute the personality of the House of Commons and endow it at once with its focus and its strength." He offered, "I am a child of the House of Commons and have been here I believe longer than anyone. I was much upset when I was violently thrown out of my collective cradle. I certainly wanted to get back to it as soon as possible." Five years after V-E day, the House of Commons had been restored to its prewar splendor, but Britain had not been, and the Empire never would be.[146]

In London that December, the weather turned depressing, and snow and ice and low temperatures persisted through the New Year. This was Churchill's travel season. He left mid-month for five weeks in Marrakech, where Clementine was to join him in early January. On Christmas Day he wrote his wife a short note from the Hotel La Mamounia, where he spent his days painting and his evenings dining on champagne and Marennes oysters. He asked after all the animals at Chartwell—the golden orfes, the Black Mollies, the black swans, and Rufus. He had no distractions, and was hard at work on the sixth and final volume of his memoirs. Of Korea, he wrote: "Much depends on the coming battle."[147]

In London, there was talk of an Eastern Munich. Harold Nicolson now regretted his switch to the Labour Party and its failing socialist experiment. On New Year's Eve Nicolson told his diary: "So ends a horrible year with worse to come.... We are all oppressed by a terrible sense of weakness and foreboding.... The year closes in a mist of anxiety. We shall be lucky if we get through 1951 without a war.... It is sad to become old amid such darkness."[148]

Harold Macmillan began expressing similar sentiments to his diary and continued to do so well into the late summer. In January: "The British Govt has almost ceased to function. The P.M. doodles or talks platitudes; the Foreign Secretary has pneumonia; there are no rearmament plans, no economic plan, and now—no coal!" As in 1947, Britons stoked their fires and pulled on another sweater in anticipation of a long, cold, lonely winter. On January 22 Macmillan wrote: "It is tragic that at such a moment we should have Attlee and Bevin.... Churchill is still painting in Marrakesh!"[149]

He was. But if he was to fight his final battle against Attlee and for the premiership, he needed his rest and his strength, which he nourished over eight days with numerous picnics, long evening meals on his veranda, and painting. Still, he managed to proof eight chapters of volume 6 of his war memoirs as well as work on the final draft of the U.S. Book-of-the-Month Club edition of volume 5. He daubed, dictated, and dined until January 20. He returned to London by way of Paris, where on the twenty-second he dined with Madame Odette Pol-Roger, the beautiful socialite whose company and champagne he thoroughly enjoyed (he later named one of his racehorses for her). Churchill arrived in London on the twenty-third, and set to work to bring down the Attlee government.

Britain by then was losing prestige along with the Empire. It could not mediate the Kashmir border dispute. It could not protect Malayan rubber plantations from roving bands of Communist guerrillas. The news from Korea only worsened. In April, the 1st battalion of the Gloucestershire Regiment was surrounded by Chinese forces and annihilated—704 of 750 men were killed or captured. The news from the Middle East became increasingly worrisome. The Egyptian government denied passage through the Suez Canal to British oil tankers bound for the refinery at Haifa, this in abrogation of international agreements.

Then, in late April, the Iranian parliament elected Mohammad Mosaddegh—Churchill called him Mousy Duck—prime minister. The Shah, whom the British and Americans had put on the Peacock Throne a decade earlier, appointed Mosaddegh premier. On May 1, Mosaddegh nationalized the British Anglo-Iranian Oil Company, including its refineries at Abadan. The Attlee government pledged to not abandon the Abadan complex, but failed to explain whether it would meet that pledge through force or negotiation. It resorted to neither.

In February, Labour won a no-confidence vote by a majority of 9. A vote on steel nationalization went to Labour by 10 votes. Remarkably, almost the entire House showed up for these sessions, and divided strictly along party lines, with the Liberals sometimes splitting their few votes. The *Times* speculated that if an influenza outbreak that was then spreading through the land kept enough Labourites from appearing in the Commons, the government might fall. Macmillan told his diary he hadn't seen such attendance—and such partisanship—since the General Strike of 1926. On the day following the steel vote, Labour won a referendum on meat rationing by eight votes. Macmillan scribbled in his diary: "The people do not go into little shops every weekend to buy a piece of steel. But they do grumble every weekend about their minute portion of meat."[150]

The Attlee government hung on, but just. When Labour came to power in 1945, the party was led by the Big Five: Attlee, Ernest Bevin (Foreign Office), Herbert Morrison (leader of the House), Sir Stafford Cripps (Board of Trade), and Hugh Dalton (Exchequer). By the end of 1947, Dalton was out, having been driven from the Exchequer for the egregious offense of leaking vital parts of HMG's budget to a reporter, before the House saw the budget and while the stock market was still open. Cripps took over at the Exchequer, where he raised taxes and forced a reduction in consumer spending, in order, he hoped, to raise exports. He failed. Morrison, who according to Colville "was not short of ambition," sought to maneuver Attlee out of the party chairmanship and himself in. Bevin, a bitter enemy of Morrison, refused to accede to that notion. After five years of marshaling nationalization schemes through the House, Morrison took over the Foreign Office when Bevin finally resigned due to ill health in March 1951. He was dead a month later. Bevin had always been on the opposite side of the House from Churchill, but like Churchill he was a great English patriot. Attlee, who was in the hospital with a duodenal ulcer, could not even pay tribute to Bevin in the House.

Cripps, too, had departed the scene. Plagued by severe digestive distress that his vegetarian diet failed to ameliorate, he resigned from Parliament and the cabinet in 1950, and took himself off to a Swiss sanatorium. He died two years later. Hugh Gaitskell, who also had his eye on the party leadership, succeeded him at the Exchequer in October 1950. When in early April 1951 Gaitskell announced plans to reel in costs associated with Aneurin Bevan's National Health Service by forcing Britons to pay half of their of eye care and dental expenses, and to contribute one shilling (about twenty-five cents) to their prescription costs, Bevan resigned in protest. Two days later, the head of the Board of Trade resigned. When Harold Macmillan heard the news, he told his diary, "If this is true, the Government must fall, and a general election follow."[151]

By the summer of 1951, in contrast to the fractious and disputatious Labour leadership, the Conservatives, led by Churchill, in harness with

Eden, Lord Woolton, Oliver Lyttelton, Rab Butler, Duncan Sandys, and Harold Macmillan, presented a unified opposition front, with Churchill firmly in the role of party leader.

By then, House debates, sometimes lasting all night, regularly descended into bitter shouting matches, with Churchill often being the object of the invective. But he gave as good as he got. When the minister of defence, Emanuel Shinwell, muttered his disagreement over re-arming Germany, Churchill shot back, "Oh shut up. Go and talk to the Italians; that's all you're fit for." That outburst resulted in one hundred Labour MPs signing and sending an apology to the Italian government, which in turn demanded an apology from Churchill, who gave one. During a May debate on the matter of the Attlee government continuing to sell Malay rubber and other raw materials to China over the strident objection of the United States (Churchill opposed the sales), a member shouted, "Do not write down [criticize] your country all the time." Churchill replied: "Will the honourable Member yell it out again?" The member did just that. *"Sit down!" "Untrue!" "Get out!"* and *"Give way!"* were regularly yelled from both benches. When Churchill once averred that he only wanted to do what was best for Britain, a member called out, *"Resign!"* An extraordinary exchange took place during a July debate on the handling of the Suez and Iranian crises, when Herbert Morrison, recently elevated to foreign secretary, interrupted Churchill with "They are laughing at the right honourable Gentleman behind him." Churchill replied, "I expect that the right honourable Gentleman wishes that he had such cordial relations with his own back-benchers." But Churchill could not leave it there, for Morrison had recently told an audience of coal miners that Churchill and the Tories sought war in both Egypt and Iran. Morrison, Churchill declared, "shows to all the world that his main thought in life is to be a caucus boss and a bitter party electioneer." Churchill added, "It is tragic indeed that at this time his distorted, twisted and malevolent mind should be the one to which our Foreign Affairs are confided."[152]

That night Macmillan told his diary that Churchill's performance was "one of his most devastating and polished efforts." Under a mass of Labour "chaff and invective," Churchill "thus established a complete ascendancy over the party and indeed over the House." He had, but although he had recovered from his hernia operation and had experienced no minor strokes for two years, such exertions took an increasing toll on his health. House debates were trying, and sessions sometimes lasted until morning, an ordeal even for a younger man. Lord Moran told his diary that if Churchill "goes back to No. 10, I doubt whether he is up to the job . . . he has lost ground and has no longer the same grip on things and events." And Moran, worried about Churchill's mental health if he did not go back to No. 10, told his diary, "When the struggle for power is at an end, and his political life is over, Winston will feel there is no purpose in his existence. I dread what may happen then."[153]

All now expected Attlee to call for a general election, with polling likely to take place in October, after the late summer vacation season.

Although Clementine wanted nothing more than to retire from political life, she did not discourage Winston in his quest for No. 10. Yet neither did she encourage him. She believed that his reputation could not be enhanced by another term at the top, and would most likely be damaged. She preferred that husband and wife live out their days at Chartwell, where she had finally found happiness. Their neighbors accepted the family now, whereas in the past they had considered Churchill something of an enfant terrible, and local merchants had considered the family a poor credit risk. All had changed, Mary later wrote. Neighbors were proud of having the Churchills in their midst, and the Churchills for their part became more outgoing and welcoming. Winston and Clementine now opened the Chartwell gardens four times each summer, admission was charged, and the proceeds donated to local charities.

Clementine, though ten years her husband's junior, lacked his energy and was easily exhausted—mentally and physically—by the strains of the political life. In May she had undergone a hysterectomy; in July she continued her convalescence near Biarritz, on the Bay of Biscay, in the company of Mary. In mid-August, with Parliament in summer recess, Churchill (and two secretaries, his valet, and Christopher Soames) set off for Paris to rendezvous with Clementine and Mary. From Paris the party traveled to the Rhone Alps region, where they planned to spend two weeks in the sun at Lake Annecy, near the Swiss border. But the sun failed to shine. Instead, a cold rain fell for a week, at which time Clementine and the Soameses returned to London, while Churchill prepared to take himself and his retinue off to Geneva by train, and from there to Venice, where he expected the bathing on the Lido would be more enjoyable. Told that the French train to Geneva did not stop at the Annecy station, Churchill instructed one of his secretaries to inform the stationmaster that Winston Churchill wishes that the train be stopped in order for Winston Churchill to board. The train was stopped. Churchill and party boarded, along with fifty-five suitcases and trunks and sixty-five smaller articles.[154]

On September 20, a week after Churchill returned to London, Attlee sent him a short note: "My dear Churchill," it read. "I have decided to have a general election in October." He added that he would issue a formal declaration after that night's nine o'clock news. The elections were set for October 25.[155]

Churchill, at seventy-six, knew that this was his final chance to attain his lifelong goal of being sent to No. 10 Downing Street by a vote of the English people. Defeat would mean retirement to the Weald. In a Tory defeat he'd likely retain his Woodford seat, but he would very likely lose the party leadership to a younger man, most likely Anthony Eden. But Eden, at fifty-four, was no longer a young man, nor with his recurring stomach ailments was he a healthy man. The results of a Gallup poll had reached Churchill in Venice: a majority of Conservatives and Liberals favored Eden over Churchill for party leadership. This general election would be Churchill's last as the Tory leader, win or lose. He had formed two governments, in 1940 and 1945, neither with a public mandate. Now, he would stake the reputation he had earned over fifty years on the final campaign. He had the nerve and sinew for the fight. Most of all he had the lion heart. All who knew him knew also that a loss would leave Churchill with little to hold on to.

The general election campaign of 1951 was a Hobbesian affair—not brutish, but nasty and short. Churchill began his campaign in early October, delivering eight speeches and two broadcasts in the three weeks up to polling day, October 25. Churchill's overall theme was the "melancholy story of inadvertence, incompetence, indecision and final collapse, which has . . . marked the policy of our Socialist rulers."

Foreign affairs offered him rich fields to plow. In late September, after Iranian prime minister Mosaddegh demanded that all British employees in Abadan leave Iran, Britain pulled its personnel out. Churchill, having negotiated the Persian oil concessions in 1914, once again, as during the war, saw events in the Middle East as not only threats to British national security but also personal affronts. During one House debate on the Iranian crisis, he managed to denigrate both the Attlee and the Iranian governments in the same sentence:

> If I may digress for a moment, it would seem that the Government have an advantage in their task in Persia in having so much in common with the Persian Government. They, like them, are holding on to office by the skin of their teeth and, like them, they are persevering in a policy of nationalization without the slightest regard for national interests.[156]

Thus, the campaign's first week found Attlee acceding to Mosaddegh's demand that the British leave Abadan. Mosaddegh, known for fits of public weeping and the occasional swoon, had actually rattled his saber. And Attlee had stood down, leading Churchill to tell a Liverpool audience that Britain had "fled the field" and had "been ejected" from Iran after "fifty years of British enterprise and management." He added a charge of appeasement: "Mr. Morrison, the Foreign Secretary, and his party associates no doubt hope to cover up their failure by saying that the Tories want war, while they are for peace at any price."[157]

Indeed, painting the Tories as warmongers, Churchill foremost among them, formed the core of Labour's strategy. Labour did not fight the election on the merits of socialism, Macmillan told his diary, but on fear—fear of unemployment, reduced wages, fewer social benefits, and, the greatest fear of all, war. During the first week of the campaign, the socialist *Daily Mirror,* with a circulation of four million, introduced a slogan that encapsulated the message: "Whose finger do you want on the trigger, Churchill's or Attlee's?" Churchill pointed out that the finger might be American, or Russian, but it could not be British, as Britain had no atomic bomb because its "influence in the world is not what it was in bygone days." All knew that to be true; and all asked, how does Churchill intend to reclaim that influence? By war, answered Labour.[158]

On the domestic front, Churchill let the Labour record speak for itself. He had stated his case for months, with feeling, but with little exaggeration. Britain's plight would have been hard to exaggerate. The country was stumbling toward financial disaster. Labour had imposed the highest tax rates in the free world. During that fourth quarter of 1951, Britain was hemorrhaging from its gold and dollar reserves at a pace never before seen in its history. At the current rate, the reserves would disappear sometime around mid-1952. The Iranian crisis meant that future oil purchases might have to be made in American dollars, a further drain of three hundred million on Britain's dollar balances. The pound had lost one-third of its value since the war ended. Internal inflation had been creeping up for six years, and was now accelerating as the Attlee government undertook to re-arm, a policy Churchill agreed with. Now, with America beginning its second year on a re-armament spending binge, worldwide commodity prices were spiraling upward, and Britain's finances were out of control. Britain was still the world's second-wealthiest country, a distant second behind the United States, but it clung to that status only because the economies of France, Germany, and Japan were just climbing out of the ruins of war. Churchill could not know it then, but that year's inflationary spike (12.5 percent) would reverse itself within months as the world's largest economies settled into the new order of the consumer society. America's new economic model, based on ever-increasing defense and consumer spending, soon begin to lift Britain from its economic mire, as a rising tide lifts all boats. It was a process that neither Attlee nor Churchill had much control over.[159]

On domestic issues, Churchill chose to tread a mostly metaphorical path during the election campaign. He gave Britons few precise details of Tory economic plans, as he told Moran: "We propose to give the people a lighthouse not a shop window." During one broadcast he averred: "The difference between our outlook and the Socialist outlook on life is the difference between the ladder and the queue. We are for the ladder. Let all try their best to climb. They are for the queue. Let each wait in his place till his turn comes." He nebulously pledged to slow the nationalization of steel and coal. Yet he did make two specific promises, which at his insistence were included in that year's Conservative manifesto. He pledged to build three hundred thousand houses, and in an adroit reading of the public mood, he proposed an excess profits tax be levied on corporations. Britain was re-arming, and would re-arm even more were he to win. Profits were being made on the stock exchanges and in boardrooms, the type of profits the common man did not partake in. Churchill, too, knew how to play the fear card. Ever unable to resist a shot at Bevan, he told an audience at Woodford: "It is certain that a vote for Bevanite Socialism is in fact, whatever its intention, a vote which increases the hazard of a world catastrophe." A return to power of the socialists, he said, would deal "a real blow to our hopes of escaping a Third World War."[160]

Several Tory and Liberal candidates volunteered not to run against each other in constituencies where a divided vote might throw the seat to Labour. One such was at Huddersfield, where Lady Violet Bonham Carter—daughter of the great prime minister H. H. Asquith—ran as a Liberal. She and Churchill had been best of friends since first meeting at a dinner party in 1906, when he was thirty-two and she nineteen. She later wrote that Churchill "seemed to me to be quite different from any other young man I had ever met." Churchill did not appear to notice her at first. When he did, he abruptly asked her age. She gave it. "'And I,' he said almost despairingly, 'am thirty-two already, younger than anyone else who *counts,* though.' Then savagely: 'Curse ruthless time. Curse our mortality. How cruelly short is the allotted span for all we must cram in.'" He then proceeded on a long discourse on the shortness of human life and the vast potential for human accomplishment, at the end of which he announced, "We are all worms, but I do believe that I am a glow worm." By the end of the dinner Bonham Carter was convinced he indeed was, "and my conviction remained unshaken throughout the years that followed." Now, speaking on her behalf at Huddersfield, Churchill reminded the crowd of his two decades as a Liberal, his service to Asquith, and his role in bringing unemployment insurance and old age pensions to Britons. He told the audience:

"'All men are created equal,' says the American Declaration of Independence, 'All men shall be kept equal,' say the British Socialist Party." He added, "Now is the time to break with these follies."[161]

Speaking in Plymouth on Randolph's behalf two days before polling day, he denounced Labour and Communist charges of warmongering as "a cruel and ungrateful accusation."

> It is the opposite of the truth. If I remain in public life at this juncture it is because, rightly or wrongly, but sincerely, I believe that I may be able to make an important contribution to the prevention of a Third World War and to bringing nearer that lasting peace settlement which the masses of the people of every race and in every land fervently desire. I pray indeed that I may have this opportunity. It is the last prize I seek to win.[162]

Max Beaverbrook predicted a Tory majority of at least one hundred. Max was well informed, but not always accurately informed, as borne out by the margin of error of his predictions in the last two elections. Moran advised Churchill not to put too much stock in Max's rosy prognostications. Churchill replied that since Max's papers were read by millions, "he must know what he's talking about." Max may be right, Moran told his diary, but on all sides Tories were worried, not only about the election results but by Churchill's age and his penchant for neither asking for nor taking advice. Churchill told Macmillan that he hoped for a majority of ninety but would settle for fifty. Macmillan also learned from Brendan Bracken that the Old Man, if victorious, planned to hold office for just one year, perhaps eighteen months at most. Churchill alluded to his planned retirement during a campaign address when he told the audience, "Mr. Eden will carry on the torch of Tory democracy when other and older hands have let it fall." Eden, though ill, was eager, his arms outstretched, to catch the torch.[163]

But Churchill was not prepared to let the torch pass until he claimed his prize—a summit at the top. That was what he sought; it was almost all he sought. Truman was still in the White House, Stalin still in the Kremlin. An election victory would turn the clock back to July 1945, to Potsdam, where the last meeting of the Big Three had been interrupted by the election.

On polling day, Thursday, October 25, the *Daily Mirror* accompanied its slogan—Whose finger on the trigger?—with a large photograph of a chubby man in half silhouette, holding a cigar. The man in the photo was not Churchill. By staging the shot, the *Daily Mirror* crossed the line. Churchill soon filed a lawsuit, and was rewarded with a full, if insincere, apology wherein the editors expressed regret if their words and photos implied in any way that Churchill did not dislike war. But the question asked by Tories on polling day was, how effective had the *Daily Mirror* been in its underhanded campaign? The answer to that question arrived overnight as the votes were counted. The Tories won, but just. Churchill did not get his hoped-for majority of 100, or even 50, but only 18, over all parties. The Conservatives finished with 321 seats, Labour with 295, the Liberals only 6. In fact, Labour, with 13,866,000 votes, outpolled the Conservatives by 229,000 votes. The results did not in any way resemble a mandate for Churchill. By noon on October 26, Attlee knew he was beaten. Early that evening he motored to Buckingham Palace to hand King George the seals of office. An hour or so later Churchill made his journey to the palace, where for the third time since 1940 he was asked by King George to form a government. Once again, as in 1939, when he was called back to the Admiralty, the signal went out worldwide: Winston is back.

The King was a very ill man, recuperating from lung surgery to remove a cancer. Weeks earlier, Churchill, shocked by the King's appearance and always anxious about all things medical, pressed Moran for details of the King's ailment and his chances for recovery. It was then that Moran understood that Churchill's anxiety had to do with his own decline, about which he received regular reminders by way of spells of dizziness, bouts of forgetfulness, numbness in his shoulders, and increasing deafness. And it was then that Moran concluded that Churchill had lost much ground along with his grip on things, and if he returned to No. 10 would not be up to the job. Clementine braced herself for the pending ordeal. Shortly after the election, she wrote a short note to Ronald Tree: "I do hope Winston will be able to help the country. It will be up-hill work, but he has a willing eager heart."[164]

Pug Ismay, happily retired from public affairs, had gone to bed early on the night of October 26. Late that night the telephone on his bedside table jangled to life. The familiar ring had heralded the invasion of the Low Countries, the death of Roosevelt, and the surrender of the German armies. Ismay lifted the receiver; a voice on the other end of the line asked him to stand by for the prime minister. A moment later: "Is that you Pug?...I want to see you at once. You aren't asleep are you?" Ismay explained that in fact he had been. "Well," said Churchill, "I only want to see you for five minutes." Ismay put his head under a cold tap, dressed hurriedly, and within fifteen minutes arrived at 28 Hyde Park Gate. There Churchill told Ismay, a career soldier, that he wanted him to take the office of secretary of state for Commonwealth relations, a political post for which Ismay considered himself totally unqualified. "I thought the cold tap had failed to do its job," Ismay later wrote, "and I was still dreaming." He accepted the position, "overjoyed at the prospect of serving under Churchill again."[165]

Jock Colville's summons arrived the next morning, as he and his wife were enjoying themselves at the Newmarket races. A steward of the Jockey Club found Colville in the crowd and told him that the prime minister was on the line and wished to speak to him. "Whatever he asks you to do," warned Colville's wife, "say no." Colville had returned to the Foreign Office after his two years in service to Princess Elizabeth and was content to finish his career there. But it was not to be. When Colville picked up the phone in the Jockey Club, the prime minister apologized for any inconvenience, and asked if Colville might be willing to meet in person. "Tomorrow?" Colville asked. "No," replied Churchill, "this afternoon." When they met, Colville asked Churchill how long he thought he'd stay on at Downing Street. The question stemmed from Colville's concern that another prolonged absence from the Foreign Office would derail his career. One year, Churchill replied. Colville signed on.[166]

At Chartwell over the next four days, the Old Man reassembled his old team. Eden would again lead the House and head the Foreign Office, the very same dual role that had exhausted him during the war. Colville came aboard as joint principal private secretary, sharing those duties with David Pitblado, an Attlee appointee. Rab Butler would go to the Exchequer, Oliver Lyttelton as colonial secretary, and Lord Woolton as lord president of the council. The Prof—Lord Cherwell—was to be paymaster general. Harry Crookshank, a party lesser light, was to take on the Ministry of Health. Harold Macmillan was to be minister of housing, with a mandate from Churchill to build the three hundred thousand houses he had promised during the campaign. When Macmillan asked Churchill what that might entail and how to go about it, the Old Man answered, "I haven't an idea." Churchill's sons-in-law were brought in, Duncan Sandys as minister of supply, Christopher Soames as parliamentary private secretary. But the nepotism did not extend to Randolph. Randolph, who had served his father during the war as adviser without portfolio and minister of provocation, no longer even served in those capacities. Churchill had grown weary of the knockdown political arguments that Randolph precipitated with regularity. Such verbal jousts had on occasion stimulated the Old Man during the war; now they tired him. One appointment raised eyebrows on both sides of the Atlantic. As he had in 1940, Churchill named himself minister of defence. "It is just folly for Churchill to become Minister of Defence," Macmillan told his diary. "It almost justifies the *Daily Mirror*.... This is a major blunder."[167]

During those autumn weeks, Dwight Eisenhower, supreme commander of NATO, set about organizing his NATO headquarters in Paris. Eisenhower sought something along the lines of his World War Two SHAEF arrangement, that is, allied countries would put their armies under NATO command in the event of war, but they would otherwise maintain sovereign control over their forces. The French Assembly and Robert Schuman, however, advocated the creation of a European Defense Community, something of a supranational military version of Schuman's Coal and Steel Community. The European army, as outlined by then–French premier René Pleven in 1950, would exist separately from the armies of the nations that contributed soldiers to it. De Gaulle, still in self-imposed exile from French politics, saw the EDC as an abdication of French sovereignty. The Scandinavian countries feared Franco-German domination if the EDC succeeded, and a German threat if it did not. Political cartoonists throughout Western Europe panned the plan, citing the absurd problems of command and control inherent in trying to guide brigades and divisions—let alone an entire army—made up of a dozen or more nationalities, all speaking different languages and carrying different weapons. The Bevan wing of the Labour Party opposed the EDC on the grounds that a European army, especially one containing Germans, would provoke Moscow. Eisenhower, too, was wary of bringing German forces into the mix, and remained so for three years. Britons were largely apathetic toward Europe, Dean Acheson later wrote, and, like the French, feared a re-armed Germany. America and NATO were where Britons beheld their salvation. For many Britons, including Churchill, the Atlantic was narrower than the English Channel.[168]

On December 6, Churchill imparted to the House his thoughts on the matter in an address that marked another milestone in the European journey toward unity, and Britain's role in that journey. Churchill told the House he foresaw "a European Army, containing a German contribution of agreed size and strength, [that] will stand alongside the British and United States Armies in a common defensive front. That, after all, is what really matters to the life or death of the free world." Then came the seeming paradox from the man who had argued for almost two decades for a united Europe: "As far as Britain is concerned, we do not propose to merge in the European Army but we are already joined to it. Our troops are on the spot." As with any future European economic union, Britain would be *in* and *out* simultaneously. But it wasn't a paradox. Unlike de Gaulle, whose loyalty was to France *alone,* Churchill was loyal to Britain *first.* It had always been so. He ended his address by declaring that the progress toward a European Defense Community (discussions Attlee had refused to join) amounted to "an enlightened if not an inspiring tale." Noting that the EDC had not yet taken its final shape, he announced that he would not make a final decision on Britain's role until it did.[169]

But the EDC never took its final shape. Churchill mocked the EDC weeks later in the private company of Truman and Acheson. The EDC talks dragged on until 1954, when France, by then losing a war in Indochina, pulled out. But by then Germany had re-armed, and NATO—including Greece and Turkey—had assumed the command structure that Eisenhower had envisioned, and had formed the defensive cordon for Western Europe, largely funded and manned by Churchill's American cousins, which was exactly what Churchill had sought since 1945.

By late 1951, Churchill had reached his goals also regarding the political and economic elements of European union. In February 1949, he had told a council of European ministers meeting in Brussels that their duty, and his, was to return to their respective countries and impress upon the leaders of their governments the wisdom of European unity: "We may even, in the form of an active, enlightened and ever more dominant public opinion, give them the fuel they need for their journey and the electric spark to set all in motion." It was now in motion.[170]

So, too, was the British atomic deterrent, another lynchpin of Churchill's European defense strategy. During the December 6 address, Churchill outlined the essence of that strategy. Having learned upon taking office that the Attlee government had been in the process of building an atomic bomb, Churchill pledged to bring it to fruition. Doing so, he warned the House, "adds to the deterrents against war, but it may throw the brunt on to us should war come." The Russians, upon learning of the American atomic bombers in East Anglia, had called Britain an "aircraft carrier." Britain, therefore, was a prime target. Yet, Churchill added, "We shall not flinch from the duty Britain has accepted."[171]

With the atomic deterrent in hand, he could then proceed to the prize he now saw as the culmination of his career; world peace brought about by a summit meeting between the American president, himself, and Joseph Stalin. He believed still that men of honor keep their word. He shocked one of his private secretaries when he declared that Stalin had never broken his word. Of course Stalin had broken his word, leading to the current state of world affairs. Churchill the romantic was overruling Churchill the statesman and ignoring Churchill the historian.

In early November, while reiterating the dangers posed by a nuclear world, he told the House: "But our great hope in foreign affairs is, of course, to bring about an abatement of what is called 'the cold war' by negotiation at the highest level from strength and not from weakness." He then read to the House the letter he had sent Stalin in 1945, in which he had warned of a dangerous world with Communists drawn up on one side against the English-speaking nations and their allies. "It is quite obvious," he had told Stalin, that such a "quarrel would tear the world to pieces and that all of us leading men on either side who had anything to do with that would be shamed before history." It had all come to pass, he told the House, "with horrible exactitude." Thus, a summit at the top, Churchill believed, was the only way to avert the ultimate catastrophe of World War Three. He also believed that only absolute Anglo-American solidarity could bring the Soviets to the table. As he put it to President Truman, the Kremlin feared a strong Anglo-American friendship, and would try to drive a wedge between Americans and Britons. But if the Soviets grew to fear the unshakable Western alliance enough, they might then see friendship with the West as more advantageous than enmity. In 1942 he told Americans, "If we are together, nothing is impossible, if we are divided, all will fail." He believed that yet.[172]

To that end, on the final day of 1951, Churchill and his retinue—including Colville, Lord Moran, Pug Ismay, Dickie Mountbatten, and the Prof—once again, as during the late war, embarked for the United States on board the *Queen Mary*. At midnight they convened in Churchill's cabin for a champagne toast and a rendition of "Auld Lang Syne." Churchill had turned seventy-seven a month earlier. Bob Boothby, who had been drummed from office in 1940 over alleged financial improprieties, had dined with him that month after the Old Man asked Boothby to lead the British delegation in talks on a united Europe, an act of magnanimity that resurrected Boothby's career. Boothby was an old, but false, friend of Churchill's, and he never forgave the Old Man for not coming to his defense in 1940. Yet on one matter Boothby shared the opinion of many of Churchill's colleagues. Boothby reported to Harold Nicolson that Churchill was getting "very, very old, tragically old." Secretary of State Dean Acheson later wrote that during the Washington meetings, he found Churchill to be "still formidable and quite magnificent," but noted, "the old lion seemed to be weakening."[173]

Acheson later wrote that the French seemed always to arrive in Washington bearing demands, while the American press believed the British did likewise, and in fact ran roughshod over American leaders. But Acheson understood that the British and Churchill had come only in search of friendship. In his third address before the U.S. Congress, an unprecedented honor for a foreign leader, Churchill made clear he had not come "to ask you for money to make life more comfortable or easier for us in Britain." Rather, he came to pledge his support for American policies in Asia, the Middle East, and in Europe. Speaking in a sense to the Kremlin, he declared, as he had many times since 1945, that Britain sought nothing from Russia. Although he regularly called Communists and communism sinister and malignant, he did not do so now. Nor did he refer to the Communists as "godless" or "atheists," as was the wont of many Americans in high office. The words, in fact, do not appear in any of his public addresses delivered between 1940 and 1961. His battle was fought not over Christian dogma, but over liberty. He ended with his favorite Bismarck quote: "Bismarck once said that the supreme fact of the nineteenth century was that Britain and the United States spoke the same language. Let us make sure that the supreme fact of the twentieth century is that they tread the same path."[174]

Harry Truman, who was not running for reelection in 1952, deferred to his successor any decision on a possible summit. That turned out to be Dwight Eisenhower. Churchill's New Year's 1952 Atlantic crossing was the first of four journeys to Washington and Bermuda that he undertook over the next three years, each one a quest for his summit prize. Implicit in that is the fact that Churchill did not leave office in a year or so as he had told his colleagues he would. Instead, he stayed on for almost four more years, in pursuit of his prize, which in the end eluded him. He never flagged in that pursuit, even as pneumonia and then a terrible stroke hobbled him, even as his colleagues, driven in part by their concern for his health, and in part by their own ambitions, sought to ease him out of Downing Street, even as Stalin and his successors rebuffed him after the ogre's death in 1953. President Eisenhower did likewise.

Truman often told Dean Acheson that Churchill was the greatest public figure of their age. Acheson thought that an understatement. Churchill's greatness, Acheson wrote, "flowed not only from great qualities of heart and brain, indomitable courage, energy, magnanimity, and good sense, but from supreme art and deliberate policy." These elements, Acheson believed, fused into a style of leadership "that alone can call forth from a free people what cannot be commanded." One would have to go back almost four hundred years, to Queen Elizabeth I, Acheson believed, to find Churchill's equal. Churchill's final battle, to bring the Americans, Soviets, and British to the conference table, fought into his eighties, was as dogged as any he ever fought. And yet, tragedy is the wasting shadow always cast, sooner or later, by towering heroism.

Jock Colville later wrote that Churchill's "return to power seemed to many to presage the recovery of hopes tarnished by the dismal aftermath of the war." Those hopes fell short of complete fulfillment during the three and one-half years of Churchill's last administration, but during those years, the austerity programs and rationing disappeared, the standard of living rose, if modestly, and Europe remained at peace, albeit an uneasy peace. The first year under Churchill remained bleak: rationing was severe, and coal still scarce. Then King George VI died on February 6, 1952. Colville found Churchill in tears that morning, staring straight ahead, reading neither his official papers nor the newspapers. The Old Man feared he could not work with the new Queen, as he did not know her and "she was only a child." But he pledged to stay on as prime minister until her coronation in mid-1953.

Here was the first delay in his promised departure; there would be more. It was much the same tactic he had used when he delayed the second front during the war: pledge support for an outcome but keep moving the timetable back. Had he announced in early 1952 that he might stay on until 1955, he'd have sparked a palace revolt by Eden, Butler, Macmillan, and most certainly by Clementine, who wanted him out of Downing Street and home in Kent.[175]

On April 24, 1953, the Queen summoned Churchill to Windsor Castle, where she conferred on him the Order of the Garter. He had declined her father's offer of the Garter in 1945. At that time, the law held that the prime minister must approve the monarch's nomination. Churchill, as prime minister, refused his own knighthood. But the law had been changed; the decision was now the Queen's alone to make. And so Churchill became Sir Winston Churchill, K.B.

The young Queen heralded a new era of youthful optimism as the old order and the old wars receded into Britain's collective memory. In early June 1953, twenty million Britons watched Queen Elizabeth's coronation on live television, mostly in pubs, but the new TV experience led to a doubling of television sales in Britain. America watched, too. For the young, a golden future beckoned, rich with promise.

But not for the old. For some weeks before the Queen's coronation, Churchill had once again, as during the war, been acting foreign minister after Anthony Eden was forced to undergo a third operation for his debilitating stomach ulcers. In his role as acting foreign minister, the P.M. concluded that the Soviets had changed their stripes following the death of Stalin in March, felled by a stroke, although rumors coming out of Moscow had it that he had been poisoned by the murderous head of the NKVD, Lavrentiy Beria, the man responsible for the Katyn forest massacres. Indeed, Beria was arrested in June. Churchill had sent friendly greetings to Stalin's apparent successor, Georgy Malenkov, who responded in kind. It was all simply diplomatic dancing in the dark, but Churchill believed the moment had arrived to "grasp the paw of the Russian bear." He had told Britons since 1950 that the goal of sitting down with the Russians was to work toward a nuclear disarmament treaty, always stressing that any such treaty must include provisions for international inspections and enforcement. Now, believing the moment had arrived, he sent preliminary feelers to Eisenhower, suggesting that they meet in order to plan the big summit. Eisenhower tentatively agreed; Bermuda was to be the place, the date not yet confirmed.

Then, on June 23, just two weeks after the Queen's coronation, Churchill went to rise from the dinner table at No. 10 and instead collapsed into his chair, unable to walk, his words slurred. Colville at first thought the Old Man had had too much to drink. Colville, Christopher Soames, and Clementine managed to get Churchill to bed. They summoned Lord Moran, who took only a few minutes to conclude that his patient had suffered a stroke. When Churchill, pale but mobile, chaired a cabinet meeting the next morning, no one present thought anything amiss. Moran moved him to Chartwell that afternoon. The next day the symptoms grew more severe, so severe that by the following day, his doctors believed the end might come within days. He lost feeling on his left side and then the ability to make a fist. Moran concluded that the "thrombosis is obviously spreading," but did not tell Churchill in so many words. The doctor ordered bed rest—no cabinet meetings, no Questions in the House, and no Bermuda. Moran drew up a medical bulletin that referenced a "disturbance of cerebral circulation." That phrase was axed by Rab Butler and Churchill. The edited bulletin simply stated the P.M. needed respite from his arduous duties. So began an almost two-month news blackout of a sort that would be impossible to pull off in this age of total media. Churchill's health improved slowly during those months. During one low point, he told Colville that he'd resign in October, as he no longer had "the zest" for the work and thought the world was in "an abominable state." He was depressed, he said, by thoughts of the hydrogen bomb.[176]

Then he changed his mind on the matter of resigning. With logic only Churchill could conjure, he told all those who believed he should resign due to his ill health—Clementine, his cabinet colleagues, and Lord Moran—that the time to leave office was not when he was weak but when he recovered. To speed that process, he informed Moran that he had given up brandy, substituting Cointreau instead, and that he had switched to milder cigars. He read a great deal: *Jane Eyre,* Trollope, *Candide, Wuthering Heights, 1984, Phineas Finn,* C. S. Forester. He edited his *History of the English-Speaking Peoples.* He banged croquet balls about on the lawn, more from frustration over his condition than from any love of the game.[177]

Churchill's spirits were boosted in early July by the prospect of Eisenhower's visiting Britain, an idea that apparently had germinated in Churchill's imagination. In fact, Eisenhower followed in the footsteps of presidents Truman and Roosevelt, footsteps that never led to London. Bitterness was Churchill's response as it dawned on him later in the month that Eisenhower was not coming to Britain and did not see eye to eye with him on a thaw in relations with Russia. The Democrats should have won the election, the Old Man told Colville, adding that Eisenhower was "both weak and stupid."[178]

Slowly, he regained his gait and powers of speech. He was cheered by the news on July 27 that the armistice was signed that day ending the Korean conflict. But there would be no V-K day celebrations; the West had not won, and the Chinese or North Koreans might at any time violate the treaty. That night he told Moran that the opportunity for peace had been within reach before the stroke, "if only, Charles, I had the strength. I'm a sort of survival. Roosevelt and Stalin are both dead. I only am left."[179]

Eden, himself frail, paid a visit to Churchill in August. By then Rab Butler was exhausting himself filling in for both Eden and Churchill. Colville noted that Eden seemed to come with one burning thought in mind: "When do I take over?" Yet it dawned on Eden that he would not be moving up to No. 10 until and unless his health improved considerably. Eden's was a family visit, in that the previous year he had married Jack Churchill's daughter, Clarissa, which made him Churchill's nephew-in-law. But the familial bonds did not guarantee a warm relationship. Churchill was growing increasingly resentful of Eden's transparent ambition. The Old Man told Colville that the more Eden tried to hustle him out, the longer he'd stay.[180]

Churchill ran only three cabinet meetings over three months, and kept his visits to No. 10 at a minimum. By late August he was on his way back. Still, one consulting physician, the aptly named neurologist Sir Russell Brain, told Lord Moran that he doubted Churchill could ever again give speeches or answer Questions in the House.[181]

Churchill proved Sir Russell's diagnosis dead wrong in early November, when, on the third, he made his first parliamentary speech since the stroke. Other than members of Churchill's cabinet, no one in the chamber knew he had been ill. Yet rumors of a stroke had percolated through the press. The *Daily Mirror* had repeated the rumor running in the American press that he had been struck down, was expected to recover, and then resign. The eyes of the world were therefore upon him that day. He covered a plethora of domestic and international matters before arriving at the root of the matter: defense. He declared that two dominant events had taken place since 1951—the shift of hostilities in Korea from the battlefield to the conference table, and the death of Stalin. He wondered aloud if the death of Stalin had ushered in a new era in Soviet policy conducive to détente, a "new look." He had no ready answer but told the House he believed all nations act in their best interest and that the Soviets might have "turned to internal betterment rather than external aggression." How could the West encourage such behavior? His proposed solution was to be found in the third dominant event of the last two years:

> I mean the rapid and ceaseless developments of atomic warfare and the hydrogen bomb. These fearful scientific discoveries cast their shadow on every thoughtful mind, but nevertheless I believe that we are justified in feeling that there has been a diminution of tension and that the probabilities of another world war have diminished, or at least have become more remote. I say this in spite of the continual growth of weapons of destruction such as have never fallen before into the hands of human beings. Indeed, I have sometimes the odd thought that the annihilating character of these agencies may bring an utterly unforeseeable security to mankind.

Churchill was unaware at the time that the United States had exploded an H-bomb on the Pacific atoll of Eniwetok in November 1952. The device was far too large—seventy tons—to fit inside an airplane. The Americans were now at work perfecting a smaller though far more powerful version. The Russians had followed in August 1953 with their own H-bomb test in Kazakhstan. Both tests had so far remained state secrets. But Churchill and the world were well aware that a hydrogen bomb would soon be exploded, somewhere, by someone, most likely the Americans.

He developed his remarkable "odd thought" further, and in doing so became the first world leader to articulate what later became known as the policy of MAD: mutually assured destruction.

> It may be that...when the advance of destructive weapons enables everyone to kill everybody else nobody will want to kill anyone at all. At any rate, it seems pretty safe to say that a war which begins by both sides suffering what they dread most—and that is undoubtedly the case at present—is less likely to occur than one which dangles the lurid prizes of former ages before ambitious eyes.[182]

Churchill left the House under his own power, strolling to the smoking room, where he drank brandy for two hours (having abandoned his experiment with Cointreau). The speech was the final hurdle, he told Moran, to restarting the Bermuda talks. Churchill fully expected to soon be meeting with Malenkov, after gaining Eisenhower's approval. He was ebullient, telling Moran, "I'm thinking of substituting port for brandy." That night, Moran said this of Churchill in his diary: "I love his guts. I think he's invincible." Macmillan committed similar thoughts to his diary: "Indeed, he [Churchill] was complete master of himself and the House. It seems incredible that this man was struck down by a second stroke at the beginning of July."[183]

Within the week, Eisenhower agreed to an early December meeting with Churchill in Bermuda, with the purpose of discussing a unified approach to the Russians, preparatory to an Anglo-American-Soviet summit. The French would attend the Bermuda meeting as well, in their role as the third Western power. Indeed, the conference had been postponed not only because of Churchill's summertime hiatus, but because the turnover in French ministers had been so great for so long that the French government at times had no one to send to conferences. Neither the P.M. nor Eden believed the French would add anything of value to the discussion. The Bermuda talks would be fly-by-the-seat-of-the-pants, always a concern to foreign ministers when their heads of state are doing the flying. Churchill's belief that Russia was ready to talk was a result, Moran believed, of Churchill existing "in an imaginary world of his own making." On December 2, Churchill, Eden, Moran, and Colville boarded the pressurized Stratocruiser *Canopus* for the seventeen-hour flight to Bermuda by way of Gander, Newfoundland. For much of the journey—a far cry from the days of rattling and unheated B-24s—Churchill read C. S. Forester's *Death to the French,* an unfortunate choice if he was seen carrying it into the conference.[184]

Clementine did not accompany Winston to Bermuda. She was in Stockholm that week to accept on Churchill's behalf the Nobel Prize for Literature, awarded for Churchill's war memoirs. The prize was £12,500, tax free, a sum that Churchill in a note to his wife declared was "not so bad!" She likely would not have made the trip to Bermuda in any event. "Her heart had never been in this second term of office," her daughter Mary later wrote. She was tired, and prone to agitation, especially around her husband, to whom she made clear that his soldiering on as P.M. imposed great burdens upon her. She was mistress of Chartwell and the Hyde Park Gate house, as well as hostess at No. 10 and Chequers, where the constant entertaining and steady streams of visitors were a strain. For Clementine, the present held no joy and the future promised only more worries.[185]

Britain had tested its first atomic bomb a year earlier. It deployed its first atomic weapons days after Churchill's November 3 address. Yet the hydrogen weapon, not the A-bomb, obsolete now in Churchill's opinion, lay at the core of Churchill's strategy to bring the Russians into disarmament talks. Soon after the Bermuda meetings began, he learned that Eisenhower did not believe likewise. As if to prove the risks inherent when heads of state sit down to talk, Churchill supported Eisenhower—in turn seconded by his secretary of state, John Foster Dulles—without hesitation when the president declared he felt "free to use," indeed was prepared to use, atomic bombs in North Korea if the Chinese violated the armistice. Eisenhower added that he intended to say just that in an upcoming speech at the United Nations, a copy of which he gave Churchill to look over. Eden was shocked, and told Churchill so in private. Churchill began to grasp Eden's point: any such declaration by Eisenhower would not help to bring the Russians to the conference table. Churchill dispatched Colville to Eisenhower's quarters at the Mid-Ocean Club with a brief note in which he suggested the president temper his language by changing "free to" to "reserved the right to" use atomic weapons. Eisenhower agreed to do so, and offered as well to call for the creation of an international atomic regulatory agency.

The president then told Colville that "whereas Winston looked upon the [hydrogen bomb] as something new and terrible," he believed it to be simply the latest "improvement in military weapons." The president implied, Colville told his diary, that "there was in fact no distinction between 'conventional weapons' and atomic weapons." Churchill had once believed likewise, in 1945, but no longer did. After Churchill at one of the plenary sessions outlined at length his "double dealing" approach to the Soviets—an atomic bomb in one hand, the other extended in friendship—Eisenhower responded with a harangue of a sort none around the table had ever heard at an international conference. As for the Soviets' "new look," Eisenhower compared Russia to a whore wearing a new dress but "it was surely the same whore underneath." The French, predictably, leaked all of this to the press.[186]

Yet Eisenhower had to step with care. Wisconsin senator Joseph McCarthy, chairman of the Senate Permanent Subcommittee on Investigations, was riding high that year, and riding roughshod over the State Department, which for three years McCarthy had alleged was rife with Communists. When, during a private lunch in Bermuda, Churchill asked Eisenhower about McCarthy's influence in America, the president suggested he pay no attention to McCarthy, just as Americans paid no attention to Aneurin Bevan. It was not an apt comparison; Bevan might be a socialist gadfly, but he was not a dangerous presence in British politics. Many Americans presumed the British Foreign Office and the British intelligence services were likewise infested with Reds, a conclusion drawn in part by the defections to Moscow by Donald Maclean and Guy Burgess in

1951, although their exact whereabouts were not ascertained until 1956. It would not do for Eisenhower to encourage the notion that the British and Churchill had bullied him into glad-handing with the godless Communists in the Kremlin. Churchill could not bring himself to condemn his old wartime colleague for bowing to anti-Communist fury. Instead, he shifted blame onto John Foster Dulles, to whom he had taken an immediate and visceral dislike the previous year. "It seems that everything is left to Dulles," Churchill told Moran. "It appears that the president is no more than a ventriloquist's doll." In any case, Churchill went home to London without his prize. There would be no Anglo-American-Soviet summit anytime soon.[187]

Soon after Churchill's return from Bermuda, the *Daily Mirror* began calling for his resignation. One *Mirror* piece, under the headline SHADOW OF A GIANT, quoted the *New York Times:* Churchill "was only the shadow of the great figure of 1940." The *Daily Mirror*'s attacks got under Churchill's skin, Moran told his diary, but an article and cartoon in *Punch* hit the Old Man harder. The article, titled "A Story Without an Ending," was written by Malcolm Muggeridge, then the editor of *Punch.* It was an allegorical tale of a fictitious Byzantine ruler who had served his nation well but had lost his once-splendid faculties to old age and decrepitude. Accompanying the piece was a cartoon that depicted Churchill with a slack jaw, the left side of his face flaccid, as if from his stroke. Churchill's hands as depicted in the cartoon—"podgy, shapeless," in Moran's description—peered out from white cuffs. Churchill held his hands up to Moran. "Look at my hands," he said, "I have beautiful hands." Then he offered that, as *Punch* goes everywhere, he must resign. Years later Muggeridge declared that statement showed that Churchill "was totally out of touch with the contemporary situation," because by 1954 *Punch* did not go everywhere. It once did, Muggeridge declared, "but only in the 19th century."[188]

On March 1, 1954, the Americans detonated a hydrogen bomb over Bikini Atoll in the South Pacific. Three months later, on June 16, Churchill convened a secret session of the Defence Policy Committee at which he and his defence ministers agreed to a dramatic new atomic policy: Britain would build its own hydrogen bomb. The decision was so secret that not even the cabinet was informed. A week later, on June 24, Churchill departed by air for Washington.[189]

It was his last official trip to the United States, his final chance to garner Eisenhower's support for a summit. The usual group attended to his needs—Eden, Moran, Colville, and Christopher Soames. His mood aboard the Stratocruiser was at first somber. To Moran he lamented the changes wrought by the Wright brothers. The world had grown smaller: "It was an evil hour for poor England." But the mood passed, and at ten in the morning British time, he told the steward to remove his whisky and bring on the champagne and caviar. Knowing that Eisenhower, guided by John Foster Dulles, would not agree to a three-party or four-party summit, Churchill arrived in Washington with a new proposal—to conduct a two-party summit, himself and Malenkov.[190]

Thus his mood improved exponentially when on Friday, June 25, shortly after arriving at the White House, Eisenhower voiced no objection to Churchill's holding bilateral talks with the Russians, and did so before Churchill had even presented his case, which he had thought would be a long and complicated process. The objective of talks with the Russians, as Churchill saw it, was to buy ten years of "easement" in relations with Moscow, such that America, Russia, and Britain could divert their monies and scientific research away from catastrophic atomic bombs and into fruitful, peaceful endeavors. Eisenhower agreed, and even suggested that he and Churchill, along with the French and Germans, hold preliminary talks in London before Churchill went off to engage the Russians. Colville noted that Dulles tried to squelch the Russian initiative, without success. Eisenhower hosted a small dinner on Sunday, described by Colville as "very gay," with Churchill and Eisenhower agreeing that Germany must re-arm, even if over French objections. The French, Eisenhower declared, "were a hopeless, helpless mass of protoplasm." In fact, within weeks, the EDC died in the French Assembly and the tri-party occupation of West Germany was lifted, and within ten months, Germany was welcomed into NATO. Another cause for cheer had been Eisenhower's reaction when Churchill told him of the British decision to build a hydrogen bomb: Eisenhower had made no objection. Churchill could return to London a victor. As well, with a summit in mind, if not in hand, he now had another reason to stay on at No. 10.[191]

This he imparted to Eden on the return voyage to Britain, aboard the Cunarder *Queen Elizabeth,* christened in 1938 in honor of the first Elizabeth. When asked by Eden when he might resign, he set September 21 as a tentative date. This was important, because British law called for a general election to be held at least every five years. That meant October 1956 at the latest. If Churchill stayed on well into 1955, Eden would have precious little time to chart the course of his new government before the election. Churchill understood that well. Yet he would not go before he met with the Russians.

On that front, while on board the *Queen Elizabeth,* Churchill dictated a telegram to Soviet foreign minister Molotov in which he proposed direct talks between himself and the Soviet leaders, talks in which the United States would not participate. When Eden objected, pointing out correctly that such a message could not be sent without cabinet approval, Churchill dismissed his rationale as "nonsense," telling Colville that if the cabinet objected, he'd resign. That, Colville told the P.M., would split the Tories and the country "top to bottom." Churchill was practicing blackmail of a sort, and it worked. Eden backed off. Churchill's approach to Eden, Colville noted, had been "ruthless and unscrupulous." Eden finally agreed under Churchill's relentless pressure to inform the cabinet that he approved of the message. The telegram to Molotov was duly sent. The Russians waited three weeks to reply, and when they did, their proposal, by its absurd demands, effectively killed any chances of bilateral talks. They demanded a thirty-two-party all-European conference, with NATO withdrawal from Germany topping the agenda. Eden had been correct: by shooting off the message, Churchill had confused the Russians, angered Eisenhower, and alienated his cabinet. They all now questioned his wisdom. Of Churchill's crusade for a summit, Macmillan told his diary: "It was his last passionate wish—an old man's dream—an old man's folly, perhaps, but it might have saved the world."[192]

Churchill admitted defeat during the cabinet meeting following the arrival of the Soviet message. There would be no talks. Churchill's official biographer, Martin Gilbert, needed only a few words to close this chapter of the Great Man's life: "Churchill's last great foreign policy initiative was at an end."[193]

By all rights, so, too, should have been his premiership. But he held on, in part to secure cabinet approval on making a hydrogen bomb, which he duly gained on July 8; four days later he told the House that decisions had been made regarding atomic weapons, but he gave no details. Earlier in the year, he had proposed to leave in June, then July, then September. In August he decided against September. As summer gave out to fall, Eden and Harold Macmillan increased their efforts to move him out, to no avail.

In late July, Macmillan approached Clementine on the matter, a tactical mistake. He should have gone directly to Churchill, but perhaps did not, knowing well the Old Man's blunt style of debate. Churchill summoned Macmillan in order to discuss the matter. Colville feared an eruption. Macmillan was ushered into Churchill's study to find the Old Man engaged with Colville in a game of bezique. Churchill offered Macmillan a whisky and cigar, and continued his game. Then he insisted the score be tallied and that he pay Colville the monies owed. They disputed the exact amount. Churchill's checkbook was sent for and a pen. The pen arrived, the wrong pen. Macmillan meanwhile was allowed to fidget for the better part of a half hour. Finally, Churchill asked if Colville would be so good as to leave the room, because it appeared Mr. Macmillan "wanted to talk about some matter of political importance." The meeting did not last long; it took Churchill only a minute to make his point, which was that he was staying, although he told Macmillan that the party leaders had the authority to replace him as leader. Macmillan knew full well that given Churchill's popularity, a coup by the Tory leadership would spell their doom, not Churchill's. "I cannot understand what all the fuss was about," Churchill told Colville after Macmillan's departure. "He [Macmillan] really had nothing to say at all. He was very mild."[194]

In early August, Macmillan told his diary: "His [Churchill's] present mood is so self-centered as to amount almost to mania. It is, no doubt, the result of his disease [his stroke]." Were Churchill a king, Macmillan wrote, he'd be deposed. When pressed by Butler, Macmillan, and Eden, Churchill replied, "You cannot ask me to sign my own death warrant." Yet by not going he was signing theirs. "All of us, who really have loved as well as admired him," wrote Macmillan, "are being slowly driven into something like hatred."[195]

Churchill's treatment of Eden became shabby. During one luncheon, he told Eden that it would all be his by the time he was sixty. For Eden, that birthday was three years away. Colville wrote that Churchill had begun "to form a cold hatred of Eden, who, he repeatedly said, had done more to thwart him...than anybody else." That was a cruel and untrue assessment. Of Churchill during these final months in office, Colville wrote: "And yet on some days the old gleam would be there, wit and good humour would bubble and sparkle, wisdom would roll out in telling sentences and still, occasionally, the sparkle of genius could be seen in a decision, a letter or a phrase." But Colville asked himself, was Churchill still the man to negotiate with the Soviets and nudge the Americans to a less militant attitude toward Russia? "The Foreign Office thought not; the British public would, I am sure, have said yes. And I, who have been as intimate with him as anybody during these last years, simply do not know."[196]

Churchill turned eighty on November 30, 1954, the first prime minister since Gladstone to hold that office at that age. He was now the Father of the House and the only MP then sitting who had been elected during Queen Victoria's reign. Parliament, to mark his birthday, presented him with the portrait painted by Graham Sutherland, for which Churchill had sat throughout the autumn. He loathed it. In public he declared that it "certainly combines force with candor." In private he called it "malignant."

Clementine thought it hideous, and soon banished it to the attic, and sometime later had it burned. It portrayed him as old, which he was, and his face as coarse and cruel, which it was not. The royal family sent a birthday gift of four silver wine coasters engraved with the signatures of those who joined in giving it. On Churchill's birthday, Clement Attlee, who now led the opposition, delivered a long and generous tribute on the floor of the House, during which he declared that Churchill's wartime speeches reflected both the will of Parliament and of the nation.[197]

Churchill replied to Attlee's address the next day:

> I was very glad that Mr. Attlee described my speeches in the war as expressing the will not only of Parliament but of the whole nation. Their will was resolute and remorseless and, as it proved, unconquerable. It fell to me to express it, and if I found the right words you must remember that I have always earned my living by my pen and by my tongue. It was a nation and race dwelling all round the globe that had the lion heart. I had the luck to be called upon to give the roar. I also hope that I sometimes suggested to the lion the right places to use his claws. I am now nearing the end of my journey. I hope I still have some services to render.[198]

His nine grandchildren and four children were on hand for the holiday season. During a family celebration that season, his daughter Diana expressed wonderment of all that he had seen and done in his life. He listened and said, "I have achieved a great deal to achieve nothing in the end."[199]

Churchill pondered his exit during the Christmas holidays and into the winter. Colville later wrote that during the long winter months, "alone with him at the bezique table or in the dining-room, I listened to many disquisitions of which the burden was: 'I have lost interest; I'm tired of it all.' " During a mid-March dinner with Rab Butler, he proclaimed: "I feel like an aeroplane at the end of its flight, in the dusk, with the petrol running out, in search of a safe landing." Finally, in late March, he told Colville that he'd leave just before the Easter recess. Easter fell on April 10 that year.[200]

Churchill made his last major address to the House of Commons on March 1, 1955, on the subject of that year's defence white paper, wherein his government announced for the first time the decision to build a hydrogen bomb. Churchill understood that Britain was indefensible against such weapons, yet he was determined that other countries—Russia—be made indefensible as well. The bomb could not help England regain its former glory but it might just offer England the means to survive. He titled his speech "The Deterrent—Nuclear Warfare." "There is no absolute defence against the hydrogen bomb," he told the House, "nor is any method in sight by which any nation, or any country, can be completely guaranteed against the devastating injury which even a score of them might inflict on wide regions." He went on to ask, "What ought we to do?"

> Which way shall we turn to save our lives and the future of the world? It does not matter so much to old people; they are going soon anyway; but I find it poignant to look at youth in all its activity and ardour and, most of all, to watch little children playing their merry games, and wonder what would lie before them if God wearied of mankind. The best defence would of course be bona fide disarmament all round. This is in all our hearts.[201]

He took care to speak of the "Soviets" and "Soviet communism," telling the House that he was avoiding the term "Russian" because he greatly admired the Russian people "for their bravery, their many gifts and their kindly nature." It was the Communist dictators who posed the threat to human survival, not the Russian people. He declared, "There is only one sane policy for the free world in the next few years."

> That is what we call defence through deterrents.... These deterrents may at any time become the parents of disarmament, provided that they deter. To make our contribution to the deterrent we must ourselves possess the most up-to-date nuclear weapons, and the means of delivering them.

Entire continents, not simply small islands such as Britain, were now vulnerable and would become more vulnerable as the Soviets developed new means to deliver atomic bombs:

> There is no reason why, however, they should not develop some time within the next four, three, or even two years more advanced weapons and full means to deliver them on North American targets. Indeed, there is every reason to believe that within that period they will.

A "curious paradox has emerged," he declared. "Let me put it simply. After a certain point has been passed it may be said: The worse things get, the better." He still believed that, as he told the House, "mercifully, there is time and hope if we combine patience and courage.... All deterrents will improve and gain authority during the next ten years. By that time, the deterrent may well reach its acme and reap its final reward." After forty-five minutes, his voice still strong, he came to the end, and his valediction to the House and to his countrymen:

> The day may dawn when fair play, love for one's fellow-men, respect for justice and freedom, will enable tormented generations to march forth serene and triumphant from the hideous epoch in which we have to dwell. Meanwhile, never flinch, never weary, never despair.[202]

Churchill's powers, declared that week's *Sunday Times,* "as he has so brilliantly demonstrated, are still of the highest order." The next day, as the defence debate continued, Aneurin Bevan accused Churchill of allowing America to dictate Britain's foreign policy, declaring that Churchill had canceled his 1953 Bermuda trip because he knew Eisenhower would not accede to a request to hold talks with the Russians. Churchill's reply stunned the House, for he revealed for the first time in public that he had not gone to Bermuda because "I was struck down by a very sudden illness which paralysed me completely. That is why I had to put it off."[203]

Moments later he tucked his reading glasses into a jacket pocket, gathered up his notes, and departed. He delivered two minor speeches in the House during his final month in office, the last a tribute to Lloyd George on March 28. Though he remained the member of Parliament from Woodford for nine more years, Churchill never again spoke in the House of Commons.

On April 4, Winston and Clementine hosted their last dinner at No. 10. Some fifty guests attended, including Queen Elizabeth and Prince Philip. The other grandees present, Colville wrote, included high government officials, members of Churchill's family, and several dukes and duchesses, including the sixteenth Duke of Norfolk, soon to chair a special top-secret government committee code-named Hope Not and vested with the task of planning Churchill's state funeral. Randolph Churchill attended, and predictably got drunk, at one point haranguing his cousin and Anthony Eden's wife, Clarissa, over a nasty article he had written about Eden for *Punch*. Sir Winston presided over all, attired in his Garter, Order of Merit, and knee breeches. His after-dinner speech took the form of a long toast to the Queen: "I used to enjoy drinking during the years when I was a cavalry subaltern in the reign of your Majesty's great-great-grandmother, Queen Victoria." At the end, he raised his glass *"to the Queen."* Later that night, after the last guests had left, Jock Colville escorted Churchill up to his bedroom. The Old Man sat on his bed, and for several minutes did not speak. Colville imagined Churchill was "contemplating that this was his last night [as P.M.] at Downing Street. Then suddenly he stared at me and said with vehemence, 'I don't believe Anthony can do it.' "[204]

The next evening, Churchill donned his top hat and the frock coat he reserved for such formal occasions and went to Buckingham Palace to resign. Ever since the nineteenth century, an earldom had been the traditional path to the peerage for retired prime ministers who aspired to such titles. But Churchill had no peers, and deserved something more. Thus, the idea of offering him a dukedom was floated, although the Queen was not enthused at creating the first nonroyal duke in eighty years. The most satisfactory outcome for the Palace would be for the offer to be made and for Churchill to decline it. Days earlier, in fact, Churchill had told Colville that if the Queen offered him a dukedom, he would not accept it. Colville passed this information along to the Palace. The Queen indeed made the offer, and Churchill, after a moment's temptation, indeed declined. The Commons was his home, not the House of Lords. He later that night told Colville that he had declined the dukedom because to accept it would have ruined Randolph's political career, for as a Lord, Randolph could not sit in the Commons, from where the sovereign chose the prime minister. In fact, after his 1951 defeat, Randolph Churchill never again stood for office. Of his father, Randolph once said, "Nothing grows under the shadow of a great tree." To the end, the father did what he could to help the son, although Churchill once told one of his private secretaries, "I love Randolph, but I do not like him."[205]

On Wednesday, April 6, Winston and Clementine hosted a tea party at No. 10 for about one hundred of the staff. Late in the afternoon, Churchill left for Chartwell. Clementine, with much to arrange at their London house, stayed behind. Churchill arrived at Chartwell in the gloaming, Mary later wrote, but appeared "in quite good form." A small crowd of neighbors and reporters had gathered outside the house. As Churchill made for the front steps, a reporter called out: How does it feel not to be prime minister?[206]

Churchill replied, "It's always nice to come home."

8

Postscript

1955–1965

Although a general election was not required until 1956, soon after Churchill departed No. 10, Anthony Eden, who wanted to take his case to the people, dissolved Parliament and scheduled elections for late May. Churchill stood for the Commons for the nineteenth time, and was returned to the House in a sweeping Conservative victory on May 27. Eden picked up forty more seats, and the Conservatives this time won a plurality of the popular vote. During the campaign, Churchill was not asked by Eden to make any of the three BBC broadcasts allotted the Tories. The torch had passed.

In mid-May, Soviet foreign minister Molotov informed Harold Macmillan, the new foreign secretary, that Molotov and Soviet premier Nikolai Bulganin, who had succeeded Malenkov, were willing to join in a four-power summit meeting in Geneva. Nikita Khrushchev, too, would attend. Khrushchev, the Ukrainian political boss who had bungled the Kharkov battle in 1942, was now effectively co-leader in the Kremlin and leader of the de-Stalinization effort—the attempt to erase Stalin from Soviet history. President Eisenhower, well aware of Churchill's feelings on the matter, wrote a letter to Churchill in which he expressed wariness of the chances of success in Geneva, adding, "Foster and I know—as does the world—that your courage and vision will be missed at the meeting." The prize Churchill had sought for so long had gone to Eden.[1]

A new man had joined Churchill's private secretariat three years earlier, Anthony Montague Browne. He was not yet thirty at the time, had flown Beaufighters in Burma late in the war, and after coming home had forged a friendship with Jock Colville. Montague Browne, who, like Colville, was officially attached to the Foreign Office, was asked by Harold Macmillan upon Churchill's retirement to stay on with Churchill in order to vet the Old Man's communications with the many foreign leaders who were sure to ask his opinions on myriad matters. The posting, Macmillan assured Montague Browne, shouldn't last more than a year or two. It lasted almost a decade, until the end of Churchill's life. Though the Foreign Office paid Montague Browne's salary, Churchill insisted on repaying the money. Recalled Montague Browne, "Churchill did not want to feel that he was indebted to the government for anything."

Montague Browne titled his memoirs of these years *Long Sunset,* a turn of phrase that applied to both Churchill and the British Empire. He called the portion of the book—about one half—that had to do with Churchill's retirement "Late Afternoon." Yet even as the shadows lengthened, Churchill could not bring himself to fully retire from politics. Montague Browne wrote, "It is undoubtedly true that WSC loved his family deeply. It is also undoubtedly true that they came second to his purposes and his political work. How could it be otherwise?" There were consequences to his wife and children, unintended of course, and it is a perverse irony that Churchill's late afternoon lasted long enough for him to witness them.[2]

After his 1951 election defeat, Randolph never again stood for public office. Instead, he followed in his father's footsteps in the family traditions of the lecture circuit, essay writing, freelance jounalism, and biography. His accomplished biography, *Lord Derby: King of Lancashire,* was published in 1959, and met with critical acclaim. The son, Montague Browne wrote, displayed the same knack for reportage and writing as the father. By then Randolph had begun assembling the papers of his grandfather, Lord Randolph Churchill, in preparation for writing Sir Winston's official biography. Although Churchill had long been inclined to allow Randolph the privilege, he had specifically instructed the trustees of the literary trust to undertake the work only after his death. Randolph, as stubborn as his father, pushed for an early start. Finally, in 1960, Churchill relented. Randolph set to work with the same military precision his father had brought to the task of writing *The Second World War,* and with much the same staff. Yet, recalled the military historian A. J. P. Taylor, Randolph "treated the researchers abominably in his usual arrogant way. He regarded them as quite indistinguishable from the domestic servants." Thus, Randolph's team of researchers underwent frequent turnovers. "They never stayed very long."[3]

The son had inherited the father's cutting wit, but Randolph's came with a serrated edge and did him little good politically, wrote Montague Browne. On one occasion, Montague Browne dissuaded Randolph from following Anthony Eden (whom he despised) to a Washington conference in order to write a no doubt negative magazine story. Randolph: "Oh well, I suppose you're right. I would be the last camel to break the straw's back." Randolph's tastes (as did his sister Sarah's) ran to the extravagant, leading to his asking regularly for financial help from his parents, which meant the Chartwell Trust. The trust purchased him a London house and a three-story redbrick Georgian country house at East Bergholt, Suffolk. Churchill had set up the trust in order to benefit his children, but Clementine resented the children's repeated trips to the well. She believed, Mary later wrote, that "the fruit of Winston's genius and generosity" was being "poured... down the drain" in service to the "fecklessness" of their children. Randolph had married June Osborne in 1948. In 1949, a baby girl arrived—Arabella, named for the First Duke of Marlborough's sister, mistress to James II. But Randolph, wrote Mary with great understatement, "does not seem to have possessed the aptitude for marriage." He and June divorced in 1962. She later committed suicide. Randolph completed two volumes of his father's biography before dying of a heart attack on June 6, 1968, aged fifty-seven. His death, like his life, took place in the shadows: Robert F. Kennedy was murdered on that day. Randolph's passing went little noted.[4]

None of the children but Mary displayed the aptitude for marriage. She remained married to Christopher Soames—made Baron Soames in 1978—for forty years, until his death in 1987. Together they had five children; the oldest, Nicholas, followed his father into government, as the Conservative MP for Bedford.

Sarah and Diana charted the course of their marriages and lives under dark stars. Asked by Montague Browne why the family called Sarah "the Mule," Churchill replied, "Because she's bloody obstinate and she won't breed." During the six years before Churchill retired, Sarah had spent a great deal of her time in the United States pursuing her stage and screen career, with success. She toured the country in a Theatre Guild production of *The Philadelphia Story,* and then appeared in the 1951 Broadway version with Jeffrey Lynn. That same year, she signed on with MGM and starred with Jane Powell, Peter Lawford, and Fred Astaire in *Royal Wedding.* Early in 1952 she made the first of several appearances on NBC's *Hallmark Hall of Fame,* the creation of Joyce Hall, founder of Hallmark Cards, and an admirer of Sir Winston Churchill, with whom Hall struck a financial deal to reproduce Winston's paintings on Hallmark cards. This was the era of live television, and Sarah excelled—in *Amahl and the Night Visitors, Joan of Arc,* and as Ophelia in Hallmark's 1953 two-hour production of *Hamlet.* She had remarried in 1949. As with her first marriage, it was an elopement in the United States, this time at Sea Island, Georgia. The new groom was Anthony Beauchamp, who had served as a war artist and photographer in Burma during the war. Upon first meeting Beauchamp in early 1949, Churchill had taken an immediate dislike to him, for reasons unknown, which may explain Sarah's decision to have the wedding ceremony performed in Georgia. Her sister Mary—Lady Soames—called Sarah the "sunshine" in her parents' lives; Anthony Montague Browne anointed her "the brightest star."[5]

But by the late 1950s, Sarah's star was dimming and her marriage to Anthony Beauchamp failing. It ended utterly in July 1957 when Beauchamp committed suicide by swallowing a fistful of sleeping pills. Beauchamp's death came almost exactly a decade after Gil Winant, hopelessly in love with Sarah, went home to America and killed himself with a gunshot to the head. Never able to control her drinking, Sarah began a long descent into alcoholism. The next year she was arrested in Malibu and fined fifty dollars for public drunkenness. Her father lived long enough to read the newspaper accounts of three more arrests for drunkenness in Britain and a ten-day stay in jail for violating her probation. In a 1959 letter to Clementine written while he was on the Riviera, he attributed Sarah's decline to "the difficulties which are common to women at the change of life." Finally, in 1962, it appeared Sarah might have found happiness when she met and married Henry Touchet-Jesson, the twenty-third Baron Audley. Fifteen months later, Audley died of a massive coronary. Sarah's film and stage career was at an end. In 1967 she wrote a short and lyrical tribute to her father: *A Thread in the Tapestry*. In 1981 she published her autobiography, *Keep on Dancing*, in which she discussed her battles with alcohol in poignant and honest terms. She died an alcoholic in 1982, aged sixty-seven.[6]

Diana suffered the same bouts of depression, fatigue, and nervous tension as her mother, yet Clementine, rather than find common cause with her daughter, had always maintained a discreet emotional distance. Diana had had a nervous breakdown in 1953 and was on the verge of another at about the time her father retired. Unlike Randolph and Sarah, she did not find release from her pain in the bottle. It was Diana who comforted Randolph and Sarah during their regular crises; it was Diana alone who attended Henry Audley's funeral. She was a steady daughter and wife, married since 1935 to Duncan Sandys, who was made minister of defence in 1957 and secretary of state for Commonwealth relations in 1960. They separated in 1956; in 1960, Sandys divorced Diana and soon remarried. Sympathetic to those in severe emotional distress, Diana joined the Samaritans in 1962, an organization dedicated to round-the-clock help for anyone contemplating suicide.

Sometime during the night of October 19–20, 1963, Diana swallowed a massive overdose of sleeping pills and died. Her sister Mary delivered the news to Clementine, herself hospitalized and under sedation that month, on the verge of a nervous breakdown. And it fell to Mary to deliver the news to her father, who, dulled now by old age, only took it in slowly and "then withdrew into a great and distant silence." Both father and mother were too weak to attend Diana's funeral, held in the little churchyard at Bladon, where Churchill's parents were buried.[7]

The theme of the latter portion of Lord Moran's memoirs, *Churchill: The Struggle for Survival, 1940–1965*, is one of Churchill brought low in his retirement years by the relentless onslaught of the Black Dog of depression. It is a tale—exaggerated and incomplete—of Churchill's journey to decrepitude and the slow wasting away of his physical and mental powers. Among the chapter headings are "Swan-song," "Depression," "The Flesh Was Weak," and "The Dying Gladiator." Moran chronicles Churchill's battle with carbuncles in 1955 (which Churchill believed were "malignant"), pneumonia in 1958, and two minor strokes in 1959. Churchill was not afraid of death, yet minor illnesses provoked bouts of anxiety. Moran, Montague Browne later wrote, was always ready and willing to treat his most important—his only—patient.

Although Moran claimed that Churchill had approved his publishing his medical memoirs, he had not secured the approval in writing. The family, then and since, has held that against Moran. His narrative of Churchill's first five years of retirement is rife with scenes depicting Churchill's loneliness and despondency. Moran called the decade of 1954–1964 "a long chronicle of despair." These were years, he wrote, that found Churchill giving up reading; he had not and in fact polished off *War and Peace, Tom Jones,* Scott's *Rob Roy,* and Macaulay's essay on Milton, among many other works. A stack of books borrowed from the local library always occupied Churchill's night table, and the turnover was swift.

Churchill loved his days outside, painting and feeding his menagerie, including Toby, a budgerigar Churchill had received on his eightieth birthday. Where Churchill went, Toby went, including the Riviera. Moran suggested that Churchill teach Toby the Chartwell phone number in case the bird escaped. Churchill replied that he did not know his own phone number. Alas, Toby gained his freedom in 1960 after finding an open window at the Hôtel de Paris. At the end of a Chartwell day, the Old Man enjoyed the movies regularly screened at 9:15 P.M. sharp: *The Bridge on the River Kwai, The Longest Day, The Guns of Navarone,* the 1958 musical *Gigi,* and all the Disney films. Moran wrote that these were the years that found the Old Man spending his days "staring into the fire, giving it a prod with his stick when the room got cold" as the Black Dog of depression hovered nearby. These were "sad years of mounting decrepitude" when Churchill became "the chief mourner at his own protracted funeral."[8]

That was largely untrue during Churchill's first five or six years of retirement, and only partially true during Churchill's last two years. Montague Browne writes that in his thirteen years of service to Churchill, he never once heard the Old Man refer to the "Black Dog." Churchill mourned the passing of the British Empire, recalled Montague Browne, and was profoundly saddened by the dangerous state of world affairs. He expressed his worries in that regard to Montague Browne as only Churchill could: "I always feared that mass pressure in the United States might force them to use their H-bombs while the Russians still had not got any. It's always been a tendency of the masses to drop their Hs." Churchill's melancholy, Montague Browne wrote, was "objective, detached, and sadly logical"; it did not stem from any sort of "subjective mood of deep depression."[9]

Retirement found Churchill busy publishing his four-volume *History of the English-Speaking Peoples*. He regularly attended dinners at his private dining society, the Other Club, and visited Harrow at least once each year. In 1956 he was invited by Eden to lunch at No. 10 in order to meet Bulganin and Khrushchev, co-leaders in the Kremlin, although Churchill told Moran that week that he thought Khrushchev would soon emerge as the real power. Meals, as always, were splendid affairs, and Churchill's intake of roast beef, brandy, whisky, and cigars remained undiminished. He painted dozens of landscapes that met with critical acclaim. The eminent British art critic and historian Ernst H. Gombrich wrote in the *Atlantic Monthly* that Churchill's essay *Painting as a Pastime* contained ideas "so acute and so profound... I could do no better than to build them into the fabric of my book, *Art and Illusion*."[10]

His wanderlust, too, remained undiminished. Churchill's post–No. 10 travels took him to Sicily, Morocco, the French Riviera numerous times, the Italian Riviera, Rome and Paris and New York. In 1959 he journeyed by jet to New York and on to Washington for another stay at the White House, and then to the Gettysburg battlefield in the company of President Eisenhower, who made his home nearby in the shadow of the Alleghenies. On that excursion, Churchill offered a running narrative of the Battle of Gettysburg as Eisenhower's helicopter hovered over the battlefield—the Old Man recounting Union and Confederate troop deployments, the names of the divisions and corps commanders, the time of day and outcome of each skirmish fought. His gait was slower, his hearing almost gone, but the great mind remained strong.

Later that year he stood for election in Woodford, and was returned to the House. And late in 1959, he went to Cambridge, where he planted two oak trees and laid the foundation stone of Churchill College. At his behest, the Prof and Jock Colville had been raising subscriptions for the college since 1955, when Churchill, with MIT in mind, proposed that a similar institution for science and technology be built in Britain. Churchill contributed the first £25,000, and by the end of the decade, more than three million pounds had been raised. Churchill College opened in 1964. The charter contained a clause—suggested by Clementine and endorsed by Churchill—calling for the admission of women on the same basis as men. In 1972 Churchill College became the first of the Oxford and Cambridge colleges to admit women on an equal basis, and allow them to take up residence at the schools.[11]

In January 1957, Queen Elizabeth summoned Churchill to Buckingham Palace to help guide her in the selection of a new prime minister—either Harold Macmillan or Rab Butler. The need to decide arose because of the resignation of Anthony Eden, whose health had collapsed, a condition brought about by the disaster that had befallen Britain during the Suez crisis of late 1956.

It began during the summer, when Egypt's President Nasser nationalized the Suez Canal in retaliation for the United States' and Britain's pulling their financial backing from the great Aswan Dam project in protest of Nasser's increasingly friendly relations with the U.S.S.R. and Egypt's recognition of the People's Republic of China in July. The nationalization of the canal was in violation of an agreement Egypt had signed with France and Britain in 1954. On October 29, the Israeli army launched a preemptive strike into the Sinai; the British and French knew and approved it in advance. Thus, with Israel and Egypt at war and the integrity of the canal zone threatened, Britain and France intervened. In fact, Eden's real objective was to depose Nasser, whom Eden hated for his pan-Arabic nationalism and the French despised for the aid he was rendering to the Algerian rebels. Forty-eight hours after the Israelis attacked, the RAF struck Nasser's forces, followed three days later by a French and British landing at Port Said, on the north end of the canal, which they quickly took. America had not been notified in advance of the operation, and President Eisenhower was furious. Within days, the United States joined the Soviet Union in voting for UN resolutions condemning the British and French. Most Britons questioned the morality of the strike, Colville later wrote, but all believed success was assured. It was not. On November 6, Eden, his cabinet cowed by the American threat to gut the value of the pound by flooding financial markets with sterling bonds, ordered a cease-fire (without informing the French).[12]

Thus Churchill's audience with the Queen. He advised her to choose Macmillan, later telling friends he did so because Macmillan was the older and more experienced man. But all knew that Butler, though loyal in his service to Churchill since 1940, had been a man of Chamberlain, and Munich, and at the time had told Colville that Churchill's criticism of Chamberlain was "vulgar." In the years since, Butler, in private conversations, had made clear his belief that Churchill was a political opportunist and that he, Butler, would be a suitable choice as prime minister. The Queen chose Macmillan. Eden retired to his country house, Rose Bower, in Wiltshire, to write his memoirs. He remained a close friend of Churchill's, and Churchill remained loyal to Eden, who, he told Moran, had "been bitched" by the cabinet when it refused to carry through on the Suez affair. Over dinner Churchill told Colville he considered the Suez operation "the most-ill-conceived and ill-executed imaginable." Asked by Colville what he would have done, the Old Man replied, "I would never have dared; and if I had dared, I would certainly never have dared stop."[13]

Nine months later, on October 4, 1957, Soviet scientists bolted a 184-pound metal sphere that had been polished to a high sheen atop a two-stage R-7 Semyorka rocket and launched it out of the stratosphere and into space, where it dutifully began to tumble around the earth, one pass each ninety or so minutes. The launch was a complete surprise; nobody in the West had seen it coming. They could see it now, overhead. The Soviets called it *Sputnik 1;* it was about the size of a soccer ball. The Western press termed the device "an earth satellite." *Sputnik* was outfitted with a radio beacon, which broadcast back to earth a steady signal. American scientists claimed it was transmitting secret messages. It wasn't. The signal was gibberish, but its message was clear: we can reach you. Several times a day *Sputnik* passed over the United States and Western Europe, just visible with binoculars at dawn and dusk (which is why the Soviets had polished it). Clementine, having returned to England from Max Beaverbrook's Riviera villa, La Capponcina, scribbled a quick note to Winston, now ensconced on the French Riviera at La Pausa, the villa of his European literary agent, Emery Reves. "What do you think of the earth satellite? I heard it on the wireless—it sounded ominous."[14]

It was. The temperature of the Cold War was approaching absolute zero. The Soviet rocket that had launched *Sputnik* had a range of five thousand miles, quite sufficient to reach London. Worse, as the Soviets demonstrated a month later with a second launch, it could carry a payload of more than one thousand pounds, the weight of a small hydrogen bomb, although the payload for this launch consisted only of a dog named Laika, whom the American press dubbed Muttnik. Harold Nicolson believed Britons cared more for the dog than for the implications—men in rockets carrying atomic bombs orbiting the earth in search of targets. Indeed, members of the Dumb Friends League proposed gathering outside the Soviet embassy and observing two minutes of silence. Such was the West's paranoia that the *New York Times* ran a story in which Dr. Fred L. Whipple, director of the Smithsonian Astrophysical Observatory in Cambridge, Massachusetts, claimed that it was "entirely possible the Russians already have a rocket on the way to the moon," where it might detonate an H-bomb during a lunar eclipse later in the week, perhaps in celebration of the fortieth anniversary of Lenin's November 1917 revolution. The Semyorka rocket's accuracy was thought to be wobbly, perhaps within three or four miles of a target at best. Yet accuracy no longer mattered. H-bombs had joined horseshoes and hand grenades, where close counts. Months earlier, President Eisenhower had asked Horace Rowan Gaither, of the Ford Foundation, to form a commission to study America's missile capabilities. One month after *Sputnik* went aloft, Gaither's recommendations were leaked to the press: build more missiles, quickly, and build fallout shelters.[15]

With *Sputnik* speeding along through the heavens, the rocket age and the atomic age had merged, as Churchill in his last major address in the House predicted would happen. But Sir Winston Churchill was no longer a participant in the unfolding of the story. In his reply to Clementine he wrote that *Sputnik* itself did not trouble him but the Soviet gains in science and technology did. "We must struggle on," he wrote, "and [look] to the union with America."

The world press did not think to ask Churchill for his opinion on the earth satellite. The press by then was interested only in news that pertained to Churchill's health. Churchill had spent his entire life creating an identity from his own audacious imagination, which, as Oscar Wilde observed, was the best way to get through life without suffering through it all. Churchill had made his dream a reality; he had imagined himself into Sir Winston Leonard Spencer Churchill, the greatest statesman of the twentieth century. He had fought the monster—Hitler—without himself becoming a monster. He had prevailed on his countrymen during his final year at No. 10 to build the hydrogen bomb, in order to keep the Soviet dictators behind their Iron Curtain. Yet by 1958, new ages and new generations—the atomic, the space, the beat, the rock and roll, the television—had overtaken and bypassed Sir Winston. With no further role to play in history's unfolding, he became a spectator.

On September 12, 1958, Winston and Clementine celebrated their fiftieth wedding anniversary at La Capponcina. Clementine had finally come to accept Max, but she despised the Riviera, especially when her husband did not fare well at the Monte Carlo casino. On September 22, Churchill and Clementine embarked on a Mediterranean cruise as the guests of Aristotle Onassis on board Onassis's yacht *Christina,* a 325-foot, 1,850-ton converted Canadian frigate—a destroyer in American parlance. Onassis, Churchill told Colville after first meeting the shipping magnate in 1956, "was a man of mark." Onassis believed likewise of Churchill. The September voyage was the first of eight cruises Churchill made aboard the *Christina* over the next five years, in the Aegean, the Mediterranean, and to the West Indies in 1960 and 1961, when Onassis set a course from the Caribbean up the U.S. east coast to New York City in order that Churchill could pay one more visit to his other country.[16]

Onassis joined the small circle of family, friends, and staff who tended to Churchill's care and comfort. Any given day might find Bernard Montgomery stopping by Chartwell for tea, Randolph and Evelyn Waugh for dinner, the "wollygogs" for a tour of the Chartwell farms. Requests for interviews, and there were many in the first years, were all screened by Montague Browne, who in the final years composed Churchill's few brief addresses and wrote letters for the Great Man's signature. Two nurses attended to Churchill's needs after 1958; two typists stood by for dictation, cleaned his brushes and palettes, and helped manage his and Clementine's social calendar. A Mr. Shaw—"a Labour man but quite a nice fellow," Churchill told a nurse—ran the Chartwell movie projector. Churchill never dined alone; if no family or friends were on hand, Montague Browne took a seat at the table, and did so for fifteen straight nights during one stretch. In the bargain he listened in awe as Churchill delivered fifteen dissertations on British history. Dinner conversation with Churchill, Montague Browne wrote, "was a wonder and a delight" and "never, ever dull." All who surrounded the Great Man were, in effect, "in service" to Sir Winston. Churchill's bodyguard, Detective Sergeant Edmund Murray, remained nearby at all times, never more than a room away. Lord Moran was expected to appear at once if summoned by Churchill, who did so frequently, often to complain of imaginary ailments. On one occasion Churchill phoned the doctor with the worrisome news that he had taken his temperature only to find it read sixty-six degrees. Montague Browne overheard Churchill's end of the conversation: "What the hell do you mean, in that case I'm dead." A long pause ensued, then, "Well, that is to say, ninety-six, but I would still like you to come around."[17]

His last charge in defense of the Empire came in November 1958, in Paris, when Charles de Gaulle (French premier at the time and elected President of the Fifth Republic in December) awarded him the Croix de la Libération. Churchill made a brief speech, telling the assembled in English that he would not "subject you to the ordeals of darker days" by making his remarks in French. He anointed de Gaulle "the symbol of the soul of France and of the unbreakable integrity of her spirit in adversity." He closed with: "The future is uncertain, but we can be sure that if Britain and France, who for so long have been the vanguard of the Western civilization, stand together, with our Empires, our American friends... then we have grounds for sober confidence and high hope. I thank you all for the honour you have done me. *Vive la France!*"[18]

His mention of "our Empires" was ironic. By 1958, the French had lost Indochina: Cambodia had gained independence in 1953; in South Vietnam the corrupt premier, Ngo Dinh Diem, was desperately trying to prop up his regime with the help of newly arrived American military advisers. Algeria, too, was violently departing the French fold. There, diverse revolutionary armies—united only by their desire to drive out the French—fought the French army from 1954 until final victory in 1962, a war that claimed the lives of at least three hundred thousand Algerians and sent at least one million descendants of French settlers into exile.

The British, meanwhile, were losing lesser jewels in their crown: in July, Iraqi army officers overthrew and murdered King Faisal II, the Hashemite king whose father the British had put on the throne in 1932. The new regime, backed by Nasser and manifesting a pro-Moscow bent, ordered the RAF out of its airbase near Baghdad. The Gold Coast had bolted the empire in 1957, and it became the independent nation of Ghana. Kenya did likewise in 1963, after the decade-long Mau Mau uprising that had claimed at least 20,000 Kenyan lives, and the lives of scores of white European settlers. Among the Mau Mau victims were thirty-two British settlers, including small children, whose deaths at the hands of the Mau Mau had inflamed Britain, and Churchill. The British response was brutal. At one point Churchill wanted to read the Mau Mau initiation oath—he called it "incredibly filthy"—in the House. It called for eating the flesh of disinterred bodies and the eyeballs of enemies, fornicating with sheep, and drinking the "Kaberichia cocktail," a mixture of semen and menstrual blood. He settled for giving MPs a printed version. In Kenya, the British made administering the oath a capital offense; more than one thousand suspected Mau Maus were hanged.[19]

Churchill remained an unrepentant champion of the British Empire to the end. Months before he retired, President Eisenhower suggested—with some nerve—that "a fitting climax" to Churchill's career would be to deliver a valedictory speech proclaiming that colonialism was "on the way out as a relationship between peoples." Churchill's reply was immediate and caustic: "I read with great interest all you have written me about what is called colonialism; namely, bringing forth backward races and opening up the jungles." He declared that in India, "with all its history, religion, and ancient forms of despotic rule, Britain has a story to tell which will look quite well against the background of the coming hundred years." He added that the sentiments and policies Eisenhower advocated "are in full accord with the policy now being pursued in all the Colonies of the British Empire." Yet: "In this I must say that I am a laggard. I am a bit skeptical about universal suffrage for the Hottentots even if refined by proportional representation."

The final few years of retirement formed "a desultory tale," wrote Montague Browne, speaking as much for himself as for Churchill. By the early 1960s, Montague Browne found that he needed only an hour or two each day to address his official, diplomatic duties in service to Churchill. As the months and years passed by, Montague Browne—and sometimes his wife and daughter, or the Colvilles—drifted with Churchill, from one Riviera villa to the next, from one port of call to the next aboard *Christina*. Onassis invited luminous muses aboard for Churchill's entertainment, including Onassis's mistress Maria Callas, Gracie Fields, and Greta Garbo. "There is no doubt," recalled Churchill's grandson and namesake, "that my grandfather enjoyed the company of beautiful women." Near the end of the previous century, Churchill had written his mother after his first Atlantic crossing: "I do not contemplate ever taking a sea voyage for pleasure." He had been especially put off on that voyage by the complete lack of any "nice people" on board. Now nearing the end of his life, he found great pleasure roaming the high seas on *Christina* in the company of his merry companions. On one voyage, Churchill proposed that all the men grow mustaches; they did. Montague Browne thought Churchill's "did not become him." On another, Montague Browne overheard Churchill address a dolphin that was swimming alongside the ship: "I do wish I could communicate with you." It was a good life.[20]

The 1961 voyage to the Caribbean on *Christina* marked Churchill's sixteenth—and last—journey to the United States. A wild storm blew off Cape Hatteras as *Christina* made for New York along the Carolina coast. Churchill, now eighty-six, insisted on sitting atop a piano in the lounge in order to witness the fury outside. He did so supported by four strong Greek seamen. He was Churchill; it could not be otherwise. When high seas struck on these voyages and made dining at a table impossible, Churchill took his meals in bed, propped up by numerous pillows, his bottle of Pol Roger held firmly between his thighs. Onassis and Montague Browne would join him, sitting cross-legged on the floor, with their bottles of Pol Roger held between their thighs. On board *Christina* Churchill could indulge in his love of long games of bezique, cigars, and postprandial brandies. Yet by 1961, Churchill's fire had dimmed enough that Montague Browne, upon *Christina*'s docking in New York City, had to politely decline when President John F. Kennedy telephoned with an invitation for Churchill to spend a few days at the White House. It was time to go home.[21]

When, in early November 1895, twenty-year-old subaltern Winston Churchill disembarked the Cunard steamship *Etruria* at a Hudson River pier and set foot for the first time in his mother's native land, horse-drawn omnibuses plied the dusty macadam roads of New York City. The Ninth Avenue and Third Avenue elevated railroads ran up the island (and spewed glowing embers upon hapless pedestrians below), but the first New York subway would not be operating for almost a decade. London was then ushering in its third decade of underground rail service between Paddington and King's Cross, but young Churchill had not availed himself of this form of public transport and would do so only once during the remainder of his life.

When Churchill first came to American shores, Henry Ford had yet to successfully propel his quadricycle by means of a gasoline engine, and the Dodge brothers were still building bicycles in Ontario, Canada. So, too, in Sheffield, England, was Thomas Humber, whose armored motorcars Churchill relied on during the Blitz, though he would rarely actually operate one in his lifetime—not because he was an aging Victorian man who did not understand the mechanics of automobiles but because he was a Victorian man who believed it only proper that liveried drivers drove carriages, including motorized carriages. Churchill was approaching early middle age when Orville Wright, at Kitty Hawk, took aloft the spruce-and-wire flying machine that he and his brother Wilbur had built. By then the earliest infernal contraptions built by Thomas Humber and Henry Ford were petrifying cows and horses and old women on both sides of the Atlantic. In the motorcar Churchill saw the genesis of the tank; in the airplane, the fighter plane and the bomber. In the early decades of the twentieth century, he mused in magazine articles on the nature of rockets, atomic power, and television. He analyzed the moral and political implications of every new technology brought forth in the first half of the twentieth century. The *Etruria* had carried sail on the 1895 voyage lest its steam engines fail during the ten-day Atlantic crossing. Churchill departed his other country for the final time on April 14, 1961, on board a Pan American World Airways Boeing 707 that, pushed along by the jet stream seven miles high, carried him home across the Atlantic at more than five hundred miles per hour.

Moran's memoir is correct in one regard; after Churchill suffered a serious bout of pneumonia in 1958, his ailments became more frequent and more serious—the 1959 strokes followed in 1960 by a hairline spinal fracture from a fall in his bedroom. Moran ordered bed rest on that occasion. Churchill refused. Caring for Churchill resulted in "open warfare" between the nurses and the patient, nurse Roy Howells recalled. A big blow came in June 1962, when Churchill slipped and fell in his suite at the Hôtel de Paris. While drifting in and out of consciousness, Churchill told Montague Brown that he wanted to die in England. Prime Minister Harold Macmillan dispatched an RAF Comet to bring the Great Man home. The press expected the worst. Montague Browne believed he would have to instruct the Duke of Norfolk to set Operation Hope Not—Churchill's state funeral—in motion. On the flight to London, Churchill, heavily sedated, awoke, and muttered to Montague Browne: "I don't think I'll go back to that place, it's unlucky. First Toby, and then this." Montague Browne had forgotten Toby, the budgerigar, but Churchill had not. The body was frail, but not the wit. On his arrival in London, he flashed the "V" sign from his stretcher. He underwent surgery to insert a pin in his hip. After three weeks in the hospital, he left for 28 Hyde Park Gate, where within three months he could stroll unaided to the little gardens behind the house.[22]

He told Moran he felt he was "lingering," and by 1962 he was. Prof—Lord Cherwell—had died in 1957, at seventy-one. He had served Churchill as science adviser and loyal friend since 1920. Brendan Bracken, fifty-seven, followed Cherwell in 1958 after suffering the horrific effects of throat cancer and botched cobalt radiation therapy. During his 1959 trip to America, Churchill visited Foster Dulles and George Marshall in the hospital, the former dying of cancer, the latter of the effects of two strokes and kidney failure. Two weeks later, Dulles—whom Churchill once described as "the only case of a bull I know who carries his china closet with him"—was dead. Marshall went in October. Alanbrooke went in 1963, but not before publishing his wartime diaries, which hurt Churchill deeply. Another, though lesser, link to the past was broken in 1964 when Montague Phippen Porch, three years Churchill's junior, died. Porch had been Jennie Churchill's third and last husband, and therefore Sir Winston's stepfather. The hardest blow—after Diana's death—came on June 9, 1964, when his friend of nearly six decades, Max Beaverbrook, died of cancer, at eighty-five. Montague Browne began his narrative of these final years: "This is a story of decline." The decline came in 1963 and 1964 in fits and starts, relapses and recoveries, but it came, relentless and unyielding.[23]

Churchill would much prefer to have someone put an old dance hall tune or martial march on the gramophone than turn on the television. He did enjoy an occasional episode of *Sea Hunt,* starring Lloyd Bridges, but otherwise believed, as he told Moran, that "this bloody invention will do harm to the society and to the race." But on April 9, 1963, he watched with satisfaction as a live satellite feed from the Rose Garden of the White House brought him images of President Kennedy bestowing upon him, by Act of Congress, honorary U.S. citizenship. Churchill became only the second person—after the Marquis de Lafayette—to be accorded the honor. The Old Man, too ill to attend the ceremony, was represented by Randolph and young Winston. Seven weeks later, he embarked on his eighth and final voyage aboard *Christina* a tour of the Aegean. On July 4 he left Athens for London by air; *Christina,* was then made ready for its next guest, First Lady Jacqueline Kennedy, who sought a peaceful autumn interlude after the death that summer of her infant son, Patrick. She also sought rest and relaxation in order to prepare herself for the fall campaign season in the United States, which would include a trip to Texas in November. And so it came to pass that Churchill's television again saw use late in the evening of Friday, November 22. That night Churchill sat in silence for a long time before the fire. Yet, as with Diana's death a month earlier, the full impact of the president's murder was dulled by Churchill's advanced age.[24]

As 1964 came on, Churchill still served as the member of Parliament from Woodford, but only infrequently took his place on the front bench, below the gangway, where he had sat during the Wilderness Years of the 1930s. He visited the House of Commons for the last time on July 27, and soon thereafter announced that he would not stand for Woodford in that October's general election. He left Chartwell for the last time in October, taking up residence at 27–28 Hyde Park Gate, where a ground-floor bedroom had been prepared for him. On November 30, he celebrated his ninetieth birthday in the company of his family, the Colvilles, and the Montague Brownes. Champagne flowed all day; a basket of Whitstable oysters was hauled in. Cakes arrived all day from well-wishers, and 70,000 cards and telegrams from around the world. By midafternoon, hundreds of Londoners crowded the street in front of the house. A news photographer snapped a shot of a smiling Sir Winston, attired in a siren suit, peering from behind a parted curtain. Dinner—and brandy and cigars—carried into the early hours of December 1. Ten days later Churchill made an appearance at the Other Club; it was to be his last.

Christmas was a subdued affair. Churchill's gift to Montague Browne was his six-volume war memoir. A few days later, Montague Browne asked the Old Man to sign the books. Churchill managed to sign his full name in the first volume; by the sixth he could only scrawl "W." They were the last papers he signed. Now the Great Man did indeed spend long hours staring into the fireplace. Yet he still took lunch with Clementine, and he still took his cigar and brandy after dinner.[25]

But on January 9 he refused both.

His nurses helped him to bed that night. He was not to leave it again.

On the twelfth—Churchill was by then unconscious—doctors Moran and Brain diagnosed a stroke, and informed the family to prepare for the worst, which the doctors believed would likely come very soon. But they underestimated the strength of their patient. Days passed, and then a week. Old friends and colleagues came by to pay their respects. Violet Bonham Carter stopped in, but only for the briefest of moments: "Goodbye, Winston," she said, standing at the foot of his bed. Then she turned and walked out.

Early on a January day about a dozen years earlier, Jock Colville brought a minor matter of state to Churchill's attention, as the Old Man shaved. Churchill turned to Colville, and said: "Today is the twenty-fourth of January. It is the day my father died. It is the day that I shall die too."

And on January 24, 1965, he did.[26]

Churchill's coffin lay in state at Westminster Hall for three days and three nights. More than 320,000 people filed past the catafalque, the silent queue of men and women and children threading through Parliament Square and on across Westminster Bridge. On the bleak, cold morning of Sunday, January 30, the coffin, covered by the Union Jack, was borne from the hall on the shoulders of eight Grenadier Guards. It was placed on a gun carriage drawn by one hundred Royal Navy seamen and flanked by the guard of honor nearly one hundred strong, in bearskins and greatcoats. Randolph and eight young Churchill men took their places behind the gun carriage. Before and behind, companies of troops from storied regiments—from the Hussars, from the RAF, from the army, in khaki, and the Royal Marines, in blue—stood at attention awaiting the order to march. The Horse Guard in their red jackets waited on their impatient steeds. Hundreds of thousands of Britons lined the Strand and Fleet Street and the roads to Ludgate Hill and to St. Paul's, where the Archbishop of Canterbury, in his purple robes, stood atop the steps and awaited the procession. Shortly after 9:45 the first of ninety cannons in Hyde Park fired its salute. The Earl Marshal of England, in greatcoat and cocked hat, raised his baton.

Then, to the haunting beat of a single drum, the procession began the journey to St Paul's. Only twice in the past 112 years had a nonroyal personage been so honored with a state funeral: the Duke of Wellington in 1852 and Gladstone in 1898. Queen Victoria attended neither funeral, but Queen Elizabeth II honored Churchill by her presence in St. Paul's. She was joined by representatives from more than 110 nations, including four kings, a queen, five heads of state, and sixteen prime ministers. Charles de Gaulle, wearing a plain kepi and simple uniform, unadorned with insignia, medals, or ribbons, stood a head taller than all present as the great imperial ceremony began.[27]

From St. Paul's, the coffin was taken by motor launch up the Thames to Waterloo Station. There it was put aboard one of five Pullman coaches hauled by the Battle of Britain–class locomotive *Winston S. Churchill* for the sixty-mile journey to the Oxfordshire village of Bladon and the little churchyard of St. Martin's, within sight of the spires of Blenheim Palace, where the story had begun. Lord Moran, finding in the end his literary voice, wrote:

> And at Bladon, in a country churchyard, in the stillness of a winter evening, in the presence of his family and a few friends, Winston Churchill was committed to the English earth, which in his finest hour, he had held inviolate.[28]

Eight months later, on the twenty-fifth anniversary of the Battle of Britain, the Dean and Chapter of Westminster Abbey, at the request of the Queen and Parliament, placed a sixty-by-seventy-six-inch polished green-marble slab in the floor of that thousand-year-old monument to English history. All who enter cannot help but to see it there, in the nave, just a few feet inside the great west doors. Engraved upon it are the words:

REMEMBER
WINSTON
CHURCHILL

SOURCE NOTES

ABBREVIATIONS AND SHORT TITLES USED IN THESE NOTES

C&R-TCC	*Churchill and Roosevelt: The Complete Correspondence,* 3 vols., edited by Warren F. Kimball. Princeton, 1984.
CAB	British Cabinet Documents, Public Record Office, Kew.
ChP	Churchill Papers, Churchill College, Cambridge, U.K.
Hansard	*Record of Parliamentary Debates* (Hansard).
NYT	*New York Times.*
Times	*The Times* of London.
TWY	*Harold Nicolson: The War Years 1939–1945,* vol. 2 of *Diaries and Letters,* edited by Nigel Nicolson. New York, 1967.
W&C-TPL	*Winston and Clementine: The Personal Letters of the Churchills,* edited by Mary Soames. New York, 2001.
WM/[name]; PFR/ [name]	Author interviews.
WSCHCS	*Winston S. Churchill: His Complete Speeches,* edited by Robert Rhodes James, vols. VI (1935–1942), VII (1943–1949), and VIII (1950–1963). London, 1974.

The Official Biography of Winston Spencer Churchill, by Martin Gilbert (Boston, 1966–1988), is cited as follows:

GILBERT 6	Volume 6. *Finest Hour 1939–1941*
GILBERT 7	Volume 7. *Road to Victory 1941–1945*
GILBERT 8	Volume 8. *Never Despair 1945–1965*
Cv/2	Companion volume to Gilbert 6 (May–December 1940)
Cv/3	Companion volume to Gilbert 6 and Gilbert 7 (1941)

The Second World War, by Winston S. Churchill (Boston, 1983), is cited as follows:

WSC 1	Volume 1. *Gathering Storm*
WSC 2	Volume 2. *Their Finest Hour*
WSC 3	Volume 3. *The Grand Alliance*
WSC 4	Volume 4. *The Hinge of Fate*
WSC 5	Volume 5. *Closing the Ring*
WSC 6	Volume 6. *Triumph and Tragedy*

Preamble

1. WM/Sir Ian Jacob, 11/12/80.
2. John Wheeler-Bennett, *Action This Day: Working with Churchill* (London, 1968), 140; Cv/3, 267, 387; Kay Halle, *Irrepressible Churchill: Stories, Sayings and Impressions of Sir Winston Churchill* (London, 1985), 171.
3. Wheeler-Bennett, *Action,* 53–56; PFR/Winston S. Churchill, 5/04 ("summer sunshine"); GILBERT 6, 1214–15 (recollection of Elizabeth Layton).
4. John Colville, *The Fringes of Power: 10 Downing Street Diaries 1939–1955* (New York, 1985), 406; Lord Moran, *Churchill: Taken from the Diaries of Lord Moran* (Boston, 1966), 451; Halle, *Irrepressible Churchill,* 133; Cv/3, 1309, 1471 (Baldwin family); TWY, 307.
5. Mary Soames, *Clementine Churchill: The Biography of a Marriage* (New York, 2003), 383.
6. Wheeler-Bennett, *Action,* 79, 140.
7. WM/Jock Colville, 10/14/80; Colville, *Fringes,* 434; WSCHCS, 7912; Winston Churchill, *My Early Life: 1874–1904* (New York, 1996), 112.
8. Colville, *Fringes,* 170–71; Wheeler-Bennett, *Action,* 93.
9. Moran, *Diaries,* 265.
10. Anthony Montague Browne, *Long Sunset* (London, 1996), 118; Walter H. Thompson, *Assignment: Churchill* (New York, 1953), 84.
11. Thompson, *Assignment: Churchill,* 84; WM/Sir Robert Boothby, 10/16/80.
12. WM/G. M. Thompson, 10/24/80; Colville, *Fringes,* 217; WSC 6, 752.
13. WM/G. M. Thompson, 10/24/80.
14. WM/G. M. Thompson, 10/24/80; Colville, *Fringes,* 136, 142–43, 231; E. L. Spears, *Assignment to Catastrophe,* 2 vols. (New York, 1955), 1:154; WM/Kathleen Hill, 11/4/80; WM/Jock Colville, 10/14/80.
15. Wheeler-Bennett, *Action,* 153; Colville, *Fringes,* 195–96; WSC 6, 733 ("foreign names were made for Englishmen . . .").
16. Robert E. Sherwood, *Roosevelt and Hopkins: An Intimate History* (New York, 1948), 688.
17. Wheeler-Bennett, *Action,* 182–83; WM/Cecily ("Chips") Gemmell, 7/10/80 (Johnnie Walker Red and daily routine); PFR/Winston S. Churchill, 3/04.
18. Colville, *Fringes,* 417; Sherwood, *Roosevelt and Hopkins,* 24; WM/Sir Ian Jacob, 11/12/80.
19. Colville, *Fringes,* 319; Alex Danchev and Daniel Todman, eds., *Field Marshal Lord Alanbrooke: War Diaries 1939–1945* (Berkeley, 2003), 637.
20. Martin Gilbert, *Winston Churchill: The Wilderness Years* (New York, 1984), 42–44; WM/Cecily ("Chips") Gemmell, 7/10/80; *NYT,* 5/5/09; Warren Kimball, *Finest Hour,* spring 2007, 31–33.
21. WM/Oscar Nemon, 1980.
22. WM/Kathleen Hill, 11/4/80; Colville, *Fringes,* 163–65.
23. WM/Kathleen Hill, 11/4/80; WM/John Martin, 10/23/80; Thompson, *Assignment: Churchill,* 179; WM/Cecily ("Chips") Gemmell, 7/10/80; Moran, *Diaries,* 360.
24. John H. Peck, "The Working Day," *Atlantic Monthly,* 3/65.
25. F. H. Hinsley et al., *British Intelligence in the Second World War,* 5 vols. (London, 1979).
26. Wheeler-Bennett, *Action,* 20, 23.
27. Colville, *Fringes,* 130.

28. Tom Hickman, *Churchill's Bodyguard* (London, 2005), 130; Colville, *Fringes,* 223.
29. WM/Jock Colville, 10/14/80; WM/John Martin, 10/23/80.
30. WM/Sir Ian Jacob, 11/12/80; Wheeler-Bennett, *Action,* 185.
31. PFR/Lady Mary Soames, letter of 9/3/07; Moran, *Diaries,* 100; Colville, *Fringes,* 416.
32. WM/William Deakin, 1980; Thompson, *Assignment: Churchill,* 178.
33. Colville, *Fringes,* 416; Halle, *Irrepressible Churchill,* 263.
34. Colville, *Fringes,* 481; Moran, *Diaries,* 111, 604; WM/Pamela Harriman ("wollygogs"), 8/22/80; Browne, *Long Sunset,* 220–21 (Sinatra).
35. WSCHCS, 6307.
36. Moran, *Diaries,* 604; Winston Churchill, *Thoughts and Adventures* (New York, 1991), 204.
37. R. V. Jones, *The Wizard War* (New York, 1978), 106.
38. Halle, *Irrepressible Churchill,* 345, 346; Moran, *Diaries,* 444.
39. H. Chartres Biron, ed., *"Sir," Said Dr. Johnson* (London, 1911), 112, 213.
40. Biron, *"Sir,"* 216; Colville, *Fringes,* 341; W&C-TPL, 111, 213.
41. WSC 5, 704; Anthony Montague Browne, speech to Churchill Society; Roy Jenkins, *Churchill: A Biography* (London, 2011), 702n; Colville, *Fringes,* 239, 578; Moran, *Diaries,* 781.
42. Colville, *Fringes,* 482; Richard Langworth, ed., *Churchill by Himself: The Definitive Collection of Quotations* (London, 2008), 463.
43. Randolph S. Churchill, *Winston S. Churchill: Youth, 1874–1900* (Boston, 1996), 208.
44. GILBERT 7, 348; Colville, *Fringes,* 526; Danchev and Todman, *War Diaries,* 690–91.
45. WSCHCS, 5818.
46. WM/Viscount Antony Head, 1980.
47. H. H. Asquith, *Letters to Venetia Stanley,* edited by Michael Brock and Eleanor Brock (Oxford, 1982), 267; WM/John Martin, 10/23/80.
48. Violet Bonham Carter, *Winston Churchill: An Intimate Portrait* (New York, 1965), 4; WSCHCS, 6250, 6264.
49. Sherwood, *Roosevelt and Hopkins,* 729; WSC 4, 796–97.
50. Sherwood, *Roosevelt and Hopkins,* 241.
51. Colville, *Fringes,* 158; WM/Jock Colville, 10/14/80; WM/John Martin, 10/23/80.
52. Moran, *Diaries,* 158; WSC 6, 115; Halle, *Irrepressible Churchill,* 257.
53. WM/Jock Colville, 10/14/80; WM/John Martin, 10/23/80; Browne, *Long Sunset,* 114.
54. GILBERT 7, 1322 ("This wicked man..."); WSCHCS, 6277; Langworth, *Churchill by Himself,* 137.
55. WM/William Deakin, 1980; WM/Jane (Portal) Williams, 1980.
56. WM/William Deakin, 1980; WM/Jane (Portal) Williams, 1980.
57. WM/Jane (Portal) Williams, 1980; GILBERT 6, 1156; Thompson, *Assignment: Churchill,* 183; *Daily Telegraph,* 3/18/09.
58. WM/Jane (Portal) Williams, 1980; WM/Jock Colville, 10/14/80; Colville, *Fringes,* 285.
59. WM/Cecily ("Chips") Gemmell, 7/10/80.
60. Vincent Sheean, *Between the Thunder and the Sun* (New York, 1943), 260; Wheeler-Bennett, *Action,* 146–47.

61. WM/John Martin, 10/23/80.
62. Wheeler-Bennett, *Action*, 139.
63. Anthony Storr, *Churchill's Black Dog, Kafka's Mice, and Other Phenomena of the Human Mind* (New York, 1973), 5, 27, 49–50.
64. W&C-TPL, 53; Moran, *Diaries*, 179.
65. Moran, *Diaries*, 112; PFR/Dr. Ron Pies (clinical psychiatrist, professor, Tufts University School of Medicine), 2007; PFR/Dr. David Armitage (Col. U.S. Army, ret.), 2007; Dr. Michael First (editor, *Diagnostic and Statistical Manual of Mental Disorders*, 4th ed., text rev. [DSM-IV-TR], lead author, *Structured Clinical Interview for DSM-IV-TR* [SCID], electronic and telephone communications, 3/07, 10/08; Browne, *Long Sunset*, 119.
66. Hastings Lionel Ismay, *The Memoirs of General Lord Ismay* (London, 1960), 155; Colville, *Fringes*, 215.
67. WM/Jock Colville, 10/14/80; Colville, *Fringes*, 578; Moran, *Diaries*, 827; Langworth, *Churchill by Himself*, 58.
68. John Keegan, *The Mask of Command* (New York, 1987), 236–38.
69. David Rising, "Hitler's Final Days Described by Bodyguard," AP, 4/24/05.
70. Hugh Dalton, *Memoirs 1931–1945: The Fateful Years* (London, 1957), 335–36.
71. David Dilks, ed., *The Diaries of Sir Alexander Cadogan, 1938–1945* (New York, 1972), 267.
72. Mollie Panter-Downes, *London War Notes, 1939–1945* (London, 1972), 62.
73. Dilks, *Diaries*, 267, 272, 283; WM/Jock Colville, 10/14/80.
74. Clare Boothe, *Europe in the Spring* (New York, 1941), 127.
75. WSC 1, 558–59.
76. Vincent Sheean, *Thunder*, 83.
77. Général André Beaufre, *Le Drame de 1940* (Paris, 1965).
78. Charles de Gaulle, *Lettres, Notes et Carnets*, vol. 2: *1942–May 1958* (Paris, 1980), 486.
79. BBC broadcast, 3/30/40; WSCHCS, 6201.
80. Colville, *Fringes*, 25–26.
81. William L. Shirer, *Berlin Diary (The Journal of a Foreign Correspondent 1934–1941)* (New York, 1941), 329–30.
82. Adolf Hitler, *Mein Kampf*, edited by John Chamberlain et al. (New York, 1939), 766.
83. René de Chambrun, *I Saw France Fall* (New York, 1940), 54–55.
84. De Chambrun, *France*, 54–55.
85. Alphonse Goutard, *1940: La Guerre des Occasions Perdues* (Paris, 1956), 131; Boothe, *Europe*, 1941.
86. William Bullitt, *Foreign Relations of the United States*, vol. 1: *1945–1950, Emergence of the Intelligence Establishment* (Washington, DC, n.d.), 469.
87. WSC 1, 454.
88. F. W. Winterbotham, *The Ultra Secret* (New York, 1974), 50.
89. GILBERT 6, 305.
90. Len Deighton, *Blitzkrieg: From the Rise of Hitler to the Fall of Dunkirk* (New York, 1979), 191.
91. Général Maurice Gustav Gamelin, *Servir*, 3 vols. (Paris, 1947), 3:389.
92. Boothe, *Europe*, 241–42.
93. Adolf Heusinger, *Befehl im Widerstreit: Schicksalsstunden der deutschen Armee 1923–1945* (Tübingen, 1950), 88.
94. Panter-Downes, *War Notes*, 56–57.
95. Dilks, *Diaries*, 277.

Cyclone

1. GILBERT 6, 313; John Colville, *The Fringes of Power: 10 Downing Street Diaries 1939–1955* (New York, 1985), 121–22.
2. John W. Wheeler-Bennett, *King George VI: His Life and Reign, 1865–1936* (New York, 1958), 443; GILBERT 6, 307, 317.
3. WM/Lady Mary Soames, 10/27/80.
4. W&C-TPL, 412; Ernst Hanfstaengl, *Hitler: The Missing Years* (London, 1957), 193–96.
5. WM/Lady Mary Soames, 10/27/80; Brian Roberts, *Randolph: A Study of Churchill's Son* (London, 1984), 181.
6. Colville, *Fringes,* 256.
7. Lord Moran, *Churchill: Taken from the Diaries of Lord Moran* (Boston, 1966), 5.
8. Mollie Panter-Downes, *London War Notes, 1939–1945* (London, 1972), 61.
9. Colville, *Fringes,* 736.
10. WSC 1, 475.
11. Brian Gardner, *Churchill in Power: As Seen by His Contemporaries* (Boston, 1970), 6; Colville, *Fringes,* 121–22; Max Plowman, *Bridge into the Future: Letters of Max Plowman* (London, 1944), 710.
12. John Wheeler-Bennett, *Action This Day: Working with Churchill* (London, 1968), 48; WM/Jock Colville, 10/14/80.
13. Wheeler-Bennett, *Action,* 51–53; WM/Jock Colville, 10/14/80; WM/John Martin, 10/23/80; WSC 2, 17.
14. Wheeler-Bennett, *Action,* 161, 195–97; Colville, *Fringes,* 289, 436.
15. Wheeler-Bennett, *Action,* 193–96; WM/Sir Ian Jacob, 11/12/80.
16. John Rupert Colville, *Footprints in Time* (London, 1976), 75–76; Wheeler-Bennett, *Action,* 147; Ian Jacob, "His Finest Hour," *Atlantic Monthly,* 3/65.
17. WSC 2, 28; GILBERT 6, 325; WM/Sir Ian Jacob, 11/12/80; Virginia Cowles, *Winston Churchill: The Era and the Man* (New York, 1953), 317.
18. TWY, 85, 99; Hansard 5/13/40 (WSC statement to House).
19. Arthur Bryant, *The Turn of the Tide: A History of the War Years Based on the Diaries of Field-Marshal Lord Alanbrooke, 1939–1943* (New York, 1957), 21.
20. WSCHCS, 6232; Henry Pelling, *Winston Churchill* (Conshohocken, PA, 1999), 437; WSC 2, 10–11; Wheeler-Bennett, *Action,* 49.
21. Colville, *Fringes,* 196.
22. GILBERT 6, 328–29; WSC 2, 13.
23. Laurence Thompson, *1940* (New York, 1966), 94.
24. GILBERT 6, 342; C&R-TCC, 1:38.
25. Thompson, *1940,* 118.
26. CAB 65/7.
27. Général C. Gransard, *Le 10e Corps d'armée dans la bataille* (Paris, 1949), 141.
28. William L. Shirer, *The Collapse of the Third Republic* (New York, 1969), 664; Charles de Gaulle, *The Complete War Memoirs of Charles de Gaulle* (New York, 1964), 39.
29. Alistair Horne, *Seven Ages of Paris* (New York, 2002), 381–402.
30. WSC 2, 42.
31. Antoine de Saint-Exupéry, *Flight from Arras* (New York, 1942), 116–33 *passim.*
32. WSC 2, 43; de Saint-Exupéry, *Flight,* 120.

33. Hastings Lionel Ismay, *The Memoirs of General Lord Ismay* (London, 1960), 127; Horne, *Seven Ages,* 381; Vincent Sheean, *Between the Thunder and the Sun* (New York, 1943), 142.
34. Ismay, *Memoirs,* 128.
35. WSC 2, 47.
36. Paul Reynaud, *In the Thick of the Fight* (New York, 1940), 323–24.
37. WSC 2, 42–43; de Saint-Exupéry, *Flight,* 120.
38. Len Deighton, *Fighter* (New York, 1977), 58; Ismay, *Memoirs,* 128.
39. Ismay, *Memoirs,* 128–29.
40. GILBERT 6, 334, 358; Colville, *Fringes,* 135.
41. John Rupert Colville, *Man of Valour: The Life of Field Marshal the Viscount Gort* (London, 1972), 204; Anthony Eden, Earl of Avon, *The Reckoning: The Memoirs of Anthony Eden* (New York, 1965), 106.
42. WSCHCS, 6222–23.
43. Jones, *Diary,* 460; W. M. James, *The Portsmouth Letters* (London, 1946), 15.
44. Panter-Downes, *War Notes,* 67.
45. William L. Shirer, *Berlin Diary (The Journal of a Foreign Correspondent 1934–1941)* (New York, 1941), 437–38.
46. WSC 2, 56; Général Maurice Gustav Gamelin, *Servir,* 3 vols. (Paris, 1947), 3:417.
47. WSCHCS, 6232.
48. Roderick Macleod, ed., *Time Unguarded: The Ironside Diaries, 1937–1940* (London, 1974), 327; Premier (Prime Minister) Papers, Public Record Office, Kew, 3/188/3, folio 18; WSC 1, 375.
49. Ismay, *Memoirs,* 131; Colville, *Fringes,* 137–38.
50. WSC 2, 64–65; Macleod, *Time Unguarded,* 328.
51. William L. Shirer, *The Rise and Fall of the Third Reich: A History of Nazi Germany* (New York, 1960), 728.
52. Colville, *Fringes,*139; GILBERT 6, 385.
53. Colville, *Fringes,* 139; GILBERT 6, 385; WSC 2, 69–70.
54. E. L. Spears, *Assignment to Catastrophe,* 2 vols. (New York, 1955), 2:120–21.
55. L. F. Ellis, *The War in France and Flanders 1939–1940* (London, 1953), 368; Macleod, *Time Unguarded,* 331–32.
56. Ellis, *France and Flanders,* 208, 389.
57. Len Deighton, *Blitzkrieg: From the Rise of Hitler to the Fall of Dunkirk* (New York, 1979), 265.
58. B. H. Liddell Hart, *History of the Second World War* (New York, 1971), 77; David Dilks, ed., *The Diaries of Sir Alexander Cadogan, 1938–1945* (New York, 1972), 289–90; CAB 65/7; Macleod, *Time Unguarded,* 332; WSC 1, 393.
59. Spears, *Assignment,* 2: 202, 236–37; WSC 1, 389; Bryant, *Tide,* 90; Macleod, *Time Unguarded,* 321.
60. *Time,* 1/23/41, 23; Roger Keyes, *Outrageous Fortune: The Tragedy of King Leopold of the Belgians 1901–1941* (London, 1984), 308–10, 396.
61. CAB 65/13.
62. Dilks, *Diaries,* 290; ChP 80/11.
63. Dilks, *Diaries,* 291.
64. WSC 2, 99.
65. Thompson, *1940,*137–38.
66. *NYT,* 5/30/40; TWY, 91; Thompson, *1940,* 133–34, 139.
67. Ellis, *France and Flanders,* 368.

68. Ellis, *France and Flanders*, 162–69; Macleod, *Time Unguarded;* WSC 2, 82; Ismay, *Memoirs*, 133.
69. Bryant, *Tide*, 101–2 *passim*.
70. Ellis, *France and Flanders*, 326.
71. Ellis, *France and Flanders*, 182; Macleod, *Time Unguarded*, 340; WSCHCS, 6225.
72. Macleod, *Time Unguarded*, 333ff.; Ismay, *Memoirs*, 134.
73. WSC 2, 100; Hugh Dalton, *Memoirs 1931–1945: The Fateful Years* (London, 1957), 335–36.
74. WSC 2, 101.
75. Thompson, *1940*, 133–36.
76. Alex Danchev and Daniel Todman, eds., *Field Marshal Lord Alanbrooke: War Diaries 1939–1945* (Berkeley, 2003), 72.
77. WSC 2, 428; War Office papers 106/1708; John Spencer Churchill, *Crowded Canvas* (London, 1961), 162–63; WM/Sir Ian Jacob, 11/12/80; Jacob, "Finest," 3/65.
78. Macleod, *Time Unguarded*, 354; Harold Macmillan, *The Blast of War: 1939–1945* (New York, 1967), 81.
79. Panter-Downes, *War Notes*, 63–66.
80. WSCHCS, 6230.
81. Colville, *Fringes*, 147–48; *News Chronicle* 6/5/40; TWY, 93; Gardner, *Churchill in Power*, 55.
82. WSCHCS, 6228.
83. George Bilainkin, *Diary of a Diplomatic Correspondent* (London, 1942), 102.
84. Chief sources for the last three meetings of the council (Paris, Briare, Tours): Spears, *Assignment;* de Gaulle, *War Memoirs;* Ismay, *Memoirs;* S. Petrie et al., *The Private Diaries of Paul Baudouin* (London, 1948).
85. Spears, *Assignment*, 1:293–94.
86. Ismay, *Memoirs*, 134.
87. Spears, *Assignment*, 1:295.
88. Spears, *Assignment*, 1:295.
89. Spears, *Assignment*, 1:295; Petrie, *Diaries*, 53–54.
90. Spears, *Assignment*, 1:314–15.
91. Spears, *Assignment*, 1:316, 2:113.
92. Panter-Downes, *War Notes*, 68; Colville, *Fringes*, 151–53.
93. Spears, *Assignment*, 2:138–39; Ismay, *Memoirs*, 139.
94. Spears, *Assignment*, 2:141–44; Eden, *Reckoning*, 133. The French minutes of the Briare meeting are given textually in Paul Reynaud, *Au Coeur de la mêlée, 1939–1945* (Paris, 1951), 823–24.
95. Spears, *Assignment*, 2:145–47; Eden, *Reckoning*, 115.
96. Spears, *Assignment*, 2:149ff.
97. Reynaud, *Au Coeur.*
98. Ismay, *Memoirs*, 140.
99. Ismay, *Memoirs*, 140–41.
100. Ismay, *Memoirs*, 140–41.
101. *Les Événements survenus en France de 1933 à 1945*, 2:343; Horne, *Seven Ages*, 546n; Shirer, *Collapse*, 618; *Histoire de l'Aviation Militaire Française* (Paris, 1980), 379–80; Deighton, *Blitzkrieg*, 269–70.
102. WSC 2, 156–57; Ismay, *Memoirs*, 142–43.
103. Spears, *Assignment*, 2:163.

104. Ismay, *Memoirs*, 141.
105. WSC 2, 158; Walter H. Thompson, *Assignment: Churchill* (New York, 1953), 194.
106. CAB 99/3; Colville, *Fringes*, 152–54.
107. Earl of Birkenhead, *Life of Lord Halifax* (London, 1965), 459; Dilks, *Diaries*, 297; Ismay, *Memoirs*, 143–44.
108. Eleanor M. Gates, *End of the Affair: The Collapse of the Anglo-French Alliance, 1939–40* (Berkeley, 1981), 250; Gordon Wright, "Ambassador Bullitt and the Fall of France," *World Politics* 10, no. 1, 87.
109. Horne, *Seven Ages*, 573.
110. Spears, *Assignment*, 2:210–13.
111. James Leasor, *War at the Top* (London, 1959), 91; Colville, *Fringes*, 152.
112. Spears, *Assignment*, 2:218–20.
113. Colville, *Fringes*, 155; C&R-TCC, 1:48.
114. Spears, *Assignment*, 2:292–93; WM/Kathleen Hill, 11/4/80; Colville, *Fringes*, 161.
115. Spears, *Assignment*, 2:292–93; WM/Kathleen Hill, 11/4/80; Colville, *Fringes*, 161.
116. L. B. Namier, *Europe in Decay* (London, 1950), 93; Spears, *Assignment*, 2:304, 310–11.
117. Spears, *Assignment*, 2:319–23; WSC 2, 218.
118. J. A. Cross, *Sir Samuel Hoare: A Political Biography* (London, 1977), 339–40.
119. Michael Bloch, *The Duke of Windsor's War: From Europe to the Bahamas, 1939–1945* (New York, 1983).
120. Colville, *Fringes*, 184.
121. ChP 20/9; C&R-TCC, 1:53.
122. ChP 20/49; WSC 1, 1091.
123. Colville, *Fringes*, 166.
124. Panter-Downes, *War Notes*, 72.
125. De Gaulle, *War Memoirs*, 76.
126. WSC 2, 230; Eden, *Reckoning*, 155.
127. William Bullitt, *Foreign Relations of the United States*, vol. 2: *The Intelligence Community 1950–1955* (Washington, DC, n.d.), 465–66.
128. WSCHCS, 6241.
129. WSC 2, 231.
130. Colville, *Fringes*, 171–72; WSC 2, 233; Warren Tute, *The Deadly Stroke*, introduction by John Colville (New York, 1973), 21–28.
131. Tute, *Deadly Stroke*, 73–87.
132. Tute, *Deadly Stroke*, 112–14; WSC 2, 234.
133. For a thorough discussion of the British attack on the French fleet at Mers-el-Kébir, see chap. 5 of Arthur Marder's *From the Dardanelles to Oran* (London, 1974).
134. Tute, *Deadly Stroke*, 148.
135. Tute, *Deadly Stroke*, 152–62.
136. Thompson, *1940*; WSCHCS, 6246.
137. Tute, *Deadly Stroke*, 17; Ben Pimlott, *Hugh Dalton* (London, 1985), 348; TWY, 100.
138. Tute, *Deadly Stroke*, 17.
139. Shirer, *Rise and Fall*, 813.
140. CAB 65/9.
141. Cv/2, 259; WSCHCS, 6287.
142. GILBERT 6, 372, 392; Macleod, *Time Unguarded*, 369; Hermann Löns, *Ein Soldatisches Vermächtnis* (1939), 85; Richard Gerlach, *Das Beste von Hermann Löns* (Hanover, 1980), 16.

143. WSCHCS, 6230.
144. Cv/2, 429.
145. Hansard 6/18/40; WSCHCS, 6238.
146. Deighton, *Fighter*, 8.
147. C&R-TCC, 1:40, 49; Cv/2, 261; Bryant, *Tide*, 151.
148. Thompson, *1940*, 149; WSC 1, 598–99, 695; Premier (Prime Minister) Papers, Public Record Office, Kew, 4/100/3; Birkenhead, *Halifax*, 458, and Llewellyn Woodward, *British Foreign Policy in the Second World War* (London, 1962), 53; Williamson Murray, *Luftwaffe* (Baltimore, 1985), 43.
149. Duff Cooper, *Old Men Forget* (London, 1954), 267; Jones, *Diary*, 465; Lloyd George, *Sunday Pictorial*, 7/28/40; Wheeler-Bennett, *King George VI*, 456.
150. Panter-Downes, *War Notes*, 83–86; Jones, *Diary*, 465–66.
151. Wheeler-Bennett, *King George VI*, 456.
152. Wheeler-Bennett, *King George VI*, 456.
153. Gardner, *Churchill in Power*, 65–66.
154. Panter-Downes, *War Notes*, 71, 91, 97, 110–11.
155. Colville, *Fringes*, 195.
156. Cv/2, 417–18.
157. Shirer, *Rise and Fall*, 798.
158. WSC 2, 286.
159. WSCHCS, 6495.
160. WSCHCS, 6234.
161. WSC 2, 282–84.
162. Colville, *Fringes*, 178–81, 182.
163. TWY, 97; Ismay, *Memoirs*, 153; Jones, *Diary*, 467–68.
164. WSCHCS, 6775.
165. Mary Soames, *Clementine Churchill: The Biography of a Marriage* (New York, 2003), 408; TWY, 100.
166. TWY, 90.
167. TWY, 89, 90, 93; WM/Kathleen Hill, 11/4/80.
168. Macleod, *Time Unguarded*, 369.
169. GILBERT 6, 478; Gardner, *Churchill in Power*, 68; Panter-Downes, *War Notes*, 66; Hansard 6/4/40; A. J. P. Taylor, *English History, 1914–45* (Oxford, 1978).
170. Colville, *Fringes*, 182; Cv/3, 445 (mustard gas).
171. Thompson, *1940*,145.
172. TWY, 101, 103.
173. WSC 2, 298; Macleod, *Time Unguarded*, 383; Danchev and Todman, *War Diaries*, 94.
174. Colville, *Fringes*, 102–3.
175. WSCHCS, 6248.
176. WSCHCS, 6250.
177. *Documents on German Foreign Policy 1918–1945*, vol. 10: *The War Years, June 23–August 23, 1940* (Washington, DC, 1957), 81; Charles Burdick and Hans-Adolf Jacobsen, eds., *The Halder War Diary, 1939–1942* (New York, 1988), 7/22/40; Führer's Conferences on Naval Affairs, 71–73; *Die Weiterführung des Krieges gegen England*, IMT, TWMC, vol. 28, 301–3.
178. Shirer, *Rise and Fall*, 754.
179. Colville, *Fringes*, 200; Leonard Mosley, *Battle of Britain* (New York, 1980), 26; WSC 2, 260.

180. Hugh Gibson, ed., *The Ciano Diaries, 1939–1943* (New York, 1946), 277–78.
181. Deighton, *Fighter,* 272; Liddell Hart, *History,* 87.
182. Klaus A. Maier et al., *Das Deutsche Reich und der Zweite Weltkrieg,* 2 vols. (Stuttgart, 1988), 2:3, 78–79.
183. Shirer, *Rise and Fall,* 752.
184. Shirer, *Rise and Fall,* 752.
185. Shirer, *Rise and Fall,* 762–63.
186. William L. Shirer, *Aufstieg und Fall des Dritten Reiches* (Cologne, 2000), 815.
187. Deighton, *Fighter,* xiv–xv; Hansard 11/10/32; WM/Sir Ian Jacob, 11/12/80.
188. Deighton, *Fighter,* xviii, 57.
189. Mosley, *Battle of Britain,* 50.
190. Mosley, *Battle of Britain,* 54; Telford Taylor, *The Breaking Wave: The Second World War in the Summer of 1940* (New York, 1967), 87; John Keegan, ed., *Collins Atlas of World War II* (New York, 2006), 38–39.
191. BA/MA RL 211/27, *Allgemeine Weisung für den Kampf der Luftwaffe gegen England,* OBDL, Führungsstab, Ia Nr 5835/40, 30.6.40; Murray Williamson, "The Battle of Britain: How Did 'The Few' Win?" *Military History Quarterly* 2, no. 2 (summer 1990).
192. WSC 2, 323.
193. Colville, *Fringes,* 213.
194. Liddell Hart, *History,* 93.
195. Liddell Hart, *History,* 93.
196. Colville, *Fringes,* 194.
197. Hansard 11/11/42; WSCHCS, 6707; Shirer, *Berlin Diary,* 467–68.
198. Deighton, *Fighter,* xvii, 218; Mosley, *Battle of Britain,* 91; A. J. P. Taylor, *Beaverbrook* (London, 1972), 422–30.
199. Colville, *Fringes,* 217; Taylor, *Beaverbrook,* 430.
200. Murray, *Luftwaffe.*
201. Deighton, *Fighter,* 217.
202. Deighton, *Fighter,* 187.
203. Len Deighton, *Unternehmen Adler. Die Luftschlacht um England,* 264–65.
204. R. V. Jones, *The Wizard War* (New York, 1978); F. H. Hinsley et al., *British Intelligence in the Second World War,* 5 vols. (London, 1979), 1:176–77; Ronald Lewin, *Ultra Goes to War* (New York, 1978); Brian Johnson, *The Secret War* (London, 1978); Harold Deutsch, "Ultra and the Air War in Europe and Africa," in *Air Power and Warfare, Proceedings of the Eighth Military History Symposium,* USAF Academy, edited by Colonel Alfred F. Hurley and Major Robert C. Ehrhart (Washington, DC, 1979), 165–66; Maier, *Das Deutsche Reich,* 2:384; Aileen Clayton, *The Enemy Is Listening* (New York, 1978).
205. Sheean, *Thunder,* 201.
206. Sheean, *Thunder,* 199.
207. Sheean, *Thunder,* 201–2.
208. Colville, *Fringes,* 236.
209. Collier, *Defence of the United Kingdom* (London, 2009), 189–90, 450; Helmuth Greiner, *Kriegstagebuch des Oberkommandos der Wehrmacht* (the *OKW* war diary) 8/15/40; Denis Richards, *Royal Air Force, 1939–1945,* vol. 1: *The Fight at Odds* (London, 1953), chaps. 6 and 7.
210. Helmuth Greiner, *Die Oberste Wehrmacht/Weltkrieg 1939–1945* (Stuttgart, 1954); Ismay, *Memoirs,* 188.

211. WSCHCS, 6265–66.
212. Edward Bishop, *The Battle of Britain* (London, 1960), 142, 149; Helmuth Greiner, *OKW*, 8/19/40.
213. Richards, *Royal Air Force*, 1:178.
214. Deighton, *Fighter*, 219.
215. Colville, *Fringes*, 234–36.
216. Collier, *Defence*, 206–7, 210; Bishop, *Battle of Britain*, 166–69; Alexander McKee, *Strike from the Sky: The Battle of Britain Story* (Boston, 1960), 197–209; Derek Wood and Derek Dempster, *The Narrow Margin: The Battle of Britain and the Rise of Air Power 1930–1949* (London, 1961), 316–25.
217. Colville, *Fringes*, 236–37.
218. Deighton, *Fighter*, 248; Collier, *Defence*, 205; Wood and Dempster, *Narrow Margin*, 332–33; WSC 2, 331–32.
219. Wood and Dempster, *Narrow Margin*, 304.
220. Taylor, *Breaking Wave*, 151; H. R. Trevor-Roper, ed., *Hitler's War Directives 1939–1945* (London, 1964), 38.
221. Helmuth Greiner, *Die Oberste Wehrmachtführung, 1939–1943* (Wiesbaden, 1951), 8/29/40, 8/31/40; Cv/2, 555.
222. Colville, *Fringes*, 230.
223. Shirer, *Berlin Diary*, 8/26/40.
224. *Frankfurter Zeitung*, 8/29/40 and 8/30/40.
225. *OKW*, 8/24/40; *Facts in Review* 2, no. 22 (5/27/40): 217.
226. Adolph Galland, *The First and the Last* (New York, 1954), 40–41.
227. Shirer, *Rise and Fall*, 777.
228. *Frankfurter Zeitung*, 9/5/40.
229. Gibson, *Ciano Diaries*, 290.
230. WSC 2, 229.
231. CAB, 79/6. The chiefs signing the order were Ismay, Pound, Dill, and Peirse, vice chief of the Air Staff.
232. McKee, *Strike*, 125.
233. Collier, *Defence*, 135–40; Wood and Dempster, *Narrow Margin*, 334–39; Mosley, *Battle of Britain*, 120.
234. GILBERT 6, 773–74; WSC 2, 312.
235. GILBERT 6, 774.
236. Danchev and Todman, *War Diaries*, 105.
237. Cv/2, 703.
238. C&R-TCC, 1:56–67; GILBERT 6, 25.
239. C&R-TCC, 1:56–67.
240. Robert E. Sherwood, *Roosevelt and Hopkins: An Intimate History* (New York, 1948), 1980; Cv/2, 255; Dilks, *Diaries*, 322–23.
241. Cv/2, 255 (letter to Mackenzie King); C&R-TCC, 1:69.
242. WSCHCS, 6266.
243. GILBERT 6, 756; WSC 2, 297.
244. WM/Sir Robert Boothby, 10/16/80.
245. Cv/2, 655; Cv/2, 748; Collier, *War in the Desert*, 18–19.
246. GILBERT 6, 756.
247. Greiner, *OKW*, 9/13/40.
248. Greiner, *OKW*, 8/30/40.
249. WSC 2, 337; Deighton, *Fighter*, 262.

250. Taylor, *Breaking Wave,* 165; *Seekriegsleitung Kriegstagebuch,* War Diary of the German Naval War Staff, Part D, Lufttage, for September 16 and 18, 1940.
251. WSC 2, 240.
252. F. H. W. Sheppard, *London: A History* (Oxford, 1998); David Johnson, *The London Blitz* (New York, 1981), 33; WSC 2, 342.
253. Cv/2, 788–89 (Ismay recollection); Thompson, *1940,* 211; Cv/2, 789.
254. Colville, *Fringes,* 192.
255. WSC 2, 343; Mosley, *Battle of Britain,* 143.
256. TWY, 111; Mosley, *Battle of Britain,* 145.
257. William K. Klingaman, *1941: Our Lives in a World on the Edge* (New York, 1989), 3, 7, 12.
258. Klingaman, *1941,* 6–7; WSC 2, 360.
259. Bertrand Russell, *Which Way to Peace?* (London, 1936), quoted in Sheppard, *London,* 262; Colville, *Fringes,* 263.
260. WSCHCS, 6277.
261. WSCHCS, 6276.
262. BBC address, 9/11/40.
263. Johnson, *London Blitz,* 39.
264. Jones, *Wizard War,* 96–97.
265. WSC 2, 384–85; Jones, *Wizard War,* 101–2.
266. Jones, *Wizard War,* 102.
267. WSC 2, 385; Tom Shachtman, *Terrors and Marvels: How Science and Technology Changed the Character and Outcome of World War II* (New York, 2002); see chap. 5 ("Battles Above Britain") for overview.
268. WSC 2, 383–84; Jones, *Wizard War,* 102.
269. Sheppard, *London,* 333.
270. Philip Ziegler, *London at War* (New York, 1995), 175.
271. WSC 2, 343.
272. WSC 2, 343.
273. Mosley, *Battle of Britain,* 138.
274. Kay Halle, *Irrepressible Churchill: Stories, Sayings and Impressions of Sir Winston Churchill* (London, 1985), 168.
275. Klingaman, *1941,* 16.
276. TWY, 115–16.
277. WM/Lady Mary Soames, 10/27/80; Soames, *Clementine,* 379.
278. Colville, *Fringes,* 240–41; Thompson, *Assignment: Churchill,* 206.
279. WM/Jock Colville, 10/14/80.
280. WM/Lady Mary Soames, 10/27/80; Soames, *Clementine,* 384–86.
281. WSC 2, 375.
282. Thompson, *1940,* 213.
283. Thompson, *1940,* 222.
284. Mosley, *Battle of Britain,* 36–37.
285. WM/Viscount Antony Head, 8/6/80.
286. *Time,* 10/3/43; *Time,* 2/1/43; Mark Mayo Boatner, *The Biographical Dictionary of World War II* (New York, 1999), 8. See also *Modern Law Review* 5, no. 3/4 (July 1942):162–73; Tim Pat Coogan, *The IRA* (London, 1971), 58.
287. *Time,* 9/23/40; Cv/2, 440, 446, 764; Colville, *Fringes,* 173; WSC 5, 680.
288. TWY, 114.
289. Mosley, *Battle of Britain,* 139.

290. TWY, 115–16.
291. WM/Jock Colville, 10/14/80; Colville, *Fringes*, 245.
292. Colville, *Fringes*, 249.
293. *Oxford Companion to World War II*, edited by I. C. B. Dear (Oxford, 1995), 179, 331.
294. Martin Gilbert, *The Second World War: A Complete History* (London, 1989), 132.
295. TWY, 121.
296. CAB 120/300.
297. Shirer, *Rise and Fall*, 778; Gilbert, *Second World War*, 128.
298. WSC 2, 584, 586.
299. WSC 2, 581.
300. Colville, *Fringes*, 214.
301. Panter-Downes, *War Notes*, 110; Klingaman, *1941*, 9.
302. Thompson, *1940*, 220; Sheean, *Thunder*, 224–25.
303. Sheean, *Thunder*, 224–25; Panter-Downes, *War Notes*, 137.
304. WSCHCS, 6287.
305. Winston Churchill, *My Early Life: 1874–1904* (New York, 1996), 62.
306. GILBERT 6, 808–10.
307. Joseph P. Kennedy, *Boston Globe* interview, 11/10/40; Victor Lasky, *JFK: The Man and the Myth* (New York, 1963), 58.
308. Colville, *Fringes*, 262, 275.
309. GILBERT 6, 816; C&R-TCC, 1:74.
310. WSCHCS, 6297.
311. WSCHCS, 6297.
312. WSCHCS, 6298; Conrad Black, *Franklin Delano Roosevelt: Champion of Freedom* (Washington, DC, 2003), 595.
313. Cv/2, 979, 985; Colville, *Fringes*, 272.
314. WM/Pamela Harriman, 8/22/80.
315. PFR/Lady Mary Soames, 6/07; WM/Pamela Harriman, 8/22/80.
316. Colville, *Fringes*, 216, 219, 248; WM/Jock Colville, 10/14/80.
317. Colville, *Fringes*, 265; Thompson, *1940;* WM/Pamela Harriman, 8/22/80.
318. Soames, *Clementine*, 387.
319. Soames, *Clementine*, 387; GILBERT 6, 793; Sarah Churchill, *A Thread in the Tapestry* (London, 1967), 56–57; *Time*, 9/30/40.
320. Thompson, *Assignment: Churchill*, 129; WM/Jock Colville, 10/14/80.
321. WM/Lord Geoffrey Lloyd, 11/27/80.
322. WM/Jock Colville, 10/14/80.
323. Mosley, *Battle of Britain*, 121.
324. WM/Jock Colville, 10/14/80; Wheeler-Bennett, *Action*, 118.
325. Churchill, *Early Life* ("being shot at without result").
326. Thompson, *Assignment: Churchill*, 211.
327. Thompson, *Assignment: Churchill*, 210–11.
328. Colville, *Fringes*, 278; Dean Acheson, *Sketches from Life of Men I Have Known* (New York, 1959), 3, 17.
329. Thompson, *Assignment: Churchill*, 211.
330. Cv/2, 907–8.
331. Cv/2, 907–8.
332. Moran, *Diaries*, 9.

333. TWY, 127.
334. Randolph S. Churchill, *Winston S. Churchill: Youth, 1874–1900* (Boston, 1996), 400, 410; Colville, *Fringes,* 273.
335. Colville, *Fringes,* 291; Thompson, *Assignment: Churchill,* 170–75.
336. WM/John Colville, 10/14/80; Thompson, *Assignment: Churchill,* 174.
337. Soames, *Clementine,* 386; Danchev and Todman, *War Diaries,* 123; Cv/2, 1069.
338. Colville, *Fringes,* 319; Moran, *Diaries,* 336; WM/Lord Soames (Pol Roger), 1980.
339. Colville, *Fringes,* 319; Shirer, *Berlin Diary,* 468.
340. PFR/Winston S. Churchill, 3/04.
341. Colville, *Fringes,* 267; Sheppard, *London,* 336; WSC 2, 370–72; Gilbert, *Second World War,* 132.
342. Ziegler, *London at War,* 119–20.
343. WSC 2, 360–61.
344. WSC 2, 360–61.
345. WM/Cecily ("Chips") Gemmell, 7/10/80; Thompson, *Assignment: Churchill,* 183; Colville, *Fringes,* 243; WM/John Colville, 10/14/80.
346. Ismay, *Memoirs,* 188–89.
347. Colville, *Fringes,* 262, 275; GILBERT 6, 862; ChP 20/13.
348. Colville, *Fringes,* 264, 280–81.
349. GILBERT 6, 835.
350. Soames, *Clementine,* 394; Colville, *Fringes,* 259; GILBERT 6, 837.
351. WCS 2, 299, 355; GILBERT 6, 886.
352. Thompson, *1940,* 221–24; Ziegler, *London at War,* 240.
353. C&R-TCC, 1:81.
354. John Keegan, *The Second World War* (London, 1989), 144–46.
355. GILBERT 6, 874–75, 877; Keegan, *Second World War,* 144–46; Cv/2, 1016.
356. Richard Collier, *Duce!* (New York, 1971), 179–80.
357. Colville, *Fringes,* 276; Keegan, *Second World War,* 145.
358. Collier, *War in the Desert;* GILBERT 6, 883–85.
359. Colville, *Fringes,* 283–84.
360. ChP 20/13.
361. Colville, *Fringes,* 224.
362. Cv/2, 1001.
363. GILBERT 6, 885, 905; WSC 2, 536–43; Eden, *Reckoning,* 195.
364. Collier, *War in the Desert,* 21–22; WSC 2, 543.
365. Gilbert, *Second World War,* 137.
366. Cv/2, 1022–23.
367. C&R-TCC, 1:81.
368. Cv/2, 1147.
369. Panter-Downes, *War Notes,* 116 ("*Eyetalian fleet . . .*").
370. Panter-Downes, *War Notes,* 114; Cv/2, 1089 ("sugar for the birds"); WSCHCC, 6309.
371. Ronald Kessler, *The Sins of the Father* (New York, 1996), 230.
372. WSCHCS, 6307.
373. Colville, *Fringes,* 294–95.
374. Colville, *Fringes,* 292.
375. WM/John Martin, 10/23/80.
376. Cv/2, 1096; WM/John Martin, 10/23/80.
377. WSC 2, 383–85.

378. TWY, 139; Panter-Downes, *War Notes,* 117.
379. Panter-Downes, *War Notes,* 117.
380. WSC 2, 384–85; Winston Churchill, *Thoughts and Adventures* (New York, 1991), 198–99.
381. WM/John Martin, 10/23/80; Colville, *Fringes,* 295; John Colville, *The Churchillians* (London, 1981), 635.
382. Thompson, *1940,* 227.
383. Public Record Office documents AIR2/5238 and AIR20/2419 indicate that Churchill and the War Cabinet did not know which city would be the target on November 15.
384. Colville, *Fringes,* 297.
385. Cv/2, 1186, 1217–18; WM/Jock Colville, 10/14/80.
386. Cv/3, 1163.
387. Soames, *Clementine,* 395.
388. Colville, *Fringes,* 167; TWY, 96–97.
389. WSC 2, 576; GILBERT 6, 939.
390. David Miller, *U-Boats* (New York, 2000), 126; C&R-TCC, 1:112; Premier (Prime Minister) Papers, Public Record Office, Kew, 3/462/2; Cv/2, 1233.
391. Roger Chesneau, *Conway's All the World's Fighting Ships, 1922–1946* (London, 1980) (HMS *Lewes*).
392. Cv/2, 780, 844–45.
393. Cv/2, 1246.
394. Shirer, *Rise and Fall,* 810–11; WCSHCS, 6269.
395. WSC 2, 556–58; C&R-TCC, 1:102–9.
396. WSC 2, 558.
397. C&R-TCC, 1:107–8.
398. C&R-TCC, 1:107–8; WM/Malcolm MacDonald, 1980.
399. C&R-TCC, 1:107–8.
400. WSC 2, 567–69.
401. GILBERT 6, 694.
402. Colville, *Fringes,* 309, 321; WSC 2, 570.
403. Colville, *Fringes,* 314.
404. C&R-TCC, 1:86.
405. WSC 2, 530.
406. WSC 3, 568–69.
407. Winston S. Churchill, *Step by Step, 1936–1939* (New York, 1959), 137.
408. WSC 2, 497, 523; Dilks, *Diaries,* 329.
409. C&R-TCC, 1:74.
410. *Time Capsule 1940: A History of the Year Condensed from the Pages of* Time, edited by Henry R. Luce (New York, 1968).
411. *Time Capsule 1940.*
412. C&R-TCC, 1:65–66; Churchill, *Early Life,* 33 (from Manchester, *The Last Lion,* vol. 1, and Cowles, *Churchill*).
413. Celia Sandys, *Chasing Churchill* (New York, 2005), 138; Shirer, *Rise and Fall,* 782–83.
414. Collier, *War in the Desert,* 26–33.
415. Collier, *War in the Desert,* 27–28; Colville, *Fringes,* 308–9.
416. Collier, *War in the Desert,* 29.
417. GILBERT 6, 935; Colville, *Fringes,* 309; Mark Mayo Boatner, *The Biographical Dictionary of World War II* (New York, 1999), 602.

418. GILBERT 6, 935; Collier, *War in the Desert*, 29.
419. Cv/2, 1204.
420. Mosley, *Battle of Britain*, 149.
421. Leonard Mosley, *Marshall: Hero for Our Times* (New York, 1982), 150–51.
422. *NYT*, 12/30/41; TWY, 132; Klingaman, *1941*, 16.
423. FDR broadcast, 12/29/40, Franklin D. Roosevelt Presidential Library and Museum.
424. FDR broadcast, 12/29/40, Franklin D. Roosevelt Presidential Library and Museum; Colville, *Fringes*, 321; C&R-TCC, 1:122–23.
425. WSC 2, 628–29.

The Rapids

1. C&R-TCC, 1:120; John Colville, *The Fringes of Power: 10 Downing Street Diaries 1939–1955* (New York, 1985), 326–27.
2. WSC 3, 540; Noel Annan, "How Wrong Was Churchill?" *New York Review of Books*, 4/8/93.
3. William K. Klingaman, *1941: Our Lives in a World on the Edge* (New York, 1989), 24, 92–93; ChP 20/36; ChP 20/21.
4. Klingaman, *1941*, 24–25; ChP 20/36; ChP 20/21.
5. Colville, *Fringes*, 145.
6. C&R-TCC, 1:121–22; Colville, *Fringes*, 327.
7. John Colville, *The Churchillians* (London, 1981), 162; Colville, *Fringes*, 653; Anthony Eden, Earl of Avon, *The Reckoning: The Memoirs of Anthony Eden* (New York, 1965), 168, 215.
8. Lewis Broad, *Anthony Eden, The Chronicle of a Career* (New York, 1955), 4–8; Eden, *The Reckoning*, 435; W&C-TPL, 408.
9. Martin Gilbert, *Churchill's War Leadership* (New York, 2004), 72; Mark Mayo Boatner, *The Biographical Dictionary of World War II* (New York, 1999), 18–19, 372–73; Colville, *Churchillians*, 156–57.
10. ChP 2/416; Colville, *Fringes*, 326; Boatner, *Biographical Dictionary*, 380.
11. Klingaman, *1941*, 90–91.
12. Klingaman, *1941*, 92; WM/Malcolm Muggeridge, 11/25/80.
13. Dwight D. Eisenhower, *Crusade in Europe* (New York, 1948), 9; Carlos D'Este, *Patton: A Genius for War* (New York, 1995), 390–91.
14. Klingaman, *1941*, 43.
15. Charles de Gaulle, *The Complete War Memoirs of Charles de Gaulle* (New York, 1964), 84.
16. Klingaman, *1941*, 44.
17. Klingaman, *1941*, 48; Brian Gardner, *Churchill in Power: As Seen by His Contemporaries* (Boston, 1970), 96; Charles Eade, ed., *Churchill by His Contemporaries* (New York, 1954), 140; William L. Shirer, *Berlin Diary (The Journal of a Foreign Correspondent 1934–1941)* (New York, 1941), 481.
18. George F. Kennan, *Memoirs: 1925–1950* (New York, 1967), 130; Klingaman, *1941*, 18; Shirer, *Berlin Diary*, 448–49, 459.
19. C&R-TCC, 1:147; CAB 65/18 (to Halifax).
20. Mollie Panter-Downes, *London War Notes, 1939–1945* (London, 1972), 122–23, 139–40; Klingaman, *1941*, 14.

21. Klingaman, *1941,* 89–90.
22. Klingaman, *1941,* 89–90.
23. Klingaman, *1941,* 90; GILBERT 6, 895; ChP 20/36.
24. TWY, 136–37.
25. Leonard Mosley, *Battle of Britain* (New York, 1980), 136–37.
26. TWY, 136–37; ChP 20/36.
27. WSC 3, 4.
28. William L. Shirer, *The Rise and Fall of the Third Reich: A History of Nazi Germany* (New York, 1960), 813, 816.
29. WM/Jock Colville, 10/14/80; Cv/3, 39, 973.
30. Colville, *Fringes,* 419.
31. Cv/3, 43.
32. Cv/3, 44; Eden, *The Reckoning,* 270–72.
33. Kennan, *Memoirs;* Cv/3, 44.
34. Cv/3, 165.
35. Cv/3, 430; Colville, *Fringes,* 209 (Operation Razzle); Cv/3, 430.
36. Cv/3, 173.
37. Cv/3, 165.
38. Margery Allingham, *The Oaken Heart* (London, 1991), 169–89.
39. ChP 20/36; WM/Lord Butler, 1980; WM/Viscount Antony Head, 1980.
40. Eden, *The Reckoning,* 203–4.
41. C&R-TCC, 1:115.
42. Robert E. Sherwood, *Roosevelt and Hopkins: An Intimate History* (New York, 1948), l, 14, 15, 234.
43. Arthur Conan Doyle, *The Great Boer War* (Charlestown, SC, 2006); Colville, *Fringes,* 330; Cv/3, 29.
44. Franklin D. Roosevelt Presidential Library and Museum, 1/6/41.
45. H. L. Mencken, *The American Language, Supplement Two* (New York, 1962), 784–85 (derivation of "Jeep").
46. WSCHCS, 6328.
47. WSCHCS, 6328; *Times,* 1/10/41; David Dilks, ed., *The Diaries of Sir Alexander Cadogan, 1938–1945* (New York, 1972), 342; Cv/2, 1268.
48. Colville, *Fringes,* 332.
49. John Rupert Colville, *Footprints in Time* (London, 1976), 153.
50. James Conant, *My Several Lives: Memoirs of a Social Inventor* (Boston, 1970), 229–31.
51. Conant, *My Several Lives,* 231.
52. WM/Sir Robert Boothby, 10/16/80 ("cool and *yella*").
53. TWY, 114; WSCHCS, 6529.
54. TWY, 136–37; Mosley, *Battle of Britain;* Cv/3, 825; Cv/2, 1314.
55. WSCHCC, 6451.
56. Shirer, *Rise and Fall,* 779; Cv/2, 1243.
57. Eade, *Churchill,* 141.
58. Colville, *Fringes,* 305.
59. Walter H. Thompson, *Assignment: Churchill* (New York, 1953), 220; WSC 3, 5; Colville, *Fringes,* 341.
60. WSC 3, 38.
61. Panter-Downes, *War Notes,* 134.
62. Klingaman, *1941,* 88.

63. Klingaman, *1941*, 127; *Time*, 3/14/41, 25; WSC 3, 112, 122.
64. Colville, *Fringes*, 358.
65. Roger Chesneau, *Conway's All the World's Fighting Ships, 1922–1946* (London, 1980), 244; WSC 3, 122.
66. Laurence Thompson, *1940* (New York, 1966), 234–35; Ian Kershaw, *Hitler: 1936–1945 Nemesis* (New York, 2000), 334; WSC 3, 12–13.
67. Shirer, *Rise and Fall*, 806; Kershaw, *Hitler*, 342–44; Adolf Hitler, *Mein Kampf*, edited by John Chamberlain et al. (New York, 1939), 959–61.
68. Shirer, *Berlin Diary*, 459–65.
69. Colville, *Fringes*, 148–49.
70. Ben Pimlott, *Hugh Dalton* (London, 1985), 296.
71. Colville, *Fringes*, 196; Hugh Dalton, *Memoirs 1931–1945: The Fateful Years* (London, 1957), 365–67.
72. Pimlott, *Hugh Dalton*, 301.
73. Pimlott, *Hugh Dalton*, 312.
74. Martin Gilbert, *The Second World War: A Complete History* (London, 1989), 161.
75. Klingaman, *1941*, 47; *NYT*, 7/21/41.
76. Colville, *Fringes*, 441.
77. Duff Cooper, *Old Men Forget* (London, 1954), 270–71.
78. WM/A. J. P. Taylor, 1980.
79. Gardner, *Churchill in Power*, 108; *Time*, 1/6/41.
80. Colville, *Fringes*, 331–33.
81. WM/Pamela Harriman, 8/22/80; WM/Averell Harriman, 8/22/80; Sherwood, *Roosevelt and Hopkins*, 203.
82. Robert E. Sherwood, *The White House Papers of Harry L. Hopkins: An Intimate History* (London, 1948).
83. Sherwood, *White House Papers*.
84. Colville, *Fringes*, 334–35; WM/Jock Colville, 10/14/80.
85. Colville, *Fringes*, 334–35; WM/Jock Colville, 10/14/80.
86. Colville, *Fringes*, 334–35; WM/Jock Colville, 10/14/80.
87. Colville, *Fringes*, 334–35; WM/Jock Colville, 10/14/80.
88. Colville, *Fringes*, 334–35; WM/Jock Colville, 10/14/80.
89. GILBERT 6, 986; WSCHCS, 7235.
90. Colville, *Fringes*, 333–34.
91. GILBERT 6, 986–87 (Lyttelton recollection).
92. Colville, *Fringes*, 331–34.
93. Colville, *Fringes*, 334–35; GILBERT 6, 987.
94. GILBERT 6, 988–89; Sherwood, *White House Papers*, 1:239–40.
95. GILBERT 6, 988–89; Sherwood, *White House Papers*, 1:239–40.
96. GILBERT 5, 990; Lord Moran, *Churchill: Taken from the Diaries of Lord Moran* (Boston, 1966), 6–7; WSCHCS, 6329.
97. Moran, *Diaries*, 6–7.
98. WSC 3, 5.
99. Richard Collier, *The War in the Desert* (New York, 1980), 26–33; John Keegan, *The Second World War* (London, 1989); ChP 20/14.
100. ChP 20/49 (cable to Wavell); Colville, *Fringes*, 329.
101. WSC to Wavell, 1/11/41, ChP 20/49.
102. William Manchester, *The Last Lion* (Boston, 1983), 1:522.

103. GILBERT 6, 988–89.
104. Collier, *War in the Desert,* 30–33.
105. WSCHCS, 6346.
106. Keegan, *Second World War,* 328; Collier, *War in the Desert,* 32–33.
107. Hastings Lionel Ismay, *The Memoirs of General Lord Ismay* (London, 1960), 190; Keegan, *Second World War,* 328; Collier, *War in the Desert,* 33.
108. Keegan, *Second World War,* 147–48, 328.
109. Ismay, *Memoirs,* 195.
110. B. H. Liddell Hart, *History of the Second World War* (New York, 1971), 118.
111. WSC 3, 757; Ismay, *Memoirs,* 270.
112. Boatner, *Biographical Dictionary,* 513–14.
113. Keegan, *Second World War,* 322–24.
114. Keegan, *Second World War,* 322–24.
115. Keegan, *Second World War,* 323.
116. WSC 3, 26–27; *Time,* 10/16/44.
117. TWY, 198; Conant, *My Several Lives,* 231.
118. Colville, *Fringes,* 773; Sarah Churchill, *Keep On Dancing* (London, 1981), 96.
119. Colville, *Footprints,* 153–55; WM/Averell Harriman and Pamela Harriman, 8/22/80; GILBERT 6, 1019.
120. Sherwood, *Roosevelt and Hopkins,* 157.
121. WSCHCS, 6347; F. W. Winterbotham, *The Ultra Secret* (New York, 1974), 99–100.
122. WSCHCS, 6346–51.
123. Dilks, *Diaries,* 353.
124. WSCHCS, 6346.
125. WSCHCS, 6346.
126. Cv/3, 395–97.
127. ChP 69/2; ChP 20/49.
128. Conant, *My Several Lives,* 254.
129. ChP 20/13.
130. Scott Berg, *Lindbergh* (New York, 1999), 414–15.
131. Gardner, *Churchill in Power,* 108.
132. Conant, *My Several Lives,* 232.
133. Steel, *Walter Lippmann,* 389.
134. Eric Sevareid, *Not So Wild a Dream,* 177, 193.
135. Cv/3, 321.
136. Colville, *Fringes,* 350; PFR/Alexander Balas (Iron Guard), 12/08.
137. *Time,* 2/3/41.
138. Colville, *Fringes,* 312–13, 403.
139. Cv/3, 204; TWY, 144–45, 186–87.
140. WM/John Martin, 10/23/80.
141. *Time,* 6/9/41 (Eden address on war aims), 26; Colville, *Fringes,* 329.
142. Colville, *Fringes,* 329; ChP 20/36; ChP 20/30.
143. Cv/3, 974.
144. Cv/3, 974.
145. Cv/3, 977.
146. Cv/3, 320–21.
147. Cv/3, 320–21.

148. Conant, *My Several Lives*, 276.
149. Conant, *My Several Lives*, 274, 277–78.
150. Conant, *My Several Lives*, 274, 277–78.
151. Colville, *Fringes*, 736.
152. Cv/3, 320–21.
153. WSCHCS, 6386.
154. Cv/3, 302.
155. WM/Viscount Antony Head, 1980; Colville, *Churchillians*, 136.
156. C&R-TCC, 1:145; Klingaman, *1941*, 127–30.
157. WM/George Thomson, 1980.
158. Klingaman, *1941*, 98–99; WM/Jock Colville, 10/14/80.
159. WM/Pamela Harriman, 8/22/80; TWY, 189.
160. TWY, 140–41.
161. *Time*, 1/20/41.
162. Conant, *My Several Lives*, 254–55.
163. Conant, *My Several Lives*, 254–55; Keegan, *Second World War*, 538.
164. *NYT*, 3/12/41.
165. *NYT*, 3/12/41.
166. *NYT*, 3/12/41; WSCHCS, 6360, 6505; CAB 115/436; Colville, *Fringes*, 343.
167. ChP 23/9; Keegan, *Second World War*, 104–6.
168. WSC 3, 111–14; Keegan, *Second World War*, 104–6.
169. Harriman and Abel, *Special Envoy*, v–vi; Sherwood, *Roosevelt and Hopkins*, 269.
170. Boatner, *Biographical Dictionary*, 206.
171. WM/Averell Harriman, 8/22/80.
172. WM/Averell Harriman, 8/22/80.
173. WM/Averell Harriman, 8/22/80.
174. Eden, *The Reckoning*, 248, 251, 253; Colville, *Fringes*, 360–61.
175. C&R–TCC, 1:144–45 (3/10/41 cable to FDR).
176. C&R–TCC, 1:144–45 (3/10/41 cable to FDR); Cv/3, 329.
177. Cv/3 (cable to Eden re Italians), 432; John Keegan, *Winston Churchill* (New York, 2002), 138–39.
178. Colville, *Fringes*, 369; Klingaman, *1941*, 194–95.
179. Dilks, *Diaries*, 365; Colville, *Fringes*, 337, 366; GILBERT 6, 1042–43.
180. Colville, *Fringes*, 367; Pimlott, *Hugh Dalton*, 309; Dilks, *Diaries*, 366.
181. Colville, *Fringes*, 367.
182. Keegan, *Second World War*, 328–29; ChP 20/49; Ismay, *Memoirs*, 201; Colville, *Fringes*, 135.
183. ChP 20/37.
184. John Keegan, *Who's Who in World War II* (London, 1995), 175.
185. Colville, *Fringes*, 369–70.
186. Dilks, *Diaries*, 367–68.
187. Cv/3, 426–28.
188. Colville, *Fringes*, 368; Cv/3, 427–28.
189. Cv/3, 447.
190. WSCHCS, 5818.
191. GILBERT 6, 1050–51; Cv/3, 447–48.
192. Winterbotham, *Ultra Secret*, 100–101.
193. Keegan, *Second World War*, 152–54; Eden, *The Reckoning*, 247.

194. Cv/3, 439.
195. Cv/3, 445.
196. Cv/3, 439.
197. Collier, *War in the Desert,* 65–67.
198. Keegan, *Second World War,* 328–29; Collier, *War in the Desert,* 65–67.
199. Colville, *Fringes,* 371; Cv/3, 448–49.
200. Cv/3, 448–49; Colville, *Fringes,* 371.
201. WSC 3, 211.
202. Colville, *Fringes,* 369–70.
203. Brown, *Suez to Singapore,* 4–5; WSC 3, 175.
204. Brown, *Suez to Singapore,* 4–6.
205. Keegan, *Second World War,* 157–59.
206. CAB 65/22.
207. Cv/3, 517–18.
208. Cv/3, 521.
209. David Irving, *Hitler's War* (New York, 1977), 1:246–47.
210. Keegan, *Second World War,* 157.
211. Sherwood, *Roosevelt and Hopkins,* 239.
212. Collier, *War in the Desert,* 67–68.
213. ChP 69/2; Cv/3, 445.
214. Berg, *Lindbergh,* 418–19.
215. Shirer, *Rise and Fall,* 824.
216. Basil Collier, *The Second World War: A Military History from Munich to Hiroshima* (New York, 1967), 186–87.
217. *Time,* 5/5/41.
218. WM/Jock Colville, 10/14/80.
219. Cv/3, 360.
220. Panter-Downes, *War Notes,* 141; Colville, *Fringes,* 374–75.
221. Dilks, *Diaries,* 372; Colville, *Fringes,* 375; WM/Jock Colville, 10/14/80.
222. Broad, *Anthony Eden,* 170; John Wheeler-Bennett, *Action This Day: Working with Churchill* (London, 1968), 77; Colville, *Fringes,* 128.
223. Colville, *Fringes,* 443–45.
224. Eden, *The Reckoning,* 295; WSCHCS, 6378.
225. Eden, *The Reckoning,* 295; WSCHCS, 6378; Winterbotham, *Ultra Secret,* 101.
226. WSCHCS, 6378.
227. WSCHCS, 6378.
228. C&R-TCC, 1:322.
229. George Orwell, "Reflections on Gandhi" (1949), in *The Orwell Reader* (New York, 1984); WSCHCS, 6378.
230. Orwell, "Reflections"; WSCHCS, 6378.
231. Harriman and Abel, *Special Envoy,* 16–17; GILBERT 6, 1018.
232. Cv/3, 560 (Wavell cable).
233. GILBERT 6, 1072; Panter-Downes, *War Notes,* 140.
234. Danchev and Todman, *War Diaries,* 154; ChP 120/10.
235. ChP 120/10.
236. ChP 120/10.
237. Colville, *Fringes,* 391.
238. Kenneth Young, *Churchill and Beaverbrook* (London, 1966), 178–79.
239. Panter-Downes, *War Notes,* 145.

240. Panter-Downes, *War Notes,* 123.
241. Panter-Downes, *War Notes,* 123, 138; Hansard 5/29/41 Oral answers (Cv/3, 735).
242. Dilks, *Diaries,* 375.
243. WSC 3, 254, 255, 265; John Keegan, ed., *Churchill's Generals* (New York, 1991).
244. *Time,* 6/2/41, 24; WSC 3, 264–66.
245. Cv/3, 560.
246. Keegan, *Second World War,* 161.
247. C&R-TCC, 1:176.
248. Keegan, *Second World War,* 161.
249. C&R-TCC, 1:172–74.
250. C&R-TCC, 1:172–74; Harriman and Abel, *Special Envoy,* 31.
251. Colville, *Fringes,* 381–82.
252. C&R-TCC, 1:181–82.
253. WSC 3, 53–55; Sherwood, *Roosevelt and Hopkins,* 293–94; *Time,* 12/27/43, 73; *Time,* 12/27/43, 73 (MacNeice).
254. WM/Pamela Harriman, 8/22/80.
255. WSC 3, 53–55.
256. WSC 3, 53–55.
257. Sherwood, *Roosevelt and Hopkins,* 294.
258. Albert Speer, *Inside the Third Reich: Memoirs by Albert Speer* (Macmillan, 1970), 174–75.
259. WM/Kay Halle, 8/6/80.
260. *Time,* 6/12/44.
261. Colville, *Fringes,* 385–86; Cv/3, 767; WSCHCS, 6399.
262. Colville, *Fringes,* 385–86.
263. Boatner, *Biographical Dictionary,* 596.
264. Keegan, *Second World War,* 166–69.
265. C&R-TCC, 1:191, 192; Colville, *Fringes,* 389.
266. Colville, *Fringes,* 389.
267. Colville, *Fringes,* 389.
268. WSC 3, 305.
269. Boatner, *Biographical Dictionary,* 328.
270. Chesneau, *Conway's;* WSC 3, 305–20.
271. C&R-TCC, 1:192; Colville, *Fringes,* 374.
272. Colville, *Fringes,* 390; Ismay, *Memoirs,* 219; ChP 4/219.
273. WM/Averell Harriman, 8/22/80.
274. WCS 6, 1094.
275. Colville, *Fringes,* 391; WSC 3, 299.
276. Colville, *Fringes,* 391.
277. Colville, *Fringes,* 391.
278. Colville, *Footprints,* 188–89.
279. WSC 3, 316–17.
280. WSC 3, 317–20; Colville, *Fringes,* 403.
281. *Time,* 6/16/41;WM/Averell Harriman, 8/22/80.
282. WSC 3, 317–20.
283. Cv/3, 761; *Time,* 6/16/41, 30; WSC 3, 304.
284. WSCHCS, 6412–15; Hansard 6/10/41.
285. WSCHCS, 6415; Hansard 6/10/41.
286. Colville, *Fringes,* 383, 393.

287. Colville, *Fringes,* 396.
288. Colville, *Fringes,* 396; C&R-TCC, 1:191.
289. Colville, *Fringes,* 382, 402; GILBERT 6, 846.
290. GILBERT 6, 1074 n1.
291. ChP 20/36.
292. Robert W. Creamer, *Baseball and Other Matters in 1941* (Lincoln, NE, 1991), 169–70.
293. Franklin D. Roosevelt Presidential Library and Museum, 5/27/41.
294. WSCHCS, 6490.
295. Cv/3, 731 (to Wavell).
296. Cv/3, 1132 (letter to Randolph); Colville, *Fringes,* 432.
297. WSC 3, 368.
298. WSC 3, 342.
299. Cv/3, 807, 830; *Time,* 3/31/41.
300. Cv/2, 1246; Colville, *Fringes,* 403–4.
301. Colville, *Fringes,* 403; Boatner, *Biographical Dictionary,* 556.
302. Colville, *Fringes,* 403.
303. Eden, *The Reckoning,* 312; Colville, *Fringes,* 403.
304. Keegan, *Second World War,* 181.
305. Keegan, *Second World War,* 181; Shirer, *Rise and Fall,* 849.
306. Keegan, *Second World War,* 180–81.
307. Keegan, *Second World War,* 178–79; WSC 3, 353.
308. Colville, *Fringes,* 403–4; TWY, 174.
309. TWY, 174.
310. Colville, *Fringes,* 402–3.
311. Colville, *Fringes,* 405.
312. Colville, *Fringes,* 405.
313. WSCHCS, 6427.
314. WSCHCS, 6427; C&R-TCC, 2:22 (Balkan proverb).
315. TWY, 174.
316. PFR/Sir John Keegan, 6/04.
317. J. Erikson, *The Soviet High Command* (London, 1962); William Taubman, *Khrushchev: The Man and His Era* (New York, 2003), 162.
318. ChP 65/19; Cv/3, 1107; C&R-TCC, 1:253.
319. Cv/3, 842.
320. Cv/ 3, 870–71.
321. C&R-TCC, 1:224.
322. Young, *Churchill and Beaverbrook,* 200; WSC 2, 577; Richard Langworth, ed., *Churchill by Himself: The Definitive Collection of Quotations* (London, 2008), 324.
323. Cv/3, 956; Cv/3, 1161.
324. WSC 3, 462–63; Cv/3, 1171–72.
325. ChP 20/44.
326. Cv/3, 1171 (to Cripps); Cv/3, 964–65 (to Stalin).
327. Cv/3, 841 (to Chiefs).
328. Cv/3, 991; Cv/3, 1236.
329. GILBERT 6, 1050–51.
330. James C. Humes, *The Wit and Wisdom of Winston Churchill* (New York, 1995), 151; Colville, *Fringes,* 309; Anthony Montague Browne, *Long Sunset* (London, 1996), 76.

331. *Time*, 6/9/41.
332. Colville, *Fringes*, 194; Colville, *Churchillians*, 144.
333. Colville, *Fringes*, 416–17.
334. Colville, *Fringes*, 419; Cv/3, 978.
335. *Brooklyn Eagle*, 8/6/41.
336. Cv/3, 1031; Colville, *Fringes*, 424; WM/Sir Ian Jacob, 11/12/80.
337. WSC 3, 429.
338. WSC 3, 425–27; *Brooklyn Eagle*, 8/6/41; GILBERT 6, 1155–56.
339. WSC 3, 445–46.
340. Cv/3, 111 (draft of threat to Japan).
341. Dilks, *Diaries*, 396–97; *Brooklyn Eagle*, 8/6/41; *Time*, 5/31/41.
342. Thompson, *Assignment: Churchill*, 230.
343. Wheeler-Bennett, *Action This Day*, 207.
344. WSC 3, 434.
345. WSC 3, 432.
346. Thompson, *Assignment: Churchill*, 234, 236, 239; ChP 4/225; Dilks, *Diaries*, 398.
347. WSC 3, 443–44.
348. WSC 4, 890; Cv/3, 1059.
349. Thompson, *Assignment: Churchill*, 271; Dilks, *Diaries*, 277, 280, 401.
350. CAB 65/19; Cv/3, 1079, 1084.
351. Dilks, *Diaries*, 402; Cv/3, 1068; Cv/3, 1079.
352. Colville, *Fringes*, 428; Cv/3, 1111; Cv/3, 1079–81; Keegan, *Second World War*, 538–39.
353. Colville, *Fringes*, 428; James MacGregor Burns, *Roosevelt: The Soldier of Freedom, 1940–1945* (New York, 1970), 118, 134.
354. Shirer, *Rise and Fall*, 854.
355. *NYT*, 9/2/41; Sherwood, *Roosevelt and Hopkins*, 369.
356. T. R. Fehrenbach, *FDR's Undeclared War 1939–1941* (New York, 1967).
357. Franklin D. Roosevelt Presidential Library and Museum, Fireside Chat, 9/11/41.
358. Klingaman, *1941*, 370.
359. War Cabinet No. 112 of 1941; C&R-TCC, 1:265.
360. War Cabinet No. 112 of 1941.
361. Franklin D. Roosevelt Presidential Library and Museum, 9/11/41.
362. C&R-TCC, 1:198.
363. C&R-TCC, 1:265.
364. Wheeler-Bennett, *Action This Day*, 202.
365. Gordon Prange, *At Dawn We Slept: The Untold Story of Pearl Harbor* (London, 1983), 37–39, 320; Liddell Hart, *History*, 227.
366. Cv/3, 236; *Time*, 1/19/42, 9.
367. WSC 3 (memo to Ismay), 177.
368. Colville, *Footprints*, 150; Cv/3, 44; Premier (Prime Minister) Papers, Public Record Office, Kew, 3/156/6.
369. Klingaman, *1941*, 346.
370. WSC 3, 580–81.
371. C&R-TCC, 1:108; ChP 20/13 (Ismay Minute, 7/25/40); Colville, *Fringes*, 335; Cv/3, 575.
372. C&R-TCC, 1:257; WSC 3, 603.
373. Cv/3, 1094.
374. Cv/3, 1555.
375. *Chicago Tribune*, 10/27/41.

376. Cv/3, 1111.
377. C&R-TCC, 1:276.
378. Cv/3, 1530–31.
379. ChP 2/416.
380. Eden, *The Reckoning*, 325.
381. Boatner, *Biographical Dictionary* 63 (Brooke); Danchev and Todman, *War Diaries*, 89–90.
382. Colville, *Fringes*, 446.
383. Cv/3, 1534; Cv/3, 1530–36.
384. C&R-TCC, 1:266.
385. Cv/3, 1530.
386. Colville, *Fringes*, 414–15; Churchill, *Keep On Dancing*, 95.
387. WM/Lady Mary Soames, 10/27/80; Mary Soames, *Clementine Churchill: The Biography of a Marriage* (New York, 2003), 403; Churchill, *Keep On Dancing*, 160.
388. Soames, *Clementine*, 404.
389. Collier, *War in the Desert*, 83–86.
390. Cv/3, 1531 (Auchinleck greetings).
391. WSCHCS, 6519.
392. TWY, 190.
393. TWY, 205.
394. Cv/3, 1534–36.
395. Keegan, *Second World War*, 538.
396. Keegan, *Second World War*, 203, 206.

Vortex

1. Walter H. Thompson, *Assignment: Churchill* (New York, 1953), 3.
2. PFR/Winston S. Churchill, 4/04 (Christmas at Chequers); WM/Pamela Harriman, 8/22/80; Martin Gilbert, *Churchill and the Jews* (New York, 2007), 2; John Colville, *The Fringes of Power: 10 Downing Street Diaries 1939–1955* (New York, 1985), 392.
3. PFR/Winston S. Churchill (Christmas at Chequers), 4/04.
4. Alex Danchev and Daniel Todman, eds., *Field Marshal Lord Alanbrooke: War Diaries 1939–1945* (Berkeley, 2003), 209.
5. Cv/3, 1553; Cv/3, 1235.
6. W. Averell Harriman and Elie Abel, *Special Envoy to Churchill and Stalin: 1941–1946* (New York, 1975), 111.
7. *Time*, 5/11/42, 90; C&R-TCC, 1:279.
8. C&R-TCC, 1:280–81; *Time*, 1/19/42, 9.
9. Arthur Bryant, *The Turn of the Tide: A History of the War Years Based on the Diaries of Field-Marshal Lord Alanbrooke, 1939–1943* (New York, 1957), 233.
10. Cv/3, 1574.
11. WM/Averell Harriman, 8/22/80.
12. Cv/3, 1576–77; WM/Pamela Harriman, 8/22/80; WM/Averell Harriman, 8/22/80.
13. Cv/3, 1576–77; WM/Pamela Harriman, 8/22/80; WM/Averell Harriman, 8/22/80; WM/John Martin, 10/23/80.
14. WSC 3, 604; Danchev and Todman, *War Diaries*, 209.

15. Cv/3, 1579.
16. ChP 20/36; Bryant, *Tide,* 226; Duff Cooper, *Old Men Forget* (London, 1954), 301.
17. William Manchester, *American Caesar: Douglas MacArthur 1880–1964* (Boston, 1978), 209–11; Samuel Eliot Morison, *The Two-Ocean War* (Boston, 1963), 82; Clay Blair Jr., *Silent Victory* (Annapolis, MD, 1975), 134, 171.
18. *NYT,* 12/12/41; Manchester, *American Caesar,* 209–11; Morison, *Two-Ocean War,* 82.
19. Eisenhower, *Crusade,* 21; Leonard Mosley, *Marshall: Hero for Our Times* (New York, 1982), 189–91.
20. C&R-TCC, 1:283.
21. WSCHCS, 6525; TWY, 194.
22. WSC 3, 611; ChP 20/46; ChP 20/20.
23. Cv/3, 1586; Anthony Eden, Earl of Avon, *The Reckoning: The Memoirs of Anthony Eden* (New York, 1965), 330–31.
24. Mary Soames, *Clementine Churchill: The Biography of a Marriage* (New York, 2003), 349–50 (Komodo); WM/Viscount Antony Head, 1980.
25. Winston S. Churchill, *A History of the English-Speaking Peoples,* 4 vols. (New York, 1993), 3:212.
26. WM/Mark Bonham Carter, 10/20/80.
27. Cv/3, 1435; Cv/3, 1455; WM/Sir Ian Jacob, 11/12/80.
28. Cv/3, 1083; WM/Sir Ian Jacob, 11/12/80.
29. WM/G. M. Thompson, 1980; WSC 3, 854; WM/Sir Ian Jacob, 11/12/80.
30. Mark Mayo Boatner, *The Biographical Dictionary of World War II* (New York, 1999), 428; Stephen Roskill, *Churchill and the Admirals* (New York, 1978), 199; Hastings Lionel Ismay, *The Memoirs of General Lord Ismay* (London, 1960), 240.
31. WM/G. M. Thompson, 1980.
32. Cv/3, 1592; Cecil Brown, *Suez to Singapore* (New York, 1942), 298.
33. WSC 3, 619; David Reynolds, *Britannia Overruled* (London, 2000), 141.
34. Brown, *Suez to Singapore,* 311–23; Cv/3, 1474.
35. Brown, *Suez to Singapore,* 311–23; Cv/3, 1474.
36. Brown, *Suez to Singapore,* 328.
37. WM/Averell Harriman, 8/22/80.
38. Cv/3, 1593; WSC 3, 620.
39. Mollie Panter-Downes, *London War Notes, 1939–1945* (London, 1972), 198.
40. Thompson, *Assignment: Churchill,* 245–46.
41. Winston Churchill, *My Early Life: 1874–1904* (New York, 1996), 19; WM/Lady Mary Soames, 10/27/80.
42. Churchill, *Early Life,* 19; WM/Lady Mary Soames, 10/27/80.
43. Hansard 12/11/41; TWY, 196–97.
44. WSC 3, 616; CAB 69/4 (Cv/3, 1651); Winston S. Churchill, *The World Crisis,* 5 vols. (New York, 1923–31), 1:212 ("gigantic castles of steel").
45. The Editors of the Viking Press, *The Churchill Years 1874–1965, with Foreword by Lord Butler of Saffron Walden* (London, 1965), 21; WM/R. A. B. Butler, 12/5/80.
46. Cv/3, 1627.
47. *Time,* 1/5/42, 13–14; *Time,* 3/2/42, 57.
48. *NYT,* 12/12/42.
49. WSCHCS, 6530; TWY, 196–97.
50. Colville, *Fringes,* 404; WSCHCC, 6531.

51. C&R-TCC, 1:286.
52. Cv/3, 1612; Danchev and Todman, *War Diaries,* 209.
53. GILBERT 7, 6–7; PFR/Lady Mary Soames, 6/07.
54. W&C-TPL, 459–61.
55. WM/G. M. Thompson, 1980.
56. *NYT,* 12/12/41.
57. Richard Collier, *The War in the Desert* (New York, 1980), 84–85.
58. Cv/3, 1657; David Dilks, ed., *The Diaries of Sir Alexander Cadogan, 1938–1945* (New York, 1972), 439.
59. PFR/Winston S. Churchill, 5/04; Soames, *Clementine,* 499.
60. WSC 3, 696; PFR/Winston S. Churchill, 4/04.
61. James MacGregor Burns, *Roosevelt: The Soldier of Freedom, 1940–1945* (New York, 1970), 551.
62. WSC 6, 400–401; C&R-TCC, 3:68–69; WSCHCS, 7117.
63. John Gunther, *Inside Europe* (New York, 1938), 464–65; WM/Averell Harriman, 8/22/80; Harriman and Abel, *Special Envoy,* 283.
64. Harriman and Abel, *Special Envoy,* 77, 220.
65. Elisabeth Barker, *Churchill and Eden at War* (New York, 1978), 233–35; ChP 20/50.
66. Cv/3, 1644.
67. Louis P. Lochner, *The Goebbels Diaries 1942–1943* (New York, 1948), 136; Charles Burdick and Hans-Adolf Jacobsen, eds., *The Halder War Diary, 1939–1942* (New York, 1988); Boatner, *Biographical Dictionary,* 200–201.
68. Panter-Downes, *War Notes,* 191.
69. Thompson, *Assignment: Churchill,* 246; WSC 3, 682.
70. Cv/3, 1344–45.
71. John Keegan, ed., *Churchill's Generals* (New York, 1991), 86; Cv/3, 1341; WSC 4, 24.
72. CAB 69/2; ChP 20/20.
73. Harriman and Abel, *Special Envoy,* 216; Bryant, *Tide,* 15.
74. Dwight D. Eisenhower, *Crusade in Europe* (New York, 1948), 22.
75. Bryant, *Tide,* 16 ("salt water" general).
76. Danchev and Todman, *War Diaries,* 281; Bryant, *Tide,* 234.
77. Edward Jablonski, *Airwar: Tragic Victories* (Garden City, NY, 1971), "American Renegades," 26–42.
78. WSC 3, 674; Bryant, *Tide,* 231.
79. WSCHCS, 6535; Written Archives Center, U.S. National Park Service.
80. William K. Klingaman, *1941: Our Lives in a World on the Edge* (New York, 1989), 449.
81. WSC 3, 666.
82. ChP 20/50; *Time,* 1/5/42, 22–23; *Time,* 8/3/42, 15.
83. *Time,* 1/5/42, 16; Moran, *Diaries,* 11; WSCHCS, 6536.
84. WSCHCS, 6537–39.
85. *NYT,* 12/27/41; ChP 20/49; Bryant, *Tide,* 229; GILBERT 7, 28–29.
86. WSC 3, 691; Lord Moran, *Churchill: Taken from the Diaries of Lord Moran* (Boston, 1966), 17–18.
87. Moran, *Diaries,* 20.
88. WSC 3, 679; Martin Gilbert, *In Search of Churchill: A Historian's Journey* (New York, 1994), 295–96.

89. Thompson, *Bodyguard,* 257; WSC 3, 680–81.
90. PFR/Brig. General Albine Irzyk (U.S. Army ret.), 12/11.
91. TWY, 199; WSC 3, 681.
92. Danchev and Todman, *War Diaries,* 217; Klingaman, *1941,* 450–51.
93. Boatner, *Biographical Dictionary,* 324; WSC 3, 682–83.
94. Boatner, *Biographical Dictionary,* 324; WSC 3, 682–83; GILBERT 7, 35; WM/Pamela Harriman, 8/22/80. This was her secondhand recollection of what Churchill said to Roosevelt when the president encountered WSC naked. Afterward Churchill disputed the recollection of his bodyguard, Inspector Walter Thompson (*Assignment: Churchill,* 248), and his secretary, Patrick Kinna, who both claimed Churchill said to the president, "You see Mr. President, I have nothing to conceal [or "hide"] from you." (GILBERT 7, 28). Churchill later told Robert E. Sherwood (*Roosevelt and Hopkins: An Intimate History* [New York, 1948], 442–43) that he in fact had secrets to keep from the Americans, and did so.
95. *NYT,* 12/12/41.
96. Mencken, *American Language,* 785–86.
97. *Atlantic Monthly,* 3/65, 79.
98. Tom Hickman, *Churchill's Bodyguard* (London, 2005), 261; WSC 3, 691, 706; Celia Sandys, *Chasing Churchill* (New York, 2005), 148; WM/John Martin, 10/23/80.
99. *Time,* 5/25/42, 22–23; The Adamic Louis Papers, Slovene American Collection, Immigration History Research Center, University of Minnesota; WM/Sir Fitzroy Maclean, 10/15/80.
100. GILBERT 6, 1215 (lisp); *Time,* 9/2/46; *Time,* 11/4/46.
101. WM/Cecily ("Chips") Gemmell, 7/10/80; WM/Jock Colville, 10/14/80.
102. WM/Cecily ("Chips") Gemmell, 7/10/80; WM/Jock Colville, 10/14/80; WM/Sir David Hunt, 1980.
103. Barbara Tuchman, *Stilwell and the American Experience in China* (New York, 1971), 296, 308–9.
104. Tuchman, *Stilwell,* 625; WSC 3, 705; WSC 4, 123.
105. WSC 3, 689–90; *Time,* 5/5/43.
106. WSC 2, 115; Morison, *Two-Ocean War,* 138.
107. WSC 3, 710–11.
108. WSC 3, 708.
109. GILBERT 7, 53–54; Eden, *The Reckoning,* 369.
110. ChP 20/23; WSC 4, 8.
111. Moran, *Diaries,* 28; WSC 4, 60–61.
112. Brian Gardner, *Churchill in Power: As Seen by His Contemporaries* (Boston, 1970), 150.
113. David Stafford, *Churchill and Secret Service* (London, 2000), 280.
114. *Time,* 3/2/42, 27 ("Christ and Carrots" Cripps); Lochner, *Goebbels Diaries,* 137.
115. Kenneth Young, *Churchill and Beaverbrook* (London, 1966), 230, 232; WSC 4, 75; Cv/3, 1373–74; Gardner, *Churchill in Power,* 183.
116. WSC 4, 61; Gardner, *Churchill in Power,* 157.
117. Gardner, *Churchill in Power,* 147.
118. John Colville, *The Churchillians* (London, 1981), 69; John Wheeler-Bennett, *Action This Day: Working with Churchill* (London, 1968), 79; Charles Eade, ed., *Churchill by His Contemporaries* (New York, 1954), 298; WM/Jock Colville, 10/14/80.

119. Brian Gardner, *Churchill in Power: As Seen by His Contemporaries* (Boston, 1970), 152; Moran, *Diaries*, 80; WSCHCS, 7269.
120. Jan Morris, *The Matter of Wales* (New York, 1984), 404, 405; Gardner, *Churchill in Power*, 152; Moran, *Diaries*, 649.
121. WM/Pamela Harriman, 8/22/80; WSC 4, 61; Gardner, *Churchill in Power*, 157; TWY, 207, 208, 209; Colville, *Fringes*, 737.
122. WM/Averell Harriman, 8/22/80; WSC 4, 61; Gardner, *Churchill in Power*, 157; TWY, 207, 208, 209.
123. Gardner, *Churchill in Power*, 158.
124. TWY, 209.
125. *Time*, 10/24/1941.
126. WSC 3, 576–77.
127. WSC 3, 576–77; W&C-TPL, 558; *Time*, 5/3/43, 40.
128. Collier, *War in the Desert*, 89; WSC 4, 21; TWY, 209.
129. *Time*, 3/2/42, 20.
130. Basil Collier, *The Second World War: A Military History from Munich to Hiroshima* (New York, 1967), 268; *Time*, 3/2/42, 20.
131. Brown, *Suez to Singapore*, 370, 392.
132. WSC 4, 50–51; Collier, *Second World War*, 273.
133. Brown, *Suez to Singapore*, 373; Cooper, *Old Men*, 305; PFR/Michael Browning, 7/04.
134. GILBERT 7, 47, 57; ChP 20/67.
135. John Toland, *The Rising Sun: The Decline and Fall of the Japanese Empire, 1936–1945* (London, 2003), 336–37; *Time*, 3/2/42, 21; C&R-TCC, 1:381; Danchev and Todman, *War Diaries*, 231.
136. WSC 3, 581.
137. John Keegan, *The Second World War* (London, 1989), 261.
138. Lochner, *Goebbels Diaries*, 81, 83.
139. WSC 3, 680; TWY, 212; Hansard 2/17/42.
140. WSC 4, 72, 113; Panter-Downes, *War Notes*, 206–7; WSCHCS, 6615 ("simpletons and dunderheads").
141. WSC 4, 81; WM/Lord Geoffrey Lloyd, 1980.
142. WM/Malcolm Muggeridge, 11/25/80; WM/Lord Geoffrey Lloyd, 1980; WSC 4, 81; Danchev and Todman, *War Diaries*, 713.
143. WSC 4, 75; W&C-TPL, 464.
144. Roy Jenkins, *Churchill: A Biography* (London, 2011), 685.
145. Panter-Downes, *War Notes*, 205.
146. Klingaman, *1941*, 215.
147. WSCHCS, 6427.
148. WSCHCS, 6527.
149. Dilks, *Diaries*, 433.
150. WSC 4, 155–56.
151. Morison, *Two-Ocean War*, 93–97.
152. Soames, *Clementine*, 415; Morison, *Two-Ocean War*, 93–97; *Time*, 3/9/42.
153. Morison, *Two-Ocean War*, 98, 100.
154. Jablonski, *Airwar*, 41–42.
155. WSC 4, 160; Keegan, *Churchill's Generals*, 108–9.
156. For a study of the Bengal famine, see Amartya Sen, *Poverty and Famines: An Essay on Entitlements and Deprivation* (New York, 1982).

157. Tuchman, *Stilwell,* 347; WSC 4, 170.
158. Tuchman, *Stilwell,* 361, 371.
159. Tuchman, *Stilwell,* 361, 371; C&R-TCC, 1:391, 423, 438, 458.
160. TWY, 221; Dilks, *Diaries,* 438.
161. C&R-TCC, 1:421–22.
162. Colville, *Fringes,* 382.
163. Danchev and Todman, *War Diaries,* 438.
164. WSC 4, 121–22.
165. WSC 4, 184.
166. C&R-TCC, 1:382–83, 443; Samuel Eliot Morison, *The Battle of the Atlantic: September 1939–May 1943* (Edison, NJ, 2001), 168; Bryant, *Tide,* 244.
167. C&R-TCC, 1:382–83, 453, 459; Harriman and Abel, *Special Envoy,* 167; Danchev and Todman, *War Diaries,* 290.
168. C&R-TCC, 1:390, 452–54.
169. WM/Jock Colville, 10/14/80.
170. Morison, *Two-Ocean War,* 142.
171. Morison, *Two-Ocean War,* 141; Hiroyuki Agawa, *The Reluctant Admiral* (Tokyo, 1979), 73, 177.
172. Morison, *Two-Ocean War,* 141; Agawa, *Reluctant Admiral,* 140–41; C&R-TCC, 1:466.
173. WSC 4, 188.
174. C&R-TCC, 1:383, 391, 392, 441.
175. WSC 4, 217; George Orwell, "Reflections on Gandhi" (1949), in *The Orwell Reader* (New York, 1984).
176. C&R-TCC, 1:446–47; Harriman and Abel, *Special Envoy,* 131.
177. Sherwood, *Roosevelt and Hopkins,* 530–31.
178. Harriman and Abel, *Special Envoy,* 131; WM/Averell Harriman, 8/22/80; WSC 4, 209; *Time,* 9/14/42, 29.
179. C&R-TCC, 2:449; WM/Lord Christopher Soames, 1980.
180. Lochner, *Goebbels Diaries,* 177.
181. WSC 4, 204–5.
182. C&R-TCC, 1:484, 491.
183. WSC 4, 219.
184. C&R-TCC, 1:441; GILBERT 7, 117.
185. Danchev and Todman, *War Diaries,* 247, 249.
186. C&R-TCC, 1:458.
187. Mosley, *Marshall,* 204–5.
188. Boatner, *Biographical Dictionary,* 1999, 305.
189. C&R-TCC, 1:460.
190. C&R-TCC, 1:494.
191. David Miller, *U-Boats* (New York, 2000), 127; WSC 4, 109; Morison, *Two-Ocean War,* 108.
192. WSC 4, 112, 118, 123; Sherwood, *Roosevelt and Hopkins,* 544; Harriman and Abel, *Special Envoy,* 169.
193. Panter-Downes, *War Notes,* 264.
194. Miller, *U-Boats,* 117–18, 134, 174–75.
195. Miller, *U-Boats,* 117–18, 134, 174–75; Dilks, *Diaries,* 433.
196. WSC 4, 112, 118, 125.
197. C&R-TCC, 1:528.

198. WSC 4, 296.
199. WSC 3, 702–3; Bryant, *Tide,* 357.
200. Ismay, *Memoirs,* 273.
201. Cv/3, 160; Lochner, *Goebbels Diaries,* 189–90; *NYT,* 4/2/08.
202. WSC 3, 702.
203. WM/Sir Ian Jacob, 11/12/80; Danchev and Todman, *War Diaries,* 187.
204. Lochner, *Goebbels Diaries,* 130, 135
205. Lochner, *Goebbels Diaries,* 189; Harold Lee Hitchens, *America Goes to War* (Chicago, 1942), 66; Danchev and Todman, *War Diaries,* 348.
206. Lochner, *Goebbels Diaries,* 179; PFR/Alexander Balas, 12/06; *Time,* 2/1/43, 33.
207. C&R-TCC, 1:382.
208. *Time,* 5/11/42, 17.
209. Collier, *Second World War,* 296; John Keegan, *The Second World War* (London, 1989), 221–22; WSC 4, 343.
210. Keegan, *Second World War,* 222–23.
211. John Keegan, *The Mask of Command* (New York, 1987), 255, 286.
212. Gardner, *Churchill in Power,* 131.
213. C&R-TCC, 1:503.
214. Harriman and Abel, *Special Envoy,* 138.
215. Harriman and Abel, *Special Envoy,* 136.
216. C&R-TCC, 1:441; WSC 4, 314, 327, 341–42; Harriman and Abel, *Special Envoy,* 136.
217. WSC 4, 336–37.
218. Danchev and Todman, *War Diaries,* 100.
219. Collier, *War in the Desert,* 90–91.
220. Danchev and Todman, *War Diaries,* 154; WM/John Martin, 10/23/80.
221. Colville, *Fringes,* 412; Kew, British Archives, Cabinet Minutes (electric chair); see George Orwell, "Politics and the English Language" (1946) in *A Collection of Essays by George Orwell* (Orlando, FL, 1970).
222. WSC 4, 334–35.
223. Colville, *Fringes,* 412; Keegan, *Mask,* 282–283.
224. *Time,* 8/17/42, 24; GILBERT 7, 75; GILBERT 6, 1205; *NYT,* 6/1/42.
225. *Time,* 7/13/42, 92; Lochner, *Goebbels Diaries,* 155.
226. Arthur Harris, *Bomber Offensive* (London, 1947), 52, 310; *Time,* 6/8/42.
227. Panter-Downes, *War Notes,* 226; *Time,* 6/12/42, 32.
228. Lochner, *Goebbels Diaries,* 229.
229. David Stafford, *Churchill and Secret Service* (London, 2000), 280; William L. Shirer, *The Rise and Fall of the Third Reich: A History of Nazi Germany* (New York, 1960), 991.
230. Shirer, *Rise and Fall,* 991–92.
231. *Time,* 6/12/42; Lochner, *Goebbels Diaries,* 147–48.
232. Stafford, *Secret Service,* 281.
233. WSCHCS, 6475.
234. Lochner, *Goebbels Diaries,* 140.
235. Morison, *Two-Ocean War,* 150–51.
236. Morison, *Two-Ocean War,* 155–61.
237. C&R-TCC, 1:510.
238. Keegan, *Atlas,* 64–65.
239. C&R-TCC, 2:510.

240. Danchev and Todman, *War Diaries,* 266; WSC 4, 375.
241. Harry C. Butcher, *My Three Years with Eisenhower* (New York, 1946), 24; Danchev and Todman, *War Diaries,* 266; WSC 4, 376.
242. Collier, *War in the Desert,* 92.
243. WSC 4, 381, 382; GILBERT 7, 426.
244. WSC 4, 383–84.
245. Collier, *War in the Desert,* 92–93.
246. Richard Collier, *Duce!* (New York, 1971), 184–85.
247. WSC 4, 386.
248. WSC 4, 386.
249. WSC 4, 386; Bryant, *Tide,* 333.
250. Harriman and Abel, *Special Envoy,* 144; Panter-Downes, *War Notes,* 232.
251. Butcher, *Eisenhower,* 13, 24.
252. Panter-Downes, *War Notes,* 233, 234, 235, 238.
253. WSC 4, 392.
254. WSC 4, 386.
255. TWY, 231; Panter-Downes, *War Notes,* 234.
256. WSC 4, 398.
257. WSC 4, 400; Boatner, *Biographical Dictionary,* 462.
258. TWY, 232.
259. Butcher, *Eisenhower,* 5, 12, 22, 28.
260. TWY, 235.
261. WSC 4, 447; Eisenhower, *Crusade,* 69; WM/Averell Harriman, 8/22/80.
262. WSC 5, 72; Panter-Downes, *War Notes,* 224.
263. Eisenhower, *Crusade,* 68; *Time,* 7/13/42, 20–21; Butcher, *Eisenhower,* 23.
264. WSC 4, 444 (Roosevelt memo to American Chiefs); Butcher, *Eisenhower,* 51; Sherwood, *Roosevelt and Hopkins,* 648.
265. C&R-TCC, 1:545; Harriman and Abel, *Special Envoy,* 171–72.
266. John Grigg, *1943: The Victory That Never Was* (New York, 1980), 156; Eisenhower, *Crusade,* 83, 85.
267. WSC 4, 529–33; Butcher, *Eisenhower,* 52.
268. Danchev and Todman, *War Diaries,* 272, 357, 358, 359, 364, 634.
269. Colville, *Fringes,* 289.
270. Mosley, *Marshall,* 202, 211; Burns, *Roosevelt,* 286.
271. WM/Sir Ian Jacob, 11/12/80.
272. Danchev and Todman, *War Diaries,* 249, 276; Sherwood, *Roosevelt and Hopkins,* 523.
273. Danchev and Todman, *War Diaries,* 588, 634.
274. Danchev and Todman, *War Diaries,* 716.
275. ChP 20/67; Viscount Montgomery of Alamein, *The Memoirs of Field Marshal Montgomery* (London, 1958), 69–70.
276. Keegan, *Mask,* 288; Keegan, *Second World War,* 226–28.
277. Keegan, *Second World War,* 228; *Time,* 1/4/43, 21.
278. Keegan, *Mask,* 265.
279. F. W. Winterbotham, *The Ultra Secret* (New York, 1974), 109; Stafford, *Secret Service,* 283–84.
280. WSC 4, 452–53; Butcher, *Eisenhower,* 12.
281. Bruce West, *The Man Who Flew Churchill* (New York, 1965), 31, 32; Sandys, *Chasing Churchill,* 152; Moran, *Diaries,* 56; WSC 4, 452–53.
282. Bryant, *Tide,* 353; Danchev and Todman, *War Diaries,* 288.

283. WSC 4, 475.
284. West, *Man Who Flew Churchill*, 104–5; W&C-TPL, 405; WSC 4, 456.
285. WSC 4, 456; Winston S. Churchill, *The River War*, edited by John Muller (London, 2003).
286. WSC 4, 456–57.
287. Danchev and Todman, *War Diaries*, 289.
288. Danchev and Todman, *War Diaries*, 293.
289. WSC 4, 465; Ladislas Farago, *Patton: Ordeal and Triumph* (New York, 1963), 179.
290. WSC 4, 467; TWY, 259; Danchev and Todman, *War Diaries*, 296.
291. TWY, 259; W&C-TPL, 467–68.
292. Colville, *Fringes*, 256; WM/Sir Robert Boothby, 10/16/80.
293. Colville, *Fringes*, 391.
294. W&C-TPL, 467.
295. Joseph M. Mueller, *Guadalcanal 1942* (Oxford, 1992), 29, 34, 35; Morison, *Two-Ocean War*, 172.
296. W&C-TPL, 466; WSC 4, 475; Danchev and Todman, *War Diaries*, 300.
297. Danchev and Todman, *War Diaries*, 297.
298. Harriman and Abel, *Special Envoy*, 165–66.
299. Harriman and Abel, *Special Envoy*, 165–66; Danchev and Todman, *War Diaries*, 300; Dilks, *Diaries*, 470.
300. Bryant, *Tide*, 375.
301. Thompson, *Assignment: Churchill*, 268–69; WSC 4, 466; Harriman and Abel, *Special Envoy*, 159; George F. Kennan, *Memoirs: 1925–1950* (New York, 1967), 279 (Stalin's yellow eyes).
302. Harriman and Abel, *Special Envoy*, 152–53.
303. Dilks, *Diaries*, 471–72.
304. Harriman and Abel, *Special Envoy*, 157–59; Thompson, *Assignment: Churchill*, 268; Martin Gilbert, *Churchill: A Life* (New York, 1992), 727–30.
305. Harriman and Abel, *Special Envoy*, 161; WSC 4, 492; Dilks, *Diaries*, 472; Danchev and Todman, *War Diaries*, 301–3.
306. Harriman and Abel, *Special Envoy*, 163; WSC 4, 499.
307. WSCHCS, 6675.
308. GILBERT 7, 211–12.
309. Boatner, *Biographical Dictionary*, 380; Danchev and Todman, *War Diaries*, 438; WM/Averell Harriman, 8/22/80; Colville, *Fringes*, 622.
310. Danchev and Todman, *War Diaries*, 317; WSC 4, 509.
311. WSC 4, 63, 471; Panter-Downes, *War Notes*, 235–36.
312. WSC 4, 523; Danchev and Todman, *War Diaries*, 313.
313. Montgomery, *Memoirs*, 100, 107; Ronald Walker, *Alam Halfa and Alamein* (Wellington, NZ, 1966), 180 ("The swine will not attack").
314. Bryant, *Tide*, 412.
315. Danchev and Todman, *War Diaries*, 326; Bryant, *Tide*, 407.
316. Joesph P. Lash, *Eleanor and Franklin* (New York, 1971), 664, 666.
317. Butcher, *Eisenhower*, 20; Philip Ziegler, *London at War* (New York, 1995), 219; *Time*, 10/19/42, 33–34.
318. W&C-TPL, 459; TWY, 198.
319. Peter Catterall, ed., *The Macmillan Diaries: The Cabinet Years, 1950–57* (London, 2003), 383; Moran, *Diaries*, 692.

320. Joseph P. Lash, *Eleanor and Franklin* (New York, 1971), 600–64, 667.
321. TWY, 258; *Atlantic Monthly,* 3/65, 79–80.
322. Desmond Young, *Rommel: The Desert Fox* (New York, 1967), 147.
323. Collier, *War in the Desert,* 109–10; Danchev and Todman, *War Diaries,* 338.
324. Bryant, *Tide,* 417, 421.
325. Moran, *Diaries,* 83–84; Bryant, *Tide,* 412, 421.
326. Collier, *War in the Desert,* 115; Montgomery, *Memoirs,* 137–40.
327. Collier, *War in the Desert,* 115; William L. Shirer, *The Rise and Fall of the Third Reich: A History of Nazi Germany* (New York, 1960), 920; Young, *Rommel,* 251; TWY, 349.
328. WSC 4, 601; TWY, 257; WSCHCS, 6694.
329. Miller, *U-Boats,* 188.
330. Kenneth Young, *Churchill and Beaverbrook* (London, 1966), 248–50; *Time,* 11/30/42, 38.
331. Eisenhower, *Crusade,* 95.
332. WSC 4, 529
333. Bryant, *Tide,* 415; Winterbotham, *Ultra Secret,* 140; Danchev and Todman, *War Diaries,* 332.
334. Eisenhower, *Crusade,* 88; Grigg, *1943,* 41; Butcher, *Eisenhower,* 145.
335. Eisenhower, *Crusade,* 99–100.
336. Jean Lacouture, *De Gaulle* (New York, 1965), 121–22.
337. Winterbotham, *Ultra Secret,* 307; Bryant, *Tide,* 423; Boatner, *Biographical Dictionary,* 9.
338. Sarah Churchill, *Keep On Dancing* (London, 1981), 111; WM/Pamela Harriman, 8/22/80.
339. GILBERT 7, 251–52; Bryant, *Tide,* 423, 424; Morison, *Two-Ocean War,* 220–24.
340. Eisenhower, *Crusade,* 105; Butcher, *Eisenhower,* 178.
341. WSC 4, 616; Lochner, *Goebbels Diaries,* 235 (Dec. 7, 1941); A. M. Sperber, *Murrow: His Life and Times* (New York, 1986), 217.
342. Butcher, *Eisenhower,* 179.
343. Collier, *War in the Desert,* 149–50.
344. Morison, *Two-Ocean War,* 82.
345. Eisenhower, *Crusade,* 104; Farago, *Patton,* 202; Morison, *Two-Ocean War,* 225, 228.
346. Carlos D'Este, *Patton: A Genius for War* (New York, 1995), 431, 435; Bryant, *Tide,* 333.
347. Eisenhower, *Crusade,* 104–5; WSCHCS, 6729 (Darlan).
348. Farago, *Patton,* 200–201.
349. Shirer, *Rise and Fall,* 922–23.
350. Panter-Downes, *War Notes,* 253; WSC 4, 632; 651; C&R-TCC, 2:7; TWY, 266.
351. WSC 4, 647; Eden, *The Reckoning,* 414.
352. C&R-TCC, 2:90, 103, 104.
353. WSCHCS, 6695.
354. Joseph P. Lash, *Eleanor and Franklin* (New York, 1971), 664; Wheeler-Bennett, *Action This Day,* 74, 75; Danchev and Todman, *War Diaries,* 474; Colville, *Fringes,* 340.
355. Wheeler-Bennett, *Action This Day,* 74; Churchill, *English-Speaking Peoples,* 1: preface; Cv/2, 925–26.
356. WSCHCS, 6499.

357. Lady Mary Soames letter to PFR, 11/07 ("un-manned him").
358. GILBERT 7, 239–40; Dilks, *Diaries,* 488.
359. Soames, *Clementine,* 419; Danchev and Todman, *War Diaries,* 338.
360. Panter-Downes, *War Notes,* 251.
361. George Orwell, "England, Your England" (1941), in *A Collection of Essays by George Orwell* (Orlando, FL, 1970).
362. George F. Kennan, *Russia and the West Under Lenin and Stalin* (Boston, 1960), 349.
363. GILBERT 7, 217.
364. GILBERT 7, 255; Martin Gilbert, *Churchill's War Leadership* (New York, 2004), 50; Danchev and Todman, *War Diaries,* 207.
365. Danchev and Todman, *War Diaries,* 345.

Crosscurrents

1. Alex Danchev and Daniel Todman, eds., *Field Marshal Lord Alanbrooke: War Diaries 1939–1945* (Berkeley, 2003), 344; GILBERT 7, 270–71.
2. Richard Collier, *The War in the Desert* (New York, 1980), 159; Robert E. Sherwood, *Roosevelt and Hopkins: An Intimate History* (New York, 1948), 659; Danchev and Todman, *War Diaries,* 342, 346.
3. John Keegan, *The Second World War* (London, 1989), 297, 312, 317; GILBERT 7, 265.
4. Samuel Eliot Morison, *The Two-Ocean War* (Boston, 1963), 199–205.
5. Sherwood, *Roosevelt and Hopkins,* 656; Morison, *Two-Ocean War,* 208.
6. GILBERT 7, 271.
7. Keegan, *Second World War,* 234, 235.
8. Keegan, *Second World War,* 231, 234.
9. Harry C. Butcher, *My Three Years with Eisenhower* (New York, 1946), 198; Arthur Bryant, *The Turn of the Tide: A History of the War Years Based on the Diaries of Field-Marshal Lord Alanbrooke, 1939–1943* (New York, 1957), 428; C&R-TCC 2:48–49.
10. Sherwood, *Roosevelt and Hopkins,* 658.
11. Danchev and Todman, *War Diaries,* 346, 347; GILBERT 7, 298.
12. C&R-TCC, 1:669, 2:11.
13. Morison, *Two-Ocean War,* 238; Butcher, *Eisenhower,* 644.
14. James MacGregor Burns, *Roosevelt: The Soldier of Freedom, 1940–1945* (New York, 1970), 314.
15. Danchev and Todman, *War Diaries,* 346, 350; C&R-TCC, 1:552; Sherwood, *Roosevelt and Hopkins,* 588, 615; Butcher, *Eisenhower,* 644.
16. *NYT,* 11/12/42; GILBERT 7, 255; Bryant, *Tide,* 428; WSCHCS, 6698.
17. Sherwood, *Roosevelt and Hopkins,* 591; WSCHCS, 7160 ("intriguers").
18. Mark Mayo Boatner, *The Biographical Dictionary of World War II* (New York, 1999), 13–14; Bryant, *Tide,* 442.
19. Danchev and Todman, *War Diaries,* 342; Louis P. Lochner, *The Goebbels Diaries 1942–1943* (New York, 1948), 160, 352.
20. Lochner, *Goebbels Diaries,* 243, 245, 250.
21. Lochner, *Goebbels Diaries,* 251, 252.
22. Leonard Mosley, *Battle of Britain* (New York, 1980), 191; Philip Ziegler, *London at War* (New York, 1995), 224; *Time,* 12/28/42.
23. WSCHCS, 6714; *Time,* 12/7/42, 40.

24. Mollie Panter-Downes, *London War Notes, 1939–1945* (London, 1972), 254, 255, 257; GILBERT 7, 264.
25. WM/Pamela Harriman, 8/22/80.
26. WM/Pamela Harriman, 8/22/80.
27. Burns, *Roosevelt,* 315; C&R-TCC, 2:73.
28. C&R-TCC, 2:109; WSC 4, 667–70; W. Averell Harriman and Elie Abel, *Special Envoy to Churchill and Stalin: 1941–1946* (New York, 1975), 177–78.
29. Danchev and Todman, *War Diaries,* 351, 451.
30. Danchev and Todman, *War Diaries,* 346; Bryant, *Tide,* 443.
31. *Time,* 12/28/42.
32. *Daily Telegraph,* 5/11/07; WM/Jock Colville, 10/14/80; Mary Soames, *Clementine Churchill: The Biography of a Marriage* (New York, 2003), 69 (pink silk underclothes); Anthony Montague Browne, *Long Sunset* (London, 1996), 219–20.
33. Tom Hickman, *Churchill's Bodyguard* (London, 2005), 219–20.
34. Tizard memo, Imperial War Museum archives; WSC 4, 679–80.
35. John Colville, *The Churchillians* (London, 1981), 35.
36. Dwight D. Eisenhower, *Crusade in Europe* (New York, 1948), 61; WSC 4, 679.
37. GILBERT 6, 1205–6; John Colville, *The Fringes of Power: 10 Downing Street Diaries 1939–1955* (New York, 1985), 563.
38. GILBERT 7, 647.
39. Dean Acheson, *Present at the Creation: My Years in the State Department* (New York, 1969), 48, 49; Browne, *Long Sunset,* 127.
40. Acheson, *Present,* 48, 49, 52.
41. Brian Gardner, *Churchill in Power: As Seen by His Contemporaries* (Boston, 1970), 211.
42. GILBERT 7, 292–93.
43. TWY, 286, 264–65.
44. *Chambers Biographical Encyclopedia* (London, 1984), 135; GILBERT 7, 367; *NYT,* 1/8/39.
45. WSC 4, 930; Edward Stettinius Jr., *Lend Lease: Weapon for Victory* (New York, 1944), 254–55.
46. Harriman and Abel, *Special Envoy,* 180; Hastings Lionel Ismay, *The Memoirs of General Lord Ismay* (London, 1960), 284–85.
47. Lord Moran, *Churchill: Taken from the Diaries of Lord Moran* (Boston, 1966), 85–86; WSC 4, 674–75.
48. Harriman and Abel, *Special Envoy,* 180.
49. W&C-TPL, 471.
50. GILBERT 7, 273.
51. *NYT,* 1/25/43; Walter H. Thompson, *Assignment: Churchill* (New York, 1953), 276.
52. Anthony Eden, Earl of Avon, *The Reckoning: The Memoirs of Anthony Eden* (New York, 1965), 398; Danchev and Todman, *War Diaries,* 338, 356.
53. Sherwood, *Roosevelt and Hopkins,* 671–73; *Time,* 2/1/42, 11.
54. Danchev and Todman, *War Diaries,* 359; Sherwood, *Roosevelt and Hopkins,* 688–89.
55. Danchev and Todman, *War Diaries,* 359.
56. GILBERT 7, 417; WSCHCS, 6785.
57. Danchev and Todman, *War Diaries,* 361; Sherwood, *Roosevelt and Hopkins,* 689; Bryant, *Tide,* 454–55.

58. Danchev and Todman, *War Diaries*, 362; Morison, *Two-Ocean War*, 239; WSC 4, 692.
59. GILBERT 7, 277; Eden, *The Reckoning*, 416–17.
60. Eden, *The Reckoning*, 420, 421.
61. Moran, *Diaries*, 88; W&C-TPL, 475.
62. Sherwood, *Roosevelt and Hopkins*, 685.
63. The American Presidency Project, 17: Excerpts from the Press Conference for the American Society of Newspaper Editors, 2/12/43.
64. *Time*, 2/5/45; Rene De Chambrun, *I Saw France Fall* (New York, 1940), 100.
65. Sherwood, *Roosevelt and Hopkins*, 695–97; WSC 4, 687.
66. WM/Averell Harriman, 8/22/80.
67. Sherwood, *Roosevelt and Hopkins*, 695–97; WSC 4, 687–88.
68. Butcher, *Eisenhower*, 386; *Time*, 5/10/43; GILBERT 7, 581; WM/Averell Harriman, 8/22/80.
69. Moran, *Diaries*, 89–90, WSC 4, 94–95; GILBERT 7, 31.
70. Danchev and Todman, *War Diaries*, 368–69.
71. Danchev and Todman, *War Diaries*, 368–69; David Dilks, ed., *The Diaries of Sir Alexander Cadogan, 1938–1945* (New York, 1972), 508, 510–11.
72. Danchev and Todman, *War Diaries*, 375.
73. Danchev and Todman, *War Diaries*, 375; WSC 4, 710–11.
74. *Time Capsule 1943: A History of the Year Condensed from the Pages of* Time, edited by Henry R. Luce (New York, 1968), 121; *NYT*, 2/9/43; Keegan, *Second World War*, 236, 237, 458; William L. Shirer, *The Rise and Fall of the Third Reich: A History of Nazi Germany* (New York, 1960), 933.
75. *Time*, 2/1/43, 33–34.
76. Dilks, *Diaries*, 511; GILBERT 7, 318–19.
77. GILBERT 7, 318–19.
78. *Time Capsule 1943*, 121.
79. Butcher, *Eisenhower*, 691; Sherwood, 677; *Sunday Telegraph*, 2/9/64, 4.
80. Danchev and Todman, *War Diaries*, 378–79.
81. Dilks, *Diaries*, 513.
82. Butcher, *Eisenhower*, 255.
83. Danchev and Todman, *War Diaries*, 380.
84. Bryant, *Tide*, 474–75.
85. W&C-TPL, 477.
86. *NYT*, 2/3/43; *NYT*, 2/9/43.
87. John Keegan, *Winston Churchill* (New York, 2002), 161.
88. C&R-TCC, 2:138; GILBERT 7, 337.
89. Moran, *Diaries*, 95–96.
90. Collier, *War in the Desert*, 162–63; John Keegan, ed., *Churchill's Generals* (New York, 1991), 114; Eisenhower, *Crusade*, 145; Thomas E. Griess, ed., *The West Point Atlas for the Second World War, Europe and the Mediterranean* (New York, 2002), 41; Butcher, *Eisenhower*, 267.
91. WSC 4, 734; GILBERT 7, 348.
92. Butcher, *Eisenhower*, 273.
93. GILBERT 7, 348, 350; WSC 4, 736–37.
94. *Time*, 5/3/43; GILBERT 7, 343; WM/Averell Harriman, 8/22/80.
95. Collier, *War in the Desert*, 168; Keegan, *Second World War*, 342.
96. *Time*, 3/22/42, 26; Lochner, *Goebbels Diaries*, 262.

97. GILBERT 7, 338, 379.
98. GILBERT 7, 352.
99. C&R-TCC, 2:161.
100. Morison, *Two-Ocean War,* 242; Harriman and Abel, *Special Envoy,* 212.
101. Morison, *Two-Ocean War,* 242–44.
102. C&R-TCC, 2:177.
103. C&R-TCC, 2:180.
104. David Miller, *U-Boats* (New York, 2000), 123–24; Morison, *Two-Ocean War,* 242.
105. *Time,* 3/22/43.
106. *Time,* 3/22/43.
107. Collier, *War in the Desert,* 171–73; Eisenhower, *Crusade,* 151.
108. WM/Sir William Deakin, 1980.
109. WSCHCS, 6755; *Time,* 4/16/43, 18–19; Sherwood, *Roosevelt and Hopkins,* 716.
110. WSCHCS, 6756.
111. TWY, 286.
112. *Time,* 3/1/43, 30.
113. *Time,* 4/16/43; WSCHCS, 6771.
114. WSC 4, 769; Panter-Downes, *War Notes,* 274.
115. Eden, *The Reckoning,* 440.
116. Eden, *The Reckoning,* 438–39; Sherwood, *Roosevelt and Hopkins,* 714–15; Harriman and Abel, *Special Envoy,* 227.
117. Colville, *Fringes,* 245, 312.
118. Eden, *The Reckoning,* 432–33; George F. Kennan, *Russia and the West Under Lenin and Stalin* (Boston, 1960), 368; John Grigg, *1943: The Victory That Never Was* (New York, 1980), 156.
119. Kennan, *Russia and the West,* 355.
120. Harriman and Abel, *Special Envoy,* 227; Danchev and Todman, *War Diaries,* 390.
121. *Time,* 3/22/43, 15.
122. Kennan, *Russia and the West,* 359–63; Harriman and Abel, *Special Envoy,* 206–7.
123. Ziegler, *London at War,* 237.
124. Ziegler, *London at War,* 238; Ernie Pyle, *Brave Men* (New York, 1944), 324; PFR/Andy Rooney, 5/08.
125. *Time,* 3/15/43, 28–29; WM/Averell Harriman, 8/22/80; Harriman and Abel, *Special Envoy,* 165–66.
126. *NYT,* 3/11/25; WSC 4, 749.
127. WSC 4, 749.
128. WSC 4, 747, 751.
129. GILBERT 7, 370; Panter-Downes, *War Notes,* 279.
130. Lochner, *Goebbels Diaries,* 387–88; Panter-Downes, *War Notes,* 282.
131. Charles Eade, ed., *Churchill by His Contemporaries* (New York, 1954), 300–301; *Time,* 5/3/43.
132. Danchev and Todman, *War Diaries,* 393.
133. GILBERT 7, 383; Danchev and Todman, *War Diaries,* 394.
134. Martin Gilbert, *The Second World War: A Complete History* (London, 1989), 421.
135. *Time,* 3/29/43, 25; Lochner, *Goebbels Diaries,* 325.
136. *Time,* 3/15/43; GILBERT 7, 676.
137. Lochner, *Goebbels Diaries,* 318, 332.

138. Dilks, *Diaries*, 520; Lochner, *Goebbels Diaries*, 348; WSC 4, 759.
139. Dilks, *Diaries*, 526; C&R-TCC, 2:194, 199; WSC 4, 759–61.
140. *Time*, 2/7/44; *Time*, 7/17/72; WM/Averell Harriman, 8/22/80.
141. C&R-TCC, 2:389, 398–99; GILBERT 7, 665.
142. Burns, *Roosevelt*, 373–74; WSC 6, 141.
143. *Time*, 2/5/43.
144. WSC 4, 783.
145. Collier, *War in the Desert*, 173.
146. TWY, 291.
147. Keegan, *Second World War*, 343; Butcher, *Eisenhower*, 285.
148. *Time*, 4/17/42, 31; *Time*, 5/10/43, 30.
149. GILBERT 7, 417–18; C&R-TCC, 2:206.
150. *Time*, 4/19/43, 32.
151. Burns, *Roosevelt*, 367–68.
152. *Time*, 5/10/43, 25; Harriman and Abel, *Special Envoy*, 201; Ismay, *Memoirs*, 294.
153. Ismay, *Memoirs*, 294.
154. GILBERT 7, 397–98.
155. Lochner, *Goebbels Diaries*, 360.
156. Harriman and Abel, *Special Envoy*, 209.
157. Harriman and Abel, *Special Envoy*, 206, 209, 211; GILBERT 7, 397–98; Danchev and Todman, *War Diaries*, 400–401.
158. Harriman and Abel, *Special Envoy*, 205; WM/Averell Harriman, 8/22/80.
159. Harriman and Abel, *Special Envoy*, 202.
160. GILBERT 7, 418; Ismay, *Memoirs*, 295.
161. *NYT*, 5/13/43, 5/14/43.
162. Harriman and Abel, *Special Envoy*, 210.
163. WSCHCS, 6782.
164. Richard Collier, *Duce!* (New York, 1971), 195.
165. W&C-TPL, 479–80.
166. Danchev and Todman, *War Diaries*, 394; GILBERT 7, 399.
167. WSC 4, 786.
168. WSC 4, 786–87.
169. Danchev and Todman, *War Diaries*, 405; Morison, *Two-Ocean War*, 244.
170. Danchev and Todman, *War Diaries*, 405; Harriman and Abel, *Special Envoy*, 210–11; Bryant, *Tide*, 540–41.
171. Danchev and Todman, *War Diaries*, 420.
172. WSC 4, 803; Eden, *The Reckoning*, 439, 461.
173. WSC 4, 801; C&R-TCC, 2:210–11.
174. Eden, *The Reckoning*, 448–49.
175. WSC 4, 811.
176. GILBERT 7, 335.
177. Danchev and Todman, *War Diaries*, 412–13; WM/Sir Ian Jacob, 11/12/80.
178. Bryant, *Tide*, 528.
179. WSC 4, 831.
180. WSCHCS, 6784; Harriman and Abel, *Special Envoy*, 215.
181. Butcher, *Eisenhower*, 318, 322–23.
182. WSC 4, 816; Danchev and Todman, *War Diaries*, 415; Butcher, *Eisenhower*, 319, 325.
183. W&C-TPL, 484; C&R-TCC, 2:230–31.

184. Ismay, *Memoirs,* 301.
185. WSC 4, 830.
186. Panter-Downes, *War Notes,* 284.
187. WSC 4, 803; Harriman and Abel, *Special Envoy,* 212–13.
188. Harriman and Abel, *Special Envoy,* 212–13.
189. Collier, *Duce!,* 195–96.
190. Eisenhower, *Crusade,* 164–65.
191. Vincent Orange, *Tedder: Quietly in Command* (London, 2004), 225.
192. Eisenhower, *Crusade,* 171–72.
193. Panter-Downes, *War Notes,* 284.
194. Panter-Downes, *War Notes,* 285.
195. Eden, *The Reckoning,* 461.
196. Eden, *The Reckoning,* 452–53, 463; Jean Lacouture, *De Gaulle* (New York, 1965), 130.
197. Danchev and Todman, *War Diaries,* 427; WSC 4, 801; C&R-TCC, 2:208.
198. Panter-Downes, *War Notes,* 285.
199. C&R-TCC, 2:328, 341.
200. GILBERT 7, 443–44.
201. Bryant, *Tide,* 552; Butcher, *Eisenhower,* 373–74.
202. GILBERT 7, 444–45.
203. C&R-TCC, 2:331, 336, 345; GILBERT 7, 443–44.
204. C&R-TCC, 2:331–32.
205. Danchev and Todman, *War Diaries,* 429.
206. Collier, *Duce!,* 226–31.
207. Lochner, *Goebbels Diaries,* 407.
208. TWY, 308–9.
209. Danchev and Todman, *War Diaries,* 433; Lochner, *Goebbels Diaries,* 417.
210. Danchev and Todman, *War Diaries,* 433.
211. GILBERT 7, 463.
212. Soames, *Clementine,* 333, 334, 338, 446; Sherwood, *Roosevelt and Hopkins,* 831; Moran, *Diaries,* 112.
213. WSC 5, 67; Moran, *Diaries,* 114.
214. Danchev and Todman, *War Diaries,* 436–37.
215. Keegan, *Second World War,* 472; Lochner, *Goebbels Diaries,* 415.
216. GILBERT 7, 464–65; C&R-TCC, 2:357; WSCHCS, 6784.
217. WSCHCS, 6778; GILBERT 7, 437, 468; Dilks, *Diaries,* 551; *Time,* 12/13/43, 36.
218. Lochner, *Goebbels Diaries,* 383.
219. Lochner, *Goebbels Diaries,* 407; Bryant, *Tide,* 555–56; WSC 5, 520–21.
220. Lochner, *Goebbels Diaries,* 419.
221. Bryant, *Tide,* 556; GILBERT 6, 468; *Daily Mirror,* 8/9/43.
222. Lochner, *Goebbels Diaries,* 429, 442; Keegan, *Second World War,* 429.
223. Trumbull Higgins, *Winston Churchill and the Second Front* (New York, 1957), 205.
224. Danchev and Todman, *War Diaries,* 405.
225. Trumbull Higgins, *Winston Churchill and the Second Front* (New York, 1957), 203; Eisenhower, *Crusade,* 160; Robert E. Sherwood, *The White House Papers of Harry L. Hopkins* (London, 1949), 2:763; WSC 3, 673.
226. WSC 5, 74–75; Ismay, *Memoirs,* 309; Basil Collier, *The Second World War: A Military History from Munich to Hiroshima* (New York, 1967), 387.

227. Danchev and Todman, *War Diaries,* 437, 439; WSC 5, 75–76.
228. Eisenhower, *Crusade,* 199.
229. Danchev and Todman, *War Diaries,* 447.
230. Ismay, *Memoirs,* 310.
231. Danchev and Todman, *War Diaries,* 431–32.
232. *Time,* 8/30/43; *Time,* 11/8/43, 8.
233. WSC 5, 82; Kay Halle, ed., *Winston Churchill on America and Britain* (New York, 1970), 263.
234. WSCHCS, 6782; Thompson, *Assignment: Churchill,* 280.
235. GILBERT 7, 397; Ismay, *Memoirs,* 310–11.
236. Sherwood, *Roosevelt and Hopkins,* 758–59; Ismay, *Memoirs,* 311; Danchev and Todman, *War Diaries,* 442; Bryant, *Tide,* 587.
237. WSC 5, 85; Ismay, *Memoirs,* 311.
238. Sherwood, *Roosevelt and Hopkins,* 759.
239. Danchev and Todman, *War Diaries,* 441–42.
240. Barbara Tuchman, *Stilwell and the American Experience in China* (New York, 1971), 489–90; Leonard Mosley, *Marshall: Hero for Our Times* (New York, 1982), 301; Danchev and Todman, *War Diaries,* 445.
241. Danchev and Todman, *War Diaries,* 444–45; Noel Annan, "How Wrong Was Churchill?" *New York Review of Books,* 4/8/93.
242. WSC 5, 106–7; Butcher, *Eisenhower,* 394–95.
243. Albert Speer, *Inside the Third Reich: Memoirs by Albert Speer* (Macmillan, 1970), 368–69; GILBERT 7, 474; David Johnson, *V-1, V-2* (London, 1981), 26.
244. Danchev and Todman, *War Diaries,* 444–45.
245. C&R-TCC, 2:369, 370.
246. Eden, *The Reckoning,* 467–68.
247. Harriman and Abel, *Special Envoy,* 225–26.
248. Harriman and Abel, *Special Envoy,* 234–35; Ismay, *Memoirs,* 367; Dilks, *Diaries,* 584–85.
249. *Time,* 10/25/43, 21; Sherwood, *Roosevelt and Hopkins,* 755.
250. Eden, *The Reckoning,* 466, 470; Harriman and Abel, *Special Envoy,* 222; Dilks, *Diaries,* 560.
251. Eden, *The Reckoning,* 468–69.
252. Dilks, *Diaries,* 556; Soames, *Clementine,* 447.
253. Eden, *The Reckoning,* 468–69; Moran, *Diaries,* 122–23.
254. Eden, *The Reckoning,* 470; Danchev and Todman, *War Diaries,* 451, 452.
255. B. H. Liddell Hart, *History of the Second World War* (New York, 1971), 456; Viscount Montgomery of Alamein, *The Memoirs of Field Marshal Montgomery* (London, 1958), 190.
256. Danchev and Todman, *War Diaries,* 448.
257. Butcher, *Eisenhower,* 386–87; Liddell Hart, *History,* 446.
258. WSC 5, 128–29.
259. WM/Averell Harriman, 8/22/80; Richard Langworth, ed., *Churchill by Himself: The Definitive Collection of Quotations* (London, 2008), 553.
260. WSCHCS, 6824.
261. Sherwood, *Roosevelt and Hopkins,* 750; GILBERT 7, 494; *NYT,* 9/8/43.
262. Dilks, *Diaries,* 560; Moran, *Diaries,* 123, 126.
263. Lochner, *Goebbels Diaries,* 444, 460; Liddell Hart, *History,* 455, 458; Gardner, *Churchill in Power,* 224–25.

264. Keegan, *Second World War,* 351; WSC 5, 114; Kay Halle, *Irrepressible Churchill: Stories, Sayings and Impressions of Sir Winston Churchill* (London, 1985), 227; WSC 5, 224–25.
265. Liddell Hart, *History,* 467; WSC 5, 662.
266. WSC 5, 141–42.
267. Moran, *Diaries,* 127.
268. Gardner, *Churchill in Power,* 225; Dilks, *Diaries,* 559.
269. GILBERT 7, 494; Martin Gilbert, *Churchill: A Life* (New York, 1992), 753.
270. Soames, *Clementine,* 448.
271. GILBERT 7, 487.
272. Dilks, *Diaries,* 554–55; Jones, *Wizard War,* 474.
273. WSC 5, 117; Lochner, *Goebbels Diaries,* 460.
274. Lochner, *Goebbels Diaries,* 457.
275. WSC 5, 10, 12, 13; Morison, *Two-Ocean War,* 376.
276. Lochner, *Goebbels Diaries,* 466; Morison, *Two-Ocean War,* 244–46.
277. PFR/Dr. Porter Crowe (private, U.S. Army, 1942–1945), 6/06.
278. Ismay, *Memoirs,* 320.
279. WSCHCS, 6855; Langworth, *Churchill by Himself,* 427.
280. WM/Jock Colville, 10/14/80; Dilks, *Diaries,* 562.
281. Liddell Hart, *History,* 455; Danchev and Todman, *War Diaries,* 466.
282. Danchev and Todman, *War Diaries,* 458–59.
283. C&R-TCC, 2:501, 504, 506; Danchev and Todman, *War Diaries,* 467.
284. Danchev and Todman, *War Diaries,* 465–66.
285. Gilbert, *Churchill: A Life,* 755; Harold Macmillan, *War Diaries: Politics and War in the Mediterranean, January 1943–May 1945* (New York, 1984), 295; WSC 5, 224–25, 326.
286. Danchev and Todman, *War Diaries,* 463, 465.
287. GILBERT 7, 530–31; Danchev and Todman, *War Diaries,* 463, 465–66.
288. Keegan, *Second World War,* 319; C&R-TCC, 2:556–57.
289. Keegan, *Second World War,* 472–74; Keegan, *Atlas,* 106–7; Liddell Hart, *History,* 481, 492.
290. Lochner, *Goebbels Diaries,* 435, 461.
291. Lochner, *Goebbels Diaries,* 464, 468, 477–79, 483.
292. Lochner, *Goebbels Diaries,* 467; C&R-TCC, 2:559–60; Dilks, *Diaries,* 573.
293. *Time,* 3/15/42, 24; Harriman and Abel, *Special Envoy,* 234–35; Joseph E. Persico, *Edward R. Murrow: An American Original* (New York, 1988), 217–18.
294. Eden, *The Reckoning,* 481; C&R-TCC, 2:545–46.
295. WSC 5, 270; GILBERT 7, 571.
296. WSC 5, 242–43, 290.
297. Harriman and Abel, *Special Envoy,* 244; *Time,* 10/25/43, 29.
298. Harriman and Abel, *Special Envoy,* 244.
299. C&R-TCC, 2:562–63; Eisenhower, *Crusade,* 190, 199, 200, 213.
300. *Time,* 2/28/44.
301. Liddell Hart, *History,* 602–3; Keegan, *Second World War,* 426–27.
302. Duff Cooper, *Old Men Forget* (London, 1954), 317.
303. GILBERT 7, 557.
304. Lochner, *Goebbels Diaries,* 522–23.
305. Moran, *Diaries,* 138–39.

306. Macmillan, *War Diaries*, 401; Danchev and Todman, *War Diaries*, 472; W&C-TPL, 485.
307. Eisenhower, *Crusade*, 195, 198–99; Butcher, *Eisenhower*, 465.
308. Danchev and Todman, *War Diaries*, 475.
309. WSC 5, 328–29; Boatner, *Biographical Dictionary*, 509.
310. C&R-TCC, 2:597; WSC 5, 328–29; Danchev and Todman, *War Diaries*, 477–81.
311. W&C-TPL, 487; Danchev and Todman, *War Diaries*, 480; Sherwood, *Roosevelt and Hopkins*, 782.
312. Ismay, *Memoirs*, 312; Mosley, *Marshall*, 262; Tuchman, *Stilwell*, 516; WM/Viscount Antony Head, 8/6/80; Danchev and Todman, *War Diaries*, 480.
313. WSC 5, 341; Danchev and Todman, *War Diaries*, 478; Dilks, *Diaries*, 578, 580, 587; Sarah Churchill, *A Thread in the Tapestry* (London, 1967), 63.
314. Churchill, *Thread*, 62–63; Sarah Churchill, *Keep On Dancing* (London, 1981), 117.
315. Eden, *The Reckoning*, 491; Moran, *Diaries*, 141; Danchev and Todman, *War Diaries*, 482; Eisenhower, *Crusade*, 199.
316. Danchev and Todman, *War Diaries*, 482.
317. Dilks, *Diaries*, 580; WSC 5, 342; Thompson, *Assignment: Churchill*, 283; Danchev and Todman, *War Diaries*, 482; Ismay, *Memoirs*, 377.
318. Harriman and Abel, *Special Envoy*, 265–66.
319. Moran, *Diaries*, 144; Harriman and Abel, *Special Envoy*, 165–66; David Halberstam, *The Best and the Brightest* (New York, 1969), 81.
320. Dilks, *Diaries*, 579.
321. W&C-TPL, 487; WSC 5, 679–80.
322. Danchev and Todman, *War Diaries*, 483; Moran, *Diaries*, 143.
323. Danchev and Todman, *War Diaries*, 483.
324. Moran, *Diaries*, 145.
325. Moran, *Diaries*, 145–46; Ismay, *Memoirs*, 338.
326. Sherwood, *Roosevelt and Hopkins*, 781.
327. Arthur Bryant, *Triumph in the West, 1943–1946* (London, 1959), 89–91.
328. Harriman and Abel, *Special Envoy*, 266–67; Bryant, *Triumph*, 89–91; Moran, *Diaries*, 145.
329. Harriman and Abel, *Special Envoy*, 268–69.
330. WSC 5, 360.
331. Gilbert, *Churchill: A Life*, 761; Moran, *Diaries*, 208; WSCHCS, 6475.
332. WSC 5, 360.
333. Sherwood, *Roosevelt and Hopkins*, 796.
334. Eden, *The Reckoning*, 494–98; WSC 5, 361–62.
335. Dilks, *Diaries*, 400; WSC 5, 362.
336. WSC 5, 362.
337. John Wheeler-Bennett, *Action This Day: Working with Churchill* (London, 1968), 209–10; WM/Sir Ian Jacob, 11/12/80.
338. *Time*, 5/10/43; *Time*, 1/4/42; *Life*, 3/29/43.
339. Wheeler-Bennett, *Action This Day*, 209–10; WM/Sir Ian Jacob, 11/12/80; Dilks, *Diaries*, 580.
340. Sherwood, *Roosevelt and Hopkins*, 785–86.
341. WSC 5, 364; Jenkins, *Churchill*, 722.

342. WSC 5, 372–73.
343. Danchev and Todman, *War Diaries,* 485; Keegan, *Second World War,* 378.
344. Moran, *Diaries,* 148.
345. WSC 5, 373–74; Harriman and Abel, *Special Envoy,* 191.
346. Harriman and Abel, *Special Envoy,* 273–74; WSC 5, 374.
347. Dilks, *Diaries,* 578; Frances Perkins, *The Roosevelt I Knew* (New York, 1946), 84; PFR/Lady Mary Soames, telephone conversation, 4/07.
348. Moran, *Diaries,* 151; GILBERT 7, 583–84; WSC 5, 383–85.
349. WSC 3, 384.
350. WSC 5, 383–85; Harriman and Abel, *Special Envoy,* 176.
351. Danchev and Todman, *War Diaries,* 486–88.
352. Danchev and Todman, *War Diaries,* 486–88; Harriman and Abel, *Special Envoy,* 276–78; Sherwood, *Roosevelt and Hopkins,* 793.
353. WSC 5, 388.
354. WSC 5, 396–97; Eden, *The Reckoning,* 496–97.
355. WSC 5, 396–97; Eden, *The Reckoning,* 496–97.
356. Sherwood, *Roosevelt and Hopkins,* 797.
357. Sherwood, *Roosevelt and Hopkins,* 799; Dilks, *Diaries,* 586.
358. Milovan Djilas, *Conversations with Stalin* (Orlando, FL, 1962), 73, 115.
359. WSC 5, 384.
360. Martin Gilbert, *In Search of Churchill: A Historian's Journey* (New York, 1994), 5; *Time,* 12/27/43.
361. WM/Jock Colville, 10/14/80; Wheeler-Bennett, *Action This Day,* 96.

Pilot

1. W. Averell Harriman and Elie Abel, *Special Envoy to Churchill and Stalin: 1941–1946* (New York, 1975), 283; WSC 5, 405.
2. C&R-TCC, 2:709.
3. Louis P. Lochner, *The Goebbels Diaries, 1942–1943* (New York, 1948), 536.
4. Lochner, *Goebbels Diaries,* 536, 540–42.
5. Robert E. Sherwood, *Roosevelt and Hopkins: An Intimate History* (New York, 1948), 802.
6. Anthony Eden, Earl of Avon, *The Reckoning: The Memoirs of Anthony Eden* (New York, 1965), 499–500; WSC 5, 467–68, 473.
7. Eden, *The Reckoning,* 498–99; David Dilks, ed., *The Diaries of Sir Alexander Cadogan, 1938–1945* (New York, 1972), 584–85.
8. John Colville, *The Fringes of Power: 10 Downing Street Diaries 1939–1955* (New York, 1985), 550.
9. Dwight D. Eisenhower, *Crusade in Europe* (New York, 1948), 206; Sherwood, *Roosevelt and Hopkins,* 803; WSC 5, 419.
10. *Daily Mirror,* 12/29/43; *Daily Express,* 11/20/43.
11. B. H. Liddell Hart, *History of the Second World War* (New York, 1971), 569, 571.
12. Harry C. Butcher, *My Three Years with Eisenhower* (New York, 1946), 456.
13. Basil Collier, *The Second World War: A Military History from Munich to Hiroshima* (New York, 1967), 386; Alex Danchev and Daniel Todman, eds., *Field Marshal Lord Alanbrooke: War Diaries 1939–1945* (Berkeley, 2003), 492;

WSC 5, 419; Viscount Montgomery of Alamein, *The Memoirs of Field Marshal Montgomery* (London, 1958), 214–15.
14. Eisenhower, *Crusade*, 199.
15. *Time*, 1/3/44.
16. Danchev and Todman, *War Diaries*, 493–94; WSC 5, 420.
17. Danchev and Todman, *War Diaries*, 496; Lord Moran, *Churchill: Taken from the Diaries of Lord Moran* (Boston, 1966), 159.
18. *Time*, 12/27/43, 86; Lochner, *Goebbels Diaries*, 546.
19. Danchev and Todman, *War Diaries*, 497; Moran, *Diaries*, 161–62; Anthony Montague Browne, *Long Sunset* (London, 1996), 142; WM/Jock Colville, 10/14/80.
20. Colville, *Fringes*, 455–56.
21. Colville, *Fringes*, 455–56.
22. Harriman and Abel, *Special Envoy*, 283; Moran, *Diaries*, 57.
23. Mary Soames, *Clementine Churchill: The Biography of a Marriage* (New York, 2003), 456.
24. Eden, *The Reckoning*, 495; *Time*, 12/27/43, 46 (Smuts); John Wheeler-Bennett, *Action This Day: Working with Churchill* (London, 1968), 104.
25. Sarah Churchill, *A Thread in the Tapestry* (London, 1967), 69.
26. WSC 6, 427.
27. Butcher, *Eisenhower*, 465; Eisenhower, *Crusade*, 212–13; WSC 6, 427, 434.
28. C&R-TCC, 2:632–33; Collier, *Second World War*, 377.
29. WSCHCS, 6880.
30. Colville, *Fringes*, 456, 464; Harold Macmillan, *War Diaries: Politics and War in the Mediterranean, January 1943–May 1945* (New York, 1984), 331–32, 335; John Pearson, *The Private Lives of Winston Churchill* (New York, 1991), 415.
31. Colville, *Fringes*, 465; WM/Lady Diana Cooper, 10/20/80.
32. Macmillan, *War Diaries*, 335; C&R-TCC, 3:626.
33. Colville, *Fringes*, 459; Montgomery, *Memoirs*, 211.
34. Colville, *Fringes*, 459.
35. Martin Gilbert, *Churchill: A Life* (New York, 1992), 765; Butcher, *Eisenhower*, 65, 473; Moran, *Diaries*, 169–70; WSC 5, 444.
36. David Johnson, *V-1, V-2* (London, 1981), 32; Butcher, *Eisenhower*, 462.
37. PFR/Lady Mary Soames, letter of 9/3/07; Colville, *Fringes*, 463.
38. Duff Cooper, *Old Men Forget* (London, 1954), 315, 319.
39. Moran, *Diaries*, 169; WM/Lady Diana Cooper, 10/20/80.
40. Danchev and Todman, *War Diaries*, 510; Soames, *Clementine*, 461.
41. C&R-TCC, 3:641, 649; Sherwood, *Roosevelt and Hopkins*, 805–6.
42. GILBERT 7, 652.
43. Eden, *The Reckoning*, 503–6; GILBERT 7, 648.
44. TWY, 344.
45. Danchev and Todman, *War Diaries*, 514–15.
46. Eisenhower, *Crusade*, 194, 225.
47. Kay Summersby, *Eisenhower Was My Boss* (2008), 125–28; Mollie Panter-Downes, *London War Notes, 1939–1945* (London, 1972), 300.
48. TWY, 292, 353.
49. Panter-Downes, *War Notes*, 322.
50. Summersby, *Eisenhower*, 125–28; Butcher, *Eisenhower*, 14 (Edward Murrow quote); John Steinbeck, *Steinbeck: A Life in Letters* (New York, 1975), 264; Colville, *Fringes*, 517.

51. Montgomery, *Memoirs,* 219–20.
52. Montgomery, *Memoirs,* 211–12; David Eisenhower, *Eisenhower at War 1943–1945* (New York, 1991), 121; Danchev and Todman, *War Diaries,* 516, 518.
53. Danchev and Todman, *War Diaries,* 519; WSC 5, 692–93.
54. Danchev and Todman, *War Diaries,* 515; Colville, *Fringes,* 476; John Keegan, *The Second World War* (London, 1989), 357.
55. Keegan, *Second World War,* 356; John Keegan, ed., *Collins Atlas of World War II* (New York, 2006), 114–15; Thomas E. Griess, ed., *The West Point Atlas for the Second World War: Europe and the Mediterranean* (New York, 2002), 49.
56. Danchev and Todman, *War Diaries,* 518.
57. Ernie Pyle, *Brave Men* (New York, 1944), 258–65.
58. *Time,* 6/12/44, 10.
59. Panter-Downes, *War Notes,* 314; Colville, *Fringes,* 475, 479.
60. Panter-Downes, *War Notes,* 312; Keegan, *Atlas,* 114–15.
61. Colville, *Fringes,* 474; WSCHCS, 6883.
62. WSCHCS, 6883; Panter-Downes, *War Notes,* 314.
63. WSCHCS, 6893.
64. Colville, *Fringes,* 473; Dilks, *Diaries,* 592.
65. WSC 5, 549.
66. C&R-TCC, 2:649–50; Danchev and Todman, *War Diaries,* 518.
67. James MacGregor Burns, *Roosevelt: The Soldier of Freedom, 1940–1945* (New York, 1970), 483.
68. *Time,* 6/12/44; WSCHCS, 6996; Danchev and Todman, *War Diaries,* 534.
69. Danchev and Todman, *War Diaries,* 534.
70. WSC 5, 689.
71. TWY, 469.
72. Cv/3, 1087; Cv/2, 1120.
73. Macmillan, *War Diaries,* 335, 382; Colville, *Fringes,* 482; Duff Cooper, *Old Men Forget* (London, 1954), 324, 336.
74. Macmillan, *War Diaries,* 409.
75. Eden, *The Reckoning,* 520; C&R-TCC, 3:109.
76. Eisenhower, *Eisenhower at War,* 260.
77. C&R-TCC, 2:527, 744, 745, 749; GILBERT 7, 700.
78. Peter Clarke, *The Last Thousand Days of the British Empire* (New York, 2008), 27–29.
79. *Time,* 5/15/44, 85.
80. C&R-TCC, 3:3.
81. C&R-TCC, 3:3.
82. Dean Acheson, *Present at the Creation: My Years in the State Department* (New York, 1969), 133–34.
83. *Time,* 5/15/44.
84. C&R-TCC, 3:140.
85. Danchev and Todman, *War Diaries,* 516; Colville, *Fringes,* 473, 476, 478, 479; C&R-TCC, 3:69.
86. Collier, *Second World War,* 376; Keegan, *Second World War,* 354–56; GILBERT 7, 526.
87. *Time,* 1/24/44; *Time,* 2/28/44.
88. Colville, *Fringes,* 474.
89. TWY, 357–58; C&R-TCC, 3:78; Colville, *Fringes,* 480.
90. Eden, *The Reckoning,* 521, 523.

91. Dilks, *Diaries,* 612, 618, 621; Colville, *Fringes,* 484; Danchev and Todman, *War Diaries,* 541.
92. Dilks, *Diaries,* 612; Colville, *Fringes,* 484.
93. Colville, *Fringes,* 477; TWY, 347, 355.
94. WSC 5, 695–97; Panter-Downes, *War Notes,* 317–18.
95. WSC 5, 694; Eisenhower, *Eisenhower at War,* 134.
96. Danchev and Todman, *War Diaries,* 519, 521, 532, 533, 534, 547; Arthur Bryant, *The Turn of the Tide: A History of the War Years Based on the Diaries of Field-Marshal Lord Alanbrooke, 1939–1943* (New York, 1957), 171.
97. Danchev and Todman, *War Diaries,* xvii, 525.
98. Eden, *The Reckoning,* 575: Colville, *Fringes,* 489.
99. Moran, *Diaries,* 763.
100. WM/John Martin, 10/23/80.
101. WSCHCS, 6913; Panter-Downes, *War Notes,* 317; TWY, 356–57.
102. Colville, *Fringes,* 483; C&R-TCC, 3:54, 74.
103. Montgomery, *Memoirs,* 247; Butcher, *Eisenhower,* 545.
104. Colville, *Fringes,* 485; C&R-TCC, 3:87; Eisenhower, *Crusade,* 243.
105. Danchev and Todman, *War Diaries,* 536; Butcher, *Eisenhower,* 509.
106. Bryant, *Tide,* 180, 183.
107. Eisenhower, *Eisenhower at War,* 190–91; *Time,* 4/24/44.
108. Eisenhower, *Eisenhower at War,* 196, 206, 207, 209.
109. Eisenhower, *Eisenhower at War,* 206; C&R-TCC, 3:133; Dilks, *Diaries,* 621.
110. Eden, *The Reckoning,* 523–24; Eisenhower, *Crusade,* 232; C&R-TCC, 3:127.
111. Eden, *The Reckoning,* 524–25.
112. Dilks, *Diaries,* 624–25; Colville, *Fringes,* 487.
113. Liddell Hart, *History,* 535; Bryant, *Tide,* 181n.
114. Dilks, *Diaries,* 566.
115. Richard Rhodes, *The Making of the Atomic Bomb* (New York, 1986), 523–24; GILBERT 7, 715; R. V. Jones, *The Wizard War* (New York, 1978), 474.
116. Rhodes, *Atomic Bomb,* 528–30; Jones, *Wizard War,* 476.
117. Jones, *Wizard War,* 477.
118. GILBERT 7, 776; WM/Viscount Antony Head, 1980.
119. Panter-Downes, *War Notes,* 319, 323–24; Pyle, *Brave Men,* 375.
120. Eden, *The Reckoning,* 520.
121. Eisenhower, *Crusade,* 134, 245; Butcher, *Eisenhower,* 539; Max Hastings, *Winston's War: Churchill 1940–1945* (New York, 2010), 361.
122. Butcher, *Eisenhower,* 535; Hastings, *Winston's War,* 361.
123. Eisenhower, *Crusade,* 246; Butcher, *Eisenhower,* 552.
124. Butcher, *Eisenhower,* 552.
125. Eisenhower, *Crusade,* 222.
126. Collier, *Second World War,* 393–94.
127. Keegan, *Second World War,* 375; Collier, *Second World War,* 394; Eisenhower, *Eisenhower at War,* 218.
128. F. W. Winterbotham, *The Ultra Secret* (New York, 1974), 185.
129. Keegan, *Second World War,* 373, 379.
130. Eisenhower, *Crusade,* 257; Winterbotham, *Ultra Secret,* 193.
131. Trumbull Higgins, *Winston Churchill and the Second Front* (New York, 1957), 199–201 (on Clausewitz); Hastings Lionel Ismay, *The Memoirs of General Lord Ismay* (London, 1960), 269–70.

132. WSC 3, 659; for an examination of Churchill and Clausewitz, see Carl von Clausewitz, *On War* (London, 1982).
133. Eisenhower, *Eisenhower at War,* 245–48.
134. Danchev and Todman, *War Diaries,* 553; Eden, *The Reckoning,* 526.
135. Cooper, *Old Men,* 329.
136. Danchev and Todman, *War Diaries,* 553; Eden, *The Reckoning,* 526; Cooper, *Old Men,* 330; de Gaulle, *War Memoirs,* 556–57.
137. Burns, *Roosevelt,* 476; Keegan, *Second World War,* 361.
138. Eisenhower, *Crusade,* 250; Butcher, *Eisenhower,* 562; Eisenhower, *Eisenhower at War,* 250–51.
139. Eisenhower, *Eisenhower at War,* 252.
140. Milovan Djilas, *Conversations with Stalin* (Orlando, FL, 1962), 81.
141. Eisenhower, *Eisenhower at War,* 260–61.
142. Danchev and Todman, *War Diaries,* 554.
143. GILBERT 7, 794; WSC 5, 631; Soames, *Clementine,* 463.
144. Collier, *Second World War,* 398.
145. Keegan, *Second World War,* 378.
146. Keegan, *Second World War,* 382; Eisenhower, *Crusade,* 240.
147. Keegan, *Second World War,* 378–79; Pyle, *Brave Men,* 381.
148. Keegan, *Second World War,* 378–79; *Time,* 6/12/44, 19.
149. Sir John Keegan, *Six Armies in Normandy* (Penguin, 1983), 132–33.
150. Pyle, *Brave Men,* 382–83.
151. Colville, *Fringes,* 492.
152. W. G. F. Jackson, *"Overlord" Normandy 1944* (Newark, DE, 1979), 179.
153. WSCHCS, 6947–48.
154. GILBERT 7, 795; WSCHCS, 6947–48.
155. Panter-Downes, *War Notes,* 329.
156. C&R-TCC, 3:147, 160–61.
157. C&R-TCC, 3:116, 155.

Anchorage

1. *Time,* 6/12/45.
2. *Life,* 6/19/44.
3. C&R-TCC, 3:153.
4. WM/Lord Soames, 11/8/80.
5. Charles de Gaulle, *The Complete War Memoirs of Charles de Gaulle* (New York, 1964), 722.
6. Walter Lippmann, *U.S. War Aims* (Boston, 1944), 134–35; Ronald Steel, *Walter Lippmann and the American Century* (Boston, 1980), 404, 408–10; *Time,* 7/17/44, 99–100.
7. David Eisenhower, *Eisenhower at War 1943–1945* (New York, 1991), 286; Alex Danchev and Daniel Todman, eds., *Field Marshal Lord Alanbrooke: War Diaries 1939–1945* (Berkeley, 2003), 556; F. W. Winterbotham, *The Ultra Secret* (New York, 1974), 196–97.
8. WM/Averell Harriman, 8/22/80; Winston Churchill, *Marlborough: His Life and Times* (London, 1947), 2:259; John Wheeler-Bennett, *Action This Day: Working with Churchill* (London, 1968), 200–202.

9. Dwight D. Eisenhower, *Crusade in Europe* (New York, 1948), 267; Eisenhower, *Eisenhower at War,* 214; John Keegan, *The Second World War* (London, 1989), 392.
10. Danchev and Todman, *War Diaries,* 556, 563.
11. Danchev and Todman, *War Diaries,* 556, 563.
12. Arthur Bryant, *Triumph in the West, 1943–1946* (London, 1959), 216–17.
13. Danchev and Todman, *War Diaries,* 557.
14. David Johnson, *V-1, V-2* (London, 1981), 40–41.
15. Duff Cooper, *Old Men Forget* (London, 1954), 333; Danchev and Todman, *War Diaries,* 560.
16. WSCHCS, 6958, 6961, 6978, 6980; Danchev and Todman, *War Diaries,* 563.
17. Danchev and Todman, *War Diaries,* 561, 563; C&R-TCC, 3:219, 223.
18. Danchev and Todman, *War Diaries,* 565; C&R-TCC, 3:226.
19. Basil Collier, *The Second World War: A Military History from Munich to Hiroshima* (New York, 1967), 386; Keegan, *Second World War,* 479.
20. Keegan, *Second World War,* 479–80; Eisenhower, *Eisenhower at War,* 325, 336; Danchev and Todman, *War Diaries,* 532.
21. *Time,* 7/17/44, 17; Keegan, *Second World War,* 390; Eisenhower, *Eisenhower at War,* 330.
22. Eisenhower, *Eisenhower at War,* 351.
23. Keegan, *Second World War,* 480; WSC 6, 128.
24. Danchev and Todman, *War Diaries,* 572–73; Harry C. Butcher, *My Three Years with Eisenhower* (New York, 1946), 618; Bryant, *Triumph,* 241.
25. William L. Shirer, *The Rise and Fall of the Third Reich: A History of Nazi Germany* (New York, 1960), 1035–36; WSCHCS, 6997.
26. Mark Mayo Boatner, *The Biographical Dictionary of World War II* (New York, 1999), 284, 467.
27. C&R-TCC, 3:254, 266.
28. C&R-TCC, 3:258–59; WSC 3, 136, 139, 145.
29. Martin Gilbert, *Churchill and the Jews* (New York, 2007), 211–13; WSCHCS, 7376.
30. *Time,* 7/17/44, 18; Charles de Gaulle, *The Complete War Memoirs of Charles de Gaulle* (New York, 1964), 574–76.
31. De Gaulle, *War Memoirs,* 574–76; Jean Lacouture, *De Gaulle* (New York, 1965), 136.
32. Lacouture, *de Gaulle,* 144; de Gaulle, *War Memoirs,* 579.
33. Eisenhower, *Crusade,* 267; Butcher, *Eisenhower,* 620–21.
34. Butcher, *Eisenhower,* 634–35, 638; C&R-TCC, 3:267.
35. WSCHCS, 6980; Cooper, *Old Men,* 335–36.
36. WM/Graham Norton, 10/8/80; TWY, 397; W&C-TPL, 498, 501.
37. Danchev and Todman, *War Diaries,* 520–21; Harold Macmillan, *War Diaries: Politics and War in the Mediterranean, January 1943–May 1945* (New York, 1984), 474.
38. W&C-TPL, 501; C&R-TCC, 3:274, 279; GILBERT 7, 910.
39. GILBERT 7, 908–9; Macmillan, *War Diaries,* 507–9.
40. GILBERT 7, 910; WSC 6, 94, 122.
41. WM/Malcolm Muggeridge, 11/25/80.
42. WSC 6, 101.
43. De Gaulle, *War Memoirs,* 648.
44. B. H. Liddell Hart, *History of the Second World War* (New York, 1971), 558; Danchev and Todman, *War Diaries,* 585; Charles B. MacDonald, *The Siegfried Line Campaign* (Washington, DC, 1990), chaps. 36–42.

45. WSCHCS, 7001.
46. C&R-TCC, 3:310–11; Lord Moran, *Churchill: Taken from the Diaries of Lord Moran* (Boston, 1966), 185; John Colville, *The Fringes of Power: 10 Downing Street Diaries 1939–1955* (New York, 1985), 507.
47. Johnson, *V-1, V-2*, 115.
48. Colville, *Fringes*, 509–11.
49. Danchev and Todman, *War Diaries*, 589; Colville, *Fringes*, 509–11.
50. Danchev and Todman, *War Diaries*, 589.
51. Danchev and Todman, *War Diaries*, 593; Colville, *Fringes*, 511.
52. Colville, *Fringes*, 513.
53. *Time*, 9/11/44.
54. Moran, *Diaries*, 190–91, 193, 208.
55. Robert E. Sherwood, *Roosevelt and Hopkins: An Intimate History* (New York, 1948), 818.
56. Mary Soames, *Clementine Churchill: The Biography of a Marriage* (New York, 2003), 475.
57. *Time*, 9/25/44, 19; Sherwood, *Roosevelt and Hopkins*, 818; Colville, *Fringes*, 517–18.
58. Colville, *Fringes*, 517.
59. Colville, *Fringes*, 520; C&R-TCC, 3:341.
60. WSCHCS, 6991, 6996.
61. C&R-TCC, 3:341, 345; W. Averell Harriman and Elie Abel, *Special Envoy to Churchill and Stalin: 1941–1946* (New York, 1975), 354–55; Colville, *Fringes*, 523.
62. David Dilks, ed., *The Diaries of Sir Alexander Cadogan, 1938–1945* (New York, 1972), 682.
63. C&R-TCC, 3:345; WSC 6, 227–28; Harriman and Abel, *Special Envoy*, 356–58.
64. Harriman and Abel, *Special Envoy*, 360.
65. WSC 6, 239.
66. Anthony Eden, Earl of Avon, *The Reckoning: The Memoirs of Anthony Eden* (New York, 1965), 563.
67. Eden, *The Reckoning*, 564; W&C-TPL, 506.
68. WSCHCS, 7015–17.
69. WSCHCS, 7067.
70. Eden, *The Reckoning*, 562.
71. Dilks, *Diaries*, 679; de Gaulle, *War Memoirs*, 723.
72. De Gaulle, *War Memoirs*, 723–24; C&R-TCC, 3:391, 395; Eden, *The Reckoning*, 574.
73. CAD 689; Eden, *The Reckoning*, 577–78.
74. WSC 6, 289; C&R-TCC, 3:458; Colville, *Fringes*, 529; Eden, *The Reckoning*, 577–78.
75. Dilks, *Diaries*, 686; Colville, *Fringes*, 533, 535.
76. WSCHCS, 7052.
77. C&R-TCC, 3:451, 456.
78. Mollie Panter-Downes, *London War Notes, 1939–1945* (London, 1972), 353, 354; Dilks, *Diaries*, 689.
79. PFR/Lady Mary Soames, letter of 9/3/07; PFR/Winston S. Churchill, 5/04; Eden, *The Reckoning*, 580.

80. Danchev and Todman, *War Diaries,* 638.
81. Colville, *Fringes,* 540, 545; Eden, *The Reckoning,* 580–81.
82. Colville, *Fringes,* 540.
83. Colville, *Fringes,* 541; WSC 5, 315.
84. Macmillan, *War Diaries,* 620; Eden, *The Reckoning,* 582.
85. Harriman and Abel, *Special Envoy,* 390; C&R-TCC, 3:476–77.
86. Sherwood, *Roosevelt and Hopkins,* 847.
87. TWY, 428; Colville, *Fringes,* 547.
88. Colville, *Fringes,* 548–50.
89. Collier, *Second World War,* 454; Danchev and Todman, *War Diaries,* 641; Colville, *Fringes,* 548–50; C&R-TCC, 3:486, 488.
90. Colville, *Fringes,* 549; C&R-TCC, 3:488.
91. Colville, *Fringes,* 555; C&R-TCC, 3:492; Harriman and Abel, *Special Envoy,* 390.
92. Eden, *The Reckoning,* 554; Panter-Downes, *War Notes,* 349; Harriman and Abel, *Special Envoy,* 390; C&R-TCC, 3:593; Colville, *Fringes,* 551.
93. Danchev and Todman, *War Diaries,* 644.
94. Danchev and Todman, *War Diaries,* 644; Collier, *Second World War,* 457; Liddell Hart, *History,* 663.
95. Collier, *Second World War,* 457–58; Shirer, *Rise and Fall,* 1091.
96. Collier, *Second World War,* 457–58.
97. Keegan, *Second World War,* 511; Shirer, *Rise and Fall,* 1097.
98. Martin Gilbert, *The Second World War: A Complete History* (London, 1989), 634.
99. Keegan, *Second World War,* 510–12; Milovan Djilas, *Conversations with Stalin* (Orlando, FL, 1962), 95, 110.
100. Keegan, *Second World War,* 510–12; Shirer, *Rise and Fall,* 1098.
101. Moran, *Diaries,* 216; Hastings Lionel Ismay, *The Memoirs of General Lord Ismay* (London, 1960), 385.
102. Ismay, *Memoirs,* 384–85.
103. Harriman and Abel, *Special Envoy,* 390; Eden, *The Reckoning,* 592.
104. Ismay, *Memoirs,* 383; Collier, *Second World War,* 454; Soames, *Clementine,* 480.
105. TWY, 433.
106. Eden, *The Reckoning,* 592.
107. Djilas, *Conversations,* 106.
108. Dilks, *Diaries,* 702; Sarah Churchill, *Keep On Dancing* (London, 1981), 128; Jim Bishop, *FDR'S Last Year* (New York, 1974), 364.
109. Bishop, *FDR'S Last Year,* 320; Harriman and Abel, *Special Envoy,* 104.
110. WSC 6, 366.
111. WSC 6, 369, 372; Harriman and Abel, *Special Envoy,* 405.
112. WSC 6, 372; Bishop, *FDR'S Last Year,* 346; Eden, *The Reckoning,* 593.
113. Harriman and Abel, *Special Envoy,* 406; WSC 6, 385.
114. WSC 6, 390; Bishop, *FDR'S Last Year,* 364; Eden, *The Reckoning,* 594.
115. WSC 6, 354; Eden, *The Reckoning,* 390.
116. Bishop, *FDR'S Last Year,* 384, 412; Dilks, *Diaries,* 707–9; Moran, *Diaries,* 247.
117. WSCHCS, 7116–18.
118. WSC 6, 353, 397; Churchill, *Keep On Dancing,* 134.
119. John Rupert Colville, *Footprints in Time* (London, 1979), 179.
120. GILBERT 6, 1161, 1165.
121. Colville, *Fringes,* 562–63.
122. GILBERT 7, 1257.

123. Colville, *Fringes,* 570.
124. Colville, *Fringes,* 576.
125. Danchev and Todman, *War Diaries,* 677, 679; WSC 6, 416.
126. Collier, *Second World War,* 465–66; Viscount Montgomery of Alamein, *The Memoirs of Field Marshal Montgomery* (London, 1958), 330.
127. C&R-TCC, 3:572, 600.
128. Danchev and Todman, *War Diaries,* 679; Montgomery, *Memoirs,* 331.
129. Shirer, *Rise and Fall,* 1105–6.
130. C&R-TCC, 3:603, 605, 608.
131. Keegan, *Second World War,* 166–67; Collier, *Second World War,* 469.
132. Colville, *Fringes,* 564.
133. C&R-TCC, 3:588.
134. C&R-TCC, 3:596.
135. C&R-TCC, 3:610, 613.
136. C&R-TCC, 3:614.
137. GILBERT 7, 1291–1293; W&C-TPL, 526.
138. TWY, 449; WSCHCS, 7140.
139. Colville, *Fringes,* 591; Randolph S. Churchill, *Winston S. Churchill: Youth, 1874–1900* (Boston, 1996), 411.
140. Colville, *Fringes,* 591.
141. Gilbert, *Second World War,* 669; WSC 6, 516.
142. Keegan, *Second World War,* 521–22.
143. Shirer, *Rise and Fall,* 1112, 1117; Albert Speer, *Inside the Third Reich: Memoirs by Albert Speer* (Macmillan, 1970), 480.
144. Shirer, *Rise and Fall,* 1114; Speer, *Memoirs,* 473.
145. Speer, *Memoirs,* 480, 485.
146. David Rising, "Hitler's Final Days Described by Bodyguard," AP, 4/24/05.
147. WSC 6, 502–3; Harry S. Truman, *Year of Decisions* (Garden City, NY, 1955), 106–7.
148. Shirer, *Rise and Fall,* 1131, 1138; Danchev and Todman, *War Diaries,* 686.
149. GILBERT 7, 1318–22; Eden, *The Reckoning,* 615–16; Colville, *Fringes,* 592.
150. Djilas, *Conversations,* 114.
151. WSC 6, 506–7; Eden, *The Reckoning,* 616.
152. Colville, *Fringes,* 596–97.
153. Shirer, *Rise and Fall,* 1133.
154. Louis P. Lochner, *The Goebbels Diaries, 1942–1943* (New York, 1948), 254.
155. Shirer, *Rise and Fall,* 1136–37; Keegan, *Second World War,* 528.
156. Colville, *Fringes,* 588, 590; TWY, 453.
157. TWY, 453; *Time,* 5/14/45, 70.
158. Colville, *Fringes,* 596.
159. Rising, "Hitler's Final Days"; Keegan, *Second World War,* 532; Mary Shelley, the final line of *Frankenstein; Time,* 5/7/45, 45.
160. WSCHCS, 7150.
161. *Times,* 5/3/45.
162. Montgomery, *Memoirs,* 335–36.
163. Danchev and Todman, *War Diaries,* 687.
164. Dilks, *Diaries,* 736, 738.
165. Ismay, *Memoirs,* 394.
166. *Time,* 5/7/45, 37; Panter-Downes, *War Notes,* 373.
167. Ismay, *Memoirs,* 395; Danchev and Todman, *War Diaries,* 687–88.

168. *The Daily Telegraph,* 5/8/45; Panter-Downes, *War Notes,* 376.
169. Cooper, *Old Men,* 325.
170. TWY, 457.
171. Moran, *Diaries,* 269.
172. WSCHCS, 7154; TWY, 457.
173. WSCHCS, 7155; Panter-Downes, *War Notes,* 377–78.
174. WSCHCS, 7161; Danchev and Todman, *War Diaries,* 689.
175. Panter-Downes, *War Notes,* 378; TWY, 459.
176. WSCHCS, 7155.
177. Soames, *Clementine,* 375; GILBERT 7, 1351.
178. My wording recalls the translation by Emily Wilson (*Six Tragedies,* Oxford, 2010).

Ebb Tide

1. WSCHCS, 7214.
2. Alex Danchev and Daniel Todman, eds., *Field Marshal Lord Alanbrooke: War Diaries 1939–1945* (Berkeley, 2003), 691; John Keegan, *The Second World War* (London, 1989), 590–91.
3. Danchev and Todman, *War Diaries,* 691.
4. WSC 6, 571, 573.
5. WSC 6, 575.
6. WSC 6, 578.
7. Keegan, *Second World War,* 592–93; Dwight D. Eisenhower, *Crusade in Europe* (New York, 1948), 439.
8. Viscount Montgomery of Alamein, *The Memoirs of Field Marshal Montgomery* (London, 1958), 356; WSCHCS, 7214.
9. WSCHCS, 7163.
10. Danchev and Todman, *War Diaries,* 598, 690, 693, 695; Montgomery, *Memoirs,* 214–15.
11. Montgomery, *Memoirs,* 336; WSC 6, 570; GILBERT 8, 1070.
12. WSCHCS, 8612.
13. WSCHCS, 5694.
14. Anthony Eden, Earl of Avon, *The Reckoning: The Memoirs of Anthony Eden* (New York, 1965), 637.
15. GILBERT 7, 972.
16. WSCHCS, 7130–33.
17. J. B. Priestley, *Letter to a Returning Serviceman* (London, 1945); *Time,* 12/31/45, 92.
18. WSCHCS, 6764.
19. WSCHCS, 7133.
20. John Colville, *The Fringes of Power: 10 Downing Street Diaries 1939–1955* (New York, 1985), 606; WSCHCS, 7170.
21. WSCHCS, 7172–73.
22. Roy Jenkins, *Churchill: A Biography* (London, 2011), 793; Colville, *Fringes,* 606–7.
23. Brian Gardner, *Churchill in Power: As Seen by His Contemporaries* (Boston, 1970), 299; TWY, 472, 475.
24. Henry Pelling, *Winston Churchill* (Conshohocken, PA, 1999), 560; Eden, *The Reckoning,* 638.
25. Colville, *Fringes,* 611; Gardner, *Churchill in Power,* 301.

26. WSCHCS, 7201–3.
27. John Wheeler-Bennett, *Action This Day: Working with Churchill* (London, 1968), 72–73.
28. Colville, *Fringes,* 610; Lord Moran, *Churchill: Taken from the Diaries of Lord Moran* (Boston, 1966), 276, 279; W. Averell Harriman and Elie Abel, *Special Envoy to Churchill and Stalin: 1941–1946* (New York, 1975), 397 (Leahy offers odds).
29. Hansard 6/14/45; Colville, *Fringes,* 611.
30. WSC 6, 637–38; Anthony Montague Browne, *Long Sunset* (London, 1996), 127.
31. Eden, *The Reckoning,* 632, 634; David Dilks, ed., *The Diaries of Sir Alexander Cadogan, 1938–1945* (New York, 1972), 765.
32. Eden, *The Reckoning,* 634.
33. Moran, *Diaries,* 291.
34. WSC 6, 642.
35. Harry S. Truman, *Year of Decisions* (Garden City, NY, 1955), 416; WSC 6, 669–70; Georgii Konstantinovich Zhukov, *The Memoirs of Marshal Zhukov* (New York, 1971), 674–75.
36. Danchev and Todman, *War Diaries,* 709.
37. WSC 6, 632; *Time,* 8/27/45; *Herald Tribune Europe,* 12/29/06.
38. WSC 6, 674–75.
39. *Time,* 7/9/45; Mary Soames, *Clementine Churchill: The Biography of a Marriage* (New York, 2003), 508–9; WSC 6, 674–75; Gardner, *Churchill in Power,* 307.
40. Soames, *Clementine,* 509; Moran, *Diaries,* 307.
41. Gardner, *Churchill in Power,* 307–9.
42. *NYT,* 1/25/65.
43. Soames, *Clementine,* 509; TWY, 479.
44. Gardner, *Churchill in Power,* 308; WSCHCS, 7204.
45. Danchev and Todman, *War Diaries,* 713.
46. Eden, *The Reckoning,* 639.
47. Soames, *Clementine,* 511.
48. Soames, *Clementine,* 511; Colville, *Fringes,* 612.
49. WSCHCS, 7505, 7257.
50. WSCHCS, 7252–53.
51. Moran, *Diaries,* 335.
52. Robert E. Sherwood, *Roosevelt and Hopkins: An Intimate History* (New York, 1948), 922, 931.
53. Dean Acheson, *Present at the Creation: My Years in the State Department* (New York, 1969), 150–51.
54. George F. Kennan, *Memoirs: 1925–1950* (New York, 1967), 290–91, 546.
55. Montgomery, *Memoirs,* 362, 454.
56. Clark Clifford, *Counsel to the President* (New York, 1991), 100–2.
57. Clifford, *Counsel,* 100; Moran, *Diaries,* 303, 350.
58. Clifford, *Counsel,* 101.
59. WSCHCS, 7286.
60. WSCHCS, 7289.
61. WSCHCS, 7286; *NYT,* 3/6/46.
62. GILBERT 8, 204–6, 211.
63. Harriman and Abel, *Special Envoy,* 550–51.
64. WSCHCS, 7382.
65. WSCHCS, 7380–82.

66. GILBERT 8, 286–88; WSCHCS, 8016.
67. WSCHCS, 7367.
68. Clifford, *Counsel,* 131; Acheson, *Present,* 217–18.
69. Clifford, *Counsel,* 138; Moran, *Diaries,* 231; Leonard Mosley, *Marshall: Hero for Our Times* (New York, 1982), 396–98.
70. Acheson, *Present,* 212.
71. Mosley, *Marshall,* 402; Acheson, *Present,* 217–18; Clifford, *Counsel,* 145.
72. Soames, *Clementine,* 522.
73. Colville, *Fringes,* 648; John Colville, *The Churchillians* (London, 1981), 156.
74. Stewart Alsop, *Stay of Execution: A Sort of Memoir* (New York, 1973); WM/Cecily ("Chips") Gemmell (German prisoners), 7/10/80.
75. WM/Cecily ("Chips") Gemmell, 7/10/80; Roy Howells, *Churchill's Last Years* (Philadelphia, 1965), 163–64; Diana Cooper, *The Light of Common Day* (London, 1959), 109.
76. GILBERT 8, 563n2; Soames, *Clementine,* 522, 564.
77. GILBERT 8, 244–45.
78. Soames, *Clementine,* 543.
79. Jenkins, *Churchill,* 824; GILBERT 8, 315.
80. W&C-TPL, 545; Moran, *Diaries,* 339.
81. Moran, *Diaries,* 341, 344, 356, 838.
82. Moran, *Diaries,* 336; *Herald Tribune Europe,* 12/29/06; WSCHCS, 7909.
83. *Time,* 6/13/45; *Time,* 9/3/45, back cover.
84. Nigel Nicolson, ed., *The Harold Nicolson Diaries: 1907–1963* (London, 2004), 346.
85. Nigel Nicolson, *Diaries,* 346; Colville, *Fringes,* 618–21.
86. Colville, *Fringes,* 620–21; GILBERT 8, 422.
87. WSCHCS, 7387–88, 7525.
88. WSCHCS, 7387.
89. Moran, *Diaries,* 336.
90. WSCHCS, 7314, 7328.
91. WSCHCS, 7376.
92. Moran, *Diaries,* 337–38.
93. WSCHCS, 7458.
94. WSCHCS, 7458.
95. WSCHCS, 7774–77.
96. WSCHCS, 7444.
97. WSCHCS, 7447, 7655 (Punjab massacres).
98. WSCHCS, 7673.
99. Martin Gilbert, *Churchill: A Life* (New York, 1992), 879.
100. WSCHCS, 7627.
101. Nigel Nicolson, *Diaries,* 361.
102. Nigel Nicolson, *Diaries,* 363.
103. David Reynolds, ed., *The Origins of the Cold War in Europe* (New Haven, CT, 1994), 13.
104. GILBERT 8, 467.
105. Colville, *Fringes,* 626.
106. *Time,* 1/5/50; WSCHCS, 7797.
107. WSCHCS, 8023.
108. Peter Catterall, ed., *The Macmillan Diaries: The Cabinet Years, 1950–57* (London, 2003), 17.

109. WSCHCS, 8023.
110. WSCHCS, 7793.
111. WSCHCS, 7653; WSCHCS, 7501.
112. WSCHCS, 7680.
113. GILBERT 8, 226; WM/Cecily ("Chips") Gemmell, 7/10/80.
114. WM/Cecily ("Chips") Gemmell, 7/10/80; WM/Jane (Portal) Williams, 1980.
115. WM/Jane (Portal) Williams, 1980.
116. Gilbert, *Churchill: A Life,* 887; WM/Jane (Portal) Williams, 1980; WM/Cecily ("Chips") Gemmell, 7/10/80.
117. WM/Cecily ("Chips") Gemmell, 7/10/80.
118. WM/Cecily ("Chips") Gemmell 7/10/80; WM/Jane (Portal) Williams, 1980.
119. Richard Langworth, ed., *Churchill by Himself: The Definitive Collection of Quotations* (London, 2008), 330; *Time,* 1/5/50.
120. James Reston, *Deadline: A Memoir* (New York, 1991).
121. W&C-TPL, 553.
122. Moran, *Diaries,* 358, 360.
123. Jenkins, *Churchill,* 829; WSCHCS, 7927.
124. WSCHCS, 7938, 7948.
125. WSCHCS, 7915.
126. WSCHCS, 7943.
127. WSCHCS, 7951.
128. Moran, *Diaries,* 359; GILBERT 8, 514.
129. WSCHCS, 7966.
130. Pelling, *Winston Churchill,* 642.
131. WSCHCS, 8236, 7897; Charles Eade, ed., *Churchill by His Contemporaries* (New York, 1954), 58, 301.
132. Eade, *Churchill,* 295.
133. WSCHCS, 8017, 8023, 8191; Jenkins, *Churchill,* 837.
134. WSCHCS, 8005, 8016, 8018, 8021, 8023, 8025, 8027.
135. WSCHCS, 8059.
136. WSCHCS, 8062.
137. WSCHCS, 7800.
138. WSCHCS, 8028, 8048; Catterall, *Macmillan Diaries,* 4.
139. WSCHCS, 8119, 8075.
140. WSCHCS, 8065; Nigel Nicolson, *Diaries,* 372.
141. WSCHCS, 8068–69.
142. Catterall, *Macmillan Diaries,* 6, 7, 10.
143. *Time,* 10/16/50, 10/30/50.
144. Acheson, *Present,* 467–69, 478; Catterall, *Macmillan Diaries,* 33.
145. Acheson, *Present,* 478, 481–82.
146. WSCHCS, 8109.
147. W&C-TPL, 558.
148. Nigel Nicolson, *Diaries,* 374.
149. Catterall, *Macmillan Diaries,* 33, 47, 49.
150. Catterall, *Macmillan Diaries,* 52.
151. Colville, *Fringes,* 759; Catterall, *Macmillan Diaries,* 63.
152. Catterall, *Macmillan Diaries,* 53–54, 90; WSCHCS, 8203, 8238, 8240.
153. Catterall, *Macmillan Diaries,* 90–91; Moran, *Diaries,* 360.
154. Soames, *Clementine,* 562; GILBERT 8, 631.

155. GILBERT 8, 638; WSCHCS, 7214.
156. WSCHCS, 8243.
157. WSCHCS, 8246.
158. WSCHCS, 8253.
159. Alec Cairncross, *The British Economy Since 1945*, 2nd ed. (Boston, 1995), 55–57, 102–3.
160. Moran, *Diaries,* 384; WSCHCS, 8256, 8261.
161. Violet Bonham Carter, *Winston Churchill: An Intimate Portrait* (New York, 1965), 4–5; WSCHCS, 8268.
162. WSCHCS, 8283.
163. Moran, *Diaries,* 366; Catterall, *Macmillan Diaries,* 105; WSCHCS, 8283.
164. Soames, *Clementine,* 429.
165. Hastings Lionel Ismay, *The Memoirs of General Lord Ismay* (London, 1960), 453.
166. Colville, *Fringes,* 631.
167. Catterall, *Macmillan Diaries,* 111, 114–15.
168. Acheson, *Present,* 608.
169. WSCHCS, 8307.
170. WSCHCS, 7793.
171. WSCHCS, 8307.
172. WSCHCS, 8297.
173. Nigel Nicolson, *Diaries,* 378; Acheson, *Present,* 595.
174. WSCHCS, 8329.
175. Colville, *Fringes,* 634, 641.
176. Moran, *Diaries,* 433, 436–37; Colville, *Fringes,* 675.
177. Moran, *Diaries,* 473.
178. Colville, *Fringes,* 672.
179. Moran, *Diaries,* 475.
180. Colville, *Fringes,* 673.
181. Moran, *Diaries,* 489.
182. WSCHCS, 8504–5.
183. Moran, *Diaries,* 527; Catterall, *Macmillan Diaries,* 272.
184. Moran, *Diaries,* 535–36; W&C-TPL, 575.
185. Soames, *Clementine,* 581.
186. Colville, *Fringes,* 683–85.
187. Moran, *Diaries,* 540.
188. Moran, *Diaries,* 557; WM/Malcolm Muggeridge, 11/25/80.
189. GILBERT 8, 593.
190. Moran, *Diaries,* 595.
191. Colville, *Fringes,* 692–93.
192. Colville, *Fringes,* 698; Catterall, *Macmillan Diaries,* 325.
193. GILBERT 8, 1036.
194. GILBERT 8, 1039.
195. Catterall, *Macmillan Diaries,* 343.
196. Colville, *Fringes,* 706–7.
197. Soames, *Clementine,* 446; GILBERT 8, 1073.
198. WSCHCS, 8609.
199. Sarah Churchill, *A Thread in the Tapestry* (London, 1967), 17.
200. GILBERT 8, 958; Colville, *Fringes,* 705.
201. WSCHCS, 8627.

202. WSCHCS, 8633.
203. *Sunday Times,* 3/6/55; GILBERT 8, 1101.
204. Colville, *Fringes,* 708.
205. Colville, *Fringes,* 708; Browne, *Long Sunset,* 148.
206. Soames, *Clementine,* 597.

Postscript

1. GILBERT 8, 1151.
2. Anthony Montague Browne, *Long Sunset* (London, 1996), 158; WM/Anthony Montague Browne, 11/15/80.
3. WM/A. J. P. Taylor, 12/1/80.
4. Browne, *Long Sunset,* 150; Mary Soames, *Clementine Churchill: The Biography of a Marriage* (New York, 2003), 545, 552.
5. Browne, *Long Sunset,* 152.
6. W&C-TPL, 628; Soames, *Clementine,* 633.
7. Soames, *Clementine,* 634–35.
8. Lord Moran, *Churchill: Taken from the Diaries of Lord Moran* (Boston, 1966), 840; Roy Howells, *Churchill's Last Years* (Philadelphia, 1965), 65.
9. Browne, *Long Sunset,* 302, 310.
10. *Atlantic Monthly,* 3/65.
11. Soames, *Clementine,* 619.
12. John Colville, *The Fringes of Power: 10 Downing Street Diaries 1939–1955* (New York, 1985), 720–21.
13. Moran, *Diaries,* 756; Colville, *Fringes,* 51, 721.
14. W&C-TPL, 621.
15. Nigel Nicolson, ed., *The Harold Nicolson Diaries: 1907–1963* (London, 2004), 412; *NYT,* 11/5/57.
16. John Colville, *The Churchillians* (London, 1981), 214.
17. Howells, *Churchill's Last Years,* 64; Browne, *Long Sunset,* 142; WM/Anthony Montague Browne, 11/15/80.
18. WSCHCS, 8687.
19. Moran, *Diaries,* 562; *Time,* 6/13/60.
20. Randolph S. Churchill, *Winston S. Churchill: Youth,* 1874–1900 (Boston, 1996), 257; Winston S. Churchill, *Memories and Adventures* (London, 1989), 115.
21. Browne, *Long Sunset,* 278, 288–89.
22. Browne, *Long Sunset,* 312.
23. Kay Halle, *Irrepressible Churchill: Stories, Sayings and Impressions of Sir Winston Churchill* (London, 1985), 325; Browne, *Long Sunset,* 312.
24. Moran, *Diaries,* 566; Howells, *Churchill's Last Years,* 128, 140.
25. Howells, *Churchill's Last Years,* 194–95.
26. Moran, *Diaries,* 840–41; Colville, *Churchillians,* 19.
27. The Editors of the Viking Press, *The Churchill Years 1874-1965, with foreword by Lord Butler of Saffron Walden* (London, 1965), 240–42.
28. Moran, *Diaries,* 842.

COPYRIGHT ACKNOWLEDGMENTS

Alan Brooke, Viscount Alanbrooke, excerpts from *War Diaries 1939–1945*, edited by Alex Danchev and Daniel Todman (Berkeley: University of California Press and London: Weidenfeld & Nicolson, 2001). Reprinted by permission of David Higham Associates, Ltd.

Alexander Cadogan, excerpts from *The Diaries of Sir Alexander Cadogan, O.M., 1938–1945*, edited by Donald Dilks (New York: G. P. Putnam's Sons, 1972). Reprinted by permission of David Higham Associates, Ltd.

Clementine Churchill and Winston S. Churchill, excerpts from letters from *Winston and Clementine: The Personal Letters of the Churchills*, edited by Mary Soames. Copyright © Clementine Churchill. Copyright © Winston S. Churchill. Reproduced with permission of Curtis Brown, London, on behalf of the Master and Fellows of Churchill College Cambridge, the Estate of Lady Clementine Churchill, and the Estate of Sir Winston Churchill.

Winston Churchill, excerpts from *The Second World War, Volume 2: Their Finest Hour; The Second World War, Volume 3: The Grand Alliance; The Second World War, Volume 4: The Hinge of Fate; The Second World War, Volume 5: Closing the Ring;* and *The Second World War, Volume 6: Triumph and Tragedy.* Copyright 1949, 1950, 1951, 1953 by Houghton Mifflin Company, renewed © 1976, 1977, 1979, 1981 by the Honourable Lady Sarah Audley and the Honourable Lady Soames. Copyright © by Winston S. Churchill. All reprinted by permission of Houghton Mifflin Harcourt Publishing Company and Curtis Brown, London, on behalf of the Estate of Sir Winston Churchill. All rights reserved.

John Colville, excerpts from *The Fringes of Power: Downing Street Diaries 1939–1955*. Copyright © 1985 by Hodder & Stoughton Ltd. Reproduced by permission of Hodder and Stoughton Limited.

Josef Goebbels, excerpts from *The Goebbels Diaries,* translated and edited by Louis P. Lochner. Copyright 1948 by The Fireside Press. Used by permission of Doubleday, a division of Random House, Inc.

William Averill Harriman and Elie Able, excerpts from *Special Envoy to Churchill and Stalin 1941–1946*. Copyright © 1975 by William Averill Harriman and Elie Able. Used by permission of Random House, Inc., and Hutchinson Publishing Group, Ltd./The Random House Group Limited.

Hastings Ismay, excerpts from *The Memoirs of General Lord Ismay.*

Published by William Heinemann. Reprinted by permission of The Random House Group Limited.

Harold Macmillan, excerpts from *Macmillan Diaries: The Cabinet Years 1950–1957*. Reprinted with permission of Macmillan.

Harold Nicolson, excerpts from *The War Years: Diaries and Letters 1939–1945*. Reprinted with permission of Juliet Nicolson.

Mollie Panter-Downes, excerpts from *London War Notes, 1939–1945*. Copyright © 1971 by Mollie Panter-Downes. Reprinted by permission of Farrar Straus & Giroux, LLC.

Seneca, excerpt from "Hercules Furens" from *Six Tragedies*, translated by Emily Wilson. Translation © 2010 by Emily Wilson. Reprinted by permission of Oxford University Press, Ltd.

Robert E. Sherwood, excerpts from *Roosevelt and Hopkins: An Intimate History*. Copyright 1948, 1950 and renewed © 1976, 1978 by Robert E. Sherwood. Reprinted by permission of Brandt & Hochman Literary Agents, Inc.

William L. Shirer, excerpts from *Berlin Diary: The Diary of a Foreign Correspondent 1934–1941*. Copyright 1941, renewed © 1968 by William L. Shirer. Reprinted by permission of Don Congdon Associates, Inc. Excerpts from *The Rise and Fall of the Third Reich: A History of Nazi Germany*. Copyright © 1960 by William L. Shirer. Reprinted with the permission of Simon & Schuster, Inc.

Walter Thompson, excerpts from *Assignment: Churchill*. Copyright © 1955 by Walter Thompson. Reprinted by permission of Farrar Straus & Giroux, LLC.

Charles Wilson, Baron Moran, excerpts from *Winston Churchill: The Struggle for Survival 1940–1965; Taken from the Diaries of Lord Moran*. Copyright © 1966 by Trustees of Lord Moran. Reprinted with permission of Constable Robinson Publishers.

INDEX

The abbreviation WSC in subheadings refers to Winston Churchill. Italic page numbers refer to figures.

ABOUT THE AUTHOR

Paul Reid is an award-winning journalist. In late 2003, Manchester, in failing health, asked him to complete *The Last Lion: Defender of the Realm.* A Boston native, Reid now lives in western North Carolina.

1937

Axis backs Spanish Fascists
Baldwin retires, Chamberlain is P.M.
Makes appeasement his foreign policy
Halifax visits Hitler — appeasement starts
WSC publishes *Great Contemporaries*

1938

Year of "The Lambeth Walk"
Il Duce's Ethiopian conquest recognized by Britain
Eden quits cabinet
ANSCHLUSS: HITLER SEIZES AUSTRIA
WSC proposes Grand Alliance to confront Hitler
Chamberlain rejects it; says Reich would be angered
WSC publishes 2 books and 59 articles, yet faces bankruptcy; proposes to sell Chartwell, quit Parliament, go into business. Saved by last-minute loan
In House Sandys documents lack of anti-aircraft defense; government wants to prosecute for revealing official secrets
MUNICH: CHAMBERLAIN SELLS OUT CZECHS
Duff Cooper resigns as first lord of the Admiralty
WSC denounces Munich Agreement
Both WSC and Hitler now travel armed
Attempt by disaffected constituents to oust WSC from House — applauded by Hitler — fails
Parliamentary inquiry exonerates Sandys
WSC compares P.M.'s judgment with his own in devastating speech at Chingford

1939

At Château de l'Horizon, WSC puts ex-king in his place
Fascists triumphant in Spain
WSC survives second attempt by appeasers to unseat him
HITLER SEIZES ALL CZECHOSLOVAKIA, ENTERS PRAGUE
Chamberlain announces Polish guarantee
Mussolini conquers Albania
WSC toils to meet debt payments
After Prague, British public begins to turn toward him
Billboards: "WHAT PRICE CHURCHILL?"
WSC suggests Britain, France, Russia form defensive alliance against Hitler
Soviet foreign commissar Litvinov formally proposes it
French enthusiastic, but Chamberlain, anti-Bolshevik, vetoes it
Stalin dismisses Litvinov, appoints Molotov
Molotov turns from Allies, signs pact with Hitler
Allies pledge support for Poland
WSC tours Maginot Line
HITLER INVADES POLAND
ALLIES DECLARE WAR ON GERMANY
Italy proclaims neutrality
WSC named first lord of the Admiralty
Nazis and Soviets partition Poland
Ark Royal torpedoed in Scapa Flow
Russia invades Finland
RN defeats *Graf Spee*

1940

British prisoners rescued from *Altmark*
Finns surrender to Soviets
Chamberlain: Hitler "missed the bus"
GERMANY INVADES DENMARK, NORWAY
WSC masterminds ill-starred Norway campaign

May 10, 1940

NAZIS INVADE LOW COUNTRIES, FRANCE
WSC BECOMES PRIME MINISTER

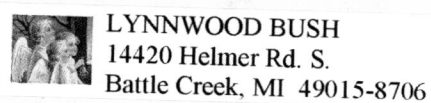

Alone
1932–1940

Books by William Manchester

Disturber of the Peace

The City of Anger

Shadow of the Monsoon

Beard the Lion

A Rockefeller Family Portrait

The Long Gainer

Portrait of a President

The Death of a President

The Arms of Krupp

The Glory and the Dream

Controversy

American Caesar

Goodbye, Darkness

The Last Lion: Visions of Glory

One Brief Shining Moment

In Our Time

The Last Lion: Alone

A World Lit Only by Fire

The Last Lion: Defender of the Realm

The Last Lion

Winston Spencer Churchill

Alone

1932–1940

William Manchester

Little, Brown and Company
New York Boston London

Little, Brown and Company
Hachette Book Group
237 Park Avenue, New York, NY 10017
littlebrown.com

First Edition: October 1988

Little, Brown and Company is a division of Hachette Book Group, Inc., and is celebrating its 175th anniversary in 2012. The Little, Brown name and logo are trademarks of Hachette Book Group, Inc.

Library of Congress Cataloging-in-Publication Data
(Revised for vol. 2)
Manchester, William Raymond.
The last lion, Winston Spencer Churchill.

Includes index.
Contents: v. 1. Visions of glory, 1874–1932—v. 2. Alone, 1932–1940.
1. Churchill, Winston, Sir, 1874–1965. 2. Great Britain—Politics and government—20th century. 3. Great Britain—Foreign relations—20th century. 4. Prime ministers—Great Britain—Biography. I. Title.
DA566.9.C5M26 1983 941.087'092'4 [B] 82-42972
ISBN 978-0-316-54512-9

"The Lion Caged" appeared in slightly different form in *American Heritage*.

20 19 18 17

RRD-C

Printed in the United States of America

To

BILL SHIRER

who saw it from the other side
and saw it first

"Ich hatt' einen Kameraden . . ."

History with its flickering lamp
stumbles along the trail of the past,
trying to reconstruct its scenes,
to revive its echoes, and kindle
with pale gleams the passion
of former day.

—Winston Churchill
Speech in the House
of Commons
November 12, 1940

Then out spake brave Horatius,
The Captain of the Gate:
"To every man upon this earth
Death cometh soon or late.
And how can man die better
Than facing fearful odds,
For the ashes of his fathers,
And the temples of his gods?"

THOMAS BABINGTON MACAULAY,
Lays of Ancient Rome
Memorized by Churchill at age thirteen

ARRAY

ILLUSTRATIONS

In the turmoil of the 1930s Churchill often found sanctuary in painting. (*The Keystone Collection*)

On July 24, 1939, a huge sign appears on the Strand. (Daily Mirror)

Churchill and Anthony Eden walk down Whitehall in late August 1939. (*The Illustrated London News Picture Library*)

Churchill is appointed First Lord of the Admiralty, September 1939. (*United Press International*)

In the first month of the war Randolph marries Pamela Digby. (*Mary Soames Collection*)

New York Times, May 11, 1940. (*Copyright © 1940 by The New York Times Company. Reprinted by permission*)

Winston Spencer Churchill becomes Prime Minister of Great Britain. (*Cecil Beaton Photograph, courtesy of Sotheby's, London*)

MAPS

AUTHOR'S NOTE

This work is a biography, not a history. The two are often confused, and understandably so, for both recount the past. But there is a distinction. History is a chronological account of prior events. Biography focuses on one figure, exploring the significance of his life by examining "the earthly pilgrimage of a man," in Thomas Carlyle's words, or, in Sir Edmund Gosse's, by presenting "the faithful portrait of a soul in adventure by life."

In the view of this writer, there can be no enlightening life which does not include an account of the man's times. This need for context is even greater when the central figure is a towering statesman. It is impossible to understand Churchill and his adversaries in the 1930s, for example, without grasping the British revulsion against the horrors of World War I. If a man casts a long shadow, as Churchill did, extensive research leads to lengthy books. I propose to cover the life of Churchill in three volumes. Three volumes is a lot. But he deserves at least a triptych if one is to meet the exacting standard set down by Paul M. Kendall of the University of Kansas. The biographer, he writes in *Encyclopaedia Britannica*,

> seeks to elicit from facts, by selection and design, the illusion of a life actually lived. Within the bounds of given data, the biographer seeks to transform plain information into illumination.... His achievement as a biographer will be measured, in great part, by his ability to suggest the sweep of chronology and yet to highlight the major patterns of behavior that give a life its shape and meaning.

My personal encounters with Sir Winston Churchill were confined to a five-day Atlantic crossing aboard the *Queen Mary* in January 1953, when he was in his last premiership. Subsequently, I visited No. 10 Downing Street. But when I undertook my present task I was remembered by members of his family and entourage. Their hospitality, when I set about the ten-year job of researching and writing *The Last Lion*, honored me and moved me. Thus began the most ambitious literary venture of my life, which included taped interviews of such diversity and length that their transcription required a full year. Those are essential to *The Last Lion*'s scholarly foundation.

I am particularly grateful to Martin Gilbert, MA, Fellow of Merton

College, Oxford, and official biographer of Sir Winston Churchill, for his time, his generosity, his kindness in guiding me toward sources, and for his invaluable narrative and document volumes.

My debt to Lady Soames, DBE, née Mary Churchill, is immense, for her recollections of her father, her patience in answering my inquiries, and her role as my tour guide through the rooms, the grounds, and the outer buildings of Chartwell, in one of which, her father's studio, I saw—perhaps gaped at would be more accurate—nearly five hundred of her father's paintings. They are stunning, and serve to confirm Sir Isaiah Berlin's conclusion that Churchill was "the largest human being of our times."

The late Sir John Colville, CB, CVO, Honorary Fellow, Churchill College, Cambridge, retired RAF fighter pilot, author, and private secretary to three prime ministers—chiefly Churchill—was cooperative, forthcoming, and encouraging throughout. To assist me he devoted hours he could have spent in more urgent causes, and did so with that understated charm which is the mark of an English gentleman, almost convincing me that there was nothing he would rather do.

Among others who were most helpful to me were surviving "Churchillians," as Sir John called them: Sir William Deakin, DSO, MA; Sir Fitzroy Maclean, CBE, MP (C); the late Lord Boothby, KBE; Sir David Pitblado, KCB, CVO; Sir John Martin, KCMG, CB, CVO; the late Lord Soames, PC, GCMG, GCVO, CH, CBE; Lieutenant General Sir Ian Jacob, GBE, KBE, CB, DL; Anita Leslie; Sir David Hunt, CBE, OBE, DFC; Lord Bonham-Carter; young Winston Churchill, MP, grandson of his namesake; the late Oscar Nemon; the late, gallant Viscount Head, PC, GCMG, KCMG, CBE; the late Lord Duncan-Sandys, who was Churchill's son-in-law; and five of Churchill's secretaries—Grace Hamblin, OBE, Jane Williams, Kathleen Hill, Vanda Salmon, and Cecily ("Chips") Gemmell. I should also express my appreciation to Wing Commander R. M. Sparkes, RAF, who took me through the Annexe—Churchill's wartime bunker and the site of the Cabinet War Room as it had been in 1945—long before it was opened to the public.

With the exception of one member of the Royal Family, no one refused to be interviewed and taped. The late Harold Macmillan (Lord Stockton) set an entire day aside for me; so did the late Lord Butler of Saffron Walden ("Rab"); so did the ineffable Malcolm Muggeridge. All questions I posed (including some which were clearly impertinent) were answered by Lady Avon, the widow of Anthony Eden; the late Lady Diana Cooper, widow of Alfred Duff Cooper, Viscount Norwich; the historian A. J. P. Taylor; Lord Strauss; Lord Hailsham; the Rt. Hon. Malcolm MacDonald, OM, PC, MP, son of Ramsay and a cabinet minister in Churchill's wartime national government; Lord Geoffrey Lloyd; R. L. James, the retired headmaster of Harrow; Lord Selkirk; Noel Mander; George Malcolm Thompson; Denis Kelly; Alan MacLean; Elizabeth Gilliatt; John Grigg; Sir Charles Martin; Richard Hill; Lord Southbridge; Graham Norton; and certain Americans who enjoyed a special relationship with Churchill: the late Virginia Cowles, Kay Halle, and the late Averell Harriman. Mrs. Harriman provided immense help and encouragement, though classifying Pamela Harriman as American or British presents difficulties. As Averell was, she is very active in the U.S. Democratic party. However, she was born Pamela Digby, the daughter of the eleventh Lord Digby, KG, DSO, MC, TD, and her first husband was Randolph Churchill. As Winston's daughter-in-law and the widow of one of the greatest statesmen in American history, she is, so to speak, an English-speaking Union unto herself.

In addition to taped interviews, the primary biographical sources for this book are specified in the back of the work. Material is cited from, among others, the 300 collections of private papers in the Churchill College Archives Centre at Cambridge University; Hansard's record of parliamentary debates; the private papers of prime ministers and the minutes of cabinet meetings now stored in the Public Record Office, Kew, Surrey; and over a hundred collections of personal papers which remain in private hands. Historical sources include British, French, German, and U.S. foreign policy documents and—in translation—those of the Polish, Italian, and Russian governments.

William L. Shirer was an indispensable source for the background of events in Germany and France during these troubled years.

On my own behalf, and that of my archival research assistants in England, I should like to express my gratitude for the assistance and advice of Correlli Barnett and Dr. Michael Hoskin (Keepers of the Archives at Churchill College, Cambridge), Sir William Hawthorne (Master of Churchill College at the time of our research), Captain Stephen Roskill, RN (Fellow of the College), and archivists Pat Bradford and particularly Marion Stewart, who seemed to have even the most elusive document at her fingertips; G. H. Martin (Keeper of the Public Record Office in Kew) and his colleagues Mrs. P. Piper, N. A. M. Rodger, and Dr. M. J. Subb; H. S. Cobb and F. Johnson (Record Office, House of Lords); Christine Kennedy (Nuffield College Library, Oxford); D. G. Vaisey (Department of Western Manuscripts in Oxford's Bodleian Library—"Bodley"); Dr. B. S. Benedikz (Special Collections, University of Birmingham); D. A. Clarke and G. E. A. Raspin (British Public Library—formerly the British Museum Library—and British Library of Political and Economic Science, University of York); Gordon Phillips (*Times* Archive); Colin Watson (Obituary

Department of *The Times*); A. E. Cormack and R. F. Barker (Royal Air Force Museum, Hendon); D. M. Smith and C. C. Webb (Borthwick Institute of Historical Research); F. Bailey (Naval Historical Society, Ministry of Defence); E. C. Blayney (Foreign and Commonwealth Office); Philip A. H. Brown, A. N. E. D. Schofield, and D. H. Bourke (British Library); Mrs. K. F. Campbell (Library and Records Department, Foreign and Commonwealth Office); Eric Ceadel (Librarian, Cambridge University Library); Jacqueline Kavanagh (Written Archives Officer, BBC Written Archives Centre); L. H. Miller (Librarian, Ministry of Defence); Margaret Townsend (Editor's Secretary, *News of the World*); Judith A. Woods (Archivist, the Labour Party Library); V. E. Knight (Librarian, University of Liverpool); L. R. Day (Science Museum Library, University of Liverpool); Kay Chapman and R. J. B. Knight (National Maritime Museum); Peter McNiven (University of Manchester); Diana Grimwood Jones and Gillian Grant (St. Anthony's College, Oxford); Patricia Methven (Liddell Hart Centre for Military Archives, King's College, University of London); R. A. W. Suddaby (Imperial War Museum); and John Spencer-Churchill, eleventh Duke of Marlborough, who gave me the freedom of Blenheim Palace.

I am indebted to T. Chadbourne Dunham, professor emeritus of German at Wesleyan University, who checked my translations from the German, and to the graceful and bilingual Kathryn I. Briggs, who performed the same service with translations from the French.

I am grateful to Peter Day, Nigel Viney, and Richard Langworth, the International Churchill Society's keeper of the flame, for their meticulous review of the final manuscript in the interests of historical accuracy, and to Perry Knowlton, Adam Deixel, and I. Gonzalez at the Curtis Brown literary agency, who provided access to Churchill's American royalty statements.

My assistant, Margaret Kennedy Rider, has been loyal and tireless, as always. As my chief researcher in England, Deborah Baker once more proved imaginative and perceptive. Betsy Pitha assisted nobly in the annotation, as did Virginia Creeden, who was also invaluable in securing permission to quote from letters, diaries, documents, and published works. The staff of the Firestone Library at Princeton University was especially helpful. I am again grateful for the support and assistance provided by the staff of Wesleyan University's Olin Memorial Library, led by J. Robert Adams, Caleb T. Winchester Librarian. Particularly helpful were Joan Jurale, head reference librarian; Edmund A. Rubacha and Suzanne Javorski, reference librarians; Margaret Halstead, reference secretary; Erhard F. Konerding, documents librarian; and Steven Lebergott, chief of interlibrary loans. Other members of the staff who were especially helpful were Alan Nathanson, bibliographer, and Ann Frances Wakefield and Dale Lee.

Finally, I once more acknowledge my gratitude to Don Congdon, my literary agent of forty years; Roger Donald, vice president and publisher of Trade Adult Books, Little, Brown and Company; and, last but foremost in the final stages of text revision, Peggy Leith Anderson, whose manuscript editing skills are unmatched in my long experience.

W. M.
Wesleyan University
December 1987

The Story Thus Far

A Synopsis of

THE LAST LION: WINSTON SPENCER CHURCHILL;

Visions of Glory: 1874–1932

The grandson of a duke, Winston Churchill was born in splendrous Blenheim Palace during the autumn of 1874, when the British Empire was the world's mightiest power. Almost immediately the infant was entrusted to his plump nanny, "Woom," who became his only source of childhood happiness. His father, Lord Randolph Churchill, a brilliant if erratic member of Parliament—he was, briefly, chancellor of the Exchequer—actually loathed Winston. The boy's breathtakingly beautiful American mother, Jennie, devoted most of her time to sexual intrigue, slipping between the sheets with handsome, powerful men in Britain, in the United States, and on the Continent. Her husband was in no position to object. He was an incurable syphilitic.

Winston rebelled against school authority, first becoming a disciplinary problem and then, at Harrow, the lowest-ranked scholar in the lower form. His dismal academic record ruled out Oxford or Cambridge, so he went to Sandhurst, England's West Point. On February 20, 1895, less than a month after his father's death from paresis, young Churchill was commissioned a second lieutenant and gazetted to the Fourth Hussars, preparing to embark for India. In Bangalore Churchill succeeded where his schoolmasters failed. During the long, sweltering siestas, he educated himself, reading Plato, Aristotle, Gibbon, Macaulay, Schopenhauer, and poring over thousands of pages of parliamentary debates. Developing a flair for the language, he found he could earn money writing newspaper and magazine articles and books. At the same time he felt strong stirrings of ambition. He would, he decided, seek a seat in Parliament. But first he must become famous. Ruthlessly manipulating his mother's lovers (who included the Prince of Wales), he managed to appear wherever the fighting was fiercest. By 1899 he was in South Africa. Taken prisoner in the Boer War by the Boers, he managed a sensational escape from a POW stockade, making his way across three hundred miles of enemy territory to freedom. His breakout made him a national figure. Returning home, he was elected to Parliament while Victoria still reigned.

In the House of Commons his rise was meteoric. At thirty-three he was a cabinet minister. Appointed president of the Board of Trade, he joined with David Lloyd George, the new chancellor of the Exchequer, in the move to abolish sweated labor despite die-hard peers in the House of Lords. In 1908, working in tandem, they conceived and then guided through the Commons an unprecedented program of liberal legislation: unemployment compensation, health insurance, and pensions for the aged, all of them to be financed by taxes on the rich and the landed gentry. Winston denounced the aristocracy in savage speeches, and titled relatives stopped speaking to him. But he had a new, exciting supporter: Clementine Hozier, who became Mrs. Winston Churchill in 1908. Long afterward the groom said that they had "lived happily ever afterwards." In fact, they remained deeply in love until his death nearly sixty years later.

When the Central Powers, led by Germany and Austria-Hungary, plunged all Europe into the Great War of 1914–1918, Churchill had anticipated it. Since 1911 he had been first lord of the Admiralty. The fleet was ready. But on the western front the great armies were locked in a bloody, hopeless stalemate. It would be years before either side could hope for victory in the west. Churchill saw a way to break the deadlock. He proposed that the Allied navies open a new front in the eastern Mediterranean, exploiting the weakness of the Central Powers' unstable ally, Turkey. If the Dardanelles strait were forced by battleships, Constantinople would fall within hours. The French and British could then join hands with their Russian ally and sweep up the Danube into Hungary, Austria, Bavaria, and Württemberg, ripping open the Second Reich's undefended southern flank.

Today military historians agree that the Dardanelles strategy could have ended the war in 1916 with a German defeat. But a timid British admiral, who had been sweeping all before him, turned tail at the first sign of resistance—even as the Turks, believing themselves beaten, abandoned their forts on the strait and began the evacuation of their capital. Then equally incompetent British generals botched the landings on Gallipoli Peninsula, which flanked the Dardanelles. The British public demanded a scapegoat, and Churchill, as the stratagem's most flamboyant advocate, was dismissed from the Admiralty. He joined the army, crossed to Flanders, and, as a lieutenant colonel, commanded a battalion in the trenches.

After the Versailles peace conference, in which he played no part, he became secretary for war and air, and established the Royal Air Force. Then, as colonial secretary, he was responsible for Britain's postwar diplomacy in the Middle East. He planned the Jewish state, created the nations of Iraq and Jordan, and picked their rulers. It was typical of Churchill, whatever the question, that he would open with a ferocious stance. Negotiations would lead to compromise and solution. Thus he responded to postwar IRA terrorism by creating a force of Black and Tans—former British soldiers who became terrorists themselves. Yet in the end it was he who befriended Michael Collins, the IRA guerrilla leader, and who piloted the Irish Free State treaty through Parliament.

In 1922 Lloyd George's coalition government fell and was succeeded by Stanley Baldwin's Conservatives. As a Liberal, and then as a Liberal Free Trader, Churchill ran for Parliament in three elections and was defeated each time. Changing parties, he won as a Tory in 1924 and was appointed chancellor of the Exchequer—traditionally, a step away from the prime ministry—by Baldwin. His appointment was in fact unwise. Rejecting the counsel of John Maynard Keynes and accepting instead the advice of the Bank of England, he returned Britain to the gold standard. Markets abroad couldn't afford British exports. A coal miners' strike led to a crippling general strike. Winston founded a strike-breaking newspaper; then, after the strike had failed, he took up the coal miners' cause and fought the mine owners, including a close Churchill relative, for higher pay and safer pits.

After Ramsay MacDonald's Labour party won the election of 1929, Winston held the Exchequer post in the Tory shadow cabinet, which would return to power when Labour's slim majority disappeared. But before that could happen, he fell again. The issue was a grant of dominion status for India, putting her on a level with Canada, South Africa, Australia, and New Zealand. He, like Disraeli, regarded the British Raj as the brightest jewel in England's imperial crown. He told Parliament that India was "a geographical term. It is no more a united nation than the Equator." Facing a stone wall of hostile Tories, Churchill resigned from the shadow government on January 27, 1931. Less than seven months later a new government was formed, and in November what might have been Churchill's place at the Exchequer was filled by Neville Chamberlain. Thrice fallen from grace—the Dardanelles, the lost elections, and now India—Churchill had become a political pariah, out of joint with the times.

In the early 1920s, a small legacy and £20,000 in royalties from sales of his six-volume history of the Great War had permitted him to buy Chartwell Manor, a country home near the small Kent town of Westerham, where he did most of his writing. John Kenneth Galbraith has pointed out that administrations suspicious of intellectuals unwittingly make substantial contributions to scholarship and writing. "It comes about," he wrote, "from not employing the scholars or scribes." During Churchill's long spell as a backbencher he wrote and published a million words.

His chief concern was that Britain might be vanquished by a tacit conspiracy between Prussian aggression and English pacifism. Typically in the House of Commons, he would contemplate his colleagues, then lower his head like a bull confronting a matador and slowly shake it. After a pitifully weak MP revolt against government policy, Aneurin Bevan encountered him in the smoking room and asked: "What have you been up to? We haven't seen much of you in the fight lately." "Fight?" growled Winston, sweeping the room with a challenging glance. "I can't see any fight. All I can see in this Parliament is a lot of people leaning against each other."

PREAMBLE

The Lion Caged

Chartwell. 1932. Early morning.

THE FIRST olive moments of daylight, anticipating the imminent appearance of the sun over the English Channel, disclose a wide, misty, green plain descending to the South Downs and the sea. This is the great Weald of Kent. It is a peculiarity of the Weald's terrain — demonstrated in the shrouded past by Romans, Saxons, and Normans — that it would be quite defenseless should an enterprising foe cross the Channel. Were any force to prepare for an invasion, its campfires on the far shore would be visible from nearby Dover. But now, fourteen years after the Armistice of 1918, the Weald is an idyll of peace, and the explorer on foot finds that it possesses camouflaged delights. Its smooth breast, for example, is not entirely unbroken. The pastureland, sloping upward toward London, is cleaved by a shallow valley. This combe rises to a timbered crest. There, among eighty sheltering acres of beech, oak, lime, and chestnut, stands the singular country home of England's most singular statesman, a brilliant, domineering, intuitive, inconsiderate, self-centered, emotional, generous, ruthless, visionary, megalomaniacal, and heroic genius who inspires fear, devotion, rage, and admiration among his peers.[1]

At the very least he is the greatest Englishman since Disraeli, a quaint survivor of Britain's past who grapples with the future because he alone can see it. His past is illustrious; in the House of Commons he has, at one time or another, held every important ministry save those of prime minister and foreign secretary. Now, however, he is a backbencher — an elected member of Parliament excluded from the cabinet. In his fifty-eighth year, he is already regarded as an anachronism. He first became a household word as a gallant young British officer, a loyal subject of Queen Victoria, handsome and recklessly brave, serving alongside the Buffs in battles on India's northwest frontier, with Kitchener at Khartoum, and in the Boer War — all symbols of the nation's imperial pride, which he fiercely defends despite flagging allegiance elsewhere in the realm. He is mocked for failures which were not his, notably his strategy to force the Dardanelles in 1915. He seems less a figure of the twentieth century (which he loathes) than of the nineteenth — or, reaching even farther back, of Renaissance versatility. The wide sweep of his interests and activities embraces literature, painting, philosophy, hunting, polo, military science, the history of the United States — even architecture, bricklaying, and landscaping. Indeed, many of the shining ponds and pools and the happy waterfalls between the Weald and the manor were created by him, wearing hip-high Wellingtons and excavating the rich earth with his hands.[2]

Tree-locked and silent at dawn, Chartwell's immediate grounds further testify to his stamina. On the south side of the mansion, a garden surrounded by pleasant red brick — walled by him — invites his guest to peer inside the "Mary Cot," a brick playhouse which he built for his nine-year-old daughter. Between the playhouse and the great house lie his orchard of fruit trees and a tennis court of barbered grass he shaped for his wife, Clementine. Eastward, the flushed sky reveals a lawn terrace; northward, his heated swimming pool and ponds inhabited by black swans and "Churchill's goldfish" (actually golden orfe). He is planning to cement into Chartwell's north wall, overlooking the pool, the family's coat of arms and its Spanish motto, so appropriate in these years of his political exile: *Fiel Pero Desdichado* — Faithful but Unfortunate.

On the grounds are various lesser buildings. A painting studio. A white cottage with two bedrooms houses Maryott White, Mary's governess — "Nana" to the little girl but "Cousin Moppet" to the others. She and Nellie Romilly, Clementine's sister, are two of Mrs. Churchill's relatives in residence, sharing the household tasks. Another cottage is planned; Winston expects to finish it in 1939; then he and Clemmie will move into it, leaving the mansion to their son, Randolph. It is startling to realize that all this is less than twenty-five miles from Hyde Park corner. There men on soapboxes tell crowds, who nod in agreement, that society is rushing toward catastrophe. In eight years it will be upon them, but here all is serene. The sound of heavy guns, the roar of hostile bomb-laden aircraft overhead, arrowing toward London, are unimaginable. Quietude lies like a comforting veil over the house and grounds; Winston's 1932 Daimler 35/120 six-cylinder Landaulette seems an intrusion. He would do without the motorcar if he could; he despises automobiles, and if he encounters a traffic jam on one of those infrequent occasions when he himself is at the wheel, he simply drives on the sidewalk.

The house is a metaphor of its squire. It is above all staunch. On the outside the red bricks meet neatly; within, the walls are upright. Studs join beams with precision, doors fit sensibly. Like the householder it is complex, and, like him, steeped in the past. Most of the existing structure dates from the fifteenth century, but annals record an owner in 1350, and the oldest part of the building, now occupied by Churchill's study, was built twenty years after the Battle of Hastings, making it ten years older than Westminster Hall. After acquiring it for £5,000 in the early 1920s, he spent £18,000 on renovations. The front is stately, almost classic in its simplicity. The door frame, which Winston acquired from a London dealer, originally belonged to some other great country home when Victoria was a very young queen; the wood is silvered by age, and its pilasters and scrolls strike a baroque note. The back of the mansion is craggy, a consequence of the master's many accretions.

At daybreak the air is fresh and cool, but by midmorning it will be uncomfortably warm, and the mullioned, transomed windows are open. There is an exception. Those in Churchill's bedroom are puttied shut. He likes the country, but not country air; drafts, he believes, invite common colds, to which he has been susceptible since childhood. There is also the matter of noise. Any noise, especially if high-pitched, is an abomination. The jangling of cowbells will destroy his train of thought. But whistling, notes W. H. Thompson, the Scotland Yard detective who serves as his bodyguard from time to time, is the worst: "It sets up an almost psychiatric disturbance in him — intense, immediate, and irrational. I have seen him expostulate with boys on the street who were whistling as he passed."[3]

Daybreak brings movement to Chartwell's grounds. Sleep still envelops master, mistress, and their four children — Diana, twenty-three and about to be married; Randolph, twenty-one and already a problem (he has been drinking double brandies since he was eighteen); titian-haired Sarah, dreaming of fame on the stage at eighteen; and, in the bedroom above her, little Mary, who mercilessly taunts Sarah about her beaux. The pets are up and about, however. Trouble, Sarah's chocolate-colored spaniel, Harvey, Randolph's fox terrier, and Mary's Blenheim spaniel Jasper, a gift of the Duchess of Marlborough, are investigating the rosebushes and anointing them. Winston's pet cat, a marmalade named Tango, stretches himself; so does Mickey, a tabby cat. A fox trots up from the studio; horses begin to snort; a small black goat strides across the orchard; a goose wanders about aimlessly.

Presently people appear. Because today is a special occasion — all the children are home — the cook is Mrs. Georgina Landemare. These days Mrs. Landemare is here on and off, but like many other Westerham folk she will eventually be absorbed by Chartwell and the needs of its master. Already there are eighteen servants, including a butler, a footman, and an assistant gardener, who now arrives from his home in nearby Westerham to prowl the grounds in his daily search for the cigar butts Winston discarded yesterday, to use in his pipe. Most of the staff are natives of nearby Westerham. Both his secretaries, Grace Hamblin and Violet Pearman ("Mrs. P."), live within walking distance. Since childhood they have known Frank Jenner, the Westerham taxi driver who sometimes carries Churchill to Parliament and back and also serves as Chartwell's handyman; and Harry Whitbread, the laborer who taught Churchill to lay bricks and returns from time to time to work beside him. All of them, regardless of political persuasion, are proud of their eminent neighbor, though far from awed. Whitbread lectures him on how workingmen see social issues; Winston is attentive and thanks him afterward. The town delights in Churchillian lore. Once a month Westerham's barber trims his fringe of hair in his bedroom. Recently a temporary replacement asked him how he would like his hair cut. Churchill replied: "A man of my limited resources cannot presume to have a hairstyle. Get on and cut it."[4]

Chartwell is Churchill's sanctuary, his great keep. All his forays into tumultuous London politics are made from this sure base. However harsh the storms in the House of Commons, or the attacks on him in the press, here he is among friends and on grounds which, to him, epitomize his island nation. To him the essence of Chartwell is that it is completely, utterly, entirely *English*.

As one of the great advocates of the British Empire, he remembers the dictum of Queen Victoria: "I think it very unwise to give up what we hold." His struggle against England's pledge to free India has cost him much. But on matters of principle he has never learned how to compromise. *He does not know how to give in.*

Had he yielded on India, he could have looked to broader, brighter horizons. But he believes in his star. And if he can be spectacularly wrong he can also be terrifically right. If we are to follow his victories and his defeats — they will be many — we must try to define him, to identify him. One way is to follow him through a typical day at Chartwell. It is worthwhile if only because he will be forever remembered, not only as a great statesman, but also as one of history's great originals.

The spacious cream drawing room overlooks the Weald. Beneath the prismatic gleams of its eighteenth-century chandeliers, an exquisite little clock stands upon a mahogany Louis XVI *bureau à cylindre*. Now, at 8:00 A.M., it chimes. Above, in the householder's study, the sound is echoed as another clock also tells the hour. Simultaneously a sibilant rustle of Irish linen sheets breaks the hush in Churchill's bedroom a few feet away, as he sits bolt upright and yanks off his black satin sleep mask. *He,* not the sun, determines when he will greet the new day. Fumbling on the bedside table, he rings the bell for his valet-cum-butler, or, as Churchill calls him, "my man."[5]

Churchill's man is called David Inches by the rest of the household, and like his master he is considered eccentric, "a tremendous character," in the words of Grace Hamblin, Winston's chief secretary, "always overworked, always perspiring, sometimes drunk!" Awaiting him, Churchill peers around, rumpled but remarkably alert in view of the fact that he retired, as is his custom, only six hours ago. Poised thus, he is surrounded by Churchilliana. Elsewhere, Chartwell's decor reflects Clementine Churchill's understated upper-class elegance; but her husband is a flamboyant swashbuckler, a throwback to the Cavaliers or the Elizabethan patriciate with its aristocratic disdain for the opinions of others. Thus this most personal part of the mansion is decorated, not with implicit grace, but with explicit flourish — an ornate Fabergé cigar box, engraved plates of gold and silver, and, standing in solitary splendor, a gold-headed walking stick engraved "to my youngest minister." This last was his wedding present from King Edward VII and a reminder of the 1880s, when Edward was Prince of Wales and he and Winston's mother, Jennie, were intimate — an evocation of the first decade of the new century, when young Winston was a rising power in the Edwardian Parliament.[6]

A minute passes; two minutes. No valet. Winston fumes; the Churchillian lower lip juts out. His bizarre daily schedule deceives visitors who think it disorderly. Those who live at Chartwell know better. Though very odd, it *is* a schedule — is, in fact, a rigid one. Young F. W. D. ("Bill") Deakin will soon leave his don's rooms at Christ Church, Oxford, and become chief researcher (at a mere £300 a year) for Winston's multivolume biography of his great ancestor John Churchill, the first Duke of Marlborough. Long afterward Deakin will recall: "He was totally organized, almost like a clock. His routine was absolutely dictatorial. He set himself a ruthless timetable every day and would get very agitated, even cross, if it was broken." He is very cross now. His valet is often dilatory, though today the blame is not his. Lately the bell has not been working properly. And though Churchill is now bellowing, his shouts are unheard. That is partly his fault. The walls in this part of the mansion are thick. By puttying all the crevices he has effectively soundproofed the room.[7]

Raging, he flings aside the counterpane, leaps out, stamps his bare foot like a spoiled child, and then stalks dramatically across the room, crossing the threshold and reaching the landing in pursuit of his man. This happens from time to time, and the effect is sometimes spectacular, for Churchill sleeps naked and remains so on such sorties. He will don a robe when visiting other homes, "in deference," as he puts it, to his hosts' "views of propriety," but at Chartwell he feels free to roam around nude; as one of his servants will later explain, it seems "completely natural to him." It did not seem natural to a young housemaid who has just left his employ. Looking up the stairwell one morning she beheld, on the top step, Winston Leonard Spencer Churchill in the buff — all 210 pounds of him, a massive pink man with a bald, smooth dome and broad if slightly stooped shoulders, glaring down at her, as one of Winston's secretaries remembers, "like a laser beam." The girl fled the house shrieking. She has sent for her belongings and her pay.[8]

At long last Inches arrives, sweating and offering profuse apologies. The Churchill children delight in mimicking him, but their father values his man; despite his tippling and other flaws, the valet knows the daily Churchillian drill. He opens the day properly, carrying in a tray bearing his master's first meal of the day: orange juice from a bottle (Winston detests freshly squeezed juice), and a cooked English breakfast, with, as the pièce de résistance, a small steak, a chicken leg, or a cutlet Churchill ordered set aside at last evening's dinner for this very purpose. There is also a small dish of jam, usually black cherry. If the jam has been forgotten Winston will lie there propped up on pillows, pouting and refusing to touch anything on the tray until it appears.[9]

Rising, he moves toward the bathroom with an alacrity surprising for his age and weight and quickly shaves himself with a safety razor while his valet draws the first of his two daily baths. Like preparing the breakfast, this requires precision. Churchill will not enter the tub until it is two-thirds full and the bath thermometer registers 98 degrees. Once in, he demands that the temperature be raised to 104 degrees. Inches, obedient, again opens the hot spigot. The water has now reached the brim. Winston likes it that way; on his instructions the bath's overflow drain has been sealed off. This is splendid hydrotherapy, but like his immodest excursions beyond his bedroom door, it invites disaster. He likes to play in his bath, and when on impulse he turned a somersault, "exactly like a porpoise," a spectator recalls, the tub overflowed, damaging the ceiling below and, worse, drenching the frock coat of an eminent Frenchman there who called to pay his respects. Now a special drain has been installed. Churchill lolls in his bath, reciting Kipling, rehearsing speeches or lectures he will soon deliver, or singing, not in the virile baritone familiar in Parliament, but in a soft, high tone.[10] Elsewhere in the great building Sarah ("Mule," he fondly calls her) has risen and is playing the most popular hit of the season on her phonograph:

Night and day
You are the one . . .

Sarah's father prefers to recall melodies which evoke the England of his youth, long before 1914 and Armageddon, when, as he wrote afterward in his history of the Great War, "the world on the verge of catastrophe was very brilliant," when "nations and empires crowned with princes and potentates rose majestically on every side, lapped in the accumulated treasures of the long peace"[11] — when young patricians like Lieutenant Winston S. Churchill, subaltern of horse in Her Britannic Majesty's Fourth Hussars, lived like gods here and throughout the vast British Empire. Talleyrand once observed that those who did not live under *l'ancien régime* did not know what true *douceur de vivre* meant. Being an aristocrat in the Victorian and Edwardian eras had been *fun,* and Winston never tires of singing the great hit of the Boer War, when his escape from an enemy prisoner-of-war camp made him a national hero:

Good-bye, Dolly, I must leave you,
Though it breaks my heart to go;
Something tells me I am needed
At the front to meet the foe!

Nor of booming out Victorian England's anthem of imperial conquest:

It's the soldiers of the Queen, my lads,
Who've been the lads, who've seen the lads,
In the fight for England's glory, lads,
Of her world-wide glory let us sing!

In the England of 1932, glory has become a discredited word. After "the glorious dead" of 1914–1918, the word "glory" now soils the air. Therefore, when he warns of a Germany obsessed with a yearning for vengeance, crowds heckle him or drift away. He is no tribune of the people now. Although he believes in radical social solutions, he remains a traditionalist in all else. And tradition, he holds, begins at home. The ritualistic unfolding of a Chartwell day, from dawn to Kent's long blue twilight, is for him a kind of private pageant. He enjoys it; he considers it as efficient as it is delightful, and he never doubts — nor does anyone else sleeping beneath this roof — that he alone is qualified to be the playwright, producer, director, stage manager, and, of course, hero of the performance.

It is time for the star to don his first costume. Emerging from his bath pink and clean, he waits impatiently until Inches has toweled him dry and then slips into one of two worn-out cherished dressing gowns. The more subdued is dark blue velvet; the other, a riot of green and gold displaying a scarlet dragon coiled sinuously around his plump torso. His valet has been busy during his bath. Churchill will remain in bed all morning, and for a man with his tender skin this invites bedsores. Therefore Inches has brought a basket of large sponges, which he now deftly thrusts between the sheet and the most vulnerable parts of the Churchillian anatomy as his master yaws this way and that.[12]

The tray has gone. Remaining within reach are the jam and a weak (three-ounce) scotch and soda — always Johnny Walker Red — which the prostrate Winston will sip occasionally over the next four hours in the tradition of Palmerston, Pitt, and Baldwin. However, the legend that he is a heavy drinker is quite untrue. Churchill is a sensible, if unorthodox, drinker. There is always some alcohol in his bloodstream, and it reaches its peak late in the evening after he has had two or three scotches, several glasses of champagne, at least two brandies, and a highball, but his family never sees him the worse for drink. He remarks: "We all despise a man who gets drunk." And, after an exchange of views on drinking: "All I can say is that I have taken more out of alcohol than alcohol has taken out of me." He encourages absurd myths about his alcoholic capacity, however, partly to furbish his macho image, which needs it because he cries so often in public ("I'm a blubberer," he cheerfully tells friends), and partly because Europeans still like to think that their leaders are men who can hold their liquor. Winston tipples off and on all day but never gets drunk.[13]

Having tasted this first scotch, he is ready for one of the children's pug dogs, who leaps upon the bed, trembling with joy, tail wagging furiously. Churchill then lights his first cigar of the day. His valet is custodian of Chartwell's cigar hoard, which will eventually grow to over three thousand, all from Havana, mostly Romeo y Julietas and La Aroma de Cubas, kept in a tiny room between this chamber and his study on shelves labeled "wrapped," "naked," and "large." Friends and admirers have sent Winston countless cigar cutters, and he carries one on his watch chain. He never uses them, however. Instead, he moistens one end of a fresh cigar, pierces it with a long match, blows through it from the other end to clear a passage, and lights it from the candle that always stands by his bed. During the course of a day he may consume ten or more cigars, but he seldom smokes one through. Indeed, most of the time they will be unlit. He simply chews them and never inhales. If one becomes hopelessly frayed, he may wrap it in gummed brown paper, calling this improvisation a "bellyband."[14]

The morning papers are neatly stacked by the bed, with *The Times* and the *Daily Telegraph* on top and the *Daily Worker* on the bottom. Editorials are read first, frequently with such intense concentration that the newsprint may become hopelessly smeared with jam. That is a servant's problem, not his; when Winston has finished a page, he simply lets it slide to the floor. All in all, he devotes two hours to the press, occasionally stepping into his slippers and striding toward his wife's bedroom to call her attention to this or that item. It may be a mere statistic representing an increase in Germany's mineral ore imports, but he sees significance in it. Or she may arrive at *his* bedside on a similar errand. Although they never breakfast together, each starts the day with the same rite.[15]

As he glares at the last pages of the *Worker,* Mrs. P. or Grace Hamblin — later to be joined by Kathleen Hill — enters the room. It is important that she do so boldly, even noisily; her employer is not deaf, but he dislikes surprises. If someone glides in, he will rise wrathfully and roar: "Goddammit!" As she prepares to take dictation, he riffles through the morning mail, which she has sorted into three piles: affairs of state, private correspondence, and letters from the general public. As a young author he had written his mother, "My hand gets so cramped. I am writing every word twice & some parts three times." Now he seldom puts a word on paper himself — except when affixing his signature, correcting galley proofs, or writing close friends and his immediate family — and he normally uses fountain pens, blue ink for correspondence, red for proofs. The humblest correspondent receives a reply, but the secretary writes it. Winston merely outlines in the most general way what he wants said and she, familiar with his style and his love of anachronistic phrases ("sorely tried," "most grieved," "keenly elated," "pray give me the facts," "highly diverted"), fills it out. Important letters require more thought and longer searches for the right word. Once the mail has been cleared away, memoranda dictated, and visitors greeted — he will receive anyone except the King in his bedchamber — he may summon a researcher after glancing through proofs, and say: "Look this up," or "Find out about this." The researcher may be asked to read certain documents aloud. Or Churchill may turn to speeches. By noon the cadences of his prose have begun to trot; by 1:00 P.M. they are galloping. In the words of Mrs. Hill, he would often be "dashing around in shorts and undershirt and a bright red cummerbund while I trotted behind him from room to room with a pad and pencil struggling to keep pace with the torrential flow of words." One has the impression of a man in a desperate hurry, not even dressed yet, already behind the day's schedule — which is, in fact, the case.[16]

❦ ❦

He is approaching his daily lunch crisis. The meal is to be served at 1:15 P.M.; often, eminent guests are arriving. And he is never there to greet them. He deplores this tardiness in himself yet cannot break it, though everyone at Chartwell knows the explanation: he systematically underestimates, usually by about five minutes, the length of time he needs to do everything, from shaving to wriggling about while his valet dresses him. Its most hair-raising consequences come while he is traveling. Once at Coventry station a close friend was pacing the platform beside an infuriated Clementine. The conductor was signaling all aboard when Winston finally came in sight. Clemmie told the friend: "Winston's a sporting man; he always gives the train a chance to get away." Even at Chartwell his dilatoriness is a source of distress for both his family and the manor's staff. Once a manservant conspired against him by setting his bedroom clock ahead. It worked for a while, because he scorned that offspring of trench warfare the wristwatch, remaining loyal to his large gold pocket watch, known to the family as "the turnip," which lay beyond his grasp. After his suspicions had been aroused, however, the game was up; he exposed it by simply asking morning visitors the time of day.[17]

Eventually a communal effort by all available servants propels their master, roughly dressed, down into the drawing room, which he enters with a beaming Here-I-am-at-last expression. If the assembled guests include newcomers under the impression that it is a normal upper-class British home, they are swiftly disillusioned by the greetings exchanged between the Churchills. Instead of "Hullo," they utter elementary animal sounds: "Wow-wow!" or "Miaow!" In the family, Christian names are replaced by exotic *petits noms*. Clementine addresses her husband as "Pug," he calls her "Cat." The children are "Puppy Kitten" (Diana), "the Chumbolly" (Randolph), "Mule" (Sarah), and "Mouse" (Mary).

At the round oaken dining room table on the floor below, Churchill chooses to sit facing eastward (making that the head of the round table), looking out across his terrace toward the largest of his artificial lakes. The servants place a candle in a silver Georgian holder by his setting. He will need it when, after one of his long monologues, he finds that his cigar has gone out. As he approaches his chair it is evident that he anticipates the meal with relish. Although he scorns exercise, his appetite is always keen. He cannot, however, be considered a gourmet. Intricate dishes are unappreciated by him; for lunch he prefers Irish stew, Yorkshire pudding with "good red beef," as he calls it, or an unsauced whiting with its tail in its mouth.

Furthermore, he is a confirmed anthropormorphist; he has adopted many of Chartwell's chickens as pets, has even given them names and speaks of them as his "friends." So there is no fowl. He would be troubled by the thought that he was devouring one of them.[18]

To Churchill a meal without wine would not be a meal at all. In his ten years as squire of Chartwell he has yet to pass a day without confronting a shining bottle of champagne, always at dinner and often at lunch also. As a youth he declared: "A single glass of champagne imparts a feeling of exhilaration. The nerves are braced; the imagination is stirred; the wits become more nimble." A bottle produces the contrary effect: "A comatose insensibility." He confines himself to a single glass now. Apart from his contempt for the fiction that red meat and white wine do not mix, his drinking habits are characteristic of upper-class Englishmen. He regards the American martini as barbaric, and when Jan Christiaan Smuts arrives and presents him with a bottle of South African brandy he takes a sip, rolls it around on his tongue, then rolls his eyes, and, beaming at his old friend, says: "My dear Smuts, it is excellent." He pauses. "But it is not brandy." At the end of lunch, after a glass of port with a plain ice and a ripe Stilton, he greets the appearance of Hine, *real* brandy, with a blissful smile and the reaming of a fresh cigar. Brandy, he believes, is essential to a stable diet, and the older the bottle the better. Although uninebriated, he becomes more genial, more affable, more expansive, radiating reassurance.[19]

Sir John Colville, who will later serve as private secretary to three prime ministers, including Churchill, may well have been right in arguing that Churchill's friends are — except for the absence of boors and the garrulous — notable for their variety. They include the witty, the ambitious, the lazy, the dull, the exhibitionists, the talented, the intellectual, and above all the honorable. But the most gifted will appear at dinner. And his guests are all *friends*. In London, even in his pied-à-terre at No. 11 Morpeth Mansions, where he stays while attending Parliament, he is embattled. He needs no snipers here.

But neither are guests confined to lickspittles and sycophants. Himself a celebrity before the turn of the century, before the word had entered common usage, Churchill relishes the company of others in the public eye. His favorite American, the financier Bernard Baruch, visits here whenever in England. T. E. Lawrence, now serving in RAF ranks under an assumed name, roars up on his motorcycle and, knowing that the spectacle will enchant Mary, appears at dinner in his robes as a prince of Arabia. Charlie Chaplin entertains them all with his pantomime and mimicry. Winston asks whether he has chosen his next role. "Yes," Chaplin replies: "Jesus Christ." Churchill pauses, then asks, "Have you cleared the rights?"

Among the regulars at the table are two MPs who remain loyal to Winston in these years of his political eclipse: the handsome young Robert J. G. ("Bob") Boothby and Brendan Bracken, a brash adventurer and self-made millionaire notable for his pug nose, granny glasses, disheveled mop of flaming red hair, and the extraordinary rumors, which he encourages, that he is his host's illegitimate son. Winston finds this gossip highly amusing. Clementine does not. (She once confronted her husband and demanded to know whether the stories were true. He replied: "I've looked the matter up, but the dates don't coincide.") Clemmie is the only participant who is never intimidated by her husband's deep frowns and hissing wrath, and her dislike of Bracken, revealed by gesture, glance, and edged voice, is stark. Churchill admires her spirit — "God," he later confides in a friend, "she dropped down on poor Brendan like a jaguar out of a tree" — but remains silent. Others at the table wonder why. Undeniably Bracken is gifted and able. But his behavior, even in this most tolerant of homes, is atrocious. Recently he went through Clementine's scrapbook with shears, scissoring out articles of Winston's career.[20]

And Winston, for reasons which reveal more about him than Bracken, enjoys the younger man's company. Men who have done something with their lives interest him — indeed, they are the only men who do. He is particularly impressed by military men; any winner of the Victoria Cross is embraced, and when he meets Sir Bernard Freyberg, the New Zealand war hero, Churchill insists that the embarrassed Freyberg strip so that his host can count his thirty-three battle scars. Similarly, men who have amassed fortunes while he has struggled year after year with creditors, hold enormous appeal for him. That is part of Bracken's charm.

It also explains, in part, Winston's fondness for Baruch, though Baruch's appeal is broader. He is an American, he is Jewish, he recognizes the menace of an aggressive Germany, and Churchill is indebted to him for an extraordinary act of shrewdness and generosity. Winston was badly hurt in the Wall Street Crash three years ago. Had it not been for Baruch, however, it would have been much worse; he could have spent the rest of his life in debt. He is not a born gambler; he is a born *losing* gambler. In New York at the time, he dropped into Baruch's office and decided to play the market, and as prices tumbled he plunged deeper and deeper, trying to outguess the stock exchange just as he had tried to outguess roulette wheels on the Riviera. In Wall Street, as in Monte Carlo, he failed. At the end of the day he confronted Baruch in tears. He was, he said, a ruined man. Chartwell and everything else he possessed must be sold; he would have to leave the House of Commons and enter business. The financier gently corrected him. Churchill, he said, had lost nothing. Baruch had left instructions to buy every time Churchill sold and sell whenever Churchill bought. Winston had come out exactly even because, he later learned, Baruch even paid the commissions.[21]

Bracken can't match that. Being British and in Parliament, however, he can serve his idol in other ways. In the House he is scorned as Winston's "sheepdog," his "lapdog," or — this from Conservative leader Stanley Baldwin — his faithful *chela,* the Hindi word for minion. But uncritical admiration is precisely what Churchill needs. He is in the third of what will be ten years of political exile to the back benches. No other statesman in the country's political history will have served so long a Siberian sentence, and he would have to have a heart of stone not to be grateful for Bracken's steadfast, unquestioning allegiance.[22]

Churchill may even be flattered by the stories that he fathered a son on the wrong side of the blanket. Those closest to him agree that he is undersexed; some suggest that the explanation lies in the promiscuity of his beautiful, wanton mother. The historian A. J. P. Taylor will reflect: "She moved from one man to another. And it's possible, I don't say this is the only explanation, that Churchill's really almost extreme chastity was a reaction to his mother's lack of it. There are other possibilities. He may have been weakly sexed biologically, or the explanation may have been psychological. He once remarked: 'The reason I can write so much is that I don't waste my essence in bed.' " Winston didn't marry until his thirty-fourth year, and there is every reason to believe that he was a virgin bridegroom. Despite frequent separations from Clemmie, who disapproves of the lush Riviera and spends her holidays with the children at spartan resorts on the North Sea, or a hotel near Rugby, he has committed but one act of infidelity, at Golfe-Juan, on the Mediterranean, with a divorced, titled Englishwoman whose seductive skills and sexual experience far exceeded his. To one who cherishes his reputation for mischievousness, whispers that a fellow MP is his bastard may not be altogether unwelcome.[23]

Bracken is one of his two most striking disciples. The other, in many ways Brendan's opposite, complements him. Born in Germany of an American mother, Frederick A. Lindemann took his doctorate at the University of Berlin in 1910, continued his scientific studies in Paris and Brussels, confirmed Einstein's refinement of Planck's quantum theory, and, as a member of the Royal Aircraft Establishment in the Great War, organized London's kite balloon barrage. After the Armistice he was appointed professor of experimental philosophy at Oxford and recognized as one of Europe's leading physicists. Now in 1932 "the Prof," as everyone in the Churchill family calls him, has just published his *Physical Significance of the Quantum Theory*. His Oxford colleagues now believe that his best work is behind him;

Professor Derek Jackson notes that the younger generation regards him "as more of a theoretical physicist devoid of experimental ability." Churchill disagrees, and so will history.[24]

Lindemann's achievements cannot be impeached, but in his own way he can be trying. Even by Chartwell's standards he is odd. Indeed, he seems to be everything Winston is not. Tobacco in any form is anathema to him. He lives largely on the whites of eggs and is a vegetarian and teetotaler, except when as a guest here, he bows to his host's insistence that he consume exactly 32 cubic centimeters of brandy a day. He always wears a bowler, even on a warship or in the cockpit of an RAF fighter. His valet and secretary, Harvey, who drives his huge, unwieldy limousine, is his double, matching his attire of the day shirt by shirt, sock by sock, and bowler by bowler.[25]

The Prof will follow Churchill anywhere. Winston's motives for cultivating him are very different. Lindemann's many talents include a matchless gift as an interpreter of science for laymen. In the words of Sir John Colville, Lindemann can "simplify the most opaque problem, scientific, mechanical or economic," translating technical jargon into language which provides "a lucid explanation" and sacrifices "nothing of importance." Churchill loathes scientific terminology. He never even mastered public school arithmetic. The Prof provides him with the essential facts when he needs them without disrupting his concentration on other matters. Like radar, Lindemann's "beautiful brain," as Churchill calls it, will prove worth several divisions in the struggle to save England from Adolf Hitler. Less than ten years from now he will arrive at No. 10 Downing Street with clear, accurate charts which, by replacing statistics, present displays showing England's stockpiles of vital raw materials, the rate at which ships are being launched on the Clyde, the Tyne, and Barrow, and Britain's production of tanks, artillery, small arms, and warplanes in terms the prime minister can understand with what Colville calls "infallible skill and punctuality."[26]

It is a measure of Churchill's own accomplishments that he can inspire a man with whom he shares little except a common affection for Americans. The Prof has little use for others. Like many of his laboratory colleagues, he never applies the scientific method in judging society. He is in fact a snarl of prejudices. So profound is his misogyny that he has not spoken to his only sister for fifteen years. His sole recreation is tennis. He is a champion of Sweden, an achievement all the more remarkable because, to discourage women from regarding him as a sex object, he plays in the hottest weather wearing thick black ribbed socks and a heavy shirt tightly buttoned at the wrists.[27]

This is not at all Churchillian, though modern feminists would regard

Winston as a stereotype of male chauvinism. He opposed woman suffrage until Clementine converted him, wouldn't dream of soliciting a woman's advice on matters of national policy, and dropped the idea of writing an article for *Collier's* on the prospects of a woman becoming prime minister of England because he thought the idea laughable. Nevertheless, he admires Englishwomen of his class and enjoys their company — provided, of course, that they are attractive and don't attempt to discuss topics reserved for members of his own sex. As a man who reached his majority in 1895, when Victorian gentlemen never used the words "breast" or "leg" if ladies were present, he assumes that they are innocents who must be shielded from the brutal facts of life and that feminine beauty is unaccompanied by carnal desire.

If Chartwell's guest book is a reliable index, the only ladies who will be invited to lunch in Churchill's heaven — with the one great exception of his longtime friend Lady Violet Bonham Carter, née Asquith — will be escorted, and even they will be required to confine themselves to smiling when their host makes a clever remark, nodding vigorously when he has expressed an opinion, and expressing no opinion of their own. This is not sexist, however, because it also applies to gentleman guests. Winston means to dominate them and cheerfully acknowledges it; his own idea of a fine meal is to dine well and then discuss a serious topic — "with myself as chief conversationalist." It isn't even conversation; unlike Lloyd George he is a poor listener, has little interest in what others have to say, and, if he is not the speaker, withdraws into silent communion with himself while his interior monologue, the flow of private rhetoric, soars on. His daughter Mary will recall that "small talk or social chitchat bored Winston profoundly — but he rarely suffered from it, since he completely ignored it, pursuing his own themes."[28]

In London he will give those who disagree with him a fair hearing; two of his favorite aphorisms are "I would rather be right than consistent" and "In the course of my life I have often had to eat my words, and I must confess that I have always found it a wholesome diet." But at Chartwell, with a pony of brandy in one hand and a cigar in the other, he is inclined to bully those who challenge him. And the fact is that few dare try. Lords Birkenhead and Beaverbrook could. Birkenhead — F. E. Smith before his ennoblement — would cross foils with Churchill and win as often as he lost. It is perhaps significant that F.E. became Winston's best friend. And the man has not drawn breath who can intimidate Beaverbrook, the great press lord, known to the Churchills as "the Beaver," who, when he first met Churchill in 1911, was plain Max Aitken, a Canadian upstart. During one visit here he declined wine with his Stilton. "Port is the brother of cheese," his host said in lordly reproach. "Yes," Max flashed back, "and the sister of gout." But Birkenhead has lain in his grave two years, and Beaverbrook, though Churchill's once and future ally, will seldom be seen at Chartwell in this decade. The feisty Beaver, for all his shrewdness, shares the almost unanimous conviction of England's ruling classes that Winston — whom he calls a "busted flush" — exaggerates the emerging Nazi menace; like his fellow press lords he believes Hitler's friendship worth cultivating and assures his readers — he will reassure them every year, even when the sands are running out in 1939 — that "there will be no war."[29]

Lacking peers in colloquy, Churchill rules his table as an absolute monarch. His expression radiates benevolence, his arms are spread to embrace everyone there; then, having opened all hearts, he speaks of today's guest of honor, usually an old friend. Then his visage darkens, he points a threatening finger, and all await the inevitable consignment of a transgressor — never present — to his doom. Today's wretch turns out to be Thomas Babington Macaulay, who dared slander John Churchill, the first Duke of Marlborough. The great duke's great-great-great-great-great-great grandson thunders his verdict: "It is beyond our hopes to overtake Lord Macaulay. We can only hope that truth will follow swiftly enough to fasten the label 'liar' to his genteel coattails."[30]

Guests say afterward that the host is so fascinating they cannot remember what they ate. Political scientist and historian Harold Laski observes that many of them, in trying to remember all Winston's mots, overlook the flaws in his reasoning. Other critics note that Churchill has no small talk, though as the American writer Virginia Cowles asks, "Why should anyone want small talk when Churchill is at the peak of his form?" Certainly no one here tries to stop him. Later, biographer Lady Longford will write that "his set-pieces were . . . so brilliant that few listeners wished to interrupt. Similarly, they recognized that he was self-centered precisely because he had an interior vision which must be brought to the light of day. They felt privileged to assist."[31]

Absolutely secure here, he can laugh at himself and encourage others to join him. "Megalomania," he says, referring to his domineering manner, "is the only form of sanity." He has just published a collection of his magazine articles under the title *Thoughts and Adventures* (*Amid These Storms* in the United States) and, as usual, he has sent copies to friends and acquaintances in high places. Opening an envelope bearing the royal crest, he reads aloud an acknowledgment from the Duke of Gloucester: "Dear Winston. Thank you for your new book. I have put it on the shelf with the others." And he relishes and retells the story of how F.E., his adversary when Winston was the Liberal member for Dundee, set a Tory rally roaring with laughter by interrupting his speech to say: "I see from the *Dundee Advertiser* — I mean the newspaper, not the politician. . . ." Like a man trying on neckties, he tests his phrases at lunch, watching faces to measure their effect. "An immense responsibility," he ruminates, "rests upon the German people for this subservience to the barbaric idea of autocracy. This is the gravamen against them in history — that, in spite of all their brains and courage, they worship power, and let themselves be led by the nose."[32]

The last drop of brandy is gone. He gives the empty bottles a glance, not of regret, but of affection; he will paint them, he announces, and call the completed canvas *Bottlescape*. Through the meal his visage has been kaleidoscopic: somber, mischievous, bored, proud, arrogant, magnanimous, despairing, indifferent, exalted, contemptuous, adoring. Now it screws up, creasing his laugh lines, and he makes a crowing, expiratory sound in his throat — signs, as his friends know, that he is about to amuse them, perhaps with that odd brand of self-mockery to which British soldiers and parliamentarians alike turn in times of adversity.[33]

They are right. He tells of taking his annual Riviera holiday without his valet. This, for a patrician of his generation, was a momentous decision. He had never even been on a bus or even seen the tube. In traveling alone he felt he was "striking a blow for equality and fraternity," but misadventures plagued him all the way, and he describes each, relishing the details. His guests laugh; it is a good story. But it is more. Winston cannot get through the day without servants, and he assumes this is true of all gentlemen. It *was* true in his youth, but is no longer. Later Colville, his assistant private secretary, will ask leave to become an RAF fighter pilot. Winston hates to see a valuable member of his staff go, but it is a request he, of all men, cannot refuse. Alone together, "Jock" and Winston *are* equals; the first Lord Colville became a peer in 1604. The younger man, like Winston, is a Harrovian; his Cambridge college is Trinity; his club, White's. Churchill, the quondam hussar, grandly declaims: "The RAF is the cavalry of modern war." But he is shocked when Colville tells him he will first serve in the ranks as an aircraftsman, second class. Winston protests: "You mustn't — you won't be able to take your man!" It hasn't crossed his mind that a civil servant earning £400 a year, about $32.30 a week, could hardly afford a valet.[34]

❧ ❧

Should his visitors include a guest of great eminence, Churchill will offer to show him round Chartwell's grounds. Otherwise, he proceeds with his first afternoon activity: feeding his golden orfe, ducks, and swans. Donning a Stetson — if there is a chill in the air, he will also wear an overcoat — he heads for a broad wicker chair beside the goldfish pond, calling ahead, "Arf! Arf!" or "Yoick! Yoick!"

They rush to greet him, though a servant, a step behind him, has what they want. Twice a month Frank Jenner collects a blue baby-food tin at the local railway station. Within, packed in sawdust, are maggots, the caviar of goldfish gourmets. Winston offers a lidful of maggots to the fish; when it is empty he holds out the lid to be refilled. Nearby a wooden box contains bread crumbs. These Churchill feeds to the ducks and swans.

The feeding is an integral part of the Churchillian day. After it, he sinks into the wicker chair, dismisses his servant, and remains, companionless and immobile, for at least a half hour. A table beside the chair bears another weak Johnny Walker and soda, a box of cigars, a pagoda-shaped ashtray, and a container of long Canadian matches, useful in a rising wind. The squire of Chartwell prefers solitude here. Long afterward, servants will recall his reciting Housman and Kipling to himself, or reading, or simply staring out across the Weald, alone with his reflections, a great hunched figure whose cigar smoke mingles with the many scents of an English country home, including, in season, the fragrance of freshly cut grass.

His interest in all creatures on his estate is unflagging. As a young Colonial Office under secretary he had been an enthusiastic hunter of wild game, but those days are past. Now he holds a kitten to his face and murmurs, "Darling." It is true that he kicked a large tabby cat who played with the telephone cord when he was speaking to the lord chancellor of England, shouting, "Get off the line, you fool!" — and hastily telling the chancellor, "Not you!" But afterward he offered the cat his apologies, which he never extends to human beings, cajoling the pet, cooing, "Don't you love me anymore?" and proudly telling his valet at breakfast next day, "My Mickey came to see me this morning. All is forgiven."[35]

In his reverence for all living creatures Churchill approaches ascetic Jainism. Butterflies are sacred. So are predators. He loses two Siberian geese to foxes, but when a fox trap is proposed, he shakes his head, saying, "I couldn't bear to think of them being hurt." Similarly, when a heron raids his ponds he merely covers them with wire netting, forbidding his staff even to scare the bird away. A sheet of frosted glass occupies one wall of the guests' bathroom in a friend's Mediterranean villa. During one of Winston's visits there, he observed that the bathroom light attracted night moths, who, fluttering against the glass, were easy prey for lurking lizards. He winced and gritted his teeth when the lizards chewed up their victims, but vetoed his valet's suggestion that the lizards be frightened away by tapping on the window. They were obeying a law of nature, he said, and ought not be punished.[36]

When a black swan falls ill, he does not hesitate to summon the keeper of the London Zoo. A goat sickens, and Whitehall's Ministry of Agriculture is consulted. Arriving home at 3:00 A.M. after a late session of Parliament and learning that there has been no afternoon feeding at the pond, he rouses a maid to hold a flashlight while he makes amends to his piscatorial friends. All this is vexing to the sleepy maid. She is relieved when a new secretary becomes an overnight heroine in Winston's eyes. Something extraordinary has been happening to the fish. They are turning white and dying. Winston is stumped; so is his gardener. Then the girl pipes up: "I know what's wrong. They have fungus." Churchill gives her a lowering look. How, he rumbles, does she know? She replies that her parents have an aquarium. He asks: "And how do you treat it?" She answers: "You put in a salt solution and gradually the fungus drops off. If you act quickly enough they can be saved." He does, they are, and during the healing period he drives up to London and consults experts at the zoological gardens in Regents Park. On his return he summons the young secretary. "Do you know what they told me?" he asks. "They said exactly what *you* said." He beams at her. "Oh, I think you are a *very clever* secretary! You know what goes wrong with fish. Henceforth, you will attend them." He is delighted, the staff is delighted. The feelings of the girl, who has been at Chartwell long enough to know that her other duties will continue, are mixed.

Winston is, among other things, a dog's best friend. Observing one manservant's poodle limping, he tells him to send it to a veterinarian, and when the pet returns well two weeks later, he pays the bill. One of Chartwell's animals vexes him; Mary's dog, it seems, has never been properly housebroken. Winston mutters darkly: "He commits at least three indiscretions a day." Mary is worried about her dog. But her father cannot bring himself to intervene, and the pug continues to enjoy his unsanitary ways.

Still recuperating from a traffic accident he suffered months before in New York, Churchill lays no bricks these days. But he cannot remain idle. He is, Bill Deakin notes, "incapable of inactivity," and Cousin Moppet writes: "Winston has so many irons in the fire that the day is not nearly long enough." During one of his Johnsonian lunches he remarks: "Broadly speaking, human beings may be divided into three classes: those who are billed to death, those who are worried to death, and those who are bored to death." Though heavily billed (he has just settled £1,600 of his son's debts), and deeply worried about the events stirring central Europe, he is never bored. To Virginia Cowles, a weekend guest, he says: "With all the fascinating things there are to do in the world, some people while away their time playing Patience. Just fancy!"[37]

Since his physician has banned bricklaying, he heads for his studio, telling a member of his staff to fetch his brushes, easel, and palette. He intends to paint "one of my beloved cats" or to re-create on canvas a still life from photographs taken from their latest visit to Cannes or Marrakech. "If it weren't for painting," he tells a friend, "I couldn't live. I couldn't bear the strain of things."

Winston designed the studio. Inside, it is small but very lofty, providing maximum light. In constructing it, he put wooden slats along the interior walls; incompleted canvases went there. Eventually the slats will become shelves, supporting some five hundred finished paintings. He paints few people and no violence, but the full body of his work provides an overview of his travels: the Acropolis, Stromboli, the canals of Amsterdam, Scandinavian fjords, Pompeii, Rome, Rotterdam, Passchendaele, Ypres, Vimy Ridge, Messines, Menin, Waterloo, Scapa Flow, Ulster, Balmoral, Devonshire, and Kent. Cathedrals fascinate him. So do ruins; he had to be dragged away from Pompeii. And he finds waterfalls irresistible. He spent days at his easel by the roaring Jordan. On his finished canvas there is an illusion of moving water; one can almost catch the sound of it.

His painting methods are purely Churchillian. Confronted by a virgin canvas, he moves rapidly and decisively, giving the scene a swift appraisal and then slapping on the oils, reacting instinctively to a single theme: a villa, a temple, sailboats at low tide. Inspector Thompson, after hours of watching him at his easel, writes: "I would think that the man's inner spirit is superbly calm and that he paints from it — never from the mind or intellect." Thomas Bodkin, director of the National Gallery of Ireland, thinks successful professional painters might learn a lot from Winston: "He does not try to say two things at the same time. . . . The dominant motive is never obscured by irrelevancies." After a careful examination of Winston's canvases, Sir John Rothenstein, director of the Tate Gallery and one of England's most eminent art critics, judges them to be works "of real merit which bear a direct and intimate relationship to his outlook on life. In these pictures there comes bubbling irrepressibly up his sheer enjoyment of the simple beauties of nature."[38]

If he has chosen not to paint this afternoon, he may summon a "Miss" and enter the study to make a start on the day's work, an article for an American magazine, perhaps, or a piece for Fleet Street. Or he may read in his bedchamber, listening to BBC music, provided it is *his* kind of music — *H.M.S. Pinafore, The Pirates of Penzance,* and *The Mikado,* or French military marches. Once more Chartwell hears the poignant counterpoint of father and daughter. Sarah is playing the nostalgic:

April in Paris —
Chestnuts in blossom . . .

while Churchill is exuberantly tapping his feet in rhythm to:

Billy McCoy was a musical boy . . .
And then the hammock starts a-swingin'
And the bells begin a-ringin'
While he's sittin' at that 'pianna'
There on the Alabama,
Playin' the Oceana Roll!

MGM pioneers the renting of films to those who can afford them, other studios follow, and Alexander Korda sees to it that Churchill has priority. His taste in films, as in music, is middlebrow — Lew Ayres in *All Quiet on the Western Front,* Fredric March in *Dr. Jekyll and Mr. Hyde,* Douglas Fairbanks, Jr., and Richard Barthelmess in *The Dawn Patrol,* and Charles Laughton, Winston's favorite actor, in *The Sign of the Cross*. His taste in literature is more eclectic. Here his interests are professional. His leisure reading, serious and frivolous, strengthens his grasp of his mother tongue. In Chartwell's library one can glimpse the landscape of his mind. Among the books he has read, and often reread, are Gibbon's five-volume *Decline and Fall of the Roman Empire,* William James's *The Varieties of Religious Experience,* J. A. Froude's *History of England,* Sir Richard Burton's sixteen-volume *Arabian Nights,* the King James Bible, and C. S. Forester's biography of Nelson. Later he will devour Forester's Hornblower novels, John Paget's *The New "Examen,"* Winwood Reade's *The Martyrdom of Mankind*. He likes to dip into books of verse and later quote them at meals. His favorite poets are Kipling, Housman, and Rupert Brooke. If in the mood for mere amusement, he plucks out novels by the Brontës, Fielding's *Tom Jones,* Scott's *Rob Roy,* Trollope's political novels (particularly *The Duke's Children*), P. G. Wodehouse's fatuities, or the tales of Kipling, R. L. Stevenson, and Somerset Maugham, the only modern novelist whose skills he admires.[39]

He enjoys being cosseted — F. E. Smith said "Winston is a man of simple tastes; he is always prepared to put up with the best of everything." But although the grandson of a duke could move in the highest social circles, his leisure is largely confined to Chartwell and its grounds. Only rarely can he be coaxed away for a weekend elsewhere. His greatest pleasures lie here. On a bright afternoon he will stroll around the grounds, greeting those who are home. He is an indulgent father. Like many another man who suffered in his childhood, he has spoiled his children, especially Randolph, despite their mother's pleading, sowing winds from which he will later reap whirlwinds. Diana is sorting out the first of her trousseau. Sarah is mooning about, playing her records, savoring memories of her success in the Kitkat Players, an amateur troupe; sulking because her parents refuse to support her yearning to become a chorus girl. Randolph is growing a beard, which, his father writes, "makes him look perfectly revolting. He declares he looks like Christ. To me he looks like my poor father in the last phase of his illness."[40]

Mary has just returned from the local school, where she is a day student; Cousin Moppet will now read to her. Like the others she hails her father as "Pa-*pah*." After replying ("Puppy Kitten," "Mule," etc.) he may examine his firearms. He likes them; he has never forgotten the Mauser that saved his life in the last great charge of British cavalrymen at Omdurman. He is also an extraordinary marksman, perhaps because a weapon, like a paintbrush, does exactly what it is told to do and never argues back. Automobiles quarrel with him; he is the worst driver in England. When he tried to fly he nearly killed himself; if he takes to the dance floor all other couples leave it. But with his Mannlicher, .32 Webley Scott, or Colt .45, which require only a keen eye and a steady hand, he is a dead shot. Later, at the age of seventy, he will challenge the accuracy of guards officers and General of the Army Dwight D. Eisenhower. Of Winston's ten shots, one will hit the fringe of the bull's-eye; the other nine will be dead center. The elite guardsmen will scatter theirs. Poor Ike will miss the target completely.

Now Churchill may withdraw and don a silk sleeping vest for a siesta, a custom he had observed in 1895 as a young war correspondent in Cuba, where the climate imposed it and custom sanctioned it. The temperature in his bedchamber is always exactly 74 degrees Fahrenheit. Yet he insists on the vest. Slipping into it, and drawing the sleep mask over his eyes, he slides between fresh linen sheets. He never requires more than a few seconds to drift off. Moments after his cheek touches the pillow, before his valet has even left the room, Winston is slumbering. He can do this almost anywhere. In automobiles or aboard planes he carries a special pillow; he dons the mask, curls his head down into his chest like a mother hen, and enjoys absolute rest until the journey's end. At Chartwell his siesta may last two hours. Refreshed, he joins his family at 5:00 P.M., usually playing cards with Clemmie or Randolph in the drawing room. Bridge is rarely played because he never wins. Furthermore, it is a relatively new game and therefore suspect. He prefers mah-jongg, backgammon, gin rummy, and bezique, a forerunner of pinochle. Usually played with two thirty-two-card packs, bezique can be traced to the 1600s; its antiquity qualifies it for Churchillian amusement.

❦ ❦

As the drawing room clock strikes 7:00 P.M., he mounts the stairs for his second daily bath. During these ablutions he likes an audience, old companions who at appropriate moments will laugh, murmur approval, express indignation, and understand his arcane references to political upheavals on the Continent and parliamentary intrigue in London. If no close friends are among his guests, he may send for a research assistant and review their progress with *Marlborough*. As a last resort, Winston will summon a Miss to sit outside and take dictation during pauses in his soaping, rinsing, and splashing. Before his valet guides him into his dinner jacket, he signs the day's mail and then dawdles, putting on another record, or fashioning a bellyband, or singing "Abdullah Bulbul Amir" to the thirty-eighth verse. Dinner, the day's main event, is scheduled to be served at 8:30. He may reach the drawing room by 8:45.

It is lunch on a far grander scale, with more guests, of greater distinction, silvery buckets of iced champagne, Churchill presiding in his grandest manner, and several courses. Among the foods likeliest to be served are clear soup, oysters, caviar, Gruyère cheese, pâté de foie gras, trout, shoulder of lamb, lobster, dressed crab, *petite marmite,* scampi, Dover sole, chocolate éclairs, and, of course, roast beef and Yorkshire pudding. Winston never eats tripe, crumpets, sausages, cabbage, salami, sauerkraut, corned beef, or rice pudding. Clemmie, who knows his preferences, has briefed the cook on what is to be on the menu. He decides when meals are to be served, he determines who is to be invited.

If he has been in London recently, different versions of his latest witticisms have been repeated in the clubs of Pall Mall and St. James's, in drawing rooms of the West End and the City's counting rooms. Asked now to confirm them, he nods as he gropes for a match or the stem of his wineglass, pausing occasionally to correct a verb or alter syntax. He tells of how, crossing Parliament Square, he ran into Lord Londonderry, his cousin and frequent adversary. Londonderry, hoping to drive home a point, had asked him: "Have you read my latest book?" Winston chortles his reply: "No, I only read for pleasure or profit." In the House of Commons he had remarked upon Sir Stafford Cripps's "look of injured guilt." So many cabinet ministers wanted ennoblement that he had protested: "They can't all have peerages; there ought to be some disappearages." One member of the government had protested that this was a slur; Churchill shot back: "I know of no case where a man added to his dignity by standing on it."[41]

It is difficult to keep up with a host who can set such a pace. Nevertheless the dinner is not a one-man show. Guests have been invited for luster, not servility. David Lloyd George has been in Parliament ten years longer than Churchill and an awesome prime minister for six. Sir Archibald Sinclair — who, when Churchill led a battalion in the trenches, served as his second in command — is about to assume leadership of the Liberal party, which, with fifty-nine seats in the House, holds the balance between Labour and the Conservatives. Alfred Duff Cooper and Anthony Eden, both of whom were decorated for bravery in France, hold subcabinet posts in the government and will soon become full-fledged ministers, Duff Cooper at the War Office and Eden as foreign secretary.

Late in life Mary will recall: "The 'basic' house party, enlarged by other guests, usually formed a gathering it would be hard to beat for value. There was little warming up; the conversation plunged straight into some burning or vital question. But the talk was by no means confined to politics; it ranged over history, art, and literature; it toyed with philosophical themes; it visited the past and explored the future. The Prof and his slide rule were much in demand on all scientific problems. Sometimes the conversation was a ding-dong battle of wits and words between, say, Winston and Duff Cooper, with the rest of the company skirmishing on the sidelines and keeping score. The verbal pyrotechnics waxed hot and fierce, usually dissolving into gales of laughter." Then, she remembers, conversation "usually dwindled" as everyone wanted to "share the main 'entertainment,' " which was almost always "a dramatic and compelling monologue from Winston." Frequently he would recite "Horatius," and "this was very popular with the children, as we could join in 'the brave days of old' bits."[42]

All his guests meet his conversational standards: "The man who cannot say what he has to say in good English cannot have very much to say that is worth listening to." None hesitates to speak up when he pauses for breath. Winston is unresentful of this. As Sir David Hunt, one of Churchill's private secretaries, will recall long afterward: "He has been accused of excessive addition to the monologue; there was certainly a tendency that way but he was always tolerant of interjections from his listeners if they were relevant or amusing." Collin Brooks, the newspaper editor, in comparing Churchill in the House with Churchill at Chartwell, notes that the style of his public speeches, "slow in pace and heavy in emphasis," yields, in the privacy of his home, to "a quicker flow." Winston's casual quips "sparkle and sting, but the talk is unhurried, with occasional pauses, for effect or to hold his listeners while he gropes for the right word." Intense or gay, he infuses his discussions of grave issues with gusto and what one guest will recall as "verbal gymnastics and mental pyrotechnics . . . often rounded off by a sudden colloquial that from most other people would be an anticlimax."[43]

Brooks sets down one of Winston's observations about politics: "Our weakness today is not in the decline of Parliament itself, but in the diminished interest which the press gives to it. It is, indeed, heartbreaking for any man to go down day after day in these turbulent times to deliver speeches which, by the content, if not by their form, are of great importance, and to realize that they are heard by but a few hundreds of his fellow Members, and read by but a scattering of people who habitually read Hansard."[44]

But he did not invite them here to complain about his political isolation. He introduces other themes, and, being completely uninhibited, will from time to time burst into song. One guest recalls attending the theatre in 1926 on the evening the general strike ended. He sat directly behind Winston and Clemmie. Now he wonders whether Churchill remembers the show. Churchill not only remembers *Lady Be Good*, starring the Astaires; he can, and does, croon the lyrics of all its tunes. His memory is extraordinary. Lady Violet will remember how "he could quote back to me words of which I had no recollection, and when I asked: 'Where does that come from?' he replied: 'You said it' or 'You quoted it to me' — sometimes remembering the time and the place. He could not forget what he liked, except occasionally on purpose, when his own past utterances conflicted with his present attitudes." To illustrate a point he quotes a poem he read in *Punch* fifty years ago and has not seen since.[45]

After the ladies have left and the men are gathered around him for port, brandy, and cigars, he will sit until 10:00 P.M., or later, talking of his school days, the great political issues of the past, the MPs who fought over them, battlefields of his youth, strategic innovations in the American Civil War. Using salt shakers, cutlery, and brandy goblets, he can reenact any battle in that war, from Bull Run to Five Forks, citing the troops engaged on either side, identifying the commanders, describing the passage at arms, the aftermath. Reflections on any conceivable subject succeed one another in his racing brain. The plight of mankind, he muses, is "all the fault of the human mind being made in two lobes, only one of which does any thinking, so we are all right-handed or left-handed; whereas, if we were properly constructed, we should use our right and left hands with equal force and skill according to circumstances. As it is, those who can win a war well can rarely make a good peace, and those who could make a good peace never win."

At least one guest finds it difficult to picture Churchill as a peacemaker, noting Winston's account "of how he first came under fire when he was twenty-one, of his boyish delight in the proximity of danger, or his glee that he was actually 'seeing the real thing.' " The hazards and discomforts of war, Winston argues, strengthen a young man's character. Certainly they had strengthened his. But war was very different then. The industrial/technological revolution had not yet cranked out the appliances of death — machine guns, shrapnel shells, land mines — which were taking so frightful a toll in the twentieth century. In South Africa, at the crucial battle of Majuba in 1881, the British lost just 92 men. By contrast, over 400,000 young British soldiers had fallen in 1916 and 1917 in the Somme and Passchendaele campaigns — in vain, with no strategic gains. In 1932 few Englishmen know that as a young war correspondent he had written: "War, disguise it as you may, is but a dirty, shoddy business, which only a fool would play at," or that he declared after the Armistice in 1918: "War, which was cruel and magnificent, has become cruel and squalid."[46]

But in his youth he *had* thought it magnificent. In his first book he wrote: "Nothing in life is so exhilarating as to be shot at without result," and "There are men who derive as stern an exaltation from the proximity of danger and ruin, as others from success." It is this very trait — and his longing to be on a battlefield, watching what he calls "the fun of the good things" — which worries all but the most devoted of his followers. His critics call him "a genius without judgment," a man with "a zigzag streak of lightning in the brain," the only cabinet minister who gloated when Britain declared war on Germany in 1914.

Because of the general revulsion against another European war, and because Churchill's judgment has been discredited since the failure of the Dardanelles campaign, men will shrug and turn away when he predicts, accurately, that Hitler will come to power in Germany, and that once Hitler has moved into the Kanzlei — the German chancellery in Berlin — their only hope of avoiding another general war will lie in following his advice: shoring up England's defenses, or, that failing, in turning to a leader who possesses not only vision and intellect, but also a capacity for brutality, faith in the superiority of his race, and a positive relish at the prospect of grappling with a nation of warriors led by a demagogue who represents everything he loathes — in short, to Winston Churchill.

The great difference between the two is that Hitler wants war and will actually be annoyed by Britons and Frenchmen who propose to give him what he wants without a fight, while Churchill, though a born warlord, is prepared to sacrifice all save honor and the safety of England to keep the peace. Hitler's *Mein Kampf* is a difficult book, but no one who has struggled through it can doubt that the author is a killer obsessed with *Blutdurst*, bloodthirstiness. Churchill, on the other hand, after telling his guests that he has already begun research on a major project which will follow *Marlborough*, a four-volume *History of the English-speaking Peoples*, gloomily adds: "I doubt if I shall finish it before the war comes." If he does and an English victory is "decisive," he says, "I shall have to add several more volumes. And if it is not decisive no more histories will be written for years."

It is eleven o'clock. Churchill sees his overnight guests to their rooms and, as they retire, begins his working day. Only after entering his employ will Bill Deakin discover, to his astonishment, that Churchill lacks a large private income, that he lives like a pasha yet must support his extravagant life with his pen. The Churchill children are also unaware that, as Mary will later put it, the family "literally lived from book to book, and from one article to the next." Her mother, who knows, prays that each manuscript will sell. Luckily, they all do, with the exception of one screenplay for Alexander Korda, and editors and publishers, both in Britain and America, pay him the highest rates. His output is prodigious. During backbencher years, from early 1931 to late 1939, he will publish eleven volumes and over four hundred articles, many of them hack work ("Sport Is a Stimulant in Our Workaday World," "The Childless Marriage Threatens Our Race," "What Other Secrets Does the Inventor Hold?") in *Strand Magazine*, *Sunday Pictorial*, *Daily Mail*, *The Times*, *Saturday Review*, *Answers*, *Sunday Telegraph*, *Sunday Chronicle*, *Collier's*, *Sunday Dispatch*, *Pictorial Magazine*, *Sunday Times*, *Pictorial Weekly*, *The Listener*, *Pearson's Magazine*, *Daily Sketch*, *Evening Standard*, *Sunday Express*, *News of the World*, *Jewish Chronicle*, and *Daily Telegraph*. His annual earnings will average £20,000, or $96,000. During the same period he will deliver 368 speeches for which he is, of course, paid nothing. He will reject some commissions: a history of Parliament because the sum is inadequate, nearly $30,000 for a speaking tour in the United States because the mounting crises on the Continent keep him in England, and $50 from William S. Paley, president of the Columbia Broadcasting System, for an appraisal of Nazi activity in Austria. Paley asks CBS correspondent William L. Shirer to make the approach. Shirer, appalled by the paltry sum, phones Winston at the House of Commons. Called out of the chamber, Churchill says he will do it for \$500. Paley decides he isn't worth it, and a fragment of history is lost.[47]

Winston's Chartwell study is a writer's dream. Entering through the Tudor doorway with its molded architrave, one looks up and up — the ceiling has been removed, revealing vaulting rafters and beams which were in place long before the Renaissance. One's second impression — and it is strong — is a reminder of the greatest enigma in Churchill's life. Despite his parents' disgraceful neglect of him in his early years, a bronze cast of Jennie's hand lies on one windowsill. The desk and the bureau-bookcase with Gothic glazing were Lord Randolph's. The most prominent painting on the walls depicts his father writing. On the level of awareness, Winston reveres the memory of both his parents, but the resentment has to be there. His suppression of it is doubtless a heavy contributor to his periodic spells of depression, and his combativeness arises from the need to find another outlet for his anger. Significantly, he works not at his father's magnificent mahogany desk with gleaming claw feet, but at a high Disraeli desk of unvarnished deal with a slanting top, designed by Winston and fashioned by a local carpenter — a reminder that Victorians liked to write standing up.

His appearance heralded by the *harff, harff* of his slippers, he enters the room in his scarlet, green, and gold dressing gown, the cords trailing behind him. Before greeting his researcher and the two secretaries on duty tonight, he must read the manuscript he dictated the previous evening and then revise the latest galleys, which arrived a few hours earlier from London. Since Churchill's squiggled red changes exceed the copy set — the proofs look as though several spiders stained in crimson ink wandered across the pages — his printers' bills are shocking. But the expense is offset by his extraordinary fluency. Before the night is out, he will have dictated between four thousand and five thousand words. On weekends he may exceed ten thousand words. Once his family presented him with a Dictaphone. He was delighted. It seemed miraculous. He could dictate alone; one of the secretaries could transcribe the Dictabelt later. After a productive session, he went to bed triumphant, only to be told upon wakening that it was all wasted. He had forgotten to turn the device on. Everything was lost. "No more gadgets!" he roared, and stuck to the old system till his death.

Churchill has developed what biographer Philip Guedalla calls a faculty for "organizing large works." If he is researching a speech, a magazine essay, or a newspaper article, he needs little help. But for a major effort — his four-volume *Marlborough* or his *History of the English-speaking Peoples* — he requires a staff, most of them young Oxford graduates to whom he assigns readings and investigations; they then submit précis or memoranda which he studies between bursts of dictation. Among those thus engaged (at very small wages — £300 to £500 a year) are Deakin, John Wheldon, Keith Feiling, Maurice Ashley, Charles Hordern, and Ridley Pakenham-Walsh, both the last two former military officers. For a man approaching sixty, Winston does a great deal of his own field work, touring Marlborough's European battlefields — he is amazed at their enormity — but he hasn't time to rummage through the archives at Blenheim, translate old Flemish documents, or pore over the dispatches of William of Orange. So his staff does it for him.

This in no way diminishes his achievements. Deakin will remember that he, Winston, and the "shorthand-typists," as Churchill calls his secretaries, would sometimes "work on Marlborough until three or four in the morning. One felt exhilarated. Part of the secret was his phenomenal, fantastic power to concentrate on what he was doing. And he communicated it. You were absolutely a part of it — swept into it. I might have given him some memorandum before dinner, four or five hours before. Now he would walk up and down dictating. My facts were there, but he had seen it in deeper perspective. My memorandum was only a frame; it ignited his imagination." Winston asks him to write a summary of the election of 1710, and, Deakin will recall, "He read this without any comment at all and then dictated what he wanted to write in his book. . . . He translated it into integral power and things he understood in contemporary terms, but it was a transformation that was very special. His penetrating insight revealed insights I had completely missed."[48]

Because tonight's major project is a parliamentary speech, the researcher's tasks are complete before midnight. Those of the shorthand-typists are about to begin. Two will be on hand, to work shifts, and they will have assembled the necessary tools: scrap paper, shorthand notebooks, pens, pencils, rulers, erasers, scissors, paste, rubber bands, copy paper, carbon paper, an assortment of green tags, a copy of Vacher's *Parliamentary Companion Guide*, and Winston's "klop" or "klopper" — a powerful paper punch. Winston despises staplers. Instead the klop perforates a batch of paper; he then threads a piece of string through the hole and attaches it to a tag. In a public address the pages must be in order, and he has an irrational fear that someone will sabotage him, reversing pages. Right up to the moment of delivery he will be nervously checking to reassure himself that they are in sequence.

Sometimes, as Cecily ("Chips") Gemmell will recall, the opening hour is "ghastly." There is no diverting him. A stenographer peers through a window and observes blithly: "It's dark outside." Churchill, giving her a bleak look, replies pitilessly: "It generally is at night." His creative flow is blocked; he will prowl around, fling himself into a chair, bury his head in his hands and mutter, "Christ, I've got to do this speech, and I can't do it,

I *can't*." On such occasions, Inspector Thompson notes, Winston is "a kicker of wastebaskets, with an unbelievably ungovernable bundle of bad temper. It is better to stay away from him at such times, and this his family seeks to do."[49]

But the help has no choice. In time a word will come; then another word; then a prolonged search for the right phrase, ending, after a prolonged mumbling to himself, with a chortle of delight as he finds it. But his pace is still halting; Sir John Martin, one of his principal private secretaries, will later recall it as a long process, "while he carefully savored and chose his words, often testing alternative words or phrases in a low mutter before coming out loudly with the final choice." He is trying to establish rhythm, and once he has it, his pace quickens. Beginning where he will begin in the House, he opens with what MP and diarist Harold Nicolson calls "a dull, stuffy manner, reciting dates and chronology," but as he progresses he takes a livelier tone, introducing his familiar quips and gestures. Most writers regard the act of creativity as the most private of moments, but for Churchill it is semipublic; not only is the staff on hand, but any guest willing to sacrifice an hour's sleep is also welcome.

In Parliament he stands when speaking. Here he paces. In the House of Commons pacing is impossible, so he has adopted a different mode of delivery there. Nicolson notes: "His most characteristic gesture is strange indeed. You know the movement that a man makes when he taps his trouser pockets to see whether he has got his latch-key? Well, Winston pats both trouser pockets and then passes his hands up and down from groin to tummy. It is very strange."[50]

In Parliament his wit will flash and sting, but members who know him well are aware that he has honed these barbs in advance, and only visitors in the Strangers' Gallery are under the impression that his great perorations are extemporaneous. F.E. once referred to "Churchill's carefully prepared impromptus." Peter E. Wright, who had been among Churchill's colleagues during the Gallipoli crisis of 1915, notes: "Mr. Churchill cannot, as is well known, improvise very easily; telling as his speeches are, they are wrought, rehearsed, and often half read. To produce it all, Mr. Churchill, in his books and in his speeches, heaves like a mountain." But so, Wright adds, do other MPs, with disappointing results, whereas, "if Mr. Churchill's throes are volcanic, so is the result — a burning flood of lava, often uneven and tumultuous, but sweeping and splendid in its general effect."[51]

It is the product of toil, sweat, and frequent tears. On the average he spends between six and eight hours preparing a forty-minute speech. Frequently, as he dictates passages which will stir his listeners, he weeps; his voice becomes thick with emotion, tears run down his cheeks (and his secretary's). Like any other professional writer, he takes his text through several drafts before it meets his standards; but even in its roughest stages it is free of cant and bureaucratic jargon. Where Stanley Baldwin has said "a bilateral agreement has been reached," Churchill makes it "joined hands together." The "Local Defence Volunteers" become the "Home Guard." One sure way of rousing his temper is to call a lorry a "commercial vehicle" or alter "the poor" to "the lower-income group." He wages a long, and, in the end, successful campaign to ban the civil service's standard comment "The answer is in the affirmative" to a simple "Yes." A Churchillian text includes such inimitable phrases as "the jaws of winter," "hard and heavy tidings," and — neither Pitman nor Gregg is equal to this — "a cacophonous chorus." In both conversation and dictation he uses words with great precision and insists that others do the same. On a trip his physician comments: "I hope you did not catch cold sitting on the balcony in the chill night air." His patient, smiling mischievously, corrects him: "Portico, not balcony, Charles."[52]

Most of the action takes place in his study, but it can be unsettling even there. Once at 3:00 A.M. Winston uncharacteristically opened a window. Immediately a bat entered. The young woman on duty, more frightened of her employer than of this new uninvited immigrant of the Chartwell pet colony, closed her eyes and kept taking down words while Churchill pursued the bat with a poker, drove it back out, and slammed the window shut — meantime not missing a phrase. Another time a fire broke out in the study. Churchill's voice continued until, enveloped in smoke, his croaks and gasps became incomprehensible. By then a half-dozen servants had arrived. The flames had been smothered and all windows opened. The secretary, who had also been on duty the Night of the Bat, as the staff now called it, vanished. ("I headed for the loo," she recalls.) Churchill convened a court of inquiry on the spot, demanding the name of the arsonist. Kathleen Hill looked at him and said evenly, "You." She pointed at the remains of the cigar butt in the charred seat of an overstuffed chair. He scowled darkly, turned, and shouted, *"Where's Miss?"*[53]

His secretaries are required to take down every audible word from him; he often changes his mind in midpassage, but he may change it back. If he says "I was going" and adds after a pause "I decided to go," they type: "I was going. I decided to go." They spell one another from time to time, not because they are exhausted; he wants to see what he had said in cold type. He will revise it in his red ink, redictate it, and scrutinize it again. Occasionally he will add a paragraph. When at last he has a final version, it will be typed, on a machine with outsized type, on small pieces of paper, eight by four inches, the whole lot klopped and strung to a tag. The speech will be set in broken lines to aid his delivery, "speech form," or "psalm form," as Lord Halifax calls it. After Hitler becomes absolute master of the Third Reich, Churchill tells the House of Commons:

> I have on more than one occasion
> Made my appeal that the Führer of Germany
> Should become the Hitler of peace.
>
> When a man is fighting in a desperate conflict
> He may have to grind his teeth and flash his eyes;
> Anger and hatred nerve the arm of strife.
>
> But success should bring a mellow, genial air
> And, by altering the mood to suit the new circumstances,
> Preserve and consolidate in tolerance and goodwill
> What has been gained by conflict.

Thus, when Churchill rises to speak in the House, he holds in his hand not notes on the issues he means to address, but the entire text of what he intends to say. To be sure, he may say a few words suitable to the occasion, commenting on the remarks of previous speakers, but the rest is a set piece, though few know it. Because his delivery gives an illusion of spontaneity and the notes include stage directions ("pause; grope for word" and "stammer; correct self"), each of his speeches is a dramatic, vibrant occasion.

It would be pleasant to report that his relationship with his staff is genial, that he treats them as he would his daughters, and that he is particularly patient with new secretaries. In fact, he is nothing of the sort. He treats them like servants. A. J. P. Taylor calls him an "atrocious" taskmaster, and his attitude toward his employees is difficult to understand or, at times, even to excuse. He can summon each of his pets by name, recite poetry by the hour, and remember the exact circumstances under which he learned of a certain event fifty years earlier, but he knows the names of only three or four of his eighteen servants and stenographers. They are "the tall Miss with blue eyes" or "the man with ginger hair." Newcomers find his lisp an obstacle — they simply do not understand what he is saying — but he makes no allowance for that. Chips Gemmell will remember that during her first session she "sat there terrified; I couldn't understand a word he was saying, and I couldn't keep up with him. I thought, this is a nightmare. This isn't happening. So I went plop, plop, quite convinced it wasn't real." Winston didn't read her typescript until the team assembled in the study the following evening. He glanced through the first two pages, his face passing through deeper and deeper shades of red and his frown growing more savage, until he rose, flung the sheets on the floor, stamped his feet, and screamed: "You haven't got one word in fifty right! *Not one word in fifty! NOT ONE WORD IN FIFTY!*"[54]

She froze. So did Elizabeth Nel, when, on the evening of her secretarial baptism, she found her machine had been set at single, not double, spacing. With Churchill rattling along, uncharacteristically fluent at this early hour, she had no time to switch. After she had passed him the first page, she will recall, "he went off like a rocket. I was a fool, a mug, and idiot: I was to leave his presence and one of the others was to appear." Later she was given a second chance, and, still later, a third. She was understandably nervous, and "my apprehensions were seldom ill-founded. More often than not it would come skimming back to me with a few red alterations on it, sometimes to the accompaniment of remarks disparaging to my education and sense of hearing."[55] Yet their misunderstandings are completely understandable. Who can blame a stenographer who types "lemons" when he means the Greek island of Lemnos, mistakes "fretful" for "dreadful," or "perfervid" for "perverted"? Winston can and does; he rages and stamps his feet. (Foot-stamping is his outlet with women, a substitute for obscenities; if only men were present he would cut loose with a string of short Anglo-Saxon oaths "mostly beginning," as he once put it, "with the earlier letters of the alphabet.") One young woman wrote home:

> Not in a very good temper this morning. He suddenly said "Gimme t—gr—spts—pk." Interpreting this as "Give me a toothpick," I leapt up, looked round and then started rummaging in the bag where such necessities should be kept. After less than 20 seconds he said, very bored and superior "now Miss Layton just stop playing the bloody ass and" . . . . Presently, after dictating something, he found I'd put "Somehow I think it right" (which was what I thought he'd said). So fairly patient, he said "no, no, I said *now the time is right*" (with accents like that). So I did it again. Gave it back. There was a roar of rage. "God's teeth, girl, can't you do it right the second time? I said *ripe ripe ripe — P P P.*" I should, perhaps, have realized, but he hadn't mentioned that "right" was "wrong." However he forgave me for the rest of the day.

Occasionally the secretaries guess at a word, trusting to chance rather than provoke certain wrath by asking: "What did you say, sir?" Any break in his creative flow is intolerable to him. When a girl reaches the bottom of a page she must remove paper, carbon, and second sheet, then insert a new set and roll it into place. Winston makes no allowance for this. He barks: "Come on! Come on! What are you waiting for?" The crackling of carbon and the flimsy second sheets is almost as intolerable to him as whistling. He splutters: "Don't fidget so with that paper! Stop it!" His tantrums would be more bearable if he apologized afterward or complimented them on work well done. He never does either. When one of the secretaries carries on the night after one of his outbursts, he may mutter, "There. I knew you could do it." Or, if one bursts into tears: "Good heavens, you mustn't mind me. We're all toads beneath the harrow, you know." Once a manservant stood up to him. The result was a blazing row. At the end of it Churchill, his lower lip jutting, said: "You were very rude to me, you know." The servant, still seething, replied: "Yes, but you were rude, too." Churchill grumbled: "Yes, but I am a great man."[56]

At Chartwell this is the last word. Later the servant will say: "There was no answer to that. He knew, as I and the rest of the world knew, that he was right." Elizabeth Nel, after reciting her very legitimate grievances, adds: "Neither I nor anyone else considered this treatment unfair. . . . I used to wonder how long his patience would last, if he would not one day say, 'Go, and never let me see you again.' " Phyllis Moir, another member of the secretarial pool, will recall Winston on the phone, telling her to fetch him certain papers: "Mr. Churchill was standing by the telephone, his face very red and very angry, stamping his feet and sputtering with rage. He literally tore the papers out of my hand and savagely stammered an incoherent answer into the mouthpiece." She adds loyally: "Mr. Churchill is not the sort of man to apologize to anyone, but he would go out of his way to say something appreciative and his whole manner made you feel he was ashamed of his bad behavior." In this instance, she explains, he expressed his shame by failing to turn on her wrathfully after he had hung up. Instead he asked her if she was enjoying the countryside.[57]

It seems hardly adequate. Neither does his forgiveness "for the rest of the day" seem appropriate redress for browbeating a girl who mistook his lisped "ripe" for "right." The blunt truth is that Winston has never considered himself a toad beneath the harrow, and for the best of reasons: he isn't one. No humble man would outflank a traffic jam by driving on pavement. He believes he is a superior being, entitled to exceptional forbearance as well as special privilege and not subject to judgment by the rules of polite society. This is, of course, arguable. What is striking is that those who work for him, toiling long hours, underpaid, and subject to savage, undeserved reprimands, agree with him. They feel the sting of his whip. Yet he continues to command their respect, even their love. Those who are shocked by Churchill's treatment of his employees all have this in common: they never worked for him.

Sometime between 2:00 and 4:00 A.M. he quits, leaving the others to sort out ribbon copies and carbons, clean up the study, and, if the night's dictation has included manuscript, prepare a packet for the London courier.

In his bedroom he divests himself of his trousers and velvet slippers; then, in one great overhead swoop, yanks the rest of his clothing up, away, and across the chamber. In a gesture that is more narcissistic than remedial, he faces the mirror in his bedroom and brushes his strands of hair straight down over his ears, saying to his valet, with dubious authority, "That's the way to keep your hair, Inches." He asks him for "my eye blinkers," slips the sleep mask in place, and is soon breathing the deep, slow breaths of the slumberer. His dreams, he tells his family, are often of his father, who died prophesying Winston would be a failure. In 1932 it would be hard to find more than a dozen men of Parliament or Fleet Street who would think that prediction laughable.

PROLOGUE

A Fever over Europe

VICTORIA Regina — "the Old Queen," still a vivid memory among Englishmen in their forties — would have been shocked speechless. Here was London, the most civilized city in the world, and there in its streets were the rabble, identifiable by their ragged clothes, their faces clenched in rage, and, when they raised their voices, the unmistakable accents of their class. To affluent spectators, the rioting seemed illusory. Many were looking at the poor, really *looking* at them, for the first time in their lives. Usually the patriciate encountered them only in servile roles, and the privileged had been raised to ignore them, even to speak of them in their presence as though they were not there. But in 1932, with the Depression at rock bottom, the poor could not escape notice. There were too many of them, and they were too angry.

A London constable needed only a brief glance to distinguish between the classes. Shaw's *Pygmalion* to the contrary, it wasn't just a matter of clothes, expressions, and accents. No speech therapist or couturier could alter their posture, mannerisms, and physique. Lower-class diets were so poor that emergency programs were needed to provide them with fruit, vegetables, and, for each schoolchild, 2.67 ounces of milk a day. Generations of malnutrition, of stooping in tunnels or bending over textile looms, had given workmen slight stature, poor posture, coarse complexions, weak eyesight, and hollow chests; and even among nubile women, breasts were small and limp. Individually they were unattractive and easily overpowered. But when they coalesced into a mob they could constitute a threat to the tall, fair, erect gentry. Of course, the gentry did not dream of meeting force with their own force. It was, as most of them said, a matter for the police.

Those of less insensitive conscience were shocked. Yet they shouldn't have been. There had been plenty of warnings. People were edgy. The city's celebrated civility was beginning to fray. Every household in Mayfair or Belgravia had its tales, hushly told, of rude beggars who had accosted ladies outside Harrods or St. Paul's and grew ugly if denied sixpence. And Whitechapel had actually insulted a member of the Royal Family. The

Prince of Wales's brother Prince "Bertie" — the future King George VI — had paid a compassionate visit to the city's starving East End. According to sworn testimony, published in *The Times,* His Royal Highness had been driven back by ragged cockneys shaking grimy fists and shouting: "Food! Give us food! We don't want royal parasites!"[1]

This lèse-majesté was the prelude to the riots of October 1932. The first seems to have been spontaneous. The cockneys who had defied royalty had been released by the magistrate with a warning. Emboldened, they decided to sortie into the city proper. The sheer size of the multitude was frightening. They poured into the streets by the thousands, and soon they were bearing down on Lambeth Bridge. Twenty times the bobbies launched truncheon charges; finally, as a last resort, they blocked their bridgehead with lorries parked hubcap to hubcap. The barricade held until the bruised, scarred, and exhausted throng fell back.[2]

The second onslaught, a march on London from the outer reaches of the country, was more menacing. Its moves had been carefully planned by a dour, disheveled youth named W. A. L. Hannington,"Wal" to his men and "Red Wal" in the London newspapers. The men behind him called their trek a hunger march. It was a long one. They had come from towns as far as western Wales and northern Scotland, bearing a petition for relief signed by a million unemployed workers, with the expectation that the prime minister would receive their delegation. In the countryside local charities fed the marchers, but after a cabinet minister told the House of Commons that Bolsheviks were behind their protest and it was "up to the Communists to feed them," they were given few handouts in the capital.[3]

Their enormous petition was too cumbersome for the street brawlers to carry, so they checked it at Charing Cross Station and then swarmed up the Strand to Trafalgar Square, stoning limousines and using tree branches — hacked off in Hyde Park — to club well-dressed men. Bobbies waded into them, swinging billy clubs, and broke their momentum at Marble Arch. England's most sacred political institutions, it seemed, were safe. Then it was learned that a second column, five thousand strong, had emerged from concealment in Green Park and was crossing St. James's Park, in their rear. Debouching by the Guards Memorial, this mob advanced on No. 10 Downing Street. The only policeman in sight was the single bobby who, by tradition, stands by the prime minister's front door.

At this point, less than four hundred yards from their objective, the marchers' luck turned against them. The open ground between the rioters and the entrance to Downing Street was occupied by the parade ground of the Royal Horse Guards. As long as anyone could remember, the only duty of these cavalrymen had been to perform ceremoniously for admiring tourists. Now, preparing to fight for King and Country, they buckled on their glittering helmets, mounted their handsome steeds, drew their gleaming sabers from their polished scabbards, and formed a very thin red line. The sheer weight of the mob could have overwhelmed them, but the marchers, most of them in London for the first time, seemed awestruck. They wavered and milled around. By the time they had regrouped, reserves from Bow Street were there in force, sending them reeling back toward Trafalgar Square. Anticlimax followed. At Charing Cross Station, where they produced their claim check, a courteous clerk explained that the petition, with its million signatures, had been classified as an incentive to riot and confiscated by Scotland Yard. Beaten and bitter, they rode home on British railroads, which, relieved to see them dispersed, charged only token fares.[4]

❦ ❦

Television did not exist, and radio news was closely monitored by Sir John Reith, czar of the BBC, so the failed demonstrations had little impact on the British public. Few, if any, could have predicted that the suppressed riots, with their threat of social upheaval, would later play a role in the formation of the most disastrous foreign policy in the history of Britain and its empire. The significance of the incidents was largely overlooked by Fleet Street. It was a dreary time; people were less interested in momentous events than in escapism.

In the early thirties, the average Englishman's exposure to American culture — and he enjoyed it immensely — was chiefly confined to motion pictures, now in the transition period between silent films and talkies. In Westerham, the local cinema was The Swan. Winston Churchill, trudging up its steps with little Mary in tow to see MGM's lavish *Ben-Hur*, was, at least in this, typical of his countrymen. Like them he loved Westerns. His favorite was *Destry Rides Again*, with Tom Mix. He favored movies featuring drama, excitement, action, slapstick — Cecil B. DeMille's *The Sign of the Cross*, Douglas Fairbanks in *The Iron Mask*, Walt Disney's anthropomorphic Mickey Mouse cartoons, and the Marx Brothers at the peak of their lunacy. With the arrival of sound had come popular music from abroad: "Singin' in the Rain," "Beyond the Blue Horizon," "Tiptoe through the Tulips," and Marlene Dietrich, at twenty-nine huskily serenading Emil Jannings with "Falling in Love Again" in Josef van Sternberg's first German talkie, *Der blaue Engel*. For Britons who preferred to buy British, homemade pickings were slim, with one shining exception: Noel Coward.

These were the years when Gertrude Lawrence, young Laurence Olivier, Beatrice Lillie, and Coward himself played roles he had created, when his name was writ large on the hoardings of four London theatres: *Private Lives* at the Phoenix; *Cavalcade* at the Drury Lane; *Words and Music* at the Adelphi; and, at His Majesty's Theatre, *Bitter Sweet*.

In the back gardens of their semidetached bungalows in Streatham or Battersea, British housewives' gossip and snobbery had always served as shields against unpleasantness. The most exciting rumors in 1932 centered around the Royal Family, especially the world's most eligible bachelor, HRH the Prince of Wales, now thirty-eight. It was no secret that King George and Queen Mary were putting heavy pressure on their middle-aged heir to marry *someone* suitable; they had just spent over £10,000 renovating and redecorating Marlborough House, at the west end of Pall Mall, making it both comfortable and elegant for their new daughter-in-law, whoever she might be. Of course the Prince would find a bride soon, the housewives told one another, hanging clothes out to dry. He knew his duty. And, they added, nodding vigorously, he would marry well, giving Great Britain a future queen who would become the pride of the Empire.

The Empire! The mere mention of it aroused patriotic Britons like Churchill, made them brace their backs and lift their eyes. If there was any fixed star in their firmament it was an abiding faith in the everlasting glory of their realm — Dominions, Crown Colonies, protectorates, Chinese treaty towns — which, in sum, was over three times the size of the Roman Empire at its height: 475 million people, 11 million square miles, ninety-one times the area of Great Britain, encompassing a quarter of both the earth's surface and its population. The fourth edition of *The Pocket Oxford Dictionary* defined "imperial" as "magnificent"; "imperialism" as the "extension of the British Empire for protection of trade, union of its parts for defence, internal commerce, etc."; and "imperialist" as an "advocate of British imperialism."

Britons still scrupulously observed Empire Day, giving schoolchildren a half-holiday. They joined or encouraged the British Empire League, the British Empire Union, the Victoria League, and the Patriotic League of Britons Overseas. They cried "Hear, hear" when the new viceroy of India, Lord Willingdon, foresaw "a Great Imperial Federation, when we can snap our fingers at the rest of the world." Baldwin declared: "The British Empire stands firm, as a great force for good. It stands in the sweep of every wind, by the wash of every sea." Colin Cross, the historian, has observed that "with authority reaching to every continent, the British Empire was literally a world power; indeed in terms of its influence it was the only world power."[5]

Historian James Morris has written of the Empire: "Most Britons still considered it, all in all, a force for good in the world. . . . The Monarchy was still immensely popular in most parts of the Empire, even in India, even in Ireland." Schoolboys in the United Kingdom and the United States alike were taught that in battle the British "always won," as indeed they had in every major war since the eighteenth century.

All the imperial trappings were kept intact. The prime ministers of the Dominions continued to meet in London, ostensibly to coordinate economic policies, though none were forthcoming. Dominion children studied books with such chapter titles as "The Thread That Binds Our Race," and Boy Scouts — not only in the Empire but also in America — wore broad-brimmed Boer War hats and shared with the South African police the motto "Be Prepared." Lord Beaverbrook's newspapers, particularly the London *Daily Express,* made expansion of the imperial domain a crusade. Graduates of "Oxbridge" — Oxford and Cambridge — still sailed abroad to spend lifetimes as imperial proconsuls, looking forward, late in life, to the rewards of CMG, KCMG, or GCMG. In New Delhi, at state banquets, the viceroy's entrance into the dining hall was preceded by two elegantly uniformed aides-de-camp; and when the orchestra played "God Save the King," the Indian servants in their gold and scarlet liveries stood poised behind each guest.[6]

And yet . . .

There were signs, for those who could read them, that the Empire was, in Churchill's gloomy words, on a "downward slurge." *La belle époque* was over. Most of the Crown's subjects, abroad as well as at home, felt comfortable with imperialism. With the exception of the *Daily Worker,* every British newspaper supported it. Few, even in Ireland, were offended when the thick voice of their sovereign was identified on radio for his annual, unbearably boring Christmas broadcast ("Another year has passed . . .") by an announcer with a plummy accent as "His Britannic Majesty, by Grace of God and of the United Kingdom of Great Britain and Ireland and of the British Dominions beyond the Seas, King, Defender of the Faith, Emperor of India." But the mystique was fading; indeed, for some it had already gone.[7]

Earlier generations of Englishmen had found colonial uprisings endlessly fascinating. They had pored over newspaper accounts (many written by young Churchill) and tacked pages of the *Illustrated London News* — depicting the Mutiny, Chinese Gordon's Last Stand, Kitchener at Omdurman, and the expeditions relieving Boer sieges of Ladysmith, Kimberley, and Mafeking — to the walls of their homes. Challenges to the supremacy of the

Union Jack had stirred their blood, and they had responded eagerly to calls to the Flag, Duty, Race, and the White Man's Burden. In the early 1930s millions of Britons, especially the elderly, members of the upper class, and those who had reached their majority before 1914, still felt that way. But imperial enthusiasm was dwindling among the working classes and the young. They were weary of the White Man's Burden. The new mood was caught by Aldous Huxley; to him the Raj resembled the Old Man of Thermopylae, who never did anything properly. "For some reason," young Jock Colville wrote in his diary, "no subject is more boring to the average Englishman than the British Empire."[8]

British imperialism was, in fact, an idea whose time was going. The issue had already been decided. In the House of Commons the master blueprint governing the imperial future, the Statute of Westminster of 1931, decreed that the Mother Country and her dominions were "autonomous communities within the British Empire, equal in status, in no way subordinate to each other in any aspect of their domestic or foreign affairs, though united by a common allegiance to the Crown, and freely associated as members of the British Commonwealth of Nations."

George V, who treasured his legacy, watched in dismay as his imperial role beyond England's shores shrank to that of a posturing mascot. Confused, he minuted in November 1929, on the eve of the Depression: "I cannot look into the future without feelings of no little anxiety about the continued unity of the Empire." His apprehensions were well founded, though perhaps for reasons too cosmic for him to grasp. Empires are the sequelae of historical accidents. England, an island and therefore a trading nation, had gained control of the high seas just as colonies became ripe for plucking. As long as sea power remained dominant, imperial institutions were invincible; under Victoria it was British policy to keep the Royal Navy — 330 warships, manned by 92,000 tars — larger than the combined navies of any other two powers.[9]

Air power would prove to be the ultimate blow to the Empire's role as the world's one superpower, but the first great blow to the imperial future had been dealt by the Great War. In the red month of August 1914, when England's poet laureate promised Oxford and Cambridge students that if they enlisted they would find "Beauty through blood," all 450 million subjects of the Empire went to war, bound by a single declaration from their king-emperor. They sprang to arms in a trance of ardor, even elation. By Armistice Day 3,190,235 of the King's subjects had fallen in the slime and gore of trench warfare, 1,165,661 killed in action, 962,661 of them from Great Britain. Over 2 million soldiers had been wounded, thousands of them crippled and maimed, destined to be public wards for the remainder of their lives. Add to these the nearly half-million young widows and fatherless children, and one finds that two years after the war 3.5 million Britons, nearly 10 percent of the population, were receiving a pension or an allowance.[10]

❧ ❧

In the year of the Wall Street Crash, when Robert Graves's American publisher issued *Goodbye to All That,* his powerful evocation of service in the trenches, the *Nation* thought it striking "not that he tells the truth about the war but that it took him so long to discover it." But the lag applied not only to Graves; it was characteristic of an entire British literary generation. The most extraordinary thing about England's disenchantment with the war is that it didn't surface for over ten years. The reading public had been fed the self-serving memoirs of those responsible for the disaster and the thin fictional gruel of Bulldog Drummond and Richard Hannay. Those who had remained home were simply incapable of absorbing the truth. Aging Tommies told them that sixty thousand young Englishmen had fallen on the first day of the battle of the Somme without gaining a single yard. *Sixty thousand!* It *couldn't* be true. Those who said so must be shell-shocked.[11]

The coalescence came in 1929. On January 21 the curtain rose on the first of what would be 594 London performances of *Journey's End,* the ultimate in antiwar plays, by Robert C. Sherriff, a thirty-three-year-old former insurance man who had served in the East Surrey Regiment's Ninth Battalion through the bloody spring of 1917. Its audiences left the Savoy Theatre stunned but primed, now, for Graves's memoir; for Edmund Blunden's *Undertones of War;* for the German novelist Erich Maria Remarque's *Im Westen nichts Neues,* which appeared that spring in Berlin and was immediately translated by a London publisher as *All Quiet on the Western Front;* and, the following year, for Siegfried Sassoon's *Memoirs of an Infantry Officer.*[12]

The Great War may have been the first historic event in which reality outstripped the imagination. In the 1980s it is difficult to grasp the public innocence of that earlier generation, and how it recoiled when confronted at last by the monstrous crimes which had been committed in the name of patriotism. As time passed, the yeast of bitterness worked in the public mind and its emotions. By 1932 readers had accepted Sassoon and Graves as sources of the revealed word, and traveling troupes were presenting *Journey's End* in every post of the Empire. Newspapers and magazines picked up the now-it-can-be-told theme; pacifism became as fashionable as war fever had been less than twenty years earlier. On February 9, 1933, the Oxford Union voted 275 to 153 to approve the resolution "that this House will in no circumstances fight for King and Country." Eight months later, in what may have been the most significant by-election of the decade, a Tory in London's East Fulham, whose Conservative majority after the last campaign had been fourteen thousand votes, was swamped by an obscure Labour challenger. Labour's man had told the constituency that he would "close every recruiting station, disband the Army and disarm the Air Force," and demanded that England "give the lead to the whole world by initiating immediately a policy of general disarmament." His victory margin was five thousand votes, representing an extraordinary swing of 26 percent. It was no accident. Over the next four months constituencies ranging widely in character but representative of the country's mood elected antiwar candidates by margins ranging from 20 to 25 percent.[13]

Churchill was alarmed. In the House of Commons he was the League of Nations' chief supporter, but the league now faced a trembling future. He became preoccupied with national security. Unilateral disarmament would be madness, he told Parliament. The by-elections also distressed Stanley Baldwin, leader of the Conservative party, but his response was very different. To him the loss of safe seats was a grave matter. If the voters wanted disarmament, he decided, that was what he would give them.[14]

The real threat to British security, His Majesty's Government held, lay within. Indeed, Conservative MPs believed that the menace faced them just across the well of the House of Commons, on the Labour benches. Actually, His Majesty's Loyal Opposition was itself a mildly conservative party, and had proved it in 1924 while occupying the front bench for nine months. Many of its members were former Liberal MPs who had switched parties once they saw that Labour was the only realistic alternative to Tory rule. Nevertheless, Conservatives believed that if England was to remain the England they knew and loved, they must remain in power.

Until now British Communists had all been members of the working class, or shabby young men wearing steel-rimmed glasses who mouthed the weary party line in Hyde Park, responding to questions with incomprehensible jargon and quotations from Marx, Engels, and Lenin. In the early 1930s communism became respectable, then fashionable, then a distinction among intellectuals and university undergraduates. Among the Communist Party of Great Britain (CPGB) members were W. H. Auden, Christopher Isherwood, and Stephen Spender. Oxford's October Club, a CPGB cell, had three hundred dues-paying students. Cambridge started later, but soon one of every five Cambridge men had signed on, among them one H. A. R. ("Kim") Philby.

Those who dismissed this as an example of British eccentricity, or of typical undergraduate irresponsibility, were silenced by news from the United States, the world's most affluent nation. Ragged mobs of the homeless and penniless were occupying U.S. public buildings — including one statehouse — and twenty-five thousand war veterans, arriving in Washington with their families to plead for relief, were routed with tear gas and bayonets. American recruits to the party included John Dos Passos, Sherwood Anderson, Erskine Caldwell, and Edmund Wilson, who called Russia "the moral top of the world, where the light never really goes out."

Every generation cherishes illusions which baffle its successors (who passionately defend their own), but intellectuals are expected to view the world with healthy skepticism. Those who visited the Soviet Union in the starkest years of the Depression were so easily deceived, so eager to accept the flimsiest evidence, so determined to believe the most transparent misrepresentations, that one feels that some of the scorn directed nowadays at the appeasers of Nazi Germany should be reserved for men who ought to have known better. Bernard Baruch asked Lincoln Steffens, "So you've been over into Russia?" and Steffens replied: "I have been over into the future, and it works."[15]

He had seen what Stalin wanted him to see, on a rigged tour, the kind generals stage for visiting politicians. Everything paraded by him had worked, but he had not seen into the future or even the present. As one of the most celebrated journalists of his time, Steffens should have investigated his host's policy of collectivization and its ghastly results. Only a willing dupe could say of such a holocaust that it worked. If it did, so did Auschwitz.

Actually, the moral top of Edmund Wilson's world, where the light never really went out, had entered a period of murk which masked monstrous crimes — crimes which were suspected but not acknowledged until Nikita Khrushchev revealed them in 1957 — all committed in the name of the people they were destroying. The catastrophe had begun with Lenin's death in 1924. Churchill, his archenemy, nevertheless recognized Lenin's greatness: "The strong illuminant that guided him was cut off at the moment when he had turned resolutely for home. The Russian people were left floundering in the bog. Their worst misfortune was his birth; their next worst — his death."[16]

Lenin had left a vague "political testament" which recommended that Joseph Stalin, then secretary-general of the Communist party's Central Committee, be dismissed. Stalin suppressed this document and, in his role as secretary-general, joined two accomplices in a ruling triumvirate which expelled Stalin's chief rival, Leon Trotsky. (Eventually, Stalin would order the murders of his accomplices and Trotsky.) Stalin consolidated his position as master of the Kremlin, and by 1932 the Soviet Union was in the grip of a reign of terror which would reach its peak in the great purges of 1934–1938. To the world, however, Stalin insisted that his rule was benign. In the early summer of 1932, interviewed by the German biographer Emil Ludwig, he denied that he was a dictator, denied that he reigned by fear, and declared that the "overwhelming majority" of the laboring population in the U.S.S.R. was behind him. Their support, he said, accounted for the "stability of Soviet power," not "any so-called policy of terrorism."

At that time no Russian translation of *Mein Kampf* existed, but in this exchange Stalin had instinctively followed a principle set down in Adolf Hitler's tenth chapter: "The great masses of the people . . . will more easily fall victims to a big lie [*eine grosse Lüge*] than to a small one." Everything the Russian dictator had told Ludwig was the exact opposite of the truth. Soviet peasants were already in the toils of a misery far more wretched than anything known under the czars. Abandoning Lenin's managed economy, with its quasi-capitalistic incentives, Stalin had launched a series of five-year plans moving twenty-five million farmers from their lands into collectives. Troops and secret police rounded up protesters and murdered, exiled, or imprisoned them in an expanding net of concentration camps which systematically worked them to death. Nevertheless, collectivism failed. The Ukrainians were devastated by famine. Stalin rejected their appeal for help and actually exported grain while ten million of them starved to death.

By the autumn of 1932 England's ruling classes were afraid of their own countrymen, and their fear alarmed Labour, whose MPs heard wild tales of plots by His Majesty's Government to turn Britain into a police state. Hugh Dalton, MP, son of a clergyman but a committed socialist, visited Stafford Cripps, a member of the Labour hierarchy. Dalton wrote in his diary that Cripps "thinks there is a grave danger of Fascism in this country," that Metropolitan-Vickers, the munitions manufacturers, "are 'probably supplying arms to British Fascists.' " Cripps, Dalton wrote, believed that "Churchill will probably defeat the Government on India next spring and form a Government of his own, with a Majority in this Parliament and then 'introduce Fascist measures' and 'there will be no more general elections.' " Dalton, appalled, thought that "this seems to me to be fantastic and most profoundly improbable." But Harold Laski echoed Cripps, telling Dalton that he had "heard 'from an inside source' that members of the [all-party national] Government are discussing the advisability of not having a General Election in 1936, nor till such later date as the Government advises the King that it would be safe to return to party politics."[17]

Cripps and Laski were looking into the wrong closets. British politics were unthreatened by communism. But the domestic disorders, the dole, and the increase in CPGB memberships profoundly affected His Majesty's Government's foreign policy. HMG's subsequent dealings with a resurgent Germany make no sense unless seen in counterpoint with Tory anxiety. The London hunger riots had, or so it seemed to them, been a sign that England's class system was disintegrating. The remarkable stability of British society was rooted in a social contract whose origins lay in the medieval relationship between lord and serf. Within the memory of living men, employees could be arrested for the most trivial of offenses, and an employer was entitled to police help in finding a runaway employee. Under the Prevention of Poaching Act, suspicious constables had possessed the power to stop and search anyone in "streets, highways, and public places."[18]

Although unwritten and largely unspoken, the terms of the social contract were handed down from generation to generation and seldom challenged. Now the hunger riots had changed all that. The precise distinctions between the classes would never be the same. If mobs could roam London, those in power reasoned, their troubles with the lower middle, working, and underclasses had just begun. They were right, but wrong to blame Moscow and its British minions. Englishmen kept their places when they and their families were fed, clothed, and housed. The unemployed, however, knew no such restraint. The man without a situation took little risk, and might attract attention to his cause, by stoning limousines, joining a demonstration — or joining the Communist party. To those in power such men, by their very numbers, were alarming. Nearly a quarter of the country's work force was jobless, and in some dark pockets the figure reached 50, 60, or even 70 percent. England had to export or die. That was the fate of an island nation. Now goods lay in mountainous stacks in warehouses or on wharves. Desperate, His Majesty's Government adopted draconian measures — £24,149,060 in new taxes and £2,344 in spending cuts.

Among those affected by the cuts were British tars. An able seaman's pay was reduced from four shillings a day (ninety-seven cents) to three shillings (seventy-three cents). Shattering three centuries of tradition, men of the Royal Navy mutinied. Over thirteen thousand of His Majesty's sailors anchored in Cromarty Firth, Scotland — men whose ships bore such proud names as *Nelson, Repulse,* and *Valiant* — defied their officers, sang "The Red Flag," and elected leaders for what can only be called their own soviet. Only a handful were punished. Their pay was restored. The Admiralty angrily denounced HMG's capitulation, calling it a ghastly precedent. The government agreed but said it had had no choice.

And, of course, the grim facts did bear political implications. In December 1929 there had been just 3,200 Communists in Britain, 550 of them organized in cells. Now the hammer and sickle was carried through the heart of London. Membership in the CPGB was growing rapidly as the Depression deepened, increasing by 140 percent, then 259 percent, then 282 percent. And these were only the hard-core, card-carrying members. The number of sympathizers was far larger; in two by-elections the Communist candidates received, respectively, 31.9 and 33.8 percent of the vote.

At the same time, Communists everywhere had become more militant and more submissive to Moscow. This was one result of the Comintern's Tenth Plenum in 1929. Stalin had decreed that local deviations from the party line be suppressed and that all loyal members move to set "class against class." They were told to fight, not only capitalism, but also the labor movement. Since the Comintern had been founded to "accelerate the development of events toward world revolution," the threat to established order everywhere was open. In London it was taken seriously; to conservative Englishmen the possibility of a Communist Britain seemed very real.

Several Tories with strong influence on their party's leadership contemplated executing a momentous pivot in the history of British diplomacy. No one spoke of it publicly, nor was it whispered in the House of Commons smoking room. Even as theory, it was still in the fetal stage, and it might never come to term. Only a few Conservatives were committed to it. But others, including members of the party hierarchy, thought it had merit.

They pondered Benito Mussolini's popularity in Italy, where, by 1932, he had been ruling for ten years. It had been a good decade for Italians. *Il Duce*'s dreams of building another Roman Empire evoked a tepid response, but his managed economy had prospered; his countrymen's standard of living had risen. His goals, a biographer notes, had "a great appeal to many people in Italy in the years immediately following World War I; the Russian Revolution had terrified the leaders of the Italian financial and industrial community, and Mussolini's program seemed to many of them to be an effective means of countering any similar development in their own country."

British intelligence reported that in Germany, also suffering from the Depression, Adolf Hitler was following the Duce's lead, presenting himself to the Ruhr's *Schlotbarone* (smokestack barons) as a shield against the Reds. Hitler's National Socialist German Workers' Party — Nationalsozialistische Deutsche Arbeiterpartei, "Nazi" for short — had remained obscure as long as the German economy flourished. Now the country's industrialists, alarmed by the growing strength of communism in the working class, looked upon the Nazis with increasing approval.

At the time, the fear of Moscow was understandable. The Soviet Comintern, dedicated to the overthrow of other governments, was not just noisy; it was working, undermining the foundations of Western civilization from within. Communism was still new, virile, and virulent; cheerful tributes to it by leftists in the democracies drove democratic rightists, who were equally blind, toward Hitler. As T. R. Fehrenbach neatly states, "The Conservative Government of Great Britain, the one real order-keeping power in the world, was too intent upon the threatened social revolution to see the imminent nationalist revolt Hitler's Germany was mounting against the democratic world." They persuaded themselves, as Fehrenbach puts it, that a Germany ruled by Nazis could become "a counterpoise against the national and revolutionary ambitions of the Soviet Union."[19]

This was the rationale for the policy emerging in Whitehall and the Quai d'Orsay, of befriending the dictator states and appeasing their resentment of their postwar plight. The signs in Germany, to the men in high Tory councils, were encouraging. They pointed to the imminent establishment of a strong anti-Soviet regime in Berlin. Should that happen, they intended to befriend its leaders. Together, they believed, Englishmen and Germans had the stamina to forge a shield Comintern agents could never penetrate.

If Britain succeeded in courting Germany, His Majesty's Government would have a lot of explaining to do, much of it to Englishmen who had been targets of Mausers and Krupp howitzers for four years and could never have prevailed without the gallant poilus who fought with them shoulder to shoulder, even when the Allied line nearly collapsed in the last spring of the war. An understanding with Berlin would mean the rejection of Britain's fellow democracy. Questions in the House would be endless. But as the new men saw it, the time had come to put wartime bitterness aside. France, they felt, lacked vigor, determination, and sound business sense.

The French *were* exhausted. In *France même* — France outside Paris — the country was quiescent. The fertile northern provinces had been transformed into a wasteland of crumbling trenches and rusting barbed wire; over half the Frenchmen between the ages of twenty and thirty-two — 1,385,000 — had been killed there between 1914 and 1918. The survivors were too maimed, or too feeble, to lift the tricolor in triumph. To be sure, the City of Light, the nation's capital, still glowed. Under the chestnut trees of the Champs Élysées, fashion reporters who had penetrated the closely guarded private openings of the city's grand couturiers forecast lower waists, straighter lines, fuller sleeves, and high, wide, and handsome shoulders.

Hats were to be saucy: Arab fezzes, clown and cossack caps. Chanel would offer gloves of 18-karat spun gold, Regny an evening gown which could be converted into a bathing suit, and Rouff a naughty evening gown, with a zipper extending from the throat straight down to the bottom hem "for moonlight bathing," or, as cynics pointed out, "swift coupling."

In all world capitals it was assumed — it had, indeed, become a newspaper cliché — that France possessed "the finest army in the world." In London those pushing for a divorce from Paris and a remarriage in Berlin spread rumors of plans for a French preemptive war against the new German state. *The Times,* possibly floating a trial balloon, warned: "In the years that are coming there is more reason to fear for Germany than to fear Germany."[20]

Actually, confidence in the army of the Third Republic had been illusionary since 1917, when fifty-four French divisions — 750,000 men — had mutinied. Officers had been beaten and even murdered; an artillery regiment had attempted to blow up the Schneider-Creusot munitions plant; trains had been derailed; 21,174 men deserted outright. Trenches were abandoned, and had the Germans known there was no one on the other side of no-man's-land, they could have plunged through and won the war. The bitterness of the poilus survived the Armistice; their leaders told them their side had won, but they knew, in Churchill's words, that victory had been "bought so dear as to be almost indistinguishable from defeat."[21]

Gallic military thinking was now wholly defensive. On January 4, 1930, both houses of the National Assembly had voted to build, on the Franco-German border, a great wall to be named for the minister of war, André Maginot. It would cost seven billion francs when completed in 1935. To be sure, the line did not protect the wooded Ardennes, but Marshal Philippe Pétain dismissed fears for the forest: *"Elle est impénétrable."* This judgment by the hero of Verdun was unchallenged. To young journalist William L. Shirer, arriving at the Arc de Triomphe in 1925, it seemed that "no other country on the Continent could challenge France's supremacy. The nightmare of the German threat, which had haunted the French for so long, had been erased." Their ancient foe, prostrate in defeat, its army reduced to a token force, its leadership "forbidden by the Versailles Treaty to build warplanes or tanks, or heavy guns or submarines or battleships, and saddled with the burden of reparations, was no longer a menace."[22]

That, too, was illusion. Germany was not the Germany the Allies thought they had created at Versailles, and France seemed to be drifting into a strengthless *oubli.* Alistair Horne, the popular British historian, saw "the urge for national *grandeur*" replaced by "a deep longing simply to be left in peace." In its capital, however, the mood quickened. It could be felt in the Café Flore and the Deux Magots, for example, the haunts of young

Jean-Paul Sartre and his mistress, Simone de Beauvoir; in the *rêves fantastiques* of Jean Giraudoux and Jean Cocteau; in the Revue Nègre, the Ballet Suedois, the Ballet Russe, the extravagant theatre of Sergey Diaghilev, the fox trot *dansomanie,* Josephine Baker, Inkichinoff's film *La Tête d'un homme,* the Prevert brothers' film *L'Affaire est dans le sac;* and — the favorites of all the left-wing critics — the new stars Gilles and Julien, a pair of pacifist anarchists who performed in a Montmartre cabaret and then on the stage at Bobino's, wearing black sweaters and making songs like *"Le Jeu de massacre"* instant hits after singing them just once. The manic mood, Horne wrote, was "Anything for *spectacle.*" This was the France of legend: the land of tumbling francs, tumbling governments, and saucy, tumbling *filles.*[23]

La Force de l'âge (*The Prime of Life*), Simone de Beauvoir's memoir of the late 1920s and early 1930s, provides a more perceptive picture. Her depiction of French intellectuals contrasts starkly with the rising Nazi *Wildheit* in Berlin, where the excesses and decadence of the postwar decade were yielding to a flirtation, and then a lethal embrace, between philistinism and savagery. To be sure, there was ferocity in the French capital, too, as Communist gangs fought with members of the Croix de Feu, the Action Française, the Jeunesse Patriotes, and, later, Le Francisme, the most bizarre of the leagues. But they were a lunatic fringe; the intelligentsia considered them vulgar and so never mentioned them or even acknowledged their existence. "Peace seemed finally assured," de Beauvoir wrote in the fall of 1929. She felt she was living in "a new 'Golden Age,' " that the swelling of the Nazi ranks across the border was "a mere fringe phenomenon, without any serious significance." She, her lover Sartre, and their friends watched the Nazi seizure of power "quite calmly," she later wrote, and while she briefly noted the Nazi expulsion of Einstein, she was more dismayed by the closing of Berlin's Institute of Sexology.[24]

"We refused," she later wrote, "to face the threat which Hitler's behavior constituted to the world." Henri Barbusse wrote in *Le Monde* that the Nazis could not possibly put Germany's economy back on its feet; it was doomed, and after the collapse the German proletariat would reclaim its heritage. *Marianne,* a radical-socialist weekly, preached a steady pacifist line, coupled with announcements that if Hitler became chancellor he would soon be overthrown. In 1932 Romain Rolland drew up a manifesto, published in *Le Monde* and *Europe* and signed by André Gide, among others, which called upon all members of the French intelligentsia to vow "resistance against war." Writers, thinkers, academicians, continued to predict — despite mounting evidence to the contrary — that the two nations were moving toward a Franco-German rapprochement. Every leftist, every intellectual, was shouting simultaneously: "Down with fascism!" and "Disarmament

NOW!" Even as Germany's army swelled with illegal recruits, France's intelligentsia, de Beauvoir wrote, saw "no threat to peace"; the only danger was "the panic that the Right was spreading in France, with the aim of dragging us into war." In 1914 "the whole of the intellectual elite, Socialists, writers, and all," had "toed a wholly chauvinistic line." Their lesson "forbade us to envisage the very possibility of a war."[25]

This perilous illusion was not limited to France's intellectual community. Barbusse's shocking novel of the trenches, *Le Feu*, reached millions who had never heard of Sartre, Romain Rolland, Louis Aragon, André Gide, or Paul Eluard. Barbusse died in 1935, just as Hitler was becoming a household name in French provinces; over 300,000 readers followed his coffin to Père Lachaise Cemetery in Paris. Insulated in their Gallic world, the people for whom the Führer and his Reich were sharpening their swords assumed that everyone who had suffered in the trenches, or knew and loved those who had, shared their disgust of fighting. They should have been more attentive. There is a revealing vignette in *La Force de l'âge*. Sartre and de Beauvoir are boating down the Elbe to the rock of Heligoland. Sartre strikes up a conversation with a fellow passenger, a forty-year-old German wearing a black peaked cap and a morose expression. The German tells Sartre that he had been a sergeant in the Great War, and, his voice rising, says: "If there is another war, this time we shall not be defeated. We shall retrieve our honor." Sartre thinks the poor fellow feels shamed because his side lost; being simple, the ex-sergeant needs reassurance that war's horrors lie in the past, never to return. He mildly remarks that there is no need of war; everyone wants peace. But he is facing a *sorte* he has never seen before: a real *Kämpfer* (warrior), incapable of forgetting or forgiving. Glaring, the man replies, "Honor comes first. First we must retrieve our honor." De Beauvoir wrote: "His fanatical tone alarmed me. . . . Never had I seen hatred shine so nakedly [*à nu*] from any human face." She tried to reassure herself "with the reflection that an ex-serviceman is bound to hold militaristic views," yet added, "How many such were there, who lived only for the moment when the great day of revenge would come?"[26]

Churchill was warning of Germany's yearning for revenge, but the casual visitor to Berlin that fall of 1932 would have seen few signs of it. The Zitadelle — the monumental government buildings over which the kaisers had reigned — seemed more effete than Paris and devoid of that indefinable tone which had once given the city its Lutheran ambience: an air of hard, clean, righteous high purpose, of noble masculinity, of spartan Prussian virtues at their most demanding and most admirable. Now all that was gone. Berlin was, in fact, conspicuous for its lack of any virtue whatever. It had become the new Babylon.

Before the Great War it had been Paris which had seethed with sinful romance, illicit intrigue; if you wanted to spend a weekend with your young secretary, you asked Cook's to book you a suite near the Place de l'Étoile. In those days Pigalle, the mean streets behind *Les Halles,* the notorious *maisons de joi* in the winding little rue de la Huchette, a block from Notre Dame, had been the most lurid attractions for those exploring what then passed for European decadence. No more: it now was Berlin. "Along the Kurfürstendamm," wrote Stefan Zweig, "powdered and rouged young men sauntered, and in the dimly lit bars one might see men of the world of finance courting drunken sailors"; while at transvestite balls, "hundreds of men costumed as women and hundreds of women as men danced under the benevolent eye of the police."[27]

Over two million young German women were destitute widows. The more desperate (and attractive) of them became prostitutes, seeking prey in the alleys near the Hauptbahnhof. Among them were muscular whores with whips and mothers in their early thirties, teamed with their teenaged daughters to offer *Mutter-und-Tochter* sex. Tourists were shocked by the more infamous night spots: the Kabarett Tingle-Tangle, the Apollo, the Monokel (*"die Bar der Frau"* — for lesbians), and the White Mouse, whose most sensational performer, and the role model for thousands of German girls in the Weimar years, was Anita Berber, who danced naked, mainlined cocaine and morphine, and made love to men and women sprawled atop bars, bathed in spotlights, while voyeurs stared and fondled one another. Anita was dead at twenty-nine. So, by then, was the Weimar Republic.

It was in these years that Europeans began importing not only movies but also the most trivial and seamiest exports of American mass culture. Everyone knew about Prohibition gangsters, and how they led to political corruption. That made them attractive, even fascinating. Viennese, Romans, Berliners, and Parisians formed cults around *les bandits américains,* as they were called in France, and, in one Lutzow-Platz graffito, *"die Häuptlinger der Chicagoer und New-Yorker Unterwelt — Al Capone, Jack Diamond, und Lucky Luciano."* So sedulously had they been aped in Italy that twenty-two-year-old Alberto Moravia devoted his first novel, *Gli indifferenti* (*The Time of Indifference*), to a devastating parable of depravity in Rome. New Orleans' Mardi Gras was the model for Germany's new *Faschingszeit;* the Tiller Girls at Berlin's Scala Theater were a frank imitation of the Ziegfeld chorus line; a clever wisecracker was a *Schnauze* (big mouth). Night clubs featured bands mimicking — and sometimes unintentionally parodying — American jazz combos. Week after week an advertisement ran in Munich's *Süddeutsche Monatshefte* crying: *"So dürfen Sie nicht Charleston tanzen!"*[28]

It had become fashionable to blame the global Depression on the collapse of the New York Stock Exchange three years earlier. Certainly the Crash was an important link in the chain; but the causes, the implications, and the sequence of events were international and too complex to be within the range of understanding then. The Great War had impoverished victors and vanquished alike. The Allies, however, believed they could recover their losses by making the losers pay. It was one of history's more tragic errors.

Once they began computing the cost of civilian property damage — not to mention what was called "the estimated capitalized value" of the five million Allied fighting men killed in the war — the Allied statesmen found themselves dealing with stupendous sums, billions of dollars. At Versailles they finally arrived at a rough figure: $31,530,500,000. This was their reparations bill, they declared, and Germany must pay it. The Allies, under the threat of renewed fighting, demanded an immediate down payment of five billion dollars — nearly thirty-three billion in 1980s currency. Also, the Germans must pay off Belgium's war loans. Also, interest on the unpaid balance. Also, a 26 percent tax on all German exports.

The terms were exorbitant, vindictive, and preposterous. John Maynard Keynes denounced Versailles as "a Carthaginian Peace." Churchill, who disapproved of the entire treaty, especially the punitive clauses, called the reparations "monstrous" and "malignant." Actually, there was no way that the leaders of the new German republic, struggling to find its feet in Weimar, could meet this absurd bill. They tried. But their government had no international credit. Germany's prewar commercial system had been destroyed by the Allied blockade. Rich Germans, anticipating heavy taxation, were fleeing abroad with their fortunes. After seven months, the mark sank to an all-time low: five million to the dollar. Then it dropped out of sight.

As the worldwide economic crisis deepened, Americans rescued the tottering German republic, first with loans and then with outright gifts of over ten million dollars. Once the New York stock market crashed, however, Wall Street had to look to its own. Helpless, Weimar staggered on the brink of ruin, maintaining the appearance of solvency by feats of legerdemain. Anti-Americans, forgetting the huge gifts, blamed Germany's plight on the United States. Some Tories even resented the fact that Churchill's mother had been American. Stanley Baldwin spoke contemptuously of "the low intellectual ability" of people in the United States; Neville Chamberlain agreed with him.

On one count Americans were guilty. European respect for U.S. diplomacy had been skidding since President Woodrow Wilson's departure from Versailles. In 1919 the U.S. Senate had rejected the Versailles covenants, including membership in the League of Nations, Wilson's creation, and his pledge to guarantee France's borders. After Wilson's death a succession of Republican presidents, reflecting the mood of U.S. voters, had been turned inward, devoting their attention to domestic issues. During the interwar years this doctrine was christened isolationism. At the same time, America's leaders kept nagging their former allies to pay their unpayable war debts. England could easily have paid her war debts to the United States had France paid *her* debts to England. But France was flat broke, which meant the British were stuck, which meant hands-across-the-sea met in a clammy grasp. Washington was unsympathetic. President Calvin Coolidge didn't want to hear about the Exchequer's problems; he wanted cash. He said: "They hired the money, didn't they?" Before the war Americans had been popular in Europe. But by the early 1930s Washington's repeated insistence that the hired money be repaid merely heightened the tension Over There.

Even more troubling was the U.S. absence from Geneva. It had dealt a devastating blow to the League of Nations. But in turning their backs on the problems of other great powers American isolationists were not alone. Immediately after the signing of the peace treaties in 1919 London drifted into a mild form of the American introversion, and one by one the chancelleries on the Continent followed their example, leaving the intricacies of external affairs to their foreign ministries.

The professional diplomats, delighted, turned to what they did best, assembling in huge conferences, immaculate in their striped trousers, wing collars, and pince-nez, solemnly initialing pacts and protocols which were later signed, on their recommendation, by their governments. By the end of the 1920s plenipotentiaries had bound the Continent in a fantastic web of signed documents bearing waxed seals and streaming ribbons, documents which, had they been honored, would have kept the peace. Czechoslovakia, Yugoslavia, and Rumania were linked in the Little Entente. France was pledged to the defense of Poland; Italy to Yugoslavia, Albania, Hungary, and Austria. The climax was the cluster of pacts solemnized at Locarno, Switzerland, in 1925. Locarno guaranteed the German-French and German-Belgian frontiers and provided for the arbitration of any disputes between Germany on the one hand, and France, Belgium, Poland, and Czechoslovakia on the other. Finally, to assure the territorial integrity of the Czechs, France signed a separate treaty promising to declare war on Germany if the Germans violated Czechoslovakia's borders. Italy and Britain joined in the mutual guarantee of peace in western Europe, and though British obligations were vague, Britain was already pledged to stand by France in any war.

The Wilhelmstrasse had sent a delegation to Locarno. Its legates moved gracefully through the great halls, elegant and charming, clicking heels, kissing hands, and in the "spirit of Locarno," as it was being hailed, added their signatures to the others on December 1, 1925. Foreign correspondents were baffled. Why were Germans there? These pacts were negotiated by nations with armies and navies. As a military power Germany had ceased to exist. The Treaty of Versailles had drawn the Junkers' teeth. Their army, or Reichswehr, as it had been renamed, could not exceed 100,000 men, including officers. Even tiny Belgium outnumbered them. They were allowed no military aircraft, no General Staff, no conscription, and no manufacture of arms and munitions without written permission from the triumphant Allies. Their navy was restricted to six battleships, six light cruisers, twelve torpedo boats — and no submarines. Weimar Germany was forbidden fortification of her own frontiers, and a demilitarized buffer zone, the Rhineland, separated her from the French and Belgians. Violation of any of these provisions were to be regarded as a declaration of war, punishable by an Allied military occupation of the German republic. Thus manacled, the defeated country constituted a threat to no one. Her delegation, the inquiring newspapermen were told, had been invited to Locarno as a gracious gesture, a sign that the wounds of 1918 were healing.[29]

Veteran correspondents were skeptical. The foreign policies of great powers, they knew, are not guided by generosity. Nor were they in this instance. The fact was that the Germans had acquired their invitations by diplomatic blackmail. Versailles had stigmatized not one, but two great nations; the victors had turned their backs on both the defeated Second Reich, excluded from the peace conference, and the new Soviet Union, which in 1917 had taken Russia — then an Allied power, fighting Germany — out of the war. Walter Rathenau, a brilliant Weimar statesman, had seized his chance. Taking advantage of a Genoa conference at which European diplomats were discussing the economic prospects of the Continent, he had slipped away to meet a Bolshevik delegation at nearby Rapallo. Since the Russians had not participated in the 1919 peace settlement, they could join Germany in renouncing all war claims. Extensive agreements, signed at the same time, drew them closer together. Two months later, on June 24, 1922, Rathenau was murdered by right-wing German nationalists. But the Rapallo Treaty stood.[30]

The Allies had been shocked. They realized, for the first time, that the independent German government could make important commitments without their consent. Thus the invitation to Locarno. There, Rathenau's successor, Gustav Stresemann, smoothly reassured them. Nervous Allied ministries were reminded that Germany was their shield against the Soviet Union.

❦ ❦

Germany's former enemies listened carefully, wanting to believe. The Second Reich was dead. They cherished the hope that a stable German republic would serve as a bulwark against Russian adventurism. Another Allied incentive was anxiety; they knew that the kaiser's embittered officer corps refused to believe their army had been defeated on the battlefield and that the fighting qualities of German men were awesome.

A third motive was guilt. The Great War, by bankrupting both sides and destroying an entire generation of future leaders, eroded the confidence of the victors. Man, shocked by his inhumanity to man, was uncomfortable; he sought ways to ease his conscience. The transformation was not achieved overnight, but as the years passed a feeling deepened in London and Paris that the Central Powers had been shabbily treated at the Versailles peace conference. Allied casualties had been appalling, but at least they knew the jubilation of winning. When Germany and the two weaker members of her alliance had laid down their arms, they had lost 3,393,193 dead and 8,267,532 wounded. In defeat every conceivable humiliation had been visited upon them. Private property abroad belonging to German citizens had been summarily confiscated. The Kiel Canal and the country's five great rivers had been designated international waterways, like the English Channel or the Mediterranean. German representatives at the peace conference had been forced to sign the treaty's Article 231, accepting responsibility "for causing all the loss and damage to which the Allied and Associated Governments and their nationals have been subjected as a consequence of the war imposed upon them by the aggression of Germany and her allies."

Friedrich Ebert, provisional president of the new Weimar Republic, had called it "unbearable." The chancellor cried: "May the hand wither that signs this treaty!" The Allies, unmoved, issued an ultimatum. If the terms were not accepted, Allied troops would invade Germany. Ebert appealed to wartime chief of staff Paul von Hindenburg. Could such an attack be resisted? No, the field marshal replied, but he could not "help feeling that it were better to perish than sign such a humiliating peace [*Schmachfrieden*]." This was an outright evasion of responsibility. Because of it, Ebert, unsupported by the officer corps — the men who had actually lost the war — approved the treaty nineteen minutes before the Allied ultimatum ran out. It was an inauspicious start for the German republic.[31]

In November 1932 Churchill urged revision of Versailles "in cold blood and in a calm atmosphere and while the victor nations still have ample superiority, [rather] than to wait and drift on, inch by inch and stage by stage, until once again vast combinations, equally matched confront each other face to face." As the searing memoirs, best-selling novels, gripping plays, and popular films put the conflict in a new perspective, newspapers on both sides revealed the vast profits reaped by munitions tycoons. Holding the Germans solely responsible for the tragedy of 1914–1918, people now realized, had distorted the truth and violated the honor of the losers. It had amounted to an imposition of vindictive conditions on helpless men, forbidden, at the time, even to protest.[32]

By the early 1930s, however, the strongest emotion aroused in Germany's neighbors was primitive terror. The Germans knew it; they had deliberately provoked it in two wars, and had even given it a name, *Schrecklichkeit* (frightfulness). The nineteenth-century Prussian strategist Karl von Clausewitz had encouraged it as a means of shortening wars by putting the enemy "in a situation in which continuing the war is more oppressive to him than surrender." Teutonic troops, armed and dangerous, *were* frightful. They had practiced *Schrecklichkeit* in 1914, when bands of French and Belgian guerrillas defending their own soil had led to German executions of civilians, hostages, and prisoners of war. "Suddenly," Barbara Tuchman writes, "the world became aware of the beast beneath the German skin."[33]

In the 1920s and 1930s, accounts of these crimes were suppressed by pacifists in *das Ausland,* that revealing German term which welded all nations outside the Reich into a single collective noun. The new line was that all tales of German atrocities in the Great War had been Allied propaganda. But Belgians who had treated their invaders with disrespect had in fact been led before firing squads as early as the second day of the war. German records proved it. If Belgian refugees slowed the German advance, hostages were picked at random and killed.[34] One can find their gravestones today, inscribed: "*1914: Fusillé par les Allemands*" — "Shot by the Germans."

It was the dread of another such nightmare which provided the more powerful drive behind the grid of interlocking treaties culminating at Locarno. Even after Versailles, Germany remained the most powerful nation in Europe, with a population exceeding that of either Britain or France by thirty million. Geographical position alone seemed fated to guarantee Germany domination of Europe. Hitler's Nazis attracted the attention of chancelleries of Europe as Hitler set forth his goals, giving priority to the union of all Germans in a greater Germany. The very idea made foreign ministries tremble. Were it achieved, the smaller nations would confront a monolith of eighty-two million Teutons. A reconstituted Reich under strong leadership could reassemble the kaiser's dismantled juggernaut.[35]

Thus German signatures on the Locarno Pact had been welcomed. Despite Germany's violation of Belgian neutrality in 1914 — dismissing the Wilhelmstrasse's written pledge not to do so as *"ein Fetzen Papier"* ("a scrap of paper") — it was still inconceivable that a civilized nation would break its word. Great powers did not invade other states until war had been formally declared. If Locarno and Weimar's other postwar commitments were to be treated as scraps, diplomacy would be meaningless. Therefore, foreign ministries watched the tumultuous course of German politics in 1932 with increasing uneasiness. The Nazis were scum, men bereft of honor as Europe's ruling classes understood it. Late in the year a French agent, burrowed in the Wilhelmstrasse, sent the Quai d'Orsay a shocking report on the ten-year-old Russo-German treaty which Walter Rathenau had negotiated in Rapallo. A secret protocol, drafted by Foreign Minister Rathenau himself, had specified that the Russians would set aside tracts of land where the Germans would lay new foundations for the development of armament technique. There, too, German bombers and fighter planes were being assembled and German pilots, navigators, and bombardiers trained. The agent in Berlin was absolutely reliable. His French control in the Deuxième Bureau was badly shaken, but after he had regained his poise he felt baffled by one detail. Rathenau's assassins had been identified and interrogated. Their militant nationalism was clear. They wanted a new, rearmed Reich. Why had they slain a diplomat who had rendered their cause so priceless a service? The decoded reply was: "Rathenau was a Jew."[36] The Quai d'Orsay was dumbfounded. Would they, they wondered, *ever* understand the Germans?

In Berlin the world's longest breadline stretched down the Kurfürstendamm. Over fifteen million Germans were on the dole. In the streets husky, brown-shirted storm troopers (*Sturmtrupper*), wearing their high-crowned caps and black-on-white-on-red swastikas (*Hakenkreuz*, literally "hooked cross"), clubbed and battered men suspected of leftist sympathies, Jews of every age and sex, and anyone who failed to raise a stiff-armed *heil* when a Nazi band marched past under the banner *"Deutschland erwache!"* ("Germany awake!")

None of this was, in itself, extraordinary. In 1932 hunger and bloodshed haunted every great capital. But there was a significant difference in German turmoil. The drafters of Versailles had mutilated the kaiser's Second Reich in every way except the one which counted most. The internal structure of Wilhelmine Germany had been left intact. Because the judges in Weimar courtrooms had belonged to the prewar privileged class and regarded the republic as a puppet regime installed by enemies of the Reich, Nazi street fighters who murdered their political opponents in broad daylight, with dozens of witnesses testifying against them, received suspended sentences and five-mark fines. At the same time, supporters of the republic were sentenced to long prison terms for revealing, in speeches or newspapers, that the Reichswehr was rebuilding the army in defiance of Germany's pledge to the Allies. Franz L. Neumann writes: "It is impossible to escape the conclusion that political justice is the blackest page [*schwärzeste Seite*] in the life of the German Republic."[37]

Leniency was extended even to those rightists for whom the aristocracy had little sympathy. After the Armistice, Munich became the center of revolutionary conspiracies, including the successful plot to kill Rathenau and Hitler's unsuccessful putsch of 1923, an act of high treason in which nineteen men lost their lives while the Nazi leader fled the scene and hid from the police. Tracked down and arrested, Hitler spent only nine months in Landsberg prison, cossetted by every comfort the warden could provide, including writing materials. When he left his spacious "cell," he carried the manuscript of *Mein Kampf* under his arm, and as he emerged from the prison gate his supporters hailed him as a victorious hero.[38]

Until the Depression the Nazis had been a lunatic fringe. In 1928 they polled some 810,000 votes — 2.6 percent of those cast. The economic crises brought them swollen rolls and made Hitler a national figure. Oswald Spengler wrote: "In the heart of the people the Weimar Constitution is already doomed!" Two elections — in 1930 and 1932 — demonstrated that the Nazis, although shy of a working majority, had emerged as the country's largest political party. It was also the most violent. "We want a dictatorship!" Hitler cried, and his deputies left no doubt of their scorn for democratic procedures. In the Reichstag and the Prussian Diet they wore their uniforms, swung their fists and clubs, and disrupted any session which seemed about to reach agreement on a substantive issue by hurling any object which came to hand, including, according to one account, "inkwells, water bottles, desk drawers, chairs, ledgers, broken table legs." Having driven all others from the chamber, the Nazis "spent the next half-hour triumphantly roaring old war songs."

With few exceptions, Churchill among them, foreign politicians were unalarmed by Hitler. To *Time,* amused by his pretentiousness, Hitler was a "bristle-lipped, slightly pot-bellied" forty-three-year-old who often "stroked his tuft of brown mustache." Those with no command of the German tongue regarded him as a comical figure bearing a close resemblance to Charlie Chaplin. Even foreign correspondents underrated him. They reasoned that the heart of the Nazi constituency lay in the lower middle class, and that the upper classes would be alienated by the party's leader, whose wartime rank had been that of corporal.[39]

Until 1932 they had been right. National Socialism had been a stigma. Among well-born Germans, the Nazi party was regarded as coarse. But that autumn they were beginning to understand that the door of history had been shut on their Augustan Age of princes and potentates and plumed marshals and glittering little regular armies — on all the fanfaronade that had marked their disciplined, secure world. In the waning autumn of 1932, when Americans were voting Franklin D. Roosevelt into the White House, the German patriciate was reassessing its view of Hitler. The eminent *Deutsche Allgemeine Zeitung*, always reflective of their opinion, abruptly abandoned its hostile treatment of National Socialism and urged Reich President Hindenburg to overcome his "strong personal dislike" of the Nazi leader and appoint him chancellor "in the interests of that tranquillity required for business revival."[40]

Once Hitler moved, he moved fast. Nazi deputies, though still short of an absolute majority, outnumbered the Social Democrats nearly two-to-one and dominated the Reichstag. Nevertheless, Field Marshal Hindenburg, Ebert's successor to the figurehead post of president, refused to appoint Hitler chancellor. The Chancellor Crisis followed. Running the government was impossible without the Nazi deputies, who, on Hitler's orders, vetoed each Hindenburg nominee for the office. Then Franz von Papen and General Kurt von Schleicher, the two strongest conservatives, agreed on a remarkable solution. Name Hitler chancellor, they told the Reich president, and they would manipulate him. Pandora's box was thereupon pried open, and on January 30, 1933, Hitler was sworn in as chancellor, or, as he preferred to be called, Reich chancellor — chancellor of the Empire. His expression, caught by a cameraman, was one of ecstasy. With his grasp of the Teutonic mind, he knew that now, having acquired *Autorität* by legal means, he would be accepted and obeyed by the German people, and that if he continued to pay lip service to Weimar's constitution, he could use it to destroy itself.[41]

He appointed Hermann Göring president of the Reichstag, and Göring moved into the Präsidentenpalast (Reichstag President's Palace). An underground passage, part of the central heating system, connected the Präsidentenpalast and the Reichstag building. Less than a month after Hitler became chancellor — five days before a new election — an arsonist or arsonists entered the Reichstag building through this tunnel and set it ablaze. Hitler swiftly exploited the tumult; he persuaded the anxious, confused Hindenburg to sign a decree for the protection of *Volk und Staat* which, in effect, put the entire country under martial law. The chancellor could and did gag his political opponents, terrorize them, and silence all but the boldest, who were arrested. Over four thousand figures in public life, including Reichstag deputies, were thrown into jail. Later the hard core of his opposition were moved to Dachau, the first Nazi concentration camp, and never knew freedom again.

As the election campaign approached its climax the Nazis, needing money, sought it from the titans of German industry. Göring invited them to the Präsidentenpalast — to respecters of *Autorität* the invitation had the force of a command — and on arrival they were seated in carefully arranged armchairs, with Gustav Krupp von Bohlen in the place of honor and four I. G. Farben directors immediately behind him. Hitler entered and faced them. "We are about to hold the last election," he began and paused to let the full implications of that sink in. Naturally, he said, the transition to National Socialism would be smoother if the party was swept in by a landslide. Therefore, he solicited their support. In backing a dictatorship they would be backing themselves: "Private enterprise cannot be maintained in a democracy." Using his "authority and personality," he assured them, he would not only eliminate the Communist threat; he would abolish the trade unions and restore the Wehrmacht to its former glory. "Regardless of the outcome" at the polls, there would be "no retreat." If he lost he would stay in office "by other means . . . with other weapons." The chancellor sat down and Krupp sprang up to express "the unanimous feeling of the industrialists in support of the chancellor." Göring reminded them of the point of the meeting. Dr. Hjalmar Schacht, the Nazi financial wizard, cried more bluntly: "And now, gentlemen, pony up!" Once again Krupp, as senior man, rose to pledge a million marks, and Schacht collected two million more from the others.[42]

Financed by German industrialists, Hitler led the bloodiest election campaign in European history. Every night trucks bearing squads of brownshirted storm troopers thundered down streets and alleys all over the country, breaking down doors, dragging away their critics to be beaten and tortured. Bonfires blazed on hilltops and the storm troopers held torchlight parades, singing the party anthem. By day other party columns marched down thoroughfares, public address loudspeakers brayed martial music. Billboards were plastered with Nazi posters. Swastikas decorated telegraph poles.

It worked. The Nazis polled 17,277,180 votes; the Social Democrats 7,181,629. With the support of sympathetic nationalist deputies, Hitler could muster an absolute majority in the Reichstag. He needed more than that, however. His immediate goal was passage of an enabling act giving him dictatorial powers. Only a constitutional amendment could grant that, and amendments required two-thirds of the deputies. To the new chancellor, this presented no obvious problem; armed with his extraordinary decree, he could bar opposition deputies from entering Reichstag sessions, or, if they became unruly, arrest them.

But Hitler, though evil, was an evil genius; he recognized the necessity of mollifying the old Wilhelmine order, particularly the officer corps. If they backed him, the country would feel a sense of continuity, strengthening the impression of Nazi legitimacy. Thus he announced that the Third Reich's first Reichstag would convene in Potsdam's Garrison Church, the very temple of Prussianism, where the Hohenzollern sovereigns had prayed and Frederick the Great lay buried. He turned the session into an obsequious tribute to Hindenburg. André François-Poncet, the French ambassador, wrote that after this performance, "how could . . . the Junkers and monarchist barons . . . hesitate to grant him their entire confidence, to meet all his requests, to concede the full powers he claimed?"[43]

Two days later, in the Kroll Opera House in Berlin, the Reichstag voted 444 to 84 to give Hitler his dictatorial powers. The Enabling Act of March 23, 1933, transferred from the deputies to their chancellor the powers to make laws, control the budget, ratify treaties with foreign countries, and initial constitutional amendments. Thus ended the fourteen-year German republic. *Autorität* had been punctiliously observed every step along the way. "It was no victory," wrote Spengler, "for enemies were lacking."[44]

In one of his more magnanimous moments, Churchill said of the Reich's future führer: "I admire men who stand up for their country in defeat, even though I am on the other side." Hitler, he added, had "a perfect right to be a patriotic German if he chose." Winston's son, Randolph, then a journalist, had accompanied the Nazi leader during his first, peaceful 1932 campaign, and later, when the returns showed a sharp increase in Nazi voters, Randolph had sent him a telegram of congratulation. His father, however, was less enthusiastic now. In Hitler's speeches, *The Times* had reported, he was demanding *Wehrfreiheit* (military freedom), a euphemism for German rearmament. Many MPs thought he might have a point, that *Wehrfreiheit* was worth discussing. In May 1932 Churchill asked them: "Do you wish for war?" Two months later he declined to join those acclaiming the Lausanne Conference, which had virtually ended reparations. How, he wondered, would Germany spend the money she owed the Allies? He felt apprehensive. Germany might rearm, he said, and cited a recent warlike statement by Hitler, "who is the moving impulse behind the German government and may be more than that soon."[45]

Churchill and Hitler almost met. Although still shaky from his New York automobile accident, Winston was moving ahead in mid-1932 with the research for his biography of his great ancestor, the first Duke of Marlborough. In the summer of 1932, he and a small entourage of friends and relatives toured Marlborough's old battlefields on the Continent. After a day on the field at Blenheim, he rested in Munich's Regina Hotel. The Nazis were, of course, aware that he was in the country. Inevitably, the Churchill party was approached, and their envoy was skillfully chosen. Ernst ("Putzi") Hanfstaengl was a Harvard graduate, a friend of Randolph's, and the millionaire son of a German father and a wealthy American mother. He was also the man who had given Hitler asylum after the aborted Nazi putsch of 1923. Putzi joined the Englishmen for cocktails. After he had played some of Churchill's favorite tunes on a lobby piano, they dined together.

The issue of German politics was raised almost immediately. Putzi offered to introduce Winston to his idol. Nothing would be easier, he said; Hitler came to the hotel every evening at five o'clock and would be delighted to meet so great a British statesman. It was all arranged, and then Churchill disarranged it. He asked Hanfstaengl: "Why is your chief so violent about the Jews? I can quite understand being angry with Jews who have done wrong or who are against the country, and I understand resisting them if they try to monopolise power in any walk of life; but what is the sense of being against a man simply because of his birth? How can any man help how he is born? Tell your boss for me that anti-Semitism may be a good starter, but it is a bad stayer."

Putzi's face fell. The next day he solemnly informed Winston that the meeting was off; Hitler had other plans. Since Churchill and his party remained at the Regina for a full week with no further overtures, he concluded that his disapproval of Nazi anti-Semitism had blacklisted him. So it had, but the story has an interesting envoi. Hitler had told Hanfstaengl: "In any case, what part does Churchill play? He is in the opposition and no one pays any attention to him." Putzi shot back: "People said the same thing about you." For this and other flippancies, Putzi, who had not only sheltered Hitler but had also given generously to his war chests, would later flee for his life, thus joining the extraordinary exodus from Germany of the blameless and the gifted. Hitler, in effect, exiled German intellectual life. During his first year in power he drove 1,600 scholars out of the country, including a quarter of the Heidelberg faculty and five Nobel laureates.[46]

In Parliament Churchill continued to urge revision of Versailles but vehemently opposed *Wehrfreiheit,* warning that accepting equality of armaments "would be almost to appoint the day for another European war — to fix it as if it were a prize-fight." Sounding the alarm even before Hitler moved into the chancellery, he wrote in the *Daily Mail* on October 17, 1932, that General Schleicher had "already declared that whatever the Powers may settle, Germany will do what she thinks fit in rearmament. Very grave dangers lie along these paths, and if Great Britain . . . encouraged Germany in such adventures, we might in an incredibly short space of time [be] plunged into a situation of violent peril." He told the House: "Now the demand is that Germany should be allowed to rearm. Do not delude yourselves. Do not let His Majesty's Government believe — I am sure they do not believe — that all that Germany is asking for is equal status. . . . That is not what Germany is seeking. All these bands of sturdy Teutonic youths, marching through the streets and roads of Germany, with the light of desire in their eyes . . . are not looking for status. They are looking for weapons."[47]

Perhaps nothing underscores the difference between German and British moods in the early 1930s so starkly as the political activities of their university undergraduates. In Oxford they were vowing never to fight, even in defense of England, while in Heidelberg, H. R. Knickerbocker of the *New York Evening Post* found, nearly three out of every four students were dues-paying Nazis. A German historian points out that Heidelberg, like Oxford, had preserved its "traditionalist, socially exclusive structure," but that the German youths from privileged families were suppressing student groups supporting the republic in Berlin by "a powerful union of nationalist, *völkisch*-oriented, and above all dueling fraternities." They campaigned strenuously against what they called the "Jewification" of the universities. Weimar's Ministry of Culture tried to end discrimination against "non-Aryan" undergraduates, but this merely brought "a further radicalization, increasing disorders and a further growth of National Socialist propaganda." Even "the majority of German writers," according to Günter Grass, "made no attempt to defend the republic, while not a few of them deliberately held it up to ridicule."[48]

The rightward drift in academe and the intellectual community was of profound significance. In Germany, as in England, most undergraduates came from upper-class families. Because their commitment to National Socialism was often decisive in determining parental commitment, the trend toward the hakenkreuz enlisted the lives, the fortunes, and the sacred honor of the country's traditional ruling oligarchies, including their children, who would inherit tomorrow's Germany.

Meantime, the Oxford Union's resolution that it would "in no circumstances fight for King and Country" had aroused Churchill's wrath. He called it an "abject, squalid, shameless avowal," a "very disquieting and disgusting symptom." Its impact abroad, he said, would be disastrous. He thought "of Germany, with its splendid clear-eyed youth marching forward . . . burning to suffer and die for their fatherland," and of "Italy, with her ardent Fascisti." He said: "One can almost feel the curl of contempt upon the lips of the manhood of all these peoples when they read this message sent out by Oxford University in the name of young England."[49]

In early 1934 Oxford's Tories invited him to speak, and he accepted — unwisely, for it was impossible for him to force entry into the locked minds of British undergraduates in the early 1930s; earlier, the Cambridge Union had voted 213 to 138 for "uncompromising" pacifism. But he couldn't resist a fight. He agreed to appear and answer twelve prepared questions. That part of the evening went well. It was afterward, during a general discussion, that he ran into trouble. Among the five hundred students present was a German Rhodes scholar, Adolf Schlepegrell. Schlepegrell pointed out that Versailles had specified a Saar plebiscite, scheduled for 1935, to determine whether it would join France or Germany. Since the population was German, the results were a foregone conclusion. Schlepegrell suggested a generous gesture — an immediate withdrawal of French troops stationed there. Churchill, in his most combative mood, rejected the idea. Germany must abide by the letter of Versailles, he said, because she "started the war," thereby "plunging the whole world into ruins." The young German quickly asked: "Does Mr. Churchill believe that the German people, the men and women who live in Germany today, are responsible for the war? Would he please answer 'yes' or 'no.' " Winston looked straight at him and replied: "Yes." The youth bowed to him and, amid tremendous applause from his fellow students, walked out of the hall.[50]

Ironically, when Schlepegrell returned to Germany — where he had become a newspaper hero — the authorities found that one of his grandmothers had been Jewish, and this disqualified him from taking a bar examination. Eventually he became a naturalized British citizen and served as a political intelligence officer during World War II. So Churchill won in the end. But that sequel lay in the future, unknown, on that evening when he walked out on Winston and humiliated him in the eyes of Oxford. Nor was that all.

Later in the discussion, after the German's departure, Churchill declared British rearmament "essential for us to be safe in our island home," and the audience, to his surprise and consternation, burst into laughter. He repeated the phrase, and the laughter grew so raucous, and so prolonged, that he could not continue.[51]

A half-century later their mirth seems incomprehensible. Yet how could a generation informed by *Journey's End* and *All Quiet on the Western Front* have responded differently? They believed that Churchill was crying wolf. And they knew his alarm was groundless. As the new year arrived, a catchy tune from Walt Disney's *Three Little Pigs* was on everyone's lips:

> *Who's a-fraid of the big bad wolf, big bad wolf, big bad wolf?*
> *Who's a-fraid of the big bad wolf? Tra la la la la!*

ONE

SHOALS

NUMBER 10 Downing Street, at that time the most famous address in the world, is one of three gracious seventeenth-century houses built by George Downing, a Harvard man who returned to the country of his birth, became a Cromwellian civil servant, and designed No. 10, No. 11, and No. 12 as "large and well-built houses, fit for persons of honour and quality, each house to have a pleasant prospect into St. James's Park." Originally the properties of the Earl of Lichfield, they passed into royal hands when his lordship was undone by reckless gambling.[1]

Not all of No. 10's subsequent occupants were people of quality. King Charles II, the most promiscuous of the Stuarts, used it to house his kept women, who, when neglected by him, solicited passersby from windows and charged them fees. In 1732 King George II presented the building to Sir Robert Walpole, Britain's first prime minister, and ever since then it has been the London home of his successors (except Lord Salisbury, who preferred to live in his magnificent London mansion), just as No. 11 is the residence of the chancellor of the Exchequer and No. 12 the workplace of government whips. Because Walpole was also responsible for the kingdom's money, the front door of No. 10 bears a worn brass plate reading: "First Lord of the Treasury."[2]

If, during Churchill's last years as tenant, you were a young American foreign correspondent bearing an invitation to call here, that plate was the first thing you would have seen after the bobby at the door confirmed your appointment and checked your identity. Inside, on the ground floor, the house at first appeared to be, not the teeming hive of a world leader, but a lovely, somewhat quaint relic of the Restoration. Jock Colville has recalled that in the 1930s the atmosphere was that of any other comfortable upper-class London home, and that even after the outbreak of World War II Neville Chamberlain "disliked being disturbed, telephonically or otherwise, at weekends or after dinner at 10 Downing Street." But in some respects appearances were deceptive. There was more to No. 10 than at first met the eye — tunnels linked the building with No. 11 and No. 12, and the rear of

No. 10 joined the much larger Lichfield House, another possession which became crown property when the cards turned against the unlucky Lichfield.[3]

State rooms occupied the floor above, and a creaking old elevator led to the top floor, where the prime minister and his wife lived in guarded privacy. Most intriguing, however, for one who cherished the past, was the Cabinet Room on the ground floor. Outside, a row of coat pegs bore the names of the cabinet ministers, and a dapper man in striped trousers checked the P.M.'s appointments and studied documents from institutions responsible to No. 10's householder — that morning the documents came from, among others, the British Museum, the Church of England, and the ancient universities. Baize double doors led to the elegant cabinet chamber, centered around a dark, gleaming table. A secretary sat at a Victorian desk near the door; tall, well-proportioned windows overlooked the Horse Guards. The cabinet met at 11:00 A.M. on Tuesdays and Thursdays, but its members waited outside until the prime minister, seated with the secretary to the cabinet beside him, summoned them.[4]

Winston had first occupied a minister's chair at this table in 1908, at the age of thirty-three, when the entire world awaited decisions made here, and the future of millions, living in British possessions which most ministers hadn't even seen, depended on their judgments. In the last quarter of the twentieth century the greatness of the British Empire is a memory shared by a fraction of the population. The world was very different in 1932. Neither the United States nor the Soviet Union was a superpower. Powerful armies were found elsewhere, but Britannia continued to rule the world's waves, and her imperial resources were almost inexhaustible. The roar of the British lion was still deafening — not only in Europe, but in every time zone. In the aftermath of Waterloo an English journalist first observed that "the sun never sets upon the Union Jack." That was still true in the twenty-one-year interwar period which followed the Armistice of 1918, when decisions around this table, counterpoised with those made in Berlin's Reich Chancellery, profoundly altered the course of history.

Over the centuries No. 10 has been the home of men whose luster was not limited to Britain and whose names are household words, among them Chatham, Pitt, Melbourne, Peel, Palmerston, Disraeli, Gladstone, and Lloyd George. Although he had earlier been regarded as a future prime minister, during the 1930s Fleet Street saw Churchill as a wine which had passed its point. Still vigorous, still brilliant, he was nevertheless out of tune with the times. He was distrusted, disliked — even hated — by those who did not share his conviction that Germany threatened the peace and England must arm to defend her shores. The leaders of England's three political parties were convinced that Hitler would never make war if his demands were met with diplomatic finesse. In those years, when Britain was losing her eminence as the world's mightiest power, Churchill was pitted against three tenants of No. 10 whom Englishmen would prefer to forget, three political mediocrities who presided over disastrous policies which reduced Britannia to an embattled island struggling to survive — a struggle that only Churchill and his small band of followers, who would finally succeed them on the first stroke of twelve, believed could be won.

Who were they?

Ramsay MacDonald was of humble origins — a bastard, actually. In his early years he joined the socialist Fabian Society, and in 1924 he became England's first Labour prime minister. All his life he had been a pacifist; in 1914 he had condemned Britain's entry into the Great War, and his foreign policy concentrated on the limitation, and then the elimination, of armaments. Bewildered by the worldwide Depression, he was, by the early 1930s, a ruin of the man he had been. "The wretched Ramsay," Churchill wrote his wife, "is almost a mental case — he'd be far better off in a Home." His most striking weakness was his vanity. Leonine, with a magnificent thatch of snowy hair, he wanted to remain prime minister despite his repudiation at the polls in 1931. Stanley Baldwin, the leader of the Conservative party, was more interested in power than titles. Baldwin suggested that MacDonald remain at No. 10 as the leader of a coalition, the "National Emergency Government," while Baldwin actually took the reins in the House as its lord president. MacDonald agreed. On June 7, 1935, however, he and Baldwin exchanged offices. Two years later he was dead.

Stanley Baldwin, "S.B.," the ultimate politician, was a plain, unsophisticated, and outwardly modest man, affectionately known to Tory ladies as the "Dear Vicar." Yet he was the most powerful prime minister since Walpole; in one form or another, either singly or jointly with MacDonald, he held supreme power, with two short intervals, for fourteen years, from 1923 to 1937. He had no interest in events on the Continent; indeed, anything beyond England's shores, including her empire, bored him. His instructions to the Foreign Office were to avoid agreements with Russia, "keep us out of war," and buy "peace at any price." Bob Boothby recalled: "If at any time after 1929 you had asked him where he was going, he would have had difficulty in answering the question." Short and thick-set, he was the personification of John Bull; in an ambiguous comment, Churchill said that Baldwin "represented in a broad way some of the strengths and many of the infirmities of our island race."[5]

"Good Old Neville," Baldwin's successor as prime minister in 1937, was the son of the great Joseph Chamberlain, who considered him "entirely unsuitable for a political career." Lloyd George declared that Neville's vision was no greater than that of "a provincial manufacturer of bedsteads," and once he had found his footing at No. 10 the French gave him the sobriquet *Monsieur J'aime Berlin*. His half brother Austen was an eminent statesman and one of Churchill's few allies in his struggle to prepare England for the coming Nazi onslaught, but Neville was the narrowest of prime ministers. He is still the least understood. His image is that of a weakling waving a frail umbrella while cowering before fearsome Hitler. In fact, he was decisive, self-confident, and — as revealed in his diaries and his letters to his two sisters — domineering. Most of his life had been devoted to business, chiefly in Birmingham. He did not stand for Parliament until his fiftieth year. Sir John Simon, an admirer, wrote that when colleagues came to Neville he would "listen in a businesslike fashion to what one had to say, and then state his conclusions with the finality of a General Manager conducting his company's affairs." Chamberlain once told Ivan Maisky, the Soviet ambassador, he felt that "if only we could sit down at a table with the Germans and run through all their complaints and claims with a pencil, this would greatly relieve all tensions." Later he said: "I don't believe myself that we could purchase peace at a lasting settlement by handing over Tanganyika to the Germans, but if I did I would not hesitate for a moment to do so." He was passionately antiwar, in large part because it meant government interference in private enterprise, and the manufacture of armaments which would be useless when peace returned. All in all he was preeminently a man of the thirties, "highly competent," in the words of Telford Taylor, the historian and lawyer, "but grim and graceless." J. C. Davidson, later Viscount Davidson, described him as "a good Lord Mayor of Birmingham in a lean year." Chamberlain, Churchill said, looked at foreign affairs "through the wrong end of a municipal drainpipe."[6]

The arena where prime ministers and other Englishmen in public life perform — and whence, in Churchill's prime, the British Empire was ruled — is astonishingly small. Its length, between Trafalgar Square and Parliament, is six hundred yards; its breadth, from the Victoria Embankment along the Thames eastward to St. James's Park, three hundred yards. Within this small neighborhood are Downing Street, the Admiralty, Westminster Abbey, Parliament, Scotland Yard, and the Palace of Whitehall, now occupied by the Home Office, Commonwealth Office, and Foreign Office (called the FO or simply Whitehall). In World War II Churchill's bunker, an underground war room, lay beneath Storey's Gate, where Birdcage Walk, flanking the park, starts. The walk ends a thousand yards

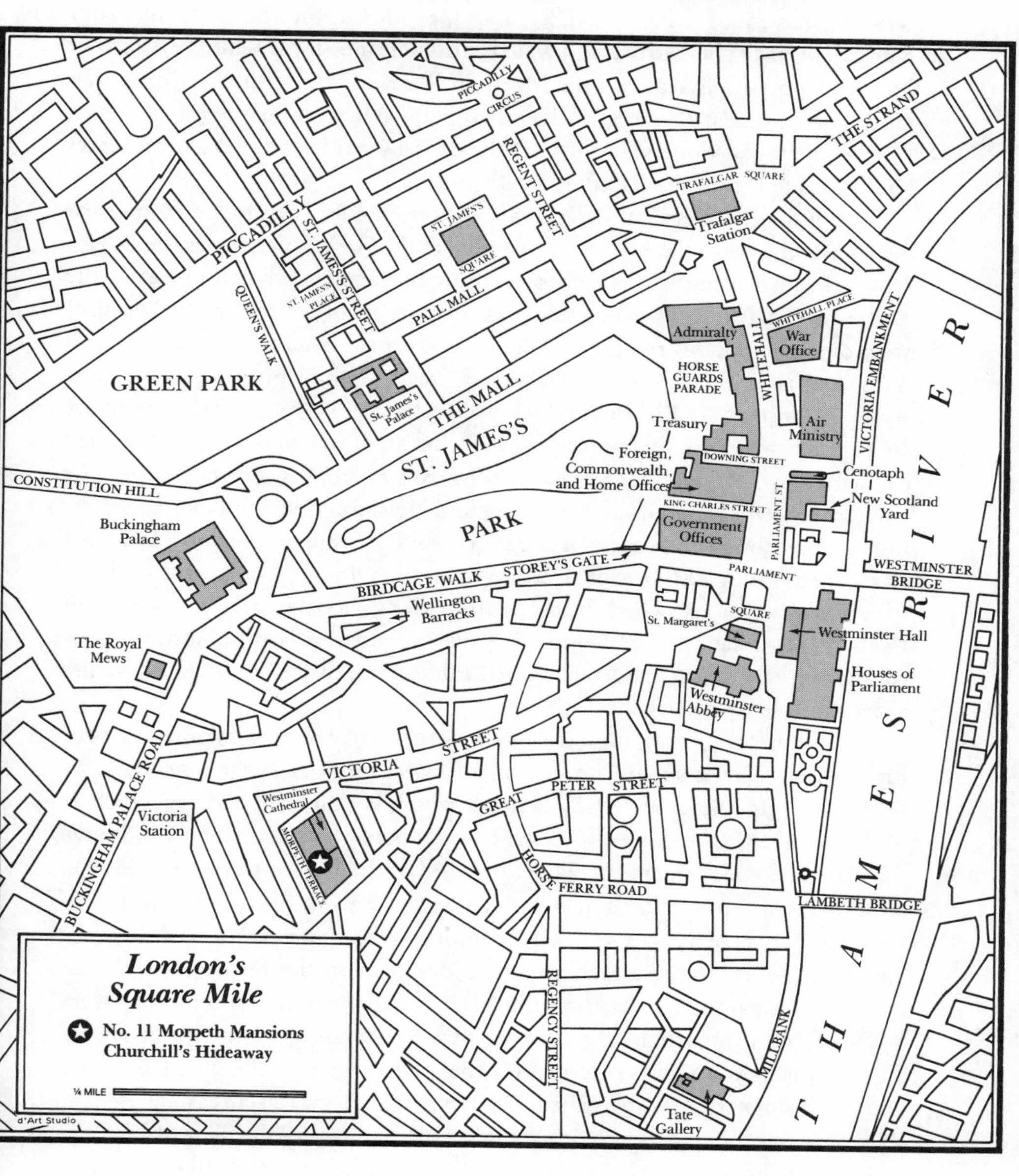

London's Square Mile
No. 11 Morpeth Mansions Churchill's Hideaway
¼ MILE
d'Art Studio
PICCADILLY CIRCUS
PICCADILLY
REGENT STREET
ST. JAMES'S SQUARE
ST. JAMES'S STREET
ST. JAMES'S PLACE
QUEEN'S WALK
PALL MALL
THE MALL
GREEN PARK
St. James's Palace
TRAFALGAR SQUARE
Trafalgar Station
THE STRAND
Admiralty
HORSE GUARDS PARADE
WHITEHALL
WHITEHALL PLACE
War Office
Air Ministry
Treasury
VICTORIA EMBANKMENT
ST. JAMES'S
PARK
Foreign, Commonwealth, and Home Offices
DOWNING STREET
Cenotaph
New Scotland Yard
KING CHARLES STREET
Government Offices
PARLIAMENT ST
CONSTITUTION HILL
Buckingham Palace
STOREY'S GATE
BIRDCAGE WALK
Wellington Barracks
PARLIAMENT SQUARE
WESTMINSTER BRIDGE
St. Margaret's
Westminster Hall
The Royal Mews
Westminster Abbey
Houses of Parliament
RIVER THAMES
VICTORIA STREET
GREAT PETER STREET
Westminster Cathedral
MORPETH TERRACE
Victoria Station
BUCKINGHAM PALACE ROAD
HORSE FERRY ROAD
LAMBETH BRIDGE
REGENCY STREET
MILLBANK
Tate Gallery

away at Buckingham Palace. On the opposite side of the park is the Mall, St. James's Palace, Pall Mall, and all the famous clubs, including White's, the Oxford and Cambridge, the Athenaeum, Brooke's, the Reform, which was the haven of Liberal MPs, and the site of the Carlton, its Tory equivalent until the Luftwaffe leveled it during the Blitz. Churchill's flat at No. 11 Morpeth Mansions on Morpeth Terrace was within walking distance of the entire area. His daughter Mary remembers it as a " 'maisonette-flat-duplex' — just off the unfashionable end of Victoria Street and opposite the Roman Catholic cathedral."[7]

Except for Buckingham Palace, whose householder is excluded from great decisions, these are the haunts of the powerful. Their epicenter is the Palace of Westminster, parts of which were built in the eleventh century after the Battle of Hastings. Westminster was a triumph of Victorian exuberance, with over a thousand rooms, a hundred staircases, over two miles of corridors, and an eight-acre roof. Towering, vast, Gothic, built in asymmetric style, and topped by Big Ben, which was installed in 1858, Westminster has an interior which is the accomplishment of an entire generation of skilled craftsmen, who embellished the palace's robing rooms, private suites for parliamentary leaders, its ancient crypt and cloisters, division lobbies, smoking rooms, libraries, processional gallery, and, of course, the two Houses of Parliament — the House of Lords, with seats for 1,100 peers, and the House of Commons, which is too small to accommodate all 635 members of Parliament. That was deliberate. Regular attendance is rare, intimacy encourages lively debate, and "a crowded House," in historic moments, creates a dramatic sense of urgency.

The Commons, now rebuilt, was Churchill's principal forum for over forty years, and it should be envisaged as he knew it, unchanged in 225 years, with its timbered ceiling beneath which lay the well and carved chair of the Speaker, who determined which members of Parliament should have the floor and could intervene when the rules of the House were violated. On either side of the Speaker's dias, stretching away from him to the far end of the chamber, rose five tiers of benches upholstered in green. An aisle — "the gangway" — cuts across each tier at midpoint. On the Speaker's right sat MPs of the party in power; on his left, facing them across the well, were MPs of the Opposition. The lowest bench extending from the Speaker's right to the gangway was reserved for the government — the prime minister and his ministers. It was called the front bench or the Treasury Bench, sharing a common ancestor with the brass plate adorning the door of No. 10.

Backbenchers — "private members" — sat wherever they liked, or, in a crowded House, wherever they could find room. Because of his past glories, however, by tacit understanding the first seat beyond the gangway on the lowest tier was reserved for Winston Churchill, the member for Epping. He cherished it; his father, Lord Randolph Churchill, also a rebel, had sat there in the 1880s. Only the width of the narrow gangway separated Winston from the governments he attacked so unmercifully throughout the 1930s. But his maxim was: "Never give in, never give in, never, never, never, never . . . never give in, except to convictions of honour or good sense."

❧ ❧

Hitler had been vexed by Putzi Hanfstaengl's jeu d'esprit, and understandably so. It was true that both Putzi's Nazi idol and his British dinner companion were out of office, and certainly no one was paying much attention to the visitor from England, either here or in his own country. But Hitler, whose political antennae were exceptionally acute, knew how anxiously informed Europeans, and particularly *Auslandspolitiker*, were following his rising star. What he did not know was the keenness with which Churchill was watching him, or how doggedly Churchill would stalk him for twelve years, until the Führer of the Third Reich lay dead by his own hand in the ruined Reich Chancellery garden, a corpse enveloped by the writhing flames of a Viking funeral, while the blackened hulks of what had once been Berlin collapsed all round him.

Precisely when Winston became aware of freedom's archenemy is uncertain. In his World War II memoirs he wrote of his stay in Munich, shortly before the Nazis came to power, "I had no national prejudice against Hitler at this time. I knew little of his doctrine or record and nothing of his character."[8] But that is an astonishing lapse of memory. By then he had been well informed about Hitler for two years, had published several appraisals of him, and had repeatedly warned the House of the imminent threat in central Europe. His perception was exceptional; an extraordinary number of his peers were completely hoodwinked.

Once he had moved into the chancellery, Hitler had let it be known that his door would be open to English political figures, and pilgrimages to him became fashionable. His guests returned glowing with optimism, reporting that the Reich chancellor, despite his savage rhetoric, was eager to reach a political settlement with other nations, an agreement exorcizing the threat of war for a decade. In retrospect this is puzzling. Diplomats had already forged such a settlement in two great treaties meant to guarantee peace, not for ten years, but for the rest of the century. The first had been signed at Versailles in 1919. Versailles was now discredited in the eyes of many, having sown seeds of resentment in Germany, but the Locarno Pact, enthusiastically signed by Germany in 1925, remained unslandered.

Yet within a decade of the Locarno agreement, Englishmen of power and influence were discussing new solutions as though this pact, despite its popularity in Germany, did not exist. Lord Lothian wrote *The Times:* "The central fact today is that Germany does not want war and is prepared to renounce it as a method of settling her disputes with her neighbors" — which is precisely what Germany *had* renounced, in writing, at Locarno. Thomas Jones, who had been in and out of Whitehall for a quarter century, wrote in his diary: "Rightly or wrongly, all sorts of people who have met Hitler are convinced that he is a factor for peace." Even after the German chancellor's aggressive intentions had become clear, Jones accompanied Lloyd George to Munich's Braunhaus — Nazi headquarters — and returned with the conviction that "Hitler does not seek war with us. He seeks our friendship. If we fail him, he will turn elsewhere and we shall be sorry to have refused him" — which, of course, was precisely the response their Braunhaus host had meant to invoke.[9]

Of greater interest, however, were the impressions of Jones's distinguished traveling companion. Meeting the press after he had been closeted with Hitler for an hour, Lloyd George said he regarded him as "the greatest living German," and had "told him so to his face." Back in England, Lloyd George wrote for the *Daily Express* — out of office like Churchill, he was struggling to make ends meet on his £300 salary as an MP, and journalism was a source of income for political celebrities — that the leader of the Nazis was "a born leader, a magnetic, dynamic personality with a single-minded purpose": to keep the peace. Lloyd George declared that with Hitler at the helm Germany would "never invade any other land." A year later he wrote to T. Philip Conwell-Evans, another admirer of the Nazis and one of Lothian's closest friends, of "the admiration which I personally feel for [Hitler]. . . . I only wish we had a man of his supreme quality at the head of affairs in our country today."[10]

No trap is so deadly as the one you set for yourself. Vernon Bartlett, a British journalist with a large following, spent forty minutes in Hitler's study. Afterward he wrote of his host's "large, brown eyes — so large and so brown that one might grow lyrical about them if one were a woman." Actually, Hitler's eyes were blue. Nazi goals were even applauded by Anglican clergymen, a group of whom expressed "boundless admiration for the moral and ethical side of the National Social programme, its clear-cut stand for religion and Christianity, and its ethical principles, such as its fight against cruelty to animals, vivisection, sexual offences, etc."[11]

Later there would be repentance, but the moving finger had writ, and neither sackcloth and ashes, nor magnums of tears could wash out a word of it. And none but Churchill, it seemed, was immune. The impressions of Sir John Simon, His Majesty's foreign secretary from 1931 to 1935, are among the most memorable. In Hitler he saw not arrogance but a man "rather retiring and bashful and of a certain mystical temperament . . . unconcerned with affairs in Western Europe." Later he described him to King George as "an Austrian Joan of Arc with a moustache." One expects more from Arnold Toynbee, but Toynbee, equally spellbound by the Reich chancellor, declared that he was "convinced of his sincerity in desiring peace in Europe and close friendship with England." The most painful toast to Hitler, for Americans, is a Walter Lippmann column which appeared in the *New York Herald Tribune* on May 19, 1933. Lippmann had heard a speech by the new chancellor, and described it as a "genuinely statesmanlike address," providing convincing "evidence of good faith." He told his readers: "We have heard once more, through the fog and the din, the authentic voice of a genuinely civilized people. I am not only willing to believe that, but it seems to me that all historical experience compels one to believe it." He went further. Persecuting the Jews served a purpose by "satisfying" Germans' yearning to "conquer somebody"; it was "a kind of lightning rod which protects Europe."[12] Walter Lippmann was a Jew.

Churchill didn't believe it. Ever since the Armistice he had been poring over reports from Berlin and Munich, winkling out evidence of a revanchist Germany. In 1924, when the future führer was still doing time after his failed putsch in Munich, Winston had warned that "the soul of Germany smoulders with dreams of a War of Liberation or Revenge." That August he told readers of the Hearst newspaper chain that "German youth, mounting in its broad swelling flood, will never accept the conditions and implications of the Treaty of Versailles." Over the years Hitler confirmed this view, and by 1930 he was declaring openly that once a National Socialist government had been formed, he and his *Strassenkämpfer* (street fighters) would "tear the covenants signed at Versailles into shreds." Then they would rearm. "I can assure you," he said in his thick, coarse voice, "that when the National Socialist movement is victorious in this struggle, the November 1918 revolution will be avenged and heads will roll."[13]

Using diplomatic channels, Churchill made his views of the Nazis clear to the Germans. Among the classified documents seized when Allied troops entered Foreign Minister Joachim von Ribbentrop's office on the Wilhelmstrasse in 1945 was a memorandum encoded K567878/A283, an appraisal written on October 18, 1930, by a German counselor posted to his government's London embassy. He reported that he had spent the past two days at a weekend house party where he had encountered "Mr. Winston Churchill." Churchill had expressed his opinions of National Socialism "in cutting terms" (*"mit schneidenem Wort"*), remarking that it had "contributed towards a considerable deterioration in Germany's external position." His indictment of Hitler was specific. He believed him to be a congenital liar and was convinced, in the diplomat's words, that although Hitler had "declared that he has no intention of waging a war of aggression, he, Churchill, is convinced that Hitler or his followers will seize the first available opportunity to resort to armed force." Later, after the Nazis had seized power, Fritz Hesse, the press attaché in Germany's London embassy, called on Winston to sound him out again. He was told that with Hitler in power there was only one solution to the "German problem" — "If a dog makes a dash for my trousers, I shoot him down before he can bite." Hitler, after reading this, muttered that Churchill was a *"Deutschenfresser"* — a devourer of the Germans. Each man, therefore, was wary of the other from the outset.[14]

Political genius lies in seeing over the horizon, anticipating a future invisible to others. Churchill first warned of the approaching war in the Hearst papers on March 31, 1931, when Berlin and Vienna had announced the formation of a customs union. He wrote: "Beneath the Customs Union lurks the *'Anschluss'* or union between the German mass and the remains of Austria." Once that happened France's dwindling population would see "the solid German block of seventy millions producing far more than twice her number of military males each year, towering up grim and grisly." Nor would France be the only nation under the Teutonic shadow. Czechoslovakia had "3,500,000 Austrian-Germans in their midst. These unwilling subjects are a care." And an Anschluss would mean that Czechoslovakia would not only be weakened by "the indigestible morsel in its interior" but would also be "surrounded on three sides by other Germans." The Czechs would "become almost a Bohemian island in a boisterous fierce-lapping ocean of Teutonic manhood and efficiency."

This was to be one of Churchill's themes throughout the 1930s. The Germans, he told readers of the *Strand* in 1935, constituted "the most industrious, tractable, fierce and martial race in the world." And Hitler, having risen "by violence and passion," was "surrounded by men as ruthless as he." Churchill wanted England to pursue a policy leading to a "lasting reconciliation with Europe." But one could not deal with men who lied and murdered, men without honor or decency, led by a ruthless demagogue upon whose orders armed men tramped "from one end of the broad Reich to another." Single-handedly Hitler was reversing the decision reached on the battlefield in 1918. "That is where we are today," Churchill concluded, "and the achievement by which the tables have been completely turned upon the complacent, feckless, and purblind victors deserves to be reckoned a prodigy in the history of the world, and a prodigy which is inseparable from the personal exertions and the life-thrust of a single man."[15]

In the House he spoke to empty seats, dozing MPs, and disapproving frowns. Once the cry "Winston's up!" had brought members scurrying from the lobby and the smoking room. Now — like Edmund Burke six generations earlier, warning Parliament that unless the government changed its policy, Britain would lose her American colonies — he was largely ignored. There is a time to be eloquent, and there is a time when eloquence is wasted. Many of his greatest addresses, writes an Oxford historian, were delivered before "inattentive or skeptical audiences." To Sir John Wheeler-Bennett, who was in Germany, the 1930s were a period in which he, "like so many others, tried desperately to convince those in authority of the growing menace of National Socialism." They "failed miserably." It was "in those days," Wheeler-Bennett recalls, that "Winston was a tower of strength and comfort to us, the one British statesman who understood the warning which we sought to give, and who perceived, in all its starkness, the danger of a fresh outbreak of the *Furor Teutonicus*."[16]

England, to paraphrase Melville, seemed cloaked in a damp, drizzly, foggy November of the soul. So did France. In his Paris home at 110, boulevard Raspail, Major Charles de Gaulle was writing *Vers l'armée de métier*, advancing his concept of a small professional army, mobile and highly mechanized, which, he believed, should replace the reigning static theories of war symbolized by the Maginot Line. In the London murk Churchill, with his moral compass, knew exactly where he was, but few Englishmen even glimpsed him. Sir Robert Vansittart, "Van," the permanent under secretary of the Foreign Office, wrote: "Left or Right, everybody was for the quiet life." To those who saw what lay ahead, the quietude was excruciating. Franklin Roosevelt, sworn in as president five weeks after Hitler became Reich chancellor, was lifting American hearts with his fireside chats, and an MP suggested to Churchill that MacDonald or Baldwin try the same thing. "If they did," said Winston, "the fire would go out."[17]

Lady Astor — née Nancy Langhorne of Danville, Virginia — was rarely reflective of the British public's mood, but threading the maze of parliamentary intrigue with consummate skill, she always knew who was welcome at No. 10 Downing Street and who was not, even when those who were not included her. Joseph Stalin, receiving a British delegation headed by Nancy and George Bernard Shaw, had bluntly asked her about Winston's political prospects. Her eyes had widened. *"Churchill?"* she had said. She gave a scornful little laugh and replied, "Oh, he's *finished.*" Afterward, in Red

Square, Shaw told the waiting press that he found the Soviet Union admirable, and would, indeed, advise young men from all over the world to pack up and settle in it. Nancy smiled and nodded, which, Virginia Cowles points out, was "reprehensible, because up until then she had been a tremendous anti-Bolshevik, denouncing the slaughter of the Russians in speech after speech." Winston's rhetorical weapons were of larger bore. He fired his broadside in the *Sunday Pictorial,* pointing out that the lady in question "denounces the vice of gambling in unmeasured terms, and is closely associated with an almost unrivaled racing stable. She accepts Communist hospitality and flattery, and remains the Conservative member for Plymouth." The Russians, he said, "have always been fond of circuses and traveling shows," and "here was the world's most famous intellectual Clown and Pantaloon in one, and the charming Columbine of the capitalist pantomime."[18]

In Parliament Churchill was supported by five MPs at most. The power of the party whips in those days was immense. Their effectiveness, Churchill wrote, combined with the "lethargy and blindness" of the three parties, made this "one of those awful periods which recur in our history, when the noble British nation seems to fall from its high estate, loses all sense of purpose, and appears to cower from the menace of foreign peril, frothing pious platitudes while foemen forge their arms." A. J. P. Taylor observes that Winston had "periods of great distinction when he seemed right at the front, and he had a gift for sliding down the ladder again. His life was one of snakes and ladders. Until the very end of the 1930s, there were more snakes than ladders. Before then, his reputation, in a sense, was at its lowest ebb." He had served twenty years in one cabinet or another, but because of his stand against independence for India, the "majority of the party," recalled Harold Macmillan, then a Conservative MP, not only "regarded his attitude as reactionary and unrealistic," but also questioned "the soundness of his judgment." The consequence, Macmillan believed, was that "all his warnings about the German threat and the rise of Nazism, as he himself has described, were in vain." Baldwin told his whips to keep a sharp eye on the outcast and to foster the view, Lord Winterton recalled, that Churchill was "an erratic genius; that he was utterly unreliable"; he had caused "unnecessary trouble to the Prime Minister and to all his colleagues in every Cabinet in which he has served by his volubility in disregarding every opinion except his own." In sum, according to Boothby, "The breach between Winston and the Conservative leaders was complete."[19]

In these years Churchill, in Lady Longford's words, was often "far away from the 'clatter and whirlpool,' beached, like one of the boats he painted."

The British left, led by Clement Attlee and pledged to pacifism and disarmament, deeply distrusted him. Thus he outraged MPs on both sides of the Commons. But in Parliament, at least, traditional civility was observed. Outside Westminster was another matter. Afterward he said there had been "much mocking in the Press" about his fall from grace. The political cartoonists in *Punch,* the *Daily Herald,* the *Express,* and above all David Low in Beaverbrook's *Evening Standard* were brutal. Public appearances became an ordeal for him. Chosen rector of Edinburgh University, he was unable to deliver his rectorial address; students hostile to his calls for a strengthened national defense repeatedly shouted him down until he gave up and left the platform. A particularly ugly book published in 1931 was *The Tragedy of Winston Churchill.* Disregarding all evidence, including the findings of the Dardanelles Commission, the author wrote: "Overriding the considered opinions of every seaman who knew his job, he [Churchill] rushed blindly into that wretched fiasco of the Dardanelles. He had great gifts but 'nothing to offer' any member of any party." The author asked, "What has been Mr Churchill's career in reality but the tragedy of the brilliant failure, of whom it has been repeatedly said that he secretly despises those who pass him on the road to office and power?"[20]

Churchillian apocrypha has it that he was unwounded by all this, that throughout he was supremely confident that his hour would strike. On the contrary, his daughter Mary remembers, he was "far from resigned to his exclusion from the exercise of power"; the slanders, libels, and the distortions of his long career "hurt him deeply." In the House an MP launched a personal attack on him, saying: "All his political life has been notorious for changing opinions, just like the weathercock, which vacillates and gyrates with the changing winds. It is about time this House took notice of this menace." When Winston cited figures on the growing (and illegal) Nazi Luftwaffe and all but begged the government to strengthen the Royal Air Force, Sir Herbert Samuel, an eminent Liberal, compared him to "a Malay running amok."[21]

His old acquaintances and former colleagues were convinced that he was misjudging the Nazis as he had India. Beaverbrook wrote that Churchill had "been everything to every party. He has held every view on every question. . . . He is utterly unreliable in his mental attitude." After Hitler became chancellor, the Beaver predicted that "Winston Churchill will retire from Parliament. It is really the best thing for him to do." Hindenburg died, Hitler's power grew, and Max convinced himself that Winston's speeches were stanzas in a swan song. "Now that he seems to have reconciled himself to the part of a farewell tour of politics, he speaks better than for years past." Beaverbrook's biographer writes: "It became clear even to

Churchill that Beaverbrook was no longer on his side, nor even sympathetic to him."[22]

Nevertheless, the two men occasionally saw one another. Beaverbrook's devotion to his newspapers approached that of a *religieux;* Churchill always produced good copy, so the Beaver paid him to write a column every other week for the *Evening Standard*. Malcolm Muggeridge was a young reporter for the *Standard;* at the next desk was Winston's son. Randolph, now in his early twenties, was already difficult, constantly quarreling with his father and nearly everyone else who crossed his path. Churchill would nod briefly at his son as he passed through the *Standard*'s office with his fortnightly piece. Muggeridge recalls that Winston "just looked awful. You'd say to yourself, 'There's a guy who's not well, or down on his luck, or dead broke.' If you knew he was a politician you'd think, 'He's washed out, he's had his chance and now he's through.' " Randolph rarely mentioned his father in the office, but one afternoon, as he watched him depart, he said to Muggeridge, "He's in a terrible state." Then, in an amused tone: "He misses his toys." Muggeridge asked, "What toys?" Randolph said: "His dispatch boxes."[23]

Even before Hitler became chancellor, British intelligence had confirmed Churchill's unofficial estimates, based on his private sources of information, that the Nazis had over 400,000 storm troopers in uniform. During the Chancellor Crisis, Churchill had told the House: "I do not know where Germany's parliamentary system stands today, but certainly military men are in control of the essentials." Each concession which had been made to them, he said, each softening of the Versailles agreement, "has been followed immediately by a fresh demand." To him the peril was clear. If the Germans were permitted to reassemble their military juggernaut, every nation bordering the Reich would be in mortal danger. These, he said, were facts. The British people were being told lies. The prime minister and his cabinet had developed a "habit of saying smooth things and uttering pious platitudes and sentiments to gain applause." He could not recall "any time when the gap between the kind of words which statesmen used and what was actually happening in many countries was so great as it is now."[24]

MacDonald and Baldwin should have been aware of the threat. The British ambassador in Berlin, Sir Horace Rumbold, was an exceptional diplomat. In early March 1933, less than four days after Hindenburg had signed the emergency decree, Rumbold sent the Foreign Office a lengthy assessment of the new regime. The Nazis, he reported, had brought out "the worst traits in German character, i.e. a mean spirit of revenge, a tendency to brutality, and a noisy and irresponsible jingoism." In the heart of the capital, whippings and clubbings could be seen in every block and every park, even the Tiergarten. Rumbold regretted the failure of foreign opinion "to have fully grasped the fact that the National-Socialist programme is intensely anti-Jewish." It was no passing phase: "The imposition of further disabilities . . . must therefore be anticipated, for it is certainly Hitler's intention to degrade, and if possible expel the Jewish community from Germany."[25]

The ambassador knew this dispatch would be unwelcome to both the prime minister and the Foreign Office, but he continued to send them stark appraisals, including an account of the March 23 Enabling Act and its immediate consequences. The Nazis, he wrote, had ordered local burgomasters to "carry on anti-Jewish propaganda among the people." Jews were being "systematically removed from their posts" throughout the civil service because of "the accident of race." Youths were being enrolled in infantry training programs, boys under sixteen were subject to military training, pilots were being recruited for a Luftwaffe — all in open defiance of Versailles. The departure of "so many writers, artists, musicians, and political leaders has created for the moment a kind of vacuum [because] they numbered among their following the intellectual life of the capital and nearly all that was original and stimulating in the world of arts and letters." Most ominous of all, Jews, together with "Social Democrats, Communists, and non-political critics of Nazi policy" were being seized and sent to "large concentration camps" which were "being established in various parts of the country, one near Munich" — it was Dachau — "being sufficiently large to hold 5,000 prisoners."[26]

The ambassador was genuinely alarmed. He told Foreign Secretary Simon that he viewed the future with "great uneasiness and apprehension. . . . Unpleasant incidents are bound to occur during a revolution, but the deliberate ruthlessness and brutality which have been practiced [here] seem both excessive and unnecessary. I have the impression that the persons directing the policy of the Hitler Government are not normal. Many of us, indeed, have a feeling that we are living in a country where fanatic hooligans and eccentrics have got the upper hand."[27]

Rumbold was quietly replaced by Sir Eric Phipps, the British minister in Vienna. But Phipps also found the Nazis outrageous. He told the American ambassador that Hitler was "a fanatic who would be satisfied with nothing less than the dominance of Europe"; that although the Nazis would not invade neighboring countries until 1935, "war is the purpose here"; and that he had actually been approached by the Wilhelmstrasse with a suggestion that Germany and England divide Europe between them, to which he replied that such an agreement would "mean the end of international morality." The Nazis, never troubled by the principle of diplomatic immunity, opened the British pouches and read these reports before they reached London. Hitler told Lord Londonderry that he hated "the looks of Sir Eric" and felt relations between the two countries would be vastly improved if Britain were represented "by a 'more modern' diplomat who showed, at least, some understanding of the changes taking place in Germany."[28]

"What are we to do?" a disconcerted Baldwin asked Thomas Jones. His predecessors would have known precisely what to do. The German führer would have been told that Great Britain did not welcome foreign advice in determining ambassadorial appointments. But Jones reflected the new statesmanship when he wrote in his diary, "If it is our policy to get alongside Germany, the sooner Phipps is transferred elsewhere the better." He should be replaced, Jones thought, by someone "unhampered by professional diplomatic tradition" who could "enter with sympathetic interest into Hitler's aspirations." A candidate had already nominated himself. He was Sir Nevile Henderson, Britain's representative in Argentina. Henderson had let the Foreign Office know that he had regarded Phipps's assignment to Germany a "most unsuitable appointment" and that wags said "there is no British Embassy in Berlin at all, only a branch of the Quai d'Orsay." So Phipps was retired "at his own request" and Henderson took over. His colleagues quickly nicknamed him "our Nazi ambassador to Berlin." Hermann Göring and he became fast friends. Labour MP Josiah Wedgwood noted how he resembled those MPs who had "flocked to Germany at Hitler's invitation, in like manner," forgetting their "duty and their country's standards."[29]

But British diplomats and visiting Englishmen were not the government's sole sources of what was happening in Berlin. In the early years of the new regime, Paul Joseph Goebbels's Propaganda Ministry concentrated on preaching its glories to the German people. Cultivation of the foreign press was of lesser concern. As it happened, this was the high summer of foreign correspondents. The best of them — who covered Europe — were intelligent, well-read men, fluent in several languages, who had developed contacts and sources across the full spectrum of society, in the Reich and beyond. Long before Hitler came to power they knew of Nazi brutality and had sent accounts of it home.[30]

Even after Goebbels decided that something must be done about the foreign press in Berlin, little was. His problem was compounded by geography. Germany's capital, like England's, represented a concentration of great power in a small neighborhood. But in London a combination of ceremonial pomp, the discouraging mazes of Whitehall, and a tradition

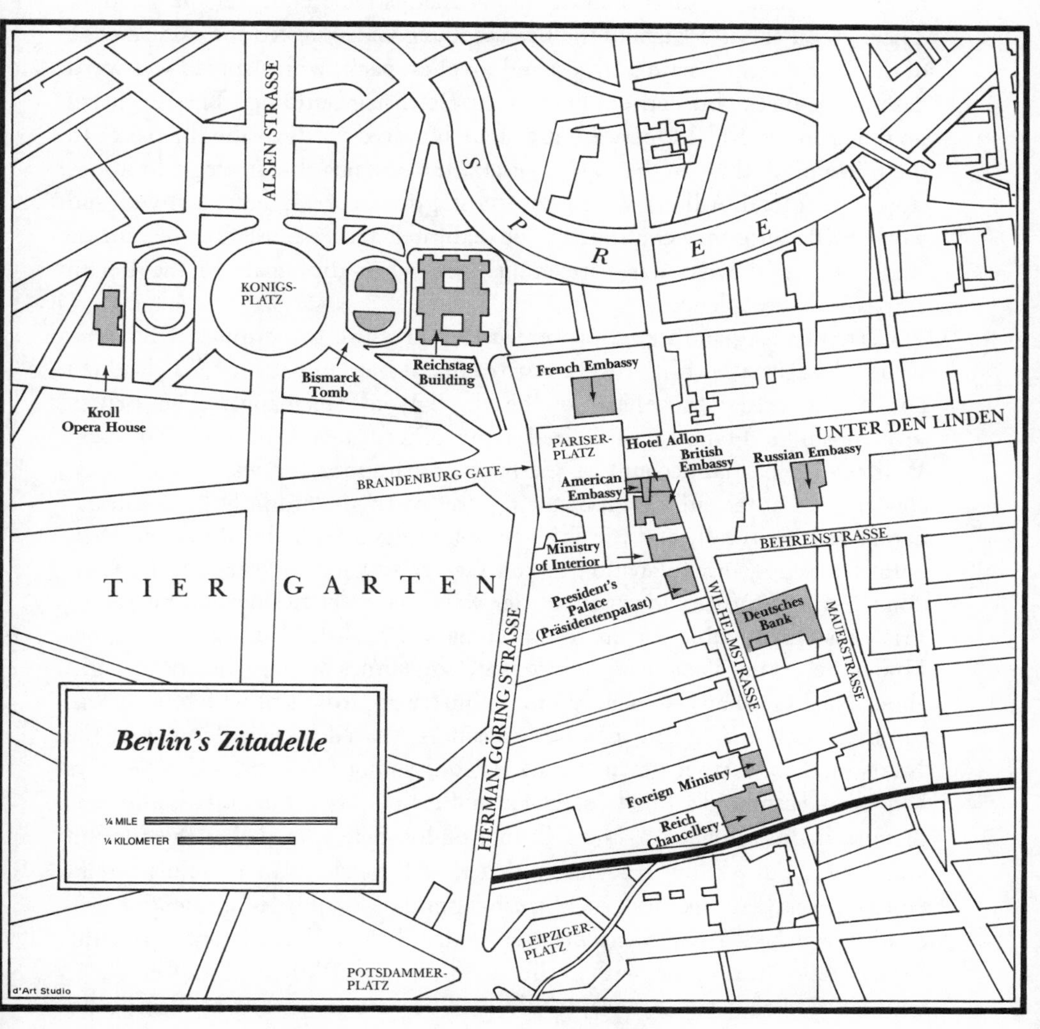

Berlin's Zitadelle
¼ MILE
¼ KILOMETER
ALSEN STRASSE
S P R E E
KONIGS-
PLATZ
Kroll
Opera House
Bismarck
Tomb
Reichstag
Building
French Embassy
PARISER-
PLATZ
Hotel Adlon
British
Embassy
American
Embassy
UNTER DEN LINDEN
Russian Embassy
BRANDENBURG GATE
BEHRENSTRASSE
Ministry
of Interior
T I E R G A R T E N
President's
Palace
(Präsidentenpalast)
WILHELMSTRASSE
Deutsches
Bank
MAUERSTRASSE
HERMAN GÖRING STRASSE
Foreign Ministry
Reich
Chancellery
LEIPZIGER-
PLATZ
POTSDAMMER-
PLATZ
d'Art Studio

of studied rudeness toward outsiders created a web of safeguards which could be penetrated only by an insider of Churchill's stature. The heart of the Reich was more vulnerable. In the Zitadelle the great ministries stood shoulder to shoulder along the Wilhelmstrasse, with Hitler's huge new chancellery at the southern end. People wandered in and out on the flimsiest of excuses. The northern end of the Wilhelmstrasse ended at the Linden. There, the Pariser-Platz and the Brandenburg Gate marked the eastern edge of the Tiergarten, Berlin's largest and loveliest park, which spread westward behind the black, burned-out hulk of the Reichstag building. The Reichstag now met in the Kroll Opera House, four hundred yards inside the park. In the midst of all this, on the Pariser-Platz, the best possible strategic location, stood the Hotel Adlon, where the most gifted correspondents lived and worked. Because they continued to be dedicated and resourceful, the outside world was told what was happening even when diplomats in the Berlin embassies were silenced.[31]

Certainly England's envoys were under pressure to be mute. Civil servants who criticized Hitler were warned that it was "unpatriotic," as Lothian put it, "to refuse to believe in the sincerity of Germany." The British vice-consul in Hanover, a retired army officer turned businessman, sent Whitehall a partial account of German preparations for war. The Nazis, concerned that the full extent of their secret rearmament might be disclosed, demanded his recall, and Sir John Simon obliged without asking the Wilhelmstrasse for an explanation or the vice-consul for his version. In London's Foreign Office, however, Hitler was beset by critics beyond his reach. His most formidable foe in the diplomatic establishment was Permanent Under Secretary Vansittart — arrogant, sometimes wrong, but dead right about Nazi Germany — who ran the ministry regardless of which party was in office. Ralph Wigram, beneath Vansittart, shared his hostile view of the Nazis, and so, farther down the ladder, did young Duncan Sandys. Sandys had been Rumbold's third secretary in Berlin. After the ambassador was dismissed, he returned to the FO in London determined that the foreign secretary should know his views. When a dispatch from Britain's Berlin embassy reached his desk — a fresh appraisal of Hitler's intentions — Sandys attached a comment proposing that FO diplomacy anticipate the future. Specifically, he wrote, the demilitarized Rhineland buffer state, between Germany and France, would soon become an issue. The Nazis were preparing to march in. Talks between Britain and France now would assure joint action when they did. If no action was contemplated, the Wilhelmstrasse should be told so now; the democracies could demand, and get, a quid pro quo. If they meant to fight, Hitler ought to know that, too; he might back away from the risk. It was a shrewd, prophetic note, but the foreign secretary rejected it with the scribble: "We cannot consider hypothetical issues." Sandys promptly resigned, entered politics, was elected to Parliament, and joined the small band of Churchillians.

Van remained in the FO, arguing that the Nazis' savagery in their own country could not be divorced from the growing possibility of aggression beyond their borders; one had only to read *Mein Kampf* to know that. The journalist Vernon Bartlett protested that it was "unfair" to judge Hitler by his book; its expansionist passages had been written ten years earlier, when the author was depressed and imprisoned. Van dismissed that as a non sequitur and went on to say that "from the very outset of the regime" in Berlin he had felt "no doubt whatever about the ultimate intentions of the Nazis." It was, in his opinion, "an open secret that anything said by Hitler is merely for foreign consumption and designed to gain time. . . . Nothing but a change of the German heart can avert another catastrophe," and that was "unlikely to come from within, for the true German nature has never changed."[32]

Any accomplished continental diplomat would have seen the significance in a Vansittart minute reporting that the Nazis were determined to make their Reich "first in Europe." England could not tolerate domination of the Continent by *any* nation. Churchill defined the principle for the Conservative Members Committee on Foreign Affairs: "For four hundred years the foreign policy of England has been to oppose the strongest, most aggressive, most dominating power on the Continent, and particularly to prevent the Low Countries" — Belgium, Luxembourg, and Holland — "falling into the hands of such a power." This had been England's guiding light in its struggles against Philip II of Spain, Louis XIV of France, Napoleon, and the kaiser. Each time, he reminded them, Britain had "joined with the less strong powers, made a combination among them, and thus defeated and frustrated the continental military power, whoever he was, whatever nation he led. Thus we preserved the liberties of Europe . . . and emerged after four terrible struggles with an ever-growing fame and widening Empire, and with the Low Countries safely protected in their independence."[33]

The House stirred uneasily when Churchill, who, whatever his flaws, had been more hostile to the Bolshevik regime than any other Englishman in public life, told them — on the very day the Enabling Act became law in the Reich — that Nazi Germany was a greater threat than the Soviet Union. "We watch with surprise and distress," he said, "the tumultuous insurgence and ferocity and war spirit, the pitiless ill-treatment of minorities, the denial of normal protections of civilized society to large numbers of individuals solely on the grounds of race."[34] In any prewar Parliament, so eloquent an appeal to the most cherished of British virtues — decency — would have touched off a demonstration. Now the chamber was silent. The difficulty was that any political coalition becomes indistinguishable from a single-party state. There is no responsible opposition. With Labour's MacDonald as the King's first magistrate, guided by the Tory Baldwin as his éminence grise, the coalition government disciplined everyone but the party mavericks, most of whom accepted Lloyd George's assessment of Hitler anyway.

The appeasers distrusted France, blamed her for the punitive Versailles clauses, felt Germany had been wronged, and were determined to make restitution. Lord Lothian declared that it was Britain's moral obligation to support the Germans in their struggle to "escape from encirclement" (the encircling powers, presumably, being France, Switzerland, Austria, Czechoslovakia, Poland, Holland, Belgium, and Luxembourg) "to a position of balance." He neglected to add that any shift in the status quo would mean the liquidation of legitimate governments. At Versailles the 1914–1918 holocaust had been blamed on the Germans. Now the fashionable scapegoat was Germany's ancient enemy. "Lady Astor," *The Week* reported, "is obsessed with a vivid personal dislike of the French." As late as November 7, 1936, a member of the cabinet told his ministerial colleagues that Francophobia was increasing in England because the French were an obstacle to Britain "getting on terms with the dictator powers."[35]

The British yearning to accommodate their former enemies took peculiar forms. Upper-class Englishmen had been bred to handle foreign affairs with grace and subtlety. But many of the new breed of German diplomats were boorish. Therefore, envoys from Whitehall, eager to court them, tried to teach the Wilhelmstrasse manners. On August 22, 1932, for example, Sir Maurice Hankey, secretary of the cabinet and of the Committee of Imperial Defence (CID), sent a long memorandum to Prime Minister MacDonald, expressing apprehension over the likelihood that the Germans' claim to *Wehrfreiheit* — the right to rearm — would be "conducted with their usual clumsy and tactless way," which "might have a disastrous effect." He proposed making a demarche, after consulting the French, urging the Germans to postpone their demands. This failing, Britain should attempt to persuade the Wilhelmstrasse "to make their proposals in as harmless a form as possible."[36]

The foreign secretary, Sir John Simon, had his own euphemism for the rebuilding of the Reich's armed might. It was "parity." His resolve — and the cabinet's — was to sanction an expanding German army while disarming the French, until, after an infinite number of carefully monitored phases, both nations possessed the same number of soldiers, tanks, artillery pieces, warplanes, and warships.

The Times thought it "essential" that the Germans be permitted "to build the forbidden weapons at once." Restoring Germany's martial might would restore her pride and strengthen her feelings of security; then Germany and England, "in company," would launch a program of genuine, large-scale disarmament. The prime minister was first impressed, then inspired. Thus was the seed of the extraordinary MacDonald Plan implanted. Its first tenet was that England, as the conscience of Europe, would divest herself of her most formidable weapons. The press, the universities, labor unions, and every sounding board of public opinion would enthusiastically endorse the plan. When the League of Nations Union conducted a nationwide poll, the Peace Ballot, it found that 10.4 million Britons favored international disarmament, while 870,000 — about 8 percent — opposed it.[37]

As Churchill later wrote, "The virtues of disarmament were extolled in the House of Commons by all parties. On June 29, 1931, Ramsay MacDonald, looking forward to the first World Disarmament Conference, had proudly announced in the House that the dismantling of England's armed forces had been "swift, patient, and persistent," and that although it had gone "pretty near the limit," he intended to make "still further reductions" once he had persuaded other European governments to follow suit. His first target would be Paris. Germany, stripped of her defenses, constituted no threat to the peace, but the huge French army could attack across the Rhine at any time.[38]

Churchill instantly replied that the French army, far from being dangerous, was the strongest guarantee of peace on the Continent. Moreover, the chancelleries of eastern Europe, from the Baltic to the Black Sea, "look to France for guidance and leadership." If the French followed MacDonald's advice and sent half their poilus home, he continued, those states between Germany and Russia would be lost, leaderless, and ripe for the plucking. Britain must be armed — "England's hour of weakness is Europe's hour of danger." He urged the prime minister to abandon his mission: "The sudden disappearance or undue weakness of that factor of unquestionable French military superiority may open the floodgates of measureless consequence."[39]

Even as he had risen to speak, other members had begun drifting out of the chamber. Winston, they told one another, had always been against disarmament. Every MP knew it; they discounted it; he would make no converts here. But he had his readers, and as the diplomats convened in Geneva, he toiled in his Chartwell study urging close scrutiny of all proposals by the conferees in Switzerland. In the *Daily Mail* he wrote that "millions of well-meaning English people" were praying for a successful conference. That, he said, was their vulnerability: "There is such a horror of war in the great nations who passed through Armageddon that any declaration or public speech against armaments, although it consisted only of platitudes and unrealities, has always been applauded; and any speech or assertion which set forth the blunt truths has been incontinently relegated to the category of 'warmongering.' "[40]

Despite MacDonald's optimism, the first round of talks at Geneva ended in July 1932 after five months of frustration. Nothing had been accomplished. Sixty nations, the United States and the U.S.S.R. among them, had sent delegations, but every session ended in a deadlock between the Germans, who insisted on permission to rearm before any other item on the agenda could be even considered, and the French, who argued that the disarmament of all European states be supervised, and then monitored, by an international police force. MacDonald, undiscouraged, laid plans for resuming the conference.

To Churchill the negotiations were highly suspect. He believed, quite simply, that military weakness invited attack, a view more controversial then than it has since become. As early as September 9, 1928, he had written a friend: "We always seem to be getting into trouble over these stupid disarmament manoeuvres, and I personally deprecate all these premature attempts to force agreements on disarmament." Was it likely, he asked in the *Daily Mail* of May 26, 1932, that France, with twenty million fewer people than Germany, and half the number of youths coming to military age every year, would deprive herself "of the mechanical aids and appliances on which she relies to prevent a fourth invasion in little more than a hundred years?" The goals of disarmament were admirable, but they would never be "attained by mush, slush, and gush." The hard and bitter truth was that lasting demilitarization of Europe could only be "advanced steadily by the harrassing expense of fleets and armies, and by the growth of confidence in a long peace."[41]

Convalescing from paratyphoid, Churchill was confined to Chartwell during the opening of Parliament's disarmament debate of November 10, 1932, and missed Sir John Simon's affirmation that it was the objective of British policy to find a "fair meeting of Germany's claim to the principle of equality." Baldwin, supporting disarmament as the only way to peace, spoke of what he called "the terror of the air." Enemy bombers, he said, could hammer London into the earth like a hot white saucer. No defense against them was possible: "I confess that the more I have studied this question, the more depressed I have been at the perfectly futile attempts that have been made to deal with this problem." He thought that "the man on the street" should "realize that there is no power on earth that can protect him from being bombed." Whatever happened, he said, "the bomber will always get through."[42]

Baldwin had raised, or perhaps stumbled upon, one of the thorniest military issues of the time. The weight of professional military opinion was on his side. In England, Italy, the United States, France, and Germany, most air strategists subscribed to what was called the Douhet Theory. Shortly before his death in 1930, an Italian airman, General Giulio Douhet, had published *The War of 19—*, in which he argued that armies and navies should be relegated to defensive roles while bomber fleets won the war. Any nation investing heavily in air defense was risking defeat, he wrote, for "No one can command his own sky if he cannot command his adversary's sky." His most important convert was Nazi air force chief Hermann Göring, the 1918 ace, with his treasured memories of the Red Baron and the wind in the wires. Unfortunately for Göring, one aging RAF officer thought Douhet's thesis fatally flawed. He was Air Chief Marshal Sir Hugh Dowding, who would later command the RAF in the Battle of Britain. Dowding and eminent British scientists, colleagues of the Prof, convinced Churchill that every offensive weapon could be countered by imaginative, intrepid defenders. They cited fast fighters and trained antiaircraft crews; later they would brief Winston on RDF, an acronym so secret that until the war only a handful of men would know of it. It represented "radio direction finding"—or, as the Americans were to christen it, radar.[43]

In the *Daily Mail* of November 17, Churchill called on the government to look to Britain's defenses: "If Geneva fails, let the National Government propose to Parliament measures necessary to place our Air Force in such a condition of power and efficiency that it will not be worth anyone's while to come here and kill our women and children in the hope that they may blackmail us into surrender." Six days later he addressed the House on the issue. He had studied Baldwin's speech and thought it needlessly pessimistic. It had "created anxiety," he said, "and it created also perplexity." S.B. had left an unjustified impression of "fatalism, and even perhaps of helplessness." The time had come not to dismantle the RAF, but to expand it. "Why should we fear the air?" he asked. "We have as good technical knowledge as any country." He pressed the government to "consider profoundly and urgently the whole position of our air defense."

Of the French, he said, "They only wish to keep what they have got, and no initiative in making trouble would come from them." He was "not an alarmist" (this drew jeers) and did not "believe in the imminence of war" (more jeers). But, he continued, "the removal of just grievances of the vanquished ought to precede the disarmament of the victors."[44]

* * *

Diplomatic conversations and disarmament pacts seemed tiresome to Britons in those years. The Depression persisted, and they sought diversion in the yo-yo craze, three trunk murders, and the exceptional seductive prowess of the middle-aged rector of Stiffkey, who prowled London teashops, persuading an astonishing number of young waitresses to slip into toilets with him, assume awkward positions, and copulate. Defrocked, the vicar found employment as a tamer of lions and was eaten by one. The popular songs of the era were played in slow, almost lugubrious measures: "How Deep Is the Ocean," "Say It Isn't So," and "With My Eyes Wide Open, I'm Dreaming," which, Churchill later suggested, ought to have been Ramsay MacDonald's theme as the prime minister crossed the Channel in February 1933 and entrained for Geneva, where the plan bearing his name would highlight the agenda of the resuming disarmament talks.[45]

Churchill was not impressed. In Parliament he produced a copy of the Swiss newspaper *La Liberale Suisse* and quoted from the leading article. Prime Minister MacDonald's call for "German equality in armaments," he said, was depicted in the Swiss paper as raising suspicions "all over the Continent" that England wanted to "help Germany at the expense of her neighbours." The Swiss, he continued, saw it as "part of a deliberate plot by which the British Prime Minister is pursuing those pro-German sympathies which he has had for so many years. It is devised in order to bring about the defeat or paralysis of France at the hands of Germany and Italy, and so to expose the small nations to the ambition of the Teuton mass." Churchill tossed the paper aside. "Of course it is not true," he told the House, but "you see how small countries work out these proposals."[46]

MacDonald had called the Continent a house "inhabited by ghosts." It wasn't, said Churchill; "Europe is a house inhabited by fierce, strong, living entities. Poland, recreated at Versailles, is not a ghost: Poland is a reincarnation." But he was anxious about Teutonic influences. Poland's national character, like Germany's, was marred by a livid streak of anti-Semitism; the "odious conditions now ruling in Germany" might spread across the border "and another persecution and pogrom of Jews [begin] in this new area." Czechoslovakia — "the land of Good King Wenceslas" — had also emerged from Versailles "with its own dignity established." To be sure, there were Germans living within its borders, but they had always lived there, as inhabitants of the Austro-Hungarian Empire. Neither they nor their ancestors had ever been citizens of the Reich.

Indeed, he continued, at the Versailles peace conference, "No division was made of the great masses of the German people. . . . No attempt was made to divide Germany. . . . No State was carved out of Germany. She underwent no serious territorial loss, except the loss of Alsace and Lorraine, which she herself had seized only fifty years before. The great mass of Germans remained united after all that Europe had passed through, and they are more vehemently united today than ever before."[47]

The response in Germany was outrage. The *Birmingham Post*'s Berlin correspondent cabled: "Today's newspapers are full with 'sharp warnings' for England, introduced by headlines about . . . Mr Winston Churchill's 'impudence.' " Winston had no intention of lowering his voice. Eleven days later he told the Royal Society of St. George that the greater peril lay not in Berlin, but in British "defeatist doctrines" arising from "the mood of unwarrantable self-abasement into which we have been cast by a powerful section of our own intellectuals." He said: "Nothing can save England if she will not save herself. If we lose faith in ourselves, in our capacity to guide and govern, if we lose our will to live, then indeed our story is told."[48]

The House did not shout him down, but it came close, when his attacks on MacDonald took a more personal turn. Returning from Geneva, all smiles, the prime minister of the coalition briefed Parliament on the various proposals he had initialed, all of immense importance, he assured them, though he astonished and embarrassed his admirers by adding, "I cannot pretend that I went through the figures myself." Winston snapped up that line, noting that though MacDonald was unfamiliar with the numbers, he had taken "responsibility for them. It is a very grave responsibility. If ever there was a document upon which its author should have consumed his personal thought and energy it was this immense disarmament proposal." This was harshly critical perhaps, but still permissible. Other of Winston's observations, however, were incendiary: speaking on March 23, Churchill described the prime minister as "our modern Don Quixote," returning with the "somewhat dubious trophies" collected among the "nervous tittering of Europe." In Churchill's opinion, the proceedings in Geneva had been "a solemn and prolonged farce." He hoped that MacDonald would now take "a good rest, of which I have no doubt he stands in need," and then devote himself to "the urgent domestic tasks which await him here," leaving "the conduct of foreign affairs, at any rate for a little while, to be transacted by competent ambassadors through the normal and regular diplomatic channels."[49]

Harold Macmillan, who was elated, later recalled "hearing the speech from the back benches and the impression made by his formidable attack," but Winston himself saw the "look of pain and aversion" on the faces round him. Even while he was in the midst of it, the protests had begun. MacDonald's four years in Downing Street, he said, "have brought us nearer to war and made us weaker, poorer, and more defenceless." This touched off cries of "No, no, no!" Turning toward those who had interrupted him, Winston replied, "You say 'No.' You have only to hear what has been said here today to know that we have been brought much nearer to war." And when they cried, "By whom?" he said sensibly that he didn't "wish to place it on one man," but when a single individual had held "the whole power of foreign affairs for four years," nothing was to be gained "by pretending that there is no responsibility to be affixed anywhere." Once he sat down MPs from all three parties rose, variously deploring "a disgraceful personal attack on the Prime Minister," which was "thoroughly mischievous," and "mean and contemptible." Winston himself was described as "a disappointed office-seeker," the pursuer of a "personal vendetta" who was trying to "poison and vitiate the atmosphere" which MacDonald and his foreign secretary had tried to create in Switzerland.[50]

As usual Winston had a bad press. The *Northern Echo* called his performance "vitriolic," one of "the most audacious he has delivered," a "furious onslaught." The *Daily Dispatch* reported: "The House was enraged, in an ugly mood — towards Mr Churchill." So it was. It was perhaps a sign of the contempt MacDonald felt for his critic that he chose a thirty-six-year-old Foreign Office under secretary to reply for the government. Churchill's fear of Germany was groundless, the young diplomat told the House; the Germans merely wanted to replace their small long-service army by a larger, short-service militia. It was unfortunate that the member from Epping had thought so solemn a matter as foreign affairs an occasion for "quips and jests." To hold the prime minister accountable for deteriorating international relations was "a fantastic absurdity."

So said Anthony Eden in the House of Commons on March 23, and under his debonair manner he seemed honestly puzzled. Eden had fought in France as a young officer in the King's Royal Rifle Corps; he had fought in the trenches, been gassed and decorated. As a Tory he disagreed with MacDonald on most domestic issues, but in pursuing a lasting European peace he felt they should "all pull together," as in the Eton boating song, "steady from stroke to bow." How could anyone misinterpret the prime minister's reply to the rising Nazis? It was certain, Eden earnestly told the House, to "secure for Europe that period of appeasement which is needed." If appeased, Hitler's anger would vanish; his fear of encirclement would disappear; the Nazis, freed from anguish and insecurity, would become sensible, stable neighbors in a Europe free of rancor. The House gave him a standing ovation — Churchill and those around him remained seated. The MacDonald Plan was supported by Conservatives, Labour, and Liberals alike. Its essence was simple. The Nazis were entitled to bear arms. At the same time, Germany's former enemies should take the first long steps toward disarmament. And the first country to spike its guns should be that aggressive, martial, bellicose country — France.[51]

> **Appease** *vt* Pacify, conciliate: *esp:* to buy off (an aggressor) by concessions usu. at the sacrifice of principles — **appeasable** *adj* — **appeasement** *n* — **appeaser** *n*

So defined, the word implies a slur, but Eden had used it in its original meaning — to bring to peace, pacify, quiet, or settle. In that sense it has been in the language for five centuries and appears in Chaucer, Spenser, and Samuel Johnson. Churchill had employed it after the general strike of 1926 in describing his approach to the negotiation of a settlement between miners and the owners of coalfields. As an aspersion, however, it had been introduced in the House of Lords on November 5, 1929. The speaker had been the dying Lord Birkenhead, F. E. Smith. Condemning Britain's conciliatory tactics toward advocates of Indian independence, F.E. called them "appeasers of Gandhi." Eventually, Telford Taylor notes, "the word became a symbol of weak and myopic yielding when resistance would be bolder and, in the long run, safer."[52]

Churchill used it as a stigma in 1933, when the coalition's determination to meet the German dictator's demands became clear to him. Appropriately, the first cabinet minister to rebuke Churchill outside the House for his attack on MacDonald was the man who would become known to history as the archpriest of appeasement. Speaking to his Birmingham constituency on March 24, Neville Chamberlain deplored Churchill's abuse of his talent "to throw suspicion and doubts in the minds of other Governments who have not expressed such feeling." He declared it England's duty to make "every effort," exert "every influence," and "act as mediators" to preserve the peace by reconciling estranged countries. The British government wanted to avoid all wars between nations because — and this was a typical Chamberlain touch — "they thereby destroy the possibility of markets for ourselves."[53]

Appeasement became evangelical; indeed, for some the line between foreign policy and religion became blurred. Thomas Jones denounced Vansittart's hostility toward the Nazis; Baldwin commented: "I've always said you were a Christian." Rage, wrote Margot Asquith, the widow of the prime minister, should be met with Christian love. "There is only one way of preserving Peace in the world, and getting rid of yr. enemy, and that is to come to some sort of agreement with him — and the *viler* he is, the more you must fight him with the opposite weapons than his." She concluded: "The greatest enemy of mankind today is *Hate*."[54]

As for mistreatment of the Jews — some said this and some said that.

After all, no one could deny that Jews were, well, *different*. Churchill, an ardent Zionist since 1908, could speak for himself, but here as in so many ways he was unrepresentative of England's upper classes. This was over ten years before the Holocaust. The martyrdom of Jews in the 1940s would strip anti-Semitism of its respectability, but in the 1930s it was a quite ordinary thing to see restaurants, hotels, clubs, beaches, and residential neighborhoods barred to people with what were delicately called "dietary requirements." As late as the 1950s the *Pocket Oxford Dictionary* defined *Jew* as "1. *n*. Person of Hebrew race; (fig.) unscrupulous usurer or bargainer. 2. *v.t.* (colloq.). Cheat, overreach." Contempt for them was not considered bad form. They were widely regarded as unlovable, alien, loud-mouthed, "flashy" people who enriched themselves at the expense of Gentiles. Some even said the Germans who abused them were only getting back a little of their own. As Martin Gilbert and Richard Gott observed: "Even England was not free of anti-semitism. Not all Hitler's criticisms of Jews were discounted. Rumbold hated the anti-semitism of the new Germany; other Englishmen were less certain in their condemnation."[55]

One of Churchill's relatives, a peer and an anti-Semite, argued that Anglo-German friendship was mandatory if Western civilization was to be preserved. Churchill replied: "You cannot expect the English people to be attracted by the brutal intolerance of Naziism." But, he was asked, how brutal *are* the Nazis? Britons wondered whether Nazi excesses were sufficiently outrageous to permit a deterioration of relations between London and Berlin — thereby forfeiting what many believed could be a lasting peace. *The Times* thought not. The "shouting and exaggeration" in the new Reich, it assured its readers, was "sheer revolutionary exuberance"; Hitler's men, feeling "themselves to be the only true patriots, are enjoying the sound of their own unrestrained voices." The trouble was that the noise, the ugly language, and the accounts of bestial conduct didn't stop. Be patient, counseled *The Times;* hysteria was un-British: "Anxious Germans may rest assured that all this is not deliberately misconstrued by foreigners." Most *Times* leaders on foreign policy were written by editor Geoffrey Dawson or Robert Barrington-Ward, a fellow Oxonian, both of whom shared Lothian's conviction that France and Russia were conspiring to deny Germany her rank among the great powers, a place, Dawson said, "to which she is entitled by her history, her civilization, and her power."[56]

Barrington-Ward told a friend that Nazi outrages were "largely the reflex of the external persecution to which Germans have been subjected since the war." Englishmen's commitment to fair play, he added, obligated them to help the victimized country "escape from encirclement" and achieve "equality," the code phrase which meant rearmament. History has credited the Nazis for the restoration of the Reich's military might, but some Englishmen had anticipated them. In the summer of 1932, Franz von Papen, then chancellor, declared that the shackles of Versailles were "*unerträglich*" ("intolerable"). *The Times* — which the Germans believed was the voice of the government — weighed the chancellor's complaint, found it justifiable, and called for "the timely redress of grievances."[57]

Once Hitler had been sworn in and his *Strassenkämpfer* began unsheathing their long knives, the British government took the remarkable position that the detailed reports from two of its most eminent ambassadors, describing conditions in the Third Reich, were based on misunderstandings, distortions, and unconfirmed rumors. Speaking in Newcastle, Lord Lothian said that the Germans "have passed through a tribulation which we have never known. We should receive in no niggardly spirit the offers" — they were, of course, demands — "made to the world by Herr Hitler."[58]

The prime minister agreed. According to one Wilhelmstrasse document which came into British hands when Berlin fell in May 1945, MacDonald assured Germany's ambassador to Britain, Leopold von Hösch, that he knew there were no atrocities, no beatings, no desecration of synagogues — that everything England's own envoys had reported, was, in short, a lie. MacDonald explained that he understood "very well the character of, and the circumstances attending, a revolution." According to *The Times,* Baldwin told Hösch that England was "entirely willing to work closely . . . with a Germany under the new order" — "*die Neuordnung.*" It is startling to read this Nazi phrase, so freighted with evil, quoted by a once and future prime minister in the columns of *The Times*. Doubtless Baldwin had not grasped its implications. But he should have. And he should have spoken out. His silence, his refusal to see, hear, and speak no evil of the Nazi chancellor was characteristic of the response among England's ruling classes. If they offended him, they told one another, he would become hostile, and his hostility would blind him to reason.[59]

Vernon Bartlett thought his countrymen altogether too smug about democracy. Although it "suits us," he wrote, it "may not suit other people." Even Bartlett could not defend the imprisonment of Jews who had committed no crime and of former Reichstag critics of National Socialism. But, he wrote, "the Government now proposes to get rid of the concentration camp [*sic*] without much delay." Sir Thomas Moore, a respectable MP with a distinguished university career behind him, was another early admirer of Hitler. He joined the Anglo-Germany Fellowship and spent half his time in Germany, where, he reported, he had been unable to find any trace of the abuses Rumbold and Phipps described. After the Nazi chancellor had been in power eight months, Moore wrote in the *Sunday Dispatch,* "If I may judge from my personal knowledge of Herr Hitler, peace and justice are the key words of his policy." The next year he wrote "Give Hitler a Chance," calling the chancellor, now führer, "absolutely honest and sincere."[60]

War between the Germans and Communist Russia was a prospect with twin appeals to Britain's upper classes, reflecting their pacifism and their fear of bolshevism. But before the two totalitarian giants could meet at a common border, momentous events would be necessary in intervening states: Poland, Czechoslovakia, Austria, Hungary, Rumania, Latvia, Lithuania, and Estonia. The appeasers thought that it would be rather a good thing if Hitler began meddling there. J. L. Garvin, editor of *The Observer*, owned by Lord Astor, wrote that before a "constructive peace" could be established, "a large part of 'Eastern Europe' proper should be reconstructed under German leadership." The extraordinary Lord Lothian, who held no office, sailed to Germany and solemnly informed Hitler that "Britain has no primary interests in Eastern Europe." This folly was summed up by the Rumanian foreign minister. He said sadly: "Germany has her plans. Do other countries have their plans? If the other powers are without plans, we will be forced to go along with Germany."[61]

Lords Astor and Lothian were not only forfeiting future allies; they were also overlooking the fact that Britain *did* have interests in the buffer states between Russia and Germany. France was bound by treaty to go to war should any other country invade Czechoslovakia. And Britain was pledged to follow France's declaration with her own. In November 1933, in the Wilhelmstrasse, Konstantin von Neurath, the Nazi foreign minister, read a minute from Hösch. MacDonald had suggested that Hitler make a state visit to England. Neurath scrawled across the memorandum: *"Unsinn!"* — "Nonsense!" And so it was. Why run such a risk when British aristocrats were already giving what even Hitler hadn't dared ask for?

❧ ❧

Churchill was right — the Geneva conference was doomed — but no one in Parliament would congratulate him on his foresight. In those days faith in disarmament was a creed, and to slight it was poor politics. But then, Churchill was a poor politician. Although the most gifted speaker of his age, he was clumsy, even inept, in manipulating the House, the intricate maneuvering of which Baldwin was master. Neither, in the opinion of prominent Labour leader Clement Attlee, was he a great parliamentarian, "mainly, of course, because he was too impatient to master the procedures." He was also capable of appalling political misjudgments. By resigning from

Baldwin's shadow cabinet in 1931 over the India issue, thereby repeating his father's aristocratic disdain for consequences, he assured his exclusion from every prewar ministry and made the eventual designation of Neville Chamberlain as prime minister — with all that entailed — inevitable.

But no British politician in this century has matched Winston's skill in keeping himself in the public eye. In 1899, when Winston was still in his mid-twenties, G. W. Steevens, the great Victorian journalist, met him on the boat home from India and wrote in the *Daily Mail* that Churchill might become, among other things, "the founder of a great advertising business." Certainly he was a matchless self-advertiser. Even as a backbencher, he made news by his dramatic presence in the House of Commons, by his soaring speeches, by parliamentary tricks which just skirted the borderline of propriety, and by his way of digging into a pocket, producing classified documents, and reading selected passages aloud, with all the gaudy panache he alone could display, to an astonished House, press gallery, and public.[62]

Now and then he would enter the chamber carrying a prop. If he had nothing else, at crucial moments he would produce his watch and play with it. Parliament was aware of his diversions, sometimes amused, often annoyed. Yet everything he did was just within the rules. Once, when an Opposition speaker had the floor, Winston lowered his great head and began to swing it back and forth in widening arcs. Backbenchers grinned and then chuckled. The victim said icily: "I see the Right Hon[orable] Gentleman shaking his head. I wish to remind him that I am only stating my own opinion." "And I," said Churchill, "am only shaking my own head." Another time, when an MP was approaching the end of a very long address and was drawing breath, pausing before his peroration, Churchill destroyed it by growling, "Rubbish." Anticipating an attack on an argument he himself had presented at the last session, he entered the chamber sucking a jujube — a lozenge — and pocketed it as he sat down. His opponent had just begun to pick up momentum when Winston began searching his jacket, vest, and trousers. At first he was surreptitious, as though anxious not to distract the listening MPs, but gradually one MP after another noticed that he was digging into his pockets, ever harder, ever more frantically. Laughter began, and the speaker, trembling with justifiable rage, asked: "Winston, what are you *doing?*" Churchill said meekly, "I am looking for my jujube."

The speaker's colleagues raised indignant shouts, but when they quieted down he reminded them that he always enjoyed a noisy House and told them why: "Honorable Members opposite will give me credit for not being afraid of interruptions and noise. It even would be much easier to be shouted down continually or booed down, because I have not the slightest doubt that I could obtain publicity for any remarks I wish to make, even if they are not audible in the House." He did not add, though they knew it, that he could also make money doing it, selling his text in Fleet Street at a handsome price. And if his tactics offended MPs on both sides of the well, he could always win back their hearts. The House of Commons is no less susceptible to flattery than each of its members, and when he digressed for a moment to recall a critical issue in the recent past, concluding, "All through these convulsions the House of Commons stood unshaken and unafraid," they felt, as Lord Chandos puts it, "that they had been in a battle and had just been decorated."

Splendid prose, wrote Hazlitt, should be accompanied by vehemence and gesture, a dramatic tone, flashing eyes, and "conscious attitude" — a precise description of Churchillian delivery. A consummate performer, he would rise, when recognized by the Speaker, with two pairs of glasses in his waistcoat. Perching the long-range pair on the end of his nose at such an angle that he could read his notes while giving the impression that he was looking directly at the House, he gave every appearance of speaking extemporaneously. If the occasion called for quoting a document, he produced his second pair and altered his voice and manner so effectively that even those who knew better believed that everything he said when *not* quoting was spontaneous.

As a youthful MP he had excelled at the set piece but faltered in the give-and-take of debate; Arthur Balfour, prime minister from 1902 to 1905, had chided him, calling his "artillery" impressive "but not very mobile." It was mobile now, and frequently sardonic. "It is wonderful how well men can keep secrets they have not been told," he said, and, "Too often the strong, silent man is silent because he has nothing to say," and, describing Lloyd George's criticism of his hostility toward Nazi Germany, "It revealed a certain vein of amiable malice." Sir Samuel Hoare, a coalition minister, was a favorite target. Winston said of him: "He never resents the resentment of those to whom he has been rude." But the coalition government must be allowed its day: "Where there is a great deal of free speech there is always a certain amount of foolish speech."[63]

Although this was said in a bantering tone, it reflected Churchill's absolute faith in democracy. If the electorate preferred to be governed by fools, they should be. Of course, that did not make folly wisdom. He did not share the view that sagacity lies in the masses, and in thwarted moments he would quote Hazlitt: "There is not a more mean, stupid, dastardly, pitiful, selfish, spiteful, envious, ungrateful animal than the Public. It is the greatest of cowards, for it is afraid of itself." The man of honor remained true to himself, even though drawn through the streets in a tumbril. He scorned opinion polls: "It is not a good thing always to be feeling your pulse and taking your temperature. Although one has to do it sometimes, you do not want to make a habit of it. I have heard it said that a Government should keep its ear to the ground, but they should also remember that this is not a very dignified attitude." He was often called irrational and cheerfully admitted it. So, he replied, was politics; so was human experience. It did not, he observed, "unfold like an arithmetical calculation on the principle that two and two make four. Sometimes in life they make five, or minus three, and sometimes the blackboard topples down in the middle of the sum and leaves the class in disorder and the pedagogue with a black eye. The element of the unexpected and the unforeseeable is what gives some of its relish to life, and saves us from falling into the mechanic thraldom of the logicians."[64]

Churchill was celebrated as a polemicist, but many of his flashing moments in the House were sheer fun. Rising to pay tribute to a fellow member on his golden wedding anniversary, Winston touched off a parliamentary cachinnation by beginning: "I rise to commit an irregularity. The intervention I make is without precedent, and the reason for that intervention is also without precedent, and the fact that the reason for my intervention is without precedent is the reason why I must ask for a precedent for my intervention." One of his baiters was Edith Summerskill, a feminist MP. Every time he said "man" during one of his addresses she interjected "or woman." After several such interruptions he paused, turned to her, and said: "It is always the grammarian's answer that man embraces woman, unless otherwise stated in the text." A rash new member called his thrusts slanders. Winston replied: "He spoke without a note and almost without a point." And after crossing foils several times with a Welsh Labour member and anticipating another demand from him to which his only response could be an unqualified negative, he had "Nothing doing" translated into Welsh and memorized it. The entire House was stunned when the Welshman, having made his claim, sat down and Churchill rose to growl: *"Dym a grbl."*

In a rare moment of humility he acknowledged to the House that it had put up with a lot from him. Since he first took his seat in the chamber, he said, "I have always said to myself one thing: 'Do not interrupt,' and I have never been able to keep to that resolution." Nor had he succeeded in curbing his savage tongue; he confessed that he could not recall "any expression of scorn or severity" used against him by his critics which "has come anywhere near the language I have been myself accustomed to use. . . . In fact, I wonder that a great many of my colleagues are on speaking terms with me."[65]

He could indeed be vicious. And he could bide his time. Ten years earlier Churchill and Michael Collins, founder of the Irish Republican Army, had established the Irish Free State, and won an Eire referendum despite opposition from Eamon de Valera. Now, with Collins and all other rivals murdered, De Valera had waded to power through their blood. In his first venture into foreign affairs he encouraged Mussolini's absurd claims in Ethiopia. Winston remarked: "Mr. De Valera, oblivious to the claims of conquered peoples, has given his croak. No sooner has he clambered into the imperial box than he hastens to turn his thumb down upon the first prostrate gladiator he sees." He prepared a trap for a Labour MP and spent four months waiting to spring it. Eventually the man stumbled, the House jeered, and the stumbler lost his temper. Winston pounced: "There is no one more free with interruptions, taunts, and jibes than he is. He need not get so angry because the House laughs at him: he ought to be pleased when they only laugh at him."[66]

Often he was at his most dangerous when he seemed bored. Hunched over in his seat below the gangway, within spitting distance of the Treasury Bench, he would appear to be inattentive to the business before the House. His eyes would close; he would breathe heavily. It was an ambush, of course, and twice MPs on the opposite side of the House lurched into it. The first asked loudly: "Must you fall asleep when I am speaking?" Winston replied: "No, it is purely voluntary." The second, more cautious, merely inquired whether he was asleep. Winston immediately answered: "I wish to God I were!" And he could stifle an effective jab with a sharper retort. As he finished a scathing attack on the cabinet, a backbencher called: "The Right Hon[orable] Gentleman, like a bad bridge player, blames his cards." Churchill snapped: "I blame the crooked deal."[67]

But these were minor prey. His great adversaries were the leaders of the national government — the coalition — who kept him out of the cabinet despite his long and brilliant ministerial career, which outshone any of theirs. Ramsay MacDonald, the prime minister, no longer spoke to him. Winston had called him "the boneless wonder," the "greatest living master of falling without hurting himself," and the man who possessed "the gift of compressing the largest number of words into the smallest amount of thought." He dismissed Neville Chamberlain as "a greater Birmingham." His chief target was Baldwin, the ringmaster of the coalition, who ruled the House as lord president, using MacDonald as a puppet and grooming Neville as his successor. Observing an elderly member listening to the lord president through an ear trumpet, Churchill rumbled: "Why does that idiot deny himself his natural advantage?"[68]

During one evening session, when it became obvious to every man in the House that the lord president had Luftwaffe and RAF production figures hopelessly muddled, Winston called him "no better than an epileptic corpse," and when asked what should be done if Baldwin died in office, he replied, "Embalm, bury, and cremate. Take no chances!"[69]

A young MP, an admirer of the lord president, delivered an emotional plea for unilateral disarmament and was so incautious as to approach Winston in the smoking room and ask his opinion of it. "Why, I thought it was very good," Winston replied. "It must have been good, for it contained, so far as I know, all the platitudes known to the human race, with the possible exceptions of 'Prepare to meet thy God' and 'Please adjust your dress before leaving.' "

His own taunts in the House were carefully prepared to observe parliamentary custom. There was a line between ridicule, which was permissible, and personal insults, which were not. Churchill had been in Parliament since 1901; he knew exactly where the line lay — knew, for example, of Parliament's list of banned words, which included "blackguard," "dog," "guttersnipe," and "swine." One young Labour MP, unaware of the list, had used all these in a ferocious assault on Churchill, thereby deeply offending not only Winston but the entire House. Attlee took the man aside; he told him he would have to go to Chartwell and apologize. The chastened MP drove to Kent and knocked on the front door. Churchill's valet answered. The man stated his name and mission and was asked to wait. Winston was in the toilet, moving his bowels. The valet stood in the hall outside, delivered his message, and waited. After a long moment Churchill said: "Tell him I'm on the privy and can take only one shit at a time."[70]

❧ ❧

On the military balance between Germany and those who had conquered her armies less than twenty years earlier, Churchill was not only the most knowledgeable backbencher in the House; he was better informed than many senior diplomats on the Wilhelmstrasse. Some of his information was acquired routinely. As one of the monarch's senior privy councillors, he was on several distribution lists. He received copies of other, more sensitive documents because in 1931 he had asked Ramsay MacDonald for access to figures on the strength of England's armed forces. MacDonald found military matters dull, even trivial; he casually approved the request and then, apparently, forgot about it. It was one of those bureaucratic decisions which become self-perpetuating, remaining in effect unless withdrawn.

Among the documents to reach Chartwell was a Foreign Office assessment of Britain's defenses. The FO had found them pitiful. To double the blow, military intelligence reports, which also found their way to Churchill in the mid-1930s, disclosed that Germany had begun to rearm even before Hitler came to power. The Weimar Republic had started it in 1929, when only 2.6 percent of the German electorate supported Hitler. British agents found that the republic had spent two million pounds more than the British on "artillery, small arms ammunition and anti-gas material." Winston learned that the British embassy in Berlin, submitting its annual report in 1929, had stated that "the necessary jigs and patterns and gauges for the manufacture of modern weapons are being prepared and stocked in various factories all over Germany."[71]

By contrast, the Royal Navy in the 1930s was, in Telford Taylor's words, "sadly down-at-the-heels." During the two interwar decades only two capital ships were commissioned, and in 1929 the Labour government cut cruiser replacement and suspended work on the Empire's Singapore base. On May 31, 1933, when the delegates in Geneva were debating reciprocal inspections of one another's military establishments, the ministers responsible for Britain's armed forces told the cabinet that such inspections would "expose to the world our grave shortage of war supplies." One of Churchill's constituents asked him: "Don't you think it high time that the British lion showed its teeth?" He growled: "It must go to the dentist first."[72]

In the beginning many of Winston's informants were obscure and had small tales to tell: men returning from Germany — engineers, foreign correspondents, bankers, salesmen, tourists, professors, British officers who had traveled in mufti — and diplomats from neutral countries who passed data and appraisals through third parties or sometimes arrived unexpectedly on Chartwell's threshold. Refugees from the new Reich were interviewed, and those with scientific backgrounds were closely questioned by the Prof, who seemed to spend less and less time at Oxford and more and more advising Winston on radar, missiles, aircraft design, and high explosives. Everything found its place in Winston's jigsaw puzzle. He even established a relationship with Maisky, the Soviet ambassador to Britain, and met with him at regular intervals until the end of the 1930s.

British contacts close to the seats of power were, of course, much more useful. It is England's homogeneity and class insularity which make it seem small; in the public school network, referrals by mutual friends to mutual friends may lead anywhere, even to the sovereign. Here, as so often in his life, Churchill's membership in the privileged class was a great advantage. His informants included his second cousin Lord Londonderry, from 1931 to 1935 secretary of state for air in the coalition cabinet; Sir Henry Strakosch, an official adviser to the cabinet; and John Baker White, director of the Economic League, who collected details about German rearmament, found the government unreceptive to them, and turned the lot over to

Churchill, who, he drily recalls, became very affable "when I made it clear that we did not want to be paid."[73]

Winston's chief secretary, Violet Pearman, befriended Wing Commander Torr Anderson, holder of the Distinguished Flying Cross. Anderson was troubled by Britain's air defenses, or lack of them, and spilled it out to Mrs. P. in a Westerham tearoom. She returned to Chartwell with him in tow, and after a long conversation with Anderson, Winston acquired a pipeline into the RAF, the service which worried him most.

Mrs. P.'s tasks included sorting the daily mail. It was enormous, it came from everywhere, and it fell into patterns. The high fever of militarism was throbbing throughout Germany. Duff Cooper, financial secretary at the War Office in the early 1930s and a parliamentarian marked for higher office, spent September of 1933 driving through Germany and Austria. He wrote Winston that throughout the Reich, "everywhere and at all times of the day and night there were troops marching, drilling, singing." Duff Cooper was convinced that the Reich was readying itself for war, preparing to fight any country at any time, "with more general enthusiasm than a whole nation has ever put into such preparation." A retired British lieutenant colonel, known for his hospitality to continental youths visiting the United Kingdom, wrote Winston: "I dined with four young Nazi students a week ago. They had been sent over to tell England what the Hitler movement was doing to the youth of Germany. It all sounded very unpleasant, though they seemed to like it. They made no secret of their belief that within three or four more years Germany would be at war."[74]

Among Churchill's chief sources was Major Desmond Morton, slim, elegant, with hooded eyes and a handsome mustache, whose country cottage conveniently lay just over the hill from Chartwell. In 1917 Morton had been shot through the heart at Arras; he had survived to join military intelligence, where, after the Armistice, he had worked under Churchill, who was then secretary for war and air. Seconded to the Foreign Office, Morton found himself idle much of the time. He knew Churchill was researching *The World Crisis,* his six-volume history of the Great War, and so, in a neighborly way, he volunteered to help. The offer was eagerly accepted; they became friends. Morton's name first appears in the Churchill papers in a letter from Clementine to Winston, then touring the United States. The brief mention is dated August 31, 1929: "Major Morton dined with us & helped keep in countenance Mr Lennox Boyd who was surrounded by a cloder of (6) cats."[75]

The reference was casual, and deliberately so. Winston shared everything with his wife — at the outbreak of hostilities in 1914, when he was first lord of the Admiralty, she had known more about Royal Navy activities than most cabinet ministers — and seven months earlier the relationship between Churchill and Morton had been transformed and was now delicate, even perilous. The major had been appointed to an extraordinarily sensitive post — chief of the Committee of Imperial Defence's Industrial Intelligence Centre, with official instructions to "discover and report the plans for manufacture of armaments and war stores in foreign countries." He shared Winston's anxiety over German militarism. Because their homes were within strolling distance of each other, the two men could meet casually. Long before Hitler unveiled the Luftwaffe, Churchill knew, through Morton, that thousands of young Nazi aviators and members of national glider clubs had been carefully organized and were prepared, on a signal from Berlin, to expand and deploy into fighter and bomber squadrons.[76]

Late in the fifth month of the Third Reich, June 1933, Morton telephoned Chartwell and suggested an immediate rendezvous. British intelligence had just received a most secret report from Group Captain J. H. Herring, the air attaché in Berlin. The Nazis had begun production of warplanes. Hitler had ordered all owners of civilian aircraft to register with his new Air Ministry, which meant, wrote Herring, that "a process of mobilisation is in progress"; in effect, Hitler was "already engaged in building an air force." The attaché added a prediction. Once the registration was over and the command structure in place, "all German aviation will remain a Government controlled branch of public life so long as the Nazi regime lasts."[77]

Morton continued to be a vital source of classified information, but he was not alone. Today Churchill's intelligence net seems amateurish; his informants would be quickly picked up by MI5, the internal security service. Luckily for them — and, later, for England — Scotland Yard had not yet formed a special branch to ferret out civil servants and military officers who became what were later described as security risks. Henry Stimson, an American patrician of the time, reasoned: "The only way to make a man trustworthy is to trust him; and the surest way to make him untrustworthy is to distrust him and show your distrust."[78] Later this article of upper-class faith would be exploited by Cambridge men who became Soviet agents, but the men who kept Churchill informed were faithful to King and Country.

It was during the disarmament talks in Switzerland that Winston hit his mother lode of intelligence. He found that although he was a pariah in the House of Commons, certain British civil servants in key positions regarded him as heroic. Equally useful was Winston's long career in the governments of Campbell-Bannerman, Asquith, Lloyd George, and Baldwin. He was known to hundreds of men in public life, the City, Fleet Street, and — most important — those who worked in shabby little offices opening off the long, bleak corridors of Whitehall. During his twenty years in office Winston had headed seven different ministries. He and Sir Robert Vansittart, for example, had been friends since 1902. The civil servants knew that soon England's survival might be at stake. As Michael Creswell, deputy head of the Foreign Office's Central Department, put it, they felt that their political leader, the foreign secretary, Sir John Simon, did not want to know "uncomfortable things."[79]

And so, even as Hitler consolidated his power, the first trickle of reports and memoranda not meant for Winston's eyes began to find their way there. It grew to a steady, broadening stream, until, as Professor Herbert G. Nicholas of Oxford puts it, Churchill, "supported by a small but devoted personal following," was able to "build up at Chartwell a private information centre, the information of which was often superior to that of the government."[80] The civil servants who were among his sources were the highly educated, well-connected, understated and underpaid men who really governed England and the Empire. The prime minister and cabinet made policy, but they relied on the briefings of their permanent under secretaries and the tiers of veteran specialists below them. Civil servants remained in place while governments came and went. They belonged to no party. But they knew when Britain's interests were in danger and Britons misinformed. Sir John Simon received daily reports from Vansittart, Ralph Wigram, and their staffs. If Simon distorted the truth in the House of Commons, the men in the FO swore and kicked their wastebaskets, but it had been happening for generations, and they had grown resigned to it. There was, however, a distinction between manipulation in the interests of political expediency and what amounted to treachery — compromising England's very existence.

The line had always existed. Every sensible man had known when it had been crossed. But in the past the incidents had been rare. Now, however, the line was being traversed so often that it had become blurred beyond recognition. The quiet men in bowlers, each with his rolled umbrella and his copy of *The Times*, became increasingly troubled. Several decided to approach Churchill. It was a momentous move. They were risking not only their careers, but also imprisonment, for, as one informant reminded Winston, the government "always has the Official Secrets Act to fall back upon." Under this remarkable piece of legislation, which would be unconstitutional in the United States, the disclosure of any government information, even if the purpose is to expose wrongdoing, is a crime. As Anthony Lewis pointed out in the *New York Times*, the act "intimidates the press and limits public discussion of policy." If the scholar of today concludes that Churchill saved England, the meticulous, often anonymous men who faced ruin and jail yet still put their country first also deserve to be remembered.[81]

Their first important contact with Chartwell came in the spring of 1933, when tension in Britain's Geneva delegation led to a split in the Foreign Office. A. C. Temperley, one of the frustrated British delegates, said aloud what had been on everyone's mind — that to talk of disarmament while Hitler secretly armed was absurd. Then he put it in writing: "Can we afford to ignore what is going on behind the scenes in Germany?" If the Nazis were unchecked, he wrote, Hitler would settle for nothing less than annexation of all of Europe. He proposed an ultimatum: tell Berlin to stop arming, and, if the Nazis balked, add a "hint of force." He was confident that it would work. At this point Nazi arrogance was all facade; Germany was "powerless before the French army and our fleet. Hitler, for all his bombast, must give way. Strong concerted action . . . should prove decisive. . . . There is a mad dog abroad once more and we must resolutely combine either to ensure its destruction or at least its confinement until the disease has run its course."

In the margin of Temperley's minute Vansittart scrawled his "entire agreement"; then he urged Eden to distribute copies to members of the cabinet and then have it read to them. It was done — "to no effect," Van wryly noted. Reginald ("Rex") Leeper, head of the FO's News Department, snatched up the fallen standard. Temperley had addressed his note to Leeper, knowing that Leeper wanted Britain to challenge Nazi rearmament. Following the cabinet's rejection of the suggested ultimatum, Leeper said he knew exactly how and when to trap the Nazis — now, at the conference in Geneva. After one of the Nazi delegates had spoken "in the best Hitlerian manner," he suggested, the Britons and Frenchmen should rise "one after another" and expose what was happening in the Ruhr. Leeper knew this was a "sensational step," he wrote, but if the Geneva talks continued on their present course, the conference would "drift to its certain death" and the munitions factories in the Ruhr would continue with increasing momentum.[82]

The prime minister and Simon had been pursuing a different approach. On June 16, 1932, MacDonald had met with Franz von Papen, then Germany's chancellor, and the result had been a reduction of the German reparations liability to a token sum — three thousand marks. Although Churchill was highly critical of the Treaty of Versailles, he believed in abiding by the rules of diplomacy; such bilateral agreements on the side, violating this or that clause, diminished the integrity of the whole. And Hitler — who was loutish even in small triumphs — roused Winston's wrath by announcing with a smirk that the three thousand marks "would be worth only a few marks in a few months." Churchill angrily told the House that the massive American loans of the 1920s, meant to support German reparations payments, had actually been used by the Germans to modernize their industries — factories which could turn out arms faster than those in Britain and France. He wanted a firm reply to the German challenge.

But the coalition was marching to the beat of a different drummer. Offending the Germans, the foreign secretary argued, would be disastrous. He and the prime minister were determined to return from Switzerland with Germany's signature on a disarmament treaty, and if there was too high a price to pay, no one sitting around the table mentioned it. Leeper's proposal was therefore rejected. The consequences of jettisoning it were graver than anyone there knew; it led to Winston's deep penetration of the Foreign Office, directly across the street from No. 10. The FO became the most valuable beam in his intelligence structure: Churchillians there included Vansittart, Rex Leeper, and — in the FO's inner sanctum, the Central Department — Ralph Wigram, the department's head, together with his immediate subordinates, Michael Creswell and Valentine Lawford.

Everyone remembers Wigram as a man of immense charm. Lawford's first impression of him was one of "gentleness, young looks, shyness, modesty, economy of language." After Eton and Oxford he had risen almost effortlessly, drawing assignments at all the choice embassies. In 1933, aged forty-three, a Commander of St. Michael and St. George (CMG), he was brought back to the Foreign Office and, the following year, appointed counsellor. Beginning on the day Hitler became dictator of Germany, Wigram and Vansittart had watched developments in the Third Reich with growing concern. Now they agreed to share their information with Churchill. On October 26, 1934, Wigram sent his first significant report to Chartwell through Creswell and Morton. The Central Department had learned, he wrote, that the Nazis were "working for an army of offensive strength; in two years they expect to have 1,000 warplanes ready for combat." The threat was not immediate. They would "have to be mad . . . to try any games in the immediate future." However, he wrote, by 1938, "we shall be faced by a very, very much stronger Germany." The Central Department had acquired a transcription of a long conversation between Hitler and Admiral Erich Raeder, dated June, and ending: "The Führer demands complete secrecy on the construction of the U-boats." By November 19, 1934, the counsellor's anxiety had further increased. Hitler now led an army of 300,000 men, and its ranks were growing every day. The kaiser's Generalstab — the army's General Staff, outlawed at Versailles — was back in power. Since Hitler took over, Wigram pointed out, the Reichswehr had stopped publishing its annual list of officers. Otherwise, their swollen rolls would betray the Reichswehr's rapid expansion.[83]

Wigram recommended that the British government begin the immediate stockpiling of strategic materials and industrial retooling for armaments manufacture. Soon the Reich's military establishment would be strong enough to defy enforcement of Versailles by the Allies. This, he predicted, would be revealed by the Germans themselves. Before their might was great enough "to wage an aggressive war," Hitler would be demanding this and that, showing off his army to blackmail other European powers. The Nazis, the counsellor's report predicted, would become "increasingly arrogant and definitely aggressive. Instead of emitting protests and airing grievances Germany will make demands and assert rights." When the Führer possessed the greatest war machine in the world, he would turn his "attention to the absorption of Austria and the penetration of central Europe." Wigram's recommendations came at the end of this minute. If Britain accepted Nazi military might as a fait accompli, France would be alienated. Once the Western democracies' front was broken, no other combination of continental nations would dare resist the Führer. Therefore he proposed that Whitehall and the Quai d'Orsay "arraign" the Reich before the League of Nations, charging it with violations of Versailles. This strategy, he suggested, would "give us an opportunity for informing public opinion clearly of the nature of German rearmament." So warned, the Belgians and the Dutch would, in Wigram's judgment, join the anti-Nazi alliance.

Read today, this yellowing document reveals a sagacity and vision seldom matched in Britain's archives. Yet after its submission to the foreign secretary, the prime minister, and the rest of the cabinet, it was returned with comments which could only be interpreted as hostile, or, at best, indifferent. Before a debate in the House senior civil servants would walk up to Parliament and enter the "briefing box." There they would respond to ministerial questions. Creswell recalls: "One felt again and again that for them the important thing was to get through the debate. . . . What was happening in the world wasn't in the forefront of their mind." They hadn't studied the FO's assessments and appreciations; at most they had glanced through them. And that was what protected the secret of the civil servants' Churchill connection. Reading the transcriptions of those parliamentary debates today, one can only imagine the ministers' astonishment as Churchill rose to face them and reel off facts and figures that seemed to have come from nowhere — but were always confirmed afterward. Had Simon, say, or Hoare done his homework, they would have realized that Churchill had access to documents stamped "Most Secret."

At first the drill was Wigram-to-Creswell-to-Morton-to-Churchill. Then Ava Wigram came to Chartwell for the weekend, bearing analyses her husband had drawn up for a government that didn't want them. In time Ralph joined his wife, staying overnight. If a matter was urgent, however, an exchange in London was quicker and safer. Wigram's home was at 4

North Street (now Great Peter Street), three blocks from Parliament and a brief stroll from Churchill's pied-à-terre in Morpeth Mansions.

Although Churchill never wrote of their meetings — their existence was unknown until Creswell revealed them nine years after Winston's death — one can surmise how they must have appealed to his romantic imagination: the furtive telephone conversation; hurrying down the foggy streets; the risk of discovery; the eager anticipation, afterward, of opening the plain unmarked buff envelope containing plans and details his foes in Parliament didn't know he had; visualizing their dismay if they knew — picturing, with ever greater gusto, the horror of Hitler if *he* knew.

Wigram's information was hard, precise, and tersely told. Churchill would read the latest FO accounts of the Luftwaffe's growing strength; reports (as early as May 1935) of Nazi propaganda campaigns among the Sudeten Germans in Czechoslovakia; columns of figures on artillery, tanks, and other Nazi armaments; and advance copies of Hitler's speeches. Winston had to disguise his sources, and sometimes lose a debate when he had the clinching facts in his hands, but in time he became as well informed as the prime minister and in some ways more so, because certain documents, inconsistent with the catechism of appeasement, were suppressed or altered before they reached the P.M.'s desk. Winston, however, had seen the originals, and seen them first. Long afterward, Sir John Colville, who became one of his principal aides, looked through Winston's papers of the 1930s and was astounded by what he found. Colville wrote: "Why the Government allowed . . . its servants to supply ammunition to its principal critic and gadfly, I have never understood." Neither the prime minister nor the foreign secretary would have approved, Colville reasoned, and after World War II, he recalled, he "asked Churchill this question direct and was given an uncharacteristically evasive answer. In fact all Winston said was: 'Have another drop of brandy.' "[84]

Although ill served by ministers who refused to recognize the truth, the British public, enjoying a free press, was aware of some of the more flagrant abuses in the Third Reich. On May 10, 1933, Nazis had celebrated their contempt for learning by building an enormous bonfire of books, incinerating all works on psychology and philosophy and all written by Jews, socialists, and liberals. On July 1 Nazi fliers began dropping leaflets and urging all Austrians to support the country's tiny Nazi party in plans to overthrow the government of Engelbert Dollfuss, which, though Fascist, had come to office through free elections. If that didn't work, Hitler confided to subordinates, he would have Dollfuss killed.

On July 14 the Reich chancellor dissolved the coalition of parties which had brought him to power. Any political speech or pamphlet not endorsed by the Nazis was verboten. Of Germany's three greatest newspapers, the 230-year-old *Vossische Zeitung,* comparable to *The Times* of London and the *New York Times,* was forced to close; the *Berliner Tageblatt*'s Jewish owner was driven out of business, and the *Frankfurter Zeitung*'s editorial hierarchy, largely Jewish, was replaced by Nazis. *Völkischer Beobachter* and *Der Angriff,* the two official Nazi organs, glorified Nazi street terrorists and ran flattering front-page pictures of those responsible for the desecration of synagogues. Germans who protested Nazi outrages were sent to Dachau or other, newer stockades. Teachers were told in the official publication of their profession, *Der Deutsche Erzieher,* that *Mein Kampf* was their *"unfehlbarer Leitstern"* ("infallible star"). Those who actually read the book could have had no doubts that the chancellor's infallible star would eventually lead their children to far-flung battlefields.

Central Europe lay under an "evil and dangerous" cloud, Churchill told an audience of his constituents in Theydon Bois after reading Group Captain Herring's report in 1933. "No one," he said, "can watch the events which are taking place in Germany without increasing anxiety about what their outcome will be. At present Germany is only partly armed and most of her fury is turned upon herself. But already her smaller neighbors, Austria, Switzerland, Belgium, and Denmark, feel a deep disquietude. There is grave reason to believe that Germany is arming herself, or seeking to arm herself, contrary to the solemn treaties exacted from her in her hour of defeat." He told the House: "At a moment like this, to ask France to halve her army while Germany doubles hers, to ask France to halve her air force while the German air force" — here he must have been sorely tempted to quote Herring — "remains whatever it is, is a proposal likely to be considered by the French Government, at present at any rate, as somewhat unreasonable."[85]

In Geneva, however, there was little support for the Quai d'Orsay's lonely stand. This may puzzle those who remember the great alliance of 1914–1918. But England and France had been enemies for nearly a thousand years before then, leaping back and forth across the Channel to fly at each other's throats. In Geneva the French believed they were conducting themselves *sans peur et sans reproche.* Actually they weren't. To their new allies in eastern Europe the delegates from Paris asked not "What can we do for you?" but "What can you do for us?" The instinctive French response to battlefield disasters, in 1870 and 1914 — it would be heard again in 1940 — was the wail: *"Nous sommes trahis!"* ("We are betrayed!"). As other nations in Geneva drew away from them, the French foreign minister declared: "Henceforth France will guarantee her security by her own means." Alistair

Horne comments: "For sheer arrogant folly [this declaration] is hard to beat."[86]

Had the Geneva disarmament talks continued, British Foreign Office documents reveal, France herself would have been betrayed by her greatest ally; but the conference never reached that point. On March 27 Japan, offended by the League of Nations' censure of her Manchurian aggression, had announced that she would quit the league. It was a precedent and Hitler liked it. He had been provoked by the conferees' decision that his storm troopers — there were now 500,000 of them — counted as fighting men, and he declared that league overflights, checking upon the Reich's compliance with any agreement, were *"beschimpfend"* ("insulting"). In the light of French provocations, said the Wilhelmstrasse, the German Reich refused to apologize for its glorious past. Nor need it give reasons for its present position. The Reich was a sovereign state, though it was not being treated like one, which was intolerable and *"unverschämt"* ("shameless").[87]

President Roosevelt had tried to free the conferees from their gridlock by suggesting a ban on all offensive weapons. Privately, Hitler was furious. Nevertheless, he saw great political possibilities in the message from the White House, and on May 17, 1933, he exploited them in a deeply moving, breathtakingly meretricious speech before the Reichstag. FDR, he said, had earned the *"warmem Dank"* of the Reich. He accepted the president's proposals and stood ready to scrap the Reich's offensive weapons the moment other powers did the same. Germany was indeed prepared to disband her entire military establishment, together with uniforms, weapons, and ammunition, under the same circumstances, and would sign any nonaggression treaty, "because she does not think of attacking but only of acquiring security." The National Socialists cherished no ambition to *"germanisieren"* ("Germanize") other nations: "Frenchmen, Poles, and others are our neighbors, and we know of no event, compatible with history, which can conceivably change this reality."[88]

The speech constituted the basic draft of what diplomats came to call Hitler's *Friedensrede* (peace speech), to be delivered before the Reichstag after each German act of aggression, assuring the world that no one wanted peace more than he did, that he had just made his last territorial claim upon Europe. His reply to Roosevelt was a fraud, of course, but it was the work of a master swindler, and it took almost everyone in. London's *Daily Herald*, the official organ of the Labour party, declared that Hitler, as a trustworthy statesman, should be taken at his word. The conservative weekly *Spectator* called him the hope of a tormented world; to *The Times* his claim was "irrefutable."[89]

But there was a catch, and Churchill had spotted it. Implicit in Hitler's offer to disarm whenever other powers did likewise was Nazi Germany's assertion of its right to rearm unchallenged by *Ausländer*. Winston made this point in the House, and after the first few minutes the chamber emptied. The German chancellor had given the MPs a present, the illusion that he had no intention of becoming a warlord, and Churchill was trying to take it away. Beaverbrook wrote a friend that "if he continues on his present course, I would not be surprised if Baldwin put a veto on him in his constituency. And believe me, Baldwin can do it."[90]

Yet every time Churchill seemed on the verge of being driven out of politics, Hitler came to his rescue by building his brutal record, outrage succeeding outrage, each a flagrant betrayal of his most recent *Friedensrede*. His lightning prewar strokes startled a sane world unable to grasp the stark fact that he was not sane. On October 14, 1933, without warning, he made three announcements. The important one was that Germany was withdrawing from both the disarmament conference and the League of Nations. But there was more. One arose from the eternal language problem. Lord Hailsham, MacDonald's secretary for war, had told Hitler that German rearmament would violate Versailles, answerable, under the treaty's terms, by sanctions. In German, *Sanktionen* implies armed invasion; therefore Hitler added that if the league attempted to impose sanctions, his new minister of defense, General Werner von Blomberg, would order German troops to fight. Blomberg did in fact instruct his soldiers to man the Reich's frontiers and "hold out as long as possible." However, as he and his fellow officers were well aware, that wouldn't be long. Serious German resistance was impossible, and they were horrified.[91]

They were not, however, politicians. Hitler, the transcendant politician, knew that he couldn't lose, because in his third and final announcement he declared that he had dissolved the Reichstag and was submitting his decision to quit Geneva to a national plebiscite. No democracy, he knew, would intervene in a German election. He could also be certain of the results. The ballots would offer a single-party Nazi slate of Reichstag nominees, and the plebiscite — which, carefully worded, omitted the disarmament issue, turning the poll into a *ja–nein* on the Versailles treaty — would be held on November 12, the day after the anniversary of the hated Armistice. *Ausländskorrespondenten* — foreign correspondents — skeptical by profession and especially distrustful of the Nazis, monitored the election and reluctantly agreed that it was fair. The results were astounding. Some 96 percent of the electorate went to the polls and 95 percent of them approved of Germany's Geneva walkout. Nazi candidates for the Reichstag received 92 percent of the vote. *Ausländspolitiker* — political leaders in other countries — could no longer speculate over whether the Nazi chancellor had the support of his people. In the entire history of the Reich, no German leader, including the kaiser, had matched his popularity.[92]

The diplomats droned on in Switzerland, and in June 1934 the last truncated session adjourned. The chairman had been Arthur Henderson, a Labour MP, who, as a tribute to his tireless efforts in Geneva, was declared winner of the Nobel Peace Prize. In his closing words, according to a contemporary account, he openly charged France with "responsibility for its failure to accomplish any practical results." The French furiously denied it, and history confirms them. Their peers, however, did not.[93]

❧ ❧

The breadline on Berlin's Kurfürstendamm had vanished. The Third Reich had become the only great power without massive unemployment, beggary, or hunger — a country freed from the shackles of the worldwide Depression. Since Hitler had moved into the Reich Chancellery on January 30, 1933, Germany's income had doubled; production had risen 102 percent; her *Volk* were riding a crest of affluence, euphoria, and throbbing patriotism not seen since their fathers had lustily marched off to war twenty years earlier. The Aladdin with the lamp was Reichsbank president Dr. Hjalmar Schacht. To foreign economists he seemed to be a magician. His genius was undeniable, but he possessed an extraordinary advantage, a gift of power from Hitler. Exercising this authority, Schacht created credit for a country without liquid capital or monetary reserves by manipulating the currency. So adroit was his jugglery that at one point bankers assigned the mark 237 different values.[94]

Europe had never seen anything like it, but Americans had. Under Roosevelt the new economists had been fueling a recovery a full year before August 1934, when Hitler appointed Schacht the Reich's economics minister. There was a difference, however. Germany was now bankrupt, and with a trade deficit approaching a half-billion marks Schacht was, under the laws of the German republic, a counterfeiter. In the City of London or in Wall Street his wizardry would have consigned him to prison. But in the Third Reich he was quite safe. Members of the government were untroubled by legalities, courts, and traditional stock trading principles. Indeed, the central fact about Nazi Germany, obvious now but visible to only a few at the time, is that it was a criminal conspiracy. When President Hindenburg died on August 2, 1934, at the age of eighty-six, Hitler announced that he was combining his office of chancellor with that of the dead president. He then appointed himself *Führer* — leader. This, unlike Hitler's appointment as chancellor, was illegal. In taking this step, Hitler committed a major felony under the German constitution, which stipulated that if a president should die while in office, his title and powers should pass, not to the chancellor, but to the president of the supreme court, to be safeguarded by him until the people could cast their votes in a new election.[95]

Laws are effective only when authorities enforce them and society submits. But in Germany the felons were the men invested with the greatest authority, and the handful of brave demonstrators who protested the transformation of a democracy into a dictatorship were beaten by the *Strassenkämpfer* and found themselves, not their assailants, facing criminal charges. The *Strassenkämpfer*, Hitler biographer Alan Bullock writes, "had seized control of the resources of a great modern State; the gutter had come to power." Hitler now announced his second nationwide plebiscite, this one on his assumption of dictatorial rule. Virtually no voices of dissent were heard from the universities, the eminent Jews having already left; from Germany's industrialists, who had in fact contributed heavily to Nazi election funds after he had promised to abolish trade unions; or from officeholders sworn to protect and defend the constitution now being raped. None even resigned in protest. On August 19, 1934, after a week of massive Nazi rallies, torchlight parades, and storm troopers marching through neighborhoods roaring, *"Wir wollen das Gesetz — sonst Mord und Totschlag!"* ("We want power — otherwise death and destruction!"), the plebiscite was held. Over 42.5 million Germans went to the polls — 95 percent of those registered — and 38 million, nine out of every ten, voted *ja*.[96]

The self-anointed Führer declared that he was now head of state and commander in chief of the country's military establishment. Every German officer was required to swear an oath of loyalty to him. The officer corps knew how momentous this step was. The kaiser had never dreamed of asking personal allegiance. The oath bound them not to the government or even the country, but to the commands of a single individual whose stability, even then, was widely questioned. Nevertheless, to their eternal shame, each of them pledged "by God" that he would "render unconditional obedience to Adolf Hitler, the Führer of the German Reich and people, Supreme Commander of the Armed Forces, and will be ready as a brave soldier to risk my life at any time for this oath." Hitler was now absolute ruler of Europe's most powerful state, a phenomenon unknown to the Continent since Napoleon.

Meanwhile, anti-Semitism, which had troubled Churchill from the outset, was becoming increasingly vicious. His informants reported that all over Germany *Bierkeller*, motion picture theatres, shops, and restaurants were displaying prominent signs reading *"Juden unerwünscht"* ("Jews not welcome"). Day-to-day existence was becoming increasingly difficult for non-Aryans. *"Für Juden kein Zutritt"* ("Jews not admitted") placards hung outside grocery and butchers' shops; they could not enter dairies to buy milk for their infants, or pharmacies to fill prescriptions, or hotels to find lodging. At every turn they were taunted: *"In dieser Stadt ist Juden der Zutritt streng verboten"* ("Jews absolutely forbidden in this city"); *"Juden bretreten diesen Ort auf eigene Gefahr"* ("Jews enter this place at their own risk"); and, at a dangerous highway curve on the west bank of the Rhine opposite Mannheim: *"Vorsicht! Scharfe Kurve! Juden 100 km!"* ("Caution! Sharp Curve! Jews 60 mph!").[97]

Visitors attending the Berlin Olympics in 1936 would ask how Germany had ended the breadlines and found jobs for the jobless. Their hosts suavely assured them that the Führer had solved the Depression in Germany by expanding public works programs and stimulating private enterprise. It sounded plausible, and the tourists left believing it. Yet any persistent searcher for the real source of the Reich's booming economy could have found it by visiting the Ruhr valley — the Ruhrgebiet — and the industrial areas of the Rhineland, where the great factories of Krupp, Thyssen, Flick, and I. G. Farben, looming like *kolossale* cathedrals through the smoke belching from their smokestacks, were working shifts around the clock. It was, for those who saw it, a vision of stark Teutonic power. In the peak years of Victorian energy, when England had been called "the workshop of the world," Londoners had a word for the sound of their toiling city. It was the Hum. Now the Ruhr was Germany's *Bienenstock* — its beehive. But the yield of a beehive is benign; the Ruhr's sweating workers were intent on building a more powerful military juggernaut than the army General Erich Ludendorff had guided in 1918.

No one who held high office in the 1920s, Churchill included, can be completely absolved of responsibility for the shocking deterioration of England's defenses between the wars. After the Armistice Lloyd George's government, at Winston's urging, had adopted a "ten-year rule" — an assumption, in drawing up service budgets, that "no great war is to be anticipated within the next ten years." Year after year the principle was reaffirmed. Ministers saw no reason to drop it. Germany was disarmed; Russia still in turmoil; France pacifistic; America isolationist. Nevertheless, as early as 1929 Basil Liddell Hart had written in the *Daily Telegraph* that "every important foreign power has made startling, indeed ominous, increases of expenditure on its army" and declared that the British government "would be false to its duty to this nation if it reduced our slender military strength more drastically." The Admiralty recommended building a submarine base at Hong Kong. "For what?" asked Winston. "A war with Japan! But why should there be a war with Japan? I do not believe there is the slightest chance of it in our lifetime."[98]

Churchill had an unusual, if unorthodox, grasp of military strategy, but was weak on tactics. In hindsight his observations of weapons seem odd. "The submarine," he wrote, "is not now regarded as the menace it used to be." Similarly, he told readers of the *News of the World* that he doubted "very much" whether the tank "will ever again see the palmy days of 1918. . . . Nowadays the anti-tank rifle and the anti-tank gun have made such great strides that the poor tank cannot carry thick enough skin to stand up to them." Anticipating "How Wars of the Future Will Be Waged," he envisioned "great prepared lines of fortifications which it will be very difficult indeed for the other army to break through. . . . The idea that enormous masses of mechanical vehicles and tanks will be able to overrun these fortifications will probably turn out to be a disappointment." He foresaw deadlock; any ground gained "will very often be only as moles." Doubtless there would be new developments, but nothing dramatic: "One thing is certain about the next war; namely, that the armies will use their spades more often than they use their bayonets."[99]

He also underestimated air power. In 1936 the first reports of civil war in Spain led him to conclude that events there demonstrated "the limitations rather than the strength of the air weapon" and proved that "so far as the fighting troops are concerned, aircraft are an additional complication rather than a decisive weapon." This, he felt, together with "the undoubted obsolescence of the submarine . . . should give a feeling of confidence and security so far as the seas and oceans are concerned, to the western democracies." On one point he had no doubt whatever. No warplane, he declared, could sink a warship. Over a decade had passed since Brigadier General William ("Billy") Mitchell, the American airman, had proved it could be done — proved it by actually doing it, sending six obsolete battleships to the floor of the Atlantic. But as late as January 14, 1939, Churchill told subscribers to *Collier's* that "even a single well-armed vessel will hold its own against aircraft."[100]

A friend of his later recalled a dinner party in the mid-1930s: "Winston was laughing at the idea that any bombers could put ships out of commission. He thought it ridiculous, so terribly funny. He said to get a ship you would have to be sure to put the bomb down the funnel. He had been told it had to go down the funnel or these armor-plated ships wouldn't blow up. . . . You know, he was making this great joke about the whole thing. I just remember how he amazed me at the time. Of course, the bomb didn't have to go down the funnel at all."

Winston's most striking tactical gaffe was a memorandum he sent to Neville Chamberlain, then prime minister, only six months before the Munich Agreement, and it sharply criticized the two fighter planes which would prove to be England's salvation in 1940. On March 12, 1938, Churchill wrote: "We have concentrated upon the forward-firing fixed gun Fighter (Hurricane and Spitfire). The latest developments increasingly suggest that hostile aircraft can only be engaged with certainty on parallel or nearly parallel courses, hence that the turret type of equipment will be paramount." This revealed a total failure to grasp the evolution of aerial rearmament. Churchill was thinking in terms of the Tiger Moth and other old wood-and-fabric two-gun biplanes. To send such slow, fragile aircraft against the Nazis' Messerschmitt fighters would have meant the sacrifice of the RAF, followed by catastrophe; the Luftwaffe's bombers, arriving in fleets, would have leveled their targets, unchallenged by a single British fighter pilot.[101]

But if he misunderstood armored warfare, so did every officer on Britain's Imperial General Staff; and if he underrated air power and believed it would be ineffective against capital ships, the Admiralty agreed with him. The essence of England's armaments dilemma was not inaccurate views on weaponry. The real problem was that the most powerful and influential men in Britain were determined not to offend Hitler. And in this matter Churchill's vision was clear. He warned that whenever absolute rulers assemble great armies, they eventually make war: "Dictators ride to and fro upon tigers which they dare not dismount. And the tigers are getting hungry." Appeasing Germany was folly, he said; Hitler would spare no one; and there was no refuge in neutrality, no sense in urging the Nazis to turn their wrath against others or pursue a policy based on the hope that the Führer would be satisfied with half a loaf — even the whole loaf would leave him unglutted; he would never stop until he was stopped by force. British rearmament was therefore essential.

After the Japanese seized Shanghai in 1932 the cabinet had quietly dropped the ten-year rule, adding, however, that expenditures on arms would be determined by existing economic conditions. Existing economic conditions being what they were, arms budgets were depressed, and England, as Churchill put it, remained a "rich and easy prey." Winston said: "No country is so vulnerable and no country would better repay pillage than our own"; with London "the greatest target in the world," Britain was "a kind of tremendous, fat, valuable cow tied up to attract the beast of prey."[102]

Yet except for Austen Chamberlain, who as foreign secretary had been the architect of Locarno, no eminent parliamentarian backed Winston's calls for rearmament and for binding military alliances with European states under the shadow of the swastika. Even England's Chiefs of Staff were wary of commitment to other states; without such pacts, they argued, Britain could choose when and where to apply pressure. Alliances — even a League of Nations alliance — would mean that each member nation would be obliged, at the very least, to apply sanctions to an aggressor, who in response could declare war on England. Anthony Eden agreed with the chiefs. Answering Churchill in the House of Commons on one occasion, he had said that "where I differ, with respect, from my Right hon Friend the Member for Epping, is that he seems to conceive that in order to have an effective world consultative system nations have to be heavily armed. I do not agree. . . . General disarmament must continue to be the ultimate aim."[103]

Labour regarded Churchill's demands for rearmament with a suspicion which can only be called paranoid. Clement Attlee, the party's deputy leader, denounced all arms appropriations and denied that Hitler's attentions were aggressive. He told Parliament: "We are back in a prewar atmosphere . . . in a system of alliances and rivalries and an armaments race," adding: "We deny the proposition that an increased British air force will make for the peace of the world." In the military estimates of HMG — His Majesty's Government, the prime minister and his cabinet — which were so inadequate in Churchill's view, Attlee discerned familiar, sinister themes. They were "nationalist and imperialist delusions . . . far more wild than any idealist dreams of the future we hold." He declared: "We on our side are for total disarmament because we are realists." When Winston recited a list of over twenty-four German factories producing airframe components and "considerably more" than eight plants turning out parts for warplane engines to be assembled by Heinkel, Junker, and Dornier, "on whose behalf the majority of other factories are working," Attlee replied that anyone could draw up lists. One Labourite suggested that Baldwin was building a force which could be sent "abroad to fight in foreign countries." Vansittart, who knew the MP had indicted the government of the wrong country, read that a Labour party conference had recommended a policy "subordinating our defense to the permission of Geneva, abolishing allegiance and loyalty to England, and pledging British citizens to a world-commonwealth which would 'override any national duty in time of war.' " They had decided to take this position, they explained to the press, because "we have abandoned the whole idea of the national order." In his memoirs Van acidly noted: "Hitler hadn't."[104]

Churchill's isolation in Parliament seems remarkable now. England was not ready for him. Whenever Hitler loomed large in headlines, Britons plunged their heads deeper into the sand. And their leaders joined them. Sir John Wheeler-Bennett, a British expatriate living in Germany, had first judged Hitler as "a man of sense . . . who does not want war," then, when his vision cleared, tried to persuade his countrymen at home that the Nazi regime was evil. He failed, he came to believe, because in Britain the "forces of apathy, of wilful myopia and of general delusion in high places were too strong for us."[105]

Neville Chamberlain told Nancy Astor that when he moved from No. 11 Downing Street to No. 10 he intended to be his "own Foreign Minister." His half brother Austen chided him: "Neville, you must remember you don't know anything about foreign affairs." Neville thought he knew a great deal, however, and his fellow ministers, especially Baldwin, found him impressive. He convinced them that Hitler would never attack France, the Low Countries, and Britain. The Führer, he said, wanted to move against Russia, not the West.

Actually, Hitler intended to turn south first. On the first page of *Mein Kampf* he had declared that a rejoining of Austria and Germany was a "goal to be pursued with every means [*mit allen Mitteln*], all our lives," and had melded both countries into a single proper noun: *Deutschösterreich*. His motive, as Churchill saw it, was to open "to Germany both the door of Czechoslovakia and the more spacious portals of southeastern Europe." His chief obstacle was Chancellor Engelbert Dollfuss, no tribune of the people but a leader who had risen through free elections. In the summer of 1934 Austrian Nazis, acting on Hitler's orders, plotted to murder Dollfuss and arrest everyone in his cabinet. At noon on July 25, ten of them, dressed in Austrian army uniforms, passed the chancellery sentries unchallenged. Bursting into the chancellor's office they shot him and left him on a sofa bleeding to death, ignoring his pleas for a priest. But their cabinet roundup was flawed; among the ministers they failed to capture was Kurt von Schuschnigg, a man of action. On Schuschnigg's orders Austrian troops overpowered the plotters. He hanged them while Mussolini, jealous of German designs on Austria, rushed fifty thousand troops to the Brenner Pass. This was the kind of language Hitler understood. He lay low, leaving Austria, in Churchill's phrase, "on the hob."

Even *The Times* commented that the assassination of Dollfuss "makes the name of Nazi stink in the nostrils of the world." But the appeasers were also shocked by the executions in Vienna and the Duce's threat of armed intervention. Somehow Schuschnigg's violence, and Mussolini's threat of it, blurred the brutal assassination of a national leader on orders from — and not even Germany's most ardent British supporters doubted the instigator's identity — another head of state. It was part of the tragedy of the 1930s that the democracies always gave Hitler a second chance, and he never failed to profit from it. Next time his plan to seize Austria would be foolproof and his armed might overwhelming.

❧ ❧

It was Ludendorff's concept of *totaler Krieg*, total war, which gave the Reich's feverish boom its identity: *deutsche Wehrwirtschaft*, or German war economy. While the House of Commons haggled over petty appropriations for the services and debated whether men in the Royal Navy should be paid a living wage, all German shops were retooling to prepare for war so thoroughly that victory would be inevitable. Within a year of Schacht's appointment his staff had completed plans to convert 240,000 plants for total war. Lord Eustace Percy later wrote in awe of how Germany succeeded, "in little more than five years, not only in mobilizing a nation and abolishing its unemployment, but in equipping a great army and bringing the dreams of a new strategy within the bounds of reality." At the time, he added, English observers, official and unofficial, had "considered this feat wholly incredible."[106]

In 1945 Georg Thomas, the German general who served as Schacht's military liaison officer, published an account of Nazi rearmament in the 1930s. He wrote: "History will know only a few examples of cases where a country has directed, even in peacetime, all its economic forces deliberately and systematically toward the requirements of war, as Germany was compelled [*sic*] to do in the period between the two world wars." The army hierarchy was grateful, and particularly aware of its debt to the Reich's economic czar. In the mid-1930s, on Schacht's sixtieth birthday, *Militärwochenblatt*, the official army periodical, paid tribute to him as "the man whose skill and great ability" had made it possible for "an army of 100,000 men" to swell to "its present strength."[107]

But what *was* its present strength? The Foreign Office was monitoring the German press and radio, studying reports from its intelligence sources in the Reich, and struggling to establish figures, or at least approximations, of Hitler's growing might. The Nazis were gambling with time. Versailles notwithstanding, on assuming the chancellorship in 1933 Hitler had told Germany's generals that he wanted heavy army recruitment to start immediately. The generals were aghast at his military goals. Walter Görlitz's history of the German General Staff clearly documents their doubts. It would be 1942 or 1943, they believed, before they could present him with a reliable military instrument. But Hitler knew them better than they knew themselves. He said he wanted the Reichswehr tripled by October 1, 1934. And the generals nearly made it.[108]

Winston's intelligence apparatus was now almost complete, and the information he assembled was somber. Others shared his alarm; Vansittart remembers that "Wigram, made desperate by our danger, asked leave to leak some of my figures. . . . After all they *were* my figures, given to me personally for the good of the world and if necessary for its enlightenment. Indeed the donor had only risked his life on condition that I use them, and the moment had come." Some of the data arriving at Chartwell were almost unbelievable. Meeting in executive session, the cabinet in early 1934 had decided to sell 118 Rolls-Royce Merlin engines to the German government. Chamberlain had declared that approval of the sale was a matter of principle; trade, like religion, should recognize no frontiers. The engines, he said, had been designed for civilian use, and he refused to yield ground when an Air Ministry minute pointed out that they could also "be used in small fighter planes." When word of this transaction first reached Churchill, he dismissed it as preposterous; but then the actual bill of lading arrived in a plain envelope. Immediately he proposed a total ban on aircraft deliveries abroad. The Royal Air Force needed every plane it could get, he said, and none should be sold to *any* other country — certainly not to Nazi Germany. Chamberlain, speaking for the cabinet, rejected his proposal because the trade policy of His Majesty's Government required that "deficiencies in the Defence Forces should be made up with the least possible interference with the export trade."[109]

It is significant that HMG thought it necessary to make a formal reply to Winston, who, on the face of it, was merely another backbencher. But in England's ruling classes, little is as it seems. Historic policy decisions, including some which Walter Bagehot incorporated in *The English Constitution*, have been made by men who never held public office or were even elected to Parliament. It is what one *is* that counts; Churchill carried with him his lineage, his former eminence, and a presence so commanding that he dominated a room the moment he entered it. He might be mocked in the House of Commons, his calls to arms dismissed as "warmongering" or "scaremongering." But he was heard; he was seen. No one, however haughty, dismissed him with one of those rude, infuriating stares which Englishmen of position hand down from generation to generation, as though by gene.

Winston himself, when aroused, could be intimidating, a tremendous advantage in a leader. Unfortunately his hubris made it impossible for him to play the sneak. Because he was the least devious of men, his informants often lost sleep wondering whether he might unwittingly betray their confidences. Vansittart, a fellow patrician (and at times an infuriating snob), was the most visible of them; to those whose spiritual homes were Lothian's Blickling Hall and the Astors' Cliveden — citadels of appeasement — his hostility to Hitler had made him the most dangerous man in Whitehall, although he was, at this time, beyond the reach of his critics. Lesser men worried about the possibility that Churchill might compromise them. Mrs. P., anxious about the informant she had recruited in Westerham, sent Winston a note: "Cmdr Anderson told me very seriously that he had never been frightened in life before, but he is of this, ie that the fact of the vast number of German pilots" — the Nazis had trained over 8,000 — "may come out. IT MUST NOT BE DIVULGED OPENLY as it would implicate not only him, but Wing Commander Goddard, whom he must not harm. The number must be camouflaged." And Major G. P. Myers, in reporting that General Aircraft Ltd. had built only twenty-three Hawker Furies (fighters), reminded Winston: "I am an employee of General Aircraft Ltd. and as such would lose my position were the source of this information disclosed by mischance."[110]

To those threatened by it, Churchill's carelessness in shielding such informants constituted a major defect. Certainly it was a flaw. So was his lack of consideration for those who served him, and (this became more conspicuous after he moved into No. 10) the callousness with which he discarded men for whom he had no further use. Ingratitude is not attractive. But the man who stood against Nazi Germany when his peers ridiculed him — and who later refused to quit when those around him believed England's cause lost, thereby saving Western civilization — is surely entitled to a few warts.

Not so Stanley Baldwin. In the mid-1930s he possessed more prestige and political power than any prime minister since the death of Queen Victoria. Yet in history he is a cypher. Clearly he relished his popularity and knew how quickly it would vanish if he warned the country to prepare for another four years in the trenches and barbed wire of France and Flanders. Everyone would turn on him, including his sovereign. In 1935, when Sir Samuel Hoare succeeded Simon as foreign secretary, Baldwin gave him one instruction — "Keep us out of war, we are not ready for it." And when Hoare kissed hands within the hour, George V urged him to resolve diplomatic crises with compromises. "I have already been through one war," he moaned. "How can I go through another? If I am to go on, you must keep us out of one."[111]

Churchill, hammering away at the need for collective security, remained far from the mainstream. Writing in the *Daily Mail* on July 13, 1934, he reaffirmed his support of the League of Nations, urging agreements, under the sanction and authority of the league, between anxious nations with standing armies: "If you want to stop war, you gather such an aggregation of force on the side of peace that the aggressor, whoever he may be, will not dare challenge. . . . It is no use disguising the fact that there must be and there ought to be deep anxiety in this country about Germany. This is not the only Germany which we shall live to see, but we have to consider that at present two or three men, in what may well be a desperate situation, have their grip on the whole of that mighty country."

In 1934 the BBC decided to broadcast a series of talks by prominent Englishmen on "Causes of War." The first two speakers declared that wars were fostered by armaments manufacturers ("merchants of death"), by "nationalism" (a perjorative alias for patriotism), and by networks of treaties, specifically the encirclement of Germany, which was called "a gratuitous affront to German pride." On Friday, November 16, when Churchill's turn came, his message was very different. Diplomatic attempts to isolate the Third Reich were "the encirclement of an aggressor," and the only alarming thing about it was that the circle seemed too fragile to contain the rising tide of Teutonic fury. If containment failed, a series of crises would "lead to war. Great Wars usually come only when both sides think they have good hopes of victory." He knew, he said, that some of his listeners would think none of this threatened them. But they must remember that only a few hours away "there dwells a nation of nearly seventy millions of the most educated, industrious, scientific, disciplined people of the world, who are taught from childhood to think of war and conquest as a glorious exercise, and death in battle as the noblest fate for man. There is a nation which has abandoned all its liberties in order to augment its collective might. There is a nation which with all its strength and virtues is in the grip of intolerance and racial pride unrestrained by law." He went on:

At present we lie within a few minutes' striking distance
of the French, Dutch, and Belgian coasts,
and within a few hours of the great aerodromes of Central Europe.
We are even within cannon-shot of the Continent.
So close as that!

Is it prudent, is it possible, however much we might desire it,
to turn our backs upon Europe and ignore what may happen there? . . .
I hope, I pray, and on the whole, grasping the larger hope,
I believe, that no war will fall upon us,

But . . . if you look intently at what is moving towards Great Britain,
you will see that the only choice open
is the grim old choice our forefathers had to face, namely,

Whether we shall submit to the will of the stronger nation
or whether we shall be prepared
to defend our rights, our liberties, and indeed our lives.[112]

By now a few elder statesmen were drifting toward his standard, and on November 28 Leopold Amery and Sir Robert Horne joined his small group of supporters when he moved to "humbly represent to Your Majesty that, in the present circumstances of the world, the strength of our national defences, and especially of our air defences, is no longer adequate to secure the peace, safety, and freedom of Your Majesty's faithful subjects." Speaking to the motion, Winston reasoned that only a strong British military presence would guarantee peace. He reasoned — and was jeered for reasoning — that "to urge preparation of defence is not to assert the imminence of war. On the contrary, if war was imminent preparations for defence would be too late." *Now* was the time for Britain to strengthen her ramparts. Parliament could not wish away the fact that German munitions factories were working around the clock — that rearmament dominated all other issues in the Third Reich, while Hitler Youth were taught "the most extreme patriotic, nationalistic and militaristic conceptions." The greatest peril to England was the Reich's building of a mighty air arm: "However calmly surveyed, the danger of attack from the air must appear most formidable." It was also unique. "Never in our history have we been in a position where we could be blackmailed, or forced to surrender our possessions, or take some action which the wisdom of the country would not allow it to do. . . . And yet, as I am going to show, this is the kind of danger which is coming upon us in a very short time unless we act upon a great scale and act immediately."

The time had arrived, he said, "when the mystery surrounding the German rearmament must be cleared up." The brutal fact was that "Germany already, at this moment, has a military air force — that is to say, military squadrons, with the necessary ground services, and the necessary reserves of trained personnel and material — which only awaits an order to assemble in full open combination; and that this illegal air force is rapidly approaching equality with our own." In less than three years the Luftwaffe would be "nearly double" the size of the RAF. And his estimate did not include some four hundred Nazi mail planes which could be converted into long-distance bombers "in a few hours" by removing passenger accommodations and fitting in bomb racks, racks which "are already made and kept in close proximity to the machines."

All Britain was vulnerable to Nazi bombers; modern aircraft traveling 200, 230, and even 240 miles an hour possessed an "enormous range. . . . The flying peril is not a peril from which one can fly. It is necessary to face it where we stand. We cannot possibly retreat. We cannot move London. We cannot move the vast population which is dependent upon the estuary of the Thames."[113]

Characteristically, Churchill had singled out one issue — air power — and would set all else aside when the RAF/Luftwaffe question arose. The year ahead would be crowded with crises, and he would play an active role in all of them, but he would always return to the question of England's strength in the air, for there England's very life was at risk. It was the linchpin of his military policy, linked to his call for collective security as diplomatic policy. If European states threatened by Nazi aggression agreed to confront Hitler with a solid phalanx of nations, as Napoleon had been confronted at Leipzig, the RAF's Fighter Command need never fly into battle.

Facing the hostility of all three party leaders — Baldwin, Attlee, even Liberal leader Archie Sinclair — the old lion braced himself and demanded emergency appropriations to establish an air force "substantially stronger" than Germany's. If Britain lost her lead, "even for a month," it should be considered "a high crime against the state." The turnout in the last election, he reminded them, was the largest in Britain's history, and the people had voted, above all things, for the maintenance and security of their native land. "That was the emotion which brought us into power, and I venture to say: Do not, whatever be the torrent of abuse which may obstruct the necessary action, think too poorly of the greatness of our fellow countrymen. Let the House do its duty. Let the Government give the lead, and the nation will not fail in the hour of need."[114]

Frances Stevenson, Lloyd George's mistress, watched the speech from the Strangers' Gallery. In her diary she wrote that she did not think Winston "spoke as well as usual. But I suppose it was the *matter* of the speech that was more important than the delivery. . . . There was imagination in it too, coupled with a patriotism that was almost imperialistic."[115]

Baldwin rose to reply for the government. He was skeptical of Winston's information. It was "extraordinarily difficult" to acquire accurate figures on German air strength; in that respect the Third Reich was "a dark continent." But in his position he had access to highly classified reports, he said, and he could assure the House that it was "not the case" that the German air arm was "rapidly approaching equality with us"; alarmists to the contrary, Germany's strength was "not fifty percent" of England's. In his reply to Churchill he said: "I cannot look further forward than the next two years," but "such investigations as I have been able to make lead me to believe that his figures are considerably exaggerated." Indeed, no other conclusion was reasonable, because "the Royal Air Force is far superior to German air power" and would hold a margin of 50 percent superiority.

Baldwin then made a formal pledge, to Parliament, his king, and his country:

> His Majesty's Government are determined in no condition to accept any position of inferiority with regard to what air force may be raised in Germany in the future.[116]

What possessed Stanley Baldwin, the shrewdest of politicians, to climb out so far on so brittle a limb — and for the second time within the year? On that earlier occasion, March 8, 1934, in the face of heated questioning from Churchill, Baldwin had assured Parliament: "Any Government of this country — a National Government more than any, and this Government — will see to it that in air strength and air power this country shall no longer be in a position inferior to any country within striking distance of our shores."[117] Now, as then, Baldwin wanted to silence Churchill, and he had, but the price was exorbitant. He had also been swayed by his craving for peace, of course, and his enjoyment of great personal popularity in the country. Still another explanation is that he ran what parliamentarians call an "easy" government, letting his ministers handle decisions in their departments while he acted as chairman of the board. So great was his indifference to diplomacy that the Foreign Office came to think of itself as a remote kingdom. Finally, the possibilities of error were multiplied by an irrational factor: Baldwin and those around him had repeatedly refused to believe that Hitler was what Hitler was. They had, in short, developed the political equivalent of a mental block.

If Baldwin had shut his mind to what was happening in Europe, however, he certainly knew the meaning of a solemn vow. No public school boy could survive the sixth form without a rigid sense of honor, and Baldwin, a Harrovian, knew how the Game was Played. But appeasement had begun to corrode the character of its evangelists. They were learning how to break promises and survive.

The immediate aftermath of Baldwin's November pledge is more interesting than the pledge itself, for it reveals the deeper motives of the men then governing England, ministers of the Crown who believed they were preserving the peace when in fact they were assuring the inevitability of war — and the end of Britain's role as a great power. When Baldwin committed his government to setting aside £130,000 for Britain's defenses, to abolish their "worst deficiencies," his own chancellor of the Exchequer cut him off at the pass. Bargaining relentlessly in cabinet meetings, Neville Chamberlain succeeded in paring down the £130,000 to £75,000 and finally to £25,000.

Although Chamberlain's position on rearmament would blur after he moved from No. 11 Downing Street to No. 10, as chancellor he fought every appeal for funds from the War Office, the Admiralty, and the Air Ministry. If Clausewitz saw war as a science, the chancellor viewed it as a business, or at any rate as an enterprise to be managed in the style of successful businessmen. When pondering decisions he liked to make a steeple of his hands and ruminate, looking out across the Horse Guards as to a mote in the middle distance. It was meaningless rite. His was a closed mind. Like Baldwin he was suspicious of innovations and of intellect. His Majesty's Government's position was that it would not prevent scientists or any other private citizens from preparing for war, provided they pay for it out of their own pockets and do nothing to obstruct the nation's business. Lord Weir, a Scottish manufacturer who also served as an adviser to the Air Ministry, said that an RAF expansion would do precisely that, so the project was shelved. Chamberlain explained to the House: "What we have to do is carry through in a limited period of time, measures which will make exceptionally heavy demands on industry and upon certain classes of skilled labour, without impeding the course of normal trade." He was willing to accept larger arms budgets, but believed that, for financial reasons, there must be a limit. That limit meant the gap between Britain's defense establishment and Germany's would continue to widen.[118]

In January 1935 two British peers visited the Reich Chancellery, on the Wilhelmstrasse, where they held vague discussions with Hitler on the subject of arms limitations. The talks were inconclusive, but since the Führer hadn't actually closed any doors, the FO was cautiously optimistic. Sir John Simon proposed that as foreign secretary he call at the chancellery and explore treaty possibilities. Arrangements were made and a meeting scheduled for March 6. Simon and Eden were packing on March 5 when the German ambassador telephoned to say that the talks would have to be postponed. The Führer had caught "a cold" (*"Erkältung"*) and was in bed, miserable and short-tempered.

The Foreign Office was familiar with diplomatic colds. Other sources in Berlin confirmed what was suspected: Hitler was furious at Britain. From

Chartwell Churchill wrote Clementine that Hitler had flown "into a violent rage and refused to receive Simon. . . . This gesture of spurning the British Foreign Secretary from the gates of Berlin is a significant measure of the conviction which Hitler has of the strength of the German Air Force and Army."[119]

There was an explanation for the Führer's *Zorn*. In London Baldwin's pledge to keep the RAF supreme in the sky had already begun to look wobbly. The fragments of information about German air strength pieced together by the Foreign Office were, as Michael Creswell put it, "most alarming." The Central Department had discussed the data, and Ralph Wigram had drawn up a memorandum for the cabinet. His latest information, assembled and analyzed, revealed that by 1936 the German air arm would surpass France's and exceed Britain's "very greatly." There was now no doubt, Wigram had concluded, that Nazi Germany was "out for superiority."[120]

Even Chamberlain had realized that something must be done. On March 4, therefore, His Majesty's Government had issued a White Paper on air defense. In it, HMG deplored the swiftness of Nazi rearmament, which, together with the belligerence of the government in Berlin, was identified as contributing to a general European "feeling of insecurity." The government therefore announced plans to expedite air force increases and proposed a major additional defense appropriation. Churchill was elated. He wrote Clementine that "all the frightened nations are at last beginning to huddle together."[121]

If Churchill was encouraged by the proposed increases, Hitler was enraged — hence his refusal to meet with Simon. Ralph Wigram wrote: "One wonders if in this 'rage' there is not also a design to make [it] difficult for the Govt here . . . to challenge the German rearmament." That, he pointed out, "would be entirely in the tradition of German diplomacy." Three days later Vansittart minuted: "All this is a far more overt German interference in British internal politics than anything the Soviets have done."[127] The Labour MPs remained pacifists to the man. Attlee moved to censure the government for recommending the increases. Though the Labour censure motion was defeated soundly, an air estimates debate was scheduled for Tuesday, March 19.

Meantime, Hitler was neither coughing nor sneezing. Instead he was unusually active, pacing his huge office in the Reich Chancellery, pondering a momentous move. Before April 1, he had promised General Ludwig Beck, an honorable officer who believed Germany's secret buildup was dishonorable, he would denounce the Versailles *Diktat* as *null und nichtig*. The time seemed ripe. The Versailles carbuncle had been festering long enough. Now he would lance it. To be sure, it would be awkward if France drew her sword. Her 352,000 poilus in metropolitan France could rout his half-formed army. But his instincts told him that they would shrink from force. He decided to test them. Air Minister Göring was told to announce the existence of the Luftwaffe. Everyone already knew it was there, but coming from a Reich minister the announcement would mean a formal, public rejection of the *Diktat*. London and Paris could either fight or submit. His instincts were right. They submitted. On March 9 Göring made his declaration, and the Quai d'Orsay was silent.

The following Saturday, March 16, with the British prime minister and his cabinet relaxing in their remote country homes, Hitler took the next step. After formally renouncing the Versailles treaty he decreed that all German youths were subject to conscription. The next day was Germany's annual Memorial Day, *Heldengedenktag*. The officer corps, wearing decorations and dress uniforms, gathered in the State Opera House to observe the occasion, the "spiked helmets of the old Imperial Army," writes William Shirer, who was there, "mingling with the . . . sky-blue uniforms of the Luftwaffe, which few had seen before."[123]

Churchill had tried again and again to tell Parliament that Germany was on a war footing. As he later wrote in the *Strand,* "the full terror of this revelation" now broke "upon the careless and imprudent world," as Hitler cast aside "concealment." He saw but one solution. France must use her superiority while she still had it.[124] But as Hitler had anticipated and Churchill had feared, France did nothing of the sort. In Geneva the French weakly lodged a protest at Germany's "violation of international law." The League of Nations condemned the Führer's decrees but rejected all proposals of punitive action, including sanctions.

In the House of Commons on March 19, Sir Philip Sassoon, parliamentary under secretary at the Air Ministry, announced that the RAF would be further strengthened by forty-one and a half squadrons over the next four years. During the past four months, he admitted, "the situation has deteriorated. There has been a great acceleration . . . in the manufacture of aircraft in Germany." However, he assured the House, "at the end of this year we shall still have a margin, though I do not say a margin of 50 percent."[125]

Churchill's sources unanimously, and vehemently, disagreed. The cabinet, he learned, was aware of the "potential superiority of German air power" but had concluded that Britain must learn to live with it. Baldwin must have known that the air debate would produce a stormy session, and any doubts he may have harbored had been dispelled by a letter from

Churchill, who bluntly told him that he meant to raise the issue of the Reich's growing strength. "I believe," he wrote, "that the Germans are already as strong as we are and possibly stronger." The March 4 White Paper, because of its inadequacy, could actually widen the gap between the two air forces. Then: "This will of course run contrary to your statement that 'this country shall no longer be in a position inferior to any country within striking distance of our shores.' " He ended ominously: "I shall argue that according to such knowledge as I have been able to acquire, this is not being made good, as will be rapidly proved by events."[126]

On Tuesday, March 19, he made this threat good. Backbenchers, he told the House, were beginning to lose faith in the credibility of His Majesty's Government. He picked up the previous day's *Daily Telegraph* and quoted: " 'Between 250 and 300 military aircraft have been added to Germany's total since November.' " At that rate, the Nazis could have another 1,500 warplanes by 1936.

> I must submit to the House that the Lord President was misled in the figures he gave last November, quite unwittingly, no doubt, because of the grave difficulty of the subject. At any rate, the true position at the end of this year will be almost the reverse of what he stated to Parliament. . . . I am certain that Germany's preparations are infinitely more far-reaching than our own. So that you have not only equality at the moment, but the great output which I have described, and you have behind that this enormous power to turn over, on the outbreak of war, the whole force of German industry.[127]

Laying before the House a string of precise figures, he went on: "At the end of the year, when we were to have had a 50 percent superiority over Germany, they will be at least three and four times as strong as we." He demanded that RAF expansion be redoubled.

Attlee's Labourites were outraged. The government's position was more nebulous. Baldwin chose Under Secretary Sassoon to answer the attack. To what extent Sassoon's reply was based on duplicity — Baldwin's duplicity or Sassoon's — and to what degree on ignorance by either or both, is matter for speculation. The record merely tells us that Sassoon rose, addressed himself to Winston, and said vaguely: "I do not think I can follow him into a morass of figures which must be, after all, very largely conjectural." Sassoon denied that the Luftwaffe would become "50 percent stronger than ours either on the basis of first-line strength or on the basis of total number of aircraft. So far as we can at present estimate, we shall still, at the end of this year, possess a margin of superiority."[128]

Baldwin again questioned Winston's evidence. It was incredible to him that the Luftwaffe could mount a serious challenge to the RAF. He could, it seemed, be convinced by only one man: Adolf Hitler. And that, amazingly, is what happened. Hitler had everything to gain by remaining silent, leaving His Majesty's Government comfortable in its false security. But in this, as in all else, he was unlike other men. Curing himself of his cold, he impulsively invited Simon and Eden to Berlin on March 25, less than a week after Parliament's air debate, and told them that the Reich had "reached parity with Great Britain as far as their respective air forces are concerned." Simultaneously, Goebbels released this electrifying news to the press. The Luftwaffe, the Führer told Simon, was a bulwark against bolshevism. He was alert to "the Russian danger," he said, though he seemed to be "a solitary prophet in the desert." He added confidently: "But later people will find out that I was right."[129]

Churchill wrote Clementine: "The political sensation of course is the statement by Hitler that his air force is already as strong as ours. This completely stultifies everything that Baldwin has said and incidentally vindicates all the assertions that I have made. I suspect in fact that he is really much stronger than we are."[130] Hitler had told Simon and Eden that according to his information the RAF had 1,045 first-line aircraft; since he was claiming parity, that, presumably, was the present strength of the Luftwaffe. But German intelligence had blundered. The British were nowhere near as formidable as he believed them to be. According to Air Ministry archives the RAF had only 453 first-line warplanes. Britain was in deep trouble unless she acted swiftly, but as summer approached and the days grew warmer it was often difficult to find any movement at all in Whitehall.

Parliament awaited a response from the front bench. And waited. And waited. In the *Daily Mail* of April 4 Churchill urged the government to make preparations for converting "the whole of our industry, should it become necessary, to various forms of munition production." Three days later Ralph Wigram arrived at Chartwell for an overnight stay. With him he brought a February 27 analysis by Creswell, comparing the relative air strengths of Britain and Germany. The Air Ministry report on RAF strength was only one of several sources; they varied greatly, but all confirmed Hitler. Actually the Führer had inflated the operational strength of his air arm, but Nazi "training, design, and production were proceeding apace and expanding rapidly," Telford Taylor writes. "The [operational] base was rapidly broadening, and by 1936 the threat of German air power would become reality."[131]

Given this momentum, and the inertia at No. 10, the threat was already real, and on May 2 Churchill spoke in the House of Commons:

> When the situation was manageable it was neglected, and now that it is thoroughly out of hand, we apply too late the remedies which then might have effected a cure. There is nothing new in the story. It is as old as the Sibylline books. It falls into that long dismal catalogue of the fruitlessness of experience and the confirmed unteachability of mankind. Want of foresight, unwillingness to act when action would be simple and effective, lack of clear thinking, confusion of counsel until the emergency comes, until self-preservation strikes its jarring gong — these are the features which constitute the endless repetition of history.[132]

He bluntly told the House: "It cannot be disputed that both in numbers and in quality Germany has already obtained a marked superiority over our Home Defence Air Force." At Chartwell Wigram had told Churchill that the Foreign Office staff was profoundly disturbed by the facts the FO was reporting to His Majesty's Government and HMG's abuse of them, and a remarkable instance of this had occurred only a few days earlier, on April 30. By April 1937, MacDonald had told the Ministerial Committee on Defence Requirements, "Germany will have 1,512 aircraft, and we shall have 740." He asked: "Is this a situation that the Government can explain and defend in the House?" Chamberlain replied firmly that they couldn't and shouldn't; if they were to remain loyal to Baldwin they were "bound to maintain the position" that his pledge had not been broken. Should they acknowledge the mistake, he said, they would "give Germany the impression that we are frightened." His proposal, which his colleagues accepted, was that air power should be judged not from the number of fighters and bombers in an air force, but by an intangible "air strength." Secretary for Air Londonderry eagerly fell in line. Luftwaffe training, he said, "is inferior to ours." RAF flying skills were so finely honed, and British airplane designers and manufacturers were so imaginative and competent, that to say "Germany is stronger" would be incorrect. Therefore Britain had, in effect, retained parity.

The Foreign Office and Air Ministry experts protested that this was mendacity. The parliamentary under secretary for foreign affairs produced a sheaf of reports demonstrating that German pilots and planes, far from being "behind in training and equipment," were in the lead. Even if Luftwaffe air expansion ended in 1937, aerodynamic engineers said, Britain might not catch up until 1942, which meant that in the interval German diplomacy could exploit the gap.

Baldwin considered a cover-up and rejected it. A parliamentary inquiry could destroy him and give Churchill a national forum from which he could emerge as Britain's hero. So, to the consternation of a majority of his ministers, he announced that he had decided to make a clean breast of things.

Addressing the House on May 22, nearly two months after Hitler's revelation, he quoted his pledge and followed it with what might be called his first confession:

With regard to the figure I gave in November of German air strength, nothing that has come to my knowledge since then makes me think that figure was wrong. I believed at the time it was right. Where I was wrong was in my estimate of the future. There I was completely wrong. . . . Whatever responsibility there may be — and we are perfectly ready to meet criticism — that responsibility is not that of any single Minister; it is the responsibility of the Government as a whole, and we are all responsible, and we are all to blame.[133]

> *"The horror of that moment," the King went on, "I shall never,* never *forget!"*
>
> *"You will, though," the Queen said, "if you don't make a memorandum of it."*

The fact that Stanley Baldwin had made a personal pledge to Parliament and England was ignored. Privately he blamed the Foreign Office. But FO figures which would have alerted him had gone to the Air Ministry. Vansittart recalled: "S.B. did not know the true position, either because the Air Ministry had not given my figures to him, or because it took them with salt, or because it had different ones of its own. Or perhaps they just got into a box and stayed there."

Intelligence, Van noted, "was becoming increasingly hard to operate in Germany, because informants, if detected, died slow and horrible deaths. Money was no longer enough for the risk of vastly improved tortures. Yet the facts were there. If S.B. had none, he was the rasher to say that we had a 50 percent margin."[134] The implications of the new situation were profoundly disturbing. Working at maximum capacity, British industry could turn out 1,250 planes in two years. Safety required twice as many.

Churchill expected a dramatic surge of public opinion, or at the very least a formal parliamentary inquiry. The conviction that he and England had been cheated burned in him. In April he had written Clementine: "How discreditable for the Government to have . . . misled Parliament upon a matter involving the safety of the country." Two days later he had written her again: "It is a shocking thing when a Government openly commits itself to statements on a matter affecting the public safety which are bound to be flagrantly disproved by events."[135]

But he had not thought it through. If the government fell, who would succeed? In other circumstances he might have expected a coalition, but both the Labour and Liberal parties had opposed *any* arms appropriations. Unmoved by Hitler's disclosures, they continued to plan waging the 1935 election campaign, now imminent, against "Tory armaments." Sinclair delivered a long speech in Parliament on "the question of private profits being made out of the means of death," and expressed astonishment at Winston's "dangerous argument" that vast sums should be spent on the RAF "in view of the financial conditions of the country and the intolerable burdens of our national debt and taxation." Lloyd George declared that Germany had been treated "as a pariah." She had, he said, been "driven into revolution" by the architects of Versailles (of whom he had been one) and demanded that her grievances be "put right."

Meanwhile, Baldwin was traveling around the country, puffing his pipe and assuring relieved audiences that England was safe. "His statements were wrong," Churchill wrote in an unpublished memorandum, "but they were everywhere accepted . . . by the British public." Winston blamed Fleet Street. His indictment was unjustified; as Lord Londonderry noted, press comment was "vehement." British reporters entering Germany confirmed the existence of the swelling army and the sense of urgency among the generals. In detailed dispatches the *Daily Telegraph* reported that the Luftwaffe was "already equipped with practically double the number of firstline military aircraft available in the country for the purposes of home defence." No sensible man could doubt now that Churchill had been right and Baldwin wrong. Londonderry wrote that the unmasking of the Baldwin pledge "came as a rude shock to the British public." In an open apology to Winston for having "ignored" his warnings, the *Daily Express* prophesied: "The reaction of the British public to the Nazi rearmament will be plain and positive."[136]

It wasn't, though. To a British colonel, a survivor of the Dardanelles expedition twenty years earlier, Churchill wrote that he was "astounded at the indifference" which had been the country's response to "the fact that the Government have been utterly wrong about the German air strength," and in a despairing note to Clemmie he said that the Nazis were "not only substantially stronger than we are," but were "manufacturing at such a rate that we cannot catch them up."[137]

By summer it was clear that the Dear Vicar had not only weathered the rearmament crisis; he was more popular than ever. Later Churchill recalled bitterly: "There was even a strange wave of enthusiasm for a Minister who did not hesitate to say he was wrong. . . . Conservative Members seemed angry with me for having brought their trusted leader to a plight from which only his native manliness and honesty had extricated him; but not, alas, his country." He wrote a friend: "When I first went into Parliament the most insulting charge which could be made against a Minister — short of actual malfeasance — was that he had endangered the safety of the country. . . . Yet such are the surprising qualities of Mr. Baldwin that what all had been taught to shun has now been elevated into a canon of political virtue."[138]

❧ ❧

The revelations emanating from Germany — the announcement of the Luftwaffe, the overt rejection of Versailles and the resumption of conscription, the claim of air parity with Britain — had shaken all Europe, and reverberations continued through the spring. Mussolini at that time was committed to neither Germany nor the democracies. The Duce admired Hitler's style but worried about Austria. He liked it as it was, a buffer between Italy and the Reich, but he knew the Führer had designs upon it. Therefore he had agreed to meet Ramsay MacDonald and Premier Pierre-Étienne Flandin for a three-power conference in Stresa, Italy. There, in April, the three leaders had declared that they would "oppose by all appropriate means any unilateral repudiation of treaties which may endanger the peace of Europe." This formation of the "Stresa Front" was followed by negotiations between Paris and Moscow for a Franco-Soviet military alliance. Stalin's foreign commissar then signed a similar pact with Czechoslovakia, though this was odd: the two countries lacked a common border; if Soviet troops were to rescue the Czechs, they would have to cross Poland or Rumania, both of whom historically regarded Russia as their bête noir.[139]

Hitler, deciding that Europe needed more reassurance, summoned the Reichstag on May 21 and delivered another *Friedensrede*, declaring that Germany would never dream of threatening other countries, that the Reich "has solemnly recognized and guaranteed France her frontiers," including the renunciation of "all claims to Alsace-Lorraine," and — at a time when Nazi *Strassenkämpfer* were storming through the streets of Vienna, clubbing Austrian pedestrians who had failed to greet them with the stiff-armed *Hitlergruss* — that "Germany neither intends nor wishes to interfere in the internal affairs of Austria, to annex Austria, or to conclude an Anschluss."[140]

In London *The Times* rejoiced. The Führer's speech was "reasonable, straightforward, and comprehensive. No one who reads it with an impartial mind can doubt that the points of policy laid down by Herr Hitler may fairly constitute the basis of a complete settlement with Germany — a free, equal and strong Germany instead of the prostrate Germany upon whom peace was imposed sixteen years ago." But the only settlement the Führer wanted was one achieved by conquest. On the evening of May 21, a few hours after his *Friedensrede,* he issued a secret decree reorganizing the Reich's military establishment. The name Reichswehr, a reminder of the hated Weimar regime, was replaced by the prouder, more aggressive Wehrmacht; the Ministry of Defense was rechristened the Ministry of War. General Blomberg, the war minister, was designated commander in chief of the armed forces. Under Blomberg, Göring headed the Luftwaffe, Raeder the navy, and Werner von Fritsch the army. Beck became chief of the Generalstab. In a few months, the War Academy would ceremoniously reopen, and the men Hitler had chosen to lead Germany in the coming war would speak eloquently of "the spirit of the Old Army." The tempo of the Reich's martial music was *accelerando.*

Had *The Times* known of this, Dawson's enthusiasm might have been tempered, but there can be little doubt that the paper's course would have remained unaltered. Very likely, excuses would have been found for Hitler. How Dawson and Barrington-Ward remained so blind to developments in central Europe is unfathomable. It is not as though information was withheld from them. Norman Ebbutt, the paper's Berlin correspondent, filed accurate, perceptive dispatches on Nazi Germany for over three years, until the summer of 1937, when the Nazis, realizing that there seemed to be virtually no limit to the humiliation and intimidation London would accept rather than risk war, expelled him. Ebbutt's editors read his stories; they knew what was happening in the Third Reich, though their readers often did not; his dispatches were frequently rewritten or suppressed by Dawson, who, after five years of jumping through Hitler's hoops, merely wondered at the man's ingratitude. He wrote H. G. Daniels, his Geneva correspondent: "I do my utmost, night after night, to keep out of the paper anything that might hurt their [Nazi] susceptibilities. I can really think of nothing that has been printed now for many months past to which they could possibly take exception as unfair comment."[141]

The Führer, meantime, had made England an offer which any proud government would have rejected. In November 1934 he had told the British ambassador that Germany, in building up her navy, would agree to limit it to 35 percent of the size of the Royal Navy, with parity, or something close to it, in submarines. He had repeated his proposal to Lord Lothian in January, to Simon again in March, and on May 21 before the Reichstag, vowing that there would be no escalation of demands. He recognized "the overpowering importance, and hence the justification of the British Empire to dominate the seas," and he was determined to "maintain a relationship with the British people and state which will prevent for all time a repetition of the only struggle there has been between the two nations." He added: *"Für Deutschland ist sie endgültig"* ("For Germany this is final").[142]

The Times found Hitler's proposal "sincere" and "well considered," and the prime minister and his cabinet agreed. Baldwin, at that point still lord president, received Joachim von Ribbentrop, the Reich's ambassador-at-large, to review the details. In less than two weeks S.B. intended to cast MacDonald aside and move into No. 10 himself. It was time he dealt directly with the Germans. He had negotiations in mind, but it turned out that there was no room for them; Hitler, Ribbentrop explained, had committed himself to the Reichstag and could not retreat. However, he quickly added, the Führer would never dream of naval rivalry with Britain, though submarines were an exception to the 35 percent ratio; there the Germans meant to limit themselves to four vessels for every five British subs, except in cases of *"Notwendigkeit"* ("necessity"). Baldwin accepted on the spot, then called in a small group of ministers and laid it all before them.[143]

Even the most devout parishioner has moments of doubt, and now and then one finds a true believer in appeasement straying, if only a few steps, from the garden path. It happened at this point to Sir John Simon. Usually Simon was among the most devout. But for a moment in 1935 he was shaken; during the opening talks with German naval officers and Wilhelmstrasse diplomats he lost his temper, delivered a heated lecture on the unwisdom of ratios, and stalked from the room. He was the only member of the cabinet who refused to endorse the treaty. His successor as foreign secretary, Sir Samuel Hoare, spoke sharply in the House on July 11 about "those people" — he meant Churchill and the Churchillians — "who seem to take a morbid delight in alarms and excursions, in a psychology, shall I say, of fear, perhaps even of brutality." He called them "alarm-mongers and scaremongers." The pact with Germany, he noted, had been greeted by the people with glee. It was "an agreement profitable alike to peace and to the taxpayer."[144]

Hoare and the rest of His Majesty's Government overlooked a great deal. Hitler had driven a wedge between the allied nations on the Reich's western front, the two powers his generals feared most. At the same time he had ended Germany's diplomatic isolation, imposed by the rest of Europe after he had quit the League of Nations and abrogated Versailles. And with a stroke of the pen England — which had nothing to gain from the naval pact — was shattering what remained of Versailles' claims to legitimacy. Germany, as she continued to rearm, could no longer be accused of breaking her word. It was perhaps true, as Eden told the French diplomat Alexis Léger, that the limitations imposed at Versailles no longer meant much. But "it should have been apparent," Telford Taylor writes, "that for the British to countenance a reborn German Navy, including U-boats, would deeply wound French and Italian feelings."[145] Moreover, with an Anglo-Italian crisis over Ethiopia imminent, the timing of the pact was atrocious.

Two backbenchers in the House saw this: Lloyd George and Churchill. The Welsh firebrand was very old now, and his flame was flickering low, but Winston was fine, fit, and fierce. Speaking immediately after Hoare, he damned the agreement. Britain, he said, had struck a very poor bargain. The assumption that the Nazis would observe the still untested rules of submarine warfare was, he said, "the acme of gullibility." He pointed out that Britain had "condoned this unilateral violation of the Treaty [of Versailles]" without conferring with any of "the other countries concerned." At the very moment when European salvation depended on a "gathering together of Powers" fearing the "rearmed strength of Germany," England had chosen "to depart from the principle of collective security in a very notable fashion." The French would moan but cling desperately to Britain, their only sure ally. The Italians could go elsewhere. And, he predicted, they would.

But the most perilous feature of the pact, said Churchill, was that it took no account of Britain's worldwide responsibilities. Germany, he reminded Parliament, had no overseas possessions. Britain had an empire. He knew there were men in the chamber who disapproved of the Empire, but it still existed, and until Parliament decided otherwise, the government was obliged to shield the Dominions, Crown Colonies, and protectorates. The 100-to-35 ratio was comforting only if the Royal Navy were confined to the North Sea.

He paused, scowled, and then lashed out: "What a windfall this has been for Japan! Observe what the consequences are. . . . The British Fleet, when this [German] programme is completed, will be largely anchored in the North Sea." Now "the whole advantage of having a great naval base at Singapore upon which a battle fleet can be based" — to protect, he pointed out, imperial domains including Australia and New Zealand — "is greatly affected by the fact that when this German fleet is built we shall not be able to keep any appreciable portion of the British Fleet so far from home." The path to peace did not lie in bilateral agreements. War could be prevented only by collective security. And now His Majesty's Government had abandoned that. Admirers of the German regime might rejoice, but he was troubled. Before he rose, he reminded the House, the right honorable gentleman preceding him had talked of alarm-mongers and scaremongers. He accepted those epithets. One could do worse. "It is better to be alarmed and scared now than to be killed hereafter."[146]

The issue rankled. Later he noted that the *Daily Herald* had quoted Baldwin as saying, "We shall have to give up certain of our toys — one is

'Britannia rules the waves.' " Here Baldwin was attacking, not only Churchill's position, but also one of the three patriotic anthems Winston treasured most, the other two being "Land of Hope and Glory" and "The British Grenadiers." Churchill drew attention to the prime minister's misquotation. "It is, 'Britannia, rule the waves' — an invocation, not a declaration of fact. But if the idea 'Rule Britannia' is a toy, it is certainly one for which many good men from time to time have been ready to die." Yet at the time he said privately that very few Britons seemed ready to die for anything anymore; the entire country seemed crippled by a national *défaillance*. He had spoken to them in the tongue of Victoria's England, itself a dead language, and there were no interpreters.[147]

The Anglo-German Naval Agreement was signed on June 18, 1935 — Hitler sent Ribbentrop to London as his personal emissary — eleven days after Baldwin succeeded MacDonald at No. 10, thereby becoming prime minister *de jure* as well as *de facto*. Less than three months had passed since the Führer made public the fact that Germany had renounced Versailles and was rearming. Europe, the United States, and Japan took note of Britain's cynical disregard of her Versailles obligations, and Mussolini, deciding he could now safely flout the League of Nations Covenant, ordered his generals to plan an invasion of Ethiopia, to take place after the rainy season ended.[148]

The most baffling aspect of this diplomatic debacle was Britain's treatment of her great ally across the Channel. In a spectacular understatement, Eden had pointed out to his ministerial colleagues that the French, when they learned of the agreement, might have "reservations." Certainly they were entitled to them. Hoare told the cabinet that it was "essential" to humor the Germans in certain small requests, among them a pledge that the French be told none of the treaty's provisions. France also had a first-class navy, and the new agreement would put her ships within range of German naval gunners. Yet His Majesty's Foreign Office could not even tell the Quai d'Orsay how many ships Hitler could build, their size, and their categories — battleships, heavy cruisers, light cruisers, destroyers, U-boats. Actually, the pact permitted the Nazis to construct five battleships whose armament and tonnage outclassed any vessels in the Royal Navy — this had been accomplished by a mistranslation of one clause — together with twenty-one cruisers, sixty-four destroyers, and, in practice, an unlimited number of submarines.[149]

French loyalty to the triumphant entente of 1914–1918 was vital to England's safety. If war were declared, it would be France's job to contain the German army; at most the British could send but five divisions to the

Continent at the outset and six later. But beginning with Hitler's defiant rejection of Versailles and continuing through the imminent crises in the Rhineland, Austria, Czechoslovakia, and Poland, France was to be the passive member of the 1918 entente, deferring to the British, accepting decisions made in Whitehall. The patriciate ruling England enjoyed their dominant role, accepting Gallic docility without question. They had never understood why anyone should question their judgment and thought the French were merely being sensible.

Churchill shared the illusion of France's defensive strength. Speaking in the House three days after Hitler's defiant acknowledgment of German rearmament, Winston said: "The frontiers of Germany are very much nearer to London than the sea-coasts of this island are to Berlin, and whereas practically the whole of the German bombing air force can reach London with an effective load, very few, if any, of our aeroplanes can reach Berlin with any appreciable load of bombs."[150] He considered this warning dire. He did not anticipate England's plight if Nazi bombers were based on *French* airfields — directly across the Channel. Carrying blockbuster bombs, they could then devastate London and Britain's great industrial cities, including their armaments factories, in the Midlands. Even Churchill's imagination could not encompass such a calamity. The possibility that the Germans could actually conquer France and overrun Paris, using over a million superb infantrymen behind a great panzer force, was never raised. He still believed that the French army was "the finest in the world."

Having predicted Hitler's outrages throughout 1935, Winston was treated with new respect in Parliament, but, he later wrote, although the House "now listened to me with close attention, I felt a sense of despair." The year had seen a series of triumphs for the Führer and humiliating defeats for the democracies. Baldwin, Churchill now knew, was hopeless. He recalled, from an 1883 issue of *Punch*, lines he had memorized as a young schoolboy in Brighton:

Who is in charge of the clattering train?
The axles creak and the couplings strain;
And the pace is hot, and the points are near,
And Sleep has deadened the driver's ear;
And the signals flash through the night in vain,
For Death is in charge of the clattering train.[151]

Baldwin was asleep at the throttle, so Winston decided that *he* must become the engineer, or at any rate the conductor or stoker — in short, a member of the government's crew and therefore a participant in the formulation of policy. On August 2, 1935, Parliament passed the Government of India Act, charting the course which would lead to Indian independence and, at the same time, ending Winston's six-year struggle to keep India in the Empire. He had quit the Tory leadership because of its decision to end the Raj, but now India was no longer an issue. He was free to concentrate on the Nazi menace, and, as he saw it, to rejoin his old cabinet colleagues. On August 25 he addressed an open letter to his Epping constituents, a eulogy to the glories of British India, which ended: "We have done our best and we have done our duty; we cannot do more."

As a propitiary gesture he invited G. D. Birla, one of Mahatma Gandhi's chief lieutenants, to lunch.* Afterward, Birla wrote Gandhi that the luncheon had been "one of my most pleasant experiences" in England. His host, he reported, had said, "Mr. Gandhi has gone very high in my esteem since he stood up for the untouchables," and had then gone on to express the hope that a Congress party regime would bring "improvement in the lot of the masses, morally as well as materially. I do not care whether you are more or less loyal to Great Britain. I do not mind about education, but give the masses more butter." Winston had told Birla: "I am genuinely sympathetic towards India. You need not expect anything but silence or help from us." Later Attlee introduced Churchill to Jawaharlal Nehru. According to him, the two old Harrovians "got on splendidly. Winston said how he had admired Nehru's courage in standing up to rioters and Nehru said he had enjoyed reading Winston's books. They chatted most amicably and something like real confidence was established, and to the best of my knowledge never diminished."[152]

In the weeks before November's general election, no Tory campaigned more tirelessly for Conservative candidates than Churchill. He offered his services to the party's central office, and they scheduled him to deliver major addresses in Wanstead, Hull, Biggleswade, Epping, Woodford, and South Chingford. He would decide his own strategy, of course, but Baldwin had chosen the ground on which the party as a whole would fight. The issues would be the Anglo-German Naval Agreement, trade and shipping, and public works. Actually, as Macmillan later recalled, Baldwin's own campaigning was "somewhat disingenuous. His speeches were admirably devised to suit all shades of opinion." He declared, *"No great armaments!"* That pleased the pacifists. Advocates of lower taxes wanted to stress the

* For a full account of Churchill's struggle against Gandhi's campaign for Indian independence, see volume one of this work, pages 830 ff.

government's refusal to join Hitler in an arms race; Baldwin preferred an agreement with Hitler, which, he said, provided solid evidence that hard-headed, no-nonsense Britons could deal with dictators.[153]

Hitler, Baldwin's audiences were reassured, was not the menace he had been made out: "There may be Governments deliberately planning the future, leading reluctant or unsuspecting people into the shambles. . . . I confess that in my own political experience I have not encountered Governments possessed of all these malevolent qualities. Most Governments seem not much better or worse than the people they govern." To those like Leo Amery, who privately predicted that appeasement might encourage dictators, Chamberlain, speaking for the prime minister, heatedly replied that this was a "mischievous distortion." The choice, he said, was "whether we shall make one last effort at Geneva for peace and security" or submit in a "cowardly surrender" to warmongerism, which would hold them up to "the shame of our children and our children's children." It was Chamberlain's strength that he never doubted that events would vindicate him; it was his fate that they would condemn him. Baldwin was the same, and the tragedy for both was that they lived long enough to know it.[154]

Churchill remained faithful to the cadence of his own drummer. Tory whips had approached him, advising him his prospects in the party would brighten if he refrained from fresh attacks on the Nazis until after the election. Winston replied that although that was the prime minister's line, it wasn't his. While Baldwin was dismissing the Nazi threat, Winston, in speeches and in articles for the *Daily Mail* and *Strand,* told his audiences the Ruhr's "great wheels revolve . . . disgorging weapons" for "the already largely war-mobilized arsenals and factories of Germany." As the campaign reached the home stretch he delivered a major address in Parliament, reminding members that Hitler was still spending £800 million a year — $3.9 billion at the then current rate of exchange — on arms. He said: "We cannot afford to see Naziism in its present phase of cruelty and intolerance, with all its hatreds and all its gleaming weapons, paramount in Europe," and he noted that he was being joined by fresh converts in the House. Only yesterday Lloyd George, finally aware of the Nazi peril, had performed an act of contrition in the House. Winston said that neither Lloyd George "nor His Majesty's Government will, I imagine, disagree today with the statement that Germany is already well on her way to becoming, and must become incomparably, the most heavily armed nation in the world and the nation most completely ready for war."[155]

There could be no doubt, he declared, that Nazi plans of European conquest existed. "Germany is an armed camp," he told Parliament. "The whole population is being trained from childhood up to war." And: "The

German air force is developing at great speed and in spite of ruthless sacrifice of life." In "The Truth about Hitler," published in the November 1935 *Strand*, he wrote of how the Führer, after secretly rearming, had "sprung forward armed to the teeth, with his munitions factories roaring night and day, his aeroplane squadrons forming in ceaseless succession, his submarine crews exercising in the Baltic, and his armed hosts trampling from one end of the broad Reich to the other." Condemning Hitler's "ferocious doctrines," and predicting that they would be carried out with "brutal vigour," he wrote that German soil was "pock-marked" with concentration camps, where masses of Germans, from "world-famous scientists" to "wretched little Jewish children," were persecuted. Nothing could save a Jew from imprisonment and torture. "No past services, no proved patriotism, even wounds sustained in war," could prevent atrocities against people "whose only crime was that their parents had brought them into the world." Churchill referred skeptics to *Mein Kampf*, where Jews were described as "a foul and odious race." But the inmates of these camps were not all Jewish. Under Hitler "the slightest criticism" of the Führer and his criminal regime was "an offence against the State."[156]

The British ambassador in Berlin reported that Churchill's attacks on Hitler were widely covered in German newspapers, some of which "point out that the speech has special importance in view of Mr. Churchill's almost certain inclusion in the next Cabinet." There was no such certainty, of course, but throughout the thirties Winston seemed more formidable abroad than in England — a consequence, perhaps, of his perception and his eloquence. On October 30 Ralph Wigram minuted: "Mr. Churchill is making himself very unpopular in Germany," and the ambassador reported that the tone of Winston's piece "is much resented here." Desmond Morton, however, cabled Chartwell that "Germany did not like it — but resentfully admires it in private. It is right that Germany should realize that we are not all lulled into weak-livered complacency."[157]

Hitler read a translation of the *Strand* piece. According to Wigram's sources, he all but flung himself on the carpet and drummed his heels on the floor. Libels against the Reich's head of state, the Wilhelmstrasse officially warned the British embassy in Berlin, were "intolerable." Wigram sent the protest to Churchill, including the infuriated Führer's question to Britain's ambassador: "What is to be the fate of the Anglo-German Naval Agreement if the writer of this article is to be the Minister of the British Navy?" When this reached Wigram he wrote in the margin: "I don't know what exactly this means: but if Churchill knew that Hitler had said this" — as though Winston wouldn't know, and within hours — "he might well say that it was only another proof of the necessity of strong armaments — otherwise we shall have Germans telling us who shall & shall not be in office in this country."[158]

An unexpected consequence of this was a clumsy Nazi attempt to discredit Churchill in his own constituency. Broadcasts by the London correspondent for *Völkischer Beobachter* identified him as "an unscrupulous political intriguer," who, unless HMG repudiated him, might become a threat to world peace. His aunt Leonie Leslie wrote him: "Oh Winston! What a grand speech and *how* I am enjoying the abuse from Germany which I hear on the wireless." The British naval attaché in Berlin wrote him from Warsaw: "I had to wait until I left Germany to write & say how wonderful I thought your speech — as the Germans are so annoyed with you for telling the truth that no letters addressed to you would ever have got out of the country." He reminded Winston of a conversation between them in the spring of 1933 and commented: "I have never forgotten what you said then about the Nazis. Two & a half years in Berlin has shown everything you said then is true today. The Germans have only learnt one thing from the War — & that is *never* to go to war again until they are absolutely ready, & certain of victory. No chances next time! The Germans fear, & I hope, you WILL be 1st Lord — or Minister of Defence! Please don't give me away."[159]

The Nazi reaction to Churchill's speeches and writings during the 1935 election campaign mirrored the future. Indeed, over the years one of the most persuasive witnesses to Churchill's effectiveness abroad was Adolf Hitler. In speeches to his people he said: "If there is any man in the world who is authorized to speak for Germany, then I am that man and no one else. . . . The German regime is entirely a matter for the German people and I will never allow any such foreign schoolmasters or governesses to interfere with it." When Winston spoke of the fate of Austria and Czechoslovakia, two democracies which lay helpless in Hitler's path, Hitler cried: "I can only ask — Good Lord [*du meine Güte*]! After all, what is a democracy? Who defines it? Has the Almighty perhaps handed the key to democracy to such people as Churchill? I am only the advocate of Germany. I am not like Churchill, and God knows what oppositionalists, who style themselves advocates of the world. If Churchill says: 'How is it that a Head of State can cross swords with a British parliamentarian?' I must say: 'Churchill, feel yourself honored.' " And: "Churchill said the German regime should be destroyed by forces within Germany. . . . I can assure this gentleman, who appears to live on the moon, that forces opposed to the regime do not exist in Germany. There is only one force — the National Socialist movement and its leadership and armed forces. I cannot stop this man from rising to high office, but I can assure you that I will prevent him from destroying Germany." And: "If Churchill came to power in Great

Britain instead of Mr. Chamberlain we know it would be his aim to unleash immediately a world war against Germany. He makes no secret of it." And: "I assume it is his desire to steal our weapons and to bring about again our fate of 1918. I can tell Churchill that it happened only once and that it will not happen again!"[160]

❧ ❧

On Thursday, November 14, Britain voted. By evening it was clear that the Conservatives, winning 432 seats, had retained their overwhelming majority in the House of Commons. Labour had won 154 seats, a gain; the Liberals 21, a loss. Churchill was among the few Conservatives actually to increase his plurality; he polled over 10,000 votes more than his two opponents combined. That evening he dropped by Albert Hall to watch the results posted. Once the outcome was certain, he took a cab to Stornoway House, where Lord Beaverbrook was throwing a victory party. Beaverbrook's first words to Churchill were: "Well, you're finished now. Baldwin has so good a majority that he will be able to do without you." Twelve years later, in an unpublished note, Winston wrote: "I was taken aback and offended by this." A "man like Mr. Baldwin," he had believed, "would not be influenced . . . about my joining the Government by the size of his majority."[161]

When he had resigned from Baldwin's shadow cabinet nearly five years earlier, Churchill had told Vansittart: "I have cheerfully and gladly put out of my mind all idea of public office." Van knew that was untrue. "Without office he was miserable," he wrote, "although I could never understand why. The big boy without a bauble had at his command every other gift in the world, and much attention if small assent. He should have been radiantly happy as the greatest of his time, probably of all time." Van had pointed out to him that should he become one of the cabinet's twenty-two ministers, the only consequence would be an increase in his frustration. Churchill believed the government thought well of him. Vansittart knew he was wrong: "Right and Left he was in bad odor for his gloomings. The Left called him 'the darling of the die-hards,' who proved too faint-hearted to back him." And the right regarded him a renegade. "The pity was great" for both Winston and himself, Van recalls, "for a lone voice can accomplish nothing, and in the last analysis a British public servant can do little to serve the State. We both pegged away, he with orations, I with comments and memoranda."[162]

In June, when Baldwin moved into No. 10, he had appointed Hoare as Simon's successor at the FO and replaced Londonderry with the abler Sir

Philip Cunliffe-Lister, an admirer of Churchill. The new air minister's greatest achievements were to be his promotion of new fighter planes: the Hawker Hurricane, first tested five months after he took office, and the Spitfire, whose prototype flew four months later. In the House Winston had continued what he later described as his "severe though friendly" criticism of the government. He supported the government's position, in Geneva and elsewhere, with increasing frequency. "It is a terrific decree in life," George Meredith wrote, "that they must act who would prevail." A backbencher could not act. Vansittart notwithstanding, a minister could. In previous cabinets Churchill had found that he could often sway decisions. As his desire for a seat on the Treasury Bench grew, so did the frequency with which he praised Baldwin in public. In October he had written him: "If yr power is great, so also are yr burdens — and yr opportunities. I think you ought to go to the country at the earliest possible moment, & I hope you will do so. . . . I will abide with you in this election, & do what little I can to help in the most serviceable way." It is impossible to miss the hunger in these last words.[163]

This, then, was how matters stood when Beaverbrook told Churchill that Baldwin didn't need him. Six months had passed since Winston had last spoken disparagingly of the P.M. His ministerial experience surpassed that of any other man in the House save Lloyd George. Despite slighting references to his age (in May a Tory MP had patronized him: "Although one hates to criticise anyone in the evening of his days . . .") he was at the height of his powers. And he yearned for office. This longing was inexplicable to Vansittart, but Winston found no pleasure in playing the independent critic. His imagination, his energy, and his capacities could be best expressed only when he occupied a seat of power. He hoped to be given the Admiralty but would take what he could get. Therefore he left London for Chartwell and awaited a call from Baldwin.[164]

It never came.

He remained near the telephone for six suspenseful days, and then, abandoning hope, sank into one of his deepest depressions, unable even to paint. Actually, Baldwin had toyed with the idea of bringing him into the government earlier, when he had reshuffled the cabinet after taking over as P.M. Dawson had talked him out of it, arguing that senior members of the party would be resentful and, moreover, that Churchill would be "a disruptive force, especially since foreign relations and defense will be uppermost."[165]

Ironically, Churchill's greatest handicap among his fellow Tories is now seen as a source of his splendor. Far more suspicion and disfavor in the party were aroused by the strength and coherence of his convictions than by his stinging phrases in the House or his undisguised lust for office. "No strongly centralized, political organization," Isaiah Berlin noted, "feels altogether happy with individuals who combine independence, a free imagination, and a formidable strength of character with stubborn faith and a single-minded, unchanging view of the public and private good."[166]

After the November 14 landslide, other Conservatives joined *The Times* editor in urging Baldwin to keep Churchill out. Nancy Astor wrote him: "Don't put Winston in the Government — it will mean war at home and abroad. I know the depths of Winston's disloyalty — and you can't think how he is distrusted by *all* the electors of the country." Three days after the election Thomas Jones wrote in his diary: "Winston will be kept out, I think." Later in the day, when the decision had been made, he noted with relief that the government had "kept clear of Winston's enthusiasm for ships and guns."[167]

To Jones, Baldwin said: "One of these days I'll make a few casual remarks about Winston. . . . I've got it all ready. I am going to say that when Winston was born lots of fairies swooped down on his cradle with gifts — imagination, eloquence, industry, ability, and then came a fairy who said 'No one person has a right to so many gifts,' picked him up and gave him such a shake and twist that with all these gifts he was denied judgment and wisdom. And that is why we delight to listen to him in the House but do not take his advice."[168]

But no fairy tale was responsible for Churchill's disappointment. Baldwin was swayed by other, less enchanting motives. One was recrimination. The Dear Vicar's geniality was legendary, but he would have been masochistic not to nurse the wounds Winston had inflicted on him in the past. In one of Baldwin's less affable moments he snapped: "Winston is part of the flotsam and jetsam of political life thrown up on the beach." Those around him agreed. Neville Chamberlain came close to the truth when, arguing against giving Churchill a ministry, he commented that his powers of persuasion might convince the cabinet to increase rearmament, which would have pressed the Treasury to produce funds. The Depression was still a grave problem. The City and the Bank of England were wedded to stable prices and a stable pound. Deficits were considered wicked, except in wartime, and deplorable even then. As A. J. P. Taylor puts it: "The secret of Pandora's box which Schacht had opened in Germany and which the American New Deal had also revealed, was still unknown to the [British] Government." Taylor believes that the MacDonald, Baldwin, and Chamberlain administrations "feared to offend economic principles even more than to offend Hitler."[169]

Apprehension over the reaction in Berlin was a factor, though Churchill's conclusion was that Baldwin had denied him office to pay "some of his debt to the pacifist deputation which he had received in the last days of the election." The truth was more ignoble. It hadn't occurred to Winston that a British prime minister, in selecting his cabinet, would bow to German sensitivities. He was wrong. According to Lady Longford, in considering a cabinet reshuffle, "Baldwin felt less inclined than ever to annoy Hitler by including the bellicose Churchill." Years later Boothby said: "Many people asked why Mr. Churchill, who had held the offices of first lord of the Admiralty, secretary of state for war, secretary of state for air, and minister of munitions, had not been appointed. The answer is quite simple. He would have roused, disturbed, and rearmed the country."[170]

Winston felt he had to leave England for at least six weeks. Afterward he wrote that he had "agreeable consolations. I set out with my paintbox for more genial climes without waiting for the meeting of Parliament."[171] Like all Churchillian holidays, this one would be a working vacation, largely devoted to writing the third volume of his Marlborough biography.

It seemed to be an excellent time for a Conservative member of Parliament to be absent from London. The situation in northeastern Africa had become critical; Italian troops massed in the horn of East Africa, on the frontiers of the Italian Somaliland, had invaded Ethiopia, or Abyssinia, as it was called then, undeterred by a commitment Sam Hoare had made to the League of Nations in Geneva. Slapping the lectern with the flat of his hand, the foreign secretary had declared: "The League stands, and my country stands with it for . . . steady and collective resistance to all acts of unprovoked aggression!" The press and the overwhelming majority of league delegates had agreed with Belgium's revered Paul Hymans: "The British have decided to stop Mussolini even if that means using force."[172] But they hadn't. In Geneva, Hoare, schooled at Harrow and Oxford, the very model of an English gentleman, had sown the seeds, not of resolve, but of hypocrisy.

TWO

REEF

SURVEYORS establishing landmarks work from several known reference points, and those who wish to view the past in perspective may adopt a similar technique. In the mid-1930s Europe's anticipation of the future began its swing from the unthinkability of war to the thinkability of it to the fatalistic acceptance of its inevitability. The omens were unmistakable. In March 1935 Hitler had announced that Germany was rearming; eleven days after Baldwin replaced MacDonald as prime minister in June the calamitous Anglo-German Naval Agreement was signed; and, after the Tory landslide in November, the redemption of Hoare's vow came due. Dead ahead lay the three pivotal crises: Ethiopia, the Rhineland, and Spain.

Using a boundary dispute as an excuse, Italy had begun its east African buildup in February 1935. Emperor Haile Selassie withdrew his troops twenty miles behind his frontier to avoid the kind of incident Mussolini was seeking, but the Duce would not be denied; he declared that he intended to use every weapon at hand, including poison gas, which had been outlawed by international convention. Hoare's warning speech in Geneva was delivered on September 11, a month before the fighting began. The historian of the league wrote that "it would be difficult to exaggerate the effect of his electrifying address, putting Mussolini on notice."[1]

It was Hoare's finest hour, though he hadn't meant it to be; to the end of his life he insisted that the world had simply misunderstood him, he hadn't intended to sound resolute. The fact is that he had been carried away by his own rhetoric. It had been his intention to suggest obliquely that if the league should censure any rupture of the Ethiopian frontier, invoking mild sanctions against Italy, the Duce might be bluffed into backing off. This, in Hoare's words, would infuse "new life" into the league's "crippled body." But bluffs work only if the other side thinks them real. And Italian intelligence agents, after burgling the British embassy in Rome, knew Britain had no intention of using force — had, in fact, no force available to use. Royal Navy ships routinely cruised the Mediterranean, but none carried ammunition. Therefore Mussolini felt quite safe when, as it was reported to

Hoare, he appeared on his balcony, jutted his jaw to the cheers of the throng below, and cried that Britain was trying to "rob" Italians of "a place in the sun."[2]

Churchill's steady eye was still fixed on Nazi Germany. England and France needed allies, and the best possible solution to that problem was a strong, united League of Nations. Compared with Hitler's Reich, he told Parliament, Ethiopia was "a very small matter." Nevertheless, he had read with pride that the foreign secretary had taken a stand for the independence of the ancient mountain kingdom confronting Italian invasion. It was, he said, a matter of honor. The League of Nations was "fighting for its life. Probably it is fighting for all our lives. But it is fighting." He believed that the league "has passed from shadow into substance, from theory into practice, from rhetoric into reality. We see a structure always majestic, but hitherto shadowy, which is now being clothed with life and power, and endowed with coherent thought and concerted action. We begin to feel the beatings of a pulse which may, we hope, some day . . . restore a greater measure of health and strength to the whole world."[3]

Actually, he was troubled. His feelings about the issue were far more ambivalent than he publicly acknowledged. In the last war the Allies had barely beaten the Germans with Italy on their side. Backing the league made sense if all the member nations observed its covenant. If they didn't, Britain's stand would prove disastrous, for Italy would be alienated. And Ethiopia was not, in his view, a moral issue. Like most men of his generation, he regarded blacks as an inferior race. In Cuba, fresh out of Sandhurst, he had written that he distrusted "the negro element among the insurgents." He never outgrew this prejudice. Late in life he was asked whether he had seen the film *Carmen Jones*. He had walked out on it, he replied, because he didn't like "blackamoors."[4]

Berlin, not Rome, remained the enemy capital. To him Ethiopia was a "wild land of tyranny, slavery, and tribal war." He later wrote: "In the fearful struggle against rearming Nazi Germany which I could feel approaching . . . I was most reluctant to see Italy estranged, and even driven into the opposite camp." Moreover, Britain and France were in an awkward position. Arguably they were Italy's accomplices, because in April at Stresa they had not done what they ought to have done. At the end of the conference Mussolini had made a point of excluding Africa from the mutual agreement to abstain from aggression. The Allied diplomats decided not to argue the point. In Churchill's words, "Everyone was so anxious for Mussolini's support in dealing with Germany that it was felt undesirable at that moment to warn him off Abyssinia, which would obviously have very much annoyed him."[5]

Now they were facing the consequences. On August 21, when east Africa's rainy season was still holding Italian troops in check, Hoare and Eden, now minister for League of Nations affairs, had approached Winston for his advice. According to Hoare's record of their talk, Churchill had "showed himself deeply incensed at the Italian action," had "urged reinforcement of Britain's Mediterranean Fleet," and, above all, had stressed the need for "collective" action — not in the service of the league's ideals, but because of his "main interest in the League as a defence against Hitler." Churchill explained, noted Hoare, that "if the League now collapsed in ignominy," it would mean "the destruction of the bond that unites British and French policy and of the instrument that might in the future be chiefly effective as a deterrent to German aggression."[6]

He said as much in Parliament, supporting Hoare's pledge because the integrity of the league was at stake, but adding that he could not envisage Haile Selassie in the role of martyr. "No one," he said, "can keep up the pretense that Abyssinia is a fit, worthy, and equal member of a league of civilized nations." The sanctity of the League Covenant was still paramount, however; he proposed that the British government leave no doubt in Mussolini's mind that England was prepared to observe the covenant "even to the point of war."[7]

The issue was moot and still is. As Telford Taylor writes: "In retrospect, it seems that the wisest course, if bold, would have been to play the game of collective security to the hilt and bring Mussolini down, even if it meant a war, in which Italy would have had no allies. But benefit might also have been derived from a more cautious, if cynical, policy of keeping the Duce on the side of the angels in Europe by allowing him a bit of deviltry in Africa."[8]

As it happened, neither course had been given a chance. In "The Hollow Men" T. S. Eliot had written:

Between the idea
And the reality . . .
Falls the shadow.

Rome's new legions struck southward from Eritrea on October 3, 1935, erupting across the frontier in a festive mood, trumpets blaring and huge battle flags rippling overhead. But even before they could reach Haile Selassie's troops the banners were discarded, the trumpets mute, and the Duce's gladiators bogged down in the wild, pathless terrain. Then the African defenders, attacking to drive them back, proved unexpectedly fierce. Evelyn Waugh described the Italian fighting, if that is the word for it, in his satirical *Scoop*. But events in the diplomatic arena were even more absurd. The British delegation in Geneva rallied the support of fifty nations in condemning Italy as the aggressor. Asked how far he would go in backing the covenant, Churchill replied, "The whole way with the whole lot."[9]

The league voted overwhelmingly to impose economic sanctions upon the Italians, but Baldwin's list of sanctions suggested that the prime minister had developed a bizarre taste for black humor. Among the items denied to the aggressor were camels, mules, donkeys, and aluminum — a metal so available in Italy that it constituted one of the country's chief exports. Unmentioned were the raw materials essential to the waging of war: steel, iron, coal, and, most remarkably, oil. Had they been deprived of petroleum, Mussolini's mechanized columns would have vanished in the ravines and chasms separating them from the Ethiopian capital, Addis Ababa. Indeed, had Baldwin been serious, he could have achieved an even quicker end to the Italian offensive by simply closing the Suez Canal to the Duce. It was suggested. Eden and his colleagues in Geneva answered that if Mussolini's patience were tried he might lose his temper and spread the war to the Continent, or launch a "mad dog" assault on His Majesty's Mediterranean Fleet.

This opéra bouffe gained in lunacy as it went along. Ice skating was Hoare's passion. En route to Switzerland, and accompanied by Vansittart, he broke his journey on Saturday, December 7, to confer with France's premier, Pierre Laval. Together they concocted a plan which would end the Ethiopian war by ceding two-thirds of the country to Italy — including vast tracts she could never win by force of arms — leaving Haile Selassie with the remainder of his territory and a corridor through Italian territory to the Red Sea. If Mussolini balked, the emperor would be given a different corridor running through the adjoining colonies of Britain or France. Elated, Hoare entrained for the Swiss village of Zuoz, laced on his skates, glided across the frozen lake, and fell, breaking his nose. Churchill, upon learning of the cynical intrigue in Paris, growled, "Too bad it wasn't his neck."[10]

The conspirators had agreed to keep their scheme secret until their governments had approved of it, but *Paris-Soir* acquired the complete text before Hoare even reached Zuoz, and on Monday the details were on every front page in the world. Churchill was in Majorca. Friends persuaded him that he was lucky to be abroad, so he decided to stay outside Barcelona, painting and writing in the serene countryside. There was no serenity in England; in the House a Labourite proposed that a new sign be erected over the league portals: "Abandon half, all ye who enter here — half your territory, half your prestige." In a letter to *The Times*, Harold Macmillan declared that were the Hoare-Laval plan approved, Britain would be party to a conspiracy "to undermine the very structure which a few weeks ago the nation authorized us to underpin. I have never attended the funeral of a murdered man, but I take it that at such a ceremony some distinction is made between the mourners and the assassins."[11]

The Hoare-Laval scheme, a loser from the beginning, now became an albatross. Mussolini, Haile Selassie, Baldwin, and Laval's cabinet all denounced it. On December 17 Randolph sent his father a full account. Relations between the two were strained — and would soon be strained further — but Churchill had found his son a resourceful reporter. Randolph wrote that "Baldwin, Hoare, and Vansittart" had "planned this shameful surrender," and "are extraordinarily confident of the outcome." Outraged public opinion on the other side of the Channel forced Laval from office, and the day after Randolph's report the British cabinet voted overwhelmingly — Neville Chamberlain was the sole exception — to demand Hoare's resignation. Desmond Morton wrote to Churchill: "Baldwin has completely lost every shred of confidence. He is believed to have sacrificed his friend, not because that friend made an error in method, but because he believed it was the only hope of saving his own skin."[12]

In hindsight it seems that Churchill's wisest course would have been to reject his friends' advice and return to London the moment the scandal broke. But he still believed his chances of reaching office were greater if he kept his sword sheathed and let others attack the prime minister. Indeed, from October 1935 to March 1936 he neither wrote nor spoke a single word criticizing the prime minister in public. Even his memoirs are bland on the Hoare-Laval deal; he merely comments that Vansittart, preoccupied with the Nazi menace, wanted to strengthen the Anglo-French entente "with Italy in their rear a friend and not a foe."[13]

Perhaps the most perceptive glimpse of Churchill during the Ethiopian crisis is provided by Vincent Sheean, the American foreign correspondent. Sheean, like Churchill, Lloyd George, the writer Michael Arlen — and, later, the Duke and Duchess of Windsor — was a friend of Maxine Elliott, a rich retired actress whose white, terraced villa in Cannes, the Château de l'Horizon, offered exotic asylum to celebrities.

"Churchill first became visible to me," Sheean wrote, "in a red bathrobe over bathing trunks; he wore a large, flopping straw hat, and slippers and a cherubic grin." He was defensive on the Ethiopia issue, but never evasive. When an elegant Frenchwoman pointed out that the British Empire had been built by the sort of small wars Italy was now waging, Winston smiled benevolently and said: "Ah, but you see, all that belongs to the unregenerate past, is locked away in the limbo of the old, the wicked days. The world progresses." That, he said, explained the purpose of the League of Nations. Winston declared that the Duce was "making a most dangerous and foolhardy attack upon the whole established structure." The results were "quite incalculable. Who is to say what will come of it in a year, or two, or three? With Germany arming at breakneck speed, England lost in a pacifist dream, France corrupt and torn by dissension, America remote and indifferent — Madame, my dear lady, do you not tremble for your children?"[14]

In such company he never criticized His Majesty's Government, but his letters are full of it. After four days with Lloyd George at the Hotel Mamounia in Marrakech, he wrote Clementine that Britain was "getting into the most terrible position, involved definitely by honour & by contract in almost any quarrel that can break out in Europe" with her "defences neglected" and the cabinet "less capable a machine for conducting affairs that I have ever seen." He believed that the "Baldwin-MacDonald regime has hit this country very hard indeed, and may well be the end of its glories."[15]

Clemmie replied that "I really would not like you to serve under Baldwin, unless he really gave you a great deal of power and you were able to inspire and vilify the Government." The political situation at home, she wrote, was "depressing." She saw, as he did not, how powerful his position would be if, when his hour struck, he were free of any tainted association with the appeasers. Afterward he agreed, writing of his years in the wilderness: "Now one can see how lucky I was. Over me beat the invisible wings." Anthony Eden, less fortunate, emerged slightly stained. He had nearly resigned when he learned of the Hoare-Laval agreement, but Baldwin persuaded him to remain and then appointed him foreign secretary. Eden was only thirty-eight. He looked like a man of the future. But Churchill thought him a poor choice. He wrote home: "I expect the greatness of his office will find him out."[16]

It was Eden, in his new role, who had to tell the House that what Austen Chamberlain had described as the Ethiopian "madness" was over. It wasn't quite; but clearly the old kingdom was doomed to become an Italian colony. Lloyd George rose in a terrible fury. He said: "I have never before heard a British Minister . . . come down to the House of Commons and say that Britain was beaten . . . and that we must abandon an enterprise we had taken in hand." He pointed at the front bench. "Tonight we have had the cowardly surrender, and there are the cowards."[17]

In itself, the seven-month Ethiopian war was of little consequence. But the implications of the Hoare-Laval fiasco were far-reaching. By the time Haile Selassie's capital fell, the League of Nations had been destroyed as a force for peace and a referee of international disputes. At the same time, British hopes for an Anglo-Italian alliance, based on Mussolini's determination to keep Austria free of Nazi rule, had vanished in the quarreling between London and Rome. Neville Chamberlain, Baldwin's designated successor, had written off collective security as a bad debt. The Stresa Front, the Duce's handiwork, lay in ruins, and though he himself was to blame, he resigned from the league in a blind rage and sent his son-in-law and foreign minister, Count Galeazzo Ciano, to Hitler's Berghof retreat on the Obersalzberg, overlooking the resort town of Berchtesgaden. Informal discussions there led to serious talks in Berlin. The climax came in a fateful speech by Mussolini, delivered in Milan's Piazza del Duomo on November 1, 1936. In it he added a phrase to history, declaring, "The Berlin conversations have resulted in an understanding between our two countries. . . . This Rome-Berlin line is not a diaphragm but rather an axis around which can revolve all those European states with a will to collaboration and peace." "Rome-Berlin Axis" would be on front pages all over the world for the next seven years. Thus Germany, though uninvolved throughout, was the one beneficiary of the Ethiopian travesty. The naval treaty with Britain had been Hitler's first giant step in freeing his country from the diplomatic quarantine imposed on it after he had violated treaties bearing the signatures of Germany's leaders. Now two clumsy Allied politicians had freed him of that odium. In foreign chancelleries, at least, the Reich was once more respected as a great power.[18]

Today Hoare's conspiracy with Laval would mean the destruction of his political career. But fifty years ago members of the old boy network could survive almost any disgrace. Hoare's career was switched to a siding, but Baldwin had already marked him down as the next first lord of the Admiralty, and subsequently he served as home secretary, lord privy seal, secretary for air, and ambassador to Spain, after which he moved over to the House of Lords as Viscount Templewood. The great mass of the British people had a short memory and paid little attention to upper-class quid pro quo. In 1935 Baldwin merely advised Hoare to lie low for the present. The future viscount understood; he knew the rules; he must stiffen his lip and do his penance when old friends declined to be seen with him just now.

He was, therefore, startled to receive a graceful letter, bearing a Morocco postmark, from Winston Churchill. Winston wrote "to congratulate you on the dignity of yr speech of resignation, & to tell you how vy sorry I am at what has happened. . . . After so much work & worry I daresay the breathing space will be welcome." Like the hypochondriac who always arrives at the bedside of the sick, Winston rarely failed to provide consolation for political casualties. But Hoare was uncomforted. That same day he had been subjected to the unkindest cut of all — and from his sovereign at that. Following the timeless custom, he had resigned his office by riding to

Buckingham Palace and surrendering his seals of office to King George V. The King said: "Do you know what they're all saying? No more coals to Newcastle, no more Hoares to Paris!" When Eden arrived to kiss hands and claim the seals, the monarch repeated his royal jest and added that he had been puzzled by Hoare's response. "You know," he said, "the fellow didn't even laugh."[19]

❦ ❦

Churchill had ended his letter to Hoare: "We are moving into a year of measureless perils." The first blow of 1936 was the death of the King, at Sandringham, in January. Winston was still in Morocco when he learned of it from a *News of the World* cable, which offered him £1,000 — three times an MP's annual salary — to write a tribute to George V. He dictated the piece to Mrs. Pearman on a train between Tangier and Marrakech and dispatched it only three days after the new monarch, Edward VIII, had begun his reign. Winston had known Edward for twenty-five years, and to his "joyous and gay" memories of their long association, as he now wrote him, there was also the "hope that Your Majesty's name will shine in history as the bravest and best beloved of all the sovereigns who had worn the island Crown."[20]

Within hours of his return to London he was engulfed in politics. Since Hitler's early days in power, Churchill had been urging Baldwin to create a new cabinet post, a minister of defense who would coordinate all three services. Support for the office had been growing in Parliament ever since, and now Baldwin agreed. But who would he name? Most MPs didn't even ask; the appointment of Churchill was assumed. Austen Chamberlain wrote his sister: "In my view there is only one man who by his studies, and special abilities, and aptitudes, is marked for it, and that man is Winston Churchill." At one time or another Churchill had borne ministerial responsibility for the War Office, the Admiralty, and the RAF. The previous November, when he had been excluded from the post-election cabinet shake-up, Harold Nicolson had written in his diary: "Clemmie tells me that Winston has not yet been approached. It looks as if he were going to be left out till February." It was February now. H. A. Gwynne of the *Morning Post*, a harsh critic of Churchill for over twenty years, nevertheless took the matter as "settled." Harold Macmillan and Lord Castlereagh were openly backing him, and *Cavalcade* magazine reported that even "left-wing Conservatives, who were hostile to Winston over the India question, now take the line that if there must be a defence minister, Winston Churchill is the man." Anthony

Crossley, a young Conservative MP, parodied the arguments against Churchill's appointment:

But Winston were worst, with his logic accursed
For he'll scorn our impartial endeavour.
He'll make up his mind, right or wrong, with the first,
And how shall we temporise ever?
Let's have soldier or sailor or peer or civilian,
Whatever his faults, so they not be Churchillian.[21]

The inner circle around Baldwin — the members, so to speak, of the Dear Vicar's congregation — were not amused. They were thinking along other lines. Secretary to the Cabinet Hankey wanted a "sound man," someone who "will work and not upset the psychology of the whole machine." Warren Fisher, permanent under secretary of the Treasury, thought that the minister "should be a disinterested type of man, with no axe to grind or desire to make a place for himself" — a qualification which would have ruled out every gifted man in the House. Hoare, untouched by the letter which had wished him well in his dark hour, sang Churchill's dispraises with the prime minister and emerged to write Neville Chamberlain jubilantly: "On no account would he [Baldwin] contemplate the possibility of Winston in the Cabinet for several obvious reasons, but chiefly for the risk that would be involved by having him in the Cabinet when the question of his (S.B.'s) successor became imminent." News of this reached Chartwell. Sir Roger Keyes wrote Churchill that, encountering Baldwin in one of Westminster's halls, he had told him that Churchill "would be a very good appointment both in your interests and those of the Country." "I cannot only think of my interests," Baldwin remarked, turning away. "I have to think of the smooth working of the machine." The two minds — one preoccupied with the country, the other with the party machine — could not meet.[22]

Churchill, at Chartwell, remained on tenterhooks. He wrote Clemmie on February 21: "There is no change in the uncertainty about my affairs. Evidently B. desires above all things to avoid bringing me in. This I must now recognize. But his own position is much shaken, & the storm clouds gather." She replied: "My darling, Baldwin must be mad not to ask you to help him. Perhaps it is a case of 'Those whom the Gods wish to destroy. . . .' " Ten days later he wrote her: "The Defence business is at its height. Baldwin is still undecided. . . . Now this morning the DT [*Daily Telegraph*] comes out as the enclosed, wh is the most positive statement yet & the latest — & from a normally well-informed quarter. Anyhow I seem to be still *en jeu*."[23]

Baldwin didn't want Churchill, but since the Ethiopian debacle his prestige had dwindled, and support for Winston was growing in the House and in Fleet Street. It was at this moment, when events hung in a delicate balance, that Winston was sandbagged by his impetuous son. Churchill had a premonition of disaster from this quarter. On the day after Christmas he had written Randolph from Rabat: "It would in my belief be vy injurious to me at this junction if you publish articles attacking the motives & character of Ministers, especially Baldwin & Eden. I hope therefore you will make certain this does not happen. If not, I shall not be able to feel confidence in yr loyalty & affection for me."[24]

Randolph honored his father's request; he wrote no pieces critical of anyone else in the government. He did something worse. He announced that he would stand for Parliament, running against the national government's incumbent — Ramsay MacDonald's son Malcolm, a member of Baldwin's cabinet. Winston wrote Clemmie that Randolph had "put a spoke in my wheel." Later he wrote her: "You will see how unfortunate and inconvenient such a fight is to me. 'Churchill v MacDonald.' " It was worse: Lord Rothermere, the press lord, had assigned Baldwin's son Oliver "to write up Randolph, which he is apparently ready to do, and to write down Malcolm. . . . So we shall have Ramsay's son, Baldwin's son, and my son — all mauling each other in this remote constituency." Churchill was apprehensive that the prime minister might interpret Randolph's candidacy "as a definite declaration of war by me." Then he surmised that no other interpretation was possible: "I should think that any question of my joining the Government was closed by the hostility which Randolph's campaign must excite." Yet he still hoped for a post.[25]

Winston did not appear in Scotland to speak for his son. He wanted to; Brendan Bracken advised against it. They compromised by agreeing that Churchill should release a brief statement to the press, concluding with the mild observation that with "parliamentary government under grievous challenge in the present age . . . undue pressure should not be put by the Central Government upon a free choice of the constituency." That fell far short of a ringing endorsement, but the assumption that he was behind his son's challenge remained. *The Times* as much as said so. Winston wrote the proprietor of the paper that he was "surprised to read in the leading article of Saturday's 'Times' on the Ross and Cromarty by election, an insinuation that I had prompted my Son's candidature. As a matter of fact, I strongly advised him to have nothing to do with it. Naturally, as a Father, I cannot watch his fight . . . without sympathy; but I am taking no part in it. . . . In these circumstances the innuendo of your leading article is neither true nor fair."[26]

But the skeptics included the Scots voters, who, when they went to the polls, turned the contest into a rout. Malcolm MacDonald's victory was extraordinary. Of the 17,343 votes cast, 2,427 — less than 14 percent — were for Randolph. Boothby wrote Winston that while he was "sorry," he believed that "a little chastening at this particular juncture will not necessarily be to his ultimate disadvantage." There was, Boothby continued, "more sympathy & friendly feeling" for Randolph "than he suspects. But, my God, you don't challenge that machine with impunity." The *Edinburgh Evening News* wrote bitingly: "By emphasizing the unpopularity of the Churchillians' attitude, the decisive defeat of Mr Randolph Churchill in Ross and Cromarty seems to be regarded as another nail in the political coffin of Mr Winston Churchill, either as a candidate for the Admiralty or Cabinet Minister charged with the coordination of Defence Services." Friends visiting Chartwell were careful to avoid any mention of the by-election, though they could see Winston's hurt, a wound sharper than any inflictable by a serpent's tooth.[27]

The prime minister thought Winston lacked judgment. Yet on his instructions, the cabinet was taking the first of the steps Churchill had demanded. On March 3, the government published a new Defence White Paper, revealing plans to build an aircraft carrier, two new battleships, and five battle cruisers; recruit six thousand Royal Navy ratings; raise four motorized infantry battalions; modernize antiaircraft defense and field artillery; and build 224 more Spitfires and Hurricanes. Fleet Street called it a bid for carte blanche, and indeed the White Paper itself declared: "Any attempt to estimate the total cost of the measures would be premature."[28]

Backbenchers were startled. It seemed hardly possible that such a program could get past the Exchequer without Neville's approval. Nor had it. He had suggested the vague wording, reasoning that "it would probably be advisable to avoid figures which could be added up to a larger amount than public opinion is expecting." The appropriation endorsed by the cabinet was £400 million, to be spread over the next five years. Since Nazi Germany was spending over twice that much on arms every year, the outlay which troubled Chamberlain seems rather less than exorbitant. It was in fact quite inadequate; RAF strength would rise from 1,512 front-line aircraft to only 1,736. To Churchill a strong England was one capable of defending itself. To Chamberlain it meant balanced budgets. "The British government," in the words of A. J. P. Taylor, "still lived in the psychological atmosphere of 1931: more terrified of a flight from the pound than of defeat in war. . . . The confidence of the City of London came first; armaments came second." Furthermore, the program outlined in the White Paper specified that it must be carried out "without impeding the course of normal trade." In other words, Britain would observe business as usual.[29]

Although the step was in the right direction, Churchill told Parliament on March 10, it was far too short. He could not feel that the new policy "has done full justice to the anxiety which the House feels about the condition of our national defences." Money was irrelevant and should not even be a consideration: "When things are left as late as this, no high economy is possible. That is the part of the price nations pay for being caught short." Churchill had been startled to read in the press, and even to hear remarks in the House smoking room, "giving a general impression that we are overhauling Germany now. . . . The contrary is true. All this year and probably for many months next year Germany will be outstripping us more and more." It would "not be possible for us to overtake Germany and achieve air parity, as was so solemnly promised," until the Germans reached a saturation point and decided to end expansion of the Luftwaffe. Then England could bridge the gap. "But this day will be fixed by Germany, and not by us, whatever we do." He believed that if London and Paris acted promptly, as he later wrote, there was "still time for an assertion of collective security." But "virtuous motives, trammelled by inertia and timidity, are no match for armed and resolute wickedness. A sincere love of peace is no excuse for muddling hundreds of millions of humble folk into total war. The cheers of weak, well-meaning assemblies soon cease to echo, and their votes soon cease to count. Doom marches on."[30]

Doom appears in many forms, but none more naked than fixed bayonets. Even as Labour and Liberal pacifists were fuming that Baldwin, prodded by the warmonger Churchill, was returning England to its militant, imperialist past, genuine militarism was forming ranks on a riverbank 375 miles to the east. On the moonbright Rhine it was Friday, March 6, 1936. Night was thickening. In London's Savoy ballroom that evening, couples were dancing to the popular American tune "Red Sails in the Sunset." Across the Atlantic, where it was still afternoon, teenagers leaving school were arguing over the Lucky Strike Hit Parade's ranking of "In the Chapel by the Moonlight," "The Way You Look Tonight," and "Pennies from Heaven." In Atlanta Margaret Mitchell, an obscure newspaperwoman, was correcting proof for her first novel — she had named her heroine Pansy and titled the book *Tomorrow Is Another Day,* but her editor had changed them to Scarlett and *Gone with the Wind.* Meanwhile, for the first time since 1918, the hobnailed boots of German soldiers would march. Adolf Hitler's first invasion would begin at daybreak.

After the failure of his Austrian coup two years earlier, the Führer had been looking for a quick military victory elsewhere, and increasingly he had found himself looking westward, toward the Rhineland. Although it was the French who had christened this seventeen-year-old state *la région zone démilitaire*, it remained a part of the Reich, inhabited by Germans and including within its borders some of their greatest cities — Cologne, Aachen, Frankfurt, and Düsseldorf — industrial hubs separated by lovely vineyards producing some of the world's finest wines. Here the Versailles peacemakers had carved out, from land on both banks of the Rhine, a strip of territory thirty-one miles wide. French troops had occupied the zone after the war but left early at British urging. Under the treaty, Germany was forbidden to billet troops or build fortifications there. The buffer had been designed to provide France and Belgium with security, or at least a warning, should the Germans decide to give the Schlieffen Plan a second try and knife swiftly westward. Even more important, the zone was the keystone to France's arch of postwar alliances with Poland and Czechoslovakia. If the Germans attacked eastward, the French could race across the Rhineland and strike at the Ruhr, the Reich's industrial heartland and the center of its armaments works, including Krupp's flagship plant, the Gusstahlfabrik, in Essen.

At Versailles the losers had had no choice, but six years later Germany had freely joined the Locarno Pact, accepting the demilitarized zone as a permanent buffer. Should German troops enter the zone under any pretext, the Locarno agreement provided, they would be guilty of "an unprovoked act of aggression," and the other European powers bound by Locarno — France, Britain, Belgium, and Italy — would have not only the right, but the duty, to expel them from the Rhineland by force. Before 1914 generations of Rhinelander children had been taught to sing *"Die Wacht am Rhein,"* with its rousing challenge: "The Rhine, the Rhine, the German Rhine! Who guards tonight our Stream Divine?" In Wilhelmine Germany the reply had always been: the Sword of Germany. But for the past eighteen years guards had been unnecessary, for under Locarno soldiers of France or Belgium who entered the buffer would also have been guilty of *une violation de propriété*. The zone was one of the few postwar political achievements blessed by the Führer; as late as his *Friedensrede* of May 21, 1935, delivered to the Reichstag, he had hailed the unarmed Rhineland as the Third Reich's "contribution" to European peace. The Reich, he had solemnly declared, would "unconditionally respect" the "territorial" provisions of Versailles and the pledge, freely made by the republic of Germany at Locarno, to honor the inviolability of the Rhineland.[31]

Europe between the Wars
Hitler's Aggressions 1936-1939
1. Rhineland (March 1936)
2. Austria (March 1938)
3. Sudetenland (September 1938)
4. a. Bohemia, Moravia (March 1939)
b. Memel Territory (March 1939)
MILES
KILOMETERS
NORTH SEA
ATLANTIC OCEAN
FINLAND
NORWAY
SWEDEN
ESTONIA
LATVIA
LITHUANIA
BALTIC SEA
SCOTLAND
GREAT BRITAIN
IRISH FREE STATE
ULSTER
WALES
ENGLAND
DENMARK
HOLLAND
BELGIUM
LUXEMBOURG
GERMANY
DANZIG
EAST PRUSSIA
POLAND
SOVIET UNION
FRANCE
Rhine River
SWITZERLAND
CZECHOSLOVAKIA
AUSTRIA
HUNGARY
RUMANIA
YUGOSLAVIA
ITALY
ADRIATIC SEA
ALBANIA
GREECE
BULGARIA
BLACK SEA
TURKEY
AEGEAN SEA
SYRIA
PORTUGAL
SPAIN
CORSICA
SARDINIA
BALEARIC IS.
SICILY
MEDITERRANEAN SEA
AFRICA
d'Art Studio

Churchill was suspicious. The Führer, he believed, was likelier to remain faithful to his "great lie" credo, set forth in *Mein Kampf*. Winston had adopted, as a working thesis, the assumption that any given foreign policy statement by Hitler was the exact opposite of the truth. On January 17, eight months after the May *Friedensrede*, he wrote Clemmie that if his intelligence sources were right, the Führer was planning a major announcement which "may well be that Germany will . . . reoccupy the neutral zone with troops and forts." Should that happen, he wrote, the French with British help would be obliged to drive the invaders out. He added: "Baldwin and Ramsay, guilty of neglecting our defences in spite of every warning, may well feel anxious not only for the public but for their own personal skins."[32]

He was wrong about the British reaction but right about Hitler's intentions. Three weeks *before* promising to respect the territorial integrity of the Rhineland, the Führer had ordered the OKW (Oberkommando der Wehrmacht), the high command of Germany's armed forces, to draw up plans for seizing it. The operation was encoded *Schulung* (Schooling) and was, according to the Führer, to be "executed by a surprise blow at lightning speed," with "only the very smallest number of officers" to be informed. Meanwhile he was building an excuse for aggression. He began with the same Reichstag speech, observing, in an aside, that the mutual assistance treaty between France and Russia, initialed two months previously but not yet ratified by the Chamber of Deputies, would alter the status of Locarno by introducing "an element of insecurity."[33]

The French government knew what was coming. As early as October 21, 1935, the Deuxième Bureau informed the ministry that German troops were "actively preparing" to invade the zone; on October 21 the French high command sent an alert to the Quai: "The hypothesis of a German repudiation of the Rhineland statutes must be envisaged before the autumn of 1936, at the latest." The most plausible warnings came from the able French ambassador in Berlin. After a lengthy talk with the Führer in November, André François-Poncet wrote that Hitler had lost his temper *"dans une longue tirade contre le pacte franco-soviétique qu'il considérait comme criminel."* François-Poncet was convinced that Hitler now awaited only the appropriate moment to attack.[34]

Laval wired the French ambassador in London on January 11, 1936, advising him that four German divisions had been moved to the Rhineland's border. In Whitehall, the FO acknowledged receipt of the message but made no comment. A week later Laval and his cabinet learned from General Maurice Gamelin, the French commander in chief, that intelligence reports left little doubt that the Germans would invade the zone "as soon as possible." Again the British were informed; again the FO was unresponsive. This silence troubled Pierre-Étienne Flandin, who had succeeded Laval as *ministre des affaires étrangères,* and in the last week in January, Flandin crossed the Channel, officially to join the mourners at George V's state funeral but actually to discuss the approaching crisis with Eden.[35]

The timing was unpropitious. During the past eight months relations between the two allies had become strained; after the Anglo-German Naval Agreement and the Hoare-Laval affair, France seethed with Anglophobia. "With Hitler against bolshevism!" cried *L'Ami du peuple,* and in *Gringoire* the fiery journalist Henri Béraud raged: "I hate England. I hate her by instinct and by tradition. I say, and I repeat, that England must be reduced to slavery!" Knowledge of all this had preceded Flandin to London, and diplomatic jargon did not ease the tension. Men charged with managing a nation's foreign affairs are expected to rise above petty bickering, but Eden's reception of Flandin on Monday, January 27, 1936, was frosty. On Tuesday the Frenchman talked to Baldwin. Flandin had come to ask precisely what Britain planned to do if Hitler attempted to seize the Rhineland. To his consternation, neither Englishman would say. When he pressed them, they countered by asking him what *France* would do. It was hardly the sort of encouragement one is entitled to expect from an ally.[36]

Eden's own account of the French minister's mission is almost self-incriminating. To Flandin's question, he wrote, he had "replied that the French attitude to a violation of the Rhineland was clearly a matter for the judgment of the French government. . . . If they wished to negotiate with Hitler, they should do so; if they intended to repel a German invasion of the zone, they should lay their military plans. Any forcible action would depend on France." His "impression" was that "while not prepared to use force to defend the zone," his French guest had been "equally reluctant to negotiate about it." The young foreign secretary even entertained the uncharitable thought that Flandin "might be tempted" to "put the blame for inaction on either count elsewhere." In a cable to the British ambassador in Paris, Eden warned against "hypothetical" discussions and added: "Taking one thing with another, it seems undesirable to adopt an attitude where we would either have to fight for the zone or abandon it in the face of German reoccupation. It would be preferable for Great Britain and France to enter betimes into negotiations with the German Government for the surrender on conditions of our rights in the zone while such surrender still has bargaining power."[37]

None of this makes sense. You cannot bargain rights over territory which you are not prepared to defend. If the Allies meant to surrender the Rhineland — and an invitation to open negotiations would tell the Germans that they did — there was nothing left to discuss. The Germans would know they could march into a void, encountering no opposition. But the appeasers assumed that everyone preferred peace to war.

In the early hours of that Saturday, March 7, 1936, darkness and patchy fog lay over long stretches of the ancient Rhine, a river beloved by German poets and a source of exasperation to foreign conquerors from Caesar to Eisenhower, Bradley, and Montgomery. Despite the hour, few Rhinelanders were asleep. All week hearsay had been spreading among them, gathering in momentum, and it was accurate to the last particular. In Germany even the rumors were precise.

As the first streaks of dawn flushed the sky they heard a faint hum coming from the direction of Berlin. It grew to a growl which reached a thundering crescendo as Messerschmitt fighters, flying in tight V formations and bearing the broken cross of the German Reich on their wings, swarmed out of the eastern sky, circled the spires of Cologne Cathedral, and raced back eastward. Then the infantry began approaching from the right bank. Brawny young soldiers in the old, familiar coal-scuttle helmets crossed the bridges on bicycles and entered the squares of cities and towns in the demilitarized zone. Crowds already gathered there murmured their approval, a susurration which rose to an ovation as German battalions wearing red carnations in their belts goose-stepped over the Rhine and into the square under the eyes of their commanding officers, who stood, in full uniform, their medals twinkling, on small platforms which had miraculously appeared to give them eminence. The *Volk* in the squares rejoiced. Local Nazi leaders, many of them *Oberbürgermeisters,* appeared in their sausage-tight *Sturmtruppen* uniforms to lead the singing:

Deutschland, Deutschland über alles . . .

And then the Nazi anthem, the "Horst Wessel Song":

Die Fahne hoch! Die Reihen dicht geschlossen.
S.A. marschiert mit ruhig festem Schritt. . . .

Raise the banners! Stand rank on rank together.
S.A. march on, with steady, quiet tread. . . .[38]

The entire Rhineland was aflame with excitement, but the world was unaware of Hitler's move until, at the stroke of noon, he addressed the Reichstag in the Kroll Opera House, his deep, resonant voice thundering that the German Reich no longer felt "bound" by Locarno. Therefore, in the "interests of the basic rights of its people to the security of their frontier and the safeguarding of their defense," he had "reestablished, as from today, the absolute and unrestricted sovereignty of the Reich in the demilitarized zone of the Rhineland." The Reichstag exploded in delirium. Its six hundred deputies stiffened their right arms in *Hitlergrussen* and bellowed "Heil! Heil! Heil! Heil! Heil!" until the Führer raised his hand to silence them. "Men of the German Reichstag!" His deep voice was throbbing now. He vowed at "this historic moment," while German troops were on the march, that he would never yield to force in *"Wiederherstellung der Ehre"* ("restoring the honor of our people"). But neither would he threaten other nations. He pledged that "now, more than ever," he would work toward understanding between the people of all European countries, "particularly our Western neighbor nations."[39]

This was Hitler at his wiliest. Here he was speaking, not to the Reichstag, but to Frenchmen, Belgians, Italians, and Britons frightened of bolshevism. In an ingenious distortion of carefully worded state documents, he embroidered his argument that the Russo-French agreement was a breach of Locarno directed against the Reich — that it might even force France to join the Soviet Union in a war against Germany. France, said the Führer, "has destroyed the political system of the [Locarno] pact, not only in theory but in fact." Then, in a characteristic *Friedensrede* touch, he offered a string of meaningless carrots: immediate negotiations for a new demilitarized zone on both sides of the Franco-German and Belgo-German frontiers; the return of the Reich to the League of Nations; a twenty-five-year nonaggression pact between France and Germany; nonaggression treaties between the Reich and France, Czechoslovakia, Poland, and the smaller countries of eastern Europe. Deeply moved, he paused, his eyes moist and his voice choked. Then he made his last two vows. First, he once more pledged: *"Wir haben in Europa keine territorialen Fordernungen zu stellen"* ("We have no territorial demands to make in Europe"). And then: *"Deutschland wird niemals den Frieden brechen!"* ("Germany will never break the peace!").[40]

The cheering went on and on, but the diplomats, who had to inform their governments, and the foreign correspondents, who had to tell the world, slipped out. Shirer was among them. He observed a few generals making their way out toward the Tiergarten. Their smiles seemed forced. Then he encountered Blomberg and was shocked at his appearance: "His face was white, his cheeks twitching." In his diary Shirer wrote: "You could not help detecting a nervousness."[41]

War Minister Blomberg, General Fritsch, General Beck, and a handful of other senior members of the army hierarchy were now convinced that Nazi Germany would collapse within a week or less. Blomberg bore the immediate responsibility; hence his pallor and his nervous tic. In deciding to invade the buffer zone Hitler had acted in defiance of their advice. The generals knew that the occupation, stripped of the Führer's thespian eloquence and his hand-picked, carefully rehearsed battalions now camped on forbidden soil, was a gigantic scam. By canceling leaves and putting every trained poilu into battle dress, France could retake the Rhineland in a matter of hours. Outnumbering the half-trained, inadequately equipped Wehrmacht conscripts ten to one, the French infantrymen would be supported by tanks and the finest artillery in the world. Blomberg had agreed to assume command only after receiving written assurance from the Führer that he could take "any military countermeasures" he felt appropriate. If he so much as glimpsed a single French bayonet, he intended to beat "a hasty retreat" back across the Rhine.[42]

And that, in the opinion of the *Militärbehörden* — the senior military authorities on Behrenstrasse — would be the end of Adolf Hitler. How many generals had discussed the approaching debacle and shared in planning how to exploit the aftermath is unknown. Blomberg and Beck were excluded; the disgrace of the Führer would also reflect on the army, they were to be the commanding officers, and if they acknowledged defeat before the operation began, their honor would be compromised. But almost certainly a majority of the Generalstab believed France was committed, by a treaty Hitler had approved, to take military action against the presence of German troops in the demilitarized zone. The moment the French infantry moved, calling his bluff, the same treaty required Britain to support France with her own armed forces. The fledgling Wehrmacht would be routed. Hitler and his Nazis would be the laughingstock of Europe. Once the German people realized that they had been betrayed, a military government would move into the Reich Chancellery pending a constitutional convention and free elections.[43]

It is impossible to overestimate the strength of the belief within Germany's officer corps that France's advantage was overwhelming. Ten years later General Alfred Jodl, who became Hitler's chief of staff, would testify to it before the Nuremberg tribunal. At the time of the Rhineland coup, he said, "Considering the situation we were in" — they knew Gamelin had thirteen French divisions near the frontier — "the French covering army could have blown us to pieces." Afterward Hitler himself acknowledged it. His interpreter, Paul Schmidt, heard him say: "A retreat on our part would have spelled collapse." Still later he said: "The forty-eight hours after the march into the Rhineland were the most nerve-racking [*die aufregendste Zeitspanne*] in my life. If the French had then marched into the Rhineland, we would have had to withdraw with shame and disgrace [*mit Schimpfe und*

Schande zurückziehen müssen], for the military resources at our disposal would have been wholly inadequate for even a moderate resistance."[44]

But in that blustery March week of 1936, Hitler, unlike his generals, saw the Rhineland as a risk worth taking. How much he knew of the democracies' impotence is unfathomable, but he had been surprised by the feeble Allied response to his earlier moves. In these years, before he became intoxicated with his own triumphs, his intuitive grasp of how far he could go with Allied leaders was uncanny.

Nearly an hour passed before François-Poncet could cable Flandin a terse summary of Hitler's new sensation. Premier Albert Sarraut immediately summoned his inner cabinet, including the minister of war, General Joseph-Léon-Marie Maurin, and the constable of France, Généralissime Gamelin. Their talks were already under way when the text of Hitler's Reichstag speech arrived.[45]

A large crowd of Parisians had begun to gather outside the Hotel de Ville. They seemed more curious than angry, though P. J. Phillips of the *New York Times* cabled his foreign editor: "Rather than submit to this last crushing piece of Teutonism France will fight." That was precisely what the premier and three of his civilian ministers wanted to do, but they had no Bonaparte, nor even a Foch, to lead the troops of their Third Republic. After setting forth the basic facts, Sarraut turned to Gamelin and asked him what the army proposed to do. According to the premier's testimony before a postwar investigating committee established by the French National Assembly at the insistence of wartime Resistance leaders, the premier expected France's commander in chief to unroll a map revealing swift, imaginative maneuvers which would drive the intruders back across the Rhine. Instead, Gamelin mildly asked permission to take "*les premières mesures de précaution*." Asked what those were, he replied that he wanted to recall soldiers on furlough, move reinforcements toward the frontier, and begin preparations to send up more troops should that seem advisable.[46]

Sarraut was aghast. Gamelin was planning the classic dispositions of a Saint-Cyr-l'École graduate whose native soil is threatened by an invasion. "Naturally," the *généralissime* said, "there is no question of forcing the Rhine, on which the Germans are virtually entrenched already." He then ran through what Sarraut later called "the whole gamut of perils." If France advanced into the Rhineland, the German riposte would be an "attack on us through Belgium, aerial bombing in Paris . . . attacks by submarines, artillery bombardment of our Rhine cities, Strasbourg, Mulhouse. . . ." He went on and on. Joseph Paul-Boncour, minister for League of Nations affairs, interrupted to tell the general that he would like to see him in

Mainz — a German industrial city ninety miles from the French border — "as soon as possible." That, Gamelin replied, was *"une autre affaire."* He would like nothing better, he added, "but first you must give me the means."

At first they didn't understand. As commander in chief he was entrusted with all the military means the country possessed. Maurin entered the discussion; presently the two generals were in animated conversation, and slowly the premier and his civilian ministers comprehended. The soldiers were discussing a *mobilisation générale,* costing thirty million francs and consisting first of putting a million men in positions which, with the Maginot Line, would permit the army to shield France. But that, the exasperated Sarraut pointed out, wasn't the problem. There were no signs that the Nazis had designs on French soil, at least not now. They *had* invaded a buffer zone where no soldier of either nation had the right to bear arms — a neutral land essential to France's survival and her diplomatic commitments in eastern Europe. The generals looked at one another, shrugged, and spread their hands in a gesture which could only be interpreted as *"Hélas, la politique!"*[47]

The baffled premier explained that he simply wanted an *opération de police,* with Gamelin using his vast superiority in infantry strength, firepower, and air power — the few Nazi aircraft, unarmed, were based on airstrips too far away to intervene in a swift expulsion. It was an *absurdité.* The invaders had three battalions; the poilus would overwhelm them. "After all," Sarraut told his commander in chief, "you have just a symbolic force in front of you."

Shirer was reporting that "for the first time since 1870 gray-clad German soldiers and blue-clad French troops face each other across the upper Rhine." The world awaited the response in Paris to this gross violation of Versailles and Locarno. Had it known the truth, it would have been incredulous. The elected leaders of France were begging their high command to put up their fists. And the generals were refusing. Gamelin and Maurin were immovable. The *généralissime,* backed by his war minister, insisted that his army was *"une force purement défensive."* Asked to propose an alternative, he suggested that the government lodge a vigorous protest with the League of Nations.

Sarraut asked Gamelin point-blank: "If we act alone against Germany, without allies, what will be the prospect?" The general said that at first, "given the present conditions," the French would have *"la prépondérance,"* but in a long war Germany's industrial power and numerical superiority might tip the balance.[48]

There was a long silence as they pondered the implications of this: another four years — perhaps more than four — of trenches, barbed wire, incessant shellfire, *attaques en masse* which gained a hundred yards at most, "leaving the dead," as Scott Fitzgerald had written, "like a million bloody rugs," and the legless or blind stumbling around the country while desperate young widows became streetwalkers. All this, and the possibility that France would be defeated in the end.

Then someone pointed out that the premier had assumed they would be acting without allies. France was allied with Britain in the west, and, in the east, with Czechoslovakia, Poland, and Russia. Locarno had specifically committed Italy, Belgium, and Britain to support the French in expelling troops or weapons Germany sent into the zone. And the Locarno powers weren't the only countries affected by Nazi aggression in the Rhineland. Aides were summoned, instructed to place telephone calls; they slipped back with promises of support from the Poles, the Czechs, and the Rumanians. Even Austria, bound to France by no pact, was ready to back her. The Belgians and the Italians had adopted attitudes of cautious reserve.[49]

France's most powerful ally, of course, lay across the Channel. "Above all," as Churchill later observed, the French "had a right to look to Great Britain, having regard to the guarantee . . . against German aggression, and the pressure we had put upon France for the earlier evacuation of the Rhineland." His Britannic Majesty's ambassador to France, Sir George Clark, didn't wait for a telephone call from a Sarraut aide. On instructions from Anthony Eden, he hastened to the Quai d'Orsay and insisted *"très vigoureusement,"* according to Flandin, that France take "no military measures which commit the future before prior consultation with the British Government." Sarraut and Flandin, trying to consult Whitehall by telephone, discovered what Hitler already knew — that on weekends most leaders of the English government were inaccessible. Eden was available but unhelpful. When Charles Corbin, France's ambassador to London, called on him he was told that no decision could be reached before Monday. Corbin reported to the Quai that Eden had "abstained, despite my insistence, from giving me any indication of his own views." Corbin had mentioned Britain's treaty commitment; Eden, he said, had "maintained silence."[50]

Sarraut was affronted, but France, lacking a moat to separate her from the Germans, needed Britain more than the British needed her, and after an interval the premier put his pride in his pocket and authorized Flandin to inform the British that rather than take an "isolated position," the French government preferred "to confer with the other powers party to Locarno."[51]

Eden handled the French with a duplicity they did not deserve. Among the information Eden withheld from Flandin was that after lunch on Saturday he had driven to Chequers, the country home of prime ministers. In Eden's words, "Baldwin said little, as was his wont on foreign affairs.

Though personally friendly to France, he was clear in his mind that there would be no support in Britain for any military action by the French. I could only agree."[52]

Back in the Foreign Office that afternoon, the foreign secretary drafted a long memorandum for submission to the cabinet Monday morning, and then a statement he would deliver in the House of Commons afterward. Any ultimatum to the Germans, he wrote, or even a strong note demanding that the Wehrmacht evacuate its troops in the buffer zone "should certainly not be made unless the powers concerned are prepared to enforce it by military action." Hitler's seizure of the zone, he felt, "has deprived us of a useful bargaining counter" — he was still trapped in that non sequitur — but above all, "We must resist any attempt to apply financial and economic sanctions" against Germany. At this point — and the situation in the zone would remain unchanged throughout the crisis — fewer than five thousand German soldiers had been posted within twenty miles of the French frontier. They were not deployed for battle, and they lacked tank support.[53]

Eden told Corbin on Sunday that there would be no British reinforcements. Reluctantly he agreed to fly over on Tuesday for talks with other Locarno diplomats, provided "it be understood" that those attending the conference would not be asked to agree "on concrete propositions." The French minister concluded that France's only hope of salvation lay in changing Eden's mind, or in persuading Englishmen who made or influenced the government's decisions to change it for him.[54]

That would be difficult. The *Daily Herald* (Labour) had already insisted that Hitler be taken at his word. Lord Lothian approved of the German invasion, remarking that, "after all, they are only going into their own back garden," a statement that has been widely, and mistakenly, attributed to *The Times*. It would not, however, have been out of place there; Dawson's editorial was headed "A Chance to Rebuild," and although it opened by describing the Nazi coup as "Herr Hitler's invasion," Dawson scorned the "sensationally minded," who had called it "an act of 'aggression.' " As he saw it, the Germans were understandably afflicted by a "deep, instinctive fear — the dread of encirclement," and the Rhineland had become, in their eyes, "more than a badge of inferior status, a source of military weakness to a Power which might one day become involved in a war on both sides again."[55]

Nancy Astor, Tom Jones, and Attorney General Sir Thomas Inskip were guests that weekend at one of Lord Lothian's house parties at Blickling Hall. The host and his party prepared a comment on Hitler's seizure of the Rhineland and telegraphed it to Baldwin. They "wholeheartedly" endorsed the Führer's act, urged that the Nazi "entrance to the zone" be ignored in the light of peace proposals before the Reichstag, and suggested that seizure of the buffer zone should be regarded as an "assertion . . . of equality and not an act of aggression." Tom Jones wrote in his diary that he intended to persuade Baldwin to accept Hitler's proposal at its face value even before discussing it with the cabinet. Harold Nicolson, a wise diarist, noted that the general mood "is one of fear. Anything to keep out of war. . . . On all sides one hears sympathy for Germany. It is all very tragic and sad."[56]

Ambassador Corbin, listening to Eden's speech in the diplomatic gallery of the House Monday afternoon, found it discouraging. Thankfully, the foreign secretary said, there was "no reason to suppose that the present German action implies a threat of hostilities." He scolded the Germans' disrespect for treaties. The invasion had "profoundly shaken confidence in any engagement into which the Government of Germany may enter" — it is a pity that Neville Chamberlain, sitting beside Eden, did not write that down and commit it to memory — but His Majesty's Government would study the Führer's new "peace proposals seriously and objectively" to see whether they would shore up "the structure of peace."[57]

Eden flew to Paris accompanied by Lord Halifax and Ralph Wigram, but the conference was sterile. The French foreign minister wanted immediate action — ejecting the Germans from the Rhineland while imposing economic, financial, and military sanctions against the aggressor. Eden noted: "The gravity of Flandin's statements exceeds anything which has been said before." He opposed meeting force with force, and to Flandin's surprise and dismay the Belgian premier agreed. The Italian ambassador, after bitterly reminding them that his country was still under league sanctions, folded his arms, lifted his chin, and spoke not another word.[58]

As they broke up, Eden said he was "glad that there was no intention of trying to reach decisions at this meeting." Flandin, who had convened the conference with precisely that intention, looked directly into Eden's eyes and said prophetically: "Negotiations will end in nothing, or rather, they will sanction a new retreat. And this time the retreat will be decisive, for it will generate a whole series of retreats."[59]

The following morning the British cabinet met to hear the foreign secretary's report. In the Quai, Eden had been bland and elusive, but in Downing Street he could be frank. He said he was convinced that if the Germans were permitted to keep the Rhineland, and to fortify it, war would be inevitable in two years — a war which "would be fought under very unfavourable conditions." The difficulty, he said, was that Sarraut and Flandin did not reflect the views of the typical Frenchman. France was "pacifist to the core"; in battle she would be an unreliable ally. Alfred Duff Cooper, the new secretary for war, disagreed. He too believed that war was inevitable, but he thought that the time to stand up to Hitler was now. French morale would rise, he thought, once the French army had received its marching orders. According to cabinet minutes, he pointed out that "in three years' time" — 1939 — "Germany would have 100 divisions and a powerful fleet." Even with Parliament's adoption of the most recent White Paper, England could not match Nazi rearmament stride for stride, and "We should not, relatively, therefore, be in a better position."[60]

But the rest of the cabinet, including the prime minister, felt otherwise. Baldwin even opposed an appeal to the League of Nations. At some point, he said, "it would be necessary to point out to the French" that intervention in the Rhineland would not only let loose "another great war. . . . It would probably . . . result in Germany going Bolshevik." The first lord of the Admiralty and the secretary for air acknowledged that their position was "a disadvantageous one." One of Baldwin's ministers observed that "public opinion" strongly opposed Allied intervention in the neutral zone. Another concurred. And this was a government whose respect for public opinion was profound. In the end they decided to do nothing. Indeed, Baldwin observed, peace was "worth taking almost any risk."[61]

Quiet and efficient, British civil servants were taken for granted by most cabinet ministers, and when political issues arose they were treated brusquely or even ignored, despite the fact that most of them belonged to the same class and had gone to the same schools. Sir Robert Vansittart, forceful, knighted, and destined for a peerage, was an exception. Ralph Wigram was farther down the ladder. In Paris he had sat behind Eden and Halifax, speaking only when asked for a date, a statistic, a protocol, or technical advice. Nevertheless, Wigram had vehemently agreed with Flandin, believing a policy of drift now would be fatal, and afterward he had a private word with him. If the Locarno powers were to reconvene in London Thursday, he asked, why not move the league council's meeting there, rather than Geneva? The hope of action was small, but whatever the Locarno decision, it would gain prestige if promptly endorsed by the League of Nations. Flandin warmly agreed, and spoke to the others. It was done. But Wigram was still troubled, and once he returned to British soil he drove straight to Chartwell.

Although he was exiled from public life in England, Churchill's political statements continued to be closely studied in foreign chancelleries by those who sensed that eventually his hour would strike. Adolf Hitler continued to be among them. The Führer loathed Churchill and always spoke of him with undisguised malice, but he could not ignore him. In the beginning his insults were merely ugly. Winston, he said, was "a nervous old hen." You couldn't "talk sense" to such a man, the Führer said; he was merely *"ein romantischer Phantast"* — a romantic dreamer. However, once Churchill opened up with his heavy rhetorical artillery, Hitler's invective also escalated. "The gift Mr. Churchill possesses is the gift to lie with a pious expression on his face and to distort the truth. . . . His abnormal state of mind can only be explained as symptomatic of either a paralytic disease or a drunkard's ravings!" After his offer of nonaggression treaties, meant to blur the jagged edge of his thrust into the Rhineland, Hitler predicted that "only the Churchill clique" would "stand in the way of peace."[62]

Actually, the Rhineland crisis had broken at an awkward time for Winston. When the Foreign Office phoned Chartwell and read him a translation of Hitler's March 7 speech, he instantly saw it for what it was: "comfort for everyone on both sides of the Atlantic who wished to be humbugged." But because he still expected a summons to No. 10 and a cabinet appointment, he suppressed his most compelling instincts and spared Baldwin's government.[63]

In public, and especially in House debates, Churchill was civil, almost subdued. Parliament was amused; Winston, for once, was maneuvering for office. He had been sounding his trumpet of alarm for over three years now. His notes had been clear and true, yet they had neither altered the government's foreign policy nor slowed the rush toward catastrophe. Since he couldn't give up, he had redoubled his efforts to wedge his way into a seat at the cabinet table, where, he thought, he could control the clattering train. Winston believed, and virtually every parliamentary correspondent and MP not in office shared his conviction, that he would soon be appointed to the office, still vacant, of minister of defense.

Yet though he had spared the prime minister, Winston had not remained mute after Nazi troops burst into the Rhineland. He and Austen Chamberlain had formed a team, working in tandem to arouse the House by spelling out the consequences if the Nazi coup were to pass unchallenged. Austria would be the Führer's next objective, Churchill predicted, and Austen pointed out that "if Austria perishes Czechoslovakia becomes indefensible." Once Hitler had mastered eastern Europe, they both told the House, he would turn westward, stalking France and Britain. Some MPs, Churchill observed, thought the French were exaggerating the danger. He told them: "If *we* had been invaded four times in a hundred years, we should understand better how terrible that injury is." In France and Belgium, he said, "the avalanche of fire and steel which fell upon them twenty years ago" was still "an overpowering memory and obsession." He asked: "How should we feel if — to change the metaphor — we saw a tiger, the marks of whose teeth and claws had scarred every limb of our bodies, coming toward us and crouching within exactly the distance of a single spring?'"[64]

In his diary Neville Chamberlain wrote that Winston had "made a constructive and helpful speech." On one point, however, Churchill had been adamant, and Neville's failure to assign it importance, or even mention it, reveals the moral gap between the two men. Both Austen and Winston emphasized Hitler's grave damage to the sanctity of treaties. Britain, they held, must remain faithful to her every vow. There was, Churchill said, much goodwill in England toward Germany, and an abiding hope that "the three great peoples of Western Europe may join hands in lasting friendship. But" — he paused — "it ought not even to be necessary to state that Great Britain, if called upon, will honor her obligations both under the Covenant of the League and under the Treaty of Locarno." In an article for the *Evening Standard* he amplified on this theme, appealing to Hitler "and the great disconsolate Germany he leads," urging them to place themselves "in the very forefront of civilisation" by "a proud and voluntary submission, not to any single country or group of countries, but to the sanctity of treaties and the authority of public law, by an immediate withdrawal from the Rhineland." It was like telling Rasputin to use his knife and fork. Still, Churchill had mentioned neither the past nor present sins of the men on the Treasury Bench.[65]

Wigram, reaching Chartwell late in the evening on Wednesday, March 11, found Churchill eager for news. After listening to an account of the Paris meeting, Winston decided he must talk to Flandin before anyone in the government saw him. Breaking the habit of a lifetime, he rose at dawn and drove to his London flat in Morpeth Mansions. Flandin arrived there by taxi at 8:30 A.M. He told Winston he intended to propose simultaneous mobilization by Britain and France of all land, air, and sea forces; producing a sheaf of papers, he read aloud what Churchill afterward called "an impressive list" of support from Poland, Czechoslovakia, Austria, Yugoslavia, Rumania, and the three Baltic states. "There was no doubt," Churchill wrote, "that superior strength still lay with the Allies of the former war. They had only to act to win." Winston told the French minister that in his "detached private position" there was little he could do, but he guided him to others, like Duff Cooper, who had a voice in the government, and that evening he gave a dinner for him. Influential Englishmen heard Flandin out and left promising to do what they could.[66]

Churchill himself had left the table earlier. The House of Commons Foreign Affairs Committee was holding a late session, and he had asked to be heard. There he repeated his insistence that Britain keep her Geneva and Locarno pledges. Alec Douglas-Home, a future prime minister, took notes at the meeting. He recorded that Winston produced Flandin's papers and then "drew a dramatic picture of all the countries of Europe hurrying to assist France and ourselves against Germany." The next speaker was Hoare, who ridiculed Churchill's argument. "As regards Winston's references to all the nations of Europe coming to our aid," he said, "I can only say that in my estimate these nations are totally unprepared from a military point of view." It was Douglas-Home's impression that after Churchill had spoken "a substantial proportion" of the committee was "prepared to see this country go to war." But Hoare, he thought, had "definitely sobered them down."[67]

It seems remarkable that no one there sought expert opinion on *Germany's* military preparedness. If they were unaware that the Wehrmacht was only a shadow of its future self, they surely knew Hitler had introduced conscription barely a year earlier. Doubtless the smaller countries were unprepared. All Europe was, even the nations that had made a fetish of rearmament; the Italians were proving that in Ethiopia. Nevertheless, all had standing armies of trained men. The MPs can hardly have doubted that Hitler would have backed down if encircled by an alliance of France, Great Britain, and the chain of states, swiftly forged by Flandin, on the Reich's eastern and southern fronts. It seems strange that Hoare, so recently disgraced, could discredit Churchill with so flimsy an argument.

But all the meetings held in London in that second week of March were peculiar. On Thursday, Neville Chamberlain entered in his diary: "March 12, talked to Flandin, emphasising that public opinion would not support us in sanctions of any kind." Flandin had replied that at the very least Britain could declare an economic boycott. Neville rejected that, though he offered to give up "a colony" in the interests of peace. The appeasers thought their empire a great bargaining counter, when in fact Hitler wanted none of it. The Third Reich, Ribbentrop had explained to Eden, wanted its *Lebensraum* (living space) in Europe, preferably to the east. In a deep leather chair at his club, Halifax reread Hitler's *Friedensrede* of March 7 and found a passage he had overlooked. In denouncing the Franco-Soviet treaty, the Führer charged that it not only violated Locarno but had also introduced "the threatening military power of a mighty empire into the center of Europe by the roundabout way of Czechoslovakia, which has signed an agreement with Russia." Halifax rang for a Carlton servant and told him he wanted an atlas with a more detailed map of Czechoslovakia. The man returned empty-handed. The map, he explained, had already been checked out by another member, Neville Chamberlain.[68]

Policy is often determined in camera, which is why contemporaneous public opinion, formed amidst the convulsion of historic events, is shaped by incomplete, often distorted, information. In London that week of conferences in St. James's Palace — one of the Locarno powers and the other of the Council of the League of Nations — the press was admitted only to the public meetings. It was at one of them that a friend saw Wigram, sitting at Eden's side, "looking increasingly disillusioned and depressed." The entire Foreign Office establishment had been shaken by the government's failure to respond to Hitler's challenge. The foreign secretary's conduct completely baffled them. And a few of them decided to tell him so. On the initiative of Rex Leeper, they converged on Eden's Whitehall office. He told them he shared their concern. But he doubted that the British people were ready for war. Most of the FO believed that Hitler's *Friedensrede* offer of nonaggression treaties was fraudulent, and that his invasion of the Rhineland was as great a threat to England as an invasion of Belgium; greater, say, than a conquest of Austria.[69]

Leeper therefore proposed a nationwide campaign to awaken all Britain to the Nazi menace, persuading the country to "abandon an attitude of defeatism vis-à-vis Germany." The need, he said, was for "bold and frank speeches, not hesitating to call a spade a spade and not shirking from unpleasant truths." Eden agreed, but on reflection decided that the idea was impractical. It would divide the country and politicize the Foreign Office. In the end Leeper and his colleagues decided to turn to Churchill. He would lead, and they would support him behind Baldwin's back.[70]

Wigram couldn't wait. Vansittart, who had given him permission to leak data to "selected publicists,"* was dismayed when Wigram gave this mandate the broadest possible interpretation. He called a press conference in his Lord North Street home and gave Flandin the floor. Abandoning diplomatic language the French minister spoke straight to the point. He said: "Today the whole world, and especially the small nations, turn their eyes toward England. If England will act now, she can lead Europe. You will have a policy, all the world will follow you, and you will thus prevent war. It is your last chance. If you do not stop Germany now, all is over. France cannot guarantee Czechoslovakia any more because that will become geographically impossible." If Britain did not act, he continued, France, with her small

* *Publicist,* one of the most abused words in the English language, means "a writer versed in international law," or, loosely, "any writer, as a journalist, on matters of public policy." Walter Lippmann was a publicist. Publicity men are *not*.

population and obsolete industry, lay at the mercy of a rearmed Germany. Franco-German friendship was impossible; "the two countries will always be in tension." He acknowledged that England could reach a fragile understanding with the Nazis now, but it would not last; if Hitler were not stopped "by force today, war is inevitable."[71]

The reporters returned to Fleet Street and wrote straightforward accounts of Flandin's appeal, which their editors buried. Everyone in Whitehall expected Baldwin to loose a lightning bolt, destroying Wigram, but his irregularity was ignored. Thoughtful Englishmen wavered, hawks one day and doves the next. Harold Nicolson summed up the quandary in a letter to his wife, Vita Sackville-West, that Thursday, March 12. "If we send an ultimatum to Germany, she ought in all reason to back down," he wrote. But what if she didn't? Then, he said, "We shall have war." He assumed that the Nazis would lose, but, he asked, what would be "the good of that? It would only mean communism in Germany and France." At that his line of reason broke. It wouldn't happen that way, he decided, because "the people of this country absolutely refuse to have a war. We should be faced by a general strike if we even suggested such a thing. We shall therefore have to climb down ignominiously and Hitler will have scored." Indecision was the equivalent of a Nazi triumph, and by the end of the week a swelling majority of MPs, diplomats, and journalists decided that Hitler would emerge the winner of the Rhineland crisis — that he had, indeed, already won.[72]

Flandin, offended and disheartened by the British press's lack of attention and the failure of his meeting with Chamberlain, again arrived at Morpeth Mansions. Churchill shared his anguish but could offer nothing but advice. As he later wrote: "I advised M. Flandin to demand an interview with Mr. Baldwin before he left." Darkness had fallen when the French minister's taxi turned off Whitehall and into Downing Street. The prime minister appeared at the threshold of No. 10 to receive his troubled guest. Baldwin was gracious. Once the amenities were over and they began to talk, however, he told his guest that his cause was lost. Explaining diffidently that he "knew little of foreign affairs" — quite true, but an astonishing admission from the leader of the world's one superpower, vulnerable, through its empire, to major disorders all over the world — he said he did know the feelings of his people, "and they want peace." Flandin protested. The peace would be unbroken. Not a shot would be fired. If faced by a police action the Germans would quickly evacuate the Rhineland. According to Flandin, the prime minister replied: "You may be right, but if there is *even one chance in a hundred* that war would follow from your police action, I have not the right to commit England."[73]

The behavior of both men is baffling. What commitment was Flandin seeking? According to his later version, he merely asked Baldwin to give the French a free hand. But France was a sovereign power. She needed no one's permission to act. Churchill had recognized this weakness in Flandin's first visit to England, before the invasion. He had thought it feckless of Flandin to come to Downing Street, cap in hand, urging the prime minister to honor England's treaty obligations and send British troops to join the French in a Rhineland counterattack. Statesmen shouldn't beg; "Clemenceau or Poincaré," he later noted, "would have left Mr. Baldwin no option." If France moved to meet her Locarno commitments — even though England refused to honor hers — Baldwin's approval would be unnecessary and irrelevant. It was the postwar verdict of the French parliamentary investigating committee that during the Rhineland crisis Premier Sarraut and his cabinet, unable to make up their own minds, were asking the British to do it for them. Churchill would have done it; Baldwin didn't. He said repeatedly: "England is not in a state to go to war." Back in the Faubourg Saint-Germain, Flandin described his call at No. 10 to Sarraut and his cabinet, concluding, "I understood that evening that I would not obtain, despite my efforts, British acceptance of our military intervention in the Rhineland." In other words, *"Nous sommes trahis."* In Berlin, Shirer scrawled in his diary: "Hitler has got away with it!" And so he had. The Führer immediately ordered a nationwide plebiscite to ask the *Volkes* whether they approved of the coup, and 98.8 percent voted *ja*.[74]

In Parliament that same month Winston reflected: "When we think of the great power and influence which this country exercises we cannot look back with much pleasure on our foreign policy in the last five years. They have certainly been very disastrous years." He spoke slowly, his voice heavy: "Five years ago all felt safe; five years ago we were all looking forward to peace, to a period in which mankind would rejoice in the treasures which science can spread to all classes if conditions of peace and justice prevail. . . . Look at the difference in our position now! We find ourselves compelled once again to face the hateful problems and ordeals which those of us who worked and toiled in the last struggle hoped were gone forever."

He summed up the outcome of the latest crisis: "What is, after all, the first great fact with which we are confronted? It is this. An enormous triumph has been gained by the Nazi regime. . . . The violation of the Rhineland is serious from the point of view of the menace to which it exposes Holland, Belgium, and France. It is also serious from the fact that when it is fortified . . . it will be a barrier across Germany's front door, which will leave her free to sally out eastward and southward by the back door."[75]

This speech was ignored. Macmillan recalls that at that time Winston's "speeches and demands . . . however effective in themselves, were injured because of the general doubt as to the soundness of his judgement," and Lady Longford described him as "the disregarded voice of Cassandra."[76]

Painter Paul Maze wrote Churchill, "Half England is hardly aware of the situation." That was understating it. The masses of the British people, few of whom knew where or what the Rhineland was, had returned with relief to their daily routines. Sir Oswald Mosley was planning an anti-Semitic demonstration, the Cunarder S.S. *Queen Mary* was ready for launching, George Orwell's *Keep the Aspidistra Flying*, having received mixed reviews, was selling poorly, and early vacationers in Brighton heard music hall "vocalists," as they were now called, croon:

These foolish things
Remind me of you . . .

Nazism had become fashionable in London's West End. Ladies wore bracelets with swastika charms; young men combed their hair to slant across their foreheads. Paul Maze continued: "*Do* write to the papers all you can. The German propaganda spread about is most harmful, especially in Mayfair society!"[77]

The Führer still had many admirers in Parliament and a lofty one (King Edward VIII) in Buckingham Palace. Germanophilia in the British upper classes had begun as an open, closely reasoned cause, but as the nature of Nazism became evident, with Churchill lifting rocks to show the creatures scurrying below, its character had changed. Martin Gilbert and Richard Gott observed that, "the more it was opposed and the more it was shown to be inadequate, if not erroneous, the more it transformed itself into a hidden obsession." The faithful plotted in the dark, behind closed doors. Sympathy for the Germans, "originally a mood to be proud of," Gilbert and Gott wrote, "became, with the brutalization of German politics, a mood of whispers and cabals." *The Times* echoed *Der Angriff* and *Völkischer Beobachter;* much was made of the joint Saxon heritage shared by pure-blooded Britons and German Aryans (and *not* by Jews). British criticism of the Third Reich was deeply resented in Berlin, and the British embassy there was always quick to apologize for it.[78]

The Quai d'Orsay and the Foreign Office, bruised and shaken, had done their best to paper over the debacle with new documents, exchanges of formal letters, and sealed covenants. Flandin wearily told the British he would accept Hitler's coup provided the reoccupation remained *symbolique* and unfortified — a provision which England could not possibly guarantee.

Nevertheless, Eden and the FO went to work, persuading the other signatories to accept the Nazi fait accompli. Meanwhile, the League of Nations council went through the motions of condemning Germany for her treaty violations. On the day of the council's finding, twelve irreclaimable days had passed since the Führer's nervous battalions had crossed the Rhine bridges. Since no one even raised the question of imposing sanctions on the aggressor, the condemnation was a meaningless gesture, serving only to demonstrate the league's hollow authority and shrunken prestige.

The repercussions were not over. In 1918, when Ludendorff was plunging his bloody fists into the snakelike line of Allied trenches winding from the Swiss border to the Channel, the northern anchor of the defense had been held by King Albert's stubborn Belgians. Now Albert had lain in his grave for two years and the country was ruled by Leopold III, frivolous, shallow, and callow. After the fall of the Rhineland, Leopold decided that Britain and France were no longer reliable allies. He renounced the military alliance Albert had signed with the democracies twenty years earlier and acquired written releases from Paris and London. This meant that at the outbreak of war French troops could not enter Belgium until a Nazi invasion had been confirmed. "In one stroke," writes Alistair Horne, the British military historian, "the whole of her [France's] Maginot Line strategy lay in fragments."[79]

By March 26, less than three weeks after a few thousand poorly equipped Wehrmacht troops had cowed the armed might of France, photographs of the rising system of concrete fortresses Hitler was building opposite the Maginot Line — the Siegfried Line — came into Churchill's possession, and during the first week in April he received detailed reports. Shielding his sources, he shared the substance of the reports with the House. In a remarkably prescient speech he pointed out that these redoubts would permit Nazi troops to be "economised on that line," enabling "the main force to swing round through Belgium and Holland." If that happened, and the two Low Countries fell "under German domination," England would be in mortal peril, a terrifying prospect, he said, which was "brought very much nearer to this island by the erection of the German fortress line." Nor was that all. "Look east," he continued. "There the consequences of the Rhineland fortification may be more immediate. . . . Poland and Czechoslovakia, with which must be associated Yugoslavia, Rumania, Austria and some other countries, are all affected very decisively the moment this great work of construction has been completed."[80]

Parliament was unmoved. It was characteristic of the late 1930s that His Majesty's Government — and the vast majority of His Majesty's subjects — assumed that each crisis was the last, and that Hitler could be taken at his word when he assured them that he would press no further claims upon Europe. Churchill warned them now: "When you are drifting down the stream of Niagara, it may easily happen that from time to time you run into a reach of quite smooth water, or that a bend in the river or a change in the wind may make the roar of the falls seem far more distant. But" — his voice dropped a register, and only those who strained could hear — "*your hazard and your preoccupation are in no way affected thereby*."[81]

On May 18 the Reich's foreign minister, Baron Konstantin von Neurath, received William Bullitt, Franklin Roosevelt's friend and the American ambassador to France. Neurath could scarcely have spoken more plainly. In his report to the State Department Bullitt quoted Neurath as declaring that it would be "the policy of the German Government" to take no new action beyond Germany's borders "until the Rhineland has been digested. . . . Until the German fortifications have been constructed on the French and Belgian frontiers, the German Government will do everything possible to prevent rather than encourage an outbreak by the Nazis in Austria and will pursue a quiet line with regard to Czechoslovakia." Neurath's parting words to Bullitt were: "As soon as our fortifications are constructed and the countries of Central Europe realize that France cannot enter German territory at will, those countries will begin to feel very differently about their foreign policies and a new constellation will develop."[82]

If public men of vision are tough, as Churchill was, they endure. If they are not, and most are not, they perish or live out their lives in lonely exile. The future may serve as an appellate court. It cannot, however, award retroactive damages, and so Ralph Wigram can never be redeemed. He was not a weak man. Nevertheless, Hitler's successful smash-and-grab coup had, in Churchill's words, dealt Wigram "a mortal blow." The crisis had subjected him to an unbearable strain. Valentine Lawford, one of Wigram's subordinates, notes that the "purely physical demands of those twelve days had been almost intolerable; and they had still further enfeebled the frail organs of a frail body." After Flandin had left London, Wigram forced himself to tour the occupied Rhineland. There he was shocked to see little children, coached by German soldiers, play "grenades" with snowballs. He returned to his Lord North Street home, as Ava Wigram later wrote Churchill, "and said to me, 'War is now *inevitable*, and it will be the most terrible war there has ever been. I don't think I shall see it, but you will. Wait now for bombs on this little house.' " He felt a sense of personal guilt. He told her, "I have failed to make the people here realize what is at stake. I am not strong enough to make the people here understand. Winston has always, always understood, and he is strong and will go on to the end." Several months later, writes

Henry Pelling, Fellow of St. John's College, Cambridge, "depression overtook him and he committed suicide."[83]

Vansittart phoned the news to Winston. Churchill wrote Clementine, "I was deeply shocked & grieved. . . . I thought him a grand fellow." Meantime Clementine, skiing in Austria, had read Wigram's obituary in *The Times*, and their letters crossed in the mail, hers reading: "He was a true friend of yours & in his eyes you cd see the spark wh showed an inner light was burning — His poor wife will be overwhelmed with grief." Bearing a wreath, Winston attended the funeral, near Hayward's Heath, with Vansittart, Bracken, and Maze. Afterward they brought the young widow and the Wigrams' five-year-old mongoloid child back to Chartwell for lunch. Churchill was amazed to learn — it is astonishing that a statesman who owed so much to civil servants should not have known — that, as he wrote Clemmie, "there appears to be no pension or anything for Foreign Office widows." In another note he added: "Poor little Ava is all adrift now. She cherished him [Ralph] & . . . he was her contact with gt affairs. Now she has only the idiot child."[84]

The last phrase jars. So does Churchill's mention of Wigram in his memoirs. To be sure, Winston wrote that his death "was an irreparable loss to the Foreign Office, and played its part in the miserable decline of our fortunes," but then he adds that Wigram "took it too much to heart. After all, one can always go on doing what one believes to be his duty, and running ever greater risks till knocked out." Churchill, Boothby noted, could be cruel. It seems less than generous thus to stigmatize Wigram, suggesting that he had deserted his post in his country's hour of need. Yet that seems to have been Winston's final opinion. One feels that in one of his combative moods, Churchill would have sympathized with General Patton for slapping a soldier broken by the shock of battle. Winston had been hammered and tempered and shaped by ordeals beyond Wigram's imagining. And, of course, Wigram would have been no match for Hitler. Churchill knew he was, or would be, if he could only reach the helm.[85]

Now, over two years since Winston had first urged the appointment of a minister of defense to preside over the three services, Baldwin prepared to make the appointment. He had been under great pressure from the press and Parliament to name Churchill. Even Neville Chamberlain, for once in agreement with his half brother, had said: "Of course, if it is a matter of military efficiency, Winston is no doubt the man." In his memoirs Churchill recalled that "I was naturally aware that this process was going on. In the debate of March 9" —Monday, two days after the Rhineland invasion, when the House first confronted the developing crisis — "I was careful not to derogate in the slightest degree from my attitude of severe though friendly criticism of Government policy."[86]

He wrote to Clemmie, insisting, "I do not mean to break my heart whatever happens," but of course he craved office. In the same letter he examined the prospects of the two candidates most prominently mentioned in the press and reported that neither really wanted the job — Neville Chamberlain "because he sees the premiership not far away" and Sir Kingsley Wood "because he hopes to be Chancellor of the Exchequer then and anyhow does not know a Lieutenant-General from a Whitehead torpedo." Thus, he reasoned, "it may all come back to your poor pig."[87]

Baldwin's reservations about Winston remained; and he had to consider his eventual successor. One of Neville Chamberlain's biographers writes: "The party would not have the immediate return of Hoare. If the new Ministry went to Churchill, it would alarm those Liberal and Central elements who had taken his exclusion as a pledge against militarism, it would be against the advice of those responsible for interpreting the party's general will, and would it not when Baldwin disappeared raise a disputed succession?'"[88]

Churchill, Neville Chamberlain, and Kingsley Wood were not the only names which were submitted for the new ministry; the secretary of state for air, Lord Swinton (formerly Philip Cunliffe-Lister), and Walter Runciman, the president of the Board of Trade, were being considered. And so, by Hoare, was Hoare. Speaking from the back benches the injured ice skater skated on very thin ice indeed by making what a friend recalls as "a curiously distasteful bid for office." Neville Chamberlain noted it in his diary: "He began well but shocked the House by an elaborate tribute to S.B. which sounded like an obvious and clumsy bid for power and created a thoroughly bad impression."[89]

Actually, the prime minister preferred Hoare for the post, but nothing could be done until he had been rehabilitated. Baldwin and those around him also shied away from the thought of what they called "a strong personality" in the new ministry. These and other "niceties and gravities," as a Chamberlain biographer called them, had been "well weighed" for a full month, the month that ended during the Rhineland crisis.[90]

Nazi aggression, one might think, should have lent support to Winston's candidacy. At this, of all times, it seems inconceivable that Baldwin would pick a weak man to supervise the defense of England. Nevertheless, that was what he did. Baldwin said outright: "If I pick Winston, Hitler will be cross." In his biography of Chamberlain, Keith Feiling writes that the Rhineland was "decisive against Winston's appointment"; it was "obvious that Hitler would not like it." As the prime minister's heir apparent,

Chamberlain encouraged Baldwin to think along these lines. He suggested that Baldwin choose a man "who would excite no enthusiasm" and "create no jealousies." The prime minister agreed. On Saturday, March 14 — exactly a week since German troops had crossed the Rhine — he announced that he was establishing, not a ministry of defense, but a ministry for coordination of defense. Its leader, the new cabinet member, would be Sir Thomas Inskip.[91]

Inskip? Fleet Street and Parliament were incredulous. The name was familiar but had been attached to no political achievements. As a youth Inskip had seriously considered becoming a missionary. Called to the bar instead, he had taken silk, and, for most of the past fourteen years, had been England's solicitor general or attorney general. Macmillan recalled that he lacked "the slightest glimmer of that ruthless determination, by which alone such an office could have been made effective at such a time." Until now he had never before been proposed or even considered for a high cabinet post. A search of *The Times* files reveals that his only notable public effort had been a successful campaign to suppress revisions of the Anglican prayer book. His appointment had been suggested to the prime minister by Chamberlain and David Margesson, the Tories' chief whip, on the ground that he was "the safest man." Now, rising from the front bench for his maiden speech as watchdog of Britain's security, Inskip confessed: "I may say, with all sincerity, that it never occurred to me — I say this in all seriousness — that I would ever be able to discharge this duty even if it were offered to me. . . . I do not claim to be a superman."[92]

In *The Gathering Storm,* the most personal of his six books on World War II, Churchill wrote that Baldwin had selected "an able lawyer, who had the advantages of being little known himself and knowing nothing about military subjects." He also set down his deeper, emotional reaction to the Inskip appointment: "To me this definite, and as it seemed final, exclusion from all share in our preparations for defence was a heavy blow." Bitterness was uncharacteristic of him, but in three acrid sentences he revealed his naked anger, his feeling that England had been placed in even greater peril, and he himself personally violated: "Mr. Baldwin certainly had good reason to use the last flickers of his power against one who had exposed his mistakes so severely and so often. Moreover, as a profoundly astute party manager, thinking in majorities and aiming at a quiet life between elections, he did not wish to have my disturbing aid. He thought, no doubt, that he had dealt me a politically fatal stroke, and I felt he might well be right."[93]

He added, accurately, that the "Prime Minister's choice was received with astonishment by press and public." Macmillan later commented that "Astonishment is almost an understatement. Even the most defeatist and most adulatory of the Prime Minister were aghast." Winston's friends were in shock. Lord Lloyd recalled Lindemann telling him that Baldwin's choice was "the most cynical thing that has been done since Caligula appointed his horse as consul." One of Lloyd George's young parliamentary protégés called it "another glaring instance of the stupidity of party politics, which always denies a nation the services of most of its best men," and Anthony Crossley added two more verses to his venomous parody:

Did you dare, Father Churchill, did you dare to expect
A summons to the Council again,
In the face of the feeling that haunts the elect
That they scoffed at your warnings in vain?

You're polite to the small and you're rude to the great,
Your opinions are bolder and surer
Than is seemly today in an office of state —
You've even insulted the Führer.[94]

Churchill had proposed a five-man cabinet team to supervise preparedness. To the three traditional posts of air, war, and Admiralty he would have added a minister of supply, with a defense minister presiding over the four. Given the complexities of total war, he argued, a ministry of supply was vital. Its responsibilities would include the manufacture of arms and equipment, the policing of profiteers, and agreements with the trade unions, who would become mutinous if, say, excessive profits for defense industries were not restrained. Baldwin, unimpressed, merely told Inskip to "coordinate" defense. He gave him no instructions on what that vague word meant, no power to enforce his decisions, and no professional advisers. It is difficult to grasp what he expected from a committed pacifist who had never worn a uniform nor heard the sound of gunfire, who — at a time when military strategy depended on an understanding of new weapons, including mastery of radar, upon which England's very survival would depend — had never even flown in an airplane, and whose only previous encounter with Britain's defense establishment had been a consequence of his opposition to rephrasing the Anglican service for burial of the dead at sea.

Alice laughed. "There's no use trying," she said; "one can't believe impossible things."

"I daresay you haven't had much practice," said the Queen.

Passed over for a cipher when he had been supremely qualified, Churchill was now free to unsheathe his broadsword again. But to sulk or fume would have diminished him. "I had to control my feelings," he later wrote, "and appear serene, indifferent, detached." Of course, he was not capable of detachment. Nor should he have been. Someone had to sound the alarm bell after Göring, contemptuous of the Allies' pusillanimity, announced that between four million and five million "active, intelligent, valiant Germans" were working "night and day" in the munitions factories of the Ruhr to arm the expanding Wehrmacht. In the *Evening Standard* Winston expressed astonishment that Parliament and the British people should ignore this boast and its implications. The Reich, he wrote, "is arming more strenuously, more scientifically and upon a larger scale, than any nation has ever armed before. . . . Surely these are facts which ought to bulk as large in ordinary peaceful people's minds as horse-racing, a prize fight or nineteen-twentieths of the current newspaper bill of fare." Over the next several days the *Standard* received a thick sheaf of letters from outraged subscribers protesting the publication of such "nationalistic" articles by England's "number one warmonger."[95]

He was in fact the country's number one peacemonger, the last champion of the League of Nations and therefore of collective security, the only policy which could have thwarted Hitler before the war which he alone wanted destroyed Europe's dominance of the globe. Once other countries had been knitted in a "strong confederacy for defence and peace," Winston told an inattentive House, "they should give Germany an absolute guarantee of the inviolability of German soil and a promise that if anyone offended her all will turn against that one, and if she strikes at anyone all will stand by and defend that victim." He ended: "Let us free the world from the approach of a catastrophe, carrying with it calamity and tribulation beyond the tongue of man to tell." Later he would be remembered as a great war leader, but no man ever fought harder for peace.[96]

Delivering the first report of progress in the new ministry, Inskip braced his stocky legs and, turning his curiously bunched face to the House, spoke confidently of "a swelling tide of production," reporting that "forty new aerodromes have been or are being acquired." In fact the new ministry had already acquired a reputation for slackness. Desmond Morton passed Winston a detailed analysis of Inskip's speech. "A swelling tide of production"? There was, said Morton, "nothing of the kind"; the only steps being taken were "to get industry into a condition *eventually* to produce what is required." Inskip's staff had contacted fifty-two firms, asking whether they would turn out armaments; fourteen agreed to manufacture munitions, "but none of them, not even the fourteen who have accepted firm contracts, have yet entered into production." The "forty new aerodromes" were simply forty fields which Inskip's staff had inspected accompanied by real estate agents. "The forty pieces of ground have not yet even been acquired."[97]

In the House in July, Inskip continued to sing hymns of exultation. To be sure, he acknowledged, Britain's heavy reliance on imported machine tools was unfortunate, and he further conceded that English factories would be unable to turn out shells for at least two years. But he felt certain that the government's "hope and trust" would assure the recruitment of enough skilled workers to man the machines. Churchill, troubled, replied that it would be unwise for him to set forth his case "in open debate in this Chamber. . . . The times have waxed too dangerous for that." Parliament's Foreign Affairs Committee, meeting behind closed doors, had heard Winston out. Harold Nicolson was there and thought his presentation unanswerable. Ranging beyond defense, Winston pointed out that were the Germans given a free hand in eastern Europe, as they had asked, within a year they would be dominant from Hamburg to the Black Sea. England, in that case, would be faced by the most formidable coalition since the fall of Napoleon. But a majority of the committee members belonged to Baldwin, and "what they would really like," Nicolson wrote, "would be a firm agreement with Germany and possibly Italy by which we could purchase peace at the expense of the smaller states. This purely selfish policy would to my mind make an Anglo-German war quite certain within twenty years."[98]

Churchill would have preferred to ignore Inskip himself, knowing that his criticism would invite charges of jealousy. But he could not remain seated when the new minister told the House that defense preparations for England would "of course" be circumscribed because interference with the country's commerce, and the everyday lives of its people, was unthinkable. Winston challenged him. Inskip, he said, had "made a very important pronouncement" in explaining that he was "working under peace conditions." There were, he pointed out, "many conditions" between peacetime and wartime: "preparatory conditions, precautionary conditions, emergency conditions." He had been under the impression that the new ministry had been created to recommend which of them should be adopted now. Churchill cited fresh data from Germany, obtained "from a source which I cannot divulge." Checking these figures against those published by the Nazi regime, he had found that they confirmed one another, revealing that Hitler had spent twenty billion marks preparing for war since coming to power, and, during 1935, another eleven billion — far in excess of Churchill's earlier estimate.

What, he asked, was England's new defense ministry doing? It was "drifting and dawdling as the precious months flow out." No member should be under the illusion, he said, that the balance could be redressed later by a massive appropriation of funds. The House had just approved the

Chartwell: Churchill's sanctuary, home, and great keep.

Churchill's study, in the oldest part of Chartwell, which dates from 1086, twenty years after the Battle of Hastings.

Churchill in his study.

The Churchill coat-of-arms, with its motto — fitting for this period of his life — "Faithful but unfortunate."

Winston, Clementine, Diana, Randolph, and friends entertain Charlie Chaplin (*far right*) at Chartwell.

Clementine bathing in Chartwell's swimming pool, one of Winston's creations.

A life mask of Clementine, taken by Paul Hamann, a German artist, in the early 1930s.

Major (later Sir) Desmond Morton, a member of Churchill's intelligence net and a Chartwell neighbor.

F. W. Lindemann, "the Prof" — later Lord Cherwell.

Brendan Bracken.

A Chartwell guest: French socialist Leon Blum, former Premier of France.

Albert Einstein (*right*), another 1930s guest, in Chartwell's rose garden.

Jack Churchill and Clementine play bezique.

Accompanied by her parents, Sarah "comes out" — is formally presented at the Court in Buckingham Palace — in 1932.

Diana and her father leaving Morpeth Mansions in December 1932 for her marriage at St. Margaret's, Westminster, where Winston and Clementine had wed on September 12, 1908. Diana's marriage ended in divorce three years later.

Winston, Clementine, and Randolph hunt with the Duke of Westminster's boarhounds in Normandy, January 20, 1933.

Mary, aged thirteen, visibly excited, is flanked by her parents en route to Westminster Hall to hear loyal addresses from both Houses of Parliament, celebrating the Silver Jubilee of King George V and Queen Mary, May 9, 1935.

Diana's second marriage, to Duncan Sandys, MP, September 16, 1935.

After electing Churchill Lord Rector of Edinburgh University, students chair him through the city streets.

A shooting party, representing the power elite confronted by the Führer of the Third Reich. *(Left to right)* Geoffrey Dawson, editor of *The Times* and an implacable foe of Churchill's; Lieutenant-Colonel R. Lane Fox, MP (later Lord Bingley); Neville Chamberlain; Lord Halifax; and Sir Roger Lumley (later Earl of Scarbrough, K.G.).

Sir Horace Wilson, Chamberlain's *éminence grise*.

David Lloyd George, Britain's World War I Prime Minister, and Churchill in November 1934. A year earlier the BBC, pandering to Nazi Germany, banned both of them and Sir Austen Chamberlain, a distinguished former Foreign Secretary, from taking part in a series of political broadcasts.

expenditure of fifty million pounds on munitions. But only twenty million could be spent because the gun and shell plants "and, above all, the aeroplane factories," had inadequate stockpiles of raw materials, lacked workers with the right skills, and hadn't retooled. One must also consider the workmen at the forges, lathes, and drills, he said, again raising the issue of profiteering. As minister of munitions in the last war he had learned that "you cannot do anything without a working arrangement with the trade unions"; they would not cooperate "so long as they think there are a lot of greedy fingers having a rakeoff." It is a measure of both the government's incompetence and its contempt for Churchill that another two years would pass before Inskip's ministry met with Labour's leaders.[99]

> *"A slow sort of country!" said the Queen. "Now,* here, *you see, it takes all the running you can do, to keep in the same place. If you want to get somewhere else, you must run at least as fast as that!"*

As usual Winston sat down to a faint ripple of applause. After the last division — MPs vote, literally, by dividing, leaving the chamber through one of two exits, "aye" or "no" — members scurried out into Parliament Square, pausing there to buy newspapers. The newsstand dealers were well stocked. As the season wore on, they had found, MPs were buying more papers every week. The news was extremely interesting, and became even more so when warm weather arrived. On May 5, the Duce's ragged legions finally straggled into the Ethiopian capital of Addis Ababa. Two months later, on Thursday, July 2, the League of Nations bowed to the inevitable, and discontinued all sanctions against Italy. Now, on July 18, Generalissimo Francisco Franco, *El Caudillo* and former chief of Spain's General Staff, broadcast a manifesto from his outpost in the Canary Islands, proclaiming a Fascist revolt against the country's republican government.

It is difficult to recapture the intense passions aroused throughout Europe and much of the United States by the bitter, bloody three-year Spanish Civil War. It was, among other things, a religious war. Loyalists, as the defenders of the republic were known, were not only hostile to the church; they tortured priests, raped nuns, and slaughtered innocents. Roman Catholics committed atrocities equally vile. The republic was Spain's legitimate government, but it had proved incapable of governing a nation in social and economic turmoil.

Labour had remained inflexibly pacifist, but in Edinburgh in October, at the party's first annual meeting after Franco's revolt, delegates were split over whether England should remain aloof in Spain. Cripps expressed the familiar Labour policy in an open letter to the Glasgow *Forward,* urging that "every possible effort should be made to stop recruiting for the armed forces. . . . Suppose you won another imperial victory, what then? British Fascism would be less brutal than German, but the world situation would be no better. Another Versailles peace, another period of acute suffering for the workers, and then the next war. That's all." On the first day of the conference Arthur Greenwood introduced a resolution calling for nonintervention in Spain, and it passed, 1,836,000 to 510,000 — 3.6 to 1.[100]

But within the party a great anguished turning had begun, a growing realization that pacifism had been discredited — that the only effective answer to Fascist and Nazi aggression was to cross swords with it. (The most astute of the pacifists, for whom George Orwell would speak two years later in his *Homage to Catalonia,* had also begun to question Moscow's motives in backing the Loyalist cause.) On October 7, 1936, two days after Greenwood's resolution, the Spanish issue was raised again, in a moment of high drama. The conference was addressed by Señora Dolores Ibarruri, celebrated by Spanish Loyalists as *La Pasionaria.* Her English was flawless — she was the daughter of a Scotswoman — and she spoke movingly of insurgent atrocities, Republican heroism, and hope for a new, socialist Spain. She ended: "We know that we are holding your hand over the distance. But if you wish this atrocious war to end soon, come and help us. Think of the precious gift that is being wasted — of the lives of our youth. Do not tarry. Now you know the truth. Now you know what the situation is. Come and help us. Come and help us. Scotsmen, ye ken noo."[101]

It was, Hugh Dalton recalled, "a magnificent performance, and it swept the whole Conference to its feet. We all rose and sang 'The Red Flag.' " Dalton then moved that Britain meet her responsibilities, as a member of the League of Nations, by preserving "the people's rights and liberties, the continuance of democratic institutions, and the observance of international law" by rearming, the quicker the better. Attlee warned the conference that if they passed the motion they would increase the risk of a general European war and Cripps tried to shelve it, but the delegates' blood was up. The measure passed, 1,738,000 to 657,000 — 2.6 to 1. Labour's parliamentary party — the MPs — did not all approve of this transformation, but Churchill's crusade for a stronger Britain no longer seemed quixotic.[102]

Awakening from their pacifist dream, Labourites and intellectuals invested the Republican cause with a romantic nimbus, reflected in their slogan, *"No pasarán!"* ("They shall not pass!"). One young Communist undergraduate came to symbolize the swing from the submissiveness of pacifism to the aggressive mood of youths prepared to sacrifice their lives in the struggle against fascism. John Cornford, returning to Cambridge from the Edinburgh meeting, called for volunteers — students who wanted to fight Franco's troops by joining the ranks of the Loyalist army. He organized them into Brigades XI and XIV (Loyalists used military terms loosely — a "brigade" could range in size from a force of thousands to a few hundred, or even less than a hundred). He himself then crossed to the Iberian Peninsula and joined 145 other Englishmen in No. 1 Company, Twelfth Battalion, XIV Brigade. On December 27, 1936, he turned twenty-one. On that day, or the following day, he was killed in action. His body was never recovered.[103]

The Loyalist leadership was infested with Communists, but as Harold Macmillan put it, "Many young men — by no means all with Socialist sympathies — joined the International Brigade to support the Spanish Government, and battled heroically for their faith." After Hitler had called them "Jews and Communists," a German staff officer advising Franco reported sardonically: "They may be Jews and Communists, but they fight like Germans and beat Italians." Spain, in the words of A. J. P. Taylor, "provided for the generation of the thirties the emotional experience of a lifetime."[104]

The young idealists did not, however, reflect the views of the older generation, particularly those guiding Britain's political destinies. Hoare, who did, hoped "Fascists and Bolsheviks would kill each other off." At the Admiralty the sea lords heartily favored Franco; Harold Nicolson, ever the moderate, considered Loyalist Madrid "a mere Kerensky Government at the mercy of an armed proletariat," though "Franco and his Moors are no better." Without waiting for action in Berlin or Rome, Eden in August announced an embargo on arms to Spain, hoping, as he wrote Baldwin, that "we might, by setting an example, do our best to induce . . . Germany and Italy to follow suit."[105]

Germany and Italy did the exact opposite. Mussolini sent Franco over sixty thousand troops. The Führer directed Göring to take the first steps in what became a half-billion-mark program, shipping tanks, warplanes, and artillery, all accompanied by German technicians. One of the Führer's motives was to use the Iberian Peninsula as a proving ground for the Reich's new weapons. Alfried Krupp first tested six batteries of his 88's as they later became known and feared by World War II Allied infantrymen, in the siege of Madrid, and was pleasantly surprised; designed as antiaircraft guns, they were also effective against tanks and infantrymen. Krupp sent prototypes of his new U-boats to Spain, including the mammoth *Deutschland*. The Italians did likewise.

That was a mistake. One or more commanders, eager for action, torpedoed British and French merchantmen. In London the sea lords, so ardently pro-Franco that they wanted Eden to join Berlin and Rome in recognizing his government, attributed the losses to submarines of "unknown origin." But their origin was unknown to no one, and nothing was surer to arouse the fury of Englishmen than firing on the red ensign. Angry questions were raised in Parliament. Chamberlain, speaking for the government, said that nothing could be done. "I have been through every possible form of retaliation," he declared on June 20, "and it is absolutely clear that none of them can be effective unless we are prepared to go to war with Franco, which might possibly lead to war with Germany, and in any case would cut right across [the] policy of general appeasement." Nevertheless, in the fall of 1937, Eden persuaded the French to join the Royal Navy in depth-charge attacks on Axis submarines. Berlin and Rome raised trivial objections, but they could do little more without confessing their guilt. Significantly, decisive action resolved the issue. As they quibbled, the Admiralty in London and the Amirauté in Paris began sweeping Spanish waters with a fleet of eighty destroyers. Overnight the submarine threat vanished. "Open piracy," Eden told the House, had ended.[106]

Hitler's most memorable contribution to the Caudillo's arsenal was the Condor Legion, a *Luftwaffeneinheit* (squadron) of bombers which inspired one of Pablo Picasso's most celebrated paintings. The civilized world was deeply shocked when it read that on April 27, 1937, nine waves of Heinkels, armed with 550-pound bombs and piloted by Germans in Spanish uniforms, had conducted a massive raid on Guernica, killing 1,654 civilians, most of them women and children. Foreign correspondents in the vicinity confirmed the early Loyalist reports. The burning question was: "Who was responsible?" Eden asked Ribbentrop whether Germany would agree to an international investigation; Hitler personally rejected the proposal as "entirely outside the bounds of possibility." Instead he blamed the Russians; Guernica, he said, was a "*bolschewistische*" outrage, whereupon Mussolini, now being gradually obscured by the Führer's lengthening shadow, called it "*bolscevico*" violence.[107]

Churchill's immediate response to the outbreak of fighting in Spain had been to damn the Loyalists as the more wicked of two wicked causes. "Naturally," he later wrote, "I was not in favor of the Communists. How could I be, when if I had been a Spaniard they would have murdered me and my friends?" In the *Evening Standard* of August 10, 1936, he wrote that the "constitutional and would-be Republic" had found itself "sliding steadily toward the Left . . . falling into the grip of dark, violent forces coming ever more plainly into the open, and operating by murder, pillage and industrial disturbance." Atrocities were being committed by both sides, he acknowledged, but he dwelt more luridly on the "nightly butcheries" of the Loyalists. Encountering the Republican ambassador at a reception, he turned away from the diplomat's outstretched hand, dramatically muttering, "Blood, blood, blood."[108]

Yet he was among the few who understood Hitler's role in Spain, and he was particularly troubled by the prospect of driving Mussolini deeper into the Nazi camp. In his view, advocating the use of British strength on any Iberian battlefield was absurd. Apart from the courting or alienating of Italy, Britain and the Empire had no stake in Spain. Indeed, Winston saw, an outright Anglo-French commitment to either side — given their military deficiencies, particularly in the air — would be madness. The "Spanish convulsion," he declared, could evoke but one response: "Send charitable aid under the Red Cross to both sides, and for the rest — keep out of it and arm." In August he added: "It is of the utmost importance that France and Britain should act together in observing the strictest neutrality themselves and endeavoring to induce it in others. This Spanish welter is not the business of either of us." He remembered what the Duke of Wellington had said: "There is no country in Europe in . . . which foreigners can intervene with so little advantage as Spain." In victory, he believed, Franco would be an ingrate, and as Hitler would discover, Winston was right.[109]

Those who regarded Churchill as a man of principle were baffled. They shouldn't have been. He had always nailed his colors to the mast, but not always to the same mast. His sole concern now was the safety of his country. William James once wrote that men of genius differ from ordinary men not in any innate quality of the brain, but in the aims and purposes on which they concentrate and in the degree of concentration which they manage to achieve. Napoleon, himself great, called it the mental power *"de fixer les objets longtemps sans être fatigué"* — to concentrate on objectives for long periods without tiring. Churchill possessed it. His eyes were focused on Hitler to the exclusion of all else. Earlier, when the Japanese invaded Manchuria, he had expressed doubts that the League of Nations "would be well-advised to have a quarrel with Japan. . . . I hope we shall try in England to understand a little the position of Japan, an ancient state, with the highest sense of national honor and patriotism and with a teeming population and a remarkable energy." One doubts that he would have been so indulgent had Malaya, Australia, and the Raj been threatened by Nipponese bayonets then.[110]

He reviled Hitler, but spoke enigmatically of Mussolini and the Caudillo. In Cannes he told Vincent Sheean that to him Ethiopia, the Rhineland, and Spain were not unrelated incidents, that they "involve the whole structure of Europe, with possibilities of realignment carrying the promise of deadly danger to England." It struck Sheean that Churchill's "patriotism was rapidly engulfing all other sentiments," that his "awareness of the danger to England drove out whatever had originally prepared him for benevolence toward the Fascist principle, and he was willing, in the end, to work with the extreme left if necessary to defeat the paramount enemy. This evolution I saw." At their last parting, with Franco on the verge of triumph, Sheean observed that Churchill, "saddened and made solemn by the whole thing, perceived the importance of the victory for Hitler and Mussolini, and regarded the fall of the Republic as a blow to England."[111]

Harold Macmillan remembered "Churchill talking to me with great energy on this [aspect] of the Spanish question. He decided to declare himself neutral, for his eye was on the real enemy." Italy, as he saw it, was not England's real enemy. In his memoirs he would write that Britain was "justified in going so far with the League of Nations against Italy as we could carry France," but he knew the French could not be carried far. At the time he said: "We are not strong enough to be the lawgiver and the spokesman of the world." There was poignance here, for in his youth — before 1914 destroyed Britain's paramountcy — they had been both.[112]

As Franco's Nationalists gained the upper hand, he urged the House not to repeat the Ethiopian fiasco: "It is no use once again leading other nations up the garden path and then running away when the dog growls." As Sheean had seen, once the tide of battle favored the Nationalists, Churchill turned away from them. In the *Daily Telegraph* he wrote on December 30, 1938, that "the British Empire would run far less risk from the victory of the Spanish Government than from that of General Franco," and a few months later he told subscribers to the *Telegraph* that "the British Conservative Right Wing, who have given him [Franco] such passionate support, must now be the prey of many misgivings." Since the German threat had absolute priority, he told the House, Britain should refuse to take sides in Spain, though "I will not pretend that, if I had to choose between Communism and Naziism, I would choose Communism." He added: "I hope I will not be called upon to survive in a world under a Government of either of these dispensations. I feel unbounded sorrow and sympathy for their victims."[113]

However qualified, this was a remarkable turnabout for the man who, in the turmoil after the Armistice, had led the attempt to stifle bolshevism in its cradle. But he had executed remarkable pivots before: in the first decade of the century, when, as a young MP, he had fought to provide the poor with unemployment insurance, pensions for the aged, and insurance for the sick;

again, by joining the IRA's Michael Collins in the early 1920s to create the Irish Free State; and yet again, after the general strike of 1926, by leading the struggle for the underpaid, ill-housed, ill-fed British coal miners. If a foolish consistency is the hobgoblin of little minds, Winston was disqualified.

At the urging of Vansittart and Leeper, Churchill in 1936 embarked on a strenuous campaign to awaken Britain through public lectures and newspaper articles, beginning on April 3 in the *Evening Standard*. His cry of alarm, published in the most prominent newspapers of fourteen countries, warned that without concerted action by the nations now lying under the shadow of the swastika, "such civilisation as we have been able to achieve" would be reduced by renewed warfare to "pulp and squalor." The peoples of Europe, "chattering, busy, sporting, toiling, amused from day to day by headlines and from night to night by cinemas," were nevertheless "slipping, sinking, rolling backward to the age when 'the earth was void and darkness moved upon the face of the waters.' " Surely, he argued, "it is worth a supreme effort — the laying aside of every impediment, the clear-eyed facing of fundamental facts, the noble acceptance of risks inseparable from heroic endeavour — to control the hideous drift of events and arrest calamity on the threshold. Stop it! Stop it! Stop it!!! NOW is the appointed time."

Time increased Hitler's momentum. His triumph in the Rhineland had heightened the Third Reich's prestige throughout Europe and dealt England and France a deep wound, all the more painful because it was self-inflicted. The damage to Britain had been particularly grievous; in 1914 the French had gone to war because, facing invasion, they had no choice, but the British, who could have remained on the sidelines — where the Germans had begged them to stay — had fought to defend Belgian neutrality. Other small countries had assumed that they too could rely on the righteous might of history's greatest empire. Now that England had shown the white feather, recruits swelled the ranks of Nazi parties in Austria, Czechoslovakia's Sudetenland, western Poland, and the Free City of Danzig. New parties raised the hakenkreuz in Bulgaria, Rumania, and Hungary; and in May a Fascist plot was exposed in Estonia. On July 11 Churchill gloomily wrote Sir Hugh Tudor, with whom he had stood shoulder to shoulder when Ludendorff launched his great triad of offensives on March 21, 1918: "Everything is getting steadily worse on the Continent. A good deal of work is of course going on here, but all about two years behind."[114]

By now Churchill had gathered a formidable mass of data about war preparedness from Morton, Anderson, and the FO. He could not reveal it in open session without further endangering the national security, however, and Baldwin refused his request for secret session. The prime minister did agree to receive a delegation representing both houses of Parliament, and they met on July 28 and 29. There Churchill presented an extraordinary array of facts detailing German air strength, identifying his sources as French to protect his informants. He went on to discuss, among other matters, "night-flying under war conditions"; the need to recruit more university graduates as pilots and to train more navigators; the gap between planning aircraft production and actual delivery; the want of spare parts; the vulnerability of England's "feeding ports" of London, Bristol, Liverpool, and Southampton; the need for an "alternative centre of Government" if London were bombed flat; proposals to build underground storage tanks to protect the country's fuel oil from attack; radar; industrial mobilization; and the shortages of machine guns, bombs, searchlights, trench mortars, and grenades. He stopped short of recommending that the nation's industry be put on a war footing, but he did suggest that "we ought not to hesitate to impinge on a certain percentage — 25 percent, 30 percent . . . and force them and ourselves to that sacrifice." He said: "The months slip by rapidly. If we delay too long in repairing our defences, we may be forbidden by superior power to complete the process. . . . I say there is a state of emergency. We are in danger as we have never been in danger before."[115]

After Churchill had finished, Tom Jones wrote in his diary, "all subsequent speeches were an anti-climax." He was wrong. The most memorable remarks were Stanley Baldwin's. The prime minister observed that he could not "deal in detail with the many points that have been raised." He and Neville had discussed the implications of an all-out effort to prepare the country for the worst, he said, and had concluded that the adverse "effect on trade" would be too high a price to pay. Any disturbance of peacetime production "might throw back the ordinary trade of the country for many years," inflicting grave damage on the nation's economic health "at a time when we might want all our credit."[116]

Winston could not imagine how British credit could be useful if Hitler's headquarters were in Buckingham Palace, the Reichstag met in the House of Commons, and all Englishmen in public life were herded into concentration camps. Baldwin assured him it would never come to that. As the City said, the prime minister was a practical man, a "sound" man. Churchill's figures, he said, were "exaggerated" — unaware that most of them had appeared in the weekly reports he initialed and passed on, apparently unread — and, raising doubts about "the peril itself," he recited the worn litany that Hitler's Reich was a shield against the Bolshevik bogey. Germany had no designs on Western Europe, he told them, because "West would be a difficult programme for her." The Führer wanted "to move East, and if he should move

East, I should not break my heart." In all events, he was not going to get England into a war "for the League of Nations or for anybody else." If war broke out, he said, "I should like to see the Bolshies and the Nazis doing it." To Churchill this begged the question. Germany, not Russia, threatened the peace. His fear was that the Tory rank and file, championing Franco's brand of Red-baiting, would join Hitler's camp followers. After the meeting broke up he wrote Corbin at the French embassy that one of his "greatest difficulties" was "the German talk that the anti-Communist countries should stand together." Should Léon Blum — the new French leader, a socialist — support the Spanish Loyalists, he said, "the dominant forces here would be pleased with Germany and Italy, and estranged from France. . . . I do not like to hear people talking of England, Germany and Italy forming up against European Communism. It is too easy to be good."[117]

The unforgivable sin of a commander, said Napoleon, is to "form a picture" — to assume that the enemy will act a certain way in a given situation, when in fact his response may be altogether different. The first Allied response to the Nazi regime had been prompted by the universal loathing among decent men of modern war's senseless slaughter. But revulsion is a frail foundation for a foreign policy. As Hitler's belligerence became clearer, Baldwin, Chamberlain, their fellow appeasers in England, and *les apaisers* in France assured one another that he would fight the Russians and leave them alone. But wishing didn't make it so, and they should have known that; Baldwin himself had described Hitler as a "lunatic" with whom "you can never be sure of anything," adding that "none of us know what goes on in that strange man's mind." Therefore, in the autumn of 1936, he called for his fiddlers three — Samuel Hoare (now first lord of the Admiralty), Lord Halifax (lord privy seal), and Neville Chamberlain (Exchequer) — and moved toward what they thought was firmer ground.[118]

It was quicksand. Their new mantra was *diplomacy* — negotiation as a sensible alternative to war. Britain's honor, they told the public, would be preserved; the negotiating table, not the battlefield, was where differences between England and Germany would be resolved. They were convinced that Hitler had his price. Some of them believed this even after all their assumptions, and much of London, lay in ruins. Devoted to peace, they could not understand that the ruler of Nazi Germany disdained negotiations, enjoyed bloodshed — including the shedding of German blood — and therefore preferred military conquest. Churchill understood because of the aggressive drives lying deep in his own complex personality. He worked tirelessly to avoid hostilities, but if the Führer was determined to fight, the prospect of unsheathing the sword of England struck no terror in Winston's heart. All other remedies having been exhausted, he would wield it with relish.

Unfortunately it was a blunt, rusting weapon in 1936, and its hilt lay beyond his reach anyhow. Those who held it despised it. And on November 7, after King Edward VIII had opened the new session of Parliament, they all but discarded it. Although the exhausted prime minister was confined to Chequers on doctor's orders — only a handful knew that the King's yearning for an impossible marriage was responsible for his exhaustion — his cabinet, meeting in Downing Street and knowing he would approve, set the course which would lead to Munich less than two years later.

Inskip was first to speak. The devout Anglican had no prayer for the League of Nations. Collective security, he said, was dead; after Ethiopia and the Rhineland, confidence in it had simply "disappeared." He proposed it be succeeded by broadening "the appeasement of Germany's economic conditions." This was the new diplomacy, which had its critics even within the government. Foreign Secretary Eden and Secretary for War Duff Cooper disagreed. The government, they argued, should give absolute priority to preparing a credible response to Nazi aggression within a year. Hoare protested that this would trigger an "immense upheaval," weakening England in the long run, and William Ormsby-Gore, the colonial secretary, remarked that Britain's close ties with France were "widely resented in the country."

Everyone awaited Chamberlain's decision. He would move into No. 10 in a few months; his voice would be decisive. After a long pause he adopted a firm, if reasonable, tone. He saw no alternative to a widening of the search for appeasement. The issue of "national safety" was hard to oppose, he said, but as chancellor of the Exchequer he was "concerned that the cost of defence programs was mounting at a giddy rate." The latest White Paper had led to the appropriation of £400 million. Should the flow of funds continue at the present rate, rumors of an unbalanced budget would spread. If that happened — and his tone left no doubt that he viewed the possibility as calamitous — they might discover that Britain's credit abroad was "not so good as it was a few years ago."[119]

In the discussion the chancellor's most enthusiastic supporter was the minister of health, Kingsley Wood. Wood's forte, and no one could do it better, was tidying files, updating appointment books, and — he was a wizard at this — keeping interoffice memos moving. After four years as Chamberlain's parliamentary private secretary, he had risen in the postal, telegraph, and telephone services. Baldwin, impressed by the alacrity with which his mail arrived, made inquiries about Kingsley Wood and was told that he was "a sound man." Soon Chamberlain would appoint him secretary of state for air, assigning him responsibility for the RAF with the enthusiastic approval of *The Times,* which hoped he would "increase the number of aeroplanes with the same bright suavity with which he has increased the number of telephone subscribers." Duff Cooper wrote of him: "He clings to the idea of friendship with Germany and hates the thought of getting too closely tied up with the French."[120]

The cabinet approved Chamberlain's position, and thus his emerging policy was established. To preserve Britain's financial resources, they would reach some sort of agreement with Hitler. The vote was not, however, unanimous. Eden, Duff Cooper, and Minister of Transport Leslie Hore-Belisha, veterans of the trenches, disagreed with the chancellor, thereby numbering their days in office, for Chamberlain had little patience with men who, after he had given them clear instructions, argued about them. Already it was said of those rallying to his standard that each was "like a naught in arithmetic that makes a place but has no value of its own."

"Reeling and Writhing, of course, to begin with," the Mock Turtle replied, "and the different branches of Arithmetic — Ambition, Distraction, Uglification, and Derision."

Kept abreast of developments at No. 10 by his FO informants, Churchill had seen Chamberlain's move coming. His intelligence net had provided new evidence that Parliament's appropriations, which Chamberlain thought improvident, would prove pitifully inadequate should Hitler let slip the dogs of war. Next to air power, a matter of life or death for Britain, Winston took a personal interest in the tank corps. The tank had been his conception, originally meant to mash German barbed wire for British soldiers swarming over their parapets and across no-man's-land; he had forced it on a reluctant War Office and seen its triumphant performance in the Great War's last battles. Although he had yet to grasp the role it would play in the next conflict, he knew Allied tanks had to be strong enough to match Germany's. On the evening of October 27, Brigadier P. C. S. Hobart, commander of England's only tank brigade, arrived at Morpeth Mansions in mufti and laid before him the full extent of Britain's mobile armor. Its medium tanks, the world's best in 1918, were now hopelessly obsolete, surpassed in quality and quantity by those of Germany, Russia, Italy, and even isolationist America.

In the air Britain continued to lag; Wing Commander Anderson, taking his greatest risk yet, sent Churchill a diagram dated October 6 and stamped "for official use only," pinpointing the exact location and strength of all RAF operational, training, and administrative units, together with its chain of command. The most dismaying report to reach Morpeth Mansions came from Squadron Leader H. V. Rowley, who had returned from the Reich only a few days earlier. He wrote: "The development of air power in Germany has left me in a somewhat dazed condition, but with one fact firmly in my mind, and that fact is that they are *now* stronger in the air than England and France *combined*."[121]

Armed with all this, Churchill struck. The cabinet had endorsed Chamberlain's proposal, thereby giving formal approval to Baldwin's meandering appeasement by adopting it as His Majesty's foreign policy. Winston laid his facts before Austen Chamberlain and other members of the delegation Baldwin had so recently received and reassured. All joined in a phalanx which petitioned the prime minister to schedule a two-day debate on the country's defenses. Since most of them were elder statesmen of his own party, he had no choice. At long last Churchill would have it out with him with the House of Commons as spectators, and, in a sense, as jurymen.

In 1897, as a twenty-three-year-old cavalry officer stationed in India, Winston had written a striking essay, "The Scaffolding of Rhetoric." Unpublished but found among his papers after his death, it dealt with diction, rhythm, accumulation of argument, analogy, and — approvingly — "a tendency to wild extravagance of language." Extravagance did not, however, mean verbosity; he preferred short words because "their meaning is more ingrained in the national character and they appeal with greater force to simple understanding than words recently introduced from the Latin and the Greek." The key to a speaker's impact on his audience, he believed, was sincerity: "Before he can inspire them with any emotion he must be swayed by it himself. . . . Before he can move their tears his own must flow. To convince them he must himself believe." If he has grasped all these, young Winston had written, his is the most precious of gifts: "He who enjoys it wields a power more durable than that of a great king. He is an independent force in the world. Abandoned by his party, betrayed by his friends, stripped of his offices, whoever can command this power is still formidable."

Now, nearly forty years later, abandoned by his party, betrayed by friends, and stripped of office, Churchill himself had grasped and mastered rhetorical skills, and in the RAF debate of 1936 his range, force, and depth held the House rapt and brought Stanley Baldwin to his knees. On November 11, the first day of the debate, Winston's hapless victim was Inskip.

Under Winston's pitiless questioning, the defense minister admitted that England could put up only 960 warplanes to match the Luftwaffe's front-line strength of 1,500. Churchill then asked him when the government proposed to reach a decision on the proposal to establish a ministry of supply. Inskip was stammering, contradicting himself, evading the issue with vague promises to "review" the matter "in a few weeks," when Hoare intervened.

Mr. Hoare: All that my right hon. Friend quite obviously meant — and I repeat it — is that we are constantly reviewing it.

Mr. Churchill: You cannot make up your minds.

Mr. Hoare: It is very easy to make interjections of that kind. He [Churchill] knows as well as anyone in the House . . . that the situation is fluid.[122]

In a lengthy exchange Hoare repeatedly used the word "fluid." It was among the notes in Churchill's hands when he rose the following afternoon. His sense of history, of irony, and of retribution prompted him to adopt a tactic which struck a profound chord among those who had followed his long struggle, including, in the Strangers' Gallery, Lady Violet Bonham Carter, with her lifelong emotional commitment to him. Exactly two years earlier Churchill had moved an amendment declaring that Britain's security from attack, especially in the air, was "no longer adequate." It was then that Stanley Baldwin had made his formal pledge — a personal commitment — to maintain British military superiority in the air. Now Winston moved the identical amendment with the same cosponsors: Amery, Guest, Winterton, Horne, and, in place of Bob Boothby, who was abroad, Colonel John Gretton.

The prime minister's vow was at forfeit, and there was no way to redeem it. Only twenty-four hours earlier Inskip had acknowledged to the House that the RAF was outnumbered by Göring's fleets of Heinkels, Messerschmitts, Junkers, and Focke-Wulfs. This was Winston's day to speak for all who knew that sooner or later England must confront Hitler, and to observe it he had worked through the night, dictating and revising passages to polish one of his most brilliant philippics. The amendment of November 1934, he reminded the House, had been "the culmination of a long series of efforts to warn the Government of looming dangers." Producing a discolored old newspaper, he quoted a *Times* account of one of his own 1933 speeches. He had said: "During the last four or five years the world has grown gravely darker. . . . We have steadily disarmed, partly with a sincere desire to give a lead to other countries, and partly through the severe financial pressure of the time. But a change must now be made. We must not continue longer on a course in which we alone are growing weaker while every other nation is growing stronger."[123]

Unheeded, he had therefore moved his amendment the following year, and exacted Baldwin's promise. In so doing, he now reminded the House, he had been "much censured by leading Conservative newspapers, and I remember that Mr Lloyd George congratulated the Prime Minister, who was then Lord President, on having so satisfactorily demolished my extravagant fears."

That was the background: his concern in 1933 and, in 1934, his warning, which had been dismissed as "alarmist." What would have been said then, he now wondered aloud, had he predicted what had actually happened since? Imagine that he had prophesied that Nazi Germany would spend billions of marks on weapons, creating a stupendous arsenal by organizing her industries for war "as the industries of no country have ever been," building "a gigantic air force," introducing conscription, occupying the Rhineland and fortifying it "with great skill," launching a large submarine fleet "with our approval, signified by treaty," and forming a standing army of thirty-nine divisions "of highly equipped troops," with another eighty divisions "rapidly being prepared" — all momentous events which threatened the peace of Europe and defied covenants signed by the German government. Assume that he had foretold the disarray of the smaller powers in eastern and central Europe, the Belgian declaration of neutrality — "which, if the worst interpretation proves to be true, so greatly affects the security of this country" — and the transformation of Italy from an Anglo-French ally to an Axis partner — "Italy, whose industry is so much smaller, whose wealth and credit are a small fraction of this country's," yet who boasts an army of "eight million bayonets."

He continued relentlessly: "Suppose all that had been forecast. Why, no one would have believed in the truth of such a nightmare tale. Yet just two years have gone by and we see it all in broad daylight. Where shall we be this time in two years? I hesitate to predict."

But some things seemed certain. During 1937 the Wehrmacht would outnumber the French and increase in efficiency. The gap between the Luftwaffe and the Allied air forces — particularly the long-range bombers — would continue to grow. The French and British rearmament programs "will not by themselves be sufficient." Therefore, the Western democracies should "gather round them all the elements of effective collective security . . . assembled on the basis of the Covenant of the League of Nations." It was his great hope that "we may succeed again in achieving a position of superior force" and "not repeat the folly which we committed when we were all-powerful and supreme," but instead "invite Germany to make common cause with us in assuaging the griefs of Europe and opening a new door to peace and disarmament."

The House was waiting, quiet but alert. They knew he had not risen to propose joining hands with Hitler. He always opened with feints, often with studied praise of those he meant to execute. No one, he said, could withhold sympathy from Inskip, who "from time to time lets fall phrases or facts which show that he realizes, more than anyone on that bench it seems to me, the danger in which we stand." One such phrase "came from his lips the other night." In justifying his weak ministerial performance, he had called the period before he had taken office "years that the locust hath eaten." Churchill intended to weave locusts in and out of his speech, but here he merely observed that "from the year 1932, certainly from the beginning of 1933, when Herr Hitler came to power, it was general knowledge in this country that serious rearmament had begun in Germany." Then, with a genial smile, he turned toward the prime minister and expressed his pleasure at seeing him back in the chamber, "restored to vigour . . . recuperated by his rest and also, as we hear, rejuvenated." Knowing Baldwin, Churchill said, he felt sure that he would not wish any "shrinking" from "real issues of criticism" over "his conduct of public affairs." At any rate, Winston intended to "proceed in that sense."

Now, like Ulysses, he bent his bow. His expression hardened; joviality faded; there was bite in his voice as, without taking his eyes off Baldwin, he declared that in matters of national security "there rests upon him inevitably the main responsibility for everything that had been done, or not done." From his waistcoat he produced a piece of paper and let the arrow fly, slowly reciting Baldwin's promise of March 8, 1934:

> Any Government of this country — a National Government more than any, and this Government — will see to it that in air strength and air power this country shall no longer be in a position inferior to any country within striking distance of our shores.

The House was still, but Churchill's voice rose, as though he meant to be heard above a din: "Well, sir, I accepted that solemn promise." He recalled that some of his friends, men less trusting than he, had demanded particulars, and Baldwin had then "showed less than his usual urbanity in chiding those Members for even venturing to doubt the intention of the Government to make good in every respect the pledge which he had so solemnly given in the afternoon." Now, cuttingly, Winston said: "*I do not think that responsibility was ever more directly assumed in a more personal manner.*"

Baldwin was set up. Everyone expected an immediate attack on him. Baldwin himself did, and of course Winston knew that, so he left him hanging there and briefly dealt with what at first seemed to be the less incendiary issue of ministerial supervision of the armed forces. "The proper organization," he said, "is four Departments — the Navy, the Army, the Air, and the Ministry of Supply, with the Minister for the Co-ordination of Defence over the four." He observed that "practically everyone in the House is agreed upon this," and — the tone was sharpening again — if Inskip "had known as much about the subject when he was appointed" as he must have learned by now, he would have insisted upon the reorganization. Now, committed, he stubbornly refused to alter his stand; he argued that a supply ministry would do more harm than good, disturb or delay military programs, upset the country, destroy trade, demoralize finance, and turn the country into "one vast munitions camp." But then, surprisingly, Inskip had told the House, " 'The decision is not final.' It would be reviewed again in a few weeks." Churchill turned on him and asked: "What will you know in a few weeks about this matter that you do not know now, that you ought not to have known a year ago, and have not been told any time in the last six months? What is going to happen in the next few weeks which will invalidate all these magnificent arguments by which you have been overwhelmed, and suddenly make it worth your while to paralyze the export trade, to destroy the finances, and to turn the country into a great munitions camp?"

In the next minute Hoare wished he had never heard the word "fluid."

> The First Lord of the Admiralty . . . said, "We are always reviewing the position." Everything, he assured us, is entirely fluid. I am sure that that is true. Anyone can see what the position is. The Government simply cannot make up their minds, or they cannot get the Prime Minister to make up his mind.
>
> So they go on in strange paradox, decided only to be undecided, resolved to be irresolute, adamant for drift, solid for fluidity, all-powerful to be impotent. So we go on preparing more months and years — precious, perhaps vital to the greatness of Britain — for the locusts to eat. They will say to me, "A Ministry of Supply is not necessary, for all is going well." I deny it. "The position is satisfactory." It is not true. "All is proceeding according to plan." We know what that means.

He was on them now, his vowels soaring and his consonants crashing as he reeled off dates, figures, and information new to those not on the front bench, revealing that 140,000 young Englishmen had volunteered for the territorials (reserves) only to find there were neither arms nor equipment for them; painting the shocking picture of the tank corps ("Nothing has been done in the years that the locusts have eaten for them"); decrying the army's lack of antitank weapons, antiaircraft weapons, wireless sets. In comic relief, he related the story that a friend of his had come upon "a number of persons engaged in peculiar evolutions, genuflections and gestures." He thought they must be gymnasts, evangelists, or "lunatics out for an airing," but found instead, they were "a Searchlight Company of the London Territorials who were doing their exercises as well as they could without having the searchlights." He waited a full moment, then ripped: *"Yet we are told there is no need for a Ministry of Supply."*

Many MPs had been in the smoking room or the lobby when he rose, but word spread that this was worth watching, and the House had become crowded. Winston had assumed an almost biblical pose, his feet planted apart, his body immobile save for his head, which slowly toiled back and forth as his eyes swept the chamber and he told off his wrath in heavy cadence: "If we go on like this, and I do not see what power can prevent us from going on like this, some day there may be a terrible reckoning, and those who take the responsibility so entirely upon themselves are either of a hardy disposition or they are incapable of foreseeing the possibilities which may arise."

Everyone anticipated what was coming next, and now, after one of those staged Churchillian entr'actes in which he feigned confusion, breaking the tension by appearing to fumble for a memorandum and then grope for a word, he resumed his stand, and, moving into another octave, turned to "the greatest matter of all, the air." On Tuesday night, he recalled, Hoare had given them "the assurance that there is no foundation whatever for the statement that we are 'vastly behindhand' with our Air Force programme. It is clear from his words that we are behindhand. The only question is, what meaning does the First Lord attach to the word 'vastly'? He also used the expression, about the progress of air expansion, that it was 'not unsatisfactory.' One does not know what his standard is. . . ."

He broke off. This pause was heavy. Other MPs, whenever within earshot of Hoare, had left his sacrifice of Ethiopia unmentioned. Winston had cared little about the African kingdom; what rankled was Hoare's mortal blow to the League of Nations, which, he believed, represented Europe's greatest hope of salvation. To him sabotaging the principle of collective security forfeited any right to pity. He glowered at Hoare across the gangway and said slowly: "His standards change from time to time. In that speech of the eleventh of September [to the League of Nations] *there was one standard*, and in the Hoare-Laval Pact *there was clearly another*."

Lowering his key Churchill told the House, in general terms, of the July deputation to Baldwin. Baldwin had said Winston's facts and figures were "exaggerated," but after checking them over the ensuing three months, Churchill had found them to be absolutely accurate, "and were it not that foreign ears listen to all we say, or if we were in secret session, I would repeat my statement here." A lucid, rapid-fire summation of Europe's balance of air power followed, comparing British and German might and reminding the House that "We were promised most solemnly by the Government that air parity with Germany would be maintained by the home defence forces. At the present time, putting everything at the very best, we are . . . only about two-thirds as strong as the German air force." Once more his baleful eye fell on Hoare. The first lord had confirmed Churchill's estimates of both Luftwaffe and RAF strength, yet said: "I am authorised to say that the position is satisfactory." Winston declared: "I simply cannot understand it. Perhaps the Prime Minister will explain the position."

The House, he submitted, had no choice but to demand an inquiry by six to eight "independent Members, responsible, experienced, discreet," who would "make a brief report to the House, whether of reassurance or of suggestion for remedying the shortcomings. That, I think" — and this was the first sign that he would not confine his fire to the Treasury Bench—"is what any Parliament worthy of the name would do in these circumstances. . . .I hope that Members of the House of Commons will rise above considerations of party discipline, and will insist upon knowing where we stand in a matter which affects our liberties and our lives." Before approaching his peroration he delivered a straight shot at Baldwin. "I should have thought that the Government, and above all the Prime Minister, whose load is so heavy, would have welcomed such a suggestion."

Then:

> Owing to past neglect, in the face of the plainest warnings, we have now entered upon a period of danger greater than has befallen Britain since the U-boat campaign was crushed. . . . The era of procrastination, of half-measures, of soothing and baffling expedients, of delays, is coming to its close. In its place we are entering a period of consequences. . . . Germany may well reach the culminating point of her gigantic military preparations. . . . If we can shorten this period in which the German Army will begin to be so much larger than the French Army, and before the British Air Force has come to play its complementary part, we may be the architects who build the peace of the world on sure foundations.[124]

Here another speaker would have ended. But Winston was not finished with them. The quintessential Churchill of the 1930s stood proudly alone. He had not been swayed by public opinion. But others had, and he meant to put them on notice. If he offended them they had it coming. One cannot imagine Franklin Roosevelt condemning Congress, or Hitler — though he could have done it with impunity — the Reichstag. Churchill could, and did, damn the House of Commons. And it was the finest passage in his speech. Harold Nicolson, watching, noted: "His style is more considered and slower than usual, but he drives his points home like a sledgehammer."[125] Even *The Times* described his coda as "brilliant":

> Two things, I confess, have staggered me, after a long parliamentary experience, in these debates. The first has been the dangers that have so swiftly come upon us in a few years, and have been transforming our position and the whole outlook of the world. Secondly, I have been staggered by the failure of the House of Commons to react effectively against those dangers. That, I am bound to say, I never expected. I would never have believed that we should have been allowed to go on getting into this plight, month by month and year by year, and that even the Government's own confessions of error would have produced no concentration of parliamentary opinion and force capable of lifting our efforts to the level of emergency. I say that unless the House resolves to find out the truth for itself it will have committed an act of abdication of duty without parallel in its long history.[126]

Baldwin's reply — halting in delivery and appalling in content — has, in the words of one historian, "haunted his reputation to and beyond the grave." "He speaks slowly," Nicolson wrote, "and with evident physical effort." One of the whips whispered: "This will take three months energy out of him." Toward the end of his speech, Nicolson thought his voice was as "limp as if he were a tired walker on a long road. The House realizes that the dear old man has come to the end of his vitality."[127]

The result was shocking. He was talking extemporarily — he usually did; that was part of his charm — but for once his celebrated candor betrayed him. He said: "I want to speak to the House with the utmost frankness. . . . The difference of opinion between Mr. Churchill and myself is in the years 1933 onwards." After reminding them of the financial crisis then, and remarking that in establishing and enforcing policy "a democracy is almost always two years behind the dictator," he declared: "I put before the whole House my own views with an appalling frankness." Speaking of 1933 and 1934, he reminded them that "at that time there was probably a stronger pacifist feeling running through the country than at any time since the war."

Suddenly he was talking, not about the threat to British lives and homes, but of votes, campaign slogans, and by-elections in which any candidate "who made the most guarded reference to the question of defence was mobbed for it." That, he said, "was the feeling of the country in 1933. My position as the leader of a great party was not altogether a comfortable one." After the East Fulham results, in which a previously safe Tory seat was lost resoundingly "on no issue but the pacifist," he had asked himself "what chance there was within the next year or two of that feeling being so changed that the country would give a mandate for rearmament? Supposing I had gone to the country and said that Germany was rearming and that we must rearm, does anybody think that this pacific democracy would have rallied to that cry at that moment? I cannot think of anything that would have made the loss of the election from my point of view more certain."[128]

From my point of view. Surely this admits of but one interpretation. Tory victories were more important to Stanley Baldwin than the specter of Luftwaffe bombers overhead. Even *The Times*, after Baldwin's death a decade later, sadly concluded in its editorial columns that "what he sacrificed to political expediency obscured the real issue, delayed the education of public opinion, and impeded the process of rearmament, on the speed of which the success of any conceivable foreign policy then depended."

Baldwin has his defenders. Had the coalition lost, they point out, power would have passed to the parliamentary Labour party, which opposed any rearmament whatsoever. It is true that Labour didn't want it done. But then, Baldwin hadn't really done it. In 1935, urging support for Conservative candidates, he had told crowds that despite the ugly stories from Germany, "I confess that in my own political experience I have not encountered Governments possessed of all these malevolent qualities," and adopted as his rallying cry, "No great armaments!"[129]

To Churchill the argument that "the Government had no mandate for rearmament until after the General Election" was "wholly inadmissible":

> The responsibility of Ministers for the public safety is absolute and requires no mandate. It is in fact the prime object for which Governments come into existence. The Prime Minister had the command of enormous majorities in both Houses of Parliament ready to vote any necessary measures of defence. The country has never yet failed to do its duty when the true facts have been put before it, and I cannot see where there is a defence for this delay.[130]

Afterward Londonderry wrote Winston: "SB's admission was a very remarkable one." The prime minister, he noted, had never acknowledged that "the country was running risks. In fact his lips were sealed. We told him and Neville of the risks, but they were too frightened of losing bye-elections." In a postscript Londonderry added: "Neville was really the villain of the piece because he as Chancellor blocked everything on the grounds of Finance." Nevertheless, Churchill's later indictment of Baldwin's confession stands: "It carried naked truth about his motives into indecency. That a Prime Minister should avow that he had not done his duty in regard to national security because he was afraid of losing the election was an incident without parallel in our political history."[131]

This second confession that he had broken his pledge, coming eighteen months after the first, shocked all England. Baldwin's prestige plummeted. William James had written: "Truth *happens* to an idea. It *becomes* true, is *made* true by events." Now it was happening to the Dear Vicar. "Today," Morton wrote Churchill, "his name is mud." Only a year earlier, Macmillan recalled, his prestige was "higher than it had ever been. He was universally trusted. He stood on a pinnacle." A few days before the general election in which Baldwin took so much pride he had delivered a memorable address to the Peace Society, speaking first of the generation shattered in France and Flanders, and then, on the issue of peace: "Everything that we have and hold and cherish is in jeopardy." He had spoken eloquently of the beauty which war could destroy. But he had not addressed the issue of how that destruction could be prevented. He was, writes Telford Taylor, "too easily swayed by the perils of the moment, too little governed by the dangers of the future."[132]

For the prime minister the past year had been a year of almost unrelieved disaster: Hoare-Laval; his unseemly reward of Hoare's groveling encomium by returning him to the cabinet; the even more unsuitable appointment of Inskip; the loss of the Rhineland; his humiliating, unsuccessful attempts to wring concessions from Mussolini and Hitler after their illegal conquests; and now Churchill's philippic, followed by his own shocking admission that he had put party before country.

Baldwin's friends were worried, concerned about both his health and his emotional stability. Distress signals had been visible for some time. Since February he had been afflicted with spells of disabling fatigue, and on April 30 Tom Jones found him swallowing pills which he told Jones relieved "nervous exhaustion." After a thorough examination, his physician found him free of functional disorders. His patient, he concluded, was simply worn out.[133]

The prime minister planned to retire, moving into the House of Lords as Earl Baldwin of Bewdley. He wanted to leave the memory of a final accomplishment before departing, but now, learning that their island's ramparts were insecure, Englishmen were outraged. He was unaccustomed to public hostility and, unlike Churchill, unprepared to face it down. To paraphrase one of sociologist David Riesman's similes, Winston was guided by a built-in gyroscope which would carry him toward his objective through tumult, while the prime minister relied on a kind of sociological radar — signals from the voters — to determine his course.

Despairing of Parliament, and hoping to form a nucleus of support beyond its walls, Winston had begun turning to tiny organizations which were struggling to waken the nation to its peril. In June 1935, at the request of

Lady Bonham Carter, he had addressed one such group, Focus, at a Victoria Hotel luncheon. Clearly Focus was not the germ cell for a mass movement. Indeed, all present agreed that it should have neither rules nor members, and only sixteen people were present anyway. Nevertheless, the meeting was important, for they were all eminent and came from varied backgrounds and political convictions — Conservatives, Liberals, Labourites, aristocrats, and a representative of the working class. Winston became the group's natural leader. As his stock rose in the aftermath of Baldwin's mortification, he became increasingly active in the World Anti-Nazi Council, whose chairman was Sir Walter Citrine, general secretary of Britain's powerful Trade Union Congress. Here, for the first time, Churchill found common cause with socialists. He urged them to spread the word that Englishmen of all classes, from "the humblest workman" to "the most bellicose colonel" must form ranks against the growing danger. To this sympathetic audience Churchill declared that the government must adopt the policy of uniting all countries from the Baltic to the Aegean, including the Soviet Union, in an agreement to "stand by any victim of unprovoked aggression," with each nation pledging "a quota of armed force."[134]

He was speaking daily now and writing for newspapers each evening, knitting into his texts information from new sources, which included Viscount Cecil of Chelwood (the former Lord Robert Cecil), a member of the League of Nations Union. At Chartwell Churchill received Robert Watson-Watt, the inventor of radar, who told him of the Air Ministry's "unwillingness to take emergency measures" to test his devices — a measure even Inskip had supported, though Baldwin and a majority of the cabinet overruled him. Each of the service ministries shared Winston's sense of urgency, though in the government, as Martin Gilbert writes, "there was increasing Cabinet resentment at what was considered interference by him and . . . his constant appeals to Ministers and civil servants for greater vigilance."[135]

At its second meeting the Anti-Nazi Council established yet another movement, the Defence of Freedom and Peace. Churchill thought he had a better name for it: Arms and the Covenant, representing a policy of rearmament and collective security under the League of Nations Covenant. Citrine and other Labourites shied away from that. They were embarrassed; the parliamentary socialists, led by Attlee, still backed the league but not rearmament. Nevertheless, they agreed that Churchill should deliver the chief address at the movement's first great rally at the Albert Hall on December 3, 1936. He wanted broad support, and he was getting it. To Austen Chamberlain he wrote of the "robust spirit" among Labour's leaders, adding, "I have been surprised to find the resolution and clarity of thought which have prevailed among them, and the profound sense of approaching danger from the growing German power."[136]

The great rally exceeded all expectations. Winston later recalled: "We had the feeling that we were on the threshold of not only gaining respect for our views but of making them dominant." Lady Violet Bonham Carter, arriving, found "huge crowds surging around Albert Hall," with "groups of communists and fascists distributing leaflets and attempting demonstrations." In the Green Room, where the speakers assembled, she found Citrine, Sir Archibald Sinclair, and three peers, including Lord Allen of Hurtwood, a conscientious objector in the last war. It was meant to be, and bore every sign of becoming, a massive demonstration demanding action and a moment of personal triumph for Churchill. With similar rallies scheduled throughout the country during the following week, the movement could hardly be ignored by the government. Arms and the Covenant — the press had adopted Winston's more striking phrase — seemed on the verge of making history. It appeared that the only man who could derail it was the King of England. And that is exactly what happened.[137]

❧ ❧

Lady Violet's "expectancy," she wrote, "was pierced by a sharp 'needle' of apprehension. I knew Winston could never think of two things at once. Would his eye be 'off the ball' tonight?" As he entered the Green Room, she later wrote, she "knew at a glance that my anxiety was justified. His face was sombre and overcast. He went straight up to Citrine and said that he felt that at this critical juncture in our affairs he must make some statement." According to Citrine, Winston said "People will expect some statement from me."[138]

Thus the curtain rose for the final act in one of the sorriest episodes in Churchill's career: the abdication crisis of 1936. Everyone within earshot knew what he meant; they had all read the lead editorial in that morning's *Times*. What they did not know was that just as he was leaving Morpeth Mansions to come here Churchill had received the text of a broadcast Edward VIII proposed to deliver to the nation. Citrine was appalled that Winston would even mention the issue in public. The audience, he replied, would certainly not expect any such statement; this meeting had nothing to do with the sovereign. "You will certainly be challenged," Citrine said, "and if no one else does I will." Winston, taken aback, said, "I must consider my position." In Violet's version Citrine went even further, declaring "quite firmly that if this was Mr. Churchill's intention, he [Citrine] could not take the chair. This cinched the matter. . . . But though Winston was obliged to bow to Citrine's ultimatum, I could see how much he minded being overridden."[139]

The press agreed that all the speakers received "a tumultuous reception." Churchill heard "prolonged cheering"; Violet felt "throughout my own speech that I had never spoken to a more responsive and inspiring audience." Churchill spoke last. Violet wrote: "He got a tremendous reception, and of course he made a good speech. (He could not make a bad one.) But many of us felt that he was not at the zenith of his form, and of course we knew why. His heart and mind were engaged elsewhere."[140]

Mystery enshrouds what happened next. Churchill later wrote that he heard a man cry, "God Save the King," and, "on the spur of the moment," told the hall: "There is another grave matter which overshadows our minds tonight. In a few minutes we are going to sing 'God Save the King.' I shall sing it with more heartfelt fervour than I have ever sung it in my life." Then, according to his version, he described Edward VIII as "a cherished and unique personality" and said he expected Parliament "to discharge its functions in these high constitutional questions." He trusted, he said, that "the British nation and the British Empire and . . . the British people" would not "be found wanting in generous consideration for the occupant of the Throne."[141]

This account has entered history virtually unchallenged. So reliable a source as Macmillan believed the fall of Winston's rising star, and Baldwin's remarkable comeback, began that night "in the Albert Hall, [when] Churchill said a few words of sympathy for the King." Lord Strauss, then an MP and later a member of Winston's wartime cabinet, recalled that "Churchill made a dramatic speech in support of the King at an Albert Hall meeting. It just killed the meeting."[142]

Yet no one who was on or near the platform that evening recalled him saying a word about the sovereign, and therefore, by implication, about what had become delicately known as "the royal marriage crisis." Citrine — who had vowed to challenge Winston if he spoke up for Edward — did not hear him do so. Nobody was standing closer to Winston, or watching him with a keener eye, than Violet. It was her recollection that "at the end of the meeting he commented to Mr. Eugen Spier on the enthusiasm with which the audience had sung the National Anthem, which he had interpreted as an endorsement of his attitude on the royal marriage issue." One can only assume that the sentiment was in Churchill's heart at the time, and that later he believed he had given voice to it. He was wrong. He was also wrong in his assumption that the lusty singing of the anthem signified support for the King. Any gathering of Britons would have done the same at the end of a patriotic rally.[143]

Actually, the sovereign's subjects were furious with him. When they learned over the next few days that Winston had decided to be his chief defender — and (inaccurately) that he had advised the King to "Raise the drawbridge, lower the portcullis, and tell them to come and get us!" — they transferred their rage to Churchill, with shattering results for the great cause he led. The elaborate schedule of rallies meant to follow the first one in Albert Hall was canceled. Chamberlain assured a relaxed cabinet that Arms and the Covenant was dead. The government would deal with Hitler, he said, not by matching him bomb for bomb, Short Lee-Enfield for Mauser, Spitfire for Messerschmitt, but by extending the hand of friendship and appeasement. Surely Hitler realized that his demands had to stop at some point. Churchill talked as though the Germans wanted all Europe. It was absurd. If they had it, whatever would they do with it? And, obviously, the wild stories of storm troopers leading anti-Semitic pogroms were rubbish. If the persecutions were as widespread as Winston claimed, Hitler would get wind of them and jail those responsible. But to hear Churchill you would think that the Führer wanted to kill every Jew in Europe![144]

Ich dien — I serve — is the motto of the princes of Wales, who mostly serve by standing and waiting for their reigning parent to die, at which instant they mount the throne, with the formal coronation following a year or so later. In the nine centuries since the Norman Conquest of 1066, thirty-five men and six women (if you include William and Mary's Mary) have reigned over England and her possessions. In Buckingham Palace, Windsor Castle, Sandringham, or any of the other royal estates, an English sovereign is an awesome personage, possessing so much wealth that no one can fix an exact sum. It fluctuates, like the stock market — or like the devotion of the Crown's subjects toward their sovereign.

In the dim, distant, blurry centuries of absolute monarchies, a king's power was exactly that: he had the absolute right to make war without consulting anyone, taxing as he pleased, raping, murdering, pillaging, and committing arson with license. This despotic rule was tempered only by his conscience, provided he had one, and the knowledge that if he alienated too many resourceful vassals, he might be overthrown. Beginning with the signing of the Magna Carta at Runnymede in 1215, the King's authority was limited by this agreement or that, with an occasional spurt of restrictions followed by generations with none. In 1837, when Victoria's delightful silvery voice was first heard at Kensington Palace, a member of Parliament could not become prime minister without "the confidence of the Crown." When Walter Bagehot's *The English Constitution* was published thirty years later, the sovereign was left with three great rights: to be consulted, to encourage, and to warn. These were deliberately vague; a great monarch like Victoria could dominate — even alter policy — by spotting opportunities with her celebrated "drill eye," by insisting on daily consultations, and by skillfully encouraging and admonishing prime ministers and their cabinets. Strong-minded as she was, however, Victoria saw the steady erosion of her power as suffrage broadened. There was little left by 1894, the fifty-eighth year of her reign, when her son's eldest son's eldest son was born and christened Edward Albert Christian George Andrew Patrick David. The House of Commons congratulated Queen Victoria on the infant's birth, but Keir Hardie, Labour's first member of Parliament, delivered a remarkable prophecy: "From childhood onward this [boy] will be surrounded by sycophants and flatterers and will be taught to believe himself as of a superior creation. . . . He will be sent on a tour round the world, and probably rumours of a morganatic marriage will follow and the end of it all will be that the country will be called upon to foot the bill."[145]

By 1911, when the youth was invested as Prince of Wales, the occupant of the throne had become a puppet. His father, George V, could not utter a public word without the prime minister's approval; when he addressed Parliament, he was handed a manuscript written by others and was warned not to stress this word or that.

Nevertheless, George V learned to enjoy his job, and like most men of his generation he had been raised to follow the path of Duty. The Prince was another matter. Edward reached maturity when the sheath of discipline, among royalty as well as commoners, was yielding to self-indulgence and the pursuit of pleasure. During Stanley Baldwin's first premiership, in the 1920s, he and the Prince exchanged sharp words on several occasions. Everything about His Royal Highness — his dress, his contempt for convention, the company he kept, his enthusiastic performances on dance floors — strengthened the doubts of those who thought him an unsuitable heir to the crown. He agreed with them. Anita Leslie, Winston's cousin, witnessed an appalling scene between the Prince and his father. The Prince screamed that he didn't want the throne, and, when his father grew angry, staged a royal temper tantrum. Deeply distressed, the monarch strode out the door. Shortly thereafter, the King died.[146]

His difficult son, now Edward VIII, became, among other things, Defender of the Faith — the faith of the Church of England, which did not recognize divorce. Britain's first bachelor king since the mad George III, 176 years earlier, Edward was now forty-two, and both his subjects and the Royal Family thought it time he acquired a queen. So did he; in his autobiography he wrote, with a careless air which would have dismayed Bagehot, that his "rolling stone was beginning to seek a resting place." He had enjoyed relationships with many women, but there was a curious pattern to them. He stared right through lovely girls and headed for their mothers. He not only sought out women whose childbearing years were over or ending; he was especially attracted to those already married.[147]

His search had ended late in his tenure as Prince of Wales, when he discovered, or was discovered by, Mrs. Wallis Warfield Spencer Simpson, a charming Baltimore adventuress of genteel if threadbare origins who had learned, like Becky Sharp, to live by her wits. Beginning her womanhood "in greatly reduced circumstances," Baltimoreans said, she supported herself "in greatly seduced circumstances." Wallis lacked beauty but possessed something rarer. She was *smart*. Violet eyes, dark hair, a magnolia complexion, and a stunning figure, combined with the great gift of being a good listener, made her popular everywhere. In 1916 she had married a naval officer. Divorcing him, she eloped with her best friend's husband, Ernest Simpson, a wealthy shipping man. Simpson's work often brought him to London; he was always accompanied by his wife, and upon being introduced to her at a garden party, the Prince of Wales found he could not take his eyes off her. How often they saw one another, or in what circumstances, is unknown, but after Edward became monarch she began divorce proceedings against her second husband. The divorce case was a seamy one of middle-aged adultery, and as it began toiling its way through His Majesty's courts of law that year, there were those who trembled at the possibility that His Majesty himself might be named in the proceedings.[148]

Early in February 1936, less than a month into the new reign, Stanley Baldwin was told that his new sovereign intended to marry Mrs. Simpson as soon as her decree was final. The bearer of the news was a third party, however, and the prime minister dismissed it as incredible. Sir Walter Monckton, Edward's chief confidant, later wrote: "I thought throughout, long before as well as after there was talk of marriage, that if and when the stark choice faced them between their love and his obligations as King-Emperor, they would in the end make the sacrifice, devastating though it may be."[149]

Nevertheless, Monckton was troubled, and on July 7 he called on Churchill to seek advice. Clementine once called Winston "the last believer in the divine right of kings." It was almost impossible for him to think unkind thoughts about any occupant of England's throne. But he was aware of Wallis. At the time of George V's death, he later wrote in an unpublished memorandum of events, "it was known through wide circles of politics and society" that Edward "had formed a deep attachment for Mrs. Simpson." However, he continued, "although branded with the stigma of a guilty love, no companionship could have appeared more natural, more free from impropriety or grossness." If the man existed with whom Wallis had enjoyed a platonic friendship, his name is lost to history. Yet Churchill wrote that first as prince, and now as king, Edward simply "delighted in her company, and found in her qualities as necessary to his happiness as the air he breathed." Winston drew the peculiar inference that her presence was "a safeguard."[150]

At No. 11 Morpeth Mansions that Tuesday evening Monckton told him all he knew, which was less than the whole truth. Mr. Simpson was now living with another woman, he said, and on the strength of that Wallis was seeking her freedom. Monckton added that while the King had no thought of marrying her, his strong "possessive sense" would be gratified were she a free woman. Indeed, even now he contemplated inviting her to Balmoral Castle, the royal residence in Scotland.[151]

Churchill frowned. His view of what happened when two worldly figures of opposite sex were alone together may have been distorted, but he knew what was and was not done in public. The divorce itself, he said, would be "most dangerous." Gossip was one thing; court proceedings were "in another sphere." If the woman gained her freedom under Wallis's circumstances, "it would be open to any Minister of Religion to say from the pulpit that an innocent man had allowed himself to be divorced on account of the King's intimacies with his wife." He urged "most strongly" that "every effort should be made to prevent such a suit." He also opposed, with all his vigor, any appearance by Mrs. Simpson at Balmoral. Edward must be reminded "that his friendship [with Mrs. Simpson] should not be flaunted in the eyes of the public." Later, he wrote, he learned that this advice "was not at all pleasing to Mrs Simpson," who had "expressed surprise that I should have been 'against her.' " Thursday evening Churchill dined with the King at York House. Edward had not yet received Monckton's report; he asked Churchill whether they had met. Winston nodded. What, asked Edward, had they discussed? Churchill answered in one word: "Gossip." Later he wrote: "His Majesty looked at me hard, but did not pursue the subject." And when Monckton did relay Winston's advice, the King ignored it.[152]

On October 4 Wallis took a house in Regents Park, and three weeks later at Ipswich she was awarded a decree nisi. It could not become absolute, and she could not remarry, until six months had passed. Nevertheless, the story was on the front page of every American newspaper. Not so in England. The British press, responding to a personal appeal from their sovereign, suppressed the story. In fact, when Churchill wrote that the affair was common knowledge among "wide circles of politics and society," he was referring to the people *he* knew, the highest reaches of the upper class. The rest of Britain was ignorant of the marriage crisis. Even Anthony Eden was unaware of it until Baldwin, returning from vacation on October 12, astonished him by asking: "Have you had any letters about the King?" The young foreign minister replied: "No, not so far as I know; why should I have?" The answer awaited Eden, he later wrote, when he returned to the Foreign Office and "found there had been letters from overseas, where there was no press restraint. . . . They wrote of the King and Mrs. Simpson and her impending divorce suit and they were critical." Throughout the summer and early autumn, the Dominions and the Americans had been following with keen interest what H. L. Mencken called "the greatest story since the resurrection."[153]

Afterward Philip Guedalla said of Baldwin that he had handled the King "with a firmer touch than [he had] the King's enemies." Weary and fragile though he was, baffled by the glowering events on the Continent, the Dear Vicar nevertheless retained his sensitive domestic antennae. "Here, indeed," Macmillan recalled, "was a matter upon which his special talents and his lovable personality had their full play. The King's problem was, at it were, a supreme 'family' problem. Nobody could handle this kind of thing more skilfully or more sympathetically than Baldwin, or with a surer touch." He had been praying for the chance to score one last triumph. He could have hoped for none greater than this.[154]

But monarchs, even constitutional monarchs, are intimidating to those who have been brought up to revere the Crown, and this sovereign was displaying a cunning, evasive side no one in Parliament had noticed in him before. He had lied to Monckton, to his solicitor, and to his own family. Despite his solemn assurances, the terrible truth was that his intentions toward Wallis were honorable. He *did* intend to marry her. Finally, he laid the awful truth before his mother. Queen Mary, seething with rage and grief, told him that it was his constitutional duty to inform the prime minister at once.[155]

On Monday, November 16, he did so. Baldwin was convinced that Britons would not have Mrs. Simpson on any terms — as queen, as titled consort, or as morganatic wife. Had he been discreet, His Majesty might have kept her as his mistress, but since she was already a household word in the United States and the Dominions, sooner or later Fleet Street would make her a British celebrity. Moreover, any surreptitious arrangement was unacceptable to the King. She must become his wife, he insisted, and must share his throne. Baldwin told him that was unthinkable. The King remained adamant. Obviously, there was only one solution. Edward VIII must abdicate and be succeeded by his brother the Duke of York, "Bertie," as King George VI. Apparently both His Majesty and the prime minister recognized the inevitability of this from the outset, but neither could mention it to the other, let alone outsiders. In Cannes, whence she had gone, "the Baltimore woman," as the press now called her, was unaware that her next name was likely to be, not Wallis Regina, but Mrs. Windsor.

Baldwin's next move was obligatory; he had to report this conversation to the cabinet, leaders of the opposition parties, elder statesmen, and key figures in the House of Lords. Thus informed, Lord Salisbury led a small group of outraged senior parliamentarians to No. 10 the next day. It was their position, Salisbury said, that though they would not be shocked by a commoner who wanted "to marry his mistress," the situation was very different when "a man born to sublime responsibilities" was "ready to jeopardize them, as it seems, in order to gratify his passion for a woman of any sort." Salisbury had invited Churchill to join this delegation, but Winston had declined. He agreed with the delegates, he explained, but were he to commit himself now, he "would lose all influence over the King." Instead, he planned a personal appeal to His Majesty, arguing that just as millions of other Englishmen in his generation had "made every sacrifice in the War, so he must now be willing to make this sacrifice for his Country." Here Winston encountered a problem. He had a good case, but to state it he must see His Majesty, and Baldwin wouldn't permit that; he was keeping Edward secluded in the royal lodge at Ford Belvedere. Anyone wanting to call on him must be screened by the prime minister, who had approved only a handful of applicants, notably the Archbishop of Canterbury and Geoffrey Dawson of *The Times*.[156]

At this point a certain illogic began to creep into Winston's thinking. On Wednesday of the following week, Baldwin, seeking nonpartisan support in Parliament, told Churchill, Attlee, and Sinclair that should the King refuse to abandon his marriage plans, he and his cabinet would resign; he asked what their response would be. Attlee and Sinclair quickly replied that neither would accept the seals of prime minister. Churchill said his attitude was "a little difficult," but he would "certainly support the Government." He was convinced that the King would abandon his marriage plans. At the same time, he saw no reason why, after Wallis was again free, they should not "continue to see one another outside marriage." Even if one accepts his view of their relationship as a sexless friendship, this would constitute an invitation to scandal which, as he himself had told Monckton, could only tarnish the Crown. Furthermore — and here he raised an issue which would loom ever larger as the crisis grew — Churchill deplored talk of a swift decision. He saw no reason to be "hasty." This was merely a royal "infatuation." In time, he predicted, two or three months at most, it would pass and His

Majesty would come to his senses. Baldwin, who had studied the expression on the King's face when he spoke of Wallis, knew better.[157]

Churchill did see that the essential "difficulty," as he wrote Salisbury, had risen since Wallis's decree nisi. It was a "point of honour that a man should marry the woman who divorces herself or is divorced on his account." This problem was "insuperable, unless the lady in question herself spontaneously gives the release." He therefore approved the dispatch of a mission to Cannes with that objective. One was formed. Lord Beaverbrook led it; he was perhaps the only man in Edward's kingdom audacious enough to ask his monarch's intended "to renounce all idea of marriage, morganatic or otherwise, with the King." All she had to do, he explained, was withdraw her petition for an absolute divorce. Winston believed that would end the crisis. His hopes were high. In a letter praising Beaverbrook he wrote: "He is a tiger in a fight . . . a *devoted* tiger! Very scarce breed." But if Beaverbrook was a tiger, Wallis was a man-eater. She coldly informed him and all the other King's men that should their sovereign decide to marry, she would place no obstacles in his path.[158]

Until now the public had been unaware of the impasse. Their ignorance ended on December 2, when the Right Reverend Alfred Blunt, bishop of Bradford, inadvertently touched off a furor by criticizing the King's poor churchgoing record. The press seized upon the occasion to comment on Wallis in Bradford, Leeds, Manchester, Nottingham, Darlington, and Birmingham newspapers. No power on earth would keep the crisis out of *The Times* the next day. The cabinet met in emergency session. Duff Cooper proposed that the coronation move forward as planned and the marriage issue be raised after the King had been crowned in May. But he was a minority of one. Were his course followed, the others told him, the monarchy, the very symbol of unity, would become the eye of a storm tearing Britain and the Empire apart, with the possibility that a King's party might be formed — a throwback to the days when the royal court vied with the House of Commons in governing the nation. Duff Cooper was also reminded that the prime minister had other duties, among them rearmament and foreign policy in Spain, Geneva, and Ethiopia. This was incontestable. Macmillan sympathized with the King, but he later emphasized that "apart from the personal problems involved, grave injury was done to the public interest from a wider point of view. During many weeks — the whole of the late summer and autumn — the Prime Minister and his leading colleagues . . . were occupied with the complications and distractions of this affair at a vital period."[159]

Baldwin declared the matter must be swiftly resolved. The cabinet agreed. That evening the King once more told the prime minister that his decision to marry Wallis was irreversible; Baldwin again replied that the government's position was unalterable. The need for a solution being urgent, there was no point in continuing the deadlock. But Churchill did not know that. As Baldwin and Edward conferred, Winston rose in the House to ask that "no irrevocable step" be taken until Parliament could be consulted. His appeal was greeted by angry murmurs. He and Beaverbrook then met with the King's solicitor and endorsed Edward's wish to address the nation. Within the hour Baldwin vetoed any royal broadcast as "thoroughly unconstitutional."

The Times leader the following morning — the day of the Albert Hall meeting — was the opening gun in Dawson's campaign against the marriage. He wrote of "a grave constitutional issue" arising from "a conflict between the KING'S intentions and the advice of his Ministers," and observed that "the high office which HIS MAJESTY holds is no man's personal possession. It is a sacred trust, handed down from generation to generation." The path of a sovereign was not easy, particularly one "who has reached middle age without the blessing of a happy marriage," but His Majesty must understand that the monarchy itself would be "weakened if ever private inclinations were to come into open conflict with public duty and be allowed to prevail." Edward was stung. In his memoirs he would write bitterly: "The press creates; the press destroys. All my life I had been the passive clay that it had enthusiastically worked into the hackneyed image of a Prince Charming. Now it had whirled around and was bent upon demolishing the natural man who had been there all the time."[160]

Emotionally, Churchill was becoming a loose cannon, making contradictory statements as he tried to reconcile the unsuitable marriage with his devotion to the Crown. Lunching with Sir Walter Citrine, he said very quietly, "I shall defend him. I think it is my duty." It was also a violation of his assurance to Salisbury, and Citrine, startled, said, "What? Irrespective of what he has done?" Winston, according to his companion, "looked grave, and, putting his hands on his breast, he said with emotion, 'He feels it here.' "[161]

Those closest to Churchill were appalled. His daughter Mary recalls that Clementine "disagreed profoundly. She saw something else very clearly, too," Mary remembers. "She realized that Winston's championship of the King's cause would do him great harm, and that he would be accused of making political capital out of this crisis." Harold Nicolson wrote that Churchill's "line" was "let the King choose his girl." But there was more to it than that. Later Winston's physician observed: "King and country, in that order, that's about all the religion Winston has." Yet he, too, missed the point. Part of it was Churchill's deep, unquestioning loyalty to those he had befriended. One of his secretaries recalls that even if a man had publicly disgraced himself, he would say, "I don't want to hear it. This man is my friend."[162]

Lady Violet Bonham Carter, after trying to reason with him about the issue and being "met by black hostility," concluded, as Clementine had, that he was "quite oblivious" to the public's distaste for "a hole-and-corner morganatic marriage." Violet wrote that "his championing of Edward VIII was inspired by a romantic loyalty. He would have been prepared to stand alone beside his King against a world of arms." Winston himself said much the same thing later: "I should have been ashamed if, in my independent and unofficial position, I had not cast about for any lawful means, even the most forlorn, to keep him on the Throne of his fathers." This was intuitive, not reasonable; it was as though the King had called: "Now who will stand on either hand / And keep the bridge with me?" Two had sprung forward: Beaverbrook and Churchill. But their incentives were very different. Later Beaverbrook said he had been trying to "get" Baldwin. Winston, aroused, hotly replied: "*I* wasn't trying to 'get' anyone. I wanted to save the King."[163]

It couldn't be done, and when, the day after *The Times* editorial and the Albert Hall rally, Edward asked the prime minister if he might see Churchill, as "an old friend" with whom he might "talk freely," Baldwin agreed. He knew he had won. He had just told His Majesty that the cabinet wanted a decision during the weekend — it was now Friday — or, if possible, this evening. Edward had replied: "You will not have to wait much longer." He hadn't wanted the crown; he wouldn't fight for it. Conservative MP Henry Channon wrote in his diary: "The King told [the Duke of Kent] that over two years ago while he knew he was an excellent Prince of Wales and liked the job, he nevertheless felt that he could never 'stick' being King as he put it, he was afraid of being a bad one. He could never tolerate the restrictions, the etiquette, the loneliness; so perhaps if the issue had not arisen something else would have."[164]

Yet His Majesty did not reveal this submissiveness to Churchill, who went to Fort Belvedere on the evening of December 4 under the impression that he could save him, nor did he mention Baldwin's time limit and his tacit acceptance of it. Churchill's impression was that Edward "wanted a fortnight to think the matter over." Winston had assumed that the prime minister would give him no less than a month. He said: "Your Majesty need not have the slightest fear about time. If you require time there is no force in this country which would or could deny it to you. Mr. Baldwin would certainly not resist you." He added a piece of advice. The King should not "on any account leave the country." That would "produce the worst possible impression"; everyone would say he had "gone to meet Mrs. Simpson." Edward demurred; he had no intention of seeing her, but thought "a complete change in the Alps" was what he needed. Nevertheless, he dropped the idea. Winston was his friend and champion; he couldn't quarrel with him. In his memoirs he would write: "When Mr Baldwin had talked to me about the Monarchy, it had seemed a dry and lifeless thing. But when Mr Churchill spoke it lived, it grew, it became suffused with light."[165]

Saturday morning Winston sent the prime minister a complete account of his audience with the King and prepared a statement for publication in the Sunday papers. It opened: "I plead for time and patience." There was no conflict between King and Parliament, he argued, because Parliament had not been consulted, nor allowed to express an opinion, and for a monarch to abdicate "upon the advice of the Ministry of the day" would be without precedent. Because Mrs. Simpson's decree would not be absolute until April 1937, the marriage could not be celebrated until spring, and "for various reasons" it might "never be accomplished at all." Surely "the utmost chivalry and compassion" should be shown "toward a gifted and beloved King torn between private and public obligations and duty."[166]

Churchill's assurance that the King "need not have the slightest fear about time" had been ill-advised. Actually, Baldwin told his senior ministers that same Sunday, "This matter must be finished before Christmas." According to Monckton, who was there, Chamberlain insisted even that was too much time; the uncertainty, he said, was "hurting the Christmas trade." And word of the King's fatalistic acceptance of dethronement was spreading. Beaverbrook had phoned Churchill with the bad news: "Our cock won't fight." Winston, refusing to give in, drafted a compromise statement for His Majesty. In it the King would give the cabinet veto power over his marital plans, should the question arise in April. Sinclair cosigned the proposal, but when it reached Fort Belvedere the King rejected it "on the grounds," as Winston later wrote Boothby, "that it would not be honourable to play for time when his fundamental resolve was unchanged, and he declared it unchangeable." After that, Churchill added, "No human effort could have altered the course of events."[167]

Unfortunately, before word of the King's response reached him, Winston had blundered into the worst political mauling of his life. Bob Boothby, one of a handful of MPs who had remained loyal to him, had been his weekend houseguest at Chartwell; there he had noted that Churchill was "silent and restless and glancing into corners," like "a dog . . . about to be sick on the carpet." Later Boothby told a friend his premonition, on Sunday, that "Winston was going to do something dreadful," but that he never dreamed he would come into the House of Commons and be "sick right across the floor."[168]

Monday, December 11, Churchill attended a meeting of the Anglo-French Luncheon Club, and, according to Boothby, arrived in Parliament "drunk, for the first and only time in his life." It was Question Time. The prime minister was at his best, patiently answering queries about the crisis. The House was friendly; MPs had spent the weekend taking the pulse of their constituencies and had found little support for Edward. "What is so tragic," Harold Nicolson wrote Vita,"is that now that people have got over the first sentimental shock, they *want* the King to abdicate. I mean opinion in the House is now almost wholly anti-King." MPs, he wrote, were saying that " 'If he can first betray his duty . . . there is no good in the man.' "[169]

As Winston took his seat Baldwin was explaining, rather disingenuously, that His Majesty was still weighing his decision and that until he reached it the government would make no move. Winston later acknowledged in his letter to Boothby that he "did not sufficiently realise how far the Prime Minister had gone to meet the views I had expressed. I ought of course to have welcomed what he said. . . ." Instead, oblivious to the proceedings he was interrupting, he rose to defend his press statement of the day before. He began: "May I ask my right hon. Friend whether he could give us an assurance that no irrevocable step will be taken before the House has received a full statement —" That was as far as he got. The House rose as one man in a spectacular display of collective fury. Macmillan recalled "the universal hostility shown to him from every quarter — Conservatives, Socialists, and Liberals." Winterton, who served in the House of Commons for forty-seven years, called the demonstration "one of the angriest manifestations I have ever heard directed against any man in the House of Commons." Individual cries were audible — "Drop it!" "Order!" "Twister!" — but most voices joined in a wordless, derisive, ear-splitting roar.[170]

In his diary Leo Amery wrote that Churchill was "completely staggered by the unanimous hostility of the House," and Nicolson noted: "Winston collapsed utterly in the House. . . . He has undone in five minutes the patient reconstruction work of two years." Winston himself felt "entirely alone in a wrathful House of Commons. I am not, when in action, unduly affected by hostile currents of feeling," but now it was "almost physically impossible to make myself heard." Nevertheless, he stood defiantly, in his familiar fighting stance, his jaw thrust forward and his expression grim, until, to his astonishment, the Speaker ruled him out of order for attempting to deliver a speech during Question Time. Flushed, he turned to Baldwin, and, according to Beaverbrook, shouted: "You won't be satisfied until you've broken him, will you?" Then he stalked out, followed only by Brendan Bracken. It was, *The Times* declared the next morning, "the most striking rebuff in modern parliamentary history."[171]

So extraordinary a spectacle suggests motivation which lay deeper than the immediate issue, in which Churchill, after all, had played a minor role, and an ineffectual one at that. Indeed, the entire response to the Simpson affair, public and private, seems to have been an overreaction. It had "completely absorbed the public interest," in Boothby's opinion, because "here, at last, was something that was moving and exciting without being dangerous." One could safely commit oneself; whichever way it went, the solution would not be a matter of life or death. Therefore, Britons could release the tension arising from frustration over rearmament and the growing likelihood of another European war. They had brooded over Churchill's recitation of alarming facts, resenting his insistence that they face the growing danger. As events vindicated him, that exasperation grew. Now, when he was clearly wrong, they made him the target of their chagrin. In raging at him they were raging at the prospect of another great conflict, one they did not deserve and for which, as they saw it, they bore no responsibility.[172]

After the Churchill shoutdown, events moved swiftly toward a denouement. On Thursday, December 10, the King signed the Deed of Abdication, stipulating that his reign would end at noon the following day. Baldwin brought it to the House of Commons that same afternoon, had it read by the clerk, and then delivered an excellent speech tracing the course of the crisis from its origins. Holding up the signed document, he declared: "No more grave deed has ever been received by Parliament, and no more difficult, I may say repugnant, task has ever been imposed upon a Minister."[173]

That last part was not entirely true. Encountering Harold Nicolson afterward, Baldwin said, "I had a success, my dear Nicolson, at the moment I most needed it." Coming after a year crowded with disappointments, the acclaim over his masterstroke can hardly have been repugnant. But no one begrudged him it. In the *Evening Standard* Churchill wrote that the prime minister had "never spoken with more force or more parliamentary skill." His own brief account to the House of his action during the crisis — pointing out that he had been acting based on the limited information then available to him, was heard next — heard first in distrustful silence, then with sympathy, and finally with what Hansard's record described as "loud cheers." In his diary Amery wrote: "Winston rose in face of a hostile House and in an admirably phrased little speech executed a strategical retreat."[174]

On Friday Churchill lunched at Fort Belvedere, working with the King on the text of his abdication broadcast. As Edward wrote in his memoirs, it was an address which any "practiced student of Churchilliana could spot at a glance," with such phrases as "bred in the constitutional tradition by my father" and "one matchless blessing, enjoyed by so many of you and not bestowed on me — a happy home with his wife and children." Afterward Winston wrote of his host, "His mettle was marvellous." So it should have been. Edward was free of duties he detested; soon he would be reunited with his love, and he could devote the rest of his life to pleasure as His Royal Highness, the Duke of Windsor, the title his brother was about to bestow upon him — although, at the insistence of the Royal Family and to Edward's anger, Wallis would be denied the honorific Her Royal Highness. But she would be a duchess, which was a lot more than anyone in Baltimore would have predicted. At the end of his luncheon with Winston, Edward glanced at his watch and realized that "I ceased to be King." As he saw Churchill off, he wrote, "there were tears in his eyes. I can still see him standing at the door; hat in one hand, stick in the other. Something must have stirred in his mind; tapping out the solemn measure with his walking stick, he began to recite, as if to himself." The something was from Andrew Marvell's ode on the beheading of King Charles I:

He nothing common did or mean
Upon that memorable scene.[175]

But in the streets of London children were chanting a different couplet:

Hark! The herald angels sing,
Mrs. Simpson pinched our King.

That was not all she had pinched. Listening to the former king's broadcast at Chartwell with Bill Deakin, Churchill was moved to tears, not by his own prose but by its implications. For him, and for those working to strengthen the defense of England, the crisis had been disastrous. Afterward he wrote: "All the forces I had gathered together on 'Arms and the Covenant,' of which I conceived myself to be the mainspring, were estranged or dissolved, and I was myself so smitten in public opinion that it was the almost universal view that my political life was at last ended."[176]

Certainly his campaign for preparedness was a casualty. Violet Bonham Carter wrote that many of his loyal followers "expressed to me (and no doubt to others) the view that if he continued to lead us our cause would be hopelessly compromised." Had it not been for the Simpson crisis, Macmillan believed, Arms and the Covenant "might have succeeded in shaking the already weakened position of the Prime Minister. We might have been able to force a change of policy or of Government or both. Alas! . . . All the effect of the Albert Hall meeting was destroyed — first by the Abdication and secondly by the catastrophic fall in Churchill's prestige."[177]

In an angry letter written immediately after the shoutdown in the House, Boothby had reminded Winston of their agreement that "you were going to use all your powers," which could have been "decisive" in a successful resolution of the royal marriage issue. "But this afternoon you have delivered a blow to the King, both in the House and in the country, far harder than any that Baldwin ever conceived of. You have reduced the number of potential supporters to the minimum possible — I shd think now about seven in all. *And you have done it without any consultation with your best friends and supporters.*" Boothby wanted "to follow you blindly" because, as he wrote in a second letter, "I believe, passionately, that you are the only man who can save this country, and the world, during the next two critical years." But now the Churchillians were under attack by men who had been on the verge of conversion to Winston's cause. One of them had been prepared "to send a series of cables to friends of his in the Australian Government . . . under the aegis of your authority," but now refused to do so. Boothby pointed out that it was "only when you rely on the power of clear disinterested argument, based on your unrivalled intellect and experience, with *the solid central mass of the House of Commons,* that you rise to the position of commanding authority which you should always occupy."[178]

At the new king's coronation in Westminster Abbey in May, Winston leaned toward Clementine and whispered: "You were right. I see now the other one wouldn't have done." But a public apology was impossible for him, and an acknowledgment of error nearly so. On Christmas Day he wrote Lloyd George, vacationing in the West Indies: "It has been a terrible time here. . . . You have done well to be out of it" — as though the Welsh radical, with his humble origin and scorn for aristocracy, would have risked his career to save a man who had abandoned a kingdom for a woman. To the Duke of Westminster, Churchill wrote: "It is extraordinary how Baldwin gets stronger every time he knocks out someone or something important to our country." But had Edward been important to England, and to the cause Churchill championed, he would not have appeared in Germany, on his honeymoon, striding down the middle of a street lined with Nazis extending their arms in a *Hitlergruss* — and returning the greeting with a stiff-armed *heil* of his own.*[179]

* A touched-up photograph of this scene, showing Edward with his right hand by his side, was published around the world. The original, described above, is in the possession of one of the American prosecutors at Nuremberg.

Churchill, the strategist and statesman, could not recognize the achievement of Baldwin, the political technician. Macmillan grudgingly admired the feat which left "Baldwin's authority . . . immensely strengthened and Churchill's fallen almost to nothing." Nicolson, singling out "the supremacy of Baldwin" as the chief consequence of the Simpson affair, quoted "a leading Labour man" as saying to him: "Thank God we have S.B. at the top. No other man could have coped with this." Nicolson was proud of "how unanimous the House really is in times of crisis. There has been no hysteria and no party politics." Actually, of course, there had been both: hysteria in the outburst against Churchill, and, in Baldwin's triumph, Tory gains equivalent to a victory at the polls.[180]

In the end Winston grasped the extent of his debacle and was plunged into gloom. In Paris after the abdication he told Beaverbrook, "My political career is over." The Beaver replied, "Nonsense," but later he wrote: "It was only by chance that he was a Member of Parliament when the war broke out." After the war Bernard Baruch reminded Churchill how, in 1936, "your political career seemed ended, and you wondered whether you should enter some business." The Albert Hall rally had turned to ashes. When Lord Davies urged Winston to rouse the nation by embarking on a public speaking campaign, Churchill replied that he thought there was a tendency to "overrate the value of public meetings," that at "the present time non-official personages count for very little," and that "one poor wretch may easily exhaust himself without his even making a ripple upon the current of opinion. If we could get access to the broadcast [*sic*] some progress could be made. All that is very carefully sewn up."[181]

Indeed it was; the appeasers, secure once more, and still convinced that Churchill was a dangerous provocateur, took every opportunity to muzzle him. The cabinet reviewed a BBC plan for a new series of broadcasts on European affairs. Duff Cooper, again a minority of one, thought all knowledgeable Englishmen should be invited to speak; the rest of the cabinet voted to exclude "independent expression of views." Secretary to the Cabinet Hankey suggested that Winston's privilege, as a privy councillor, to see copies of Air Ministry replies to his criticisms of the RAF be discontinued. "So far as I can see," he said, "there is no advantage in continuing this controversy with Mr Churchill." Baldwin approved, then quickly reversed himself when Winston phoned threatening to circulate his own memoranda "to any of my friends I might think fit." The government knew how accurate Winston's information was, though as yet none of them had made it a major issue.[182]

He knew — and told Inskip — that Britain's rearmament was falling "ever more into arrears," and that the country's weakness in the air was "marked and deplorable." Lord Rothermere, who had been staying at

Berchtesgaden as the Führer's first overnight foreign guest, wrote Churchill that the Führer "professes great friendship for England but it will be friendship on his terms and not ours." Rothermere predicted that "even without a great war Britain and France will be practically vassal states before the end of the present decade. The idea that we cannot fight is spreading all over England." In the *Evening Standard* on February 5, 1937, Winston wrote that fifteen million Czechs now lived "under the fear of violent invasion, with iron conquest in its wake." There the Goebbels "hate-culture continues, fostered by printing press and broadcast," and at any time Berlin's propaganda might be directed against Belgium, Holland, Sweden, Switzerland, even Britain.[183]

All this deepened his melancholy. Clementine and fourteen-year-old Mary were staying at the Flexen Hotel in Zürs am Arlberg, skiing in the Austrian Alps. Winston was alone at Chartwell with Deakin, working on *Marlborough,* and, as he wrote his wife, turning out "articles to boil the pot." Yet they weren't enough; unpaid bills lay in a heightening pile on his desk. Even the weather was cheerless — bleak and gray, with a heavy, pounding rain which confined him and his easel to one end of the drawing room, where he erected dust sheets to protect the furniture and peered out, painting what he could see. At last it cleared. Cecil Roberts, a journalist and an old acquaintance, called and found him seated by Chartwell's lake, hunched over, staring at his swans. Winston spoke mournfully of the imminent changing of the guard at No. 10, with Baldwin moving out and Chamberlain in. He said, "There's no plan of any kind for anything. It is no good. They walk in a fog. Everything is very black, very black."[184]

And as his debts mounted and his gloom deepened, England's indebtedness to Stanley Baldwin rose. He had kept that undesirable woman out of Buckingham Palace, and now, in his final deed for his homeland, he joined Chamberlain in telling Tory MPs that if they felt they must deplore totalitarianism and aggression, they must not name names. It was important, he said, to avoid "the danger of referring directly to Germany at a time when we are trying to get on terms with that country."[185]

Fleet Street cheered. So did Britain. These were men of *peace.*

> *"When* I *use a word," Humpty Dumpty said, in rather a scornful tone, "it means just what I choose it to mean — neither more nor less."*
>
> *"The question is," said Alice, "whether you* can *make words mean so many different things."*
>
> *"The question is," said Humpty Dumpty, "which is to be master — that's all."*

THREE

UNDERTOW

CHURCHILL'S popularity touched bottom in the months following the royal marriage crisis. After the holidays Randolph brought the American writer Virginia Cowles to a Chartwell lunch. Late in life she recalled: "The year 1937 was one of the most painful in Churchill's life. His influence had fallen to zero, partly because of the Abdication Crisis, partly because Hitler and Mussolini remained quiet and people began to feel that perhaps there would not be a war after all." Exploring the grounds, she found him "down by the pond, in a torn coat and battered hat, prodding the water with a stick, looking for a pet goldfish which seemed to have disappeared." The goldfish was retrieved; his prestige in London was not.[1]

On May 27, 1937, six days after the coronation of George VI in Westminster Abbey, Stanley Baldwin resigned, departing, wrote Churchill, "in a glow of public gratitude and esteem." Harold Nicolson noted in his diary, "No man ever left in such a blaze of affection." At the abbey the applause for Baldwin had rivaled that for the King. Dawson's editorial declared that the Dear Vicar had "revealed himself as the authentic spokesman of the nation" — a startling accolade; until then Dawson had reserved that role for *The Times* — and, he continued, the crowds had "cheered him just because they had come to look upon him as the embodiment of their own best interests." At No. 10 that evening, as the maids packed, the departing P.M. became Earl Baldwin of Bewdley, Knight of the Garter, while his lordship's ladyship was invested as a Dame of the British Empire. "All hearts seem open at the moment," S.B. wrote Halifax. "It is wonderful. I feel tired, happy, and at peace." Churchill, of course, did not join the chorus. Instead he said: "Well, the light is at last out of that old turnip."[2]

History has coupled Baldwin's name with Neville Chamberlain's, though they were very different men, leaving No. 10 with different legacies. S.B. approved of appeasement, but passively; unsure of himself in foreign affairs, he waited for other governments — particularly Germany's — to take the initiative. Chamberlain, never troubled by self-doubt, gave the policy drive. As Churchill later wrote, S.B.'s "vague but nonetheless deep-seated intuition" had been succeeded by the "narrow, sharp-edged efficiency" of an "alert, businesslike, opinionated, and self-confident" man. Macmillan thought the new P.M. "only too sure that he was right on every question. Baldwin's attitude to problems was largely one of temperament and feeling; Chamberlain approached them with a clear, logical mind. The only trouble was that when he was wrong he was terribly wrong."[3]

Part of Baldwin's charm had been his air of boundless tolerance; he had refused openly to take offense even when offense was deliberate. Chamberlain, on the other hand, "was resentful of criticism even from his supporters," Leo Amery wrote in his memoirs. "It seemed to him akin to insubordination, and no team could get on without discipline." Eden and Duff Cooper, outspoken men with independent minds, were all but ignored in cabinet meetings. At first Eden had been delighted by Chamberlain's ascent of what Disraeli called "the greasy pole." He had told Halifax that it would be a great relief "to have a Prime Minister who would take some interest in the foreign side." Eden was less pleased when he learned that Neville meant to be his own foreign minister, and that when the P.M. did seek advice on foreign affairs, he sought it from two other ministers who had presided over the Foreign Office: Simon and Hoare. Simon, Hoare, Halifax, and Chamberlain himself formed what Fleet Street called "the Big Four." The lesser three refrained from contradicting Chamberlain or challenging his judgment. "Both by instinct and training," wrote Hoare, "I was bound to find myself in accord with Chamberlain's ideas." In other words, if you wanted to get along, you went along.[4]

As they veered away from traditional British foreign policies and turned down the garden path, the appeasers seemed wholly unaware of Hitler's great design, blueprinted in *Mein Kampf* and now emerging as an alarming reality. They preferred to concentrate on political intrigue. Halifax, lord president in Chamberlain's cabinet, had his eye on Eden's office at the FO, and Chamberlain was seriously considering the switch, despite the fact that in the first year of the new government Halifax demonstrated how imperfect his grasp of diplomacy was. On November 17, 1937, he became the first member of a British cabinet to call on the Führer at Berchtesgaden, accepting an invitation which had pointedly excluded the French. When the car arrived he remained seated. Viscounts do not open doors for themselves. He saw a man's black trousers just outside. Assuming they were those of a footman, he muttered impatiently about the delay until the shocked chauffeur whispered hoarsely, *"Der Führer! Der Führer!"* Wrenching the door open, Halifax made matters worse by explaining why he had not done what he ought to have done. Adolf Hitler was the last man to enjoy being mistaken for a servant, and he glared as only he could. The noble lord laughed heartily. It was not a propitious overture. When Halifax reported back to No. 10 the P.M. agreed that the misunderstanding was a great joke, however, and that, for Halifax, was what counted. He told Chamberlain of Hitler's solution for the turmoil in India: "Shoot Gandhi." That, too, amused the P.M. It occurred to neither of them that the Führer had been serious.[5]

Chamberlain was appalled when the House of Commons voted to debate Halifax's trip. Determined to forge bonds of friendship and trust with the Third Reich, he was dismayed by the possibility that the Führer, who understood neither a free press nor parliamentary debates, might be offended by critics over whom the P.M. had no control. He sent Eden word that he hoped nothing would be said to "upset the dictators." It was a vain hope; on December 21, 1937, Winston delivered a powerful speech. Twice, he noted, the Nazi foreign minister had been invited to London; twice the invitation had been rejected. Halifax's mission, Churchill said, was an unseemly response to obduracy and bound to offend the French. He attached "the greatest significance to the relations we have with France." The security of the two democracies was "founded upon the power of the French Army and the power of the British Fleet." Noting that since Hitler had become Reich chancellor and Führer "the Germans in Czechoslovakia" had loudly denounced "the form of government under which they have to live," he expressed the hope that no more Europeans would come under Nazi rule; they would suffer for it — "particularly the Jews." It was unspeakable, he said, the timbre of his voice rising, that Hitler should plot to exterminate a race from the society "in which they have been born," or that, from their earliest years, "little children should be segregated, and that they should be exposed to scorn and odium. It is very painful."[6]

Chamberlain had been following a different line of thought. Over the holidays he read Stephen Roberts's *The House That Hitler Built*, a powerful indictment of National Socialism by an eminent Australian scholar, but he wrote his sister Ida: "If I accepted the author's conclusions I should despair, but I don't and won't. Fortunately I have recently had a 'scintillation' on the subject of German negotiations. It has been accepted promptly and even enthusiastically by all to whom I have broached it and we have sent for [Nevile] Henderson [the British ambassador in Berlin] to come and talk it over with us."[7]

Churchill watched the evil stirring in central Europe and felt strengthened in his conviction that it was time, and past time, that Britain looked to her defenses. An unimpeachable source had sent him a tentative draft of the Führer's *Fall Grün*, or Case Green, a plan to invade Czechoslovakia with three Wehrmacht corps in two or three months. Another informant had written Chartwell of the frantic attempts in eastern Europe's capitals "not to provoke Germany" and how the Nazi hierarchy was "convinced that we would be neutral if they attacked Czechoslovakia." Still another had provided him with figures on the RAF's loss of new aircraft due to inexperienced pilots and incompetent, untrained mechanics.[8]

But Chamberlain, certain there would be no war, saw no future for the armed forces. Churchill was standing against the tide, and on March 16, 1937, he had lost his most prestigious ally in the campaign to waken England when Sir Austen Chamberlain died. "Nothing can soften the loneliness or fill the void," he wrote Lady Chamberlain. "In this last year I have seen more of him and worked more closely with him that at any time in a political and personal association of vy nearly forty years."[9]

As the character of Neville's foreign policy emerged — alliances with Italian fascism and German Nazism, leaving France out and thus, by washing England's hands of old quarrels, assuring peace for Britain — ministers would hear less and less of it from the prime minister himself. The new householder at No. 10 rarely received anyone. Visitors appearing at the door were greeted by Sir Horace Wilson, a deferential man of hooded eyes and soft voice who had entered the civil service at the time of the Boer War. As chief industrial adviser to the government he had proved indispensable to Chamberlain during Neville's six years as chancellor of the Exchequer. On taking over the reins from Baldwin, the new P.M. appointed Sir Horace head of the civil service and head of the Treasury. Although never elected to office and unknown to the British public, Chamberlain's adviser held more power than most members of the cabinet, and he served his master as Rasputin had served the last czar. By the end of 1937 he would build for himself, writes W. J. Brown, "a more powerful position in Britain than almost anybody since Cardinal Wolsey. . . . His influence was almost wholly bad. . . . In all the critical years, when swift, bold, strong action alone could have served our need, Wilson's temporising, formula-evolving mind reinforced and emphasized the weakness of the Prime Minister." The Big Four made headlines, but it was Wilson, working through Chamberlain — whose faith in him was boundless — who became the high priest of appeasement.[10]

In a spirit of reconciliation Churchill had volunteered to appear at the Conservative convention to second the nomination of Chamberlain as leader of the party, but it was a wasted gesture. He was never a bearer of grudges; nevertheless, Sir John Colville recalled, he always retained "some bitterness toward 'the caucus' which, first under Baldwin and then under Chamberlain," had kept him "out of office throughout the nineteen-thirties." His nominating speech, delivered at Caxton Hall on May 31, 1937, was not quite what the Tories had come to hear. After paying ritualistic tribute to Neville's accomplishments as chancellor in stimulating foreign trade and restoring England's foreign credit ("a memorable achievement"), he put the Conservatives on notice: he intended to continue on his lonely, unpopular path. The role of leader, he said, had never been interpreted as "dictatorial or despotic"; the House "still survives as the arena of free debate." He felt confident, he said — though he felt no such thing — that Chamberlain, "as a distinguished Parliamentarian and House of Commons man," would "not resent honest differences of opinion," and that party opinion would "not be denied its subordinate but still rightful place in his mind." In his diary one Tory MP described it as "an able, fiery speech not untouched by bitterness."[11]

Even Nicolson chose not to march under Churchill's banner. To his wife, Vita, he wrote: "Don't be worried, my darling. I'm not going to become one of the Winston brigade. My leaders are Anthony [Eden] and Malcolm [MacDonald]." Eden's following outmatched Churchill's, still limited to Boothby, Bracken, and Duncan Sandys, Winston's son-in-law since his 1935 marriage to Diana.[12]

There can be little doubt that Chamberlain was the choice not only of Conservative MPs but of the general public, and that Churchill was seen as a scaremonger. Sir John Reith saw to it that he was seldom heard over the BBC, and in that Reith had the full backing of the prime minister; twice in one week Horace Wilson summoned Reith to No. 10 to warn him that Chamberlain disapproved of broadcasting excerpts from parliamentary speeches critical of the government. Excerpts in which the P.M. chided his critics were another matter. Like all evangelists he observed two standards, arrogating all power to himself when his own cabinet disagreed with him, and, whenever possible, gagging eloquent critics.[13] But he could never have got away with it had his countrymen disagreed. The voices of 1930s appeasement fall strangely on the ear today; at the time a consensus of Englishmen not only thought them sensible, but those who argued otherwise were scorned, vilified, and even accused of treason. That same year British crowds packed cinemas to see Frank Capra's *Lost Horizon,* based on the novel by James Hilton. Early in the film the protagonist, Robert Conway — memorably played by Ronald Colman — bitterly reproaches himself for his flawed character. As a pacifist he had believed that Great Britain should dismantle her army, scuttle the Royal Navy, destroy all RAF bombers and fighter planes, and beat her swords into plowshares. Should hostile troops arrive on English soil, he had argued, they should be greeted politely and asked what they wanted, and be immediately given it. But when he was appointed foreign secretary with extraordinary powers, his nerve had failed him. When the movie was shown to Tommies and GIs in the early 1940s it required heavy editing. The uniformed audiences knew what Hitler would have done had he stumbled upon Shangri-La, whose inhabitants were clearly non-Aryan.

Early in 1938, as he had intimated to his sister, Neville struck out boldly. The prime minister's inspiration was christened "colonial appeasement." In *Mein Kampf*, and in his demagogic speeches to Nazi mass rallies, the Führer had bitterly denounced the "theft" of Germany's pre-1914 colonies at Versailles. Chamberlain believed that if the colonies were returned, Hitler would stop plotting to seize neighboring countries on the Continent. He presented his idea to the cabinet as a plan to court Nazi friendship by opening "an entirely new chapter in the history of African colonial development," under which the Reich would be "brought into the arrangement by becoming one of the African Colonial Powers . . . by being given certain territories to administer." Henderson and Halifax enthusiastically backed it. Eden's support was muted. The P.M. looked at him sharply. It was an omen.[14]

Horace Wilson assembled a task force of civil servants to draft documents for the transfer of colonial possessions. Halifax told Ribbentrop, Hitler's ambassador to the Court of St. James's, that England was "urgently trying to make concessions"; Eden, still loyal to Chamberlain, assured the Nazi ambassador that His Majesty's Government's "earnest desire" was a quid pro quo — colonies for the Reich and, for England, "a greater feeling of security," which would require some kind of arms agreement.[15]

At this point, the French, alarmed at reports from London, challenged the concept of colonial appeasement and Colonial Secretary Ormsby-Gore put a spoke in its wheel. Eden had pointed out that Britain's moral superiority would be less plausible if, like Hitler and Mussolini, she shredded agreements and flouted compacts — which, Chamberlain's colonial secretary now reminded him, would be entailed in such a deal. The territories which had once belonged to Germany flew the Union Jack now, but that didn't mean that they belonged to Britain; the League of Nations had mandated them to the English with the understanding that Englishmen would better the lot of the native populations. That pledge would clearly be shattered if they were turned over to the Third Reich, which had withdrawn from the league and taken the official view that blacks, like Jews, belonged to an inferior race and should be so treated.

But the appeasers, like all fundamentalists, held facts in contempt. One of England's most respected intellectuals, R. W. Seton-Watson, wrote heatedly that "the convenient thesis of Germany's unfitness to administer colonies is as untrue as it is insulting, and should be recanted." After Hitler's Rhineland coup and the Anglo-German Naval Agreement, it was argued, the Versailles treaty and the League of Nations had become feeble precedents. Dawson, back in his role as self-appointed spokesman for forty million Britons, wrote that "British public opinion is probably far ahead of the Government" in its conviction that a stable relationship with Germany should be the sole objective "of our foreign policy." Englishmen, he declared, had "little sympathy with the view" that the Third Reich should be bound by "limits imposed twenty years ago."[16]

Now a rift appeared among the appeasers. Hitler refused the quid pro quo on armaments. Eden argued that that should be the end of it. So did Churchill's cousin Lord Londonderry, who thought all Germany's former colonies should be returned but believed it essential that Britain get something in exchange. He was, he told a friend, "very anxious lest our conciliatory trend" be interpreted in Berlin as weakness, and he feared that when the Germans became strong enough they would seek to redress their grievances "by force of arms. . . . It appears to me that by the shilly-shallying policy of the Government we are slowly but surely drifting toward this position."[17]

Actually that was already Chamberlain's position. By February 1938, two years after the House of Commons had first debated the issue of German colonial claims — and despite the vehement protests of Eden — he cabled Nevile Henderson in Berlin that he would accept less quid than quo. To "justify" the exchange to the British public, he wanted the Nazis to offer something "towards safeguarding the peace of Europe." He withdrew his request for a broad limitation of armaments and said an agreement on aerial bombing would be enough. When Ribbentrop rejected that, too, Chamberlain caved in. They could settle the colonial issue now. It wouldn't even be used as a bargaining chip in future negotiations.[18]

Chamberlain sent Hitler a new offer. African colonies which had never belonged to Germany — and had therefore been unmentioned at Versailles — would be "redistributed." They were now the property of France, Belgium (the Congo), and Portugal (Angola), but they would be a present from England to the Reich. Hitler understood this kind of language. It was his own. Intrigued, he asked what would happen if the Belgians and Portuguese objected. Chamberlain replied that not only Portugal and Belgium but also "presumably" France would "in the end cooperate in the settlement." At present, however, it was essential that no word of his new plan reach Paris, "much less" Lisbon or Brussels. They would "merely be informed" that talks had been held to discuss issues "concerning Germany and England." Unfortunately for this scheme, Britain had a free press. Henderson explained to the Führer that Chamberlain lacked his absolute control over newspapermen. However, the ambassador continued, he had spoken to "about eighty" men from Fleet Street and had "earnestly emphasized" the need for discretion. At the same time Halifax happily sent the Wilhelmstrasse word that "measures taken" by the BBC guaranteed that broadcasts "eliminated discussion regarding colonies." In London Horace Wilson noted that Halifax had taken "special pains" to keep the country ignorant of the deal. Wilson expressed "hope that he has been successful."[19]

Chamberlain was running fantastic risks. In exchange for a phantom promise to calm British nerves, he was laying territories belonging to three imperial powers — none of which had been consulted, or would be told of the decision until it had been made — on the diplomatic table. Luckily for him, the Reich chancellor rejected his proposal. Once again Hitler fooled everyone, including his own diplomats. As late as November 10, 1937, Baron Ernst von Weizsäcker, the Wilhelmstrasse's equivalent of Vansittart, had written: "From England we want colonies. . . . The British need for tranquillity is great. It would be profitable to find out what England would be willing to pay for such tranquillity." And so it was. Hitler had begun to acquire a sense of Chamberlain, a feel for his weaknesses. As for the colonies, he brusquely told the amazed Henderson on March 3, he had no use for them. They "would only be a burden for me." The colonial question, he said, "can wait for four, six, eight, or even ten years." The British ambassador asked for something more definite, and Hitler promised a written reply, but Henderson, as he wrote in his memoirs, "left Berlin a year and a half later without having received it." Belatedly Henderson realized that the issue of Germany's prewar colonies had been a red herring, that it was not "understanding with Great Britain" that Hitler wanted; it was "dominion in Central and Eastern Europe."[20]

❧ ❧

The P.M. had been courting Mussolini, hoping to sign him up before Hitler could, but the Führer was a more skillful seducer. Eden knew it, and so did Kurt von Schuschnigg, the Austrian minister who had hanged the Nazi murderers of Chancellor Dollfuss in 1934 and had now himself become chancellor. Schuschnigg had been the object of both Hitler's and Mussolini's manipulations. In the summer of 1936 the Duce had persuaded him that a rapprochement with the Third Reich was desirable, and the result — a joint communiqué published on July 11, 1936 — declared that Austria would "maintain a policy based on the principle that Austria acknowledges herself to be a German State," while the Reich recognized "the full sovereignty of the Federal State of Austria." It was a bad bargain. Secret clauses stipulated the muzzling of the Viennese press and amnesty for Nazi "political prisoners" in Austrian jails — many of them storm troopers convicted of murdering Jews and critics of the Führer.[21]

A devout Catholic and a born leader, Schuschnigg nevertheless knew that his small army would be helpless against Hitler's Wehrmacht and Luftwaffe. And Mussolini, when asked whether he could continue to guarantee the Austrian frontiers, was now evasive. Schuschnigg was pondering a restoration of the Hapsburg dynasty as his last available safeguard when, on February 12, 1938, Hitler summoned him to the Berghof, his villa in the Bavarian mountains. Berlin had announced that the meeting had been called to foster better relations between the two countries; nonetheless, Schuschnigg was wary. He was not a man to be intimidated, but the Führer had yet to meet the man he couldn't break.

The Führer's methods were rarely subtle. Wearing the brown tunic of a Nazi storm trooper and flanked by German generals — a shocking breach of protocol, particularly to an Austrian of impeccable old-world Viennese manners — he led his uneasy guest to his second-floor study, with its enormous picture window overlooking the snow-capped Alps. In his later account of the meeting, *Ein Requiem in Rot-Weiss-Rot* (Red-White-Red, the national colors of Austria), Schuschnigg described what followed as "somewhat one-sided [*einseitig*]."[22]

Actually it was outrageous. The Austrian addressed Hitler as "Herr Reichskanzler," as diplomatic courtesy required; the Führer rudely referred to him as "Schuschnigg." Hitler spoke in harsh and contemptuous tones. Gazing out beyond the Alps, toward Austria, he declared: "I have a historic mission, and this mission I shall fulfill because Providence has destined me to do so. . . . Who is not with me will be crushed [*kommt unter die Räder*]." Austria was too weak to defend herself against his Wehrmacht and would be without allies. Italy? He and Mussolini saw things "eye to eye [*im reinen*]." France could have stopped him at the Rhineland; now "it is too late for France." And England? He had an understanding with the British; "England will not lift one finger for Austria [*keinen Finger für Österreich rühren*]." To Schuschnigg it seemed that Hitler might as well be speaking Hindustani; he was "a man from another world."

But in the end his tremendous, hypnotic force won. After eleven hours of insults and threats — at one point Hitler screamed: "I have only to give an order, and your ridiculous defenses will be blown to bits [*zerstoben*]!" — Schuschnigg crumbled. He accepted the Führer's ultimatum, signing a two-page "agreement" drafted by Ribbentrop. All jailed Austrian Nazis were to be freed, their party was recognized as legitimate, and three pro-Nazis were to become members of the cabinet, including the infamous Arthur Seyss-Inquart, who, as minister of the interior, would wield dictatorial powers over the police and security.[23]

Hitler reported all this to a cheering Reichstag, praising Schuschnigg's "understanding" and his "warmhearted willingness" to bring Austria and the Reich closer. This provoked a snort from Churchill: "When a snake wants to eat his victims he first covers them with saliva." The repercussions were felt in every world capital, though not by every world leader. On February 16, the day the Austrian cabinet was rebuilt to suit Hitler, Chamberlain's cabinet met to consider an RAF appeal for larger appropriations. Foreign Secretary Eden and First Lord of the Admiralty Duff Cooper thought it overdue. Chancellor of the Exchequer Simon argued against it on the ground that higher taxes would imperil Britain's "present standard of financial prosperity." Chamberlain agreed. So did Inskip; though responsible for defense coordination, he took the line that the Foreign Office should set about "reducing the scale of our commitments and the number of our potential enemies." This could only mean continued appeasement of Germany and Italy, and when Chamberlain said, "Hear, hear," Eden flushed.[24]

Relations between the prime minister and his young foreign secretary were approaching the breaking point. In January President Roosevelt had cabled Chamberlain, proposing that European leaders convene in Washington to discuss their differences. The prime minister was annoyed — according to Sir Alexander Cadogan, Vansittart's deputy at the Foreign Office, Chamberlain "had an almost instinctive contempt for the Americans" — and he rejected Roosevelt's offer without consulting Eden, stiffly replying that he believed he could reach agreements with the dictators, with Mussolini first. His Majesty's Government was prepared "to recognise *de jure* the Italian occupation of Abyssinia, if they found that the Italian Government on their side were ready to give evidence of their desire to contribute to the restoration of confidence and friendly relations."[25]

In Churchill's opinion Chamberlain's rebuff to the president's overture effectively ended, as he wrote in his memoirs, "the last frail chance to save the world from tyranny other than by war." If this seems extravagant, one must reflect on Churchill's reasoning, which Eden had adopted. Roosevelt, as Churchill wrote, was "running great risks in his own domestic politics by deliberately involving the United States in the darkening European scene."

And he knew the democracies could not survive in Europe without American support. Roosevelt was not a man you could insult twice. His message had been graceful, even deferential; now he knew he and Neville Chamberlain could never mesh. FDR realized that at some time Hitler must be turned back. If Great Britain fell, FDR could buy peace for a generation, but by then the position of the United States would be hopeless. Already local admirers of the Nazis were swinging clubs in the streets of Latin American capitals. Therefore the president, like Churchill, was determined to establish a special relationship between England and America.[26]

Chamberlain preferred agreements with Germany and Italy to America's goodwill. And he and those around him saw the foreign secretary as an obstacle to this policy. This is somewhat puzzling. To the British and American publics, Eden later came to be regarded as a shining figure overshadowed only by Churchill. Actually, he was more cautious than ambitious; until late in the decade there was little difference in principle between him and the prime minister whose friendship and confidence he had enjoyed. With Hitler threatening Austria, he told the cabinet, he did not want to put himself "in the position of suggesting a resistance which we could not in fact furnish." Nevertheless, Chamberlain persuaded Hankey that Eden had been "swayed by a lot of sloppy people in the F.O." In Rome, Lady Ivy Chamberlain, Austen's widow, proudly wearing a new Fascist party badge, reported that Eden was regarded there "with strong dislike and distrust." The prime minister was turning to people like her for private diplomacy, or sending messages abroad over his own name, thus bypassing and humiliating the foreign secretary. Why? The likeliest explanation is that Chamberlain, as Eden had told a friend, had a certain sympathy for dictators, "whose efficiency appealed to him."[27]

The climax came in late February. Hitler had browbeaten Schuschnigg on a Saturday. Eden's turn came the following week. He had invited the Italian ambassador to England, Dino Grandi, to confer with him at the Foreign Office. Acting on instructions from Rome, Grandi refused and asked for a meeting with Chamberlain to discuss the Führer's insistence on further concessions from Schuschnigg. The prime minister agreed and sent Eden instructions to join them when they met on Friday, February 18. Thus the British foreign secretary was in the extraordinary position of facing a de facto alliance between the envoy of a potential enemy and his own prime minister, which, as Telford Taylor suggests, "must be well-nigh unique in diplomatic annals."[28]

British intelligence had informed Eden that Hitler had decided to seize Austria by force and Mussolini had agreed not to intervene. Grandi, prompted by the P.M., denied that there was any such understanding and added that unless Britain were sympathetic toward Mussolini's policies, Italian hostility toward His Majesty's Government would harden. After Grandi left, Eden wrote in his diary: "N.C. became very vehement . . . and strode up and down the room saying with great emphasis 'Anthony, you have missed chance after chance. You simply cannot go on like this.' " After following the star of appeasement for five years, Eden had found it to be tinsel. Only a week earlier he had promised an audience in Birmingham that he would agree to "no sacrifice of principles and no shirking of responsibilities merely to obtain quick results," that peace could be preserved only "on a basis of frank reciprocity with mutual respect." Now, unless he broke that vow, he had to quit. On Saturday the prime minister told his cabinet that he had decided to open direct negotiations with the Duce. Eden resigned in disgust the next day, and his under secretary quit with him.[29]

Halifax, appointed to succeed him, was delighted. Chamberlain was relieved, and no one in Parliament was surprised. Chamberlain filled the under secretary's void by appointing R. A. ("Rab") Butler. Butler called at the German embassy, described his close relationship with Sir Horace Wilson, told Hitler's diplomats that his primary objective was "close and lasting cooperation" with the Reich, and said he would "do all I can" to promote it. The embassy, which had reported to the Wilhelmstrasse that Wilson was "decidedly pro-German," now sent word that Butler also "has no prejudices against us."[30]

Readers of *The Times* were under the impression that anyone who spoke out in Eden's behalf would be a lone voice. Actually, the country was more divided than Dawson acknowledged. As England's most eminent journalist, he came under fire in Oxford. A young Fellow asked him why the FO, with *The Times*'s approval, devoted so much space to Mussolini and other Fascists when "It isn't they who are the danger. It is the Germans who are so powerful as to threaten all the rest of us together." Dawson revealed the depth of the void left when honor had been abandoned: "To take your argument at its own valuation — mind you, I'm not saying I agree with it — but if the Germans are so powerful as you say, *Oughtn't we to go in with them?*"[31]

Winston had reservations about Eden — he thought him weak at times and capable of unsound judgment — but he knew he had been a brave officer in France and would never compromise England's honor in the name of a sham peace. Later he described the impact of the news on him:

> Late in the night of February 20, a telephone message reached me as I sat in my old room at Chartwell . . . that Eden had resigned. I must confess that my heart

sank, and for a while the dark waters of despair overwhelmed me. In a long life I have had many ups and downs. During all the war soon to come and in its darkest times. . . . I slept sound and awoke refreshed, and had no feelings except appetite to grapple with whatever the morning's boxes might bring. But now, on this night of February 20, 1938, and on this occasion only, sleep deserted me. From midnight till dawn I lay in my bed consumed by emotions of sorrow and fear. There seemed one strong young figure standing up against long, dismal, drawling tides of drift and surrender, of wrong measurements and feeble impulses. My conduct of affairs would have been different from his in various ways; but he seemed to me at this moment to embody the life-hope of the British nation, the grand old British race that had done so much for men, and had yet some more to give. Now he was gone. I watched the daylight slowly creep in through the windows, and saw before me in mental gaze the vision of Death.

He sent Eden a note, advising him on what line to take in his resignation speech and urging him not to "allow your personal feelings of friendship to yr late colleagues to hamper you in doing full justice to yr case."[32]

Hurt and angry, Eden spoke to the House on February 21: "I should not be frank if I were to pretend that it is an isolated issue. It is not." Without actually mentioning the rebuff to Roosevelt or Hitler's designs on Austria, he said slowly: *"Within the last few weeks upon one most important decision of foreign policy which did not concern Italy at all the difference was fundamental."* His peroration was a paraphrase of the speeches Winston had been delivering for over five years: "I do not believe that we can make progress in European appeasement if we allow the impression to gain currency abroad that we yield to constant pressure. . . . I am certain in my own mind that progress depends above all on the temper of the nation, and that temper must find expression in a firm spirit. That spirit I am confident is there. Not to give voice to it is I believe fair neither to this country nor to the world."[33]

Churchill spoke the next day. Citing recent "acts of bad faith" by Fascists and Nazis, he said he thought "this was an inopportune time for negotiations with Italy." Furthermore, "the dictator Powers of Europe are striding from strength to strength and from stroke to stroke, and the Parliamentary democracies are retreating abashed and confused." All in all, he said, "This has been a good week for the Dictators. It has been one of the best they have ever had. The German Dictator has laid his hand upon a small but historic country, and the Italian Dictator has carried his vendetta to a victorious conclusion against my right Hon friend the late Foreign Secretary. . . . All the might, majesty, dominion and power of the British Empire was no protection to my right Hon friend. Signor Mussolini has got his scalp." The prime minister's contempt for Americans was widely known. Churchill foresaw the time when the United States might be desperately needed as a

British ally. But after this disgraceful episode, "millions of people there who are our enemies have been armed with a means to mock the sincerity of British idealism, and to make out that we are all Continental people tarred with the same brush." That, he said, was a staggering blow. Britain's old policy, he noted, had been to build up the League of Nations. Chamberlain openly scorned the league. Churchill asked: "Is the new policy to come to terms with the totalitarian Powers in the hope that by great and far-reaching acts of submission, not merely by sentiments and pride, but in material Factors, peace may be preserved?" He reminded them of Britain's weak defenses, of the loss of the Rhineland, of the drama in Austria, now approaching a tragic climax, and added: "We do not know whether Czechoslovakia will not suffer a similar attack." To turn away from the Americans was folly, he said, facing Chamberlain and concluding: "I predict that the day will come when at some point or other, on some issue or other, you will have to make a stand, and I pray God that when that day comes we may not find that through an unwise policy we are left to make that stand alone."[34]

After thirty years of marriage the Churchills had reached the age at which familial bonds loosen. All the children except Mary, now in her midteens, were grown. Diana, nearly thirty, had married the son of Sir Abe Bailey, a wealthy South African and a friend of Winston's; three years later she divorced him and married Duncan Sandys. Now she was the mother of two. Randolph, in his late twenties, had been engaged to a girl from Cleveland, Ohio, until his mother talked him out of it. Her motive had been his happiness, but the real winner was the girl. Despite his distinguished name and his leonine features, the Churchill's only son was a grim prospect for any bride, or, indeed for anyone who crossed his path. Already he had as many enemies as his father. The constitution of one club had actually been amended to read: "Randolph Churchill shall not be eligible for membership." During one dinner-party argument he shouted at an executive of British Petroleum: "You have nothing to contribute to this. You are only a clerk in an oil store." He was a chain-smoker, and late in his life, when a tumor was discovered in his alimentary canal, many hoped for the worst. They were disappointed. It was benign. Lord Stanley of Alderly learned of the surgery while standing at the bar in White's. "What a pity," he said, "to remove the one part of Randolph that is not malignant." Both parents shared the responsibility for having raised a cad, though Winston's guilt was more conspicuous. Remembering his own wretched school years, he had approved of his son's contempt for Etonian discipline. After only four terms at Christ Church, Randolph came down from Oxford to launch his public career by a lecture tour of the United States. Everyone in the family except Winston, Mary recalls, thought the scheme "a hare-brained adventure."[35]

Eventually — and perhaps inevitably — the youth turned on his father. One mealtime after another erupted in terrible rows between the two, often in the presence of eminent guests. It became, in Colville's words, "a sad and sorry relationship." The climax followed a January 1938 visit to Chartwell by Leslie Hore-Belisha, the war minister. A few weeks later Churchill sent him a small gift. It was a typical Churchillian gesture — magnanimity toward a man whose company he enjoyed despite their disagreements on the government's defense policy. One evening during dinner *en famille* he was highly critical of Hore-Belisha's role in shaping that policy. Randolph interrupted to say that since he felt that way, the invitation to the war minister and the gift must have been meant to curry favor. The rest of the family gasped. Young Churchill meant to be ironic, but he must have known that his father's personal honor was no joking matter. Outraged, Winston stopped speaking to his son. Randolph wrote him the next day, not to apologize, but to reproach him for "relapsing into moody silence." Churchill replied: "I thought yr remark singularly unkind, offensive, & untrue; & I am sure no son shd have made it to his father. Your letter in no way removes the pain it has caused me, not only on my own account but also on yours, & also on account of our relationship. . . . I really cannot run the risk of such insults being offered to me, & do not feel I want to see you at the present time."[36]

As the years passed, Colville recalled, "the worm turned, and when Randolph arrived, resolved to be good and peaceful, it would be Winston who launched an attack." Thus their relationship deteriorated, never sinking to the depths of Winston's with his own father but nevertheless a source of pain for the entire family. The intriguing question arises: Where was Randolph's mother? The answer is that she was there but might just as well not have been. Aloof, silent, eyes averted, Clementine by her whole manner proclaimed that she had warned her husband, he hadn't listened, and this was the result. But the son felt uncomfortable with his mother, too. Later, after he had married Pamela Digby, he told her that Clementine "hated" him. That was absurd, but friends of the family thought her an unusual mother. Until the last quarter of the twentieth century, the wives of Britain's public men balanced their obligations to their husbands against those to their children. Most compromised. To Clementine, Winston always came first. Mary recalls that he and his career "consumed the cream of her thought and energy." That was not entirely true. She "never became a yes-woman," in

Mary's words, "or lost her capacity for independent thought." Certainly she had a strong mind of her own. When Pamela was having difficulties with her young husband, Clemmie advised her: "Pack up, take the children, leave *and don't tell him where you're going*. You can't imagine how kind and sweet he'll be when you return."[37]

In all events, the Chumbolly — his *petit nom* in childhood — had become a problem. So had "Mule," Sarah, now in her early twenties, green-eyed and stunning, with titian hair and milk-white skin. Her mother wrote a friend: "Sometimes she looks absolutely lovely — but on the other hand she can look like a moping raven." She moped when she didn't have her way. In the end she always had it; she was her father's favorite; he could deny her nothing. She decided on a theatrical career and got it, beginning in the chorus line of C. B. Cochran's "Young Ladies," which, according to Pamela, was "a London revue of girls who danced fairly naked — as naked as you could get in those days. That was not really what her parents had in mind for their daughter." Then, while playing in *Follow the Sun,* she fell in love with a music hall comedian, Vic Oliver, a thirty-three-year-old Viennese, thought to be Jewish, who had already been married twice. The response of her parents was a vehement *No*. They wouldn't budge; neither would she. After a year of quarreling she bolted to New York, where Vic was working. Winston sent Randolph after her and engaged American lawyers to stop the marriage, but since she was legally of age, they were helpless. On Christmas Eve, 1936, two weeks after Edward's abdication, Sarah became Mrs. Victor Oliver. The newspapers made a carnival of the affair, and Randolph's public denunciation of them made everything worse. Hankey wrote Chartwell, "We both sympathise with you two," and even Baldwin wrote that he wanted Churchill "to know that I felt with you from my heart when I read in the papers of certain domestic anxieties that must have caused you pain. I know you well enough to realize how closely these things touch you." In the end, a family friend says, "Sarah broke Winston's heart, and he hers."[38]

That left Mary, the Chartwell child — unlike the others, she could remember no other home — with the companionship of an astonishing array of pets: lambs, bantams, a Blenheim spaniel, a beige-colored pug dog, and a marmalade cat, two fox cubs, and three goats, one of whom produced twins while the other gave birth to triplets, and all of whom ate the cherry trees, to Clementine's indignation. Sarah had learned French in a Paris finishing school from Georges Bidault, then obscure but later foreign minister of France; Mary was taught at Chartwell during school holidays by Madame Gabrielle l'Honoré, a discovery of Clemmie's. A nearby riding school provided Mary with mounts. Her relationship with her mother, she now recalls, was "respectful and admiring rather than close," though Clementine had taken her skiing in the Arlberg mountains. After ten days, Winston received a report on their first Zürs expedition: "Mary fell down 19 times. . . . Today I am going in a sleigh as I am really bored with tumbling down!" The letter was signed: "Your bruised & struggling but undaunted Clemmie."[39]

Sometimes husband and wife spent holidays together. They were welcomed at Blenheim and Lou Sueil by the Marlboroughs; at Taplow by Lord and Lady Desborough; at Trent Park by Sir Philip Sassoon; and the Duke of Westminster (known as Bendor to his friends) was their host at his several homes in England, France, and Scotland. But these were relatives or very old friends. Other patricians felt awkward with them. Winston's criticism of the new Germany was considered bad form — even disloyal to His Majesty's Government. And his manners were odd. How could you entertain a man who wouldn't laugh at anti-Semitic jokes? His wife was almost as bad, and in some ways worse. She would even walk out on her own guests at Chartwell, something one didn't *do*. Mary recalls that "her victims were never the timid, however tedious, but the brash and powerful," and her "basic and undying radicalism also made high Tories and most very rich people potential targets for her scorn." Twice at Chartwell she humbled a British general. Leaving her guests to bathe before dinner, she told his aide-de-camp that she looked forward to seeing him in a half hour. The general said that his ADC didn't dine with him. Clementine turned on him and said: "In my house, General, I invite whom I wish and I don't require your advice." The ADC dined. The second time, the general muttered the threadbare old military myth that all politicians are dishonest. She rose starchily and said: "If that is your view, General, you should leave Chartwell at once. I shall arrange to have your bags packed." He stammered his apologies.[40]

Usually, however, the Churchills took separate vacations. Winston's painting was his release, his escape valve, and he found the "paintatious" Riviera, as he called it, irresistible. "I paint all day, and so far as my means go, gamble after dark," he happily wrote the former Edward VIII, now Duke of Windsor, in the early spring of 1937. He was seeing a lot of Edward and Wallis. To Clemmie he wrote from Maxine Elliott's Château de l'Horizon:

> The Windsors dine here and we dine back with them. They have a lovely little palace next door to La D [La Dragonnière, Lord Rothermere's villa at Cap Martin]. Everything extremely well done and dignified. Red liveries, and the little man himself dressed up to the nines in the Balmoral tartan with dagger and jabot etc. . . . I am to dine with him tomorrow night with only Rothermere. No doubt

to talk over his plans for returning home. They do not want him to come, but they have no power to stop him.[41]

British expatriates on the Mediterranean liked to think of their society as neo-Edwardian, and those who could afford it were as idle as only the idle rich can be. But Churchill was a working man. Typically, he wrote his wife: "I have stayed in bed every morning and made great progress with the book. We have averaged fifteen hundred words a day, though nominally on vacation. I shall have a lot for you to read when you come home." His occasional forays into Riviera diversion were, almost without exception, disappointing. He was taking lessons in what he called a "very pretty dance. We take three steps and give a hop." He added ruefully: "I always hop at the wrong time, which, I am afraid, provokes small minded people to laugh."[42]

Nevertheless, the creature comforts of the expatriate society appealed to the hedonistic streak in him; if he was well supplied with Pol Roger, fed by a great chef, and offered his choice of the best cigars, the identity of his suppliers was of little interest to him. As a statesman he was fiercely incorrupt, but on holiday he could be had — for a stiff price, to be sure — by women like Maxine Elliott and "Daisy," the daughter of the Duc de Decacazes, known in newspaper columns as "Mrs. Reginald Fellowes," though Mr. Fellowes was invisible. Daisy spent a great deal of her valueless time trying to seduce Winston, but between his paint box, printers' galleys, losing money on the green baize of the Riviera's gaming tables, monologues over brandy, and the pleasures of the table, he had no time for the pleasures she had in mind and may indeed have been unaware of her intentions. He would always find women mysterious. He had Clementine; that was enough for him.

It was not always enough for her, however. Late in life she told Mary, "It took all my time and strength just to keep up with him." This was hyperbole. Certainly, being Mrs. Winston Churchill required rare stamina. Fortunately, Clemmie had it. Indeed, she had enough to pursue her own pleasures, which were very unlike his. She didn't write, paint, gamble, or enjoy the company of *gens du monde;* she didn't like Maxine and wouldn't speak to Daisy. "Her favorite holiday," her youngest daughter recalls, "was to stay in a modest but comfortable hotel in some beautiful or interesting place," where, in the company of congenial people, she would "spend a week or two sightseeing and gallery visiting in an unhurried fashion." Winston disliked sightseeing, and he loathed being part of a tour group which would pause, in this gallery or that museum, while a guide explained what the tourists should appreciate and why. If so trapped, Churchill would stand on the outer fringe of the party, seething with frustration because he wasn't talking, couldn't even interrupt, and therefore wasn't the center of attention.[43]

Ambitious politicians try to project an image of radiant health, and to his admirers Churchill was the robust personification of John Bull. But he had been prey to ills since childhood. Some of his vacations were taken on doctor's orders; others were interrupted by bouts of influenza or infectious fevers. Once, when en route to Venice — where he expected to holiday with Clemmie, Randolph, Sarah, and the Prof — he had been stricken by paratyphoid in Bavaria. His condition was grave; a return to England was out of the question; he lay in a Salzburg sanitarium for two weeks, unable even to raise his head. His confinement continued through a third week, and he abandoned all hope of reaching Italy. He could write, however, and his bank balance, which was always in and out of the red, made work essential. Still in the sanitarium, he began a series of twelve articles on "The World's Great Stories," commissioned by Lord Riddell for *News of the World*. Back at Chartwell he wrote his cousin the Duke of Marlborough that he was "rather battered, but in another week I shall be alright. It was an English bug which I took abroad with me, and no blame rests on the otherwise misguided continent of Europe."[44]

Clementine, now moving gracefully into her fifties, shared with her husband the same peculiar mélange of exceptional energy and an unreliable constitution. As the Chamberlain government approached the end of its first year, with Halifax and the prime minister negotiating agreements with Italy — thus assuring Mussolini's support in any future European conflict, they confidently told the House — Clemmie took the cure in the Pyrenees at Cauterets, near Lourdes. Winston celebrated the following Christmas without her; she was resting on a South Pacific beach in the French colonial archipelago Îles sous le Vent. Perhaps enforced pleasure whetted her appetite for more. A splendid horsewoman, she rode often, and she played tennis with increasing skill, often with the Prof, who had made her an exception to his misogyny. She swam, hunted boar at Bendor's invitation, and beginning in 1936, the year of the Rhineland crisis, had improved her skiing while holidaying with her sister-in-law Lady Gwendeline ("Goonie") Churchill and Venetia Montagu, spending long hours après-ski by firesides in Zürs or Lenzerdeide, trying to forget the troubling present with tales of the serene past.[45]

Her most cherished memories of those interwar years were of a spectacular voyage halfway round the world in the second winter of the Third Reich, roughly the period between the Nazis' murder of Austrian chancellor Dollfuss and Hitler's announcement that Germany was rearming in defiance of Versailles. Clementine was an enchanted guest aboard Lord Moyne's yacht *Rosaura*. Moyne — who would be assassinated ten years later in Cairo by Jewish terrorists — was sailing off on one of those whimsical adventures, evocative of *King Kong,* which spiced the idle life of wealthy Englishmen between the wars. His destination was Komodo, an obscure island in what is now Indonesia, reportedly inhabited by "dragonlike monster lizards." Moyne intended to capture some for the London zoo. These creatures actually existed — one member of the party photographed a twelve-foot lizard with a pig in its jaws, and Moyne brought back two smaller specimens — but the real purpose of the trip was to visit exotica and to escape the gloom and vulgarity of Europe. Her husband and children saw her off at Victoria Station, and in her first letter she wrote that at the moment of departure, seeing "you all collected on the platform, I thought how much I love you all, and above and more than them all *you* my darling Winston. . . . You all looked so sweet and beautiful standing there, and I thought how fortunate I am to have such a family. Do not be vexed with your vagabond Cat — She has gone off toward the jungle with her tail in the air, but will return presently to her basket and curl down comfortably. . . ."

Clementine on the high seas was — at least at the outset — the quintessential Clementine. As she lay in her stateroom, she wrote home, she could "contemplate the photographs of my family erected on the chest of drawers." She had begun "an enormous piece of needlework which Venetia made me bring. I have got 144 reels of silk with which to quilt it & I calculate that even if I sew all day & never catch a butterfly or dragon I could not finish it before my return!" After thirty years of marriage her intimate letters to Churchill, and his replies, were as charming as an exchange between honeymooners. On New Year's Day she wrote from Madras: "Oh my Darling, I'm thinking so much of you & how you have enriched my life. I have loved you very much but I wish I had been a more amusing wife to you. How nice it would be if we were young again." He replied that she had written

> some words vy dear to me about my having enriched yr life. I cannot tell you what pleasure this gave me, because I always feel so overwhelmingly in yr debt, if there can be accounts in love. It was sweet of you to write this to me, & I hope & pray I shall be able to make you happy & secure during my remaining years, and cherish you my darling one as you deserve, & leave you in comfort when my race is run. What it has been to me to live all these years in yr heart & companionship no phrases can convey. Time passes swiftly, but is it not joyous to see how great and growing is the treasure we have gathered together, amid the storms & stresses of so many eventful & to millions tragic & terrible years?[46]

Winston's domestic stresses, during his wife's absence, were trivial but irksome to a man trying to sway Parliament and write the opening passages of his next Marlborough volume. His eminent ancestor fascinated him, though he saw some of his warts; Marlborough had "far less pride than the average man," he wrote Clemmie, and was in fact capable of "grovelling." It was "only in the field and in his love for Sarah that he rises to the sublime. Still Mars and Venus are two of the most important deities in the classical heaven." It was maddening to descend from the eminence of character analysis to cope with the fox who was devouring his geese, an astonishing explosion among Chartwell's canine population, and feverish young Churchills who, he reasoned, ought to be too old to catch infectious childhood diseases. Discovering that every bitch on the grounds was giving birth to litters of puppies, Winston unmasked the culprit. He was Mary's pug, a slave of lust. But Mary couldn't be admonished; she had whooping cough. Randolph was home with a severe case of jaundice. Sarah was pale and tired, a consequence, her father wrote her mother, of "dancing practically four hours a day as well as going to balls. . . . I have therefore told her that she must not go to balls on any night when she practises dancing." As to the puppies, he had "banished all dogs from our part of the house. . . . I really think you will have to buy a new strip of carpet outside my landings."[47]

Another writer would have cut his schedule to the bone and concentrated on his manuscripts. But it was part of the Churchill syndrome that despite diversions he had absolute concentration during the hours set aside for work, and that other activities were actually necessary to fuel this power. One activity was social intercourse; he needed people as ships need water. The Prof's arrival for a two-day visit delighted him. So did the unexpected appearance of his eldest daughter at a moment when she was most needed. "I was sitting down last night to eat my New Year's dinner as I thought in solitude," he wrote his wife, "and in marched Diana looking absolutely lovely. She had come on her own to keep me company."[48]

Working with his hands was equally important. Every day he laid bricks, building a wall which, he promised Clemmie, would be completed when she arrived home. That ought to have been enough, but he also launched two major landscaping projects: turning a peninsula on one Chartwell lake into an island, where the geese could nest safe from the fox, and creating a ha-ha, or sunk fence, beyond the swimming pool to permit one's eye to plunge "across a valley of unbroken green." All this was to be accomplished in one week by hiring an enormous mechanical digger for twenty-five pounds. He assured his wife the digger would "do more than forty men do." Indeed, he added, it was capable of feats beyond the competence of people "as he is a caterpillar and can walk over the most sloppy fields without doing any harm."[49]

Note: the contraption was a "he." Winston, the ultimate anthropomorphist, invested every object, animate or inanimate, with a personality and assigned it a personal pronoun. Mary simply described the contrivance as "the monster." And she was right. The "digger drama," as it came to be known at Chartwell, began when the machine clanked into view with all the grace of a heavy tank. Winston regarded the creature with admiration, which was transformed into uneasiness, alarm, pity, and, finally, fury. In his next letter to Clemmie he wrote that the project was proving "a bigger and longer business than I had expected. It will take a fortnight in all." Nearly a month later he reported in exasperation that the digger had broken down, had fallen into a pit and, despite his heroic efforts to extricate it, had been idle for three weeks. Four hydraulic jacks were rented; with their help "the animal emerged from his hole." Churchill doubted "if I shall get out of it under £150." Altogether the mechanical digger was on his property, with its expenses mounting, for ten weeks. As the day for its departure approached, it became the object of a profound Churchillian study, the results of which were reported to Chartwell's absent mistress: "The animal is very strong with his hands but feeble with his caterpillar legs, and as the fields are sopping, they had the greatest difficulty in taking him away. They will have to lay down sleepers all the way from the lake to the gate over which he will waddle on Monday. I shall be glad to see the last of him."[50]

At last, on March 8, he wrote: "The digger has gone, thank God." His wife knew how to restore his spirits. From Singapore she wrote: "What tremendous works you are doing. . . . I'm *delighted* about the Ha-ha. Please do *not* throw back *too* much earth on the garden side or the slope might look too sudden. . . . How lovely it will be when your beautiful wall reaches the end." Thus far in her trip she had been playing a familiar role as Winston's eyes and ears; she had inspected the great Singapore dockyard and noted how the government's cuts in defense spending had reduced its effectiveness, and she had marched into the city's largest bookshop and asked "if there were a brisk demand for your books." She was told that a condensed version of *The World Crisis,* his history of World War I, had "gone very well," and the second Marlborough volume was "going better than the first. They had sold 12 sets of Marlborough & had 5 more on order. I think this is rather good when you realise how expensive it is."[51]

At about this time Clementine left civilization, put away the needlework, turned away from her family photographs, and forgot her straightlaced upbringing. The *Rosaura* was headed for the most exotic islands in the world: Borneo, Celebes, the Moluccas, New Caledonia, the New Hebrides,

New Britain, and the Solomons. "This is the genuine article!" she wrote in a euphoric burst, "unchartered [*sic*] seas, unexplored territory, stark naked savages." Churchill, vaguely troubled, perhaps goaded by a flicker of intuition, replied that it made him gasp "to look at the map & see what enormous distances you have covered . . . and it depresses me to feel the *weight* of all that distance pressing down upon us both. How glad I shall be when you turn homewards, & when the mails will be closing up together, instead of lagging & widening apart!" He had reason for anxiety. Clementine was in the presence of danger. That included physical danger; at one point she became separated from the rest of the party, lost in an almost impenetrable patch of dense tropical jungle; she was soaked in a sudden rainstorm, terrified of the lizards and snakes around her, her screams unheard until the yacht's second officer came crashing through the undergrowth to rescue her. She wrote: "I almost kissed him."[52]

She was, in fact, in a kissing mood. And the greater peril lay there. Among the unhappier facts of life is that desire peaks in the two sexes at disparate ages. "The elementary notion of standardization," Mencken noted, "seems never to have occurred to the celestial Edison." A male is lustiest at fifteen; the average female reaches the heights of passion in her mid-thirties. Churchill had always been a sublimator. All who were close to him agree that he was weakly sexed, even in youth, and in his sixties his volcano was virtually extinct. In Parliament a fellow MP whispered to him that his trousers were unfastened. "It makes no difference," Winston replied wryly. "The dead bird doesn't leave the nest."[53]

Clementine, however, was vulnerable. The setting conspired against her. Cruising through tropical seas, past lush, nameless islands heavy with the scent of exotic flowers, she felt transported. Like a Maugham heroine — strong-minded, puritanical, even prim — she met a romantic unattached man and fell in love. The man was Terence Philip, a handsome, wealthy art dealer seven years younger than she. In any affair, La Rochefoucauld observed, one partner is the lover and the other the beloved. Philip was the beloved. Long afterward Clementine conceded that the initiative had been hers, adding, "But he made me love him." Mary compares the relationship between them to "a fragile tropical flower which cannot survive in grayer, colder climes." Clementine came to her senses. She was not meant for enchantment; her destiny was inseparable from Churchill's. Late in life, in a nostalgic letter, she summed up the magic of those three months beneath the Southern Cross, saying, in effect, that she had briefly known the transient rapture of Cinderella at the ball; then the clock struck and she fled. Of course, she missed Philip. They met several times, and that summer she suggested to Churchill that she take another trip. She wrote a friend: "It's very nice to be back but Oh Dear I want to start out again very badly! Mr. Pug is very sweet but now he says 'NO.' . . ." Even before she returned he had written her: "I think a lot about you my darling Pussie . . . and rejoice that we have lived our lives together; and have still some years of expectation in this pleasant vale. . . . I feel this has been a gt experience and adventure to you & that it has introduced a new background to yr life, & a larger proportion; and so I have not grudged you your long excursion; but now I do want you back."[54]

She brought back one souvenir, an exquisite Bali dove which lived, at Chartwell, in a lovely wicker cage. It could not last there long; perhaps she had known that. After its death she buried it in the walled garden, beneath the sundial. Today one can read the epitaph she had carved round the sundial's base:

HERE LIES THE BALI DOVE

It does not do to wander
Too far from sober men
But there's an island yonder,
I think of it again.

By 1937 Churchill's isolation in the House of Commons was almost complete; as his daughter Mary notes, "his gradual estrangement from the Conservative party's leadership, due to his . . . campaign for rearmament and confrontation with the growing power of Germany, made the probability of his being offered office increasingly remote." The quarantine of him was effective among and in the organs of entrenched power, notably *The Times* and the BBC. But Winston reached millions of readers with his powerful articles — over a hundred in 1937 alone, including fortnightly pieces in Beaverbrook's *Evening Standard*, which were syndicated in the *Glasgow Evening News*, the *Aberdeen Evening Express*, the *Belfast Telegraph*, the *Adelaide Advertiser*, the *East African Standard*, and the *Madras Mail;* translations in Brussels, Rotterdam, Copenhagen, Stockholm, Oslo, Tallinn, Kaunas, Zurich, Lausanne, Prague, Bucharest, Cracow, Buenos Aires, Trondheim, Lucerne, Budapest, and Belgrade; and a weekly essay in *News of the World*. *News of the World* was disdained by the mighty for its sensationalism and its pandering to the working class, but with an audience of four million members it could not be scorned by a man struggling to rouse the country, and Churchill was in no position to pick his forum anyhow. On November 3, 1937, he wrote the *News*'s publishers, grandly describing it as "a wonderful platform from which to address the stable, sagacious, good-humoured, kind-hearted mass of the British nation, and I value the opportunity of doing so, quite apart from the handsome payments which you make."[55]

Handsome was the right word; on December 18, 1937, after he had agreed to write sixteen *News of the World* articles in 1938, he received a check for £4,500. William L. Shirer knew Randolph as a fellow journalist in the late 1930s and learned something of Winston's finances from his son. Randolph, he writes, explained that "his father lived mainly from a syndicated weekly [*sic*] newspaper column sold around the world. There were over two hundred subscribers, he said, who paid a total of around $2,000 a week, of which Churchill received some £300, or $1,500, a fairly comfortable income. But not one that was making him really rich." Yet Winston insisted upon continuing to live as though he were, and most Englishmen, including some who knew him well, would have been astounded to know that all his life he had been just a few steps — sometimes very few — from his creditors.[56]

Abroad he was taken more seriously than in Parliament. He was, as he described himself, "a private member of Parliament, but of some prominence." Newspaper publishers who held him in contempt would have preferred to ignore him, but their reporters gave him celebrity status, knowing he always made good copy. At one time or another, photographs of him laying bricks must have been seen by every Briton. When a British tailors' magazine deplored his wardrobe, it was news, even in the United States. Léon Blum, the French statesman, visited Chartwell to ask his advice. French generals invited him to tour the Maginot Line. He went and, after inspecting it, painted it. His following in France was large; when George VI and his queen made a state visit to Paris, the Churchills were invited to all the royal functions, always *bien placés* — better seated, indeed, than the British ambassador. Among Clementine's papers, when she died, was a Versailles menu dated July 21, 1938, and signed by her partners on both sides: M. Gabriel Hanotaux, a celebrated author, now forgotten, and Marshal Philippe Pétain, the hero of Verdun, whose performance in World War II would be less illustrious.[57]

Among those who recognized Churchill's potential should war come was the man who was going to make it all happen. Several months before Eden's resignation Ambassador Joachim von Ribbentrop, on Hitler's instructions, asked Winston to call on him at the German embassy in London. The excuse was one of Churchill's columns in Beaverbrook's *Evening Standard;* Winston had written that a recent speech by Ribbentrop had been misrepresented. But there was more to it than that. Envoys of great powers did not deign to discuss articles in newspapers of their host country; lesser men on their staffs did it for them. And when Churchill appeared at the German embassy on May 21, 1937, the column wasn't even mentioned. The matter discussed was so momentous that they were closeted for over two hours. The Führer, his ambassador said, proposed to guarantee the integrity of the British Empire. Churchill replied that the Royal Navy had been doing that for centuries and needed no help. Nevertheless, Ribbentrop declared that the Third Reich would "stand guard" over it; all he asked in return was a "free hand" in eastern Europe. The Reich, he explained, needed lebensraum for its increasing population. Winston, intrigued, asked how much living space Hitler wanted.[58]

Strolling up to a wall map, the Nazi blandly ticked off the Reich chancellor's shopping list: all of Poland, all of the Ukraine, and the Soviet republic of Byelorussia, including the Pripet Marshes. Churchill stared at the map. The Reich's land mass would be quintupled, from 182,000 square miles to 760,000. Great Britain had less than 89,000. After a long pause he replied that although Britons were "on bad terms with Soviet Russia" and "hated Communism as much as Hitler," they didn't hate it *that* much. He could only speak for himself, but he felt certain that no British government would tolerate German "domination of Central and Eastern Europe." According to Churchill, Ribbentrop "turned abruptly away" and said, "In that case, war is inevitable. The Führer is resolved. Nothing will stop him and nothing will stop us." Churchill urged him not to "underrate England," and particularly not to "judge by the attitude of the present administration." Britain, he said, "is a curious country, and few foreigners can understand her mind. . . . She is very clever. If you plunge us all into another great war, she will bring the whole world against you like last time." The Nazi said heatedly, "Ah, England may be very clever, but this time she will not bring the world against Germany." Because he thought the incident should be "put on record," Churchill later wrote, he "reported it at the time to the Foreign Office."[59]

It was not news there. The FO was, however, surprised by Hitler's decision to approach Churchill, his most implacable enemy, apparently in the belief that he could frighten him with Teutonic *Schrecklichkeit*. It was also noted wryly that this was one of those rare occasions in which Winston arrived in Whitehall as the bearer of news. Usually it was the other way round; the situation map he kept at Chartwell was almost as detailed, and as accurate, as those in Whitehall. He had begun on a small scale, but now his business as the receiver of stolen goods — state secrets not meant for the eyes of a private MP, however prominent — was booming. At Chartwell and in his Westminster flat he pored over classified British documents and reports on the latest developments in eight continental capitals. In London his informants included three members of Chamberlain's cabinet; in the world of science, technology, and the intelligentsia were Sir Eustace Tennyson-d' Eyncourt and Sir William Beveridge; in the War Office, the chief of the Imperial General Staff (first Sir Cyril Deverell, and then, in 1939, Sir Edmund Ironside), a brigadier, and two colonels; in the RAF, an air chief marshal, a wing commander, a group captain, and a squadron leader; and in the Admiralty, a vice admiral (Sir Reginald Henderson), a rear admiral, a captain, and a brilliant young commander, Lord Louis Mountbatten. He had the support of almost every man in the top echelon of the Foreign Office. Ribbentrop had thought his message would stun Winston, and had been taken aback by his ready reply. In fact, he had only confirmed what Churchill had already known — from Vansittart's agent in Göring's office — for several months.

He relied on Van for material from the Wilhelmstrasse, but his data on the RAF's inadequacies, which created such consternation on the front bench, came directly from officers who were risking court-martial if found out. Group Captain Lachlan MacLean, who had commanded a company of Gurkha Rifles in France before transferring to the Royal Flying Corps in 1916, had drawn up a savage indictment describing the RAF's obsolete equipment and concluded that were war to come in the next three or even five years, "We shall be powerless to retaliate, at any rate in the air." Wing Commander Anderson acquired a copy and sent it to Churchill, who replied that he would like to meet the author. According to MacLean's account, "Accompanying Anderson I was introduced to Winston in his flat in Westminster and he congratulated me on the paper and we discussed the air rearmament." Subsequently Anderson would tell MacLean that Churchill needed data for a speech in the House. MacLean would prepare a memorandum "and I would let him have these papers and would perhaps go to Churchill's flat for a discussion." The arrangement evolved, he recalled, "into my sending to Winston's personal secretary, Mrs Pearman, papers on the more significant events in the air rearmament." In less than seven months the two RAF officers met Churchill, either in Morpeth Mansions or at Chartwell, seven times. Inevitably, they met Lindemann. Papers were exchanged on such arcane topics as RDF and "Times of Flight and Trajectory Tables" — dull to the layman, but essential to Britain's survival three years later.[60]

Eminent guests from abroad whose names are inscribed in Chartwell's guest book include the Rumanian foreign minister Nicolae Titulescu; former

German chancellor Heinrich Brüning; Pierre Cot, the French air minister; and Britain's ambassador to Belgrade, who approved Churchill's plan to visit Yugoslavia and urge the formation of a European alliance to confront Nazi aggression. These visitors would stay for dinner. British civilian informants would arrive for tea at Chartwell or "elevenses" in his London flat, leaving behind them, when they departed, copies of blueprints, charts, diagrams, minutes of cabinet meetings, and confidential reports to the prime minister, all of which belonged in locked, guarded files at the War Office, the Admiralty, the Air Ministry, or Downing Street.

In bed the following morning, sipping his breakfast highball, Winston would compare them with information from the Wilhelmstrasse and the Linden; reports from the mistresses of the Duce's intimate advisers; foreign ministries from Helsinki to Athens; and straightforward *en clair et net* dispatches from the French. Churchill regularly exchanged data with three successive prime ministers, Blum, Flandin, and Édouard Daladier. Typically, he wrote Daladier in early 1938, asking for a cross-check of "information I have been able to gather from various sources about the present and prospective strength of the German Army." He put it at forty divisions "now at full war-strength," four of them armored, with another twenty divisions ready by October 1, and still another thirty-six in trained reserves. This represented a sevenfold jump in one year, an expansion of military strength without precedent in peacetime. Moreover, another twelve Austrian divisions would be added if Hitler's Anschluss succeeded and was followed by conscription there. Daladier consulted his War Office in the rue St. Dominique, checked the Deuxième Bureau, and replied that they were "entirely in accord with you." Even Desmond Morton was impressed. "I am astonished," he wrote to Winston, "by your knowledge of detail on Defence matters."[61]

All this did not pass the Treasury Bench unnoticed. Nor was it meant to. Espionage is usually covert. Information so acquired is exploited without the knowledge of the spies' victims; if made public it becomes valueless, and agents may be blown. But Churchill's motives were political; he meant to reverse the course of Britain's military policy. Throughout the fall of 1937 and into 1938 he continued to receive disturbing reports from Anderson, Morton, and, through MacLean, Air Chief Marshal Sir Edgar Ludlow-Hewitt of the RAF. In the House of Commons his remarks on Britain's lack of preparedness grew sharper. So did the criticism of his criticism, but as Morton wrote him, he was "not the first to have told the truth and become heartily unpopular for it." Even if prophecies proved true, Morton continued, men had "the habit of crucifying the prophet or . . . they exterminate him with a gas cloud — of propaganda. However, they have not silenced you yet, so there is some hope for the Empire still."[62]

In the eyes of His Majesty's Government, press lords like Beaverbrook, and most members of Parliament, Churchill's concerns were largely irrelevant. To them, war between Britain and Nazi Germany wasn't even a remote possibility. Differences between the British Empire and the German Reich would be resolved at negotiating tables. Since Britain was prepared to give Hitler whatever he wanted, why should a drop of blood be spilled, or England's rising productivity be threatened by a bloated arms budget?

Churchill was painfully aware that His Majesty's Government regarded him as a meddler and a Cassandra. Yet his figures — which were also HMG's figures — cried for action. In the fall of 1937 the Air Ministry, looking ahead to December 1939, had found that the RAF would have only 1,736 aircraft as against Germany's 3,240. More urgently, Chamberlain had invited a Luftwaffe mission headed by General Erhard Milch to spend a week inspecting the RAF's latest models on the ground and reviewing a fly-past. On October 12, Group Captain MacLean sent word of this to Chartwell. MacLean had inferred, not unreasonably, that the Nazis, suspecting the inadequacies of England's air force, were coming "to find confirmation of their suspicions." Once they had grasped Britain's weakness in the air — and they could scarcely miss it; the aircraft they would be examining weren't even fully equipped — their discovery, MacLean wrote, "must inevitably influence German policy. . . . We are bluffing with the sky as the limit, without holding a single card, and we have then invited our opponents to come round and see what cards we hold, trusting to sleight of hand to put across a second bluff."[63]

Alarmed, Churchill was also in a quandary. There was no way to withdraw the invitation to Germany without making things worse. But it was time the government moved quickly to heal its sickly air force. His latest data, as he wrote Sir Maurice Hankey, could not be discussed in the House of Commons because "of the present dangerous world situation." He had decided to lay the facts before Hankey, who, as secretary to both the cabinet and the Committee of Imperial Defence, carried weight in the government. Hankey was aware of the problem; he had written Inskip that if the country realized how vulnerable Britain was to aggression HMG would be "forced to undertake late in the day panic measures." On October 16 Winston sent him MacLean's report, omitting the author's name and identifying him only as "a high staff officer of the RAF." He added, "I trust to our friendship and your honour that its origin is not probed. But look at the facts!"[64]

To his dismay, Hankey chose to ignore the facts. Instead he replied with an unexpected, lengthy rebuke. He was, he said, "a good deal troubled by the fact of your receiving so many confidences of this kind," particularly since Winston was "a critic of the Departments under whom these Officers serve" and they were ignorant "of the wider factors" in national policy. If they had grievances, they should speak to their senior officers or to the cabinet minister representing their service. "Backstairs" information, he wrote, should be discouraged "because it breeds distrust and has a disintegrating effect on the discipline of the Services." In a stiff reply, Churchill said he had not expected a "lengthy lecture," and "you may be sure I shall not trouble you again in such matters."[65]

By now His Majesty's Government was aware that Churchill had become a spymaster, and the hunt for his sources within the government — the "rotten apples," as Horace Wilson called them — was on. Not long after Churchill's exchange with Hankey, MacLean resigned from the RAF, reportedly under pressure. But those pursuing a military alliance were after bigger game. In the Foreign Office, Vansittart, with his swagger and arrogance, was the apple likeliest to be tainted. Since moving into No. 10 with Chamberlain, Wilson had been stalking the FO's permanent under secretary, judging him, Churchill wrote in his war memoirs, "as hostile to Germany." In HMG's view criticism of the Third Reich blackened a man's name. The prime minister had dismissed Van's warnings of German aggression as "hysterical," and Wilson had called the under secretary "an alarmist" who "hampers all attempts of the Government to make friendly contact with the dictator states," adding that "his influence over Anthony Eden is very great."[66]

At that time Eden, still foreign secretary, could have fought for Vansittart, and his decent instincts prodded him to do it. But as Gilbert and Gott put it, he "unwisely and rashly bowed to the wind" when Chamberlain declared that Van must be replaced by Sir Alexander Cadogan, a protégé of Horace Wilson. Vansittart had thirty-six years of diplomatic experience, but Cadogan, as a zealous believer in appeasement and the promise of an Anglo-German alliance, was likelier to sympathize with Chamberlain's conviction that the Third Reich should become Britain's most favored nation.[67]

On January 1, 1938, Vansittart was kicked upstairs and given the empty title of chief diplomatic adviser to the government. Cadogan would run the Foreign Office. The Germans were delighted; Ernst von Wörmann, chargé d'affaires at Hitler's London embassy, minuted that Van could no longer issue instructions to British envoys in foreign capitals, nor would classified material be channeled through him; he would see documents only "as required" by Cadogan. The fact that he was permitted to remain in his old office deceived no one. His "dismissal," as Churchill rightly called it, stunned Whitehall. There was no precedent for it; traditionally, permanent under secretaries held office until they died or chose to retire. Winston heard the news in Paris, where, after a month's holiday at the Château de l'Horizon, he was staying at the British embassy, conferring with Daladier, who would be premier in the next French government, and Alexis Léger, secretary general at the Quai d'Orsay. The fall of his great FO ally left Churchill distraught. The British ambassador, Sir Eric Phipps, reported to London that Winston could "hardly talk of anything else," that he "thought Van's displacement was a very dangerous thing, that it would be represented as a victory for pro-Germans in England, that it would arouse the suspicions of the French, etc etc." Phipps, himself an appeaser, wrote Hankey that he was "honestly perturbed at the fuss over Van's appointment." But Churchill saw the significance of Vansittart's fall. "No one more clearly realised or foresaw the growth of the German danger," he later wrote, "or was more ready to subordinate other considerations to meeting it," and now "the whole responsibility for managing the Foreign Office passed out of his hands."[68]

Emboldened, a few months later the appeasers actually tried to imprison one of Churchill's few parliamentary followers. Duncan Sandys had his own clandestine sources; on June 17, 1938, armed with facts and figures, he sent the War Office a question — concerning London's air defenses — which clearly revealed access to classified information. Summoned by the attorney general, he was told that unless he disclosed the name of his informant, he would be prosecuted under the Official Secrets Act. Sandys told his tale in Parliament and requested the appointment of a select committee to study the applicability of the act to MPs carrying out their official duties. Winston delightedly wrote Lord Hugh Cecil, one of his oldest friends — he had been best man when Churchill married Clementine thirty years earlier — "The fur is going to fly."[69]

Tempers were up, and skyrocketed the next day when Sandys informed a crowded House that as a reserve officer he had been ordered to appear, in uniform, before a court-martial. This, he submitted, was a "gross breach" of Parliamentary privileges. He was backed by Attlee and Sinclair, the Labour and Liberal leaders, and, of course, by his father-in-law, who tartly remarked that an act designed to protect the national defense should not shield ministers who had neglected national defense. When the House cleared Sandys without dissent, Oliver Harvey of the Foreign Office noted in his diary, "I hear Winston is in the highest spirits over it." The appeasers, unchastened, reopened the inquiry on a technicality. It compounded the original blunders; Churchill took advantage of every opportunity to maul his critics. To a fellow MP he wrote that he was "quite content with my corner seat."[70]

Of course he wasn't, but a political outcast enjoys a freedom denied those charged with responsibility, and this was particularly true in Winston's case; even Hankey had conceded that he was "a leading Statesman . . . patriotic beyond criticism." As such he had been visited by the German air mission and briefed by Ambassador Joachim von Ribbentrop.[71]

❧ ❧

Central to the appeasers' creed was the assumption that no one wanted war. They did not know, or refused to believe, that the German chancellor was an exception. Thus the victorious allies of 1918 "slept," as Churchill put it, while Germany, not answerable to voters, trained armies, built ships, and sent swarms of bombers and fighter planes into the sky. On November 5, 1937, Hitler had summoned his generals and senior diplomats to announce an irrevocable decision. Germany must make war. He was not getting any younger, and he wanted to fight, wanted to see his armies take action while he was still vigorous and capable of exercising direct command. The Wehrmacht and Luftwaffe were ordered to prepare for battle, which could come "as early as 1938."

In the Reich Chancellery that day he had rambled on for four hours and fifteen minutes, raising the possibility of war between Japan and France; denouncing France and England, the two "hate-filled" (*"hasserfüllte"*) countries; and sounding the ritualistic demand for lebensraum. He had chosen to prolong the war in Spain, he said, because among other things, the issue might bring Italy into armed conflict with Britain and France. This would open the way for Germany to resolve the Czech and Austrian questions. He added that "annexation of Czechoslovakia and Austria" would mean improved strategic frontiers, new sources of food, the assimilation of twelve million more "Germans," and, best of all, enough young men to form twelve new divisions. Of course, if Germany were to make use of this war between Italy and the democracies, "the attack on the Czechs" (*"Überfall auf die Tschechei"*) would have to be carried out with "lightning speed" (*"blitzartig schnell"*). Then — for the last time, as it turned out — he had agreed to answer questions from his subordinates.[72]

Three men stood up to him: Generals Blomberg and Fritsch and Foreign Minister Neurath. They pointed out what everyone there knew: to predict war between Britain and Italy was absurd. Moreover, Czechoslovakia had been supported by a military alliance with France since 1925 — and by the Franco-Soviet alliance since 1936. Less than two months earlier the French foreign minister had stressed that France would fulfill her obligations "whatever the form of the aggression if the aggression is certain"; unofficially, the Foreign Office had let it be known that a British declaration of war on Germany would follow.[73]

Hitler ignored all this. Within three months the dissenters had all been dismissed. Neurath was replaced as foreign minister by Ribbentrop, though (like Vansittart) he was given an impressive new title to save his prestige abroad. But Blomberg and Fritsch, the leaders of Germany's military elite, were destroyed, and Hitler, being Hitler, did it in the coarsest possible way. Blomberg was cashiered on the ground that his wife had once been a prostitute; Werner von Fritsch, the Wehrmacht's commander, was disgraced by a preposterous assertion that he was a homosexual who practiced sodomy in a dark alley near Berlin's Potsdam Hauptbahnhof on a demimonde figure known as Bayernsepp (Bavarian Joe). Stunned, too proud even to dignify such an accusation with an answer, the aristocratic officer told the Führer that he would respond only to a court-martial. Hitler had no evidence — there was none to be had — and he had no intention of letting the officer corps caste pass judgment on one of its own. He simply ordered Fritsch to retire, and the general, having taken the oath to obey his führer under all circumstances, vanished into obscurity. On February 4, 1938, Hitler proclaimed himself *Kriegsherr* (warlord), assuming personal command over Germany's armed forces. His dictatorial powers would remain unchecked until his death.[74]

It was time, the Führer decided, for Austrian independence to mount the scaffold. In the Berghof he had granted Schuschnigg's homeland a reprieve, but it was short; he was not a patient man. Eight days after the distraught Austrian chancellor returned to Vienna, the Führer staged one of his frenzied performances before the Reichstag. He raved that "political separation from the Reich must not lead to the deprivation of rights — that is, the general rights of self-determination [*Selbstbestimmung*]. . . . To the interests of the German Reich belongs the protection of those German peoples who are not in a position to secure, by their own efforts, their political and spiritual freedom." He ordered Jodl and Göring to mobilize their men and call up the reserves, confronting Schuschnigg with 4,126,200 superbly trained men — Versailles, had it been enforced, would have limited them to 100,000 — against Austria's 38,000 soldiers, many of German stock and therefore of doubtful loyalty.[75]

But how many Austrians wanted to join the Third Reich? In the *Evening Standard* on March 4 Churchill estimated that two-thirds of Schuschnigg's countrymen were prepared to defend their independence. The following day he was challenged by Unity Mitford, his wife's cousin. Unity had strong

Nazi sympathies. She had been among Hitler's traveling companions since he became Reich chancellor five years earlier. Now she wrote "Dear Cousin Winston" that he, like most Englishmen, was "very misinformed about Austrian affairs, which are consistently misrepresented by the British press." She had been in Vienna when her führer had torn his strip off the Austrian chancellor, and she wrote:

> The jubilation which broke out among all classes must have been one of the most tremendous demonstrations of belief the world has ever seen. . . . Everyone looked happy & full of hope for the future. . . . In Graz, Linz, and Vienna I witnessed demonstrations in which the people went mad with joy and one could not move in the streets for people shouting "Heil Hitler! Anschluss!" & waving Swastika flags. By night, the hills around Vienna were ablaze with bonfires in the shape of Swastikas.

She predicted that "a free plebiscite would result in *at least* 80% for the Nazis."[76]

Churchill passed this along to Georg Franckenstein, a veteran diplomat and Austria's envoy in London, asking for advice and assuring him that his reply would be confidential. Franckenstein pointed out that the Austrian Nazis were purposefully noisy and highly visible because they wanted to create the impression that they formed a majority, and he agreed that "there was much jubilation among the National Socialists after Hitler's speech." But while the Nazis were "displaying the greatest possible activity," the majority of people, at Schuschnigg's expressed wish, were remaining quiet and orderly "to avoid conflict and bloodshed which might lead to German intervention." Franckenstein had consulted several informed, objective observers about Nazi strength in Austria; "some suggested 25%, others 35%, but all were agreed that the majority in the country is in favor of an independent Austria."[77]

Chamberlain had applauded the "negotiations," at the Berghof. To what extent the P.M. was misled by his hopes and his advisers can never be determined, but the documents prove that in crises he was capable of lying to Parliament and the country. Once back in Vienna, Schuschnigg and Guido Schmidt, his under secretary of foreign affairs, had described their ordeal in detail, including the Führer's ultimatum. They had briefed envoys of all the powers, particularly England's, and William L. Shirer, who was there at the time, read the British legation's unsparing account before it was cabled to London. Even Ambassador Henderson, whose admiration for the Third Reich approached Unity Mitford's, wrote that Austria's chancellor had been "threatened and browbeaten, and under menaces accepted an arrangement of which he thoroughly disapproved." Furthermore, the Viennese correspondents of the *Daily Telegraph* and *The Times* had telephoned accurate reports of Hitler's *Schrecklichkeit* in the Berghof. Dawson didn't always print dispatches from his correspondents in Europe, but those he suppressed he sent to No. 10. Thus it is impossible to argue that the prime minister did not really know what had happened at the Führer's alpine retreat. On the contrary, he was keenly aware that Austria's independence was gravely imperiled. Nevertheless, he told the House on March 2 that

> what happened was merely that two statesmen had agreed upon certain measures for the improvement of relations between their two countries. . . . It appears hardly likely to insist that just because two statesmen have agreed on certain domestic changes in one of two countries — changes desirable in the interest of relations between them — that one country renounced its independence in favor of the other. On the contrary, the Federal Chancellor's [Schuschnigg's] speech of February 24 contained nothing that might convey that the Federal Chancellor himself believed in the surrender of the independence of his country.[78]

Actually, Schuschnigg's address to the Austrian Bundestag, delivered after his return from the Berghof, had been an act of desperate courage. The federal chancellor declared that Austria would make no more concessions to the Nazis. "We must," he declared, "call a halt and say 'Thus far and no farther [*Bis hierher und nicht weiter*].' " He swore that the country would never surrender its independence, giving it a rallying cry: *"Rot-Weiss-Rot bis in den Tod!"* ("Red-White-Red till we're dead!").[79]

Obviously, defying Hitler was highly dangerous. He had already murdered one Austrian chancellor. His Austrian Nazis, who were if anything more brutal than the Reich's, roamed the streets in mobs — twenty thousand in Graz alone — hauling down their nation's flags and raising hakenkreuz banners. The police, acting on instructions from Seyss-Inquart, made no attempt to restrain them. In Vienna, the Karlsplatz was swarming with hysterical Nazis screaming *"Sieg Heil! Heil Hitler!"* and demanding that Schusschnigg be lynched. But the federal chancellor was made of sterner stuff than the men then ruling the British Empire, who were afraid to challenge Hitler. On March 9 Schuschnigg announced a national plebiscite to be held on Sunday, March 13. His countrymen would be asked whether or not they wanted a free, independent, Christian, united Austria: *Ja oder Nein?*[80]

In a note to Churchill, Ambassador Franckenstein jubilantly wrote that the Austrian voters would settle the "'duel' between Miss Mitford and myself." But the next day — Thursday, March 10 — the ambassador was less sanguine. Leo Amery gave a lunch for him at 112 Eaton Square. Harold Nicolson noted that the Austrian seemed "anxious and depressed." They congratulated him, Nicolson continued, upon "Schuschnigg having declared a plebiscite and having been so brave as to stand up to Hitler," but "he does not seem to think that his courage will avail very much."[81]

Until the plebiscite issue arose, Hitler had not planned an immediate Anschluss, an outright annexation of Germany's southern neighbor; he merely wanted Austria as a vassal state. Hitler's goal had been to dominate Austria by undermining Schuschnigg, overthrowing him, and installing a government of Austrian Nazis. Schuschnigg's radio broadcast Wednesday evening, the ninth, announcing the plebiscite, was one of three developments which led Hitler to decide that Austria must and *could* be annexed, abolished as a nation, and integrated as part of the Reich.

The other two developments were the reactions to the broadcast in Rome and London. Before perpetrating the outrage, the Führer had to be certain Austria would be isolated. His brag to Schuschnigg about Austria's lack of allies had been equivocal; at that time he had no assurance that Italy, France, and Britain would remain aloof. In the case of France it hardly mattered. Churchill had warned his guests from Paris that their unstable governments gravely diminished their prestige in foreign chancelleries. Camille Chautemps's regime fell that Thursday; the country would lack a premier for a month; meantime, action was impossible.

Schuschnigg had hoped for more from Italy — four years earlier Mussolini had helped abort the Nazi coup when Dollfuss was murdered — but when he consulted him about the plebiscite, the Duce replied: *"C'è un errore!"* Hitler didn't know that, however, and on Thursday, as his troops deployed on the southern border of the Reich in attack formation, he sent Mussolini a preposterous letter, declaring that Austria was in "a state of anarchy," that the Austrians and Czechs were plotting to invade Germany with "at least twenty million men," and that Schuschnigg's failure to meet his "more than moderate" demands "made a mockery" of "a so-called plebiscite." Friday the Duce, still smarting from Anglo-French attempts to thwart his conquest of Ethiopia, sent word that Austria would be "immaterial" to him. The Führer danced with joy and told the messenger: "Tell Mussolini I will never forget him for this. . . . Never, never, never, no matter what happens!"[82]

The dictators, unanswerable to public opinion, could act like that. British statesmen couldn't; they had to satisfy their colleagues, their consciences, and, ultimately, their constituents. So the Chamberlain government resorted to hypocrisy. HMG took the position that Britain's armed forces were too weak to challenge the rearmed Reich (overlooking its responsibility for that weakness) and that Hitler's feelings of insecurity must be stroked with reassurances. In Berlin, Henderson wrote, "The big question which all Germans asked themselves was, 'What will England do?' " His own recommendation was: Nothing. "His Majesty's Government," he explained in his memoirs, was in no "position to have saved Austria by [its] actions." Besides, he added — and here his rationalization is remarkable — "the case against Hitler was not yet a cast-iron one. Austria was German, and many Austrians were wholeheartedly in favor of union with the Reich." Determining *how* many had been the purpose of the plebiscite, but Henderson dismissed the plebiscite as Schuschnigg's "final mistake" and "the throw of a desperate gambler." It apparently occurred to none of the appeasers that the chancellor of an independent country, in resolving to poll his countrymen on whether they wished to surrender their independence, might be acting, not only within his rights — the legality of his move could scarcely be challenged — but wisely. Henderson triumphantly concluded, "The love of peace of the British public was too great for it to approve of a war in which the moral issue was in any possible doubt."[83]

Within an hour of Schuschnigg's broadcast on Wednesday, Goebbels had been whipping up German rage against him, and Churchill gloomily told a Manchester audience the next evening: "The horizon has not lightened in the last few months — or in the last few hours." By Thursday the question of what England would do had become urgent, and the ball was in the foreign secretary's court. Halifax and Ribbentrop were closeted for several hours, after which Ribbentrop sent a telegram which surfaced after the war among other German foreign policy documents in Nuremberg. "England will do nothing with regard to Austria," Ribbentrop reported, even if Germany resorted to naked force, provided there was "a very quick settlement."[84]

That was straightforward, if ignoble. More humbug began Friday morning. Ribbentrop breakfasted at his London embassy with Thomas Jones, Astor, Inskip, and a German diplomatic aide. The guests had been carefully picked; all were eager to hear Ribbentrop's justification of whatever Hitler was going to do, as were many others in England. As early as 1936, when Ribbentrop was the Reich's new ambassador to the Court of St. James, he had been approached by Lord Lothian, who expressed the hope that German seizure of Austria, despite the attendant battles and bloodshed, would not lead to a "breach of faith" between His Majesty's Government and the Wilhelmstrasse.[85]

Thomas Jones, typically, had written Lady Grigg: "I keep on and on and on, preaching against the policy of ostracizing Germany, however incalculable Hitler and his crew may be. . . . We have abundant evidence of the desire of all sorts of Germans to be in friendly terms with us." Jones, it should be noted, had been elected to no office; in 1930 he had retired as deputy secretary to the cabinet, far below Vansittart in official protocol. Astor had been a delegate to the League of Nations seven years earlier and had retired to private life. Inskip, foundering in a job for which he was so singularly ill suited, was the only cabinet member at the breakfast. But Ribbentrop knew these men made vital decisions and would be fertile ground for his rationalizations.[86]

After the Friday breakfast Jones noted in his diary that Ribbentrop "was clearly in a state of active apprehension. . . . He did tell us that Schuschnigg had acted without consultation with his Nazi colleagues and this rankled." No one had pointed out that Schuschnigg, remembering Dollfuss, may have assumed that any such consultation would have ended with himself a cadaver. But Ribbentrop's breakfast guests were not completely gulled. "Walking away," Jones wrote, "we said to each other that R. had not been frank about the Berchtesgaden [Berghof] interview"; they had heard "the account given by Schuschnigg to our Austrian ambassador — that the interview was the most terrible experience of his life." Yet Jones remained convinced that England had to go "to absurd lengths" in offering Hitler the other cheek. This reasoning had lost the Rhineland; now Austria was sliding down the Nazi maw.[87]

Ribbentrop was, in fact, only in town to wind up his London affairs, as Hitler had appointed him foreign minister of the Third Reich. Breakfast at the Reich embassy was followed by a farewell lunch at No. 10, with Ribbentrop as the P.M.'s guest of honor and Churchill as an impotent if bemused spectator. Because Winston was the most unpopular Englishman in the great stone piles lining the Wilhelmstrasse, Chamberlain would have enjoyed omitting his name from the guest list, but that was impossible. The prime minister could hardly give the Nazis veto power over visitors to his home. And Churchill was a world celebrity who had been a member of six British cabinets; if he were cut, there would be an uproar in the House.

There were sixteen at the table, including Winston and Clementine. About halfway through the meal an FO messenger brought Cadogan an envelope. Van's successor read it, walked round the table, and handed it to Chamberlain. By now Churchill was alert, sensing danger. Afterward he recalled: "I could not help noticing the Prime Minister's evident preoccupation." On a signal from her husband, Mrs. Chamberlain rose, saying, "Let us *all* have coffee in the drawing-room." Winston felt that "a kind of restlessness pervaded the company, and everyone stood about ready to say good-bye to the guests of honour." The Ribbentrops were merry and voluble, however; Churchill guessed that this was a "manoeuvre to keep the

Prime Minister away from his work and the telephone." Finally the P.M. said: "I am sorry. I have to go now to attend to urgent business." In parting, Churchill bowed to Gertrud von Ribbentrop and "in a valedictory vein" murmured: "I hope England and Germany will preserve their friendship." She gave him a rude stare and snapped: "Be careful you don't spoil it."[88]

Placed as far as possible from the guest of honor, Churchill had been beyond earshot of the exchanges between Chamberlain and Ribbentrop and left No. 10 under the impression that the diplomatic transaction, whatever it had been, was over. Within an hour, however, even without Van, he knew the contents of the FO luncheon message. Two telegrams from the British delegation in Vienna had reported that at 5:50 A.M. the Germans had closed their Austrian border at Salzburg, that Wehrmacht divisions were massed all along the frontier between the two countries, and that at 10:00 A.M. Seyss-Inquart, on instructions from Hitler, had appeared in Schuschnigg's office to insist that plans for the plebiscite be canceled. Told that the alternative would be bloodshed, Schuschnigg, with his pitifully small army, capitulated. But yielding to one Nazi ultimatum quickly led to another. The Führer now followed with demands that Schuschnigg resign, that Seyss-Inquart succeed him as federal chancellor, and that his first official act be an appeal to the Reich Chancellery in Berlin, asking that the Wehrmacht enter Austria to "restore order." One way or another, 100,000 German troops would cross the border at 10:00 P.M. and move swiftly to envelop Vienna.

Churchill missed fireworks at No. 10 — a row which sharply defined the cultural abyss between the appeasers and the appeased — and the rainbow that followed. Englishmen cherished civility and good manners as social lubricants. German aristocrats — often cousins, several times removed, of their counterparts in England — shared their conviction. Until Hitler moved into the Reich Chancellery, the men in striped *Hosen* from the Wilhelmstrasse were celebrated for their breeding, their mastery of exquisite diplomatic language, and their meticulous observance of international treaties. Elaborate, almost choreographed manners had always graced relations between powers, however bloody the deeds. "When you have to kill a man," as Churchill later said, "it costs nothing to be polite."[89]

But the division between the Old Boys lunching at No. 10 that Friday, March 11, 1938, and the Nazi foreign minister representing his omnipotent führer cut deep. For the first time in history, the power of a European state was rooted in its lower middle class. Ribbentrop had appropriated his "von" from a distant aunt and affected noble origins. His sole distinction, before he caught the Führer's eye, had been his matinee profile, which had won him the hand of his boss's daughter, thereby ending his drab, ill-paid, exhausting career as a commercial traveler roaming Europe and hawking wines. Had he been an Englishman, he could never have been admitted to a London club, not to mention to a Tory cabinet. To Chamberlain and his cabinet, trying to persuade one another that he was acceptable in their circle, he remained an enigma, entertained by them only because he had been designated the formal representative of what was, by the third month of 1938, the greatest military power in the world. England's patricians had never dealt with such Europeans in affairs of state.

Before arriving for lunch, Ribbentrop knew of Hitler's first ultimatum to Schuschnigg — call off the plebiscite or face a German invasion. And shortly afterward word reached him of the second ultimatum, demanding that Seyss-Inquart replace Schuschnigg as chancellor. Yet he had given no indication that anything was amiss when, moments before Cadogan handed Chamberlain news of these developments from the British legation in Vienna, the prime minister told him of his "sincere wish and firm determination to clear up German-British relations." After studying the two telegrams the prime minister gave his honored guest a quizzical look and asked why German troops were massing on their Austrian border. With a straight face Ribbentrop replied that he believed they were there for "spring training." Clearly Chamberlain was unsatisfied, but it was not the sort of conversation a prime minister pursues over lunch, particularly when the most eloquent English critic of his foreign and defense policies is at the other end of the table, gazing at him intensely.[90]

Only after the others had departed did Chamberlain invite Ribbentrop and Halifax into the drawing room. By then additional reports of the Führer's ultimatum and its sequelae had arrived from Vienna. Chamberlain read them aloud. "The discussion," as Ribbentrop reported to the Führer afterward, "took place in a tense atmosphere." To his surprise, Halifax, who had been so unctuous at the Berghof, was "more excited than Chamberlain, who outwardly at least appeared calm and cool-headed." The Nazi statesman responded by doing what Nazis did best; rather than defend the indefensible, he simply denied "the truth of the reports." The Englishmen asked no questions, accepted the remarkable charge that British diplomats in Vienna had concocted everything, and cheerfully accompanied Ribbentrop to the door. His "leave-taking," he reported to the Führer, "was entirely amiable, and even Halifax was calm again."[91]

In an attempt to make Hitler's strong-arm diplomacy seem less brutal, Ribbentrop had not only lied to his hosts; he had also underestimated them. Accepting Austria as a state within the Reich's sphere of influence was one thing; naked bayonets were another. By the time the Nazi foreign minister had returned to his embassy, it had occurred to Chamberlain and Halifax that their guest had been less than candid with them. It was Ribbentrop, they recalled, who had denounced the Schuschnigg plebiscite as "a fraud and a swindle" and "a violation of the letter and spirit of the Berchtesgaden agreement." Within an hour they learned that Seyss-Inquart had proclaimed himself chancellor of Austria, that Hitler was preparing a broadcast promising his new subjects "a real plebiscite" to be supervised by the SS (the Führer's private army) and the Gestapo (state secret police), and declaring that Schuschnigg was a fugitive. Halifax persuaded a reluctant Geoffrey Dawson to condemn what was now clearly a coup, and in an emergency cabinet meeting Chamberlain expressed shock at the "manner" of the annexation, calling it "distressing" and "a typical illustration of power politics." Henderson was instructed to deliver a formal note to the Wilhelmstrasse declaring that "His Majesty's Government feel obliged to register a protest in the strongest possible terms."[92]

But Henderson had already sandbagged British objections by telling Göring that Austria had fallen victim to "Schuschnigg's ill-conceived and ill-prepared folly." And words after an event have little force anyhow. Before the Anschluss, Halifax had encouraged it, and during Schuschnigg's last bitter hours in office he had telegraphed him that he could not "take the responsibility" of advising him to take measures "which might expose [your] country to dangers against which His Majesty's Government are unable to guarantee protection" — this despite Britain's Stresa pledge to guarantee Austrian independence.[93]

In Berlin, Neurath accepted the British note. Long afterward, Henderson acknowledged that "protests without the resolute intent to use force if they were disregarded were not going to stop the German troops, which were already on the march." Considering the Rhineland fiasco two years earlier, he realized "Germany had become too strong to be impressed by empty gestures, which merely confirmed those like Ribbentrop in their opinion that Britain would put up with anything rather than fight. Lung power was no match for armed power."[94]

In Nicolson's diary one senses the momentum, the rush of events that weekend. On Friday evening, March 11, he noted Schuschnigg's capitulation after "a pathetic farewell broadcast saying that he is yielding to 'brutal force.' " Saturday Hitler crossed the border and entered Linz, where he had spent his boyhood. Göring, reproached by the vacillating Henderson, replied with "a diatribe against Schuschnigg's lack of good faith." Nicolson, mingling with his working-class constituents, wrote: "They are all anti-Chamberlain, saying 'Eden has been proved right.'"[95]

At No. 10 on Saturday Chamberlain told the cabinet that Eden, in opposing friendly approaches to the Duce, had been proved wrong: "It might be said that we were too late in taking up the conversation with

Italy. . . . Signor Mussolini would have moved troops to the Brenner Pass at the time of the Berchtesgaden talks, but he had not felt sure of his position in the Mediterranean." Cadogan blamed his predecessor, Vansittart ("an idiot with an idée fixe — all facade and nothing else"), for being obsessed with Austria "when we can't do anything about it." But to the prime minister, Eden remained the scapegoat. Writing his sister the next day Chamberlain reflected that "very possibly this might have been prevented if I had had Halifax at the Foreign Office instead of Anthony." He added: "What a fool Roosevelt would have looked like if he had launched his precious proposal. What would he have thought of us if we had encouraged him to publish it, as Anthony wanted us to do? And now we too would have made ourselves the laughing stock of the world." Chamberlain did not consider that a prime minister who had wined and dined with the Nazi foreign minister while Hitler was seizing Austria might look like a bigger fool and a greater laughingstock.[96]

Mapping out strategy for a forthcoming parliamentary debate on military policy, Horace Wilson had written to Chamberlain on Thursday predicting that Churchill would demand an air defense inquiry. Now he noted that at the cabinet meeting the P.M. decided that "an enquiry should be refused and refused flatly and firmly, the decision to be adhered to notwithstanding any criticism that may be raised during the debate." According to the meeting's official minutes, all present were informed "that the Right Hon Winston Churchill was intending to attack the Government on the inadequacy of their Air Force programme, and to support the motion of the Opposition for an enquiry into the Air Ministry. It was suggested that a speech belittling our efforts might have a very adverse effect on the international position just now," when dealings with Germany might be better served "by creating the impression of force." How the Nazis could be gulled when they already knew the frailty of Britain's defenses — particularly the RAF — was among the questions unraised by the cabinet.[97]

It is Sunday, March 13, the day Schuschnigg had set for his plebiscite, but 100,000 German troops, led by General Heinz Guderian's Second Panzer Division and the SS *Leibstandarte Adolf Hitler* are being pelted with flowers by their Austrian admirers — Goebbels calls it a "*Blumenkrieg*" ("flower war"). Seyss-Inquart presents his führer with a proclamation declaring that Austria no longer exists. It is now the Ostmark, "a province of the German Reich."

By Monday the Austrian scene is clearer. The enthusiasm of the crowds cheering Wehrmacht and Waffen SS troops is beyond doubt, but they are a minority. Churchill writes Unity Mitford: "It was because Herr Hitler feared the free expression of opinion that we are compelled to witness the present dastardly outrage." The Führer has added another seven million subjects to his expanding Reich, while seizing a military position of priceless strategic value without the firing of a single shot.[98]

In permitting the Führer to take Austria, the governments of Europe have betrayed tens of thousands of anti-Nazis, not only Austrians but also German citizens of Austria. Many have fled for their lives and choke the roads to Czechoslovakia, Poland, and Hungary. Some are turned back at the border; others, more affluent, possess passports and are passed through the frontier roadblocks, only to be rejected because they have no visas. Acquiring these documents is, for thousands, a matter of life or death. When they return to the Austrian capital their visa applications at the British and French consulates are rejected. In Vienna alone seventy thousand are arrested. Before the month is out virtually all who tried to flee have been shot by SS firing squads, have died by their own hands, or have been sent to the Reich's new Austrian concentration camps.

No photographs of the refugees appear in *The Times*. Instead, Dawson runs pictures of Austrian Nazis beaming on Wehrmacht battalions, creating an impression of a tumultuous, wildly enthusiastic welcome from all their countrymen. It is a shocking distortion; foreign tourists and foreign correspondents, particularly the Americans, give it the lie. Shirer is among them. Later he will recall that "the behavior of the Vienna Nazis was worse than anything I had seen in Germany. There was an orgy of sadism."[99]

In one of his syndicated newspaper columns Churchill writes, "The Austrian Nazis are a peculiarly virulent type who carried pillage, corruption and brutality beyond the wide limits of political discretion." Reports reaching Chartwell from his Austrian informants confirm him. An emaciated, haggard Schuschnigg will spend the next seven years in Dachau and then Neiderdorf, a concentration camp in the South Tyrol, whence he will be rescued by American troops just as a Gestapo guard is about to execute him. The litany of misery which will end there may be glimpsed in Churchill's post-Anschluss mail from Austrian informants: "My many friends in this city are in the depths of despair"; ". . . many sickening incidents. A family of six Jews have just shot themselves, a few houses down the street"; "Yesterday morning I saw two well-dressed women forced to their knees to scrub out a 'Heil Schuschnigg!' on the pavement." Churchill writes Dawson, asking why this side of the story is unreported and is frostily told: "There is no doubt, I think, that the impression of jubilation was overwhelming."[100]

That would have been enough to satisfy his readers two years earlier. But the mood of the British public has shifted since the Rhineland. MPs hear from their constituents: even if most Austrians wanted to live under the swastika, those who don't have rights, too; are they being persecuted? Replies from the Foreign Office are vague. The temper of the upper classes has also changed. Their wealth has permitted them to visit the Continent often. The Rhineland was declassé; one couldn't have been seen there by one's equals, gaping at the Cologne Cathedral like shopkeepers' wives on tour. Hitler's seizure of it menaced few of their peers. Austria is another matter. They have friends there, even cousins, in Vienna, in lodges on the slopes of the Austrian Alps, and in shooting boxes in the deep, dark evergreen woods. And now they are worried about them. Among the worriers are Lady Londonderry, Lady Halifax, and the wife of the British prime minister. Ambassador Henderson cannot fob these people off with excuses. They send him names. He submits the lists to Ribbentrop, inquiring as to their whereabouts. The Reich's foreign minister replies that he finds their interest "incomprehensible. The British Government never lifted a finger for the victims of the Schuschnigg regime." It is an insolent note, and inauspicious. The Germans are beginning to feel like Germans again — like the Germans of the Second Reich, Bismarck's great creation in the wake of Prussia's victory over Louis Napoleon's France in 1871, memorable for its faith in Blood and Iron, its allegiance to *ein Volk, ein Kaiser, ein Reich,* the pigheadedness of its Junker leaders, and the rising hauteur of their officers, monocled and rude, who slapped "insolent" civilians in Alsace-Lorraine, and expected even German ladies to step in gutters and let them pass.[101]

Neurath strengthens this impression of arrogance by returning Henderson's initial note of protest with the comment: "Relations between the Reich and Austria can only be regarded as an internal affair of the German people which is no concern of third powers. . . . For this reason the German Government must from the outset reject as inadmissible the protest lodged by the British Government." If His Majesty's envoy wants proof of Seyss-Inquart's telegram inviting the Führer's troops into the Ostmark, he will find it "already published in the German press."[102]

❧ ❧

On Monday, March 14, Nicolson heard the P.M. make "a dry statement" in the Commons, "giving little indication of real policy." The House had expected to hear more about Austria, but there seemed to be a conspiracy on the Treasury Bench (and in the FO, under its new permanent under secretary) to sidestep the Anschluss and turn to other matters. Of Hitler's conquest the prime minister declared: "The hard fact is that nothing could have arrested what actually happened — unless this country and other countries had been prepared to use force." A backbencher called: "What about rearmament?" Chamberlain's reply was evasive; the government "would make a fresh review" of the subject and "in due course we shall announce what further steps we may think it necessary to take." Nicolson wrote: "There is a sense of real national crisis." But it was felt in neither Downing Street nor the corridors of Whitehall.[103]

Since the defrocking of Vansittart the Foreign Office had drifted under uncertain leadership. Cadogan, whose office gave him such wide discretionary powers that they rivaled Halifax's, seemed incapable of contemplating meeting force with force. As early as Saturday, March 12, he wrote in his diary: "We are helpless as regards Austria — that is finished. We *may* be helpless as regards Czechoslovakia. . . . Must we have a death-struggle with Germany again? . . . I'm inclined to think not. But I shall have to fight Van . . . and all the forces of evil. God give me courage. So far we've not done wrong."[104]

A month before the crisis, after Schuschnigg's mortification at Berchtesgaden, Cadogan had "almost" wished that "Germany would swallow Austria and get it over," and now that Hitler had devoured it he wrote Nevile Henderson: "Thank goodness, Austria's out of the way. I can't help thinking we were very badly informed about that country. . . . We should evidently have been very wrong to try to prevent *Anschluss* against the wishes of a very considerable proportion of the population. After all, it wasn't our business: We had no particular feelings for the Austrians: We only forbade *Anschluss* to spite Germany."[105]

Churchill was ready with an answer for both the prime minister and the Foreign Office during that same House session Monday. Nicolson wrote: "Winston makes the speech of his life." Churchill's instinctive response to the Anschluss had been that the issue should be laid before the League of Nations. He and Lord Cecil had approached Halifax with that suggestion, but the foreign secretary told them that "such procedure would be of no practical advantage in redressing the present situation." So Churchill offered the House of Commons a foreign policy which, we now know, would almost certainly have led to a military coup in Berlin, toppling the Nazi regime.[106]

Churchill saw the need for British unity, British action, and a firm policy to discourage new aggression. He surveyed the wreckage in Austria, submitting that the damage had been great. Nazi mastery of Vienna, "the center of all the communications of all the countries which formed the old Austro-Hungarian Empire, and of all the countries lying to the southeast of Europe," threatened the entire Danube basin, particularly Czechoslovakia, which had been "the greatest manufacturing area" in the Austro-Hungarian

Empire. No doubt its name "sounds outlandish" to English ears, he said, but the Czech army was "two or three times as large" as Britain's, its munitions supplies were triple Italy's, and "they are a virile people; they have their treaty rights, they have a line of fortresses, and they have a strongly manifested will to live freely." At present, however, they were isolated.[107]

As Leo Amery had pointed out earlier in the day, England lacked a foreign policy. The country should acquire one, Churchill said, and swiftly. "Why," he asked the House, "should we assume that time is on our side?" Each day dawned on a Reich stronger than the day before. Parliament was "in no position to say tonight, 'The past is the past.' We cannot say 'The past is past' without surrendering the future." Churchill's proposed geopolitical concept, he declared, would assure peace for Britain and indeed for all European nations alarmed by Hitler's huge, teeming Wehrmacht.[108]

Winston told the House that England's neglected defenses were too shaky for her to stand alone against the pullulating Reich and the lands it dominated: "Over an area inhabited perhaps by 200,000,000 people Naziism and all it involves is moving on to absolute control." Even a rearmament crash program would be inadequate. Britain, he said, needed allies. The House was alert. They knew where Winston's line of thought was leading, and a few catcalls were heard from Tory backbenchers. He said quickly: "I know that some of my hon. Friends on this side of the House will laugh when I offer them this advice. I say, 'Laugh, but listen.' "[109]

Those who listened heard an imaginative, closely reasoned plan to confront Nazi aggression with an interlocking alliance of nations, each country inadequate in itself, but together mighty enough to give pause to Hitler's generals, if not to Hitler himself. Churchill directed their attention to the three states of the Little Entente: Czechoslovakia, Rumania, and Yugoslavia. Each was a power of the second rank, "but they are very vigorous states, and united they are a Great Power." The first had the Skoda munitions plants, the second oil, the third minerals and raw materials — and all had large armies. The Anschluss had driven "a wedge" into the Little Entente, but if that had roused them, perhaps the price was not exorbitant. Each faced a simple choice: "to submit, like Austria, or else to take effective measures while time remains to ward off the danger and, if it cannot be warded off, to cope with it." Coping, he said, could include widening the Little Entente by offering membership to other Danube countries lying in Hitler's path: Hungary and Bulgaria. That would thwart the Reich's drive for lebensraum in the east. Meantime Britain, with France, should vow to declare war on Germany if Hitler attacked any country in eastern Europe. Should Churchill's alliance become a reality, Germany's Generalstab would face the specter they had sworn to avoid since 1918: a two-front war. Winston turned on the jeering backbenchers; his voice rose: "Our affairs have come to such a pass that there is no escape without running risks. On every ground of prudence as well as of duty I urge His Majesty's Government to proclaim a renewed, revivified, unflinching adherence to the Covenant of the League of Nations. What is there ridiculous about collective security? The only thing that is ridiculous about it is that we haven't got it."

But Churchill knew that restoring the balance of power, however practical, reasonable, and even essential, would not in itself satisfy a British public still haunted by the memory of a million British corpses in the trenches. Winston believed in statecraft on a higher level, and he believed the British public could be swayed at this level. He insisted that there must be a "moral basis" for British rearmament and foreign policy, that only on those terms could the British people be united. Parliament could on this basis "procure their wholehearted action, and" — Churchill, typically, included America in his plan — "stir the English-speaking people throughout the world."

Meantime, he argued for the virtual encirclement of the Third Reich. Treaties binding Europe's Western democracies and the Danube states in a united front would turn back German aggression, and England would regain the security she had lost in 1914. He closed:

> If a number of states were assembled around Great Britain and France in a solemn treaty for mutual defence against aggression; if they had their forces marshaled in what you may call a Grand Alliance; . . . if all this rested, as it can honourably rest, upon the Covenant of the League of Nations, in pursuance of all the purposes and ideals of the League of Nations; if that were sustained, as it would be, by the moral sense of the world; and if it were done in the year 1938 — and, believe me, it may be the last chance there will be for doing it — then I say that you might even now arrest this approaching war. Then perhaps the curse which overhangs Europe would pass away. Then perhaps the ferocious passions which now grip a great people would turn inwards and not outwards in an internal rather than an external explosion, and mankind would be spared the deadly ordeal towards which we have been sagging and sliding month by month. . . . Before we cast away this hope, this cause and this plan, which I do not at all disguise has an element of risk, let those who wish to reject it ponder well and earnestly upon what will happen to us if, when all else has been thrown to the wolves, we are left to face our fate alone.[110]

Such a speech, and such a proposal, coming from a senior statesman known throughout Europe, could not be ignored or set aside for future "study" and "discussion." In Moscow, Maksim Litvinov, the Soviet foreign commissar, praised the Grand Alliance strategy, condemned the Anschluss as an act of aggression and a threat to the chain of small countries between the Soviet Union and the Reich, and — though Churchill had not mentioned Russia as a grand ally — declared that his government was ready "to participate in collective actions . . . checking the further development of aggression and eliminating the increased danger of a new world massacre." The U.S.S.R., he said, was "prepared immediately to take up in the League of Nations or outside of it the discussion with other Powers of the practical measures which the circumstances demand."[111]

Ambassador Maisky delivered Litvinov's statement to the Foreign Office, which, by diplomatic custom, was bound to respond within a week. France was also heartened; Joseph Paul-Boncour, the minister now presiding over the Quai d'Orsay, submitted a similar demarche through Corbin, his ambassador in London. Halifax received these overtures with elegant courtesy, expressing a gratitude for Russian and French interest which he did not feel. The noble lord despised Bolsheviks and was a lifelong Francophobe. "The French are never ready to face up to realities," he remarked after Corbin had departed; "they delight in vain words and protestations." Cadogan agreed. Although Paul-Boncour had been in politics since 1899 — serving variously as minister of war, minister of labor, and premier except between 1914 and 1918, when he had commanded an infantry battalion and won the Croix de Guerre — Cadogan thought him "not a Foreign Minister who at so serious a moment could be a worthy partner in a discussion of the European crisis."[112]

Nicolson despaired. "A sense of danger and anxiety hangs over us like a pall. Hitler has completely collared Austria; no question of an *Anschluss*, just complete absorption." Later in the same entry he noted, without dissent, a colleague's argument that "the Government have betrayed the country and that the Tories think only of the Red danger and let the Empire slide. I am in grave doubts as to my own position. How can I continue to support a Government like this?" Looking back, Lord Boothby damned sheep and shepherds alike:

> From 1935 to 1939 I watched the political leaders of Britain, in Government and in Opposition, at pretty close quarters; and I reached the conclusion, which I have not since changed, that with only two exceptions, Winston Churchill and Leopold Amery, they were all frightened men. On four occasions Hitler and his gang of bloody murderers could have been brought down, and a second world war averted, by an ultimatum. . . . Every time we failed to do it. And four times is a lot. The reasons for it, I am afraid, can only be ascribed to a squalid combination of cowardice and greed; and the British ministers responsible, instead of being promoted, should have been impeached.[113]

Nevertheless, Churchill's vision — challenging Hitler with a broad coalition of nations threatened by Nazi aggression — reached the hearts of millions. In London the *Star* expressed gratitude that "one man spoke out in Parliament last night, and made a speech which fitted the hour." Liddell Hart sent the War Office a memorandum pointing out that "we are blind if we cannot see that we are committed to the defence of Yugoslavia," adding that the French "military situation largely turns on the existence of a Czechoslovakian distraction to Germany's power of concentration in the West." According to minutes of a March 16 meeting, Halifax told the cabinet that "public opinion was moving fast in the direction of placing the defences of the country more nearly on a war footing." The prime minister, nodding slowly, replied that he was well aware of the nation's mood, and knew it was entitled to a statement or broadcast from him, but "at the moment he himself did not feel clear how far we are to go, or in what direction."[114]

Chamberlain was, in fact, tempted by Churchill's soaring proposal. Napoleon had been overwhelmed by a coalition of allied powers led by England; why not crush Hitler by the same strategy? But forming an alliance wasn't Chamberlain's style. Like Baldwin he felt uncomfortable with foreigners; he didn't really trust them, and their differences in national character seldom stirred his curiosity. On March 21, scarcely nine days after the Anschluss, Dawson quoted the P.M. as saying he had "come clear around from Winston's idea of a Grand Alliance to a policy of diplomatic action and no fresh commitments."[115]

The eight days in between had been filled with debate — Churchill and his supporters on one side, HMG on the other. Austria had gone down almost unnoticed, it seemed, and while Churchill's idea of a Grand Alliance had been aimed at securing the future of all Europe, in those eight days the spotlight was turned upon one country, Hitler's next target: Czechoslovakia.

❧ ❧

By universal agreement the Reich's warlord was either a madman or a genius. In neither case could he be expected to behave like ordinary men, and he rarely did. General Alfred Jodl, the Wehrmacht's chief of operations, had worked with him for five years. He believed that at last he understood him. Yet when the Anschluss had been accomplished, Jodl wrote in his diary: "After the annexation, the Führer indicated that he is in no hurry to solve the Czech question." In fact, Hitler was rapidly revising *Fall Grün*, Case Green, the plans for a surprise attack on Czechoslovakia first drafted by Blomberg nine months earlier.[116]

How Case Green could have surprised anyone now seems inexplicable. In his Reichstag speech of February 20, when he declared that "over ten million Germans live in two of the states adjoining our frontiers," Hitler was including the three million Czechoslovakians of German descent — the *Sudetendeutsche* — living in the northern part of the country, in the shadow of the Sudeten (Sudetic) Mountains. Prague had trembled when he warned: "It is unbearable for a world power to know there are racial comrades at its side who are constantly being afflicted by the severest suffering for their sympathy with the whole nation. . . . The German Reich intends to protect those German peoples who live along its frontiers and cannot, by their own efforts, secure their political and spiritual freedom [*ihre politische und geistige Freiheit*]."[117]

London newspapers had carried brief accounts of disturbances in the Sudetenland, but British opinion was not, at this time, concerned with Czechoslovakia as a whole. Nor, until then, was Hitler. It was on his hit list, but rather far down. Now the Sudetendeutsche were forcing his hand. Their part of Czechoslovakia had never belonged to Germany. Nevertheless, the Führer's intoxicating performance had spawned five pseudo-Nazi parties in the Sudetenland, of which the noisiest, and probably the largest, was the Sudetendeutsche Heimatfront (Sudeten German Home Front) with its political arm, the Sudetendeutsche Partei (SDP), led by one Konrad Henlein, an otherwise unprepossessing gymnastics teacher with a fanatical loyalty to Germany's charismatic leader. One of the Heimatfront's most effective talents was to send gangs of SDP bullies into Czech communities and deliberately create *Grenzzwischenfälle* (border incidents). These scuffles revealed the Heimatfront's ardor (and violence); they also won broad sympathy for the group among the Germans. Hitler's countrymen remembered his campaign pledge to unshackle Germans enslaved in other countries. He was under pressure to deal with Czechoslovakia — but he was not irked; this was the kind of pressure he liked.

Actually, the Czechs had been extraordinarily tolerant of the boisterous Nazis who lived under their flag and were spoiling for a fight. In recent years President Eduard Beneš had been wary and tactful, but he was unreassured by Göring's "word of honor" ("*Ehrenwort*") that the Czechs had nothing to fear from the Reich. In the Third Reich, Beneš knew, honor had acquired new meanings. The word was, for example, engraved on the daggers of SS men. He believed the Sudetenland riots were being orchestrated in Berlin as pretexts for intervention by Reich troops, and by the spring of 1938 he was absolutely right.

Churchill had long foreseen a jeopardized Czechoslovakia should a vindictive, rearmed Germany emerge in central Europe. As early as February 13, 1925, he had urged a redrawing of national borders in eastern Europe, contending that "real peace" would be elusive as long as regions with large German populations lay outside Germany's borders, only to be told that any change in frontiers would mean "tearing up" the Versailles treaty. On March 31, 1931 — two years before Hindenburg appointed Hitler chancellor — he told readers of the Hearst papers that Tomáš Masaryk, the country's first president, and Beneš had "refounded an ancient nation. . . . They have established a strong state on the broad basis of social democracy and anti-communism." But if Germany and Austria were reunited, "Czechoslovakia would lie in dire peril."[118]

The more Hitler pondered Czechoslovakia, the more he concluded that its very existence was an affront to him. Its birth at Versailles was enough to condemn it. Moreover, it lacked ethnic integrity; Hungarians, Ruthenians, Slovaks, Germans, and Czechs had all been spliced into the ancient Kingdom of Bohemia, and, if that weren't enough, the splicers had been Masaryk and Beneš, both intellectuals and believers in democracy. These men had then committed the ultimate sin in the Führer's eyes: they had transformed their country into the most prosperous, progressive, and enlightened nation in eastern Europe.

Until 1938 neither Hitler nor Henlein contemplated outright annexation. Most Sudeteners — about 18 percent of the country's fifteen million people — had intermarried with Czechs of other ethnic stock. Henlein could not speak for them; indeed, thousands of them were refugees from the Reich he admired, and thousands of others thanked God they didn't live under the hakenkreuz. Nevertheless, the Führer had concluded that the SDP had a future and he would invest in it. Beginning in 1935 the Sudeten party received fifteen thousand marks a month from the Wilhelmstrasse.

On May 19, 1935, the SDP had shown astonishing strength at the polls, winning 1,250,000 votes, three out of every five German votes cast, making it the second largest party in the national parliament. In the House of Commons Churchill called this demonstration of support "a very considerable fact, having regard to the energy which the German people, when inspired by the Nazi spirit, are able to exercise." It was, he said, one of several alarms set off by the success of the German dictatorship; "not only [was] the supreme question of self-preservation" involved, "but also the human and the world cause of the preservation of free Governments and of Western civilisation against the ever-advancing forces of authority and despotism."[119]

There was cause for alarm: by the summer of 1936 Nazi parties had appeared in Poland, the Baltic States, and the Free City of Danzig, where men wearing the swastika in their lapels held all key positions in the government. On July 21 Churchill wrote Lord Rothermere: "My information tallies with yours, that Czecho-Slovakia will soon be in the news." It was; the Czechs were rapidly rearming and building a powerful line of fortifications along the German frontier. Goebbels accused them of letting the Russians build military airfields on their soil, opening a campaign of denunciation and recrimination resembling his attacks on the Austrian government on the eve of Chancellor Dollfuss's murder. On February 5, 1937, Churchill wrote in the *Evening Standard* that "at any moment a quarrel may be picked with [the Czechs] by a mighty neighbor. Already they see the directions given in the regimented German press to write them down, to accuse them of being Communists, and, in particular, of preparing their airports for a Russian assault upon Germany. Vain to protest their innocence, vain to offer every facility for German or neutral inspection of their arrangements."[120]

In June 1937 Winston received a long report from one of his most reliable informants, Sheila Grant Duff, a cousin of Clemmie's and an Oxford graduate who was living in Prague. Western Czechoslovakia, she wrote, was kept in constant turmoil by gangs of Sudeten Germans who roamed the streets at night, clubbing Jews, looting their shops, and desecrating synagogues. She cited two of Henlein's Nazis, who claimed they had been ill-treated by Czech policemen: "This could be used to launch the '*Gegenmassnahmen*' [countermeasures] which the German press has threatened." Sheila was worried about the future of the Czech state. She implored Winston to "do everything in your power to make our attitude firm and unfaltering. The crisis has never been so great and I am convinced that only a stand on our part can overcome it. Czechoslovakia is, for the moment, almost entirely dependent on us." Writing in October to Lord Londonderry — who continued to believe that Anglo-Nazi friendship was possible — Winston pointed out that any arrangement with the Germans would entail giving them a "free hand so far as we are concerned in Central and Southern Europe. This means that they would devour Austria and Czecho-Slovakia as a preliminary to making a gigantic middle Europe-block. It would certainly not be in our interests to connive at such policies of aggression."[121]

The Chamberlain government, however, clearly agreed with Lord Londonderry, and continued to refuse to allocate adequate funds for defense. In February 1938, the secretary for air, Lord Swinton, having been blocked in his earlier proposals, again submitted an RAF budget, this one representing "the minimum for security." Attempts to match the Luftwaffe's overwhelming superiority in fighter planes were abandoned; the RAF would settle for enough aircraft to meet German "bombers that could be used against this country." Inskip said that would be too expensive. He proposed cutting back not only Britain's first-line air strength but also the reserve. Halifax, supporting him, stressed "every possible effort to get on good terms with Germany," which, as a code phrase of the time, meant refraining from war preparations which might arouse the Führer's wrath. Summing up the discussion, Chamberlain told his ministers what they already knew — that he attached "great importance to . . . the maintenance of our economic stability." Despite Swinton's appeal for a swift decision, the record shows that "no final decision was reached on policy for expansion of the Air Force." Action on the Admiralty budget was also deferred for a year.[122]

Meanwhile, the Czechoslovakian bomb continued to tick. One of Churchill's sources, traveling through eastern Europe, sent Chartwell an appraisal underscoring the determination of small countries not "to provoke Germany," while the Germans themselves "are convinced that we would be neutral if they attacked Czechoslovakia." The Czechoslovakian mood was described as "desperate." In Prague, Beneš reflected bitterly on a Versailles misjudgment, the drawing of his country's frontiers. The Sudeten Mountains, which he had fortified to repel a German attack, were an integral part of the very region inhabited by Henlein's Teutonic constituents. If they were annexed by Hitler, those strongholds would become part of the Reich, leaving the rest of Czechoslovakia defenseless.[123]

The tumultuous events in Vienna in March set off huge demonstrations in the Sudetenland, irresponsible talk of "going home to the Reich," and heightened harassment, including Sudetendeutsche clubbing of Czechs living along the German border. At Eger twenty-five thousand Sudetendeutsche demonstrated as church bells pealed; at Saaz fifteen thousand paraded down streets chanting, *"Ein Volk, ein Reich, ein Führer!"* Until now the Germans had enjoyed prosperity and peace in Czechoslovakia, but the Führer would tell the world that they were martyrs, that they were "subjected to unspeakable suffering at the hands of Prague sadists because Aryan blood coursed through their veins." And decent Englishmen in public life, including a decent prime minister and his decent cabinet, would hesitate to challenge this absurd indictment because open disbelief would "provoke" Hitler. In reality, Hitler needed no provocation. He now meant to destroy the Czech state and incorporate it into the Reich.[124]

Immediately after Churchill's proposal for a Grand Alliance, Cadogan had discussed it with Chamberlain and Halifax, and had left with the impression that they were giving it serious consideration. He disagreed, and his report to the FO reflected it. His position was not, however, acceptable to his colleagues, among them his assistant under secretary, Sir Orme Sargent, a protégé of Vansittart. In a memorandum to Cadogan, Sargent saw the Anschluss as the first step in a Nazi "policy of expansion" which would reduce "all the weak and disorganized countries of the Danubian basin . . . to a position, both politically and economically, of vassal states."[125]

It became the task of William Strang, Ralph Wigram's successor as head of the FO's Central Department, to sort it all out. Strang proposed three possible courses of action, ending with a wretched alternative, "a negative one," in his words, "not advanced on its own positive merits," but on the assumption that England was too weak to make any other response. In that event, Britain should "try to persuade France and Czechoslovakia that the best course would be for the latter to make the best terms she can with Germany while she can perhaps still do so in more favorable conditions than would obtain later."[126]

That was the option Cadogan found most appealing. He recommended that Britain make no commitment to support France in fulfilling her pledge to join the Czechs if they were attacked. In his diary that night, March 16, he wrote: "I shall be called 'cowardly' but after days and nights of thinking, I have come to the conclusion that it is the least bad. We *must* not precipitate a conflict now — we shall be smashed. . . . That is the policy of the line of least resistance, which the Cabinet will probably take." He was right. After Churchill's speech Chamberlain wrote his sister Ida that "the plan of the 'Grand Alliance,' as Winston calls it, had occurred to me long before he mentioned it. . . . I talked about it to Halifax." They had found it "a very attractive idea," he continued; "indeed, there is almost everything to be said for it until you come to examine its practicability. From that moment its attraction vanishes. You have only to look at the map to see that nothing that France or we could do could possibly save Czechoslovakia from being overrun by the Germans." He had reached the conclusion that "we could not help Czechoslovakia — she would simply be a pretext for going to war with Germany." But he intended to remain flexible. Should the Sudeten Germans agree to a sensible solution, he was "not sure that in such circumstances I might not be willing to join in some joint guarantee with Germany of Czech independence." Here, surely, was foreign policy with a clogged drain. Chamberlain refused to join France in defending the integrity of Czechoslovakia, but he might sign on with the Nazis. In Berlin, Henderson spoke as though a Nazi-British alliance were already a reality. He openly referred to "those blasted Czechs," and, when a diplomat on his staff began a dispatch to the Foreign Office, "There is no such thing as Czechoslovakia," made a marginal note agreeing that this was "largely true."[127]

The Times urged the Czechs to negotiate with Hitler; Czech stubbornness, it declared, could lead to war. *The Times* also reported a speech by Alan

Lennox-Boyd, one of Winston's personal friends, who had told an audience in Biggleswade that Hitler could "absorb Czechoslovakia and Great Britain would remain secure." Boothby sent Churchill a cutting of this story and called it "an incitement to Germany to get on with the job."[128]

Even as Lennox-Boyd spoke, Churchill flung down his own gauntlet in the *Evening Standard*. Obviously, he wrote, Prague must make every effort to provide its Germanic minority with "every form of good treatment and equal citizenship, not incompatible with the safety of the State," but he had every reason to believe that this was being done already. The real danger, as he saw it, was that the Germans might create incidents and use them to justify an invasion of Czechoslovakia. He therefore welcomed the French reassurance that France would keep her word and fulfill treaty obligations to support the Czechs if they were victims of an unprovoked attack. He added: "A further declaration of the intentions of the British Government in such an event must be made."[129]

Thus, at the inner cabinet meeting of March 18, the government faced two Churchillian challenges: his call for a Grand Alliance and a demand that the government join France in a defensive alliance with Czechoslovakia. Chamberlain had asked the military Chiefs of Staff whether they were ready for war. He knew the answer; though his rearmament record was better than Baldwin's, it could hardly be compared to Hitler's. Production of the Hawker Hurricanes had begun five months earlier; the gull-winged Spitfire, now being redesigned to accommodate four additional machine guns (for a total of eight), had followed. Both were superior to the Luftwaffe's best fighters, but tightfisted budgets meant only a handful could be put in the sky now. Therefore, the Air Ministry's reply to the prime minister concluded that the RAF "cannot at the present time be said to be in any way fit to undertake operations on a major war scale." The Admiralty and the War Office agreed that Britain was "at a stage of rearmament when we are not ready for war." After these précis had been reviewed by the inner cabinet, according to the minutes summarizing the meeting, Halifax said they demonstrated "conclusively" that it "behooved us to take every step that we could and to use every argument that we could think of to dissuade France from going to the aid of Czechoslovakia."[130]

But this argument was specious in itself. The questions the P.M. had put to the chiefs had been highly selective, and minority reports had been suppressed. For example, Air Chief Marshal Sir Hugh Dowding, who headed the RAF's Fighter Command and would lead it during the Battle of Britain, believed that the speed and high rate of climb which marked Britain's new fighters, combined with the chain of radar towers now rising along England's southeast shores, demonstrated that hostile bombers could be intercepted in clear weather, when 60 percent of enemy raids could be expected. Radar also meant that continuous fighter patrols could be discontinued, and radar accuracy was improving every day.

Halifax had previously told his FO advisers that negotiations for Churchill's alliance would by their very nature be protracted, proving "both a provocation and an opportunity for Germany to dispose of Czechoslovakia" before the ink had dried. Colonial Secretary Ormsby-Gore thought the commitment would be "bad and dangerous"; Lord President Hailsham believed it would "hasten an attack" on the Czechs; Minister for Defence Inskip called Czechoslovakia "an unstable unit in Central Europe"; and Chancellor of the Exchequer Simon, agreeing, added that it was a "very artificial creation with no roots in the past." (The border between Germany and the Sudetenland had endured for two hundred years.) The decisive voices, however, were those of the foreign secretary and the prime minister. Halifax advanced the remarkable argument that without a formal commitment both France and Germany would be kept "guessing," and would be less inclined to precipitate a general war. Chamberlain agreed. England, he told the cabinet, was "in no position from the armament point of view" to go to war — the responsibility for that plight was unmentioned — and France was "in a hopeless position. . . . No effective help could be swiftly brought to Czechoslovakia," and if the Reich could get what it wanted through negotiation, there was "no reason to suppose that [it] would reject such a procedure in favor of one based on violence." The British should take the initiative in pursuing a solution "more acceptable to Germany." The cabinet agreed that it would be "a mistake to plunge into a certain catastrophe in order to avoid a future danger that might never materialize." Bringing pressure on Prague to yield to Sudetendeutsche demands was, Halifax acknowledged, "a disagreeable business" to be accomplished "as pleasantly as possible." He endorsed the prime minister's conclusion "that we must decline to undertake any fresh commitment in regard to Czechoslovakia and that we must try and persuade Dr. Beneš and also the French Government that the best course would be for Czechoslovakia to make the best terms she could with Germany," meanwhile "impressing on the French . . . the imperative necessity . . . of arriving at some amicable and permanent settlement."[131]

Afterward Halifax told Cadogan that the members had been "unanimous" in agreeing that "Czechoslovakia is not worth the bones of a single British grenadier." That was not entirely candid. Duff Cooper, first lord of the Admiralty, had protested the note to the French as a "cold refusal to give any support to France" which "read like a declaration of isolation." If France and Germany went to war, he argued, "we should have to fight too, whether we like it or not, so we might as well say so."[132]

To the world outside No. 10 and even to backbenchers, Chamberlain and his cabinet gave the impression that they believed that the Germans and Czechs would reach a sensible settlement of their differences. In such a tangled web England could not be blindly committed by French decisions, but should war come, the Union Jack would fly beside the tricolor — or so the world outside supposed. In fact, the prime minister and his foreign secretary were determined that *under no circumstances* should England and France go to war to save Czechoslovakia. On March 21 Halifax told Foreign Office aides that the great thing was "to dissuade France from going to the aid of Czechoslovakia." Or, as Hilaire Belloc put it while lunching with Duff Cooper, Chamberlain's policy was:

Dear Czecho-Slovakia,
I don't think they'll attack yer
But I'm not going to back yer.[133]

❧ ❧

As part of their report to the prime minister, the combined chiefs, in an assessment which would have amazed their counterparts in Berlin, had declared it to be "certain that Germany could overrun the whole of Czechoslovakia in less than a week." That Friday, March 18, Chamberlain told the cabinet of his conviction that Hitler's concern was limited to the Sudetenland — that he had no designs on the rest of the country because it was his policy "to include all Germans in the Reich but not to include other nationalities." It was not one of Neville's more prescient statements, but he enlarged upon it the following Thursday afternoon in a House of Commons foreign policy debate. His Majesty's Government, he said, had decided to stand aloof from continental alliances. If France chose to go to war over the Sudetenland, Britain would not be committed to join her. In Czechoslovakia, the prime minister said, British "vital interests" were not concerned. Of course, the French had been told that legalities were irrelevant "in the case of two great countries like Britain and France, with long associations of friendship, with interests closely interwoven, devoted to the same ideals of democratic liberty, and determined to uphold them." An aide-mémoire to that effect had been sent to the British ambassador in Paris. The Russians had received no such assurance.[134]

As Churchill rose to respond, Virginia Cowles, in the Strangers' Gallery for the first time, "looked down," she wrote, "on the sea of black coats and white faces." To her Winston first "seemed only one man of many; but when he spoke his words rang through the House with terrible finality." As he often did, he attributed to Chamberlain opinions Chamberlain did not hold. He was glad to hear that Britain's arrangements for mutual defense with the French republic amounted to a defensive alliance. But "why not say so?" he asked. "Why not make it effective by a military convention of the most detailed character?" A similar commitment might be made to the Czechs, not "a permanent or automatic pledge," but one contingent upon "an act of violent aggression" by the Germans. Unless the Nazi pressure on Prague were counterbalanced by other great powers, the democratic state Beneš and Masaryk had founded "will be forced to make continuous surrenders, far beyond the bounds of what any impartial tribunal would consider just or right, until finally her sovereignty, her independence, her integrity, have been destroyed." It was absurd, said Churchill, to pretend that England could remain detached, and naive to believe that the Sudeten crisis would be Hitler's last: "The might behind the German Dictator increases daily. His appetite may grow with eating. The forces of law and freedom have for a long time known nothing but rebuffs, failures, and humiliations. Their influence would be immensely increased by any signs of concerted action and initiative and combination." England should be committed not only to Paris and Prague but to the integrity of every state which might come within range of Wehrmacht artillery.[135]

Great danger lay, he continued, in growing complacent during lulls in Hitler's demands: "After a boa constrictor has devoured its prey, it often has a considerable digestive spell." Each Nazi outrage — the defiant unveiling of the Luftwaffe and conscription, the seizure of the Rhineland and then its fortification — had been followed by a pause. "Now," he said,

> after Austria has been struck down, we are all disturbed and alarmed, but in a little while there may be another pause. . . . Then people will be saying, "See how the alarmists have been confuted; Europe has calmed down, it has all blown over, and the war scare has passed away." The Prime Minister will perhaps repeat what he said a few weeks ago, that the tension in Europe is greatly relaxed. *The Times* will write a leading article to say how silly those people look who on the morrow of the Austrian incorporation raised a clamor for exceptional action in foreign policy and home defence, and how wise the Government were not to let themselves be carried away by this passing incident.

To take such an attitude, he said, was indefensible, a flagrant defiance of the facts. Every day, every week, the people of Austria were being subjected "to the rigors of Nazi domination." Every hour, every minute, the forces "of conquest and intimidation" were regrouping for another assault. Soon "another stroke" would fall. "What I dread," he told the House, "is that the impulse now given to active effort may pass away when the dangers are not diminishing, but accumulating and gathering, as country after country is involved in the Nazi system, and as their vast preparations reach their final perfection."

He was nearing the end. The Commons was still as still. He lowered his head and continued, the slight impediment in his speech adding to the drama of his delivery as he followed the psalm form of his notes:

> For five years I have talked to the House
> on these matters — not with very great success.
>
> I have watched this famous island
> descending incontinently, fecklessly,
> the stairway which leads to a dark gulf.
>
> It is a fine broad stairway at the beginning,
> but after a bit the carpet ends.
>
> A little farther on there are only flagstones,
> and a little farther on still
> these break beneath your feet. . . .[136]

Then, in measured tones:

> If mortal catastrophe should overtake the British Nation and the British Empire, historians a thousand years hence will still be baffled by the mystery of our affairs. They will never understand how it was that a victorious nation, with everything in hand, suffered themselves to be brought low, and to cast away all that they had gained by measureless sacrifice and absolute victory — gone with the wind!
>
> Now the victors are the vanquished, and those who threw down their arms and sued for an armistice are striding on to world mastery. That is the position — that is the terrible transformation that has taken place. . . . Now is the time at last to rouse the nation. . . . We should lay aside every hindrance and endeavour by uniting the whole force and spirit of our people to raise again a great British nation standing up before all the world; for such a nation, rising in its ancient vigour, can even at this hour save civilisation.[137]

As he took his seat, the House broke into a hubbub of noise; members rattled their papers and shuffled their way to the lobby. Virginia Cowles was in the House lobby, awaiting a prominent Conservative MP who had invited her to tea. As he strode up she asked him his opinion of Winston's speech. He replied: "Oh, it was the usual Churchillian filibuster; he likes to rattle the sabre and he does it jolly well, but you always have to take it with a grain of salt." She recalls: "That was the general attitude of the House of Commons in those days." Even Churchill realized that Chamberlain's determination not to "rouse the nation" was echoing the mood of countrymen who did not want to be roused. Fleet Street, in step with its readers, ignored Churchill's speech and reported Chamberlain's. The liberal *Manchester Guardian* declared, "Mr. Chamberlain has overcome the enemies in his own camp," and in the *New Statesman* John Maynard Keynes urged the Czechs to negotiate a settlement with Hitler. The Chamberlains and the Cadogans drove to Cliveden for a weekend party with, as Cadogan put it, an "ordinary sort of crowd." The P.M. won the after-dinner game of musical chairs every time. They always let him win. It meant so much to him.[138]

The morning after his dire warning to the House, Churchill received an unexpected, dismaying, and most unwelcome letter from the editor of Beaverbrook's *Evening Standard,* terminating his contract — in effect, firing him. Thus ended two years of fortnightly columns, depriving him of his most valuable public rostrum, because, the editor wrote, "it has been evident that your views on foreign affairs and the part this country should play are entirely opposed to those held by us." Winston replied that his "divergence from Lord Beaverbrook's policy" had been "obvious from the beginning, but it clearly appears to me to be less marked than in the case of the Low cartoons." Then, scathingly: "I rather thought that Lord Beaverbrook prided himself upon forming a platform in the *Evening Standard* for various opinions including of course his own."[139]

It was a setback, an annual loss of £1,820 — about $9,000 at the then prevailing rate of exchange — and the timing could scarcely have been worse. He was broke. He sat in his Chartwell study, staring at columns of figures which should have made him blush. As chancellor of the Exchequer in the 1920s he had presided over England's fiscal affairs for nearly five years, yet his personal finances were hopelessly muddled. Few writers could match his income; during the past eight years he had earned £102,102, an annual average of £12,763, the equivalent of about $62,000. Chartwell, his London flat, and general expenses alone exceeded £10,000 each year, and his travels, secretaries, researchers, and the lavish lunches and dinners he gave for colleagues and visitors from the Continent drove him deeper and deeper into the red.[140]

The year before, he had faced his first real financial crisis. His letters to Clementine in the first weeks of 1937 are shadowed by a veiled and then explicit preoccupation with money which was wholly out of character — small attempts at economizing while he spread himself elsewhere. He had set up Randolph and Sarah in Westminster Garden flats and had "told Sarah I will give her £200 toward expenses." But, he added defensively, he was only fulfilling promises made long before. Fuel for Chartwell, delivered "in five ton batches at £9.11.0 each . . . used to last a fortnight," he reminded her, but the last load kept them warm for three months, despite weather that was "raw and generally damnable." Moreover, he had lost only £12 at bezique, he wrote, and "the wine has been very strictly controlled and little drunk." Also, telephone bills showed "a marked reduction. We are having fortnightly accounts from the Post Office which enables us to check it." Finally, he wrote, on a note of triumph, "I am not taking Inches with me abroad."[141]

Clemmie knew that the little saved by leaving his valet behind would shrink to insignificance beside his Riviera expenses. And indeed, he glumly wrote on February 2 that he had been talking to a Mr. Frank Capon, a real estate agent. Capon "tells me," he wrote, "that there is a lady nibbling around for a house like Chartwell, and even mentioning Chartwell." The agent said he would "on no account mention any figure less than £30,000. If I could see £25,000 I should close with it. If we do not get a good price we can carry on for a year or two more. But no good offer should be refused, having regard to the fact that our children are almost all flown and my life is probably in its closing decade."[142]

Experience had taught him that budgets did not work with his family. The reason — though he would never have acknowledged it — was that *he* was the family spendthrift. Nevertheless, in April he drew up a balance sheet cutting their personal expenses to £6,000, solemnly telling them: "This cannot on any account be exceeded." In that year, as in the years preceding, it was exceeded by over £4,000. The flaw in the budget was that the head of the household was exempt; and Churchill had no intention of curtailing his own extravagant life-style. Indeed, no one except Clemmie dared raise the question. By the process of elimination, therefore, he concluded that he would have to work harder. He wouldn't rattle a tin cup, but he could no longer turn his back on lecture fees, though earning them meant a loss of time better spent working toward the strengthening of England's defenses.[143]

Now, a year later, he seemed to have no choice — his home and its eighty acres must be sold. Even so, it appeared he would have to quit Parliament to make money, as a writer, lecturer, and/or businessman. His security had lain in his reserve of American stocks. It was from there, where he felt safest, that the blow fell. Early in March 1938 the U.S. recession hit Wall Street. Stock prices plummeted so swiftly, and so deeply, that Churchill's brokers, Vickers da Costa, told him that his American investments had been wiped out. In fact, it was worse than that — his share account owed the brokerage firm £18,000. Where could he find so tremendous a sum? After his *History of the English-speaking Peoples* was finished — but only then — he would be paid £15,000. Even so he would be £3,000 in the red. His earnings as a journalist were high; but they weren't large enough to meet Britain's income tax and supertaxes. Chartwell must be put on the market.

In his youth Churchill had been the highest-paid correspondent in the Empire; perhaps the world. His articles still brought premium rates from newspapers and magazines, but he knew little of modern journalism. He decided to buy a full page from *The Times* to advertise Chartwell's attractions and availability. It was scheduled to run on April 2. He expected, at most, that the fact of his putting up his home for sale might merit a discreet paragraph in *The Times*'s "Londoner's Diary." But famous writers often forget that they are famous, and the malice of political enemies slips the memory of statesmen who hold no grudges themselves. Thus Winston was unprepared for what actually happened. Beaverbrook's *Daily Express* picked up the story immediately, and Winston's once and future friend, now a devout appeaser, managed to insinuate that Churchill was irresponsible, telling the *Express*'s readers that he was auctioning off his home while attempting to sabotage Chamberlain's thrifty budgets. The paper's March 17 headline read: "CHURCHILL FOLLOWING L.G. TO PARIS." To the Beaver, Paris meant intrigue with a weak ally when the sound course was to embrace virile Nazi Germany. The story beneath the head drove in this long needle: "In some quarters there has been a disposition to question the desirability of British politicians visiting Paris at this juncture." Hearst never sank lower. And *The Times* ran an account on its main news page — in those days its front page was still all ads — headed: "MR CHURCHILL'S HOME IN KENT FOR SALE," and including personal details which deeply offended Winston.[144]

Meantime he moved to close one hole in his dike — the loss of earnings from the *Standard*. He wrote Lord Camrose, proprietor of the *Daily Telegraph*, explaining the circumstances of his departure from the *Standard* and proposing to write now for the *Telegraph*. Attached to his letter were three lists of newspapers which carried his syndicated columns: the first list was of papers in Great Britain, the second of English-language papers around the world, and the third of papers which published them in translation. His agent, Imre Revesz, had drawn up the last list; they meant that Churchill's views and disclosures — chiefly from his intelligence net — reached readers in seventeen languages. "As you will see it is a very fine platform," he noted dryly, "though as Nazi power advances, as in Vienna, planks are pulled out of it." Camrose agreed to a six-month trial, paying Winston £70 a piece. The arrangement continued for fourteen months, until the *Daily Mirror* offered him better terms.[145]

This was an important step but in itself would not have been enough to save Chartwell. The fact is that Churchill never understood money and was awed by those who did. They in turn were captivated by him, which was fortunate, for his profligate ways would have driven him from Parliament long before he became the only man who could save England. Bernard Baruch had rescued him in 1929, but Winston couldn't go to the same well twice. Besides, Baruch was in America. The only wealthy member of his inner circle was Brendan Bracken, and the origin and extent of Bracken's holdings were unknown; he cultivated his reputation as a man of mystery. In any event, few men possessed the enormous liquidity Churchill needed, and Brendan wasn't one of them.

But he knew men who *did*. The day after the *Daily Express* story Winston told Bracken that he wanted someone to take over his portfolio for three years, with the power to buy or sell holdings, provided his debt not deepen. He expected to pay interest on the loan — about £800 a year. Afterward he wrote Bracken: "If it were not for public affairs and my evident duty I shd be able to manage all right." He thought it "unsuitable as well as harassing" to have to follow the market "from day to day when one's mind ought to be concentrated upon the great world issues now at stake. I shd indeed be grateful if I cd be liberated during these next few critical years from this particular worry, wh descended upon me so unexpectedly [and to] which I shall certainly never expose myself again. I cannot tell you what a relief it would be if I could put it out of my mind; and take the large decisions wh perhaps may be required of me without this distraction and anxiety."[146]

Bracken was alarmed. Austria had just fallen; Czechoslovakia lay between the Nazi jaws; Chamberlain was rejecting defense spending, which Berlin might misunderstand. To Brendan — and he knew he was not alone — Churchill was the one leader standing against the black tide, contemptuous of HMG, Cliveden, and Blickling Hall. The thought of him spending his energy on potboilers for *Collier's* and *News of the World*, leaving his corner seat in the House of Commons to speak in provincial lecture halls — of Churchill absent from the center of action when the future of civilization hung in the balance — was unbearable. Among Bracken's acquaintances in the City were wealthy men — many, but not all, Jews — who were outraged by Chamberlain's policy of courting Hitler. He circulated a memorandum among them, explaining Churchill's quandary. If Winston absented himself from public life he could pay his debts and build an estate. "But how is he to do this," Brendan asked, "while events run at this pitch?" One man took him aside; they talked quietly and shook hands; it was done.[147]

Told of the transaction, Churchill sent Brendan a note: "Enclosed is a letter wh you can show to our friend. This is only to tell *you* that as Hitler said to Mussolini on a recent and less worthy occasion, 'I shall never forget' this inestimable service." The "friend" was Sir Henry Strakosch, an industrialist in the City, who had been mining gold in South Africa for over forty years. Winston knew him; he was part of Churchill's intelligence net; since the Führer's decision to rearm the Reich, the expatriated South African tycoon had been an invaluable source of facts and figures in Germany's military budgets. Churchill's pride prevented him from begging; therefore Bracken, his most loyal follower, had done it for him. Strakosch agreed to cover Churchill's losses, buying his deflated U.S. securities at the price he had paid for them. He wrote Winston that he would "carry this position for three years, you giving me full discretion to sell or vary holdings at any time, but on the understanding that you incur no further liability."[148]

Chartwell had been saved (the *Times* advertisement was withdrawn after a single appearance) and Churchill had been granted a reprieve — not a gift, but a loan. He would have refused charity, and Strakosch had not amassed his fortune by playing the samaritan to improvident statesmen. Winston could remain a member of Parliament, provided he met his publishing deadlines — chiefly those for the last volume of his Marlborough biography and for *A History of the English-speaking Peoples* — and sent payments to Strakosch as they came due.

As Europe toiled slowly toward its next butchery — never was there a war so hard to start, nor a warlord more frustrated than the *Kriegsherr* in Berlin — the quintessential Churchill, the Winston the public never saw, prowled his study night after night, an inner shutter drawn in a private blackout of the mind, excluding everything but the topic before him. His prose grew in intensity as though controlled by a rheostat, as he used the language to express his wrath, a fury matched only by that of Hitler, who was free to act while Churchill, who couldn't even control his own spending, saw himself approaching senescence with no prospect of any change in his reputation as the leper of Parliament.

Meantime, he limited his attendance in Westminster to great debates and crucial votes. While his colleagues slept in London, in Kent he paced about in his loud dressing gown, scanning précis from his researchers, dictating, sending the typed manuscript to the printer by courier, and revising the galleys in red ink — "playing with the proofs," as he called it, a very expensive amusement, since extensive changes in the galleys were charged to the author. The grammar and spelling were subjected to a final, rigorous check by Eddie Marsh, his private secretary in earlier years, now recently knighted; then the courier reappeared and the job was done. The front bench was often critical of Churchill's absenteeism, but had he been faithful in his attendance, what would he have accomplished? In November and December of 1937 he had been completely absorbed in writing his Marlborough biography. During that time the prime minister and his cabinet had, in the name of economy, permitted England's military strength to lag farther and farther behind Germany's. Yet had Churchill been in Parliament he could have done nothing; His Majesty's Government did not need the approval of the House; it was under no obligation even to inform Parliament, and it didn't. Much of the caviling about Winston's truancy was disingenuous; when he was at Chartwell, they were safe from his biting wit. Writing Maxine Elliott in February 1938 he said he was determined to finish the book "by the end of the month. I am therefore not paying much attention to the House of Commons, at which I expect the Ministers will not be at all vexed!"[149]

Furthermore, his was the most persuasive rhetoric in England, and while speeches in Parliament were heard only by those within earshot, the written word may reach anywhere. Years later the White House revealed that a copy of *While England Slept*, the American edition of Churchill's *Arms and the Covenant*, had lain on President Roosevelt's bedside table, with key passages, including an analysis of the president's peace initiative, underscored. Churchill's prose, so rhythmic that it can be scanned, was vibrant with the terrific energy that can hold and sway vast audiences. Its vitality is remarkable, and in the late 1930s, because of his continuing financial obligations, his output became prodigious. In late 1937 he published *Great Contemporaries*, which was published in a revised and expanded edition the following year, along with *Arms and the Covenant* and the fourth and last volume of *Marlborough: His Life and Times*. *Step by Step* appeared in mid-1939. During 1938, while working on his four-volume *History of the English-speaking Peoples*, he also turned out fifty-nine magazine articles on subjects as diverse as "Would I Live My Life Again?" and "Women in War." Two of the books — *Great Contemporaries* and *Step by Step* — were collections of pieces written for newspapers and magazines, and *Arms and the Covenant* presented key foreign policy speeches; but even they required revision and rewriting. After reading the fourth volume of *Marlborough*, Maxine Elliott wrote him from the Riviera: "It is incredible to me that one man can possess the genius to write a book like this and at the same time pursue his ordinary life which is a thousand times fuller of grave duties and obligations than that of lesser men."[150]

* * *

He paid a price. In a life crowded with incident, familial obligations, recreation, and public service, he published forty-four books, five of them during Victoria's reign, when both his writing style and political philosophy were formed. Except for the small legacy which he had used to buy Chartwell, writing had been his sole source of income, but he had never written under such pressure, and at an age when other writers slow down or retire altogether.

At times the sheer volume of his research notes and the goading of his agent, his publishers, and magazine editors were exasperating. "I am toiling double shifts," he wrote Clementine, away on holiday; "it is laborious: & I resent it and the pressure." Like any other writer, he hoped for windfalls. Now and then an unexpected check arrived, to be greeted with a radiant grin and instructions to Mrs. Landemare for a lavish spread that evening. But at least once he was cruelly disappointed. He had written Clemmie: "To-morrow the Daily Herald begin distributing the new cheap edition of the World Crisis wh Odham's have printed. It can be sold for 3/9 for each of two volumes — a miracle of mass production. They expect to sell 150,000! I like to feel that for the first time the working people will hear my side of the [Gallipoli] tale." The royalty check, which would have exceeded £1,000, would have been equally welcome, but the cheap book was not an idea whose time had come. The workmen remained unenlightened and Churchill uncompensated. So he returned to double shifts. He was irked by deadlines, believing he could do a better job if given more time. He wrote Clemmie: "I should be able to do my books more slowly and not have to face the truly stupendous task like Marlborough IV being finished in 4 or 5 months," only to face another urgent date for the *History*, "worth £16,000, but entailing an immense amount of reading and solitary reflection if justice is to be done to so tremendous a topic."[151]

The consequences of such a grind have not enhanced his literary reputation. His masterpiece is *The World Crisis*, published over a period of several years, 1923 to 1931, a six-volume, 3,261-page account of the Great War, beginning with its origins in 1911 and ending with its repercussions in the 1920s. Magnificently written, it is enhanced by the presence of the author at the highest councils of war and in the trenches as a battalion commander. "After it," the British historian Robert Rhodes James writes, "anything must appear as anticlimax."[152]

Certainly *Marlborough* and *A History of the English-speaking Peoples* are heavy with what Philip Guedalla called "the lullaby of a majestic style." The second Lord Birkenhead, son of Churchill's old friend F.E., deplored "his lack of historic objectivity, of the fact that he is usually justifying a policy or a cause, and that his perception of the feelings and motives of others is dim and uncertain." Ironically, it was Churchill himself who had diagnosed part of his difficulty when, as a young man, he had written: "Few authors are rich men. Few human beings are insensible to the value of money. . . . Hurried style, exaggerated mannerisms and plagiarism replace the careful toil. The author writes no more for fame but for wealth. Consequently his books become inferior. All this is very sad but very true." In his contributions to periodicals, however, it is fair to add that he may have had a second, higher motive. Events were moving swiftly in Europe; lacking power in Parliament, he made the press his megaphone. He believed he could arouse the nation by his prose, even though it was not his best. He was right. He did.[153]

❦ ❦

After the slaughter of ten million young men twenty years earlier, a renewal of the struggle seemed incomprehensible. The German people hated war as passionately as their once and future enemies, but in the Reich public opinion was forged by the state to an unprecedented degree. The Nazi Reichskulturkammer determined what was taught in the schools, the music people heard, the content of radio broadcasts, the books they read, what was published in newspapers, the churches they attended, and the plays and films they saw. The Führer, they were told over and over, was working toward noble goals and making a supreme effort to save the peace. Those who threatened it, who hated Germans because the Aryan race was superior to their own, were unmasked each year on the anniversary of the Nazi party — the Nuremberg *Reichsparteitag*, held in September.

The average Briton was better informed. To be sure, *The Times* was not the only paper in which rogue editors disgraced their craft by the distortion or outright suppression of the facts. Nevertheless the truth was there for those who cared to know. A majority chose to ignore it. Confronted with the prospect of another world war, they sought refuge in escapism. Londoners whose dreams were haunted by Nazi storm troopers could leave their nightmares in the checkroom at the St. James's Theatre, while they watched Terence Rattigan's *After the Dance;* or at the Duchess, where Emlyn Williams's *The Corn Is Green* was playing to packed houses; or at His Majesty's Theatre, where the high point of the evening would be hearing a quartet sing "The Stately Homes of England" in Noel Coward's *Operette,* which ran through 133 performances.

If you wanted to forget Japanese aggression in China and mutual aggression in Spain, a smorgasbord of entertainment lay before you: Len Hutton scoring 364 runs against Australia in the Oval Test Match; or, in the book department of Harrods, P. G. Wodehouse's *The Code of the Woosters*, Evelyn Waugh's *Scoop*, and Graham Greene's *Brighton Rock*. From across the Atlantic came new works by Faulkner, Hemingway, Steinbeck, and Nathanael West. The United States also presented, to enthusiastic theatre audiences, *Life with Father* and Rodgers and Hart's *The Boys from Syracuse;* and, on what was then called the silver screen, *Gone with the Wind, The Wizard of Oz,* and Walt Disney's *Snow White and the Seven Dwarfs.*

In 1938, the year of the Anschluss and Munich, the British produced a tune and a dance step that swept all Europe and the United States:

Any time you're Lambeth way,
Any evening, any day,
You'll find us all
Doin' the Lambeth walk.
Hey!

But Britain's greatest accomplishments in the lively arts would follow World War II. In the 1930s her entertainers remained loyal to the traditional, rollicking music hall songs. Yet the huge halls were barely half full now, relics, really; houses haunted by memories of Harry Lauder, Lillie Langtry, and George "Champagne Charlie Is My Name" Leybourne. The brash Americans rushed into the vacuum. *Snow White* alone provided three hit songs; other imported popular songs of 1938–1939 were "Over the Rainbow," three inanities — "Three Little Fishes," "A-Tisket A-Tasket," "Flat Foot Floogie with the Floy Floy" — and "Are You Having Any Fun?"[154]

Among those not having any fun were over two-thirds of Czechoslovakia's population. The country's prominence in the news from May 1938 to March 1939 may explain the immense popularity of an old Czech drinking song, "Roll Out the Barrel." In the popular view, World War II had not yet begun, but that would have been news to the Chinese, the Ethiopians, and the Spaniards. The greatest sufferers, of course, were the Jews. Nicolson, meeting an Austrian "who had just got away from Vienna," set down the man's account:

They rounded up the people walking in the Prater on Sunday last, and separated the Jews from the rest. They made the Jewish gentlemen take off all their clothes and walk on all fours on the grass. They made the old Jewish ladies get up into the trees by ladders and sit there. They then told them to chirp like birds. The Russians never committed atrocities like that. You may take a man's life; but to destroy all his dignity is bestial. This man told me that with his own eyes he had seen Princess Stahremberg washing out the urinals at the Vienna railway-station. The suicides have been appalling. A great cloud of misery hangs over the town.[155]

The situation of the German Jews was desperate. In every community, posters declared that they had been stripped of their civil rights and were forbidden to seek employment of any kind; Jewish shops and homes were plundered by Nazi storm troopers. Among the victims were the parents of Herschel Grynszpan, a seventeen-year-old refugee living in Paris. On November 7, 1938, after learning of this, Grynszpan murdered Ernst vom Rath, a third secretary at the German embassy in Paris. Senior Nazis, SS officers, and Gestapo agents instantly saw this as an outrageous opportunity. On November 9 Goebbels issued instructions that "a spontaneous demonstration of the German people" (*"eine spontane Reaktion des deutschen Volkes"*) was to be "organized and executed" that night. No one knows how many acts of murder, rape, and pillage were carried out during *die Kristallnacht*, as it came to be called — Crystal Night, or the Night of Broken Glass — but the pogrom was the greatest in history. Reinhard Heydrich, Heinrich Himmler's second in command at the SS, reported that the number of Jewish shops smashed and looted was 7,500.[156]

❧ ❧

On May 10, 1938, Ambassador Henderson's first secretary, Ivone Kirkpatrick, lunched with Prince Bismarck. Kirkpatrick had a specific proposition, of which the French, he said, were unaware. In his report to Ribbentrop, Bismarck quoted Kirkpatrick as saying: "If the German Government would advise the British Government confidentially what solution of the Sudeten German question they were striving after, the British Government would bring such pressure to bear in Prague that the Czechoslovak Government would be compelled to accede to the German wishes."[157]

If one assumes that men in public life are guided by patriotism, reason, or even political survival, the conduct of His Majesty's foreign policy defies understanding. It makes sense, however, if one grasps the fact that HMG and the key diplomats who owed their rise to the men in Downing Street believed that England should sever her bonds with leftist France and form a new alliance with Hitler's Germany, thereby forming a solid front against the Soviet Union. It is a historic irony that Churchill, Britain's original anti-Bolshevik, should have fought them every inch of the way.

He could do little beyond sending Bill Deakin as his personal representative, to ask Prague whether the Czech government approved of his plan for a Grand Alliance — which it did — and to inquire about reports of disorders in the Sudetenland. In the spring of 1938 the Czechs were breaking up the Sudetendeutsche riots but treating the ringleaders with kid gloves, determined to give the Reich no excuse for intervention. On March 12 — the day Hitler annexed Austria and Churchill unsuccessfully urged Halifax to protest his conquest in Geneva — the Czech foreign minister, Dr. Kamil Krofta, instructed his ambassadors "to avoid all unnecessary criticism, and to make every effort to avoid being involved." His envoy in London was Jan Masaryk, the son of Tomáš. Jan was worried about London's vocalizing its support of the Czech cause. On the evening of March 13, a crowd gathered in Trafalgar Square and cheered a proposal that they stage a sympathetic demonstration outside his home in Grosvenor Place. He protested that he was "a good deal disturbed," and the demonstration was quietly canceled. It was a measure of Hitler's power that the mere possibility of annoying him was enough to quash a peaceful show of friendship — for a country he had not yet threatened — in the capital of the world's greatest empire.[158]

In newspaper accounts of the Czech disturbances, the German führer was reported to be upset by them. The British public did not suspect his complicity. For better or for worse, but mostly worse, Woodrow Wilson had sown the seed of self-determination at Versailles, and enlightened Europeans sympathized with the discontented Sudeten Germans. If German observers were to be believed — and German credibility was very high among those determined never to fight another war — the Czech government was subjecting the demonstrating Sudetendeutsche to outrageous brutality. As Harold Macmillan later pointed out: "It is a falsification of history to suggest that appeasement up to the time of Munich was not widely supported, either openly or by implication. It was only as the relentless march of events revealed the true character of the man who had seized control of Germany that opinion in Britain began to change."[159]

It was going to take a lot of havoc to turn people around, and except for Churchill few were trying. The London press was disenchanted with the French. The *Observer* commented: "We cannot allow the British Empire to be dragged down to disaster by the separate French alliances with Moscow and Prague." Kingsley Martin, then editor of the liberal *New Statesman*, later reflected on the pessimism in Whitehall and at No. 10. It began, he thought, toward the end of the 1920s, when Germany was still ruled from Weimar and almost every well-informed Englishman "regarded the French notion of keeping Germany as a second-class power as absurd, and agreed that the Versailles Treaty must be revised in Germany's favor." But France wouldn't have it, and Weimar, unarmed but still suspect, was impotent. By 1938, however, Martin felt that "things had gone so far that to plan armed resistance to the dictators was now useless. If there was a war we should lose it. We should, therefore, seek the most peaceful way of letting them gradually get all they wanted."[160]

One of the most outspoken of the appeasers was an Anglican bishop, the Reverend Morley Headlam, who defended Hitler's suppression of religious freedom before a church assembly, arguing that it was "only fair to realize that a great majority" of the Nazis believed that their cause "represented a strong spiritual influence" and looked upon it as "a real representation of Christianity." A visiting Nazi told the Anglo-German Fellowship: "Herr Hitler has given the Church a free hand . . . he is a very religious man himself." There was "no persecution of religion in Germany," said Bishop Headlam, merely "persecution of political action." Geoffrey Dawson published the bishop's sermons in full while consigning dispatches from his own Berlin correspondent, describing the imprisonment of German clergymen, to the wastebasket.[161]

The curtain rose on what would be the first Czech crisis when Konrad Henlein addressed a Sudeten German party rally in Karlsbad on April 24. He read a list of eight demands for action in Prague. They bore Hitler's stamp; two weeks after the Anschluss, on March 28, Henlein had been rushed to Berlin for a three-hour session in which he was coached by Hitler and his foreign minister. Hitler's closing words to the SDP leader were found among the Wilhelmstrasse debris in 1945 and submitted as an exhibit in Nuremberg. The Führer had told his Sudeten puppet that "demands should be made by the Sudeten German party which are unacceptable to the Czech government." Accordingly, sandwiched between innocuous demands at Karlsbad were two which any Prague government would reject. One was the recognition of the Sudeten Germans as autonomous within the state, and the other provided them "complete freedom to profess adherence to the German character and ideology." Later Henlein added another demand: a revision of Czech foreign policy, which had "hitherto placed the [Prague regime] among the enemies of the German people" and had considered it "the particular task of the Czech people to form a Slav bulwark against the so-called *Drang nach Osten,*" the Reich's "thrust to the east."[162]

This was provocative and, at the time, puzzling. If Hitler had the best interests of the Sudeten Germans at heart, or even if he intended to annex the Sudetenland — in short, if he intended anything except the incitement of riot leading to bloodshed — he was going about it the wrong way. Two days earlier President Beneš had told the British minister, Basil Newton, that he planned to open "serious negotiations" with Henlein and his party during May and June and, once they had reached an agreement, to pass the necessary legislation through the Czech legislature in July. Now Prague canceled this program. The Czech press was outraged. Foreign Minister Krofta called Henlein's program "far-reaching and dangerous"; among other things, it could be used to restrict equality and freedom for other minorities — specifically Jews. The demand that the Sudeten Germans be given a separate "legal personality," he added, was totally unacceptable. Nevertheless, the coalition government led by Premier Milan Hodža, a Slovak with broad popular support, left the door to negotiations ajar, though he told Newton that he doubted anything "serious" would be possible until after the local elections.[163]

Another French government had fallen in mid-April, and on April 28, four days after Henlein's Karlsbad speech, the new premier arrived in London for two days of conferences between the allies of the last war. He was Édouard Daladier. Accompanying him was Georges Bonnet, France's tenth foreign minister in less than six years. Daladier — not yet defeatist — was determined to honor his country's commitment to the embattled Czechs. Like Churchill, he believed Hitler's objective was nothing less than the "destruction of the present Czechoslovakian State." To block him Daladier wanted a joint declaration, putting the Führer on notice that a Nazi invasion of Czechoslovakia would trigger declarations of war in Paris and London. But when he arrived at No. 10 Downing Street he found that if he wanted to form a solid anti-Nazi front he had come to the wrong address. On March 20 Chamberlain had written his sister Ida: "I have therefore abandoned any idea of giving guarantees to Czechoslovakia, or the French in connection with her obligations to that country." He repeated this to Daladier, who left disappointed.[164]

Bonnet, whom Churchill called "the quintessence of appeasement," was secretly delighted, and, in fact, he represented the mood of French politicians and the Paris press. The Army of the Third Republic was ready to fight the Boche; so were the people, with their bitter memories of 1914–1918. But their leaders and their journalists were preparing to turn them round. Professor Joseph Barthélemy, who later served in Pétain's Vichy government as minister of justice, argued in *Le Temps* that the frequent violations of Locarno freed France from her treaty commitments. *Paris-Soir*, *Le Matin*, *Le Figaro*, *Paris-Midi*, *Information*, *L'Action Française*, *Le Temps*, *Petit Parisien*, the Socialist *Le Populaire* — every daily in the capital except the chauvinist *Epoque* and the Communist *L'Humanité* — opposed defending democratic Czechoslovakia.[165]

Churchill's financial straits kept him at Chartwell most of the time, working to keep faith with Sir Henry Strakosch. Chamberlain's tenure faced no strong challenge, and his most visible rival was the "Eden Group," as Fleet Street called them, between twenty and thirty MPs who met regularly at various homes with Eden presiding. Churchill's followers were the "Old Guard," never more than four or five at this time. His absences from London were too frequent and too long to attract and hold a large number of supporters, while "Eden's resignation," as Harold Macmillan recalled, "had at least produced a pivot round which dissenting members of the Conservative Party could more readily form."[166]

Visitors to Chartwell, correspondence, and frequent telephone conversations brought Churchill abreast of developments in the capital, however, and since public men of that generation kept meticulous accounts of public activities and personal impressions, Churchill's growing role in British affairs can be traced and documented with confidence. His intellect and will had been recognized since his first years in Parliament nearly forty years earlier, yet his contemporaries continued to charge that he lacked sound judgment. Isaiah Berlin later commented: "When biographers and historians come to describe and analyse his views . . . they will find that his opinions on all these topics are set in fixed patterns, set early in life and lately only reinforced."[167]

Whenever he was in London, Winston stopped in Whitehall to see Vansittart. Though stripped of power and influence, Van kept in touch with his sources abroad and accumulated inside information in Whitehall through friends and former subordinates. He was troubled, as was Winston, by the rot of defeatism among Englishmen, particularly among British diplomats. In Paris, Sir Eric Phipps told Bonnet that the Czechs, by declaring they would fight if invaded, had "put themselves in the wrong." Basil Newton, in Prague, consistently supported Nazi demands. If the French believed it "worthwhile to try to perpetuate the *status quo* in [their] own interests," he advised the FO, Britain should stand aside. As early as March 13, 1938, the day after the Anschluss, Newton counseled London: "If I am right in thinking that Czechoslovakia's present political position is not permanently tenable, it will be no kindness in the long run to try to maintain her in it."[168]

The most egregious of all His Majesty's emissaries was Sir Nevile Henderson. Duplicity had won him his appointment in Berlin, and any other foreign secretary — or prime minister — would have dismissed him long before he could inflict a mortal wound on European peace. When, in the

House of Commons, Duff Cooper described him as "violently anti-Czech and pro-German," no one rose to Henderson's defense; no other interpretation of his record was possible. He described the Czechs as "a pigheaded race"; Beneš, their president — a graduate of the universities of Prague, Paris, and Dijon — was "the most pigheaded of the lot." As His Britannic Majesty's official representative, he informed the Germans: "Great Britain would not think of risking even one sailor or airman for Czechoslovakia and . . . any reasonable solution would be agreed to, so long as it were not attempted by force."[169]

Putting all other work aside to back the Czechs, Churchill was writing and speaking in their behalf at Manchester, Bristol, Sheffield, and Birmingham, trying to rouse Britain to the great peril Chamberlain and those around him could not see. In the May 1, 1938, issue of the *News of the World* he opened a new series of articles with a piece on "Future Safeguards of National Defence." Predicting that Britain's chances of surviving the approaching conflict depended upon the extent and efficiency of her air-raid precautions, he called for a crash program to bring nearer the day "when the accursed air-murderer, for such I must judge the bomber of civilian populations, meets a sure doom." The "greatest safety," he argued, "will be found in having an air force so numerous and excellent that it will beat the enemy's air force in fair fight"; therefore continued study, expenditures, and preparations were essential. Chamberlain was infuriated; he regarded the article as an attack on His Majesty's foreign policy, a foul blow at the fragile arch of understanding the prime minister and foreign minister were trying to build between London and Berlin.

Recriminations over what had been done and what had been left undone were futile. Unlike Baldwin, Chamberlain believed in rearmament within limits. The chief limitation arose from his greater concern for Britain's economic prosperity. As he saw it, the practice under which the cabinet approved estimates submitted by the three services endangered the country's fiscal security. His solution was to fix a ceiling for defense spending and then let the services distribute it among themselves.

This was a businessman's way of defending a nation, but to others it made no sense. Duff Cooper attacked "the absurd new system of rationing the defence departments"; the "sensible plan," he argued, "must be to ascertain your needs for defence first, and then inquire as to your means for meeting them." Soldiers were even more vehement. Lieutenant Colonel Henry Pownall of the Committee of Imperial Defence wrote in his diary that the prime minister's theory of "limited liability in war" was "a most dangerous heresy"; the politicians "cannot or will not realize that if war with Germany comes again . . . we shall again be *fighting for our lives*. Our efforts *must* be the maximum, by land, sea, and air. . . . In God's name let us recognize that from the outset — and by that I mean *now*."[170]

Chamberlain told his cabinet that British production could not match Germany's "unless we are prepared to undertake the tremendous measure of control over skilled labour, as in Germany." He preferred "voluntary" cooperation by arms manufacturers, though such firms had not been noted in the past for their patriotism. The fact was that the bill for years of neglecting the nation's defenses, most of it during the ministries of MacDonald and Baldwin, was coming due. The people were uneasy; a scapegoat was needed, and the prime minister's eye fell on the secretary for air, Lord Swinton, who had neglected to show enthusiasm for appeasement policies. Later Churchill wrote of an Air Defence Research Committee meeting of May 12, 1938, at which "we were all busily engaged" discussing "technical problems, when a note was brought in to the Air Minister asking him to go to Downing Street." Swinton left at once and "never returned. He had been dismissed by Mr. Chamberlain."[171]

There was speculation, though not among those in a position to know, that Churchill might be appointed in his place. Instead, the prime minister announced a reshuffling of his cabinet, with Swinton replaced by Minister of Health Sir Kingsley Wood, the P.M.'s oldest and most faithful supporter, a Francophobe and the most fervent of appeasers, more eager even than Chamberlain for friendship with Nazi Germany. Kingsley Wood had never worn a uniform; his career had been devoted to health, education, and welfare. Nicolson wrote Vita: "We had an excitement yesterday, Swinton sacked. At once I telephoned or rather got Duncan [Sandys] to telephone to Winston. . . . How silly the whole thing is! Here we are at the greatest crisis in our history, with a genius like Winston doing nothing and Kingsley Wood as our Minister for Air." Other changes in the cabinet seemed just as baffling, Nicolson wrote. He blamed Chief Whip David Margesson ("not . . . a good Cabinet-maker") but conceded in the end that in such a hodgepodge it was impossible to assign responsibility. (He overlooked the prime minister.) "Nobody understands anything," he concluded. "There is a real impression that the whole show is going to crack up. This view is held, not only by protagonists like Winston, but by the silent useful members of whom nobody ever hears. They think that a new Government will emerge on a far wider basis, possibly a Coalition Government." Nicolson was two years — almost to the day — ahead of time.[172]

The RAF leadership, first under Sir Hugh ("Boom") Trenchard and then under Lord Weir, still held sacred the doctrine that "the bomber will always get through." Holding this principle sacred, Trenchard and Weir believed that Britain's only hope of survival lay in devastating retaliation against an enemy. Every RAF plan had called for two or three times as many bombers as fighter planes. Since bombers cost more, and required larger crews, both in the air and on the ground, the waste, in retrospect, is obvious. In the spring of 1938 Dowding's reply to this theory — radar and fast fighters to intercept hostile bombers — won acceptance. Before the shift could be reflected in the sky, however, Britain was confronted with a surplus of bombers and a scarcity of Spitfires and Hawker Hurricanes.

The imbalance, the loss of faith in their striking force of heavy bombers, wild exaggerations of Luftwaffe strength, and the deleterious implications of rationing on the service which most needed reequipment crippled RAF morale. It seemed at its lowest point in 1938, urged there by the most famous aviator of his time. Colonel Charles Lindbergh's impact had first begun to be felt in early 1936; he had just left Germany and was reappearing in London at the invitation of U.S. ambassador Joseph Kennedy, who squired him around as he shared his views with Chamberlain, his cabinet, Fleet Street, and virtually every other Briton who possessed power and made decisions. Göring, General Ernst Udet, and the rest of the Luftwaffe hierarchy had done a job on the Lone Eagle, but there had been more to it than that. Like many other visitors to Berlin, he and his wife had been impressed by the energy and self-confidence of the Führer and his people. She wrote: "There is no question of the power, unity, and purposefulness of Germany. It is terrific." Nothing they learned in subsequent visits to the Reich caused them to change that opinion. In April 1938 Lindbergh wrote in his diary: "England seems hopelessly behind in military strength in comparison to Germany" and "the assets in English character lie in confidence rather than ability; tenacity rather than strength; and determination rather than intelligence. . . . It is necessary to realize that England is a country composed of a great mass of slow, somewhat stupid and indifferent people, and a small group of geniuses."[173]

At the American embassy in September he told a select group of Englishmen, presumably those he would include among the geniuses (Kennedy had not invited Churchill), that they couldn't "realize the change aviation has made" and that "this is the beginning of the end of England as a great power." He thought that "German air strength is greater than that of all other European countries combined" and that "she is constantly increasing her margin of leadership." England and France, he believed, "are far too weak in the air to protect themselves. . . . It seems to me essential to avoid a general European war in the near future. I believe that a war now might easily result in the loss of European civilization."[174]

At Cliveden, where Lindbergh was guest of honor, Thomas Jones and

Lord Astor said it was "necessary for England to fight if Germany moves into Czechoslovakia." The others, led by Nancy, shouted them down. Later Jones wrote that after reflecting upon what Lindbergh had said, "I've sided with those working for peace at any price in humiliation, because of the picture of our relative unpreparedness in the air and on the ground which Lindbergh painted, and because of his belief that the democracies would be crushed absolutely and finally."[175]

After Roosevelt had publicly branded him "defeatist," Lindbergh's prestige began to shrink, and when Wilhelmstrasse documents became available to historians during the war crimes trials at Nuremberg, his prewar evaluation of Nazi air strength was discredited. It is a measure of Lindbergh's prewar renown, however, that Roosevelt found it necessary to take such a step. In 1938 he was at his peak. A. L. Rowse recalls: "Great play in those days, I remember, was made of Lindbergh, treated as omniscient in air matters. . . . Dawson quoted Lindbergh to me: he was made much of by the Cliveden set." As Sheila Grant Duff reported to Churchill from central Europe, Lindbergh buttressed the German conviction that England "would be neutral if they attacked Czechoslovakia." On October 18, 1938, three weeks after the Munich Agreement, Hitler would decorate the American aviator with the highest award Germany could confer upon an *Ausländer* — the Service Cross of the German Eagle with Star — accompanied by a citation declaring that he "deserved well of the Reich." The Lone Eagle had earned his Nazi medal.[176]

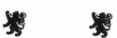

On Friday, May 6, when America's 1938 recession touched bottom and Churchill found his wallet empty, Lord Rothermere told readers of his *Daily Mail* that "Czechoslovakia is not of the slightest concern to us. If France likes to burn her fingers there, that is a matter for France." Bonnet, who was prone to nausea, read it over breakfast and became ill. On Saturday, May 7, French and British diplomats in Prague presented a formal demarche to Foreign Minister Krofta. Hitler already knew the gist of it; four days earlier Halifax had told the new German ambassador to the Court of St. James's, Herbert von Dirksen, that the demarche would "aim at inducing Beneš to show the utmost measure of accommodation to the Sudeten Germans." (The foreign secretary had not extended the same courtesy to Czechoslovakia's Ambassador Masaryk.) The Czechs were asked to make a "supreme effort" to go to "the utmost limit" to meet the Henlein demands of April 24, with the hope of reaching a "comprehensive and lasting settlement" with the Sudetendeutsche. Dirksen reported to the Wilhelmstrasse that Chamberlain and his government regarded the possibility of military action "doubtful," though the French, more optimistic, were ready to march.[177]

Henderson gave the Germans his personal view: "France is acting for the Czechs and Germany for the Sudeten Germans. Britain is supporting Germany." He "urgently hoped" that the Führer would "not refuse some kind of cooperation with Britain in this matter, which might then, perhaps, lead to cooperation in other matters also." Ribbentrop quickly replied that after this question was solved, the Reich would be *"durchtränkt"* — saturated.[178]

Any doubts about HMG's position were resolved by the prime minister. Lady Astor had given Chamberlain a luncheon on May 10; his fellow guests were American and Canadian foreign correspondents. The P.M. was accustomed to the deference of British newspapermen. He also put some of his remarks on the record and some off, a dangerous format, vulnerable to misunderstandings. On May 14 the *Montreal Star* and the *New York Times* broke the story, the *Star* reporting, "Nothing seems clearer than that the British do not expect to fight for Czechoslovakia. . . . That being so, then the Czechs must accede to the German demands, if reasonable." The *New York Times* man, formerly a diplomatic correspondent for *The Times,* went further: "Mr. Chamberlain today . . . certainly favors a more drastic measure — namely, separation of the German districts from the body of the Czechoslovak Republic and the annexation of them to Germany."[179]

The British press picked the story up. In less than a week the German embassy learned that the articles had been based on the P.M.'s remarks at Nancy Astor's luncheon. Dirksen advised Berlin that Chamberlain would approve of the Sudetenland's secession from Czechoslovakia, provided the wishes of the people were determined in a plebiscite "not interrupted by forcible measures on the part of Germany."

Hitler had hesitated to threaten Czechoslovakia. The Anschluss, he knew, had been much simpler. Austria had lacked allies and a strong military presence; nor did she have a defensive position which, if forfeited, would undermine Anglo-French security. Because the Czechs had all these, deliberate provocation of a crisis would risk a general European war or a humiliating withdrawal. Everything would depend on speed. He needed a fait accompli, before sympathy for the underdog mounted in the democracies, where public opinion counted, and the Russians seized the opportunity to become a European power through intervention. Hitler had wanted reassurance before he took such risks. And now he had it — from Britain.

* * *

Although Chamberlain had eased Hitler's doubts, the Führer had a backup plan. Colonel Malcolm Grahame Christie was an enigmatic figure similar to those found in Eric Ambler novels and Alfred Hitchcock films of the time. Educated in Germany and trained as an engineer, he had been a British fighter pilot in the last war and, afterward, an embassy attaché in Washington and Berlin, where he had become a friend of Göring. In 1930 he had retired from the RAF, ostensibly to become a businessman whose work required frequent trips to Germany. Actually, he was an intelligence officer gathering data on the Luftwaffe and the Reich's military plans. Vansittart — kicked upstairs, but still serving the FO in an advisory role — was his control. When Van received a message from Henlein, asking for an interview, he asked Christie to make arrangements for him to visit London and return. If shown British resolve, Van reasoned, the Sudeten Germans might think twice before flouting Prague again. He seems not to have considered the possibility that Henlein, an ardent Nazi, might be acting on orders from Berlin.[180]

He was. On May 12, exactly two months after the Anschluss, he had stopped at Berlin on his way west, was admitted to the Foreign Ministry through a seldom-used door, and was ushered into the office of Baron von Weizsäcker, Ribbentrop's under secretary, for his final instructions. Most important, said Weizsäcker, would be British questions suggesting, or assuming, that he had been briefed by anyone in the government of the Third Reich, such as, say, Weizsäcker. Great weight was attached to his meeting with Churchill. The Führer believed that either Churchill or Eden would head the next government in England. Lastly, and this was a matter of judgment, he was expected to determine the temper of the men now in office. Were they as weak and incompetent as they seemed? Or was it all a trap? The Führer, himself a builder of traps, often thought he saw them in other countries, always with himself as their purported victim.[181]

Van minuted for the FO record afterward that as "it was impossible for members of the Government to see Herr Henlein lest some sort of negotiations be suspected, it was necessary to arrange that Herr Henlein should see not only myself but some persons of consequence in the House of Commons." Here Churchill was indispensable. The visitor wanted to sample British opinion; a meeting with Winston might persuade him that the British lion could still roar. Churchill, told of the plan, agreed to give Henlein a lunch at Morpeth Mansions. "His visit is being kept a secret," Winston wrote Archibald Sinclair. "His wish to come to London to see Van and a few others is a hopeful sign." The other guests were Sinclair, Christie, and the Prof, who served as interpreter and took notes.[182]

Henlein's theatrical talents were effective. They listened gravely, nodding in approval as he told them the excessive demands in his Karlsbad speech were not to be taken seriously; they were "bargaining points" from which he was "prepared to recede." He felt he was entitled to embrace the Nazi ideology but not "to impose it on others." Questioned over whether he might be used as a pawn in Hitler's *Drang nach Osten*, he swore on his word of honor that he had never received orders, or even "recommendations" ("*Weisungen*"), from Berlin. Asked whether he had claimed a veto power in Czechoslovakia's foreign policy, he vigorously denied it. Churchill wondered whether he realized that an incident in the Sudetenland "might easily set Europe alight" — that "if Germany marched," for example, "France would come in and England would follow."

Henlein replied that he had known that from the outset and had, in fact, avoided incitements, even when he "believed he was in the right." Looking ahead, he saw three paths: "Autonomy within the Czech State," a plebiscite which would probably lead to an Anschluss, and war. His followers, who were "impatient," preferred an Anschluss. If Prague ignored their appeals, they would ask Europe's great powers for a plebiscite "under international supervision."[183]

Police, railway, and postal workers in the Sudetenland would be required to speak German and the Sudeten Germans would be entitled to their own town and county governments, but "the frontier fortresses could be manned by Czech troops, who would, of course, have unhindered access thereto." As he left — not for his homeland, as his hosts assumed, but for Berchtesgaden, where he would report to Hitler — one of the others called out: "We hope you're not another Seyss-Inquart!" Over his shoulder he called back: "No chance of that!" Churchill immediately laid Henlein's terms before Jan Masaryk, who, as Winston later noted in his memoirs, "professed himself contented with a settlement on these lines." On May 16, three days after his luncheon for Henlein, Churchill told an audience in Bristol that he saw "no reason why the Sudetendeutsche should not become trusted and honored partners in what is, after all, the most progressive and democratic of the new States of Europe."[184]

Weizsäcker's coaching of Henlein — exploiting Britain's traditional championing of fair play — had been brilliant. The issue in Czechoslovakia had previously been depicted simply, as an unequal struggle in which the huge Reich was intimidating a plucky but outgunned neighbor. Now there was concern over a minority whose rights were being ignored or trammeled by insensitive Prague. In the Berghof, Henlein told Hitler that "no serious intervention in favor of the Czechs was to be feared from England or probably from France."[185]

* * *

The lunch in Morpeth Mansions had been on Friday, May 13, and Churchill had spoken in support of Henlein on the following Monday. Now, on Wednesday, a Leipzig newspaper published an account of Wehrmacht assault divisions moving into position on the Czech frontier. Thursday the British consulate in Dresden reported that there was "strong reason to believe that German troops are concentrating in southern Silesia and northern Austria." Later in the day a similar report arrived from Bavaria, together with a cable from Henderson adding: "My French colleague has also heard rumors of concentration of troops on the [Czech] frontier." The following day Krofta, alarmed, phoned Ernst Eisenlohr, the German minister in Prague, to protest; on his desk were several reports, each confirming the others, of heavy German troop concentrations in Saxony. Thus the stage was set for the May crisis.[186]

Czech municipal elections were to be held on Sunday. Since Henlein's return the Sudetenland had been chaotic. Gangs of Sudetendeutsche youths wearing swastika brassards had attacked neighbors of Slavic descent, marched through streets carrying torches, and held rallies which culminated in chants of *"Sieg Heil!"* and *"Wir wollen heim ins Reich!"* ("We want to go home to the Reich!"). Goebbels, meantime, had stepped up his denunciation of "Czech terror." The parallels with Austria were unmistakable. Any incident might touch off an invasion, and Friday, May 20, one made to order occurred when two Sudeten German motorcyclists were shot dead after ignoring a Czech policeman's whistle. After an emergency cabinet meeting in Hradschin Palace, President Beneš approved an urgent recommendation of the Czech General Staff, calling up reservists and specialist troops to man the Sudetenland garrisons.

In Berlin Ribbentrop heatedly denied hostile Wehrmacht concentrations, but when Eisenlohr and his military attaché called on General Ludvik Krejcí, the Czech chief of staff, they were shown an impressive collection of what he called "irrefutable evidence that in Saxony a concentration of from eight to ten divisions has taken place," with another twelve on the Czech frontier "ready to march within twelve hours." All the pieces of what had seemed a puzzle were falling into place. Krejcí's army believed it could hold the Wehrmacht in check long enough for France, Britain, and the Russians to intervene, provided its fortress line was manned and ready. The country would, however, be particularly vulnerable to a surprise attack by Nazi forces assembled and deployed under what Beneš's General Staff called "the guise of training purposes."[187]

"Training" was indeed the explanation the German high command (OKW) gave Weizsäcker, who passed it on to a skeptical world. But for once it was true. The Wehrmacht wasn't ready. A scrupulous examination of OKW and German foreign policy documents at Nuremberg after the war revealed that there had been no aggressive concentrations in Silesia or Austria that May. The OKW's statement that the Nazi troops along the Czech border were assembled for "peacetime maneuvers" was accurate. To foreigners the number of German soldiers near the frontier would have been disquieting, but such numbers could be seen nearly anywhere in the Reich. Germany had become a highly militarized nation; its economy was on a war footing. Hitler did intend to invade Beneš's country. And these were the soldiers who would form the point of his spearhead. But not yet.

In the spring of 1938, however, the truth was unknown. In Paris and London the men responsible for crucial decisions had every reason to believe that Hitler might be poised to unleash another bolt of lightning from his aerie above Berchtesgaden. Daladier staked out the French position by inviting the German ambassador to his home and speaking "frankly as a French ex-serviceman to his German comrade," warning him that should Hitler invade Czechoslovakia "the French would have to fight as they did not wish to be dishonored," and that the result could be the utter destruction of European civilization. Halifax, out of character but acting in the finest tradition of British diplomacy, sent the unhappy Henderson to the Wilhelmstrasse twice with personal messages from him to Ribbentrop. In the first he declared that "His Majesty's Government could not guarantee that they would not be forced by circumstances to become involved" if France, following her treaty obligations, intervened. The second note warned that if the Nazis resorted to force, "it is quite impossible for me to foretell results that might follow, and I would beg him not to count on this country being able to stand aside."[188]

Now there was no way Germany could avoid an enormous loss of face. Because the Wehrmacht was unprepared, Hitler could not attack, and since he did not, the Allies concluded that he had backed down. That was Churchill's interpretation. The Czechs, he wrote in the *Daily Telegraph* of June 23, had seemed doomed "to be swallowed whole by Berlin and reduced to shapeless pulp by the close-grinding mandibles of the Gestapo." Now Hitler knew Czechoslovakia would not "be left to struggle week after week against an avalanche of fire and steel."

Churchill thought the incident a triumph for England, but His Majesty's Government did not see it that way. For men who had presumably won a victory of diplomacy, they took no heart from it. In fact, they were badly frightened. Still convinced that the Germans had been intent on military action, they thought of the peril they had skirted and mopped their brows. Chamberlain wrote his sisters: "The more I hear about last weekend, the more I feel what a damned close run thing it was." In another letter to them, he wrote, "The Germans, who are bullies by nature, are too conscious of their strength and our weakness, and until we are as strong as they are" (which, if his defense policies were unaltered, would be never) "we shall always be kept in a state of chronic anxiety." After reviewing the cable traffic, Halifax and Cadogan vowed never again to approach the brink and, accordingly, sent Paris a telegram warning the French not to be "under any illusion" about the possibility of British help "against German aggression."[189]

The May crisis had arisen from a misunderstanding; if the Führer had been a sane man, he would have counted himself lucky to be out of it. Hitler, not sane, personifying the underside of the Teutonic character and four horrible years which had ended in the defeat, not just of Germany, but of *him*, saw a wrong crying for redemption. The fact that he had been planning the invasion of Czechoslovakia — that the only real misunderstanding in May had been over timing — somehow made it worse. "Injustice is relatively easy to bear," wrote Mencken. "What stings is justice." On May 28 the Führer suddenly appeared in Berlin and summoned the hierarchies of the OKW, the party, and the government to the chancellery. His voice still choking with rage, he said that the Sudeten question would be solved "once and for all, and radically." Preparations for military action must be completed by October 2, the Siegfried Line would be extended by workers toiling around the clock, and ninety-six divisions were mobilized immediately. The execution of *Fall Grün* "must be assured by October 1, 1938, at the latest." In his hoarse, staccato delivery, his voice sounding like a bearing about to go, he roared: *"Es ist mein unerschütterlicher Wille, die Tschechoslowakei von der Landkarte auszulöschen!"* ("It is my unshakable will to wipe Czechoslovakia off the map!").[190]

Churchill, unaware of Hitler's resolution, shared a fresh sense of relief with his *Daily Telegraph* readers on July 6. The Anschluss, he had decided on reflection, was not the Nazi triumph it had seemed to be. At the time, he recalled, he had told Parliament that

> after a boa-constrictor has devoured a goat or a deer it usually sleeps the sleep of repletion for several months. It may, however, happen that this agreeable process is disturbed by indigestion. . . . If the prey has not been sufficiently crushed or covered with slime beforehand, especially if it has been swallowed horns and all, very violent spasms, accompanied by writhings and contortions, retchings and gaspings, are suffered by the great snake. These purely general zoological observations . . . suggest a parallel — no doubt very remote — to what has happened since Austria was incorporated into the German Reich.

Extrapolating from "a continuous stream of trustworthy information" he said that the German Nazis were bedeviled by "Jews in very large numbers . . . Catholics by the million . . . Monarchists faithful to a Hapsburg restoration . . . strong Socialist and Left-wing elements in every working-class district . . . numerous remnants of what was once the high society of the Austro-Hungarian Empire." There was also, in Austria, "the strongest and the only covert resistance to the Nazification" which "oddly enough" came from the "Austrian Nazis who were the prime cause and pretext of the invasion." Churchill was delighted to describe their fury at finding themselves "excluded from all positions of power, profit, and control," and their resulting rebellion.

By custom, newspaper columnists are entitled to an occasional romp in fantasy, and Churchill's optimistic picture of the Austrian situation was, unfortunately, that. On the whole, Churchill was a highly reliable journalist. His innumerable informants assured the accuracy of his information, at least eventually. In his *Daily Telegraph* piece of July 6 he was, however, guilty of another lapse, flagrant now but invisible at the time. "A settlement and reconciliation in Czechoslovakia would be no humiliation to Herr Hitler," he wrote. The Führer could take pride in having won for the Sudeten Germans "honorable status and a rightful place in the land of their birth," reforms which would have "strengthened rather than shaken the foundations of European peace." Churchill had been Konrad Henlein's mark in a kind of diplomatic confidence game, generating Churchillian warnings to Prague over its treatment of the restless citizens in the Sudetenland and this mild assessment of Hitler's goals. As late as July 26, Churchill was still lecturing Prague, writing in the *Daily Telegraph* that "The Czech Government owe it to the Western Powers that every concession compatible with the sovereignty and integrity of their State shall be made, and made promptly." Englishmen who demanded that "Germany not stir up strife beyond her border" should, to be consistent, offer "no encouragement to obduracy on the part of a small state."

In midsummer Sheila Grant Duff put Churchill straight. She wrote him of "the use which the Germans and Sudeten Germans are making of your words and actions. They claim to have your support against the Czechs and this is used by the more extreme to force the more moderate to raise their claims." She reminded Winston that Henlein had "shown himself to be most moderate in his conversation with you and that he had told you that the fulfillment of *all* his Carlsbad [*sic*] demands was not the necessary condition of agreement with the Czechs." But, "since his return to Prague," she wrote, "he has in fact raised his original demands." She believed Churchill was "the one British statesman of whom the Germans are afraid. If you are conciliated, they consider that they can expect much greater support from the British Government, whom they think are afraid. . . . Henlein is much more radical since he saw you." Indeed he was. Under great pressure from Halifax, Beneš offered the Sudetens "cantonal self-government" — a concession far exceeding the Sudeten German leader's most extravagant hopes when he had laid his case before Churchill in Morpeth Mansions. His followers rejoiced, but after conferring with Hitler at Berchtesgaden, Henlein rejected the offer, insisting on full independence, including sovereignty over the Czech fortress line in the Sudeten Mountains.[191]

Churchill's informants continued to be of a much higher caliber than the government's. Men unavailable to any other correspondent came to Chartwell to be interviewed by him. As early as July 14, 1938, less than eight weeks after the May crisis and a year before Hitler got round to Poland, Winston interrogated Albert Förster, *Gauleiter* (Nazi district leader) of Danzig and the Führer's man, in his sitting room. Many of Chartwell's visitors came at grave personal risk, though none graver than Major Ewald von Kleist-Schmenzin.

On August 18, 1938, Major von Kleist, in mufti, registered incognito at the Park Lane Hotel and was driven to Kent by Frank Jenner, the Westerham taxi driver. As the German talked, Randolph took notes; his father listened and interrupted from time to time with comments and questions. Kleist described an attack on Czechoslovakia as "imminent." He believed it would come between the annual Nazi rally at Nuremberg in the first week of September and the end of the month. "Nobody in Germany," Randolph's notes read, "wants war except H." The generals were for peace, "convinced that an attack upon Czechoslovakia would involve Germany in war with France and Britain." They were prepared to disobey the Führer, even overthrow him, but needed "a little encouragement." Churchill replied that though many Englishmen were unprepared to advocate war "in cold blood," few would "stand by idly once the fighting started." He emphasized that he and those who shared his view on this point were "anti-Nazi and anti-war but not anti-German." Kleist replied that he would share this message with his friends and colleagues but would welcome some gesture, even from "private members of Parliament," to help consolidate the "universal anti-war sentiment in Germany." After Kleist departed Chartwell, his host consulted Halifax, and when Kleist left London on August 23, he carried with him a letter signed by Churchill declaring that the crossing of the Czech frontier by German troops or warplanes "in force" would mean the renewal of the world war, which would be fought out "to the bitter end," with all the nations engaged in the struggle fighting on "for victory or death."[192]

When Winston received information that could not be published, he usually sent it to men in power. Usually they disregarded it. Kleist could have been invaluable, but when a summary of his message reached the prime minister, Chamberlain waved it away, saying, "I take it that von Kleist is violently anti-Hitler and is extremely anxious to stir up his friends in Germany to make an attempt at its [*sic*] overthrow. He reminds me of the Jacobites at the Court of France in King William's time, and I think we must discount a good deal of what he says."[193]

Like Churchill, who also traveled armed now, Hitler worried that before he could play out his role in history "something might happen" to him. It would be tragic, he told his generals, if, after so much toil in so just a cause, the war were to be fought without him. He knew they were worried about war on two fronts, and so on June 18, when he had drawn up his final directive for the invasion of Czechoslovakia, he had assured Field Marshal Wilhelm Keitel, chief of the OKW, that he would sign the order to march "only if I am firmly convinced, as in the case of the [Rhineland] demilitarized zone and the entry into Austria, that France will not march, and that therefore England will not intervene."[194]

Keitel was a lickspittle, but other OKW commanders were not reassured. On June 12 Daladier had renewed France's 1924 guarantee of Czech borders, saying it was "sacred and cannot be evaded." The commanders were depressed further by Kleist's failure in August in England; the letter Churchill had given Kleist had been invigorating, but he was out of power and likely to remain there. Hitler therefore gave his General Staff additional grounds for concern at the Kummersdorf Proving Ground, delivering one of his fulsome autopanegyrics: "Fortune must be seized when she strikes, for she will not come again! . . . I predict that by the end of the year we will be looking back at a great success!" The Siegfried Line, growing stronger with each passing hour, could hold the French and British in check, if it came to that, while they and their men overran Czechoslovakia. The man who couldn't hold the line against odds was "a scoundrel." At this point Major Helmuth Groscurth, an intelligence officer, scribbled in his diary that the Führer was spouting "*völliger Unsinn*" ("total nonsense").[195]

Europe's statesmen, if frozen in time during that late summer and early fall period in 1938, would resemble characters in a grotesque Friedrich Dürrenmatt play, each acting on assumptions the others would find startling or even preposterous. In Paris the prospect of another great war dismays Daladier, but he has faith in his British ally and the greatness of his army, and the mere suggestion that France might break her word is unthinkable. Bonnet, who breaks his own word almost daily, thinks of little else. In

London His Majesty's Government still dreams of scuttling France and forming a new alliance with the Germans. Many powerful Germans would like to reciprocate, but only one of them counts and he is demented. He has told Keitel that the Western democracies won't fight, but even he doesn't believe it, and neither does the chief of the German General Staff, General Ludwig Beck, who resigns on August 27. Unless one shares the Führer's superstitious belief in intuition, his plans are ludicrous. In Beck's words, he has put himself in an "untenable position." William L. Shirer will write: "Germany was in no position to go to war on October 1, 1938" — the date Hitler had set, and would cling to — "against Czechoslovakia *and* France and Britain. . . . Had she done so, she would have been quickly and easily defeated, and that would have been the end of Hitler and the Third Reich."[196]

It wouldn't even have gone that far. Conspirators in the OKW would have intervened. At Nuremberg eight years later Field Marshal Keitel was asked to describe the Generalstab's reaction to Chamberlain's Munich sell-out, and replied: "We were extraordinarily happy [*ausserordentlich glücklich*] that it had not come to a military operation because . . . we had always been of the opinion that our means of attack against the frontier fortifications of Czechoslovakia were insufficient." General Franz Halder, interrogated by an American officer toward the end of the Nuremberg trials, testified that the Czech issue inspired the German generals' plot against Hitler. Had the Führer ordered the attack in 1938, he said, "It had been planned to occupy by military force the Reich Chancellery and those government offices, particularly ministries, which were administered by party members and close supporters of Hitler, with the express intention of avoiding bloodshed and then trying the group before the whole German nation."[197]

Meanwhile, the Czechs, trusting their formidable defenses and their two fellow democracies in the west, were ready for anything — anything, that is, except betrayal by those two. The Poles and the Hungarians were plotting ignobly; if the Germans took part of Czechoslovakia, they wanted some, too. In Rome, Mussolini imagined that the others were wondering which way he would pounce. Actually, they weren't thinking of him at all. Since the Ethiopian fiasco the Duce's legions had been heavily discounted.

But what of the Russians? The fate of Czechoslovakia had the highest strategic consequences for the Soviet Union. If Hitler seized the Sudetenland and the Czech fortifications, the Soviets would lose the outer bastion of their defense system. Hitler understood that; he called Beneš's country "the Soviet Russian Aircraft Carrier." The Foreign Office in Whitehall was aware of these implications; its career diplomats had repeatedly urged their political overseers to open "conversations" with the Russians, but although

Litvinov had been trying to shoulder his way into an anti-Nazi alliance since the fall of Austria, the appeasers kept pretending the U.S.S.R. didn't exist.[198]

One incident reveals how far certain men in London and in France would go to stifle an alliance with the Soviet Union. Speaking to the French chargé d'affaires in Moscow, Litvinov proposed "immediate staff talks between the Soviet, French and Czech experts." Bonnet buried the chargé's report in a locked file and mentioned it to no one. Two days later he misled the British ambassador in Paris, telling him that the Rumanians would not permit Russian warplanes to violate their air space in support of the Czechs. But the secretary general at the Quai, the incorruptible Alexis Léger, had already informed Phipps that permission *would* be granted. Despite Bonnet, the facts reached R. A. Butler, Halifax's young new under secretary, who promptly spiked them, remarking, "Let us hope no more will come of this idea."[199]

Churchill prayed that something *would*. Hitler had massed at least 1.5 million soldiers on Czechoslovakia's borders and Churchill felt Russia's help was essential. On the last day of August he wrote Halifax to advise delivery of "a joint note" to Hitler from Britain, France, and Russia expressing their "desire for peace," their "deep anxiety at the military preparations of Germany," their common interest in "a peaceful solution of the Czechoslovak controversy," and their conviction that "an invasion by Germany of Czechoslovakia would raise capital issues." Ambassadors for the three powers, he said, should hand the note to President Roosevelt, "and we should use every effort to induce him to do his utmost upon it." To Winston it seemed "not impossible" that the president "would then address H. emphasising the gravity of the situation . . . saying that a world war would inevitably follow from an invasion of Czechoslovakia, and that he earnestly counselled a friendly settlement." The "peaceful elements in German official circles" — and no one in the Foreign Office was more aware of their strength — would "make a stand," forcing the Führer to "find a way out for himself by parleying with Roosevelt." This sequence of events was conjectural, Churchill granted; "one only sees them as hopes." But any hope was better than none.[200]

He drove to Whitehall and handed his letter to Halifax, who went across Downing Street to No. 10. There, like every other communication to the prime minister, including those bearing the royal seal, it came under the shifty eyes of Sir Horace Wilson. At his peak Rasputin was known to all Moscow. Wilson was more like one of the burrowing insectivores. A nation in peril, with hundreds of thousands of lives in jeopardy, does not refuse to answer the doorbell when a well-muscled neighbor, feeling his own future darkened by the same shadow, comes to make common cause. But that, in effect, was Horace Wilson's advice to his patron. When Churchill's proposal reached Chamberlain, attached to it was an admonition in his seneschal's neat handwriting condemning it in every particular. Wilson described it as "a mixture of diplomacy and threat" which would enrage Hitler by including Russia in the coalition confronting him. He predicted that if Winston's proposal were adopted, England would be carried closer to a situation in which "we might find ourselves . . . tackling Germany single-handed" — which was, of course, the one thing it would *not* have done.[201]

Winston, meantime, was receiving confirmation that his plan would have had a warmer reception elsewhere. On September 2 the Russian ambassador sent Chartwell word that he would like to drive down and discuss "a matter of urgency." Maisky's mission was to inform him of conversations which had taken place in Moscow the previous day between the French chargé d'affaires and Foreign Commissar Litvinov, the essence of which was that the Soviet Union wanted to stand shoulder to shoulder with the British and French against Hitler. Churchill later recalled: "Before he had got very far, I realized that he was making a declaration to me, a private person, because the Soviet Government preferred this channel to a direct offer to the Foreign Office which might have encountered a rebuff." He felt this implication strengthened, he wrote after the Russian had left, "by the fact that no request for secrecy was made." Considering the matter of signal importance, Winston composed a detailed account of the conversation for Halifax, taking special care not to use language which might "prejudice its consideration by Halifax and Chamberlain." This report, too, was received unenthusiastically by HMG; Halifax replied, Winston later wrote, "in a guarded manner, that he did not feel that action of the kind proposed . . . would be helpful, but that he would keep it in mind."[202]

Nonetheless, when Churchill's August 31 proposal was returned to the Foreign Office with Wilson's comment endorsed by Chamberlain, Halifax had been uneasy. If Hitler was Britain's enemy, then so was time; the government should make some clear statement of policy before the Reich chancellor delivered another of his incendiary speeches to the Reichstag, touching off rioting among Henlein's Sudeten Nazis. To restore order Prague would be obliged to use force; Hitler would rant about Czech police brutality, and the cycle would be repeated again, until a single swing of an impatient policeman's club could bring the Wehrmacht surging across the border. Therefore, the foreign secretary decided he himself should speak, establishing Britain's disapproval of Sudeten German incidents. He sent his text across the street, and back it came, with its own Wilson critique embellished by the prime minister's approval.

Wilson liked this even less than Winston's. He declared that "any intelligent journalist . . . could draw but one deduction, namely that we were threatening Germany." Patiently, Halifax sent over a new draft. Chamberlain himself commented on this one, and he could find nothing good to say about it. One paragraph was sure to "draw protests from the Dominions," another was "clearly a threat"; all in all it was "out of place till after Nuremberg." The whole point of it had been to put His Majesty's Government on record *before* the Führer's annual diatribe at the Nazis' September rally. Ambassadors Henderson and Newton were also critical, and Halifax wrote Henderson that he had "more or less given up the idea of making a public speech."[203]

Others, even champions of the new Germany, shared his concern. Henderson reported that Ribbentrop believed England would not "move under any circumstances," and Under Secretary Weizsäcker had pointedly remarked that "war in 1914 might possibly have been avoided if Great Britain had spoken in time." In a general FO discussion on September 4, support grew for what one participant called "a *private* warning" to the Führer, a plain statement "that we should have to come in to protect France." Cadogan thought this had merit because "Hitler has probably been persuaded that our March and May statements are bluff, and that's dangerous." Yet nothing was done. They drifted.[204]

British policy had evolved subtly since late March, when the prime minister had barred commitments to, or even concern over, political events in Europe. Chamberlain was now concentrating on two objectives which were mutually exclusive: establishing a special relationship with the Reich and, at the same time, preserving England's longtime friendship with France. Together they were impossible, but *some* tie with the Continent was necessary. Otherwise England was merely an island country off the Continent's coast, at the mercy of any dominant continental power. So now, when Lord Maugham, Somerset Maugham's brother, said that "no vital British interest is involved" in the Sudetenland, Duff Cooper fiercely reminded him that "the main interest of this country has always been to prevent any one power from obtaining undue predominance in Europe," that in Nazi Germany they faced "the most formidable power that has ever dominated Europe," and that resistance to power "is quite obviously a British interest." No one in the cabinet disagreed. Yet as the crisis escalated, no statement of policy was made, publicly or through private diplomatic channels.[205]

The one British voice which had been heard through the summer was Geoffrey Dawson's. On June 3, in his lead editorial he had pondered the advisability of permitting "the Germans of Czechoslovakia — by plebiscite or otherwise — to decide their own future, even if it should mean secession to the Reich." Indeed, he wondered whether it might be sensible to allow other minorities inside the country to take the same course. It would be, he acknowledged, "a drastic remedy for the present unrest, but something drastic may be needed."

Drastic was not the word; it would be catastrophic. The nation Beneš and Masaryk had founded was a polyglot state, a reflection, in microcosm, of the Austro-Hungarian Empire from which it had derived. Within its borders were communities of Czechs, Slovaks, Germans, Magyars, Ruthenians, Poles, and Bohemians. That hardly meant that it was doomed. Dawson was writing *völliger Unsinn*. But many Europeans had once more concluded that *The Times* was the voice of Downing Street, and as September 1938 opened, no spokesman of His Majesty's Government denied this. Since no one in Whitehall was making foreign policy, a newspaper editor had done it.

The prime minister was assigning greater priority to an exercise in personal diplomacy.

❧ ❧

There is something almost touching about Neville Chamberlain's faith in his cherished Plan Z, a simple scheme, redolent of those *Chatterbox* volumes in which the Chamberlain boys, like so many young Victorians of their class, had lost themselves on long Saturday afternoons when there were no playmates and Nanny was busy elsewhere. Pen-and-ink drawings identified the handsome, mesomorphic heroes, the helpless but winning heroines, and the scowling ruffians doomed, in issue after issue, to be foiled in the last paragraph. And how had they been outwitted? By Plan Z! Or Plan X, or Q, or whatever — a simple ruse, harmless to others but fatal for the wicked. The first we know of its reappearance in the mind of Neville, grown up and grown old, is a memorandum by Sir Horace Wilson, written after the adjournment of a cabinet meeting on August 30, 1938. He and the prime minister had discussed the matter two or three days earlier, and now he wrote: "There is in existence a plan, to be called 'Plan Z,' which is known only to the Prime Minister, the Chancellor of the Exchequer, the Foreign Secretary, Sir Nevile Henderson and myself."[206]

The procedure's success, he continued, depended upon "its being a complete surprise, and it is vital nothing should be said about it." A second Wilson memorandum, filed the following day, gives the whole thing away: "On being told that Plan Z is emerging, Henderson will ascertain where

Hitler is, but will not say why he wants to know." If time permitted, HM's ambassador in Berlin would receive another message indicating time of arrival; he would pass this along to Ribbentrop. Again, time permitting, "we would like to do this before we make public announcement here that Plan Z has been put into operation. Place of arrival must be Berlin connecting with Henderson and Ribbentrop. (Schmidt is reliable.)"[207]

Wilson's emphasis on time is subject to but one interpretation; the plan anticipated a supreme crisis, with a German invasion of Czechoslovakia imminent — perhaps but a few hours away. The need to know Hitler's whereabouts, and the reference to Paul Otto Schmidt, the Führer's personal interpreter, contemplated a surprise call on him — uninvited, with no prior arrangements. Presumably the P.M. planned to land in Germany and tell wide-eyed Germans, "Take me to your leader," though that would have been difficult because he, like Hitler, spoke only his native language.

On September 3 Chamberlain wrote his sister Ida: "I keep racking my brains to try and devise some means of averting catastrophe, if it should seem to be upon us. I thought of one so unconventional and daring that it rather took Halifax's breath away. But since Henderson thought it might save the situation at the 11th hour, I haven't abandoned it, though I hope all the time that it won't be necessary to try it." If, as Horace Wilson had written, success of the operation depended upon "complete secrecy," its chances were slim, since Henderson was notorious for sharing confidences with his Nazi friends Göring and Ribbentrop. The circle of those informed widened; Hoare and Simon were also told of it. No one remembered that it was illegal for a prime minister to leave the country without the King's permission, but the matter of cabinet approval arose. It was, they decided, unnecessary. Chamberlain's power to commit his country was beginning to rival Hitler's.[208]

The year which had begun with Vansittart's dismissal and Eden's resignation had now reached the first lovely week of September, and if the Wilhelmstrasse of 1914 had been confused by England's intentions, the Nazi generation was utterly baffled. The Quai d'Orsay had made it as clear as diplomats can that the French would fight if the Czech frontier were ruptured, and Britain was France's ally. Yet, after a long cabinet meeting in Downing Street, Henderson told Ribbentrop that "the Sudeten Germans and the Czechs are a matter of complete indifference to Great Britain. Great Britain is only concerned with the attitude of France."[209]

It was time to read *The Times* again. It is in keeping with the bizarre patterns of the Big Czech Crisis, now looming, that the author of the paper's September 7 leader has never been identified. Dawson would spend the rest of his life explaining that he had returned late from his country weekend, insisting that he didn't reach the office until late Tuesday afternoon, September 6. He read an incomplete draft of an editorial on Czechoslovakia, cut a paragraph, ordered it rewritten, and, apparently exhausted by this effort, left for dinner. Returning at 11:45 P.M. he had misgivings. A Francophile colleague, solicited for advice, urged further surgery. It would have been more useful, for those who wanted to avoid another great war, if they had burned every copy of the paper and then burned the building. One paragraph, in the words of Martin Gilbert, "gave its support to what was, in effect, the extreme Henlein position, unacceptable not only to Beneš, but also to that large number of Sudeten Germans for whom union with Germany would mean the loss of all liberty, swift imprisonment, forced labour, and death." It ran:

> If the Sudetens now ask for more than the Czech Government are ready to give . . . it can only be inferred that the Germans are going beyond the mere removal of disabilities for those who do not find themselves at ease within the Czechoslovak Republic. In that case it might be worth while for the Czechoslovak Government to consider whether they should exclude altogether the project, which has found favour in some quarters, of making Czechoslovakia a more homogeneous state by the cession of that fringe of alien populations who are contiguous to the nation to which they are united by race.[210]

Considering the unique relationship between *The Times* and the government, it would be difficult to find a more irresponsible passage in the history of journalism. The unknown author — his identity shielded by Dawson, who either wrote it himself or knew who did — betrayed a staggering ignorance of geography, history, and both the ethnic diversity and range of political persuasions of the people living in the shadow of the Sudeten Mountains. As Churchill wrote the following day, in a letter which Dawson refused to publish, *The Times*'s proposal "would have the effect of handing over to the German Nazis the whole of the mountain defence line which marks the ancient boundaries of Bohemia, and was specially preserved to the Czechoslovak State as a vital safeguard of its national existence." German propaganda had created the impression that everyone living in the Sudetenland was German, and that Henlein was their spokesman. Neither was true; four other political parties strongly opposed his Sudetendeutsche Nazis, and at least a quarter-million voters were German fugitives from the Third Reich. Like their Austrian comrades in terror, they knew that the names of their leaders were on Gestapo lists. For them, the *Times* editorial was at the very least the first draft of a death warrant.[211]

Jan Masaryk had to pay two visits to Whitehall that morning before the

Foreign Office agreed to announce that the *Times* proposal "in no way represents the view of His Majesty's Government." By then every capital in Europe was convinced that it did. In Blackpool the Labour party's National Executive issued a formal statement declaring that "the British Government must leave no doubt that they will unite with the French and Soviet Governments to resist any attack on Czechoslovakia." Halifax agreed — he was vacillating, not for the last time, on the Czech issue, and like many appeasers he was occasionally discomfited by flecks of doubt about the wisdom of endlessly yielding to Hitler's demands.[212]

By now the Czech border was swarming with German assault troops, and London knew that this time they weren't there for maneuvers. Theodor Kordt, the chargé d'affaires at the German embassy in the absence of Dirksen, had arrived in Downing Street the night of September 6 and entered No. 10 through the garden gate and the Horse Guards Parade. There he told Horace Wilson, and then Halifax, who came hurrying over from the FO, that he had come, "putting conscience before loyalty," as "a spokesman for political and military circles in Berlin who desire by every means to prevent war." He and his associates wanted a blunt warning that England would fight for the Czechs. "Hitler," he said, had "taken his decision to 'march in' on the nineteenth or twentieth."[213]

Kordt was confirmed by an equally sensational development. Dr. Karl Burckhardt of the League of Nations had given the British ambassador in Berne a message from Weizsäcker, second only to Ribbentrop in the Wilhelmstrasse, confirming Kordt in every particular and underscoring the need to warn the Führer that the invasion of Czechoslovakia meant war. Halifax, with Chamberlain's reluctant approval, drafted a sharply worded note for delivery to the German government: if the Czech frontier were breached France would declare war on Germany, touching off "a sequence of events" resulting in "a general conflict from which Great Britain could not stand aside." But Ambassador Henderson — who had no authority whatever to pass judgment on the foreign secretary's instructions — refused to deliver the note, on the ground that it would only inflame the Führer. Besides, he said, he had already made the British position "as clear as daylight to people who count." With this assurance, and because of the difficulty of communicating with Henderson, who was living aboard a train for five days while he attended the Nuremberg rally, Halifax, "on understanding that you have in fact already conveyed to Herr von Ribbentrop . . . [the] substance of what you were instructed to say," agreed that Henderson need make no further representation.[214]

Precisely what His Majesty's ambassador to the Reich may have said to Ribbentrop is unrecorded; but the SS officer who served as Henderson's escort at Nuremberg later said that during his stay he "remarked with a sigh that Great Britain was now having to pay for her guilty part in the Treaty of Versailles" and "expressed his aversion to the Czechs in very strong terms."[215]

On the third day after the *Times* editorial, Göring spoke to the vast, hysterical mass at Nuremberg, calling the Czechs a "miserable pygmy race . . . oppressing a cultured people" and fronting for "Moscow and the eternal mask of the Jew Devil." The Führer's turn at the rostrum came, as always, on the last night of the rally, Monday, September 12. Bathed in spotlights, pausing after each scream of invective as the huge, packed stadium roared, *"Sieg Heil! Sieg Heil! Sieg Heil!"* he shouted his distorted version of the May crisis, raging at the recollection of Germany's humiliation then, which he blamed on Beneš and his "Jew plotters." Sweating till his cowlick was plastered across his forehead, he called Czechoslovakia a "monstrous formation" and demanded that the Sudetendeutsche be granted the "right of self-determination" and "justice" ("*Gerechtigkeit*"), adding in a flash of arrogation: "Germans of Austria know best how bitter a thing it is to be separated from the Fatherland. They will be the first to recognize the significance of what I have been saying today." They would indeed. And so would Winston Churchill. According to the cabinet minutes, Halifax reported that he and the prime minister had seen Churchill on the previous day (Sunday), and said that "Mr. Churchill's proposition was that we should tell Germany that if she set foot in Czechoslovakia we should at once be at war with her. Mr. Churchill agreed that this line of action was an advance on the line of action which he had proposed two or three weeks earlier, but he thought that by taking it we should incur no added risk."[216]

Yet while Winston saw an Anschluss replay thundering toward them, the edgy cabinets in Paris and London, listening to Hitler's Nuremberg speech over radios, heard only wind. They awaited what the FO called "triggers," vows and demands which could only be resolved by German bayonets slashing toward Prague. Since the Führer was unspecific, however, the prime minister, the premier, and their ministers felt relieved. Misunderstanding him and his genius, they erred. This was his milieu, and he knew, as they did not, that his wild gestures and mindless raving were enough to set off bloody rioting in the Sudetenland. Prague declared martial law and rushed in convoys of troops. *"SCHRECKENHERRSCHAFT!"* ("REIGN OF TERROR") shrieked *Der Angriff*, and Henlein fled into Germany. Then, abruptly, the storm ended. Thursday morning everything in the Sudetenland was normal.[217]

At No. 10 Downing Street and the Paris home of the French premier, things were not. Premier Daladier wired Chamberlain, proposing that France, Britain, and Germany convene for a discussion *à trois*. But the P.M. had anticipated him. With the Sudetenland rioting approaching its peak, Chamberlain decided the time for Plan Z had arrived. Bypassing Henderson, he cabled Hitler during the night of September 13 that in the light of "the increasingly critical situation I propose to come over at once to see you with a view to trying to find a peaceful solution." He intended to fly, could "start tomorrow," asked for the "earliest time" they might meet and "a very early reply." Chamberlain was eager. And anxious. It was the sort of mood that sales clerks recognize in the customer who has decided to buy even before entering the store, and to pay any price.[218]

Churchill's *Daily Telegraph* column of September 15 predicted bloodshed; the Czechs, he wrote, possessed "an absolute determination to fight for life and freedom." If not "daunted by all the worry and pressure to which they have been subjected," they would inflict 300,000 or 400,000 casualties, but the world would hold them blameless. It was German aggression which would be condemned; "from the moment that the first shot is fired and the German troops attempt to cross the Czechoslovakian frontier, the whole scene will be transformed, and a roar of fury will arise from the free peoples of the world, which will proclaim nothing less than a crusade against the aggressor."

He could still sound his bugle, but the rest of the orchestra was following a different score. In the Foreign Office, Oliver Harvey wrote: "British press receives news of PM's visit with marked approval. City is much relieved. Reaction in Germany also one of relief. In America it looks as if it were regarded as surrender. Winston says it is the stupidest thing that has ever been done." Churchill knew what the prime minister was planning. He had learned that nearly a year earlier Chamberlain had written what he really wanted to tell the Nazis: "Give us satisfactory assurance that you won't use force to deal with the Austrians and Czechoslovakians and we will give you similar assurance that we won't use force to prevent the changes you want, if you can get them by peaceful means." Declining Lord Moyne's invitation to join him on a Caribbean cruise, Winston wrote: "Alas, a cloud of uncertainty overhangs all plans at the present time. . . . We seem to be very near the bleak choice between War and Shame. My feeling is that we shall choose Shame, and then have War thrown in a little later on even more adverse terms than at present."[219]

The prime minister, of course, saw matters differently. In his eyes the choice lay between peace and devastation, and he saw nothing shameful in buying peace by coercing a pretentious little state on the far side of Germany. Late in life R. A. Butler, who had watched him prepare for his historic trip, described his mood as "exalted." Some Britons were worried by the loss of a strong ally — Czechoslovakia, whose army was described by the British military attaché in Prague as "probably the best in the smaller states of Europe," could field thirty to forty divisions after manning her fortress line. Others were troubled by the moral implications, and by the sloughing off of British pride. Winston's sixteen-year-old daughter, Mary, wrote him: "I have been following the Czechoslovakian problem with keen interest. I think we are making things more difficult by declaring such a feeble policy."[220]

Chamberlain, who distrusted public opinion, the press, and to some extent, the House of Commons and even the cabinet, had taken steps to free himself of unwanted advice while he practiced his personal diplomacy. Parliament was not sitting and would not convene in the immediate future. (They were "being treated more and more as a kind of Reichstag," Harold Macmillan complained.) The cabinet's Foreign Policy Committee had last met three months before; the next meeting was a month away.[221]

Those familiar with later conferences between world leaders, particularly Churchill's, may be surprised by the fact that apart from two typists and two bodyguards — who would travel in a separate plane — the prime minister took with him only three companions: the ubiquitous Sir Horace Wilson and two young FO diplomats. Like their leader, none in the party spoke a word of German. Henderson, who would join them in Munich, was fluent in German, but of course he also spoke in tongues. Chamberlain and Hitler would talk *à deux,* aided only by an interpreter. The prime minister had no strategy, no proposals, no conversational lines to fall back upon if confronted by an unexpected proposal requiring thought. As he said afterward, he regarded himself as a one-man mission of inquiry to determine "in personal conversation whether there was any hope of saving the peace." Horace Wilson had made some notes on reciprocal suggestions, but the P.M., it seems, was prepared only to accept the Führer's terms. This was his virgin flight, and he had been told to anticipate a bumpy three-hour trip to Munich. Understandably he was nervous, and he had therefore asked Geoffrey Dawson to ride with him to Heston airstrip. At such a time it was comforting to be accompanied by a friend who would console you with reasonable answers to unreasonable doubts, someone who understood you, someone you could trust.[222]

Hitler was guilty of treason, incest, incitement to riot, and the murder of millions. In small matters, however, he was a prig: a vegetarian who scorned nicotine, and was offended by foul language. *"Um Himmel willen!"* ("For heaven's sake!") was about as strong as he got, and he fairly sputtered it when told that the prime minister of Great Britain, the leader of the greatest empire in history, was coming to him, like the English pilgrims in the early days of the Third Reich. Landing at Munich about noon on September 15, Chamberlain enjoyed reviewing an honor guard whose members, Wilson noted without comprehension, wore skulls and crossbones on their caps. Though none of the English visitors knew it, these were members of the *Totenkopf* (Death's Head) SS, recruited from Dachau guards. It was not an auspicious greeting.

Chamberlain wrote Ida that he "felt quite fresh" during the ride from the airport to the train station, and was "delighted with the enthusiastic welcome of the crowds . . . all the way to the station." A three-hour train ride brought him to Berchtesgaden; then he and his entourage were driven up to the Berghof. There, Chamberlain later wrote, "Halfway down [the] steps stood the Führer, bareheaded and dressed in a khaki-coloured coat of broadcloth with a red armlet and a swastika on it, and the military cross on his breast." Except for this costume, the prime minister thought, "he looks entirely undistinguished. You would never notice him in a crowd, and would take him for the house painter" — Chamberlain had swallowed this whopper — "he once was."[223]

The prime minister had been traveling since dawn, and it was nearly 5:30 P.M. when, after tea, he and the Führer, accompanied by Schmidt, Hitler's interpreter, climbed the stairs to the Berghof's study, where Schuschnigg had been browbeaten seven months before. Hitler dominated the conversation, running on and on about how he had vowed to solve the Czech issue "one way or another." The Sudetenland's three million Germans must "return" (*"zurückkehren"*) to the Reich. He was "prepared to risk a world war rather than allow this to drag on." Chamberlain had tried again and again to comment; now he succeeded in interrupting Hitler — something one did not *do* — and said that if the Führer had decided to resolve the issue by force, "why did you let me come? I have wasted my time." Hitler calmed down and suggested they examine "the question of whether a peaceful settlement is not possible after all." Would Britain agree to a *"Loslösung"* ("liberation") of the Sudetenland, one based on the right of *"Selbstimmungsrechts der Volker"* ("self-determination")? That was the trap. Chamberlain went for it. He was pleased, he said, that they "had now got down to the crux of the matter." Of course, he would have to sound out his cabinet and confer with the French, he said, adding, according to Schmidt's shorthand notes, that "he could personally state that he recognized the principle of the detachment of the Sudeten area. . . . He wished to return to England to report to the Government and secure their approval of his personal attitude." That, so to speak, was the ball game. The prospect had been hooked.[224]

At Chartwell, Winston was writing A. H. Richards, general secretary of the Anti-Nazi Council, "If, as I fear, the Government is going to let Czechoslovakia be cut to pieces, it seems to me that a period of very hard work lies before us all." Hard work lay ahead for Chamberlain, too. The betrayal of a nation requires just as much paperwork, conferring, and arguing over obscure points as its salvation. But the prime minister believed that *he* was the savior. He asked for, and was given, Hitler's promise that Germany would launch no attack until they had held a second summit sometime in the next few days. Departing Berchtesgaden, Chamberlain later wrote Ida, he felt he had "established a certain confidence, which was my aim, and, on my side, in spite of the hardness and ruthlessness I thought I saw in his face, I got the impression that here was a man who could be relied upon when he had given his word."[225]

In London on September 17 Chamberlain described Hitler to the cabinet as "the commonest little dog," and a "most extraordinary creature," but repeated his conviction that he would be "rather better than his word," adding that he had been told (presumably by Henderson) that the Führer had been "most favourably impressed." This, he said, was "of the utmost importance, since the future conduct of these negotiations depends mainly upon personal contacts." Hitler had assured him, he emphasized, that he wanted "no Czechs in the Reich"; he would be satisfied once he had included the Sudeten Germans. "The impression left on me was that Herr Hitler meant what he had said. . . . My view is that Herr Hitler is telling the truth."[226]

Having given this testimonial to the Führer, the P.M. assumed that his ministers would approve of ceding the Sudetenland to the Reich. To his surprise and dismay, several declined endorsing the German claim pending further discussion. In Paris there was also what Phipps described as "considerable heart-burning." Léon Blum wrote in *Le Populaire* that war would probably be avoided, but "under such circumstances that I, who for many years dedicated my life to [the struggle for peace], cannot feel joy. I feel myself torn between a sense of cowardly relief and shame."[227]

Churchill's feelings were unmixed; he was outraged. He sent his agent, Revesz, a statement for distribution to the European press. "The personal intervention of Mr Chamberlain and his flight to see Herr Hitler," he wrote, "does not at all alter the gravity of the issue at stake. We must hope that it does not foreshadow another complete failure of the Western Democracies to withstand the threats and violence of Nazi Germany." Phipps reported to Halifax that Churchill had telephoned the Quai d'Orsay, noting caustically that Winston "presumably . . . breathed fire and thunder in order to binge Bonnet up."[228]

But France was already committed to the Chamberlain solution. A delegation headed by Daladier and Bonnet reached Whitehall on September 18. The French premier's chief concern was to avoid the proposal of a plebiscite, "a weapon with which the German Government could keep Central Europe in a constant state of alarm and suspense." Chamberlain assured him that he had discarded that possibility — he knew Hitler would reject it since if the polling was supervised, he might lose. Yet the French were still uneasy; they could not walk away from their treaty with the Czechs. They wanted the British to join them in guaranteeing the borders of the mangled Czechoslovakia that the cession would leave. Chamberlain and Halifax tried to avoid that, but after nearly three hours of discussion they yielded, the P.M. taking consolation in Hitler's Berghof assurance that he was solely interested in the Sudeten Germans. The issue was absurd. If England had been unwilling to fight for a defensible Czechoslovakia, why should she agree to rush to the aid of the indefensible remnant? Beneš saw that; when the Anglo-French proposal was presented to him by Basil Newton, he rejected it, on the ground, reported Newton, that "guarantees which he already possessed had proved valueless."[229]

The Times, on September 20, in massive understatement, observed that the Anglo-French proposal, giving Hitler what he would otherwise have found very expensive, "could not, in the nature of things, be expected to make a strong *prima facie* appeal to the Czech Government, and least of all to President Beneš." It didn't, and at 8:00 P.M. on the twentieth the Czech government refused to agree to the annexation of its sovereign territory, explaining that as leaders of a democracy they could not make such an enormous decision without the approval of their parliament. Furthermore, they declared, submission to the Führer's demands would not solve the "question of peace" because they would face minority unrest elsewhere in their country. Lastly, Europe's "balance of power would be destroyed."[230]

This was one of those mysterious historical moments in which events acquire a momentum all their own and begin to exert an irresistible pressure. There was no reason to hurry; Ribbentrop told Paris, London, and Prague that the Führer could wait, and at his suggestion the next Hitler-Chamberlain meeting was postponed from Wednesday, September 21, to Thursday. Nevertheless, Phipps suggested to Bonnet that they tell Beneš that unless his reply constituted a complete, immediate acceptance of what amounted to an

Allied ultimatum, England and France would "wash their hands of Czechoslovakia in the event of a German attack."[231]

In Prague the British minister, Newton, advised Whitehall that if he could deliver an "ultimatum to President Beneš," then "he and his Government will feel able to bow to a *force majeure.*" That, more or less, is what happened. At 2:00 A.M. on the twenty-first Newton and his French counterpart, Victor de Lacroix, delivered a démarche informing Beneš that surrender of the Sudetenland to the Reich was "the only means of averting war and the invasion of Czechoslovakia," and that if he persisted in refusing it he would "bear the responsibility for the war," which would divide France and England, because the English would declare themselves neutral. British neutrality meant further that when "war starts, France will not take part, i.e. she will not fulfill her treaty obligations." They argued with the old man for an hour and a half; then he threw in his hand. Jan Masaryk sent the text of the Anglo-French ultimatum to Hugh Dalton, a Labour MP and a Churchill ally. When Dalton read it in the House of Commons, Sir Samuel Hoare solemnly replied that it was "in almost every respect a totally inaccurate description of the representations that we made to the Czechoslovak Government." Among the signs of moral disintegration in Chamberlain's clique was the adoption, by Hitler's British admirers, of the Big Lie.[232]

Roosevelt, summoning the British ambassador in Washington, told him that the Anglo-French proposal was "the most terrible remorseless sacrifice that has ever been demanded of a State" and predicted that it would "provoke a highly unfavorable reaction in America." The president again suggested a conference of world leaders — not in Europe, but in the Azores or some other Atlantic island — which he would attend. Roosevelt's proposal was swept from the prime minister's desk into his wastebasket.[233]

The P.M. was equally unresponsive to FDR's humanitarian appeal for the Czechs who would be dispossessed and were already well into the early stages of panic. The Sudetenland's anti-Nazis were hopelessly trapped. Wednesday evening Wenzel Jaksch, the leader of Czechoslovakia's 400,000 German Social Democrats, told John Troutbeck, the first secretary of the British embassy in Prague, that his followers had nowhere to go; the Czechs, overwhelmed by the mass of Sudeten refugees of their own race, were turning Sudeten Germans away. Therefore, Jaksch told Troutbeck, they "must lay their lives in the hands of the British and French Governments and ask for advice as to what was to be done for them." But the Allied embassies were mute. It was Vienna all over again. Jaksch's followers applied for British and French visas and were rejected. They returned to their homes to await the Gestapo, which would not keep them waiting long.[234]

* * *

Churchill had been active from the beginning of the crisis, using every weapon he could lay hands on to subvert Chamberlain. He tried to work behind the scenes, but in a nation with a free press, that was impossible; on Tuesday September 6, to his chagrin, the *Daily Express* had reported that Heinrich Brüning, the former Weimar chancellor, had visited Chartwell, asking his host to urge His Majesty's Government to "speak plainly to Hitler." After *The Times* ran its disastrous editorial of September 7 proposing a partition of Czechoslovakia, Winston had repeatedly called on Halifax, trying to find out what was happening and then to influence policy. On Thursday, September 15, when Chamberlain departed for Berchtesgaden, Winston devoted his *Daily Telegraph* column to the Czechs.[235]

He bitterly rued his resignation, on a matter of principle, from the Conservative party's hierarchy in 1931. Like his father, who had surrendered his seals as chancellor of the Exchequer fifty years earlier on another issue, he had been ostracized ever since. Now he was alarmed by news that two strong members of Daladier's cabinet, Paul Reynaud and Georges Mandel, planned to quit their offices unless France honored her pledges to the Czechs. Churchill had immediately flown over on September 20 to point out that if they quit they would forfeit their roles as shapers of another, more rational foreign policy. Either the force of his argument, his powerful presence, or his position as Hitler's greatest enemy in Europe — or perhaps all three — brought them round. They agreed to stick it out.[236]

His plane brought him back on September 21. Upon returning to Morpeth Mansions he issued a statement denouncing plans to balkanize Czechoslovakia. Partition, he said, would amount "to the complete surrender of the Western democracies to the Nazi threat of force," putting England and France in an "ever weaker and more dangerous situation." A neutral Czechoslovakia would free at least twenty-five German divisions to threaten France and the Low Countries while opening up "for the triumphant Nazis the road to the Black Sea." It was "not Czechoslovakia alone which is menaced," he said, "but also the freedom and the democracy of all nations." The conviction that security could be bought "by throwing a small State to the wolves" was "a fatal delusion."[237]

On the twenty-second Chamberlain was on his way to his second airplane trip, with Dawson again alongside to see him off. At Heston Airport the prime minister was irritated by the presence of a small group which had gathered there, not to wish him well, but to boo. The German crowds were friendlier. The second summit was to be held in the small town of Godesberg, on the Rhine, and at the Petersberg Hotel elegant suites overlooking the river had been reserved for *die Engländer* — the P.M. and his small entourage, which included two British diplomats who had met his plane: Ambassador Henderson and Ivone Kirkpatrick. All that the German people knew of Chamberlain was that he was trying to preserve the peace, but it was enough; they had brought a band, and standing beneath his windows they serenaded him with the rollicking London hit:

Kommt ihr je nach Lambeth-Stadt
Nich nur abends, auch em Tag,
Findet ihr uns dabei,
Beim tanzen des "Lambeth Walks,"
Hei!

Even as the P.M., Kirkpatrick, and Henderson crossed the Rhine for talks with Hitler in the Hotel Dreesen, Churchill, having left Downing Street, was hailing a cab for 11 Morpeth Mansions. He had called at No. 10 to ask precisely what Chamberlain would propose at Godesberg, and five peers along with three MPs — Bracken, Sinclair, and Nicolson — were gathering in his flat to hear what he had learned. Nicolson, the last to arrive, was waiting for the lift when Winston paid the cabbie and hurried in. As they ascended together, Nicolson said: "This is hell." Churchill muttered: "It is the end of the British Empire." According to Nicolson's diary, Churchill told the group that the cabinet had demanded "a firm stand" on Chamberlain's part, insisting on German demobilization, supervision of the Sudetenland transfer by an international commission, a refusal to discuss Polish or Hungarian claims on Czech territory, and a German guarantee of the new Czech borders. Almost in chorus, his guests said: "But Hitler will never accept such terms!" Winston replied, "In that case, Chamberlain will return tonight and we shall have war." In that event, one peer pointed out, "It will be inconvenient having our Prime Minister in German territory." Winston shook his massive head and growled, "Even the Germans would not be so stupid as to deprive us of our beloved Prime Minister."[238]

Hitler neither accepted nor rejected the cabinet's terms, because Chamberlain never gave them to him. He never had a chance. Expecting to please the Führer, he told him of the Anglo-French agreement to the Sudeten annexation. To his dismay, Hitler replied brusquely, *"Ja, es tut mir leid, aber das geht nicht mehr"* ("Yes, I am very sorry, but that is no longer possible "). He had decided to raise the stakes, indifferent to the outcome; war was his objective, and this old man was obstructing that. The Führer now said he thought Warsaw and Budapest were right in advancing claims on Czech territory, and peace could "not be firmly established until these claims had been settled." Furthermore, the Sudetenland problem must be completely solved by October 1 — there would be no time to adhere to the idea of self-determination. The Führer produced a marked map defining the area which must be occupied at once by German troops. Chamberlain, Kirkpatrick's notes recorded, professed himself "disappointed and puzzled." He had, he told Hitler, "risked his whole political career" to obtain his cabinet's approval of the principles agreed to at Berchtesgaden. After three hours of inconclusive and, as Chamberlain reported by telephone to London that night, "most unsatisfactory" talks, the meeting was adjourned, to be resumed the next day.[239]

Meanwhile, German troops were reported to have entered Egerland, on the Czech side of the Ohre, and Prague wanted to mobilize. As a sovereign power, Czechoslovakia needed no one's permission to take defensive measures, but Beneš sought the advice of the two great democracies, if only because alienating them was unthinkable. The Czech request to mobilize was forwarded to Godesberg and answered by Henderson, who, predictably, replied: "Wait awhile." The exchange had been relayed to London, however, and the cabinet, overruling Henderson, gave Beneš a green light. It was promptly changed back to red on instructions from Sir Horace Wilson in Godesberg, who had consulted no one. But the French told the Czechs to proceed. Prague, understandably confused, hesitated.

Phipps, in Paris, was indignant. "All that is best in France is against war," he wired Whitehall. "His Majesty's Government should realize extreme danger of even appearing to encourage small, but noisy and corrupt war group here." Cadogan, in the unaccustomed role of a hawk, angrily rebuked him: "By war group you surely do not include all those who feel that France must carry out her treaty obligations to Czechoslovakia." Phipps, equally angry, answered wildly: "I meant the communists who are paid by Moscow and have been working for war for months."[240]

Halifax was not a Communist, but he had begun to think seriously about approaching the Russians. In London he was encouraged by Winston Churchill, uninvited but nevertheless welcomed in this anxious hour when all lines to Godesberg seemed dead. The talks between the Führer and the prime minister had been suspended until Friday the twenty-third. War seemed very near. At 1:15 P.M. on Friday the foreign secretary instructed Butler, in Geneva: "It would be useful if you would have a conversation with M. Litvinov on the present situation, and endeavour to elicit from him anything concerning the views and intentions of his Government."[241]

At 10:00 P.M. Halifax, with the approval of the cabinet, sent Chamberlain word that the "great mass of public opinion seems to be hardening in sense of feeling that we have gone to the limit of concession and that it is up to the Chancellor to make some contribution. . . . From point of view of your own position, that of Government, and of the country, it seems to your colleagues of vital importance that you should not leave without making it plain to Chancellor if possible by special interview that, after great concessions made by Czechoslovak Government, for him to reject opportunity for peaceful solution . . . would be an unpardonable crime against humanity." Godesberg was again quiescent. An hour passed; two hours. Then, to Halifax's astonishment, Chamberlain sent him a brief report, assuring the nervous FO that Hitler's demands and a lasting European peace were reconcilable. Whitehall wondered what had happened. The answer was that the prime minister had been duped.[242]

The Friday meeting between Chamberlain and Hitler, originally scheduled to begin at 11:30 A.M., had been several times delayed while the two exchanged letters and notes laying out their positions. It was not until 10:30 P.M. that Chamberlain again crossed the Rhine; the German chancellor was waiting at the water's edge to meet the ferry and accompany the prime minister into the hotel lounge. But the cordial atmosphere soon evaporated as the British party studied the lengthy memorandum the Germans had prepared detailing the Führer's final position.

The document demanded that the Czechs begin evacuating the Sudetenland at 8:00 A.M. September 26, with the process to be completed two days later. Any who remained would be arrested or shot as trespassers, because the region would be Reich soil. During the two days of evacuation German troops would be moving in to "protect" the area and to "restore order."[243]

Chamberlain was appalled; the talks became agitated and had reached an impasse when an adjutant entered with word that Beneš had just announced Czech general mobilization over the radio. According to Schmidt, the room was "deadly still" (*"totenstill"*). Suddenly, it erupted in furious argument. One of the few German words the prime minister knew was *Diktat,* and after rereading Hitler's memorandum and conferring with Schmidt about the translation, which was still incomplete, he said heatedly: "But this is an ultimatum!" Not at all, snapped the Führer. Pushing the paper under the P.M.'s eyes, he invited him to see for himself. It wasn't a *Diktat* at all, he said: *"Es steht ja 'Memorandum' darüber"* ("It is headed by the word 'Memorandum' "). Chamberlain ignored this childish duplicity and rose, saying he would fly home with a heavy heart. Hitler, determined to keep him hooked, quickly offered a *Konzession,* something, he said, he had never done before. The Czech evacuation needn't end till October 1. This was flimflam; Chamberlain did not know that the Generalstab had told the Führer that they couldn't possibly move in before the first of the month. But the prime minister was impressed, and expressed his appreciation. When the meeting broke up about 1:30 A.M., noted Schmidt, "Chamberlain bid a hearty farewell to the Führer." As he left the Dreesen, a newspaperman intercepted him to ask: "Is it hopeless, sir?" Chamberlain replied: "I would not like to say that. It is up to the Czechs now." In other words, peace was possible unless the Czechs stubbornly insisted on defending their homeland.[244]

When the Führer's terms became known in London, they were met with consternation. "Hitler's memo. now in," wrote Cadogan in his diary. "It's awful." Over the past week, he noted, they had "moved from 'autonomy' to cession," and "we salved our consciences, at least I did, by stipulating it must be an 'orderly' cession." This meant "safeguards for the exchange of populations, compensation, etc. Now," Cadogan continued, "Hitler says he must march into the whole area *at once* (to keep order!) and the safeguards — and plebiscites! can be held *after!* This is throwing away every last safeguard we had. The P.M. is transmitting this 'proposal' to Prague. Thank God he hasn't yet recommended it for acceptance."[245]

The prime minister arrived in London on Saturday afternoon, carrying with him Hitler's memorandum, a map showing which regions would pass into the hands of the Wehrmacht (followed by the Gestapo), and an evacuation timetable for the Czechs. At 5:30 P.M. he met with an anxious cabinet. At first, he told them, he had been "indignant" that Hitler was "pressing new demands on me." Eventually, however, "I modified my view on this point." The prime minister added that he thought he had "established some degree of personal influence over Hitler," who had told him, " 'You are the first man for many years who has got any concessions from me.' " Hitler had told him, he said, that if they "solved this question without conflict, it could be a turning-point in Anglo-German relations." The Führer had voluntarily added that (as he had already said several times) the Czech problem was "the last territorial demand" which he had to make in Europe. The prime minister thought this so important that he had instructed a bilingual young diplomat to write it out in German, and here it was: "*die letzte territoriale Forderung*." Chamberlain stressed that the Führer had not been prompted and had spoken "with great earnestness." (As Eden said later, "Chamberlain knew that Hitler lied. He just could not believe that Hitler would lie to *him*.") Now it was Chamberlain's conclusion that "We should accept those [Hitler's] terms and should advise the Czechs to do so."[246]

Duff Cooper protested. Hitherto, he said, they had faced the unpleasant alternatives of peace with dishonor or war. He now saw "a third possibility, namely war with dishonor, by which I mean being kicked into war by the boot of public opinion when those for whom we were fighting have already been defeated." But the other ministers endorsed the prime minister's view.

Czechoslovakia's leaders could hardly believe that Chamberlain had done what he had done. In France, Daladier was still troubled by "the moral issue," as he called it. Churchill wanted him to stay on that course. On Monday, September 26, Winston called on Halifax at the FO, asked that Rex Leeper be summoned, and with the foreign secretary's tacit agreement, stood over Leeper dictating a Churchillian communiqué: "If . . . a German attack is made upon Czechoslovakia . . . France will be bound to come to her assistance, and Great Britain and Russia will certainly stand by France." It is a measure of Churchill's powerful presence that Halifax then "authorized" the communiqué. As A. J. P. Taylor has observed, Halifax approved this announcement "but did not sign it. In this roundabout way, he secured his position both present and future: he retained Chamberlain's confidence, yet was later the only 'Man of Munich' who continued to stand high in favor with Churchill."[247]

The communiqué was ineffective. In Paris, Bonnet dismissed it as a forgery, and Chamberlain quashed it that evening by issuing a statement reaffirming his vow to meet all Hitler's demands. On Sunday an FO minute had set forth Britain's new stance vis-à-vis the Czechs: "It can be taken for granted that the only hope of preventing or at least localizing war is for His Majesty's Government . . . to make it absolutely clear that they [the Czechs] must accept German plan or forfeit claim to further support from Western Powers." Nevertheless, Jan Masaryk formally rejected the memorandum that Hitler had handed to Chamberlain, describing it as "a *de facto* ultimatum of the sort usually presented to a vanquished nation and not a proposition to a sovereign state. . . . The nation of St. Wenceslas, John Hus and Thomas Masaryk will not be a nation of slaves." Chamberlain sent Horace Wilson to Germany on Monday as his personal envoy, asking that the details of the annexation be settled by a commission of Germans, Czechs, and English. If Hitler rejected this proposal, Wilson was authorized to inform him that France and England would fight with the Czechs. The request was a bad idea. In his one concession at Godesberg, the Führer had specified that the annexation be complete by October 1. When Sir Horace brought up the commission, Hitler told him that acceptance of the memorandum was a precondition and must be received by 2:00 P.M. on Wednesday, September 28. Wilson called this a "very violent hour." To his horror Hitler fell to the floor, writhing in one of his famous fits. Henderson, who had accompanied Wilson, noted that the Reich chancellor "shrieked a good deal." It was effective. Following Henderson's example, Sir Horace decided not to deliver Chamberlain's warning.[248]

That night Hitler, still raging, delivered a venomous attack on Beneš in Berlin's Sportpalast. William L. Shirer thought he had "completely lost control of himself." On orders from the Czech president, the Führer charged, "whole stretches of country were depopulated, villages burned down, attempts were made to smoke out Germans with hand grenades and gas." He paused. "Now two men stand arrayed against one another: there is Mr. Beneš and here stand I." Another pause. Then: "Now let Mr. Beneš make his choice."[249]

Chamberlain's reaction to the Sportpalast speech was, even for him, extraordinary. Hitler had referred to him in passing, and now he told the press: "I have read the speech of the German Chancellor and I appreciate his references to the efforts I have made to save the peace." He stood ready, he said, to make further efforts. Wilson paid a farewell call on the Führer on Tuesday, and, according to Schmidt, the interpreter, he told him: "I will try to make those Czechos sensible." Hitler, in turn, handed him the Reich's final concession to England, a letter to Chamberlain offering a formal guarantee from him, as Führer, of truncated Czechoslovakia's new frontiers. That evening of the twenty-seventh the prime minister spoke to the country over the BBC, a speech most memorable for a single sentence which might be called the epitome of defeatism. "How horrible, fantastic, incredible it is that we should be digging trenches and trying on gas masks here because of a quarrel in a faraway country between people of whom we know nothing."[250]

If Chamberlain knew nothing of Czechoslovakia after the past five months, he was a very slow learner. And, as Harold Macmillan later pointed out, "In this message to the nation, nothing was said of the sufferings of the Czech people, only sympathy with Hitler 'and his indignation that German grievances had not been dealt with before this,' together with an offer to 'guarantee' that the Czech Government would 'carry out their promises.' "[251]

The people of Britain and France, conditioned by ghastly descriptions of what another European war would be like, were genuinely frightened. Macmillan recalled that "In the last few days of September — the five days that followed Chamberlain's return from Godesberg — they were grimly . . . making up their minds to face war," the "unthinkable" which was now "round the corner." Air attacks, they had been told, would wreak destruction "beyond all imagination," and they must "expect civilian casualties on a colossal scale." Baldwin had predicted sixty thousand Londoners dead after the first Luftwaffe offensive. (In fact, ninety thousand Britons were killed by Nazi bombers during the entire war.) Given these astounding figures, the mind-set of Londoners and Englishmen living in the great industrial cities of the Midlands can be compared to that of Americans in the 1980s if told that missiles with nuclear warheads were on their way to major U.S. cities. His Majesty's Government did not handle it well. Panic was the inevitable consequence of official notice instructing parents of infants under two years to bring their children to designated centers where they would be "fitted with helmets for protection against the effects of gas." There were even rumors, some of which found their way into print, that trenches were being dug in Hyde Park.[252]

As September 28 dawned, war seemed very near; the Führer's ultimatum would expire at 2:00 P.M. But late that morning, Chamberlain, through his ambassador in Rome, asked Mussolini to save the peace by intervening. The Duce telephoned Berlin, and within an hour Hitler had agreed to see the British prime minister again. He invited Mussolini to join them, and the Duce, flattered, replied that he was "willing to be present."[253]

The scene in Parliament later in the day was a piece of stage management from the people who had brought Britain to the brink of catastrophe. At about noon Hitler's invitation to Chamberlain had reached the German embassy in London, where it was immediately decoded and dispatched to No. 10. Three hours passed. Chamberlain, addressing the House of Commons in its first session since the August adjournment, was describing the tangled diplomatic skein when a messenger arrived. Normally so important a dispatch would have been taken straight to the front bench. This one was delivered to Halifax, seated in the Peers' Gallery. He passed it down to Simon, who read it and pushed it in front of the prime minister. The House watched all this with mounting interest. In a voice that could be heard throughout the hall, Chamberlain asked: "Shall I tell them now?" and, when Simon smiled and nodded, announced: "Herr Hitler has just agreed to postpone his mobilisation for twenty-four hours and to meet me in conference with Signor Mussolini and [Monsieur] Daladier at Munich." One independent MP, a diarist, described what followed as "one of the most dramatic moments which I have ever witnessed. For a second, the House was hushed in absolute silence. And then the whole House burst into a roar of cheering, since they knew that this might mean peace." Harold Macmillan remembered that "I stood up with the rest, sharing the general emotion."[254]

Some were undeceived by the contrivance. Macmillan recalled that "Eden just could not bear it; he got up and walked out of the Chamber. Another Member sat bravely still and refused to rise. It was Harold Nicolson." Amery also remained in his bench, arms folded. Men all round them were shouting "Get up! Get up!" and "Thank God for the Prime Minister!" Then, Macmillan recalled, "I saw one man silent and seated — with his head sunk on his shoulders, his whole demeanour depicting something between anger and despair. It was Churchill." But Winston, ever magnanimous, rose as Chamberlain passed him, shaking his hand, wishing him "Godspeed."[255]

The German army's anti-Nazi conspirators had been about to spring. The order to arrest Hitler and occupy all government buildings, including the chancellery, had been on General Franz Halder's desk at noon, and General Erwin von Witzleben was standing by to witness his signature, when his orderly entered with a bulletin: Chamberlain and Daladier would travel to Munich for further talks. Halder later testified: "I therefore took back the order of execution because, owing to this fact, the entire basis for the action had been taken away." The next day, as Telford Taylor writes, "the four men of Munich danced their quadrille."[256]

Webster defines "munich" as "an instance of unresisting compliance with and capitulation to the demands of an aggressor nation." Actually, nothing of great consequence happened at the Munich Conference. The Czechs' fate had been decided at Berchtesgaden and Godesberg. Britain's participation was a gross violation of parliamentary government. Unnoticed after the prime minister had been swept out of the chamber by hysterical MPs was a singular omission. His (and Horace Wilson's) inconclusive, ambiguous, highly questionable exchanges with the German führer had never been subjected to a House debate. The entire cabinet assembled at the airport the next morning to wish him luck, but neither the cabinet (including the foreign secretary) nor Parliament had shared in the formation of the policy that led to Munich.

At Munich the prime minister was clearly delighted to see Hitler again, eager to stand at his side. Here he made a cardinal error. Afterward he happily wrote his sister that the Astors' son William, recently returned from a trip to Berlin, had the impression that "Hitler definitely liked me & thought he could do business with me." This was true in the sense that an armed robber thinks he can do business with a bank teller. In fact, Hitler had taken a strong personal dislike to Chamberlain, who impressed him as an "insignificant" man. The Führer dealt with him because he believed him to be infinitely malleable. Other men in Parliament, he knew, were dangerous. On the eve of Munich he said he was "fully aware" that one day Chamberlain might be replaced by Churchill, whose "aim would be to unleash at once a new world war against Germany."[257]

* * *

The Führer was right. He had never met Churchill, but he understood him, as Winston understood Hitler. Walter Lippmann observed that the supreme qualification for high office is temperament, not intellect, and on that level the two men had more in common than either would have acknowledged. The countless millions spellbound by Winston's genius would angrily reject any comparison of the two. Nevertheless they were mirror images of one another. Since the embattled defender of Western civilization was the one who was ultimately successful, his vision has prevailed. What would have happened had victory gone to the Nazi leader doesn't bear thinking about. In the mid-1980s a poll reported that a large majority of *Germans* believe the worst thing that could have happened to them would have been the triumph of the Third Reich.[258]

Satan was once angelic; he and God had much in common. Similarly, both the Führer and his English nemesis were born demagogues. Each believed in the supremacy of his race and in national destiny; each had artistic talent — Churchill had more, but Hitler, though dismissed as a shallow painter of picture postcards, was a charismatic figure moved by dark but profound passions, the man whose voice at Nuremberg inspired men to lay down their lives, shouting *"Heil, Hitler!"* as they died. The inescapable fact is that Hitler and Churchill both were ruled not by reason but by intuition.

Chamberlain, the businessman, accustomed to the friendship of other good fellows who met on the level and parted on the square, understood neither man. The P.M. respected success. He assumed that any man who had risen to rule the most powerful nation on the Continent was a man with whom he could deal. Neville seems to have been oblivious to the fact that nearly everyone who had tried to bargain with this extraordinary man had been murdered, sent to a concentration camp, or hounded into exile.

Chamberlain could not have comprehended the depth of the horrors plumbed by the Third Reich. The Führer vowed that restoring their beloved homeland to the mistreated Sudetendeutsche was his last claim, and Chamberlain believed him. The P.M. had not been deceptive in his "faraway country" broadcast. Although the "Czech problem" had been on his desk for months, to him Czechoslovakia remained precisely that: a problem, not a land inhabited by real people. He knew nothing of eastern European geography, not to mention the Serbs, Croats, Slavs, Slovaks, Czechs, Poles, and gypsies inhabiting the region; he disregarded all the warnings of the FO and swallowed everything he was told by the Reich's *Kriegsherr*.

Churchill knew better. He had studied Adolf Hitler's career with intensity, and remembered his remarkable history of broken promises. When the

Führer broke the Versailles treaty he promised to honor Germany's signature on Locarno; when he broke the Locarno Pact — long before the Sudetenland became a synonym for crisis — he had sworn that the Rhineland would be his last territorial claim. When he sent Wehrmacht bayonets into Austria he grandly guaranteed Czechoslovakia's borders. His position had subtly evolved; he was interested only in Germans, he said — including, of course, Germans living beyond the borders of the Reich. But over the past two thousand years Europe had become a mix, racially, culturally, and ethnically. As Duff Cooper observed, "There are Germans in Switzerland, in Denmark, and in Alsace; I think that one of the few countries in Europe in which there are no Germans is Spain, and there are rumors that Germany has taken an interest in that country."[259]

Churchill's sources in the Reich reported that the great Ruhr munitions factories, on orders from Berlin, continued to work around the clock. In Kiel and Hamburg new U-boats slid into the water like the litters of an incredibly fertile sea monster; Luftwaffe observation planes, equipped with long-range cameras, overflew eastern Europe, Scandinavia, the Low Countries, even France. Churchill carried graphs when he entered the House of Commons now. They revealed that the gap between British and German arsenals was widening. Since fighting was inevitable, he argued, better that it come now, with France prepared to meet her treaty obligations to Czechoslovakia, thus confronting German strategists with the specter of a two-front war.

Now the crisis had reached its climax. Violet Bonham Carter recalled Churchill's mood then. "He rightly mistrusted Chamberlain, who, he was convinced, was still searching desperately for a way out" when no honorable way existed. That same September 29, as the so-called Four-Power Meeting began in Bavaria, the Focus group lunched in the Savoy's Pinafore Room. Violet saw that "Winston's face was dark with forboding. I could see he feared the worst, as I did. I finally suggested that during the afternoon a few of us should draft a telegram to the Prime Minister adjuring him to make no further concessions at the expense of the Czechs and warning him that if he did so he would have to fight the House of Commons on his return." The wire was to be signed by, among others, Churchill, Lord (Robert) Cecil, Attlee, Archie Sinclair, Eden, Liddell Hart, Lloyd George, and Lord Lloyd.[260]

It was drafted — after eliminating the threat — and at 7:00 P.M. they again met at the Savoy. Winston then called for the signatures, and Sinclair, Lloyd, and Cecil came quickly forward. But some who had said they would come had not. Eden, reached by telephone, declined to permit the use of his name. Attlee was then phoned. He, too, refused; he said he would need the approval of his party. As Nicolson wrote in his diary, they "sat there gloomily realising that nothing could be done. Even Winston seemed to have lost his fighting spirit. . . . So far as one can see, Hitler gets everything he wants."[261]

It was decided to send no telegram. One by one the group drifted away. Violet wrote: "Winston remained, sitting in his chair immobile, like a man of stone. I saw the tears in his eyes. I could feel the iron entering his soul. His last attempt to salvage what was left of honor and good faith had failed." She spoke bitterly of those who refused to put their names to their principles. Then Churchill spoke. He said: *"What are they made of?* The day is not far off when it won't be signatures we'll have to give but lives — the lives of millions. Can we survive? Do we deserve to do so when there's no courage anywhere?"[262]

Shortly after noon that Thursday — as Churchill, heavy with despair, lunched at the Savoy — Hitler led his guests from a buffet at the Führerbau (the working headquarters of the Nazi party) and into his private office, to determine the future of a country in a conference from which that nation's elected leaders had been excluded. Two Czechs — Hubert Masařík and Vojtech Mastny — were in the city as "observers" attached to the British delegation, but when Chamberlain weakly suggested they attend the discussions the Führer had said *"Nein!"* The issue was then dropped, with the tacit understanding that the delegation from Prague would be informed of the Hitler-Chamberlain-Mussolini-Daladier decisions later.

"O Oysters, come and walk with us!"
The Walrus did beseech.
"A pleasant walk, a pleasant talk,
Along the briny beach."

Mussolini produced a memorandum, ostensibly drawn up by him but actually the work of Göring, Neurath, and Weizsäcker. The Englishmen — Horace Wilson had again accompanied Chamberlain — assumed that it was a base for negotiations, but Hitler did not negotiate. He simply repeated, over and over, what he was going to take, when he would take it, and what he might or might not do with it. Nevertheless, the men from Paris and London kept battering away, through the evening and past midnight. At 1:00 A.M. Chamberlain capitulated. Virtually all of the claims Hitler had made in the past were accepted, including many he could never have won by force of arms. He now held the strategic center of Europe. The agreement signed in the early hours of September 30 (though it was dated September 29) specified that Czechoslovakia should begin evacuation of the Sudetenland at once. All Czechs in the Sudetenland must be gone — no one thought to ask where they might go — by October 10. Their departure would be supervised by an international commission which would also decide when plebiscites should be held, determine where the borders of the rump Czech state should be drawn, and see to it that all "existing installations" remain intact in Czechoslovakia's lost territories. Poland, exploiting the turmoil, was placated by a slice of the pie, some three hundred square miles of Teschen Silesia. If other "problems of Polish and Hungarian minorities in Czechoslovakia" were not settled by negotiations with Prague, they would "form the subject" of another four-power meeting.[263]

The proceedings ended briskly, with efficient young German diplomats tidying up and disposing of loose strings. It had been a disgraceful business, but only Daladier and François-Poncet saw it for what it really was. The French premier was glum and silent; his ambassador to Germany, mortified by his country's sellout of a faithful ally, was overheard by Ciano as he spoke in a voice broken by shame: *"Violà comme la France traite les seuls alliés qui lui étaient restés fidèles."* ("See how France treats the only allies who remained faithful to her.")[264]

As they were about to break up Horace Wilson gave a little start and asked: "What to do about the Czechs?"[265]

"But wait a bit," the Oysters cried,
"Before we have our chat;
For some of us are out of breath,
And all of us are fat!"

While others discussed who was to inform the Czechs and how to assure their cooperation, the P.M. and Hitler discussed the Reich's economic difficulties. Then the Führer consented to glance at a joint declaration regarding future Anglo-German relations which the prime minister had brought with him. This, for Chamberlain, was the high point in the conference. According to him, "As the interpreter translated the words into German, Hitler frequently ejaculated *'Ja, Ja,'* and at the end he said, 'Yes, I will certainly sign it; when shall we do it?' I said 'Now,' and we went at once to the writing table, and put our signatures to the two copies which I had brought with me." Neither Schmidt nor Alec Douglas-Home, Chamberlain's parliamentary private secretary, who were looking on, shared the prime minister's conviction that the Führer was as elated as Chamberlain thought him to be. Schmidt wrote afterward that Hitler agreed to sign "with a certain reluctance," because the wording was too vague to be described as a commitment, and "to please Chamberlain." Douglas-Home thought he signed "perfunctorily." Compared with his signature on other documents, this one was careless, even sloppy.[266]

At 2:30 A.M. the P.M. joined a delegation to tell the Czechs — who were being held in the Regina Hotel, prisoners, in effect, of the Gestapo — the fate of their country. Hubert Masařík, who was given the text to read aloud, later said that the French seemed "embarrassed." Certainly the agreement was an occasion for Allied embarrassment. To the Czechs the terms were shocking. Yet Chamberlain, according to Masařík, "yawned without ceasing and with no show of embarrassment." Both he and Daladier said Czech approval was not, strictly speaking, necessary. It was indeed irrelevant; the agreement was final. According to Horace Wilson's later notes, Mastny was given "a pretty broad hint that . . . the best course for his Government was to accept what was clearly a considerable improvement upon the German Godesberg memorandum." It wasn't. Hitler had yielded nothing. Every outrageous demand he had made at Godesberg had been meekly met.[267]

As the Czechs were facing those who had betrayed them, Churchill had returned to the Savoy, joining fellow members of the Other Club for a very late dinner, to be followed by a meeting. Sleep was out of the question. According to Colin Coote, a member of the Other Club and also a member of the *Times* staff, they were awaiting the first editions of London's newspapers, which were expected to be carrying the Munich settlement. In the meantime, Coote remembered, discussion of the Godesberg terms and whether the P.M. would succeed in modifying these demands sparked "a violent argument. One began to understand why, in the House of Commons, a red line on the carpet, just beyond rapier reach of the opposite bench, marks the limit beyond which the speaker must not stray." One defender of Chamberlain was insulted so grossly that he left the table and, upon reaching home, sent a letter of resignation from the club.[268]

"Winston," Coote remembered, "was snarling and clawing at the two unhappy ministers [First Lord Duff Cooper and Walter Elliot, secretary for Scotland]. . . . One could always tell when he was deeply moved, because a minor defect in his palate gave an echoing timbre to his voice. On this occasion it was not an echo, but a supersonic boom." He asked them: "How could honourable men with wide experience and fine records in the Great War condone a policy so cowardly? It was sordid, squalid, sub-human, and," he said, "suicidal. . . . The sequel to the sacrifice of honour" would be "the sacrifice of lives, our people's lives." In his memoirs Cooper charges, quite rightly, that Churchill was fouling him. He agreed with Winston, but since he was still a cabinet minister, he felt it was "honorable to defend them for the last time."[269]

At last one man produced his watch and remarked that the early papers must be on the streets. The member pocketed his watch, left, and returned with a stop press. Duff Cooper snatched it from him and read the terms out loud, according to Coote's account "with obvious anger and disgust." Then he rose and departed without a word. Behind him he left silence. In Coote's words: "Nobody attempted to defend them. Humiliation took almost material shape." Churchill left with Richard Law, a young Tory MP. They passed the open door of a restaurant, from which issued the sounds of loud laughter. It was "packed," Law remembered long afterward, "and everyone was very gay. I was acutely conscious of the brooding figure beside me." As they turned away Winston muttered: "Those poor people. They little know what they will have to face." In the darkness they may have passed E. M. Forster, an English writer who resembled Churchill in only two traits: both possessed genius and remarkable intuition. Forster heard of the agreement in Munich and wrote that he "trailed about reading the notices, some of which had already fallen into the gutter." It was "good news," he wrote, "and it ought to have brought great joy; it did bring joy to the House of Commons. But unimportant and unpractical people often foresee the future more clearly than do those who are engaged in shaping it, and I knew at once that the news was only good in patches. Peace flapped from the posters, and not upon the wings of angels."[270]

Later in the morning, still September 30, Winston, Clemmie, and Lord Cecil seriously discussed gathering a group of friends who shared their wrath, marching to No. 10, and heaving a brick through a window. By then the two Czech delegates in the Regina had agreed not to fight. The need for their approval was urgent. By 5:00 P.M. that day an international commission would convene in Berlin to fix the details for evacuation of the first zone of the Sudetenland, which was to commence October 1, and the transfer of policing power from local officials to the German Wehrmacht.

The Czechs were angry, of course — they would have been certifiable otherwise — and the Frenchmen were the focus of their wrath. Chamberlain, to them, was contemptible. Masařík's narrative concluded: "The atmosphere was becoming oppressive for everyone present. It had been explained to us in a sufficiently brutal manner, and that by a Frenchman, that this was a sentence without right of appeal and without possibility of modification. Mr. Chamberlain did not conceal his fatigue. After the text had been read, we were given a second slightly corrected map. We said 'Good-bye' and left. The Czechoslovak Republic as fixed by the frontiers of 1918 had ceased to exist."[271]

"I weep for you," the Walrus said:
"I deeply sympathize."
With sobs and tears he sorted out
Those of the largest size,
Holding his pocket-handkerchief
Before his streaming eyes.

Masařík had not, however, formally accepted Czechoslovakia's subjugation. Nor could he; that decision had to be made in Prague. But he knew all hope had fled. The Führer didn't even have to send an ultimatum to Prague — Englishmen did it for him. Frank Ashton-Gwatkin, the member of the British delegation who had been given this dubious honor, arrived from Munich September 30, breakfasted with Lieutenant Colonel H. C. T. Stronge, the British military attaché, and showed him the Munich Agreement. Stronge said Czechoslovakia could never accept such terms; it would mean a sacrifice of their defenses, leaving them helpless. Ashton-Gwatkin said they *had* to accept. Stronge, to use his own word, was "staggered."[272]

Later in the day, after heated arguments with his advisers, military and civilian, Beneš capitulated. He also resigned five days later, but decided, at the urging of his ministers, to speak to the entire nation in a 7:00 P.M. broadcast, telling them what lay in the hearts of those they had elected to govern them. "They wished," Churchill later wrote, "to register their protest against a decision in which they had no part." On the air Beneš said that he remained "what I have always been, a convinced democrat." That was why he was stepping down; he thought it "best not to disturb the new European constellation which is arising." (He would be succeeded by an anti-Semitic banker who, in the words of one newspaper, "enjoys the confidence of Germany.") Beneš said: "Do not expect from me a single word of recrimination. But this I will say," — here he came as close to bitterness as a gentle man could — "that the sacrifices demanded from us were immeasurably great, and immeasurably unjust. This the nation will never forget, even though they have borne these sacrifices quietly." He departed to set up a government-in-exile in London. The SS moved in swiftly. No one knows how many Czechs were murdered in the week that followed, though it has been estimated that more than half of them were Jews. Exact figures were unavailable; with the Führer's men reigning over the Sudetenland, the news blackout was absolute.[273]

But answer came there none —
And this was scarcely odd, because
They'd eaten every one.

* * *

The German generals, who had been sweating blood, could scarcely believe their good luck. They were unanimously agreed that had the British and French stood up to Hitler, and had Hitler invaded Czechoslovakia, the Reich would have been swiftly defeated. All this came out at Nuremberg. Keitel, chief of the OKW, testified: "From a purely military point of view we lacked the means for an attack which involved the piercing of the [Czech] frontier fortifications." Fritz Erich von Manstein, Germany's most brilliant field commander (and not a defendant at Nuremberg), said that "had Czechoslovakia defended herself, we would have been held up by her fortifications, for we did not have the means to break through." And Alfred Jodl, the key general at OKW, taking the witness stand in his own defense, told the International Military Tribunal: "It was out of the question with five fighting divisions and seven reserve divisions in the western fortification [Siegfried Line] . . . to hold out against 100 French divisions. That was militarily impossible." Churchill later wrote that he had "always believed that Beneš was wrong to yield. He should have defended his fortress line. Once fighting had begun, in my opinion at that time, France would have moved to his aid in a surge of national passion, and Britain would have rallied to France almost immediately." The chance had been tragically missed.[274]

Nevertheless, Hitler, returning from Munich on his private train, was not rejoicing. To his SS honor guard he ranted that Chamberlain had *"meinen Einzug in Prag verdorben"* ("spoiled my entry into Prague"). In his grand strategy the seizures of Austria and Czechoslovakia were to be the opening moves in a tremendous campaign for lebensraum in the east, to be followed in the west by the conquest of the Low Countries and France. Only ten days earlier he had told the Hungarian prime minister that the wisest course was *"die Tschechoslowakei zu zerschlagen"* ("to destroy Czechoslovakia"). The sole danger was that the Czechs might buckle at the first threat. Now the British had done the buckling for them; Chamberlain had deprived the *Kriegsherr* of his first battlefield victory.[275]

On his flight home Daladier was also out of sorts, desolate and despairing. He later told Amery that as they landed in Paris and taxied toward the terminal he turned up his coat collar, to protect his face from the rotten eggs he expected when he came within range of the crowd. To his astonishment there were no eggs, no offensive shouts of *"Merde!"* and *"Nous sommes trahis!"* He paused halfway down the steps, dumbfounded. They were actually cheering him — shouting *"Vive Daladier!" "Vive la Paix!" "Vive la France!"* — greeting him as though he had won a great victory. Daladier was a man completely without vanity. He turned to Léger and whispered,

"Les cons!" ("Fools!"). There were a few grumblers; one man muttered, *"Vive la France malgré tout."* Yet for the most part the gaiety was unqualified. It was also mindless. Because the Reich no longer need face the formidable Czech army in the east, Munich had been a catastrophe for France. Hitler's empire had increased its strength, and could quickly field twice as many soldiers. Nevertheless, the Chamber of Deputies ratified the Munich Agreement 535 to 75. Bonnet told an interviewer: "Yes, we have a treaty with the Czechs, and France remains faithful to her sacred word. Czechoslovakia wasn't invaded, was she?"[276]

Nestling in Chamberlain's pocket was the document he prized; today it lies in an obscure file at the Imperial War Museum, possibly the last place he would have had in mind. At the time that it was famous, Harold Nicolson denounced it in Parliament as "that bit of paper" which had betrayed the Reich's neighbors and threatened the security of England. In reality the document was meaningless. That was why Hitler had signed it. The first paragraph declared that Anglo-German relations were "of the first importance for the two countries and for Europe"; the second that the Munich Agreement and the Anglo-German Naval Agreement of 1935 were "symbolic of the desire of our two peoples never to go to war with one another again"; and the third that both the prime minister of Great Britain and the Führer of the Third Reich intended to use the "method of consultation" in questions "that may concern our two countries," because of their mutual determination "to continue our efforts to remove possible sources of difference, and thus to contribute to assure the peace of Europe." That is all. It lacked even the ringing affirmation of nonaggression treaties; instead it expressed the *desire* of their peoples not to war on one another. But for a few days in the quirky autumn of 1938 — the same season that Orson Welles's radio drama of Martians landing in New Jersey sent thousands of Americans heading for the hills — people believed that Chamberlain had done rather a good thing. Britons, haunted by the dread that war might be declared at any hour, felt that they had been granted a reprieve. They cast about for ways to express their gratitude. Some became hysterical.[277]

The P.M. had been "pleasantly tired" during the flight home, but once he saw the size of the crowd awaiting him at Heston Airport, he felt as though he had shed fifty years. To his entourage he seemed as excited and energetic as a youth returning from an adventure. They cheered. He read his three pitiful paragraphs, and they cheered louder, shouting, "Good old Neville!" and singing, "For he's a jolly good fellow." Then a courier wearing royal livery appeared and handed him a message from the King, asking him to come straight to Buckingham Palace, "so that I can express to you personally my most heartfelt congratulations. . . . In the meantime, this letter brings the warmest of welcomes to one who, by his patience and determination, has earned the lasting gratitude of his fellow-countrymen throughout the Empire." Afterward, Neville wrote Ida: "Even the descriptions of the papers give no idea of the scenes in the streets as I drove from Heston to the Palace. They were lined from one end to the other with people of every class, shouting themselves hoarse, leaping on the running board, banging on the windows, and thrusting their hands into the car to be shaken."[278]

But it was in Downing Street that the adulation peaked, and there — though it was not immediately obvious to the crowd — Chamberlain overreached himself. In the lore of every nation there are scenes, phrases, and deeds which live in the popular imagination. But an event, a speech, or a legend can never be repeated, for part of its appeal is that it is unique. That is why there cannot be another Arthur, another Joan of Arc, another Lincoln. It also explains why Chamberlain's last public act on his day of glory was a blunder.

Benjamin Disraeli's supreme diplomatic triumph came in 1878, at the Congress of Berlin. Unlike Chamberlain's Munich, Berlin was a genuine contribution to European peace. The states of eastern Europe were at each other's throats; the Russian diplomats were bumbling from bad to worse; even Bismarck couldn't broker a general settlement. Disraeli could and did. His mastery of divergent cultures permitted him to take the map apart and rebuild it, throttling several wars before they could break out and ending a full-fledged conflict between the Russians and the Turks. The memory of that feat sixty years earlier was on many minds that fall evening in 1938, including Chamberlain's. He wrote his sister that he spoke to the great crowd below "from the same window, I believe, as that from which Dizzy announced peace with honour 60 years ago." (He was wrong; Disraeli's declaration was made in the House of Commons on July 16, 1878.) Now his wife said, "Neville, go up to the window and repeat history by saying peace in our time." He replied icily, "No, I do not do that kind of thing." Then he did it. Waving the piece of paper he and Hitler had signed, he called to the dense throng below: "My good friends, this is the second time in our history that there has come back from Germany to Downing Street peace with honor. I believe it is peace for our time." On the whole, public men are wise to avoid extravagant predictions. Very soon Chamberlain would have reason to regret this one.[279]

Meanwhile, however, the combers of admiration and praise continued to break at his feet. "No conqueror returning from a victory on the battlefield," *The Times* trumpeted, "has been adorned with nobler laurels." *Paris-Soir* offered him "a corner of French soil" where he could cast for trout, his favorite sport, than which "there could be no more fruitful image of peace." Fifty Englishmen wrote to Printing House Square, calling for a national fund in Chamberlain's honor. Those who had cheered his departure for Munich felt vindicated. Nicolson wrote of an exchange with Margot Asquith. She had said: "Now, Harold, you must agree that he is a great man." He replied, "Not at all." "You are as bad as Violet," she snapped; "he is the greatest Englishman that ever lived." Yet even Nicolson confessed in his diary that he momentarily felt "an immense sense of *physical* relief, in that I shall not be afraid tonight of the German bombs."[280]

But, he added "my moral anxieties are in no way diminished." After the cheering, a few thoughtful men, in the quietude of reflection, read the terms of Munich and were troubled. Halifax had sensed what was coming; in the triumphant ride from Heston he had astounded the prime minister by suggesting that he form a national government, bringing Churchill and Eden back and inviting Labour to join. Chamberlain replied that he would "think it over," but there is no evidence that he did. Lord Lloyd, who had been in the roaring throng outside No. 10, remembered feeling "elated" until Chamberlain said "peace with honor." Then "my heart sank; it was the worst possible choice of words, for I realized that he had sold honor to buy peace."[281]

The most sensational defection from Chamberlain's entrenched majority was that of his first lord of the Admiralty, Alfred Duff Cooper, "the pioneer," Conservative backbencher Vyvyan Adams called him, "along the nation's way back from hysteria to reason." Revolted by Chamberlain's fawning over Hitler, his sellout of the Czechs, and his smug pride in the piece of trumpery he and Hitler had signed, on Saturday, October 1, the day after the prime minister's return, Cooper resigned. Chamberlain, Duff Cooper wrote, was "as glad to be rid of me as I was determined to go." Lady Diana Cooper recalled that she "telephoned the news to Winston. His voice was broken with emotion. I could hear him cry." Churchill exulted that "one minister alone stood forth. . . . At the moment of Mr. Chamberlain's overwhelming mastery of public opinion, he thrust his way through the exulting throng to declare his total disagreement with its leader."[282]

The first doubts were struggling to the surface, but it was too soon for them to coalesce. Although some MPs were already wrestling with their consciences, they would have to put themselves on record in just five days, the evening of October 5, at the close of a three-day debate, when the issue before them would be: "That this House approves the policy of His Majesty's Government by which war was averted in the recent crisis and supports their efforts to secure a lasting peace." The vote was never in doubt, with the huge Conservative margin Baldwin had won three years earlier. But even those Conservatives who had remained doggedly faithful to their leader were becoming troubled. After the vote, Sir Alan Herbert, an independent member, wrote: "My soul revolted at the thought of another, and, I was convinced by many expert opinions, a much worse war. . . . But, 'wishful thinker,' 'anxious hoper,' 'old soldier,' or 'Christian believer' — what you will — I wanted Mr. Chamberlain to be right, and keep the peace successfully. . . . I voted sadly for Munich; and the whole thing made me ill."

FOUR

VORTEX

On the Saturday before Parliament's Munich debate, Winston was at Chartwell, vigorously slapping bricks into place and awaiting a visitor, a twenty-six-year-old BBC producer, unknown then but destined to become infamous in the early 1950s. He was Guy Burgess, who with Kim Philby and Donald Maclean — all three upper class, all Cambridge men — would be cleared to review the U.S. government's most sensitive documents, including the Central Intelligence Agency's daily traffic and dispatches from Korea. In fact they would be Soviet intelligence agents. Burgess's notoriety lay far in the future that sunbright morning, however, when Churchill, in a blue boilersuit (a forerunner of his wartime "siren suit"), left his bricks to greet his visitor, a trowel still in one hand. The meeting was purposeless; Winston had been scheduled to give BBC listeners a half-hour talk on the Mediterranean, but when the Czech crisis erupted he had asked that the program be canceled. Burgess was keen to meet him anyhow, however, and Churchill, feeling that was the least he could do, had agreed.

In the beginning he was gruff. He complained, Burgess recollected afterward, that he had been "very badly treated in the matter of political broadcasts and that he was always muzzled by the BBC. . . . He went on to say that he would be even more muzzled in the future, since the BBC seemed to have passed under the control of the Government." According to Burgess, Winston said he had just received a message from Beneš — he always called him "Herr Beans" — asking for his "advice and assistance." But, he asked, "what answer shall I give? — for answer I shall and must. . . . Here am I, an old man without power and without party. What advice can I give, what assistance can I proffer?" Burgess stammered that he could offer his eloquence. Pleased, Winston said: "My eloquence! Ah, yes . . . that Herr Beans can rely on in full and indeed" — he paused and winked — "some would say in overbounding measure. That I can offer him. But what else, Mr. Burgess, what else can I offer him?" Burgess, usually garrulous, was tongue-tied. Moment succeeded moment, but he could think of nothing to say. He saw a great man, the scourge of fascism, caged by frustration. Then Churchill spoke. "You are silent, Mr. Burgess. You are rightly silent. What else can I offer Herr Beans? Only one thing: my only son, Randolph, who is already training to be an officer."[1]

Throughout 1938 Churchill's warnings had grown more and more persistent, and less and less effective. His mots were seldom passed along now because his targets, the "Men of Munich," as Fleet Street called them, were believed to have prevented a general European war. In almost any gathering, it would have been indiscreet to remark: "Have you heard what Winston says about Neville? 'In the depths of that dusty soul there is nothing but abject surrender.' " Or: "Churchill says the Government had to choose between war and shame. They chose shame. They will get war, too." Yet some hit home. Malcolm MacDonald, son of Ramsay and minister for the colonies and Dominions under Chamberlain, recalls with discomfort but also amusement how, during a speech on the future of Palestine, he was moved to say that "I cannot remember a time when I was not told stories of Jerusalem and Bethlehem, the birthplace of the Prince of Peace." And as he paused for breath Churchill muttered: "I always thought he was born in Birmingham."[2]

At 3:34 P.M. on Monday, October 3, 1938, Parliament opened its debate on the Munich Agreement. In the observance of custom, Duff Cooper, as a resigning minister, spoke first. "The Prime Minister," he said, "has believed in addressing Herr Hitler through the language of sweet reasonableness. I have believed that he was more open to the language of the mailed fist. . . . We have taken away the defences of Czechoslovakia in the same breath as we have guaranteed them, as though you were to deal a man a mortal blow and at the same time insure his life."

Chamberlain, he noted, attached "considerable importance" to the document he and Hitler had signed at Munich. "But," he asked, "what do those words mean? Do they mean that Herr Hitler will take 'no' for an answer? He has never taken it yet. Or do they mean that he believes that he will get away with this, as he has got away with everything else, without fighting, by well-timed bluff, bluster and blackmail? Otherwise it means very little." Duff Cooper ended: "I have ruined, perhaps, my political career. But that is a little matter. I have retained something which is to me of great value. I can still walk about the world with my head erect."[3]

The House was deeply moved by Cooper's resignation speech. Antony Winn, the *Times* lobby correspondent, reported that it had been well received. Dawson, who hadn't been there, tore up Winn's piece and wrote an account of his own, dismissing the speech as "a damp squib," and headed the story "From our lobby correspondent." Winn resigned.[4]

The prime minister, following Duff Cooper, paid ritualistic tribute to him and ignored his arguments. Chamberlain had already set forth his own views to the cabinet earlier in the day, and the kindest interpretation of his position is that he had forgotten he was prime minister and thought himself once more watchdog of the Treasury. Ever since his stewardship as chancellor of the Exchequer, he had told the cabinet, he had been haunted by the possibility that "the burden of armaments might break our backs." Therefore he had sought "to resolve the causes . . . responsible for the armaments race." Now, after his agreement with the German führer, England was in "a more hopeful position." The next steps would be further agreements "which would stop the arms race." The effort to strengthen the country's defenses should proceed, but that was "not the same thing as to say that as a thank offering for the present détente we should at once embark on a great increase in our armaments programme." His goal, he now told the House, had been "to work for the pacification of Europe, for the removal of those suspicions and those animosities which have so long poisoned the air. The path which leads to appeasement is long and bristles with obstacles." Czechoslovakia had been "the latest and perhaps the most dangerous" of these obstacles, but "now that we have got past it, I feel that it may be possible to make further progress along the road to sanity."[5]

The House did not hear him in silence. When he spoke proudly of the release by the Czechs of Sudetendeutsche prisoners, one MP called: "What about the kidnapped Czechs?" When he spoke of his "profound feeling of sympathy" for Czechoslovakia, several members cried, "Shame!" He replied: "I have done nothing to be ashamed of. Let those who have, hang their heads. We must feel profound sympathy for a small and gallant nation in the hour of their national grief and loss." A backbencher interrupted him: "It is an insult to say it." He told the House that "the real triumph" of Munich "is that it has shown that representatives of four great Powers can find it possible to agree on a way of carrying out a difficult and delicate operation by discussion instead of by force of arms, and thereby they have averted a catastrophe which would have ended civilisation as we have known it."[6]

Watching the prime minister, Harold Nicolson thought: "He is obviously tired and irritable and the speech does not go down well. Then up gets Anthony Eden. I felt at first that he was not coming out strongly enough, but he was getting the House on his side before opening the attack. When it came, it was superb." Eden doubted that "the events of the last few days . . . constitute the beginning of better things, as my right honorable friend

[Chamberlain] hopes." Instead, he believed, "they only give us a breathing space, perhaps of six months or less, before the next crisis is upon us."[7]

Attlee, coming next, declared that they were "in the midst of a tragedy. We have felt humiliation. This has not been a victory for reason and humanity. It has been a victory for brute force." Sinclair noted that the P.M. had called the Munich terms a victory for self-determination; it was, he said, "a plain travesty of self-determination," because although the areas ceded were inhabited by "a substantial minority" of Germans, they *were* a minority, and many of them wanted no part of the Reich. The "irruption of German troops," he predicted, accurately, "will sweep before them a whole crowd of refugees who certainly would have been in favour of remaining in those territories. There is no justice or self-determination about that." Attacks on the settlement by Amery, Macmillan, and Bracken followed.[8]

Churchill sat, silent and immobile, for nearly three days of debate. He was scheduled to speak Wednesday after Sir John Simon, the chancellor of the Exchequer, wound up for the government. Simon declared that Chamberlain would be vindicated by time: "It can only be for history to decide hereafter whether the things done in Munich the other day lead . . . to better things, or whether the prognostications of increasing evil will prove to be justified." The crisis, he said, had been a splendid experience for the British people. Next time they would know precisely what to do. The Munich terms were "a vast improvement over the Godesberg Memorandum," he insisted. Everyone in the chamber knew that was untrue, and he finally acknowledged that His Majesty's Government was "deeply conscious today that while war has been avoided, Herr Hitler has again achieved the substance of his immediate and declared aim without declaring war."[9]

It was 5:10 P.M. when the Speaker recognized Churchill, and as Winston rose the mood of the House resembled that of Spaniards when the bull lunges into the arena. Before he had spoken a dozen words the turmoil began, and because nothing he said was conciliatory, it continued throughout the forty-nine minutes of his speech, led by Nancy Astor's cries of "Rude! Rude!" Sweeping the House with a hard stare, chin down, thumbs in his waistcoat pockets, feet solidly planted far apart, he declared that he would begin by saying "the most unpopular and most unwelcome thing. . . . We have sustained a total and unmitigated defeat, and . . . France has suffered even more than we have." Nancy called out, "Nonsense," and he whirled on her: "When the Noble Lady cries 'Nonsense' she could not have heard the Chancellor of the Exchequer admit in his illuminating and comprehensive speech just now that . . . the utmost . . . the Prime Minister has been able to secure by all his immense exertions, by all the great efforts and mobilisation which took place in this country, and by all the anguish and strain through which we have passed in this country, the utmost he has been able to gain has been —" He was interrupted by cries of "Peace!" ". . . the utmost he has been able to gain for Czechoslovakia and in the matters which were in dispute has been that the German dictator, instead of snatching his victuals from the table, has been content to have them served to him course by course." He saw no point in distinguishing between the positions reached at Berchtesgaden, Godesberg, and Munich. "They will be very simply epitomized, if the House will permit me to vary the metaphor. One pound was demanded at the pistol's point. When it was given, two pounds were demanded at the pistol's point. Finally, the dictator consented to take one pound, seventeen shillings and sixpence and the rest in promises of good will for the future." The terms Chamberlain had brought back with him could have been reached "through the ordinary diplomatic channels at any time during the summer. And I will say this, that I believe the Czechs, left to themselves and told they were going to get no help from the Western Powers, would have been able to make better terms than they have got."

He reviewed Hitler's successive aggressions and why all efforts to check him had failed: "There can never be absolute certainty that there will be a fight if one side is determined that it will give way completely." He himself had "always held the view that the maintenance of peace depends upon the accumulation of deterrents against the aggressor, coupled with a sincere effort to redress grievances." France and Britain — "especially if they had maintained a close contact with Russia, which certainly was not done" — could have influenced the "smaller States of Europe, and I believe they could have determined the attitude of Poland." Indeed, their impact would have been felt in the Reich, giving "strength to all that intense desire for peace which the helpless German masses share with their British and French fellow men, and which, as we have been reminded, found a passionate and rarely permitted vent in the joyous manifestations with which the Prime Minister was acclaimed in Europe."

Alliances and deterrents "of Powers, great and small, ready to stand firm upon the front of law and for the ordered remedy of grievances . . . might well have been effective." He did not "think it fair to charge those who wished to see this course followed, and followed consistently and resolutely, with having wished for immediate war. Between submission and immediate war there was this third alternative, which gave a hope not only of peace but of justice." Naturally, for such a policy to succeed, Britain "should declare straight out and a long time beforehand that she would, with others, join to defend Czechoslovakia against an unprovoked aggression. His Majesty's Government refused to give that guarantee when it would have saved the situation, yet in the end they gave it when it was too late, and now, for the future, they renew it when they have not the slightest power to make it good.

All is over.
Silent, mournful, abandoned, broken,
Czechoslovakia recedes into darkness.

She has suffered in every respect
by her association with the Western democracies.

Plebiscites, he said, as defined in Hitler's Munich office, could not "amount in the slightest degree to a verdict of self-determination. It is a fraud and a farce to invoke that name. We in this country, as in other liberal and democratic countries, have a perfect right to exalt the principle of self-determination, but it comes ill out of the mouths of those in totalitarian States who deny even the smallest element of toleration to every section and creed within their bounds." In any event "this particular block of land, this mass of human beings to be handed over, has never expressed the desire to go under Nazi rule. I do not believe that even now, if their opinion could be asked, they would exercise such an option."

He asked: "What is the remaining position of Czechoslovakia? Not only are they politically mutilated, but, economically and financially, they are in complete confusion." Their banking and railroad nets were "severed and broken, their industries are curtailed, and the movement of their population is most cruel." He gave an example: "The Sudeten miners, who are all Czechs and whose families have lived in that area for centuries, must now flee into an area where there are hardly any mines left for them to work." He doubted — prophetically — that "in future the Czechoslovak State" could be "maintained as an independent entity. You will find that in a period of time which may be measured by years, but may be measured only by months, Czechoslovakia will be engulfed by the Nazi regime."

As a true Conservative, Churchill sought guidance "in the wisdom of the past, for all wisdom is not new wisdom." On holiday he had studied the reign of King Ethelred the Unready, and particularly "the rugged words of the Anglo-Saxon Chronicle, written a thousand years ago." He quoted a sentence: "All these calamities fell upon us because of evil counsel, because tribute was not offered to them at the right time nor yet were they resisted; but when they had done the most evil, then was peace made with them." So it was now: "We are in the presence of a disaster of the first magnitude which has befallen Great Britain and France. Do not let us blind ourselves to that. It must now be accepted that all the countries of Central and Eastern Europe will make the best terms they can with the triumphant Nazi Power." The democracies' loss of prestige, he told the House, beggared description. In Warsaw the British and French ambassadors sought to visit Colonel Józef Beck, Poland's foreign minister. "The door was shut in their faces." And what, he wondered, would be "the position of France and England this year and the year afterwards?" The German army probably outnumbered that of France now, "though not nearly so matured or perfected." There were, he said, unexplored options; unfortunately, none were encouraging. But what he found "unendurable" was "the sense of our country falling into the power, into the orbit and influence of Nazi Germany, and of our existence becoming dependent upon their good will or pleasure. . . . In a very few years, perhaps in a very few months, we shall be confronted with demands" which "may affect the surrender of territory or the surrender of liberty." A "policy of submission" would entail "restrictions" upon freedom of speech and the press. "Indeed, I hear it said sometimes now that we cannot allow the Nazi system of dictatorship to be criticised by ordinary, common English politicians."

He did not "grudge our loyal, brave people . . . the natural, spontaneous outburst of joy and relief" when they learned that war was not imminent, "but they should know the truth. They should know that there has been gross neglect and deficiency in our defences; they should know that we have sustained a defeat without a war, the consequences of which will travel far with us along our road; they should know that we have passed an awful milestone in our history, when the whole equilibrium of Europe has been deranged, and that the terrible words have for the time being been pronounced against the Western democracies: 'Thou art weighed in the balance and found wanting.'

And do not suppose that this is the end.
    This is only the beginning of the reckoning.

This is only the first sip —
    the first foretaste of a bitter cup
        which will be proffered to us year by year —

Unless —
    by a supreme recovery of our moral health and martial vigour,
        we arise again and take our stand for freedom,
            as in the olden time.[10]

❧ ❧

Lord Maugham called Churchill an "agitator" who should be "shot or hanged." *The Times* reported that Churchill had "treated a crowded House to prophesies which made Jeremiah appear an optimist" and referred patronizingly to his "dismal sincerity." His speech, according to the *Daily Express*, was "an alarmist oration by a man whose mind is soaked in the conquests of Marlborough," and his failure to support the government "weakens his influence among members of the Conservative Party." It did indeed; Robert Rhodes James notes that "the feeling against him in the party was now intense."[11]

Parliament was still dominated by the privileged classes and their dread of the Soviets, a fear which Hitler played like a Stradivarius, repeatedly citing as his principal aim *"zur Bekämpfung des Bolschewismus"* ("the fight against bolshevism"). But out beyond Westminster and Whitehall — in the Midlands, the mines, the Lake District; the tributaries of the Thames, Humber, and Severn; and the commercial cities of Liverpool, Manchester, Birmingham, Sheffield, Leeds, and Bristol — there, once the first flush of gratitude for peace had passed, Munich became more controversial. In the House of Commons, once the big guns of Chamberlain's critics had ceased fire — Duff Cooper, Eden, and Churchill as anchor man — the debate would proceed languidly.

In humbler neighborhoods it was another story, now that Spain had taught rank-and-file workmen that fascism could not be stopped without bloodshed. This awareness was by no means confined to them. In Mayfair, Park Lane, and Bloomsbury, the wives of many Conservative MPs denounced their husbands' support for Chamberlain's appeasements.

These heated exchanges were not confined to the United Kingdom — England, Scotland, Wales, and Northern Ireland. Britain was still the world's sole superpower. The repercussions of decisions made in Whitehall and Downing Street were felt almost everywhere — throughout the Dominions and even in the United States, which was bumbling about, playing blindman's buff with the twin games of pacifism and isolationism. Churchill afterward wrote: "Among the Conservatives, families and friends in intimate contact were divided by a degree the like of which I have never seen. Men and women, long bound by party ties, the social amenities, and family connections, glared at one another in scorn and anger." His daughter Mary remembers: "Looking back, it is difficult to describe the feelings of anger, shame, and bitterness felt by those who opposed the Munich Agreement." And Lady Diana Cooper recalled that "husbands and wives stopped speaking to one another, fathers and sons said unforgivable things to one another; it was as if the entire country was in labor, straining to give birth. And in a way it was."[12]

Harold Macmillan believed that the new, proud Britain was two years in gestation and had been conceived in the summer of 1938, when dissident Tories, mostly young, began to form factions critical of the Chamberlain government. The followers of Leo Amery were stronger once he broke with HMG, but the most visible group was still Eden's. Eden's followers were pursued by the press; many of their leaders had distinguished themselves in the war, and they were commonly regarded as the next generation of ministers. Taken as a whole, however, they were altogether too civil, too respectful of their elders, too reluctant to take firm stands, and far too unimaginative to acquire the élan and vigor of successful Young Turks. They avoided offending the prime minister; they carefully disassociated themselves from Churchill and his tiny band; when Duncan Sandys expressed interest in attending one of their meetings, he was told that his presence was not required. In these weaknesses they reflected the flaws of their leader. Eden's departure from the Foreign Office had been the political sensation of the season, but his resignation speech was so crafted to avoid affronting anyone that, as Macmillan noted, it "left Members somewhat uncertain as to what all the row was about." At a Queen's Hall rally protesting Munich, Eden's discretion, according to Liddell Hart, irritated the audience, which grew restless. As he sat down, Violet Bonham Carter proposed the ritualistic vote of gratitude, but later she said she felt more like moving a vote of censure. Eden's chief asset then was that he was neither Neville Chamberlain nor Winston Churchill.[13]

In retrospect it seems that once Britain had grasped the price Chamberlain paid for Hitler's signature, the people should have turned to Churchill. In time they did, but public opinion is slow to coalesce, and as winter deepened and 1939 arrived, England vacillated. Certainly the average Briton was appalled by the Czech sellout. A poll taken after Godesberg showed that two out of every three Englishmen had disapproved of the Anglo-French proposals as too generous to Germany. Walking home on the evening of September 22, Duff Cooper had encountered a "vast procession . . . marching down Whitehall crying 'Stand by the Czechs' and 'Chamberlain must go.' " Yet England was not ready for Churchill. Capitulation to Hitler was unpopular, but the revulsion against a renewal of trench warfare remained. Although Winston's repeated calls for a defense buildup had been intended to avoid war, it was clear to all that, once committed, he would relish a good fight. As a Labour candidate had charged in 1923, he was "militant to the fingertips." In the wake of Munich a House critic effectively quoted A. G. Gardiner's comment made thirty years earlier: "Churchill will write his name in history; take care that he does not write it in blood."[14]

* * *

Macmillan recalled that "Everyone knew that so great was the strength of the Government in the country that nothing could seriously shake them in Parliament. At our almost daily conferences with our friends, we had the gloomiest forebodings. The tide was, at present, too strong. It was flowing against us — especially Churchill." Increasingly the dissidents' meetings were furtive, almost conspiratorial. Nicolson confided to his wife that he had attended "a hush-hush meeting" of a dozen MPs, including Eden, Amery, Macmillan, Sidney Herbert, and Duff Cooper. They had "decided that we should not advertise ourselves as a group or even call ourselves a group." It is difficult to understand what they hoped to accomplish; they would "merely meet together from time to time, exchange views, and organise ourselves for a revolt if needed." But they were too timid and far too respectable to rebel; Nicolson characterized them as "all good Tories and sensible men. This group is distinct from the Churchill group. . . . I feel happier about this."[15]

Part of Churchill's particular alienation may be traced to his megalomania, a source of strength in public life but distasteful to many in private. Boothby remarked that " 'Thou shall have no other gods but me' has always been the first, and the most significant, of his Commandments." Desmond Morton wrote a journalist long afterward: "The full truth, I believe, is that Winston's 'friends' must be persons who were of use to him. The idea of having a friend who was of no practical use to him, but being a friend because he liked him, had no place." To be sure, Morton's comment was made late in life, when he had become embittered because Churchill had not given him a more prominent role in the wartime government. But even Violet Bonham Carter, who adored Winston, conceded that "He demanded partisanship from a friend, or, at the worst, acquiescence."[16]

However, that was not why parliamentarians who had come to share his views avoided him in the House. Churchill was considered dangerous. If an MP had ministerial ambitions, association with Winston could kill his chances, and what could be the point of that? Because Churchill always seemed confident, strong, and self-assured, it never occurred to them that he might welcome a pat on the back, or a few pleasant words commending him for a great speech, despite the editorials, despite the lord chancellor's opinion that he should be introduced to a firing squad, or the noose of hemp, for having delivered it. The prime minister might notice, or hear of it. Since his acclamatory reception at the airport and at Downing Street, Chamberlain had acquired messianic airs.

On Thursday, the day after Churchill had spoken, the prime minister moved for an adjournment of the House until November 1. Attlee, Sinclair, and several Conservatives — Macmillan the most vehement of them —

strongly protested. Churchill urged a two-day session in mid-October; it was "derogatory to Parliament," he said, "that it should be thought unfit, as it were, to be attending to these grave matters, that it should be sent away upon a holiday in one of the most formidable periods through which we have lived." Chamberlain replied shabbily that the Speaker decided when the House would be recalled, to which Winston instantly retorted: "But only on the advice of His Majesty's Government." Every MP knew that. Chamberlain called his remark "unworthy . . . tittle tattle," and now it was between the two of them; Winston, desperately in need of support, got none. He wrote No. 10, protesting the prime minister's slur, and the P.M. responded: "I am sorry if you think my remarks were offensive, but I must say that I think you are singularly sensitive for a man who so constantly attacks others. I considered your remarks highly offensive to me and to those with whom I have been working. . . . You cannot expect me to allow you to do all the hitting and never hit back."[17]

Churchill returned to Chartwell profoundly depressed. He canceled a lecture at the Imperial Defence College, explaining, "I am so distressed by the change in the situation that I haven't the heart to address myself to the task to which you invited me at present." Paul Reynaud and Georges Mandel, outraged by Munich, had resigned from the French cabinet, and Winston wrote Reynaud: "I cannot see what foreign policy is now open to the French Republic. No minor State will risk its future upon the guarantee of France. I am indulging in no pretensions upon our own account. . . . Can we make head against the Nazi domination, or ought we *severally* to make the best terms possible with it — while trying to rearm? Or is a common effort still possible?" His nephew John George Churchill later told Martin Gilbert: "The gloom after Munich was absolutely terrific. At Chartwell there were occasions just alone with him when the despondency was overwhelming." To an old Canadian friend Winston wrote on October 11: "I am now greatly distressed, and for the time being staggered by the situation. Hitherto the peace-loving Powers have been definitely stronger than the Dictators, but next year we must expect a different balance."[18]

He thought he had touched bottom when Edward abdicated, but this was worse. *That,* however, was part of *this*. In 1936, A. J. P. Taylor writes, "Churchill had seemed the rallying point for patriotic and democratic opinion," but Winston's ambiguous position on the Spanish Civil War and his championing of a discredited monarch eroded his support, and "his prestige ran downhill," particularly on the left. The conventional explanation for his continued isolation is that he had outraged Parliament by his long losing battle for the Indian Raj; but Chamberlain had deplored the parliamentary maneuvers which led to dominion status for India. Labour approved of

Winston's support of the League of Nations but recoiled from his calls for collective security. He "estranged the idealists," as Taylor puts it, "and so remained until the outbreak of war a solitary figure, distrusted by both sides." After Britain's disillusionment with Munich — and the "first ecstasy," noted Muggeridge, "soon passed" when Englishmen realized that the agreement would "involve still further concessions to Germany" —reasonable men might at the very least have acknowledged that Churchill had been right. But politics is never reasonable. Having denied, ridiculed, and scorned his accusations and impeachments, the cabinet could not indemnify him without confessing to its own incompetence.[19]

As the last weeks of 1938 skulked away, anyone wagering that the member from Epping would still be in his corner seat a year hence would have been entitled to ask for odds. Two exits were available. He could quit, or his constituents could recall him. He had hung on for nine years, hoping for a responsible post, but the chances of that were as remote as ever. He was still urging the strengthening of Britain's defenses, and that, in the eyes of the appeasers, was enough to disqualify him, despite his great abilities. Furthermore, as Chamberlain noted in his diary, recognition of Churchill was out of the question as long as friendship with Hitler and Mussolini seemed possible: "I wouldn't risk it by what would certainly be regarded by them as a challenge." Macmillan told Hugh Dalton that in Parliament or out, Churchill was "in danger of relapsing into a complacent Cassandra. He would say: 'Well, I have done my best. I have made all these speeches. Nobody has paid any attention. All my prophecies have turned out to be true. I have been publicly snubbed by the Government. What more can I do?' "[20]

In London it seemed inconceivable that Churchill could be forced to resign his seat in Parliament. But in the aftermath of Munich, during those weeks in which it seemed that Chamberlain had actually succeeded in buying peace, the rank and file of Conservative voters, proud of the party's leader, were aroused by any criticism of him. In this political climate the *Sunday Express* ran a brief item under the head: "Trouble is being made for Churchill in Epping. The campaign is strong, the campaigners determined." Winston sent Beaverbrook a note of protest; the story, he wrote, was "misleading as to the true state of affairs: & certainly most unhelpful to me." It was unhelpful, but it was also accurate. Two of his loyal constituents, Sir Harry Goschen and Sir Colin Thornton-Kemsley, had been dismayed by his Munich speech. Goschen wrote to the chairman of the Epping Conservative Association, Sir James Hawkey, that he could not "help thinking it was rather a pity that he broke up the harmony of the House by the speech he made. . . . I think it would have been a great deal better if he had kept quiet and not made a speech at all."[21]

Goschen decided to stick with Churchill; but Thornton-Kemsley wanted him repudiated and replaced by someone who would "support the Conservative administration, not . . . discredit them." On November 4, in a public meeting, Churchill defended his position on Munich. Then Thornton-Kemsley spoke, arguing that Winston's attempts to contain Germany with a "ring of strongly armed powers" had floundered. There was, he said, no conflict between British and German goals, and if the four nations represented at Munich could "agree upon a policy of friendship," no other nation would dare touch off a war. The audience seemed equally divided, but Hawkey lent his support to Winston, and his constituents passed a resolution regretting the failure of His Majesty's Government to respond to their member's warnings "given during the last five years" and declaring that had the prime minister and his cabinet followed Churchill's advice, Chamberlain "would have found himself in a far better position to negotiate with the heads of the dictator States."[22]

Churchill was once more secure in Epping — or so it seemed in November 1938 — but as Sarah later wrote him: "What price politics since they won't listen to you?" The one who listened least was the one who mattered most.[23]

Neville Chamberlain believed that Munich was the triumph of his career. Intolerant of dissent, a believer in strong party discipline, he was vain, rude, and vindictive. These unattractive traits were balanced by terrific energy, a powerful intellect, and an even stronger gift for command. William Strang, of the Foreign Office, who was outraged by the Munich settlement, nevertheless saw him as "a man of cool, calm mind, strong will, decisive purpose, wholly devoted to the public cause and with a firm confidence in his own judgment."[24]

If he had a sense of humor, it is unrecorded. In any event, he did not think public business and national institutions subject to levity. He had detested Rugby as much as Winston had Harrow; nevertheless, he believed that public schools were part of the social order and should not be mocked. When Churchill told the House that "Britain is like a Laocoön strangled by old school ties" and compared England's public school system to "feeding sham pearls to real swine," Neville scowled. An incapacity for the droll and the whimsical is typical of fanatics — and the prime minister now resembled a skipper who has set his bearing and lashed himself to the wheel. After Munich he should have given England's security overriding priority, but on Christmas Day, 1938, Oliver Harvey, a senior civil servant in the Foreign Office, noted despondently in his diary that Chamberlain was not pressing on with rearmament, that under Inskip the Committee of Imperial Defence "goes slower and slower," and that "Inskip must certainly go. A much more vigorous and imaginative man should be there. Winston is the obvious man, but I believe the PM would rather die than have him."[25]

That much seemed clear. In November, addressing the House of Commons from the front bench, the P.M. had scorned Winston, repeating the old accusation of Churchillian instability. It was the same old wine from the same dirty bottles, but no one could remember a British prime minister turning on one of his own party's private members. It simply wasn't done. And it was particularly unwise to do it to Churchill, as Chamberlain learned when Winston, speaking to 1,200 of his constituents in Chingford on December 9, noted that the P.M. had told Parliament "that where I failed, for all my brilliant gifts, was in the faculty of judging. I will gladly submit my judgement about foreign affairs and national defence during the last five years in comparison to his own."[26]

It was a devastating speech. In 1934, he recalled, Chamberlain had been chancellor of the Exchequer when Winston warned Stanley Baldwin that "the Germans had a secret Air Force and were rapidly overhauling ours. I gave definite figures and forecasts. Of course, it was all denied with all the weight of official authority." He had been derided as a "scaremonger." In less than six months, he reminded his audience, Baldwin "had to come down to the House and admit he was wrong and he said, 'We are all to blame.' " Baldwin had "got more applause for making this mistake, which may prove fatal to the British Empire and to British freedom," than most Englishmen who rendered a great service to the nation. "Mr Chamberlain was, next to Mr Baldwin, the most powerful Member of that Government. . . . He knew all the facts. His judgement failed just like that of Mr Baldwin and we are suffering from the consequences of it today." That blunder had been only the beginning. A year later Winston had asked that the RAF be doubled and redoubled, which prompted Lord Samuel, who shared Chamberlain's faith in appeasement, to say he thought "my judgement so defective that he likened me to a Malay running amok. It would have been well for him and his persecuted race if my advice had been taken. They would not be where they are now."

He then turned to Chamberlain's record as prime minister over the past two years. In his early days at No. 10 "the Prime Minister made a heart-to-heart settlement with Mr de Valera, and gave up to him those fortified ports on the South Coast of Ireland which are vital to our food supply in time of war." The P.M. led Englishmen to believe that "the country now called Eire were reconciled to us in friendship, but I warned him with my defective judgement that if we got into any great danger Mr de Valera would demand the surrender of Ulster as the price of any friendship or aid." And this, he said, "fell out exactly." Recently De Valera had announced that he could give England neither friendship nor aid while any British troops remained in Northern Ireland.

Next, in February 1938, Churchill continued, Chamberlain had said that

> tension in Europe had greatly relaxed. A few weeks later Nazi Germany seized Austria. I predicted that he would repeat this statement as soon as the shock of the rape of Austria passed away. He did so in the very same words at the end of July. By the middle of August Germany was mobilising for those bogus manoeuvres which after bringing us all to the verge of a world war, ended in the complete destruction and absorption of the Republic of Czechoslovakia. At the Lord Mayor's Banquet in November at the Guildhall, he told us that Europe was settling down into a more peaceful state. The words were hardly out of his mouth before the Nazi atrocities upon the Jewish population resounded throughout the civilised world.

These "proved errors of judgement in the past," Winston ended, should be weighed carefully when pondering "some of the judgements which have been passed upon the future, the results of which have not yet been proved."[27]

The Treasury Bench excepted, Churchill *did* have an attentive audience in Parliament, and they were its elite, men of eminence and accomplishment in other fields, backbenchers many of them, not because they lacked ministerial talent but because their time for public affairs was limited. In the division over the Munich Agreement, MPs, following their ancient ritual, had left the chamber to vote for or against it. Thirty eminent Conservatives remained seated, however, signifying abstention. This, wrote Nicolson, "must enrage the Government, since it is not our numbers that count but our reputation." Among the abstainers were Churchill, Eden, Duff Cooper, Leo Amery, Roger Keyes, Macmillan, Sandys, Bracken, and Boothby. This was a sign of party disarray. Rank and file MPs, Nicolson noted, realized that these dissidents "know far more about the real issue than they do." It was clear that "the Government were rattled by this. . . . The House breaks up with the Tories yelling to keep their spirits up. But they well know that Chamberlain has put us in a ghastly position and that we ought to have been prepared to go to war and smash Hitler. Next time he will be far too strong for us." On November 17 Churchill wrote in the *Daily Telegraph:* "Everyone must recognize that the Prime Minister is pursuing a policy of a most decided character. . . . By this time next year we shall know whether the Prime Minister's view of Herr Hitler and the German Nazi Party is right or wrong. By this time next year we shall know whether the policy of appeasement has appeased, or whether it has only stimulated a more ferocious appetite." Privately he wrote Lord Wolmer on December 12: "Neville leads us from bad to worse."[28]

Certainly he had presided over a series of disastrous defeats in 1938, altering the European balance of power and putting in jeopardy nations in eastern Europe which were friendly to France and Britain. The Anschluss and Munich had swollen the Reich's population by 10,250,000 — conscripts for the Wehrmacht, toilers in arms factories, drudges for the expanding empire. But it had already become clear that the safeguards adopted at Munich — the international commission and the guarantee of Czechoslovakia's new borders — were worthless. The commission met in the Wilhelmstrasse, under Ribbentrop's eye; the British and French delegates were under instructions, from Halifax and Bonnet, to yield to Hitler whenever possible. Their request for a definition of the impossible was unanswered. And Churchill's prediction that the Czech state could not survive the butchery of its frontiers in the Führerbau had been swiftly realized. With Beneš gone, the Czech defensive forts in Nazi hands, and ethnic minorities at each other's throats, the only democracy in eastern Europe was disintegrating. The Slovaks made the first move toward autonomy on October 6; three days later the Ukrainians followed their example; and on November 2 German and Italian arbitrators awarded Hungary nearly 4,600 square miles of Czechoslovakian soil. That left the Czech rump of Bohemia and Moravia, vaguely associated with the independent governments of Slovakia and Ruthenia.

At Chartwell, Churchill read reports of anti-Nazi fugitives from the Sudetenland. They echoed the tales Viennese had told earlier: midnight arrests, Gestapo firing squads, respectable leaders of their communities vanishing into concentration camps. On October 7 Halifax sent Berlin a note citing press accounts of such ill-treatment; he would be grateful, he said, for information "to combat such assertions, the spreading of which might in fact hamper the advocates of Anglo-German relations in the realisation of their aspirations." Hitler's response gave Britain's foreign secretary a lesson straight from *Mein Kampf:* anyone who agreed to negotiate with Nazis emerged a loser, his wounded pride treated with vigorous applications of salt. Speaking at Saarbrücken two days later, the Führer angrily declared: "We cannot tolerate any longer the tutelage of governesses. Inquiries of British politicians concerning the fate of Germans within the frontiers of the Reich — or of lands belonging to the Reich — are none of their concern."[29]

On the last evening of 1938 Nicolson wrote: "It has been a bad year. . . . A foul year. Next year will be worse." Churchill, more optimistic, told his constituents in January that while Englishmen like himself doubted that

Munich had "purchased a lasting peace," they felt that at least a "breathing space" had been won. He said: "Let us make sure that this breathing space is not improvidently cast away." Later, after the Men of Munich had been discredited, that became the keystone of their cover-up; they had, they said, bought time to rearm. It wouldn't wash. The day after Churchill's speech, Chamberlain rejected Secretary for War Hore-Belisha's request for a larger army budget, playing the same weary tune the cabinet had heard so often before, telling them that "finances cannot be ignored, since our financial strength is one of our strongest weapons in any war which is not over in a short time." As a former chancellor, he said, he thought Britain's financial position looked "extremely dangerous." Other ministers argued that Hitler would be shocked by British rearmament, interpreting it as inconsistent with the spirit of Munich, asking why, if the two countries were trusted friends, England was arming to the teeth. Hore-Belisha proposed conscription. He was denied it. Kingsley Wood wanted air parity with Germany. His request was also denied, but because he invested everything he was given in new, superior fighter planes — while the bloated Luftwaffe remained content with what it had — the number of Spitfire and Hurricane squadrons jumped from five to forty-seven in a year. Antiaircraft batteries also multiplied, but "these improvements," as Churchill later wrote, "were petty compared with the mighty advance in German armaments."[30]

In every other category — artillery, tanks, and equipped divisions — Nazi gains were overwhelming. While Chamberlain was lecturing his ministers on the military value of stocks and bonds and spending £304 million on arms, German arms expenditures exceeded £1.5 billion — a fivefold gap. The number of Nazi divisions jumped from seven to fifty-one. By calling up trained reserves, the Reich could field an army of over seven million men, outnumbering the armies of France and England combined, and the Führer, unlike the democracies, did not have troops tied down in colonial possessions overseas. Vis-à-vis France, Churchill found, with every month that passed from 1938 onward the German army not only increased "in numbers and formations . . . but in quality and maturity." He believed that "in morale also the Germans had the advantage," and he attributed the ebbing of French martial resolve to Munich: "The desertion of an ally, especially from fear of war, saps the spirit of any army."[31]

Less than two months after Munich, Churchill entered his sixty-fifth year, and some parliamentarians, including friends, thought he was beginning to show his age. On Monday, December 5, the House of Commons received its long-awaited report on the preposterous attempt to court-martial Duncan Sandys. Everyone was exonerated; "misunderstandings" were blamed. Churchill rose. He started brilliantly, and everyone, Nicolson wrote, was "expecting a great speech." Then:

> He accuses Hore-Belisha of being too complacent. The latter gets up and says, "When and where?" Winston replies, "I have not come unprepared," and begins to fumble among his notes, where there are some press-cuttings. He takes time. He finds them. But they are not the best cuttings, and the ones he reads out tend to excuse rather than implicate Hore-Belisha. Winston becomes confused. He tries to rally his speech, but the wind has gone out of his sails, which flop wretchedly. "He is becoming an old man," says Bill Mabane beside me.[32]

It wasn't age, and he was capable of rebounding. The fact is that he was simply attempting to do too much. Indeed, the wonder is that he found time to appear in the House at all. His writing schedule continued to be punishing, and even as he struggled to meet it, Grace Hamblin recalls, Chartwell was being inundated by a blizzard of invitations to speak. As the taste of Munich turned to ashes, people wanted to see and hear the vindicated Ishmael. He was sensible enough to decline these, though some were tempting: the League of Nations Union, the Oxford Union (from its young president Edward Heath, a future prime minister), and a Jewish Youth Rally for National Service ("because of your courageous defence of freedom and denunciation of Nazi-ism [*sic*] you are held in the very highest esteem by all sections of Jewry"). He even turned down a dinner invitation from General Edward L. Spears, a fellow officer in Flanders twenty years earlier, explaining that "It is absolutely necessary for me to be in the country every possible night this year in order to complete the history I am writing."[33]

By day, however, he entertained visitors: French politicians, men who had held high posts in Vienna and Prague, and German anti-Nazis, many of them, like Count Lutz Schwerin von Krosigk, the Führer's finance minister, members of the old Wilhelmine aristocracy. In January a high French source sent Chartwell, in great confidence, information unknown to anyone in the British government. Deuxième Bureau agents were reporting that German munitions convoys were moving across Czechoslovakia, from the Sudetenland to the Hungarian frontier. Churchill immediately took this to the Foreign Office, where it was confirmed and then dismissed as part of a program to execute maneuvers and rearm the Austrian army on "the German scale and with German weapons."[34]

Of course, Winston could not hew to a spartan regimen. No one could work harder — while writing longer and more strenuously than ever before, he was also in one of his periods of intense bricklaying — but he had no intention of abandoning his sybaritic life-style. In the House of Commons he defended it with wit. Among the unhappiest victims of his gibes was Sir Stafford Cripps. Cripps was one of the very few on Labour's side of the House who shared Churchill's contempt for appeasement; he begged the front bench to rearm before Hitler struck. But he was also ascetic, a vegetarian, a man who shunned coffee and tea and quit smoking cigars because he thought the habit vulgar. "My God," said Churchill when told of this. "Cripps has cut his last tie with human civilization." On another, later occasion, Churchill was airborne over the Sahara Desert when his plane had to land for an emergency repair. Winston stretched his legs and gazed in all directions. "Here we are marooned in all these miles of sand — not a blade of grass or a drop of water or a flower," he said. "How Cripps would have loved it."[35]

Churchill did not propose to slacken his pace, but experience had taught him that he could be equally productive, and more comfortable, on the Riviera. Thus, in the first week of January, 1939, after an interview with Kingsley Martin of the *New Statesman* — "War is horrible," he told Martin, "but slavery is worse, and you may be sure the British people would rather go down fighting than live in servitude" — he was off for Maxine's Château de l'Horizon. Changing trains in Paris, he read in the papers that the Germans had announced a vast plan to expand their submarine fleet. Before unpacking in Cannes he wrote and cabled home a *Daily Telegraph* column, calling the Nazi U-boat program "a heavy blow to all international cooperation in support of public law." It meant, he said, that England was imperiled by an "avoidable danger" which could only be mastered after great "loss and suffering." The *Telegraph* was unread in Cannes, but a local newspaper subscribed to his syndicate, and there was a stirring in the lush villas when the same paper ran an earlier piece in which Churchill pondered an Anglo-Soviet détente. Among its readers was the quondam king of England, now Duke of Windsor, and he was splenetic.[36]

To Churchill, Edward's wrath, once majestic, now seemed more like petty whining. By now Winston had shed all illusions about the man he had championed, at such cost to his career and the cause he led. There was, he noted, no depth to the man; he never read a serious book, never gave the world's affairs profound thought, and what he presented as opinion was merely narrow, ill-informed prejudice. He doted on his wife, who ordered him about, apparently to his delight. Winston was amused by Wallis's sartorial influence on her husband. On the memorable night when the Duke crossed swords with Churchill in Maxine's white-and-gold dining room he was wearing a Stuart tartan kilt. He was lucky Winston didn't leave him without a fig leaf, according to the account of Vincent Sheean, who kept notes when, as he wrote,

> the Duke of Windsor and Mr. Churchill settled down to a prolonged argument, with the rest of the party listening in silence. . . . We sat by the fireplace, Mr. Churchill frowning with intentness at the floor in front of him, mincing no words, reminding HRH of the British constitution on occasion — "When our kings are in conflict with our constitution, we change our kings," he said — and declaring flatly that the nation stood in the gravest danger of its long history. The kilted Duke . . . sat on the edge of the sofa, eagerly interrupting whenever he could, contesting every point, but receiving — in terms of the utmost politeness as far as the words went — an object lesson in political wisdom and public spirit. . . . There was something dramatically final, irrevocable about this dispute.[37]

According to Sheean and their hostess, those who thought of Winston as doddering should have been there that evening. Afterward Maxine wrote Churchill, "Never have I seen you in such good form. . . . You are the most enormously gifted creature in the whole world and it is like the sunshine leaving when you go away." England was not like sunshine to him. "People talk of how brave Winston was in 1940," Lady Diana Cooper observed, "but his highest courage, and it was his *moral* courage, shone through when he saw war coming, England virtually helpless, and himself impotent — when he spoke the truth and men he had entertained in his home cut him in Parliament Square." He took it; he had to take it, but he didn't have to like it. Writhing in the bonds of his frustration he reminded Virginia Cowles of "a mighty torrent trying to burst its dam."[38]

That was one aspect of him, and to all but the few close to him it was the intrinsic Churchill, his quiddity and diathesis. Most public men have one personality for the world and another in private. Winston Churchill was an exception. In his greater speeches he could hold Parliament spellbound; at Chartwell his guests were entranced as he used the same language, mannerisms, and expressions. He could reminisce with old comrades, and the emotional undercurrent was always there. His eyes would fill, but like a sun shower the misty moment passed. The only people who saw the intimate Churchill — who knew the power and depth of his love, which lay within him like a vast reservoir eternally replenishing itself, available to them in boundless measure when they were parched or careworn — those few whom he cherished, were his family. His awareness of them was constant. In the middle of a letter on another topic in early 1939, he interpolated: "Mary has been . . . vy sweet to me and is growing into her beauty." His son had tried him as few fathers have been tried; nevertheless, it was understood that once Randolph married and began his own family, Chartwell would be his: his parents would move into more modest quarters. Creating those quarters was the impulse behind Churchill's renewed interest in bricklaying. Some diversion from his writing was essential, and he was aware of it. There were only so many productive working hours in a day; anything written beyond that was chaff. So he painted, fed his goldfish, savored his Pol Roger, and laid his bricks, letting his mind drift and rejuvenating his powers of thought.[39]

As usual, he had a new Chartwell improvement in progress. He was, he wrote Clemmie on January 28, supervising the tiling of roofs, putting down new floors, and "the joinery of the doors, cupboards, etc." Any other country squire at his age might have been overseeing such projects. But Churchill, as always, had grander plans. He was already building one cottage on the grounds with his own hands and planning another — for Clemmie and himself — when he retired and Randolph became Chartwell's householder. He wrote her: "In the summer when I am sure the book will be finished, I think I will build a house." It would stand on ten acres far from the mansion, he wrote, and would "cost about three thousand pounds." This was reasonable. Assuming he met the terms of his continuing contract for the *English-speaking Peoples* and completed assignments for *Collier's*, *News of the World*, the *Daily Mirror*, and his fortnightly syndicated columns, his literary earnings for 1939 would be £15,781. But knowing her dread of debt, he assured her that "we could sell it for five or six thousand pounds." After he had met all his writing deadlines he planned to ask Sir Edwin Lutyens, the eminent architect, for appraisals and opinions, hastily adding: "He will do this for nothing, I am sure, as he has always begged to give advice." For Winston the immediate value of the construction would be recreational: "It would amuse me all the summer and give me good health." To further soothe her he promised that "downstairs you will have one lovely big room" and "you may be sure that nothing will be done until you have passed the plans. I have at least two months work ahead on the present cottage." He had already christened it "Orchard Cottage."[40]

This letter reached her in Barbados. The year just passed, so disastrous for British diplomacy, had also been wobbly for her. A succession of minor ailments discouraged activity, and in July she had spent nearly three weeks alone in the French Pyrenees "taking the cure." In Paris she had broken her toe, a minor affliction but painful and slow to heal. Then came Munich and Winston's denunciation of it. Early in their marriage, as the wife of a politician who took unpopular stands, she had known that part of the price he paid — social opprobrium — must be shared by her. At first, when old acquaintances crossed the street to avoid greeting her, she had been shocked and hurt. She had been young and resilient then, however; tempered by her own anger, she had learned to take such shabby partisanship in her stride. It had seemed a small sacrifice; she shared her husband's convictions and was proud to be his wife. The pride was still there, but she was older now, and slights were harder to bear. Her spirits were at their lowest when deliverance, or what looked like it, appeared in the form of an invitation from Lord Moyne, suggesting that she join him and his friends for another voyage on the *Rosaura*, this time in the Caribbean. She loved the yacht and loved the idyllic islands, but her hopes of recapturing the ecstasy of their South Seas cruise four years earlier were crushed. As an unreconstructed Liberal she was outraged by conditions in the British West Indies. "These islands," she wrote Winston, "are beautiful in themselves but have been desecrated & fouled by man." Starchy food kept the population "alive but undernourished — eighty percent of the population is illegitimate, seventy percent (in several islands) have syphilis and yaws." There was no sanitation of any sort, not even earth latrines. "And this," she bitterly concluded, "is a sample of the British Empire upon which the sun never sets."[41]

She felt he was neglecting her. In the past, when they were parted he had sent her long, clever holographs, decorated with drawings of pigs or pug dogs. Now, preoccupied with his manuscripts, avalanches of mail, and the recurring crises in Parliament, he dictated notes or cables. She responded tartly: "*Please* don't telegraph — I hate telegrams just saying 'all well rainy weather love Winston.' " The news he did send was worse than none: an obituary of Sir Sidney Peel, who had fallen in love with her when she was eighteen, just after the turn of the century. She had nearly married him; twice they had been secretly engaged. Winston commented: "Many are dying that I knew when we were young. It is quite astonishing to reach the end of life & feel just as you did fifty years before. One must always hope for a sudden end, before faculties decay." By the time the *Rosaura* approached Nelson's old dockyard on Antigua, Clemmie was plainly homesick. "I miss you & Mary & home terribly," she wrote, "& although it is a boon to miss the English Winter & to bask in this warmth, I really think I should come home — only that I hope this prolonged voyage in warm weather will really set me up in health — I do not yet feel very strong, but I am sure I shall."[42]

She found strength when, following the news and reading Winston's letters — now frequent, long, and penitent — she realized how lonely and embattled he must be. In the February 9 *Daily Telegraph* he had ruefully conceded that support for a firm stand against Nazi aggression was still weak, that "ripples of optimism" to the contrary were, "alas," based on "insufficient justifications." He pointed out that the press had reported long troop trains passing through Vienna and Munich and asked "What is their destination? What is their purpose?" Obviously, the British public didn't care. Mussolini was mobilizing for an invasion of Albania, and Hitler had announced that Germany would support the Duce: "Indeed, it is clear that the German dictator could not afford to witness the downfall of his Italian colleague."

Nevertheless, England remained lethargic. In an attempt to rouse it, he had left his Disraeli desk for a whirlwind lecture tour, but his audiences had been small and tepid. To a friend he wrote: "Nothing but the terrible teaching of experience will affect this all-powerful, supine Government. The worst of it is that by the time they are convinced, or replaced, our own position will be frightfully weakened." Hitler appeared determined to fight on one issue or another; it hardly seemed to matter which. And each fresh concession by Chamberlain and Halifax debilitated Britain as the inevitable showdown approached.[43]

In the middle of one letter home Clementine blurted out, "O Winston, are we drifting into War?" England, it seemed, yearning for peace and all but defenseless, was nevertheless tottering toward the brink "without the wit to avoid it or the will to prepare for it." Then she scrawled across the page: "God bless you my darling." Thus clouds were gathering within her, and sooner or later Clementine's overcast moods led to an outburst. One that entered Churchill family lore occurred when Moyne and his guests were listening to a BBC political broadcast. The speaker was vehemently pro-appeasement — Sir John Reith banned any arguments from the other side — and when Churchill was attacked by name, Lady Vera Broughton, another member of the party, cried: "Hear, Hear!" Clementine awaited a conciliatory word from her host, but he compressed his lips and remained silent. That put the wind in her sails. She flew to her cabin, wrote him a note of explanation, and packed. Lady Broughton arrived, begging Clemmie to stay, in vain; Winston Churchill had been insulted, and Mrs. Winston Churchill would accept no apologies. Ashore, she booked a berth on the *Cuba,* which was sailing for England in the morning.[44]

As she entered Chartwell's front hall she cried their old mating call: "Wot!" And from deep within the mansion came the delighted echo: *"Wot!"* He embraced her, heard her story with pride and pleasure, described his progress on the manuscript, and then broke the news, as gently as possible, of a new attempt to expel him from Parliament. This second campaign, four months after the first, was again led by Thornton-Kemsley. But "Peace for our time," which had pealed across the land then, now had a hollow ring.

Winston knew he had but to hire a hall or two, give tongue to what was in his heart, and his constituents would come gamboling to him.

That was his strategy, and it worked, first in Chigwell, on March 10, 1939, and then at Waltham Abbey four days later. He was in fine, fiery form at Chigwell, repeating his indictment of Munich ("I do not withdraw a single word"), declaring that he would "cordially support" larger defense appropriations, approved of a recent Chamberlain call at the Soviet embassy "to show the world" that Britain was prepared to cooperate with Moscow "so long as Russia continues to show herself an active friend to peace," and — this was mendacious — saying, "I have been out of office for ten years, but I am more contented with the work I have done in these past five years as an Independent Conservative than of any other part of my public life." He asked them: "What is the use of Parliament if it is not the place where true statements can be brought before the people?"[45]

Winston was confident, and no wonder. In the months following Munich, Hitler himself had entered the fray on behalf of those working against Churchill. No doubt the Führer had felt provoked: "When you look long into an abyss," Nietzsche wrote, "the abyss also looks into you." Churchill had been glaring at the Reich since the birth of the Nazi regime, and as the Führer looked up and their eyes locked, staring across the North Sea, Hitler impulsively decided to hound his gadfly from public life. The Führer had been nettled by the attempts of Britons, and particularly Winston in his syndicated columns, to arouse anti-Nazi Germans. Speaking at Weimar he said: "If Mr. Churchill had less to do with traitors and more with Germans, he would see how mad his talk is, for I can assure this man, who seems to live on the moon, that there are no forces in Germany opposed to the régime — only the force of the National Socialist movement, its leaders and its followers in arms." If Churchill returned to office, he predicted that his "aim would be to unleash [*loslassen*] at once a new world war against Germany."[46]

Churchill immediately issued a statement expressing surprise that "the head of a great State" should attack private members of Parliament "who hold no official position and who are not even leaders of parties." He said: "Such action on his part can only enhance any influence they may have, because their fellow countrymen have long been able to form their own opinions about them, and really do not need foreign guidance." As A. J. P. Taylor puts it, Hitler tried to "split British opinion." Assuming that Englishmen could be manipulated like Germans, he believed that advocacy of British rearmament would raise opposition among England's pro-Germans — whose number he vastly exaggerated, and whom he expected to sway by denouncing Winston as a "warmonger" (*"Kriegshetzer"*). This, he thought, would be Churchill's undoing. It was a *kolossal* error. The voters, in Taylor's words, "resented Hitler's interference in their affairs. They believed in non-interference. Hitler could do what he liked in Eastern Europe; he could demolish Czechoslovakia or invade the Ukraine. But he must leave British politicians alone." His demands that Churchill be routed gave the English *Kriegshetzer*s, Taylor observes, "a popularity which they could not have won for themselves."[47]

One wonders who, or what, was behind the challenges to Churchill. Obscure backbenchers are voted in and out of the House, but no one could remember a concerted attempt to unseat an eminent statesman known and respected in every European capital. There was gossip of German money being distributed among Winston's critics, but this lurid version is wholly without evidence. Thornton-Kemsley hinted at a more plausible source of support when he said that unless Winston was prepared to work with "our great Prime Minister, he ought no longer to shelter under the goodwill and name which attaches to a great Party." Later he added: "It was made clear to me that the growing 'revolt' in the Epping Division . . . was welcomed in high places."[48]

How high he did not say, but it was hardly a secret that the P.M. would be glad to see his eloquent critic retired; he had written his sister that Winston was "carrying on a regular campaign against me with the aid of [Jan] Masaryk, the Czech minister. They, of course, are totally unaware of my knowledge of their proceedings." He said he had "information of their doings & sayings which for the nth time demonstrated how completely Winston can deceive himself when he wants to, & how utterly credulous a foreigner can be when he is told the things he wants to hear." It seems unlikely that Chamberlain would instigate a plot against Churchill, but it is even unlikelier that Tories "in high places" would encourage Thornton-Kemsley without the knowledge and even the support of the party's national leader. Viewed in any light, the effort to unseat Churchill is depressing, a symptom of the squalid political intrigues which afflicted England as her hour of peril approached — and a direct consequence, ironically, of a selfless but mindless crusade for peace.[49]

Entering Waltham Abbey for his speech on March 14, Winston was handed a report that Nazi troops were massing along the frontiers of mutilated Czechoslovakia. At the lectern he departed from his notes to say: "The Czechoslovakian Republic is being broken up before our eyes. They are being completely absorbed; and not until the Nazi shadow has finally been lifted from Europe — as lifted I am sure it will eventually be — not until then will Czechoslovakia and ancient Bohemia again march into freedom." But, he added, to suppose that this new aggression did not threaten

England was "a profound illusion." Although Britain could "do nothing to stop it," Britons would suffer "on a very great scale." Not only would they have to make financial sacrifices, which "would have been unnecessary if a firm resolve had been taken at an earlier stage," but English lives would be forfeit, and for the same reason.[50]

Late that night, after a BBC broadcast announced that Hitler had annexed Bohemia, Churchill — who was at the time writing about the late seventeenth century — told his son: "It's hard to take one's attention off the events of today and concentrate on the reign of James II — but I'm going to do it." It was perhaps the most remarkable example of his genius for concentration. Randolph stared in astonishment as his father rose and plodded up the stairs to his study. The reports were, in fact, extraordinary, and the following day they were confirmed. Barely three years earlier, in the *Friedensrede* following his Rhineland coup, the Führer of the Third Reich had assured the world that he had "no territorial demands" to make in Europe, and that "Germany will never break the peace!" At Munich he had told Chamberlain that he wanted no Czechs in his realm and had even joined the British prime minister in guaranteeing the frontiers of the truncated Czech state. Now, on March 15, he was entering its capital at the head of his troops, standing erect in an open Mercedes, beaming and extending a stiff-armed *Hitlergruss*. But here, unlike Vienna and the Sudetenland, few arms rose in response. The Czechs were stunned. So was all Europe. So was Neville Chamberlain.[51]

HITLER IN PRAGUE!" screamed the newspaper posters on kiosks throughout England. What, outraged Englishmen asked one another, was he doing there? They had read his personal pledges to Chamberlain at Munich and his promise to be guided by the international commission, which would recognize Reich sovereignty only in "predominantly German" areas. Most Britons were unaware that Germany had ignored the commission with the connivance of London and Paris, unaware of Czechoslovakia's slow disintegration, unaware that the Nazis had, in defiance of the Munich Agreement, "awarded" Hungary and then Poland large tracts of Czech territory, inhabited by over one and a quarter million citizens of Czechoslovakia, none of them German, now made citizens of other states. These ominous events, heavy with implications, had been reported in the British press, but only briefly and obscurely.

His Majesty's Government had not prepared their countrymen for this blow. The fact is that they, too, were unprepared for the Prague invasion.

In Hitler's most recent speech he had reflected upon how fortunate the world would be if Britons and Germans could unite "in full confidence with one another." On March 10, only five days before Hitler's Prague coup, the P.M. had told the House of Commons that the Continent was now "settling down to a period of tranquillity." Hoare, speaking next, had predicted that if Hitler, Mussolini, Franco, Chamberlain, and Daladier were to work in tandem they could banish nightmares of war and burdens of armament and thus "in an incredibly short space of time transform the whole history of the world." As a consequence of this joint effort, Hoare had envisioned a new "Golden Age," whose promise would be realized if the "jitterbugs" — singling out those who had appealed for a stronger British military presence: Churchill, Eden, Duff Cooper, Bracken, Amery, Boothby, Sandys, Nicolson, Macmillan, and Keyes — were denied their goals.[52]

A backbencher softly quoted Shakespeare:

That England, being empty of defense
Hath shook and trembled at the ill neighborhood. . . .

Hoare was fatuous, and Churchill knew it, but he could not deliver a plausible rebuke without exposing informants already being tailed by the Gestapo. Two weeks after Munich, Hitler had summoned Frantisek Chvalkovsky, Prague's new pro-German foreign minister, and told him that Czechoslovakia must abandon her cordial relationship with Britain and become reconciled to her "proper place" as a colony of the Reich. The Czechs must "not play any tricks with Germany." If they did, "in twenty-four hours — no, in eight hours — I'll finish her off [*mache ich Schluss*]!" The following month one of Winston's sources sent him a secret memorandum in which the Führer had described the next phase of his foreign policy to Ribbentrop and Weizsäcker. Britain, he had said, "must be attacked with speeches and in the press . . . first the Opposition, and then Chamberlain himself." Munich had taught him "how to deal with the English — one had to move aggressively [*vor den Bauch treten*]." His objective, he declared, was "to overthrow Chamberlain." The Opposition, he assumed — an absurd assumption, revealing his ignorance of parliamentary rule — "would not then be capable of forming a new government, and the same would occur as in France. The political strength of Great Britain would be paralyzed" and "Fascism would gain the upper hand."[53]

On March 12, three days before Hitler's rape of the rump Czech state, Chartwell had received another report from an agent in Brno, Moravia. "Hitler," Winston had learned, "is coming to Vienna" — fifty miles from Prague — "this week." Swastika banners "lavishly decorated" a "great many public buildings," and each evening Czech Nazis "gathered in or around the Deutsches Haus to sing and demonstrate." One night a procession of anti-Nazis paraded by the German House; the men wearing the hakenkreuz brassards shouted *"Sieg Heil!"* and sang the "Horst Wessel Song." These Nazis had been told that "Hitler will come on March 15 and the greeting 'Heil Marz!' instead of 'Heil Hitler!' has been quite common for some weeks."[54]

On the morning of March 14 the Slovakian legislature, which had been quarreling with the national government in Prague, had declared its independence. This presented the Führer with his opportunity. Obviously, he declared, Prague could not control its people. The Czechs were informed of his displeasure by Ribbentrop, who stressed the need for an immediate solution. At 10:40 P.M. — just as Churchill's meeting at Waltham Abbey was breaking up — a train bearing Chvalkovsky and Dr. Emil Hácha, formerly a judge of Czechoslovakia's supreme court and now the country's president, drew into Berlin's Anhalt Station. An SS guard of honor escorted them to the Hotel Adlon and then the Reich Chancellery, where the Führer kept them waiting until 1:15 A.M. Hácha was no Masaryk, no Beneš; he had come prepared to grovel. He denounced his great predecessors and actually said that after Munich "I asked myself whether it was a good thing for Czechoslovakia to be an independent state at all." He realized that the destiny of his country lay "in the Führer's hands, and I believe it is in safekeeping in such hands." He knew that the Czechs had a bad reputation in the Wilhelmstrasse. His explanation was that "there still exist many supporters of the Beneš regime." But, he was "trying by every means to silence them." He meekly added that he hoped the Führer "will understand my holding the view that Czechoslovakia has the right to live a national life."[55]

Hitler didn't understand it, however. Hácha's "Rump State" (*"Rest-bestand"*), he said, owed its very existence to his indulgence. At Munich he had hoped that the Czechs, under new leadership, would mend their ways, but he had also resolved that "if the Beneš tendencies did not completely disappear he would completely destroy this state." It was now obvious that they had not disappeared. Therefore, last Sunday, March 12, *"die Würfel waren gefallen"* ("the die was cast"). He had issued the orders for the invasion by German troops and for the incorporation of Czechoslovakia into the German Reich. Schmidt, his interpreter, noted that the Czechs "sat as though turned to stone. Only their eyes showed that they were alive." Hitler told them that at 6:00 A.M., on his orders, his armies would cross their borders near points where the Luftwaffe had already seized Czech airfields. Any attempts at defense would be broken by *"rohe Gewalt"* ("brute force").

He paused. Of course, he said, they had a choice. If the defenders laid down their arms the Führer would treat them with generosity, assure their autonomy, and even grant them a certain measure of freedom. He suggested they step into the next room and talk it over.[56]

Awaiting them there were Göring and Ribbentrop, who literally chased them around a table strewn with documents, thrusting the papers at them, pushing pens into their hands, shouting that if they refused to sign, within two hours half of Prague would be bombed to ruins and their families slain. Suddenly Schmidt heard Göring shout: *"Hácha hat einen Schwächeanfall bekommen!"* Hácha, who had a heart condition, had indeed fainted, and a single thought crossed the minds of the Germans: the world would say that Czechoslovakia's president had been murdered in the Reich Chancellery. Then Dr. Theodor Morell — Hitler's personal physician, whose strange drugs later addicted the Führer — gave Hácha an injection. A special telephone line to Prague had been rigged up; over it, in a slurred voice, the revived president advised the cabinet to capitulate. Morell gave him another shot, and both Czechs signed the papers. It was 3:55 A.M. Two hours later German troops swarmed over the shrunken Czech frontier. Hácha was appointed governor of the German Protectorate of Bohemia and Moravia. But the world already knew who really ruled the country now. Hitler had told them. Before retiring for the night in Hradschin Palace he issued a triumphant statement: *"Die Tschechoslowakei existiert nicht mehr!"* —"Czechoslovakia has ceased to exist."[57]

That evening, as Hitler slept in his hijacked palace, Churchill dined at the Grillions Club with Sir Horace Rumbold, formerly His Majesty's ambassador to Berlin, who had been dismissed after the Nazis, opening his pouches, found he was reporting the facts about Hitler's regime and demanded an envoy more sympathetic to the Führer's policies. Rumbold was in low spirits. Learning that Hitler was in Prague, he concluded that "Even Chamberlain's eyes must now be opened to the fact that Hitler's statements and assurances are not worth the breath with which they have been uttered. . . . I confess that I have never in my life been so disheartened as I am now." He was angry that the Foreign Office had ignored his warnings six years before and that Chamberlain had been so gulled by Hitler. Over the past few months, however, he had begun to note "increasing disgust with Germany" on all levels of British society and "a growing conviction that there is nothing to be done with the Nazis."

This, he told Churchill, gave him a flicker of hope. And yet there were Englishmen who were still working toward an Anglo-German alliance. One, he said, was Lord Brocket, whom he regarded as "among the most gullible of asses." Brocket had been shooting with Göring. Göring had entrusted him with news of great importance: "Neither he [Göring] nor Hitler had any knowledge of the recent Nazi action against the Jews." On reflection Rumbold became convinced that further aggression by Nazis in 1939 was inevitable. The following day he wrote to his brother: "This year . . . is their last opportunity of doing so with any chance of success." There was a general feeling of uneasiness, he wrote Churchill that same afternoon. "You asked me last night what I thought of the present situation. I replied that I was profoundly disheartened. This was an understatement. . . . I have never felt so depressed or so nauseated as I feel now and this because it seems to me that our Government have, for a year or more, failed to look ahead or to understand the character of the man with whom they are dealing. . . . I only hope that it will not enter into the PM's head to pay Hitler another visit." On March 20 Churchill replied, thanking Rumbold for his letter and adding: "Since you wrote it events have told their unanswerable tale."[58]

"The blow has been struck," Churchill told his readers on March 24. Hitler had "broken every tie of good faith with the British and French who tried so hard to believe in him. The Munich agreement which represented such great advantages for Germany has been brutally violated." British confidence in the Nazi hierarchy

> can never again be mended while the present domination rules in Germany. . . . A veritable revolution in feeling and opinion has occurred in Britain, and reverberates through all the self-governing Dominions. Indeed, a similar process has taken place spontaneously throughout the whole British Empire. This mass conversion of those who had hitherto been hopeful took place within a single week, but not within a single day. It was not an explosion, but the kindling of a fire which rose steadily, hour by hour, to an intense furnace heat of inward conviction.[59]

That, or something like it, had indeed happened. A profound shift in public opinion was noted all over Britain. Hitler's Prague coup — which was followed, in a week, by his annexation of Memel, part of Lithuania — was the pivotal event in turning round British public opinion. The spirit of friendship between London and Berlin, which Chamberlain believed had been the fruit of Munich, had, in A. J. P. Taylor's phrase, "lost its glitter." And Robert Rhodes James, after reviewing the period, concludes:

> All that can be said, and said with absolute justice, is that after the annexation of Czechoslovakia in March 1939, the possibility of averting war with Germany was entertained only by a minority in Britain. By some strange process which is inex-

plicable to those who were not alive that year, the fear of war which had been so evident in 1938 seemed to evaporate. The British did not want war, but . . . there was a weariness with procrastination, an aversion to false promises and wishful thinking, and a yearning for a simple, clear solution.[60]

Later in the year a scrap-iron drive was launched, but an exception had to be made for Lord Baldwin; the wrought-iron gates leading to his estate were needed to control angry men who, only two years before, had cheered his every appearance. Malcolm Muggeridge bitterly recalled Chamberlain's return from Munich and his response to the airport crowd: "He showed them the very document, pointed to the signature upon it; then told them to go home and sleep quietly in their beds, confident that they were secure against molestation, not just for that night and tomorrow night, but for many nights, perhaps for ever. Peace in our time; peace in his time — not even that. The first ecstasy soon passed."[61]

Muggeridge was considered a crank and was disregarded by the House because of his contempt for everything trendy. But for once he was in the mainstream; MPs knew it because their constituents told them so in every mail delivery. Only the prime minister remained blind to the shift in the national mood. Addressing the House of Commons on March 15 he ignored the Nazis' exploitation of ethnic feuds which had always riven eastern Europe. Slovakia, he solemnly noted, had proclaimed her "independence." What had happened in Bratislava hardly resembled the American Declaration of Independence — in fact the proclamation had been issued by an extremist band of Slovakian Fascists — but you would never have known it from the prime minister's remarks to the House. He said: "The effect of this [Slovakian] declaration put an end by internal disruption to the State whose frontier we had proposed to guarantee. His Majesty's Government cannot accordingly hold themselves any longer bound by this obligation."[62]

Back in Downing Street his ministers told him this made no sense. He turned away, refusing to concede that the issue which had made him a national hero had boomeranged. But his cabinet persisted, and he was under growing pressure from his whips, his closest colleagues, even from the King. Finally, on March 17, Chamberlain grasped the humiliating fact that the Führer had deceived him, exposing the paper they had signed for the placebo it was.

Another statesman might have abandoned his discredited policies, and at first it seemed that the P.M. had decided to do precisely that. Actually his commitment to appeasement lay too deep, and he could never entirely relinquish his conviction that the path to enduring peace lay through continuing compromise. So his public positions became schizoid, swinging from one extreme to another. That Friday he was decidedly hawkish. The Prague betrayal had angered him, and speaking before a large crowd in Birmingham, the arena most sympathetic to Joe Chamberlain's son, he executed what was, for the moment at least, an about-face. He believed, he said, that most Englishmen had not only approved of the Munich Agreement but had "shared my honest desire that that policy be carried further." Now he shared "their disappointment," their "indignation." Hitler claimed that his ingestion of what was left of Czechoslovakia was "justified by disturbances [there]. Is this the last attack upon a small state or is it to be followed by another? Is this in fact a step in the direction of an attempt to dominate the world by force?" If so, he said, Britain would take part "in resisting the challenge to the utmost of her power."[63]

Halifax told Dirksen: "In Anglo-German relations the clocks [have] been put back considerably." But Chamberlain did not let a formal protest leave the FO until March 18, three days after the occupation of Prague. Bonnet, having been put under similar pressure, did the same. Couriers from the French and British embassies sped along the Wilhelmstrasse bearing stiffly worded notes protesting the "denial of the spirit of Munich" to the Foreign Ministry. Ribbentrop discarded them unread.[64]

Ribbentrop's contempt was deserved. There had been so many such notes, deploring Hitler's seizure of the Rhineland and then its fortification, objecting to the Anschluss, remonstrating against the *Kristallnacht* and subsequent anti-Semitic pogroms. Ribbentrop knew the drill. Presently Henderson would appear and explain that friendship between the two countries must not be jeopardized, that mistakes would be resolved by negotiation. And, sure enough, the British envoy arrived within the hour.

Meantime a meeting in Düsseldorf between British and German industrialists had been scheduled to open on March 15. It went ahead as planned. Even as Hitler rode through Prague, the participants signed a preliminary agreement, one clause of which permitted Germany to spend the foreign exchange resources of the country he had just seized — in short, providing the Reichsbank with stolen funds to finance Hitler's regime.[65]

The disposition of Czech gold deposited abroad soon became the focus of heated disagreement in England. Though the Bank of England quickly froze its Czech assets, some of the Czech gold it held — six million pounds' worth — was controlled by the Bank for International Settlements, which wanted it transferred to the Reichsbank. By mid-May rumors were rife that a German representative was in London to conclude negotiations — and HMG was refusing to intervene. The House of Commons erupted on May 26. Where, indignant MPs asked, was the six million pounds in gold? Why was the government willing to permit its transfer to Germany? Chancellor of the Exchequer Simon replied that he was not sure he was even entitled to ask the bank about Czech deposits. But MPs were persistent. After the Anschluss, Vienna's Threadneedle Street had been a gold mine for Hitler, transferring all Austrian assets to the Nazis, and Parliament wanted no encore. "Really," said Bracken, "this is the most squalid form of appeasement . . . appeasing the Germans with the money of the unfortunate Czechs."[66]

Chamberlain was evasive, Churchill apoplectic. British rearmament was picking up speed; the lag with the Germans continued, but an effort had begun at last. He told the House:

> Here we are going about urging our people to enlist, urging them to accept new forms of military compulsion; here we are paying taxes on a gigantic scale to protect ourselves. If at the same time our mechanism of government is so butter-fingered that this £6,000,000 can be transferred to the Nazi Government of Germany, which only wishes to use it and is only using it, as it does all its foreign exchange, for the purpose of increasing its armaments, if this money is transferred out of our hands, to come back in certain circumstances quicker than it went, it stultifies the efforts people are making in every class and in every party to secure National Defence and rally the whole forces of the country.[67]

The prime minister flushed when Winston added that he could not understand how this matter could have escaped him. Churchill demanded that he put a halt to "the transference of this £6,000,000 of Czech money into the hands of those who have overthrown and destroyed the Czech republic." This, in Chamberlain's view, was another example of Churchill's lack of judgment, of his misunderstanding of the business world. Sentiment had no place in the City. The government in Prague had changed legally, since the Czech government had signed Hitler's documents, and Hácha had a perfect right to the gold Beneš had deposited here in the name of Czechoslovakia.[68]

Because of legerdemain — a hasty change in the Bank of England's bookkeeping methods — and the fact that vital Reichsbank records were later lost in the bombing of Berlin, to this day no one knows the degree to which the Nazis succeeded in obtaining these Czech assets. Gilbert and Gott state that Germany "never claimed the gold." But even if Nazi Germany lost a windfall, the Reich kept most of its powerful British friends.[69]

In London, Hitler was praised — praise which was entirely unmerited — for his generosity and restraint in suppressing violence in Prague. During the months following his entry into the city, 250,000 Czechs were killed, over half of them Jews. That was unknown at the time, for it was extremely difficult to get precise accounts of German behavior in Prague. The Nazi grip there had begun to tighten even before the coup. "Everywhere the Nazi salute and 'Heil Hitler' are to be found," one of Churchill's sources had written, "with pictures of the Führer in German restaurants." Nazis insulted young Czechs and clubbed them, Jews were required to register, and — a glint of black humor — "At the Capitol Cinema here [he was reporting from Brno] the German film 'Olympia' is showing. All the Nazis are itching to go, but there is a Nazi picket outside . . . because the cinema is owned by a Jew!" The same source described the Nazis' arrival: "I saw the first German troops entering the town. . . . The local Germans were very enthusiastic, but the rest of the population has been extremely and amazingly quiet. Everything is now draped in swastikas. Yesterday morning Hitler paid a surprise visit; the reception was very cool, and he drove straight back and did not make his intended speech here this evening. Few people saw him or even recognized him."[70]

Although the full scope of Nazi atrocities in Czechoslovakia was concealed from foreign correspondents, they could not be prevented from witnessing clubbings, the persecution of Jews, and the disappearance of Czech intellectuals once concentration camps had been built, wired, and equipped with watchtowers for machine guns and searchlights. There was no blinking the fact that this time Hitler had acted not as the champion of Germans living in a neighboring country but as a Genghis Khan bent upon pillage, enslavement, slaughter, and destruction. The Czechs were the first Slavs he had subjugated. He frequently broke his promises; his threats he always made good. In a secret *Führerordnung* he decreed that the Czechs were to be *"assimiliert,"* chiefly as *"Sklavenarbeit"* ("slave labor") in the Reich; the others, *"besonders die Intellektuellen"* ("particularly the intellectuals"), were to be *"entmanntet und ausgeschaltet"* ("castrated and eliminated"). All this had been set forth in *Mein Kampf*, the best-seller read by few and dismissed by most of them as ravings. Churchill, virtually the only public man who had taken Hitler at his word, published a collection of his own *Evening Standard* and *Daily Telegraph* columns under the title *Step by Step*. Clement Attlee wrote him, "It must be a melancholy satisfaction to see how right you were," and Lord Wolmer wrote: "The book is a record of perspicacity and courage on your part."[71]

Powerful Nazis had become British celebrities, however. On March 18, R. H. S. Crossman, a future cabinet member, spoke in the House of Göring's "courage and capability." "Apart from Hitler," he said, "he is the only statesman of any caliber in the Third Reich. . . . Moreover, it was his energy in reorganizing the Prussian police and establishing the Gestapo which enabled Hitler to consolidate his position in 1933, and since then the triumphs of the Nazi foreign policy would have been impossible without his work."[72]

Parliament's indifference to the lot of the Czech Jews infuriated Churchill. Dispossessed by the Nazis, they wandered the roads of eastern Europe. Photographs of their ordeal were profoundly moving, but Dawson refused to run any of them in *The Times;* he couldn't help the victims, he explained to his staff, and if they were published Hitler would be offended. Then, nine weeks after Prague, the Chamberlain government announced that British policy in Palestine had been changed. Unlimited Jewish immigration was over; strict limits would be imposed on the number entering Palestine for the next five years, and after that all Jews would be turned away "unless the Arabs of Palestine are prepared to acquiesce in it." This closed the chief refuge for European Jews fleeing the growing Nazi empire, and it gave the Arabs veto power over the eventual establishment of a Jewish state.[73]

This was popular in the Reich. But it was also a renunciation of the Balfour declaration, which in 1917 had promised British support in "the establishment [in Palestine] of a national home for the Jewish people." To Churchill, who had been a Zionist for thirty years, it constituted a shocking act of treachery and a violation of his personal honor. In 1921, as colonial secretary, he had committed Britain to the founding of a homeland for the Jews; it would be called "Judea" or "Israel." And in 1937, he had reaffirmed his support of such a nation publicly and, privately, to Chaim Weizmann, president of the World Zionist Organization, who had become a close friend. In May 1939, the new Middle Eastern policy was defended in the House by Malcolm MacDonald, who now presided over the Colonial Office. Amery denounced it in blistering terms, and Churchill, after reviewing his speech with Weizmann (who said he wouldn't change a word; he thought it perfect), addressed the issue in Parliament on May 22.

As one "intimately and responsibly concerned in the earlier stages of our Palestine policy," he could not "stand by and see solemn engagements into which Britain has entered before the world set aside." Perhaps the government's purpose was "administrative convenience." It was unlikely. No one had suggested it. Or perhaps — and here Winston hinted at the darker, more obvious, and most reprehensible motive, an attempt by His Majesty's Government to ingratiate itself with the Führer — it was being done "for the sake of a quiet life," which, he predicted, would be "a vain hope." Of the Arab veto he said, "There is the breach; there is the violation of the pledge; there is the abandonment of the Balfour Declaration; there is the end of the vision, of the hope, of the dream." He asked: "What will our potential enemies think? . . . Will they not be tempted to say: 'They're on the run again. This is another Munich.' " At the end he stared straight at the prime minister's eyes and recalled that twenty years earlier, in this chamber, Chamberlain had said — he was quoting him directly — "A great responsibility will rest upon the Zionists, who, before long, will be proceeding, with joy in their hearts, to the ancient seat of their people. Theirs will be the task to build up a new prosperity and a new civilisation in old Palestine, so long neglected and misruled." Churchill closed with three shattering sentences: "Well, they have answered his call. They have fulfilled his hopes. How can he find it in his heart to strike them this mortal blow?"[74]

The House witnessed its first sign of revolt by Tory MPs against their leadership on March 28, when thirty distinguished Conservatives — among them Churchill, Eden, Duff Cooper, and Macmillan — appealed for a new national government, with ministers drawn from the benches of all three parties.

Chamberlain, a better politician than a statesman, was ready for them. He knew the country no longer shared his faith in Munich. Indeed, it was apparent to all the appeasers that they could not survive another such sellout. Daladier told a secret meeting of his Foreign Affairs Commission that all agreements between France and Germany were *"en ruines."* He said that "if France does not face up to the consequences there will be a stampede among friendly countries which until now have been firm. It will be a rush toward servitude [*à la servitude*]. And we must have no illusion as to what will happen thereafter. New invasions will come to our country and threaten to submerge it [*risqueront de le submerger*]." At both No. 10 and in the Élysée Palace it was agreed that the Führer's next victim must be identified and bound to the democracies in a tight military alliance.[75]

It is a marvel that the Third Reich, now in its seventh year, had survived without precipitating a general conflict. It was coming now; historian Brian Gardner recalls that "While nations busily armed themselves for the war which statesmen said they had averted, there was a sort of political hush in Europe. Where would Hitler strike next, and when?" Appropriately, the answer found in London and Paris reflected their diplomatic incompetence. They picked the wrong country.[76]

Less than two weeks after the Führer had devoured Czechoslovakia the prime minister wrote one of his sisters: "There is always the possibility that Germany will act more cunningly & that instead we shall be faced with a new 'commercial agreement' which in effect puts Roumania at her mercy." Although the Rumanians shared no common border with the Reich, Hungary did; the government in Budapest was hostile toward Bucharest and would not object — in fact, would not *dare* object — if Nazi panzers raced across Hungarian soil to penetrate Rumania, a primitive Balkan country which was nevertheless rich in oil and controlled the mouth of the Danube.[77]

In Paris, Phipps asked Bonnet whether he thought Rumania would be "the next course on the Nazi menu." Bonnet told the British ambassador that he thought it "very likely." He was in fact convinced of it; his prediction was later found in Quai d'Orsay files. Henderson agreed that Hitler's next target would be "domination by force of the whole Danube basin." All this seemed supported by Virgil Tilea, the Rumanian minister in London. Tilea called at the Foreign Office on Thursday, March 16, the day after Prague fell. He told his tale to an FO assistant under secretary, then to Halifax and Cadogan — and, going public, to *The Times* and the *Daily Telegraph*. The gist of it was that his government, "from secret and other sources," had learned that the Germans planned to overrun Hungary and "disintegrate Roumania in the same way as they had disintegrated Czechoslovakia . . . establishing a German protectorate over the whole country." Their greatest prize would be the oil fields at Ploesti. He asked for a loan of ten million pounds to strengthen his country's defenses, emphasizing the "extreme urgency" of a "precise indication" of Britain's position "in the event of Roumania becoming a victim of German aggression." The "gravity" of the "imminent danger" was heightened by new German demands that the Reich receive preferred treatment in trade between the two countries, terms set forth in such language that they "seemed very much like an ultimatum," an impression reinforced by Wehrmacht troop movements along the Rumanian border. The eruption of hostilities "might possibly be a question of days."[78]

Halifax was alarmed. He seems to have accepted the Rumanian minister's apprehension at face value. But Tilea's account should have been examined more carefully. Had the Wilhelmstrasse conceived so bold a stroke, Rumania's government would have known of it, and an appeal to Britain would have been made on the very highest level. Instead, Halifax and Cadogan — without consulting first with Sir Reginald Hoare, their envoy in Bucharest — sent cables to Britain's ambassadors in Paris, Moscow, Warsaw, Ankara, Athens, and Belgrade, spreading Tilea's story and instructing them to ask what the leaders in these capitals would do if events confirmed it. Sir Reginald, when informed of Tilea's story, requested that these distress signals be withdrawn; he found the tale "utterly improbable" and the Rumanian foreign minister denied it in every particular. Sir Howard Kennard, His Majesty's ambassador to Warsaw, cabled that Poland's Ministry of

Foreign Affairs was "highly skeptical," and so, it developed, were other foreign ministries throughout Europe.[79]

Tilea had been discredited. Nevertheless, he retracted nothing, and the response of His Majesty's Government was exactly what it would have been had he been confirmed. Chamberlain convened an emergency meeting of the cabinet on Saturday, the eighteenth. Halifax reported that Rumania's foreign minister, Grigore Gafencu, denied that there was a word of truth in what Tilea had said and affirmed that relations between his government and the Reich were "proceeding on completely normal lines as between equals." Therefore, said the foreign secretary, the matter was "probably" not "immediately threatening," as they had thought. But, as they all knew, he continued, the Führer was capable of anything. He proposed that they anticipate the next crisis and ponder what HMG's position should be. His own opinion was that "if Germany committed an act of naked aggression on Roumania, it would be very difficult for this country not to take all the action in her power to rally resistance and to take part in that resistance herself."[80]

They discussed how to go about ascertaining which countries might be willing to join Britain in standing up to Nazi Germany. At the time that Churchill had urged a Grand Alliance in Parliament, such a coalition had been feasible, but since Munich Britain had few friends in eastern Europe. His Majesty's Government simply wasn't trusted. Other ministers suggested the obvious course — to court the Soviet Union, Nazi Germany's sworn enemy and the most powerful military force in eastern Europe. But Chamberlain, as he wrote his sister, held "the most profound distrust of Russia." He concluded that Saturday meeting by saying that "the real point at issue" was whether Britain could persuade "sufficient assurances from other countries" to justify "a public pronouncement that we should resist any further act of aggression on the part of Germany."[81]

It was Tilea who suggested that Britain's position would be strengthened if Poland joined them as a third ally. Halifax and Chamberlain found the prospect appealing. Poland shared a common border with Rumania and, according to British intelligence (whose agents cannot have been on speaking terms with Churchill's informants), was "in a strong position with regard to Germany." The governments in Warsaw and Berlin were much alike. Both persecuted Jews; both despised Soviet Russia; both had conspired against the Czechs — during the Munich crisis and its aftermath Ribbentrop had worked in tandem with Colonel Józef Beck, Poland's foreign minister. The Poles had left nothing undone to weaken Prague's position and, with Hitler's approval, had annexed Czech territory. In 1934 the Reich and Poland had signed a ten-year nonaggression treaty proclaiming mutual respect for existing territorial rights, the first breach in France's structure of alliances in eastern Europe. Since then Beck had toiled strenuously — and, it seemed, successfully — to remain on the best possible terms with Germany.[82]

To be sure, the port of Danzig was a potential sore spot. But the city's Polish commissioner, asked about the possibility of a German coup, "definitely" discounted it. In London, Dirksen, the German ambassador, assured Halifax that although the Reich intended to pursue a new role for the city, Hitler's means would entail neither threats nor violence. Instead, he would propose "consultation with the Polish government." (The anesthetic effect of German promises to negotiate in these years was extraordinary. Hitler never negotiated. He lied, he bluffed, he blackmailed, but serious negotiation was a skill he despised, a refuge for weaklings.) The last and decisive card in Poland's deck was her military reputation. Unlike her neighbors — and Great Britain — she boasted a field strength that was, at least on paper, immense: a million men under arms and another 800,000 reserves.[83]

The man who might well determine if these troops would be sent into battle was an enigmatic Polish colonel who in some ways resembled the Führer. No one questioned Józef Beck's ability. His remarkable diplomatic skills had led to his appointment, at the age of thirty-eight, as Poland's foreign minister. Respected for his intellect and powerful will, he was also distrusted — even detested — for his duplicity, dishonesty, and, in his private life, depravity. In Rome, where he had spent an extended visit-cum-vacation, the Princess of Piedmont had said of him that he had "the sort of face you might see in a French newspaper as that of a ravisher of little girls." Ciano thought him "an unsympathetic character who produces a chill around him." On one of his visits to London that spring, HMG gave him a lunch at the Savoy. Churchill thought him "cynical" and "coldhearted." Winston was watching him carefully, because he knew more about the strain between Warsaw and Berlin than anyone else there except the guest of honor. He casually asked Beck: "Will you get back all right in your special train through Germany to Poland?" The colonel gave him a sharp look and replied quietly: "I think we shall have time for that."[84]

Léger had advised the FO not to trust Beck because, to deflect Hitler southward, "he betrayed Rumania or is in the process of doing so." The very premise of Halifax's stratagem was false; it was Beck who fostered the notion that Poland was safe from Germany and did all he could to make it plausible. His ambassador in London told Halifax that Beck would "go a long way" to avoid a quarrel with the Reich. Beck himself, in conversation with Halifax, said that he and Ribbentrop would soon open negotiations over Danzig and he had decided to offer the Germans "magnanimous" terms. It would be his posture to do "nothing provocative." Pressed for details, he replied that he "did not propose to trouble" the British with an analysis of the Danzig dilemma. The problem was local, he said, and easy to solve; the possibility that it might grow into an international issue was inconceivable.[85]

Polish support of Rumania was indispensable, Halifax believed; however, on March 19, when he asked Beck to join a four-power declaration to warn the Germans against aggression in eastern Europe — the four being Britain, France, Poland, and Russia — Beck declined. Such a move would only provoke Germany, he said, and Poland did not want to associate herself in any way with the Soviet Union. In Warsaw, Ambassador Kennard asked Beck to "ponder" the matter, and within five days the Polish foreign minister came back with a counterproposal, relayed to Halifax by Beck's London ambassador, Count Edward Raczyński. Beck suggested that the two countries sign a bilateral convention that would call for Britain and Poland to "consult" in the event Germany threatened Poland. This should be kept a secret, Raczyński said, to avoid antagonizing the Reich. Halifax and Chamberlain were cool to the idea. For one thing, it made no mention of Rumania, which was the locus of Britain's concern. Besides, a secret convention would offend the French, whom the British had been consulting regularly, and would have no impact as a deterrent to the Nazis. A public pronouncement was needed.[86]

Halifax now conceived of another approach, which he proposed to the P.M.: What if Britain took matters a step further and offered to guarantee Poland? That might persuade Beck to reciprocate by joining Britain in guaranteeing Rumania. Chamberlain thought it was worth a try; after all, the Führer had no designs on territory governed by the Poles. What could be the harm? On his instructions, therefore, Halifax, Cadogan, and Butler spent the evening drafting a declaration of England's commitment. After consultation with the Quai d'Orsay, the consequence was an Anglo-French offer to rescue Poland or Rumania if either were attacked by Germany and resisted, although the commitment to Bucharest was contingent upon Warsaw's also agreeing to intervene — support the P.M. and his foreign secretary were confident they could secure. On March 27 the proposal was transmitted to Warsaw and Bucharest.[87]

As soon as reactions were received from these capitals, it was thought, negotiations to refine the details could proceed apace. The Continent was quiet. Nothing seemed particularly urgent. And then, suddenly, everything did. One reason was Chamberlain himself. Despite his hard-headed businessman's approach to issues, he had a hidden mercurial streak; he blew hot and cold, destroying a defensible Czechoslovakia one year and now guaranteeing Poland — which would prove far less defensible — the next. He had been misled by rumors all month, and this was dangerous, because his decisions were often based on fragile, unconfirmed evidence. Tilea's false alarm was one example.

Ian Colvin's warning was another, and in this instance the consequences were far graver. Colvin, Berlin correspondent for the London *News Chronicle,* was among the most astute newspapermen in Europe. His sources lay deep in the Nazi hierarchy; he was, indeed, part of Churchill's intelligence net. More than once he had sent to Chartwell directives from the Führer that were distributed to only three or four Nazi leaders. Repeatedly the correspondent's prophecies had proved true, and when he flew to London and conferred with Halifax and Cadogan late in the afternoon of Tuesday, March 28, he had their undivided attention.[88]

In January, he told them, "a victualling contractor to the German army" had received instructions to provide "the same amount of rations he had supplied in September 1938, and to have them ready by March 28, 1939." They were to be delivered "in an area of Pomerania which forms a rough wedge pointing to the railway junction of Bromberg [Bydgoszcz] in the Polish corridor." That was sinister enough, but Colvin's flight to London had also been inspired by the previous day's issues of *Völkischer Beobachter, Der Angriff,* and the *Berliner Tageblatt.* All had carried inflammatory accounts of "incidents" on the German-Polish frontier, assaults on Reich customs posts and even German civilians by Polish *Schweine,* some of whom had confessed they had been acting on orders from Warsaw. No one in the Foreign Office needed to be reminded that the Nazis had manufactured similar border clashes before each of their earlier invasions. Colvin was taken across Downing Street; Chamberlain heard his tale and agreed with the FO's recommendation — an immediate public declaration binding Britain to the defense of Poland.[89]

In the morning the cabinet cabled an approved text to the Poles and the French, who promptly endorsed it. Parliament was less docile. Critical MPs elicited acknowledgment that British intelligence had found nothing to confirm Colvin's suspicions. This was no reflection on him; the standards for a good newspaper story are quite different from those required of a prime minister committing his country's military forces. As it happened, Colvin had misinterpreted his data. The facts were right, but they were part of a German contingency plan whose date had since been set back. The spurious "incidents" were meant to build a case against Poland, and Hitler was indeed planning to move against the Poles; but his Wehrmacht directive specified action in September, not March. He wasn't ready now; after touring Memel, his latest conquest, he had stopped briefly in Berlin and entrained for Munich, leaving the OKW various instructions, including: "The Führer does not wish . . . to solve the Danzig problem forcefully. He does not wish thus to drive Poland into England's arms. . . . However, it should now be worked on. A solution in the near future would have to be based on especially favorable political conditions. In that case Poland shall be knocked out so completely that it will not be a political factor for the next decades."[90]

His staff knew he meant to hoist the hakenkreuz over all Poland before the first snow fell. Chamberlain was therefore aiming at the right target — though both his weapon and his ammunition were pitifully small — when he told the House on March 31:

> I now have to inform the House that . . . in the event of any action which clearly threatens Polish independence, and in which the Polish Government accordingly considers it vital to resist with their national forces, His Majesty's Government will feel themselves bound at once to lend the Polish Government all support in their power. They have given the Polish Government an assurance to this effect. I may say that the French Government have authorised me to make it plain that they stand on the same ground in this matter as do His Majesty's Government.[91]

Thus Chamberlain reversed the British policy, adopted in 1918, of avoiding continental commitments. He had not — yet — signed a formal military alliance, but he had taken a long step in that direction. All evidence to the contrary, he believed he could discourage Hitler from forcing himself upon the Poles. He was also convinced that Poland was a powerful military nation. In both instances he was wrong.

France, already committed to Poland's defense, was greatly relieved. But Englishmen who possessed strategic vision were, with few exceptions, appalled. Boothby told Churchill: "This is the maddest single action this country has ever taken." Not only was the policy crazy, he said; so was the man with whom they were dealing. He had talked with Hitler for over an hour, and when the Führer told him that the Reich meant to use Poland as a staging area for a Nazi invasion of the Soviet Union, he said he saw in Hitler's eyes "the unmistakable glint" of dementia. The Führer had assured Boothby that he did not "wish to attack Britain and the British Empire but of course if England became a Polish or Russian ally, he would have no choice." Now, to Boothby's horror, Chamberlain had given "a sudden, unconditional guarantee to Poland, without any guarantee of Russian support." Basil Liddell Hart agreed that the Polish guarantee was "foolish, futile, and provocative . . . an ill-considered gesture" which "placed Britain's destiny in the hands of Poland's rulers, men of very dubious and unstable judgment." To dramatize his protest, he resigned as military correspondent of *The Times*. In the House, Lloyd George asked, and was not answered, whether the General Staff had agreed to defend this country which they could not reach under any conceivable circumstances. Duff Cooper noted in his diary: "Never before in our history have we left in the hands of one of the smaller powers the decision whether or not Britain goes to war."[92]

Churchill's reaction to the Polish guarantee was ambivalent. In his postwar memoirs he wrote of Poland's "hyena appetite" in joining in the "pillage and destruction of the Czechoslovak State." In 1938, with the Czechs as allies, fighting would have made sense, he said; now, after six years of "placatory appeasement," they were asking their young men "to stake their lives upon the territorial integrity of Poland." He wrote: "Here was decision at last, taken at the worst possible moment and on the least satisfactory ground, which must surely lead to the slaughter of tens of millions of people." That is not what he said at the time, however. He told the House of Commons: "The preservation and integrity of Poland must be regarded as a cause commanding the regard of all the world," and added that Chamberlain's declaration meant there was "almost complete agreement" between the prime minister and critics of his foreign policy: "We can no longer be pushed from pillar to post." This approached a blanket endorsement. The most generous explanation for the chasm between these two Churchillian positions is that in 1939 he was inspired by the discovery that Chamberlain would fight for *something*. It is also fair to add that within a week Winston was raising doubts about the Polish guarantee.[93]

Poland, Chamberlain had told the cabinet, was "very likely the key to the [European] situation." But Poland wasn't. It was true that the Poles were brave beyond belief, and that the million men in uniform, splendidly uniformed, were formidably organized in thirty infantry divisions and twelve large cavalry brigades — gallant horsemen all. Unfortunately, they would be useless against Nazi panzers. The Germans planned to invade Poland with ninety-eight divisions. They were the best fighting men in Europe, and their leaders understood the mobile, armored warfare of the future. Halifax, according to Liddell Hart, "believed that Poland was of more military value than Russia, and preferred to secure her as an ally." Actually, Liddell Hart continues, Poland's generals "still pinned their trust to the value of a large mass of horse cavalry, and cherished a pathetic belief in the possibility of carrying out cavalry charges. In that respect . . . . their ideas were eighty years out of date, since the futility of cavalry charges had been shown as far back as the American Civil War."[94]

Nevertheless, Józef Beck carried himself as though he were — and doubtless he believed himself to be — the representative of a first-rate military power. Swaggering, chain-smoking, and leering at young women, he arrived in London on April 3 to negotiate the details of Britain's new pledge to Poland. Though HMG expected that it would lead to a Polish guarantee of Rumania's frontiers, the FO had not secured an assurance from Warsaw on this point. Now, alone with Beck in Whitehall — Chamberlain, after welcoming his guest, had stepped across Downing Street to No. 10 — Halifax brought it up.

To his dismay Beck declined to commit himself. Any such maneuver by Poland, he said, would increase tension in eastern Europe; it would, moreover, "automatically" link Hungary and Germany in a military alliance. Halifax heatedly replied that the link was already there, de facto if not de jure, and with the menacing cloud of approaching conflict already darkening the Continent, "the lack of 'concerted plans' would be calamitous." Beck suavely countered by paraphrasing a recent Chamberlain warning in the House against the establishing of "opposing blocs" of nations; "rigid political systems," he said, were equally dangerous. At this point the prime minister rejoined them, and the more he listened to Beck the more alarmed he became. Poland alone was pointless, the P.M. said; Rumania was the "vital spot." The colonel lit a cigarette and repeated his objection to "too rigid a system." The prime minister tried to scare him. If Nazi troops occupied Rumania, he said, "Poland would have a longer frontier with Germany." Beck smoothly replied that "the additional frontier would be quite short," adding that it would be in the mountains, which could be held "with quite a small force."[95]

Chamberlain — apparently grasping, for the first time, the implications of Britain's commitment to Warsaw — expressed anxiety that a German invasion of Poland might involve Great Britain. Beck said nothing; there was nothing to say. Chamberlain naively asked where Hitler would strike next. The Pole sardonically replied that if Nazi statements were to be believed, "the gravest question is the colonial question." Chamberlain asked about Russia, pointing out that the Reich and the U.S.S.R. shared no common border; to fight Nazis the Red Army would have to cross Polish or Rumanian soil. Beck replied that "any association between Poland and Russia" would mean war between Poland and the Reich; whatever Britain and the Soviet Union decided to do, Poland would "keep clear." The issue of Rumania was raised for the third time, and Beck declared that Rumania should be left to her own devices "until the Danubian problem has cleared itself up." He then reeled off a series of outright fabrications. Germany had "never contested" Polish rights in Danzig; indeed, Ribbentrop had "recently reaffirmed them." He doubted that the Führer would "risk a conflict" over "local matters," or that "any serious danger" of Nazi aggression existed. The prime minister suggested that Poland had been weakened by Germany's seizure of Czechoslovakia's Skoda Works. Beck replied that Poland was "not at all" dependent on Skoda's factories. In munitions she was "largely self-supporting"; indeed, the Poles exported weapons and "even supplied guns to Great Britain."[96]

That was too much for Chamberlain. As a man of commerce, he kept a sharper eye on England's trade balance than any prime minister in memory. He knew what Britain imported, where it came from, the quantities and the prices, particularly goods bought by His Majesty's Government. Polish arms weren't on the list. The illustrious Colonel Beck was a liar. Chamberlain and Halifax were beginning to understand why this man was a legend. They had been had. HMG's negotiations with him, and the culminating guarantee, had been a blind. Europe's security had not been strengthened. Instead Britain's vulnerability had grown.[97]

In politics the squeaky wheel gets little grease. This is particularly true when a public figure challenging the leader carries a controversial reputation in train. The mass distrusts controversy. Reluctant to reconsider its convictions, superstitions, and prejudices, it rarely withdraws support from those who are guiding its destinies. Thus inertia becomes an incumbent's accomplice. So does human reluctance to admit error. Those who backed the top man insist, against all evidence, that they made the right choice.

Chamberlain was still basking in the glow of the reception that had greeted his return from Munich. Having saved the peace then, he believed he could do it again. And in their hearts Englishmen still yearned for abiding peace. Chamberlain thought he had time. He could avoid a general election until 1942. By then, his loyal admirers believed, the old man could pull one more rabbit out of his hat, and the old man thought so, too. Something had gone wrong. If he could identify it and find it, he could set the world right again. But he was puzzled. What was it? Where had it gone?

The source of his greatest anxiety could be found in the Reich Chancellery, but now Hitler's fellow dictator in Rome had decided that he had better start grabbing while the grabbing was good. Brooding on his balcony above the huge sign *"Il Duce ha sempre ragione!"* ("The Duce is always right!") Mussolini had decided the Führer had been upstaging him. The surest way to reach the world's front pages was to break the peace. Therefore, the Duce would dazzle the international press by avenging a personal insult: the Albanians, under King Zog, had objected to the bullying tactics of the local Fascist party. The tattered banners that Italian legions had dragged through Ethiopia were unfurled and mended; Italian warships bombed Zog's coast, causing him and his queen to flee to Greece first, and then to Turkey. On April 7, Good Friday, the first wave of legionnaires waded ashore, some of them drowning in a treacherous undercurrent, and the natives fled inland.

Enough of them were assembled to vote for union with Italy. King Victor Emmanuel reluctantly accepted the crown. It was an infamous victory.

Churchill dryly observed: "The British habit of the week-end, the great regard which the British pay to holidays which coincide with festivals of the Church, is studied abroad." He then pointed out that this was not all opéra bouffe. Despite its Ruritanian appearance, the mountainous little country was a strategic springboard for an invasion of Greece. Mussolini's operation had been anticipated for weeks — every Italian embassy was like a sieve — but Churchill was the only English statesman who had worked out what he regarded as England's most appropriate response. The evening before the Duce launched his Albanian adventure, Winston had dined at Cherkeley, Beaverbrook's country home near Leatherhead. While the others were playing backgammon, he had approached a fellow guest — Arthur Christiansen, editor of the *Daily Express* and until now a stranger to him — to talk. He was feeling histrionic, and, as Christiansen put it in his memoirs, he seemed to be "rolling the words around his palate and licking them before they [were] uttered." He asked: "Where is the — ah — the British Fleet tonight? It is lolling in the Bay of Naples. No doubt the — ah — the Commander of the British ships at Naples is — ah — being entertained ashore, entertained no doubt on the orders of — ah — Mussolini himself at the Naples Yacht Club." Winston's demeanor changed; he glowered, chewed his cigar, then growled: "And where *should* the British Fleet be tonight? On the other side of that longheel of a country called Italy, in the Adriatic Sea, not the Mediterranean Sea, to make the rape of Albania impossible."[98]

At dawn the Duce's men were on the beaches. Churchill was at home in Kent when news of the Italian assault reached Chartwell. He sent word to No. 10: "Hours now count." Parliament, he wrote, ought to be "recalled at the latest on Tuesday," and he hoped Chamberlain would form a united parliamentary front, "as in the case of the Polish Agreement." As Churchill saw it, "It is imperative for us to recover the initiative in diplomacy. . . . What is now at stake is nothing less than the whole of the Balkan Peninsula. If these states remain exposed to German and Italian pressure while we appear, as they may deem it, incapable of action, they will be forced to make the best terms possible with Berlin. How forlorn then will our position become!"[99]

He proposed, as a first step, a British occupation of the Greek island of Corfu, "of course with Greek consent." If the Royal Navy were there first, an Italian attack "even upon a few British ships would confront Mussolini with beginning a war of aggression upon England. This direct issue gives the best chance to all the forces in England which are opposed to a major war with England. So far from intensifying the grave risks which are now open, it diminishes them. But action ought to be taken tonight." Chamberlain replied that this maneuver had found no support in the cabinet. Winston was not easily put off; the following week the P.M. wrote his sister that Churchill had been "at the telephone all day urging that Pmt should be summoned for Sunday & that the Fleet should go & seize Corfu that night!" If Winston were given an office, "would he wear me out resisting rash suggestions of this kind?"[100]

It was in fact rash. Churchill had proposed a classic exercise of sea power, ignoring the havoc Italian warplanes could wreak upon the British Fleet. Later he would learn not to underrate air power at sea. But the cardinal point is that he was urging action — while the prime minister was above all a man of inaction who would move only when, as at Munich, he was menaced by the threat of greater involvement. Harold Macmillan, a luncheon guest at Chartwell that Good Friday, later recalled, "It was a scene that gave me my first picture of Churchill at work. Maps were brought out; secretaries were marshalled; telephones began to ring." The estate had been transformed into a state within a state, with advisers, researchers, filing cabinets, and mounted charts. Approaching the end of his life, Macmillan would remember: "I shall always have a picture of that spring day and the sense of power and energy, the great flow of action, which came from Churchill, although he then held no public office." In London's ministries everyone seemed indecisive, vacillating. But not here with the master of Chartwell. To Macmillan, "He alone seemed to be in command, when everyone else was dazed and hesitating."[101]

Winston's proposals to Chamberlain seemed presumptuous, but no other living Englishman, in uniform or mufti, possessed so profound a knowledge of the Royal Navy. The effort which dazzled Macmillan continued to annoy Chamberlain, however. To his sister the P.M. complained that "It doesn't make things easier to be badgered . . . by the two Oppositions & Winston who is the worst of the lot, telephoning almost every hour of the day."[102]

Actually the prime minister ought to have been seeking advice; he had a great deal at stake in the Adriatic. Ever since moving into No. 10 he had been courting Mussolini, trying to drive a wedge between the Duce and the Führer. In January he and an FO entourage had journeyed to Rome and appealed for the good offices of "Musso," as Chamberlain called him in his diary. Specifically, he hoped that the Duce could be persuaded "to prevent Herr Hitler from carrying out some 'mad dog' act." Mussolini asked the P.M. whether he wanted to raise any specific point. Chamberlain replied that German rearmament and Wehrmacht troop moves were "giving rise to a great deal of anxiety and doubt . . .

all over Europe." According to Ciano, his father-in-law thought this sounded like a whine; he had been listening for a trumpet call, but that was an instrument Neville Chamberlain did not know how to play. "The talks with the English are finished," wrote Ciano, dismissing them as "nothing of consequence." Churchill had anticipated Chamberlain's failure. Earlier, dining with Vansittart and Duff Cooper, he had remarked: "Mussolini, like Hitler, regards Britannia as a frightened, flabby old woman, who at worst would only bluster, and was anyhow incapable of making war. She certainly looks the part."[103]

Bismarck, when told that Romans dreamed of a second empire, remarked: "The Italians have a big appetite and poor teeth." That was rather brutal, but it described Musso to a T. Tiny Albania, like tiny Ethiopia, was about all that the new Italian army, straining every muscle and summoning that last desperate erg of effort, could manage to conquer. Still, his attack on King Zog's realm was aggression and therefore had to be condemned by Parliament, ending the possibility, once real, that Italy might again march with the democracies. This was a good time for wise British statesmen to say nothing. But Chamberlain, who brandished an olive branch when the flashing blade of a saber was needed, had a genius for flexing Britannia's muscles at the wrong time. On the following Thursday, April 13, he informed a startled House of Commons that His Majesty's Government had decided to guarantee the frontiers of Greece, Turkey, and, once more, Rumania.

Winston was already having second, third, and fourth thoughts about the Polish guarantee, in part because he learned that the prime minister was also having them. On Monday, April 3, three days after Chamberlain had announced Britain's new relationship with the Poles, Churchill had told the House that "this is no time for negotiation. After the crime and treachery committed against Czechoslovakia, our first duty is to reestablish the authority of law and public faith in Europe." Members were beginning to wonder about the relevance of this when he drew their attention to "a sinister passage in *The Times*' leading article on Saturday, similar to that which foreshadowed the ruin of Czechoslovakia." Dawson had written: "The new obligation which this country yesterday assumed does not bind Great Britain to defend every inch of the present frontiers of Poland. The key word in the statement is not 'integrity' but 'independence.' " The prime minister's statement, the editorial continued, "involves no blind acceptance of the *status quo*. . . . This country" — the confidence of *The Times*'s editor in assuming that he always spoke for Britain is a source of endless amazement — "has never been an advocate of the encirclement of Germany, and is not now opposed to the extension of Germany's economic pressure and influence, nor to the constructive work she may yet do for Europe."[104]

Churchill was unaware that this passage actually reflected Chamberlain's views. Earlier that same Monday, before Winston spoke, the prime minister had written his sister that his statement linking England's fortunes with Poland was "unprovocative in tone, but firm, clear but stressing the important point (perceived alone by *The Times*) that what we are concerned with is not the boundaries of States, but attacks on their independence. And it is we who will judge whether this independence is threatened or not." Reports that appeasement was dead, it seemed, had been greatly exaggerated. But it was dying. Only a few weeks earlier Margot Asquith had declared that anyone "who is against the Gvts. Peace policy" was guilty of treason. But she had been among those who were completely turned round by the Nazi rape of Prague. After the prime minister's Birmingham speech protesting Hitler's betrayal of the Munich accord, she had written to Winston: "We are *old* friends (I, *very* old!). I think you sd go to 10 Downing Street & offer yr services, in whatever the PM wishes to place you. We *must* show Germany that we are united against her wish to dominate Europe."[105]

If so proud a woman could be humbled by Prague, as she was, if she could reject her convictions of yesterday and campaign for stronger British defenses, a hard line with Hitler, and, above all, Churchill's return to power — if that single event could reconcile Margot and her stepdaughter Violet, who had long believed Churchill alone could save England, to the point that they wept and embraced — then it is hardly surprising that their reconciliation was repeated in millions of homes, as those who had believed Munich meant "peace for our time" turned volte-face, boxing the compass as their long winter of feuding ended. Churchill, then Chamberlain, and then Margot prayed for "unity," for "union" — an end to the dissension which enervated England and succored only Hitler.

Their yearning for a single national purpose was not self-fulfilling. England was not marching in lockstep toward a single goal. Democracies do not work that way. Churchill's proposed policies, in the prime minister's view, would split the country into flinders. Nevertheless, one or the other must prevail. The question was which, and as England struggled toward a consensus, Englishmen had a lot of catching up to do. For six lost years the British public had been misled and misinformed. To be sure, it had been a public willing, even eager, to be deceived, but leaders bred in British public schools were expected to achieve more than popularity. Now, and throughout 1939 and into 1940, as the transfiguration of an England disenchanted with appeasement picked up momentum, the long pendulum swung back toward honor.

The swing was neither smooth, swift, nor uninterrupted. A vague uneasiness had been perceptible even before Munich; after the prime minister departed London for his confrontation with the Führer at Godesberg, the German chargé d'affaires had wired the Wilhelmstrasse: "Chamberlain and his party have left under a heavy load of anxiety. . . . Unquestionably opposition is growing to Chamberlain's policy." But then the P.M. had brought back what the British public thought was peace with honor, and the pendulum had been arrested. After Prague, its motion resumed, only to slow when the Polish guarantee was announced.[106]

It went like that, in fits and starts. The British people remained deeply respectful of authority, and Neville Chamberlain continued to control the institutions of government. Fleet Street, in the beginning, was deeply divided. And those who wanted to see His Majesty's Government replaced could not agree on who should lead them. In retrospect Churchill seems to have been inevitable, but that was not so at the time. As the prime minister's popularity ebbed, senior Conservatives, led by David Margesson, the chief Tory whip, began casting about for a successor. Almost to a man, they preferred Halifax. Chamberlain himself favored his foreign secretary; so did the King; so did *The Times*. Outside the establishment, however, Halifax was discredited. If a new tenant were to move into Downing Street, most of the great London dailies — and, if the polls were accurate, most Englishmen — wanted a man untainted by a record of truckling to Hitler and unstained by responsibility for the shabby state of Britain's defenses.

The shoe fitted Winston, and he was an obvious candidate. Yet claims were advanced for others. Eden and Duff Cooper, disillusioned, had resigned from the cabinet. Amery was also fearless. Nevertheless, each of Churchill's rivals was vulnerable. Eden and Cooper had waited too long to quit. And Amery, who had misjudged the Führer in the beginning, had gone along with Baldwin's draconian cuts in Britain's defense estimates during the years when rearmament was vital.

Those who wanted a new broom in Downing Street sought a man of political stature who had opposed HMG's policies and attempted to reverse their course. Eden in particular had problems here. Even before his appointment as foreign secretary, he had been an ardent appeaser. To his mortification, his role in forfeiting the Rhineland, which he had thought forgotten, was exhumed. Duff Cooper, on the other hand, was unpredictable and guilty of lapses in judgment. As relations deteriorated between Whitehall and the Wilhelmstrasse he wrote seventy-two-year-old Earl Baldwin of

Bewdley, the one man no other Conservative wanted to remember, with a singular proposal. "If the international situation deteriorates, which I believe it will," he wrote, "we shall be forced to have a Coalition Government." Duff Cooper doubted "that Neville could ever lead such a Government," and then dealt with the two likeliest successors — "Halifax or Winston." He didn't believe the first was "up to it," and Churchill "has too many and such violent enemies." Many Englishmen, he added, "don't trust him." Having set up the retired P.M., who was even more responsible than Chamberlain for the neglect of the country's defenses, Duff Cooper propositioned him: "I am wondering whether after two years' rest you feel you could come back." Since Earl Baldwin of Bewdley's image had been tarnished beyond restoring, he replied that no, he did not think he could.[107]

But there were doubts about Churchill, too. Amery, Eden, and Duff Cooper at least spoke in the idiom of their time, and until now each had attracted more supporters in Parliament than the lonely, eccentric genius whose star was just beginning to rise. In 1932 Nancy Astor had written him off as "finished"; his denunciation of Munich had been regarded as political suicide. Moreover, at this time the fall of Chamberlain, though in many minds, was not an immediate issue. Because of his party's large majority, only an uprising among Conservative backbenchers could drive him from No. 10. He was in trouble, but not that much trouble. Those who wished him ill could not move until he had suffered an accumulation of defeats. And the House knew that Churchill would not be satisfied with a cabinet post. He wanted office only as a springboard to the premiership, which raised other questions. On a superficial level, Churchill in the 1930s seemed almost vestigial. Approaching his late sixties, eligible for a pension, he was anachronistic in manner, dress, and speech. He could actually remember Gladstone recalling youthful memories of the bonfires celebrating Waterloo. Churchill's eclipse in the party, indeed, had been a direct consequence of his conviction, an article of faith in the nineteenth century but widely disputed in the twentieth, that the British Raj should continue to rule India.

Since his exile from power, he had campaigned against his own party's imperial, defense, and foreign policies, with a signal lack of success. To a people still haunted by the slaughter of trench warfare he had called for rearmament, declared that courage on the battlefield was a virtue, and gave "the world at large," in Samuel Hoare's words, the impression that he was "the very embodiment of a policy of war." He was also immovable. Any other politician twice faced with uprisings in his own constituency would have trimmed his sails, if ever so slightly. Churchill had known that the Munich Agreement, before the seizure of Prague, was popular. But he wouldn't retract a word. He delivered scathing speeches on appeasement and

HMG's failure to rearm to audiences who felt otherwise, and whose votes he needed if he was to keep his seat. He didn't enjoy it. More than most public men, he reveled in applause. He just didn't know how to compromise. In *Great Contemporaries* he had written: "Politicians rise by toil and troubles. They expect to fail; they hope to rise." Perseverance is the worthiest of political traits, and certainly the most difficult; a British historian who takes a jaundiced view of Winston acknowledges that "To persist in a political career that appears to others, and even on occasion to the politician himself, as finished, demands exceptional strength of character in a sensitive and proud man." As Ralph Waldo Emerson pointed out, there is a distinction between intellect and character. Intellect had won Churchill acclaim; character prevented him from exploiting it. He yearned for a ministry, but only on his own terms. Had his constituents rejected him, his response would have echoed an Emerson couplet: "Good-bye, proud world! I'm going home; / Thou art not my friend and I'm not thine."[108]

Yet Prague had undeniably transformed Churchill's political weaknesses into strengths. The policies he had attacked were exposed, overnight, as bankrupt. England had been hoodwinked, and Englishmen wanted no Dear Vicar or Good Old Neville. Martin Gilbert observes: "With the shock of Hitler's occupation of Prague, pressure mounted for . . . a decisive change in British policy." Britons listened with a thirsty ear for a call to arms, but Chamberlain, like Baldwin before him, lacked the voice for that. They heard it loud and clear in Churchill's rhetoric, however, and his appeal for a "recovery of moral health." As a contributor to the *Yale Review* has pointed out, this was "his way of saying that the English after Munich had to learn all over again to recognize evil. They had lost the sense of villainy; they had no solid principles, unshakable convictions."[109]

Chamberlain still held the House of Commons. It is a peculiarity of the British parliamentary system that in insulating Parliament from mass hysteria or chimerical shifts in the public mood, the House may also ignore an aroused electorate and remain loyal to its leader, particularly if he is strong, determined, and clever. Each MP could be held accountable only to his constituency, and then only in general elections. Hitler had touched a nerve when he said on November 8, 1938: "After all, Churchill may have 14,000, 20,000, or 30,000 votes behind him [actually he had 34,849] — I am not so well informed about that — but I have 40,000,000 behind me." Since he had banned elections, there was no way to confirm that. Yet even in democratic England, Tory MPs were subject to pressure, not from the voters, but from Margesson and his fellow whips, who worked at No. 12 Downing Street and received their instructions from No. 10.[110]

Eventually, of course, the House must reckon with the public temper. So must a prime minister, though a stubborn man, which Chamberlain was, may act without parliamentary approval — even without the approval of his cabinet. After Prague, the tide of opposition to the P.M. rose throughout 1939, and it began with Churchill's readers, whose number multiplied week by week. His pieces were appearing in the *Daily Telegraph*, *Picture Post*, the *Illustrated London News*, the *Daily Mail*, and — in the United States, where he was sowing the seeds of a future alliance — *Collier's*. The titles speak for themselves: "Let the Tyrant Criminals Bomb!" "What Britain's Policy Should Be," "War, Now or Never," "Towards a Pact with Russia," "Bombs Don't Scare Us Now," "Germany's Use of Tactics of Encirclement," and "No Blood Will Flow Unless . . . ."

Churchill's prose was but one of many forces hammering on the consciences of the British public — Hitler's actions were the most effective — but the phenomenon of a militant Britain could not have been shaped as it was without him. The "gathering storm," as he later called it, became apparent to men in pubs, women pushing prams, greengrocers, drummers, lorry drivers, businessmen, shop stewards; to everyone, in short, except the oligarchy in power, which need not face the voters again for three years. Slowly the prevailing opinion of fifty million Englishmen would turn round until Britain became a mirror image of the country whose throne Edward VIII had rejected, a valiant nation glorying in everything it had scorned after Munich. This reversal was far more profound than the Führer's arousal of his *Volk* earlier in the decade. The Germans, after all, had been belligerent for two thousand years; British public school boys were taught that "Civilization stops at the Rhine and the Danube, the frontiers of the Roman Empire," or, as Winston put it, "A Hun alive is a war in prospect." In the past seventy years Germany had writ her name large on battlefields, while the British Empire had endeavored to impose a Pax Britannica on the world.[111]

Once appeasement was discredited, the scapegoating began. Like Gallipoli it became a political weapon, a lash to flog the Conservative party. Michael Foot and two collaborators later published a devastating Labour attack on the appeasers. Titled *Guilty Men*, it singled out fifteen Tories, among them Chamberlain, Simon, Hoare, MacDonald, Halifax, and Baldwin, indicting each for neglecting England's defenses and failing to alert and prepare the country for the inevitable conflict. *Guilty Men* received an enthusiastic press. The *Atlantic Monthly* called it an irrefutable exposure of Baldwin's "blunder and blindness"; the *Spectator* thought it persuasive evidence that coalition and Conservative ministries "were deceived by Hitler and did not, when awakened to realities, apply themselves with vigour to the task of restoring our defences"; and the *Boston Transcript* found the book's arguments "unanswerable."[112]

But they weren't. Throughout the 1930s Foot, a socialist who had cheered pacifist speeches, following Attlee's pacifist lead, had opposed *any* appropriations for the British army, the Admiralty, and the RAF. If the Tories had taken his line, Britain would have faced the Nazis naked. The MacDonald-Baldwin-Chamberlain triumvirate never went that far. At least they left the infrastructure intact. Indeed, it may almost be said that *Guilty Men* was written by guiltier men.

Churchill was still beleaguered by both sides of the House as the sands ran out, but "the public," as Brian Gardner notes, "were beginning to think otherwise; for someone who was meant to be an adventurer, his warnings had been going on a remarkably long time, and with strange consistency, determination, and integrity." J. B. Priestly, whose politics lay in deep left field, wrote that there were three urgent reasons for appointing Churchill to the cabinet: his "outstanding ability and experience," which Chamberlain's ministers conspicuously lacked; the emerging realization that "the people want him there"; and the fact that "his presence will at least do something to show the world, which has no confidence whatever in our statesmen, that we are in earnest."[113]

In a country enjoying freedom of speech, shifts in public opinion are first sensed by the press. Lord Boothby believed that until the great awakening which followed Prague most of the London press, "with the shining exception of the *Daily Telegraph*, was bright yellow," with editors following Geoffrey Dawson's lead. "Fleet Street," according to Boothby, "did everything in its power to help Neville Chamberlain and his wretched Government turn the whole country yellow." The campaign to depict Chamberlain as heroic and Churchill as a blackguard peaked in the weeks immediately following Munich. Even Kingsley Martin, the left-wing editor of the *New Statesman*, who had indicted His Majesty's Government for failing to stand up to Fascist and Nazi aggressors, was deceived by the Munich hoax and later felt shame. Sir John Reith at the BBC continued to gag Hitler's critics — Sir Horace Rumbold and Harold Nicolson were denied airtime because they were "anti-German."[114]

Nevertheless, London newspapermen remained objective. Jaded by their government's duplicity, half-lies, and distortion, and by the gullibility of their readers, they were surprised to find growing support for Churchill among the middle, lower middle, and working classes — the yeomanry of England, and now, it seemed, her spine. These people wanted Winston in the government, with power to act and persuade — in short, with a ministry. His supporters could even be found in the cabinet. Malcolm MacDonald recalls that "the government was divided over whether Churchill should come in. On balance the younger members were for him, the older members skeptical. . . . We had begun to think this is war, we must get Churchill in, not as P.M. but as a very important war minister, or war-to-be minister, but Neville was reluctant."[115]

Chamberlain believed war ministers unnecessary because he remained convinced that he had brought Englishmen peace in their time, and this became clear as debate over establishment of a ministry of supply — first proposed by Churchill three years earlier, on April 23, 1936 — approached its climax. Without such a minister, an economic czar empowered to mobilize British industry and provide a national arsenal, future recruits would lack rifles, even uniforms. It was no longer enough for a nation to spring to arms. Artillery, tanks, and warplanes, decisive in modern war, must also be there. Such complicated weapons required lead time. On October 28, a month after Munich, the Air Ministry's director of plans had expressed doubts that RAF reserves would "last for more than a week of warfare on a modern scale." Churchill's intelligence net had seen to it that a copy of this report reached Chartwell, and he had written a friend that such failure "strips Ministers of all credentials to be judges of the national interests."[116]

Two days earlier the prime minister had told his cabinet he was ruling out a ministry of supply. No one could shake his faith in appeasement, not even Adolf Hitler. On November 14 Halifax, at a meeting of the cabinet Committee on Foreign Policy, had quoted the Führer as saying: "If I were Chamberlain I would not delay for a minute to prepare my country in the most drastic way for a 'total' war and I would thoroughly organize it. If the English have not got universal conscription by the spring of 1939 they may consider their world empire as lost. It is astounding how easy the democracies make it for us to reach our goal." The P.M., after a moment of stony silence, took up the next item on the agenda.[117]

To Churchill the need for the new ministry was compelling. That same week he had risen in the House of Commons to propose an amendment calling for its immediate establishment: "I put it as bluntly as I possibly can. If only fifty members of the Conservative Party went into the Lobby tonight to vote for this amendment, it would not affect the life of the Government, but it would make them act." The rapid production of munitions, he declared, should have begun long ago, and on a scale immensely greater than anything the War Office now contemplated. HMG's reply was that a ministry would "seriously dislocate" British industry, that it was wiser "to trust to cooperation than to compulsion." The House was still Chamberlain's, and Winston's rebuff was stunning. Not fifty MPs, but just two —

Bracken and Macmillan — joined him. Berlin rejoiced. "GREAT DEFEAT OF CHURCHILL!" read one Nazi headline. Another trumpeted: "CHURCHILL'S INTRIGUES COLLAPSE / EVEN DUFF COOPER AND EDEN COULD NOT BE ROPED IN."[118]

As late as March 2, 1939, the prime minister's own secretary for war, Leslie Hore-Belisha, told him that if the government was serious about defending the country, something had to be done to arm and equip its fighting men, and Britain's industrial titans would listen to no one without a seat at the cabinet table. Wearily the P.M. cut him off in mid-argument. They were already "getting the goods," he said, and "now that public opinion is becoming satisfied on this point I think the demand for a Ministry will die down."[119]

But it didn't, and Hore-Belisha kept hammering away at cabinet meetings, citing desperate, unmet needs and how a supply minister could resolve them. He met Churchill in Morpeth Mansions for strategy meetings, and once, when Winston had hurt his foot in yard work, he drove to Chartwell for advice. This was risky; in a cabinet dominated by sycophants, the rebellious war minister was isolated.

Yet the Ministry of Supply had become inevitable, and presently even Chamberlain knew it. In April 1939, after the German occupation of Prague, his panel of industrialists — the men he admired most and had sought to shield from bureaucracy — reported that their chief recommendation, an urgent question to be met squarely "at the first possible opportunity," was "the establishment of a Ministry of Supply." Brendan Bracken wrote Bernard Baruch: "Winston has won his long fight. . . . No public man of our time has shown more foresight, and I believe that his long, lonely struggle . . . will prove to be the best chapter in his crowded life."[120]

It had been assumed by the public, Fleet Street, Parliament, and most of the cabinet that Churchill would be the man appointed to the new office. No one in the country could match his experience as the czar of war industry twenty years earlier. On April 19 Nicolson wrote in his diary: "The feeling that Winston is essential is gaining strength, and we shall probably see him in the Cabinet within a short time." Writing Winston, Lord Rothermere predicted "a great responsibility" falling on his shoulders "at an early date" and offering him £600 if he quit drinking brandy for a year; all England, he added, "including especially myself, will wish you to be in the finest fettle when the day arrives."[121]

The new post went, however, not to the superbly qualified man who would have served England best, but to Leslie Burgin, the minister of transportation, an obscure man whose only other appointment had been parliamentary secretary to the Board of Trade. Nicolson set down two reactions in the House of Commons: "a gasp of horror" and "a deep groan of pain." The *British Weekly* noted: "There was much disappointment on both sides of the House that the changes in the Cabinet did not include such out-standing figures as Mr. Winston Churchill and Mr. Anthony Eden." Samuel Hoare later attributed Churchill's exclusion to his repeated calls to arms, which had stigmatized him as a warmonger, and the prime minister, according to his biographer, was "anxious that Hitler not think of [Winston] as a spokesman for His Majesty's Government."[122]

Chamberlain's decision to bypass Winston and appoint Burgin had been made with an eye on the Wilhelmstrasse, and in his diary the prime minister justified it: "If there is any possibility of easing the tension and getting back normal relations with the dictators, I wouldn't risk it by what would certainly be regarded by them as a challenge." But he paid a price in Parliament. There, Nicolson noted, the general "impression was deplorable." Independent MPs, he wrote, had "hoped that the P.M. would take this opportunity of broadening the basis of his Cabinet. There is a very widespread belief that he is running a dual policy — one the overt policy of arming, and the other the *secret de l'Empereur*, namely appeasement plus Horace Wilson. Chamberlain's obstinate refusal to include any but the yes-men in his Cabinet caused real dismay."[123]

On March 18 Neville Chamberlain celebrated his seventieth birthday. He was exhausted, and the seeds of personal tragedy were beginning to take root. After two grueling years at No. 10, signs of stress were evident. Rab Butler had been in the country on Good Friday. Learning that the Italians had invaded Albania he hurried to Downing Street, and long afterward he recalled being led upstairs to a small room overlooking a garden, which the P.M. used as a study. The window was open; bird food was strewn on a shelf outside. Chamberlain appeared annoyed by Butler's arrival and expressed amazement at his distress. He said: "I feel sure Mussolini has decided not to go against us." Butler recalled: "When I started to talk about the threat to the Balkans, he dismissed me with the words: 'Don't be silly. Go home and go to bed,' and continued to feed the birds."[124]

Writing his sister of the Duce's Albanian adventure, Chamberlain complained, not of Italian aggression, but of duplicity: "What I had hoped when I went away on Thursday was that Musso would so present his coup as to make it look like an agreed arrangement & thus raise as little as possible questions of European significance." In a strange admission — coming so late, after so many broken promises in Rome and Berlin — he wrote: "Such faith as I ever had in the assurances of dictators is rapidly being whittled away."[125]

Before Parliament's Albania debate, on April 13, the P.M. sent for Winston "in the hope of keeping the House as united as possible." In the debate Churchill did endorse Chamberlain's guarantee to Rumania and Greece and said he anticipated "even more effective arrangements with Turkey." If a "great design" of binding alliances were achieved, he said, "even now, at the eleventh hour," the world could be spared "the worst of its agonies." At the same time, however, he wondered how His Majesty's Government could make such wide-ranging commitments when Britain's defenses were so weak — how they could speak so loudly when carrying so small a stick. At the very least, he argued, Parliament should be asked to approve the conscription of British youth. He could not understand why the government had remained silent on this pressing issue. He asked: "How can we bear to continue to lead our comfortable, easy lives here at home, unwilling even to pronounce the word 'compulsion,' unwilling even to take the necessary measure by which the armies that we have promised can alone be recruited and equipped?"[126]

He then raised an issue which MPs had discussed among themselves in the smoking room or lobby, but never in the chamber itself. It was the unique position of Sir Horace Wilson, known to insiders for his influence on Chamberlain, his sympathies for the Third Reich, and his unscrupulous intervention between the prime minister and other government advisers, including senior members of the cabinet. Without naming names, Churchill wondered how anyone on the Treasury Bench could indulge in "sunshine talk," predicting "the dawn of a Golden Age" only five days before Hitler raped what was left of Czechoslovakia. Yet it was now obvious that "something of a very exceptional character, the consequences of which could not be measured, was imminent." Why, then, was the government unprepared? "After twenty-five years' experience in peace and war, I believe the British Intelligence Service to be the finest of its kind in the world. Yet we have seen, both in the case of the subjugation of Bohemia and on the occasion of the invasion of Albania, that Ministers of the Crown had apparently no inkling, or at any rate no conviction, of what was coming. I cannot believe that this is the fault of the British Secret Service."

Churchill knew "very well," he continued, "the patriotism and sincere desire to act in a manner of perfect rectitude which animates Ministers of the Crown, but I wonder whether there is not some hand which intervenes and filters down or withholds intelligence from Ministers." More than once "the facts were not allowed to reach high Ministers of the Crown until they had been so modified that they did not present an alarming proposition."[127]

* * *

Chamberlain was vexed. April was turning into the cruelest month of his prime ministry. He had expected an altogether different sequel to Munich: growing friendship with Germany and Italy, trade agreements reviving British industries still sunk in the Depression, and, once Hitler and the Duce realized that the British could be trusted, worldwide disarmament. Instead, he had seen his diplomatic strategy collapse with the Nazi conquest of Czechoslovakia, the Italian invasion of Albania, threats to the Balkans, intrusions into Europe's affairs by Russia, and, most alarming of all, Nazi pressure on Poland, England's one hostage in eastern Europe — pressure suspiciously like Hitler's modus operandi in the opening moves of the Anschluss and the Czech crisis.

Moreover, Roosevelt had interceded. The American president's concern over Europe's murky future had been crystallized by the Italian landings in Albania. The week after the invasion the president had sent a personal message to Mussolini and Hitler, asking them to pledge not to undertake further aggression for ten "or even twenty-five years, if we are to look that far ahead." Both dictators ridiculed it. The Duce called it "a result of infantile paralysis." Göring suggested that Roosevelt was "*im Anfangsstadium einer Geisteskrankheit*" ("in the early stages of a mental disease"), and on April 28 Hitler cruelly mocked the president before the Reichstag — and then renounced both the Anglo-German Naval Agreement of 1935 and the German-Polish agreement of 1934, charging that Poland and Britain were conspiring to encircle the Reich.[128]

Chamberlain's response to Roosevelt's initiative was to denounce "Yankee meddling." He was sympathetic toward Berlin, indifferent or hostile to Washington; he believed Hitler, not Roosevelt. As Sidney Herbert had written Churchill: "One of the things which the Prime Minister appears consistently to ignore is American public opinion." He also tried to disregard British opinion, but his choices were narrowing. Events were in the saddle, riding Neville Chamberlain and driving him toward the one measure he had vowed he would never take: conscription.[129]

Churchill had been accused of living in the past. Actually that was what HMG was doing; in dodging the draft the appeasers were ignoring Britain's altered status as a world power. For generations the Continent had listened to British prime ministers with respect and had given their advice great weight because behind them ranged the great British Empire, ready to spring to arms — as in 1914 — when the sovereign, on instructions and without consulting his dominions, committed his vast realm to global war. Victoria had spoken of those dwelling in imperial possessions as "my people." But her great-grandson's relationship with their great-grandchildren had been altered by parliamentary statute. Although the Dominions would probably declare war if England did, they couldn't be counted on.

This massive fact, together with the neglect of the island's armed forces by MacDonald, Baldwin, and Chamberlain, meant that Britain could no longer expect the Continent to catch cold when the prime minister sneezed. Chamberlain had treated the Czechs as pawns. In reality their military presence — forty trained, well-equipped divisions — had dwarfed Britain's. As of this moment, Europe's great standing armies were the French and Italians, each with about one hundred divisions; the Germans, with over two hundred; and the Red Army — which Chamberlain slurred — with three hundred. Britain's potential might was great, and had the front bench responded to Churchill's appeals over the past six years the country might have had a strong force-in-being. He had been ignored. If asked to field an expeditionary force now, the chief of the Imperial General Staff could have sent two regular divisions right away, another two later, and four divisions of territorials.

Even Chamberlain had to recognize the discrepancy. In late March he took a half step toward conscription, increasing the territorials by 210,000 (unequipped) and therefore, theoretically, doubling the army reserve. No one was deceived. Now, on April 24, after introducing the new Ministry of Supply, he renounced his past pledges and proposed a draft. The pressures of an aroused country, the press, his own party, and even the King had played roles in turning him around; but the main force goading him was the persistence of Hore-Belisha, who "took his political life in his hands," Winston later wrote. "Several of his interviews with his chief were of a formidable character. I saw something of him in this ordeal, and he was never sure that each day in office would not be his last."[130]

Churchill, the *Daily Telegraph* reported, "was in his most striking and effective form" during the conscription debate. "To hear him, Members hurried in, filling the Chamber and side galleries." He not only approved of the draft; he said it should have been introduced immediately after Munich. Pacifists had denounced the measure as "peacetime conscription." His eyes sweeping the benches, he asked, "Is this peace?" and answered his own rhetorical question: "We have had three disastrous campaigns and the battles, the actions of the war have gone not only against us but against the principles of law and freedom, against the interests of the peaceful and progressive democracies. Those battles already make a long catalogue — the Rhineland, Abyssinia, Austria, Munich, Prague and Albania [Hon Members 'And Spain'].... We are all, then, agreed that circumstances are analogous to war actually prevailing."[131]

But now he saw "a common cause in this House," and, indeed, throughout Western Europe: "The impulse, the main impulse, to resist the Nazi principles comes from the mass of the people." Doubtless many members voting for the bill would feel a wrench inside. He, too, had reservations, but his were different. He thought the measure inadequate. It provided for the induction of 200,000 twenty-year-old youths, but they would be issued neither equipment nor supplies until the Ministry of Supply persuaded British manufacturers to turn them out. It was the story of the reserves all over again; young Englishmen were to surrender their liberty and later, perhaps, their lives, but the production schedules of English factories still had priority. In effect this bill was a gesture, Churchill said, and "a gesture is not sufficient; we want an army and we may want it soon." He said he believed that "everyone is baffled by the now rapid changes of policy upon fundamental issues" in the government, switches which suggested that decisions were being made, "not after mature planning, but in a hurry, not from design, conviction, or forethought," but in response to initiatives in Berlin and Rome. This was consistent with the theme he had been sounding for years, but Chamberlain now suspected malice in all Churchill's criticism of him. He had heard, he wrote his sister, that Winston "thought I was going to offer him the Ministry of Supply & he was therefore smarting under a sense of disappointment, only kept in check by his unwillingness to do anything which might prevent his yet receiving an offer to join the Govt."[132]

The relationship between the Duce and the Führer was warmer. Within a month of the conscription debate, Mussolini yielded to Hitler's cajoling and agreed to join Germany in a military alliance. On May 22, 1939, the two dictators signed their Pact of Steel, agreeing to use force in acquiring "living space" for their peoples. If one of the two went to war, the other would "immediately come to its assistance as an ally and support it with all its military forces on land, at sea, and in the air." In the event of war neither nation would conclude a separate armistice or peace. General Ironside told Churchill that England and France were "in for a bad time."[133]

What the prime minister failed to grasp was that with all Europe rushing headlong into a maelstrom, the readings on traditional political barometers were meaningless. Normally, crises in public life peaked and passed, the issues quickly forgotten. Instead, all spring and throughout the summer Churchill and Chamberlain moved in elegant counterpoint, as though cast in one of those skillfully plotted Wilkie Collins novels in which the narrative moves among several sets of characters, some evil, some benign, with the reader unaware of which will win, or how. But among the British public in 1939 there was little doubt about which of the duelists aroused the greater enthusiasm. All over England, on posters, billboards, and cartoons, the theme echoed: *Winston must come back.*

The prime minister's manner toward Churchill was unchanged — civility masking hostility. This disturbed Churchill. It was not in the parliamentary tradition; Winston's differences with Neville's father had been many and had cut deep, yet outside the House chamber they had been on good terms, and had frequently dined together. The prime minister's coldness toward him derived in part from the reversal of their standing in the public opinion polls. Winston's popularity was rising; one letter to *The Times,* which even Dawson hadn't dared suppress, was signed by 375 professors, faculty members of every British university, "strongly urging" Churchill's appointment to an important cabinet post.

It is impossible to say precisely when the yearning for Churchill first took hold, but even before Prague the turning toward him had begun. His foreign policy views had been set forth in the February 25, 1939, issue of *Picture Post,* which predicted that "the greatest moment of his life is still to come." A second piece trumpeting him had appeared in the March 4 *Picture Post,* and in a third, on March 11, Churchill answered thirteen questions put to him by the magazine's editor, calling for a new government and cabinet seats for Labour. Newspapers ran letters or even editorials calling him "The Only Man"; an *Evening Advertiser* cartoon had depicted him camping outside No. 10, awaiting appointment as minister of supply.

By April demands that he be brought into the government were being published almost daily. On Friday, April 21, the *Daily Telegraph* ran an especially poignant one from an Oxford don whose father had been killed at Gallipoli. Saturday's *Evening News* called for his appointment "as soon as possible," and the day after that the *Sunday Pictorial* devoted its first two pages to Churchill, telling readers: "The jealousy and suspicion of others compel him to stand idly aside." On Tuesday the editor wired Chartwell: "Huge mail has reached me this morning following my Churchill article Sunday. Letters are overwhelmingly in your favour." Wednesday he sent word that he had received 2,400 responses from subscribers, 97 percent agreeing that Winston must return to office. Of the majority, he wrote: "I have never known such an unqualified response." They came from all classes: ex-soldiers, men still in uniform, and especially the young. Typical comments, he said, were "No more boot-licking to Hitler," and "We want a strong man who is not afraid." The editor ended: "Your name on our street placards aroused tremendous interest, and there is not the slightest doubt of the overwhelming view of the country on this issue."[134]

"WE NEED CHURCHILL" cried a page-one headline in *Time and Tide* on May 6. Four days later the *News Chronicle* published the results of a straw vote reporting that 56 percent of those polled wanted Winston in the cabinet, 26 percent were opposed, and 18 percent expressed no opinion. Horace Wilson destroyed No. 10's copy of this edition before it reached the prime minister's desk. It was a futile gesture; there was no way to keep Chamberlain ignorant of the massive shift in Fleet Street's coverage of Churchill. After Munich speeches praising him had frequently gone unreported; all were covered now, and often published on front pages. On July 1 Archibald Sinclair told an enthusiastic audience that the prime minister should bring Churchill and Eden into his "inner counsels." The *Yorkshire Post* carried a full account of the meeting. The *Star* assumed Winston's appointment to office — "Mr Chamberlain will shortly strengthen his Cabinet. It is expected that he will invite Mr Churchill to join the Government" — and reported that Margesson, taking "soundings" among Tory backbenchers, had found that "in nearly every case the Chief Whip was told that the appointment of Mr Churchill to one of the key posts in the Cabinet would create fresh confidence." The *Sunday Graphic* on July 2 predicted that Churchill would be named first lord of the Admiralty.[135]

Editorials became bolder. The *Observer* thought it incredible that Churchill, with "so firm a grasp of European politics," should be excluded from office, adding that the phenomenon "must be as bewildering to foreigners as it is regrettable to most of his own countrymen." On July 3 the *Manchester Guardian* urged the prime minister to put patriotism above personal rancor and use Winston's gifts "in any capacity," because England needed "Ministers of vision and power as well as administrators." The *Daily Telegraph* agreed. That same week calls for Churchill's return to office appeared in the *Daily Mirror*, the *Evening News*, the *News Chronicle*, and even the *Daily Worker*, on the ground that Churchill had been "the outstanding opponent of the 'Munich policy.' " The *Mirror* described Winston as "the most trusted statesman in Britain . . . the watchdog of Britain's safety. For years he warned us of dangers which have now become terrible realities. For years he pressed for the policy of STRENGTH, which the whole nation now supports." The following day the *Daily Mail* and the *Evening Standard* joined the recruits; so, on July 7, did the *Spectator*, declaring that giving Churchill and Eden seats at the cabinet table would constitute "a decisive contribution to our cause" and might persuade Hitler to pause before sending his troops into yet another country.[136]

"Oh Winston dear," Maxine Elliott wrote from the Riviera, "was there ever such a triumph for a public man! Press and public alike hotly demanding its one man who has told them the frightening truth all these years and now they run to him to try and pull their burning chestnuts out of the fire." Leo Amery wrote him that he hoped the newspaper push "will result in your being brought in to the Government," and Stafford Cripps asked: "Could you not make a public statement . . . stating your preparedness to give your services to the country. . . . I feel it would make a tremendous impact just now on the country and would intensify enormously the demand that is growing everywhere for your inclusion in the Government."[137]

But Churchill replied that he was "quite sure that any such demarche would weaken me in any discussion I might have to have with the gentleman in question." And he was right. In Hoare's words, Chamberlain "resented outside pressure. The more, therefore, the Press clamoured for Churchill's inclusion, the less likely he was to take any action." Colin Coote at *The Times* — Winston called him his "friend in the enemy's camp" — wrote Boothby that the "agitation" favoring Churchill would fail: "I will offer you a small bet that the other Mr. C. won't listen to it for a moment; for his motto is still peace at any price except loss of office, and he is rightly sure that the inclusion of Winston means his own proximate exclusion."[138]

Probably nothing would have stopped Hitler at this point. By the first anniversary of Munich he would have 7,188,000 Germans in Wehrmacht and Luftwaffe uniforms. Orders for the destruction of Poland had been cut, and although rebel generals were still scheming against him, five years would pass before they made their move. But Winston was the last Englishman the Führer wanted in office. In the early summer of 1939 the Foreign Office received an account of a conversation between James Marshall-Cornwall, a British general, and Count Schwerin von Krosigk, Reich finance minister and a member of the German cabinet. Krosigk had told the general that Chamberlain should "take Winston Churchill into the Cabinet. Churchill is the only Englishman Hitler is afraid of." Marshall-Cornwall added that Krosigk had said that Hitler "does not take the PM and Lord Halifax seriously, but he places Churchill in the same category as Roosevelt. The mere fact of giving him a leading ministerial post would convince Hitler that you really mean to stand up to him."[139]

But Chamberlain still did not believe in standing up to him. All evidence to the contrary, he remained convinced that if the Führer were treated with generosity, he could become Britain's best friend. Therefore Churchill remained in Coventry. Lord Camrose, proprietor of the *Daily Telegraph*, called at No. 10 to state the case for Winston. The press lord did not represent himself alone. He spoke for a select group of the most astute and distinguished Conservatives and independents, all of them known to Chamberlain and most of them friends of his. One of them was Harold Nicolson, a disaffected National Labour member, and on June 30, four days before Camrose's meeting with the P.M., he had noted in his diary: "The vital thing is to bring into the Cabinet people who are known abroad to be pledged to a policy of resistance and whose willingness to enter the Cabinet would show to the whole world that there can be no further Munichs." Briefing Camrose, the group had discussed "how far the Prime Minister would be opposed to bringing in Winston Churchill and Anthony Eden. . . . Camrose says that Winston is the vital figure. . . . The difficulty is that the Prime Minister himself, as well as Hoare and Simon, are terrified of Winston and will put up the strongest resistance. It would be much easier for them to accept Anthony, Amery or Duff Cooper." Camrose, however, was adamant. "You must have Winston," he said, and a majority of the group agreed.[140]

That was the centerpiece of the case he put to Chamberlain. According to Camrose's account, the prime minister replied that "while he appreciated Churchill's ability, his own experience in Cabinet work with him had not been such as to make him feel that his (Churchill's) inclusion in the Cabinet would make his own task any easier." Over the years, Chamberlain said, "he had had two discussions with him which had ended in rather violent disagreement." Anthony Eden's name had also been put forward, Camrose reminded the P.M. "Well, Winston was Public Enemy No 1 in Berlin, and Eden was the same in Italy. Their inclusion in the Cabinet might strike both ways." Chamberlain was cautious about Eden; his case was "not of the same consequence as that of Winston." Ministers, he conceded, made mistakes. "Simon's judgment, and Hoare's, might have been wrong at times, but Winston's was notorious." Camrose did not mention the notoriety of Hoare's deal with Laval, a far greater blunder than anything in Churchill's career.[141]

By the third week in July the Men of Munich thought "the Churchill flurry," as they called it, had ended. Halifax's chief aide wrote in his diary: "Pro-Churchill campaign dying down; no sign whatever of a move in No 10." Chamberlain wrote his sister: "As for the Churchill episode it has in Joe Kennedy's picturesque phrase 'Fallen out of bed.' . . . Even Camrose has now dropped it in the Telegraph." In another letter he wrote Ida that "the drive to put Winston in the government" had merely "enlivened" the week. "Anyway they have as usual over-played their hand," he said, and Hoare, echoing him in a letter to Lady Astor's son — she had startled Parliament by coming out for Churchill — wrote that "I was convinced that the attempt would fail. Anything that Winston attempts is overdone, and in this case it was so overdone that it has stirred up a great reaction against him."[142]

Winston hadn't had a thing to do with it; despite pleas from his supporters, he had remained aloof. At one point he drafted a statement: "I have taken no part in the movement in favour of broadening His Majesty's Government, in which my name has been mentioned." On second thought he decided not to make it public. On April 24, before the press campaign to put him in the cabinet had picked up momentum, he had spoken to a large gathering of city workers in the East End: "Those who now come forward to join the Territorial Army are discharging the highest duty of citizenship." That was hardly incendiary, but once the press lords had tossed his hat in the ring he canceled all public addresses and spoke only in the House of Commons.[143]

Actually, he had no time to mount a major political campaign. He faced publishing deadlines, and the need to meet them was more urgent than ever. His income from newspaper syndication had dropped sharply, and the blow was not softened by the fact that Hitler was to blame. As the Axis empire grew — and the smaller states bordering the bloated Reich frantically followed pointed advice from the Wilhelmstrasse — editors dropped Winston's column. Since the fall of Albania, for example, the government in Athens had prohibited publication of any article criticizing fascism or Nazism — this despite Britain's guarantee of Greece's frontiers. In Rumania, Imre Revesz wrote him in May, twenty-two newspapers were "controlled directly by the Propaganda Ministry in Berlin." Poland was now Britain's ally, but Warsaw authorities had suppressed his piece on the Nazi threat to the Poles. Churchill sent an account of all this to Cadogan at the Foreign Office. He was not the only victim of Goebbels's strategy: articles by Duff Cooper, Attlee, Eden, and Henry Wickham Steed, Dawson's predecessor at *The Times*, had also been rejected. It was "a serious matter," Winston submitted to Cadogan. "A net is closing round our activities," he wrote to Revesz, "through fear of Germany." The literary agent, ever resourceful, opened negotiations with American networks for ten-minute Churchill broadcasts once or twice a month. Responding to this news, Winston wrote him on May 8, congratulating him for having "called in the New World to redress the balance of the Old." In little more than a year his use of that cluster of prepositional phrases, slightly altered, would arouse an embattled free world.[144]

* *

As the dreary decade approached its close, Winston's main effort, the key to his financial survival, was directed toward completion of his *History of the English-speaking Peoples*, the linchpin of his agreement with Sir

Henry Strakosch. The grand design was totally Churchillian: "I have all that in my head," he explained to one researcher. So was the prose; the entire text came from his muttering lips or, if he was revising galleys, from his fountain pen. He needed a supporting cast, of course, and he picked a first-rate troupe — Bill Deakin, Maurice Ashley, C. C. Wood, Ridley Pakenham-Walsh, John Wheldon, and three scholars who would one day become illustrious biographers of his most famous foes: Keith Feiling (Neville Chamberlain), Alan Bullock (Hitler), and G. M. Young (Stanley Baldwin, perhaps the most hostile official biography ever published). Eddie Marsh once more came aboard to read proofs and make general comments on syntax and grammar; Brigadier Sir James Edmonds, the official historian of the Great War, was recruited because his knowledge of the American Civil War was profound. Considering their skills and the immense amount of time each devoted to his assignments, they can scarcely be said to have been overpaid; the researchers received fifty pounds a month and Marsh twenty pounds per 100,000 words — less than twenty-eight cents a page. But, of course, they weren't in it for the money. Other scholars would have done it for nothing.[145]

Winston's correspondence during these months reveals a quicksilver gift for bounding back and forth across nearly twenty centuries, from 55 B.C., when "the Proconsul of Gaul, Julius Caesar, turned his gaze upon Britain," to the Boer War, an adjournment chosen, perhaps, because it was then that the author himself appeared as a historical figure. Churchill opened with the broadest of themes:

> Our story centres in an island, not widely sundered from the Continent, and so tilted that its mountains lie all to the west and north, while south and east is a gently undulating landscape of wooded valleys, open downs, and slow rivers. It is very accessible to the invader, whether he comes in peace or war, as pirate or merchant, conqueror or missionary. Those who dwell there are not insensitive to any shift of power, any change of faith, or even fashion, on the mainland, but they give to every practice, every doctrine that comes to it from abroad, its own peculiar turn and imprint. . . .[146]

To an exceptional degree he enjoyed writing and was even invigorated by it. Few writers of depth are actually exhilarated by creativity; it drains them; at the end of a session most are exhausted. In many ways he was an exception. "Writing a long and substantial book," he said, "is like having a friend and companion at your side, to whom you can always turn for comfort and amusement, and whose society becomes more attractive as a new and widening field of interest is lighted in your mind." His letters seem to reflect the excitement of a writer rejoicing in the power of his inimitable style; to Clementine, skiing in Austria, he wrote: "The days pass quickly for I have so much to do."[147]

One senses his delight in his own virtuosity as, moving from informal to formal English, he shifts tone and syntax. Writing Clementine of his progress with the *History*, he tells her:

I have just finished writing about Joan of Arc. I think she is the winner in the whole of French history. The leading women in those days were more remarkable and forceful than the men.

Then, in his manuscript, we see the magic, his bold strokes, the might he could always invoke:

There now appeared on the ravaged scene an Angel of Deliverance, the noblest patriot of France, the most splendid of her heroes, the most beloved of her saints, the most inspiring of all her memories, the peasant Maid, the ever-shining, ever-glorious Joan of Arc.[148]

Eden wrote that he read Winston's accounts of the past "to forget the haunting apprehensions of our present days." His historical works appeared to offer Churchill the same asylum. "It has been a comfort to me in these anxious days," he wrote Mortimer Wheeler, keeper of the London Museum, "to put a thousand years between my thoughts and the twentieth century." On July 10, 1938, he had written Keith Feiling:

I have definitely plunged into the "English Speaking Peoples" and am now rollicking with the "Piltdown Man," Cassivalanus, Julius Caesar, the Scribe Gildas, the Venerable Bede and other hoary figures. How to make anything of this that is (a) readable, (b) original, (c) valuable and (d) true, is known only to the presiding genius of Britain who has not yet imparted his secrets to Yours most sincerely, Winston S. Churchill.[149]

And yet . . .

It was anything but a lark. Ten days later he wrote Eddie Marsh, "I am staggering along to the end of this job, and am glad to have found the strength to have accomplished it." Over half the present volume was in galleys, but ahead lay the insertion of special studies by Deakin and Bullock, checking facts, and soliciting comments from scholars who were expert in various areas. "I have had to work very hard," he wrote his publisher, "and many a night have sat up until two or three in the morning." In early 1939 he wrote Clemmie, "I have been leading a life of unbroken routine at

Chartwell — and have now got into print no less than 220,000 words i.e. 63 days ahead of the vy hard task I prescribed of 1,000 a day from August 1. At this rate I shd cover the whole ground by May, wh wd leave 7 months for polishing. It is a formidable grind; but if accomplished will put things in a vy satisfactory basis."[150]

The strain was evident to those closest to him. Grace Hamblin recalls him as "a very hard taskmaster. He drove us." Kathleen Hill recollects that he "could be very ruthless." But he was exciting, too. Mrs. Hill was now living at Chartwell, and she remembers her first impressions of it: "I had never been in a house like that. It was alive, restless. When he went away it was still as a mouse. When he was there it was vibrating." In retrospect she sees him as "a disappointed man who was waiting for the call to serve his country."[151]

Pride and drive, that inner gyroscope which never failed, spurred him on. His remarkable output is even more extraordinary when seen in the context of the time. As events accelerated in central Europe he continued to be the best-informed private citizen in the country. Following his instructions, foreigners arriving in London would take the Oxted train from Victoria Station and detrain to find Winston himself there to greet them. Flattered, they would enter his car, sublimely unaware that they were putting their lives in the hands of the worst driver in the British Empire.

Vansittart, fuming under the meaningless title Chief Diplomatic Adviser to the Foreign Secretary, had become his silent partner. But Van remained on His Majesty's payroll; he had no establishment to support and could devote all his working hours to gathering and analyzing the European situation, which grew in complexity and frightfulness after the Anschluss, as Hitler led the Continent from crisis to crisis. Somehow Churchill kept all that in one part of his mind and his work in another. Only the first Queen Elizabeth could check his creative flow. In August 1939 he wrote to G. M. Young, the Oxford historian and Fellow of All Souls College. Young had agreed to vet parts of the work, and Winston now wondered "how you are getting along with the proofs I sent you." He himself, he added, had "completed the Commonwealth story (Lambeth and Monk), but have still not cleared away the Queen Elizabeth block. I am now working on the Chatham period, which is very inspiriting." He overcame the Queen's intimidation after the war, when his work was published. And that block stands alone. If in his long career he ever again struggled with anyone more complex, there is no record of it. And if he had, there would be.[152]

The Lambeth Articles of 1595 can scarcely be regarded as possessing great historical significance. There were nine articles, and they were meant to express Calvinist doctrine in such weighty matters as predestination and justification. Since they were never adopted by the church in any synod, they lacked ecclesiastical authority and are interesting to us only because they interested Churchill. Nor could George Monk, a Devonian soldier, be regarded a key figure in the vastness of history, though he was certainly more engaging. At the outbreak of the English Civil War he fought for the King; captured by Roundheads, he was imprisoned in the Tower for two years, emerged as an admirer of Cromwell, fought hard for him while intriguing for the reestablishment of the monarchy, and became a duke. During the plague of 1665 and the great fire a year later, he restored order in London; he wound up fighting the Dutch as a British admiral. In the long reach of history, he deserves a footnote at most; his prominence in Churchill's work is startling.

But history, like beauty, lies in the eye of the beholder. If it happened, and if the writer believes it to be consequential, in it goes. To the dismay of the dons advising him, Churchill overruled their recommendation that he cut the tale of King Alfred burning the housewife's cakes, on the ground that myths are as important as facts in the memory of a people. Actually, the weight of four thousand years was on his side. In ancient Greece and Rome historical accuracy was subordinate to style and dramatic tone. During the millennium which followed, theological historians — there were no others — sought evidence of divine motives, intervention, and design. This was the evocation of Saint Augustine's *City of God* and, in 1681 — a thousand years later — Jacques-Bénigne Bossuet's *Discours sur l'histoire universelle*. Interpreting human experience was considered the function of religion or philosophy — even of poetry or other imaginative works. Modern historiography, constructing a documented record of mankind's activities and then interpreting it, did not emerge until early in the nineteenth century. By 1900, however, it had emerged as a distinct discipline, the preserve of academicians who, jealous of their hard-won recognition, regarded interlopers like Churchill as trespassers.

Yet despite jeers that Churchill was shallow, volatile, the Barnum of politics, Sir Isaiah Berlin, singling out a 1928 condemnation of Winston's style, comments that "the stern critic and his audience were . . . mistaken. What he and they denounced as so much tinsel and hollow pasteboard was in reality solid; it was this author's natural means for the expression of his heroic, highly coloured, sometimes over-simple and even naive, but always genuine, vision of life." Both as a politician and as a historian he was an unrepentant romantic. He did indeed divide those of whom he wrote into white hats and black hats. But that is how he saw life, as a struggle between the forces of light and the powers of darkness. He never tried to hide it, or veil it, or hoodwink or mystify or dupe his audiences. It was an authentic view of life; there was and is no need to justify it.[153]

His grand vision, as the *History* testifies, was of an expanding British Empire governed by Great Britain and the United States, ruling in tandem. A. J. P. Taylor comments that while this theme "has a few merits . . . he never considered how far England and America had been associated, which was very little, and — particularly — how far they could be associated in the future." To Churchill, it is clear, the great thing, apart from the fact that the two countries shared the same language, was that they had fought side by side. Wars, to Winston, were of immense historic importance; like Carlyle and Nietzsche, he believed that armed conflict was a natural state of man. Although one may argue that events since 1945 have vindicated him, this viewpoint put him on a collision course with mainstream intellectuals of his time. His derogators declared that he was a boy who had never outgrown playing with toy soldiers.This denied him not only maturity but also the high seriousness to which he was entitled.[154]

Nevertheless, his zest for combat *was* excessive. In a revealing comment to Lord Moran he complained that 1830–1860, when England and the United States were at peace, were "thirty years when nothing happened." So marked was his lack of balance that in his second part, dealing with the era between 1485 and 1688, Shakespeare was not even mentioned in the index, and in the third the Industrial Revolution was disposed of in a single paragraph. His trivial dismissal of those who abhor war is jarring, as is his later remark, in the 1940s, to a British general: "Cheer up! We can't have a war every day." It was Crane Brinton, an American historian, who observed that the fourth part, covering the years between Waterloo and the end of the nineteenth century, gave "disproportionate attention" to the bloody struggle between America's North and South, while the development of the British Dominions received "comparative brevity."

In part this imbalance was a reflection of the tumultuous times in which he lived. Moreover, he was writing — particularly toward the end of the *History* — under tremendous pressure. And in fact it would not be published until after the coming war. But the wonder is not that his text was incomplete and flawed, but that he got most of the job done when he did. Part of the explanation was his skill in dictation; part was his memory, which one survivor of those days calls "Napoleonic"; part his prowess in commanding his team of researchers; and part his proficiency in gathering a chaos of material in his mind, mastering it, assembling it in an inner prism, and then refracting it in a terrific, blinding beam. Of course, he could have improved upon it had he had time, but with an eye on central Europe he did his best, and Churchill's best was very, very good. If his reach exceeded his grasp, it was because he was intent upon more than literary achievement in the first eight months of 1939. Had he not been the preeminent leader in the struggle against Hitler during this time, the results would doubtless have been very different.

Certainly his understanding of Britain's political history was remarkable. In the first week of January his mind had leaped nimbly back 216 years from Joan of Arc's execution to the Magna Carta (1215), then leapfrogged four centuries to the Petition of Right (1628) and the Habeas Corpus Act (1679). In sending Wheldon a check for £52.10 he asked him to read, "for a similar fee," chapters he had written spanning 1455 to the death of Henry VIII in 1547. Back at Chartwell on April 6, the eve of Mussolini's invasion of Albania, he wrote Wheldon: "I send you herewith Richard III, Henry VII, Edward VI, Mary and Elizabeth." All except Elizabeth were in a "very rudimentary form"; he would be "most grateful" for "any improvements and expansions you can make to them." The manuscript was moving swiftly between the 1400s and 1500s at a time when events in the 1930s begged for his attention, and it was a strain, even for him. On March 24, when Hitler wrenched Memel from Lithuania, he wrote Ashley: "It is very hard to transport oneself into the past when the future opens its jaws upon us."[155]

April had brought conscription, Roosevelt's appeal to Hitler and Mussolini, and the introduction of anti-Semitic laws, based on those of the Reich, in Hungary. Winston was asking Bullock for "two or three thousand words" of English social history which "I could then interweave . . . with the text as it stands"; he was also thanking G. M. Young "for your invaluable notes on the Stuart period," and sending him five thousand words on the opening of Charles II's reign, including an analysis of the Protestant status under the Clarendon Code.[156]

In May the Axis powers had signed the Pact of Steel, while the Japanese, threatening British communications between Hong Kong and Singapore, blockaded the British and French concession at Tientsin, and demanded British withdrawal of support for the Chinese. Winston sent Young revisions of his seventeenth-century chapters, including one on the Restoration (1660) but "omitting the Cromwell period which I am going to reconsider later." A week later he executed a mighty leap, in time and place: "I have the American Civil War on my hands now, which should take me about a fortnight." Actually four weeks passed before he reported again. It was June 11 — Britain and France were trying to form a "peace front" against Nazi aggression — before he sent Civil War galleys to Brigadier Edmonds, and even then he had only reached the Battle of Chancellorsville (1863). He hoped, however, "to complete the tale to the death of Lincoln in 40,000 words." Simultaneously, he was revising the text on the 1400s, four centuries earlier. Even as he wrote about Gettysburg, he was dictating passages on the Norman Conquest of 1066. And four days later he was deep in chapters on the reigns of King John (1199–1216), Edward the Confessor (1042–1066), and Canute (1016–1035).[157]

By July the war fever had reached Washington, and Churchill's determination to stand by his Disraeli desk night after night approached the heroic. Roosevelt had asked Congress for a repeal of the arms embargo and revisions in the Neutrality Act; at the same time he announced that he would abrogate the U.S. 1911 trade treaty with Japan. Chamberlain maundered on, defending his foreign policy. The urge to shred it in a major speech was almost irresistible, but Churchill could do nothing for England if broke. Nevertheless, he attended all significant sessions of Parliament; his presence was felt in the service ministries, the Foreign Office, on the Continent, and even in Washington and Moscow.

His manuscript, however, had absolute priority, and he believed he was going to meet his deadline. On July 9 he wrote his publisher: "You will be glad to know that the 'Story of the English Speaking Peoples' is now practically complete. Four hundred and sixty thousand words are actually in print" — Churchill used galley proofs when a thriftier writer would use typists — "and more than half has gone a second revise. I hope, therefore, to let you have the work ready for publication in plenty of time before the end of the year." He thought the "American side has been very well treated, and the story of the American Civil War is a small book in itself." But he had far to go. The following day he was back in the 1300s with John Wycliffe and Richard II, then in the 1200s with Henry III and Edward I. A week later he decided to redraft forty-seven thousand words; then he sent Bullock his Henry III galleys, asking him to "kindly read it again for accuracy, challenging any points on which you do not agree." Style ("Will you think over some rules to be given to the printer about Capitals?") had to be settled with Eddie Marsh. It was mid-August before his treatment of the Victorian Age was complete, and at the end of the month he confronted Deakin with a major problem, the organization of the work. "What we want is a chronological account of the Seven Years War, featuring the rise of Chatham. This will include the 'Continental Struggle' and 'Frederick the Great.' . . . Will you let me have some books on the period covered by Chapter VII 'The Great Pitt'? While you are sending them to me, I am going on with 'Queen Elizabeth.' "[158]

It may be argued that if Churchill had not been a virtual prisoner in his Chartwell study during those critical months, England might have been better prepared in September, but he was still far from power, virtually impotent in the House of Commons. Only catastrophe could place England's fate in his hands. Yet because of the very men who had ignored or mocked him in the years since Hitler became Reich chancellor and führer, catastrophe was ineluctable. Some of the appeasers showed signs of uneasiness. Even *The Times,* while belittling public support for him, nevertheless commented on July 13: "Mr Churchill may well be needed in a Government again."

To Chamberlain this was heresy; his conviction that he would be vindicated was unshakable. Two days later, on July 15, he wrote his sister Ida: "If I refuse to take Winston into the Cabinet to please those who say it would frighten Hitler, it doesn't follow that the idea of frightening Hitler or rather of convincing him that it would not pay him to use force need be abandoned." On July 23 he again wrote her: "One thing is I think clear namely that Hitler has concluded that we mean business and that the time is not ripe for the major war. Therein he is fulfilling my expectations. Unlike some of my critics I go further and say the longer the war is put off the less likely it is to come at all as we go on perfecting our defences and building up the defences of our allies. That is what Winston and Co never seem to realise."[159]

They didn't realize it because it wasn't true. Churchill knew that Hitler's huge army and the Ruhr's smokestack barons were widening their lead over Britain and France. He wasn't speculating; he had the facts, and was sending them to the P.M. and the cabinet, hoping to rouse them before the blow fell. He was still recruiting new informants in Whitehall or the Wilhelmstrasse. A March 21 letter to Chamberlain urging a crash antiaircraft program, for example, had been provoked by Major F. L. Fraser, who probably knew more about AA than anyone else in England. Fraser's reason for joining the net sheds light on why career officers volunteered to flout the Official Secrets Act. "In 1916 when you were commanding a battalion of the Royal Scots Fusiliers," he had written Winston on March 15, "I was GSO 3 of the 9th Division; in 1917, when I was wounded, you were kind enough to come & see me in hospital. . . . I am now Chief Intelligence Officer of the ARP [Air Raid Precautions] Dept and have been with the Dept since 1936. I should be most grateful if you could spare me a few minutes, as I should like to discuss certain matters with you." Chamberlain's chief accomplishments during the Great War had been serving as lord mayor of Birmingham and then as director-general of National Service. He had no concept of the bond between men who have worn the same uniform and survived heavy fighting together.[160]

In June the secretary for air, Kingsley Wood, offered Churchill a tour of airfields where radar was being installed. After inspecting the towers at Biggin Hill, Bawdsey, and Martlesham, Churchill wrote Wood that his trip had been "profoundly interesting, and also encouraging." He then anticipated Hermann Göring by over a year by noting: "These RDF stations require immediate protection." He had thought of "erecting dummy duplicates and triplicates of them at little expense" but "on reflection it seems to me that here is a case of using the smoke-cloud." He ended: "We are on the threshold of immense securities for our island. Unfortunately we want to go further than the threshold and time is short."[161]

The prime minister, too, was concerned about time, but he lacked Winston's sense of urgency. Chamberlain wrote his sister: "As always I want to gain time for I never accept the view that war is inevitable," and, in a letter to the Archbishop of Canterbury, he predicted that "some day the Czechs will see that what we did was to save them for a happier future." Sacrificing them, he believed, had "at last opened the way to that general appeasement which alone can save the world from chaos." Halifax, addressing the House of Lords in early June, declared that "the really dangerous element in the present situation . . . is that the German people as a whole should drift to the conclusion that Great Britain had abandoned all desire to reach an understanding with Germany and that any further attempt at such a thing must be written off."[162]

Winston wrote Halifax that he had been "a little disturbed" by his remarks, which suggested more appeasement. He called the foreign secretary's attention to the "very bad reports" of "bloody episodes," including "oppression and terrorism" in Bohemia, Moravia, and Slovakia. Because of these outrages, he continued, "I am sure you realise that to talk about . . . *lebensraum*, or any concession, while nine million Czechs are still in bondage, would cause great division among us." But defeatism seemed to lie over Whitehall like a dense pea-souper. In public appearances Joseph Kennedy, Hitler's best friend in the diplomatic community, was loudly cheered by Londoners. Churchill was confronted by the American ambassador's views at a dinner party given by Harold Nicolson and his wife, Vita Sackville-West. The American publicist Walter Lippmann, a fellow guest, recounted his afternoon with Kennedy, who had left the impression that he was pro-Nazi, anti-Semitic, and convinced that war was inevitable, and that Britain would be defeated. Nicolson noted: "Winston is stirred by this defeatism into a magnificent oration. He sits hunched there, waving his whisky-and-soda to mark his periods, stubbing his cigar with the other hand." According to his host's diary, Churchill said:

> It may be true, it may well be true . . . that this country will at the outset of this coming and to my mind almost inevitable war be exposed to dire peril and fierce ordeals. It may be true that steel and fire will rain down upon us day and night

scattering death and destruction far and wide. It may be true that our sea-communications will be imperilled and our food-supplies placed in jeopardy. Yet these trials and disasters, I ask you to believe me, Mr Lippmann, will but serve to steel the resolution of the British people and to enhance our will for victory. No, the Ambassador should not have spoken so, Mr Lippmann; he should not have said that dreadful word. Yet supposing — as I do not for one moment suppose — that Mr Kennedy were correct in his tragic utterance, then I for one would willingly lay down my life in combat, rather than, in fear of defeat, surrender to the menaces of these most sinister men. It will then be for you, for the Americans, to preserve and maintain the great heritage of the English-speaking peoples. It will be for you to think imperially, which means to think always of something higher and more vast than one's own national interests. Nor should I die happy in the great struggle which I see before me, were I not convinced that if we in this dear dear island succumb to the ferocity and might of our enemies, over there in your distant and immune continent the torch of liberty will burn untarnished and — I trust and hope — undismayed.[163]

But Churchill was always more than a rhetorician. Lippmann had been seated beside him at dinner, and the American's notes made later that night reveal Winston's grasp of global politics and his plan for victory:

Would cut losses in Far East; no dispersion of the fleet; settle with Japan after the war. Central Europe mobilized as a unit in 1914. Then Germany had ten divisions from Czechoslovakia; now they need six to hold it. Hungary, Jugoslavia, Rumania, dangerous and unreliable. Poland, a new force, and behind it the Russian pad. No use to say to Germany they are not being encircled. Better to overwhelm them with righteous indignation. Only argument that counts is force. No use shaping policy in accordance with Goebbels' propaganda. Take your own line and make them follow. In event of German mobilization, mobilize fleet; at first provocative action, cut German railway communication with Europe and defy them to do anything about it. . . .[164]

It is impossible to put a good face on war, but war, Churchill argued in the *News of the World* on June 18, did not mean annihilation. Even the "atrocity" of bombing civilians could be met by evacuations, RAF attacks on the bombers, antiaircraft — he couldn't mention radar, which was still highly secret — and shelters. Nevertheless, defeatism and the policy to which it gave voice — peace at any price — still flourished at the highest levels of English society. Hitler had betrayed Chamberlain in Prague and Chamberlain had struck back blindly, but appeasement remained his faith. He was also a loyal subject of the Crown, and this was one of those rare moments when a constitutional monarch could have influenced policy. Victoria had done so repeatedly, simply by speaking out forcefully. But this chance was missed. George VI, reticent, said little, and his sympathies lay with Chamberlain. The Queen Mother, in a letter to the King, had expressed the Royal Family's reaction to Munich: "I'm sure you feel as angry as I do at people croaking as they do at the P.M.'s action; for once I agree with Ly. Oxford who is said to have exclaimed as she left the House of Commons yesterday, 'He brought home Peace, why can't they be grateful?' "

Churchill yearned to finish his manuscript and do things which ought to be done and no one else was doing. He knew, from his informants in Whitehall, that the prime minister and his foreign secretary had been treating their French ally shabbily, dealing directly with Hitler and Mussolini without even informing the French. To be sure, those holding political power in Paris almost seemed to encourage this. At Munich, Daladier had played second fiddle to Chamberlain. The agreement had dismayed him but he failed to protest, despite the fact that he was among the more assertive premiers of the tottering Third Republic. But if war came again, poilus, not Tommies, would bear the heavier burden on the battlefield. Winston felt that it was time fences between the allied democracies were mended. Chamberlain and Halifax, however, still dreamed of a London-Berlin-Rome axis.

FIVE

SURGE

CHASING deadlines, Churchill was pushing himself and his secretaries ruthlessly, but when an important guest arrived he gave them, their silent typewriters, and himself a rest. As Chartwell moved through spring and high summer, it became the chief watering place for parliamentarians, flag officers, generals, air marshals, members of the established government, and even cabinet ministers haunted by nightmares of triumphant Nazis marching through the streets of London.

Among those who put their careers at risk to seek Winston's advice was a future chief of the Imperial General Staff, Tiny Ironside, now Sir Edmund Ironside, inspector-general of overseas forces. The general not only shared his host's concerns; they had been friends since the Boer War, and he regarded him with genuine affection. In his diary he wrote that the two of them "made a night of it"; after dining alone they "sat talking till 5 am this morning." The talk was of this and that. Churchill said he would have to "pull in my horns considerably" if he were returned to office, because he "would have to cease making money by writing." Ironside speculated that had last year brought war instead of Munich, his host would at the very least be first lord or war minister, and possibly P.M. But Winston had made friends in the cabinet, particularly "Belisha because . . . it was Belisha who got conscription through." They agreed that "Neville Chamberlain is not a war Prime Minister. He is a pacifist at heart. He has a firm belief that God has chosen him as an instrument to prevent this threatened war." In Winston's opinion, the general noted, it was "now too late for any appeasement. The deed was signed and Hitler is going to make war." Ironside concurred, and the prospect troubled him, for he knew that despite Hore-Belisha's efforts the General Staff had "no considered plans, no plans to deal with the war in general."[1]

Unlike the War Office, Churchill had plans. In a paper he had written on stratagems for the Royal Navy, he proposed, among other moves, that the Admiralty put "a Squadron of battleships into the Baltic. It would paralyse the Germans and immobilise many German divisions." The following day

Ironside noted: "It ran through my head that here was a grand strategist imagining things, and the Navy itself making no plans whatever." When the present first sea lord had commanded the Mediterranean Fleet, Ironside had asked him for "any offensive plan for dealing with Italy." He had none then, and, the general added: "I am sure there is none now."[2]

Insofar as England's political leaders had plans, many surmised that Germany and Britain were virtually allied. One of them was Lord Kemsley, brother of Lord Camrose and a Fleet Street tycoon in his own right. Even as Winston and Ironside parted after a hearty breakfast, Kemsley was in Germany meeting a series of Nazi leaders, including Alfred Rosenberg, editor of the anti-Semitic Nazi *Völkischer Beobachter,* and Baron von Weizsäcker at the Foreign Ministry. Both asked about the strength of Chamberlain's critics in England, particularly Mr. Winston Churchill. On Thursday, July 27, when Hitler received Kemsley at Bayreuth, he, too, asked about Churchill "and his powers of expression." According to Kemsley's notes, he replied that in his opinion "far more notice was taken abroad of the Opposition than in England," and he reminded the Führer that "Mr. Churchill had been unfortunate in his campaigns on at least four occasions in the past, starting with the Abdication of King Edward VIII."[3]

This is shocking, and it served England ill, encouraging the Nazi conviction that England would not fight under any circumstances — that Churchill was an eccentric without a following, who spoke only for himself. A few months earlier that had been true. But as a publisher of newspapers Kemsley must have known how public opinion had changed since Prague, and how Churchill's stock had soared. It was now summertime 1939. By now Winston could have spoken anywhere in England, on any topic, for any fee. Ironside wrote in his diary on July 27: "I keep thinking of Winston Churchill down at Westerham, full of patriotism and ideas for saving the Empire. A man who knows that you must act to win. You cannot remain supine and allow yourself to be hit indefinitely. Winston must be chafing at the inaction. I keep thinking of him walking up and down the room."[4]

One of the more insidious consequences of Munich was a sharp erosion in Britain's credibility, a suspicion on the Continent that His Majesty's Government would respond to future Nazi demands by diplomatic talks leading to capitulation. Churchill warned the House that " the slightest sign of weakness will only aggravate the dangers which concern not only us, but the whole world." He begged the prime minister: "Do not yield another yard."[5]

Britain's guarantee to the Poles was, he felt, one promissory note which was certain to be called. "The glare of Nazi Germany," he predicted in the *Daily Telegraph*, would soon "be turned on Poland." His great worry was that Chamberlain would refuse to redeem his pledge. The prime minister's betrayal of the Czechs had established a pattern. The first transgression is always the most difficult; the second is relatively easy. If forced to choose between breaking his word and breaking the peace, the P.M., Winston suspected, would not hesitate to scuttle his vow to rescue Poland, and that, Churchill believed, would lead to an irrevocable disaster. Britain's honor would be forfeit. Hitler's mastery of the Continent would be absolute. Freedom would vanish from Europe.[6]

But what if the P.M. acted out of character? Suppose he kept his word, and took Britain and France into war? He could do it; the French had permitted the initiative to pass to London and were a silent, acquiescent partner. Then diplomatic problems would be replaced by strategic questions. At Chartwell, Churchill studied his map and recalled the lessons inherent in *The World Crisis*. During the first three years of trench warfare, the Allied armies had kept the enemy at bay only because the czar's huge forces had tied a million Germans down on the eastern front. After the Bolsheviks had overthrown the Romanov regime in 1917 and signed a draconian peace with the kaiser's generals, the million Germans on the eastern front, no longer needed there, were rushed to the west for a knockout blow. In 1918 they had nearly achieved total victory. Only the last-minute arrival of a huge American army had rescued the weary Allies from defeat.

Now the Americans were committed — legally, by an act of Congress — to a policy of neutrality. Churchill doubted that Poland could hold the Wehrmacht at bay. It would be 1918 all over again, except that the Western democracies would lack not only the Yanks but also the Italians. This time the Germans looked like winners, and the future would be an unsurpassed horror for any people who lost a war to Adolf Hitler.

The destruction of Czechoslovakia and the subsequent demoralization among her neighbors to the south had left Britain and France without any strong ally in the east. Poland by herself was inadequate. What the democracies needed, Churchill concluded, was an eastern European ally more powerful than Poland — a nation strong enough to hold the Wehrmacht at bay, forcing the Führer to fight a two-front war. They couldn't choose; only one great power lay east of the Reich. He would have preferred almost any other country, but the long years of appeasement, pacifism, defeatism, and threadbare military budgets had reduced the democracies to the role of beggars, or at any rate petitioners. Moscow, however, had every reason to be responsive to Western overtures. The Soviet Union lay directly in Hitler's path of conquest. He meant to crush her; *Mein Kampf* testified to his intent, reaffirmed in a hundred Führer speeches since.

To Winston the solution to the Anglo-French dilemma was obvious: détente with Russia should become Whitehall's primary goal. Yet he knew that the chances of persuading the men ruling Britain to embrace Bolsheviks were exceedingly small. Therefore, when Labour adopted a policy of recriminations, reciting all the ways in which Baldwin and Chamberlain had played into Hitler's hands, he aligned himself with the government. Opening a major address on Monday, April 3, he described the Polish guarantee as "splendid," declaring his "full support" for the prime minister's policies. Chamberlain eyed him warily. Such ringing Churchillian affirmations were often followed, not by sly attacks — his rhetoric was nothing if not straightforward — but by the introduction of a new proposal which the P.M. liked even less. Actually, Winston began by reintroducing an old proposal of his own; he quoted a passage he had delivered in this chamber a year earlier: "If a number of States were assembled around Great Britain and France in a solemn treaty for mutual defence against aggression; if they had their forces marshalled in what you may call a Grand Alliance; if they had their staff arrangements concerted . . . then I say that you might even now arrest this coming war."[7]

Since then "the situation has deteriorated." And one of Hitler's excuses for the enslavement of millions had been his paranoid claim that Germany's enemies were trying to "encircle" her. In fact, Churchill said, he and his supporters had been urging "the encirclement of an aggressor." Collective security reassured nations which felt threatened, and all were entitled to it, including the Third Reich: "If Herr Hitler feels that he will be overrun by Russia, that he will be fallen upon by Poland, that he will be attacked by Belgium, Holland, or Switzerland, he has only to declare his anxiety open to the world in order to receive the most solemn international guarantees. We seek no security for ourselves that we do not desire Germany to enjoy as well." But providing that security for all countries deserved absolute priority, he said; halfway measures were more dangerous than none: "To stop here with a guarantee to Poland would be to halt in no-man's-land under fire of both trench lines and without the shelter of either. . . . We must go forward now until a conclusion is reached. Having begun to create a Grand Alliance against aggression, we cannot afford to fail." Nor, he warned the House, could they exclude unsavory regimes, provided those who ruled them sought peace.

As the P.M. had feared, Winston was proposing a fresh policy, a British tie with the one great power Chamberlain detested. Churchill's loathing of bolshevism was more famous, and had certainly been more memorably expressed; he had described Lenin as a "plague bacillus"; he had denounced "the Bolshevik cancer eating into the flesh of the wretched being" and had reviled "the bestial appetites and passions" of Communist Russia, a "tyranny of the vilest kind," where "thousands of people have been executed or murdered in cold blood." But he had also declared that when the safety of Britain and her empire stood at risk, his conscience became "a good girl"; and it happened now. He wanted the five million men of the Red Army marching against the Wehrmacht, and he told the House of Commons why.[8]

"Russia," he said, "is a ponderous counterpoise in the scale of world peace. We cannot measure the weight of support which may be forthcoming from Soviet Russia." Labour had proposed that "the attitude of His Majesty's Government towards Russia" be summed up in the phrase "The maximum cooperation possible." Winston thought this "a very accurate and convenient phrase." But, he added, "to find any guidance as to where we stay with Russia, one must ask what is the interest of the Russian people." He asked: "Why should we expect Soviet Russia to be willing to work with us? Certainly we have no special claims upon her good will, nor she upon ours." The answer, he said, was that "Soviet Russia is profoundly affected by German Nazi ambitions." He reeled off Nazi objectives which menaced the U.S.S.R.: the Danube Valley, the Black Sea (a "conquest of the Ukraine by Nazi Germany, upon which such covetous eyes have been avowedly set, would be a direct assault upon the life of the Russian Soviet State"), and targets in the Far East. Thus, "No one can say that there is not a solid identity of interest between the Western democracies and Soviet Russia, and we must do nothing to obstruct the natural play of that identity of interest. . . . The worst folly, which no one supposes we should commit, would be to chill and drive away any natural cooperation which Soviet Russia in her own deep interests feels it necessary to afford." The wisest course was to forget the Bolshevik past and forge Britain, France, and Russia in a "Triple Alliance."[9]

The Men of Munich thought the folly was Churchill's. The prime minister, gazing into his foggy crystal ball, appraised potential Soviet military contributions in a war against Germany and wrote, in a private letter on March 26: "I have no belief whatever in her [Russia's] ability to maintain an effective offensive, even if she wanted to." And even if she wanted to and could, he wasn't sure he would welcome her help. In his mind Bolsheviks, not Nazis, were still the greater threat to Western civilization. Here Chamberlain represented the opinion of Britain's ruling classes. As Winston later observed in the House, during his April 3 speech he "heard a sort of commotion behind me. I heard the Noble Lady the Member for the Sutton Division of Plymouth (Viscountess Astor) express her dislike of any contact with Bolshevik Russia." He asked pointedly: "Where was this dislike when she paid a visit to Soviet Russia with Mr Bernard Shaw?" Lady Astor interrupted: "I have had the great advantage of going to Russia and seeing it; you have only had the advantage of hearing about it from the outside." The point, Winston replied, was that "the time when she went to Russia and gave all her applause and credit to Russia was the time when the influence was deeply detrimental to the interests of this country."[10]

The need for a bond with the U.S.S.R. was "very serious," he said, "and I hope I shall be able to put it without any offense." Nevertheless, it *was* offensive; the thought of shaking hands with what he himself had once called the "bloody paws" of the czar's murderers shocked all the Conservatives from front bench to backbenchers. But he wasn't speaking to them now, or to Nancy Astor; or even, at that evening session, to the House of Commons. His audience was in the Kremlin. Ivan Maisky was in the gallery, and his presence cannot have been coincidental. It was customary, when foreign powers were being discussed, for His Majesty's Government to suggest that their envoys attend Parliament. For a private member to extend such an invitation was highly irregular, but that is the only way the Russian ambassador could have got one that Monday; he and Halifax were on the worst of terms. After Munich, the foreign secretary wrote, Maisky's "attitude seemed to me . . . one of some suspicion." The ambassador, for his part, had come to regard the appeasers as Hitler's "accomplices."[11]

In this he reflected the views of his superior in Moscow, Maksim Litvinov, the Soviet commissar for foreign affairs. Litvinov and Churchill had been thinking along the same lines, and on March 18, three days after the destruction of Czechoslovakia, the commissar had made his first diplomatic move toward rapprochement, proposing an immediate conference in Bucharest of six powers — Russia, Rumania, Poland, Britain, France, and Turkey — to form a "peace front" against the expanding Reich. In the Quai d'Orsay files there is no record of any response from Bonnet, and the Soviet overture is not even mentioned in his capacious (and self-serving) memoirs. Halifax and Chamberlain read the Litvinov initiative, but the prime minister dismissed the plan as "premature" and the Foreign Office told the Russians that it was "not acceptable." On March 19 Maisky called at the FO to ask why. Halifax told him that he was short-handed; no minister of the Crown could be spared for the Bucharest meeting. Even though Litvinov had issued a public statement explaining that no Soviet guarantees of Poland

and Rumania would be forthcoming unless their governments asked for them — they didn't ask; they were terrified by the prospect of Nazi reprisals — Chamberlain told the House of Commons on March 23 that His Majesty's Government took a dim view of establishing "opposing blocs" in Europe, the very argument Beck would use in refusing to guarantee Rumania. After a frustrating session with Halifax, Maisky told Boothby that this rebuff to the Russian proposal had dealt "another smashing blow to the policy of collective security."[12]

Churchill's relationship with the Soviet envoy was very different. They had been meeting regularly for seven years to discuss diplomatic moves which could contain or discourage Nazi aggression. After Churchill concluded his speech suggesting British overtures to Moscow, the House broke up, and Maisky came down to the smoking room to talk to Churchill and other MPs he knew. According to Nicolson's diary: "The House rises at 10.50 pm and I am seized upon by Winston and taken down to the lower smoking room with Maisky and Lloyd George. Winston adopts the direct method of attack [upon Maisky]. 'Now look here, Mr Ambassador, if we are to make a success of this new policy, we require the help of Russia.' " He said: "Now I don't care for your system and I never have, but the Poles and the Rumanians like it even less. Although they might be prepared at a pinch to let you in, they would certainly want some assurances that you would eventually get out. Can you give us such assurances?" Although the question was highly pertinent, it was not one an envoy could answer, and they were interrupted anyway. Nicolson noted: "Lloyd George, I fear, is not really in favour of the new policy and he draws Maisky on. . . . Winston rather objects to this and attacks Lloyd George. 'You must not do this sort of thing, my dear. You are putting spokes in the wheel of history.' "[13]

This does not ring true. It seems inconceivable that Churchill had not consulted Maisky, with whom he was on such close terms, before his speech. As early as February 9 Maisky had been entertaining writers and independent MPs, encouraging the belief that Britain and Russia should put aside ideological differences and face the common enemy together. Boothby, J. B. Priestly, and Nicolson had attended such a luncheon at the Soviet embassy, and Nicolson noted that evening: "Maisky says that Russia was obviously much wounded by Munich and that we can expect no advance from her side. But (and here he became serious) if *we* made approaches, we should not find Russia as aloof or offended as we might have supposed. Bob Boothby and I have an eye-meet like a tennis-ball across a net."[14]

After Prague the Russians had, in fact, made a major advance, the six-power proposal at Bucharest. Then, and throughout the spring and summer of 1939, Churchill's son was seeing a great deal of the Soviet ambassador — Chamberlain wrote his sister of "a regular conspiracy in which Mr Maisky has been involved as he keeps in very close touch with Randolph" — and it is reasonable to assume that when Winston rose on the evening of April 3 he had Russian assurances that his seed would not fall on barren ground. No doubt prodding from Maisky contributed to his proposal, though he alone would have been inadequate. Churchill would have sought, or been offered, encouragement from a Soviet leader of higher rank.[15]

Almost certainly it came to him from Litvinov. The Soviet Union's commissar for foreign affairs held a curious position in Kremlin intrigues. He had become a revolutionary in 1898, was arrested and imprisoned in 1901, but escaped to England and became a Bolshevik in 1903. As a party member he was actually senior to Stalin. But he had never been admitted to the Kremlin hierarchy. He was a Jew, he had been abroad during the 1905 uprising, his wife was British, and during the great revolt in 1917 he had been in London — as Lenin's representative, to be sure, but Communists with an eye on the future made sure they were seen on the barricades. Nevertheless, Litvinov had been foreign commissar since 1930. Stalin trusted him, and was persuaded by Litvinov's argument that the Soviet Union would be wiser to pursue closer ties with England and France than to seek Hitler's good graces. Hitler, Litvinov said, had none. Thus, in Harold Macmillan's words, it became Russian policy "to seek security through the League and by alliances with the western democracies."[16]

The Soviets' chief obstacle continued to be what Thomas Jones called Chamberlain's "Russian complex." Late in November 1938 Bernard Shaw had given a lunch at his flat for Maisky and Jones, and in his diary Jones set down Maisky's summary of the blows Litvinov — and his policy — had suffered during the year. Immediately after the Anschluss, he said, Litvinov had approached Paris, proposing a joint declaration, vowing to fight for Czechoslovakian independence. In the Quai d'Orsay his demarche had been ignored. The foreign commissar had tried again on September 2. Bonnet suppressed his note, whereupon Maisky went to Whitehall. There, too, he was disappointed. "Beyond expressing an interest in the views of Russia," Jones wrote, "Halifax made no sign." The Soviets' exclusion from the Munich Conference had meant an immense loss of prestige for Litvinov and Maisky in the Kremlin; the Anglo-French rejection of Litvinov's proposal for a six-power conference was a further blow. Nevertheless, Stalin permitted him to prepare another tremendous move in 1939, which was in its final stages when Churchill on April 3, knowingly or unknowingly, fired the first gun in Parliament.[17]

Ten days later, on Thursday, April 13, in the debate following the invasion of Albania, Winston fired a second gun, warning Parliament that the peril is "now very near. A great part of Europe is to a very large extent mobilised. Millions of men are being prepared for war. Everywhere the frontier defences are manned. Everywhere it is felt that some new stroke is impending." Should war come, he asked, "can there be any doubt that we shall be involved?" Three months earlier, Britain, free of commitments, could stand aloof, but now His Majesty's Government had provided guarantees "in every direction, rightly in my opinion, having regard to all that has happened." Before Munich, when prospects were brighter, Britain had backed away from the growing tension on the Continent. "Surely then," he said, "when we aspire to lead all Europe back from the verge of the abyss onto the uplands of law and peace, we must ourselves set the highest example." But if they were to "rescue our people and the people of many lands from the dark, bitter waters which are rising fast on every side," they must seize every opportunity, or create opportunities where none existed.

Turning again to the need for an approach to the Soviets, he said:

> The other day I tried to show the House the great interest that Russia has against further Eastward expansion of the Nazi power. It is upon that deep, natural, legitimate interest that we must rely, and I am sure we shall hear from the Government that the steps they are taking are those which will enable us to receive the fullest possible cooperation from Russia, and that no prejudices on the part of England or France will be allowed to interfere with the closest cooperation between the two countries, thus securing our harassed and anxious combinations the unmeasured, if somewhat uncertain, but certainly enormous counterpoise of the Russian power."[18]

Two days later he got action — of sorts. England and France could not reject Russia's Bucharest proposal outright; it would have been bad manners, bad diplomacy, and bad politics — the British people were beginning to anticipate the time when they would need every friend they could get. On April 15, therefore, the Soviets received formal proposals from Whitehall and the Quai. They found them disappointing. The British merely asked Russia to follow their example and affirm the independence of Poland and Rumania. The French had wanted more. They had proposed that Britain, France, and the Soviet Union come to one another's aid should Germany make war on any one of them, but Chamberlain and Halifax weren't prepared to go that far.[19]

Litvinov wanted them to go much further. The following Monday he rocked the chancelleries of Europe by handing Sir William Seeds, the

British ambassador in Moscow, a formal proposal which, if it succeeded, would assure that any Wehrmacht offensive in the east would be met not only by Poland but also by the much larger resources of the Soviet Union, including the Red Army. What Stalin's foreign commissar had submitted was, in fact, nothing less than a blueprint for a triple alliance — a re-creation of the entente which had declared war on the kaiser's Second Reich in 1914 and which would have defeated Germany and Austria, without American help, had the Bolshevik revolution not shattered it three years later.

In Litvinov's draft agreement, England, France, and Russia would not only provide mutual assistance if attacked by Hitler; the treaty would be backed by a specific commitment defining the strength and objectives of their armies, navies, and air forces. This alliance, which Poland could join if she chose, would bind the signatories to "render mutually all manner of assistance, including that of a military nature, in case of aggression in Europe" against any member of the alliance or against "Eastern European States situated between the Baltic and Black Seas and bordering on the U.S.S.R." Further, the signing parties would neither negotiate nor make peace "with aggressors separately from one another and without common consent of the three Powers."[20]

The encirclement of Germany, a myth spun by the Führer at Nuremberg rallies, would be real, and it would be awesome. Any Wehrmacht thrust, anywhere, would trigger retaliation from every country on the Reich's borders except Switzerland and Italy, whose legions, after their performances in Ethiopia and Albania, counted for very little. Swift action was essential, however; with Germany on a war footing Hitler could strike while the alliance was being negotiated. Moreover, Litvinov was aware that Stalin would be highly suspicious of Allied delay. Therefore the commissar stipulated that military conversations between the three powers begin immediately. It was his last bid for a united anti-Nazi front with the West. He was staking his career on it. And he believed it would work.[21]

In London the critics of the Chamberlain government agreed. Macmillan recalled: "This was Litvinov's last chance. It was also ours." Later Churchill summed up the situation: "If . . . Mr. Chamberlain on receipt of the Russian offer had replied: 'Yes. Let us three band together and break Hitler's neck,' or words to that effect, Parliament would have approved, Stalin would have understood, and history might have taken a different course. At least it could not have taken a worse." Robert Coulondre, formerly France's ambassador in Moscow and now her envoy in Berlin, thought Litvinov's offer was almost too good to be true. He cabled Paris, urging instant acceptance.[22]

His advice was rejected. As Thomas Jones wrote, in both Paris and

Churchill votes in the General Election, November 14, 1935.
The Baldwin victory keeps him in political exile.

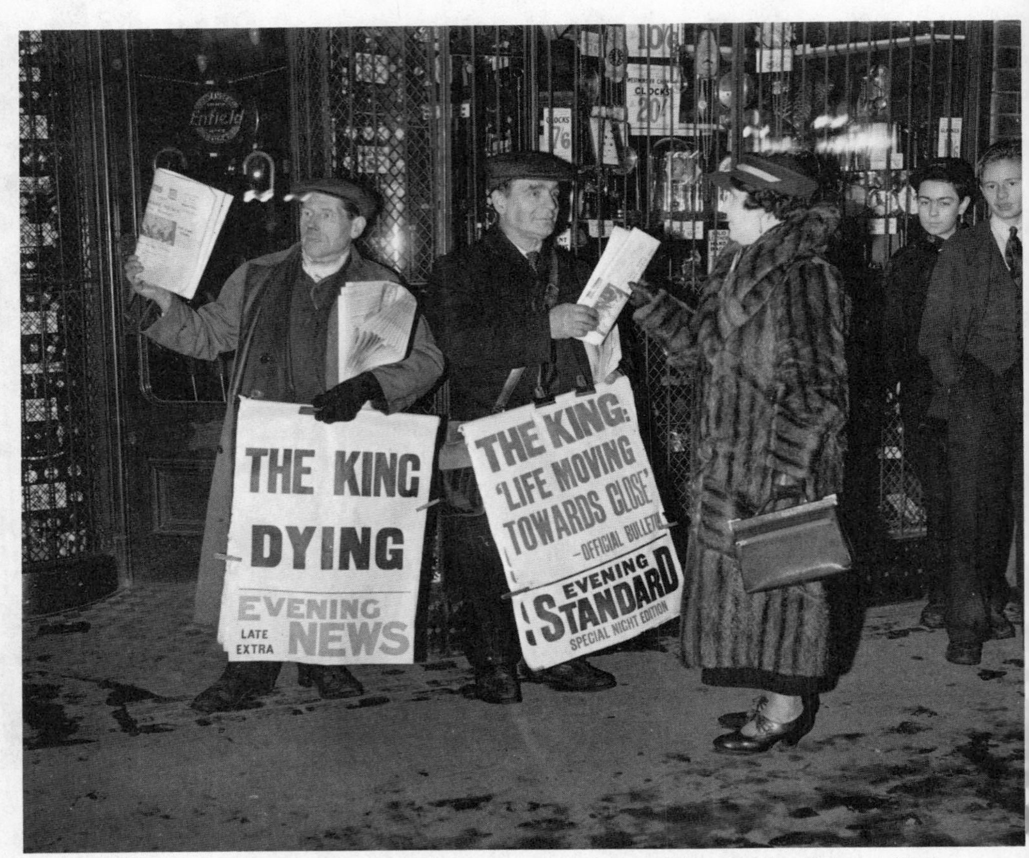

King George V dies on January 20, 1936. His son succeeds him as King Edward VIII.

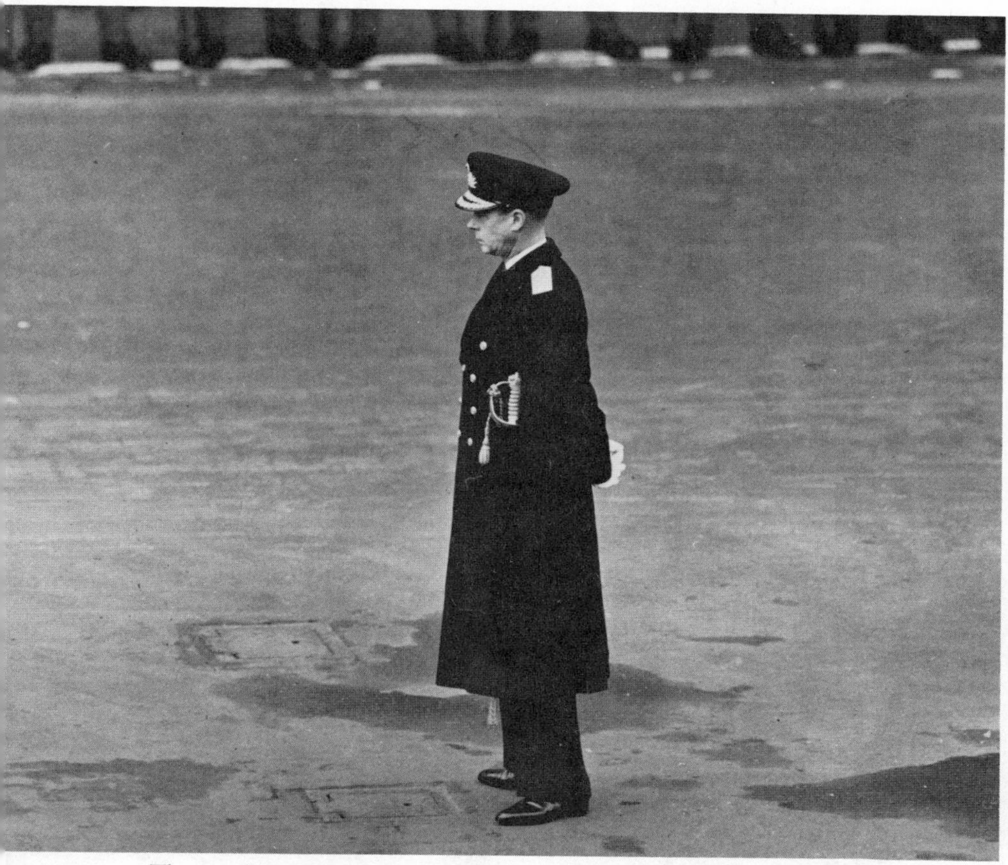

The new king stands somberly at the Cenotaph, November 11, 1936.

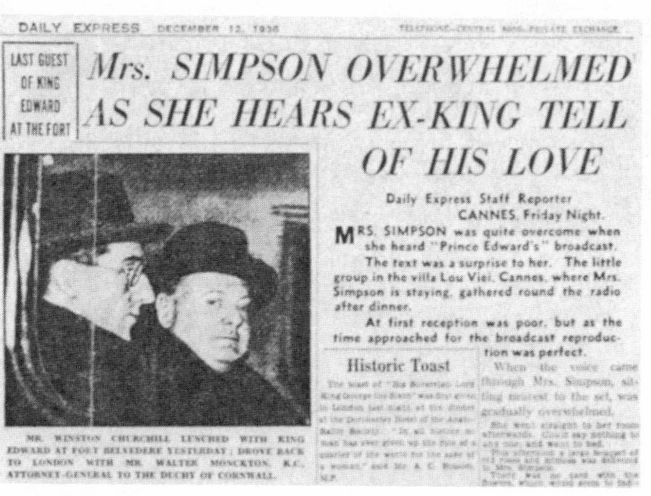

DAILY EXPRESS DECEMBER 12, 1936

LAST GUEST OF KING EDWARD AT THE FORT

Mrs. SIMPSON OVERWHELMED AS SHE HEARS EX-KING TELL OF HIS LOVE

MR. WINSTON CHURCHILL LUNCHED WITH KING EDWARD AT FORT BELVEDERE YESTERDAY; DROVE BACK TO LONDON WITH MR. WALTER MONCKTON, K.C., ATTORNEY-GENERAL TO THE DUCHY OF CORNWALL.

Daily Express Staff Reporter
CANNES, Friday Night.

MRS. SIMPSON was quite overcome when she heard "Prince Edward's" broadcast.

The text was a surprise to her. The little group in the villa Lou Viei, Cannes, where Mrs. Simpson is staying, gathered round the radio after dinner.

At first reception was poor, but as the time approached for the broadcast reproduction was perfect.

When the voice came through Mrs. Simpson, sitting nearest to the set, was gradually overwhelmed.

Historic Toast

Edward VIII insists upon marrying an American woman with a tarnished past. Churchill, in a highly unpopular stand, supports him. Lord Beaverbrook's *Daily Express* tells the tale.

Hermann Göring *(right)* with one of his warmest admirers,
Sir Nevile Henderson, His Majesty's ambassador to Nazi Germany.

As Hitler overruns the Rhineland, Sir John Simon, Anthony Eden, and Sir Robert Vansittart follow the coffin of Leopold von Hösch, the German ambassador to Britain.

Discussing Hitler's Austrian Anschluss, Churchill and Foreign Secretary Lord Halifax walk from the Foreign Office to Parliament, March 29, 1938.

Alfred Duff Cooper, First Lord of the Admiralty, resigns from Chamberlain's cabinet in disgust over Munich.

At the peak of the Munich crisis, September 1938, Winston Churchill gloomily leaves No. 10 Downing Street after conferring with Prime Minister Neville Chamberlain.

At Chartwell in early 1939 Winston nails tiles to the roof of Orchard Cottage, which he designed and largely built as a retirement home for Clementine and him.

Clementine in 1939 with one of Chartwell's two fox cubs, Charles-James and Victoria. With war imminent, both cubs were turned loose in the wild.

As Honorary RAF Commodore, Winston flies as copilot at Kenley, April 16, 1939.

Why Not Mr. Churchill?

In an article in this page on Thursday last, Percy Cater, "Daily Mail" Parliamentary Correspondent, asked the question, "Why Not Mr. Baldwin?" and contended that he was the best leader of the country at the present time.

To-day F. G. Prince-White, "Daily Mail" Special Correspondent, retorts with "Why Not Mr. Churchill?"

★

IT has been said of William Pitt that he became Prime Minister at the moment when his leadership was a *tactical* necessity.

Great tasks awaited the hands of Chatham's brilliant son; there were vast responsibilities to be borne. England was soon to be shaken by the convulsions of a politically epileptic Europe. The timber for the tumbrils of the French Revolution was seasoned; in Paris the Little Corsican was finishing his military studies, oblivious yet of his dazzling destiny.

By

F. G. PRINCE-WHITE

At such a time no ordinary voice could speak the country's will — nor could a weakling's hand steady the State in the fast oncoming day of upheaval among the neighbour nations.

have been errors inseparable from the exercise of great gifts. And even Mr. Churchill's bitterest opponents cannot but own that he is uncommonly gifted.

To younger students of politics it is a most puzzling mystery that Mr. Churchill was not Prime Minister long ago. They look at his record and discover that he has occupied almost every other Government position.

In 1906, when he was only 32, he was given the post of Under-Secretary of State for the Colonies. Two years later he was President of the Board of Trade, and two years after that found him Home Secretary. From 1911 until 1915 he was First Lord of the Admiralty, from which office he passed to that of Chancellor of the Duchy of Lancaster.

In 1917 he followed Mr. Lloyd George in that supremely important Department, the Ministry of Munitions. Next he figured on the Governmental stage as Secretary for War and for Air, and after that as Secretary of State for the Colonies.

For five years—from 1924 to 1929—he was Chancellor of the Exchequer.

Here is no mediocre experience, but such as might well stand a Prime Minister in good stead.

Brilliant Oratory

IT has been Mr. Churchill's incomparable eloquence in the House of Commons that has crystallised most perfectly the nation's inmost thoughts and feelings in this prolonged season of international fear and distrust.

One could have believed, listening the other day to the climax of his speech on the Budget, that his voice belonged to one of the great masters of oratory and statecraft whose statues now stand silently amid Westminster Abbey's shadows:

" Either there will be a melting of hearts and a joining of hands between great nations, and they will set out on realising the glorious era of prosperity and freedom now within the grasp of millions of toiling people, or there will be an explosion and catastrophe the course of which no imagination can measure,

Demands that Churchill be brought into the government had been swelling for three years. The *Daily Mail* ran this article on May 11, 1936, in reaction to Hitler's seizure of the Rhineland.

"BRING HIM BACK–IT'S YOUR LAST CHANCE"

By the spring of 1939, the dictators were overrunning Europe; Memel, Albania, and what was left of independent Czechoslovakia fell to Hitler and Mussolini. Now most of Fleet Street sounded the alarm.

Churchill appeals for Territorial Army recruits at the Mansion House, April 24, 1939.

CALLING MR. CHURCHILL

The press heightens its demands; this cartoon appeared in the *Daily Express* on July 6, 1939.

THE OLD SEA-DOG

"Any telegram for me?"

Six days later this cartoon appeared in *Punch*.

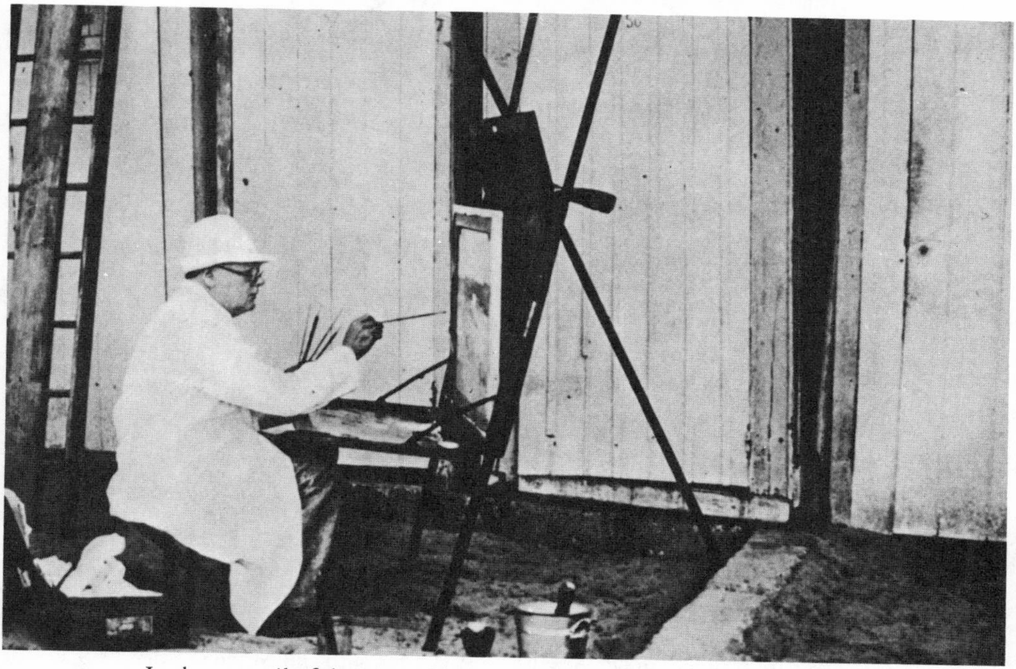

In the turmoil of the 1930s Churchill often found sanctuary in painting.

On July 24, 1939, a huge sign, paid for by an anonymous backer of Churchill, appears on the Strand.

War is imminent in late August 1939, as Churchill and Anthony Eden walk down Whitehall to the House of Commons. Both are still treated as lepers by Chamberlain.

On September 1, 1939, the Germans invade Poland, and that same day Chamberlain appoints Churchill First Lord of the Admiralty. On September 3 Britain declares war on Germany. This photograph was taken on September 4, Churchill's first full day at the Admiralty.

In the first month of the war Randolph, serving in his father's old regiment, the 4th Hussars, marries Pamela, the daughter of Lord and Lady Digby.

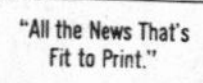

"All the News That's Fit to Print."

The New York Times.

LATE CITY EDITION

VOL. LXXXIX...No. 30,058. NEW YORK, SATURDAY, MAY 11, 1940 THREE CENTS

DUTCH AND BELGIANS RESIST NAZI DRIVE; ALLIED FORCES MARCH IN TO DO BATTLE; CHAMBERLAIN RESIGNS, CHURCHILL PREMIER

COALITION ASSURED

Labor Decides to Allow Leaders to Join New National Cabinet

OLD MINISTERS STAY

Churchill Asks Them to Remain Until They Can Be Replaced

The text of Chamberlain's statement is printed on Page 9.

By RAYMOND DANIELL

Special Cable to THE NEW YORK TIMES.

LONDON, May 10—In the gravest crisis Great Britain has faced since the World War, Winston Churchill became Prime Minister tonight as Allied armies raced across Belgium again for a death grapple with invading German armies.

Neville Chamberlain, who had headed the government since just after King George VI ascended the throne, resigned early in the evening after convincing himself that it was impossible to remain and give the country the truly national government that the people want.

A genuine coalition Cabinet was assured when the executive committee of the Labor party declared that it would accept a share in a government headed by a new Prime Minister who had the nation's confidence. This is expected also to result in the entry of Liberals into the government.

Invasion Fails to Save Cabinet

The German invasion of Belgium, the Netherlands and Luxembourg,

The International Situation

The War in the Low Countries

The Netherlands—The defenders claimed to be holding the Germans along the lines of the Yssel and Maas Rivers. At Delfzijl, across the River Eems from the German stronghold of Emden, the Netherland troops appeared still to be in command, despite strong German attacks. [Page 1.] German troops, landed by air transports and parachute at Rotterdam, did not succeed in seizing the city; Rotterdam officials said the invaders there had been pressed into dangerous positions. [Page 6.] The Netherland Commander in Chief summed up: "The surprise attack is a failure." [Page 1.]

Belgium—Although dispatches agreed that in most places the Belgians had stopped the Germans at the frontier, it was reported that Limburg Province, in the northeast, had been overrun. Brussels, Antwerp and other important centers were bombed; in Greater Brussels forty-one persons were reported killed, eighty-two wounded. German troops were landed by parachutes extensively in the eastern part of the country, but no accounts of outstanding success at this kind of Blitzkrieg were received. The attitude in Belgium was that the army could hold out for a time, but help was needed quickly. King Leopold was at the front. [Page 1.]

Luxembourg—This small and armyless duchy was overrun by the Germans.

Allied Help—Paris emphasized that two hours after German troops had crossed neutral borders, meeting strong resistance, French and British troops had crossed into Belgium, receiving enthusiastic welcome.

Battle was engaged at many points. The French put the German attacking force at twenty-nine divisions. On both banks of the Moselle, which separates Luxembourg from Germany, a German operation was under way which, the French said, might be the beginning of a large-scale attack. French air fields, railways, coal mines and factories were attacked by air raiders. Generalissimo Gamelin said: "Germany has engaged us in a struggle to the death. The watchword is: 'For France and all her Allies: Courage, energy, confidence.'" [Page 1.]

Germany—Berlin made no great claims of immediate victory, aside from the general statement that enemy resistance in the border region had been broken. [Page 1.] In an Order of the Day to his troops, Chancellor Hitler said: "The fight beginning today decides the fate of the German nation for the next 1,000 years. Do your duty now!" [Page 4.]

The War Elsewhere

Britain changed pilots, Neville Chamberlain stepping down in response to popular demand, and Winston Churchill taking over. Mr. Churchill is expected to have full Labor and Liberal support; he asked all Ministers to carry on until he could form a new government. It was believed

hint that Mussolini would enter the war. [Page 5.]

At Vatican City the Pope was reported deeply shocked at the German invasion. He is expected to issue a formal condemnation today. [Page 4.]

At Washington President

AID IS SENT AT ONCE

French Enter Belgium—Britons Cross Sea to Netherlands

CONTACT SOON MADE

AlliesHelpLowCountries Meet First Thrust of 29 German Divisions

By G. H. ARCHAMBAULT

Wireless to THE NEW YORK TIMES

PARIS, May 10—Two hours after the Germans invaded the Low Countries, French and British forces were crossing the border to help the Netherland and Belgian Armies withstand the shock of at least twenty-nine German divisions. Contact was made without delay, and by nightfall the battle had been engaged at many points.

(The landing of British troops by transport at Netherland ports was reported by The Associated Press from Amsterdam.)

On broad lines both the Netherlanders and the Belgians are resisting with determination on positions already prepared. Farther south, what may turn out to be an operation on a large scale is in its preliminary phase on both banks of the Moselle River.

The Germans also made a demonstration in the extreme north at the mouth of the Ems River. Progress thence southward through the Netherlands would be impeded by marshes.

von Epp Plan Believed Used

The Germans apparently are put-

THE FIRES OF WAR LEAP ACROSS THE LOW COUNTRIES

Following upon Germany's lightning invasion there were no connected battle fronts yesterday, but many scattered points of major fighting. The main battle sectors in the Netherlands were at Delfzijl (1) and along the Yssel River (2) and the Maas River (4), while a struggle raged in the city of Rotterdam (3). In Belgium the Germans claimed to have advanced to the Albert Canal and taken Maastricht fortress (6), although there was stiff fighting along the canal. Brussels and Antwerp (5) were both attacked by Nazi bombers. Luxembourg (7) was overrun by the invaders, but the Allies were apparently engaging the Germans west of the Moselle River.

BELGIUM REPORTS NAZIS ARE HALTED

Leopold Is at Front as Active Commander—41 Killed, 82 Wounded in Brussels Raid

Bulletins on European Conflict

Special Cable to THE NEW YORK TIMES

AMSTERDAM, the Netherlands, Saturday, May 11—Amsterdam was bombed shortly after dawn today. The raid lasted twenty-five minutes, during which a number of heavy bombs fell. No casualties were immediately reported. Another wave of German bombers passed over the city a half hour later.

Widespread French Air Alarms

PARIS, Saturday, May 11 (AP)—Widespread air alarms

HOLLANDERS FIRM

Report 100 Nazi Planes Shot Down as Troops Strike at Invaders

BOMBERS RANGE LAND

Air Attacks Continuous—Parachutists Land at Strategic Spots

By OSCAR MOHR

Wireless to THE NEW YORK TIMES.

AMSTERDAM, the Netherlands, May 10—The German invaders of the Netherlands are being held in check and the surprise element of their attack can be considered a failure, Lieut. Gen. Henri Gerard Winkelman, the Netherland supreme commander, declared tonight.

"In all parts of the country our forces stand firm in their positions as far as this is required by orders," General Winkelman said in an order to his troops, "and they even attack the enemy intrepidly and successfully where necessary for preventing execution of the enemy's plans."

General Winkelman's statement followed a High Command communiqué declaring that the Netherland forces were offering "serious resistance" along the Maas and Yssel Rivers and were maintaining their positions at Delfzijl "in spite of strong German attacks."

Heavy Toll of Planes Claimed

At least seventy German airplanes were shot down during the day as they attacked airdromes or attempted to land, the communiqué said. (A later communiqué raised

New York Times, May 11, 1940.

As France collapses and all seems lost,
Winston Spencer Churchill becomes Prime Minister of Great Britain.

London the Men of Munich were "much more optimistic than I am about the behavior of the dictators" — Hitler and Mussolini — and far more wary of the despot in the Kremlin. Jean Montigny, a Radical-Socialist, had warned the Chamber of Deputies on "the error and the illusion of any foreign policy based even partly on confidence in the power of the Russian army outside its frontiers and on the loyalty of the Soviet government." Many deputies were concerned about Poland's willingness to accept Soviet aid; as Poland's ally, France had to deal with it. Nevertheless, on April 22 the French cabinet, albeit without enthusiasm, agreed to Litvinov's proposal as a basis of negotiation, and so informed the British. The Quai declared, Whitehall delayed.[23]

On April 19 the cabinet's Foreign Policy Committee considered the Litvinov initiative. The Foreign Office was startled by its airtight language; by contrast — and by design — Britain's Polish guarantee was a sieve of loopholes. Litvinov took Horace Wilson's breath away; what if a copy of this document fell into the Führer's hands? Suppose he blamed England for it? The consequences didn't bear thinking about, and so, instead of thinking about them, Cadogan, in the absence of Halifax, described the Russian plan as "extremely inconvenient," suggested that Soviet military strength was trivial, and declared that "from the practical point of view there is every argument against accepting the Russian proposal." As a civil servant, however, the under secretary had to recognize that England had more than one party. Politically, the issue could become a quagmire. Thus, "there is great difficulty in rejecting the Soviet offer. . . . The left in this country may be counted on" to exploit a refusal. There was also a "very remote" possibility that the Russians might join hands with the Germans. Nevertheless, Cadogan ended, "on balance" Litvinov's offer should be turned down on the ground that it might "alienate our friends and reinforce the propaganda of our enemies without bringing in exchange any real material contribution to the strength of our Front." One wonders who, in Cadogan's opinion, England's "friends" and "enemies" were.[24]

The situation, as one cabinet member pointed out, was "very awkward." The French cabinet, however reluctantly, had voted to accept the plan. Churchill, Lloyd George, Eden, Duff Cooper, Labour, and the Liberals would raise Cain if His Majesty's Government rejected it. The Poles and the Rumanians, *per contra*, would be up in arms if Litvinov's offer were accepted. Finally — and this was decisive — Chamberlain, Halifax, Wilson, Cadogan, Inskip, and Simon were revolted by the prospect of an alliance with Bolsheviks. The Russians, as Thomas Jones wrote in his diary, "made our flesh creep." Looking for a way out, the P.M. solicited the views of the Chiefs of Staff and seized upon one point in their report. The military support the U.S.S.R. could provide to Poland or Rumania, they wrote, "is not so great as might be supposed generally."[25]

Chamberlain ignored what followed, which was the chiefs' conclusion that "Russian cooperation would be invaluable in that Germany would be unable to draw upon Russia's immense reserves of food and raw materials and should succumb more quickly to our economic stranglehold." He also suppressed the chiefs' supplementary appraisal, which concluded:

> A full-blown guarantee of mutual assistance between Great Britain and France and the Soviet Union offers certain advantages. It would present a solid front of formidable proportions against aggression. . . . If we fail to achieve any agreement with the Soviet, it might be regarded as a diplomatic defeat which would have serious military repercussion, in that it would have the immediate effect of encouraging Germany to further acts of aggression and of ultimately throwing the U.S.S.R. into her arms. . . . Furthermore, if Russia remained neutral, it would leave her in a dominating position at the end of hostilities.[26]

According to Cadogan, this passage "annoyed" Chamberlain. Privately he threatened to "resign rather than sign an alliance with the Soviet." Admiral of the Fleet Lord Chatfield, whose commitment to defend Britain eclipsed his hostility to bolshevism, pointed out that the chiefs were "very anxious that Russia should not under any circumstances become allied with Germany. Such an eventuality would create a most dangerous situation for us." In the Foreign Office this minute was the source of great amusement. The admiral was informed that Communists and Nazis were as unlikely a combination as oil and water. If he would look after the Royal Navy, he was politely told, Whitehall would tend to foreign affairs.[27]

After a fortnight of silence from London, Stalin, not a man of great patience, lost the little he had. On the back page of *Pravda*'s May 3 issue a small item appeared in the "News in Brief" column: "M. Litvinov has been released from the Office of Foreign Commissar at his own request."

The significance of Litvinov's dismissal passed almost unnoticed in the Western democracies. Because of an intelligence failure in MI6 and the Deuxième Bureau, Allied governments did not know, as Churchill later wrote, that Vyacheslav Molotov, Litvinov's successor, "had always been favourable to an arrangement with Hitler," that he had been "convinced by Munich and much else that neither Britain nor France would fight until they were attacked, and would not be much good then." Like the FO diplomats, ordinary citizens never dreamed that a treaty binding Moscow and Berlin was possible. Eventually, it was assumed, the two would go to war.[28]

But it would not be Molotov who would make the final decision as to which way the Soviets turned; that power belonged exclusively to Joseph Stalin. Exploring the mind of a psychotic is impossible — the shortest distance between two points becomes a maze — yet as Churchill perceived, there was method in Stalin's dementia. In his own twisted way he was a patriot; like Winston he saw the peril in the Reich and wanted his country to survive it. That was his end. Any means was acceptable to him. He was quietly searching for one that would work.

Doubtless he would have preferred to avoid allies altogether. If he was viewed with suspicion in the capitals of Europe, his suspicions of their leaders ran to paranoia. Nevertheless, the necessity of making a choice, however distasteful, was becoming clear to him, and although Litvinov was in disgrace, an attachment to Britain and France was still preferable to a loathsome alliance with Berlin. Therefore the new foreign commissar, despite his Germanophilia, was instructed not to abandon discussions with Halifax and Bonnet.

Coulondre was encouraged by Molotov's accession. Molotov, he cabled the Quai from Berlin, was chairman of the Council of People's Commissars and a "member of the Politburo, depositary of the thoughts of Stalin"; his appointment meant "Soviet foreign policy can only gain in clarity and precision, and France and England will have no reason to regret it." Bonnet wrote in his memoirs that he was "quite satisfied by the assurances" of the Russian ambassador in Paris that the switch in foreign commissars "does not denote any change in Soviet foreign policy," and that diplomatic discussions between envoys of the three nations could open whenever Britain and France were ready. Maisky brought the same message to Chamberlain and Halifax, who protested that they weren't ready.[29]

In fact, the democracies had every reason to regret the departure of their champion in the Kremlin. The Germans realized that they had gained ground. To drive the point home, the Russian chargé d'affaires in Berlin called at the Wilhelmstrasse to stress "the great importance of the personality of Molotov" — a curt, mulish man who spoke only Russian and held the Western Allies in contempt — and his "importance for future Soviet foreign policy." A dispatch from Warsaw reported that Litvinov had resigned after Marshal Kliment Voroshilov had told him that the Red Army was not prepared to fight for Poland and had denounced, in the name of the Russian General Staff, "excessively far-reaching military obligations." The *Frankfurter Zeitung* commented that Litvinov's fall was a serious setback for Anglo-French plans to "encircle" the Reich. The German chargé in Moscow cabled the Wilhelmstrasse:

> Since Litvinov had received the English Ambassador as late as May 2 and had been named in the press of yesterday as guest of honour at the parade, his dismissal appears to be the result of a spontaneous decision by Stalin. . . . At the last Party Congress, Stalin urged caution lest the Soviet Union should be drawn into conflict. Molotov (no Jew) is held to be "the most intimate friend and closest collaborator of Stalin." His appointment is apparently the guarantee that the foreign policy will be continued strictly in accordance with Stalin's ideas.[30]

Some Englishmen were apprehensive. In London, Nicolson noted in his diary that "the left-wing people" in particular were "very upset. . . . They are not at all sure that Russia may not make a neutrality pact with Germany. I fear this terribly." In his memoirs Churchill would write scathingly of Litvinov's dismissal: "The eminent Jew, the target of German antagonism, was flung aside for the time being like a broken tool, and, without being allowed a word of explanation, was bundled off the world stage to obscurity, a pittance, and police supervision."[31]

The extent of Churchill's information about Kremlin infighting is unknown. But the Soviet envoy Maisky was almost certainly his chief confidant. It can hardly have been coincidence that he renewed his campaign for the triple alliance on May 4, the day after Litvinov was sacked. The chief stumbling block, he knew, was Poland. The Poles were adamant that Russian troops never be permitted to cross their territory, not even, say, if Germany attacked France and the Red Army lunged westward to support the French. Beck and his fellow officers in Warsaw not only persisted in regarding the Russians as lepers; they resented anyone who suggested that they be treated as anything else.

Churchill believed the moment must be seized despite the fears in Warsaw. He pointed out in the *Daily Telegraph* that "Ten or twelve days have passed since the Russian offer was made. The British people . . . have a right, in conjunction with the French Republic, to call upon Poland not to place obstacles in the way of a common cause." Hitler's prey needed not only "the full cooperation of Russia" but also the three Baltic states, who, with arms and munitions from the Soviet Union, could provide "perhaps twenty divisions of virile troops." He appreciated the Polish policy of "balancing between the German and Russian neighbour," but now that "Nazi malignity is plain, a definite association between Poland and Russia becomes indispensable." Otherwise, war would be certain, and a German victory likely, with Poland in chains. The British and French could hold the Wehrmacht in the west, he wrote, but without the Red Army, the eastern front would collapse. He believed the Soviet Union would be responsive to overtures.

> Russian interests are deeply concerned in preventing Herr Hitler's designs on Eastern Europe. It should still be possible to range all the states and peoples from the Baltic to the Black Sea in one solid front against a new outrage or invasion. Such a front, if established in good heart, and with resolute and efficient military arrangements, combined with the strength of the Western Powers, may yet confront Hitler, Goering, Himmler, Ribbentrop, Goebbels and Company with forces the German people would be reluctant to challenge.[32]

Unmentioned in his column, but of greater concern, was his knowledge that his own government was as hostile to the triple alliance as Beck. Britain had yet to issue a formal reply to Litvinov's proposal. That same day Lord Camrose, acting, in effect, as Winston's representative, called at the Foreign Office for a lord-to-lord talk with Halifax. Camrose reviewed all the reasons for establishing the peace bloc. After leaving the FO he wrote an account summing up the foreign secretary's counterarguments. Halifax thought such an alliance would be ill-received in Tokyo. Rumania, as well as Poland, would oppose it. England's Roman Catholics would be offended. Spain might react by joining the Axis, Italy would be alienated, the Portuguese might object, and Hitler might be driven into undertaking "desperate measures." Camrose had patiently replied that all these points were trivial or irrelevant — the Italians were already German allies — when balanced against the need to halt Nazi aggression in its tracks, defend Britain, and avert a general European war. Halifax listened politely but was unmoved.[33]

On May 8, three weeks after the Soviet Union had made its great move, London replied to it. "The response," William Shirer notes, "was a virtual rejection. It strengthened suspicions in Moscow that Chamberlain was not willing to make a military pact with Russia to prevent Hitler from taking Poland." His Majesty's Government did leave the door ajar — a few inches. The proposal would be restudied. A flame of hope gleamed, but it was faint and flickering.[34]

Chamberlain did not reveal his opinion of the Russian proposal in the House of Commons until May 19, and then only after Churchill, Lloyd George, and Eden had, in Winston's words, "pressed upon the Government the vital need for an immediate arrangement with Russia of the most far-reaching character and on equal terms." For an hour Lloyd George appealed for decision, a clear policy to succor England's friends and confound her enemies. Churchill described the prime minister's speech on the Soviet proposal as "cool, and indeed disdainful." Chamberlain's view, he later wrote, showed "the same lack of proportion as . . . in the rebuff to the Roosevelt proposals a year before." The P.M. insisted that "the suggestion that we despise the assistance of the Soviet Union is without foundation." If the government could "evolve a method by which we can enlist the cooperation and assistance of the Soviet Union . . . we welcome it; we want it; we attach value to it." It would be foolish, he said, to suppose that Russia, "that huge country, with its vast population and enormous resources, would be a negligible factor." Talks between British and Soviet diplomats had, he said, already begun. Unfortunately, they had bogged down. He acknowledged that he was reluctant to join hands with Moscow, but insisted that his position was based "on expedience and not on any ideological ground." There was, he said, "a sort of veil, a sort of wall, between the two governments which is extremely difficult to penetrate."[35]

Churchill thought the veil was in the P.M.'s mind. His skepticism was justified; two months earlier, commenting on the Soviet Union, Chamberlain had written his sister: "I must confess to the most profound distrust of Russia. . . . I distrust her motives, which seem to me to have very little connection with our ideas of liberty, and to be concerned only with getting everyone else by the ears. Moreover, she is both hated and suspected by many of the smaller States, notably by Poland, Roumania, and Finland." Significantly, he was untroubled by Nazi Germany's ideas of liberty, though at that time Hitler's concern with getting everyone by the ears had been far more conspicuous, and certainly more successful, than Stalin's. Colin Coote wrote Churchill that the prime minister "fundamentally wants Nazi ideas to dominate Europe, because of his fantastic dislike of Soviet Russia."[36]

French *députés* in Paris's *quartier des ministères* found an alliance with Moscow more attractive — no Channel separated them from the Wehrmacht — but ministers like Bonnet also regarded the Soviet Union as an evil empire, and made no effort to conceal it. In neither capital were the men in office aware that their personal opinions were irrelevant. Men who control great states must deal with their peers abroad, whatever their opinions of them; the Allies' studied rudeness toward the U.S.S.R. in the spring and summer of 1939, when Russia was offering them collective security, was inexcusable. Certainly it was no service to the millions they governed. It is arguable that Litvinov, had he met with civility and those supple conversations *à deux* in which trained diplomats excel, might have stopped the war that all Europe, with the exception of the Führer and his co-conspirators, dreaded. The fact that they did not understand Litvinov's policy and the inner workings of the Soviet bureaucracy does not brighten their memory.

Winston, looking beyond ideologies, saw England in danger; her survival, for him, outstripped everything else. He doubted, he told the House on May 19, that Chamberlain's speech had contributed to the task before Parliament. "Nor has it, I venture to say, reassured those who feel deep misgivings about the present situation." He was, he said, "quite unable to understand what is the objection to making the agreement with Russia. . . . The alliance is solely for the purpose of resisting further acts of aggression. I cannot see what is wrong with that." Turning toward the front bench, he told the prime minister: "When you come to examine . . . the interest and loyalty of the Russian Government in this matter, you must not be guided by sentiment. You must be guided by a study of the vital interests involved. The vital major interests of Russia are deeply engaged in cooperation with Great Britain and France to prevent further acts of aggression." He asked: "If you are ready to be an ally of Russia in time of war" — as Chamberlain had said he was — "why should you shrink from becoming an ally of Russia now, when you may by that very fact prevent the breaking out of war? I cannot understand all these refinements of diplomacy and delay. If the worst comes to the worst you are in the midst of it with them, and you have to make the best of it with them. If the difficulties do not arise, well, you will have had the security in the preliminary stages."[37]

Of course, Winston told the House, there were complicated side issues in any treaty, but here, surely, the issue could hardly be simpler.

I should have thought that this plan of a triple alliance is a preliminary step, and an invitation to other countries in danger on this front to come under its protection, was the most straightforward and practical manner of approaching the subject. I do not know whether I can commend it to my right hon. Friend by adopting a simile selected as a special compliment to him. It is like setting up an armoured umbrella, under which other countries will be invited to take shelter as and when they seek to do so. But we cannot exclude from our minds the fact that we are in a deadlock at the moment. What are the differences? We have already given guarantees to Poland and Rumania, and the Government tell us that they would be glad if Russia would give similar guarantees. Consequently, if Poland and Rumania are attacked we shall be in the war, and so will Russia. It is almost axiomatic that those who are allies of the same Power are allies of one another.

"Clearly," he went on, "Russia is not going to enter into agreements unless she is treated as an equal, and not only treated as an equal, but has confidence that the methods employed by the Allies — by the peace front — are such as would be likely to lead to success." Vague policy and wavering leadership discourage nations otherwise attracted to a coalition, and Chamberlain "must realise that none of these States in Eastern Europe can maintain themselves for, say, a year's war unless they have behind them the massive, solid backing of a friendly Russia, joined to the combination of the Western Powers." Then Churchill raised what, for Englishmen, was the ultimate issue: "Unless there is an Eastern front set up, what is going to happen to the West? What is going to happen to those countries on the Western front to whom, if we have not given guarantees, it is admitted we are bound — countries like Belgium, Holland, Denmark, and Switzerland? . . . How are they to be defended if there is no Eastern front in activity?"

He ended:

> It is a tremendous thing, this question of the Eastern front. I am astonished that there is not more anxiety about it. Certainly, I do not ask favours of Soviet Russia. This is no time to ask favours of countries. But here is an offer, a fair offer, and a better offer, in my opinion, than the terms which the Government seek to get for themselves; a more simple, a more direct and a more effective offer. Let it not be put aside and come to nothing. I beg His Majesty's Government to get some of these brutal truths into their heads. Without an effective Eastern front, there can be no satisfactory defence of our interests in the West, and without Russia there can be no effective Eastern front. If His Majesty's Government, having neglected our defences for a long time, having thrown away Czechoslovakia with all that Czechoslovakia meant in military power, having committed us without examination of the technical aspects to the defence of Poland and Rumania, now reject and cast away the indispensable aid of Russia, and so lead us in the worst of all ways into the worst of all wars, they will have ill-deserved the confidence and, I will add, the generosity with which they have been treated by their fellow-countrymen.[38]

Winston — and by now the weight of British public opinion — thought this reasoning unanswerable. Bowing to the storm of criticism, the prime minister on May 23 grudgingly agreed to negotiate with the Soviets on the basis of a British-French-Soviet alliance. He remained unpersuaded that such an alliance was necessary, however. And perhaps there was a certain logic in the argument that a strong ally on Germany's eastern front — or her western front, for that matter — was unnecessary if the intention was to meet Hitler's demands anyway. That, after all, had been the pattern; capitulation was inherent in the character of the British prime minister. The Führer's minister of propaganda, certain beyond doubt that the P.M. would yield, openly said so. The *Observer* quoted Goebbels as predicting that "Herr Hitler will secure peace with triumph because Mr. Chamberlain will force the Poles to give way."[39]

Give way where? Over what?

After Chamberlain's vow of support for Polish independence, Daladier had told his cabinet that the British now regarded the Vistula, not the Rhine, as their frontier. At the mouth of the Vistula stood the Free City of Danzig, a free state created by the Treaty of Versailles; the city's real significance arose from the fact that it lay on the Baltic Sea. Because the port could be approached through the Polish Corridor — another creation of Versailles — it gave the Poles access to the sea and world trade. Like almost every memorable Versailles gift, however, the transformation of the city's sovereignty had been made at the expense of the Germans. Until the 1919 peace treaty, it had been part of the Second Reich. Danzig, in fact, is a German name. After 1945 the Poles renamed it Gdańsk.

In 1939 it was not Polish territory, though *führertreu* readers of *Völkischer Beobachter* and *Der Angriff* had been led to believe that it was. The victors of 1918 had designated it a free state, to be administered by the Poles, but because the population remained overwhelmingly German, Germans dominated its legislative assembly. Even in the late 1920s friction between administrators and legislators had been frequent, and beginning in 1933, when Hitler moved into the Reich chancellery, it had intensified each year. Elected officials, proud of their membership in the local Nazi party, wore swastikas on their sleeves. On orders from Berlin, they could stage a full-fledged riot within an hour.

The dispute over Danzig was destined to launch World War II, but it had long lain quiescent, like a silent fracture in the earth's crust which, when it ruptures, will generate an earthquake. The Foreign Office had been largely unaware of the gravity of the problem until the spring of 1939, a shattering example of incompetence in both Whitehall and MI6, Britain's secret intelligence service. Danzig's tremors had been perceptible long before the *Volksdeutsche* made their grievances known in the Sudetenland; the Führer's plan to exploit them had been inscribed in *Mein Kampf*. Yet even after the issue emerged, His Majesty's Government believed it was manageable. It wasn't, because Hitler wasn't. The assumption that he was — the root of the government's foreign policy failures in the prewar years — was to persist through August 1939. Even after hostilities had actually begun, Chamberlain would cling to it, like an old dog worrying a naked bone.

The British might have been more alert had Colonel Beck not obscured the issue during his visit to London in April 1939. Danzig, the suave colonel had assured his hosts, was nothing to worry about; he would not even "trouble" them over it. Beck had been mendacious; the issue of the free city's future was in fact deeply troubling, and shadows had been darkening over it as early as November 5, 1937, when Konstantin von Neurath had told Józef Lipski, Poland's ambassador to the Reich, that "the Danzig question" would "permanently disturb German-Polish relations" until solved, and that the only possible solution would be "the restoration of German Danzig to

. . . the Reich." The following year, in the aftermath of Munich, Ribbentrop had summoned Lipski to Berchtesgaden for a three-hour luncheon discussion about Danzig. It should, he said, be returned to Germany. In addition, Germany wanted extraterritorial rights in the Polish Corridor and a Polish denunciation of Russia. Chamberlain had committed himself to Poland initially because he thought Rumania was next on Hitler's hit list and he wanted the Poles to join him in pledging support of Rumanian independence. Actually, Poland had been — and still was — in far greater danger than Rumania.[40]

After Prague Ribbentrop had drawn the Poles deeper into the vortex of power politics. On Tuesday, March 21, he had again summoned Lipski, repeating his Danzig and corridor demands and adding complaints: anti-Nazi demonstrations by Poles must be crushed, and criticism of the Führer in Polish newspapers suppressed. The lack of a "positive reaction" to the Danzig issue had made "an unfavorable impression on the Führer," he said darkly; Hitler now "felt nothing but amazement over Poland's strange attitude on a number of questions." It would be wise, he suggested, for Colonel Beck to discuss these matters with the Führer, who might otherwise conclude that Poland "simply was not willing" to accommodate the Reich.[41]

Lipski had flown home, received instructions from Beck, and reappeared at the Wilhelmstrasse on Sunday with a memorandum from the colonel. Stripped of its elaborate periphrasis, it was a courteous rejection of all Hitler's demands, coupled with a refusal to visit Berlin until "the questions [have] been prepared, in advance, according to diplomatic custom." Ribbentrop, flushed with anger, replied that this response "could not be regarded by the Führer as satisfactory." If matters continued this way, he warned, "a serious situation might arise." Monday's papers carried accounts of anti-Nazi rioting in Bydgoszcz — a city in western Poland whose population was largely German. Ribbentrop exploited the disorders by summoning Lipski, implying that Bydgoszcz's Poles were to blame, and declaring that he could "no longer understand the Polish government." He added: "An evasive answer has been given to the generous proposal Germany made to Poland. . . . Relations between the two countries are therefore deteriorating sharply."[42]

The Foreign Office had first heard this ticking time bomb in the second week of April, when Goebbels spread rumors that Germany planned a Danzig coup on the Führer's birthday, six days away. When this hearsay reached Halifax he wondered how Poland would respond to a staged "internal revolt" in the city, and asked HM's ambassador in Warsaw to clarify the question, which to him was "by no means clear." It seemed to him that if the Poles were "prepared to treat" with the Reich, they would "cut the ground from under the German Government by showing their disposition to negotiate." Beck curtly disagreed. He felt the time was not "opportune" for Warsaw to approach Berlin. If the Germans wanted to alter the status quo, they should take the initiative and state their claims; the Polish government would then consider them. It would not, however, agree to negotiate. Danzig, the Poles insisted, must remain a free city, their only major port, administered by them, as specified in the Versailles treaty. To turn it over to the Nazis would be interpreted as a sign of weakness and would invite further German claims. Halifax, unconvinced, continued to hint at the desirability of negotiations. Beck's principal private secretary told a British diplomat that these hints "tend to create an element of doubt as to the fixity of [Britain's] purpose." They evoked memories of Munich, he added, which was "not a good precedent."[43]

The Danzig crisis became public knowledge on the last Friday in April, when Hitler revealed to the Reichstag and the listening world — including the dismayed governments in London and Paris — that the Wilhelmstrasse had been negotiating with Beck over German claims against Poland for the past six months. Danzig was a German city, the Führer shouted; it must "*zurückkehren*" ("revert") to the Reich. He also demanded the right to build an autobahn and a double-track railroad across the Polish Corridor to East Prussia. Finally, Poland must join the Anti-Comintern Pact. Hitler called his Polish proposals "the greatest imaginable concession in the interests of European peace." Yet, he added in a sinister note, the Poles had refused "my one and only offer."[44]

All this was stage business. The OKW and the inner Nazi circle knew that the Führer had already decided to invade Poland whatever happened. Nearly a month earlier, he had issued to his high command copies of *Fall Weiss* (Case White), each numbered and labeled *Geheimhaltungsstufe* — Most Secret. "The task of the Wehrmacht," he had written, "is to destroy the Polish armed forces. To this end a surprise attack is to be aimed at and prepared." He added: "Surprise occupation of Danzig may become possible independently of Case White by exploiting a favorable political situation."[45]

He had created that situation by one of his cleverest strokes. Danzig now had the undivided attention of *Ausländspolitiker*. The free city, they were convinced, was his next objective. Meantime he would exploit their preoccupation as he prepared to achieve his real goal: the seizure of all Poland. He knew his Chamberlain. "Danzig at present is the danger spot," the prime minister wrote his sister, thrusting aside all warnings of a larger onslaught. He was "thinking of making a further proposal to Musso that he should move for a twelve months truce to let the temperature cool down." The Duce, eager to fuel the myth that Hitler took his advice seriously, wrote the Reich chancellor that "the British requests" for a cooling-off period over Danzig "contain the prerequisites . . . for reaching a solution favorable to Germany" which would not disturb the "rhythm of your splendid achievements . . . and you will add a fresh indubitable success to those you have already obtained."[46]

But a Danzig solution — incorporating the city in the Reich — would deprive Hitler of an excuse to invade Poland. On May 23 he summoned all OKW commanders in chief and Chiefs of Staff, each Generalstab officer with the distinctive red stripe running down his field gray trousers, to tell them they would "attack Poland at the first opportunity." There would be "no repetition of the Czech affair," the *Kriegsherr* warned them; instead, "There will be war." He was convinced that the British guarantee of Poland's frontiers was a bluff. Several weeks later in Zossen, twenty miles southeast of Berlin, where he had established General Staff headquarters and a small chancellery for himself, he assembled his generals and told them that they should not flinch "from solving the Eastern questions even at the risk of complications in the West," because he was sure the democracies would not fight, that such "complications" would never arise.[47]

Zossen thought him wrong, but he wasn't; throughout the summer of 1939 the appeasers remained in firm control of HMG's foreign policy. Lord Rothermere wrote Churchill on July 17: "Carefully handled I don't think there will be war over Danzig. Hitler left upon me the indelible impression that overtly he will never take the initiative in resorting to bloodshed. I suppose when I had my long talk with him he mentioned this matter at least a dozen times." Yet, he wrote, England was going on "arming night and day using up if necessary whatever available resources we can lay our hands on." Rothermere thought Hitler had been "badly handled. Instead of the language of reproach and rebuke constantly applied to him, I should have tried out the language of butter. . . . The language of guns may not go nearly as far as the language of butter." He ended, memorably, "I have never yet seen an authoritative statement made in England complimenting Hitler on his tremendous record of achievement in Germany."[48]

Churchill replied two days later: "You may well be right about Danzig; but does it really matter very much what the thing is called? Evidently a great 'crunch' is coming, and all preparations in Germany are moving ceaselessly to some date in August. Whether H. will call it off or not is a psychological problem which you can probably judge as well as any living man. I fear he despises Chamberlain, and is convinced that the reason he does not broaden his Government is because he means to give in once Parliament has risen [adjourned]." Plugging away at his book, Winston was, he said, "remaining entirely quiescent at the present time. . . . I have given my warnings, and I am consoled for being condemned to inaction by being free from responsibility." But of course he would never be free from responsibility. The pressure from without — to remain silent — was overpowered by the pressure from within. His conscience, his very essence, compelled him to shoulder his way into the public forum again and again.[49]

The first occasion was a 1900 Club dinner on June 21. Lord Londonderry, Winston's Germanophile cousin, was in the chair, and the guest of honor was Halifax. After his ritualistic, oleaginous tribute to those with whom he differed profoundly on the issues of the hour, Winston reminded Londonderry of "the flagrant and brutal manner in which the Munich agreement has been torn to pieces by the Nazi Government" and "the folly or villainy of the Nazi outrage" upon the rump Czech state. Summing up the case for the triple alliance, he concluded: "I believe most who are here tonight approve and endorse the willingness of His Majesty's Government to make an alliance with Soviet Russia, without which no effective stability can be created or long maintained in the East."[50]

Privately he was discouraged. Cripps visited him at his flat the following afternoon and stayed for over an hour. In his diary he noted that Winston "inveighed strongly against the PM, said he and Eden had been ready to join the Cabinet since Hitler went into Prague but would not be admitted as it would stop all possibility of appeasement." He agreed with Cripps that Parliament needed a coalition government "but despaired of any way of getting rid of or convincing Chamberlain." Cripps added with relish: "Amongst other things he pointed out that but for Chamberlain's shift on Foreign Policy after Prague, the Popular Front [left-wing] movement would have swept the country and I gather he could have supported it!" On Thursday, June 22, Churchill warned readers of the *Daily Telegraph* that reports of German troops massing on the Slovak frontier meant the Wehrmacht was intent on driving in Poland's "southern flank," and that Hitler wanted Danzig in order "to cut Poland [off] from the sea." The following day, Winston wrote G. M. Young: "I am afraid I continue to take a sombre view of our affairs," but in public he kept his spirits high. On Tuesday, June 27, he spoke to the Carlton Club before what the *Yorkshire Post* called "the largest audience ever gathered there on such an occasion" and appealed for "a full and solid alliance" with Russia. He told his audience that he wished he "could convince Herr Hitler of the fact that the British nation and, surely also, the British Empire, have reached the limit of their patience. We have receded and acquiesced time after time in breaches of solemn promises and treaties. Herr Hitler would make a profound mistake if he persuaded himself that all these retreats were merely the results of cowardice and degeneracy."[51]

However, that was precisely what Hitler thought. Moreover, successful criminals rarely change their M.O. — their method of operation. The Germans in the Sudetenland had led to Chamberlain's surrender at Munich, and there was a larger percentage of Germans in Danzig than in Czechoslovakia. He would stick to his M.O. He thought the British prime minister would come round to his way of thinking. And he was right. To Ida Chamberlain, Neville wrote that "should the [Danzig] issue come to a head now" he doubted that "any solution short of war is practicable," but if the Führer "would have a modicum of patience I can imagine a way could be found of meeting German claims while safeguarding Poland's independence and Economic Security." He listened again, with thirsty ear, for the cheers acclaiming his return from Munich. His M.O. had been established, too.[52]

Late in June another Goebbels rumor predicted a coup in Danzig for the weekend. He was testing British resolve, and he found it weak. Ribbentrop's under secretary, Weizsäcker, told Ambassador Coulondre: "We know you [France] would fight, but we are not sure about England." Daladier, disturbed, advised the British that "only a declaration couched in very energetic terms . . . will stop the Danzig coup," and in Warsaw a member of the ruling military junta told Clifford Norton, chargé d'affaires at the British embassy, that if Britain and France remained "unshaken," there would be no coup. At the same time, the British consul general in Danzig let the Foreign Office know that Germans there were saying that the Western Allies "will leave Poland in the lurch by not fighting on account of Danzig."[53]

The consul general recommended a strong stand by Britain, and Halifax dismissed him. The foreign secretary had no intention of fighting for Danzig. On July 1 the French, acting alone, informed Ribbentrop: "Any action, whatever its form, which would tend to modify the *status quo* in Danzig, and so provoke armed resistance by Poland, would bring the Franco-Polish agreement into play and oblige France to give immediate assistance to Poland." Bonnet suggested that Halifax take a similar step "at an early date." Halifax refused. In Parliament on July 10 Chamberlain declared that a Danzig coup "would involve a menace to Poland's independence which we have undertaken to defend," but added that future negotiations "ought to be possible . . . as the atmosphere cools."[54]

Churchill knew that the prime minister was putting pressure on the Poles; J. L. Garvin, editor of the *Observer*, had repeatedly accused him of it, and presently it became common knowledge. As Chamberlain wrote his sister on July 23, he had "heard last week that Hitler had told Herr Förster, the Danzig Nazi Leader, that he was going to damp down the agitation. True, the German claim that Danzig should be incorporated in the Reich was to be maintained, but that could wait until next year or even longer." Meantime "the city would be demilitarized and the press muzzled, but particular stress was laid on the need for secrecy at present and for restraint on the Polish side." Chamberlain had undertaken to send "all sorts of warnings to the Poles accompanied by exhortations to let nothing leak out." Unfortunately, the Germans had "let the cat out of the bag," giving "all my enemies" a chance "to say 'There I told you so. He means to sell the Poles,' and [making] it impossible for me to enter into conversations with Germans on any subject."[55]

That was shading the truth. He was talking to both the Germans and the Poles through Halifax, and he was consistently taking the Nazis' side, with his foreign secretary concurring. A remarkable example of their double standard arose when the Poles asked for a loan to buy arms. Colonel Adam Koc, a member of the Warsaw junta, had arrived in London on June 14 with a financial commission. The British had pledged a "general decision on principle," but during Koc's first ten days in England he was received but once by England's chief economic adviser, and that meeting was "purely nominal." Two weeks later the Treasury offered the Poles eight million pounds. It was far less than they needed, and was accompanied by so many strings that Koc returned to Warsaw alarmed and depressed. The Poles, after deliberations, decided with "great reluctance" that they could not accept the terms. Koc then requested a loan convertible into dollars, permitting Poland to buy weapons in the United States. Chancellor of the Exchequer Simon, who had been willing to let Czech gold slip through his "butter-fingers," as Churchill called them, replied that because "this would seriously affect our own financial position," he "could not agree." Yet at the same time, as Gilbert and Gott found in their study of these transactions, "Treasury officials were offering the Germans widespread economic advantages in return for an Anglo-German non-aggression pact." Sir Orme Sargent, who had become the strongest Foreign Office opponent of appeasement since the fall of Vansittart, thought it lunacy to extend such privileges to Nazi Germany while Poland was so "roughly handled." During that summer one of those catchy, anonymous phrases which arise in times of great stress was heard on the lips of Englishmen who agreed with him: "It is better to die on your feet than live on your knees." Proud men all, His Majesty's Government never dreamed of living on their knees, but they believed that peace would be their reward if they answered the polemics of the Führer by keeping their other cheek turned and extending boundless generosity to Berlin. Meanwhile the Poles, who had been encouraged to entrust their independence to England, were consigned to march into battle carrying obsolete weapons and defective ammunition.[56]

❧ ❧

The present is never tidy, or certain, or reasonable, and those who try to make it so, once it has become the past, succeed only in making it seem implausible. Among the perceptive observations and shrewd conclusions of the Churchills and Sargents were clutters of other reports and forecasts, completely at odds with them. All of it, the prescient and the cockeyed, always arrives in a promiscuous rush, and most men in power, sorting through it, believe what they want to believe, accepting whatever justifies their policies and convictions while taking out insurance, whenever possible, against the possibility that the truth may lie in their wastebaskets.

Neville Chamberlain required a very large wastebasket, for he was stubborn and strong-willed, and long after his subordinates had abandoned their faith in appeasement he clung to the conviction that if he could just put the proper deal together, Hitler would buy it. "Hitler," Macmillan recalled, "was always regarded by British politicians as if he were a brilliant but temperamental genius who could be soothed by kindness or upset by hard words. It was this fearful misconception about the nature of dictators that was . . . the root-cause of much that went amiss in these tragic years." Somehow an excuse had been found for every wild threat and instance of extravagant behavior in the Reich Chancellery. Karl Burckhardt, the League of Nations high commissioner of Danzig, who later wrote *Meine Danziger Mission 1937–1939,* told Halifax that the Führer had said to him: "If the slightest incident happens now, I shall crush the Poles without warning in such a way that no trace of Poland can be found afterwards. I shall strike with the full force of a mechanized army, of which the Poles have no conception." Burckhardt thought the Führer's "boasting" arose from "fear," and Halifax accepted that explanation as reasonable.[57]

By the end of May virtually every powerful *Ausländpolitiker* in Europe had endorsed the triple alliance except the British prime minister. He wrote his sisters that Halifax had written that he had been "unable to shake Maisky on his demand for the 3 party alliance & Daladier had insisted that it was necessary, Poland had raised no objection. . . . It seemed clear that the choice lay between acceptance & the breaking off of negotiations," which "no doubt" would "rejoice the heart of Berlin & discourage Paris." There was "no sign of opposition to the Alliance in the Press & it was obvious that refusal would create immense difficulties in the House even if I could persuade my Cabinet." Nevertheless, he still distrusted the Russians, still lacked faith in the Red Army, and still thought it disastrous to divide Europe into two armed camps. The only supporter he could find, he wrote, was

"Rab Butler & he was not a very influential ally." The P.M. was searching for an escape hatch, instructing Horace Wilson to work out a plan which would give the Russians "what they want" but avoid "the idea of an Alliance" by substituting "a declaration of *intentions* in certain circumstances."[58]

That was on May 28, 1939. Churchill's repeated calls for swift execution of the alliance were a growing irritant to Chamberlain, a variant of the Chinese water torture; another of them appeared in the *Daily Telegraph* of June 8, and this time Winston struck a new, somber note. There was, he wrote, reason to doubt that His Majesty's Government was negotiating in good faith. This opinion seemed confirmed by HMG's response to a suggestion from the Kremlin that Britain send a special envoy to Moscow. Eden quickly volunteered. He would have been an excellent choice; he was a former foreign secretary, he had met Stalin several times under agreeable circumstances, and his resignation from the cabinet on a matter of principle had enhanced his prestige on the Continent. Instead, Chamberlain sent William Strang, "an able official," as Churchill described him, "but without any standing outside the Foreign Office." It was, as Winston called it, "another mistake. The sending of so subordinate a figure gave actual offence." The Russians were highly sensitive on matters of protocol, and the junior diplomat from Whitehall, having presented his credentials, was ignored by the new commissar for foreign affairs. On June 19 Nicolson wrote: "Strang has not seen Molotov again since Friday. Yet . . . Halifax told Winston yesterday that all was well. I confess I am most uneasy."[59]

In Parliament the prime minister repeated his pledge to stand by Poland if she were invaded. Nevertheless, Churchill felt a thickening sludge of defeatism. As so often in moments of despair, he looked westward across the Atlantic toward the one power which, if aroused and armed, could crush Nazi Germany without mortgaging Europe's future to Stalin. In *News of the World* on June 18, after outlining ways in which the "atrocity" of bombing civilian targets could be countered, he wrote: "Of these grievous events the people of the United States may soon become the spectators. But it sometimes happens that the audience becomes infuriated by a revolting exhibition. In that case we might see the spectators leaving their comfortable seats and hastening to the work of rescue and of retribution."

Britain and France, however, seemed to be losing their audience. The diplomatic conversations in Moscow were not revolting, but they had certainly become tiresome. The negotiations were wallowing. After a brief spurt of activity at the bargaining table, Halifax, on Chamberlain's instructions, permitted the talks to lapse again. This was dangerous, raising questions in other capitals over England's resolution and strength. On July 7

Mussolini, the poseur of machismo, summoned His Majesty's ambassador in Rome, Sir Percy Loraine, and said loftily, "Tell Chamberlain that if England is ready to fight in defense of Poland, Italy will take up arms with her ally, Germany."[60]

Actually, this was the hollowest of threats. Despite the Pact of Steel, the Italian end of the Axis was tin. Mussolini's men weren't ready. However, Whitehall was unaware of that (so was Hitler), and in any event Chamberlain's extravagant efforts to keep Italy in the Anglo-French entente had already failed.

The defection of Belgium was more serious. Three years had passed since the Belgians' announcement that they would no longer participate in staff talks with officers from the War Office and the French Ministère de Guerre. Instead they would, in any future conflict in Europe, remain strictly neutral. But Belgium now, as in 1914, did not enjoy the freedom to make that choice. If Hitler's powerful new Wehrmacht chose to knife through the Low Countries into France, it would drive a bloody blade into the same scar over the same wound the kaiser had opened a quarter-century earlier, and a nation which has been invaded cannot remain neutral. All the callow sovereign in Brussels had accomplished was to ease the task of Hitler's Generalstab. King Leopold III had reached his decision, Churchill commented, "in a spirit of detachment from the facts." He lived to see his people subjugated by the Wehrmacht, the young men forced to work as slave labor in Ruhr munitions factories, the old subject to execution as hostages whenever Belgian freedom fighters struck. They would still be bowed beneath the Third Reich's yoke when he died in 1944.[61]

Despite Hitler's shredding of the Munich Agreement, despite daily reports of Nazi outrages in Austria and shattered Czechoslovakia, and despite brutal incidents on the borders between Germany and Poland (the beatings of civilian Poles by Nazi thugs), Neville Chamberlain remained serene in his stateroom on the *Titanic*. And his troika — Halifax, Simon, and Hoare — was equally tranquil. Churchill, untranquil but helpless as Europe blundered toward the brink of war, toiled away at Chartwell or sat brooding by his fish pond, his hands in his lap, like weapons put to rest. The Chamberlain government ignored him, but he remained a public figure; J. L. Garvin wrote and published in the *Observer* an editorial stating that were Churchill taken into the cabinet the decision "would be accepted" throughout Europe as "conclusive proof of national efficiency and resolution." *Pravda,* arguing that the Baltic states must not fall into Nazi hands, noted on July 22 that "The security of such states" was of prime importance for Britain and France, "as even such a politician as Mr. Churchill has recognized."[62]

Churchill's rare disclaimers of ambition, his affecting to enjoy the squire's life in Kent, were merely the palaver expected of any political figure excluded from power. His lust for office remained undiminished. He yearned to be in the cockpit of action, not only for the excitement — though that would always be there, and was part of his charm; his expressions, gestures, and swings in mood evoked images of the mischievous small boy at Harrow. He relished the prospect of glory, and, if he made it to the top, of more decorations and honors, of audiences with his sovereign, and motorcycle escorts as he raced about serving the monarch and his people. But he was driven by deeper motives. He was, and proudly proclaimed himself to be, an egoist. He wanted, he *needed* power. He knew his worth, and suffered when he saw mediocrities, men without imagination, vision, or honor, betraying his England. Egoism and grandeur are so close that they may merge in one man, and he was such a man. Like Lord Chatham, prosecuting the Seven Years' War in the eighteenth century, Churchill could say: "I believe I can save this country and no one else can."[63]

Clearly Neville Chamberlain couldn't. His indifference to the Russian proposal proved that. The talks in Moscow remained stalled, and on July 13, nearly three months after the Soviet offer to Britain and France, Winston wrote in the *Daily Mirror* that there could be no excuse for the "unaccountable delay" in signing "a solid, binding, all-in alliance" between Moscow, Paris, and London. Such procrastination, he declared, "aggravates the danger of a wrong decision by Herr Hitler. It is lamentable indeed that this broad mainsail of peace and strength, which might carry the ship of human fortunes past the reef, should still be flapping half-hoisted in the wind."

The prime minister was unmoved. He wrote Ida: "I am so sceptical of the value of Russian help that I should not feel that our position was greatly worsened if we had to do without them." This was a stunning misjudgment. Hitler had told his interpreter that if Britain and France accepted the Soviet offer and formed the triple alliance which had been Litvinov's dream, he would be outmanned, outgunned, and outwitted; he would be forced to cancel his war plans and bide his time. Churchill later wrote that the three-power coalition "would have struck deep alarm into the heart of Germany." With "superior power on the side of the Allies," countries the Führer had marked as future victims would have regained the diplomatic initiative and "Hitler could afford neither to embark upon the war on two fronts . . . nor to sustain a check. It was a pity not to have placed him in this awkward position, which might well have cost him his life." Winston concluded: "Having got ourselves into this awful plight of 1939, it was vital to grasp the larger hope."[64]

Throughout July the three-power talks flickered, sputtered, and guttered, like the last candle in a darkening house. *Pravda* reported that "in the circles of the Soviet Foreign Ministry, results of the first talks are regarded as not entirely favorable." Actually Maisky had told the ministry that he believed the men from London "want the talks to fail," that Chamberlain was a creature of the "Cliveden set" whose only reason for entering negotiations had been to mollify his critics in Parliament. The distrust was mutual. Cadogan was developing a profound hatred for the Soviet delegation. Their chairman was particularly easy to hate. Churchill, who later encountered him at several official functions, described Molotov in vintage Chartwell prose: He was "a man of outstanding ability and cold-blooded ruthlessness. He had survived the fearful hazards and ordeals to which all the Bolshevik leaders had been subjected in the years of triumphant revolution. . . . His cannonball head, black mustache, and comprehending eyes, his slab face, his verbal adroitness and imperturbable demeanour, were appropriate manifestations of his qualities and skill. He was above all men fitted to be the agent and instrument of the policy of an incalculable machine. . . . I have never seen a human being who more perfectly represented the modern conception of a robot."[65]

But during the Moscow talks Molotov also had reason to fume. Cadogan wrote: "We give them all they want, with both hands, and they merely slap them." That was absurd; how could they be giving the Russian negotiators "all they want" when, despite repeated Soviet entreaties, they refused to exert pressure on Poland — whose best interests would be served, since the Poles would be trapped in any war between Russia and Germany — to become party to the agreement? The Anglo-French delegates rejected the simple, comprehensive Soviet proposal, suggesting instead unilateral guarantees by individual nations. The Englishmen parried and thrusted, immunized to boredom by their profession and doubtful that Britain had anything to gain or lose here. Like Chamberlain and Halifax, most of them doubted that the Red Army would be any match for the Wehrmacht. And, like them, they believed nothing else was at stake.[66]

Here their error was not only spectacular, it was historic. Harold Macmillan, one of the handful who suspected what was coming, was puzzled by their blindness. In part they were victims of a distorted self-image, an illusion common among superpowers; like Americans a generation later, they assumed that all other countries held them in high regard. Actually, the men in the Kremlin bore malice toward the Western Allies, and with reason.

Both England and France had intervened in the Russian Civil War after the Armistice of 1918 and had sent troops to fight the Bolsheviks; both had imposed diplomatic sanctions on Russia's new regime; and they had deprived the Soviet Union of Russian territories in postwar treaties. Postwar Germany had, on the other hand, shared in none of these actions. Even after the Nazi rise to power, Macmillan noted, "German-Russian relations had been good and even cordial." To be sure, "Hitler's violent and offensive anti-Communist propaganda no doubt angered Stalin, but he was not a man to be deterred by words from any action that he deemed advantageous."[67]

Yet what diplomatic action, in the growing European crisis, would be to Russia's advantage? War was coming, the Reich would be the aggressor, and Hitler did not wish Stalin well. If Russia allied herself with the democracies, the Führer would be forced to fight on two fronts. On the other hand, such a treaty would mean war between Germany and the Soviet Union. Britain and France could not guarantee Stalin peace — but Hitler could. A Nazi-Soviet nonaggression pact would mean peace for a Russia which chose to remain neutral, and would bring about, without the loss of a single Red soldier, the recovery of the lost lands surrendered to Rumania, Poland, and the Baltic states twenty years ago at the insistence of the Western powers. If he chose that course and the Allies were defeated, eventually he would have to face Germany alone. But Hitler might be dead by then, or overthrown; or Germany might be defeated. The temptation to withdraw from the imminent maelstrom, to buy time to arm, was enormous.

Meantime, the talks with the Allies were permitted to continue, in the hope that they would give him reason to turn away from what would, in the long run, be the greater peril. Long afterward, Churchill wrote: "It is not even now possible to fix the moment when Stalin definitely abandoned all intention of working with the Western democracies" and turned his attention to "coming to terms with Hitler." Maisky told Boothby he thought the die had been cast on March 19, when Halifax sandbagged Moscow's Bucharest conference, but the evidence strongly suggests that a firm Anglo-French commitment could have saved the triple alliance as late as mid-August. Nevertheless Stalin was keeping his German option open.[68]

How long had it been open? After the war Russian expatriates published *Notes for a Journal*, identifying the author as Maksim Litvinov. Establishing its authenticity is impossible, but according to this source, the Soviet dictator had pondered a détente with Germany as soon as he read the Munich Agreement. He is quoted as having told Litvinov toward the end of 1938: "We are prepared to come to an agreement with the Germans . . . and also to render Poland harmless." According to a journal entry dated January 1939, Stalin had instructed Alexei Merekalov, the Russian ambassador in

Berlin, to open talks with Weizsäcker, telling him "in effect" that "We couldn't come to an agreement until now, but now we can."[69]

Almost certainly this, or a variant of it, is close to the truth. If Munich had been a battle, it would have been among the most decisive in history. Walter Lippmann wrote: "In sacrificing Czechoslovakia to Hitler, Britain and France were really sacrificing their alliance with Russia. They sought security by abandoning the Russian connection at Munich, in a last vain hope that Germany and Russia would fight and exhaust one another." Stalin was aware of that. On March 10, five days before Prague, he had savaged the democracies for sacrificing Austria and Czechoslovakia and accused them of trying to "embroil" the Reich in a war with the U.S.S.R., "pushing the Germans further eastward, promising them an easy prey and saying: 'Just start a war with the Bolsheviks, everything else will take care of itself!' "[70]

Whitehall saw no shadows cast by coming events, but Gallic suspicions had begun well before Prague, when Coulondre had warned the Quai that a Nazi-Soviet rapprochement was in train; its objective, he said, would be to divide Poland between them. On May 9 he cabled the Quai: "For the last 24 hours Berlin is full of rumors that Germany has made, or is going to make, proposals to Russia leading to a partition of Poland." On May 22 he reported that Ribbentrop had said that Poland "sooner or later must disappear, partitioned again between Germany and Russia. In his mind this partition is closely linked with a rapprochement between Berlin and Moscow." Later Coulondre told Paris that the Führer "will risk war if he does not have to fight Russia. On the other hand, if he knows he has to fight her too he will draw back rather than expose his country, his party, and himself to ruin."[71]

Daladier, having studied the cable traffic from Coulondre, afterward wrote: "Since the month of May [1939] the U.S.S.R. had conducted two negotiations, one with France, the other with Germany. She appeared to prefer to partition rather than to defend Poland." Chamberlain seems to have been the last politician in Europe to discover that the Russians were keeping two sets of books. In late May, when the P.M. finally agreed to negotiate with the Russians largely on the basis of the terms embodied in Litvinov's original proposal, Dirksen, the Führer's envoy to the Court of St. James, advised the Wilhelmstrasse that Chamberlain had taken this step "with the greatest reluctance," prompted by reports to the Foreign Office of "German feelers in Moscow." Chamberlain and Halifax, according to Dirksen, were "afraid that Germany might succeed in keeping Soviet Russia neutral or even inducing her to adopt benevolent neutrality."[72]

By then the two dictators were in fact on the way to the altar. Churchill observed afterward: "It is a question whether Hitler or Stalin loathed it most." But marriages of convenience are not expected to be joyous. The one mot which won universal acceptance in the democracies and the United States was "They deserve each other." Certainly the Führer, until now regarded as the new Machiavelli, had met his match in duplicity. It was characteristic of Stalin's amorality that on the day after Litvinov had invited England and France to join Russia in an anti-Nazi alliance, Merekalov called on Ernst von Weizsäcker at the Wilhelmstrasse, ostensibly to discuss commercial issues arising from Czechoslovakia's incorporation into what was now known as *Grossdeutschland*, beginning with a request for sales to Russia from the Skoda Works, now a Nazi arsenal.[73]

In fact the ambassador's objectives transcended trade. His appearance in the office of Ribbentrop's under secretary marked the beginning of a dramatic shift in relations between the two dictatorships. On that day Weizsäcker responded to the Skoda issue first. He told his visitor that reports of Soviet negotiations with Britain and France, looking toward a military alliance, did not create "a favorable atmosphere for the delivery of war materials to Soviet Russia." But he knew that trade, even trade in arms, could not be the real reason for this visit. The ambassador had presented his credentials nearly a year ago, and this was the first time he had entered the Foreign Ministry. Weizsäcker, unlike Ribbentrop, was a trained diplomat; he had a pretty good guess at what was coming. To encourage Merekalov to get to the point, he remarked that the Russian press was not "fully participating in the anti-German tone of the American and some of the English papers."[74]

At that, his visitor spoke up: "Ideological differences of opinion had hardly influenced the Russian-Italian relationship," he said, "and they need not prove a stumbling block for Germany either. . . . There exists for Russia no reason why she should not live with Germany on a normal footing. And from normal, relations might become better and better." This groundbreaking ceremony was followed, first, by two meetings between Dr. Julius Schnurre of the Wilhelmstrasse and Georgi Astakhov, the Russian chargé d'affaires, and second, on May 20, by a long talk in Moscow between Molotov and Ambassador Friedrich Werner von der Schulenburg. Schulenburg found the foreign commissar *"sehr freundlich"* ("very friendly") and ready to discuss both economic and political agreements between the two powers. Thus the seeds were planted. They might never blossom. Russian diplomats were still courting Britain and France. But if those talks fell through, Stalin had established an alternative.[75]

On July 24 prospects for an accord between the Reich's three most powerful adversaries seemed to brighten. Molotov, summoning the British and

French negotiators, was conciliatory; clearly he had received fresh instructions from the Kremlin. Since the political matters still to be thrashed out were technical, he said, he recommended that they draw up the related military convention spelling out the obligations of each nation, under the mutual assistance pact, in meeting Nazi aggression. The Foreign Office and the Quai were consulted; the French agreed enthusiastically, the British less so. Dirksen reported to the Wilhelmstrasse — now genuinely alarmed by the prospective alliance — that His Majesty's Government regarded the military talks "skeptically."[76]

Events swiftly confirmed the German ambassador. In diplomacy great importance is attached to the prestige of the men a nation sends to represent it. For these talks the Russians chose officers holding the highest ranks in the U.S.S.R.: Marshal Voroshilov, Russia's commissar for defense; the chief of the Red Army's General Staff; and the commanders in chief of the air force and the navy. To lead the French delegation Daladier picked General of the Army André Doumenc, formerly Maxime Weygand's deputy chief of staff, regarded throughout France as one of the most brilliant officers to serve under the tricolor. Chamberlain, however, repeated the Strang snub, deliberately offending the Kremlin. A month earlier, when Anglo-Polish military talks were held in Warsaw, Britain had been represented by Tiny Ironside. This time Tiny was kept home. Instead, an obscure and undistinguished British party was led by Admiral Sir Reginald A. R. Plunkett-Ernle-Erle-Drax, of whom Dirksen wrote that he was "practically on the retired list and was never on the Naval Staff."[77]

So slipshod were Whitehall's arrangements for the talks that Plunkett-Ernle-Erle-Drax wasn't even given written authority to negotiate — a serious breach of diplomatic courtesy — though he had been instructed to be discourteous anyway; British foreign policy documents reveal that he had been told to be vague and "go very slowly." As a final slight to the Russians, the British, who were handling transportation for the Allied teams, rejected the suggestion that they fly to Moscow, which would have taken a day. They boarded the nine-thousand-ton passenger-cargo ship *City of Exeter*, an ancient vessel whose top speed, Molotov's deputy foreign commissar found, was thirteen knots. They left England on August 5 and did not reach Leningrad until very late on August 9; they arrived in Moscow August 11. The *Queen Mary* would have brought them to New York in less time. And in this August, like that other August a quarter-century earlier, every hour counted. The triple alliance now had Hitler's undivided attention; he knew how formidable it would be and had ordered Ribbentrop to break it up. Joachim von Ribbentrop may have been only a wine salesman, but he had been a very good salesman, and he knew Molotov would be an eager customer. The only obstruction was Stalin. That was enough to discourage any diplomat except one who would have to return to the Führer empty-handed. The German's main hope lay in the possibility that the Anglo-French officers would bungle their assignment.[78]

That is precisely what they — or, more accurately, their governments — did. The military talks in Moscow got off to a wobbly start. Marshal Voroshilov was offended by the failure of Plunkett-Ernle-Erle-Drax to produce credentials signed by Chamberlain. Soviets put a premium on form; they interpreted the lapse as a sign that Britain did not regard the occasion as grave. General Doumenc, on the other hand, was on excellent terms with the Russians from the start. His *Ordre de Service*, signed by Daladier, was flawless; he had impressed the Red Army's leaders by his knowledge of Russian military traditions; he sympathized with their painful memories of Allied hostility to the Bolshevik cause in their struggle of 1918–1920 and was tactfully silent about Stalin's purges of the Red Army. In his determination to impress the Russians in their talks, he had, as one of his subordinates put it, "stretched the truth a little." The Maginot Line, he said, now extended "from the Swiss frontier to the sea." As any newspaper correspondent could have told the Soviets — and as their own intelligence service doubtless had — it was less than half that long. In Doumenc's defense, it should be noted that the French delegation, like Britain's, had been instructed by its senior officers to gloss over military weaknesses. The British were poorer liars. Their army spokesman blithely declared that Britain could field sixteen divisions "in the early stages of the war." The French were "astounded," one of their delegates later wrote; this was "three or four times" greater than Ironside's figure in the most recent Anglo-French staff talks. Voroshilov, suspicious, pressed the issue, asking, "How many divisions will you have if war breaks out soon?" The embarrassing answer was that England's standing army at present consisted of "five regular divisions and one mechanized division." At that moment, one French officer later wrote, "the Soviet delegation understood better than it had the immense weakness of the British Empire."[79]

The Russians' crucial question was asked by Voroshilov late in the afternoon of Sunday, August 13. The Soviet Union, he pointed out, had no common frontier with the Reich. What, he inquired, did the French and British General Staffs think the Red Army could do if Poland or Rumania were attacked, since the Soviet troops could not take action without entering "the territory of other states?" There was silence. Doumenc and Plunkett-Ernle-Erle-Drax replied that they would answer in the morning. That bought them a reprieve, but next day the marshal's questions were more specific: Would Soviet forces be allowed to move against the Wehrmacht through Poland's Wilno Gap and Polish Galicia? He said flatly: "We ask for straightforward answers to these questions. In my opinion, without an exact, unequivocal answer, it is useless to continue these military conversations." It was up to the Allies to secure permission for the passage of Russian troops, he said, because they, not the Soviet Union, had guaranteed Poland and Rumania. For the next two days the military talks got nowhere, as Allied diplomats sought to win the cooperation of the Poles. By the seventeenth Voroshilov had run out of patience. He demanded that the meetings adjourn until a definite reply from Warsaw had been received. The negotiators agreed to reassemble on Monday, August 21.[80]

The British and French ambassadors in Warsaw approached Beck on August 18. He told them that Soviet troops were of "no military value." The chief of the Polish General Staff agreed; he could see "no benefit to be gained by Red Army troops operating in Poland." Two days later the Polish foreign minister formally rejected the Anglo-French requests. Moreover, he added, he didn't want to hear any more about it: "I do not admit that there can be any kind of discussion whatever concerning the use of part of our territory by foreign troops." If Poland agreed, he said, "this would lead to an immediate declaration of war on the part of Germany." Hitler frightened him, but Stalin terrified him.[81]

The provocative question is why Paris and London did not put Beck to the ultimate test. Under these extraordinary circumstances they were entitled to declare that unless Poland agreed to let the Red Army help, Britain and France no longer felt bound to go to war in defense of Poland. Actually this dilemma had been anticipated in April when, four days after Chamberlain announced England's unilateral guarantee of Poland, Churchill and Lloyd George, speaking in the House, had both urged that the Soviet Union be encouraged to join an entente of countries threatened by Nazi aggression. Lloyd George, and then Churchill, had demanded that Chamberlain's guarantee be provisional, valid only if the Poles agreed to accept help from the U.S.S.R. Lloyd George had predicted:

> If we are going in without the help of Russia, we are walking into a trap. . . . I cannot understand why, before committing ourselves to this tremendous enterprise, we did not secure beforehand the adhesion of Russia. . . . If Russia has not been brought into this matter because of certain feelings the Poles have that they do not want the Russians there, it is for us to declare the conditions, and unless the Poles are prepared to accept the only conditions with which we can successfully help them, the responsibility must be theirs.[82]

The option was still there. The Anglo-Polish mutual security pact had not yet been signed. Britain's foreign secretary could have taken the simple step of making Beck's acceptance of Russian aid a condition of signature. Bonnet actually proposed this stratagem. Halifax sent Bonnet's proposal across Downing Street; Chamberlain frostily replied that he declined to be party to such a "maneuver." "Maneuver," like "creatures," was one of his pet pejoratives, but in this context it was meaningless. The prime minister had to have had another motive. The likeliest, though he did not cite it, was his visceral dislike of the Soviet Union.

Daladier, more tenacious and dismayed by the loss of a powerful ally on Germany's other front, was slow to accept diplomatic defeat. After a final appeal to Warsaw, which was brusquely rejected, the premier cabled Doumenc on the morning of August 21, instructing him to sign a military convention with Russia under the best terms possible, with the sole provision that it must be approved by the cabinet. The French premier also wired his ambassador in Moscow, authorizing him to tell Molotov that France approved "in principle" the right of Russian soldiers to cross Poland if Hitler attacked. But these telegrams did not arrive in the Soviet capital until late in the evening, and by then the drama was over.

Pressed to accept Soviet help in the event of trouble, the Poles were also being urged to yield on the Danzig issue, to placate the Führer and alleviate the mounting tension in Europe. In the final British negotiations over Danzig, a key figure, and at times *the* key figure, was Churchill's mirror image — the Nazis' favorite diplomat, Sir Nevile Henderson, His Majesty's ambassador to the Third Reich. Henderson defended the anti-Semitic pogroms of Danzig Nazis, opposed any link between London and Warsaw, thought the Poles should "talk a little less" about their courage and think "a little more" about the "realities" of their position on the eastern fringe of *Grossdeutschland*. He criticized his own country, telling Cadogan that England had led Poland "far up the garden path" by her pledges. Britain, he thought, should cede Danzig to Hitler. His great fear was that Beck, Koc, and their fellow colonels might arouse the German's temper. Danzig, he told Halifax in late July, ought to be declared a "*German* Free City," forcing Poles living there to leave. Until then, he predicted, "there will be no real peace" in eastern Europe.[83]

Clifford Norton, Britain's chargé in Warsaw, strenuously attacked Henderson in his dispatches. He thought it unlikely that "the present moment is a good one" for negotiations between Germany and the Poles. Before any talks began, he wrote, Poland's strength, and the justice of her cause, should be "visible and apparent not only to its partners, but also to its opponents." Actually, he doubted the value of negotiations under any circumstances: "Even if Danzig were removed from the front of the stage . . . there is little basis for hopes that such a settlement would introduce the millennium." When Henderson criticized this as "rather hypothetical," Norton replied that the Führer and his Nazi hierarchy were "imbued with the desire to dominate all Eastern Europe." That being true, he wrote, "no difficulties . . . should be allowed to shake the firmness of the Anglo-Polish alliance."[84]

Reading British foreign policy documents of that summer — Henderson's dispatches, the memoranda of Halifax, the prime minister's papers — it is startling to recall that Britain had made a commitment to Poland, not Germany. Norton reminded the foreign secretary of that. In consequence, Halifax tried to bypass him, and in Downing Street he was dubbed "pro-Polish." It was meant as a slur. His Majesty's Government was determined to prevent the Poles from embarrassing Britain by dragging her into war. Henderson thought that was their intention. Their objective, he cabled home, was to "humiliate" the Third Reich.[85]

Clearly humiliation was to be the lot of *some* powers. Governments were taking positions from which retreat without loss of face was impossible. Britain was committed to Poland; if the European balance of power shifted dramatically, and the Polish position became untenable, England would be in the soup. If that thought crossed Henderson's mind, he made no record of it. Probably it didn't; as a diehard appeaser, he refused to admit the possibility of a showdown, even to himself. If matters reached an impasse, the disciples of appeasement reasoned, they would negotiate a new settlement and their armies would stand down.

The Wehrmacht wasn't going to stand down. The Führer had made that clear at Zossen. Germany was going to march into Poland, and the dying would begin, whatever the diplomats did. The Reich's hopes for victory, however, relied heavily on its chief diplomat. Ribbentrop was doing both his best and his worst to achieve a pact with the Soviet Union, though he had had problems with his führer. Hitler loathed Slavs almost as much as he hated Jews, and while he had known a triple alliance would present the gravest of threats to him and his Reich, he had vacillated through May and June.

In late May the Führer had instructed the Wilhelmstrasse "to establish more tolerable relations between Germany and the Soviet Union," and said he wanted Count von der Schulenburg, his ambassador in Moscow, to convey this to Molotov "as soon as possible." Four days later he canceled this and said he preferred a "modified approach." Trade talks had begun, but in June Hitler suddenly repudiated them. On July 18 they were resumed after the Soviets had said they were prepared to extend and intensify economic relations between the two countries. Hitler's munitions buildup was suffering from a lack of raw materials; he told Schulenburg to sign a trade agreement at the earliest possible moment and *"den Faden wiederaufnehmen"* ("again take up the thread") of political discussions with the foreign commissar. Suddenly, Russians and Germans began talking about power plays in Poland and the Baltic states — grabbing territories by joint aggression — coups elected leaders in democracies would not dare hatch, knowing that a free press and an aroused public would force them to withdraw.[86]

Englishmen were proud of their customs and traditions, some of which bordered on the eccentric. To Churchill's exasperation, Britain's ruling class continued "to take its weekends in the country," as he put it, while "Hitler takes his countries in the weekends." This was no small matter. It meant that crucial decisions could not be made because those with the authority to make them were beyond the reach of telephones. Suggestions that country weekends be shortened, or that provisions be made for emergencies, were met with icy stares. Britain's leaders detested being pushed; one of their chief complaints about Americans was that they always seemed to be in a hurry. Haste was somehow regarded as un-British. The ruling class was not called the leisured class for nothing.[87]

The timetable of events, as July melted into August, suggests the price England paid for Edwardian manners when trying to outwit and outmanipulate a twentieth-century Attila. On July 31, the day Chamberlain told Parliament that an Allied military mission would be sent to Moscow, the Reich's ambassador to Russia received an "urgent and secret" telegram from the Wilhelmstrasse, instructing him to see Molotov immediately. Three days later, *before the Anglo-French mission sailed for Leningrad,* the Russo-German talks became more specific. Ribbentrop, carrying out his *Blitzwerbung,* had told Schulenburg to present "more concrete terms . . . in view of the political situation and in the interests of speed." The Führer was no longer irresolute.[88]

He had scheduled his invasion of Poland for late August; the Wehrmacht had to overwhelm Poland before the October rains made the unpaved roads impassable for his panzers. He had to outbid the Allies in Moscow quickly, and price was no object. On August 12, toward the end of a meeting with the Italian foreign minister, Hitler said he had just received "a telegram from Moscow. The Russians have agreed to a German political negotiator being sent to Moscow."[89]

This may have been a trick to impress Ciano — no such cable was found among the German documents captured in 1945 — but other documents leave no doubt that on that same day Molotov agreed to discuss issues Schulenburg had raised, including Poland. The foreign commissar stressed the Soviet view that such talks must "proceed by degrees." When word of this was relayed to the Reich Chancellery, Hitler replied that protracted talks were out of the question. He didn't explain his reason — that German troops would march in less than three weeks. And the triple alliance was a harrowing possibility: that same afternoon in Moscow, Anglo-French military conversations with the Russians had begun.[90]

Hitler, in his summer headquarters on the Obersalzberg, made his great move on Monday, August 14. He told his court: "The great drama is now approaching its climax!" He was confident that neither Britain nor France would sacrifice a single soldier for Poland. The Quai d'Orsay was deferring to London, he said, and England "has no leaders of real caliber. The men I got to know at Munich are not the kind to start a new world war." Still, he knew how edgy his generals were about a two-front war, and so, on his instructions, Ribbentrop sent Schulenburg a "most urgent" cable directing him to "read it to Molotov."[91]

In his telegram to the Kremlin, Ribbentrop said the Reich was prepared to send him to Moscow to settle all outstanding problems "from the Baltic to the Black Sea." At the same time, he played to Stalin's paranoia. Britain and France, he said, were "trying to drive Russia into war with Germany" — Stalin, he knew, had used those very words in a speech to the Communist Party Congress. Tuesday evening Molotov greeted Ambassador Schulenburg warmly and asked whether the Nazis would join him in a joint "guarantee" of the Baltic states and — this was completely unexpected — a nonaggression treaty between the Soviet Union and the Reich. Hitler was ecstatic; Stalin was offering to play the role of spectator while the Wehrmacht took Poland. Wednesday Ribbentrop cabled the Führer's reply: "Germany is prepared to conclude a nonaggression pact with the Soviet Union . . . and to guarantee the Baltic States jointly." His foreign minister was ready, bags packed, to travel to Moscow "by airplane," bearing "full powers from the Führer . . . to sign the appropriate treaties."[92]

Stalin knew what he was giving Hitler. He also knew what he would get — all that Russia had lost at Versailles and more: vast tracts of Estonia, Latvia, Lithuania, Poland, Rumania, and what Ribbentrop's August 14 telegram had described as "Southeastern questions," i.e., the Balkans. The Western democracies couldn't match that. If the Russians signed the triple alliance Nazi panzers might rip through Poland and, without stopping, into the Soviet Union. Nevertheless, when Schulenburg passed along Ribbentrop's request that he be received on Friday, August 18, the foreign commissar, after consulting with the general secretary, replied this was too soon: the meeting would require "thorough preparation." But his manner was encouraging. He told the German envoy that he was "highly gratified" by the prospect of a visit by the foreign minister of the Reich; it stood, he said, "in marked contrast to England, which, in the person of Strang, has sent only an official of second-class rank to Moscow." Meantime, he was directing his military negotiators to ask the Allies, in effect, what Russia would get out of an alliance with Britain and France.[93]

The tyrant in Moscow continued to play with the tyrant in the Berghof. The Führer's eyes were on the calendar and on the clock. If the war was to start as planned, OKW orders had to be cut quickly: two huge army groups had to deploy on Poland's waters while fleets of U-boats sailed for British waters. Stalin and Molotov, sensing the Führer's anxiety, decided to let him hang. On the night of Friday, August 18, Schulenburg was sent another urgent cable from the Obersalzberg; he must insist that Molotov see Ribbentrop immediately, must refuse to take no for an answer, and must repeat that the German foreign minister had been authorized by the Führer "to settle fully and conclusively the total complex of problems." Ribbentrop was, for example, prepared "to sign a special protocol regulating the interests of both parties," including "the settlement of spheres of interest in the Baltic area."[94]

This cable arrived in the Reich's Moscow embassy at 5:45 A.M. on Saturday, and the German ambassador made a 2:00 P.M. appointment with Molotov. But when they met, the foreign commissar refused to make a date for Ribbentrop's trip; he repeated that "thorough preparations" would be required. Depressed, Schulenburg returned to his embassy, wondering how he could break the news to a despot who never accepted excuses and ruthlessly punished failure. So fearsome were the consequences that — blasphemous in a servant of the Führer — he prayed. And his prayers were answered. At 4:30 P.M. his telephone rang. It was Molotov, asking him to return. Emerging from the commissar's office, the elated ambassador returned to his embassy and sent the Wilhelmstrasse a triumphant wire. "The Soviet Government agree to the Reich Foreign Minister coming to Moscow," it began. The Soviet foreign commissar had stated that Ribbentrop "could arrive in Moscow on August 26 or 27. Molotov handed me a draft of a nonaggression pact." Hitler was elated, but he had by now set August 26 as the date for the attack on Poland. Drastic measures were necessary. Overcoming his distaste for Bolsheviks, on the twentieth the Führer sent a personal cable to Stalin, accepting the general terms of the nonaggression treaty and urging that final negotiations take place as soon as possible.[95]

Late the next night, Berlin radio interrupted a musical program for an announcement: "The Reich government and the Soviet government have agreed to conclude a pact of nonaggression with each other. The Reich Minister for Foreign Affairs will arrive in Moscow on Wednesday, August 23, for the conclusion of the negotiations." It was nearly midnight, Monday, August 21, 1939. Europe had ten slaughterless days left.[96]

* * *

This conspiracy against peace — for that is what the pact amounted to — was a cynical deal, and Russia would pay a terrible price for it. But the British and French governments had played a sorry role. Over four months had passed since Litvinov had made his proposal to them. Had the opportunity been seized — had Eden, say, arrived in the Soviet capital with plenary powers — Hitler might never have had his chance. Russia needed peace; everyone knew that; but the democracies were insensitive to it. Three years later Stalin explained to Churchill: "We formed the impression that the British and French Governments were resolved not to go to war if Poland were attacked, but that they hoped the diplomatic line-up of Britain, France, and Russia would deter Hitler. We were sure it would not." Later Winston wrote: "Thus Hitler penetrated with ease into the frail defences of the tardy, irresolute coalition against him."[97]

Bonnet, as he later wrote in his memoirs, realized that *"pour France c'était un désastre."* At a bleak convocation of the Conseil de la Défense Nationale a pall of defeatism hung heavy over the council table. Gamelin, the most spineless generalissimo, said the army would not be ready for war until 1942; the most France could do now was mobilize, bringing "some relief to Poland by tying down a certain number of large German units on our frontier." Bonnet said flatly that they should ponder whether to ignore their treaty commitment and leave the Poles to their fate.[98]

Only Daladier's peasant strength suppressed Bonnet's pusillanimity. France's commitment to Poland, the premier reminded him, was a matter of honor and had been since Marshal Foch's secret military agreement with the Poles in 1921. If either a German hobnail or a Russian boot set foot on Polish soil, France had agreed, the Army of the Third Republic was pledged to attack the aggressor. Therefore, at the premier's insistence, the Conseil de la Défense decided that *"la seule solution"* in the present crisis was to adhere to *"nos engagements vis-à-vis de la Pologne."* In a public statement the French government reconfirmed its alliance with Poland, with each party guaranteeing the other "immediately and directly against any menace, direct or indirect, threatening their vital interest." The formal language of exchanges between governments could be no more precise.[99]

But the triple alliance which Russia had proposed and Churchill had enthusiastically endorsed — which conceivably could have averted war, or at the very least given the Germans less than an overwhelming margin — had become another of history's colossal Ifs. England and France were in the position of disappointed fiancées. The Soviets, in need of a spouse, had asked for their hand. They, also lacking a strong partner, had reluctantly approached the altar. There the ritualistic question had been raised: whether anyone had just cause to object to the union. And the Poles, at that crucial moment, had rudely spoken up, leaving the Russians in the embarrassing position of rejected suitors. Ribbentrop, having caught them on the rebound, rejoiced. His glee is understandable. The jubilation of Beck is harder to grasp, but he certainly felt triumphant. Ordinarily, he ran his office like a martinet, his face stiff and expressionless. But all that critical week his smile was vulpine, a smile of malice, the smile of a man who relished revenge. In the Russo-Polish War of 1920 the Bolsheviks had driven deep into Beck's homeland, to the gates of Warsaw. Now they had thought they could do it again, but he had outwitted them. This, he told his staff, was his greatest success. If he were to be remembered, it would be for barring the Red Army from Polish soil. He had saved Poland from the Communists.

So Nazis and Communists, until now sworn enemies, had been meeting secretly, frequently, and with growing confidence while the frustrated British public watched the Moscow-London-Paris entente, imaginatively conceived, struggling vainly to avoid stillbirth. Churchill's breathing spells from his book had been rare and brief. Any major issue brought him up to the House of Commons, however, and the prime minister created one when he decided to adjourn Parliament for two months — from August 4 to October 3. Chamberlain wrote his sister from Chequers that "all my information indicates that Hitler now realises that he can't grab anything else without a major war and has therefore decided to put Danzig into cold storage." If Parliament urged a show of Britain's growing military strength, however, the Führer would feel that "he must do something to show he is not frightened. I should not be at all surprised therefore, to hear of movements of large bodies of troops near the Polish frontier. . . . That is part of the war of nerves and [would] no doubt send Winston into hysterics." Provocative speeches in the House of Commons and demands for military maneuvers would, Chamberlain wrote, "play straight into Hitler's hands and give the world [the impression] that we are in a panic."[100]

Churchill — anxious, not panicky — feared, as a friend put it, "that Neville, having got rid of the House, proposed to do another Munich." Therefore, he decided to protest Chamberlain's decision to adjourn Parliament. General Spears, who had been staying at Chartwell that last weekend in July, told Harold Nicolson: "The old boy is determined to speak with great violence and to vote against, arguing, 'It is no good Chamberlain saying he will summon Parliament "if there is any change of situation." He must promise to summon if any cloud rises at all.' " Churchill told Spears that the motion for recess was a profound mistake because it would convince Hitler that Britain would be slow to act in a crisis, and give Russia the impression that Britain was not serious about collective security. "The scattering of Parliament," he wrote to Lord Wolmer, "is a serious snub."[101]

Most Tory critics of appeasement agreed, but thought the issue not worth another vote against their party leader. Harold Macmillan felt that way and phoned Churchill, asking him to reconsider. Winston bluntly refused. Eden also suggested that they let Chamberlain have this one and "toe the line," as Nicolson noted in his diary, adding: "I would do so were it not that Winston refuses, and I cannot let the old lion enter the lobby alone. But apart from this I do feel very deeply that the House ought not to adjourn for the whole of two months. I regard it as a violation of constitutional principle and an act of disrespect to the House."[102]

"This House," Churchill opened on August 2, "is sometimes disparaged in this country, but abroad it counts." Its debates and motions were particularly weighed by dictators "as a most formidable expression of the British national will and an instrument of that will in resistance to aggression." Winston had "the feeling that things are in a great balance." Certainly it was an "odd moment" for a parliamentary vacation "when the powers of evil are at their strongest." Berlin said the Reich had two million men under arms — the real figure was at least triple that — and another half million would be added this month.[103]

He had learned that public schools in large parts of Czechoslovakia, especially Bohemia, were being cleared and prepared for accommodation of wounded Germans. There was "a definite movement of supplies and troops through Austria towards the east" and a "strained situation in the Tyrol." The elements of crisis were there, and "all these are terribly formidable signs." Thus, he said, "At this moment in its long history it would be disastrous, it would be pathetic, it would be shameful for the House of Commons to write itself off as an effective and potent factor . . . against aggression." Then he delivered his heaviest blow:

> It is a very hard thing, and I hope it will not be said, for the Government to say to the House, "Begone! Run off and play. Take your masks with you. Do not worry about public affairs. Leave them to the gifted and experienced Ministers" who, after all, so far as our defences are concerned, landed us where we were landed in December of last year, and who, after all — I make all allowances for the many difficulties — have brought us in foreign policy at this moment to the point where we have guaranteed Poland and Rumania, after having lost Czechoslovakia, and not having gained Russia.[104]

Amery and Macmillan joined in arguing against such a long adjournment, but Chamberlain was unmoved. Nicolson noted in his diary: "To the astonishment of the House the Prime Minister gets up and after saying that he will not give way an inch, he adds that . . . he wished it to be clearly understood that he regarded the vote as a vote of confidence in himself. . . . The general impression is that Chamberlain has in fact missed an opportunity and outraged the feelings of the House." Party strength prevailed, although forty Conservatives abstained; on that sour note the House dispersed for the summer.[105]

The following Tuesday Winston delivered a broadcast to the United States. Once more he was looking westward, convinced that the hope of England's security and, if it came to that, her deliverance lay across the Atlantic, in the vast untapped power of the United States. The fact that his mother had been American in no way diminished his loyalty to the Crown — he had been called "fifty percent American and one hundred percent British" — but he believed in bloodlines, was proud to have cousins across the sea, and admired the United States as Baldwin and Chamberlain did not. Furthermore, Franklin Roosevelt was president. Churchill would have regarded most occupants of the White House as lesser men than himself, but Roosevelt was not among them. Like Churchill, he was a great statesman. The two men were very different in other ways, but both possessed intellect, vision, courage, and the conviction that if civilization was to survive, Adolf Hitler must be destroyed. Roosevelt's handicap was that his people were overwhelmingly isolationist. Refugees from Europe, or descended from refugees, they wanted no part of "Europe's wars." Roosevelt and Churchill saw that the German demagogue was the enemy of freedom for all men. In his broadcast Churchill tried to plant the seed of that thought in the minds of his U.S. listeners, there to be nourished by Roosevelt.

His opening chord was unfortunate. In his hands the rapier of wit or the broadsword of ridicule was deadly, but on this occasion he was awkward, even embarrassing, with the hacksaw of sarcasm. He began heavily: "Holiday time, ladies and gentlemen! Holiday time, my friends across the Atlantic! Holiday time, when the summer calls the toilers of all countries for an all too brief spell from the offices and mills and stiff routine . . ." This went on. And on. He rumbled: "Let me look back — let me see. How did we spend our summer holidays twenty-five years ago?" Millions of listeners were too young to remember, and the rest had no recollection, as he had, of Germans "breaking into Belgium and trampling down its people." He had forgotten that the United States hadn't declared war on Germany until three years later, and that another year passed before U.S. doughboys, most of whom had never heard of Belgium, filed into the trenches.[106]

In the same vein of ponderous japery, he said that to believe Dr. Goebbels, "you would suppose that it was . . . this wicked Belgium," with "England and the Jews," who attacked Germany, which in its righteous might fought manfully for four years and was about to win an overwhelming victory when "the Jews got at them again, this time from the rear. Armed with President Wilson's Fourteen Points they stabbed, we are told, the German armies in the back."

Dropping his caustic tone, Churchill became Churchillian once more, rousing and persuasive. Now, he said somberly, "There is a hush all over Europe, nay, over all the world." What kind of hush? "Alas, it is the hush of suspense, and in many lands it is the hush of fear." But, he said, almost whispering, if you listened carefully you could hear "the tramp of armies crunching the gravel of the parade grounds, splashing through rain-soaked fields, the tramp of two million Germans and over a million Italians." He recited their conquests — Austria, Czechoslovakia, Abyssinia, Albania — noting that the Duce and the Führer called them "liberations," and commented: "No wonder there is such a hush among the neighbors of Germany and Italy while they are wondering which one is going to be 'liberated' next."

Once more he appealed for collective security, once again he disposed of the Nazi charge of "encirclement." Then he drew a striking parallel between the American and British constitutions. "It is curious," he observed, "how the English-speaking peoples have always had [a] fear of one-man power," or "handing themselves over, lock, stock and barrel, body and soul, to one man, and worshipping him as if he were an idol." Tradition in the Reich was different: "In Germany, on a mountain peak, there sits one man who in a single day . . . can plunge all that we have and are into a volcano of smoke and flames." If that man "does not make war there will be no war. No one else is going to make war. . . . No one has ever dreamed of attacking Germany."

Approaching the end he said: "It is not, believe me, my American friends, from any ignoble shrinking from pain and death that the British and French peoples pray for peace." He was wallowing again; everyone shrinks from pain, and there is nothing ignoble about it. Yet, as always, he came on strong at the end:

> But whether it be peace or war — peace with its broadening and brightening prosperity, now within our reach, or war with its measureless carnage and destruction — we must strive to frame some system of human relations in the future which will put an end to this prolonged hideous uncertainty, which will let the working and creative forces of the world get on with their job, and which will no longer leave the whole life of mankind dependent upon the virtues, the caprice, or the wickedness of a single man.[107]

Even when off his form, Churchill was a powerful broadcaster, and getting better all the time. By now informed Americans were beginning to realize it. As early as October 1938, he had told U.S. listeners why Munich had been a disaster and the perils it had spawned. Thomas Jones wrote a friend in the United States: "Churchill's speech to America, brilliant as it was in phrasing, is criticised here as not likely to be helpful on your side. I should have thought that for the present we ought to leave America alone."[108]

British opinion had reversed itself since Munich. Chamberlain, however, had not, and the country's new mood was not reflected in his policy. The public — even the House of Commons — knew very little of the decisions and commitments being made in the name of their king and affecting their future, or indeed, whether they would have one. Fleet Street had kept them informed of negotiations looking toward an alliance with the Soviets, because Litvinov had announced his plan to foreign correspondents. No Englishman — including, for a time, the country's leaders — knew of the talks between Berlin and Moscow, but England's Polish policy should have been known everywhere in Britain. At the very least it ought to have been debated in Parliament. In practice, it was conducted in secret by a handful of men, led by Chamberlain, Halifax, and Horace Wilson. They withheld news of the moves and countermoves in London, Warsaw, and Berlin because they knew their countrymen would disapprove. They were still the Men of Munich. Their higher loyalty was to appeasement. That policy continued to entail duplicity, lies, a stronger Reich, and a further weakening of the Führer's enemies in the coming conflict. His Majesty's Government had sold out the Czechs; now, if they thought it would keep them out of war, they would sell out the Poles, too.

Hitler and Stalin could gag their newspapermen; in the democracies that was impossible. Foreign correspondents from the United States and every European capital were aware of the developing tension between London and Warsaw, and although they only picked up fragments of the story, they gave the Poles a forum for their grievances, which were found to be completely justified when the forty volumes of *Documents on British Foreign Policy 1919–39* were published after the war. The issue was whether England would or would not fight for Poland. One of the first journalists to put it bluntly was Garvin, who noted in the *Observer* that summer that Chamberlain's reputation was reflected in the greeting now exchanged by passing acquaintances on the streets of Warsaw. They simply said: "Remember Munich."[109]

On Monday, August 14, the day Ribbentrop cabled Schulenburg that he wanted to fly to Moscow "in the name of the Führer" with the object of "restoring German-Russian friendship," Churchill left England for a three-day tour of the Maginot Line. His mission was an exercise in personal diplomacy, obsolescent then, illegal today, and rarely productive. At the time of Winston's departure, Chamberlain and his cabinet were unaware that he had left the country; only the Imperial General Staff, whose blessing he had, knew where he was going, and why. His name and his reputation were familiar to every Frenchman in authority.[110]

Political relationships between the two Western allies had soured; the Warsaw junta had driven a wedge between them. To Churchill's consternation, the rift between London and Paris was matched by chilliness on the military level. The Conseil Supérieur de la Guerre, France's high command, was altering its military plans, but Tiny Ironside had been provided with no details. He hoped they were better than Britain's.

Winston's prestige across the Channel made him an ideal choice to do what Britain's Imperial General Staff could not: talk to the French high command, question them, reassure them. In 1936, as their guest, he had toured Verdun, Metz, and the famous line named after André Maginot, a politician who believed good fences made neighbors who are not good friends keep their distance. Winston's letters then had been notable for their lack of opinion. To Clementine he had written: "There was nothing to see as all the troops were hidden in holes or under bushes. But to anyone with military knowledge it was most instructive." Now he was going to take a closer look. To Ironside he wrote that he was "off tomorrow" for the Rhine sector. "Generals Georges and Gamelin are very kindly going to come with me part of the time, and I expect we shall be able to have some talks on the matters we discussed."[111]

Accompanied by General Spears, he landed at Le Bourget and was greeted personally by Gamelin's deputy, General Joseph Georges, who had cleared his crowded calendar to serve as Churchill's guide. Winston was flattered; as he wrote Clementine that evening from the Ritz, "Georges will command the army in a war." After they had left the airport, he wrote, the general drove him and Spears "to the restaurant in the Bois where in divine sunshine we lunched & talked 'shop' for a long time." As they ate wood strawberries soaked in white wine, the French commander said the French thought "nothing will happen till the snow falls in the Alps & gives to Mussolini protection for the winter." Churchill agreed. "This looks like early or mid-September, wh wd still leave Hitler two months to deal with Poland, before the mud season in that country. All this of course is speculation, but also reasonable. It seems to fit the German programme so far as it has been published."[112]

As the tour progressed — they traveled, Winston proudly wrote Clementine, "in a special Michelin train of extreme speed, dining en route" and spent "2 vy long days on the line" — their host's feeling grew that hostilities were inevitable. According to Spears's notes, Georges said he was "convinced that war was almost upon us, and that the Germans, unless given all they wanted, were prepared to launch it." Spears wrote, "It emerged that there was no more doubt in General Georges' mind than in ours that it was the Germans rather than we who had benefited by the time gained at Munich, always supposing that they had really intended fighting then, which he doubted. He thought Hitler had been bluffing." A year ago, he told them, the Nazis had no elaborate defenses facing France; now they had built their *Westwall*, the Siegfried Line, "a formidable obstacle built according to modern ideas, in great depth, whereas the Maginot Line was linear." A year earlier, French artillery had been "incomparably superior"; the Germans, whose Munich spoils included Czechoslovakia's vast Skoda munitions works, were now masters of the big guns. Moreover, Georges said, the Nazis had built a long lead in the air, "and all we could do was to build and build, and place the largest possible orders in the United States."[113]

Churchill's second tour of the Maginot Line confirmed his new views of modern tactics and strategy. After he had lunched with General Gamelin, chief of the French General Staff and commander in chief–designate (Georges would be the field commander), Gamelin left instructions that Winston and Spears were to be shown parts of the intricate defense system never revealed before to any foreign visitor — strong points along the Rhine, ingenious new antitank obstacles, underground railroads opposite the *Westwall*, and, should Hitler decide to attack through Switzerland, heavy artillery sited on Swiss road junctions. And so it was that on Tuesday, August 15 — as Anglo-French diplomats tried in vain to get Poland to agree to let Soviet troops cross Polish territory — Churchill and Spears, led by Georges, began a grueling exploration of the line's eighty-seven "fortified" miles, completed four years earlier.

Shielded by ten feet of cement, each casemate housed grenade throwers, machine guns firing out of underground slits with a fifty-degree arc, and rapid-firing antitank guns. Every casemate was manned by twenty-five men who moved through tunnels and down elevators to sleeping quarters deep below the earth. Skillfully camouflaged, the casemates were invisible to intruders in the forest, save only for the two observation cupolas above each.

Five miles behind these outer strong points, spaced every three to five miles, were steel-and-concrete forts housing as many as twelve hundred poilus, who were transported from their subterranean barracks to gun turrets by electric trains. Ventilation was provided by compressors which could screen out poison gas. A major fort consisted of from fifteen to eighteen concrete blocks, each bristling with guns — ranging from 37 millimeters to 135 millimeters — bolted to disappearing turrets. Each block was split into two sections linked by underground galleries, some over a mile long. If half the fort were captured, the other half could fight on, bringing down heavy fire on the enemy. At Verdun in 1916 two forts, Douamont and Vaux, had been lost to Germans who infiltrated their superstructures and fought their way downward. To prevent this, the designers of the Maginot Line had provided for "interval troops," special forces complete with their own field artillery, which could be shifted to any fort under heavy attack. "These," Alistair Horne explains, were meant "to compensate for what, by definition, the Line lacked: mobility."[114]

On Wednesday, August 16, accompanied by a *Times* correspondent, Winston and his party drove right up to the front line, within shouting distance of Nazi troops on the right bank of the Rhine. *The Times* reported that Winston was "amazed" to see an enormous sign opposite Neufbrisach reading: *"Ein Volk, ein Reich, ein Führer,"* and, on the left bank, a French billboard replying: *"Liberté, Égalité, Fraternité."* Churchill was amazed — but not by this very ordinary sport of idle soldiers. He was startled by the naked intent of the German deployment, invisible to the reporter's untrained eye but recognized immediately by him and his companion. "The trip," Spears wrote, "tore to shreds any illusion that it was not Germany's intention to wage war and to wage it soon. There was no mistaking the grim, relentless and barely concealed preparations she was making."[115]

That evening they joined French officers for a long discussion of the new threat posed by parachute troops, of tank traps, of assaults screened by artificial fog — Winston thought this very important — and of the need for heavier tanks, upon which all were agreed. As Spears listened, his mind drifted back to Vimy Ridge in 1915. Winston had earnestly explained his theory of "land cruisers" then to a French general and his staff. Spears had lingered after Churchill departed, and he remembered "how heartily they had laughed" at "this absurd idea." They had told Spears: "Your politicians are even funnier than ours."[116]

Thursday, when Ribbentrop's Luftwaffe pilot was instructed to prepare a flight plan for imminent departure to Moscow's Khodnynka Airport, Churchill and Spears were back in Paris, registering at the Ritz. Long afterward Spears said that what had impressed him most during their tour was "Winston's incredible vitality." Nearly sixty-five, he would have been entitled to bypass some of the line's lesser features, but he had insisted on stumbling over every pillbox in sight, scrutinizing antitank obstacles in front of the main line of resistance (repeatedly ensnaring himself on barbed wire), climbing in and out of antitank ditches, and striding in and out of the reinforced barracks, known as *maisons fortes*, for troops who must remain on the surface. He had been on the go for three days, hurrying through tunnels and sleeping bays, arguing over whether certain stretches could support the weight of tanks, and being manhandled down the slopes of the Rhine's banks so he could stand, arms akimbo, staring at the German soldiers on the far shore.

And he was not finished. In his room he prepared a report, to be dispatched by courier to the War Office. He thought it might be useful, he began, "to set down some of the points in my mind as a result of my long talks here." The coming war, he believed, ought to be better managed than the last, and to that end he recommended "a liaison between British and French supply organizations." In his opinion German regulation of industry "is the greatest advantage they possess." The Allies "should match it."[117]

He thought the possibility of any "heavy German effort" in the west during the "opening phase" of the war extremely unlikely. The Wehrmacht's strategy would be to crush Poland first. Preventing this was essential; if the Poles were overwhelmed the Germans could turn and hurl their full might against the Allies. Eventually France could put six million men in the field, but her present strength was only a fraction of Germany's. To "take the weight off Poland" the French should be prepared "to engage actively all along the line and . . . force the Germans to man their lines heavily." Since the German border on that front "extends so many miles, it ought to be possible to hold a very large number of German divisions in the West." The thought that England and France might remain idle, leaving the Poles to their fate in the hope of a negotiated peace with Hitler, never crossed his mind.[118]

However, his misgivings about the French static strategy were grave. The Paris dailies called the line "France's shield." But, Winston noted, the great advantage of a shield is that it may be moved to defend any part of the soldier's body. The Maginot Line was immovable. It was incapable of protecting the French from Germany's classic invasion route over the Belgian plains — "the pit of the French stomach," as Clausewitz had called it. Churchill recalled an old Whitehall joke: "The War Office is always preparing for the last war." Now, he thought, it was "certainly true of the French." In his report to Tiny Ironside he wrote that while "the French Front cannot be surprised . . . the flanks of this front . . . rest upon two small neutral states." He was satisfied that the French had "done everything in their power to prepare against an invasion through Switzerland," but "the attitude of Belgium," on the other hand, "is thought to be profoundly unsatisfactory. At present there are no military relations of any kind between the French and the Belgians."[119]

He had begun to understand the Maginot mind. It was the mind of a nation which did not want to lose a war, but didn't much want to win either. The French soldiers of 1914 had lusted for revanche, the return of Alsace and Lorraine, lost when their grandfathers had been overwhelmed in the Franco-Prussian War. The two provinces had been made French again at Versailles, and now the country had no war aims. In denying an appropriation to enlarge the republic's tank corps in 1935, the minister of war had asked a wildly cheering Chamber of Deputies, "How can we still believe in the offensive when we have spent milliards to establish a fortified barrier? Would we be mad enough to advance beyond this barrier upon God knows what adventure?" Yet everyone — including the Generalstab plotters meeting beneath the murmuring pines and hemlocks in Zossen — knew France's basic war plan. Because the minister of war had discounted the threat through Switzerland, the Maginot Line was expected to hold the enemy at bay while other poilus valiantly drove into Belgium to counterattack the attacking Germans. But if the counterattacking poilus lacked élan vital, their assault would fail. Feeling safe behind the line, "like the lotus-eating mandarins of Cathay behind their great Wall," as one writer put it, France had lapsed into languor, a spiritless lassitude which was the exact obverse of the lusty, singing, marching young Nazi soldiers across the border.[120]

During his tour of the line Churchill, like most visiting VIPs, confined his remarks to senior officers. Indeed, he would have given grave offense had he done otherwise. Spears tells us that he was "pleased with the aspect of the men. . . . He knew how to look every man in the eyes as he passed him, thus convincing him he had been recognised by someone already known, even in France, to be a very important person." But it is a pity Winston could not have talked to them, too, and later he said as much. The spirit of the Marne had, he realized, "exhausted its mission and itself in victory." It was as though the Third Republic had become a different country. Bravery, he noted, was now associated in the great majority of French minds with the futile butchery of 1914–1918. In metropolitan France alone 27 percent of the country's young men between the ages of eighteen and twenty-seven had not returned from the trenches. Simone de Beauvoir tells of a Dr. Lemair, who had operated on countless poilus under appalling conditions and who, on returning home, "took to his bed and never got up again."[121]

No one knew how many of the survivors of the war, the men who should have been guiding France in 1939, had been drained, exhausted, broken at the front. But the deterioration in the army's leadership had been shocking. The Conseil Supérieur de la Guerre, whose members would become senior generals when war broke out, was hopelessly entangled in red tape and bureaucratic muddle — *paperasse,* as the French call it. Tanks were despised (as mortars, machine guns, and warplanes had been despised in 1914). In 1921 Marshal Pétain, then supreme commander, had dismissed the future of armored warfare in nineteen words: "Tanks assist the advance of the infantry by breaking static obstacles and active resistance put up by the enemy." His successors endorsed this finding. As Charles de Gaulle had discovered in the early 1930s, no one in the Conseil Supérieur understood revolutionary air power and the implications of armored vehicles which could now "be made capable of withstanding artillery fire and could advance a hundred miles a day." Indeed, not a single French general had wanted to know. De Gaulle's memoranda had been returned to him unread, and when he published his controversial views in *Vers l'armée de métier* his name had been struck from the promotion list.[122]

During his glimpse of the Maginot Line in 1936, Churchill had thought the Conseil's doctrine sound. He later wrote that, lacking "access to official information for so many years," he had not comprehended "the violence effected since the last war by the incursion of a mass of fast-moving enemy armour. I knew about it, but it had not altered my convictions as it should have done."[123]

Indeed it should. He had fathered the tank in 1915, when it had been ridiculed as "Winston's Folly." And he was the last man in Parliament to plead backbencher lack of "access to official information." It is doubtful that any man at the cabinet table, including the prime minister, was as well-informed about the War Office, Admiralty, and RAF, all of which he had headed at one time or another, and whose staffs included officers who saw to it that he was kept abreast of the latest military developments. Moreover, as chancellor of the Exchequer he had witnessed the spectacular maneuvers of Britain's Experimental Armoured Force on Salisbury Plain in 1927, which vindicated advocates of high-speed tank forces. Nevertheless, as late as 1938 Churchill had written that "the tank has, no doubt, a great part to play; but I personally doubt very much whether it will ever again see the palmy days of 1918. . . . Nowadays the anti-tank rifle and the anti-tank gun have made such strides that the poor tank cannot carry thick enough skin to stand up to them."[124]

Other views had been suggested to him. The most imaginative came from Captain Basil Liddell Hart. After the Armistice, Liddell Hart had served on the team which drafted the new infantry training manual. Then, and later as military correspondent of *The Times*, he had set forth the first practical alternative to the entrenched, deadlocked siege warfare he had survived. In its place he proposed an "expanding torrent" offensive, spearheaded by swift, mobile masses of heavy tanks and backed by equally versatile self-propelled guns and infantry, bound for the enemy's rear aboard armored carriers. Liddell Hart urged abandonment of methodical siege techniques, which involved hitting the enemy where he was strongest. Instead, attackers would search for a weak spot in the foe's defenses and pour through it with mobile firepower, creating new fronts deep in the enemy's rear.

Churchill's French was weak, and he had not been exposed to de Gaulle. But he and Lloyd George had met Liddell Hart in Morpeth Mansions and heard him out. At least, Lloyd George had. In his memoirs Liddell Hart wrote: "It was . . . very noticeable that Churchill's mind was apt to focus on a phrase, while Ll. G. seized the point and followed on to the next point. . . . Moreover, Churchill liked to do most of the talking in any discussion." Winston was usually hospitable to military innovations. If he had been slow to grasp the new role of air power, he understood the fragility of England's air defenses. On the ground, however, he still clung to the continuous front school of military thought, remembering when it broke Ludendorff's line and forgetting the four years of heartbreaking, bloody failures before. Perhaps the answer to his inconsistency lay in his youth and his romantic idealization of it ("Twenty to twenty-five!" he often said. "Those are the years!"). Tanks were replacing horses, and at heart he remained a young officer of hussars. In a nostalgic chamber of his mind, Victorian colonial wars, with their negligible casualties — negligible, that is, for the British — would always glitter. He rejoiced in the memory of magnificence and turned away from the squalid, forgetting that the only moral judgments in war are made by the victors, and victorious armies are led by those who have mastered the latest, most efficient tools of their trade.[125]

Nevertheless, he possessed a rare gift for strategy, and he had been more attentive in Morpeth Mansions than Liddell Hart had thought. Spears's most vivid recollection of their eve-of-the-war examination of the Maginot Line, with long sessions of men bowed over map tables, was of Churchill spotting the great weakness in the French defense system. His mouth pursed, his gaze was fixed "as if," Spears wrote in his account, "he were crystal-gazing." He had been smiling; now the smile vanished and he shook his head ominously as he put his finger on the shoulder of the Maginot, where it ended near Montmedy and was extended by field works opposite the Ardennes forest. "He observed," recalled Spears, "that he hoped these field works were strong." He understood that Marshal Pétain had once remarked that the Ardennes was "impassable to strong forces." That view, said Winston, was now "very unwise." He asked Georges to "remember that we are faced with a new weapon, armour in great strength, on which the Germans are no doubt concentrating, and that forests will be particularly tempting to such forces since they will offer concealment from the air."[126]

Spears could not remember Georges's reply, but neither Georges nor Weygand acted upon, or even made note of, Churchill's advice. Yet in its heavily guarded headquarters outside Berlin, the German high command was studying that same spot in the Ardennes. Using tanks, the generals believed, they could outflank the Maginot Line, take Paris, and force the French to their knees — accomplishing in six weeks what their fathers had vainly sought in four years of bloody, frustrating siege warfare.

On Friday, August 18, when Ambassador Schulenburg was climbing walls in Moscow, trapped between his führer's demand for a windup of treaty negotiations with Russia and Stalin's dawdling, Spears and Churchill parted, Spears returning to London and Winston traveling fifty miles north of Paris to Dreux and the château of Consuelo Balsan, born a Vanderbilt and for twenty-six years a duchess of Marlborough. Her 1921 divorce from Charles ("Sunny") Marlborough had been amicable, and the door to her home was always open to Winston and his family. Churchill was aware that galleys and even page proofs were accumulating on his Chartwell desk, but despite his outward display of vigor, he was weary. Believing as always that "a change is as good as a rest," he had decided to paint. Clementine and Mary, now approaching her seventeenth birthday, awaited him there. Because they were "conscious that the sands of peace were fast running out," Mary recalls, their "appreciation of those halcyon summer days was heightened: there was swimming and tennis (so greatly enjoyed by Clementine) and *fraises des bois;* Winston painted a lovely picture of the exquisite old rose-brick house; we visited Chartres cathedral and were drenched in the cool blueness of the windows." As with a song that runs through one's mind, she kept remembering a line from Walter de la Mare: "Look thy last on all things lovely."[127]

Among Consuelo's other guests was Paul Maze, the professional painter and an old friend of Winston's. In his diary Maze noted: "We talked about his visit to the Maginot Line with Georges — very impressed by what he saw." At dinner he was cross, "but with reason," Maze thought, "as the assemblée didn't see any danger ahead. As [Sir Evan] Charteris was walking up the stairs to go to his bed he shouted to me, 'Don't listen to him. He is a warmonger.' " On two successive days he and Winston painted together. Maze wrote that as he worked alongside him, Churchill "suddenly turned to me and said: 'This is the last picture we shall paint in peace for a very long time.' What amazed me was his concentration over his painting. No one but he could have understood more what the possibility of war meant and how ill-prepared we were." As they worked, Winston would remark from time to time on the relative strength of the opposing armies. "They are strong, I tell you, they are strong." Then, Maze wrote, "his jaw would clench his large cigar, and I felt the determination of his will. 'Ah,' he would say, 'with it all, we shall have him.' "[128]

After three days at Consuelo's château Winston suddenly left. Later, in his memoirs, he wrote that he "decided to go home, where at least I could find out what was going on," promising "my wife I would send her word in good time." It was August 22; the Germans and the Russians had announced that final negotiations for their nonaggression pact would begin tomorrow. Now it was official: the triple alliance was dead. The Allies could expect no support from the U.S.S.R. The situation was even worse than they thought. Not only would the pact provide that if either country should "become the object of belligerent action by a third party," the other country would "in no manner lend its support to this third power"; in a secret protocol the signatories agreed to respect each other's "spheres of influence in Eastern Europe" — the basis, a month later, for the division of conquered Poland between the Soviet Union and the Reich. Even so, the impact of the impending treaty on Englishmen may be roughly compared to that of Pearl Harbor upon Americans. Nicolson, learning of it over the 6:00 P.M. BBC news, described Britain's shock: "This smashes our peace front and makes our guarantees to Poland, Rumania and Greece very questionable. How Ribbentrop must chuckle. I feel rather stunned. . . . I fear that it means we are humbled to the dust." Malcolm Muggeridge wrote: "Groping down darkened streets, dimly it was felt that a way of life was failing, its comfortable familiarity passing away never to reappear."[129]

Churchill paused in Paris to lunch with Georges, who produced figures on the strength of the opposing armies, including their fighting spirit. "The result impressed me so much," Winston later wrote, "that for the first time I said: 'But you are the masters.' " The general replied: "The Germans have a very strong army," adding cryptically: "We shall never be allowed to strike first." French politics, in short, ruled out a French preemptive strike into the Ruhr after war had been declared — Poland's only hope and also, as it turned out, France's. Apparently Winston missed these implications; he left Paris in a cheerful mood. Leaving Dreux, he had seemed depressed, and Maze had given him a note to be read after he was on his way: "Don't worry Winston. You *know* that you will be Prime Minister and lead us to victory."[130]

"That night," Churchill wrote in his memorandum of events, "I slept at Chartwell." He did not sleep unguarded. In *The Gathering Storm* he later wrote: "There were known to be twenty thousand organised German Nazis in England at this time, and it would only have been in accord with their procedure in other friendly countries that the outbreak of war should be preceded by a sharp prelude of sabotage and murder." In February he had spent six pounds, fifteen shillings, on his two guns, having them stripped, cleaned and oiled, fitted with new trigger blades and cross pins, and the two pairs of barrels rejointed. He had hired Inspector W. H. Thompson, the retired Scotland Yard detective who had served as his bodyguard in the 1920s, to resume his old duties. Thompson recalled that in the car on his way home from Croydon Airport, "Mr. Churchill grew graver and graver as he sat wrapped in thought, and then said slowly and thoughtfully: 'Before the harvest is gathered in — we shall be at war.' "[131]

Winston had not asked for official protection, as he wrote afterward, but "I had enough information to convince me that Hitler recognised me as a foe." At Chartwell he and Thompson planned vigils. "While one slept," Churchill wrote, "the other watched. Thus nobody would have had a walk-over." He knew "a major burden" would fall upon him if war came — "and who could doubt its coming?" His wife and daughter had no doubts. They followed him to England a few days later, passing through Paris. "On that golden summer evening," Mary recalls, "the Gare du Nord teemed with soldiers: the French army was mobilizing."[132]

In the morning Churchill felt refreshed, and was off to London. Nicolson noted that he "has just returned from Paris and is in high fettle. The French are not at all perturbed by the Russo-German Pact and are prepared to support Poland nonetheless." Winston had "just rung up Paul Reynaud who asserts that all is going well: by which he means war, I suppose." He did, but only because there was no honorable alternative. A year ago the pied piper at No. 10 had thought there was. This new crisis was the bitter price they must pay for that error. Their exigency had worsened. There were no Czech divisions to march with them now, and the Russians — who had been ready to fight for Czechoslovakia — had shifted sides. Churchill believed that if the Allies had taken a firm stand at Munich, it "would have prevented war," and "if worse had come to worst, we should have been far better off than we may be at some future date."[133]

This was that future date. He devoted the night of his return to writing an article for the *Daily Mirror* — "At the Eleventh Hour" — which appeared on August 24. In the light of the "intrigue" between the Nazis and the Communists, he wrote, it was becoming "increasingly difficult to see how war can be averted." Events, he stated, were "moving forward from every quarter and along all roads to catastrophe. The German military preparations have already reached a point where action on the greatest scale is possible at any moment." That afternoon, August 24, Chamberlain recalled Parliament — to reach the House of Commons MPs had to pass through a line of pickets carrying signs bearing the single name CHURCHILL in a blue circle. The House approved an emergency war powers bill; the Royal Navy was ordered to its war stations, reservists were called up, twenty-five merchantmen were requisitioned for conversion to armed merchant cruisers, leaves were canceled, the Dominions alerted, and twenty-four thousand reservists ordered to man ack-ack batteries, radar stations, and balloon stations.

Britain was springing to arms, but not eagerly. In 1914, London, including Parliament, had thrilled with war fever. Now — and this was also true of Paris and Berlin — the mood was somber and resigned. Victor Cazalet wrote in his diary that the House had been "very full" and that Chamberlain had made "a good but not very impressive speech." Afterward, he added, "I sat in Smoking Room with LG and Winston. Both v anti-Chamberlain. Think he has led us into this mess. We ought never to have given guarantees to Poland unless they had consented to allow Russian army across their frontiers." Nicolson joined the group in the smoking room; he had heard rumors that the P.M. had offered to resign if war came and that the King would refuse to accept. That evening Churchill dined at the Savoy with Duff Cooper, Eden, Sandys, and Sinclair. In his diary Duff Cooper noted: "We were all very gloomy."[134]

On August 25, His Majesty's Government, recognizing the gravity of Poland's peril in light of the Nazi-Soviet Pact, signed a formal treaty of alliance with the Poles, turning a unilateral guarantee into a bilateral pact. Britain's obligation to Poland was now far more binding. The next Tuesday, after talking to Churchill on the telephone, Eddie Marsh noted in his diary that Winston had said "Hitler was evidently rattled, but he didn't see how he could climb down, which would cost him his life." That same day the FO also sent Berlin a note urging Germany not to attempt a Danzig coup. Churchill read it before it was sent — he always managed to be in the Foreign Office at critical moments, alerted by his informants there — and doubted that the message was strong enough. Duff Cooper, another diarist, noted that Vansittart had assured them that "HMG's note to Hitler was everything that could be desired. Winston rang up the Polish ambassador while we were there, who said that he was now completely satisfied with the support he was receiving from our Government."[135]

On Saturday, Ironside, driving down to Chartwell for lunch, had found Winston "full of Georges, whom he had seen over in France. I found that he had become very French in his outlook. . . . The burden of his song was that we must have a great Army in France, that we couldn't depend upon the French to do our effort for us." He wanted twenty British divisions across the Channel by Christmas. Before Ironside left Chartwell, Winston observed that His Majesty's Government, in trying to sway European events, was taking a far more imperious pose than its military establishment warranted — that, as Ironside paraphrased him, "We were trying to get as much control in the conduct of affairs as if we had an Army of one and a half millions."[136]

Churchill thought HMG still did not fully appreciate that the great danger on the Continent required urgent measures. The prime minister and members of the cabinet, apparently believing this was just one more crisis which could be solved by deferring to the Führer, continued to be relatively passive as the week unfolded. With a few outstanding exceptions — Shirer, Colvin, Sheean, John Gunther, and the best of the London press corps — press dispatches from the Continent did not reflect a need for speed. One of Winston's most reliable sources was Geoffrey Parsons of the *New York Herald Tribune*. On Sunday Parsons wired Chartwell: "Send you this by telegraph since hours are numbered. Impossible to exaggerate confidence of Hitler and German people that British will capitulate. . . . Nobody has expected anything but swift easy victory over Poles, having been fed idea British would never fight over Danzig or Poland. . . . General cynicism toward British attitude amazes me after visit to London. But it exists in opinion of American observers in Britain."[137]

Chamberlain seems to have sensed as much, and, within the bounds of his desire to avoid offending the Führer, had been taking steps to counter this impression. On August 22 he had written a personal letter to Hitler, informing him that Britain was now on a war footing. This alert, he said, was the result of German troop movements and the assumption "in some quarters in Berlin" that since the announcement of Germany's agreement with Russia "intervention by Great Britain on behalf of Poland is no longer a contingency that need be reckoned with. No greater mistake could be made." Whatever the nature of Hitler's pact with Stalin, the P.M. wrote, "it cannot alter Great Britain's obligation to Poland, which His Majesty's Government have stated in public repeatedly and plainly, and which they are determined to fulfill."[138]

Ambassador Henderson flew to Berchtesgaden, arriving at Hitler's mountain retreat about noon on Wednesday, the twenty-third, to deliver the P.M.'s letter. Hitler was on edge — thirty Wehrmacht divisions were moving toward the Polish frontier — and his response, according to Henderson's cable to Halifax, was "excitable," couched in language "violent and exaggerated both as regards England and Poland." The situation of Germans in Poland had become intolerable, he shouted; *Polendeutsche* were even being subjected to *"kastrieren"* ("castration"). If Britain did not force the Poles to stop these outrages, the Reich would be forced to begin *"Gegenmassnahmen"* ("counter measures"). Later that day, he again received Henderson. This time his temper was under control, which made what he had to say all the more appalling. He was "fifty years old," he said, and "preferred war now" to when he "would be fifty-five or sixty." It was "surely quite clear to everyone that the World War would not have been lost" had he "been Chancellor at the time." In his formal, uncompromising reply to Chamberlain, he declared that the Reich had displayed "unparalleled magnanimity" in its attempts to settle the Danzig and Polish Corridor problems. Then, in what Churchill later called "a piece of lying effrontery," the *Kriegsherr* charged that England's "unconditional assurance" to Poland "could only be interpreted in that country as an encouragement henceforward to unloose, under cover of such a charter, a wave of appalling terrorism against the one and a half million German inhabitants living in Poland."[139]

In Danzig and Poland, local Nazis were following the modus operandi which had played so well in Austria and Czechoslovakia. Local Nazi storm troopers in uniform sacked stores owned by Jews, painted huge yellow swastikas on synagogues, and assaulted critics of their führer in the streets. In Polish communities where Germans were a majority, policemen cheered them on. Meantime German newspapers were telling their readers the exact opposite — that the victims were *Polendeutsche*, stalked by Polish terrorists. In Karlsruhe the daily paper carried the headline "WARSAW THREATENS BOMBARDMENT OF DANZIG — UNBELIEVABLE AGITATION OF THE POLISH ARCHMADNESS! [POLNISCHEN GRÖSSENWAHN]." "POLEN, GIB ACHT!" ("POLAND, LOOK OUT!") warned the *Berliner Arbeiterzeitung;* "ANSWER TO POLAND, THE RUNNER-AMOK [AMOKLÄUFER] AGAINST PEACE AND RIGHT IN EUROPE!" On Saturday, August 26, the *Zwölf-Uhr Blatt* reported: "THIS PLAYING WITH FIRE GOING TOO FAR — THREE GERMAN PASSENGER PLANES SHOT AT BY POLES — IN CORRIDOR MANY GERMAN FARMHOUSES IN FLAMES!" The banner headline in the *Berliner Arbeiterzeitung* that day read, "COMPLETE CHAOS IN POLAND — GERMAN FAMILIES FLEE — POLISH SOLDIERS

PUSH TO EDGE OF GERMAN BORDER!" Goebbels saved his masterpiece for the Sunday *Völkischer Beobachter:*

ALL OF POLAND IN A WAR FEVER! 1.5 MILLION MEN MOBILIZED!
UNINTERRUPTED TROOP TRANSPORT TOWARD FRONTIER!
CHAOS IN UPPER SILESIA![140]

William L. Shirer notes dryly: "There was no mention, of course, of any German mobilization." Germany had been fully mobilized for two weeks, but the Poles, anxious to avoid provoking the Reich, and on British advice, had actually delayed their mobilization. Only thirty Polish divisions were in position to defend their frontiers. The Germans had massed fifty-six divisions, including nine armored, on Poland's borders. Two great pincer movements were prepared to overwhelm the defenders, troops whose leaders had no plan and cherished an absolute faith in the power of cavalry charges to defeat modern tanks.[141]

The Anglo-Polish Treaty of Mutual Assistance, as announced in London and Warsaw that last Friday in August, was a model of clarity. Article One clearly stated that should either country fall victim to aggression, the other would declare war on the offenders. To strengthen this, Article Two provided that this action would be triggered in the event of "any action by a European Power which clearly threatened, directly or indirectly, the independence of one of the contracting parties."

That was the way to handle Hitler. Yet despite Chamberlain's firm words in Parliament, the indecisiveness and yearning for German friendship were still there. When Hitler studied the text of the pact, he found no mention of Danzig. Since the free city was not Polish soil, he assumed that England was not committed to its defense. Actually England *was,* but Halifax had been unwilling to commit himself openly, and so — in an act of prodigious diplomatic incompetence — the guarantee to defend Danzig's status quo had been entered in a secret clause of the treaty. It would have been better to omit it entirely. As Duff Cooper had written in July: "Lack of decision is the worst fault from which a policy can suffer. So soon as a decision has been taken no time should be lost in announcing it. . . . It is of the first importance that we should know our own minds; it is of almost equal importance that the world should make no mistake about our intentions." Halifax, by clouding HMG's intentions, should have forfeited his office on this issue alone.[142]

Misunderstandings between the dictators and the democracies were inevitable anyhow; never, in the long reach of European history, had two more disparate cultures coexisted. The Nazis and Fascists were convinced that they were, as an admiring Anne Morrow Lindbergh called them, "the wave of the future." To celebrities from the West the societies created by the Duce and the Führer were impressive. They seemed efficient. There were no strikes, no demonstrations, no disrespect for authority. The *Gleichschaltung* — political coordination and the elimination of opponents — of Hitler's new order meant more productive assembly lines, organized holidays for workers, and an inspired, patriotic youth. It was heartening to see blond Aryan boys in short leather pants running through the fields hand-in-hand with blond, buxom Aryan girls, though visitors were seldom told why they were so enthusiastic. Once they were out of sight, the boy's lederhosen were shucked while his companion, as a loyal member of the Bund Deutscher Maedel, hoisted her skirts to enjoy Strength through Joy, pleasing the Führer by increasing the population of his Reich, which, he said, would always need soldiers. The young were the most ardent Nazis, but enthusiasm for the regime was found among Germans of every age and on every social level. They had always been a regimented people, and did not seem to mind the loss of personal freedom. They rallied to the slogans *"Gemeinnutz vor Eigennutz"* ("The Common Interest before Self-interest") and *"Kanonen statt Butter"* ("Guns instead of Butter"). Those who preferred liberty and butter absconded or remained silent. In the Third Reich *Gleichschaltung* wasn't for everybody, just everybody who wanted to live.

Nothing in the democracies, including the United States, matched the euphoria of this lusty carnival, these vigorous folk who never jaywalked, never argued with their superiors, who listened meekly when upbraided by policemen yet turned viciously on those they considered *Untermenschen*, their inferiors. They seemed to spend an inordinate amount of their time marching, and singing stirring songs as they marched: *"Die Wacht am Rhein,"* *"Bomben auf Polen,"* the *"Horst Wessel Lied,"* and *"Deutschland über Alles"* (". . . *über alles in der Welt*").

Since the United States was among *alles in der Welt*, and Franklin Roosevelt was determined not to see the swastika hoisted in Washington, the president asked Congress for $552 million to strengthen American defense. He also appealed to Hitler to keep his sword sheathed. The Führer ignored him; he held all democracies in contempt, seeing them as weak, indecisive, and easily bullied. Many in England, France, and the United States agreed with him. Each democracy now had its strong, local Fascist movement, and even those who scored dictatorships wondered whether their countrymen had gone "soft."

In the Nazis' book burning of May 10, 1933, Goebbels, who had struck the first match, had declared: "The soul of the German people can again express itself." Implicit here was the Nazi conviction that beneath the veneer of modern culture was the primitive vigor of a warrior race; of noble savages, supple and powerfully built; of those ancient Germans who, Tacitus had written, were conspicuous for their "fierce blue eyes, red hair, tall frames," and whose loyalty to their chieftain was absolute. Strip away that veneer, the Nazi ideologues told one another, and Germany, redeemed, would be invincible. What they overlooked was that it was true of all civilized nations. Deutschland was not the only European nation with proud military traditions. British soldiers had been winning battles, and the Royal Navy sinking ships, three centuries before Bismarck welded the three hundred states of central Europe into the German Empire. Churchill was putting it on record every night. It was Britain's misfortune, and the world's, that the men at the helm of His Majesty's Government in 1939 had lost England's compass and, lacking the wisdom of Caesar, thought you could strike a deal by shaking hands with barbarians.

Britain was by treaty committed to the defense of Danzig, but in fact HMG's position was very different. Immediately after signing the Anglo-Polish treaty on Friday, August 25 — the first day of the last week of peace — Halifax told the Polish ambassador that while he recognized "how vital to Poland was the position in Danzig," he did not feel that "if there were ever any opportunity of conversations being held about Danzig, the Polish Government would be right or wise to reject it." Indeed, he thought the Poles "would make a great mistake if they sought to adopt a position in which discussions of peaceful modifications of the status of Danzig were ruled out." Despite Daladier, members of the French government were frantically trying to abandon their ally in the east; a member of Daladier's cabinet said publicly: "There is nothing to be done but to allow Germany to have her way." To further enfeeble opposition to Hitler, England and France were trying to approach the Führer through Mussolini, although neither democracy was informing the other.[143]

The Poles, wary of yielding an inch to the Germans, believed that any concession over Danzig would lead to new Nazi demands. In Warsaw the British ambassador, Sir Howard Kennard, had returned from leave, to the relief of his exhausted chargé. Kennard was blessed with clearer vision than any senior diplomat in Whitehall except the shelved Vansittart. To the Foreign Office he explained that "if Hitler decides on war, it is for the sole purpose of destroying Polish independence."[144]

But HMG was sure Hitler could be bought off for less, if only they could get him to state his price. Hitler, too, with the invasion of Poland nearly at hand, needed to know what Britain would do. On August 25, the Führer summoned Henderson to the chancellery. There Hitler told him, as the ambassador afterward reported to Whitehall, that he "accepts the British Empire and is willing to pledge himself personally for its continued existence." Once "the problem of Danzig and the Corridor" was resolved, Hitler would convey "an offer" detailing how his few colonial demands could be "negotiated by peaceful methods." But first, HMG must inform him of its attitude toward the Polish problem.[145]

Meantime the Duce was trying desperately to stop the Nazi juggernaut from rolling into Poland, not to spare the Poles or avert another general war, but because, as Germany's ally, he was pledged to fight beside Hitler and couldn't do it. On the morning of August 25 he found himself in an unaccustomed state of acute embarrassment. The Führer had sent him an urgent personal letter, alerting him to the Wehrmacht's imminent plunge into Poland. The Führer had written: "In case of intolerable events in Poland, I shall act immediately."

Mussolini's reply reached Hitler at about 6:00 P.M. According to Schmidt, it staggered him. He had not asked for Italy's help; under the three-month-old Pact of Steel it was taken for granted. But Hitler and Chamberlain were not the only European statesmen prepared to break their word. In his answer to Hitler's letter, the Duce said flatly that if the Reich made war on the Poles, Italy must be counted out. "The Italian war preparations," he said, were not complete; he was unprepared to "resist the attack which the French and English would predominantly direct against us." It had been his understanding "at our meetings [that] the war was envisaged for 1942, and by that time I would have been ready." After Hitler read it, he summoned Keitel and shouted: "Stop everything! At once!" Thus the invasion of Poland — *Fall Weiss* — was postponed to September 1.[146]

As Europe slept, Churchill stood hunched over his Disraeli desk, correcting galleys, revising passages with his red pen, or dictating inserts to Mrs. Hill, who sat over the keyboard of a silent typewriter, her fingers at the ready. He was telling the tale of an earlier Britain, when, in time of war or the threat of war, pusillanimous officials were flogged or hung. He went back to the birth of Britain, to the Roman occupation, the departure of Rome's legions, and the chaos that followed in the fifth century when, as the Welsh monk Nennius recorded, invading Saxons ("Sessoynes") from Germany plundered the island's quilt of little kingdoms, raping, looting, and spreading disease. The desperate kings turned to a dux bellorum *— no monarch, but in those times something far more prestigious: a* *military commander of great gifts and courage — known to history as Arthur. Arthur brought England a century of peace by defeating the Saxons in twelve mighty battles, the greatest of which, "the crowning mercy," as Churchill called it, was fought on Mount Badon at some time between 490 and 503. Now in 1939, at Chartwell, he invested Arthur with a crown and wrote that his "name takes us out of the mist of dimly remembered history into the daylight of romance. There looms, large, uncertain, dim but glittering, the legend of King Arthur. . . . Somewhere in the Island a great captain gathered the forces of Roman Britain and fought the barbarian invaders to the death. Around him, around his name and deeds shine all that romance and poetry can bestow."*[147]

In London three days were devoted to preparing an official reply to Hitler's insolent offer to "accept" the British Empire once Polish problems were solved. Horace Wilson and Rab Butler completed the first draft that Friday. Chamberlain reworked it until late in the evening. At 6:30 P.M. Saturday it was presented to the full cabinet, with Henderson present, presumably to offer the views of the German führer. There was, it turned out, nothing in it which he would have found objectionable. The reply was largely devoted to the need for Polish concessions, or the lack of them. Hitler had been insisting that they must give way, and HMG agreed. Hore-Belisha thought this first draft "fulsome, obsequious and deferential." He wrote in his diary that he had "urged that our only effective reply was to show strength and determination — that in no circumstances" should England "give the impression that we would weaken in our undertaking to Poland. Kingsley Wood supported me." Discussion continued awhile longer, then the group adjourned for the night.[148]

To Frenchmen it is *La Manche*, to Germans *der Ärmelkanal*, but Britons and Americans know it as the English Channel, and with some justification; it has long served the British as a formidable moat, the equivalent, in military terms, of perhaps a hundred divisions. It is not, however, unbridgeable. The Romans, Saxons, and Normans hurdled it. Philip II, Louis XIV, and Napoleon tried and came close. Concern about invasion fueled "isolationism," as the Victorians called it, three generations before Americans thought the concept theirs; and until Neville Chamberlain decided to chart his own foreign policy, it served as the keystone of British foreign policy in Europe. The island's safety, it was held, rested upon two stout principles. First, no nation possessing a great army would be permitted to seize the lowlands, Belgium and Holland. It was Germany's violation of Belgian territory which had triggered England's declaration of war in 1914. Second, power on the Continent would be shared by two or more nations. Chamberlain was the first prime minister to encourage domination by one, believing that Anglo-German friendship would guarantee peace, and — until Ribbentrop and Molotov signed their treaty of alliance in Moscow — that the Third Reich was a bulwark against Soviet imperialism. However, England's encouragement of balanced power in Europe had been challenged in every century, most frequently by France, but most memorably, perhaps, by Spain.

Prowling back and forth in his study — muttering while Mrs. Hill's fingers flew over her keyboard — Churchill reworked the story of Philip II's Great Armada. Philip II of Spain, envisaging his empire as the worldly arm of the Roman Catholic church, and himself as its sword, had plunged into all the religious wars of the time, guided by the faith that the Reformation could be undone and all Europe reunited in a single faith, regardless of the cost. Henry VIII had led England out of the church. Now his daughter Elizabeth was defending her father's Reformation. Philip, honing his blade, became obsessed with England, and when the northern Netherlands broke loose from Catholicism in 1581, he began building his "invincible Armada," over 132 vessels bearing 3,165 cannon and 30,000 men, intent upon the conquest of Britain. Lord Leicester could muster but 20,000 untrained men. This force could not defend the beaches, and the fate of the island therefore rested with the fleet.

If the British prevailed, rule of the seas would pass from Spain to England. There, too, however, prospects seemed dim. Only 34 of the Queen's ships were seaworthy, all of them smaller than the enemy's galleons. They were joined by 36 privately owned vessels. It didn't seem enough. But the Royal Navy was led by captains like John Hawkins and Francis Drake, the finest seamen the world had known. The size of their craft was misleading; based on his experience as a buccaneer in colonial waters, Hawkins had radically altered the design of English ships, cutting down the castles which had towered over decks, mounting heavier, long-range guns, and deepening keels and concentrating on seaworthiness and speed.

Perhaps the island's greatest weapon, however, was its sovereign. Now in her mid-fifties, she had ruled England for thirty years, as long as Philip had Spain, and was as skilled in the use of power. She knew how to wear the crown, how to use it, and, in this hour of national peril, how to arouse her people in its defense. "The nation was united in the face of Spanish preparations," Churchill wrote. "While the Armada was still off England Queen Elizabeth reviewed the army at Tilbury and addressed them in these stirring words:

"Let tyrants fear. I have always so behaved myself that, under God, I have placed my chiefest strength and safeguard in the loyal hearts and goodwill of my subjects; and

therefore I am come amongst you, as you see, resolved, in the midst and heat of the battle, to live or die amongst you, to lay down for my God, and for my kingdom, and for my people, my honour and my blood, even in the dust. I know I have the body of a weak and feeble woman, but I have the heart and stomach of a king, and of a king of England too, and think foul scorn that Parma or Spain or any prince of Europe should dare to invade the borders of my realm; to which, rather than any dishonour shall grow by me, I myself will take up arms, I myself will be your general, judge and rewarder of every one of your virtues in the field."[149]

The first appeaser Hitler had laid eyes on had been Halifax, when the noble lord had visited the Berghof nearly two years earlier and had mistaken the master of the Reich for a servant. The Führer, skilled at taking a man's measure, told his guest that all SS men were shown the film *Lives of a Bengal Lancer* because it depicted "a handful of Englishmen holding a continent in thrall." It was then that he had recommended that Gandhi be shot. Halifax's lack of enthusiasm, Hitler told his interpreter, triggered his first suspicion that the heirs to the British Empire were weak and irresolute. In mid-August, with the crisis over Poland growing, he had decided to probe. To Karl Burckhardt of the League of Nations he expressed "great sympathy" for Halifax: "I thought he was a man who saw things on a big scale and desired a peaceful solution. I hope one day to see him again." Burckhardt sent London an account of these remarks and Halifax began "considering" sending a member of His Majesty's Government to talk to the Führer. Another Munich seemed to be shaping up.[150]

On August 27 the P.M. met with Birger Dahlerus, a Swedish businessman and friend of Göring who served as an unofficial go-between that week. Dahlerus, who had arrived in London from Berlin that afternoon, told Chamberlain, Wilson, Halifax, and Cadogan that Danzig and the corridor were indeed Hitler's targets. To Dahlerus, Halifax emphasized the necessity of "direct discussions" between the Germans and the Poles. Now that HMG "knew" that Danzig was the Nazi objective, England could force Beck to yield it. This should be construed, the foreign secretary told Dahlerus, not as England's final position, "but rather to prepare the way for the main communication" — to establish, in short, a procedure for meeting further Nazi demands. In Berlin the Swede saw Göring that evening, but not the Führer: "Hitler too tired," he wired the Foreign Office. Halifax said he understood; the Führer had many burdens. In the morning — it was now Monday, August 28 — Dahlerus was granted an audience in the chancellery. To Halifax he quoted the chancellor: "Great Britain must persuade Poland to negotiate with Germany." It was "most important," Hitler said, that "Sir N. Henderson" bring him a statement affirming that England had undertaken to so persuade the Poles. The desirability of this was underscored after a cabinet meeting that afternoon, when the foreign secretary received a telegram from Sir George Ogilvie Forbes, counsellor in Britain's Berlin embassy. Ogilvie Forbes quoted Dahlerus as saying: "Herr Hitler suspects that the Poles will try to avoid negotiations. Reply should therefore contain a clear statement to the effect that the Poles have been strongly advised *immediately to establish contact* with Germany and negotiate." Halifax now took a step without precedent. He wired Kennard in Warsaw: "His Majesty's Government earnestly hope that . . . Polish Government . . . is ready *to enter at once into direct discussion* with Germany. Please endeavour to see M. Beck at once and telephone reply." Thus, without consulting or even informing the cabinet, Halifax turned a Nazi demand into British foreign policy, thereby weakening Britain's sole ally in the east. If the Wehrmacht crushed Poland, Hitler could turn and hurl the full fury of his might against France, Britain's only ally in the west. Should France be overwhelmed, England would stand alone, facing the first European power in a century to threaten the very existence of Britain by vaulting the Channel.[151]

At Chartwell Churchill was writing Bill Deakin: "I have tried to fit these Galleys together. The present arrangement is quite impossible. I send you my own copies, where the Galleys are arranged more or less in chronological order. I see no use mixing up sections about Pitt and George III with separate studies of the American colonies." The Canadian section was "more or less complete"; so was the one on India. All that would be gathered together under the heading "The First British Empire," to be followed by a chapter called either "The Great Pitt" or "The Seven Years' War," describing "the position of the First British Empire as it stands at the Peace of Paris 1763." The next would be "The Quarrels of the English Speaking Peoples," covering "the reign of George III." George III is not remembered as an admirable sovereign, and not only because of his madness; but his years on the throne were marked by stirring events and the deeds of great men, among them the greatest military hero in the history of England. Winston had told his tale, and it lay in the galleys he was correcting before their dispatch to Deakin.[152]

By the autumn of 1805 Napoleon had massed his invasion barges at Boulogne. The Royal Navy's blockade of the Continent, built around nearly forty ships of the line, had frustrated French plans to cross the Channel in force, but now, Churchill wrote, "Napoleon . . . believed that the British fleets were dispersed and that the moment had come for invasion."

The decisive battle took place in the waters off Cape Trafalgar, Spain. Nelson was outnumbered and outgunned. At daybreak on October 21 he saw, "from the quarterdeck of the Victory, *the battle line of the enemy" — an advance squadron of twelve Spanish ships and twenty-one French ships of the line under Villeneuve. He signaled his captains to form for the attack in two columns. Then:*

Nelson went down to his cabin to compose a prayer. "May the Great God whom I worship grant to my country and for the benefit of Europe a great and glorious Victory. . . . For myself, I commit my life to Him who made me, and may His blessing light upon my endeavours for serving my country faithfully."

The fleets were drawing nearer and nearer. Another signal was run up upon the Victory, *"England expects every man will do his duty. . . ."*

A deathly silence fell upon the fleet as the ships drew nearer. Each captain marked down his adversary, and within a few minutes the two English columns thundered into action. . . . The Victory *smashed through between Villeneuve's flagships, the* Bucentaure, *and the* Redoutable. *The three ships remained locked together, raking each other with broadsides. Nelson was pacing as if on parade on his quarterdeck when at 1:15 p.m. he was shot from the mast-head of the* Redoutable *in the shoulder. His backbone was broken, and he was carried below amid the thunder of the* Victory*'s guns. . . . In the log of the* Victory *occurs this passage, "Partial firing continued until 4.30, when a victory having been reported to the Right Hon. Lord Viscount Nelson, K.B. and Commander-in-Chief, he then died of his wound."*[153]

Chamberlain and Henderson were to die of cancer, Chamberlain in the autumn of 1940, Henderson two years later. Halifax spent the war years as Britain's ambassador in Washington, was created an earl in 1944, and died, aged seventy-eight, on December 23, 1959, thus surviving for over fourteen years the 357,116 Britons killed during the war.

The pressure on Warsaw worked. Two hours after receiving Halifax's wire, Kennard replied to the FO: "Poland is ready to enter at once into direct discussions with Germany." His instincts had told him that negotiations with the Nazis could lead only to disaster, but disaster lay at the end of every turning. Now, at last, HMG could give Hitler the reply he wanted, and that evening Ambassador Henderson met with Hitler to deliver the British note. Poland had given assurances that she was ready to "enter into discussions." The next step should now be to initiate negotiations between Germany and Poland. Instead of responding directly to the suggestion of negotiations, Hitler extended the limits of absurdity by asking whether Britain "would be willing to accept an alliance with Germany." An abler diplomat would have realized that Hitler was muddying the waters and raising a question of future policy while they were in the midst of a crisis requiring immediate solution. Beyond that was the fact, noted by Vansittart, that "an alliance means a military alliance if it means anything. And against whom should we be allying ourselves with such a gang as the present regime in Germany? The merest suggestion of it would ruin us in the United States." It would also have destroyed British credibility in countries to whom England was committed: France, Poland, Rumania, Turkey, and Greece. But Henderson's answer to the Führer, as he reported it to the FO, was that "speaking personally I did not exclude such a possibility."[154]

For an ambassador to express an opinion on such an issue was inexcusable. The FO sharply told Henderson that he had gone too far and turned the offer down. Incredibly, Henderson failed to tell the Führer that Britain had rejected his proposal. During their talk Hitler had spoken of "annihilating Poland," which ought to have alerted anyone, much less a diplomat, to the momentous fact that he would not be satisfied with Danzig. Yet Halifax ordered the reference deleted from the account of Henderson's meeting that was sent to Warsaw.[155]

Hitler wanted this problem, which he had created, to be resolved by bloodshed, but the Poles must be made to appear culpable. Receiving Henderson on Tuesday, the twenty-ninth, the Führer dispensed with the tact, civility, and outward show of mutual respect required in discourse between civilized nations. Instead, he demanded the appearance in Berlin of a Polish negotiator "with full powers" the following day.[156]

Even Henderson was astonished. He blurted out that this was *"ein Diktat."* Hitler and Ribbentrop, he later reported to Halifax, "strenuously and heatedly" denied it. The British ambassador left the chancellery "depressed by my own inadequacy" and "filled with the gloomiest foreboding." Danzig, he told Whitehall, "must revert to Germany."[157]

Halifax's response was a procedural suggestion. He, too, saw the Führer's demands as an ultimatum and suggested that instead they be called "proposals," offered as "a basis for discussion." Hitler agreed to this meaningless rephrasing, but it would still be necessary, he insisted, for a Pole qualified to speak for his government to appear in Berlin immediately. This was a problem. The Poles, under pressure and against their better judgment, had agreed to discussions with the Reich, but they balked at the Nazi demand that they send a negotiator, armed with full powers, on the next plane to Berlin. For them to do otherwise would have been madness; Hitler had yet to set forth formal proposals. Until he had, and until Warsaw had studied them, talks between the two sovereign powers would be meaningless — unless, of course, the Poles capitulated, which, they suspected, was what the Führer wanted.[158]

That the Poles continued to assert their rights was considered by Britain's ambassador to the Reich a sign of exaggerated "prestige" and *"amour propre."* Henderson advised Robert Coulondre, his French counterpart, "strongly to recommend" to Paris that France advise the Polish government "to propose the immediate visit of M. Beck as constituting in my opinion the sole chance now of preventing war." He "implored" the Polish ambassador in Berlin, Lipski, to ask the immediate dispatch of a negotiator from Warsaw, as commanded by the Führer and chancellor of the Greater German Reich.[159]

The pressure on the Polish government was becoming massive. At noon Wednesday Henderson, in one of his unauthorized trespasses into areas where he did not belong, approached the papal nuncio in Berlin and suggested that the pope put forward some "definite impartial solution," such as a neutral frontier patrolled by Catholic priests. The papal nuncio replied that he thought laymen would be more suitable. Unknown to either Henderson or the nuncio, the pope, after talking to Mussolini, was already in touch with Warsaw. He believed, he told the Poles, that prospects of peace would improve if they surrendered Danzig. Then, he reasoned, Hitler would be willing to negotiate over the corridor and minority problems. The pontiff thought this suggestion should receive the "most careful consideration of the Poles."[160]

Polish obstinacy, Chamberlain concluded, was the greatest obstacle to peace. Ambassador Joseph Kennedy wired the State Department: "Frankly he is more worried about getting the Poles to be reasonable than the Germans." At the cabinet meeting that Wednesday morning, only Hore-Belisha opposed pressing Beck to dispatch a negotiator to Germany. He thought it "important," he said, "to make it clear that we are not going to yield on this point," and he opposed any negotiations, anywhere, while the Führer was threatening Warsaw and massing his troops in Poland's borders. The cabinet agreed that Hitler's ultimatum was "wholly unreasonable." But the "really important thing," Halifax told them, was the German agreement to negotiate. The Polish government should "be prepared to do so without delay."[161]

Forcing the weak to submit is clearly easier than confronting the strong, particularly if you have persuaded yourself that the weak deserve what is coming to them. At Berchtesgaden, Godesberg, and Munich, Chamberlain had discovered flaws in the Czechs which had previously escaped his attention. So it was now with the Poles. Henderson worried that the Poles might provoke the Führer's wrath and "force" the Nazis to move against Poland. Actually, all the provocation had been on the other side, though the Nazis had gone to great lengths to make it appear otherwise. On Hitler's orders the

Sicherheitsdienst, the SS security service, had dressed a dozen German prisoners in Polish uniforms. Identical uniforms were to be worn by SS men who would "lead" them in a simulated attack on a German radio station near the Polish border, holding it long enough for a Nazi fluent in Polish to announce Poland's invasion of the Reich. The criminals — whose code name was *Konserven* (Canned Goods) — would be given lethal injections by an SS doctor and then shot; their bloody bodies would be shown to the foreign press as evidence of Polish aggression.[162]

To the appeasers, efforts to avoid war were, ipso facto, virtuous, and they assumed that all sensible men would agree. But in Berlin making war was a virtue, and those who shrank from it were base. The Men of Munich never grasped this, and Henderson was staggered when the Nazis, whom he had regarded as his friends and future allies, decided that the time had come to humiliate him. On the evening of Wednesday, August 30, a German courier summoned Henderson to the Foreign Ministry. He expected the best. The Führer's diplomats were assumed to have drawn up proposals for a solution, and these, he hoped, would be the subject of their discussions.

There were no discussions. It was after midnight when Ribbentrop ordered him into his office. "From the outset," Henderson wrote in his memoirs, "his manner was one of intense hostility, which increased in violence. . . . He kept jumping up to his feet in a state of great excitement, folding his arms across his chest, and asking if I had anything more to say." He then interrupted each attempt to reply — though Henderson was trying to tell him that HMG had "consistently warned" the Poles against "all provocative action." The bewildered ambassador did manage to say that if the Reich's proposals were ready, HMG "could be counted upon to do their best in Warsaw to temporise negotiations." At this, the Nazi minister produced a long document and read it aloud "as fast as he could," Henderson wrote, "in a tone of utmost scorn and annoyance." There were sixteen points — the return of Danzig, a plebiscite in the corridor, sovereignty over Gdynia, a redrawing of boundaries, and on and on — but Henderson, as he wrote afterward, "did not attempt to follow too closely," assuming the paper would be handed to him at the end.[163]

It wasn't. Ribbentrop pocketed it, saying that since no Polish negotiator had come to Berlin, the proposals were "now too late." It was now the last day of August, the last day of peace. Henderson spent it frantically trying to get Beck, Lipski, or some senior Polish official to call on Ribbentrop. It is unlikely that any of them would have been received. Hitler admitted to Schmidt, his interpreter, that his offer to negotiate was a pretext. "I needed an alibi," he said, "especially with the German people, to show them that I had done everything to maintain peace." That, he said, explained his "generous offer" to settle *"die Danziger und Korridor-Frage."* In any event, the Poles, proud and defiant, were not much interested in the advice of Henderson or any well-meaning go-between. Dahlerus told Horace Wilson that it had become "obvious to us" that the Poles were "obstructing" possible negotiations.[164]

Indeed they were. They didn't trust England anymore, though Wilson, Henderson, Halifax, and Chamberlain couldn't imagine why. Churchill could have told them, and later did. Ribbentrop's lies about Polish brutality had been believed; Beck's reports of Nazi atrocities rejected. Halifax and Chamberlain had confided in Dirksen, yet were evasive, not only with the Polish ambassador, Raczyński, but also with the French. They were violating, both in letter and spirit, solemn treaties they themselves had drafted and signed a few days earlier. The prospect of fighting was unthinkable to them, unimaginable and inconceivable, and it had unmanned them. In their desperate attempts to avoid it they had resorted to trickery and deception. And they were still in business. As Hoare had told the cabinet on Monday, should German troops invade Poland they could "always fulfil the letter of a declaration without going all out." In short, declare war but not wage it. The *dux bellorum* Arthur, Elizabeth I, Hawkins, Drake, and Nelson wouldn't have known what he was talking about, and Churchill would be slow to grasp it.[165]

As Henderson desperately tried to overcome what Chamberlain called "Polish stubbornness" and paced his embassy office struggling to remember the sixteen points the foreign minister had read to him at top speed, Churchill was at Chartwell dictating letters to Chamberlain, Kingsley Wood, his publisher, and G. M. Young ("It is a relief in times like these to escape into other centuries"). The note to Chamberlain urged him to take stern measures because there seemed to be no way "Hitler can escape from the pen in which he has put himself," but afterward Winston decided not to mail it. The caution was sound; the P.M. had become increasingly unresponsive to his suggestions, and if, as Churchill believed, his prospects of a cabinet seat were at last brightening, sending unsought advice to a suspicious prime minister was clearly impolitic.[166]

He could be frank with Secretary for Air Kingsley Wood, and he was. Flying home from Consuelo Balsan's château he had found that the buildings and concrete aprons at Croydon Airport had not been camouflaged, that airport authorities were "obstructing" the digging of trenches for pilots and crews during enemy air raids, and that construction of underground shelters was "proceeding far too slowly." Remarking upon these details was characteristic of him. So, at that time, was the lethargy of

Croydon authorities and construction workers. British newspapers had reported the Nazi-Soviet Pact, and the public had been alarmed by it. But the ominous diplomatic exchanges between governments, and the growing momentum of the rush toward war, were known to very few. Only Chamberlain, Horace Wilson, and Halifax were in possession of all the facts, and the complete story of Hitler's actions, including the murders of the Canned Goods, would not emerge until the postwar Nuremberg trials, where Ribbentrop was candid, obsequious, and hanged. Civilians in England had not even been told that their government was committed to the defense of Danzig, that Danzig was in grave peril, and that war was therefore imminent.[167]

Churchill was probably better informed than anyone outside the inner circle, but the windup of his book preempted his attention. While Ribbentrop was affronting Henderson and telling him it was "too late," Winston was reworking his manuscript and writing Sir Newman Flower at Cassells, thanking him "for procuring this extra time for the Preface to the Life of Sir Austen Chamberlain" and adding:

> I am, as you know, concentrating every moment of my spare life and strength upon completing our contract. These distractions are very very trying. However, 530,000 words [1,621 pages of manuscript] are now in print, and there is only cutting and proof reading, together with a few special points, now to be done.
>
> You will understand, more than anyone else, how difficult it is for me to spend a night upon another form of work. However, I still hope I may be able to serve you.[168]

At 8:30 Friday morning Churchill was awakened by a telephone call from Raczyński, who told him that at 4:00 A.M. fifty-six German divisions, nine of them panzers, had crossed the Polish frontier in darkness from Silesia, Cracow, and the Carpathian flank. After he had bathed and breakfasted Winston received another call from Raczyński. Two Luftwaffe air fleets — sixteen hundred aircraft — had begun bombing Polish cities; civilian casualties were heavy. It was ten o'clock, and it occurred to Winston that the War Office might have fresh details. The War Office didn't even know Poland had been invaded. As Ironside noted in his diary, he reached "the Horse Guards as 10 A.M. was striking and was immediately rung up by Winston from Westerham who said 'They've started. Warsaw and Kracow are being bombed now.' " Ironside phoned Lord Gort, chief of the Imperial General Staff, "who didn't believe it." Ironside urged him to tell Hore-Belisha; Gort called back to report that "Belisha was seen rushing off to Downing Street." Ironside "rang Winston and he said he had the news definitely from the

Polish Ambassador 1½ hours ago. . . . How could the War Office possibly be ignorant of this?"[169]

The answer was that Raczyński, a graduate of the London School of Economics and a twenty-year veteran of diplomacy, was familiar with the intricacies of English politics. He knew Winston could be trusted but was unsure of the others, and events swiftly confirmed him. Despite their treaty obligations, the unprovoked German invasion of Poland produced, not declarations of war by Britain and France, but an awful silence. On Hore-Belisha's return from No. 10 the War Office dispatched telegrams ordering full mobilization at 2:00 P.M., and France followed suit. But instead of planning to break through the Siegfried Line — a golden opportunity, for Hitler, confident that the democracies' fear would restrain them, had left only ten divisions to defend it — both Paris and London expressed their readiness to negotiate if the Führer's troops withdrew from Poland. For Berlin, this Allied betrayal of the Poles more than compensated for Mussolini's declaration of Italian neutrality less than an hour later.[170]

Churchill, outraged, was writing a blistering attack on the Chamberlain government. His voice counted now. Herbert Morrison, the leading Labourite, had once called him "a fire-eater and a militarist." But after Prague, Morrison saw him as England's last hope. The *Daily Telegraph*, *Manchester Guardian*, and *Daily Mirror* had become the most vehement forums demanding Winston's recall to the government. As long as the struggle between Churchill and his critics had remained confined to the House of Commons he was hopelessly outnumbered, but Fleet Street had laid his case before the people of England, who now saw him as their champion. That may have explained, at least in part, Chamberlain's call to Chartwell that noon. Parliament had been summoned for 6:00 P.M. Churchill would be driving up to London, and the prime minister said he would be grateful if, before entering the House of Commons, Winston would stop at No. 10 for a few minutes.

In the Cabinet Room, Chamberlain told Churchill that he saw "no hope of averting war." He proposed to form "a small War Cabinet of Ministers without departments" to conduct it. This would exclude the war, Admiralty and RAF ministers, which he thought wise. He had hoped to form a national coalition, but Labour had declined to join it. Churchill later recalled that the prime minister "invited me to become a member of the War Cabinet. I agreed to his proposal without comment, and on this basis we had a long talk on men and measures." The P.M. repeated that he had abandoned his long quest for peace. "The die," he said, "is cast." The Foreign Office had informed Berlin that unless the Germans suspended "all aggressive action against Poland" and were prepared "to withdraw their forces" already there, His Majesty's Government would fulfill its obligations to the Poles "without hesitation."[171]

This was considerably less than candid. Chamberlain had not abandoned hope of preserving the peace, did not believe the die was cast, and was prepared to hesitate indefinitely before fulfilling HMG's obligations to the Poles. To Parliament early that evening the prime minister announced that the government was preparing a White Paper which would "make it perfectly clear that our object has been to bring about discussions about the Polish-German dispute between the two countries themselves on terms of equality, the settlement to be one which safeguarded the independence of Poland," an agreement buttressed "by international guarantees." The P.M. had his eye on history now; he was trying to launder it. His attempt was doomed. By drafting an apologia instead of fighting, he himself was flouting such guarantees. British and German foreign policy documents would provide a day-by-day account of his stewardship, and Churchill, not Chamberlain, was to be the first writer of that history. Furthermore, the last thing the Poles needed in this hour of desperation was a White Paper exonerating the Chamberlain government. Lacking tanks and divisions which could be moved on trucks, very short of antiaircraft and antitank guns, they had rashly decided to make their stand on Poland's frontiers, meeting the enemy columns with massed cavalry charges. The strongest enemy force, the army group under Field Marshal Gerd von Rundstedt, attacking from Moravia and Slovakia as well as Silesia, had overwhelmed the gallant but ill-starred defenders and was now roving through open country. Defiant but tragic Poles were being mashed beneath panzer treads of Generals Heinz Guderian and Paul von Kleist as the Wehrmacht drove across the corridor. The Poles' Field Marshal Edward Rydz-Smigly had no reserves because the corridor forced him to fight a two-front war, sending the reserves to check another German army group striking southward from East Prussia.[172]

At 10:00 A.M., as Churchill had been breaking the news to an incredulous Ironside, Raczyński had met his official obligation by calling on Halifax and delivering a formal notice of the Nazi invasion. It was, he said, "a plain case as provided for by the treaty." The foreign secretary replied that he had no doubt of the facts — he was reluctant to discuss the treaty — and at 10:50, after Raczyński had departed, Halifax summoned the German chargé d'affaires, Theodor Kordt, and asked if he had any news which might interest HMG. Kordt replied that he knew nothing of a German attack and had received no instructions from the Wilhelmstrasse. The foreign secretary murmured that reports reaching his desk "create a very serious situation." He said no more. Kordt reported their brief meeting to Berlin by phone at 11:45 A.M.[173]

In this new situation, one of the few civilians who seemed to be himself — if indeed he was a civilian — was Adolf Hitler. After describing the bogus Polish attack on the German radio station to the Reichstag, he received Göring, accompanied by the ubiquitous Dahlerus. The Führer had been at ease with the Reichstag, but now, Dahlerus thought, his manner was "exceedingly nervous and very agitated." He had always suspected that England wanted war, he said — believing his own lies — and now he knew it. He would crush Poland; he would crush England; he would destroy anyone who tried to stop him. The Führer "grew more and more excited and began to wave his arms," Dahlerus noted; he shouted, and the shout rose to a scream; the "movements of his body began to follow those of his arms," and "he brandished his fist and bent down so that it nearly touched the floor as he shrieked: '*Und wenn es erforderlich ist, will ich zehn Jahre kämpfen!*' ['And if necessary I will fight for ten years!']."[174]

Henderson was another exception to the rule. Everyone else in his embassy was anxious, but he followed the course that had contributed so much in leading Europe to the cataclysm now upon them. At 10:45 A.M., while the War Office in London was sending mobilization telegrams and Kordt was on his way to the FO, His Majesty's envoy in Berlin had phoned Halifax: "I understand that the Poles blew up the Dirschau bridge during the night." It was their bridge; they had the right to blow it, and, with German troops in their coal-scuttle steel helmets swarming on the far bank, would have been fools not to, but Henderson appears to have thought it aggressive. "On receipt of this news," he said, "Hitler gave orders for the Poles to be driven back from the border line and to Göring for destruction of the Polish Air Force along the frontier."[175]

The ambassador ended his report: "Hitler may ask to see me . . . as a last effort to save the peace." The fact that peace could no longer be salvaged — that World War II had begun, that borders guaranteed by his own government had been violated on a clumsy, vaudevillian excuse, that Poles of both sexes and all ages had been dying for nearly seven hours — was ignored. Josiah Wedgwood, an MP who despised appeasement and had visited Germany, recalled now in bitter contempt how Henderson had "smiled [and] fraternized with evil." Like Chamberlain, Halifax, and Horace Wilson, Henderson was among that group of Englishmen who had, in Wedgwood's words, mistaken Hitler "for a new crowned head at whose fancy cruelties they might giggle and from whom they might not differ with propriety."[176]

Hitler did not ask to see the British ambassador. After Britain's declaration of war Henderson would return to London and volunteer to serve His Majesty in another diplomatic post for which his experience made him suitable. The Foreign Office would reply that there was none.

In London parents of small children were studying a notice from the town clerk of Westminster instructing them to bring "infants up to two years of age" to designated centers "between the hours of 10.p [*sic*] and 6.0 p.m., to be fitted with helmets for protection against . . . gas." This time the gas threat was real. John Gunther, until recently the London correspondent of the *Chicago Daily News*, told Americans in an NBC broadcast that Friday evening, September 1: "It's a strange face that London wears tonight. It's a dark face. We're having a blackout here. The streets are black, the houses are black." In the entire length of Piccadilly he had seen fewer than a half-dozen cars; the only Londoners in sight were workmen carrying sandbags into position; indeed, already "the whole town looks sandbagged." Although "what may be the second world war began today," London was "quiet and confident. The British take even such a supreme moment of crisis as tonight with good humor, quietly. A few moments ago I saw something highly typical on the news ticker: 'The Football Association announces that a message received stated that the situation at present does not warrant the cancellation of tomorrow's matches.'."[177]

That sort of thing was taken as an illustration of British phlegm, and therefore encouraging. In fact, it was a sign that in their hearts and minds Britons were still at peace and expected to remain so. They were following their prime minister, matching their government's mood. Under the agreement Poland and Britain had signed the previous Friday, England was pledged to act "at once" with "all the support and assistance in its power," to make war on Germany. The status of Danzig alone was no longer an issue. Polish sovereignty had been violated. Without either an ultimatum or a declaration of war — shocking in those days — the Wehrmacht had invaded Poland on all fronts, and the Luftwaffe was bombing every Polish city, including Warsaw. No one could doubt now that the Führer's objective was the military conquest of the entire country. Legally, under her covenant, Great Britain had no choice; she was bound to declare war on Germany immediately. But she hadn't; the bold note to Berlin which Chamberlain had quoted to Churchill, and then in the House of Commons, was inadequate.[178]

Even so, there was less there than met the eye. Halifax sent Henderson, who would deliver the Foreign Office's message to Ribbentrop, a note explaining that it was "in the nature of a warning and is not to be considered as an ultimatum." At the same time, the Foreign Office asked Dahlerus: "Could you limit the hostilities until you had been to London?" Obviously, the invasion of Poland was not considered casus belli. Assured of some "limit," His Majesty's Government stood ready to negotiate. But any negotiations now would be cramped; the only alternative to declaring war was to insist that the Wehrmacht withdraw from Poland. Roger Cambon, of the French embassy, told Halifax that such a demand for a withdrawal "ought to be accompanied by a time limit." Halifax replied that it was an interesting question, but at this point the matter was "moot." How it could be moot confounded Cambon, but his position was weak. He couldn't be sure his own government would back him. France's response to the invasion of her ally had been waffly; the Quai d'Orsay had expressed its "willingness to negotiate" if the Wehrmacht pulled back but, like Whitehall, had specified no time limit.[179]

Churchill's situation was now uncomfortable. He had accepted a position in a War Cabinet, and this shackled him from public criticism of HMG's foreign policy. Shortly after midnight, in the early hours of Saturday, September 2, he wrote the prime minister from his Morpeth Mansions flat. It was a careful, crafted letter, opening with a minor issue and building toward his chief point. "Aren't we a very old team?" he asked at the outset. "I make out that the six you mentioned to me yesterday aggregate 386 years or an average of over 64!" Labour's refusal to join a coalition — which, though he did not mention it, was understandable; Chamberlain had not offered them a single cabinet post — meant "we shall certainly have to face a constant stream of criticism, as well as the many disappointments and surprises of which war largely consists." It was, therefore, "all the more important to have the Liberal Opposition firmly incorporated in our ranks," and because of Eden's popularity there, he suggested that a place on the front bench be found for him. Then Winston rolled up his heavy guns. "The Poles," he reminded the prime minister, "have now been under heavy attack for thirty hours, and I am much concerned to hear that there is talk in Paris of a further note. I trust you will be able to announce our Joint Declaration of War at *latest* when Parliament meets this afternoon." He closed: "I remain at your disposal."[180]

All day Saturday he awaited a summons from No. 10. Mrs. Hill recalls him "pacing up and down like a lion in a cage. He was expecting a call, but the call never came." At a suggestion from No. 10 Lord Hankey, who would also be included in the new cabinet, called at Morpeth Mansions for a visit. Hankey wrote his wife the following day: "As far as I can make out, my main job is to keep an eye on Winston! . . . He was brimful of ideas, some good, others not so good, but rather heartening and big. I only wish he didn't give one the impression that he does himself too well!"[181]

It was a time when men in public life — and their wives — kept diaries, wrote letters, and filed memoranda to themselves against the day they wrote their memoirs. Because of this, we know far more about their observations and opinions than future writers will know of ours. But it is important to remember that Churchill's popularity in the country was never matched in Parliament. In justifying him, events had discredited most of his colleagues. Being decent men, they tried to suppress their resentment. But they were not always successful. Hankey had been an appeaser. When Winston was down he had said hard things about him. Now Winston was up, and when Hankey told his wife about encountering him later that same day, his letter bore a faint taint of malice. In the House of Commons smoking room, Hankey wrote, "the amount of alcohol being consumed was incredible! Winston too was in a corner holding forth to a ring of admiring satellite MPs! He has let it get into the Press that he will be in the War Cabinet — to the great annoyance of many."

Certainly, Churchill had not kept the news of his impending appointment to himself. Lord Camrose's diary entry for that day opens, "Winston called me up at 11.30 and told me he had accepted a place in the Cabinet and was to be a Minister without portfolio." Telling a press lord was like making an announcement over the BBC. But to keep mum would have been wholly out of character for Churchill. Thirty years earlier, when he proposed to Clementine, he had promised to keep her acceptance secret until she could tell her mother; ten minutes later he had shouted it out to everyone within earshot. After ten years in the wilderness, he could hardly be expected to keep his new appointment to himself. The indiscretion, if any, was slight. It seems fairer to infer that the motives of those who were "greatly annoyed" are suspect.[182]

The real indiscretion that evening was historic, and it was committed by Neville Chamberlain. When the cabinet met at 4:30 P.M., the Poles' situation was desperate. The superior training, equipment, and strategy of the Germans had already brought Rydz-Smigly's troops to the brink of collapse. They had lost all the frontier battles. The Luftwaffe's Stuka dive-bombers were spreading chaos in the Polish rear, destroying communications and preventing the movement of replacements. German troops were already over the River Warta and approaching Cracow. In the north the Fourth Army, driving eastward, had linked up with another force, striking southward from East Prussia. If ever an embattled nation needed allies, it was Poland, and now. The French, fully mobilized, could have lunged into the Ruhr and the Saar upon the issuance of a single command. Hitler had rejected Anglo-French notes urging him to abort his attack; he blamed the British for encouraging the Poles in a policy of "persecution and provocation." Some French leaders, ever distrustful of perfidious Albion, believed him. Others, grasping at straws, found merit in Mussolini's proposal, earlier in the day, for a five-power conference. The French government, appalled at the prospect of facing the Wehrmacht alone, awaited a British initiative.

It was well that the MPs in the smoking room were fortifying themselves with drink. The session that lay ahead of them was going to be grim. In his note to Berlin, Halifax had been unwilling to set a time limit; now, in the Cabinet Room, he claimed this was the *French* position, though he supported it. The Germans, he thought, ought to be given till Sunday noon to accept or reject a conference with France and Britain. Raczyński, who had been waiting in an anteroom, was invited to address the ministers. The Polish ambassador told them that the Nazi offensives, slashing deep into his country from all sides, had been "violently resumed" at dawn, and since noon all large Polish cities had been subjected to "heavy bombing from the air."[183]

Hore-Belisha, deeply moved, spoke immediately after Raczyński's departure. As he recorded in his diary, he told his colleagues that "I was strongly opposed to further delay, which I thought might result in breaking the unity of the country. Public opinion was against yielding an inch." He proposed that His Majesty's Government immediately send Hitler an ultimatum which would expire at midnight. The discussion was lively, with several vehement conversations going on at once, but in the end all were won over, and Hore-Belisha recorded the final decision, binding on all ministers, including the prime minister: "*Unanimous decision was taken that ultimatum should end at midnight.*" Halifax agreed to tell the Germans that what had been a warning was now in fact an ultimatum, and that it would end at the stroke of twelve. They rose. Parliament awaited them. The prime minister would make the announcement in the House. When the clock struck, Great Britain and Germany would be at war.[184]

The sequel to this meeting is baffling, even incomprehensible. With the exception of one telephone call, *no one outside the Cabinet Room was ever told of the decision*. Halifax, his faith in negotiations undiminished, broke his word to his colleagues and did nothing — did, in one instance, worse than nothing: he told Ciano that Britain saw her role as that of a "mediator" and, flatly contradicting the cabinet, repeated the line that HMG's warning "was *not* an ultimatum." The phone call was made by Cadogan. After the cabinet had adjourned he spoke to Bonnet in Paris and informed him of its resolution. Why he bypassed Ambassador Phipps is inexplicable. So is his choice of Bonnet, the arch appeaser ("*Votre Chamberlain, il est faible* [weak]," Georges Mandel told Duncan Sandys. "*Mais notre Bonnet, il est lâche* [a coward].") Bonnet did not repeat the conversation. He himself had not decided whether a conference of the great powers should be made conditional on the withdrawal of Nazi troops from Poland. The French cabinet, he had told Cadogan, was "going to deliberate" that point, but in any event they were "firmly decided" that any ultimatum "must be of forty-eight hours."[185]

At 7:30 P.M. a crowded House awaited the prime minister's announcement. Parliament, like the British press and public, was ready for war. The secret conduct of foreign policy was past. The country knew of HMG's commitment to Poland, knew how deeply the German army had penetrated the Polish defenses, knew England's delay in declaring war was responsible for Luftwaffe supremacy in the skies over Poland, and was ready to come to her aid. Spears had never seen Parliament "so stirred, so profoundly moved. . . . The benches were packed. The unbearable suspense was about to be relieved. One and all were keyed up for the announcement that war had been declared."[186]

To Churchill there was "no doubt that the temper of the House was for war. I even deemed it more resolute and united than in the similar scene on August 2, 1914, in which I had also taken part." As the prime minister rose another MP felt that "most [members of the House] were ready to show their intense relief that suspense was ended by cheering wildly."[187]

"But as we listened," Spears wrote, "amazement turned to stupefaction, and stupefaction into exasperation." Chamberlain was speaking, not of Nazi crimes, nor of suffering Poland, nor Britain's honor, but of "further negotiations," or rather of their possibility, since the German government had rejected HMG's last such proposal. But, the prime minister said to the staring, straining, immobile House, that was not necessarily a reason for discouragement. The Führer of the Reich was a very busy man. It was not impossible that he was pondering the Italian government's suggestion for a conference. Chamberlain affirmed HMG's demand that German troops leave Poland but — despite the unanimous vote of his own cabinet, and his pledge to report it here — he mentioned no deadline for their departure. "If the German Government should agree to withdraw their forces, then His Majesty's Government would be willing to regard the position as being the same as it was before the German forces crossed the Polish frontier." Then, he said triumphantly, "the way would be open to discussion" between Poland and the Reich, in which case Britain would be willing "to be associated with such talks."[188]

He sat down. No one cheered. Instead, Hugh Dalton heard what he called "a terrific buzz." Margesson signaled his whips to brace themselves for physical violence, and with reason. Duff Cooper and Amery, Dalton saw, were "red-faced and almost speechless with fury." Cooper himself had "never felt so moved." Spears saw the House "oozing hostility." Two MPs actually vomited. Churchill, for once understating the hostility to Chamberlain merely noted that "the Prime Minister's temporising statement was ill-received by the House," but Amery wrote that Parliament "was aghast.

For two whole days the wretched Poles had been bombed and massacred," and here was the prime minister of Great Britain discussing how "Hitler should be invited to tell us whether he felt like relinquishing his prey! And then there were all these sheer irrelevancies about the terms of a hypothetical agreement between Germany and Poland." Amery wondered whether Chamberlain's "havering" was "the prelude to another Munich." On that occasion, Parliament had given the prime minister a standing ovation, but "this time any similar announcement would have been met by a universal howl of execration." When Arthur Greenwood rose to reply for the Opposition, Amery, fearing a "purely partisan speech" shouted, "Speak for England!" Greenwood, not known for his eloquence, stammered and said of Chamberlain, "I must put this point to him. Every minute's delay now means the loss of life, imperilling of our national interest —" He hesitated, and Boothby called: "Honour." Greenwood said: "Let me finish my sentence. I was about to say imperilling the very foundations of our national honour."[189]

Parliament adjourned, Amery wrote, in "confusion and dismay." In the prime minister's private room behind the Speaker's chair, Greenwood angrily told him that unless "the inevitable decision for war" had been announced before they gathered for tomorrow's session, "it will be impossible to hold the House." According to Ivone Kirkpatrick, Margesson, following on Greenwood's heels, confirmed him, "warning him," in the strongest possible language, that "unless we act tomorrow," Parliament would "revolt," and Spears wrote that Chamberlain could now entertain no doubts that "the House would accept no further procrastination." Chamberlain knew it. Back at No. 10 he phoned Halifax, who had been preoccupied with telegrams from his ambassadors. The prime minister said his statement "had gone very badly." Halifax hurried across the street and found him distraught. Later he wrote that he had "never known Chamberlain so disturbed." The P.M., insisting that he stay for dinner, said Parliament had been "infuriated"; if they were unable to "clear the position" by tomorrow, he doubted that his government would be able "to maintain itself."[190]

The foreign secretary was sympathetic. Yet even as Chamberlain recoiled from the House's hostility, Halifax had been pursuing the squalid policy which had led them to this dead end. Among the cables to reach his desk late that afternoon had been a report, from Ambassador Kennard in Warsaw, that Polish forces were severely handicapped by the Luftwaffe's mastery of the air. Beck had "very discreetly" suggested "some diversion as soon as possible in the west," hoping that the RAF would "draw off a considerable proportion of the German aircraft" at the eastern front. Kennard, endorsing this, thought that "every effort ought to be made to show activity on the western front." But there was no western front, and could be none until Britain and France, now neutral, became belligerents. The ambassador knew that. He ended: *"I trust I may be informed at the earliest possible moment of our declaration of war."*[191]

Halifax had ignored the telegram. Instead, he had instructed Henderson "immediately" to hand the text of the prime minister's statement in Parliament — the same statement which now threatened to split Chamberlain's government — "to certain quarters," among them Dahlerus and Göring. And now, despite the uproar in the House, and the abundant evidence to support the contrary position, Britain's foreign secretary returned to his office believing that the Nazi juggernaut could be halted and thrown into reverse gear by the prospect of conversations.

At ten o'clock that night he received the Polish ambassador, who told him that since noon the Luftwaffe had been bombing the center of Warsaw. "The position of Poland," Raczyński said, was "getting bad with the delay." What deadline, he asked, had Britain given the Germans? The noble lord replied that he was "not in a position" to divulge that information. The Pole was dumbfounded. If the Anglo-Polish alliance meant anything, the Poles were entitled to this vital information. He could not imagine why it was being withheld, never dreaming that a deadline could not be revealed because it did not exist. Yet Halifax knew the price of this last-ditch stand under the banner of appeasement, now stained with the blood of Austrians, Czechs, and Poles. To a fellow diplomat he acknowledged that "the moral effect of this delay on Poland [is] devastating."[192]

The Germans were fully aware of the situation — and of their thin line of field gray facing France. Saturday evening two of Dirksen's diplomats had approached Horace Wilson, asking what England's attitude would be if the Wehrmacht pulled back; specifically, whether Britain would approve of a German road across the Polish Corridor and the incorporation of Danzig into the Reich. Glossing over the situation in Poland, where, after forty-two hours of enemy assault, Polish casualties were approaching 100,000, Chamberlain's creature answered that once the Wehrmacht was back where it belonged, "the British Government would be prepared to let bygones be bygones." His visitors had told him that the question was not asked lightly. It was a formal "proposal" from the Wilhelmstrasse.[193]

It wasn't, nor could it have been; had Ribbentrop approved such a suggestion, and had Hitler heard of it, the Reich's ambassador to the Court of St. James would have been repudiated, recalled, and sent to a *Konzentrationslager*. Why did Wilson not only listen to such tripe, but pass it along to the Foreign Office with an endorsement from No. 10? There is only one possible answer. It was still HMG's policy to believe anything the Germans said and disregard reports critical of them. Göring denied that his Luftwaffe was bombing cities, thereby killing or maiming civilians. Kennard, His Majesty's envoy in Warsaw, said it was happening all over Poland; he could see it from his embassy window. Halifax was doubtful. He asked for fuller accounts, adding: "In the meantime it is accepted Germans are attacking only military objectives."[194]

Among the deeply troubled men in London that Saturday evening was Duff Cooper, formerly first lord of the Admiralty and now, by choice, a private member. After Parliament broke up, Cooper and his wife — the striking Lady Diana, a public figure in her own right and much admired by Churchill — had walked along the Embankment to the Savoy. Cooper had dined here with Churchill the previous evening, and he was still fuming over an ugly exchange with the Duke of Westminster after they had parted. For over thirty years Winston and Bendor had been friends; but Westminster's virulent anti-Semitism and his admiration for Hitler had ruptured their friendship. Cooper had encountered him while leaving the Savoy, and in his diary he recorded that the Duke began by "abusing the Jewish race" and "rejoicing that we were not yet at war," adding "Hitler knew after all that we were his best friends." Infuriated, Cooper had replied: "I hope that by tomorrow he will know we are his most implacable and ruthless enemies."[195]

But this was tomorrow, and Duff Cooper's hope had been dashed. He lacked appetite. As he stared morosely at his plate two junior members of the government, Harold Balfour, the under secretary for air, and Euan Wallace, the minister of transport, passed the table. Cooper asked Balfour whether he was still in office; the answer was a gesture "of shame and despair." Wallace said nothing — later he explained that he was afraid that Cooper would cut him if he spoke — but he sent him word, via a waiter. The prime minister's statement, he said, had taken "the whole Cabinet by surprise," and they were demanding another meeting before midnight. Cooper was startled. The *whole* cabinet? Surely Wallace was exaggerating. Of course, there must have been some dissenters on the front bench, but it hardly seemed possible that the King's first minister would abrogate a commitment to another nation in defiance of a unified cabinet. Duff Cooper, like Eden, knew the strength of Neville Chamberlain's will, but Chamberlain was no Hitler. Wallace's implication didn't seem possible, Cooper thought, deciding that it wasn't. Shortly after 10:00 P.M. a messenger brought him another note: Conservative MPs distressed by the afternoon's events were meeting in Winston Churchill's flat opposite Westminster Cathedral; Churchill would like him to join them. Asking Diana to excuse him, Duff Cooper hurried to the turnaround in front of the Savoy and hopped into a cab: "Number eleven Morpeth Mansions."[196]

Eden, Sandys, Bracken, and Boothby were already there. Duff Cooper joined them "in a state of bewildered rage." Churchill himself afterward wrote that "all expressed deep anxiety lest we should fail in our obligations to Poland," but his account omits a basic disagreement over the course they should follow. If Churchill turned against the prime minister, Chamberlain's government would fall, and that was what his guests wanted. Boothby, Duff Cooper recorded in his diary, thought the prime minister had "lost the Conservative Party forever"; it was, he said, "in Winston's power to go to the House of Commons tomorrow and break him and take his place." If Winston failed to act, that would save Chamberlain, which was unthinkable; Churchill would be given office, but at an exorbitant price: "In no circumstances now should Winston consent to serve under him."[197]

The difficulty was that he already had, or thought he had. It was a nice point. The prime minister had offered him a place and he had accepted it. However, the place was to be in a *War* Cabinet. If there was no war there would be no office for Winston to hold; therefore he could not be part of the government and need not muffle his thunder. But Churchill, always sensitive about honor, believed that he must keep his word, even when, as in this case, it seemed unreasonable. His position was unmitigated by the fact that since their talk Chamberlain's behavior had been anything but gentlemanly. Drawing Duff Cooper aside, he told him, according to Cooper's diary, that he "considered that he had been very ill-treated, as he had agreed the night before to join the War Cabinet but throughout the day he had not heard a word from the Prime Minister." He said he had "wished to speak" to the House that afternoon, but "feeling himself already almost a member of the Government had refrained from doing so." Churchill's grievance was real. Nevertheless, he refused to split the country. The public images of political leaders were often volatile. Chamberlain was down now, but until recently he had been a national hero. He represented peace, and it was hard to quarrel with that; if overthrown now he would be martyred, and a divided England would be no match for Hitler.[198]

Outside, an electrical storm was rising. Distant thunder became less distant; suddenly, the cars parked outside were wrapped in sheets of heavy rain, and a servant hurried around closing windows. To the others Churchill seemed "very undecided," and Duff Cooper wrote that he "said that he had no wish to be Prime Minister, doubted his fitness for the position." This has a hollow ring. Churchill had never doubted his aptitude for Parliament's highest office and had been longing for it since the first decade of the century. It is, of course, very common for men confronted by the imminence of great responsibility to cloak themselves in humility. Winston, however, was not such a man. Perhaps Duff Cooper misunderstood him. It doesn't fit. It is a riddle without solution, but then, it had been a day of riddles, the greatest being the prime minister's behavior in the Commons.[199]

The men in Morpeth Mansions had many contacts, and they took turns phoning them. All cabinet ministers appeared to be unavailable. Churchill phoned the French embassy and "was told," one of his guests wrote, "that all was well — that we should see the situation from quite a different angle tomorrow which sounded very ominous to us." Whom Churchill had spoken to was unknown, but his source proved unreliable; at that hour no Frenchman, in the embassy or in France, knew what would happen in the morning. Other calls were made to senior civil servants. These yielded little. Eden, perplexed and disappointed, learned that he was scheduled to be Dominions secretary and excluded from the War Cabinet. According to Duff Cooper, "We all argued that Winston should refuse to serve unless Anthony was included in the War Cabinet as otherwise he would be a minority of one. Brendan pressed that he should also insist on my inclusion." At length Churchill left them all and withdrew into another room. He told them he was going to write Chamberlain. Before sending the letter to No. 10, he would read it to them.[200]

The letter began with a subtle reproach: "I have not heard anything from you since our talks on Friday, when I understood that I was to serve as your colleague, and when you told me that this would be announced speedily." In offering him office, he recalled, Chamberlain had said that war was inevitable. The recollection puzzled him: "I really do not know what has happened during the course of this agitated day; though it seems to me that entirely different ideas have ruled from those which you expressed to me when you said 'the die was cast.' " He realized that "with this tremendous European situation changes in method may become necessary," but felt "entitled to ask you to let me know how we stand, both publicly and privately, before the debate opens at noon." This was neither an ultimatum nor even a warning, but the steel beneath the velvet was unmistakable, and so was the time limit. Chamberlain might give Hitler forever to respond; Churchill was giving Chamberlain till lunch. He went on to offer advice. With both Labour and the Liberals "estranged," forming an effective war government would be "difficult." The only solution, it seemed to Winston, was to reconcile the other two parties by offering to share power with them.[201]

That brought him to the uproar in Parliament. There was a "feeling . . . in the House," he wrote, "that injury had been done to the spirit of national unity by the apparent weakening of our resolve." Winston did not "underrate the difficulties you have with the French" — this was a shrewd guess — but England must reach her decision "independently, and thus give our French friends any lead that may be necessary." To do that "we shall need the strongest and most integral combination" possible. Then came the final thrust: "I therefore ask that there should be no announcement of the composition of the War Cabinet until we have had our talk." On Friday he had accepted Chamberlain's offer without comment, but only after the prime minister had told him that Britain was going to war. Now the situation had changed, and Churchill was commenting, making conditions. He would enter the cabinet only if assured — before the deadline — that Chamberlain's policy toward Nazi Germany was consistent with Churchillian principles. He added a final sentence: "As I wrote to you yesterday morning, I hold myself entirely at your disposal, with every desire to aid you in your task." Then he signed his name and rejoined his guests.[202]

Unknown and unsuspected by any of the men in Churchill's flat — including Duff Cooper, despite Wallace's hint at the Savoy — Chamberlain's cabinet was in a state of mutiny. To them his volte-face, coming only three hours after he had accepted their unanimous decision, was a gross betrayal. Everyone was in it, including Simon and Hoare. With the exception of Halifax, who had been absent during the afternoon meeting, they were the two most powerful men in the cabinet and the closest to the prime minister. As chancellor of the Exchequer, Simon, like Chamberlain, had a private room in Parliament. That was the mutineers' headquarters, and there they chose Simon as their leader. "The Cabinet," writes Robert Rhodes James, "was now in a state of acute tension." The prime minister's statement had left it, as one minister later recalled, "completely aghast." Hore-Belisha told them: "We are weakening on our undertaking to Poland and the French are ratting." The rebellious ministers intended to approach Chamberlain, but not to bargain with him; at No. 10 they had voted for an ultimatum to Germany, and they wanted it handed to Ribbentrop in Berlin *now*. Sir Reginald Dorman-Smith, minister of agriculture, later recalled that they voted to march on Downing Street and deliver "a plain *Diktat*."[203]

Simon was on the phone, trying to get through to No. 10. He couldn't manage it. The house had been inhabited by prime ministers for over two hundred years, but now, it seemed, no one was home. The chancellor's room was crowded; in Dorman-Smith's words, "we got scruffier and sweatier," but "my colleagues . . . had decided they would not leave that room until such time as war had been declared. As we sat there and waited by the phone and nothing happened, I felt like a disembodied spirit. It didn't seem real; we were 'on strike' — like those poor little miners down there, you know."

The dinner hour came and passed; there was no food, and the only water arrived in little cardboard cups borne by secretaries. At 9:00 P.M. Simon, Hore-Belisha, and two other ministers "sent PM a letter," as Hore-Belisha put it, "rehearsing our points." Eventually Simon was connected with Chamberlain, however, and they were all invited to No. 10. Outside it was raining, hard. Some had cars, some found cabs, some actually hitchhiked. "By now," Dorman-Smith remembered, "*all* of us [were] actually scruffy and smelly, and it rather shook us to find Halifax, who had been dining with the PM, and Cadogan in evening clothes."[204]

Chamberlain had not dressed for dinner. He had been too busy, and as he led his ministers into the Cabinet Room they began to understand, from exchanges between him, Halifax, and Cadogan, why he had failed to answer Simon's calls. As late as 9:30 P.M., shortly after he had received the cabinet ultimatum signed by four senior members of his government, he had been on the phone with Rome, trying to turn Mussolini's proposal for a five-power conference into a reality, with the understanding that the talks could not begin until the German troops now in Poland were back in Germany. Ciano's final message had torpedoed the prime minister's hope. The Italians, the Duce's son-in-law had told him, "do not feel it possible" to ask the Reich to join such a conference; the British insistence on a Wehrmacht withdrawal would merely arouse the Führer's celebrated wrath. If Hitler decided "on his own" to pull out the Wehrmacht, Ciano said, "well and good," but Mussolini did not "feel able to press him to do so."[205]

This was the final blow to appeasement. Chamberlain bleakly acknowledged that his long struggle to keep the peace had failed. Halifax was not so sure, but the responsibility was not his, and he had not been in the House of Commons that afternoon. The decision was Chamberlain's, and, having made it, his next step was to inform Paris and arrange for a joint declaration of war. Shortly before 10:00 P.M., while dissident conservatives were conferring at Morpeth Mansions, the prime minister phoned Daladier and told him that there had been "an angry scene in the House of Commons," adding that his "colleagues in the Cabinet are also disturbed." The premier replied that the French government had decided to present the Germans with a forty-eight-hour ultimatum which would begin at noon tomorrow, Sunday, September 3. Out of the question, said the prime minister; if he agreed "it would be impossible . . . to hold the situation here." He wanted an Anglo-French ultimatum which would be issued at 8:00 A.M. tomorrow and expire at midday. Daladier, distressed, replied that he would confer with his ministers and reply through the Quai d'Orsay.[206]

In the Cabinet Room, Cadogan was also talking to Paris, telling Bonnet that His Majesty's Government would, of course, prefer simultaneous declarations of war by the two democracies, but England could not wait until noon Tuesday. If the German offensive maintained its momentum, Poland's position would be hopeless by then. Bonnet replied that it was all very well for England to set a Sunday deadline; the British had evacuated London's children to the country, but "we cannot get our young people out of Paris" on such short notice. This issue was new. The French could have followed the British example. They had overlooked it, and now, in the last-minute rash of calls to No. 10 and the Foreign Office, it obsessed them. According to Dorman-Smith's recollection they were "convinced Paris would be bombed as soon as war was declared . . . horrified and terrified at our determination for an immediate ultimatum and saying: 'Are you going to have all our women and children killed?' " HMG was unmoved. The French were indignant and surprised, and they sulked through most of Sunday. Yet their able ambassador in London, Charles Corbin, had alerted them to the fact that if HMG did not deliver an ultimatum in Berlin before Parliament met, "They risk overthrow," and French politicians, with their history of tumbling cabinets, should have understood that.[207]

In the past Chamberlain had tried to accommodate the French whenever possible, and he had usually found it possible. The renitent cabinet — representing, in Gilbert and Gott's felicitous phrase, England's "revolt of conscience" — had stiffened the backbones of its leaders. The decisive conversation was between the two foreign ministers. Halifax had crossed the street to take the call in his own office, but the prime minister, with an aroused Hore-Belisha at his elbow, had given him precise instructions. Chamberlain had not yet decided how he would yield to the cabinet, but he wanted the French to know that the British were prepared to act independently of Paris. Thus Halifax informed Bonnet that the British government would send Berlin an ultimatum, with a deadline, before they went to bed. They had no choice, "owing to the difficult position which has arisen in the House of Commons." And hesitation by Chamberlain now would make it "very doubtful" he could "hold the position" of His Majesty's Government. If France wanted to delay its ultimatum later than 8:00 A.M. that was up to the French. Great Britain would already be at war.[208]

Returning to No. 10 with Ivone Kirkpatrick, Halifax encountered Hugh Dalton and greeted him almost as a colleague; though Dalton represented Labour in Parliament, he was also a graduate of Eton, King's College at Cambridge, and the London School of Economics, and under MacDonald he had served two years as parliamentary under secretary in the FO. Halifax told him that France was vacillating and asked whether he thought Labour would "favor our declaring war alone." Dalton said he couldn't speak for the party, and in fact it was unnecessary; Greenwood had already gone on record with the prime minister. Kirkpatrick said he could speak for himself and then did. Public opinion, he said, was "bewildered and disturbed. Unless we go to war we are sunk."[209]

After a long meeting with Margesson — who once more advised that he could not answer for the consequences should Parliament meet tomorrow without a declaration of war — Chamberlain finally joined his ministers in the Cabinet Room. It was 11:00 P.M. They were hungry and tired, but none had left, or forgotten why they had come, or the strategy adopted in Simon's office. To Dorman-Smith "the PM was calm, even icy-cold." He told them of the French pleas and said they had not left him unmoved; he was, in fact, "terribly worried that Paris might indeed be attacked from the air." No one commented. However, when he pointed out that should an ultimatum be sent, they must agree on its timing, they broke their vow of silence. Hore-Belisha thought Henderson should deliver it at 2:00 A.M., less than three hours from now, and that it should expire four hours later. "The less time involved, the better," he argued. Many heads nodded in agreement, and Halifax left the room to cable Henderson: "I may have to send you instructions tonight. . . . Please be ready to act." But Chamberlain's implicit acceptance of war had dulled the edge of the mutineers' resolve. They were vulnerable to manipulation. In the end they agreed on a 9:00 A.M. delivery and an 11:00 A.M. expiration. Thus, by failing to stand by Hore-Belisha, Britain gave the advancing Nazi troops another five hours, and in the new mobile warfare that counted heavily. When time ran out and this final deadline passed, the Germans would be on the Vistula.[210]

It was nearly midnight. Outside, the storm was mounting, the lightning bolts coming ever closer; there was scarcely any interval now between the flash and the thunder pealing across St. James's Park. Simon and Sir John Anderson of the Home Office were in a corner, conferring. Chamberlain *seemed* determined, but he had seemed no less in earnest only seven hours earlier, in this very room, when he had approved of the "immediate fulfilment of British obligations to Poland" and declared his agreement with those in favor of a midnight ultimatum. This time they wanted his sworn word; either he promised to respect the decision of the cabinet now reassembled or they would carry their fight to the people. They approached him and told him that. Chamberlain nodded and said quietly: "Right, gentlemen. This means war."[211]

He had scarcely said it, Dorman-Smith recalled, "when there was the most enormous clap of thunder and the whole Cabinet Room was lit up by a blinding flash of lightning. It was the most deafening thunder-clap I've ever heard in my life. It really shook the building."[212]

* * *

The same stunning thunderclap shook Churchill's flat, and there, too, the timing was dramatic. Winston had just finished reading his letter to the prime minister aloud. Dazzled by the lightning bolt, his friends took a sharp breath, agreed that his message was splendid — and began arguing loudly over what should be added and what stricken out. This was scarcely practical, since the letter, if it was to be effective, must be sent to No. 10 immediately. Winston let them fuss. He had no intention of altering a comma. And he was quite pleased by the lightning. Its timing could scarcely have been improved upon.

Actually he was entitled to another dramatic moment. At intervals, between writing paragraphs, he had been placing more phone calls, and now he reached one of the insurgent ministers at No. 10. He told his guests that someone — he mysteriously described him as "a friend" — would call back and tell him what had been decided. "Unfortunately," Duff Cooper noted with amusement, "his secretary gave the show away by coming in and saying, 'Mr. Hore-Belisha is on the telephone.' Churchill was much annoyed. He came back with the information that it had been decided 'to deliver the ultimatum next morning.' " This changed the situation. The quarreling ended; the men in Morpeth Mansions recovered their poise. After a moment of reflection he decided to send his letter to Chamberlain anyway. Then he rooted around, producing items he had had the foresight to order a year earlier, before the Munich crisis. It was all on a list in his pocket: "1 Torch for Mrs. Churchill; dark material for door; Adhesive tape, gum and black paper." His departing guests had taken no precautions, "and so," Duff Cooper wrote, "we wandered through the dark streets."[213]

Halifax had cabled Henderson to request a 9:00 A.M. appointment with Ribbentrop, and then — since the ultimatum need not be drafted until morning — went to bed. To Kirkpatrick he had "seemed relieved" that the waiting was over and his role as an appeaser was finished. That was not true of his French counterpart. As the British foreign secretary slept, the French foreign minister made one last absurd attempt to avoid fighting Hitler's Germany. Telephoning Ciano, Bonnet asked whether "*un retrait symbolique*" ("a symbolic withdrawal") of German troops was possible. Ciano knew Hitler would scorn not only the idea, but also anyone who brought it to his attention. In his diary he wrote: "Nothing can be done. I throw the paper in the wastebasket without informing the Duce."[214]

Henderson delivered the ultimatum but he was heartbroken. Awaiting a reply that never came — Hitler would deliver his answer with his U-boats, now patrolling the sea lanes around Britain — he said farewell to Dahlerus, who noted that the British ambassador could not hide "his profound grief and disappointment." Dahlerus later wrote that "certain circles in England regarded him with scepticism and considered him susceptible to Nazi influence," but the Swede thought that unjust; he had "never found him a dupe of German policy." Since Dahlerus himself was a dupe, his judgment here carries little weight. But if Henderson's dreams lay in ruins, they were not only his dreams; they were shared by his superiors in London. He had not served King and Country well. Neither had they. And none of his acts diminishing England's prestige, and weakening her in the years before her people faced the greatest challenge in her history, would have been possible without the connivance and even the encouragement of Chamberlain, Halifax, and Cadogan.[215]

The British ultimatum expired (the French declaration of war would follow at 5:00 P.M., six hours later) and at 11:15 A.M. September 3 the prime minister spoke to the nation over the BBC, telling them that England and Germany were once again at war. His address was neither memorable nor inspiring; Boothby wrote Churchill: "Your immediate task seems to have been made much easier by the PM today. His was not the speech of a man who intended to lead us *through* the struggle." Winston and Clementine had heard over their Morpeth Mansions radio, and hardly had Chamberlain's voice died away than the piercing wail of air-raid sirens, later to become so familiar to an entire generation of Englishmen, sounded all over the city. Winston, Clementine, and Inspector Thompson hurried toward the door. "You know, you've got to hand it to Hitler," said Churchill — heading for the roof, not the shelter — "The war is less than a half-hour old, and already he has bombers over London." Actually, the alarm was false, though Churchill didn't know it as he gazed out, as he put it, "in the clear, cool September light" to watch "thirty or forty cylindrical balloons" slowly rising above the city. "It was with difficulty," Inspector Thompson recalled, "that we prevailed upon him to enter an air-raid shelter. He only agreed to go when it was pointed out to him that it was up to him to set an example. Down we went . . . the Old Man with a bottle of brandy under his arm."[216]

They made their way, Churchill wrote, "to the shelter assigned to us." It lay a hundred yards down the street, "an open basement, not even sandbagged," as he described it, already occupied by the tenants of a half-dozen flats. "Everyone was cheerful and jocular," he recalled, "as is the English manner when about to encounter the unknown." But according to Fritz Günther von Tschirschky, a German refugee, Churchill himself was less than jolly. Tschirschky remained outside the shelter, feeling a German would not be welcome, until Clemmie, who knew him, insisted he come down. There he found Churchill "in a great state of indignation, stamping his foot, complaining that there was no telephone and no portable wireless, and saying the Germans would have much better organized air raid shelters." Tschirschky volunteered that there was a portable radio in his flat, and Churchill said: "You Germans are so damned efficient — please be kind enough to fetch it." But just then the wailing was heard again. Churchill afterward remembered that he "was not sure that this was not a reiteration of the previous warning, but a man came running along the street shouting 'All Clear.' "[217]

Parliament met at noon, and as Churchill crossed the lobby he was handed a note from the prime minister asking him to call on him "as soon as the debate died down." It wasn't much of a debate. The issue which had divided them had been resolved. The prime minister, speaking first, called the day "a sad day"; then, having turned overnight from dove to hawk, added: "I hope I may live to see the day when Hitlerism has been destroyed." Greenwood, speaking for Labour, told the House that the "intolerable agony of suspense" had ended and saluted the gallant Poles, "now fighting for survival." More cheers. Churchill, scheduled as the third speaker, wrote afterward that "as I sat in my place, listening to the speeches, a very strong sense of calm came over me, after the intense passions and excitements of the last few days. I felt a serenity of mind and was conscious of a kind of uplifted detachment from human and personal affairs. The glory of Old England, peace-loving and ill-prepared as she was, but instant and fearless at the call of honour, thrilled my being and seemed to lift our fate to those spheres far removed from earthly facts and physical sensation. I tried to convey some of this mood to the House when I spoke."[218]

Parliament remembered his years of warnings, his denunciation of Munich, the countless scenes in which he had been hooted and jeered and mocked when he tried to tell them of Nazi Germany's growing military superiority and the threat to them and their island. He had anticipated this more than six years ago and never was a man more entitled to remind them that he had told them so. But his friends knew him incapable of that. "If we quarrel with the past," he had said, "we may lose the future." It is fair to add that he had high hopes of his imminent meeting with the prime minister. Bitterness now could sour his prospects then. So he began by declaring: "In this solemn hour it is a consolation to recall and to dwell upon our repeated efforts for peace. All have been ill-starred, but all have been faithful and sincere. . . . Outside, the storms of war may blow and the lands may be lashed with the fury of its gales, but in our own hearts this Sunday morning there is peace. . . . Our consciences are at rest."[219]

He warned them to expect "many disappointments, and many unpleasant surprises," but added, "We may be sure that the task which we have freely accepted is not one beyond the compass and strength of the British Empire and the French Republic." It was hardly true that Chamberlain had freely accepted it, and at hour four France was still at peace, but mention of the Empire was greeted with a murmur of approval; within the hour Australia and New Zealand had declared war on Germany while the other Dominions prepared to follow. Churchill noted that the prime minister had said it was "a sad day," and so it was, but "there is another note which may be present," a sense of gratitude that a new generation of Britons was "ready to prove itself not unworthy of the days of yore and not unworthy of those great men, the fathers of our land, who laid the foundations of our laws and shaped the greatness of our country."

Few cheered that. It was prophetic, but on that first day of the war the older generation's thoughts about England's youth were anxious thoughts. The Oxford Oath was still popular. Hitler was wicked; they knew that. He had forced this hated war on England. But fighting for the Union Jack, so powerful an incentive in 1914, had little appeal now. Vision was necessary, and in his closing remarks Churchill recognized that. Over the past few days, he observed, Parliament had passed bills entrusting "to the executive our most dearly valued traditional liberties," but they would be safe there; no British government would use them "for class or party interests"; it would instead "cherish and guard them." England's dream was of a world in which all governments could be so trusted, the dignity of all people respected.

> This is not a question of fighting for Danzig or fighting for Poland. We are fighting to save the whole world from the pestilence of Nazi tyranny and in defence of all that is most sacred to man. This is no war of domination or imperial aggrandisement or material gain; no war to shut any country out of the sunlight and means of progress. It is a war, viewed in its inherent quality, to establish, on impregnable rocks, the rights of the individual, and it is a war to establish and revive the stature of man. . . . We look forward to the day, surely and confidently we look forward to the day, when our liberties and rights will be restored to us, and when we shall be able to share them with the peoples to whom such blessings are unknown.[220]

There was no standing ovation; whips on both sides of the House, wary of Churchill's rhetoric, had seen to that. But after Lloyd George had delivered the day's final speech, MPs of all parties surged toward Winston, their hands extended congratulating him. Comparison with the prime minister's remarks was inevitable. In his diary Amery described Chamberlain's address as "good, but not the speech of a war leader." He added: "I think I see Winston emerging as PM out of it all by the end of the year."[221]

If the prime minister overheard such invidious comparisons, he gave no sign of it. Cordially welcoming Churchill, he told him he had considered his letters and then told him the cabinet was being reshuffled. The Liberals had declined to join the government, and until now he had seen no role in the War Cabinet for the three service ministers. They had urged him to change his mind, however, and he had relented, which brought the average age of cabinet members — a matter which had troubled Winston — below sixty. Hore-Belisha would continue at the War Office, and Kingsley Wood would remain as secretary for air. However, Chamberlain proposed to transfer the Earl of Stanhope, now first lord of the Admiralty, to another post, and give the Admiralty to Churchill.

Thus, at a stroke, Winston was given a place in the War Cabinet and the responsibility of a ministry — the one he cherished most. He was "very glad of this," he wrote, "because, though I had not raised the point, I naturally preferred a definite task to that exalted brooding over the work done by others which may well be the lot of a Minister, however influential, who has no department." Had Chamberlain given him a choice between the War Cabinet and the Admiralty on Friday, he wrote, "I should, of course, have chosen the Admiralty. Now I was to have both." Clementine was waiting in the car outside No. 10, and Winston told her: "It's the Admiralty. That's a lot better than I thought."[222]

He would have preferred hurrying straight to his new post, because "the opening hours of war may be vital with navies," but the first meeting of the War Cabinet was scheduled for 5:00 P.M. It would be largely a formality; nevertheless, he had to be there. Thus he sent word to the Admiralty Board — "I shall take charge forthwith and arrive at six o'clock" — and headed for Downing Street. Newspaper opinion, led by *The Times*, had favored direction of the war by a small group, not more than five or six members. But counting the home secretary (Sir John Anderson) and the new Dominions secretary (Eden), Chamberlain's War Cabinet had eleven, the other nine being himself, Halifax, Hoare (privy seal), Simon (Exchequer), Hore-Belisha (war), Kingsley Wood (air), Hankey (without portfolio), Churchill, and Lord Chatfield (coordination of defense). Of these, Chamberlain, Halifax, Hoare, and Simon were still the Big Four; they had been in the public eye so long that if England's fortunes failed her, the British public would hold them accountable, even though the leaders had stayed in front by following public opinion. Every newspaper reader was familiar with them — Good Old Neville, as the crowds called him at his peak, the archetypical British businessman; Halifax, master of foxhounds, with the patrician's gift for backing into the limelight; dapper, fussy Hoare, the cabinet's fixer of Fleet Street opinion; Simon, the pedantic lawyer, of whom it was said that at the Exchequer he was chiefly concerned with making certain that Britain had enough money to pay the indemnity after losing the war.[223]

If, as Chamberlain put it a week later, righteousness was "a tremendous force on our side," no one else felt it. The British were depressed. *The Times* cheerfully reported that an eighty-six-year-old shepherd had presented the prime minister with a walking stick in the form of a rolled-up umbrella, whittled out of elm wood with a pocketknife; but shepherds were unthreatened by massive Luftwaffe bombings which, according to a Committee of Imperial Defence estimate, would last sixty days, leaving 600,000 dead and 1.2 million wounded. The committee had issued a statement, for reasons which defy understanding, that every possible precaution had been made: hospital beds had been prepared for the injured, thousands of papier-mâché coffins were stacked and then photographed for the press, and over a million burial forms were in the mail. The British public — remembering Baldwin's warning that "the bomber will always get through" — already lacked a once-more-into-the-breach spirit, and this did not develop it.

Winston's critics had predicted that if given a cabinet role he would be divisive, and now they observed with schadenfreude that he already was. The War Cabinet's first duty was to choose a new chief of the Imperial General Staff, since Secretary for War Hore-Belisha wanted to replace Gort. The War Office preferred Ironside, and so did Hore-Belisha. But Tiny had remained aloof from political maneuvering; other generals had courted ministers who now nominated them. Churchill intervened vigorously, and as Hore-Belisha wrote in his diary that evening, "There was some opposition to Ironside's appointment, but Winston came down on my side and strongly supported it; and that settled it." Churchill also asked for a survey of British gun production, and during the discussion Major General H. L. Ismay, secretary to the Committee of Imperial Defence, entered the room with an air reconnaissance report: a German *Flotte* — four or five battleships, four cruisers, and five destroyers — had weighed anchor and put out to sea. As first lord, Churchill was particularly alert to any threat, by submarines or surface ships, to merchant vessels, England's lifeline. If that was the *Flotte*'s mission, he said, they would be headed for the Baltic. Kingsley Wood, the air minister, agreed that the RAF could not ask for a "fairer target." An air attack was authorized, by twenty-seven Blenheim bombers and nine Wellingtons.

But here, as in so many other ventures early in the war, nothing went right for the British. Sir Ian Jacob, then a field-grade officer seconded to No. 10, recalls that the RAF mission, which failed, "showed how ineffective and ill-designed our aircraft and bombs were against strong defences and well-armoured ships." Their mission unaccomplished, the British planes were downed by flak.[224]

The meeting over, Churchill headed for the Admiralty — which had already signaled the fleet: "Winston is back"— crossing the Horse Guards Parade with a young friend. Winston observed that to improve British morale, the public's conception of the country's military establishment must be revised upward. Between 1914 and 1918 London's chauvinistic press had elevated general and flag officers to the level of deities, and when the truth about the butchery in France and Flanders had eventually emerged, the crash in their status had been deafening. World War II restored dignity to the military profession, but it was not retroactive; it is still generally believed that during the interwar years English officers were insensitive, unimaginative Colonel Blimps. They weren't. Churchill had found them to be keen, anxious observers of the Luftwaffe and Wehrmacht buildups, and among them were the officers who, by coming to him, had risked their careers to prepare England for the ordeal they — but few civilians — knew was coming.

One of their projects, undertaken by those who anticipated the bombing of London, had been construction of a shelter for the country's leaders at Storey's Gate, two blocks south of Downing Street. Commonly described by the few who knew of it as the CWR, short for Cabinet War Room, it was actually an underground warren of drab rooms, including a bedroom for the P.M., whose sparse furnishings included a desk and a BBC microphone through which the P.M. could address the nation. Construction of this shelter — which might more properly be called a bunker, for its purpose, like that of the *Führerbunker* in Berlin, was to safeguard the leader's life — had begun in 1935, after the War Office pointed out that No. 10 was far too fragile to survive heavy bombardments undamaged. Millions of Londoners, allies, and an unknown number of enemy spies, passed the CWR daily without knowing it. The drab stone building above it, facing St. James's Park, bore a dull plaque reading CENTRAL STATISTICAL OFFICE.

Another precaution, anticipated long before the English public would even acknowledge a renewal of the conflict with Germany, was more conspicuous — was, indeed, spectacular. Every major governmental building was surrounded by huge concertinas of barbed wire — coils twelve feet high, with barbs as thick as a man's thumb. They had lain in warehouses for years and were produced when Britain's ultimatum was delivered in Berlin.

The instant war was declared, up went the wire. The facade of Admiralty House was hidden by intervening buildings until Winston and his companion were almost upon it. Churchill and his companion turned a corner, and there it was, with its vast new concertinas and thousands of barbs gleaming in the late afternoon sun. "Great God!" said Winston's young friend. "What's *that* for?"

Churchill replied, "That's to keep me out."[225]

SIX

CATACLYSM

At the Admiralty he was expected, recognized, and saluted as he passed through a gap between concertinas. No guide was necessary, of course; the once and present first lord went straight to a concealed entrance where Kathleen Hill, summoned earlier by telephone, and Captain Guy Grantham, who would be his aide, awaited him. Inside, Churchill raced up the stairway, with Mrs. Hill and the captain panting at his heels, and burst into his old lair, the first lord's office, known to those who had served under Winston between 1911 and 1915 as "the private office." Swiftly crossing the room, he "flung open a hidden panel," as Mrs. Hill put it, revealing "a secret situation map" on which he had last plotted the locations of Allied and enemy ships on that long-ago day when he had last worked here. "The ships," Mrs. Hill remembers, "were still there" — exactly as he had left them on May 22, 1915, when his daring Dardanelles strategy was, as he later wrote, "ruined irretrievably" by incompetent subordinates, and he himself was generally regarded as a ruined politician. Now, he reflected, "a quarter of a century had passed, and still mortal peril threatened us at the hands of the same nation. Once again defence of the rights of a weak state, outraged and invaded by unprovoked aggression, forced us to draw the sword. Once again we must fight for life and honour against the might and fury of the valiant, disciplined, and ruthless German race. Once again! So be it."[1]

Churchill's early start at the Admiralty accomplished little; he was adrift in memories of the past — "filled with emotion," in the words of Rear Admiral Bruce Fraser, the third sea lord. That evening the first sea lord, Admiral Sir Dudley Pound, introduced him to the senior men with whom he would be working, and in the boardroom Winston took the first lord's chair, as of old. Pound formally welcomed him; Churchill, according to one of the admirals, "replied by saying what a privilege and honour it was to be again in that chair. . . . He surveyed critically each of us in turn and then, adding that he would see us all personally later on, he adjourned the meeting. 'Gentlemen,' he said, 'to your tasks and duties.' " They left quietly.

"Everybody," one of them later recalled, "realized what a wider responsibility he had" — his duties as a member of the War Cabinet and its Land Forces Committee, and his concern over the fighting in Poland and the strange lack of it in France.[2]

His original instinct had been correct; in the war at sea the early hours were crucial. Yet it is hard to see how anyone in the Admiralty could have prevented the war's first sea tragedy. When hostilities were declared late that morning, Admiral Karl Dönitz had thirty-nine U-boats cruising outside British seaports. One, the *U-30*, was lurking 250 miles off the Irish coast. At 7:45 P.M., as Pound was introducing Churchill to his fellow sea lords, the submarine's commander sighted the S.S. *Athenia*, no warship but an unarmed ocean liner carrying 1,103 passengers, most of them European refugees heading for asylum in the United States. Hitler had vetoed unrestricted submarine warfare in the early stages of the conflict, but the commander of the *U-30*, mistaking the liner for a British auxiliary cruiser, had torpedoed her. The 112 dead included 28 U.S. citizens. Two British destroyers and a Swedish yacht picked up the survivors, who signed affidavits testifying that the U-boat had circled the sinking steamship without offering assistance, though by then the sub's commander knew he had blundered. The Americans among them demanded transportation home shielded by a convoy of U.S. warships, which was not possible. Ambassador Kennedy sent his twenty-two-year-old son John F. Kennedy, a Harvard senior, to defuse their anger, reassure them, and find them safe passage to New York.

Hitler was indifferent to American public opinion, but Goebbels, as the Reich's minister of propaganda, could not be, particularly after Churchill publicly declared: "The *Athenia* was torpedoed without the slightest warning. She was not armed." Goebbels interrupted a Radio Berlin broadcast to call Churchill "*ein Lügenlord*" ("lying lord") and denied Nazi responsibility for the sinking, saying the only source for such reports was "your impudent lies, Herr Churchill, your infernal lies!" Learning that in English Winston's initials stood for what Germans called *Wasserklosett*, zealous Nazis painted them on latrines. Berlin announced that Churchill had personally ordered a bomb placed aboard the *Athenia*. "This falsehood," Winston noted, "received some credence in unfriendly quarters." In the House of Commons he said the passenger ship "was not defensively armed — she carried no guns and her decks had not even been strengthened for this purpose." He added that he had expressed his "profound sympathy with the relatives of those who may be bereaved by this outrage." Privately, he told the War Cabinet, "The occurrence should have a helpful effect as regards public opinion in the United States."[3]

* * *

He did not, however, expect a call from the White House. Nevertheless, in early October, while he was dining in Morpeth Mansions with two Admiralty guests, the phone rang, and a few moments later his valet-cum-butler entered to summon him. Churchill asked who was calling. "I don't know, sir," his man replied. "Well," said Winston, "say I can't attend to it now." To his surprise, the butler said: "I think you ought to come, sir." Annoyed, Churchill went, and it was his guests' turn to be perplexed, at his answers to his caller: "Yes, sir. . . . No, sir." One of them later recalled that there were "few people whom he would address as 'sir' and we wondered who on earth it could be. Presently he came back, much moved and said: 'Do you know who that was? The President of the United States. It is remarkable to think of being rung up in this little flat in Victoria Street by the President himself in the midst of a great war.' He excused himself, saying, 'This is very important. I must go and see the Prime Minister at once.' "[4]

Roosevelt had told him of a strange warning from Admiral Raeder, commander in chief of the Kriegsmarine. The *Grossadmiral* had informed the Americans that his agents had discovered a British plot: the U.S.S. *Iroquois,* which had sailed from Cork the day war was declared, would be sunk "in similar circumstances to the *Athenia,*" which, according to the current Nazi line, meant by the Royal Navy, on Churchill's orders. The implication was that England would try to blame the Reich for the ship's loss and thus get the U.S. into the war. After consulting No. 10 and his sea lords, Churchill cabled the White House: "*Iroquois* is probably a thousand miles West of Ireland. . . . U-boat danger inconceivable in these broad waters. Only method can be time-bomb planted at Queenstown. We think this not impossible." Roosevelt agreed and warned the ship's commander, who quickly sought, and found, safe harbor. But a stem-to-stern search produced nothing. The British accused Germany of trying to spread propaganda against England, and Raeder was embarrassed. The truth is that despite all these hypotheses of Byzantine intrigue, no one in high position was to blame.[5]

The real significance of this minor contretemps was that Roosevelt had taken the initiative in establishing a bond with a belligerent power — despite official U.S. neutrality, a policy which enjoyed the overwhelming support of the American people — and had cooperated with the British to a remarkable degree, even following up the first lord's suggestion that the Germans might have smuggled a bomb aboard the ship. With few exceptions the British people, unfamiliar with U.S. politics and the mood of the American public, were unaware of how grave a political risk the president was taking. One British historian observes that from the outset

Roosevelt's idealism was clear-sighted. He was well aware that at least four out of five Americans were unwilling to be involved in what they saw as the Quarrel of European states, the very lands from which their ancestors had fled in search of freedom and prosperity. He was equally aware that the Nazi threat was of greater than local significance. . . . He was determined to spare nothing in his endeavors to sustain the West European democracies . . . and he had the vision to determine that whatever advice he might receive to the contrary from his Ambassador in London, Joseph P. Kennedy, Churchill was and would remain the standard bearer of resistance.[6]

In bypassing No. 10 Downing Street, the Foreign Office, and his own embassy in London, the president had established a direct tie with the only man, in his view, who could save Europe from Hitler. And since Roosevelt had made this extraordinary move entirely on his own, Churchill was the passive partner in the establishment of the most momentous relationship in his life. Of course, on their level each man was known to the other. Six years earlier, as a rapt admirer of FDR's New Deal, Winston had sent a copy of his first *Marlborough* volume to the White House, inscribed, on October 8, 1933: "With earnest best wishes for the success of the greatest crusade of modern times."[7]

Actually they had met once, at Gray's Inn, London, on July 29, 1918, when both were guests at a dinner for the War Cabinet, though Churchill — to FDR's annoyance — did not remember it. Roosevelt professed to have enjoyed Churchill's subsequent books, and, as noted earlier, he had read *While England Slept,* though the president rarely read anything except newspapers; he liked to learn the views of contemporary writers by inviting them to his home and listening to them. Considering Churchill's present responsibilities that was impractical now, but already Roosevelt was pondering ways to manage a rendezvous, the more dramatic the better. He never doubted he could do it. After overcoming his appalling paralysis to become the greatest figure in American political history, he felt he could do anything. If he wanted something, he reached for it. No president has ever had a broader reach, and now his hand was extended across the Atlantic.[8]

He knew he could buy peace for a generation of Americans, but the more he pondered the character of the regime in Berlin, the more convinced he became that the next U.S. generation would lie at Hitler's mercy. On September 1, as the Wehrmacht's panzer tracks chewed their way toward Warsaw, Phelps Adams of the *New York Sun* had asked FDR: "Can we stay out of it?" Privately, Roosevelt was doubtful, but after a long pause he had replied: "I not only sincerely hope so, but I believe we can, and every effort will be made by this Administration to do so." This amounted to duplicity, but the president could not become a great wartime leader unless he won a third term the following year. If he were blunt now he would lose then. However, on Sunday, the day Britain entered the war, he had sounded an unmistakable knell. It was "easy for you and me to shrug our shoulders," he told his countrymen in a fireside chat, and to dismiss "conflicts thousands of miles from the continental United States" as irrelevant to Americans. But "passionately though we may desire detachment, we are forced to realize that every word that comes through the air, every ship that sails the seas, every battle that is fought does affect the American future." In 1914 Woodrow Wilson had told the Senate that the "United States must be neutral in fact as well as in name. . . . We must be impartial in thought as well as in action." FDR now declared that impossible: "The nation will remain a neutral nation, but I cannot ask that every American remain neutral in thought as well. Even a neutral cannot be asked to close his mind and conscience."[9]

His own mind was open and his conscience at peace. In time his commitment would be clear to the entire world. He had already planned one of his bold, ingenious strokes, renouncing freedom of the seas for Americans. "Danger zones" would be proclaimed, and U.S. citizens and ships would be barred from them; there would be no *Lusitania* this time. The isolationism bloc could find no flaw in that. But if they mulled it over, they would see that the policy in effect gave a free hand to Britain and France, who were controlling the seas despite German submarines. A further step came in November 1939, when the U.S. Neutrality Act was amended to permit the sale of arms to belligerents on a cash-and-carry basis. Although theoretically applying equally to all, cash and carry in fact favored whoever dominated the seas; now the Allies could place large orders with American munitions manufacturers and then sail over to take delivery. The impact of cash and carry on the Reich would be anything but neutral, and the orders would mean thousands of jobs for Americans. In all events, FDR intended to intervene personally whenever he could help the democracies and hurt Hitler.[10]

If Roosevelt had judged him right, Churchill was the man with whom he could join hands. Even before his phone call to Morpeth Mansions, he had sent the Admiralty's first lord an overture via the American diplomatic pouch. Dated September 11 it began: "My dear Churchill: — It is because you and I occupied similar positions in the World War [FDR had been assistant secretary of the U.S. Navy] that I want you to know how glad I am that you are back again in the Admiralty." Winston — and of course Chamberlain, he added as an afterthought — should know that "I shall at all times welcome it, if you will keep me in touch personally with anything you want me to know about," sending "sealed letters through your pouch or my pouch." The president ended gracefully, "I am glad you did the Marlborough volumes before this thing started — and I much enjoyed reading them."[11]

To Winston, who had looked westward when the appeasers were looking to Berlin, this letter bore enormous implications. Laying it before the War Cabinet, he pointed out that the president, as commander in chief, controlled the movements of all American naval vessels and could "relieve the Royal Navy of a great load of responsibility." By executive order he could declare a safety belt around the Americas, which would make it impossible for the Germans to attack His Majesty's merchantmen "approaching, say, Jamaica or Trinidad, without risking hostilities with the United States." The War Cabinet approved his reply, the first of 1,688 exchanges between the two men. It opened, "The following from Naval Person," and that would continue to be his salutation until he took over the government of Great Britain, when he altered it to "former Naval Person."[12]

Now that he was first lord, Churchill saw no reason to alter his daily regimen. He knew that his late hours, a consequence of his siestas, were a trial for his subordinates. But most of them were career officers; they knew the need for sacrifices in wartime. He had followed the same schedule the first ten months of the last war, and the Admiralty had adjusted to it. He had been forty then; now, at sixty-five, he found the nap an absolute necessity, permitting him, he said, "to press a day and a half's work into one." Mary remembers that after an hour's rest he "awoke a giant refreshed." If he could work sixteen or seventeen hours a day, he reasoned, they could adjust to his eccentric hours. At one time or another all those officers directly under him tried to sleep in the early afternoon. Somehow they couldn't drift off. The only exception was the first sea lord. Pound developed a habit of sleeping while sitting bolt upright. The only difficulty was that it became involuntary. Winston would pace the private office, delivering precise, detailed instructions on a matter of considerable importance, only to discover that the Royal Navy's senior admiral of the fleet was, and for a time had been, dead to the world.[13]

Winston's typical Admiralty day began at six or seven in the morning and continued, broken only by his rest after lunch, through a two-hour evening conference and on until two or three the next morning. Of course, this was not Chartwell; his first visitor each morning was Captain Richard Pim, RN, arriving to brief the first lord on overnight developments in the war at sea. Pim always began by describing changes in the Admiralty's situation map. He did this slowly; Winston carried a rough map around in his head, and he needed time to switch, say, the little flag for this cruiser from here to there, or to remove — with great satisfaction — the pin representing a Nazi

U-boat sunk by a British destroyer. Should Winston ever be captured by the enemy and successfully interrogated, using torture or drugs, the results would be catastrophic for the navy. Therefore, he never left Admiralty House without his pistol and a suicide pill in his pen.

During the first week of the war, while the first lord and his lady stayed in Morpeth Mansions, the Office of Works converted the nurseries and attics on the two top floors of Admiralty House into a flat for them. Clementine decided to keep the gay chintz curtains, hung by Lady Diana Cooper during Duff Cooper's tenure as first lord, but transformed the rest, as Lady Diana discovered when she came calling. In her diary she wrote: "O what a change . . . from my day!" She mourned her bed, which "rose sixteen feet from a shoal of gold dolphins and tridents; ropes made fast the blue satin curtains; round the walls Captain Cook was discovering Australia. Now all has suffered a sea change. The dolphins are stored away and on a narrow curtainless pallet bed sleeps the exhausted First Lord. My gigantic gold-and-white armoire holds his uniform. The walls are charts."[14]

First in Morpeth Terrace and then Admiralty House, Pim had to do a bit of shouting to make himself heard while Winston splashed about in his bath. The new first lord was eager to leave Morpeth Mansions; he disliked sleeping so far from his maps, framed in wood and hung on the walls of Admiralty House's elegant, 217-year-old library, which overlooked the Horse Guards Parade. This became the upper war room, a floor beneath the flat, created by Pim as directed in one of Churchill's first wartime orders. It was soon the nerve center of the navy. The maps — covered with black cloth to hide them from unauthorized Admiralty personnel passing through — bore small pins with flags which identified the last known position of His Majesty's warships, convoys, enemy vessels which had been spotted, and — with the help of Lloyd's of London — all British merchantmen. Details were at the fingertips of the Prof, who occupied an office next to the war room.[15]

This was in Lloyd's interest. Submarines were not the only peril awaiting British ships which left home waters. German raiders also lurked over the horizon: enemy warships and armed steamships disguised as peaceful freighters. A British skipper spotting a tramp steamer in the South Atlantic could send the Admiralty a coded inquiry and, within minutes, receive a reply telling him whether the vessel was registered and, if so, her mission and whether she was supposed to be where she was. "If a Raider was reported in any specific area," Pim wrote in his unpublished memoirs, "we were able in a few minutes to say what British ships were in the vicinity and what was their speed so that a wireless message could be sent ordering them, if necessary, to alter course to avoid the danger."[16]

Pim's assignment was formidable. Thousands of merchantmen flew the red ensign, feeding and arming England, and at any given moment at least half of them were at sea. Pim recalled how, when he believed the war room was ready, he sent word to the first lord. "Very good," said Churchill after inspecting it, "but the maps will all have to be replaced. When you know me better you will know that I only paint in pastel shades, and those strong colours under the lamps would give me and you a headache." Churchill required Pim and his staff to check the position of all known ships and convoys every twelve hours and replot them on the maps. The plotting was determined by a stream of signals, arriving around the clock, reporting losses of shipping to enemy attacks, details of attacks by Allied warships and aircraft, tonnage sunk by both sides, and graphs of imports arriving safely in England. If any signal of importance arrived after Winston was installed in his flat over the upper war room, Pim wrote,

> a very few moments would elapse before he arrived in the War Room and was in complete possession of all the facts. I had always heard that he was an indefatigable worker and there is no other word to describe his activities. His day started with a visit in his multi-coloured dressing gown to the War Room generally soon after seven — although often it was a far earlier hour. . . . With the exception of about two hours' rest each afternoon he continued hard at it with a short respite for meals until one or two o'clock next morning when he used to pay us a final visit on his way to bed.[17]

The evening conference usually began at 9:00 P.M.; two hours later the first lord would start dictating speeches. ("Are you ready?" he might remark to his typist. "I'm feeling very fertile tonight.") The Prof would arrive in the private office around midnight, settle on a sofa in front of the fire, and remain until Churchill retired. Before bed Winston would tour the operational rooms in the basement — "terribly good for the naval staff," a private secretary recalls — and end his day with a final visit to the war room. Sir Geoffrey Shakespeare, parliamentary secretary to the Admiralty, writes that once, well after midnight, Winston asked a secretary, "Where is the OIL?" Baffled, the secretary replied, "What OIL?" Churchill said: "I want Admiral the OIL" — he meant "Earl" — "of Cork and Orrery." Shakespeare adds: "It was nearly 3 A.M. We were dropping with fatigue."[18]

Although the King waited patiently in Buckingham Palace, ready to present the Admiralty's seals to his new first lord, Churchill did not kiss hands until the third day after his appointment. He was far too busy. His prewar informants had kept him apprised of urgent naval issues, and as a critic of Anglo-German naval treaties, he had undertaken a detailed study of Raeder's new Oberkommando der Kriegsmarine (navy high command). But now he had to explore the whole of his new realm, launch projects, devise strategies, propose offensive operations, assign priorities, prepare defenses for the vast arsenal of challenges Raeder — after six years of planning aggressive naval war — was hurling at the Admiralty around the clock. Moreover, he had his other War Cabinet responsibilities, and was deeply involved in plans for the expansion of the army.

Nevertheless, if the Admiralty did not have his undivided attention, he gave it far more than any of Chamberlain's other ministers could have done. "His energy and stamina were prodigious," the historian Arthur Marder writes. "A stream of memoranda, virtually ultimata, issued from the Private Office covering every aspect of the war at sea and leaving the recipient in no doubt as to what the First Lord wanted." These memoranda became irreverently known as the First Lord's Prayers because they frequently opened with "Pray inform me . . ." or "Pray why has . . . not been done." Captain G. R. G. Allen recalls that the "one thing that remains firmly in my mind about Winston's arrival in the Admiralty was the immediate impact which his personality made on the staff at all levels, both service and civilian." Allen was among those who "began to receive little notes signed 'WSC' from the private office demanding weekly reports of progress direct to him. If the required report was a good one . . . one might get a reply in red ink: 'v.g. press on.' It was like the stone thrown in the pond, the ripples got out in all directions, galvanising people at all levels to 'press on' — and they did." He adds: "The same stimulation was at once felt in the fleet."[19]

The most fundamental source of conflict between Churchill and his staff would arise from polar opposites — his instincts and their traditional discipline. In peacetime the gravest sin a captain can commit is to lose his ship. If the vessel lost is a British or American warship, a court-martial is mandatory. Naval officers know that some ships must be lost in wartime, but their early training makes them cautious strategists, shrinking from risky plans and daring maneuvers. The battle of Jutland, in 1916, wasn't really a battle. On both sides the officers making the decisions were intent upon returning home with the fewest possible losses. Both succeeded — historians called Jutland a draw — because neither put up a real fight. If the man on the bridge believes, even on a subliminal level, that sinking is, for him, the ultimate disaster, he will remain secure in his command. He will also remain a cypher. Jellicoe and von Hipper, the commanders at Jutland, are forgotten. Nelson, Farragut, and Yamamoto will be remembered as long as fighting men go down to the sea in ships.[20]

Churchill loved risks and always sought ways to carry the war to the enemy. On the evening of his second day he again gathered his senior subordinates and subtly let them know, in a deceptively offhand talk, that his grasp of the Royal Navy was profound. His predecessor, the languid Lord Stanhope, had been a Gilbert and Sullivan first lord, celebrated for his ignorance of ships, of naval strategy, even of the sea. "Tell me," he once asked a sea lord, "what is a 'lee' *exactly*?" Winston's very language was nautical. He casually mentioned that after the naval treaties of 1930 and 1935, which he had opposed in Parliament, he had studied the design of the new German cruisers; and, as the admirals took notes, he reeled off figures and concise analyses of gunnery, engine room pressures, and keel design which would have been the envy of a flag officer lecturing at the Royal Naval College. He told them he was studying a convoy system to protect merchant shipping and was considering the laying of a mine barrage between Scotland and Norway; that he believed twelve destroyers could be "scraped" from other theaters for the Atlantic, where the enemy's "prime attack" could be expected, and that trawlers he had ordered reconditioned were being equipped with antisub devices, including Y-guns for firing depth charges. Since the Admiralty had assumed responsibility for the safety of merchantmen, they must faithfully follow zigzag courses to foil U-boats. Royal Navy officers would examine their logs and charts when they docked, and captains who had not zigzagged as instructed would be deprived of their papers. At present the war's big question mark was Italy. Her intentions were obscure. As long as they remained so, merchant shipping must avoid the Mediterranean by taking the long Cape route to India. But Mussolini could not drift forever. Churchill felt the Admiralty should "press" the government to bring the situation "to a head . . . as soon as possible." Rising, he said that "the First Lord submits these notes to his naval colleagues for consideration, *for criticism and correction*." He wanted them treated as bases for discussion, he explained, not as direct orders.[21]

Admiral Sir William M. James thought Churchill displayed a "remarkable grasp of sea warfare," and that this mastery was also evident "in the numerous minutes he wrote." These memoranda, which would grow in fame as the war progressed, were described by one of his staff officers. "The First Lord," he wrote, "devised special red labels with just three words printed on them: 'ACTION THIS DAY.' This ensured that any important document . . . would be dealt with at once, and the reply was expected to be on not more than 'one sheet of paper.' " Winston also stressed that instructions from him were to be obeyed only if he put them in writing, immediately or immediately thereafter.[22]

During his years out of office, Churchill had, of course, been preoccupied with the widening gap between the Luftwaffe and the RAF. He had anticipated the need for an expanded army, and urged that plans be made to raise and equip one. The service which had troubled him least was the navy. It was still the most powerful fleet in the world, the "senior service" in an island nation which had dominated the high seas for over three centuries. When Stanley Baldwin, slashing naval estimates, had told Parliament that Britain's might at sea was an "expensive toy" and Churchill had rebuked him, for once in those lonely years he had heard an approving murmur of "Hear, hear" on both sides of the House. Winston had denounced the Anglo-German Naval Agreement of 1935, but its provision that the Nazi navy be permitted to build two warship tons for every seven built by Britain did not alarm the Royal Navy. Even the navies of other countries thought Admiralty hubris, though infuriating, was justified. On the first day of the new war Admiral Raeder had written that the Führer's Kriegsmarine was "in no way" prepared "for the great struggle with Great Britain." He thought his surface forces were "so inferior in number and strength to those of the British fleet" that they "can do no more than show that they know how to die gallantly"; and *"die U-bootwaffe"* — the submarine arm — was "still much too weak to have any *decisive* effect on the war."[23]

German admirals had always suffered from an inferiority complex; in their country the army was the senior service. But Hitler knew how dependent England was upon imports, and how close she had been brought to her knees in 1917, nearly starved into submission by German submarines lying athwart Britain's sea lanes and sinking all ships approaching England, regardless of nationality. To Birger Dahlerus he swore that he would create a great *U-bootwaffe* and destroy first the Royal Navy and then the merchant ships flying the red ensign. When the Swede looked skeptical, the Führer had given history one of its unforgettable moments. Flinging out his right arm and striking his breast with his left, he had cried: "Have I ever told a lie in my life?"[24]

If the Führer's confidant and the head of his navy expected little from the Reich's forces at sea, it is unsurprising that England's peril there was unknown to Churchill. He wasn't even aware of Germany's new naval strength. Here his intelligence had failed him. In the early summer of 1934 Hitler had given secret orders for the construction of the *Scharnhorst* and *Gneisenau*, battle cruisers of 26,000 tons, exceeding by 16,000 tons the limit imposed on Germany at Versailles. By 1939 the yards at Kiel and Bremen had built three battleships, eight heavy cruisers, an aircraft carrier, thirty-four destroyers and torpedo boats, and, at Krupp's Germania shipyard, the first litter of the Kriegsmarine's newly designed U-boats, vastly improved over those of the last war. Two vessels of particular interest to *Jane's Fighting Ships,* the celebrity register of warships, were the *Graf Spee* and the *Deutschland*. The Germans called them *Panzerschiffe* (armored ships); to *Ausländer* they were "pocket battleships."

The *Panzerschiffe* were masterpieces of miniaturization. Powered by diesel engines, which gave them a range of 21,500 miles, each carried six eleven-inch guns and was capable of a 28-knot top speed. In the view of *Jane's,* they were mightier than almost any warship fast enough to overtake them. Moreover, at the outbreak of the war shifts of German shipbuilders were working around the clock to finish a battle cruiser, two battleships with tonnages of 41,700 — British, French, and American capital ships were limited to 35,000 tons — and the *Bismarck*, a superbattlewagon of 45,000 tons. Some military experts thought that in challenging Britain's naval superiority, the Führer was repeating the kaiser's mistake. They underestimated him. The British Admiralty's classic strategy had been the blockade. It had defeated Napoleon and the kaiser. The German counter to this was to sink ships provisioning Britain. Their argument was that sinkings were no more monstrous than a blockade which starved German children — they never answered the charge that leaving the survivors of the ships they sank to drown was another matter — and in any event they intended to launch torpedoes whenever they thought the loss of a target vessel would hurt England.[25]

One would have expected that the Royal Navy, after its harrowing duel with German submarines in the last war, would have been alert for signs that the Nazis were plotting a rematch. But all British naval glory seemed to lie in the past, and not the recent past. During the interwar years the sea lords had been refighting, not Jutland, but Trafalgar. They still glowed in anticipation of battles between ships of the line, firing broadsides that raked the enemy's decks and maneuvering to cross his T. The U-boat threat, they assured their civilian superiors, had been solved by surface ships in 1918, and, besides, they had a new secret weapon. This was the asdic, "the name," Churchill wrote, for "the system of groping for submarines below the surface by means of sound waves through the water which echoed back from any steel structure they met. From this echo the position of the submarine could be fixed with some accuracy." Lord Chatfield, the first sea lord, had driven him to Portland for a demonstration on June 15, 1938. Afterward Winston wrote excitedly, "I could see and hear the whole process, which was the sacred treasure of the Admiralty." He wrote Chatfield: "What surprised me was the clarity and force of the [asdic] indications. I had imagined something almost imperceptible, certainly vague and doubtful. I never imagined that I should hear one of those creatures asking to be destroyed. It is a marvellous system and achievement."[26]

It wasn't, not then. Later versions, which Americans came to know as sonar, fulfilled the promise of the primitive device Churchill saw and would prove valuable antisub weapons, but during Churchill's tenure as first lord the asdic was almost worthless. The clarity with which he had heard its unmistakable "ping" derived from the fact that its target subs were far from the transmitter. The shorter the range, the weaker the ping, and if a U-boat approached within fifteen hundred yards — the lethal range for torpedoes — the asdic signal was lost completely. U-boat commanders could hear the ping, too, and they would quickly learn how to take evasive action and approach at a deadlier angle. These problems challenged the most experienced asdic operators, of which there were very few in 1939; in the opening phase of the war at sea the transmitter-receivers would be in the hands of civilians who had been rushed through a three-month training course and assigned a task they simply could not grasp. Finally, the asdic could only be operated underwater. Admiral Karl Dönitz, a heroic submariner in the last war and now *Befehlshaber der U-boote,* simply ordered his commanders to attack at night from the surface. In the Royal Navy the asdic would be discredited, and its return to favor, like Churchill's, came slowly.

Dönitz, who knew the weaknesses of 1918 U-boats from personal experience — his had been sunk in the Mediterranean, and he had escaped drowning only to serve ten months of POW imprisonment — had devoted the 1920s to designing a tougher, more versatile underwater vessel. Ten days after the Anglo-German pact became effective in 1935 he had launched his new *U-1* from a tightly guarded shed in the Kiel shipyard. Unlike its predecessors, the *U-1* was equipped with heavy-duty batteries, which meant she could hide underwater for a much longer time. Of even greater importance was the revolutionary design of her torpedoes. Electrically powered, they left no telltale wakes, and each bore a magnetic firing mechanism which exploded it directly under the target vessel's keel, where a ship is most vulnerable.

If he had a fleet of a hundred U-boats, Dönitz believed, he could paralyze England by waging what he called a "tonnage war" — sinking all merchantmen carrying cargoes to England, whatever flag they flew. And with three hundred of them, organized in "wolf packs," he could sink over 700,000 tons of shipping a month in the Atlantic, even if the merchantmen sailed in convoys, escorted by warships. Events later in the war proved he could have done it in the first year of hostilities, but Dönitz was plagued by Hitler's chimerical moods and by interservice rivalry. Despite his vow to Dahlerus, the Führer blew hot and cold on submarine warfare. Yet sinking ships, particularly when civilians were aboard, appealed to the broad nihilist streak in him, and in that regard he found the reasoning of his *Befehlshaber der U-boote* flawless. In that last meeting with Dahlerus he had screamed: *"Ich U-boote bauen, U-boote bauen, U-boote, U-boote, U-boote, U-boote!"* ("I shall build U-boats, build U-boats, U-boats, U-boats, U-boats, U-boats!").[27]

Had he followed through and given Dönitz his three hundred submarines, it is hard to see how England could have avoided starvation. But the *Kriegsherr* liked the idea of powerful warships flying the swastika even more; when they sailed into European ports they contributed to the Third Reich's intimidating image. Furthermore, the senior admirals in Berlin, as in London, preferred to envision battles between surface ships, with enormous battleships trying to huff and puff and blow their enemies into submission. So Hitler let Britain's misfortune slip from his hands.

Even so, the war on the Atlantic shipping lanes opened with a series of savage, unexpected jolts for Britain. In the first week eleven merchantmen — 65,000 tons of shipping — were sunk, half the weekly losses of April 1917, the peak month of U-boat attacks that year, when England's Admiral John Jellicoe confided in his American counterpart that one freighter in four was going down, there was six weeks' supply of corn in the country, and he expected an Allied surrender by November 1. By the end of September 1939, twenty-six ships had been sunk by torpedoes. The fighting at sea, Churchill told the House of Commons on September 26, had "opened with some intensity," but, he assured the House: "By the end of October we expect to have three times the hunting force which was operating at the beginning of the war."[28]

At the same time, he felt he ought to inform Parliament that German *Schrecklichkeit* had reared its loathsome head. The Royal Navy had scrupulously observed the "long acquired and accepted traditions of the sea." When the RN sunk enemy vessels, their crews were picked up. Even when German ships had deliberately sunk themselves to avoid the formalities of the prize court, the Royal Navy had rescued their crews, and no ship flying the flag of a neutral nation had been attacked. "The enemy, on the other hand," said Churchill, had behaved very differently; in their zeal to prevent supplies from reaching England, the Nazis had torpedoed Finnish, Dutch, Swedish, Greek, Norwegian, and Belgian vessels "on the high seas, in an indiscriminate manner, and with loss of life." Churchill acknowledged that "from time to time the German U-boat commanders have tried their best to behave with humanity. . . ." But many cruel and ruthless sea crimes had been committed. They all remembered the *Athenia*. Her "tragic end" had been followed by the loss of the *Royal Sceptre,* "whose crew of 32 were left in open boats hundreds of miles from land and are assumed to have perished. Then there was the *Hazelside* — only the day before yesterday — twelve of whose sailors were killed by surprise gunfire, in an ordinary merchant ship." His Majesty's Government "cannot at all recognize this type of warfare . . . as other than a violation of the laws of war, to which the Germans themselves have in recent years so lustily subscribed." Such, he said, "is the U-boat war — hard, widespread and bitter, a war of groping and drowning, a war of ambuscade and stratagem, a war of science and seamanship."[29]

Speaking over the BBC a few days later, he described the first U-boat onslaught — how "they sprang out upon us as we were going about our ordinary business with two thousand ships in constant movement . . . upon the seas," and how, in consequence, "they managed to do some serious damage." But Britain was meeting the challenge with a threefold response: convoys, the arming of merchantmen and fast liners, and, "of course," the "British attack upon the U-boats." The *Athenia* had scarcely disappeared beneath the waves when "the Royal Navy . . . immediately attacked the U-boats and is hunting them night and day — I will not say without mercy, for God forbid we should ever part company with that — but at any rate with zeal and not altogether without relish."[30]

His voice vibrated with confidence, but in fact he was uneasy. Because the navy occupied a special place in the hearts of Englishmen, the Exchequer's knife, which had slashed so deeply into War Office and Air Ministry budgets in the 1930s, had been relatively gentle with Admiralty estimates. But since prime ministers, Fleet Street, and the public had been united in their scorn for all uniformed men, morale had slumped throughout the services. At the docks, ports, and naval bases Churchill inspected, he saw tarnished brass, scuffed shoes, and sagging coils of rope — insignificant in themselves but symptomatic of an institutional *défaillance.* If Nelson had relied on men like these he would have lost the battles of the Nile, Copenhagen, and Trafalgar, and Napoleon would have galloped up the Mall at the head of his *vieille garde* to demand the palace keys.

Nor was the fleet the force-in-being Churchill had ruled a quarter-century earlier. All that had been needed to keep it supreme had been hospitality to innovative ideas, supported by simple maintenance. The one new concept which both he and his admirals largely rejected was the enormous limits air power now placed on sea power. In all her wars till now, England had been able to control an island simply by stationing a warship offshore, or bottling up the enemy by sending a flotilla to bar a strategic strait. The kaiser's Kriegsmarine, for example, had been confined to the Baltic Sea during most of the last war because British warships had guarded the Skagerrak, the narrows separating the Baltic from the North Sea, thus keeping Germany from, among other possible objectives, the long coast of Norway. But if the fleet was vulnerable to Luftwaffe bombers, which the Admiralty would not concede, German ships could no longer be denied passage through the Skagerrak. Under an umbrella of Nazi planes, they could steam through unchallenged. Because the first lord and his sea lords would not fully accept this in 1939, within eight months the lesson would be forced upon them, and at a bitter price.

Maintenance was another matter. It seemed inconceivable that equipment vital to the navy should have been permitted to rust away, but that had happened. The sea lords blamed the small Admiralty appropriations under MacDonald, Baldwin, and Chamberlain. That wasn't good enough. During the 1930s their budgets had been large enough to build five new battleships, six aircraft carriers, and nineteen heavy cruisers. They just let small matters slide. In the first war Lord Kitchener of Khartoum, trying to console Winston in the dark hour of his dismissal from the Admiralty, had reminded him of his thorough preparations for the war. "There is one thing at any rate they cannot take from you," K of K had said. "The fleet was ready." This time, Churchill was discovering, the fleet was not.[31]

On the evening of September 15 he boarded a London train with Bracken, Sinclair, and Lieutenant Commander C. R. ("Tommy") Thompson, the first lord's flag commander. Their destination was Scotland and the sea anchorage of England's Home Fleet — the sea basin of Scapa Flow in the Orkney Islands. There, if anywhere, the Royal Navy should be buttoned up. Later he recalled how "on two or three occasions" in the autumn of 1914, most memorably on October 17, "the alarm was given that there was a U-boat inside the anchorage. Guns were fired, destroyers thrashed the waters, and the whole gigantic armada put out to sea in haste and dudgeon." Scapa was that important.[32]

Anxiety over the sea basin had returned, and this time the threat was real. In his lap lay a locked box of secret documents, among them a shocking report from the Chiefs of Staff Committee revealing that Scapa's defenses would not be ready until the spring of 1940. Arriving, he called on Sir Charles Forbes, the commander in chief, aboard H.M.S. *Nelson,* the admiral's flagship. Sir Charles confirmed that the basin's entrance channels were "not properly netted." The old steel webs had rusted, rotted, broken up, and drifted away. Winston immediately issued an order, stamped "urgent," calling for nets, booms, blockships (sunken ships barring entrance channels), antiaircraft guns, patrol craft, balloons, and searchlights. Until they were in place Scapa was insecure, an inviting target for daring German submarine commanders.[33]

And U-boat *Kapitäns*, so successful in sinking merchantmen, were now turning their periscopes toward Britain's ships of war. The enemy had actually laid a minefield across the mouth of the Thames, disabling one warship. After a second RN ship was sunk, the government, worried about civilian morale, had suppressed news of the loss. Two days before Churchill entrained for Scotland a U-boat had fired a salvo of torpedoes at H.M.S. *Ark Royal*, an aircraft carrier; they missed, and the carrier's destroyer escort sank the sub, but it was disquieting to know that Dönitz's vessels were lurking in British waters, capable of striking one of His Majesty's capital ships at any hour.

Indeed, it happened while Churchill was slumbering aboard H.M.S. *Nelson*, as he learned the next day. He and his party returned from Inverness to London aboard an overnight sleeper, and "as we got out at Euston," Winston wrote, "I was surprised to see the First Sea Lord on the platform. Admiral Pound's look was grave. 'I have some bad news for you, First Lord. The *Courageous* was sunk yesterday in the Bristol Channel.' " The ship had been an aircraft carrier, "a very necessary ship at this time," as Churchill wrote, and Bristol Channel, lying between South Wales and Somerset, was very close to home. Churchill told Pound, "We can't expect to carry on a war like this without these sorts of things happening from time to time. I have seen lots of this before." But within he was seething. He knew there would be questions in the House of Commons. To bring unconvoyed merchantmen into port he had been using carriers as escorts. *Courageous* had been attended by four destroyers, but two of them had been detached to hunt a Nazi submarine elsewhere. As the carrier turned into the wind to receive her aircraft, another U-boat *Kapitän* ran up his periscope and saw her naked flank in his cross hairs. He emptied his torpedo tubes and 518 Englishmen drowned, including the captain, who chose, as captains in those days did, to go down with his ship.[34]

Churchill's anxiety over Scapa Flow continued and mounted after His Majesty's Government spurned a peace feeler from Hitler. The offer had reached London via Birger Dahlerus. In Göring's presence, the Führer had proposed that a British representative — Ironside's name was mentioned — meet Göring "in some neutral country." Halifax on October 5 told the War Cabinet that "We should not absolutely shut the door"; Hoare suggested that Britain "damp down" her "anti-Göring propaganda"; Kingsley Wood also thought Göring the man to back, because "he would be glad to secure the removal of Herr Hitler." They had learned nothing, could not grasp the strength of the Führer's hold on his people, did not realize that the life expectancy of any German who moved against him would be measured in minutes. Churchill swiftly disposed of their arguments. If the overture was insincere its "real object might be to spread division and doubt amongst us"; if sincere, it had been inspired "not from any sense of magnanimity, but from weakness." The war, he suggested, might not be so popular in Germany as Goebbels insisted. On October 12 Chamberlain rejected the Nazi approach in the House. Winston had written the firmer parts of his speech, and afterward he told Pound that "one must expect a violent reaction from Herr Hitler. Perhaps quite soon." He ordered "special vigilance," suggested that "the Fleet at Scapa should be loose and easy in its movements," and concluded: "Pray let me know anything else you think we can do, and how best to have everything toned up to concert pitch. The next few days are full of danger."[35]

Danger appeared outside Scapa Flow at seven o'clock the following evening in the form of *U-47*, commanded by a thirty-one-year-old Dönitz protégé, Lieutenant Commander Günther Prien. In the first war, Dönitz knew, two U-boats had attempted to penetrate the deep, almost landlocked basin, and neither had returned. But studying aerial photographs of the anchorage, Dönitz reached the conclusion that an adroit navigator could thread his way past the three sunken ships meant to block Holm Sound.

Prien was his best U-boat *Kapitän*, and he almost failed. It took him nearly six hours to do it — at one point he seemed hopelessly ensnarled in a cable from one of the blockships — but at 12:30 on the morning of October 14 he was inside the basin. Dead ahead, at four thousand yards, lay the battleship *Royal Oak*. His first salvo missed, but the second time his spread of four torpedoes exploded in concert, mortally wounding the capital ship. In his log Prien wrote: "There is a loud explosion, roar and rumbling. Then come columns of water, followed by columns of fire, and splinters fly through the air." Thirteen minutes later *Royal Oak* rolled on her side and sank, carrying with her 833 officers and men, among them their captain and the rear admiral commanding the Second Battle Squadron.[36]

"Poor fellows, poor fellows," Churchill said when told, "trapped in those black depths." He wept, then thought of the unknown submariner's achievement and murmured: "What a wonderful feat of arms." It was not so wonderful for him, however. He "understood," he wrote, "how First Lords of the Admiralty are treated when great ships are sunk and things go wrong. If we were in fact going over the same cycle a second time, should I have once again to endure the pangs of dismissal? Fisher, Wilson, Battenberg, Jellicoe, Beatty, Pakenham, Sturdee, all gone!" He set down some lines of the nineteenth-century Irish poet Thomas Moore:

I feel like one
Who treads alone
Some banquet hall deserted,
Whose lights are fled,
Whose garlands dead,
and all but he departed.[37]

Hoare wrote His Majesty's ambassador in Washington: "Winston has been through some rough moments over the Scapa incidents. Being for the moment the war hero, he has come through it fairly well. I shudder to think what would have happened had there been another First Lord and he had been in Opposition." Exactly. Chamberlain could hardly dismiss the chief critic of the prewar governments which had been responsible for Scapa's vulnerability; the whole country knew that Winston bore no responsibility for the peacetime Royal Navy. Nevertheless, he took the setback personally, and took it hard. In the House he tried to balance the loss against the number of U-boats the navy had destroyed, but the books wouldn't balance. Germany's submarines were expendable; British warships were her lifeline. After informing the War Cabinet that the Home Fleet was being moved to the Clyde estuary in southwest Scotland as a "temporary disposition" prior to a move into an east coast base, Rosyth, he declared that the loss of the *Royal Oak*, "though an extremely regrettable disaster, does not materially affect the general naval position."[38]

It did, though. Germany was jubilant, Hitler ecstatic, Lieutenant Commander Prien a national hero. Even William L. Shirer was impressed, writing in his diary that the British battleship had been sunk in "the middle of Scapa Flow, Britain's greatest naval base!" Dönitz had scored a coup for *U-boote*. At the outset of hostilities the Führer had instructed U-boats to conform to the Hague Convention, which prohibited attacks without warning on enemy passenger and merchant ships. Prien's achievement opened Hitler's eyes to the possibilities of submarines and their lethal torpedoes. On October 16 Grossadmiral Raeder, speaking in Hitler's name, formally announced that "All merchant ships definitely recognized as enemy can be torpedoed without warning." So, it developed, could those flying neutral flags — except those of the United States — if their destinations were English ports. Neutral shipping had been sunk before, inadvertently or by reckless commanders. Now it was Kriegsmarine policy.[39]

All the billboards urging Englishmen to "Talk Victory" seemed to mock the Admiralty, and Clementine Churchill wrote her sister Nellie at Chartwell: "The war news is grim beyond words. One must fortify oneself by remembering that whereas the Germans are (we *hope*) at their peak, we have only just begun. Winston works night & day — He is well Thank God & gets tired only when he does not get 8 hours sleep — He does not need it at a stretch but if he does not get that amount in the 24 then he gets weary."[40]

England needed, not talk of victory, but the real thing. Any bright news would almost have to come from the high seas; there was no fighting, nor the prospect of any, on land or in the air. So out of this nettle, frustration, the navy must pluck this flower, triumph. The issue was not merely civilian morale. Captain Pim's maps told a sad tale, growing gloomier as autumn waned. Britain's loss of shipping would approach 745,000 tons by spring — over two hundred vessels. On November 21 H.M.S. *Belfast*, a new cruiser just launched, was gravely damaged by a mine in the Firth of Forth; two days later the British merchant cruiser *Rawalpindi*, armed with only four six-inch guns, was destroyed by the *Scharnhorst*, which then returned safely home with her sister ship, *Gneisenau*. But the Admiralty's greatest worry lay in the South Atlantic, where the pocket battleship *Graf Spee* was running amok. There, on the hundredth day of the war, an England famished for glory was about to be fed.

During the first weeks of the war Hitler had held back his fast, lethal *Panzerschiffe*, hoping to impose his peace terms upon a dispirited England. Once it became clear that His Majesty's Government meant to stay the course, he unleashed them as surface raiders. Of his two pocket battleships, *Deutschland* proved a disappointment. She was recalled after sinking only two merchantmen, one a neutral, and capturing a third, the U.S. freighter *City of Flint*, a prize Hitler did not need. *Flint* became the eye of a diplomatic storm which ended only after a Norwegian vessel intercepted her and returned her to her American crew. The tale of *Graf Spee* was very different, however. Commanded by Hans Langsdorff, a gallant, Wilhelmine anachronism, *Spee* had sent nine British cargo ships to the bottom without the loss of a single German life.

His adversary now was Commodore Henry Harwood, RN, and His Majesty's South Atlantic Fleet. Finding a single ship in so broad a vastness was almost impossible, but it was also crucial; *Graf Spee* was not only terrorizing merchant captains; the hunt for her was tying down over twenty Allied warships badly needed elsewhere, among them the carrier *Ark Royal*, the battle cruiser *Renown*, and the French battleship *Strasbourg*. Harwood believed that sooner or later Langsdorff would be irresistibly drawn to the fat, rich merchantmen emerging from the broad estuary of the River Plate, bound for England. He was right. Unfortunately, when the *Spee* hove into view at 5:52 on the morning of December 13, Harwood's force was no match for her. His heavyweights were elsewhere, too far to be recalled in time. He commanded three vessels: the British heavy cruiser *Exeter*, with six eight-inch guns; and two light cruisers, *Ajax* (his flagship) and the New Zealand *Achilles*, with six-inchers. The range of the German battleship's eleven-inchers was fifteen miles.

The commodore had issued a standing order to all RN vessels in the South Atlantic; should they find a Nazi battleship they were to "attack at once by day or night." Now, after scattering his small command so that Langsdorff would confront warships from three different directions, he sent *Exeter* racing toward Langsdorff at flank speed, 33 knots. Because the enemy was lunging forward at 28 knots, the two vessels were approaching one another at 50 miles an hour. *Ajax* and *Achilles* were also pouring it on, but *Exeter* was the first to come within range of Langsdorff's guns, and moments after she did, a 670-pound shell killed the crew manning the starboard torpedo tubes and crippled both communications and the ship's gun control.

But *Exeter* kept closing. Her gunners had just straddled the German ship when another huge shell demolished the wheelhouse and tore away one of the British gun turrets. Still she continued to close. The captain, though wounded, took a compass from one of the lifeboats and organized a line of tars to relay his orders to the helmsman abaft, where the strongest men in the crew, straining aching muscles, turned the cruiser's rudder by hand. They did it, to no avail; two more German shells hit the *Exeter*, one tearing up the deck and gouging out a huge gash on a flank, just above the waterline, while the other left a gaping wound in her port flank. Several fires had broken out in the ship; she was enveloped in smoke; fifty-one seamen lay dead. But *Exeter* had done her job, for *Ajax* and *Achilles* now had the *Panzerschiffe*. They were within range, their gunners were skilled veterans, and their six-inch shells were riddling the *Graf Spee*. After ninety minutes of continuous combat, with the pocket battleship swinging about, trying to decide which of the three attackers threatened her most, Harwood ordered his captains to make smoke and break off action.

The mauled *Exeter* headed for the Falkland Islands and repair. *Ajax* and *Achilles* were less battered, though the captain of the *Achilles* had been wounded in both legs and *Ajax*'s after gun turrets had been knocked out. The real loser, however, was Langsdorff. He himself had been hit by one British shell; his casualty list included thirty-seven men killed in action. His ship was a wreck. She had been hit eighteen times. Gaping holes had been opened in the deck and both flanks, several guns no longer functioned, her galleys were ruined, and she was almost out of ammunition. A voyage home was out of the question; even if unchallenged she could never make it. Repairs were essential. He limped into neutral — but anti-Nazi — Uruguay and asked for two weeks to put his ship in shape. He was given seventy-two hours. *Ajax* and *Achilles*, he knew, would be radioing for reinforcements. He did what he thought was sensible. His men were given berths on German freighters in the port, his ship was scuttled, and he himself, after wrapping himself in an old banner of imperial Germany — *not* the Nazi swastika — shot himself. He left a note: "For a captain with a sense of honor, it goes without saying that his personal fate cannot be separated from that of his ship."

The Royal Navy's triumph, wrote Churchill, "gave intense joy to the British nation and enhanced our prestige throughout the world. The spectacle of the three smaller British ships unhesitatingly attacking and putting to flight their far more heavily gunned and armoured antagonist was everywhere admired." His youngest daughter remembers: "It was a glorious victory, and brought a gleam of light into a dark December." Harwood was knighted and made an admiral. The sea lords proposed to leave *Exeter* in the Falklands, unrepaired, until the end of the war, but Winston would have none of it. Instead, he proposed to bring Sir Henry and his British ships home. He had not exaggerated the country's elation; acclaiming the heroes would guarantee their remembrance and give civilian morale a badly needed lift.[41]

By now Churchill had established his authority over the Admiralty. "Conveniently forgotten," one historian writes, was "his role in scaling down the navy's cruiser-building programme when Chancellor of the Exchequer in 1924–29. Remembered was his experience of the Admiralty, his love of the sea and the navy, his deep knowledge of the role of sea power in British history, and his reputation for getting things done." His weakness was his love of gadgetry and wildly improbable schemes. Admiral J. H. Godfrey notes: "Anything unusual or odd or dramatic intrigued him: Q ships, dummy ships, the stillborn operation 'Catherine' " (of this, more presently), "deception, sabotage, and, no doubt influenced by Professor Lindemann, the application of novel scientific methods."[42]

In retrospect some of his projects seem absurd. "White Rabbit Number 6," as he called it, was a "trench-cutting tank," capable of excavating an earthwork six feet deep and three feet wide at a rate of one mile an hour. Weighing 130 tons, standing eight feet tall, and stretching eighty feet long, it was to be used at night, penetrating the enemy's lines and taking him by surprise. The cabinet approved it; no one seems to have asked how surprise could be achieved by a device whose noise would be deafening. At the Admiralty, according to Godfrey, these schemes were regarded as outlets for the first lord's "demonic energy and extraordinary imagination," and generally tolerated, though some were considered "offensive." One pet project was an antiaircraft device which he called the Naval Wire Barrage (NWB). It looked like a large umbrella stand. In reality it was a multiple launcher into which were crammed fourteen three-inch projectiles, each carrying two thousand feet of wire with a small parachute at one end and a two-pound bomb at the other. Once the launcher had been rocketed aloft, the projectiles would be ejected at four thousand feet downward, their descent slowed by the parachutes. If an aircraft struck a wire, the bomb would be drawn upward and explode when it hit the plane's wing. It was the Prof's idea. Churchill thought NWBs marvelous, and despite his Ordnance Department's advice he ordered forty of the ungainly contraptions mounted on forty RN ships. They proved worthless. Rear Admiral R. D. Nicholls puts it bluntly: "The NWB was considered by everyone except Winston as plain crazy." Then he takes the larger view: "It was just part of the price — and not a very high one — that had to be paid to keep Winston going. Without him Britain and the Free World were sunk."[43]

In fact, as the war progressed, many of his ideas were to generate highly useful innovations: "Window" (strips of tinfoil dropped by bombers to confuse enemy radar), "Pluto" (a pipeline under the Channel), "Gee" (a device for guiding pilots), and "Mulberry" (the artificial harbors used in the D day invasion of Hitler's Europe).

What was needed now was a concept, a device, *something* that would make submarining so dangerous that Karl Dönitz would be walking the Kurfürstendamm looking for a job. Thus far, nothing had been found that surpassed the last war's answer to the U-boat, the destroyer. Unfortunately, the Royal Navy was incredibly short of destroyers — and the prospects for more were dim. "It is most disconcerting," Winston wrote Rear Admiral Fraser at the start of the war, "that we only get six destroyers in the present year, then no more for nine months, and only three more in the whole of 1940. Nine destroyers in sixteen months," he declared, "cannot possibly be accepted." Later, in his memoirs, he wrote: "Destroyers were our most urgent need, and also our worst feature."[44]

Here was a void that wanted filling. He hadn't forgotten the Nazi peril in the sky, so he called for the design and mass production of an "antisubmarine and anti-air vessel," built with "the greatest simplicity of armament and equipment" to free the few destroyers in commission for duty elsewhere. The ships he had in mind, he wrote in an Admiralty memorandum, "will be deemed 'Cheap and Nasties' (cheap to us, nasty to the U-boat)." Because they would be "built for a particular but urgent job," they would be useless once their mission was accomplished. Not to worry; the important thing was to "get the job done." The Prof, now working full time at the Admiralty, told him modern warfare could certainly be nasty, but never inexpensive. The *Unterseewaffe* threat would continue to grow. The Admiralty would have to fight back with its very thin line of destroyers.[45]

Most senior naval officers who worked with Winston allude to this quintessential Victorian trait — the late Victorians believed inventors could accomplish anything, and in the world of their limited imagination they were right. Yet these same officers had exaggerated claims for asdic before Winston saw or heard it. And he and the Prof (whom the admirals had come to detest) *did* contribute to technological warfare. One early contribution was Britian's effective response to the magnetic mine. Here Churchill revealed the double standard found in all warriors; a weapon is admirable if his side has found it first, despicable if found first by the enemy. In a memorandum to Inskip a year earlier, he suggested that disabling the Kiel Canal would be a prime objective in any war with the Reich, and recommended that "*special fuses with magnetic actuation*" be considered. But while the British were still studying the problem, the Germans solved it. In the first weeks of the war their magnetic mines, dropped by parachute in shallow waters of channels and harbors and activated when a ship passed over them, became a nightmare for merchantmen.[46]

Winston was outraged. The "Nahrzees" (he was working on that idiosyncratic delivery, and each time, he came closer to making "Nazi" sound like an unspeakably vulgar moist petard) had stolen his idea. Briefly he persuaded himself that the device itself was criminal. The new mines, he said, were "contrary to the accepted rules of sea warfare," and he told the House of Commons: "This is about the lowest form of warfare that can be imagined. It is the warfare of the I.R.A., leaving the bomb in the parcels' office at the railway station. The magnetic mine . . . may perhaps be Herr Hitler's much vaunted secret weapon. It is certainly a characteristic weapon, and one that will no doubt be for ever associated with his name." Lacking a specimen of the mine, no counter could be devised. Then, as Churchill wrote, "fortune . . . favoured us." The night of November 22 a Nazi plane was seen dropping a large object, attached to a parachute, into the mud of the Thames estuary off Shoeburyness. Before dawn two RN officers skilled in underwater weapons retrieved the device, which, as suspected, turned out to be a magnetic mine. Here the Prof intervened, devising a method of demagnetizing ships by girdling them with an electric coil — degaussing, as it is called. Before the winter was out, Winston had his own magnetic mines and had forwarded a plan to sow the Rhine with ten thousand fluvial mines, only to have it vetoed in the spring by the French, who feared Nazi reprisals.[47]

Franklin Roosevelt later said: "Winston has fifty ideas a day, and three or four are good." He was no crank; when he hit the jackpot it was the mother lode. Although the Germans were the first to produce the magnetic mine, their very success demonstrated that his conception had been sound. Most of his schemes were politely discussed and then dropped. The difficulty was that his Admiralty staff was dealing with genius, with a man who thought in cosmic terms, and that the price for some of these excursions was beyond the grasp of career naval officers.

So it was with "Catherine," named after Catherine the Great, "because," he explained, "Russia lay in the background of my thought." Churchill introduced this proposed operation to his closest advisers in a five-page outline on September 12, Britain's tenth day at war. Unlike the rest of the Admiralty, Churchill had stopped speculating over where the Kriegsmarine would strike next and instead considered a Royal Navy counteroffensive. Thinking defensively, his admirals had assumed that if they could keep U-boat sinkings of Britain-bound merchantmen to a minimum and blockade enemy ports, they would have done their job, leaving it up to the soldiers to do theirs. But the first lord was taking a very different line. He was talking about a naval strategy which had never entered their minds, and as he talked, they wished it hadn't entered his. The command of the Baltic Sea, as he later pointed out in his memoirs, was "vital to the enemy. Scandinavian supplies, Swedish ore, and above all protection against Russian descents on the long undefended northern coastline of Germany — in one place little more than a hundred miles from Berlin — made it imperative for the German Navy to dominate the Baltic." Moreover, as he had noted earlier, an "attack upon the Kiel Canal" would render "that side-door from the Baltic useless, even if only at intervals."[48]

Churchill was contemplating an imaginative — and perilous — action: the seizure of the entire Baltic, the Reich's only sea link with Norway, Finland, and especially Sweden, the Ruhr's chief source of iron ore. He knew it would be difficult, but no one could doubt that success would bring Hitler to his knees. His source of raw materials for tanks, artillery, mortars, and rifles would be cut off.

A critical challenge lay in the narrow waters joining the North Sea and the Baltic; navigation of them by a strong fleet would attract swarms of Luftwaffe bombers. Winston had already discussed possible solutions with the Admiralty's director of naval construction. "It would . . . be necessary," he noted in his September 12 memorandum, "to strengthen the armour deck so as to give exceptional protection against air attack." He planned to commit two British battleships ("but of course 3 would be better") with fifteen-inch guns; "their only possible antagonists" would be the *Scharnhorst* and the *Gneisenau*, "the sole resources of Germany" in the battleship class. Both would be destroyed by the heavier guns of the British battleships, which would outrange them and "would shatter them." Escorting them, and shielding them, would be a dozen vessels yet to be built, "mine bumpers," he called them, with "a heavy fore end to take the shock of any exploding mine." Confiding only in Pound, he set down the five-page précis of his plan, marked "Most Secret." He wrote: "I commend these ideas to your study, hoping that the intention will be to solve the difficulties." Distribution of Catherine was confined to eight copies, "of which all except one," he wrote, "will be destroyed after the necessary examination has been made."[49]

Pound commented: "There can be little doubt that if we could maintain control of the Baltic for a considerable period it would greatly enhance our prestige." But the first sea lord saw difficulties. If the Soviet Union became a Nazi ally, the operation was doomed. The "*active* cooperation of Sweden" in providing a base, repair facilities, and oil must be assured, and the British ships committed must be expendable, "such that we can with our Allies at that time win the war without [them], in spite of any probable combination against us." Winston scrawled, "I entirely agree." To him Catherine had become "the supreme naval offensive open to the Royal Navy." Others receiving Winston's presentation studied it seriously and thought it feasible if . . . And then they, too, saw problems. The decisive problem was air power. Even admirals who underrated it had to consider the Luftwaffe threat. Battleships could be taken into the Baltic, but RAF fighters could not accompany them; the ships would be under constant, heavy attack from land-based enemy aircraft. Churchill dismissed the Luftwaffe. He wrote Roosevelt: "We have not been at all impressed by the accuracy of the German air bombing of our warships. They seem to have no effective bomb sights." In any event, he held, the ship's antiaircraft gunners could eliminate the air threat.[50]

He convinced no one. The support for Catherine, never strong, faded away. Moreover, it seems not to have occurred to Winston that the Nazis could occupy Denmark, move heavy artillery to the shore, and lay mines in the Kogrund Channel. Catherine died a slow, quiet, expensive death. Apart from preempting the time of Britain's best naval minds, twelve million pounds was spent on special equipment for the battleships' escorts. Churchill was disappointed, but because the entire plan had been highly classified he faced no barrage of criticism. Indeed, his reputation at the Admiralty shone as brightly as ever. The general verdict among the sea lords and other senior officials was that Catherine had been brilliantly conceived, that it could have ended the war if successful, but that too much had been at stake — and the ice too thin for skating.

Slowly the Admiralty came to realize that while the first lord might be dissuaded from this or that, he never lost because he never quit; his mind had many tracks, and if one was blocked, he left it and turned to another, the very existence of which was unknown until he chose to reveal it. Admiral Fraser, the flag officer responsible for naval construction, later wrote how Winston stunned him by asking him point-blank: "Well, Admiral, what is the navy doing about RDF?" Fraser was tongue-tied. Radar was the most closely guarded secret in the British military establishment, roughly comparable to America's Manhattan Project three years later. "A number of able officers were working on the problem," Fraser later wrote, "but to make any real progress a high degree of priority — especially in finance — was essential."[51]

Fully developed RDF had been a casualty of Chamberlain's cuts in military spending. England should have had a long lead with this extraordinary defensive weapon; Englishmen had discovered and perfected it, and Zossen didn't even know it existed. Yet not a single vessel in the Royal Navy had been equipped with it. After a long silence Churchill said, "Well, Admiral, it is very important," and later sent Fraser an instruction that all British warships, particularly "those engaged in the U-boat fighting," be provided "with this distinguishing apparatus." Fraser wondered how Churchill, a backbencher until the day England declared war on Germany, had heard about RDF. His bewilderment would have deepened had he known that Winston's knowledge of radar dated from July 25, 1935 — within twenty-four hours of Robert Watson-Watt's completion of experiments proving that the distance and direction of approaching aircraft could be pinpointed by using radio waves.[52]

If all the views of Churchill's months at the Admiralty are pooled — Winston seen in the letters, diaries, memoirs, and recollections of those who worked under him then and were close enough to reach informed judgments — a striking portrait emerges. It is distorted as Picasso's *Les Demoiselles d'Avignon* is distorted, complex and defying proportion but recognizable as the powerful image of an emerging warlord. The approval or disapproval of the witnesses is essentially irrelevant. They see him differently because he is different to each, possessing a plural, kaleidoscopic personality. His guise depends upon the man confronting him, and what he wants that man to see.

The first sea lord outranks the others and is closest to him. His admiration for Churchill is almost unqualified. No one in the Royal Navy can launch a direct attack on the first lord because Sir Dudley Pound, a great sailor and a man of absolute integrity, will deflect the blow. Pound's loyalty is reinforced by the first lord's popularity in the fleet. Captain S. W. Roskill, the distinguished naval historian, challenges this popularity, noting that "There was not one Admiral in an important sea command . . . whom Churchill, sometimes with Pound's support, did not attempt to have relieved." But admirals are not the fleet. Below decks, support for the first lord is strong. The ratings admire a fighter; they have heard of his concern for their welfare, which is genuine, and see him as a stimulating, inspiring first lord. Winston's constituency, then, is solidly behind him.[53]

He needs that support because a warlord, by definition, is a man with enemies. His natural aggression, curbed in peacetime, a stigma only a year earlier, is now a virtue. He cannot compromise, nor should he. Leaders in battle are guided less by reason than by instinct. He has always distrusted Eamon de Valera, and now in the War Cabinet he proposes that England reclaim her former bases in Eire, by force if necessary. Even Pound knows that the navy has no use for the bases and can easily deny them to the Germans. Churchill is wrong. Nevertheless, Englishmen approve, remembering: *Churchill stood up to the IRA*. Sir Andrew Cunningham, the RN's Mediterranean commander in chief, protests the first lord's repeated interference in tactical issues, telling him not only what to do, but how to do it. Commanders in chief in other theaters have the same grievance but wisely remain silent. Cunningham wins little sympathy in England. *Churchill has shown him who's in charge*. Winston has issued an order — "Plan R" — for strengthening the defenses at Scapa Flow. Contracts are signed. Nothing happens. He issues a general order to the Admiralty, reminding all hands of the time lag since Plan R was approved, and asks: "What, in fact, has been done since? How many blockships sunk? How many nets made? How many men have been in work for how many days? What buildings have been erected? What gun sites have been concreted and prepared? What progress has been made with the run-ways of the aerodrome? I thought we settled two months ago to have a weekly report. . . . Up to the present I share the Commander-in-Chief's anxieties about the slow progress of this indispensable work."[54]

That is on a Monday. On Tuesday Scapa is a hive of construction activity. R. D. Oliver, the officer responsible for Plan R, recalls: "With his backing it was amazing how bureaucratic obstruction melted." The impression: *Churchill gets things done*.[55]

In the House of Commons he consistently overstates the number of Nazi U-boats destroyed. His old adversaries make much of that, but this is war; facts are its first casualties. Leaders exaggerate the enemy's losses and inflate their own triumphs. To do otherwise would be interpreted, in the eyes of his people and his foes, as a sign of weakness. Donald McLachan, who understands this, writes afterward: "The First Lord had a morale role to play. The

Navy was the only Service which was fully engaged at the time; it must not be discouraged by too rigorous a method of assessing 'kills'; it was essential that the nation should have some sense of action and success and achievement; and the only material that was readily available at that time came from the U-boat war. It was essential to make the most of what was happening [though] in the process truth suffered." Significantly, in less than a year the RAF will play faster and looser with *its* kill figures, but its records will go virtually unchallenged. There is no Churchill at the Air Ministry to incite critics.[56]

Nevertheless Churchill is disqualified, by temperament, from waging an effective campaign against U-boats. He has known from the beginning that if Britain loses the duel with Nazi submarines she cannot survive. The high priority he gives to converting trawlers into antisub vessels and his emphasis on destroyer production will contribute to the Admiralty's eventual success. The difficulty is that all this is *defensive,* and he is comfortable only when carrying the war to the enemy. He overrates the asdic. Worse, he withdraws destroyers from convoys to form "hunting groups" or "attacking groups," directing them to seek and destroy U-boats. This is "aggressive," he argues; convoy duty, on the other hand, is "passive." He minutes to Pound — who agrees — that "Nothing can be more important in the anti-submarine war than to try to obtain an independent flotilla which could work like a cavalry division." He is dead wrong; weakening convoys to permit offensive sweeps fails on both counts — no U-boats are sunk, and their elusive commanders, seizing opportunities while the destroyers are looking for them elsewhere, penetrate convoys with alarming results. Yet Churchill will stick to his "hunt 'em down" strategy after he becomes prime minister. Not until 1942, when the effectiveness of the convoy strategy has been demonstrated beyond all doubt, does he accept it without reservation.[57]

Meetings of the full cabinet, the War Cabinet, and the Land Forces Committee engage him in frequent and often lengthy colloquies with men against whom he has been waging parliamentary guerrilla warfare for the better part of a decade. He bears no grudges — "The only man I hate is Hitler," he says, "and that's professional" — but some of his adversaries are less generous. Although the year since Munich should have humbled them, humility is a rare virtue among men of this class, especially at this time. Sam Hoare was first lord in 1936 and 1937; he cannot evade some of the responsibility for the neglect of Scapa's defenses, without which Lieutenant Commander Prien's feat would have been impossible. Yet if Hoare has ever suffered a pang of guilt, no one has heard him acknowledge it. In the first days of the war he *was* heard describing Churchill as "an old man who easily gets tired," a judgment which would startle those at the Admiralty trying to match the old man's pace. According to John Reith, whom Chamberlain brings into the government as minister of information, the prime minister says Churchill's reputation is "inflated," largely "based on broadcasts." Reith, who would have prevented those broadcasts if Winston hadn't been a minister, agrees, and notes in his diary that there is "no doubt" about how the P.M. "feels about Churchill." Early in the war Hoare tells Beaverbrook that at meetings Winston is "very rhetorical, very emotional, and, most of all, very reminiscent." Actually, the Cabinet Papers show that Churchill, like everyone else at the time, is trying to understand what is happening in Poland.[58]

❧ ❧

blitz · krieg . . . [G, lit., lightning war, fr. *blitz* lightning + *krieg* war]. . . .

So the word appears in *Webster's Third New International Dictionary*, presented as a term borrowed from the German. The anonymous journalist who first used it in an English periodical clearly agreed. "In the opening stage of the war," he wrote in the October 7, 1939, issue of *War Illustrated*, "all eyes were turned on Poland, where the German military machine was engaged in *Blitz-Krieg* — lightning war — with a view to ending it as soon as possible." In fact, the term "lightning war," like the concept itself, was of British origin. The bloody stalemate of 1914–1918 had bred pacifism and isolationism among civilians. Professional soldiers — and one statesman, Churchill — agreed that a reprise of trench warfare, with its adumbrations of stalemate and lethal attrition, was unthinkable.

They doubted, however, that it could be abolished; like Plato they believed that only the dead have seen the end of war. Therefore, men like Major General J. F. C. Fuller and Captain Basil Liddell Hart, searching for an alternative, studied Great War engagements in which tanks had been used successfully. Working out the theoretical possibilities of a totally mechanized offensive, they evolved the doctrine of mobile warfare, combining tanks and tactical aircraft. Commenting on the Wehrmacht's Polish campaign Liddell Hart wrote: "When the theory had been originally developed, in Britain, its action had been depicted in terms of the play of 'lightning.' From now on, aptly but ironically, it came into worldwide currency under the title of 'Blitzkrieg' — the German rendering."[59]

It might also have been christened *guerre d'éclairs*, for in Paris Colonel Charles de Gaulle, working independently, as always, had reached the same conclusion: "*la fluidité*" would be imperative on battlefields of the future and must be achieved, for "the sword is the axis of the world." But neither England nor France was interested in military innovation between the wars. Victors rarely are. Professional soldiers are wedded to tradition and resent change; politicians and the public flinch at the prospect of slaughter.[60]

The Conseil Supérieur had dismissed de Gaulle as an eccentric; Fuller, who had a knack for rubbing people the wrong way, was forced into early retirement; Liddell Hart was regarded as an entertaining writer with beguiling but impractical ideas.

Colonel Heinz Guderian, an enthusiastic reader of Fuller and Liddell Hart, was luckier. In the years before the Republic of Germany became the Third Reich, Guderian's superiors, like their fellow generals in England and France, were skeptical of mobile warfare. But he was among the ablest officers in the Reichswehr, the Wehrmacht's precursor, and so they threw him a sop — command of an armored battalion. He had no tanks, only automobiles with canvas superstructures identified by cardboard signs, PANZER or PANZERWAGEN, and aircraft had to be imagined. Then came Hitler. Like Churchill, the new Reich chancellor was fascinated by technical innovation. He first visited army maneuvers in the spring of 1933, and while other spectators were amused by Guderian's performance, Hitler instantly grasped its possibilities. He cried: "That's what I need! That's what I want!"[61]

Later Goebbels tried — with considerable success — to convince the world that every German division invading Poland was armored. Actually only nine were; the other forty-seven comprised familiar, foot-slogging infantrymen, wearing the same coal-scuttle helmets, the same field gray uniforms, and equipped much as their fathers had been on the Somme, in Flanders, and in the Argonne. That does not slight them; the Führer's soldiers were the best fighting men in Europe, and their morale was now at fever pitch. But it was the panzers which were terrifying. Each of Guderian's divisions was self-contained, comprising two tank regiments, self-propelled guns, and supporting units — engineers, reconnaissance companies, antitank and antiaircraft batteries, signalmen, and a regiment of infantry — transported on trucks or armored half-tracks. The Poles prayed for rain; commentators talked about "General Mud," as though World War II might be called off because of bad weather. But God wasn't riding at the Poles' stirrups that golden month. In 1870 and 1914 men in spiked helmets had talked of *Kaiserwetter*. Now it was *Hitlerwetter*, and Guderian's men found the dry, rolling plains of Poland ideal for maneuver.

The Poles were confident; they were overconfident; they were eager for battle, buoyed by Radio Warsaw, which played the national anthem, Chopin, and martial music, over and over. By the standards of 1920, when Poles had last seen action — against the Bolsheviks — they possessed a fine army: two million men under arms, with another million hurrying to the front. Twelve splendid brigades of horse cavalry were the pride of Poland. But they had only one armored brigade. Its tanks were obsolete. So were the air force's warplanes. And the battle plan of Marshal Edward Rydz-Smigly was a bad Polish joke. Since the Nazi occupation of Czechoslovakia had left the Poles with an immensely long frontier, it would have been prudent — it would have been sane — to assemble farther back. Instead, Rydz-Smigly decided to fight on the frontier, with no reserves behind his men and no defensive preparations. Their defense, he told incredulous military attachés from the Allied embassies, would be the counterattack.

Indulging his national pride, which his troops shared, over a third of his troops were concentrated in the Polish Corridor, exposed to Germans attacking from both east and west. Because of this stratagem, tracts more vital to Poland's defense were left thinly manned. Perhaps the mind-set of the Polish military on the eve of battle is best illustrated by Rydz-Smigly's high hopes for one unit, the crack Pomorska Cavalry Brigade. As the spearhead of Guderian's First Panzer Division appeared in the valley below, white-gloved officers signaled trumpeters, who sounded the charge. Down the slope rode the Pomorskas, sabers gleaming, pennons waving, moving at a steady gallop, their lances at the ready. And then, as they were preparing for the final irresistible surge, the Germans squeezed their triggers. The limbs, viscera, and skin — of men and horses, inextricably tangled — spewed gorily for over a mile. The few Polish survivors were taken prisoner. They were seen rapping hard on the tanks' armor. Somebody had told them German armor, like Guderian's mock panzers of 1933, was cardboard, and someone had been wrong.

Elsewhere Poles heard an ominous hum and looked up to see squadron after squadron of bombers — nearly four thousand of them — headed for Warsaw, where, by midafternoon, they annihilated the Polish air force, such as it was, on the ground. Poland's one million reservists never reached their units; the Luftwaffe blew up the railroad stations where they waited, or the trains they had already boarded. Then it bombed radio stations, bridges, factories, barracks, and public buildings. Before heading home to the Reich the bombers sowed incendiary and high-explosive bombs among the densest concentrations of civilians, including children's playgrounds. Farmers who had never held a weapon larger than a shotgun saw rapid-firing, self-propelled guns rolling down the rutted dirt roads at forty miles an hour. What they did not see, and would not have believed if they saw it, was the intricate communications net — telegraph, telephone, and radio — which coordinated the huge juggernaut.

The Polish soldiers on the frontier, each standing in front of a single hastily strung strand of barbed wire, each assuming that the high-level, Warsaw-bound bombers had been the entire Luftwaffe, were in for a shock. It was *half* the Luftwaffe. Now came the rest of it, meant for them, led by the Junkers 87 dive-bombers — the Stukas. The Stuka was more than a bomber; it was also an instrument of fear. Many had sirens attached to their undercarriages, and as the plane dove vertically, the ear-splitting siren convinced every Pole that it, and its bomb load, was headed straight for him. The Ju 87s left. It was time for the invading army to launch its ground attack. Guderian's panzers came in the first wave — motorcycles followed by armored cars, then tanks, then trucks bearing artillery and infantry. To the Poles' bewilderment, these Germans were not seeking a fight. They deliberately avoided pitting strength against strength, preferring to probe for soft spots. Eventually, given Rydz-Smigly's dispositions, they would find one, lunge through, and fan out, destroying communications, machine-gunning Poles who thought themselves safe behind the front, and — here tactics merged with strategy — splitting the Polish army into fragments, each out of touch with the others. When the marshal's headquarters tried to maneuver the troops, either the lines were dead or troop movement was impossible because panicky Polish civilians had choked the roads. This frenzy was encouraged by Nazis who, simulating Polish news programs with German commentators fluent in Polish, told the people to flee down the very roads Rydz-Smigly most needed. The Germans had enlarged the compass of military science. They had discovered how to exploit the very people defending armies are supposed to protect — the young, the aged, the women trembling at the prospect of rape — by encouraging them to ensnarl the defenders' rear.

By Sunday, September 3, when England and France finally declared war on Germany, the fighting in Poland was in its third day, and the situation of the defenders was critical. The Poles now had no air force. The country's railroad grid was in ruins. All bridges, except those which were useful to the Nazis, had been demolished. The Wehrmacht's troops, healthy and strong, were led by some of the greatest generals in German history — Gerd von Rundstedt, Heinz Guderian, Walter von Reichenau, Fedor von Bock, Paul von Kleist, Günther von Kluge, Georg von Küchler — all, indeed, except Erich von Manstein, who was planning the invasion of the Low Countries and France. Already the Polish frontier had been deeply penetrated by three great German drives, each advancing on Warsaw: eight divisions from East Prussia, twelve from Pomerania, and another seventeen — the main thrust,

886,000 men — heading straight for the capital from Silesia in the south. That Sunday, after the British declaration of hostilities but before France's, Kluge's 630,000 men had cut off the corridor and were advancing southeastward along both banks of the Vistula, toward the capital. All other commanders had reached their objectives and were engaged in complex envelopments, double envelopments, and encircling movements, incomprehensible to laymen in other countries, who nevertheless grasped their essence — that with the war less than seventy-two hours old, the defense of Poland was already disintegrating.

In London it was *hot*. Churchill could not recall a more pitiless heat wave. He wore a black alpaca jacket over a linen shirt and reflected that this was "indeed just the weather that Hitler wanted for his invasion of Poland. The great rivers on which the Poles had counted in their defensive plan were nearly everywhere fordable, and the ground was hard and firm for the movement of tanks and vehicles of all kinds." The War Cabinet, he wrote, stood "around the Cabinet table," witnessing the beginnings of "the swift and almost mechanical destruction of a weaker state according to Hitler's method and long design."[62]

It was hard to believe that the Poles actually had a quarter-million more men under arms than the invaders. "Each morning," Churchill later recalled, "the CIGS, General Ironside, standing before the map, gave long reports and appreciations which very soon left no doubt in our minds that the resistance of Poland would speedily be crushed. Each day I reported to the Cabinet the Admiralty tale, which usually consisted of a list of British merchant ships sunk by the U-boats." On Monday spearheads of Reichenau's panzers — which had jumped off from Jablunkov Pass in the Carpathian Mountains only three days earlier — reached and crossed the Pilica, fifty miles behind the Polish frontier. On Tuesday, the day Dönitz's submarines sank the *Royal Sceptre* and the *Bosnia*, Ironside told them that several panzer divisions had overrun the Poles' defenses at Czestochowa — a breakthrough "that might result in Germany capturing Poland's main industrial area" and the withdrawal of Rydz-Smigly's army to the line of the Vistula. Even now, however, no one in the Cabinet Room envisaged the disappearance of organized Polish resistance. They were remembering how the great German offensive of 1914 had been stopped in the Battle of the Marne and wondering when and where the Poles would roll back the field gray tide. But this was not 1914, and the Vistula was not the Marne.[63]

London newspapers on September 4 reported another bombardment of Warsaw; civilian casualties were said to be heavy. Labour MPs, remembering Guernica, were calling for British action. So, within the government, was Churchill. That morning, at the second meeting of the War Cabinet, he pointed out that the "main German effort" was against the Poles and proposed that "every means possible should be employed to relieve the pressure," starting with an immediate attack on the Siegfried Line carried out by French infantry and the RAF. The rest of the War Cabinet agreed that such a move was "a vital necessity."[64]

It was indeed. To do otherwise would be dishonorable; the world would conclude that pledges by His Majesty's Government and the Third Republic were as worthless as Hitler's. The first article of the Anglo-Polish treaty signed ten days earlier specified: "Should one of the contracting parties become engaged in hostilities with a European Power in consequence of aggression by the latter . . . the other contracting party will at once give the contracting party engaged in hostilities all the support and assistance in its power," and the second paragraph stipulated that each country was committed to the use of force even in the absence of aggression, in the event of "any action . . . which clearly threatened, directly or indirectly, the independence of one of the contracting parties."[65]

The rub was that Britain, an island, shared no border with Germany. It had the Royal Navy and the RAF, but the Poles had not been challenged at sea, and the limited range of aircraft then ruled out intervention by Britain-based warplanes in the skies over Poland. Poland needed an army, and England didn't have one. On land, writes Telford Taylor, Britain was "still almost in the position of a nineteenth-century Asiatic state challenging with the traditional arms of the past a European power armed with modern artillery and machine guns." In 1914 Churchill, as first lord, had ferried seven superbly trained British divisions across the Channel. He was preparing to repeat this feat, but it was impossible now; the men weren't there; Britain's standing army was so small as to be embarrassing. All the War Office could send now was four divisions. Winston noted that at best this could be called "a symbolic contribution." He had been appalled to find that although England had been "the cradle of the tank in all its variants," the "awful gap" in this symbolic contingent was "the absence of even one armoured division in the British Expeditionary Force."[66]

The War Cabinet's Land Forces Committee met September 7, on what Winston called a "sweltering afternoon," at the Home Office with Hoare in the chair, and decided, after hearing the views of the army's high command, to "forthwith begin the creation of a fifty-five division army," hoping that "by the eighteenth month, two-thirds of this . . . would either already have been sent to France or be fit to take the field." The Air Ministry protested; it planned to build an enormous air force in two or three years, and "the full army programme could not be realized in the time limits of two years without serious interference with the air programme." That took a moment to sink in. The protester — a veteran civil servant who had been permanent under secretary to the Air Ministry when Winston was its minister between 1919 and 1920 — was objecting to army expansion before 1942. Now, in 1939, it was too late to save Poland, but a gesture should be made. To leave the French army standing alone was unthinkable. London was blacked out; Britain could not tell when her turn would come, but expected a massive Luftwaffe raid at any time, and here were the service bureaucracies talking of three-year plans, five-year plans, unaware that by 1942 all London might be reduced to an unrecognizable, uninhabited scene of desolation. In a meeting of the full War Cabinet, Kingsley Wood repeated the Air Ministry argument: the RAF insisted upon priority; the army would have to wait. Churchill vigorously replied to this position and set down his thoughts in a secret memorandum: "I cannot think that less than twenty divisions by March 1, 1940, would be fair to the French army. . . . We must take our place in the Line if we are to hold the Alliance together and win the war."[67]

It was a sensible point, but Chamberlain's men had developed a habit of attributing the lowest motives to him. In his diary Hoare noted that one man had whispered to him, "He is writing his new memoirs," and Oliver Stanley, president of the Board of Trade — in a reference to *The World Crisis,* Churchill's history of the last war — said bitingly, "Why did he not bring his *World War?*" Chamberlain hesitated; he finally endorsed the recommendations of the Land Forces Committee, but the committee's report contained some disquieting predictions. The French army, it said, would probably "require assistance" in equipping its men "after the first four months of the war." And yet, the report went on to say that perhaps France could help in remedying certain of *Britain's* deficiencies. Clementine Churchill, reading the War Office's shopping list later, commented: "It shews the interminable distance we had to travel before we could fight."[68]

Before England could fight she needed, not only troops and arms but also a government of fighting ministers, men prepared — as soldiers must be — to sacrifice everything, including their lives, toward a great objective, the destruction of Nazi Germany. Churchill was such a man. Despite his membership in the cabinet, however, he was virtually alone. The rest of the government was schizoid. Their faith had failed; they were like simple folk who have been told yesterday that the world would end today and have found the prophecy a fraud. Nevertheless, they remained evangelists. The appeasers were still devout, still hopeful that the shopworn messiah at No. 10 would be vindicated. But now England was at war, a war she could lose — would certainly lose if their advice prevailed.

Friday morning, September 8, the war was five days old, and in his briefing Ironside told the War Cabinet that the Poles were "fighting well and had not been broken." Another War Office summary added that although the Poles were "not demoralized," their movements were "much impeded by the overwhelming German superiority in the air and in armoured vehicles." They wanted to know what their allies in the West were doing. The Air Ministry had already received a message from the Polish air attaché in London asking for the "immediate" bombardment of German industries and airports within reach of the RAF. He received no satisfactory reply. That same day Leo Amery approached Kingsley Wood and asked if the government was going to help Poland. Amery suggested dropping incendiary bombs on the Black Forest. "Oh, you can't do that," the air minister said, "that's private property. You'll be asking me to bomb the Ruhr next." Essen's Gusstahlfabrik, the flagship of the Krupp munitions works, should have been leveled already, Amery said, but Kingsley Wood told him that should he do so, "American opinion" would be alienated. In his memoirs Amery wrote that he "went away very angry." Hugh Dalton raised the same question; Kingsley Wood replied that such a mission would be a violation of the Hague Convention, that the RAF must concentrate on "military objectives."[69]

It was still His Majesty's Government's policy to avoid offending Germany; although Great Britain and the Third Reich were at war, Reith's BBC was uncomfortable with criticism of the enemy regime. Reith, now minister of information, denied air time to eminent Englishmen on the ground that they were too critical of Germany. As a cabinet minister Hore-Belisha could not be denied BBC time, and in October he delivered a superb speech on British war aims. They were not fighting to reconstitute Czechoslovakia or Poland, he said: "We are concerned with the frontiers of the human spirit. . . . Only the defeat of Nazi Germany can lighten the darkness which now shrouds our cities, and lighten the horizon for all Europe and the world." Hore-Belisha's days were numbered. Next to Churchill he was the ablest member of the War Cabinet, advocating vigorous prosecution of the war; nevertheless, in January 1940 the prime minister asked for his resignation. Chamberlain wanted to offer him the Ministry of Information, but Halifax objected to the appointment; it would have a "bad effect among the neutrals," he said, "because HB [is] a Jew." Being a Jew was worse in Germany, of course, but under His Majesty's Government at the time it was no character reference.[70]

On Wednesday, September 6, His Majesty's Government assured the House of Commons that the Luftwaffe was bombing "only Polish military objectives." Yet three days earlier the Warsaw government had informed

HMG that twenty-seven towns had been bombed by Nazi planes and over a thousand civilians killed. Edward Spears decided to raise in the House "the question of the lack of support we are giving the Poles," but changed his mind when Kingsley Wood told him the reply would involve "questions of strategy" and to discuss them in public would be "most dangerous." On Saturday, Beck cabled Raczyński, instructing him to raise the issue in Whitehall. On Monday, the Polish ambassador told Cadogan: "This is very unfair to us. The least that we can ask is, what are you prepared to do?" Cadogan promised him an answer by the end of the day. But Raczyński never heard from Cadogan, then or later.[71]

Chamberlain saw the growing anger in the House. He believed he fathomed it. "The Amerys, Duff Coopers, and their lot," he wrote, "are consciously swayed by a sense of frustration because they can only look on." He added: "The personal dislike of Simon and Hoare has reached a pitch which I find difficult to understand." There was a great deal he did not understand; he was neither the first nor the last leader to lose his touch, his feeling for the temper of his people. Once war has been declared, the slate is wiped clean. A leader's peacetime policies are forgotten, even those which led the country into a war it did not want, unless, of course, he is so unwise as to bring them up. Even after the fall of Poland, after Fleet Street had printed evidence of Nazi crimes in Poland — the random murders, then mass executions; the tortures and the seizure of Poles to work in German munitions factories — the prime minister seriously considered a negotiated peace with a Reich purged of the more extreme Nazis. He had a "hunch," he wrote, that the war would end in the spring of 1940. "It won't be by defeat in the field," he wrote, "but by German realization that they *can't* win and that it isn't worth their while to go on getting thinner and poorer when they might have instant relief." If negotiations were successful the Germans might "not have to give up anything they really care about." One pictures Neville Chamberlain in hell, sitting at one end of a table with Satan at the other, each checking off items on his agenda, and a slow, awful expression of comprehension crossing the late P.M.'s face as he realizes that he has just traded his soul for a promise of future negotiations.[72]

One issue which eluded him completely was that the plight of the Poles could not be relieved by Allied defensive warfare in the west. An offensive, or a series of offensives, should be launched, and launched *now,* while the Wehrmacht was committed in Poland. Blood had to be spilled in a drive against the Siegfried Line or in bombing the Reich. An infantry attack on the western front depended upon France. Although the British Expeditionary Force (BEF) was growing in strength every week, the overwhelming majority of the troops there were French, and their decisions would determine the Allied strategy there. The RAF could bomb, but here again France, because of her proximity to the Reich, could cast the decisive vote.

France did. The vote was a veto. The French had ruled out bombing, Chamberlain explained to the War Cabinet, because the Nazis might retaliate by an air attack on one of the Seine bridges. Churchill was aroused, but "I could not move them," he wrote. "When I pressed very hard, they used a method of refusal which I never met before or since. [On one occasion in Paris] M. Daladier told me with an air of exceptional formality that 'The President of the Republic himself had intervened, and that no aggressive action must be taken which might only draw reprisals upon France.' " In his memoirs, Winston commented:

> This idea of not irritating the enemy did not commend itself to me. Hitler had done his best to strangle our commerce by indiscriminate mining of our harbours. We had beaten him by defensive means alone. Good, decent civilised people, it appeared, must never strike themselves till after they have been struck dead. In these days the fearful German volcano and all its subterranean fires drew near to their explosion point. There were still months of pretended war. On the one side endless discussions about trivial points, no decisions taken, or if taken, rescinded, and the rule "Don't be unkind to the enemy, you will only make him angry." On the other, doom preparing — a vast machine grinding forward ready to break upon us![73]

The prime minister, it developed, had decided to avenge the Poles killed in Luftwaffe raids on Warsaw, Cracow, and Katowice by punishing the Reich with "truth raids." In truth raids, leaflets were to be substituted for bombs. This strategy assumed that once Germans read the leaflets describing Hitler's atrocities, they would rise up and overthrow their Nazi leadership. After the first mission over Germany, Kingsley Wood revealed that this ingenious approach had been his inspiration, and that the Nazis in Berlin were deeply troubled by them. They were not without peril for the RAF; German antiaircraft gunners could not distinguish between Blenheims dropping explosives and those distributing the pamphlets threatening the stability of the regime in Berlin; hence British planes were lost. Hoare paid tribute to the truth-raiders. They wrote, he said, "a chapter of heroic bravery, of forlorn hopes, of brilliant improvisation."[74]

Ironside's optimistic briefing of the War Cabinet had been inspired more by the Poles' valor than their military prospects. Yet their élan *was* astonishing. That same Friday the Fourth Panzer Division, attacking Warsaw's southeastern suburbs, was thrown back and Polish divisions around Kutno rallied, counterattacked across the Bzura, and drove the German Eighth Army back for three straight days. It would be a long time before any troops, under any flag, would do anything like that again. They were inspired not solely by determination to preserve their honor — though their gallantry still gleams across nearly a half century — but because they believed they were going to win. They knew they couldn't do it by themselves. That, they thought, was unnecessary. England and France were bound to them in ironclad military alliances. Both powers had declared war on Nazi Germany. The British, they assumed, had unleashed an all-out bombing of the Ruhr, and the French army, the world's strongest, must have penetrated deep into western Germany. If they pinned down the Wehrmacht here, the Poles reasoned, their allies would soon force Hitler to sue for peace.

RAF bombers had been rendered impotent by French fear of Luftwaffe reprisals. Where was the French army? Here the Poles' nemesis was the same officer who three and a half years earlier had, in effect, awarded Hitler the Rhineland by default. Gustave-Maurice Gamelin, a short, timid, rabbity man in his late sixties, was a former aide to Marshal Joseph-Césaire Joffre who had toiled his way upward through the maze of military politics to become *généralissime* of the enormous French army, constable of France, and leader of the combined Anglo-French high command. His rise had been extraordinary, not because he was eccentric — in mufti he was just another nondescript *fonctionnaire* — but because under pressure he became everything a commander ought not to be: indecisive, given to issuing impulsive orders which he almost always countermanded, and timid to and beyond a fault. Illustrative of his unpredictability was his proposal, at the outbreak of war, to invade Germany by lunging across neutral Belgium and Holland, and then, when a shocked cabinet rejected the plan, declaring that any French offensive would be doomed, that the poilus in the Maginot and their comrades above it should sit out the war. There would be more of this sort of thing later. And more. And more.

His performance during the Rhineland crisis should have revealed his incompetence to his civilian superiors. They had asked him for action then, and he had given them excuses. After that he ought to have been relieved of all responsibility for the defense of French soil. But like the rest of the senior officers in their army he had his *patron*, who in his case was Premier Daladier. So he had remained at his high post, and now the price must be paid, not by him, not by Daladier, but by the Poles. The issue of Polish survival was a matter of days, if not hours. France possessed the only force strong enough to save Poland by attacking Germany now. Furthermore, the Franco-Polish Military Convention of May 19, 1939, was more precise than Britain's agreement with the Poles. Drafted by Gamelin and two Polish generals, the convention provided that "the French army shall launch a major offensive in the west [*lancerait une grande offensive a l'ouest*] if the Germans attack Poland." The Poles had asked how many poilus would be available for this drive. "Between thirty-five and thirty-eight divisions," Gamelin had replied. The Poles had also wanted to know what form the attack would take. It was spelled out in the convention: the French army would "progressively launch offensive operations . . . the third day after General Mobilization Day." Yet that deadline had passed without action in Paris.[75]

On August 23, when the German invasion of Poland was imminent, the irresolute French commander in chief — without telling the Poles — had reappraised the military prospects of nations who offended the Führer. As a result, his faith in his army had been shaken, and his confidence in France's political leaders, and himself (this was justifiable), had shrunk. He hoped that by the spring of 1940, with British concurrence and the support of "*matériel américain,*" France would be capable of fighting, if necessary, "*une bataille défensive.*" Then — this from a man who had promised the Poles offensive operations on the third day after mobilization — "My opinion has always been that we could not take the offensive before roughly 1941–1942." The French, in short, had unilaterally renounced the Franco-Polish Military Convention. Despite the fact that his signature was on the document, Gamelin concluded in his memoirs, "Our military protocol had no meaning and [did] not bind us." In his heart, therefore, he was "*satisfait.*" Among other things, he had overlooked an earlier military treaty — still an absolute commitment by the French government — which Marshal Ferdinand Foch had negotiated with the Poles on February 19, 1921, pledging "*effectif et rapide*" support should Poland be confronted by German aggression.[76]

Generals are seldom afflicted by nagging consciences, but then, they seldom betray an embattled ally. Perhaps a pang of guilt moved this commander in chief to point out that French mobilization in itself would bring some relief to Poland "by tying down a certain number of large German units on our frontier." Daladier asked him how long the Poles, abandoned by their allies, could hold out. The *généralissime* replied that he believed they would put up "*une résistance honorable*" which would prevent "*la masse des forces*" of the Reich from turning against France until the English were "*effectivement à nos côtés*" — standing beside them, shoulder to shoulder.[77]

Between them the Poles and the French had 130 divisions against Germany's 98 — really 62, because 36, as Liddell Hart put it, were "virtually untrained and unorganized." Rydz-Smigly's army had but to hold up the Wehrmacht divisions on the eastern front; the French, meantime, could overwhelm the green, second-rate German divisions across the Rhine. The challenge should have daunted no one. Gamelin's forces in the west outnumbered the Germans by at least two to one — four to one, if one is to believe the Nuremberg testimony of OKW General Alfred Jodl, who told the International Military Tribunal that he had expected the Third Reich to collapse in 1939. He attributed its survival "to the fact that during the Polish campaign the approximately 110 French and British divisions in the West were held completely inactive against the 23 German divisions."[78]

Most of the Zossen generals were appalled at Hitler's gamble. To blitz Poland he had stripped the Siegfried Line defenses of armor, artillery, warplanes, and reliable troops, leaving a skeleton force to face Germany's ancient foe in the west. It seemed inconceivable that the French would let so golden an opportunity pass, knowing that a quick Nazi conquest of Poland would free the German Generalstab of its greatest nightmare — a two-front war — and permit the Führer to concentrate the full might of the Wehrmacht in a massive attack, knifing through the Low Countries, into France. Field Marshal Wilhelm Keitel, head of the OKW, recalled that "We soldiers always expected an attack by France during the Polish campaign, and were very surprised that nothing happened. . . . A French attack would have encountered only a German military screen, not a real defense."[79]

General Franz Halder agreed — up to a point. He testified: "The success against Poland was only possible by completely baring our western border." If the French had attacked, he added, "they would have been able to cross the Rhine without our being able to prevent it" and taken the Ruhr area, "the most decisive factor" in the German conduct of the war. Yet Halder, who had greater respect for Hitler's military intuition than his fellow members of the officer corps, was unsurprised by the inertia on the western front; on August 14 his first entry in his war diary noted that he considered a French offensive "not very likely," that France would not attack across the Low Countries "against Belgian wishes," and that the French would probably "remain on the defensive."[80]

At the time Halder was the only senior general in Zossen to endorse the Führer's prediction. On September 7, with the issue of whether to send Wehrmacht divisions to the west being discussed seriously, Halder's diary entry ended with a few lines summing up Hitler's views: "Operations in the West not yet clear. Some indication that there is no real intention of waging war." The Generalstab couldn't believe it. They remembered the indomitable poilus who had fought under Joffre and Galliéni in the early years of the last war, who had always counterattacked when attacked, whose line was never broken, whose "*Ils ne passeront pas*" denied Verdun to Germany's finest regiments through seven terrible months, and who paid an unprecedented price — four million casualties, one out of every four of them dead — for victory in 1918.[81]

But Joffre, Galliéni, Pétain, and Foch were gone, and in their place stood — though not particularly tall — Gamelin. As Halder recorded the Führer's thoughts, the French *généralissime* prepared to launch the only offensive of his career, a piece of opéra bouffe which mocked the memories of Verdun. *"L'offensive de la Sarre,"* as he grandly called it, was in fact a pitiful sortie. Of his 85 heavily armed divisions he committed 9 to an advance on a fifteen-mile front southeast of Saarbrücken. Moving slowly, taking every precaution, the infantry occupied twenty deserted villages and gained five miles. Here and there were reports of skirmishes, but the German response was to give ground, withdraw — and pray that the *généralissime* did not commit another fifty divisions to a full-scale attack. Of the Germans' total strength, all but eleven divisions were untrained and the rest lacked adequate arms and ammunition. Nevertheless, on September 12 Gamelin commanded a halt. He congratulated his men on their victory and instructed them to make preparations for a retreat into the security of the Maginot Line if a German offensive came roaring down through Belgium. The next day the Polish military attaché, on orders from an alarmed Rydz-Smigly, asked Gamelin whether French warplanes had attacked their mutual enemy, and whether he could accelerate his infantry advance. Later that same day the architect of the Saar "offensive" replied mendaciously, in writing: "More than half of our active divisions on the northeast front are engaged in combat." The Boche, he said, were responding with *"vigoureuse résistance."* Interrogation of enemy prisoners revealed that the Germans were "pouring in reinforcements" — all of this, every word, pure fiction — and French warplanes had been in action from the outset, tying down *"une part considérable"* of the Luftwaffe. He had gone "far beyond" his pledge, he concluded. *"Il m'a été impossible de faire plus"* ("It has been impossible for me to do more").[82]

The ground gained in the Saar was lost when Gamelin, on September 30, ordered a retreat. The only achievement of his so-called Saar offensive was to reveal France's persistent confidence in outdated tactical ideas, notably the doctrine that any drive against a defended position must be preceded by a massive artillery bombardment, the "tin-opener," as it had been called in 1918. General André de Beaufre, then a captain, said that Gamelin's action, in character, had been a meaningless gesture (*"Voilà notre aide à la Pologne!"*), and Colonel de Gaulle dismissed *"l'offensive"* contemptuously as *"quelques démonstrations."*[83]

* * *

By the tenth day of fighting, the Polish cause was lost, and Rydz-Smigly, who had read the heartbreaking dispatches from Beck's diplomats in Paris and London, knew it. He ordered a general withdrawal into southeastern Poland, planning to organize a defensive position on a narrow front to prolong resistance. But the Generalstab had thought of everything. Already over half of the marshal's remaining forces had been trapped before they could retreat across the Vistula. Cut off from their bases, running out of ammunition, this remnant was caught in a vise between two German armies. And before Rydz-Smigly could reach his redoubt in the southeast, he, too, was encircled.

On September 17 two Soviet army groups, in accordance with the secret clause in the Nazi-Soviet Pact, invaded Poland from the east. Ribbentrop and Molotov had fixed the demarcation line along the river Bug, but there are always soldiers who don't get the word; shots were exchanged between some Germans and Russians, and a few men were wounded. Then all was quiet along the Bug. Both foreign armies were in Poland, but the Poles were forgotten; the fate of their homeland had been decided in the first three days of the Nazi invasion — actually, given the fourth color Gamelin had added to the French tricolor, before the fighting had begun.

By all precedents the Poles, in extremis, should have yielded once they found that they faced both the Wehrmacht and the Red Army. The Germans had them checked; now they were in checkmate. It was time to quit. They were victims of a squalid deal worked by two despots whose hands reeked of innocent blood, and they had been betrayed by two allies whose leaders had been regarded as honorable men. No indignity had been spared them. In London — where their cause found little sympathy — a cabinet minister had declared that after Nazi Germany had been crushed, "a Polish state would be reconstituted"; *the* Polish state to whose defense England had been committed was unmentioned. The Poles would gain nothing if they made a messy exit; they would merely forfeit the claims they had upon the world's compassion. It was far more sensible to go along quietly.

But the Poles didn't want pity, and while quietude may be good form among Anglo-Saxons in exigency, the Poles are traditionally noisy. Newspaper photographs showed German and Russian officers shaking hands, elated that the battle was over. Except that it wasn't; there were no pictures of Poles shaking hands with anyone. Their government and high command had left Warsaw for Rumania, leaving orders to fight to the bitter end. The Poles did; fueled by patriotic fervor, they barricaded streets with streetcars, stopping Reichenau's tanks; his infantry was forced into the ugliest and most dangerous close combat — house to house, room by room. By that mysterious process which telegraphs news throughout a country, even after its communications system has been destroyed, all Poland knew what was happening in Warsaw, and thousands of Poles followed its example. Guderian plunged deep through the Polish rear to Brest-Litovsk, but when he tried to storm the town's ancient citadel, he found an obsolete Renault tank had been jammed, and then welded, into the doorway. Warsaw, starving, lacking water, pounded around the clock by Nazi planes and artillery, finally capitulated ten days after the Russian invasion. Pockets of resistance fought on, though the last major stronghold — 17,000 men in Kock, a village southeast of the capital — did not lay down their arms until October 7. Meanwhile, 100,000 Polish soldiers and pilots had escaped to Rumania and made their way to England, where they would fight in Free Polish battalions beside the British, French, and later, the Americans; Polish destroyers and submarines reached the Orkneys and joined the Royal Navy.

Stalin left central Poland to Hitler. In return he got the eastern provinces, a free hand in Lithuania, and the oil fields of southeast Poland, with the understanding that he would ship thirty thousand tons of crude to the Reich every year. Hitler annexed part of Poland and established the rest as a Nazi vassal state, the General Government of Poland, whose governor-general was Hans Frank, a feisty, dapper young Nazi lawyer, the adoring father of five children, who began braiding his Nuremberg rope by announcing: "The Poles shall be the slaves of the Third Reich." He also became expert in carrying out programs whose euphemistic names masked some of the vilest crimes in history. Polish intellectuals, professional men, and anyone possessing leadership qualities — men and women who might subvert Frank's authority — were marked for slaughter. This operation, in which 3,500 persons were actually executed, persons who had committed no crime, who were singled out precisely because they had led distinguished careers, was encoded *Ausserordenliche Befriedigungsaktion* (Extraordinary Pacification Program). In another Frank campaign, all Jews were grouped together for his *Flurbereinigungs-Plan* (Housecleaning Plan). Later, after other code words had been tried, the Nazis settled on *Endlösung*, the Final Solution, to represent the destruction of the European Jews. Their time had come.[84]

And so had Western civilization's hour of maximum danger. Hitler was free now to turn the full fury of his might on England and France. Churchill had repeatedly spoken — mostly to empty seats — on the need to confront Nazi Germany with collective security. Above all, he had said, the Reich must be bracketed by strong nations, east and west, so that Hitler would know German aggression would mean a two-front war. When the Führer came to power the safeguards had seemed solid: France, England, and the Rhineland on the west, and Czechoslovakia and Poland to the east, with Russia, alienated by Nazi murders of German Communists and Hitler's anti-Soviet polemics, frowning behind them. One by one Hitler had eliminated these threats. He could not have done it alone. He had needed help — and found it in London and Paris. The Polish army had been a disappointment. But France, whose army was vital to the security of free peoples, hadn't even tried to exploit the period of grace — at least three weeks — when the German armies were tied down in the east. Now the democracies must face him alone — him and, in all probability, Italy, for the unprincipled Duce wanted to be on the winning side, and the Anglo-French alliance had been losing, losing, losing for nearly seven years. In England the iconoclastic General Fuller declared that France must be ruled by lunatics. There they had been in September, he wrote, with "the strongest army in the world, facing no more than twenty-six divisions, sitting still and sheltering behind steel and concrete while a quixotically valiant ally was being exterminated!" In Paris Léon Blum was recalling his conversation with a nonconformist French officer when they met in 1936. The Socialist leader had asked: "What would France do if Hitler should march on Vienna, Prague, or Warsaw?" Charles de Gaulle had replied: "According to circumstances, we shall have a limited call-up or full mobilization. Then, peering through the battlements of our fortifications, we shall watch the enslavement of Europe." Vienna, Prague, and Warsaw had fallen. Now Blum was wondering whether those battlements and fortifications were strong enough to save France herself from bondage.[85]

Hitler had not expected France and England to go to war over Poland. After they had yielded the Rhineland, Austria, and Czechoslovakia, he had assumed that appeasement would continue to be the keystone of their foreign policy. He still doubted that they intended to fight. The French failure to attack the Siegfried Line when it was at its weakest had, in his view, confirmed him. The first inkling that he might have misjudged the British had been Churchill's appointment to the War Cabinet. Told of it, Hermann Göring had dropped into a chair and said heavily: "Churchill in the Cabinet. That means war is really on. Now we shall have war with England."[86]

The Nazi hierarchy had long been aware of Churchill. That included the Führer, which made Winston an exception. It is a remarkable fact that Hitler knew almost nothing of his enemies and even brushed aside information made available to him, preferring to rely on his instincts, which included contempt for all *Ausländer*. He did regard England as "our enemy

Number One," however, and Churchill as the symbol of British militancy. After the fall of Poland he lost little time in singling him out. Making his ritualistic peace offering, the sequel to all Nazi conquests, he declared that Poland was dead; it would never rise again; therefore why fight about it? "I make this declaration," he said, "only because I very naturally desire to spare my people suffering. But should the views of Churchill and his following prevail, then this declaration will be my last. We should then fight. . . . Let those repulse my hand who regard war as the better solution!"[87]

As a cabinet minister, Churchill could now speak over the BBC whenever he chose, and on October 1, in his first wartime broadcast, he had told Britain: "Poland has again been overrun by two of the great powers which held her in bondage for a hundred and fifty years but were unable to quench the spirit of the Polish nation." The heroic defense of Warsaw had shown that "the soul of Poland is indestructible, and that she will rise again like a rock, which may for a spell be submerged by a tidal wave, but which remains a rock." He was more intrigued by "the assertion of the power of Russia." He would have preferred that the Russians "should be standing on their present line as the friends and allies of Poland instead of invaders. But that the Russian armies should stand on this line was clearly necessary for the safety of Russia against the Nazi menace." Ribbentrop, he noted, had been summoned to Moscow last week to be told that "the Nazi designs upon the Baltic States . . . must come to a dead stop." He continued:

> I cannot forecast to you the action of Russia.
> It is a riddle
> wrapped in a mystery
> inside an enigma;
>
> But perhaps there is a key.
> That key is Russian national interest.
>
> It cannot be in accordance
> with the interest or safety of Russia
> that Germany should plant itself
> upon the shores of the Black Sea
>
> Or that it should overrun the Baltic States
> and subjugate the Slavonic peoples
> of southeastern Europe.[88]

He announced with pride — not pardonable, because he still distrusted the convoy policy — that "a week has passed since a British ship, alone or in convoy, has been sunk or even molested by a U-boat on the high seas," and he closed with one of those passages which men in public life later wish could be expunged from the record. "Rough times lie ahead," he said, "but how different is the scene from that of October 1914!" Then the French front "seemed to be about to break under the terrible impact of German Imperialism. . . . We faced those adverse conditions then; we have nothing worse to face tonight."[89]

They faced something far worse, of course, but no one can hold a mirror up to the future, and the speech was well received in England. The prime minister's junior private secretary, Jock Colville, wrote in his diary that Churchill "certainly gives one confidence and will, I suspect, be Prime Minister before this war is over." Colville thought he might "lead us into the most dangerous paths. But he is the only man in the country who commands anything like universal respect, and perhaps with age he has become less inclined to undertake rash adventures." Hoare, another diarist, noted that Churchill seemed "very exhilarated" and that "the Press talked of him as Prime Minister." It was not just the press; Sir John Wheeler-Bennett was among those establishmentarians who, listening to Winston, "first realized that Churchill was 'the pilot of the storm' who was needed to lead us through the crisis of the Second World War." That thought did not occur to Neville Chamberlain, but he was impressed; to his sister he wrote that he took "the same view as Winston, to whose excellent broadcast we have just been listening. I believe Russia will always act as she thinks her own interests demand, and I cannot believe she would think her interests served by . . . German domination in the Balkans."[90]

In Berlin, William Shirer wrote: "The local enthusiasm for peace a little dampened today by Churchill's speech last night." Goebbels suppressed references to Winston's comments on Russia, but his allusion to the Admiralty's success in shielding merchantmen from Nazi submarines had touched a nerve. Led by *Der Stürmer*, *Völkischer Beobachter*, and *Deutsches Nachtrichenbüro*, the German press had made a great thing out of the U-boat campaign; U-boat captains were the toast of the Reich, and cartoonists had pictured Winston as a battered, cornered prizefighter and as a drowning man surrounded by periscopes. His announcement that the subs had let a week pass without a victory enraged Hans Fritzsche, director of the Nazi broadcasting services. Fritzsche interrupted a program to deliver a thirteen-minute polemic denouncing Winston, quoting him and then raging: "So that is what the dirty gangster thinks! Who does that filthy liar think he is fooling? . . . So Mr. Churchill — that bloated swine [*aufgeblasenes Schwein*] — spouts through his dirty teeth that in the last week no English ship has been molested by German submarines? He does, indeed? . . .

There you have the twisted and diseased mind of this infamous profiteer and specialist in stinking lying. Naturally those British ships have not been molested; they have been sunk."[91]

It is possible to be more overbearing in German than in any other tongue, but only if one has mastered it as Winston had mastered English. In any duel of denigration he was bound to leave Fritzsche far behind, and he did it in November, in his second wartime address over the BBC. Germany, he said, was more fragile than it seemed. He had

> the sensation and also the conviction that that evil man over there and his cluster of confederates are not sure of themselves, as we are sure of ourselves; that they are harassed in their guilty souls by the thought and by the fear of an ever-approaching retribution for their crimes, and for the orgy of destruction in which they have plunged us all. As they look out tonight from their blatant, panoplied, clattering Nazi Germany, they cannot find one single friendly eye in the whole circumference of the globe. Not one![92]

Russia, he said, "returns them a flinty stare"; Italy "averts her gaze"; Japan "is puzzled and thinks herself betrayed"; Turkey, Islam, India, and China "would regard with undisguised dread a Nazi triumph, well knowing what their fate would soon be"; and the "great English-speaking Republic across the Atlantic makes no secret of its sympathies." Thus "the whole world is against Hitler and Hitlerism. Men of every race and clime feel that this monstrous apparition stands between them and the forward move which is their due, and for which the age is ripe." The "seething mass of criminality and corruption constituted by the Nazi Party machine" was responsible for the power of its führer, "a haunted, morbid being, who, to their eternal shame, the German people in their bewilderment have worshipped as a god."[93]

Jock Colville wrote that he had "listened to Winston Churchill's wireless speech, very boastful, over-confident and indiscreet (especially about Italy and the U.S.A.), but certainly most amusing." If Colville was condescending, Harold Nicolson sometimes turned his thumb down on a Churchill broadcast. After listening to one of the early radio addresses, Nicolson observed in his diary that Winston "is a little too rhetorical, and I do not think that his speech will really have gone down with the masses. He is too belligerent for this pacifist age, and although once anger comes to steel our sloppiness, his voice will be welcome to them, at the moment it reminds them of heroism which they do not really feel."[94]

One hesitates to gainsay Harold Nicolson; he was one of the shrewdest observers of his time, and his lapses were rare. But this may have been one of them. Nicolson, with Amery and Spears, was a member of the Eden group and continued to attend their Carlton meetings well into 1940. More important, he — like Colville — belonged to the upper class, and carried all its paraphernalia with him. His credentials as an analyst of "the masses" are therefore thin; as he himself acknowledged, he misinterpreted the feelings of his own constituents. Now that the issue with Hitler was joined and English blood was flowing, Churchill had become the most overstated member of His Majesty's Government. Clearly that troubled Nicolson; men with his background prized understatement and recoiled from its opposite. Elsewhere on England's social spectrum, however, that was not true. Among the middle and lower classes, pacifism had begun to fade when Hitler entered Prague, and once war was declared it was replaced by patriotism. Before the war became dreary and stale, the signs of the nation's shift in mood had been unmistakable. The jubilant response to the naval victory off Montevideo had been one. Another had appeared when the people learned — from accounts of a Churchill speech in Parliament — that Luftwaffe pilots were machine-gunning the crews of unarmed fishing vessels and "describing on the radio what fun it was to see a little ship 'crackling in flames like a Christmas tree.' " Winston was swamped with mail from clerks and miners, waitresses and small businessmen, demanding reprisals. Of course, he refused; he was a gentleman. But *they weren't,* and they vastly outnumbered those who were.

There was talk — more out of Parliament than in it — of Churchill as prime minister. It was, and for thirty years had been, the only job which clearly suited him. That does not mean he was ineffectual elsewhere. He had always been able, and often brilliant, in other ministries, and even his Admiralty critics conceded that no other man in public life could match his performance in the private office. But given the broad reaches of his mind, his knowledge of the entire government, and his inability to hold his tongue in check, he often exasperated the cabinet by trespassing in departments which were the preserve of other men round the table. So it was in his BBC broadcasts. Although he began by confining himself to the war at sea, sooner or later he was bound to touch upon issues which could not be remotely construed as naval. If his touch had been light, the encroachment would have been ignored, but it was also characteristic of him that he was incapable of subtlety. His third major broadcast raised an issue which was clearly the special concern of the Foreign Office. He tore into Europe's neutral nations. By now none could doubt that the German führer had plans for their future, yet like Scarlett O'Hara they seemed to be promising themselves they would think about it tomorrow, while every tomorrow darkened their prospects. In a BBC broadcast on January 20, 1940, Churchill said:

All of them hope that the storm will pass
before their turn comes to be devoured.
But I fear — I fear greatly —
the storm will not pass.

It will rage and it will roar,
ever more loudly, ever more widely.
It will spread to the South;
it will spread to the North.

There is no chance of a speedy end
except through united action;

And if at any time, Britain and France,
wearying of the struggle,
were to make a shameful peace,

Nothing would remain for the smaller states of Europe,
with their shipping and their possessions,
but to be divided between the opposite, though similar,
barbarisms of Nazidom and Bolshevism.[95]

Hoare commented in his diary: "Winston's broadcast to the neutrals. Bad effect." One consequence of the broadcast, unknown in London, was a *Führerordnung* to restudy possible operations in Scandinavia. Hitler guessed — correctly — that the first lord of the Admiralty had his eye on Norway. The Foreign Office was more concerned about the reaction in neutral capitals. In a pained note Halifax wrote Churchill: "I am afraid I think the effect of your broadcast in the countries which you no doubt had principally in mind has been very different from what you anticipated — though if I had seen your speech myself, I should have expected some such reactions." Among the newspapers which had bridled were *Het Handelsblad* in Holland, *Journal de Genève*, Denmark's *Politiken*, and Norway's *Morgenbladet*. Halifax complained that it "puts me in an impossible position if a member of the Gov. like yourself takes a line in public which differs from that taken by the PM or myself: and I think, as I have to be in daily touch with these tiresome neutrals, I ought to be able to predict how their minds will work." Churchill answered at once: "This is undoubtedly a disagreeable bouquet. I certainly thought I was expressing yr view & Neville's. . . . Do not however be quite sure that my line will prove so inconvenient as now appears. What the neutrals say is vy different from what they feel: or from what is going to happen." In fact Hitler had designs on most of them, and before spring ended the swastika would float over all their capitals but Switzerland's.[96]

Halifax had passed over the one paragraph in the broadcast with momentous implications. It was a reference to the fighting going on in Finland, part of a complex issue which no one in England, including Churchill, understood. The Russo-German marriage of convenience had scarcely been consummated in Poland before divorce proceedings were quietly begun. Stalin, anxious to guard his Baltic flank from a future Nazi attack, signed pacts with Estonia, Latvia, and Lithuania, permitting Moscow to garrison Red Army troops in each. He then turned to Finland. Among his objectives, all of which were defensive, was blocking the Gulf of Finland with artillery on both coasts, thus protecting the entrance to Leningrad. The Soviet Union offered Helsinki 2,134 square miles in exchange for the cession of 1,066 Finnish square miles. National sentiment — and fear of a German reprisal — barred an agreement. The Russians, desperate, offered to buy the territory. Helsinki still refused, and on November 30, 1939, the Red Army invaded Finland. To outsiders the invasion was an atrocity as black as the Nazi seizure of Poland. In retrospect, however, the difference is obvious. Russia's need to defend Leningrad is clear. The city came perilously close to conquest by the Germans later, and would certainly have fallen to the Nazis without the strip taken from the Finns.

The necessities of war modify principle; the hand of a country whose existence is threatened is not stayed by the rules of war. Churchill, at this very time, was telling the War Cabinet that "We must violate Norwegian territorial waters"; and Pétain, worried about the stretch of French frontier undefended by the Maginot Line, had told the Conseil Supérieur de la Guerre that if France was to remain faithful to the principle which had saved her in the last war ("the defensive and continuous front"), she must face the fact that the one stretch of her frontier unprotected by the Maginot Line was the classic invasion route followed by Germans for nearly two thousand years. Consequently, he concluded: *"Nous devons entrer en Belgique!"* — "We must go into Belgium!" Winston agreed that Belgium could not possibly remain neutral, that it was essential to erect "a shield along the Belgian frontier to the sea against that terrible turning movement" which had "nearly encompassed our ruin in 1914."[97]

To the astonishment of the world, tiny Finland threw the Russians back. Beginning with the Japanese conquest of Manchuria eight years earlier, the aggressor powers had repeatedly overwhelmed weak, poorly led defenders. Now a small country with one-fortieth the strength of the Soviet Union was humiliating a great power, sending the invaders reeling from the Mannerheim Line, named for their leader, Field Marshal Carl Gustaf Emil von Mannerheim. The Finn victories seemed miraculous, but there were several explanations. One was Mannerheim himself. Before the Russian Revolution, when Finland belonged to the czar, he had served as a lieutenant general; he had fought the Bolsheviks to a standstill then, and now, aged seventy-two, had come out of retirement to do it again. Stalin was holding his crack divisions in reserve should Hitler strike. He had sent the Red Army's poorest troops, ill-trained and sorely lacking in fighting spirit, against the Finns. Mannerheim led men fueled by the incentive of soldiers defending their homeland. He blinded the Russians with superior tactics, the use of superbly trained ski troops, a thorough knowledge of the lakes and forests constituting the terrain's natural obstacles, and a strategy peculiarly suitable to arctic warfare — cutting the enemy's line of retreat, waiting until the Russians were frozen and starved, and then counterattacking. The paralyzed invaders were not even properly clothed for the bitter Finnish winter. Churchill had spoken for tens of millions when, in his indictment of neutrals, he made an exception: "Only Finland — superb, nay, sublime — in the jaws of peril — Finland shows what free men can do. The service rendered by Finland to mankind is magnificent. They have exposed, for all the world to see, the military incapacity of the Red Army and of the Red Air Force. Many illusions about Soviet Russia have been dispelled in these few fierce weeks of fighting in the Arctic Circle."[98]

The British and the French — seeing the opportunity for a pretext to cross northern Sweden, and, in passing, to seize the Swedish iron mines at Gällivare, vital to the Third Reich's war effort — were about to send "volunteers" to aid the Finns when the tide turned. After two months of frustration the Russians secured their communications from the Leningrad-Murmansk frontier, which they should have done before the invasion, and launched a major assault on the Mannerheim Line with fourteen divisions of sledge-borne infantry supported by heavy artillery, tanks, and warplanes. The Finns stood up to it for five ferocious weeks, counterattacking the tanks with what Churchill called "a new type of hand-grenade" — bottles filled with gasoline and topped by wick, lit at the moment of hurling — which they audaciously christened Molotov cocktails. They gave ground slowly, but they gave it. Vyborg, vital to the defense, was threatened by frontal assault and, from the rear, by troops crossing the icebound Gulf of Finland and the icebound island of Hogland. On March 6, 1940, the Finns sued for peace and the Allies disbanded their expeditionary force. The repercussions of this — for England, and particularly for Churchill — were almost immediate. Winston felt he now had an excellent precedent for intervention in Scandinavia. The greatest sequel, however, was taking shape in the minds of Hitler and the German General Staff in Zossen. Like Britain's first lord of the Admiralty, they underestimated Soviet military strength "with," as Liddell Hart writes, "momentous consequences the following year."[99]

Churchill was not the first man in European public life to exploit the possibilities of radio. Hitler had been doing it for seven years. But Winston was the first British statesman to reach people in their homes and move them even more deeply than Roosevelt had in his fireside chats. Because the BBC had gone to great lengths to avoid controversy, its interwar programs were extraordinarily dull — "Arranging a Garden" and "Our Friends at the Zoo" were typical. So was Churchill's scheduled talk on the Mediterranean, which had brought Guy Burgess to Chartwell in 1938. Public issues had been discussed over the BBC, and earlier in the decade Winston had managed to get a word in now and then, but as the crises mounted on the Continent and tensions increased, Reith screened participants in debates, approving only those who presented bland views, offending no listeners, particularly those occupying the front bench in the House of Commons.

Until he entered the War Cabinet, Churchill's audiences had been largely confined to the House, lecture halls, and, during elections, party rallies. Suddenly that had changed. England was at war; the only action was at sea, and millions whose knowledge of Churchillian speeches had been confined to published versions heard his rich voice, resonant with urgency, dramatically heightened by his tempo, pauses, and crashing consonants, which, one listener wrote, actually made his radio vibrate. Churchill had been a name in the newspapers, but even his own columns lacked the power of his delivery. He found precisely the right words for convictions his audiences shared but had been unable to express. He spoke of "thoughtless dilettanti or purblind worldlings who sometimes ask us: 'What is it that Britain and France are fighting for?' To this I answer: 'If we left off fighting you would soon find out.' " His elaborate metaphors, simplistic but effective, fortified his argument, and were often witty: "A baboon in a forest is a matter of legitimate speculation; a baboon in a Zoo is an object of public curiosity; but a baboon in your wife's bed is a cause of the gravest concern."[100]

After the fall of Poland, when Hitler told the Western democracies to choose between a negotiated peace with him or "the views of Churchill and his following," Chamberlain gave him the official reply (which Churchill helped draft), but England heard Winston's, on the evening of November 12, 1939:

We tried again and again to prevent this war, and for the sake of peace we put up with a lot of things happening which ought not to have happened. But now we are at war, and we are going to make war, and persevere in making war, until the other side have had enough of it. . . . You may take it absolutely for certain that either all that Britain and France stand for in the modern world will go down, or that Hitler, the Nazi regime, and the recurring German or Prussian menace to Europe will be broken or destroyed. That is the way the matter lies and everybody had better make up his mind to that solid, somber fact.[101]

Like a thespian, Churchill began to receive critical notices. When he rose from the front bench to address the House of Commons, Beverley Baxter, an MP and a writer for the Beaverbrook press, compared him to "the old bandit who had been the terror of the mountain passes . . . the fire in him was burning low. His head was thrust forward characteristically, like a bull watching for the matador. He squared his shoulders a couple of times as if to make sure that his hands were free for the gestures that might come." When Winston told BBC listeners that "Now we have begun; now we are going on; now with the help of God, and the conviction that we are the defenders of civilisation and freedom, we are going on, and we are going on to the end," Virginia Cowles wrote that he was "giving the people of Britain the firm clear lead" they needed and "had not found elsewhere."[102]

In December, the war's fourth month, a public opinion poll reported that barely half of the British people had expressed confidence in Chamberlain — one disillusioned Conservative described him as "hanging onto office like a dirty old piece of chewing gum on the leg of a chair" — and Churchill, right behind him, was gaining. In the House of Commons smoking room, and in the lobby, predictions that Winston would succeed Chamberlain, once shocking, were no longer whispered; they were legitimate speculation. The theme is an undercurrent in Nicolson's diaries, returning whenever disaster looms. The first cluster of references begins early, as on September 17, when he writes, "At 11 am. (a bad hour) Vita comes to tell me that Russia has invaded Poland and is striking toward Vilna. . . . It may be that within a few days we shall have Germany, Russia and Japan against us." At the end of the entry, clearly a frightened man, he writes: "Chamberlain must go. Churchill may be our Clemenceau or our Gambetta. To bed very miserable and alarmed." Nine days later, in the House, Nicolson watches as "The Prime Minister gets up to make his statement. He is dressed in deep mourning. . . . One feels the confidence and spirits of the House dropping inch by inch. When he sits down there is scarcely any applause. During the whole speech Winston Churchill had sat hunched beside him looking like the Chinese god of plenty suffering from acute indigestion." Then Churchill rises. Nicolson is euphoric: "The effect of Winston's speech was infinitely greater than could be derived from any reading of the text. . . . One could feel the spirits of the House rising with every word. . . . In those twenty minutes Churchill brought himself nearer the post of Prime Minister than he has ever been before. In the Lobbies afterwards even Chamberlainites were saying, 'We have now found our leader.' " And then, in early October — at a meeting of the Eden group — Nicolson hears the second Lord Astor tell members that he "feels it is essential that the Prime Minister should be removed and that Winston Churchill should take his place."[103]

In Winston's place another ambitious politician hearing such praise — and it was coming to him from many sides — might have taken the pulse of the House, seeking to put together a coalition to topple the government and then form one of his own. Although members of this House of Commons, elected in 1935, were no longer reflective of the national mood, they too had built high hopes in the aftermath of Munich only to see them dashed; many felt betrayed; many others had heard from constituents who felt so. But plotting wasn't Churchill's style. He owed the Admiralty and his seat on the War Cabinet to the prime minister. Moreover, Chamberlain hadn't bullied him, called him on the carpet, or interfered in any way with his administration of the country's naval policy, though he may have been tempted; Winston, being Winston, had critics among naval officers of flag rank.[104]

Chamberlain did visit the upper war room frequently, but was always cordial and left expressing gratitude — if he knew that Sinclair and Beaverbrook were also shown the Admiralty maps (though neither was a member of the government), he kept it to himself. In the House Winston loyally supported the government's policies — was indeed their most forceful advocate — and praised the P.M. from time to time. In one of his broadcasts he said: "You know I have not always agreed with Mr. Chamberlain, though we have always been personal friends. But he is a man of very tough fiber, and I can tell you that he is going to fight as obstinately for victory as he did for peace." The war had, in fact, brought out an unexpected streak of belligerence in the prime minister. "Winston, for his part," Colville noted, "professes absolute loyalty to the P.M. (and indeed they get along admirably)," while Chamberlain wrote: "To me personally Winston is absolutely loyal, and I am continually hearing from others of the admiration he expressed for the P.M."[105]

It was the same in Churchill's private life. Virginia Cowles, lunching at Admiralty House, was startled by Winston's reaction when one of the children attempted a mild jest at Chamberlain's expense. In the past, she remembered, jokes at the prime minister's expense had been featured at almost every meal, but this time she saw "a scowl appear on the father's face.

With enormous solemnity he said: 'If you are going to make offensive remarks about my chief you will have to leave the table. We are united in a great and common cause and I am not prepared to tolerate such language about the Prime Minister.' " Similarly, when he received Lady Bonham Carter, née Violet Asquith — "Well, here we are back in the old premises after a short interval of twenty-five years," he said in greeting — her criticism of "the old appeasers" still in the government sparked a Churchillian rebuke. In a vehement defense of Chamberlain, he said: "No man is more inflexible, more single-minded. He has a will of steel."[106]

On Friday the thirteenth of October, Churchill recorded, "my relations with Mr. Chamberlain had so far ripened that he and Mrs. Chamberlain came to dine with us at Admiralty House, where we had a comfortable flat in the attics. We were a party of four." During Stanley Baldwin's first prime ministry the two men had been colleagues for five years, yet they had never met socially. Churchill, "by happy chance" — one doubts that luck had anything to do with it — mentioned the Bahamas, knowing Chamberlain had spent several years there. Winston was "delighted to find my guest expand . . . to a degree I had not noticed before." Out came the long, sad story; Neville's father was convinced that the family fortune could be enriched, and an Empire industry developed, if his younger son grew sisal on a barren island near Nassau. Neville spent six years trying. Buffeted by hurricanes, struggling with inadequate labor, "living nearly naked," as Churchill paraphrased him, he built a small harbor, wharf, and a short railroad. But those were ancillary; his objective was to produce sisal, and although he tried every known fertilizer he found it could not be done, or at any rate not by him. "I gathered," wrote Winston, in one of his wonderfully wry curtain lines, "that in the family the feeling was that although they loved him dearly they were sorry to have lost fifty thousand pounds." And then a thought flashed across his mind: "What a pity Hitler did not know when he met this sober English politician with his umbrella . . . that he was actually talking to a hard-bitten pioneer from the outer marches of the British Empire!"[107]

But that was not the height of the evening. During dinner an officer came up from the war room immediately below them to report that a Nazi submarine had been sunk. He reappeared during dessert with news that a second U-boat had been sunk, and yet again, just before the ladies left the prime minister and first lord to their brandy, to announce, rather breathlessly, that a *third* sub had been sunk. Mrs. Chamberlain asked Winston: "Did you arrange all this on purpose?" Her host "assured her," as he put it, "that if she would come again we would produce a similar result."[108]

As ruler of the King's navy, Winston was paid £5,000 a year and found;

Admiralty House was an absolute defense against creditors. Clementine felt like a young woman again. She hadn't christened a ship in over twenty-six years, but she remembered the drill when invited to launch the aircraft carrier *Indomitable* at Barrow-in-Furness. Winston was there, and a photograph — taken at the instant she was gaily waving the ship away — became his favorite picture of her; years later, when he returned to his easel, he sketched an enchanting portrait from it. Lord Fraser, watching him during the launching, observed first "his cheers" as the long vessel slid free of the ways, "and then the grave salute," perhaps prompted by thoughts of the ordeals *Indomitable* "would have to face in the future."[109]

Once the first lord and his lady had settled in topside at Admiralty House, Clementine's friends — and some acquaintances who weren't — came calling, wide-eyed ladies who could scarcely wait to see how she had done over the attics. Unwilling to offend them, she took them on tour, though she felt martyred; she had good taste, knew it, and didn't need confirmation. The only one qualified to judge was Diana Cooper, and she confined her criticisms to her diary. Even there she added that she was glad that the Churchills were in Admiralty House: "Winston's spirit, strength and confidence are . . . a chime that wakes the heart of the discouraged. His wife, more beautiful now than in early life, is equally fearless and indefatigable. She makes us all knit jerseys, for which the minesweepers must bless her."[110]

Winston hadn't time to miss Chartwell, but something had to be done; it was impractical to keep the mansion open and prodigal to continue paying servants when only maintenance was necessary. In the early days of the war it seemed destined for a humanitarian purpose. In anticipation of heavy, continuous bombing of British cities, the evacuation of over 1,250,000 women and children, particularly those living near London's East Side docks, had begun in August. Members of the upper class, their attitudes formed in abstract discussion of "the underprivileged" and "depressed areas," flung open the doors of their great country homes and received the evacuees with a compassion and a hospitality that was frequently, and swiftly, regretted. Two cultures clashed; the young strangers had never seen or even heard of underwear; many would neither eat at tables nor sleep in beds; they were accustomed to doorways and alleys. Others brought lice which often spread to a horrified hostess and her own children. The unbridgeable gap was reflected in the remark of a Whitechapel mother to her six-year-old: "You dirty thing, messing the lady's carpet. Go and do it in the corner."[111]

Chartwell had welcomed two East End mothers and their seven children. But like most other evacuees they drifted back to the docks, homesick and weary of the green country landscapes. Clemmie conferred with Winston. After two years' work he had nearly finished Orchard Cottage, to which they intended to retire while Randolph — who had joined his father's old regiment, the Fourth Hussars, and married the lovely Pamela Digby — moved into the big house. The cottage's three bedrooms were quite livable; if the first lord yearned for a weekend, they could stay there. Cousin Moppet agreed to serve as caretaker. She moved into what had been the chauffeur's cottage and was presently joined by Diana's two small children and their nannie. They had been evacuated but did not miss London, where their mother was serving as an officer in the Women's Royal Naval Service (WRNS). Duncan Sandys, Diana's husband, had been called up by his territorial unit and was stationed in London with an antiaircraft battery. Sarah and Vic Oliver had taken a flat in Westminster Gardens. "Darling Papa," Sarah wrote Winston,

> . . . wherever I go, people rush up to me and shake me by the hand, congratulate me, and smile on me — because of you, and I felt I must pass on some of their wishes and good will to you.
>
> There was such a lovely picture of you on the Newsreel the other day, and the buzz and excitement that swept through the theatre, suddenly made me feel so inordinately proud that I was your daughter, and it suddenly occurred to me that I had never really told you, through shyness and inarticulateness — *how much* I love you, and how much I will try to make this career that I have chosen — with some pain to the people I love, and not a little to myself — worthy of your name — one day — [112]

The note was signed, "Your loving Sarah." She was his favorite, and he needed her now. Security was so tight that every servant had to be investigated and cleared; even conversations with most friends and relatives were tense. Discussions of nearly everything now on Winston's mind was forbidden, so Clementine entertained less and less, grouping "outsiders," as the Churchills called them, together at dinner parties. Mary, seventeen and just out of school, lived with her parents, worked in a canteen and Red Cross workroom, and was enjoying her first taste of London society. Not everyone, she recalls, was barred from discussions of restricted information: "There was the small golden circle of trusted colleagues known to be 'padlock,' and to whom, of course, that trust was sacred." Nevertheless, the circle was very small. In wartime every cabinet member had to be careful in conversation, and this was especially true of the Admiralty's first lord. As Winston had said of Jellicoe in the first war, he was the only minister who could lose the war in an afternoon. Even the list of outsiders was short, excluding many with whom they had been close in the past.[113]

It certainly did not include Unity Mitford, who arrived back in England with a self-inflicted bullet wound in her neck. She had not cared to live through a war between her homeland and her beloved führer. The government did what it could to protect the privacy of her return, posting a guard with a fixed bayonet at the dock gate — "Nazi methods," fumed an *Express* reporter — but when her father protested that the whole family was being persecuted as Nazi sympathizers, Winston declined to intervene. Lord Redesdale and his talented daughters would have to muddle through on their own.[114]

The knitting bee into which Lady Diana had been drafted was only one of Clementine's projects. Life aboard the small boats which had been commandeered by the Admiralty and transformed into minesweepers was spartan and uncomfortable; therefore Clemmie made a successful public appeal for contributions to the Minesweepers and Coastal Craft Fund. She also served as a volunteer at the Fulmer Chase Maternity Home for officers' wives. By now she had become resigned, if not reconciled, to the company of Brendan Bracken and the Prof, and invited them to join other "padlock" friends, relatives, and "Chartwell regulars" in celebrating Christmas at Admiralty House. For Churchill it was a rare moment of relaxation; even so, he disappeared from time to time to check Pim's maps, aware that on this most sacred of holidays there were Britons who could not observe it, whose duties kept them at peril on the sea.[115]

❦ ❦

In the United States thirty years later, Americans protesting the Vietnam War displayed bumper stickers asking: "What if they gave a war and nobody came?" The answer is that the war would become inconvenient, depressing, vexing, and, most of all, a bore — which is what Britons called World War II's first eight months: the Bore War. To Chamberlain it was the Twilight War, to Churchill the Sinister Trance, to Frenchmen the *Drôle de Guerre*, to Germans the *Sitzkrieg*, and to U.S. Senator William Borah and his fellow Americans the Phony War. But for the average Englishman it remained a bloody bore.[116]

In that strange lull following the fall of Poland a state of war existed between the Third Reich and the Anglo-French forces confronting them, but after Gamelin's *offensive de la Sarre* the only Allied casualty on the Continent was a British corporal who suffered a flesh wound while cleaning his rifle. Britain had been psyched up in September, ready for sacrifice; two stock comments at the time were, "We can't let old Hitler get away with it again, can we?" and "It's got to come, so we might as well have it and have done with it." An Englishwoman wrote that "we seemed to me to be going to war as a duty," because "it was the only wise course to take. . . . I began to hope (feeling very glad nobody knew) that the air raid would begin at once and the worst happen quickly." After Chamberlain's broadcast declaring war on Germany, a young office girl in Sheffield stood with her parents as the national anthem was played; she had "a funny feeling inside. . . . I know we were all in the same mind, that we shall and must win." A middle-aged schoolmistress noted: "At 11:15 I went up, and we sat round listening to Chamberlain speaking. I held my chin high and kept back the tears at the thought of all that slaughter ahead. When 'God Save the King' was played we stood."[117]

The country had braced itself to withstand a shock, believing its cause just, and then — nothing happened. As one Englishman put it: "The sense of mission turned sour." Chamberlain, demanding that the wage claims of workers be withdrawn, insisted that the wealthy had already made voluntary sacrifices. Audiences, even in Birmingham, laughed at him. Admiralty control of merchantmen often determined what was imported and what was not, and the first lord's ruling that all ships must zigzag to evade U-boats — a carryover from the last war — doubled the length of voyages. As a result there were shortages of everything: food, coal, and — though the government had encouraged householders to keep backyard hens — grain to feed poultry. Sugar, bacon, ham, and butter were rationed: by the fifth month of the war forty-eight million ration books had been issued in the United Kingdom. Mutton, smoked to look like bacon, became known as "macon"; native and imported butter were lumped together and officially designated "nation butter." In London Gracie Fields bellowed out a new hit:

They can muck about
With your Brussels sprout,
But they can't ration love!

There was even a shortage of noise. Under the Control of Noises (Defence) Order, ambulance sirens, factory whistles, and automobile horns were prohibited. Later, church bells were added. The thought behind this was that such sounds might alarm citizens or confuse those responsible for defending the city. It does not seem to have occurred to the authorities that Britons who had been hearing these noises all their lives might find *silence* alarming. In the territorials ammunition for rifles and Bren guns was rationed, and frequently officers, whose only personal weapons were their pistols, were unable to fire a single practice round. MPs like Sandys who were also reserve officers were accosted, at officers' mess, with complaints and questions. One question which they themselves would have liked to raise in the House irked property owners, which many of them were. In the first week of the war the government had requisitioned private property for wartime use. Tenants were evicted, warehouses emptied, livestock ousted from barns which were then locked. Winter deepened, spring approached, and the housing, warehouses, and barns stood empty. What had the government wanted them for? And where were the evacuees, now streaming back into London, going to live?[118]

Doubt, suspicion, and distrust of authority — the mood known as "bloody-mindedness" in the British army — appeared and spread. The lower classes were especially restive. As late as May 3, when all continued quiet on the western front, Jock Colville's Downing Street diary noted "a somewhat alarming report from the Conservative Central Office. . . . It seems that the war is not popular among the lowest sections of the community, that there is a suspicion it is being fought in the interests of the rich, and that there is much discontent about the rising cost of living." He added perceptively: "This is but a slight foretaste of what we shall have to face after the war." But the discontent was everywhere. A public opinion poll found that 46 percent of the British people were gloomy, 20 percent saw "a dark future" which would eventually reveal "a silver lining," 22 percent were fatalistic, and only 12 percent were optimistic. Churchill belonged with those believing in a silver lining. At the end of the war's first week he wrote Ambassador Corbin that "if there is full comradeship I cannot doubt our victory"; and, in another letter, he reaffirmed his conviction that — quoting his Boer War captors, who had given him a lifelong maxim to live by — "all will come right if we all work together to the end."[119]

But Winston, whose home and office were in the same building, did not have to cope with the blackout, the most exasperating irritant of a war in which the enemy had yet to appear. On Christmas Day, King George VI, following precedent, addressed his people over the BBC. He had inherited his father's gift for tedium — "A new year is at hand," he said. "We cannot tell what it will bring" — and his closing remark was more appropriate than he knew. "Go out into darkness," he told them, "and put your hand into the hand of God. That shall be to you better than light, and safer than a known way." Englishmen knew bloody well they were going out into darkness, but they preferred the known way, believing it safer, and were convinced that after nightfall nothing was better than light.[120]

In the beginning the impenetrable darkness had been rather exciting, like Guy Fawkes Day. But it could also be dangerous. In January a Gallup poll reported that since the outbreak of war about one Briton in five had been hurt in blackouts: bowled over by invisible runners, bruised by walking smack into an Air Raid Precautions post, stumbling over a curb, or being knocked down by a car without lights when they were on a street or road and didn't know it. Criminals appeared in the Square Mile, the heart of London, and even sortied into the West End. Just before Christmas some shopping centers tested what was known as "amenity lighting" — equivalent to the glow of a single candle seen seventy feet away. It was judged more depressing than utter darkness. Youth had fun with it, as youth always does. In the tube they merrily sang bawdy music hall ballads popular when Churchill was a handsome young cavalry officer — "Knees Up, Mother Brown" was a hit once more. Mass Observation reported a new fashion; a young couple would enjoy "intercourse in a shop doorway on the fringe of passing crowds, screened by another couple waiting to perform the same adventure. It has been done in a spirit of daring, but is described as being perfectly easy and rather thrilling."[121]

When war broke out, or was reported to have broken out, Air Raid Precautions wardens had been popular. Usually they were kindly, avuncular neighbors, looking a bit sheepish at first in their helmets as they went from door to door testing gas masks and explaining that no chink of light should escape a dwelling. But as time passed people grew tired of waiting for the Luftwaffe. One man told an interviewer that he felt like a patient in a dentist's waiting room: "It's got to come and will probably be horrible while it lasts, but it won't last forever, and it's just possible these teeth won't have to come out after all." It was just possible that Nazi Heinkels or Junkers would never appear in the night skies over England, so Mum or Dad might carelessly leave a shade up an inch or two, or a door ajar. Then the fatherly wardens turned into monsters. Their shining hour would come, and soon; in the Bore War, however, many of them were stigmatized to a degree which is puzzling today. But it should be remembered that in those days an Englishman's home was considered his castle; a premium was placed on privacy. And many men in tin hats were seen as a threat to it.[122]

In one remarkable instance a hundred-watt bulb had been left burning in an unoccupied house. The warden, a young, powerfully built man, found himself eyeball to eyeball with a double-locked mahogany door, framed in oak and set in concrete. He left, returned with a long iron bar, and, gathering his muscles for one heroic effort, burst into the room and turned off the lamp. The damage was fifteen pounds. An understanding magistrate reduced the usual two-pound fine to one pound. One outraged Londoner said he hated wardens more than Nazis and wanted to strangle them. If the German bombers had come it would have been different, but they hadn't. "What was the *point* of it?" asked Laurence Thompson, speaking for countless thousands. The English people, he wrote, were "a decent, puzzled, discontented people who had braced themselves to withstand Armageddon, and found themselves facing the petty miseries of burst water pipes, a shortage of coal, verminous evacuees, and the dim spiritual erosion of the blackout."[123]

The burst pipes, amounting to an epidemic, derived from the coldest European winter in forty-five years, an act of God which did not strengthen confidence in the King's endorsement of His benevolence. The coal shortage contributed to it, of course, but even without the inconveniences of wartime, Britain and the Continent would have suffered. Trains were buried under thirty-foot drifts; snowplows dug them out, but even so they were over twenty-eight hours late in reaching their destinations. Among civilians communications were often impossible. You couldn't phone, you couldn't send a wire; hundreds of miles of telephone and telegraph wires were down. In Derbyshire the drifts towered over cottage roofs. The Thames was solid ice for eight miles — from Teddington to Surbury. And the Strait of Dover was frozen at Dungeness and Folkestone. Afterward, one editorial surmised: "It is probable that on January 29, when chaotic transport conditions prevailed over a large part of England, due to snow and ice, Berlin had little idea of the extent of our wintry weather."[124]

It did not occur to that insular editor that the Continent might be sharing Britain's misery. Actually, the Continent was just as frigid. Even the Riviera was desolate, and Berlin, like London, was snowbound. The weather, which had not saved Poland, gave the Allies a reprieve. Seldom, if ever, have meteorological conditions so altered the course of a war, though the issue of who benefited most is debatable. Telford Taylor believes that because "the extremity of that bitter winter alone prevented Hitler from launching [an attack] against an ill-equipped and ill-prepared Anglo-French army . . . the weather saved the British army, which at that time had only half the strength it was to attain by spring." Certainly they felt blessed at the time. But afterward, when the OKW hierarchy was interrogated at Nuremberg, it became clear that during that arctic hiatus the Führer, in a brilliant stroke, completely changed his western strategy and thereby gained his margin of victory. How the Allies would have fared in the autumn of 1939 is moot. The fact that the French collapsed in the spring of 1940 is not, and the fewer troops the BEF had when France fell, the better, for in the ultimate crisis all of them had to be rescued.[125]

Hitler's military genius in the war's early years — his gift for reviewing the choices presented by *die Herren Oberbefehlshaber* (the commanders in chief) and unerringly selecting the right one — can hardly be exaggerated. Later, after his victories persuaded him that he was invincible, he provided the same generals with evidence to support their contention that his strategy was a succession of blunders. It wasn't; he achieved his remarkable triumphs despite them, in part because he understood them, and, more important, their soldiers, better than they did. Most of the world outside the Reich assumed that the Wehrmacht would rest after overwhelming Poland while the Führer digested his new conquest. Ironside disagreed. On September 15 — twelve days before the surrender of Warsaw — the CIGS told the War Cabinet that the French believed the Wehrmacht "would stage a big attack on the Western Front" within a month, and he himself thought a German offensive possible before the end of October. It seemed improbable. Even Churchill wrote Chamberlain later that same Friday that in his view a German attack on the western front "at this late season" was "most unlikely." A turn eastward and southward through Hungary and Rumania made more sense to Winston. He doubted that the Führer would turn westward until "he has collected the easy spoils which await him in the East," thereby giving his people "the spectacle of repeated successes."[126]

His vision was clouded there. However, no one outside the War Office and the Conseil Supérieur de la Guerre, and very few in them, matched his analysis of the Polish campaign. In that same letter he wrote that he was "strongly of the opinion that we should make every preparation to defend ourselves in the West." In particular, French territory on the border "behind Belgium should be fortified night and day by every conceivable resource," including "obstacles to tank attack, planting railway rails upright, digging deep ditches, erecting concrete dolls, land-mines in some parts and inundations all ready to let out in others, etc.," which "should be combined in a deep system of defence." The panzers which were overrunning Poland, he wrote, "can only be stopped by physical obstacles defended by resolute troops and a powerful artillery." If defenders lacked those, he warned, "the attack of armoured vehicles cannot be resisted."[127]

Hitler shared Churchill's admiration for tanks, and for that very reason he wanted to invade the neutral Low Countries before such obstacles could be built. He also assumed — illustrating his ignorance of how democracies work — that the Allies would soon occupy Belgium and Holland. Two days after Ironside's presentation to the War Cabinet and Churchill's advice to the prime minister, the Führer told the OKW commanders in Zossen that immediately after the Polish surrender he wanted to move the entire Wehrmacht across Germany and strike at the Allied forces. The Generalstab was shocked. They had been counting on several months of positional warfare in the west while they retrained their men and planned the army's order of battle. He was adamant; a few weeks later, on October 10, he issued his Directive No. 6, ordering immediate preparations for an attack through

Luxembourg, Belgium, and Holland "at as early a date as possible" with the objective of defeating the French and establishing "a base for conducting a promising air and sea war against England." To his staff he said he wanted the invasion under way by November 12.[128]

Ten days after his directive, the generals submitted their plan for invasion in the west. In Hitler's view, and in history's, it was remarkable for its mediocrity and lack of imagination. They proposed a frontal assault driving head-on across the Low Countries to the Channel ports. Six days later the Führer suggested that the main thrust drive across southern Belgium and through the forested Ardennes toward Sedan. Their reply echoes Pétain's view; the hills and thick woods of the Ardennes were "*unmöglich*" ("impossible"). The Führer made no further comment then. He hadn't dismissed the idea, but had the fine weather held, the unimaginative attack would have proceeded. Although the Allied armies were not up to strength, that was the plan they expected, and they would have met it with everything they had. They did so seven months later, when they had much more. Unfortunately, the German plan of attack had changed; while they were rushing to bar the front door, the enemy slipped in the back.

The weather, responsible for the long delay, persuaded Hitler to postpone his assault nine times. Each time, he reconsidered lunging through the Ardennes with a panzer corps. His aides were instructed to bring him aerial photographs and detailed topographic maps of the terrain. Studying them, he felt confirmed; much of it was good panzer country, fields and roads; the forested areas which discouraged generals could be used to advantage, camouflaging tanks from aerial surveillance. In fact, although this was unknown to him, in 1939 when the Conseil Supérieur had staged a seven-division German drive in the French Ardennes with armored support, the "enemy" had put the defenders to flight. Field Marshal Walther von Brauchitsch, army commander in chief, was unconvinced, and protocol required the Führer to deal directly with him. However, a handful of his most gifted generals, Manstein, Rundstedt, and Guderian among them, believed that a massive panzer *Sichelschnitt* (scythe-cut) in the south, with a far stronger force than Hitler had proposed, could slice through the Ardennes, drive to the sea, and trap the Allied armies in the north, where the Germans were expected. On February 17, in a traditional ceremony, five generals promoted to corps commanders were invited to dine with the Führer. Manstein was among them. He gave his host a detailed account of the plan he, Rundstedt, and Guderian had developed. Hitler was ecstatic. At noon the next day he issued a new *Führerordnung*, incorporating all Manstein's points. By February 24, Hitler, Halder, and the OKW in Zossen, working round the clock, had completed the final orders for their Ardennes offensive. The blow would fall in May.

* * *

The British military presence in France, so slight before winter closed down Hitler's plan for a lightning stroke in the west, grew through the bitter winter, until Lord Gort, the BEF commander, had nearly 400,000 men dug in. Unlike their fathers in 1914, they were not eager to fight, but they were ready. Morale was high; the British spit-and-polish traditions were observed; so were training schedules; and officers organized games, the more vigorous the better, to keep the men fit. Gracie Fields's ration song was unheard here. The music halls had given the BEF a rollicking anthem which enjoyed tremendous popularity until events soured its lyrics.

We're gonna hang out the washing on the Siegfried Line.
Have you any dirty washing, Mother dear?

Soldiers given leave headed for Paris, where the season's hit shows were *Paris, Reste Paris,* at the Casino de Paris, starring Maurice Chevalier and Josephine Baker; Lucienne Boyer at her *boîte de nuit* in the rue Volney; and revivals of *Cyrano de Bergerac* and *Madame sans Gêne* at the Comédie Française. But on the whole Tommies found the City of Light disappointing. The attitude of the French puzzled them. They seemed surly, hostile, smoldering with grievances. And so they were. Some of their anger was intramural; they held their leaders in contempt. After the Russians had picked up their winnings in Poland and declared themselves at peace, France's powerful Communist party took the position that the war was a "capitalist-imperialist project" in which workers had no stake. At the other end of the political spectrum, the extreme French right still yearned for an understanding with the Reich; with Poland gone, they argued, the need for an anti-Bolshevik bulwark was all the greater. To them, German National Socialism was preferable to French socialism; their rallying cry was "Better Hitler than Blum." Lucien Rebattet, a gifted writer for the Fascist weekly *Je Suis Partout,* wrote that the war had been launched "by the most hideous buffoons of the most hideous Jewish and demagogic regime. . . . We are supposed once more to save the Republic, and a Republic worse than the one in 1914. . . . No, I do not feel the least anger against Hitler, but much against all the French politicians who have led to his triumph."[129]

However, the chief target of French discontent was Britain. Although the British were allies, they were treated with scorn. Until Tommies began manning sectors of the Maginot Line, a brigade at a time, most poilus were unaware that the British Expeditionary Force even existed. Certainly their newspapers didn't tell them. The Parisian press, reinforcing the public mood, was resentful not of Nazi aggression, the root cause of the war, but of *l'Albion perfide*. England, in the popular French view, had forced France into unnecessary hostilities, and there was widespread suspicion that the British had no intention of fighting — that when battle appeared imminent they would withdraw to their island, shielded by the Royal Navy, while poilus were slaughtered. Daladier told William Bullitt, the American ambassador, that he was convinced Britain intended to let the French do all the fighting. At the Quai d'Orsay, Alexis Léger spoke as though Britain were uncommitted, telling Bullitt: *"La partie est perdue. La France est seule."* Holding his first staff meeting as supreme commander of Allied troops, Gamelin revealed his opinion of his ally by neglecting to bring an interpreter and speaking so rapidly that less than half of what he said was understood by the British officers.[130]

We're gonna hang out the washing on the Siegfried Line
'Cause the washing day is here.

Churchill had been visiting France since childhood, and despite his atrocious accent, he spoke the language fluently. Hitler spoke only German. He had never been abroad. Yet Churchill's Francophilia was a romantic illusion, while the German führer's evaluation of the people who had been Germany's foe for over two thousand years was penetrating. "Hitler," Churchill later wrote, "was sure that the French political system was rotten to the core, and that it had infected the French Army." Whatever the reason, the rot was there. And Joseph Goebbels knew how to make it fester. The Luftwaffe, like the RAF, staged truth raids. They were, however, far more clever than England's. Their contribution to what one French officer called "*une guerre de confettis*" was not leaflets but single slips of paper that fluttered down round the French lines. Resembling colored leaves, they bore on one side the message: "In the autumn the leaves fall. So fall the poilus, fighting for the English." The obverse read: "In the spring the leaves come again. Not so the poilus."[131]

The leaflets were followed by beguiling enticements from French-speaking Germans using bullhorns and large signs taunting poilus at the front, asking why they should die for Danzig, the Poles, or the British (*"Ne mourez pas pour Danzig, pour les Polonais, pour les Britanniques!"*). Nazi propagandistic statements quoted by Molotov, effective among French Communists, assigned to *"la France et la Grande-Bretagne la responsabilité de la poursuite des hostilités."* On September 26, with Poland vanquished, the Germans opened a new propaganda campaign: "Why do France and Britain want to fight now? Nothing to fight about. Germany wants nothing in the

West. [*L'Allemagne ne demande rien à l'ouest*]." The most effective line was the assurance that if the French didn't open fire, German guns would remain silent. *Time* reported a version of this: "We have orders not to fire on you if you don't fire on us." Soon poilus and *Soldaten* were bathing in the Rhine together. *Time* readers unfamiliar with the fighting spirit essential in infantry combat — not only for victory but also for the survival of the individual infantryman — might have thought this harmless. But it served the Führer in two ways. In the first week of the war civility between men on both sides would permit his thin screen of troops on the Reich's western front to hold while the Wehrmacht finished off the Poles. And idle soldiers, especially those doubtful of their cause, deteriorate under such circumstances; their combat efficiency loses whatever edge it had, and when the balloon goes up, they find it almost impossible to kill the likable, fair-haired youths on the far shore, which means the youths on the far shore, no longer under orders to appear likable, are far likelier to kill *them*.[132]

British soldiers appeared to be immune to the contagion. Their commanders were not defeatist, neither their great-grandfathers nor their fathers had been routed by German troops in 1870 and 1914 — and besides, whoever heard of Blighty losing a war?

What though the weather be wet or fine,
We'll just travel on without a care.

British officers, however, were worried. One of their strengths, and a source of impotent rage among those who lived under other flags and had to deal with them, was that Englishmen with their background could not be offended by pomposity because their own capacity for arrogance was infinite. In 1914 British officers had told their men, "The wogs" — a pejorative for subjects of the Empire — "begin at Calais." They were still saying it in 1939, distinctly pronouncing the final *s* in *Calais* while natives gnashed their teeth. Gamelin, reading French aloud at top speed, could never win playing this game with them. They had invented insolence and would leave his hauteur a thing of shreds and patches.

They were, however, concerned about the poilus' morale. If the Germans came — and despite enemy propaganda no one in authority doubted that they would — these French soldiers would be on the British right. Should they break, the BEF's flank would be left hanging on air, the ultimate horror of a generation of soldiers wedded to the doctrine of *le front continu*. Again and again they had been told that the French army was "matchless," a word, it now occurred to them, subject to two interpretations. Certainly few of them could recall seeing its equal in carelessness, untidiness, and lack of military courtesy. General Sir Alan Brooke, a future CIGS now commanding a BEF corps, attended a ceremony as the guest of General André-Georges Corap, commander of the French Ninth Army. In his memoirs he would recall taking the salute: "Seldom have I seen anything more slovenly and badly turned out. Men unshaven, horses ungroomed, clothes and saddlery that did not fit, vehicles dirty, and a complete lack of pride in themselves and their units. What shook me most . . . was the look in the men's faces, disgruntled and insubordinate looks, and although ordered to give 'Eyes left,' hardly a man bothered to do so." It would be a distortion, however, to indict the conscripted French soldier for his reluctance to defend the soil of France. The blight went all the way to the top. It was their *généralissime* who expressly forbade poilus from firing on German working parties across the river. *"Les Allemands,"* he said, *"répondront en tirant sur les nôtres"* ("The Germans would only respond by firing on us").[133]

Sumner Welles, the American under secretary of state, accepted an invitation to inspect the Allied front. Welles was touring Europe as a special emissary of FDR, and in Washington he reported that French officers had privately complained to him that their men were undisciplined; unless the Germans attacked soon, they predicted, the poilus would spontaneously disband and go home. If an army's leaders take a foreigner aside to criticize their own men, something is very wrong. Vigilant French leaders knew it. Not only was there no training; neither Gamelin nor General Georges, Churchill's friend, ordered exercises at divisional strength to make commanders familiar with the problems of handling large units in the field. General André-Charles-Victor Laffargue later wrote: "Our units vegetated in an existence without purpose, settling down to guard duty and killing time until the next leave or relief." Longer leaves were granted more frequently, recreation centers established, theatrical troupes summoned from Paris to entertain the troops.[134]

Nothing worked. Morale continued to decline. General Edmond Ruby, commander of the First Army, was alarmed to find "a general apathy and ignorance among the ranks. No one dared give an order for fear of being criticized. Military exercises were considered a joke, and work unnecessary drudgery." The next step down was alcoholism. It appears to have descended upon the whole army overnight. *"L'ivrognerie"* — drunkenness — "had made an immediate appearance," General Ruby noted, "and in the larger railroad stations special rooms had to be set up to cope with it — euphemistically known as 'halls of de-alcoholizing.' " So many men were so drunk in public that commanders began to worry about *civilian* morale.[135]

Although Churchill believed that the French army would never break, however strong the German assault, in January 1940 he crossed the Channel for a visit to the front. He did not return reassured. The French artillery, he was pleased to find, had been improved "so as to get extra range and even to out-range, the new German artillery." But he was deeply troubled by "the mood of the people," which "in a great national conscript force is closely reflected in its army, the more so when that army is quartered in the homeland and contacts are close." During the 1930s, he later wrote, "important elements, in reaction to growing Communism, had swung towards Fascism," and the long months of waiting which had followed the collapse of Poland had given "time and opportunity" for "the poisons" of communism and fascism "to be established." There could be "no doubt," he observed, that "the quality of the French army" was being "allowed to deteriorate during the winter." Sound morale in any army is achieved in many ways, "but one of the greatest is that men be fully employed at useful and interesting work. Idleness is a dangerous breeding-ground." He had observed "many tasks that needed doing: training demanded continuous attention; defences were far from satisfactory or complete, even the Maginot Line lacked many supplementary field works; physical fitness demands exercise." He had been struck by the "poor quality of the work in hand, by the lack of visible activity of any kind," and thought the "emptiness of the roads behind the line was in great contrast to the continual coming and going which extended for miles behind the British sector."[136]

Colonel de Gaulle also believed the troops needed training and exercise, and urged it in a vigorous report to his superiors. He thought programs should be both intensive and exhausting, partly because the men weren't fit but also to raise their spirits. Somewhere on its way up to high command his recommendation was lost, which was no surprise to those familiar with the system. In combat a leader's greatest need is information, and if he is competent he does everything possible to establish a communications system that will survive in the chaos of battle, and, if possible, at least one backup net, for what works well in peacetime maneuvers may disintegrate and vanish when great armies clash in the fog of war.

Gamelin seems not to have anticipated this obstacle. Indeed, it was almost as though he set out to frustrate his own chain of command and assure his isolation when he was most needed. Poring over documents in Vincennes, on the outskirts of Paris, he never established means of keeping in touch with field commanders. There was no radio at Vincennes. He could telephone Georges, the commander of all forces at the front, whose headquarters were at La Ferté-sous-Jouarre, thirty-five miles away, but he preferred to drive, an hour each way on roads swarming with suburban

Paris traffic. In the age of radio and the teletype, it took six hours for an order from Gamelin to reach an air force command — by which time the target would be gone — and *forty-eight hours* to issue a general order to all commands. One French officer described his remote headquarters as a "submarine without a periscope," and later de Gaulle wrote bitterly: "There he was, in a setting as quiet as a convent [*silencieux comme un couvent*], attended by a few officers, working and meditating without mixing in day-to-day duties. In his retreat at Vincennes, General Gamelin gave the impression of a savant testing the chemical reactions of his strategy in a laboratory."[137]

Sir John Slessor of the Air Ministry, one of a series of visitors from London, described the supreme commander as a "nice old man not remotely equal to his enormous job." Why, then, didn't the British move to thwart the debacle that lay dead ahead? One reason was that the British troop commitment was much smaller than the French. Another was that in the last war it had taken four years to establish a unified command under Foch. Furthermore, Gamelin had served ably on Foch's staff. Most members of His Majesty's Government were Francophiles; they refused to credit the tales of Anglophobia across the water. All, Churchill included, retained their blind faith in the French army, which had taken the worst the Germans could throw at them between 1914 and 1918 and always came back. The poilus of this war were the sons of those in the last. Surely they had inherited the same fighting qualities. But they hadn't. Unlike their fathers, they preferred to live.

There was also the Maginot Line. Those whose memories do not reach back to the 1930s cannot grasp its enormous reputation before its hour struck. *La Ligne* was considered one of the world's wonders, and the French never lost an opportunity to polish its image. The French high command celebrated the first Christmas of the war by announcing that they had completed a staggering "work of fortification." Their goal had been "to double the Maginot Line" and it was "virtually complete. . . . From the first of this month our new line of fortifications seems to have removed any hope the enemy may have entertained either of crossing or flanking the Maginot Line."[138]

We're gonna hang out the washing on the Siegfried Line.
Have you any dirty washing, Mother dear?

An American foreign correspondent asked about the Ardennes. Every staff officer was aware that the forest was unfortified; Hitler knew; Manstein, Guderian, Halder, and Rundstedt knew; and Liddell Hart had known of it for over eleven years. But the American public, the British public, and the French public did not know. A majority were under the impression that the Maginot shielded France from every possible German thrust. At Vincennes an officer in a kepi and flawless uniform of sky blue quoted Pétain — *"Elle est impénétrable"* — with the proviso that "special dispositions" must be made there. The edges on the enemy side would be protected; some blockhouses would be installed. The war was nearly four months old, the Maginot Line had been doubled, but the dispositions were not complete. The American asked why. Because at this point the front would not have any depth, he was told, the enemy would not commit himself there. Finally: *"Ce secteur n'est pas dangereux."*[139]

We're gonna hang out the washing on the Siegfried Line

Walter Lippmann was received as though he were a head of state; a dozen colonels took him on a tour of the Maginot Line, then accompanied him to Vincennes. Lippmann commented that there was only one thing wrong with the line: it was in the wrong place. The *généralissime* did not understand. What would happen, the American publicist asked, if the enemy attacked in the north, where the line ended at the Belgian frontier? Gamelin was glad he had asked. He was *hoping* the Germans would try that. "We've got to have an open side because we need a *champs de bataille,*" he explained. "The Maginot Line will narrow the gap through which they can come, and thus enable us to destroy them more easily."[140]

'Cause the washing day is here.

Colonel de Gaulle was a *peste*. He had been repeatedly referred to the army manual *Les instructions pour l'emploi des chars* — tanks — which clearly stated that "Combat tanks are machines to accompany the infantry. . . . In battle, tank units constitute an integral part of the infantry. . . . Tanks are only supplementary means. . . . The progress of the infantry and its seizing of objectives are alone decisive." The role of the tank was to accompany infantry *"et non pour combattre en formations indépendantes."* Could anything be clearer? He was worse than the aviators, who at least had the decency to remain silent after General Gamelin had told them: "There is no such thing as the aerial battle. There is only the battle on the ground." Yet here was de Gaulle, turning up in Montry at general headquarters, where most of the General Staff and staff officers could be found, with another of his reports, this one on *les leçons* to be learned from the blitzkrieg in Poland. He wrote: "The gasoline engine discredits all our military doctrines, just as it will demolish our fortifications. We have excellent material. We must learn to use it as the Germans have."[141]

At present, de Gaulle pointed out, French tanks were dispersed for infantry support. It would be wiser, he submitted, to follow the example of the Germans, forming them in armored divisions as the Wehrmacht had done in its Polish campaign, and, indeed, before the Anschluss. His proposals were rejected by two generals — one of whom predicted that even if Nazi tanks penetrated French lines they would face *"la destruction presque complète."* To this snub the high command added mortal injury to the France de Gaulle loved. Despite the vindication of Guderian's prewar book *Achtung, Panzer!* in Poland, the French high command decided to sell its tanks abroad. The R-35 was a better tank than any German model. Of the last 500 produced before May 10, 1940, nearly half — 235 — were sold to Turkey, Yugoslavia, and Rumania, with the result that when the Germans struck only 90 were on the French front. Moreover, while Nazi troops, Stukas, and armored divisions were massing in the Rhineland for their great lunge westward, the generals charged with the defense of French soil gathered representatives of countries not regarded as unfriendly to France and auctioned off 500 artillery pieces, complete with ammunition, and 830 antitank guns — at a time when the French army was desperately short of both weapons.[142]

The French Ministry of War announced that 100,000 pigeons had been mobilized and housed inside the Maginot Line to carry messages through artillery barrages.

We're gonna hang our washing on the Siegfried Line —
If the Siegfried Line's still there!

The brief struggle in Finland had drawn the world's attention to Scandinavia, a development deplored by the Scandinavians, who, like other neutrals, hoped they would be overlooked until the war was over. Norway's yearning for obscurity — which was inevitably shared by Denmark, as it was situated between the Norwegians and the Reich — was frustrated by the Royal Navy on Friday, February 16, in an action which thrilled all England, widened the war, increased Churchill's popularity, and, in its sequel, almost led to his ruin.

Probably Oslo's desperate attempts to remain a spectator were doomed. A country's neutrality cannot always be determined by its own government. If it is violated by one warring power, the country is like the ravished maiden in the Nibelungenlied legend who immediately becomes available to all others, and the Germans had been exploiting Norway's territorial waters since the outbreak of the war. Swedish iron ore from Gällivare was "vital for the German munitions industry," as Churchill had told the War Cabinet on September 19, and while in summer German ships could transport this ore across the Gulf of Bothnia, between Finland and Sweden, in winter it had to be moved westward to Narvik, a Norwegian port, and then down the length of the Norwegian coast through the Leads, a deep-water channel running parallel to the shore. Germany wasn't the only country with U-boats; British submarines could have littered the floor of the North Atlantic with the sunken hulks of enemy freighters.[143]

It hadn't done so because their captains had remained within Norway's three-mile limit, and the government in Oslo, fearful of Nazi reprisals, had decided not to protest. If this use of Norwegian territorial waters could not be stopped "by pressure on the Norwegian government," said Churchill, it would be his duty to propose "the laying of mines" inside Norway's "territorial waters." There was precedent for this. The Admiralty had done it in 1917, and had successfully drawn the German ships out beyond the Leads. After the meeting broke up, he sent Pound a minute advising him that the War Cabinet, including Halifax, "appeared strongly to favor this action." Therefore, he wrote, he wanted Admiralty staff to study the minelaying operation, adding: "Pray let me be continually informed of the progress of this plan, which is of the highest importance in crippling the enemy's war industry." A further decision of the War Cabinet would be made "when all is in readiness."[144]

Pound had seen to it that all was soon in readiness, but other members of the cabinet had not really shared Churchill's sense of urgency, and when the project was mooted in Whitehall, the Foreign Office and the Dominions emitted sounds of alarm. After discussion a majority of the War Cabinet had decided that immediate action was unnecessary, and the matter had been set aside. This seemed to be the fate of every imaginative proposal Winston laid before them, and his sense of frustration is evident in a letter to a colleague. His "disquiet," he wrote, was mainly due to "the awful difficulty which our machinery of war conduct presents to positive action. I see such immense walls of prevention, all building and building, that I wonder whether any plan will have a chance of climbing over them."[145]

The issue had remained on Churchill's mind, however, and had been one of his motives in drafting Operation Catherine. Now in February a flagrant Nazi trespass inside the three-mile limit called for an instant response by the Admiralty. Before *Graf Spee*'s last battle, the captured crews of the British merchantmen she had sunk had been transferred to her supply ship, the *Altmark*. Over three hundred of these English seamen had been locked in *Altmark*'s hold, and they were still there, because after *Graf Spee* went down the smaller *Altmark* had escaped from the battered British warships. For nine weeks she had been hiding in the vastness of the South Atlantic; now, running out of fuel and provisions, with no safe haven elsewhere, she was bringing the British crews home to the Reich for imprisonment. On the morning of February 16 Winston was told that an RAF pilot had sighted her, hugging the Norwegian coast and heading south. Immediately he decided to rescue the men in her hold. Ordering all British warships in the area to "sweep northwards during the day," he directed them "to arrest *Altmark* in territorial waters should she be found. This ship is violating neutrality in carrying British prisoners of war to Germany. Surely another cruiser or two should be sent to rummage the Skagerrak tonight? The *Altmark* must be regarded as an invaluable trophy."[146]

That afternoon H.M.S. *Cossack,* Captain Philip Vian commanding, sighted the German vessel. She fled into Jösing Fjord. Vian blocked the mouth of the fjord and sent in a destroyer with a boarding party. Two Norwegian gunboats intercepted them, and the captain of one of them, the *Kjell,* arrived by barge on the *Cossack*. Vian wrote afterward that he told the Norwegian that he "demanded the right to visit and search, asking him to come with me." The Norwegian officer replied that the *Altmark* had been searched three times since her entry into Norwegian waters and that "no prisoners had been found. His instructions were to resist entry by force: as I might see, his ships had their torpedo tubes trained on *Cossack*. Deadlock."[147]

Vian signaled the Admiralty for instructions. Churchill had left word that any message concerning *Altmark* should be sent directly to him. The incident offers an excellent illustration of what General Sir Ian Jacob has called "the fury of his concentration." On such occasions, Jacob writes: "When his mind was occupied with a particular problem, however detailed, it focused upon it relentlessly. Nobody could turn him aside." Marder adds: "With a display of energy and his imagination, Churchill sometimes carried his offensive ideas too far. . . . The Baltic, and increasingly the Norwegian facet, became almost an obsession with him." There were those in the Foreign Office who thought his reply to Vian was too aggressive; they were the same people who, after his broadcast criticizing neutral countries, had issued a gratuitous statement declaring that the first lord had not represented HMG policy.[148]

In fact his instructions to Vian were almost flawless — "almost," because he should have sent them through Admiral Sir Charles Forbes, Vian's superior. He *did* phone Halifax and told him what he proposed to do. The foreign secretary hurried over to the Admiralty, where Winston and Pound lectured him on the "Law of Hot Pursuit" at sea. Halifax suggested giving the Norwegian captain an option — taking *Altmark* to Bergen under joint escort, for an inquiry according to international law. His suggestion was adopted, and then the order was radioed to *Cossack*. If the Norwegians refused to convoy *Altmark* to Bergen, Vian was told, he was to "board *Altmark*, liberate the prisoners, and take possession of the ship." If a Norwegian vessel interfered she should be warned off, but "if she fires upon you, you should not reply unless the attack is serious, in which case you should defend yourself using no more force than is necessary, and ceasing fire when she desists."[149]

That night, as the first lord and the first sea lord sat up in the war room — "in some anxiety," as Churchill wrote — Vian boarded *Kjell* and proposed the Halifax option. The Norwegian captain declined; he repeated that the German ship had been searched, that she was unarmed, and that she carried no British prisoners. These were all lies, but as Churchill pointed out, "Every allowance must be made" for the Norwegians, who were "quivering under the German terror and exploiting our forbearance." Already the Nazis "had sunk 218,000 tons of Scandinavian ships with a loss of 555 Scandinavian lives." Vian said he was going to board *Altmark*. He invited the Norwegian officer to join him. The invitation was declined; henceforth he and his sister ship were passive spectators.[150]

So the *Cossack* entered the fjord alone, searchlights blazing, knifing through the ice floes until Vian realized that *Altmark* was under way and attempting to ram him. Luckily the German at the helm was a poor seaman. He ran his vessel aground. Vian forced his way alongside; his crew grappled the two ships together, and the British boarding party sprang across. The Nazi vessel *was* armed, with two pom-poms and four machine guns. The tars seized those and turned on *Altmark*'s crew; in a hand-to-hand fight four Germans were killed and five wounded; the others fled ashore or surrendered. No Norwegians had searched the ship. In battened-down storerooms and in empty oil tanks, 299 Britons awaited rescue. The boarding party was flinging open hatches; one of them called, "Are there any English down there?" There was a shouted chorus of "Yes!" and a boarder shouted back, "Well, the navy's here!" By midnight Vian was clear of the fjord, racing home to England.[151]

The news reached Admiralty House at 3:00 A.M., and Churchill and Pound were jubilant. Randolph's wife, Pamela, saw *Cossack* land the rescued prisoners at Leith, on the Firth of Forth, where doctors, ambulances, press, and photographers awaited them. She wrote her father-in-law: "You must have had a very thrilling & anxious night on Friday. It's comforting to know we can be ferocious." In his Downing Street diary, Jock Colville's Saturday entry began: "There was great excitement at No. 10 over the *Altmark* affair, news of which reached us early in the morning. It is a perfect conclusion to the victory over the *Graf von Spee*." The King sent a congratulatory note to his Admiralty's first lord, who replied at once: "It is a vy gt encouragement & gratification to me to receive Your Majesty's most gracious & kindly message. . . . By none is Your Majesty's compliment more treasured than by the vy old servant of Your Royal House and of your father & yr grandfather who now subscribes himself / Your Majesty's faithful & devoted subject / Winston S. Churchill."[152]

Arthur Marder speaks for RN professionals when he writes of the *Altmark* incident: "It was a minor operation of no significance save for its considerable moral effects." The episode had repercussions, as we shall see, but the casual reference to its impact on the British public reflects the attitude of military professionals. In wartime they are condescending toward civilians, although public opinion, as France was already demonstrating, can determine what kind of war will be fought, and, to a considerable extent, whether it will be won or lost. Blackouts without bombers were merely exasperating; it was after the *Altmark* that people began to hate. Not all the people — the well-bred still recoiled from the chauvinism without which great victories are impossible. As late as April 26, 1940, Jock Colville saw "a group of bespectacled intellectuals" in Leicester Square's Bierkeller "remain firmly seated while God Save the King was played. Everybody looked but nobody did anything, which shows that the war has not yet made us lose our sense of proportion or become noisily jingoistic." The lower classes were less tolerant, and the newspapers fed their wrath. Churchill had found the rescued men "in good health" and "hearty condition," but Fleet Street rechristened *Altmark* "The Hell-Ship"; those rescued were encouraged to exaggerate their ordeal, and their stories gained in the retelling. Public opinion was developing genuine hostility toward Nazi Germany. People *wanted* to believe in atrocities. Even after four of the men saved had appeared on a platform in the East End, looking well-fed and ruddy, a woman in the audience was quoted as saying: "If I saw a German drowning, I wouldn't save him. Not after that, I couldn't."[153]

Churchill, no hater, used the brief clash in the fjord to build patriotism and confidence in men like Vian and his crew. The House of Commons liked that. On Tuesday, February 20, Harold Nicolson noted: "Winston, when he comes in, is loudly cheered." Admiral Keyes had been in the war room that night, Nicolson's diary entry continued, and had told him how "Winston rang up Halifax and said, 'I propose to violate Norwegian neutrality.' The message was sent and they waited anxiously in the Admiralty for the result. What a result! A fine show. Winston, when he walks out of the House, catches my eye. He gives one portentous wink."[154]

Churchill wanted to squeeze every last drop out of it. The war hadn't been much of a war thus far. The Germans, he knew, were refitting for an offensive somewhere, and the Allies — who should have been giving them no rest — remained passive. He had no authority over the other services, but he could make the navy fight. The battle off Montevideo had given England its first real news to cheer about, and on February 15, just one day before the *Altmark* triumph, he had greeted *Exeter* as she arrived at Plymouth. Now, on February 23, he gathered the heroes of the River Plate in the great hall of the Guildhall, the focal point for the government of London for over a thousand years. There, beneath the Gothic facade, beneath the four fantastic pinnacles, the exuberant coat-of-arms, and the monuments to Chatham, Nelson, and Wellington, he reminded those present — and the nation beyond — that the brunt of the war thus far had been borne by sailors, nearly three thousand of whom had already been lost in the "hard, unrelenting struggle which goes on night and day." He said:

> The spirit of all our forces serving on salt water has never been more strong and high than now. The warrior heroes of the past may look down, as Nelson's monument looks down upon us now, without any feeling that the island race has lost its daring or that the examples they set in bygone centuries have faded as the generations have succeeded one another. It was not for nothing that Admiral Harwood, as he instantly at full speed attacked an enemy which might have sunk any one of his ships by a single salvo from its far heavier guns, flew Nelson's immortal signal.[155]

He was gathering himself for the final flourish, shoulders hunched, brow lowered, swaying slightly, holding them all in his stern gaze. It wasn't a Bore War when Churchill spoke of it; it wasn't squalid or demeaning; it wasn't, in fact, like modern war at all. Destroying the Nazis and their führer became a noble mission, and by investing it with the aura of heroes like Nelson, men Englishmen had honored since childhood, he made the Union Jack ripple and St. George's sword gleam. To the action off the Plate, he said, there had recently been added an epilogue, the feat of "the *Cossack* and her flotilla," a gallant rescue, "under the nose of the enemy and amid the tangles of one-sided neutrality, of the British captives taken from the sunken German raider. . . . And to Nelson's signal of 135 years ago, 'England expects that every man will do his duty,' there may now be added last week's no less proud reply: '*The Navy is here!*' "[156]

The Guildhall exploded in a roaring, standing ovation.

In his diary Hoare grumbled about "Winston overbidding the market in his speeches," but it was a popular speech. No one had fewer illusions about combat than Siegfried Sassoon, who had been court-martialed for publishing his powerful antiwar poems while serving as a junior officer in the first war. Now he wrote Eddie Marsh: "What an apotheosis Winston is enjoying! I suppose he is the most popular — as well as being the ablest — political figure in England. He must be glorying in the deeds of the Navy, who are indeed superb. And W himself has certainly put up a grand performance."[157]

His last four words — "The Navy is here!" — wrote Laurence Thompson, "gripped the public mind. It was felt that, dull and unenterprising though the conduct of the war might be on land and sea, the navy was eternally there; and so it heroically was, bearing with the Merchant Navy the heaviest burden of the war." England had gone to war no more eagerly than the French, and as a people the British were less vulnerable to slogans and political melodrama. But as divisions deepened in Paris and the rest of France, Britons grew more united. If they had to fight they would. And though it seemed on that Friday that the Royal Navy had preempted the national consciousness, British soldiers were about to take the field against Nazi troops for the first time. It was to be an inauspicious opening.[158]

For Hitler the Royal Navy's coup de main in Jösing Fjord was "*unerträglich*" — "intolerable." He was enraged that the German seamen on the *Altmark* had not fought harder. According to Jodl's diary he raved, "*Kein Widerstand, Keine engl. Verluste!*" ("No resistance, no British losses!"). This seems hard on the four Germans who had been killed in the firefight, but the Führer had his own yardstick of valor; he reserved his approval for men who had been worthy of *him*. Two days later, on February 19, Jodl's diary reveals, "The Führer pressed energetically" for the completion of *Weserübung* — the code name for plans to occupy Norway — issuing orders to "equip ships; put units in readiness." To lead this operation he summoned a corps commander from the western front, General Nikolaus von Falkenhorst, who had fought in Finland at the end of the last war. Later, under interrogation in Nuremberg, Falkenhorst said he had the impression that it was the *Altmark* incident which led Hitler to "carry out the plan now."[159]

The origins of *Weserübung* were more ambiguous than might appear to be the case. In his war memoirs Churchill wrote that "Hitler's decision to invade Norway had . . . been taken on December 14, and the staff work was proceeding under Keitel." The only relevant event on December 14 had been a meeting between Hitler and Major Vidkun Quisling, a former

Norwegian minister of defense, who had fallen under the Nazi spell and whose present ambition was to betray his country to the Reich. Admiral Raeder had urged the Führer to exploit this man's twisted allegiance, and Hitler had scheduled the interview because he wanted "to form an impression of him." Afterward, the Führer had put him on the payroll "to combat British propaganda" and strengthen Norway's Nazi party, an organization which existed almost entirely in Quisling's imagination. But *Weserübung* had not been Hitler's idea. In fact it was the only unprovoked Nazi aggression which wasn't. It was drawn up by the Oberkommando der Kriegsmarine on orders from Raeder alone, which also made it unique; the Wehrmacht high command and its Generalstab were not consulted, and Göring wasn't even told until the execution of the plan was hours away.[160]

Hitler was aware of it, of course; to embark on so ambitious a venture without keeping the chancellor fully informed would have been worth an officer's life. Hitler also knew how the kaiser's Imperial Fleet had been frustrated in the last war, bottled up in the Baltic by the British blockade, with no access to the high seas; and he knew his navy was determined to thwart the Royal Navy in any future conflict by establishing bases in Norway. In October, during a long report to the Führer on Kriegsmarine operations, Raeder had mentioned this objective, and according to Raeder's Nuremberg testimony, Hitler "saw at once the significance of the Norwegian operation." After the outbreak of the Russo-Finnish war several weeks later, the Führer also became alert to the danger implicit in reports that the Allies were forming expeditions to support the Finns, a pretext which threatened the lifeblood of his munitions factories in the Ruhr valley, where the smokestack barons needed fifteen million tons of iron ore every year and counted on Sweden for eleven million tons of it. The existence of *Weserübung* could be misinterpreted by civilians as proof of planned aggression. It wasn't; professional soldiers in every nation know that during peacetime general staffs draw up plans contemplating hostilities with other powers, even though the likelihood that they will ever be needed is very small. The War Department in Washington, for example, had drafted detailed instructions for invasions of virtually every country on the Continent.[161]

The fact — established beyond doubt at Nuremberg and in captured documents — was that Hitler did not *want* to occupy Norway. During his interview with Quisling, which was recorded in shorthand and transcribed, he said that he "would prefer Norway, as well as the rest of Scandinavia, to remain completely neutral"; he was not interested in schemes which would "enlarge the theater of war." A neutral Norway meant the Reich could import Swedish ore without British interference. There is strong evidence that he impressed this on Raeder; on January 13, the official war diary of the

Kriegsmarine mentioned Scandinavia in passing and noted that "the most favorable solution would be the maintenance of Norway's neutrality." But both the Führer and his naval staff established caveats. "If the enemy were preparing to spread the war" in Scandinavia, Hitler said, he would "take steps to guard against that threat." Similarly, the Kriegsmarine's war diary expressed anxiety that "England intends to occupy Norway with the tacit agreement of the Norwegian government." The dubious source for this was Quisling, who also told Hitler that the *Cossack*'s boarding of the *Altmark* had been prearranged. The government in Oslo, he said, was England's willing accomplice; the Norwegian gunboats had been ordered to take no action, thereby hoodwinking the Third Reich and its führer. That was the kind of meat upon which this Caesar fed, but the records of his conferences with Raeder show that he was still hesitant, still convinced that "maintenance of Norway's neutrality is the best thing," and — this on March 9 — that so perilous an operation, pitting his small fleet against the legendary might of the Royal Navy, was "contrary to all the principles of naval warfare." Yet in that same conference he called the occupation of Norway *"dringend"* — "urgent." Ambivalence was not characteristic of the Reich's supreme *Kriegsherr*, but he seems to have been indecisive here.[162]

On the last Thursday in March William L. Shirer observed in his diary: "Germany cannot stay in the war unless she continues to receive Swedish iron, most of which is shipped from the Norwegian port of Narvik on German vessels which evade the blockade by feeling their way down the Norwegian coast. . . . Some of us have wondered why Churchill has never done anything about this. Now it begins to look as if he may." It was reported in Berlin that "a squadron of at least nine of HM's destroyers was concentrated off the Norwegian coast and that in several instances Nazi freighters carrying iron had received warning shots." The Wilhelmstrasse told Shirer they would "watch" Churchill, and a key source assured him that "if British destroyers go into Norwegian territorial waters Germany will act." Act how? he wondered. "The German navy is no match for the British."[163]

Evidence that the Royal Navy was closing in had been accumulating since March 13, when a concentration of RN submarines had been reported off Norway. The next day the Germans had intercepted a message alerting all Allied transports to prepare to sail on two hours' notice; the day after that a party of French officers arrived in Bergen. Hitler did not reach his final decision, however, until Monday, April 1. Signals from Oslo, picked up by Germans monitoring all radio traffic in northern Europe, revealed that Norwegians manning coastal guns and antiaircraft batteries were being instructed to open fire on any unidentified vessels without asking permission from their superiors. Obviously Norway was expecting action and preparing for it. If *Weserübung* was to achieve surprise — essential to success — the Führer would have to move fast; the invasion was ordered to begin April 9. He prepared his explanation to the international audience: "The government of the Reich has learned that the British intend to land in Norway."[164]

The world outside the Reich, jaded by his *grosse Lügen*, would dismiss this new accusation as another absurd Nazi lie. But for once the Führer was telling the unvarnished truth.

Easter had arrived a week before Hitler's decision, and after the harsh winter England was celebrating an unseasonably warm four-day weekend. Traffic to Brighton was heavy. Over two hundred visitors were turned away from a hotel in Weston-super-Mare, and Blackpool landladies enjoyed one of their most profitable holidays in memory. Seaside resorts were unusually crowded; Britons hoped to hear warlike sounds over the water, the eruption of an exploding torpedo, perhaps, or the rattle of machine-gun fire. They heard none. Europe was at war but peaceful. The ominous news from Scandinavia attracted little attention. Hitler take Norway? With the Royal Navy barring the way? What a hope! And if he got it, what would he do with it? The British public, editors had learned, regarded Scandinavia as boring.

What they *did* want was summed up in a *Daily Express* story headed "COME ON HITLER! DARES IRONSIDE." The six-foot-four CIGS was in hiding, suffering the mortification of a man blindsided by a clever newspaperman. Reith's Ministry of Information had persuaded him to grant an interview to an American reporter, suggesting that he paint the rosiest possible picture. Tiny had thought he was talking off the record, and was staggered to learn that the *Express* owned British rights to whatever the American wrote. And so, to his horror, he found himself quoted as yearning for a clash with the Führer: "We would welcome a go at him. Frankly, we would welcome an attack. We are sure of ourselves. We have no fears." Actually, he spoke for millions of Englishmen weary of waiting for the monster to make his next move. At No. 10 Colville had wondered, a month after the fall of Poland, "whether all that has happened has been part of a gigantic bluff." Three months later he noted that a "number of people seem to be thinking that Hitler will not take the offensive, but may even be in a position to win a long war of inactivity — or at least to ruin us economically. . . . There is thus, for the first time, a feeling that we may have to start the fighting, and Winston even gave a hint to that effect in his speech on Saturday."[165]

In the teeth of vehement Foreign Office opposition, led by Halifax,

Churchill since late September 1939 had sought cabinet approval of his plan to mine the Leads "by every means and on all occasions," as he later put it. The farthest his colleagues would go was on February 19, when they authorized the Admiralty "to make all preparations" to lay a minefield in Norwegian territorial waters so that, should he be given actual approval, "there would be no delay in carrying out the operation." But ten days later, the authorization was rescinded. The tide turned for Winston on March 28, when the Allied Supreme War Council approved the plan, and on April 1 — the day Hitler, unknown to them, gave the green light to *Weserübung* — the War Cabinet set April 5 for the operation. Churchill decided that because it was "so small and innocent," the mining operation should be called "Wilfred" — the name of a comic strip character in the *Daily Mirror*. He pointed out that the minelaying "might lead the Germans to take forcible action against Norwegian territory, and so give us an opportunity for landing forces on Norwegian soil with the consent of the Norwegian government"; and he proposed that "we should continue in a state of readiness to despatch a light force to Narvik." The Supreme War Council went farther; on April 8 a British brigade and a contingent of French troops would be sent to Narvik to "clear the port and advance to the Swedish frontier." Other forces would land at Stavanger, Bergen, and Trondheim "to deny these bases to the enemy."[166]

Had this schedule been followed, the Allies would almost certainly have scored a resounding triumph. On April 3 Oliver Stanley, who had succeeded Hore-Belisha at the War Office, received "a somewhat garbled account" that the Germans had "a strong force of troops" at the Baltic port of Rostock. Halifax noted that this "tended to confirm" the latest report from Stockholm, that large German troop concentrations were boarding transports at Stettin and Swinemünde. An assistant military attaché at the Dutch legation in Berlin passed along the same information to the Danes and Norwegians. The Danish foreign minister concluded that the Germans were headed for Norway but would bypass the Danes. The Norwegians believed the Nazis had decided to seize Denmark.[167]

On Saturday, April 6, Churchill later wrote, RAF reconnaissance pilots spotted "a German fleet consisting of a battle cruiser, two light cruisers, fourteen destroyers and another ship, probably a transport . . . moving towards the Naze across the mouth of the Skagerrak." Churchill wrote: "We found it hard at the Admiralty to believe that this force was going to Narvik. In spite of a report from Copenhagen that Hitler meant to seize that port, it was thought by the Naval Staff that the German ships would probably turn back into the Skagerrak."[168]

Actually, the British were involved in making adjustments to their plans because of a serious disagreement with the French, which had stalled Wilfred at a critical juncture. Churchill said that whatever the French did, England should proceed with the minelaying in Norway, and Chamberlain agreed. "Matters have now gone too far," he said, "for us not to take action." One more attempt would be made to reconcile differences with the French. If they continued to be fractious, Britain would go it alone.[169]

The row with France arose from French determination to avoid any move which might invite German retaliation. For over seven years they had been trying to wish Hitler away, and the habit was hard to break. Eventually they were bound to disagree with Churchill, who spent most of his waking moments trying to find new ways of making life miserable for the Nazis. One operation, whose potential exceeded Wilfred's, had been encoded "Royal Marine." During the winter he had studied mines. Among the various types, he had found, was a fluvial mine which floated just below the surface of water. The possibility of paralyzing all traffic on the Rhine — Germany's main artery of transport and communications — excited him. Among the river's many uses was sustaining the Reich's huge armies on the French frontier. Large numbers of fluvial mines which exploded on contact would be launched on that stretch of the river which lay just inside French territory, below Strasbourg. Among the targets would be tankers, barges, and floating bridges. Winston had conceived this scheme during his visit to the Rhine on the eve of war, but he had hesitated to lay it before the War Cabinet because neutral shipping also used the river. His mind had been changed by the "indiscriminate warfare" of U-boats, magnetic mines, and machine-gunning of crews in lifeboats, all of which had victimized neutrals as well as Britons. Then and later he insisted that, as he wrote General Gamelin, "the moral and juridical justification" for Royal Marine "appears to be complete." The Germans had "assailed the ports of Great Britain and their approaches with every form of illegal mining," had attacked unarmed fishing boats, and "waged a ruthless U-boat war on both belligerents and neutrals." Against such an enemy, he submitted, "stern reprisals are required." On November 19, 1939, he had proposed that "a steady process of harassing this main waterway of the enemy should be set on foot. . . . Not a day should be lost."[170]

Months, not days, were lost, for although the War Cabinet endorsed his recommendations "in principle" eight days later, the plan had to work its way through both the British and French bureaucracies. Meantime Royal Marine was expanding; by January the Admiralty had stockpiled ten thousand fluvial mines, the RAF had been brought into the picture as sowers of them, and not only the Rhine, but all major German rivers and canals were to be their targets. Churchill was captivated by his scheme; if padlock visitors called at the private office, one of his aides wrote, Winston would produce "a bucket full of water and insist that everyone should watch the model [of a fluvial mine] work." The War Cabinet finally approved Royal Marine on March 6, and detailed plans provided for floating the first two thousand mines; three hundred or four hundred would be loosed each night thereafter, and eventually the number would stabilize at two thousand a week. Admiral Jean Darlan, commander in chief of the French navy, declared himself "enthusiastically in favor" of the project and predicted that it would have "a decisive effect" on the war in less than a year. Only pro forma consent of the French government remained.[171]

It was not forthcoming. Daladier's government fell on March 20, several days after the Finnish surrender — he had been accused of tardy, inadequate aid to the Finns — and Paul Reynaud became premier. Though no longer premier, Daladier retained his post as minister of defense, and in that office he had the power, which he now exercised, of vetoing Royal Marine. According to gossip at No. 10, Daladier "does not want Reynaud to get the credit, or possibly . . . the French fear instant retaliation which they are not in a position to withstand." The second motive was the one given the British. The minister of defense, they were told, flinched from the possibility of reprisals in the form of Luftwaffe attacks on French air factories. The factories were especially vulnerable now. In two months they would be dispersed and the mines could be launched. On March 28, at the same meeting of the Supreme War Council at which Wilfred was approved, Chamberlain intervened, and his powerful promotion of Royal Marine persuaded the French to float the mines on April 4. Back in Paris they changed their minds and demanded a three-month postponement. Colville wrote, "Winston is going over to Paris to do a little personal persuasion. We are trying to blackmail the French by maintaining that we may not undertake the Norwegian territorial waters project unless we can combine it with the other."[172]

Churchill once observed: "There is only one thing worse than fighting with allies, and that is fighting without them." Yet it is hard to think of any substantial blow struck for Allied victory by the Third Republic. They were, of course, very *courtois* when Winston arrived in Paris the evening of April 4; the premier and most of his cabinet dined with the first lord at the British embassy. Unfortunately, the *ministre de guerre,* "the stumbling-block," as Churchill called him, did not find it convenient to attend. Next day Winston sought him out and cornered him in the rue St. Dominique. He "commented," as he later wrote, on Daladier's "absence from our dinner the night before. He pleaded his previous engagement." That was the war minister's last opportunity to say anything else for quite some time, for Churchill unloosed a torrent of arguments in favor of his project: melting snow in the Alps made this the most favorable time of year for the mines; the Rhine traffic was heavy; if the Germans possessed retaliatory weapons they would have used them by now. Nothing worked. The German reaction would be violent, Daladier said when Winston had finished, and the blow would "fall on France." Churchill reluctantly phoned London and told his colleagues he had decided that to press the French harder would be "a very great mistake." In reality, a far greater mistake had already been made. Operation Wilfred, the mining of Norwegian ports, had been scheduled for Friday, April 5, with Anglo-French landings to follow. Because of Winston's trip to Paris, the dates had been set back three days, to begin Monday, April 8. It is startling to read his postwar apologia: "If a few days would enable us to bring the French into agreement upon the punctual execution of the two projects, I was agreeable to postponing 'Wilfred' for a few days." Yet neither project was dependent upon the other; French reluctance to endorse one should not have held the other back, and "punctual execution" was precisely what his trip to Paris lost Wilfred.[173]

The delay proved fatal. Though each was only vaguely aware of the other, the British and the Germans were in a crucial race for Norway, and Falkenhorst and the Kriegsmarine won it in a photo finish. Hankey, then a member of the War Cabinet, later wrote that in their designs on Norway "both Great Britain and Germany were keeping more or less level in their plans and preparations. Britain actually started planning a little earlier. . . . Both plans were executed almost simultaneously, Britain being twenty-four hours ahead in the so-called act of aggression, if the term is really applicable to either side." But Germany's final surge made the difference.[174]

Unaware of Nazi intentions, Chamberlain delivered a major political address on Thursday, the day Wilfred was put on hold while Winston traveled to Paris, ending it with four words which were to haunt him and, ultimately, to serve as powerful ammunition in the Tory uprising which would drive him from office. Germany's preparations at the war's outbreak, he told a mass meeting of Conservatives, "were far ahead of our own," and His Majesty's Government had assumed that "the enemy would take advantage of his initial superiority" and "endeavour to overwhelm us and France" before they could catch up. "Is it not a very extraordinary thing that no such attempt was made? Whatever may be the reason — whether it was that Hitler thought he might get away with what he had got without fighting for it, or whether it was that after all the preparations were not sufficiently complete — however, one thing is certain: he missed the bus."[175]

Hitler had already boarded another bus, which followed its timetable with Teutonic precision on Tuesday, April 9, and at 4:10 A.M. began dropping off its passengers — elements from three Wehrmacht divisions — at their destinations: Denmark and the chief ports of Norway from Oslo right up to Narvik, twelve hundred miles from the nearest Nazi naval base and well above the Arctic Circle. Denmark was overrun in twelve hours. The Norwegian government was busy lodging protests against the British minelaying, which had begun a day earlier — and which Ribbentrop had called "the most flagrant violation of a neutral country [since] the British bombardment of Copenhagen in 1801" — but German landings there were not unopposed. At Oslo alone, shore batteries — ancient 28-centimeter guns built, ironically, by Krupp before the turn of the century — sank the heavy cruiser *Blücher,* permanently damaged the cruiser *Emden,* and destroyed auxiliary ships.

In London the first reaction to German audacity had been confusion and disbelief. That afternoon in Parliament, Chamberlain confirmed newspaper accounts of enemy landings at Bergen and Trondheim and added: "There have been some reports about a similar landing at Narvik, but I am very doubtful whether they are correct." It seemed unbelievable that Hitler could have committed himself so far north, particularly when he knew the Royal Navy was present in strength. The Admiralty suggested that "Narvik" must be a misspelling of Larvik, a community on Norway's south coast. But by evening they knew that forces of the Reich held all major Norwegian ports, including Narvik and Oslo, the country's capital. Two days later Churchill, his confidence in British sea power undiminished, told the House of Commons that it was his view, "shared by my skilled advisers," that "Herr Hitler has committed a grave strategic error," and that "we have greatly gained by what has occurred in Scandinavia." Having seized defenseless ports, the Führer "will now have to fight" against "Powers possessing vastly superior naval forces." Winston concluded: "I feel that we are greatly advantaged by . . . the strategic blunder into which our mortal enemy has been provoked."[176]

Liddell Hart comments: "The dream-castles raised by Churchill" were doomed to "come tumbling down." To be sure, in almost every surface battle the Royal Navy crippled the fleet Hitler had put at risk. But victory at sea was no longer determined solely by surface engagements. Churchill thought it still was, and so did Admiral Sir Thomas Phillips, who would sacrifice his life for this precept twenty months later in the waters off

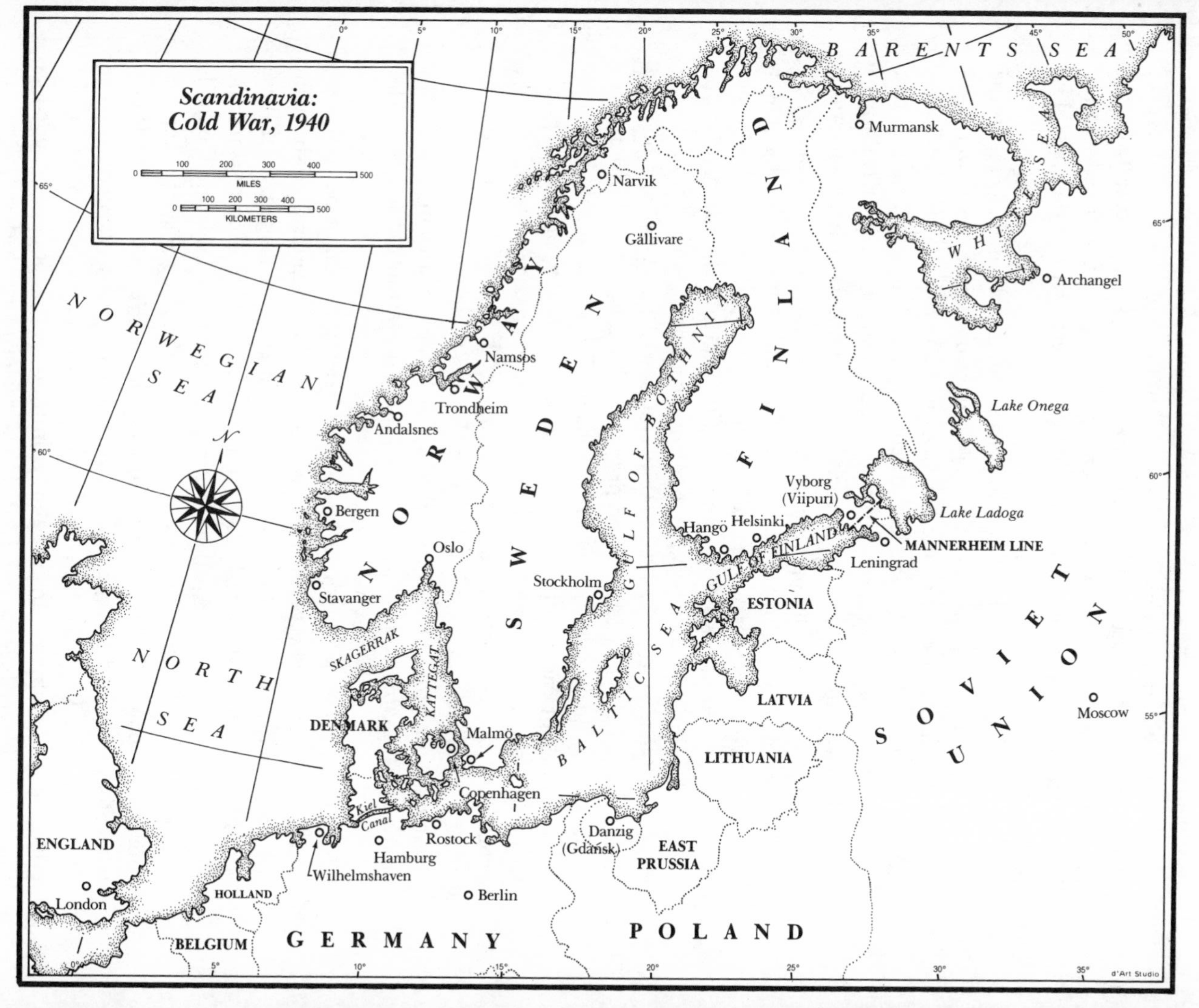
Scandinavia: Cold War, 1940
MILES
KILOMETERS
BARENTS SEA
WHITE SEA
NORWEGIAN SEA
NORTH SEA
SKAGERRAK
KATTEGAT
GULF OF BOTHNIA
GULF OF FINLAND
BALTIC SEA
NORWAY
SWEDEN
FINLAND
SOVIET UNION
DENMARK
ENGLAND
HOLLAND
BELGIUM
GERMANY
POLAND
EAST PRUSSIA
LITHUANIA
LATVIA
ESTONIA
Murmansk
Archangel
Narvik
Gällivare
Namsos
Trondheim
Andalsnes
Bergen
Oslo
Stavanger
Stockholm
Malmö
Copenhagen
Kiel Canal
Rostock
Hamburg
Wilhelmshaven
Berlin
London
Danzig (Gdańsk)
Hangö
Helsinki
Vyborg (Viipuri)
Leningrad
MANNERHEIM LINE
Lake Ladoga
Lake Onega
Moscow
d'Art Studio

Malaya. Rear Admiral J. H. Godfrey comments: "Both W.S.C. and Tom Phillips were obsessed with the idea that a fleet or a big ship could provide complete aerial protection with its own A.A. guns." A vice admiral believes that Pound "was quite as ignorant as we all were before the Second World War as to what aircraft could do to ships. This was quite clear from the Norwegian campaign, where we intended . . . to send a squadron into Trondheim with no reconnaissance, and with the certainty that they would be bombed."[177]

Strategic thinking at the Admiralty had foundered on this reef — the conviction that in this war, as in the last, superior British sea power foreclosed a German invasion of the Norwegian coast. Admiral Forbes, commander in chief of the Home Fleet, discovered that "the scale of attack that would be developed against our military forces on shore and our naval forces off the Norwegian coast were grievously underestimated when the operations were undertaken." In the opinion of S. W. Roskill, the naval historian, those most blind in their conviction that Britannia's traditional sea power ruled the waves were the Chiefs of Staff, particularly Pound and Ironside. But the first lord of the Admiralty should be added to the list. Churchill, being Churchill, did not hesitate to assume command when he deemed it necessary. Godfrey refers to "Churchill's dictatorial behavior" and quotes a senior officer as saying that "Pound proved unable to prevent Winston from running wild during the Norwegian campaign." These, it should be noted, are the views of career officers, united in their loyalty to one another. Sir Eric Seal, who was Churchill's principal private secretary at the Admiralty, vehemently denies Admiral Godfrey's charges: "It is perfectly true that he spent a good deal of time in the War Room, which had a tremendous fascination for him. To infer from this that he assumed control is, in the circumstances, almost malicious. It is certainly unwarranted, and false."[178]

There was a bedrock issue here, and it transcended a clash of personalities, which can almost always be assumed in assessing relationships between Churchill and those who differed with him. War had changed. And those who had seen the Luftwaffe knew it in their bones. According to Gamelin, who was in London on April 26 for a meeting of the Supreme Council, Pound told him: "It is impossible to do anything against the enemy's superior air power." The first sea lord had told the *généralissime* that Polish tales of the Nazis' fearsome bomber fleet had not been exaggerated. The following day, Reynaud said, he found the Admiralty "terrorized by the effects of the bombing." In citing the Admiralty he cannot have included its first lord. Nevertheless, the Luftwaffe's performance had so impressed England's military establishment — less at sea than by its tactical support of

Wehrmacht infantry — that they felt the French needed to prepare for it.[179]

But something else is wrong here. What the admirals say and write about air power in the Norwegian campaign is not consistent with what was done. Ships were *not* sacrificed to aircraft in the name of sea power. The Luftwaffe had confirmed conclusions already reached. With very few exceptions, Churchill among them, flag officers had been alert to the peril in the sky long before war was declared. Perhaps the most significant military event in the struggle for Norway was the decision — made in the first hours of the German attack — to send no British vessels except submarines into the Skagerrak. All German shipping had to pass through this channel between the Baltic and North seas. If it had been barred, neither supplies nor reinforcements could have been sent to German troops already committed. It is only seventy miles wide, and in Nelson's day, or even Jellicoe's, Britain's ships of the line would have annihilated them. But now in 1940 the Nazis quickly seized all usable Norwegian airfields, which meant that the Luftwaffe, with over a thousand planes committed to the operation, dominated the sky over the Skagerrak, and the admirals refused to risk their battlewagons to air power. In the 135 years since Trafalgar, sea power had permitted a small island to control its future and build the greatest empire in history. Now tiny little craft, hardly more expensive than ammunition for an 18-inch gun, could deny strategic waters to the mightiest navy the world had ever known.[180]

Weserübung, as conducted by Falkenhorst, was marked by meticulous planning, speed, and professionalism. German captains, entering Norwegian ports in the predawn darkness, answered gunners' challenges in English. One parachute battalion floated down to take the airstrips at Oslo and Stavanger — the first use of paratroops in war, and it was very impressive. Narvik had been taken by what Colville called "a Trojan Horse manoeuvre"; freighters which usually bore iron ore carried Nazi soldiers in their holds. ("Very clever," said a cabinet minister, "and we were ninnies, we were ninnies!") Hitler's naval commitment had been large, but only 8,850 troops had been sent north in the first wave, and no landing was made by more than 2,000 men. Except for elements from a mountain division, none of Falkenhorst's soldiers came from elite units. Yet once dug in, they were almost impossible to dislodge. In Narvik 2,000 Austrian alpine troops, reinforced by another 2,000 German seamen, held off a British force — at one point 25,000 troops — week after week. In their lightning stroke the Nazis had not only occupied every major Norwegian airfield; they had also taken over the country's radio and telephone networks and seized all five major ports. The *Völkischer Beobachter* ran a banner headline in red ink and end-of-the-world type: "GERMANY SAVES SCANDINAVIA!" Churchill seemed stunned. He told Pound, "We have been completely outwitted." Thursday, April 11, he prepared an account of these tumultuous events for Parliament. The *Daily Mail* reported that "A thousand people packed the pavements outside the House of Commons. 'Where's Winnie?' they asked after other Ministers had arrived. 'Wonder if he'll be smiling. You can always tell what's in the air by Winnie's face.' " But when he appeared his expression was forbidding, and inside, as he arose, he faced what he later described as "a disturbed and indignant House of Commons." Nicolson, watching from his backbencher seat, wrote that the House

> is packed. Winston comes in. He is not looking well and sits there hunched as usual with his papers in his hand. When he rises to speak it is obvious that he is very tired. . . . I have seldom seen him to less advantage. The majority of the House were expecting tales of victory and triumph, and when he tells them that the news of our reoccupation of Bergen, Trondheim, and Oslo is untrue, a cold wave of disappointment passes through the House. He hesitates, gets his notes in the wrong order, puts on the wrong pair of spectacles, fumbles for the right pair, keeps on saying "Sweden" when he means "Denmark", and one way and another makes a lamentable performance.[181]

Colville disagreed. Although Churchill was "less polished than usual," he wrote, he was "witty," causing "amusement by saying that Denmark had had most to fear from Germany of all the neutrals, because she had been the most recent to negotiate a non-aggression pact with her. He wisely damped down the absurd over-optimism of this morning's newspapers, but made a good case for the navy's achievements during the past few days." The public preferred the jingoism of Fleet Street, however, and was slow to accept the emerging truth. All they knew, or wanted to know, was that the Nazi navy was at loose along the thousand-mile Scandinavian peninsula, stopping here and there to leave contingents of troops, and the Royal Navy, led by Admiral Forbes, was in hot pursuit. No true Englishman could doubt which force would emerge triumphant. Even Churchill, rallying, told the War Cabinet, "We have the Germans where we want them." Colville noted: "The First Lord (who at last sees a chance of action) is jubilant and maintains that our failure to destroy the German fleet up to the present is only due to the bad visibility and very rough weather in the North Sea, while if the German ships fly for home they will leave their garrisons exposed to our expeditionary forces." *The Listener* quoted an enraptured Hoare as having told the nation over the BBC: "Today our wings are spread over the Arctic. They are sheathed in ice. Tomorrow the sun of victory will touch them with its golden light, and the wings that flashed over the great waters of the North will bear us homewards once more to the 'peace with honour' of a free people and the victory of a noble race."[182]

The Times was reminded of Napoleon's (Iberian) peninsula war. The *Express* wrote of the British storming of Narvik, which the British had not stormed, that it had "an Elizabethan ring to it. It ranks with Cadiz where we singed the King of Spain's beard." The *Daily Mirror* told its readers that despite the need for a speedy response to the German challenge, all cold-weather gear had been provided, including pack saddles for reindeer; and the *Daily Mail* reported: "The British Navy has embarked on a glorious enterprise. Hitler is shaken by the hammer blows of our sailors and airmen."[183]

In his memoirs Gamelin writes that upon hearing that German ships were on the move, he urged Ironside to hurry the dispatch of troops to Norway — Gamelin approved of fighting Germans anywhere except in France — but the CIGS replied: "With us the Admiralty is all-powerful; it likes to organize everything methodically. It is convinced that it can prevent any German landing on the coast of Norway." Churchill confirmed him. On the second day after the German landings, Shirer noted in his diary: "The BBC quotes Churchill as having said in the House of Commons today that 'Hitler committed a grave strategical error' and that the British navy will now take the Norwegian coast and sink all the ships in the Skagerrak and the Kattegat. God, I hope he's right." He was wrong. No one doubted that Raeder's fleet paled beside the Royal Navy, but the Norwegian coastline is 2,100 miles long, deeply incised by fjords, some several miles deep, fringed with thousands of islands, and throughout April a heavy mist lay over all of it. Except in contested ports the RN couldn't *find* all the German ships.[184]

They found some, though, and the early days shone with tales of heroism. In the first confrontation between ships of the two navies, the Nazi heavy cruiser *Admiral Hipper* (13,000 tons) bore down on the British destroyer *Glowworm* (1,350 tons), all guns firing. In a magnificent beau geste the destroyer, hopelessly trapped, turned as if to flee, threw out a smoke screen, and when the *Hipper* charged into it, rammed her at flank speed, tearing away 130 feet of her armor belt and her starboard tubes. As the gallant *Glowworm* went down, her crew could see the huge heavy cruiser beginning to list under 500 tons of ingested seawater. And the British failure to take Narvik wasn't the navy's fault. On Wednesday, April 10, the day after ten German destroyers had taken Narvik and landed two battalions commanded by General Eduard Dietl, five British destroyers entered the harbor, sank two of the enemy destroyers, damaged the other three, and sank all but one of the Nazi cargo vessels. As they were leaving the harbor, the RN ships sighted the other five German destroyers. This time the British were outgunned. One of their destroyers was sunk, a second beached, and one of the three surviving vessels was damaged.

Three days later the Royal Navy was back, this time with a battleship and a flotilla of destroyers. Every enemy vessel still afloat was sent to the bottom. The commander of the RN task force radioed that Dietl and his men, stunned and disorganized, had taken to the hills. Since Narvik was wide open, he suggested, it should be occupied at once "by the main landing force." The next day an advance part of three infantry battalions arrived. Unfortunately, they were led by Major General P. J. Mackesy, a windy officer cast in the same mold as those who had lost Gallipoli in the first war. Mackesy decided landing at Narvik was too perilous; instead he went ashore at Harstad. There were no Germans in Harstad, only friendly Norwegians. But it was thirty-five miles north of Narvik, his objective.

The *Daily Mail*'s guess that Hitler had been badly shaken was not wide of the mark. Jodl's diary quivers with phrases describing Hitler's loss of self-control, his terror that he might lose his gamble, how he was always trembling on the verge of hysteria and sometimes plunged into it. *"Führer ist zunehmend beunruhigt über die englischen Landungen"* ("Führer is increasingly worried about the English landings") reads one of the milder entries. The Royal Navy's Narvik victory and the flight of Dietl, one of Hitler's old Bavarian cronies, led to "terrible excitement." Hitler demanded that Dietl and his men be "evacuated by air — an impossibility." Then: "Renewed crisis . . . an hysterical attack." "Chaos of leadership is again threatening." "Each piece of bad news leads to the worst fears." Hitler never had been able to take the rough with the smooth, and as the war proceeded his violence increased. As campaigns go, *Weserübung* had entailed no great risks except to Raeder's surface vessels, which were considered expendable, and setbacks had been few. Between the lines of Jodl's diary one reads the anxious question: If the Führer carries on like this in what is almost a textbook victory, how might he behave in the face of defeat?[185]

In overplaying local successes and ignoring Britain's strategic dilemma, Fleet Street was merely following the line taken by briefing officers at the Admiralty, War Office, and Air Ministry — a press policy usually adopted by military men who are losing a struggle and cannot understand why. Totalitarian regimes can suppress bad news to the end, until the civilian comes to find his home in flames and his wife raped by an enemy he thought was about to surrender. In democracies the lid cannot be kept on long. Editors and publishers are willing to play the game in wartime, but when they send trusted correspondents to the front they will print their dispatches. And soldiers write home. Censors may cut military information which the enemy would find useful, but excluding details of the men's day-to-day life is impossible, and it was precisely there that the British people began to grasp the unwelcome fact that those responsible for the Norwegian campaign were mismanaging it.

Nearly three weeks of action had passed before Englishmen became aware of a cold, cruel shaft of light they recognized as truth. It arrived when several British newspapers quoted the distinguished U.S. foreign correspondent Leland Stowe. Stowe was in Norway, and he had described the plight of an English battalion dumped into Norway, untrained, poorly armed, lacking artillery, antiaircraft weapons, or fighter cover. After four days' fighting, half of the men had been killed, wounded, or captured by the Germans; the rest had fallen back. An officer had told Stowe, "We've simply been massacred." The War Office dismissed the dispatch as "an obvious distortion of the facts." But the English newspapermen in Norway also were talking to soldiers, and they were confirming the American.

Some of the unpleasant news was inherent in the War Office's disposition of forces, and it had little choice there. The country's trained troops were all in France. Those sent to Norway were largely territorials who had been called up only eight months earlier — salesmen, bank tellers, farmers, truck drivers, haulage contractors: men who knew very little about infantry combat. Their grievances were harder to explain. Along the line that started with the CIGS and descended to the rifle company commander, mismanagement had been, at times, scandalous. The territorials were equipped to fight Germans who had been under fire in Poland and carried complete equipment, including sealskin caps and uniforms lined with sheepskin. Pack saddles for reindeer may have been provided the Tommies (though they would have been useless, the reindeer having sensibly retreated inland) but no Tommy had been issued the one piece of gear essential in Norway: skis. Every Norwegian civilian, every enemy soldier had them. So did the French *Chasseurs Alpins*, trained for this sort of fighting, but once ashore they discovered that the navy had neglected to land their bindings, without which the skis were useless.

This kind of elementary error multiplied as time passed. Two territorial battalions were issued a dozen tourist maps of all Norway; their objective wasn't on them. Admiralty orders were often slow, hesitant, countermanded, reissued, and countermanded again. One cruiser squadron was about to depart Rosyth with an expeditionary force when the Admiralty learned Nazi battle cruisers had been spotted nearby; the squadron commander was ordered to put "the soldiers ashore, even without their equipment, and join the Fleet at sea." By the time the soldiers were reunited with their ships, their original objective was in enemy hands.

The worst blunders were committed in an operation Churchill had opposed, a stratagem designed by civilians sitting around the cabinet table fifteen hundred miles from the scene of action. The leadership in Whitehall had been weakened by divided counsel from the beginning, and basic disagreements surfaced over what Britain's chief military objective in Norway should be. Churchill argued that it had been, and should continue to be, Narvik. That was why the Germans were there; that was where the Allies wanted them out. But other members of the War Cabinet, and soon they were a majority, had favored throwing the Nazis out of Trondheim, Norway's ancient capital, nearly halfway between the peninsula's southern tip and Narvik. King Haakon VII and his government, fleeing from Oslo, begged the British to take Trondheim back, thereby giving them a rallying point to organize Norwegian resistance to the Nazi occupation. Halifax, as a peer, took royal requests very seriously. He buttressed his case: Trondheim would provide the Allies with a superb harbor, a base for the buildup of fifty thousand troops, a nearby airfield which would support several fighter squadrons, and direct railway contact with Sweden, which — a non sequitur he did not attempt to unravel — would "greatly improve the chances of Swedish intervention." The possibility of Sweden declaring war on the Reich was zero. Hitler had warned the Swedes of dire consequences if they abandoned strict neutrality and, Shirer wrote on Wednesday, April 10, "As far as I can learn the Swedes are scared stiff [and] will not come to the aid of their Norwegian brethren."[186]

On Saturday, April 13, with troop transports crossing the North Sea toward Narvik, Halifax told the War Cabinet they should be diverted to Trondheim because "The most important point is to seize Trondheim and the railways leading from that port across the peninsula." Ironside vigorously disagreed; Churchill also opposed the switch, protesting that Trondheim, unlike Narvik, was "a much more speculative affair." But only Secretary for War Stanley supported him. Simon joined Halifax and Chamberlain; otherwise, Simon said, the Norwegians and Swedes would believe they were "only interested in Narvik." When the War Cabinet had decided to mine Norwegian territorial waters — clear evidence that Britain's intent in Norway was confined to crippling the Reich's war effort — Simon had not raised this novel proposition that public relations should play a role in fixing military objectives. He and his colleagues now rejected Churchill's proposal that no further commitment be made.[187]

The attack on Trondheim, it is now clear, derived from the lack of policy. At the outset, Britain's goal had been to stop the Swedish ore shipments. To reach their objective they needed Narvik. Implicit in the decision to take

Trondheim was a decision to retake all Norway. The country's strategic value was small. And whether it could be conquered by anyone is doubtful; of its 119,240 square miles only 4 percent was inhabitable. Seizing its chief ports was one thing; keeping them, as Hitler was to discover, was another. That required the consent of the Norwegian people, and it was not forthcoming. The country had been taken by fewer than 10,000 German soldiers. Then the Norwegian underground began to organize, and it began its work by killing Nazi sentries. Despite the conquerors' policy of killing one hundred civilians for every murdered German, nearly 400,000 Nazi troops were tied down in Norway when Hitler's need for them elsewhere would be urgent.

"Although Narvik was my pet," Churchill wrote, he was serving "a respected chief and friendly Cabinet"; since they had decided to make the effort at Trondheim, he threw himself "into this daring adventure, and was willing that the Fleet should risk the weak batteries at the entrance to the fiord, the possible minefields, and, most serious, the air." The British ships' "very powerful antiaircraft armament" would be, he believed, equal to the Luftwaffe. But on April 18 the Chiefs of Staff, wary of the Luftwaffe, decided the risks of a frontal assault were too great. Therefore, Trondheim was to be enveloped by two forces already put ashore at ports still in Norwegian hands. One ("Sickleforce") was at Andalsnes, a hundred miles southwest of the city; the other ("Mauriceforce") at Namsos, far to the northeast. Originally they had been landed as diversions. Now, as Churchill wrote, they would "develop a pincer movement on Trondheim from north and south."[188]

Neither Trondheim pincer had a chance. The British were relying on the Norwegians for their information, and the Norwegians either blundered or were cleverly misled by the Germans, who were expecting an attack at this strategic harbor. Had the attackers known that Trondheim was now defended by 120,000 Nazi troops, outnumbering them six to one and reinforced with tanks and several Luftwaffe squadrons, they would have kept their distance. To do the job properly, six or seven divisions would have to have been withdrawn from France. Moreover, there were difficulties with the terrain. And the Germans were not likely to be deceived by the two-pronged attack; it was the textbook alternative to a frontal assault, and they knew where the British would be coming.

Reinforcing the small forces already ashore at Namsos and Andalsnes presented other problems. Namsos in particular looked forbidding. Later there would be questions in Parliament over why the troop transports did not carry the infantry all the way in to the Namsos docks; the implication was that the War Cabinet had overruled the navy. No one who had seen Namsos would have asked. Only one approach was possible: a fifteen-mile-long fjord, too narrow and winding for any ships but destroyers, to which the assault brigades were transferred. Furthermore, the transfer was an invitation to confusion, and confusion resulted. The transports departed with Mauriceforce's ammunition, rations, heavy weapons — and the brigade's commanding officer.

None of the planners seem to have given much thought to the weather at that latitude. Churchill did; Namsos, he found, was "under four feet of snow and offered no concealment from the air." Indeed, at each of their Norwegian objectives meteorologists forecast further "dense falls of snow" which could "paralyse all movement of our troops, unequipped and untrained for such conditions." They were waging war in a very cold climate. The men had mistakenly been left with only two days' supplies. The distance was long, movement was clogged by snowdrifts, and the reinforced German garrison, when told the British were ashore in force, landed parties to intercept them. Mauriceforce Tommies could only hope that Sickleforce's luck was better.[189]

It wasn't. It was worse. Afterward, Hoare said that one reason for the Trondheim operation was to secure airfields; but the Germans had taken them all, and therefore the RAF could not challenge the Luftwaffe. "In that case," Lloyd George acidly observed in the House of Commons, "we ought to have had picked men, and not a kind of scratch team . . . because the Germans had picked men, as is generally accepted. We sent there, I think, a Territorial brigade, which had not had much training." The territorials were in fact only part of the force put ashore at Andalsnes — a small fishing port unsuitable for the debarkation of soldiers and equipment — but their experience was typical. They lacked mortar ammunition, radios, accurate maps, or fire-control equipment for their antiaircraft weapons. Their orders called for a northward march toward Trondheim, but the Norwegian commander who met them, and who had participated in planning the mission in London, persuaded their brigadier to reinforce exhausted Norwegian forces in Lillehammer, eighty miles to the southeast. An eighty-mile march with combat gear is grueling for veteran infantrymen in suitable terrain. The territorials, whom one Norwegian officer described as looking like "untrained steel workers from the Midlands" — which some of them were — reached Lillehammer wearier than the men they were reinforcing. And before they could be billeted the Germans pounced on them.[190]

Quickly outflanked, they fell back. That night a panzer battalion seized Lillehammer. Once more they fell back, to the banks of a river, where the enemy tanks routed them. Once more the territorials retreated, forty-five miles this time, and along the way units became separated from the rest of the brigade. Their plight was pitiable. Now and then they would spot a lone Norwegian on a nearby crest, staring down, in amazement or contempt, at their lack of skis. Wading through the deep snow was like crossing a bog, and because they lacked compasses, they dared not leave roads, which sometimes took them in strange directions. In the early hours of April 20 two companies, staggering slowly through a dense snowstorm, reached a town which natives identified as Nykirke. The Norwegians produced a map. Studying it, the soldiers discovered that they were now two hundred miles from Trondheim, which they were supposed to capture, and were moving in the opposite direction.

Risking security, they phoned a hotel which the Norwegians told them was battalion headquarters. "Lucky you rang," said a cheerful English voice on the other end. "We were just wondering what was happening to you." Keeping in touch now, they set off with new instructions. Along the way they learned that the freighter carrying their transport and Bren carriers had been torpedoed and that the Royal Navy had been unable to prevent the Germans from landing tanks. They thought themselves lost again, but the panzers quickly tracked them down, whereupon they learned that their antitank gun, with its brutal kickback, did not penetrate enemy armor. They withdrew into a forest, but the enemy mortared them into the open, where the tanks machine-gunned them. Having achieved nothing, they had ceased to exist as a fighting force.

That was also true of the main body. Of the original force under his command, the brigadier could count only 300 soldiers and nine junior officers. He sent the survivors back to Andalsnes for evacuation. It was not that easy. The enemy followed the column, as vultures do; stragglers, moving in groups of two or three, roamed the hills, hoping to find sympathetic Norwegians, but most were found first by unsympathetic Germans. A few reached Sweden and were interned. By now the War Cabinet and the Chiefs of Staff were aware of the disaster. Mauriceforce and Sickleforce had been in Norway ten days; neither had gained a yard; between them they had lost 1,559 men. Those who had succeeded in eluding capture were in danger. Those in London who had sent them there had no choice; as many as possible had to be evacuated. Thanks to the Norwegians — who paid a terrible price when the Nazis tracked them down — 1,800 Sickleforce troops stumbled aboard blacked-out transports on the night of April 30. In the morning, under constant Luftwaffe attack, another 1,300 men were picked up, and, that night, 1,000 more. Mauriceforce, more fortunate, had lost only 157 troops. But the sacrifice there had been equally pointless.

Hitler scorned Britain's Trondheim adventure as *"ein Fall von leichtsinnigem Dilettantismus"* ("a case of frivolous dilettantism"). At the Supreme War Council on April 27, Reynaud had predicted that an Allied failure in central Norway "would come as a great shock to public opinion," and might be followed by an Allied capitulation to the Reich. However, the council had agreed that the Trondheim plan must be abandoned because of the enemy's air superiority. On May 1 Nicolson noted having "a talk with Buck De la Warr and Stephen King-Hall in former's room at the House of Lords. Buck seems to think that if Norway is lost, the P.M. will have to resign." The next day, when the evacuation from Andalsnes was announced, Amery telephoned Hoare and angrily told him: "The government must go."[191]

On the western front of the Third Reich lay the greatest army Germany had ever mobilized to lunge into Belgium, Holland, and France: 136 divisions, ten of them panzer divisions, with virtually every aircraft in the Luftwaffe ready to darken the sky as the tanks and the infantry advanced. On May 1 the Führer, with his penchant for weekend invasions, set Sunday, May 5, as the day for *Fall Gelb* — Case Yellow — the assault on the Low Countries and France.

In Berlin, Shirer, listening to a 6:00 P.M. BBC news broadcast on May 2, heard "the bad news" that "Chamberlain had just announced in the Commons the awful [Scandinavian] reverse." Two days later he wrote in anguish: "The British have pulled pell-mell out of Namsos to the north of Trondheim, thus completing the debacle of Allied aid to the Norwegians in central Norway. Where was the British navy which Churchill only a few fortnights ago boasted would drive the Germans out of Norwegian waters?" And on May 4 Nicolson wrote that "there is grave suspicion of the Prime Minister. His speech about the Norwegian expedition has created disquiet. The House knows very well that it was a major defeat. But the P.M. said that 'the balance of advantage rested with us' and that 'Germany has not attained her objective.' . . . If Chamberlain believed it himself, then he was stupid. If he did not believe it, then he was trying to deceive. In either case he loses confidence."[192]

On May 3, a Friday, the day the men of Mauriceforce swung down an English gangplank, carrying the equipment they had never had a chance to use, Colonel Hans Oster of OKW intelligence (Abwehr) dined in the secluded Berlin suburb of Zehlendorf, at the home of one of his closest friends, Colonel G. J. Sas, military attaché in Holland's Zitadelle embassy and an ardent anti-Nazi. Oster had provided his host with earlier Nazi plans to overrun The Hague, and ten days before Germany's seizure of Denmark and Norway had given him OKW's plans and the exact date for *Weserübung*. Now Sas listened intently as the Abwehr colonel told him that fifty Wehrmacht divisions were concentrated on the Reich's western borders and the long-expected German offensive there would begin in a week — May 10. Actually, the offensive had been scheduled to begin in two days, but on that Friday the Führer set *der Tag* back to May 6, partly because of bad weather but also because the Foreign Ministry advised him that his pretext for invading the neutral Low Countries wasn't good enough. The Dutch attaché sent Oster's information home in the next day's pouch. It reached The Hague within an hour of another coded warning from Holland's envoy at the Vatican. The Dutch immediately passed this warning along to the Belgians, but not to the British or the French. Even at this late hour the Low Countries believed neutrality was possible.

How much of this information was in Churchill's hands is unknown, but over a month earlier he had warned Britain: "More than a million German soldiers, including all their active divisions and armored divisions, are drawn up ready to attack, at a few hours' notice, along the frontiers of Luxembourg, of Belgium, and of Holland. At any moment these neutral countries may be subjected to an avalanche of steel and fire." Ten days later he had written Admiral Forbes: "It seems to me very likely that the great land battle in the West will soon begin."[193]

On the French side of the Franco-Belgian border a brief argument enlivened the Sedan sector. General Charles Huntziger, responsible for it, was so convinced that the enemy would not strike there that he ordered the demolition of antitank obstacles which had been erected on the initiative of a major. Pierre Taittinger and another deputy, both members of the Chamber of Deputies' Army Committee, inspected the position and were shocked at its vulnerability to enemy attack. In their report they wrote that the high command gave "*une importance exagérée*" to "the natural obstacles of the Ardennes forest and the Meuse river." They "trembled" they wrote, at the thought of what a German attack could do to this strategic position and recommended urgent measures to strengthen it. Huntziger replied: "I believe that there are no urgent measures to take for the reinforcement of the Sedan sector."[194]

On May 4 Hitler postponed *Fall Gelb* to May 7 and Premier Reynaud took the first steps toward dismissing General Gamelin from all his commands. Gamelin, though supreme commander of all Allied troops, had been completely ineffectual in the Norwegian campaign. Asked by the British how many troops he could send for the assault on Trondheim, he had replied, "One division per month." Reynaud exploded. He said: "It would be a crime to leave this gutless man [*cet homme sans nerfs*] as head of the French army."[195]

In parliamentary crises — one of which was shaping up in Westminster, though the prime minister didn't seem to realize it — precedents are worthless. A real political donnybrook bears less resemblance to *Robert's Rules of Order* than to a typhoon, in which water piles up behind a ship's keel, baffling the screws and forcing the helmsman to violate every principle of seamanship to avoid broaching to. Winston had never been a shrewd manipulator of votes. If he ever held a serious conversation with David Margesson, the chief Tory whip, one wonders what they could have discussed. At 11:00 P.M. on Saturday, April 27, he sent for Bill Deakin. Over the last several months he had done this often. Conscious of his contract with Cassell & Company and his obligation to finish his *History of the English-speaking Peoples* if possible, he had, according to Deakin, asked him "to spend an hour or so in the afternoon or in the early morning hours completing his chapters on the Norman Conquest and mediaeval England."[196]

This, surely, was unique in the history of statesmanship. That Saturday evening the Admiralty was sending ships to rescue the survivors of the ill-starred Trondheim expedition — "ramshackle" was Winston's word for it — while reinforcing the British force besieging Narvik. His Majesty's cruiser *Glasgow* was headed for Molde to evacuate King Haakon, his government, and Norway's gold reserves. The U-boats had sunk 101 merchant ships, and new corvette escort vessels intended to cut the German score — Winston's "cheap and nasties," nasty if not cheap — were doing the job, though the first lord was pondering, and would soon approve, closing the Mediterranean to normal British shipping. In the private office, Deakin recalls,

> Naval signals awaited attention, admirals tapped impatiently on the door of the First Lord's room, while on one occasion talk inside ranged round the spreading shadows of the Norman invasion and the figure of Edward the Confessor who, as Churchill wrote, "comes down to us faint, misty, frail." I can still see the map on the wall, with the dispositions of the British Fleet off Norway, and hear the voice of the First Lord as he grasped with his usual insight the strategic position in 1066. But this was no lack of attention to current business. It was the measure of the man with the supreme historical eye. The distant episodes were as close and real as the mighty events on hand.[197]

Churchill knew the government was in trouble and might fall. His wisest course would have been to play the lonely role which had been his lot for so long, behaving correctly but keeping his distance from a prime minister who might be on his way out. He couldn't do it. Even when those in trouble were adversaries — for example, Hoare when his deal with Laval was exposed — Winston consoled them and, if it was in his power, helped them. He sensed that Chamberlain was in trouble. Plainly, the prime minister was overworked. When Chatfield resigned as minister for the coordination of defense his office was abolished; Churchill, at the prime minister's request, took up part of the burden, and since early April had presided over the War Cabinet's Military Coordination Committee. A *Daily Mail* headline on April 4 read: "MR CHURCHILL BECOMES SUPER WAR CHIEF," and a columnist wrote that Winston had become "in effect, Britain's Supreme Defence Minister." Berlin radio broadcast on April 3 that Winston had been "elevated from warmonger to grand warmonger." One of Churchill's oldest friends wrote him: "You have indeed great responsibility now, you are practically at the top of the tree." However, he went on: "What a terrible job you have Winston. Your helpmates do not strike me as being very good." Another friend, suspicious, wrote that he couldn't help "wondering whether it isn't deliberately calculated . . . so as to load you with work as to make things impossible."[198]

Separate forces were rallying round the prime minister and round his first lord, and there was very little either could do short of renouncing the premiership, which would have been absurd, since each felt himself the better man. One side whispered, *Gallipoli*; the other, *Munich*. On May 1 Harold Nicolson noted: "The Tapers and Tadpoles" — Taper and Tadpole were party hacks in Disraeli's novel *Coningsby* — "are putting it around that the whole Norwegian episode is due to Winston. There is a theory going round that Lloyd George may head a Coalition Cabinet. What worries people is that everybody asks, 'But whom could you put in Chamberlain's place?' " Clearly it would require someone who would take a sacred oath never to say that Hitler had "missed the bus." That slight remark rankled all England. Clementine called it "a monument to ignorance and obstinacy," and the rage it sparked seems to us now to be all out of proportion to the offense. The P.M. was simply a victim of very poor timing, over which he had no control.[199]

But the anger was there; a Gallup poll early in May, after the defeat in Norway, shocked No. 10. Chamberlain's supporters were vanishing. Only 32 percent of those polled backed him; 58 percent were vehement in their opposition. Nicolson went "to Arlington Street for the Watching Committee" and found "a glum crowd," he wrote on April 30. "The general impression is that we may lose the war. The tanks position is appalling and we hear facts about that. We part in gloom. Black Week in the Boer War can hardly have been more depressing."[200]

Henry Channon, a Tory MP loyal to Chamberlain, noted in the April 30 entry in his diary that he had heard "more talk of a cabal against poor Neville." Then, turning caustic: " 'They' are saying that it is 1915 all over again, that Winston should be Prime Minister as he has more vigour and the country behind him." On May 3 Ironside wrote in his diary: "I hear there is a first-class row commencing in the House, and that there is a strong movement to get rid of the PM." He added a backhanded endorsement of Churchill: "Naturally the only man who can succeed is Winston and he is too unstable, though he has the genius to bring the war to an end." This much was certain: Churchill's steadfast stand against Hitler was all that kept his candidacy alive — in Clementine's words, "Had it not been for your years of exile & repeated warnings re. the German peril, Norway might well have ruined you." Typically, a Liberal peer wrote him May 2: "You, I believe, are the only person in the Cabinet who is not responsible for this War. You are not tarred with the Munich brush. Your advice to re-arm went unheeded. You did not let down the small nations or throw our friends to the wolves."[201]

Later Winston wrote: "Failure at Trondheim! Stalemate at Narvik! Such in the first week of May were the only results we could show to the British nation, to our Allies, and to the neutral world, friendly or hostile. Considering the prominent part I played in these events . . . it was a marvel that I survived." Like Clemmie and others, he attributed his durability to "the fact that for six or seven years I had predicted with truth the course of events, and had given ceaseless warnings, then unheeded but now remembered."[202]

Churchill was trying desperately to salvage something from the wretched campaign in Norway, to depart with dignity and a small victory — something to justify the casualties, the anxieties, the expenses, and the hopes of England. He could not mourn Trondheim. He had been against it from the start. All he had ever wanted was Narvik. But although Winston was farsighted, his vision did not extend into the Arctic Circle, where Admiral of the Fleet Lord Cork and Orrery was trying to reconcile his own aggressive instincts, Churchill's prods, the lethargic general commanding the Tommies, and the fact that some of the general's reasons for his immobility were quite sound. Major General Pierse Joseph Mackesy had drawn up a battle plan which he considered flawless. He would wait until the snow melted and then attack. According to his calculations, that would happen sometime in the summer. Cork didn't believe that at this latitude the earth was ever entirely free of snow, though certainly it was too deep now. And it was growing deeper; more snow fell almost every day. It was "exasperating," he wrote Winston, "not being able to get on, & I quite understand your wondering why we do not, but I assure you that it is not from want of desire to do so."[203]

Taking Narvik became a matter of face, though after the major German offensive erupted across the Channel on May 10, no one in His Majesty's Government seriously considered trying to hold the town. On May 24 the cabinet voted to abandon it as soon as it was in Allied hands. That happened four days later, when it fell to British, French, and Polish troops. On Tuesday, June 4, the evacuation began; by Saturday the last Allied soldier had left. England scarcely noticed. Interest in Norway had dropped sharply; attention was riveted upon the Low Countries and northern France. In 1914, Churchill had written, the cabinet had been preoccupied by the Irish question when "a strange light began immediately, but by perceptible gradations, to fall and grow upon the map of Europe." Now that light had reappeared.[204]

In Berlin it was impossible to forget that one was in the capital of a nation at war. Bands blared *"Heil Hitler Dir,"* headlines preached rage, enormous banners displaying the hakenkreuz streamed down tall buildings from roofs to the street, and posters demanded *"Deutschland Erwache!"*, *"Die Fahne Hoch!"*, and *"Gemeinnutz vor Eigennutz!"* ("The Common Interest before Self-interest!"). On Saturday, May 4 — the day Hitler again postponed *Fall Gelb* — Shirer noted in his diary: "The German papers are full of accusations that *Britain* now intends to 'spread the war' in the Mediterranean or Balkans or *somewhere else*, by which I take it they mean Holland." May 5 was a Sunday, "and as the week began to unfold," Shirer later recalled, "it became pretty clear to all of us in Berlin that the blow in the West would fall within a few days."[205]

That same Saturday His Majesty's Loyal Opposition asked for a debate on the war situation. It was scheduled for May 7. The prime minister wasn't concerned or even particularly interested; on Saturday, May 4, he noted: "I don't think my enemies will get me this time." By "enemies" he meant his critics in the House of Commons, not Nazis, though a state of war had existed between Great Britain and the German Reich for eight months, and he himself had declared it. But in London it was easy to forget. Here there were no parading bands, no marching soldiers, no banners, and no posters. In the first weeks of the war people had talked of little else; now, except among those complaining about the blackout, it was scarcely mentioned.[206]

Winston in the cabinet was Winston gagged, so even politics was a bore. There was the usual maneuvering behind the scenes. The Watching Committee to which Nicolson had referred was led by Lord Salisbury, son of the turn-of-the-century prime minister. Now seventy-eight, the frock-coated marquess had been lord privy seal and the leader of the House under Baldwin. He was a man of convictions — his denunciation of Munich had been so savage that one of Chamberlain's supporters had physically assaulted him.

On May 5 the noble lord wrote: "The Sunday papers are excited, as I knew they would be, about Norway and the reconstruction of the Government. A good deal of this inspired by personal prejudice against the P.M. I fancy the movement for including Labour will grow, but whether they will serve under him [Chamberlain] or not remains to be seen." Actually, it was the other way round; the prime minister was not interested in leading a cabinet with Labour ministers. But Chamberlain's popularity had dropped so far and so fast that even Conservatives were speculating about his successor. Halifax was no speculator, not even in his diary, because his name was the one mentioned most often as the next prime minister. Geoffrey Dawson had been promoting him since March. And on Monday, May 6, the *Evening Standard* observed that "an all-party group of critics" wanted some ministers dropped and replaced by Liberals and Socialists. "If Mr Chamberlain refuses to make the changes," the *Standard* declared, "they say there should be a new Prime Minister. And the man they select is Lord Halifax." Halifax's only comment in his diary that evening was: "Considerable political clamour, but I doubt whether this, at present in all events, will amount to much."[207]

The following day was Tuesday, May 7, 1940.

The debate which opened that day was to be one of the most memorable in British history, but no one planned it so, or even expected it. Like a runaway grand jury, it was moved by forces deep within the House of Commons, views vehemently held by individual MPs who had been unaware, till now, that so many fellow members shared them and felt just as strongly. They were to address the formal motion, "That this House do now adjourn," though in fact they would be debating the prosecution of the war. Chamberlain had chosen to open for the Conservatives; Churchill would close the following day. Labour had wanted Winston first — "We took the view that the First Lord was the Prime Minister's principal witness," Herbert Morrison said — but the prime minister knew Churchill was his most effective speaker and could draw all the government's arguments together as no other minister could.[208]

The government's most ineffective speaker was Chamberlain himself. "The House is crowded," Nicolson wrote, "and when Chamberlain comes in, he is greeted with shouts of 'Missed the bus!' He makes a very feeble speech and is only applauded by the Yes-men. He makes some reference to the complacency of the country, at which the whole House cheers vociferously and ironically, inducing him to make a little, rather feminine, gesture of irritation." As always Neville was coldly logical, but he seemed to lack his usual easy control of the House; his heart wasn't in it. Norway was no Gallipoli, he said — a comparison Winston may have wished he had found unnecessary, though the P.M. defended his first lord by dismissing as "unworthy and unfounded" the suggestion that one minister was more responsible than his colleagues for what had happened. Plainly, he was off his form. It may have been at this point that he realized for the first time that a shadow lay over his government.[209]

Attlee also made "a feeble speech" in Nicolson's opinion, but "Archie Sinclair a good one." Sinclair said the Norwegian operation had failed because "there had been no foresight in the political direction of the war and in the instructions given to the Staffs." He added: "In the first major effort of this war . . . we have had to creep back to our lairs, which is against the spirit of the men who are over the waters." Such damaging words were rarely heard in the Commons, but the pyrotechnics had only started. Another slashing speech followed, and yet another by the Labour MP Josiah Wedgwood, which was very odd. Nicolson wrote that he said "everything that he ought not to have said" and gave "the impression of being a little off his head. At one moment he suggests that the British Navy have gone to Alexandria since they are frightened of being bombed."[210]

This led to the first sign that a real tempest loomed. As Wedgwood wound up, Roger Keyes entered the chamber. At Duff Cooper's suggestion Keyes was in full uniform, gold braid up to his elbows and six rows of ribbons, topped by the Grand Cross of the Order of Bath, glittering on his chest. Here was a genuine naval hero, the man who had led the gallant raid against the German U-boat pens at Zeebrugge and Ostend in 1918. Nicolson handed him a note quoting Wedgwood's remark about the navy. The old admiral immediately rose, went straight to the Speaker's chair, was recognized at once, and began by calling the previous speaker's remark "a damned insult" — unparliamentary language, but the Speaker did not call him on it, and the House, noted Nicolson, "roars with laughter, especially Lloyd George who rocks backwards and forwards in boyish delight with his mouth wide open."[211]

But Keyes had not come to amuse Parliament. He had brought a speech. His appalling delivery was known to everyone in the chamber, so at Harold Macmillan's suggestion he had written everything out. It was a devastating attack on the naval conduct at Narvik; the chamber was completely silent when he declared that a naval assault at Trondheim would have succeeded but had been canceled because of lack of nerve at the Admiralty. This was a blow at Churchill, doubly so because he and the admiral were old friends. It was probably unjustified; nevertheless, when Keyes sat down Chamberlain knew he was in real trouble. Nicolson described the reaction: "There is a great gasp of astonishment. It is by far the most dramatic speech I have ever heard, and when Keyes sits down there is thunderous applause."[212]

Now it was Leo Amery's turn. The Speaker called him during the dinner hour, and the House was no longer crowded, but Clement Davies, a Liberal MP and the unofficial whip of the dissident factions, toured the dining room, lobbies, and smoking room, drumming up an audience for him. They found him worth it. Amery was a senior parliamentarian; he had been an admirer of old Joe Chamberlain's and a friend of both Joe's sons. With great skill he moved the target of the government's critics away from the navy — and by implication, Churchill — and toward Chamberlain and the conduct of the war. "Somehow or other," he said, "we must get into the Government men who can match our enemies in fighting spirit, in daring, in resolution and in thirst for victory." Approaching the end he said: "Some 300 years ago, when this House found that its troops were being beaten again and again by the dash and daring of the Cavaliers, by Prince Rupert's cavalry, Oliver Cromwell spoke to John Hampden. In one of his speeches he recounted what he had said. It was this: 'I said to him, "Your troops are most of them old, decayed serving men and tapsters and such kind of fellows." You must get men of a spirit that are likely to go as far as they will go, or you will be beaten still.' "

Amery paused. He said: "We are fighting today for our life, for our liberty, for our all. We cannot go on being led as we are." Again he paused, assessing the mood of the House. He had them rapt. In his research he had come upon another quotation. It was brutal; he might lose his converts if he used it, but he was carried away, and looking toward the front bench he plunged ahead:

> I have quoted certain words of Oliver Cromwell. I will quote certain other words. I do it with great reluctance, because I am speaking of those who are old friends and associates of mine, but they are words which, I think, are applicable to the present situation. This is what Cromwell said to the Long Parliament when he thought it was no longer fit to conduct the affairs of the nation:

"You have sat too long here for any good you have been doing. Depart, I say, and let us have done with you. In the name of God, go."[213]

In the opinion of some close to Chamberlain, Amery's pitiless attack shattered him. Churchill later wrote: "These were terrible words coming from a friend and colleague of many years, a fellow Birmingham Member, and a Privy Councillor of distinction and experience." In Nicolson's opinion the general impression left by the debate was that "we are unprepared to meet the appalling attack which we know is about to be delivered against us." The response was "something more than anxiety; it is one of actual fear, but it is a very resolute fear and not hysteria or cowardice in the least. In fact I have seldom admired the spirit of the House so much as I did today." He believed "there is no doubt that the Government is very rocky and anything may happen tomorrow." In his diary the loyal Henry Channon noted of the first day's debate: "The atmosphere was intense, and everywhere one heard whispers: 'What will Winston do?' "[214]

There is a jeu d'esprit that Frenchmen tell — though only to one another — of how, when God created the earth, he wanted one perfect place, so he made France. Then, seeing what he had done, he decided he had gone too far, so he made Frenchmen. At times foreigners also repeat the story, and it was enjoying an exceptional vogue in early May 1940. Anyone who has studied the fighting which was about to begin as the Wehrmacht surged into France cannot doubt that Reynaud was justified in his determination to cashier the indecisive, almost inaccessible Généralissime Gamelin. However, the premier's timing was poor. It may be that having no commander in chief was preferable to the French Hamlet in Vincennes, but the problem was larger than that. It was political, because Gamelin's champion, the republic's minister of defense, was Daladier, who wanted to be premier again and was awaiting only an opportunity to strike. Cashiering the *généralissime* would provoke Daladier's resignation and, therefore, a cabinet crisis. France could survive without a government now, but not if she were invaded. But Reynaud's mind was made up. By May 8 the document of indictment was ready; the premier called a cabinet meeting for the following day. The prospect, for everyone except Germans, was depressing. Marianne would face a powerful foe with her leaders quarreling among themselves. Once again poilus would reel backward shouting, *"Nous sommes trahis!"* and in a sense they would be right, though the betrayers would be *les députés* they had elected to office.

But Paris in the spring! In that second week in May the place God had made was a poem of beauty. The gardens of the Luxembourg and the

Tuileries were in full blossom; so were the chestnut trees along the Seine; the overarching sky was unflawed by a single cloud, and on the boulevards and the Champs Élysées one could meditate or amuse oneself with friends in what Henri de Kerillis later remembered as "a bath of sun." The Duchess of Windsor worked at a canteen for poilus; Clare Boothe Luce, who had come to see her, thought the capital "insanely beautiful," with "unstartled birds singing in the gardens" and the flower market at the Madeleine "madly colorful." Theatres, cinemas, and nightclubs were packed; so were the stands at the Auteuil for spring racing; so were the halls of the Grand Palais, where the annual art exhibition was on display. In the rue de la Paix the windows of the great gem stores glittered with rubies, garnets, diamonds, jade, opal, sapphires, and emeralds, and business was brisk. On the Place Vendôme elegantly dressed women moved through the gilded corridors on their way to tea or lunch. Afterward de Kerillis would remember "how carefree and lighthearted" Parisians were.[215]

London is less celebrated for its beauty, though there are those who prefer it because, among other reasons, it never occurred to Londoners — and certainly not to Churchill — that England's capital should be surrendered rather than be submitted to the ravages of battle. The British were prepared to sacrifice London house by house, to be destroyed rather than dishonored. The French loved honor, but loved Paris more, as they would demonstrate before summer arrived. On Wednesday, May 8, the second day of the Norway debate in the House of Commons, Hitler set the final date for *Fall Gelb*. It would begin at 5:35 A.M. on Friday. This would be confirmed Thursday when he flashed the irrevocable code word "Danzig" to his commanders. Meantime, the Führer boarded his special train for his headquarters, Felsennest (Aerie), near Münstereifel, twenty-five miles southwest of Bonn. That Wednesday, as the House of Commons gathered, with its leaders feeling they were on the verge of something tremendous, though none could identify it, Shirer was cabling New York from Berlin. As he later wrote, he advised his home office "to hold one of our correspondents in Amsterdam instead of shipping him off to Norway, where the war had ended anyway." That evening his military censors "allowed me to hint in my broadcast that there would soon be action in the West, including Holland and Belgium." Only later did he learn why. The Nazis were deliberately focusing attention on the northern and western parts of the Low Countries, in the hope that no one would notice the German troop concentrations around the Ardennes.[216]

Wednesday morning Labour's leaders were busy. Hugh Dalton breakfasted with Hugh Gaitskell, who told him that "high Foreign Office officials are leaking very freely." Halifax, he had learned, had threatened to resign unless Trondheim were attacked, and Lord Cork and Orrery had said that "in the first twenty-four hours" — before the Germans arrived — "I could have taken Trondheim with my bare hands." His request to do so had been denied, not by Churchill, but by Whitehall.[217]

That morning's *Daily Herald*, the voice of Labour, reported that the party's Parliamentary Executive would meet before noon to determine its tactics in the concluding day of the debate. The *Herald*'s political correspondent, Maurice Webb, predicted "sweeping reconstruction of the Government, involving the possible resignation of Mr. Chamberlain . . . in the near future." Webb doubted, however, that events would "take this drastic turn at once. Indeed, as I have previously stated, the Government will get through the present debate without immediate disaster." He noted suggestions "that the Labour Party should either put down a vote of censure or force a division on a motion for the adjournment, a motion which, if passed, would bring the Government down." To his subsequent regret, he called this "an unwise tactic. . . . The view taken by the most experienced critics of the Government is that the debate should be allowed to end without any direct challenge."[218]

Herbert Morrison and Dalton had given Webb their assurance that there would be no call for a vote. However, he had not talked to Clement Attlee. Throughout Tuesday's session Attlee had kept a sharp eye on the benches opposite. He had observed the hostility toward their prime minister, and he meant to measure it. The leadership meeting, which he chaired, opened at 10:30 A.M., and he proposed that the Opposition force a division. Several of his colleagues were reluctant, arguing, as Dalton did, that "a vote at this stage" would "consolidate the Government majority," that it was precisely what Chamberlain and Halifax wanted. Nevertheless, Attlee's motion carried and was ratified at a later meeting of Labour backbenchers. Labour therefore prepared to make the first move when Parliament assembled. Morrison rose, as usual, to bait the front bench. At last, he observed, the prime minister had found a newspaper endorsement outside Britain and her commonwealth. It was the official organ of Franco's Spanish Falangists. He also read a few lines from Hoare's Norway speech from the BBC in *The Listener*. "Today our wings are spread over the Arctic. They are sheathed in ice. . . ." Hoare flushed crimson as the House roared. Morrison said: "Hon. Members understandably laugh, but I am not quoting this for the purpose of arousing amusement, because it really is serious, for it is an indication of the delusions from which the Government are suffering." He then announced that "in view of the gravity of the events which we are debating . . . every Member has a responsibility to record his particular judgment upon them." Therefore, "we feel that we must divide the House at the end of our debate today." The Opposition was calling for a censure of the government.[219]

Chamberlain was startled, then angry. The cockiness of Morrison's manner — he always seemed to be lecturing a particularly stupid child — was enough to get under anyone's skin. Moreover, the prime minister had not expected this. There was an understanding between whips that if either party planned to ask for a vote, the other would be told, although recently Sir Charles Edwards, Labour's chief whip, had warned Margesson, his Tory counterpart, that he couldn't always carry out his side of the bargain, explaining apologetically, "It's a very difficult party to manage, you know."[220]

Thus taken unaware, the prime minister miscalculated. He jumped up and sputtered: "The words which the right hon. gentleman has just uttered make it necessary for me to intervene for a moment or two at this stage." Dalton thought he showed "his teeth like a rat" as he cried, "It may well be that it is a duty to criticise the Government. I do not seek to evade criticism, but I say to my friends in the House, *and I have friends in the House*" — here, according to Nicolson, his expression became "a leer of triumph" — "[that] no Government can prosecute a war efficiently unless it has public and parliamentary support. I accept this challenge. I welcome it indeed. At least I shall see who is with us and who is against us, and I call on my friends to support us in the Lobby tonight."[221]

Churchill described this as "an unfortunate passage"; his fellow Tories, he noted, "sat abashed and silenced." "Friends," in the context and idiom of the time and place, meant members of the P.M.'s party. Thus, in a partisan stroke, he had reduced the debate to the lowest level of politics, demanding that men belonging to the majority vote for him, regardless of how they felt about his prosecution of the war. It led to an unforgettable speech. Churchill called it "the last decisive intervention of Mr. Lloyd George in the House."[222]

He was now approaching eighty, and the awesome fire which had fueled the passion of the young Welsh crusader for justice had been reduced to embers. But Chamberlain, by cheapening the office Lloyd George had held in the last war, kindled them; in a final pyrotechnical display he evoked memories of the days when he was in his forties and Churchill in his thirties and the two radicals, the older as chancellor and the younger as president of the Board of Trade, had forged an alliance to emasculate the House of Lords and bring England a maximum work day for miners, pensions for the aged, free meals and free medical attention for all British schoolchildren, and insurance for the jobless and the sick. Violet Bonham Carter, whose father was then the prime minister, had watched them both, and now in 1940, sitting in the Strangers' Gallery, she thought this, Lloyd George's last bow, "the most deadly speech I have ever heard from him — voice, gesture, everything was brought into play to drive home the attack."[223]

He tried to exculpate Churchill — "I do not think the First Lord was responsible for all the things that happened in Norway" — but Churchill immediately interrupted him: "I take full responsibility for everything that has been done by the Admiralty, and I take my full share of the burden." After warning Winston not to allow himself "to be converted into an air-raid shelter to keep the splinters from hitting his colleagues," Lloyd George turned on Chamberlain:

> It is not a question of who are the Prime Minister's friends. It is a far bigger issue. He has appealed for sacrifice. The nation is prepared for every sacrifice so long as the Government show clearly what they are aiming at, and so long as the nation is confident that those who are leading it are doing their best. *I say solemnly that the Prime Minister should give an example of sacrifice, because there is nothing which can contribute more to victory in this war than that he should sacrifice the seals of office.*[224]

Now the outcome of the House vote was a source of speculation. Labour could not win. They held 166 seats to the Conservatives' 387. Many men could not switch; commitments had been made, papers signed, obligations incurred. To many others, casting a Conservative vote was a sacrament. And still others knew that if they broke with the party they would be pariahs in their own constituencies, even their own homes. But Chamberlain, smug only yesterday, began to feel uneasy. If the great Tory majority thinned perceptibly, his problems could become grave. Keyes, Amery, and Lloyd George had stirred the House. He was lucky Churchill was on the front bench and would anchor the government's position in the last speech of the evening.

As the debate continued into evening it became obvious that Winston would not be called before 10:00 P.M. He wandered into the smoking room, and was poking a hole in a new cigar when he glanced up and saw Harold Macmillan. Macmillan recalled long afterward: "He beckoned to me, and I moved to speak to him. I wished him luck, but added that I hoped his speech would not be too convincing. 'Why not?' he asked. 'Because,' I replied, 'we must have a new Prime Minister, and it must be you.' He answered gruffly that he had signed on for the voyage and would stick to the ship. But I don't think he was angry with me."[225]

Churchill was, however, worried. After Lloyd George's valediction he had been heard to say to Kingsley Wood, "This is all making it damned difficult for me tonight," and to Walter Elliott that the old man had been "absolutely devastating." Nevertheless, when the Speaker recognized him shortly after ten o'clock, he squared away like a prizefighter, assuming his most pugilistic stance. He had taken the queen's shilling, had signed on for the cruise, and intended to give the captain his best possible performance. In his diary Channon observed, "One saw at once that he was in a bellicose mood, alive and enjoying himself, relishing the ironical position in which he found himself: i.e. that of defending his enemies, and a cause in which he did not believe." Channon called the speech "slashing, vigourous . . . a magnificent piece of oratory. I was in the gallery behind him, with Rab" — R. A. Butler — "who was several times convulsed with laughter."[226]

Winston said he understood Keyes's "desire to lead a valiant attack" but regretted "that this natural impulse should have led him to cast aspersions upon his old shipmates and his old staff officers, Sir Dudley Pound and Vice-Admiral Phillips." Then he turned on those who had deplored the prime minister's appeal to his friends. He had shared their dismay, but he wasn't going to let that prevent him from having fun with them. "He *thought* he had some friends," he said, "and I *hope* he has some friends. He certainly had a good many when things were going well." At one point he said that Allied shipping losses had almost been redeemed by new shipbuilding and the capture of German ships. "Oh!" cried Emanuel Shinwell, an exasperated socialist and a favorite Churchill target. Winston rounded on him. "I daresay the hon. Member does not like that. He would like me to have a bad tale to tell. That is why he skulks in a corner." A Labour MP, "rather the worse for drink," according to Channon, had never heard the word "skulks"; he thought Winston had said "skunks" and protested, with the support of several colleagues who had it aright, that he had used unparliamentary language. The brief exchange in Hansard is hilarious:

[*Interruption*]

Mr. Churchill: What are we quarreling about? [HON. MEMBERS: "You should withdraw that."] I will not withdraw it.

Mr. Sloan (South Ayreshire): On a point of order — [*Interruption*]

Mr. Maclean: On a point of order. Is "skulk" a Parliamentary word? The right hon. Gentleman used the word "skulk" and I am asking whether it is a Parliamentary word to use to another Member?

Mr. Speaker: It depends whether it applies accurately or not.

Mr. Maclean: Further to that point of order — [*Interruption*]

Mr. Churchill: Finally — [*Interruption*] — Hon. Members dare not listen to the argument.

Mr. Maclean: Are we to understand, Mr. Speaker, that a word becomes Parliamentary if it is accurate?

Mr. Churchill: All day long we have had abuse, and now hon. Members opposite will not even listen. . . .[227]

He had a knack for that — drawing them out and then playing the outraged injured party. "How much of the fire was real, how much ersatz, we shall never know," Channon wrote, "but he amused and dazzled everyone with his virtuosity." John Peck, a young civil servant who had recently joined Winston's staff, was fascinated — and troubled. Winston, he later wrote, "was constantly heckled by the Labour opposition, and he tore into them vehemently and often angrily. I had never heard him in action in the House of Commons and I was strangely uneasy." Somehow, he felt, "it did not ring entirely true." Actually, he reflected, it was impossible to offer "a completely sincere and heartfelt reply" to the attacks on the government. "Churchill knew that he was defending positions which were in many respects, indefensible. He knew that if the bitterest critics had their way, Chamberlain would resign. He knew that, in that case, he would probably become Prime Minister himself. But throughout the entire political crisis he never spoke or acted except in absolute loyalty to his Prime Minister." The fact was that the more eloquent his defense of Chamberlain, the more Chamberlain's chances shrunk. After this no one would ask: "If not Chamberlain, who?"[228]

The House was blinded, and beguiled, by the skyrockets and pinwheels, but in solemn moments Churchill, though entertaining, was never a mere entertainer. He knew serious men would pore over Hansard, looking for a chain of logic, and he provided them with it. He did not lie, he did not distort. But it was sophistry all the same. He omitted certain facts; since they reflected well upon him, it would have been difficult for anyone to argue that he had deliberately remained mute. Among his omissions was the fact that he had spent seven months trying to persuade the War Cabinet that they must move on Narvik (though he *did* say, "My eye has always been fixed on Narvik"), nor did he reveal his original doubts about Trondheim. Once the Nazi invasion had begun, he said, no one could "dispute that we were bound to go to the aid of the Norwegians and that Trondheim was the place." Not a voice in the chamber cried: "Why?" Yet that was his one weak point; had he been challenged here, the whole structure of his presentation could have collapsed.

But he got by it and was home free. He conceded that Trondheim had been "a hazardous operation," but could have succeeded had the Norwegians not neglected to blow key bridges, destroy railroad junctions, hold the mountain passes, or block the Nazi advance north of Oslo. All these delaying tactics having failed, the British commanders were left with a Hobson's choice: either evacuate their troops "or leave them to be destroyed by overwhelming force." Could they have been strengthened? They could — by ignoring the military maxim "Never reinforce failure" and by withdrawing divisions from the BEF in France. Escalation in Norway would have led to "a forlorn operation on an ever-increasing scale." Perhaps he was thinking of Gallipoli. Here he added a warning; he had not abandoned his illusion that sea power was omnipotent, but he foresaw the danger of recklessly committing the RAF unless the need for it became absolute: "We must be careful not to exhaust our air force, in view of the much graver dangers which might come upon us at any time."[229]

The prime minister was pleased and grateful. Then the House voted, and he was shocked to discover that over a hundred of those he had counted among his friends weren't friendly anymore. Despite the Conservative whips, 41 Chamberlain supporters had defected to the Opposition and another 60 had abstained — 26 of them Tories whose constituencies included the territorials martyred at Andalsnes. A united party vote would have given the P.M. a majority of 213. Instead, the final tabulation was 281 for the government, 200 against it — a majority of 81. It was a stinging rebuke, wholly unforeseen. And for many the decision had been excruciating. Duff Cooper saw "a young officer in uniform, who had been for long a fervent admirer of Chamberlain, walking through the Opposition lobby" — voting against the government — "with tears streaming down his face." Churchill had always voted as he pleased, but he was an exception; others faced punishment from Margesson and the party machine. They knew that if they appeared at No. 11 Downing Street's patronage office now they would be turned away. To abandon their leader had required considerable courage, but they had done it, and now he was in the deepest trouble of his political career.[230]

His spirits cannot have been raised by Parliament's response to the announcement of the vote. "Up to the last moment," Nicolson wrote, "the House had behaved with moderation," but "during the last twenty minutes . . . passions rose." The figures "are greeted with a terrific demonstration," he continued, "during which Joss Wedgwood starts singing *Rule Britannia*, which is drowned in shouts of 'Go, go, go, go!' " Some were waving handkerchiefs at the fleeing P.M. To counteract their jeers, Nicolson noted, "Margesson signals to his henchmen to rise and cheer the departing Prime Minister, and he walks out pale and angry." Hugh Dalton was asked: "What next?" He replied: "The Old Man must go to Buckingham Palace and hand them [the seals of office] in."[231]

At 11:13 P.M., May 8, 1940, when the House of Commons adjourned, thousands of Dutch, Belgians, and Luxembourgers had less than forty-eight hours to live, though they were unaware of it; in those days civilized nations mobilized, exchanged hostile notes, and then formally declared war. Nevertheless, guards on the borders of each of these small countries were puzzled and troubled by the total silence on the German side of their frontiers. Hitler had signed nonaggression pacts with each and repeatedly and solemnly reaffirmed them, vowing that not a single hobnailed Wehrmacht boot would ever touch their soil. They had taken little comfort from that; he had told too many *grosse Lügen*; his credibility had vanished and been replaced by fear. The Third Reich, possessing the most powerful military juggernaut Europe had ever known, was recognized as a terrorist nation, the very essence of *Schrecklichkeit*, the stuff of nightmares.

Luxembourg was not going to win this war. Her army comprised four hundred infantrymen and twelve cavalrymen. But she had already taken the first step in a campaign which would cripple the Wehrmacht in every conquered country. Luxembourgers had erected barbed wire barricades on frontier roads, evacuated border towns, and closed bridges across the duchy's river border with the Reich. They called it "passive defense," but the world would adopt the French name: *La Résistance*.

❦ ❦

As he rose to leave the chamber, the prime minister had motioned to Churchill, an invitation to join him in his private room. There Winston "saw at once," as he later recalled, "that he took the most serious view of the sentiment of the House toward himself. He felt he could not go on. There ought to be a National Government. One party alone could not carry the burden. Someone must form a Government in which all parties would serve, or we could not get through."[232]

Churchill's reply was the last response one would have expected. He could have relished the moment. He had every right. "If [a prime minister] trips," he later observed, "he must be sustained. If he makes mistakes, they must be covered. If he sleeps he must not be wantonly disturbed. If he is no good he must be pole-axed." If ever a man deserved retribution, it was Neville Chamberlain. More than any man except Hitler — and Hitler could not have done it without him — he was responsible for the transformation of Germany into the most powerful military state in Europe, which had begun, with Teutonic efficiency, the destruction of all European Jews and had turned the Slavs in the vast lands it conquered into *Sklavenarbeiter* — slave laborers. Young Colville, who scorned those who condemned all Germans per se, had nevertheless reflected in March: "I suppose there is a natural strain of brutality in the German character and as great an insensitivity to human suffering as there is a sensitivity to beauty." The Nazis had unleashed the brutality, but had Chamberlain not embraced their führer at Munich, their government would have fallen as his was now falling.[233]

It would have been almost instinctive in any other member of Parliament to ponder the implications of the House vote for his own career. Every speech denouncing the government over the past two days had been an echo of the speeches Churchill had been delivering for years — often to empty seats. The awakening of Parliament's conscience had vindicated the torch he had held aloft, alone, at great personal cost. It was savage irony that he now found himself among the crew of a ship being sunk by torpedoes he had designed. Since he first won election to Parliament forty years earlier, his objective had been to become prime minister. Here, writhing on the rack of humiliation, was the man who had been his chief adversary during the three crucial years before the outbreak of the war. Knowing Neville, he was sure he would not throw in his hand voluntarily, but now the choice might no longer be his. Had Winston connived for office, as was his right — some would have said, his duty — he would have suggested various lines of action, or at the very least have remained silent.

But Churchill was never a rational man. His conduct often seemed to run at cross-purposes with what was best for him and best for England. His magnanimity, so often extended to those who least deserved it, might have led him to console Chamberlain by making some wildly generous, completely ruinous gesture, volunteering to accept, for example, blame that was not his. Instead, he yielded to another Churchillian impulse — to stand with Chamberlain, as though he were Horatius, to defend the indefensible bridge. "Aroused by the antagonisms of the debate," as he later wrote, he urged the prime minister to "fight on. 'This has been a damaging debate, but you have a good majority. Do not take the matter grievously to heart. . . . Strengthen your Government from every quarter, and let us go on until our majority deserts us.' " At midnight he left the P.M. unconvinced, uncomforted. Winston wondered why the man would "persist in his resolve to sacrifice himself." The answer was that although Chamberlain had never backed away from a fight, logic told him that if he were to survive this moral defeat, he would have to search for compromises. Churchill had never compromised. And in moments of crisis he sought guidance not by reasoning but by intuition.[234]

After baring his soul to Churchill, the prime minister reverted to type, trying to find a way out of the trap. Although it was midnight, the King readily agreed to see him. The audience was brief. Smiling, the prime minister said he had not come to resign; he hoped to restructure his government as a coalition, with Labour participation. Later a reliable source reported that George VI offered to intervene with Attlee. It seems implausible, a dubious move for Britain's constitutional monarch. In all events, the prime minister said that Attlee would have a better understanding of his party's attitude after its annual meeting, about to begin in Bournemouth. He had not yet grasped the nature of the crisis; he thought it would develop slowly, giving him time to negotiate.[235]

Chamberlain's critics have held that his sole object after the disastrous debate was to cling to office — "The Old Man is incorrigibly limpet," wrote Dalton, "always trying new tricks to keep himself firm upon the rock." It is unlikely that his motives were overtly selfish; able politicians always regard themselves as indispensable, and once Chamberlain realized that the country's fortunes were likely to improve under another leader, he devoted himself to an orderly transition. That light did not dawn on him until late Thursday morning, but he never sacrificed or bargained or wheedled to stay at No. 10, as Ramsay MacDonald had done ten years earlier.[236]

Churchill was shaving the following morning when Eden called at the Admiralty. Flourishing his safety razor, Winston predicted, as Eden wrote in his diary, that the P.M. would "not be able to bring in Labour and that a National Government must be formed." Eden returned early in the afternoon for lunch, and was startled to find that Kingsley Wood was also a guest. Just as Bracken was Churchill's satellite, so Wood was Chamberlain's. The prime minister trusted him and respected his advice; in turn, he had raised him from parliamentary secretary to cabinet rank, first as minister of health and now air minister. The RAF had doubled its strength during the past year, but that was not his doing; he was defeatist and had enthusiastically supported appeasement. Why was he at the Admiralty? He wanted to tell Churchill what Chamberlain had been doing. Eden was appalled. Churchill wasn't. With England in danger, personal loyalties went over the side. Winston may have assumed that his visitor was concerned about the nation's survival, not his cabinet seat, though later events demonstrated that his visitor's tale-bearing would not go unrewarded.[237]

The previous evening, it seemed, no member of the House had gone straight home. Factions and cabals had met in Westminster chambers, Whitehall offices, and private apartments. The largest group, sixty rebel Conservatives, had elected Amery as their chairman and voted, unanimously, that none of them would join or support any government which did not include Labour and Liberals. Downing Street had been informed of this, of course, and at 8:00 A.M. Amery had been summoned to No. 10. Chamberlain had offered him the choice of any cabinet ministry — the Foreign Office and the Exchequer were expressly offered — if he would bring his rebels back into the fold. Amery had asked whether the rebuilt government would include members of the other two parliamentary parties. The prime minister had said bleakly: "I hope that will not be necessary." In that event, Amery had said, he could not accept the P.M.'s generous offer, and expressing his regrets he had departed.[238]

At 10:00 A.M., Kingsley Wood went on, Lord Halifax had appeared. There is something intriguing about the Halifax candidacy. The prime minister urged him to be his successor, implying that he would serve under him. Chamberlain's biographer leaves no doubt that the foreign secretary was his first choice. Back in his office Halifax dictated a note to Cadogan, commenting on the P.M.'s offer: "The evident drift of his mind left me with a bad stomach ache." Yet from the moment knowledgeable Englishmen had begun talking about a new prime minister, Halifax's name had led all the rest. On May 6, the day before the crucial two-day debate, he had quietly conferred with Morrison about the possibility of a Conservative-Labour coalition. His diary merely notes the appointment; neither his papers nor Morrison's mention what was said or decided. And the following day, before the debate began, the *Daily Mail* had published a letter from Sir Stafford Cripps, KC, which *The Times* had rejected. Signed "A British Politician," it had called for an all-party government, with a small cabinet — Churchill, Eden, Lloyd George, Morrison, and Attlee were mentioned — led by Halifax as prime minister.[239]

Dalton, like Morrison a member of the Labour hierarchy, was open in his support of Halifax. After Chamberlain's humiliation in the House, Dalton had told Rab Butler that "provided Chamberlain, Simon and Hoare disappeared" Labour might join a coalition, that if asked who should be the new P.M., "I thought, and a number of others shared this view, that there was much to be said for Halifax." Given the lopsided Tory majority in the House, the hard fact was that no one could form a government without the support of Tory backbenchers. Dalton told Attlee: "Given the strength of parties in the House, the P.M. *must* be a Conservative. He quite agreed. We thought it lay between Halifax and Churchill, and that either, if other conditions were right, would be a possible leader of a Coalition which we might join."[240]

Halifax had left the door ajar, or Chamberlain thought he had, and the P.M., a man of heroic doggedness, refused to accept the noble lord's rejection. In any event, he himself would resign. In his diary Eden noted that at luncheon with Wood and Churchill, "They told me that Neville had decided to go. The future was discussed. Kingsley thought that W. should succeed, and urged that if asked he should make plain his willingness." But Wood warned Winston that the P.M. wanted Halifax and would ask Churchill to agree. "Don't agree," Wood said, "and don't say anything." In his memoirs Eden commented: "I was shocked that Wood should talk in this way, for he had been so much Chamberlain's man. But it was good counsel and I seconded it."[241]

For a party holding only 27 percent of the seats in the House, Labour was courted with extraordinary ardor. During the debates, Harold Macmillan later remembered, there was apprehension on the part of Churchill's supporters over Winston's role as the last speaker — concern that by giving a fighting speech, he might alienate Opposition leaders who would then veto his bid to succeed Chamberlain. "We were determined to bring down the Government," Macmillan recalled, but "if the chief issue of the first day had been the overthrow of the Government, the chief anxiety of the second was the rescue of Churchill." In fact, he wrote, Chamberlain was convinced that Winston's spirited defense of his government meant "Labour hostility to Churchill in forming a National Government." But Bracken, anticipating this, had entertained Attlee at dinner Tuesday evening. Attlee thought Halifax would move into No. 10 with Winston as his minister of defense. His people, he said, "have never forgiven Churchill for Tonypandy."*[242]

Bracken, on his own initiative, insisted that Churchill would never serve under Halifax, "incurring all the blame if things went wrong and with no real control of the situation." He then exacted a pledge from Attlee: if Churchill came to power, Attlee would not refuse to join the government. The irony here is that while Morrison and Dalton found Halifax acceptable — they barred only Chamberlain, Simon, and Hoare — the rest of the party leadership and virtually all the rank and file were less tolerant. On Thursday the ninth Clement Davies reported to Bob Boothby that "Attlee & Greenwood are unable to distinguish between the PM & Halifax & are *not* prepared to serve under the latter." That same evening Boothby — who had been in the House all day, drumming up support for Churchill — passed this information along to Churchill with the comment: "Opinion is hardening against Halifax as Prime Minister. I am doing my best to foster this, because I cannot feel he is, in any circumstances, the right man." The Halifax boomlet was doomed; he could never have formed a coalition government — the only government that Parliament would accept.[243]

Kingsley Wood's visit was enormously useful to Winston. As Churchill put it, over lunch he "learned that Mr. Chamberlain was resolved upon the

* The location of a riot by striking Welsh miners in November 1910. Churchill, then home secretary, restored order and actually saved miners' lives. But "Tonypandy" had a memorable ring to it; union leaders made it pejorative and — like "Gallipoli" — it stuck.

formation of a National Government and, if he could not be the head, he would give way to anyone commanding his confidence who could. Thus, by the afternoon, I became aware that I might well be called upon to take the lead. The prospect neither excited nor alarmed me. . . . I was content to let events unfold." He was back in his office, scanning staff reports, when the call came from No. 10. Arriving, he found Halifax with Chamberlain; very soon, the prime minister told him, Attlee and Greenwood, Labour's deputy leader, would arrive. The socialists arrived late, though they could scarcely reveal why. Stopping at the Reform Club, they had met with Clement Davies to review their position. A German attack on the Low Countries was believed imminent. Because of it, Attlee favored keeping Chamberlain in office until the crisis passed. The other two disagreed. Eventually they had brought him round, but it had taken them two hours. In the Cabinet Room he and Greenwood sat on one side, the three Tories on the other, Chamberlain in the middle.[244]

Chamberlain asked whether Labour would serve under him, or, if not, under another Conservative prime minister. Their formal response, they said, would depend upon the views of the party, now convening in Bournemouth, but they believed the reply to the first question would be "almost certainly, 'no' "; to the second "probably 'yes.' " Both Halifax and Churchill loyally urged support for Chamberlain, but just as Winston was beginning to work himself up toward a cadenza, Greenwood cut in: "We haven't come here to listen to you orating, Winston." Whatever their feelings, they said, they lacked the power to make decisions "because members of our party have got absolutely no confidence in the Prime Minister." Attlee was even more blunt: "I'm bound to tell you, Prime Minister, that in my view our party will not serve under you, nor does the country want you." Serving under another Conservative prime minister was another matter; they would lay it before the Labour Party Executive at Bournemouth tomorrow and Attlee would telephone yes or no. He and Greenwood then withdrew. Chamberlain, Halifax, and Churchill remained in the Cabinet Room; because this was a political matter, David Margesson joined them. If Kingsley Wood had been right, this was the time to be on the qui vive.[245]

Chamberlain told them he was now convinced that forming a national government was beyond his power. Attlee and Greenwood had tied the knot of that shroud. Margesson, asked for his opinion, agreed. Unity was indispensable, he said, and as long as Chamberlain remained in power it would be beyond reach. He added that he was not prepared — at the moment — to comment on the political strengths of Churchill and Halifax among Conservative backbenchers, at which, Halifax noted in his diary, "my stomach ache continued." Chamberlain's task now was to tell the King who should be sent for after he had surrendered the seals of office. He seemed calm, cool, almost detached. But he looked across the table at both of them.[246]

At this point we must choose between Churchill's recollection and Halifax's. Winston's account, the more engaging, has been almost universally accepted and presented in various stage, television, and film dramas. In this version he remembered Kingsley Wood's admonition to say nothing — advice far more difficult for Winston to follow than most men — and sat immobile while "a very long pause ensued. It certainly seemed longer than the two minutes which one observes in the commemorations of Armistice Day." Then, he tells us, Halifax said he couldn't possibly lead a government because, being a peer, he sat in the House of Lords.[247]

But Winston's tale, as it appears in *The Gathering Storm*, the first volume of his World War II history, does not bear close scrutiny. The meeting in the Cabinet Room occurred on May 9. He puts it on May 10. The difference between the two is huge; on May 9 the borders of France and the Low Countries were inviolate. The great surge of the Wehrmacht came on May 10, and Churchill tells us that upon returning to the Admiralty from the Cabinet Room, he found that "the Dutch Ministers were in my room. Haggard and worn, with horror in their eyes, they had just flown over. . . . Their country had been attacked without the slightest pretext or warning." The day before, when Chamberlain actually faced Halifax and Winston, Holland had been peaceful. Churchill got it wrong. And no wonder. He was dictating it six years after the event — six of the most crowded years any man had endured. To acquire some inkling of what that pressure did to his memory, one need only reflect upon what the first year did to it. Millions remember, and can recite, lines from his great speeches of 1940: "Their finest hour," "We shall fight on the beaches," and his tribute to the RAF after the Battle of Britain. Yet twelve months later, in 1941, Winston himself couldn't remember any of them.[248]

The more plausible account, and unquestionably the correct one, lies in these notes which Halifax scribbled upon returning to his office on the other side of Downing Street, and then turned over to Cadogan:

PM said I was the man mentioned as the most acceptable. I said it would be hopeless position. If I was not in charge of the war (operations) and if I didn't lead the House, I should be a cypher. I thought Winston was a better choice. Winston did *not* demur. Was very kind and polite but showed that he thought this right solution.

The PM, Winston, David Margesson and I sat down to it. The PM recapitulated the situation, and said he had made up his mind that he must go, and that it must be either Winston or me. He would serve under either. . . . I then said that I thought for the reasons given the PM must probably go, but that I had no doubt at all in my own mind that for me to take it would create a quite impossible position. . . . Winston, with suitable positions of regard and humility, said he could not but feel the force of what I had said, and the PM reluctantly, and Winston evidently with much less reluctance, finished by accepting my view.[249]

Margesson had been unwilling to comment on the popularity of the two among Tories until the decision had been made; now he could, and he observed that they had been "veering towards" Winston. Halifax had noted the same trend and remarked upon it to Cadogan, adding that if Chamberlain were to remain in the government, "as he is ready to do," his advice and judgment "would steady Winston." The prime minister had left them, explaining that he had to see someone else. The man who felt himself dispensable and the man who knew he was indispensable were left alone. They decided to have tea. "It was a bright, sunny afternoon," Churchill wrote, "and Lord Halifax and I sat for a while . . . in the garden of Number 10 and talked about nothing in particular." They then parted, each to his office. Winston knew Chamberlain could not move until Attlee called, and in the Cabinet Room he had said that he would "have no communication with either of the Opposition Parties until I had the King's commission to form a Government. . . . I then went back to the Admiralty."[250]

At "about 8 o'clock," Channon's diary entry read, he called at No. 10 and left with the impression that "Neville still reigns, but only just." A half-hour later, on the other side of the Horse Guards Parade, Churchill sat down to dinner in Admiralty House with four guests: the Prof, Bracken, Anthony Eden, and Archie Sinclair. He told them, Eden wrote, that he thought it "plain" that Chamberlain would advise the King to send for him, because Halifax, his only rival, "did not wish to succeed." As the evening lengthened, Winston slowly absorbed the massive fact of his position. During the evening Randolph called from his battalion, billeted in Northamptonshire, some seventy miles northwest of London. He asked if there was any news. His father replied: "I think I shall be Prime Minister tomorrow."[251]

On the evening of May 9, as Churchill entertained his friends at dinner, Labour's leaders in the palm courts of Bournemouth pondered whether to serve under him in an all-party government, and the London *News Chronicle* went to press with a banner story reporting that "Mr Chamberlain's early

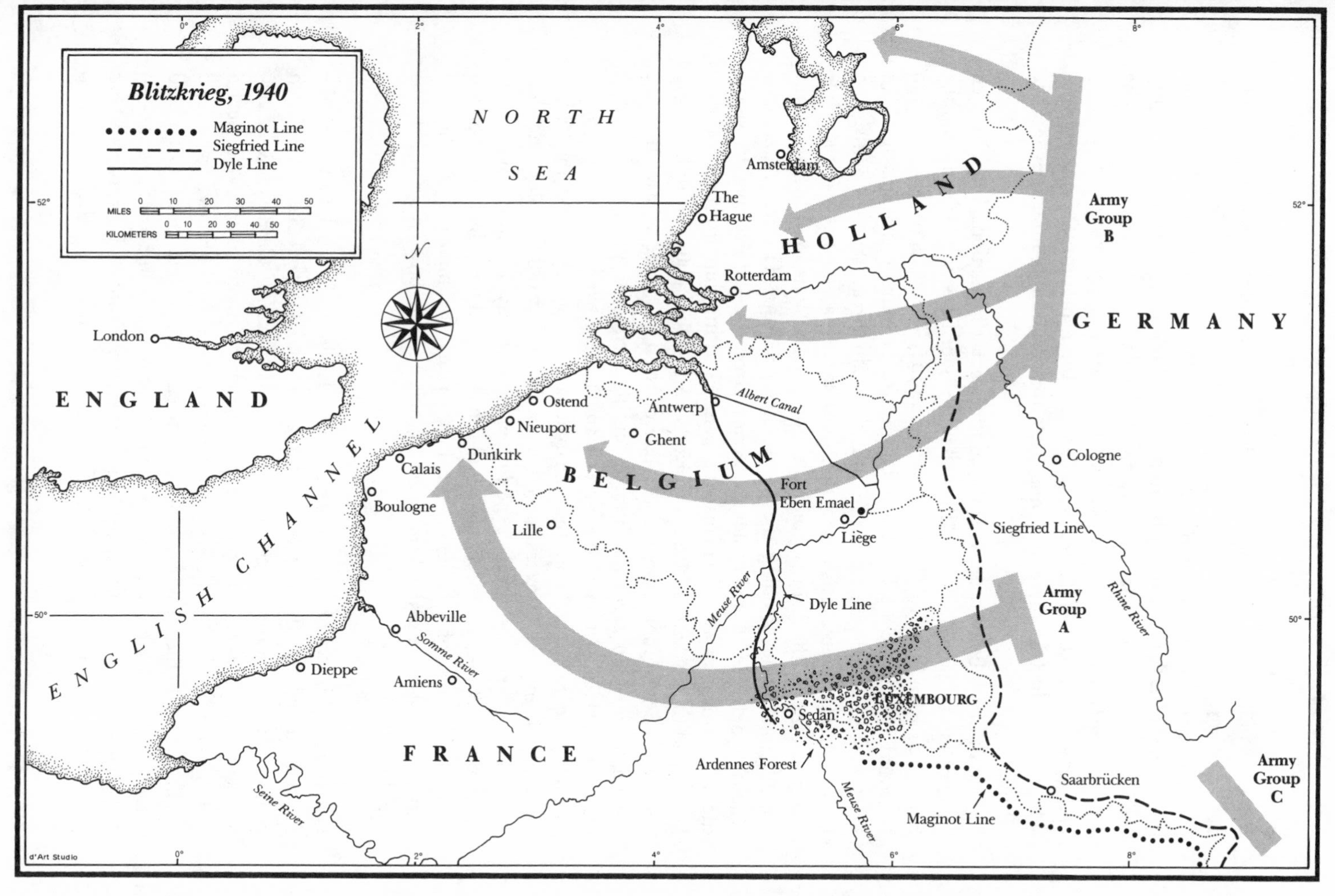
Blitzkrieg, 1940
Maginot Line
Siegfried Line
Dyle Line
MILES 0 10 20 30 40 50
KILOMETERS 0 10 20 30 40 50
NORTH SEA
ENGLAND
ENGLISH CHANNEL
HOLLAND
BELGIUM
GERMANY
FRANCE
LUXEMBOURG
Army Group B
Army Group A
Army Group C
London
Amsterdam
The Hague
Rotterdam
Antwerp
Albert Canal
Ostend
Nieuport
Ghent
Dunkirk
Calais
Boulogne
Lille
Fort Eben Emael
Liège
Cologne
Siegfried Line
Dyle Line
Meuse River
Rhine River
Abbeville
Somme River
Amiens
Dieppe
Seine River
Sedan
Ardennes Forest
Saarbrücken
Maginot Line
d'Art Studio

resignation is now certain" — the Bore War, in short, continued to bore. But developments across the Channel continued to foreshadow England's approaching peril.

On Germany's side of the Rhine, the Führer had assembled 136 divisions and their reserves — two million men, including a contingent wearing uniforms of the Netherlands army and fluent in the Dutch language. The Low Countries would be overwhelmed by vast surging waves of infantry and armor "unprecedented for size, concentration, mobility," Shirer wrote, which "stretched in three columns back for a hundred miles beyond the Rhine."[252]

The Führer's bold strategy deployed three great formations, one of which was meant to persuade the Allies that the Germans were following the Schlieffen Plan of 1914. In the north, the thirty divisions of Army Group B would strike into Holland and Belgium in a four-pronged assault. To meet what they were meant to think was the main threat, the best British and French troops would rush into Belgium, taking a stand along the Dyle River. In the south, Army Group C's nineteen divisions would feint toward the Maginot Line, keeping the poilus there tied up. The real Nazi blow would be delivered in the center, by Army Group A — forty-five divisions, including most of the Wehrmacht's panzers. Plunging through Luxembourg and the Ardennes, these motorized units would pour through the gap between the Maginot Line and the line of the Dyle, race westward to the Channel, and then pivot northward, joining Army Group B in the encirclement and destruction of the French and British troops.

Thus, the main body of the German army, cutting across the Allied rear, and using the panzers as it had in Poland, would exploit the new concept in warfare — deep penetration into enemy territory by mobile armored forces — a concept as revolutionary, Liddell Hart has pointed out, as "the use of the horse, the long spear, the phalanx, the flexible legion, the 'oblique order,' the horse-archer, the longbow, the musket, the [artillery] gun."[253]

On May 9, in the Berlin suburb of Zehlendorf, Colonel Oster of the Abwehr dined for the last time with his friend Colonel Sas, the Dutch military attaché. Oster once more confirmed that *Fall Gelb* would be unleashed at daybreak. To double-check, he drove them to OKW's Berlin headquarters in the Bendlerstrasse after their coffee and brandy. Sas waited in the car while the Abwehr colonel inquired within. Returning, Oster said there had been no changes. He added: *"Das Schwein ist zur Westfront"* — "The swine [Hitler] has gone to the Western Front." They parted. Sas passed the new information to the Belgian military attaché, then crossed to his own legation and called The Hague to transmit, in simple code, the message: "Tomorrow at dawn!"[254]

At 10:20 that Thursday morning, when Chamberlain was offering the prime ministry of England to Halifax, Paul Reynaud announced that he would present the premiership of France to anyone who could form a government, unless his cabinet agreed with his indictment of Gamelin, commander in chief of the French army; supreme commander of the Allied forces, British as well as French; and the officer who presided over both the Conseil Supérieur de la Guerre and the Haut Comité Militaire. This was not Reynaud's first attempt to sack him — nor was Reynaud the first to try — but it was by far the most vigorous. The premier, though suffering a sore throat, spent over two hours reading his presentment. French military appointments were determined to a remarkable degree by an officer's politics and religion, and Gamelin had been a beneficiary of that *drôle* system, having served as France's senior soldier for five years. Afterward, after the calamitous spring of 1940, he and his officers bitterly complained that the Chamber of Deputies never gave them the arms to fight with. An audit revealed that each year Gamelin returned appropriations unspent — as much as 60 percent of his budget. He hated allies because they entailed the possibility of bloodshed, and would go to great lengths to avoid a fight, but the last straw, for Reynaud, had been the Norwegian operation. Gamelin had exercised none of his powers as supreme commander, and the first French force of any size — two demibrigades of *Chasseurs Alpins* and a third of foreign legionnaires — had not arrived in Norway until April 27, when the issue had already been decided. It is extraordinary to reflect that his name was never mentioned in newspaper accounts of the struggle there, never raised during the two-day debate in the House. He had participated in the plan to mine Norwegian waters. When the Germans swooped down on Norway, Reynaud had asked what he proposed to do. Mine the waters, Gamelin replied; that was the plan, and he meant to carry it out. The sudden appearance of the Germans was, to him, irrelevant.

Paul Baudouin, who kept the minutes, noted that throughout most of the premier's arraignment of the country's most prestigious military figure the cabinet observed *"un silence total. Personne ne dit mot."* As Reynaud went on and on, piling up his case, one minister whispered to another, *"C'est une exécution."* At 12:30 P.M. Reynaud finished, commenting that if France continued with such a supreme commander, she was sure to lose the war. The minister of finance was convinced, he said, of *"l'impossibilité de laisser le général Gamelin à la tête des armées françaises."*[255]

Everyone turned to Daladier. He was minister of defense; he had defended Gamelin in the past. This was not the Daladier who had once been ready to fight for Czechoslovakia. He was defeatist now, infected with the spiritual corruption which had infected the government, the army, and virtually the entire infrastructure of French society. Replying to the premier, he blamed the British for the failure in Norway. Gamelin, he said, bore no share of the responsibility. He believed Gamelin was *"un grand chef militaire,"* a soldier with tremendous prestige and a fine military record. Everyone acknowledged his superior intelligence. True, he was seventy, but he was more active than many men his age. Daladier opposed "the desire of the premier to replace the generalissimo."[256]

Reynaud appealed to other ministers to speak up. Surely they had formed opinions; duty required that they voice them. But these were frightened little men. If one took a position, one might offend a powerful figure; by remaining silent, one lost nothing. Reynaud, however, wasn't going to let them off that easily. Their failure to speak, he said, meant they opposed him; since the government could not survive such a loss of confidence, therefore, "I consider the government as having resigned." They were dismayed. None had thought he would actually dissolve the government. Now they were all ex-ministers, as he was an ex-premier.[257]

During the afternoon Gamelin, glooming around in his Vincennes dungeon, learned of the bill of particulars Reynaud had drawn up against him. Indignant, *he* resigned.

At 1:00 A.M. he was awakened. A French agent behind the German lines had sent an urgent signal: *"Colonnes en marche vers l'ouest"* — "Columns marching westward."

Hitler was on his way.

France had no government. The French army had no commander.

The telephones began ringing in Whitehall as the first olive moments of daybreak revealed the majestic buildings towering against a darkling, still starry sky — vast cathedrals of an empire whose celebrants had been dwindling year by year since what had been called, and was now known to be, the Armistice.

Shortly after 5:30 A.M. Churchill was wakened and told the first, fragmentary reports. Before the mists of legend envelop him, before he comes to power and assumes leadership of the struggle to crush the monster in central Europe — while he is still, so to speak, Drake bowling when informed that the Armada has been sighted — it is useful to glimpse the entirely mortal Winston. The vision is less than inspiring; unlike some earlier heroes, Winston is engaged in no mundane but memorable act when the news arrives. Instead, wearing his blue dressing gown and carpet slippers, he stumbles down to the upper war room and is told that thus far the attack is "on Holland alone." Assuming, like everyone else in His Majesty's Government, that the main Nazi thrust will come here, he phones Charles Corbin, the French ambassador. He asks: Will the Allied armies move into Belgium on the strength of the little now known?

At 6:20 Corbin called back. German troops were now across the Belgian border, he said, and Brussels had "asked for help." Therefore, Gamelin had been told to invoke Plan D — the advance of the French Seventh Army and the British Expeditionary Force to the line of the Dyle River, there to join the Belgian and Dutch forces. Randolph Churchill, breakfasting in his camp, had heard a radio bulletin. He phoned his father, asking: "What's happening?" Winston replied: "Well, the German hordes are pouring into the Low Countries." He told him of the Allied countermove, adding, "In a day or two there will be a head-on collision." His son asked him about his reference the previous evening to "you becoming Prime Minister today." Churchill said, "Oh, I don't know about that. Nothing matters now except beating the enemy."[258]

In this crisis Sam Hoare and Oliver Stanley, the other two service ministers, appeared with their chief advisers at Admiralty House. Later Hoare would remember, "We had had little or no sleep, and the news could not be worse, yet there he was, smoking his large cigar and eating fried eggs and bacon, as if he had just returned from an early morning ride." He was surrounded by yesterday's newspapers. The *Times* leader that morning rebuked Labour for dividing the House, since it had been obvious that Chamberlain intended to rebuild his cabinet when "the Labour Party ran up its flag," throwing the prime minister's plans "into confusion." The *News Chronicle* — which had championed Lloyd George — more accurately reported that since neither Liberal nor Labour leaders were willing to serve under Chamberlain, "a new Premier will thus have to be found. He is more likely to be found in Mr Winston Churchill than anyone else." Winston swept the papers to the floor with one vigorous arm, rose, and suggested they meet in the war room downstairs. There, with him in the chair, they agreed that two RAF squadrons should be sent to France "in accordance with the prearranged plan." Then orders to execute Royal Marine, his plan to mine the waters of the Rhine, were issued at long last.[259]

The first casualty of the Nazi offensive was the feud between Reynaud and Gamelin. The premier sent Vincennes a message: "The battle has begun. Only one thing counts: to win it." Gamelin agreed, replying: *"Seule la*

France compte" — "Only France counts." His Majesty's Government, preoccupied with its own political crisis, had known nothing of the impasse in Paris. It had little meaning now anyway; what mattered was news of the enemy's penetration. Minute by minute information was accumulating. German paratroopers had landed in Belgium, the Luftwaffe was bombing airfields in France and the Low Countries, and the British and French were marching into Belgium — the last thing, we now know, that they should have done. The Führer's Army Group B had their undivided attention. Nothing much was happening to Army Group C, holding the frontier opposite the Maginot Line, and nothing was known of Rundstedt's Army Group A. Allied intelligence wasn't even aware that it was by far the largest, dwarfing the other two.[260]

During the night the first of Rundstedt's tanks had negotiated the minefields near the German-Belgian border, and at daybreak three panzer corps were driving hard, intent upon maneuvering through the wooded ravines of the Ardennes and crossing the Meuse near Sedan in forty-eight hours. Even the few French officers who doubted that the Ardennes were *impénétrable* believed the enemy could not possibly reach the river in less than ten days, by which time reinforcements could be brought up to dig in along the Meuse, swift and narrow, running between steep banks and therefore easy to defend. Yet already Rundstedt's armor had easily thrown aside the defense behind the mines — a thin screen of French cavalry, backed by light motorized forces. Thus, while the Allied right wing remained idle in the bowels of the troglodytic Maginot Line, and the left advanced toward what was expected to be the decisive encounter, the center was already gravely threatened. In the confusion of their rout the officers there neglected to send the bad news winging to Vincennes, La Ferté, or Montry. The fox was among the chickens, but the farmer, out in the pasture, didn't even know he had a problem.

At No. 10 the first of the War Cabinet's three meetings that day began with the Chiefs of Staff present. They were dazed, in the state of confusion which was the first reaction to blitzkriegs. Reports were accumulating faster than they could be skimmed. H.M.S. *Kelly* had been torpedoed off the Belgian coast. The Wehrmacht was in Luxembourg. Nazi paratroops had been dropped at three strategic locations, in the area between The Hague and Leiden, and near Rotterdam; Nancy had been bombed; the Luftwaffe was dropping magnetic mines in the Scheldt to disrupt Dutch and Belgian shipping. Churchill, the ministers were relieved to hear, had already sent sweeping gear to clear it.[261]

According to Reith's diary, Chamberlain "did not refer to Amery or any of the other Conservatives who had attacked him. He was in good form; the news from the Low Countries had stimulated him"; the German invasions had found him "ready for action if encouraged and authorized to act." He was a new man; he told his sister many of those who had voted against him had written to say "they had nothing against me except that I had the wrong people in my team." He had, indeed, convinced himself that in this crisis the country would be much better off if he remained as prime minister. Halifax noted in his diary: "The P.M. told the Cabinet . . . that he thought all would have to wait until the war situation was calmer." Privately he told his foreign secretary that "he had a feeling that Winston did not approve of the delay, and left me guessing as to what he meant to do."[262]

Reith's diary, which is confirmed by Eden's, notes that the prime minister had seen Attlee and Greenwood and understood that they were prepared to defer the political crisis, though the final decision would have to be made in Bournemouth. Hoare later wrote: "Chamberlain's first inclination was to withhold his resignation until the French battle was finished." Nicolson and his friends were among the outsiders who learned of this, and they were aghast. One of them phoned Salisbury, who replied, wrote Nicolson, "that we must maintain our point of view, namely that Winston should be made Prime Minister during the course of the day."[263]

Churchill's feelings about Chamberlain's switch of mood can only be imagined, but anxiety must have been among them. He was somewhat reassured by Kingsley Wood. At about 10:00 A.M. Wood once more crossed the Horse Guards Parade to report, as Winston later wrote, that the prime minister "was inclined to feel that the great battle which had broken upon us made it necessary for him to remain at his post." Hoare had encouraged him in this, but Wood's emphatic comment — which Horace Wilson, embittered, later damned as an act of "betrayal" — was that "on the contrary, the new crisis made it all the more necessary to have a National Government, which alone could confront it." Wood, wrote Churchill, had told him that Chamberlain had "accepted this view." But that was not the end of it. Shortly before the second meeting of the War Cabinet, at 11:00 A.M., Simon approached Eden and Hankey. He told them, Eden wrote, that he had heard that "despite the attacks in Flanders, Churchill was pressing for early changes in the Government." Simon was "indignant," but Hankey commented "quietly and firmly: 'Personally, I think that if there are to be changes, the sooner they are made the better.' "[264]

At this second meeting Winston pointed out that Roger Keyes was a close personal friend of the Belgian king; the admiral was eager to serve his country and might be useful in Brussels. The War Cabinet approved. The ministers were also pleased to learn that Churchill had given instructions "for the removal of the gold still left in Holland." They were less enthusiastic when Winston, explaining, "It won't take a minute," insisted that the war wait while they watch the Prof, who was sitting at a side table, demonstrate an antiaircraft homing fuse. According to Reith, "Ironside, very snotty," whispered to him, "Do you think this is the time for showing off toys?" This shirtiness sounds more like Reith than Ironside, who, noting the incident in his diary the following day, wrote of Churchill: "I have seldom met anybody with stranger gaps of knowledge or whose mind worked in greater jerks. Will it be possible to make it work in orderly fashion? On this much depends."[265]

During this second meeting of the War Cabinet, Chamberlain had continued to be very much the prime minister. Despite his assurance to Kingsley Wood he made no reference to surrendering his seals. Actually, the crucial decision could not be made by any member of His Majesty's Government. It rested with the men in Bournemouth; Chamberlain had agreed to abide by their finding. Labour's national executive, meeting in a basement room of the Highcliff Hotel, resolved that the party was "prepared to take our share of the responsibility, as a full partner, in a new Government, which, under a new Prime Minister, commands the confidence of the nation." Dalton was responsible for inserting "under a new Prime Minister." Some of the others doubted its necessity. He told them: "If you don't make it absolutely plain, the Old Man will still hang on." Attlee and Greenwood were about to drive to London with the signed document when the prime minister's private secretary phoned from Downing Street to ask whether Labour had reached a decision. Attlee read the resolution over the telephone.[266]

It was now 5:00 P.M. The War Cabinet's third meeting of the day had begun a half-hour earlier. The private secretary entered the Cabinet Room and handed the typewritten transcript of Labour's verdict to Horace Wilson, who read it and wordlessly slipped it in front of the prime minister. Chamberlain glanced at it and continued with his agenda. The Germans had bombed a dozen objectives and had dropped incendiaries in Kent; the Rotterdam airfield was in the hands of the Nazis, who were landing troop-carrying aircraft there; six Blenheims had been sent to intercept the troop carriers and five of them had been lost; the BEF had reached the line of the Dyle. After a lengthy discussion the ministers decided not to bomb the Ruhr. More paratroopers had landed in Belgium and the ministers decided to warn British troops in the United Kingdom "against parachutists attempting to land in this country." Then Chamberlain came to the last item on his agenda: the political situation.[267]

He read the Labour resolution aloud and said that "in the light of this answer" he had decided that he should "at once" tender his resignation to the King. It would be "convenient," he suggested, for the new prime minister to assume that "all members of the War Cabinet" were placing their resignations at his disposal, though there was no need "for this to be confirmed in writing." The minutes of the meeting ended: "The War Cabinet agreed to the course suggested." He had not told them whom he preferred as his successor, nor had he mentioned his meeting with Halifax and Churchill the day before. He proposed "to see the King this evening" — that was all.[268]

Actually, the prime minister, in his last act as prime minister, was on his way to the palace in less than half an hour. In his diary George VI recorded how he saw Chamberlain "after tea. I accepted his resignation, & told him how grossly unfairly I thought he had been treated, & that I was terribly sorry." They then talked informally about his successor. "I, of course, suggested Halifax," His Majesty wrote, "but he told me that H was not enthusiastic, as being in the Lords he could only act as a shadow or a ghost in the Commons, where all the real work took place." His royal host was "disappointed . . . as I thought H was the obvious man." Before the former prime minister could mention another name, George "knew that there was only one other person whom I could send for to form a Government . . . & that was Winston." He said so; Chamberlain confirmed his judgment. The King "thanked him for all his help to me, and repeated that I would greatly regret my loss at not having him as my P.M. I sent for Winston & asked him to form a Government."[269]

They didn't get to it straightaway. The monarch enjoyed a bit of regal byplay first. "His Majesty received me most graciously," wrote Churchill, "and bade me sit down. He looked at me searchingly and quizzically for some moments, and then said: 'I suppose you don't know why I have sent for you?' Adopting his mood, I replied: 'Sir, I simply couldn't imagine why.' He laughed and said: 'I want you to form a Government.' I said I would certainly do so." Since the King had made no stipulation about the government being national in character — apparently Chamberlain had not mentioned this, an unaccountable lapse — Winston felt his commission "was in no formal way dependent upon this point. But in view of all that had happened, and the conditions which had led to Mr. Chamberlain's resignation, a Government of national character was obviously inherent in the situation." However, if he failed to come to terms with the Liberal and Labour parties, he believed, "I should not have been constitutionally debarred from trying to form the strongest Government possible of all who would stand by the country in the hour of peril, provided that such a Government could command a majority in the House of Commons."[270]

He told the King that he would "immediately send for the leaders of the Labour and Liberal Parties, that I proposed to form a War Cabinet of five or six Ministers, and that I hoped to let him have at least five or six names before midnight." On this he took his leave. His sole companion was his bodyguard, W. H. Thompson. As Thompson later recalled, their ride back to Admiralty House was made "in complete silence," but as the new prime minister was leaving the car he asked: "You know why I have been to Buckingham Palace, Thompson?" The former Scotland Yard inspector said he did and congratulated him, adding, "I only wish the position had come your way in better times, for you have an enormous task." Churchill's eyes filled. He said: "God alone knows how great it is. I hope that it is not too late. I am very much afraid that it is. We can only do our best."[271]

While Churchill had been with the King, Randolph found a message in the adjutant's office asking him to phone the Admiralty. He did, and asked why he was wanted. The private secretary in the private office replied: "Only just to say that your father has gone to the Palace and when he comes back he will be Prime Minister."[272]

Early in the evening Attlee, accompanied by Greenwood, called on Churchill. They talked easily; during the eleven years before the war's outbreak, Winston had crossed swords with the Conservative and national governments far more often than with Labour. He proposed that Labour should have "rather more than a third of the places, having two seats on the War Cabinet of five, or it might be six." He asked Attlee for a list of names — they could then discuss "particular offices" — and mentioned Labour MPs he admired: Morrison, Dalton, Ernest Bevin, and A. V. Alexander.[273]

As they conferred, Harold Nicolson was on his way to King's Bench Walk, passing posters saying "BRUSSELS BOMBED," "PARIS BOMBED," "LYONS BOMBED," "SWISS RAILWAYS BOMBED." That evening he joined his wife at Sissinghurst, their home forty miles southeast of London. They dined together and "just before nine, we turn on the wireless and it begins to buzz as the juice comes through and then we hear the bells" — the BBC identification signal. "Then the pips sound 9.0 and the announcer begins: 'This is the Home Service. Here is the Right Honourable Neville Chamberlain M.P., who will make a statement.' I am puzzled by this for a moment, and then realise that he has resigned." Addressing the nation, the fallen prime minister told the people that the events of the past few days had shown that a coalition government was necessary, and since the only obstacle to such a coalition was himself he had resigned. The King had "asked my friend and colleague, Mr. Winston Churchill, to form a truly National Government." For the moment, acting ministers "will carry on." He himself had agreed to serve under Churchill. Nicolson noted: "He ends with a fierce denunciation of the Germans for invading Holland and Belgium. It is a magnificent statement, and all the hatred I have felt for Chamberlain subsides as if a piece of bread were dropped into a glass of champagne."[274]

"Thus," wrote Winston, "at the outset of this mighty battle, I acquired the chief power in the State. . . . As I went to bed at about 3 A.M., I was conscious of a profound sense of relief. At last I had the authority to give directions over the whole scene." He felt, he said,

> as if I were walking with Destiny, and that all my past life had been but a preparation for this hour and for this trial. Eleven years in the political wilderness had freed me from ordinary party antagonisms. My warnings over the last six years had been so numerous, so detailed, and were now so terribly vindicated, that no one could gainsay me. I could not be reproached either for making the war or with want of preparation for it. . . . Therefore, although impatient for the morning, I slept soundly and had no need for cheering dreams. Facts are better than dreams.[275]

Labour endorsed the decision of its leaders to support Churchill by a lopsided vote: 2,450,000 to 170,000 — a 93 percent victory — and when a pacifist MP demanded a division of the House on the question of whether Churchill should be prime minister, the vote was 380 to 0, the pacifist presumably abstaining. Winston possessed one great advantage which no other eminent parliamentarian could claim; as the historian Cyril Falls puts it, "His record was completely clean and satisfactory in those years when the Government had been hiding its head in the sand and . . . simultaneously voting against every attempt to arm the British forces." But his mood had not yet been synchronized with that of the powerful, including his sovereign. In his diary entry the following day — Saturday, May 11 — the King noted: "I cannot yet think of Winston as P.M. . . . I met Halifax in the garden" — the noble lord had been granted permission to walk through the palace garden en route from his Belgravia flat to the Foreign Office — "and told him I was sorry not to have him as P.M." George still felt uncomfortable with Winston. There was a generational gap between them. When they had first met in 1912 Winston was first lord of the Admiralty and the future monarch a young naval cadet. By normal reckoning Winston's political career ought to have ended ten years earlier. He had turned sixty-five the previous November; five months before he became prime minister he had been eligible to draw an old-age pension. Indeed, he was to be the senior statesman of the war — four years older than Stalin, eight years older than Roosevelt, nine years older than Mussolini, fifteen years older than Hitler. The King also liked Tories to be orthodox, conventional, loyal party men, and Churchill was none of those.[276]

That same Saturday, Margot Asquith, writing a letter to Geoffrey Dawson at *The Times,* told how, on impulse, she had taken a taxi to No. 10 the previous evening; she had looked at Chamberlain's "spare figure and keen eye and could not help comparing it with Winston's self-indulgent rotundity." R. A. Butler called Churchill "a half-breed American." And that evening young Colville, at No. 10, wrote in his diary: "There seems to be some inclination in Whitehall to believe that Winston will be a complete failure and that Neville will return." Long afterward Colville observed: "Seldom can a Prime Minister have taken office with the Establishment . . . so dubious of the choice and so prepared to have its doubts justified." Only a month earlier Eden's followers in Parliament had outnumbered Churchill's, and some of Winston's closest friends preferred Lloyd George as an alternative to Chamberlain.[277]

Among the general public it was different. Even so, the *News Chronicle* had reported that according to an opinion poll, his principal support was among "those in the lower income groups, those between 21 and 30, and among men." A prime minister should enjoy broader approval, particularly among the sophisticated, and a Conservative prime minister, in the House of Commons, ought to receive more cheers from Tory benches than from Labour. In his May 13 diary entry Nicolson noted: "When Chamberlain enters the House, he gets a terrific reception, and when Churchill comes in the applause is less. Winston sits there between Chamberlain and Attlee" — Attlee was now lord privy seal and, in effect, deputy prime minister — "[and then] makes a very short statement, but to the point." The only tribute to the new prime minister came from Lloyd George, who spoke of his "glittering intellectual gifts, his dauntless courage, his profound study of war, and his experience in its operation and direction." Winston wept.[278]

What Nicolson called Churchill's "very short statement" and Geoffrey Dawson described patronizingly as "quite a good little warlike speech from Winston" included five words now known to millions who were unborn at the time, who have never seen England, and do not even speak English.

I would say to the House,
as I have said to those who have joined this Government:
"I have nothing to offer but blood, toil, tears, and sweat." . . .

You ask, what is our policy?
I will say: It is to wage war, by sea, land and air,
with all our might and with all the strength God can give us. . . .
That is our policy.

You ask, what is our aim?
I can answer in one word: It is victory,
victory at all costs, victory in spite of all terror,
victory however long and hard the road may be;
for without victory, there is no survival.[279]

The mighty Belgian fortress of Eben Emael, with its garrison of 1,200, fell on Saturday, May 11, the second day of the great Nazi offensive, captured by only 78 parachute-engineers led by a lieutenant. Landing in gliders on the unguarded roof, they blew up the armored cupolas and casemates of the fort's guns with a new, highly intensive explosive kept secret until now. Belgian frontier guards were prepared to blow up the bridges of the King Albert Canal, blocking the Nazi advance, but another small Nazi detachment, dropping silently out of the night sky, massacred them. In Holland the French Seventh Army engaged the Germans and was flung back. Liège fell to blond young Nazis shouting "*Heil Hitler!*" as they threw their bodies on the muzzles of Belgian machine guns, sacrificing themselves to maintain the blitzkrieg's momentum. On Tuesday, Rotterdam was the target of a massive Luftwaffe terror attack; thousands of 2,200-pound delayed-action bombs gutted the center of the city, destroyed 25,000 houses, and left 78,000 civilians homeless and a thousand dead. Rotterdam capitulated. The Dutch commander in chief surrendered his entire army. Queen Wilhelmina and the Dutch government fled to London.

That was the small shock. The great shock came in barely coherent dispatches from the Meuse. Guderian, leading mechanized spearheads of Rundstedt's army group, had been racing through Luxembourg and Belgium's Luxembourg Province. After rocking and tilting and pivoting their way through a seven-mile stretch of the Ardennes — they had been elaborately rehearsed in the Black Forest — these forces had entered France Sunday, right on schedule. Before Churchill had completed the formation of his cabinet, the Germans had seven tank divisions on the Meuse near Sedan. The heights on the far side of the Meuse were forbidding. The French had rushed heavy artillery there, and after firing a few rounds at the panzers, the artillery officer predicted that the Nazis would try to cross elsewhere. But the Germans had rehearsed this, too, and Rundstedt was a master at integrating his commands, including the use of tactical air. At first light on Monday, Stukas and low-level bombers began pounding the French batteries; by 4:00 P.M. every field piece, every enemy howitzer on the heights, had been destroyed. Nazi rubber boats reached the far shore unmolested; beachheads were established; pontoon bridges spanned the river, then heavy bridges — and finally, lumbering and growling, German tanks.

French tanks appeared to challenge them. They were superior to the Germans' in design and armament, and history's first great tank battle seemed imminent. But the outcome, to use a word that was on everyone's lips that week, was *une débâcle*. The French tank commanders weren't to blame. Their high command, having ruled that armor was to be used only in support of infantry, had gone to extraordinary lengths to discourage attacks by armored formations. The installation of radios in turrets had been forbidden. The French drivers, assembled from different units and unable to communicate with one another, could not coordinate a counterattack. In two hours Guderian's panzers had blown up fifty of them. The rest fled. Among the frustrated Frenchmen was Colonel de Gaulle. To his astonishment, dismay, and *effroi*, he saw shuffling mobs of poilus without weapons. The Germans had no time to take prisoners; they had disarmed the men and left them to blunder about. Meantime, the panzers had made a second crossing of the Meuse at Dinant. German armor was now pouring across the river. In Vincennes, however, concerned French officials calling upon Généralissime Gamelin found him still confident. He did ask if they had any news of the fighting. Apparently all the dispatches sent to him had gone astray.

Guderian's tanks had reached Montcornet, less than fifteen miles from Laon; they were plunging down the valley of the Somme toward Abbeville on the English Channel. Aghast, the Allied forces in Belgium, including the BEF, realized that the great German scythe slicing across France was slicing behind them. Already they were cut off from the main French armies in the south. On the nineteenth Reynaud dismissed Gamelin from all commands; his predecessor, seventy-three-year-old Maxime Weygand, was brought out of retirement to take over, but Weygand was helpless; events were beyond his control; the Nazis seemed to be everywhere, and everywhere victorious. Thus, only a few days after their advance into Belgium, the French and British divisions in the north disengaged and retreated behind the line of the Scheldt. Lord Gort was poring over a map, studying routes to the Channel ports, where the Germans planned to turn the last key in the last lock.

On May 19, Churchill addressed the nation over the BBC:

> I speak to you for the first time as Prime Minister
> in a solemn hour for the life of our country,
> of our Empire, of our Allies,
> and above all of the cause of freedom.

A tremendous battle is raging in France and Flanders.
The Germans, by a remarkable combination
of air bombing and heavily armoured tanks,
have broken through the French defences
north of the Maginot Line,

And strong columns of their armoured vehicles
are ravaging the open country,
which for the first day or two
was without defenders.

They have penetrated deeply
and spread alarm and confusion in their track.

Behind them there are now appearing
infantry in lorries,
and behind them, again,
the large masses are moving forward.

He had received, he said, "the most sacred pledges" from the leaders of the French Republic, "and in particular from its indomitable Prime Minister, M. Reynaud . . . that whatever happens they will fight to the end, be it bitter or glorious." Then, a typical Churchill touch: "Nay, if we fight to the end, it can only be glorious."

Since receiving the King's commission, he told the country, he had formed a government "of men and women . . . of almost every point of view.

We have differed and quarreled in the past;
but now one bond unites us all —
to wage war until victory is won,
and never to surrender ourselves to servitude and shame,
whatever the cost and agony may be.

If this is one of the most awe-striking periods
in the long history of France and Britain,
it is also, beyond doubt, the most sublime.

Side by side . . . the British and French peoples have advanced
to rescue not only Europe but mankind
from the foulest and most soul-destroying tyranny
which has ever darkened and stained the pages of history.

Behind them, behind us —
behind the armies of Britain and France —
gather a group of shattered states and bludgeoned races:
the Czechs, the Poles, the Norwegians,
the Danes, the Dutch, the Belgians —

Upon all of whom a long night of barbarism will descend
unbroken even by a star of hope,
unless we conquer, as conquer we must;
as conquer we shall.[280]

Despite the "most sacred pledges" from Paris, the possibility loomed that France might not fight "to the end." The leaders of a nation verging on collapse cannot commit their countrymen if the army can no longer defend them. In capitals around the world leaders and newspapers wondered whether, if France fell, England would also quit. The prime minister again went on the air, on June 18, the day after Pétain sued for peace, to discount such speculation — to vow that England would continue the battle alone:

Upon this battle depends the survival of Christian civilisation.
Upon it depends our own British life,
and the long continuity of our institutions and our Empire. . . .

Hitler knows that he will have to break us on this island
or lose the war.

If we can stand up to him all Europe may be free
and the life of the world may move forward
into broad, sunlit uplands.

But if we fail, then the whole world,
including the United States,
including all we have known and cared for,

Will sink into the abyss of a new Dark Age
made more sinister, and perhaps more protracted,
by the lights of perverted science.

Let us therefore brace ourselves to our duties,
and so bear ourselves
that if the British Empire and its Commonwealth
last for a thousand years,

Men will still say:
"*This* was their finest hour."[281]

He had come to power because he had seen through Hitler from the very beginning — but not, ironically, because his inner light, the source of that insight, was understood by Englishmen. Churchill's star was invisible to the public and even to most of his peers. But a few saw it. One of them wrote afterward that although Winston knew the world was complex and in constant flux, to him "the great things, races, and peoples, and morality were eternal." Isaiah Berlin, the Oxford philosopher, later observed that the Churchill of 1940 was neither "a sensitive lens, which absorbs and concentrates and reflects . . . the sentiments of others," nor a politician who played "on public opinion like an instrument." Instead Berlin saw him as a leader who imposed his "imagination and his will upon his countrymen," idealizing them "with such intensity that in the end they approached his ideal and began to see themselves as he saw them." In doing so he "transformed cowards into brave men, and so fulfilled the purpose of shining armour."[282]

Churchill's mood seemed to confirm this. He possessed an inner radiance that year and felt it. In his memoirs he wrote that "by the confidence, indulgence, and loyalty by which I was upborne, I was soon able to give an integral direction to almost every aspect of the war. This was really necessary because times were so very bad. The method was accepted because everyone realised how near were death and ruin. Not only individual death, which is the universal experience, stood near, but, incomparably more commanding, the life of Britain, her message, and her glory."[283]

To him, Britain, "her message, and her glory," were very real. At times he would address his country as though she were a personage. After he had comprehended the revolution wrought at Kitty Hawk he said (to the astonishment of his companion, who had thought they were alone), "You came into big things as an accident of naval power when you were an island. The world had confidence in you. You became the workshop of the world. You populated the island beyond its capacity. Through an accident of airpower you will probably cease to exist." It sounded quaint, and it was. Churchill was not a public figure like, say, Roosevelt, who thought and spoke in the idiom of his own time. He was instead the last of England's great Victorian statesmen, with views formed when the British lion's roar could silence the world; he was the champion of the Old Queen's realm and the defender and protector of the values Englishmen of her reign had cherished, the principles they held inviolate, the vision which had illumined their world, which had steadied them in time of travail, and which he had embraced as a youth.[284]

He was ever the impassioned Manichaean, seeing life and history in primary colors, like Vittore Carpaccio's paintings of St. George; a believer in absolute virtue and absolute malevolence, in blinding light and impenetrable darkness, in righteousness and wickedness — or rather in the forces of good *against* the forces of evil, for the two would always be in conflict and be therefore forever embattled. He had been accused of inconsistency and capricious judgment. Actually, it was MacDonald and Baldwin and Chamberlain who tailored their views to fit the moment. Churchill's binnacle remained true. "Death and sorrow will be the companions of our journey," he told the House of Commons; "hardship our garment, constancy and valour our only shield."[285]

And, he might have added, grief as their reward. He was sure Britons could take it. Despite his high birth he had an almost mystical faith in the power of the ordinary Englishman to survive, to endure, and, in the end, to prevail. "Tell the truth to the British people," he had begged the shifty prime ministers of the 1930s; "they are a tough people, a robust people. . . . If you have told them exactly what is going on you have ensured yourself against complaints and reproaches which are not very pleasant when they come home on the morrow of some disillusion."[286]

But in those shabby years His Majesty's Governments believed that there were some things the country ought not to know, and that their policy of duplicity — which at times amounted to conspiracy — would be vindicated in the end. Chamberlain would be the scapegoat of appeasement, and before the year was out sackcloth would be his shroud, but he was only one of many. Baldwin, for example, bore a greater responsibility for weakening Britain's defenses while Hitler built his military juggernaut. The appeasers had been powerful; they had controlled *The Times* and the BBC; they had been largely drawn from the upper classes, and their betrayal of England's greatness would be neither forgotten nor forgiven by those who, gulled by the mystique of England's class system, had believed as Englishmen had believed for generations that public school boys governed best. The appeasers destroyed oligarchic rule which, though levelers may protest, had long governed well. If ever men betrayed their class, these were they.

Because their possessions were great, the appeasers had much to lose should the Red flag fly over Westminster. That was why they had felt threatened by the hunger riots of 1932. It was also the driving force behind their exorbitant fear and distrust of the new Russia. They had seen a strong Germany as a buffer against bolshevism, had thought their security would be strengthened if they sidled up to the fierce, virile Third Reich. Nazi coarseness, anti-Semitism, the Reich's darker underside, were rationalized; time, they assured one another, would blur the jagged edges of Nazi

Germany. So, with their eyes open, they sought accommodation with a criminal regime, turned a blind eye to its iniquities, ignored its frequent resort to murder and torture, submitted to extortion, humiliation, and abuse until, having sold out all who had sought to stand shoulder to shoulder with Britain and keep the bridge against the new barbarism, they led England herself into the cold damp shadow of the gallows, friendless save for the demoralized republic across the Channel. Their end came when the House of Commons, in a revolt of conscience, wrenched power from them and summoned to the colors the one man who had foretold all that had passed, who had tried, year after year, alone and mocked, to prevent the war by urging the only policy which would have done the job. And now, in the desperate spring of 1940, with the reins of power at last firm in his grasp, he resolved to lead Britain and her fading empire in one last great struggle worthy of all they had been and meant, to arm the nation, not only with weapons but also with the mace of honor, creating in every English breast a soul beneath the ribs of death.

SOURCE NOTES

Primary Biographical Sources

By far the largest single source for *les justifications*, as the French call scholarly citations, is the Churchill College Archives Centre at Cambridge University, the repository of 300 collections of private papers, including those of Baroness Spencer-Churchill (Clementine), Bracken, Violet Pearman, Bevin, Grigg, Keyes, E. L. Spears (partial), Hankey (partial), Phipps, Lord Lloyd, Lord Thurso (Sinclair), Christie, Page Croft, Margesson, Attlee, and Halifax (on microfilm — the originals are in the India Office Library, the Public Records Office, and the estate of his heir). Papers of Viscount Templewood (Hoare, partial), Baldwin, and Crewe may be found in the Cambridge University Library; those of Beaverbrook, Lloyd George, and Samuels —until their recent transfer to the Jerusalem Archive —were available in the House of Lords Library; those of Austen and Neville Chamberlain in the Birmingham University Library; those of Lothian and Margo Asquith in the National Library of Scotland, Edinburgh; Derby's in the Liverpool Public Record Office; Henry James Scrymgeours-Wedderburn's in the Dundee Archives; Hankey's (partial) in the Public Record Office; Marsh's in the New York Public Library; Dalton's diary and papers, as well as those of Cherwell (partial) in the British Library of Political and Economic Science; and Baruch's in the Princeton University Library.

Over a hundred collections of papers remain in private hands, including some of Spears's, Camrose's, some of Cherwell's, some of Halifax's, Amery's, Lord Lloyd's, Lord Southborough's, Butler's, Lothian's, Boothby's, Geoffrey Dawson's, J. L. Garvin's, Sheila Grant Duff's, Ironside's, Thomas Jones's, Harold Laski's, Paul Maze's, Harold Nicolson's, those of Viscount Norwich (Duff Cooper), Major General Pakenham-Walsh, Selborne, Vansittart, Weir, Chaim Weizmann, William Heinemann Ltd., Cripps, Rumbold, Salisbury, Swinton, Thornton-Kemsley, Ramsay MacDonald, Cecil, and the Blenheim Palace Archive.

Primary Historical Sources

British Documents

British Cabinet Documents, Premier (Prime Minister), and Foreign Office Documents are catalogued at the Public Record Office in Kew, Richmond, Surrey, under "Records of Interest to Social Scientists." Guidance is necessary; the records of the Committee of Imperial Defence, for example, are filed under twenty-one different categories.

Published material may be found in *Documents on British Foreign Policy 1919–1939*, particularly the second and third series, edited by E. L. Woodward, MA, FBA, and Rohan Butler, assisted by Anne Orne, MA, and issued by Her Majesty's Stationery Office in 1952. Other unpublished official material concerning Churchill is in the archives of the Air Ministry, the Committee of Imperial Defence, the Treasury, Documents on International

Affairs, and *Documents Concerning German-Polish Relations and the Outbreak of Hostilities between Great Britain and Germany*, London: His Majesty's Stationery Office, 1939 (The British Blue Book). Verbatim accounts of all proceedings in both the House of Commons and the House of Lords are published in *Parliamentary Debates* (Hansard), England's equivalent of America's *Congressional Record*.

French Documents

Le Livre Jaune Français. Documents diplomatiques, 1938–1939 (Paris: Ministre des Affaires Étrangères (The French Yellow Book).

Documents Diplomatiques Français, Première Série and *Deuxième Série: Les Événements survenus en France de 1933 à 1945*, a postwar investigation of French policy in the 1930s conducted by the *Assemblée Nationale* and published (a two-volume report supported by nine volumes of testimony) in 1947.

German Documents

Dokumente der deutschen Politik, 1933–1940; Akten zur Deutschen Auswürtigen Politik 1918–1945 (German Foreign Policy Documents), published jointly by the Foreign Office and the U.S. State Department; issued in Baden between 1950 and 1956. These documents are divided into *Serie C* (four volumes, covering January 30, 1933, to October 31, 1933) and *Serie D*, thirteen volumes which are arranged, not chronologically but by subject, but generally running from September 1937 to December 1941. There is an eleven-month gap here, but there are gaps in the Allied documents, too.

Nuremberg Documents (ND)

Nuremberg seems far in the future to those who have turned the last page of this book, but it was there that all the secret papers of the interwar years — some dating from 1919 — first appeared, and in documents which could not be explained away. They may be found in *Trial of the Major War Criminals:* forty-two volumes covering the proceedings and exhibits — mostly in German — before the International Military Tribunal; *Nazi Conspiracy and Aggression:* ten volumes of additional interrogation transcripts and affidavits, in English; *Trials of War Criminals before the Nuremberg Tribunals:* fifteen volumes of selected material from the twelve Nuremberg trials following the adjournment of the IMT.

Other Published Documentary Material

I documenti diploma italiani; Ottavo series, 1935–1939, Rome, Liberia della Stato, 1952–1953; *Official Document Concerning Polish German and Polish Soviet Relations 1933–1939*, London, 1939 (The Polish White Book); *Documents and Material Relating to the Eve of the Second World War*, 1937–1939, two volumes, Moscow, Foreign Language Publishing House, 1948; *Soviet Documents on Foreign Policy*, three volumes, London, Royal Institute of International Affairs, 1931–1953.

Citations from British manuscript collections are puzzling, or rather are a series of puzzles, because each archive makes its own rules. In some instances the archive is not large enough to require extensive cataloguing. With eminent men it is not so simple. However, there are certain constants. The figure or code to the left of the slash — e.g., "123" in "123/456" — identifies the section or shelf where a document may be found. The figure to the right usually identifies the specific box number, or, if the entry is large, such as a scrapbook, the file number which houses the document. See Janet Foster and Julia Sheppard, *British Archives: A Guide to Archive Resources in the United Kingdom* (London, 1982).

The first of the three major documents centers for this work is the Churchill College Archives Centre, Churchill College, Cambridge; Correll Barnett, the learned Keeper of the Archives, was ably assisted, during my early visits, by Archivist Marion Stewart, who has since been succeeded by Leslie James. The Centre contains 300 accessions of diplomatic, political, military, scientific, and naval papers, most of them twentieth-century. Everything has been done to make document retrieval simple; even so, the researcher must dig. To take one example, the Spears papers in the Centre comprise four sections. The first number following the code abbreviation gives the section number. Section 1 (300 files) is correspondence, A to Z. The second code number identifies the file number. The papers in Spears's code 2 (thirty-five files) pertain to personal and family matters. Section 3 (sixty-five boxes) has no material about Churchill and is restricted to scholars. Section 4 (seven files) contains miscellaneous papers.

The second mother lode of documents is the Public Record Office in Kew, Surrey, safe in the hands of Alfred Knightbridge, head of the search department. Here a letter code (CAB for cabinet papers, PrP for Prime Minister's papers, etc.) opens each citation. The second part, in numbers, breaks down the mass of materials by dates: the date of a cabinet meeting, or of events between meetings. The slash comes next, then the "piece number" identifying a given document.

The third trove of documentary material is the British Library's reference division in Great Russell Street (D. A. Clark and G. E. A. Raspin in charge). Much of the most valuable material here is kept in the Woolwich Repository; delivery is normally a day after application. British newspapers since 1801 are filed in the library's Newspaper Library, at Colindale Library, London.

Abbreviations and Short Titles Used in the Notes

BSCP	Papers of the Baroness Spencer-Churchill (Clementine Churchill).
CAB	British Cabinet Documents, Public Record Office, Kew.
ChP	Churchill Papers.
DBFP	*Documents on British Foreign Policy 1919–1939*, edited by E. L. Woodward and Rohan Butler, assisted by Anne Orne. London, 1952.
DDF	*Documents Diplomatiques Français, Première Série, Deuxième Série.*
DGFP	*Dokumente der deutschen Politik 1933–1940; Akten zur Deutschen Auswürtigen Politik 1918–1945.* Series C, D.
Événements	*Les Événements survenus en France de 1933 à 1945.*
FCNA	Führer's Conferences on Naval Affairs.
Hansard	*Record of Parliamentary Debates* (Hansard).
ND	Nuremberg Documents (see also NCA, TMWC, and TWC below).
NCA	*Nazi Conspiracy and Aggression,* 10 volumes of interrogation transcripts and affidavits; in English.
NYT	*New York Times.*
Prp	Premier (Prime Minister) Papers. Public Record Office, Kew.
Times	*The Times* of London.

TMWC	*Trial of the Major War Criminals*; 42 volumes covering the proceeding and exhibits (mostly in German) before the International Military Tribunal in Nuremberg.
TWC	*Trials of War Criminals before the Nuremberg Tribunals*; 15 volumes of selected material from the twelve Nuremberg trials following the adjournment of the International Military Tribunal.
WM/[name]	Author's interviews.
WSCHCS	*Winston S. Churchill: His Complete Speeches*, edited by Robert Rhodes James.

The Official Biography of Winston Spencer Churchill, by Martin Gilbert (Boston, 1966–), is cited as follows:

WSC V	Volume V. *The Prophet of Truth, 1922–1939* (biography)
CV V/1	Companion Volume V, part 1 (1922–1929, Documents)
CV V/2	Companion Volume V, part 2 (1930–1935, Documents)
CV V/3	Companion Volume V, part 3 (1936–1939, Documents)
WSC VI	Volume VI, *Finest Hour 1939–1941*

Preamble

1. WM/Lady Soames (at Chartwell), 10/27/80; Robin Fedden, *Churchill and Chartwell* (Westerham, Kent, 1968), 13 ff.
2. Walter Henry Thompson, *Assignment Churchill* (New York, 1955), 92.
3. Walter Thompson, 183.
4. Mary Soames, *Clementine Churchill: The Biography of a Marriage* (Boston, 1979), 352; Adam Sykes and Iain Sproat, eds., *The Wit of Sir Winston* (London, 1965), 85.
5. WM/Lady Soames (at Chartwell), 10/27/80; Fedden, 25–26, 43–44. R. Howells, *Simply Churchill* (New York, 1965), 19.
6. WM/Grace Hamblin, 11/4/80, and letter of 9/12/87; Hamblin, letter to Martin Gilbert, 6/12/78; WM/Lady Soames (at Chartwell), 10/27/80; Fedden, 27; Kay Halle, *The Irrepressible Churchill: A Treasury of Winston Churchill's Wit* (New York, 1967), 109.
7. Howells, 41, 36; WM/Sir William Deakin, 10/5/80.
8. Howells, 36; Elizabeth Nel, *Mr. Churchill's Secretary* (New York, 1958), 33.
9. Norman McGowan, *My Years with Churchill* (London, 1958), 86–87; Howells, 19.
10. Howells, 19–20, 49; Halle, 313.
11. Winston S. Churchill, *The World Crisis*, 5 vols. and *The Aftermath* (New York, 1923–1931), V, Afterword.
12. Bruce West, *Churchill's Pilot: The Man Who Flew Churchill* (Canada, 1975), 6; McGowan, 93; Howells, 110.
13. Fedden, 50–51; Howells, 37–39; WM/Lieutenant General Sir Ian Jacobs, 11/12/80; Sir John Wheeler-Bennett, ed., *Action This Day: Memoirs* by Lord Normanbrook, John Colville, Sir John Martin, Sir Ian Jacobs, Lord Bridges, Sir Leslie Rowan (London, 1968), 183; Charles Eade, ed., *Churchill by His Contemporaries* (London, 1953), 309.
14. Howells, 36, 138; McGowan, 92–93.
15. Howells, 20.
16. Howells, 138; CV I/2 996; Phyllis Moir, *I Was Winston Churchill's Private Secretary* (New York, 1941), 1, 89–90; WM/ Deakin; WM/Kathleen Hill, 11/4/80.
17. WM/Sir John Colville, 10/8/80; Sarah Churchill, *A Thread in the Tapestry* (New York, 1967), 38.

18. Fedden, 49.
19. Fedden, 49; Sir David Hunt, *On the Spot: An Ambassador Remembers* (London, 1975), 63; Colin Coote and Denvil Batchelor, *Maxims and Reflections* (London, 1947), 36; Viscount Chandos, *Memoirs* (London, 1962), 167; Howells, 150.
20. WM/Virginia Cowles, 10/15/80; WM/George Malcolm Thompson, 10/13/80; WM/Lord Geoffrey Lloyd, 11/27/80, WM/Deakin; WM/Lady Soames, 10/9/80; WM, personal information.
21. Wheeler-Bennett, ed., 87.
22. WM/Lord Lloyd; WM/Lord Boothby, 10/16/80.
23. WM/A. J. P. Taylor 12/1/80; WM, personal information.
24. Second Earl of Birkenhead, *The Professor and the Prime Minister* (Boston, 1962), 27–35, 36.
25. Birkenhead, 129–159 *passim.*
26. Sir John Colville, *Footprints in Time* (London, 1976), 100; WM/Colville.
27. Birkenhead, 38.
28. WM/Lady Soames, 10/9/80; Halle, 263; Wheeler-Bennett, ed., 25–28.
29. Kenneth Young, *Churchill and Beaverbrook: A Study in Friendship and Politics* (New York, 1966), 130.
30. Coote and Batchelor, 44.
31. WM/Cowles; WM/Kay Halle, 8/6/80; WM/Pamela Harriman, 8/22–23/80; Elizabeth Longford, *Winston Churchill: A Pictorial Life Story* (Chicago, 1974), 87, 130–131.
32. Sykes and Sproat, eds., 70, 71; Eade, ed., 307; Coote and Batchelor, 119–120.
33. Lord Moran, *Churchill. Taken from the Diaries of Lord Moran: The Struggle for Survival. 1940–1965* (Boston, 1966), 198; Halle, 152.
34. WM/Colville; Wheeler-Bennett, ed., 59–60.
35. McGowan, 72.
36. McGowan, 70; WM/Vanda Salmon, 11/26/80.
37. WM/Salmon; Martin Gilbert, *Winston Churchill: The Wilderness Years* (London, 1981), 28; Virginia Cowles, *Winston Churchill, The Era and the Man* (New York, 1953), 11.
38. Walter Thompson, 94; Eade, ed., 356–357; McGowan, 60.
39. John Paget, *The New "Examen"* (London, 1934).
40. Halle, 263; Soames, 323; Gilbert, *Wilderness*, 129.
41. Hunt, 77.
42. Soames, 301.
43. Eade, ed., 300, 309.
44. Eade, ed., 305.
45. Violet Bonham Carter, *Winston Churchill: An Intimate Portrait* (New York, 1965), 151, 152; Moran, 449.
46. Kenneth Young, *Churchill and Beaverbrook: A Study in Friendship and Politics* (New York, 1966), 26.
47. Soames, 305; WM/Deakin; Moran, 420; Winston S. Churchill, *Young Winston's Wars; The Original Despatches of Winston S. Churchill, War Correspondent 1897–1900*, edited by Frederick Woods (New York, 1972), xiii; WM/William L. Shirer, 7/20/74.
48. WM/Deakin.
49. WM/Cecily Gemmell, 7/10/80; Walter Thompson, 45.
50. Wheeler-Bennett, ed., 144; Harold Nicolson, *Diaries and Letters*, II, edited by Nigel Nicolson, 3 vols. (London, 1966), 320–321.
51. Peter Stansky, ed., *Churchill: A Profile* (New York, 1973), 38.
52. Robert Rhodes James, *Anthony Eden* (London, 1980), 229; Moran, 604.
53. WM/Hill, 11/4/80.
54. WM/Gemmell, 7/10/80.
55. Nel, 31.
56. Moir, 2, 58; Howells, 61.
57. Nel, 32; Moir, 88.

Prologue

1. *Times* 11/12/32.
2. *NYT* 10/19/32; *Times* 10/31/32.
3. *NYT* 10/6/32, 10/25/32, 11/1/32; *Time* 11/7/32.
4. *Time* 11/14/32.
5. James Morris, *Farewell The Trumpets: An Imperial Retreat* (New York, 1978), 314, 311; Colin Cross, *The Fall of the British Empire* (New York and London, 1968), 216.
6. Morris, 313–314; *Time* 3/21/32.
7. Morris, 362; *Time* 4/11/32, 4/18/32.
8. Sir John Colville, *The Fringes of Power: 10 Downing Street Diaries, 1939–1955* (New York, 1985), 71.
9. Morris, 335
10. *Times* 8/18/14; Robert Rhodes James, *Memoirs* (New York, 1970), 110.
11. *NYT* 11/18/29; *Nation* 2/12/30.
12. *Times* 1/22/29; *Book Review Digest* 433–434, 792–793; Siegfried Sassoon, *Siegfried's Journey, 1916–1920* (New York, 1946), 116–119.

13. Harold Nicolson, *Public Faces* (London, 1932), 16–17; Richard Kenin and Justin Wintle, eds., *The Dictionary of Biographical Quotations* (New York, 1958), 35.
14. Winston S. Churchill, *Amid These Storms: Thoughts and Adventures* (New York, 1932), 15–16; Telford Taylor, *Munich: The Price of Peace* (New York, 1979), 204.
15. Lincoln Steffens, *The Autobiography of Lincoln Steffens* (New York, 1931), 131.
16. Winston S. Churchill, *The World Crisis*, 5 vols. and *The Aftermath* (New York, 1923–1931), V, 66.
17. Hugh Dalton, *The Fateful Years* (London, 1957), 41–42.
18. William Manchester, *The Last Lion: Visions of Glory* (Boston, 1983), 76.
19. T. R. Fehrenbach, *F.D.R.'s Undeclared War 1939 to 1941* (New York, 1967), 22.
20. Telford Taylor, 107; Alistair Horne, *To Lose a Battle* (Boston, 1969), 22–23.
21. Churchill, *Crisis, The Aftermath*, 156.
22. William L. Shirer, *The Collapse of the Third Republic* (New York, 1969), 137.
23. Alistair Horne, *To Lose a Battle* (Boston, 1969), 56–57; Simone de Beauvoir, *La Force de l'âge* (Paris, 1961), 116–117.
24. Shirer, *Collapse*, 203; Beauvoir, 120–121; Horne, 57.
25. Beauvoir, 120–121.
26. Horne, 52; Beauvoir, 155.
27. Robert T. Elson and the editors of Time-Life Books, *Prelude to War* (New York, 1976), 47.
28. Elson et al., 74–79.
29. *NYT* 12/2/25.
30. *Berliner Tageblatt* 6/25/22.
31. *Frankfurter Zeitung* 12/2/25; *The New Encyclopaedia Britannica*, 15th ed. (Chicago, 1974), XIX, 966–967; *Berliner Tageblatt* 5/9/19; *NYT* 6/25/22.
32. WSCHCS 5197–5206; J. D. Scott, *Vickers: A History* (London, 1962), 86–87, 150–151; Otto Lehmann-Russbüldt, *Die blutige Internationale der Rüstungen* (Berlin, 1933), 50.
33. General Karl von Clausewitz, *On War*, trans. Col. J. J. Graham, 3 vols. (London, 1911), I, 5: Barbara Tuchman, *The Guns of August* (New York, 1962), 314.
34. Hugh Gibson, *A Journal from Our Legation in Belgium* (New York, 1917), 324.
35. Adolf Hitler, *Mein Kampf* (Munich, 1932), 369–370; Konrad Keiden, *Geschichte des Nationalsozialismus* (Berlin, 1932), 36.
36. *Living Age* 12/12/25; WM/Tilo Freiherr von Wilmowsky, 5/30/63 (Essen); *Der Spiegel* 6/5/63; Tilo von Wilmowsky, *Rückblickened möchte ich sagen . . .* (Hamburg, 1961), 178–181; *The New Encyclopaedia Britannica*, XIX, 969.
37. Hans Kohn, *The Mind of Germany, The Education of a Nation* (New York, 1960), 308; Franz L. Neumann, *Behemoth* (New York, 1942), 23.
38. *Süddeutsche Monatshafte* 12/21/24.
39. *Time* 8/22/32, 10/17/32.
40. *Time* 9/5/32, 11/28/32.
41. *Times* 2/2/32; Arnold Brecht, *Prelude to Silence* (New York, 1944), 35.
42. ND 203, 204, 37–25 PS.
43. André François-Poncet, *The Fateful Years: Memoirs of a French Ambassador in Berlin 1931–1938* (New York, 1949), 61.
44. *NYT* 3/25/33; Oswald Spengler, *Jahre der Entscheidung* (Munich, 1933), xiii.
45. Winston S. Churchill, *The Gathering Storm* (Boston, 1948), 84; Hansard 5/13/32, 7/11/32.
46. Churchill, *Storm*, 84; Ernst Hanfstaengl, *Hitler, The Missing Years* (London, 1957), 193–196.
47. Hansard 11/23/32; *Daily Mail* 10/17/32; WSC V, 627.
48. Günter Grass, *On Writing and Politics 1957–1983*, trans. Ralph Manheim (San Diego, 1985), cited in *NYT Book Review* 6/23/85.
49. *Times* 2/18/33.
50. *Times* 2/24/34; WSC V, 545; Christopher Hollis, *The Oxford Union* (London, 1955), 184–193.
51. Churchill, *Storm*, 85 fn.; WSC V, 504–505.

Shoals

1. *Fodor's London 1984* (New York, 1984), 152.
2. WM, personal information (1/30/53).
3. WM, personal information (1/30/53); Sir John Colville, *The Fringes of Power: 10 Downing Street Diaries, 1939–1955* (New York, 1985), 36.
4. Sir David Hunt, *On the Spot: An Ambassador Remembers* (London, 1975), 30–31.
5. Lord Boothby, *I Fight to Live* (London, 1947), 38.
6. Telford Taylor, *Munich: The Price of Peace* (New York, 1979), 549, 550, 555.
7. WM/Lady Soames, 10/9/80.
8. Winston S. Churchill, *The Gathering Storm* (Boston, 1948), 83.
9. Thomas Jones, *A Diary With Letters, 1931–1950* (Oxford, 1954), 239–265.
10. Frank Owen, *Tempestuous Journey: Lloyd George, His Life and Times* (London, 1954), 737; *Daily Express* 9/16/36.

11. DBFP series 2, vol. IV, no. 265; Vernon Bartlett, *Nazi Germany Explained* (London, 1933), 517–522.
12. Telford Taylor, 217 fn.; *New York Herald Tribune* 5/19/33, 5/12/33.
13. *München Süddeutsche Zeitung* 9/26/30; *Frankfurter Zeitung* 9/26/30.
14. Fritz Hesse, *Hitler and the English* (England, 1954), 11–12; WM/R. A. Butler, 12/5/80.
15. *Strand* 11/35.
16. Sir John Wheeler-Bennett, ed., *Action This Day: Memoirs* by Lord Normanbrook, John Colville, Sir John Martin, Sir Ian Jacobs, Lord Bridges, Sir Leslie Rowan (London, 1968), 11.
17. Lord Vansittart, *The Mist Procession* (London, 1958), 482; WM/R. A. Butler.
18. *NYT* 7/30/31; Lord Moran, *Churchill, Taken from the Diaries of Lord Moran: The Struggle for Survival, 1940–1965* (Boston, 1966), 65; Virginia Cowles, *Winston Churchill; The Era and the Man* (New York, 1953), 285.
19. WM/A. J. P. Taylor, 12/1/80; WM/Harold Macmillan, 12/4/80; Harold Macmillan, *Winds of Change* (London, 1966), 291; Charles Eade, ed., *Churchill by His Contemporaries* (London, 1953), 67.
20. Elizabeth Longford, *Winston Churchill: A Pictorial Life Story* (Chicago, 1974), 84; Macmillan, 437; Victor Wallace Germains, *The Tragedy of Winston Churchill* (London, 1931).
21. WM/Lady Soames, 10/9/80; Macmillan, 113.
22. Kenneth Young, *Churchill and Beaverbrook: A Study in Friendship and Politics* (New York, 1966), 120–122.
23. WM/Malcolm Muggeridge, 11/25/80.
24. Hansard 11/23/32.
25. DBFP series 2, vol. IV, nos. 263, 30.
26. DBFP series 2, vol. V, nos. 5, 2229.
27. DBFP series 2, vol. V, no. 2229.
28. William E. Dodd, *Ambassador Dodd's Diary, 1933–1938,* edited by William E. Dodd, Jr., and Martha Dodd (London, 1941), 239 (4/15/35); Foreign Relations of the U. S., 1937, I, 84.
29. Jones, 180; Josiah Wedgwood, *Memoirs of a Fighting Life* (London, 1941), 225.
30. WM/William L. Shirer, 7/5/83.
31. WM/Shirer.
32. Vernon Bartlett, 242–243.
33. Churchill, *Storm*, 207.
34. Winston S. Churchill, *While England Slept* (New York, 1938), 35.
35. Claud Cockburn, *The Week*, No. 166, June 17, 1936; Martin Gilbert, *Winston Churchill: The Wilderness Years* (London, 1981), 165; CAB 23/86.
36. Stephen Roskill, *Hankey: Man of Secrets*, vol. III, *1931–1963* (London, 1974), 53.
37. A. L. Kennedy, *Britain Faces Germany* (London, 1937), 83–86; Gilbert, *Wilderness*, 136.
38. Hansard 6/29/31; Gilbert, *Wilderness*, 37.
39. Hansard 6/29/31.
40. WSC V, 445; *Daily Mail* 5/26/32.
41. ChP 18/75; *Daily Mail* 5/26/32.
42. Hansard 11/10/32.
43. Len Deighton, *Fighter* (New York, 1977), 39.
44. *Daily Mail* 11/17/32; 11/23/32.
45. Alistair Horne, *To Lose A Battle* (Boston, 1969), 22; WM/Lady Soames; WM/R. A. Butler.
46. ChP 9/103; *Times* 4/13/33.
47. Hansard 4/13/33.
48. *Birmingham Post* 4/19/33.
49. WSC V, 460–461.
50. Macmillan, 354; Hansard 3/23/33.
51. Hansard 3/23/33.
52. Hansard 11/5/29 (Lords); Telford Taylor, 249.
53. *Birmingham Post* 3/28/33.
54. Jones, 129; Murray Papers.
55. Martin Gilbert and Richard Gott, *The Appeasers* (Boston, 1963), 11.
56. ChP 2/266; *Times* 9/27/33, 6/17/36; J. R. M. Butler, *Lord Lothian* (London, 1960), Appendix IV, 354–362.
57. Cowles, 293.
58. *Times* 6/26/33.
59. *Times* 6/26/33.
60. Vernon Bartlett, 242–243.
61. Gilbert, *Wilderness*, 161; Norman Angell, *The Defence of the Empire* (New York, 1937), 183–184; Kennedy, 83–86.
62. Eade, ed., 44.
63. Kay Halle, *The Irrepressible Churchill: A Treasury of Winston Churchill's Wit* (New York, 1967), 37, 181, 323.
64. Halle, 268, 322.
65. Hansard 7/10/35, 6/25/41.
66. Colin Coote and Denvil Batchelor, eds., *Maxims and Reflections* (London, 1947), 53–54; Hansard 12/8/44.
67. Halle, 269; Coote and Batchelor, eds., 142.
68. Hansard 1/21/31; Halle, 125, 257.
69. Halle, 131, 133.
70. William Safire, "Banned Words," *NYT* 10/28/84.
71. Gilbert, *Wilderness*, 132.
72. Telford Taylor, 205; CAB 23/76.
73. John Baker White, *True Blue* (London, 1970), 161.
74. ChP 2/201.

75. BSCP 8/31/29.
76. Cowles, 296; Gilbert, *Wilderness*, 15.
77. Foreign Office Papers 371/16733.
78. *Harper's*, March 1946.
79. Gilbert, *Wilderness*, 120.
80. *The New Encyclopaedia Britannica*, 15th ed. (Chicago, 1974), VII, 4, 597.
81. DBFP series 2, vol. V, no. 127; *NYT* 2/17/85.
82. Vansittart, 478.
83. Gilbert, *Wilderness*, 118, 119.
84. Hansard 5/11/35; Sir John Colville, *Footprints in Time* (London, 1976), 95; WM/Sir John Colville, 10/8/80.
85. *Epping West Essex Gazette* 8/13/33; Hansard 8/23/33.
86. Horne, 38 *passim*.
87. Oswald Spengler, *Jahre de Entscheidung* (Munich, 1935), viii; TMWC XXXIV.
88. *Völkischer Beobachter* 5/18/33.
89. Hermann Rauschning, *Gespräche mit Hitler* (Munich, 1940), 55; Franz von Papen, *Der Wahrheit eine Gasse* (Munich, 1953), 330–333.
90. Beaverbrook Papers.
91. Blomberg's directive, TMWC, XXIV, 487–491.
92. William L. Shirer, *The Rise and Fall of the Third Reich: A History of Nazi Germany* (New York, 1960), 212.
93. Gottfried Benn, *Der neue Staat und die Intellecktuellen* (Stuttgart/Berlin, 1933), 576.
94. André François-Poncet, *De Versailles à Potsdam* (Paris, 1948), 107; ND 2001-PS; Alan Bullock, *Hitler —A Study in Tyranny* (New York, 1952), 199; ND EC-419.
95. Wolfgang Foerster, *Ein General kaempft gegen den Krieg* (Munich, 1949), 70–73.
96. NCA, VII, 335; Foerster, 122; *Völkischer Beobachter* 8/20/34; *Frankfurter Zeitung* 8/20/34; *Berliner Tageblatt*, 8/20/34.
97. ND C-100.
98. Telford Taylor, 205; CV V/1, 306, 307.
99. Robert Rhodes James, *Churchill: A Study in Failure, 1900–1939* (New York, 1970), 262; "How Wars of the Future Will Be Waged," *News of the World* 4/24/38.
100. Ronald H. Bailey and the editors of Time-Life Books, *The Air War in Europe, 1940–1945* (Chicago, 1981), 26.
101. PrP 1/237; Bailey et al., 43; Deighton, 78.
102. Churchill, *Storm*, 116, 127, 128.
103. WSC V, 553.
104. Hansard 3/11/35; Vansittart, 509.
105. Wheeler-Bennett, ed., *Action This Day*, 11.
106. Lord Eustace Percy, *Some Memories* (London, 1958), 187.
107. General Georg Thomas, *Basic Facts for a History of German War and Armament Economy* (mimeographed) (Nuremberg, 1945), cited in Shirer, *Rise and Fall*, 259; NCA, I, 827–830.
108. Walter Görlitz, *History of the German General Staff 1657–1945* (New York, 1953), 299.
109. Vansittart, 226; Gilbert, *Wilderness*, 108; Telford Taylor, 591–592; CAB 23/83–86.
110. ChP 2/271; WM/Kathleen Hill 11/4/80.
111. Templewood Papers.
112. *Times* 11/17/34; WSCHCS 5433 (verse form added).
113. Hansard 11/28/34.
114. Hansard 11/28/34.
115. Frances Stevenson, *Lloyd George: A Diary by Frances Stevenson*, edited by A. J. P. Taylor (New York, 1971), 294.
116. Hansard 11/28/34.
117. Hansard 3/8/34.
118. Telford Taylor, 246.
119. BSCP 3/8/35.
120. Foreign Office Papers 371/18828.
121. White Papers Cmd. 5107; BSCP 3/8/35.
122. Foreign Office Papers 371/18828.
123. *NYT* 3/17/35; Telford Taylor, 98; Shirer, *Rise and Fall*, 284.
124. *Strand* 11/35.
125. Hansard 3/19/35.
126. ChP 4/143.
127. Hansard 3/19/35.
128. Hansard 3/19/35.
129. Foreign Office Papers 371/18828.
130. BSCP 4/5/35.
131. Telford Taylor, 218.
132. Hansard 5/2/35.
133. Hansard 5/22/35.
134. Vansittart, 497–498.
135. BSCP 5/11/35, 5/13/35.
136. *Daily Telegraph* 4/26/35; *Daily Express* 5/3/35.
137. ChP 8/503; BSCP, 4/11/35.
138. Churchill, *Storm*, 126; Coote and Batchelor, 158–159.
139. Telford Taylor, 123.
140. *NYT* 5/23/35; *Times* 5/23/35.
141. John Evelyn Wrench, *Geoffrey Dawson and Our Times* (London, 1955), 361.
142. Shirer, *Rise and Fall*, 287–288.
143. Telford Taylor, 222–223; CAB 23/82, 6/19/35.
144. CAB 23/82, 6/19/35; Hansard 7/11/35.
145. Telford Taylor, 223.
146. Hansard 7/11/35.
147. *Daily Herald* 3/27/36; Halle, 299.
148. Telford Taylor, 97.
149. Telford Taylor, 222.
150. Hansard 3/19/35.
151. Churchill, *Storm*, 123.

152. Birla Papers; Martin Gilbert, *Churchill's Political Philosophy* (Oxford, 1981), 85–88; Peter Stansky, ed., *Churchill: A Profile* (New York, 1973), 201.
153. Robert Keith Middlemas and John Barnes, *Baldwin* (London, 1969), 868; WM/Macmillan; Macmillan, 395–397; A. W. Baldwin, *My Father: The True Story* (London, 1956), 242.
154. Middlemas and Barnes, 867; *Times* 11/1/35; L. S. Amery, *My Political Life*, 3 vols. (London, 1953), III, 75, 170; Middlemas and Barnes, 369.
155. *Strand* 11/35; Hansard 10/24/35.
156. *Strand* 11/35.
157. Foreign Office Papers 371/18878, 371/18880; ChP 2/237.
158. Foreign Office Papers 371/18880.
159. WSC V, 680; ChP 2/237.
160. Eade, ed., 171; DNB 11/8/38, 11/6/36, 9/9/38.
161. Henry Pelling, *Winston Churchill* (New York, 1974), 373; ChP 4/141.
162. Vansittart, 497.
163. Churchill, *Storm*, 128, 200; Baldwin Papers, 47, 113.
164. Hansard 5/2/35.
165. Wrench, 322.
166. Isaiah Berlin, *Mr. Churchill in 1940* (Boston, 1964), 16.
167. Jones, 157.
168. Jones, 203.
169. Brian Gardner, *Churchill in Power* (Boston, 1970), 6; WM/A. J. P. Taylor, 12/1/80; A. J. P. Taylor, *Origins of the Second World War* (New York, 1961), 116.
170. Churchill, *Storm*, 181; Longford, 86; Boothby, *I Fight to Live*, 137; WM/Lord Boothby 10/16/80.
171. Churchill, *Storm*, 181.
172. Robert T. Elson and the editors of Time-Life Books, *Prelude to War* (New York, 1976), 149.

Reef

1. Francis Paul Walters, *A History of the League of Nations* (New York, 1952), 648.
2. Harold Macmillan, *Winds of Change* (London, 1966), 383; Robert T. Elson and the editors of Time-Life Books, *Prelude to War* (New York, 1976), 150–151.
3. Hansard 10/24/35.
4. Lord Moran, *Churchill. Taken from the Diaries of Lord Moran: The Struggle for Survival, 1940–1965* (Boston, 1966), 692.
5. Macmillan, 386; Winston S. Churchill, *The Gathering Storm* (Boston, 1948), 133–134, 166–169.
6. Templewood Papers; Martin Gilbert, *Winston Churchill: The Wilderness Years* (London, 1981), 137.
7. Robert Rhodes James, *Churchill: A Study in Failure, 1900–1939* (New York, 1970), 286; *Times* 9/27/35.
8. Telford Taylor, *Munich: The Price of Peace* (New York, 1979), 233.
9. *Times* 10/4/35; Hansard 10/24/35.
10. Rhodes James, *Failure*, 283; Macmillan, 402; Elson et al., *Prelude*, 152; Earl of Avon, *Facing the Dictators* (Boston, 1962), 303.
11. *Paris-Soir* 12/9/35; Macmillan, 408; *Times* 12/18/35.
12. ChP 2/238.
13. Churchill, *Storm*, 183.
14. Vincent Sheean, *Between the Thunder and the Sun* (New York, 1943), 30, 42.
15. BSCP 12/30/35.
16. BSCP 1/7/36; Churchill, *Storm*, 181; BSCP 12/26/35.
17. Hansard 6/10/36; Telford Taylor, 232-233.
18. Telford Taylor, 169; *NYT* 11/2/36.
19. Templewood Papers; Avon, 355.
20. ChP 1/284.
21. Gilbert, *Wilderness*, 145; Harold Nicolson, *Diaries and Letters*, edited by Nigel Nicolson, 3 vols. (London, 1966), I, 228; WSC V, 709.
22. CAB 21/424; Templewood Papers; ChP 2/251.
23. BSCP 2/21/36, 2/27/36, 3/3/36.
24. Randolph Churchill Papers.
25. BSCP 1/8/36, 1/15/36; WM/Malcolm MacDonald, 11/6/80.
26. Beaverbrook Papers; ChP 2/28.
27. ChP 2/251; *Edinburgh Evening News* 2/13/36.
28. *Time* 3/16/36.
29. White Papers Cmd. 5107; WSC V, 711–712, 727; Hansard 3/10/36; A. J. P. Taylor, *Origins of the Second World War* (New York, 1961), 117.
30. Hansard 3/10/36; Churchill, *Storm*, 190.
31. Churchill, *Storm*, 191–192; *NYT* 5/22/35.
32. BSCP 1/17/36.
33. William L. Shirer, *The Collapse of the Third Republic* (New York, 1969), 251–252; General Maurice Gustave Gamelin, *Servir*, 3 vols. (Paris, 1947), II, 194–195; *Événements*, I, 138.
34. André François-Poncet, *The Fateful Years: Memoirs of a French Ambassador in Berlin 1931–1938* (New York, 1949), 188–189;

ND C-159; William L. Shirer, *The Rise and Fall of the Third Reich: A History of Nazi Germany* (New York, 1960), 288, 291.
35. Shirer, *Collapse*, 253.
36. Shirer, *Collapse*, 250; Avon, 373, 376.
37. Avon, 373–376.
38. *Time* 3/16/36.
39. William L. Shirer, *Berlin Diary* (New York, 1941), 52–53.
40. Telford Taylor, 99–100; *NYT* 3/8/36.
41. Shirer, *Berlin Diary*, 51–54.
42. DGFP series D, vol. XI, no. 411.
43. Paul Schmidt, *Statist auf diplomatischer Buehne 1923–1945* (Bonn, 1945), 320.
44. Shirer, *Rise and Fall*, 294; TMWC XV, 352.
45. François-Poncet, *Fateful Years*, 192–193.
46. *NYT* 3/8/36.
47. *Événements*, III, 722.
48. *Événements*, I, 157–158; Gamelin, II, 212–218; Shirer, *Berlin Diary*, 49–50; *Événements*, I, 201; François-Poncet, *Fateful Years*, 190, 194–195.
49. Telford Taylor, 135.
50. Churchill, *Storm*, 193; *Événements*, I, 20.
51. DDF, I, Doc. No. 301, 413–414; I, Doc. No. 316, 426–427.
52. Avon, 385.
53. Avon, 388, 387.
54. *Événements*,. III, 591–592.
55. *Times* 3/9/36.
56. Thomas Jones, *A Diary with Letters, 1931–1950* (Oxford, 1954), 180; Nicolson, I, 248–249.
57. Hansard 3/9/36.
58. Avon, 394.
59. Pierre-Etienne Flandin, *Politique française 1919–1940* (Paris, 1947), 202–204, 207–208.
60. Gilbert, *Wilderness*, 148–149; CAB 23/83.
61. CAB 23/83.
62. Shirer, *Rise and Fall*, 779, 828.
63. Churchill, *Storm*, 192–193.
64. Hansard 3/36.
65. N. Chamberlain Papers, diary; Hansard 3/36; *Evening Standard*.
66. WSC V, 712–713; Churchill, *Storm*, 195.
67. Foreign Office Affairs Comm. minutes; PrP 1/194.
68. N. Chamberlain Papers, diary, 3/12/36; WM/R. A. Butler, 12/5/80.
69. Gilbert, *Wilderness*, 152–153.
70. Gilbert, *Wilderness*, 152–153.
71. Churchill, *Storm*, 196.
72 Nicolson, ed., *Diaries and Letters*, I, 249–250.
73. Churchill, *Storm*, 195–196.
74. Churchill, *Storm*, 198, 197; Flandin, as quoted in Shirer, *Collapse*, 277; Shirer, *Berlin Diary*, 55; WM/William L. Shirer, 7/5/83; *NYT* 3/20/36.
75. Hansard 3/26/36.
76. Macmillan, 291; Elizabeth Longford, *Winston Churchill: A Pictorial Life Story* (Chicago, 1974), 84.
77. ChP 2/252.
78. Martin Gilbert and Richard Gott, *The Appeasers* (Boston, 1963), 48.
79. Alistair Horne, *To Lose a Battle* (Boston, 1969), 41.
80. Hansard 4/6/36.
81. Hansard 3/26/36; WM/Harold Macmillan, 12/4/80.
82. NCA, VII, 890; ND I-150.
83. Lord Vansittart, *The Mist Procession* (London, 1958), 497, 499; Gilbert, *Wilderness*, 268; Churchill, *Storm*, 152–153.
84. WSC V, 833–834.
85. Churchill, *Storm*, 198.
86. Churchill, *Storm*, 200.
87. Gilbert, *Wilderness*, 146; BSCP.
88. Sir Keith Feiling, *The Life of Neville Chamberlain* (London, 1946), 278.
89. Macmillan, 431; Iain Macleod, *Neville Chamberlain* (London, 1961), 193; Gilbert, *Wilderness*, 146.
90. Feiling, 278.
91. Feiling, cited by Churchill, *Storm*, 200; Macleod, 193; Brian Gardner, *Churchill in Power: As Seen by His Contemporaries* (Boston, 1970), 5.
92. Macmillan, 432; Macleod, 193, Robert Rhodes James, *Memoirs* (New York, 1970), 410; *Times* 3/16/36; Inskip, quoted in Gilbert and Gott, 365.
93. Churchill, *Storm*, 200.
94. Gardner, 5; Churchill, *Storm*, 200; Macmillan, 432; WM/Lord Geoffrey Lloyd, 11/27/80; ChP 2/330.
95. Churchill, *Storm*, 201; Gardner, 5; *Evening Standard* 5/4/36.
96. Hansard 3/26/36.
97. ChP 2/268.
98. Hansard 7/20/36; Nicolson, I, 269.
99. Hansard 4/23/36.
100. *Glasgow Forward* 10/3/36; *Times* 10/6/36.
101. *Times* 10/9/36. Ibarruri (born 1895) was still alive in 1988.
102. Hugh Dalton, *Memoirs, 1931–1945: The Fateful Years* (London, 1957), 97–104.
103. Peter Stansky and William Abrahams, *Journey to the Frontier. Julian Bell and John Cornford: Their Lives and the 1930s* (London, 1966), 315–316, 387, 390.
104. Macmillan, 436; WM/Macmillan; A. J. P. Taylor, *Origins*, 395; Wm/A. J. P. Taylor, 12/1/80.

105. Telford Taylor, 538; Nicolson, I, 270; Avon, 453.
106. Macmillan, 438; Foreign Relations of the U.S., 1938, I.
107. Telford Taylor, 286.
108. Churchill, *Storm*, 214; *Evening Standard* 8/10/36.
109. Macmillan, 435.
110. Hansard 2/12/33.
111. Sheean, 59–60.
112. WM/Macmillan; Churchill, *Storm*, 144.
113. *Daily Telegraph* 12/30/38, 4/20/39; Hansard 4/14/37.
114. ChP 2/266.
115. PrP 1/193.
116. Jones, 233; Gilbert, *Wilderness*, 160–161.
117. Gilbert, *Wilderness*, 160–161; ChP 2/356.
118. Jones, 191.
119. CAB 23/86.
120. Alfred Duff Cooper, *Old Men Forget* (New York, 1954), 220.
121. ChP 2/271.
122. Hansard 11/11/36; Sir John Wheeler-Bennett, ed., *Action This Day: Memoirs by Lord Normanbrook, John Colville, Sir John Martin, Sir Ian Jacobs, Lord Bridges, Sir Leslie Rowan* (London, 1968), 242–243.
123. Hansard 11/12/36.
124. Hansard 11/12/36.
125. Nicolson, I, 278.
126. Hansard 11/12/36.
127. Nicolson, I, 278–279.
128. Hansard 11/12/36.
129. *Times* 11/1/35.
130. Hansard 11/12/36.
131. ChP 2/267; Churchill, *Storm*, 216.
132. Macmillan, 400; WM/Macmillan; Telford Taylor, 252–253, 254.
133. Telford Taylor, 535.
134. Eugen Spier, *Focus* (London, 1963), 9, 25; Gilbert, *Wilderness*, 153.
135. Gilbert, *Wilderness*, 156, 157, 158.
136. Winston S. Churchill, *While England Slept* (London, 1938), 302–303; ChP 2/283.
137. Churchill, *Storm*, 217; *Daily Telegraph* 3/1/65.
138. *Daily Telegraph* 3/1/65; Walter M. Citrine, *Citrine; Men and Work, An Autobiography* (London, 1964), 357.
139. Citrine, 357; *Daily Telegraph* 3/1/65.
140. Churchill, *Storm*, 217; *Daily Telegraph* 3/1/65.
141. Churchill, *Storm*, 217–218.
142. Macmillan, 441; WM/Macmillan; WM/Lord Strauss, 10/13/80.
143. *Daily Telegraph* 3/1/65.
144. Kay Halle, *The Irrepressible Churchill: A Treasury of Winston Churchill's Wit* (New York, 1967), 132; WM, private information.
145. Hansard 6/28/1894.
146. WM/Anita Leslie, 10/1/84.
147. Duke of Windsor, *A King's Story: Memoirs of the Duke of Windsor* (New York, 1947), 237.
148. Francis F. Beirne, *Amiable Baltimoreans* (New York, 1951), 297, 119.
149. Robert Keith Middlemas and John Barnes, *Baldwin* (London, 1969), 280; Lord Birkenhead, *The Life of Walter Monckton of Trenchley* (London, 1969), 123.
150. ChP 2/264.
151. Lord Birkenhead, *Monckton*, 130; ChP 2/264.
152. ChP 2/264.
153. *NYT* 10/4/36, 10/15/36, 11/18/36; Telford Taylor, 541.
154. Macmillan, 440; WM/Macmillan.
155. Lord Beaverbrook, *The Abdication of King Edward VIII* (London, 1966), 37; WM/Lady Diana Cooper, 10/20/80.
156. ChP 2/264.
157. Middlemas and Barnes, 999; Gilbert, *Wilderness*, 169.
158. ChP 2/264; Kenneth Young, *Churchill and Beaverbrook: A Study in Friendship and Politics* (London, 1966), 123.
159. Macmillan, 440; WM/Macmillan.
160. *Times* 12/3/36; Duke of Windsor, 358.
161. Citrine, 328.
162. Mary Soames, *Clementine Churchill: A Biography of a Marriage* (Boston, 1979), 359; Telford Taylor, 542; Nicolson, I, 282; Lord Moran, *Churchill*, 207.
163. *Daily Telegraph* 3/1/65; Hansard 12/9/36.
164. WSC V, 814; Channon Papers.
165. ChP 2/264; Duke of Windsor, 381.
166. *Times* 12/6/36.
167. WM/Lloyd; Walter Monckton, quoted in WSC V, 820; WSC V, 820; Boothby Papers 12/11/36.
168. WM/Lord Boothby, 10/16/80.
169. WM/Boothby; Nicolson, ed., *Diaries and Letters*, I, 283–284.
170. Boothby Papers; WM/Macmillan; WM/Boothby; WM/Lloyd; Macmillan, 441; WSC V, 821; Hansard 12/7/36.
171. Hansard 12/7/36; Nicolson, I, 284; Churchill, *Storm*, 218–219; WSC V, 822.
172. WM/Boothby.
173. Hansard 12/11/36.
174. Nicolson, I, 286; *Evening Standard* 12/28/36; Amery Papers.
175. Duke of Windsor, 407; ChP 2/264.
176. WM/Sir William Deakin, 10/5/80; Churchill, *Storm*, 219.
177. *Daily Telegraph* 3/1/65; Macmillan, 441.
178. ChP 2/264.

179. Soames, 360; ChP 2/264.
180. Macmillan, 441; Nicolson, I, 289, 284.
181. Young, 123; Bernard Baruch, "A Birthday Letter," Sir James Marchant, ed., *Winston Spencer Churchill: Servant of Crown and Commonwealth* (London, 1954), 166; ChP 2/312.
182. WSC V, 835–836 fn; Hankey Papers.
183. ChP 2/306; WSC V, 849–850.
184. Soames, 361 fn; Roberts Papers.
185. CAB 23/87.

Undertow

1. WM/Virginia Cowles, 10/15/80; Virginia Cowles, *Winston Churchill: The Era and the Man* (New York, 1953), 307; Henry Pelling, *Winston Churchill* (New York, 1971), 410.
2. Winston S. Churchill, *The Gathering Storm* (Boston, 1948), 220; Harold Nicolson, *Diaries and Letters, 1930–1962*, edited by Nigel Nicolson, 3 vols. (London, 1966), I, 301; Lord Halifax, *Fullness of Days* (England, 1957), 182–183; Kay Halle, *The Irrepressible Churchill: A Treasury of Winston Churchill's Wit* (New York, 1967), 135.
3. Churchill, *Storm*, 221–222; Harold Macmillan, *Winds of Change* (London, 1966), 467.
4. L. S. Amery, *My Political Life*, 3 vols. (London, 1955), III, 226; Thomas Jones, *A Diary with Letters, 1931–1950* (Oxford, 1954), 350; Viscount Templewood, *Nine Troubled Years* (London, 1954), 257.
5. *NYT* 11/19/37; Martin Gilbert, *Winston Churchill: The Wilderness Years* (London, 1981), 210; Ivone Kirkpatrick, *The Inner Circle* (London, 1959), 97.
6. Hansard 12/21/37; Gilbert, *Wilderness*, 210–211.
7. Templewood Papers.
8. ChP 2/341, 2/328.
9. A. Chamberlain Papers.
10. Gilbert, *Wilderness*, 210; W. J. Brown, *So Far* (London, 1953), in Martin Gilbert and Richard Gott, *The Appeasers* (Boston, 1963), 377.
11. WM/Sir John Colville, 10/8/80; *Times* 6/1/37; Hansard 5/31/37; Channon Papers.
12. Nicolson, I, 328.
13. J. C. W. Reith, *Into the Wind* (London, 1949), 307–308.
14. CAB 27/623; PrP 1/27/38.
15. Churchill, *Storm*, 222–223; Earl of Avon, *Facing the Dictators* (Boston, 1965), 587–588.
16. R. W. Seton-Watson, *Britain and the Dictators* (Cambridge, 1938), 77; *Times* 10/28/37.
17. DGFP series D, vol. I, nos. 108, 104.
18. DGFP series D, vol. I, no. 131.
19. DGFP series D, vol. I, nos. 138, 148.
20. DGFP series D, vol. I no. 40; Sir Nevile Henderson, *Failure of a Mission: Berlin 1937–1939* (New York, 1940), 119.
21. *NYT* 7/12/36.
22. TWC XII, 761–764; Kurt von Schuschnigg, *Ein Requiem in Rot-Weiss-Rot* (Zurich, 1946), 109–111.
23. TWC XII, 761–764; NCA III, 409–413, NCA III, S. 690–693; NCA III, S. 716–717; NCA VII, S. 300; NCA V, S. 378; Paul Schmidt, *Statist auf diplomatischer Buehne, 1923–1945* (Bonn, 1949), 449.
24. Halle, 138; CAB 23/92.
25. Churchill, *Storm*, 251; David Dilks, ed., *The Diaries of Sir Alexander Cadogan O.M. 1938–1945* (New York, 1972), quoted in Telford Taylor, *Munich: The Price of Peace* (New York, 1979), 767 fn; Avon, 626.
26. Churchill, *Storm*, 254–255.
27. DDF-2e-V, no. 429; DDF-2e-VI, nos. 249, 482, 465; DDF-2e-VII, nos. 28, 137, 198.
28. Robert Rhodes James, *Anthony Eden* (London, 1986), 192–193; Telford Taylor, 566.
29. Rhodes James, *Eden*, 193–195, *Times* 2/14/38.
30. DGFP series D, vol. I, nos. 128, 750.
31. A. L. Rowse, *All Souls and Appeasement* (London, 1961), 28.
32. Churchill, *Storm*, 257–258.
33. Hansard 2/21/38.
34. Hansard 2/22/38.
35. WM/Kay Halle, 8/6/80; Sir John Colville, *The Churchillians* (London, 1981), 24; Harold Balfour, *Wings over Westminster* (London, 1973), 230; Mary Soames, *Clementine Churchill: The Biography of a Marriage* (Boston, 1979), 24.
36. Colville, *Churchillians*, 24; ChP 1/325.
37. WM/Colville; WM/Pamela Harriman, 8/22/80; Soames, 309.
38. Soames, 321–325; WM/Pamela Harriman; ChP 8/531.
39. WM/Lady Soames, 10/9/80, 6/25/85; Colville, *Churchillians*, 565; Soames, 325–326; BSCP 1/11/36.
40. Soames, 303.
41. ChP 1/344.
42. ChP 1/344.
43. WM/Lady Soames, 10/9/80; Soames, 339.
44. ChP 8/315.
45. Soames, 365, 369, 326.

46. Soames, 343–344.
47. WSC V, 589; Soames, 352–353.
48. Second Earl of Birkenhead, *The Professor and the Prime Minister* (Boston, 1962), 442; BSCP 1/1/35.
49. Soames, 345.
50. Soames, 345.
51. Soames, 347.
52. Soames, 349.
53. Willi Kerr, *Times Literary Supplement*.
54. Soames, 351, 354–355.
55. Soames, 356; WSC V, 933 fn; Gilbert, *Wilderness*, 209; ChP 8/551, 1/300.
56. William L. Shirer, *20th Century Journey: The Nightmare Years 1930–1940. A Memoir of the Life and the Times* (Boston, 1984), 311.
57. *Time* 2/13/39; Soames, 361.
58. Churchill, *Storm*, 222–224.
59. Churchill, *Storm*, 222–224.
60. ChP 2/303, 2/327.
61. Churchill, *Storm*, 236–237, WSC V, 853.
62. ChP 8/599.
63. ChP 2/304, 9/129.
64. Gilbert, *Wilderness*, 182–184; CAB 21/626; Hankey Papers.
65. ChP 2/304.
66. Churchill, *Storm*, 241; Avon, 447–448.
67. Gilbert and Gott, 69.
68. Dirksen Papers, vol. II. Appendix; DGFP series D, vol. I, nos. 95, 101; ChP 2/299, 2/302; Phipps Papers; Churchill, *Storm*, 241.
69. Quickswood Papers.
70. Hansard 6/30/38; WSC V, 952; John Harvey, ed., *The Diplomatic Diaries of Oliver Harvey* (London, 1970), 7/2/38.
71. Hankey Papers.
72. TMWC XXV, 402–13 (in German); DGFP series D, vol. I, nos. 29–39; William L. Shirer, *The Rise and Fall of the Third Reich: A History of Nazi Germany* (New York, 1960), 307.
73. DGFP series D, vol. II, no. 21.
74. Franz von Papen, *Der Wahrheit eine Gasse* (Munich, 1952), 456; DDF-2e-I, doc. 425, 549–552; Avon, 400, 402, 403; *Événements*, I, 157–158; Bernd Gisevius, *Bis zum bittern Ende* (Zurich, 1946), 229.
75. *Berliner Tageblatt* 2/21/38, and from Shirer's notes at the time.
76. *Evening Standard* 4/4/38; ChP 2/328.
77. ChP 2/328.
78. TMWC XVI, 193; WM/William L. Shirer, 7/20/80; Henderson, 120; Hansard 3/2/38.
79. *NYT* 2/25/38.
80. *Frankfurter Zeitung* 3/4/38.
81. ChP 2/328; Nicolson, I, 330.
82. Shirer, *Rise and Fall*, 335, 336, 343.
83. Henderson, 124.
84. WSC V, 910; DGFP series D, vol. I, no. 146.
85. Jones, 208.
86. Jones, 175.
87. Jones, 395–396.
88. Churchill, *Storm*, 271.
89. Winston S. Churchill, *The Grand Alliance* (Boston, 1950).
90. DGFP series D, vol. I, 273–275; Churchill, *Storm*, 271–272.
91. DGFP series D, vol. I, 273–275.
92. DBFP series D, vol. I, nos. 138–151, 578.
93. WSC V, 911.
94. Henderson, 124–125.
95. Nicolson, I, 330–331; Henderson, 311.
96. CAB 23/91; Templewood Papers.
97. PrP 1/238; CAB 23/91.
98. ChP 2/328; Shirer, *Rise and Fall*, 353.
99. WM/Shirer; Shirer, *Rise and Fall*, 351.
100. Winston S. Churchill, *Step by Step: 1936–1939 Articles* (London, 1939), 227; *NYT* 5/5/45; ChP 2/328.
101. DGFP series D, vol. II, no. 278.
102. NCA, I, 501–502.
103. Nicolson, I, 331; Hansard 3/14/38.
104. Dilks, ed., 3/12/38.
105. Dilks, ed., 2/12/38, 4/22/38.
106. Nicolson, I, 331; DBFP series 3, vol. I, no. 57.
107. Hansard 3/14/38.
108. Hansard 3/14/38.
109. Hansard 3/14/38; WM/Lord Boothby, 10/16/80.
110. Hansard 3/14/38.
111. *NYT* 3/18/38; DBFP series 3, vol. I, no. 107.
112. DBFP series 3, vol. I, no. 107; Dirksen Papers.
113. Nicolson, I, 331; Lord Boothby, *Recollections of a Rebel* (London, 1978), 134–135; WM/Boothby.
114. *Star* 3/15/35; Liddell Hart Memorandum, "Defence of Britain," 63–74, CAB 23/93.
115. Alfred Duff Cooper, *Old Men Forget* (New York, 1954), 218.
116. DGFP series D, vol II.
117. *Frankfurter Zeitung* 2/21/38.
118. Balfour Papers.
119. Hansard 5/31/35.
120. ChP 2/266.
121. ChP 2/307, 2/299.
122. CAB 23/93.
123. ChP 2/341.
124. WM/Shirer.
125. DBFP series 3, vol. I, no. 86; Foreign Office Studies, C 1865/132/18.
126. Foreign Office Studies, C 1865/132/18.

127. Foreign Office Studies, C 1865/132/18; Dilks, ed., 63; Sir Keith Feiling, *The Life of Neville Chamberlain* (London, 1946), 347–348; Robert Keith Middlemas and John Barnes, *Baldwin* (London, 1969), 188; DGFP series D, vol. II, 776.
128. *Times* 3/19/38. ChP 2/328.
129. *Evening Standard* 3/18/38.
130. CAB 53/27; Foreign Policy Committee Meeting 3/21/38.
131. CAB 27/623; CAB 27/627; Feiling, 347–348.
132. Duff Cooper, 218.
133. Duff Cooper, 218.
134. DBFP series 3, vol. I, nos. 106–110, 112, 116; CAB 27/623; Hansard 3/24/38.
135. WM/Cowles; Cowles, 308–309; Middlemas and Barnes, 206–207; Hansard 3/24/38.
136. Hansard 3/24/38 (verse form added).
137. Hansard 3/24/38.
138. WM/Cowles; Cowles, 308–309; Middlemas and Barnes, 206–207; Dilks, ed., 3/26/38.
139. ChP 8/600.
140. WSC V, 835.
141. BSCP 2/2/37.
142. BSCP 2/2/37.
143. BSCP 4/8/37.
144. *Daily Express* 3/17/38; *Times* 4/1/38, 4/2/38.
145. Camrose Papers.
146. ChP 1/328.
147. Lord Vansittart, *The Mist Procession* (London, 1958), 477, 499; ChP 1/328.
148. J. Baker White, *True Blue* (London, 1970), 161.
149. ChP 1/323.
150. Frederick Woods, *A Bibliography of the Works of Sir Winston Churchill KG, OM, CH* (London, 1963), 75–79, 83, 221–268; ChP 8/596.
151. Soames, 366; ChP 8/626; BSCP 2/2/37.
152. Robert Rhodes James, *Churchill: A Study in Failure, 1900–1939* (London, 1970), 340.
153. WM/John Grigg, 10/15/80; Rhodes James, *Failure,* 340.
154. WM/Lady Soames; WM/Lord Geoffrey Head, 11/19/80.
155. Nicolson, I, 347.
156. Shirer, *Rise and Fall,* 430–433.
157. DGFP series D, vol. II, no. 151.
158. Hansard 3/17/38; *NYT* 3/14/38.
159. Macmillan, 495.
160. *Observer* 11/29/37; Kingsley Martin, *Editor* (London, 1968), 50; Hugh Dalton, *Memoirs, 1931–1945: The Fateful Years* (London, 1957), 162.
161. *Times* 2/27/37, 6/23/37.
162. *NYT* 4/24/38; DGFP series D, vol. II, nos. 197–198; ND 388-PS item 2.
163. DBFP series 3, vol I, no. 158.
164. DBFP series 3, vol. I, no. 164; Templewood Papers.
165. *Le Temps* 4/12/38; Telford Taylor, 778.
166. WM/Harold Macmillan, 12/4/80; Macmillan, 495–496.
167. Isaiah Berlin, *Mr. Churchill in 1940* (Boston, 1964), 16–17.
168. DBFP series 3, vol. I, no. 98.
169. DBFP series 3, vol. II, no. 337.
170. Telford Taylor, 638; Lieutenant General Sir Henry Pownall, *Chief of Staff,* vol. 1, *1933–40,* edited by Brian Bond (London, 1972), 80.
171. Churchill, *Storm,* 231–232.
172. Balfour, 99–110; Nicolson, I, 341–342.
173. Telford Taylor, 759; Anne Morrow Lindbergh, *The Flower and the Nettle: Diaries and Letters of Anne Morrow Lindbergh 1936–1939* (New York, 1976), 100; Charles A. Lindbergh, *The Wartime Journals of Charles A. Lindbergh* (New York, 1970), 22.
174. Charles Lindbergh, 73.
175. Jones, 409–411.
176. Telford Taylor, 851; Shirer, *Nightmare Years,* 238.
177. DBFP series 3, vol. I, nos. 171, 170.
178. DGFP series D, vol. II, no. 154.
179. *Times* 6/3/38; Shirer, *Rise and Fall,* 376.
180. ChP 2/329.
181. DBFP series 3, vol. I, no. 219, app. III.
182. Foreign Office Papers 271/1719; ChP 2/329.
183. ChP 2/340.
184. ChP 2/340; Churchill, *Storm,* 286; *Times* 5/17/38.
185. DGFP series D, vol. II, no. 13.
186. DBFP series 3, vol. I.
187. DBFP series 3, vol. I; DGFP series D, vol. II.
188. Telford Taylor, 392–393.
189. Telford Taylor, 655.
190. H. L. Mencken, *On Being an American,* 1923; NCA, V, 743–744.
191. *Daily Telegraph* 7/6/38, 7/26/38; ChP 2/330.
192. ChP 2/340, 2/331.
193. DBFP series 3, vol. II, app. IV.
194. ND II, 10.
195. Helmuth Groscurth, *Tagebücher eines Abwehroffiziers 1938–1940,* edited by Helmut Krausnick and Harold Deutsch (Stuttgart, 1970), 9/2/38; 9/4/38.
196. Shirer, *Rise and Fall,* 426.
197. TMWC X, 509.

198. Hermann Förtsch, *Schuld und Verhangnis* (Stuttgart, 1951), 173–174.
199. Dalton, 182.
200. ChP 2/331.
201. PrP 1/266.
202. Churchill, *Storm*, 293–294.
203. PrP 1/265.
204. Telford Taylor, 670; Dilks, ed., 95.
205. CAB 23/95.
206. PrP 1/266.
207. PrP 1/266.
208. Feiling, 357.
209. DGFP series D, vol. II, no. 42.
210. WSC V, 969; *Times* 9/7/38.
211. ChP 2/331.
212. Dalton, 174–175.
213. Dilks, ed., 95.
214. DBFP series 3, vol. II, nos. 775, 815, 818, 819, 823, 825; Dilks, ed., 96; Gilbert and Gott, 138; Harvey, 172–173.
215. DBFP series 3, vol. II, no. 482.
216. *Standard* 9/13/38; CAB 23/95.
217. Telford Taylor, 676–677.
218. DBFP series 3, vol. II, no. 862.
219. Harvey, 9/15/38; Feiling, 333; ChP 2/331.
220. WM/R. A. Butler 12/5/80; DBFP series 3, vol. I, no. 120; ChP 1/325.
.221. WM/Macmillan.
222. Sir John Wheeler-Bennett, *Munich: Prologue to Tragedy* (New York, 1948), 108; Feiling, 366.
223. N. Chamberlain Papers, in Feiling, 366.
224. Shirer, *Rise and Fall*, 335, 386; DGFP series D, vol. II, no. 487.
225. ChP 2/343; N. Chamberlain Papers.
226. Duff Cooper, 229; CAB 23/95.
227. DBFP series 3, vol. II, no. 907; *Le Populaire* 9/20/38.
228. ChP 8/612; DBFP series 3, vol. II, no. 907.
229. DBFP series 3, vol. II, nos. 928, 951, 952, 961.
230. *Times* 9/20/38; DBFP series 3, vol. II, no. 978.
231. DBFP series 3, vol. II, no. 973.
232. Dalton, 196.
233. Foreign Relations of the U.S., 1938, III.
234. DBFP series 3, vol. II, no. 1008.
235. ChP 2/331.
236. ChP 4/92.
237. ChP 9/132.
238. Nicolson, I, 363–364.
239. Telford Taylor, 806 fn; DBFP series 3, vol. II, no. 1033.
240. DBFP series 3, vol. II, no. 1076.
241. DBFP series 3, vol. II, no. 1043.
242. DBFP series 3, vol. II, no. 1058.
243. DBFP series 3, vol. II, nos. 463, 773, 499–508.
244. Paul Schmidt, *Hitler's Interpreter* (New York, 1951), 95–102; Henderson, 156–162; *Times* 9/24/38.
245. Dilks, ed., 9/24/38.
246. CAB 23/95, Duff Cooper, 234.
247. Duff Cooper, 234; A. J. P. Taylor, *Origins of the Second World War* (New York, 1961), 177.
248. DBFP series 3, vol. II, no. 1092.
249. Shirer, *Berlin Diary*, 141–142.
250. *NYT* 9/28/38.
251. WM/Macmillan; Macmillan, 507.
252. Macmillan, 505, 507; WM/Macmillan; E. S. Turner, *The Phoney War* (London, 1961), 55.
253. DBFP series 3, vol. II, no. 1231.
254. *Times* 9/29/38; Kirkpatrick, 124–125; Nicolson, I, 370–371; Macmillan, 506.
255. Macmillan, 506; WM/Macmillan.
256. Shirer, *Rise and Fall*, 411; Telford Taylor, 897.
257. Templewood Papers; Peterpaul Donat, *"Das Munchener Abkommen vom 29. September 1938," Deutsches Adelsblatt* no. 6 (1971), 82; Brian Gardner, *Churchill in Power: As Seen by his Contemporaries* (Boston, 1970) 11.
258. WM/Walter Lippmann, 10/10/64.
259. Hansard 10/3/38.
260. *Daily Telegraph* 3/1/65.
261. Nicolson, I, 372.
262. WSC V, 988.
263. Telford Taylor, 50–53.
264. Count Galeazzo Ciano, *The Ciano Diaries, 1939–1943*, edited by Hugh Wilson (New York, 1946), 166.
265. DBFP series 3, vol. II, no. 1210.
266. Feiling, 376.
267. Telford Taylor, 48–49.
268. Colin Coote, *A Companion of Honour: The Story of Walter Elliot* (London, 1965), 174.
269. Coote, 174.
270. Coote, 174; Gardner, 13.
271. Telford Taylor, 49.
272. Wm/Shirer; Boothby, *Rebel*, 130.
273. G. E. R. Gedye, *Fallen Bastions* (London, 1939), 488–489; Churchill, *Storm*, 322.
274. International Military Tribunal, X, 572, 600, 772; Churchill, *Storm*, 302.
275. IMT, XIII, S. 4; ND 739–PS.
276. Amery, III, 337; J. P. Sartre, *The Reprieve* (London, 1947), 398.
277. Gilbert and Gott, 179; Middlemas and Barnes, 179; Telford Taylor, 64–65.
278. Shirer, *Berlin Diary*, 147–148; N. Chamberlain Papers.
279. Feiling, 376.
280. Nicolson, I, 371.
281. Halifax, 200; WM/Lord Lloyd, 11/27/80.
282. Rhodes James, *Failure*, 373; Duff Cooper, 243; ChP 2/350; Churchill, *Storm*, 234.

Vortex

1. ChP 2/350; WSC V, 991–992.
2. Hugh Dalton, *Memoirs, 1931–1945: The Fateful Years* (London, 1957), 198; WM/Malcolm MacDonald, 11/6/80; Hansard 11/24/38.
3. Hansard 10/3/38.
4. John Evelyn Wrench, *Geoffrey Dawson and Our Times* (London, 1955), 378.
5. CAB 23/95; Hansard 10/3/38.
6. Hansard 10/3/38.
7. Harold Nicolson, *Diaries and Letters, 1930–1962*, edited by Nigel Nicolson, 3 vols. (London, 1966), I, 374.
8. Hansard 10/3/38.
9. Hansard 10/5/38.
10. Hansard 10/5/38.
11. Brian Gardner, *Churchill in Power: As Seen by His Contemporaries* (Boston, 1970), 11; Robert Rhodes James, *Churchill: A Study in Failure, 1900–1939* (London, 1970), 373.
12. WM/Lady Soames, 10/9/80; Mary Soames, *Clementine Churchill: The Biography of a Marriage* (Boston, 1979), 363; WM/Lady Diana Cooper, 10/20/80.
13. WM/Harold Macmillan, 12/4/80; Harold Macmillan, *Winds of Change, 1914–1939* (London, 1966), 485; B. H. Liddell Hart, *The Memoirs of Captain Liddell Hart*, 2 vols. (London, 1965), II, 211.
14. Alfred Duff Cooper, *Old Men Forget* (London, 1953), 232.
15. WM/Macmillan; Nicolson, I, 377–378.
16. WM/Lady Soames.
17. Hansard, 10/6/38; ChP 2/332.
18. ChP 2/336, 2/332; WSC V, 1006.
19. A. J. P. Taylor, *The Origins of the Second World War* (New York, 1962), 123, 96, 116; Martin Gilbert, *Churchill's Political Philosophy* (Oxford, 1981), 910.
20. Sir Keith Feiling, *The Life of Neville Chamberlain* (London, 1946), 406; Dalton, 202.
21. Kenneth Young, *Churchill and Beaverbrook: A Study in Friendship and Politics* (New York, 1966), 128–129; WSC V, 1012.
22. WSC V, 1012, 1014–1015.
23. ChP 1/344.
24. Lord Strang, *Home and Abroad* (London, 1964), cited in Telford Taylor, *Munich: The Price of Peace* (New York, 1979), 549.
25. Kay Halle, *The Irrepressible Churchill: A Treasury of Winston Churchill's Wit* (New York, 1967), 140–141; Oliver Harvey, *The Diplomatic Diaries of Oliver Harvey 1937–1940*, edited by John Harvey (London, 1970), 12/25/38.
26. Hansard 11/17/38; WSCHCS 6046–6048.
27. WSCHCS 6046–6048.
28. Nicolson, I, 375–376; ChP 8/597.
29. DGFP series D, vol. IV, no. 249.
30. Nicolson, I, 384; CAB 23/97; Winston S. Churchill, *The Gathering Storm* (Boston, 1948), 329.
31. Churchill, *Storm*, 329–330.
32. Nicolson, I, 382.
33. WM/Grace Hamblin, 11/4/80; ChP 8/624.
34. Foreign Office Papers 371/22963.
35. Halle, 255.
36. *Daily Telegraph* 1/12/39.
37. Vincent Sheean, *Between the Thunder and the Sun* (New York, 1943), 73–74.
38. ChP 1/343; WM/Lady Diana Cooper; Virginia Cowles, *Winston Churchill: The Era and the Man* (New York, 1953), 307.
39. BSCP 1/8/39.
40. Perry Knowlton, Adam Deixel, and Iam Gonzales at Curtis Brown; ChP 1/344; WM/Lady Soames.
41. Soames, 364.
42. Soames, 367; BSCP 12/20/38.
43. ChP 2/378.
44. ChP 1/332; Soames, 368.
45. WSC V, 1044.
46. F. Nietzsche, *Beyond Good and Evil*, trans. Hellen Zimmern (London, 1923), IV, 146; *Frankfurter Zeitung* 11/5/38.
47. ChP 9/133; WM/A. J. P. Taylor, 12/1/80.
48. WSC V, 1043.
49. N. Chamberlain Papers.
50. WSC V, 1045.
51. Phyllis Moir, *I Was Winston Churchill's Private Secretary* (New York, 1941), 100.
52. Martin Gilbert, *Winston Churchill: The Wilderness Years* (London, 1981), 248.
53. DGFP series D, vol. IV, nos. 55, 61; ChP 2/340.
54. ChP 3/12/39.
55. *NYT* 3/17/39.
56. William L. Shirer, *The Rise and Fall of the Third Reich: A History of Nazi Germany* (New York, 1960), 445–446.
57. Shirer, *Rise and Fall*, 445–446; Dalton, 226–227.
58. Martin Gilbert, *Sir Horace Rumbold: Portrait of a Diplomat* (London, 1973), 442.
59. Winston S. Churchill, *Step by Step: 1936–1939 Articles* (London, 1939), 302–303.
60. A. J. P. Taylor, 192; WM/A. J. P. Taylor; Rhodes James, *Failure*, 377.
61. Gardner, 9–10.
62. Hansard 3/15/39.
63. *Times* 3/18/39.
64. DGFP series D, vol. IV, no. 244.
65. Martin Gilbert and Richard Gott, *The Appeasers* (Boston, 1963), 209–210.
66. Hansard 5/26/39.
67. Hansard 5/26/39.

68. WM/Lord Boothby, 10/16/18; Hansard 5/26/39.
69. Gilbert and Gott, 212.
70. ChP 2/358.
71. ND UdSSR-172; ChP 8/628.
72. Hansard 3/18/39.
73. WSC V, 1069.
74. WSC V, 1070.
75. William L. Shirer, *The Collapse of the Third Republic* (New York, 1969), 418.
76. Gardner, 12.
77. N. Chamberlain Papers.
78. DBFP series 3, vol. IV, nos. 288, 298, 390, 397, 398, 395.
79. DBFP series 3, vol. IV, nos. 298, 390, 397, 398.
80. DBFP series 3, vol. IV, nos. 298, 390, 397, 398.
81. DBFP series 3, vol. IV, nos. 298, 390, 397, 398.
82. DBFP series 3, vol. IV, no. 395.
83. Leon Noèl, *L'Agression allemande contre la Pologne* (Paris, 1946), 326 note 1.
84. Telford Taylor, 421; Churchill, *Storm*, 350.
85. DBFP series 3, vol. IV, no. 433.
86. DBFP series 3, vol. IV, nos. 433, 447; Józef Beck, *Final Report* (New York, 1957), 187–189.
87. Gilbert and Gott, 240; CAB 27/624; DBFP series 3, vol. IV, nos. 515, 516.
88. ChP 2/340.
89. Ian Colvin, *The Chamberlain Cabinet* (London, 1971), 194–198; Ian Colvin, *None So Blind* (New York, 1965), 298–311.
90. ND R-100, C-120.
91. Hansard, 3/31/39.
92. WM/Boothby; Lord Boothby, *Recollections of a Rebel* (London, 1978), 132; B. H. Liddell Hart, *History of the Second World War* (New York, 1971), 11; Alfred Duff Cooper, *The Second World War: First Phase* (New York, 1939), 320.
93. Churchill, *Storm*, 347; Hansard 4/3/39.
94. CAB 23/98; Liddell Hart, *Second World War*, 16.
95. Lord Halifax, *Fullness of Days* (London, 1957), 206.
96. Lord Vansittart, *The Mist Procession* (London, 1958), 430; Gilbert and Gott, 245.
97. DBFP series 3, vol. V, no. 207.
98. Churchill, *Storm*, 350, 352; Arthur Christiansen, *Headlines All My Life* (New York, 1962), 89.
99. Churchill, *Storm*, 350–351.
100. N. Chamberlain Papers.
101. Macmillan, 539; WM/Macmillan.
102. Templewood Papers.
103. N. Chamberlain Papers, diary; DBFP series 3, vol. III, nos. 477, 495, 496, 500, 502; Count Galeazzo Ciano, *The Ciano Diaries 1939–1943*, edited by Hugh Wilson (New York, 1946), 1/11–14/39.
104. Hansard 4/3/39; *Times* 4/1/39.
105. N. Chamberlain Papers; Murray Papers; ChP 2/358.
106. Shirer, *Rise and Fall*, 341.
107. Gardner, 17.
108. Gilbert, *Political Philosophy*, 376.
109. Gilbert, *Wilderness*, 249; Reed Whittemore, "Churchill and the Limitations of Myth," *Yale Review*, Winter 1955.
110. WSC V, 1016.
111. Sir John Colville, *The Fringes of Power, 10 Downing Street Diaries, 1939–1955* (New York, 1985), 260, 264.
112. *Atlantic Monthly*, October 1940; *Spectator* 7/12/40; *Transcript* 9/26/40.
113. Gardner, 16, 17.
114. WM/Boothby; Lord Boothby, *Rebel*, 182; E. L. Spears, *Assignment to Catastrophe*, 2 vols. (New York, 1955), I, *Prelude to Dunkirk*, 38–39.
115. WM/MacDonald.
116. ChP 2/332.
117. CAB 27/624.
118. Hansard 11/18/38.
119. PrP 3/2/39.
120. PrP 1/358; Baruch Papers.
121. Nicolson, I, 398; ChP 2/360.
122. Nicolson, I, 398–399; *British Weekly* 4/27/39; Feiling, 386.
123. Feiling, 406; Nicolson, I, 399.
124. DGFP series D, vol. VI, no. 169; WM/R. A. Butler 12/5/80.
125. N. Chamberlain Papers.
126. Hansard 4/13/39.
127. Hansard 4/13/39.
128. Churchill, *Storm*, 355; *Frankfurter Zeitung*, 4/29/39.
129. ChP 2/322.
130. Churchill, *Storm*, 353.
131. *Daily Telegraph* 4/28/39; Hansard 4/27/39.
132. WSC V, 1065–1066; N. Chamberlain Papers.
133. *NYT* 5/23/39; Ironside Papers.
134. ChP 2/350, 8/264.
135. WSC V, 1068, 1080; WM/Butler.
136. WSC V, 1080, 1082, 1084.
137. ChP 2/371, 2/364, 8/628.
138. Viscount Templewood, *Nine Troubled Years* (London, 1954), 378; ChP 2/363.
139. Foreign Office Papers 371/22974.
140. Camrose Papers; Nicolson, I, 6/30/39.
141. Camrose Papers.
142. WSC V, 1086; N. Chamberlain Papers.

143. ChP 2/360, 2/343.
144. ChP 8/638.
145. ChP 8/217, 8/626.
146. Winston S. Churchill, *A History of the English-Speaking Peoples,* 4 vols. (London, 1956–1958), I, 1.
147. ChP 2/302; BSCP 1/7/37.
148. ChP 1/325.
149. ChP 8/596, 8/597.
150. ChP 8/626.
151. WM/Hamblin; WM/Kathleen Hill, 11/4/80.
152. ChP 8/625.
153. Isaiah Berlin, *Mr. Churchill in 1940* (Boston, 1964), 9.
154. WM/A. J. P. Taylor.
155. ChP 8/626.
156. ChP 8/626.
157. ChP 8/626.
158. ChP 8/626.
159. N. Chamberlain Papers.
160. ChP 2/358.
161. Air Ministry Papers 19/26, 19/29.
162. *Yorkshire Post* 6/28/39; Hansard (Lords) 6/11/39.
163. ChP 2/359; Nicolson, I, 403.
164. Walter Lippmann notes, Lippmann Papers, as cited in WSC V, 1074–1075.

Surge

1. Ironside Papers.
2. Ironside Papers.
3. PrP 1/332.
4. Ironside Papers.
5. Hansard 4/3/39.
6. *Daily Telegraph* 5/4/39.
7. Hansard 4/3/39.
8. *Sunday Express* 12/5/30; *Times* 1/21/27.
9. Hansard 4/3/39.
10. Keith Feiling, *The Life of Neville Chamberlain* (London, 1946), 603; Hansard 4/13/39.
11. DBFP series 5, vol. II, no. 1222, 623–624; Ivan Maisky, *The Origins of the Second World War,* broadcast talk, 1961, cited in Martin Gilbert and Richard Gott, *The Appeasers* (Boston, 1963), 31.
12. DBFP series 5, vol. II, no. 1221; DBFP series 5, vol. IV, no. 433; Hansard 3/23/39; WM/Lord Boothby, 10/16/80; Lord Boothby, *I Fight to Live* (London, 1947), 189.
13. Harold Nicolson, *Diaries and Letters, 1930–1962,* edited by Nigel Nicolson, 3 vols. (London, 1966), I, 394.
14. Nicolson, I, 391.
15. N. Chamberlain Papers.
16. Harold Macmillan, *Winds of Change* (London, 1966), 542.
17. Thomas Jones, *A Diary with Letters, 1931–1950* (Oxford, 1954), 418–419.
18. Hansard 4/13/39.
19. *Times* 4/16/39.
20. David Dilks, ed., *The Diaries of Sir Alexander Cadogan O.M. 1938–1945* (New York, 1972), 4/19/39; Lord Halifax, *Fullness of Days* (London, 1957), 206–207; DBFP series 3, vol. V, nos. 228, 229.
21. DBFP series 3, vol. I, no. 107.
22. WM/Harold Macmillan, 12/4/80; Macmillan, 542; Winston S. Churchill, *The Gathering Storm* (Boston, 1948), 365.
23. Jones, 418; *Le Monde* 3/28/39.
24. Dilks, ed., 175; CAB 23/98.
25. Jones, 210; CAB 27/624, 27/627.
26. CAB 27/624, 27/627.
27. Dilks, ed., 180; WM/Duncan Sandys, 11/7/80.
28. Churchill, *Storm,* 366.
29. Robert Coulondre, *De Staline à Hitler: Souvenirs de deux ambassades, 1936–1939* (Paris, 1950), 270; Georges Bonnet, *De Munich à la guerre* (Paris, 1967), 184.
30. Telford Taylor, *Munich: The Price of Peace* (New York, 1979), 975; William L. Shirer, *The Collapse of the Third Republic* (New York, 1969), 428; Churchill, *Storm,* 366, 367; *Frankfurter Zeitung* 5/7/39.
31. Nicolson, I, 401; Churchill, *Storm,* 366.
32. *Daily Telegraph* 5/4/39.
33. Camrose Papers.
34. William L. Shirer, *The Rise and Fall of the Third Reich: A History of Nazi Germany* (New York, 1960), 481.
35. Churchill, *Storm,* 371, 373–374; Hansard 5/19/39; Feiling, 603.
36. Feiling, 603; ChP 2/332.
37. Hansard 5/19/39.
38. Hansard 5/19/39.
39. *Observer* 7/22/39.
40. Richard M. Watt, *Bitter Glory: Poland and Its Fate 1918–1939* (New York, 1974), 389–390; DBFP series 3, vol. VI, nos. 104–107; DGFP series D, vol. V, no. 13; Dilks, ed., 163–164; CAB 27/624.
41. Józef Beck, *Dernier Rapport: politique polonaise 1926–1939* (Neuchatel, 1951), 187–189; DBFP series 3, vol. IV, no. 518.
42. DGFP series D, vol. IV, no. 518.
43. DBFP series 3, vol. V, no. 163; vol. VI, no. 16.
44. *NYT* 4/29/39; Shirer, *Rise and Fall,* 455, 471.
45. NCA, VI, 916–928.
46. N. Chamberlain Papers; DGFP series D, vol. VII, no. 417.

47. DGFP series D, vol. IV, no. 513; vol. VII, no. 307, ND TC-73.
48. ChP 2/360.
49. ChP 2/367.
50. ChP 9/137.
51. ChP 4/19; *Yorkshire Post* 6/28/39; WSCHCP 6141–6142.
52. N. Chamberlain Papers.
53. DBFP series 3, vol. VI, nos. 289, 197, 198.
54. DBFP series 3, vol. VI, no. 212; Hansard 7/10/39.
55. N. Chamberlain Papers.
56. DBFP series 3, vol. VI, nos. 176, 222, 327; Gilbert and Gott, 256.
57. WM/Macmillan; Macmillan 542; DBFP series 3, vol. VI, no. 659.
58. N. Chamberlain papers.
59. *Times* 6/13/39; Churchill, *Storm*, 389; Nicolson, I, 404.
60. Churchill, *Storm*, 387–388.
61. DDF-2e-II, III, IV, V; Earl of Avon, *Facing the Dictators* (Boston, 1962), 547–548.
62. *Observer* 7/22/39.
63. WM/Boothby.
64. Templewood Papers; Churchill, *Storm*, 363.
65. *Pravda* 6/16/39; Churchill, *Storm*, 390, 365, 368.
66. Telford Taylor, 976; Dilks, ed., 189.
67. WM/Macmillan; Macmillan, 542.
68. Churchill, *Storm*, 363; Boothby, *I Fight to Live*, 189.
69. Shirer, *Collapse*, 428fn.
70. WM/Walter Lippmann, 10/10/64; "The Reminiscences of Walter Lippmann," 191–193, in Oral History Collection, Yale University Walter Lippmann Collection; Shirer, *Collapse*, 426.
71. *Le Livre Jaune Français. Documents diplomatiques, 1939–1940*, No. 120, 153–155.
72. Churchill, *Storm*, 367–370; DGFP series D, vol. VI, nos. 616–617.
73. Churchill, *Storm*, 393–394.
74. DGFP series D, vol. VI, no. 429.
75. ND 1526-PS, 084-PS, 288-P; *Nazi-Soviet Relations, 1939–1941. Documents from the Archives of the German Foreign Office* (Washington, 1948), 5–7, 8–9.
76. Shirer, *Rise and Fall*, 503.
77. DGFP series D, vol. VI, nos. 1033–1035.
78. Shirer, *Rise and Fall*, 673; DBFP, Appendix V, 763.
79. Shirer, *Collapse*, 454, 455–456; DBFP series 3, Appendix II, nos. 558–614; *Événements*, I, 39ff.
80. Shirer, *Collapse*, 454–456.
81. Shirer, *Rise and Fall*, 714.
82. Hansard 4/3/39.
83. DBFP series 3, vol. V, Appendix I (i); vol. VI, nos. 458, 460.
84. DBFP series 3, vol. VI, no. 461.
85. DBFP series 3, vol. VI, no. 585.
86. Shirer, *Collapse*, 451.
87. Several of the author's interviewees have cited WSC's quip about weekends.
88. Shirer, *Collapse*, 451–455.
89. DGFP series D, vol. VII, nos. 49, 58–59, nn. 13, 48.
90. Shirer, *Collapse*, 452.
91. ND 1618–PS; DGFP series D, vol. II, nos. 67–68.
92. DGFP series D, vol. VII, no. 75.
93. DGFP series D, vol. VII, no. 105.
94. Shirer, *Collapse*, 463; DGFP series D, vol. VII, no. 113.
95. DGFP series D, vol. VII, no. 125.
96. Shirer, *Collapse*, 465.
97. Churchill, *Storm*, 391, 380.
98. Bonnet, 301–302; General Maurice Gustave Gamelin, *Servir*, 3 vols. (Paris, 1946), I, 23–24.
99. DBFP series 3, no. 212; *Événements*, II (Docs.), 276–278; Bonnet, 305–308.
100. N. Chamberlain Papers.
101. Selborne Papers; Nicolson, I, 8/1/39; WSC V, 1095.
102. Nicolson, I, 407.
103. Hansard 8/2/39.
104. Hansard 8/2/39.
105. Nicolson, I, 407–408.
106. ChP 9/137.
107. ChP 9/137.
108. Jones, 419.
109. *Observer* 7/22/39.
110. DGFP series D, vol. VII, nos. 62–64.
111. ChP 2/365.
112. BSCP 8/14/39.
113. BSCP; E. L. Spears, *Assignment to Catastrophe*, 2 vols. (New York, 1955), I, 5.
114. Alistair Horne, *To Lose a Battle* (Boston, 1969), 29.
115. Spears, I, 9.
116. Spears, I, 10.
117. ChP 2/371.
118. ChP 2/371.
119. See Churchill, *Storm*, 474–475; ChP 2/371.
120. Shirer, *Collapse*, 186.
121. Spears, I, 9; Horne, 18; Churchill, *Storm*, 474; Simone de Beauvoir, *The Prime of Life*, trans. Peter Green (New York, 1962), 33.
122. Churchill, *Storm*, 474; Horne, 72.
123. Winston S. Churchill, *Their Finest Hour* (Boston, 1949), 36–37.
124. *News of the World* 4/24/38.
125. B. H. Liddell Hart, *The Memoirs of Cap-*

tain Liddell Hart, 2 vols. (London, 1965), I, 373.

126. Spears, I, 7.
127. WM/Lady Soames, 10/9/80; Consuelo Balsan, *The Glitter and the Gold* (New York, 1952), 298.
128. Maze Papers, Maze diary.
129. Churchill, *Storm,* 400; Nicolson, I, 411; Brian Gardner, *Churchill in Power: As Seen by His Contemporaries* (Boston, 1940), 18.
130. Churchill, *Storm,* 400–401.
131. Churchill, *Storm,* 401.
132. Churchill, *Storm,* 401; Mary Soames, *Clementine Churchill: The Biography of a Marriage* (Boston, 1979), 369.
133. Nicolson, I, 411; ChP 1/344.
134. Churchill, *Storm,* 396; CV V/3, 1597; Nicolson, I, 413; Norwich Papers.
135. WSC V, 1105; Norwich Papers, Duff Cooper diary.
136. Ironside Papers.
137. ChP 2/361.
138. Churchill, *Storm,* 396.
139. The British Blue Book, 98–104; DGFP series D, vol. VII, nos. 210–219; Churchill, *Storm,* 396–397.
140. Shirer, *Rise and Fall,* 564.
141. Shirer, *Rise and Fall,* 564; Churchill, *Storm,* 442–443.
142. C. Roberts, *The Nazi Claim to Colonies,* Introduction by Alfred Duff Cooper (London, 1939).
143. DBFP series 3, vol. VII, no. 309.
144. DBFP series 3, vol. VII, no. 367.
145. The British Blue Book, 120–123.
146. Shirer, *Rise and Fall,* 479–480.
147. Winston S. Churchill, *A History of the English-Speaking Peoples,* 4 vols. (London, 1956–1958), I, 58–59.
148. R. J. Minney, *The Private Papers of Hore-Belisha* (London, 1960), 220.
149. Churchill, *English-Speaking Peoples,* II, 125–126.
150. DBFP series 3, vol. VII, no. 3.
151. DBFP series 3, vol. VII, no. 349, note 7; no. 402, note 3; nos. 406, 411.
152. ChP 8/626.
153. Churchill, *English-Speaking Peoples,* III, 306–308.
154. DBFP series 3, vol. VII, nos. 420, 426, 455.
155. DBFP series 3, vol. VII, no. 455.
156. DBFP series 3, vol. VII, no. 508.
157. DBFP series 3, vol. VII, no. 508; Sir Nevile Henderson, *Failure of a Mission: Berlin 1937–1939* (New York, 1940), 266.
158. DBFP series 3, vol. VII, no. 519.
159. DBFP series 3, vol. VII, nos. 501, 493; Henderson, 267–268.
160. DBFP series 3, vol. VII, nos. 523, 526.
161. Foreign Relations of the U.S., Kennedy to Hull, 8/30/39; Minney, 223–224; DBFP series 3, vol. VII, no. 539.
162. ND 2751-PS.
163. Henderson, 270.
164. Paul Schmidt, *Statist auf diplomatischer Buehne* (Bonn, 1949), 460; DBFP series 3, vol. VII, no. 589.
165. DGFP series D, vol. VII, no. 405.
166. ChP 2/364.
167. ChP 8/626, 8/624.
168. ChP 8/624.
169. Ironside Papers.
170. *Daily Mirror* 7/13/39; Churchill, *Storm,* 405.
171. Churchill, *Storm,* 405; Martin Gilbert, *Winston Churchill: The Wilderness Years* (London, 1981), 262.
172. Hansard, 9/1/39.
173. Shirer, *Rise and Fall,* 602.
174. Shirer, *Rise and Fall,* 500; Birger Dahlerus, *The Last Attempt* (London, 1947), 120; TMWC IX, 471.
175. DBFP series 3, vol. VII, no. 644.
176. DGFP series D, vol. VII, nos. 509–510; Josiah Wedgewood, *Memoirs of a Fighting Life* (London, 1941), 225.
177. Gardner, 17–18.
178. Command Paper 6144.
179. DGFP series D, vol. VII, nos. 664, 639, 648.
180. ChP 4/96; Churchill, *Storm,* 406.
181. WM/Kathleen Hill, 11/4/80.
182. Camrose Papers; Hankey Papers.
183. Minney, 225.
184. Minney, 225, 226.
185. DBFP series 3, vol. VII, no. 731, 713.
186. Spears, I, 18.
187. Churchill, *Storm,* 406; Spears, I, 20.
188. Spears, I, 20; Hansard 9/2/39.
189. Hugh Dalton, *Memoirs, 1931–1945: The Fateful Years* (London, 1957), 264–265; Alfred Duff Cooper, *Old Men Forget* (London, 1953), 259; Spears, I, 21; Churchill, *Storm,* 406; L. S. Amery, *My Political Life,* 3 vols. (London, 1953), III, 324; Hansard 9/2/33.
190. Amery, III, 324; Ivone Kirkpatrick, *The Inner Circle* (London, 1959), 143–144; Spears, I, 22; Halifax, 210.
191. DBFP series 3, vol. VII, no. 734.
192. DBFP series 3, vol. VII, no. 751.
193. DGFP series D, vol. VII, no. 558.
194. DBFP series 3, vol. VII, nos. 740, 743.
195. Lady Diana Cooper, *The Light of Common Day* (Boston, 1959), 257; WM/Lady Diana Cooper, 10/20/80.

196. WM/Lady Diana Cooper; Duff Cooper, 259.
197. Duff Cooper, 259; Churchill, *Storm*, 407; Norwich Papers.
198. Norwich Papers.
199. Norwich Papers.
200. Norwich Papers.
201. ChP 4/96; Churchill, *Storm*, 407.
202. ChP 4/96; Churchill, *Storm*, 407.
203. Minney, 226; *Sunday Times* 9/6/64; Robert Rhodes James, *Churchill: A Study in Failure, 1900–1939* (London, 1970), 379; Amery, III, 324.
204. *Sunday Times* 9/6/64; Minney, 227.
205. DBFP series 3, vol. VII, no. 739.
206. DBFP series 3, vol. VII, no. 740.
207. *Sunday Times* 9/6/64; Bonnet, 364.
208. Gilbert and Gott, 308; DBFP series 3, vol. VII, no. 741.
209. Kirkpatrick, 143–144.
210. *Sunday Times* 9/6/64; Minney, 227; DBFP series 3, vol. VII, no. 746.
211. *Sunday Times* 9/6/64.
212. *Sunday Times* 9/6/64.
213. Norwich Papers, Duff Cooper diary; ChP 8/639.
214. Kirkpatrick, 144; Bonnet, 363; Count Galeazzo Ciano, *The Ciano Diaries, 1939–1943*, edited by Hugh Wilson (London, 1946), 137.
215. Dahlerus, 109.
216. ChP 2/363; Churchill, *Storm*, 408; W. H. Thompson, *Sixty Minutes with Winston Churchill* (London, 1953).
217. W. H. Thompson; Martia Russell Papers; Churchill, *Storm*, 408.
218. Hansard 9/3/39; Churchill, *Storm*, 409.
219. Hansard 9/3/39.
220. Hansard 9/3/39.
221. Amery Papers, Amery Diary.
222. Churchill, *Storm*, 409; Gilbert, *Wilderness*, 267.
223. Churchill, *Storm*, 419–420; Laurence Thompson, *1940* (New York, 1966), 31.
224. CAB 65/1; Churchill, *Storm*, 442; Minney, 228–230; WM/Sir Ian Jacob, 11/1/80; Jacob to Martin Gilbert, 7/1/82.
225. WM/Lady Diana Cooper.

Cataclysm

1. WM/Kathleen Hill, 11/4/80; Winston S. Churchill, *The Gathering Storm* (Boston, 1948), 409–410.
2. Churchill, *Storm*, 410; CAB 100/1; Admiral of the Fleet Lord Fraser of North Cape, "Churchill and the Navy," in Sir James Marchant, ed., *Winston Spencer Churchill: Servant of Crown and Commonwealth* (London, 1954), 78–79; John Higham recollections in conversation with Martin Gilbert, 3/1/82.
3. Hansard 9/6/39; Churchill, *Storm*, 331; CAB 16/11.
4. Fraser, in Marchant, 81.
5. ChP 4/123.
6. Sir John Colville, *The Churchillians* (London, 1981), 88.
7. T. R. Fehrenbach, *F.D.R.'s Undeclared War 1939–1941* (New York, 1967).
8. Francis L. Loewenheim, Harold D. Langley, and Manfred Jonas, eds., *Roosevelt and Churchill: Their Secret Wartime Correspondence* (New York, 1975), 5.
9. *New York Sun* 9/2/39; *NYT* 8/20/14, 9/4/39.
10. Fehrenbach, 42–43.
11. Churchill, *Storm*, 440–441.
12. Admiralty Papers 199/1928; ChP 4/123.
13. Churchill, *Storm*, 421; WM/Lady Soames, 10/9/80; Mary Soames, *Clementine Churchill: The Biography of a Marriage* (Boston, 1979), 372.
14. Diana Cooper, *Trumpet from the Steep* (London, 1960), 37.
15. Pim Papers; Arthur Marder, *From the Dardanelles to Oran* (London, 1974), 29; Fraser, in Marchant, 87.
16. Pim Papers.
17. Pim Papers.
18. Recollections of Bernard Sendall in conversation with Martin Gilbert, 11/14/79; Shakespeare Papers.
19. Churchill, *Storm*, 411; Fraser, in Marchant, 79–80; Arthur Marder, "Winston Is Back: Churchill at the Admiralty," *English Historical Review*, Supplement 5 (Aberdeen, 1972), 2; Marder, *Dardanelles*, 106–107.
20. Turner Catledge, *My Life and the Times* (New York, 1971), 157.
21. Marder, *English Historical Review*, 2; Admiralty Papers 205/2.
22. Charles Eade, ed., *Churchill by His Contemporaries* (New York, 1954), 121; Fraser, in Marchant, 78–80.
23. Führer's Conferences on Naval Affairs, 1939 (mimeographed by British Admiralty, London, 1947), 13–14.
24. DBFP series 3, vol. VII, no. 283.
25. ND C-189, C-190.
26. Churchill, *Storm*, 163–164.
27. DBFP series 3, vol. VIII, no. 283.
28. Hansard 9/26/39.
29. Hansard 9/26/39.
30. WSCHCS 6160–6164 (10/1/39).
31. Winston S. Churchill, *The World Crisis*, 5

vols. and *The Aftermath* (New York, 1923–1931), II, 391.
32. Churchill, *Storm*, 429.
33. Chiefs of Staff, 17 of 1939; CAB 79/1; Stephen Roskill, *The War at Sea*, 3 vols. (London, 1954), I, 78–80.
34. Churchill, *Storm*, 433–444.
35. CAB 65/1; Admiralty Papers 205/2.
36. William L. Shirer, *The Rise and Fall of the Third Reich: A History of Nazi Germany* (New York, 1960), 646.
37. Churchill, *Storm*, 433.
38. Brian Gardner, *Churchill in Power: As Seen by His Contemporaries* (Boston, 1970), 27; Hansard 11/8/39; CAB 65/1.
39. William L. Shirer, *Berlin Diary* (New York, 1941), 237.
40. WM/Lady Soames; Soames, 372.
41. Churchill, *Storm*, 528, 527; Soames, 374; Templewood Papers.
42. Marder, *English Historical Review*, 2; J. H. Godfrey, *Naval Memoirs of Admiral J. H. Godfrey* (privately printed, 1964–1965), I, vi, 35.
43. Marder, *English Historical Review*, 9.
44. ChP 19/3; Churchill, *Storm*, 465.
45. ChP 19/3; Churchill, *Storm*, 465.
46. Captain J. S. S. Litchfield to the author; Marder, *English Historical Review*, 3; Churchill, *Storm*, 414.
47. Hansard 12/6/39; Churchill, *Storm*, 414, 505–508, 706–711; Marder, *English Historical Review*, 10, 28; CAB 65/6.
48. Admiralty Papers 199/1928; Churchill, *Storm*, 413–414.
49. Admiralty Papers 205/5, 199/19.
50. Admiralty Papers 199/1928, 205/5; Marder, *English Historical Review*, 31–38; WSC VI, 26–27, 37–38.
51. Fraser, in Marchant, 78.
52. Fraser, in Marchant, 78; ChP 19/3, 25/4; CAB 16/132; Weir Papers.
53. S. W. Roskill, "Marder, Churchill, and the Admiralty 1932–42," RUSI *Journal*, December 1972.
54. Admiralty Papers 205/6.
55. Vice-Admiral R. D. Oliver to the author; Marder, *English Historical Review*, 22.
56. Donald McLachan, "Naval Intelligence in the Second World War," RUSI *Journal*, 112, August 1967, 244.
57. CAB 66/1; Admiralty papers 199/1928.
58. Charles Stuart, ed., *The Reith Diaries* (London, 1975), 249; CAB 132/33.
59. B. H. Liddell Hart, *The Memoirs of Captain Liddell Hart*, 2 vols. (London, 1965), II, 27.
60. Charles de Gaulle, *Le fil de l'épée* (Paris, 1932).
61. Robert Wernick, *Blitzkrieg* (New York, 1976), 24.
62. Churchill, *Storm*, 450, 442.
63. Churchill, *Storm*, 451.
64. CAB 61/11.
65. CAB 65/1; Command Paper 6144 (Treaty Series No. 58) 1939.
66. B. H. Liddell Hart, *History of the Second World War* (New York, 1971), 18; William L. Shirer, *The Collapse of the Third Republic* (New York, 1969), 519; Churchill, *Storm*, 558.
67. Churchill, *Storm*, 451; CAB 83/3, 92/111; WSC VI, 15.
68. Hoare Diary, Templewood Papers; CAB 66/1; ChP 4/131.
69. CAB 65/1, 100/1; L. S. Amery, *My Political Life*, 3 vols. (London, 1953), III, 330; E. L. Spears, *Assignment to Catastrophe*, 2 vols. (New York, 1955), I 31–32; Hugh Dalton, *Memoirs, 1931–1945: The Fateful Years* (London, 1957), 274.
70. R. J. Minney, *The Private Papers of Hore-Belisha* (London, 1960), 251; Iain Macleod, *Neville Chamberlain* (New York, 1962), 286.
71. Hansard 9/6/39; Spears, I, 29; Dalton, 274, 277.
72. Sir Keith Feiling, *The Life of Neville Chamberlain* (London, 1946), 440.
73. Churchill, *Storm*, 574–575.
74. Dalton, 292; L. F. Ellis, *The War in France and Flanders* (London, 1953), 30–31; Viscount Templewood, *Nine Troubled Years* (London, 1954), 428.
75. General Maurice Gustave Gamelin, *Servir*, 3 vols. (Paris, 1947), II, 413–416, 424–425; Sir Lewis B. Namier, *Diplomatic Prelude* (London, 1948), 459–460.
76. Gamelin, I, 23–24; *Événements*, II, 276–278.
77. Gamelin, I, 24.
78. Shirer, *Rise and Fall*, 840.
79. TMWC XI, 350; TMWC X, 519.
80. TWC XII, 1086.
81. Franz Halder diary, 9/7/39.
82. Jacques Minart, *P.C. Vincennes Secteur 4*, 2 vols. (Paris, 1945), I, 19–20; Gamelin, III, 60–61, 55.
83. Général André Beaufre, *Le Drame de 1940* (Paris, 1965), 189; Général Charles de Gaulle, *Mémoires de Guerre*, 3 vols. (Paris, 1954), I, 22.
84. TMWC I, 257.
85. Shirer, *Rise and Fall*, 744.
86. A. J. P. Taylor, *The Origins of the Second World War* (New York, 1962), 228 fn. 4.
87. Virginia Cowles, *Winston Churchill: The Era and the Man* (New York, 1953), 313.

88. WSCHCS 6160–6164 (10/1/39; verse form added).
89. WSCHCS 6160–6164.
90. Sir John Colville, *The Fringes of Power: 10 Downing Street Diaries 1939–1955* (New York, 1985), 29; Templewood Papers; Chamberlain Papers.
91. Shirer, *Berlin Diary,* 229; *Time* 10/16/39.
92. WSCHCS 6171–6175 (11/12/39).
93. WSCHCS 6171–6175 (11/12/39).
94. Colville, *Fringes,* 50; Harold Nicolson, *Diaries and Letters, 1930–1962,* edited by Nigel Nicolson, 3 vols. (London, 1966), II, 59.
95. WSCHCS 6183–6186 (1/20/40; verse form added).
96. Hoare diary, Templewood Papers; ChP 23/3.
97. CAB 11/39; Général Paul-Emile Tournoux, "Les origines de la ligne Maginot," *Revue d'Histoire de la Deuxième Mondiale,* No. 33, January 1959, 14.
98. WSCHCS 6183–6186 (1/20/40).
99. Churchill, *Storm,* 541; Liddell Hart, *Second World War,* 45.
100. Kay Halle, *The Irrepressible Churchill: A Treasury of Winston Churchill's Wit* (New York, 1967), 153.
101. WSCHCS 6171–6175 (11/12/39).
102. B. Baxter, *Men, Martyrs, and Mountebanks* (London, 1940), 251; Cowles, 312–313.
103. Nicolson, II, 34–35, 37, 38.
104. Laurence Thompson, *1940* (New York 1966), 32.
105. WSCHCS 6171–6175 (11/12/39); Colville, *Fringes,* 108; N. Chamberlain Papers, diary.
106. Cowles, 311; Gardner, 21.
107. Churchill, *Storm,* 495.
108. Churchill, *Storm,* 494–495.
109. Soames, 374; Fraser, in Marchant, 81.
110. Soames, 374; Diana Cooper, 37; WM/Lady Soames; WM/Lady Diana Cooper.
111. Thompson, 24.
112. *Times* 10/5/39; ChP 1/355.
113. WM/Lady Soames.
114. Thompson, 17.
115. WM/Lady Soames.
116. Feiling, 424; Churchill, *Storm,* 549; Fehrenbach, 45.
117. T. Harrison and C. Madge, eds., *War Begins at Home* (London, 1940), 39; Margery Allingham, *The Oaken Heart* (London, 1941), 84; Thompson, 14.
118. *Time* 1/22/40.
119. Colville, *Fringes,* 116; Thompson, 15; ChP 19/2.
120. *Times* 12/26/39.
121. Thompson, 13–28 *passim.*
122. Thompson, 13–28 *passim.*
123. Thompson, 13–28 *passim.*
124. Thompson, 16.
125. Telford Taylor, *The Breaking Wave: The Second World War in the Summer of 1940* (New York, 1967), 39.
126. CAB 65/3.
127. ChP 19/2.
128. ND L-52; DGFP series D, vol. VIII, no. 224.
129. WM/William L. Shirer, 7/20/71; Emmanuel Beau de Loménie, *La Mort de la Troisième République* (Paris, 1951), 128–129.
130. Foreign Relations of the U.S., 1940, I, 107.
131. Churchill, *Storm,* 479.
132. *Time* 9/18/39; Shirer, *Berlin Diary,* 9/26/39.
133. Alphonse Goutard, *1940: La Guerre des Occasions Perdus* (Paris, 1956), 234.
134. Shirer, *Collapse,* 535–536.
135. Goutard, 132–133.
136. CAB 83/3; Churchill, *Storm,* 558–559.
137. *Événements,* III, 690, Beaufre, 232; Shirer, *Collapse,* 620–621.
138. Shirer, *Collapse,* 183–187.
139. *Time* 12/18/39.
140. Ronald Steel, *Walter Lippmann and the American Century* (Boston, 1980), 381.
141. Goutard, 131.
142. Goutard, 131; *Événements,* II, 281–282; Shirer, *Collapse,* 533–534.
143. CAB 65/1.
144. CAB 65/1; ChP 19/3; Eade, ed., 122.
145. CAB 65/1; ChP 19/3; Churchill, *Storm,* 554.
146. Churchill, *Storm,* 561–562.
147. Sir Philip Vian, *Action This Day: A War Memoir* (London, 1960), 26.
148. Marder, *English Historical Review,* 31 fn.
149. Churchill, *Storm,* 561–562; Nicolson, II, 59.
150. Churchill, *Storm,* 562, 564.
151. Churchill, *Storm,* 564; Vian, 26; ChP 19/5.
152. WSC VI, 154.
153. Churchill, *Storm,* 563; Marder, *English Historical Review,* 30; Thompson, 51.
154. Nicolson, II, 59.
155. ChP 9/143.
156. ChP 9/143.
157. Templewood Papers; ChP 8/658.
158. Thompson.
159. ND 004-PS; DGFP series D, vol. VIII, no. 663–33; ND C-63; NCA, Suppl. B, 1543–47.
160. Churchill, *Storm,* 564; ND C-66.
161. ND CD-170, C-166; FCNA, 1939, 27, 51.
162. FCNA, 1939, 51, 53–57; Jodl diary,

12/13/39; Halder diary, 12/14/39; Liddell Hart, *Second World War*, 54–55.
163. Shirer, *Berlin Diary*, 307.
164. Liddell Hart, *Second World War*, 56; ND 063-C; DGFP series D, vol. VIII, no. 644.
165. Thompson, 56; Colville, *Fringes*, 40, 76.
166. Churchill, *Storm*, 571–581; CAB 66/5, 65/11; Admiralty Papers 1/10795; CAB 65/12; Chief of Staff 64 (40); CAB 79/85; CAB 65/12.
167. John Elting and the editors of Time-Life Books, *Battles for Scandinavia* (Chicago, 1981), 47.
168. Churchill, *Storm*, 591–592.
169. Churchill, *Storm*, 582; CAB 65/12; Liddell Hart, *Second World War*, 58.
170. Admiralty Papers 205/2.
171. Admiralty Papers 116/4240; CAB 65/12.
172. Colville, *Fringes*, 94–95; CAB 65/6.
173. Churchill, *Storm*, 583, 582; Colville, *Fringes*, 95.
174. NCA, Supplement B, 1543–477; Liddell Hart, *Second World War*, 58.
175. *Times* 4/6/40.
176. Hansard 4/ 11/40.
177. Liddell Hart, *Second World War*, 52; Marder, *English Historical Review*, 55.
178. Roskill, *War at Sea*, I, 179; CAB 65/11; Sir Eric Seal's letter to the author, 9/8/71; Marder, *English Historical Review*, 57.
179. Gamelin, III, 866; Paul Baudouin, *The Private Diaries of Paul Baudouin* (London, 1953), 41.
180. Liddell Hart, *Second World War*, 62; Churchill, *Storm*, 624–627.
181. Shirer, *Berlin Diary*, 314; Admiralty Papers 116/4471; Churchill, *Storm*, 601; Nicoson, II, 70.
182. Colville, *Fringes*, 101; *The Listener* 5/6/40.
183. CAB 65/6; Colville, *Fringes*, 90; Thompson, 57; *Daily Mail* 4/11/40.
184. Shirer, *Berlin Diary;* Liddell Hart, *Second World War*, 59.
185. Jodl diary in Shirer, *Rise and Fall*, 709.
186. Churchill, *Storm*, 619; Shirer, *Berlin Diary*, 315, 320.
187. CAB 65/12, 21/1388; Churchill, *Storm*, 614.
188. Churchill, *Storm*, 624, 626–627.
189. Churchill, *Storm*, 623.
190. Hansard 5/8/40.
191. Shirer, *Collapse*, 569; Nicolson, II, 74.
192. CAB 99/3; Shirer, *Berlin Diary*, 324–326; Nicolson, II, 74–75.
193. Hansard 3/3/40; Seal Papers.
194. *Événements*, II, 359–360, 361–363.
195. Baudouin, 25.
196. WM/Sir William Deakin, 10/5/80; F. W. Deakin, "Churchill The Historian," *Schweizer Monatshefte* Nr. 4 (Zurich, 1970).
197. F. W. Deakin.
198. *Times* 4/4/40; *Daily Mail* 4/4/40; ChP 2/392, 2/395.
199. Nicolson, II, 74–75.
200. Nicolson, II, 74–75; ChP 4/131; Thompson, 70.
201. Robert Rhodes James, *Chips, The Diaries of Sir Henry Channon* (London, 1967), 243; Col. Roderick Macleod and Denis Kelly, eds., *The Ironside Diaries 1937–1940* (London, 1962), 293.
202. ChP 3/131, 2/393.
203. ChP 19/2.
204. ChP 1/99/1929; CAB 79/4.
205. Shirer, *Rise and Fall*, 944; WM/William L. Shirer, 7/20/80.
206. N. Chamberlain Papers, diary.
207. *Evening Standard* 5/6/40; Halifax Papers, diary.
208. Hansard 5/7/40.
209. Nicolson, II, 76; Hansard 5/7/40; Thompson, 80.
210. Nicolson, II, 76; Hansard 5/7/40.
211. Hansard 5/7/40; Nicolson, II, 77.
212. Nicolson, II, 77.
213. Hansard 5/7/40 (italics added).
214. Churchill, *Storm*, 659; Nicolson, II, 77; Rhodes James, *Chips*, 243, 245.
215. Henri de Kerillis, *Français, voici la vérité* (New York, 1942), 247; Clare Luce, *Europe in the Spring* (New York, 1940), 246, 126–127.
216. Shirer, *Rise and Fall*, 716.
217. Dalton, 304–305.
218. *Daily Herald* 5/8/40.
219. WM/Malcolm MacDonald, 11/6/80; Dalton, 305–306; Hansard 5/8/40.
220. Thompson, 82–83.
221. Nicolson, II, 78; Hansard 5/8/40.
222. Churchill, *Storm*, 659.
223. F. Owen, *Tempestuous Journey* (London, 1954), 748.
224. Hansard 5/8/40 (italics added).
225. WM/Macmillan; Harold Macmillan, *The Blast of War 1939–1945* (London, 1967), 74.
226. Dalton, 306; Rhodes James, *Chips*, 246; WM/R. A. Butler, 12/5/80.
227. Hansard 5/8/40; Rhodes James, *Chips*, 246.
228. Rhodes James, *Chips*, 246; John Peck, "Bull and Benediction," unpublished typescript, 96–97 (published in WSC VI, 298–299).
229. Hansard 5/8/40.
230. Alfred Duff Cooper, *Old Men Forget* (New York, 1954), 279.
231. Nicolson, II, 79–80; Dalton, 306.
232. Churchill, *Storm*, 661.

233. Adam Sykes and Iain Sproat, eds. *The Wit of Sir Winston* (London, 1965), 75; Colville, *Fringes*, 89.
234. Churchill, *Storm*, 661.
235. Thompson, 82, 83.
236. Dalton, 310.
237. Earl of Avon, *The Reckoning* (London, 1965), 96.
238. Dalton, 308; Thompson, 88.
239. Thompson, 89.
240. Thompson, 78–80; Dalton, 306–307, 309.
241. Avon, *Reckoning*, 96–97.
242. WM/Macmillan; Macmillan, *Blast*, 72; Amery, III, 361.
243. ChP 2/392.
244. Churchill, *Storm*, 661; Thompson, 91–92.
245. Churchill, *Storm*, 661–662; Thompson, 91–92.
246. Halifax Papers, diary, 5/9/40.
247. Thompson, 90; Churchill, *Storm*, 662–663.
248. Churchill, *Storm*, 662–663; WM/Viscount Head, 11/19/80.
249. Earl of Birkenhead, *Life of Lord Halifax* (London, 1965), 454.
250. David Dilks, ed., *The Diaries of Sir Alexander Cadogan O.M. 1938–1945* (New York, 1972), 280; Birkenhead, 454; Churchill, *Storm*, 662–663.
251. Rhodes James, *Chips*, 248; WM/Kathleen Hill, 11/4/80; ChP 2/413; Avon, *Reckoning*, 97; WSC VI, 305.
252. Shirer, *Rise and Fall*, 723.
253. Liddell Hart, *Second World War*, 66–67.
254. Allen Dulles, *Germany's Underground* (New York, 1947), 58–61. According to W. L. Shirer, Sas personally confirmed this account with him after the war.
255. *Événements*, IX, 2758–2760; Anatole de Monzie, *Ci-devant* (Paris, 1942), 44; Baudouin, 44–48.
256. Baudouin, 44–48.
257. Paul Reynaud, *Au Coeur de la mêlée, 1930–1945* (Paris, 1951), 412.
258. Churchill, *Storm*, 662; CAB 64/7; WSC VI, 306.
259. Templewood, 431–432; *Times*, *News Chronicle* 5/10/40; CAB 83/3.
260. Shirer, *Collapse*, 605.
261. CAB 65/7.
262. J. C. Reith, *Into the Wind* (London, 1949), 382; Halifax Papers, diary, 5/10/40.
263. Avon, *Reckoning*, 97–98; Templewood, 432; Nicolson, II, 82.
264. Churchill, *Storm*, 662; Avon, *Reckoning*, 94–98.
265. CAB 65/7; Stuart, 250; Macleod and Kelly, 303–304.
266. Dalton, 311–312.
267. CAB 65/7.
268. CAB 65/7; Avon, *Reckoning*, 98.
269. John W. Wheeler-Bennett, *King George VI, His Life and Reign* (London, 1958), 443–444.
270. Churchill, *Storm*, 665.
271. Churchill, *Storm*, 665; W. H. Thompson, *Sixty Minutes with Winston Churchill* (London, 1953), 44–45.
272. WSC VI, 311.
273. Churchill, *Storm*, 666.
274. Nicolson, II, 83–84.
275. Churchill, *Storm*, 666–667.
276. Reed Whittemore, "Churchill and the Limitations of Myth," *Yale Review*, Winter 1955; Wheeler-Bennett, *George VI*, 446.
277. John Evelyn Wrench, *Geoffrey Dawson and Our Times* (London, 1955), 415; Colville, *Fringes*, 122; WM/Sir John Colville, 10/8/80.
278. *News Chronicle* 1/1/40; Nicolson, I, 85.
279. Hansard 5/13/40 (verse form added).
280. WSCHCS 6220–6223 (5/19/40).
281. WSCHCS 6231–6238 (6/18/40).
282. ChP 4/194; Isaiah Berlin, *Mr. Churchill in 1940* (London, 1940), 26, 29.
283. Winston S. Churchill, *Their Finest Hour*, (Boston, 1949), 21–22.
284. Lord Moran, *Churchill. Taken from the Diaries of Lord Moran: The Struggle for Survival (1940–1965)* (Boston, 1966), 959.
285. Hansard 10/8/40.
286. Hansard 11/23/32.

INDEX

COPYRIGHT ACKNOWLEDGMENTS

The author is grateful to the following publishers, individuals, and companies for permission to reprint excerpts from selected material as noted below.

Quotations from the letters of Neville Chamberlain are reprinted by kind permission of the Head of Special Collections, University Library, University of Birmingham.

Quotations from the letters in the Baroness Spencer Churchill collection are reprinted by kind permission of Curtis Brown Ltd., London, on behalf of Lady Mary Soames. Copyright Mary Soames.

Quotations from the letters of Randolph Churchill are reprinted by kind permission of Curtis Brown Ltd., London, on behalf of the Estate of Randolph Churchill. Copyright the Estate of Randolph Churchill.

Winston S. Churchill from *A History of the English-Speaking Peoples*, reprinted by permission of Dodd, Mead and Co., Inc., the Canadian Publisher McClelland & Stewart, Toronto, and Cassell Publishers Ltd.

Winston S. Churchill from *The Second World War: Volume I, The Gathering Storm*. Copyright 1949 by Houghton Mifflin Company, Copyright © renewed 1976 by Lady Spencer Churchill and the Honourable Lady Sarah Audley, the Honourable Lady Soames. Reprinted by permission of Houghton Mifflin Company and Cassell Publishers Ltd.

John Colville from *The Fringes of Power: 10 Downing Street Diaries 1939–1955*. Copyright © 1985 by Hodder and Stoughton Ltd. Reprinted by permission of W. W. Norton & Company, Inc., and Hodder and Stoughton Limited.

Anthony Eden from *Facing the Dictators*. Copyright © 1962 by the Times Publishing Company, Ltd. Reprinted by permission of Houghton Mifflin Company, Macmillan London, and Times Newspapers Ltd.

Excerpt from "The Hollow Men" in *Collected Poems 1909–1962* by T. S. Eliot, copyright 1936 by Harcourt Brace Jovanovich, Inc., copyright © 1963, 1964 by T. S. Eliot. Reprinted by permission of Harcourt Brace Jovanovich, Inc., and Faber and Faber Limited.

Martin Gilbert from *Winston S. Churchill: Volume V, The Prophet of Truth 1922–1939*. Copyright © 1976 by C & T Publications, Ltd. Reprinted by permission of Houghton Mifflin Company and William Heinemann Ltd.

Martin Gilbert from *Winston S. Churchill: Volume VI, Finest Hour 1939–1941*. Copyright © 1983 by C & T Publications, Ltd. Reprinted by permission of Houghton Mifflin Company and William Heinemann Ltd.

Kay Murphy Halle from *The Irrepressible Churchill*. Reprinted by permission of the author.

Thomas Jones from *A Diary with Letters 1931–1950* (Oxford University Press, 1954). Reprinted by permission of Oxford University Press.

Harold Macmillan from *Winds of Change*. Copyright © 1966 by Thompson Newspapers Ltd. Reprinted by permission of Harper & Row Publishers, Inc. and Macmillan London.

Harold Nicolson from *Harold Nicolson: Diaries and Letters, 1930–1939*. Volume I, edited by Nigel Nicolson. *Harold Nicolson's Diaries and Letters* copyright © 1966 by William Collins Sons & Co. Ltd. Introduction and Notes to this volume copyright © 1966 Nigel Nicolson. V. Sackville-West's Letters copyright © 1966 by Sir Harold Nicolson. Reprinted with the permission of Atheneum Publishers, an imprint of Macmillan Publishing Company, and William Collins Sons & Co. Ltd.

Harold Nicolson from *The War Years, 1939–1945*. Volume II of *The Diaries and Letters of Harold Nicolson* edited by Nigel Nicolson. *Harold Nicolson's Diaries and Letters* copyright © 1967 by William Collins Sons & Co. Ltd. Introduction and Notes to this volume copyright © 1967 Nigel Nicolson. V. Sackville-West's Letters copyright © 1967 by Sir Harold Nicolson. Reprinted with the permission of Atheneum Publishers, an imprint of Macmillan Publishing Company, and William Collins Sons & Co. Ltd.

Material from the Royal Archives reproduced with the permission of the Controller of Her Majesty's Stationery Office.

Mary Soames from *Clementine Churchill: The Biography of a Marriage* copyright © Mary Soames 1979. Reproduced by permission of Curtis Brown Ltd., London, on behalf of Lady Mary Soames and Houghton Mifflin Company.

"Lambeth Walk" written by Noel Gay and Douglas Furber. Copyright © 1937 Richard Armitage Ltd. Copyright Renewed. All rights managed in the U.S. by Bibo Music Publishers (c/o The Welk Music Group, Santa Monica, CA 90401). International Copyright Secured. All Rights Reserved. Used by Permission.

"WE're Gonna Hang Out The Washing on the Siegfried Line" by Jim Kennedy and Michael Carr. © 1939 by Skidmore Music Co., Inc. for the territories of the United States and Canada. Copyright renewed. Used by permission. United Kingdom, © 1939 Francis Day & Hunter Ltd. Reproduced by permission of EMI Music Publishing Ltd., London, WC2H OLD.

CHRONOLOGY

1932

MacDonald is puppet P.M.; Tories, led by Baldwin, have power
Depression; hunger riots; Royal Navy mutiny
Roosevelt elected president of U.S.
Nazis lack majority in Reichstag
WSC researches *Marlborough* in Germany
His meeting with Hitler canceled after WSC criticizes Nazi anti-Semitism
WSC publishes *Amid These Storms*
His daughter Diana marries
Son Randolph quits Oxford for journalism

1933

Named chancellor, Hitler seizes power
Reichstag destroyed by fire
British leaders begin visits to Hitler; see Germany as shield against U.S.S.R.
Toynbee, Lippmann also among his admirers
British policy: unilateral disarmament
Eden enthusiastically supports it
WSC publishes first *Marlborough* volume
He builds intelligence network in London and Berlin
Cites German rearmament in Parliament, is labeled "scaremonger"

1934

Hindenburg dies; Hitler becomes Führer, spends ten billion pounds yearly on arms
The Times kills stories that might offend him
WSC's first major speech on air defense
Baldwin pledges RAF will never be No. 2
WSC creates a lake at Chartwell
Publishes second *Marlborough* volume
Clementine's South Seas voyage

1935

Hitler repudiates Versailles, signs naval treaty with Britain, invokes anti-Semitic laws
Labour denies Hitler aggressive, opposes rearmament
Baldwin's first confession: admits Luftwaffe stronger than RAF, but his popularity unaffected
Baldwin becomes P.M.
Mussolini invades Ethiopia
General election — Tory victory
Randolph runs as Tory at West Toxteth, is defeated
Hoare-Laval deal exposed
Diana divorces, marries Duncan Sandys, MP
Her sister Sarah becomes chorus girl

1936

King George V dies; Edward VIII is King
Randolph loses by-election at Ross and Cromarty; his candidacy an embarrassment to WCS
SMALL NAZI FORCE INVADES RHINELAND
FRENCH, WITH 350,000 TROOPS, BACK OFF
Cliveden/Blickling set rejoices
WSC: "Stop it! Stop it! NOW is the appointed time!"
Civil war in Spain
WSC publishes third *Marlborough* volume
Baldwin's second confession: he concealed RAF inferiority to win election
Hitler and Mussolini form Axis, opposing democracies
WSC leads huge Albert Hall rally to support rearmament and League of Nations
He errs, backing King in marriage crisis
Shouted down in Parliament; his movement falters
King abdicates; WSC is discredited
Sarah marries vaudeville performer

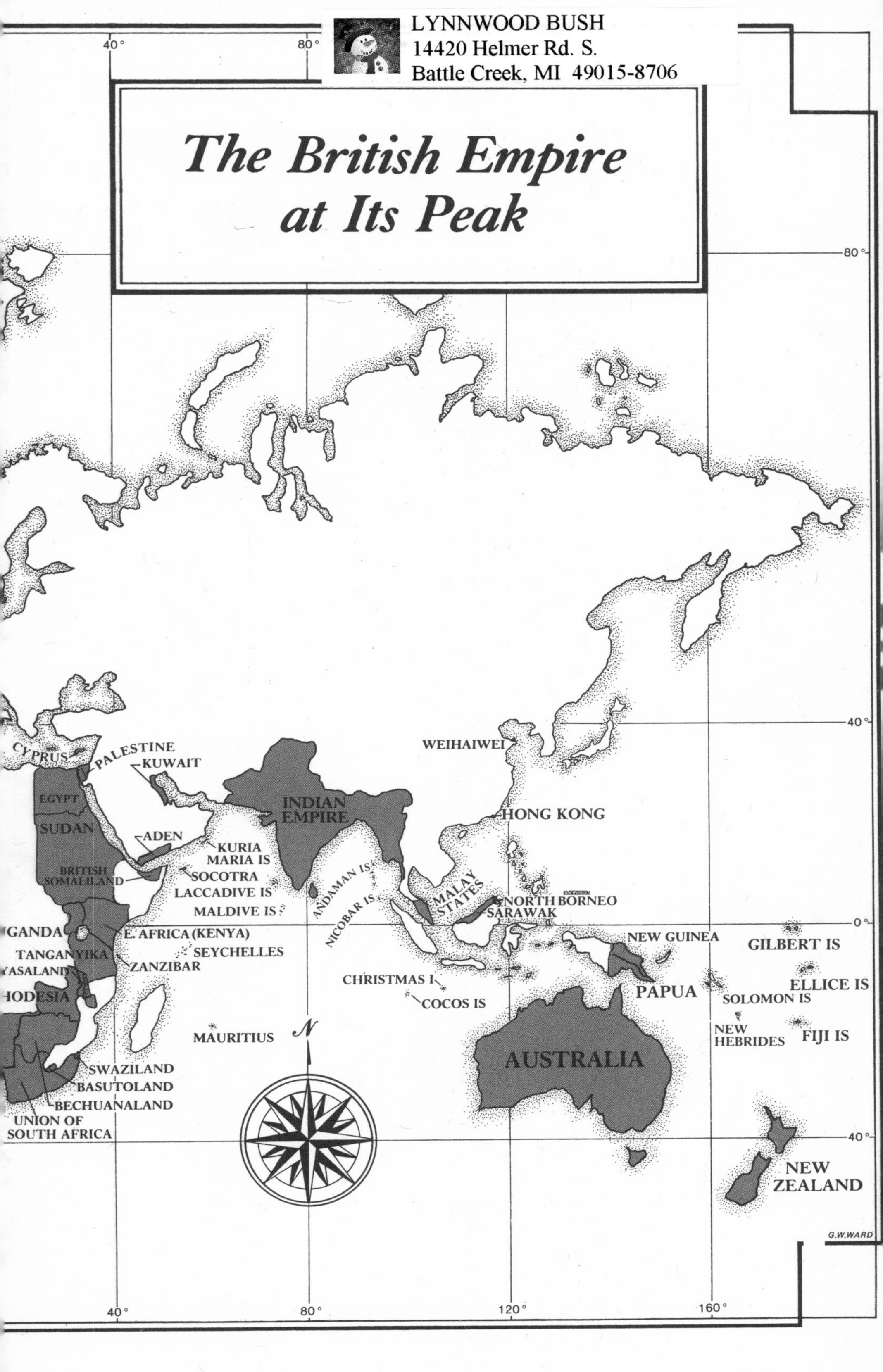
The British Empire at Its Peak
CYPRUS
PALESTINE
KUWAIT
EGYPT
SUDAN
ADEN
BRITISH SOMALILAND
KURIA MARIA IS
SOCOTRA
LACCADIVE IS
MALDIVE IS
INDIAN EMPIRE
ANDAMAN IS
NICOBAR IS
MALAY STATES
WEIHAIWEI
HONG KONG
NORTH BORNEO
SARAWAK
UGANDA
E. AFRICA (KENYA)
SEYCHELLES
TANGANYIKA
ZANZIBAR
NYASALAND
RHODESIA
CHRISTMAS I
COCOS IS
MAURITIUS
NEW GUINEA
PAPUA
GILBERT IS
ELLICE IS
SOLOMON IS
NEW HEBRIDES
FIJI IS
AUSTRALIA
SWAZILAND
BASUTOLAND
BECHUANALAND
UNION OF SOUTH AFRICA
NEW ZEALAND
N
40°
80°
120°
160°
0°
G.W.WARD

Visions of Glory
1874–1932

Books by William Manchester

Disturber of the Peace

The City of Anger

Shadow of the Monsoon

Beard the Lion

A Rockefeller Family Portrait

The Long Gainer

Portrait of a President

The Death of a President

The Arms of Krupp

The Glory and the Dream

Controversy

American Caesar

Goodbye, Darkness

The Last Lion: Visions of Glory

One Brief Shining Moment

In Our Time

The Last Lion: Alone

A World Lit Only by Fire

The Last Lion: Defender of the Realm

THE LAST LION

Winston Spencer Churchill
Visions of Glory
1874–1932

William Manchester

Little, Brown and Company
New York Boston London

Little, Brown and Company
Hachette Book Group
237 Park Avenue, New York, NY 10017
littlebrown.com

First Edition: October 1983

"The Lion Caged" appeared in slightly different form in *American Heritage*.

Photographs appear after pages 198 and 454.

Library of Congress Cataloging-in-Publication Data
Manchester, William Raymond, 1922–2004.
The last lion, Winston Spencer Churchill.
Bibliography: p.
Includes index.
1. Churchill, Winston, Sir, 1874–1965.
2. Great Britain—Politics and government—1901–1936.
3. Great Britain—Foreign relations—1901–1910.
4. Great Britain—Foreign relations—1910–1936.
5. Prime ministers—Great Britain—Biography. I. Title.
DA66.9.C5M26 1983 941.084'092'4 [B] 82-24972
ISBN 978-0-316-54503-7

20 19 18 17 16 15 14

RRD-C

Printed in the United States of America

To

MARY

and

CHARTWELL

The credit belongs to the man who is actually in the arena, whose face is marred by dust and sweat and blood, who knows the great enthusiasms, the great devotions, and spends himself in a worthy cause; who at best, if he wins, knows the thrills of high achievement, and, if he fails, at least fails daring greatly, so that his place shall never be with those cold and timid souls who know neither victory nor defeat.

—John F. Kennedy *on Theodore Roosevelt*
New York City, December 5, 1961

Lieutenant Winston S. Churchill, Subaltern of Horse, Fourth Hussars, 1896

ARRAY

ILLUSTRATIONS

MAPS

PREAMBLE

The Lion at Bay

THE French had collapsed. The Dutch had been overwhelmed. The Belgians had surrendered. The British army, trapped, fought free and fell back toward the Channel ports, converging on a fishing town whose name was then spelled Dunkerque.

Behind them lay the sea.

It was England's greatest crisis since the Norman conquest, vaster than those precipitated by Philip II's Spanish Armada, Louis XIV's triumphant armies, or Napoleon's invasion barges massed at Boulogne. This time Britain stood alone. If the Germans crossed the Channel and established uncontested beachheads, all would be lost, for it is a peculiarity of England's island that its southern weald is indefensible against disciplined troops. In A.D. 61, Queen Boudicca of the Iceni rallied the tribes of East Anglia and routed the Romans at Colchester, Saint Albans, and London (then Londinium), cutting the Ninth Legion to pieces and killing seventy thousand. But because the nature of the southern terrain was unsuitable for the construction of strongpoints, new legions under Paulinus, arriving from Gaul, crushed the revolt, leaving the grief-stricken queen to die by her own hand.

Now the 220,000 Tommies at Dunkirk, Britain's only hope, seemed doomed. On the Flanders beaches they stood around in angular, existential attitudes, like dim purgatorial souls awaiting disposition. There appeared to be no way to bring more than a handful of them home. The Royal Navy's vessels were inadequate. King George VI has been told that they would be lucky to save 17,000. The House of Commons was warned to prepare for "hard and heavy tidings."[1] Then, from the streams and estuaries of Kent and Dover, a strange fleet appeared: trawlers and tugs, scows and fishing sloops, lifeboats and pleasure craft, smacks and coasters; the island ferry *Gracie Fields;* Tom Sopwith's America's Cup challenger *Endeavour;* even the London fire brigade's fire-float *Massey Shaw* — all of them manned by civilian volunteers: English fathers, sailing to rescue England's exhausted, bleeding sons.

Even today what followed seems miraculous. Not only were Britain's soldiers delivered; so were French support troops: a total of 338,682 men. But wars are not won by fleeing from the enemy. And British morale was still unequal to the imminent challenge. These were the same people who, less than a year earlier, had rejoiced in the fake peace bought by the betrayal of Czechoslovakia at Munich. Most of their leaders and most of the press remained craven. It had been over a thousand years since Alfred the Great had made himself and his countrymen one and sent them into battle transformed. Now in this new exigency, confronted by the mightiest conqueror Europe had ever known, England looked for another Alfred, a figure cast in a mold which, by the time of the Dunkirk deliverance, seemed to have been forever lost.

England's new leader, were he to prevail, would have to stand for everything England's decent, civilized Establishment had rejected. They viewed Adolf Hitler as the product of complex social and historical forces. Their successor would have to be a passionate Manichaean who saw the world as a medieval struggle to the death between the powers of good and the powers of evil, who held that individuals are responsible for their actions and that the German dictator was therefore wicked. A believer in martial glory was required, one who saw splendor in the ancient parades of victorious legions through Persepolis and could rally the nation to brave the coming German fury. An embodiment of fading Victorian standards was wanted: a tribune for honor, loyalty, duty, and the supreme virtue of action; one who would never compromise with iniquity, who could create a sublime mood and thus give men heroic visions of what they were and might become. Like Adolf Hitler he would have to be a leader of intuitive genius, a born demagogue in the original sense of the word, a believer in the supremacy of his race and his national destiny, an artist who knew how to gather the blazing light of history into his prism and then distort it to his ends, an embodiment of inflexible resolution who could impose his will and his imagination on his people — a great tragedian who understood the appeal of martyrdom and could tell his followers the worst, hurling it to them like great hunks of bleeding meat, persuading them that the year of Dunkirk would be one in which it was "equally good to live or to die" — who could if necessary be just as cruel, just as cunning, and just as ruthless as Hitler but who could win victories without enslaving populations, or preaching supernaturalism, or foisting off myths of his infallibility, or destroying, or even warping, the libertarian institutions he had sworn to preserve. Such a man, if he existed, would be England's last chance.[2]

In London there was such a man.

Now at last, at last, his hour had struck. He had been waiting in Parliament for forty years, had grown bald and gray in his nation's service, had endured slander and calumny only to be summoned when the situation seemed hopeless to everyone except him. His youngest daughter, seventeen-year-old "Mary the Mouse" — her family nickname — had been sunning herself at Chartwell, their country home in Kent, during the first hours of the German breakthrough, when the music on her portable radio had been interrupted by a BBC bulletin: "His Majesty the King has sent for Mr. Winston Churchill and asked him to form a government." Mary, who adored her father, prayed for him and assumed that he would save England. So, of course, did he. But among those who fully grasped the country's plight, that was a minority view. The Conservative party leadership, the men of Munich, still controlled the government — Lord Halifax, Sir Horace Wilson, Sir Kingsley Wood, Sir John Simon, Sir Samuel Hoare, and, of course, Churchill's predecessor as prime minister, Neville Chamberlain, who detested him and everything he represented. Even George VI hadn't wanted Chamberlain to quit No. 10 Downing Street; he thought his treatment had been "grossly unfair." The King suggested Halifax as his successor. Labour's erratic Stafford Cripps had already come out for Halifax. That suited the Tory hierarchy, but only a coalition could govern the nation, and the National Executive of the Labour party, meeting in a basement room of the Highcliff Hotel in Bournemouth, sent word that they would serve under no Conservative except Churchill. So Chamberlain persuaded the reluctant King to choose the man neither wanted.[3]

Not that it seemed to matter much. Churchill had said that "the Germans are always either at your throat or at your feet," and as a hot May melted into a hotter June it appeared that their stranglehold was now unbreakable. Hitler was master of Europe. No one, not even Caesar, had stood so securely upon so glittering a pinnacle. The Führer told Göring: "The war is finished. I'll come to an understanding with England." On May 28, the first day of the Dunkirk evacuation, Halifax, speaking for the Conservative leadership, had told Churchill that a negotiated peace was England's only alternative. Now, as the new prime minister's foreign secretary and a member of his War Cabinet, the Yorkshire nobleman was quoted by the United Press as inviting "Chancellor Hitler to make a new and more generous peace offer." It was, he said, the only reasonable course, the only decision a stable man of sound judgment could reach.[4]

He was quite right. But Winston Churchill was not a reasonable man. He was about as sound as the Maid of Orleans, a comparison he himself once made — "It's when I'm Joan of Arc that I get excited." Even more was he an Elijah, an Isaiah; a prophet. Deep insight, not stability, was his forte. To the War Cabinet he said, "I have thought carefully in these last days whether it was part of my duty to consider entering into negotiations with that man," and concluded: "If this long island story of ours is to end at last, let it end only when each one of us lies choking in his own blood upon the ground." He spoke to them, to the House, and then to the English people as no one had before or ever would again. He said: "I have nothing to offer but blood, toil, tears, and sweat." Another politician might have told them: "Our policy is to continue the struggle; all our forces and resources will be mobilized." This is what Churchill said:

> Even though large tracts of Europe and many old and famous states have fallen or may fall into the grip of the Gestapo and all the odious apparatus of Nazi rule, we shall not flag or fail. We shall go on to the end. We shall fight in France, we shall fight on the seas and oceans, we shall fight with growing confidence and growing strength in the air, we shall defend our island, whatever the cost may be, we shall fight on the beaches, we shall fight on the landing grounds, we shall fight in the fields and in the streets, we shall fight in the hills; we shall never surrender.

"Behind us," he said, ". . . gather a group of shattered states and bludgeoned races: the Czechs, the Poles, the Danes, the Norwegians, the Belgians, the Dutch — upon all of whom a long night of barbarism will descend, unbroken even by a star of hope, unless we conquer, as conquer we must, as conquer we shall." That was the language of the Elizabethans, and of a particular Elizabethan, the greatest poet in history: "This England never did, nor never shall, / Lie at the proud foot of a conqueror."[5]

Now, fired by the conviction which could only belong to one who had faced down inner despair, Churchill defied the "celestial grins" of Britain's enemies, said peace feelers would "be viewed with the greatest disfavor by me," and said he contemplated the future "with stern and tranquil gaze." Free Englishmen, he told his people, would be more than a match for the "deadly, drilled, docile, brutish mass of the Hun soldiery plodding on like a swarm of crawling locusts." But he warned his family to prepare for invaders. His son's bride Pamela protested: "But Papa, what can *I* do?" He growled: "You can always get a carving knife from the kitchen and take one with you, can't you?" To the demoralized

French he declared: "Whatever you may do, we shall fight on forever and ever and ever." General Maxime Weygand replied by asking what would happen if a hundred Nazi divisions landed at Dover. Churchill told him: *"Nous les frapperons sur la tête"* — they would be hit on the head as they crawled ashore. Visiting Harrow, he heard the boys sing an old school song rewritten in his honor:

> *Not less we praise in darker days*
> *The Leader of our Nation,*
> *And Churchill's name shall win acclaim*
> *From each new generation.*

He suggested a change. "Darker," he said, should be "sterner." These were no dark days, he told them. Indeed, they would be remembered as great days, provided this "island race" followed his watchword: "Never, never, never, never give in."[6]

And so he saved Western civilization when men considered its redemption worth any price. The Nazi stain was spreading into the Balkans, into the Middle East, into Brazil; the German-American Bund was staging mass rallies in Madison Square Garden; the *New York Times* reported in front-page headlines: URUGUAY ON GUARD FOR FIFTH COLUMN, NAZIS TAKE BOLD TONE IN ECUADOR, and ARGENTINE NAZIS RALLY. Men who think of themselves as indispensable are almost always wrong, but Winston Churchill was surely that then. He was like the lion in Revelation, "the first beast," with "six wings about him" and "full of eyes within." In an uncharacteristically modest moment on his eightieth birthday he said: "It was the nation and the race dwelling all round the globe that had the lion's heart; I had the luck to be called upon to give the roar." It wasn't that simple. The spirit, if indeed within them, lay dormant until he became prime minister and they, kindled by his soaring prose, came to see themselves as he saw them and emerged a people transformed, the admiration of free men everywhere.[7]

At the height of the Battle of Britain, when Hitler tried to win in the air over London what he had expected to gain in a negotiated peace, the prime minister's headquarters lay in a drab brick bunker two blocks south of Downing Street, beneath a stone government building which bears the plaque CABINET OFFICE / CENTRAL STATISTICAL OFFICE. The bunker is still there — nothing in it, not even the pins in the maps, has been changed since V-E Day — and you can descend a cellar stair into the past, emerging into what was known as "the Annexe," or "the CWR," short for "Cabinet War Room." In fact there are many rooms, including a rather barren cell containing a desk bearing the microphone which the prime minister used for his broadcasts and the bed into which his wife could tuck him at night. All messages reached him here through the No. 10 switchboard; an aide could be put through anywhere in England by dialing the magic number: Rapid Falls 4466.

Churchill hated the Annexe's cramped quarters. Donning his zippered blue Siren Suit, as he called it (it looked like a workman's boiler suit; the staff called it his "Rompers"), he would mount the stairs to visit his family in their ground-floor flat, or stroll over to No. 10, or cross the street into St. James's Park to feed the ducks and pelicans in the lake despite reports, taken seriously, that German agents lurked there. At night he was even more incautious. During raids he would dart out after close hits to see the damage. Sometimes he climbed up to the roof and squatted there on a hot-air vent, counting the Heinkel 111's as the searchlights picked them up. He wanted to be wherever the bombs were falling. It is a lie that he knew Coventry would be destroyed on November 14, 1940, and didn't alert the city because the Germans would have known their code had been broken. Sir John Martin was with him that evening. They were driving out of the capital when a motorcyclist stopped them; word had just arrived that the Luftwaffe was headed for London. So the prime minister ordered the car turned around. It was early morning before he knew that the real target had been Coventry.

All his life he was a man of extraordinary personal courage. As a youth he sought danger in Cuba, on India's North-West Frontier, on the Nile, and in South Africa. Each battle found him recklessly exposing himself to gunfire. In the Sudan in 1898 he was a subaltern and Herbert Kitchener was Anglo-Egyptian commander in chief (Sirdar), but he attacked Kitchener, in print, for "the inhuman slaughter of the wounded" and the desecration of the tomb of the Mahdi, the natives' idol. Then, in Natal, the Boers captured Churchill. He escaped and later rode a bicycle in civilian clothes through the Boer stronghold of Johannesburg, risking execution as a spy had he been caught. Elected to Parliament at the age of twenty-five, he defended the enemy in his maiden speech — and then savaged Britain's war minister, a senior statesman of his own party. At sea in 1943 he awoke Averell Harriman to tell him that a U-boat had them in its sights. He said: "I won't be captured. The finest way to die is in the excitement of fighting the enemy." After a moment's thought he added:

Churchill among the ruins of the House of Commons, 1941

"It might not be so nice if one were in the water and they tried to pick me up." Harriman, frightened, said, "I thought you told me that the worst a torpedo could do to this ship . . . was to knock out one engine room." Churchill grinned and replied, "Ah, but they might put two torpedoes in us. You must come with me . . . and see the fun."[8]

The harder question is whether he enjoyed war too much. He denied it. He called it a "dirty, shoddy business, . . . disguise it as you may." On September 4, 1898, after he had survived the dreadful battle of Omdurman on the Nile, he wrote his mother that the scenes he had witnessed "made me anxious and worried during the night and I speculated on the shoddiness of war. You cannot gild it. The raw comes through." At Tehran in 1943 he said to his daughter Sarah: "War is a game played with a smiling face, but do you think there is laughter in my heart?" And he said: "War, which used to be cruel and magnificent, has now become cruel and squalid. In fact it has been completely spoilt."[9]

But this assumes that there was something magnificent to spoil. The implication is ineluctable: he saw chivalric, Arthurian, *brioso* aspects of war; it was to him, as life was to Peter Pan, "an awfully big adventure." As a young war correspondent he reported the death of a young peer in battle as "a sad item, for which the only consolation is that the Empire is worth the blood of the noblest of its citizens." In 1914, the diarist Frances Stevenson, Lloyd George's mistress, noted that the outbreak of war found the British cabinet sunk in gloom, whereupon "in burst Churchill, radiant, smiling, a cigar in his mouth and satisfaction upon his face. 'Well!' he exclaimed, 'the deed is done!' " Lloyd George, who was also there, told Margot Asquith that "Winston was radiant, his face bright, his manner keen. . . . You could see he was a really happy man," and Churchill himself wrote his wife: "I am interested, geared up & happy. Is it not horrible to be built like that?" During World War II he liked to cap his day by watching captured German combat films. After the second Quebec conference in 1944 he told the press that he would visit the battlefronts soon because he did not wish to miss any of the "fun" of "the good things." The *New Statesman* acidly commented that these were "strange words for a process whereby human beings are being disembowelled, roasted to death, drowned, blown into fragments, or are dying slowly of agonizing wounds." But the prime minister was unchastened. Six months later he stood on Xanten hilltop, watching British regiments cross the Rhine. The spectacle, he complained, was insufficiently dramatic. He said: "I should have liked to have deployed my men in red coats on the plain down there and ordered them to charge."[10]

Red coats, which the army had doffed for khaki in the late 1890s, obviously belonged to the wars of earlier times. But so did he. He liked panoply, bugles, drums, battle flags, British squares. He said: "It is a shame that War should have flung all this aside in its greedy, base, opportunistic march, and should turn instead to chemists in spectacles, and chauffeurs pulling the levers of aeroplanes or machine guns." At times he believed it a shame that technology had altered peace, too. "In the nineteenth century," he observed, "Jules Verne wrote *Round the World in Eighty Days.* It seemed a prodigy. Now you can get around it in four, but you do not see much of it on the way." He thought that "the substitution of the internal combustion machine for the horse marked a very gloomy milestone in the progress of mankind" and that it was "arguable whether the human race have been the gainers by the march of science beyond the steam engine." The real point here was that steam had opened up the British Empire; air power, and then the atom, had closed it down. Lord Moran, his physician, wrote that "Winston is a proud man, and it hurts him to think how vulnerable, in the atomic age, a small, densely populated island like Britain has become." It was to Moran that Churchill said glumly: "I wish flying had never been invented. The world has shrunk since the Wrights got into the air; it was an evil hour for poor England." And addressing England as though it were a colleague — he was apt to do this — he said: "You came into big things as an accident of naval power when you were an island. The world had confidence in you. You became the workshop of the world. You populated the island beyond its capacity. Through an accident of airpower you will probably cease to exist."[11]

In a thousand little ways he revealed his preference for the past and his reluctance to part with it. Victorian expressions salted his speech: "I venture to say," "I am greatly distressed," "I rejoice," and "I pray"; so many of his memos began "Pray do," "Pray do not," or "Pray give me the facts on half a sheet of paper" that they became known among his staff as "Churchill's prayers." If it was time to leave Chartwell for London, and he wanted to know if his chauffeur was behind the wheel, he would ask: "Is the coachman on his box?" After the House of Commons snuffbox was destroyed in the Blitz, he replaced it with one from his family's ancestral home of Blenheim, explaining, "I confess myself to be a great admirer of tradition." He frankly preferred "the refinements of Louis XIV" to the modern "age of clatter and buzz, of gape and gloat." He also thought that "bad luck always pursues peoples who change the names of their cities. Fortune is rightly malignant to those who break with the customs of the past." Accordingly, Istanbul was Constantinople to him; Ankara was Angora; Sevastopol was Sebastopol; and in a directive to his minister of information dated August 29, 1941, he wrote: "Do try to blend in without causing trouble the word Persia instead of Iran." As for Cambodia and Guatemala, they didn't exist for him; he had got this far without having heard of them and saw no need to change now. He spoke of Sir Walter Raleigh, Henry VIII, and James I as though they were his contemporaries. Anthony Montague Browne recalls walking into Churchill's office after Harold Macmillan had been chosen over R. A. ("Rab") Butler as the new Conservative leader. Churchill was muttering, "Intelligent, yes. Good looking, yes. Well-meaning, yes. But not the stuff of which Prime Ministers are made." Montague Browne asked: "But would Rab have been any better?" Churchill looked at him blankly. He said: "I was thinking of Melbourne."[12]

Like Melbourne and all other Victorian prime ministers, Churchill never attended Parliament, or called at Buckingham Palace, wearing anything but a frock coat. It was sometimes difficult for those around him to remember that he had fought his first election in the nineteenth century and had been, by the time of the old Queen's death, one of the highest-paid newspaper reporters in the world. Some thought his viewpoint and attitudes reached even farther back in history; Harold Laski called him "a gallant and romantic relic of eighteenth-century imperialism." Churchill replied: "I like to live in the past. I don't think people are going to get much fun in the future." The older he grew, the stronger the bond he felt between himself and others who had reached manhood before the turn of the century. When he was told that a Londoner over seventy-five years of age had been arrested in Hyde Park for making improper advances toward a young girl in subzero weather, he chortled: "Over seventy-five and below zero! Makes you *proud* to be an Englishman!"[13]

But to those who chided him for being preoccupied with earlier ages, he answered: "The longer you look back, the farther you can look forward. This is not a philosophical or political argument — any oculist can tell you it is true." Certainly it was true of him. He was no mere fogy. Clement Attlee, his great Labour adversary, compared him to a layer cake: "One layer was certainly seventeenth century. The eighteenth century in him is obvious. There was the nineteenth century, and a large slice, of course, of the twentieth century; and another, curious, layer which may possibly have been the twenty-first."[14] Churchill may have lacked sympathy for inventive contributions to warfare, but he understood them and even anticipated them. In World War I he was the father of the tank. As early as 1917 he conceived of vessels which would serve as landing craft for tanks. In the late 1930s he became interested in rockets and showed friends graphs illustrating their ballistic characteristics. And in the war against Hitler his genius was responsible for "Window," strips of tinfoil dropped by bombers to confuse enemy radar; "Pluto," a pipeline under the ocean; "Gee," a device for guiding pilots; and the artificial harbors used at Normandy.

All these, of course, were weapons. Martial strains reverberated throughout his career as a kind of background score. In the House his rhetorical metaphors were those of the battlefield — events marched, political flanks were turned, legislative skirmishes fought, ultimata delivered, and opponents told to surrender, to strike their colors, to lay down their arms. More than half of the fifty-six books he published were about war and warriors; the two he most regretted not having found time to write were biographies of Caesar and Napoleon. Partly this was because he knew that peace hath not her heroes, and he meant to be heroic. In part it was because of his combative spirit. He agreed with George Meredith: "It is a terrific decree in life that they must act who would prevail." There is no doubt that he enjoyed peril and delighted in battle. In his last days he said that 1940 and 1941 had been the best years of his life, despite the fact that for other Englishmen they had been incomparably the worst.

It is equally true that throughout his life he retained the small boy's glee in making mischief, in dressing up, in showing off. He was probably the only man in London who owned more hats than his wife — top hats, Stetsons, seamen's caps, his hussar helmet, a privy councillor's cocked hat, homburgs, an astrakhan, an Irish "paddy hat," a white pith helmet, an Australian bush hat, a fez, the huge beplumed hat he wore as a Knight of the Garter, even the full headdress of a North American Indian chieftain. He had closets full of costumes. When his grandchildren visited him, he appeared as an ape, snarling. Dressing for dinner when he traveled abroad, he wore the decorations awarded him by whatever country he was visiting — his favorite was the Danish Order of the Elephant — together with his sash. If nothing else was suitable, he would don his uniforms as RAF air commodore, as colonel of the Queen's Own Fourth Hussars, as Lord Warden of the Cinque Ports, or as Elder Brother of Trinity House, England's first lighthouse and pilotage authority, chartered by Henry VIII in 1514. His fame had eclipsed the medals; his figure had outgrown the uniforms; it didn't matter. Once in Strasbourg Lord Boothby entered wearing a Légion d'Honneur rosette. Churchill glared, pointed at it, and demanded: "What's that in your buttonhole?" Told, he scowled, then brightened. "I've got something better than that," he said. He disappeared and reappeared, proudly wearing the *médaille militaire.*[15]

In the House he expressed this side of himself by thumbing his nose at the Opposition, or sticking out his tongue, or, when he had enraged them and they looked apoplectic, by blowing them a kiss. He once wrote of his childhood that he had been "so happy in my nursery with all my toys." He still was; the imp lurked within. As home secretary before World War I he refused to prohibit roller-skating on sidewalks; pedestrians might be bowled over, but boys must not be deprived of their fun. Once during World War II, vacationing in Florida, he disguised himself as "a Mr. Lobb, an invalid requiring quiet." His principal private secretary, Sir John Martin, was registered as the invalid's butler. Security officers, after thinking it over, encouraged the prime minister to use pseudonyms when phoning. So he used Martin's name, with the consequence, Sir John wryly recalls, that "I received a rocket from Censorship." Despairing, the security men begged Churchill at least to keep his movements secret. He then telephoned Franklin Roosevelt before a Washington summit meeting: "They won't let me tell you how I'm going to travel. You know security measures. So all I can say is that I'm coming by puff-puff. Got it? *Puff-puff.*" Once during the height of the Blitz, Mrs. Kathleen Hill, one of the prime minister's secretaries, was visited by her son Richard, an army private on leave. She sent him out on a personal errand for the prime minister — buying an electric train for his first grandson. Hill had just finished assembling it on the rug of a first-floor room at No. 10 when he became aware of an august presence hovering over him. "You've got two locomotives," Churchill rumbled. "Have you got two transformers?" Private Hill nodded dumbly. "Good!" boomed Churchill, clapping his hands together. "Let's have a crash!"[16]

That, too, was a part of him, but to leave it there would be to trivialize him. On a deeper level his aggressive, let's-have-a-crash manner was rooted in his vision of statesmanship. That vision is difficult to grasp today. It is wholly at odds with a central doctrine of his contemporaries, sanctified by the conventional wisdom of generations since. They hold that peace is the norm and war a primitive aberration. Churchill held otherwise. As a youth he concluded that the great issues of his time would be decided on the battlefield, that Nietzsche, Carlyle, and Gobineau had been right: that war was a legitimate political instrument, that it was by no means the worst that could happen; that conflict, not amity, would be the customary relationship between great states. He reconciled himself to it — as did Hitler, Stalin, Mao Tse-tung, and the Zionists — and began a lifelong study of strategy.

Although he was diametrically opposed to the prevailing attitudes in Western Europe and the United States, it is arguable that events have vindicated him. In this century every world power has been engulfed by war in Europe, Asia, the Middle East, and Africa. Latin America has not known a year of silent guns. Australia was threatened by Japanese invasion. Indians have fought Pakistanis, Arabs have fought Israelis, Danes and Norwegians have fought Germans; Spaniards have fought Spaniards and Burmese, Burmese. Emerging nations have acquired independence only to cross the frontiers of their newly independent neighbors. Cuba became a missile base, then a port nursing Soviet submarines. Even the remote, barren Falkland Islands saw Britons and Argentinians slay one another. The United States has seen no fighting on its mainland, but American soldiers and airmen have died in France, Belgium, the Netherlands, Germany, Sicily, Italy, North Africa, China, the Pacific islands, Japan, Korea, Vietnam, and Cambodia, and U.S. warships lie rusting on the bottom of every ocean. Russia and the West are locked in a truce of terror, held in check only by the fear of mutual annihilation.

Having accepted what was unacceptable to others, Churchill devoted his remarkable gifts to martial arts at an early age. His aim was always victory, but victory at the least possible cost in suffering, at the lowest price in casualties. The proper course for Britain, he reasoned, was to follow the principle of Chatham — the Elder Pitt — and hold continental enemies in the grip of English sea power, sapping their strength at the distant fringes of their dominions. In 1915 this led to the most controversial, most misunderstood decision of Churchill's career. He meant to break the stalemate in France by forcing the Dardanelles, the narrow strait between the Sea of Marmara and the Aegean which separates Europe and Asia, knocking Turkey out of the war and joining British and French forces with their Russian ally. Because of blunders in the field, the stratagem failed. That failure, which drove him from office and nearly ended his career, haunted him all his years. Today the wisdom of his plan then is obvious. "In the whole of the First World War," Attlee has written, there was "only one brilliant strategical idea — and that was Winston's: the Dardanelles."[17]

Still, in the age of nuclear weapons, which Churchill did not anticipate, even the most humane of warriors is suspect. The London *Observer* declared in 1951: "Any consideration of Mr Churchill's career as a whole brings one up against the extraordinary fact that, for all its majestic scope, it remains to this day tragically unfulfilled and fragmentary. His political role has not been meteoric and disastrous, like Napoleon's or Hitler's. But neither has it been linked to a definite achievement, like Richelieu's or Chatham's, Washington's or Lincoln's, Bismarck's or Lenin's." An American is struck by the facility with which so many British intellectuals slight the man who saved their country. In fact, Churchill was more than an exponent of Mars. His ultimate goal was the "broad, sunlit uplands" of a time when all swords became plowshares. Even in the grim days after Dunkirk he looked westward and saw hope. If the British Isles were conquered by the Germans, he said, then the struggle would continue abroad "until, in God's good time, the new world, with all its power and might, steps forth to the rescue and liberation of the old." He had faith in eventual peace, and he believed he knew how it could be achieved: by combining the might of the English-speaking peoples in so strong a defense of the United States and the Commonwealth that the rest of the world would be held at bay, as it had been held by the British Empire in the relatively quiescent nineteenth century. Then, from that absolute base, freedom would expand outward. He cherished the possibility of a world order, a kind of Renaissance pageant to be accomplished, not by emerging states squabbling on United Nations Plaza in Manhattan, but by the Americans and the great powers of Europe, including Germany but not, significantly, the Russians, whom he "always looked on," in Sir Isaiah Berlin's words, "as a formless, quasi-Asiatic mass." His dreams of a tranquil global civilization in many ways resembled the exotic mysticism of Cecil Rhodes, Alfred Milner, and Joseph Chamberlain, but they never turned westward. To Churchill, the "Great Republic," as he called it, was the key. This, as he readily acknowledged, was partly because of his origins. The blood in his veins was as American as English. His mother was a New Yorker. He always kept a cast of her hand, molded in copper, on his desk. It was an exact replica of his own.[18]

He adored her and she neglected him. He later wrote: "She shone for me like the Evening Star. I loved her dearly — but at a distance." She later told friends she ignored Winston until he grew older and became "interesting." That was an improvement on the attitude of her husband, who didn't even like his son, but young Winston's happiness among his nursery toys derived from neither parent but from his nanny, Elizabeth Everest — "Woom." He recalled: "My nurse was my confidante. . . . [At her death she was] my dearest and most intimate friend." Wrenched from her while still a child, he was sent to a brutal boarding school in Ascot, where the sadistic headmaster caned him until his back was a mass of welts. His treatment at the hands of the other boys was, if anything, worse. Toward the end of his life, in halting tones, he told his doctor about it. Sickly, an uncoordinated weakling with the pale fragile hands of a girl, speaking with a lisp and a slight stutter, he had been at the mercy of bullies. They beat him, ridiculed him, and pelted him with cricket balls. Trembling and humiliated, he hid in a nearby woods. This was hardly the stuff of which gladiators are made. His only weapons were an unconquerable will and an incipient sense of immortality. Already he was memorizing Macaulay's tale of a man with two comrades barring a bridge to an army:[19]

Then out spake brave Horatius,
The Captain of the Gate:
"To every man upon this earth
Death cometh soon or late.
And how can man die better
Than facing fearful odds,
For the ashes of his fathers,
And the temples of his gods?"

Beginning at the age of seven, Churchill deliberately set out to change his nature, to prove that biology need *not* be destiny. Anthony Storr, the English psychiatrist and author of *Human Aggression,* concludes that he "was, to a marked extent, forcing himself to go against his own inner nature."[20] As a Victorian, Churchill believed he could be master of his fate, and that faith sustained him, but everything we have learned about human motivation since then underscores the immensity of his undertaking. W. H. Sheldon has delineated three dominant physiques, each with its concomitant personality traits. Of the three — ectomorphic (slight), mesomorphic (muscular), and endomorphic (fat) — Churchill clearly fell in the third category. His head was ponderous, his limbs small, his belly tumescent, his chest puny. His skin was so sensitive that he broke into a rash unless he slept naked at night between silk sheets. By day he could wear only silk underwear against his skin. Endomorphs are characteristically lazy, calculating, easygoing, and predictable. Churchill was none of these. He altered his emotional constitution to that of an athlete, projecting the image of a valiant, indomitable bulldog.

At times along the way he despaired. In 1893 he wrote, "I am cursed with so feeble a body, that I can hardly support the fatigues of the day." Yet he was determined to prove just as hardy as any mesomorph. In his teens he nearly killed himself while leaping from a bridge during a game of tag; he pitched down almost thirty feet and lay unconscious for three days. He fell again steeplechasing at Aldershot, and yet again when disembarking at Bombay, where he permanently injured a shoulder; for the rest of his active life he played polo, off and on, with his arm bound to his side. As a child he caught pneumonia. He suffered from chest ailments the rest of his life. He was allergic to anesthetics and periodically erupted in boils. Nevertheless, he refused to yield to human frailty. In his inner world there was no room for concessions to weakness. He never complained of fatigue. In his seventieth year he flew to councils of war overseas sprawled across a tick mattress on the floor of an unheated World War II bomber. During the ten years after V-E Day he suffered a heart attack, three bouts of pneumonia, two strokes, and two operations. Nevertheless, he continued to build the image of a tireless embodiment of machismo who ate, smoked, and drank, all to excess. It survives to this day. Actually, most of the stories about his alcohol intake are myth. It is true that he started each day with a scotch and soda. What is not generally known is that he made that drink last until lunch, and that the amount of liquor he put away over a twenty-four-hour day was surprisingly modest. You would never have known it to hear him talk. He wanted to be remembered as a two-bottle man, like Pitt, and he cultivated the yarns about his drinking with characteristic aplomb. Once he asked Frederick Lindemann — "the Prof," a scientific wizard who later became Lord Cherwell — how many boxcars could be filled with the champagne he had drunk in his lifetime. The Prof replied: "Only part of one." Churchill sighed. He said: "So little time and so much to achieve."[21]

In his most famous photograph he is seen glaring at the camera, his jaw jutting like the butt end of a ham, the incarnation of defiant Britain. The Canadian photographer Yousuf Karsh, who understood him, caught the expression by a trick. Just before he triggered the shutter, he reached out and yanked Churchill's cigar from his mouth. What you really see in that picture is an endomorph rudely deprived of his pacifier. If you look closely, however, you may catch a glimpse of something else: a man ruled by his instincts. In triumphing over his physiognomy Churchill had become an aggressive extrovert, but at the same time he had developed into a rare type — C. G. Jung called it the "extroverted intuitive" — and it was that, not his surface toughness, which changed the history of the world. Jung wrote: "The intuitive is never to be found among the generally recognized reality values, but is always present where possibilities exist. He has a keen nose for things in the bud, pregnant with future promise. . . . Thinking and feeling, the indispensable components of conviction, are, with him, inferior functions, possessing no decisive weight: hence they lack the power to offer any lasting resistance to the force of intuition." That, or something like it, was what C. P. Snow had in mind when he wrote: "Judgment is a fine thing: but it is not all that uncommon. Deep insight is much rarer. Churchill had flashes of that kind of insight. . . . When Hitler came to power Churchill did not use judgment but one of his deep insights. . . . *That* was what we needed. . . . Plenty of people on the left could see the danger; but they did not know how the country had to be seized and unified." The answer was found by an extroverted intuitive. In Jung's description of the type, "his capacity to inspire his fellow-men with courage, or to kindle enthusiasm for something new, is unrivalled." Field Marshal Alanbrooke, Churchill's chief of the Imperial General Staff, was constantly astonished by his "method of suddenly arriving at some decision as it were by intuition, without any kind of logical examination of the problem. . . . He preferred to work by intuition and by impulse." Jan Christiaan Smuts said: "That is why Winston is indispensable." A colleague described it as his "zigzag streak of lightning in the brain."[22]

Political genius, said Bismarck, consists of hearing the distant hoofbeat of the horse of history and then leaping to catch the passing horseman by the coattails. The difficulty is that one may hear the wrong horse, or lunge for the wrong horseman. As Jung pointed out, the extroverted intuitive lacks judgment. Churchill was right about the Dardanelles, right about Ireland, right about Munich, right about stripping England of tanks to defend the Suez Canal in 1940, and, as the Third Reich crumbled, supremely right about the menace of the rising Russian empire in Eastern Europe. However, he had not been right about fascism; at first, his conservative instincts and his allegiance to tradition had led him to apologias for strong men who posed as defenders of the established order. In 1926 he told Italian journalists that he had been "charmed . . . by Signor Mussolini's gentle and simple bearing." Resisting British opposition to Franco, he recommended instead that England "send charitable aid under the Red Cross to both sides." And while loathing Nazism, he once remarked that he "admired" Hitler for being a "champion" of his nation's pride. As his friend F. E. Smith put it, "Winston was often right, but when he was wrong, well, my God."[23]

Despite his versatility, vitality, and fertile mind, his belligerent instincts led him to fight Gandhi's campaign for Indian independence, to oppose the abdication of Edward VIII, and, in the heat of the 1945 political campaign, to predict that a Labour party victory would bring Britain "a Gestapo apparatus." In January 1938 he wrote: "The air menace against properly armed and protected ships of war will not be of a decisive character." This conviction, stubbornly held, led to the sinking of the *Prince of Wales* and *Repulse* by the Twenty-second Japanese Air Flotilla on December 10, 1941. In the opening months of the war, when he was first lord of the Admiralty, he was responsible for England's intervention in Norway, a fiasco which was mercifully overlooked when he became prime minister. Anzio was his idea; later he admitted that "I had hoped that we were hurling a wildcat onto the shore, but all we got was a stranded whale." Diversionary attacks, however impractical, always had his support. Late in the war he still wanted to land in Norway. At his insistence amphibious assaults were attempted on Rhodes and other Greek islands. All failed. In 1944 he even wanted to seize the tip of Sumatra, which was wholly without strategic value. George C. Marshall said, "His planning was all wishing and guessing." Actually, it wasn't. Had the combined chiefs adopted his grand proposal to sail up the Adriatic and invade Europe through the Ljubljana Gap, some military historians believe, British Tommies and American GIs, not Russians, would have been the liberators of Budapest, Prague, Vienna, and Warsaw, with all that would have entailed for the postwar world. But by then his stock had fallen because he had championed so many impractical schemes.[24]

That had been the story of much of his public life. His career passed through three stages: from 1900 to 1915, when his star rose to a dizzy height; from then until 1940, when he achieved little and failed often; and from Dunkirk to the end, when he became a legend. The legend obscures what was a patchy record. Again and again he was rejected by his countrymen; he never won their love and confidence until they faced disaster. His following was limited to a few personal friends. He lost more elections than any other British politician of his time. Twice he switched parties, and although he wound up leader of the Conservatives, he spent three-quarters of his political life battling Tory leaders. His brilliance was recognized from the first, but he was regarded as erratic, unreliable, shallow, impetuous, a hatcher of "wildcat schemes." In 1915, Liberal Prime Minister Herbert Asquith observed of Churchill that "to speak with the tongue of men and angels, and to spend laborious days and nights in administration, is no good if a man does not inspire trust." Instead, he inspired suspicion. His love of adventure, it was said, ran away with his discretion. He was put down as an opportunist, a swashbuckler, a man who was "jaywalking through life." He was labeled a man incapable of party loyalty. In the House of Commons he wasn't even a good listener; he "lacked antennae." Once his mind was set, he wouldn't budge an inch. Nor could he judge men. He was easily taken in by quacks and charlatans; in the words of Air Chief Marshal Charles Portal, "Winston was a bad picker." By the 1930s it was generally felt that the people were wise to him at last, that he was a figure from the past, out of touch with reality. A newspaper editorial described him as a "genius without judgment." Prime Minister Stanley Baldwin, who watched Germany rearm and crushed all proposals for British military expenditures, said that although Churchill had a "hundred-horsepower brain," he didn't know how to harness it. Harold Begbie wrote: "Mr. Churchill carries great guns, but his navigation is uncertain. His effect on men is one of interest and curiosity, not of admiration and loyalty. His power is the power of gifts, not character. Men watch him but do not follow him. He beguiles their reason but never warms their emotions."[25]

Margot Asquith had sized him up in 1908 as a man of "transitory convictions." Later, the Tories reached the same conclusion; they accused him of inconstancy, of veering opinions. In fact, it was the other way around. It was Baldwin and Chamberlain who were the trimmers, switching their policies when public opinion shifted. Except in the 1920s — when, as Baldwin's chancellor of the Exchequer, he withheld criticism of some questionable policies — Churchill never changed at all. He could misjudge others, but his own principles were a rock. This, in fact, is what offended traditional party politicians. If one reads the letters he wrote as a subaltern, his dispatches as a war correspondent, his speeches as a young MP, his cabinet papers, his books, and his "Action-This-Day" memoirs of the early 1940s, it will be clear that his views, once formed, were immutable. Here and there one encounters surprises. In the Edwardian era he and David Lloyd George were the most effective champions of the working class in the cabinet. Churchill's sympathy for workmen had been engaged by the humble circumstances of Mrs. Everest, who had given him the love his mother withheld, and by reading early sociological studies of the desperate poverty in the lower classes. Despite his wealthy friends and relatives and his allegiance to the Empire, he denounced "our unbridled Imperialists who have no thought but to pile up armaments, taxation, and territory." He invented the excess-profits tax. Yet more than thirty years later he bitterly fought Labour's cradle-to-grave welfare legislation. The explanation is intriguing. He wasn't opposed to the substance of Labour's bills; what he found objectionable was the *way* the thing was being done. Labour held that the people had an absolute right to these comprehensive benefits. Churchill thought they should be gifts from a benign upper class to grateful lower classes. It was characteristic of him that in 1944, when Harold Laski proposed raising a fund as a token of the nation's gratitude to him, he demurred, then added: "If, however, when I am dead people think of commemorating my services, I should like to think that a park was made for the children of London's poor on the south bank of the Thames, where they have suffered so grimly from the Hun." Subscriptions were admirable. Taxes were an affront.[26]

His concept of magnanimity is among his more fascinating and, if you disregard the overtones of noblesse oblige, more endearing traits. He was always being excoriated in print or on the platform, and one of his sources of income was damage suits for libel or slander. He always won, and he always felt genuine pity for the loser. He wrote: "I have always urged fighting wars and other contentions with might and main till overwhelming victory, and then offering the hand of friendship to the vanquished. Thus I have always been against the Pacifists during the quarrel, and against the Jingoes at its close." It was a pattern with him. Defeat had to precede conciliation. He refused to negotiate until his adversary had capitulated. Revenge afterward, however, was to him unmanly and ungentlemanly. It was Kitchener's vindictiveness on the Nile, his total lack of generosity toward the routed natives, which infuriated young Churchill. After Chamberlain's fall, which was swiftly followed by his death, Churchill rose in the House of Commons to pay him tribute. He said Chamberlain's hopes had been foiled by events, then asked: "But what were these hopes in which he was disappointed? . . . They were surely among the most noble and benevolent instincts of the human heart — the love of peace, the pursuit of peace, even at great peril." He was a ferocious enemy of Germany in both world wars, yet after each he begged the British government — in vain — to dispatch emergency shipments of food to its starving people. However high he rose, the man who as a boy had been bullied and bruised could always identify with the underdog.[27]

In a profound sense, he himself always remained the underdog. All his life he suffered spells of depression, sinking into the brooding depths of melancholia, an emotional state which, though little understood, resembles the passing sadness of the normal man as a malignancy resembles a canker sore. The depressive knows what Dante knew: that hell is an endless, hopeless conversation with oneself. Every day he chisels his way through time, praying for relief. The etiology of the disease is complex, but is thought to include family history, childhood influences, biological deficiencies, and — particularly among those of aggressive temperament — feelings of intense hostility which the victim, lacking other targets, turns inward upon himself. Having chosen to be macho, Churchill became the pugnacious, assertive fighter ready to cock a snook at anyone who got in his way. That was why he began carrying a Bren gun in his car when he became prime minister, then took bayonet lessons, and insisted that his lifeboat on the wartime *Queen Mary* be equipped with a mounted machine gun. But in peacetime he often lacked adequate outlets for his aggression. The deep reservoir of vehemence he carried within him backed up, and he was plunged into fathomless gloom.

Depression is common among the great; it may balance their moods of omnipotence. Among its sufferers have been Goethe, Lincoln, Bismarck, Schumann, Tolstoy, Robert E. Lee, and Martin Luther. To these should be added Churchill's father and five of the seven dukes of Marlborough, his ancestors, for it should be remembered that genes, too, play a depressive role. The personality traits are unmistakable; it is impossible to imagine Franklin Roosevelt offering blood, toil, tears, and sweat, but the expression would have come naturally from Lincoln. We first encounter Churchill's awareness of his illness in a letter, written when he was twenty, complaining of "mental stagnation" and a "slough of despond." The note is sounded again in his second book, a novel. The hero drops into a chair and asks himself: "Was it worth it? The struggle, the labour, the constant rush of affairs, the sacrifice of so many things that make life easy, or pleasant — for what?" Later, "a sense of weariness, of disgust with struggling, of desire for peace filled [the hero's] soul. The object for which he had toiled so long was now nearly attained and it seemed of little worth." An echo of this is heard more than a half-century later. It was Churchill's birthday. Glasses were raised to honor his accomplishments. He muttered to his daughters Diana and Sarah: "I have achieved a great deal to achieve nothing in the end."[28]

"What a creature of strange moods he is," Max Aitken, later Lord Beaverbrook, wrote, "always at the top of the wheel of confidence or at the bottom of an intense depression." In times of disappointment, rejection, or bereavement, feelings of hopelessness overwhelmed him. Thoughts of self-destruction were never far away. He told his doctor: "I don't like standing near the edge of a platform when an express train is passing through. I like to stand back and if possible to get a pillar between me and the train. I don't like to stand by the side of a ship and look down into the water. A second's action would end everything." He also disliked sleeping near a balcony. He explained: "I've no desire to quit this world, but thoughts, desperate thoughts, come into the head."[29]

To a remarkable degree he coped successfully with "Black Dog," as he called his depressive spells. He sought flamboyant, stimulating, zestful company. He avoided hospitals. And like Cuchulain, the Hound of Ulster, he found solace in incessant activity. He told Violet Asquith* that unless he was perpetually active he relapsed into "dark moments of impatience and frustration." Sir George Riddell wrote in his diary in January 1915 that Churchill "is one of the most industrious men I have ever known. He is like a wonderful piece of machinery with a flywheel which occasionally makes unexpected movements." He would tell his family, "A change is as good as a rest," and then set about laying bricks at Chartwell or painting landscapes at Marrakesh. After the Dardanelles he crossed into France, fought in the trenches as a battalion commander, and set up his easel just behind the front line. And he always pursued acclaim. Depressives, more than most people, are dependent upon external sources of self-esteem. Churchill was never bashful about soliciting applause. As a youth, mailing a manuscript to his mother, he sought from her what she had not given him in childhood. He wrote: "Write to me at great length about the book and be nice about it. Don't say what you think, but what I . . . should like you to think." If friends suggested that this book or that speech might be improved, he reproached them: "You are not on my side." He expected total, uncritical loyalty. And he reciprocated. Brendan Bracken, one of the few who stood by him in the 1930s, said: "He would go to the stake for a friend."[30]

Nothing, however, could match the satisfaction of directing his hostility outward, toward a great antagonist, a figure worthy of massive enmity. But as the years rolled by and he approached old age, the possibili-

* The prime minister's daughter. In November 1915 she became Violet Bonham Carter, but since she was single during the years when she knew Churchill best, her maiden name is used in this volume.

ties of finding such an object became remote. The strain began to tell. Anthony Storr writes: "In day-to-day existence, antagonists are not wicked enough, and depressives suffer from pangs of conscience about their own hostility."[31] Then Churchill's prospects were dramatically altered. Adolf Hitler entered his life. It would be fatuous to suggest that the Nazi dictator's only significance for Churchill was as an answer to an emotional longing. Churchill was no warmonger. He was a statesman, a humanitarian, a thinker in cosmic terms; he would have been profoundly grateful if Hitler had strangled on his own venom. But the Führer's repeated lunges across the borders of peaceful neighboring states did arouse a Churchillian belligerence far beyond the capacity of ordinary men. His basic weakness became his basic strength. Here, at last, was pure evil, a monster who deserved no pity, a tyrant he could claw and maim without admonishment from his scruples. By provoking his titanic wrath, the challenge from central Europe released enormous stores of long-suppressed vitality within him. In the beginning Hitler responded in kind. He, too, was a hoarder of rage, and he was a great hater. He may have felt that Britain's prime minister met an ache in him, too. As it turned out, he needed Churchill the way a murderer needs a noose.

Hitler's archenemy was not a man of small ego. It is an egalitarian fiction that the great are modest. They haven't any right to be, and they aren't. He said to Attlee: "Of course I am an egotist. Where do you get if you aren't?" In 1940 he believed that he had been destined for the extraordinary role he must now play. He declared to Lord Moran: "This cannot be accident, it must be design. I was kept for this job." It didn't surprise him. Determined to prove himself unworthy of parental neglect, he had lived much of his life in a world of fantasy centered on the conviction that something special lay ahead for him. He wasn't vain; merely self-centered. As a young war correspondent in the midst of combat he called to the soldiers around him: "Keep cool, men! This will make great copy for my paper!" Later, he liked to lie in bed listening to recordings of his speeches. Once he and his valet had words. Afterward Churchill rumbled: "You were rude." His manservant, forgetting his station, said, "You were rude, too." Churchill pouted. After a moment he said: "But I am a great man." His idea of a good dinner, he said, was to dine well and then "to discuss a good topic — with myself as chief conversationalist." After one meal his son, Randolph, was trying to make a point. Churchill broke in with a comment of his own. Randolph tried to pick up the thread of his argument. His father barked: "Don't interrupt me when I am interrupting!" In 1945, after the collapse of the Third Reich and his electoral defeat, he said: "For my part, I consider that it will be found much better by all parties to leave the past to history, especially as I propose to write that history myself."[32]

Some of the most moving passages in his historical accounts pay tribute to England's common man, but he never really understood his constituents' minds, and in fact he didn't much care. During one campaign he described his audience as "a sea of hard little hats on hard little heads." Lloyd George, who cared very much about the voters' dreams, was saturated with class consciousness; Churchill, as Attlee once observed, would have been content in a feudal society. He never grasped the revolution of rising expectations in the Birmingham mills and the bazaars of New Delhi. He thought Labour unfit to govern, and his early appeals for laborers' votes were almost absurd in their condescension. (In 1900 he told them: "I like the British working man and so did my father before me.") This insensitivity is one explanation for the periodic eclipse of his political fortunes. It is indeed singular that a man so remote from commonality, so completely out of touch with his times, could have become a national hero. Eventually he became beloved for his courage, his humor, his bulldog image, and such touches as his V-for-Victory sign, his ritualistic circumcision of cigars, and his deliberate mispronunciation of *Nazis* — it came out of the Churchill euphonium as "Nahrzees." But he never mastered the British political mood. Instead, he repeatedly misjudged it. Except in national emergencies, at the hour of fate or the crack of doom, he was largely ignored. People didn't identify with him because he never reciprocated.[33]

In his personal life he was the complete patrician. F. E. Smith said: "Winston is a man of simple tastes. He is always prepared to put up with the best of everything." Churchill's wife, Clementine, told Lord Moran that at home "Winston is a pasha." If no servant responded when he clapped his hands upon entering the house, he would immediately call for his valet. The valet dressed him right down to the pulling on of his socks, and ran his bath — twice a day — almost to the brim, at a precise temperature. Churchill's nanny had begun ministering to him; she had been succeeded by his manservants, batman, wife, secretaries, footmen, doctors, and attendants. He was inconsiderate of them; impatient, arrogant, unfeeling. Why did they put up with it? Dr. Storr suggests that "men who demand and need a great deal of attention from others are manifesting a kind of childlike helplessness, which evokes an appropriate response, however difficult they may be." Churchill could be very difficult. When a plane was preparing to land and the NO SMOKING sign flashed on, he would light up a cigar. If he found himself driving in a traffic jam, he wheeled his car out on the shoulder or sidewalk and drove to the head of the line. He rarely traveled with fewer than sixteen pieces of matched baggage. Once, according to Vincent Sheean, he arrived by himself at Maxine Elliott's Riviera villa and told her: "My dear Maxine, you have no idea how easy it is to travel without a servant. I came here all the way from London alone and it was quite simple." She murmured: "Winston, how brave of you."[34]

Reminiscing, he once said: "I was not twenty at the time of the Cuban War, and was only a Second Lieutenant, but I was taken to an inspection at West Point and treated as if I had been a General. I was brought up in that state of civilization when it was everywhere accepted that men are born unequal." This explains, in foreign affairs, the ferocity of his attacks on bolshevism well into the 1920s, long after his intransigence had become embarrassing to the government, and in domestic politics it accounts for his distrust of Labour. Late in life he read that Christopher Mayhew, one of Attlee's junior ministers, had walked out during the arena scene in the film *Quo Vadis.* Winston ordered the picture screened at Chartwell and intently watched the scenes of mayhem in the arena. After it was over, he rose and told his family: "Do you know why Mr. Mayhew walked out? It was because his socialist, egalitarian principles were outraged. There was one poor lion who hadn't got a Christian."[35]

But if Churchill's blind spots are often attributable to his aristocratic heritage, so are many of his successes. His career would have been impossible without preferential treatment. His name, not academic competence, got him through Harrow and Sandhurst. Then his mother, finally taking an interest in his affairs, began pulling strings for him. There were a great many available to her. She had been intimate with many influential men in America, on the Continent, in the British establishment; even in the royal family. Theoretically, her son was subject to army discipline in his youth. Actually, he moved around the world as he pleased. There is a stunning line in his book *The River War:* "With the design of thereafter writing this account, I moved to a point on the ridge which afforded a view of both armies." Here are two mighty forces preparing to do battle, and here is a lowly subaltern riding off to get the best perspective. A fellow war correspondent in South Africa pointed out that Churchill had the assurance, arrogance, and bravado that one found in the British ruling classes, "the conviction that he belongs to the best group in the world." He never doubted it. Nor did his mother. In 1900 other Englishwomen yearned to see their sons, off fighting the Boers. Jennie Churchill simply outfitted a hospital ship and sailed down to Cape Town to see how Winston was doing.[36]

She didn't pay for the vessel herself. She raised the funds by subscription. Her name wasn't even among the subscribers'. She couldn't afford it. She was always just a jump ahead of her creditors. So, for most of his life, was her son. To be sure, neither of them ever came close to a soup kitchen. Winston often complained of being broke, but that did not mean to him what it meant to most of his countrymen. He had expensive tastes, and he always indulged them. Consequently, he was often short of funds. In the desperate 1930s he was reduced to writing, for *Collier's* and other popular magazines on both sides of the Atlantic, such pieces as "The American Mind and Ours," "Is There Life on the Moon?" and "Under the Microscope." (His most striking idea was an article to be titled "Will There Be a Woman Prime Minister?" Editors vetoed it on the ground that it was too fantastic.) He would ask editors for payment, "if possible, by Monday morning." Six months before Munich, when he was waiting in the wings to stride out on the stage of history, he was so deep in red ink that he contemplated resigning from Parliament. He — and all he represented — was saved only when a wealthy friend settled his debts. On August 31, 1939, he wrote his publisher, "I am, as you know, concentrating every minute of my spare life and strength upon completing our contract. These distractions are trying." The distractions were German troop movements along the Reich's eastern border. That night, as he stood at his high desk in Chartwell, correcting proofs, Hitler invaded Poland.[37]

At Harrow he had first learned that he had a remarkable memory. Aged thirteen, he recited, without a slip, the twelve hundred lines of Macaulay's *Lays of Rome.* And once he had committed something to memory, he rarely forgot it. In the autumn of his life he quoted verses he had read in *Punch* as a boy. Riding through the Maryland countryside, during World War II, he declaimed the whole of Whittier's "Barbara Frietchie." In 1953, after he had suffered a stroke, he recited the thirty-four lines of Longfellow's "King Robert of Sicily," which he had last read fifty years earlier, while his doctor followed the text. Moran found that "here and there he got a word wrong: priests became monks and lamps candles; perhaps half a dozen words out of three hundred and fifty." This writer met him that same year — my stateroom was next to his suite on the *Queen Mary* — and when he learned that I was a fledgling foreign correspondent on my way to Egypt and India, he reeled off amazingly detailed accounts of his own experiences as a correspondent there in the 1890s. At about the same time he asked Sir David Hunt: "Can you look up the exact words of this quotation from Aristophanes: 'The qualities required for writing tragedy and comedy are the same, and a tragic genius must also be a comic genius'?" Hunt told him he must mean Aristotle. Churchill indignantly denied it. "Light began to dawn," Hunt recalls. He checked the Loeb Classical Library in the Cabinet Room at No. 10 and found the line at the end of the *Symposium,* in Plato's imaginary dialogue with Aristophanes. Awed, he asked the prime minister how recently he had read it. In Bangalore, Churchill said, in 1896. Hunt notes: "He was then twenty-two; at the time he recalled these words with perfect accuracy he was seventy-eight." Hunt was among those who suffered through the showing of *Quo Vadis* but thought it worth it when, later that evening, Churchill recited the entire fourteenth chapter of Gibbon's *Decline and Fall of the Roman Empire.* That, too, had been among the books he had read at Bangalore.[38]

He had also discovered at Harrow that he had a flair for the language. Although rated the stupidest boy in the school, he scribbled off essays for classmates who had difficulty writing. His later years as a newspaperman, and his early books, showed him that he could make a good living with his pen. His work was not universally admired; in *English Prose Style,* published in 1928, the eminent Oxford literary critic Sir Herbert Read declared that it revealed "aggrandisation of the self," that "such eloquence is false because it is artificial . . . the images are stale, the metaphors violent," and that a typical passage "exhales a false dramatic atmosphere . . . a volley of rhetorical imperatives." But Churchill wasn't writing for critics. He was addressing the world, and to that end he had fashioned a soaring, resonant style, sparkling with eighteenth-century phrases, derivative of Gibbon, Johnson, Macaulay, and Thomas Peacock, throbbing with classical echoes of Demosthenes and Cicero, but uniquely his own. It is impossible to imagine him employing a ghost writer. No one but Churchill could write Churchillian prose. The stamp of the man is on everything he wrote or uttered, whether pondering the lessons of the past ("the grievous inquest of history"), or describing Roosevelt's polio ("his lower limbs refused their office"), or those who feigned contempt for public affairs because they dared not commit themselves ("flaccid sea anemones of virtue who can hardly wobble an antenna in the waters of negativity"). It made Sir Herbert wince, but its author won the Nobel Prize in literature.[39]

Churchill's feeling for the English tongue was sensual, almost erotic; when he coined a phrase he would suck it, rolling it around his palate to extract its full flavor. On first meeting Violet Asquith he told her that words had "a magic and a music" all their own. That was what troubled Lloyd George, another critic of his rhetoric; he protested that to call Mussolini's conduct in Ethiopia "at once obsolete and reprehensible," as Winston had, was meaningless. Unchastened, Churchill replied, "Ah, the b's in those words: 'obsolete, reprehensible.' You must pay attention to euphony." He said, "I like short words and vulgar fractions." When short words hit hard he used them. Needing military equipment after Dunkirk, he told the United States, "Give us the tools and we will finish the job." He did not declare that the Allies had "consented to a coalition" or "agreed to cooperate." Instead, they had "joined hands." But on other occasions he did not hesitate to dip into his enormous vocabulary. Once he dictated a note to the Admiralty: "Must we have this lugubrious ingemination of the news of our shipping losses?" At first the sea lords thought his secretary had mistyped "insemination." Then they consulted the *Oxford English Dictionary* and found that *ingemination* means "redundancy."[40]

Like all writers, he had his favorite words: *unflinching, austere, somber, squalid.* He said *aircraft,* not *aeroplane,* and *airfield,* never *aerodrome.* He also liked to gather his adjectives in squads of four. Bernard Montgomery was "austere, severe, accomplished, tireless"; Joe Chamberlain was "lively, sparkling, insurgent, compulsive." He would open a speech with a sluggish largo tempo, apparently unsure of himself; then he would pull out his organ's Grand Swell and the Vox Humana, and the essence of his prose would be revealed; a bold, ponderous, rolling, pealing, easy rhythm, broken by vivid stabbing strokes. It gained force by its participatory character. He himself was part of the great events he described; he could say, with Aeneas, *"Quorum pars magna fui."* It is an advantage given to few, and those few have usually bungled it, resorting, among other things, to euphemisms, which Churchill scorned. He derided bureaucrats who called the poor the "lower income group," or lorries "commercial vehicles," or homes "accommodation units" — once he astonished the House of Commons by bursting into song: "Accommodation unit, sweet accommodation unit, / There's no place like accommodation unit." One of his first acts when he took over as prime minister in 1940 was to change the name of the "Local Defense Volunteers" to the "Home Guard." Words like *adumbrated* and *coordination* do not appear in his work. Of an MP who strung together phrases of jargon, Churchill said: "He can best be described as one of those orators who, before they get up, do not know what they are going to say; when they are speaking, do not know what they are saying; and when they have sat down, do not know what they have said." Of another, who had been defeated at the polls, he said, "Thank God we've seen the last of that Wuthering Height."[41]

He loved books and wrote of them: "If you cannot read all your books, at any rate handle, or, as it were, fondle them — peer into them, let them fall open where they will, read from the first sentence that arrests the eye, set them back on their shelves with your own hands, arrange them on your own plan so that if you do not know what is in them, you will at least know where they are. Let them be your friends; let them at any rate be your acquaintances." But he hated verbosity. "This paper, by its very length," he told a cabinet meeting, "defends itself against the risk of being read." And he despised pedants. A junior civil servant had tortuously reworded a sentence to avoid ending with a preposition. The prime minister scrawled across the page: "This is nonsense up with which I will not put." His profound knowledge of Latin and Greek was acquired through translations; he had been a miserable classics student. Labour MPs, most of whom lacked public-school educations, objected to classical phrases in the House for the very sensible reason that they couldn't understand them. During a discussion of this Churchill rose to a point and began, "As to the chairman of this committee, he should be not *facile princeps,* but *primus inter pares,* which for the benefit of any . . ." He paused while the Opposition MPs, anticipating insult, struggled to their feet. Then he broke up the House by continuing, ". . . for the benefit of any Old Etonians present, I should, if very severely pressed, venture to translate." His insularity, his feigned ignorance of all foreign tongues, was a source of popularity with the masses and served as antidote to his elitism. He told Jack Seely, later Lord Mottistone, "Jack, when you cross Europe you land at Marsai, spend a night at Lee-on and another in Paree and, crossing by Callay, eventually reach Londres. *I* land at Marsales, spend a night in Lie-ons, and another in Paris, cross by Calase, and come home to London." He believed that of all languages, English was incomparably superior. On his tongue, it was.[42]

Throughout his youth, he once said, "it was my only ambition to be master of the spoken word." He glittered as a young MP, speaking after elaborate preparation but — like his father before him — without a note.

Then one spring evening, in the middle of an address on a trade-union bill, he discovered that he couldn't recall a word of his peroration. Speechless, he sank down on the bench and buried his head in his hands. Thereafter, when delivering a major speech, he came armed with everything he was going to say, including the pauses and the pretended fumbling for the right phrase in the first few sentences and anticipating "Cheers, 'Hear, hears,' " "Prolonged cheering," and even "Standing ovation." He said accurately, "I am not an orator. An orator is spontaneous." William Hazlitt wrote that the first duty of an orator is to echo back the feelings of his audience. Pitt translated a Latin epigram: "Eloquence is like a flame: it requires fuel to feed it, motion to excite it, and it brightens as it burns." But Churchill was no echo; he needed neither fuel, motion, nor reflected glow. His speeches were one-way. Their luster owed nothing to his listeners. F. E. Smith said: "Winston has spent the best years of his life writing impromptu speeches." Many of them were written in the bathtub. Norman McGowan, one of his valets, was surprised on his first day to hear his master's voice rumbling from the bathroom. He put his head in and asked: "Do you want me?" Churchill rumbled, "I wasn't talking to you, Norman. I was addressing the House of Commons." Harold Nicolson congratulated him upon a remark to a small audience, apparently improvised as he left the podium. Churchill snapped, "Improvised be damned! I thought of it this morning in my bath and I wish now I hadn't wasted it on this little crowd."[43]

He estimated that the preparation of a forty-minute speech took between six and eight hours. The actual writing of it wasn't writing at all, at least not by him. He made his living, he said, "from mouth to hand." He prowled back and forth in his study, head down, hands clasped behind his back, dictating to a secretary at a typewriter. That became the first of several drafts, the basis for his preliminary revisions. Scissoring and pasting came next. He despised the thump of staplers — the only sound he hated more was whistling — so in fastening pages he used a paper punch and threaded tape through the holes. He called the punch his "klop" or "klopper." "Bring me my klop," he would tell a secretary. (There was a memorable day at Chartwell when a new girl left and returned staggering under the weight of Onno Klopp's fourteen-volume *Der Fall des Hauses Stuart.*) Eventually, when the address reached its penultimate form, he would add the asides and "RHGs" (Right Honourable Gentlemen), underlining certain sentences, capitalizing others, and spacing the lettering to indicate words which were to be stressed or spoken slowly. In the last stage a special typewriter with large type was wheeled out. The speech was ready to be set down in what the staff called "psalm form" because it looked as though it were being pointed for singing. This is what Churchill would see when he stood in the House, arranged his two pairs of spectacles, and glanced down at the final draft:[44]

We cannot yet see how deliverance will come
or when it will come.

but nothing is more certain
than tt every trace of Hitler's footsteps,

every strain of his infected
and corroding fingers,

will be sponged and purged
and, if need be, blasted
fr the surface of the earth.

He was never a man for small talk, and during his early, awkward years, the cut and thrust of House debates found him wanting. Painfully aware of this weakness, he blamed it on his lack of a university education, during which such skills would have been developed and honed. His manner, haughty even then, invited merciless attack. Arthur Balfour taunted him: "The Right Honourable Gentleman's artillery is very powerful but not very mobile." Slowly Churchill realized that while he was a born writer, he would have to make himself a great parliamentarian. He did it by practicing endlessly in front of mirrors, fashioning ripostes to this or that parry. He would never be comfortable listening to others speak, but over the years he came to relish Question Time in the House. And though his monologues were always more brilliant than his exchanges across the aisle, he developed a wit which has become an authentic part of his legend. It was not always good for him. As Harold Laski pointed out, people were so anxious to remember what he said that they didn't drive him to defend his positions. Yet we can only be grateful to them for setting down his gibes. He shone and would have shone in any company — Falstaff in Eastcheap, say, or Ben Jonson at the Mermaid, or Johnson and Burke at the Mitre. Watching him build up to a quip was an entertainment in itself. Hugh Massingham recalls: "One always knew it was coming. His own laughter began somewhere in the region of his feet. Then a leg would twitch; the bubble of mirth was slowly rising through the body. The stomach would swell; a shoulder heave. By this time, the audience would also be convulsed, although it had no idea what the joke was going to be. Meanwhile, the bubble had ascended a little further and had reached the face; the lips were as mobile and expressive as a baby's. The rich, stumbling voice would become even more hesitant. And finally there would be the explosion, the triumphant sentence of ridicule."[45]

Like all true wits, he knew the tickling quality of the unexpected. One day in the White House, according to Harry Hopkins, Churchill stepped naked from his bathroom just as Roosevelt was wheeling his chair into the room. This was always happening to him; the maids in his household and at No. 10 had grown accustomed to his nudity. In this case FDR apologized and turned to go, but Churchill held up a detaining hand. He said solemnly: "The Prime Minister of Great Britain has nothing to hide from the President of the United States." Before the battle of El Alamein, he summoned General Montgomery and suggested that he study logistics. Montgomery doubted that he should become involved in such technical matters. "After all, you know," he said, "they say that familiarity breeds contempt." Churchill replied: "I would like to remind you that without a degree of familiarity we could not breed anything." On his seventy-fifth birthday a photographer said: "I hope, sir, that I will shoot your picture on your hundredth birthday." Churchill answered: "I don't see why not, young man. You look reasonably fit and healthy." On his eighty-fifth birthday a back-bencher in the House, assuming that Churchill was out of earshot, told the MP beside him: "They say the old man's getting gaga." Without turning, Winston said: "Yes, and they say he's getting deaf, too."[46]

More in character, his wit was usually aggressive. Sometimes he chose the rapier. Lady Astor neither gave nor asked for quarter, and she got none from him. At a dinner party she told him: "Winston, if I were your wife I'd poison your soup." He replied, "Nancy, if I were your husband, I'd drink it." But he was at his best baiting public men who crossed broadswords with him. It was Churchill who called John Foster Dulles "the only bull who brings his own china shop with him," and who coined the progression, "dull, duller, Dulles." The austere Sir Stafford Cripps was a favorite target. In North Africa in World War II the prime minister said: "Here we are, marooned in all these miles of sand — not one blade of grass or drop of water or a flower. How Cripps would love it." After Cripps gave up smoking cigars, Churchill remarked that he was sorry to hear it: "The cigar was his last contact with humanity." As leader of the Opposition, Attlee could hardly escape, though the Labour leader, with his strong ego, enjoyed Churchill's jabs at him. When Attlee was in Moscow, Churchill said of the Labour MPs he had left behind, "When the mouse is away, the cats will play." He called Attlee "a sheep in sheep's clothing," and "a modest man with much to be modest about," and he drove a sharp needle into Labour policy one day when he met him in the House's men's room. Attlee, arriving first, had stepped up to the urinal trough when Churchill strode in on the same mission, glanced at him, and stood at the trough as far away from him as possible. Attlee said, "Feeling standoffish today, are we, Winston?" Churchill said: "That's right. Every time you see something big, you want to nationalize it."[47]

His niche in history — it is a big one — is secure. And so is his place in our affections. He will be remembered as freedom's champion in its darkest hour, but he will be cherished as a man. He was a feast of character, a figure emanating parochial grandeur like King David, and he also belonged to that rare species, the cultivated man of action, the engagé intellectual. Attlee said: "Energy and poetry . . . sum him up." But nothing sums him up. He was too many people. If ever there was a Renaissance man, he was it. In the age of the specialist, he was the antithesis, our Leonardo. As a writer he was a reporter, novelist, essayist, critic, historian, and biographer. As a statesman he served, before becoming His Majesty's first magistrate, as minister for the colonies and for trade, home affairs, finance, and all three of the armed forces. Away from his desk he was at various times an airplane pilot, artist, farmer, fencer, hunter, breeder of racehorses, polo player, collector of tropical fish, and shooter of wild animals in Africa. One felt he could do anything. That was why he seemed inevitable in 1940. Bernard Shaw said: "The moment we got a good fright, and had to find a man who could and would do something, we were on our knees to Winston Churchill."[48]

It is pointless to expect balance and consistency in genius. Churchill was not made like other men. Among his many traits was a kind of built-in shock absorber which permitted him to survive his repeated defeats and concomitant depressions. Going through his papers one is struck by his resilience, his pounding energy, his volatility, his dogged determination, and his utter lack of humility. He said: "I am not usually accused, even by my friends, of being of a modest or retiring disposition."[49] In the thousands of photographs of his face you will find every expression but one. He never looked apologetic. He had the temperament of a robber baron. As Walter Bagehot said of Palmerston, "His personality was a power." In World War I John Maynard Keynes singled out as his most striking virtue his intense concentration on the matter at hand — precisely the quality which, in the opinion of William James, identifies men of genius. In games he was a consistent winner. Like his distant cousin Douglas MacArthur, he was satisfied by nothing short of victory.

He was formidable, but he was also cherubic. That was what made him lovable even to those who recoiled from his benevolent despotism. He said, "All babies look like me." They did, and he looked like, and sometimes acted like, them. He enjoyed a child's anthropomorphism — finishing a book, he would put it aside and say: "I don't want to see his face again." His chief playthings were his seven-inch cigars, Romeo y Julietas and La Aroma de Cubas. Most of the time they were unlit; he liked to chew and suck them anyway, and when an end grew soggy, he would fashion mouthpieces — "bellybandos," he called them — from paper and glue. Mornings he worked in bed wearing a scarlet and green-dragon silk bed jacket, with papers strewn around him, and his play in the bath was an important part of his daily ritual; on long flights his luggage included a portable canvas bathtub. Dictating, or just puttering around his study, he wore a bright quilted dressing gown, which had been originally designed for a character playing Pooh-Bah in a production of *The Mikado,* and gold-embroidered slippers bearing his initials, a gift from Lady Diana Cooper. In his Siren Suit, Lady Diana recalls, he looked "exactly like the good little pig building his house with bricks."[50]

He was the absolute romantic. His paintings reflect this. There are no monotones — each stroke of his brush added shimmering light and color. And everything he painted or wrote, his very gestures, was invested with emotionalism. "I've always been blubbery," he said. No man wept more easily. His tears flowed at the mention of gallantry in battle, the thought of "invincible knights in olden days," victims of anti-Semitism, Canadian loyalty to the Empire, the death of George VI, Elizabeth II's kindnesses toward him, or the name of Franklin Roosevelt — "the best friend Britain ever had." He never tried to hold back the teardrops because he never knew any inhibitions. In the middle of a 3:00 A.M. wartime conference at Chequers, the prime minister's country home, his generals took a smoking break. One started playing "The Blue Danube" on a piano, and to their amazement their host, all alone, started waltzing dreamily around the floor. His feelings about his family were laced with sentimentality. His home was an independent kingdom, with its own laws, its own customs, even its own language. "Wow!" one of them would say in greeting another. When Churchill entered the front door he would cry: "Wow! Wow!" and his wife would call back an answering "Wow!" Then the children would rush into his arms and his eyes would mist over. Except when they lived at Chequers, their closest moments were at Chartwell.

He tried never to miss a weekend there. It says much for his belief in privilege, and for his staff's unquestioning acceptance of it, that No. 10 observed two distinct standards at Christmas, 1940. He was asked if the staff would have any time off. He said, "Yes, an hour for divine services." Then they all applauded as he flourished his V sign and left to spend a working holiday with his family.[51]

The Churchill children were never spanked. The worst that could happen to them, according to Sarah, was banishment from his presence. Like many another great captain who has sent thousands of men to their deaths, he shrank from personal violence. This was most striking in his treatment of animals, even of insects. Since he detested fresh air — he had his bedroom windows sealed with putty — it was hard for bugs to get at him. But sometimes a bee, wasp, or moth flew in from another part of the house. "Don't kill him," he would tell his valet. "Make sure you put him out the window." Once, during a division in the House, Anthony Head, the first man out of the chamber, spied a ladybug on the carpet. Realizing that a thunder of MP feet would soon pass this way, he bent down to rescue it. At that moment the prime minister arrived and instantly grasped the situation. Taking charge, he said, "Put her out the window." But since the introduction of air conditioning the windows had been permanently locked. "Use the Chancellor's office," he said, "and report back to me." Head did, but when he returned Churchill was in conference with the French foreign minister. The secretary told him he could look in for a moment. Head did and told Churchill: "She escaped. I let her out through Macmillan's window. Nobody touched her." "Good, good!" the prime minister boomed. To this day Head wonders what must have passed through the foreign minister's mind.[52]

"Poor fox," Churchill said brokenly when an MFH presented him with a mounted fox head. En route to Chartwell one night, his car ran over a badger. He ordered the car stopped, picked up the shattered animal, and carried the dead, bleeding body home in the lap of his striped pants. He would cry over the death of a swan or a cat; would leave the House chamber to telephone Chartwell, asking about the health of his goldfish. But his favorite pet was his little poodle Rufus. More accurately, there were two of them, Rufus I and Rufus II; the first was run down when a maid left him off his leash. (Churchill never spoke to her again.) Sometimes the Rufuses slept with him. After taking dictation — it might be 3:00 or 4:00 A.M. — his secretary would take the dog for his nightly walk. As Winston was about to drift off he would ask, "Did Rufus do his business?" and, assured that he had, would sleepily congratulate him. The poodle ate in the dining room with the rest of the family. A cloth was laid for him on the Persian carpet beside the head of the household, and no one else ate until the butler had served Rufus's meal. One evening at Chequers the film was *Oliver Twist.* Rufus, as usual, had the best seat in the house, on his master's lap. At the point when Bill Sikes was about to drown his dog to put the police off his track, Churchill covered Rufus's eyes with his hand. He said, "Don't look now, dear. I'll tell you all about it afterwards."[53]

Predictably, Churchill's taste in entertainment was unpredictable. In literature it was excellent, though of course he preferred British authors. Music was another matter; aged eleven, he had asked his parents for cello lessons, had been turned down, and had developed instead a fondness for what his daughter Mary calls "somewhat primitive" tunes — such music hall favorites as "Daddy Wouldn't Buy Me a Bow-wow," "Ta-ra-ra-boom-der-ay," "Hang Out the Washing on the Siegfried Line," and a curious ballad about a husband who discovers that his bride has a wooden leg: "I Married Half a Woman and Half a Tree." He enjoyed any movie about the Royal Navy; otherwise, his preference in films was less discriminating than one might expect. When he learned that Rudolf Hess had parachuted into Scotland, for example, he was watching the Marx Brothers. His favorite star was Deanna Durbin. His favorite motion picture — he must have seen it twenty times — was *That Hamilton Woman* with Laurence Olivier playing Lord Nelson and Vivien Leigh as his mistress. He was always lachrymose at the end of it. But probably the trashiest movie he ever watched was a sentimental pastiche based on a novel by Paul Gallico. Entitled *Never Take No for an Answer,* its chief character was a little Italian orphan whose donkey, named Violetta, helped him run a grocery stand. Violetta sickened. She could be healed, the boy believed, if he could take her to that hub of miracles, the Shrine of Saint Francis. So the orphan embarked on a journey, appealing in vain to a series of clerics: priests, archdeacons, bishops, archbishops, cardinals. Each time the boy was turned down the camera would flash back to Violetta, sprawled in her stable, ready for the last rites. Churchill wept inconsolably. "Oh, the donkey's dead!" he would sob. The others would reassure him: "No, no, Prime Minister, she's still alive." Churchill would recover and declare firmly: "If the donkey dies, I shan't stay. I shall go out." Finally the boy, in his finest hour, was granted an audience with the pope. The pontiff reversed the lower rulings and made an appointment at the shrine for Violetta. In the last scene a blazing cone of light, slanting down from heaven, revealed the donkey, bursting with health, beside her loyal, trudging little friend. The prime minister arose slowly from his chair, his eyes luminous and his cheeks streaming.[54]

Joyously human, anachronistic and wise, capable of willful misjudgment and blinding vision, dwarfing all those around him, he was the most benevolent of statesmen and the most gifted. Today the ordinary Englishman lives a better life than his fathers did, and for that he is largely indebted to Labour. But the extraordinary man has a harder time of it. He is trapped in regulations, his rise is impeded; his country pays a price. And even the masses seem to sense that while the socialists love ideas, Churchill, the unrepentant Victorian Tory, loved life. Since that love was balanced by a hatred of injustice, the average Briton owes him more than a higher standard of living. He owes him his very liberty.

"History," wrote Aristotle, "is what Alcibiades did and suffered." Social scientists impeach that, but Churchill never doubted it. Because the man was matched by his times, he achieved immortality and changed the world, for good or for ill — though not as he had expected or would have wanted, for he was not the only giant in the century. In the long reach of events the impact of the Churchillian era upon his island was decidedly mixed. Hitler lost the war but he didn't lose it to Britain alone. Churchill, in desperate need of allies, forged a coalition with the United States and the Soviet Union and then had to make concession after concession to them. They emerged in 1945 as superpowers, while Britain, formerly Great Britain, lost its Empire, lost its independent and decisive role in world affairs, and sank to the level of a second-rate power. Of course, that, too, was Aristotelian. Alcibiades routed the Spartans, but in the end he was dismissed and fled to Asia Minor, where he was murdered by Spartan agents. Tragedy is the wasting shadow always cast, sooner or later, by towering heroism. Therein lay the terrible grandeur in Churchill's funeral, a quarter-century after Dunkirk. The nation was bidding farewell both to a great Englishman and to the greatness of England. When his flag-draped coffin moved slowly across the old capital, drawn by naval ratings, and bareheaded Londoners stood trembling in the cold, they mourned, not only him and all he had meant, but all that they had been, and no longer were, and would never be again.

PROLOGUE

LAND OF HOPE AND GLORY

On February 4, 1874 — the year of Winston Churchill's birth — British troops led by General Sir Garnet Wolseley entered the small African city of Kumasi, now part of central Ghana, and put it to the torch, thereby ending the Second Ashanti War and winning the general a handsome spread on the weekly page devoted to the Empire in the *Illustrated London News.* He had worked for it. A melancholy martinet with spaniel eyes and a long drooping mustache rather like that of Lord Randolph Churchill, Winston's father, Wolseley had joined Victoria's army — "putting on the widow's uniform," as they later said — while still in his teens. Convinced that the surest way to glory lay in courting death at every opportunity, he had been felled by a severe thigh wound in the Second Burmese War, lost an eye to a bursting shell in the Crimea, and survived hairbreadth escapes while relieving Lucknow in the Indian Mutiny, capturing the Ta-ku Forts and Peking during Britain's 1860 dispute with the Chinese, and suppressing an insurrection in Canada. After finishing off the Ashantis he fought Zulus and dervishes, and organized campaigns against Boer guerrillas. His concern for soldiers' welfare won him a reputation among England's upper classes as a dangerous radical. London's cockneys loved him, however; their expression for topnotch was "all Sir Garnet." His great ambition was to die a heroic death in action against the French. That failing, the general, who ended up a viscount, planned to enrich his heirs by writing his memoirs after his retirement. Unfortunately, by then he had completely lost his memory. Visitors who mentioned his conquests to him were met by blank stares. He died in 1913, the last year of England's golden age.

Wolseley was one of the country's imperial heroes — others included Clive, Stamford Raffles, Chinese Gordon, Richard Burton, and, of course, Cecil Rhodes — whose feats were held up to the nation as examples of how men of courage and determination could shape the destiny of that noblest achievement of mankind, the Empire. If their lives were metaphors of the Empire's rise, that of Churchill, their rapt pupil, was the other way around. He entered the world in 1874, when the royal domain was approaching flood tide, and left it in 1965, as the last rays of imperial splendor were vanishing. That is one way of summing him up; it is, in fact, one of the ways he saw himself. Toward the end of his life he told Lord Boothby: "History judges a man, not by his victories or defeats, but by their results."[1] Yet the vitiation of the Empire does not diminish his stature. Alexander was driven out of India; Genghis Khan was undone by his sons; Napoleon lost everything, including France. Indeed, it may be argued that the greater the fall, the greater was a man's height. If that is true, then Churchill's stature rises above that of all other statesmen, for no realm, past or present, can match the grandeur of imperial Britain at its sublime peak.

It was the Tory journalist John Wilson of *Blackwood's Magazine* who first observed, in 1817, that "the sun never sets upon the Union Jack." At any given moment, wherever dawn was breaking, Britain's colors were rippling up some flagpole. If one could have ascended high enough in one of those balloons which fascinated Jules Verne and were actually used in the Franco-Prussian War, the view of Britain's colonial sphere would have been breathtaking. Victoria reigned over most of Africa, both ends of the Mediterranean, virtually all that mattered in the Middle East; the entire Indian subcontinent, from Afghanistan to Thailand, including Ceylon, which on a map appeared to be merely the dot below India's exclamation mark but which was actually the size of Belgium; Malaya, Singapore, Australia, islands spread all over the Pacific and the Atlantic, and Canada. The Canadians, proud of their loyalty to the Queen, issued a stamp depicting a world map with the Empire's lands colored red. It was a study in crimson splotches. Although the British Isles themselves were dwarfed by czarist Russia, and were smaller than Sweden, France, Spain, or Germany, their inhabitants ruled a quarter of the world's landmass and more than a quarter of its population — thrice the size of the Roman Empire, far more than the Spanish Empire at full flush, or, for that matter, than the United States or the Soviet Union today.

To its classically educated patricians, London was what Rome had once been: *caput mundi*, the head of the world. The popular aristocrat

Lord Palmerston said that colonies were multiplying so rapidly that he had to "keep looking the damned places up on the map." Disraeli said: "No Caesar or Charlemagne ever presided over a dominion so peculiar. Its flag floats on many waters, it has provinces in every zone, they are inhabited by persons of different races, . . . manners, customs." All this had been acquired by imperial conquest, and young Winston Churchill, writing for the *Morning Post* from a colonial battlefield on September 12, 1898, took note of "the odd and bizarre potentates against whom the British arms continually are turned. They pass in a long procession. The Akhund of Swat, Cetewayo brandishing an assegai as naked as himself, Kruger singing a Psalm of Victory, Osman Digna, the Immortal and the Irrepressible, Theebaw with his umbrella, the Mahdi with his banner, Lobengula gazing fondly at the pages of *Truth,* Prompeh abasing himself in the dust, the Mad Mullah on his white ass and, latest of all, the Khalifa in his Coach of State. It is like a pantomime scene at Drury Lane."[2]

All these suzerains lost, and all England rejoiced — loudly. The British were very vocal in their allegiance to their Empire. In public schools and public houses boys and men responded to "Three cheers for India!" and roared, to the music of "Pomp and Circumstance," Edward Elgar's patriotic hymn, composed in the last weeks of the old Queen's reign:

Land of hope and glory, mother of the free,
How shall we extol thee, who art born of thee?
Wider still and wider shall thy bounds be set;
God who made thee mighty, make thee mightier yet;
God who made thee mighty, make thee mightier yet!

On declamation days children recited, from Kipling:

Dear-bought and clear, a thousand year,
Our fathers' title runs.
Make we likewise their sacrifice,
Defrauding not our sons.

Music hall favorites were "The Death of Nelson," by S. J. Arnold and John B. Raham; "Annie Laurie," the great hit of the Crimean War; and, later, the rousing "Soldiers of the Queen." Today their great-grandsons wince at the public displays of patriotism, but the Victorians responded quickly to calls of Duty, the Flag, the Race, the White Man's Burden; the lot. Far from feeling manipulated — which they were; most Victorians gained nothing from the nation's foreign conquests — they memorized lines from W. E. Henley, the balladeer of England's colonial wars:

What if the best our wages be
An empty sleeve, a stiff-set knee,
A crutch for the rest of life — who cares,
So long as One Flag floats and dares?
So long as One Race dares and grows?
Death — what is death but God's own rose?

Her Britannic Majesty was "by the Grace of God of the United Kingdom of Great Britain and Ireland and of the British Dominions beyond the Seas, Queen, Defender of the Faith, Empress of India." In thatch-roofed villages of British North Borneo and the steamy jungles of Sierra Leone, her primitive vassals regarded her as divine and slit the throats of propitiatory goats before her image, usually a drab statue of a dowdy woman wearing a tiny crown and holding an orb and scepter. Elsewhere Anglican missionaries prevailed and read their Book of Common Prayer in hundreds of languages and dialects, from Swahili to Urdu, from Maori to Bugi, from Kikuyu to Mandarin, and even, in remote valleys on the Isle of Man, the ancient tongue of Manx. Information from Victoria's twenty-five turbulent tribal possessions in the Middle East reached Britain from their only contact with the outside world, Aden, on the tip of the Arabian Peninsula, which had been acquired as a coaling station for the British fleet. There an Englishman perspiring beneath a gyrating punkah sent the Queen all the news she needed from the sheikhs: "They are content to be governed from London." No one in Whitehall paid much attention. The only resource the Arabs could offer the Empire was an unpleasant liquid, of limited value, called oil.

Most Englishmen were familiar with scattered facts about the Empire. They had only the haziest idea of where Borneo was, but they had seen its Wild Man exhibited in a traveling cage. They knew the silhouette of lion-shaped Gibraltar, knew the legend that if Gibraltar's monkeys vanished from its caves, the Empire was finished. (In the midst of World War II Churchill found time to replenish the Rock's supply of monkeys.) They were proud of the Suez Canal, then considered an engineering marvel, and they were under the impression that all Egypt belonged to them, too. That wasn't strictly true; Egypt still flew its own flag and paid homage to the sultan of Turkey, but after the Queen's fleet had pounded Alexandria into submission, the country was run by the British agent and consul general. Thomas Cook and Son, booking clerks for the Empire, reserved Shepheard's Hotel's best rooms for Englishmen on official business. Cook's also ran steamers up the Nile for English tourists, though pilots turned back short of the Sudan border in 1885, after fanatic tribesmen of the Mahdi butchered Chinese Gordon in Khartoum. This tiresome restriction ended in 1898 when Kitchener routed and humiliated the tribesmen under the critical eye of young Churchill.

The British public was aware of the tiny island of Saint Helena, in the middle of the Atlantic, because that was where imprisoned Napoleon spent his last years, but such possessions as Ascension isle, Saint Helena's neighbor, which provided the turtles for the turtle soup at the traditional banquets of London's lord mayor, and Tristan da Cunha, the most isolated of the Empire's outposts, twelve hundred miles south of Saint Helena, in the broadest and most desolate reaches of the Atlantic, were virtually unknown outside the Colonial Office. Yet if ordinary Englishmen were confused about details of their realm, they can scarcely be blamed. The Empire itself was the vaguest of entities. Legally, under the British constitution, it did not exist. It was a kind of stupendous confidence trick. By arms or by arrogance, Englishmen had persuaded darker races that Britain was the home of a race meant to dominate the world. Therefore they ruled by consent. So successful was this bluff that the Mother Country held its possessions with an extraordinarily thin line of bwanas and sahibs; in India, for example, the rule of the Raj was administered by roughly one member of the Indian Civil Service for every 200,000 subjects.

Unless one counts Ireland, England's first imperial conquest was Newfoundland, discovered by John Cabot in 1497. The East India Company was chartered in 1600, and thereafter explorers like Captain James Cook, roaming the South Pacific, were followed by missionaries and merchants who ruled and exploited the new lands. It is true that the newcomers introduced natives to law, sanitation, hospitals, and, eventually, to self-government, but Dickens's Mrs. Jellyby, neglecting her family while "educating natives of Borrioboola-Gha, on the left bank of the Niger," was deceiving herself about her country's chief imperial motive. Palmerston, under no such illusion, said it was the government's goal to "open and secure the roads for the merchant," and Joseph Chamberlain said Whitehall must "find new markets and defend old ones."[3] Expansion of Britain's maritime strength had led to settlements on America's east coast and the hoisting of the Union Jack over the West Indies. The conquest of India had begun with a small trading station at Surat, on the west coast. Canada had been an acquisition of the Hudson's Bay Company, a firm just as zealous in its pursuit of profits as the East

India Company. Victorian Australia was built on the need for cargoes of gold and wool. And each new territory meant a further boost of England's entrepôt trade, expansion of markets for the coal of Wales, the textiles of Lancashire and Yorkshire, and the steel of Sheffield and Birmingham. By Churchill's youth the nation's foreign trade had reached the astounding total of £669,000,000 a year.

As James Morris pointed out in his masterful *Pax Britannica,* the Empire's growth had been "a jerky process," a formless, piecemeal advance which leapfrogged across continents and was never static. Sometimes imperial possessions were lost — Manila and Java were once British, and so, of course, were the American colonies — but the realm always waxed more than it waned. The great prize, "the brightest jewel in the imperial crown," as Englishmen said then, was the Indian Empire, comprising the modern nations of India, Burma, Pakistan, Sri Lanka, and Bangladesh. It was the need to secure their ties to India which, they said, justified holding the southern tip of Africa, Gibraltar, Malta, Cyprus, Port Said, and Aden. But the brightest jewel could also be approached from the other direction, so they had to have Sarawak, the Straits Settlements, and Malaya, too. The fact is that just as all roads had once led to Rome, so did all sea-lanes lead to India. When that argument seemed strained, as in Africa, the Queen's statesmen explained that they had to move in before other great powers did. With this excuse, Victoria's Lord Salisbury gobbled up the lion's share of Africa without igniting a European war.

Imperial unity was a fiction proclaimed every time colonial officials visited London. Usually all they had in common were hats bought in St. James's Street and gloves and spats from Dents'. Each possession had its own degree of freedom, its own language and customs, its own vision of God. The stable Dominions, Canada, Australia, and New Zealand, governed themselves, and Australia even ran its own colonies, the Cook Islands in the Pacific. Most possessions of the Queen were protectorates, territories, or Crown Colonies. Running these was the responsibility of His Excellency, the local governor, who had all the trappings of royalty. On ceremonial occasions he wore a gaudy uniform with a cocked hat sprouting ostrich feathers; he was entitled to a seventeen-gun salute; men bowed to him; and women, including his own wife, curtsied as he led a party into his dining room, where he was served before anyone else. His reward for good and faithful service was inclusion on the Honours List at home. (The irreverent said that CMG stood for "Call Me God," KCMG for "Kindly Call Me God," and GCMG for "God Calls Me God.") This, subscriptions to *The Times,* the stiff upper lip, the legends of Nelson and the Charge of the Light Brigade, faith in the pound sterling, "Abide with

Me," and a passion for cricket were among the frail linchpins linking imperial lands. Yet even on the administrative level there were exceptions to the colonial pattern. One Asian state was governed from a private office at 37 Threadneedle Street in London. Another, Sarawak, in Borneo, was an independent, third-generation despotism whose 600,000 people were ruled by an Englishman, the "White Raja." The White Raja, Charles Brooke, had his own flag; national anthem; newspaper, the *Sarawak Gazette;* and army, the Sarawak Rangers. Since he accepted British "protection" — permitting Whitehall to handle his foreign affairs — Sarawak was considered part of the Empire. Similarly, Nepal had a native sovereign, but the Nepalese cavalry pledged allegiance to the British Resident and bore his personal crest. Native sultans and rajas were accepted as aristocrats and were usually addressed as "Your Exalted Highness." For diplomatic reasons, however, the islands of Tonga were recognized as an independent kingdom. Tonga's queen was greeted as "Your Majesty." When Edward VII, who took the matter of royal blood very seriously, was told that he was about to meet the sovereign of Tonga, he asked suspiciously, "Is she a real queen or just another damned nigger?"[4]

By then the Empire was on an ebb tide, but even at its peak it was a lurching, reeling contraption, riddled with contradictions and inequities. Matthew Arnold knew how vulnerable it was:

. . . she
The weary Titan, with deaf
Ears, and labour-dimm'd eyes,
Regarding neither to right
Nor left, goes passively by.
Staggering on to her goal;
Bearing on shoulders immense,
Atlantean, the load,
Well-nigh not to be borne,
Of the too vast orb of her fate.

And yet the thing worked. In those days before the Wright brothers began the annihilation of distance, sea power was everything, and no other nation could match Britain's. Altogether there were 330 imperial warships, manned by over 92,000 tars, policing the world's waterways and keeping trade free. Spangling all oceans with their coaling stations and strategic forts, they were the strongest guarantee of the Empire's integrity, and their men spoke of its far-flung domains with the affectionate familiarity of men supremely confident of their national strength: the sacred Swami Rock in Ceylon was "Sammy Rock"; Barbados was "Bimshire"; Kuala Lumpur was "K.L."; Johannesburg was "Joburg"; Alexandria was simply "Alex." When the mighty British Mediterranean Fleet sighted Malta, the whole population turned out for the spectacle. The ships were painted silver, with tars in white in rigid formation on the decks; the procession was led by destroyers, followed by cruisers and then the battleships. Royal Marine bands played "Hearts of Oak" and the ships anchored with their prows pointing seaward, baring their teeth to any challenger.

Britannia ruled the waves, and Britons knew how important that was; every family with the means clothed its children in sailor suits and sailor dresses, their caps bearing the name of the Queen's latest battleship. And the warships were only part of it. The other part was the merchant marine. At the peak of its glory, England was launching a thousand merchant ships every year, most of them on the Clyde. More than half the world's maritime vessels flew the red ensign of British merchantmen; at any given moment they were carrying 200,000 passengers. The Peninsula and Oriental Steam Navigation Company's four-week voyage between the Mother Country and Calcutta, then India's capital, had become a legend. The worst part of the passage was the crossing of the Red Sea. Those who could afford relative comfort bought — for fifty pounds each way, not counting deck-chair rental — port-side cabins going out to India and starboard cabins for the trip home; in time "Port Out, Starboard Home" became the acronym *POSH.* Unfortunately the service was anything but posh. Kipling wrote that P & O crewmen behaved "as though twere a favour to allow you to embark."[5]

But if the crews seemed high-handed to their British passengers, all Britons had that reputation in other nations. Robert Laird Collier, an American touring England in the 1880s, wrote: "No people are so disliked out of their own country. . . . They assume superiority, and this manner is far from pleasant to other people. . . . They are overbearing, and haughty. . . . I have never seen among any people such rudeness and violation of good breeding. . . . As a nation they are intensely selfish and arrogant." In their "Splendid Isolation" — isolationism was British before it became American — Englishmen looked disdainfully across their Channel and said: "The wogs begin at Calais." Thomas Cook lectured the French on the cancan as a sign of national decadence, performed with "an unnatural and forced abandon," and when a dispatch from Africa reported a French colonial claim, Joe Chamberlain, the very model of an imperial statesman, scrawled in the margin: "Cheek!" England issued the first postage stamp, the "Penny Black," in 1847, and in an act of conceit undiminished by the fact that it was unintentional, the stamp bore a cameo of the Queen and nothing else — identification of the country seemed superfluous. Yet sometimes British contempt could be magnificent. Dressed to the nines, buttons glittering and collar starched, Captain William Packenham went ashore to deal with a gang of cutthroats who were massacring Armenians. The leaders of the pogrom gathered around him, glowering and fingering the edges of their bloody knives. Packenham stroked his beard and told the interpreter: "Let us begin. Tell these ugly bastards that I am not going to tolerate any more of their bestial habits."[6]

Britons were so sure of themselves. Like today's Americans, who are also disliked abroad, their dominance was the consequence of a cluster of accidents, among them their tremendous deposits of coal and iron ore — one-third of all the miners on earth were British — and England's role as the birthplace of the Industrial Revolution. Thus, Britain had naturally become the world's manufacturer, merchant, shipper, and banker — "the workshop of the world." Not only were Britons certain that they would keep all they had; they expected more and more — "wider still and wider." Already English economists were managing Siam's foreign trade. There were two British colonies, British Honduras and British Guiana, in Latin America. More important, Hong Kong and Weihaiwei were on the Chinese coast; in London, men speculated over when Victoria's other titles would be joined by "Empress of China." They also dreamed of a Cape-to-Cairo railway, just as Germans looked toward a Berlin-to-Baghdad railway. Englishmen had expelled officious Chinese from Tibet, and the Indian Ocean was already an English lake. Southeast Asia's future was pretty much settled. The Bank of Persia was a British firm. In Italy, the cable car route up Mount Vesuvius was owned outright by Cook's. Constantinople had its own judge and jail for Englishmen. The inspector general of Chinese Customs was Irish, and the military adviser to the sultan of Morocco was a Scot. Foreign governments were told where and when to build new lighthouses, and if they weren't prompt, the British solved the problem in their own way; the P & O put one up in the Red Sea on Dardalus Reef — foreign soil — and hired Englishmen to man it.

London was not only the capital of the world; it was the largest metropolis history had ever known, bigger than most imperial possessions or even some European powers. As we shall see, in matters of sex the Victorians should be judged, not by what they said, but by what they did; during the century before Churchill's birth the population of the island tripled — then a reproductive record — and London grew from two million souls to five million. (It was also the favorite of expatriates. Over thirty thousand Germans lived there, over fifteen thousand Americans, and more Irishmen than in Dublin.) The advent of trains and steamships had seen London rise as England's greatest port and the largest exporter on earth. The clocks of the world were measured from Greenwich. The Near East and the Far East were so called because they were near and far from London. Lloyd's was the world's insurance agent, and had been for two hundred years. In the vaults beneath the City's banks, gold bars rose in gleaming stacks; British securities were worth an astounding £11,333,000,000. The interest on foreign investments alone exceeded £100,000,000 a year. The gold sovereign was the strongest currency on earth; the City, the world's center of finance, commerce, and banking. London was the center of much else. Here, at the time of Churchill's birth, Joseph Lister was pioneering antiseptic surgery. Here Bessemer had perfected his process. Here Darwin, Tennyson, Browning, and Trollope were at the height of their careers. Dickens had been in his grave only four years; John Stuart Mill less than one. And if distant natives became restless, British ingenuity could be counted on to solve the problem:

Whatever happens, we have got
The Maxim gun and they have not.

In London there were ten mail deliveries a day. "Communications," Morris wrote, "were the first concern of [the] late Victorian rulers."[7] Letters reached Melbourne in four weeks, and British lines of communications, which had begun with cables to India and the United States in 1866 and were now spanning Australia, would soon gird the entire world. Distant outposts still depended upon native runners, trotting through jungles or over highlands with forty-five-pound leather pouches slung over their shoulders, but the days of isolation for months or sometimes years were past. Lebensraum was one of the Empire's driving forces; millions of Englishmen lived under its mandates, and serving them was a major industry. If you were posted near one of the population centers, the free ports of Aden, Gibraltar, Singapore, or Hong Kong, for example, you lived in style. The ubiquitous Cook's would provide you with poultry, vegetables, rowboats, donkeys, servants wearing Cook's livery, and even the Oxford Marmalade of which Victorians were so fond. Cook's made the arrangements for Gordon's and Kitchener's military expeditions on the Nile and also for troops fighting on India's frontiers. Cook's planned Moslem pilgrimages to Mecca and arranged Queen Victoria's own travels. On one occasion Cook's mapped out a European trip for an Indian maharaja whose baggage train included twenty chefs, ten elephants, thirty-three tigers, and a Krupp cannon.

Except for the time lag for news from home, which the cables would soon close, Englishmen in the Empire's settled possessions were well informed about the world's goings-on. In Cairo, say, you could read the *Egyptian Gazette,* or in Lahore the *Civil and Military Gazette,* subedited by young Kipling. The reading room of your club carried *Punch,* the *Book of Horse, Blackwood's, Wisden,* and *Country Life.* The favorite London paper was the archimperialist *Daily Mail,* which, typically, said of lascars: "It is because there are people like this in the world that there is an Imperial Britain. This sort of creature has to be ruled, so we rule him, for his good and our own." Doing so required preservation of the myth of white supremacy; of what we call racism. (Significantly, there was no such word then.) Conditions had improved since pre-Victorian days, when a native could be castrated for striking a white man or hanged for the theft of one shilling and sixpence. Certainly the average Indian or African toiling beneath the Union Jack was far better off than the average Chinese under his warlords, but British colonial hotels still found it necessary to display notices reading: "Gentlemen are requested not to strike the servants." English soldiers arriving in imperial cantonments were coached in how to avoid inflicting blows on the face, where the bruises would show. And Africans were caned frequently, like unruly boys.[8]

Playing the role of an *Übermensch* wasn't always pleasant. You paid the price of the myth. In Calcutta it meant wearing a frock coat and top hat in the punishing heat. Even the white linen suits and cork topees worn inland could be cruelly uncomfortable. Emotional discomfort could be worse. For loving parents the hardest moment came when a boy reached his seventh birthday, time for him to be sent home to school, never again to be seen as a child. Health was also a problem. Every newcomer could expect to be laid low by diarrhea — "Delhi Belly." Old-timers suggested Cockle's Pills, and they seemed to work for some. Others suffered from intestinal upsets, off and on, throughout their colonial years, attended by the native "wet sweepers" who serviced the privies known as "gulkskhanas" or, more vulgarly, as "thunder boxes." It didn't help that snakes were said to slither inside sometimes and lurk within the thunder box, coiled there, waiting to bite the next visitor.

The penultimate sin for an Englishman, in all imperial possessions, was to go broke. If it happened, the hat was passed for passage home, and the penniless offender was dumped on the dock like trash, which was how he was regarded. Only cowardice was worse than indigence. Showing a yellow streak was the greatest threat to rule by consent of the ruled, the surest way to shatter the image, and the man guilty of it was lucky to escape unflogged. Absolute fearlessness was assumed. Death in battle was the noblest of ends. In Africa, men's eyes misted over and their voices grew husky in speaking of Major Allen Wilson's Last Stand on the bank of the Shangani River during the wars against the Matabele tribesmen in 1896. When Wilson and his thirty-two men had run out of ammunition, the story ran, they shook hands, sang "God Save the Queen," and stood shoulder to shoulder to meet their doom. There were many similar examples. The Last Stand — resistance to the last man — was in fact a kind of rite, a tableau vivant celebrated in Victorian yarns and ballads, and in Wilson's case by a famous painting, Allan Stewart's *There Was No Survivor,* depicting dauntless men veiled in gunsmoke, surrounded by their dead horses, with their leader stage front, bareheaded, a sublime expression on his face. Such accounts were particularly popular in *Chatterbox,* a magazine favored by genteel children; they were probably a secular expression of the evangelical Christianity which swept England in the 1870s and 1880s.

Chinese Gordon was the most heroic martyr. His hour of glory struck on January 28, 1885, when Winston was ten. According to one popular account, Gordon waited until the Arabs were storming his Khartoum palace. Then, knowing all was lost, it was said, he changed into his white uniform at daybreak and took up a position at the head of the stairs, "standing in a calm and dignified manner, his left hand resting on the hilt of his sword." Racing upward, one sneering Arab shouted, "O cursed one, your time has come!" Gordon, according to this version, "made a gesture of scorn and turned away." Moments later he was impaled upon a half-dozen spears. Queen Victoria wrote his sister: "*How* shall I write to you, or how shall I attempt to express *what I feel?* To *think* of your dear, noble, heroic Brother, who served his Country and his Queen so truly, so heroically, with a self-sacrifice so edifying to the World . . . is to me *grief inexpressible!*" What is peculiar about this is that Gordon's garrison, like Wilson's, had been wiped out. As there were no survivors, there had been no one to tell the world how either had actually ended.[9]

In India, Last Stand immortality was attained in Burma or on the North-West Frontier, among the Afghans and the warring tribes of the Waziris, the Mahsuds, and the Afridis. It was in Kabul, on September 3, 1879 — the year Winston began reading *Chatterbox* — that Arabs invaded the British legation and put Sir Louis Cavagnari and his staff to the sword. Disraeli had assured the Commons that the position was impregnable, and Gladstone never let him forget it. Yet turning the brittle pages of old newspapers one has the distinct impression that the sentimental Victorians enjoyed their sobs. They erected statues of Sir Louis and went about rejuvenated. The following year they put up another after a gallant young officer named Thomas Rice Henn and eleven men forfeited their lives while covering the retreat of an entire British brigade. Wolseley wrote of Henn: "I envy the manner of his death. . . . If I had ten sons, I should indeed be proud if all ten fell as he fell."[10] Horatius had held the Sublician Bridge over the Tiber to the last, or so Macaulay had said, and now, over two thousand years later, soldiers of the Queen were inspired by a similar code of valor:

The sand of the desert is sodden red —
Red with the wreck of a square that broke —
The Gatling's jammed and the Colonel dead,
And the regiment blind with dust and smoke,
The river of death has brimmed his banks,
And England's far, and honour a name,
But the voice of a schoolboy rallies the ranks:
"Play up! play up! and play the game!"

This famous stanza strikes an odd note. The typical British soldier, if he had any education at all, had attended a "Ragged School" for the poor, where there were no games and certainly no concept of fair play. Those were the legacy of the public schools — Eton, Harrow, Winchester, Westminster, Charterhouse, Rugby, Shrewsbury — in whose forms the future rulers of the Empire were trained. The Victorian age was the Indian summer of homage, before wars, depressions, and nuclear horrors had destroyed faith in all establishments. The social contract was everywhere honored. England was guided by the self-assured men of the upper classes. They thought themselves better than the middle and lower classes, just as those classes assumed that they were better than the *fellahin* and the *dukawallahs.* In both cases the presumption was rarely challenged.

The selection of the Queen's proconsuls in the colonies was oligarchic, a product of what later generations would call "the old-boy network" or — to use an allusion they would have understood — a philosophic vision not unlike that of Er the Pamphylian in Plato's *Republic,* who, watching the souls choosing their destiny, saw the noblest pick power. There were two ways to enter the autocracy of colonial Britain. If you were recommended by your tutor at Oxford, say, or at Cambridge or Edinburgh, and were between the ages of twenty-one and twenty-three, you could make an appointment at the India Office, situated along one side of the Foreign Office quadrangle at the corner of Whitehall and Downing Street. There you were given the Indian Civil Service examination on subjects ranging from Sanskrit to English literature, and if you passed you were tested on another spectrum of topics, including Asian languages and horsemanship, a year later. Candidates who were accepted were off to Calcutta, Bombay, or Madras on the P & O, probably for good. The "Indian Civil," or "ICS," was a much stiffer hurdle than that at the Colonial Office, on another side of the quadrangle. Applicants there needn't be brilliant; indeed, those with a first-class degree were suspect. The emphasis was on "character" and the "all-rounder," on being "steel-true and blade-straight." You were interviewed by the colonial secretary's assistant private secretary, who never saw a British colony in his life. The atmosphere in his homey office was convivial, clublike, manly. One talked of mutual acquaintances, friends, headmasters, tutors, and engaged in similar rituals of self-reference. In this crucial stage it was important to have the backing of someone whom the interviewer considered a keen judge of men — someone like Benjamin Jowett, the cherubic master of Balliol College, Oxford. Jowett's maxims tell us much about his protégés. He said: "Never retract. Never explain. Get it done and let them howl." And: "We are all dishonest together, and therefore we are all honest." And, on Darwin's *Descent of Man:* "I don't believe a word of it." He was partial to peers and noble families on the ground that "social eminence is an instrument wherewith, even at the present day, the masses may be moved." If Jowett or his sort approved, a stripling just out of the university might find himself ruling a territory twice the size of Great Britain, acting as magistrate, veterinarian, physician, resolver of family quarrels, and local expert on crop blight. The similarity of officials' backgrounds gave the realm a certain cohesiveness. Morris observed: "All over the Empire these administrators, like members of some scattered club, shared the same values, were likely to laugh at the same jokes, very probably shared acquaintances at home. . . . Place them all at a dinner table, and they would not feel altogether strangers to each other."[11]

It was collusion, of course, and it could lead to highly unsuitable appointments, particularly when a great family wanted to rid itself of a black sheep. But most of the youths grew into shrewd men; the level of performance was very high. And many of them could scarcely be envied. Often they started out living in leaky mud huts, rarely seeing anything of their countrymen except for an occasional trader or missionary with whom, under other circumstances, they would have had nothing in common. They often had only the vaguest idea of the boundaries defining their territories, or the size of the populations for which they were responsible. In Uganda, six months was added to home leave because an Englishman had to walk eight hundred miles to reach civilization. While on leave he had to choose an English wife in a hurry, because it might be years before he saw another white woman. With grit, that quality much prized among the Victorians, he stuck it out, sometimes leaving a benign stamp on his tract of the wild. In Nyasaland, England's deepest penetration into Africa, you can still find natives who, because their overlord was Scottish, recite Christian prayers with a Scot's burr: "The Lor-r-r-d is my shepherd . . ."[12] It is difficult to condemn men who followed their star when the temptation to slacken was immense, who daily wore their quaint little uniform of white shorts and white stockings into which the traditional pipe was stuffed, but dressed for dinner whenever possible, to keep a sense of order, and carried collapsible little flagpoles wherever they went, so that the fluttering Union Jack would always remind their wards of their distant Queen.

Uganda and Nyasaland were hardship posts. Elsewhere life was more agreeable. In Kenya, British residents stocked streams with trout, and all the great imperial cities had racecourses and polo fields. John Stuart Mill called the whole Empire "a vast system of outdoor relief for the British upper classes."[13] That was misleading — by their sheer numbers, non-U voices were more audible than the accents of the U — but it was the highborn British who set the tone, which, by the time young Winston Churchill reached India, had become disturbingly insular. In the beginning white men had adopted local ways, learning that in Kerala, for example, it was polite to cover one's mouth when talking to an Indian of high caste. In 1859 Samuel Shepheard, who built Shepheard's Hotel, was photographed on an Egyptian divan, wearing a fez, with a glittering brass hookah at one elbow and a parrot at the other. Then, with the invasion of English wives, the memsahibs, all this began to change. Potted plants arrived, and whatnots, and acres of that printed fabric so popular among the natives that its admirers gave it the Hindi name of chintz. The metamorphosis reached its culmination in the hill station of Simla, the cool summer capital of the Raj, in the foothills of the Himalayas, with its Scottish-baronial palace for the viceroy and his vicereine; tea shops; bandstands where Gilbert and Sullivan airs were played; and the Anglican tower of Christ Church, whose bell had been fashioned from a mortar seized in the Second Sikh War.

Churchill, writing from Bangalore, told his brother Jack: "Labour here is cheap and plentiful — existence costs but little and luxury can be easily obtained. The climate is generous and temperate. The sun — even in the middle of the day — is not unbearable and if you wear a 'Solar topee' or a cork hat — you can walk out at any time." And then he reported: "I have just been to luncheon at the Western India Club — a fine large building where every convenience can be obtained."[14] The Raj was beginning to sink its hooks into him. He had been disarmed "up at the Club," a phrase familiar all over the Empire. There, surrounded by paneled walls, deep leather chairs, and cut-glass decanters, a fresh subaltern like Winston could step up to the bar and find himself, if not among friends, at least among friends of friends. It was an important moment in Churchill's life. Only by understanding the spell of the Empire, and particularly the Raj, can one begin to grasp the Churchillian essence.

It is a way of life which has vanished, and now, in the heyday of liberal piety, it is considered disreputable, even shameful. Yet there was an attractive side to the Raj, and its vitality is preserved in our language, in such words as *bazaar, bungalow, pajamas, punch, dinghy, khaki, veranda, sandals, gingham, shampoo, jodhpurs,* and *chit.* For young patricians who had passed the Indian Civil, or, like Churchill, had passed out of Sandhurst, the adventure began in London, with a shopping expedition in Oxford Street. There you bought your topee, in white or tan, at Henry Heath's Well Known Shoppe for Hattes. Also available were clever contrivances for coping with the tropics — Churchill had been wrong about the heat, and soon acknowledged it ("Imagine . . . a sun 110 in the shade!").[15] Among these were antitermite matting, mosquito netting, thorn-proof linen, canvas baths, and patent ice machines. Quinine was essential, but the thrifty postponed ordering tropical clothing until they docked in India, where they would also hire a tropical servant, the first of as many as twenty-five servants. Help was cheap, as Churchill had observed; a lower-middle-class mem who had slaved over a washtub at home would supervise a whole staff, and even British privates had bearers who polished their brass and boots and blancoed their webbing. Once ready for the next leg of his journey, the tyro would travel by train, chugging along at twenty miles per hour, his blinds securely locked at night, telegraphing ahead for a light breakfast (which he would learn to call *chota hazri*) and for lunch (tiffin). Detraining, he might cover as much as a hundred miles on horseback before reaching his appointed bungalow or, if he were a serving officer, his cantonment. By then he might be ready for his first trip to the thunder box, but if he still felt fit he would be introduced to the more welcome ritual of the "sundowner." This was the daily drink, and it was served in style by a bearer in a gown and turban. His tray would support a variety of paraphernalia: a carafe, linen napkin, gasogene, and ice bucket. Seasoned sahibs might add a nip of their quinine, as insurance against fever. Indeed, that is how the sundowner custom had begun, when men believed that alcohol was preventive medicine in the tropics.

It was an exotic, colorful life, and at a time when masculinity was valued, its greatest appeal was to men. The mems established their own conventions, their weekly At Homes and dances, their solemn talks with the C of E vicar, and, during the lawn tennis craze of the 1870s, a little exercise. But it was their husbands and the bachelors who thrived in India. They could retreat to their club, where women were of course forbidden, and they had polo, tiger hunting, golf, and all the glory, fireworks, and bunting that were manifestations of virile patriotism. If they were lucky and industrious, one day their names would appear on an Honours List. They were absolutely incorrupt, and the best of them were devoted to the natives in their charge. They adored their Queen, they knew that God was an Anglican, they believed in courage, in honor, in heroes. They could no more have identified with an antihero than with the Antichrist. In retrospect they all appear to have been gallant figures in one of history's greatest Last Stands. Of course, they didn't think of it that way. It never occurred to them that they, and all they represented, would one day be disowned, as the result of a national *défaillance,* within the lifetime of young Lieutenant Churchill, the polo star in Bangalore.

If you were passed back through a time warp and set down in Victorian London, your first impressions would depend upon where in the city you were, and under what circumstances. Henry James saw it at its most inhospitable, while riding in a "greasy four-wheeler to which my luggage had compelled me to commit myself" from the Euston train station to Morley's Hotel in Trafalgar Square. Night had fallen. It was a cold, damp March Sunday. Recalling the scene in 1888, James wrote: "The weather had turned wet. . . . The low black houses were as inanimate as so many rows of coal-scuttles, save where at frequent corners, from a gin-shop, there was a flare of light more brutal still than the darkness." He felt "a sudden horror of the whole place . . . like a tiger-pounce of homesickness which had been watching its moment. London was hideous, vicious, cruel, and above all overwhelming."[16]

The city itself was also overwhelmed, engulfed by changes with which it had not learned to cope, and which were scarcely understood. Some were inherent in the trebling of the population, some consequences of the Industrial Revolution. Particles of grime from factory smokestacks, blending with the cold fogs that crept down from the North Sea channel, produced impenetrable pea-soupers which could reduce visibility to a few feet — "London particulars," Dickens called them in *Bleak House.* They could be dangerous; it was in one of them that Soames Forsyte's wife's lover was run down by horses and killed. Much of London stank. The city's sewage system was at best inadequate and in the poorer of neighborhoods nonexistent. Buildings elsewhere had often been constructed over cesspools which, however, had grown so vast that they formed ponds, surrounding homes with moats of effluvia. Thoroughfares were littered with animal excrement. Gaslight was not yet the clear piped white light which arrived with the invention of the incandescent mantle in the 1890s. It was smokier, smellier, and yellower; some smudged lanterns dating from the reigns of George IV and William IV may still be found in Regent's Park. And the narrow, twisted streets were neither sealed nor asphalted. Victorians are often mocked for locking their windows, even in summer, but they had a lot to keep out: odors; dust; gusts of wind that could turn the open flames of candles or kerosene lamps into disastrous conflagrations.

In affluent neighborhoods windows were barred during most of the Queen's reign, for no policemen pounded beats until late in the century. James recoiled from the gin shops, but he didn't see the worst of it. The worst was in the blackened, brooding slums of Bluegate Fields, Cheapside, Wapping Docks, Bleeding Heart Yard, Mile-End Road, Maiden Lane, Paddington; St. Giles's, along Saffron Hill; Westminster ("the Devil's Acre"); Granby Street, beneath what is now Waterloo Station, with its bolt-holes for criminals; and Whitechapel, where the heaviest concentration of London's eighty thousand prostitutes lived and Jack the Ripper stalked his prey. At night the East End was eerie. Here the bricks which built the rising city were hardened in kilns like those in *Bleak House* and in Trollope's *Last Chronicle of Barset,* where fugitives found warmth at night. Workingmen were no longer paid in pubs, but that was where many headed when they had their money. There cheap gin, the curse of their class, fueled murderous fights and, by blurring judgment, converted men into easy recruits for criminal schemes — burglaries, typically, or pocket picking in Piccadilly. London's vast slums terrified respectable Londoners. Even the huskiest gentlemen refused to enter them without a heavy police escort.

The center of London was a hive of hyperactivity. If, like Henry James, you were an American who had spent his first night beneath Nelson's column and rose in the morning for a stroll along the Embankment, you might first become aware of a familiar quickness in the air. "*Mon Dieu, ces anglais, comme ils travaillent!*" wrote a French tourist.[17] London then had the push and bustle foreign visitors began to note in New York in the 1920s. You could hear it; Londoners called it "the Hum." This was the busiest metropolis in the world; men were all in a hurry, doing the world's work. And in this part of the city they *were* men. If you wanted to see women you would have to stroll toward the shopping district and its center, Piccadilly Circus, then named Regent Circus, with its beguiling statue, now called *Eros* but then, more primly, *Charity.* Wealthy ladies would be accompanied by servants carrying their parcels and followed, at a respectful distance, by their carriages (hence "the carriage trade"), which, if they were upper class, bore heraldic crests on the doors and were driven by coachmen wearing livery. Middle-class women hired their "Parcels Men" by the hour and usually shopped in pairs. An extraordinary number of them were pregnant, though propriety forbade them from venturing out in public after their third month. Whatever their condition, they would be tightly corseted in armor of whalebone and steel, a cruel fashion which was responsible for internal injuries even among women not carrying children. The point was to show the world that your husband had a comfortable income, that you didn't have to work. So styles were wildly impractical: great loops of ribbon, hoopskirts, lacy caps, silken parasols, dangling ringlets, blunt bustles, frills, petticoats, and layers of silk and satin heavily trimmed with bugles and beads.

None of them made women attractive to men. That was, or was thought to be, their last objective. Men were "the coarser sex"; women, as Janet Horowitz Murray found in her study of gender attitudes in nineteenth-century England, were thought to be "softer, more moral and pure." The very existence of sexual desire was denied. It says much about the Victorians that none of them recognized the Ripper murders as sex crimes. This was part of what O. R. MacGregor calls "the Victorian conspiracy of silence about sex." Occasional male lubricity was grudgingly accepted for the future of the race, though men who lacked it were reassured by William Acton, a distinguished surgeon of the day: "No nervous or feeble young man need . . . be deterred from marriage by any exaggerated notion of the duties required of him." For a wife, her husband's animal drive was a cross to be borne. Dr. Acton wrote: "As a general rule, a modest woman seldom desires any sexual gratification for herself. She submits to her husband but only to please him; and, but for the desire for maternity, would far rather be relieved of his attentions." A Victorian mother prepared her daughter for the marriage bed with the advice: "Lie still, and think of England." It was in this spirit that Thomas Bowdler, earlier in the century, had published *The Family Shakespeare,* bearing the subtitle: "In which nothing is added to the Text; but those Words and Expressions are omitted which cannot with Propriety be read aloud in a Family." By contrast, the distributors of a pamphlet which advised couples not ready for children to practice douching were indicted for scheming "to vitiate and corrupt the morals of youth as well as of divers other subjects of the Queen and to incite . . . to indecent, obscene, unnatural, and immoral practices" by publishing an "indecent, lewd, filthy, bawdy, and obscene book." During the year before their trial, the pamphlet, which the jury agreed was salacious, had sold 700 copies. In the four months of notoriety, sales leapt to 125,000. The issue, it should be noted, was a middle-class issue. Sex was one of the few pleasures not denied to working-class women, and they hadn't the slightest intention of abandoning it. (Their word for lustful was *gay.*) As for the patricians — ladies like Winston's mother — the upper class had, as it had always had, a moral code all its own.[18]

Identifying a stranger's class has always been a social challenge for Londoners. Today it is a matter of vowels. In those days it was far easier, and would usually be accomplished by a glance. J. M. Bailey, an American visitor to London in the 1870s, wrote that he could find "traces of nobility" in an aristocrat's "very step and bearing." He asked mischievously: "Can you conceive of a bowlegged duke? Or is it possible for you to locate a pimple on the nose of a viscount? And no one, however diseased his imagination, ever pictured a baron with an ulcerated leg, or conceived of such a monstrous impossibility as a cross-eyed duchess."[19] That was Yankee wit, but the plain fact was that you *could* tell. At least you could tell the difference between a gentleman and a man who was not. Partly it was a matter of genes. The Normans had introduced high cheekbones, Roman noses, an abundance of equine chin, and hooded, sardonic eyes to the Anglo-Saxon nobility. Diet was more important. Generations of malnutrition and, more recently, of stooping in mines or bending over looms had given workmen's descendants slight stature, poor posture, and coarse complexion. They aged prematurely; they needed the attention of doctors they could seldom afford. The gentry were tall, fair, and erect. Although they may not have been godlike, they were certainly far healthier than their social inferiors, and by today's standards, even the genteel were sick a great deal. The groaning tables on Victorian Christmas cards groaned beneath platters of food that would be condemned as unfit by modern public-health officials. Preventive medicine was in its infancy. The twentieth-century visitor to the Strand would be startled by the number of pitted faces there. Smallpox was still rife. There were far more pocked features among the workmen, however. They simply lacked the resistance to affliction. They also lacked running water. Cholera hit them harder; so did diphtheria; so did infant mortality. In all of London, more babies died than adults. We cannot even guess at the toll in the slums, but it must have been appalling.

Gentlemen, no less than ladies, could be identified by their clothing. They wore top hats, indoors and out, except in homes or churches. Cuffs and collars were starched, cravats were affixed with jeweled pins, waistcoats were white, wide tubular trousers swept the ground at the heel but rose in front over the instep, black frock coats were somber and exquisitely cut. Swinging their elegant, gold-headed canes, gentlemen swaggered when crossing the street, dispensing coins to fawning men who swept the dung from their paths. (These men were followed by nimble boys with pans and brushes, who collected the ordure and sold it in the West End for fertilizer.) Bowlers were worn by clerks and shopkeepers and caps by those below them. Switching hats wouldn't have occurred to them, and it wouldn't have fooled anyone anyway. Despite advances in the mass production of menswear, dry cleaning was unknown in the London of the time. Suits had to be picked apart at the seams, washed, and sewn back together. Patricians wore new clothes or had tailors who could resew the garments they had made in the first place. The men in bowlers and caps couldn't do it; their wives tried but were unskillful, which accounts for their curiously wrinkled Sabbath-suit appearance in old photographs. Toward the end of Victoria's reign games and cycling modified gentlemen's dress. The Prince of Wales introduced the lounge coat. Short loose breeches and Norfolk jackets were worn on bikes, football players and runners and jumpers appeared in shorts, and cricketers and tennis players adopted long pants of white flannel. Except at regattas, none of this was matched in feminine fashions. Not only were bustles worn on the tennis court; a woman had to use her free hand to hold her trailing skirt off the ground. And the lower classes were unaffected because they had neither the money for fashions nor the time for sports.

Social mobility, as we understand it today, was not only unpursued by the vast majority; it had never existed. For centuries an Englishman's fate had been determined at birth. The caste system was almost as rigid as India's. Obedience to the master had been bred in childhood, and those who left the land for the mills as the agricultural class seeped into the cities were kept in line by custom and the example of all around them. Successful merchants were an exception, and a significant one. They built mansions, bought coaches, and hired servants, yet they were never fully accepted by the patriciate. As late as the spring of 1981 a *New Yorker* writer attributed Britain's sagging economy to the fact that a stigma was still attached to men "in trade." Similarly, the British trade unions' twentieth-century truculence may arise from the lower classes' inability to transfer their allegiance from aristocrats to merchants. In Victorian England, the chimney sweeps, ragpickers, chip sellers, dustmen, coachmen, and sandwich-board men who hired out at one-and-six a day were no more rebellious than the serfs from whom they were descended. They did what they did well, and that was enough for them. Richard Harding Davis wrote from England: "In America we hate uniforms because they have been twisted into meaning badges of servitude; our housemaids will not wear caps, nor will our coachmen shave their mustaches. This tends to make every class of citizen look more or less alike. But in London you can always tell a 'bus-driver from the driver of a four-wheeler, whether he is on his box or not. The Englishman recognizes that if he is in a certain social grade he is likely to remain there, and so, instead of trying to dress like some one else in a class to which he will never reach, he 'makes up' for the part in life he is meant to play, and the 'bus-driver buys a high white hat, and the barmaid is content to wear a turned-down collar and turned-back cuffs, and the private coachman would as soon think of wearing a false nose as a mustache. He accepts his position and is proud of it, and the butcher's boy sits up in his cart just as smartly, and squares his elbows and straightens his legs and balances his whip with just as much pride, as any driver of a mail-cart in the Park."[20]

London's massed horsepower made a lively spectacle, bewildering and even frightening to visitors. Each morning some twenty thousand vehicles drawn by steeds lumbered and surged over the toll-free London Bridge — Tower Bridge would not be ready until 1894 — and fanned out into the wakening city. The rigs varied. At this hour, in this tumult, you would see few private carriages. They sat parked in the West End and could be seen in large numbers only when they assembled for such liturgical upper-class ceremonies as the annual Eton-Harrow cricket match at Lord's, in St. John's Wood, where over six hundred of them were counted in 1871. Much of the bridge traffic carried essentials. There were convoys of carts bearing galvanized tanks, headed for neighborhoods which still had no running water. Produce and livestock accompanied them, including, once a year, sheep on their way to an enclosure near Kensington Palace. A contemporary account tells of the annual sheepshearing: "Thousands of sheep are brought from Scotland and distributed over London wherever grazing can be obtained. After the shearing, the sheep are kept awhile in the park for fattening, and thence gradually find their way to the butchers' shops."[21]

In the city these wagons mingled with public transport and cabs. The first electric tramcar was built in 1883 — electric lights had made their appearance two years earlier, for the Savoy Theatre's premiere of Gilbert and Sullivan's *Patience* — but London wasn't introduced to trolleys until 1900. Before that, horse-drawn streetcars crawled along tracked paths in the center of the streets, maddening obstacles to the faster hansoms, growlers, and flys. Flys were usually rented. The Coupé and Dunlop Brougham Company in Regent Street would hire one out at seven shillings and sixpence for the first two hours. But the smartest and fastest way to travel was in the two-wheeled hansom cabs, "the gondolas of London," as Disraeli called them. Harnesses jingling, horses trotting briskly, and lamps and brass work polished to a blazing finish, there were over three thousand hansoms in London, charging a shilling for two miles and sixpence a mile over that, though the driver could charge more if he traveled beyond the "Four Mile Radius" from Charing Cross, which was (and still is) the geographic center of the city. The cabman sat high in the back, holding reins which passed through a support on the front of the roof, and the front of the cab was open except for two folding doors which came halfway up and protected the passenger from dust and mud. This feature was important. Trains had been so successful that other forms of transportation had hardly changed since Victoria's coronation. Country roads were surfaced with grass, earth, and stones. Downtown London's streets were cobbled, but unless you were in an enclosed coach you were lucky to arrive at your destination unstained.

Alighting at Charing Cross, a visitor from the 1980s would quickly become aware of a gamy tang in the air — blended aromas of saddle soap, leather, brass polish, and strong tobacco; scents of wood fires; the fragrance of baking bread and roasting meat manipulated by street chefs. All sorts of entrepreneurs were active on the pavements, and they fascinated Gustave Doré, who executed a series of engravings of them in the early 1870s: dog sellers, flower girls, flypaper merchants (who wore fly-studded samples on their dilapidated top hats), hardware dealers, tinkers, ragmen, knife grinders, ginger-beer men, apple sellers, oyster men, match vendors, "lemonade" men who mixed their chemicals on the spot in portable tubs, and some four thousand hawkers of oranges. The popularity of oranges was due less to their taste than to their smell. Even where sanitation existed, not all street odors were pleasant. Deodorants were unknown. The poor reeked, which was why they were unwelcome in Victorian churches. Nell Gwyn had carried oranges to cut the stench of sweat, vermin, and manure. Before that, the Elizabethans had used pomanders, small balls of pierced metal packed with fragrant herbs. To this day, London judges mount their benches bearing nosegays — hence the name — and once a year herbs are scattered in courtrooms.

Among the other peddlers were salesmen exhibiting great bolts of black broadcloth. The Victorians were very open about death. Today people die in hospitals, where children are "shielded" or "protected" from them; graveyards are landscaped like parks, and mourning is seldom worn. In those days a demise was an important, fascinating event. Typically it occurred in the home, in bed, with the whole family in attendance and little ones held up for a final embrace from the departing parent or grandparent. The pavement chapmen made garments of deep mourning available to the lower classes. Patricians bought their black, gray, and deep purple clothes and black ostrich feathers in Oxford Street shops devoted solely to that trade. Men draped sashed crepe "weepers" around their hats. Even cousins sewed black armbands on their sleeves. Englishmen were more preoccupied with death then than we are, partly because there was much more of it. In 1842 a royal commission had found that the average professional man lived thirty years; the average laborer, seventeen. By the year of Churchill's birth about fifteen years had been added to these, but it was still not unusual for a middle-class man to die at thirty-nine, as Arthur Sullivan's brother Fred did in 1877, inspiring Sullivan to write "The Lost Chord." Another reason for bereavement had nothing to do with delicacy of feeling. The loss of a father was disastrous. There was seldom any financial net beneath the survivors of a wage earner. Jobs were at a premium; artisans provided or rented their own tools, and one mill outdid Scrooge, issuing the notice: "A stove is provided for the clerical staff. It is recommended that each member of the clerical staff bring four pounds of coal each day during cold weather."[22] Except for the thriftiest of savers, however, no class was immune to the catastrophe which followed the passing of a head of household. If a man had been a successful physician, say, or a respectable barrister, his family might have belonged to the upper middle class as long as he was alive, living in the Wordsworthian tranquillity of a leafy Georgian square, with a coach in the mews and a boy at Winchester. All that vanished with his last breath. The family was evicted from the house; the son took a job as a clerk; his mother made what she could as a seamstress, or, in that bitterest refuge of shabby gentility, as a governess in a bourgeois home.

Prosperous homes could be identified by their bay windows, as much a status symbol as the eight-paned window had been a century earlier. The skyline was dominated by St. Paul's, Wren's fifty other baroque churches, Big Ben, and the Gothic Houses of Parliament. In Pall Mall were the Athenaeum and the Reform Club, the home of the Liberal party; the Conservatives' Carlton Club; and the great imperial clubs: the Oriental, the East India, and the Omar Khayyam. The city was a mass of poles and crossbars that bore telegraph wires and the boisterous excesses of Victorian advertising. Napoleon had scorned England as *"un pays de marchands."* Actually, it was more a nation of hucksters. Billboards, or "sky-signs," celebrated the virtues of Salada Tea, Waltham Watches, Cook's Tours, Thurston's Billiard Tables, Brinstead Pianos, and Goddall's Yorkshire Relish. Bumping down London's streets came remarkable vehicles shaped like Egyptian obelisks, cabbages, and huge top hats, each of them bearing a brand name. The front of opticians' shops looked like the lenses of gigantic spectacles. Of all the forms of ads, the cheapest and wildest was the "fly-poster," which could be plastered on any "dead wall" in public view. Gangs pasted these up at night, so that early risers would be greeted, typically, with: "Good morning! Have you used Pears' Soap?" Sometimes householders would find their windows, even their doors, papered over. Other times gangs from different agencies would clash in the dark, tearing down the others' posters or obliterating them with buckets of black tar.

Optical illusions, red puzzle signs, posters gummed to public monuments or the hulls of ships anchored in the Thames — anything went. A young advertising man said: "Any fool can make soap. It takes a clever man to sell it." One innovation, still with us, was the endorsement of a product by a celebrity, which in those days meant such notables as Eugene Sandow, the German strong man, and Captain Webb, the Channel swimmer. Ambitious copywriters aimed even higher than that. We think of the Victorians as deferential toward the royal family. So they were, but some admen, who weren't, exploited that deference. The Queen was depicted holding a cup of Mazawatta Tea or presiding over the legend: " 'The Subject's Best Friend' — HUDSON'S DRY SOAP — Home and Clothes as Sweet as a Rose." The Prince of Wales was shown handing a glass of Bushmills Whiskey to the shah of Persia at the Paris Exhibition in 1889, and saying: *"This, your Majesty, is the celebrated Bushmills Whiskey which you tasted in England and liked so much.* I feel sure it will win the Gold Medal." A florist, pushing corsages, quoted the Duchess of York — without her approval; none of the luminaries were consulted — "She thinks the Flower Shield a most ingenious invention and wishes it success." Even the pontiff was identified as an admirer of a popular drink: "Two Infallible Powers. The Pope and Bovril." The soap manufacturers knew no shame. Sir John Millais, a successful artist, painted a portrait of a boy making soap bubbles with a clay pipe. The boy's bar of soap lay on the ground. To Sir John's astonishment, the picture was reproduced all over the country with "Pears" painted on the bar. In Berlin, Heinrich von Treitschke told a class: "The English think soap is civilization."[23]

One device the advertisers missed was the jingle, and this is puzzling, because Victorians loved melodies. Garibaldian organ-grinders stood on every downtown London street corner, bawling ballads. Gilbert and Sullivan were national figures. Not counting the Salvation Army and the military, there were over five thousand bands in the country, and on holidays Londoners crowded around the bandstands in their parks. This was the golden age of the music halls. Between 1850 and 1880 about five hundred new ones were built — with the city's fifty theaters, this meant that 350,000 Londoners were entertained every night — of which the most famous were the Alhambra, the London Pavilion, the Empire, and the Tivoli. Each hall had its portentous chairman, with his candle, his gavel, and his vast expanse of shirtfront; each encouraged its audiences to join the choruses. The stars were famous enough to endorse soap and whiskey, though unlike the eminent they expected their cut and got it. (Lillie Langtry got it and lost it; her signature was reproduced in an ad, and a forger copied it and cleaned her out.) High on the lists of sightseers arriving from the far reaches of the Empire were evenings hearing the "lion comiques": Harry Clifton singing "Knees Up, Mother Brown,"

George Layborne leading "Champagne Charlie Is My Name," Jenny Valmore whispering "So Her Sister Says," and Marie Lloyd:

Only fancy if Gladstone's there,
And falls in love with me;
If I run across Labouchère
I'll ask him home to tea.
I shall say to a young man gay,
If he treads upon my frock,
"Randy pandy, sugardy pandy,
Buy me some Almond Rock."

Henry du Pré Labouchère was an advocate of Home Rule for Ireland. And "Randy pandy" was Lord Randolph Churchill. Music hall performers were keenly aware of politicians and public events, of England's power around the world, of London's role as an imperial capital. Britain was hardly a democracy, at least as we understand it; only 16.4 percent of the people could vote. But Britain's people counted because they, like the distant races toiling beneath the same flag, consented to be ruled as they were. Not the Queen, not peers, not the Commons, and not public-school men wrote the ditties that celebrated the nation's glory and defied those who sought to curb the growth of an Empire which they believed belonged to them. It was G. H. "the Great" Macdermott, the most celebrated of the music hall performers, who, singing the lyrics of George William Hunt, gave voice to their determination in the 1878 crisis which arose during the Russo-Turkish War:

We don't want to fight, but by jingo, if we do,
We've got the ships, we've got the men, we've got the money, too.
We've fought the Bear before,
And while Britons shall be true,
The Russians shall not have
Constantinople.

The British soldier was given a small island for his birthplace and the whole world as his grave. Including Indian sepoys, there were about 356,000 soldiers in the army — at the time of Marcus Ulpius Trajanus, Rome's legions had numbered 300,000 men — including 55 line battalions scattered about India, Ireland, Hong Kong, Bermuda, Ceylon, Malta, Egypt, Gibraltar, Canada, Singapore, the West Indies, South

Africa, Barbados, and Mauritius. Their epitaph may be found today on sinking gravestones: "For Queen and Empire." It is inadequate. They died for more than that. So vast an Empire, so vigorous a society, could have been neither built nor held without staunch ideological support, a complex web of powerful beliefs, powerfully held. Alfred North Whitehead defined a civilization in spiritual terms, and Christopher Dawson, in *The Dynamics of World History,* said: "Behind every great civilization there is a vision." What was the vision of imperial Britain?

Jingoism was part of it, or rather one of its outward manifestations, and it wasn't confined to the music halls. On the slightest excuse, Londoners in the city's rookeries hung out bunting and gay streamers, crisscrossing mews and alleys where washing was usually hung to dry. Behind the calls to honor, duty, and glory lay the Victorians' firm belief in obedience — absolute obedience to God, the Queen, and one's superiors, in the family as much as in the army. It was a time of pervasive authoritarianism. The Baptist preacher C. H. Spurgeon wrote of the Victorian wife that her husband "has many objects in life which she does not quite understand; but she believes in them all, and anything which she can do to promote them, she delights to perform."[24] Unquestioning submission to orders was taught to schoolboys as soon as they reached the age of awareness; they recited "The Death of Nelson," "Drake's Drum," "The Boy Stood on the Burning Deck," "The Wreck of the Hesperus," and "The Charge of the Light Brigade." Every story for Victorian children had a point, a moral; usually one of dutifulness. Winston Churchill was four years old when the most popular glorifier of discipline, G. A. Henty, published the first of his eighty novels for children. With loyalty went courage, as witness Red Riding Hood, Hansel and Gretel, Alice, the Ugly Duckling, and Tom Thumb.

War was Henleyized, and such ancient institutions as the Crown, the aristocracy, and the Church of England were venerated. This allegiance to tradition accounts for the immense popularity of Tennyson's *Idylls of the King* and the flood of best-selling historical novels: Scott's *Ivanhoe,* Bulwer-Lytton's *Last Days of Pompeii,* Robert Louis Stevenson's *Kidnapped,* Charles Reade's *Cloister and the Hearth,* Stanley Weyman's *Under the Red Robe,* Charles Kingsley's *Westward Ho!* and Harrison Ainsworth's *Old St. Paul's.* Reverence for the past was especially strong in the church. The devout took the Bible literally, assumed the existence of an afterlife, and believed that the only significance of life on earth was as a preparation for eternity. That blind faith could have flourished in an age of intellectual ferment may be puzzling, but the Victorians could rationalize anything; for them, doubts raised by evolution, for example, were resolved by Tennyson's *In Memoriam.* By the time a youth of good family had reached manhood, he had heard more than a thousand sermons. He could not matriculate at Oxford, or graduate from Cambridge, until he had signed the church's Thirty-Nine Articles. Days of Humiliation, such as the one commemorating the Mutiny martyrs, signified national atonement. The Sabbath was sacred. To be sure, half the population stayed away from weekly services — when the Archbishop of Canterbury grieved that the church was losing the working people, Disraeli replied, "Your Grace, it has never had them" — but this was a matter of propriety, not piety.[25] The poor were only too well aware that they were unwelcome. Nevertheless, they knew their Bible, knew their hymns; the ancestors of workmen who read nothing today were familiar with *Pilgrim's Progress* and *Paradise Lost* and could quote from them.

The middle classes, who were always in their pews, if not singing in choirs, cultivated evangelical seriousness, Arnoldian earnestness, and the eagerness of Bagehot. They loved maxims. "Attend church, abstain from drink, read a serious newspaper, put your money in the bank," they told one another. And:

> *Staid Englishmen, who toil and save*
> *From your first childhood to your grave,*
> *And seldom spend and always save —*
> *And do your duty all your life*
> *By your young family and wife.*

Carlyle implored them to devote themselves to work, which was sending coals to Newcastle. They had already made a cult of toil. It dominated their lives, and not just in London. A French visitor to the Midlands in the 1870s wrote: "On entering an office, the first thing you see written up is: 'You are requested to speak of business only.' " *Bradshaw's Handbook to the Manufacturing Districts* described "the utmost order and regularity" in the enormous textile mills of Ancoats and Chorlton, and said that visitors were discouraged because they "occupy the time of an attendant, and disturb the attention of operatives throughout the mill. The loss accruing from this cause is frequently more than can be readily estimated." Until the year of Churchill's birth, working-class children started in the mills on their ninth birthday; then the age was raised to ten. When Parliament passed a "short-time" bill limiting workers to a sixty-hour week, employers were outraged. Safety measures, as the term is understood today, were unknown. This led to what Professor Geoffrey Best calls "Death's continuing Dance around the scene of labour."

Toilers in phosphorus factories suffered from "fossy jaw." A thousand miners were killed each year, and more than three thousand railway workers killed or maimed. The proliferation of moving parts was lethal, but mill owners airily dismissed the problem: "Workers *will* be careless." Protests were few and unheard. Writing in *The Uncommercial Traveller,* Dickens quoted a Shoreditch woman: "Better be ulcerated and paralyzed for eighteenpence a day . . . than see the children starve." Yet, astonishingly, she made no complaint. Like her Queen, she believed that all work, even drudgery, was sacred. The Victorians were never more Victorian than when they stood in church, or around a Salvation Army band, belting out "Art Thou Weary?"[26]

Though safer than mill hands, the middle classes drove themselves just as hard in pursuit of "respectability," which was not, as Shaw acidly noted, the same thing as morality. Gilbert's Pirate King sang that piracy was more honest than respectability, and in *H.M.S. Pinafore* the reproachful Captain Corcoran tells Buttercup that it would have been "more respectable" if she had gone ashore before nightfall. Respectability, in short, was largely a matter of appearances. It was fragile; the slightest lapse could shatter it. Those who retained it were, in G. M. Young's words, forever fearful that "an unguarded look, a word, a gesture, a picture, or a novel, might plant a seed of corruption in the most innocent heart, and the same word or gesture might betray a lingering affinity with the class below." Ridiculing the Victorians is easy, and nearly everyone who has written of them since their departure has done it. They were hypocritical, snobbish, maudlin, fanatical about "moral rectitude" and the superiority of the British "race," devoted to Augustan "order, regularity, and refinement of life."[27] The books on their shelves told you that they played their games according to Hoyle, toured England as directed by *Bradshaw's Weekly Guide to the Railways,* were instructed in housekeeping by Mrs. Beeton and guided abroad by Baedeker and Cook. Always deferential (Bagehot's favorite word), they dreamed that their daughters might marry someone in *Who's Who* or, even better, in Burke's *Peerage* and *Baronetage.* At the table they watched their tongues. Legs were "limbs," and anyone wanting to use such words as "disemboweled" or "pelvis" employed another language or remained silent.

Palmerston had pointed the way for those who obeyed the rules; he extolled the nation's social system as one "in which every class of society accepts with cheerfulness the lot which providence has assigned to it; while at the same time each individual is constantly trying to raise himself, not by violence and illegality, but by preserving good conduct and by the steady and energetic exertion of the moral and intellectual faculties with which his creator has endowed him." This sent them to public reading rooms, Mechanics Institutes, mutual improvement groups, and public lectures and displays. Not only did they intend to better themselves; they insisted that the lower classes follow their example, until Dickens protested: "The English are, so far as I know, the hardest worked people on whom the sun shines. Be content if in their wretched intervals of leisure they read for amusement and do no worse. They are born at the oar, and they live and die at it. Good God, what would we have of them!"[28]

Yet even Dickens believed that true love and marriage led to a horse and carriage — that respectability was rewarded by a rise in social standing. The nouveaux riches Victorians, with their sudden access to prosperity and power, were certainly naive, and often vulgar. They worshiped false gods (the theme of *Dombey and Son*) and they failed to meet the standards they set for themselves. But certainly that is loftier than the abandonment of all standards. The stars of social navigation which they tried to follow were stars — genuine ideals, even if unattainable. Their "civilizing mission" in far lands was not only well-meant; at its best it was also noble. The English way of life, which they believed was exportable, was at least as estimable as the way of life the Americans tried to export a century later, with less success. When the Romans conquered a province, the glories of Roman citizenship were slow to follow. The moment the Union Jack raced up a colonial flagstaff, speech was free and habeas corpus the right of all. Among distant people a parliament became a status symbol, like having a national airline today, but more admirable. And if the Victorians' system was flawed, they knew it. Believing in individual and collective reform, the best of their intellectuals, like the Americans who followed them, practiced vigorous, often savage, self-criticism. In the fine arts, London was a suburb of Paris and Berlin, but in literature it led the way. Carlyle, Dickens, John Ruskin, Samuel Butler, Herbert Spencer, and the contributors to *Yellow Book* were all Victorian rebels.

The chief difference between rebels then and rebels now is that they saw the world as rational, harmonious, teleological. Cartesians to a man, they believed that life was rational and mechanical and that progress was as inevitable as evolution and moved in the same direction. Their world, in Hans Koning's happy phrase, was "an unthreatened world." The earth seemed to be on the verge of being totally understood. Its flora, fauna, tides, and mountain ranges had been catalogued, measured, and minutely described. Some parts were still unexplored, but steamships would soon fix that. So the Victorian intellectuals felt a sense of confidence and optimism. They never doubted that the globe would always be dominated by Caucasian men. If the white masters differed among themselves, their governments would resort to arms. That prospect didn't alarm them. "Unwarlike," indeed, was a pejorative. It signified vitiation. The prime weakness of the darker races was their lack of martial spirit. Kipling urged England's youth: "Bite the bullet, old man, and don't let them think you're afraid." Not that there was much to fear; the Industrial Revolution had not yet caught up with weaponry. The Gatling and the Maxim were clever gadgets but, it was thought, without potential. Bloodshed in Britain's little colonial wars was relatively light. The eleventh edition of the *Encyclopaedia Britannica* actually told its readers that "losses in battle are . . . almost insignificant when compared with the fearful carnage wrought by sword and spear."[29]

If any Victorian institution was cherished above all others, it was the home. "Home Sweet Home" — which sold 100,000 copies in its first year — was the most popular song of the century, even among workingmen who sang it in pubs because their own homes were unbearable. When an Englishman crossed his threshold he was in his castle, with almost absolute power over everyone within. That wasn't true of his wife, but if diaries and letters are to be trusted, she enjoyed their hearth even more than he did. It was a good thing they liked it. They hadn't much choice. Divorce usually meant ruin. It was almost impossible to obtain; a woman had to prove, not only that her husband was an adulterer, but that he was also guilty of desertion, cruelty, incest, rape, sodomy, or bestiality. Simple infidelity on his wife's part was all a man need show. However, the moment he picked up his decree, he was an outcast. Victoria dismissed one divorced member of her court even though he was the injured party. Often families turned a divorced relative's picture to the wall and spoke of him, if at all, as though he were dead.

Home was sanctuary, a place of peace and stability with sturdy furniture, in which evenings were spent reading aloud, whence the family departed for church and reunions with grandparents, uncles, aunts, and cousins, and where children were trained to assure the continuity of generations to come:

sic fortis Etruria crevit,
scilicet et facta est rerum pulcherrima Roma.

Keeping the Empire growing "strong and most beautiful" would be the solemn legacy of these children. Middle-class Victorian parents had no Rousseauistic illusions about youthful innocence; their young were never allowed to stray from adult supervision. The inference of repression is not necessarily justified. Children were taken to Punch-and-Judy shows, "suitable" plays in Drury Lane, and summer holidays at the seashore. But their lives revolved around the family. London evenings found them in the parlor, the boys in Norfolk jackets and the girls in beribboned bonnets and buttoned boots, joining in indoor games, handicrafts, watercolors, tableaux vivants, and, most colorfully, standing around the cheap upright pianos which began to be mass-produced in the 1870s, singing ballads. Over seven hundred publishers thrived in the city selling sheet music, including such favorites as "Danny Boy," "I Dreamt I Dwelt in Marble Halls," "Yes, Let Me Like a Soldier Fall," "I'll Sing Three Songs of Araby," "Annie Laurie," "Oft in the Stilly Night," "Come into the Garden, Maud" (from Tennyson), selections from Handel's *Messiah* and Mendelssohn's *Elijah,* and Sullivan's "Onward, Christian Soldiers" and "The Lost Chord," which sold a half-million copies before Victoria's death.

The music would be read — and everyone with social aspirations could read music — by gaslight. By the 1880s gas had been installed in most middle-class neighborhoods. (Lower-class illumination was still provided by wax, oil, and tallow; penny-in-the-slot meters did not arrive until 1892.) The light flickered on gleaming brass coal scuttles and much that would seem stifling today: heavy repp curtains; reproductions of pre-Raphaelite paintings; patterned carpets, patterned wallpaper, even patterned ceilings; overstuffed Tavistock chairs with the new coiled springs; ebonized Chippendale music stools; and almost unbelievable clutter, with whatnots displaying bric-a-brac, ostrich feathers in vases, fans fastened to the walls, and marble-topped tables crowded with family photographs, china nodding cats, vases of flowers, and, on the mantel, a "Madeleine" clock in black marble with bronze columns from Oetzmann's which cost thirty-two shillings and sixpence.

All this required a great deal of dusting. That was the point of it. Keeping it clean, and polishing the brass knockers, bedsteads, taps, and andirons, required servants, and the number of servants was a sign of status. They were cheap. A clerk making seventy or eighty pounds a year could afford a charwoman or a scullery maid ("skivvy") at twelve pounds a year, less than five shillings a week, plus such fringe benefits as broken dishes and cast-off clothes. At the very least, a middle-class family would have a staff of four — cook, housemaid, parlormaid, and kitchen maid — and many homes would have six or seven bustling around in their lavender-print dresses and freshly laundered Breton caps. There were also butlers, footmen, and coachmen, but most domestic servants were young women. In 1881 there were 1,545,000 Englishwomen "in service"; one of every three girls between fifteen and twenty years of age was waiting on someone. Their employers complained endlessly about their dishonesty, their incompetence, and the expense of them. (A first-class cook made nineteen pounds a year, ninety dollars, though experienced lady's maids earned more.) *Punch* was always having fun with them, depicting them as insolent and pretentious. Actually, they were almost pathetically servile. They had little choice. To be dismissed without a reference was a girl's nightmare. Moreover, in her situation she was learning domestic arts and might attract the eye of a promising footman. If that led to matrimony it meant a step up. It was the responsibility of the butler, or the housekeeper, to see that it led nowhere else, though sometimes it did. One's heart is wrung by the plea of a maid begging her mistress to let her keep her illegitimate baby: "It's only a little one, ma'm."

Doubtless many of them did steal from the pantry. They would have been inhuman not to have done it; outside in the dark and cold were relatives who had left the land, like them, and had found no jobs. These were the drifting poor who could not even afford a twopence Whitechapel breakfast and whom Shaw and H. G. Wells would soon discover. During the day they lived in London's parks, but when the parks closed at sunset they would shuffle out and huddle in doorways or on Embankment benches, wrapped in rags and newspapers against the cold, until 4:15 A.M., when the gates of the first to open, Green Park, were unbolted. Primitive as street life was, it was considered preferable to the desperate workhouses. Now and then these institutions created by the Poor Law were humane; Maggie, Little Dorrit's protégée, was so thankful for her treatment in a workhouse hospital that she called all kindness "hospitality." But to most of the suffering masses they meant pitilessness and terror and were a major reason for the emigration of nearly three million Englishmen between 1853 and 1880. The system was against them. The purpose of law enforcement was the protection of property. Policemen deferred to top-hatted gentlemen and hounded wretches in ragged clothes. Under the Master and Servant Law, employees could be arrested in the dead of night for disobeying the most outrageous of orders, and under the Prevention of Poaching Act, suspicious constables could stop and search anyone in "streets, highways, and public places." The woman in a middle-class servant's hall, warm and well fed, not only knew her place but was grateful for it.

Her mistress had solved the middle-class woman's greatest challenge just by reaching the altar. With so many men of her social standing abroad in the Empire, the supply of bachelors was limited, and marriage was the only respectable occupation open to her. Failing that, she was doomed to lifelong submissiveness in her parents' home, serving as an unpaid servant. There were many like her. Indeed, W. L. Burn noted in *The Age of Equipoise* that "the dependent daughter was one of the fundamentals on which the mid-Victorian home was based." Not all daughters suffered in silence; Florence Nightingale denounced "the petty grinding tyranny of a good English family. What I complain of . . . is the degree to which they have raised the claims upon women of 'Family.' It is a kind of Fetichism."[30] Miss Nightingale is one of the few women whose names have survived, an outrider of twentieth-century feminism. Another, who was actually more useful to her sisters, was Isabella Beeton, born within the sound of London's Bow Bells and therefore a cockney. Like Florence, Isabella was a human dynamo. Before her death at twenty-eight of puerperal fever, that assassin of Victorian mothers, she had given birth to four children, served as fashion editor for her husband's periodical, the *British Domestic Magazine,* and produced a tremendously successful volume of her own, her 1,111-page *Household Management,* with fourteen color plates and hundreds of black-and-white illustrations. (It weighed two pounds and cost seven shillings and sixpence.) By 1871, six years after her funeral, two million copies had been sold.

"Mrs. Beeton," as Englishwomen called the book, was to them what "Dr. Spock" became for American mothers four generations later. The needs it filled tell us a great deal about their circumstances. As wealth poured into England from its colonial possessions abroad, the waves of growing affluence enriched and complicated life in a nation arriviste. Brides had no precedents for orchestrating sophisticated social skills; their mothers, having lived in simpler times, were of little help. So Mrs. Beeton explained when to wear gloves, how to maneuver on the pavement so that gentlemen escorts walked on the street side, and what the French names for courses of food meant. The British were still an insular people. (A headline of the period was FOG IN THE CHANNEL, CONTINENT CUT OFF.) And serving as hostess at dinner parties was a wife's most important role. Ladies did not eat out until the Savoy Hotel opened in 1889, with César Ritz as the headwaiter. Entertaining was done at private residences only. Mrs. Beeton told her readers, in extraordinary detail, which wines to serve with meat and fish, when the ladies should leave the gentlemen to their brandy, and how to cope with a party of three dozen, counting the coachmen who had to wait for their masters and mistresses. She provided recipes, information on how much to order, and what to do with the leftovers. One entry was: "Bill of Fare for a Picnic for Forty Persons." It recommended, among other things, 122 bottles of refreshment for the entire group, including servants, coachmen, and lady's maids. The food was absurdly cheap, but the logistics were staggering. Moreover, this was a *middle-class* affair. The upper class entertained on a scale unmatched today. It was expected of them, which sometimes presented difficulties. Winston Churchill, born to a noble family, simply could not afford it. He had to live by his wits most of his life.

Upper-class hostesses had no need to plan picnics in the country. They were already there. They had London mansions, too, but the soul of the leisure class was in the land. It always had been. Chaucer wrote of his medieval franklin, or landowner, that "It snewed in his hous of mete and drinke, / Of alle deyntees men coude thinke." Arundel Castle, in Sussex, goes back even farther. It is mentioned in the will of King Alfred, who reigned eleven centuries ago. An ancestor of the present tenant, the sixteenth Duke of Norfolk, won it when an arrow from the bow of one of his archers pierced the eye of Harold in the Battle of Hastings. Socially, a duke in the country has always had the best of all possible worlds. In the British aristocracy the twenty-seven dukes are outranked only by members of the British royal family; the College of Arms advised a hostess, who was worried about seating arrangements for her dinner party, that "the Aga Khan is held to be a direct descendant of God," but "an English Duke takes precedence." The other degrees of the British peerage, in descending order, are marquess, earl, viscount, and baron, and though these don't carry as much weight as they once did, in Victoria's time to be titled, in most instances, still meant to be landed. On the estates of the nobility stood the great country houses, where England's three hundred ruling families celebrated the weekly three-night British holiday, which is popularly thought to have been a brainchild of the Queen's hedonistic Prince of Wales, but which was actually created by, of all people, Oliver Cromwell; in 1899 one of Cromwell's biographers, S. R. Gardiner, found that "Oliver . . . may be regarded as the inventor of that modified form of enjoyment to which hard-worked citizens have, in our day, given the name of 'week-end.' "[31]

But upper-class Victorians weren't hard-worked. Most of them didn't work at all. That was what set the upper class apart from the upper-middle class. The two mingled, but never as equals; as Lady Warwick explained to Elinor Glyn, "Doctors and solicitors might be invited to garden parties, though never of course to luncheon or dinner." The elite kept themselves to themselves. This small, select, homogenous patriciate, this "brilliant and powerful body," in Churchill's admiring phrase, passed most of their time by passing the port, sherry, and claret; by discussing cricket; by playing billiards, admiring their horses, and shooting grouse — a thousand grouse were felled in a single shoot attended by Churchill's mother. Unlike the French, they did not cultivate tête-à-têtes; Robert Laird Collier found that "they are poor talkers as a rule, and conversation seems to be a labor to most of them," that they "never express the least feeling in their social intercourse," and that "all the social talk is stupid and insipid." In an age which cherished the Latin motto *laborare est orare,* when Samuel Smiles's *Self-Help* could be found in almost every middle-class home, an idle nobility seemed an affront to social critics. In Edward Lear's *Book of Nonsense* the likable figures are Floppy Fly and Daddy Long Legs, who are ejected from court because their legs are ill-made. Lewis Carroll depicted patricians as tyrants and muddlers. Gilbert and Sullivan's *Iolanthe* described the House of Lords as a body that "did nothing in particular and did it very well." But the ruling class was unperturbed. Ideas bored them. "As a class," Lady Warwick said, "we did not like brains." A contemporary work, *Kings, Courts and Society,* saw Britain comprising "a small, select aristocracy, booted and spurred to ride, and a large, dim mass, born, saddled and bridled to be ridden." On Sunday the weekenders gathered in the chapels found under every country-house roof and sang:[32]

The rich man in his castle
The poor man at his gate
God made them high and lowly
And orders their estate.

Later Churchill wrote: "The old world in its sunset was fair to see." It doesn't seem very fair to us. In their portraits titled Victorians, particularly the men, seem to be oozing complacency and self-esteem, wholly indifferent to the fact that 30 percent of the inhabitants of their capital city were undernourished while they feasted, at a typical lunch for six, on cold pheasant, a brace of partridges, a pair of roast fowls, steak, salmon, and a choice of two soups. As late as 1940 Clare Boothe Luce, though an anglophile, fumed: "Sometimes they are so insolent, so sure of themselves, so smug, I feel as though it would do them good for once to be beaten." But by then they had become an anachronism, and the brightest among them knew it. To put them in context is to see them against the background of nineteenth-century Eurasia. From the Barents Sea to the Mediterranean, from the Rhine to Vladivostok, monarchs not only reigned but ruled through bewildering hierarchies of grand dukes, archdukes, princelings, and other hereditary nobles — twenty-two dynasties in Germany alone. The masses having accepted the saddles and bridles, threadbare commoners also sang about God making men high and lowly. It was, James Laver writes, "probably the last period in history when the fortunate thought they could give pleasure to others by displaying their good fortune before them." Bagehot wrote: "The fancy of the mass of men is incredibly weak; it can see nothing without a visible symbol. . . . Nobility is a symbol of mind." So ingrained was the habit of forelock-tugging that by 1875, when Trollope wrote *The Way We Live Now*, that society accepted the exploitation of titles by impecunious nobles who sold their prestige by consenting to serve as directors of businesses in wobbly shape.[33]

This did not declass them. Their social status was their birthright, and nothing could deprive them of it. Even if a peer committed murder, he was entitled to a trial by the House of Lords, and if sentenced to the gallows he was hanged with a silken rope. Of course, most of the upper class was merely related to peers. Given primogeniture, with all property going to the eldest son, including the title, the patriciate was heavily populated with younger sons who had inherited nothing and usually entered the navy, army, church, or diplomatic corps — the traditional order of preference. (Two generations passed before a descendant became a commoner. The firstborn son of the seventh Duke of Marlborough was his heir. The second son was called Lord Randolph Churchill. Randolph's wife was Lady Randolph Churchill. *Their* son was simply Mr. Winston Churchill.) Yet all retained the life-style of the aristocracy. Characteristically, members of the upper class never lifted an unnecessary finger. It was said of Lady Ida Sitwell that she not only did not know how to lace up her own shoes; she would have been humiliated by the knowledge. Churchill's cousin, the ninth duke, while visiting friends and traveling without his valet, or "man," complained that his toothbrush didn't "froth properly."[34] He had to be told gently that toothpaste had to be applied to the brush before it would foam. His man had always done that, and he hadn't realized it. Winston himself lived ninety years without once drawing his own bath or riding on a bus. He took the tube just once. His wife had to send a party to rescue him; helpless, he was whirling round and round the tunnels under London. And all his life he was dressed and undressed by someone else, usually a valet, though during one period by a secretary in her twenties. There are those among his friends who believe that this sort of thing taught him how to use people properly.

It was during the London "Season" — from the Queen of Charlotte's Ball in mid-spring to the Goodwood races in midsummer — that the great peers were to be found in their town houses. These were surrounded by barbered gardens, high walls, and gates manned by gatekeepers who fought off beggars and other street people. Sometimes they shot them. This aroused neighbors, who knew their station but believed a line should be drawn short of homicide. Actually, the very sites of many of the huge homes were outrageous. In Mayfair, Belgravia, Marylebone, and St. Pancras, streets maintained at public expense had been included within such walls, which meant that fire engines were blocked and buildings burned down. All attempts at legislation outlawing this extraordinary practice were defeated in Parliament.

In London the upper classes had their stylized rituals, most of them frivolous. Every morning after breakfast processions of victorias — low four-wheeled carriages with folding tops — debouched from the West End and trotted along Park Lane, gay harnesses tinkling and erect postilions wearing uniforms, glistening high boots, and varnished, high-crowned hats. Daughters were presented at court; the ladies, *en grande toilette,* wore three ostrich feathers in their hats if married, two feathers if not. Wasp-waisted, their gowns off the shoulder, skirts voluminous and rustling, the debutantes would be waited upon by uniformed members of the Corps Diplomatique, Gentlemen of the Household in full court dress, and Yeomen of the Guard in scarlet and gold. The fathers of the girls being brought out would be absent, loitering in their clubs: the Athenaeum, White's, the Carlton, the Reform, and the rest. They did not care to be "seen" then. But the sexes did mingle on other public occasions. Everyone enjoyed the royal enclosure at Ascot, gorging on champagne, strawberries, and lobster mousse. And — rowing being considered manly — it was rather a good thing to turn out for the Henley Regatta. Dress there was about as informal as it ever got for that class. Ladies appeared in blouses and long linen skirts; their husbands, in straw boaters, blazers, and flannels.

The best club in London was Parliament, which, by no coincidence, held its key sessions between Easter and August — in effect, the Season. At the time of Winston Churchill's birth, MPs were not only unpaid; they were expected to contribute generously to charities in their constituencies. So the upper class controlled both the Lords *and* the House of Commons. B. Cracroft, analyzing the House in his *Essays on Reform,* found that 326 members were patricians, including 226 sons or grandsons of peers, and a hundred others "connected with the peerage by marriage or descent." Over a hundred more belonged "substantially to the same class," which meant that three out of every four MPs were linked to each other and to the older generation in the Lords by blood as well as by conservative outlook. Between a third and a half of all cabinet members were from the upper house — six of Disraeli's thirteen ministers, five of Gladstone's fourteen. As we have seen, their hold on key posts in the Empire was even greater. Every viceroy of India was a peer by inheritance. In *Little Dorrit* Dickens wrote caustically of the Barnacle "clan, or clique, or family, or connection" that "there was not a list, in all the Circumlocution Office, of places that might fall vacant anywhere within half a century, from a Lord of the Treasury to a Chinese Consul, and up again to a Governor-General of India, but, as applicants for such places, the names of some or every one of these hungry and adhesive Barnacles were down."[35]

So the opening of Parliament, or a heralded debate in the Commons, was not unlike a family reunion. Broughams, landaus, barouches, victorias, and hansoms tingling their unmistakable bells clattered over the cobblestones of New Palace Yard and drew up in front of the Westminster Hall entrance. Men in striped trousers and frock coats descended carrying bulky red leather boxes stuffed with state papers, then disappeared into lobbies brightened by flaring gas jets. In the Strangers' Dining Room wives and daughters awaited them, wearing flowing skirts of tulle and hats as large as the displays at the Chelsea Flower Show. Gossip was exchanged, outcomes predicted, Liberals scorned by Tories or Tories by Liberals — it scarcely mattered, since their interests and social positions were virtually identical. The mighty seemed completely secure. Yet there were those who worried. Macaulay had warned against "the encroachments of despotism and the licentiousness of democracy." Bagehot said "sensible men of substantial means are what we wish to be ruled by" and cautioned that "a political combination of the lower classes . . . is an evil of the first magnitude. . . . So long as they are not taught to act together there is a chance of this being averted, and it can only be averted by the greater wisdom and foresight in the higher classes." The Queen, alarmed, let it be known that "a democratic monarchy is what she will never belong to."[36] Skittish patricians held their breath when the franchise bill of 1884 swept away 216 seats in rotten boroughs and increased the electorate. One man in five now had the vote — but at the next election the Conservatives were returned to power, with Lord Salisbury succeeding Disraeli. Salisbury was eminently a patrician of his time. A descendant of the two Cecils who had been Elizabeth I's and James I's chief ministers, he was a towering, massive man — acerbic, gauche, preoccupied, disdainful, and possessed of a penetrating intellect. He declined to live at 10 Downing Street, preferring his own more elegant London home, in the chapel of which he prayed each morning upon arising. He suffered spells of depression which he described as "nerve storms." It was Salisbury's firm belief that only uncontentious legislation should be brought before Parliament. If it was controversial, England wasn't ready for it.

In one of those little paragraphs that illumine the era, *The Times,* reporting on a public trial, noted that "Viscount Raynham, MP, and other gentlemen present were accommodated with seats on the bench."[37] Given the system, it is unsurprising that the judge moved over for men whose social rank was equal to, or more likely greater than, his own. The key word is "gentlemen." What was a gentleman? Even then the term was inexact, and it has been the despair of sociologists ever since. Some cases were easy. Phileas Fogg in Jules Verne's *Around the World in Eighty Days* was almost an archetype. In 1872 he lived in Burlington Gardens, in the house at No. 7 Savile Row — flats didn't become respectable till the mid-1870s — and he was a member of the Reform Club. His financial independence permitted him to be indifferent to public opinion (though not to his conscience and his fellow gentlemen) and his arrogance and eccentricity arose naturally from his absolute security. Other cases were marginal. You could be a gentleman in one place but not in another. In a small community the word would be applied to a physician, a lawyer, a country squire, a master of foxhounds, or just a man who had a little money and good manners. In London, or in the great country homes, that wasn't enough. Samuel Smiles to the contrary, the mantle did not fall upon every responsible, brave, selfless Englishman. If gentlemen were those who were treated as such — the best definition — the standards were usually higher than that.

The high-born and members of the landed gentry were gentlemen by birthright. Stupidity — even illiteracy — did not disqualify them. But they were exceptions. It was generally understood that a "gentleman's education" meant Oxford or Cambridge, admittance to which was still largely limited to public-school boys. During their heyday, roughly from

Waterloo to the outbreak of World War I, the self-contained public schools were the ruling class's boot camps. Their autocratic headmasters, Church of England clerics, taught austerity, loyalty, honor, and the virtue of "service." Theoretically this meant serving those not lucky enough to see the inside of a public school; in practice it came down to defending the established order. Since the tuition exceeded the annual income of the huskiest workman, the pool of applicants was limited, as it was meant to be, to the affluent. The teaching of Latin and Greek was thought useful in disciplining young minds, but the playing fields were at least as important. The Duke of Wellington had said that the schools should produce the kind of youth who could go straight from his sixth form to a convict ship and, with the help of two sergeants and fifteen privates, transport a shipload of convicted criminals to Australia without incident. Thomas Arnold of Rugby told his faculty: "What we must look for . . . is, first religious and moral principles; secondly, gentlemanly conduct; thirdly, intellectual ability." At Harrow it was said that a boy might spend fifteen hours a week at cricket or, if he took "every opportunity," twenty hours. Sports were believed to be peculiarly suitable to the building of character. A small boy learned to submit to the authority of older boys because they were physically stronger than he. As he moved up through the higher forms, it was reasoned, he himself matured and became a "natural ruler," a self-reliant gentleman, disciplined by what Irving Babbitt later called the "inner check." Thus, though his family may have had no aristocratic connections, he joined the gentry and was accepted as a member of the ruling class. Merchants couldn't make it, but their sons could.[38]

In a revealing aside, John Buchan wrote: "In the conventional sense, I never went to school at all." In fact, he had received an excellent education in a Glasgow day school, but socially that didn't count. Yet Buchan rose to become Lord Tweedsmuir, governor-general of Canada. So it was possible to bypass the Etons and Harrows. Even an American could do it; in 1879 Henry James dined out 107 times. There were a thousand little ways, some of them extraordinarily petty, by which one gentleman identified another. One's vocabulary was important. Mantelpieces were "chimney-pieces," notepaper was "writing paper," mirrors were "looking glasses." But there was a catch. If you worried about such things, your concern showed, and you were dismissed as a swot. The true gentleman emanated a kind of mystique. He always belonged wherever he was. If he was intellectual he did not hide it; in *Paracelsus* Browning had told him: "Measure your mind's height by the shadow it casts." And somehow he always recognized his equals, whatever the circumstances or attire. When two strangers meet in *Doctor Thorne,* Trollope says of one: "In spite of his long absence, he knew an English gentleman when he saw one." Even penury was no obstacle. At the end of Trollope's *Last Chronicle of Barset* Josiah Crawley meets Archdeacon Grantly. The archdeacon is about to become Crawley's daughter's father-in-law. Crawley is wearing seedy clothes and "dirty broken boots." He is suspected of being a thief. He is quirky and perverse. But he was a scholar at Oxford and has "good connections," and when he apologizes because he is too impoverished to provide a dowry, the archdeacon replies: "My dear Crawley, I have enough for both." Crawley says: "I wish we stood on more equal grounds." Rising from his chair, the archdeacon tells him: "We stand on the only perfect level on which such men can meet each other. We are both gentlemen." Crawley, also rising, replies: "Sir, from the bottom of my heart I agree with you. I could not have spoken such words; but coming from you who are rich to me who am poor, they are honourable to the one and comfortable to the other."[39]

The Barsetshire novels are set outside London, which was one reason for their popularity in the upper class. Out of season, thoroughbreds found the capital's social life stifling. They felt more comfortable in their country houses, surrounded by parks landscaped in the eighteenth century, where fountains danced, deer darted, and, in the case of Blenheim, peacocks strutted. On foxhunts they galloped past villages whose inhabitants' forebears had toiled as serfs for their own ancestors — ancestors who now lay in village churchyards beneath marble armor with marble basset hounds at their feet. And the great houses were communities unto themselves, where servants might be waited upon by their own servants and hospitality was almost a secular religion. Chatworth, seat of the Duke of Devonshire, accommodated almost five hundred guests, but the finest view in England was found at Blenheim, set among the thousand-year-old oaks of what was once a royal forest. When George III saw Turner's painting of its great lake, its poplared island, and the hanging beeches beyond, he said: "We have nothing to equal this!"[40]

This was the home of the Duke of Marlborough, head of the Churchill family. Winston once described it as "an Italian palace in an English park."[41] A stupendous castle of almost ominous power, buttressed by massive towers, it is surrounded by courtyards, formal gardens, and 2,700 acres of parkland. Beneath its roof — which covers an incredible 7 acres — lie 320 rooms: bedrooms, saloons, cabinets, state apartments, drawing rooms, a conservatory, the obligatory chapel, and a library 183 feet long. The lock on the main door, copied from the one on the old Warsaw Gate, is turned by a brass key weighing 3 pounds. Within, busts of deceased dukes and duchesses stand in a grand hall whose 67-foot-high ceiling, supported by Corinthian columns, is embellished by a remarkable allegorical painting showing the first duke, John Churchill, kneeling before a figure of Britannia, who is seated on a globe, one hand resting on a lance as the other extends a wreath to him, while a figure holds fire and sword at John's feet, a white horse prances alongside, and trumpeters hover all around him.

Today Blenheim and other such shrines of the advantaged, with their marble halls and vast distances, seem intimidating. Their inhabitants didn't feel that way. On the contrary, they found them warm and convivial, bright, for some of them, with the promise of the greatest social gift they could imagine. It was illicit love. Here, too, the privileged enjoyed special privileges. Seen through the prism of a long century, they are hard to comprehend. Nineteenth-century sex, between thoroughbred lovers, was extremely complex, but like everything else they enjoyed, it had its precedents. The British aristocracy had always gloried in its sexual prowess. Exceptional concupiscence was rewarded; John Churchill, the first Duke of Marlborough, first rose to prominence because his sister Arabella, maid of honor to the Duchess of York, became the duke's most passionate mistress. When Marlborough returned from European battlefields at an advanced age, his wife Sarah proudly wrote: "Today the Duke returned from the war and pleasured me twice in his top boots." Had she sought lovers during his absence, the social risk would have been slight. For generations before Victoria's coronation the patriciate had tolerated promiscuity among its more hot-blooded members. Byron wrote his shortest and most eloquent poem as a testament to a titled woman who had taken leave of her husband for a nine-month romp with him:

Caroline Lamb,
Goddamn.

The Duke of Wellington had his pick of ladies when he returned from his various triumphs, and two of his bedmates expressed their appreciation to him in their memoirs. The duke's sister-in-law, Lady Charlotte Wellesley, the mother of four young children, left them to sleep with Lord Paget, himself the father of four children by his wife, Lady Caroline Villiers, daughter of Lady Jersey, who was the former "favorite," as it was then put, of the Prince of Wales. At Waterloo the duke made Paget his chief of cavalry. An aide protested: "Your Grace cannot have forgotten the affair with Lady Charlotte Wellesley?" The duke: "Oh, no!

I have not forgotten that." Aide: "That is not the only case, I am afraid. At any rate [he] has a reputation of running away with everybody he can." Duke: "I'll take good care he don't run away with me. I don't care about anybody else."*[42] During the Regency, upper-class sexual conduct became particularly flagrant. It was then that ladies diverted themselves with the best-selling *Memoirs of Harriet Smith,* which opened with the gripping line: "I will not relate the exact circumstances by which at the age of thirteen I became the mistress of the Earl of Croydon."

The tradition has continued to flourish in the twentieth century, a colorful example being the beautiful and wanton Edwina Ashley, Lady Mountbatten. When Lord Louis Mountbatten was viceroy of India, negotiating the terms for Indian independence, the sessions went much more smoothly because the vicereine, with her husband's resigned knowledge, was sleeping with Jawaharlal Nehru. Earlier she had been even more headstrong. At one point she vanished from London society for four months. Friends in Park Lane found Louis extremely vague when asked his wife's whereabouts. Actually, he didn't know. Later he learned that Edwina had shipped aboard a fifty-ton trading schooner, bound for the South Seas, as an ordinary seaman. Night after night, as they cruised among the lush islands, she gratified herself with her fellow crewpersons.

Victoria's reign was a hiatus, not in extracurricular upper-class ardor, but in the flagrant practice of it. Her ascent saw the triumph of the puritans — of what Melbourne called "that d——d morality." In the 1840s and 1850s debauchery went underground. By the time of Winston Churchill's childhood and early youth it had become prudent to keep mum about your love affairs. Gladstone in a candid moment said he had known "eleven prime ministers and ten were adulterers"; nevertheless, he joined in the persecution of Charles Stewart Parnell, an Irish MP who had been the lover of Kitty O'Shea with Mrs. O'Shea's husband's consent. In 1887 Sir Charles Dilke, at one time regarded as a future prime minister, was ruined by a divorce trial. He lost his cabinet post, then lost his seat, and eventually became a social pariah. One modern British scholar is convinced that "Disraeli slept his way to the top," but Dizzy was too crafty to be caught. Gladstone made a curious practice of prowl-

* Apocrypha has it that the two commanders did not speak during the battle. Actually, they were mounted side by side when a ball passed over the neck of Wellington's horse and hit Paget. "By God, sir," Paget cried, "I've lost my leg!" Wellington looked over and replied: "By God, sir, so you have!" (From *Waterloo: Day of Battle* by David Howarth [New York, 1968], page 186.)

ing the London streets at night and holding long, intimate conversations with prostitutes. Sometimes he brought them home and Mrs. Gladstone gave them hot chocolate. It was assumed that he was trying to convince them to mend their ways. If so, he doesn't appear to have been discouraged by his failure to produce a single convert. Indeed, after these talks he always appeared beaming, animated, and flushed. No one thought that odd. Nor could anyone pass judgment on affairs of which they knew nothing. The key to successful extramarital sex, therefore, was discretion. Mrs. Patrick Campbell, perhaps the most outspoken woman in polite society, said dryly: "It doesn't matter what you do in the bedroom, as long as you don't do it in the street and frighten the horses."[43]

The difficulty lay in finding the bedroom. Mrs. Campbell also said, after maneuvering one man out of his marriage to a Churchill and up the aisle with her: "Ah, the peace of the double bed after the hurly-burly of the chaise longue!" It was all very well for a Forsyte to tuck away a common mistress in Chelsea, but that couldn't be done with a lady. In the city she was under observation all the time. Her gown, her coif, her bearing, gestures, and diction testified to her class, and she couldn't be seen outside her aerie. Her very presence in a hotel lobby would invite scandal. Thus the preference of the aristocracy and gentry for their homes in the country. London society was too ritualized; there was little privacy, unless you were an unmarried bachelor, like young Freud, who informed his housekeeper that he expected a woman for tea and was told: "Right, sir, I'll change the sheets on the bed."[44]

The servants knew of most dalliances. They even understood why there was one standard for their masters and mistresses and another for the rest of England. Victorian morality arose from the needs of the new middle class. As the lord chancellor explained when divorce courts were established in 1857, a woman lost nothing by her husband's infidelity and could absolve him "without any loss of caste," while "no one would venture to suggest" that he could pardon her adultery, which "might be the means of palming spurious children upon him." This was important; such children shared a middle-class legacy. In titled families it was meaningless. Only the legitimacy of the first patrician child counted. Professor McGregor writes: "The sexual waywardness of aristocrats . . . did not endanger the integrity or succession of family properties regulated by primogeniture and entail. Countless children of the mist played happily in Whig and Tory nurseries where they were no threat to the security of family property or to the interests of the heirs." Pamela Harriman, a

Digby who was Winston Churchill's daughter-in-law before she married New York's former governor, takes the traditional light view of such sex: "They went to bed a lot with each other, but they were all cousins, so it didn't really count." It was their insularity that largely limited them to cousins; among the great families, Barbara Tuchman notes, "everyone knew or was related to everyone else. . . . People who met each other every day, at each other's homes, at race meetings and hunts, at Cowes, for the Regatta, at the Royal Academy, at court and in Parliament, were more often than not meeting their second cousins or brother-in-law's uncle or stepfather's sister or aunt's nephew on the other side."[45]

One area of scholarly inquiry being explored by today's sexologists is how the voluptuaries of the Victorian upper class led such colorful sex lives and produced so little issue. The average British wife then conceived ten times during her childbearing years. But the great thoroughbred beauties, who treasured their figures, carried far less often. After giving birth to Winston, Jennie Churchill was in and out of lovers' beds all her life, yet she bore only one more child. And she was not exceptional.

It is worth noting that these small victories of desire were achieved, not by men, but by prudent women. One would expect that Victorian gentlemen, proud of their protective instincts, would have shielded their mistresses from impregnation. The means were at hand. Condoms, originally thin sheaths made from the visceral tissue of sheep, had been used for two centuries; Casanova mentions them, and so does Boswell. ("French letter" was the term used in England; across the Channel it was "*la capote anglaise.*") But Victorian males were also romantics, and they found condoms distasteful. Therefore their partners turned to faithful douching with a solution of sulfate of zinc or alum, rigid austerity during their ripe periods each month, beeswax disks which blocked the entrance to the uterus, sponges moistened with diluted lemon juice and inserted into the vagina, and, increasingly, the Dutch cup, a primitive diaphragm designed to fit longitudinally in the vagina with the forward end under the pubic bone and the back end in the posterior fornix. Aletta Jacobs introduced this device in the Netherlands in the early 1880s. The cup comprised a steel ring with rubber stretched across it — a painful expedient, but passion overrode the discomfort. Mere possession of a Dutch cup was a sign of privilege in London. The vast majority of Englishwomen didn't know they existed and would have had difficulty acquiring one anyhow; the cups were available, only to those who furnished respectable references, at a Mayfair bookshop.

Partly because they bred less, ladies flourished. They were so much healthier and more active than their unprivileged sisters that they almost seem to have belonged to a different species. Lower-class women weren't envious; they adored them. An article in *Graphic Magazine* described in the saccharine prose of the time how such social celebrities were regarded:

> For the fashionable beauty, life is an endless carnival, and dress a round of disguises. She does everything and the wings of Mercury might be attached to her tiny bottines, so rapid are her changes of scene and character. She is a sportswoman, a huntress, a bold and skillful swimmer; she drives a pair of horses like a charioteer, mounts the roof of a four-in-hand, plays lawn tennis, is at home on a race course or the deck of a fast yacht. She is aware of the refinements of dining and has a pretty taste in vintages. She is a power at the theater or the Opera; and none is more brilliant at a supper party. Of the modern young lady a la mode, who wields alike the fiddle-bow, the billiard-cue, and the etching-needle, who climbs mountains and knows the gymnasium, none but herself can be the prototype.[46]

Among the most sophisticated of these women, often bored partners in arranged marriages, the affairs which were joyously celebrated during weekends were sometimes launched in wife-to-wife conversations. "Tell Charles I have designs on him," one would tell Charles's lady, who would acknowledge the proposal with a nod and an amused smile; she herself already had a lover or had designs of her own on someone else's husband. But you had to be very secure to take that approach — had to be, say, one of that select circle of ladies who took turns sleeping with Victoria's eldest son. More often an understanding would have been reached in advance between the primary partners. Some affairs were known to everyone. General Sir Neville Bowles Chamberlain, for example, always slept with the Duchess of Manchester, and the Duke of Marlborough with Lady Colin Campbell. Of course, they didn't cross a bedroom threshold together. On Thursdays each of the hundred-odd guests was assigned a room; a tiny brass frame on the door held a card with his or her name written on it. Wise and worldly hostesses knew who should be paired with whom. Vita Sackville-West later described how they served as accomplices to Victorian and later Edwardian intrigue: "This question of the disposition of bedrooms always gave the . . . hostesses cause for anxious thought. It was so necessary to be tactful, and at the same time discreet. The professional Lothario would be furious if he found himself in a room surrounded by ladies who were all accompanied by their husbands. Tommy Brand, on one such occasion, had been known to leave the house on the Sunday morning. . . . Tommy's motto was 'Chacun a sa chacune.' Then there were the recognised lovers to be considered; the duchess herself would have been greatly annoyed had she gone to stay at the same party as Harry Tremaine, only to find that he had been put at the other end of the house. . . . It was part of a good hostess' duty to see to such things; they must be made easy, though not too obvious." After lights were out, shadowy figures would glide through the darkened hall and everyone would settle in for the night's pleasure. An hour before dawn the butler would appear in the hall bearing a gong. He would strike it once and depart. The same tiptoeing figures would reappear. Presently they would all meet at the breakfast table.[47]

Breakfast could be bewildering to outsiders. At the table you were expected to be brusque, even rude, to your companion of the night. "Pass the toast," you would say crossly, or "I want the salt." The upper class was always very direct ("I want to pee"), but this went beyond that. It was important to sort out your different roles, to let it be known that you weren't going to break the rules by being demonstrative, or eloping, or doing anything else rash. One-night stands were very rare, but now and then they happened. The story of one, involving a young Frenchwoman, survives. During an evening musicale a handsome gentleman propositioned her. She accepted, and a memorable night followed. Two hours later she was cracking a soft-boiled egg downstairs when he appeared, took a seat, and arranged his napkin. Still aglow with romance, she bestowed a tender smile upon him. He glowered and growled: "Are you going to hog the butter all day?" She was shocked, then enraged. Hurling the butter in his face, she flew upstairs, summoned her maid, packed, and demanded that she be driven to the station at once. She told their stunned hostess that she would never again visit *atroce* England. She didn't. She wasn't invited.[48]

The casual promiscuity of the English patriciate over the centuries suggests the need for caution in tracing the bloodlines of Winston Churchill. He himself, while researching his biography of the great duke — the income from which went far toward supporting his family in the 1930s, when pleas for resistance to Hitler made him a political pariah — found "disquieting" evidence of "a rather shady phase" in the 1500s, when the duke's great-grandmother so forgot herself in the early years of her marriage that she presented the family blacksmith with a sturdy son. On a loftier scale, the duke's sister gave birth to a bastard son of James

THE CHURCHILL FAMILY

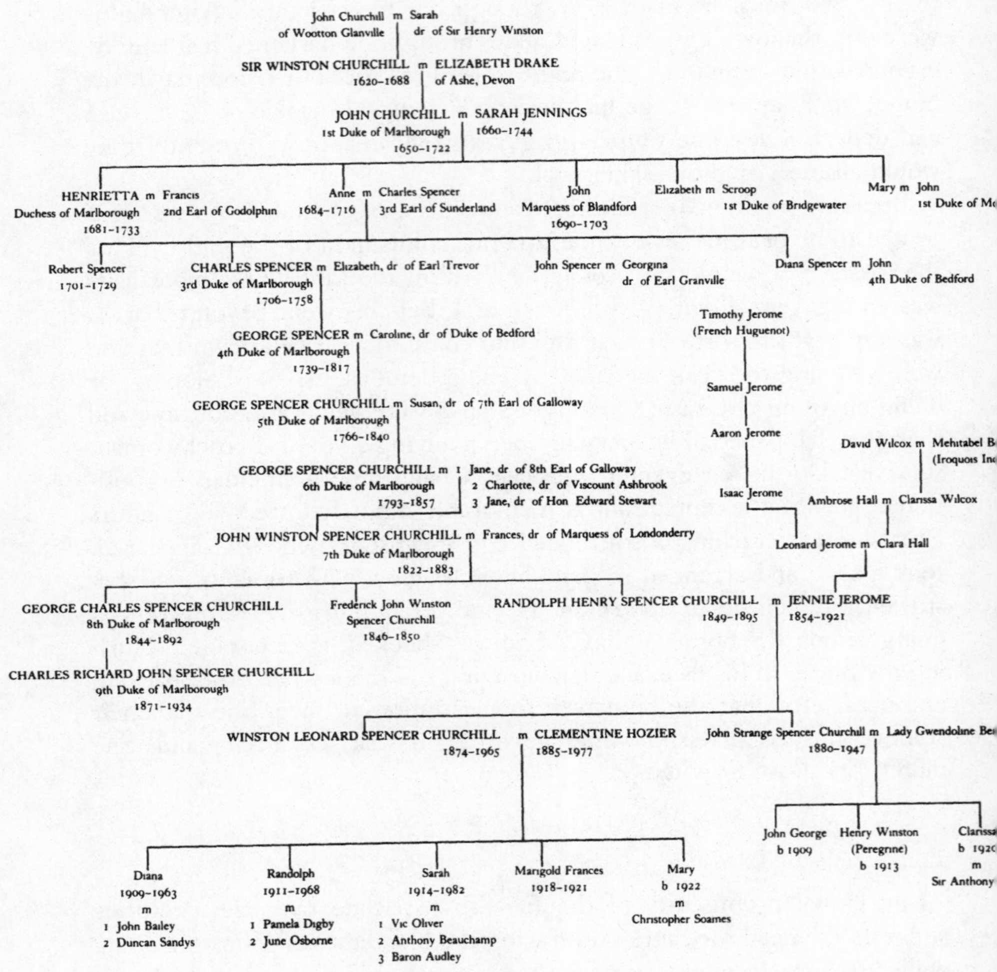

John Churchill m Sarah
of Wootton Glanville
dr of Sir Henry Winston
SIR WINSTON CHURCHILL m ELIZABETH DRAKE
1620–1688
of Ashe, Devon
JOHN CHURCHILL m SARAH JENNINGS
1st Duke of Marlborough
1660–1744
1650–1722
HENRIETTA m Francis
Duchess of Marlborough
2nd Earl of Godolphin
1681–1733
Anne m Charles Spencer
1684–1716
3rd Earl of Sunderland
John
Marquess of Blandford
1690–1703
Elizabeth m Scroop
1st Duke of Bridgewater
Mary m John
1st Duke of Mo
Robert Spencer
1701–1729
CHARLES SPENCER m Elizabeth, dr of Earl Trevor
3rd Duke of Marlborough
1706–1758
John Spencer m Georgina
dr of Earl Granville
Diana Spencer m John
4th Duke of Bedford
GEORGE SPENCER m Caroline, dr of Duke of Bedford
4th Duke of Marlborough
1739–1817
Timothy Jerome
(French Huguenot)
GEORGE SPENCER CHURCHILL m Susan, dr of 7th Earl of Galloway
5th Duke of Marlborough
1766–1840
Samuel Jerome
Aaron Jerome
David Wilcox m Mehitabel B
(Iroquois Ind
GEORGE SPENCER CHURCHILL m 1 Jane, dr of 8th Earl of Galloway
6th Duke of Marlborough
2 Charlotte, dr of Viscount Ashbrook
1793–1857
3 Jane, dr of Hon Edward Stewart
Isaac Jerome
Ambrose Hall m Clarissa Wilcox
JOHN WINSTON SPENCER CHURCHILL m Frances, dr of Marquess of Londonderry
7th Duke of Marlborough
1822–1883
Leonard Jerome m Clara Hall
GEORGE CHARLES SPENCER CHURCHILL
8th Duke of Marlborough
1844–1892
Frederick John Winston
Spencer Churchill
1846–1850
RANDOLPH HENRY SPENCER CHURCHILL m JENNIE JEROME
1849–1895
1854–1921
CHARLES RICHARD JOHN SPENCER CHURCHILL
9th Duke of Marlborough
1871–1934
WINSTON LEONARD SPENCER CHURCHILL m CLEMENTINE HOZIER
1874–1965
1885–1977
John Strange Spencer Churchill m Lady Gwendoline Ber
1880–1947
John George
b 1909
Henry Winston
(Peregrine)
b 1913
Clarissa
b 1920
m
Sir Anthony
Diana
1909–1963
m
1 John Bailey
2 Duncan Sandys
Randolph
1911–1968
m
1 Pamela Digby
2 June Osborne
Sarah
1914–1982
m
1 Vic Oliver
2 Anthony Beauchamp
3 Baron Audley
Marigold Frances
1918–1921
Mary
b 1922
m
Christopher Soames

II, and the family genes were quickened by the passionate George Villiers, the first Duke of Buckingham and the confidant of two Stuart sovereigns, whose descendants included both Pitts and several mistresses and lovers in royal households. So although it is theoretically possible to trace our Winston Churchill's lineage back at least to 1066, here and there skepticism is advisable. As Sarah, the first duchess, said, upon reading an account of her husband's forebears, "This History takes a great deal of Pains to make the Duke of Marlborough's Extraction very ancient. That may be true for aught I know. But it is no matter whether it be true or not in my opinion" — the customary riposte when a defense of legitimacy became hopeless. Thus one should, as far as possible, stick to what can be confirmed.[49]

One may as well begin with the first Sir Winston Churchill (1620–1688), for whom his great-great-great-great-great-great-great-grandson was named. A scholar, this earlier Winston left Oxford to bear arms for Charles I in the struggle between the Royalists and the Roundheads. Wounded after several ferocious battles, he found asylum in the castle of his mother-in-law, Lady Drake, a firm supporter of Cromwell and therefore above Puritan suspicion. After the Restoration, Charles II knighted Churchill. As Sir Winston he became MP for Weymouth, then a fellow of the Royal Society, meanwhile supervising the raising of five children who, because of their mother's bloodline, were descendants of Sir Francis Drake. One of the five was John Churchill, the future duke. John is one of the great figures in English history, glorious as a soldier, statesman, and diplomat. Though frequently the victim of court intrigue — in 1692 he was arrested, locked up in the Tower of London, and charged with high treason — he was always forgiven by William III and Queen Anne because of his remarkable military conquests. John fought ten campaigns on the Continent and never lost a battle, never even failed to take a fortress to which he had laid siege. His mightiest victory was at Blenheim, on the Danube, in Bavaria. On August 13, 1704, he and Eugene of Savoy risked everything, ignoring a formidable threat to their rear, and led the allied English, Germans, Dutch, and Danes to a historic triumph over the French. Blenheim is regarded as one of the world's ten most decisive engagements. John had become a duke in 1702. Now he was made a Knight of the Garter and given a palace, which he named after the battle.

This first Marlborough left no sons. The dukedom therefore passed through his daughters to his grandson, a Spencer. The Spencer family had become notable in 1504, when one of them acquired estates in Warwickshire and at Wormleighton and received a grant in arms. Henry VIII knighted him; our Winston Churchill became his direct male descendant through fifteen generations. In his *Memoirs of My Life and Writings,* Gibbon would write: "The nobility of the Spencers has been illustrated and enriched by the trophies of Marlborough; but I exhort them to consider the Fairy Queen as the most precious jewel of their coronet." Like many another historian, Gibbon skidded from time to time. There was no relationship between the poet and these Spencers. But they were remarkable in other ways. One served as ambassador to Spain and France. Another, a contemporary of Robert Walpole, England's first prime minister, was first lord of the Treasury between 1718 and 1721. A third, the second Earl Spencer, was first lord of the Admiralty in Nelson's great years. The next earl was one of the authors of the reform bill of 1832, and his son became viceroy of Ireland and then Gladstone's first lord.

In 1817, by royal license, the fifth Duke of Marlborough changed his family name to Spencer-Churchill. The arms were quartered beneath two crests, a griffin's head for the Spencers and a lion for the Churchills. The lion is the traditional symbol of England's greatness, and a duke outranks an earl, but for over a century the Spencers had outperformed the Churchills as servants of the Crown. One Duke of Marlborough became a mere brigadier of foot guards; another, during his fifty-eight years as master of Blenheim, simply collected pictures. During the Regency, two dukes succumbed to that gambling fever which afflicted so many members of the aristocracy in those raffish years. Rees Howell Gronow, a gossip writer of the early nineteenth century, told of a coach ride with a Marquess of Blandford (the title of the elder son of the Duke of Marlborough before his succession). The marquess produced a wad of fifty thousand-pound notes. He had just borrowed them. He said: "You see, Gronow, how the immense fortune of my family will be frittered away; but I can't help it; I must live. My father inherited five hundred thousand pounds in ready money and seventy thousand pounds a year in land; and in all probability when it comes my turn to live at Blenheim I shall have nothing left but the annuity of five thousand pounds a year on the Post Office." When he did become duke, we are told, "he lived in one remote corner of his magnificent Palace, a melancholy instance of extravagance."[50]

It was his son, John Winston, who began restoration of the Churchill pride. He and his successors added such luster to the family's reputation that recent generations have used Spencer only as a middle name or dropped it altogether. John Winston entered politics, was elected MP for Woodstock, and sat in the Commons for fifteen years. Becoming the seventh duke, he moved to the Lords and served as a cabinet minister under Lord Derby and then Disraeli. His elder son, George, was a disappointment. So, at first, was George's brother Randolph. Randolph was a poor student at Eton. He failed his first examinations at Oxford. But then he picked up. At Merton College he left a creditable record, marred only by an arrest for drunkenness and assault. After the ceremonial grand tour of Europe which had become customary for upper-class youths, and after a brief period as an idler and carouser, he stood for Parliament in 1874 and was elected to his father's old seat. His first speech went well; Disraeli wrote the Queen: "Lord Randolph said many imprudent things, which is not very important in the maiden speech of a young member and a young man, but the House was surprised, and then captivated, by his energy, and his natural flow, and his impressive manners. With self-control and study he might mount. It was a speech of great promise."[51]

Dizzy's unerring eye had caught the flaws, however. Randolph was "imprudent," lacking in "self-control." Later, after disaster had overwhelmed him — after he had first been marked as a future prime minister and had then lost everything — that was all which would be remembered. It is easy to withhold sympathy from him. Surviving pictures do not help. His most striking feature was his eyes. They were not attractive; he suffered from exophthalmos, and his protruding eyeballs seem to have surveyed the world with a supercilious, offensive stare. His walrus mustache draws attention to a large head set on a short, frail body. He looks pompous, curt, and rude. And so he was, to those who bored him. Yet his friends have left eloquent testaments to his jauntiness, wittiness, and charm. He was an enthusiastic foxhunter, a splendid horseman. His mind and tongue were quick. He was courtly with the ladies. He had little money; Disraeli, who made it his business to know such things, told the Queen in another letter that Randolph's father was "not rich for a Duke," and virtually everything would pass to the new MP's elder brother anyhow.[52] Nevertheless, "Randy," as he was known to the whispering galleries and sounding boards of London society, was a popular member of the "fast" set headed by the Prince of Wales. Randy's chief attractions were his social standing, his eligibility, and his faultless dress, for he was very much the dandy. And he enjoyed his kaleidoscopic social role. He detested dancing, yet he never turned down an invitation to a ball.

In time he might have overcome his youthful impetuosity, but time

Lord Randolph Churchill at the time of his marriage

was denied him. His greatest misfortune, though he didn't know it then, was a consequence of what was surely the cruelest of all Oxford pranks. Years later he described it to Louis Jennings, a close friend, and Jennings passed it along to another of Randy's friends, Frank Harris, editor of the *Fortnightly Review.* One evening at Merton a small group of students were discussing a favorite undergraduate topic: the relationship between masters and servants. Randy had firm views on this. He believed the aristocracy knew instinctively how to handle menials and that the rising merchants — he once told Harris that he regarded them as "jumped-up grocers from Ballarat and shopkeepers from Sydney" — would never learn. That evening he was eloquent; he was applauded; a fellow student handed him an enormous stirrup cup of champagne; he drank it off. It had been drugged. He awoke at daybreak with a ghastly taste in his mouth. He was in a strange room. The wallpaper, in his words, was "hideous — dirty." He turned his head and sat bolt upright, gasping. There was an old woman lying beside him; "one thin strand of dirty grey hair" lay on the pillow. His hopeless questions to Jennings evoked the chilling horror and the pathos of his plight: "How had I got there? What had happened to bring me to such a den?" Did he remember anything? *Pas trop;* the stirrup cup, and now this. Rising quietly, he slid into his trou-

Lord Randolph Churchill in his prime

sers. Abruptly, the hag awoke and grinned. She asked hoarsely: "Oh, Lovie, you're not going to leave me like that?"[53]

Randolph vividly recalled that she had "one long yellow tooth in her top jaw that waggled as she spoke." Obviously, she expected to be paid — this was the ultimate master-servant relationship. Emptying his pockets, he threw all the money he had on the bed. Her leer grew. Speechless, he struggled into his waistcoat and coat and bolted. As he slammed the door he heard her call, "Lovie, you're not kind!" Then, said Randolph, "Downstairs I fled in livid terror."* He knew his peril; he made for the nearest doctor's office. There he was treated with a strong disinfectant, but three weeks later a venereal sore appeared on his genitals, followed by lesions elsewhere. He returned to the physician, who treated him with mercury, warned him to abstain from alcohol, and told him he had nothing to worry about. It was a lie. Victorian medicine, confronted with such symptoms, was helpless. Thus it was that at the height of the 1873 Season, even before his entrance into public life, the elegant twenty-four-year-old bachelor son of a duke, the cynosure of aspiring debutantes and their ambitious mothers, was a doomed syphilitic.[54]

* In his *Lord Randolph Churchill* (Oxford, 1981) R. F. Foster discounts Harris's "almost completely unlikely assertion of the manner in which he [Randolph] contracted syphilis." Foster does not say why. The account does not seem unlikely to this writer, and Harris, as Foster concedes, enjoyed a relationship with both Lord Randolph and Winston which "was both genuine and appreciably close" (page 389).

To meet
Randolph
Their Royal Highnesses the Prince and Princess of Wales
and
Their Imperial Russian Highnesses the
Grand Duke Cesarewitch and Grand Duchess Cesarevna.

Captain Carpenter and the Officers of H.M.S. "Ariadne"
request the honour of the Company of

Mrs & Misses Jerome

On board, on Tuesday, August 12th, from 3.30 to 7.30, p m.

Boats will be in attendance at the R.Y.C. Landing Place.

DANCING. R.S.V.P.

On this deckle-edged invitation — it still exists; the Churchills, the biographer ardently notes, saved everything — a feminine hand later wrote, below "To meet," the name "Randolph." Certainly Clarissa ("Clara") Jerome hoped that she and her three daughters would meet *someone* interesting. Lately Europe had been a disappointment to them. Clara had begun to long for Newport, or even the Jeromes' New York mansion on Madison Square. She took the Franco-Prussian War as a personal affront. She and her daughters — Clarita, Leonie, and Jeanette ("Jennie") — had adored the Paris of the Second Empire. Beginning in 1858 they had lived in a palatial apartment on the Champs-Elysées. Clarita had made her debut at the Tuileries and had been the guest of Napoleon III and Eugénie at Compiègne. Jennie had been scheduled to come out in 1870. She had already been fitted for her gown when Louis Napoleon sent Wilhelm a rude note. Wilhelm of Prussia replied — at Bismarck's urging — with the ruder Ems telegram, and suddenly the two armies were lunging at each other. In the beginning Clara saw no need for alarm. French confidence was boundless. And neutral observers thought it fully justified. The *Pall Mall Gazette* of July 29, 1870, predicted that the first Napoleon's triumphs were about to be repeated. *The Times* felt an Englishman would be justified in laying his "last shilling on Casquette against Pumpernickel." The élan of Louis Napoleon's soldiery could scarcely have been higher. They pored over the maps of Prussia which had been issued to them, studied German phrase books, and eagerly looked forward to heroic attacks gallantly carried out by them and their comrades crying *"En avant! A la baïonnette! A Berlin!"* to the strains of "La Marseillaise."[55]

It was "unthinkable," the *London Standard* said, for the Prussians "to take the offensive."[56] General Helmuth von Moltke and his general staff disagreed. They had built their railroad grid with war in mind, had profited by William T. Sherman's brilliant use of railways in Tennessee, and had mastered the coordination of telegraph lines and troop trains. Three weeks after war had been declared, Moltke had efficiently mobilized 1,183,000 Germans, backed by more than 1,440 Krupp cast-steel cannon. The French, who regarded efficiency as a pedestrian virtue, weren't ready. They collided with massed battalions wearing spiked helmets and uniforms of Prussian blue singing "Die Wacht am Rhein" and "Deutschland über Alles" and chanting *"Nach Paris!"* While their deadly artillery, outranging Louis Napoleon's obsolete bronze guns, flung shattering barrages ahead of them, they blazed a trail which would be followed by their grandsons in 1914 and their great-grandsons in 1940. Suddenly news reached the Champs-Elysées that half the French army was bottled up in the mighty fortress of Metz. At Sedan the other half, led by Louis Napoleon himself, laid down their arms and accepted humiliating surrender terms. Paris lay open to the invader.

Clara and her daughters fled to Cowes, the fashionable British seaside resort on the Isle of Wight. They moved back to Paris the following spring, taking a house in the boulevard Haussman, but the city had been devastated by the Commune, the leftist regime which had defied the Prussians and their own countrymen until starved into submission. Returning to Cowes, the Jeromes leased what Clara called a "sweet little cottage" and were frequently seen there and in London, attending balls, recitals, receptions, and musicales, and other highlights of the Season. Most weekends found them on the great country estates. Unlike the Frenchwoman whose naiveté spoiled a perfectly good English breakfast, they were not shocked by careless interpretations of the marriage sacrament. Clara's husband slept with many women in New York; she knew it, knew that he had sired several illegitimate children, and was indifferent. Her grandson Winston relished telling of a meeting between Clara and one of Leonard Jerome's mistresses; Clara said: "My dear, I understand how you feel. He is *so* irresistible." But a lady's sexual emancipation was possible only after matrimony. As long as the Misses Jerome remained single, they must also be maidens. At least one of them was straining at the leash. A photograph of the mother and her daughters, taken at about this time, shows her seated, facing left, regarding the world with a resolute jaw and eyes like

Mrs. Jerome and her daughters (from left): Leonie, Clara, and Jennie

raisins. Clarita, also seated, is holding her mother's hand and searching her face, as though for guidance. Leonie, standing, leans on her mother's shoulder for support. Jennie, however, doesn't seem even to be a part of the group. She was already known as "a great show-off." Here the show is well worth watching. Dark, vivacious, and magnificent, she stands alone, staring boldly at the photographer, her left arm outflung, the hand atop a furled umbrella, her hips cocked saucily. It is almost a wanton pose, the posture of a virgin who can hardly wait to assume another position.[57]

Their Cowes home was a "cottage" in the sense that the sprawling Newport châteaux were called cottages. Leonard was seldom there, but when he crossed the Atlantic — usually at the helm of his own yacht — he expected to find his family living in style. He was an American type peculiar to his time, a vigorous, handsome man, a brokerage partner of William R. Travers and a member of the New York Stock Exchange who repeatedly amassed, and then spent, enormous portfolios of wealth. As Winston told the story, "My grandfather would devote himself to work and in a short time make a fortune. Then he would give up the life completely, disappearing for a year or two, generally to Europe. When he came back to New York he might have lost the fortune he had made, and at once set about piling up another. Money poured through his fingers. He generally had an income of about £10,000, perhaps equal to £40,000 now. My grandfather thought nothing of spending $70,000 on a party, where each lady found a gold bracelet, inset with diamonds, wrapped in her napkin."[58]

In his careening career, Leonard seems to have succeeded at almost everything he tried. He founded the American Jockey Club, built a racetrack in the Bronx, supported an opera house, was for a time a part-owner of the *New York Times,* participated in politics, spent eighteen months as American consul in Trieste, gambled heavily and successfully, and was the first man to drive a team of racing horses four-in-hand down Broadway. Like many other Wall Street millionaires of that period, he held mixed feelings about the English aristocracy. He envied their power; Britain was a mightier nation than the United States, and an English peer was a great figure throughout the Empire and beyond. But Americans were also proud, especially self-made men. Having reached the top of a mobile society, they scorned those whose future had been assured at birth. After all, Britain's patricians and New York's financiers came from the same stock. Leonard was the great-great-grandson of a Huguenot who had arrived in what were then the American colonies in 1710. Leonard's wife's family had settled in Connecticut by 1650. There was one faint blemish in Clara's otherwise pure Anglo-Saxon blood, one which later delighted Winston: her grandmother had been an Iroquois Indian. But that merely made her more colorful. Both Leonard and Clara were descended from American officers who had fought in the War of Independence. One, a major in the Fourth Massachusetts Regiment, had served with Washington at Valley Forge. To be sure, the Jeromes would be unlikely to place obstacles in the path of a titled British son-in-law. Palmerston had predicted: "Before the century is out, these clever and pretty women from New York will pull the strings in half the chancelleries in Europe."[59] Louisa Caton, the daughter of a Baltimore merchant, had been Lady Hervey-Bathurst and then, after her first husband's death, Duchess of Leeds. Minnie Stevens became Lady Paget; Mrs. Arthur Post, Lady Barrymore; Mary Leiter of Chicago, Lady Curzon and vicereine of India. And Consuelo del Valle, who had been Jennie's schoolmate, would soon be Duchess of Manchester. So a Jerome girl wouldn't find herself in altogether unfamiliar company. Leonard and Clara might have been pleased by the thought. At the same time, they would have bridled at the suggestion that she was marrying up.

The shipboard dance at Cowes aboard the cruiser *Ariadne* was considered a major social event and even a historic occasion, for the guests of honor were the future Czar Alexander III and his czarina, Maria Feodorovna. Today they are forgotten, part of the legacy which was destroyed with the last of the Romanovs, but one question asked that evening by an acquaintance of the Jeromes, by an obscure dandy named Frank Bertie, is memorable. Although Jennie had a full dance card, she happened to be standing alone, watching the bobbing Chinese lanterns and the entwined British and Russian flags overhead and listening to the Royal Marine band, when Bertie appeared at her elbow with a pale youth. Bertie said: "Miss Jerome, may I present an old friend of mine who has just arrived in Cowes, Lord Randolph Churchill." Jennie inclined her lovely head. Randolph stared. She was nineteen, at the height of her glory, bare-shouldered and sheathed below in a flowing white gown with flowers pinned to the bosom. After some hesitation, he invited her to dance. The quadrille proved to be beyond him; he tripped and suggested they sit this one out. They did. Her dance card notwithstanding, they sat out the next one, and then the next, talking of horses and mutual friends until Clara, wondering uneasily where her daughter might be among all these virile naval officers, sought her out. Before leaving, Jennie persuaded her mother to invite Randolph to dinner the following evening, accompanied by a British colonel for the sake of appearances. At the dinner Randolph seems to have tried hard to be clever, without much success. Afterward Jennie and Clarita played piano duets. Randolph whispered to the startled colonel: "If I can, I mean to make the dark one my wife." They left, and Jennie asked her sister what she thought of Randolph. Clarita wasn't impressed. She thought his manner pretentious and his mustache absurd. She doubted she could learn to like him. Jennie said: "Please try to, Clarita, because I have the strangest feeling that he's going to ask me to marry him." If he did, she said, "I'm going to say 'yes.' " Her sister laughed, but in three days, during a stroll in the Cowes garden, the two became engaged.[60]

Leonard's first response was apprehension. When Jennie wrote him the news he replied, "You quite startle me. I shall feel very anxious till I hear more. If it has come to that — that *he* only 'waits to consult his family' you are pretty far gone. . . . I fear if anything goes wrong you will make a dreadful shipwreck of your affections. I always thought if you ever did fall in love it would be a very dangerous affair." Letters from her and her mother brought him around, however. Once persuaded, his optimism was irrepressible. In Wall Street the panic of '73 was at its peak. He had been all but wiped out. But he never doubted that he would win it all back — as he did — and on September 11, giving the marriage his blessing, he wrote Jennie: "I must say I have been very happy all day long. I have thought of nothing else. I telegraphed your mother immedi-

Jennie as drawn by John Singer Sargent

ately that I was 'delighted' and that I would arrange £2,000 a year for you which she says in her letter will do. The letter I recd from you the other day only filled me with anxiety. I feared nothing would come of it and that you would be left shipwrecked. The situation as related by you today leaves no reasonable doubt of the accomplishment of your hopes. The consent of his paternal [sic] I should say must follow when he learns that moderate provision can be made for you and that our family is entirely respectable — all that can be said for any American family."[61]

It wasn't enough. At Blenheim the duchess was muttering angrily about "dollars and impudence." On August 25 Randolph's brother had written him: "I tell you that you are mad simply mad. I don't care if *la demoiselle* was the incarnation of all moral excellences & physical beauties on God's earth. My opinion is the same." If he wanted to run off with a married woman, George said, that would be one thing. "But my friend *le mariage!* It is a delusion and a snare like all the rest, and in this disagreeable addition [sic], that it is irrevocable. . . . You really only want to marry because you are in love with *an idea 'une phantasie. . . .'* " Meanwhile, Randolph had written his father of his plans. He told him: "I love her better than life itself," then added with exasperating vagueness: "Mr. Jerome is a gentleman who is obliged to live in New York to look after his business. I do not know what it is."[62]

The duke meant to find out. He wrote Randolph: "I can't say that what you have told me is reassuring. . . . This Mr. J. seems to be a sporting, and I should think vulgar kind of man. I hear he drives about 6 and 8 horses in N.Y. (one may take this as a kind of indication of what the man is). I hear he and his two brothers are stock brokers, one of them bears a *bad* character in commercial judgement in *this* country, but which of them it is, I do not know, but it is evident he is of the class of speculators; he has been bankrupt once; and may be so again: and when we come to think of N.Y. speculators & their deeds look at Fisk and *hoc genus omne.*"[63]

Randolph besieged Blenheim. A month later he wrote Clara that although his father still deplored "the suddenness & rapidity of the attachment formed . . . he wld give his consent if we were of the same mind in a year hence." Neither Randolph nor Jennie would agree to wait. They were both hot-blooded and impatient; with each passing day they wanted each other more. Weeks dragged on, and then months. Randolph's election to Parliament in February seems to have improved his standing in his father's eyes, and presently the duke, mollified if not reconciled, was getting down to the bedrock issue. It was money. He had decided to give Randolph £1,000 a year, which, with the £2,000 from Leonard, seemed ample for the couple. The issue was who should control it. Lawyers were consulted. The Churchill family's solicitors took the position that settling any money on the bride was inconsistent with English practice. The groom, they said, should get everything. Leonard offered a split between husband and wife, writing: "My daughter although not a *Russian* princess is an American and ranks precisely the same and you have doubtless seen that the Russian settlement recently published" — this was between the Grand Duchess Marie Alexandrovna and Victoria's second son, the Duke of Edinburgh — "claims *everything* for the bride." It was now April 7, and Jennie and Randolph could scarcely control themselves. Indeed, as we shall see, they probably couldn't, and didn't. A compromise was reached involving settlements on children to be born of the union. On April 14, 1874, Randolph wrote his mother: "Things are now going as merrily as a marriage bell. I expect the settlements over tonight and they will be signed tomorrow."[64]

They were. The next day, Wednesday, April 15, the Reverend Dr. Edward Forbes united them during a ceremony in the British embassy in Paris — Paris, which had become civilized once more, having been Clara's suggestion. Present were the bride's parents, the groom's brother George, and Francis Knollys, private secretary to the Prince of Wales. Absent were the Duke and Duchess of Marlborough. This was an extraordinary snub, for Randolph was their favorite son. But they had made it quite clear that they had no intention of attending the service. Leonard had sent the duke a chilly note the previous Tuesday. ("I am very sorry you are not able to come over to the wedding. We had all hoped to have had the pleasure of seeing both yourself & the Duchess.") There is no record of a reply. But the inhabitants of Woodstock — which lies outside Blenheim's grounds and was the new constituency of Randolph Churchill, MP — were overjoyed. When the couple arrived there on Monday, May 25, the train station was decorated with bunting and crowded with well-wishers. Cheering broke out as Jennie appeared carrying a lacy parasol mounted on a tortoiseshell rod trimmed with gold, a present from her father. ("Just the sort of bit of nonsense you like," he had said.) The parasol was inadequate that day. A heavy rain was falling, split by bolts of lightning. Nevertheless, the throng, undaunted, unhitched the horses from the carriage which had been sent from the palace and pulled it through the narrow streets. They paused at the Bear Hotel, where the mayor spoke briefly, telling them that Woodstock "cannot be unmindful of anything which concerns the happiness of the noble house of Churchill," and wishing them many years of "unclouded" joy. Then they were off again, through the triumphant arch dividing the town from the

Blenheim Palace

palace grounds. “As we passed through the entrance archway and the lovely scenery burst upon me,” Jennie later wrote, “Randolph said with pardonable pride, ‘This is the finest view in England.’ Looking at the lake, the bridge, the miles of magnificent park studded with old oaks . . . and the huge and stately palace, I confess I felt awed. But my American pride forbade the admission.”[65]

Another admission, which she preferred to keep from her husband’s family, was that she was bearing their grandchild. Indeed, it is virtually certain that she had been pregnant for three months, and soon it would begin to show. Randolph had leased a house in Mayfair, at 48 Charles Street, off Berkeley Square; they planned to return to London and await the delivery there, explaining, when invited to Blenheim, that his political duties required his presence in town. But when Parliament rose, the duke and duchess would hear no excuses. Having accepted the marriage grimly, they wanted a long close look at their new daughter-in-law. As the weeks passed, they were pleasantly surprised. They found her charming. The increase in her girth appears to have been slight; the time for consulting the calendar hadn't yet arrived. Ironically, she no longer cared. Free of her cloying mother, she also felt free of her in-laws. By October she was her own woman, independent and headstrong. She would never change again. It would be characteristic of her that she would always do exactly as she pleased, flouting convention and tossing her head when met by disapproval. Expectant mothers — she was very heavy by now — were supposed to remain quiet and, so far as was possible, immobile. But she was her father's daughter; she had always been lively; she loathed inactivity, and gave it the back of her hand now. On Tuesday, November 24, she left the palace on a shooting party, stumbled in a field, and fell. Shaking off anxious hands, she said she was fine. On Saturday, as Randolph later wrote Clara, she took "a rather imprudent & rough drive in a pony carriage." That evening the annual St. Andrew's Ball was held in the palace. To the astonishment of everyone, including her husband, she appeared in a loose gown, holding a dance card. She was actually on the floor, pirouetting, when the pains started. Randolph wrote his mother-in-law: "We tried to stop them, but it was no use." It was, in fact, time to choose a birthplace. Her grandniece, Ann Leslie, afterward described Jennie's search for one. Attended by servants and by Randolph's aunt Clementina, Lady Camden, she stumbled away from the party — which seems to have proceeded gaily without her — and lurched "past the endless suite of drawing-rooms, through the library, 'the longest room in England,' " toward her bedroom.[66]

She didn't make it. She fainted and was carried into a little room just off Blenheim's great hall. Once it had belonged to the first duke's chaplain; tonight it was the ladies' cloakroom. Sprawling, she lay on velvet capes and feather boas, which were deftly drawn from beneath her when the ball ended and the merry guests departed. It was a long night, with servants hurrying in and out with poultices and towels. The pains, Randolph told Clara, "went on all Sunday." He had telegraphed the London obstetrician Jennie had consulted, but, Sunday train schedules being what they were, the doctor couldn't arrive until Monday. Thus, the historic role of delivering England's greatest prime minister fell to Frederic Taylor, a Woodstock physician. "The country Dr is . . . a clever man," Randolph reported, "& the baby was safely born at 1.30 this morning after about 8 [sic] hrs labour. She suffered a good deal poor darling, but was vy plucky & had no chloroform. The boy is wonderfully pretty so everybody says dark eyes and hair & vy healthy considering its prematureness."[67]

Premature? *The Times* bought it. At the head of its birth notices it reported: "On the 30th Nov., at Blenheim Palace, the Lady Randolph Churchill, prematurely, of a son." But no one believed it, not the patrician friends of the family, chuckling over the announcement, nor even the yeomen of Woodstock who, the *Oxford Times* reported, rang "a merry peal on the church bells . . . in honour of the event." Winston was full-term. It was generally believed that sometime the previous February, during the maddening negotiations over the marriage settlement, Jennie had eluded her mother, divested herself of the incredible layers of clothing then worn by young ladies, and received Randolph's seed. Indeed, it was thought the duke and duchess had known Jennie was pregnant at the time of the wedding; that was why they had boycotted it. Sly allusions to the circumstances of his birth followed Winston all his life. He enjoyed them. He would reply: "Although present on the occasion, I have no clear recollection of the events leading up to it."[68] Of course, it is possible that his parents have been slandered. Periods of gestation do vary. He may have been premature. It would have been just like him. He never could wait his turn.

ONE

HEADWATERS

1874–1895

WINSTON'S early appearance, despite its implications, actually improved Jennie's relationship with her mother-in-law. Frances, Duchess of Marlborough — the "Duchess Fanny" — was a formidable, domineering woman, at the rustle of whose skirt all Blenheim trembled. Had she elected to make an issue of Winston's conception, life would have been difficult for the young couple. She did the exact opposite. Jennie was now accepted as a full-fledged member of the family. Like many another grandmother the duchess had taken one adoring look at her grandson and capitulated. The infant was no beauty — he had an upturned nose, red curls, and what his daughter Sarah later called "strange pallid eyes" — but Fanny thought him stunning, and she briskly set about seeing to his needs. Someone had to see to them. There had been no preparations for his advent: no diapers, no cradle, nothing. Fannie borrowed these from the wife of the village solicitor, whose baby was not expected until late in January, and dispatched orders for others from London. At the end of the first week Randolph wrote Clara: "The *layette* has given great satisfaction but the little shawls with *capuchons* have not arrived. Jennie says they are much wanted, also the pillow cases have not come."[1] By Christmas the crisis was past, however. On December 27 the duke's chaplain baptized the infant in the palace chapel, naming him Winston Leonard Spencer Churchill.

New Year's Day found the Randolph Churchills back in Charles Street. Ladies did not feed their babies then, and one of Fanny's first tasks had been to hire a wet nurse. The nurse was swiftly followed by Elizabeth Anne Everest. Plump, calm, vehemently Low Church, and proud of her origins in Kent, "the garden of England," as she called it, "Mrs." Everest — she had no husband; nannies, like cooks, received the honorific as a courtesy — entered Winston's life when he was a month old. That was the custom. "I had him from the month" was a nanny's equivalent of "He is my own child." Violet Asquith wrote: "In his solitary childhood and unhappy school days Mrs. Everest was his comforter, his strength and stay, his one source of unfailing human understanding. She was the fireside at which he dried his tears and warmed his heart. She was the night light by his bed. She was security." Except at bedtime, when mother appeared for good-night kisses, nurseries, like kitchens, were rarely visited by upper-class parents then. Like popes granting audiences, they received their children at appointed times, when the small ones, scrubbed and suitably dressed, presented themselves for inspection while their nannies reported on their deportment. Randolph and Jennie appear to have omitted even these token meetings. They had no time for them. Every hour appears to have been devoted to the pursuit of pleasure. Randolph all but abandoned politics; in two years he delivered just two speeches in Parliament. Thirty years afterward Jennie wrote in *The Century:* "We seemed to live in a whirl of gaieties and excitement. Many were the delightful balls I went to, which, unlike those of the present day, lasted till five o'clock in the morning." The Churchills were also lavish hosts. In Winston's words, "They continued their gay life on a somewhat more generous scale than their income warranted. Fortified by an excellent French cook, they entertained with discrimination. The Prince of Wales, who from the beginning had shown them much kindness, dined sometimes with them."[2]

In London, His Royal Highness, the Prince of Wales, was the key to social success. Since the Queen had withdrawn from fashionable gatherings after her husband's death, His Royal Highness and Alexandra, Princess of Wales, had assumed the social duties of royalty. Great prestige therefore accompanied acceptance into HRH's entourage. The "Marlborough House Set," to which the Randolph Churchills belonged, was simply a clique of HRH's friends and their wives or, in several instances, HRH's mistresses and their husbands. In their dissipation of leisure they seem to have been both vigorous and inane. They studied the finer points of the Venetian quadrille, the Van Dyke quadrille, and — Jennie's favorite — the cancan. At fancy balls, prolonged discussions examined the merits of holding one's partner's hand high, in the polonaise fashion. In Mayfair the Churchills gave grand dinners, hired expensive orchestras, spent fifteen pounds on masked-ball costumes, journeyed to Hurlingham to watch the pigeon shooting, and attended the Derby and races at Goodwood and Ascot. Later Jennie would remember how dinners, balls, and parties succeeded one another without intermission, and "how we all laughed at M. de Soveral, because he looked like a blue monkey and was always called the blue monkey," and laughed again when "the Grand Duke poured the chocolate sauce over his head," and applauded HRH's spectacular attire: "The doublet and cloak were of light maroon satin embroidered in gold, the large black felt hat . . . had a white feather, and the dress was completed with loose buff boots, steel spurs, and a long sword. On the left shoulder was a diamond star, and the Prince wore the Order of the Garter hanging from a blue riband round his neck. Fair cavalier curls flowing down his shoulder somewhat distinguished H.R.H. [and] were the finishing touch to a very splendid and perfect costume." In those giddy years, Jennie later recalled, they were confronted by only one serious misfortune: "it was no less than the sudden illness of the greatest hairdresser of his day."[3]

But a genuine crisis loomed in 1876. What HRH gave, HRH could take away. It was in his power to consign any member of his set to social oblivion. It happened to the Churchills. In his biography of his father, Winston wrote: "Engaging in his brother's quarrels with fierce and reckless partisanship, Lord Randolph incurred the displeasure of a great personage . . . London became odious to him."[4] Or vice versa. The fact is that Randolph had acted badly, as a consequence of his brother George's having acted badly, which was a result of Lady Aylesford's having acted badly and the Prince of Wales, impetuously. All of them had broken the thin membrane of contrived deceit which permitted adultery and civility to coexist. Since the details became public in subsequent divorce proceedings, it is possible to reconstruct the chain of events which led to the Churchills' exile and meant that Winston's first childhood memories would be of Dublin.

On October 11, 1875, when Lord Heneage, Earl of Aylesford, left England with the Prince of Wales to hunt in India, his wife, Edith, Countess of Aylesford, moved to Packingham, the family seat, with their two daughters. George Churchill was living in a nearby inn. As heir to the dukedom, George bore the title Marquess of Blandford and lived more or less independently. Each evening he entered an unused wing of the hall, using a key which, in the words of the divorce court, he "had obtained . . . with the knowledge and sanction of Lady Aylesford, with whom he passed many nights." There was nothing indiscreet here. As a marquess, George was a suitable lover for a lonely countess. Unfortunately, the two of them couldn't leave it at that. In February they decided to leave the children with Edith's mother-in-law and elope. Edith imprudently wrote her husband, telling him this, and he hurried home from India. Meanwhile, the Duke of Marlborough sent one of his sons-in-law to persuade his son to abandon the impossible affair. The emissary reported: "I think that any steps you may take to influence Blandford to give up Lady Aylesford would be for the present at any rate entirely thrown away."[5]

Edith's brother then challenged George to a duel, and that brought Randolph, as George's brother, into the drama. Randolph told all interested parties that his brother could be called out by Lord Aylesford and no one else. Then he hired private detectives to watch both George and his challenger, "to prevent," he said, "a breach of the peace." Had he stopped there, his social position would have remained intact. But Randolph discovered that George's predecessors in Edith's bed included none other than the Prince of Wales. The breakdown in decorum was complete; Edith had saved HRH's love letters, which she turned over to Randolph. Incredibly, Randolph then called upon Alexandra, Princess of Wales, asking her to use her influence with the prince and see to it that Lord Aylesford canceled plans to divorce his erring wife. Whether he showed her the love letters is unknown, but he did tell friends about them, boasting that "I have the Crown of England in my pocket." Victoria heard of this; indignant, she wrote her son: "What a dreadful disgraceful business!" But her anger was a moonshadow on that of the prince. Enraged, HRH arrived home and wrote the Earl of Beaconsfield — Disraeli — that "Ld B. and Ld R.C." were spreading lies about him and that "it is a pity that there is no desert island to which these young gentlemen (?) could be banished." He then settled for the next best thing. Lord Blandford and Lord Randolph Churchill, he announced, were in Coventry. Not only would he refuse to see them; he would not enter the home of anyone who had entertained them. Socially they had ceased to exist. Jennie was grief-stricken. She wrote her husband: *"C'est trop fort* — my own darling dear Randolph I shd give anything to have you here tonight I feel so wretchedly." As for Randolph, Winston wrote, "The fashionable world no longer smiled. Powerful enemies were anxious to humiliate him. His own sensitiveness and pride magnified every coldness into an affront. . . . A nature originally genial and gay contracted a stern and bitter quality, a harsh contempt for what is called 'Society,' and an abiding antagonism to rank and authority."[6]

Even Randolph realized that he had gone too far, however. He turned the letters over to a royal emissary, Lord Hartington, later Duke of Devonshire. Hartington — who himself had been sleeping with another duke's duchess for thirty years — burned them in Randolph's presence. But HRH was unappeased. To untangle the mess, he sent another letter to Disraeli, the wisest man in the kingdom, begging his advice. Dizzy told Duchess Fanny, "My dear Lady, there's but one way: make your husband take the Lord Lieutenancy of Ireland and take Lord Randolph with him. It will put an end to it all." Randolph, he said, could leave Parliament to serve as his father's unpaid secretary. At first the duke said no.

He was loath to move from Blenheim to Dublin, which he regarded as a primitive outpost of Empire, and an expensive one at that, but he had never been able to deny Disraeli anything. As Winston once said, "He always did whatever Lord Beaconsfield told him to do." On July 22 he wrote Beaconsfield from his town house in St. James's Square: "The acceptance of such a high office, is as you say a matter of much moment, and the change, I may almost say the sacrifice of one's ordinary habits and engagements in England is not an insignificant one, but as you have again done me the honour to repeat the offer, you previously made, I should not feel it my duty on the present occasion to stand aloof, and I shall be therefore happy to place myself at the disposal of the Queen's service."[7]

That settled it. On a bitter morning the following winter the duke, Fanny, Randolph, Jennie, and various other relatives — *The Times* incorrectly identified the youngest of them as "Lord Winston Spencer Churchill" — left London in a private saloon carriage attached to the Irish Mail. At Holyhead they boarded the mail steamer *Connaught* and crossed to Kingstown, where a delegation greeted them and led them to a special train. In Dublin the duke was greeted by a salute of twenty-one guns, invested with the Collar and Insignia of the Order of Saint Patrick, and installed in the Vice Regal Lodge. The Randolph Churchills moved into the Little Lodge nearby. Back in London the bad Aylesfords left England forever. Lord Aylesford sailed off to America, bought twenty-seven thousand acres at Big Spring, Texas, and flourished as a dude rancher until his death, at thirty-five, of cirrhosis of the liver. As Miss Edith Williams — her divorce had gone through — Lady Aylesford emigrated to Paris, where she bore George's child. She had wanted to marry him, but he had grown weary of her, and she died an unwed mother.

Volatile Ireland was enjoying one of its periods of quiescence. The problems were there, and Randolph, for whom these were maturing years, began a serious study of the social unrest. Jennie didn't. During her three years there it is doubtful that she saw a typical Irishman, except when trampling potato fields beneath the hooves of her favorite stallion. The Dublin she beheld was a creation of the Anglo-Irish aristocracy. To her surprise and delight, she found it very like Mayfair: balls, theaters, dinner parties every evening, amusing friends to be made, and splendid steeplechasing, point-to-points, and foxhunting. Winston's picture of her in Ireland was "in a riding habit, fitting like a skin and often beautifully spotted with mud. She and my father hunted continually on their large horses; and sometimes there were great scares because one or the other did not come back for many hours after they were expected."[8]

His mother was only in her early twenties, approaching the height of her beauty. Viscount D'Abernon, seeing her for the first time in the Vice Regal Lodge, wrote that although the duke sat at one end of the room on a dais, "eyes were turned not on him or on his consort, but on a dark, lithe figure, standing somewhat apart and appearing to be of another texture to those around her, radiant, translucent, intense. A diamond star in her hair, her favourite ornament — its lustre dimmed by the flashing glory of her eyes. More of the panther than of the woman in her look, but with a cultivated intelligence unknown to the jungle." Later Margot Asquith met her at a racecourse and thought: "She had a forehead like a panther's and great wild eyes that looked through you." Pantherlike women do not project maternal images, and two notes she wrote Randolph when he was absent from Dublin reinforce the impression that she had grown no closer to her son. In the first she reported: "Winston is flourishing tho' rather X the last 2 days more teeth I think. Everest has been bothering me about some clothes for him saying that it was quite a disgrace how few things he has & how shabby at that." In the second she wrote: "Winston has just been with me — such a darling he is — 'I can't have my Mama go — & if she does I will run after the train & jump in' he said to me. I have told Everest to take him out for a drive tomorrow if it is fine — as it is better the stables shd have a little work."[9]

The shabby clothes are insignificant, except in revealing what came first for Jennie; she wore a diamond in her hair but didn't see to it that her son was dressed properly. But childish fears of being abandoned are easily aroused. Staying away on horseback until the entire household is fearful of an accident, and telling a little boy that you are about to leave on a train — information he does not need — are bound to unsettle him and leave scars afterward. It is in this context that his relationship with his nanny assumed such importance. Her role in his childhood cannot be overemphasized. She was the dearest figure in his life until he was twenty; her picture hung in his bedroom until he died. He wrote: "Mrs. Everest it was who looked after me and tended all my wants. It was to her I poured out my many troubles." After reading Gibbon's memoirs he wrote: "When I read his reference to his old nurse: 'If there be any, as I trust there are some, who rejoice that I live, to that dear and excellent woman their gratitude is due,' I thought of Mrs. Everest; and it shall be

Jennie in Ireland, about 1877

her epitaph." An even more revealing tribute appeared in his second book, the novel *Savrola.* He wrote of the hero's nanny:

> She had nursed him from his birth up with a devotion and care which knew no break. It is a strange thing, the love of these women. Perhaps it is the only disinterested affection in the world. The mother loves her child; that is maternal nature. The youth loves his sweetheart; that, too, may be explained. The dog loves his master, he feeds him; a man loves his friend, he has stood by him perhaps at doubtful moments. In all these are reasons; but the love of a foster-mother for her charge appears absolutely irrational.[10]

Why irrational? Childless women have maternal feelings, too; surely it is understandable that they should lavish affection on other women's children entrusted to them. Anthony Storr comments upon this passage: "Churchill is showing surprise at being loved, as if he had never felt he was entitled to it." This is part of the depressive syndrome. Most infants are loved for themselves; they accept that love as they accept food and warmth. But in Winston's case, as his son later observed, "The neglect and lack of interest in him shown by his parents were remarkable, even judged by the standards of late Victorian and Edwardian days." That anyone should love him became a source of wonder. The uncritical devotion of "Woom" (derived from an early attempt to say "woman") was

Mrs. Everest

inadequate. He could hardly have failed to sense that the woman was a servant. Affection from others had to be earned; eventually he would win it by doing great things. At the same time — and this would cripple his schooling — the deprivation of parental attachment bred resentment of authority. One might expect that his mother and father, the guilty parties, would be the targets of his hostility. Not so. The deprived child cherishes the little attention his parents do give him; he cannot risk losing it. Moreover, he blames himself for his plight. Needing outlets for his own welling adoration, he enshrines his parents instead, creating images of them as he wishes they were, and the less he sees of them, the easier that transformation becomes. By this devious process Lord Randolph became Winston's hero, and his mother, as he wrote, "always seemed to me a fairy princess: a radiant being possessed of limitless riches and power." His resentment had to be directed elsewhere. Therefore he became, in his own words, "a troublesome boy." His mother called him "a most difficult child to manage." Toward the end of their years in Ireland Jennie engaged a governess for him. He couldn't stand her. He kicked, he screamed, he hid. There is a story that one day a parlormaid was summoned to the Little Lodge room where he was having his lessons. The maid asked the governess why she had rung. Winston said: "*I* rang. Take Miss Hutchinson away. She is very cross."[11]

That was precocious. He was just approaching the age of assertiveness, with consequences which would not be realized until he was ready for boarding school. Most of his Irish memories were passive. There was the mist and the rain and the red-coated British soldiers and the breathtaking emerald greenery. There was the time in Phoenix Park when he ran away into the woods, or what he thought were woods; actually, he had just crept under some shrubbery. Once Woom organized an expedition to a pantomime show. When they arrived at the Theatre Royal it had burned down; the mournful manager said all he had left was the key to the front door. Already insatiably curious, Winston demanded to see the key and was awarded a black look. Another day the duke unveiled a statue of Lord Gough, and his grandson would remember "a great black crowd, scarlet soldiers on horseback, strings pulling away a brown shiny sheet, the old Duke, the formidable grandpapa, talking loudly to the crowd. I even recall a phrase he used: 'And with a withering volley he shattered the enemy's line.' "* Woom dressed him in a sailor suit and took him to a photographer. Freckled, redheaded, and pug-nosed, the likeness gives the impression of violent motion suddenly arrested, and in fact he was already hyperactive; from the time he had learned to talk his lips had been moving almost incessantly. Woom, the nanny-cum-chauvinist, kept him quiet with chilly tales about the "wicked Fenians." They were not wholly fanciful. The ancestors of the Irish Republican Army were active, and they were a murderous gang; two years after the duke's successor arrived in Dublin, his under secretary and a companion were hacked to death with long surgical knives within sight and hearing of the Vice Regal Lodge. Mrs. Everest had good reason to be wary, and she was. One afternoon when Winston was riding a donkey beside her she saw some soldiers in the distance and mistook them for Irish rebels; she screamed and frightened the donkey, which reared up, unseating its young mount. Winston recalled: "I was thrown off and had concussion of the brain. This was my first introduction to Irish politics."[12]

In the early 1880s the Churchills' banishment ended. Randolph had laid low when visiting in London, but he had never really abandoned politics; three years earlier he had slipped across the Irish Sea and spoken to his Woodstock constituency, attacking Disraeli's lackluster Irish policy.

* That was close. The actual line was: "And with a crashing volley the enemy was fiercely beaten back." Winston was five years old at the time. Actually, his version is an improvement on the original.

("The only excuse I can find for Randolph," his mortified father had written a Tory leader, "is that he must either be mad or have been singularly affected with local champagne or claret.") Now he ran for Parliament again in the family borough and was elected by 60 votes — something of a triumph, for there were only 1,071 voters in the borough, compared with today's typical constituency of 50,000. Moreover, he was bucking the tide; Gladstone had overthrown Disraeli and would be prime minister for the next five years. That meant a new viceroy in Dublin. Back in London, Randolph moved his small family into a new house at 29 St. James's Place, next door to Sir Stafford Northcote, the leader of the Conservative opposition in the House, and opened negotiations for his reentry into the Prince of Wales's favor. Victoria approved. She had already told her son that she could not continue to exclude Randolph from court festivities. Sir Stafford approached Disraeli and wrote in his diary: "I asked him whether Randolph Churchill was forgiven yet in high quarters. He said he was all right so far as the Queen was concerned, but that the Prince of Wales had not yet made it up with him." Four years were to pass before HRH and Randolph sat at the table together, at a dinner given by Sir Henry James, MP (the future Lord James of Hereford), in March 1884. Afterward the prince sent word to Sir Henry that "R. Churchill's manner was *just* what it ought to have been." Yet all bygones were not to be bygones. *Vanity Fair* reported the "full and formal reconciliation" between the two but added: "It is understood, however, that while Lord Randolph feels much satisfaction at being again on friendly terms with the Heir-Apparent, he does not propose to become intimate with all the Prince's friends." Randolph would never forgive those Tories who had turned their backs when HRH had ostracized him. He would remain a member of the Conservative party, but would be a rebel within it. After his death his son would step into the same role. Thus, in a sense, one source of Winston's rebellious stand against Neville Chamberlain in the 1930s lay in Lady Aylesworth's bed.[13]

Randolph's brief but spectacular political career was just beginning when Winston reached the age of full awareness, first at St. James's Place, then at Beech Lodge in Wimbledon after Randolph and Jennie had toured the United States, and, finally, at 2 Connaught Place, a block from Hyde Park and Marble Arch and the first house in Mayfair to be equipped with electricity. All three homes had large nursery wings; Winston lost himself in fantasy there, playing with his steam engine, his magic lantern, and his toy soldiers. Already he had more than a thousand lead soldiers. Year by year the collection would grow. It is not clear who first gave them to him — Randolph, perhaps, or perhaps Mrs. Everest, who was provided with cash to be used at her discretion — but relatives learned that, when in doubt about presents, a gift of tiny dragoons or lancers would be prized by him. He now had a brother, or half-brother, Jack. Six years separated them, however, and there appears to have been no attempt to find playmates for Winston. Woom took him to pantomimes, Drury Lane, Madame Tussaud's, and for walks in the park. But mostly he was alone. He loved it. The time flew — "It is the brightest hours," he wrote of these years, "that flash away the fastest."[14]

In *Cradles of Eminence,* their study of childhood patterns found in the lives of men who later distinguished themselves, Victor Goertzel and Mildred George Goertzel found that Winston's family provided "multiple examples of the qualities in parents and other relatives which seem to be related to the production of an eminent man. There was respect for learning, an experimental attitude, failure-proneness, a plentitude of opinionated relatives, and turbulence in the family life as a result of the erratic behavior of his irrepressible uncle and father. During the time that Winston was thought dull, he was, like other boys, evidencing qualities which presaged ability." But that was hindsight. It was no consolation to Woom. She worried about her charge. When not lost in thought, he was in constant motion, jumping up and down, leaping from chair to chair, rushing about, and falling and hurting himself. He seemed to have no sense of personal safety. His love of martial poetry was obsessive. He had a speech defect, and one miserable cold after another. But his interest in politics was, for a boy his age, decidedly precocious. When Disraeli sickened in March 1881 and died six weeks later, Winston could talk of nothing else. He later recalled: "I followed his illness from day to day because everyone said what a loss he would be to his country."[15] In one way, his anxiety for Disraeli was a boon to Woom. It gave him an incentive to read. She had given Winston a book, *Reading without Tears.* Soon he was forming letters. His first letter, undated, was to his mother:

My dear mama
I am so glad
you are coming
to see us I had
such a nice
bathe in the
sea to day.
love to papa
your loving
winston

His second, also to her, was written on January 4, 1882, at Blenheim, where he was visiting his grandmother:

My dear Mamma
I hope you are quite
well I thank you
very very much
for the beautiful
presents those
Soldiers and
Flags and Castle
they are so nice
it was so kind
of you and dear
Papa I send
you my love
and a great
many kisses
Your loving
Winston

Still at Blenheim — Jennie was in a frenzy of preparation for the Season — he learned on March 20 that his father was afflicted with a serious infection. He wrote another note: "My dear Papa, I hope you are getting better. I am enjoying myself very much. I find a lot of primroses every day. I bought a basket to put them in. I saw three little Indian children on Saturday, who came to see the house. Best love to you and dear Mamma. I am, Yr loving son Winston." Very likely Woom helped guide his hand in these first attempts; his subsequent childhood correspondence, scrawled while he was away from her, is peppered with misspellings. But writing already came easily to him; his fluency would grow year by year, undiscouraged by the infrequency of replies from his parents. Arithmetic was another matter. His struggles with it seemed hopeless, and led to his only real battle with his nurse. He remembered afterward: "Letters after all had only got to be known, and when they stood together in a certain way one recognized their formation and that it meant a certain sound. But the figures were tied into all sorts of tangles and did things to one another which it was extremely difficult to forecast with complete accuracy. You had to say what they did each time they were tied up together. It was not any use being 'nearly right.' In some cases these figures got into debt with one another: you had to borrow one or carry one, and afterwards you had to pay back the one you borrowed." He tried, he tried again, and again; he gave up, threw down his pad and paper and stamped on them. Patiently Woom explained. Impatiently he shook his head. He fled; she pursued him. He threatened to attack her with his toy soldiers. She wasn't intimidated by that, but she did surrender when he shouted that unless she quit he would bow down and worship graven images. In time his grasp of numbers improved, yet he never fully mastered them, as England would learn to its sorrow when he became chancellor of the Exchequer.[16]

He was seven years old and his parents decided it was time he left home. On November 3, 1882, five weeks after the start of the autumn term, he was enrolled as a boarder at St. George's School near Ascot, a place famous for its women and horses. St. George's was an expensive school — fifty-two pounds for the first month, payable in advance — which prepared boys for Eton. Winston wept when told he must go. "I had been so happy in my nursery," he wrote later; ". . . now it was to be all lessons." Precisely how he traveled there is unclear. Jennie rode with him to Paddington Station in Randolph's private hansom, but on the train platform they parted; she gave him three half crowns and sent him on alone. He lost the coins, panicked, found them, and arrived trembling. It was late afternoon, and dark. A master led him to a desk, handed him a thin, brown-green Latin grammar, told him to memorize the declension of *mensa,* and departed. When the teacher returned, Winston reeled off a perfect recitation. The man seemed satisfied, and Winston, encouraged, asked, "What does it mean, sir?" He was told, "*Mensa* means a table." Winston pointed out that according to the book, one of the forms would then be translated as "O table." He asked why. The master explained that this was the vocative case, that "you would use that in addressing a table." Astonished, the boy blurted out: "But I never do." The master snapped: "If you are impertinent, you will be punished, and punished, let me tell you, very severely."[17]

That was the quintessential St. George's, the school in microcosm. Churchill would remember "how I hated this school, and what a life of anxiety I lived there for more than two years. I made very little progress at my lessons, and none at all at games. I counted the days and the hours to the end of every term, when I should return home from this hateful servitude and range my soldiers in line of battle on the nursery floor." However, he did not tell his parents that. At the end of his first month there he wrote his father, "I am very happy at [s]chool. You will be very plesed to hear I spent a very happy birthday," and the same day he wrote Jennie, "I hope you are quite well. I am very happy at school." But this is unsurprising. Boarding-school boys who feel wretched and badly treated seldom mention it in letters home. They think the flaw is in them, and they hide it. He doubtless assumed that his father would have snorted had he complained, and he was probably right. Like all Victorian children of his class, he had been taught to keep a stiff upper lip, so he did. Now and then he hinted at his immense yearning to quit St. George's. In March he wrote: "30 day [sic] more and the *Holidays* will be *Here.*" Then: "Only 18 more days." And then, on the eve of his next vacation: "I am comeinge home *In a month.*" He dragged out the end of his letters, as though he could not bear to break this frail tie with his family:[18]

...W...I...T...H
love & kisses
I
Remain
your
loveing
Son
W.L.S. Churchill

Mostly he wrote of trivia. "We went to hampton cort palace." "We went to see the picture gallry." "Give my love to my ants." He had caught another cold, but wrote, "My cough is nearly well now." Still another cold followed six months later; it hung on and on before he could report: "I am all wright and well. I have been allowed to go back into my own room." It is doubtful that his mother had known he had a room. Certainly she didn't know what it looked like. She never came. And he mourned her absence. That is the one thread that runs through his pathetic little correspondence: he desperately wanted visitors. "It was so kind of you to let Everest come," he wrote in the summer of 1883, but Woom, and then Woom and Jack, seem to have been the only ones who came. Ascot was a short hansom ride from Mayfair — trains from Paddington were even quicker — but neither Jennie nor Randolph found the trip convenient. So his pathetic pleas were unanswered. He begged his mother to "come and see me soon," to "Come & see me soon dear Mamma." He wrote, "I am wondering when you are coming to see me?" and, "You must send somebody to see me." The least she could have done was reply. She seldom did. On June 8, 1884, when he was nine, his accumulating resentment flared briefly: "It is very unkind of you not to write to me before this, I have only had one letter from you this term." The back of one of his notes tells us something about her priorities. On it are scribbled lists of guests for two dinner parties. She had time to entertain "Sir R. Peel," "Consuelo," "Duke of Portland," "Ld Marcus," and sixteen others, but she couldn't spare a few minutes to slake her small son's thirst for a line or two of love. She planned feasts for her friends. Winston asked for bread, and she gave him a stone.[19]

Randolph, surprisingly, did send him a gift that year. It was a copy of *Treasure Island.* Winston devoured it and promised to be worthy of it: "I will try to be a good boy." Most boys at St. George's tried to be good, though, and without incentives from home. The penalties for failure were dire. Since the Churchills were not the only influential family to be gulled into sending their son there, we know a good deal about the school. It was an upper-class version of Dotheboys Hall in *Nicholas Nickleby.* The regimen was fierce: eight hours a day of lessons, followed by football and cricket. There was fagging, and there were floggings almost every day, the chief whipper being the Reverend H. W. Sneyd-Kynnersley, a sadistic headmaster who would lay as many as twenty strokes of birch on a boy's bare rump. Given Winston's extremely sensitive skin, this must have been excruciating. Yet he became, and remained, the school's chief rebel. He excelled in history, but refused to learn Latin verses he did not understand; in his words, "Where my reason, imagination or interest were not engaged, I would not or I could not learn." Pitted against authority for the first time in his life, he defied it, refused to curry favor, and was, as a consequence, beaten until he shrieked. He later wrote: "My teachers saw me at once backward and precocious, reading books beyond my years and yet at the bottom of the Form. They were offended. They had large resources of compulsion at their disposal, but I was stubborn."[20]

His rebelliousness did not arise from the dignified resolution of a mature man standing on principle. Principles were indeed at stake, but he couldn't have known that. He was less than ten years old. His behavior was intuitive. To others he simply seemed a disobedient, mischievous little boy. Maurice Baring, who entered St. George's shortly after Winston left it, wrote: "Dreadful legends were told about Winston Churchill, who had been taken away from the school. His naughtiness appeared to have surpassed anything. He had been flogged for taking sugar from the pantry, and so far from being penitent, he had taken the Headmaster's sacred straw hat from where it hung over the door and kicked it to pieces. His sojourn at this school had been one long feud with authority." His masters and even his schoolmates, with the conformity of youth, were appalled. Baring said: "The boys did not seem to sympathise with him. Their point of view was conventional and priggish."[21]

One afternoon Sir Henry Drummond Wolff, a political ally of Randolph's and a founder of the Tory Primrose League, called at Connaught Place and asked Jack if he was good. Jack said, "Yes, but brother is teaching me to be naughty." Actually, Jack would never be naughty. Though he was born of the same mother and shared the same family life, his development was the opposite of Winston's. He resisted nothing, accepted what he was given, turned inward, and grew up to be an inoffensive man from whom little was expected or given. Boys like Jack create no difficulties for their parents. He was the kind of son Jennie wanted, and the contrast with his sibling pained her. As early as December 26, 1882, she wrote Randolph at Monte Carlo — the familial Christmas rites, so beloved by other Victorians, seem never to have been celebrated at Connaught Place — "As to Winston's improvement I am sorry to say I see none. Perhaps there has not been time enough. He can read very well, but that is all, and the first two days he came home he was terribly slangy and loud. Altogether I am disappointed." Sneyd-Kynnersley, she said, had assured her that the masters intended "to be more strict with him." She meant to try her own hand anyhow; "it appears that he is afraid of me." That was an odd admission from a mother, but perhaps it was true; a fearsome mother was at any rate preferable to maternal indifference. But she failed. Nothing intimidated him, certainly not St. George's. One riffles through his report cards there with mounting rage and amazement. It seems to have occurred to no one that a fresh approach might improve the behavior of this very difficult child. In his first accounting to Jennie the headmaster noted that Winston "has been *very* naughty." Then: "He is still troublesome." Next: "He is, I hope, *beginning* to realize that school means work and discipline." And then: "He is rather greedy at meals" — a peculiar description of a youthful appetite. After that, according to Sneyd-Kynnersley's comments, it was all downhill. His conduct was "very bad"; he was "a constant trouble to everybody and is always in some scrape or other"; he could not "be trusted to behave himself anywhere"; he had "no ambition"; he gave "a great deal of trouble." There is a sense of impending crisis in all this, and it crystallized when Winston, flayed beyond endurance, fled home to Mrs. Everest. Woom undressed him and recoiled when she saw his back and bottom crisscrossed with welts. She summoned Jennie, and the sight of his wounds told her what he, in the mute, tortuous language of a child, had been trying to tell her for two years. She immediately removed him from St. George's and entered him in a small school run by two maiden sisters in Brunswick Road, Brighton. It is unclear what, if anything, passed between her and the headmaster. Very likely Randolph knew nothing of the incident; his own letters show that he did not even know how old Winston was. But it is satisfying to report that two years later Mr. Sneyd-Kynnersley, aged thirty-eight, dropped dead of a heart attack.[22]

Brighton, with its sea air, chalybeate springs, colorful architecture, and general atmosphere of freedom, was a distinct improvement on St. George's, but Winston continued to play the imp. Any form of discipline still incensed him. The word *permissiveness* cannot be found in any dictionary of the time; as a concept it did not exist. Even if it had, Kate and Charlotte Thomson would have condemned it. They expected docility from their wards, and the record shows that they did not get it from their new boy; in his first term, when he passed his tenth birthday, his conduct was ranked twenty-sixth in a class of thirty-two. By the next term he was at the bottom, and there he remained. Charlotte Thomson wrote Jennie in her first report that "frequent absence from the schoolroom made competition with other boys very difficult." His dancing teacher, Vera Moore, later depicted him as "a small, red-haired pupil, the naughtiest boy in the class; I used to think he was the naughtiest small boy in the world." Even the indulgent Duchess Fanny, in whose Grosvenor Square home he spent holidays from time to time, wrote to Randolph: "Winston is going back to school today. Entre nous I do not feel very sorry for he certainly is a handful."[23]

Yet the Thomson sisters treated him with kindness and understanding, and he began to respond. At the end of his second term they noted "very satisfactory progress," and, after the third, "very marked progress." He was first in his classics class and near the top in English, French, and Scripture knowledge. He began to enjoy school: "We are learning Paradise Lost for Elocution, it is very nice." He was "getting on capitally in Euclid. I and another boy are top of the school in it we have got up to the XXX Proposition." In French they were rehearsing "Molière's *'Médecin Malgré lui.'* I take the part of 'Martine.' " In Greek, he wrote, "I have at last begun the verbs in 'μι' of which the first is 'ιστημι' " He proudly wrote his mother: "I have got two prizes one for English Subjects & one for Scripture." He even wrote Jack, aged six: "When I come home I must try and teach you the rudiments of Latin." In later life he recalled: "At this school I was allowed to learn things which interested me: French, History, lots of Poetry by heart, and above all Riding and Swimming. The impression of those years makes a pleasant picture in my mind, in strong contrast to my earlier schoolday memories."[24]

Collecting stamps, autographs, and goldfish, he began to share the interests of the other boys. He even tried sports — "We had a game of Cricket this afternoon, I hit a twoer, as the expression goes, my first runs this year" — though that didn't last long. He was now reading every newspaper he could find, poring over accounts of the Belgian conquest of the Congo, the Haymarket riot in Chicago, the death of Chinese Gordon, the erecting of the Statue of Liberty, and, in Germany, Gottlieb Daimler's invention of the first practical automobile. (These years also saw the founding of the Fabian Society and the Indian National Congress, both of which were to play major roles in his life, but London editors had dismissed them as insignificant.) In the spring of 1885 he was aroused by the uproar in Paris over whether or not Victor Hugo should receive a Christian burial and wrote his mother: "Will you send me the paper with Victor Hugo's funeral in it?" *King Solomon's Mines,* published during his first year in Brighton, held him mesmerized. He begged Jennie to send him everything Rider Haggard wrote, and was transported when her elder sister Leonie, who knew the author, took the boy out of school to meet him. Afterward he wrote Haggard: "Thank you so much for sending me *Allan Quatermain;* it was so good of you. I like *A.Q.* better than *King Solomon's Mines;* it is more amusing. I hope you will write a good many more books."[25]

The visit with Haggard, though unusual, was not unique; teachers and relatives were taking the restless boy off the school grounds on frequent trips. He saw what he described as "a Play called 'Pinafore' " with Leonie's daughter Olive, and, with Randolph's sister Cornelia, heard Samuel Brandram recite *Twelfth Night.* Then came electrifying news. "Buffalow Bill," he wrote home, was bringing his show to London; Bill was a friend of Clarita Jerome's husband, Moreton Frewen, who owned a Montana ranch. Queen Victoria's Golden Jubilee was to be celebrated the Monday after that weekend, and Winston was determined to see both of them. He wanted to come home to Connaught Place on Saturday and stay until Wednesday. The Thomsons discouraged him, explaining that there would be no place for him in Westminster Abbey and his mother would be far too busy to look after him. Predictably, Jennie agreed with the sisters; she rejected his first appeal. He wouldn't give up: "I can think of nothing else but Jubilee. Uncertainty is at all times perplexing write to me by return post please!!! I love you so much dear Mummy and I know you love me too much to disappoint me. Do write to tell me what you intend to do. I must come home, I feel I must. . . . Please, as you love me, do as I have begged you." Before she could reply, he wrote again: "Miss Thomson says that she will let me go if you write to ask for me. For my sake write before it is too late. Write to Miss Thomson by return post please!!!" In the end, his mother relented. A seat for him in the abbey was in fact out of the question — though Jennie had a good one — but he did see Buffalo Bill and all the rest. Thus it was that Winston Churchill stood among the cheering throngs on June 21, 1887, as the old Queen rode by, crowned by a coronet-shaped bonnet of lace studded with diamonds, her hands folded, her head bowed, her cheeks glistening with tears. Afterward Jennie and the Prince of Wales took him for a ride on the royal yacht, where he met the future King George V. It would be pleasant to report that his conduct was exceptional. It wasn't. He was loud, he stunted, he showed off. Back in Brighton he apologized to his mortified mother: "I hope you will soon forget my bad behavior . . . and not . . . make it alter . . . my summer Holidays."[26]

He feared a summer tutor. One tutor had spoiled a seaside holiday at Cromer, then as now a watering place on the North Sea coast; Winston had complained that she was "very unkind, so strict and stiff, I can't enjoy myself at all." But the reports of improvements in Brighton had lifted that threat. He was free to play, and in his choice of games we see the growth of his combative instincts. Once he talked Woom into taking him and his cousins to the Tower of London, where he delivered, with great relish, a lecture on medieval tortures. Pencil sketches of cannon and soldiers adorned the margins of his letters. His cousin Clare Frewen recalled in her memoirs that when the Churchills rented a summer house in Banstead, Winston erected a log fort with the help of the gardener's children, dug a moat around it, and, with Jack's help, built a drawbridge that could be raised and lowered. Then, she said, the children were divided into two rival groups and "the fort was stormed. I was hurriedly removed from the scene of the action as mud and stones began to fly with effect. But the incident impressed me and Winston became a very important person in my estimation." Shane Leslie, Leonie's son, remembered that "we thought he was wonderful, because he was always leading us into danger." There were the fort struggles, fights with the village children, and raids on the nests of predatory birds. In Connaught Place he had converted the entire nursery into a battlefield. According to Clare Frewen, "His playroom contained from one end to the other a plank table on trestles, upon which were thousands of lead soldiers arrayed for battle. He organized wars. The lead battalions were maneuvered into action, peas and pebbles committed great casualties, forts were stormed, cavalry charged, bridges were destroyed. . . . Altogether it was a most impressive show, and played with an interest that was no ordinary child game." It impressed Lord Randolph. One day he put his head in the door and studied the intricate formations. He asked his son, then in his early teens, if he would like to enter the army. In Winston's words: "I thought it would be splendid to command an Army, so I said 'Yes' at once: and immediately I was taken at my word. For years I thought my father with his experience and flair had discerned in me the qualities of military genius. But I was told later that he had only come to the conclusion that I was not clever enough to go to the Bar."[27]

On such slender evidence was so weighty a verdict reached. Winston was clearly ready for intellectual stimulation, and one might expect that he would have found it in the home of a lord who was also a member of Parliament and a charismatic MP at that. Instead, the boy's mind was fired by, of all people, Mrs. Everest's brother-in-law, John Balaam, a senior warden at Parkhurst Prison. British workmen in the nineteenth century, undiverted by mass media, often read deeply and thoughtfully. The family of Woom's sister Mary lived in the coastal town of Ventnor, on the Isle of Wight, and she took him there on holiday. It was the first time Winston had seen a humble English home. The experience was worthwhile for that alone, but the old warden, after holding the boy spellbound with tales of prison mutinies, produced a worn copy of Macaulay's *History of England.* He read passages aloud; Winston listened, rapt, to the cadences of the majestic prose. Later in India he remembered those evenings in the cottage on the sea. He acquired his own Macaulay and, in his words, "voyaged with full sail in a strong wind."[28]

Woom never let him down, but her health did. During the Christmas holidays at the end of 1887, while Jennie and Randolph were abroad, she contracted diphtheria, then a fearsome disease and often fatal. Dr. Robson Roose found two bad patches of false membrane in her throat and moved the two boys from Connaught Place to his own home. "It is very hard to bear — we feel so destitute," Winston wrote. "I feel very dull — worse than school." Duchess Fanny whisked them off to Blenheim, and Leonie telegraphed the news to their parents. Fanny, very much in charge, wrote to Randolph: "I fear you will have been bothered about this misfortune of Everest having diphtheria but she appears to be recovering & the 2 children are here safe & well." Blandford (George) offered to take them into his London house. Fanny wrote: "They leave here & go to Grovr Sq tomorrow so you might write (or Jennie might in your name) a line to B for having had them here. It has done them good & I keep Winston in good order as I know you like it. He is a clever Boy & not really naughty but he wants a firm hand. Jack requires *no* keeping in order. They will stay at 46 till you return."[29]

By January 12 Winston could write his mother: "Everest is much better — thanks to Dr Roose. My holidays have chopped about a good deal but . . . I do not wish to complain. It might have been so much worse if Woomany had died."[30] There seems to have been a tacit acceptance by the relatives of both parents that Randolph and Jennie were not really responsible for their children. As a consequence, Winston's awareness of his grandparents, uncles, aunts, and cousins deepened; they move in and out of his early life like characters in a Pirandello play. Had his immediate family been more self-sufficient, he might have been less conscious of his Marlborough heritage on one side and his American roots on the other. Jennie, by now, was indistinguishable from the titled Englishwomen of her social circle. She had no interest in Buffalo Bill. But her sisters were vibrant with the U.S. chauvinism of the time. Jennie, a purebred American, had become indifferent to the fact. Her son was half American, was constantly reminded of it by his maternal aunts, and never forgot it.

Winston's own illnesses, with one important exception, were normal for children of the time. He caught mumps ("My mumps are getting smaller every day the very thought of going home is enough to draw them away") and, later, measles, which — to his mother's intense annoyance — he passed along to her current lover, the dashing Austrian sportsman Count Charles Kinsky. The important exception was double pneumonia. All his life he would be plagued by recurrences of bronchial infections; his consequent indispositions would play a role in World War II. He was first stricken in his twelfth year, on Saturday, March 13, 1886. The danger was clear from the outset; Jennie and Randolph arrived separately in Brighton, and Dr. Roose, who kept a house there, remained by the boy's side, sending them bulletins after they had departed. These survive. At 10:15 P.M. Sunday he scrawled: "Temp. 104.3 right lung generally involved. . . . This report may appear grave yet it merely indicates the approach of the crisis which, please God, will result in an improved condition should the left lung remain free. I am in the next room and shall watch the patient during the night — for I am anxious." Infection of the left lung swiftly followed. At 6:00 A.M. Monday he wrote: "The high temp indicating exhaustion I used stimulants, by the mouth and rectum. . . . I shall give up my London work and stay by the boy today." Then, at 1:00 P.M.: "We are still fighting the battle for your boy. . . . As long as I can fight the temp and keep it under 105 I shall not feel anxious." At 11:00 P.M.: "Your boy, in my opinion, on his perilous path is holding his own well, right well!" Tuesday: "We have had a very anxious night but have managed to hold our own. . . . On the other hand we have to realise that we may have another 24 hours of this critical condition, to be combatted with all our vigilant energy." By Wednesday the worst was over. At 7:00 A.M. Roose scribbled: "I have a very good report to make. *Winston has had 6 hours quiet sleep.* Delirium has now ceased." Later in the day he wrote from the Brighton train station: "Forgive my troubling you with these lines to impress upon you the absolute necessity of quiet and sleep for Winston and that Mrs Everest should not be allowed in the sick room today — even the excitement of pleasure at seeing her might do harm! and I am so fearful of relapse knowing that we are not quite out of the wood yet."[31]

But they were, and the suggestion that Woom might constitute a threat is curious. Duchess Fanny agreed. "I hope Everest will be sensible," she wrote Jennie, "and not gushing so as to excite him. This certainly is not wise." His nurse was entrusted with his love, but not his health. In an emergency, it was thought, women of her class could not be depended upon to remain stoical. A display of affection could endanger him; only patricians could be counted on to remain poised. Jennie, certainly no gusher, was admitted to the sickroom (Randolph sent her sandwiches and sherry) while the woman who had saved him from emotional starvation was deliberately excluded. A child of the aristocracy was in jeopardy, and the Churchills' peers were closing ranks. Because Randolph was at the pinnacle of his career that year, powerful men were concerned for Winston's survival. Sir Henry James prayed for him; so did Sir Michael Hicks-Beach. Lord Salisbury, who had succeeded Disraeli as the Tory leader, wrote of his anxiety from Monte Carlo, and Moreton Frewen told Jennie that the Prince of Wales had "stopped the whole line at the levée" to ask after Winston. In a sense, the boy's recovery was an affair of England's ruling families, and the humble people whose lives had touched his did not belong.[32]

At Brighton, in his later words, "I got gradually stronger in that bracing air and gentle surroundings." Meanwhile, his relatives sententiously vowed to cherish him the more now that he had been saved and urged Jennie to do the same. Frewen thought of "poor dear Winny, & I hope it will leave no troublesome after effects, but even if it leaves him delicate for a long time to come you will make the more of him after being given back to you from the very threshold of the unknown." Duchess Fanny was "so thankful for God's Goodness for preserving your dear Child," and Jennie's own mother, in London but sick herself, wrote her, "I can't tell you how anxious we have all been about poor little Winston. And how delighted & thankful now that he is better. And what a relief for you my dear child. Yr whole life has been one of good fortune & this the crowning blessing that little Winston has been spared to you. You can't be too *grateful* dear Jennie."[33]

Jennie had been scared, and was doubtless relieved, but if gratitude meant changing her life-style, she wouldn't have it. These were the busiest years of her life, and she was enjoying them immensely. In those days an ambitious woman — and she was very ambitious — could express her drive only by advancing her husband's career. In the year of Winston's pneumonia, Anita Leslie writes, "Jennie took it for granted that her husband would reach the post of Prime Minister," but she was leaving nothing to chance.[34] She was active in the Primrose League; she campaigned for Randolph in a smart tandem with the horses beribboned in pink and chocolate, his racing colors; she gave endless dinner parties. No one declined her invitations, for she had become a celebrity in her own right. In the England of the 1880s and 1890s beautiful young genteel ladies diverted the public as film stars do now; their photographs were displayed in shop windows and sold as pinups. Jennie's was among the most popular. She was also recognized as a gifted amateur pianist, always in demand for charity concerts. In addition there were her social schedules. It was a grand thing to leave each autumn on her annual tour of Scotland's country houses, grand to receive the Order of the Crown of India from the Queen's own hands, grand to be courted by Europe's elegant gallants. There were hazards, to be sure, but they merely added to the excitement. Ironically, the only public embarrassment to arise from Jennie's catholicity of friendships among the eminent had nothing to do with her role as a romantic adventuress. She cultivated both Oscar Wilde and Sir Edward Carson. Later this proved awkward when Wilde and

Carson faced each other in the Old Bailey with the ugly charge of sodomy between them.

In short, Jennie had her priorities to consider, and while the frail child in Brighton was not at the bottom of the list, he scarcely led it. She wrote him, but except when he lay at death's door and propriety gave her no choice, she avoided the school. Pleas continued to pepper his letters: "Will you come and see me?" "When are you coming to see me?" "It was a great pity you could not come down Sunday," *"I want you to come down on some fine day and see me,"* he would give her billions of kisses if she came. She never found time. He had the chief role in a class entertainment, and he wanted her in the audience — "Whatever you do come Monday please. I shall be miserable if you don't." He was miserable. Another entertainment was planned — "I shall expect to see you and shall be very disappointed indeed if I do not see you, so do come." He was very disappointed. They were going to perform *The Mikado* — "It would give me tremendous pleasure, do come please." He forwent tremendous pleasure. He ached for the sight of her — "Please do do do do do do come down to see me. . . . Please do come I have been disappointed so many times." He was disappointed once more. Learning that a dinner party at Connaught Place conflicted with a school play, he begged her to cancel the dinner — "Now you know I was always your darling and you can't find it in your heart to give me a denial." Nevertheless, she found it in her heart to do just that.[35]

At times the breakdown in communications was total. He made elaborate plans for Christmas in 1887, only to discover at the last minute that both his parents were away on a seven-week tour of Russia. Jennie's sister Clarita — now called "Clara," like her mother — invited him to her home but then fell ill, so he spent the holiday with his brother, Woom, Leonie, and his uncle Jack Leslie. Once he wanted to write his mother but didn't have her address, didn't even know which country she was visiting. He was too young to travel in London alone, yet he couldn't even be sure there would be anyone to greet his train when he arrived: "We have 19 days holiday at Easter. I hope you will send some one to meet me at the station." Astonishingly, Randolph met an appointment in Brighton a short walk from the school but didn't bother to cross the street and call on his son. Winston found out about it. "My dear Papa," he wrote, "You never came to see me on Sunday when you were in Brighton." It happened again: "I cannot think why you did not come to see me, while you were in Brighton, I was very disappointed but I suppose you were too busy to come."[36] There was a note of resignation here. He was disappointed, but he was not surprised. His father was too busy. His father would always be too busy. Indeed, unlike his wife, he rarely wrote Winston. Jennie was a lax mother, but later, when her situation altered, she became a loving one. In Randolph's case that was impossible. Randolph actually disliked his son.

It is impossible to say exactly when a diagnostician told Lord Randolph Churchill that he was hopelessly afflicted with venereal infection and could not possess his wife without risking her health, too. Before meeting her he had passed through the first two stages of syphilis — the penile chancre and the body rash. After his wedding, according to Frank Harris, he told Louis Jennings that he had followed the physicians' medical advice for a while, "but I was young and heedless and did not stop drinking in moderation and soon got reckless. Damn it, one can't grieve forever. Yet I have had few symptoms since." He added, "The Oxford doctor and the London man said I was quite clear of all weakness and perfectly cured." Frank Harris asked Jennings if he thought Randolph's optimism unfounded. Jennings said, "I'm sure of it. He has fits of excessive irritability and depression which I don't like. In spite of what he told me, I don't think he took much care. He laughed at the secondary symptoms."[37]

Randolph's assumption that he had emerged from the sinister shadow of the disease was shattered in 1881, when, at the age of thirty-two, he suffered his first paralytic attack. His speech and gait were affected, though at first almost imperceptibly. The following year, however, he was mysteriously absent from London for seven months, and when he returned in October, gaunt and grim, he evaded all questions about where or why he had gone. The fact was that he had entered the third phase of syphilis; the deadly spirochetes had begun their invasion of his blood vessels and internal organs. Less than two months later, on December 12, the London newspapers announced that on the advice of his doctors he was sailing off again, to stay in Algeria and Monte Carlo until February. A remission brought him back, outwardly healthy, apparently his old self.

By now, however, Jennie, too, knew everything. Her source may have been Randolph; it could have been their family physician, Dr. Roose, who had made his own examination of her husband. Henry Pelling of St. John's College, Cambridge, observes: "The nature of Randolph's illness, once it had been diagnosed, was such that he could no longer claim his conjugal rights, and it is not surprising that Jennie began to seek the company of other men."[38] She may have begun to seek it earlier in their marriage. Indeed, one of her first admirers, Lieutenant Colonel John Strange Jocelyn, had found her receptive when the Churchills were still in Ireland. Jennie was Jocelyn's guest on his 8,900-acre Irish estate. She became pregnant in the summer of 1879, and when Winston's brother was born in Dublin the following February 4, he was christened John Strange Spencer Churchill.

That would not do; it was not done. Back in England, older and more experienced women counseled her in discretion. One disguise for affairs was to effect a lively interest in the arts and so encounter others similarly inclined. So she joined an artistic set called "the Souls." Reporting one of their parties at the Bachelor's Club, the London *World* told its readers: "This highest and most aristocratic cult comprises only the youngest, most beautiful and most exclusive of married women in London." Lady Warwick thought they were "more pagan than soulful." Sir William Harcourt said, "All I know about The Souls is that some of them have very beautiful bodies," and George Curzon wrote an ode to them called "The Belles" — a parody of "The Bells" by Poe — which ended: "How delicious and delirious are the curves / With which their figure swells / Voluptuously and voluminously swells / To what deed the thought impels." Marriage vows were certainly broken, but the fact was not advertised. After Ireland, Jennie never flaunted her lovers. Neither, however, was she furtive. She had superb legs, and she found a way to display them; *Town Topics* quoted a footman who had seen her dance the cancan at a ball: "She suddenly touched the mantelpiece with her foot, making a dreadful exposé." *Town Topics* also wrote that "Society has invented a new name for Lady R. Her fondness for the exciting sport of husband-hunting and fiancé-fishing has earned her the title 'Lady Jane Snatcher.' " Later she herself published an article slyly observing that some aristocratic wives could "live down scandals, whereas the less-favored go under, emphasizing the old saying, 'One may steal a horse while another may not look over the wall.' "[39]

She was a cunning thief, and at times piratical, but she learned to observe the rules. If a prospect was happy in marital harness, she did not tempt him to leave it. She was careful to point out that at the time she was meeting Paul Bourget he was "then unmarried." When another Frenchman married an American girl, she left his bed, though only temporarily; he implored her not to be puritanical, and perhaps because he was charming and a magnificent horseman, she returned. He was a diplomat, with a reputation to guard. That was important. She had an instinct for men who were dangerous. Sir Charles Dilke was attractive, engaging, and apparently on his way to high office. He seemed to have his pick of Souls. When Mrs. J. Comyns-Carr told Lady Lindsay that she was interested in Dilke, she was told: "There's a waiting list, you know." But Jennie wasn't on it. He sank to his knees and beseeched her to become his mistress. She refused, and described the preposterous scene to Lord Rosebery, who put it in his papers. Afterward, when Dilke was trapped in a public scandal woven of testimony about brothels, exotic sex, and some of Jennie's friends, her foresight was remembered. She always knew just when to stop. It was one of her many rare traits. Shane Leslie recalled: "She didn't seem to be like other women at all."[40]

Toward the end of her life, the novelist George Moore said that she had slept with two hundred men. That is absurd. She was far too fastidious for that, and only she would have known the figure anyhow. But though far from promiscuous, she had certainly led an active romantic life. Her lovers are known to include Kinsky, Henri Breteuil, Thomas Trafford, Baron Hirsch, Sir Edgar Vincent (later Viscount D'Abernon), Lord Dunraven, Herbert von Bismarck, Henri le Tonnelie, Norman Forbes Robertson, Hugh Warrender of the Grenadier Guards, a cavalry officer named Kinkaid Smith, the American Bourke Cockran, Bourget, William Waldorf Astor, Harry Cust, a soldier named Taylor, a man called Simon, an Italian named Casati, and Albert Edward of the house of Saxe-Coburg, eldest son of Queen Victoria, Prince of Wales and later King Edward VII.

Jennie was one of those favored ladies who, invited to dinner by His Royal Highness, found that she was the only guest. HRH usually made his royal conquests in a private dining room over a fashionable restaurant; one paneled wall swung down at the touch of a button, exposing a double bed. There was also a settee on one side which was adequate for most lovers, but HRH needed more room; Rudyard Kipling described him as "a corpulent voluptuary." Jennie was more than paramour to him. He granted her the rare privilege of using Buckingham Palace's private garden entrance. According to Ralph G. Martin, "she had a significant and lasting influence on him because he respected her judgment. He also knew he could rely on her. If he wanted a small private party arranged, he often asked her to oversee the compiling of the guest list and decide on the menu. Jennie knew his particular friends as well as his favorite foods. She knew what kind of music he liked. She knew the level of his impatience and boredom, the danger point of his anger, and what to do about them. In return, he was lavish in his gifts and in his open affection for her."[41] On his coronation in Westminster Abbey, she sat in the

King's Box with the other women he loved, including Mrs. George Keppel, his current mistress, all wearing diamond tiaras. Edward saw to it that pleasure was not sin's only reward. So did his wife; like Jennie's mother, Princess Alexandra understood and forgave her husband. She was on the best of terms with Mrs. Keppel, and always kind to Jennie.

Randolph had been less forgiving. He had put up with a lot from the prince; first Ireland, and now this. In 1889, when he had nothing left to lose, he ordered HRH out of his Mayfair house. On another occasion, after hearing from Rosebery that Dilke had propositioned Jennie, Randolph attacked him with his fists. This was rather hard on Dilke, who hadn't even made it into Jennie's arms, but he seems to have been a chronic loser. So was the man who hit him. And apart from these two episodes, Randolph, at least in his marriage, appears to have accepted his lot. He dined with men who had lain between his wife's thighs; he played cards with them; he rode to hounds with them and entertained them in his club. There were those who wondered why. Some speculated that he had become homosexual. That might explain his antagonism toward Winston, but there is no evidence of it. All we can say with certainty is that Winston knew about Jennie's affairs. The question is when. There is a story, probably apocryphal, that he first learned of her waywardness as a small boy because of a flaw in one of her stockings. In the late 1870s fashionable women in London wore red hose. Red was his favorite color. As she left home one noon, according to this account, he noticed a blemish in her left stocking, just above her shoe, and when she returned several hours later he saw the imperfection had moved from her left ankle to her right. But he would have become aware of her lovers anyhow. He could not have avoided it. In one of his schoolboy letters to his brother he wrote that upon arriving in London for a weekend, "I went, as Mamma had told me to Aldford Street, where I found Mamma & Count Kinsky Breakfasting." Visiting France, he was entertained by three of his mother's gallants: Trafford, Hirsch, and Breteuil. In *Savrola* the character based on Jennie is presented as an adulteress whose husband saw her less and less frequently. Not all this should be entered in the debit column: Jennie's men, including Edward VII, were to help Winston enormously during his struggle to establish himself. But his knowledge of her guilt undoubtedly contributed to his adolescent turmoil. Even in his early thirties he would have difficulty establishing relationships with young women. "Ambitions I still have: I have always had them," says *Savrola*'s hero, "but love I am not to know, or to know it only to my vexation and despair."[42]

His knowledge of romantic love came later, and it was glorious. Because Jennie lived until his late forties, he resolved his relationship with her. It was otherwise with his father. Here the grave denied him any opportunity for reconciliation; his image of Randolph was arrested in time. The crucial years were 1884 to 1886, roughly from Winston's tenth to twelfth birthdays, when he was in Brighton and beginning to take a serious interest in current events. Randolph was in the news constantly. Paresis, which progresses very slowly, had only just begun to cripple him. Outwardly he was vigorous, witty, powerful; the most spectacular man of the day. Newspapers called him "Gladstone's great adversary," and described workmen smiling at his mustache and doffing their caps as his carriage passed by. Winston clipped these stories and cartoons of his father and pasted them in scrapbooks. He next memorized his speeches verbatim. To his father he wrote: "I have been out riding with a gentleman who thinks that Gladstone is a brute and thinks that 'the one with the curly moustache ought to be Premier.' The driver of the Electric Railway said 'that Lord R. Churchill would be Prime Minister.' . . . Every body wants your Autograph but I can only say I will try, and I should like you to sign your name in full at the end of your letter. I only want a scribble as I know that you are very busy indeed."[43]

Long afterward he recalled that his father seemed to him "to own the key to everything or almost everything worth having." He could imagine nothing more exalted than to stand in the House of Commons, guiding the course of England and Empire. Taken to Marylebone swimming baths, he asked the attendant whether he was a Liberal or a Conservative. The unfortunate man replied that he didn't "bother myself about politics." Winston was outraged. "What?" he cried. "You pay rates and taxes and you don't bother yourself about politics?" He broke off his friendship with a playmate. The playmate's father asked his son why. The boy answered, "Winston says you're one of those damned Radicals and he's not coming over here again." Probably the man believed in nothing more rabid than Gladstonian liberalism, and possibly the bath attendant wasn't even allowed to vote, but a boy couldn't be expected to know that. He was his father's staunchest supporter. He yearned to battle for him. He was obsessed with his image. He had placed him on a high pedestal. He worshiped at the altar of a man he did not, in fact, even know.[44]

He tried to know him; tried, in his childish way, to draw Randolph into the family. "We had a Christmas tree and party here this year," he wrote, "which went off very well. My Stamp Book is gradually getting filled. . . . Jack had such a beautiful box of soldiers sent him from Lady de Clifford." Winston might have been a foreign correspondent sending word of developments from abroad, and indeed at times Randolph was a stranger to Connaught Place. Once he arrived home with a full beard — "a horrid beard so raged [ragged]," Jack wrote his brother at Brighton, and Jennie wrote that "his beard is a 'terror.' I think I shall have to bribe him to shave it off." Most of the time Winston could keep track of him in the newspapers. Apparently he did not find it peculiar that Randolph, who had been too occupied to visit him in Brighton, should have journeyed to speak to another school: "I went to see Grandmamma a fortnight ago, & she read me your speech on the Distribution of Prizes at the school of Art, it was just the sort of speech for school boys." Then, wistfully: "You had great luck in Salmon fishing. I wish I had been with you I should have liked to have seen you catch them."[45]

To a ten-year-old English boy in the 1880s, India was enthralling, and Winston was transported by news that his father was actually on his way there. "Will you write and tell me all about your voyage, was it rough at all?" he asked. "I wrote to you once when the ship stopped at Gibraltar. How nice for sailing all over the sea." Then, six weeks later: "I hear you have been out shooting at Calcutta and shot some animals. When are you coming home again. I hope it will not be long. I am at school now and am getting on pretty well. Will you write and tell me about India what it's like. . . . Will you go out on a tiger Hunt while you are there? Are the Indians very funny? . . . Try and get me a few stamps for my stamp album, Papa. Are there many *ants* in India if so, you will have a nice time, what with *ants mosquitos* [sic]. . . . I am longing to see you so much."[46]

At the end of this letter he again raised the question of autographs, asking, "Every body wants to get your signature will you send me a few to give away?" How anxious the other boys were is moot. We do know that later, at Harrow, subjects which interested schoolmates and those Winston thought should interest them were not always identical. It seems unlikely that many could have shared his passion for politics. Boys aren't like that now; they weren't then. But Winston was rapt in the world he had fashioned for himself, surrounded by scrapbooks, pastepots, scissors, and cuttings. His father thought he would have to go for a soldier, that he was too stupid for anything else. Yet politics already held him in its spell. He wrote his mother: "I am very glad Papa got in for South Paddington by so great a majority" — Randolph had polled 77 percent of the vote — "I think that was a victory. I hope the Conservatives will get in, do you think they will?" And three months later, on October 19, 1886, he wrote his father, "I hope you will [be] as successful in your speech at Bradford as you were at Dartford, and regularly 'cut the ground from under the feet of the Liberals.' " That winter he campaigned tirelessly among the other boys, bullying or cajoling them into making a Conservative commitment, and a handful yielded. The following May 24 he jubilantly informed Jennie that "about a dozen boys have joined the Primrose League since yesterday. I am among the number & intend to join the one down here, and also the one which you have in London. Would you send me a nice badge as well as a paper of Diploma, for I want to belong to yours most tremendously."[47]

It was an act of faith in his father's destiny, and it came too late. Not for the last time in his life, Winston had boarded a sinking ship. Randolph's political career had ended five months earlier.

Disraeli, whose memory the Primrose League was meant to perpetuate — it had been his favorite flower — had in his last days pointed Randolph out to a young colleague and said: "He can have anything he asks for, and will soon make them take anything he will give them." Gladstone had called him the greatest Conservative since Pitt. Lord Hartington had said that Randolph knew the House of Commons better than it knew itself; it always filled to hear him speak. Harris thought that "from his entrance into the House till 1886, it was Randolph's courage chiefly that commended him to the House of Commons. It may have been mainly aristocratic *morgue,* but Englishmen liked it none the less on that account." After a century which has seen countless changes in oratorical style, it is difficult to account for his appeal, but men of all political persuasions testified to it. He wrote his speeches out and learned them by heart; then he spoke at great speed, with daunting vehemence and compelling intensity. In debate his acid tongue set the House roaring. Once the Liberals thought he was napping. They introduced a specious motion, concealing a trap. He said: "Surely in vain is the net spread in the sight of any bird." In a typical thrust he attacked George Sclater-Booth, a ponderous Liberal minister: "I don't object to the Head of the Local Government Board dealing with such grave questions as the salaries of inspectors of nuisances. But I have the strongest possible objection to his coming down here with all the appearance of a great law-giver to repair, according to his small ideas and in his little way, breaches in the British Constitution." Then, almost as though speaking to himself, he added: "Strange, strange how often we find mediocrity dowered with a double-barreled name."[48]

He was at his sharpest when he took the offensive. At Blackpool, early in 1884, he turned one of Gladstone's endearing little traits into a sharp jab at the Grand Old Man. The GOM and his son enjoyed felling trees together. Randolph told his audience how a delegation of workingmen arrived at Gladstone's home and were led out into the grounds, where "all around them" lay "the rotting trunks of once umbrageous trees; all around them, tossed by the winds, were boughs and bark and withered shoots. They came suddenly on the Prime Minister and Master Herbert, in scanty attire and profuse perspiration, engaged in the destruction of a gigantic oak, just giving its last dying groan." The workmen were "permitted to gaze and worship and adore"; then each was "presented with a few chips as a memorial of that memorable scene." Randolph swiftly developed his theme, which was that the GOM had given the delegation exactly what he had given the Empire: "Chips to the faithful allies in Afghanistan, chips to the trusting native races of South Africa, chips to the Egyptian fellah, chips to the manufacturer and the artisan, chips to the agricultural laborer, chips to the House of Commons itself. To all who leaned on Mr. Gladstone, who trusted him, and who hoped for something from him — chips, nothing but chips — hard, dry, unnourishing, indigestible chips."[49]

The self-righteous GOM was particularly vulnerable to satirical oratory, and it was Randolph's great good fortune that the Liberals should have been in power when he returned from Dublin to make his way in the House as a Tory MP. Gadflies like him flourish in opposition. It was Winston's boyhood impression, he later wrote, that "Dizzy had been thoroughly beaten by Mr. Gladstone, so we were all flung out into Opposition and the country began to be ruined very rapidly. Everyone said it was 'going to the dogs.'" Afterward, looking back, he wrote that the position of the Conservatives, as a result of that beating, had "become weak and miserable in the extreme. . . . Outmatched in debate, outnumbered in division, the party was pervaded by a feeling of gloom." Dispirited, many stopped attending Parliament altogether. But for Randolph, the moment and his own mood were matched. His resentment of the men who had cut him after his row with HRH had infused him with a Jacobin spirit. The membership of the House was divided into Liberals, Conservatives, and Irish Nationalists; Randolph, without relinquishing his Tory label, founded what he called "the Fourth Party." There were four members: himself, Sir Henry Wolff, Sir John Gorst, and Arthur Balfour. Salisbury picked up the torch of Conservative leadership after Disraeli's death, but in his grasp it flickered low. The four free lances concentrated their fire on Gladstone and his ministers, but they did not spare the Tories' shadow government. They dubbed Tory insiders "the

Old Gang"; Salisbury's weaker colleagues were "the Goats." Nothing was sacred to the four, not even Disraeli's spirit. Dizzy's policy had been *Imperium* abroad and *Libertas* at home. Randolph challenged both. He attacked Gladstone's occupation of Egypt and embarrassed both Gladstone and Salisbury by squaring off against Charles Bradlaugh, a professed atheist who, when elected to Parliament by Northampton, refused to take the religious oath of allegiance. There was a fiery scene in the House on February 21, 1882, when Bradlaugh appeared, produced a book, identified it as "a Testament," and swore himself in. Randolph bounded up from his corner seat below the gangway and called the oath a farce. The book could have been anything, he said; "it might have been *Fruits of Philosophy*" — an appeal for birth control of which Bradlaugh was coauthor. After a series of complicated parliamentary maneuvers, Randolph persuaded the House to expel the member from Northampton. It was a brilliant coup, but it left a bad taste. Disraeli, wiser men knew, would never have permitted it. Then they remembered that Randolph, unlike his father, had never deferred to Disraeli — had, in fact, scarred him with the same rapier he was brandishing now.[50]

The week after his "chips" speech, Randolph stunned England by announcing that in the next election he would contest John Bright's Birmingham seat. This was carrying the battle into the very stronghold of liberalism, the home ground of the mighty Joe Chamberlain.* He had no chance of winning, but his audacity invigorated his party and brought it recruits in workmen's pubs, where spirit was admired. Winston, of course, was too young to appreciate this strategy. He wrote Jennie from Ascot: "Mrs Kynnersley went to Birmingham this week. And she heard they were betting two to one that Papa would get in for Birmingham." In fact, he polled 4,216 votes to Bright's 4,989. It was an impressive moral victory, and the next day an admirer stepped down in South Paddington, giving Randolph his seat. Randolph, by now, was the fighting heart of his party. As he moved from triumph to triumph, the House came to realize that eventually he would challenge Salisbury's role as Conservative leader. He was still in his thirties, his following in the country was growing, and he had a rallying cry: "Tory democracy." The party, he argued, needed new blood and wider popular appeal. *Democracy* was less than a charmed word among entrenched Tory diehards. The mere mention of it made Salisbury shudder, and he rejected Randolph's proposal to bring more rank-and-file members into the party's

* Father of Neville, Winston's great adversary. This marked the beginning of the on-and-off feud between the Chamberlains and the Churchills — a dispute which, in the tradition of British politics, was conducted with great civility.

inner councils. The two split in 1884 in a struggle for control of the National Union of Conservative Associations. Winston, aged nine, wrote to Jennie, "Has Papa got in I hope he has. You must let me no if he does." Papa did get in; he and Salisbury then staged a public reconciliation, each giving a little. Salisbury was still the leader, but the challenger was inching closer. "Trust the people, and the people will trust you!" Randolph told an enthusiastic crowd in Birmingham that same year. It sounded selfless. It wasn't. Randolph had become a shrewd campaigner. The Liberals were winning elections, he concluded, because the workmen felt closer to them than to the aristocratic Conservatives. "But," he said, "my feeling is that this earl or that marquis is much more in sympathy with the working man than the greedy nonconformist butcher or baker or candlestick maker. I want you to seize my point because it explains what I have always meant when I speak of myself as a Tory-democrat. The best class and the lowest class in England come together naturally. They like and esteem each other. They are not greasy hypocrites talking of morality and frequenting the Sunday school while sanding the sugar. They are united in England in the bonds of a frank immorality."[51]

If this was devious, it wasn't a patch on his Irish policy, which had ripened slowly during the early 1880s and was held in abeyance, to be revealed at the right moment. As Randolph's gibes wore Gladstone down, Home Rule became the key issue in Parliament. In a close election between the two major parties, the Irish Nationalists would hold the balance of power. It says much for England's ignorance of Ireland that Randolph's three years in Dublin made him an expert on the country in the eyes of Parliament, even though his knowledge of the people was largely confined to glimpses from the saddle while foxhunting. Thus his exile there, which had been looked upon as punishment, turned out to be a political asset. Gladstone, whose whole career would eventually hinge on this one question, had spent only three weeks in Ireland. Yet he was on good terms with Parnell, the Nationalists' militant leader, and he regarded that as his trump card when, on June 8, 1885, his government fell over a minor budget bill. Salisbury formed a caretaker government, but both sides knew that was of small consequence. The main event was the imminent general election.

Gladstone had miscalculated. Unable to pry an acceptable Home Rule pledge from him, Parnell issued a "Vote Tory" manifesto. Salisbury, meanwhile, had appointed Randolph to his first office. Denying him a post was impractical; his strength had been evident for a year. He had been told in camera that he would become secretary of state for India — hence his trip there, to get ready — but a problem now arose, and it was revealing. Randolph was sulking. He refused to be sworn in until he had been assured that a rival, Sir Stafford Northcote, would be denied the office of leader of the House in the caretaker government. The Queen was shocked. She wired Salisbury: "With due consideration to Lord R., do not think he should be allowed to dictate entirely his own terms, especially as he has never held office before."[52] Salisbury sought a meeting. Randolph refused; he had taken his stand, and that was that. Yielding, the new prime minister sent the rival to the House of Lords as the Earl of Iddesleigh, and Randolph received his seals of office from the Queen. Then, to the astonishment of all London, the man who had denounced imperialism in Egypt launched the Third Burmese War and annexed the country. Aristocratic disdain for consequences was common, but this went beyond that. The first rumors about Randolph's unreliability and bad judgment spread through Parliament and beyond.

In effect, the election was a dead heat. The voters returned 335 Liberals, 249 Conservatives, and 86 Irish Nationalists. Salisbury and Parnell could lock the GOM in stalemate. But after the results were in, Gladstone's youngest son revealed that his father did in fact favor Home Rule. The Irish then swung behind him, and he was again prime minister. Randolph now played a deep game. He courted the support of Irishmen on both sides of the Home Rule issue. His fight against Bradlaugh had won him the admiration of Catholics; that was one reason he had fought it. Privately, he assured Parnell that he favored Irish self-government on the local level and would oppose the coercion bill, which permitted the arrest and detention of Irish suspects without trial. Publicly, however, he became the most eloquent of Unionists; that is, opponents of Home Rule. Speaking in Belfast's Ulster Hall, he told Irish Unionists — Protestants — that he would stick with them to the end. By now he had had a great deal of experience in demagoguery and had got into the way of it. He compared Gladstone to Macbeth before the murder of Duncan and predicted that if politicians "should be so utterly lost to every feeling and dictate of honour and courage as to hand over coldly . . . the lives and liberties of the Loyalists of Ireland to their hereditary and most bitter foes, make no doubt on this point: Ulster at the proper moment will resort to the supreme arbitrament of force; *Ulster will fight, Ulster will be right.*"[53] This mischievous slogan was to be his chief contribution to history. It outlived him and his son. People are still dying for it in Northern Ireland.

Parliament rejected Gladstone's Home Rule bill in June 1886 — a quarter of his Liberals defected — and the country went to the polls again. This time the result was a Conservative landslide. The Tories held a clear majority of 118 seats over the Liberals, Irish Nationalists, and Unionists combined. Salisbury was now prime minister with a clear mandate, but as Randolph's grandson wrote, "It had been Lord Randolph's victory. He had pioneered it, engineered it and executed it. His exceptional services to the Party had to be recognised. He was indispensable to it." Harris observed, "When the House met again Lord Randolph's power had grown: he had deposed Gladstone, had won a greater position in the House than Gladstone himself." Sir Michael Hicks-Beach, offered the post of party leader of the House by Salisbury, insisted on stepping aside for the Tories' most brilliant campaigner. He wrote: "I felt that Lord Randolph Churchill was superior in eloquence, ability and influence to myself; that the position of Leader in name, but not in fact, would be intolerable; and that it was better for the party and the country that the Leader in fact should also be Leader in name." Randolph was good in the job. He was always in his seat, always informed, always an able tactician. And he could be charming when he chose. Margot Asquith boldly invited both him and Gladstone to her Grosvenor Square home. Randolph, she recalled afterward, "had made himself famous by attacking and abusing the Grand Old Man with such virulence that everyone thought it impossible that they could ever meet in intimacy. . . . I was not awed by this but asked them to a luncheon-party; and they both accepted. I need hardly say that when they met they talked with fluency and interest, for it was as impossible for Mr Gladstone to be gauche or rude as it was for anyone to be ill at ease with Lord Randolph Churchill. The news of their lunching with us spread all over London; and the West End buzzed round me with questions: all the political ladies, including the Duchess of Manchester, were torn with curiosity to know whether Randolph was going to join the Liberal Party."[54]

And yet . . .

Everyone who had worked closely with Randolph knew that he had a dark underside. Certainly Salisbury was aware of it. He would have disputed Mrs. Asquith; he was always ill at ease with Churchill. He had found him rude, peevish, temperamental, and, much of the time, unapproachable. The four crosses he bore, he said, were "the Prime Ministership, the Foreign Office, the Queen, and Randolph Churchill — and the burden of them increases in that order." Randolph had been an exasperating colleague in the India Office the year before. Salisbury's friends were appalled, therefore, when he appointed him chancellor of the Exchequer, the second most powerful position in the government. Even Randolph's friends were apprehensive. Lord Rosebery wrote that the new chancellor had displayed "certain defects of brain and character which are inconsistent with the highest statesmanship." And the Exchequer was the last place where he might succeed. Commenting on the columns of decimals in his budget, he growled, "I could never make out what those damned dots meant." But Salisbury knew what he was doing. He owed his landslide to Randolph. No one could say he was ungrateful now. At the same time, he was alert to the fact that Randolph was after his job. So he had put him into an impossible position and then sat back, waiting for him to destroy himself.[55]

It took six months. "Very soon," Harris heard, "there were rumors of disputes in the Cabinet."[56] Churchill was restive in harness; being a critic had been more fun. Tiring of the damned dots, he took a subversive interest in the affairs of other ministers. On October 3, without consulting Salisbury, he delivered a sensational speech before fourteen thousand people at Oakfield Park, Dartford, demanding more sovereignty for local governments in England, close ties with Germany and Austria-Hungary, and stiff protests against Russian influence in the Balkans — all at odds with the prime minister's programs. Next he submitted a startling budget to the cabinet. He proposed to reduce taxes and military spending: a plank right out of Gladstone's platform. Salisbury calmly rejected it. Churchill then decided to force his hand. He did it in the worst possible way.

His relationship with the Queen had been improving steadily. Victoria admired success. And he had been courting her. She disliked the patronizing Gladstone — "He always addresses me as though I were a public meeting," she complained — and was pleased by Randolph's more graceful approach. He wrote to her constantly, explaining political developments without a flicker of condescension. On September 22 she had expressed her gratitude to him: "Now that the session is over, the Queen wishes to write and thank Lord Randolph Churchill for his regular and full and interesting reports of the debates in the House of Commons, which must have been most trying. Lord Randolph has shown much skill and judgement in his leadership during the exceptional session of Parliament." She asked him to dine with her at Windsor Castle on December 20. He was immensely pleased; it was his first royal invitation since the row over her son's love letters to Lady Aylesford. The dinner went exceptionally well. On his return he glowed. Victoria, he told Harris, had called him "a true statesman." He in return felt that she was "a great woman, one of the wisest and best of women." What he did not tell Harris was that he had used the Queen's letter paper to write a letter of resignation from the cabinet. He had shown it to a fellow guest at the castle, Lord George Hamilton, the first lord of the Admiralty. Hamilton had remonstrated: "You cannot send a letter like that to Salisbury. Won't you consult somebody?" Randolph had replied, "No, I won't consult anybody." Nor had he. By Tuesday, December 21, the letter was in the prime minister's hands.[57]

On Wednesday evening, while Churchill was dining at the Carlton Club with Sir Henry Wolff, a messenger handed him Salisbury's reply. His resignation had been accepted. As Winston later wrote, Salisbury was doubtless "glad to have the whole power in his hands, instead of dividing it with a restless rival, entrenched in the leadership of the House of Commons and the control of the public purse." Randolph hadn't expected this — he had come to think of himself as indispensable — but he wasn't dejected. Indeed, he seemed strangely euphoric. Taking a cab to Connaught Place, he and Sir Henry picked up Jennie, and the three of them proceeded to the Strand Theatre. The play was Sheridan's *School for Scandal,* a theme of special interest to Jennie. She knew nothing of his letter. As they settled in the stalls, she mentioned the guest list for an official reception she was planning. He said enigmatically, "Oh, I shouldn't worry about that if I were you. It probably will never take place." Before she could ask him what he meant, the curtain rose, and when it fell on the first act, he excused himself, saying that he was returning to the club.[58]

Actually, he went to *The Times* and gave the editor copies of his correspondence with the prime minister, including a final, savage note from him to Salisbury. The editor read this last and said, "You can't send that." Lord Randolph said, "It has already gone." He then said he expected, in exchange for the scoop, editorial support from *The Times.* Nothing doing, the editor replied; indeed, the paper would attack him. That jarred Randolph, but not much; he was under the illusion that the party would rise up, depose Salisbury, and make him Salisbury's successor. He told a friend, "There is only one place, that is Prime Minister. I like to be boss. I like to hold the reins." In the morning he welcomed Harris to Connaught Place with the merry cry: "What do you think of it? More than two hundred and fifty Tory members come to attest their allegiance to me. I've won! The Old Gang will have to give in." But when Harris returned a few days later, Randolph said gloomily, "The rats desert the sinking ship."[59]

In fact, he had come closer to bringing Salisbury down than most commentators realized. It took the prime minister twelve days to find another Conservative willing to serve as chancellor. But with that, the crisis was over. Randolph was finished. In a moment of arrogance and folly he had gambled everything and lost. He was thirty-seven years old. He would never hold office again.* Jennie was bitter: "It was gall and wormwood," she said, "to hear Randolph abused in every quarter," often by men who owed "their political existence to him." Randolph himself wrote vainly, "What a fool Lord S. was to let me go so easily." For a time he affected gaiety. His appearances on the back benches became infrequent. He was seen more often at racecourses, where he entered horses from his own stable and bet heavily. He won often. "People smiled," wrote Harris, "as at the aberrations of a boy."[60]

Did you go to Harrow or Eton?" Winston wrote Randolph the following October. "I should like to know." It is extraordinary that he did not know already. Since 1722, Churchill boys — six generations of them — had been Etonians. But Dr. Roose urged a break in the tradition. Eton, hard by Windsor Castle, often cloaked and soaked in the fogs rolling off the Thames, was highly unsuitable for a boy with a weak chest. Randolph's brother had sent his son Charles ("Sunny") to Winchester. The cousins had been playmates; Sunny liked the school; it seemed the logical choice for Winston. On May 30, 1885, when he was ten, Winston wrote that he was "rather backward with Greek, but I suppose I must know it to get into Winchester so I will try and work it up," and as late as the summer of 1887 he was still bearing down on Greek because it was "my weak point & I cannot get into Winchester without it." But then Randolph and his brother quarreled. Their father had died. George was duke. Like his predecessors, he was improvident; to pay his debts he sold the family library, paintings, and jewels. Randolph denounced George with his customary venom and the two stopped speaking. Dr. Roose then recommended Harrow — "Harrow-on-the-Hill" — as best for Winston's health, and the boy was piloted in that direction. On October 8 Winston wrote his father: "I am very glad to hear that I am going to Harrow & not Winchester. I think I shall pass the Entrance Examination, which is not so hard as Winchester."[61]

It was characteristic of him in his teens that he always approached tests of his learning with breezy confidence and, in the breach, always per-

* Writing of this in 1930, his son commented: "It is never possible for a man to recover his lost position. He may recover another position in the fifties or sixties, but not the one he lost in the thirties or forties" (*Roving Commission*, page 47). Perhaps Winston was thinking of himself. He had been dismissed as first lord of the Admiralty in 1915, when he was forty-one. But *never* is a treacherous word. In 1939 Winston was again appointed first lord.

formed wretchedly. In this instance Brighton may have been partly responsible for his failure. He had just won two more prizes there, in English and Scripture, but the level of instruction was perhaps not all it might have been: "A master here is going to give a lecture on Chemistry, is it not wonderful to think that water is made up of two gases namely hydrogdgen and nitrodgen, I like it, only it seems funny that two gases should make water." But to scapegoat the Thomson sisters would be unfair. The pattern continued until the end of his school days. He was not, as many have assumed, a victim of dyslexia. Nor could he have been as stupid as he seemed. Confronted with the testing ritual, he seemed stricken by the kind of paralysis that can afflict men in moments of unbearable stress, when the mind seems fathoms down, like some poor land creature entangled in the weeds of the sea. Later he would write poignantly of his entrance into "the inhospitable regions of examinations, through which, for the next seven years, I was destined to journey. These examinations were a great trial to me. The subjects which were dearest to the examiners were almost invariably those I fancied least. . . . I should have liked to be asked to say what I knew. They always tried to ask what I did not know. When I would have willingly displayed my knowledge, they sought to expose my ignorance. This sort of treatment had only one result: I did not do well in examinations."[62]

The explanation, of course, was hostility, and it angered his parents, who never dreamed that they themselves, by their rejection of him, might have been responsible for it. They assumed that he was lazy. But he really wanted to get into Harrow. He boned up weeks in advance; on February 28, 1888, he wrote Jennie, "I am working hard for Harrow," and a week later he wrote his father, "I am working hard for my examination which is a very Elementary one, so there is all the more reason to be careful & not to miss in the easy things." On Friday, March 16, a day of shocking weather — the roads, in his words, "were in a horrible condition mud & water & in some places the road was covered with water which reached up to the carriage step and extended for over 200 yrd" — Charlotte Thomson accompanied him to Harrow, where they were received by the headmaster, J. E. C. Welldon. Winston thought Welldon "very nice," but then he was led into a classroom and the ordeal was upon him. There were no questions about the subjects he felt he had mastered: grammar, history, French, geography. Instead, he was asked to translate passages in Greek and Latin. His mind went blank. He couldn't even remember the Greek alphabet. Then, as he recalled afterward, he found himself "unable to answer a single question in the Latin paper. I wrote my name at the top of the page. I wrote down the number of the question, 'I.' After much reflection I put a bracket round it, thus, '(I).' But thereafter I could not think of anything connected with it that was either relevant or true. Incidentally there arrived from nowhere in particular a blot and several smudges. I gazed for two whole hours at this sad spectacle; and then merciful ushers collected up my piece of foolscap and carried it up to the Headmaster's table."[63]

In the corridor he was near hysteria. He told Miss Thomson that he had never been asked to render Latin into English before. She knew he had been translating Vergil for a year and Caesar longer, but, wisely, did not contradict him. To their mutual astonishment, Harrow accepted him. She wrote Randolph, "I hear from Mr Welldon today that Winston passed the examination yesterday." She didn't try to camouflage the truth: "My worst fears were realised with regard to the effect the nervous excitement would produce on his work: and he had only scraped through. . . . He had a severe attack of sickness after we left Harrow and we only reached Victoria in time for the 7.5 train. If Mr Welldon would allow him to try again on the 18th April, I believe that Winston would do himself more justice; but I think the permission would be difficult to obtain." It was, in fact, denied. Winston didn't think it mattered. He wrote: "I have passed, but it was far harder than I expected. . . . However I am through, which is the great thing."[64]

It wasn't that simple. Had he been another boy, he would have been automatically rejected. His sole qualification was that he was the son of a former cabinet minister. Thus, even before he was enrolled, the masters at Harrow regarded him as a special problem. On April 17, after a holiday at Blenheim with Duchess Fanny, he arrived at the school with his baggage and wrote his mother: "I will write tomorrow evening to say what form I'm in. It is going to be read out in the speech room tomorrow." The news was crushing. He was assigned to the lowest form. Only two boys in all Harrow were below him, and when both withdrew he was left as the school dunce. On visitors' days, the roll ("Bill") was called outside the Old School, and boys filed past in the order of their scholastic record. Other parents, curious about the son of the famous Lord Randolph, would await Winston's appearance and then whisper to one another: "Why, he's the last of all!"[65]

Today Harrow is part of Greater London, but in the 1880s it stood in open country. Peering toward the city from Headmaster's House you saw nothing but green fields, and the churchyard provided an unbroken view of rolling English landscape as far as Windsor, which could be seen on a clear day. Old Boys muttered indignantly about the Metropolitan Railway, which had begun to inch this way, and the new bicycle craze, which, in the phrase of the day, was "annihilating distance." Proud of their school, conscious of its role in English history, which to them meant the history of the world, they wanted nothing to change there. Strangers were shown the flat churchyard tombstone where Byron had brooded beneath the elms and the Fourth Form Room, dating from 1609, whose walls were inscribed with the names of Harrow boys who had made their mark. The Bill was followed closely for pupils of promise; already two of Winston's contemporaries, John Galsworthy and Stanley Baldwin, had been marked for future greatness. Harrovian traditions, encrusted by generations of observance, were considered sacred. Some seem odd. The food was inedible. Boys needed generous allowances to survive; such delicacies as eggs and sardines were available only in the private "tuckshops" in High and West streets. If you wanted to read anything but classical literature, you had to buy it in J. F. Moore's bookshop. And masters were regarded as the natural enemies of boys, though Welldon, then in his third year as head of the school, was personally popular. In appearance he resembled the twentieth-century British actor Jack Hawkins. One of Winston's classmates later wrote that the headmaster's "great massive form, as he swung into Fourth Form Room or Speech Room to take prayers or introduce a lecturer or ascended the pulpit to deliver one of his impressive sermons, produced a feeling of confidence."[66] Most important, in tracing Harrovian influences on Winston, were the school's patriotic songs:

So today — and oh! if ever
Duty's voice is ringing clear
Bidding men to brave endeavour —
Be our answer, "We are here."

And:

God give us bases to guard or beleaguer,
Games to play out whether earnest or fun;
Fights for the fearless and goals for the eager,
Twenty and thirty and forty years on.

In 1940 Churchill revisited Harrow and heard these stanzas again from another generation. Afterward he said: "Listening to those boys singing all those well-remembered songs I could see myself fifty years before, singing with them those tales of great men and wondering with intensity how I could ever do something glorious for my country." Here his memory was perhaps selective — songfests were not typical of his Harrow experience — but that is true of most Old Boy memories. Moreover, when one of their number becomes famous, many former schoolmates tend to edit their recollections, or even to distort them. It happens to old retainers, too. In the aftermath of Dunkirk, when Churchillian rhetoric seemed Britain's only shield against Nazi conquest, a reporter interviewed Wright Cooper, whose confectioner's store had been Harrow's most popular tuck-shop of the 1880s and 1890s. Cooper said:

> Churchill was an extraordinarily good boy. He was honest and generous in a day when robust appetites were not always accompanied by well-lined pockets. My family lived over the shop, and when Churchill was downstairs we all knew it. Boys crowded round his table. . . . He was witty and critical and kept the other boys in roars of laughter. He was exceedingly popular and even the seniors sought his company. He was well behaved and had the ear of everyone. When his father or his mother came to see him, he used to book a table in the tuck shop, and that was a great occasion for him. He was extremely happy at Harrow and full of high spirits. I knew him well in the tuck-shop days and it is one of the proudest memories of my life that I should have known the Prime Minister when he was preparing for his great career.[67]

So much for the infallibility of eyewitnesses. It would be difficult to find a statement more riddled with falsehood. He wasn't a good boy; he was a disciplinary problem. He wasn't generous; he couldn't afford to be — "I am afraid I shall want more money," he wrote on his third day at the school, and he never had enough to cover his debts. Other boys disliked him; Sir Gerald Wollaston, a classmate, later recalled that those who "had not met him personally soon heard about him, and what we heard created a somewhat unfavourable opinion." Most seniors sought his company only when they wanted him to black their boots or make their beds; he had to fag for three years, performing menial tasks until he was nearly seventeen. Each of his parents visited him but once, and were never there together. And he was wretched most of the time. He himself said later that he was, "on the whole, considerably discouraged" during his Harrow years, and in another reminiscence he wrote that he had been "just a pack-horse that had to crop what herbage he could find by the roadside in the halts of long marches, a bit here and there."[68]

"High spirits," however, rings true. His letters attest to his misery, but he concealed it from his masters and the other boys. They saw him as an energetic, abrasive, insolent miscreant who, in Sir Gerald's words, "broke almost every rule made by masters or boys, was quite incorrigible, and had an unlimited vocabulary of 'backchat' which he produced with dauntless courage on every occasion of remonstrance." The most frequent target of his back talk was Harrow's ultimate authority figure, the headmaster. Once Welldon told him sternly, "Churchill, I have grave reason to be displeased with you." Winston instantly replied, "And I, sir, have grave reason to be displeased with you." Another time the headmaster, hearing reports that the boy was using bad language, called him on the carpet. He said: "Now, my boy, when was the last time you used bad language." Winston had developed a stammer — which should have triggered suspicions that his self-confidence was frailer than it seemed — and he replied: "W-ell, sir, as I en-entered this r-room, I tr-tr-tripped over the do-do-or m-mat, and I am afr-fr-aid I s-s-said D-d-damn." Pets were strictly forbidden, but he kept two dogs in a kennel on West Street. Parts of the town were out-of-bounds for Harrovians. He made it a point to trespass there. Once he tried to blow up an out-of-bounds building, Roxreth House on Bessborough Road, which was said to be haunted. Using gunpowder, a stone ginger-beer bottle, and a home-made fuse, Winston built a bomb, lit it, and lowered it into the gloomy cellar. When nothing happened, he peered down. At that instant it exploded. His face scorched and his eyebrows singed, he was rescued by a neighbor; she bathed him and sent him back to school. As he left he cheerily told her, "I expect this will get me the bag." He wasn't expelled, but he was birched. It wasn't the first time for him. Harrow wasn't Ascot, and Welldon was no sadist, but all public schools practiced corporal punishment then. Guilty Harrovians were birched before breakfast in the Fourth Form Room. In most cases it didn't come to that. Usually it was enough for the headmaster to warn a boy that unless he mended his ways, "It might become my painful duty to swish you." Winston, however, ignored these threats and was a frequent swishee. He didn't seem to care. Perhaps the Reverend Sneyd-Kynnersley had hardened him to beatings.[69]

Once he had a bad accident when playing and had to be confined to bed. Lord Salisbury heard about it from the father of another Harrow boy and asked how it had happened. "It was during a game of 'Follow the Leader,' " he was told. Salisbury muttered, "He doesn't take after his father." But that is precisely what he *was* trying to do. During his first day at the school he tried to engage a master in political debate. The master may have been embarrassed; by then Randolph had tumbled into public disgrace. But Randolph was still his son's idol. During his infrequent visits home, Winston begged his mother to introduce him to men prominent in Parliament. This, at least, was something Jennie could enjoy doing for her son. Invitations went out, and among the guests

Winston met were three future prime ministers: Rosebery, Balfour, and Asquith. He later wrote: "It seemed a very great world where these men lived; a world in which high rules reigned and every trifle in public conduct counted; a duelling ground where although business might be ruthless, and the weapons loaded with ball, there was ceremonious personal courtesy and mutual respect." During the convalescence after his fall, Sir Edward Carson, one of Jennie's beaux, took Winston to dinner and then to the Strangers' Gallery overlooking the House of Commons. There the boy peered down and listened, in his later words, to "the great parties ranged on each side fighting the Home Rule controversy." Gladstone, he thought, resembled "a great white eagle, at once fierce and splendid." He also witnessed the Grand Old Man's tribute to Joe Chamberlain after the maiden speech of Joe's son Austen. "It was," the Grand Old Man said, "a speech which must have been dear and refreshing to a father's heart." The boy saw how moved Joe was: "He was hit as if a bullet had struck him." Winston was touched, too. He thought how proud his own father would be if he were elected to Parliament and spoke well. Back at Harrow, he stood before a mirror, trying to imitate Randolph's style and delivery. Except for his stammer, a speech impediment which was just becoming evident, and a certain guttural quality which was developing in his reedy adolescent voice, it went well.[70]

It went too well. He was modeling his tone and phrases after those of an embittered man who denounced "a government which has boycotted and slandered me" and used the language to inflict painful wounds on the men who, he thought, had betrayed him. In the mouth of an adolescent who was already thought odd by his peers, Randolph's studied invective and biting sarcasm were bound to alienate other boys. During his entire time at Harrow he made but one friend, an older boy, John — later Sir John — Milbanke. Even those who admired his nerve were put off by his truculence; one of them would recall in his memoirs how "this small red-haired snub-nosed jolly-faced youngster" darted up "during a house debate, against all rules, before he had been a year in the house, to refute one of his seniors." He was also becoming cheeky at home. In the kitchen he taunted Rosa Ovenden, the Churchills' cook, until she took a broom to him, shouting, "What the devil are you messing about here for? Hop it, copper-nob." Clara Jerome came to see her grandson and left describing him as "a naughty, sandy-haired little bulldog."[71]

In his first letter to Jennie from Harrow, he had told her: "I want to learn Gymnastics and carpentering." Later he also became interested in fencing, but most of the time he was alone, sawing and hammering with the intensity of purpose he would later show in laying bricks; collecting mulberry leaves for a colony of silkworms he kept; poring over his stamp album; or going on long walks with his dogs, sometimes accompanied by a town detective he had befriended. He hated cricket, hated football, hated field days. He liked boxing in the gym and swimming in Ducker, the school swimming pool, and might have developed warm relationships with other boys there, but he would only box with a master, and his manner elsewhere discouraged intimacy. After Churchill had become prime minister, J. E. B. Seely, by then Lord Mottistone, recalled setting eyes on him for the first time at Ducker. Winston was trying unsuccessfully to push a floating log toward the bank. A Sixth Former said, "You see that little red-headed fellow having a row with the log? That's young Churchill." His companion called, "Hi, Churchill, I bet you two buns to one you don't get it out." Winston, said Seely, "bent his head down and appeared to be thinking deeply," as he later did "in the House of Commons." Then he turned his back on Seely, thereby snubbing a popular boy who could have helped him. On another occasion at Ducker, he sneaked up behind a slight figure and pushed him into the water. As the indignant boy climbed out, another swimmer said, "Now you're for it. That's Leo Amery, a Sixth Former." Realizing that he had gone too far this time, Winston apologized ineptly: "I thought you were a Fourth Former because you are so small." Sensing his blunder, he bit his tongue and added what, for him, was the supreme compliment: "My father is small, too, and he is a great man."[72]

As editor of the school paper, the *Harrovian*, Amery got even. Using the pseudonym "Junius Junior," Winston sent, as a letter to the editor, an attack on the school's gym policy. Amery thought part of it too abusive to print. He cut it, adding the note: "We have omitted a portion of our correspondent's letter, which seemed to us to exceed the limits of fair criticism." Winston was in tears; his best paragraphs, he protested, had been deleted. Actually, he should have been grateful for the blue-penciling. Even expurgated, the letter aroused Welldon; he resented its implied criticism of his authority. Amery quite properly refused to identify "Junius Junior." The headmaster knew his boys, however; Winston was summoned and threatened with another swishing. By now he was regarded as the school subversive, a hoarder of grievances and defier of conventions. But some of his grievances were justified. Unreasonably, the school insisted upon listing him alphabetically under *S* — Spencer-Churchill instead of Churchill. Before his arrival, he had been promised a room in Welldon's house; he had to wait a year for it. And in at least one instance his defiance was admirable. Public-school boys then were ashamed of their nannies. They would no sooner have invited one to

Harrow than an upper-class American boy today would bring his teddy bear to his boarding school. Winston not only asked Woom to come; he paraded his old nurse, immensely fat and all smiles, down High Street, and then unashamedly kissed her in full view of his schoolmates. One of them was Seely, who later became a cabinet colleague of Winston's and won the DSO in France. Seely called that kiss "one of the bravest acts I have ever seen."[73]

Churchillian stubbornness, which would become the bane of Britain's enemies, was the despair of his teachers. He refused to learn unless it suited him. Welldon put him in what today would be called a remedial reading class, where slow boys were taught English. He stared out the window. Math, Latin, Greek, and French were beneath his contempt. Questions "about these Cosines or Tangents in their squared or even cubed condition," as he later called them, were in his opinion unworthy of answers. He repeated Horace's *Odes* four times and remained ignorant of it. Looking back on those days, the man Churchill would write: "If the reader has ever learned any Latin prose he will know that at quite an early stage one comes across the Ablative Absolute. . . . I was often uncertain whether the Ablative Absolute should end in 'e' or 'i' or 'is' or 'ibus,' to the correct selection of which great importance was attached. Dr. Welldon seemed to be physically pained by a mistake being made in any of these letters. . . . It was more than annoyance; it was a pang." His French accent was atrocious. It would *always* be atrocious. During World War II he remarked that one of the greatest ordeals of the French Resistance was hearing him address them in their own tongue over the BBC.*[74]

He had scarcely settled in at Harrow when he was put "on reports." That meant that he had to acquire weekly accounts of his progress in each subject and discuss them with the headmaster. He begged his mother to come and "jaw Welldon about keeping me on reports for such a long time." For once Jennie came, but the headmaster was immune to her charm; Winston's status remained unchanged. The following week he wrote her: "It is a most shameful thing that he should keep me on like this. . . . I am awfully cross because now I am not able to come home for

* "*Prenez garde!* I am going to speak to you in French, a formidable undertaking and one which will put great demands upon your friendship for Great Britain."

an absit [overnight leave] on Thursday which I very much wanted to do. I hope you don't imagine I am happy here. It's all very well for monitors & Cricket Captains but it is quite a different thing for fourth form boys. Of course what I should like best would be to leave this *hell of a* [italicized phrase underlined, then struck out] place but I cannot expect that at present."[75]

One member of the faculty who looked forward to seeing the last of Winston was H. O. D. Davidson, who, as his housemaster, was responsible for discipline and therefore his natural enemy. On July 12, when Winston had been enrolled less than three months, Davidson sent his mother an extraordinary complaint. He was a seasoned teacher, and had been a champion shot-putter at Oxford, but this thirteen-year-old boy was clearly beyond his competence. "After a good deal of hesitation and discussion with his form-master," he wrote Jennie, "I have decided to allow Winston to have his exeat ["day out"]; but I must own that he has not deserved it. I do not think, nor does Mr [Robert] Somervell, that he is in any way *wilfully* troublesome; but his forgetfulness, carelessness, unpunctuality, and irregularity in every way, have really been so serious, that I write to ask you, when he is at home to speak very gravely to him on the subject." New boys, he conceded, needed "a week or two" to adjust to Harrow. But "Winston, I am sorry to say, has, if anything got worse as the term passed. Constantly late for school, losing his books, and papers and various other things into which I need not enter — he is so regular in his irregularity that I really don't know what to do; and sometimes think he cannot help it. But if he is unable to conquer this slovenliness . . . he will never make a success of a public school. . . . As far as ability goes he ought to be at the top of his form, whereas he is at the bottom. Yet I do not think he is idle; only his energy is fitful, and when he gets to his work it is generally too late for him to do it well." Davidson thought it "very serious that he should have acquired such phenomenal slovenliness." He felt "sure that unless a very determined effort is made it will grow upon him." Winston, he concluded, "is a remarkable boy in many ways, and it would be a thousand pities if such good abilities were made useless by habitual negligence. I ought not to close without telling you that I am very much pleased with some history work he has done for me."[76]

Clearly there was something odd here. Winston, Davidson had conceded, was the ablest boy in his form. He was, in fact, remarkable. His grasp of history was outstanding. Yet he was considered a hopeless pupil. It occurred to no one that the fault might lie, not in the boy, but in the school. Samuel Butler defined genius as "a supreme capacity for getting

Winston at Harrow in 1889

its possessors into trouble of all kinds," and it is ironic that geniuses are likeliest to be misunderstood in classrooms. Studies at the University of Chicago and the University of Minnesota have found that teachers smile on children with high IQs and frown upon those with creative minds. Intelligent but uncreative students accept conformity, never rebel, and complete their assignments with dispatch and to perfection. The creative child, on the other hand, is manipulative, imaginative, and intuitive. He is likely to harass the teacher. He is regarded as wild, naughty, silly, undependable, lacking in seriousness or even promise. His behavior is distracting; he doesn't seem to be trying; he gives unique answers to banal questions, touching off laughter among the other children. E. Paul Torrance of Minnesota found that 70 percent of pupils rated high in creativity were rejected by teachers picking a special class for the intellectually gifted. The Goertzels concluded that a Stanford study of genius, under which teachers selected bright children, would have excluded Churchill, Edison, Picasso, and Mark Twain.

None of this was known to Welldon and his staff, but as term succeeded term an awareness grew among them that Winston was a baffling boy. He couldn't, or wouldn't, learn the ablative absolute — a minor feat of memory — but he could recite twelve hundred lines of Macaulay without missing a word, and at no one's urging he memorized whole scenes from three Shakespeare plays: *A Midsummer Night's Dream, Henry VIII,* and *The Merchant of Venice.* There are learned men who do not know that *byss* is the opposite of *abyss.* He knew it; he had been haunting J. F. Moore's bookshop and the school library. Teachers who misquoted English poets were corrected by him. He sat rapt through a lecture on the battle of Waterloo and then delivered a stunning critique of it, citing sources which were unknown to the lecturer but which, when checked, were confirmed. This merely convinced his masters that he could do the work if he wanted to and didn't do it because he was obstinate. One of them would recall, "I formed the highest opinion of his abilities and never ceased to wonder why he did not rise higher in the School. But he hated the Classics, and in his time that kept him down. . . . On one field-day he came and asked me to let him act as my *aide-de-camp,* and his alertness and zeal for action were amazing." Another wrote: "He was plainly uninterested in the academic subjects." A third teacher came close to the truth; with a fine disregard for prepositional precedence he observed that "he was not an easy boy to deal with. Of course he had always a brilliant brain, but he would only work when he chose to and for the matters he approved of."[77]

That would have been the solution: to put him under the spell of gifted teachers who, shunning pedantry, could engage his interest and persuade him that the challenge of some courses, at least, deserved his best response. It was pointless to scold him, as Jennie did in her letters: "Your report which I enclose is as you see a *very* bad one. You work in such a fitful inharmonious way, that you are bound to come out last — look at your place in the form! . . . If only you had a better place in your form, & were a little more methodical I would *try* & find an excuse for you. Dearest Winston you make me very unhappy. . . . Your work is an insult to your intelligence." He could only reply: "I will not try to excuse myself for not working hard, because I know that what with one thing & another I have been rather lazy. Consequently when the month ended the crash came I got a bad report & got put on reports etc. etc. . . . My own Mummy I can tell you your letter cut me up very much. . . . I knew that work however hard at Mathematics I could not pass in that. All other boys going in were taught these things & I was not, so they said it was useless." Such sterile exchanges merely led him farther down the low road. Luckily there were three masters at Harrow who knew how to guide him upward. One taught math, the very subject Winston thought hopeless. In afterlife Churchill wrote: "All my life from time to time I have had to get up disagreeable subjects at short notice, but I consider my triumph, moral and technical, was in learning Mathematics in six months. . . . I owe this achievement not only to my own 'back-to-the-wall' resolution — for which no credit is too great; but to the very kindly interest taken in my case by a much respected Harrow master, Mr. C. H. P. Mayo. He convinced me that Mathematics was not a hopeless bog of nonsense, and that there were meanings and rhythms behind the comical hieroglyphics."[78]

Robert Somervell deserves a footnote in history. When Winston was about to go down for the third time, this perceptive young master — "a most delightful man, to whom my debt is great," Winston said of him — took over the remedial English class. His pupils were considered dolts too simple to learn Latin and Greek. They must continue to try, but Harrow would be satisfied if they mastered their own language. Usually such assignments fall to teachers who are inept themselves, and had that been true of Somervell, Winston's life might have taken a different turn. But not only was he not dull; he thought English inspiring, and his enthusiasm was infectious. In the words of Churchill: "He knew how to do it. He taught it as no one else has ever taught it." First they learned to parse sentences thoroughly. Then they practiced continuing grammatical analysis, using a system of Somervell's which appealed to the playful instinct in every boy: using a spectrum of inks, he would score a long sentence, breaking it up into subject, verb, object; relative clauses, conditional clauses, conjunctive and disjunctive clauses. Each had its color and its bracket. "It was a kind of drill," Churchill recalled. "We did it almost daily." Since Winston remained obdurate in his refusal to study the classics, he remained in Somervell's class for three terms. As a man he would write that he went through the drills "three times as long as anyone else. I had three times as much of it. I learned it thoroughly. Thus I got into my bones the essential structure of the ordinary British sentence — which is a noble thing. And when in after years my schoolfellows who had won prizes and distinction for writing such beautiful Latin poetry and pithy Greek epigrams had to come down again to common English, to earn their living or make their way, I did not feel myself at any disadvantage."[79]

At Harrow his lifelong fascination with words grew. He was thirteen, and Somervell was introducing him to literature. Except for best-sellers like Wilkie Collins's *Moonstone,* few Harrovians read for pleasure. Winston was soon deep in Thackeray, Dickens, Wordsworth, and every biography he could lay his hands on. He knew what was good and found he liked it. Inevitably his vocabulary increased. In his letters he wrote of a toy given him by his aunts as "a source of unparalleled amusement," his funds needed "replenishing," welcome news was "pleasing intelligence." The bookseller Moore, who saw him almost daily, noticed that he was displaying "evidences of his unusual command of words. He would argue in the shop on any subject, and, as a result of this, he was, I am afraid, often left in sole possession of the floor."[80] At this point another teacher, L. M. Moriarty, Winston's fencing master, suggested that he drop in on him evenings at home to discuss essays and history. They talked, not only of content, but also of form, particularly essay techniques then being developed by Stevenson, Ruskin, Huxley, and Cardinal Newman. None of this was reflected in the report cards sent to Connaught Place, but the autodidactic pattern was forming. Winston was being taught to teach himself. He would always be a dud in the classroom and a failure in examinations, but in his own time, on his own terms, he would become one of the most learned statesmen of the coming century.

Aware of his growing intellect and increasing flair for expression, he was exasperated by his dismal marks. Welldon was also frustrated, and for the same reason. Shortly after Winston's fourteenth birthday, the headmaster told Seely that he had never seen a boy with "such a love and veneration for the English language."[81] When he received a sparkling paper from a Sixth Former who was a brilliant classicist but clumsy with his native tongue, Welldon called the boy in. He told him he didn't believe he had written the theme. Churchill, he said, was the only pupil who wrote that well. Confession followed. Welldon had uncovered a conspiracy. The Sixth Former had been translating Winston's elementary Latin assignments. Then he had sat at his desk with paper and pencil while Winston, pacing back and forth, dictated the theme. There is no record of disciplinary action, but the incident is striking. It is the first known instance of the technique Churchill would use in writing his greatest books. And it is a devastating comment on public-school values. Eloquent and lucid in living English, Winston was a scholastic failure because of his disdain for two languages which would be almost useless to him.

He was writing now, submitting further contributions to the school paper as "Junius Junior." They seldom appeared. He didn't fit here, either. A fellow Old Boy recalled: "From time to time he sent notes on current events to *The Harrovian;* these could not always be printed, but they were extraordinarily witty and well expressed, and often caused the editors to roar with laughter." This is reminiscent of the nineteenth-century Krupp cannon which was sent to Saint Petersburg as a sample in the hope of stimulating sales. It fired so well that the Russians put it in a museum. Laughing editors spiked Winston's copy because they felt that passing their amusement along to their readers would be undignified. Of his contributions which were accepted, only one survives, a lugubrious poem inspired by an epidemic of influenza raging on the Continent:[82]

And now Europe groans aloud
And 'neath the heavy thunder-cloud
Husked in both song and dance:
The germs of illness wend their way
To westward each succeeding day
And enter merry France.

The flu hit Winston during his first Christmas holidays from Harrow. On December 30 Randolph peevishly wrote his sister-in-law, "Of course the boys have made themselves ill with their Christmassing, & yesterday both were in bed with [Dr.] Roose and [Dr.] Gordon hopping in & out of the house. Jack is better this morning but Winston has a sore throat & some fever. I hope it is nothing but biliousness & indigestion." He and Jennie didn't hover around to find out. They left that day on a vacation of their own. Meanwhile, Winston worsened. Two days later he wrote his mother: "My throat is still painful & swelled — I get very hot in the night — & have very little appetite to speak of. . . . It is awful 'rot' spending ones holidays in bed or one room." Another letter followed a few days later. He was "tired of bed and slops." His new magic lantern didn't work. The "Dr says I ought to go to the seaside, & then *I shan't see you at all.*" He calculated that "1 week at the seaside leaves 1 week & that 1 week you will be away. It is an awful pity. I don't know what to do." Woom knew. She bundled him off to her brother-in-law's cottage at Ventnor. Back at Harrow he wired her: "Am quite well."[83]

But he wasn't. Suffering a relapse the following month, he wrote his mother that he was "still far from well & am in bed because I can hardly stand. I am so weak as I have had very [little] food for 4 days." Woom had come, and Mrs. Davidson had told him that "she hopes you will let Woomany come [again] tomorrow, because she says the company will do me good. I do not know how the day would have passed but for Woomany. I have had another big poultice on my liver to-day to make it worse [sic]. I hope you will allow Woomany to come tomorrow as I shall certainly be very disappointed if she does not turn up." His need for his nurse is a thread running through his correspondence with his mother:

"Thank you so much for letting Woom come down." "Do let Woom come down tomorrow." "Thanks awfully for letting Woom come down today." Mrs. Everest, for her part, wrote him faithfully, but she couldn't grasp his adolescent problems; she still thought of him as a small boy. She sent him "some fine flannel shirts to sleep in" and a new suit: "Winny dear do try to keep the new suit expressly for visiting, the brown one will do for everyday wear, please do this to please me. I hope you will not take cold my darling take care not to get wet or damp." And: "I hope you have recovered from the effects of your dental operation deary. . . . I hope you wear your coat in this wet weather & change your Boots when they are damp, that is what gives you tooth ache sitting in wet boots."[84]

Woom alone attended to his errands. She was anxious about his well-being and missed him terribly; in her long, gushing letters she told him again and again that she was always at his beck and call. She asked, "Did you get your luggage alright to Harrow this time it is always best to take it with you from the Station. . . . Have sent you 3 Black Waistcoats let me know dear also if you receive a small parcel of 2 shirts &c I sent off yesterday. I am sending you 1 dozen new Handkerchiefs on Monday with the hamper. Are you always going to have the room to yourself or is it only temporary. Old Mr Wickes sent me a lot of lovely grapes from Ventnor out of his green house. I am so glad you are well my sweet mind & try to get through the exam my precious loving darling old lamb — much love & kisses from Your old Woom." If he neglected to write her, she was reproachful: "My darling Lamb, I have been looking for a letter from you all last week. I never have heard anything about you for a whole week. Are you well dear. . . . Did you get a Pocket Book or a Memorandum Book from me I sent you one. . . . Do send me a line there's a dear Boy & tell me what you are going to do. Did Mamma bring you a Birthday present. I have no news to tell you so with fondest love to you my darling. I am ever your loving W."[85]

His mother had not brought him a present. Unlike her husband, Jennie remembered Winston's age, but she doesn't appear to have been much more thoughtful. "His Lordship has postponed his arrival for a fortnight, so you will not see him," Woom wrote in a typical midweek letter to Winston; "Mamma has been away since Saturday." Except for two years when Randolph rented a house at Banstead — it was here that Winston built his great fort, together with a homemade catapult which hurled green apples at a nearby cow — Winston and Jack spent their long holidays with Woom, often in the Balaam cottage at Ventnor. Even at Banstead, Woom was usually in loco parentis, the only adult on the spot. She wrote Jennie from there in 1891: "I hope you got Master Winston's letter he wrote last evening. They are both so happy & delighted & in towering spirits. . . . They are so happy and well I should like to keep Master Jack here until Mr Winston returns from Canford. . . . It is so much better for them than London. I am desired to enclose drawings of last night with their best love & kisses. Your ladyship's obednt servant E. A. Everest."[86]

Lord Randolph was usually to be found these days at the Jockey Club. His most successful horse was a yearling he named "Abbess" after a French novel Jennie happened to be reading at the time. Abbess won, among other races, the Oaks at Epsom, the Manchester Cup, and the Hardwicke Stakes — over £10,000 in prize money. Unfortunately for her owner, when she won the Oaks at twenty-to-one, Randolph, convinced she couldn't do it, had bet all his money on another horse. The story went around the London clubs; it was regarded as characteristic of his recidivous disloyalty. He was down now, and his critics were kicking him mercilessly. The *Spectator* reported that parliamentary debates showed "that Lord Randolph's power to impress, if not to interest the House of Commons, is dwindling rapidly. The House watch his gyrations with languid curiosity or mild amusement. . . . Most of them probably think that it was indeed a memorable, a very memorable, mistake to put so feather-headed a politician as Lord Randolph Churchill in the position in which he was expected to counsel gentlemen on the Ministerial side of the House, and did counsel them with more or less cleverness for a few weeks." To escape this sort of thing — and perhaps to flee from the winks of London society, which saw Jennie openly reaching for younger and younger men — Randolph decided to try his hand at journalism. He sailed to Cape Town for three months, after reaching an agreement with the *Daily Graphic*, which would publish his letters from there. Even these pieces vexed the *Review of Reviews*: "Lord Randolph Churchill in his time has played many parts, but not even in the famous somersault which terminated his career as leader of the House of Commons and possible leader of the Conservative party has he afforded the public a more unseemly exhibition of irresponsibility than in his letters from South Africa. They furnish the culminating evidence, if further evidence were necessary, as to the impossibility of Lord Randolph Churchill as the leader of men."[87]

Such a man, in such straits, is ever alert for slights. When Abbess won the Manchester Cup, again at twenty-to-one, Randolph harvested £2,202 in prize money plus his enormous winnings from his bets. He sent Winston a five-pound note. When instant gratitude was not forthcoming from Harrow, he was furious. Jennie wrote: "Your Father is very angry with you for not acknowledging the gift of the £5 for a whole week, and then writing an offhand careless letter." Of course, money wasn't what Winston wanted from his father. Welldon knew that, and he wrote Lord Randolph, tactfully suggesting that it might "perhaps not be disagreeable" to His Lordship and Her Ladyship to come to Harrow sometime and take "at least the opportunity of seeing what Winston's school life is like." Winston hoped they would come for Speech Day, when he would be honored for his feat of memory with Macaulay's *Lays.* He checked timetables and wrote his father: "If you take the 11.7 from Baker Street you will get to Harrow at 11.37. I shall meet you at the station with a fly, if I can get one. . . . You have never been to see me & so everything will be new to you." He wrote his mother: "Do try to get Papa to come. He has never been." Papa refused. The relationship between these two had long been doomed. Randolph had sent him a bicycle, but Welldon wrote Jennie the following month: "I am sorry to say Winston has fallen off his bicycle and hurt himself. . . . The Doctor calls it 'slight concussion.' " Later Winston wrote his mother that he had decided to have the bike fixed and then exchange it for a bulldog. Jennie didn't care — "Do as you like about yr bicycle" — but Woom foresaw trouble if Randolph found out: "What on earth is the good of your having a Bull Dog unless it is to keep us all in terror of our lives. . . . Besides His Lordship gave you the Bicycle & he would not like you to part with it." Winston found her argument persuasive. Offending his father was the last thing he intended. Randolph's African journey excited him. He wrote him in Johannesburg: "Have you shot a lion yet?" He was still Randolph's most loyal partisan.[88]

His father's criticisms of conditions in South Africa, brought on by commercial exploitation, were appearing in the *Daily Graphic.* Savage rebuttals of them had spread from the *Spectator* and the *Review of Reviews* to virtually every serious newspaper. Winston excitedly wrote him: "You cannot imagine what vials of wrath you have uncorded [sic]. All the papers simply rave. Shareholders, friends of the company, and directors from Sir Donald Currie to the lowest Bottle Washer are up in arms. *Truth,* the *Speaker, Standard* and others including even the *Harrow Gazette* devote a column to 'Lord Randolph's Grumbles.' The *Standard* quotes the *Speaker* & is particularly offensive. It states that — but oh I will not bore you with the yapping of these curs hungry for their money bags." Winston's vows of filial loyalty seem to have brought father and son to the brink of cordiality. Randolph replied to one of them, "You cannot think how pleased I was to get your interesting & well written letter." But the moment swiftly passed. It was like that flash of green in tropical sunsets just before the sun vanishes over the horizon. It lasts but a microsecond and is followed by total darkness. Randolph was approaching the last stages of his terrible disease. Ahead, for his family, lay horror.[89]

Jennie flourished during her husband's South African absence. She was deeply in love with Count Kinsky, and when not sleeping with him she spent virtually every moment entertaining friends. No. 2 Connaught Place was always full. Then, to her annoyance, the annual Eton-Harrow cricket match rolled around. Cricket still bored Winston, but the match at Lord's was an annual social ritual, a great occasion for the boys at both schools to wear top hats, ride around in glittering coaches with the aristocracy, and feast on strawberries and cream. To Winston's consternation, his mother told him that her social calendar was full; there was no room for him at the Connaught Place house. Indeed, there was no room for *her*. She had invited so many guests that she had been obliged to move in with her sister Clara at 18 Aldford Street. Unappeased, he wrote her: "Think how unhappy I should be being left at Harrow when 90 out of every hundred boys are enjoying themselves. You promised I should come. . . . I was terribly frightened when I got your letter this morning. The Possibility of my not being able to come being to my mind entirely out of the question. Could you not ask Grandmamma Marlborough to let me come stay with her (at least). . . . My darling Mummy I am sure you have not been very much troubled about me this term. I have asked for no visits & I forfeited the pleasure of seeing you on Speech Day therefore I do hope you will endeavour not to disappoint me utterly with regard to July 11th and 12th." Two days later she replied: "Oh! dear oh! You silly old boy I did not mean that you would have to remain at Harrow only that I cld not have you here." She suggested that Clara might "put you up." That proved impossible, and Woom wrote him the next day: "Well my dearest the reason Mamma cannot have you at home is the house is to be full of visitors for the race week which commences on the Tuesday tomorrow week. But I don't see why you could not go from Friday till Monday because you could go by yourself." Since she herself would be billeted elsewhere, he could stay with her "and then perhaps Aunt Clara or some one would see you off to Harrow." That evening it was settled. He would stay with Duchess Fanny on Grosvenor Square.[90]

Actually, it turned out to be Winston's most memorable boyhood weekend. Despite Jennie's lack of maternal instincts, her strong erotic drive assured a constant string of sensitive suitors, some of whom sensed Winston's loneliness, understood his yearning for an affectionate father figure, and were eager to give him strong arms to lean on. On the morning of Friday, July 10, 1891, sixteen-year-old Winston arrived at Baker Street Station, watched the early innings at Lord's, took a hansom to Grosvenor Square, and lunched with Duchess Fanny. That evening John Milbanke took him to dinner at the Isthmian Club; afterward they attended the Naval Exhibition. ("Most beautiful models & guns of every description," Winston wrote Jack. "Got home at 11:45.")[91] His great treat, however, came the following day. Kaiser Wilhelm II, emperor of Germany's Second Reich and now in the fourth year of his reign, was visiting Queen Victoria, his grandmother. All London knew he would be appearing at the Crystal Palace, where a special exhibition awaited him, and that the public was invited. Count Kinsky decided to take Winston.

Charles Andreas Kinsky, son of an Austrian prince and a Liechtenstein princess, was then thirty-five, two years younger than Jennie. In appearance he was the apotheosis of what a man of the world should be. Tall, powerfully built, handsome, with a bristling mustache, he wore his top hat at a jaunty angle and, superbly tailored, glided across drawing rooms with effortless grace. Nine years earlier, riding against heavy odds, he had become the first amateur to win the Grand National. Disdainful of danger, he repeatedly risked his life steeplechasing. In 1881, the year he met Jennie, he had been appointed honorary attaché at the Austro-Hungarian embassy. Since then he had become an imperial chamberlain. Impetuous and hot-tempered, he was as much in love with Jennie as she with him. Now he meant to charm her son. Back at Harrow afterward, Winston would write Jack, for whom he set down all his experiences on that glorious day, that he spent part of the morning at Lord's. "Of course you know Harrow won by five wickets. I could not 'smash an Eton hat' as I had to leave the ground early to go to the Crystal Palace." Then Kinsky picked him up and "drove me in his phaeton."[92]

The palace, a glass-and-iron conception of Joseph Paxton and Victoria's Albert, had been built in Hyde Park for the Great Exhibition of 1851 and then moved to Penge, in South London. From Lord's it was an eight-mile ride, but Kinsky had brought a copy of the July *Strand Magazine,* which carried "A Scandal in Bohemia," the first of Conan Doyle's Sherlock Holmes short stories. Winston thought it a capital yarn and Kinsky a capital fellow. After he had finished the tale of Irene Adler's ingenuity, they sang that year's most popular song, already a hit though still only in rehearsal at London's Gaiety Theatre:

Ta-ra-ra-boom-der-ay:
Did you see my wife today?
No, I saw her yesterday:
Ta-ra-ra-boom-der-ay!

And then they were there. The first sight to greet Winston was a menagerie of "Wild Beasts. (wonderful never seen anything like them.)" Next came a parade, before the seated spectators, of two thousand firemen and a hundred engines, marching past the kaiser and his kaiserin to the music of a military band. Winston was especially interested in the guest of honor. He had brought a sketchbook, and there, in the crowd beside Kinsky, he made his first surviving attempt in the arts. He wrote Jack: "I must describe the Emperor's uniform. A helmet of bright Brass surmounted by a white eagle nearly 6 inches high." Wilhelm also wore "a polished steel cuirass & a perfectly white uniform with high boots."[93]

After "the Engines trotted past & finally all the lot Galloped past as hard as they could go," the count took Winston to dinner. The maître d' told them the restaurant was full, that he couldn't possibly seat them, but "Count K. spoke German to him & it had a wonderful effect." The dinner was "very tolerable," with "lots of champagne which pleased your loving brother very much." More fun lay ahead. The major event that evening was to be a display of fireworks for Wilhelm. Finding time on their hands before it began, Kinsky took Winston to another exhibition, which, when they arrived, turned out to be closed. Instead, they visited a nearby feature attraction, an "Aerial Car," which raced along a wire rope "nearly 300 yards in length & awfully high." They waited in line ten minutes. Then the car broke down, and a distant cannon signaled the start of the fireworks. The count led Winston over a rail and was preparing to leave when "a half breed sort of Kaffir who was in charge" tried to stop them by grabbing Kinsky's coattails. The count, "whom you know is immensely strong," grabbed "the blackguards hand" and crushed his fingers. At that "the Mulatto" dropped the coattails, swore, and told Kinsky he should think himself " 'd——d lucky' " that he wasn't pitched over the banisters. " 'By ——' said Count Kinsky 'I should like to see you touch me.' 'You go and learn manners,' retorted the cad. 'But not from you' said Count K." Then the crowd howled down "the scoundrel" and "we went on our way angry but triumphant." It is an incident right out of *Chatterbox,* Nick Carter, or Karl May. The uppity ruffian of inferior race accosts our hero, is defied by him, and slinks away. Boys of Winston's class believed that sort of thing happened all the time, that it was the classic confrontation between the wicked and the just. And because Winston never entirely put away childish things, part of him would go on believing it to the end.[94]

The kaiser, whose image would later alter in Winston's eyes, was in all his splendor that night. Pyrotechnists opened their display with volleys of rockets. Next came "two great set pieces of Cornflowers & Roses (the Emperors Favourit Flowers) which afterward changed to the heads of the Emperor & Empress." Then the battle of the Nile was refought in the sky. "The ships actually moved & the cannonading was terrific. Finally L'Orient blew up." It was an ironic moment, though they did not appreciate it. That was how they saw war then: brilliant girandoles, flares, Catherine wheels, candlebombs, and whizbangs, celebrating the feats of daring of the intrepid Nelson and his "band of brothers" aboard the *Vanguard* while honoring the gallant French squadron who went down nobly — and apparently bloodlessly — when thirteen of Napoleon's men-of-war were annihilated and strewn across the waters of Abukir Bay. No horror, no agony, no bestiality; just puffs and streaks of blinding color against the serene night sky. No spectator was more deceived than the guest of honor, and Winston, grown to manhood, would be among those who had to cope with the consequences of his deception. But he himself had been dazzled, that evening; he too had believed in what the French called *la Gloire.* The day, he thought, had been perfect, and when the display ended "we went & got our coat & had each an American drink & then we went to our carriage. Count K. drives beautifully & we passed with our fast pair of horses everything on the road."[95]

If that was the high point of his Harrow years, the low point came five months later. Jennie was becoming increasingly exasperated with the reports from Welldon. Again and again she tried to convince Winston that his record now could affect his whole life, pleading with him to "stop and think it out for yourself and take a good pull before it is too late." Now from Paris, now from Monte Carlo, now from Mayfair ("I would go down to you — but I have so many things to arrange about the Ascot party next week that I can't manage it"), she implored him to tackle and master languages, his biggest bugbear. He was by turns contrite, confident that next term his marks would soar (which they never did), or teasing. His sense of timing was poor. When he learned that her purse had been snatched at Monte Carlo, he wrote carelessly: "C'est Dommage, because at the same moment I must put in a request for 'un peu plus d'argent.' . . . Don't go to that Casino. Invest your money in me, its safer. . . . You are a bird." She was not amused. She had also begun to find his company irritating. He was an awkward teenager; in a letter she described him as "just at the 'ugly' stage — slouchy and tiresome." Something drastic, she decided, must be done. A hint of what it would be came in a letter she wrote Randolph during Winston's Kinsky weekend: "Welldon says W should have special help for the French this summer."[96]

He was to be taught a lesson, and not just in French. Jennie and Welldon worked it out together. He would be sent across the Channel to learn the language by speaking with Frenchmen. The first plan was to board him with a family in Rouen. Winston objected violently: "No family! No family! Ugh!" he wrote Jennie. "I beg and Pray that you will not send me to a vile, nasty, fusty, beastly French 'Family,' " adding — a sign that he knew the company his mother was keeping — that "even if the worst comes to the worst you could send me to some of your friends & not to 'respectable creatures.' " That was in July, when he assumed that the distasteful experience would be behind him by autumn. Then the blow fell. He was told he would spend Christmas at the Versailles home of one of Harrow's French masters. He was accustomed, if by no means reconciled, to his parents' absence over the year-end holiday. But at least he could count on the company of Woom, Jack, his aunts, and his grandmother. Now he would be alone, in a foreign country, trying to cope with a language he detested. He fought back with everything he had. "Darling Mummy," he wrote on December 6, "I shall think it will be very unkind and unnatural of you . . . to do me out of my Christmas. Out of all this school not 5 boys are going away at all. . . . Mummy don't be so unkind and make me unhappy. . . . If you in spite of my entreaties force me to go I will do as little as I can and the holidays will be one continual battle."[97]

Jennie struck back savagely: "Quite apart from other considerations, the tone of your letter is not calculated to make one over lenient. When one wants something in this world, it is not by delivering ultimatums that one is likely to get it." She told him that he was "old enough not to play the fool" for "the sake of a few days pleasure," and that "you can be quite certain my darling that I will decide for what is best, but I tell you frankly that *I* am going to decide not *you.*" Replying, he reproached her for being "so sarcastic to me since it is I not you who have to make the sacrifice. . . . You say it is for you to decide. I am required to give up my holidays — not you. I am forced to go to people who bore me excessively — not you. You were asked to give up a short part of the year to take me abroad — you promised — refused & I did not press the point. . . . Please do have a little regard for my happiness."[98]

She returned this note without comment. He wrote again, asking why, and she told him: "I have read only one page of yr letter and I send it back to you — as its style does not please me. . . . My dear you won't gain anything by taking this line." It was now December 16, and he was close to panic. "Never," he wrote her, "would I have believed that you would have been so unkind. I am utterly miserable. That you should refuse to read my letter is most painful to me. There was nothing in it to give you grounds for rejecting it. . . . Oh my Mummy!" Next: "I am more unhappy than I can possibly say. . . . Darling Mamma if you want me to do anything for you, especially so great a sacrifice don't be so cruel to Your loving son Winny." Then, the next day: "Please don't be so unkind. Do answer my letter." Then, the day after that — with Christmas a week away — he made his last pitiful effort: "Darling Mummy do attend to my letter. I am so wretched. Even now I weep. Please my darling Mummy be kind to your loving son. Don't let my silly letters make you angry. Let me at least think that you love me. — Darling Mummy I despair. I am so wretched. I don't know what to do. Don't be angry I am so miserable. . . . Please write something kind to me. I am very sorry if I have 'riled' you before I did only want to explain things from my point of view. Good Bye my darling Mummy. With best love I remain, Ever your loving son Winston." It availed him nothing. Jennie was adamant. She booked second-class passage for him for a December 21 crossing and wrote Randolph, "I can't tell you what trouble I have had with Winston this last fortnight he has bombarded me with letters, cursing his fate and everyone. Of course it is a great disappointment to him not being home for Xmas but he makes as much fuss as tho' he were going to Australia for 2 years."[99]

Debarking, he telegraphed Woom: "Arrived safe. Good passage." Putting a brave face on what remained a desolate business, he jauntily wrote his mother, to convince her that his French needed no improvement: "We arrived at Dieppe où nous partook of de bon Café au lait. Le chemin de fer etait très incommode. Pour quatres heures I waited having nothing to do. Nous arrivames au gare St Lazare. J'ai déclaré ma boite des cigarettes. But they did not charge me anything nor did they open mon mal." He rode three hours on hired hacks ("chevaux de louage");

then his host, M. Minssen, met him with a spare mount and led him to his Versailles home at 18, rue de Provence. "M.M. rides very well & very hard at full gallop on the 'ard 'igh road. Les chevaux ne sont pas mal. Ils son véritablement rossés. Mme Monsieur M's mère ne dit rien que 'Son progrés est marveilleux.' 'N'est ce pas extraordinaire' etc. etc." Christmas was quiet at Versailles, but Minssen *mère* turned out to be English, so they had turkey and plum pudding. "Also," Winston acknowledged, "a little fun on Christmas Eve." He went to the theater to see Michel Stroghoff, learned to skate, rode a great deal — once, with M.M., for three hours: "The horses are very good considering." But his chief excitement was the "Bon Marche," which sold toy soldiers. He wrote Jack that the shop carried French and Russian infantrymen, artillerymen, and black cannon. "They were in all positions for loading & firing. Ramming home, etc. Only 7 francs=5/–." The soldiers were two francs for a dozen. "When I return we will have much fun and great games with the army." He was "longing to return. . . . I count the hours. I won't travel 2nd again by Jove."[100]

He wrote his mother daily, heard nothing from her, and protested: "It seems to me that with you 'out of sight is out of mind' indeed. Not a line from anybody. You promised to write 3 times a week — I have recd 1 letter." Jennie didn't even acknowledge his present to her. The fact was that she couldn't have received either letters or gift; she was away at Penn, the ancestral home of Lord and Lady Howe, preparing a party for the Prince of Wales. Winston's one letter had been from Mrs. Everest. He had picked a good time to be away, Woom said; the electricity had failed, there was no gas, so for five days she and Jack had lived in utter darkness "in this room with a candle until I am half blind." On Christmas Day she and the servants, in the tradition of the time, "drank to the health and happiness of Mamma and Papa"; then, after supper, "we went into the kitchen & they put aside the table & danced for dear life. There was no music, so Edney [the butler] whistled & I played the comb with a piece of paper & comb like we used to do in our good old nursery days." Of Winston's present to her she wrote: "It is very kind of you but you know my Lamb I would rather you did not spend your money on me." Woom had mailed him a gift and hoped his spirits picked up: "Cheer up old Boy enjoy yourself try & feel contented you have much to be thankful for if you only consider & fancy how nice it will be to be able to parlez vous francais." His glumness troubled her, and, nannylike, she suspected an earthy cause: "I should buy plenty of fruit & eat it if I were you keep you *regular you know dear.*"[101]

Lack of congeniality, not constipation, was Winston's chief complaint.

Before leaving England he had exacted from his mother a pledge that he would be entertained by three of her continental admirers. He wanted another Kinsky. Unaware that she was absent from London, he had written her on Christmas Eve: "Write to Baron Hirsch. Do! I have not heard a word from those 'friends' you spoke about." Three days later he sent another reminder: "Not a word from Baron Hirsch — not a line from M. de Breteuil — Not a sound from Mr. Trafford. I don't know any of their addresses, so what can I do?" He waited two more days and wrote again: "I wish you would try my mummy to fulfill your promise. Baron Hirsch may be in Jericho for all I know." He needn't have worried. Jennie was an adroit manipulator of men. Approaching her fortieth birthday, she still had the figure of a young girl, coupled with extraordinary social skills, and when she gave her lovers marching orders, they leapt to obey. At the bottom of a letter to Jack, Winston scrawled: "N.B. Invitations have come. Baron Hirsch Friday last Mr Trafford Sat yesterday. Baron Hirsch Tomorrow M. de Breteuil Tuesday." They moved in a Paris unknown to Winston's French master; they entertained him at the best restaurants, taught him wines, and introduced him to the recherché society of continental gentlemen. He also saw his first corpses: "Last Monday I went to M. de B. and B. Hirsch after. He took me to the morgue. I was much interested. Only 3 Macabres — not a good bag." One suspects adolescent bravado here. At the age of seventeen he could scarcely have coped with massed cadavers.[102]

Another pledge from his mother was of a different order. Jennie had given him her word that upon his return from Versailles he would be kept out of school for a week, to provide him a decent vacation at Connaught Place. He wrote her from France on December 27: "I will remind you of the promise you made me at Harrow of an extra week [at home] if I gave up my Christmas. A promise is a promise & as I have fulfilled my part I rely on you my darling mummy to do the rest. I know you won't chuck me like that." On January 13 he again told her that he meant to hold her to her commitment: "I am of course counting, my Mummy, on you to fulfil your promise which was more than anything the reason of my coming here willingly." He was nailing her to her vow, and his very vehemence suggests an uneasiness, a growth of doubt. But cutting even a day of classwork was a serious matter for a boy with his academic record. Mothers in Victorian families lacked the authority to make so grave a decision, and Winston, sensing that, decided to lay the matter before Randolph. He pointed out to him that "I have missed everything this year. Christmas, New Years Day etc." Then he wrote:

"The chief inducement Mamma held out for me to go to France was the promise of an extra week. Please do see what you can arrange for me."[103]

His father was in no mood to arrange any such thing. He was in a foul temper. The party at Penn had collapsed because the Duke of Clarence had chosen this extremely inconvenient moment to die, causing HRH to cancel all his social engagements. But even if Randolph had been in the best of spirits, he believed he had the best of reasons for pulling the rug from under his wife. He wrote Winston, "I think I will not try and get you an extra week because really every moment is of value to you now before you go up for your examination in June. The loss of a week now may mean your not passing, which I am sure you will admit would be very discreditable and disadvantageous. . . . I do pray you my dear boy to make the most of every hour of your time so as to render your passing a certainty. . . . I hope you will work like a little dray horse right up to the summer examination, only about four months off." Winston was bitter. He wrote: "How I have been tricked!" Jennie wrote him: "Papa showed me his letter to you. He won't hear of yr asking for an extra week. I am very sorry." So she should have been. Robert Rhodes James concludes that "behind Lady Randolph's vivid beauty and warm vivacity there lay an essentially selfish and frivolous character."[104] That is hard but just. Winston rightly felt betrayed. Yet his affection for her did not diminish. And such is the wonder of human relationships that soon she would reciprocate. Jennie was not a faithful wife, but in other ways she was a loyal one. As the final stages of Randolph's paresis overtook him — as he became less endearing each day — she would slowly transfer her devotion to her brilliant, eccentric elder son. Her passion would run deep and strong, and it would be of immeasurable benefit to him, though it could never be mistaken for maternal love.

The examination, a screening of candidates for admission to the Royal Military College at Sandhurst, had been looming before Winston ever since his father's decision, based on a display of toy soldiers in a nursery, to make his son an army officer. Other Harrovians were following the same star — so many, indeed, that Welldon had created a special Army Class. Winston had joined it in September 1889, when he was fourteen. In effect these boys were cramming for military exams. Moriarty and another master decided early that Winston's math was too poor for Woolwich, the academy that prepared cadets for commissions in the artillery and engineers. Instead, they piloted him toward Sandhurst, which turned out subalterns of infantry and cavalry.

After four months in the Army Class, Winston had written his mother, "I am getting along capitally. . . . I am going up for my 'preliminary Exam' for 'Sandhurst' in June." His confidence, here as so often before, was wholly unjustified. Welldon withdrew his name, explaining to him that he wasn't ready for the test; among other things, his grasp of geometrical drawing was hopelessly deficient. But the headmaster gave him the green light six months later, and then Winston had three pieces of good luck. This was the last Sandhurst preliminary in which Latin was an optional subject. Second, an essay question dealt with the American Civil War, and Jennie's mother had seen to it that he knew a great deal about that long before he entered Harrow. The third stroke of fortune was remarkable. He had known there would be a map question, but did not know of which country. Therefore, he wrote the names of twenty-five countries on scraps of paper the night before the exam, put them in a hat, and drew one. He had picked New Zealand. He memorized it. And in the morning the geographical problem was: "Draw a map of New Zealand." So he passed all subjects, becoming one of twelve out of the twenty-nine Harrow candidates to succeed. He wrote his mother: "I have received congratulations from scores of boys and many masters. Dudley" — Dudley Marjoribanks, the son of Randolph's sister Fanny — "has not spoken to me. Vive la joie! He has not passed and is furious." Jennie wrote her husband: "I think you might make him a present of a gun as a reward. He is pining for one, and ought to have a little encouragement."[105]

No gun arrived, there was no pat on the back from Randolph, and the edge of Winston's enthusiasm for a military career was briefly blunted. He toyed with the notion of taking holy orders. In a postscript home he wrote: "Really I feel less keen about the Army every day. I think the church would suit me better." Looking back long afterward, he reflected that "I might have gone into the Church and preached orthodox sermons in a spirit of audacious contradiction to the age." But it had been a preposterous notion; while Churchill can easily be pictured in a pulpit, one cannot imagine him on his knees. As a boy, he would say in later life, he had to go to church every week and "this was very good. I had accumulated in those years so fine a surplus in the Bank of Observance that I have been drawing confidently upon it ever since. Weddings, christenings, and funerals have brought in a steady annual income, and I have never made too close enquiries about the state of my account. It might well even be that I should find an overdraft." He wrote trenchantly of World War I: "Religion, having discreetly avoided conflict on the fundamental issues, offered its encouragement and consolations through all its forms impartially to all the combatants." Toward the end of his life he said: "I am ready to meet my Maker. Whether my Maker is ready to meet me is another question." To those who pressed him, he quoted Disraeli: "Sensible men are all of the same religion." Asked what that was, he quoted him again: "Sensible men never tell."[106]

But Disraeli had also said that "what we anticipate seldom occurs, what we least expected generally happens," and this was Winston's immediate problem in the summer of 1892, when he was seventeen. Having leapt over the preliminary hurdle, he assumed that he was as good as accepted by Sandhurst. Thus he was rudely shaken when, having taken the main entrance examination, he learned that he had flunked, and flunked badly. Not only had he failed to qualify for an infantry cadetship; his marks were also inadequate for the cavalry, which accepted lower performances. He had scored 39 percent in freehand drawing, 30 percent in Latin, and 28 percent in math, and had excelled only in English composition. Counting French, English history, chemistry, and geometry, he was 300 marks below the minimum and 700 below his cousin Dudley, who had caught up with the other successful applicants. Moriarty consoled Winston — "I think your marks and place very creditable for your first try" — but Welldon was brusque: "I feel it essential that in coming back to school you should come resolved to work not by fits and starts but with regular persistent industry." The headmaster considered recommending a free-lance tutor, then decided against it. Randolph, predictably, was disgusted. He was also unsurprised. On the few occasions he had questioned his son about his education, he had been distinctly unimpressed. Once he had turned on him and suddenly asked: "What was the Grand Remonstrance against Charles I?" This had been a complicated issue in 1641, turning on parliamentary influence in the monarch's court and the Anglican church. Winston's reply was: "Parliament beat the king and cut his head off." (Decapitation "seemed to me," he later said wistfully, "the grandest remonstrance imaginable.") But his father had sworn to himself and turned away. Now, with the results from Sandhurst, Randolph felt confirmed. He glumly awaited Winston's second attempt to matriculate, writing Duchess Fanny that his "next try is on Nov. 24th. If he fails again I shall think about putting him in business." Trade would have been even less suitable for Winston than the ministry, and he knew it. Thus, his last term at Harrow was clouded by the possibility of an aborted career. Welldon kept giving him pep talks and seems to have convinced himself that they were justified; on the eve of the second exam he wrote Randolph that the boy's "work this term has been excellent. He understands now the need of taking trouble, and the way to take it. . . . It is due him to say that of late he has done all that could be asked of him."[107]

One bright spot for Winston that fall was that Jack was now a twelve-year-old Harrovian, and the brothers were allowed to share a room. ("We have now quite settled down," he wrote home. "The room is very beautiful. We purchased in London sufficiency of ornaments to make it look simply magnificent.") Moreover, Winston had finally mastered skills which won him the admiration of his peers. He made the swimming team, led the School Rifle Corps, starred in boxing, and became the fencing champion of Harrow. "I have won the fencing," he wrote his mother, then in Monte Carlo. "A very fine cup. I was far and away first. Absolutely untouched in the finals." Then he accomplished something spectacular. He was chosen to stand for Harrow in a tournament at Aldershot, the winner to be England's public-school fencing champion. He wrote excitedly: "My fencing is now my great employment out of school as now that I represent the School it behoves me to 'sweat up.' " On the great day he crossed foils with boys from Eton, Winchester, Bradfield, and Tonbridge and beat them all. His victory, the *Harrovian* reported, "was chiefly due to his quick and dashing attack which quite took his opponents by surprise." The school paper commented: "Churchill must be congratulated on his success over all his opponents in the fencing line, many of whom must have been much taller and more formidable than himself."[108]

He ought to have left Harrow on a rising tide of hope. Instead, he departed in despair. The second Sandhurst examination had not gone well. Traditionally, seniors passing out entertained their friends at a "Leaving Breakfast" in Hance's Tuck Shop: mutton cutlets, steak and onions, ham, mushrooms, eggs, sausages, and deviled kidneys — all for sixpence. Winston wouldn't have it. In December he quietly bade farewell to Jack and then slunk off to the station alone, like a fugitive. Sandhurst posted the exam results the next month; they then appeared in *The Times.* As he feared, he had failed again. His performance had actually worsened in Latin, French, and — the cruelest cut — English composition. It is astonishing that in this, of all subjects, the boy who would become one of the greatest masters of his native language scored 53 percent. Randolph pondered putting him out as a commercial apprentice to Rothschild, Farquharson, or Cassel, but relented when Welldon told him that he felt certain Winston would make it on the third try. The headmaster urged tutoring. There was no disgrace in this. In 1870 Lord Dufferin's Royal Commission on Military Education had "earnestly" deprecated "the irregular system of 'cramming' " because, as one member explained, they feared that the acceptance "of such a large proportion of crammed candidates would cause the Army to lose its 'tone.' " Nevertheless, in Winston's day seven out of every ten successful candidates for admission to Sandhurst had been rigorously tutored. Spencer Coyle, in Henry James's story "Owen Wingrave," was a typical Victorian crammer. The character was inspired by Captain Walter H. James, who, Welldon wrote Lord Randolph, was "the most successful 'crammer' for the Sandhurst Examination." Randolph approved, and James then wrote him from 5 Lexam Gardens, London: "I shall be very happy to receive your son and should be pleased to see you at 12:30 on Monday next."[109]

Winston didn't keep the appointment. He was near death. In their study of boys marked for future greatness, the Goertzels found that among adventurous youths "there is almost always a history of accident-proneness." Sometimes the youthful Winston seemed to move from crisis to crisis, risking his life in pointless adventures. That was true of him that year. His second failure as a Sandhurst candidate had left him tense and distraught, which probably contributed to his flirtation with disaster. Randolph's sister-in-law, the "Duchess Lily," had given his family the run of Deepdene, her estate at Branksome Dene, near Bournemouth, for the winter. Its fifty acres of pine forest, sloping down to the Channel, offered endless opportunities for the daring games Winston loved to play in the woods. Each morning he briefed Jack and a fourteen-year-old cousin on his newest game plan while the servants, Woom among them, wrung their hands and prayed for the children's safety. In the wildest corner of the estate, a thicket was split by a deep cleft called the "chine." The chine was bridged by a crude fifty-yard bridge. The boys were playing fox and hare, with Winston the hare, when he found himself in the middle of the bridge with a foe at either end. He contemplated jumping down into the cleft. It was thick with fir trees; he thought he might leap to one and slide down, snapping off tiers of branches as he descended and thus breaking his fall. In his words: "I looked at it. I computed it. I meditated. Meanwhile I climbed over the balustrade. My young pursuers stood wonderstruck at either end of the bridge. To plunge or not to plunge, that was the question! In a second I had plunged, throwing out my arms to embrace the summit of the fir tree. The argument was correct; the data were absolutely wrong." He tumbled twenty-nine feet to hard ground and lay insensible. Jack and their cousin ran back to the mansion, crying, "He won't speak to us!" This was real trouble, and it brought his parents flying. Jennie arrived first; Randolph, who had been spending Christmas at one of Lord Fitzgibbon's interminable wild parties in Ireland, took the next express from Dublin. Dr. Roose appeared with Dr. John Rose, a Harley Street specialist. They found, among other things, that Winston had a ruptured kidney. He did not recover consciousness for three days. The physicians recommended three months in bed, Rose adding that "young Mr. Churchill should not return to hard study any more than he should take vigorous exercise."[110]

Unfortunately, abstinence from study was out of the question. Winston's last chance at Sandhurst loomed in June, and in Lexham Gardens Captain James sat waiting, pencils sharpened, textbooks open. Some forty years later Winston decided that he understood why this obscure half-pay officer had stood at the top of his small, curious profession. James, he wrote, had studied the minds of the men who drew up civil service examinations and could predict "with almost Papal infallibility the sort of questions which that sort of person would be bound on the average to ask on any of the selected subjects." His skill lay in anticipating such questions and how best to answer them. He was "really the ingenious forerunner of the inventors of the artillery barrages of the Great War," Churchill wrote. "He fired from carefully selected positions upon the areas which he knew must be tenanted by large bodies of enemy troops. . . . He did not need to see the enemy soldiers. Drill was all he had to teach his gunners. Thus year by year for at least two decades he held the Blue Ribbon among the Crammers."[111]

But he had never dealt with anyone remotely like Winston. The crammer represents everything the creative youth despises: drill, contempt for intuition, slavish fixation on meaningless, unrelated facts. Winston, in his own words, found himself in "an 'Alice-in-Wonderland' world, at the portals of which stood 'A Quadratic Equation,' " followed by the "dim chambers" inhabited by the "Differential Calculus" and then a "strange corridor" of sines and cosines "in a highly square-rooted condition." Of mathematical skills he wrote: "I am assured they are most helpful in engineering, astronomy and things like that. It is important to build bridges and canals and to comprehend all the stresses and potentialities of matter, to say nothing of counting all the stars and even universes and measuring how far off they are, and foretelling eclipses, the arrival of comets and such like. I am glad there are quite a number of people born with a gift and a liking for all this." He, however, was not one of them. The Goertzels found that most boys pregnant with genius have serious problems with school curricula and dull, irrational teachers. James was a distillate of these. He was concentrating on the courses Winston had found pointless, using the very methods Winston hated most. By March he must have wished that this exasperating boy had killed himself in his fall. Reporting to Randolph on March 7, he deplored his pupil's "casual manner." Winston was "distinctly inclined to be inattentive and to think too much of his abilities." He had been "rather too much inclined up to the present to teach his instructors instead of endeavouring to learn from them." In fact, "he suggested to me that his knowledge of history was such that he did not want any more teaching in it! . . . What he wants," he concluded, "is very firm handling." Unfortunately, James could not provide it for the moment. He was literally sick of Winston, "confined to my room."[112]

Staggering to his feet, he plodded on. But he deceived neither himself nor his ward's father. He was making little progress. In an April 29 report he gloomily warned his employer: "I do not think that his work is going on very satisfactorily." Although the boy "has good abilities he does not apply himself with sufficient earnestness to his reading" and "I doubt his passing if he does not do this." James delicately hinted at one difficulty. Randolph was making his last attempt at a political comeback, and his son could think of little else. The crammer realized that "at a time like the present it is difficult for him not to take an interest in current political topics, but if this be done to an extent which takes his mind away from his studies, the result is bad for the latter." Every attempt must be made to impress upon him "the absolute necessity of single-minded devotion to the immediate object before him, and the extreme desirability of thoroughness and detail [sic] attention to all he attempts."[113]

The break came sometime in May. Winston gave ground. He yielded as little as possible, but he knew what was at stake, and though the job revolted him, he set his jaw and made some progress. Not much; just enough. On June 19, James wrote: "Without saying that your son is a certainty I think he ought to pass this time. He is working well and I think doing his best to get on but, as you know, he is at times inclined to take the bit in his teeth and go his own course." The exam was upon them then, and this time Winston squeaked by. He came in too low to become an infantry cadet, but was admitted to the cavalry. He hadn't changed much, even under his crammer's pressure; most of the spring, when he should have been doing James's lessons, he had been reading English history for pleasure, with the jarring effect — jarring for James, who had abandoned attempts to drill him in history — that he far outscored every other candidate in that subject. When the list of those who had passed was announced, Winston had left on a hiking trip in Switzerland with Jack and J. D. G. Little, a young Eton master. He was in Lucerne when he learned he had made it. Immediately he wired his father and then wrote him from the Schweizerhof Hotel: "I was so glad to be able to send you the good news on Thursday. I did not expect that the list would be published so soon & was starting off in the train, when Little congratulated me on getting in. I looked in the paper & found this to be true." It was only fitting, he thought, that he should celebrate his achievement in such "a splendid hotel — lifts, electric light, & fireworks (every Saturday)."[114]

Other congratulations arrived from grandparents, aunts, uncles, and cousins, but there was an ominous silence from Bad Kissingen, where Lord Randolph and Jennie were taking the cure. Unknown to his son, Randolph had been counting heavily on an infantry cadetship. That would have relieved him of the cost of horses. It would also have brought a social dividend; a friend of his, the aged, royal Duke of Cambridge, commander in chief of the army, had promised, once Winston had been commissioned, to find a place for him in the crack Sixtieth Rifles. Now the humiliated father had to tell His Grace that his boy was too stupid to become an infantry officer. Jennie saw the storm gathering in her husband. She sent a warning to Lucerne: "I am glad of course that you have got into Sandhurst but Papa is not pleased at yr getting in by the skin of yr teeth & missing the Infantry by 18 marks. He is not as pleased by yr exploits as you seem to be!"[115] That was putting it gently. A week later, in Milan, Winston received an extraordinary letter from his father.

Randolph was surprised that he had expressed "exultation over your inclusion in the Sandhurst list" instead of being ashamed of "your slovenly happy-go-lucky harum scarum style of work." It was the same old story: "Never have I received a really good report of your conduct in your work from any master or tutor you had from time to time to do with. Always behind-hand, never advancing in your class, incessant complaints of total want of application, and this character which was constant in yr reports has shown the natural results clearly in your last army examination." Thus "you have failed to get into the '60th Rifles' one of the finest regiments in the army." Furthermore, as a cavalry cadet, "you have imposed on me an extra charge of some £200 a year." It got worse: "Do not think I am going to take the trouble of writing to you long letters after every failure you commit and undergo . . . I no longer attach the slightest weight to anything you may say about your own acquirements & exploits." Randolph predicted that "if you cannot prevent yourself from leading the idle useless unprofitable life you have had during your schooldays & later months, you will become a mere social wastrel one of the hundreds of the public school failures, and you will degenerate into a shabby unhappy & futile existence. If that is so you will have to bear all the blame for such misfortunes yourself." He ended venomously: "Your mother sends her love."[116]

Little wrote Randolph that Winston had showed him this letter and "was a good deal depressed." Actually, he was stunned. It never occurred to him that this philippic might be the work of an unstable mind. He considered his father's judgment above reproach, and believed that he had failed him again. In his reply he wrote that he was "very sorry indeed that you are displeased with me," that he would "try to modify your opinion of me by my work at Sandhurst," that "my extremely low place in passing *in* will have *no* effect whatever on my chance there," and that Randolph needn't worry about expenses there because "all the necessary equipment & outfit are supplied at Sandhurst at a charge of £30." Here he erred. All cadets were charged £120 tuition, in addition to the cost of their mounts, to screen out applicants who were not considered suitable. But in a larger sense he was right. Sandhurst fees were a pittance when set against the costs Randolph's own father had paid for his Oxford education; Randolph had raised the issue only to justify his wrath. Winston closed his own letter pathetically: "Thank you very much for writing to me." And, once again, "I am very sorry indeed that I have done so badly." Yet on a deeper level he may have smoldered. At the bottom he wrote: "P.S. Excuse smudge &c as pens & blotting paper are awfully bad." The page was a mess. Hostility, though repressed, must have been there. By now it should have been clear that the relationship between father and son would be abrasive for both until one of them lay in his grave.[117]

Winston almost died first. His second skirting of the Styx immediately followed the posting of this response. He and a companion hired a boat on the shore of Lake Geneva and rowed out a mile. Stripping, they dove in for a swim. Suddenly a breeze sprang up and carried the boat away from them. Striking out desperately, Winston just managed to reach the hull, hoist himself aboard, and return for his friend. Afterward he wrote that he had seen Death "as near as I believe I have ever seen Him. He was swimming in the water, whispering from time to time in the rising wind." Either because of this or because of Randolph's tirade, he was still upset when he returned to London and found that the row over his poor showing in the exam had been entirely unnecessary. At 50 Grosvenor Square a letter from the military secretary awaited him, disclosing that several boys with higher scores than his had dropped out, so he needn't go into the cavalry. He wrote his father: "I have no doubt that you will be pleased to find that I have got an Infantry cadetship and shall be able, after all, to enter the 60th." Randolph's pride enjoined an acknowledgment, but he wrote Duchess Fanny — as he had grown apart from Jennie, his mother had become the only woman he fully trusted — that "I am very glad Winston has got an infantry cadetship. It will save me £200 a year."[118]

On the afternoon of Friday, September 1, 1893, Winston switched from train to carriage in the village of Camberley and rode into the grounds of the Royal Military College, passing through a forest of pine, birch, and larch before debouching on the plain where, every year since 1812, young members of England's upper classes had been certified as "officers and gentlemen." The landscape was inviting: two lakes, athletic fields, rifle and revolver ranges, and, of course, parade grounds. As a "junior," or plebe, he was assigned to "E" Company, led to the long, low, white stone building which would be his barracks for the next sixteen months, and measured for his cadet uniform, a gaudy costume featuring gold lace, pantaloons, and a pillbox cap. He studied the daily schedule he would be expected to meet, worried about his physical frailty, and wrote his mother, with a confidence he did not feel: "I suppose I shall get stronger during my stay here."[119] His physique was in fact unimpressive. He was only five feet, six and a half inches tall, and his chest measured but thirty-one inches, with an expansion of two and a half inches — inadequate, unless he could improve upon it, for a commission. To succeed at Sandhurst he would summon strengths which, until now, had been unrevealed.

Even before the tailor had finished outfitting him, he had again incurred his father's displeasure. Lord Randolph had decided to give him a ten-pound monthly allowance and little leave. "I wont have any running backwards & forwards to London," he wrote Duchess Fanny. "He shall be kept to his work so that he may acquire the elementary principles of a military education." But since his arrival on the post, Winston had discovered that his financial expectations required revision. He needed a batman to black his boots, pipe-clay his belt, clean his rifle, and carry away slops. He thought he ought to have a horse; other cadets had them. His room needed furnishing, and he not only wanted to visit the capital regularly — "going up to town," as they said at Sandhurst — he also meant to join clubs there. His father would have none of it. To Duchess Fanny, Randolph explained: "I have demurred to 'unrestricted leave,' and have told him he can come to town when his mother is there. I have declined paying for horses. . . . Winston's letters are generally full of requests for unnecessary things and articles." The youth begged his mother to intervene. Without a horse, he said, he would be excluded from polo classes. "As to leave — it is very hard that Papa cannot grant me the same liberty that other boys in my position are granted. It is only a case of trusting *me.* As my company officer said, he 'liked to know the boys whom their parents could trust' — and therefore recommended me to get the permission I asked for. However, it is no use trying to explain to Papa, & I suppose I shall go on being treated as 'that boy' till I am 50 years old."[120] Actually, it would be only a short time longer. But Winston had been kept at such a distance from his family that he knew nothing of the tensions within it. He couldn't understand the niggling over money. He was keenly aware of his father's reentry into politics. He did not, however, grasp the futility of it.

In the summer of 1892, when Winston was beginning his struggle to enter Sandhurst, the voters narrowly rejected Salisbury's Conservatives, giving Gladstone the chance to form his last government. His position in the House of Commons was fragile. Even with the support of eighty Irish Nationalists, the Liberal majority was only forty. In 1886 Joe Chamberlain had deserted the Grand Old Man on the question of Home Rule and joined the Ulster Unionists, whom he would eventually leave to become a full-fledged Tory. The cabinet differed sharply among themselves on key issues. Obviously the Tories would soon return. But Randolph didn't see it that way. He thought they needed his help. When Parliament met the following summer — the summer Winston scraped through his third examination — the political configuration looked like 1885 all over again. The GOM sat on the government bench, and Churchill, the master of invective, was preparing to display his brilliant talent once more. In Winston's words, "It was thought that he would in Opposition swiftly regain the ascendancy in Parliament and in his party which had been destroyed by his resignation six years before. No one cherished these hopes more ardently than I. . . . We all looked forward to his reconquest of power. . . . Although he was only a private member and quite isolated, everything he said even at the tiniest bazaar was reported verbatim in all the newspapers, and every phrase was scrutinized and weighed. Now it seemed that his chance had come again."[121]

Only rarely could Winston observe the parliamentary maneuvering from the Strangers' Gallery, and even then he deferred to his father's wishes, asking his permission to attend: "I have had a letter from Mr

Carson inviting me to dine with him at the House on Friday evening. I have accepted as I have very little work on Saturday. If you would rather I would not go Please send me a line." He was fascinated by the civility between adversaries; at table "not only colleagues, but opponents, amicably interchanged opinions on the burning topics of the hour." Apart from newspapers, his sources of information on what was happening behind the scenes in the House were his mother and his father's brother-in-law Edward Marjoribanks, who, as Gladstone's chief whip, was on the other side. Political civility also prevailed within the family, though Winston enjoyed trying to pin Marjoribanks down. He wrote his father: "Uncle Edward has been here to dinner. He spent nearly half an hour after dinner explaining to me the methods by which the Opposition of the House of Lords was going to be overcome. I wish you had been there to answer him, as I am sure there was an answer though I could not think of it."[122]

Jennie and Uncle Edward gave him accounts of Randolph's progress. They said he was doing well, and in the beginning they were right. Even the *Spectator,* the Conservative organ, which had abused him so cruelly, reported: "The chief feature of this Session . . . has been the return of Lord Randolph Churchill to active political life, and his successful reassertion of himself as a force to be reckoned with in party warfare. Lord Randolph has seen his opportunity in the crusade against the Home-rule Bill . . . we rejoice that the party has recovered the services of a man with such excellent fighting qualities. . . . More than any of the Unionist leaders, Lord Randolph possesses the faculty of speaking to uneducated men in the style which they understand and admire. . . . We wish Lord Randolph every success."[123]

Suddenly it was all over. Although Home Rule passed the Commons, it was rejected by the Lords. The Grand Old Man, half blind and half deaf at eighty-five, rode up Birdcage Walk to the Queen who had never liked him and resigned. Randolph had been deprived of his prey. But even before then it had become evident that he, like Gladstone, was not the man he had been. Winston noted: "I could not help feeling that my father's speeches were not as good as they used to be. There were some brilliant successes; yet on the whole he seemed to be hardly holding his own. I hoped of course that I should grow up in time to come to his aid. . . . I thought of Austen Chamberlain who was allowed to fight at his father's side, and Herbert Gladstone who had helped the Grand Old Man to cut down the oak trees and went everywhere with him, and I dreamed of days to come when Tory democracy would dismiss the 'Old Gang' with one hand and defeat the Radicals with the other." Randolph, however, found the very thought of a mature relationship between himself and Winston repellent. "If ever I began to show the slightest idea of comradeship," Winston wrote, "he was immediately offended." Once, when "I suggested that I might help his private secretary to write some of his letters, he froze me into stone."[124]

Now that we have the son's life spread before us, the father's behavior seems monstrous. But Randolph could not hold a mirror up to the future. He only saw what was there to be seen, and it was anything but encouraging. His letter from Bad Kissingen had been unforgivably brutal, but it had not been an exercise in fantasy. Winston's school records *were* a catalogue of misconduct and scholastic failure. Even when seen through the kindest eyes — those, say, of Mrs. Everest — he was a redheaded, puny little swaggerer who was always in trouble, always disobedient, always making and breaking promises. Unquestionably parental negligence had contributed to his many fiascos. Undoubtedly his father bore a thinly veiled animosity toward him. But Randolph had his own troubles. Although stricken with a vile disease through no fault of his own, he had achieved a certain position in public life. He was, in fact, the most successful Churchill since the first duke. A proud man, he yearned for parental pride and was thwarted. If he had little faith in his son's potential, there was precious little there to inspire faith. He wrote Duchess Fanny in August 1893: "I have told you often & you would never believe me that he has little [claim] to cleverness, to knowledge or any capacity for settled work. He has great talent for show off exaggeration & make believe."[125] Sending his son to a military academy was the wisest decision he ever made, but he had no way of knowing that then. At one point he even asked a friend about career opportunities in South America. Winston, he was convinced, would never make good in England.

Recognizing that an upper-class father had certain obligations to a son who had become a gentleman cadet, responsibilities which could not be slighted without offending society, he invited Winston to join him for weekends with his racing cronies and fellow MPs. Winston enjoyed the company of the friends and parliamentarians, but the man he really wanted to talk to was his father. That was not possible. Randolph could write Duchess Fanny, "He has much smartened up," but the closest he came to a public compliment was in introducing Winston to Bram Stoker, Sir Henry Irving's secretary and the future author of *Dracula.* "He's not much yet," he told Stoker, "but he's a good 'un." Winston, immensely pleased, hoped that intimacy would follow. It didn't. He felt that "I would far rather have been apprenticed as a bricklayer's mate, or run errands as a messenger boy, or helped my father to dress the front windows of a grocer's shop. It would have been real; it would have been natural; it would have taught me more; and I should have got to know my father, which would have been a joy to me." Later, when Herbert Asquith was prime minister, his daughter Violet quoted Asquith's views on issues and public men to Winston. Winston was amazed. He said: "Your father told you that? He talks to you about such things quite freely? I wish I could have had such talks with mine." In middle age he told his own son, home from Eton, "I have talked to you more in this holiday than my father talked to me in his whole life." He wrote of Lord Randolph that "only once did he lift his visor in my sight." Vacationing with his family in the country, Winston fired a double-barreled gun at a rabbit which had appeared beneath his father's window. Randolph raged at him; then, seeing that he had upset him, backed down and explained that old people, absorbed in their own affairs, sometimes spoke rudely to their children. He said: "Do remember things do not always go right with me. My every action is misjudged and every word distorted. . . . So make some allowances."[126]

Winston's later view of Lord Randolph was ambivalent. To Violet Asquith he spoke of him with "glowing pride." He liked to call on Lord Rosebery, encouraging him to reminisce about Randolph, whom Rosebery had known well and Winston hardly at all, and Winston's two-volume biography *Lord Randolph Churchill* is a tribute to filial devotion. Yet he was bitter when he told Frank Harris that whenever he tried to open serious conversations with his father, he was snubbed pitilessly. He recalled: "He wouldn't listen to me or consider anything I said. There was no companionship with him possible and I tried so hard and so often. He was so self-centered no one else existed for him." Harris asked: "You didn't like him?" Winston replied: "How could I? . . . He treated me as if I had been a fool; barked at me whenever I questioned him. I owe everything to my mother; to my father, nothing." Actually, he owed him a great deal, much of which he could have done without, for when he himself entered politics he felt obliged to pay off Randolph's old scores. But there was no real love lost between them. In Winston's books one may trace a steady theme: great men are frequently products of boyhood loneliness. Three years after his father's death he wrote of the Mahdi, leader of Sudanese tribesmen: "Solitary trees, if they grow at all, grow strong; and a boy deprived of a father's care often develops, if he escapes the perils of youth, an independence and vigour of thought which may restore in after life the heavy loss of early days." And in his biography of the first Duke of Marlborough he observed that "famous men are usually the product of an unhappy childhood. The stern compression of circumstances, the twinges of adversity, the spur of slights and taunts in early years, are needed to evoke that ruthless fixity of purpose and tenacious mother wit without which great actions are seldom accomplished."[127]

It is difficult to resist the tide of Churchillian eloquence. Yet every author, as Cicero observed, is wise and forbearing in his own eyes. The fact is that at Sandhurst, as at Harrow, Winston could be a vexing son, though now his growing flair for seizing command of situations — and perhaps a ripening imagination — added a lively touch to his explanations. These were summed up in the remarkable case of the gold watch. When Winston settled in at the military academy, his father presented him with a fine watch, made by Dents'. Later, dropping into the London shop to see about his own timepiece, Randolph was "annoyed and vexed," in his words, to learn that Winston's watch had twice been sent back for repairs, first after it had been "dropped . . . on a stone pavement & broken," and, second, when it had been immersed in water, with the result that "the whole of the works were horribly rusty & that every bit of the watch had had to be taken to pieces." Mending it after it had been dropped had cost three pounds, seventeen shillings. At the time of Randolph's infelicitous visit it was still in the shop from the submersion. He scribbled off a furious note to Sandhurst. He "could not believe that you could be such a young stupid. It is clear you are not to be trusted with a valuable watch & when I get it back from Mr Dent I shall not give it back to you." Then he wrote the details to Jennie in Paris, adding that Winston "wont forget my letter for some time & it will be a long time before I give him anything worth having. I wanted you to know this as he may tell you a vy different story."[128]

Winston told a vy different story indeed. "The first accident," he wrote, "was not my fault at all." He hadn't been careless; quite the contrary. Shielding the Dent watch from harm had, it seemed, been a major concern of his, almost a mission. To that end, he had had a special leather case made for it. He was holding it in this protective case when a rude cadet ran into him, dislodging it from his grasp with such force that, to his horror, it crashed on the surface of the parade ground, emitting a discordant tintinnabulation, a knell of ruin. The dunking had been more complicated. Cadets' tunics, unlike waistcoats, lacked deep pockets. He had been strolling along the bank of Sandhurst's Wish Stream when he stooped to pick up a stick. Out popped the watch, sinking into six feet of water, "the only deep place for miles." Instantly he stripped and dove after it, trying again and again until exhaustion raised the possibility that he might drown. "The next day I had the pool dredged — but without result," he wrote. Therefore, obtaining official permission for a major effort, he borrowed twenty-three infantrymen, "dug a new course for the stream," rerouted it, acquired a fire engine from the nearest village, "pumped the pool dry and so recovered the watch." It was irresistible. Jennie wrote: "Oh! Winny what a harum scarum fellow you are!" Even Randolph relented: "You need not trouble any more about the watch. It is quite clear that the rough work of Sandhurst is not suitable for a watch made by Dent." He sent an inexpensive substitute.[129]

Bills, Winston's allowance, expenses — throughout 1893 Randolph was increasingly preoccupied with the disagreeable subject of money. To trim his budget, he sold the Connaught Place house and moved his family in with his mother in the ducal mansion on Grosvenor Square. With Jack away at Harrow, Elizabeth Everest stepped into a new role, becoming Duchess Fanny's housekeeper. Randolph continued to write for the *Daily Graphic,* but he still couldn't make ends meet. On October 6, when his elder son was entering his sixth week as a cadet, he wrote Jennie that "I am vy sorry but I have no money at the present moment & balance overdrawn at bank." He had some South African mining shares for which he had paid £10,000 two years earlier, and was putting them on the market, "but it is vy difficult to get 4½ for them now, & I must not sell more than £500. I will try & send you £105 to Hotel Scribe." He turned to his mother for help. The duchess, however, was having financial difficulties of her own. She, too, had to economize. She decided she needed less domestic help. She fired Mrs. Everest.[130]

If ever a servant was a member of a family, Woom was she. She had been with the Churchills for nineteen years, and she had few savings. Randolph knew that, because she had entrusted them to him; he had driven her down to the City in his private hansom and turned them over to Lord Rothschild at New Court for investment. The return was a pittance. By the time Winston learned of her dismissal, she had been gone for three months. Aghast, he wrote his mother, who replied that it was none of his business and she would refuse to read anything further he wrote her about it. He begged her to listen to him out of "common decency." He felt that if he allowed Woom "to be cut adrift without protest" he would be "extremely ungrateful — besides I should be very sorry not to have her at Grosvenor Square — because she is in my mind associated — more than anything else with home." She was an old woman; to be "packed off" in this way "would possibly, if not probably break her down altogether. . . . At her age she is invited to find a new place & practically begin over again. . . . I think such proceedings cruel & rather mean." Of course, the duchess had "every right to discharge a servant for whom she has 'no further use.' " But at the very least

Woom should be kept on until she found another job or "be given a pension — which would be sufficient to keep her from want — & which should continue during her life." He told Jennie: "It is in your power to explain to the Duchess that she *cannot* be sent away until she has got a good place." He posted this letter on October 29. There was no reply. Randolph sent Woom seventeen pounds. Other "presents" followed from time to time, but apart from that, she had been discarded like a shabby cradle. Her sisters kept her from destitution. In the little time left her, she continued to write Winston and Jack faithfully, and to remember them with little gifts on their birthdays and Christmas.[131]

Winston had entered Sandhurst ninety-second in a class of 102. Immediately he had trouble with parade-ground drill — his officers were dumbfounded to find that he wanted to argue about commands — and was put in the awkward squad. But within a fortnight he had grown to love the life. He felt himself "growing up every week." Gone, he later wrote, were Harrow's "unending spell of worries that did not then seem petty, and of toil uncheered by fruition; a time of discomfort, restriction and purposeless monotony. . . . At Sandhurst I had a new start. I was no longer handicapped by past neglect of Latin, French or Mathematics." Instead, there were just five subjects to master: fortification, tactics, topography, military law, and military administration. In retrospect it seems inadequate preparation for England's greatest war leader. "We were never taught anything about bombs or hand-grenades," he would recall, "because of course these weapons were known to be long obsolete. They had gone out of use in the eighteenth century, and would be quite useless in modern war." And though Winston would be disdainful of the U.S. Military Academy when he visited there two years later, West Point without math would have been unthinkable even then.[132]

But Sandhurst was *fun.* He particularly liked the exercises in field fortification. They dug trenches, built breastworks, and revetted parapets with sandbags, heather, fascines, and "Jones' iron-band gabions" — cylinders filled with earth. Chevaux-de-frise were constructed, and *fougasses,* a kind of primitive land mine in which the charge was overlaid with stones. Using slabs of guncotton, they blew up simulated railroad tracks and masonry bridges; then they erected pontoon or timber substitutes. All the hills around Camberley were mapped. Roads were reconnoitered. Picket lines were established and advance and rear guards posted. It was like being back at Banstead with Jack and their cousins, building the castle with its moat and drawbridge and using the homemade elastic catapult to hurl green apples at the cow. In a revealing comment on his cadet days, Winston later said he thought it "a pity that it all had to be make-believe, and that the age of wars between civilized nations had come to an end for ever. If only it had been 100 years earlier what splendid times we should have had! Fancy being nineteen in 1793 with more than twenty years of war against Napoleon in front of one!"[133]

Sandhurst, like West Point, divided cadets into companies. There were six, each commanded by a commissioned officer, regular army NCOs, and cadet corporals; each with its own quarters, mess, and billiard room; each fielding athletic teams against the others. The year after he was commissioned, Winston wrote an article about the academy for the *Pall Mall Magazine.* He used the pseudonym "Cornet of Horse,"* and he described a typical day at Sandhurst. Reveille sounded at 6:00 A.M. and forty-five minutes later the study halls were filled with cadets in immaculate blue uniforms, "deep in the wiles of tactics or the eccentricities of fortification."[134] Breakfast was served at 8:00 A.M. Morning parade came an hour later, followed by gymnastics, the formation of skirmishers beyond the cricket pavilion, bayonet practice, lectures on outposts and attacking enemy positions, and lunch. Riding school was held in the early afternoon and was mandatory, even for infantry cadets; those who lacked mounts, like Winston, hired "screws" at the local livery stables. Sports began at 4:00 P.M. Tea and study preceded mess, the school's only formal meal. Evenings were devoted to reading, talking, playing whist and billiards, and, sometimes, watching a boxing match between cadets. The bugler played "lights out" at 11:00 P.M.

Winston became a passionate horseman. He was the liveryman's steadiest customer. Gradually, he wrote, he developed "a tolerably firm seat," learning to saddle his mount, to ride without stirrups or reins, to ride bareback, to leap fences, and to mount and dismount while his horse was trotting, a "feat very easily performed." He became Sandhurst's second-best rider. "I enjoyed the riding-school thoroughly," he wrote, "and got on — and off — as well as most. . . . Horses were the greatest of my pleasures. . . . Young men have often been ruined through owning horses, or through backing horses, but never through riding them; unless of course they break their necks, which, if taken at a gallop, is a very

* The rank held by Chatham (the Elder Pitt). Sir Robert Walpole, his political adversary, said, "We must muzzle this terrible young Cornet of Horse," and Chatham was expelled by the army.

good death to die." In idle hours he organized races and point-to-points. His sole complaint about Sandhurst was that "polo for the last two years has been relegated to the limbo of prohibited pleasures," despite the fact that "if there is a game which could prepare a youth for a soldier's life, that game is polo." The argument against it was that some officers would be unable to afford it. "This levelling-down doctrine," he concluded, "is pure Socialism." Thus, in the first piece he sold to a newspaper, he identified his parliamentary enemies of the coming century.[135]

He was now an eager student of war. Lord Randolph had instructed his bookseller to send Winston any books he needed for his studies, and presently the young cadet was devouring Maine's *Infantry Fire Tactics,* Prince Kraft's *Letters on Infantry, Cavalry, and Artillery,* and Sir Edward Bruce Hamley's 1866 classic, *Operations of War.* Days passed pleasantly. He was surrounded by his peers. As Byron Farwell observes in *Mr. Kipling's Army,* a youth arriving at Sandhurst or Woolwich "found himself surrounded by others with backgrounds similar to his own. . . . Officer-instructors and cadets spoke the same language in the same accents, possessed similar vocabularies, had the same set of attitudes and beliefs." Lieutenant General Brian Horrocks, looking back, wrote: "We regular army officers of those days might all have come out of the same mould. We had been to identical public schools. . . . We . . . were, I'm afraid, terribly dull." Winston, though his social position was loftier than most, didn't think them at all dull. After the long dreadful years of being bullied and taunted, he was accepted here as a comrade, and he rejoiced.[136]

In his early cadet days his father had written him: "Mind you if you do well at Sandhurst & get good reports good positions in your classes & even the good conduct medal you would go to your regiment so much higher in credit & more thought of. So if you feel at times like giving way or falling off 'Don't.' " Winston had been getting these goads for twelve years. They hadn't worked then, and now they were unnecessary. In the examinations at the end of his first term, he scored near the top of his class, his strongest subjects being tactics and military law. Under "Conduct" the official verdict was "Good but unpunctual." He would always be unpunctual, always missing trains, ships, and, later, planes, until he reached a station so exalted that they all waited for him. But he excelled so in every other Sandhurst course that his tardiness was overlooked. His earlier status of public-school dolt was forgotten now that he was an admirable young soldier with a brilliant career ahead of him. This showed, he wrote, "that I could learn quickly enough the things that mattered." He was growing stronger physically. Furthermore, he was popular with his fellow cadets. Randolph, astounded by all this, lifted the restrictions on his leave, and Winston began entraining for Waterloo Station in London with his new friends.[137]

The imperial capital was then approaching its prime, and for privileged youths who knew they would inherit it one day, the city was a source of endless wonder and ebullience. The metropolis of the 1870s, when Winston had played in Mayfair and Hyde Park, had been transformed. London was gay; it was, by earlier Victorian standards, permissive. These were the 1890s, the Naughty Nineties, the Mauve Decade, the best time, Churchill would later write, in his entire life: "Twenty to twenty-five — those are the years!"[138] It was almost as though the capital was preparing for the momentous events which lay ahead. Popular institutions which would flourish in the next century, and which later generations of Englishmen would come to regard as the very essence of the British way of life, were just then arriving on the national stage. The first white-fronted J. Lyon's Teashop had just opened at 213 Piccadilly. Harrods had newly installed display windows. Marks and Spencer had opened their Penny Bazaar ("Don't ask the price, it's a penny") at Cheetham Hill, Manchester, and were building a branch in London. Londoners of the upper and middle classes had plenty to spend; that year the capital of England's limited liability companies exceeded £1,000,000,000 — one and a third times that of France and Germany combined. At the five-year-old Savoy, Auguste Escoffier had created the Peach Melba, honoring Madame Nellie Melba, who was singing Wagner's *Lohengrin* at Covent Garden. Piccadilly Circus was acquiring its fountain. In Langham Place, Queen's Hall had replaced old St. James's Hall as the home of the capital's orchestral music; it would be famous for its Promenade Concerts until Nazi bombers leveled it in 1941. The Tower Bridge had just been completed. Strolling along the Embankment from Westminster Bridge, the cadets from Sandhurst could see New Scotland Yard rising, a creation of the architect Norman Shaw, who contrived to give the police station the appearance of a French Renaissance château transplanted from the Seine to the Thames.

If they were in the mood for a play, the Sandhurst cadets could see Oscar Wilde's *Woman of No Importance* at the Haymarket Theatre, George Bernard Shaw's *Arms and the Man* at the Avenue, *Charley's Aunt* at the Royalty, and, at the St. James's, Arthur Wing Pinero's *Second*

Mrs. Tanqueray, starring that acrobat of the chaise longue, Mrs. Patrick Campbell. The hit songs likeliest to be hummed by passersby in the street were Dvořak's "Humoresque"; or "Happy Birthday to You," a curious tune composed by a Kentucky kindergarten teacher; or, if the pedestrian had just returned from Paris, the theme of Debussy's *Après-midi d'un faune*. Lounge suits, worn with bowlers in winter and boaters in summer, were frequently seen here in the center of town, but in the West End the cadets' fathers were loyal to their frock coats and toppers. Women's fashions were another matter. The bustle had disappeared four years earlier. Leg-of-mutton sleeves had arrived, and so had separate blouses and skirts, a by-product of lawn tennis's popularity, though the blouses were worn with stiff collars. Hems were higher, always a source of pleasure for the coarser sex, and boys who could divert chaperons and make exceptional progress with a cooperative girl were delighted to find that knickers had replaced thick petticoats. This was a tribute, not to sexual emancipation, but to the bicycle craze, which dated from J. K. Starley's invention of the Rover "Safety" bike and J. B. Dunlop's patenting of the pneumatic tire. The most startling switch in women's appearance, which did nothing for anyone, was in hair and hats. During Jennie's youth, hair had been plaited and coiled in a knob at the back of the neck; bonnets were then arched over the knob and tied under the chin. Now hair was brushed forward from the back of the neck and massed on top. Hatpins became indispensable. Hatpin hats, floating on top of the coiffures, might be toques, miniature straw hats, or wide-brimmed picture hats. Many pins were required to anchor them. Keeping them in place discouraged motion, a handicap to a youth intent upon exploring his date's knickers, and the pins themselves were long and deadly, which, if push came to shove on a park bench, could be lethal.

Had Winston but known it, the change with the greatest significance for his future was the appearance on London streets of W. H. Smith's newsstands. Once Richard Hoe's steam-powered rotary "lightning" press had replaced flatbed presses, vast supplies of fodder were needed to feed it. The answer, a German discovered, was cheap groundwood pulp. Readers were ready. W. E. Forster's Compulsory Education Act of 1870, followed by compulsory schooling ten years later, had raised the entire nation's level of literacy. In 1858 only 5 percent of the army's recruits had been able to read and write. But by Churchill's time the figure was 85.4 percent. Civilians had made similar progress. Reading materials began to be available to them. The 1880s had brought free libraries; Parliament had then abolished the newspaper tax and the excise duty on paper. That cleared the way for what can only be called an explosion in journalism. W. T. Stead's *Pall Mall Gazette,* which was founded in 1892 and cost a penny, was one of the first eruptions. Others were the *Daily Chronicle,* the *Daily Mail,* George Newnes's *Tid-bits,* and, from the Harmsworth Brothers, *Answers to Correspondents, Comic Cuts* (for children), the *Evening News,* and, the year after Winston left Sandhurst, the *Daily News,* which, at a halfpenny, would reach a circulation of a half-million, twice as high as that of any other paper. Five years later Alfred Harmsworth would become Lord Northcliffe, and three years after that he would acquire *The Times* and begin trumpeting the danger of war with Germany.

Because of this print revolution, Winston would reach millions of the newly literate, like Mrs. Everest's brother-in-law, and, with checks from editors and book royalties, support his political career. He would also become a lifelong omnivorous reader of newspapers and one of the most well-informed men in the world on the events of his times. At Sandhurst, as at Brighton, he was scanning column after column of newsprint every evening. Among his discoveries, during his three terms at the school, were the passage of woman suffrage in New Zealand, the election of Keir Hardie as the first MP to represent Britain's workingmen, and the court-martial conviction, in France, of Captain Alfred Dreyfus, after which a mob outside chanted, "Death to the Jews!" Winston approved of none of these. He was more pleased by the West African explorations of the English naturalist Mary Kinsley, who traveled through cannibal country protected by Fan tribesmen, and by the expansion of French imperialism in Laos, French Guiana, and Dahomey; by Belgian imperialism in the Congo; by American imperialism in Hawaii; and by British imperialism in South Africa, where Cecil Rhodes and Leander Starr Jameson had just suppressed a native revolt. (Already they were plotting the fateful Jameson Raid, to be carried out a few months after young Churchill had passed out of Sandhurst.) Czar Nicholas II had succeeded his father in Russia and seemed to be settling in for a long, stable reign. Winston liked that, too, and because he was fascinated by the trivial as well as the momentous, he was gratified by descriptions of the new Winchester rifle; by the first striptease, at the Bal des Quatre Arts in Paris; by the defeat of John L. Sullivan by James Corbett; and by the invention of the safety razor by an American bottle-stopper salesman named King Gillette.

Hubert Gough, recalling his own early days in uniform, wrote that on weekends he and his friends rode by "coach, with four horses and two men, all taken from the ranks, to almost every race meeting round London."[139] Winston liked horses, but he was developing other interests. On each excursion to the city he browsed through bookstores. The expansion of the publishing industry, he found, had not been confined to penny dailies. New magazines were also flourishing, from the popular *Strand Magazine* and the *Review of Reviews* through W. E. Henley's *National Observer* and C. H. Pearson's *National Life and Character,* both journals of imperialist thought, to the avant-garde *Yellow Book,* which carried Aubrey Beardsley's black-and-white "art nouveau" drawings. The book counters offered a feast: Thomas Hardy's *Tess of the D'Urbervilles* and *Jude the Obscure,* Marie Corelli's *Sorrows of Satan,* Kipling's *Jungle Book,* Robert Louis Stevenson's *Ebb-Tide,* Anthony Hope's *Prisoner of Zenda,* H. G. Wells's *Time Machine,* volumes of poems by A. E. Housman, Yeats, and Hardy; Robert Blatchford's *Merrie England,* which sold over a million copies; A. Conan Doyle's *Memoirs of Sherlock Holmes* (in the December 1893 issue of the *Strand,* Conan Doyle had contrived to kill Holmes in the Reichenbach Falls, but his public successfully demanded a resurrection); and, if you were more fluent in continental languages than Winston was, Emile Zola's *Débâcle,* just off the Paris presses, and thirty-nine-year-old Sigmund Freud's *Studien über Hysterie.*

In knowledgeable circles *Yellow Book,* Oscar Wilde, and *fin de siècle* were code words. They signaled flagrant vice in the West End and, among most educated Englishmen, a collapse of morals. In the upper classes extramarital coitus was acceptable, but sodomy and fellatio were literally unmentionable. Everyone knew that certain public-school boys became confused about sexual roles. You didn't talk about that. You didn't let the side down. But these new people were advertising it. "Art for Art's Sake" meant more than it said. Polite critics called it decadence, which was accurate, though hedonism, a broader term, was more applicable. What few grasped was that this was one of but three new forces which, by the 1890s, had evolved from the religious evangelism of Victoria's prime years. The other two were Anglo-Catholicism — "High Church," or "Ritualistic," Christianity — and rationalism. Rationalism was the wave of the future. Charles Booth had begun his nine-volume inquiry into London poverty when eleven-year-old Winston caught double pneumonia in Brighton. Booth was still at it, and now, while Cadet Churchill was galloping across the meadows around Camberley, Sidney and Beatrice Webb brought out their *History of Trade Unionism.* Conscience, until now the province of men of the cloth, had found secular forms of expression. When Randolph had gone up to Oxford, the brightest students had been preparing for the ministry. Hardly any were now. Church attendance had dropped sharply all over England. Family prayers in upper-class households, though still prevalent, began to decline. One casualty of this shift was the Victorian Sabbath. Sunday papers were frowned upon, and public restaurants were closed on that day, but it was difficult to defend the old values when all London knew of the Prince of Wales's showy Sunday dinner parties. Throughout the decade society receded from the old Sabbath observance. Museums and art galleries were thrown open on Sunday afternoon. The National Sunday League urged healthy Sunday recreation and organized Sunday railway excursions at cheap rates. The railroads, unwilling to haggle over old values when profits loomed, accommodated them.

The lower classes couldn't afford the excursions, even at half price. Instead, they crowded into the music halls, which, responding to the new moral climate, permitted their comedians' humor to grow broader and broader. This was the halls' Augustan age. The stars, like their audiences, were mostly cockneys: Marie Lloyd, George Robey, Albert Chevalier, Little Titch, Dan Leno, Harry Champion. They sang "My Old Dutch," "Don't Dilly Dally," "Two Lovely Black Eyes," "Oh, Mr Porter," "One of the Ruins That Cromwell Knocked About a Bit," and England's greatest hit of 1892:

After the Ball is over, after the break of morn;
After the dancers' leaving, after the stars are gone;
Many a heart is aching, if you could read them all;
Many the hopes that have vanished, After the Ball.

Sometimes celebrities paraded across the stage: Eugene Sandow, the German strong man; Blondin, the tightrope walker; Captain Webb, the Channel swimmer. Audiences were intensely patriotic, cheering every glimpse of the Union Jack and, when the chairman thumped his gavel and gave them their cue, belting out "Tommy, Tommy Atkins," and "The Union Jack of Dear Old England." The best of the halls were in the heart of London. The Eagle, the Alhambra, and the Empire in Leicester Square were the most popular. It was in the Empire, of all places, that Winston Churchill delivered his first speech. The date was Saturday, November 3, 1894. He was defending prostitution.

Mrs. Ormiston Chant, a crusader against vice, had been eyeing the theater with disapproval for some time. The management, like those of most of the halls, had built a promenade beside the men's bar, and it was along this walk, as patrons emptied their glasses, that elegant doxies strolled back and forth, describing their specialties and citing their prices in stage whispers. Winston, now a Sandhurst senior, was not among their customers. He, like many of his peers, sublimated his sex drive and idealized women. He had a crush on Mabel Love, a performer at the Lyric, and at his written request she had sent him an autographed photograph; but his feelings for her were nothing if not chaste. His band of cadets regularly toured all London's great music halls, however, and he was stung when he read that, at Mrs. Chant's insistence, a "barricade" had been erected between the Empire and its promenade. Instinctively hostile toward authority, he wanted to lash out. He wrote, and then thrice rewrote, a speech which, Churchill the man would recall, was "a serious constitutional argument upon the inherent rights of British subjects; upon the dangers of State interference with the social habits of law-abiding persons; and upon the many evil consequences which inevitably follow upon repression not supported by healthy public opinion." Reading in the *Daily Telegraph* that champions of the harlots were forming an "Entertainments Protective League" to defend their dishonor, he resolved to join up. The meeting was held in a seedy London hotel. When he arrived by hansom, he found there was only one other member. The man said sadly, "It's very difficult to get people to do anything in England now. They take everything lying down. I do not know what's happened to the country; they seem to have no spirit left."[140]

Winston felt that someone had to speak for freedom. But organization needed funds. In the Strand he spotted the three golden balls hanging over Attenborough's celebrated moneylending shop and hocked his watch, reflecting that, "after all, the Crown Jewels of great kingdoms [have] been pawned on hard occasions." Three days later he rounded up fellow cadets out for lark, led them to the Empire, and found that the "barricade" was merely a canvas screen supported by a wooden framework. He had come prepared to incite a riot. The elements were there. The men already in the bar agreed with him and his friends that the barrier was a bloody shame. A silence spread among them, like the thickening in the air before a storm. One man poked a hole through the screen with his cane. A cadet gave it a shove. Someone else kicked it, and it moved. In a flash the whole crowd, suddenly excited and infuriated, rushed at the flimsy encumbrance and demolished it. Amid the din Winston shouted: "Ladies of the Empire! I stand for Liberty!" It turned out that there were no ladies present, soiled or otherwise; the prostitutes had prudently decamped. That ought to have been a letdown, but he felt flushed with victory. Leaping on a chair — his text, revised, was in his hand — he cried: "Where does the Englishman in London always find a welcome? Where does he first go when, battle-scarred and travel-worn, he reaches home? Who is always there to greet him with a smile and join him with a drink? Who is ever faithful, ever true? The ladies of the Empire promenade!"[141]

It was in vain. The London County Council, as licensing authority for the music halls, supported Mrs. Chant. Trollops were banned from all of them. Nonetheless, Winston felt a sense of achievement. He wrote Jack, at Harrow: "It was I who led the rioters — and made a speech to the crowd. I enclose a cutting from one of the papers so that you may see." After the council had acted he wrote a formal denunciation of its decision and sent it to his father, who, though he didn't know it, had strong personal reasons for favoring the suppression of tarts. "I am sure," Winston wrote him, "you will disapprove of so coercive and futile a measure." He wrote his aunt Leonie: "It is hard to say whether one dislikes the prudes or the weak-minded creatures who listen to them most. Both to me are extremely detestable. In trying to be original they have merely lapsed into the aboriginal. The 'new woman' is merely the old Eve in a divided skirt." He also wrote an open letter to the *Westminster Gazette,* submitting that the only way to lasting reform lay in "educating the mind of the individual and improving the social conditions under which he lives," but the editor refused to print it, hoping, perhaps, to conceal the identity of the crowd's ringleader. If so, he failed. Mandel Creighton, the bishop of London, found out. He wrote *The Times:* "I never expected to see an heir of Marlborough greeted by a flourish of strumpets."[142]

Winston, satisfied that he had at least drawn blood, continued to drop into music halls whenever he had a free evening. Shortly after he had been commissioned, he was at the Alhambra with a fellow officer when a flag-waving entertainer, inspired by a disagreement between Salisbury and the new czar over the Armenian crisis of 1896, sang:

Cease your preaching! Load your guns!
Their roar our mission tells,
The day is come for Britain's sons
To seize the Dardanelles!

Winston leaned toward his friend and asked: "Where are the Dardanelles *exactly?*"[143]

He reached the pinnacle of his Sandhurst days on December 2, 1894. Fifteen of the 127 seniors who had qualified to receive the Queen's commission were chosen to compete for the school's annual riding prize, and he was among them. He wrote his father, who was abroad with Jennie,

"Well we rode — jumped with & without stirrups & with out reins — hands behind back & various other tricks. Then 5 were weeded out leaving only ten of us. Then we went in the field & rode over the numerous fences several times. 6 more were weeded out leaving only 4 in. I was wild with excitement and rode I think better than I have ever done before but failed to win the prize by 1 mark being 2nd with 199 out of 200 marks. I am awfully pleased with the result, which in a place where everyone rides means a great deal, as I shall have to ride before the Duke and also as it makes it very easy to pick regts when the Colonels know you can ride. I hope you will be pleased."[144]

It was unlikely. By the time this letter reached Randolph he was in no condition to express pleasure or displeasure. Winston knew, however, that his riding skills had reopened the sore subject of whether he should enter the cavalry or the infantry. Earlier in the year, when they had last exchanged views on the subject through Jennie, his father had still been strong for the Sixtieth Rifles. But Winston now wanted nothing to do with foot soldiering. The man responsible for this view was, ironically, an old friend of Randolph's, Colonel John Brabazon, an impoverished Irish landlord who had seen action during the Afghan War in 1878 and 1879 and during the fierce fighting around Suakin, on the Red Sea, in 1884. Brabazon now commanded the Fourth Queen's Own Hussars — light cavalry. During Winston's first months at Sandhurst, this regiment had been transferred from Ireland to Aldershot, and Brabazon had invited Winston to ride over and dine with him in the regimental mess. The young cadet was dazzled. Some thirty officers, magnificently uniformed in blue and gold, gathered around a table which bore the shining plate and trophies won by the Fourth Hussars during two hundred years of campaigning. In Winston's words: "It was like a State banquet. In an all-pervading air of glitter, affluence, ceremony and veiled discipline, an excellent and lengthy dinner was served to the strains of the regimental string band." Even the imperfections were charming; the colonel's lisp, he was delighted to find, was worse than his own. By the time the vintage port was passed, he had lost his heart to his hosts. Brabazon invited him back several times. Early in 1894 Winston had decided that he wanted a commission in the regiment. He had asked his mother to write the Duke of Cambridge, requesting that he be released from his commitment to the Sixtieth Rifles. The duke, however, had been incensed by the threat of defection, and Randolph had sent word to him that "Brabazon, who I know is one of the finest soldiers in the army, had no business to go and turn that boy's head about going to the 4th Hussars."[145]

But turned it was, and it wouldn't be turned back. When Jennie had reproached him for continuing to accept invitations to the regimental mess, he had replied: "I should not think that Papa would object to my having stayed with Col Brab at Aldershot. How I wish I were going into the 4th instead of those old Rifles. It would not cost a penny more & the regiment goes to India in 3 years which is just right for me. I hate the Infantry — in which physical weaknesses will render me nearly useless on service & the only thing I am showing an aptitude for athletically — riding — will be no good to me." There was another reason. Ambition was beginning to flame in him. "Promotions much quicker in Cavalry than in Infantry (60th Rifles slowest regiment in the army)." Nevertheless, his father, unconvinced, had closed the subject in May. Now, seven months later, he passed out of Sandhurst with honors, twentieth in a class of 130. He wrote afterward that he passed out "into the world. It opened like Aladdin's Cave . . . an endless moving picture in which one was an actor. . . . All the days were good and each day better than the other. Ups and downs, risks and journeys, but always the sense of motion, and the illusion of hope."[146]

What is baffling about this passage is that the weeks after he left Sandhurst were among the most terrible of his life. His parents were away; he had no home. He drifted from his aunt Leonie's London house at 53 Seymour Street to Deepdene, his aunt's estate; to his grandmother at Blenheim; to the home of a friend at Bayham; to the estate of Lord Hindlip, another friend; and then back to Deepdene. He had not yet been commissioned. That would come only when he had been gazetted. Eventually he was to serve in nine different British regiments — the Fourth Hussars, the Thirty-first Punjab Infantry, the Twenty-first Lancers, the South African Light Horse, the Oxfordshire Hussars, the Oxfordshire Yeomanry, the Grenadier Guards, the Royal Scots Fusiliers, and the Oxfordshire Artillery — but in that winter of his twenty-first year he was an upper-class vagabond, a wanderer with no place to hang his top hat. Not that it much mattered. He was in a state of shock, trying to come to terms with the shattering fact that his father, whom he cherished despite the sad history of their relationship, was about to die.

By 1885, when Winston was ten, his father had entered the fourth syphilitic stage, the slow invasion of the nervous system, in which the microorganisms successively attack the membranes, the spinal cord, and, finally, the brain, producing general paresis — total paralysis. Lord Rosebery began to notice physical impairment in his friend early in the year. That summer other friends became disturbed. Dilke, Chamberlain, and Lord James put their heads together in September, shared observations, and broke up after realizing that it was beyond them. Labouchère sent Rosebery a note: "R. Churchill is in a very bad way. . . . He says he cannot sleep after 6 in the morning and breaks down if he does not go to bed early." In August and again in November Randolph was confined to his bed. He confided to Lord Dufferin that sessions in the House entailed strain "and the constant necessity of trying to say something new makes one a drivelling idiot."[147]

By now Dr. Roose had thrown in his hand. Although chiefly known in the West End for his successful treatment of gout, Roose had also researched neurasthenic diseases and was, for his time, an accomplished diagnostician. He had bluntly told Randolph that he believed his disease to be incurable, then sent him to Dr. Thomas Buzzard, a VD specialist, for another opinion. Buzzard shared Roose's pessimism. In the 1880s anyone who had reached the quaternary stage of syphilis was beyond hope. The two doctors proscribed alcohol and tobacco, and prescribed early bedtimes and doses of potassium iodide, mercury, and digitalis. They might as well have done nothing. Except for the digitalis, which fought the cardiac weakness accompanying the affliction, their drugs merely produced embarrassing side effects: hoarseness, dizziness, darkened skin, and progressive deafness — all of which were observed by Randolph's acquaintances in subsequent years and noted in their diaries and letters.

Paresis, though fatal in the end, is interrupted by frequent remissions, thereby encouraging false hope. It is also characterized by spells of feverish energy alternating with despair; by poor judgment, violent rages, and moodiness. In 1892, as general paralysis slowly approached, these were joined, in Randolph's case, by palpitations and slurred speech. Jennie was in torment. She was nursing her husband, keeping up a brave front, trying to pretend that life was normal, and wondering what to tell the children. Her sons were not only unaware that their father had an irremediable social disease; they didn't even know he was seriously ill. On the face of it this is inexplicable. Others watched Randolph's deterioration for ten years. But the boys rarely saw him. Most of what Winston knew about his father's activities now came from his mother. Randolph did write to him from time to time, and with hindsight we can trace his deterioration in those letters. Winston didn't, or couldn't. There had always been a wild streak in his father's scrawled notes to him anyhow. Those who saw Randolph more frequently, however, had long since despaired of him. It had been more than a year since his friends had been able to endure hearing him speak in Parliament. "R. C. terrible," James wrote Chamberlain after one scene in the House. After another, *The Times* parliamentary correspondent wrote that "nothing more tragical has been seen in the House of Commons in our generation." Randolph became completely unpredictable. In a shrewd moment he drafted an amendment to the Parnell Report, shifting responsibility for the witch-hunt from the government to one of his favorite bêtes noires, *The Times.* Louis Jennings was to speak first; Randolph was to follow. The House was full. Before the Speaker could recognize Jennings, Randolph was on his feet, denouncing the government in the crudest language members had heard there. Jennings never spoke to him again. Others left the chamber whenever he rose, not out of anger, but because they knew they could not suffer what they knew would follow. Rosebery said: "There was no curtain, no retirement. He died by inches in public."[148]

The final symptoms were now evident. As his brain and spinal cord rotted, he became subject to unexpected attacks, facial tremors, tremors of the lip and tongue, abrupt changes in the pupils of his eyes, impaired vision, splitting headaches, lapses of memory, delusions, depressions, and dementia. At times he could not engage in coherent conversation. William H. Rideing, who sat at his right during a dinner party, later recalled: "Lord Randolph was plainly a doomed man. He shook as if in a palsy; his voice was woolly and stuttering, almost unintelligible." On May 27, 1894, Wilfrid Scawen Blunt wrote in his diary: "Wednesday I called on Randolph Churchill in Grosvenor Square (his mother's house) and had some political talk with him. He is terribly altered, poor fellow, having some disease, paralysis, I suppose, which affects his speech, so that it is painful to listen to him. He makes prodigious efforts to express himself clearly, but these are only too visible. . . . As he came to the door with me he tried again to explain to me what he wanted to tell me about Egypt, but broke down and said, almost in tears, 'I know what I want to say, but damn it, I can't say it.' " Frank Harris, another caller at 50 Grosvenor Square, wrote of Randolph that he was "appalled by his appearance. In a couple of years he had changed out of character, had become an old man instead of a young one. His face was haggard; his hair greyish and very thin on top; his thick beard, also half-grey, changed him completely. . . . As I took his hand and looked at him I felt sick: the deep lines on his face, the heavy gummy bags under his miserable eyes, the shaking hand. . . . A moment later he put his hand over his eyes and sat down heavily. 'I have slept badly and I don't feel well today,' he went on in trembling, indistinct tones. . . . He filled me with pity and regret — such an end to such a great career!"[149]

Shortly afterward, Harris was a guest at one of Sir Henry Thompson's "octave" dinners, so called because of the number of guests. He sat almost opposite Randolph. "His face was drawn and his skin leaden grey," he wrote; "there were gleams of hate, anger, and fear in his eyes, the dreadful fear of those who have learned how close madness is." After one course Randolph pointed at grouse on the sideboard and squealed, as if in pain, "E-e-e-e-e-e!" Sir Henry asked quietly, "What is it, Lord Randolph?" Randolph squealed "E-e-e-e!" again, pointing at the footman who was carving. "I want that — e-e-e! Some of that — e-e!" Sir Henry said, "It shall be brought back. I'm very glad you like it." Served, Randolph ate greedily, then suddenly dropped his knife and fork and glared at each face in turn around the table. Harris was convinced he had seen "what I called 'the malignant monkey stage' of insanity. His shrill prolonged squeal is always in my ears when I think of him." But Harris, though a gifted editor and confidant of gentlemen, was a native of Ireland and a naturalized American. In a word, he was not British. The distinction became apparent to him when, after the dinner, he approached a fellow guest and asked whether he had noticed the incident with the game. The man replied, "No, I didn't remark anything, but the grouse was excellent." Harris then asked another man whether he had thought anything strange in Randolph's behavior. "No," he was told, "except that he seems to be in a d——d bad temper." Harris persisted: "Didn't you notice how he squealed and pointed? He's mad!" The man chuckled and asked lightly, "Was he ever sane?"[150]

If Randolph's friends refused to discuss his deterioration with one another, they certainly weren't going to acknowledge it in front of his son. The fact that others, including Jennie, treated his conduct as normal, and that Winston apparently never witnessed one of his father's seizures, contributed to the boy's inability to grasp the gravity of his illness until the end approached. He was solicitous, but not alarmed, when Jennie told him that his father's doctors had recommended that he take a long sea voyage, and that she would accompany him. Actually, there was more to it than that. The doctors' chief concern had been persuading Randolph to give up politics for a year, and this was the solution. At the last minute they worried about losing touch for so long. Therefore, a young physician, Dr. George Keith, would accompany the Churchills. The family was worried for another reason. Jennie's presence at his side troubled them; as Marjoribanks wrote Rosebery, she "always grates on his

Lord Randolph in later years

nerves." Nevertheless, she was going. Her marriage to this strange man had become a brittle shell, but she felt she owed him this. They would circumnavigate the globe via the United States, Canada, Japan, Burma, India, and the P & O route home, with frequent stops along the way. Winston, Jack, and Rosebery, now prime minister, saw them off at the station, and they sailed aboard the S.S. *Majestic* on June 27, 1894. Their first stop was New York, where reporters met them. One observed that Randolph, who had appeared "gay, clever and vivacious" when he had visited the city a decade earlier, was now "restless, nervous and irritable, and walks feebly, with jerky steps, like a man uncertain of where he is putting his feet. His whole manner indicates a painful nervousness and mental irritation, from the querulous tones of his voice to his compressed lips, which he keeps drawn over his teeth in an apparent effort to control their trembling." After that it was all downhill. By the time they reached Asia, *Harper's Weekly* reported, it was the opinion of his fellow passengers "that he would not leave Japan alive. He grew very much worse on the voyage. At the outset he was petulant and irritable, but soon an ominous calmness, at times almost a lethargic quietness, grew upon him. His malady was one of the forms of softening of the brain, and this change was called a very bad symptom. His face, thin and wrinkled, was pitiful to look upon." Sometimes, behind closed doors, his lethargy vanished. Jennie later told Leonie that her husband, now paranoid, had come to believe that she was his persecutor. Once in their cabin he produced a loaded revolver and threatened her; she grabbed it, shoved him on his berth, and left, locking the door behind her. She later said: "At first, when he was practically a maniac and very strong, it was bad, but as soon as he became weak and idiotic, I didn't mind."[151]

She minded very much. The trip was a six-month ordeal for her. She wrote her sister Clara aboard ship on the Bay of Bengal, after a week in Rangoon: "I cant tell you how I pine for a little society. . . . And yet the worst of it is that I dread the chance even of seeing people for his sake. He is quite unfit for society. . . . One never knows what he may do. At Govt House Singapore he was very bad for 2 days and it was quite dreadful being with strangers. Since then he has become quieter & sometimes is quite apathetic but Keith thinks it a bad sign." She felt that it was "quite impossible for us to go travelling about in India. It means staying with people all the time & R is too unfit for it. . . . Dearest Clarinette I cannot go into all the details of his illness but you cannot imagine anything *more* distracting & desperate than to watch it & see him as he is." As if this weren't enough, she had received a further jolt in Burma. Of all her men, the one she had loved most deeply was Charles Kinsky. For years he had remained single, hoping that one day she would be free. Now he had given up; he had found another woman, a countess twenty years younger than Jennie: "I had a telegraph from Charles at Rangoon telling me of his engagement. *I hate it.*"[152]

Dr. Keith blew the whistle in Madras. On November 24 he wired Roose that their patient had begun to sink and the party would return to London as soon as possible. Six days later Keith wrote Randolph's sister Cornelia from Bombay: "I regret extremely that we have to come home but for everyone's sake I know it is the only thing to do. Lord Randolph is in no condition to continue his journey: it is the worst thing for him, he gets no pleasure out of it, and did he understand how he is he would be the last person to wish it. . . . It may seem that rather a cruel way has been taken to prevail on Lord Randolph to return but he really does not think about it much and it does not strike him in the way it would do if he were well. We ought to reach Marseilles on the 20th of next month and our subsequent movements must be entirely guided by Lord Randolph's condition. He stood the journey from Madras very well, it certainly did him no harm. I will write you again from Port Said."[153]

Winston's awareness of what was happening seems to have come to him in fits and starts. He would accept the situation, reject it, accept it again, and reject it again — the cycle was repeated over and over. Nearly a month earlier, before his parents had even reached Yokohama on the *Empress of Japan,* he had confronted Roose and demanded to know the facts about the state of his father's health. He wrote his mother on November 2, "I thought it was only right that I should know exactly how he was progressing. You see I only hear through grandmamma Jerome who does not take a very sanguine view of things — or through the Duchess who is at one extreme one minute and at the other the next. So I asked Dr Roose and he showed me the medical reports. . . . I need not tell you how anxious I am. I had never realised how ill Papa had been and had never until now believed that there was anything serious the matter. I do trust & hope as sincerely as human beings can that the relapse Keith spoke of in his last report was only temporary and that the improvement of the few months [sic] has been maintained. Do, my darling mamma when you write let me know *exactly* what you think." He suggested that she and Keith "write nothing but good to the Duchess" because "she lives, thinks, and cares for nothing in the world but to see Papa again."[154]

Six days later, after Keith had sent Roose his report from Japan, Winston had written Jennie: "I am very very sorry to hear that so little improvement has been made, and that apparently there is not much chance of improvement." Yet a few lines later he suggested, "If I were you I would always try and look on the bright side of things and endeavour perpetually to derive interest from everything." In addition, as we have seen, he had not only sent his father a cheery report on the Sandhurst riding competition but felt the world opening for him "like Aladdin's cave." And by then he had known the worst. Upon receiving Keith's Madras telegram, Roose had summoned Winston from Hindlip Hall and informed him that his father's life was approaching its end. On Christmas Eve his parents reached London. "For a month," Winston wrote in his biography of Randolph, "he lingered pitifully." Most of the time he was in a stupor. His son had by now become reconciled to the inevitable. He saw his father only as "a swiftly-fading shadow." In the early hours of Thursday, January 24, 1895, Winston was roused in the mansion of a neighbor, where he had been sleeping. "I ran in the darkness," he wrote, "across Grosvenor Square, then lapped in snow." It was all over. Three days later Randolph was buried in Bladon churchyard — the bells overhead, which had pealed merrily at Winston's birth, now tolled slowly — and a memorial service was held in Westminster Abbey.[155]

Behind him Randolph left disorder. His career had been one long strife, and it did not end at the Bladon grave. He had his defenders. The *Saturday Review* thought him "the greatest elemental force in English politics since Cromwell," and Sir Herbert Maxwell wrote in the *National Review:* "Reckless beyond all men's reckoning in prosperity, he was wont to be swift and dangerous when hard pressed. . . . Lord Randolph remained, to the last, first favourite among his party with a very large section of the people. No one can doubt that, who was in London during the closing weeks of his life, for one had only to lend an ear . . . to hear anxious discussion of the latest bulletins about 'Randy,' as he was affectionately called." But *de mortuis nil nisi bonum* was not observed by his enemies. Other obituaries described him as a man lacking in delicacy, subtlety, or decency — the *Outlook* said that he represented "the coarser qualities of his race . . . his defect was his lack of power of subordination." An officious young man from the Treasury even appeared at the Grosvenor Square portal and demanded the return of the robes Randolph had worn as chancellor of the Exchequer. His widow replied superbly — and prophetically — "I am saving them for my son." Jennie's demeanor was the subject of much comment. *Harper's Weekly* had reported on the fateful last trip: "Lady Churchill's devotion to her husband won for her the admiration of all who saw them abroad. Vigorous and active, and still a great beauty, she gave up every other pleasure to give him constant and loving care." That wasn't the half of it. She had vowed that the nature of his disease should remain forever secret. To Leonie she wrote that "up to now the General Public and even Society does not know the real truth, and after *all* my sacrifice and the misery of these 6 months it would be hard if it got out. It would do incalculable harm to his political reputation and memory and be a dreadful thing for all of us."[156] Nevertheless, there was some ill feeling toward her in her husband's family. Duchess Fanny felt that her mourning for Randolph was inadequate. There was some truth in this. Jennie was grief-stricken, but it was for Count Kinsky, who had been married just two weeks before she returned to England. The duchess extended her resentment to Winston, however, and that was unjust, for he was, and would continue to be, obsessed with the memory of his father. Seldom, indeed, has a man invested so little affection in a son and reaped such dividends of posthumous loyalty.

It is clear now that Randolph, had he lived, would have been a crushing burden for Winston's parliamentary ambitions. But the boy did not see it that way. He never would. At the funeral he felt that his task was "to lift again the flag I found lying on a stricken field." Over thirty years later he would write: "All my dreams of comradeship with him, of entering Parliament at his side and in his support, were ended. There remained for me only to pursue his aims and vindicate his memory." Unfortunately, aspiring politicians needed money — even ambitious cavalry officers needed it — and although his father had left an estate of £75,951, debts claimed most of that. Winston's pay as a subaltern would be £120 a year. Fortunately Jennie received $10,000 a year from the rental of the Jerome family home on Madison Square in New York, and she told Winston she would provide him with another £300. It wasn't nearly enough, but a dim plan was forming in his mind. He must take his father's place in Parliament. To be elected he would have to become famous. The quickest way to popular acclaim, he believed, was to acquire a reputation for military heroism. This, he knew, would be difficult. He wrote afterward: "In the closing decade of the Victorian era the Empire had enjoyed so long a spell of almost unbroken peace, that medals and all they represented in experience and adventure were becoming extremely scarce in the British Army." Still, there were always small wars here and there. Someone was always fighting someone else. He would shop around. There was nothing to stop him. Here, at least, he was realistic about Randolph's death: "I was now in the main the master of my fortunes."[157]

Among his father's last words to him had been: "Have you got your horses?" Winston interpreted this to mean an end to talk of the Sixtieth Rifles and approval of the cavalry. Jennie agreed. Their relationship had changed. "My mother was always at hand to help and advise," he later recalled, "but I was now in my twenty-first year and she never sought to exercise parental control. Indeed, she soon became an ardent ally, furthering my plans and guarding my interests with all her influence and boundless energy. She was still at forty young, beautiful and fascinating. We worked together on even terms, more like brother and sister than mother and son." Jennie had been indifferent toward him in his childhood, but she knew men. Now she wired Brabazon, who suggested she reopen negotiations with the Duke of Cambridge, which she did. In less than two weeks Winston's orders were cut. On February 18 he reported to the Fourth Hussars, and two days later he was awarded his commission, informing him: "VICTORIA by the Grace of God of the United Kingdom of Great Britain and Ireland, Queen, Defender of the Faith, Empress of India, & To Our Trusty and well beloved Winston Leonard Spencer Churchill, Gentleman, Greeting: We, reposing especial Trust and Confidence in your Loyalty, Courage and Good Conduct, do by these Presents Constitute and Appoint you to be an Officer in Our Land

Forces from the twentieth day of February 1895. You are therefore carefully and diligently to discharge your Duty as such in the Rank of 2nd Lieutenant. . . ."[158]

Discomfort has always been the lot of men being initiated into professional soldiering, and Sandhurst graduates were not exempt. Winston's first six months were to be spent in the company of enlisted recruits, drilling under the command of the regimental riding master, a fiery tyrant nicknamed "Jocko." After the glamour of the regimental mess, this was a comeuppance. The life, Winston wrote Jennie, "is fearfully severe and I suffer terribly from stiffness — but what with hot baths and *massage* I hope soon to be better. At present I can hardly walk. I have however been moved up in the 2nd Class recruits which is extremely good. The horses are very different to [sic] the Sandhurst screws. Rather too broad I think for me." Jocko's taunts were humiliating for a green officer, and were meant to be. Early in the course Winston strained a thigh muscle, necessary for gripping a horse; the choice was to suffer tortures or be thought wet, so he suffered, and sometimes fell. He later wrote: "Many a time did I pick myself up shaken and sore . . . and don again my little gold braided pork-pie cap, fastened on the chin by a boot-lace strap, with what appearance of dignity I could command, while twenty recruits grinned furtively but delightedly to see their Officer suffering the same misfortunes which it was their lot so frequently to undergo." But he was a good horseman, and it began to show. In a break with precedent, his time of indoctrination was cut to three months. He began to like Jocko, though not the drill, "which as usual I loathe and abominate."[159]

He was still drilling, and still under Jocko's eye, when older officers invited him to ride in the regiment's annual point-to-point for subalterns. Jennie had tried to discourage him from steeplechasing — Kinsky had nearly come to grief that way — telling him it was "idiotic" and could be "fatal." As yet he had no horse of his own, and had therefore reassured her that his participation was out of the question, but when another subaltern offered to lend him a charger, he couldn't resist. Afterward he wrote his brother: "It was very exciting, and there is no doubt about it being dangerous. I had never jumped a regulation fence before and they are pretty big things as you know. Everybody in the regiment was awfully pleased by my riding, more especially as I came in third. They thought it very sporting. I thought so too." Jennie was reproachful. So was Woom, and for the same reason. She wrote him: "I hope you will take care of yourself my darling. I hear of your exploits at steeple chasing. I do so dread to hear of it. Remember Count Kinsky broke his nose once at that."[160]

His mother had scarcely recovered from this, and he had hardly seen the last of the bull-lunged Jocko, when real trouble loomed, a scandal which could have ruined him. Alan Bruce, a Sandhurst classmate, was about to join the Fourth Hussars. He had been an unpopular cadet, as ill-adjusted there as Winston had been at Harrow. Winston and his new confreres in the officers' mess decided they didn't want him; they took him to dinner at the Nimrod Club in London and told him that his father's allowance of £500 would be inadequate. That was preposterous, and he said so. Since he had failed to take their hint, they discouraged him in other ways. The details are unclear, but it is not a pretty story. Bruce was accused of using foul language, of being familiar with enlisted men, of abusing regimental sergeants. The upshot was that he was asked to resign from the army. His infuriated father, A. C. Bruce-Pryce, persuaded the weekly review *Truth* to mount a press crusade against an "undisguised conspiracy formed against this subaltern before he joined to have him out of the regiment unless he consented to go voluntarily." That was the last way to engage the affections of those who had maneuvered Bruce's dismissal, and the incident would have been swiftly forgotten if Bruce-Pryce hadn't taken leave of his senses. He charged that Winston Churchill had been guilty of "acts of gross immorality of the Oscar Wilde type."[161]

Winston moved fast. He hired the Holborn solicitors Lewis and Lewis, who, four days later, issued a writ demanding damages of £20,000. Within a month he got £500, an apology, and a complete withdrawal: "I unreservedly withdraw all and every imputation against your character complained of by you in paragraph 2 of your Statement of Claim and I hereby express my regret for having made the same." *Truth* howled on, now charging that the point-to-point had been rigged, but the great reef had been skirted. Except for an absurd remark by Lord Beaverbrook — that Winston had told him he once went to bed with a man to see what it was like — nothing in Churchill's life offers the remotest ground for intimations of homosexuality. At the time, however, the barest rumor of it, unless instantly suppressed, could have been calamitous. As Brabazon wrote him, expressing "very great relief" at the outcome, "one cannot touch pitch without soiling one's hands however clean they may originally have been and the world is so ill natured and suspicious that there would always have been found some ill natured sneak or perhaps some d——d good natured friend to hem & ha! & wink over it — perhaps in years to come, when everyone even yourself had forgotten all about the disagreeable incident. You took the only line possible. . . . For malignant, preposterous as it was, it would have been impossible to have left such a charge unchallenged." Thus, with the colonel's sanction, the regiment regarded Winston as a martyr. The triumph of irony was complete. The Harrovian who had been at odds with his peers and a rebel against school authority was now accepted, and content with his acceptance, in an authoritarian sodality.[162]

Hubert Gough, later recalling his days at Aldershot as a subaltern in the Sixteenth Lancers, said: "We led a cheerful, care-free life; what duties we had to do . . . did not call for much mental effort. Afternoons were usually free for most officers." Winston's life there followed a relaxed routine. His batman brought him breakfast in bed. A subaltern's only obligations in a typical day were to spend two hours riding, an hour with the horses in the stables, and ninety minutes drilling. The rest of his time was his own. If he remained in barracks, Winston might play bezique for threepence a point, "a shocking descent from the shillings at Deepdene," he wrote, or whist, "a most uninteresting game and one at which I have but little luck." He liked games he could win. He described golf, one of his failures, as "a curious sport whose object is to put a very small ball in a very small hole with implements ill-designed for the purpose." Polo and steeplechasing occupied him more and more, though he paid for his recklessness; after one fall, which confined him to bed for three days, he explained to his mother that at a jump "the animal refused and swerved. I tried to cram him in and he took the wings. Very nearly did he break my leg, but as it is I am only bruised and stiff." Another young officer might have kept that information to himself. Winston didn't; he was still an egotistical, bumptious, rude youth. But these traits were common among young Victorian officers. Besides, he was witty, daring, generous, entertaining. Jennie had found the right word for him. He was *interesting*.[163]

Because Aldershot was only thirty-two miles from London, celebrities often visited to take the salute. Once the hussars rehearsed in the Long Valley under the scrutiny of a rising cavalryman, Captain Douglas Haig. It was "a very fine thing," Winston wrote, to see "a cavalry division of thirty or forty squadrons" maneuvered "as if it were one single unit. . . . When the line was finally formed and the regiment or brigade was committed to the charge, one could hardly help shouting in joyous wrath." As the grandson of a duke, Winston was chosen to escort the Prince of Wales, the Duke of Cambridge, the Duke of Connaught, Field Marshal Lord Roberts, and the Duke and Duchess of York (later King George V and Queen Mary). Best of all were the "splendid parades when Queen Victoria sat in her carriage at the saluting point and . . . the whole Aldershot garrison, perhaps 25,000 strong, blue and gold, scarlet and steel, passed before her, Horse, Foot, and Artillery . . . in a broad and scintillating flood." The purpose of all this was obscure. Winston later wrote: "Certainly no Jingo Lieutenant or Fire-eating Staff Officer in the Aldershot Command in 1895, even in his most sanguine moments, would have believed that our little army would ever again be sent to Europe."[164]

Any member of England's ruling families was, by that very fact, welcome in the London mansions and country homes of the aristocracy. Even Lord Randolph, diseased and mad, had not been excluded. And his son was not only a Churchill; he was also an eligible bachelor. "A gay and lordly life," he wrote, "now opened upon me." He had "a great many invitations and could go to a ball every night should I wish to." The greatest affairs that Season were held in Stafford House and Devonshire House, and he was always present. "Everywhere one met friends and kinfolk," he wrote. "The leading figures of Society were in many cases the leading statesmen in Parliament." Present were "all the elements which made a gay and splendid social circle in close relation to the business of Parliament, the hierarchies of the Army and Navy, and the policy of the State." It was almost always urbane; only once was he obliged to step between two men lunging at each other, one a participant in the Jameson Raid then on trial in Bow Street, the other a former Liberal minister who regarded the raid as an outrage. Neither thought it incongruous that a mere subaltern should step between them. It was Winston's social standing, not his rank, which counted.[165]

In his regiment, he was glad to find, virtually all the officers were Conservatives, and since the country was going to the polls that summer, there was much talk of politics. Rosebery, though a Liberal, was personally popular, particularly with Winston, for he had been a good friend to the Churchills. But everyone agreed that he had fallen among bad companions; as prime minister he owed his office to the Irish Nationalists and hence was tainted with the Fenian brush. His government fell in June because, it was said, he had permitted the country's stocks of cordite to run low. Why England needed cordite just then was unmentioned, and it wasn't true anyway, but there were cheers in Aldershot when Salisbury was returned with a majority of 150. Winston attended a party at Devonshire House and found that the other guests included Salisbury's new ministers, looking smart in their new blue-and-gold uniforms. "These uniforms were not so magnificent as ours," he wrote, "but they had a style about them which commended them to my eye." He fell into conversation with George Curzon, the new under secretary for foreign affairs. Curzon outlined his duties. In the House of Commons he would explain and defend Britain's foreign policy. More important, in Whitehall he would share in making that policy. Specifically, he expected to guide Britain's conduct toward other European powers. That was very different from galloping about and parading in an army which, everyone agreed, would never see action on the Continent. The difference between him and Curzon, Winston reflected gloomily, had nothing to do with braid and frogging. One had power and the other only the illusion of it. He studied the under secretary as he listened to him, looked around at the other ministerial uniforms, and "felt free to give rein to jealousy."[166]

It was a year of funerals. His father had slipped away in January, his grandmother Clara died in April, and as hot weather approached he learned that Elizabeth Everest lay stricken with peritonitis. They had kept in touch; she was living with her sister Emma at 15 Crouch Hill in the Islington district of North London. On April 1 she had written him: "My darling Precious Boy, I have just recd £2. 10s from Cox & Co. Charing Cross on your account. I thank you very much indeed dearest it is awfully kind & thoughtful of you. My dear dear Boy you are one in ten thousand but I am afraid you will find your income not any too much for your expenses dear. It really is too good & kind of you I don't know how to thank you enough. I am afraid Her Ladyship will think me a terrible imposter [sic]."[167]

Late in June her sister wrote him that Woom was ill, and he hurried to Islington. She knew her condition was grave, but Woom's only anxiety was for him. He had passed through a heavy shower, his jacket was wet; she told him he might catch cold and would not rest until he spread out the jacket to dry. He had to return to Aldershot by the midnight train for an early parade, and he was there when a telegram arrived from Emma. His old nurse's end was very near. Winston fetched Dr. Keith, engaged a private nurse, and hurried to Woom's side. She recognized him, but as she spoke she sank into a coma. He sat there, holding her hand, until she died at 2:15 the following morning. He wrote: "Death came very easily to her. She had lived such an innocent and loving life of service to others and held such a simple faith, that she had no fears at all, and did not seem to mind very much."[168]

He organized the funeral. Knowing that she had nursed the children of an archdeacon in Cumberland, he wired him, and the clergyman agreed to come and read the service. Winston didn't want to telegraph Jack; he went to Harrow and told him, and they traveled together to London's

Manor Park cemetery. Jennie was in Paris and saw no reason to return, but Winston ordered a wreath in her name. He was surprised at the number of mourners. He wrote his mother: "All her relations were there — a good many of whom had travelled from Ventnor overnight — and I was quite surprised to find how many friends she had made in her quiet and simple life. The coffin was covered with wreaths & everything was as it should be." Afterward he paid for a headstone:

Erected in Memory
of
Elizabeth Anne Everest
who died 3rd July 1895
Aged 62
by
Winston Spencer Churchill
Jack Spencer Churchill

Then he made arrangements with the local florist for the upkeep of the grave. "I feel very low," he wrote Jennie, "and find that I never realized how much poor old Woom was to me." It was "indeed another link with the past gone — & I look back with regret to the old days at Connaught Place when fortune still smiled." Depressed, he made a pilgrimage to his father's grave in Bladon and wrote his mother, who had never been there, that he "was so struck by the sense of quietness & peace as well as by the old world air of the place — that my sadness was not unmixed with solace . . . I think it would make you happier to see it."[169] The real source of his solace, although he could not have recognized it, was that all his links with the past were well broken. Except for his hours in the nursery with Woom, his early years had brought him very little pleasure and much pain. But they had fashioned him into a strong young man possessed of immense drive, ready to mount the steep slopes of challenge ahead.

TWO

STREAM

1895–1901

QUEEN Victoria's army, which would leave a lasting impression upon Churchill, was an eccentric, insular institution that had changed little since Waterloo, a battle some men still alive could remember clearly. The troops were led by patricians: Wellington had decreed that English gentlemen made "the best officers in the world, and to compose the officers from a lower class would cause the Army to deteriorate." Military leaders, it was held, should be men with "a stake in the country." Only WASPs need apply; there were few Disraelis or Rothschilds wearing epaulets. Apart from that, public-school boys were accepted if they were "sound," were "of the right sort," and came from "good families." (You could quickly identify those with classical educations; they swore "By Jove," an oath never heard in Other Ranks.) In endorsing an application, one colonel scrawled across it, "The son of a good soldier, his mother is a lady." It was common to note on reports as a recommendation: "A good man to hounds." Lord Roberts always checked the bloodlines of a man applying for an appointment, and according to the career officer Ian Hamilton, if Roberts thought the candidate "owned a good grandmother he would give him a trial."[1] Gentlemen were expected to guard zealously their regiment's "tone," a Victorian word freighted with class consciousness. The army counted on them to live by the gentleman's code, and if they didn't know what that was, they weren't commissioned in the first place. In some ways the code was peculiar. Gambling debts were always settled promptly, but those to tradesmen weren't. Six years after joining the Fourth Hussars, Churchill still hadn't paid the tailor who made his first uniforms. But once you were in, you could stay in forever. Some officers who had reached their eighties retained their commands. Nor were crippling wounds disqualifying. Two generals, Roberts and Wolseley, were one-eyed. Hamilton's wrist had been shattered at Majuba.* Lord Raglan had been one-armed.

* On February 27, 1881, Boer troops fighting for their independence had defeated a British force under Sir George Colley and killed Sir George at Majuba Hill.

So was Samuel Browne, who invented the Sam Browne belt so he could draw his sword swiftly with his remaining hand.

By continental standards, the number of men in uniform was tiny. Asked what he would do if the British army landed in Prussia, Bismarck replied: "Send a policeman and have it arrested." There were no corps, no divisions, nor even brigades. Everything was built around the regiment. An infantry regiment might have a single battalion of seven hundred men divided into five or six companies. An entire cavalry regiment like Winston's — hussars, dragoons, or lancers — numbered from three hundred to five hundred men, led by its colonel, four majors, eight captains, and fourteen or fifteen subalterns. There were just thirty-one cavalry regiments in the whole of the British Empire. Seniority — which determined which outfit was stationed on the right in an attack — was jealously guarded in both the cavalry and the infantry. The Coldstream Guards went back to 1661, the Grenadier Guards to 1656, the Scots Guards to 1633, the Buffs to 1572, and the Honourable Artillery Company, which was neither a company nor confined to ordnance, to 1537. Each of them cherished drums and flags captured in battles, some long forgotten, and each dressed officers and ranks in absurd uniforms. *The Times* had reported on the regalia of the Eleventh Hussars: "The brevity of their jackets, the irrationality of their headgear, the incredible tightness of their cherry-colored pants altogether defy description." The man responsible was George IV, who had never been near a battlefield but who, as Prince Regent, had designed uniforms so tight that men could hardly get into them. In his opinion, "A wrinkle is unpardonable."[2]

These zany costumes had become preposterous with the invention of smokeless gunpowder in 1886, but the British didn't like smokeless powder, and wouldn't accept it until their enemies had shown them how effective it could be. It was new; therefore, it was suspect. So were the breech-loading fieldpieces Krupp had introduced; Britain was the last European power to abandon muzzle-loading cannon. So were carbines; those issued to one cavalry regiment were dumped on the stable manure pile. The Duke of Cambridge protested that he wasn't against change. He favored it, he said, when there was no alternative. But encroachments on tradition, if avoidable, were fiercely resisted. Enlisted men were called Tommy Atkins because that was the name of the private Wellington had picked for a specimen signature on an army identity card. Officers drank wine, brandy, and whiskey, and Other Ranks drank gin and beer, because it had always been that way. Regulation bugle calls, though difficult for some buglers, were defended on the ground that they were quintessentially British, though in fact they had been composed by Franz Joseph Haydn.

The citadel of custom, charmingly described in Byron Farwell's *Mr. Kipling's Army,* was the regimental mess. This, thought Captain R. W. Campbell, was "the school for courage, honour, and truth"; there, Hamilton wrote, one understood the "Chivalry of Arms"; there, in the opinion of Major General George Younghusband, "The prig ceases to be priggish: it isn't good enough. The cad, if by chance he has slipped in, ceases to be caddish: it isn't good enough. The real 'bad hat,' or 'untamable bounder' quietly disappears."[3] Meals were rituals. You wore a proper mess jacket, which varied from one regiment to another. New subalterns did not speak until spoken to, never expressed opinions, and, in at least one regiment, did not stand on the hearthrug in front of the fire until they had completed three years' service. The first toast of the evening was to the Queen. Thereafter the port was passed from right to left, and no one smoked until the decanter had circulated twice, or, as they put it, "when the cloth was removed." Those who broke the rules were fined, and the rules were so numerous, and so divorced from reality, that one wonders when they had time to ponder the profession of arms. Not at mess; shoptalk was forbidden there. So were discussions of politics, religion, and women. Therefore, they rambled on about sport and horses, particularly hunting, where they shot hares, plover, quail, stags, grouse, partridges, ducks, snipes, woodcocks, pigeons, and, occasionally, through error, one another.

What did their countrymen think of them? It is difficult to say. "Victorian England," Brian Bond writes, "was simultaneously jingoistic and anti-militarist." A visiting foreigner observed: "How this blind glorification and worship of the Army continues to co-exist with the contemptuous dislike felt towards the members of it, must remain a problem of the national psychology." They were paid almost nothing. Regimental rates, established in 1806, varied from £95 for a subaltern to £365 for a lieutenant colonel — less than half the wages of War Office clerks — and they would remain unchanged until 1914. No man could afford a commission unless he possessed a private income of at least £150 a year for an infantry office and as much as £700 in the cavalry. Enlisted men received eleven shillings and fourpence per week, twopence less than the most exploited rural laborer in England. Edward Spiers quotes a recruiting sergeant: "It was only in the haunts of dissipation or inebriation, and among the very lowest dregs of society, that I met with anything like success."[4]

Yet these men had conquered an Empire. Under Victoria one regiment or another had been in action every year, somewhere on five continents, fighting from Aden and Afghanistan to Zululand and the Zhor Valley. They were almost always victorious. One reason was their sublime, unfathomable courage. Braver officers never led men into battle. They marched at the head of their columns, disdaining weapons for themselves, brandishing only cigars or swagger sticks. At the battle of Isandhlwana every officer had a horse and could have escaped with his life. Not one did; all remained and died with their men. Under fire, they refused to "bob" — to duck bullets and shells. An astonishing number actually enjoyed courting death. Of his first wound Wolseley wrote: "What a supremely delightful moment that was!" A captain in the First Royal Dragoons wrote his mother: "I *adore* war. It is like a big picnic. I have never been so well or happy." Chinese Gordon, seeing combat for the first time in the Crimea, found it "indescribably exciting."[5] If officers found themselves in peaceful billets, they looked for war elsewhere, took leave to get there, and paid their own expenses. The colonel commanding the Fourth Dragoon Guards enlisted as a private in the King's Own Scottish Borderers so he could join the storming of the Malakand Pass. The commander of the Tenth Hussars fought under the Turkish and Egyptian flags. Younghusband, having vanished from his post, was next seen standing rapturously in the middle of a Philippine bloodletting. And in November 1895 Second Lieutenant Winston Churchill went to embattled Cuba via the United States.

His motives were mixed. He wanted to see a real war. He was curious about New York, his mother's home. And he was bored. Anticipating its move to India, the Fourth Hussars had been giving its officers ten weeks' leave. They were expected to spend it yachting, racing, steeplechasing, and riding to hounds. The War Office assumed that, as gentlemen, they all had independent incomes and could afford such diversions. Being broke was bad form. The Manchester Regiment had the lowest status in the army because it was said that its officers could live on their pay. But a young cavalry subaltern needed a charger, two hunters, and three polo ponies. Buying them had exhausted Churchill's funds and his mother's patience. Therefore, as he put it, he "searched the world for some scene of adventure or excitement."[6] Spain was making its last attempt to quell the insurrection led by José Martí and Máximo Gómez, and 200,000 Spanish troops were tied down in Cuba. Both sides were murdering civilians and putting towns to the torch. That, and its proximity to America, appealed to Churchill. Moreover, he could manage some of the expenses. The *Daily Graphic*, which had published Randolph's letters from Africa in 1891, agreed to pay Winston five guineas for every dispatch from the front. He persuaded one of his regiment's senior subalterns, Reginald Barnes, to accompany him.

At that time there were no restrictions on officers' writing for the press. Brabazon had no objections to the trip. Neither had Jennie. She sent ninety pounds and wrote: "I understand all right — & of course darling it is natural that you shd want to travel & I won't throw cold water on yr little plans." Next Winston wrote Lord Randolph's old friend Sir Henry Wolff, now the British ambassador in Madrid, applying for permission from the Spanish military authorities to visit the war zone. It was granted instantly, almost eagerly. The fighting in Cuba had given Spain a terrible image. The press in both England and the United States ardently supported the rebels. This briefly became an issue. Churchill needed one more endorsement, from the War Office. He called on the commander in chief, Wolseley, who seemed embarrassed by the request and hinted that it would be better if Winston went without asking him; newspapermen might misinterpret his sanction of two British officers marching with the Spanish troops. But he couldn't deny a Churchill. He sighed, nodded, and, Winston wrote, added that "if I worked at the military profession he would help me in every way he could & that I was always to come and ask when I wanted anything." Then Wolseley sent Winston to his director of military intelligence. This officer, unlike his commander, saw no need for discretion. He provided Churchill with maps and a full briefing. In addition, Winston wrote, he and Barnes were "requested to collect information and statistics on various points and particularly as to the effect of the new bullet — its penetration and striking power. This invests our mission with almost an official character & cannot fail to help one in the future."[7]

On November 2 they sailed aboard the Cunard Royal Mail Steamship *Etruria.* The voyage was "tedious and uncomfortable . . . & I shall always look upon journeys by sea as necessary evils." But in New York they forgot their grievances. Originally they had scheduled three days in the city, and, aboard ship, had considered cutting this in half. Actually, they were there a week. The man responsible for this revision in plans was Bourke Cockran, a wealthy Irish-American lawyer, congressman, and power in the Tammany wigwam. Cockran was one of Jennie's men — at one time he had been her favorite — and like the rest he cut a remarkable figure, towering, leonine, with deep-set eyes and a massive forehead. His mobile features gave a contemporary the impression of "something Spanish, Celtiberian as well as Celtic."[8] His oratory was remarkable. Twice, in 1884 and 1892, his deep, resonant brogue had held

Jennie and two of her lovers (Count Kinsky on left)

Democratic national conventions spellbound. Churchill was to be one of his early conquests. Among the last was Adlai Stevenson, who modeled his rhetoric on Cockran's. In the early 1950s Churchill would astound Stevenson by quoting long passages from Cockran speeches.

Churchill and Barnes were Cockran's guests in his sprawling apartment at 763 Fifth Avenue, on the corner of Fifty-eighth Street. Jennie had written him that they would be calling, and he made wonderful things happen. Her son wrote her that he had "engagements for the next few days about three deep. It is very pleasant staying here as the rooms are beautifully furnished and fitted with every convenience & also as Mr Cockran is one of the most charming hosts and interesting men I have met." Twelve judges, including a Supreme Court justice, came to dine with them the first evening. The two young English officers dined out at the Waldorf, were entertained at Koster and Bial's, toured the harbor in a tugboat, attended the annual horse show, were shown around the iron-clad cruiser *New York,* attended five fires with the fire commissioner, were received by the Cornelius Vanderbilts — whose niece would be the next Duchess of Marlborough — and visited West Point. Winston wrote: "We are members of all the Clubs and one person seems to vie with another in trying to make our time pleasant."[9]

He was not an uncritical tourist. To Jack he wrote that West Point discipline was so strict as to be "positively disgraceful." He wrote his aunt Leonie that he had paid his fare across the eleven-year-old Brooklyn Bridge "with a paper dollar," which he thought "abominable currency." It seemed to him that "the essence of American journalism is vulgarity divested of truth." Considering the character of Pulitzer's *World* and Hearst's new *Journal,* this was not unjust. Besides, he qualified it: "I think mind you that vulgarity is a sign of strength. A great, crude, strong, young people are the Americans — like a boisterous healthy boy among enervated but well bred ladies and gentlemen." And New Yorkers, by their treatment of him, won his heart. "What an extraordinary people the Americans are! Their hospitality is a revelation to me and they make you feel at home and at ease in a way that I have never before experienced." He adored America's most popular song that year:[10]

When you hear dem a bells go ding, ling ling,
All join 'round and sweetly you must sing,
And when the verse am through, in the chorus all join in,
There'll be a hot time in the old town tonight!

But there is no doubt about which New Yorker impressed him most. He wrote: "I have great discussions with Mr Cockran on every conceivable subject from Economics to yacht racing. He is a clever man and one from whose conversation much is to be learned." Night after night, long after Barnes had retired, they sat in the flat's large library, sipping brandy, smoking cigars — Churchill's first — and talking, talking, talking. Jennie's intimate admirer introduced her son to the works of Edmund Burke. He told him: "Burke mastered the English language as a man masters the horse. He was simple, direct, eloquent, yet there is a splendor in his phrases that even in cold type reveals how forcibly he must have enthralled his visitors." Churchill was enthralled by his host's fire, vision, vigor, and, most of all, by his own mastery of English. In speaking, Cockran advised him, one should avoid scurrility, affectations, and cant. He said: "What people really want to hear is the truth — it is the exciting thing — speak the simple truth." All his life Winston would remember, and frequently quote, some of the phrases he heard by the fire in that Fifth Avenue apartment. Cockran said: "The earth is a generous mother. She will provide in plentiful abundance food for all her children, if they will but cultivate her soil in justice and peace." He also said: "In a society where there is democratic tolerance and freedom under the law, many kinds of evils will crop up, but give them a little time and they usually breed their own cure." Thirty-seven years later Churchill would write of Cockran: "I have never seen his like or, in some respects, his equal. His conversation, in point, in pith, in rotundity, in antithesis and in comprehension, exceeded anything I have ever heard."[11] By then Winston knew scores of great men. But even in 1895 he had met Rosebery, Salisbury, and Balfour. The difference was that they had all regarded him as his father's misfit son. In New York, for the first time, he found himself in the company of a distinguished man who treated him as a peer. Today Bourke Cockran's papers gather dust in the New York Public Library. He is forgotten in his own city. Yet a man who aroused young Churchill, and inspired Stevenson's gallant campaign in 1952, deserves remembrance.

Cockran seemed omnipotent in New York. At a word from him, the two English lieutenants had a private compartment for the thirty-six-hour train trip through Philadelphia, Washington, Savannah, Tampa Bay, and Key West, where they boarded the steamer *Olivette.* In the early hours of Wednesday, November 20, they sighted Havana and the rugged coast outlined against the deep blue horizon. Winston felt "delicious yet tremulous . . . I felt as if I sailed with Long John Silver and first gazed on Treasure Island. Here was a place where anything might happen. Here was a place where something would certainly happen. Here I might leave my bones." In his first dispatch as a war correspondent he wrote:

> High up on the cliffs, as the ship enters the narrows, one sees the fortress of El Moro, formerly a place of great strength, and commanding the channel to the port. It is now only used as a prison for political and military offenders, and an occasional place for execution. Here it was that the sentence of death on Lieutenant Gallegos was carried out in May last. This officer had the charge of a small post with some fifty soldiers, and was unfortunate enough to be breakfasting in a café when the insurgents happened to pass.[12]

A carriage carried them to the Gran Hotel Inglaterra and then to the office of Alexander Gollan, the British consul general. Everything had been arranged. In the morning they would leave the capital for a twelve-hour train trip to Santa Clara, the headquarters of Captain General Arsenio Martínez de Campos. Unfortunately, they could not be guaranteed a safe passage. Rebels frequently used passing trains for target practice.

Sometimes they set them afire, or blew up the tracks. Winston was excited. He told readers of the *Graphic* that the train preceding theirs, carrying a Spanish general, "had been thrown off the line a few miles beyond Santo Domingo, and . . . fifteen of its occupants had been severely injured." Their train, however, completed the trip without incident. "Marshal Campos, to whose headquarters we went, received us very kindly, and readily gave us the necessary passes and letters."[13]

Campos turned them over to Lieutenant Juan O'Donnell, son of the Duke of Tetuán. The lieutenant was fluent in English. Unfortunately, he had a sad tale to tell. Churchill was introduced to the most exasperating problem of correspondents covering a guerrilla war — finding the front. A Spanish mobile column was camped twenty miles away, pursuing a force of four thousand insurgents, but the jungle between here and there was "infested by the enemy." To get there, Churchill and Barnes must take another train to Cienfuegos, proceed by steamer to Tuna, and then travel, again by train, to Sancti Spiritu. "Though this route forms two sides of a triangle, it is — Euclid notwithstanding — shorter than the other, and we shall catch the column there."[14]

Altogether he filed five "Letters from the Front" for the *Graphic*, each of which ran under the head "The Insurrection in Cuba," was bylined "From Our Own Correspondent," and concluded with the initials "WSC." They show a keen eye for detail, a gift for clarity, and a sure grasp of tactics. The fourth was the best. By November 30 — his twenty-first birthday — he had joined troops commanded by General Juarez Valdez in the fortified village of Arroyo Blanco. At 5:00 A.M., wearing his British uniform, he accompanied two battalions, seventeen hundred men, who were feeling their way toward a band of rebels led by Gómez. "No sooner had we got clear of the town than we heard the sound of firing." To deceive Gómez's scouts, the Spaniards retraced their steps and approached from a different direction, "through swampy meadows of coarse grass traversed by frequent water-courses." At 10:00 A.M., to his astonishment, they halted and everyone except sentries slept for four hours. This was his introduction to the siesta, a custom which he would appropriate and use during both world wars to turn one working day into two. Rising, they advanced and came upon a rebel encampment; the enemy's line of march could be traced "by broken branches and trampled grass, and this line the column followed." At 5:00 P.M. the Spaniards found rebel campfires "still smouldering, and signs of a hasty departure were to be seen on every side." Here they dug in for the night, with four companies of infantry posted as sentinels. "The whole scene, bathed in brilliant moonlight — in strong contrast to which the tall palm trees and the surrounding woods showed in deepest black" — was compared with "the numerous watch fires, against whose glaze the figures of the soldiers were silhouetted."[15]

At 5:15 A.M. they were off again. "The sun had not yet risen, and a mist hung over all the low-lying ground." The path ahead "lay through the thickest and most impenetrable forest." Until now Valdez's plan had been to throw one battalion ahead, with two extended companies guarding each flank, but here the flank guards had to be abandoned; the dense jungle confined them to a narrow path. "Daylight slowly broadened, and the long Spanish column insinuated itself like a snake into the endless forests and undulations of a vast, lustrous landscape dripping with moisture and sparkling with sunshine." Their siesta was interrupted by rebel sharpshooters. Back on the trail Winston lit a Cuban cigar — he had the habit now — and noted that the bush here "gave place to a forest of extraordinary palm trees of all possible sizes and most peculiar shapes." The column forded a river and camped at a place called Las Grullas, where he persuaded two officers to join him in a swim. As they were dressing, "suddenly we heard a shot fired. Another and another followed; then came a volley. The bullets whistled over our heads." Like Chinese Gordon and George Washington, he found it thrilling to be under fire: "There is nothing more exhilarating than to be shot at without result." He coolly observed that while Valdez's men carried Mausers, the enemy used Remingtons, "and the deep note of their pieces contrasted strangely with the shrill rattle of the magazine rifles of the Spaniards."[16]

That night a bullet passed through the thatched hut in which he was sleeping and another wounded an orderly just outside. Battle — the battle of La Reforma — was joined in the morning. The Spanish column debouched into open country, and the general, scanning the field through his field glasses, saw the enemy's main position. He ordered an attack. His infantry advanced three hundred yards in silence; then "from the distant crest line came a lot of little puffs of smoke, followed immediately by the report of the insurgent rifles." The Spaniards' rifles replied as the infantrymen continued their advance. "The firing on both sides became heavy." There was "a sound in the air sometimes like a sigh, sometimes like a whistle, and at others like the buzz of an offended hornet." Valdez, "in his white uniform and gold lace, mounted on a grey horse, was a mark for every sharpshooter," yet he rode up to within fifty yards of the firing line, urging his men on while bullets felled staff officers riding on either side of him. "Presently the sound of the Mauser volleys began to predominate and the rebel fire to slacken, till finally it ceased altogether." Churchill saw "figures scurrying to the shelter of the woods," then silence. Spanish troops occupied the enemy's position. They had but one day's rations left, however, and pursuit of the insurgents "was impossible owing to the impenetrable nature of the woods." Valdez, triumphant but foiled, returned to his base in Cienfuegos.[17]

Campos — who was about to be relieved by Veleriano Weyler, whose suppression of rebellious Cuban civilians helped precipitate the Spanish-American War — awarded Churchill and Barnes the Red Cross, a Spanish decoration for officers. In London the War Office announced that they wouldn't be permitted to wear it, however; sympathy for the insurrection was still strong on both sides of the Atlantic. New York newspapers reported that Winston had fought under the Spanish colors. In Tampa he hotly denied it: "I have not even fired a revolver. I am a member of General Valdez's staff by courtesy only." But in England the *Newcastle Leader,* ignoring British army precedents, observed that "spending a holiday in fighting other people's battles is rather an extraordinary proceeding even for a Churchill," and the *Eastern Morning News* predicted that "difficulties are certain to arise and Lord Wolseley will probably order him to return at once and report himself." Wolseley did no such thing; if he reprimanded officers for serving in foreign armies, he would lose his best men. American editors were more cutting; the two subalterns were described as "emissaries of the British Government sent to teach Campos how to whip the secessionists" and proof that England was "throwing more bricks at the Monroe doctrine."[18]

Back in Cockran's flat, Churchill, stung, held his first press conference. Some of his remarks were foolish. If Campos took two Cuban strongholds before spring, he said, "he will, in my judgment, break the back of the revolution." The rebels might then "carry on the war for a year or two longer, but ultimately they will be forced to accept virtually dictated terms." Campos was, "in my judgment, one of the most distinguished men that Spain has ever produced," a leader of "rare judgment and great humanity." The rebels were "not good soldiers, but as runners would be hard to beat." That inspired derisive headlines across the United States. He was described as a "pleasant faced young officer" wholly lacking in judgment. Yet he had qualified his predictions. If the Cubans held their present gains, he said, they would "be in a position to demand more favorable terms in the event of any attempt at settlement or arbitration." The Spaniards were valiant and energetic, "but the nature of the country is against them, and, furthermore, there is too little combination in the movements of their various columns." This could turn the tide. Indeed, "If the insurgents hold out until the spring rains set in, they may yet win."[19]

He and Barnes sailed home on the *Etruria,* but the Cuban dilemma still weighed heavily upon him. He dashed off a piece for the *Saturday Review* denouncing rebel cruelty and adding, "They neither fight bravely nor do they use their weapons effectively." Bad as the Spanish administration was, "a Cuban Government would be worse, equally corrupt, more capricious, and far less stable. Under such a Government revolutions would be periodic, property insecure, equity unknown." The best solution, he wrote Cockran, would be an American takeover of the island: "I hope the United States will not force Spain to give up Cuba — unless you are prepared to accept responsibility." If the rebels won, the government would be dominated by "the negro element among the insurgents," who would "create renewed and even more bitter conflict of a racial kind."[20]

Cuba had been the first test of his courage and his sagacity. He had handled himself well under fire, inviting death near the firing line when, as a nonbelligerent, he might honorably have sought safety in the rear. His reportorial skills were already remarkable. On the other hand, he had failed to grasp the essential nature of guerrilla warfare, so important to an understanding of the century ahead. He had been, and in some respects always would be, a defender of the established order. *Imperialism* would never be a pejorative for him. Of the infamous Jameson Raid, which took place a week after his return from New York, he later wrote, "I was all for Dr. Jameson and his men. I understood fairly well the causes of the dispute on both sides. I longed for the day on which we should 'avenge Majuba.' I was shocked to see our Conservative Government act so timidly in this crisis. I was ashamed to see them truckling to a misguided Liberal Opposition and even punishing these brave raiders, many of whom I knew so well." His forecasts of Cuba's immediate future would soon be discredited. But in the long run his pessimism about the island would be vindicated. He had just reached his majority. He had been growing in acumen since his father's death, and was continually revising his judgments. Little more than a year after his return from embattled Cuba, he expressed misgivings over his first interpretation of the revolution there. "I reproach myself somewhat," he wrote, "for having written a little uncandidly and for having perhaps done injustice to the insurgents. I rather tried to make out, and in some measure succeeded in making out, a case for Spain. It was politic and did not expose me to the charge of being ungrateful to my hosts, but I am not quite clear whether it was right. . . . I am aware that what I wrote did not shake thrones or upheave empires — but the importance of principles do not [sic] depend on the importance of what involves them." One principle was clear. It was inconceivable to him that a colony could survive as a sovereign state. After the *Maine* blew up, he told a reporter that "America can give the Cubans peace, and perhaps prosperity will then return. American annexation is what we must all urge, but possibly we shall not have to urge long." To him the very thought of Cuban independence was as absurd as, say, an independent India.[21]

India now loomed. The Fourth Hussars marched from Aldershot to Hounslow, paraded past the retiring Brabazon for the last time, and began packing leisurely for the long voyage eastward in the autumn. Churchill later recalled: "I now passed a most agreeable six months; in fact they formed almost the only idle spell I have ever had." It was the year of Victoria's Diamond Jubilee; fashionable London celebrated with balls, receptions, recitals, and dinner parties. Jennie was back after nine months of dalliance on the Continent, including a marathon romp with Bourke Cockran in a Champs-Elysées apartment, and vexed only by pursuing, jealous little notes from the Prince of Wales, who typically speculated on "where your next loved victim is. . . ?" Winston had also missed her. "My darling Mamma," he had written her from Aldershot, "I am longing for the day when you will be able to have a little house of your own and when I can really feel that there is such a place as home." Now she had taken, not a little house, but a seven-story Georgian mansion at 35A Great Cumberland Place, near Hyde Park and within sight of Marble Arch, and using London's six-year-old "electric deep-level" subway, the precursor of the modern tube, he commuted between there and Waterloo, taking the train on to his barracks. Once Duchess Lily invited him to join a weekend party at Deepdene given for the prince. Colonel Brabazon would also be present. Churchill realized, he wrote, that "I must be upon my best behaviour: punctual, subdued, reserved, in short display all the qualities with which I am least endowed." Unforgivably, he missed the six o'clock train to Dorking. That delayed him by an hour and a quarter. In his railway compartment, he frantically changed to full dress — to the dismay of the man who shared it — and a servant, meeting him at the station with a brougham, lashed the horses into a gallop. Nevertheless, he was late. He hoped to slip into the dining room unnoticed and apologize afterward. Instead, he found the entire company assembled in the drawing room. Without him there were only thirteen in the party, and the royal family was superstitious about that. As Winston bowed, HRH said shirtily with his German accent: "Don't they teach you to be punctual in your regiment, Winston?" He glared at Brabazon, who glared at Winston, who was, for once, mute.[22]

It didn't last. Before the meal ended he was chatting amiably with the prince. Duchess Lily reproachfully called him incorrigible; he cheerfully acknowledged it. Among the other guests he had met Sir Bindon Blood, an influential veteran of colonial wars, so he counted the weekend a triumph. In his letters of those months one has the feeling that skies were always blue. He danced, he hunted, he devised clever masquerades for fancy-dress balls, and he evaded creditors. His means during this period are in fact mysterious. Messrs E. Tautz, breeches and trousers makers, were dunning him for nearly forty guineas. He now had "five quite good ponies" and owed payment for them. Wine bills, book bills, saddler's bills — they accumulated, were stuffed away and ignored. His attitude toward them was insouciant. He left a note for his mother: "Our finance is indeed involved! If I had not been so foolish as to pay a lot of bills I should have the money now."[23]

She wrote him tautly: "I assure you unless something extraordinary turns up I see ruin staring me in the face." Jennie was as improvident as Winston — she would spend £200 on a ball dress — but after he left she would be in London to face the consequences of his extravagance, and her alarm mounted. She borrowed from friends. She borrowed £17,000 from a bank, using her life insurance as collateral. She raised money on her jewels and juggled balances. Still the drain continued. She wrote: "My darling boy, you can't think how all this worries me. I have so many money problems of my own I feel I cannot take on any others"; and, "What an extraordinary boy you are as regards yr business affairs." Her annual income had fallen to £900, out of which she had to provide allowances for both her sons. She explained this to Winston, and he replied: "The situation as described by your letter is appalling. As you say it is of course impossible for you to live in London on such a pittance." Then he hinted unscrupulously: "I hate the idea of your marrying — but that of course would be a solution." It was indeed the eventual solution. Meanwhile, she made ends meet by taking over houses, redecorating them, and selling them for a profit. Winston remained indifferent to her struggle. Once one of his checks actually bounced. She told him: "I marvel at their allowing you to overdraw as you do. Neither the Westminster or the

National Bank will let me overdraw £5 without telling me at once." She sounded envious.[24]

He remitted thirty pounds of the forty-five she had paid on his account and vaguely assured her he would send the rest "when my ship comes home." He did not mean the ship to India. He had decided that he wanted to miss that one. The Fourth Hussars would be there nine years, and the more he thought about that, the less he liked it. The fact was that he wasn't really cut out to be a professional officer. His father's impression that he was, fragilely based on a boyhood infatuation with toy soldiers, had been whimsical. Winston was brave, and would distinguish himself in battle, but the long droughts of peacetime service could only frustrate him. He wanted to get on. Barracks life in the East would be dull, confining, dispiriting — Harrow all over again. England was the place to be; here he could find a constituency and run for office. Money would be necessary, of course, but he was an experienced journalist now; surely some newspaper would pay for his by-line. Crete was going through one of its periodic upheavals. He approached the *Daily Chronicle* with the suggestion that the paper send him there as its correspondent. The editor replied that they would pay him "at the rate of ten guineas a letter" if he got there on his own. He couldn't afford it. In Fleet Street he floated other proposals. He offered to cover the Nile expedition Kitchener was organizing, or Sir Frederick Carrington's expedition in Matabeleland, or the Ninth Lancers' adventures in Rhodesia. There were no takers. He urged relatives and powerful friends to intercede on his behalf. They failed, and Lord Lansdowne, the secretary of state for war, wrote Jennie that Winston's importuning was causing talk. His duty, Lansdowne said, lay with his regiment. There were rumors that he was trying to dodge it. "There are plenty of ill natured people about," Lansdowne wrote, "and it is just conceivable that an attempt might be made to misrepresent his action."[25]

Churchill was unchastened. By now it was August, and they would be sailing for Bombay in a month. He leaned on his mother. He leaned hard. Perhaps he sensed that she, ashamed of her early neglect of him, was vulnerable to pressure. Surely, he felt, one of her many contacts could solve his problem. Writing from Hounslow he begged her to find "places where I could gain experience and derive advantage — rather than to [sic] the tedious land of India." If he went he would be losing a "golden opportunity" and "guilty of an indolent folly that I shall regret all my life. A few months in South Africa would earn me the S.A. medal and in all probability the company's star. Thence hot foot to Egypt — to return with two more decorations in a year or two — and beat my sword into an iron despatch box." He turned the screw: "I cannot believe that with all the influential friends you possess and all those who would do something for me for my father's sake" something could not be done. It was "useless to preach the gospel of patience to me. Others as young are making the running now and what chance have I of ever catching up. I put it down here — definitely on paper — that you really ought to leave no stone unturned to help me at such a period." He begged her: "Three months leave is what I want & you could get it for me."[26]

She couldn't, or at any rate didn't; no reply from her survives. The army had been lenient with him, and what he was asking of her was probably impossible. Later she would move mountains for him, but he could not avoid India now. On September 11, 1896, he and a hundred other officers sailed from Southampton aboard the S.S. *Britannia.* Twelve days later, at Balmoral, Queen Victoria celebrated the sixtieth year of her reign. Churchill, who would do more to preserve and protect the Victorian legacy than any of her other subjects, was on the Red Sea, at midpoint in the twenty-three-day voyage. He played chess with a fellow officer that afternoon and listened to a string band that evening. His spirits were low. He wrote home: "The weather is beginning to get hot and the troop decks are awful." His only good news was that he had reached the semifinal of a shipboard chess tournament: "I have improved greatly since the voyage began, and I think I shall try to get really good while I am in India." But that was the limit of his expectations there. He had no inkling that India, far from dooming his future, would be the first crucial experience of his youth.[27]

In 1896 the British Raj had reached flood tide. It lay halfway between the Mutiny forty years earlier, which had seen the transfer of power from the Honourable East India Company to the Crown, and the great days of that improbable, bespectacled nationalist who wore only a homespun dhoti and was known as Mahatma Gandhi. In the interval English dominance over the subcontinent flourished. The Indian Empire was a jigsaw of 602 states, ranging in size from Kashmir and Hyderabad to tiny holdings of a few acres. All were ruled from London under the principle of "paramountcy." This was paternalism at best, and at worst, dictatorship, but the British argued, not unreasonably, that India had never been democratic, had never even been a country, and had always been governed by rajas, whose rights were respected by the Queen's viceroy. As Englishmen saw it, they had rescued the people from pagans and savagery and introduced them to a better way of life. This was not entirely hypocritical. At the time of the Mutiny they had founded three Indian universities. Qualified natives, though few in number, had been admitted to the Indian Civil Service since 1864. Irrigation, railroads, newspapers, and the concept of Western justice and its quaint trimmings had been introduced and accepted. Solicitors wore white collar-tabs, like lawyers in Lincoln's Inn; barristers wore wigs; judges wore imperial ermine. Hospitals, physicians, and public-health officials treated black and white patients alike.

Nevertheless, the Union Jack flew over all public buildings. Englishmen could, with impunity, strike natives who offended them. The pukka sahib and the burra sahib were masters to be respected and feared. By no means did all of them abuse their privileges. Those who came to love India, and they were many, treated its people with respect and civility. To them the Raj was a gigantic humming chromoscope providing endless, delightful, exotic sights and sounds: the sullen red glow growing in the bazaars and the little compounds crayoned with light at dawn, and equestrian statues of British generals staring blankly at the alien sunshine; the rhinestone eyes of plodding bullocks, and chuprassies fussing busily about in their gold-frogged *chamras,* and red *tikkas* on the foreheads of Brahmin women; dholl *banyas* beating their gongs and chewing blood-red pan supari; the fierce *dadu* wind blowing down the Himalayas and the contrasting hot puff of a sultry *loo* breeze; the fabrics of Mysore silk and Travancore coir and khuskhus screening from Bombay; the strumming of sitars, the quiet green maidans, the pye-dogs, the *ita'at* festivals of holy sadhus, the *did-you-do-it did-you-do-it* of lapwings perched on the branches of gigantic haldu trees, and the choruses of doves weeping piteously in scented foliage overhead, throbbing like a fever in the night. Britons who had found a home here ("Ah India, my country, my country," Kipling had scribbled in the middle of an essay) rejoiced in the land's eccentricities: the sacred elephants with their embroidered howdahs, the big fruit bats which flapped home at daybreak and hung upside down in trees by day; the fields of steaming white where dhobis' sheets lay drying; the native railway engineers who rode around seated beneath umbrellas on their little inspection trolleys; the paddle-wheelers of the Ganges; the "*kala* memsahibs," or black ladies, who could be just as arrogant as the most insensitive English mems; and the obscene carvings on the Nepalese temple of Benares, of which *Murray's Handbook* chastely observed, "visitors need not see them if the attendant is discouraged from pointing them out." Visits to rajas' palaces could be stunning; one might see strutting peacocks, figures of four-armed goddesses in marble courtyards, gardens of brilliant melon-flowers, displays of star rubies, Kashmir sapphires, and emeralds like eggs — visions of the ancient, merciless India of priceless jewels and slave girls. Performing scorpions were to be found in the streets. So were snake-charmers, and fakirs, and freak shows, and the indescribable scent of communal India, a complex compound of kerosene, burned ghee, rose, dung, and dahlia. Excitement could be found in just sitting on your veranda at teatime, sipping whiskey in the heat, your legs propped up on the long arms of your wicker chair, awaiting the first mango showers and watching the fading of daylight, so unlike the long blue twilights of England, when the sun plunged behind the Arabian Sea with dramatic swiftness, and darkness fell on the vast Hindustan plain before you could grope your way inside.

This was the India Kipling loved, but it was known to too few of the new arrivals of the 1890s. A majority of them ignored the magic of India, eschewed curry, tried to re-create English suburbs in their cantonments, and watched regimental cricket matches while bands played Gilbert and Sullivan airs. Among themselves they laughed heartily, slapped one another on the back, and called each other "old chap" while completely ignoring the Indians, or, as they called them, the "wogs."* They traveled like lords. Short distances were covered in horse-drawn tongas, in coolie-drawn rickshas, or in sedan chairs, where you sat on a *dholi*, a small stool suspended from poles carried on the shoulders of two natives. Long trips were by train, in coaches reserved for the English; at stations there were rest rooms for First Class Gents, even special ones for Officers. On Saturday evenings subalterns got drunk, played rugger for regimental trophies, and sobered up in the morning over mulligatawny soup — all without leaving the post to explore the mysteries beyond the gate. It was assumed that the greatest possible achievement of an Indian youth would be to be accepted by a British public school. Natives believed it, too. Jawaharlal Nehru, Gandhi's greatest protégé, became, and remained, a loyal Harrovian.

That did not, however, entitle him to enter a Raj club. It was said that the only difference between the Bengal Club and the Bombay Club was that one excluded Indians and dogs while the other admitted dogs. These were sahib bastions. A member sat at a little table, rang a silver bell with the reproduction of a cobra as a handle, and ordered a chota peg, a small whiskey, secure in the knowledge that no one of inferior blood could approach. Reading matter was all from home: *Punch, Country Life,* the

* Originally an acronym of Worthy Oriental Gentlemen.

Book of the Horse, The Times, Blackwood's Magazine, and, of course, the *Queen's Regulations, Hart's Army List,* and, later, *Jane's Fighting Ships.* In the clubs, members of the ascendant race planned war memorials, fountains, and statues honoring great Anglo-Indians. Memsahibs concentrated on converting hill stations — cooler because of their altitude, and therefore summer refuges — into a bit of the Mother Country. Naini Tal, Mussoorie, Ootacamund, and Darjeeling were popular hill stations, but the greatest was Simla, to which the viceroy and his court repaired when thermometers began to soar. Simla's English parks and its half-timbered cluttered homes, shrines of Victorian materialism, testified to the insularity of the Raj. There one could sit by evening fires, breathe deeply of moist, cool air, ride bridle paths, and pretend that the real India did not exist.

Architecture reflected the confusion of disparate cultures, no more so than in Bombay, the destination of the Fourth Hussars before they moved south to permanent quarters outside Bangalore in the Madras Presidency. Here, where Kipling was born nine years before Churchill, you could find Moslem and Hindu and Occidental architectural principles warring with one another in the Municipality, erected in 1893, and in the Victoria Terminus, the central train station, which Nicholas Wollaston called "pure imported ingenuity, a fantasy of spikes and pillars full of grime and purple gloom."[28] The Mint was Ionic. The Town Hall was Doric outside and Corinthian inside. The Old Secretariat was Venetian Gothic. The university library and clock tower, fourteenth-century Gothic, were the work of Sir Gilbert Scott, who had built the Albert Memorial. You couldn't miss the similarity; it was awesome. University Hall, fifteenth-century French Decorative, was named, appropriately, after Sir Cowasjee Jehangir Readymoney, an Indian who had met the standards of success recognized in the Victorian Midlands. The telegraph office was Romanesque; the High Court, Early English. Various monuments, in indescribable styles, saluted the military virtues, commerce, and equity. The identity of the designer of Bombay's Sassoon Dock has not survived, luckily for his reputation. It is a triumph of incompetence, so ill-suited to disembarkation that impatient immigrants often chose to come ashore in skiffs, a risky procedure which could cripple a man before he set foot on Indian soil.

It happened to Churchill. Let him tell it: "We came alongside of a great stone wall with dripping steps and iron rings for hand-holds. The boat rose and fell four or five feet with the surges. I put out my hand and grasped at a ring; but before I could get my feet on the steps the boat swung away, giving my right shoulder a sharp and peculiar wrench. I scrambled up all right, making a few remarks of a general character, mostly beginning with the earlier letters of the alphabet, hugged my shoulder and soon thought no more about it." He was reminded of it in Poona, where the regiment spent the night under double-fly tents and then tried out the polo ponies of the Poona Light Horse. On his mount he found he could not swing a polo stick unless his right arm was strapped to his side. He procured a leather harness. That would come and go, but tennis was out forever. Indeed, his injury was to plague him in various maddening ways all his life. His shoulder would go out at unexpected moments, while he was taking a book from a shelf, swimming, sleeping with his arm under a pillow, or slipping on a stairway. Once the capsule that held the joint together nearly tore loose during an expansive gesture in Parliament, and he thought "how astonished the members would have been to see the speaker to whom they were listening, suddenly for no reason throw himself upon the floor in an instinctive effort to take the strain and leverage off the displaced arm bone."[29]

But he reflected little then on what seemed a temporary disability. He was too caught up in the new life that lay before him. India, "that famous appanage of the Bwitish Cwown," as Brabazon had called it, overwhelmed him. He thought he might have landed on "a different planet." That first morning he acquired his staff, or, as he came to call it, his "Cabinet." All salaamed and presented recommendations from the homeward-bound regiment the Fourth Hussars was replacing. For a few pice he hired a dressing boy, who would be responsible for his uniform and clothing; a butler, who would manage his money; a syce, or groom, who would handle his ponies; various bearers; a wet sweeper; and, to be shared with two officers, two gardeners, three water carriers, four dhobis, and a watchman. "Princes," he wrote, "could live no better than we." That noon, after he had completed his only official task of the day — reprimanding troopers who weren't wearing their cork helmets in the beating heat — he and another subaltern were approached by a messenger in a red-and-gold frock coat carrying an envelope with a puissant crest. It was an invitation to dine with William Mansfield, Baron Sandhurst, governor of Bombay.* At the table Winston, cocky as ever, overrode his host and dominated the conversation. Afterward he put it charmingly: "There were indeed moments when he seemed willing to impart his own views; but I thought it would be ungracious to put him to so much trouble. He kindly sent his aide-de-camp with us to make sure we found our way back to camp all right. On the whole, after forty-eight

* Lady Sandhurst was a daughter of the fourth Earl Spencer, and thus great-great-great-great-grandmother of Lady Diana, who became Princess of Wales in 1981.

hours of intensive study, I formed a highly favourable opinion about India." Hugo Baring, the young officer who had accompanied him, told the tale to the regimental mess. Their comrades were amused but unsurprised. They had grown accustomed to the strutting, slim, freckle-faced, irrepressible youth so quick to resent a slight, but quicker to offer the hand of friendship. Their favorite word for him was, and would continue to be, *bumptious.* Repeatedly, and unsuccessfully, they had tried to put him in his place. Once, aboard the *Britannia,* they had shoved him, struggling, under a huge couch, and then piled themselves upon it, but while they were still sorting themselves out he crept from beneath, rumpled but crowing: "You can't keep me down like *that!*"[30]

Darkness still lay over Poona the following morning when the bugles sounded reveille, rousing them in time to catch the 5:10 for a thirty-six-hour, twenty-mile-per-hour trip aboard a typical troop train "where the 'eat," as Kipling wrote, "would make your bloomin' eyebrows crawl." But Bangalore, on the great triangular plateau of southern India, was worth the discomfort. It was a coveted station, three thousand feet above sea level. Days were fierce, but nights, except in the months preceding the annual monsoon flowering, were fresh and cool. The cantonment lay six miles from the city. Troops were housed in spacious, colonnaded barracks. Officers were paid a lodging allowance and left to find their own quarters. Churchill, Barnes, and Baring rented an enormous bungalow, a pink-and-white structure with a heavy tile roof supported by white plaster columns and broad verandas, the whole enlaced with purple bougainvillea and surrounded by two acres of gardens. He wrote his mother: "My writing table at which I now am — is covered with photographs and memories of those in England. The house is full of you — in every conceivable costume and style. My cigarette box that you brought me from Japan — my books — and the other Lares and Penates lie around and I quite feel at home — though 6,000 miles away."[31]

Days began just before dawn, when, he wrote, one was "awakened by a dusky figure with a clammy hand adroitly lifting one's chin and applying a gleaming razor to a lathered and defenceless throat."[32] Morning parade formed at 6:00 A.M. Mounted, they drilled and maneuvered for an hour and a half. Baths followed, and then breakfast. After that they were free until 5:00 P.M., the hour of polo. Despite his shoulder, he rode in every chukker, or playing period, he could find. As shadows crossed the field they broke up, bathed again, and dined at 8:30 P.M. to the strains of the regimental band. Subalterns fortunate enough to avoid being drafted for after-dinner whiskey by garrulous senior officers smoked and talked until 11:00 P.M. and lights out.

Every reveille found him ready for the new day. He was a keen soldier. His troop sergeant later recalled in the regimental history that "after a field day Mr Churchill would arrive at stables with rolls of foolscap and lots of lead pencils of all colours, and tackle me on the movements we had done at the exercise." Both sergeant and subaltern were detailed to attend a course on musketry; Churchill passed out first in the class. He was happy, at least in the beginning, to be ignorant of political crises and social gossip. Long afterward he would say: "If you liked to be waited on and relieved of home worries, India thirty years ago was perfection." He seldom gave money a thought. In addition to his lodging allowance, he was paid fourteen shillings a day, and three pounds a month to keep two horses. This, with his allowance from Jennie, constituted his income. Each month the paymaster handed him a string bag about the size of a turnip, filled with silver rupees. He immediately turned it over to his butler and forgot about it. This lofty disdain was irresponsible; his mother, her sister Clara, and several friends had just been defrauded of over £4,000 by an American confidence man. Jennie wrote, begging him to practice thrift. Instead, he lived beyond his means, borrowing from native moneylenders. He would recall: "Every officer was warned against these gentlemen. I found them most agreeable; very fat, very urbane, quite honest and mercilessly rapacious. All you had to do was to sign little bits of paper, and produce a polo pony as if by magic. The smiling financier rose to his feet, covered his face with his hands, replaced his slippers, and trotted off contentedly till that day three months."[33] Somehow Jennie managed to cover their debts. Her admirers were still many, and rich.

Romance first reared its violin-shaped head in Winston's life on November 3, 1896. He wrote home from Trimulgherry that he had just been introduced "to Miss Pamela Plowden — who lives here. I must say that she is the most beautiful girl I have ever seen — 'Bar none' as the Duchess Lily says. We are going to try and do the City of Hyderabad together — on an elephant." Pamela would be in and out of his life for years. Other girls did not attract him. Returning from a racecourse he reported that he had seen "a lot of horrid Anglo-Indian women" there, and that "nice people in India are few & far between. They are like oases in the desert. . . . I have lived the life of a recluse out here. The vulgar Anglo-Indians have commented on my not 'calling' as is the absurd custom of the country. . . . I know perhaps three people who are agreeable and I have no ambitions to extend my acquaintance." But there were other diversions. For a time he collected butterflies in the gardens around his bungalow — swallowtails, white admirals, purple emperors, and rare species. He sent home for nets, collecting boxes, pins, boards, and a killing tin. Barnes and Baring protested that he was turning the house into a taxidermist's shop. Then disaster struck. "My butterfly collection," he mournfully wrote Jack, "which included upwards of 65 different sorts, has been destroyed by the malevolence of a rat who crawled into the cabinet and devoured all the specimens." Undaunted, he cultivated roses: Maréchal Niel, La France, Gloire de Dijon — "over 50 different kinds of roses," he wrote his mother, adding, "if it would not worry you I would like you very much to send a few English seeds — Wallflowers, Stocks, Tulips etc."[34]

Winston's one great passion in those first months continued to be polo. His fellow officers shared it, and they concocted a plan. Never in the history of the Raj had a cavalry regiment from southern India won the Indian Empire's Regimental Cup. But the officers of the Fourth Hussars, pooling their resources, helped to break this precedent. Their scheme was to approach the Poona Light Horse. Because this regiment was permanently stationed in the country, the Poona sepoys, largely officered by Britons, had a clear advantage in securing the Arabian ponies so prized by polo players. Specifically, they had first choice of mounts arriving at the Byculla stables in Bombay, where Arab steeds were imported. During the Fourth Hussars' pause in Maharashtra, Churchill and his comrades had admired these animals. Now they bought an entire stud of twenty-five ponies from the Poona Light Horse. Ordinarily two or three years' practice was believed essential before a regiment could field a passable team, but six weeks after their landing they challenged the Nineteenth Hussars for the Golconda Cup in Hyderabad. Although the match was considered a joke — and the laughter grew when the crowd saw that one subaltern from Bangalore had to ride one-armed — it was preceded by customary ceremonies. The native army of the nizam of Hyderabad paraded in full dress. The British troops followed. Elephants hauling cannon raised their trunks in salute as they passed the reviewing stand. After tiffin the game began, and the lithe, darting Nineteenth Hussars, as expected, quickly scored three goals. They were held to that, however, while the Fourth Hussars, with the one-armed officer leading them, scored nine times, thus establishing a record, never broken, of a regiment's winning a major tournament within fifty days of landing in India. One of Churchill's contemporaries, Patrick Thompson, believed that if you wanted to understand him, you had to see him play polo. "He rides in the game," Thompson said, "like heavy cavalry getting into position for the assault. He trots about, keenly watchful, biding his time, a master of tactics and strategy. Abruptly he sees his chance, and he gathers his pony and charges in, neither deft nor graceful, but full of tearing physical energy — and skillful with it, too. He bears down opposition by the weight of his dash and strikes the ball. Did I say 'strikes'? He *slashes* the ball."[35]

Apart from polo, he had acquired a taste for horse racing, with himself as jockey. Duchess Lily had promised him a pony, and he had expected to find it waiting for him in Bombay. It wasn't there. He wrote Jennie of his disappointment. She was unsympathetic: "It may be dead for all I know, but if it is not I want you to promise me to sell it." She and the Prince of Wales had discussed it, "& he begged me to tell you that you ought not to race . . . it is next to impossible to race in India & keep clean hands." Winston bridled: "I do not at all want to sell it — and I cannot see that it is unwise of me to keep it. . . . Everyone out here possesses an animal of one sort or another which they race in the numerous local meetings. . . . Now I cannot believe that all who race — *on this small scale* — must necessarily soil their hands." He scoffed at HRH: "He always loves 'glittering generalities' and it is so easy to say, 'They are all cheats in India.' Such a statement is of course nonsense and I am sure you will not believe it." His mother shot back, "They all tell me that the racing in India is a very shifty unsatisfactory thing." He boldly retorted: "You should tell His Royal Highness, if he says anything further about racing in India, that I intend to be just as much an example to the Indian turf as he is to the English as far as fair play goes."[36] Anticlimax followed. The pony, which arrived in November, was a lemon. Riding it, he came in third three times, and, of course, even second place would have been unacceptable to him. But in London his second cousin, the Marquess of Londonderry, put him up for the Turf Club; Brabazon seconded the nomination, and he was in. Loyally he registered his father's old racing colors, chocolate and pink.

Comradeship, ease, butterflies, roses, horses — obviously his new life was enchanting. But a new hunger was growing within him. That appetite, and the means he took to satisfy it, marks the end of his youth and the incipient signs of his emergence as an exceptional man. The transformation began with early pangs of intellectual curiosity. He found that he had "a liking for words and for the feel of words fitting and falling into their places like pennies in the slot. I caught myself using a good many words the meaning of which I could not define precisely. I admired these words, but was afraid to use them for fear of being absurd." On the day his troopship left Southampton a friend had told him, "Christ's gospel was the last word in ethics." Churchill had been puzzled. What, he wondered, were ethics? Judging from the context, he assumed they meant the Public School Spirit, Playing the Game, honorable behavior, or patriotism. Then someone else remarked to him that ethics dealt, not merely with what you ought to do, but with why it ought to be done, and that there was a vast literature on the subject. He knew tactics, he had some grasp of politics, but "here in Bangalore there was no one to tell me about Ethics for love or money." Next he remembered his father's gibe about the Grand Remonstrance during the reign of Charles I. It occurred to him that his knowledge of history was limited and something ought to be done about it. He overheard a man using the phrase "the Socratic method." Churchill wondered who Socrates was, or had been. He made inquiries. They were unsatisfactory. He was told that Socrates was a contentious Greek, hounded by a nagging wife, who became so troublesome that he was forced to take his own life. But Winston knew there must have been more to it than that. More than twenty-three hundred years had passed since the Greek's death, and people were still arguing about it. "Such antagonisms," Churchill reasoned, "do not spring from petty issues. Evidently Socrates had called something into being long ago which was very explosive. Intellectual dynamite! A moral bomb! But there was nothing about it in *The Queen's Regulations.*"[37]

In the winter of 1896, as he approached his twenty-second birthday, he "resolved to read history, philosophy, economics, and things like that; and I wrote to my mother asking for such books as I had heard of on these topics." He began with Gibbon's eight-volume *Decline and Fall of the Roman Empire.* At Harrow his history text had been *The Student's Hume,* and he had found it dull. Now, "all through the glistening middle hours of the Indian day, from when we quitted stables till the evening shadows proclaimed the hour of Polo, I devoured Gibbon. I rode triumphantly through it . . . and enjoyed it all. I scribbled all my opinions on the margins of the pages." On January 14, 1897, we find him writing Jennie, "The eighth volume of Gibbon is still unread as I have been lured from its completion by [Winwood Reade's] *The Martyrdom of Man* & a fine translation of the Republic of Plato: both of which are fascinating." Then, remembering Woom's brother-in-law by the fire at Ventnor, he tackled twelve volumes of Macaulay. On March 17 he wrote, "I have completed Macaulay's History and very nearly finished his Essays." He thought that Macaulay "is easier reading than Gibbon and in quite a different style. Macaulay crisp and forcible, Gibbon stately and impressive.

Both are fascinating and show what a fine language English is since it can be pleasing in styles so different." He was covering "fifty pages of Macaulay and twenty-five of Gibbon every day. There are only 100 of the latter's 4,000 odd left now."[38]

The scope of his explorations was broadening — "I read three or four books at a time to avoid tedium" — and he was poring over Schopenhauer, Malthus, Darwin, Aristotle (on politics only), Henry Fawcett's *Political Economy,* William Lecky's *European Morals* and *Rise and Influence of Rationalism,* Pascal's *Provincial Letters,* Adam Smith's *Wealth of Nations,* Bartlett's *Familiar Quotations,* Liang's *Modern Science and Modern Thought,* Victor-Henri Rochefort's *Memoirs,* the memoirs of the Duc de Saint Simon, and Henry Hallam's *Constitutional History.* Incredibly, he asked his mother to send him all one hundred volumes of the *Annual Register,* the record of British public events founded by Burke. He explained that he wanted to know "the detailed Parliamentary history (Debates, Divisions, Parties, cliques & caves)* of the last 100 years." Jennie balked at the expense — fourteen shillings a volume — but she did send twenty-seven. In using them, he first set down his opinion of an issue, then studied the debates. By this practice he hoped "to build up a scaffolding of logical and consistent views which will perhaps tend to the creation of a logical and consistent mind. Of course the *Annual Register* is valuable only for its facts. A good knowledge of these would arm me with a sharp sword. Macaulay, Gibbon, Plato etc must train the muscles to wield that sword to the greatest effect."[39]

He was scrawling letters to Jennie, Jack, Welldon, and Cockran, rekindling issues which had fired Parliaments of the past but were now resolved or at least dormant. Disraeli's support for the popular election of Scottish clergymen won his approval; Gladstone's opposition to parliamentary reform, his disapproval. He thought Lord Northbrook right in banning the export of Indian grain during the famine of 1873–1874. He favored the Irish Coercion Laws, advocated the establishment of a criminal appeals court in England, came down hard on the side of slum clearance, death duties, compulsory vaccination, and capital punishment in public ("Justice in every form should not shrink from publicity"), and rejected the charge that newspapers fanned the flames of war — a curious inference from one who knew the role of Pulitzer's *World* and Hearst's *Journal* in Cuba. What sort of education, he asked rhetorically, could a pupil anticipate in a tax-supported school? "Reading and writing, the knowledge of sufficient arithmetic to enable the individual to keep his

* In British politics a cave is a group of MPs who quit their party. Here Churchill was anticipating himself.

accounts; the singing of patriotic songs and a gymnastic course is all that he may expect." Woman suffrage was ridiculous, "contrary to natural law and the practice of civilized states." Wives were "adequately represented by their husbands." Spinsters would back religious intolerance and "every kind of hysterical fad." Admit females to the polls and "all power passes to their hands." Indeed, "if you give women votes you must ultimately allow women to sit as members of Parliament." It was, he darkly prophesied, "only the thin end of the wedge."[40]

His autodidacticism precipitated a religious crisis. At Harrow he had attended daily prayers and Sunday services; in the army he participated in church parades. Until now he had never doubted their value. The anticipation of a hereafter, he had assumed, justifiably disciplined the lower classes and served as an incentive for middle-class morality. Indian sects were similarly useful, provided they did not degenerate into fanaticism. But the books he was now reading challenged the underpinning of everything he had learned since childhood. Gibbon, Reade, and Lecky convinced him that he had been gulled, and as a consequence he "passed through a violent and aggressive anti-religious phase which, had it lasted, might have made me a nuisance." This, of course, is a common experience among the self-educated. But Churchill's resolution of it was unusual. In moments of danger in Cuba and later, he instinctively recited prayers he had learned at Woom's knee. He survived. He asked for lesser gifts, "and nearly always in these years, and indeed throughout my life, I got what I wanted. This practice seemed perfectly natural, and just as real as the reasoning process which contradicted it so sharply." In a book of quotations he had read: "*Le coeur a ses raisons que la raison ne connaît point.*" Why, he asked himself, should he discard the reasons of the heart for those of the head? Why not enjoy both? He therefore adopted "quite early in life a system of believing whatever I wanted to believe, while at the same time leaving reason to pursue unfettered whatever paths she was capable of treading."[41]

"I have hardly looked at a novel," he wrote on March 31, 1897. He was sticking to tough reading and writing letters meshed with abstruse allusions. His brother officers wondered how he did it. The climate was punishing. This was the Raj in its heroic period, without air conditioning, refrigerators, or even electric fans. One thinks of Kipling in the Punjab only a few years earlier, sweating and scribbling under the same sun through long afternoons in his darkened bungalow, struggling to immortalize the age. Churchill was writing, too, but his was a genius of a different order, and he had not found his medium. He was writing his first book, and only novel, *Savrola,* though he had not yet settled on that title.

Once it had begun to take shape he wrote Jennie: "I think you will be surprised when you get the MS. It is far and away the best thing that I have ever done. I have only written 80 MS pages — but I find a fertility of ideas that surprises me. . . . It is called 'Affairs of State,' a political romance. Scene Plot a hypothetical Republic. . . . I am quite enthusiastic about it. All my philosophy is put into the mouth of the hero. But you must see for yourself. It is full of adventure."[42]

He added a postscript: "Do try to get me up to the war if you can possibly." He meant the imminent clashes along India's North-West Frontier, but it is clear from his correspondence that year that the prospect of fighting anywhere would have been welcome. The first flush of his enthusiasm for Bangalore had faded. He had become restless; his temperament cried for action. India had become "an abominable country to live long in. Comfort you get — company you miss. . . . There is every temptation to relapse into a purely animal state of existence." He and Baring had spent Christmas in Bengal, but he had concluded that "Calcutta is full of supremely uninteresting people endeavouring to assume an air of heartiness"; he was glad to have seen it only because "it will be unnecessary ever to see it again." Yearning for a stimulating environment, he wrote that if he could "only get hold of the right people my stay here might be of value. If I had come to India as an MP — however young & foolish, I could have had access to all who know and can convey. As a soldier . . . I vegetate." Without his books, he felt, he would stagnate. "The Indian press is despicable — being chiefly advertisements." All sorts of complaints crowded his letters now. "My face is blistered by the sun so badly that I have had to see a doctor," he wrote after one field exercise, and when he was appointed acting adjutant he had to write "so many memos etc that to touch a pen is an effort."[43]

His first chance to break free from this oppression came in the spring of 1897. The Greeks had sent a small expeditionary force to fight rebellious Turks on Crete. The British Mediterranean fleet, joining those of five other nations, was blockading the island to prevent the landing of Greek reinforcements. Churchill was indignant: "What an atrocious crime the Government have committed in Crete! That British warships should lead the way in protecting the blood bespattered Turkish soldiery from the struggles of their victims is horrible to contemplate." His mother disagreed: "The Concert of Europe were *obliged* to act as they did altho' they certainly were slow in making up their minds." He was unconvinced: "We are doing a very wicked thing in firing on the Cretan insurgents . . . so that she [Greece] cannot succour them." He saw the whole thing as a devious Salisbury plot to strengthen the Turks and thereby deny Constantinople to the Russians. He was right there, but wrong in an aside which, in the light of subsequent events, has a haunting ring: Salisbury's policy was "foolish because, as surely as night follows day — the Russians are bound to get Constantinople. We could never stop them even if we wished. Nor ought we to wish for anything that could impede the expulsion from Europe of the filthy Oriental."[44]

All this laid the groundwork for his letter to Jennie of April 21. "I am afraid you will regard this letter somewhat in the aspect of a bombshell," he began. He proposed to cover the Cretan fighting as a war correspondent, and he didn't care which side accepted his credentials. "Of course all my sympathies are entirely with the Greeks, but on the other hand the Turks are bound to win — are in enormous strength & will be on the offensive the whole time." It didn't matter, really; "if you can get me good letters to the Turks — to the Turks I will go. If to the Greeks — to the Greeks." He thought her close friend Sir Edgar Vincent "could probably do everything for me in Constantinople & could get me attached to some general's staff etc as in Cuba. On the other hand you know the King of Greece and could of course arrange matters in that quarter." Jennie, he was confident, could also find a newspaper which would hire him. He expected to be paid ten or fifteen pounds for each piece but would meet his own expenses, and he asked her to manage a loan — "Lord Rothschild would be the person to arrange this for me as he knows every one." His mother, he felt certain, would "not stand in my way in this matter but will facilitate my going just as you did in the case of Cuba." He misjudged her. In London she described his design to friends as "a wild scheme" and told Jack that the men she knew in the Foreign Office thought the war would end soon anyhow. This being true, his plan, far from being a bombshell, would end rather "like a damp firework," which is precisely what happened.[45]

He had been checked. But not mated. Considering the powerful men who had been enticed by his mother's beauty — the Prince of Wales, the Duke of Cambridge, Salisbury, Vincent, Sir Evelyn Wood, Kitchener, Lord Cromer, Sir Bindon Blood — Winston concluded that she could surely exploit at least one of her relationships to his advantage. He had no compunctions about twisting her arm, thereby persuading her to twist theirs. But he could not do it from six thousand miles away. Luckily he would soon be at her side. As the hot season of 1897 approached, the officers of the Fourth Hussars were offered what was called "three months' accumulated privilege leave" in England. Most declined on the ground that they had just settled in, but "I," Churchill would recall, "thought it was a pity that such good things should go a-begging, and I therefore volunteered to fill the gap." On May 8 he sailed from Bombay aboard the *Ganges.* The trip was an ordeal: "sweltering heat, rough weather and fearful seasickness." At Aden he was greeted by bitter news. The Greeks had sued for peace. His disappointment was shared by a fellow passenger, Colonel Ian Hamilton, a romantic who dreamed of Greece's past glories and would later encounter Churchill again and yet again, but Winston, unconsoled, left the ship when it reached Naples, dawdled in Pompeii, Rome, and Paris, and reached home only just in time to attend society's annual fancy-dress ball at Devonshire House in Piccadilly. Jennie went as Theodora. Of Winston we know only that he wore a sword. He had, he said, returned to enjoy "the gaieties of the London Season," but he had other matters on his mind.[46] War, any war, was one. Politics was another. After the ball he dropped into the St. Stephen's Chambers office of Fitzroy Stewart, secretary of the Conservative Central Office and a distant cousin, and told him he wanted to stand for Parliament as a Conservative.

No seats were vacant, Stewart explained, but he wrote Henry Skrine, the party's agent in Bath, asking: "Will you allow the late Lord Randolph Churchill's son, Mr Winston S. Churchill . . . to speak at your gathering on the 26th? He is very keen about politics and about the Primrose League and has told us he would like to address a few political meetings before rejoining his regiment. . . . He is a clever young man and his presence would no doubt be of some interest to the Bath Conservatives." Thus it was that Churchill delivered his first political address at Claverton Manor, now England's American Museum, in a park near Bath, in the high summer of 1897. Newspapers then devoted roughly the same space to politics that they give to sports today, and both the *Bath Daily Chronicle* and London's *Morning Post* ran full accounts of his performance. The speech was enthusiastically received — he was interrupted by cheers forty-one times — but that may have arisen in part from sympathy for his inexperience; he began by telling his audience that the timeworn "unaccustomed as I am to public speaking" should be pardoned in this instance, because this was, in fact, his maiden effort.[47]

Not much was happening in politics just now, he said, which was dull for the politicians but probably a relief to the people. Then he launched into a spirited defense of the Conservative party and an attack on its critics. Liberals were "always liberal with other people's money." Radicals — "the dried-up drain-pipe of Radicalism" — reminded him of "the man who, on being told that ventilation was an excellent thing, went and smashed every window in his house, and died of rheumatic fever." Conservative policy, on the other hand, was "a look-before-you-leap policy

. . . a policy of don't leap at all if there is a ladder." He praised the Tories' bill to compensate workers injured in industrial accidents, regretted a recent strike, and took the position, always popular with politicians courting the average voter, of damning both labor and capital. Ultimately, he believed, "the labourer will become, as it were, a shareholder in the business in which he works," though he hastily added that this solution would become practical only "in the distant future." The greatest achievement of the Conservatives, he said, had been teaching "the people of Great Britain the splendour of their Empire, the nature of their Constitution, and the importance of their fleet." This was the heart of his message, a paean to imperialism, and his peroration, throbbing with the rhythms of Gibbon, is both a tribute to his imperial faith and a demonstration of his beginning struggle toward eloquence:

> There are not wanting those who say that in this Jubilee year our Empire has reached the height of its glory and power, and that we now should begin to decline, as Babylon, Carthage, and Rome declined. Do not believe these croakers, but give the lie to their dismal croaking by showing by our actions that the vigour and vitality of our race is unimpaired and that our determination is to uphold the Empire that we have inherited from our fathers as Englishmen, that our flag shall fly high upon the sea, our voice be heard in the councils of Europe, our Sovereign supported by the love of her subjects, then shall we continue to pursue that course marked out for us by an all-wise hand and carry out our mission of bearing peace, civilisation, and good government to the uttermost ends of the earth.[48]

On the day that Churchill spoke in Bath, news reached England of a Pathan uprising in the Swat Valley, on India's North-West Frontier. This had been smoldering for some time, and was a direct consequence of Whitehall's policy in that harsh, craggy corner of Asia. The British, having conquered the plains of India, had paused at the foothills of the Himalayas and turned back to develop the lands they had taken. The mountains formed a natural barrier as definite, and as unbridgeable, as the English Channel. But in the northwest the peaks trailed off. There, in 1893, an Anglo-Afghan frontier had been demarcated; Britain intended to build Afghanistan up as a buffer between the Raj and the Russians, Asia's other great power. Meanwhile, they went about enrolling the tribesmen on their side of the frontier as subjects of the Queen. And there lay the rub. These clansmen — Pathans, Swatis, Waziris, Mahsuds, Afridis, Bunerwalis, Chitralis, and Gilgitis — had lived in remote independence since the dawn of time. Now bands of pale aliens were moving among them, building roads, putting up signs, establishing outposts and blockhouses. They were bewildered, then angry. They knew almost nothing of what was happening in the rest of the world, but now they were being informed, and misinformed, by a Moslem rabble-rouser whom the British called the Mad Fakir and Churchill later described as "a priest of great age and of peculiar holiness."[49] This mullah told the tribesmen of victories by their fellow Moslems — the Turks on Crete and the Mahdi in the Sudan — and spread wild tales. Turks had captured the Suez Canal, he said, explaining what it was, and he assured them that the British bullets could not harm men faithful to Mohammed, displaying as proof a small bruise on his leg which, he said, was the only consequence of a direct hit by an English cannonball. The viceregal staff in Calcutta was not unaware of this agitation. Word of it came to them through networks of — readers of *Kim* will have guessed — informers. Punitive expeditions were organized; reinforcements of Tommies were on their way from other parts of the Empire. London was particularly worried by the isolation of the Raj's key frontier fort, Chitral, far to the north, a miniature Gibraltar situated on an eminence commanding the great passes into Afghanistan. A Swati revolt threatened the British garrison holding the Malakand Pass and, specifically, a long wire-rope *jhula*, or swinging bridge, needed to provision Chitral. Whitehall reacted by announcing that a field force of three brigades would put down the uprising. It would be led by General Sir Bindon Blood.

Churchill was standing on the lawn at the Goodwood races, enjoying balmy weather and winning money, when the report of this decision buzzed through the crowd. He was electrified. On meeting Sir Bindon at Deepdene the year before he had extracted a promise that, should the general take the field again, Winston would join him. Churchill had three weeks of leave left, but he instantly wired Blood, reminding him of his pledge, and caught the next boat to India, the S.S. *Rome,* leaving behind, in his haste, a batch of new books, his polo sticks, his pet dog Peas, a Primrose League badge old Mr. Skrine had lent him in Bath, and, of course, a sheaf of bills. At each port of call he looked, in vain, for a reply from Blood. This P & O voyage was even worse than the last, particularly on the Red Sea: "The temperature is something like over 100 ° and as it is damp heat — it is equal to a great deal more. . . . It is like being in a vapour bath. The whole sea is steamy and there is not a breath of air — by night or day." Finally, at Bombay, a telegram from Upper Swat awaited him: "Very difficult. No vacancies. Come as correspondent. Will try to fit you in. B.B."[50]

A four-day detour to Bangalore was necessary; he needed his colonel's permission to join Blood. Newspaper credentials came next. Jennie tried *The Times,* without success, but the *Daily Telegraph* contracted to pay Winston five pounds a column, and in India the Allahabad *Pioneer,* which had published much of Kipling's early work, agreed to run a three-hundred-word telegram from him every day and pay accordingly. At the Bangalore train station he pushed a small sack of rupees across the counter and asked, out of curiosity, how far north his journey would take him. The ticket babu checked a timetable and told him 2,028 miles — a five-day trip through the worst of the summer heat. But there were compensations. He had bought a bag of books, and the first-class, leather-lined, heavily shuttered railway compartment carried a circular wheel of wet straw which the passenger could turn from time to time. Thus, he proceeded, as he put it, "in a dark padded moving cell, reading mostly by lamplight or by some jealously admitted ray of glare."[51] He broke his trip at Rawalpindi to visit a friend in the Fourth Dragoon Guards. The dragoons were preparing to be sent to the front; officers expected the order to grind their swords any day. That evening he joined a sing-along in the sergeants' mess. Long afterward he would remember roaring out:

And England asks the question
When danger's nigh
Will the sons of India do or die?

And:

Great White Mother, far across the sea,
Ruler of the Empire may she ever be.
Long may she reign, glorious and free,
In the Great White Motherland!

A photograph of Churchill taken at the time shows him faultlessly turned out in the romantic uniform of that period: spurred cavalry boots, whipcord jodhpurs, and military tunic with choker collar, Sam Browne belt, and the swooping khaki topee which will forever be identified with Victorian colonial wars. Wearing it, with a Wolseley valise for paper and pencils slung over his shoulder, he stood on the platform at Nowshera, the railhead of Blood's Malakand Field Force, and arranged for transportation for the last leg of his journey: forty miles across a scorching plain and then up the steep, winding ascent to Malakand Pass, the general's headquarters. Upon arrival Winston learned that Blood himself was off with a flying column, putting down a local mutiny by the Bunerwal tribe. Yellow with dust, Churchill was provided with a tent, a place in the staff mess, and a tumbler of whiskey. He took this last only to be polite. He had long enjoyed the taste of wine and brandy, but until this moment the smoky taste of whiskey had turned his stomach. Here, however, he faced a choice of tepid water, tepid water with lime juice, and tepid water with whiskey. As he put it, he "grasped the larger hope." In the five days Blood was away he conquered his aversion. "Nor was this a momentary acquirement," he later wrote. "Once one got the knack of it, the very repulsion of the flavour developed an attraction of its own. . . . I have never shrunk when occasion warranted it from the main basic refreshment of the white officer in the East." Thus fortified, he contemplated his immediate future. He cherished few illusions about warfare; he had, after all, come under fire in Cuba. Aboard the train to Nowshera he had warned his mother that danger lay ahead for him. Nevertheless, "I view every possibility with composure. It might not have been worth my while, who am really no soldier, to risk so many fair chances on a war which can only help me directly in a profession I mean to discard." That, at least, was settled. "But I have considered everything and I feel that the fact of having seen service with British troops while still a young man must give me more weight politically — must add to my claims to be listened to and may perhaps improve my prospects of gaining popularity with the country." Now he wrote her again, more somberly: "By the time this reaches you everything will be over so that I do not mind writing about it. I have faith in my star — that is that I am intended to do something in the world. If I am mistaken — what does it matter? My life has been a pleasant one and though I should regret to leave it — it would be a regret that perhaps I should never know."[52]

General Blood returned, magnificently erect on his charger, mustache bristling, snorting with triumph. The Bunerwalis were vanquished. Moreover, during his absence the Eleventh Bengal Lancers and the Guides Cavalry had driven the Swatis from Chakdara and chased the tribesmen up and down the valley. Everyone was ready for more action. Several officers had been killed in local skirmishes, and their effects, in accordance with Anglo-Indian campaigning custom, had been auctioned off. Winston had bought two horses, hired a groom, and acquired a kit. He was now fully equipped. In the morning Blood welcomed him, motioned him to his side, and then led an expedition of twelve thousand men

Lieutenant Winston Churchill in India

and four thousand animals over the bridge, into the valleys where lurking tribesmen, armed with long rifles, lay in wait. In describing the enemy's practice of hiding in the hills and firing down at the moving British column, Churchill introduced his readers to a new word. Such a rifleman, he wrote, was "a 'sniper,' as they are called in the Anglo-Indian army."[53]

While pursuing tribesmen, the Malakand Field Force also carried out punitive missions: destroying crops, driving off cattle, putting huts to the torch. The Pathans were a pitiless foe, but the British perpetrated atrocities, too. Winston wrote Reggie Barnes in Bangalore: "After today we begin to burn villages. Every one. And all who resist will be killed without quarter. The [tribesmen] need a lesson — and there is no doubt we are a very cruel people. At Malakand the Sikhs put a wounded man into the cinerator & burnt him alive. This was hushed up. However I will tell you more stories — some queer ones I have heard too — when we meet." He wrote his mother: "The danger & difficulty of attacking these active — fierce hill men is extreme. They can get up the hills twice as fast as we can — and shoot wonderfully well. . . . It is a war without quarter. They kill and mutilate everyone they catch and we do not hesitate to finish their wounded off. I have seen several things wh. have not been very pretty since I have been up here — but as you will believe I have not soiled my hands with any dirty work — though I recognise the necessity of some things." Long afterward he recalled that "it was all very exciting and, for those who did not get killed or hurt, very jolly." His newspaper dispatches do not reflect this. Even less so do his letters. He was ill. It cannot have been pleasant to remain on the line at Inayat Kila with a 103-degree fever. "Here I am," he wrote miserably, "lying in a hole — dug two feet deep in the ground — to protect me against the night firing — on a mackintosh with an awful headache — and the tent & my temperature getting hotter every moment as the sun climbs higher and higher."[54]

Most war correspondents hover around headquarters, writing dispatches based on communiqués; in World War II they reported the fighting on the island of Okinawa, in the Pacific, while sitting at typewriters on Guam, fourteen hundred miles away. Churchill went into the field. Indeed, as Sir Bindon's officers fell, he found himself leading troops. At one point he commanded a company of the Thirty-first Punjab Infantry, sepoys whose language he didn't even speak. (He learned two words, *maro* ["kill"] and *chalo* ["get on"], and introduced them to an English one, "Tallyho!") There can be no doubt that he was remarkably brave, at times even rash. After closing within forty yards of the enemy he wrote, "I felt no excitement and very little fear." Like Nelson, he freely admitted that he was chiefly driven, not by patriotism, but by ambition. He wrote Jennie: "I rode on my grey pony all along the skirmish line where everyone else was lying down in cover. Foolish perhaps but I play for high stakes and given an audience there is no act too daring or too noble. Without the gallery things are different." This, he was convinced, was advancing him another step toward the House of Commons. "I shall get a medal and perhaps a couple of clasps," he wrote at one point, and, at another, "I should like to come back and wear my medals at some big dinner or some other function." The awful thought crossed his mind that no medal might be struck for this expedition. He told Jennie, "Here out of one brigade we have lost in a fortnight 245 killed and wounded and nearly 25 officers," suggested a comparison with "actions like Firket in Egypt — wh are cracked up as great battles and wh are commemorated by clasps & medals etc etc," and concluded, "I hope you will talk about this to the Prince and others." But apart from its political value, physical courage had an intrinsic value in his eyes, and the lack of it was shameful. To his "intense mortification" he saw men of the Royal West Kents "run and leave their officer on the ground." He added: "I know the Buffs wd never have done this." Despite the heavy casualties, when he thought of "what the Empire might have lost I am relieved."[55]

He wrote Reggie: "It is bloody hot." You could "lift the heat with your hands, it sat on your shoulders like a knapsack, it rested on your head like a nightmare." The worst scorcher was Thursday, September 16. It also saw the heaviest fighting — "16th was biggest thing in India since Afgan [sic] war," he wrote his mother. Judging from his letters and dispatches, it was a harrowing day for him. On its eve Sir Bindon ordered Brigadier Patrick Jeffreys, commanding his Second Brigade, to enter the Mamund Valley, a cul-de-sac, and clear it out. Swinging around in his saddle, the general told Churchill, "If you want to see a fight, you may ride back and join Jeffreys." A troop of Bengal Lancers was headed that way, so Winston mounted and accompanied them as they gingerly picked their way through the ten miles of broken ground between the general's camp and the brigadier's. They reached Jeffreys at dusk. "All night long the bullets flew across the camp; but everyone now had good holes to lie in, and the horses and mules were protected to a large extent."[56]

At the instant of dawn the entire brigade, preceded by a squadron of lancers, moved in warlike formation into the valley, Lee-Enfields at the ready. The Mamund basin widened as they entered it, and when they fanned out in three separate detachments, Churchill chose to ride with the center column. As they advanced not an enemy shot was fired. The slopes above were silent, watchful. But the natives were there. Approaching the far end of the valley, Churchill raised his field glasses and saw "a numerous force of tribesmen on the terraced hillsides . . . they appeared seated in long lines, each with his weapon upright beside him. . . . The sun threw back at intervals bright flashes of steel as the tribesmen waved their swords." At 7:30 A.M. the lancers, trotting a hundred yards forward, opened fire with their carbines. Martini-Henrys immediately replied. Churchill wrote: "From behind rocks and slopes of ground, on spurs, and from stone houses, little puffs of smoke darted. A brisk skirmish began." He accompanied about fifteen men around him who rode up, dismounted, and opened fire at seven hundred yards. They, too, came under fire. Then the British infantry, the bulk of Jeffreys's brigade, toiled up and reached them. The Thirty-fifth Sikhs split into small parties and attacked various hills, hummocks, and a village. Churchill picked the one heading for the village. Enemy fire died away; they reached their objective without incident. But once there, he looked back and saw no brigade. He searched the valley with his glasses. Jeffreys's force had simply disappeared. Although he did not realize it then, they were in fact enveloped in folds of the vast terrain. He and his people were equally invisible to the brigade; geography was the Pathans' great ally. It occurred to Winston that his was a very small troop: five officers, including him, and eighty-five Sikhs. He recalled Sandhurst warnings about "dispersion of forces," and was grateful when the company commander relayed word from a lieutenant colonel down below to withdraw because "we are rather up in the air here." Churchill noted on his pad that this was "a sound observation." Then the officer said: "You stay here and cover our retirement till we take up a fresh position on that knoll below the village."[57]

Winston's small rear guard waited uneasily for ten minutes. They were about to depart when the mountain above them sprang to life. Sabers flashed, gun muzzles erupted, bright flags appeared, and figures dressed in white and blue began dropping down from ledges hundreds of feet overhead, shrieking, "Yi! Yi! Yi!" A group of Pathans began to assemble in a clump of rocks about a hundred yards from Churchill, and as they fired, Winston, borrowing the rifle of a Sikh, squeezed off answering shots while the Sikh handed him cartridges. This continued for five minutes; then the battalion adjutant scrambled up and panted: "Come on back now. There is no time to lose. We can cover you from the knoll." Churchill pocketed his ammunition — it was a standing order to let no bullets fall into the hands of the tribesmen — and was about to leave when an enemy fusillade killed the man beside him and hit five others, one of whom "was spinning around just behind me, his face a mass of blood, his right eye cut out." Recovering wounded was a point of honor; torture was the lot of those who fell into the hands of the Pathans. Carrying their casualties, they were halfway down the slope when a force of thirty tribesmen charged them. Chaos followed. More Sikhs fell. The adjutant was hit; Churchill stayed behind to rescue him, but a Pathan swordsman, getting there first, butchered the dying officer. At this point Winston remembered that he had won the public-school fencing championship. He drew his cavalry saber. "I resolved on personal combat *à l'arme blanche.*" But he was all alone, and other clansmen were hurrying up. These were not public-school boys. "I changed my mind about cold steel." Instead, "I fired nine shots from my revolver" and leapt down the hill, gratefully finding refuge with the Sikhs on the knoll nearest the plain.[58]

But they were being outflanked. And they were demoralized. As Winston wrote his "Uncle Bill," Lord William Beresford, a winner of the Victoria Cross, "The men were completely out of hand. The wounded were left to be cut up. We could do nothing. . . . Of course I had no legal status but the urgency was such that I felt bound to see the affair out. . . . Martini rifles at 80 yards make excellent practice and there were lots of bullets. At last we got to the bottom in great disorder, dragging some wounded with us, and the men loosing off wildly in all directions — utterly out of hand with a crowd of Ghazis at our heels." During the descent, he himself got off thirty or forty shots ("I am sure I never fired without taking aim") before they joined the battalion. There the lieutenant colonel drew them up two deep, shoulder to shoulder, while hundreds of firing Pathans, "frenzied with excitement," streamed around their flanks. In that formation the Sikhs presented a tremendous target, but anything was preferable to scattering. British officers shouted above the din: "Volley firing. Ready. Present. Fire!" Tribesmen were toppling, but their numbers were overwhelming. The lieutenant colonel told Churchill: "The Buffs are not more than half a mile away. Go and tell them to hurry or we shall all be wiped out." Winston was turning away when he had a vision of himself as the sole, fleeing survivor of a massacre. That was *not* the way to Parliament. He turned back and said, "I must have the order in writing, sir." Startled, the commander fumbled in his tunic and began to write. Then they heard the distant notes of a bugler sounding the Charge. "Everyone shouted. The crisis was over, and here, Praise be to God, were the leading files of the Buffs."[59]

His ranks swollen, the lieutenant colonel ordered a counterattack to recover the wounded, the adjutant's body, and his own prestige. They retook the knoll (all the wounded had been slain and mutilated) but not till 5:00 P.M. Then they fell back. In the confusion Winston had lost his mount, "but I borrowed a mule — I was too blown to walk and rode up again. We were attacked coming down but the Buffs were steady as rocks and hence lost very little." Meanwhile, another company of Sikhs, on their right, had been driven to the plain with even heavier casualties. "Well then we found the [brigadier Jeffreys] had split up his force and that odd companies were cut off and being cut up etc and it got pitch dark and poured with rain." It had been a calamitous day, and it wasn't over. Winston had been in action for thirteen hours, but before he could fall asleep he heard the boom of a fieldpiece three miles away, followed by twenty more booms, followed by silence. It had to be Jeffreys; he had the only battery in the valley. But why should his cannon be fired at night? There was only one explanation — he, his staff, his sappers, and miscellaneous headquarters personnel must be fighting at very close quarters. The battalion officers, including Churchill, conferred. Sending a rescue party in the dark would be an invitation to disaster. The brigadier and those with him must fight it out where they were with what they had. At daybreak a squadron of lancers galloped across the open pan of the valley and found them dug in around the battery. They had taken heavy casualties in hand-to-hand fighting. Jeffreys himself had been wounded in the head, though not seriously; he reported by heliograph to Sir Bindon Blood. Sir Bindon and the brigade with him had also been heavily engaged. Blood ordered that the valley be laid waste. "So long as the villages were in the plain, this was quite easy," Winston wrote. "The tribesmen sat on the mountains and sullenly watched the destruction of their homes and means of livelihood. When however we had to attack the villages on the sides of the mountains they resisted fiercely, and we lost for every village two or three British officers and fifteen or twenty native soldiers." He commented dryly: "Whether it was worth it, I cannot tell. At any rate, at the end of a fortnight the valley was a desert, and honour was satisfied."[60]

He saw action again with Jeffreys's brigade at Domodoloh, with the Buffs at Zagia, with the Mohmands in a minor engagement, and, after Sir Bindon had succeeded in getting his leave from the Fourth Hussars extended for two more weeks, at Agrah and then with the Thirty-first Punjab Infantry. Twice more he rode his gray pony along skirmish lines. Jeffreys mentioned him in dispatches, praising "the courage and resolution of Lieutenant W. L. S. Churchill, 4th Hussars, the correspondent of the *Pioneer* newspaper with the force who made himself useful at a critical moment," and Sir Bindon wrote Brabazon predicting that Winston "if he gets a chance will have the VC or a DSO." He received neither, partly because his reports were creating considerable discomfort at the highest levels of the Indian army in Simla. In a cable from Nowshera he had commented that "the power of the Lee-Metford rifle with the new dum-dum bullet — as it is called, though officially, the 'ek dum' bullet — is tremendous," a fact Simla would have preferred not to see in print. And he grew increasingly free with his criticisms of the British military establishment, condemning the manner in which sympathetic civilians were put in jeopardy, the failure to cover retreating soldiers with continuous fire, the "short service" system of recruitment, and the lack of proper rations for soldiers on long marches. Defiant of the wrath he knew this would arouse, he wrote: "There will not be wanting those who will remind me that in this matter my opinion finds no support in age or experience. To such I shall reply that if what is written is false or foolish, neither age nor experience should fortify it; and if it is true, it needs no such support."[61]

On October 12 he wrote his mother "one line to let you know that I am across the frontier and rejoining my regiment," and nine days later he followed this with news that "once again I write to you from my old table and my own room here in Bangalore." His first impression, when he leafed through back copies of the *Daily Telegraph,* was that his vivid reporting had been wasted in England. His stories had carried the anonymous by-line, "From a Young Officer." A letter from Jennie explained that the editor had "begged me not to sign yr name. He said it was very unusual & might get you into trouble." Winston indignantly replied: "I will not conceal my disappointment at their not being signed. I had written them with the design, a design which took form as the correspondence advanced, of bringing my personality before the electorate." He believed that "if I am to do anything in the world, you will have to make up your mind to publicity and also to my doing unusual things. Of course a certain number of people will be offended. I am afraid some people like Brab will disapprove. . . . But I recognise the fact that certain elements must always be hostile and I am determined not to allow them to interfere with my actions. I regard an excellent opportunity of bringing my name before the country in a correct and attractive light — by means of graphic & forcible letters, as lost."[62]

It was not lost. Jennie was more experienced in these matters than her son, and she had seen that everyone who mattered, from the Prince of Wales down, learned the identity of the Young Officer writing in the distant passes and gorges of the North-West Frontier. They even knew at Harrow. Welldon wrote her: "I have been much interested in seeing Winston's articles. I think he possesses in a high degree the special correspondent's art of seizing the picturesque and interesting features of a campaign. Really he is very clever, and must make a mark in the world." Voyages to India took over three weeks, and it was November before Churchill realized how deep an impression he had made. "I am very gratified to hear that my follies have not been altogether unnoticed," he wrote. His flair for the language was responsible, but he persisted in his belief that his valor, implicit in the pieces, would count far more among the Tory elders. He told his brother: "Being in many ways a coward — particularly at school — there is no ambition I cherish so keenly as to gain a reputation of personal courage."*[63]

Despite his daring and acclaim, Winston's standing in the army was not enhanced by all this. Generals were not alone in their disapproval. In the Fourth Hussars his brother officers were civil but cool. There was a vague feeling that what he had done was, by Victorian standards, "un-

* To the end of his life Churchill would believe that men who had performed well in combat held a great political advantage. In 1945 he urged Conservative friends to campaign in uniform and persuaded holders of the Victoria Cross and the Distinguished Service Order to stand for office. According to his son, Randolph, those who wore uniforms and won were convinced that it had made no difference. The heroes, almost without exception, were rejected at the polls.

gentlemanly." Regimental messes elsewhere put him down as a "medal-hunter," "self-advertiser," and "thruster." One officer would note in his memoirs that Churchill "was widely regarded in the Army as super-precocious, indeed by some as insufferably bumptious." Why, it was asked, should a subaltern praise or deprecate his seniors? Why should he write for newspapers while wearing the uniform? How did he get so much leave? Who was indulging him? The resentment was real, and became an obstacle to his plans. Sir Bindon asked that he be made his orderly officer. The adjutant general in Simla refused. Surely, Churchill thought, Lord Roberts could clear this up. The omnipotent Roberts, now in Ireland, had been a friend of his father's, and now Jennie, at his urging, wrote the field marshal, reminding him of past favors. But the old man declined to intervene. Churchill wrote bitterly: "I don't understand Lord Roberts' refusal. A good instance of ingratitude in a fortunate and much overrated man." Spurred by his mother, the *Daily Telegraph* appointed him a permanent correspondent, but the high command continued to deny him access to all battlefields. He complained to her: "The Simla authorities have been very disagreeable to me. They did all they could to get me sent down to my regiment. . . . I . . . invite you to consider what a contemptible position it is for high military officers to assume — to devote so much time and energy to harrying an insignificant subaltern. It is indeed a vivid object lesson in the petty social intrigue that makes or prevents appointments in this country." He added: "Talk to the prince about it." She did. Ian Hamilton also got busy, and finally, the morning after a polo match in Meerut, Churchill was gazetted to the staff of Sir William Lockhart. Sir William was organizing a punitive expedition into the Tirah, where the Afridi and Orzkzai tribes had risen. "Red tabs sprouted on the lapels of my coat," Winston wrote. For once, "I behaved and was treated as befitted my youth and subordinate station. I sat silent at meals or only rarely asked a tactful question." It was all for nothing. The tribesmen begged for peace; the expedition was abandoned; he boarded a train for the long ride back to Bangalore.[64]

Calling him a "publicity hound" — another epithet heard in the messes — seemed cruel. It was not, however, inaccurate. His correspondence admits of no other explanation. He had no interest in a military career, and meant to use the service to advance his prospects in public life. Peace having broken out on the frontier, he returned to his pen. He had several projects in mind: finishing his novel, writing a biography of Garibaldi, a "short & dramatic" history of the American Civil War, and a volume of short stories to be called, obscurely, "The Correspondent of the *New York Examiner.*" He wanted recognition, but he also expected to be paid. The *Telegraph* had sent him five pounds an article, and he felt that wasn't enough. "The pinch of the whole matter is we are damned poor," he wrote his mother. He sent her a short story "wh I want you to sell, signed, to one of the magazines. I think the *Pall Mall* wd like it & would pay my price. You should not get less than £20 for it, as it is a very good story — in my opinion. So don't sell it without a good offer." Financial relief was on its way, however. His first major effort to reach the British public was, in fact, ready: an account of his frontier adventures with Sir Bindon Blood, largely a paste-up of his frontier dispatches. This has become a common journalistic practice today, but he became one of its pioneers with *The Story of the Malakand Field Force.* Working five hours a day, he had dashed off a draft in two months before his posting to Sir William in Peshawar, where, he confessed, it had occupied his thoughts "more than . . . anything else." He had "affected the style of Macaulay and Gibbon, the staccato antitheses of the former and the rolling sentences and genitival endings of the latter; and I stuck in a bit of my own from time to time." Later he would say that writing a book "is an adventure. To begin with it is a toy and an amusement. Then it becomes a mistress, then it becomes a master, then it becomes a tyrant. The last phase is that just as you are about to be reconciled to your servitude, you kill the monster and fling him to the public." This monster was almost ready to be flung on December 22, 1897, when he wrote his mother: "I hope you will like it. I am pleased with it chiefly because I have discovered a great power of application which I did not think I possessed." Nine days later he mailed her the manuscript — "Herewith the book" — accompanied by maps and, for the frontispiece, a photograph of Sir Bindon Blood.[65]

There were details, as there always are, to be cleared up before publication. Quotations had to be verified; some sentences were awkward; here and there he had repeated himself. But "I don't want anything modified or toned down in any way. I will stand or fall by what I have written." Revisions and proofreading, he decided, would be entrusted to his uncle Moreton, who, on the frail strength of a monograph on bimetallism, was the only member of the family with literary pretensions. Churchill told his mother that he thought he ought to get at least £300 for the first edition, with royalties, "but if the book hits the mark I might get much more." There was one problem. Another author was writing a book on the same subject. That called for haste: "Do not I beg you lose one single day in taking the MS to some publisher. [Lord] Fincastle's book may for all I know be ready now." On reflection he decided to "recommend Moreton's treating with the publishers, it is so much easier for a man." Here he misjudged both uncle and mother. The first edition, to Winston's horror, would contain some two hundred misprints. "A mad printer's reader," one reviewer would write, and Winston would add sadly, "As far as Moreton is concerned, I now understand why his life has been a failure in the city and elsewhere." Jennie, on the other hand, had very sensibly gone to Arthur Balfour, who had referred her to A. P. Watt, the literary agent. Watt negotiated the terms with Longmans. *Malakand,* appearing in March 1898, sold eighty-five hundred copies in nine months. It was priced at six shillings; the royalty was 15 percent. Winston had earned more in a few weeks (£382) than he could in four years as a subaltern.[66]

But far more welcome was the book's enthusiastic reception. Moreton's disgraceful performance did not pass unnoticed: the *Athenaeum* observed that "one word is printed for another, words are defaced by shameful blunders, and sentence after sentence ruined by the punctuation of an idiot or of a school-boy in the lowest form." But the same reviewer predicted that the author might become as great a soldier as the first Marlborough and "a straighter politician." The *Pioneer* found "a wisdom and comprehension far beyond his years." The *Spectator* agreed. It was hailed as a minor classic, the debut of an exciting new talent, and, in the *Times of India,* the *Madras Mail,* and Delhi's *Morning Post,* a penetrating study of Raj policy. Churchill's response to all this is curiously moving. He was "filled with pride and pleasure. . . . I had never been praised before. The only comments which had ever been made upon my work at school had been 'Indifferent,' 'Slovenly,' 'Bad,' 'Very bad,' etc. Now here was the great world with its leading literary newspapers and vigilant erudite critics, writing whole columns of praise!"[67]

The Prince of Wales read *Malakand,* sent a copy to his sister, the Empress Dowager Victoria of Germany, and wrote "My dear Winston" on April 22: "I cannot resist writing a few lines to congratulate you on the success of your book! I have read it with the greatest possible interest and I think the descriptions and the language generally excellent. Everybody is reading it, and I only hear it spoken of with praise." HRH thought Churchill probably wanted to see more combat, and he approved: "You have plenty of time before you, and should certainly stick to the Army before adding MP to your name." He had, of course, misread the author. Winston wanted to be where the fighting was thickest, but as a correspondent, not as a junior officer. He had vowed to "free myself from all discipline and authority, and set up in perfect independence in England with nobody to give me orders or arouse me by bell or trumpet." Besides, the struggle on the Indian frontier was over. Everyone knew that the next excitement would be in Africa. Sir Herbert Kitchener's campaign to reconquer the Sudan had begun two years earlier; he had been moving slowly, building a railroad as he went, but now in April 1898 his major victory over sixteen thousand dervishes on the Atbara River signaled the beginning of the end. Churchill longed to be at his side. Once more he implored his mother to yank strings. "You must work Egypt for me," he told her. "You have so many lines of attack. . . . Now I beg you — have no scruples but worry right and left and take no refusal." He wanted her to "stimulate the Prince into writing to Kitchener." Two months later he wrote: "Oh how I wish I could work you up over Egypt! I know you could do it with all your influence — and all the people you know. It is a pushing age and we must shove with the best."[68]

Unfortunately Kitchener, at that time, detested Churchill. He had been outraged by his book; it was bad for discipline, he believed, for subalterns to chide their superiors. In any event, he felt that Winston already had had a good run for his money in India; the Nile was out of bounds for him. "It was," Churchill later said, "a case of dislike before first sight." Jennie and her influential friend Mary, Lady Jeune, were wining and cajoling everyone in the War Office — Winston later said that they "left no wire unpulled, no stone unturned, no cutlet uncooked" — but while guests were susceptible to petticoat diplomacy, Kitchener, as Egyptian commander in chief, or Sirdar, had the final say, and in Winston's case he said it over and over. It was *no.* Lady Jeune wired him: "Hope you will take Churchill. Guarantee he wont write." She couldn't guarantee it, and the Sirdar knew it. Sir Evelyn Wood, the adjutant general and an admirer of Lady Jeune's, was recruited to the Churchill cause. Lady Jeune and Jennie lunched with Wood and the Prince of Wales, and Wood then cabled the Sirdar: "Personage asked me personally desires you take Churchill." Kitchener was adamant: "Do not want Churchill as no room." Jennie knew Kitchener, of course; she knew everyone. Winston asked her to write him directly: "Strike while the iron is hot and the ink wet." She did, and he replied with elaborate courtesy. He had too many officers as it was, he was overwhelmed with applications from men more qualified than her son, but if at some future time an opportunity arose he would be pleased, et cetera, et cetera. Really challenged now, she decided to go to Egypt herself. Winston wrote: "I hope you may be successful. I feel almost certain you will. Your wit & tact & beauty — should overcome all obstacles." They didn't. Setting up headquarters in Cairo's Continental Hotel with her current lover, Major Caryl John Ramsden, she bombarded the Sirdar with letters. The best reply she got was: "I have noted your son's

Jennie in her prime

name and I hope I may be able to employ him later in the Sudan." All Jennie had to show for her pains was humiliation, from Kitchener and then, unexpectedly, from Major Ramsden, who jilted her; returning to her hotel room on an impulse after she had left it for Port Said, she found Ramsden in bed with Lady Robert Maxwell, the wife of another army officer. HRH sent her a teasing note: "You had better have stuck to your old friends than gone on your Expedition to the Nile! Old friends are the best!"[69]

On June 18 Churchill sailed from Bombay, taking leave to plead his cause in person. But at the War Office he found several hundred officers on similar errands. He ran up against one blank wall after another. Kitchener's general advance on Khartoum was scheduled for early August. Time was short, and Winston seemed beaten when, out of the blue, he received a note from the prime minister's private secretary. Lord Salisbury had read *Malakand* with great pleasure and wanted to discuss it. An appointment was set for the following Tuesday, July 12. Salisbury received him at the Foreign Office with elaborate old-world courtesy and led him to a small sofa. He praised the book, "not only for its manner but for its style," told him that it had provided him with greater insight into the frontier fighting than any parliamentary debate, and said, as he saw him to the door, "If there is anything at any time that I can do which would be of assistance to you, pray do not fail to let me know."[70]

Back at Great Cumberland Place, Churchill seized the opportunity. He wrote Salisbury: "I am vy anxious to go to Egypt and to proceed to Khartoum with the Expedition. It is not my intention, under any circumstances to stay in the army long." He wanted to cover the Sirdar's battles as he had covered Sir Bindon's. Sir Evelyn had written a letter approving his plan. Churchill enclosed it, explaining that Sir Evelyn had "tried his best — so he assures me — on my behalf. My mother has exerted what influence she can for two years. Even HRH has allowed his name to be used as a recommendation. All have failed." One hope remained: Lord Cromer, British agent and consul general in Egypt. Winston was "convinced," he told the prime minister, "that if you will write a letter to Lord Cromer and say that on personal grounds you wish me to go — the affair will be immediately arranged." He was "loth to afflict you with this matter. Yet the choice lies between doing so, and abandoning a project which I have set my heart on for a long time. . . . The affair is after all of extreme insignificance to any but me."[71]

Salisbury saw nothing wrong in this brazen manipulation; it was common among "young men with suitable introductions," to use Churchill's delicate phrase. The prime minister wrote Cromer, suggesting that he approach Kitchener, but as he told Winston in his reply, "I cannot advise you to rely too confidently on the result of his letter." Wheels were turning in the bureaucracy. Salisbury's role, here as in so much else, is unclear. All we know is that nothing happened before Churchill's visit to the Foreign Office and that something happened soon afterward. Sir Evelyn told Lady Jeune that the Sirdar was going too far in picking his officers and ignoring recommendations from London. He could do as he liked with his Egyptian troops, but British regiments remained under the control of the War Office. Lady Jeune repeated this to Winston, who asked: "Have you told him that the Prime Minister has telegraphed personally on my behalf?" She hadn't. "Do so," he said, "and let us see whether he will stand up for his prerogatives." Conveniently, a young officer in the Twenty-first Lancers, a regiment of English cavalry, died in Cairo that day. The Sirdar routinely informed the War Office of the vacancy, and the War Office routinely replied that another officer would be on his way. It was left to Cromer to suggest Churchill as the replacement. Kitchener, we are told, "simply shrugged his shoulders and passed on to what were after all matters of greater concern." Meanwhile, fresh orders had been delivered to Winston by courier at 35A Great Cumberland Place. He had been "attached as a supernumerary Lieutenant to the 21st Lancers for the Soudan Campaign" and would report to the Abbasiya barracks, Cairo. It was understood that he would pay his own expenses and that the government would not be liable if he were killed or wounded. He immediately took a hansom to his solicitors, Lumley and Lumley, and then, with their approval, borrowed £3,500 at 4½ percent interest from the Norwich Union Society, using as collateral an insurance policy bequeathed him by his grandfather. Then he called on Oliver Borthwick of the *Morning Post.* Borthwick agreed to pay him £15 apiece — his value was rising — for a series of Nile dispatches which, to avoid ruffling Kitchener further, would be disguised as letters to "Dear Oliver." Winston told Aylmer Haldane, a friend, "If you look at the *Morning Post* it is possible that you will see that one of my friends has committed and continues to commit an unpardonable breach of confidence by publishing letters of mine. Don't give away the pious fraud as I do not want to be recalled."[72]

He was not yet in the clear. He needed official permission from the Fourth Hussars. But that didn't trouble him; his future didn't lie there. It lay in public life, and so, while packing, he decided to deliver a political address. He spoke at Bradford and wrote afterward: "The meeting was a complete success. The hall was not a vy large one — but it was closely packed. I was listened to with the greatest attention for 55 minutes at the end of which time there were loud & general cries of 'Go on.' . . . All of which was vy gratifying. . . . The conclusions I form are these — with practice I shall obtain great power on a public platform. My impediment is no hindrance. My voice sufficiently powerful, and — this is vital — my ideas & modes of thought are pleasing to men." R. B. (later Lord) Haldane, a leading Liberal MP, read the speech in the *Morning Post* the next day and wrote Jennie: "I thought it very good — broad in tone — fresh & vigorous. I hope he will soon be in the House."[73]

After Bradford, Churchill vanished. Once in Cairo, he reasoned, he would be beyond reach of the Fourth Hussars. Indeed, unless the War Office proved uncharacteristically helpful, Bangalore wouldn't even know where he was. Ignoring the swift, comfortable steamers of the P & O and Australian Lloyd, he took the train to Marseilles and boarded the freighter *Sindh,* "a filthy tramp," he wrote in a note on July 30, manned by "detestable French sailors." On August 2 he reached Cairo and took a carriage to the cavalry barracks. "All was hustle and bustle" there. "Two squadrons of the 21st Lancers had already started up the Nile." He paid forty pounds for a charger and paraded that evening with "A" Squadron, to which he was attached, in the uniform of the day: khakis, topee, Sam Browne belt, field glasses, revolver — he had forgotten his regular one, with its lucky silk lanyard, and had to buy a new Mauser pistol — and Stohwasser gaiters. The band struck up "Auld Lang Syne," and they were off. That was on a Tuesday. On Friday he was "toiling slowly up the rising river — against a 6 knot current with only a balance of speed of 4 miles an hour," pausing briefly in Luxor, on the east bank of the Nile, where he paid "a flying visit" to the ancient temple and was reminded of Rider Haggard's *Cleopatra.* He felt like a fugitive from the Fourth Hussars, which he was. He had "heard nothing definite about my leave being sanctioned by India — but as there has been no canceling order & a fortnight has already passed I think I may now conclude . . . that 'silence has given consent.' " The trip was proving "delightful," though the boat was a strange troop transport, one of Cook's, painted alabaster white, with chintz curtains in the saloon windows and flowered toiletries in every cabin. Winston, interested in everything, noted that it was powered by steam-driven pistons which turned "a great paddle-wheel which protrudes from the stern. The appearance is peculiar." He had found "many old friends in the regiment." He had also learned that never, in its entire history, had the Twenty-first Lancers seen action. Indeed, other regiments gibed that its motto was "Thou Shalt Not Kill." The taunt was of long standing, but in a month it would be forgotten.[74]

What were the British doing on the Nile? To the public at home, and to Churchill, who wrote ardently of Queen, Empire, and Flag, the answer was obvious. They were there, he wrote, to assure the destruction of an autocracy, "a state of society which had long become an anachronism — an insult as well as a danger to civilisation; the liberation of the great waterway; perhaps the foundation of an African India; certainly the settlement of a long account." That long account was the martyrdom of Chinese Gordon in Khartoum at the hands of the Mahdi's howling dervishes. After Khartoum had been retaken, Churchill thought, it would be rather a good thing to "tell some stonemason to bring his hammer and chisel and cut on the pedestal of Gordon's statue in Trafalgar Square the significant, the sinister, yet the somehow satisfactory word, 'Avenged.' "[75]

But over thirteen years had passed since Gordon had been butchered. The Mahdi, as inscrutable as his victim, had died suddenly (and mysteriously) five months later. Before his death he had chosen Abdullah Ibn Mohammed as Khalifa — literally "successor" — to lead the forces in Mahdism. Under the Khalifa the Sudanese situation had been transformed. After suppressing a conspiracy by the Mahdi's relatives and disarming the forces of other leading emirs, he had sought to accomplish the Mahdi's dream of a universal jihad, or holy war, reforming Islam throughout the Moslem world. Although the Sudanese people were of mixed Arab, Hamitic, and Negro ancestry, all of them were, and are, commonly called Arabs, and their devotion to the Prophet Mohammed approached the absolute. The Khalifa's hordes attacked north, south, east, and west. They were checked everywhere, notably by the Belgians in the Congo and the British in Egypt. Then the Mahdist Sudan entered a three-year period of great suffering. Almost no rain fell. Crops shriveled, herds grew emaciated, dervishes starved, epidemics broke out, thousands died. Eventually the rains returned; improved harvests brought prosperity. The Khalifa became a popular leader. He was an autocrat, but his people had never known democracy, and in any event the charge of autocracy was hardly one to be flung about carelessly by a twenty-three-year-old youth who was deftly exploiting his own membership in a privileged class to build popular support among his fellow countrymen.

England's real enemy on the Nile was France. Now that the British held Egypt, they wanted to insulate the length of the river, without which Egypt could not survive. "The Nile is Egypt," said Roberts, "and

Egypt is the Nile." The Italians, the Belgians, and the Germans agreed to stay out of the river's valley. The French declined. Instead, they sent an expedition to Africa under Captain Jean-Baptiste Marchand, whose orders were to land on the continent's west coast, march inland, and seize Fashoda (now Kodok) on the upper Nile, where, it was believed, a dam could be built to shut off Egypt's water. Fashoda, not the ruins of Gordon's Khartoum, would be Kitchener's ultimate destination. The Khalifa's tribesmen merely lay between him and his objective. Since all this was beyond Churchill, it was probably beyond the Khalifa, too. All he knew was that an army of British and Egyptian troops, led by the Sirdar, was coming after him. He sat in the Mahdist capital of Omdurman, built opposite Khartoum after Gordon's death, and plotted the movements of his sixty-thousand-man army. His confidence was sky-high. Kitchener, after all, had only twenty thousand men, counting his Egyptian Camel Corps and the disaffected Sudanese he had enlisted. What the Khalifa did not realize was that the new technological superiority of European armies — resulting from such innovations as shrapnel, magazine rifles, and Maxim guns — had rendered his passionate masses, clad in their patched blue-and-white jibbas, or smocks, waving their obsolete weapons and their banners inscribed with passages from the Koran, almost meaningless. And logistics, another technological development, solved the Sirdar's supply problems, permitting him to plan the orderly arrival of reinforcing troops like the Twenty-first Lancers, setting out from Cairo, fourteen hundred miles away.

The journey took two weeks: by steamer to Aswân, where they led their horses around the cascading water at Philae and reembarked; on to Wadi Halfa, a four-day trip by boat; then four hundred miles by military railroad to Kitchener's main camp, where the waters of the Atbara flow into the vast, brown, muddy, fifteen-hundred-foot-wide Nile. Many of the place-names in Churchill's dispatches are meaningless today: Shellal, Metemmeh, Wad Habeshi, Wad Bishara, and, nine miles above the main camp, the Shabluka gorge and cataract, beyond which long, low heights overlooked Omdurman and the ruins of Khartoum. But Winston's reportorial skills were growing. A *khor,* he carefully explained to his readers, "is a watercourse, usually dry. In India it would be called a *nullah*; in South Africa a *donga*; in Australia a *gully.*" A *zareba* was a hedgehog. He described the lovely gazelles running along the riverbanks, and the Sirdar's telegraph wires, strung above them; how, where the Nile narrowed to two hundred yards, "great swirls and eddies disturb its surface"; the disembarkation of an entire division — with fifteen hundred horses, mules, camels, and donkeys — and how, when ashore, "our line of march

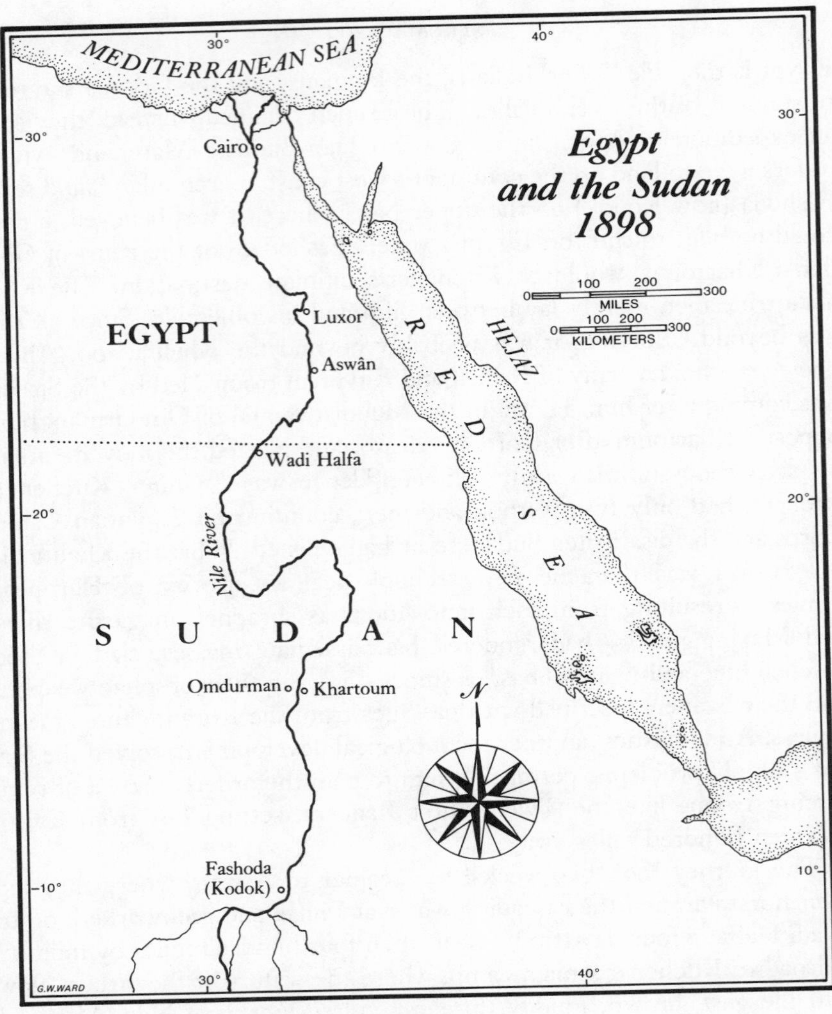

lay partly in the desert and partly along the strip of vegetation by the Nile, to which we returned every evening to water, and by which we camped at night."[76]

It was serene, hardly like war at all, and he commented on that. Ordinarily one might expect patrols, sniping, skirmishing, preludes to a major operation: "Usually the game gets warmer by degrees." The enemy lurked near Omdurman but had sent no one, except perhaps lone horsemen, to investigate the British approach. Not a shot had been heard. The British and Egyptian camps were "as peaceful as Aldershot or Bisley." And yet they knew that one day the guns would "begin to fire and a big battle open." At Wad Habeshi he wrote his mother: "We are but 60 miles from Khartoum and on the 27th we march 21 miles putting us in front of the infantry and in full contact. Within the next ten days there will be a general action — perhaps a vy severe one. I may be killed. I do not think so." He was more worried about his other enemy, the Sirdar. Nothing could be easier for the commander than to send Churchill back and say, "Let him come on with the remounts after the battle." At every stage along the way Winston half expected to be detained by a staff officer. "I suppose," he wrote, "a criminal flying from justice goes through the same emotions at every stopping-point." Toward the end hope replaced fear, though he knew his presence was resented at the top. He wrote home that Frank Rhodes, the *Times* correspondent, had "talked to the Sirdar about me. Kitchener said he had known I was not going to stay in the army — was only making a convenience of it; that he had disapproved of my coming in place of others whose professions were at stake & that E. Wood had acted wrongly & had annoyed him by sending me. But that I was quite right to try my best." Churchill concluded that Kitchener "may be a general — but never a gentleman." That was arrogant. But Churchillian swagger was almost always redeemed by his boyish charm and the quickness with which he could laugh at himself. He captured an Arab who turned out to be a British intelligence agent. Lionel James of Reuters wanted to write a story about it, "but I prevailed on him not to do so," Winston wrote, "having a detestation of publicity."[77]

Before they even reached the battlefield he had a bad fright. From Atbara the Twenty-first Lancers marched to Shabluka, bandoliers filled, lances with pennons tightly rolled, ready for action. Various duties kept Winston behind on the river's east bank; he had been told to join the column that evening at its first camp, fifteen miles away. His chores took longer than he had expected, and it was late afternoon before the ferry steamer *Tahra* carried him over to the west shore. He asked for directions and was told: "It is perfectly simple. You just go due south until you see the campfires and then turn towards the river." He nodded and left. An hour later the sun sank; darkness enveloped him. To avoid the thorny bushes on the Nile bank he struck inland and rode down through the desert, steering southward by keeping his back to the North Star. After two hours of trotting he paused for a drink and rations. To his dismay, clouds drifted across the star, and the pointers of the Great Bear became invisible. He was lost. Unless the overcast lifted, he would have no choice but to wait. Picking a spot, he passed the reins around his waist, leaned against a rock, and tried to sleep. The night was sultry; "a hot, restless, wearing wind blew continuously with a mournful sound"; slumber was

Churchill in Cairo, 1898

impossible. Then, at 3:30 A.M., the sky cleared and "the beautiful constellation of Orion came into view. Never did the giant look more splendid." He rode toward it, and after two hours he found the Nile. He and his mount drank deeply. But it was broad daylight before he found the lancers' camp, and the regiment had gone. Nearby villagers spoke no English; he made himself understood, indicating hunger by pointing to his mouth and stomach, but nothing happened until he uttered the magical Arabic word *baksheesh.* Now that they knew he was going to give them money, everything changed; "all difficulties melted." Three women appeared to serve him dates and milk. His pony was fed *doura.* What he now needed was information. Using the point of his sword, he sketched a profile of a lancer on the red mud wall. A man wearing a fez nodded excitedly, made lapping motions with his tongue to convey the fact that the troopers had watered their horses here, and pointed southward. "Then he gazed hard at me, and, with an expression of ferocious satisfaction, pronounced the word 'Omdurman.'" Thus Churchill first learned where battle would be joined.[78]

He caught up with the column at its camp that evening. By August 27 all Anglo-Egyptian forces, both the army in the desert and the gunboats on the Nile, were concentrated south of the Shabluka Hills. The following morning they began their final advance, covering only eight to ten miles a day to save their strength. The heat was "intense. In spite of thick clothes, spine pads, broad-brimmed pitch helmets, one felt the sun leaning down upon one and piercing our bodies with its burning rays." But that was the only enemy Churchill saw. Omdurman seemed undefended. He began to doubt the villager in the fez. The crisp surface of the desert plain, through which the Nile meandered in its broad sweeps, stretched wide and vacant: "Everyone in the British cavalry had made up his mind that there was to be no battle," that " 'we shall be marching like this towards the Equator for months and months.' " At nine o'clock on the morning of September 1, the Twenty-first Lancers, riding ahead as scouts, sighted Omdurman. If the Khalifa meant to fight, he would fight here. Winston was studying the city's mud huts and the dome of the Mahdi's tomb — and trying to ignore a hundred vultures circling overhead, which made him extremely uncomfortable ("It would be difficult," he told readers of the *Morning Post,* "to assign limitations to the possibilities of instinct") — when another subaltern motioned toward a ridge ahead and cried: "Enemy in sight! They haven't bolted!"[79]

Churchill squinted at the ridge. It lay three miles away, between them and the city. At first he saw only "a long black line with white spots." The white spots appeared to be dervishes, perhaps "three thousand men behind a high dense zareba of thorn bushes." They thought this "better than nothing. There would in any case be a skirmish." They rode closer for a better view. At 11:00 A.M., to his astonishment, "the whole black line, which seemed to be zareba, began to move. It was made of men not bushes. Behind it other immense masses and lines of men appeared over the crest, and while we watched, amazed by the wonder of the sight, the whole face of the slope became black with swarming savages." It crossed his mind that this was what the Crusaders had seen. The Khalifa's army, five miles from end to end, advanced while the sun, glinting on over forty thousand spear points, "spread a sparkling cloud. It was, perhaps, the impression of a lifetime, nor do I expect ever again to see such an awe-inspiring and formidable sight."[80]

"Mr. Churchill!" called Colonel Rowland Martin, the Twenty-first's commander. Winston cantered up and was told to first take a long look "and then go back as quickly as you can without knocking up your horse and report personally to the Sirdar. You will find him marching with the infantry." So there it was. He was going to meet Kitchener after all. After further scrutiny of the enemy position, it took him forty minutes to cover the six miles separating his advance party from the main body of the army, and on the way he appraised the Anglo-Egyptian formation: five solid brigades in open columns, with the gray and chocolate mass of the Camel Corps on his left below the rocky Kerrari Hills, and, to his right, seven or eight large white British gunboats on the river. He found the Sirdar riding between the Union Jack and the flag of the Egyptian khedive. Reining in, he identified himself as an officer from the Twenty-first — but gave no name — and described the situation. Kitchener said: "You say the Dervish Army is advancing. How long do you think I have got?" In a rough calculation, Churchill estimated that the enemy was jog-trotting at four miles an hour and had another seven miles to cover. He said, "You have got at least an hour — probably an hour and a half, sir, even if they come on at their present rate."[81]

There followed an interval which would have been impossible for any youth who was not a member of the Victorian privileged class. Kitchener gave no sign of knowing who Winston was, but his chief of intelligence, Sir Reginald Wingate, recognized him and invited him to lunch. They dined on a white picnic cloth with knives and forks and what was, under the circumstances, remarkable nonchalance. The outcome of the imminent battle was by no means certain. Dervishes had overwhelmed Egyptian troops in several encounters. At Abu Klea and Tamai they had broken British squares, and only seven thousand of the Sirdar's bayonets were British anyway. Moreover, the enemy was armed with more than spears; twenty thousand of the Khalifa's men were equipped with old Martini-Henrys. Yet Sir Reginald and his guests were, Winston wrote, "in the highest spirits and the best of tempers. It was like a race luncheon before the Derby." They watched, as interested but detached spectators, while the infantry formed a defensive arc and the leading brigade built a thorn-bush zareba. A young lieutenant on a passing gunboat shouted: "How are you off for drinks? We have got everything in the world on board here. Can you catch?" It was David Beatty — like Ian Hamilton he would play a larger role in Churchill's later career — and he tossed Winston a large bottle of champagne.[82]

No engagement was fought that day. The dervishes halted. Kitchener's howitzers pounded Omdurman, and Churchill returned to his regiment, which pitched camp that night inside the zareba, under the steep bank of the river. Reports, considered reliable, predicted that the enemy would attack that night. They were wrong, but the threat was real. Churchill defied it, strolling around in the moonlight to inspect the Sirdar's defenses, and when the Twenty-first's buglers blew at 4:30 A.M., he swung into his saddle, ready to join the spray of officers' patrols which would serve as Kitchener's eyes at dawn. Daybreak arrived and revealed the enemy. Churchill was delighted. "This," he wrote, "is an hour to live." He mounted a ridge which had been christened Heliograph Hill.

Afterward, writing Ian Hamilton of that morning's events, he said that he believed he was "the first to see the enemy — certainly the first to hear their bullets. . . . I and my little patrol felt very lonely." At 5:50 A.M., kneeling, he scribbled in his field service notebook the first of two messages to the Sirdar, both of which survive.

Dervish army, strength unchanged, occupies last nights [sic] position with their left well extended. Their patrols have reported the advance and loud cheering is going on. There is no *zeriba.*

Nothing hostile is between a line drawn from Heliograph Hill to the Mahdi's tomb, and river. Nothing is within three miles from the camp.

WINSTON S. CHURCHILL
Lieut 4th Hussars
attd 21st Lancers

Handing this to a corporal, he climbed for a better view. The sun was high now. Scarcely four hundred yards away he beheld the humps and squares of the Khalifa's multitude, bright with glittering weapons and iridescent standards. He wrote: "Talk of fun! Where will you beat this? On horseback, at daybreak, within shot of an advancing army, seeing everything, and corresponding direct with Headquarters." He was a target now; enemy bullets were swatting sand around him. The corporal, spurring his weary horse to a full gallop, returned with a request from the Sirdar's chief of staff for word of new developments. It was 6:20 A.M. Winston scrawled his second report:

About ¼ Dervish army is on their right which they have refused at present. Should this force continue to advance it would come the South side of Heliograph Hill.

Most of the Cavalry are with this force.

Duplicate to Col Martin

WINSTON S. CHURCHILL
Lieut 4th Hussars

By now, he wrote Hamilton, "the fire was for the time being as hot as anything I have seen — barring only those 10 minutes with the 35th Sikhs — a year ago today." An enemy patrol of three horsemen approached him: "They were dark, cowled figures, like monks on horseback — ugly, sinister brutes with long spears. I fired a few shots at them from the saddle, and they sheered off." But the enemy mass was coming on like a sea. "The tide was rising fast. One rock, one mound of sand after another was submerged by that human flood. It was time to go." Still he was reluctant. Then a major appeared and ordered him to withdraw; the British infantry was about to open fire. Back he scampered then, to watch, from the flank, the Sirdar's response to the challenge and, opposite him, "all the pride and might of the Dervish Empire . . . on this last great day of its existence."[83]

Unlike twentieth-century warfare, nearly everything at Omdurman was visible, if distorted, to the naked eye. As Churchill wrote, "the whole scene lay revealed in minute detail, curiously twisted, blurred, and interspersed with phantom waters by the mirage." It quickly became apparent that the Khalifa had now committed every man he had, including his reserves, hoping to overwhelm the infidels. His sacred black flag floated above the bright banners of lesser emirs and the white standards bearing Mohammed's most stirring passages in Arabic script. Shrieking as they ran, these troops dipped beneath a swell of ground which briefly concealed the main bodies of the rival armies from one another and then swept up, over, and down into the arena where the invaders of their soil stood shoulder to shoulder, braced to receive them. But the two never met. Lashed and scythed by storms of Lee-Enfield dumdums, by four batteries of howitzers, and by shells from at least seventy big guns on the Nile bank and in the gunboats, the dervishes faltered seven hundred yards from their objective, the last of them stumbling and sprawling over the bodies of seven thousand of their fallen comrades. Kitchener then wheeled his five brigades into echelon formation and prepared to move on Omdurman. That would cut the enemy off from his base and force him into the desert. The fifty-three thousand remaining dervishes regrouped and attacked again. This time they came within a hundred yards of the Anglo-Egyptian lines, but at the appalling cost of twenty thousand men. The Sirdar's force was virtually unblooded. The city was still accessible to the Khalifa's survivors, however, and despite their casualties, numbers were still on their side. Kitchener believed that he had to occupy Omdurman before the enemy could flee there. His army, as Churchill noted, "could fight as many Dervishes as cared to come in the plain; among the houses it was different." But before the Anglo-Egyptian infantry could advance, the Arabs must be driven from the intervening ground. That was a cavalry task. The Twenty-first Lancers, on the spot, waiting in a little hollow, stood to their horses. Then the heliograph at Kitchener's side instructed them, in flashes of reflected sunlight: "Advance — clear the left flank — use every effort to prevent the enemy entering Omdurman." The stage was set for Britain's last great cavalry charge, and Churchill, leading twenty-five troopers, would be in the thick of it.[84]

Scrambling into their saddles, the massed lancers walked forward at a deliberate pace, stepping over the crisp desert toward the city, stirred by what Churchill called "a high state of excitement." Presently they noticed, three hundred yards away and parallel to their course, a long row of blue-black objects, two or three yards apart. At that moment the bugles sounded Trot, and the regiment began to jingle and clatter across the front of these crouching dervishes. It was a lull in the battle. Except for the sound of the harnesses, silence was near perfect. Abruptly the Arabs broke it, firing a volley; three horses and several lancers toppled to the ground. Until then the colonel had intended to swing around the flank of the enemy riflemen, but now he decided to attack them head-on. The bugles sounded Right Wheel into Line. There was no further order. As Winston wrote Hamilton: "Gallop & Charge were understood."[85] In a solid line, the regiment lunged toward what appeared to be 150 dervish riflemen.

At this critical moment, Winston became preoccupied with a personal problem. He had every confidence in his gray polo pony, but until the regiment wheeled he, like the other officers, had been carrying a drawn sword. Because of his bad shoulder, he had decided early in the campaign that if hand-to-hand combat loomed, he would rely on his pistol. At full gallop, he had to return his sword to its scabbard and fumble for his wooden holster. He explained to Hamilton: "I drew my Mauser pistol — a ripper — and cocked it. Then I looked to my front. Instead of the 150 riflemen who were still blazing I saw a line nearly (in the middle) — 12 deep . . . of closely jammed spearmen — all in a *nullah* with steep sloping sides 6 foot deep & 20 foot broad."[86] The lancers found themselves heading into a mob of nearly three thousand dervishes led by mounted emirs waving bright flags. What had happened? The Khalifa's black flag, which had moved to within five hundred yards of this dry watercourse, should have told them. He had anticipated the flanking movement and reinforced the *khor*. Thus, the 310 shouting lancers, plunging furiously ahead in crescent formation, their overlapping flanks curving inward like the horns of a moon, their helmets bowed against the enemy musketry like the cuirassiers at Waterloo, were hurtling toward a wall of human flesh.

The collision was tremendous. Nearly thirty lancers and their horses, Churchill wrote, "fell knocked A.O.T. [arse over tip]." Some two hundred dervishes were down. Winston himself had passed between two riflemen; both had fired at him, missed, and hit the trooper just behind him, who was immediately stabbed to death as he slid from his mount. But most of the dervishes — and the British — were too stunned to fight. "For perhaps ten wonderful seconds no man heeded his enemy." Terrified horses were wedged in the mob. Bruised men lay in heaps, dazed and astonished. Several lancers, unhorsed but alert, had time to remount. Then the Arabs began to come to their senses. They threw spears at their enemies, swung heavy swords, cut reins and stirrup leathers, and tried to hamstring horses. Troopers jabbed back with their lances, officers with their sabers. Churchill saw his men being "dragged from their horses and cut to pieces by the infuriated foe." Finding himself "surrounded by what seemed to be dozens of men," he "rode up to individuals firing my pistol in their faces and killing several — 3 for certain — 2 doubtful — one very doubtful." One was swinging a gleaming, curved sword, trying to hamstring the pony. Another wore a steel helmet and chain-mail hangings. A third came at him "with uplifted sword. I raised my pistol and fired. So close were we that the pistol itself actually struck him." The dervish mass, he saw, was re-forming. At this point, he later recalled, "The whole scene seemed to flicker." He looked around. His troop was gone. His squadron was gone. He could not see a single British officer or trooper within a hundred yards. Instead, "I saw two or three [dervish] riflemen crouching and aiming their rifles at me."[87]

In a letter to his mother two days later (headed "Khartoum and be damned to it") he wrote: "I never felt the slightest nervousness and felt as cool as I do now." But in another account he was more candid. Staring at the Martini-Henry muzzles, he wrote, "for the first time that morning I experienced a sudden sensation of fear." And he told Hamilton: "I looked at them stupidly for what may have been 2 seconds." He thought: "What a fool I was to loiter in the midst of the enemy." The dervish riflemen fired together and missed. Hunching down over his pommel, he spurred his pony free and found his squadron two hundred yards away, faced about and already forming up. His own troop had just finished sorting itself out, but as he joined it a dervish sprang out of a hole in the ground and into the midst of his men, lunging about with a spear. They thrust at him with their lances; he dodged, wheeled, and charged Churchill. "I shot him at less than a yard. He fell on the sand, and lay there dead. How easy to kill a man! But I did not worry about it. I found I had fired the whole magazine of my Mauser pistol, so I put in a new clip of ten cartridges before thinking of anything else." It occurred to him that if he hadn't injured his shoulder in Bombay, he would have had to defend himself with a sword and might now be dead. Afterward he reflected: "One must never forget when misfortunes come that it is quite possible they are saving one from something much worse." He wrote Jennie: "The pistol was the best thing in the world."[88]

He was ready to charge again; they all were; several of his troopers asked permission to discard their lances and draw their swords. Then they looked back at where they had been, and their blood cooled. Winston saw, coming from the direction of the enemy, "a succession of grisly apparitions; horses spouting blood, struggling on three legs, men staggering on foot, men bleeding from terrible wounds, fish-hook spears stuck right through them, arms and faces cut to pieces, bowels protruding, men gasping, crying, collapsing, expiring."[89] Attending to these came first. As they finished improvising bandages, the colonel, apparently for the first time in the action, remembered that his men carried carbines. Bugles sounded and they trotted off to the flank, where they could enfilade the *khor* from three hundred yards. This forced the dervishes to retreat toward the ridge where the Khalifa's black flag still waved. Twenty minutes after the British had wheeled into line and charged, they occupied the watercourse and were breakfasting there, in sole possession of the field.

The question is whether it was worth it. Churchill wrote Hamilton: "It was I suppose the most dangerous 2 minutes I shall live to see. Out of 310 officers & men we lost — 1 officer and 20 men killed — 4 officers and 45 men wounded and 119 horses of which 56 were bullet wounds. All this in 120 seconds!" He told his mother that he was "about the only officer whose clothes, saddlery, or horse were uninjured." In the final reckoning it was found that Kitchener had lost fewer than 3 percent of his troops in the entire battle of Omdurman. Yet the Twenty-first Lancers' casualties, in their brief encounter, had exceeded 22 percent. Churchill conceded in the *Morning Post* that this isolated engagement "did not greatly influence the fortunes of the battle."[90] Actually, it had no impact whatever. The Sirdar's fears of house-to-house fighting in the city proved groundless. To be sure, the Khalifa did everything he could to arouse his people there. He ordered the Mahdi's great war drum beaten, the martial *ombya* blown, and his sole Krupp gun wheeled into position and fired, while exhorting the inhabitants to prepare for a last stand. But his troops wanted none of it. They had seen enough of pointless slaughter. Disregarding his summons and the pleas of their emirs, they faded into the desert or surrendered. As the Sirdar approached Omdurman's walls, three men emerged, knelt before him, and presented him with the keys to the city. British soldiers then marched through it, end to end. All this would have happened without the lancers' charge. The evidence is overwhelming: the blood of Colonel Martin's men had bought nothing.

The survivors of heavy fighting always try to justify the cost, however, and Churchill was no exception. He reasoned in his dispatches that the regiment had faced "no choice but to charge or gallop away. The definite orders excluded the latter alternative. In any case there was no time to argue. At that close range it was impossible so heavy a fire could be ineffective." Actually, the lancers had proceeded to outflank the position after the charge, which proves that the enemy could have been outmaneuvered without it. Churchill offered his readers other arguments, which, though irrational, tell much about the era and his enthusiasm for its values. The regiment's feat, he said, "was of perhaps as great value to the Empire as the victory itself." It was important that untested British troops show "those intrinsic fighting virtues without which no race can long continue to rule." Because of the Twenty-first Lancers at Omdurman, he concluded, England "may rise refreshed and, contemplating the past with calmness, may feel confidence in the present and high hope in the future. We can still produce soldiers worthy of their officers — and there has hitherto been no complaint about the officers."[91]

There was more of this, most of it, by today's standards, deplorable. He rejoiced to see that the Union Jack hoisted over the ashes of Khartoum was four times the size of the Egyptian khedive's flag. He wept over the new English graveyard on an eminence overlooking the desert, with its "protecting crosses which the living raised as a last tribute to those who had paid the bill for all the fun and glory of the game." To Hamilton he wrote that after his experience in the *khor,* "my faith in our race & blood was much strengthened." "Perhaps," he told his readers with heavy humor, "to these savages with their vile customs and brutal ideas, we appeared as barbarous aggressors" — which is, of course, precisely how they were regarded, and understandably so. After the guns had fallen silent he wrote in the *Morning Post,* "I raised my voice and helmet in honour of that persevering British people who, often affronted, usually get their own way in the end." And although he had assured his mother that war could not be gilded, he tried to do it himself; brave deeds, he told his newspaper's subscribers, "brighten the picture of war with beautiful colours, till from a distance it looks almost magnificent, and the dark background and dirty brown canvas are scarcely seen." David Beatty's eye was clearer. He had watched the lancers' charge from his gunboat. Years later he told Churchill he had seen it, and Churchill eagerly asked him what his impression had been. "It looked," Beatty said, "like plum duff: brown currants scattered about in a great deal of suet."[92]

Churchill's impressions of the dervish rout were melodramatic because he was, and always would be, a romantic. In this he was a man of his time. He was no more persuaded of war's ennobling virtues than Sir Henry Newbolt or Tennyson in *Maud* (". . . hail once more to the banner of battle unroll'd!"), or Thomas Hughes. *Fighting,* to Hughes, was one of the most honorable words in the language, "the real, highest, honestest business of every son of man." As late as August 24, 1914, when the British cavalry flung itself against a sleet of German bullets, John Buchan felt exalted. He knew that this suicidal act was "as futile and gallant as any other like attempt in history on unbroken infantry and guns in position. But it proved to the world that the spirit which inspired the Light Brigade at Balaclava . . . was still alive in the cavalry of today." Somehow carnage had been transformed by concepts of Saint George, the Holy Grail, and "playing the game," as though butchery were a manlier form of rugby. "Victorian and Edwardian chivalry," Mark Girouard notes, "produced its own world of myth and legend, just as much as medieval chivalry."[93]

Young Winston had fallen under this dark enchantment, and he would never be entirely free of it. But even at Omdurman he was his own man, undazzled by rank and quick to accuse those who betrayed the code of honor, which, he realized, must be observed by all or none. Kitchener soon discovered this. Despite his lordly bearing and his impeccable guardsman's mustache, the Sirdar was a man of primitive, inclement instincts. On his orders the Mahdi's tomb was desecrated, the corpse ripped from its shroud, and the head lopped off and dumped in a kerosene can to be "preserved for future disposal" — an official phrase which, the outraged Churchill wrote, could only be interpreted as meaning that it would be "passed from hand to hand till it reached Cairo," where it would be treated as "an interesting trophy."[94]

Lord Cromer read this and had the gruesome relic sent back for reinterment. Kitchener seethed. Then Churchill found evidence of battlefield atrocities. He wrote his mother that the triumph had been "disgraced" by atrocities, and that "Kitchener is responsible for this." Most of the guilty had been Egyptians and Sudanese fighting under the khedive's colors, but some had been Englishmen. No blind chauvinist would have acknowledged that. Winston accepted it and wrote about it, and that took courage. "The sentiment that the British soldier is incapable of brutality," he told his readers, "is one which never fails to win the meed of popular applause; but there are in fact a considerable proportion of cruel men in any army." Kitchener now erupted. Winston wrote Hamilton: "I am in great disfavour with the authorities here. . . . Generally things have been a little unpleasant." The Sirdar tried to punish him by putting him in charge of a band of sick camels limping wearily back to Cairo. Churchill tore up the orders, took the next launch north, and reached England in time to join the lancers' triumphant London parade. A "general officer" testily wrote to the *Army and Navy Gazette:* "What is the position of Lieut. Spencer Churchill in Her Majesty's Army?" Here he was, a subaltern with less than four years' service, "acting as special correspondent here, there, and everywhere. Now, as a special correspondent he has, as a matter of course, to criticise general officers highly placed in authority and to influence public opinion. Can it be for the good of the Service . . . ?" Even the Prince of Wales was offended. He wrote Winston: "I fear that in matters of discipline I may be considered old fashioned — and I must say that I think an officer serving in a campaign should not write letters for newspapers or express strong opinions of how the operations were carried out." HRH said he now realized why the Sirdar "viewed your joining his force with dislike — it is I am sure merely because he knows you write, for which he has the greatest objection I understand — and I cannot help agreeing with him."[95]

Winston was unruffled. This was one test for which his pathetic school years had prepared him. He knew how to stand alone. As for the controversy and evidence of his independence, he welcomed them; they would be useful in Parliament. At the same time, he was developing political acumen in other, subtler ways. Earlier he had missed the significance of the French troops on the upper Nile, but now, as Kitchener led a force there, he noted "rumours about Fashoda" in a dispatch and predicted that "the Battle of Fashoda will be fought in Westminster, that tempers rather than lives will be lost, and ink rather than blood expended." And so it happened. Five days later the Sirdar confronted Captain Marchand and demanded he leave. Paris was furious, but the deputies were split by the growing Dreyfus crisis, and Théophile Delcassé, the foreign minister, ordered Marchand to withdraw. As compensation, the British generously gave France an expanse of Sahara Desert. That was how the Empire did things under Victoria, and Churchill would go to his grave believing that it was the best way, not just for England, but for all mankind. He could hardly wait to get his own hands on the reins of some of this vast power.

The lancers' charge had been less than forty-eight hours old when, itching to reach the hustings, he had written Jennie: "Arrange me some good meetings in October, Bradford & Birmingham. Sunny will help." He was still obsessed with medals. After he had left Kitchener's command, to the vast relief of both, he wrote a superior: "I naturally want to wear my medals while I still have a uniform to wear them on. They have already sent me the Egyptian one. I cannot think why the Frontier one has not arrived. Young Life Guardsmen on Sir B. Blood's staff in Buner have already got theirs. Do try and get mine for me as soon as possible."[96]

In Egypt he felt he had mounted another rung on his ladder to the House of Commons. He had even acquired a sort of vicarious wound. Having floated down the Nile with the Grenadier Guards, he had encountered a fellow officer in Cairo, a subaltern who had charged the *khor* with him and had emerged with a severe sword cut above his right wrist. A doctor, coming to dress the wound, said a skin graft would be necessary. Winston rolled up his sleeve. The doctor warned him that he would feel as though he were being flayed alive, and Churchill later recalled, "My sensations as he sawed the razor slowly to and fro fully justified his description of the ordeal." At the end of it Winston was missing a piece of skin about the size of a shilling with a thin layer of flesh attached to it. "This precious fragment was then grafted on to my friend's wound. It remains there to this day and did him lasting good in many ways. I for my part keep the scar as a souvenir." One has the distinct impression that he believed that this, like his decorations, would win votes.[97]

Ironically, he had overlooked his greatest achievement on the Nile, a propitious sign of what was to come. It lay in the sinew of his dispatches. His mastery of the language was growing. The fruits of his formal schooling had been negligible. He had entered the army an ignorant youth. Now, less than four years later, his command of English distinguished him from every other correspondent in the field and won the admiration of readers accustomed to the finest Victorian prose. He had arrived in Bangalore without knowing who Sophocles was or what ethics were, yet he could write, speculating about the Khalifa's men meeting Kitchener's first storm of fire: "What must the Dervishes have heard? Only those who were with the Prussian Guard on the glacis of St. Privat, or with Skobeleff in front of the Grivica Redoubt, can know." He could capture, as few writers can, moments of utter horror. Of a sergeant trying to collect his troop after the charge, he wrote: "His face was cut to pieces, and as he called on his men to rally, the whole of his nose, cheeks, and lips flapped amid red bubbles." He described the abandoned battlefield as looking "like a place where rubbish is thrown, or where a fair has recently been held. White objects, like dirty bits of newspaper, lay scattered here and there — the bodies of the enemy. Brown objects, almost the colour of the earth, like bundles of dead grass or heaps of manure, were also dotted about — the bodies of soldiers. Among these were goat-skin water-bottles, broken weapons, torn and draggled flags, cartridge-cases. In the foreground lay a group of dead horses and several dead or dying donkeys. It was all litter."[98]

As magnanimous to the enemy as he was rebellious toward his commander, he paid tribute to the slain Arabs:

> When the soldier of a civilised power is killed in action his limbs are composed and his body is borne by friendly arms reverently to the grave. The wail of the fifes, the roll of the drums, the triumphant words of the Funeral Service, all divest the act of its squalour, and the spectator sympathises with, perhaps almost envies, the comrade who has found this honourable exit. But there was nothing *dulce et decorum* about the Dervish dead. Nothing of the dignity of unconquerable manhood. All was filthy corruption. Yet these were as brave men as ever walked the earth. The conviction was borne in on me that their claim beyond the grave in respect of a valiant death was as good as that which any of our countrymen could make. . . . There they lie, those valiant warriors of a false faith and of a fallen domination, their only history preserved by their conquerors, their only monument their bones — and these the drifting sand of the desert will bury in a few short years. Three days before I had seen them rise eager, confident, resolved. The roar of their shouting had swelled like the surf on a rocky shore. The flashing of their blades and points had displayed their numbers, their vitality, their ferocity. They were confident in their strength, in the justice of their cause, in the support of their religion. Now only the heaps of corruption in the plain and fugitives dispersed and scattered in the wilderness remained. The terrible machinery of scientific war had done its work. The Dervish host was scattered and destroyed. Their end, however, only anticipates that of the victors, for Time, which laughs at Science, as Science laughs at Valour, will in due course contemptuously brush both combatants away.[99]

The Prince of Wales, though he felt his rebuke justified, added thoughtfully: "Your writing a book with an account of the campaign is quite another matter." Such a work, HRH said, would have his blessing, and he hoped Winston would "come & see me & tell me all about the recent campaign & about your future plans." Then, revising his earlier advice, he observed: "I cannot help feeling that Parliamentary & literary life is what would suit you best."[100] Winston agreed, of course. And he was in a hurry. He had reached the odd conclusion that he was destined to die, like his father, at forty-six, that whatever he did must be done by 1920. He had already anticipated the prince's literary advice and was at work on a new manuscript. Its working title was *The War for the Waterway.* He believed it would be ready for publication in a year, and he was right. What he did not anticipate was that he would be unable to read the reviews, because by then, still racing the calendar, he would be a prisoner of war in another part of Africa.

Back in England he was all business. In Rotherhithe, Dover, and Southsea he addressed cheering Tories. "To keep the Empire you must have the imperial spark," he said. And: "To keep our Empire we must have a free people, an educated and well fed people." And: "The great game will go on until we are come through all the peril and trial, and rule in majesty and tranquillity by merit as well as by strength over the fairest and happiest regions of the world in which we live." Turning a room at 35A Great Cumberland Place into a study, he started the new book; then, taking a break, he finished his novel, *Savrola,* and sent the completed manuscript to his grandmother for comment. Duchess Fanny thought it had "much merit and originality," but she noted shrewdly that the character based on Jennie "is a weak and uninteresting personality. It is clear you have not yet attained a knowledge of Women — and it is evident you have (I am thankful to see) no experience of Love!"[101]

Pamela Plowden could have told her that. As the daughter of Sir Trevor John Chichele-Plowden and granddaughter of a general, Pamela was eminently suitable for Winston, and he had written his mother that he thought her "the most beautiful girl" he had "ever seen," but although they had been meeting and corresponding for two years now, their relationship was going nowhere. One has the feeling that Miss Plowden, like Eliza Doolittle, was ready for action and was becoming exasperated as she got only words, words, words. She as much as told him so. He admitted it and promised to "try and take your advice," telling her that he had met a girl "nearly as clever & wise as you," which meant "I rank her one above Plato." Pamela, who plainly did not relish a comparison with Plato, at least not in this situation, accused him of lacking ardor, thus offering him a classic opening. But Winston was merely wounded: "Why do you say I am incapable of affection? Perish the thought. I love one above all others. And I shall be constant. I am no fickle gallant capriciously following the fancy of the hour. My love is deep and strong. Nothing will ever change it."[102]

In a sense this was true, but the object of his designs was not the marriage bed but political office. Pamela can scarcely be blamed if she found this unflattering. In retrospect Winston appears to have been a very eligible bachelor. Yet vaunting ambition can be unattractive in a young man. It can even be unpleasant for him. In a revealing note, Churchill wrote that though tempted, "I have no right to dally in the pleasant valleys of amusement." Then, in gnawing terror: "What an awful thing it will be if I don't come off. It will break my heart for I have nothing else but ambition to cling to." So he turned from arms which would have welcomed him and sought hands that could help him up. He lunched at the Carlton Club with rising Tories of his generation: Ian Malcolm, Lord Hugh Cecil, Lord Percy, and Lord Balcarres. The discussion was sharper and far more clever than anything he had heard in his regimental mess; he felt like an "earthen pot among the brass" and considered attending Oxford or Cambridge — until he learned he must first pass examinations in Latin and Greek. Then he discovered that companions at the Tory club possessed another political asset he lacked. They were rich. At Conservative party headquarters Fitzroy Stewart introduced him to Richard Middleton, "the Skipper," or party manager. Middleton greeted him warmly. He said the party would certainly find him a seat, and soon. Then he delicately raised the question of money. How much could Churchill pay for a constituency? Winston, taken aback, replied that he could meet his campaign expenses and no more. The Skipper grew distant. Safe seats, he said, cost MPs as much as £1,000 a year; "forlorn hopes" were cheap, but few were free. Churchill had already decided that he could not afford to serve HRH's mother as an army officer — "Her Majesty was so stinted by Parliament," he later said, "that she was not able to pay even a living wage" — and this strengthened his resolve. His pen had already brought him five times as much as his soldier's salary. His Sudan dispatches alone had produced £300. Now the *Pioneer* was offering him £3 a week for letters from London. That in itself would be more than the income of a subaltern. As he wrote Duchess Fanny: "I can live cheaper & earn more as a writer, special correspondent or journalist: and this work is moreover more congenial and more likely to assist me in pursuing the larger ends of life."[103]

He would have quit the army then, while his *Morning Post* pieces were still the talk of Fleet Street, had it not been for India's annual Inter-Regimental Tournament, now imminent. It may seem strange that a young man afire with ambition should journey halfway around the world to play a game, but to Churchill polo was "the emperor of games," almost a religion. So he sailed the first week in December aboard the S.S. *Osiris* and rejoined the Fourth Hussars just before Christmas. The trip north from

Pamela Plowden, 1892

Bangalore to the tournament ground at Meerut was another fourteen hundred miles by special train, with a two-week pause spent as guests of Sir Pertab Singh, regent of Jodhpur. They practiced there with local players, though it was eerie; the field was constantly enveloped in clouds of red dust, through which turbaned figures galloped at full speed, following the ball by the sound of its whistle. Then, the night before they were to leave for Meerut, calamity befell them. Churchill slipped on a stone staircase, and out went his shoulder. The team was dismayed. He was their No. 1. They had brought along an extra player, and he suggested a substitution, but they voted to keep him in, his elbow bound to his side. The weather was fine, the crowd huge, and their opponents, in the final, the formidable Fourth Dragoon Guards. In a close, furious match, the Fourth Hussars won the cup, 4–3. And Churchill, despite his disability, was the star. He wrote his mother from Calcutta on March 3: "I hit three goals out of four in the winning match so that my journey to India was not futile as far as the regiment was concerned."[104]

After a week in Calcutta as the guest of the new viceroy (the vicereine, Lady Curzon, wrote Jennie, "People in India have an immense opinion of Winston & his book"), he returned to Bangalore, forwarded his resignation papers to London, and sat misty-eyed while his fellow officers drank his health for the last time. "Discipline and comradeship" were the lessons he had learned in the regiment, he wrote, and "perhaps after all they are just as valuable as the lore of the universities. Still," he added, "one would like to have both." His university continued to be his books — he could now read at great speed — and his writing had become his livelihood. *Macmillan's Magazine* was paying a hundred pounds for serial rights to *Savrola.* For *The River War,* as he now called his new manuscript, he had even greater expectations. He had worked on it during the voyage over, in Jodhpur, in Meerut, and Calcutta; he continued writing it in Bangalore and on the trip home. To his mother he wrote that he was at it "all day & every day. . . . My hand gets so cramped. I am writing every word twice & some parts three times. It ought to be good since it is the best I can do."[105]

He was still learning. Macaulay was the real architect of *The River War,* and the balanced and ironical apothegms which appeared from time to time were borrowed from Gibbon. But his own style was nearly formed now. It was evident, not only on paper, but also in conversation, a fact noted during his trip homeward by a fellow passenger, the gifted G. W. Steevens of the *Daily Mail.* When they docked, Steevens filed a story about him, prophesying that he might become "a great popular leader, a great journalist, or the founder of a great advertising business." He said Churchill was "born a demagogue, and he happens to know it. The master strain in his character is the rhetorician. Platform speeches and leading articles flow from him almost against his will. At dinner he talks and talks, and you can hardly tell when he leaves off quoting his one idol, Macaulay, and begins his other, Winston Churchill. . . . We shall hear more about this in the course of ten years. . . . At the rate he goes there will hardly be room for him in Parliament at thirty or in England at forty."[106]

Kitchener tried to see to it that there was hardly room for him in Cairo, where he broke his journey to deepen his research on the Nile. The Sirdar had forbidden Major James Watson, his aide-de-camp in the Sudan, to furnish Churchill with any documents. Winston solved the problem, as many another writer has, by simply interviewing Watson. He also lunched with Lord Cromer, who "afterwards did me the honour of talking to me about the Soudan, its past and its future with reference to my book for more than two hours and a half." Cromer saw him twice more, provided him with letters of introduction to everyone of importance in Egypt, and introduced him to the khedive. Winston's letter to Jennie written at Cairo's Savoy Hotel immediately afterward serves as a vintage example of the British contempt which outraged the Empire's darker subjects. "I was much amused," he told her, "by observing the relations between the British Agent and the *de jure* Ruler of Egypt. The

Khedive's attitude reminded me of a school-boy who is brought to see another school-boy in the presence of the head-master. But he seemed to me to be an amiable young man who tries to take an intelligent interest in the affairs of his kingdom, which, since they have passed entirely beyond his control is, to say the least, very praiseworthy."[107]

He finished the manuscript — now destined to be two fat volumes, running, with maps, to nearly a thousand pages — in Great Cumberland Place. On May 3, 1899, he noted: "Miss P. has been vy much impressed with the Proofs of the first two chapters of *The River War.*" Pamela was still trying. Jennie, on the other hand, was busy pursuing literary ambitions of her own, launching a competitor to *Yellow Book* called the *Anglo-Saxon Review,* which, at a price of five dollars in the United States and a guinea in England, was destined to last eleven issues before she ran out of money. Winston's own finances were unchanged. He had high and, as it turned out, justifiable hopes for his new work, but nothing in hand except the *Macmillan's* check. Nevertheless, he was determined to stand for office now. He would, of course, run as a Conservative. It didn't matter that Gibbon had been a protégé of a renegade Tory and Macaulay a Whig, a precursor of the Liberals, or that all the indignation over Kitchener's profanation of the Mahdi's remains lay on the Liberal side of the House of Commons, while the Conservatives, as he noted from the Strangers' Gallery, seemed to think it "rather a lark." The explanation, of course, is that to desert the Tories would have been to betray his father's memory. He couldn't do that, at least not in 1899.[108]

The constituency chosen for him was Oldham, a working-class district in Lancashire, and the chooser, at the outset, was Robert Ascroft, one of the two Tory MPs who represented it. Ascroft wanted Churchill to run with him. Suddenly he died. Oldham's other MP resigned. That called for a double by-election. The Skipper expected to lose both seats, hoping he would win them back on the rebound in the next general election, and he picked Winston and a radical Conservative for the sacrifice. Winston knew how small his chances were, but reasoned that any fight was better than none. On June 20 he wrote Miss Plowden: "I have just returned from Oldham overnight. The whole thing is in my hands as far as the Tory Party there go." He wanted her to campaign with him. She refused; reading proofs was one thing, sweaty politics quite another. She sent him encouragement, a charm, and word that she would remain in London. In his reply he said he understood; "it would perhaps have been a mistake — but I shall be sorry nevertheless." He was still drawn to her, and kept her posted with bulletins on his progress. His left tonsil became inflamed; Dr. Roose, ever reliable, put a throat spray in the mail. On

Churchill in his first, unsuccessful, campaign for Parliament

June 28 Winston wrote that "the big meeting was a great success and although I spoke for fifty minutes my throat is no worse — but rather better. We are now in the middle of the fight." Four days later he reported, "A vy busy week has closed. I now make speeches involuntarily. Yesterday I delivered no fewer than eight." He felt he was improving: "At each meeting I am conscious of growing powers and facilities of speech, and it is in this that I shall find my consolation should the result be, as is probable, unfortunate. But I still wear your charm — so who can tell. Write to me Pamela — I have had you in my mind more perhaps this week than ever." The London papers had predicted his defeat. He didn't doubt it, or resent it; "after all," he told her, "the battle in the end must be to the strong."[109]

This Nietzschean sloganeering, though in high favor at the time — Winston was actually quoting John Davidson, a popular poet of the 1890s — begs the question. The fact is that while he spoke well, he was not yet a competent politician. Disraeli had warned Conservatives never to neglect social issues when soliciting blue-collar votes; so, in fact, had Lord Randolph Churchill. Winston was addressing undernourished, underpaid textile workmen, most of whom still wore wooden clogs. He told them: "Never before were there so many people in England, and never before have they had so much to eat." He praised the status quo, the Conservatives, Irish policy, "pride in our Empire," and "love for the ancient traditions of the realm." Although he also urged provisions for the poor — Woom was not forgotten — he was vulnerable to the charge that he represented the vested interests, despite the fact that both Liberal candidates were wealthy men. He even ran afoul of his own party. Salisbury had introduced a bill increasing government support of the Anglican church. Three days before the election Churchill announced that, if elected, he would vote against it. His words were flung at the embarrassed Tories in Parliament. Arthur Balfour, the Conservative leader in the Commons — "the divine Arthur" of the fashionable Panshanger set — said, "I thought he was a young man of promise, but it appears he is a young man of promises."[110]

To Winston's delight, his mother appeared on polling day, "dressed entirely in blue," according to a newspaperman, ". . . in a landau and pair with gaily ribboned and rosetted postillions." Pamela Plowden might recoil from electioneering, but for Jennie it evoked memories of the early years of her marriage. Nevertheless, Winston lost. She was at his side when the returns came in. The Liberals had taken both seats; his margin of defeat was 1,293 votes out of 48,672 cast. The *Manchester Courier* reported that Churchill "looked upon the process of counting with amusement, and the result of the election did not disturb him. He might have been defeated, but he was conscious that in this fight he had not been disgraced." He had, however, been wounded. Tory newspapers concluded that it had been a mistake to field a green youth in a working-class district. Word reached him that in the Carlton Club members were shaking their heads over the fact that he had run in tandem with a radical: "Serves him right for standing with a Socialist. No man of any principle would have done such a thing!" He later wrote dryly: "Everyone threw the blame on me. I have noticed that they nearly always do. I suppose it is because they think I shall be able to bear it best. . . . I returned to London with those feelings of deflation which a bottle of champagne or even soda-water represents when it has been half emptied and left uncorked for the night. No one came to see me on my return to my mother's house."[111]

He did, however, receive a letter. It was from Balfour, who regretted his slight and was now "very sorry to hear of your ill success at Oldham, as I had greatly hoped to see you speedily in the House where your father and I fought many a good battle side by side in days gone by. I hope however you will not be discouraged. . . . This small reverse will have no permanent ill effect upon your political fortunes." And later in July, Lady

Jeune brought Churchill and Joe Chamberlain together in her home on the Thames. They talked of South Africa. Now secretary of state for colonies, "Pushful Joe" was negotiating the government's growing dispute with the Boers, the Dutch farmers in South Africa. At one point he offered Winston a bit of political advice. He told him: "It's no use blowing the trumpet for the charge and then looking around to find nobody following."[112]

Chamberlain and Sir Alfred Milner, the British high commissioner in Cape Town, were preparing to blow the trumpet for a showdown with South Africa's Boers, and they wanted the backing of all England. Over the next two months, while Churchill was making his final changes in *The River War,* they carefully built it. By the end of September hostilities were imminent. Obviously Winston would go as a war correspondent. Harmsworth's *Daily Mail* and Borthwick's *Morning Post* were bidding for him, but in the end he stayed with Borthwick, who offered him unprecedented terms: expenses, protection of his copyright, and £250, roughly $1,250, a month. He wired news of his coming departure to Chamberlain, who replied from Birmingham on October 4: "I have your telegraph & will write to Milner tonight asking his good offices for the son of my old friend. . . . I shall be in London on Monday but I gather that you leave before then. If so good luck & best wishes!" In fact, Milner was to receive two letters recommending Winston; Chamberlain's, which was tepid ("He has the reputation of being bumptious. Put him on the right lines."), and a warmer one from George Wyndham, the under secretary of state for war: "He is a very clever fellow & is bringing out an unprejudiced mind."[113]

Actually, Winston wasn't due to sail until Saturday, so he saw Chamberlain once more. The autocratic colonial secretary invited him to share his morning hansom ride from the Chamberlain house at Prince's Gardens to Parliament. That morning he was the very quiddity of Joe, "Joe the Brummagem screw-maker," the self-made manufacturer from the Midlands: the diamond pin in his stock, the homegrown orchid in his buttonhole, his monocle in his eye, and, with the inevitable cigar in his teeth, as calm and self-assured as a slab of his Birmingham steel. "Buller," he said of General Sir Redvers Buller, the new commander in chief for South Africa, who was still in England, "would have been wiser to have gone out earlier. Now, if the Boers invade Natal, Sir George White with his 16,000 men may easily settle the whole thing." Sir George was in Ladysmith, which, with Kimberley and Mafeking, was regarded as one of the three keys to English defense. Churchill asked about

Mafeking, close to the border. "Ah, Mafeking, that may be besieged," Chamberlain said airily, "but if they cannot hold out for a few weeks, what is one to expect?" He added prudently, "Of course, I have to base myself on the War Office opinion. They are all quite confident. I can only go by what they say."[114]

On Thursday, when the first Boer shots were fired at Kraajpan, Churchill was packing his black tin steamer trunks with Thomas Walden, who had been Lord Randolph's valet and was now his son's. Winston had just submitted his first expense account, for £30 18s. 6d. Clearly he had no intention of living a Spartan life at the front. In addition to a compass, a new saddle fitted with a pigskin case, and his Ross telescope and Voigtlander field glass, repaired at Borthwick's expense, he was taking thirty bottles of 1887 Vin d'Ay Sec, eighteen bottles of St. Emilion, eighteen of ten-year-old scotch, a dozen bottles of Rose's Cordial Lime Juice, six bottles of light port, six of French vermouth, and six of Very Old Eau de Vie 1866.* Every evening that week he attended a dinner party in his honor. Since the election he had been trying, without much success, to grow a guardsman's mustache, and his touchiness about it inspired what may have been the first faint flash of Churchillian wit in London society. A friend of Jennie's, seated next to him at one of the dinners, told him she liked neither his politics nor his mustache. He replied, "Madame, I see no earthly reason why you should come in contact with either."[115]

The Royal Mail steamer *Dunottar Castle* was to sail at 6:00 P.M. Saturday, October 14, 1899, from Southampton docks. Churchill arrived early, jaunty in a yachting cap, but the huge crowd, perched on roofs and cranes, hadn't gathered for him. It was there to cheer his most distinguished fellow passenger, Buller, and Buller's staff. A fleet of civilian liners would follow with forty-seven thousand volunteers, but Sir Redvers was the man of the hour. The general's special train arrived at the wharf two hours before the *Castle* weighed anchor. Everyone was ready to follow Chamberlain's trumpet now. The throng sang "Rule Britannia," "For He's a Jolly Good Fellow," and "God Save the Queen." Men shouted, "Remember Majuba!" "Pull old Krojer's whiskers!" and "Give it to the Boers!" The ship's foghorn blew. A pioneer newsreel cameraman from the Biograph Company cranked his camera. From the head of the gangplank Sir Redvers thanked everyone and said he hoped he would not be away long. His hope was to be dashed. So were their hopes in him.

* This seems extraordinary today. It was less remarkable then. In the Sudan campaign Major Haig's personal pack train had included "one camel, laden with claret."

Eight years earlier Lord Randolph, during his own trip to South Africa for the *Daily Graphic,* had acquired five thousand shares in Rand Mines. They had been sold to cover his debts, but had he held them their value would have been increased by twenty times at his death, and, shortly thereafter, by fifty or sixty times. That was the key to the Boer issue. After Majuba, Gladstone had negotiated the London treaty of 1884, which had granted limited self-government to the two Boer republics, the Transvaal and the Orange Free State; the two South African colonies, Natal and Cape Colony, were to remain British. Then gold had been discovered in the Transvaal — diamonds had already been found near Kimberley — and Empire builders like Cecil Rhodes wanted the Transvaal and the Orange Free State back. At that time the world's monetary systems, chiefly British, were dependent on gold. The Empire builders thought they saw a way to regain power over the Boer lands. The gold rush of the 1880s had brought the Transvaal a tremendous influx of Englishmen, or Uitlanders ("Outlanders" — foreigners), as the Boers called them: so many that by the mid-1890s they probably formed a majority of the republic's inhabitants. To British imperialists they seemed exploitable.

President Paul Kruger — "Oom Paul," that strong Brueghel peasant whom Chamberlain had called an "ignorant, dirty, cunning" old man — was uncowed. He refused to give these British immigrants the vote. That was what the Jameson Raid had been all about; the raiders had hoped to spark an uprising by the English settlers. Badly planned, the plot had failed. Nevertheless, Rhodes and Chamberlain, who had been implicated in it, were determined to answer the Uitlander's *cri de coeur.* The fact that this was a violation of the 1884 pact, in which the British had agreed not to intervene in the Transvaal's domestic affairs, was ignored. Imperialists continued to speak ominously of "consolidating the Empire." On the eve of the first Boer crisis Gladstone had warned against "the fascinations of passion and of pride," but his voice had been stilled in 1898. Thousands of young Englishmen agreed with the more strident advocates of expansion; in India, Churchill had written: "Imperial aid must redress the wrongs of the Outlanders. Imperial troops must curb the insolence of the Boers." He thought the issue was the persecution of his countrymen, not gold. Chamberlain himself regretted that there was "too much of 'money-bags' about the whole business." Still, he and Milner kept nagging Oom Paul in Pretoria. The Boers refused their de-

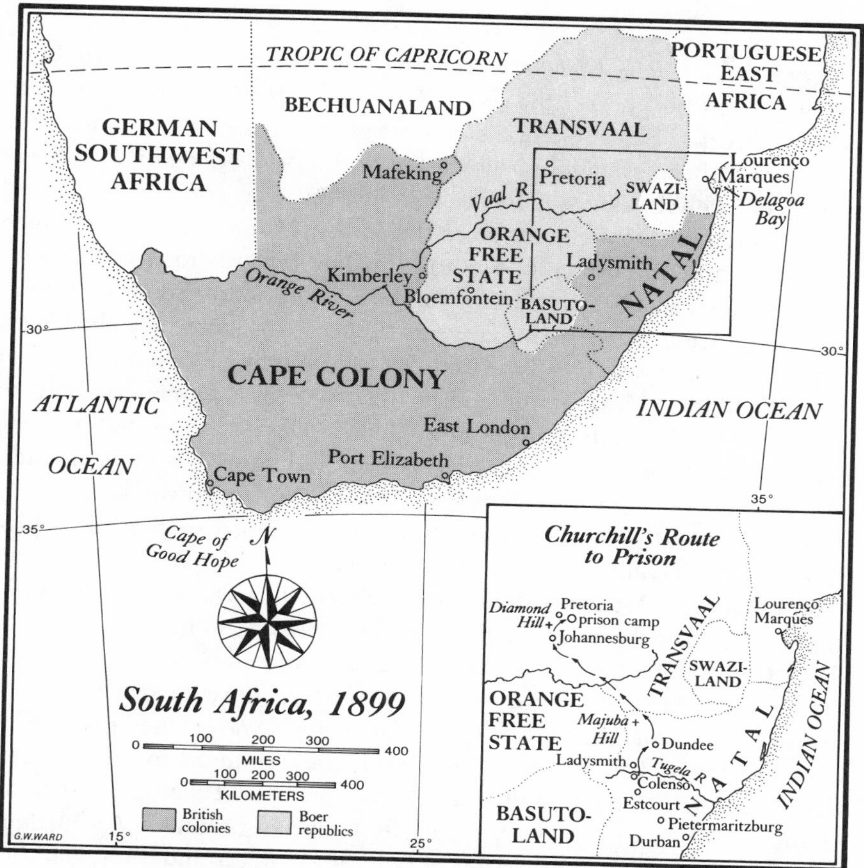

mands, and when the British began pouring reinforcements into Cape Colony and Natal, became alarmed. Unless the Afrikaners struck back, they realized, their forces would soon be outnumbered. Kruger, who understood the impact of technology on warfare, decided to put his faith in "God and the Mauser" — the Mauser, his Krupp howitzers and 75-millimeter field guns from the Ruhr, his 155-millimeter "Long Toms" from Schneider-Creusot in France, and, from Britain itself, his Maxim "pom-poms." He issued an ultimatum. If Chamberlain didn't stop his troop buildup, the Transvaal would fight. On October 11, 1899, three days before the *Dunottar Castle* sailed, the ultimatum expired and the war began.[116]

At the last minute the Orange Free State Boers had thrown in their lot with their Transvaal brothers. The British were surprised, but undaunted. Supremely self-confident, they were sure it would all be over by Christmas. *The Times* thought the ultimatum an "infatuated step" by a "petty republic," the *Globe* was irked by this "trumpery little state" and its "impudent burghers," the *Daily Telegraph* was "in doubt whether to laugh or weep." Since Victoria's coronation two generations earlier, her subjects had been swaggering down the highways of the world, fighting short, relatively bloodless colonial wars at almost no cost; the army had fought only two engagements since the Indian Mutiny of 1857 in which more than a hundred men had been lost. The rewards for this insignificant sacrifice had been immense; Rosebery had told an Edinburgh audience that during the past twelve years 2,600,000 square miles had been added to the Empire, chiefly in Africa. That might be called the end of the red-coat era. Now, at the end of the 1890s, the army was about to fight its first big conflict in its new khaki uniforms. Churchill and the *Dunottar Castle* were heading for the last of the Victorian wars, England's costliest struggle between Waterloo and Sarajevo, which would drain the Empire of a half-million men and bring down upon London the opprobrium of the civilized world. "If there was a good case for the Boer War," Margot Asquith would later write in her diary, "it was indifferently put, and I doubt if a single nation understood it." The war was about to give England, in Kipling's phrase, "no end of a lesson."[117]

Plunging through high seas and what Churchill called "grey storms" — as usual he was ill — the *Dunottar Castle* lurched toward the Canary Islands. Cut off from the world, they endured more than two weeks of what Winston called a "heavy silence"; it was, he wrote his mother, "a long time in war, especially in the beginning." At Madeira they learned nothing, which was "very hard to understand. Why did they declare war if they had nothing up their sleeves? Why do they waste time now?" On their sixteenth day they passed a tramp steamer, the *Australian,* whose crew held aloft a crude white-on-black sign: BOERS DEFEATED. THREE BATTLES. PENN SYMONDS KILLED.[118]

They took this to mean that the enemy had been routed in three engagements, though the loss of Symonds, a Natal general, was difficult to reconcile with victory. Winston heard an aide tell Buller, "It looks as if it will be over, sir." Sir Redvers replied, "I dare say there will be enough left to give us a fight outside Pretoria." The soundness of this military judgment was confirmed when, two days later, on October 31, they anchored in Table Bay and a launch sped out bearing, in Winston's words, a "Man Who Knew." All the tidings were grim. Mafeking and Kimberley were surrounded by Boers — had been, in fact, since the *Dunottar Castle* left Southampton. After Symonds's death General Sir George White had begun retreating into Ladysmith, which was itself threatened with encirclement. The enemy had been defeated nowhere. So much for the reliability of tramp steamers as news media. Ashore, Winston interviewed a distraught Milner and sent off a report: "We have greatly underestimated the military strength and spirit of the Boers. I vy much doubt whether one army Corps will be enough to overcome their resistance." Moreover, Kruger wasn't the only man with troublesome immigrants. Milner had told Winston that the Boers who lived here in Cape Colony under the Union Jack were "trembling on the verge of rebellion." Winston concluded that the British government could, "for the moment, be sure of nothing beyond the gunshot of the Navy."[119]

Buller intended to remain in Cape Town, pondering his choices and awaiting the arrival of his troop transports. At home, Salisbury was telling a Guildhall audience that his confidence in the British soldier "is only equalled by my confidence in Sir Redvers Buller." Churchill wasn't so sure. The general struck him as the kind of man who plodded "on from blunder to blunder and from one disaster to another." It was, Winston felt, time to leave him. During the voyage he and J. B. Atkins of the *Manchester Guardian* had agreed to knit their fortunes; now they decided to reach Ladysmith before the enemy slammed the door. On inquiry at the Mount Nelson Hotel they learned that by taking a train to East London, seven hundred miles away, and continuing by small mail boat or tug to Durban, they could beat other correspondents to the front by four days. It would be risky; the railroad skirted Boer strongpoints and was undefended. They caught the last express to get through safely and reached Durban, but the sea leg was an ordeal. Their ship, a steamer of about 150 tons, had to fight its way through a howling Antarctic gale. Between waves Winston could see "rocks which showed their black teeth endlessly a bare mile away upon our port beam." The seasickness, however, was far worse. He lay in his bunk "in an extreme of physical misery while our tiny ship bounded and reeled, and kicked and pitched, and fell and turned almost over and righted itself again . . . through an endless afternoon, a still longer evening and an eternal night."[120]

Arriving at midnight, they slept six hours and awoke only to be told that they were too late; Ladysmith was invested. The disappointment was deep, but they resolved to get as close to it as possible. Another train, zigzagging up and down hills and negotiating hairpin curves, took them sixty miles to Pietermaritzburg and on to Estcourt, a town of about three hundred stone-walled houses roofed with corrugated iron. Estcourt was the end of the line. They could hear the Ladysmith cannonade from there. While his valet pitched his tent, Winston uncapped his pen and began to write. All along the way he had been interviewing everyone who had fought or seen the Boers, beginning, in Durban, with Reggie

Barnes, his companion in Cuba and polo teammate later. Barnes had been wounded in the groin storming a hill at Elandslaagte; his colonel had fallen beside him; sixty-seven of their men had been killed or wounded in the assault. He had said: "All these colonials tell you that the Boers only want one good thrashing to satisfy them. Don't you believe it. They mean going through with this to the end." Again, Churchill's instincts told him Barnes was right. They betrayed him, however, when he talked to Uitlander refugees. On November 5 he reported "the fullest confirmation of the horrible barbarities perpetrated by the Boers," telling of a woman who had been flogged across the breasts and commenting: "Such is the Boer — gross, fierce, and horrid — doing the deeds of the devil with the name of the Lord on his lips. It is quite true that he is brave, but so are many savage tribes."[121]

One is struck, in reading Churchill's accounts from the South African battlefields, by the frequency with which he encountered old friends and acquaintances. Barnes was one. Ian Hamilton commanded troops nearby. Brabazon, back in uniform, was on his way. Leo Amery, Winston's fellow Harrovian, was the *Times* correspondent in Estcourt, and among the officers there was Captain Aylmer Haldane, whom he had known in India. On the night of November 14 the captain was ordered by his commanding officer, Colonel Charles Long, to lead two companies aboard an armored train and probe the Boer lines. As he later wrote in his memoirs, he was leaving headquarters when he noticed Churchill "hanging about to pick up such crumbs of information for his newspaper as might be available." Haldane described his mission to Winston and "suggested that he might care to accompany me next day. Although he was not at all keen he consented to do so, and arranged to be at the station in time for the start."[122]

Churchill's lack of enthusiasm was sensible. Buller, when he heard of Long's decision, called it "inconceivable stupidity." Winston had already described the armored train. It was "cloaked from end to end with thick plates and slabs of blue-grey iron." Slits permitted soldiers aboard to fire out. It looked formidable but was, as Thomas Pakenham puts it, "a parody of modern mobile war: an innovation that was already obsolete." All the Boers had to do was blow up a bridge or sabotage the rails; the locomotive would then be immobile and helpless. Winston should have turned Haldane down. He didn't, he wrote afterward, "because I thought it was my duty to gather as much information as I could for the *Morning Post*" and he was "eager for trouble." On those grounds it was justified. The trip would produce plenty of news and danger. It would do more;

before the adventure was over, his name would be a household word throughout England. Although it almost cost him his life the decision was, by the light of his flaming ambition, well worth the risk. He would have but one regret. Only yesterday he had posted a letter to the War Office in London, and before he saw another sunset he would wish he had left it unmailed. He had written: "There has been a great deal too much surrendering in this war, and I hope people who do so will not be encouraged."[123]

Louis Botha, the swarthy Boer general besieging Ladysmith, overestimated the number of British troops in Estcourt. Apprehensive that they might be preparing to break his grip on the town, Botha, on the day Churchill agreed to join Haldane, led a column of five hundred mounted raiders southward to investigate, and the next morning, standing in his stirrups atop a ridge, he sighted the armored train steaming north. After the lumbering monstrosity had passed, he ordered rocks strewn on the rails just around a curve and then awaited its return. As the engine reappeared, headed back toward the British lines, his gunner fired two shells at it. Peering out from inside his car, or truck, as they were called, Churchill had just spotted a clump of Boers on a nearby knoll. At that instant he was dazzled by a flash of light and jarred by the sound of steel fragments rattling on the train's iron shield: "It was shrapnel," he later wrote — "the first I had seen in war." He thought the train might be headed into a trap and turned to Haldane to say so. Simultaneously the engineer up ahead, frightened by the shells, rocketed around the curve at full throttle and crashed into the rocks. Before Churchill could speak "there was a tremendous shock, and [Captain Haldane] and I and all the soldiers in the truck were pitched head over heels on to its floor."[124]

Scrambling up, Winston saw scores of Boers lying on the grass outside, delivering heavy and accurate rifle fire upon one side of the train. He and Haldane ducked and put their heads together. The captain, they agreed, should move to the rear and order his troops to pin down the Boer riflemen while Churchill inspected the damage and tried to repair it. Winston found the locomotive still on the rails. The next three cars had been derailed, however, and the civilian engineer, bleeding from a superficial face wound, was on the verge of hysteria. Churchill lectured him on duty. Then he congratulated him. This, he told him, was the chance of a lifetime. He might even be rewarded for "distinguished gallantry." Besides, he assured him, no man could be hit twice in one battle. This absurd fiction quieted the driver and they went to work.

It was the subsequent recollection of all the survivors, including the Boers, that Winston was under intermittent fire for the next seventy minutes. He himself would remember the "soft kisses" of bullets as they "sucked in the air" around him, but he was completely engrossed in "the heat and excitement of the work"; his choice, he felt, lay between "danger, captivity and shame on the one hand, and safety, freedom and triumph on the other." It was just possible, he thought, that the engine could be used as a ram to clear the wrecked cars from the line. He darted back and forth, straining at car couplings, conferring with Haldane, and calling for volunteers from the troops in the cars behind. Few responded. His own conduct is best described in Haldane's official report, written after he and Winston had fallen out. The captain noted that "owing to the urgency of the circumstances," he formally placed Churchill on duty. He added: "I would point out that while engaged on the work of saving the engine, for which he was mainly responsible, he was frequently exposed to the full fire of the enemy. I cannot speak too highly of his gallant conduct." As a good valet, Walden was on the spot. Afterward he wrote Jennie: "the driver was one of the first wounded, and he said to Mr Winston: 'I am finished.' So Mr Winston said to him: 'Buck up a bit, I will stick to you,' and he threw off his revolver and field-glasses and helped the driver . . . knock the iron trucks off the road by running into them with the engine."[125]

It proved impossible to link the locomotive and the rear cars. Yet the situation wasn't entirely hopeless. Just ahead lay a railroad trestle and, beyond that, safety. Churchill herded Walden and forty Tommies, many of them wounded, aboard the engine and its tender, and took up a position behind the engineer until they had crossed the bridge. There he left them. He was returning to Haldane, on foot, trying to think how he might bring more men out, when two men in mufti arose from the bushes beside the tracks, "tall figures," he would later remember, "full of energy, clad in dark, flapping clothes, with slouch, storm-driven hats, poising on their levelled rifles hardly a hundred yards away." His mind flashed: "Boers!" He tried to climb the railroad embankment; they fired and missed. Next he turned to dash back to the bridge. A Boer horseman came galloping from that direction, shaking a rifle and shouting. Churchill decided to kill him. He reached for his pistol — and realized that he had left it on the locomotive. The horseman — it was Botha himself — now had him in his sights. Winston remembered a quotation from Napoleon: "When one is alone and unarmed, a surrender may be pardoned." He raised his hands and stepped forward, a prisoner of war.[126]

He was prodded toward Haldane and the cowering British troops, who had already been rounded up. Churchill blurted out to Atkins when next he met him that the soldiers had indeed been rounded up "like cattle," and that this had been "the greatest indignity of my life." A heavy rain had begun to fall, and Churchill was drenched, wading through a patch of high grass, when "a disquieting and timely reflection" crossed his mind. In the breast pocket of his khaki jacket were two clips of Mauser ammunition from Omdurman, politely known in army quartermaster manifests as "MK IV and MK V issue" but notorious to the public as dumdum cartridges — soft-nosed or expanding bullets which disintegrated when they hit a man's body. Dumdums had been outlawed at the Hague Conference the previous July, and Churchill knew it. As his guard turned to open an umbrella he managed to drop one clip unseen. He had the other in his fist when the Boer, looking down from his horse, said sharply in English: "What have you got there?" Winston opened his hand and asked, "What is it? I just picked it up." Botha took the clip, glanced at it, and tossed it in the grass. It is sad to note that the following March 9 Churchill indignantly informed his *Morning Post* readers that the Boers were using "expansive" bullets and piously commented that "the character of these people reveals in stress a dark and spiteful underside. A man, I use the word in its fullest sense, does not wish to lacerate his foe, however earnestly he may desire his death."[127]

Even without the dumdums he was anxious about his fate. He ranged himself in line with the other prisoners but was brusquely picked out by the Boers and told to stand apart. It was an ominous order. He "had enough military law," as he put it, "to know that a civilian in a half uniform who has taken an active and prominent part in a fight, even if he has not fired a shot himself, is liable to be shot at once by drumhead court martial." Then, just as curtly, he was directed to rejoin the others; an enemy officer came over and told him they knew who he was and regarded him as a prize: "We don't catch the son of a lord every day." Churchill, in his own phrase, felt "quite joyful" at the realization that he would live. His euphoria lasted during the subsequent three-day trek north, on foot sixty miles around the booming cannons pounding Ladysmith and then by train from Elandslaagte to their prisoner-of-war camp in Pretoria's State Model Schools. Once there behind wire, however, he forgot his gratitude for escaping a firing squad and he convinced himself that his captivity was illegal.[128]

An artist's reconstruction of the armored-train ambush, in the Daily News Weekly *of November 25, 1899*

Winston's response to imprisonment tells a great deal about him. He felt disgust, despair, rage. This is not a universal reaction to restraint. Many public men have adjusted to it without great difficulty; it has served as a temporary refuge for them, a place for reflection, study, and writing. Mohandas Gandhi, now toiling in South Africa as a leader of Indian stretcher-bearers, would later flourish in British prisons. But not Churchill. He found, he wrote, "no comfort in any of the philosophical ideas which some men parade in their hours of ease and strength and safety." His wrath and tremendous frustration probably arose from his depressive nature. He needed outer stimuli, the chances for excitement and achievement which were his lifelong defenses against melancholia. The prisoner-of-war camp was like being back in the harness of school. It was worse; their long tin POW dormitory was enclosed by a ten-foot corrugated iron fence rimmed by barbed wire, watched by armed guards fifty yards apart, and brilliantly illuminated at night by searchlights on tall standards. Elsewhere the war continued, great events were in progress, but here he was penned in, entirely in the power of the Boers. He owed his life to their mercy, his daily bread to their compassion, his movements to their indulgence. In this atmosphere he found himself picking quarrels with other British officer inmates over trivial matters — he couldn't tolerate their whistling — and took no pleasure from their company. He felt, he wrote, "webbed about with a tangle of regulations and restrictions. I certainly hated every minute of my captivity more than I have ever hated any other period in my whole life."[129]

At the end of his first week behind wire he wrote the Transvaal authorities, demanding his release as "a non-combatant and a Press correspondent." He argued disingenuously that he had taken "no part in the defence of the armoured train," had been "quite unarmed," and had merely done "all I could to escape from so perilous a situation and to save my life." Unfortunately, his fellow war correspondents had interviewed survivors of the wreck, and British newspapers were reporting details of his audacity under fire; the Natal *Witness* of November 17 had carried a statement by the railwaymen expressing their "admiration of the coolness and pluck displayed by Mr Winston Churchill . . . who accompanied the train, and to whose efforts . . . is due the fact that the armoured train and tender were brought successfully out." Churchill, it was reported, was being considered for the Victoria Cross. Under these circumstances, the Kruger government endorsed the recommendation of their commandant-general, Piet Joubert, who, upon hearing of his application, urged that he be "guarded and watched as dangerous for our war; otherwise he can still do us a lot of harm. In a word, he must not be released during the war. It is through his active part that one section of the armoured train got away." Winston protested that because he was well known the world would regard him "as a kind of hostage" and that this would "excite criticism and even ridicule." If given his freedom, he said, he would "withdraw altogether from South Africa during the war." The Boers were unimpressed. He wrote his mother and the Prince of Wales, begging for help. They could do nothing. In a darker mood he wrote Pamela ("Not a vy satisfactory address to write from — although it begins with P. . . . I write you this line to tell you that among new and vivid scenes I think often of you") and, on November 30, to Bourke Cockran: "I am 25 today — it is terrible to think how little time remains!"[130]

His weeks in prison would have been limited, whatever happened. Somehow, one feels, powerful friends of Jennie's, HRH's, or even Cockran's found a way to intervene successfully on his behalf. There is simply no other explanation for the extraordinary judgment Joubert rendered on December 12, completely reversing himself. Pondering Winston's denial that he played an active role in the events which followed the train wreck, and having decided (he didn't say why) that he was an honorable English gentleman and could therefore be only truthful, the commandant-general wrote: "I have to accept his word in preference to all the journalists and reporters." Their accounts, he said, must have been "exaggerated." He therefore concluded: "I have no further objections to his being set free."[131]

Had it ended there, the incident would have had little effect on Churchill's political fortunes at home. But before this order could reach the POW camp, he had taken matters into his own hands. Like his lie about the wreck, the story of his breakout from Pretoria is not entirely creditable, but a special tolerance has always been extended to prisoners of war bent on freedom, and there is no reason to withhold it from him, particularly in light of the courage and imagination with which he carried out the escape plan. The plan was not, however, his. It was the brainchild of Haldane and one A. Brockie, a regimental sergeant major, who, to get better quarters, had passed himself off as an officer. In the back of the enclosure, shielded from the searchlights, stood a circular toilet. The night sentry there seemed lax. Brockie spoke both Afrikaans, developed from seventeenth-century Dutch, and the native Bantu language. If he and Haldane could jump the wall there unobserved, he might be able to talk their way across the countryside to Portuguese East Africa — "Portuguese East" — and freedom. Churchill, overhearing them, insisted that they take him with them. He would see to it, he said, that Haldane's before the moon rose, Haldane and I both got into the roundhouse and waited for a chance of climbing over; but after much hesitation we thought it too dangerous; and came back to the veranda. Brockie then came up and asked us why we had not got over. Haldane explained the difficulty of the sentry's position, and Brockie said; "You're afraid". Haldane replied: "You can go and see for yourself". Brockie then went across the yard, got into the roundhouse, and remained there some time. Then I said: "I will go back again". I went across the yard, and at the entrance to the roundhouse I met Brockie coming out, but we dare not speak to each

From Churchill's later version of the escape

name appeared in headlines all over the world. Brockie didn't want him; he thought him unpredictable and believed another fugitive would increase their risks. But although the key to the scheme, the sergeant major was an enlisted man; his opinion didn't count for much. Haldane, having invited Winston aboard the train, felt a certain responsibility for his plight. He would include him, he said, provided he "conform to orders."[132]

Their chances of success were slight, and were to become slighter, but Winston, ever confident, wrote an impudent letter to the Boer under secretary of war on Monday, December 11, and left it in his bunk. It was headed "p.p.c." —*pour prendre congé* (to take furlough). "I do not concede," he began, "that your Government was justified in holding me . . . and I have consequently resolved to escape." Friends "outside," he said, were "making this possible." Before leaving he wanted to "place on record my appreciation of the kindness which has been shown to me," promised to "set forth a truthful and impartial account of my experiences in Pretoria," expressed the hope that "this most grievous and unhappy war" would end the enmity between the Boers and British "races," and ended: "Regretting the circumstances have not permitted me to bid you a personal farewell, believe me, Yours vy sincerely, Winston S. Churchill."[133]

Tuesday night, unaware of Joubert's order, which had gone out that afternoon, the three donned civilian suits acquired by barter and awaited their chance. Haldane and Churchill entered the latrine and returned, discouraged by the sentinel's unexpected vigilance. Brockie accused them of timidity, but when he went in, he, too, was thwarted. Churchill reentered alone, passing Brockie coming out. Once inside, he saw his chance — the guard had turned to light a pipe — and leaping to the top of the wall he dropped into a garden on the other side. There he crouched, awaiting the others. But they were luckless. At one moment Haldane was in the toilet, ready to jump, when the sentry stirred and leveled his rifle at him. Churchill waited for an hour and a half, then decided to go on alone. He left behind two very resentful countrymen. The idea, after all, had been theirs. Haldane was "bitterly disappointed to find that Winston had gone," he would later write in his memoirs, adding, "I resist the temptation of stating what Brockie had to say on the subject."[134] Yet it is difficult to see what else Winston could have done. A ledge on the outer side of the wall prevented him from climbing back. His prospects in any case were extremely dim. Ahead of him lay three hundred miles of wild and hostile country. He didn't know the language. He lacked a compass and a map — Brockie had those. His pockets contained seventy-five pounds in British money, four slabs of chocolate, and a few biscuits. Believing he had no other choice, he rose from the garden, making no attempt at concealment, and strode past another sentry, unchallenged, into the moonlit evening.

Pretoria was crowded with burghers. He strode right through them, humming to himself until he reached the suburbs, where he sat on a little bridge to reflect. At dawn he would be missed; pursuit would be immediate. At any rate he was free, "if only for an hour." Wandering about, he found a railroad track and followed it to the nearest station. There he waited in a ditch until the next train arrived. It paused five minutes and started moving again. He had no idea where it was going, but it offered the only way out of town. As the locomotive passed him he saw the engineer "silhouetted against the furnace," the "black profile of the engine," and "clouds of steam." His moment was now. Twice he hurled himself at cars and fell back; on the third try he found a handhold and vaulted into a mass of empty coal bags. Burrowing into them, he fell asleep.[135]

The sky was still dark when he awoke. Remaining aboard till daybreak was out of the question; his presence would be betrayed when the bags were unloaded. He had to alight quickly, find water, and hide, awaiting the return of night and another train. Springing from the speeding car, he took two gigantic strides and sprawled in a shallow trench. Then, finding a pool in a nearby gully, he forced himself to drink all he could hold because he had no way of knowing when he would find more. Dawn broke and he felt jubilant: the train tracks ran straight toward the sunrise and Portuguese territory. That day was spent huddled in a ravine, nibbling at chocolate; his sole companion was "a gigantic vulture, who manifested an extravagant interest in my condition, and made hideous and ominous gurglings from time to time."[136] As dusk deepened he crawled out and made his way to a point where the tracks lay uphill and on a curve, reasoning that a train would slow there, permitting him to hop aboard. But no train came. Sometime after midnight, having waited six hours in vain, he struck out on foot, hoping to put ten or fifteen miles of roadbed behind him before another day dawned. Presently he saw the flaw in this plan. Every railroad bridge was guarded by armed men. To avoid them he had to creep across the moonlit veld or detour through bogs, swamps, and streams. A station loomed. On a siding lay three long strings of freight cars. He was studying their markings, hoping to learn their destinations and then hide in one which seemed promising, when loud voices came toward him, scaring him away and driving him out into the grass of the boundless plain.

By now he was exhausted, wandering aimlessly. Out in the darkness to his left gleamed what appeared to be the fires of a Kaffir kraal, a native village. It occurred to him that the Kaffirs, who were said to be disillusioned with the Boers, might be cooperative. He spoke no Bantu tongues, but perhaps sign language would do; it had worked when he was lost in the Sudanese desert. There seemed to be no alternative, so he turned that way. As he approached the settlement, he saw he had been mistaken. It wasn't a kraal at all. The lights came from furnace fires outside several stone houses clustered around what could be identified, by the wheel of a winding gear, as a coal mine. He felt a flicker of hope. In the POW pen he had heard that a few Englishmen, needed by the Boers for their skills, had been permitted to remain in some of the Witbank and Middelburg mining districts, seventy-five miles east of Pretoria. This might be one of them. But which houses would be British, and which Boer? He would have to guess. If he picked a wrong one he would produce his bank notes, explain who he was, and promise to pay anyone who would help him another thousand pounds later. Striding out of the veld and past the furnace fires, he chose a darkened home at random and knocked. A light sprang up. A man's voice called, *"Wie is daar?"**

Churchill's heart sank. He spoke no Afrikaans. He said, "I want help;

* In his subsequent accounts, Churchill wrote that he had heard *"Wer ist da?"* But that is German. The above is Afrikaans.

I have had an accident." The door opened and he saw a tall, pale, mustachioed figure, hastily attired and holding a revolver. The man said in English, "What do you want?" Winston improvised a story: he was a burgher en route to join his commando at Komati Poort, on the Portuguese frontier; he and some friends had been skylarking on their train; he had fallen off and dislocated his shoulder. Obviously the man didn't buy it. He stared hard, backed into the house, and roughly demanded details. Winston decided to throw in the towel. Stepping inside he said, "I think I had better tell you the truth," and, after his host had nodded grimly, "I am Winston Churchill, war correspondent for the *Morning Post.* I am making my way to the frontier" — as he said it, he reflected bitterly on how wretchedly he had done — "and I have plenty of money. Will you help me?"[137]

A silence grew, and grew uncomfortable. The tall man continued to stare, as though struggling to make up his mind. Suddenly he closed the door behind them, thrust out his hand, and blurted: "Thank God you have come here! It is the only house for twenty miles where you would not have been handed over. But we are all British here, and we will see you through." Churchill sagged with relief. Wringing the man's hand he felt, as he later put it, "like a drowning man pulled out of the water and informed he has won the Derby." His savior introduced himself as John Howard, manager of the Transvaal Collieries. He led the way to the kitchen, produced whiskey and a leg of mutton, and explained their situation. Within were his British secretary, a mechanic from Lancaster, and two Scottish miners. All four had given the Boers their parole to observe strict neutrality. Howard himself was a Transvaal citizen; if caught harboring an escaped prisoner, he would be shot for treason. But the prospect didn't seem to alarm him. He vanished while Winston ate, consulted the others, and returned to say that the five of them had agreed that the best course, for the time being, was to hide their fugitive in the mine. Howard led him out to the winding wheel. There, to Churchill's astonishment, the mechanic introduced himself as a prospective constituent — Dan Dewsnap of Oldham. Gripping his arm, Dewsnap whispered: "They'll all vote for you next time."[138]

The Scotsmen were waiting at the bottom of the shaft with a mattress and blankets. By lantern light Howard gave Winston two candles, cigars, and the whiskey bottle. He warned him not to move until they returned the next night; blacks would be around during the day, and if they saw him, they would talk. Winston, weary but elated, "saw myself once more rejoining the Army with a real exploit to my credit." Then he had misgivings. He was putting these men in real danger. He offered to move on alone; he asked only for food, a pistol, a guide, and, if possible, a pony. He wouldn't have a chance, the departing Howard told him. Only that afternoon a Boer officer had been there, asking about him. "They have got the hue and cry out all along the line," he said, "and all over the district."[139]

Back at the camp the previous morning Churchill's absence had been discovered, his letter found. Its reference to friends "outside" had led his guards to believe, as he had meant them to, that he had accomplices in Pretoria. Warrants were issued, houses searched; nothing was found. This being the capital of the republic, correspondents from neutral countries heard of the hunt. Then the name of the missing man leaked out. Borthwick sent Jennie word: "Just received the following from Reuter, 'Churchill escaped.' " The *Daily Telegraph* speculated: "If Mr Churchill is caught the Boers won't let him have the privileges of being a prisoner-of-war again. He cannot be shot unless he uses arms to resist capture, but he may be subjected to confinement rigorous enough to control the innate daring and resourcefulness of which he inherits his full share." He wasn't expected to reach the frontier; within forty-eight hours two papers reported he had been seized, first at Waterval-Boven and then at Komati Poort. The Boers were certainly determined to find him. Joubert felt betrayed. He furiously wired Kruger's state secretary: "With reference to Churchill's escape I [wonder] whether it would not be a good thing to make public the correspondence about the release of Churchill to show the world what a scoundrel he is."[140]

Despite the *Daily Telegraph*, a newsman in Pretoria cabled that on recapture he "may probably be shot," and one London paper, the *Phoenix*, actually thought that reasonable, commenting that "the Boer General cannot be blamed should he order his execution. A non-combatant has no right to carry arms. In the Franco-Prussian War all non-combatants who carried arms were promptly executed." A. E. Brofman, the Boer deputy superintendent of police, posted notices all over the Transvaal describing the fugitive as: "Englishman 25 years old, about 5 ft 8 in tall, average build, walks with a slight stoop, pale appearance, red brown hair, almost invisible small mustache, speaks through the nose, cannot pronounce the letter 'S', cannot speak Dutch, during long conversations occasionally makes a rattling noise [*voggeld*] in his throat, was last seen in a brown suit of clothes." Boers were asked "to remain on the alert and in case aforementioned Churchill appears to arrest him at once." Presses were rolling with a police photograph of him, and a price was set on his head.[141]

Brofman's quarry awoke the following afternoon, reached for the candles, and found nothing. It would be dangerous, he knew, to blunder around the shaft in the dark, so he lay still until, several hours later, a faint gleam of lantern light heralded the return of Howard, bearing a chicken and several books. The chicken, he explained, came from the home of an English physician who lived twenty miles away. It was a necessary precaution; Howard's Boer servants had been inquisitive about the missing mutton. Policemen were knocking on every door here. The presence of English residents in the mining district made it a natural focus of suspicion. But he assured Churchill he was safe. He could pass the time reading. Where, by the way, were his candles? Winston told him they had vanished. His host gave him a half-dozen replacements and apologized; he should have warned him to keep them under the mattress. If left out, he explained, they would be devoured by the swarms of savage white rats in the mine.

Fortunately Churchill did not share the common revulsion for rats. During his three days in the mine they were his biggest problem, pulling at his pillow when he stored the candles beneath it, scurrying around him whenever he blew the flame out, and even wakening him from a doze by running across his face. Once the two miners came down and led him on a tour of the shaft's subterranean tunnels and galleries; Winston, ever interested in new experiences, questioned them closely about their work. But mostly he glared at rats and read. On the fourth day Howard visited him and said the manhunt seemed to be losing its momentum. The police were combing Pretoria again, convinced he could not have left the town, that a British sympathizer there must be harboring him. He was brought up for a walk on the veld that night and then moved into new quarters behind packing cases in Howard's office. There he remained for three more days, and was frightened but once, when intermittent rifle fire broke out in the neighborhood. A Boer police officer was in fact there, but the shots had been the result of a ruse of Howard's. To draw the man away from the house, he had challenged him to a rifle match, shooting bottles. The gullible policeman had won and left no wiser.

Howard now had an escape plan. He had recruited another plotter, Charles Burnham, a local shipping agent.* On Tuesday, December 19, Winston's seventh day of freedom, a consignment of wool was to be

* Churchill was always under the impression that Burnham was "a Dutchman" named "Burgener."

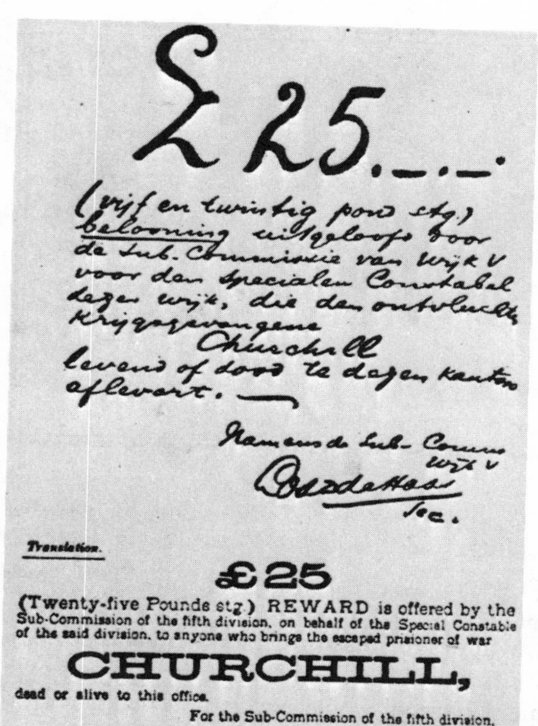

£25.—.—

(vijf en twintig pond stg.)
belooning uitgeloofd voor
de Sub-Commissie van wijk V
voor den specialen Constabel
dezer wijk, die den ontvluchte
krijgsgevangene
Churchill
levend of dood te dezen kantoor
aflevert. —

Namens de Sub-Comm.
wijk V
Lodk de Haas
Sec.

Translation.

£25

(Twenty-five Pounds stg.) REWARD is offered by the Sub-Commission of the fifth division, on behalf of the Special Constable of the said division, to anyone who brings the escaped prisioner of war

CHURCHILL,

dead or alive to this office.

For the Sub-Commission of the fifth division,
(Signed) LODK de HAAS, Sec.

Notice of reward for Churchill's return to prison

loaded on the mine's railroad branch and sent, via the main line at Balmoral, to Lourenço Marques in Portuguese territory. Churchill would be hidden among the bales. At first, curiously, he balked. He said he would rather cross the veld with directions and a horse. Imprisonment, he later reflected, had warped his judgment. He was reading Stevenson's *Kidnapped* at the time, identifying with David Balfour and Alan Breck in the glens. Like them, he was a victim of his need for concealment and deception, which, he later concluded, "breeds an actual sense of guilt very undermining to morale. Feeling that at any moment the officers of the law may present themselves or any stranger may ask the questions, 'Who are you?' 'Where do you come from?' 'Where are you going?' — to which questions no satisfactory answer could be given — gnawed at the structure of self-confidence." He agreed to the trip but dreaded it.[142]

Tuesday dawned. Howard led him to the car, and he squeezed through a tunnel in the wool to an enclosed space among the bales large enough for him to lie and sit. On the floor were a pistol, two roast chickens, several slices of meat, bread, a melon, and three bottles of cold tea. He had memorized the names of the train stations they would pass and hoped to follow their progress through a chink in the bales. A tarpaulin was tied

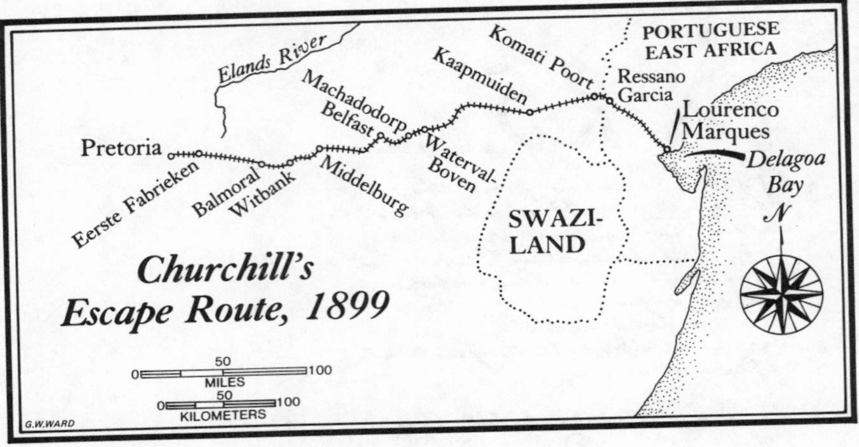

over the car; they rumbled off. But Winston found his chink inadequate. He saw few signs. The couplings and uncouplings of cars, the banging and jerking in freight yards, the long waits on sidings, baffled and exasperated him.

It was just as well he knew no more. Burnham had decided to accompany the train in one of the passenger cars, and before the trip was over he felt he had aged a lifetime. Churchill would never have made it without him. At Middelburg, their second stop, a trainman wanted to shunt the wool car off on a sidetrack and leave it there overnight; at Waterval-Boven a railroad agent ordered it sidetracked because of a petty regulation; an armed Boer started to untie the tarpaulin when they paused in Kaapmuiden; and when they reached Komanti Poort and the frontier, a detective stepped forward to search the entire train. Burnham dissuaded all of them with bribes and drinks until they had crossed the border and reached Ressano Garcia, where, for the first time, he encountered an honest man. The stationmaster, refusing his money, said the wool could not proceed with the passenger cars. The best he would do was promise it would follow within a half hour. Burnham therefore reached Lourenço first, bribed another policeman — who wanted to arrest him for "loitering with intent" — and was waiting when his cargo arrived. According to Burnham's account in the Johannesburg *Star* twenty-four years later, "The truck had not been stationary a minute when Churchill, black as a sweep by reason of the coal-dust which was in the bottom of the truck, sprang out." Meanwhile, Winston, squinting through his peephole, had already seen a Portuguese place-name painted on a board. He was so carried away that he shoved aside the bale overhead and "fired my revolver two or three times in the air as a *feu de joie.*"[143]

Burnham led him out of the station, around several corners, and

Churchill addressing the crowd at Durban

paused. He looked up silently at the roof of a building opposite. Winston followed his gaze "and there — blest vision! — I saw floating the gay colours of the Union Jack. It was the British Consulate." A piece of opéra bouffe ensued. At the door a minor official took one look at his filthy clothes and snapped: "Be off. The Consul cannot see you today. Come to his office at nine tomorrow if you want anything." Churchill stepped back, threw back his head, and shouted at the upper stories: "I am Winston Bloody Churchill! Come down here at once!" An upstairs window flew open; it was the startled consul, Alexander Ross. Ross called hurried instructions to the man downstairs, and within a quarter hour Winston was lolling in a hot bath. In borrowed clothes he accompanied Burnham to a store, where, Burnham recalled, "he bought a rigout and a cowboy hat." Back at the consulate, after an enormous dinner, Churchill dispatched a sheaf of telegrams to London. At Great Cumberland Place Jennie picked up the telephone and heard a reporter shouting into the mouthpiece: "Hurrah! Hurrah!" Miss Plowden sent a three-word telegram: "Thank God — Pamela."[144]

Winston meanwhile was devouring newspapers. All the news was bad. During what was being called Black Week, December 10–15, British forces had suffered appalling casualties and three staggering defeats, including a rout of an attempt by Buller to relieve Ladysmith by frontal attack up the railway line. Churchill, chagrined, wanted to rejoin the army as soon as possible. Ross was equally anxious to see him go; Lourenço Marques was a hotbed of Boer partisans, and there were rumors that his guest was about to be kidnapped and returned to the Transvaal. On December 21, nine days after Churchill's escape, a party of armed Englishmen escorted him from the consulate garden to the waterfront, where he boarded the steamer *Induna.* Two days later he docked at Durban. An enormous, cheering crowd awaited him. The entire harbor was decorated with bunting and flags; bands were playing; the mayor, an admiral, and a general leapt up the gangplank to embrace him. After Black Week, the British had been yearning for a hero, and here was a handsome young patrician who had broken out of a Boer prison and made his way across three hundred miles of hostile territory to freedom. The mob whirled him along on its shoulders, deposited him on the steps of the town hall, and demanded a speech. His remarks have not survived, but the mood of the moment, the vitality, confidence, and innocence of the English in that last month of the nineteenth century, are caught in the lively strains of the war's hit song, trumpeted by the bands as he finished:

Goodbye, Dolly, I must leave you
Though it breaks my heart to go
Something tells me I am needed
At the front to fight the foe

See the boys in blue are march-ing
And I can no longer stay
Hark! I hear the bugle call-ing
Goodbye, Dolly Grey!

And then, as he climbed down, they struck up that spine-tingling anthem of Victorian conquest:

Britons always loyally declaim
About the way we rule the waves
Every Briton's song is just the same
When singing of her soldiers brave . . .

We're not forgetting it
We're not letting it
Fade away or gradually die!

So when we say that England's master
Remember who has made her so!

It's the soldiers of the Queen, my lads,
Who've been the lads, who've seen the lads
In the fight for England's glory, lads —
Of her world-wide glory let us sing!

And when we say we've always won
And when they ask us how it's done
We'll proudly point to every one
Of England's soldiers of the Queen!

That afternoon he caught a train to Pietermaritzburg, where he remained overnight as the guest of Sir Walter Hely-Hutchinson, governor of Natal, and picked up more disquieting information. The kaiser had written his grandmother the Queen, threatening to side with the Boers. ("I cannot sit on the safety valve forever. My people demand intervention.") Buller had cabled the War Office that the investment of Ladysmith could not be lifted without further reinforcements. More troopships were on their way to him, but he had been demoted. Although he would retain command of the Natal forces, Lord Roberts was sailing down to take over as commander in chief, with Kitchener, Winston's nemesis, as chief of staff. Back at the front, Churchill celebrated Christmas Eve with the rest of the press corps, scarcely a hundred yards from the site of the armored-train ambush. In a flush of patriotism he cabled the *Morning Post:* "More irregular corps are wanted. Are the gentlemen of England all fox-hunting? Why not an English Light Horse? For the sake of our manhood, our devoted colonists, and our dead soldiers, we must persevere with the war." Buller wrote Lady Theresa Londonderry: "Winston Churchill turned up here yesterday escaped from Pretoria. He really is a fine fellow and I must say I admire him greatly. I wish he was leading irregular troops instead of writing for a rotten paper. We are very short of good men, as he appears to be, out here." He then sent for Churchill and questioned him closely about conditions in the Transvaal. All he got were impressions Winston had gleaned by looking through a tiny crack between bales of wool, but at the end he said: "You have done very well. Is there anything we can do for you?"[145]

To his delight, Winston asked for a commission. The general said, "What about poor old Borthwick?" and his face fell when Churchill replied that he couldn't possibly break his contract with the *Morning Post.* It might be a rotten paper to the general, but it paid twelve times as much as the army. That put Buller in a dilemma. After the Nile expedition, the War Office had ruled that no soldier could double as a war correspondent. Now Churchill, whose dispatches had been responsible for the ruling, was asking that he be made an exception to it. The general circled the room three times, worried an ear, and said: "All right. You can have a commission in Bungo's regiment. You will have to do as much as you can for both jobs. But you will get no pay for ours." Winston quickly agreed, and "Bungo" — Colonel Julian Byng, commanding the South African Light Horse, an Uitlander regiment — appointed him assistant adjutant, with the understanding that while not actually fighting he could go where he liked. Happily stitching his badges of rank on his khaki jacket, Churchill stuck the SALH's long plume of "cockyolibird" feathers in his hat and headed toward the sound of the guns.[146]

In London, Borthwick raised no objection — since the escape his circulation had soared — but the arrangement was a poor one. Taken as a whole, Churchill's youthful war correspondence reveals a remarkable grasp of strategy and tactics and an admirable readiness to criticize senior officers. He felt indebted to Buller, however, and here, as in Cuba, gratitude warped his judgment. He wrote: "If Sir Redvers Buller cannot relieve Ladysmith with his present force we do not know of any other officer in the British Service who would be likely to succeed." That was absurd, and in moments of clarity he knew it. On January 10, after a bloody reverse on the Tugela River, he wrote Pamela: "Alas dearest we are again in retreat. Buller started out full of determination to do or die but his courage soon ebbed and we stood still and watched while one poor wretched brigade was pounded and hammered and we were not allowed to help them. . . . And the horrible part of it all is that Ladysmith will probably fall and all our brave friends be led off to captivity and shame." In the aftermath of another disaster — the general had delegated authority to a weak officer, then relieved him — Churchill pictured Buller at last gripping "the whole business in his strong hands." He failed to note that by then it was too late for the men who had died in vain.[147]

The toll was mounting. And the British, including Churchill, were shocked and bewildered. None of them had ever known anything like this slaughter. Even Majuba, fought near here, had been relatively tame. In their defeat there the British had lost just ninety-two men. The Boer bullet which had crippled Ian Hamilton's left wrist — Winston called it Hamilton's "glorious" deformity — had been enough to distinguish him. Now, abruptly, everything had changed. This time the Boers, unlike the Pathan and Omdurman tribesmen, were armed with weapons just as modern as Buller's. Machine guns shredded the Queen's dense khaki ranks. Distant Long Toms, sited far beyond the reach of the English cavalry, fired 40-pound, 4.7-inch shrapnel shells that dismembered men or even obliterated them. Barbed wire had appeared, and sandbagged entrenchments. The Boers understood the new warfare. They told one another: "Dig now, or they'll dig your grave later."[148] The baffled British clung stubbornly to their Sandhurst principles. Cavalrymen like Major Douglas Haig assured one another that their *arme blanche,* the lance and sword, would winkle out the foe. They tried and failed and tried and failed and learned nothing. In British regimental accounts one finds the first pathetic strains of a theme which would be sounded throughout all the wars of the twentieth century, now less than a month old. This or that local engagement was "imperishable," or "immortal"; it would "go down in history," "enshrined forever" in the records of the past. So it was said in South Africa that winter of Hussar Hill, Mount Alice, Conical Hill, Aloe Knoll, and Potgeiter's Ferry. So it would be said of Broodseinde in 1917, Galloping Horse Ridge in 1942, the Punchbowl in 1951, and Pleiku in 1965. Eventually all would be forgotten, even by the descendants of those who had fought there.

The first of the century's butcheries was Spion Kop, or Spion Mountain, and Churchill was there, as was Gandhi with his stretcher-bearers. Abandoning the plan of forcing the Tugela at Colenso, Buller tried to turn Botha's right flank by fording the river upstream and seizing this 1,470-foot height, the hub of the range of hills between Buller and Ladysmith. On the night of January 23 his men stealthily mounted the steep slopes, scarred with huge rocks. They achieved total surprise. The enemy's defenses were thin here, and a dense mist covered the flat crest; it was 4:00 A.M. before a Boer picket on the summit challenged them: "*Wie is daar?*" He was answered by hoarse yells of "Waterloo!" and "Majuba!," a zigzag line of Lee-Enfield flashes, and a charge which took the kop at a cost of ten casualties. The victors held the key to the Ladysmith lock. But before they could turn it they had to face the greater challenge of holding it.

Botha, roused in his tent and told "the Khakis" were on the height, called for long-range rifle fire and salvos from his five Krupp field guns and two pom-poms. Presently Boer shells were bursting over the hilltop, seven every minute. The effect was devastating. By now the summit, an area about the size of Trafalgar Square, was packed with Uitlanders. They had no cover. One survivor later described the peak as "the most awful scene of carnage." Atkins, the *Guardian*'s correspondent, perched on a nearby ridge, reported that it was becoming an "acre of massacre."[149] Buller had expected to support this embattled force with an assault on the other Boer flank, but now the necessary men couldn't be found. One Uitlander raised a white flag; an officer furiously tore it from his hand. He was right to do so. Their position was precarious, but far from desperate. Around midnight Botha's artillery commander panicked and fled with his guns. The first wave of counterattacking Boer commandos was driven off the kop's reverse slope. At this point the obvious move for the British was to renew their drive, clearing a knoll and a spur just ahead. Their problem was that no one seemed to be in charge.

Into this muddle, out of breath but full of resolution, climbed Lieutenant Winston Churchill. He had been waiting in the vicinity with his regiment, hoping to be sent up the hill. Lacking orders and impatient, he had galloped over here on his own, tethered his horse at the bottom, and ascended on foot, gripping boulders and struggling through "streams of wounded." Soldiers, he wrote, were "staggering along alone, or supported by comrades, or crawling on hands and knees, or carried on stretchers. Corpses lay here and there. Many of the wounds were of a horrible nature. The splinters and fragments of the shell [sic] had torn and mutilated in the most ghastly manner." To Pamela he wrote: "The scenes on Spion Kop were among the strangest and most terrible I have ever witnessed." He had, he said, been "continually under shell & rifle fire and once the feather in my hat was cut through by a bullet. But — in the end I came serenely through."[150]

He came through and went back again, though hardly with serenity. He was rushing around the front in complete violation of regulations, intent on rescuing the situation by sorting everything out personally and then persuading nearby commanders to intervene. Incredibly, no one put him in his place; superior officers, distraught in the confusion, heard him out and pondered his advice. Night fell and he toiled back up the hill, which in his words was now "hopelessly congested" with stragglers and casualties, toward "an intermittent crackle of musketry at the top." Battalions were intermingled. Regimental officers, he noted, were "everywhere cool and cheery, each with a little group of men around him, all full of fight and energy. But the darkness and the broken ground paralysed everyone." He was off again, rounding up sappers and miscellaneous troops. Finding the senior officer, a newly promoted brigadier, he explained what he had done and what he proposed be done next. The brigadier, in shock, on the verge of a complete breakdown, mumbled that it was all hopeless and he had decided to withdraw: "Better six good battalions safely down the hill than a bloody mop-up in the morning." Churchill insisted the gains could still be consolidated — military historians agree with him — and harangued the brigadier about "Majuba" and "the great British public." It was in vain; the order to retreat went up. Down the Uitlanders came, leaving their dead three deep. In the first olive moments of dawn Churchill glowered up, his thumbs in his braces and his lower lip thrust out in that way he had, and saw two of Botha's burghers standing jubilantly on the pinnacle. They were waving their rifles and slouch hats, shouting that the Khakis had been "*kopschuw*" — routed.[151]

His bitterness over the loss of Spion Kop was relieved by the arrival in South Africa of Lady Randolph Churchill. Jennie had solicited £41,597 from wealthy Americans and commissioned a hospital ship, the *Maine*, named after the U.S. warship lost in Havana harbor. In the forecastle were an American flag, sent by Theodore Roosevelt, and, from Queen Victoria, a Union Jack. (Jennie chose to fly the British colors.) Accompanying her on the voyage was Jack, just nineteen, whose brother had obtained a commission for him in the SALH. They had learned of Winston's escape the day before they sailed, and he met them on the Durban docks. After they had killed a bottle of '25 brandy, Jennie mounted a wild horse, tamed it, and rode it into the regiment's camp. At forty-five her beauty had reached its autumnal glory, and if she seemed determined to prove that she retained the energy of youth, there was reason: she had decided to marry George Cornwallis-West, an impecunious junior officer just Winston's age. There is no record of her sons' reaction to this. Her friends, however, were appalled. Jennie didn't care. She told one of them: "I suppose you think I'm very foolish, but I don't care. I'm having such *fun.*"[152]

Winston's family was well represented in South Africa now. There was his mother; his brother; his bland, mustachioed cousin Sunny, the young duke, serving in Cape Town as Lord Roberts's military secretary; and, among the civilians in besieged Mafeking, his aunt Lady Sarah Wilson, Randolph's glamorous thirty-five-year-old sister, who, bored by London, had come down here for excitement and found it. Captured in the Transvaal during a clumsy attempt at spying, she had been exchanged for a Boer cattle thief and now held court in a luxurious, white-paneled bunker hewn out of Mafeking's red soil, the walls decorated with African spears from the Matabele War and a huge Union Jack. Lady Sarah was a survivor; no one seems to have been concerned about her. Winston was worried about Jack, however. He felt responsible for him, and almost immediately his fears were justified. In action for the first time on Hussar Hill, Jack was wounded in the calf. To Atkins, "It seemed as though he had paid his brother's debts." Winston thought it "an instance of Fortune's caprice." Jack, he wrote Pamela, had been "lying down. I was walking about without any cover — I who have tempted fortune so often. Jack was hit." To his mother he wrote: "It is a coincidence that one of the first patients on board the *Maine* should be your own son . . . but you may be glad with me that he is out of harm's way for a month. There will be a great battle in a few days and his presence — though I would not lift a finger to prevent him — adds much to my anxiety when there is fighting."[153]

The great battle, for Vaal Krantz, was fought and succeeded by another, and then another. Slowly the weight of British numbers began to tell. Kimberley, 240 miles to the west, was relieved by Major General John French, while here in Natal, Botha fell back on Hlangwane Hill, then in further retreats on Inskilling Hill, Pieters Plateau, Railway Hill, and Hart's Hill. Churchill was in action almost every day, and on the historic evening of February 28, the one hundred eighteenth day of Ladysmith's investment, he rode with the first two squadrons to enter the beleaguered town, galloping "across the scrub-dotted plain, fired at only by a couple of Boer guns. Suddenly," he wrote, "from the brushwood up rose gaunt figures waving hands of welcome. On we pressed, and at the head of a battered street of tin-roofed houses met Sir George White on horseback, faultlessly attired. . . . It was a thrilling moment." That night he dined with White and Ian Hamilton on champagne and a roast from the garrison's last trek-ox, saved for this occasion. But "better than feast or couch" was the reward, "which was all the more splendid since it had been so long delayed — victory."[154]

Churchill remained in Ladysmith over a month, feverishly writing a new book, *London to Ladysmith via Pretoria.* His escape had fueled sales of his earlier works — 8,000 copies of *Savrola,* 3,000 of the two-volume *River War* at 36 shillings ($9), and 600 of the *Malakand Field Force* — bringing him about £1,500 in royalties. This, with the checks from Borthwick, went into his political war chest. Already Tories in Southport had invited him to run in their constituency, but he wanted vindication in Oldham. When Joe Chamberlain sent him a long letter, inviting a discussion of public affairs, he cannily replied that, while he hoped "to find a seat before the dissolution, as I should like to record a vote on many points," he could not return to England "until the end of the war or at least until the Transvaal is in our hands." His Oldham defeat had taught him the need for planning. He meant to build a financial base, at the same time cultivating readers with his vivid prose — "Winston's graphic tongue," as Jennie called it. Yet he could never be a cautious politician. With casualty lists lengthening, the last thing his readers wanted from him was a plea for magnanimity toward the enemy. Nevertheless, he wrote: "Peace and happiness can only come to South Africa through the fusion and concord of the Dutch and British races, who must forever live side by side," and "I earnestly hope, expect and urge that a generous and forgiving policy will be followed." Angry subscribers disagreed, and his own paper ran an editorial demanding punishment of the Boers. Hely-Hutchinson wrote him that Boers who sought to return to Natal "shd be tried & punished. . . . You must remember that the Natal Dutch have been treated with special consideration in the past, and that if what we hear from many sources is true they have been the ringleaders in the looting & destruction that has been going on in Natal." What looting? Winston asked. What destruction? It appeared to him that this was based on unconfirmed rumors. He refused to retract; indeed, with each Boer defeat his appeals for mercy and compassion grew stronger.[155]

As a suitor, on the other hand, he continued to be both indecisive and inept. He wrote his mother: "I think a great deal of Pamela; she loves me vy dearly." Yet a considerate young man would have spared his beloved the grisly details of his brushes with death. Winston kept Pamela fully informed on every bullet, every shell fragment that came his way, reminding her over and over that each breath might be his last, that even as she read this he might already be a decomposing cadaver. "I was very nearly killed two hours ago by a shrapnel," he wrote her in a typical missive, and, on the eve of a battle, "I pray to God that I may have no thoughts of myself when the time comes — but for you my darling always." Unquestionably he missed her. Indeed, when Jennie had arrived he wrote Pamela: "Oh why did you not come out as secretary? Why did you not come out in the *Maine* so that I should be going to meet you now." Then, as after her refusal to campaign in Oldham, he backed off: "Perhaps you are wise." He didn't understand women; he compared them with his eccentric mother and was puzzled by the variance. When Pamela, like Joe Chamberlain, hinted that he had done his part and ought to come home now, he bridled. "I do not know whether I shall see the end or not," he replied, raising that specter again, "but I am quite certain that I will not leave Africa till the matter is settled. I should forfeit my self-respect forever if I tried to shield myself behind an easily obtained reputation for courage. No possible advantage politically could compensate — besides believe me none would result." That was the nub of it. He was convinced he was making political capital down there and was therefore content. The possibility that he might make better time with her by leaving the front seems never to have occurred to him.[156]

The limelight, which he craved more than any woman's company, now faded from Natal and shone down upon the Cape Colony, where England's shortest and most popular soldier was preparing to move through the Orange Free State and into the Transvaal. Kipling understood the popularity of the diminutive Field Marshal Lord Roberts, KCB, GCB:

What 'e does not know o' war,
Gen'real Bobs,
You can arst the shop next door —
can't they, Bobs?

O 'e's little but 'e's wise,
'E's a terror for 'is size,
An' — 'e — does — not advertise

Do yer, Bobs?

Churchill, forgetting his earlier bitterness, described him as "this wonderful little man." Bobs, however, did not reciprocate. Kitchener, bitter over Winston's criticisms at Omdurman, had deepened the field marshal's distrust of this impudent subaltern who presumed to pass judgment on his commanding officers. Moreover, Bobs had been outraged by a Churchillian critique of a church parade on the eve of the assault on Vaal Krantz. Over five thousand men had assembled, awaiting inspiration. "The bridegroom Opportunity had come," Winston had written. "But the Church had her lamp untrimmed." Instead of a rousing sermon, the chaplain "with a raucous voice" had preached dully on Jericho, freezing the soldiers "into apathy." Bobs was sensitive to criticism of army chaplains, who had come to South Africa in response to a War Office call for volunteers. But Hamilton and Sir William Nicholson, another of Winston's friends from India, interceded on his behalf, and on April 11 a colonel wrote Churchill from Bloemfontein, the Orange capital: "Lord Roberts desires me to say that he is willing to permit you to accompany this force as a correspondent —*for your father's sake.*"[157]

Winston seethed over Bobs's "making me accept as a favour what was already mine as a right," as he put it in a letter home.[158] There was a marvelous inconsistency here. He had, after all, thrived on favors at every step on his journey to fame, and he continued to enjoy them by joining Hamilton, now an acting lieutenant general, and Sunny, who had become Hamilton's aide, on the flank of Bobs's drive across the Vaal River toward Pretoria. By choosing to remain among friends, he missed the relief of Mafeking by two flying columns on May 17; London's hysterical joy added a verb to the language, *maffick,* "to indulge in extravagant demonstrations of exultation on occasion of national rejoicing," and the release of Aunt Sarah, not to mention that of the heroic Colonel R. S. S. Baden-Powell, commander of the garrison, would have been worth columns of soaring copy which might have swung more than a few votes in Oldham. Yet he was flourishing where he was. By now he had become adept at creating his own dramas, investing skirmishes and patrols with a Churchillian aura that depended less on the news than the reporter.

The Prince of Wales, writing that he was a rapt follower of "all yr accounts fr the front," had permitted himself a feeble little royal joke: "It is to be hoped you will not risk falling again into the hands of the Boers!" In fact, after attaching himself to Brabazon's brigade in the open countryside around Dewetsdorp, forty miles from Bloemfontein, Winston risked precisely that. A party of mounted British scouts decided to beat the enemy to an unoccupied white stone kopje, or hillock, and Winston impetuously joined them "in the interests of the *Morning Post.*" They had dismounted 120 yards from the crest, and were cutting through a wire fence there, when they found they had lost the race. Over the top, Churchill wrote luridly, loomed the heads and shoulders of a dozen Boer riflemen — "grim, hairy and terrible." The British captain called: "Too late; back to the other kopje. Gallop!" His scouts leapt on their mounts and bounded off, but just as Winston put his toe into his stirrup the riflemen opened fire, and his terrified horse, plunging wildly, slipped the saddle and ran off. He was alone, a mile from cover, an easy target. As he reached for his Mauser he saw a mounted British scout to his left, a tall man on a pale horse, and he thought: "Death in Revelation, but life to me!" He ran toward him, shouting, "Give me a stirrup!" The rider paused and Churchill vaulted up behind him. As they rode toward safety Winston wrapped his arms around his rescuer and gripped the mane. His hand came away soaked with blood. The animal had been badly hit, Churchill wrote, "but, gallant beast, he extended himself nobly." His rider cried: "My horse, oh, my poor bloomin' horse; shot with a dum-dum! The bastards! Oh, my poor horse!" Churchill, realizing that they were out of range now, consoled him: "Never mind, you saved my life." "Ah," said the rider, "but it's the horse I'm thinking about." And that, Winston wrote, "was the whole of our conversation." He never saw the man again.[159]

Poring over his dispatches, one feels that war had become like that to him, a great Hentyan adventure, heightened, here and there, by breathtaking flirtations with death, threats always turned aside at the last moment. The gore on Spion Kop, though faithfully chronicled at the time, had been forgotten; it was nasty, but not so nasty as its sequel, defeat. If Englishmen showed pluck and daring, if they were loyal to their Queen and their manhood, Britain would always win through; Saint George was sure to slay the dragon in the end. The facts, however ugly, were laundered to suit the Churchillian preconception. Those who have other memories of combat turn away troubled. Yet these incidents were real. The tall man on the pale doomed horse left no version of the episode, but the captain of the scouts made a full report, and it confirmed Winston. Virtually every event he described in South Africa, as in Cuba, on the North-West Frontier, and at Omdurman, was witnessed by others whose recollections were consistent with his. The difference, of course, lay in interpretation. Winston fashioned his own reality, created his own life. "I had thrown double sixes again," he wrote after he had been saved from the kopje riflemen.[160] He did it over and over. He had reached the prison latrine just as the sentry was lighting his pipe, had found the one train which passed through Pretoria that night, had blindly knocked on the door of the one man in the mining district who could and would help him through to the Portuguese border, and had been spared a thousand times in battle since then while the first bullet had found poor Jack. So it would continue throughout the march with Roberts, and if his view of life under Bobs seems fantastic, one can only observe that in his case life was, and continued to be, remarkably melodramatic.

Just once was he vouchsafed a glimpse of what the South African war was all about. On the last day of May, Roberts took Johannesburg, in the heart of the Witwatersrand, the "Rand," that sixty-three-mile-long ridge, seamed with auriferous rock, which constitutes the world's richest goldfield. After gazing down at the gray-stockinged feet of eighteen Highlanders awaiting burial, Churchill wrote, he found himself "scowling at the tall chimneys of the Rand." But the moment passed. England wouldn't send men to die for *that.* He turned away and presently found himself with Hamilton, Sunny, and the exhilarating advance of the eleven-thousand-man flank force's move northward. The weather was magnificent, the scenery stunning. In later life he told his doctor, "I loved it: all movement and riding." He spent £1,000 of *Morning Post* expense money on a pair of horses, a team of four oxen, and a wagon whose false bottom was crammed with liquor and Fortnum and Mason groceries. They almost lost the wagon fording a stream, but naturally Winston guided the team through the current. One night they found a flock of geese on a pond. Sunny shepherded them toward his cousin, who felled one with a flying kick. They ate it that night, and they let General Hamilton have some.[161]

Counting the main force under Roberts, Johannesburg and then Pretoria were the objectives of over 200,000 British troops. The Boers never had more than 88,000 men under arms on all fronts, and they prudently prepared to abandon the Transvaal capital and withdraw eastward. On June 2 they were still there, however, standing between Hamilton's column and the main army under Roberts. Hamilton had just crushed an enemy force at Doornkop; he wanted Bobs to know of it. He was only twenty miles from the field marshal by direct route, but a courier avoiding Johannesburg would have to cover an eighty-mile detour over rough country. Churchill, as it happened, had just finished interviewing a

Frenchman who had left the town only hours before on his bicycle. Boer security was lax there, said the Frenchman; he was certain Winston could safely cycle right through. He offered to lend him his bike, even volunteered to borrow another from a friend and act as his guide. If a Boer became suspicious, they would chat in French.

Here, surely, was temptation. Less than six months earlier, against all odds, Winston had fled prison just north of here. Then he had been merely a war correspondent. Now he held a Queen's commission. He would have to travel in a civilian suit. In his pocket he would be carrying an urgent report from one British commander to another. Even the debonair Frenchman — if indeed he was what he said he was; Winston, with his own atrocious French, was no judge of that, and no one else here had ever laid eyes on the man before — conceded that armed Boers were thick in the streets. A simple search by any one of them and Winston would be shoved against the nearest wall and executed by an ad hoc firing squad. Nevertheless, he agreed. He took the plan to Hamilton, who, amused, gave him a copy of the dispatch he was sending by orderlies the long way. Changing clothes, Winston shoved it into the jacket with his *Morning Post* telegrams and cycled off with his carefree guide.

In Johannesburg they had one bad moment. They were pushing their bikes up a long steep street when a slowly trotting Boer horseman drew abreast, reined in his mount, and walked alongside, carefully scrutinizing them. The rider had a rifle slung on his back, a pistol in a holster, and three bandoliers of ammunition dangling from his shoulder. Altering their pace would have been a grave mistake. Turning away, Winston said as much in French, sounding all the final consonants as usual — his companion flinched — and the Boer trotted off. Encountering no enemy picket line, another stroke of luck, they reached Roberts's advance patrols without further incident. Churchill was taken directly to Bobs. The commander in chief read the dispatch. Then he looked up and asked: "How did you come?" "Through Johannesburg," Churchill said, and explained. The little man's eyes twinkled. Winston wrote gaily, "Lord Roberts had very remarkable eyes, full of light. I remember being struck by this at the moment." Bobs's chilliness toward him had disappeared. Kitchener remained distant, but Winston's new source of news and favors was at the very top.[162]

The first fruit of this conversion followed within seventy-two hours. Bobs permitted him to canter into Pretoria, with Sunny at his side, at the head of the lead column. They galloped toward the POW camp in the State Model Schools. It looked exactly as it had when he left nearly six months before, a long tin building surrounded by dense wire, and the

Boer guards, still on watch, brought their rifles to the ready. "Surrender!" cried Sunny, and after an uneasy pause the commandant appeared and capitulated. Prisoners had rushed to the fence. Haldane and Brockie were gone — they had finally made it to the British lines on their own — but the others were all there. One of them, Lieutenant Thomas Frankland of the Second Dublin Fusiliers, had been wondering if the sound of distant gunfire meant approaching freedom. He wrote, "Who should I see on reaching the gate but Churchill, who, with his cousin, the Duke of Marlborough, had galloped on in front of the army to bring us the good tidings." Another prisoner, a Yorkshire engineering officer named Melville Goodacre, recorded in his diary how he had been washing clothes in the compound "when suddenly Winston Churchill came galloping over the hill." Goodacre watched, astonished, a wet shirt still in his hand, as Winston pushed past the guards — Sunny was giving the commandant a receipt for their rifles — and made for the flagpole. He produced a Union Jack. Then, Goodacre's diary continues, he "tore down the Boer flag and hoisted ours amidst cheers," whereupon "the Boer guards were put inside and our prisoners guard over *them!*" It was, the diarist thought, "roarable and splendid." It was also the first time the British colors had flown over Pretoria since April 5, 1881, immediately after Majuba.[163]

Churchill saw action once more, a week later, in the battle of Diamond Hill. Kruger, brokenhearted, was preparing to leave the country aboard a Dutch cruiser, but Botha defiantly rallied seven thousand burghers fifteen miles outside the capital and dug in on a height athwart the railroad tracks leading to Portuguese East. Roberts sent Hamilton against them. The army's elite infantry regiments, the Coldstream Guards and the Scots Guards, were bogged down on the lower slopes when Winston, according to Hamilton's memoirs, *Listening for the Drums,* saw the key to victory — a path to the crest — and realized that most of it was dead ground to the Boers because they had their heads down, seeking cover from the heavy British fire. He headed that way, having managed "somehow," Hamilton wrote, "to give me the slip." Presently the amazed British troops saw him mounting the trail alone. "He climbed this mountain," Hamilton recalled, "as our scouts were trained to climb on the Indian frontier and ensconced himself in a niche not much more than a pistol shot directly below the Boer commandos — no mean feat of arms in broad daylight and one showing a fine trust in the accuracy of our own guns. Had even half a dozen of the Burghers run twenty yards over the brow they could have knocked him off his perch with a volley of stones." Waving a handkerchief on a stick, he signaled that this was the way up.

The general sent men to the path; they rushed the summit and took the hill. Citing Winston's "conspicuous gallantry," Hamilton recommended him for the Victoria Cross, but, he wrote, "Bobs and K" vetoed it; Churchill "had only been a Press Correspondent — they declared — so nothing happened." It must have hurt. The VC was the award Winston coveted above all others. To friends, however, he assumed a philosophical air. He said of war correspondents: " 'All the danger and one-half percent of the glory': such is our motto, and that is the reason why we expect such large salaries."[164]

Churchill assumed that the war was over. By the rules of traditional warfare, it should have been; once the enemy's capital had fallen and his army had been beaten in the field, he was supposed to quit. Winston therefore began packing. "I need not say how anxious I am to come back to England," he wrote his mother. "Politics, Pamela, finances and books all need my attention."[165] But the Boers disregarded the rules. Like the Cuban insurrectionists, they ignored Roberts's demand for unconditional surrender and then dispersed into guerrilla commandos, the South African conflict's last contribution to twentieth-century warfare. Their bands, brilliantly led, continued to fight for nearly two more years; one force under Jan Christiaan Smuts raided deep into the British colonies, striking within fifty miles of Cape Town. Suppressing them, and pacifying the countryside, fell to the ruthless Kitchener — Bobs had sailed back to Europe, calling the war "practically over" — with Hamilton as his chief of staff. "K" built blockhouses along the railways, burned the guerrillas' farms, slaughtered their livestock, and penned Boer women and children in concentration camps, where over twenty thousand died. In the end the guerrillas capitulated, bitter but helpless. The two Boer republics were dissolved and incorporated in the Empire. That action could be reversed, however, and in time it was. England's losses, on the other hand, were irreplaceable. The Boer blitz of 1899 had destroyed the myth of British invulnerability; now, in this final *fin de siècle* convulsion, Britain's moral position was also crippled.

Winston missed all this. After interviewing Milner in Cape Town and spending a day foxhunting with the Duke of Westminster, he boarded the *Dunottar Castle* and set to work on a new book, *Ian Hamilton's March,* a paste-up of his dispatches since leaving Buller. *London to Ladysmith* had appeared five days before the relief of Mafeking; the two books were to sell twenty-two thousand copies in England and the United States, the equivalent of over seventy thousand today. He was also planning his entrance into public life. He hoped his mother would tell him of the country's political temper when he docked in Southampton July 20. To his consternation, she wasn't there; she was busy preparing for her wedding and had let the house in Great Cumberland Place, which Winston regarded as his home as well as hers. Sunny rescued him, assigning him the lease of a spacious flat at 105 Mount Street in Mayfair. Winston bought furniture at Maples and asked his aunt Leonie to redecorate the rooms — "you cannot imagine how that kind of material arrangement irritates me; so long as my table is clear and there is plenty of paper I do not worry about the rest."[166]

During the next seven months he was seldom there. Public interest in him was almost overwhelming. Eleven Conservative constituencies now sought him as their candidate, but he made straight for Oldham, which gave him a tremendous welcome. A band played "See the Conquering Hero Comes" as he entered the town in the midst of a procession of ten landaus. Shopkeepers and factory hands lined the streets, some shouting, "Young Randy!" At the Theatre Royal he addressed a full house. They wanted to hear of his escape, and when he responded, telling them of his arrival at the mine and mentioning Dan Dewsnap — British troops had occupied the Witbank colliery district, so he could name names — voices shouted: "His wife's in the gallery!" Mrs. Dewsnap took a bow, plump and blushing; Winston, bowing back, was cheered to the rafters. A chorus of mill girls stood and sang the music hall ditty sweeping England that summer:[167]

You've heard of Winston Churchill;
This is all I need to say —
He's the latest and the greatest
Correspondent of the day.

If this mood held, he would be swept into office. But it didn't hold; it couldn't. The Liberal incumbents were popular, well financed, and well organized, and when he declared his candidacy on September 19, two days after the dissolution of Parliament, it was clear that the race would be fought at concert pitch. "The excitement is already great," he wrote his mother after his first day on the stump, "and I have no doubt that before the end of the campaign the town will be in a state of frenzy." Twice he appealed for her help ("I need not say that it would be very pleasing to me"; "I write again to impress upon you how very useful your presence will be") but Jennie declined. She was enjoying her extended honeymoon; he would have to win by himself. Actually, no candidate in that election, "the khaki election," as it became known, was to be judged by his own merits. Party tactics guaranteed that. Chamberlain had set the tone with his slogan, "Every seat lost to the Government is a seat gained to the Boers." One poster declared: OUR BRAVE SOLDIERS IN SOUTH AFRICA EXPECT THAT EVERY VOTER WILL DO HIS DUTY. . . . REMEMBER! TO VOTE FOR A LIBERAL IS A VOTE TO THE BOER. Churchill himself was not above this. One of his Oldham hoardings read: "Be it known that every vote given to the radicals means 2 pats on the back for Kruger and 2 smacks in the face for our country." He was stung when the Liberals retaliated with a whispering campaign, describing him as a fake and a cashiered officer. The *Daily Mail* of September 27 reported: "In nothing does Winston Churchill show his youth more than in the way he allows slanders to affect him. . . . They deeply wound him and he allows men to see it. When some indiscreet supporter brings these stories to him, his eyes flash fire, he clutches his hands angrily, and he hurries out to find opportunity of somewhere and somehow bringing his traducers to book." He wrote the opposition in protest; their reply expressed "extreme regret," but added, not unreasonably, that Liberals had been exasperated by the character of the Tory campaign and "the ill-advised attempt of your political friends to run this election on the question of your undoubted physical courage instead of upon the political issues involved."[168]

Balfour had agreed to come and speak for him "if I could manage it." Now he found he couldn't. Chamberlain came, however, even though it meant a four-hour return train trip at night. They rode through Oldham together in an open carriage, with loud hurrahs rising on both sides, and afterward Winston wrote: "He loved the roar of the multitude. . . . The blood mantled in his cheek, and his eye as it caught mine twinkled with pure enjoyment." It is doubtless true, as Violet Asquith wrote, that at this time Joe had "a genuine affection and admiration" for Churchill. But as party strategist he had a special interest in his campaign. In those days of "hammer and anvil politics," as Winston called them, England did not vote in a single day. Voters went to the polls over a period of six weeks. On October 1, Oldham's thirty thousand workmen would be almost the first to poll, and the results would affect Conservatives still on the stump. Thus, Churchill's victory — his margin was only twenty-two votes, but it represented a crossover of fifteen hundred voters, and he had won a seat from a strong Liberal — instantly put his party in his debt. Salisbury personally telegraphed his congratulations. All over the country Tories in tight contests (including a penitent Balfour) begged him to come and campaign for them before their constituents voted. He went, he received standing ovations, and he was elated when victories followed in his wake. "I have suddenly become one of the two or three most popular speakers in this election," he wrote Cockran, "and am now engaged on a fighting tour, of the kind you know — great audiences (five and six thousand people) twice & even three times a day, bands, crowds and enthusiasm of all kinds."[169]

Politically, he had arrived. And his party still ruled England. Chamberlain's tactics, however dubious, had worked. The khaki election assured the future of Salisbury's Tory-Unionist coalition; it now held a solid majority of 134 seats over the Liberals and the Irish Nationalists combined. But when the new House of Commons met on December 3, its newest star was absent. Winston Churchill, MP, had decided to postpone his maiden speech until next year. His finances had priority. Sunny had contributed £400 to his campaign, and would pay £100 a year toward his constituency expenses, and Winston had his royalties and the checks from Borthwick, but he wanted more. He knew this wave of popularity would not last. He meant to cash in on it now, with lecture tours of England, the United States, and Canada. Beginning in late October, accompanied by Sunny, he covered more than half of Great Britain in a month, speaking for an hour or more almost every night except Sundays, and often twice a day, traveling ceaselessly, usually at night, seldom sleeping twice in the same bed. Because he was working with his tongue now, not his pen, he tried to master his stubborn speech between lectures by muttering under his breath such exercises as, "The Spanish ships I cannot see for they are not in sight." Violet Asquith has left an endearing portrait of his weary figure as he trudged from hall to hall, his magic lantern under his arm, the profile already unmistakable by virtue of "the slightly hunched shoulders from which his head jutted forward like the muzzle of a gun about to fire."[170] He reached his objective; by December 8, when he sailed westward on the *Luciana,* he had made £4,500 and turned it over with the rest of his savings to Sir Ernest Cassel — who had been a friend of his father's — for investment in consols.

On the whole his American tour was a disappointment. Cockran saw to it that he met President McKinley and Senator Chauncey Depew, and dined in Albany with Governor Theodore Roosevelt, the vice-president-elect. He was delighted when Mark Twain, one of his boyhood heroes, inscribed a limited edition of his works for him, writing on the first flyleaf: "To do good is noble; to teach others to do good is nobler, and no trouble." But then Twain, introducing him to his first audience, in Manhattan's Waldorf-Astoria on December 12, 1900, made it clear that he thought the British treatment of the Boers ignoble. Describing the speaker as the son of an English father and an American mother, and therefore "the perfect man," he said bluntly: "I think England sinned when she got herself into a war in South Africa which she could have avoided, just as we have sinned in getting into a similar war in the Philippines." The listeners murmured in agreement, then sat on their hands when Winston described his flight across the Transvaal. Afterward he turned to his host and growled: "My country right or wrong." But he was not yet Twain's match. "Ah," the old man nimbly replied, "when the poor country is fighting for its life, I agree. But this was not your case." Churchill, writing home, complained about his U.S. lecture agent, J. B. Pond: "First of all the interest is not what Maj Pond made out and secondly there is a strong pro-Boer feeling, which has been fomented against me by the leaders of the Dutch, particularly in New York." Yet Baltimore and Chicago audiences were colder than New York's, and beginning in Chicago, Irish-Americans, indignant over the Tory policy toward Ireland, came to boo. To quiet them, he would describe a dramatic crisis on a South African battlefield. The British position had been desperate, he would tell them, when "the Dublin Fusiliers arrived, trumpeters sounded the charge, and the enemy were swept from the field." A newspaperwoman reported: "Suddenly the balconies grew silent, then thundered with cheers."[171]

But that was cheap, and he knew it. He wrote his mother that the tour was "vy unpleasant work. For instance, last week, I arrived to lecture in an American town and found Pond had not arranged any public lecture but that I was hired out for £40 to perform at an evening party in a private house — like a conjurer. Several times I have harangued in local theatres to almost empty benches. I have been horribly vulgarised by the odious advertisements Pond and Myrmidons think it necessary to circulate — and only my cynical vein has helped me go on." He described the agent as "a vulgar Yankee" who had "poured a lot of very mendacious statements into the ears of the reporters." Moreover, "Pond's terms are vy grasping compared to Christie's." Christie, in England, had given him a generous share of the receipts: £220 in Cheltenham, £265 6s. 2d. at St. James's Hall, and £273 14s. 9d. in Liverpool. Under Pond he made $330 in Boston, $175 in Baltimore, $150 in Springfield, and just $50 in Hartford. His total American earnings were $8,000, or £1,600. It was a glum start for the man who would one day become the first Honorary Citizen of the United States.[172]

Canada, on the other hand, was a ten-day triumph. In Ottawa he was the guest of the governor-general, Lord Minto — Pamela, to his surprise, appeared as a fellow guest — and in Ulster Hall, Lord Dufferin, introducing him, said: "This young man, at an age when many of his contemporaries have hardly left their studies, has seen more active service than half the general officers in Europe." (Winston noted, "I had not thought of this before. It was good.") The audiences were adoring and huge. In Winnipeg alone he made $1,150 (£230). On New Year's Day he totted up his income since leaving the Fourth Hussars, deducted income tax — eleven pence to the pound, or 4.5 percent — and wrote his mother: "I am vy proud of the fact that there is not one person in a million who at my age could have earned £10,000 without any capital in less than two years." She could, he told her, discontinue his allowance "until old Papa Wests [sic] decides to give you and G more to live on." Henceforth, as long as he remained a bachelor, he could live on dividends and interest and devote all his energy to politics.[173]

On January 22, 1901, when Victoria breathed her last at Osborne, he was still in Canada. That night he wrote Jennie: "So the Queen is dead. The news reached us at Winnipeg and this city far away among the snows — fourteen hundred miles from any British town of importance began to hang its head and hoist half-masted flags." But the sadness did not touch him. He was young, flushed with new wealth, and full of his recent accomplishments. His tone was jaunty. The end of a sixty-four-year reign was, to be sure, "a great and solemn event, but I am curious to know about the King. Will it entirely revolutionise his way of life? Will he sell his horses and scatter his Jews or will Reuben Sassoon be enshrined among the crown jewels and other regalia? Will he become desperately serious?" Then, more delicately: "Will he continue to be friendly with you? Will the Keppel" — Mrs. Alice Keppel — "be appointed 1st Lady of the Bedchamber?"[174]

He sailed homeward aboard the S.S. *Etruria* on February 2, the day five kings and forty members of Europe's royal families followed the Queen's coffin down London streets, and a week later he was in his Mount Street rooms, working on his maiden speech. Around him the city still grieved. Every shop window was streaked with a mourning shutter. Crossing sweepers carried crepe on their brooms. Women of all ages were veiled; some had gone into perpetual mourning. Even the prostitutes, whose existence Victoria had denied, were dressed in black. Churchill ignored them; all his thoughts were of the future. Steevens of the *Daily Mail* — poor Steevens, who had died of fever in besieged Ladysmith — had said of him: "He has the twentieth century in his marrow."[175] Winston had liked that. But Steevens had been wrong. As time would prove with growing clarity, it was the nineteenth century that was in Churchill's bones. He would become the most eloquent defender of its standards, the apotheosis of its ideals, the resolute champion of its institutions and values. They were his priceless legacy; he was their fortunate heir. His career would be inconceivable today. And it would have been equally unthinkable before Victoria came to the throne, when England had been an agricultural island, lacking in industry and without an Empire. Native drive, wise legislation, an educated and enlightened oligarchy ingeniously harnessed to genuine democracy, sea power, skillful diplomacy, faith in the supremacy of its island race — these had made imperial Britain, which, in that first Edwardian winter, despite the stigma of South Africa, continued to glitter on its splendid pinnacle, the envy of the world's chancelleries.

Could any other nation in 1901 offer its young politicians the chance for greatness which was now his? Not the insular United States of nineteen-year-old Franklin Roosevelt, then an immature, unpromising Harvard freshman in a country of fewer than 76 million — less than a fifth of the Empire's 412 million — which largely ignored the rest of civilization. Not the vast China of thirteen-year-old Chiang Kai-shek; its few pretensions to a national identity had been shattered with the crushing of the Boxer uprising the previous summer. Certainly not the locked medieval oriental kingdom of sixteen-year-old Hideki Tojo's Japan. The domain of the Turk — the home of nineteen-year-old Mustapha Kemal — was an empire in name only. Czarist Russia seethed with anarchy, terror, despotism, nihilism, and intrigue, and was constantly menaced by uprisings in the Ukraine, the Baltic states, Finland, Poland, and Georgia, where Joseph Stalin, then Josif Vissarionovich Dzhugashvili, aged twenty-one, had just been fired from the only nonpolitical job he ever held, a clerkship in the Tiflis observatory. In Vienna, capital of the Austro-Hungarian dual monarchy, the Hapsburg emperor presided over an equally unstable polyglot of Serbs, Croats, Poles, Magyars, Czechs, Yugoslavs, and Austrians, including, in the Austrian town of Linz, a sullen eleven-year-old schoolboy named Adolf Hitler. Italy, where Benito Mussolini, seventeen, was the quarrelsome son of the Predappio blacksmith, had repeatedly tried to play the part of a world power under a recent series of ineffectual rightist premiers and had been humiliated every time. Italy was blinded by an *idée fixe,* the recovery of lost territories, *Italia irredenta;* the France of Charles de Gaulle, who had just celebrated his tenth birthday in Lille, by a yearning to settle the scores of 1871, which had marked the beginning of the Gallic decline in growth and prestige. Only Wilhelmine Germany loomed as an immediate rival to Britain, and the character of the kaiser's regime excluded any commoner from a distinguished career in public life. Thus England alone could offer young Churchill the role he sought, and its prospects seemed certain to remain unique, barring monumental English folly, or loss of will, or the abandonment of such Victorian principles as disdain for continental alliances. The mere suggestion of any of these lapses would, in 1901, have evoked global laughter.

THREE

RIVER

1901–1914

KING Edward VII, stout and florid, personally opened the new session of Parliament, renewing a custom his mother had discontinued after his father's death forty years earlier. It was Valentine's Day, an occasion linked with his royal presence in the hearts and loins of an astonishing number of titled Englishwomen, all of whom had turned out to see him mount his throne. They were proud of him, and he was proud of himself; having waited a half century to wear the crown, he meant to carry out the ceremony with panache. Shortly after 2:00 P.M. his huge state chariot, drawn by eight cream-colored Hanoverians draped with trappings of morocco and gilt, emerged from Buckingham Palace accompanied by Life Guards wearing dazzling silver breastplates and by postilions in red-and-gold liveries. The monarch and his cortege rode past dense masses of roaring Londoners along the broad Mall, the Horse Guards, Whitehall, and Parliament Square, where the carriage turned in and His Majesty descended, paused in the robing room, and entered the packed House of Lords. There his eminent subjects performed their obligatory gestures of homage, the ladies with curtsies, their masters with deep curvatures of the spine. The *New York Times* correspondent noted "the curious reversal of the customary appearance of the sexes. Here, for once, the women were sombre looking, in black . . . while the men, usually in black, were radiant with brilliant robes of scarlet and ermine." But one lady was not drab: "The Duchess of Marlborough was a conspicuous figure. She wore all the famous Vanderbilt pearls in ropes around her neck, a high 'dog' collar of pearls and diamonds around her throat, and a tiara of diamonds with enormous diamond tips."[1] Sunny's first duchess, the former Consuelo Vanderbilt, had never slept with HRH, now HM, and she wasn't present to honor the King. She wanted to watch Winston take the oath as a member of the House of Commons afterward, and she meant to enter the gallery in style.

Edward tried to look disconsolate. This, he told the assembled lords and commoners, was "a moment of national sorrow, when the whole country is mourning the irreparable loss we have so recently sustained, and which has fallen with peculiar severity on myself. My beloved mother during her long and glorious reign has set an example of what a monarch should be. It is my earnest desire to walk in her footsteps." Then, brightening, he turned from "this public and private grief" to other matters. The drought in his Indian Empire was over. Australia had been a commonwealth for six weeks; he planned to sail there, and to visit New Zealand and Canada. Peking having been captured, the Boxers were no more. His victorious troops were mopping up in South Africa; soon, he erroneously predicted, "the fruitless guerrila warfare maintained by Boer partisans in the former territories of the two republics" would end. Like his predecessors since the rout of Catholicism he assured his people that he would never be a vassal of the pope, and he entrusted the management of his crown revenues to the House of Commons.[2]

In the House, Churchill, sworn, took a back-bench seat, tilted his top hat over his forehead, and, doubling up his figure in the crouched attitude assumed by seasoned parliamentarians and plunging his hands in his pockets, studied the chamber which was to be the arena of his political life for the next sixty-three years. The House dated from 1708, and its decor had not changed since the eighteenth century. Directly beneath the timbered ceiling lay the well, with the carved chair of the Speaker, who determined which members should have the floor. On either side of him the benches, upholstered in green, rose in five tiers. Those to the Speaker's right were occupied by the party in power; the Opposition sat to his left. Each tier was separated at midpoint by an aisle, the "gangway." The front government bench, extending from the Speaker's chair to the gangway, was reserved for the prime minister and his cabinet; it was also called "the Treasury Bench" because the first prime minister, Sir Robert Walpole, had also been first lord of the Admiralty and chancellor of the Exchequer. Two red stripes on the well carpet marked the point beyond which no front-bencher could advance in addressing the House; the distance between the stripes was the length of two drawn swords. There were not enough seats for all elected members; this permitted the conversational style and avoided an impression of emptiness during routine sittings. "A crowded House" gave an air of urgency to dramatic moments.

Churchill knew all this; had known it since boyhood. He was also familiar with the customs of the House. Savage, even cruel words could be exchanged between members who, off the floor, were on the best of terms. Any speech made off the floor was said to be given "out of doors." The House of Lords was "another place." Committee meetings were held "upstairs." Leaders of one's own party were addressed as "my right honorable friend"; an Opposition leader was "the right honorable gentleman." The dominant figures in the chamber were, for the most part, the same men who had prevailed during his father's last days here. The Tories had remained in power, and the destroyer of Lord Randolph's career, Robert Cecil, Marquess of Salisbury, was still prime minister. Salisbury's grip on the controls had in fact tightened; he had maneuvered so many members of his family into key posts that wits called the House "the Hotel Cecil." No fewer than seven Salisbury sons, nephews, and cousins sat on the Conservative benches. Four were in the government, and one, Arthur J. Balfour, "AJB," leader of the House, was preparing to take over as prime minister when his uncle retired. As a youthful MP, AJB had belonged to Lord Randolph's Fourth Party, but now he had put all that behind him and was as rock-ribbed a supporter of Tory policies as Joseph Chamberlain. The entire Tory-Unionist hierarchy stood foursquare and was prepared to defend the established order down to the last desperate inch. Leaders of the Liberals, on the other side of the House, had been split over foreign policy since the Jameson Raid. The ablest of them — Rosebery, Herbert Asquith, Edward Grey, and R. B. Haldane — had become "Liberal Imperialists": supporters of the Boer War. But a majority of the party's MPs disagreed, remaining faithful to the Gladstonian tradition. The Liberal center was led by Sir Henry Campbell-Bannerman ("C-B"). If the party was returned to power, C-B would become prime minister. His followers included a group of antiwar radicals from the Celtic fringe, among them the charismatic young Welshman David Lloyd George, who wanted to geld the House of Lords and follow the lodestar of *la carrière ouverte aux talents.* Since only men of means could afford to enter Parliament, the left was underrepresented. Just two workingmen, supported by union dues, sat as MPs. These "Lib-Labs," as they were popularly known, were identified in the House as members of the Labour Representative Committee; five years would pass before the committee was renamed the Labour party.

Mastery of the House has been given to few. Its moods arch the British spectrum, from cockney vulgarity through Midlands stolidity and Scottish skepticism to Welsh emotionalism and, in those days, Irish mysticism. It can be frivolous, irresponsible, and grave on occasions which any other body would treat with hilarity. No new member can be expected to hold it spellbound, but on the evening of February 18, 1901, when Churchill's maiden speech was scheduled, the chamber was full. Campbell-Bannerman, Asquith, and Grey faced him on the front Opposition bench. Balfour and Joe Chamberlain sat on the Treasury Bench. Mrs. Chamberlain was in the gallery. So were Jennie and four of her sisters-in-law — Lady Howe, Lady Tweedmouth (Fanny Marjoribanks), Lady de Ramsey, and Lady Wimborne — and the Duchess Consuelo. Winston was known as "Randy's Boy," and, in his own right, as a gifted journalist and a hero of the South African war. Moreover, in his first "division," or vote — MPs vote by streaming from the chamber and into two different lobbies, Yes and No — he had sided with the radicals and the Irish. At home, as abroad, he was already magnetic. The *Morning Post* reported that his audience was one which "very few new members have commanded." The *Yorkshire Post* observed: "In that packed assembly, everybody a critic, watching to see what sort of start he made in politics, Winston Churchill made his debut."[3]

He had decided to speak on the war, ignoring the advice of older Tories who had warned, "It is too soon; wait for a few months till you know the House," and crossing the lobby he had been disconcerted to learn that, contrary to his assumption, not all these people were here just to hear him. Lloyd George was also expected to rise. He would, indeed, be Churchill's immediate predecessor. Winston suffered from a parliamentary weakness and knew it: "I had never had the practice which comes to young men at the University of speaking in small debating societies impromptu upon all sorts of subjects." He had spent days in front of a mirror, committing every word he intended to say to memory as his father had. But a House speech cannot stand alone; it must dovetail into the previous remarks, and Lloyd George, as usual, was unpredictable. He had been called to move an amendment, which would have been an easy thread for Winston to pick up. Instead, he was delivering a wide-ranging attack on the government's record in South Africa. Its truce terms were vague: "Does anyone think the Boers will lay down their arms merely to be governed from Downing Street?" Losses were appalling: "There have been 55,000 casualties; 30,000 men are in hospital." Kitchener's burning of Boer barns was barbarous: "It is not a war against men but against women and children." Every time Winston prepared an appropriate opening, the Welsh firebrand, egged on by radicals and Irish Nationalists, switched to a new tack. Churchill felt "a sense of alarm and even despair." At that point an elderly member beside him whispered: "Why don't you just say, 'Instead of making his violent speech without moving his moderate amendment, he had better have moved his moderate amendment without making his violent speech'?"[4]

When Lloyd George sat down Churchill said precisely that, drawing chuckles. His spirits rising, he continued: "I do not believe that the Boers would attach particular importance to the utterances of the hon[orable] member. No people in the world received so much verbal sympathy and so little support. If I were a Boer fighting in the field . . ." He paused dramatically. Then: *"And if I were a Boer, I hope I should be fighting in the field . . ."* Balfour groaned; Chamberlain muttered, "That's the way to throw away seats."* The radicals cheered, then found he had trapped them, for he went on, "I would not allow myself to be taken in by any message of sympathy, not even if it were signed by a hundred hon[orable] members." The Tories laughed — four years earlier a hundred radical MPs had sent an ineffectual cable of support to the king of Greece, immediately after which he had been obliged to capitulate to the Turks. Winston advocated a generous peace in South Africa, drawing a scowl from the Conservatives around him. Of course, he quickly added, the Boers might reject the offer "and stand by their old cry, 'Death or Independence.' " This drew applause from the Irish Nationalists. But he had set another trap: "It is wonderful that hon[orable] members who form the Irish party should find it in their hearts to speak and act as they do in regard to a war in which so much has been accomplished by the courage, the sacrifices, and, above all, by the military capacity of Irishmen." Kitchener's scorched-earth policy was no worse, he said, than the German practice in the Franco-Prussian War of "throwing shells into the dwelling houses of Paris and starving the inhabitants of that great city to the extent that they had to live upon rats and like atrocious foods in order to compel the garrison to surrender." Indeed, the British under Kitchener had done nothing not "justified by precedents set by European or American generals during the last fifty or sixty years." Not that he thought Britain wholly in the right. He took a middle course: "I do not agree very fully with the charges of treachery on the one side and barbarity on the other." Having established his independence — he had deftly said that the Boers were not traitors, that they were right to fight, that they deserved mercy — he drew to a graceful close, evoking his father's name by attributing "the kindness and patience with which the House has heard me" to "a certain splendid memory which many hon[orable] members still preserve."[5]

Older members led him to the House bar, where, in his words, "Everyone was very kind. The usual restoratives were applied, and I sat in a comfortable coma till I was strong enough to go home." Before he left, Lloyd George told him, "Judging from your sentiments, you are standing against the Light," and Churchill replied, "You take a singularly detached view of the British Empire" — an inauspicious opening to what

* "If I were an American, as I am an Englishman, while a foreign troop was landed in my country, I would never lay down my arms — never — never — never!" (The Earl of Chatham in Parliament, November 20, 1777.)

would become the strongest political friendship of Churchill's early career. Lloyd George had missed the mutinous notes in the speech. So had most of the press. The Liberal (anti-imperialist) *Daily Chronicle* dismissed the new member as "a medium-sized, undistinguished young man, with an unfortunate lisp in his voice." The Conservative papers approved of his remarks. He had "held a crowded House spellbound," said the *Daily Express,* had "satisfied the highest expectations," said the *Daily Telegraph,* had delivered a speech "worthy of the traditions of the House," said Borthwick's *Morning Post.* But Hugh Massingham noted in the Liberal (imperialist) *Daily News* that "this young man has kept his critical faculty through the glamour of association with our arms." Not only had he kept it; it grew. As the weeks passed, and he listened to the Opposition members, he felt himself drifting steadily to the left, feeling, as Simone Weil did, that "one must always be ready to change sides with justice, that fugitive from the winning camp." To intimate friends he confided that he now thought barn burning in the Transvaal and Orange Free State was "a hateful folly." He had come to feel "sentimental about the Boers" and was both in revolt against jingoism and "anxious to make the Conservative party follow Liberal courses." Outside his circle this was unknown. In public he remained a staunch Tory back-bencher. Yet all the while, cold as malice, unsuspected but deadly, the vengeful hand of Lord Randolph Churchill was reaching out of the grave to smite those who had struck him down fifteen years earlier, when his son had been twelve years old.[6]

Over the next three months Winston established himself as a rising political star. In the House he spoke frequently, with wit and apparent ease — few knew in those early days of the exhausting rehearsals in Mount Street, the infinite pains that went into each polished performance — and his fame grew. He became one of those rare celebrities who are identified by first names alone; "Winston said," like "Jackie wore" in America seventy years later, brought instant recognition. Gossips were alert to news of him. *Punch* and *Vanity Fair* cartoons depicted him as a slight, fastidious youth with an impish smile. A *Daily Mail* parliamentary reporter noted that "he follows every important speech delivered from the Opposition with an alertness, a mental agility," that he often scribbled notes and passed them forward to Tory ministers about to speak, that "occasionally a mischievous, schoolboy grin settles over his face as he listens to some ridiculous argument." Julian Ralph, an American jour-

Spy cartoon in Vanity Fair, *July 10, 1900*

nalist, prophesied: "Already Mr. Churchill's head is carried with a droop which comes to those who read and study hard. When he is thinking he drops his head forward as if it were heavy. That is how you see him at one moment, a pose prophetic of what is too likely to fasten itself upon him before he reaches middle age. But . . . the next time you look at him he has sprung to his feet with the eagerness of a boy, his pale blue eyes are sparkling, his lips are parted, he is talking a vocal torrent and hands and arms are driving home his words." The Press Gallery delighted in his mots. Already he was displaying a puzzling contradiction which would endure throughout his public life. He could not address the House without intensive preparation. Yet no member could be quicker on his feet. He said: "Politics is like waking up in the morning. You never know whose head you will find on the pillow." And, in another moment, he described the plight of the *genus politicus:* "He is asked to stand, he wants to sit, and he is expected to lie."[7]

Diarists began to take note of him. Beatrice Webb thought him "restless, egotistical, bumptious, shallow-minded and reactionary, but with a certain personal magnetism, great pluck and some originality — not of intellect but of character." Dilke, who had depicted Rosebery in his diary as "about the most ambitious man I had ever met," now added: "I have since known Winston Churchill." Rosebery, ironically, found Churchill's emerging zeal distasteful. But he was far from alone; in the opinion of Robert Rhodes James, Winston was "brash, assertive, egocentric, wholly absorbed in himself and his own career, and unashamedly on the make." Lloyd George misjudged him, however, when he wrote that "the applause of the House is the breath of his nostrils. He is just like an actor. He likes the limelight and the approbation of the pit." Churchill wanted, not approval, but attention. He didn't mind boos. He expected them, for he was preparing to hoist the banner of rebellion. Wilfrid Blunt, no parliamentarian, may have sensed this in describing Winston in his diary: "In mind and manner he is a strange replica of his father, with all his father's suddenness and assurance, and I should say more than his father's ability." There was, he added, "just the same *gaminerie* and contempt of the conventional." One would think Randolph's old colleagues might have seen that. But having taught the mutinous father a lesson, they hardly expected that they would have to teach it again to the son. Besides, until now Winston had performed the rites of Tory loyalty. He had dedicated *The River War* to Salisbury, "under whose wise direction the Conservative Party have long enjoyed power and the nation prosperity." Lord Randolph, the insurgent, had sat below the gangway, the customary seat for independent MPs. After being sworn in, Winston had chosen a spot directly behind the front government bench.[8]

With the arrival of spring, however, he moved. The alert correspondent for the *Daily Mail* noticed that the member for Oldham was now "sitting in the corner seat from which his father delivered his last speech in the House of Commons" and observed "a startling resemblance" between Winston and Randolph — "the square forehead and the full bold eye of his father," and "the hurried stride through the lobby." The lobby correspondent for *Punch* wrote that the resemblance lay "less in face than in figure, in gesture and manner of speech. When the young member for Oldham addresses the House, with hands on hips, head bent forward, right foot stretched forth, memories of days that are no more flood the brain." The son now began to advocate tight budgets and isolation from quarrels outside the Empire. References to Secretary for War William Brodrick began to appear in his speeches — Brodrick, under secretary in 1886, had been an enemy of Randolph's — and they were caustic. He was deeply offended, and said so, when Brodrick told the House: "It is by accident that we have become a military nation. We must endeavour to remain one." Salisbury had grown inattentive in his seventies, but Joe Chamberlain observed Winston often conferring with Sir Francis Mowatt, who had been his father's Exchequer colleague. Winston himself wrote: "Presently I began to criticize Mr. Brodrick's Army expansion and to plead the cause of economy in Parliament. Old Mowatt said a word to me now and then and put me in touch with some younger officials, afterwards themselves eminent, with whom it was very helpful to talk." Speaking to the Liverpool Conservative Association on April 23, Randolph's son fired his first heavy warning shot. He deplored the large sums earmarked for army expansion. "Any danger that comes to Britain would not be on land," he said; "it would come on the sea. With regard to our military system we must be prepared to deal with all the little wars which occur continually on the frontiers of the Empire. We cannot expect to meet great wars . . . for I think our game essentially is to be a naval and commercial power. I cannot look upon the army as anything but an adjunct to the navy. . . . I hope that in considering the lessons of the South African war we shall not be drawn from our true policy, which is to preserve the command of markets and of the seas."[9]

At 11:00 P.M. on Monday, May 13, he opened his offensive in the House. Realizing that this would be a watershed speech for him, he had been working and reworking it for six weeks, and like his father he had sent advance copies to the press, committing himself before he rose. Reminding them of "a half-forgotten episode" — his father's fall — he read a few lines from Randolph's letter of resignation and said he proposed "to lift again the tattered flag of retrenchment and economy." In less than eight years, he noted, army costs had risen from seventeen million pounds to nearly thirty million. He wryly congratulated the secretary for war. This, surely, was a triumph of acquisitiveness. But now the minister had come to the well again. The House was being asked to vote on yet another rise, this one of five million pounds. Churchill's voice rose: "Has the wealth of the country doubled? Has the population of the Empire doubled? Have the armies of Europe doubled? Is there no poverty at home? Has the English Channel dried up and are we no longer an island?" It was time "a Conservative by tradition, whose fortunes are linked indissolubly to the Tory party," should protest this increase of the public burden. Brodrick wanted three army corps. Why? "A European war can only end in the ruin of the vanquished and the scarcely less fatal commercial dislocation of the conquerors." Besides, the minister must know that "if we went to war with any great Power his three Army corps would scarcely serve as a vanguard. If we are hated they will not make us loved, if we are in danger they will not make us safe. They are enough to irritate; they are not enough to overawe. Yet while they cannot make us invulnerable, they may very likely make us venturesome. . . . We shall make a fatal bargain if we allow the moral force which this country has so long exerted to become diminished, or perhaps even destroyed, for the sake of the costly, trumpery, dangerous military playthings on which the Secretary for War has set his heart."[10]

His friend Atkins described him in the *Guardian* as "a lonely but self-possessed figure as he stood there reproducing the sentiments which caused the dramatic resignation of his father." *Punch* was jubilant. And the Opposition, of course, was elated; Massingham predicted that one day he would be prime minister. His own party was discomfited and resentful. The next day a Tory MP icily noted that it was a mistake "to confuse filial piety with public duty." Brodrick, scornful, observed that the party, having survived without the father, could part company with the son, too. He hoped Winston would "grow up" to regret "the day when he came down to the House to preach Imperialism without being able to bear the burden of Imperialism, and when the hereditary qualities he possesses of eloquence and courage may be tempered also by discarding the hereditary desire to run Imperialism on the cheap." Some Conservatives dismissed the speech as a publicity stunt. Violet Asquith heard talk that his conduct had been "based on an almost slavish imitation" of Lord Randolph. But the general feeling, once tempers had cooled, was that the incident was best forgotten and soon would be. A gifted young Tory had felt compelled to pay peculiar tribute to an unfortunate memory. Now that he had got it out of his system, he could move forward with his own career, unfettered by the awkward past.[11]

Not so. Churchill had believed every word in his speech. He himself insisted on pointing out that it marked "a definite divergence of thought and sympathy from nearly all those thronging the benches around me." The government seemed shaky to him; he was convinced he could influence it. To his mother he wrote: "There is a good deal of dissatisfaction in the party, and a shocking lack of cohesion. . . . The whole Treasury Bench appear to be sleepy and exhausted and played out." He meant to rouse it by deliberately adopting an offensive manner, singling out a major minister, Brodrick, and baiting him. Once at Question Time the secretary for war was asked how many horses and mules had been shipped to the Boer War. He replied and Winston innocently raised a supplementary question: "Can my right honorable friend say how many asses have been sent to South Africa?" To those who cried foul, he said: "Criticism may not be agreeable, but it is necessary; it fulfils the same function as pain in the human body, it calls attention to the development of an unhealthy state of things." He called Brodrick's army plan "a humbug and a sham," a "total, costly, ghastly failure," "the Great English Fraud." Several other young Tories joined him, and they spoke in relays. Sir James Fergusson, a die-hard Conservative, was so upset that he wrote the *Daily Telegraph,* protesting that he had never known "an attack upon a Government so organized, and pressed with so much bitterness and apparent determination by members elected to support it."[12]

Sir James implied pettiness. That was unjust. Churchill's motives were noble, and so was his rhetoric. It was also extraordinarily effective. One of its strengths, the perceptive Violet Asquith thought, was his lack of formal education. His colleagues, steeped in classical erudition and experience, were intellectually jaded, but "to Winston Churchill," she wrote, "everything under the sun was new — seen and appraised as on the first day of Creation. His approach to life was full of ardor and surprise. Even the eternal verities appeared to him to be an exciting personal discovery." He was unashamed, she noted, of speaking simple truths which, from others, would have been truisms. "Nor," she continued, "was he afraid of using splendid language. . . . There was nothing false, inflated, artificial in his eloquence: It was his natural idiom. His world was built and fashioned in heroic lines. He spoke its language." Other MPs, unaware how effective his eloquence would be forty years later, thought his speeches merely a last glow of Britain's Antonine age of parliamentary oratory. In fact they were mature, powerful, and, coming from a man not yet thirty, extraordinarily foresighted:

> Europe is now groaning beneath the weight of armies. There is scarcely an important Government whose finances are not embarrassed; there is not a Parliament or people from whom the cry of weariness has not been wrung. . . . What a pity it would be if, just at the moment when there is good hope of a change, our statesmen were to commit us to the old and vicious policy! Is it not a much more splendid dream that this realm of England . . . should be found bold enough and strong enough to send forth for the wings of honest purpose the message which the Russian Emperor tried vainly to proclaim: that the cruel and clanking struggle of armaments is drawing to a close, and that with the New Century has come a clearer and calmer sky?[13]

Astonishingly, his campaign against Brodrick succeeded. He won what was, for a new MP, a major triumph. The cabinet accepted his argument that three corps couldn't "begin to fight Europeans." The plan was shelved. The minister resigned and was moved to the India Office. But Churchill's victory was illusory. His premise, that "the honour and security of the British Empire do not depend, and can never depend, on the British Army," that "the only weapon with which we can expect to cope with great nations is the Navy," was rejected. In the House a senior Tory scathingly asked him if he really believed that "in future all that would happen in the case of war with a Continental power would be our magnificent fleet pursuing an inferior fleet?" The MP said: "Such a state of things is unthinkable and I cannot imagine a war between Britain and a Continental power in which the British Army would not be required." Winston, irrepressible, swiftly interjected, "Not in Europe," but the army budget passed easily. His father's battle could not be refought on this ground and won. Wilhelm II, aged twenty-nine, had just been crowned in Königsberg when Randolph left Salisbury's cabinet. Now he was powerful, aggressive, and a clear threat to British interests.[14]

Another vernal politician would have congratulated himself for having scored an important point, counted his change, and returned to the fold. But once Churchill had taken a position, no one but himself could persuade him to abandon it. He would be among the last of the Edwardians to appreciate the menace of the kaiser. In the House he distrusted every authority except his own — as, when he finally came to power, he would ruthlessly crush everyone who revolted against *him.* Yet such was his charm and intellect, even in those early days, that he could always find recruits to his cause, sometimes against their own best interests. After Brodrick's defeat he formed a society of Conservative back-benchers in their twenties, enrolling Lord Percy, the Duke of Northumberland's heir; Ian Malcolm, Lillie Langtry's son-in-law; Arthur Stanley, a son of the Earl of Derby; and, a real coup, Lord Hugh "Linky" Cecil, one of the prime minister's sons. They were called "the Hooligans," or "Hughligans," after Lord Hugh, but Winston was their undisputed leader. Every Thursday they dined together in the House, and he laid down their first principle: issues would not be discussed until after the meal — "It shall be High Imperialism nourished by a devilled sardine." Hooligans were pledged to outrageous parliamentary manners, but each week they invited a distinguished guest, and such was the prestige of their family names that no one refused them, though Salisbury insisted that they dine with him at his home in Arlington Street, a block from Green Park. Their most memorable guest was Joe Chamberlain. He joined them after a stormy House session. An English newspaperman had been imprisoned in South Africa for writing what was considered a seditious article about the war. Having served his sentence, he had been denied the right to return home on the ground, stated from the Treasury Bench, that it was "undesirable to increase the number of persons in England who disseminated anti-British propaganda." The Liberals had leapt to their feet, shouting objections, and the Hooligans had joined them, Winston crying,

"Where else can anti-British propaganda be less harmful at this time than in Great Britain?"[15]

Over soup Chamberlain eyed them challengingly. He growled: "I am dining in very bad company." They expostulated; the government's stand was arrogant, absurd, and ineptly defended. How could they be expected to support it? He shot back: "What is the use of supporting your own party only when it is right? It is just when it is in this sort of pickle that you ought to come to its aid." Churchill's reply is unrecorded, but he must have kept himself in check, for Joe thawed; he became mellow and then, according to Winston, "most gay and captivating. I never remember having heard him talk better." As he rose to leave, he turned at the door and said with great solemnity: "You young gentlemen have entertained me royally, and in return I shall give you a priceless secret. Tariffs! There are the politics of the future, and of the near future. Study them closely and make yourselves masters of them, and you will not regret your hospitality to me."[16]

They didn't, but he bitterly regretted his advice, for Churchill took it, studying tariffs and then rejecting them, thereby contributing heavily to Chamberlain's political ruin and the fall of the Tory government. The issue, dear to the heart of this self-made businessman, was rooted in the British economy and in his dream of Empire. Victorian prosperity had peaked in the early 1870s. Since then the country's annual growth rate had sunk below 2 percent. The problem was foreign competition, which, with improved transport and more efficient machinery, had deeply penetrated the English market. Wheat was down ten shillings, the textile industry was in straits, and both the United States and Germany had surpassed Britain's steel production. Because of the country's heavy investments abroad, particularly in the United States, these losses had been unfelt by the public. Indeed, per capita income actually continued to grow, a tribute to the Empire's vast wealth. But the deficit could not be camouflaged indefinitely. Chamberlain believed the answer was imperial preference. After touring South Africa late in 1902 — the Boer treaty had been signed at Vereeniging in May — he returned home to propose a tariff scheme which, he was convinced, would unite the Mother Country and her colonies and Dominions in a common market. Imposing heavy taxes on imports from outside the Empire, while establishing preferential tariffs for territories within it, the union would shield imperial industry and agriculture from foreign competitors while strengthening British security and providing funds for social programs at home.

This was logical, sensible, and political dynamite. Free Trade had been the keystone of English economic policy for a half century. Its obvious advantage, for the middle and working classes, was an abundance of cheap imported food, but to them it represented more than that; they believed that it meant peace with the rest of the world, while protective tariffs led to war. Campbell-Bannerman — who believed that Chamberlain, before turning his coat, had wrecked the Liberal party by fighting Home Rule in the 1880s — now wrote a friend: "This reckless criminal escapade of Joe's is the great event of our time. It is playing Old Harry with all Party relations." The Liberal Violet Asquith thought the issue "money for jam."[17] The ruling coalition was deeply split; three members of the cabinet resigned in protest. A lull followed. On July 11, 1902, in the middle of a conference of colonial leaders considering the tariff proposal (they favored it), Salisbury stepped down as prime minister. Balfour then succeeded him. The new leader needed time to settle in. Chamberlain welcomed the break; given time, he believed, he could bring the party around. And he was largely successful. The Conservative newspapers and the constituency committees rallied to him. At Sheffield a party conference voted overwhelmingly to support protectionism, backing it with almost ideological fervor as a way to bind the Empire together.

Nevertheless, there were a few important holdouts, among them Linky Cecil and his brother Robert — and Winston Churchill. At the beginning of the controversy Winston's position had been unclear. He believed colonies should stand alone economically — earlier in 1902 he had voted against a West Indian sugar subsidy because "I object on principle to doing by legislation what properly belongs to charity" — but the following summer, in his annual report to Oldham Conservatives, he had cautiously noted that he was merely looking into "the question of what is called Fair Trade," adding, noncommittally, "Time is, I think, coming near when men will have to make up their minds on this great issue, to formulate their opinions, and set them forth without hesitation or doubt." This sounds casual. Actually, he was examining the matter with great care. He knew that his father's old friend Sir Michael Hicks-Beach, who had been Salisbury's chancellor of the Exchequer, was an ardent Free Trader. This, however, was something he had to think through for himself. "First," he told Violet Asquith afterward, "I had to learn economics. I had to learn economics in eight weeks." She asked how he set about it. He had gone to Mowatt, he said, and Mowatt, risking dismissal as joint permanent secretary of the Treasury, "coached and grounded me with facts and general principles and arguments and gave me half a dozen books to read. He girded on my armor and equipped me for a fight. And then," he concluded with relish, "I found no difficulty in doing the rest myself." Thereafter his faith in Free Trade, Violet wrote, became "a passionate conviction, perhaps the only economic conviction he ever held, and it was upheld and reinforced by the assurance" — given him by Hicks-Beach, Mowatt, and Sir Edward Hamilton, another elderly civil servant at the Treasury — "that his father would have shared it." By the autumn of 1902 his position was firm and irreversible. On November 14 he wrote an Oldham constituent that he believed protection "a fantastic policy to endeavour to shut the British Empire up in a ringed fence. . . . Why should we deny ourselves the good and varied merchandise which the traffic of the world offers, more especially since the more we trade with others, the more they must trade with us; for it is quite clear that we give them something else back for everything they give to us."[18]

On May 15, 1903, confident that his troops were in line, Chamberlain renewed his campaign for imperial preference with a forceful address in his political stronghold of Birmingham, dismissing Free Traders as "a small remnant of Little Englanders, of the Manchester school." The Cecils and other dissidents having chosen to remain silent out of loyalty to him, Joe thought himself the party's spokesman on the issue. He found otherwise when, six days later, Churchill told a crowd at Hoxton that he could not believe anyone would "persuade the British people to abandon that system of free trade and cheap food under which they have thriven so long." A few days later Winston rose from his House seat below the gangway to deliver a fighting speech, charging that protectionism "means a change, not only in the historic English Parties but in the conditions of our public life. The old Conservative Party with its religious convictions and constitutional principles will disappear and a new party will rise . . . perhaps like the Republican Party in the United States of America . . . rigid, materialist and secular, whose opinions will turn on tariffs and who will cause the lobbies to be crowded with the touts of protected industries." If a European war broke out, he asked, would it not be "very much better that the United States should be vitally interested in keeping the English market open," rather than be indifferent to the fate of "their present principal customer?"[19]

He now took a momentous step. In a May 25 letter to the new prime minister marked "Most Private," he promised "absolute loyalty" to the party — "I would even swallow six army corps" — if Balfour pledged support of Free Trade. "But if on the other hand," he added ominously, "you have made up your mind & there is no going back, I must recon-

Joseph Chamberlain

sider my position in politics." By now, after watching Churchill in the House for two years, AJB must have known that he did not make idle threats. At the very least Winston was entitled to a frank statement of his leader's stand on this issue. So, for that matter, was the public. Balfour, incredibly, had left tariff policy to Chamberlain. Although he had been prime minister for ten months, and had urged new policies, he had taken no stand on this crucial point. Sphinxlike, leonine, outwardly a model of poise, and apparently bereft of personal ambition, Salisbury's nephew and political heir was in reality a gifted but unpredictable statesman, best remembered for a declaration in which he gave away Palestinian land Britain did not own. His answer to Winston, dictated on May 26, was tortuous and weak. Unbelievably, he wrote: "I have never understood that Chamberlain advocated protection." As he perceived it, his colonial secretary was recommending "a duty on food-stuffs," which might "incidentally be protective in character" but whose main purpose was "to provide an instrument for fiscal union with the colonies." Then, absurdly: "This is a very different thing from protection, both in theory and in practice. But undoubtedly the matter is one of difficulty, and requires the most wary walking."[20]

Undoubtedly Balfour was wary of Churchill. Shrinking from controversy, he was inviting deeper trouble. There was another possible answer

Arthur Balfour

to Winston's challenge, however, and many Tory colleagues had expected him to make it before now. Traditionally, observes Colin Coote, managing editor of the *Daily Telegraph,* "there are two ways of getting on in the House of Commons — by being very naughty, and by being very good. If you are very naughty, your party says, 'Give the puppy a nice bone to keep him quiet.' " In short, the able young critic of his elders is assigned responsibility and thus silenced. Some MPs thought such a possibility was what Churchill had had in mind when he attacked Brodrick. He had shown parliamentary ability, and he had changed Salisbury's mind. But Balfour was not Salisbury. Dissent within Conservative ranks alarmed him, and he had been offended by Winston's tactics. He may also have recalled his uncle's reply when asked why, after Lord Randolph's humiliation, he had not invited him back into the government: "When you have got rid of a boil on your neck, you don't want it back." In reshuffling his cabinet, Balfour had found room for one Hooligan, appointing Lord Percy under secretary of state for India, but in his view Winston was an even bigger boil than Randolph.[21]

Everyone knew Churchill was searching for a shortcut to office. Political tacticians had predicted that he would adopt one of two courses. Either he would try to talk Balfour into disowning Chamberlain, hoping to replace him as the party's strong man, or he would follow Lord Randolph's example and organize a revolt against the prime minister. His

May exchange of letters with Balfour represents the failure of the first. But there is reason to believe that he had already tested the possibility of a coup. On March 4, 1905, J. L. Wanklyn, MP for Central Bradford, told an audience of constituents that more than two years earlier Winston had approached him with a scheme to unseat the Balfour leadership, replacing it with a weak ministry of Tory radicals, which in turn would be succeeded by a Churchill government. According to Wanklyn, Winston already had a list of men he would appoint to his cabinet, including Hugh Cecil as education minister. *The Times* carried Wanklyn's speech and, the next day, Winston's statement that the charge was "devoid of the slightest foundation. . . . The whole story from beginning to end is a pure invention of his own, and, if not a hallucination, can only be described as a wilful and malicious falsehood."[22] Nevertheless, Wanklyn stuck to his guns. He invited Winston to sue him. The offer was declined, and the story credited, for by then the House believed that to reach his ends Winston would stop at nothing, that he was even prepared, if necessary, to bolt his party.

Churchill always nailed his colors to the mast, but not always to the same mast. He "did not," he later said, "understand the importance of party discipline and unity, and the sacrifices of opinion which may lawfully be made in their cause." The issue was everything. Less than forty-eight hours after receiving Balfour's squelch, he wrote another confidential letter, this time to Campbell-Bannerman. Describing his position on tariffs as "one of great difficulty and danger," he nevertheless proposed a joint strategy to prevent "an immense victory for Chamberlain." C-B swiftly agreed, and thenceforth Winston was increasingly drawn into Opposition councils. He felt comfortable there. He found John Morley, Asquith, Haldane, and Grey attractive. And he approved of their legislative program: wider suffrage, an eight-hour day, a graduated income tax, and less expenditure on foreign and imperial affairs. Most significant, he had become an advocate of Irish Home Rule. Violet Asquith wrote that "Irish self-government might well have stuck in his throat, for to Lord Randolph Home Rule had become anathema. But he swallowed it, apparently without effort. His filial piety had ceased to be his sole directing light. He was now charting his own course."[23]

As early as 1901, a few months after entering Parliament, he had flirted with the thought of switching parties. His motives then had been less than lofty. Lady Warwick held a long political discussion with him at Cecil Rhodes's Scottish home on Loch Rannoch. She wrote that Winston "had just been on a visit to Lord Rosebery, and he said he was inclined to leave the leadership to Mr. Balfour and proclaim himself a Liberal. He wanted power and the Tory road to power was blocked by the Cecils and other brilliant young Conservatives, whereas the Liberal path was open. Cecil Rhodes was all in favour of his turning Liberal." Winston had written his mother: "I am a Liberal in all but name." He was corresponding with Bourke Cockran, who was campaigning against Republican tariffs in Washington, and he knew that Cockran, still one of his heroes, had left Tammany on a matter of principle in 1896 to support McKinley for President. His aunt Cornelia begged him to cross the floor: "Of one thing I think there is no doubt & that is that Balfour & Chamberlain are one, and that there is no future for Free Traders in the Conservative party. Why tarry?"[24]

He tarried because he wasn't so sure about Balfour's position. On this issue the man was a Hamlet. Thus far the duel had been between Churchill and Chamberlain, and in the House, Winston had more Conservative followers than Joe; when he launched his Free Food League on July 13, 1903, sixty Tory MPs signed up, while the rival Tariff Reform League enrolled only thirty. Outside Parliament, however, Chamberlain was much stronger among the party rank and file. He was a hero to the constituency committees, the men who got out the vote. That summer he crisscrossed the country, speaking fervently for imperial preference. Churchill, fighting it, made the same tour, matching him speech for speech. Both sides were still civil. Winston's sharpest barb was: "Mr. Chamberlain loves the working man. He loves to see him work." On July 26 Sir Edward Hamilton wrote in his diary: "W.C. is taking a very devoted line against C. . . . It is the fashion to run him down — but I think there is a great deal in him and that he is bound to win in the end." On August 12 Churchill and another MP entertained several members of the party leadership, including the prime minister, at a dinner in the House. Afterward he wrote his mother, "A.B. was most amiable and very good humoured" even though "I had been very rude to him in the House of Commons in the afternoon." Leaving the dinner he "ran straight into J.C. who gave me an extraordinary look of reproach as much as to say 'How could you desert me' and I confess I felt very sorry for him indeed. . . . I cannot help admiring Chamberlain's courage. I do not believe he means to give way an inch, and I think he is quite prepared to sacrifice his whole political position . . . for the cause in which he is so wrapped up." Yet Winston came to regard Joe as the turncoat, the subversive, the renegade. In early September the *Pall Mall Gazette* quoted Churchill as saying: "Some of us were born in the Tory Party and we are not going to let any aliens turn us out." The *Gazette* reporter asked him about rumors that he would cross to the Opposition, and he replied: "Oh, absurd. I am a Tory and must always remain a Tory." The article concluded: "He is a Tory by birth and inheritance. Toryism possesses him. . . . It is with him something of a religion."[25]

It wasn't, really. He was on the verge of sacrilege. The turning point came that month. On September 12, 1903, Chamberlain quit the cabinet to devote himself to his crusade. Momentarily it seemed that the prime minister might be able to ignore the issue. It was an illusion. The tension was still there, and it was growing. Two days after Joe had stepped down, Churchill wrote his mother: "I fancy a smash must come in a few days. Mr Balfour is coming to Balmoral on Saturday. Is he going to resign or reconstruct? . . . If he reconstructs — will it be a protectionist reconstruction of a cabinet wh does not contain the free trade Ministers, or a free trade reconstruction of a Cabinet from which J.C. has resigned? All these things are possible." But there was no ministerial reshuffle. Two weeks later a second Conservative conference at Sheffield strongly reaffirmed imperial preference as a means of strengthening the Empire. In his speech to them, Balfour then tumbled off the fence and, with some characteristic reservations, declared himself to be on their side. This, to Winston, meant the time had come to take off his gloves. He wrote (but did not mail) a letter to Linky Cecil, declaring that "to proceed making perfervid protestations of loyalty to the 'party' & yet to trample on the dearest aspirations of the party & thwart its most popular champions is to court utter ruin." He added, bitterly: "I am an English Liberal. I hate the Tory party, their men, their words & their methods." Even so, he was not yet ready to make his change of heart public: "Nothing need happen until December at any rate, unless Oldham explodes."[26]

But Oldham did explode. Despite promises to jump to the Tory whip, he endorsed the Liberal candidate in a Ludlow by-election on the ground that "Free Traders of all parties should form one line of battle," and at a Free Trade rally in Halifax he cried: "Thank God we have a Liberal Party." On December 23 Oldham's Tory executive committee resolved that he had "forfeited" their confidence and could not expect their support in the next election. The resolution would be laid before the full body on January 8, 1904. In a spirited defense, Churchill wrote them that he was responding to a higher loyalty: "When Mr Balfour succeeded Lord Salisbury, he solemnly pledged himself at the Carlton Club that the policy of the party should be unchanged. And yet at Sheffield, only a year afterwards, he declared for a 'fundamental reversal of the policy of the last fifty years.' Therefore it is not against me that any charge of breaking pledges can be preferred." He said he meant to continue representing the thirteen thousand men who had voted for him, doing his best "to oppose all protectionist manoeuvres in Parliament and to explain to the electors of Oldham how closely Free Trade and cheap food are interwoven with the welfare of the Lancashire artisan." The committee was unconvinced. The resolution carried with but one dissent. He offered to resign, which was crafty of him; in a by-election he would either split the vote with their candidate or win as a Liberal — a Tory loss either way. So his original Oldham sponsors fumed, impotent, while he continued to sit on the Conservative side of the House, savaging his leaders day after day.[27]

Not even the oldest MPs could remember a more brilliant, more acrimonious performance. The *Daily Mail* commented that since Sheffield "his speeches have been almost without exception directed against the policy of the Government. They have been clever, severe, biting in their sarcasm, full of sneers and scorn for Mr Balfour and his Ministers." The Conservative party, Churchill said, had become "the slave of great interests." The Tory flaw was "a yearning for mediocrity." The party's members were "ready to make great sacrifices for their opinions, but they have no opinions. They are ready to die for the truth, if only they knew what the truth is." He cried: "To keep in office for a few more weeks and months there is no principle which the Government is not prepared to abandon, and no quantity of dust and filth they are not prepared to eat." Balfour was guilty of "gross, unpardonable ignorance" and a "slipshod, slapdash, haphazard manner of doing business." Winston said that "the dignity of a Prime Minister, like a lady's virtue, is not susceptible of partial diminution." Balfour, however, had "flouted the traditions of Parliament and dishonoured the service of the Crown." When one of the prime minister's supporters protested this outrageous language, Churchill wrote *The Times,* accusing the man of trying to gag him, and adding: "While Mr Balfour silences his followers in the House of Commons Mr Chamberlain is busy with their constituencies" disseminating "protectionist propaganda." The prime minister was only a puppet, a fool; the real Tory leader was Chamberlain, and Winston described Joe's vision of the party: "Over all, like a red robe flung about the shoulders of a sturdy beggar, an extravagant and aggressive militarism, and at the top, installed in splendour, a party leader, half German Chancellor, half American boss." Chamberlain's insistence that tariffs would enrich Britain was "a downright lie." When another Free Trader resigned from the party, Tory MPs hissed his speech explaining why. Churchill shouted: "Mr Speaker, I rise on a point of order. I am quite unable to hear what my honourable friend is saying owing to the vulgar clamour of the Conservative Party." Sir Trout Bartley, a Balfour supporter, leapt up, pointed at Churchill, and shrieked: "The vulgarest expression came from this honourable gentleman!"[28]

The prime minister tut-tutted and looked away. Most of the time he ignored Churchill, but sometimes he was drawn. What galled him most was the knowledge that while the wounding slurs of other MPs arose from the heat of battle, Churchill coldly honed and barbed his insults each evening in Mount Street. It was premeditated, ungentlemanly. Once he deeply angered Balfour. In tones dripping with malice Churchill said, "We have been told *ad nauseam* of the sacrifices which the Prime Minister makes. I do not deny there have been sacrifices. The House ought not to underrate or deny those sacrifices." He ticked them off: "sacrifices of leisure," "sacrifices of dignity," "the sacrifice of reputation." He quoted the prime minister's supporters as saying that he stood "between pride and duty." Winston sarcastically commented: "Pride says 'go' but duty says 'stay.' The Right Honourable Gentleman always observes the maxim of a certain writer that whenever an Englishman takes or keeps anything he wants, it is always from a high sense of duty." AJB rose, shaking, and accused him of poor taste. He said: "It is not, on the whole, desirable to come down to this House with invective which is both prepared and violent. The House will tolerate, and very rightly tolerate, almost anything within the rule of order which evidently springs from genuine indignation aroused by the collision of debate; but to come down with these prepared phrases is not usually successful, and at all events, I do not think it was very successful on the present occasion. If there is preparation there should be more finish, and if there is so much violence there should certainly be more veracity of feeling."[29]

Churchill did not hang his head. "I fear I am still in disgrace," he cheerfully wrote Jennie, and, in a letter to Cockran, predicted more "stormy times ahead." Margot Asquith thought his problem was a lack of empathy, that he tended "to ignore the need to feel his way about other minds," but he didn't think he had a problem at all. He was releasing his inner aggression and enjoying it enormously. He later said: "I did not exactly, either by my movement or my manner, invite any great continuing affection." He didn't want it. Earl Winterton recalled: "Churchill made no attempt to dispel the suspicion and dislike with which he was regarded by the majority of the House of Commons. He seemed to enjoy causing resentment. He appeared to have, in modern parlance, a 'chip on his shoulder,' when in the Chamber itself or in the Lobbies." Winston jovially told a reporter, "Politics are almost as exciting as war and quite as dangerous." The newsman asked, "Even with the new rifle?" Churchill replied, "Well, in war you can only be killed once, but in politics many times."[30]

Though he was to prove that repeatedly, expressions of his unpopularity in the spring of 1904 were uglier and more strident than anything his father had endured. Shouted down by his own party, he was called "wickedly hypocritical," the "Blenheim Rat," and a "Blackleg Blueblood." In a rare affront, the Hurlingham Polo Club blackballed his application for membership. He seemed unrepentant. And he offended men who might have befriended him. One contemporary noted in his diary on March 5: "Went to the Speaker's Levée . . . Winston Churchill was there in a cavalry uniform with a long row of medals. He is a most astounding person. His speeches in the House this session have been very fine." But in a fortnight the diarist changed his mind; Churchill, he had decided, was "a most infernal nuisance." *Punch* reported: "His special enmity for Chamberlain and all his works is hereditary. . . . Winston is a convinced Free Trader. But he enters with lighter, more fully gladdened heart into the conflict, since Protection is championed by his father's ancient adversary." Earl Winterton thought him "too eager to hunt down his father's old enemies." MacCallum Scott, another contemporary, wrote that "the followers of Mr Chamberlain repaid his [Winston's] hostility with a passionate personal hatred over which they vainly endeavoured to throw a mask of contempt. There was no better hated man in the House of Commons." He was shunned. Only Tories who felt absolutely secure dared be seen with him. On Good Friday, Linky Cecil suggested that "the town council of Oldham give Winston Churchill the freedom of the borough as a mark of his independence and public spirit. As he is not going to stand for Oldham again it could not be mixed up with local party politics and it would be a fitting rebuke to ill-mannered persons in the House. He is I think being abominably treated. For he is very honest and very good-hearted." But Linky was Lord Salisbury's son. Had this come from an MP less well connected, it could have been a note of political suicide.[31]

The beginning of the end came on March 29, 1904. At 5:00 P.M. Churchill rose to follow Lloyd George in debate. At that point Balfour left his seat and met Austen Chamberlain, Joe's son and chancellor of the Exchequer, beyond the glass door behind the Speaker's chair. Winston, offended, objected to the prime minister's departure just as he was about to speak; he called it an astonishing "lack of deference and respect." At that, the cabinet rose from the Treasury Bench and walked out to the smoking room, followed by almost all the back-benchers, who paused at the door to jeer and count the number of Tories left. There were fewer than a dozen, all Free Traders. One, Sir John Gorst, who had belonged to Randolph's Fourth Party, denounced his fellow Conservatives for treating Winston "with the most marked discourtesy which I think I have ever seen." That merely put Gorst, too, in Coventry. The morning edition of the *Daily Mail* carried the headlines: CHILLING REBUKE. UNIONISTS REFUSE TO HEAR MR CHURCHILL. STRANGE SCENE IN THE HOUSE OF COMMONS. The *Mail* reported: "The merry jest, the sparkling epigram and the ironical sally departed . . . from Mr Churchill's oration. He never speaks unless there is a full house. The full house had melted away under his spell. It was a chilling rebuke, crushing, unanswerable. He complained bitterly at the slight, and murmured some phrases about shifty policy and evasion. There were only the crowded benches of the Liberals to cheer. Behind him was silence and desolation." He was not yet the Winston Churchill of the 1930s; the strain of his solitary struggle had begun to tell; he was vulnerable to sudden, uncontrollable attacks of depression and had not yet learned to hide them until alone. Next day the *Pall Mall Gazette* told its readers that "in appearance there is nothing of 'the Boy' left in the white, nervous, washed-out face of the Member for Oldham. He walks with a stoop, his head thrust forward. His mouth expresses bitterness, the light eyes strained watchfulness. It is a tired face, white, worn, harassed. . . . There is, indeed, little of youth left to the Member for Oldham." He was going through the political equivalent of a divorce suit, and approaching the brink of a breakdown.[32]

On Friday, April 22, he went over the brink. He had read Benjamin Seebohm Rowntree's *Poverty: A Study of Town Life* on Morley's recommendation. The book impressed him immensely, and marked the beginning of his radical period. Trade unions, he decided, must be recognized and their rights defined. This message — "Radicalism of the reddest type," the *Daily Mail* called it — was the burden of his remarks for forty-five minutes that Friday, and he was approaching his peroration when calamity struck. He was speaking with his customary fire, and was about to strike his right fist into his left palm, clinching his argument, when his mind went completely blank. He had just said: "It lies with the Government to satisfy the working classes that there is no justification . . ." His voice trailed off. He groped. The studied phrases, laboriously composed and learned by heart, had fled from his memory. He began again: "It lies with them . . . . What?" he asked, as though someone had suggested a cue. He hesitated, frowned, looked confused, and fumbled in the pockets of his frock coat, as though looking for notes. There were none; until now he hadn't carried any. The MP beside him picked some paper scraps from the floor; there was nothing on them.

Winston made one more try: "It lies with them to satisfy the electors . . ." Some members cheered encouragingly, but it was no good. He sat down abruptly, buried his face in his hands, and muttered: "I thank honourable members for having listened to me." The next day a headline read: MR CHURCHILL BREAKS DOWN, DRAMATIC SCENE IN THE HOUSE OF COMMONS.[33]

One name was on the lips of upper-class London: *Lord Randolph*. Less than ten years earlier Winston's father, occupying the same seat, had broken down in the same way, signaling his slide down into oblivion and death. To his family and friends the parallel was appalling. The next day Shane Leslie called at Mount Street and found his cousin huddling with his brother, Jack, and Sir Alfred Harmsworth. Winston asked Leslie to make inquiries about Pelmanism, the memory training system. It was unnecessary. His memory had been, and would again be, phenomenal; he had merely suffered a temporary lapse. In the future he would seldom speak without a text, but he rarely seemed to glance at it. Over the weekend his spirits, and his confidence, rebounded. He had passed the crisis of party renunciation. A correspondent in the Press Gallery noted the return of his "unmistakably schoolboy grin" in House shouting matches, "not the assumed smile so often seen in Parliament, but the real grin of one who is alive to all the fun of things." On May 16 he delivered his last speech as a Tory, envisioning the fall of the Conservative government: "Extravagant finance was written on the head of their indictment, and it will be written on the head of their tombstone." The Boer War had been an "immense public disaster." He was partly to blame, "tarred" in a small way "with responsibility," but the heavier guilt fell upon Chamberlain and his "New Imperialism . . . that bastard Imperialism which was ground out by a party machine and was convenient for placing a particular set of gentlemen in power." The *Manchester Guardian* reported that "his neighbours melted away till scarcely a Protectionist was left in the House." This time he beamed at their retreating backs.[34]

Early in April, over Easter weekend, he had been adopted by northeast Manchester as its Liberal candidate in the next election. On the last day of May he crossed the floor. It was low-key; there was no ceremony. *Punch* reported: "House resumed to-day after Whitsun holidays. Attendance small; benches mostly empty. Winston, entering with all the world before him where to choose, strides down to his father's old quarters on the front bench below the gangway to the left of the Speaker, and sits among the ghosts of the old Fourth Party." It was here, when the Tories were in opposition, that Randolph had stood in 1885, waving his handkerchief to cheer the downfall of Gladstone. The seat beside it was now occupied by Lloyd George, who gripped Winston's hand. Rosebery and Grey also welcomed him, none of them, of course, mentioning the invective he had once poured on their party, calling them "prigs, prudes, and faddists," describing liberalism as "hiding from the public view like a toad in a hole," and predicting that "when it stands forth in all its hideousness the Tories will have to hew the filthy object limb from limb."[35]

His former colleagues on the other side of the House hadn't forgotten, however. They had agreed with him then, and now regarded him as the filthiest of toads. Henry Lucy, "Toby, MP" of *Punch* (like the *New Republic*'s later TRB), wrote in his diary: "Winston Churchill may be safely counted upon to make himself quite as disagreeable on the Liberal side as he did on the Unionist. But he will be handicapped by the aversion that always pertains to a man who, in whatever honourable circumstances, has turned his coat." However, Lucy had no control over another *Punch* correspondent, who wrote: " 'He's gone over at last, and good riddance,' say honest hacks munching their corn in well-padded stalls of Government stables. They don't like young horses that kick out and cannot be safely counted upon to run in double harness. 'Winston's gone over at last,' they repeat, whinnying with decorous delight."[36]

Afterward they had long second thoughts. Chamberlain confided to Margot Asquith: "He was the cleverest of all the young men. The mistake Arthur made was in letting him go." F. E. Smith, the brilliant young Conservative who became Churchill's closest friend, wrote: " 'He can wait' has always been the Tory formula which has chilled the hopes of young and able men. . . . And so chance after chance of modest promotion went by . . . Winston characteristically jumped the whole fence." Winston himself, of course, denied that ambition had played any role in his decision. "Some men change their party for the sake of their principles," he said; "others their principles for the sake of their party." He quoted Pope: "Sworn to no master, of no sect am I / As drives the storm, at any door I knock."[37]

But he knew that in switching parties he was joining the future. For a generation the Liberal party had carried the cross of Home Rule. Now, in part due to him, Free Trade had replaced it as the central issue before the country. And Joe Chamberlain's exhortations to working- and middle-class audiences, his pleas to "think imperially," had failed. He was booed, or addressed empty halls. That debacle, public disillusionment with the Boer War, and scandalous reports that Chinese coolies were being treated as slave labor in South African mines — charges also laid at the former colonial secretary's door — had shifted England's balance of

Churchill in 1904, when he joined the Liberals

political power. The historian D. C. Somervell has concluded that "from 1903 onwards, it seemed certain, and not only to those who wished it, that Balfour's Government would be defeated at the next election." On December 12 of that year Churchill wrote Cockran: "I believe that Chamberlain will be defeated at the General Election by an overwhelming majority."[38] And so he was. After the votes had been counted, Joe suffered a paralytic stroke and lived out his life a tragic invalid. His children carried on the family's parliamentary tradition. In subsequent governments the elder boy, Austen, went on to become foreign secretary, chancellor of the Exchequer, and first lord of the Admiralty. The other son, Austen's half brother, was Neville Chamberlain.

It was Disraeli's cynical conviction that "no man is regular in his attendance at the House of Commons until he is married." Churchill had disproved that, but there were those who felt that he might have been a dash less abrasive, a shade more conciliatory, had he shared his bed. Unfortunately he continued to be an inept suitor. His romance with Pamela Plowden had died in Canada. His mother had entertained high hopes for their meeting there. "Pamela is devoted to you," she had written him. His reply had been guarded, and Lord Minto, who had been their host, had written Jennie: "Everything seemed to me . . . platonic"; indeed, it was hard to imagine "any other feelings than those of Plato" between them. For Pamela, that was the last straw. Back in England, she managed to get engaged to two other men in a fortnight. She chose between them and became Lady Lytton the following year.[39]

Jennie wrung her hands. She told him that if he wanted a wife he must first propose. So he did — twice. First he courted the beautiful, twenty-four-year-old American actress Ethel Barrymore; he besieged her with notes and flowers, took her to Claridge's for supper every evening after her performance, and, on July 13, 1902, entertained her at Blenheim. But Miss Barrymore, having faced the footlights since the age of fourteen, knew all the stagecraft of lovemaking. Winston had mastered none of it, and she gracefully declined his hand, explaining that she felt she "would not be able to cope with the great world of politics." Next he wooed Muriel Wilson, a handsome young heiress. Privately he admitted that he was after her money. Perhaps she sensed that; after an automobile tour of Italy with her and another girl in Lionel Rothschild's motorcar, he wrote glumly: "Nothing could exceed the tranquil *banalité* of my relations with M." Halfheartedly he pressed his suit and she, to his evident relief, rejected it. She gently told him that she didn't think he had much of a future.[40]

Part of his difficulty was inherent in his upbringing. As Lord Boothby points out, in their class "the sexes were completely segregated from the age of ten to twenty-two." Yet Boothby, who shared that handicap, managed to find his way into a remarkable number of beds, partly because he genuinely liked women. Winston didn't, at least not those outside his family. He was the kind of chauvinist feminists love to hate. During his bachelor days, he and Eddie Marsh, his private secretary, would arrive early at a party and watch each lady make her entrance. Recalling "the face that launched a thousand ships," Churchill would ask, "How many ships do you think she would launch?" Marsh would hazard, "Two hundred ships, or perhaps two hundred and fifty?" Winston would reply decisively: "By no means. A small gunboat at the most." He complained that the United States "is too cluttered up with women. They are everywhere. They control eighty percent of the country's wealth. They wield enormous power — and they bully their husbands." The only person to succeed in frightening him was the American Mrs. O. H. P. Belmont, who always referred to him as "that dreadful man." He growled that she was the least feminine woman he had ever met.[41]

But he was at a loss even with the mannequins of young Edwardian womanhood. He didn't know what to say to them. The only subject which really interested him was himself. He knew none of the delicate moves that could lead to intimacy; for example, "peering down Pennsylvania Avenue," as it was called — discreetly glancing down a girl's décolletage to admire her breasts. In mixed society he was a combination of Wellington and Peel — "I have no small talk," the great duke had said, "and Peel has no manners." If Churchill felt cordial, he might ask a woman her age. Sometimes he didn't even speak. In 1904, during a dance at Salisbury Hall given by Lady Crewe, Jennie introduced him to the lovely Clementine Hozier. Clementine said, "How do you do?" In her words: "Winston just stared. He never uttered one word and was very gauche — he never asked me for a dance, he never asked me to have supper with him. I had of course heard a great deal about him — nothing but ill. I had been told he was stuck-up, objectionable etcetera. And on this occasion he just stood and stared." In the beginning, Violet Asquith, sitting beside him at dinner for the first time, found him equally uncommunicative. She wrote: "For a long time he remained sunk in abstraction. Then he appeared to become suddenly aware of my existence. He turned on me a lowering gaze and asked me how old I was. I replied that I was nineteen. 'And I,' he said almost despairingly, 'am thirty-two already.' " On reflection he added thoughtfully, "Younger than anyone else who counts, though." Then, savagely: "Curse ruthless time! Curse our mortality. How cruelly short is the allotted span for all we must cram into it!" He burst into a diatribe about the brevity of life and ended: "We are all worms. But I do believe that I am a glowworm."[42]

Later Violet observed that his "inner circle of friends contained no women. They had their own place in his life. His approach to women was essentially romantic. . . . Their possession of all the cardinal virtues was assumed as a matter of course." She, knowing how rare purity was in his mother's set — they openly despised "middle-class virtue" — accused him of "innocence." He was offended, but he was aware that his perception of girls was flawed; comparing himself to his cousin Sunny, he wrote: "He is quite different from me, understanding women thoroughly, getting into touch with them at once, & absolutely dependent upon feminine influence of some kind for the peace & harmony of his soul." Later, after marriage, he developed a glorious dependence upon his wife, but outside his home he was never really comfortable in the company of women. One explanation may lie in his mother's affairs. He knew of her relationship with the King, which appears to have resumed after his coronation. In one postscript he wrote her: "I have been reading 'An English Woman's Love Letters.' Are all Mothers the same?"[43]

Certainly they weren't in the lower classes. The nine-year reign of Edward VII saw vast technological advances, but the only sexual innovations were the brassiere, invented by Charles R. Debevoise in 1902, and the perfection of the Wassermann test in Germany four years later. Few could afford, or even knew about, the expensive Dutch cup. Contraception was largely limited to withdrawal or, for the unfastidious, such abortifacients as lead-plaster. Outright abstention was surprisingly common. Paul Thompson concludes that "the cumulative weight of three generations of Victorian puritanism, affecting the working classes directly through church and chapel teaching and indirectly through middle-class influence," led to "striking self-restraint among young adults." The average bride was twenty-six. One Englishwoman in every five did not marry at all, and those who did were often parsimonious with their favors. A pioneer sex researcher, interviewing Edwardian workmen, found them bitter about their wives' unresponsiveness in bed. One wife, during the throes, kept reminding her husband not to forget to leave twopence for the gas; another chewed an apple during sexual intercourse; a third kept her clothes on (her spouse said, "It's about as exciting . . . as posting a letter"); and a fourth, "a sad little man, complained that not only did his wife take no interest in the proceedings, but she also insisted on a regular emolument of sixpence per session."[44]

The liberal recommendations of the Royal Commission on Marriage and Divorce were ignored, and adultery still meant social ruin, but upper-class women, like their mothers in the 1880s — and often with their mothers' advice — had learned to manage complex intrigues. In public they were angelic. On Sundays they joined the black-bonneted, black-robed processions setting off for church. Mornings they trotted through the park in their gleaming victorias, parasols held over their heads and, on the seat opposite, card cases and pink leather address books from Dreyfous. They might sneak cigarettes in bedrooms, but in sitting rooms they merely wiggled crochet hooks or perched sedately behind teapots, and in dining rooms, their lovely faces illumined by candelabra, they sat erect and decorative, their piled hair crowned by gems and their bare, magnificent shoulders arising from clouds of tulle. An Edwardian lady in full dress was a wonder to behold, and her preparations for viewing were awesome. Silk stockings, carefully smoothed, went on first. Then she would rise in her chemise while her lady's maid fitted the long stays of pink coutil, heavily boned, around her hips, fastening the busk down the front, anchoring the garters to the stockings and tightening the silk lacings. Pads of pink satin would be affixed on the hips and under the arms, to stress the narrow waist. Drawers came next, after which the maid would spread the petticoat in a ring on the floor, and the lady, now wearing high-heeled shoes, would step into it. Buttons would be buttoned, tapes tied; then she would dive into the massive gown of taffeta and tulle and stand rigid while the maid laced up the bodice. Jewels went on last: rubies at the waist, dog collars of rubies and diamonds around the neck, and the tiara on top. As she sailed forth from her boudoir, you would never have guessed how quickly she could strip for action.

Assignations depended on circumstances. Vita Sackville-West explains in *The Edwardians:* "The code was rigid. Within the closed circle of their own set, anybody might do as they pleased, but no scandal must leak out to the uninitiated. Appearances must be respected, though morals might be neglected." The King's mistresses had an easy time of it. No one would question a royal command, and few husbands, even in the aristocracy, were prepared to challenge His Majesty's droit du seigneur. Indeed, some women wore, pinned to their blouses, the little watches he gave them, bearing a true lover's knot of mauve enamel ribbon, and, on the back, the crown and the interlaced *E.R. VII.* "Of course I don't *like* it," they would say, "but it's a good little timekeeper, and so I wear it." Actually, HM's watches gained, on the average, about an hour a day.[45]

Amants de coeur of lesser rank had to be more discreet. Luckily transportation was slow; if His Lordship was off shooting partridge in September, or pheasant in October, or attending to fillies and paddocks, Her Ladyship could safely conclude that the coast was clear. It was then, after darkness had gathered, that a one-horse, rubber-tired brougham would draw up outside her private entrance and her lover, using the key she had given him, would stealthily enter. (It never seems to have occurred to them that the brougham and the horse, standing there patiently throughout the evening, or even the night, were a dead giveaway.)

They were lusty in bed and rapacious at table. Meals were enormous, beginning, typically, with ortolan within quail, a truffle within the ortolan, pâté de foie gras within the truffle — on and on, until the pallor of the exhausted diners reminded one observer of the Roman vomitoria. "Dinners," wrote George Cornwallis-West, "were Gargantuan affairs . . . champagne, port and old brandy were the order of the day, or, rather, night." No one shrank from self-indulgence, and all but a few disdained work. They played tennis and auction bridge, which was invented in 1904; they attended races, amateur theatricals, elaborate teas, private recitals, and on one occasion a private circus engaged by an imaginative host. Sackville-West quotes an elderly peeress who defended all this: "We lead the country, don't we? People who lead deserve their privileges. What would happen to the country, I should like to know, if the people at the top enjoyed no leisure? What would happen to the dressmakers, if your mother had no more pretty frocks?" Then, defending the Victorian precept that ostentation was a form of altruism, the peeress added: "Besides, the country likes it. Don't you make any mistake about that. People must have something to look up to. It's good for 'em; gives 'em an ideal. They don't like to see a gentleman degrading himself."[46]

That was not entirely preposterous. During Victoria's reign each new extension of the franchise to the working class had led to Tory gains at the polls. Protestant textile hands in Lancashire were particularly ardent in their conservatism, partly because Irish Catholics were Liberals but also out of loyalty to the Empire. And most of them appear to have enjoyed the ostentation of the more fortunate. The addition of South Africa's 3,106-carat Cullinan diamond to the crown jewels, and the creation of twenty-seven diamond tiaras for the King's coronation by Louis Cartier, whose brother Jacques had just opened a London branch in New Bond Street, were sources of national pride.

But while the lower classes admired the glittering peak of Britain's social pyramid, and did not begrudge the lords their silks and feasts, they were not prepared to see their own children go hungry without protesting. Of course, hunger among England's poor — or the world's poor, for that matter — was nothing new. But the London press and the emerging sociological studies informed Britain's victims of their victimization. One such survey disclosed that in the bleakest neighborhoods of the capital, the richest city in the world, one infant in four died because mothers were incapable of producing milk. Another study, in Leeds, showed that half the children of the destitute were marked by rickets, and 60 percent had bad teeth. Workmen learned that 1 percent of the country's population controlled 67 percent of the nation's capital, while 87 percent of the people were left with 8 percent of the wealth. The average laborer earned one pound a week. At Victoria's death, Benjamin Rowntree found, 28 percent of rural York lived in chronic poverty. In the year of her son's coronation, Charles Booth, a rich shipowner, published *The Life and Labour of the People in London,* revealing that 30 percent of all Londoners suffered from malnutrition. The following year Jack London's *People of the Abyss* appeared; London had lived in the city's slums, and he described lodgings in which beds were let on a system of rotation, three tenants to a bed, each occupying it for eight hours. And in 1906 — the year Rolls-Royce was incorporated and Charles Nestle, a London hairdresser, introduced the permanent wave to fashionable ladies, charging £200 each — the *Daily News* exposed the perilous conditions and pitiful wages paid in England's sweated industries.

Wealthy Edwardians, like the peeress quoted by Vita Sackville-West, were untroubled by all this. It was the will of God; it was all in Malthus — the supply of food would never match population growth. They seldom visited slums. The only hunger most of them saw was that of beggars and the rheumy old women who sat under arches selling matches; to them they contributed a few coppers, a shilling, or even a half crown. Yet had they but investigated their own homes, they would have seen signs of economic distress. Butlers and lady's maids were well fed, but scullery maids and other "under" servants were emaciated and sickly. They slept in attics, in basements, or on cots set up in pantries, and they never slept long; there was too much for them to do. Before dawn they were up raking leaves, rolling lawns, lighting fires, drawing curtains, filling vases with flowers, and bringing up breakfasts. Foreign visitors marveled at the miracles wrought by unseen hands before 8:00 A.M., before the households' masters and mistresses arose, though one Frenchman, E. D. Gramont, found that "this majestic silence got on my nerves. Those great mute corridors, those never-raised voices made me homesick for the Latin hurly-burly; servants shouting, banging pots and pans, slamming doors."[47] But Edwardian hosts enjoyed quietude. Few of them thought of the toil which made it possible. If they did discuss their menials, they were as likely as not to do it in the presence of the help. Domestics were not supposed to have feelings.

Before the ascendancy of Churchill and Lloyd George, all legislative attempts to provide relief for the unfortunate had failed. In 1905 the government established a royal commission on the Poor Law; the members included the Webbs, but both its majority and minority reports were tabled. Parliament outlawed compulsory trade-union contributions to Labour party candidates. MPs were not salaried until 1911. Financing a campaign cost about £1,000, nearly ten times the annual income of a skilled worker, so that even Liberals tended to champion the lot, not of workmen, but of the middle classes. In the radical Parliament that replaced Balfour's House, nearly half the MPs were businessmen or financiers, one in six was an Etonian, one in three was a graduate of Oxford or

Cambridge, and only one in ten represented the working class. During the thirty years before 1916, half of all cabinet ministers were peers or members of peers' families. It was, for them, a splendid time, when everyone knew everybody, and gentlemen still wore toppers and ladies wore ostrich-plume bonnets, and there were always fresh strawberries in season on the House terrace, and waltz time was unthreatened by ragtime, and there were more hansoms than automobiles. A defender of Britain's oligarchic democracy wrote that MPs "have an extraordinarily wide acquaintance with one another from one end of the land to the other. They are connected by marriage, by early association at the public schools and at Oxford or Cambridge, and they are brought constantly together by entertainments in the capital, and visits at country houses. Such a constitution gives to society great solidity and great influence, without the narrowness and rigidity that attends a purely hereditary caste."[48]

That did not satisfy Churchill, who, despite his loyalty to his new party, would be no more a Liberal sheep than he had been a Conservative sheep. He noted that a Liberal party rule enjoined any cabinet member from serving as a director of a public company, yet thirty-one out of fifty-five Liberal ministers were directors, holding among them sixty-eight directorships — a "laxity of principle," he said, which "is a sign of the degeneration of the day," reflecting the creed of politicians "who go about preaching the gospel of Mammon advocating the 10 percent commandments, who raise each day the inspiring prayer, 'Give cash in our time, O Lord.' "[49] He raised the specter of class warfare, and with justification. The Edwardian sky grew redder each year. In 1902 the British economist John Atkinson Hobson had published *Imperialism: A Study,* which had an immense impact on Rosa Luxemburg and Rudolf Hilferding in Germany and, through them, influenced Lenin. At the same time, the new British custom of the Pleasant Sunday Afternoon, the P.S.A., was providing expectant audiences for lay speakers who could entertain and divert them: journalists, humanitarians, adventurers, authors, hobbyists — and, more and more, radical propagandists intent upon exploiting forums to spread a secular faith subversive of the established order.

The P.S.A., innocuous on the surface, was actually an institution of immense social significance. Its roots were the decline of the Victorian Sabbath and shrinking Anglican congregations — which in turn weakened the Tories, the Church of England's most ardent supporters. The solid core of agreed religious belief was gone. The Bible had lost its grip on Englishmen. People were groping for a substitute. *Fin de siècle* ideas had become unfashionable — the Boer War had tarnished Kiplingesque imperialism even as Oscar Wilde had discredited *Yellow Book* aestheticism. The new vogues were popular psychology, pragmatism, Nietzscheanism, and, toward the end of Edward's reign, the philosophy of Henri Bergson and the autosuggestivism of Emile Coué ("Every day, in every way, I'm growing better and better"). But perhaps the most influential ideological works were William James's *Varieties of Religious Experience,* appearing in 1902, and Sir James Frazer's eleven-volume *Golden Bough,* which was published intermittently, in revised editions, throughout the decade. Guided by James and Frazer, the children of nineteenth-century Christian evangelism moved toward a broadening tolerance of all creeds — which is to say, a vulnerability to radical speakers whose dogma provided hard, specific, simple answers to all complex questions.

That vulnerability was enhanced by a growing concept of a mechanistic universe — the obverse of traditional faith in the soul — which was an unanticipated by-product of the era's scientific and technological triumphs. Edwardians were bombarded by news of discoveries: glands, hormones, vitamins, genes, Einstein's $E=mc^2$, Pavlovian conditioned reflexes, Röntgen's X rays, Madame Curie's radium, and the subconscious as revealed by Freud, Adler, and Jung. Fruits of inventive genius promised more excitement to come. Because of Guglielmo Marconi, the King talked to President Roosevelt in 1903 by wireless. That same year two Americans flew the first heavier-than-air machine, and Eric S. Porter produced the first feature-length film, *The Great Train Robbery.* The British formed the Bristol Aeroplane Company; the *Daily Mail* sponsored the first international aircraft race. The Russians completed the trans-Siberian railway. Sleeping cars were introduced on Egypt's Cairo-to-Luxor Express. The production of Austin motorcars began in 1905; the following year the Royal Automobile Club turned its attention from steam-powered trucks to internal-combustion engines. In 1904 heels clicked all over Germany when the North German Lloyd steamer *Kaiser Wilhelm II* set a new transatlantic record of five days, eleven hours. Britons agreed that that would not do, and the Cunarder *Mauretania* made the trip in four days, twenty hours, and forty-one minutes. The Clyde was turning out bigger and bigger ships. The *Lusitania,* launched in 1907, was the largest yet: 31,550 tons, 790 feet long, with four screws and staterooms for 2,000 passengers. Meanwhile, the battleship H.M.S. *Dreadnought* had been launched. She carried ten twelve-inch guns. The kaiser, chagrined, announced that he would not only match her; he would widen the Kiel Canal to permit passage of the huge new fleet he was building. *"Dem Deutschen gehört die Welt"* ("The world belongs to Germans") was the slogan of the Alldeutsche Verband (Pan-German

League). The British public, however, couldn't take it seriously. To them it was as free of menace as that catchy tune written in 1908 by the English songwriters Harry Williams and Jack Judge, "It's a Long Way to Tipperary."

But the cumulative effect of all this change, which should have broadened the human vision, gave men a sense of confinement and helplessness. There were new powers at large, many of them incomprehensible, none in accord with the tidy, distinct images of reality they had been taught as children. Apparently there were no limits to the ways in which the world could be transformed. The Empire had provided their parents with a boundless frontier. Now, with the conquest of northern Nigeria in 1903, the map had filled up; Britain's new imperial challenge was not to get, but to hold. That stifled initiative abroad, and turned frustrated energy inward, into increased demands for innovation at home. The long peace of domestic law and order was shattered, the framework of Edwardian society shaken. Union organizers, reformers, and agitators told workmen of their plight. The mass-circulation newspapers — owned, ironically, by die-hard Tories — confirmed it. Labor struck, in the mines, on the docks, on the railroads; even in the newspaper composing rooms. In 1907 the Sinn Féin ("Ourselves Alone") was formed in Dublin, and Ireland flamed anew.

Finally, the balance between the sexes, the linchpin of the English home, came under ferocious attack. The attackers were idealistic wives. Their issue was the vote. Fewer than a third of all Edwardian Britons were entitled to go to the polls. Voters had to be heads of households, lodgers unencumbered by debts, owners of property, or educated. And they had to be male. In 1903 three militant feminists, Emmeline Pankhurst and her daughters Christabel and Sylvia, launched a crusade against sexism by founding the Women's Social and Political Union. The "Suffragettes," as the *Daily Mail* christened them in 1906, never attracted mass support, but they were alarmingly vocal and, in their campaign of civil disobedience, extraordinarily violent. One of them, Emily Davison, made the supreme sacrifice by throwing herself under the hooves of the King's horse at the Derby. Her comrades smashed shop windows, chained themselves to the gates of Buckingham Palace, bombed monuments, and burned down public buildings. Women like Jennie, who had flourished in the roles men had assigned them, thought that the "female suffrage women" were, as she put it, "too odious." But other upper-class women were the movement's backbone. Their husbands were shocked. Some became converts, though enough remained obdurate to defeat a woman suffrage bill in the House. Churchill spoke for them when, reviving a word which had passed out of the language, he said he refused to be "henpecked on a question of such grave importance."[50]

These shadows cast by coming events were very real, and are defined here to qualify the general impression of the Edwardian era as one of absolute serenity. Yet they did not long darken the days of the favored few. In his Mount Street rooms Churchill knew a tranquillity and security unavailable anywhere today. He did not appreciate it, of course; men rarely understand the sources of their strength. His inspiration continued to be the man who had abused him most. Memorabilia of his father dominated the flat. The walls were hung with pictures of Randolph, cartoons of Randolph from *Vanity Fair* and *Punch,* and a photograph of Randolph's champion horse Abbesse de Jouarre — "Abscess of the Jaw," the jockeys had called it. Winston sat in his father's carved oak chair behind his father's immense desk, dipped his pen in his father's brass inkwell, and toiled nearly every evening on his current work in progress, a two-volume biography entitled *Lord Randolph Churchill.*

His baths were drawn, his boots polished, his clothes laid out, and his small cellar of J. and C. Clark wines inventoried by his current valet, George Scrivings. A maid swept the gray pile carpet and dusted the gleaming, dark, heavy furniture, which, this being a typical Mayfair flat, required a lot of dusting. There were petit point chairs, a large Coromandel screen, a "sociable" on which two people of opposite sexes might sit, facing each other but properly divided by the arm; tortured carvings of ebony, Benares brass, a red-and-gold Crown Derby tea set; and mahogany tables littered with family and polo-team photographs, silver cannon models, model soldiers, jade ashtrays, Indian and Egyptian carvings, celadon bowls, a Fabergé cigar box, twin candelabra, and a small clock. The air was exotic with the scents of wax and furniture oils. Books were everywhere. There were even bookshelves in the bathroom. Hugh Massingham, coming to call, found the occupant literally "sleeping with encyclopedias." Pasted in huge scrapbooks were newspaper clippings on every public topic and on prominent men, particularly Winston S. Churchill. In an unguarded moment he mentioned these to Balfour, explaining that they were useful for reference. AJB's lip curled. He said disdainfully that he could not see the point of "rummaging through a rubbish heap on the problematical chance of finding a cigar butt."[51]

Impressions of Churchill at this time are varied but vivid. Wilfrid

Blunt, meeting him for the first time, described him as "a little, square headed fellow of no very striking appearance, but of wit, intelligence, and originality." On the other hand, Leslie Hore-Belisha, who was ten years old when Churchill called on his father in Manchester, thought him very striking indeed; Winston was wearing "a frock coat with silk facings and below his chin was a large winged collar with a black bow tie. . . . I went so far as to buy — and wear in private — a large winged collar. Thus the imagination of a small boy was captured." Directly after her first dinner-party encounter with him, Violet Asquith had gone to her father and told him that for the first time in her life she had seen genius. Asquith chuckled and said, "Well, Winston would certainly agree with you there — but I am not sure you will find many others of the same mind." Then he added, "Still, I know exactly what you mean. He is not only remarkable but unique." Jennie's new sister-in-law, Daisy Cornwallis-West, was uncharmed; her brother's marriage, she wrote, "made Winston Churchill a connection of ours, a prospect we viewed with somewhat mixed feelings. I cannot honestly say I ever cared for him very much." The same trait attracted and repelled: his brilliant, compulsive conversation. His critics called it "bombast," the "self-advertisement" of an "arriviste." His admirers delighted in what they regarded as genuine wit. Lloyd George told him he was against the social order. Winston replied: "You are only against those parts of it that get in your way." Churchill described F. E. Smith's debating skills: "The bludgeon for the platform; the entangling net and unexpected trident for the Courts of Law; and a jug of clear spring water for an anxious, perplexed conclave." "The difference between Balfour and Asquith," he said, "is that Arthur is wicked and moral, while Asquith is good and immoral."[52]

Churchill's capacity for work was remarkable. His appointment book shows that in his first two weeks as an MP he dined out eight times, attended a trade conference, conducted an inquiry at the Treasury, called on the prime minister, delivered three speeches in the House, campaigned for a Conservative candidate in Manchester, and was there to congratulate him on his victory. One friend recalled in his memoirs that Winston "gave himself to work. When he was not busy with politics, he was reading or writing. He did not lead the life of other young men in London. He may have visited political clubs, but I never met him walking in Pall Mall or Hyde Park where sooner or later one used to meet most friends. I never met him at a dinner-party that had not some public or private purpose."[53]

Once he began writing his father's biography he attended even fewer parties, and was never seen at dances. The rest of his set hummed Franz

Lehár's new waltzes; Churchill was reluctant even to learn the step. In *Anglo-American Memories,* George Smalley, a journalist from the United States, described a weekend as Churchill's fellow guest at Dunrobin, the seat of the Duke of Sutherland. Winston invited him into his bedroom, and Smalley gaped. The room, he wrote, "had been turned into a literary workshop, strewn with books and papers and all the apparatus of the writer. He had brought with him a tin box, some three feet square, divided into closed compartments. This was his travelling companion on journeys of pleasure. . . . His hostess had provided him with a large writing-table. This was covered with papers, loose and in docketed bundles, but all in exact order for ready reference. . . . When we left Dunrobin we found that Winston had reserved a compartment in the railway train for himself and for his big tin case of papers. He shut himself up there, and during that long journey read and wrote and worked as if a Highland railway train were the natural and convenient laboratory in which literature of a high order was to be distilled."[54]

Yet this view of Churchill may have been exaggerated. Like most men of affairs, he had learned to use his time efficiently, and in London he was all business. But he was not what today would be called a workaholic. Many of his leisured friends, it must be remembered, did not work at all; very little dedication was necessary to impress them. His appetite for statecraft did not prevent him from playing when he chose. He followed the races — at a Warwick Castle house party he astounded his fellow guests by reciting the names of the last fifty Derby winners and their breeding — and he always found time for polo, boar hunting, duck shooting, and holidays abroad. In Egypt he sailed up the Nile on a dahabeah with his aunt Leonie, Hicks-Beach, Sir John Gorst, the Duke and Duchess of Connaught, and Alice Keppel. In Switzerland he was the guest of Sir Ernest and Lady Cassel, and at Balmoral he stalked stags with His Majesty. ("You will see the King on Weds when he comes to Invercauld," he wrote his mother; "mind you gush to him about my having written to you saying how much etc etc I had enjoyed myself here.") After observing German military maneuvers as the guest of another personage, HM's nephew the kaiser, he traveled by stages through Breslau, Vienna, Venice, Bologna, Ravenna, Rimini, Urbino, San Marino, Perugia, Siena, and Eichorn. "Such a lot of churches we have seen and saints and pictures 'galore,' " he wrote. "It has been vy pleasant."[55] Similar expeditions were always available to him; indeed, he had difficulty avoiding them. He knew so many members of society, and was such an eligible bachelor, that he had to go into hiding to finish his father's biography. Sunny, not yet troubled by his growing radicalism, turned Blenheim over to him for three or four months each year. The book was completed in the palace and, when published, was well received, though Balfour found the passages mentioning him objectionable. In the first four months the set sold 5,827 copies. An American edition, and then a one-volume British edition, were equally successful.

Churchill was the most active member of every social gathering, and to the annoyance of other young men he never hesitated to take charge. As a guest at the seaside, one hostess wrote, he "flung himself with zest into our favorite and most perilous pastime of rock climbing, reveling in the scramble up crags and cliffs, the precarious transition from ledge to ledge, with slippery seaweed underfoot and roaring seas below. Though we considered ourselves salted climbers of four weeks' experience and he was a raw novice, he always took command of every operation, decreeing strategy and tactics and even dictating the correct position of our arms and legs. He brought to every ploy the excitement of a child and, like a child, he made it seem not only exciting but serious and important." Even more revealing was his response to a terrible fire which followed his brother's wedding. The bride and groom having departed, the rest of the party stayed in Burley-on-the-Hill, an ancient country home near Oakham famous for its paneling, tapestries, and priceless Elizabethan manuscripts. In the middle of the night a newly installed heating system burst into flames. Awakening to screams, in smoke and darkness, the guests fled to the lawn. There, Eddie Marsh wrote, "Winston commandeered a fireman's helmet and assumed the direction of operations." F. E. Smith's wife remembered Churchill on the roof, shouting down orders, trying to quench the blaze with a tiny fire engine which had been brought from Oakham. Unfortunately, nothing could be saved. The owners were in tears.[56]

Churchill wasn't. He wrote Miss Hozier: "The fire was great fun & we all enjoyed it thoroughly. It is a pity such jolly entertainments are so costly. Alas for the archives. They roared to glory in about ten minutes. . . . It is a vy strange thing to be locked in deadly grapple with that cruel element. I had no conception — except from reading — of the power and majesty of a great conflagration. Whole rooms sprang into flames as if by enchantment. Chairs and tables burnt up like matches. Floors collapsed and ceilings crashed down. . . . Every window spouted fire, & from the centre of the house a volcano roared skyward in a whirlwind of sparks." As descriptive writing, this is splendid, but as a response to tragedy it is neither pleasant nor wholesome; that the others "enjoyed it thoroughly" is doubtful — Marsh, for one, had lost his Perceval gold watch, gold chain, and three tiepins, all heirlooms. One can understand why many men distrusted Churchill. "It is no disparagement of Winston's extraordinary qualities," wrote Almeric Fitzroy, "to say that his judgement is not quite equal to his abilities." Destruction, like war, enthralled the mischievous boy in him, and he would never entirely outgrow that fascination. Yet he alone had climbed to the roof and tried to extinguish the flames.[57]

England in those years, "lapped in the accumulated treasures of the long peace," as he wrote, was like Burley-on-the-Hill before the fire: precious, deeply loved, apparently safe, unaware of its deadly peril.[58] The world's diplomats still set their clocks by Big Ben. Because the British government permitted it, Turkey ceded the Sinai to Egypt and Greece annexed Crete. Little importance was attached to the decision, made the year after Victoria's death, to end her policy of "splendid isolation." Actually, it was a move of enormous consequence. From Canning to Salisbury, isolationism had served Britain well, keeping it aloof from a whole series of continental wars. The Royal Navy was its mighty shield; for a century after Nelson's victory at Trafalgar no nation had attempted to build a competitive fleet. In 1870 Gladstone's announcement that England would intervene if Belgium's neutrality were violated had kept both the French and the Germans from crossing Belgian frontiers.

The first break with isolationist policy was made by Lord Lansdowne, the Tory foreign secretary from 1900 to 1905. Armed forces had grown all over the world, he pointed out, and at the very least England should have understandings and defined friendships with other great powers. The United States was his first choice, but America had its own isolationist tradition. Moreover, millions of new U.S. citizens were refugees from European conflicts, and this alone made an Anglo-American alliance a political impossibility. So Lansdowne signed up Japan and, in 1904, joined France in the Entente Cordiale, an agreement to settle colonial differences between the two countries. No one, not even his fellow cabinet ministers, was informed in 1906 when Sir Edward Grey, Lansdowne's successor at the Foreign Office, assumed a "moral obligation" to defend France should it be attacked by Germany, thus adding a military dimension to the Entente. Grey had been provoked by Germany's Wilhelm II. The previous March 31 the kaiser had appeared in Tangier, the chief Moroccan port on the Mediterranean, to declare that he regarded the local sultan as an independent sovereign, thereby offending the French, who had colonial designs there. Knowing the strength of British isolationist sentiment, Grey kept his pledge from his colleagues for five years. By then the Anglo-French relationship had, with the inclusion of Russia, ripened into the Triple Entente. No promises had been made to

Saint Petersburg. Still, the links had been forged, if not joined. Germany, Austria-Hungary, and Italy had been united in central Europe's Triple Alliance since 1882. The implications of this are clear now. They weren't then. An open rupture was considered inconceivable. Indeed, the balance was regarded as a guarantee of peace. The nations, Churchill wrote, "were fitted and fastened, it seemed securely, into an immense cantilever. The two mighty European systems faced each other glittering and clanking in their panoply, but with a tranquil gaze. A polite, discrete, pacific, and on the whole sincere diplomacy spread its web of connections over both. A sentence in a dispatch, an observation by an ambassador, a cryptic phrase in a Parliament seemed sufficient to adjust from day to day the balance of the prodigious structure."[59]

London had never seemed so secure, or so prodigious. The city's population had reached 6,600,000; New York, its closest rival, had 3,440,000; Tokyo, 1,450,000; and Los Angeles, just 103,000. Although its architecture was largely Victorian (it still is), the inhabitants believed they were leading the world into the future, literally lighting the way — the city's Inner Circle rail lines were electrified in 1905. Businessmen who wanted their firms to become household words came to London. The Italian Auguste Oddenino, determined to own the finest restaurant on earth, built it in Regent Street. In 1902 the Ritz had opened in Piccadilly, followed by Dunhill's in Duke Street, near Piccadilly Circus, Selfridge's in Oxford Street, and, in the last year of Edward's reign, the 2,500-seat London Palladium. Lord Northcliffe was Britain's most exciting press lord. Having transformed the *Daily Mail,* he turned the *Daily Mirror* into a halfpenny picture paper, drove its circulation to a million, and bought *The Times.* He introduced sports pages for a nation of innovative sportsmen. The world's affluent became small-boat enthusiasts; an English publisher gave them *The Riddle of the Sands.* Leisure time increased in industrial countries; their sportsmen turned to lawn tennis and football, both invented in Britain. A wave of nostalgia for an idealized childhood spread across Europe and North America. English writers quickly took it over. On December 27, 1904, James M. Barrie's *Peter Pan; or, The Boy Who Would Not Grow Up* opened at the Duke of York's Theatre with Maude Adams in the lead, and it has been playing in one hall or another ever since. Kipling wrote *Kim* and *Just So Stories for Little Children;* Beatrix Potter, *Peter Rabbit;* Kenneth Grahame, *The Wind in the Willows;* and Sir R. S. S. Baden-Powell, the hero of Mafeking, published *Scouting for Boys* in 1906 and founded the Boy Scout movement with the motto "Be Prepared," based on his initials. Boys around the globe enrolled, 11,000 of them coming to convene in the Crystal Palace.

In music and art the British were less successful. Sir Thomas Beecham was a gifted conductor and the London Symphony a distinguished orchestra, but Elgar was the only memorable composer. The best native tunes were heard in London's music halls, and the liveliest of these, "Waltzing Matilda," was written by an Austrialian, Marie Cowan, in 1903. John Singer Sargent, an American, was commissioned to paint *The Marlborough Family; Westminster Bridge, The Houses of Parliament,* and *Port of London* were the work of France's André Derain. London painters were indeed inhospitable to foreign genius. They jeered at the first major London exhibition of Postimpressionists, Derain among them; even Sargent said, "I am absolutely sceptical as to their having any claim whatever to being works of art, with the exception of the pictures by Gauguin that strike me as admirable in colour — and in colour only." In literature, however, the English scene glowed. The number of books published annually soared from 5,971 to 9,541. A certain sacrifice was made for wider audiences. Before the Edwardian era, authors could assume that their readers knew Latin and the Bible. The mass-circulation newspapers had altered their vocabulary for subscribers lacking a classical education, and this was reflected in the new books, including serious fiction. R. C. K. Ensor has noted that this created "a distinct barrier of language between the modern Englishman and most of his country's greater literature from Milton down through Burke to Macaulay."[60]

Yet the gain was greater than the loss. Edwardian writers possessed a vitality unmatched in England before or since, and this is reflected in the files of the *Times Literary Supplement,* whose first issue was dated January 17, 1902. In poetry these were the years of Masefield and Alfred Noyes's "Highwayman" ("The wind was a torrent of darkness among the gusty trees, / The moon was a ghostly galleon tossed upon cloudy seas . . ."). Drama apart, the novel was the only popular literary form, and it glittered with the works of Kipling, George Moore, Samuel Butler (*The Way of All Flesh,* 1903), Arnold Bennett, H. G. Wells, Conrad, the early Maugham, Henry James, Saki, W. H. Hudson (*Green Mansions,* 1904), John Galsworthy (Soames Forsyte arrived in *The Man of Property,* 1906), and Bloomsbury's E. M. Forster, whose most fruitful years these were (*Where Angels Fear to Tread,* 1905; *The Longest Journey,* 1907; *A Room with a View,* 1908; and his masterpiece, *Howards End,* 1910). Fictive entertainment also flourished. This period saw the appearance of Conan Doyle's *Hound of the Baskervilles;* the first Edgar Wallace thriller, *The Four Just Men;* and the debut of P. G. Wodehouse, whose *Pothunters,* astonishingly, was published in 1902.

But it was the English stage that captivated the literary world. London's dramatic renaissance, the fruit of twenty years of brilliant criticism and experiment, reached its culmination during Edward's reign; for the first time since Shakespeare, British plays were being translated into all continental languages, and the city's little theaters were packed almost nightly throughout the decade. At His Majesty's Theatre you could see Clyde Fitch's *Last of the Dandies* and John Millington Synge's *Tinker's Wedding.* The Royal Court Theatre produced Galsworthy's *Silver Box* and seven Shaw plays: *Candida, John Bull's Other Island, Man and Superman, Major Barbara, Captain Brassbound's Conversion, The Doctor's Dilemma,* and *The Philanderer.* Shaw's *Getting Married* could be seen at the Haymarket, Masefield's *Tragedy of Man* at the New Royalty. If you liked Barrie, and he was more popular then than now, you went to the Duke of York, which staged, in addition to *Peter Pan, The Admirable Crichton, Alice Sit-by-the-Fire, What Every Woman Knows, Old Friends,* and *The Twelve-Pound Look.* The Duke of York also showed Galsworthy's *Justice* and Shaw's *Misalliance.* Quite apart from artistic merits, Edwardian playwrights dealt with the absorbing social and political issues of the time — labor unions, feminism, criminal justice, the prison system, the Irish question, imperialism, armaments, socialism, salvationism, syndicalism, property, marriage, and divorce — and they therefore found Churchill in their audiences. He met most of them and knew Shaw well. When rehearsals for *Pygmalion* ended at His Majesty's Theatre (with Mrs. Patrick Campbell, Jennie's husband's mistress, playing Eliza Doolittle) GBS wired Winston: "Am reserving two tickets for you for my premiere. Come and bring a friend — if you have one." Churchill wired back: "Impossible to be present for the first performance. Will attend the second — if there is one."[61]

Winston was a Liberal back-bencher for eighteen months and, most of the time, an inconspicuous one. The larger part of his time was devoted to writing and building a Manchester constituency for the coming general election. In the House he tried to steer a careful course between the left and right wings of his new party, speaking on the safe subjects of army reform and the economy. But he was never completely himself unless in the center of the firing line, and Balfour, dodging on and off the floor to avoid taking stands which would further split his Tories, was an irresistible target. Churchill mocked his "miserable and disreputable shifts" of principle and "his gross and flagrant ignorance." *Punch* reported Balfour's reaction: "Prince Arthur lolls on the Treasury Bench looking straight before him with studious indifference, betrayed by a countenance clouded with rare anger." Other Conservatives were less aloof. They published an anonymous pamphlet quoting the turncoat's past attacks on his new colleagues. It was headed: "Mr Winston Churchill on the Radical Party Before he donned their livery and Accepted their Pay."[62]

Balfour decided to resign as prime minister before the country went to the polls. On December 4, 1905, dispirited, lacking in legislative goals, and unable to reestablish a working relationship with Chamberlain, AJB stepped down over a minor issue, and the King asked Campbell-Bannerman to form a new government. Edward gave C-B a free hand in his appointments. The new prime minister offered Churchill a choice of posts and Winston asked to be named under secretary of state for the colonies; the secretary of state would be the Earl of Elgin, and since Elgin sat in the House of Lords, Winston would handle colonial matters in the Commons. C-B agreed and it was announced. The Tories, predictably, were outraged. Now the truth was out, they cried. The renegade had changed his party to reach office; he stood exposed as "a political adventurer who would do anything for his own advancement." Actually, he was something of an ingrate. Members of the government were entitled to wear the uniforms of privy councillors. In those days secretaries, having ministerial rank, belonged to the first class, others were second-class, the difference between them being marked by the gold embroidery on the collar and cuffs — a plain edge for ministers and a serrated edge for the others. Sir Herbert Samuel later recalled accompanying Churchill to the investiture ceremony. "Winston," he wrote, "was by no means pleased at being no more than an Undersecretary, young as he was and even as a first step in office. Suddenly, pointing to his sleeve, he said to me: 'The badge of shame!' "[63]

In his first official act he picked as his private secretary Edward Marsh, a casual acquaintance who, until now, had been a well-connected but obscure clerk in the West African department. Eddie Marsh's life and Churchill's would be closely intertwined for the next thirty years. Max Beerbohm caught the essence of Eddie in one of his pencil sketches: the head cocked like a bird's, bushy eyebrows arched eagerly, monocle twinkling. He frequently removed the monocle to wipe away a tear — like Churchill, he was emotional — and his falsetto, slate-squeak voice reminded Violet Asquith of "a high-pitched chirrup." Eddie was nervous about his new job. He wasn't sure he liked Winston. In his memoirs he wrote that he was "a little afraid of him" and doubted "we could ever have anything in common."[64]

On December 12, however, Eddie was Winston's guest in Mount Street. The next morning he wrote Leonie Leslie: "Such an excitement. I *must* tell you. Your nephew has asked me to be his private secretary for 6 months or so. It will be the most interesting thing I've ever done but I'm most terribly afraid of not being the right person and turning out a failure. . . . I've just dined alone with Winston. He was most perfectly charming to me but made it quite clear what he would expect in the way of help and I almost *know* I can't do it — it's awful!" Churchill, however, had decided that this was his man. When he was determined to be fascinating, he could dispel virtually all misgivings. He had a way of tossing off lapidary epigrams as though they had just occurred to him, and he now flashed such a jewel before Marsh, describing the proper spirit for a great nation: "In war, resolution; in defeat, defiance; in victory, magnanimity; in peace, good-will." ("I wish," Eddie wrote, "the tones in which he spoke this could have been 'recorded' — the first phrase a rattle of musketry, the second 'grating harsh thunder,' the third a ray of the sun through storm-clouds; the last pure benediction.")* Marsh, still anxious, awoke in the morning, presented himself to Winston, and whispered worriedly, "I'm afraid I shan't be much use today, as I've lost my voice." Churchill looked up. "What?" he boomed. "Is that resonant organ extinct?" By then they were firm friends. Jennie, however, remembering that ugly business at Sandhurst, was troubled by this appointment; according to Douglas Plummer, Marsh was known to be "the center of a large homosexual artistic colony." But there is no evidence that his deviance was overt, and Churchill, vastly tolerant in his friendships, doubtless regarded the matter as none of his business.[65]

Three weeks later the two men checked into Manchester's Midland Hotel, which would be Winston's base for his first campaign as a Liberal candidate. That evening they toured the slums. Churchill "looked about him," Marsh wrote, "and his sympathetic imagination was stirred. 'Fancy,' he said, 'living in one of these streets, never seeing anything beautiful, never eating anything savoury, *never saying anything clever!*' " He meant to be clever here, but not alarming. The city had become a Conservative stronghold — all nine seats were held by Tories — and apart from ringing tributes to Free Trade, he skirted controversy just

* Churchill used them forty years later as the theme for his history of World War II.

twice. Courting workingmen's votes, he promised that the Liberals would remember England's "left-out millions," and, less honorably, assured Protestant Unionists that he would "support no legislation which I regard as likely to injure the effective integrity of the United Kingdom." Hecklers distributed copies of the pamphlet quoting his past scorn for his present party; one thrust it in his hands while others cried, "Answer it!" He did: "I said a lot of stupid things when I worked with the Conservative Party, and I left it because I did not want to go on saying stupid things." Then, amid loud cheers, he tore the leaflet to shreds and, a newspaperman reported, "flung it from him with a dramatic gesture, expressing . . . contempt for the cause he had once espoused."[66]

He was the most exciting candidate in the city. "There is no question about it," wrote Charles E. Hands of the Tory *Daily Mail;* "the public interest of Manchester in the General Election is centred and focussed on the personality of Mr Winston Churchill. You can hardly see the rest of the political landscape for this dominant figure." Men discussed his alliterative rhetoric, the mammoth posters bearing his name in letters five feet high, the reviews of his new book, and the startling youthfulness of his mother, who was stumping for him every day. He was billed to speak in the Manchester Coal Exchange one afternoon at three o'clock. "At half past two," the *Guardian* reported, "the hall was packed with a struggling crowd; a second crowd was struggling on the staircase leading to the hall; and a third crowd [was] jostling for standing room on the pavement in the street." The *Mail* noted that he was "wearing a new old-fashioned hat, a flat-topped sort of felt hat, and already the hatters are having enquiries for articles of that pattern." In addition, "Ladies who have been privileged to speak to him are envied of their sex."[67]

Among the enviers of their sex were the Pankhursts. In late 1905, even before the campaign had begun, Christabel Pankhurst and her friend Annie Kenney had been arrested for disrupting a Churchill speech in northwest Manchester; Churchill had offered to pay their fifteen-shilling fine, but they chose a week's martyrdom in a cell. Emmeline Pankhurst now interrupted one of his speeches repeatedly until stewards lured her into a side room and locked the door. Winston, who thought she had left the meeting, said he had voted for the one woman suffrage bill to come before the House but deplored disturbances at political rallies. Someone shouted: "That's right, don't be henpecked, Winston!" At St. John's Schools, Gartside, he had to deal with Sylvia Pankhurst. She raised a sign bearing the slogan "Votes for Women," but she had it upside down, and Churchill mildly pointed that out. She called: "Will you give us a vote?" He invited her to join him on the platform; she did, and he asked the crowd: "Will everybody please be quiet. Let us hear what she has to say." They refused; they chanted: "We want to hear Churchill!" He tried again and failed. The hall was in an uproar. According to the *Guardian,* he then said: " 'We should be fair and chivalrous to ladies. They come here asking us to treat them like men.' (Laughter) 'That is what I particularly want to avoid. We must observe courtesy and chivalry to the weaker sex dependent upon us.' (Hear hear.)" Sylvia, furious, stalked out. Like her mother, she had found that in one respect Churchill was like Arthur Balfour. He could adroitly avoid making a commitment under the wrong circumstances.[68]

Manchester voted on January 13; the results were announced two days later. All nine Liberals had won. Balfour was among the losers. Winston, whose margin of victory was over 1,200 votes, took Hands to supper at the hotel. The reporter called it "a grand slam in doubled no trumps."[69] Churchill agreed. Bridge was never his game, but this time he was on the money; he sensed the mood of the entire country. When the last votes were counted it was clear that the Liberals had won a historic landslide. They had swept 377 seats; of the Tories, who had gone into the fight 400 strong, only 157 survived. In addition, there were 83 Irish Nationalists, and — portentous, though few noted their significance — 53 Labour members. Campbell-Bannerman and his men could alter the face of England. Churchill confronted a personal challenge. He had been a formidable critic; now, holding office in a secure government, he must be constructive. But political tempers are slow to change. Men long in opposition cannot easily break habits of cavil, particularly when they have mastered the art, nor are they adept at the compromises and jugglery which are the plain handmaidens of responsibility. Winston was now answerable to the House for the administration of the King's colonies, and the first issue he faced would have taxed a seasoned veteran of the Treasury Bench, which he, at this time, clearly was not.

It was an ugly business. Sir Alfred Milner, last seen in this narrative being interviewed by Churchill in Cape Town, had been elevated to the peerage, and the month after the Liberal sweep he made his maiden speech in the House of Lords. A lot of men wanted to question Milner. As high commissioner in South Africa he had imported some fifty thousand Chinese coolies to work the Rand gold mines. Their contracts ran for three years; they were not permitted to bring their families, they were penned in camps, and reportedly they were subjected to corporal punishment. In one of his first acts as prime minister, Campbell-Bannerman had announced that the leasing of Chinese would be discontinued. Licenses for fourteen thousand more coolies had already been issued the previous November, however, and the matter of their treatment in the past was therefore a burning question. Documents acquired by the new government revealed that mine bosses had been meting out punishments without trial, flogging the Chinese indiscriminately. This was a gross violation of London's instructions to the high commissioner and of Whitehall's assurances to authorities in China. A fellow lord asked Milner if he had sanctioned this. Milner confessed that he had, adding, "I think, in the light of subsequent events, that I was wrong."[70]

The Liberal press, led by Massingham and the *Guardian,* was in full cry. Radical Liberals demanded Milner's head. Churchill agreed that his conduct had been reprehensible and said: "I should not put myself to any undue or excessive exertion to defend Lord Milner from any attacks which might be made upon him." At Question Time, replying to Hilaire Belloc, a new Liberal MP, he added: "Lord Milner committed a grave dereliction of public duty and at the same time an undoubted infringement of the law." Belloc and others drafted a motion of censure. Chamberlain, whose man Milner had been, protested that it was "despicable" to "persecute him for a single error of judgment in a long course of public service." Winston accused Joe of abusing the Boers, and then Free Trade. The only difference between the two, he said, was that "whereas the first enterprise of the right honourable gentleman has had the effect of nearly ruining South Africa, the second enterprise has had the effect of politically ruining himself." Chamberlain hotly replied that it was Churchill's duty, as "head of a department," to "defend the servants of the department." At this point senior Liberals decided to put out the fire. Milner had a large following in the country; making a martyr out of him would be both pointless and risky. Churchill had to tell the House that in the interests of peace and conciliation, he would oppose the censure motion. He was uncomfortable in this position, however, and his defense of it was deplorable. "Lord Milner," he said, "has gone from South Africa, probably for ever. The public service knows him no more. Having exercised great authority he now exerts none. Having held high employment he now has no employment. . . . He is today a retired Civil Servant, without pension or gratuity of any kind whatever. It is not worth while to pursue him any further."[71]

The Conservatives were outraged, the Liberals embarrassed. Margot Asquith called the speech "ungenerous, patronising, and tactless." Even Eddie Marsh, who had thought it impressive in rehearsal, now concluded that his new employer "appeared to be taunting a discredited statesman." A Tory MP moved to reduce Winston's salary for "embittered and empoisoned language" on coolie labor and above all for insulting Milner, "a man whom so many of us esteem, honour, and love." Kipling, an admirer of Milner, never forgave Winston. Sir William Anson, the warden of All Souls, Oxford, wrote that Churchill had seemed "both pompous and impertinent. It is terrible to think what harm that young jackanapes may do with a big majority behind him and an incompetent Prime Minister to look after him." The House of Lords passed, 170 to 35, a resolution expressing its gratitude to Milner for his service in South Africa. The King wrote the Liberal Marquess of Crewe: "It is a pity that Lord Elgin does not seem to be able to control the violent and objectionable language of his Parliamentary Under-Secretary." To Lady Londonderry, a kinswoman of Churchill's, he remarked that "the conduct of a certain relation of yours is simply scandalous. It is indeed hard on Lord Milner to be treated in such a manner."[72]

This was hard on Elgin. The secretary of state for colonies could hardly be expected to control events in the House of Commons when, as a peer, he could not even be admitted to the chamber. A shy man, bereft of social graces — Marsh described him as "a rugged old thane of antique virtue and simplicity" — he nevertheless possessed administrative abilities and had acquitted himself well as viceroy of India. Later he wrote: "When I accepted Churchill as my Under Secy I knew I should have no easy task." He had decided to show Winston all documents, let him join all policy discussions, always give him the benefit of the doubt, "but to keep control." Austen Chamberlain, in *Politics from Inside,* tells the story that Churchill submitted a long memorandum to his minister, ending, "These are my views," and Elgin sent it back with the notation, "But not mine." No doubt the under secretary tried the secretary's patience at times. He also bemused him. To his wife, Elgin wrote, "Winston is a curious impulsive creature." He described how, when he mildly criticized a paper, Churchill apologized profusely, "seized the paper and tore it up." It was Elgin who coined the phrase "Winston's latest *volte face.*" The fighter of Boers had become the champion of Boers. The critic of military budgets would soon become the most ardent advocate of rearmament. The arch-Tory was now a passionate Liberal. In each instance the shift could be supported by argument, and no one ever argued more persuasively than Churchill, but those who thought him mercurial had a case.[73]

In the Colonial Office he seemed to be a combination of Pitt and Puck. Inexhaustible, frequently carried away by his own soaring rhetoric, exaggerating his importance, he was criticized by colleagues for his heavy, "ministerial" manner. Sometimes he seemed to make work for himself and others. It is a definition of an egoist that whatever occupies his attention is, for that reason, important. The results can be hilarious. An African, one Sekgoma, had proclaimed himself chief of Batawana in Ngamiland, Bechuanaland. He was unpopular, and he was not the legal heir. When the legitimate chief came of age, the tribe crowned the youth. Sekgoma objected and was jailed. Civil servants responsible for the colony decided that the best solution was to deport Sekgoma to the Seychelles. Indeed, they seemed to have no choice. But their under secretary fiercely disagreed. To imprison or deport the deposed chief, he wrote, would be a "flat violation of every principle of British justice." In fact, he could not even begin to defend the lawless treatment of an innocent man upon "an informal *lettre de cachet.*" He asked: "If we are going to embark upon this sort of law-breaking and autocratic action, where are we going to stop? What kind of injustice is there that would not be covered by precedents of this kind?" Indeed, if men who had committed no crime could be deprived of trial by jury, exiled, and condemned to lives of penal servitude, "why stop there? Why not poison Sekgoma by some painless drug?" Since medieval practices were to be revived, "at least let us show medieval courage and thoroughness. Think of the expense that would be saved. A dose of laudanum, costing at the outside five shillings, is all that would be required. There would be no cost of maintenance, no charges for transportation, no legal difficulties, no need to apply to the Portuguese, no fear of the habeas corpus." Having made his point, and believing it safe from refutation, he ended grandly: "If however as I apprehend, Secretary of State would be averse to this procedure, the next best thing would be to obey the law, and to act with ordinary morality, however inconvenient."[74]

Elgin was nettled. He replied shirtily that he had no intention of sending to the chemist for a five-shilling dose of laudanum. The file on Sekgoma was clear: "This man is a savage — and is said to be contemplating proceedings in defiance of all law to disturb the peace." In fact, he had been plotting to behead his successor. If he were released, blood would be shed, including, probably, his own. His Majesty's government could hardly encourage that. However, the minister agreed that deportation was troublesome and objectionable in principle; another African home would be found for the dethroned chief. As an episode in the history of the British Empire, this approaches the far reaches of trivia, but it is also vintage Churchill — his memo was impudent, witty, and superbly written. Ronald Hyam commented that "Churchill exaggerated the importance of everything he touched. Every speck on the horizon, he assumed, would turn out to be a Cunarder, not a cockleshell."[75]

If others wondered at Elgin's patience with him, they did not realize how grateful the colonial secretary was to have such a lieutenant. Tirelessly drafting answers to parliamentary questions, a gifted writer of arresting minutes, he defended colonial policy in the House with a sharpening wit; to Andrew Bonar Law, a Tory who accused him of twisting the meaning of a Tory document, he replied: "The words which you now tell me you employed and which purport to be a paraphrase, if not an actual quotation, are separated by a small degree of inaccuracy and misrepresentation from the inaccuracy and misrepresentation of the condensed report." He also carried a burden of day-to-day decisions which was immense because of the Empire's immensity. He negotiated with Cypriots over pledges of financial assistance, spoke up for Jewish immigrants embittered by what he regarded as a "very harsh and quite indefensible measure," recommended reductions of naturalization fees, advocated help for Zulu tribes mistreated by the Natal government, urged Campbell-Bannerman to invite all six of Australia's state premiers to a colonial conference, and mediated a dispute in India between Curzon, the viceroy, and Kitchener, commander in chief of His Majesty's forces there. (He sided with Curzon, but Kitchener won.) Most of the matters brought before him were insignificant even then, but two weren't. The South African mining magnates were persuaded to repatriate their Chinese workers. And the Boers, at last, were given a just political settlement.[76]

Churchill played an active role in drafting the provisions for the Transvaal constitution, and later that of the Orange River Colony, and piloted them through the House. The former republics were to be granted self-government with universal manhood suffrage, an approach to the "one vote, one value" principle which even England lacked. The revered name "Orange Free State" was then restored and a limited ban on the Afrikaans language lifted; members of both Boer parliaments could address their colleagues in either English or Afrikaans. Indeed, British colonial officials posted there would be expected to master Dutch dialects, "for," Winston wrote, "if the people like to talk to him in Volapuk, he must learn Volapuk. If they have a weakness for Sanskott, it must become his study. By humouring them, and understanding them, he will be able very often to make their wishes and their welfare coincide." "We are prepared," he told the House, "to make this settlement in the name of the Liberal Party. This is sufficient authority for us; but there is a higher authority which we should earnestly desire to obtain." He asked the Tories to "join with us to invest the grant of a free Constitution to the Transvaal with something of a national sanction. With all our majority we can only make it the gift of a Party. They can make it the gift of England." But Balfour, who had found another seat in a by-election, wanted no part of it. He called the bill "a dangerous, audacious and reckless experiment." Milner condemned it in the Lords. *The Times* prophesied the doom of the Empire, and the *Daily Mail* ran the headlines: ANOTHER MAJUBA — TRANSVAAL GIVEN BACK TO THE BOERS — FRUITLESS SACRIFICES OF THE WAR — 22,000 LIVES AND £250,000,000 FOR NOTHING.[77]

Nevertheless, the measure was a triumph. Botha became prime minister, first of the self-governing Transvaal, and then after 1910 of the new Union of South Africa. When they met as fellow statesmen, he recognized Churchill as his armored-train prisoner, whereupon Winston complained that the reward for his recapture had been stingy. In 1914 Botha and his followers chose to fight side by side with the British, something not foreseen only a few years earlier, and Churchill's fellow Liberals, among others, recognized the wisdom and generosity of his terms. His "shame" was past; he was appointed a first-class member of the Privy Council, a rare honor for a man below cabinet rank. Now he stood in the party's front echelons. The next vacancy on the government's front bench would be his. Meanwhile, he decided to have some fun and possibly make money, too. In the summer of 1907, after a colonial conference at which he beat back appeals for imperial preference by arguing that tariffs would lead to "a deep feeling of sullen hatred of the colonies and of colonial affairs among the poorer people in this country," he left England for five months. He and F. E. Smith attended French military maneuvers, joined Sunny for a partridge shoot in Moravia (now part of Czechoslovakia), and then separated, Winston making his way in easy stages, by Vienna and Syracuse, to Malta, where he rendezvoused with Eddie Marsh, George Scrivings, and a distant Churchill relative. The four of them boarded the cruiser *Venus,* which, Winston wrote, was "lying obedient and attentive in the roads." The Admiralty had put it at his disposal for a tour of the east African domains.[78]

On Cyprus they were greeted by a mass demonstration favoring Enosis, complete union with Greece. That was the last flicker of controversy on the journey. The rest was an idyll, impossible now and possible then only because of the unchallenged might of the Empire. The party "threaded the long red furrow of the Suez Canal," as Churchill wrote afterward, and "sweltered through the trough of the Red Sea" to Aden.

Pausing in Mombasa, they traveled up-country on a special train provided by the Uganda Railway; two of them, he told his mother in a long letter home, sat "on a seat in front of the engine with our rifles & as soon as we saw anything to shoot at — a wave of the hand brought the train to a standstill & sometimes we tried at antelope without even getting down." They found zebras, lions, rhinoceroses, antelopes of every kind, ostriches, and giraffes. He wrote: "On the first day I killed 1 zebra, 1 wildebeeste, two hartebeeste, 1 gazelle, 1 bustard (a giant bird)," and he had also sighted "a vy fine kind of antelope with beautiful straight horns." He was nearly run down by a rhino, "a survival of prehistoric times," whose charge was halted when he fired "a heavy 450 rifle & hit her plumb in the chest."[79]

Everywhere Africans waited to pay the bwana tribute: "I was presented by the various chiefs with 108 sheep, 7 Bulls, about £100 worth of ivory, an ostrich egg, many fowls & some vy good leopard skins." A glimpse of "the mighty snow-clad peak of Mt Kenya" was followed by stops at Nairobi, Lake Victoria, Kampala, the Ripon Falls, Gondokoro, and, after a leisurely journey by train and steamer, Khartoum, where, to Churchill's dismay, his manservant fell ill with choleraic diarrhea and died. The Dublin Fusiliers, at Winston's request, gave Scrivings a military funeral; "we all walked in procession to the cemetery as mourners, while the sun sank over the desert, and the band played that beautiful funeral march you know so well." That put a damper on the rest of the trip; they hurried to Wadi Halfa, Aswân, Cairo, and home. But on balance the expedition had been a great success. Churchill felt fit and was in fact wealthier. After the last election he had left Mount Street and rented a small house at 12 Bolton Street, just off Piccadilly, two blocks from the Ritz, and during his absence his brother had sublet it for him. The *Strand* paid him £750 for four articles on his tour; Hodder and Stoughton advanced £500 against royalties for a book, *My African Journey.* Solvent and radiant, he was guest of honor on Saturday, January 18, 1908, at a dinner given by the National Liberal Club to welcome him home. He told them: "I come back into the firing line in the best possible health, and with a wish to force the fighting up to the closest possible point."[80]

That wish was swiftly granted. During his absence Campbell-Bannerman's health had deteriorated alarmingly. Aware that he had only a few weeks to live, C-B resigned on April 3. Asquith succeeded him — he crossed to Biarritz for his sovereign's permission to form a new government; Edward let nothing interrupt his holidays — and on April 8 he wrote Churchill: "With the King's approval, I have the great pleasure of offering you the post of President of the Board of Trade." Thus Winston, at thirty-three, reached cabinet rank. Since the Restoration in 1660, custom had required newly appointed ministers to stand for reelection in their constituencies. The seat Winston had won two years earlier was traditionally Conservative. Now he had to run for it again. The Tories were elated. They had been waiting with red-baited breath for this chance to humiliate the "bounder," the "opportunist," the "traitor to his class." The suffragettes also had him in their sights. His provocative wit was partly to blame. Although he had become an ardent social reformer, he said: "I refuse to be shut up in a soup kitchen with Mrs. Sidney Webb." And when a militant feminist asked him what should be the role of women in the future, he replied: "The same, I trust, as it has been since the days of Adam and Eve." She glared. Swiftly moving to recover lost ground, he assured her and her sisters that he was a convert to their cause. "Trust me, ladies," he begged. They refused. They would campaign against him, they said, unless he could guarantee Asquith's support of votes for women. He tried to explain that he could hardly speak for the new prime minister. They jeered; they didn't believe it; they vowed to give him no peace.[81]

And they did. "Painful scenes," he wrote, "were witnessed in the Free Trade Hall when Miss Christabel Pankhurst, tragical and dishevelled, was finally ejected after having thrown the meeting into pandemonium." This continued to be their most dramatic stratagem. His speeches were interrupted by hisses and even physical assaults, his rallies thrown into turmoil by women hurling rotten eggs and ripe fruit. Sometimes they waited until he was approaching his peroration, or the most intricate point in his argument. Then feminine voices would shriek: "What about the women?" "When are you going to give women the vote?" He wrote: "It became extremely difficult to pursue connected arguments." He toiled eighteen hours a day, organizing canvassers when he wasn't on the stump, and when the feminists allowed it, he gave the opposition as good as he got. He pictured himself arrayed against "all the forces of reaction" and "every discontented irresponsible element in the community," notably "old doddering peers, cute financial magnates, clever wirepullers, big brewers with bulbous noses . . . weaklings, sleek, smug, comfortable, self-important individuals." The situation was complicated by a third candidate, representing the Marxist Social Democratic Federation. In an open letter, H. G. Wells, whom socialists trusted, urged workingmen to back Churchill, but the Liberal vote split. Winston lost by 529 votes. As he left the town hall a suffragette grabbed his arm and cried: "It's the women who have done this, Mr Churchill! Now you will understand that we must have our vote."[82]

The real victors, of course, were the Tories. In what passed for humor in Balfour's set, an ill-wisher wired him: "What's the use of a W.C. without a seat?" The *Morning Post* rejoiced that Winston, "though a Cabinet minister, is a political Ishmaelite wandering around as an object of compassion and commiseration. Manchester has washed its hands of him. The juveniles have for days past been singing to a popular air 'Good-bye, Winnie, you must leave us,' and Winnie has gone. On the whole Manchester appears to be taking the sorrowful parting with composure." So was Churchill. Even before he left the city, telegrams had arrived offering him eight safe Liberal seats. He chose Dundee, one of whose MPs had just been elevated to the peerage. To his mother he wrote: "It's a life seat and cheap and easy beyond all experience." The Manchester defeat didn't rankle. He wrote a woman friend, not a militant feminist, who mourned his loss: "It was a real pleasure to me to get your letter & telegram. I am glad to think you watched the battle from afar with eyes sympathetic to my fortunes. . . . How I should have liked you to be there. You would have enjoyed it I think. We had a jolly party and it was a whirling week. Life for all its incompleteness is rather fun sometimes."[83]

The friend was Clementine Hozier, whom he had disconcerted with his rude, silent stare four years earlier. Now twenty-three, Clementine was at the height of her beauty. Violet Asquith, seeing her for the first time, thought she had "a face of classical perfection" and "a profile like the racing cutter in George Meredith's novel *Beauchamp's Career,*" or "the prow of a Greek ship."[84] Her social credentials were acceptable, if not spectacular. She belonged to one of those landed gentry families which lived on tight budgets. Descended from Scots whose lineage could be traced back to the twelfth century, she was a granddaughter of the Countess of Airlie. Jennie had once known her mother well; Winston's uncle Jack Leslie had been one of her godfathers. Men said she was a good hunter for a woman; women said that she had rightly decided her hair was her crowning glory, and on formal occasions she always wore it up. But there was much more to Clementine than that. The child of a shattered marriage, educated at the Sorbonne, she was a strong-minded young woman of firm likes and dislikes (she did not like Jennie), and her politics were rather to the left of the Liberal establishment. Although she never invited arrest or shouted down cabinet members, she believed women were entitled to the vote and was prepared to say so anywhere, to anyone, at any time. She was not, in short, a paradigm of an upper-class Englishwoman. Most youthful patricians would have found her a difficult wife, and she had already broken an engagement she knew was unwise. Yet there were deep reservoirs of love in her. For the right husband, she would be magnificent.

"Where does the family start?" Winston once asked rhetorically. "It starts with a young man falling in love with a girl. No superior alternative has yet been found." But first they must be thrown together, and both he and Clementine almost missed their second meeting. It came in March 1908, two months after his return from Africa. They had been invited separately to a dinner being given at 52 Portland Place by her aunt, Lady St. Helier, formerly Lady Jeune, who had been Winston's benefactress when he wanted to ride with Kitchener to Khartoum. At the appointed hour, however, he was in his bath. Eddie, bursting in on him, said: "What on earth are you doing, Winston? You should be at dinner by now!" Churchill said he wasn't going, that it would be a great bore; Eddie told him he couldn't do that to Lady Jeune, and, grumbling and scowling, Winston emerged from the tub, dressed, and caught a cab. Meanwhile, at 51 Abingdon Villas in Kensington, Clementine and her mother had exchanged similar words. Clementine had spent the afternoon giving French lessons at a half crown an hour. She was tired and didn't want to go out, but Lady Blanche scolded: "That is very ungrateful of you. Your Aunt Mary has been extremely kind to you. Let's have no more nonsense; go upstairs straight away and get dressed."[85]

So the two unwilling guests arrived late. Seated next to Clementine, Winston was all courtesy this time, though as usual he wanted to talk about himself. He asked her if she had read his biography of Lord Randolph. She hadn't. He promised to send her a copy and then forgot. But he didn't forget Clementine. He asked his mother to invite her and her mother for a weekend at Salisbury Hall, the Cornwallis-West country home. Clementine was impressed with him; in her letter thanking Jennie, she wrote of his "dominating charm and brilliancy." Maddeningly, Lady Blanche, who couldn't afford it, chose this spring to take her daughter abroad for six weeks. Winston's letters pursued her. Having just called on the King to "kiss hands" — receive royal sanction for his new office — he seized "this fleeting hour of leisure to write & tell how much I liked our long talk on Sunday and what a comfort & pleasure it was to me to meet a girl with so much intellectual quality & such strong reserves of noble sentiment." He wrote her of his brother's marriage to Lady Gwendeline Bertie, or "Goonie," as everyone in the family called her; he wrote of

Clementine Hozier at the time of her wedding

politics and the fire at Burley-on-the-Hill. To this last, Clementine replied: "I have been able to think of nothing but the fire & the terrible danger you have been in. . . . My dear my heart stood still with terror."[86]

Thus interest grew on both sides, fomented by aunts and cousins, Lady this and Lady that, until, on August 7, the Duke of Marlborough invited Clementine to a small party at Blenheim. The same mail brought a note from Winston. He hoped she would come because "I want so much to show you that beautiful place & in its gardens we shall find lots of places to talk in, & lots of things to talk about." His mother would act as chaperon — there were royal chuckles when the King heard that — with F. E. and Margaret Smith the only other guests. The next day he wrote her again; he thought she would like Sunny, and would "fascinate him with those strange mysterious eyes of yours, whose secret I have been trying so hard to learn. . . . Till Monday then & may the Fates play fair." Clementine could have had little doubt of what awaited her at the palace, and she felt, she later said, a "sudden access of shyness." She was down to her last clean cotton frock. The other women would have maids, and she would have to stand for fear of crumpling her skirt. Nevertheless, she arrived at Blenheim outwardly poised on Monday, August 10. That evening the stage for his proposal was set. After breakfast in the morning they would walk in the rose garden.[87]

In later years Churchill said that "at Blenheim I took two important decisions: to be born and to marry. I am happily content with the decision I took on both those occasions."[88] He neglected to mention that Clementine had had something to say about the second, and that his dilatoriness had nearly lost her. Always an early riser, she was prompt at breakfast Tuesday. Winston wasn't there. She waited for him. And waited. He was fast asleep. Mortified, she considered returning to London immediately, and no one who knew her doubts that she meant it. Luckily, Sunny intervened. The duke sent his cousin a sharp note and, in his role as host, asked her to join him in a buggy ride around the grounds. They returned a half hour later to find Churchill yawning at the horizon.

The walk was postponed until late afternoon. They were in the middle of it, and Winston was just about to clear his throat, when the skies opened and wrapped them in sheets of rain. Fortunately an ornamental little Greek temple overlooking the palace's great lake offered refuge, and there, drenched and shivering, he asked her to marry him. She said yes, but swore him to secrecy until she had her mother's consent. He couldn't keep his word. The skies cleared, they strolled back to the palace, and the moment he saw his friends he broke into a run, waving his arms and shouting the news. That night in her bedroom Clementine wrote him a love letter, addressing it by drawing a heart with "Winston" lettered inside it — the first of the endearing missives they would exchange throughout the rest of their long life together. The next day he picked a bouquet of roses for her to take home and, to make amends for breaking his pledge, wrote his future mother-in-law asking her "consent & blessing." He told her, "I am not rich nor powerfully established, but your daughter loves me & with that love I feel strong enough to assume this great & sacred responsibility; & I think I can make her happy & give her a station & career worthy of her beauty and her virtues." He never mailed the letter — he was apt to do this — but Lady Blanche took him into her heart anyway. She wrote Wilfrid Blunt: "He is gentle and tender, affectionate to those he loves, much hated by those who have not come under his personal charm." At the moment he was also busy; the wedding was scheduled for Saturday, September 12, less than three weeks after the formal announcement, and there was much to do. Congratulatory notes required answers (two were from Pamela Plowden and Muriel Wilson). He picked Linky Cecil as his best man, and asked Welldon to speak at the service. Presents had to be acknowledged. In the happy English tradition of political civility, gifts arrived from Balfour and the Chamberlains. The King sent a gold-headed walking stick; Sir Ernest Cassel, £500.[89]

On the appointed Saturday the guests, including Sir Bindon Blood, Ian Hamilton, and Lloyd George, gathered in St. Margaret's Church, Westminster. Even here the groom could not elude controversy; *Tailor and Cutter* described his attire as "one of the greatest failures as a wedding garment we have ever seen, giving the wearer a sort of glorified coachman appearance." Blunt wrote in his diary that Churchill had "gained in appearance since I saw him last, and has a powerful if ugly face. Winston's responses were clearly made in a pleasant voice, Clementine's inaudible." Appropriately, the reception was held in Lady St. Helier's home. In his new post Churchill had defended the right of costermongers to trade in the street, and "Pearly Kings and Queens," cockneys whose costumes were adorned with pearl buttons sewn in elaborate patterns, danced outside in Portland Place.[90]

Winston later wrote that he and Clementine "lived happily ever afterwards." It was, in fact, a great marriage, but few brides have had to adjust so quickly to their husband's careers. She was given a glimpse of the future immediately after the wedding ceremony, when she found him with Lloyd George in the church vestry, earnestly talking politics. At Blenheim, where their honeymoon began, he revised the final text of his book on Africa, and in Venice, their last stop, he was toiling away at official papers and memoranda, belying his letter to his mother from there: "We have only loitered & loved — a good & serious occupation for which the histories furnish respectable precedents." In Eichorn on the way back they stayed with an old friend of Winston's, the Austrian Baron Tuty de Forest, who had been educated in England. Winston and the baron had a marvelous time shooting, but Clementine found the household stiff and the baroness dull. She was glad to be headed home, and was excited by the prospect of being presented to her husband's constituents in Dundee. Her oddest experience on the wedding trip had been her first encounter with Winston's underwear. She wore cheap chemises, but his underclothes, she whispered to a wide-eyed Violet Asquith when they returned and dined at Downing Street, were made of pale pink, very finely woven silk; they came from the Army and Navy Stores and "cost the eyes out of the head" — about eighty pounds a year, she calculated. When Violet "taxed him with this curious form of self-indulgence, he replied: 'It is essential to my well-being. I have a very delicate and sensitive cuticle which demands the finest covering.' " He invited her to examine the texture of the skin on his forearm. It was, he proudly told her, "a cuticle without a blemish, except for one small portion of my anatomy where I sacrificed a piece of my skin to accommodate a wounded brother officer on my way back from the Sudan campaign."[91]

Like other lovers, they invented pet names for each other. Clementine was "Cat" or "Kat"; Winston was "Pug," then "Amber Pug," then "Pig." Drawings of these animals decorated the margins of their letters to each other, and at dinner parties Winston would reach across the table, squeeze her hand, and murmur, "Dear Cat." After a garden luncheon, Blunt entered in his diary: "He is *aux plus petits soins* with his wife, taking all possible care of her. They are a very happy married pair. Clementine was afraid of wasps, and one settled on her sleeve, and Winston gallantly took the wasp by the wings and thrust it into the ashes of the fire." She became pregnant the month after the wedding. Not knowing the child's sex, they created the name "Puppy Kitten," then shortened it to simply "P.K." The imminent arrival of the P.K. made a move from the little house on Bolton Street imperative, and early in 1909 Churchill took an eighteen-year lease, at £195 a year, on a house at 33 Eccleston Square, in Pimlico, between Victoria Station and the Thames. Clementine was economizing wherever possible; on April 27 she wrote Winston: "I had a long afternoon with Baxter & carpets. The green carpet is lovely & will do beautifully for the library. It looks like soft green moss . . . I tried hard to make the red stair carpet do for the dining room, but it is really too shabby." A "green sickly looking carpet" from Bolton Street "does

Puppy Kitten's room." One servant's room could "be done for about £2." She had "written to the people who are making the blue stair carpet to ask what it will cost to cover dining room entirely with the blue — (4/6 a yard)."[92]

In May they moved in, and three months later Clementine gave birth to a girl, whom they christened Diana. Away watching army maneuvers that September, Winston wrote his "dear Kat," begging her to "try to gather your strength. Don't spend it as it comes. Let it accumulate. . . . My darling I so want your life to be a full & sweet one, I want it to be worthy of all the beauties of your nature. I am so much centered in my politics, that I often feel I must be a dull companion, to anyone who is not in the trade too. It gives me so much joy to make you happy — & often wish I were more various in my topics." Diana was followed, less than two years later, by their son, Randolph, "the Chumbolly." Winston wrote from Blenheim: "My precious pussy cat, I do trust & hope that you are being good & not sitting up or fussing yourself. The Chumbolly must do his duty and help you with your milk, you are to tell him so from me." She replied, "I am very happy here, contemplating the beautiful Chumbolly who grows more darling & handsome every hour, & puts on weight with every meal; so that soon he will be a little round ball of fat. Just now I was kissing him, when catching sight of my nose he suddenly fastened upon it & began to suck it, no doubt thinking it was another part of my person!'"[93]

These notes are only partly attributable to his travels. She was a lark, he a nightingale; they tried having breakfast together two or three times, he later said, "but it didn't work. Breakfast should be had in bed alone." Since one was often bustling about while the other slept, they left hundreds of these missives for each other. All testify to a devotion that never flagged, though, like every other couple, they had their edgy moments. In the beginning his sudden and unexpected absences made her wonder if there were other women in his life. Her challenge does not survive, but we have his reply: "Dearest, it worries me vy much that you should seem to nurse such absolutely wild suspicions wh are so dishonouring to all the love & loyalty I bear you & will please god bear you while I breathe. They are unworthy of you & me. And they fill my mind with feelings of embarrassment to wh I have been a stranger since I was a schoolboy. I know that they originate in the fond love you have for me and therefore they make me feel tenderly towards you & anxious always to deserve that most precious possession of my life. But at the same time they depress me & vex me — & without reason. We do not live in a world of small intrigues but of serious & important affairs. . . . You ought to trust me for I do not love & will never love any woman in the world but you and my chief desire is to link myself to you week by week by bonds which shall ever become more intimate & profound. Beloved I kiss your memory — your sweetness & beauty have cast a glory upon my life. You will find me always your loving & devoted husband, W."[94]

He once said: "It is hard, if not impossible, to snub a beautiful woman; they remain beautiful and the rebuke recoils." Clementine's acquaintances forgot that at their peril. Her response to slights was swift and literally unanswerable, for she simply departed. Once, when they were playing bridge at Canford Manor, Ivor Guest, one of Winston's cousins, lost his temper and threw his cards at her head. She rose from the table, went to bed, and in the morning, ignoring Guest's profuse apologies, left for London with her dismayed husband in tow. Again, she was in the Green Room at Blenheim, replying to a letter from Lloyd George, when Sunny said: "Please, Clemmie, would you mind not writing to that horrible little man on Blenheim writing-paper?" She flew upstairs and packed. Sunny begged her to stay, but she was off on the next train from Woodstock. Winston, who hadn't been with her, was tepid in his defense of her, and she resented that; she believed she had hoisted the Liberal banner against Tory spite. When she had calmed down she wrote him: "My sweet and Dear Pig, when I am a withered old woman how miserable I shall be if I have disturbed your life & troubled your spirit by my temper. Do not cease to love me. I could not do without it. If no one loves me, instead of being a Cat with teeth & Claws, but you will admit soft fur, I shall become like the prickly porcupine outside, & inside so raw & unhappy." He replied that "I loved much to read the words of your dear letter," and this was followed by a rare Churchillian admission of self-doubt: "At times, I think I cd conquer everything — & then again I know I am only a weak vain fool. But your love for me is the greatest glory & recognition that has or will ever befall me: & the attachment wh I feel towards you is not capable of being altered by the sort of things that happen in this world. I only wish I were more worthy of you, & more able to meet the inner needs of your soul."[95]

Clementine was as complex as her husband, but in many ways his antithesis: less gregarious, always reserved, often lonely in the midst of people, and far more critical of others. In those days she admired Lloyd George — many women did, and he exploited them; his promiscuity was so extraordinary that it had won him the sobriquet "Goat" — but she didn't like Guest or F. E. Smith, who went on to be Lord Birkenhead, lord chancellor of England; or the young Canadian millionaire Max Aitken. It puzzled her that "F.E.," as everyone called him, should be Winston's best friend. His brilliance and dazzling wit were lost on her. She saw him as simply an archconservative Tory. Yet Winston and F.E. went on summer cruises together and founded the Other Club (the House of Commons being *the* Club), where bitter political rivals dined amicably in one another's company and took up their weapons again afterward, the constitution providing that "nothing in the rules or intercourse of the Club shall interfere with the rancour or asperity of party politics." Churchill later wrote of F.E. in *Great Contemporaries:* "Never did I separate from him without having learnt something, and enjoyed myself besides." He and F.E. were also fellow officers in the QOOH, the Queen's Own Oxfordshire Hussars, and took the field each spring in the regiment's annual camp, held in Blenheim Park. He and Clementine would engage in bantering correspondence during these gentlemanly maneuvers. "We are going to bathe in the lake this evening," he told her in a typical note. "No cats allowed! Your pug in clover, W." And she would assure him that while he was gone, "your lazy Kat sits purring and lapping cream and stroking her kittens."[96]

Certainly Winston needed the exercise. In 1909 newspapers noted that his stoop had grown more pronounced, and that he was getting fat. Nevertheless, the QOOH outings made Clementine uneasy. She believed that F.E. kept her husband up late and encouraged him to play poker. Winston always stayed up late and always gambled, but her anxiety was understandable; he couldn't afford the high stakes of his rich friends. At the time of his appointment, Asquith had written him that as president of the Board of Trade he would be "on the same level, as regards salary & status," as a secretary of state. That would have brought in £5,000 a year, on which the family could have lived comfortably. As it turned out, he was paid only half that. The money he had invested with Cassel was gone; so were the royalties from his later books. Clementine had grown up learning to live on little money, but she became haunted by the need to make ends meet. Her husband was loving but inconsiderate. On very short notice he would send word that he was bringing friends home to dinner. If she asked what she was expected to feed them, his answer was always the same: "Let's have Irish stew with lots of onions." She waved handfuls of bills at him and he turned away shrugging, though once he suffered pangs of remorse. At their wedding his aunt Cornelia had given her a diamond necklace; later Winston had had rubies set around the diamonds. Beset by creditors, she impulsively sold it. When she told him, he rushed to the jeweler to buy it back, but he was too late; it was gone.[97]

Being Winston Churchill's wife was sometimes embarrassing and even dangerous. In November 1909 the Churchills, arriving at Bristol railway station, were leaving their car when a suffragette, Theresa Garnett, ran up and tried to lash his face with a whip. He grabbed her wrists and she tugged him toward the tracks and the path of a moving train. At the last moment Clementine grabbed his coat and pulled both of them back to safety. A few months later he faced another whip, this one in the hands of a suffragette's male relative who cried: "Take that, you dirty cur!" Winston took evasive action instead. He warned his wife against opening "suspicious parcels arriving by post without precautions. . . . These harpies are quite capable of trying to burn us out." By 1912 he would be a supporter of their cause, but as long as their assaults on public men continued, he refused to commit himself in Parliament. Clementine's feelings were mixed. She said publicly that she was "ardently in favour of votes for women," and privately she believed feminism needed champions willing to break the law. On the other hand, she certainly didn't want Winston maimed or killed. No such ambiguity troubled her on other issues, however. As his advocacy of Liberal reforms grew more passionate, Tory homes were closed to the Churchills, and some die-hard acquaintances would cross the street rather than greet her. She gloried in their animosity, for in these years, when Winston's radicalism crested, his most enthusiastic supporter was Clementine Churchill.[98]

Even before he left the Colonial Office, Winston had become a thunderer on the left. He had urged the South Africans to adopt a program of unemployment compensation, and in a letter from Africa on December 22, 1907, he had proposed parliamentary bills establishing minimum wages, insurance against sickness, and old-age pensions in England. Back in London he gave Charles Masterman, himself a reformer, the impression that he was "full of the poor whom he has just discovered. He thinks he is called by Providence — to do something for them. 'Why have I always been kept safe within a hair's breadth,' he asked, 'except to do something like this?' " Writing in the *Nation* of March 7, he recommended that men without jobs be "treated as if they were hospital patients" and that the economy be managed through a "network of state intervention and regulation"; he saw "little glory," he had said, "in an Empire which can rule the waves and is unable to flush its sewers." In Glasgow he had delivered a historic speech, declaring that "the fortunes and interests of Liberalism and Labour are inseparably interwoven. They rise by the same forces, they face the same enemies, they are affected by the same dangers." The state, he said, must "concern itself with the care of the sick and the aged, and, above all, of the children." The government should get "the railways of this country in our hands" and become "the reserve employer of labour," establishing public-works projects to "spread a net over the abyss."[99]

All this was breathtaking in 1908. Beatrice Webb revised her early judgment of him; she wrote: "He is brilliantly able — more than a phrase-monger, I think." But the upper classes, Churchill's relatives and the people he had lived among all his life, were flabbergasted. This was the man who, as a Sandhurst cadet, had approved of churchgoing for workmen on the ground that "nothing can give them a good time here, but it makes them more contented to think that they will get one hereafter." At heart he was a traditionalist who loved the Shakespearean "tide of pomp/That beats upon the high shore of this world." Except by reading, or strolling through the Manchester slum with Eddie Marsh, he knew nothing of real poverty. Clementine's small economies were hardly comparable to the destitution of jobless Britons. The Churchills always had servants. Winston never packed a bag; it was simpler to ring a bell. It never occurred to him to travel third-class. Eddie Marsh wrote that until he married, Winston had never even heard of such things as "lodgings." He once told Violet Asquith: "I have always had to earn every penny I possessed, but there has never been a day in my life when I could not order a bottle of champagne for myself and offer another to a friend."[100]

Why, then, had he chosen to become a tribune of the oppressed? Doubtless his resentment of the Tory hierarchy was one reason; as he saw it, they had ruined his father, driven Winston himself out of their party, and treated him viciously since he had crossed the House floor. He was an intuitive rebel. But being humane, he was also genuinely appalled by the plight of the downtrodden as he discovered it through reading and in talks with the Webbs, Shaw, and Wells. Another explanation is political. The Liberals, though apparently invincible, felt menaced by the burgeoning Labour party, which threatened to steal their thunder and their strong radical wing. An increase in Lib-Lab strength was the result. Asquith made their triumphs possible, though he himself was no ideologue. Silver-haired, with a small, thin-lipped, stubborn-looking mouth and a thick Yorkshire accent which had survived the City of London School and Balliol College at Oxford, he had displayed little political imagination in the past, but he grasped his party's need for movement to the left, shrewdly sensing the necessity for some official response, however limited, to the outcry over the public and private exposés of working-class

Churchill and David Lloyd George, Budget Day, 1910

destitution. One of his first acts had been to provide free meals and free medical attention for schoolchildren. Winston's combative spirit was stirred when these mild measures provoked violent Tory protests. "Party animosity," Lord Campion wrote nearly a half-century later, "reached a degree of virulence which is hardly conceivable in the present generation."[101] Finally, all these motives for the liberation of Churchill from patrician dogma were immeasurably strengthened by the charisma and leadership of his colleague Lloyd George, his senior by eleven years.

Churchill at the Board of Trade, Lloyd George at the Exchequer — this was the team which really drove the Asquith government in its first surge of reform. It was an unlikely alliance. The younger man, born to a ducal family, weaned on privilege, had been boosted to fame by influential relatives and friends, including England's present King, and had, for all his brushes with death on battlefields, led a sheltered life. Lloyd George had been a penniless Welsh boy, raised by a widowed mother, articled to a solicitor at sixteen, and introduced to the practice of law by defending poachers in local courts. One wore a top hat in town, the other, except on extraordinary occasions, a crumpled fedora. Yet each was an impulsive political genius, fired by idealism, joined to the other by common goals. "Both," wrote Elie Halévy, "were opposed to a policy of heavy expenditure on the Army and the Navy, both advocates of a policy of social reform which, they maintained, the Liberal Party must pursue with unprecedented daring, if the Labour Party were not to grow strong on its left. They came forward as the two leaders of the radical group of pacifists and advanced social reformers as opposed to the three Imperialists, Asquith, Grey, and Haldane."[102]

If it is difficult to accept Churchill as a grandfather of the welfare state, it is even harder to picture him fighting plans to arm England against saber-rattling Germans. Nevertheless, that was his position in the summer of 1908. In this he was once more his father's son, a co-conspirator with Lloyd George against military estimates. Reginald McKenna, first lord of the Admiralty, wanted to lay keels for six dreadnoughts; Sir John Fisher, the first sea lord, wrote: "*Six in the estimates w/o any doubt is an irreducible minimum — no qualifying statement.*" Lloyd George, who regarded the navy as a toy for the rich — and called the War Office the "Ministry of Slaughter" — thought four of the ships was enough. Winston agreed with him. Speaking to miners in south Wales on August 14, he ridiculed the notion of war with the kaiser. "I think it is greatly to be deprecated," he said, "that persons should try to spread the belief in this country that war between Great Britain and Germany is inevitable. It is all nonsense." There was nothing to fight about, he added, "although there may be snapping and snarling in London clubs."[103]

"What are Winston's reasons for acting as he does in this matter?" Lord Knollys later wrote Lord Esher. "Of course it cannot be from conviction or principle. The very idea of his having either is enough to make one laugh." That is a fair sample of the kind of judgments Tories passed on Churchill then. Neither peer could see the obvious: money spent on warships couldn't go into social programs. The militants in the cabinet wanted six keels, but Asquith complained to his wife: "Winston and Ll. G. by their combined machinations have got the bulk of the Liberal press in the same camp . . . there are moments when I am disposed summarily to cashier them both." He couldn't; his back-benchers wouldn't have stood for it; of 377 Liberal MPs, over 200 had joined the League of Liberals Against Aggression and Militarism — the "LLAAMs," or "Lambs." The issue was in doubt when Lloyd George sent Winston word "that the Admiralty have had very serious news from their Naval attaché in Germany *since our last Cabinet Committee* & that McK is now convinced we may have to lay down *8* Dreadnoughts next year!!!" The news leaked to the press; in music halls jingoes sang a new ditty: "We want eight and we won't wait." They had to wait, but they got them. The two radical ministers accepted an Asquith compromise: four keels were to be laid now, and another four later if the German naval program made it absolutely necessary. Berlin obliged. "In the end," Churchill therefore wrote later, "a curious and characteristic solution was reached. The Admiralty had demanded six ships: the economists offered four and we finally compromised on eight." He added that "although the Chancellor of the Exchequer and I were right in the narrow sense, we were absolutely wrong in relation to the deep tides of destiny."[104]

Despite this channeling of money into armaments, Churchill passed most of his program through the House. A maximum workday was established for miners. Sweated labor was attacked by establishing trade boards which fixed minimum wages. In each city he set up a labor exchange where employment would be sought for the jobless, trade-union leaders could meet, and all visitors would be provided with "facilities for washing, mending, and non-alcoholic refreshments."[105] He also drafted an unemployment-insurance bill. At the same time, Lloyd George, as chancellor, was introducing a measure providing for old-age pensions and an expanded National Health Insurance Act — his slogan was "ninepence for fourpence," the difference between the two figures being the contributions from employers and the government. The latter bill didn't become law until 1911, because the House of Lords balked at it. The solution which broke the legislative impasse, and which was designed by Lloyd George and Churchill, altered the historical balance between the two Houses of Parliament.

At that time the Lords, the "upper house," could veto bills passed by the Commons, the "lower house," though since 1660 money matters, by custom, had been left to the commoners. Until now there had been few confrontations between the two because members of both houses had come from the same background, and within a fairly narrow range they shared the same political convictions, regardless of party. But Asquith's Liberals were introducing new concepts of government. The burning question, said Balfour, was whether the Conservatives "should still control, whether in power or whether in opposition, the destinies of this great Empire." The upper house, AJB pointed out, still had a heavy Tory majority. They could block or mutilate social legislation. He urged them to do it, and they did. An education bill was so maimed by the Lords that Asquith had to drop it. A voting bill was rejected outright. A land-reform program met the same fate, and so did a liquor-licensing bill. This last was a favorite of Winston's. Among the radical causes he had embraced — this from Churchill! — was temperance. Lucy Masterman was with him on November 26, 1908, when word arrived that the Lords had killed the measure. She wrote in her diary: "Churchill was perfectly furious at the rejection . . . stabbed at his bread, would hardly speak: murmured perorations about 'the heart of every Band of Hope in this country sinking within them.' He went on: 'We shall send them up a budget in June as shall terrify them, they have started a class war, they had better be careful.' "[106]

Actually, the "People's Budget" of 1909 came in April. Its essence was a revolutionary concept. Until now, with the exception of progressive death duties the taxing power had been used solely to raise revenues for the government. Now it would also redistribute the wealth. Churchill and Lloyd George drafted the budget together. On Tuesday, April 27, Winston wrote Clementine: "Tomorrow — Sweated Trades! Thursday — the deluge [the budget]!!! Thus the world wags — good, bad, & indifferent intermingled or alternating, & only my sweet Pussy cat remains a constant darling." The next day he reported that his minimum-wage bill had been "beautifully received & will be passed without division," but: "Tomorrow is the day of wrath! I feel this budget will kill or cure. Either we shall secure ample funds for great reforms next year, or the Lords will force a Dissolution in September." Clementine, replying from Blenheim, noted that "Sunny is much preoccupied about the Budget." She predicted: "It will make politics vy bitter for a long time." She was right, but it is an astonishing fact that scarcely anyone realized the budget's implications when the chancellor introduced it in the House. He began by stating his intention to "wage implacable warfare against poverty and squalidness" and went on for more than four hours while "Churchill," according to Virginia Cowles, "watched him like an anxious nannie." As a performance, Violet Asquith wrote, "it was a flop. I went to the House of Commons, agog to hear it, and I failed to sit it out. . . . It was read so badly that to some he gave the impression that he did not himself understand it." Even the press missed its implications; the following day *The Times,* the trumpet of the Conservative establishment, dismissed it as "unadventurous."[107]

It was hardly that. Taxes were raised on everything: whiskey, gasoline, pub licenses. But the stinger, cloaked in elaborate periphrases, provided that the rich, for the first time, be singled out for special treatment. Death duties were up, the aristocracy's great estates were assessed whether their land was used or not, capital gains were taxed if the land was sold, and everyone who received over £3,000 a year was subject to a supertax. Only some 11,500 Englishmen had that much, but they were the people who ran the country, including members in the House of Lords. The aristocracy was enraged — Winston and Sunny were estranged — and they decided that if Liberals could break precedents, so could they. Against the advice of wiser Tories, the peers vetoed the People's Budget. This created a constitutional crisis. Winston's dander was up; he relished the fight ahead. As early as June 1907 he had described the Lords as "one-sided, hereditary, unpurged, unrepresentative, absentee. Has the House of Lords ever been right?" he had asked. "I defy the Party opposite to produce a single instance of a settled controversy in which the House of Lords was right."[108] Until now their blunders had been borne. But never before had they usurped the lower house's power of the purse. He meant to right this wrong by taking the issue to the country, and he meant to pour it on.

So did Lloyd George, who went for the dukes, the leaders of the peerage. The economy was flourishing under the Liberal administration, he said; "only one stock has gone down badly; there has been a great slump in dukes. A fully-equipped duke costs as much to keep up as two dreadnoughts; and dukes are just as great a terror and they last longer." A nobleman's elder son, he said, was merely "the first of the litter." Since that definition fitted Sunny, Winston was expected to curb Lloyd George's invective. Instead, he matched it. In a speech which the *Daily Express* headed HIS OWN RECORD FOR ABUSE OUTDONE, he pictured "the small fry of the Tory party" falling back on their dukes, from whom nothing could be expected but childish behavior. "These unfortunate individuals," he said, "who ought to lead quiet, delicate, sheltered lives, far from the madding crowd's ignoble strife, have been dragged into the football scrimmage, and they have got rather roughly mauled in the process. . . . Do not let us be too hard on them. It is poor sport — almost like teasing goldfish. These ornamental creatures blunder on every hook they see, and there is no sport whatever in trying to catch them. It would be barbarous to leave them gasping upon the bank of public ridicule upon which they have landed themselves. Let us put them back gently, tenderly in their fountains; and if a few bright gold scales have been rubbed off in what the Prime Minister calls the variegated handling they have received they will soon get over it. They have got plenty more."[109]

Lloyd George was forgiven because of his background, Churchill condemned because of his. Cartoons depicted him denouncing the aristocracy and then retiring to Blenheim for the weekend. A Manchester Tory said that what was "neither excusable nor permissible is the lack of common decency shown by vulgar abuse of the dukes on the part of a man who is the grandson of one duke, the nephew of another, and the cousin of a third; who belongs to a family which has produced nine dukes; who figures in Debrett* as boasting a dozen titled relatives; and who owes every advantage he possesses over those whom he contemptuously calls 'the small fry of public life' to his aristocratic connections." In the great country houses during that summer of 1909 venomous gossips agreed that the Churchill family, for all its power and glory, had never produced a gentleman; the first Duke of Marlborough had been a rogue, Lord Randolph a knave; Sunny's duchess had left him because he was a cad — actually, Consuelo had left him for a lover — and now Winston had revealed himself as "utterly contemptible." For a traditionalist like Churchill, with his great pride in his family, this was bitter medicine. Once he hesitated. He wrote Clementine that he was working on a speech "and am gradually getting some material together but of doubtful merit. I cannot make up my mind whether to be provocative or conciliatory and am halting between the two." She stiffened his spine. Again and again, in these stormy years, she warned him not to be seduced by those Tories like F.E. who, even when public abuse was thickest, dined and drank with him. One morning she wrote him: "My dear Darling Amber Pug — Do not let the glamour and elegance & refinement & the return of old associations blind you. The charming people you are meeting today — they do not represent Toryism, they are just the cream on the top. Below, they are ignorant, vulgar, prejudiced. They can't bear the idea of the lower classes being independent & free. They want them to sweat for them when they are well & to accept flannel & skilly [cheap clothes and thin soup] as a dole if they fall ill, & to touch their caps & drop curtsies when the great people go by — Goodbye my Darling. I love you very much. Your Radical Bristling" — here she drew an indignant cat.[110]

Probably he would have rejected propitiation anyway. Once committed to battle, he was almost incapable of restraint. Asquith complained that Winston's letters to him were all "begotten by froth out of foam." Asquith's wife, Margot, wrote Churchill: "Believe me cheap scores, hen-roost phrases & all oratorical want of dignity is out of date." He was unrepentant and untamed. "The House of Lords," he told his audiences, was "not a national institution but a party dodge"; the peers had been "tolerated all these years because they were thought to be in a comatose condition which preceded dissolution." All they could do, "if they go mad," was "to put a stone on the track and throw the train of state off the line and that is what we are told they are going to do." He was ready for bloodshed, if it came to that: "If the struggle comes, it will be between a

* John Debrett's *Peerage, Baronetage, Knightage and Companionage.*

representative assembly and a miserable minority of titled persons who represent nobody, who are responsible to nobody and who only scurry up to London to vote in their party interests, their class interests and in their own interests." Then, savagely, to a huge crowd in Inverness: "Just as they clutched greedily at the last sour, unpalatable dregs of the bottle before it was torn away from them at the last election, so now when they see a possible chance of obtaining power and place, they kick over the whole table in an ugly wish to jam their noses in the trough."[111]

The King, dismayed, directed his secretary, Lord Knollys, to write *The Times* deploring Churchill's diatribes. This was unconstitutional; flagrantly so. Winston wrote Clementine that Edward "must really have gone mad. The Royal Prerogative is always exercised on the advice of ministers, and ministers and not the Crown are responsible — and criticism of all debatable acts of policy should be directed to ministers. . . . This looks to me like a rather remarkable Royal intervention and shows the bitterness which is felt in those circles. I shall take no notice of it. It will defeat itself." He sent Asquith a memo: "The time has come for the total abolition of the House of Lords." But the prime minister wasn't prepared to do that. Indeed, he felt that under these extraordinary circumstances, he could no longer claim the Liberal victory of 1906 as a mandate. In January 1910 he called for a general election; the party slogan would be "The People versus the Peers." Churchill was the most popular campaigner in the election, but the results were disappointing. The Conservatives picked up 116 seats, reducing the Liberal majority to 2. The *Annual Register* called the verdict "obscure and indecisive." Nevertheless, with the support of Labour MPs and Irish Nationalists, the Asquith government still held the field. Then, on May 6, 1910, Edward VII suddenly died. There was just enough time for Queen Alexandra to send a brougham to fetch Mrs. Keppel so she could be at the bedside of her royal lover when he breathed his last.[112]

Margot Asquith dined at Jennie's home that evening. Winston was there, and at the end of the dinner he rose and said: "Let us drink to the health of the new King." Lord Crewe added: "Rather to the memory of the old." Jennie, her face puffy from weeping, gave Crewe a grateful look. She and Edward's other mistresses knew now that their long social reign had ended. Some hoped that the younger generation would pick up their torch. Alice Keppel told Clementine that if she really wanted to advance Winston's career, she would take a wealthy, influential lover. Mrs. Keppel even offered to act as procuress and, when Clementine declined, called her "positively selfish." But other faded beauties realized that this was, in the words of the song they had adored, After the Ball. They stood forlornly, sobbing among a quarter-million other grievers as the gun carriage bearing Edward's coffin passed them on the Mall, between St. James's Park on one side and the stately buildings, including St. James's Palace, on the other, Big Ben tonguing with muffled clapper, the cortege led by the new King, George V, flanked by his uncle the Duke of Connaught and, wearing the scarlet uniform of a British field marshal, Kaiser Wilhelm II, to whom, said *The Times,* "belongs the first place among all the foreign mourners," because "even when relations are most strained [he] has never lost his popularity amongst us." Later Edward's mistresses paid him their own tribute. Jennie, Alice, Lillie Langtry, and the others celebrated that year's Ascot as Black Ascot, standing in their old box wearing black feathers and ribbons on enormous black hats — wrinkled, graying women in their late fifties, but still slender, still pert, still flirtatious, and, in Jennie's case — her marriage to Cornwallis-West was headed for the divorce court — still available.[113]

Winston's mother was not invited to the new King's coronation, but her daughter-in-law was. George sent Clementine a ticket to the Royal Box in Westminster Abbey, and when he learned that she was indisposed, he made special arrangements for her to arrive just before the crown was set on his head and then be whisked away. Her husband was another matter. Churchill tactlessly insisted that the King name a new battleship the *Cromwell,* which George flatly refused to do. Worse, when the King told him that he felt Asquith was "not quite a gentleman," Winston repeated it to Asquith.[114] The big issue facing the new monarch, however, was the unresolved People's Budget. The Liberals urged him to appoint enough new peers to swing the House of Lords' vote their way. He hesitated, and the country prepared to go to the polls again. Andrew Bonar Law, who would succeed Balfour as the Conservative leader, tried to exploit Churchill's gambling instincts by proposing that he and Winston run for the same constituency in Manchester, with the understanding that the loser would stay out of the next Parliament. Winston declined to abandon his safe seat, preferring to spend his time and energy campaigning for other Liberal candidates. He was a political celebrity now. Crowds gathered wherever he spoke, eager to hear his biting wit and pitiless philippics.

The second election confirmed the close results of the first. Still the Lords refused to budge. Winston wrote Clementine: "Things are tending to a pretty sharp crisis. What are you to do with men whose obstinacy & pride have blinded them to their interests and to every counsel of reason? It would not be surprising if we actually have to create 500. We shall not boggle about it when it comes to the pinch." Three weeks later

Winston and Jennie, 1912

he wrote her: "If anything goes wrong we make 350 Peers at once." It proved unnecessary. Lloyd George had derided the upper house as "Mr. Balfour's poodle," and on this issue it was; they would take their cue from him. Asquith wrote Balfour, telling him the King would pack the Lords with new peers. The diehards — originally a regimental nickname, the word entered the language at this time — were finished. Balfour resigned his post as party leader, signifying defeat, and in the sweltering summer of 1911 the upper house passed a parliamentary reform act, emasculating their powers, by the thin margin of 131 to 114. The Liberals, however, had paid a price. During the campaign Austen Chamberlain had predicted that Asquith's government, if kept in office, would "establish Home Rule in Ireland." Churchill later wrote of Austen: "He always played the game, and he always lost." But this time he was right. To win the backing of the Irish MPs in the "People versus the Peers" struggle, the Liberals had agreed to introduce a new Home Rule bill, thus reviving that old and bitter quarrel.[115]

Winston's parliamentary skills and his services to the party entitled him to a promotion — a long step toward the prime ministership which, it was generally agreed, would be his before long. Even the Tories believed it; Balfour told him: "Winston, I believe your hour has come." Churchill never waited for recognition. When the polls closed on the first of these two elections, he wrote Asquith that "Ministers should occupy positions in the Government which correspond to some extent with their influence in the country." He wanted, he said, "to go either to the Admiralty (assuming that place to become vacant) or to the Home Office." He was advised that "the First Lord could not be changed . . . without being slighted. But if you cared for the HO, no doubt it would be at your disposal." He cared for it, and on February 14, 1910, he was appointed home secretary. He was thirty-five. Only one home secretary, Sir Robert Peel, had been younger.[116]

Churchill's salary now reached the promised £5,000, and he was working hard for it. His responsibilities included the welfare of seven million factory workers and a million miners, national security, England's police force, immigration, and law and order. Every evening when the House was in session he had to write a longhand report on its proceedings for the King. He was answerable for conservation, the censorship of stage plays, regulations governing automobile mudguards, the licensing of Italian organ-grinders — everything, in short, which directly involved the people living in the United Kingdom. His view of the office was liberal and humanitarian. He said: "There is no finer investment for any community than putting milk into babies."[117] Bills drafted by him limited the hours of shop assistants and introduced safety measures in the mines. Most important, at the outset, were his role in guiding Lloyd George's National Health Insurance Act through the House and his penal reforms.

On his appointment he told Violet Asquith that he was less interested in his policemen than in their quarries. Memories of his POW imprisonment in Pretoria were still vivid. Prisoners, he said, must have entertainment, "plenty of books, that's what I missed most," and anything else which would relieve their feelings of confinement, "except of course the chance of breaking bounds and getting out of the damned place — I suppose I mustn't give them *that!*" She said she would prefer hanging to a life sentence; he vehemently disagreed: "Never abandon life. There is a way out of everything except death." He soon found that the duty he liked least was signing execution warrants; after visiting him, Blunt noted in his diary that it had "become a nightmare to him to have to exercise his power of life and death in the case of condemned criminals, on an average of one case a fortnight." One death warrant which did not trouble him was that of Dr. H. H. Crippen, who had left his wife's dismembered remains in the cellar of his London home and boarded a transatlantic steamer with his mistress, only to be intercepted on the other side by Canadian Mounties — the first fugitive to be caught by a wireless alert. Crippen was hanged at first light in Pentonville Prison on October 18, 1910. Churchill celebrated with a champagne breakfast.[118]

His predecessor, in handing over the seals of office, had told him: "As regards prisons, it won't be a bad thing to give a harassed department some rest." Winston gave it no rest. Beginning a series of visits to penitentiaries, he abolished floggings and introduced libraries and lecture programs. Of Britain's 184,000 prisoners, he found, a third had been committed for drunkenness and more than half for failure to pay fines. Imprisonment for debt, theoretically abolished, was still common: "We are confronted annually with an ever increasing number of committals to prison and hence of failures to recover debt. A vicious system of credit, based on no real security, is increasingly involving working class families in domestic disputes, extravagance, embarrassment and ultimate disgrace, and is sapping thrift and honesty." Here again he could identify with the men in cells; he, too, knew the burden of debt. He instituted a "time-to-pay" program for debtors and replaced the jailing of drunkards with fines. The number of debtors behind bars dropped from 95,686 to 5,264; of drunks, from 62,822 to 1,670. At the same time, he moved to deprive suffragettes of their martyrdom. They were, he said, "political prisoners." As such they were neither searched nor forbidden to bathe; they could wear their own clothing, receive food and parcels from outside, and talk to one another. His explanation for this leniency was that "prison rules which are suitable to criminals jailed for dishonesty or cruelty or other crimes implying moral turpitude should not be applied inflexibly to those whose general character is good and whose offences, however reprehensible, do not involve personal dishonour."[119]

He had been impressed and influenced by John Galsworthy's *Justice.* Galsworthy now wrote *The Times:* "These changes are one and all inspired by imagination, without which reform is deadly, and by common sense, without which it is dangerous." But a penal official warned that England should not "ignore the poorer classes outside the prison walls while we do so much for the worst classes of our population," and the Tories were delighted when one case of clemency backfired. On a prison visit, accompanied by Lloyd George, Winston met the "Dartmoor Shepherd." This unfortunate man had been in and out of prison since 1870. Once he had been sentenced to ten years for stealing a watch and chain; another time to five years for stealing £1 6s. 6d.; and, most recently, to three years for taking two shillings from a church box. He had never been guilty of violence. At Dartmoor he tended the penitentiary's flock of sheep. Winston described him in a minute as a man who "enjoyed a melancholy celebrity for the prodigious sentences he had endured, for his good behaviour and docility in prison, and for his unusual gift of calling individual sheep by name." On the stump Lloyd George contrasted him with the peers, "plunderers of the poor." Churchill ordered him released. It was a mistake. The man was a recidivist. He promptly left the job the warden had found for him and, three months later, was arrested while breaking into a house. Winston reported to the King that the incident had received its "mead of merriment" in the House. The Tories formally moved a reduction of £500 in his salary, and, Churchill wrote in another report to the King, "as the Irish members were away, half the Labour members absent, ministers at the gala and holiday moods in the air, this flagitious proposal was rejected only by a majority of 32."[120]

Why weren't all the Liberals and their allies there to save him from this humiliation? The answer lies in the letter's date: June 27, 1911. By then MPs on the left had begun to qualify their admiration of Churchill. Actually, it had never been wholehearted. His colleagues in the Liberal hierarchy had always had reservations about him. Asquith complained that he "thinks with his mouth"; his wife wrote in her diary, "Winston has a noisy mind"; Lloyd George compared him to "a chauffeur who apparently is perfectly sane and drives with great skill for months, then suddenly takes you over a precipice." Almeric Fitzroy thought that "his defect is that he sees everything through the magnifying-glass of his self-confidence." Another Liberal leader came closer to the deepest source of their misgivings when he told A. G. Gardiner: "Don't forget that the aristocrat is still there — submerged but latent." Charles Masterman put it bluntly a few years later: "He desired in England a state of things where a benign upper class dispensed benefits to an industrious, *bien pensant,* and grateful working class." There was an undefined feeling that his social legislation smacked of paternalism and had been a gesture de haut en bas; that, in Margot Asquith's words, he had merely learned "the language of Radicalism. It was Lloyd George's native tongue, but it was not his own, and despite his efforts he spoke it 'with a difference.' " In point of fact there *was* a difference. Beatrice Webb remarked upon Winston's "capacity for quick appreciation and rapid execution of new ideas, whilst hardly comprehending the philosophy beneath them." But in time he did comprehend the philosophy of the extremists. And when he understood it, he recoiled. He put his trust in social evolution, not upheaval. England's class distinctions suited him. He saw no need to efface them, or even blur them. Only when reactionaries refused to budge, as in the struggle with the Lords, would he endorse sweeping action. Rejected by

Tories because he had betrayed his class, he was distrusted by radical reformers because his conversion had been incomplete. He couldn't win.[121]

He was likeliest to lose in the Home Office. The first duty of the home secretary was maintenance of order, and beginning in the year he took over the ministry, organized workingmen suddenly turned to violent tactics. In the beginning the prospect of labor strife didn't daunt him. Three weeks after taking over the Board of Trade he had settled a shipbuilding lockout on the Tyne to the satisfaction of both parties. But in the two years since then battle lines had been drawn between capital and labor, and as a moderate he occupied no-man's-land. In union chapels his ritualistic denunciations of socialism were resented — though, curiously, Lloyd George's, just as vehement, were not — and his attempts to be evenhanded failed. He compared irresponsible workmen to irresponsible peers and succeeded only in irking the new King, who felt he had insulted the aristocracy. Replying to the sovereign, Winston said that the home secretary had received "with deep regret the expression of YM's Displeasure wh has reached him through the PM . . . with regard to the particular phrase wh has caused YM's displeasure, wh Mr Churchill understands is 'It should be remembered that there are idlers at both ends of the social scale.' Mr Churchill cannot understand why this shd be thought Socialistic in character. . . . To say this is not to attack the wealthy classes, most of whom as Mr Churchill knows well have done their duty in many ways: but only to point to those particular persons whose idle and frivolous conduct and lack of public spirit brings a reproach to the meritorious class to wh they belong." George was unmollified. And the left, judging Winston by his acts, found him wanting.[122]

In the first week of November, 1910, over 25,000 coal miners walked out at Rhondda, in south Wales. Riots followed; several mines were flooded, and the disorders culminated in the battle of Glamorgan Valley, after which the miners smashed shop fronts in the town of Tonypandy. The local chief constable, unable to cope, asked for troops. Aware that sending soldiers against strikers was bad politics, Churchill kept the number of troops to a minimum of four hundred, sent three hundred London policemen, and made sure that the commanding officer was reponsible to him. Afterward the officer said: "It was entirely due to Mr Churchill's foresight in sending a strong force of Metropolitan Police, directly he was made aware of the state of affairs in the valleys, that bloodshed was avoided."[123] Strikers charged the bobbies, but the policemen swung rolled-up mackintoshes and beat them off. Elsewhere, however, two miners were killed, and when a unit of soldiers was stoned, they fixed bayonets and prodded the strikers into retreating.

In light of the fact that the wrecked stores in Tonypandy were looted during what *The Times* called "an orgy of naked anarchy," the use of force does not seem excessive. The troops had been sent in response to an appeal from the Glamorgan law-enforcement official, and Churchill had had no part in that decision. But the fact that they had been called out, and had unsheathed bayonets, infuriated union leaders. Churchill firmly told them that the soldiers now in position would remain there until he judged that troops were "no longer necessary." They then blamed the two deaths on him. He called this "a cruel lie," which it was. Keir Hardie, maddened beyond reason, declared that the Liberals "will give you Insurance Bills, they will give you all sorts of soothing syrups to keep you quiet, but in the end your Liberal Party, just like your Tory Party, is the Party of the rich and exists to protect the rich when Labour and Capital come into conflict."[124]

The Conservatives turned this inside out. If troops had been sent in earlier, they said in the House, there would have been no looting and no property damage. An appeal from Winston, urging the strikers to renounce violence, was ridiculed by *The Times* as showing "a somewhat maudlin tone. . . . Mr Churchill hardly seems to understand that an acute crisis has arisen, which needs decisive handling. The rosewater of conciliation is all very well in its place, but its place is not in the face of a wild mob drunk with the desire of destruction." The *Daily Express* was even harsher: "Nothing was ever more contemptible in childish and vicious folly than Mr Churchill's message to the miners. . . . It is the last word in a policy of shameful neglect and poltroonery which may cost the country dear." To the King, Winston reported: "The insensate action of the rioters in wrecking shops in the town of Tonypandy, against which they had not the slightest cause for animosity, was not foreseen by anyone on the spot, and would not have been prevented by the presence of soldiers at the colliery itself." Nevertheless, the two myths endured. Tories thought he had acted spinelessly. Labor believed he had overreacted, and for more than forty years he would be heckled by workingmen who were convinced that he had led a bloody massacre of miners at Tonypandy.[125]

Less than two months later he was in his bathtub — it is extraordinary how many crises found him bathing — when he was summoned to the telephone, "dripping wet and shrouded in a towel," as he later recalled, to be told that members of a gang of Latvian anarchists had been trapped at 100 Sidney Street in Whitechapel. This was welcome news, exciting and important. Churchill wanted these men badly. They were not only criminals; the Liberal government was responsible for their presence in England. The city's East End, inhabited by nearly two million poor Londoners, had always seethed with crime. But since the abortive Russian uprising of 1905 and the Liberals' refusal to restrict immigration, Whitechapel, Stepney, Shadwell, and Bethnal Green had also become asylums for political refugees from the czar's Okhrana, or secret police. Joseph Stalin had briefly lived in Whitechapel in June 1907, sharing a tiny room with Maxim Litvinov. In their homeland these anarchists — today they would be called urban guerrillas — had supported their causes by robberies, and they continued to do so here, treating bobbies as they treated the Okhrana. Among them was a band of Letts led by Peter Piaktow, alias "Peter the Painter," so christened because when not ambushing bank messengers or holding up shopkeepers at pistol point, he worked as a house painter. The men trapped in the Sidney Street house were part of this gang. Heavily armed, they had already murdered three policemen; Winston and Clementine had attended the funerals in St. Paul's ten days earlier. Now the bobbies holding them at bay wanted the assistance of troops; hence the phone call to the home secretary. "Use whatever force is necessary," he said, promising that a detachment of Scots Guards from the Tower would be there within the hour. Then, dressing and donning his top hat and astrakhan-collared coat, he hurried by cab to the Home Office in search of more information. There was none there, so at noon he decided to take an official car to the scene because "I thought it my duty to see what was going on myself. . . . I must, however, admit that convictions of duty were supported by a strong sense of curiosity which perhaps it would have been well to keep in check."[126]

In Whitechapel he found high drama. Spectators and men in uniform were crouching behind buildings on both sides of the street while the killers and their besiegers blazed away at one another — the anarchists in their hideout firing Mausers; the Scots Guards, Lee-Enfields; and the sixty policemen, obsolete Morris-tube rifles. A *Daily Chronicle* reporter perched on the roof of the Rising Sun pub estimated that in the past hour and a half several thousand bullets had been exchanged without result. Churchill realized that he had made a mistake in coming: "It was not for me to interfere with those who were in charge on the spot. Yet . . . my position of authority, far above them all, attracted inevitably to itself direct responsibility. I saw now that I should have done much better to have remained quietly in my office. On the other hand, it was impossible to get into one's car and drive away while matters stood in such great uncertainty, and, moreover, were extremely interesting." Crossing the street for a better view, he sheltered in a warehouse doorway. Senior officers believed the house should be stormed, and he agreed; his "instincts," he later wrote, "turned at once to a direct advance up the staircase behind a steel plate or shield, and a search was made in the foundries of the neighborhood for one of suitable size." None was found, but the idea had lodged in his mind. In Sidney Street his concept of the tank was born.[127]

At one o'clock thin wisps of bluish smoke curled upward from a garret window of the embattled hideout, and within a half hour it was burning fiercely. The London fire brigade clattered up. Firemen and policemen argued. The bobbies refused to let the men with hoses approach the building; the firemen insisted that extinguishing the flames was their duty. At this point Churchill intervened. "I thought it better to let the house burn down," he explained afterward, "than spend good British lives in rescuing those ferocious rascals." So it blazed for an hour. "Then at last," reported the *Daily News,* "Mr Churchill stepped to the middle of the street and waved his arms . . . firemen appeared and regardless of possible bullets poured water on the burning house . . . and policemen led by Mr Churchill rushed forward to the door." Inside they found nothing but charred bodies.[128]

All this was recorded by cameramen. Eddie Marsh, dropping into the Palace Theatre, saw flickering newsreels, captioned "Mr Churchill directing the operations," and heard them greeted by boos, hisses, shouts of " 'E let the bastards in the country!" and "Shoot 'im!" More embarrassing, Balfour rose in the House to ask caustically: "We are concerned to observe photographs in the illustrated newspapers of the Home Secretary in the danger zone. I understand what the photographer was doing, but why the Home Secretary?" The Conservative press agreed that it was absurd. Churchill noted that "*The Times* blamed me for stopping the soldiers going to Tonypandy and now blames me for sending them to Sidney Street. Their doctrine is now apparent, that soldiers should always be sent to put down British miners in trade disputes but never to apprehend alien murderers engaged in crime. This is on a par with Tory thought in other directions." It was not only Tory thought, however. Liberals were equally troubled; his recent conduct seemed inconsistent with their serene slogan: "Peace, Retrenchment, and Reform." A. G. Gardiner wrote in the *Daily News:* "He is always unconsciously playing a part — an heroic part. And he is himself his most astonished spectator. He sees himself moving through the smoke of battle — triumphant, terrible, his brow clothed in thunder, his legions looking to him for victory, and not looking in vain. . . . It is not make-believe, it is not insincerity; it is that in this fervid and picturesque imagination there are always great deeds afoot, with himself cast by destiny in the Agamemnon role. Hence that portentous gravity that sits on his youthful shoulders so oddly, those impressive postures and tremendous silences, the body flung wearily in the chair, the head resting gloomily in the hand, the abstracted look." Thus, Gardiner accounted for his "tendency to exaggerate a situation" and dispatch "the military hither and thither as though Armageddon was upon us." Other Liberals believed that he had shown he lacked a sense of proportion, using "a steamhammer to crack a nut." Charles Masterman, returning from holiday, demanded: "What the hell have you been doing now, Winston?" Churchill, lapsing into his lisp, replied: "Now, Charlie. Don't be croth. It was such fun."[129]

The "Siege of Sidney Street," as the press called it, was followed by the hottest summer on record, and, with it, a wave of industrial unrest. The disturbances began in June, when dockers walked out in Southampton, and swiftly spread to other ports. Then transport workers struck to show that they sided with the longshoremen. Churchill observed that "a new force has arisen in trades unionism, whereby the power of the old leaders has proved quite ineffective, and the sympathetic strike on a wide scale is prominent. Shipping, coal, railways, dockers etc etc are all uniting and breaking out at once." The head constable in Liverpool reported to the Home Office that rioters had built barricades of dustbins and wire entanglements in side streets, lured policemen there, and stoned them from windows and housetops. The King wired Churchill: "Accounts from Liverpool show that situation there more like revolution than a strike. . . . Strongly deprecate half-hearted employment of troops: they should not be called on except as a last resource but if called on they should be given a free hand & the mob should be made to fear them."[130]

The immediate threat was famine. On August 9 the London meat and fruit markets shut down; they had nothing left to sell. Then, a week later, the railwaymen gave notice of a national strike. The railway companies had refused to recognize their union as a bargaining agent. Food shortages were imminent in the great quadrilateral of British industrialism, from Liverpool and Manchester in the west to Hull and Grimsby in the east, from Newcastle down to Birmingham and Coventry. Asquith offered the trainmen an inquiry by a royal commission. When they turned it down on the ground that such a commission would take too long, he reportedly said: "Then your blood be on your own head." That night every member of the union received a wire from its leadership: "Your liberty is at stake, all railwaymen must strike at once."

Churchill told the House that "no blockade by a foreign enemy" could be so perilous. If unchecked it would lead, he said, "to the starvation of great numbers of the poorer people."[131]

Violence erupted in Llanelly when rioters stormed a train and two were shot. The lord mayor of Liverpool telegraphed Churchill, asking him to requisition a warship and bluejackets to man the Mersey River ferries. H.M.S. *Antrim* was dispatched. But the larger issue was the railroad strike. Until August 17 the home secretary, though goaded by Tories and his sovereign, clung to the same position he had held at Tonypandy. Law enforcement was the responsibility of policemen, who were encouraged to enroll special constables. This attitude was not unappreciated; Ben Tillet, the leader of the London longshoremen, called Winston's influence moderating and responsible. In his "History of the London Transport Workers' Strike," a leaflet published by the transport workers' union in 1911, Tillet wrote that before the crisis he had thought of Winston as a "ferocious man of blood and iron," but when they met in the lobby of the House he found him "as amiable as the gentlest shepherd on earth," a man who "in quite convincing manner assured us he heartily agreed with all our views." Tillet added: "If patience and courtesy, if anxious effort and sincerity count for respect, then Winston Churchill is entitled as a man to gratitude. . . . We found an urbane young Cabinet Minister apparently fully alive to the duties and responsibilities of his office."

Unfortunately, Churchill's approach had produced no results. He was in a dilemma. Liberal politicians, including every member of the cabinet except the chancellor of the Exchequer, shied away from the use of force, and soldiers could not be legally used in any domestic dispute without specific requests from local authorites. On August 19 Winston decided to break this precedent. He alerted fifty thousand troops and announced: "The Army Regulation which requires a requisition for troops from a civil authority is suspended." Asquith remained silent. Lloyd George acted; he persuaded the railroad employers to recognize the union, and the men went back to work. Churchill believed his own order had cut the knot because it proved "that any Government must exert itself to prevent . . . catastrophe, and because it was certain that in taking such action they would be supported by the good sense and resolution of the whole mass of the people." King George concurred; he wired him: "Feel convinced that prompt measures taken by you prevented loss of life in different parts of the country."[132]

Nonetheless, he had set a questionable example. In addition, he had again offended the left, whose powerful ally he had been at the Board of Trade. Masterman charged Churchill with "whiff-of-grapeshot" tactics, even with a "longing for blood." Labour MP Ramsay MacDonald called the mobilization "diabolical" and went on: "This is not a mediaeval state, and it is not Russia. It is not even Germany. . . . If the Home Secretary had just a little bit more knowledge of how to handle masses of men in these critical times, if he had a somewhat better instinct of what civil liberty does mean . . . we should have had much less difficulty during the last four or five days in facing and finally settling the problem." One observer concluded that Churchill's "reputation with organized labour suffered a severe blow." Even the *Manchester Guardian,* until now Winston's warmest admirer in the press, was outraged when, despite the absence of any request from the lord mayor, troops appeared and occupied Manchester's railroad stations.[133]

The speed with which Churchill's reforms were forgotten is puzzling. It is almost as though the radicals had felt uncomfortable with him in their midst. Henceforth he would be regarded as a conservative. He had always felt ties to the past, and there is an inevitable connection between a public man's performance and the psychic baggage which is his unshakable companion. But the politicians of the left had pushed him rightward, just as the Tories had pushed him in the opposite direction seven years earlier. His own view was evocative of Robert E. Lee's: "True patriotism sometimes requires of men to act contrary, at one period, to that which it does at another." Essentially Churchill was unaltered. It was England which had shifted direction. The awakening of the working class, which he himself had stirred, had altered the political climate. In Victoria's reign, or even during her son's early years on the throne, workmen would never have conspired to bring the country to its knees over a union issue. But neither would a chancellor have imposed a supertax on the rich, nor a party have humiliated the peers. Social stability was wobbly, and civility diminished. The easy cordiality which had marked the rivalry between Joe Chamberlain and young Winston would soon be a rarity. Enemies were implacable. Friendships became exhausted, reservoirs of goodwill drained, public men used up. The disturbances of 1910–1911 had damaged Churchill's credibility in the Home Office, and Asquith decided to shake up his cabinet. The rift within the Liberal-Labour coalition over the use of force in industrial disputes was one reason. The other lay in Europe. The kaiser, so welcome at Edward's funeral, had been behaving outrageously. Germany was now regarded as a menace to the long European peace.

Churchill had met the kaiser on September 8, 1906, when he was still undersecretary at the Colonial Office. He had sought an invitation to the German army's military maneuvers that year in Silesia, and as a member of Britain's ruling class he was welcome. Count von der Schulenberg, military attaché at the emperor's London embassy, informed him that an officer would meet his train in Breslau; he would stay at the Hofmarschallamt as the personal guest of *Seine Majestät.* Winston didn't speak a word of German — "I'll never learn the beastly language," he growled, "until the Kaiser marches on London" — but like most upper-class Britons of the time, he assumed that every civilized man knew English.[134] His chief problem was finding an appropriate uniform. Von der Schulenberg had specified levee dress for a state dinner, and he hadn't any. He thought he could borrow the leopard skin and plume of the Oxfordshire Hussars from his brother, but Jack had turned the skin into a hearthrug six years earlier. Finally Sunny rooted around in Blenheim's attic and found his.

Winston witnessed the kaiser's "entry into the city of Breslau at the beginning of the manoeuvres. He rode his magnificent horse at the head of a squadron of cuirassiers, wearing their white uniform and eagle-crested helmet . . . surrounded by Kings and Princes while his legions defiled before him in what seemed to be an endless procession." On September 14 Churchill wrote Elgin from Vienna: "I had about 20 minutes talk with H.I.M. at the Parade dinner. He was vy friendly & is certainly a most fascinating personality." They had bantered over a recent issue. Rebellious natives in German Southwest Africa had recently fled into the Cape Colony; German police had crossed the frontier in hot pursuit, and the kaiser, Churchill told Elgin, "was pleased to be sarcastic about 'his design of flying across the deserts to seize Cape Town' wh he suggested we attributed to him; & he said that if a native rising took place all over S.A. 'those people (in Cape Town) would be vy glad of my troops.' He enlarged on the fighting qualities of the Hereros, & I said in reply that in Natal on the contrary our chief difficulty had not been to kill the rebellious natives, but to prevent our Colonists (*who so thoroughly understood native war*) from killing too many of them." Still, Winston had been impressed by the "massive simplicity & force" of the Prussian military machine. He told his aunt Leonie: "I am very thankful there is a sea between that army and England."[135]

Wilhelm remembered him, and was aware of the Churchills' prestige

Churchill and Kaiser Wilhelm at German maneuvers in 1909

in England. Over a year later, in December 1907, Jennie wrote Winston that the kaiser, meeting Leonie at a Clarence House luncheon, "asked a great deal after me & said he remembered me in Berlin with R[andolph]. He also spoke of you." In the summer of 1909, with his reputation growing, Churchill was asked to return to Germany for another visit. He wrote his mother: "The German Emperor has invited me to the Manoeuvres as his guest, and I am to be at Wurzburg, in Franconia, on the 14th of September." He wrote Clementine that the kaiser, who appeared "vy sallow — but otherwise looks quite well," was "vy friendly — 'My dear Winston' & so on." His imperial host warned him "to guard against 'disagreements on party politics' & chaffed about 'Socialists' in a good-humoured way." Winston was treated as an exalted guest: "I have a vy nice horse from the Emperor's stables, & am able to ride about wherever I choose with a suitable retinue. As I am supposed to be an 'Excellency' I get a vy good place."[136]

He was troubled by the Teutonic character: "These people are so amazingly *routinière* that anything at least [sic] out of the ordinary — anything they have not considered officially and for months — upsets them dreadfully. . . . With us there are so many shades. Here it is all black & white (the Prussian colours). I think another 50 years will see a wiser & gentler world. But we shall not be spectators of it. Only the P.K. will glitter in a happier scene." This time he was even more awed by the kaiser's martial juggernaut. He described it as "a terrible engine. It marches sometimes 35 miles in a day. It is in number as the sands of the sea — & with all the modern conveniences. . . . How easily men could make things better than they are — if they only all tried together! Much as war attracts me & fascinates my mind with its tremendous situations — I feel more deeply every year — & can measure the feeling here in the midst of arms — what vile & wicked folly & barbarism it all is." He treasured his family all the more: "Sweet cat — I kiss your vision as it rises before my mind. Your dear heart throbs often in my own. God bless you darling & keep you safe & sound. Kiss the P.K. for me all over. With fondest love — W."[137]

Back in England he once more persuaded himself that war between the two empires was unthinkable; it would be too ghastly; no sane authority could countenance it. He counseled the new King to take a conciliatory line, writing him on May 13, 1911, "Mr Churchill thinks that Your Majesty's references on Tuesday next to the German Emperor will be very warmly welcomed by the Peace party in the country, & will do a lot of good to public sentiment here & in Germany."[138] Then, less than seven weeks later, came Churchill's greatest volte-face, transforming him from a dove into a hawk. It was triggered that July by the incident at Agadir, an obscure port on the Atlantic coast of Morocco.

The Germans had been late entrants in the race for colonies, and by the time they reached Africa all the prizes were gone. After the Tangier incident in 1905, Germany and France had agreed that neither would annex Morocco, but unrest there spread into French Algeria, and French troops, in another hot pursuit, crossed over onto Moroccan soil. The kaiser, on the advice of his aggressive foreign minister, decided to make an issue of it. He dispatched a gunboat, the *Panther,* to Agadir. Wilhelm expected the French to grab Morocco, which they did, and had no intention of contesting it; his goal was acquisition of a bargaining chip which would win him concessions in the Congo. He got them, but the arrival of the *Panther* on July 1, 1911, was destined to set off a murderous chain reaction. While Paris and Berlin were haggling, the Italians took advantage of the diversion by invading Tripoli. Tripoli was part of the Turks' Ottoman Empire. Discontented nationalities in the Balkans decided that if Italy could take on the Turks, so could they. The immediate results were the Balkan wars of 1912 and 1913, followed by the rise of Serbia, Austria-Hungary's fear of a strong Serbia, and Russia's alliance with the Serbs, a consequence of the czar's determination to preserve his credibility in the Balkans. Russia's growing military presence in the region threatened Austria-Hungary and Germany, Austria-Hungary's powerful ally. The kaiser liked his cousin in Saint Petersburg, but he believed that if he ever allowed him time to mobilize and arm Russia's countless millions, they would be unbeatable. Therefore he began to contemplate preemptive war. Meanwhile, all the great European powers, engaging in a deadly quadrille, rearmed at a furious pace.

These sequelae were unrevealed to the Britons of 1911. No man, not even the wisest statesman, can see across the horizon, and in the barbarous 1980s the appearance of a small warship in an African harbor does not seem provocative. But it was then. Diplomacy was different in the years before 1914. A studied insult, even an unanswered note, could make governments tremble. The display of naked force — the *Panther* — had been shocking. It simply was not done. By doing it, the Germans changed a lot of minds, among them that of Lloyd George. Obviously, George told Churchill, Berlin believed that London would never intervene, whatever the kaiser did. He said, "People think that because I was pro-Boer I am anti-war in general, and that I should faint at the mention of a cannon." He meant to correct that impression at once, and he did, in the chancellor's annual address to the City bankers at the Mansion House. He said: "If a situation were forced upon us in which peace could only be preserved by the surrender of the great and beneficent position Britain has won by centuries of heroism and achievement, by allowing Britain to be treated where her interests were vitally affected as if she were of no account in the Cabinet of nations, then I say emphatically that peace at that price would be a humiliation intolerable for a great country like ours to endure." The German ambassador, who had described George as a pacifist, was recalled in disgrace.[139]

Churchill was also reappraising his position. His opposition to the Admiralty's dreadnought program had been based upon his faith in Germany's good intentions. Now, in an undated memorandum on Home Office stationery, he set down his thoughts. "Germany's action at Agadir," he wrote, "has put her in the wrong & forced us to consider her claims in the light of her policy & methods." He believed that England must give France diplomatic support. "If no settlement is reached between F. & G. & deadlock results we must secure Brit interests independently. . . . If Germany makes war on France in the course of the discussion or deadlock (unless F. has meanwhile after full warning from us taken unjustifiable ground) we shd join with France. Germany should be told this now." Asquith appointed him to the cabinet's Committee of Imperial Defence, formed in 1904. There Sir Edward Grey revealed his

1906 pledge to defend France. On August 30 Winston wrote Grey that if "decisive action" became necessary, Britain should join France and Russia in "a triple alliance," guarantee Belgium's frontiers, "aid Belgium to defend Antwerp," and plan "a blockade of the Rhine."[140]

Beginning that summer of 1911, after the disappointments of Tonypandy, the siege of Sidney Street, and the railroad strike, preparation for war was never far from Churchill's thoughts. "Once I got drawn in," he later wrote, "it dominated all other interests in my mind."[141] He was horrified when, at a Downing Street garden party, the commissioner of police informed him that the Home Office was responsible for guarding the magazines in which all England's reserves of naval cordite were stored. Rushing from the party to the War Office, he persuaded the duty officer to post sentries at the depots until he could organize parties of constables. In mid-August he sought peace in the country. He was sitting on a hilltop, overlooking green fields, when he realized that lines from Housman's *Shropshire Lad* were running through his head:

On the idle hill of summer,
Sleepy with the flow of streams,
Far I hear the distant drummer
Drumming like a noise in dreams.
Far and near and low and louder
On the roads of earth go by,
Dear to friends and food for powder,
Soldiers marching, all to die.

On August 23 he submitted a prescient memorandum to the Imperial Defence Committee. Assuming that Britain, France, and Russia were attacked by Germany and Austria-Hungary, he predicted that on the twentieth day of the war the kaiser's armies in France would break through the Meuse defense line. The French would then fall back on Paris. By the fortieth day, however, Germany would "be extended at full strain both internally and on her war fronts," and with each passing hour this pressure would become "more severe and ultimately overwhelming" unless they could force an immediate decision. Denying them that would require "heavy and hard sacrifices from France." Whether France could make them would depend on British military support, "and this must be known beforehand." He proposed a contingency plan under which Britain would send 107,000 troops across the Channel at the outbreak of war, with another 100,000 men from India reaching Marseilles by the all-important fortieth day. General Henry Wilson told the committee

Churchill at British army maneuvers, September 1913

that Winston's prediction was "ridiculous and fantastic — a silly memorandum." But three years later the Germans lost the battle of the Marne on the war's forty-second day.[142]

By September 1911 Churchill had tired of the Liberals' growing polarization between left and right, the internal struggle in which he was being ground up, and was again pondering the Victorian policy of Splendid Isolation. He had cherished it as part of his political legacy. But now he studied a Foreign Office paper written in 1907 by Eyre Crowe. Crowe had held that England must preserve Europe's balance of power by forging an alliance with the second-strongest nation on the Continent. Brooding over this thesis, Winston was struck by the thought that although earlier generations of Englishmen had never put it on paper, they had in fact always pursued it. This grand strategy, he believed, had been the key to the Elizabethans' rout of the Spaniards, Marlborough's defeat of Louis XIV, and Wellington's triumph over Napoleon. Following the same line of reasoning, he concluded that England must now embrace France, even hold joint maneuvers with France. As a candidate three years earlier, he had told audiences in Manchester and Dundee that the German threat was a figment of Tory imagination. After Agadir he became the cabinet's most ardent advocate of intervention.

Another prime minister might have resented his home secretary's active interest in military issues. Asquith didn't. Indeed, he had good reason to encourage it. Churchill, one of his ablest ministers, was no longer comfortable or suitable in the Home Office, and the Royal Navy needed a forceful hand at the tiller. As first lord of the Admiralty, Reginald McKenna was far too easygoing; he had been unable to overcome the resistance of his first sea lord — the equivalent of the U.S. chief of naval operations — to the formation of a naval war staff. Asquith pondered having them switch jobs. Apart from Churchill, the only other strong candidate for the Admiralty was the secretary for war, Lord Haldane, who had just completed a brilliant reorganization of the army. In September 1911 the prime minister invited both men and their wives to be his guests at Archerfield, his Scottish estate on the East Lothian coast. The Churchills would arrive late, because Winston had to visit Balmoral first. It was customary for each senior minister to spend a few days there with the King each year. Clementine passed those days with her grandmother in Airlie Castle — wives were not received at Balmoral on such occasions — and on September 25 she wrote: "I hope you are happy my sweet Pug and that you are being properly petted, & that you will secure a huge stag. I am very happy here — Granny is become much kinder with age. . . . She sends her love & is looking forward to seeing you on Wednesday for luncheon which is at 1.30 *to the second by Greenwich time.* Afterwards we fly away to Archerfield in the new motor." The automobile, a £610 red Napier, had been delivered to Churchill at Balmoral. He drove over to pick Clementine up, and before they left the castle he told her he was afraid Asquith would pick Haldane. She opened her grandmother's Bible to the one hundred seventh Psalm. "I know it's all right about the Admiralty," she said, and read: "They that go down to the sea in ships, that do business in great waters; these see the works of the Lord, and his wonders in the deep."[143]

She was right. Asquith had already made his decision. Churchill would run the navy. Asquith wrote Haldane: "The main and, in the longer run, the deciding factor with me has been the absolute necessity for keeping the First Lord in the Commons." Clementine was absent at the great moment. After a round of golf with Asquith, Winston approached Violet, who was just finishing tea, and asked her to join him for a walk. In his face, she wrote, she saw "a radiance like the sun." Did he want tea? she asked. He shook his head. They had hardly left the house when he blurted out: "I don't want tea, I don't want anything — anything in the world. Your father has just offered me the Admiralty." He looked seaward, and in the fading light of evening watched the silhouettes of two battleships steaming slowly out of the Firth of Forth. It was a full moment for him. He said: "Look at the people I've had to deal with so far. Judges and convicts! This is a big thing — the biggest thing that has ever come my way — the chance I should have chosen before all others. I shall pour into it everything I've got!" Just as Clementine had opened a Bible in Airlie Castle, so, that night at Archerfield, did he. He found himself reading from the ninth chapter of Deuteronomy: "Hear, O Israel: Thou art to pass over Jordan this day, to go in to possess nations greater and mightier than thyself. . . . Understand therefore this day, that the Lord thy God is he which goeth over before thee; as a consuming fire he shall destroy them, and he shall bring them down before thy face: so shalt thou drive them out, and destroy them quickly, as the Lord hath said unto thee."[144]

The next day he and Clementine rode to London in the Napier, and in the morning he and McKenna changed guard. McKenna came over to the Home Office and Churchill introduced him to everyone there; then they crossed to the Admiralty, where Winston met his new board, senior officers, and departmental heads. That afternoon he convened a board meeting. The secretary read the letters patent confirming the new first lord's appointment. Thereupon Churchill, in the words of the order-in-council, became "responsible to Crown and Parliament for all the business of the Admiralty." In 1923 he would write: "I was to endeavour to discharge this responsibility for the four most memorable years of my life."[145]

His new office was accompanied by many perquisites, in all of which he reveled. There has always been a certain panache to England's service ministries, and because the Admiralty is the senior service, the navy, in an old expression, "always travels first class." Among other things, the first lord decides who launches ships. Seven weeks after his appointment Clementine christened the battleship *Centurion* at Devonport, and shortly thereafter Jennie baptized its sister ship, the *Benbow*. The first lord had at his disposal a luxurious steam yacht, the *Enchantress*. In Churchill's words, this vessel became "largely my office, almost my home." His time aboard was mostly work time; he visited every important ship and every dockyard, shipyard, and naval establishment in the British Isles and the Mediterranean. But for Clementine it was mostly fun. There was one memorable cruise up the coast of Scotland, on which her sister Nellie and her sister-in-law Goonie accompanied them. Another took them to Venice, where the crew caught a huge turtle; the cook asked, "Which evening would madam prefer turtle soup?" and was dismayed when his mistress, as fond of pets as her husband, ordered the tortoise returned to the sea. On a third voyage, they anchored in Cardigan Bay and visited the Lloyd Georges in Criccieth, their Welsh home. Because Clementine knew that Winston hated meals at which nothing of importance was accomplished, most guests were men who could be useful to the Admiralty, and she scored a real coup by suggesting they entertain Kitchener, now a field marshal and agent-general in Egypt. "By all means ask K to lunch," Winston said. "Let us just be *à trois.* I have some things to talk to him about." So the long feud finally ended.[146]

These were golden days for Clementine. Motherhood had brought her a new tranquillity, and she had learned to suppress her objections to some of her in-laws. Winston wrote that they had received an invitation from Lady Wimborne, and asked her to accept: "I have a great regard for her — & we have not too many friends. If however you don't want to go — I will go alone. Don't come with all your hackles up & your fur brushed the wrong way — you naughty." She replied: "I will write tomorrow to Aunt Cornelia — I would like to go, & I will be very good I promise you, especially if you stroke my silky tail." She didn't even demur when seated next to Asquith at meals, though the prime minister was a notorious peerer down Pennsylvania Avenue. Now in her late twenties, Clementine attracted many a lustful eye. After a day at Broadstairs with the Churchills, an artist friend wrote: "Winston went off to dig castles in the sands and the rest of us bathed. It was a broiling day and the water was heavenly. Clemmie came forth like the reincarnation of Venus re-entering the sea. Her form is most beautiful. I had no idea she had such a splendid body."[147]

Yet she was jealous of Violet Asquith, feeling, according to her daughter Mary, "an understandable reserve toward this well-ensconced friend of Winston's." And soon Violet would be practically living next door. In addition to his yacht, the first lord was provided with a magnificent eighteenth-century residence, Admiralty House, with a superb view of St. James's Park. Winston wrote Clementine: "I am sure you will take to it when you get there. I am afraid it all means vy hard work for you — Poor lamb." Sir Edward Grey wanted to sublet their Eccleston Square house, but she fought the move, pleading economy. Because the government was providing them with a home, Churchill's salary was cut by £500, and Admiralty House meant increasing their servants from five to eleven or twelve. Confronted with this argument, he was, as always, vulnerable. In one helpless note he agreed with her that "money seems to flow away." A few days later he cheerfully wrote that he was "preparing a scheme which will enable us to clear off our debts & bills & start on a ready money basis. We shall have to pull in our horns." He couldn't do it, though. That same week she was off to visit France, and he wrote: "If you have anything left out of the £40, spend it on some little thing you like in Paris." Finally, after she had reduced the staff to nine by sealing off the first floor of Admiralty House, the move was made. Violet rejoiced. Winston, she wrote, had now become "our nearest neighbor. Only the width of the Horse Guards Parade separated the Admiralty from the garden door of No. 10 and it was often crossed hot-foot. It was a joy to see him buoyantly engaged in his new context, tasting complete fulfillment. I remember telling him that even his brooding had assumed a different quality. He travailed almost with serenity. 'That is because I can now lay eggs instead of scratching around in the dust and clucking. It is a far more satisfactory occupation. I am at present in process of laying a great number of eggs — good eggs, every one of them.' "[148]

He spent long days in his new nest. Eddie Marsh wrote a friend: "Winston stays until at least 8 every day. . . . Even Sundays are no longer my own, as I have spent 3 out of the last 4 on the *Enchantress.* We have made a new commandment. 'The seventh day is the Sabbath of the First Lord, and on it thou shalt do all manner of work.' " Officers at the Admiralty were on duty twenty-four hours a day, alert for a surprise attack. In Churchill's office hung a large chart of the North Sea with flag pins marking the position of every German warship; he studied it each morning on first entering the room "to inculcate in myself and those working with me a sense of ever-present danger." The *Pall Mall Gazette* described him as "quite" a naval enthusiast, and after he had visited a submarine the *Daily Express* reported: "He had a yarn with nearly all the lower deck men of the ship's company, asking why, wherefore, and how everything was done. All the sailors 'go the bundle' on him, because he makes no fuss and takes them by surprise. He is here, there, and everywhere." Everything about the Admiralty excited him, from the twin stone dolphins guarding the building's entrance to the furniture within, each piece of which was adorned with golden dolphins dating from Nelson's time. His delights, like Antony's, were "dolphin-like."[149]

Like Antony he was also accustomed to infusing his public roles with high drama. But this time it was appropriate. What had been absurd at the Colonial Office — depicting a dubious African chief as a martyr — became sublime at the Admiralty. It is arguable that the first lord's burden was greater than the prime minister's. He was answerable for

England's safety. Only the fleet could protect the island from invasion, move British troops to the Continent, bring regiments home from India, replace them with territorials, and prevent what an Admiralty paper called Britain's likeliest peril: "the interruption of our trade and destruction of merchant shipping." Two-thirds of England's food was imported. The British merchant vessels which fetched it still accounted for over half the world's seaborne trade. Enemy sea raiders, unless held at bay, could sink every one of them. Afterward Churchill wrote of the Royal Navy that its ships "were all we had. On them, as we conceived, floated the might, majesty, dominion and power of the British Empire. All our long history built up century after century, all the means of livelihood and safety of our faithful, industrious, active population depended on them. Open the sea-cocks and let them sink beneath the surface . . . and in a few minutes — half an hour at the most — the whole outlook of the world would be changed. The British Empire would dissolve like a dream; each isolated community struggling by itself; the central power of union broken; mighty provinces, whole Empires in themselves, drifting hopelessly out of control, and falling a prey to others; and Europe after one sudden convulsion passing into the iron grip of the Teuton and of all that the Teutonic system meant."[150]

He had no doubts about the identity of England's enemy. His mission, he said at the outset, was to put the fleet into "a state of instant and constant readiness for war in case we are attacked by Germany." Looking back, he wondered how he could ever have been gulled by Berlin's protestations of peaceful intent. In 1900, when he had been first elected to Parliament, the kaiser already presided over the most powerful army in Europe. That year *Seine Majestät* had proclaimed: "In order to protect German trade and commerce under existing conditions, only one thing will suffice, namely, Germany must possess a battle fleet of such strength that even for the most powerful naval adversary a war would involve such risks as to make that Power's own supremacy doubtful." Nautically, only one nation could be this "most powerful adversary." Since 1889 Britain had been committed to what was called the "two-power naval standard," meaning that England's navy must be as great as any two other navies combined. Its supremacy posed no threat to the Second Reich. England had nothing to gain on the Continent. But sea power was its lifeline, and throughout the Edwardian years the kaiser's shipbuilding program had put it at increasing hazard. In a note to Grey on January 31, 1912, four months after taking over as first lord, Churchill wrote that while "at present . . . several of the German Dreadnts are vy often the wrong side of the Kiel Canal wh they can't pass & therefore must make a long detour," that consolation was only temporary: "The deepening of the Canal by 1915 will extinguish this safety signal." Then he submitted a formal memorandum to the Committee of Imperial Defence: "The whole character of the German fleet shows that it was designed for aggressive and offensive action of the largest possible character in the North Sea or the North Atlantic. . . . The structure of the German battleships shows clearly that they are intended for attack and for fleet action. They are not a cruiser fleet designed to protect colonies and commerce all over the world. They have been preparing for years, and continue to prepare . . . for a great trial of strength."[151]

To end this insanity, Haldane visited Berlin early in 1912. He seemed the right man to send; a barrister with a passion for German philosophy, he was known at the War Office as "Schopenhauer among the generals." But the first lord was better informed about the Reich's new naval program, due to be introduced in May. The kaiser, in the naive assumption that their friendship transcended geopolitics, had sent him a copy via Sir Ernest Cassel. On February 7, with Haldane still on the Wilhelmstrasse, the Churchills were in Victoria Station, waiting for a train, when Winston picked up the late edition of an evening newspaper and read the German emperor's speech opening the Reichstag. One sentence struck him: "It is my constant duty and care to maintain and strengthen on land and water the power of defence of the German people, which has no lack of young men fit to bear arms." Two days later, after comparing this with the kaiser's May plan, Churchill spoke out in Glasgow. "This island," he said, "has never been, and never will be, lacking in trained and hardy mariners bred from their boyhood up in the service of the sea. . . . We will face the future as our ancestors would have faced it, without disquiet, without arrogance, but in stolid and inflexible determination." He could not understand the kaiser's motives: "The British Navy is to us a necessity and, from some points of view, the German Navy is to them more in the nature of a luxury."[152]

Had he understood their beastly language, he would have used another word. The German press translated it as *Luxus,* which has other implications; it denotes extravagance, or sumptuousness. In the Reich, as Churchill later wrote, it became "an expression passed angrily from lip to lip." In London the Tories were critical; even the *Daily News,* which had been one of his most ardent supporters, commented: "It is difficult to reconcile Lord Haldane's mission with Mr Churchill's speech at Glasgow. . . . Lord Haldane is on a mission to cultivate good feeling between the Governments and peoples of England and Germany. . . . Mr Churchill will pass and be forgotten. What we trust will remain and work is Lord Haldane's mission and determination to come to an understanding with Germany which doubtless it represents." The kaiser, told of Winston's statement, realized that he had miscalculated. Feeling betrayed by a former guest and protégé, he demanded an apology. None was forthcoming. Asquith said that although his first lord's choice of language had perhaps been unfortunate, he had nevertheless made "a plain statement of an obvious truth." And Haldane, upon his return from Berlin, told the cabinet that, "so far from being a hindrance" in his negotiations, "the Glasgow speech had been the greatest possible help."[153]

Regrettably, he added bleakly, it had not been enough to crown his efforts with success. He had talked to the emperor, to Chancellor Theobold von Bethmann-Hollweg, and to Grossadmiral Alfred von Tirpitz. Their price for accepting Britannia's rule of the waves had been exorbitant — an English pledge of neutrality in the event of war between Germany and France. Haldane had concluded that once "the war party got into the saddle" in Berlin, they would push "not merely for the overthrow of France or Russia but for the domination of the world." None of them seemed to realize that the English were as sensitive on the naval issue as the French on Alsace-Lorraine. They vigorously supported the German Navy League, whose hundred thousand members, corps of paid lecturers (paid by Krupp, shipbuilders to *Seine Majestät*), and magazine *Die Flotte* were flooding the Reich with chauvinistic literature and posters with such slogans as "England the Foe!" "Perfidious Albion!" "The Coming War!" "The British Peril!" "England's Plan to Fall on Us in 1911!" Apparently Bernard Shaw was right; the Germans were a people with contempt for common sense.[154]

Or perhaps their problem was their critical adoration of authority. Haldane was convinced that the root of it was the kaiser, *der hohe Herr*. It was he who had told them: "Germany's future is on the water." Apparently someone had given him a book by an American, Alfred Thayer Mahan's *Influence of Sea Power upon History*. Reading it, he had become convinced that his empire could never be truly great until it had mastered the seas. In addition, *der hohe Herr* had become paranoid. That was the explanation for his mischief-making and saber rattling. He believed his enemies were encircling the Reich and saw a powerful German fleet as a cleaver to cut through that investment. His navy, he predicted, "will bring the English to their senses through sheer fright," after which they would "submit to the inevitable, and we shall become the best friends in the world."[155]

Winston sat stone-faced through Haldane's report and, at the end, gloomily commented that the secretary for war had confirmed his worst suspicions. The German shipbuilding program scheduled to start in May, he pointed out to the cabinet, represented an "extraordinary increase in the striking force, in ships of all classes," providing Tirpitz with five fresh battle squadrons, each attended by flotillas of destroyers and submarines, each "extremely formidable."[156]

Meeting this challenge — keeping England afloat — was Churchill's responsibility, but first he had to make peace within the Admiralty, a task he compared to "burrowing about in an illimitable rabbit-warren." The relationship between civilian administrators and naval officers could hardly have been worse. The first called the second "boneheads"; the second referred to the first as "frocks" and shared the conviction of Douglas Haig, now a lieutenant general, that the word *politician* was "synonymous with crooked dealing and wrong values." Admiral Sir Arthur Wilson, the first sea lord, had been McKenna's undoing. Wilson was, among other things, the chief obstacle to the creation of a naval war staff. He thought it would undermine his authority. The admiral was nearly twice Churchill's age, but Winston was unintimidated. Believing that Wilson dwelt "too much in the past" and was "not sufficiently receptive of new ideas," the new first lord decided to fire the old first sea lord. He didn't know whom to appoint in his place, so he sent for Lord Fisher.[157]

Admiral Sir John Arbuthnot Fisher — "Jacky" Fisher to England's adoring masses — had retired to Lake Lucerne with a peerage four years earlier. He was a legend, "the greatest sailor since Nelson," and he was immensely old. In 1854, when he had joined the navy as a midshipman, British men-of-war still carried sails. He had been a captain, commanding a battleship, when Winston was born. His great period had been between 1904 and 1910, when, as first sea lord, he had scrapped ships which he said could "neither fight nor run," conceived the dreadnoughts, introduced submarines and 13.5-inch guns, revised the naval educational system, and built 161 warships, including 22 battleships of over 16,000 tons. Quick-tempered, emotional, with burning black eyes and a curiously Mongoloid face, he liked to portray himself as "ruthless, relentless, and remorseless." The description was accurate. Officers who had questioned his policies had been ruined professionally; he had branded them traitors and declared that "their wives should be widows, their children fatherless, and their homes a dunghill." Nevertheless, he was indisputably a genius. If Germany and England went to war, the navy Tirpitz would fight would be Fisher's creation.[158]

Churchill had met him in 1907, when both were visiting Biarritz. They had begun corresponding that April, and Fisher's first letter, inspired by a sugar strike in the British West Indies, provides a fair sample of his style: "St Lucia quite splendid! Dog eat dog! You are using niggers to fight niggers! For God's sake don't send British Bluejackets inland amongst sugar canes on this job or we shall have to set up a War Office inside the Admiralty & goodness knows *one* War Office is enough! I enclose a very secret paper. *Don't let anyone see it.* The best thing ever written in the English language bar the Bible & Robertson's Sermons & letters from a Competition Wallah. Kindly return the print with your improvements in the margin — study it closely."[159] The enclosure has not survived. It could have been anything. The admiral was given to superlatives and overstatements; his letters were peppered with exclamation marks and words underscored two or three times. A prudent minister would have shunned him, but Winston was never that; he believed that his own vision, married to Fisher's experience, would make a brilliant union.

In the beginning he was right. The admiral came hopping home in response to Churchill's summons, and they talked for three days. Winston found him "a veritable volcano of knowledge and inspiration; and as soon as he learnt what my main purpose was, he passed into a state of vehement eruption. . . . Once he began, he could hardly stop. I plied him with questions, and he poured out ideas." Fisher, for his part, was so excited that he ran a fever. His chief recommendations were to arm Britain's battleships with fifteen-inch guns, increase their speed, convert the entire navy from coal to oil, and shake up the senior officers: "The argument for a War Staff is that you *may* have a d——d fool as First Sea Lord, and so you put him in commission, as it were." Churchill adopted all these proposals, though his attempt to put the war staff under himself failed when Haldane persuaded the cabinet that a sailor, not a politician, should head it. The fuel conversion was a difficult step. Having made it, he took another, inducing the House to invest £2,000,000, later increased to £5,000,000, in the Anglo-Persian Oil Company, thus assuring adequate reserves in the event of war.[160]

Handling the admirals was easier, but more delicate. The war staff was established in January 1912 and Wilson was relieved of his post. Winston had considered bringing Fisher back as first sea lord, then rejected the idea because another retired admiral, Lord Charles Beresford, the old salt's sworn enemy, had become powerful in Parliament. At

Churchill and Lord Fisher, 1913

Fisher's suggestion he settled on Admiral Sir Francis Bridgeman. As second sea lord — Bridgeman's prospective successor — he chose Admiral Prince Louis of Battenberg, a relative of the royal family. It was not a foresighted move. Prince Louis was a naturalized British subject and proud of it; when one of Tirpitz's officers had reproached him at Kiel for serving under the Union Jack, he had stiffened and replied: "Sir, when I joined the Royal Navy in 1868, the German Empire did not exist." Still, he spoke with a heavy German accent, and the time was coming when that would be enough to discredit him. Winston appointed one friend, David Beatty of his Sudan days, to be rear admiral and his personal naval secretary. His key decision was naming Admiral Sir John Jellicoe as second in command of the Home Fleet and thus heir to England's most crucial seagoing command. Jellicoe was Fisher's candidate for Nelsonhood. The old admiral wrote Churchill: "He has all the Nelsonic attributes. He writes me of new designs. His *one, one, one* cry is SPEED! *Do lay that to heart!* Do remember the receipt for jugged hare in Mrs. Glasse's Cookery Book! *First catch your hare!*" After leaving London he wrote a friend: "I'll tell you . . . the whole secret of the changes! *To get Jellicoe Commander-in-Chief of the Home Fleet prior to October 21, 1914* — which is the date of the Battle of Armageddon." That was vintage Fisher. One moment he sounded demented and the next he came uncannily close to guessing the date of the approaching war.[161]

Back in Lucerne, he wrote of Churchill: "So far every step he contemplates is good, *and he is brave, which is everything. Napoleonic in audacity, Cromwellian in thoroughness.*" He peppered Winston with letters signed, typically, "Yours till Hell freezes," "Yours to a cinder," and "Till charcoal sprouts." But he was quick to turn. Three appointments offended him, and his response was savage. "I fear," he wrote Winston, "this must be my last communication with you in any matter at all. I am sorry for it, but I consider you have betrayed the Navy." The officers were close to the King; on no evidence whatever he blamed Clementine, saying she feared "the social ostracism of the Court," and called the first lord, no longer his to a cinder, "a Royal pimp." It is a sign of Churchill's faith in Fisher that he ignored this. In reply, he sent him a stream of flattering billets-doux and telegrams. The old man boasted to his son, "I sent him an awful letter, and he really has replied very nicely that no matter what I say to him, he is going to stick to me and support all my schemes and always maintain that I am a genius and the greatest naval administrator, etc. etc. . . . However, there is no getting over the fact that he truckled to Court influence . . . and I have rubbed this into WC and he don't like it!" Doubtless he loathed it, yet he persisted in his suit. By the spring he had decided that if Fisher wouldn't come to him, he would go to Fisher. He, Asquith, and their families were planning a May cruise on the *Enchantress;* he asked Fisher to meet the yacht in Naples, where they could have "a good talk."[162]

The voyage was one of Churchill's working vacations. He inspected the Gibraltar defenses, conferred with his admiral on Malta, and then docked at Naples. When his quarry came aboard, Violet Asquith thought Fisher's eyes, "as always, were like smouldering charcoals." Then "Lord F. and W. were locked together in naval conclave. . . . I'm sure they can't resist each other for long at close range." Lord F. did. He resisted the prime minister, too. His "advice wasn't followed," he said, so why should he give it? Yet he stayed. Violet's next day's diary entry opened: "Danced on deck with Lord Fisher for a very long time before breakfast. . . . I reel giddily in his arms and lurch against his heart of oak." The turning point came on Sunday. Churchill had stage-managed the church service. The chaplain riveted his eyes on the seventy-one-year-old admiral and said solemnly: "No man still possessing all his powers and full of vitality has any right to say 'I am now going to rest, as I have had a hard life,' for he owes a duty to his country and fellow men." Fisher wrote his wife, "It was an arrow shot at a venture [sic] like the one that killed Ahab." The Fisher-Churchill axis was reestablished. In letters to the Admiralty, Fisher continued to protest, "I have had my hour," but he was slowly being drawn back from retirement, and soon the first lord would conclude that despite all arguments against it, in a crisis he would want the eccentric old prodigy at his right hand.[163]

Through dynamic energy and a genius that surpassed Fisher's, Churchill mastered the Admiralty and was ready when Armageddon, as the admiral had foreseen, arrived. By then, Winston wrote, he knew "what everything looked like and where everything was, and how one thing fitted into another. I could put my hand on anything that was wanted and knew the current state of our naval affairs." He had been appalled to find that no plan existed for transporting a British expeditionary force to France. He drew one up. England's Grand Fleet had no sequestered wartime anchorage. He chose Scapa Flow, a remote shelter among the Orkney Islands at the northernmost tip of the British Isles, where Britain's dreadnoughts could keep an eye on Heligoland Bight, through which Tirpitz's *Flotte* must pass in any sortie. In Parliament he won approval of his appropriation bills by vivid, lucid descriptions of abstruse technical matters. Describing the impact of a shell upon a warship, he told the House: "If you want to make a true picture in your mind of a battle between two great modern iron-clad ships, you must not think of it

Churchill and Asquith at Camberwell Green

as if it were two men in armour striking at each other with heavy swords. It is more like a battle between two egg-shells striking each other with hammers. . . . The importance of hitting first, and hitting hardest and keeping on hitting . . . really needs no clearer proof."[164]

His inspections of ships continued to be popular with bluejackets. After his first year in office the monthly magazine *Fleet,* which echoed forecastle views, commented: "No First Lord in the history of the Navy has shown himself more practically sympathetic with the conditions of the Lower Deck than Winston Churchill." The brass took another view. Churchill's predecessors had given the sea lords free rein, but he regarded them as subordinates and issued them blunt instructions. When Bridgeman rebelled, he was swiftly retired, ostensibly on grounds of poor health, with Prince Louis replacing him. Tories protested in the House, and career officers were scandalized. Rear Admiral Dudley de Chair, who succeeded Beatty as navy secretary, was shocked by the first lord's cursory judgment of men, often based on a few minutes of conversation. De Chair found him "impulsive, headstrong and even at times obstinate." His tours of the fleet were also controversial. He encouraged junior officers and ratings to criticize their commanding officers. When a commander dared complain of this, Churchill proposed to relieve him and was dissuaded only when the second, third, and fourth sea lords threatened to resign in protest. At the end of a strategy conference, one of the admirals accused the first lord of impugning the traditions of the Royal Navy. "And what are they?" asked Winston. "I shall tell you in three words. Rum, sodomy, and the lash. Good morning, gentlemen."[165]

No profession is more wedded to the folklore of the past than the armed services. Since the last major conflict on the Continent, technology had clanked out an astonishing array of contraptions suitable for war, and the generals and admirals of Europe, regardless of national allegiance, viewed them all with deep distrust. They belonged to that generation which called electricity "the electric," and regarded it as newfangled. Being new was enough to make a device suspect. Haig thought the machine gun "a much over-rated weapon," and believed "two per battalion should be sufficient." Joffre of France refused to use a telephone, pretending that he did not "understand the mechanism." The Stokes mortar was twice rejected at the British War Office and finally introduced by Lloyd George, who begged the money for it from an Indian maharaja and was as a consequence considered "ungentlemanly" by British officers. Kitchener dismissed the tank as a "toy." It was, in fact, a pet project of Churchill's. Winston wasn't always right, however; Jellicoe was impressed by a flight in a zeppelin, and at his urging Churchill approved pilot models. Then he lost interest. As he said later, "I rated the Zeppelin much lower as a weapon of war than almost anyone else. I believed that this enormous bladder of combustible and explosive gas would prove easily destructible." As a result, in 1914 the navy had no reconnaissance airships. He also failed to provide adequate submarine defenses in Scapa and the Firth of Forth, but that was because he became entangled in red tape; unlike H. G. Wells, who predicted that the "blind fumblings" of U-boats would limit them to the torpedoing of hulks in harbors, he was fully aware of their minatory potential.[166]

The new weapon which fascinated him most was the airplane. In 1910 General Ferdinand Foch had spoken for most professional officers when he ridiculed the idea of an air force in wartime. *"Tout ça, c'est du sport,"* he said contemptuously; as far as the French army was concerned, *"l'avion c'est zéro!"* In the British navy it was otherwise. As early as February 25, 1909, when he was still at the Board of Trade, Churchill had told the cabinet that aviation would be "most important" in the future and suggested that "we should place ourselves in communication with Mr [Orville] Wright and avail ourselves of his knowledge." The following year he presented a *Daily Mail* check for £10,000 to two airmen who had taken off from the Dominion of Newfoundland and landed on a field in, as he put it, "the future equally happy and prosperous Dominion of Ireland" — poor political prophecy, but no other national figure had come to greet them. Arriving at the Admiralty, he had sought out the small band of adventurous officers who were the pioneers of naval aviation. In 1912 he founded the Royal Naval Air Service — a precursor of the Royal Flying Corps and, later, the Royal Air Force — to provide "aerial protection to our naval harbours, oil tanks and vulnerable points, and also for a general strengthening of our exiguous and inadequate aviation." A larval helicopter was built; he inspected it. In tests it proved unstable, and prone to crash, after it had risen about three hundred feet. Winston proposed a hollow propeller containing a parachute. The suggestion was completely impractical, but his encouragement of experimentation elsewhere led to breakthroughs. Because of his efforts, England became the first country to equip a plane with a machine gun, and the first to launch an airborne torpedo. He coined the words *seaplane,* and *flight* to designate a given number of aircraft, usually four.[167]

To Clementine's alarm, he decided to fly himself. He regarded his first ride, in 1912, as a matter of duty. Discovering that he enjoyed it, he made repeated ascents. The craft were primitive, the techniques slapdash. On one bumpy trip, in the teeth of a gale, nearly three hours were required to cover the sixteen miles from Gravesend to Grain, and "after landing Churchill safely," the pilot reported, "my seaplane 'took off' again, landing trolley and all over the sea wall, as it was being brought up the slipway, and was more or less wrecked." The hazards whetted Winston's appetite. In October 1913, at the Eastchurch naval flying center, he went up in three different craft. That evening he wrote Clementine: "Darling, We have had a vy jolly day in the air . . . it has been as good as one of those old days in the S. African War, & I have lived entirely in the moment, with no care for all those tiresome party politics & searching newspapers, and awkward by-elections. . . . For good luck before I started I put your locket on. It has been lying in my desk since it got bent — & as usual it worked like a charm." She wired her dismay from the *Enchantress* and then followed up with a note: "I hope my telegram will not have vexed you, but please be kind & don't fly any more just now."[168]

It was a postage stamp wasted. Churchill with the bit in his teeth was incorrigible. Deeply as he loved his wife, at that moment he loved the excitement of flying more. To the consternation of the barnstormers who had been taking him up, he declared that he wanted to be a pilot himself. He was too old, they protested; thirty-two was regarded as the top age for a novice, and he was thirty-eight. He invoked his powers as first lord, ordered them to shut up, and began taking lessons in managing controls at Apavon. One of his instructors, Ivon Courtney, later recalled: "Before our first flight together he said to me: 'We are in the Stephenson age of flying. Now our machines are frail. One day they will be robust, and of value to our country.' He had already done a lot of flying. 'I want some more instruction,' he said." Aircraft were not equipped with headphones then; the two men sat in separate cockpits, Churchill in the rear, and shouted at each other, hoping their voices would carry above the wind. The instruments were encased in a box, but most airmen scorned them, preferring to rely on what they called "ear." Winston, however, was fascinated by the dials and needles. He would crouch down, peering at them, "and," Courtney wrote, "he was right to do so. He saw that one day the box of instruments would be more important than the pilot's ear."[169]

They went up as often as ten times a day. Every officer on the instruction staff worried about their eminent student. "We were all scared stiff," said Courtney, "of having a smashed First Lord on our hands."

Churchill in pilot's gear for a practice flight

Eugene Gerrard, later air commodore, said: "WSC has had as much as twenty-five hours in the air, but no one will risk letting him solo; if anything happened to WSC the career of the man who had allowed him a solo flight would be finished." Sir Philip Joubert de la Ferté, later air chief marshal, remembered Winston as "a very fair pilot once he was in the air, but more than uncertain in his take-off and landing. His instructors usually took over the controls to make the final approach and touch-down." Another future RAF marshal, Hugh Trenchard, gave him lower marks. After watching him "wallowing about the sky," as he put it, he decided Winston was "altogether too impatient for a good pupil."[170]

But Churchill persevered. He spent the afternoon of Saturday, November 29, 1913, in the air with Captain Gilbert Wildman-Lushington of the Royal Marines. After they had parted, the captain wrote his fiancée: "I started Winston off on his instruction about 12.15 & he got so bitten with it, I could hardly get him out of the machine, in fact except for about ¾ hour for lunch we were in the machine till about 3.30. He showed great promise, & is coming down again for further instruction & practice." Winston himself was dissatisfied. Once he had set his mind on an objective, anything short of total conquest was unacceptable. Back in his Admiralty office that evening he wrote Lushington: "I wish you would clear up the question of the steering control and let me know what was the real difficulty I had in making the rudder act. Probably the explanation is that I was pushing against myself. . . . Could you not go up with another flying officer and, sitting yourself in the back seat, see whether there is great stiffness and difficulty in steering, or whether it was all my clumsiness." Then he dropped Clementine a line: "I have been very naughty today about flying. . . . With twenty machines in the air at once and thousands of flights made without mishap, it is not possible to look upon it as a vy serious risk. Do not be vexed with me."[171]

She wasn't vexed; she was frantic. By the time this letter reached her, Lushington was dead; coming in to land at Eastchurch on Sunday, he sideslipped and crashed. F.E. wrote Winston: "Why do you do such a foolish thing as fly repeatedly? Surely it is unfair to your family, your career & your friends." It was; it was thoughtless, the act of a supreme egoist. H. G. Wells wrote: "There are times when the evil spirit comes upon him and I think of him as a very intractable, a very mischievous, dangerous little boy, a knee-worthy little boy. Only thinking of him in that way can I go on liking him." The fact is that His Majesty's first lord of the Admiralty deserved a good spanking. Despite his instructor's death and his wife's appeals, he refused to stay on the ground. At Easter Clementine wrote him from Spain, where she and Mrs. Keppel were Cassel's guests: "I have been seized by a dreadful anxiety that you are making use of my absence to fly even more often than you do when I am there — I beg of you not to do it at all, at any rate till I can be there." It was a shrewd guess. That very day he had not only flown; he had been shaken up when engine failure forced his new instructor to make an emergency landing. Undaunted, he took off again two days later. Clementine and the children were now staying with her mother in Dieppe, and on May 29, 1914, he wrote her there: "I have been at the Central Flying School for a couple of days — flying a little in good & careful hands & under perfect conditions. So I did not write you from there as I knew you would be vexed."[172]

She replied: "I felt what you were doing before I read about it, but I felt too weak & tired to struggle against it. It is like beating one's head against a stone wall. . . . Perhaps if I saw you, I could love and pet you, but you have been so naughty that I can't do it on paper. I must be 'brought round' first." She signed the letter with the sketch of a cat, its ears down. She did see him the following week; he crossed on the *Enchantress* to spend a day with her and the children. They discussed his flying, and he assured her that the airfield he was using, at Sheerness in Kent, had every modern facility. Yet in her next letter the tension was still there: "I cannot help knowing that you are going to fly as you go to Sheerness & it fills me with anxiety. I know nothing will stop you from doing it so I will not weary you with tedious entreaties, but don't forget that I am thinking about it all the time & so, do it as little & as moderately as you can, & only with the *very best* Pilot. I feel very 'ears down' about it." Her fear haunted her; she was five months pregnant with their third child — it would be another daughter, Sarah — and thought, not unreasonably, that she was entitled to more consideration from her husband. In her next letter she described a nightmare. She had dreamed she had had her baby, but the doctor and nurse hid it. Finding the infant in a darkened room, she feverishly counted its fingers and toes only to find that it was a gaping idiot. "And then the worst thing of all happened — I wanted the Doctor to kill it — but he was shocked & took it away & I was mad too." The evening before, she had received a cable from Winston, telling her he was safely home. "Every time I see a telegram now," she wrote, "I think it is to announce that you have been killed flying. I had a fright but went to sleep relieved; but this morning after the nightmare I looked at it again for consolation & found to my horror it was from Sheerness & not from Dover where I thought you were going first — so you are probably at it again at this very moment. Goodbye my Dear but Cruel One, Your loving Clemmie."[173]

Winston instantly replied: "My darling one, I will not fly any more until at any rate you have recovered from your kitten." He had been callous, but he recognized a cry of despair when he heard it. Mulling it over, he realized that her anxiety had been fully justified. Prewar aviation was, in fact, a risky business, even for skillful airmen; only a few days earlier, Gustav Hamel, a celebrated monoplane aviator and a friend of both the Churchills, had disappeared over the Channel. Abandoning flight was "a wrench," Winston wrote Clementine, "because I was on the verge of taking my pilot's certificate; & I am confident of my ability to achieve it vy respectably. I shd greatly have liked to reach this point wh wd have made a suitable moment for breaking off. But I must admit that the numerous fatalities of this year wd justify you in complaining if I continued to share the risks — as I am proud to do — of these good fellows. So I give it up decidedly for many months & perhaps for ever. This is a gift — so stupidly am I made — wh costs me more than anything wh cd be bought with money. So I am vy glad to lay it at your feet, because I know it will rejoice & relieve your heart. Anyhow I can feel I know a good deal about this fascinating new art. I can manage a machine with ease in the air, even with high winds, & only a little more practice in landings wd have enabled me to go up with reasonable safety alone. I have been up nearly 140 times, with many pilots, & all kinds of machines, so I know the difficulties the dangers & the joys of the air — well enough to appreciate them, & to understand all the questions of policy wh will arise in the near future. . . . You will give me some kisses and forgive me for past distresses — I am sure. Though I had no need & perhaps no right to do it — it was an important part of my life during the last 7 months, & I am sure my nerve, my spirits & my virtue were all improved by it. But at your expense my poor pussy cat! I am so sorry."[174]

It is astonishing to reflect that Churchill was flying over Kent before the young RAF pilots who won the Battle of Britain, dogfighting in those same skies, were even born. By then, of course, no one questioned the absolute necessity of a strong air arm. In Winston's cockpit days it was regarded as a frill, however, and he was hard put to justify it in an Admiralty budget already swollen by the need to stay ahead of Germany. Alarmed by the expensive arms race, in April 1912 he had proposed a "Naval Holiday," during which both nations would suspend the laying of new keels. The kaiser rejected the idea; such an agreement, he said, could be reached only between allies. But Albert Ballin, director of the Hamburg-American Steamship Line, told Cassel that the "frankness and honesty" of Churchill's offer had "flustered . . . the leading parties in Germany, and has caused a torrent of [comment] in the Press." Winston wrote Cassel a conciliatory letter, meant for *der hohe Herr*'s eyes. It accomplished nothing. Ballin thought Churchill should visit Berlin; he believed he would be well received, and could "have some useful conversation with Admiral Tirpitz." Winston declined on the ground that "all that could be said on our part wd be that till Germany dropped the naval challenge her policy wd be continually viewed here with deepening suspicion and apprehension; but that any slackening on her part wd produce an immediate *détente,* with much good will from England. Failing that I see little in prospect but politeness and preparation." On October 24, 1913, he again suggested a shipbuilding suspension, forwarding the recommendation to *der hohe Herr* through Ballin and advising the cabinet: "The simultaneous building by so many powers great and small of capital ships, their general naval expansion, are causes of deep anxiety to us. . . . Naval strength to other powers is a mere panache. But as the frog said to the boy in the fable 'It is sport to you: it is death to us.' " This time his proposal wasn't even acknowledged.[175]

All overtures to the kaiser having failed, he and Jack Seely, who had succeeded Haldane as war minister, pushed for higher military appropriations. At the end of the year Churchill submitted his naval estimates for 1914. They were shocking: £50,694,800 — the largest in British history, the largest in the world. The chancellor of the Exchequer was stunned. Winston and Lloyd George were still friends, but they were no longer partners in political counterpoint. The first lord had become militant, even belligerent; the chancellor, whose own position was softening again, complained that Churchill was "getting more and more absorbed in boilers." The cabinet was divided. Asquith accepted the estimates, but Margot wrote Lloyd George: "Don't let Winston have too much money — it will hurt our party in every way — Labour and even Liberals. If one can't be a little economical when all foreign countries are peaceful I don't know *when* we can."[176]

The split was deep, and involved more than money. Asquith, Churchill, Seely, and Grey believed that the integrity of France was vital to England's national interest; that, as Grey put it, "if Germany dominated the Continent it would be disagreeable to us as well as to others, for we should be isolated." The Tories agreed, but among Liberals, even within the cabinet, it was a minority view. Their leader there, Lord Morley, believed he could count on "eight or nine likely to agree with us" in opposing the policies being advanced by Grey with "strenuous simplicity" and by Churchill with "daemonic energy." Morley described himself as "a pacifist at heart." He had been Gladstone's friend and biographer, and he and those who agreed with him believed they were acting on Gladstonian principles. The fights they loved were those fought for Free Trade, social reforms, Irish Home Rule, and the defeat of the arrogant dukes. They were unmoved by France. Only an appeal for help from a little country like Belgium could reach their hearts, and even that was uncertain.[177]

Thus Lloyd George had friends in power when, on New Year's Day, 1914, he told a *Daily Chronicle* reporter that Churchill's plan for "exorbitant expenditure on armaments" violated Lord Randolph's memory. Replying, Winston rebuked him; he said he never granted newspaper interviews "on important subjects of this character while they are under the consideration of the Cabinet." One of the two ministers, it seemed, would have to resign. While refusing to be quoted, Churchill became the source of sensational rumors. He was pondering a return to the Conservative party; he had become doubtful about Home Rule; if he left the Admiralty, the four sea lords would quit in protest. As tempers rose, the two principals sat down for five hours of what Winston called "polite but deadly" negotiation. The prime minister joined them, and his strong support of the estimates decided the issue. To save Lloyd George's face, 2 percent was cut from the naval budget, further economies were promised for the following year, and expensive maneuvers planned for the following summer were canceled, to be replaced by a trial mobilization of the fleet. George avoided mortification by pretending that he had changed his mind. He invited Churchill to breakfast at No. 11 Downing Street, the traditional home of the chancellors. He said his wife had told him that he ought to let "that nice Mr Churchill" have his dreadnoughts, arguing that it would be better to have too many than too few. "So," he said, "I have decided to let you build them. Let's go in to breakfast." Winston wrote his mother: "I think the naval estimates are now past the danger point & if so the situation will be satisfactory. But it has been a long and wearing business wh has caused me at times vy gt perplexity."[178]

In March he presented his naval estimates to the House. The Liberals were tepid, the Conservatives enthusiastic. The *Daily Telegraph* hailed his address as "the most weighty and eloquent speech to which the House of Commons have listened [from a first lord of the Admiralty] during the present generation."[179] This was praise Churchill didn't need. Indeed, though Tories publicly approved of his naval expansion, behind his back they said it was inspired by a personal pursuit of glory. Winston's defection from their ranks, his humiliation of Joe Chamberlain, and his corrosive invective in political campaigns and parliamentary struggles could be neither forgotten nor forgiven. His political advancement — even survival — depended on his strength with his adopted party, where, more and more, MPs on the back benches were saying: "He's not really a Liberal." He had to prove that he was. In that four-year interval between the end of the Edwardian era and the outbreak of the Kaiser's War there were many disputes between the Asquith government and the Opposition, but Churchill needed a dramatic issue. One appeared. It seemed ideal: explosive, emotional, and above all a matter of principle. And it was unavoidable. The eighty-four Irish Nationalist MPs had presented their bill for services rendered in unmanning the House of Lords, and payment was now due.

By later Irish standards they were mild — "Gentlemen first, Irishmen second" had been their muted war cry — and as gentlemen they had been patient. Their cause had been hopeless in the fourteen years between Parnell's death in Kitty O'Shea's arms and the fall of the Balfour government, but the Liberals had been in power since 1906 and had done nothing to redeem Gladstone's promise. Winston had prodded the cabinet; on February 13, 1910, Blunt had noted in his diary that

Churchill had said it was "the ambition of my life to bring in a Home Rule Bill." But neither Asquith nor Lloyd George found the issue appealing, and even Winston, who had been offered the post of chief secretary for Ireland, had turned down what was known as the "hoodoo job of the Cabinet." Ireland had always been a political minefield, and it had been doubly treacherous since Lord Randolph had played what he called his "ace of trumps, the Orange card."[180]

Ulster — the nine counties around Belfast, in northern Ireland — was largely populated by Protestants, descendants of Scots who had settled there before the *Mayflower* sighted Plymouth. Under Home Rule, the entire island would be ruled by a parliament in Dublin. Inevitably Catholics from southern Ireland would dominate it. Before they would accept that, Ulstermen swore, they would die fighting. "Home Rule," they said, meant "Rome Rule." The differences between the northern Unionists and the southern Nationalists had been, were, and always would be irreconcilable. The southerners found the status quo intolerable. For nearly eight centuries they had been governed like serfs by English viceroys entrenched in Dublin Castle. The finest estates in what is now Eire then belonged to an Anglo-Irish aristocracy, the Protestant Ascendancy. Gladstone had told these overlords again and again that the southern yearning for freedom was an indestructible passion, but they preferred to quote Queen Victoria: "I think it very unwise to give up what we hold." After the coronation of George V, however, the Irish Nationalists, under pressure from home, prepared to drop their genteel manners. They wanted their own parliament, and they wanted it immediately. "The Irish question," Churchill wrote afterward, "now cut jaggedly across the British political scene." By this time, he had completely emerged from his father's shadow and was one of the most vigorous champions of a united Ireland, governed from Dublin. Because he was Randolph's son as well as the ablest parliamentarian in the cabinet, Asquith chose him as point man for the issue. In Dundee, on October 4, 1911, Winston declared: "Next year we propose to introduce the Home Rule Bill, and we propose to carry it forward with all our strength." The crowd, knowing he had been born and bred a Unionist, was taken aback. Someone called: "Ulster will fight, Ulster will be right!" Churchill snapped: "That is a slogan from which every street bully with a brickbat and every crazy fanatic fumbling with a pistol may draw inspiration."[181]

Early the following year he announced that he had accepted an invitation from the Ulster Liberal Association to speak in Belfast's Ulster Hall, where Lord Randolph had spoken, on February 12. The Irish Unionist party erupted. "What a man to select!" thundered Sir Edward Carson, former solicitor general and a leader of the Ulster Unionists in the House. "The most provocative speaker in the whole party, going under the most provocative circumstances to a place where the words of his own father are still ringing in the ear!" Death threats arrived at Admiralty House by post and telephone. One Unionist warned him in an open letter: "The heather is on fire and Belfast today is the rallying ground of the clans. The fiery cross has sped through hill and glen, and with the undying spirit of their forbears the Ulstermen are answering to the message. . . . It would be well if Mr Churchill would read the writing on the wall, for there is great fear that harm may happen to him." Clementine decided to accompany her husband, hoping that would discourage violence. At the last minute Winston's cousin Freddie Guest joined the party, carrying a revolver in his pocket.[182]

Crossing the Irish Sea, the Churchills were kept awake all night by women who stood outside their cabin window chanting: "Votes for women! Votes for women!" Policemen patrolled the eighteen-mile railroad line from Larne, where they docked, to Belfast. Arriving at Belfast Station, Churchill was told that four infantry battalions — thirty-five hundred troops — had been called up to line his route. Even so, the risks were grave; glass had been removed from the windows of their car because demonstrators were carrying stones. The drive to the Grand Centre Hotel was a tribulation in itself. Winston stared out at a burning effigy of himself. At one point, the *Guardian* reported, the mob lifted the car's back wheels eighteen inches off the ground. The *Times* correspondent wrote that "men thrust their heads in and uttered fearful menaces and imprecations. It seemed to me that Mr Churchill was taking a greater risk than ever he expected. . . . Yet he never flinched and took hostility visualised as well as vocalised calmly and no harm befell him." This observer noted that he "smilingly raised his hat whenever the crowd groaned." Clementine, badly frightened herself, thought that "the opposition and threats seemed to 'ginger him up.' "[183]

Nevertheless, it was clear that he had misjudged Ulster's mood. A hostile throng of ten thousand awaited them at the hotel. Businessmen in the lobby angrily shook their fists. The windows of their suite were heavily draped; when Winston tried to peek out, a roar of boos and oaths swelled up from below. Meeting in Ulster Hall was out of the question. The local Unionist Council, which had resolved to prevent his appearance "in the centre of the loyal city of Belfast," had occupied it with armed "Hooligan Corner Boys," as they were called. Evicting them would cost the lives of at least six policemen. A dozen plots were afoot to murder Churchill if he even approached the hall. The rally was therefore moved to Celtic Park in the Falls neighborhood, a Catholic stronghold, where a heavy rain began falling at 2:00 P.M. as Winston, standing beneath a leaking canvas marquee, rose to address a drenched crowd of five thousand Irish Nationalists and a handful of Unionist hecklers. The Tories, he told them, were trying to regain office by using Ireland as a cat's-paw, but "the flame of Irish nationality is inextinguishable." Of his father he said: "The reverence which I feel for his memory, and the care with which I have studied his public life, make me quite content to leave others to judge how far there is continuity or discontinuity between his work and any I have tried to do." Then he ended audaciously, ringing a change on Lord Randolph's most famous words: "If Ulster would fight for the honor of Ireland, for reconciliation of races and for forgiveness of ancient wrongs, for the consolidation of the Empire, then indeed Ulster will fight, and Ulster will be right."[184]

The apologetic Liberals of Ulster presented Winston and Clementine with blackthorns, stout walking sticks — a pleasant gesture which was swiftly forgotten when, as they mounted the Larne gangplank for the journey home, dockers pelted them with rotten fish. It was a fitting farewell; in the eight centuries since Pope Adrian IV gave Ireland to Henry II, the relationship between England and Ireland had been marked by wave after wave of violence, and now new fury was rising. Churchill wasn't even safe in the House of Commons. In June, Ronald MacNeill, a prominent Unionist MP, picked up a copy of the House's standing orders from the ledge of the Speaker's chair and flung it at the first lord, cutting him in the forehead. Next day MacNeill apologized. Churchill assured him he hadn't minded at all, which was true; he was enjoying the battle, and if tempers on the other side grew frayed, he was the first to admit that his own remarks were incendiary. His treatment in Ulster, he said, was proof that Carson and Bonar Law, leader of the Tories in the House, had plotted war on the British army and had "even suggested that this process in Ireland should be accompanied by the lynching of His Majesty's Ministers." Captain James Craig, an Ulster MP, called him "contemptible." Winston replied: "If I valued the honourable Gentleman's opinion I might get angry." He enjoyed a studied insult, even when he was its victim, and chortled when he read that Lord Charles Beresford, during a Hyde Park rally, referred to him as a "Lilliput Napoleon — a man with an unbalanced mind, an egomaniac whose one absorbing thought is personal vindictiveness towards Ulster." He didn't even mind when feelings ran so high in the House that only a quick-thinking Labour

MP, who started everyone singing "Auld Lang Syne," prevented fist-fights on the floor.[185]

He was, however, troubled by talk of Belfast's gutters running red with British blood. Abuse was tolerable only up to a certain point. Carson passed it when he called him "Lord Randolph's renegade son, who wants to be handed down to posterity as the Belfast butcher who threatened to shoot down those who took his father's advice." Though his language was less blistering, Law went even farther. He said: "Ireland is two nations. The Ulster people will submit to no ascendancy, and I can imagine no lengths to which they might go in which they would not be supported by the overwhelming majority of the British people." This was an open invitation to revolt, from the man who would be prime minister in a Conservative government. Such speeches were fanning the flame of discord in northern Ireland. Protestant volunteers were already forming insurgent regiments. Law warned the House that Ulster might explode at any moment; if blood were shed, he said, the cabinet would be answerable for it. Winston retorted that "those who talk of revolution ought to be prepared for the guillotine." In a letter to *The Times* he said: "Mr Bonar Law and his lieutenant Sir Edward Carson have . . . incited the Orangemen to wage civil war. . . . All this talk of violence, of bullets and bayonets, of rebellion and civil war has come from one side alone." He wouldn't budge: "Whatever Ulster's rights may be, she cannot stand in the way of the whole of the rest of Ireland."[186]

One reason the Irish crisis grew is that it was given time to grow. Asquith introduced his Home Rule bill on April 11, 1912, two months after Churchill's Belfast speech, and the issue was still before the country in the summer of 1914. The House of Lords was responsible for the delay. The peers no longer possessed an absolute veto, but they retained some power to obstruct; if they stonewalled, as they did in this instance, they could force the House of Commons to pass a bill in three successive parliamentary sessions. As the seasons passed, the Orangemen's enmity hardened. For more than two years, Churchill later calculated, the question "absorbed nine-tenths of the political field." Meanwhile, he and his fellow ministers were struggling to find a compromise which would give Ireland both Home Rule and peace. His first proposals were naive. He saw the Transvaal constitution as a sound precedent, though it would be hard to imagine two breeds less alike than the Boers and the Irish. Lloyd George suggested a "referendum . . . each of the Ulster counties is to have the option of exclusion from the Home Rule Bill," which was equally impractical. The idea of partition was first mooted in June 1912, when two MPs introduced an amendment to the bill exempting four

Ulster counties from Home Rule. Carson, believing that "if Ulster were left out, Home Rule would be impossible," supported their measure in the hope of defeating the bill in its entirety.[187]

It was rejected, but the idea remained. On August 31 Churchill wrote John Redmond, the leader of the Irish Nationalists, that "something should be done to afford the characteristically Protestant and Orange counties the option of several years before acceding to an Irish Parliament." This was the first indication that he might be receptive to partition. At the time he thought of it as a temporary measure. With the Ulster Volunteers drilling, and Carson designated head of a "provisional government," he appealed for a fresh approach at Dundee in October 1913. By this time Home Rule had passed the Commons twice and been spurned twice by the Lords. Its enactment was now certain. Churchill, however, was looking beyond that, to the practical problems of enforcement. The Unionists' claim for special treatment, he said, was "very different from the claim to bar and defer Home Rule and block the path of the rest of Ireland." He added significantly: "Our bill is not unalterable." The Liberals could pass it without a single Tory vote, "but it will take more than one party to make it a lasting success. A settlement by agreement . . . would offer advantages far beyond anything now in sight. Peace is better than triumph provided it is peace with honour. . . . Only one thing would make it worth while or even possible to recast a measure on which so much depends: It is a very simple thing — good will." Redmond, afraid that his most powerful ally might be weakening, denounced the "two-nation theory" as "an abomination and a blasphemy." Carson was scornful. One solitary Conservative, F. E. Smith — who, astonishingly, remained close to Winston through all this — said he had "shown a grasp of those facts which are fundamental which none of his colleagues, at least in public, has displayed."[188]

If his motive in entering this donnybrook had been political — and surely that was among his reasons — he had chosen the wrong arena. To be sure, he was reestablishing his credentials as a Liberal, but the cost was prohibitive. By agreeing to be Asquith's chief spokesman on Home Rule, he had added his name to that long list of English public men who had intervened in the Irish question and emerged bloodied. Other members of Asquith's cabinet could speak out in support of Winston when his decision was popular and remain silent when it wasn't. This was even true of the prime minister. Eventually Asquith would have to commit himself, but in the interim he could leave the stump to Churchill. Moreover, Winston couldn't confine himself to polemics. He had to search for a solution, a hopeless task which was bound to antagonize partisans in both

Belfast and Dublin. Twice in the autumn of 1913 he conferred with Conservative leaders in the hope of finding middle ground, talking to Bonar Law at Balmoral in September, and then to Austen Chamberlain aboard the *Enchantress* in late November. Chamberlain's memorandum on their discussion, written immediately afterward, shows how far Churchill was prepared to go at that time to reach a settlement: "In answer to W's opening remark I said that I had assumed that . . . he was prepared to [exempt] Ulster. He replied: 'We have never excluded that possibility — never.' Of course Redmond hated it, but they were not absolutely bound to R. and he was not indispensable to them. They would not allow Ulster to veto Home Rule, but they had never excluded the possibility of separate treatment for Ulster. This was repeated more than once in the course of our talk."[189]

Winston was still not considering permanent partition. His papers leave no room for doubt on that point. He was merely contemplating a transition period for the northern counties. Yet it hardly seemed to matter. Neither side was interested in finding a middle course. Right or wrong, Ulster was preparing to fight. On September 12, 1912, Carson had drawn up a covenant, not against Home Rule for Ulster, but against any version of Home Rule, and a half-million Orangemen had signed it, some in their own blood:

> Being convinced in our consciences that Home Rule would be disastrous to the material well-being of Ulster as well as the whole of Ireland, subversive to our civil and religious freedoms, destructive of our citizenship, and perilous to the unity of the Empire, we whose names are undersigned, men of Ulster, loyal subjects of His Gracious Majesty King George V, humbly relying on the God whom our fathers in days of stress and trial confidently trusted, do hereby pledge ourselves in solemn Covenant throughout this our time of threatened calamity to stand by one another in defending for ourselves and our children our cherished position of equal citizenship in the United Kingdom, and in using all means which may be found necessary to defeat the present conspiracy to set up a Home Rule Parliament in Ireland. And in the event of such a Parliament being forced upon us we further solemnly and mutually pledge ourselves to refuse to recognize its authority. In sure confidence that God will defend the right we hereto subscribe our names. . . . God save the King.

Now, a year later, the deterioration of the situation was alarming. The month after the *Enchantress* conference, Belfast police reported that British army depots there might be raided. Carson publicly boasted that the soldiers would neither resist such raids nor fire on Orangemen. "The Army," he said, "are with us." General Henry Wilson, Seely's director of military operations, agreed; should the army be ordered to coerce Ulster, he said, there would be "wholesale defections." Law told the House: "If Ulster does resist by force, there are stronger influences than Parliamentary majorities . . . no Government would dare to use their troops to drive them out." Then, speaking to a massive Unionist rally at Blenheim, he declared: "I can imagine no length of resistance to which Ulster will go in which I shall not be ready to support them."[190]

Lloyd George warned: "We are confronted with the gravest issue raised in this country since the days of the Stuarts."[191] The signers of the Belfast Covenant had pledged armed resistance to the last man. And they had arms. In the early spring of 1914, a German lighter bearing 25,000 Mauser rifles and 2,500,000 rounds of ammunition had slipped out of Hamburg port and transshipped its cargo to a Norwegian tramp, the *Fanny.* Before Danish Customs officials could inspect the *Fanny* at the Kattegat, between Sweden and Denmark, the skipper had made a run for it and disappeared into the mists of the North Sea. Anchoring in a remote cove, the crew changed the steamer's appearance and renamed her the *Doreen.* Danish Customs having raised the alarm, Churchill had patrol boats searching these waters, but as the *Doreen* the renegade ship reached Yarmouth, then Lundy Island in Bristol Channel, and finally, on the night of April 19, Tuskar Rock off county Antrim in the Irish Sea. There she rendezvoused with the *Clydevalley,* an ancient collier black with coal dust and red with rust. The two masters lashed the hulls together and ran a single set of navigation lights as crewmen heaved the deadly crates from one hold to the other. On April 25 the *Clydevalley* groaned its way into Larne, the very harbor through which the Churchills had passed. Orangemen in the town had cut telephone wires and organized a convoy of trucks. Between 11:00 P.M. and 2:30 A.M. volunteers sweating under rigged lights lugged the guns and ammunition from the collier to waiting trucks. By dawn they had fanned out all over northern Ireland. Now, if Home Rule were forced upon them, they could field an army.

By the end of the month fifty thousand Orangemen, aged seventeen to sixty-five, had joined the Ulster Volunteer Force. Their morale was excellent, and they were superbly led. England's best generals were backing them. Kitchener belonged to the Protestant Ascendancy; so did Lord Roberts. Kitchener's duties in the Middle East ruled him out, but Roberts declined the UVF command only because, at eighty-five, he was too old. More and more one heard the name of General Henry Wilson, who had been appointed Britain's chief of military operations despite the fact that as an Ulsterman he had signed the covenant. Tall, lanky, with a look of despondent fidelity which was entirely misleading, Wilson was one of many establishmentarians whose names gave the incipient revolt an aura of respectability. Others included Lord Rothschild, Edward Elgar of "Land of Hope and Glory," and Rudyard Kipling. Kipling had contributed £30,000 to the UVF and published a poem honoring it — not in *The Times,* which supported Home Rule, but in the archconservative *Morning Post:*

The blood our fathers spilt,
Our love, our toils, our pains,
Are counted us for guilt,
And only bind our chains.
Before an Empire's eyes,
The traitor claims his price.
What need of further lies?
We are the sacrifice.

Even the King had doubts about using force against the Orangemen. He asked Bonar Law: "Will it be wise, will it be fair to the Sovereign as head of the Army, to subject the discipline and indeed the loyalty of his troops to such a strain?" Law, a Canadian who had become an adopted Orangeman, exploited the King's discomfort. At stake, he told the monarch, was not merely Ulster, but the entire British Empire. Home Rule would be the thin end of the wedge for His Majesty's fractious subjects all over the world. He should refuse to recognize it, whatever Parliament did. Law said: "You will save the Empire by your example."[192]

Meanwhile, the tale of the twenty-five thousand smuggled Mausers had leaked out. The possibility of a Belfast-Berlin collaboration seemed very real, and was discussed in the House. Liberal back-benchers demanded prosecution of Orangemen negotiating with the Germans. Asquith refused; he was vacillating. Churchill spoke out: "We have," he said, "been confronted with an avowed conspiracy to defy Parliament and the law, leaving a great army practising preparations for rebellion and for the setting up of a provisional Government, which would be an outrage against the realm and the Empire." England, he said, would not be intimidated by plots to raise a revolt "greater than the police could cope with."[193] He was not speaking only to Belfast; Redmond and his fellow Irish Nationalists had been desperately worried about the response to all this among their own people in the south, and their nightmares were being realized. Riots were reported in Dublin. Catholic youths were flocking to join the Irish Nationalist Volunteers. Irish MPs who were counselors of moderation were losing their followers. In 1913 a militant working-class movement had forged a tight alliance with the Sinn Féin, who regarded themselves as Irishmen first and last and gentlemen never, and wearers of the green were turning to these champions of violence.

By March 1914, with final passage of the Home Rule bill less than two months away, the strain was becoming insupportable. Asquith, with Redmond's reluctant consent, promised that Ulster would be permitted to vote itself out of Home Rule for six years, or until two successive general elections had been held. Carson angrily rejected this as "a sentence of death with a stay of execution for six years." Churchill decided to take his gloves off. He had been conciliatory at Dundee. Now he would swing over to the attack. At Bradford on March 14 he called Bonar Law "a public danger seeking to terrorize the Government and to force his way into the Councils of his Sovereign" by exploiting the issue for partisan purposes. "Behind every strident sentence which he rasps out," he said, "you can always hear the whisper . . . 'Ulster is our best card; it is our only card.' " That was fair. The Tories had asked for it. But then, carried away by his own rhetoric, he blundered, salting the Unionists' wounds with sarcasm. Having raised troops, he said, Ulster seemed anxious for battle "so that her volunteers could assert themselves." But the proposed moratorium would deprive them of that test. He put words in their mouths: " 'Now the Government have had the incredible meanness to postpone all possible provocation for six long years.' " Bitterly he commented: "Coercion for four-fifths of Ireland is a healthful, exhilarating, salutary exercise, but lay a finger on the Tory fifth — sacrilege, tyranny, murder!" The Liberals were not cowed, he said: "There are worse things than bloodshed. . . . We are not going to have the realm of Britain sunk to the condition of the Republic of Mexico." The issue, for him, was "whether civil and Parliamentary government in these realms is to be beaten down by the menace of armed force." If Orangemen would extend the hand of friendship, it would be eagerly clasped by Liberals and Irish Nationalists, but "if every effort to meet their views is only to be used as a means of breaking down Home Rule . . . if the civil and Parliamentary systems are to be brought to the crude challenge of force . . . then I can only say to you: Let us go forward and put these grave matters to the proof." Lord Fisher wrote him: "I should say it's probably the best speech you ever made." But *The Times* commented the next day that, having carried his naval estimates over the protests of rank-and-file Liberals, he "seemed to think it necessary to show that on occasion he could shout defiance with the rest," and another critic called his remarks redolent of "cheap champagne made of gooseberry juice and vitriol, exhilarating at the moment but nauseating sooner or later."[194]

It was quickly forgotten, for within a week Churchill found himself in deep trouble. He and Seely were worried about the loyalty of British soldiers in Ireland. A high proportion of them were natives of Ulster. Moreover, they were badly deployed for the approaching climax; of the twenty-three thousand regulars on the island, only nine thousand were stationed in the north. Mutinous mutters had met proposals for a redistribution which would transfer troops billeted on the Curragh plain, outside Dublin, to Belfast. Even if the men remained subordinate, it was reported, Ulster officials of the Great Northern Railway might refuse to carry them northward. However, it was feasible to send them up by sea. Encouraged by Lloyd George, the two service ministers, with the approval of Asquith and the King, decided to take precautionary steps. Guards at the Ulster arms depots of Armagh, Omagh, Enniskillen, and Carrickfergus were doubled. Winston signaled the vice admiral commanding his Third Battle Squadron: "Admiralty, 19 March 1914. Secret. Proceed at once at ordinary speed to Lamlash. . . . Acknowledge and report dates of arrival. WSC." This would put eight battleships, a cruiser, and three destroyers in Irish waters.[195]

The warships never reached the North Channel. General Henry Wilson sent word of their destination to Brigadier General Hubert Gough, commander of the Curragh garrison. Gough resigned his commission, whereupon fifty-seven of his seventy officers resigned, whereupon Sir John French, the chief of the Imperial General Staff, also resigned. The prime minister faced an army revolt. He countermanded Churchill's orders and canceled Seely's plans to reinforce Ulster. That wasn't enough for Gough. He sent Asquith a message through Wilson: "In the event of the present Home Rule Bill becoming law, can we be called upon to enforce it under the expression of maintaining law and order?" To make certain that his position was understood, he came to London and demanded assurances in writing. He got them. The prime minister wrote that it had all been "a misunderstanding"; that, though His Majesty's government had the right to employ crown forces anywhere, it had "no intention of taking advantage of this right to crush political opposition to the policy or principles of the Home Rule Bill." Gough and his officers then withdrew their resignations. Timothy M. Healy, an Irish Nationalist MP, concluded: "Asquith threw over Churchill, Seely and Lloyd George and refused to back up their actions."[196]

Wilson leaked all this to Bonar Law, and there was a storm in the House. The Tory press was jubilant over Asquith's "complete surrender"; the Liberals and Irish Nationalists were furious. Scapegoats were needed, so Seely and his two chief advisers resigned. The prime minister — who had initialed all the military arrangements — claimed ignorance of them. That left the first lord of the Admiralty to face the music. It would seem that twenty-five thousand rifles in the hands of Orangemen justified precautions of some sort, but the Tories believed that he had been trying to goad the Ulster Volunteers into open rebellion. One Conservative MP accused him of hatching a "plot" designed to create an excuse for an "Ulster pogrom." Balfour added scathingly: "There is one character disgusting to every policeman and which even the meanest criminal thinks inferior to himself in point of morals, and that character is the *agent provocateur.*"[197]

On April 28 Churchill blazed back: "What we are now witnessing in the House is uncommonly like a vote of censure by the criminal classes upon the police." A Tory interjected: "You have not arrested them." He replied: "Is that the complaint — that we have been too lenient?" He declared that the Conservatives, "the party of the comfortable, the wealthy . . . who have most to gain by the continuance of the existing social order," were now "committed to a policy of armed violence and utter defiance of lawfully constituted authority . . . to tampering with the discipline of the Army and the Navy . . . to overpowering police, coastguards and Customs officials . . . to smuggling in arms by moonlight." If this was an example of "how much they care for law, how much they value order when it stands in the way of anything they like," what would be the impact on England's impoverished millions, on "the great audiences that watch in India," on the Germans who believed that Britain was paralyzed by factions "and need not be taken into account as a factor in the European situation?" He said: "I wish to make it perfectly clear that if rebellion comes we shall put it down, and if it comes to civil war, we shall do our best to conquer in the civil war. But there will be neither rebellion nor civil war unless it is of your making."[198]

At this point he altered his tone dramatically and ended on a propitiatory note. He appealed directly to Carson: "The right honourable Gentleman . . . is running great risks in strife. Why will he not run some risk for peace? The key is in his hands now. Why cannot the right honourable and learned Gentleman say boldly: 'Give me the Amendments to this Home Rule Bill which I ask for, to safeguard the dignity and the interests of Protestant Ulster, and I in return will use all my influence and good will to make Ireland an integral unit in a federal system'?" The House was stirred. Balfour, while describing Churchill's earlier remarks as "an outburst of demagogic rhetoric," declared that he was "heartily in sympathy with the First Lord's proposal," and Carson went so far as to say that he was "not very far from the First Lord." Negotiations were reopened. Liberals and Irish Nationalists, who insisted that northern Ireland must yield, protested angrily. Winston's position in the party was still shaky; he wrote Clementine that his plea for a truce was "the biggest risk I have taken." His cabinet colleagues, generous with their "hear, hears" when he had taken the offensive, had sat on their hands when he offered Carson an olive branch.[199]

But the negotiations stalled and were again discontinued. The general feeling was that it was too late for one man to halt the drift toward fratricide. Churchill himself said wearily, "A little red blood had got to flow," though he quickly added: "We shall give no provocation. The Ulstermen will have no excuse, and we think that public opinion will not support them if they wantonly attack." On May 26 the Home Rule bill passed for the third and last time. Officially it was now law. The possibility of enforcing it, however, was as remote as ever. Each side was still waiting for the other to shoot first. On July 20 the King intervened, summoning an all-party conference to Buckingham Palace. The Speaker of the House presided as the delegates wrangled for four days. Winston wrote Clementine: "We are to go ahead with the Amending Bill, abolishing the time limit and letting any Ulster county vote itself out if it chooses. The [southern] Irish acquiesced in this reluctantly. We must judge further events in Ulster when they occur."[200]

Asquith's cabinet met on the afternoon of Friday, July 24, 1914, to discuss the final conclusions of the King's conference. The report was sterile; absolutely nothing had been accomplished. It was at this point that the Irish issue, foremost in everyone's mind, so certain to burst into flames at any moment, was unexpectedly deferred, destined not to reemerge for years, by which time the whole cast of characters would have changed. The ministers were about to break up when Grey began reading in quiet, grave tones a document which had just been sent in to him from the Foreign Office. It was an Austrian note to Serbia. Churchill was very tired; several minutes passed before he could disengage his mind from the tedium which had just ended. Gradually the phrases and sentences began to take shape and meaning. The foreign secretary was reading an ultimatum. Winston had never heard anything like it. He did not see how any country could accept it, or how any acceptance, however abject, could satisfy the government which had sent it. He later recalled: "The parishes of Fermanagh and Tyrone faded back into the mists and squalls of Ireland, and a strange light began immediately, but by perceptible gradations, to fall and grow upon the map of Europe."[201]

Churchill later blamed three men for the outbreak of the Great War: the Serb assassin, the Austrian foreign minister who had written that first ultimatum, and the kaiser, who could have stopped the chain reaction of governments bound by military alliances. But the initial culprit was an incompetent chauffeur whose name has not survived. On June 28, 1914, four weeks before the delivery of the fateful note to Serbia, Austrian Archduke Franz Ferdinand and his morganatic wife, Sophie, had been riding through the Bosnian capital of Sarajevo when the driver took a wrong turn. Realizing his mistake, he came to a dead halt — right in front of a Serbian fanatic armed with a revolver. Franz Ferdinand and Sophie were shot dead on the spot. In Vienna the toils of vengeance, like everything else in the Austro-Hungarian Empire, moved very slowly. But they were moving. Meanwhile, Britain stood aside. There was every reason to believe Britain would remain there. It had nothing at stake. Grey's "moral obligation," assumed eight years earlier, had been given privately and was not binding. Britain's only commitment on the Continent was to defend Belgian independence, which hardly seemed threatened then, and even that was vague. Winston didn't care for the Belgians; he thought their behavior in the Congo disgraceful. At the Admiralty he lunched with Kitchener, on leave from Egypt and soon to be Seely's successor at the War Office. Both suspected the existence of a secret agreement between Brussels and Berlin which would permit German troops to cross Belgium on their way to France. For England, they agreed, such an "invasion" would be an inadequate casus belli. But it was all very speculative, very remote, quite nebulous.

The Admiralty's trial mobilization had begun, as scheduled, in the middle of July, over two weeks after the Sarajevo murders. The grand review was held on July 18. Churchill called it "incomparably the greatest assemblage of naval power ever witnessed in the world" — 223 battleships, armored cruisers, light cruisers, destroyers, minesweepers, and submarines parading past the royal yacht and the *Enchantress* at Spithead, with the King and his first lord taking the salute. Normally, the next step would have been demobilization of all three fleets, accompanied by liberty for the regular tars and tickets home for the reservists. It wasn't taken. Churchill, concerned about rumors from central Europe, published an Admiralty notice in the newspapers of July 20: "Orders have been given to the First Fleet, which is concentrated at Portland, not to disperse for naval leave at the present. All vessels of the Second Fleet are remaining at their home ports in proximity to their balance crews." Yet he was confident that negotiations would settle the differences between Vienna and Belgrade. In a letter to Grey two days later, drawing an analogy between that problem and the more urgent situation in Ulster, he wrote that if the question were how to uphold British interests on the Continent, "you wd proceed by two stages. First you wd labour to stop Austria & Russia going to war: second, if that failed, you wd try to prevent England, France, Germany & Italy being drawn in." In either instance, mediation was the solution. The following day Lloyd George, who concurred, assured the House that "civilization" would have no difficulty in regulating disputes which arose between nations, by means of "some sane and well-ordered arbitrament."[202]

After studying the note Grey had read to the cabinet, however, Churchill wrote Clementine: "Europe is trembling on the verge of a general war, the Austrian ultimatum to Servia [sic] being the most insolent document of its kind ever devised." It was in fact remarkable. Serbia was required to suppress all criticism of Austria-Hungary in newspapers, magazines, societies, and schools; Serbian officials and teachers who had spoken unfavorably of Austrians were to be dismissed; certain Serbs known to be unfriendly to Austria were to be arrested at once; and Austrian officers were to enter Serbia to enforce all these demands and investigate the Sarajevo assassinations. Belgrade must reply to this ultimatum within forty-eight hours. A request for an extension was denied. In Vienna the foreign minister acknowledged that the tone of the note was "such that we must reckon on the probability of war."[203]

"Happily," Asquith wrote the King, "there seems to be no reason why we should be anything more than spectators." Churchill shared his view. At Overstrand, on the Norfolk coast, he had rented a little holiday house called Pear Tree Cottage for Clementine and the children — Goonie Churchill and her two young sons had taken nearby Beehive Cottage — and Friday evening he postponed an Admiralty meeting which had been scheduled for Saturday morning, preferring to spend the weekend at the shore. He wrote: "My darling one, I have managed to put off my naval conference and am coming to you & the kittens tomorrow by the 1 o'clock train." Before he left London, good news arrived: Serbia had accepted all demands upon it except the supervision of compliance by Austrian officers, and Belgrade offered to submit that question to the Hague Court. Even the kaiser believed this reply had removed "every reason for war." Winston told Prince Louis to run the Admiralty in his absence; he would stay in touch by phone. On the beach he organized the children, distributed buckets and spades, and directed them while they built

Europe, 1914
0 100 200 300 400 500
MILES
0 100 200 300 400 500
KILOMETERS
ATLANTIC
OCEAN
NORWAY
Christiania
SWEDEN
Stockholm
FINLAND
St. Petersburg
SCAPA FLOW
NORTH
SEA
SCOTLAND
Edinburgh
GREAT
BRITAIN
IRELAND
Dublin
WALES
Cardiff
ENGLAND
London
DENMARK
Copenhagen
BALTIC SEA
Tannenberg
Elbe River
Berlin
Warsaw
POLAND
R U S S I A
NETHERLANDS
Amsterdam
BELGIUM
Brussels
LUXEMBOURG
LORRAINE
ALSACE
G E R M A N Y
Prague
CARPATHIAN
MOUNTAINS
Paris
Danube River
Vienna
Budapest
Nikolayev
Odessa
Sevastopol
SWITZERLAND
AUSTRIA-HUNGARY
Piave R.
Venice
FRANCE
RUMANIA
Bucharest
I T A L Y
Sarajevo
Belgrade
SERBIA
BULGARIA
MONTE-
NEGRO
ADRIATIC SEA
ALBANIA
Constantinople
OTTOMAN EMPIRE
(TURKEY)
DARDANELLES
GREECE
AEGEAN SEA
Athens
CORSICA
Rome
Madrid
Lisbon
PORTUGAL
SPAIN
BALEARIC
ISLANDS
SARDINIA
MEDITERRANEAN
SICILY
SEA
CYPRUS
Nicosia
10°
0°
10°
20°
40°
50°
40°
10°
20°
30°

a sand castle against the rising tide. The surf leveled it. As he remembered later: "We dammed the little rivulets which trickled down to the sea as the tide went out. It was a very beautiful day. The North Sea sparkled to a far horizon."[204]

Pear Tree Cottage had no telephone, but their nearest neighbor, Sir Edgar Speyer, a rich German Jew, had offered the use of his. It was here, at noon on Sunday, that Churchill heard the latest development from Prince Louis. Vienna had declared the Serbian response unsatisfactory, severed diplomatic relations with Belgrade, and ordered partial mobilization against the Serbs — who had already mobilized their army. Winston was on the next London train. There newsboys were hawking extras; Vienna had "burst into a frenzy of delight, vast crowds parading in the streets and singing patriotic songs." At the Admiralty he learned that the first sea lord had anticipated him; the Third Fleet had completed its test mobilization and was scheduled to disperse, but Prince Louis had ordered it to remain ready for battle, and at 4:05 P.M. he had telegraphed: "Admiralty to C in C Home Fleets. Decypher. No ships of First Fleet or Flotillas are to leave Portland until further orders. Acknowledge." Churchill approved and began a ten-day shuttle between his office, Whitehall, No. 10, and Admiralty House, catching sleep in brief naps. Other ministers grew wan. He thrived.[205]

The following morning, Monday, July 27, the cabinet met for the first discussion of the crisis on the Continent. Clearly the Austrians meant to invade Serbia. That might bring in Russia, the Serbs' ally, which might bring in Germany, Austria's ally, which might bring in France, Russia's ally. The kaiser, aware of the threat on his western frontier, might launch a preemptive strike into northern France. If that happened, the Liberal militants thought, England might become involved. A majority of the ministers disagreed. The Entente Cordiale of 1904 was not binding, they pointed out; it was merely "a sentimental liaison." Grey's assurance to the French had been unofficial. In an unpublished note Churchill wrote afterward: "The Cabinet was absolutely against war and would never have agreed to being committed to war at this moment." A message arrived from Pear Tree Cottage: "Goodnight my Dearest One. I trust the news may be better tomorrow. Surely every hour of delay must make the forces of peace more powerful. It would be a wicked war." Winston had no intention of making it wickeder by being caught off guard. That night he telegraphed all British fleets, squadrons, and flotillas, scattered over five oceans: "European political situation makes war between Triple Alliance and Triple Entente Powers by no means impossible. This is *not* the Warning Telegram but be prepared to shadow possible hostile men-of-war. . . . Measure is purely precautionary. The utmost secrecy is to be observed and no unnecessary person is to be informed."[206]

Austria-Hungary declared war on Tuesday, July 28, and bombed Belgrade. Both Winston and Prince Louis were worried about the position of the First Fleet, now anchored off the Isle of Wight. It was vulnerable there, and a navy's primary duty, as Mahan had written, was to remain "a fleet in being"; Churchill pointed out that the admiral commanding the Home Fleet was the only man in Europe who could "lose the war in the course of an afternoon." The ships' war station was Scottish waters, where they would be secure and a deterrent to any sudden German attack, at the same time serving notice that England was prepared. Yet Winston "feared to bring this matter before the Cabinet," he wrote, "lest it should be mistakenly considered a provocative action likely to damage the chances of peace." Instead, he went to No. 10 and told Asquith he was going to act on his own authority. The prime minister, he recalled, "looked at me with a hard stare and gave a sort of grunt. I did not require anything else." That night, on his instructions, an eighteen-mile-long procession of darkened ships steamed through the Strait of Dover. Dawn found the battleships in Scapa Flow and the battle cruisers off Rosyth, in the Firth of Forth. "A surprise torpedo attack," wrote Winston, was "at any rate one nightmare gone forever."[207]

By Wednesday both Grey and Churchill had recommended to the cabinet, which now met daily, that England take the lead in proposing a conference of great powers to avert catastrophe. Germany had the Continent's strongest army, so Berlin was approached first. The kaiser wouldn't discuss it. Until now Winston had believed that peace was possible; Albert Ballin's biographer describes how, when he took leave of Ballin, Churchill "implored him, almost with tears in his eyes, not to go to war." But Thursday morning, when seventy-three-year-old Lord Fisher called at the Admiralty to see what was happening, he found the first lord in high spirits, persuading Asquith to approve the warning telegram to all warships, supervising the general alert, and swiftly retiring senior officers he felt were unfit for war service. His most controversial move, applauded by Fisher but resented by almost every other flag officer, was the replacement of Sir George Callaghan, commander in chief of the Home Fleet, by Sir John Jellicoe. Callaghan was sixty-one and in robust health. David Beatty told Churchill that dismissing him was a mistake, and Jellicoe himself sent Winston six telegrams, begging him to change his mind. He wouldn't do it. He was very sure of himself, making crucial decisions every hour and feeling remarkably euphoric. To Clementine he wrote: "The preparations have a hideous fascination for me. I pray to God to forgive me for such fearful moods of levity. Yet I wd do my best for peace, & nothing would induce me wrongfully to strike the blow."[208]

But the blow, he decided Friday, must be struck. That afternoon Grey cabled Paris and Berlin, asking for formal assurances that they would respect Belgium's neutrality "so long as no other power violates it." France agreed; Germany did not reply. That was enough for Winston. Asquith and Kitchener joined him for lunch at the Admiralty. He listened attentively when Kitchener argued that "if we don't back France when she is in real danger, we shall never . . . exercise real power again." Asquith nodded in agreement. The prime minister still did not reflect the opinion of his cabinet, however. Churchill and Grey were with him — Grey intimated he would resign if they abandoned France — but the rest remained adamant. Churchill asked the cabinet to approve the final steps in naval mobilization and was refused. The strongest voice for British neutrality was Lloyd George, who had reconsidered his impulsive response to the Agadir incident three years earlier. Lord Hugh Cecil, the best man at Winston's wedding, was one of the few Tories who agreed with George. England, they said, should remain aloof. After the meeting Churchill wrote "My dear Linky" that "divergent views are certainly to be expected in the grt issues now afoot. But you will be wrong if you suppose that this country will be committed to any war in wh its profound national interests — among wh I include its honour — are not clearly engaged." In a discreet letter to Arthur Ponsonby that same afternoon he revealed where he thought Britain's honor lay. "Balkan quarrels are no vital concern of ours," he wrote. "But the march of events is sinister. The extension of the conflict by a German attack upon France or Belgium wd raise other issues." And, in a third note, to Lord Robert Cecil, Linky's brother: "If we allowed Belgian neutrality to be trampled down by Germany without exerting ourselves to aid France we shd be in a very melancholy position both in regard to our interests & our honour."[209]

At the Admiralty he anxiously watched the moving flags and pins on his chart of the Mediterranean, now the scene of many French troop movements. The Germans had two capital ships there: the 23,000-ton battle cruiser *Goeben* and the 4,500-ton light cruiser *Breslau*. The *Goeben*, the size of a dreadnought, with a speed of 27.8 knots and immense firepower, "would easily be able," Winston had noted, "to avoid the French battle squadrons and brushing aside or outstripping their cruisers, break in upon the transports and sink one after another of these vessels crammed with soldiers." He notified his Mediterranean commander, Admiral Sir Berkeley Milne, that his first mission in the event of war would be to shield French troopships "by covering and if possible bringing into action individual fast German ships, particularly *Goeben.*" Milne was reminded that "the speed of your Squadrons is sufficient to enable you to choose your moment." The first lord's tone left no doubt; if the admiral failed, his career would be over. Churchill could put it no stronger than that. If the *Goeben* survived he could not be blamed.[210]

The controversy over two Turkish warships was, however, another matter. He mentioned it casually at the end of a letter to Clementine, written that Friday evening after he had dined with Asquith. "There is still hope although the clouds are blacker & blacker," he began. "Germany is realising I think how great are the forces against her & is trying tardily to restrain her idiot ally. We are all working to soothe Russia. But everybody is preparing swiftly for war and at any moment now the stroke may fall. We are ready." A maelstrom had enveloped London's financial markets: "The city has simply broken into chaos. The world's credit system is virtually suspended. You cannot sell stocks & shares. Quite soon it will not perhaps be possible to cash a cheque. Prices of goods are rising to panic levels." That reminded him of the July expenses for Pear Tree; he thought £175 too high and wanted to see the bills. Almost as an afterthought he mentioned that "I am forcibly detaining the 2 Turkish Dreadnoughts wh are ready." It was one of the most fateful sentences written in that fateful year.[211]

Turkey had joined no alliance. In 1911 its leaders had wanted to ally themselves with the British Empire, but Churchill, with the arrogance of his class in that time, had replied that they had ideas above their station. He had merely advised them not to alienate Britain, which "alone among European states . . . retains supremacy of the sea." But the vigorous Young Turks, tired of hearing the Ottoman Empire scorned as the "Sick Man" of Europe, had raised £6,000,000 by popular subscription, with every Anatolian peasant contributing at least one coin, and made a down payment for two battleships, to be built in British shipyards and armed with 13.5-inch guns. Both vessels were ready by July; they had been christened the *Sultan Osman* and the *Reshadieh;* officers and sailors from Constantinople were on hand to take delivery. Now, at 12:30 A.M. on the last day of the month, Churchill wrote the King that he had "taken the responsibility" of forbidding their departure. The Turkish commander was told his ships had been "requisitioned." When he threatened to lead his men aboard, Churchill ordered that they be repelled "by armed force if necessary." The Turkish naval minister protested. International law was moot on this point, but to the Turks it was outright piracy. Grey, as imperious as Winston, responded that England had appropriated the vessels to meet its "own needs in this crisis." Applications for indemnification would be given "due consideration," but there was no offer of compensation. The warships were summarily rechristened the *Agincourt* and the *Erin.* Turkey then turned to Germany, which eagerly grasped its hand. On August 2 the two countries signed a secret agreement. Churchill would write: "Ah! foolish-diligent Germans, working so hard, thinking so deeply, marching and counter-marching on the parade grounds of the Fatherland . . . how many bulwarks to your peace and glory did you not, with your own hands, successively tear down!" But in this case it was the diligent Churchill, in an almost unbelievable act, who tore down what could have been a British bulwark and thereby set the stage for a disaster whose chief victim would be he himself.[212]

Russia was mobilizing against Austria-Hungary. Germany, as Austria's ally, therefore proclaimed a "threatening state of war." At midnight on Thursday, July 30, the kaiser demanded the Russians demobilize at once, giving them twenty-four hours to stop and "make us a distinct declaration to that effect." In England it was Bank Holiday Weekend. Saturday morning the governor of the Bank of England called on Lloyd George with the message that the City was "totally opposed to our intervening" in the coming conflict. In the Foreign Office, Grey was reluctantly informing the French ambassador, Paul Cambon, that thus far the dispute on the Continent had been "of no interest" to England, though "Belgian neutrality might become a factor." Asquith wrote in his diary: "Of course everybody longs to stand aside."[213]

Not everybody. His first lord of the Admiralty now relished the prospect of a fight — Jennie wrote Leonie that he now thought war "inevitable" — and the cabinet meeting that day was, as a consequence, tumultuous. Sir Maurice Hankey later wrote: "Winston Churchill was a man of a totally different type from all his colleagues. He had a real zest for war. If war there must needs be, he at least could enjoy it." Asquith described him in that session as "very bellicose. . . . It is no exaggeration to say that Winston occupied at least half the time." When he wasn't talking, he was passing notes to Lloyd George, trying to persuade him to change his mind. Churchill wanted the cabinet to authorize full mobilization of the navy, including a call-up of all naval reserves. After what one minister called "a sharp discussion," he was refused on the ground that such a move might, under the circumstances, be considered incendiary. Grey suggested that preliminary plans be drawn up for the dispatch of an expeditionary force to France. He, too, was turned down.[214]

Of the eighteen ministers present, twelve went on record as being opposed to any support of France. Morley, John Burns, Sir John Simon, and Lewis Harcourt threatened to resign if they were overruled. Because of his seniority, Morley was their acknowledged leader, but the most vociferous pacifist was Lloyd George. George wasn't even sure he would fight over Belgium. If the Germans took the direct route to France, he said, they would only cross a corner of the little country; it would just be a "little violation." (Berlin would soon describe its earlier guarantee of Belgian neutrality as "a scrap of paper.") Liberal back-benchers were even more vehement. That afternoon, in an informal caucus, they voted four to one for neutrality, "whatever happens in Belgium or elsewhere." When news of the vacillation at No. 10 reached Printing House Square, the editor of *The Times* wrote his aunts: "Saturday was a black day for everyone who knew what was going on — more than half the Cabinet rotten and every prospect of a complete schism or a disastrous or dishonouring refusal to help France. . . . Winston has really done more than anyone else to save the situation." But in doing it he was once more alienating members of his party, who had, Hankey wrote his wife, "not the smallest enthusiasm for war."[215]

Churchill had invited Bonar Law and Grey to join him for dinner that Saturday evening. The Tory leader declined and Grey then withdrew, so Winston dined alone in Admiralty House. At 9:30 P.M. F. E. Smith and Max Aitken dropped in; two Admiralty officials joined them, and they sat down to bridge, Aitken being odd man out. The cards had just been dealt when a messenger arrived with a large red dispatch box. Winston produced his key, opened it, and drew out a single sheet of paper bearing six words: "Germany has declared war against Russia." Showing it to the others, he gave Aitken his cards and rang for a servant to bring him a lounge coat. He was going to No. 10. Aitken observed: "He left the room quickly. . . . He was not depressed; he was not elated; he was not surprised. . . . Certainly he exhibited no fear or uneasiness. Neither did he show any signs of joy. He went straight out like a man going to a well-accustomed job."[216]

In Downing Street he told Asquith that he intended to issue an immediate order for full naval mobilization: summoning forty thousand reservists to the colors to man the Third Fleet, putting all dockyards on a war footing, and directing cruiser squadrons and armed auxiliaries to police the world's trade routes. That was precisely what the cabinet had forbidden him to do. Once more the prime minister gave silent consent. In Churchill's words, he "simply sat and looked at me and said no more. No doubt he felt himself bound by the morning's decision of the Cabinet. I certainly, however, sustained the impression that he would not put out a finger to stop me. I then walked back to the Admiralty and gave the order." On the way he met Grey, who said: "I have just done a very important thing. I have told Cambon that we shall not allow the German fleet to come into the Channel." At 1:00 A.M., Winston wrote Clementine: "Cat-dear, it is all up. Germany has quenched the last hopes of peace by declaring war on Russia, & the declaration against France is momentarily expected." He knew that she, like most Liberals, was praying for peace. "I profoundly understand your views," he continued. "But the world is gone mad — & we must look after ourselves — & our friends. . . . Sweet Kat — my tender love — Your devoted W." He added a postcript: "Kiss the kittens."[217]

Years later, Churchill pointed out to Aitken that "the mobilization was actually ordered against Cabinet decision and without legal authority." On Sunday Asquith's ministers faced a hard choice. Either they ratified the actions taken by the first lord and the foreign secretary during the night, or the government fell. Reluctantly, they gave their approval, though Grey was instructed to tell the French that no British troops could be sent across the Channel. Thus England, carrying the whole Empire with it, slowly tilted toward France. No overt action was authorized — the British fleet would intervene only if the Germans tried to attack France by sea — but the Liberal rift nevertheless deepened. Morley and Burns resigned; Lloyd George abstained. Asquith said: "We are on the brink of a split." After they broke up, Winston, with a careless disregard for party loyalty, approached F. E. Smith and said the Liberals were seriously divided. Would the Conservatives consider the formation of a coalition government? F.E. sounded out Bonar Law, who sensibly replied that any such proposal should come from the prime minister. He did, however, empower F.E. to tell Churchill that the overwhelming majority of Tory MPs favored backing France to the hilt.[218]

"Urgent. German ship *Goeben* at Taranto," read a telegram to Winston from the British consul in that Italian seaport. Churchill instantly wired Milne: "*Goeben* must be shadowed by two battle cruisers." But the admiral bungled the job; the German ship reached Messina a few hours after Italy's declaration of neutrality, fueled, and steamed westward toward Turkey. Everything now was being cut very fine. By a little maneuvering the kaiser could still have kept England out of the war. Instead, he declared war on France on Monday and informed the Belgians that German troops would enter their country within twelve hours. That turned Lloyd George around. He decided that British public opinion wouldn't stand for it. If the Germans refused to withdraw their threat to Belgium, he said, England must fight. There were more resignations from the cabinet, and Morley bitterly accused George of succumbing to "the influence of the splendid condottiere at the Admiralty," but Redmond guaranteed the support of the Irish Nationalists, and when the prime minister, chancellor, foreign secretary, and first lord entered the House, they received a standing ovation. Pale and haggard, Grey declared that if England deserted Belgium, "we should, I believe, sacrifice our respect and good name and reputation before the world." As they left the Treasury Bench together, Churchill asked him, "What happens now?" "Now," Grey replied, "we shall send them an ultimatum to stop the invasion of Belgium within twenty-four hours." Back in the House the member for Burnley, Philip Morrell, rose to protest the abandonment of neutrality. He was drowned out by shouts of "Sit down! Sit down!" Morrell's wife, Lady Ottoline, and her lover, Bertrand Russell, glumly walked the streets of Bloomsbury, trying to console each other. Most other Bloomsbury intellectuals were despondent. Lytton Strachey was an exception. "God has put us on an island and Winston has given us a navy," he said. "It would be absurd to neglect those advantages." The most prescient remark, oddly, came from Grey, that elegant, childless widower who had done more than anyone else to commit Britain's youth. Standing at a window with a friend that evening, watching the street-lamps being lit, he said: "The lamps are going out all over Europe. We shall not see them lit again in our lifetime." It was an epitaph with special application to 750,000 English boys, children only yesterday, soon to be slain in battle:[219]

For we are very lucky, with a lamp before the door
And Leerie stops to light it as he lights so many more;
And O! before you hurry by with ladder and with light,
O Leerie, see a little child and nod to him tonight!

Thus the rush of cataclysmic events came down to Tuesday, August 4, 1914, when at midnight Berlin time — 11:00 P.M. in London — Grey's ultimatum to Germany would expire. In Pear Tree Cottage, Clementine, troubled by the peremptory retiring of Admiral Callaghan, was writing her husband, begging him to consider "the deep wound in an old man's heart. . . . *Please* see him yourself & take him by the hand and (additional) offer him a seat on the Board, or if this is impossible give him *some* advisory position at the Admiralty. . . . Don't think this is a trivial matter. At this moment you want everyone's heart & soul." It was excellent advice; Winston had made altogether too many enemies, some on matters of principle but others through sheer thoughtlessness, and the moment was rapidly approaching when he would need every friend he could find. That Tuesday was not the day to start making them, however. There wasn't time. He was alerting the captains of all British merchant ships, which flew the red ensign, and he was engrossed in the movements of the *Goeben.* Two British warships had sighted her at 9:30 A.M. He wired: "Very good. Hold her. War imminent." He wanted to attack at once. "Winston with all his war paint on," Asquith wrote Clementine's cousin, the beautiful, worldly young Venetia Stanley, with whom he was infatuated, "is longing for a sea fight to sink the *Goeben.*" The prime minister had no objection, but the cabinet vetoed the firing of a single shot before the expiration of Grey's deadline. Prince Louis pleaded with Churchill to give the British gunners a green light before dusk, but the first lord felt he had been insubordinate enough. Night fell and the enemy battle cruiser escaped.[220]

Winston dined at Admiralty House with his mother and brother. Heavy fighting was reported in Belgium. Berlin had ignored Grey's note. The largest human event since the French Revolution was now imminent. The last minutes of peace were ticking away, and vanishing with them, though no one knew it, was England's century of security and supremacy — its "intolerable hegemony" in world affairs, as the German Matthias Erzberger called it. Churchill left the table to give a council of admirals and captains their final instructions. Big Ben struck the fatal hour. The message went out:[221]

Admiralty to all HM ships and Naval
Establishments

Signal

4 August 1914
11 pm

Admiralty

COMMENCE HOSTILITIES AGAINST GERMANY

It was a warm night. Through open windows Churchill could hear a throng outside Buckingham Palace, cheering and singing "God Save the King." Custom required that he now report to the prime minister. All the other ministers were already there, sitting in a glum circle around the green baize of the cabinet table. Margot Asquith had been waiting with them. She had just decided to retire, and was pausing at the foot of the stairs, when she saw Winston entering No. 10 and, "with a happy face, striding towards the double doors of the Cabinet room."[222]

FOUR

CATARACT

1914–1918

IN that first week of the war six million European soldiers sprang to arms with medieval ardor, and a month passed before anyone knew what had happened to them. The void was quickly filled by wild rumors, especially in Britain, which was spending less of its revenues on the army, proportionately, than in 1901. Other belligerent nations had military objectives, conscription, programs for mobilizing civilian efforts. England had only the "War-Book" of 1911, prepared by the Committee of Imperial Defence at Haldane's insistence. It was inadequate, and so the country was particularly vulnerable to sensational talebearers. The most extraordinary story, almost universally accepted at the time, described a force of between 70,000 and 100,000 Russians who were said to have landed in Scotland on their way to reinforce the Allies in France. An Edinburgh railway porter told of sweeping the snow from their boots. No one seems to have reminded him that they were in the middle of an August heat wave. Instead, otherwise responsible people chimed in; a laird swore that the czar's soldiers had marched across his estate, and an Oxford scholar declared that one of his colleagues was acting as their interpreter.

Spy stories flourished on the Norfolk coast. "Foreign-looking" men were reported almost every day. Clementine wrote Winston about them. She said that Goonie had seen a British soldier corner a suspect and "give him a small prod with his bayonette," which, "tho' very exhilarating to the pursuers had the effect of making the 'spy' run so fast that Goonie fears he got away." Another time "one of the cottager's wives" saw two men walking along a cliff with odd bulges in their coats. They gave her evil glances "& spoke to each other in a foreign tongue." Following furtively, she watched them "open their jackets & let fly 4 carrier pigeons!" Policemen, alerted, "pursued the men & caught them." Clementine learned that a decoded message retrieved from one of the pigeons revealed details of a plan to kidnap her and fly her on a German plane to Berlin, where she would remain until her husband had paid a ransom of several dreadnoughts. She wasn't intimidated: "If I *am* kidnapped I beg of you not to sacrifice the smallest or cheapest submarine or even the oldest ship. . . . I could not face the subsequent unpopularity whereas I should be quite a heroine & you a Spartan if I died bravely & unransomed." Winston was alarmed, and his concern deepened when he learned that their car had broken down. "It makes me a little anxious," he wrote her on August 9, "that you should be on the coast. It is 100 to one against a raid — but still there is the chance, and Cromer has a good landing place near. I wish you would get the motor repaired and keep it so that you can whisk away at the first sign of trouble."[1]

Churchill himself caught the spy fever. Driving to the Loch Ewe anchorage of the Grand Fleet with two admirals and two commodores, he spotted a searchlight on the roof of a large private house. There were no Admiralty spotlights in the neighborhood. Conceivably, he reasoned, this one was being used to send the Germans information about fleet movements. They drove on, but when they arrived and Jellicoe told them an unidentified aircraft had been seen in the vicinity, Winston returned to the house at the head of a party armed with pistols and ammunition from H.M.S. *Iron Duke.* He was now convinced that he had discovered a nest of secret agents. At the door the butler told him that this was the home of Sir Arthur Bignold, a founder of the Kennel Club and former Tory MP. Sir Arthur himself appeared, was questioned, and gave an unlikely explanation for the searchlight; he used it, he said, to catch the gleaming eyes of deer on a nearby hillside so he would know where to stalk them in the morning. To his indignation, Churchill ordered the light dismantled and its vital parts taken away. Back at the Admiralty, Winston demanded that "the fullest report be made on the circumstances in which this searchlight came to be placed into position, together with all other facts about Sir Arthur Bignold, his guests, friends and servants."[2] The improbable deer-stalking story proved to be true. Apart from its revelation of England's preoccupation with intrigue, even on the highest levels, this incident, like the Sidney Street siege, adds further testimony to Churchill's affinity to danger. The light might have aroused the suspicions of other ministers, but they would have sent subordinates to the scene. Only the first lord of the Admiralty would have arrived in person, gun in hand.

"I am writing in the Cabinet room, at the beginning of twilight," Asquith wrote Venetia Stanley, "and thro' the opposite window across the Parade I see the Admiralty flag flying & the lights 'beginning to twinkle' from the rooms where Winston and his two familiars (Eddie and Masterton) are beating out their plans." Winston had already established the routine which would become part of the Churchill legend in World War II. Adopting the Cuban siesta, he worked until 2:00 A.M. each day, woke at 8:00 A.M., and went through correspondence without rising. To

Vice Admiral Sir Douglas Brownrigg he presented "a most extraordinary spectacle, perched up in a huge bed, with the whole of the counterpane littered with dispatch boxes, red and all colours, and a stenographer sitting at the foot — Mr. Churchill himself with an enormous Corona Corona in his mouth."[3]

He was invigorated with immense gusto, enjoying his awesome responsibilities and volunteering to take over any that other ministers found burdensome. As many as twenty major Admiralty enterprises, all of them entirely dependent on sea power, were, he noted, "proceeding simultaneously in different parts of the globe." Under his direction, the 70,000 men of Field Marshal Sir John French's first British Expeditionary Force (BEF) were virtually secure from invasion because British warships were patrolling the 200,000 square miles of sea between Scotland and Norway, and both sides of the Strait of Dover had been mined. German and Austrian merchant ports were blockaded. Fast cruiser squadrons hunted down German sea raiders. The kaiser's colonies overseas were seized or besieged with almost larcenous zest — "A month ago," he remarked to the cabinet, "with what horror and disgust would most of those present have averted their minds from such ideas!" The body of a drowned German signalman yielded a secret cipher book; as a consequence, Winston and his staff in Room 40 at the Admiralty could track the movements of German ships. But the sea wasn't large enough for him. Land and air warfare must also feel the Churchillian presence. He established a Royal Naval division of infantry. ("A band must be provided," he minuted in a typical touch. "The quality is not important.") His seaplanes hunted U-boats. The pilots who had been his flight instructors were directed, on August 27, to establish their own air base on the Continent at Dunkirk. Other naval fliers carried out, on his orders, a series of stunning raids on zeppelin sheds at Cologne, Cuxhaven, Düsseldorf, and Friedrichafen and shot down six of the German airships. When Kitchener became minister for war on August 5, he asked Churchill to take over the air defense of Britain, and Winston instantly agreed. He even found time for wartime diplomacy. At Asquith's request, the first lord served on a war council whose other cabinet members were the prime minister, the foreign secretary, the chancellor, and the war minister. He secretly bargained with Italy and Japan over the terms under which they would join the Allies. "What should we do to bring the Japanese into the war?" he was asked. He replied grandly: "They can have China." Grey said: "Winston very soon will become incapable, from sheer activity of mind, of being anything in the Cabinet but Prime Minister." At a birthday party featuring a band and a magician, Chur-

A morning ride

chill's son, Randolph, the Chumbolly, shouted at the magician: "Man, stop! Band, play!" A relative sighed: "Just like Winston."[4]

The new secretary of state for war was the man of the hour. He had just been raised to an earldom, and on August 7 the blazing eyes, broad guardsman's mustache, and pointing finger of Kitchener of Khartoum — "K of K," the people now called him — appeared everywhere on a recruiting poster above the riveting message: YOUR COUNTRY NEEDS YOU! Some colleagues worried about the relationship between this hard, enigmatic man and the ebullient Churchill. Kitchener was twenty-five years older than the first lord and at one time had regarded him as an insubordinate pest. But Winston was another man now, and K of K, recognizing it, dropped him a note: "My dear Churchill. . . . Please do not address me as Lord as I am only yours, Kitchener." Winston later wrote: "I found him much more affable than I had been led to expect. . . . In those early days we worked together on close and cordial terms. He consulted me constantly on political aspects of his work, and increasingly gave me his confidence in military matters. Admiralty and War Office business were so interlaced that . . . we were in almost daily personal consultation." Later, after everything had gone wrong, it was Kitchener who gave Churchill the consolation he would treasure during the bleakest years of his life: "There is one thing at any rate they cannot take from you. The fleet was ready."[5]

Churchill's pace was exhausting. On August 9 he wrote Clementine: "I am over head & ears in work & am much behindhand." Two days later he wrote her: "This is only a line from a vy exhausted Winston. . . . I wish I cd whisk down to you & dig a little on the beach. My work here is vy heavy & so interesting that I cannot leave it." In her reply she warned of fatigue and urged him to remember: "1) Never missing your morning ride. 2) Going to bed well *before* midnight & sleeping well & *not* allowing yourself to be woken up every time a Belgian kills a German. (You *must* have 8 hours sleep every night to be your best self.) 3) Not smoking too much & not having indigestion. Now shall I come up for a day or two next Monday & tease you partly into doing these things?"[6]

The fact is that she was dying for an excuse to be in the thick of it. Understanding that, and anxious to appease her appetite for news, Churchill took what was, under the circumstances, a remarkable risk. He sent her classified information by post. "My darling one," he wrote. "The enclosed will tell you what is known officially. It is a good summary. You must *not* fail to burn it at once. . . . Kiss the Kittens for me. Tender love to you all. Your fondest & devoted W." She consigned it to the flames and begged for more. Over the phone — in the Speyers' cottage — she elicited his consent to put more in the mail. After hanging up she wrote him: "I am longing to get your letter with the secret news. It shall be destroyed at once. I hope that in it, you tell me about the expeditionary force. Do I guess right that some have gone already? Be a good one and write again & feed me with tit-bits. I am being so wise & good & sitting on the Beach & playing with my kittens, & doing my little housekeeping, but how I long to dash up & be near you and the pulse of things." Apparently the letter, when it arrived, was a letdown. "It was most interesting," she wrote him on August 10, "but I was disappointed because I hoped you were going to tell me about the Expeditionary Force. Do send me news of it. When it is going, where it will land, which regiments are in the first batch, etc. I long for it to arrive in time to save the Liège citizens from being massacred in their houses."[7]

Even Winston couldn't tell her that. And until the BEF saw action, the public couldn't even be told of its existence. If the Germans knew of its presence in France, they would alter their plans accordingly. It was indeed inherent in most of the Admiralty's accomplishments that everything known about them had to be highly restricted. The transport of troops, the charting of courses for warship patrols, negotiations with the

Japanese and Italians, Room 40 — all these would have been compromised if revealed. Information about engagements at sea could be disclosed, but in the first phase of the war most of this news was bad. The *Goeben* and the *Breslau* entered the Dardanelles, and the sequel was worse than anything Churchill had imagined. The kaiser grandly announced that he was selling both vessels to Turkey as replacements for the two Winston had virtually buccaneered. The crews, however, remained German. They led the Turkish fleet across the Black Sea to bombard the Russian Black Sea ports of Odessa, Nikolayev, and Sevastopol. Russia, in retaliation, declared war on Turkey; England and France were then obliged to do the same. That was the price the Allies paid for Churchill's high-handed "requisition" of July 28. If he had let the Turks have their ships their country might have remained neutral or even come in on England's side.

In late August the sky briefly brightened. Beatty entered German home waters and won the war's first naval battle, sinking three of Tirpitz's cruisers, damaging three more, and killing or capturing a thousand men at a cost of one damaged ship and thirty-five British bluejackets. Clementine, back in Admiralty House with the children, sent Kitchener the news while Churchill dressed for dinner. "Winston," she wrote, "thinks this is rather a 'Coup.' " Then the Germans went underwater. Churchill, addressing an all-party recruiting rally in Liverpool, said he hoped "the navy will have a chance of settling the question of the German Fleet," then added, "if they do not come out and fight in time of war they will be dug out like rats in a hole." That was tempting fate. The British cruisers *Aboukir, Hogue,* and *Cressy* were patrolling the Dutch coast. Feeling "constant, gnawing anxieties about the safety of the Fleet from submarine attack," he had ordered them withdrawn, but they were still there when, the morning after his Liverpool speech, a U-boat sank all three in less than an hour, taking 1,459 tars with them.[8] And that was only the beginning. Another U-boat entered Loch Ewe and torpedoed the cruiser *Hawke.* Next the dreadnought *Audacious* went down, followed by the *Formidable.* Clearly Scapa Flow was insecure; Churchill ordered the Grand Fleet to sea while the Orkney defenses were strengthened. During their absence, three battle cruisers of the German High Seas Fleet under the command of Franz von Hipper emerged from their Baltic Sea sanctuary, bombarded the British ports of Hartlepool, Whitby, and Scarborough, and sailed away without a scratch. Overseas, a squadron of fast cruisers under Maximilian von Spee roamed the Pacific Ocean, sinking British freighters almost at will. The cruiser *Emden* steamed into the Bay of Bengal, shelled Madras, prowled around the approaches to Ceylon, and destroyed fifteen Allied merchantmen. When a British force under Sir Christopher Cradock attacked von Spee off the Chilean coast, the Germans wiped out the British in a sensational battle and drowned Cradock.

In time all these would be avenged. Von Hipper would be intercepted on his next sortie and so badly mauled that he would never reappear on the high seas. Von Spee and his entire squadron would be sunk in the waters off the Falkland Islands. An Australian cruiser would annihilate the *Emden*. Only the U-boats would venture to take the offensive after that, and while their toll was spectacular, their torpedoing of American merchantmen trading with England would eventually bring the United States into the war. But in late 1914 all that lay in the future. The Admiralty's initial defeats shocked Britons. They had thought their navy invincible. The shelling of their coast, the threat to transports bringing Indian troops back to fight in France, the sinking of their proud warships, evoked cries of pain and anger. Inevitably the Admiralty's first lord, the most visible member of the government, paid a price for his flamboyance.

The lord mayors of Hartlepool, Whitby, and Scarborough demanded coastal artillery and dreadnoughts anchored off their beaches. The Indian government telegraphed that Madras must be protected. The *Morning Post* found that "grave doubt is expressed on every hand" about Churchill's competence: "In the War Office we have a soldier in whom the Army and the nation have confidence. In the Admiralty, upon the other hand, there is a First Lord who is a civilian, and cannot be expected to have any grasp of the principles and practice of naval warfare." Thomas Bowles, a former Tory MP, published a pamphlet charging that the three cruisers had been lost off the Netherlands "because, despite the warnings of admirals, commodores and captains, Mr Churchill refused, until it was too late, to recall them from a patrol so carried on as to make them certain to fall victims to the torpedoes of an active enemy." The House was hostile; when he triumphantly announced the naval fliers' air raids on Germany, he was castigated for violating Swiss airspace. "What's the Navy doing?" hecklers cried, and he could not reply without jeopardizing missions and men. "In spite of being accustomed to years of abuse," he later wrote, "I could not but feel the adverse and hostile currents that flowed about me."[9]

Some flowed very close. Lloyd George told his secretary and mistress, Frances Stevenson, who kept a diary, "Churchill is too busy trying to get a flashy success to attend to the real business of the Admiralty. Churchill blames Admiral Cradock for the defeat in South America — the Admiral presumably having gone down with his ship & so unable to clear himself.

This is characteristic of Churchill." Asquith wrote the King that the cabinet felt the naval losses were "not creditable." The King, who already regarded Churchill as unreliable and irresponsible, was disgusted with his Liverpool speech. After the loss of the three cruisers, His Majesty's private secretary, Lord Stamfordham, wrote: "Indeed seeing what alas! happened today when the rats came out of their own accord and to our cost, the threat was unfortunate and the King feels it was hardly dignified for a Cabinet Minister." Even Kitchener, usually steadfast, despaired during one cabinet meeting, saying that a German invasion was not only possible, but that England would not be able to stop it. Churchill challenged him to have the brightest experts in the War Office pick any British beach, any day, and work out the logistics of landing 150,000 men. The Admiralty would then show how they could hurl those men back into the sea.[10]

Nevertheless, someone's head had to roll. It was scapegoating time again, and the choice of the victim reflects ill upon all who participated in his undoing. Since the outbreak of the war the first sea lord had been the target of a vicious witch-hunt. The press had hounded him, and every minister had been inundated with anonymous letters questioning his loyalty. Lord Charles Beresford, Fisher's bête noire, told the House that while Prince Louis was an "exceedingly able officer," nothing could alter the fact that he was a German, had German servants, owned property in Germany, "and as such should not be occupying his present position." Churchill warned Beresford not to repeat those remarks: "The interests of the country do not permit the spreading of such wicked allegations by an officer of your rank, even though retired." Violet Asquith wrote that her father's reaction to the smear campaign was one of "disgust." That is not the impression left by his letters to Venetia Stanley, however. He wrote her that he was not, "entre nous, very trustful of the capacity of Prince Louis." Then: "Our poor blue-eyed German will have to go." And then: "He *must* go."[11]

He went. Churchill told the King that the attacks on the first sea lord's "name and parentage" had subjected Louis to an intolerable strain: "The exacting duties and heavy responsibilities of his office have no doubt affected his general health and nerves, so that for the good of the service a change has become necessary." Back at the Admiralty, he wrote Louis that he and Asquith agreed that "a letter from you to me indicating that you felt in some respects yr usefulness was impaired & that patriotic considerations wh at this junction must be supreme in yr mind wd be the best form of giving effect to yr decision. To this letter I wd on behalf of the Govt write an answer." There was more of this, all of it lamentable. He closed: "No incident in my public life has caused me so much sorrow." Their parting interview may have caused him more. The prince had just learned that his young cousin, Maurice, a grandson of Queen Victoria and an infantry lieutenant, had been killed in France. With great dignity the grieving father said that "as a loyal subject of His Majesty" he was leaving "the great service to which I have devoted my life" to ease "the burden laid on His Majesty's Ministers." Thus Louis Alexander of Battenberg, GCB, GCVO, KCMB, PC, was evicted from office on shabby charges of disloyalty to which a Liberal government capitulated. At the King's request Louis changed his name to Mountbatten. One day his younger son, Dickie, then fourteen, would vindicate him.[12]

The question of his successor was a momentous one. Haldane had written Churchill that if Lord Fisher were returned to active duty, it would "make our country feel that our old spirit of the Navy was alive and come back." Violet Asquith had "not a shadow of doubt that Winston would wish to appoint Lord Fisher. . . . There was a magnetic mutual attraction between these two and they could not keep away from one another for long." The old salt had been bombarding Churchill with advice, sometimes on profound matters, sometimes on trivia: "Why is standard of recruits raised 3 inches to 5 feet 6? . . . What d——d folly to discard supreme enthusiasm because it's under 5 feet 6. *We are a wonderful nation!* astounding how we muddle through! There's only one explanation — We are the lost 10 Tribes!" He was now seventy-four. On his frequent visits to the Admiralty, Winston, in his words, "watched him narrowly to judge his physical strength and mental alertness" and had "the impression of a terrific engine of mental and physical power burning and throbbing in that aged frame." He sounded him out "and soon saw he was fiercely eager to lay his grasp on power." No one else would do, Winston told Asquith. When the prime minister agreed, the first lord was elated. Violet, seeing him immediately afterward, said: "No one knows his weather better than you do — and you are no doubt prepared for squalls ahead." Winston said: "I know him — and I know that I can manage him."[13]

The difficulty was that Fisher felt the same way about Churchill. And there were doubters even then. Clementine was apprehensive; she was afraid the old admiral would be "like the curate's egg." Beatty wrote his wife: "The situation is curious; two very strong and clever men, one old, wily, and of vast experience, one young, self-assertive . . . but unstable." Aitken believed that Churchill had "co-opted Fisher to relieve the pressure against himself," but had no "intention of letting anyone else rule the roost." He foresaw a duel between a first lord and a first sea lord "both bent on an autocracy." Admiral Rosslyn Wemyss predicted: "They will be thick as thieves at first until they differ on some subject, probably as to who is to be Number 1, when they will begin to intrigue against each other." The most determined opponent of the appointment was George V. The "Sailor King" had served fifteen years before the mast, and he distrusted Jacky Fisher. He summoned Churchill to Buckingham Palace, where, according to Stamfordham's account of their conversation, the King said that Winston's choice was "a great surprise." His Majesty thought that "Lord Fisher has not the confidence of the Navy; he is over 73 years of age. When First Sea Lord . . . he created a state of unrest and bad feeling among the officers of the service." Churchill replied that no other admiral was fit for the job. The King ended the audience by saying that he could not approve until he had seen Asquith. Stamfordham bore the sovereign's message to No. 10: "The proposed appointment would give a shock to the Navy which no one could wish to cause in the middle of this great War." Lord Fisher, the royal message continued, had become aged; he talked and wrote a great deal, but his opinions changed "from day to day." Asquith himself was troubled by Fisher's "strangely un-English" face, with its "twisted mouth" and round eyes, "suggesting the legend (which I believe quite untrue) that he had a Cingalese mother," but he replied that he supported Churchill's decision. The King, having done all a constitutional monarch could do, signed the appointment but wrote the prime minister: "I do so with some reluctance and misgivings."[14]

He then sent for the appointee. Churchill had coached Fisher carefully. The meeting lasted an hour, and afterward the King wrote in his diary: "He seems as young as ever." The two agreed to meet once a week. Winston wrote Asquith and Grey that the old admiral "is already a Court Favourite." The choice seemed inspired. It was immensely popular with the country. Since the old admiral usually awoke at 4:00 A.M., between them he and Churchill could keep an almost unsleeping watch at the Admiralty. Winston loved Fisher's wit, his contempt for pomp, his devotion to the service. He wrote him: "Contact with you is like ozone to me." To Clementine he wrote: "Tomorrow old Fisher comes down to the yacht with me. This always has a salutary effect." Certainly Fisher's energy was astounding. He wrote a friend: "Thanks for your dear letter! Isn't it fun being back? Some d——d fools thought I was dead and buried! I am busy getting even with some of them! I did 22 hours work yesterday but 2 hours sleep not enough so I shall slow down! SECRET. The King said to Winston (I suppose dissuading) that the job would kill me. Winston was perfectly lovely in his instant reply: 'Sir, I cannot imagine a more glorious death'! Wasn't that delicious? But burn please!" He wrote Jellicoe: "Let everyone be optimistic, and shoot the *pessimists!*" To Beatty he said: "It's not numbers that tell, but GUNNERY! *Gunnery, gunnery, gunnery!* All else is twaddle. Hit the target!"[15]

At the outset the first sea lord's relationship with the first lord was as Wemyss had predicted: superb. In Churchill's words, "As long as the port and starboard lights shone together all went well." The old man proposed a daring plan to force an entry into the Baltic Sea and secure command of it, cutting Germany off from its Scandinavian supplies and freeing Russian troops for an amphibious assault on Berlin. Winston, with his love of adventure, was delighted. He authorized the building of landing craft. Then he questioned Fisher about details. Before the Baltic could be entered, the Elbe River must be blocked. How could this be done? Could British warships enter the Baltic while Tirpitz's fleet was free to sortie from the Kiel Canal and attack the ships left behind in Scapa Flow? How could the Baltic islands be seized while barring the Elbe? The admiral was vague; clearly he hadn't thought it through. Slowly Churchill began to realize that the King had been right, that the aged first sea lord "was very old. In all matters where naval fighting was concerned he was more than usually cautious. He could not bear the idea of risking ships in battle." Winston had trapped himself. Fisher was his man, confirmed despite the protests of, among others, the sovereign. If the old salt turned on him, Churchill would be alone. And they were bound to find themselves on a collision course eventually, for Winston believed in taking chances — "It is not right to condemn operations of war simply because they involve risk and uncertainty," he told the cabinet — while his first sea lord, so audacious in conversation and letters, was transformed into an archconservative when the prospect of action loomed. "He settled," Churchill wrote bleakly, "upon a doctrine widely inculcated among our senior naval officers, that the Navy's task was to keep open our communications, blockade those of the enemy, and to wait for the Armies to do their proper job."[16]

But the armies were not doing their proper job. The assumption had been that Belgium would be the battleground. That was the gist of the War Office summary Winston had sent Clementine on August 9. Three days later *Punch* had run its first wartime cartoon, showing a brave little Belgian boy in wooden shoes barring the way to a fat German trespasser, with the caption "No Thoroughfare!" Heavy casualties had not been expected. When Winston learned that his young cousin Norman Leslie had been killed in action he thought it bad luck. Even in South Africa death had come to relatively few. He had no way of knowing that fifteen thousand British soldiers had fallen in five days — and that their losses had been light compared to those of the French. On the morning of August 24, three weeks after Germany had declared war on France, he looked up from his desk and saw Kitchener standing in the doorway. K of K's face was peculiar. Winston had "the subconscious feeling that it was distorted and discoloured as if it had been punched with a fist. His eyes rolled more than ever." Wordlessly he held out a telegram from the commander of the BEF, Sir John French. The Belgian fortress of Namur had fallen to the enemy. At the time this was considered a disaster. Namur was fifty-seven miles from the German frontier and the gateway to France. Neither Kitchener nor Churchill could have envisioned what lay ahead: a further BEF retreat of 157 miles, putting the Tommies just outside the suburbs of Paris before they rallied. To cheer up the war minister, Winston took him to the Other Club and proposed, after dinner, his intention to break the club rule forbidding any toast but that to the King; with a flourish he raised his glass to "success to the British arms." He beamed at Kitchener, who drank but still looked pummeled.[17]

Five days later another member of the club suffered a similar shock. That Saturday afternoon F. E. Smith, the official press censor, was handed a dispatch from Arthur Moore, the war correspondent of *The Times.* Moore had written that the Allied forces had virtually disintegrated under an "immediate, relentless, unresting" enemy advance. He was awed by the "irresistible vehemence" of the Germans, whose numerical superiority was so great that "they could no more be stopped than the waves of the sea." The BEF, a "retreating, broken army," was being "forced backwards, ever backwards," suffering "very great losses" reducing it to "bits of broken regiments" that were "grievously injured" and some divisions which had "lost nearly all their officers." F.E. suspected that the correspondent was simply windy. Nevertheless, he passed what became known as "the Amiens dispatch" in the shrewd belief that it would make excellent recruiting propaganda. Thus it was that members of the English establishment sat down to breakfast Sunday morning and found themselves confronting a front-page headline, FIERCEST FIGHT IN HISTORY, followed by the subheads *Heavy Losses of British Troops — Mons and Cambrai — Fight Against Severe Odds — Need for Reinforcements.* In a box the editor explained that the story was being run to alert the country to the "extreme gravity of the task before us." H. G. Wells

F. E. Smith

thought: "It was as if David had flung his pebble — and missed!" Asquith indignantly scolded the paper, but F.E. had been right; Monday morning recruiting posts were packed with young men eager to rescue their brothers in France. "Kitchener's Army" had begun to form.[18]

What had happened? Part of the explanation is Gallic stupidity. There is a theory that the last competent French general lies in Napoleon's tomb, and nothing that happened on the fluid front that summer refutes it. Ever since Louis Napoleon's defeat at the hands of the Prussians a generation earlier, cadets at Saint-Cyr-l'École had been imbued with the belief that, as General Ferdinand Foch put it, "There is only one way to defend ourselves — to attack as soon as we are ready." This was the doctrine of the *offensive à outrance,* of *cran,* of charging mindlessly while shouting: *"Vite, vite! Allez, allez!"* Field regulations stipulated that "the French Army henceforth admits no law but the offensive . . . the offensive alone leads to positive results." The bible of this faith was the general staff's Plan XVII, its blueprint for an irresistible march to the Rhine. The instant war was declared, they would invade German-occupied Lorraine with their right wing and advance through Alsace. As the Germans met the threat by transferring troops from their center, the French would hit the center with everything they had. *Voilà:* a quick, decisive victory.[19]

Plan XVII was hopelessly flawed. It assumed parity in the populations of the two countries, and there was none. Since 1871 German Fraus had been conceiving far more frequently than Frenchwomen; despite the Reich's commitment in the east, against Russia, the kaiser had mobilized over 1.5 million men in the west, enough to guarantee superiority in the first clash. The French plan's total commitment to massed attacks overlooked the changes in warfare wrought by modern technology — the machine gun, heavy artillery, barbed wire — all of which had been obvious to European observers of the Russo-Japanese War ten years earlier. Most grievous of all, the French generals were guilty of what Napoleon had called the cardinal sin of commanders: "forming a picture" — assuming that the enemy will act in a certain way in a given situation when in fact his behavior may be very different. It seems never to have occurred to them that the Germans, too, might have a plan. But they did. It was the Schlieffen Plan, completed in 1906 by Count Alfred von Schlieffen, then the kaiser's chief of staff. The count had anticipated Plan XVII. He intended to draw the French right into Lorraine in a "sack maneuver" while his own right wing, a million *Soldaten,* swept down through Belgium like a swinging scythe, cutting a swath seventy-five miles wide and enveloping France's extreme left flank.

Germany's enemies should have been aware of this. In 1912 Henry Wilson, cycling through the Low Countries, saw that all new German railroad construction in the area converged on Aachen and the Belgian frontier. But Joseph Jacques Césaire Joffre, constable of France and the French commander in chief, was blind to it. Immediately after the declaration of war he marched triumphantly into Lorraine, not suspecting that the slowly retreating enemy was luring him into a trap. Meanwhile, Alexander von Kluck, commanding the German right, wheeled down through Belgium, overwhelming the fortresses of Liège and Namur. His men, their *feldgrau* uniforms coated with white dust from shattered buildings, advanced across Belgium almost unopposed, burning villages and shooting hostages as they went. General Charles Lanrezac commanded the French left wing, lying in Kluck's path. As early as August 8 Lanrezac warned Joffre's headquarters, *Grand Quartier Général* (GQG), that he might be flanked. His concern, he was told, was "premature." GQG informed him that a flanking maneuver was "out of proportion to the means at the enemy's disposal," that the enemy columns his scouts had sighted must be on some "special mission," probably serving as a screen. As evidence of their strength accumulated, Joffre actually rejoiced. It meant, he said, that they were thinning their ranks in the center, where he was about to strike.[20]

He struck on August 21 in the wilderness of the Ardennes. As American GIs discovered thirty years later, the Ardennes is ill-suited to fighting. Thickly forested, slashed with deep ravines, and fogged with mists rising from peat bogs, it resembles a scene in a Hans Christian Andersen tale. Caesar, who took ten days to cross it, called it a "place of terrors." Moreover, its slopes were such that the French would be charging uphill. They found the Germans dug in and ready. Bayonets fixed, Joffre's men lunged upward in an *attaque brusque*. Machine gunners slaughtered them. During the four-day battle of the Frontiers, of which this was a part, 140,000 Frenchmen fell. Yet even this massacre failed to discourage Joffre. The British, who had lost only 1,600 at Mons, were defeatist, but the word from GQG was that although Joffre's drive in the center had been "momentarily checked," he would "make every effort to renew the offensive."[21] That was fantasy. The German right, outnumbering the defenders two to one, was about to roll up Joffre's left, and if he didn't know it, Lanrezac did. Learning that the French attackers in the Ardennes not only had failed but were actually retreating, Lanrezac saw himself facing encirclement. On the evening of August 23 he ordered a general retreat. It spread along the entire Allied line. Plan XVII had crumbled. The last chance for a short, victorious war had vanished. Urgency, even panic, was in the air. The French fell back and back. The German advance was relentless. The Allies would be lucky to save Paris. Actually, they didn't; it was Kluck who saved it for them. He blundered, swinging east of the capital on September 3 and thereby offering his flank to Joseph-Simon Gallieni, the retired officer charged with the city's defense. After the first skirmishes there the exhausted German infantrymen gave ground. The French rallied on the Marne, and after a seven-day battle involving more than 2,000,000 men, Kluck recoiled and dug in. Then the sidestepping began, the lines of the opposing armies extending westward and then northward as each tried to outflank the other in a "race to the sea." The possibility that eventually they might run out of land seems never to have occurred to them. The sacrifices in the opening battles had been so great on both sides — in August the French alone had lost 206,515 men — that the thought of stalemate was unbearable.

The Germans were masters of northern France, but the Belgians still held out. In Brussels on August 17 their premier, Count de Broqueville, had reported to King Albert that the enemy, outnumbering his forces four or five to one, were attacking across the Gette River, fifteen miles away. Liège had fallen; Namur was doomed. During the night of August 18 the king, executing a skillful disengagement maneuver, withdrew his five divisions from Brussels and the Gette and retreated into the great port of Antwerp, Belgium's strongest fortress. They reached there, intact, two days later. The disappointed Kluck reported to *Oberste Heeresleitung,* the kaiser's headquarters, that Albert's army had "managed to escape our grasp." He was forced to leave two corps — 60,000 men, badly needed on the Marne — to invest Antwerp. Even so, on August 25 the Belgians sortied and fell on the rear of Kluck's army, driving it back on Louvain. Shots were fired, and Kluck's men shouted: *"Die Engländer sind da!" "Die Franzosen sind da!"* General von Luttwitz, the military governor of Brussels, summoned the American minister and told him that Louvain civilians had either fired on the Reich's troops or signaled the attackers. "And now of course," he explained, "we have to destroy the city." It was burned to the ground as an example for those who felt tempted to defy German might.[22]

Zeppelins bombed Antwerp, but until the second month of the war the fortified city faced no serious threat. On September 5, however, de Broqueville warned the British Foreign Office that the enemy troops besieging the port were being heavily reinforced. He asked for weightier artillery, aircraft, and antiaircraft guns. Four days later the kaiser ordered the capture of the city whatever the cost, and on September 28, 420-millimeter Krupp howitzers began pounding the outworks with 2,000-pound shells. The question of Antwerp's value to the Allies now arose. Was its defense vital? The cabinet was indecisive. In 1911 Fisher, then in full possession of his faculties, had written that in the event of war between Germany and an Anglo-French alliance, the "overwhelming superiority" of the British navy, not Britain's army, would "keep the German Army out of Paris. . . . It is Antwerp we shall seize," he concluded, "and not go fooling on the Vosges frontier." But provisioning Antwerp was a logistical nightmare. The port's link with the North Sea was the Scheldt River, which belonged to the Netherlands, and the frightened Dutch, determined to remain neutral, were turning back all incoming ships except those bearing food and medicine. With Antwerp's sea approach barred, the only other route open was a thin, exposed, fifty-mile-long land corridor. Kitchener, replying to the September 5 note, said he had no munitions to spare and even doubted the port was in danger. "I expect they will hang on to Antwerp," he wrote. On the second day of the war Churchill had vetoed sending an expeditionary force there on the ground that while he could guarantee a safe passage across the Strait of Dover, he couldn't protect troop transports taking

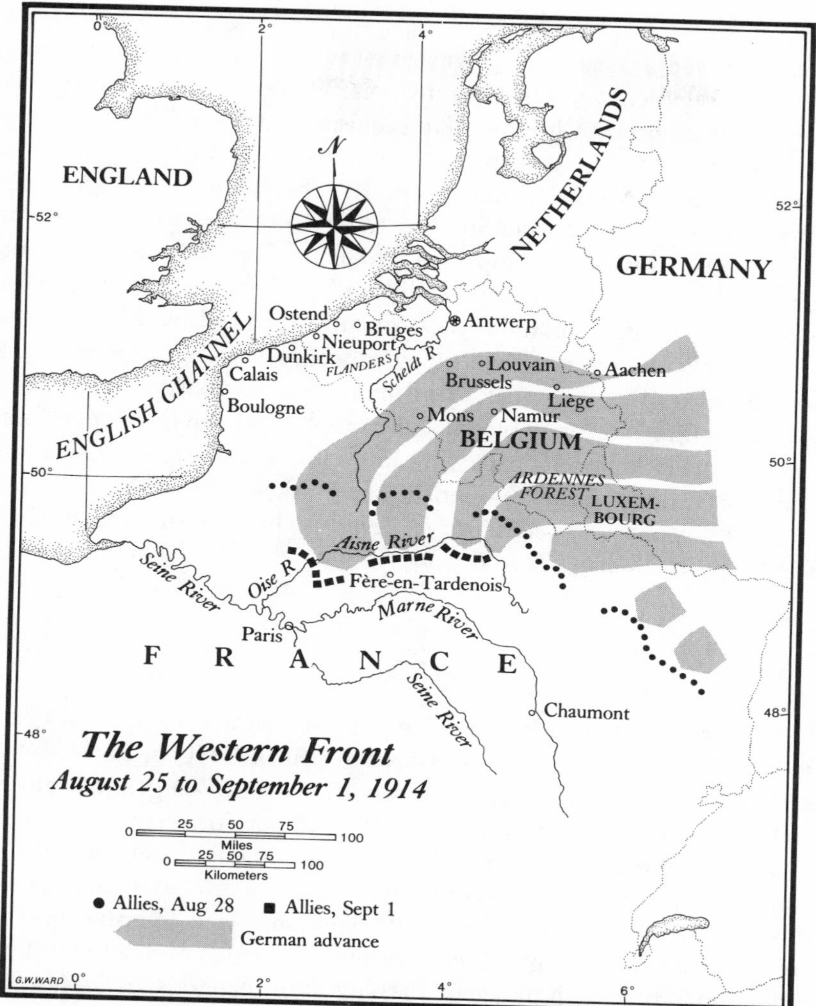

The Western Front
August 25 to September 1, 1914

the longer route across the North Sea to the Scheldt, then still open.[23]

Winston had not yet grasped the connection between Antwerp's resistance and holding the Channel ports — Dunkirk, Calais, Boulogne — but he was alert to the necessity of denying the ports to Kluck. So was Joffre. Early in September the constable had asked that British infantry be landed at Dunkirk, to make a demonstration on the Germans' right flank. Churchill's naval fliers were already based there, and Kitchener asked him to supervise the landing party. His departure was kept secret; even the cabinet wasn't told. Asquith wrote Venetia on September 9: "Winston is just off to Dunkirk . . . he will be back by lunch tomorrow. Don't say anything of this, as he doesn't want the colleagues to know."

He commanded a detachment of marines and the Oxfordshire Hussars, his reserve regiment, of which Sunny was colonel in chief. The episode reflects little credit on Churchill. He requisitioned several naval vehicles and eight three-ton trucks to provide Sunny and his officers with all the comforts of their Blenheim maneuvers. "Probably no other regiment," wrote Adrian Keith-Falconer in *The Oxfordshire Hussars in the Great War*, "went to France accompanied by such a fleet of motor transport solely for its own personal use." Winston's orders were: "Select your point and hit hard." His men were joyously received by villagers, but their feint left no impression on the enemy; Kluck wasn't even aware of their existence. The Tommies called them the "Dunkirk Circus." And Churchill, with his incorrigible love of panoply, lent the ineffective foray a touch of opéra bouffe by appearing in the full-dress regalia of an Elder Brother of Trinity House. A French officer asked him what uniform he wore. *"Je suis un Frère Aîné de la Trinité,"* he replied. *"Mon dieu!"* gasped the Frenchman. *"La Trinité!"*[24]

The moth could not resist the flame. Less than a week later Winston was back in France, driving from Calais to British GHQ in Fère-en-Tardenois with the Duke of Westminster. To avoid being swept up by Kluck's advance, they had to take a wide detour, traversing the entire British front. Near Soissons, Churchill had a long talk on a haystack with a major general, Sir Henry Rawlinson. Winston wrote afterward: "I saw the big black German shells, 'the coal boxes' and 'Jack Johnsons' as they were then called, bursting in Paissy village. . . . When darkness fell I saw the horizon lighted with the quick flashing of the cannonade. Such scenes were afterwards to become commonplace: but their first aspect was thrilling." Four days later he returned to Dunkirk, kibitzing at air-raid briefings. He had scarcely returned to London when he alerted the light cruiser *Adventure* to take him over again. The cabinet was beginning to mutter about his absences. Clementine warned him: "Now please don't think me tiresome; but I want you to tell the PM of your projected visit to Sir John French. It would be very bad manners if you do not & he will be displeased and hurt. . . . Of course you will consult K. Otherwise the journey will savour of a week-end escapade & not a mission. You would be surprised & incensed if K slipped off to see Jellicoe on his own." He took her advice, and K of K, more tolerant than his colleagues, replied: "No objection — I hope you will counteract any wild talk." Nevertheless,

Churchill was trifling with fate. Having made so many unnecessary appearances at the front, he would be hard pressed later to defend trips which were essential.[25]

By now he saw the strategic significance of Antwerp. Grey had sent identical notes to the Admiralty and the War Office: "Time presses for the Belgians. I am afraid we can do very little if anything, but if we can do nothing the Belgians may surrender Antwerp very soon." Kitchener was as yet unalarmed. Churchill, however, drew up a list of equipment he could dispatch at once and ended: "WE MUST HOLD ANTWERP." Even though the Germans were retreating from the Marne to the Aisne, the release of their two corps, still tied down by the entrenched camp at Antwerp, would permit Kluck to dash to the Channel ports and seize them before English troops were dug in. By September 29 Winston had converted Kitchener. The war secretary was ready to send men and field guns. "We had a long Cabinet this morning," Asquith wrote his beloved the following afternoon. "The Belgians are rather out of 'morale,' & are alarmed at the bombardment of Antwerp. . . . They are sending their archives & treasure over here, & talk of moving the seat of Government to Ostend. Kitchener has given them some good advice . . . to entrench themselves with barbed wire &c in the intervening spaces, & challenge the Germans to come on."[26]

The following morning de Broqueville described his situation as "very grave"; only Allied troops could "save Antwerp from falling." Asquith sent Venetia a note: "The fall of Antwerp would be a great moral blow to the Allies, for it would leave the whole of Belgium at the mercy of the Germans. The French telegraph that they are willing to send a division (of 15,000 to 20,000) & put it under a British general. . . . We resolved at the Cabinet to-day that, if the French cooperation is satisfactory, we would divert our 7th Division (of the finest troops) wh was just going to join Sir J. French." The next day, Friday, October 2, he wrote her: "The news from Antwerp this morning is far from good & gives me some anxiety. The Germans battered down 2 of the forts, and what is worse got in between them & drove a lot of Belgians out of their entrenchments." He was pessimistic: "It is a very difficult situation — particularly as our officer reports that it is the morale of the Belgian commanders rather than of the men wh shows signs of collapse." He wanted to boost their spirits. "But it is no good to lure them with false hopes." With that, he left for Cardiff to make a speech at a recruiting rally. Thus he was absent when the crisis came.[27]

The Belgian government, despairing, had resolved to pack up and leave for Ostend Saturday morning. They predicted that their troops in

Antwerp would hold out for another five or six days, but the British ambassador there, Sir Francis Villiers, thought it "unlikely that when the Court and Government are gone resistance will be much prolonged." Antwerp was the only Allied fortress left between Kluck and the Channel. If the enemy reached Calais, Kitchener thought, an invasion of England would be feasible. That evening he and Grey conferred at Kitchener's house in Carlton Gardens, between Pall Mall and St. James's Park. With the prime minister away, they needed the opinion of another senior minister, so they decided to consult Churchill. He was aboard a train, bound for Dover. On their orders, the engineer reversed direction, and from Victoria Station a waiting car drove Winston to Carlton Gardens. After listening to their analysis he recommended sending the Admiralty's marine brigade to the city. Then he volunteered to go to the beleaguered city himself and report to them by telephone and telegraph. They agreed, and shortly after midnight he was off again. Grey wired Sir Francis: "First Lord of the Admiralty will be at Antwerp between 9 and 10 tomorrow. He is fully acquainted with our views, and it is hoped he may have the honour of an audience with the King before a final decision as to the departure of the Government is taken." Sir Francis wired back that the evacuation had already begun, but de Broqueville would summon an emergency cabinet meeting now to reconsider that decision. As a result of the meeting, all Belgian troops were ordered to remain at their posts. In London that morning Asquith, returning to the fait accompli, wrote Venetia that he was "anxiously awaiting Winston's report. I don't know how fluent he is in French, but if he was able to do himself justice in a foreign tongue, the Belges will have listened to a discourse the like of which they have never heard before. I cannot but think that he will stiffen them up to the sticking point."[28]

Churchill's car, roaring up to Antwerp's hôtel de ville in a cloud of dust, reminded one observer "for all the world of a scene in a melodrama where the hero dashes up bare-headed on a foam-flecked horse, and saves the heroine, or the old homestead, or the family fortune, as the case may be." In undress uniform — no epaulets, no cocked hat — he conferred with de Broqueville and assured him that, in addition to the two thousand seasoned marines who would arrive that evening, he was sending for his two naval brigades, two million rounds of ammunition, and five days' rations. Albert and the Belgian premier, much moved, promised to defend the city for at least ten more days provided the Allies launched a major relief operation within seventy-two hours. Winston cabled Kitchener and Grey: "I must impress on you the necessity of making these worn and weary men throw their souls into it, or the whole thing will go with a run." Sunday morning he toured the city's outer forts in a Rolls-Royce. Henry Stevens, the naval rating who drove him, later recalled that although he was out of earshot most of the time, he could see that "Mr Churchill was energetic and imperative. He discussed the situation with his own Staff and some of the Belgian officers, emphasising his points with his walking stick. . . . His actions were emphatic. He appeared on occasions to criticise the siting and construction of the trenches. . . . Mr Churchill dominated the proceedings and the impression formed that he was by no means satisfied with the position generally. He put forward his ideas forcefully, waving his stick and thumping the ground with it. . . . At one line of trenches he found the line very thinly held and asked where 'the bloody men were.' He certainly was not mollified when he was told that was all that were available at that point." Winston was in fact deeply disappointed. Back at the hôtel de ville he telegraphed Kitchener that the defenders were "weary and disheartened," that because many of the outworks had been flooded to thwart the Germans, only shallow trenches could be scooped out of the waterlogged earth, furnishing little shelter "to their worn out and in many cases inexperienced troops."[29]

The marines landed and were greeted by ecstatic Belgian citizens. Kitchener cabled that the cabinet approved of the immediate dispatch of the naval brigades. He had formed these units, first called "Churchill's pets" and then "Churchill's innocent victims," just before the war. They were green and largely untrained. The officers lacked revolver ammunition. Many of the men had neither fired rifles nor dug trenches. Among their officers were Asquith's son Arthur ("Oc") and the young poet Rupert Brooke, whom Eddie Marsh had introduced to Winston in quieter days. Churchill had been unwise to ask for them and his colleagues had been unwise to agree, but it was a heady moment; the prime minister wrote Venetia: "I have a telegram from Oc sent off from Dover pier on Sunday evening: 'Embarking to-night: love.' I suppose most of the territorials & recruits would envy him, being sent off after 3 days to the front! I am sure he will do well, but it is a hazardous adventure." It was also an uncomfortable one. Brooke, who had assumed that after crossing the Channel they would spend a month "quietly training," wrote home that they bivouacked their first night under shellfire in the deserted garden of a château and were awakened at 2:00 A.M. "So up we got — frozen and sleepy — and toiled off through the night. By dawn we got into trenches — very good ones — and relieved Belgians."[30]

By sheer force of will, Churchill had taken charge of Antwerp's defense. He was rounding up men, searching for weapons and ammunition, directing troops, siting guns, and telegraphing the Admiralty for high-explosive shells, shell fuses, fire-control balloons, steel rope, entrenching tools, field telephone sets, and "30 Maxim guns on tripod mountings, with establishment of proportionate ammunition." Excited, aroused, even elated, he sent Asquith a remarkable wire early Monday, suggesting that he quit the cabinet and lead troops: "If it is thought by HM Government that I can be of service here, I am willing to resign my office and undertake command of relieving and defensive forces assigned to Antwerp in conjunction with Belgian Army, provided that I am given necessary military rank and authority, and full powers of a commander of a detached force in the field."[31]

The prime minister was astounded. At the end of a letter to King George, in which he reported that "Mr Churchill has been in Antwerp since Saturday afternoon & has successfully dissuaded the King & his Ministers from retiring to Ostend," he noted that he had "this morning received from Mr Churchill a patriotic offer to resign his office & take command of the forces at Antwerp," but, while appreciating the first lord's "zeal and skill," he had replied that "his services could not be dispensed with at home." To Venetia, Asquith was more frank. He thought the proposition "a real bit of tragi-comedy." His response to Winston had been "a *most decided* negative." When he read it to the cabinet, "it was received with a Homeric laugh." Kitchener, the only soldier in the cabinet, did not join in the laughter. He thought the idea sound and was prepared to commission Winston a lieutenant general.[32]

Asquith wouldn't hear of it. The command would go to General Rawlinson, now in Dunkirk. Rawlinson was having difficulty getting through, however, and Winston telegraphed Kitchener: "In view of the situation and the developing German attack, it is my duty to remain here and continue my direction of affairs unless relieved by some person of consequence." The British marines went into action that Monday afternoon and threw back an enemy attack. Early in the evening Churchill inspected their lines. They were, he told Kitchener, "cheerful and well dug in." Gino Calza Bedolo, war correspondent for the *Giornale d'Italia,* was visiting a position near Lier, southeast of Antwerp, when he saw a striking figure standing in the midst of a group of officers. "He was still young," Bedolo told the London Lyceum Club several weeks later, "and was enveloped in a cloak, and on his head wore a yachtsman's cap. He was tranquilly smoking a large cigar and looking at the progress of the battle under a rain of shrapnel, which I can only call fearful. It was Mr Churchill, who had come to view the situation himself. It must be confessed that it is not easy to find in the whole of Europe a Minister who would be capable of smoking

Churchill at Antwerp, October 1914

peacefully under that shellfire. He smiled, and looked quite satisfied."[33]

That night Rawlinson couldn't get closer than Bruges, fifty-one miles away. The Belgians and the Royal Marines were exhausted. Churchill's only reserves were the six thousand inexperienced men in the naval brigades. He didn't want to use them now, and was determined not to expose them to the ferocity of the enemy's storm troops, so he assigned them to a defensive position between the front and the city. At 1:00 A.M. he wired London: "All well. I have met Ministers in Council, who resolved to fight it out here, whatever happens." In the early hours of Tuesday, October 6, the weary Belgians actually counterattacked, but were quickly beaten off. Asquith wrote that "under Winston's stimulus the Belgians are making a resolute stand. I have just seen a telegram which shews that this morning both the Belgians & our Marines were pushed back. The inner forts (it says) are being held by our naval brigade [sic] — which shows that Oc & his companions have arrived & are already within range." Rawlinson was "expected shortly." Presumably the British "7th Division & Cavalry & the French Marines" were on their way. "It is to be hoped that they will arrive in time, but it is an anxious situation. Winston persists in remaining there, which leaves the Admiralty here without a head. . . . I think that Winston ought to return now that a capable General is arriving. He has done good service in the way of starching & ironing the Belges."[34]

At 5:00 P.M. Rawlinson finally arrived. But he was alone, and his forty thousand men had not even come ashore. For the king and his ministers, that was the last straw. Already the Germans were close enough to pulverize the city with their howitzers. Because of the Belgians' "complete exhaustion and imminent demoralisation," Churchill wired, they were evacuating Antwerp. The eight thousand British troops would hold the inner line of defense as long as possible and then follow. Churchill toured the three brigades, one marine and two naval, for the last time. His reception was mixed. Green troops are always shocked by the primitive conditions of life in the field and usually blame those who put them there. These boys had shivered all night in thin oilskins, and one wrote his father: "We cursed a car containing Churchill who came out to see what was going on & we were glad when he departed." After hearing from his son, Asquith wrote Venetia: "Strictly between ourselves, I can't tell you what I feel of the *wicked* folly of it all. The Marines of course are splendid troops & can go anywhere & do anything: but nothing can excuse Winston (who knew all the facts) from [sic] sending in the other two Naval Brigades."[35]

Churchill reached Dover Tuesday night. There he learned that all three brigades of the naval division were fighting in the front line, that Rawlinson had moved his headquarters back to Bruges, and that Clementine had given birth to a daughter. Thursday morning, when he reported to the cabinet, Asquith thought him "in great form & I think he has thoroughly enjoyed his adventure. He is certainly one of the people one would choose to go tiger-hunting with. . . . He was quite ready to take over in Belgium, and did so in fact for a couple of days, the army the navy & the civil government." Grey wrote Clementine: "I cant tell you how much I admire his courage & gallant spirit & genius for war. It inspires us all." Haldane called the journey "a great and heroic episode." Lloyd George told him it was a "brilliant effort" and then asked: "What are the prospects?"[36]

The prospects were wretched. Kluck's bombardment was shattering the center of Antwerp. The French had decided not to send reinforcements. The marine brigade commander was preparing to abandon his trenches. On Saturday the Belgians surrendered while the British troops escaped along the narrow land corridor. Some wandered over the Dutch border and were interned. For the others, Rupert Brooke wrote, the flight "was like several different kinds of Hell — the broken houses and dead horses lit by an infernal glare. The refugees were the worst sight.

The German policy of frightfulness had succeeded so well that out of that city of half a million, when it was decided to surrender, not ten thousand would stay. . . . I'll never forget that white-faced endless procession in the night, pressed aside to let the military — us — pass, crawling forward at some hundred yards an hour, quite hopeless, the old men crying and the women with hard drawn faces. What a crime!" Asquith wrote: "Poor Winston is very depressed, as he feels that his mission has been in vain."[37]

Others put it much more strongly. The previous Sunday, when prospects seemed relatively bright, Captain Herbert Richmond, the navy's assistant director of operations and a venomous critic of the first lord, had written in his diary at the Admiralty: "The siege of Antwerp looks ugly. The 1st Lord is sending *his* army there; I don't mind his tuppenny untrained rabble going" — he meant men like Brooke and young Asquith — "but I do strongly object to 2000 invaluable marines being sent. . . . It is a tragedy that the Navy should be in such lunatic hands at this time." Now, after the capitulation, the Tory press was in full cry, led by H. A. Gwynne, the editor of the *Morning Post.* A *Post* leader called the stand at Antwerp "a costly blunder, for which Mr W. Churchill must be held responsible. . . . We suggest to Mr Churchill's colleagues that they should, quite firmly and definitely, tell the First Lord that on no account are the military and naval operations to be conducted or directed by him." Gwynne wrote six members of the cabinet that Antwerp was proof "that Mr Churchill is unfitted for the office which he now holds," excoriating him as "a man who has shown most signally his incompetence at least in time of war." There were vehement denunciations in *The Times,* and the *Daily Mail,* reprinting the *Post* attack, described the operation as "a gross example of mal-organization which has cost valuable lives and sacrificed the services during the continuance of the war not only of a considerable number of gallant young Englishmen but also of a considerable section of the Belgian Army."[38]

Extraordinary stories were circulated. Sir Francis Hopwood, a civil lord of the Admiralty, wrote Lord Stamfordham that Winston had been aboard a train Friday evening when "somewhere along the way he heard that the Belgian Government intended to evacuate Antwerp. He rushed back to London and saw K and E. Grey in the small hours of the morning. Then in spite of their remonstrances he left for Antwerp." Stamfordham, believing it, replied: "Our friend must be quite off his head." Beatty wrote his wife: "The man must have been mad to have thought he could relieve [Antwerp] . . . by putting 8,000 half-trained troops into it." The next day he wrote her again, prophesying that "this flying about and putting his fingers into pies which do not concern him is bound to lead to disaster." Bonar Law called Antwerp "an utterly stupid business"; the first lord, he believed, had "an entirely unbalanced mind, which is a real danger at a time like this." Even Churchill's cabinet colleagues were critical. After reflecting upon the expedition, Lloyd George told Frances he felt "rather disgusted" with Winston. "Having taken untrained men over there, he left them in the lurch. He behaved in rather a swaggering way when over there, standing for photographers and cinematographers with shells bursting near him." Asquith, smarting over his son's discomfort, told his wife that the first lord was "by far the most disliked man in my Cabinet by his colleagues." Margot wondered why. "He is rather lovable I think," she said, "and though he often bored me before the war I've liked him very much since. I *love* his spirit of adventure — it suits me — and I love his suggestiveness." Asquith replied irritably: "Oh! He is intolerable! *Noisy,* longwinded and full of perorations. We don't want suggestion — we want wisdom."[39]

Because the strategic consequences of Antwerp were being worked out in high secrecy, Churchill could not defend himself in public or in the House. In private letters he pointed out that he had acted with the fullest authority and could hardly be held responsible for the French failure to reinforce the garrison. Welcoming home the brigades on October 18, he pointed out that untrained troops had been used because the need "was urgent and bitter" and they "could be embarked the quickest" — an explanation that Asquith, in a letter to the King, had endorsed at the time. The real justification for Antwerp, however, was that, far from being an exercise in futility, it had provided an invaluable contribution to the Allied cause. Asquith knew it, and once his private grievance had healed, he wrote that Churchill, by delaying the fall of the city by at least a week, had "prevented the Germans from linking up their forces." On October 29 he added: "The week at Antwerp was well spent, & had a real effect on the general campaign." Afterward the British *Official History of the War* found that while "the British effort to save Antwerp had failed" it had "a lasting influence on operations. Until Antwerp had fallen the troops of the investing force were not available to move forward on Ypres and the coast . . . they were too late to secure Nieuport and Dunkirk and turn the northern flank of the Allies as was intended." And in March 1918 King Albert told a British officer: "You are wrong in considering the RND [Royal Naval Division] Expedition as a forlorn hope. In my opinion it rendered great service to us and those who deprecate it simply do not understand the history of the War in its early days. Only one man of all your people had the prevision of what the loss of Antwerp would entail and that was Mr Churchill." The delay, the king continued, "allowed the French and British Armies to move northwest. Otherwise our whole army might have been captured and the Northern French Ports secured by the enemy."[40]

In the autumn of 1914 this was unknown. The British public wasn't even aware that Rawlinson had brought the Belgian army out intact, covering their escape along the Flanders coast, to fight beside the Allies for the next four years. They only knew that the first lord was acquiring a reputation for designing madcap schemes and interfering with the duties of other ministers. Winston himself later concluded that he had erred in taking the field: "Those who are charged with the direction of supreme affairs must sit on the mountain-tops of control; they must never descend into the valleys of direct physical and personal action." But at the time the fight for the city had merely whetted his appetite. Believing that the enemy was most vulnerable on his northern flank, he drew up plans for assaults on Borkum and Amesland in the North Sea and a proposal to "attack with explosives the locks of the Kiel canal or vessels in the canal." His imagination ranged elsewhere, however; he envisioned campaigns on the Danube or amphibious landings at the Austrian seaport of Kotor on the Adriatic. He even contemplated violations of Dutch neutrality.[41]

Asquith described a long session with Winston, "who, after dilating in great detail on the actual situation, became suddenly very confidential, and implored me not to take a 'conventional' view of his future. Having, as he says, 'tasted blood' these last few days, he is beginning like a tiger to raven for more, and begs that sooner or later, & the sooner the better, he may be relieved of his present office & put in some kind of military command. I told him he could not be spared from the Admiralty, but . . . his mouth waters at the sight & thought of K's new armies. Are these 'glittering commands' to be entrusted to 'dugout trash,' bred on obsolete tactics of 25 years ago — 'mediocrities, who have led a sheltered life mouldering in military routine' &c &c. For about ¼ of an hour he poured forth a ceaseless cataract of invective and appeal, & I much regretted that there was no short-hand writer within hearing. . . . He is a wonderful creature, with a curious dash of schoolboy simplicity (quite unlike Edward Grey's), and what someone said of genius — 'a zigzag streak of lightning in the brain.' "[42]

In assuming that statesmen could conduct the war, Winston was dwelling in a world of illusion. The politicians having lost control of events and precipitated a general war, the professional militarists of every belligerent nation were in the saddle. The officer classes were declaring that no one should have a voice in the war unless he had spent forty years in uniform — which, as B. H. Liddell Hart acidly observed, would have disqualified Alexander, Hannibal, Caesar, Cromwell, Marlborough, and Napoleon. Antwerp, they said smugly, was an example of what you might expect if civilians were in command. The British public believed them. It was generally assumed in England that Churchill had been responsible for a pointless bloodletting in Belgium. The casualty lists told another story: 57 Englishmen had died at Antwerp; 158 had been wounded. In France, by the end of 1914, the cost was 95,654 British soldiers killed in action.

The race to the sea was over and no one had won it. A week after the Germans seized Antwerp, they reached the Channel coast and overran Ostend. There they pivoted, to turn the Allied flank. Joffre, however, asked the British to thwart them, and Churchill, in response, ordered heavy shelling from English warships offshore. It worked. Now the Allies attempted to turn the Germans, but by the end of the month it was obvious that the enemy could not be dislodged either. The front was deadlocked. A wavering seam of trenches, within which troops huddled, began on the Swiss border and ended 466 miles away on the shore at Nieuport, just below Ostend. Because the armies on both sides were enormous, the density of human concentration was unprecedented: there was one soldier for every four inches of front. Mobility, and the opportunity for maneuver, were gone. The deadlock was as obvious as it was intolerable. Surely, people thought, with the expensive and ingenious arsenals available to general staffs, an early breakthrough was inevitable. It wasn't. It wasn't even possible, because offensive weapons were no match for the weapons available to defenders. And whenever a position was in peril it could be swiftly reinforced; troop trains could rocket to the tottering sector, while the attacking infantrymen could plod no faster than soldiers in the Napoleonic wars.* The British Tommies, bewildered and increasingly fatalistic, turned a gay song into a dirge:

* Astonishingly, all this had been predicted in 1899 by a Polish financier named Jean de Bloch. He published a book, *Is War Impossible?*, prophesying that war, "instead of being a hand-to-hand contest . . . will be a kind of stalemate. . . . Everybody will be entrenched in the next war. It will be a great war of entrenchments. The spade will be as indispensable to the soldier as his rifle. . . . All wars will of necessity partake of the character of siege operations. . . . Your soldiers may fight as they please; the ultimate decision is in the hands of famine. . . . That is the future of war . . . the bankruptcy of millions and the break-up of the whole social organization" (Wolff, page ix).

It's a long way to Tipperary,
It's a long way to go

They were the first men to be exposed to poison gas, massed machine-gun fire, and strafing airplanes, and they lived with rats and lice, amid the stench of urine, feces, and decaying flesh, staring up at the sky by day and venturing out only by night. Separated by the junk of no-man's-land, the great, impotent armies squatted month after month, living troglodytic lives in candle-lit dugouts and trenches hewn from Fricourt chalk or La Bassée clay, or ladled from the porridge of swampy Flanders. In the north the efficient Germans tacked up propaganda signs (*Gott strafe England; Frankreich, du bist betrügen*) and settled down to teach their language to French and Belgian children while the Allies counterattacked furiously. These titanic struggles were called battles, but although they were fought on fantastic scales, strategically they were only siege assaults. Every Allied wave found the kaiser's defenses stronger. The poilus and Tommies crawled over their parapets, lay down in front of the jump-off tapes, and waited while their officers studied the new gadgets called wristwatches before blowing their zero-hour whistles. Then the men arose and hurtled toward as many as ten aprons of ropy wire, with barbs thick as a man's thumb, backed by the pullulating Boche. *Morituri te salutamus.* A few trenches would be taken at shocking cost — the price of seven hundred mutilated yards in one attack was twenty-six thousand men — and then the beleaguerment would start again. In London, newspapers spoke of "hammer blows" and "the big push," but the men knew better; a soldiers' mot had it that the war would last a hundred years, five years of fighting and ninety-five of winding up the barbed wire.

Keep the home fires burning
Though the hearts are yearning

It was a weird, grimy life, unlike anything in their Victorian upbringing except, perhaps, the stories of Jules Verne. There were a few poignant reminders of prewar days — the birds that caroled over the lunar landscape each gray dawn; the big yellow poplar forests behind the lines — but most sounds and colors were unearthly. Bullets cracked and ricochets sang with an iron ring; overhead, shells warbled endlessly. There were spectacular red Very flares, saffron shrapnel puffs, and snaky yellowish mists of mustard gas souring the ground. Little foliage survived here. Trees splintered to matchwood stood in silhouette against the sky. Newcomers arriving from Blighty ("The necessary supply of heroes must be maintained at all costs," said Carson) were shipped up in boxcars built for *hommes* 40 or *chevaux* 8 and marched over duckboards to their new homes in the earth, where everything revolved around the trench — you had a trench knife, a trench cane, a rod-shaped trench periscope, a trench coat if you were an officer, and, if you were unlucky, trench foot, trench mouth, or trench fever.[43] In the course of an average day on the western front, there were 2,533 men on both sides killed in action, 9,121 wounded, and 1,164 missing.

Domine Deus, Agnus Dei, Filius Patris:
qui tollis peccata mundi, miserere noblis.

Even in quiet sectors there was a steady toll of shellfire casualties — the methodical War Office called it "normal wastage." The survivors were those who developed quick reactions to danger. An alert youth learned to sort out the whines that threatened him, though after a few close ones, when his ears buzzed and everything turned scarlet, he also realized that the time might come when ducking would do no good. If he was a machine gunner he knew that his life expectancy in combat had been reckoned at about thirty minutes, and in time he became detached toward death and casual with its appliances: enemy lines would be sprayed with belt after belt from water-cooled machine guns to heat the water for soup. Hopes for victory diminished and then vanished. After one savage attempt at a breakthrough Edmund Blunden wrote that "by the end of the day both sides had seen, in a sad scrawl of broken earth and murdered men, the answer to the question. No road. No thoroughfare. Neither race had won, nor could win, the War. The War had won, and would go on winning."[44]

There's a long, long trail a-winding
Into the land of my dreams

A month after Antwerp, Churchill received a letter from Valentine Fleming, an MP and fellow officer in the QOOH, now serving in France: "First and most impressive," Fleming wrote, were "the absolutely indescribable ravages of modern artillery fire, not only upon all men, animals and buildings within its zone, but upon the very face of nature itself. Imagine a broad belt, ten miles or so in width, stretching from the Channel to the German frontier near Basle, which is positively littered with the bodies of men and scarified with their rude graves. . . .

Day and night in this area are made hideous by the incessant crash and whistle and roar of every sort of projectile, by sinister columns of smoke and flame, by the cries of wounded men. . . . Along this terrain of death stretch more or less parallel to each other lines of trenches, some 200, some 1,000 yards apart. . . . In these trenches crouch lines of men, in brown or grey or blue, coated with mud, unshaven, hollow-eyed with the continual strain and unable to reply to the everlasting run of shells hurled at them from 3, 4, 5 or more miles away and positively welcoming an infantry attack from one side or the other as a chance of meeting and matching themselves against *human* assailants and not against invisible, irresistible machines. . . ." Winston sent this to Clementine with a note: "What wd happen I wonder if the armies suddenly & simultaneously went on strike and said some other method must be found of settling the dispute! Meanwhile however new avalanches of men are preparing to mingle in the conflict and it widens and deepens every hour."[45]

Asquith felt desperate. "I am profoundly dissatisfied with the immediate prospect," he wrote his beloved on December 30. He saw the war as "an enormous waste of life and money day after day with no appreciable progress." Over the holidays Lloyd George drew up a memorandum predicting that a few more months of trench warfare "will inevitably destroy the *morale* of the best of troops" and "any attempt to force the carefully-prepared German lines in the west would end in failure and in appalling loss of life." Under these conditions, Churchill believed, victory would be "bought so dear as to be almost indistinguishable from defeat." There was, however, a difference between his mood and that of the rest of the cabinet. They felt desperate; he felt challenged. The answer to immovable defense, he reasoned, was irresistible assault employing new tactics. He suggested what he described as "the attack by the spade" — some three hundred interconnected tunnels dug over a two-mile front toward the enemy's lines and emerging within sixty yards of his trenches, where they would be inaccessible to his artillery. Then he proposed a collective metal shield, "pushed along either on a wheel or still better on a Caterpillar," behind which several men could hide while crossing no-man's-land.[46]

The War Office dismissed these as absurd, and in fact they were impractical. But he was groping toward something effective. His search had begun on September 23, before the Antwerp crisis, when he had been looking for a way to protect his airmen at Dunkirk. Buying up all available Rolls-Royces, he had ordered them clad in improvised armor. "It is most important," he wrote, "that the . . . armed motor-cars should be provided to a certain extent with cars carrying the means of bridging small cuts in the road, and an arrangement of planks capable of bridging a ten- or twelve-feet span quickly and easily should be carried with every ten or twelve machines." The bridging apparatus didn't work; it couldn't reach across a double line of trenches. But an army colonel attached to GHQ in France believed it could be made to work. He approached Sir Maurice Hankey, secretary to the cabinet. Hankey approached Churchill, and on January 5, 1915, Winston sent Asquith a memorandum. It would be simple, he wrote, to quickly "fit up a number of steam tractors with small armoured shelters, in which men and machine guns could be placed, which would be bullet-proof." A "caterpillar system would enable trenches to be crossed quite easily, and the weight of the machine would destroy all wire entanglements." A fleet of them could make "many *points d'appui* for the British supporting infantry to rush forward and rally on them. They can then move forward to attack the second line of trenches." The cost would be slight. "If the experiment did not answer, what harm would be done? It should certainly be done now."[47]

The idea was not new. H. G. Wells had conceived it in 1903. But it had been science fiction then. Now, with superior steel plating, improved internal-combustion engines, and caterpillar tracks, it was practical. Asquith forwarded Winston's memo to Kitchener, who passed it along to his ordnance general, who pigeonholed it. In February, however, the matter came up again. Dining at the home of the Duke of Westminster, Churchill met Colonel Ernest Swinton, an officer fresh from the BEF who believed a large cross-country armored car could scale almost any obstacle. The following morning Winston summoned Captain Eustace Tennyson D'Eyncourt, an Admiralty designer, and asked him to devise a "land ship" using caterpillar treads. Secrecy was urgent; to mislead the Germans, everyone connected with the project would tell others in the Admiralty that they were making "water carriers for Russia" — vessels to carry large vats of drinking water into the czar's front lines. Colonel Swinton predicted that the War Office would designate them "WCs for Russia." He suggested they be called "tanks" and Churchill agreed.[48]

On February 20 Winston had the flu, so the first meeting of the "Land Ship Committee" was held in his Admiralty House bedroom. Four days later he initialed its recommendations "as proposed & with all despatch." An order for a prototype was placed with Messrs. Fosters of Lincoln, which suggested using a tractor as a model. By the end of the month Churchill had persuaded Asquith to earmark £70,000 for the committee. On March 9 Winston was shown the first designs. He minuted: "Press on." Eleven days later D'Eyncourt asked him to approve manufacture of eighteen tanks. Churchill wrote him: "Most urgent. Spe-

"Winston's Folly"

cial report to me in case of delay." His one fear was that the invention would be disclosed prematurely, before enough of them were ready, thereby destroying the element of surprise and alerting the enemy to the new weapon. But when the first one clanked weirdly across the Horse Guards Parade under his eager eyes, observers from the War Office said tanks weren't wanted at all; they would be unable to cope with mud. Even in the Admiralty the project was called "Winston's Folly."[49]

Meanwhile, the insensate killing in France continued. By the end of November, 1914, Britain and France had suffered almost a million casualties. Their leaders were trapped by geography and the sheer mass of the men mobilized. What was needed, *The Times* suggested, was strategy with a "touch of imagination."[50] *Vision,* perhaps, would have been a better word. Certainly the cabinet, preferring another battleground, almost *any* other battleground, was straining to look in all directions. Visible and close at hand was the North Sea island of Borkum, which, if seized, could be used in a variant of Fisher's suggestion — as a staging area for an amphibious invasion of the German coast, twelve miles away. Violations of

Dutch and Danish neutrality, regarded as unconscionable earlier, were now debated. The only other possibilities lay in the eastern Mediterranean, on the vulnerable edges of the tottering Turkish empire: Salonika in northeastern Greece, Syria, Gallipoli, and the Dardanelles, the strait separating Europe from Asia. Here in southeastern Europe, England might find new allies. Greece, Bulgaria, Rumania, and Montenegro shared a common hatred of the oppressive Turks. Farsighted British imperialists had long dreamed of a Balkan league, a union of Christian states federated with the Empire. Now it seemed to be within reach. In the second week of the war Eleutherios Venizelos, the anglophilic Liberal Greek premier, had proposed an Anglo-Greek alliance and volunteered to send sixty thousand men to occupy Gallipoli. The War Office was enthusiastic; in peacetime, Britain's general staff, like Greece's, had studied the peninsula and concluded that it was ripe for plucking. But Grey, wary of extending England's commitments, and believing he could change his mind later, rejected Venizelos's overture.

If one conceives of the waters in that part of the world as a listing stack of irregular glass globes — the kind of weird, bubbling apparatus Dr. Frankenstein used in infusing life into his monster — the vessel on top would be the Black Sea. The Black Sea empties through a bottleneck, the nineteen-mile-long Bosporus, into the Sea of Marmara. Constantinople stands on both banks of the Bosporus strait. The Sea of Marmara, continuing downward, drains through a second channel, the thirty-eight-mile-long Dardanelles, into the Aegean Sea, an arm of the Mediterranean. Until the end of 1914, over 90 percent of Russia's grain and half its exports had passed through the Bosporus and the Dardanelles, also known as the Hellespont. For ships approaching from the south, the Dardanelles is the key to Constantinople. It is astonishingly slim. Viewed from a height, it looks more like a river, and is in fact no wider than the Hudson at Ossining. At its mouth, by Cape Helles on the Aegean, on the tip of Gallipoli peninsula, it is four thousand yards wide. The banks open up as you proceed upward but then close again at the Narrows, where the channel is less than a mile across. Byron swam it easily in March 1810. Gallipoli forms the western shore of the strait. A military force holding the peninsula would dominate the Dardanelles. In the autumn of 1914 it was defended by a skeletal garrison of Turks.

Churchill was keenly aware of the position's military significance. On August 17, when Turkey was neutral, Asquith had written his wife: "The Turk threatens to give trouble in Egypt and elsewhere, and the Germans are doing all they can to get hold of him. Winston is quite pre-

The Turkish Theater 1915

pared to send a swarm of flotillas into the Dardanelles to torpedo the 'Goeben' if necessary." Two weeks later, before the battle of the Marne had even begun and with Turkey still a nonbelligerent, Churchill had persuaded Kitchener to send him two generals, who, with two admirals, would "examine and work out a plan for the seizure by means of a Greek army of adequate strength of the Gallipoli peninsula, with a view to admitting a British Fleet into the Sea of Marmara." The following day, with Turkey still neutral, the cabinet had agreed to help Serbia and Rumania and, in Asquith's words, "to sink Turkish ships if they issue from the Dardanelles." The prime minister wanted to frighten the Turks out of the war. His first lord expected them to come in. At that same meeting, according to the diary of Joseph Pease, a fellow minister, Churchill proposed that once the first shots had been fired the Admiralty should concentrate on "landing Greek force on isthmus on west side of Dardanelles [Gallipoli] & controlling Sea of Marmara." Grey, troubled, wrote him four days later: "I dont like the prospect in the Mediterranean at all, unless there is some turn of the tide in France." Churchill replied: "There is no need for British or Russian anxiety abt a war with Turkey. . . . The price to be paid in taking Gallipoli wd no doubt be heavy, but there wd be no more war with Turkey. A good army of 50,000 & sea-power — that is the end of the Turkish menace."[51]

In the last week of September 1914 a British squadron lying off Cape Helles had stopped a Turkish torpedo boat and, finding German soldiers aboard, turned it back. Learning of this, the German officer who had assumed command of the strait had mined the Dardanelles, ordered that all lighthouses be darkened, and erected signs on precipices declaring that the channel was closed. This had been a flagrant violation of an international convention guaranteeing free passage of the strait. Its sequel, the attack on the czar's Black Sea ports by German cruisers flying the Turkish colors, had brought Turkey in as a formal belligerent. Worried about the security of Egypt, Churchill asked Fisher to investigate "the possibility & advisability of a bombardment of the sea face forts of the Dardanelles."[52] Fisher found the prospects excellent, and during a ten-minute shelling by British warships, a lucky shot hit the magazine of the enemy position at Sedd-el-Bahr, destroying the fort and most of its guns. The wisdom of this strike is doubtful, however. The Turks, warned, withdrew their big guns to the two ancient, crenellated fortresses guarding the channel's Narrows at Chanak. Later in this campaign the same sin would be repeated again and again. The British would strike a heavy blow. It would be effective but indecisive. They would return to find the enemy alerted and strengthened.

In London the War Council met for the first time on November 25.* Churchill, according to Hankey's notes, urged "an attack on Gallipoli peninsula. This, if successful, would give us control of the Dardanelles, and we could dictate terms at Constantinople." Fisher spoke up, asking "whether Greece might not perhaps undertake an attack on Gallipoli on behalf of the Allies." Grey then delivered a rueful report. King Constantine, nagged by his German wife, unwilling to fight his cousin the kaiser, and worried about Bulgarian intentions, had vetoed Premier Venizelos's troop offer. Winston, undiscouraged, pointed out that Constantine's throne was wobbly. Surely he could be subverted. They must not give up. Before them lay a chance to execute the greatest flanking movement in history. He felt military greatness stirring within him. "I have it in me," he had confided to a friend, "to be a successful soldier. I can visualize great movements and combinations." In private he repeated his arguments to Asquith, pressing him to open a new front in the Balkans. On December 5 Asquith wrote Venetia, "His volatile mind is at present set on Turkey & Bulgaria, & he wants to organise a heroic adventure against Gallipoli and the Dardanelles: to wh I am altogether opposed."[53]

By Christmas Winston had reluctantly changed his mind. The troops were unavailable, and he assumed the strait couldn't be taken until they held the peninsula. To be sure, the Dardanelles had been forced by ships alone in 1807, when Napoleon was advancing eastward. Seven British men-of-war under Admiral John T. Duckworth had run the gauntlet, reached the Sea of Marmara, and returned through the channel a week later without losing a single vessel. But twentieth-century fortifications were more imposing. In his early years as first sea lord, Fisher had pondered the Dardanelles problem twice and concluded that it would be "mightily hazardous." On March 15, 1911, Winston himself had written the cabinet: "It is no longer possible to force the Dardanelles . . . nobody would expose a modern fleet to such perils." Now, on December 22, 1914, he wrote Fisher: "The Baltic is the only theatre in wh naval action can appreciably shorten the war." The old admiral continued to look eastward. "I CONSIDER THE ATTACK ON TURKEY HOLDS THE FIELD!" he replied, "but ONLY if it's IMMEDIATE." However, his plan called for 75,000 British soldiers now in French trenches, plus the Indian and Egyptian garrisons, none of which were available. Similarly, when Lloyd

* The War Council had succeeded the Committee of Imperial Defence. In May 1915 the council was dissolved and then replaced, a month later, by the Dardanelles Committee. The committee, in turn, was supplanted by the War Cabinet, which held its first meeting on December 9, 1916. In October 1919 the War Cabinet went the way of the others, and the peacetime cabinet was restored to full authority.

George wanted to land 100,000 men in Syria or Salonika, the men were not to be had. On December 30 Asquith noted that he had received "two very interesting memoranda" from Hankey and Churchill. Both wanted to end the senseless slaughter in the trenches. Hankey pointed out that the BEF was not advancing in France and the British were losing more men than the Germans. He proposed a broad flanking movement through the Balkans. Churchill's minute opened with a ringing cry that the new armies Kitchener was forming ought not to be sent to "chew barbed wire." He then renewed his proposal to storm Schleswig-Holstein via Borkum. In his diary Captain Richmond wrote: "It is *quite mad*. . . . It remains with the army, who I hope will refuse to throw away 12000 troops in this manner for the self-glorification of an ignorant and impulsive man." Refuse they did, and the ministers' frantic search for a better battlefield continued. On New Year's Day the prime minister found two more propositions on his desk, from Lloyd George and, again, from Winston. He noted: "They are both keen on a new objective & theatre as soon as our troops are ready. W., of course, for Borkum and the Baltic: LG for Salonica to join in with the Serbians, and for Syria!"[54]

The Russians forced their hand. They, too, had lost a million men, and had suffered crushing defeats at Tannenberg and the Masurian Lakes. Their rifles and ammunition were in short supply. Now the Turks were threatening the Caucasus. Grand Duke Nicholas summoned the chief British observer accompanying his army and told him that if the Turkish drive continued, he would have to wheel southward to meet it, reducing his commitment to the German front. This was grave. If the Russians fell back, German troops now fighting in the east could be moved into France. The threat brought Kitchener, until now obsessed with the trenches, into the debate over grand strategy. He came to the Admiralty to suggest a naval "demonstration at the Dardanelles." Winston replied that if any such move were to be effective, an infantry commitment would be necessary. When Kitchener returned to the War Office, his staff told him that every English soldier who could be mustered was required on the western front — another standoff. On January 4 Churchill expressed reservations about any attack on Turkey; he still favored the Baltic. The War Council met repeatedly, pondering plans to relieve the pressure on their harried Russian ally. Kitchener opened the January 8 session with a depressing report: a new German drive in France was imminent. Lloyd George interrupted to say heatedly that trench fighting would never lead to victory. Was there, he asked, no alternative theater "in which we might employ our surplus armies to produce a decisive effect?"[55]

Kitchener could think of only one, and he asked the others to support him in backing it. "The Dardanelles," he said, "appear to be the most suitable objective, as an attack here could be made in co-operation with the Fleet. If successful, it would re-establish communications with Russia; settle the Near Eastern question; draw in Greece and, perhaps, Bulgaria and Rumania; and release wheat and shipping now locked up in the Black Sea." Hankey added that a Dardanelles victory "would give us the Danube as a line of communication for an army penetrating into the heart of Austria and bring our sea power to bear in the middle of Europe." The first lord was skeptical. When he asked about troops, the minister for war was evasive. The attack, it seemed, would have to be by ships alone. Churchill therefore rejected it. As late as January 11 he was still pressing for action in the North Sea. The following day, however, events took a sudden, unexpected turn.[56]

Napoleon had written: "Essentially the great question remains: Who will hold Constantinople?" It does not seem essential today, but before the advent of air power the lovely, decaying, sprawling, 2,600-year-old capital of Byzantium was as vital to control of the world's trade routes as it had been in 85 B.C., when the Roman general Sulla signed a famous treaty with Mithridates VI, king of Pontus, in the ancient city of Dardanus, thereby giving the nearby strait its name. As recently as 1886, Lord Salisbury, when he was successfully negotiating free passage to Constantinople for British ships of the line, had written Winston's father: "You are naturally sarcastic about my Dardanelles, and I hope the matter will not come up in our time. . . . I consider the loss of Constantinople would be the ruin of our party and a heavy blow to the country."[57]

Exotic, vaguely sinister with its skyline of onion-domed mosques and slender minarets, its ornate Topkapi Palace housing the sultan's seraglio, its noisome Haydarpasar stews, the luxury hotels overlooking the Bosporus, the Golden Horn separating the city from its wealthy suburbs, Constantinople had seen Saracens and Crusaders eviscerate one another, had watched red-bearded Sultan "Abdul the Damned" butcher his subjects in the streets, and seemed stained by its memories. Abdul's successors, the Young Turks, were a small improvement on him. Their leader, Enver Pasha, was a vain, shallow, cruel megalomaniac who strutted around in a dandy's uniform, fingering his sword hilt. He and his fellow pashas didn't even treasure their own past; if the British approached, they planned to demolish Constantinople out of spite. Saint Sophia, Hagia Sophia, the Blue Mosque, and other priceless buildings were primed with dynamite. Henry Morgenthau, the American ambassador, begged them to save Saint Sophia at least, but a Young Turk told him: "There are not six men in the Committee of Union and Progress who care for anything that is old. We all like new things."[58] They thought of themselves as modern politicians, but they were politically inept. The people mistrusted them deeply; every neutral diplomat believed that at the first sight of a British warship off the Golden Horn, the masses would rise. The Young Turks were proud of their militarism. Yet the country's defenses were in wretched shape — obsolete, undermanned, badly led. Actually, the army's officers included a military genius: thirty-three-year-old Mustapha Kemal. But Kemal despised the Germans. Therefore he was banished from Constantinople. As a sign of his low station he was ordered to defend remote Gallipoli.

"I *loathe* the Turk," Margot Asquith wrote in her diary on November 9, "and really hope that he will be wiped out of Europe." Young men of her class saw it rather differently. They held no brief for the country's present rulers, but Asia Minor fascinated them. Classically educated in England's public schools, they had an almost mystical regard for the heroes who had dominated it in its days of greatness. The city of Troy had stood not four miles from the southern entrance to the Dardanelles. Around it lay the once embattled Troad, now called the Troas Plain. And high above loomed Mount Ida, from whose 5,800-foot peak the gods were said to have witnessed the Trojan War. Upon learning that he was bound for the Bosporus, Rupert Brooke wrote: "It's too wonderful for belief. I had not imagined Fate could be so benign. . . . Will Hero's Tower crumble under the 15-inch guns? Will the sea be polyphloisbic and wine-dark and unvintageable? Shall I loot mosaics from St. Sophia, and Turkish Delight and carpets? Shall we be a Turning Point in History? Oh God! I've never been quite so happy in my life I think. Never quite so pervasively happy; like a stream flowing entirely to one end. I suddenly realize that the ambition of my life has been — since I was two — to go on a military expedition against Constantinople." It was Brooke, the symbol of the idealistic generation now being fed to the guns, who had just written:[59]

If I should die, think only this of me:
That there's some corner of a foreign field
That is forever England.

Even Churchill, who had despised his Greek classes at Harrow, confronted the Turkish challenge with a quickening pulse; at the climax of his novel, *Savrola,* an admiral had led his ships past a gauntlet of blazing forts. That, however, had been fiction. To the Admiralty, Kitchener's insistence upon a naval attack, unsupported by infantry on Gallipoli, seemed futile. Nevertheless, Churchill summoned his senior admirals and asked their opinion. As he expected, they were pessimistic. Yet he was reluctant to leave the issue there. It was crucial, and not only because of the need for Grand Duke Nicholas to keep Germany's eastern armies tied down. Russia's grain was wanted to feed the Allies; 350,000 tons of it were piled up in the Black Sea ports. Any action in Asia Minor would have to be confined to old battleships not needed by Jellicoe in the North Sea. England's security could not be compromised. As it happened, old battleships were available; in his last naval estimates Winston had provided funds to keep such vessels in commission. There was another factor. "Like most people," he testified before a commission investigating the campaign in 1916, "I had held the opinion that the days of forcing the Dardanelles were over. . . . But this war had brought many surprises. We had seen fortresses reputed throughout Europe to be impregnable collapsing after a few days' attack by field armies without a regular siege." Before he broke the bad news to Kitchener, he decided, he would send a query to Vice Admiral Sackville Carden, commanding the blockading squadron off Cape Helles. He wired him: "Do you consider the forcing of the Dardanelles by ships alone a practicable operation. It is assumed that older battleships fitted with mine-bumpers would be used preceded by colliers or other merchant craft as bumpers and sweepers. Importance of results would justify severe loss. Let me know your views."[60]

Admiral Carden's reply reached the Admiralty on the morning of January 5, 1915, and it was electrifying. "With reference to your telegram of 3rd instant," it began, "I do not consider that the Dardanelles can be rushed. They might be forced by extended operations with large number of ships." He outlined four phases of action: leveling defenses at the entrance, clearing the channel up to the Narrows, reducing the Narrows forts, and the "final advance to Marmara." As Churchill later testified, this was "*the* most important telegram. Here was the Admiral, who had been for weeks sitting off the Dardanelles, who presumably had been turning this thing over in his mind again and again, wondering on the possibilities of action there, who produced a plan, and a detailed plan and a novel plan." He showed it to the sea lords, who were as startled as he was; Fisher enthusiastically volunteered to send Carden his newest superdreadnought, the *Queen Elizabeth,* whose fifteen-inch guns had not even been fired yet. Churchill testified: "We all felt ourselves in the presence of a 'new fact.' Moreover, the *Queen Elizabeth* came into the argument with a cumulative effect." He replied to Carden: "Your view is agreed with by high authorities here. Please telegraph in detail what you think could be done by extended operations, what force would be needed, and how you would consider it should be used." In his answer, which arrived in London on January 11, the admiral asked for twelve battleships, three heavy cruisers, three light cruisers, sixteen destroyers, six submarines, four seaplanes, twelve minesweepers, and a score of miscellaneous vessels. He planned to open with a long-range bombardment of the forts; then, with minesweepers leading the way, to sail close and destroy them seriatim. At the same time, the Turks would be misled by diversionary shelling on both coasts of Gallipoli. He wanted a great deal of ammunition, and once he had broken through to the Sea of Marmara, he intended to keep the Dardanelles clear by constant patrolling. "Time required for operations," he concluded, "depends greatly on morale of enemy under bombardment; garrison largely stiffened by the Germans; also on weather conditions. Gales now frequent. Might do it all in a month about." He proposed to start the operation on February 1 with hull-down fire from the *Queen Elizabeth.*[61]

Churchill laid all this before Asquith and Kitchener early in the afternoon on January 12. He had been particularly pleased with Fisher's response, writing him how glad he was that, as a result of the first sea lord's initiative, the mighty new ship would be "firing all her ammunition at the Dardanelles forts instead of uselessly into the sea." At noon the next day he put the War Council in the picture. Sir John French was there. After discussing the progress of plans for an amphibious attack on the German U-boat pens in Zeebrugge, Belgium, which he favored, Winston stepped up to a map and described Carden's proposal, arguing, as Lloyd George put it, "with all the inexorable force and pertinacity, together with the mastery of detail he always commands when he is really interested in a subject." He said the Admiralty could spare the twelve old battleships Carden wanted and add three modern dreadnoughts "without reducing our strength in the main theatre of war." Then he said: "Once the forts are reduced, the minefields will be cleared and the Fleet will proceed up to Constantinople and destroy the *Goeben.*" According to Hankey's memoirs, *The Supreme Command,* "The idea caught on at once. . . . The War Council turned eagerly from the dreary vista of a 'slogging match' on the Western Front to brighter prospects, as they seemed, in the Mediterranean." Asquith liked it now. Lloyd George agreed, and so did Kitchener. Arthur Balfour, present as a senior statesman, thought it would be hard to imagine a more useful operation. K of K said that if the bombardment proved ineffective, they could cancel the rest of the operation. The decision was unanimous: "That the Admiralty should prepare for a naval expedition and take Gallipoli with Constantinople as its objective."[62]

Fisher said nothing. The sea lords made a point of never speaking up at these meetings. As he once explained: "When sailors get round a Council Board they are almost invariably mute. The politicians who are round the Board are never mute; they would never have got there if they had been mute." Yet even when he was silent his presence was felt, and an understanding of him and the minister for war, the two professionals on the War Council, is essential to a grasp of what was happening and, more important, to what lay ahead. Both were immensely popular with the British public, so much so that the cabinet members, their nominal superiors, would go to almost any lengths to avoid antagonizing them. Erratic and peppery, the old admiral seemed the very personification of English sea traditions, a dauntless figure who ranked with Drake and Nelson. Churchill compared him to "a great castle, which has long contended with time; the mighty central mass of the donjon towered up intact and seemingly everlasting." But the mightiest castle crumbles in time, and probably no septuagenarian could have borne the strain of serving as first sea lord in 1915. Moreover, Fisher's temperament was ill-suited to working in harness with Churchill through an endless series of crises. Violet Asquith wrote of the admiral: "He lived by instincts, hunches, flashes, which he was unable to justify or sustain in argument. Though words poured from his lips and from his pen he was no match for Winston as a dialectician. In trying to defend his own position he trumped up reasons and pretexts of no substance which Winston easily demolished. . . . His personal intimacy with Winston and affection for him increased his sense of helplessness in standing up to him."[63]

Kitchener was underrated by the rest of the cabinet. Like Fisher, he had predicted the year of the war's outbreak, and he had been among the first to see the possibilities of the Dardanelles. It was his tragedy, and England's, that no one dared say no to him. As Churchill testified a year later, "His prestige and authority were immense. He was the sole mouthpiece of War Office opinion in the War Council. . . . He was never, to my belief, overruled by the War Council or the Cabinet, in any military matter, great or small. . . . Respect for the man, sympathy for his immense labours, confidence in his professional judgment, and the belief that he had plans deeper and wider than any we could see, silenced misgivings and disputes, whether in the Council or at the War Office. All-powerful, imperturbable, reserved, he dominated absolutely our counsels at this time." Sir Osbert Sitwell thought he knew why. Six months earlier, at the time of Sarajevo, Sitwell had written that Kitchener "plainly belonged to some different order of creation from those around him . . . he could claim kinship to the old race of gigantic German generals, spawned by Wotan in the Prussian plains, and born with spiked helmets ready on their heads . . . he sat there with the same suggestion of immense strength and even of latent fury."[64]

Kitchener was caught in a bloody debate between the "Westerners," as they were called — those who believed the war could be won only in France — and the "Easterners," who were convinced that the solution lay in Asia Minor, the Balkans, Italy, or the Baltic. Almost without exception, the Westerners were crusty, stubborn, conservative regular army officers who had been posted to France because that was where the fighting had begun, and whose professional reputations could be made only there. If France became a dead end, their sacrifice of all the lives there would have been made in vain. Haig said the key to victory was "attrition," which, his general staff explained, meant "wearing down the Boches." But this assumed that more Germans were dying than Englishmen. And it wasn't true. In the struggle for Flanders, three British soldiers fell for every two Germans. In the battle of the Somme, the figures were two British to one German. Incessant shelling back and forth across no-man's-land meant that even in the quietest sector more than a thousand Britons died every week. Sir John French admitted to the War Council that "complete success against the Germans in the Western theatre of war, though possible is not probable." When his subordinates heard of this they turned mutinous and began to plot against him. Henry Wilson was alarmed by news of the Dardanelles preparations. He wrote Bonar Law that "the way to end this war is to kill Germans, not Turks. The place where we can kill most Germans is here, and therefore every man and every round of ammunition we have got in the world ought to come here. All history shows that operations in a secondary and ineffectual theatre have no bearing on major operations — except to weaken the force there engaged. History, no doubt, will repeat her lesson once more for our benefit."[65]

This was poppycock. The way to end a war is to win it — defeating the enemy by superior strategy, not by counting his dead, especially when, as in this case, his count is lower than yours. And history refutes Wilson. Day by day, in World War I English losses in France were triple those in World War II, when, with Churchill as prime minister, British armies were fighting all over the world. Between 1914 and 1918 Britain's generals slaughtered the most idealistic generation of young leaders in the history of England, and all to no purpose. Never in the field of human conflict have so many suffered so much to gratify the pride of so few. And this was clear to some men at the time. Those not blinded by chauvinism were shocked and incredulous. Siegfried Sassoon, a decorated hero of the trenches, threw his medal away and wrote: "Pray God that you may never know / The hell where youth and laughter go." "How long," D. H. Lawrence wrote Asquith's daughter-in-law Cynthia, "will the nations continue to empty the future?"[66]

Lord Salisbury had warned the generation of parliamentarians who would succeed him: "No lesson seems to be so deeply inculcated by experience of life as that you should never trust experts. If you believe doctors, nothing is wholesome; if you believe theologians, nothing is innocent; if you believe soldiers, nothing is safe." They hadn't forgotten, but they were bullied by the military experts' doctrine of attrition. Thus cowed, they writhed and protested. Lloyd George wept over the millions of youths who did "their intrepid best to obey the fatuous orders," advancing "against the most terrible machine-gun fire directed against troops." Churchill pointed out: "A policy of pure attrition between armies so evenly balanced cannot lead to a decision. . . . Unless this problem can be solved satisfactorily, we shall simply be wearing each other out on a gigantic scale and with fearful sacrifices without ever reaping the reward."[67]

These civilian ministers knew the military hierarchy didn't have the answers. But neither did they. Like animals trapped in a maze they scurried this way and that, so confused that they wouldn't have recognized a way out if they had stumbled upon it. In that same War Council meeting which adopted the Dardanelles plan, orders were issued to draw up plans for operations in Salonika, the Netherlands, Rumania, and the Gulf of Kotor on the Adriatic. Lloyd George wanted rolling stock built for the Salonika railroad "and perhaps barges built for the Danube." Churchill agreed. "At the worst," he said, "they would be a good feint." Then he himself, who had just delivered a brilliant presentation of the flanking movement through Turkey, said: "We ought not to go South until we can do nothing in the North. Is there, for example, no possibility of action in Holland?"[68] Grey replied that there was none. Nothing could be done there until the War Office could provide at least 300,000 soldiers for an expedition. Winston said no more. Calls for troops stopped every ministerial discussion. Troops had to come from Kitchener. Kitchener would have to get them from the BEF, and there would be hell to pay in France. He would have paid if he were sure an operation would succeed. But in this new war, with its machines and gas and mines and land ships that sailed underwater, nothing could guarantee success. Inertia bound him; he sided with his brother officers across the Channel while Fisher, similarly torn, fell back on the peacetime axiom that a good naval commander doesn't risk the vessels entrusted to him.

Actually, Fisher was more confused than Kitchener. Later his conduct would raise questions about his sanity, but his bewilderment on January 13 is understandable. The council had decided that the Dardanelles task force should "take Gallipoli with Constantinople as its objective." How could a fleet "take" a peninsula? How could it occupy a great city? As we know now, the occupation of Constantinople would have been unnecessary; the dissident Turkish mobs would have done the job for them. At the time, however, no one in London could have guessed that. Nevertheless, the plan pleased everyone. Grey saw neutral states lining up to join the Allies. Arthur Balfour, who had been invited to join the council, not as a member of the Opposition, but as an elder statesman, thought everything about the Dardanelles sounded splendid. The French, similarly enchanted, offered four battleships. The Russians hinted that they might send troops, which was impractical. Kitchener, who did not know that, was delighted.

Churchill now set aside all thoughts of a Baltic campaign and concentrated on the Dardanelles. He believed the battle was as good as won, always a dangerous assumption in war. By coincidence January 13 was the Russian New Year, and he had sent an extravagant holiday message to Saint Petersburg: "Our resources are within reach and inexhaustible; our minds are made up. We have only to bend forward together laying aside every hindrance, keeping nothing back, and the downfall of German ambition is sure." For the next week he and an ad hoc Admiralty war group examined every particular detail of the coming attack, sending and receiving telegrams from Carden almost hourly. Each instruction, each technical problem, was read, endorsed, and initialed by the first sea lord with the famous scrawled green *F.* Yet the old admiral was seething. Like a tumor, an irrational terror was growing in him — the fear that the Aegean expedition would weaken the Home Fleet, encouraging Tirpitz to steam into Scapa Flow with a superior force, sink every British warship left there, and win the war. In that case Jellicoe would become the defeated admiral. But he did not share the first sea lord's doubts. He kept sending him reassurances. Fisher was unconsoled. On January 19, six days after the decision, he wrote Jellicoe that the ships sailing to the eastern Mediterranean were *"all urgently required at the decisive theatre at home!* There is only one way out, and that is to resign! But you say *'no,'* which simply means I am a consenting party to what I absolutely disapprove. *I don't agree with one single step taken,* so it is fearfully against the grain that I remain on in deference to your wishes." The next day he wept on Hankey's shoulder. Hankey told Asquith, who wrote Venetia that the old man was "in a very unhappy frame of mind," that he "likes Winston personally" but was frequently overruled ("he out-argues me") on purely "technical naval matters."[69]

The Dardanelles assault had been approved, not by Churchill, but by the entire War Council. Fisher had participated in every step taken since then. Winston had no inkling of his anxiety until, eight days after the arrival of Carden's plan of attack, the first sea lord urged the recall of a destroyer flotilla and an Australian submarine which had been sent to the Aegean from Scapa Flow. He himself had suggested the dispatch of the *Queen Elizabeth,* but on January 21, in another letter to Jellicoe, he wrote that its transfer was "a serious interference with our imperative needs in Home waters, and I've fought against it 'tooth and nail.' . . . I just abominate the Dardanelles operation, unless a great change is made and it is settled to be a military operation, with 200,000 men in conjunction with the Fleet. I believe that Kitchener is coming now to this view of the matter." But Kitchener wasn't, at least not yet. Thus far the War Office had not been drawn in. Churchill would have been elated had K of K offered 200,000 men, or even a fraction of that. Lacking troops, Winston was moving forward on the strength of Carden's professional opinion. All of them had endorsed it, including Fisher. Yet the old salt continued to have second thoughts. His blaming Churchill was a consequence of senility. Matters had to come to a head; even he recognized that, and so, on January 25, he submitted a rebellious memorandum to the first lord, with a request that it be printed and circulated among members of the War Council before their next meeting, scheduled three days hence. His paper was a flat renunciation of the entire Dardanelles plan. "We play into Germany's hands," he wrote, "if we risk fighting ships in any subsidiary operations such as coastal bombardments or the attack of fortified places without military co-operation, for we thereby increase the possibility that the Germans may be able to engage our Fleet with some approach to equality of strength. The sole justification of coastal bombardments . . .

is to force a decision at sea, and so far and no further can they be justified." Therefore, the Admiralty should be satisfied with blockading the enemy: "Being already in possession of all that a powerful fleet can give a country we should continue quietly to enjoy the advantage without dissipating our strength in operations that cannot improve the position."[70]

Churchill was stunned. He immediately drew up a table comparing the naval strengths of Britain and Germany, pointing out that England's domination of the North Sea would be unweakened by the Dardanelles task force. Jellicoe concurred. Fisher wouldn't budge. Asquith refused to circulate either his memorandum or Winston's table. On the morning of the next War Council meeting Churchill found Fisher's resignation on his desk. "I entreat you to believe," he said in part, "that if as I think really desirable for a complete *'unity of purpose'* in the War that I should gracefully disappear and revert to roses at Richmond (*'The heart untravelled fondly turns to home'*) that there will not be in my heart the least lingering thought of anything but regard and affection and *indeed much admiration* towards yourself."[71]

Winston hurried across the Horse Guards Parade to No. 10. Asquith, furious, summoned Fisher to his upstairs study, heard his version and Churchill's, and told them his decision. As a sop to Fisher, the Zeebrugge operation was shelved. The Dardanelles plan would stand unchanged. The three men then descended to the Cabinet Room to join the council. Fisher remained taciturn as usual until Churchill mentioned French and Russian reactions to Carden's coming campaign in Turkey. At that he spoke up, saying he had "understood that this question would not be raised today, and the Prime Minister is well aware of my views in regard to it." With that, he rose, left the table, and stood at a window with his back to the others. Kitchener went to him. Fisher, tight-lipped, said he was leaving the Admiralty. Kitchener pointed out that everyone else believed in the plan, that the prime minister had issued the directive, and that it was the first sea lord's duty to follow orders. Reluctantly the old admiral returned to his seat. As he himself said later, "Naval opinion was unanimous. Mr. Churchill had them all on his side. I was the only rebel." Asquith told the meeting that Churchill was anxious to have everyone's views on the importance of the coming campaign. Kitchener considered the naval attack to be "vitally important. If successful, its effect would be the equivalent of a successful campaign fought with the new armies." Grey said it would settle the situation in the Balkans, particularly in Bulgaria. Balfour was rhapsodic. He thought it would cut Turkey in half, turn Constantinople into an Allied base, provide them with

Russian wheat, and open a passage to the Danube. "It is difficult," he said, to "imagine a more helpful operation."[72]

During these cheerful forecasts, Asquith scribbled a note to Venetia: "A personal matter which rather worries me is the growing friction between Winston and Fisher." As the council broke for lunch, the prime minister called the old salt to his study, and, after a turbulent hour, persuaded him to support it. Fisher, indeed, seemed to have been transformed into an enthusiast. He even suggested — and the offer was accepted — that Carden be reinforced by two 1908 battleships from Scapa Flow, the *Lord Nelson* and the *Agamemnon.* "When I finally decided to come in," he later testified, "I went the whole hog, totus porcus." Churchill sprang a surprise during that afternoon's session. He announced that he didn't want troops even if Kitchener offered them. "A landing in force under fire on the Gallipoli peninsula" once the Turks were "fully awakened," he argued, would involve "a greater stake." A successful naval action could produce "revolutionary effects at Constantinople and throughout the Balkans." The prospects for success were so bright that he believed it worthwhile "to try the naval plan" even though, if it failed, "a subsequent military operation" would be rendered "more difficult." If a brigade of Tommies was available, he suggested, it should be sent to Salonika, where, he believed, the appearance of no more than 10,000 British soldiers would bring Greece's 180,000 troops into the war. As the dinner hour approached, he conferred with Fisher and Vice Admiral Henry Oliver, chief of the Admiralty War Staff, then told the council, with Fisher's approval, that the Admiralty was united in its determination to "make a naval attack on the Dardanelles." Oliver said: "The first shot will be fired in about a fortnight."[73]

Actually, it would not be fired for over three weeks. Meanwhile, misunderstandings and disagreements, inherent in war by committee, multiplied. "No single man," Robert Rhodes James has observed, "can, or should, bear responsibility for the series of decisions, half-decisions, and evasions of decisions that marked the initiation of the Gallipoli campaign. The manner in which the Asquith Government drifted into this vast commitment of men and resources . . . condemns not any individual but rather the system of war government practiced by the Administration." Churchill, however, had become the operation's most visible advocate and its most eloquent spokesman. As he saw the situation in early 1915, France had become an abattoir, the Russians were bogged down, the German fleet refused to come out and fight, and the world's finest military instrument, the Royal Navy, was idle. Therefore, as Asquith noted, "Winston is for the moment as keen as mustard about his Dardanelles adventure." It had become *his* Dardanelles adventure. Even the prime minister now thought of it that way. As such, it would become a cross he bore for years. Later it was seen as a monument to his genius. In *Through the Fog of War,* Liddell Hart wrote: "Everyone realizes that, in the words of the German official account, 'Churchill's bold idea was not a finespun fantasy of the brain.' We too now know, as the Germans did in the War, how feasible was the Dardanelles project, and how vital its effect would have been." Another writer, Edward Grigg, declared that had Churchill's advice been followed — had he had the power of the prime minister — "not only the entire development of the First World War but also the fate of Britain, and Europe, too, would have been different."[74]

But he was *not* prime minister. In attempting to reshape the entire direction of the war from the Admiralty, he was headed for rocks and shoals. It was Antwerp again — in spades. As he recalled in 1949: "I was ruined for the time being over the Dardanelles, and a supreme enterprise cast away, through my trying to carry out a major and combined enterprise of war from a subordinate position." Ian Hamilton described him as "one who has it in him to revive the part of Pitt, had he but Pitt's place." Lacking it, he was unable to force, not the Dardanelles, but Britain's naval and military commanders. Moreover, being wholly competent himself, he assumed that they were, too. They weren't. Hindenburg called the British soldiers of that war "lions led by donkeys."[75] Some were stupid; others were devious. Haig told the War Office that the Germans being taken prisoner were in wretched condition, proof that the enemy was scraping the bottom of the barrel; when the prime minister crossed the Channel to see for himself, Haig packed a POW camp with sick, scrawny captives. Able politicians should see through such scams. They are, or ought to be, shrewd judges of men, and Churchill's continuing misjudgment of Fisher, his failure to realize that his first sea lord was a Judas, spelled trouble ahead. So did his puzzling claim that he didn't need troops on Gallipoli.

At first it passed unnoticed. At the next meeting of the War Council, on February 9, Churchill informed them of a dazzling *coup de maître.* Venizelos had been persuaded to defy his king and turn the Greek island of Lemnos over to the British as a base for operations against Turkey. It was a masterstroke, accomplished with tact and restraint — Winston had overruled Fisher's preposterous proposal that they annex Lemnos and Lesbos — and the ministers were too elated to question this intrusion into Grey's domain. It was four days later, when the warships detailed to shell the Dardanelles had assembled off Cape Helles, and Carden was awaiting the last minesweepers before attacking, that Hankey became the first to challenge Winston's position on troops. He approached Asquith, who wrote Venetia that Hankey "thinks very strongly that the naval operations of which you know should be supported by landing a fairly strong military force. I have been for some time coming to the same opinion, and I think we ought to be able without denuding [Sir John] French to scrape together from Egypt, Malta & elsewhere a sufficiently large contingent." Others were reaching the same conclusion independently. The next day Richmond sent Hankey a memorandum arguing that "the bombardment of the Dardanelles, even if all the forts are destroyed, can be nothing but a local success, which without an army to carry it on can have no further effect." Hankey replied, "Your Memo. is absolutely A.1 . . . I am sending it to Jacky." Fisher wrote Richmond: "YOUR PAPER IS EXCELLENT." That same day Admiral Sir Henry Jackson submitted a minute to the first lord: "The naval bombardment is not recommended as a sound military operation unless a strong military force is ready to assist in the operation, or, at least, follow it up immediately the forts are silenced."[76]

All this gave Churchill pause. In first broaching the subject of the Dardanelles, he had specified the need for infantry; his switch had been based on Carden's assurance that warships could do the job alone. Now, a month later, he belatedly roused himself and cast about for sources of troops. As it happened, the very day he received Jackson's opinion, the Greeks rejected Grey's offer of a Salonika expedition. That meant a first-class division, the Twenty-ninth, was available for assignment elsewhere. Asquith called an emergency meeting of the War Council. Kitchener agreed that the Twenty-ninth should sail to Lemnos "at the earliest possible date." There they would be joined by a marine brigade and the Australian and New Zealand troops now in Egypt, all of which would be available "in case of necessity to support the naval attack on the Dardanelles." The first lord was directed to assemble sufficient transports to carry "a force of 50,000 men at any point where they might be required." The attempt on the strait was now imminent. K of K passed Winston a note: "You get through! I will find the men."[77]

The bond between Churchill and Kitchener was vital to the campaign, and at this very unfortunate moment it was cut. The origins of the dispute are unclear. Apparently Winston, on one of his visits to France, had told Sir John French that he might be in a position to lend him some Admiralty troops and equipment. It had been an informal remark. It was also ill-advised. K of K was sensitive about his prerogatives. When French sent the War Office a written request for the men and matériel

Churchill had so unwisely dangled before him, the war minister went straight to the prime minister. Asquith wrote Winston: "Kitchener has just been to see me in a state of some perturbation. He has just received two official letters from French, in which he announces that you have offered him a Brigade of the Naval Division, and 2 squadrons of armoured cars. Kitchener is strongly of the opinion that French has no need of either. But, apart from that, he feels (& I think rightly) that he ought to have been told of, & consulted about, the offer before it was made." That evening Margot Asquith wrote in her diary: "Of course Winston is intolerable. It is all *vanity* — he is devoured by vanity. . . . It's most trying as K and he had got a modus vivendi." Churchill explained that it was all a misunderstanding, but in the morning Asquith wrote Venetia: "I am rather vexed with Winston who has been tactless enough to offer Sir John F (behind K's back & without his knowledge) a brigade of his Naval Division, and 2 squadrons of his famous Armoured Cars which are being hawked about from pillar to post."[78]

On such petty quarrels did the fate of millions hang. Winston wrote Kitchener on February 19, attempting a reconciliation. It wasn't enough. The war minister's rage was still glowing when the War Council met that afternoon to confirm its decision, made three days earlier, to send the Twenty-ninth Division to Lemnos. K of K bluntly told the dismayed ministers that he had changed his mind. He had decided to withhold, not only the nineteen thousand trained men of the Twenty-ninth Division, but also the thirty thousand Australians and New Zealanders in Egypt. Asquith, Churchill, and Lloyd George protested — Lloyd George thought even these wouldn't be enough; he wanted to reinforce them with the ten-thousand-man Royal Naval Division, fifteen thousand Frenchmen, and ten thousand Russians. Grey's support was tepid; Lemnos rankled, after all. Kitchener said he would think it over. But four days later when Winston repeated his request for men — it was "not a question of sending them immediately to the Dardanelles," he explained, "but merely of having them within reach" — K of K replied that the Twenty-ninth still could not be spared. The Russian front was fluid, he had said; if disaster struck there, the men of the Twenty-ninth were "the only troops we have available as a reserve to send over to France." It was his impression that the Dardanelles had been conceived as a naval attack; did Churchill plan to lead an army, too? Not at all, said Winston. He could, however, imagine a situation in which victory was within reach "but where a military force would just make the difference between success and failure." One senses his frustration when Lloyd George, his strongest supporter in the last discussion, now warned against using troops "to pull the chestnuts out of the fire for the Navy," suggesting that if the Dardanelles miscarried, "we ought to be immediately ready to try something else" in the Middle East — presumably Syria, his pet idea. Kitchener was immovable. He doubted the Turks would try to defend Gallipoli. Churchill said they might have forty thousand men there already. If so, Kitchener predicted, they would evacuate the peninsula after the bombardment.[79]

The War Council voted to postpone further discussion of the division's destiny until the next meeting. Winston, appalled and angry, demanded that his objection be entered in the council's minutes, and so it was: "MR CHURCHILL said that the XXIX Division would not make the difference between failure and success in France, but might well make the difference in the East. He wished it to be placed on record that he dissented altogether from the retention of the XXIX Division in this country. If a disaster occurred in Turkey owing to the insufficiency of troops, he must disclaim all responsibility." That evening he wrote his brother that this "was vy vexatious to me, & hard to bear. . . . The capacity to run risks is at famine prices. All play for safety. The war is certainly settling on to a grim basis, & it is evident that long vistas of pain & struggle lie ahead. The limited fund of life & energy wh I possess is not much use in trying to influence these tremendous moments. I toil away."[80]

Asquith shared his chagrin, but such was Kitchener's power to intimidate that even the prime minister wasn't prepared to risk offending him. Of this pivotal meeting he wrote Venetia: "We are all agreed (except K) that the naval adventure in the Dardanelles shd be backed up by a strong military force." Kitchener was being "very sticky," he thought, because "he wants to have something in hand, in case the Germans are so far successful against Russia for the moment, as to be able to despatch Westwards a huge army — perhaps of a million — to try & force Joffre & French's lines." Asquith himself felt that "one must take a lot of risks in war, & I am strongly of the opinion that the chance of forcing the Dardanelles, & occupying Constantinople . . . presents such a unique opportunity that we ought to hazard a lot elsewhere rather than forgo it. If K can be convinced, well & good: but to discard his advice & overrule his judgment on a military question is to take a great responsibility. So I am rather anxious."[81]

Churchill at any rate could send the Royal Naval Division, survivors of Antwerp. For the first time in his life he joined a royal entourage; he and the prime minister accompanied George V to Blandford, where the King reviewed the men before they shipped out. Oc Asquith was there, and Rupert Brooke. Margot wrote in her diary: "The whole 9,000 men were drawn up on the glorious downs and Winston walked round and inspected them before the King arrived. I felt quite a thrill when I saw Oc and Rupert with walking sticks standing in front of their men looking quite wonderful! Rupert is a beautiful young man and we get on well, he has so much intellectual temperament and nature about him. He told Oc he was quite *certain* he would never come back but would be killed — it didn't depress him at all but he was just *convinced* — I shall be curious to see if this turns out to be a true instinct. . . . *They marched past perfectly.* I saw the silver band (given to the Hood Division by Winston's constituents) coming up the hill and the bayonets flashing — I saw the uneven ground and the straight backs — "Eyesssssss RIGHT!" — and the darling boy had passed. The King was pleased and told me they all marched wonderfully." Brooke wrote:[82]

> *Now, God be thanked, Who has matched us*
> *with His hour,*
> *And caught our youth, and wakened us from*
> *sleeping.*

His instinct turned out to be true. In two months he was dead. He had been twenty-seven years old. Winston wrote his obituary in *The Times:* "This life has closed at the moment when it seemed to have reached its springtime. A voice had become audible, a note had been struck, more true, more thrilling, more able to do justice to the nobility of our youth in arms engaged in this present war, than any other — more able to express their thoughts of self-surrender, and with a power to carry comfort to those who watched them so intently from afar. The voice has been swiftly stilled. Only the echoes and the memory remain."[83]

It wasn't much. His father, a housemaster at Rugby, where Rupert had been so popular, drew small comfort from it. His dons at King's College, Cambridge, wondered instead what he would have become. Oc grieved for a year. Then he himself, having survived the Dardanelles, was killed in France.

But they had marched well at Blandford. Even the King had remarked on it.

Sackville Hamilton Carden was not the ideal commander for the Aegean squadron. Approaching sixty, he had been superintendent of the

Malta dockyards until the outbreak of the war and lacked the temperament of a fighter. Churchill's candidate for the appointment had been Sir Arthur Limpus, a younger, more aggressive admiral who had studied the Dardanelles for years, but in early September, when Turkey had still been neutral, Grey had felt that naming Limpus would provoke the Turks. Carden was an able strategist. His plan to rush the Dardanelles was sound. But he was a worrier. He worried about the heavy concentration of enemy guns on the banks of the strait and was uncomforted by assurances that they were small, obsolete, and poorly sited. Driftage in the channel troubled him; although there was no tide in the strait, tributaries and melting snows produced a five-knot current, and chunks of floating ice could be expected at this time of year. Vessels which could navigate the Orkney Islands, however, would have no problems here. The danger of minefields preyed on his mind. This was a real hazard, but the Admiralty had judged the risk acceptable and provided him with sufficient minesweepers. None of these objections mattered in themselves. Carden's weakness was that, faced with an operation requiring exceptional daring, he was unsure of himself. It was a disease among military leaders in that war, and it was catching. Confronted by so many martial innovations, most senior officers had by 1915 become excessively cautious and easily discouraged. Bravery had nothing to do with it. Carden's second in command, Vice Admiral John de Robeck, was brave in battle, but faced with crucial decisions, he would prove to be of the same stripe.

Their long-awaited attack opened at 9:51 on the blustery morning of Friday, February 19, 1915. The Allied task force — eight British battleships, four French — approached the mouth of the strait and opened fire on the Turkish forts guarding its lips, Kum Kale and Cape Helles. It was no contest. The range of the defensive batteries was so short that their shells couldn't even reach the ships. At two o'clock that afternoon the warships closed to six thousand yards; at 4:45 P.M. de Robeck led *Vengeance, Cornwallis,* and *Suffren* closer still. Most of the blockhouses, shrouded in smoke, appeared deserted. Then night fell. High seas, snow, and sleet prevented further action until the following Thursday. But in the interim Carden, encouraged by the one-sided duel, telegraphed the Admiralty: "I do not intend to commence in bad weather leaving result undecided as from experience on first day I am convinced given favourable weather conditions that the reduction of the forts at the entrance can be completed in one day."[84] When the weather cleared, de Robeck carried the assault up to the very muzzles of the blockhouses. The remaining Turkish and German gunners fled northward. Royal Marines landed on Gallipoli, spiking guns and destroying searchlights. Another party went ashore at Kum Kale. Minesweepers penetrated the strait six miles upstream, to within three thousand yards of Kephez Point, without meeting significant resistance. Carden wired London that he expected to reach Constantinople in two weeks.

The War Council was ecstatic. Fisher wanted to hurry to the Aegean and lead the next assault, on the Narrows. The export of Russian wheat seemed imminent; in Chicago the price of grain fell sharply. Churchill, meanwhile, was counting all his unhatched chickens. At the end of February he cabled Grand Duke Nicholas: "The progress of an attack on Dlles is encouraging & good & we think the Russian Black Sea Fleet shd now get ready at Sebastopol to come to the entrance of the Bosporus at the right moment, of wh we will send notice." Asquith wrote Venetia: "Winston is breast high about the Dardanelles." That same evening the political climate in Athens went through yet another transformation. King Constantine was having second thoughts. Like the rest of the Balkan rulers, he wanted to be on the winning side. Violet Asquith was "sitting with Clemmie at the Admiralty when Winston came in in a state of wild excitement and joy. He showed us, under many pledges of secrecy, a telegram from Venizelos promising help from the Greeks. . . . Our joy knew no bounds." Violet asked if Constantine knew of this. "Yes," said Churchill, "our Minister said Venizelos had already approached the King and he was in favour of war." Moreover, he went on, Bulgaria, Rumania, and Italy were all "waiting — ready to pounce — all determined to play a part in the fall of Constantinople." Violet recrossed the Horse Guards "treading on air. Turkey, encircled by a host of enemies, was doomed, the German flank was turned, the Balkans for once united and on our side, the war shortened perhaps by years, and Winston's vision and persistence vindicated."[85]

He was already contemplating peace terms. To Grey he wrote two days later: "We must not disinterest ourselves in the final settlement of this region. . . . I am having an Admy paper prepared abt the effect of a Russian control of the Straits and Cple. I hope you will not settle anything further until you can read it. English history will not end with this war." Others were also looking to the future. Fisher wrote Winston: "*Moral: — Carden to press on!* and Kitchener to occupy the deserted Forts at extremity of Gallipoli and mount howitzers there! . . . Invite Bulgaria by telegram (direct from Sir E. Grey) to take Kavalla and Salonica provided she *at once* attacks Turkey and tell Greece *'Too late'!* and seize the Greek Fleet by a 'coup' later on. They wd probably join us now *if bribed!* All the kings are against all the peoples! Greece, Bulgaria, Rumania! *What an opportunity for Democracy!*" Asquith told Venetia that one of his ministers had written "an almost dithyrambic memorandum urging that in the carving up of the Turks' Asiatic dominions, we should take Palestine, into which the scattered Jews cd in time swarm back from all the quarters of the globe, and in due course obtain Home Rule. (What an attractive community!)" Hankey had prepared a seven-page paper: "After the Dardanelles: The Next Steps." He advocated a broad drive by British, Serbian, Greek, Rumanian, and Russian troops, targeted on the Carpathian Mountains between what are now Czechoslovakia and Poland. Others wanted to follow the Danube from the Black Sea through Austria-Hungary, into Germany's Black Forest. Churchill, to whom the War Council now listened with great respect, disagreed. "We ought not to make the main lines of advance up the Danube," he said on March 3. "We ought not to employ more troops in this theatre of war than are absolutely essential in order to induce the Balkan states to march." He still believed that the proper strategy was an "advance in the north through Holland and the Baltic."[86]

During this euphoric interlude, Kitchener's Twenty-ninth Division shrank in significance. Churchill told the War Council that in exploiting Constantinople's capitulation they could count on 140,000 men: the British troops in Egypt, the Royal Naval Division now at sea, 2,000 Royal Marines already on Lemnos, a French division, the three Greek divisions Venizelos had promised, and a Russian corps preparing to embark at Batum, the Black Sea port near the Russo-Turkish border. He hadn't even counted the Rumanians, Bulgarians, and Italians waiting in the wings. Greece's 60,000 troops alone could seize and fortify Gallipoli. But speed, as Fisher had noted, was essential. On March 4 Winston wrote Grey: "Mr Venizelos shd be told *now* that the Admiralty believe it in their power to force the Dardanelles without military assistance, destroying all the forts as they go. If so, Gallipoli Peninsula cannot be held by Turks, who wd be cut off & reduced at leisure. By the 20th inst 40,000 British Infantry will be available to go to C'nople, if the Straits have been forced, either by crossing the Bulair Isthmus, or going up the Dardanelles. A French Divn will be on the spot at the same time. M. Venizelos shd consider Greek military movements in relation to these facts."[87]

It was at this point that what he later called "the terrible Ifs" began to accumulate. If Greece had entered the war then, everything would not have hinged on Carden's conquest of the Narrows. The forts there could have been taken from the rear, by land. Churchill warned Grey two days later: "If you don't back up *this* Greece — the Greece of Venizelos — you will have another wh will cleave to Germany."[88] Precisely that happened. It wasn't Grey's fault. The blame lay in Saint Petersburg. Both London and Paris agreed that King Constantine should receive Constantinople's surrender. The czar, who more than anyone else needed a victory on this front — whose very life depended upon it — refused even to discuss the idea. The Bosporus was *his,* he told the incredulous British ambassador on March 3; once Constantine entered it in triumph he would never leave. When word of this reached Athens three days later, the Venizelos government fell and was replaced by German sympathizers led by M. Zaimis, who held that Greece must remain neutral because it was threatened by an invasion of Bulgarians. The first domino had failed to topple. The others awaited events in the Dardanelles.

That same day Carden began to encounter difficulties — nothing serious, but enough to exasperate him and temper the enthusiasm at home. Turkish riflemen reappeared at Cape Helles and Kum Kale and drove off the British landing parties. Gales and another storm developed on March 8, and when the sky cleared the admiral's battleship captains, ordered to silence the land batteries between Kephez Point and Chanak, reported that they couldn't get within range of them. Minefields barred the way. It was then that the admiral discovered his Achilles' heel. By tradition, British trawlers used for minesweepers were manned by civilians, fishermen recruited in England's commercial ports. The Turkish guns couldn't reach the warships, but they were raking the trawlers, which backed away. One trawler officer told Commodore Roger Keyes, Carden's chief of staff, that his men "recognize sweeping risks and don't mind getting blown up, but they hate the gunfire, and point out that they aren't supposed to sweep under fire, they didn't join for that."[89]

Keyes, the ablest officer in the operation, called for volunteers from his Royal Navy tars. Meanwhile, he offered the fishermen bonuses. That night the trawlers tried again. The enemy surprised them with huge searchlights from Germany, uncrated that very afternoon. Blinded by their glare, the sweeper crews turned tail. Keyes pointed out that the enemy fire, though deafening, was wild. He persuaded them to try again the following night. Again they fled. As he wrote afterward: "I was furious and told the officers in charge that they had had their opportunity. . . . It did not matter if we lost all seven sweepers, there were twenty-eight more, and the mines had got to be swept up. How could they talk of being stopped by heavy fire if they were not hit? The Admiralty were prepared for losses, but we had chucked our hand in and started squealing before we had any."[90]

In London, Churchill agreed. That same day — March 11 — he wired Carden: "Your original instructions laid stress on caution and deliberate methods, and we approve highly the skill and patience with which you have advanced hitherto without loss. The results to be gained are, however, great enough to justify loss of ships and men. . . . We do not wish to hurry you or urge you beyond your judgment, but we recognise clearly that at a certain period in your operations you will have to press hard for a decision, and we desire to know whether you consider that point has now been reached." There was no reply — Winston terrified Carden — but in forty-eight hours the bluejacket volunteers were ready, and despite the arrival of new German searchlights and more accurate fire, the sweepers persevered. In the morning shoals of mines, cut adrift by the trawlers' kites, floated southward with the current. In four or five days, Carden's staff believed, they would be ready to assault the Narrows. But Churchill was impatient. And his query was still unanswered. He telegraphed again: "I do not understand why minesweeping should be interfered with by firing which causes no casualties. Two or three hundred casualties would be a moderate price to pay for sweeping up as far as the Narrows. . . . This work has to be done whatever the loss of life and small craft and the sooner it is done the better. Secondly, we have information that the Turkish forts are short of ammunition, that German officers have made desponding reports and have appealed to Germany for more. Every conceivable effort is being made to supply ammunition. It is being seriously considered to send a German or Austrian submarine, but apparently they have not started yet. Above is absolutely secret. All this makes it clear that the operations should now be pressed forward methodically and resolutely by night and day. The unavoidable losses must be accepted. The enemy is harassed and anxious now. The time is precious as the interference of submarines would be a very serious complication."[91]

The first lord's information about the enemy's ammunition shortage was accurate. German messages had been intercepted and decoded. As he testified the following year, it was this intelligence coup "that led Lord Fisher and me, with the assent of those whom we were consulting over it, to change the methodical advance and the step-by-step bombardment . . . into a more decided and vehement attempt to quell and smash up the fortresses at the Narrows and force them to use their ammunition." At the time, however, security precautions prevented him from revealing his source to Carden. The strain and suspense were too much for the admiral. He replied that he expected to lunge at the Narrows on March 17, but he was exhausted. On the morning of March 15, after two sleepless nights, he told Keyes that he could not survive more pressure from Churchill. He had decided to resign his commission. His staff tried to argue him out of it, but a Harley Street neurologist serving with the fleet examined him and said the admiral was near collapse; his nerves were shot; he must be sent home immediately. Thus, less than two days before the critical attempt on the Narrows, the command devolved on de Robeck. The Admiralty telegraphed him: "Personal and Secret from First Lord. In entrusting to you with great confidence the command of the Mediterranean Detached Fleet I presume . . . that you consider, after separate and independent judgment, that the immediate operations proposed are wise and practicable. If not, do not hesitate to say so. If so, execute them without delay and without further reference at the first favourable opportunity. . . . All good fortune attend you."[92]

The date was Wednesday, March 17, 1915. De Robeck replied that he would attack in the morning.

It was a day out of season: pleasant, warm, with bright sunshine and a flawless overarching sky. De Robeck's attacking fleet, the mightiest ever seen in the Mediterranean, was spearheaded by four dreadnoughts, flanked by two battleships. A mile behind them came the four French men-of-war, also flanked by British battleships. Six more battleships, surrounded by destroyers and trawlers, were held in reserve; they were to clear away the last obstacles, sail through the Narrows, and enter the Sea of Marmara the following morning. Twelve hours later the Union Jack and the French tricolor would fly over Constantinople.

A morning fog rose at 10:30, revealing the enemy forts, and the first six warships, taking the bone in their teeth, sailed toward them. After twenty-five minutes of maneuvering, each captain picked his target, half of them facing the Chanak, or Asian, side of the Narrows, and the other half facing the Kilid Bahr, or European, side. Once more the warships were beyond the range of the frustrated Turkish and German gunners. Howitzers on the cliffs downstream could hit the ships, but their shells bounced harmlessly off the thick steel armor. Meanwhile, the forts were being systematically demolished. Ten minutes before noon a British gunner hit the magazine of a key Chanak blockhouse; it erupted in a single sheet of flame. It was the turn of the French. At eight bells, noon, de Robeck signaled Admiral Emile-Paul-Aimable Guépratte to come forward. The *Suffren, Bouvet, Charlemagne,* and *Gaulois* fanned out and continued the terrific bombardment for another forty-five minutes. Both banks now resembled a tortured Dantean vision: billowing clouds of dense,

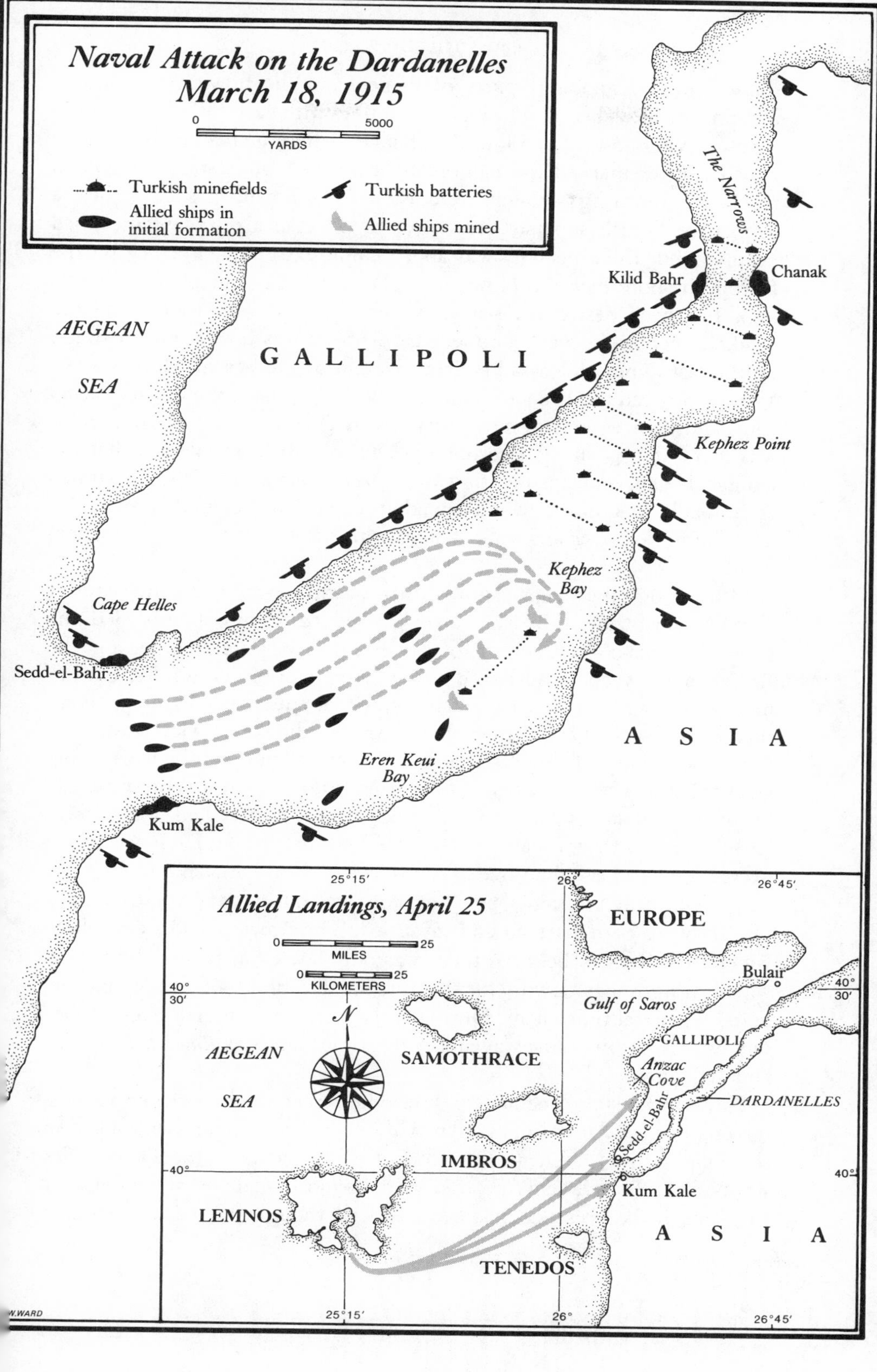
Naval Attack on the Dardanelles
March 18, 1915
0
5000
YARDS
Turkish minefields
Turkish batteries
Allied ships in initial formation
Allied ships mined
The Narrows
Kilid Bahr
Chanak
AEGEAN
SEA
GALLIPOLI
Kephez Point
Kephez Bay
Cape Helles
Sedd-el-Bahr
ASIA
Eren Keui Bay
Kum Kale
Allied Landings, April 25
25°15′
26°
26°45′
EUROPE
0
25
MILES
0
25
KILOMETERS
Bulair
40° 30′
Gulf of Saros
GALLIPOLI
N
AEGEAN
SEA
SAMOTHRACE
Anzac Cove
DARDANELLES
Sedd-el-Bahr
IMBROS
40°
Kum Kale
LEMNOS
ASIA
TENEDOS
W.WARD

roiling smoke, stabbing spurts of flame from the howitzers; roars of bursting shells; debris that heaved and shifted with each hit, dismembered corpses flying upward and into the channel, where ineffectual little fountains of water marked the failure of the fortress guns still in action to reach the towering warships. Occasionally a howitzer shell struck a French or British superstructure, but fewer than a dozen seamen had been wounded. The enemy was approaching extremity. Fort 13 on the European shore had also blown up. The forts' fire-control communications had been destroyed. Batteries were covered with rubble and the dead. Breechblocks were jammed. De Robeck was now ready to sweep up the last mines and pass his fleet through to the Sea of Marmara. At 1:30 he ordered the French to move aside and signaled the last six battleships and their escorts to move forward past the defeated enemy, and it was then, at 1:45 in the afternoon, a hairbreadth from victory, that the trouble began. *Bouvet,* pivoting in *Suffren*'s wake close to the strait's Asian bank, was rocked by a tremendous explosion. In less than two minutes she heeled over and sank, taking with her the captain and 639 seamen.

Officers on other ships assumed that a lucky howitzer gunner had hit *Bouvet*'s magazine. The six newly arrived battleships bombarded the banks; by four o'clock enemy fortress fire had ceased altogether and the British minesweepers advanced. They were working skillfully, cutting mine cables with their kites, when a howitzer shell landed among them; then they panicked and turned about. Another line of trawlers advanced; the same thing happened. This was irritating, but hardly worrisome. Graver by far was the misadventure of *Inflexible,* which was mysteriously hit at 4:41 P.M. not far from the place where *Bouvet* had gone down. Listing heavily to starboard, *Inflexible* left the battle line. De Robeck suspected a mine. Less than five minutes later a third battleship, *Irresistible,* was struck near the same spot. She, too, was out of action. Now senior officers were both alarmed and mystified. The trawlers had swept these waters. De Robeck believed there was only one explanation: the enemy was floating mines down with the current. He broke off action and ordered a general retirement. During the withdrawal a fourth man-of-war, *Ocean,* was lost the same way and in the same waters as *Bouvet, Inflexible,* and *Irresistible.*

Keyes, who stayed behind to direct the rescue of the stricken vessels, moving back and forth in a cutter by the light of a few surviving Turkish searchlights, was far from discouraged. Both banks of the Dardanelles were quiet. He had, he wrote afterward, "a most indelible impression that we were in the presence of a beaten foe. I thought he was beaten at 2

P.M. I knew he was beaten at 4 P.M. — and at midnight I knew with still greater certainty that he was absolutely beaten; and it only remained for us to organize a proper sweeping force and devise some means of dealing with the drifting mines to reap the fruits of our efforts. I felt that the guns of the forts and batteries and the concealed howitzers and mobile field guns were no longer a menace. Mines moored and drifting about could, and must, be overcome."[93] Returning to the *Queen Elizabeth,* he was, therefore, astounded to find de Robeck distraught. His career was ruined, the admiral moaned; his losses would never be forgiven; as soon as the Admiralty saw his action report, he would be relieved and dismissed from the service. Keyes replied that Churchill would never act like that. The day had been anything but a disaster. Except for the crew of *Bouvet,* fewer than seventy sailors had been hit. The disabled ships could be repaired; all were destined for the scrap heap anyway. Obviously the next step was to convert British destroyers into sweepers — the tackle, wire mesh, and kites were available on Malta — and continue the attack. They were bound to break through.

The enemy agreed. De Robeck's misfortune, they knew, was a freak. His four unlucky ships had been hit because they had sailed too close to shore. Ten days earlier a Turkish colonel had supervised the laying of a string of twenty mines parallel to the Asian bank of the Dardanelles, just inside the slack water. The British sweepers had missed them, but they weren't much of an obstacle; in skirting them the Allied warships would still have an eight-thousand-yard-wide channel in which to maneuver. Surely, the Turks reasoned, the English admiral would not repeat his error. British fleets had ruled the world's waves for two hundred years. They could hardly be stopped by the shattered defenses left at the Narrows. The Turkish guns still in service were almost out of ammunition — some were *completely* out — and no more shells were available. Once the Allies were past Chanak they would face nothing but a few ancient smooth-bore bronze cannon aimed in the wrong direction. Mines would not trouble them. The Turks had none left. Those which had been laid in the Dardanelles had been collected from mines which the Russians had been floating down the Black Sea in hopes of blowing up the *Goeben* and *Breslau.*

Already the exodus from Constantinople had begun. Gold, art treasures, and official archives had been moved to Eskişehir, in western Turkey. Two special trains, their fires banked, stood ready in the station at Uskudar, just across the Bosporus, to carry the sultan, his harem, his suite, foreign ambassadors, and wealthy pashas and beys into the interior. There was an air of panic in the streets. The city's two arsenals, visible from the water, could be easily destroyed by naval gunfire. After the war the Turkish general staff declared that "a naval attack executed with rapidity and vigor" would have found the capital's garrison "impotent to defend it," and Enver Pasha, Turkey's wartime military dictator, added: "If the English had only had the courage to rush more ships through the Dardanelles they could have got to Constantinople." The *Goeben* and *Breslau* had weighed anchor and were preparing to steam away across the Black Sea. Otto Liman von Sanders, the senior German general on this front, said afterward that if de Robeck had ordered a renewal of his attack on March 19, he would have found the city undefended. "The course of the World War," he said, "would have been given such a turn in the spring of 1915 that Germany and Austria would have had to continue the struggle without Turkey." Keyes steamed through the strait in 1925. His eyes filled. He said: "My God, it would have been even easier than I thought. We simply *couldn't* have failed . . . and because we didn't try, another million lives were thrown away and the war went on for another three years."[94]

He had sensed this at the time. So had Churchill. Far from recalling de Robeck, when Winston read his report of the March 18 action he immediately dispatched four more battleships to his command. The French similarly replaced the *Bouvet* with the *Henry IV*. The French admiral, unlike the British, was eager to return to the Narrows. Jacky Fisher was not. He had waxed hot and cold on the operation, and Winston never knew, from one day to the next, what stand his first sea lord was going to take. Before the struggle in the Narrows he had grumbled, "The more I consider the Dardanelles, the less I like it." Yet after the battle it was Fisher, not Churchill, who first proposed to make good the British losses with new battleships. "De Robeck is really better than Carden," he said, "so Providence is with us." On the afternoon of March 19, when the Admiralty's director of naval intelligence brought them newly intercepted German messages, providing details of the shell shortage in the Narrows forts, Fisher read the report aloud, waved it over his head, and shouted: "By God, I'll go through tomorrow!" Winston scanned it and said: "That means they've come to the end of their ammunition." Fisher danced a jig and cried again: "Tomorrow! We shall probably lose six ships, but I'm going through!" Yet a few hours later, at a somber meeting of the War Council, he declared that it was impossible to "explain away" the losses of such great vessels, that he had always feared that the price of forcing the Dardanelles would be twelve sunken battleships, and that he would prefer to lose them elsewhere.[95]

What troubled him? It was Gallipoli. He cried to Lloyd George: "The Dardanelles! Futile without soldiers!" And he said: "Somebody will have to land on Gallipoli sooner or later." Before the attack he had sent Churchill a memorandum: *"Are we going to Constantinople or are we not?* If NOT — then don't send half a dozen battleships to the bottom which would be better applied at Cuxhaven or Borkum. If YES — then push the military co-operation with all speed & make the demonstration with all possible despatch at *both* extremities of the *Gallipoli* Peninsula." Admiral Jackson concurred and set forth his reasons: "To advance further with a rush over unswept minefields and in waters commanded at short range by heavy guns, howitzers, and torpedo-tubes, must involve serious losses in ships and men, and will not achieve the object of making the Straits a safe waterway for the transports. The Gallipoli peninsula must be cleared of the enemy's artillery before this is achieved. . . . The time has now arrived to make use of military forces to occupy the Gallipoli peninsula, and clear away the enemy on that side. With the peninsula in our possession, the concealed batteries on the Asiatic side, which are less formidable, could be dealt with more easily . . . and the troops should be of great assistance in the demolition of the fortress's guns."[96]

This was, of course, a gross distortion of the situation. No one had suggested rushing over unswept minefields, the battleships were invulnerable to the shore batteries in the Narrows, and the artillery at the mouth of the strait, which had been cast in the days of sailing ships, was useless even against trawlers, whose helmsmen could steer beyond their range. Nevertheless, Fisher had a point. Eventually someone *would* have to occupy Gallipoli. That was why Churchill, supported by a majority of the cabinet, had wanted to send out the Twenty-ninth Division and the Australians and New Zealanders (Anzacs) in February. After Kitchener had vetoed that, the operation became what Winston called "a legitimate war gamble." It was a good gamble. Liddell Hart has described it as a "sound and far-sighted conception, marred by a chain of errors in execution almost unrivalled even in British history." Once Constantinople fell, the Turks would have been unable to fortify the peninsula. Russians — and, almost certainly, new Balkan armies — would have been lunging across their frontiers. Had the czar not been a dolt, the conquest of Gallipoli would by now have been complete. Peter Wright, a member of the War Council, later wrote: "Our navy was in command of the sea; the Greeks were eager to join us and attack in the peninsula with their whole army. The Gallipoli campaign should have succeeded without the loss of a single English soldier."[97]

Before the year was out it would cost over a quarter-million Allied casualties, counting 47,000 Frenchmen sacrificed in support operations. All were lost in vain; every inch of the peninsula would remain in enemy hands. The lion's share of the blame must be laid at the door of Lord Kitchener. Unlike French, Haig, and Wilson, mesmerized by the butchery in France, K of K grasped the possibilities in the east. He had told the War Council that if the fleet could not "get through the straits unaided, the Army ought to see the business through."[98] Yet he had been evasive when Churchill argued passionately for a combined military and naval operation, and, at a time when a relatively small British expedition could have done the job, he had mulishly refused to release the idle Twenty-ninth Division. Gallipoli was no natural fortress. Except for a series of jutting heights known as Sari Bair, it was relatively flat and largely barren, covered with stony soil, coarse scrub, a few olive trees, and scattered flocks of sheep and goats. Thinly held, as it was before the tumult in the Narrows alerted the Turks, Gallipoli could have been seized in a few days, almost without bloodshed.

Now that England was committed in the Mediterranean, with Grey telling the council that failure there "would be morally equivalent to a great defeat," Kitchener, speaking as secretary for war, told the startled cabinet that "the military situation is now sufficiently secure to justify the despatch of the XXIX Division." The trench fighting at Neuve Chapelle was at its height; barring unexpected developments there, nineteen thousand Tommies could embark five days hence. The war minister, a firm believer in locking the barn door after the horse has escaped, had also decided to commit the Anzacs to Gallipoli. Altogether, counting the Egyptian garrison and the Royal Marines, the "Mediterranean Expeditionary Force," as he called it, would number over seventy thousand. The council was excited; as Churchill wrote afterward, "Everybody's blood was up." The commanding general would be Kitchener's protégé and Winston's old friend, Ian Hamilton. K of K told Hamilton: "If the Fleet gets through, Constantinople will fall of itself and you will have won, not a battle, but the war."[99]

Asquith thought Hamilton "a sanguine enthusiastic person, with a good deal of *superficial* charm . . . but there is too much feather in his brain." His performance in small wars had been superb. He had fought well at Majuba, on India's North-West Frontier, and in South Africa, and had been a keen military observer in Manchuria during the Russo-Japanese War in 1904. None of this was evident in his appearance. He

Roger Keyes, John de Robeck, and Ian Hamilton

was scrawny, bowlegged, and birdlike in his movements, and his manner was almost effeminate. He also wrote poetry and kept a voluminous, gossipy diary, which diminished him in the eyes of bluff officer types. Clementine disliked him, but Winston regarded him as dashing and chivalrous; he wrote Kitchener of the appointment: "No choice could be more agreeable to the Admiralty, and to the Navy."[100] Churchill wanted him in the eastern Mediterranean, and he wanted him there fast; on the first lord's orders, a special train would take the general to Dover, he would cross the Channel on H.M.S. *Foresight,* another special train would rush him from Calais to Marseilles, and there H.M.S. *Phaeton,* a fast cruiser, would pick him up and carry him to his command. Churchill saw him off at Charing Cross Station, whence Chinese Gordon had left on his own fateful journey to Egypt over thirty years earlier. Because of Kitchener's touchiness, Hamilton explained, there would be no communication between him and the Admiralty. Winston said nothing, but it was a deplorable decision. The train pulled away amid gay shouts, and the dainty general settled down to study a prewar report on the Dardanelles, an out-of-date Turkish army handbook, and a highly inaccurate map of Gallipoli.

Heavy seas kept de Robeck's fleet idle on March 19, but he and Keyes put the time to good use; on the following day the admiral reported to Churchill that sixty-two destroyers were being converted into mine-sweepers, all to be crewed by bluejacket volunteers, and steel nets would soon be laid across the strait to catch any loose mines. The French, de Robeck reported to London, had been "quite undismayed by their loss." On all Allied warships "officers and men are only anxious to re-engage the enemy." He ended: "It is hoped to be in a position to commence operations in three or four days." Keyes wrote his wife from the *Queen Elizabeth:* "I am spoiling to have at it again." The War Council had authorized Churchill to tell de Robeck that he could "continue the operations against the Dardanelles" provided he thought it "fit." Clearly he did, but the first lord goaded him just the same: "*Queen* and *Implacable* should join you very soon; and *London* and *Prince of Wales* sail tonight. . . . It appears important not to let the forts be repaired or to encourage enemy by an apparent suspension of the operations. Ample supplies of 15-inch ammunition are available for indirect fire of *Queen Elizabeth* across the peninsula."[101]

Everything was proceeding smoothly until Hamilton sailed up on the *Phaeton,* studied the Gallipoli shore through field glasses, ventured into the mouth of the Dardanelles, and then sailed off to establish his headquarters on Lemnos. De Robeck wrote him there: "We are all ready for another go, and not the least beaten or down-hearted." The general took another view. He inspected the crippled *Inflexible,* talked to several army officers on the island, and telegraphed Kitchener: "I am most reluctantly driven to the conclusion that the straits are not likely to be forced by battleships, as at one time seemed probable, and that, if my troops are to take part, it will not take the subsidiary form anticipated. The Army's part will be more than mere landing parties to destroy forts; it must be a deliberate and prepared military operation, carried out at full strength, so as to open a passage for the Navy." This was an extraordinary rush to judgment. He hadn't seen the Narrows, was unaware of the devastation there, and knew almost nothing about the capabilities of huge naval guns. Kitchener replied immediately: "You know my views, that the Dardanelles must be forced." If troops were needed "to clear the way," such operations, he said, "must be carried through." On March 22, four days after the ship-to-shore fight in the Narrows, de Robeck anchored off the island to confer with the Mediterranean Expeditionary Force's commander in chief, who at this point had no army, no plan, but a strong distrust of swift action. Afterward they disagreed on who had said what.

According to the general: "The moment he sat down de Robeck told us that he was now quite clear *he could not get through without the help of all my troops.*" According to the admiral, Hamilton spoke first, and having "heard his proposals, I now considered a combined operation essential to obtain great results and object of campaign. . . . To attack Narrows now with Fleet would be a mistake, as it would jeopardize the execution of a bigger and better scheme."[102]

De Robeck's account is more convincing — until now he had never considered discontinuing his assault — but doubtless he was easily seduced. To naval officers who had risen to flag rank during the long peace, losing ships was a crime, and he had already blurted out to Keyes that he felt guilty. Moreover, he knew that Fisher, the very symbol of the Royal Navy, disapproved of the Dardanelles operation. Churchill backed it, but Churchill was a politician; politicians moved from one ministerial post to another, or dropped out of the cabinet altogether. At the Admiralty, first lords came and went, while the Royal Navy lasted forever. If the army wanted to take over here, de Robeck could only feel a sense of deliverance. He asked Hamilton if the troops would be put ashore on Bulair Isthmus at the top of the peninsula. No, said Hamilton, he would land on the southern tip and fight his way up from there. De Robeck asked when. Hamilton said he needed a little over three weeks. In that case, the admiral said, he would suspend his own drive until the fighting began on Gallipoli. He telegraphed the Admiralty that the army "will not be in a position to undertake any military operations before 14th April. . . . It appears better to prepare a decisive effort about the middle of April rather than risk a great deal for what may possibly be only a partial solution."[103]

Keyes felt "fearfully disappointed and unhappy." Churchill was dumbfounded. As he later testified, he believed "that we were separated by very little from success. Although at the outset I should have rejoiced at the provision of an army, I saw the disadvantages which would attend its employment after what had happened. . . . Landing and storming the Gallipoli Peninsula, now that the Turks were fully alarmed, seemed a formidable business. It seemed to me a far more serious undertaking than the naval attack. It would commit us irrevocably if it failed, in a way no naval attack could have done. The risk was greater. The stakes were far higher . . . and above all I feared the inevitable delay." Fisher, backed by Admirals Sir Arthur Wilson and Sir Henry Jackson, disagreed. Up to this point, they said, they had supported the attempt to force the strait because the commander on the spot had recommended it. But now that de

Robeck and Hamilton had agreed on a joint effort, the Admiralty, in Fisher's words, was "bound to accept their view." Churchill later recalled: "For the first time since the war began, high words were used around the octagonal table." He drafted a telegram to de Robeck, ordering him to break through to the Sea of Marmara, but it was never sent, because he had to consult the War Council first, and although Asquith — and Kitchener — agreed with him, the prime minister refused to overrule three distinguished admirals.[104]

The next day Winston drafted a personal telegram to de Robeck. Fisher wrote him: *"Send no more telegrams! Let it alone!"* It went out anyway. "What has happened since the 21st," he asked, "to make you alter your intention of renewing the attack as soon as the weather is favourable?" The answer was ambiguous. Churchill lowered his sights, hoping that the delay would be temporary. Then events conspired against him. Word reached London from Constantinople that "during the last fortnight about 150 mines, any amount of ammunition, guns, &c, have been coming through Roumania from Germany. . . . The ammunition comes through quite openly, and there is nothing to prevent the Germans from bringing in even big guns." To Winston this was a spur to instant action. The admirals, on the other hand, argued that it meant greater danger for their ships in the Dardanelles. Churchill urged Grey to protest this abuse of Rumanian neutrality. Grey said it would be useless. Then, on Friday, March 26, the British consul general cabled from Rotterdam that Dutch troops were massing on their frontiers; a German invasion was expected hourly. It was a false alarm, but it triggered anxiety about the strength of the Home Fleet. The second, third, and fourth sea lords took the extraordinary step of demanding written assurance from Fisher that the force in Scapa Flow was adequate to meet all challenges. Captain Richmond was spreading his poison in the Admiralty. The first lord's "personal vanity," he wrote typically, "occupies so large a place in the arrangements that the operation is either a fiasco or is most wasteful in lives or matériel — or both." Finally, Grey urged caution. Italy was on the verge of declaring war on Germany. An unsuccessful attempt to break through the Narrows might discourage it.[105]

Shortly before dawn on Saturday a long message from de Robeck reached the Admiralty. As a study in stagnation it is a remarkable document. Silencing the forts, he said, would require "an excessive expenditure of ammunition," which "cannot be spared." Complete conquest of the blockhouses on either side of the strait would require "demolishing parties. To cover these parties at the Narrows is a task General Hamilton is not prepared to undertake and I fully concur with his view." The "mine menace" was "even greater than anticipated." As he saw it, "the result of a Naval action alone might in my opinion be a brilliant success or quite indecisive." It was a risk, and he wasn't prepared to take it when the army could "occupy the Peninsula which would open up the Strait as guns on Asiatic side can be dominated from the European shore sufficiently to permit ships to pass through." He concluded: "With Gallipoli Peninsula held by our Army and Squadron through Dardanelles our success would be assured. The delay possibly of a fortnight will allow co-operation which would really prove factor that will reduce length of time necessary to complete the campaign in Sea of Marmara and occupy Constantinople."[106]

When Kitchener told the War Council that the army was now prepared to take over the job of opening the Dardanelles, Winston knew he was beaten. Though he felt, as he said, "grief-stricken," he gracefully replied to de Robeck: "I had hoped that it would be possible to achieve the result according to original plan without involving the Army, but the reasons you give make it clear that a combined operation is now indispensable. . . . All your proposals will therefore be approved." De Robeck now became Hamilton's subordinate, providing naval support when and where requested. Every subsequent decision in the theater was made by either Kitchener or Hamilton. The navy never again tried to sweep mines, reduce forts, or break through the Narrows to the Sea of Marmara. Day by day the vision of victory receded, though Churchill was slow to abandon hope. On April 29 Sir George Riddell found him studying a map. In his diary Riddell set down Winston's remarks. "This," Churchill had said, "is one of the great campaigns of history. Think what Constantinople is to the East. It is more than London, Paris, and Berlin rolled into one are to the West. Think how it has dominated the East. Think what its fall will mean. Think how it will affect Bulgaria, Greece, Rumania, and Italy, who have already been affected by what has taken place. You cannot win this war by sitting still. We are merely using our surplus ships in the Dardanelles. Most of them are old vessels. The ammunition, even the rifle ammunition, is different from that which we are using in France — an older type — so there is no loss of power there." Then he said: "I am not responsible for the Expedition. . . . I do not shirk responsibility, but it is untrue to say that I have done this off my own bat."[107]

Nevertheless, the British public believed he had done it all off his own bat. Most of them think so today.

Silence descended upon the strait. As the weeks passed, the Turks realized that they had been granted a reprieve. In time they persuaded themselves that they had triumphed. The Westerners, to whom they had felt inferior, had been routed. Islamic xenophobia stirred in them; they wanted to express their savage new strength on any available enemy. The Armenians were available. They were Christians, they were clever, they prospered as moneylenders in cities and villages, and they were suspected of sympathizing with the Russians. Rumors spread. They were sending information to the czar's troops, it was said; they were smuggling in arms and plotting a revolt. So a pogrom began. The men were tortured and shot; the women were recruited for harems; the very young and very old were sent down the roads to Syria, Persia, and Mesopotamia, where robbers stripped them naked and left them to die of hunger and exposure. Before it was over, 750,000 Armenians were dead.

Barbarism was one expression of the new Turkish mood. Another, which boded ill for Hamilton's troops, was the soaring morale of the *askar,* or private soldier. The *askari* were in a fighting temper, and they knew where they were going to fight; Turkish spies were active in Cairo, watching British officers scour shops for Gallipoli guidebooks. British soldiers cruising in the waters off the peninsula watched the entrenchments grow there. Every morning found them higher and wider. By the middle of April — Hamilton had set his landing date back eleven days — Von Sanders had sixty thousand men behind barbed wire and machine guns, backed by heavy Skoda artillery from Bohemia. His field general would be Mustapha Kemal. Von Sanders was aware of Kemal's Germanophobia, but he also knew he was fiercely patriotic and the best combat commander in the country. Both leaders were exceptionally talented. Their troops were ready. And they had plenty of time; five precious weeks intervened between the break-off of de Robeck's naval attack and the arrival of Hamilton's transports off the peninsula.

Gallipoli offers the invader four beaches: Bulair, at the neck, where de Robeck wanted Hamilton to land; Suvla Bay, halfway down the peninsula; Ari Burnu, south of there; and at Cape Helles, on the toe, where Royal Marines had walked in complete safety a month earlier. Five major landings were made on the cape, near the village of Sedd-el-Bahr. Casualties were heavy. A naval aviator flying overhead looked down on the Aegean, usually a brilliant shade of blue. He saw a strip "absolutely red with blood . . . a horrible sight to see" between the beach and fifty yards out.[108] The Anzacs were supposed to come ashore at Gaba Tepe, in the vicinity of Ari Burnu. A navigation error put them a mile to the north, where they faced precipitous cliffs from whose scrub-covered ridges the Turks could deliver a murderous, scything fire. Ian Hamilton remained at sea, riding around in the conning tower of the *Queen Elizabeth,* out of touch with his shore commanders and his staff. He refused to intervene, even when it became apparent that everything had gone wrong; officers on the spot, he said, were better qualified to make decisions. They, playing for safety, tried to establish beachheads — venturing inland was considered either impossible or too hazardous — while each evening their commander in chief, before retiring to his bunk on the battleship, wrote five-thousand-word entries in his diary, reflecting upon the mysteries and ironies of life.

Later another landing was made at Suvla. It was the same story. The force commander was an elderly, ailing officer who had made his reputation as a teacher of military history and had never commanded troops in war. Coming ashore, he sprained his knee. He sent word to Hamilton that "if the enemy proves to be holding a strong line of continuous entrenchments I shall be unable to dislodge him till more guns are landed. All the teaching of the campaign in France proves that continuous trenches cannot be attacked without the assistance of large numbers of howitzers."[109] There were no trenches and very few Turks. He had twenty thousand men ashore. Still, he was reluctant to advance. Following his commander in chief's example, he returned to his ship and spent a safe, comfortable night aboard. Meanwhile, Mustapha Kemal arrived and occupied the heights overlooking the beach.

Winston's brother, Jack, who had seen action as a major at Ypres and was now serving on Hamilton's staff, wrote him from Helles that Gallipoli was "siege warfare again as in France. Trenches and wire beautifully covered by machine gun fire are the order of the day. Terrific artillery fire against invulnerable trenches and then attempts to make frontal attacks in the face of awful musketry fire, are the only tactics that can be employed." In the first month Hamilton lost forty-five thousand men. The pattern continued. It was over-the-top carnage, with no gains of consequence. Jack wrote: "I don't think another big push will be attempted until reinforcements arrive. We shall have to dig in and await the Turks' attacks." Gallipoli had become a mere extension of the deadlock on the western front. Hamilton knew it. He telegraphed Kitchener that he was watching his attack "degenerate into trench warfare with its resultant slowness."[110]

"Damn the Dardanelles," said Fisher. "They will be our grave."

Churchill had told Riddell that "Fisher and I have a perfect understanding." In fact, they had no such thing. The old admiral had raised no objections to Hamilton's landings, but the general's subsequent frustration had depressed him. Winston kept trying to stir Fisher's fighting spirit. "It is clear," he wrote him on May 3, "that the favourable turn to our affairs in S. E. Europe arose from the initial success of our attack on the Dardanelles, was checked by the repulse of the 18th, & can only be restored by the general success of the operation. It is thus necessary to fight a battle, (a thing wh has often happened before in war) & abide the consequences whatever they may be." The old salt was unconvinced. And he was beginning to recite his litany of complaints to outsiders. One afternoon at No. 10 Margot Asquith faced him down. She bluntly told him: "You know you have talked too much — all London knows you are against the Dardanelles expedition. Why didn't you resign?" He muttered: "It's a lie — I've seen no one, been nowhere, I'm far too busy." But it was true. Word of the rift at the Admiralty had reached backbenchers in the House. An MP asked "whether Lord Fisher was consulted with regard to the March action on the Dardanelles by the Fleet; and whether he expressed the opinion that the attack ought not to be made in the circumstances in which it was made." Winston replied: "If the insinuation contained in the question were correct Lord Fisher would not now be at the Admiralty." Asquith had asked Churchill to carry on secret negotiations with the Italians on the terms under which they would enter the war against Germany. This entailed commuting to Paris, and during one of his absences Clementine, hoping to perk up the old salt, invited him to lunch at Admiralty House. It went well until, after Clementine thought he had left, she found him lurking in a corridor. She asked: "What is it?" He said: "You are a foolish woman. All the time you think Winston's with Sir John French he is in Paris with his mistress." Clementine was speechless. She was convinced Fisher was losing his mind. When Churchill returned, she told him what had happened. Fisher, she said, had been "as nervous as a kitten."[111]

In Hamilton's failure Roger Keyes saw opportunity. Four days after this remarkable scene in London, the commodore persuaded de Robeck to convene all his admirals in the *Queen Elizabeth*'s wardroom. There he unveiled a new plan of naval attack. Leaving older battleships to shield the army's beachheads, the destroyers which had been refitted as minesweepers would lead the Allies' most powerful dreadnoughts through the Narrows. It would be accomplished in a single day. All those present, including de Robeck, enthusiastically endorsed the operation; Guépratte telegraphed his minister of marine: *"A fin d'assister l'Armée dans son action énergique et rude, nous méditons vive action flotte dans détroit avec attaque des forts. Dans ces conditions il me faut mes cuirassés* Suffren, Charlemagne, Gaulois *dans le plus bref délai possible."*[112] The plan was forwarded to London for approval, which they took for granted. Fisher didn't like it, of course; he wanted no part of any further action in the strait. And Churchill, from whom one would expect support, had a problem. Assuming that all hopes of forcing the Dardanelles had been abandoned, he had agreed to provide Italy with four battleships and four cruisers from de Robeck's fleet. Yet the idea of reaching Constantinople was still exciting. He believed something could be worked out. He was arguing the issue with Fisher when an aide brought them word that a daring Turkish submarine commander had sunk H.M.S. *Goliath* south of the Narrows.

The loss could be borne. *Goliath* was no Goliath. She was a small, senectuous battleship which had been launched when Victoria was still Queen. But the presence of an enemy submarine in these waters frightened Fisher. There might be others. (There weren't.) He insisted that *Queen Elizabeth* leave the Mediterranean at once. To appease him, Winston agreed. The meeting of the War Council the next day, on Friday, May 14, was, in Churchill's word, "sulphurous." Kitchener was infuriated. He had sent an army to Gallipoli with the understanding that the navy would force the Dardanelles, he raged; the first lord had enticed him by dwelling upon "the marvelous potentialities of the *Queen Elizabeth,"* and now Hamilton was being left in the lurch. K of K's "habitual composure in trying ordeals left him," Winston wrote. "He protested vehemently against what he considered the desertion of the army at its most critical moment." At this, Fisher flared up. The ship "will come home," he declared; "she will come home at once; she will come home tonight or I shall walk out of the Admiralty then and there." He added that he was "against the Dardanelles and have been all along." That enraged Churchill. "The First Sea Lord," he retorted, "has agreed to every executive telegram on which the operations have been conducted." Sending out the *Elizabeth,* indeed, had been his idea. The wounding words flew back and forth, and Asquith couldn't stem them. To calm Fisher, the prime minister, on Hankey's advice, had promised the old admiral on Tuesday that no action would be taken in the eastern Mediterranean without his consent. The *Elizabeth* would be recalled; two battleships, *Exmouth* and *Venerable,* would replace her.[113]

Back at the Admiralty that evening Winston went over the details with Fisher in the first sea lord's office. They reviewed the entire operation. New orders would be drawn up for de Robeck. Churchill confined his recommendations to matters he knew the old admiral would accept. As he left, an aide heard him say: "Well, good night, Fisher. We have settled everything, and you must go home and have a good night's rest. Things will look brighter in the morning and we'll pull the thing through together." Working later, as was his custom, he put everything in writing. At the last moment he added two submarines, which de Robeck had requested, to the Dardanelles naval reinforcements. He left the papers for the first sea lord with a note: "I send this to you before marking it to others in order that if any point arises we can discuss it. I hope you will agree."[114]

At nine Saturday morning, May 15, he called at the Foreign Office to put the final touches on the Italian treaty. He was returning across the Horse Guards when his private naval secretary hurried up and said: "Fisher has resigned, and I think he means it this time." He handed him the brief note from the first sea lord: "After further anxious reflection," it began, "I have come to the regretted conclusion I am unable to remain any more as your colleague. . . . As you truly said yesterday I am in the position of constantly veto-ing your proposals. This is not fair to you besides being extremely distasteful to me. I am off to Scotland to avoid all questionings." Churchill wasn't perturbed; Fisher had submitted eight previous resignations. But when he discovered that he was nowhere to be found — that he had literally deserted — Winston took the letter to No. 10. Angered, Asquith instantly wrote Fisher: "In the King's name, I order you to return to your post." Delivering this command was another matter. That afternoon the old admiral was run to ground in a dingy Charing Cross hotel room. After a long argument, he agreed to see the prime minister. Lloyd George, encountering him in the No. 10 waiting room, was struck by the "dour change in him. . . . A combative grimness had taken the place of his usual genial greeting; the lower lip of his set mouth was thrust forward, and the droop at the corner was more marked than usual. His curiously Oriental features were more than ever those in an Eastern temple, with a sinister frown. 'I have resigned!' was his greeting, and on my inquiring the reason he replied, 'I can stand it no longer.' " He had made up his mind, he said, "to take no further part in the Dardanelles foolishness." Lloyd George begged him to wait until Monday, when he could put his grievances before the War Council. Fisher refused to wait "another hour." He told the prime minister the same thing. After a long argument, Asquith wrung from him a promise to remain in London, but the old man flatly refused to withdraw his resignation, to return to the Admiralty, or to see Churchill.[115]

He went back into hiding. At 10:00 P.M. a mutual friend brought him a letter from Winston, who was trying to find out what this was all about. The answer, in Fisher's reply through their intermediary, was the two submarines. He wrote that "the series of fresh naval arrangements you sent me yesterday morning convinced me that the time had arrived for me to make a final decision — there being much more in those proposals than had occurred to me the previous evening when you suggested some of them." This was absurd, of course; the vessels were insignificant, and Churchill had offered to talk it over. But Fisher had been looking for an excuse, and his hand shook as he scrawled on: "YOU ARE BENT ON FORCING THE DARDANELLES AND NOTHING WILL TURN YOU FROM IT — NOTHING — I know you so well! . . . *You will remain* and I SHALL GO — It is better so. . . . You say with much feeling that *'it will be a very great grief to you to part from me.'* I am certain you know in your heart no one has ever been more faithful to you than I have since I joined you last October. *I have worked my very hardest.*" He moved to the Ritz and wrote Reginald McKenna, Winston's predecessor at the Admiralty, that while he wouldn't quote Churchill's letter, "it absolutely CONVINCES me that I am right in my UNALTERABLE DECISION to resign! *In fact I have resigned!* . . . At every turn he will be thinking of the military and not the naval side — *he never has done otherwise.* His heart is ashore, not afloat! *The joy of his life is to be 50 yards from a German trench!* . . . I am no longer First Sea Lord. *There is no compromise possible!*"[116]

Well, there was, and he was angling for it. He very much wanted to be back at the Admiralty, but with dictatorial powers. This surfaced in his subsequent attempts to negotiate with Asquith. He would serve under McKenna or Grey, he said, but not Churchill or Balfour. Admiral Wilson must leave the Admiralty, Fisher must be empowered to appoint his own Admiralty Board, the first lord would "be absolutely restricted to policy and parliamentary procedure," and "I shall have complete professional charge of the war at sea, together with the absolute sole disposition of the Fleet and the appointment of all officers of all ranks whatsoever, and absolutely untrammelled sole command of all the sea forces whatsoever." In a postscript he added that these conditions "must be published verbatim so that the Fleet may know my position." Hankey, to whom he delivered these terms, told him they were impossible. Asquith said the old man was either "traitorous" or "unhinged." Fisher then sent word of his resignation to Bonar Law. That was malicious. His sole motive now was to ruin Churchill.[117]

After nine years in power the Liberal government was shaky, and frustration over the bloody, interminable war was at the root of it. Fisher wasn't the only officer playing politics. Sir John French needed an excuse for the failure, the previous Sunday, of his offensive against Aubers Ridge, where 11,000 men fell without gaining a single yard. The newly knighted Henry Wilson had noted in his diary: "Sir J told me he thought it quite likely that K's second army would go to Gallipoli. This *must* be stopped." Churchill's strongest argument for strengthening the drive against Turkey was that of the 644,000 Englishmen in uniform, 560,000, or 87 percent, were fighting in France, and, as he had told the War Council, he could not see "the smallest reason for believing" that there would be any change in "either the British or French lines." To keep its flow of reinforcements coming from home, the BEF badly needed an alibi. Therefore French told Colonel Charles à Court Repington, the haughty military correspondent for the Northcliffe newspapers, that the politicians in London were mismanaging their end of the war. It was a lack of high-explosive shells, he said, which had prevented him from breaking through. On Friday *The Times* carried scare headlines: NEED FOR SHELLS. BRITISH ATTACK CHECKED. LIMITED SUPPLIES THE CAUSE. A LESSON FROM FRANCE. The problem, according to this line of reasoning, was that inadequate munitions were being sent to the western front. "British soldiers," said *The Times,* "died in vain on Aubers Ridge on Sunday because more shells were needed. The Government, who have so seriously failed to organize our national resources, must bear their share of the grave responsibility." Their error, it was argued, had been compounded by the creation of a second, pointless front. Of Gallipoli *The Times* declared: "The novel interests of that enterprise cannot be allowed to distract us from what is, and will remain, the decisive theatre of operations. Our first thoughts must be for the bent but unbroken line of battle in the West." The Liberal editor of the *Westminster Gazette* agreed that "the war will be ended by killing Germans and in no other way."[118]

Churchill was slow to grasp the threat to him. Gallipoli, after all, was Kitchener's responsibility. But he was being held responsible for the entire campaign, land as well as sea. "Mr Churchill's characteristics," said the *Morning Post,* "make him in his present position a danger and an anxiety to the nation," and, in another editorial, "Mr Churchill's instincts for the melodramatic have blossomed into megalomania." *The Times* charged that "the First Lord of the Admiralty has been assuming responsibilities and overriding his expert advisers to a degree which might at any time endanger the national safety. . . . When a civilian Minister in charge of a fighting service persistently seeks to grasp the power which should not pass into his unguided hands, and attempts to use that power in perilous ways, it is time for his colleagues in the Cabinet to take some definite action." His absences from the Admiralty were noted and criticized. The government could not reveal that he was negotiating Italy's entrance into the war, and when Tories in the House asked why he wasn't at his desk, and Asquith evaded the question, they shouted: "Joy ride!" Rumors spread that he was intriguing against Kitchener. Lord Esher's son wrote his father from Paris: "Why can't he stick to his own job? He is becoming an object of amusement and some scorn here. The French are beginning to shrug their shoulders when he is mentioned — a bad sign." Esher passed this letter along to the King. Winston continued to be unpopular among Liberal back-benchers, who now, according to *The Times*'s parliamentary correspondent, considered him to be "the author of all their ills." Even in the cabinet and the War Council he had become a controversial figure. That Saturday evening when Fisher resigned, Lloyd George told his mistress that if the resignation were accepted, Winston would have to surrender his office. After George had left her, Frances rose from bed and committed his hard words to her diary. Political ruin, Lloyd George had said, would be "the Nemesis of the man who has fought for this war for years. When the war came he saw in it the chance of glory for himself, & has accordingly entered on a risky campaign without caring a straw for the misery and hardship it would bring to thousands, in the hope that he would prove to be the outstanding man in this war."[119]

Lloyd George did not speak for the prime minister. But Asquith's emotional stability, unknown to his colleagues or even his family, had just been dealt a cruel blow. All these months he had been sustained by his love for Venetia Stanley. It was a sign of his dependence upon this sophisticated but shallow young woman that he had disclosed every state secret to her; indeed, it is arguable that she had become England's greatest security risk. And Venetia, unlike Lloyd George's Frances, was not constant. She had finally decided that the disparity between her age and Asquith's — thirty-five years — was too great. That Friday, May 14, she had told him that their relationship was over. She intended to marry Edwin Montagu, a future cabinet minister. Only the week before he had written her, "You give me the life blood of all that I do, or can ever hope to do," and that if anyone wanted to destroy him, he could do it "effectively, & without a moment's delay, when any veil is dropped between me & you — soul of my life." Now, after reading her crushing letter, he wrote her brokenly: "This is too terrible; no hell could be so bad." When Bonar Law confirmed Fisher's elopement and threatened a major debate in the House, Asquith refused to pick up the gauntlet. He lacked the strength. Afterward he wrote the young woman he still adored: "You alone of all the world — to whom I have always gone in every moment of trial & trouble, & from whom I have always come back solaced and healed & inspired — were the one person who could do nothing, & from whom I could ask nothing. To my dying day, that will be the most bitter memory of my life. . . . I am on the eve of the most astounding and world-shaking decisions — such as I wd never have taken without your counsel & consent. It seems so strange & empty & unnatural: yet there is nowhere else that I can go, nor would I, if I could."[120] Bonar Law proposed a coalition, and Asquith listlessly agreed. Ironically, Churchill had been advocating this new step for several weeks. It never occurred to him that he might not be a part of a new cabinet. But the Tories had eyed his scalp too long. The exclusion of Churchill was Bonar Law's price for Conservative participation in the government; Balfour must become first lord.

Winston, who knew none of this, had realized that Fisher's departure would precipitate an uproar in the House. He had prepared a stout defense of his Dardanelles record; he meant to deliver it from the front bench, presenting, at the same time, his nominees for a new Admiralty Board. "I had," he later recalled, "prepared for a Parliamentary inquiry of the most searching character." He meant to summarize the navy's record of achievement, of which "I shall always be proud to have had a share," declaring: "The terrible dangers of the beginning of the war are over, the seas have been swept clear; the submarine menace has been fixed within definite limits; the personal ascendancy of our men, the superior quality of our ships on the high seas, have been established beyond doubt or question; our strength has greatly increased, actually and relatively from what it was in the beginning of the war, and it grows continually every day by leaps and bounds. . . . On the whole surface of the seas of the world no hostile flag is flown."[121]

Although exhausted by the Italian negotiations — Sir Henry Wilson had noted in his diary on May 7 that he "looked ill and unhealthy" — Churchill polished this speech all day Sunday, May 16. Monday morning, as a matter of form, he went to the prime minister for clearance. It was then that he learned he would not be permitted to speak. There would be no debate. Asquith, reading it, slowly shook his head. "No," he said, "this will not do. I have decided to form a National Government, and a very much larger construction will be required." He looked up and asked: "What are we to do for you?" This was Churchill's first inkling that his reign as first lord of the Admiralty was over. He was thunderstruck. He had assumed that the prime minister, who had shared all his decisions, would stand by him. Asquith asked him whether he wanted another post in the cabinet or would "prefer a command in France." Before Winston could answer, Lloyd George entered the room. George, who had been deeply involved in the negotiations with Law — "LG," Sunny wrote Winston, "has done you in" — asked the prime minister: "Why do you not send him to the Colonial Office? There is great work to be done there." Winston said numbly that he would refuse any office which cut him off from the conduct of the war. That evening he put it in writing, sending a note to No. 10: "So far as I am concerned if you find it necessary to make a change here, I shd be glad — assuming it was thought fitting — to be *offered* a position in the new Government. But I will not *take* any office except a military department, & if that is not convenient I hope I may be found employment in the field."[122]

By Tuesday morning, however, the prospect of leaving the Admiralty had become unbearable to him. That evening F. E. Smith and Max Aitken called, and Aitken wrote later that Winston "was clinging to the desire of retaining the Admiralty as if the salvation of England depended upon it," that he would "even have made it up with Lord Fisher" if he could have remained as first lord. He talked wildly of soliciting support among the Tories. Aitken bluntly told him he had no hope there. Nevertheless, on Wednesday, Churchill sent Bonar Law documents to justify his pride in his record as first lord. "Now that there is I rejoice to think good prospect of our becoming colleagues," he wrote his most implacable political enemy, "I feel entitled to send you the enclosed papers." In a postscript he added that "this great event of a National Government must be made lasting."[123]

If only the facts were known, he believed, he would be kept on. He prepared a long statement for the press, defending his Dardanelles role, and showed it to Lloyd George. George, minister of munitions in the new government, was appalled. This material was classified, he said; if it appeared, the troops on Gallipoli would be compromised. Both he and Grey, Churchill suddenly realized, were treating him as though he had already left the government. He lost his temper. Turning on Lloyd George, he snapped: "You don't care. You don't care if I am trampled underfoot by my enemies. You don't care for my personal reputation." His old ally broke in: "No, I don't. I don't care for my own at the present time. The only thing I care about now is that we win in this war." That was cant. He, too, was a political animal. Had he been in Winston's plight he would have been at his wits' end. George is a key figure in the history of that time, but his position during that turbulent week is murky. He cynically told his mistress, "The situation for Churchill has no meaning but his own prospects," and she, who always reflected his views, wrote in her diary of Winston's fall: "I am rather sorry for him, as it must be a terrible experience for one who has had so much power in his hands. But all the same I think he deserves it." It was the chancellor who, upon learning of Fisher's departure for Scotland, had told Asquith: "Of course, we must have a coalition, for the alternative is impossible." Clementine regarded that as a piece of "Welsh trickiness." She told Winston she thought Lloyd George a Judas. Yet afterward George called Churchill's dismissal "a cruel and unjust degradation. The Dardanelles failure," he said later, "was due not so much to Mr. Churchill's precipitancy as to Lord Kitchener's and Mr. Asquith's procrastination."[124]

Churchill set his jaw. He wouldn't quit. He was ready to pay almost any price rather than surrender the Admiralty. "In the evening," Hankey wrote in his diary that Wednesday, "Churchill offered Fisher any terms he liked including a seat in the Cabinet, if he would stay with him at the Admiralty." An intermediary carried the message, as before, and Fisher again played the informer, sending the letter to Bonar Law and scribbling across it: "I rejected the 30 pieces of silver to betray my country." It seems never to have occurred to him that he was betraying the friend who had brought him back from retirement. Sir Arthur Wilson, who had succeeded Fisher as first sea lord, said he would refuse to serve under any first lord except Churchill. "This," Winston wrote Asquith, "is the greatest compliment I have ever been paid." Heartened, he wrote Law again. "The rule to follow," he began, "is what is best calculated to beat the enemy, and not what is most likely to please the newspapers." The conduct of the Dardanelles operation "should be reviewed by the new Cabinet. Every fact should be laid before them." He himself bore "a tremendous responsibility" for the campaign against the Turks. "With Sir Arthur Wilson's professional aid I am sure I can discharge that responsibility fully. In view of his statement to the Prime Minister and to the naval Lords that he will serve as First Sea Lord under me, and under no one else, I feel entitled to say that no other personal combination will give so good a chance." At stake was "the safety of an Army now battling its way forward under many difficulties." For nearly four years Churchill had been, "according to my patent, 'solely responsible to Crown and Parliament' and have borne the blame for any failure: and now I present to you an absolutely secure naval position. . . . Therefore I ask to be judged fairly. . . . I do not ask for anything else."[125]

He wrote that "if the Admiralty were in uninstructed or unfriendly hands" it might "lead to the abandonment of the Dardanelles operation" which "otherwise is a certainty," and asked Asquith to "fancy my feelings if, at this critical moment — on mere uninformed newspaper hostility — the whole intricate affair is to be taken out of my hands & put in the hands of a stranger without the knowledge, or worst of all in the hands of a deadly foe of the plan." He was "clinging to my *task* & to my *duty.*" He could not defend himself without putting England's security at hazard. The Conservatives knew only what they had read in the press. "But *you* know. You alone know the whole situation and that it is my duty to carry this burden safely: and that I can do it. Let me stand or fall by the Dardanelles — but do not take it from my hands." Clementine also took the remarkable step of writing the prime minister. Her husband, she told him, had mastered "every detail of naval science. There is no man in this country who possesses equal knowledge capacity & vigour. If he goes, the injury to Admiralty business will not be reparable for many months — if indeed it is ever made good during the war. Why do you part with Winston? unless indeed you have lost confidence in his work and ability? But I know that cannot be the reason. Is not the reason expediency — 'to restore public confidence.' I suggest to you that public confidence will be restored in *Germany* by Winston's downfall. . . . If you send him to another place he will no longer be fighting. If you waste this valuable war material you will be doing an injury to this country."[126]

To swallow pride and crawl thus must have been excruciating for both Winston and Clementine. And it was all for nothing. Asquith wrote Venetia that he had received "the letter of a maniac" from her cousin Clementine. Bonar Law — who said privately that Winston "seems to have an entirely unbalanced mind" — replied to Churchill that his removal as first lord was "inevitable." Asquith wrote Winston: "You must take it as settled that you are not to remain at the Admiralty." There could be no appeal from that. Winston, who like other critics of Asquith had taken to calling him "The Block" in private, replied: "All right, I accept your decision. I shall not look back. . . . I must wait for the march of events at the Dlles." On the next Saturday, May 22, Winston saw the prime minister briefly. Asquith called it "a most painful interview to me: but he was good & in his best mood. And it ended all right." Yet there was still no place for him in the new cabinet. Two days later Margot wrote in her diary: "What a satire if the coming Coalition Government of which Winston has gassed so much should not contain him! I know Henry [Asquith] too well to suppose this but there is no doubt if Henry wanted to make himself supremely popular with every party *ours and the others* he would exclude Winston. I would not wish this, there is something lovable in Winston and he is a real pal but I should not be surprised if he wrecked the new Government."[127]

How unpopular *was* Churchill in the spring of 1915? He was controversial, of course; he always had been. But he himself believed he was now friendless. Asquith's daughter, who loved him as her father loved Venetia, came to him in tears. They "slipped away" together, she wrote, and he "took me into his room," whereupon he collapsed in a chair, "silent, despairing — as I had never seen him. He seemed to have no rebellion or even anger left. He did not even abuse Fisher, but simply said, 'I'm finished.' " She protested; he said, "No — I'm done." Yet the day after his final dismissal Italy had entered the war, and he more than anyone else had been responsible for England's new ally. His most loyal supporters remained steadfast. Virtually all the younger flag officers went on record as supporting him. At Gallipoli, Hamilton discovered "in the Air Service the profound conviction that, if they could only get in touch with Winston Churchill, all would be well. Their faith in the First Lord is, in every sense, *touching.*"[128]

But Englishmen demanded a whipping boy. If they couldn't beat the Germans, they could turn on one of their own, and Churchill, the ostentatious poseur, was the obvious choice. Sir Henry Wilson wrote Bonar Law: "A man who can plot the Ulster Pogrom, plan Antwerp, & carry out the Dardanelles fiasco is worth watching." In some vague way Winston was held accountable for everything that had gone wrong, from the shell crisis to the hopeless seesaw in the trenches. He had lost ships. He had frequently been away from his desk — on urgent missions, though they didn't know that. He had ignored expert advice — even the counsel of Fisher, England's greatest admiral. He was a reckless adventurer, a man loyal only to his own ambition. The Dundee *Advertiser* reported that many of his Liberal constituents believed that he "should be excluded altogether from the Cabinet on the ground, as they contend, that he is in a large measure responsible for precipitating the present state of affairs." Admiralty diehards, impotent during his early naval reforms, now struck out savagely. Captain Richmond called him "ignorant." Admiral Sir Henry Jackson, who was appointed first sea lord when Balfour replaced Churchill, described the attempt to force the Dardanelles as "a mad thing to do." The naval correspondent of *The Times* reported: "The news that Mr Churchill is leaving the Admiralty has been received with a feeling of relief in the Service, both afloat and ashore," and commented that while he had brought a "breezy atmosphere" with him, he had also created "a sense of uneasiness lest those very qualities of his which might be of advantage to the State in other circumstances, should lead him into making some false step, which, in the case of the Fleet, upon which our all depends, would be irretrievable." On May 24 Frances Stevenson wrote in her diary: "There is no section of the country, so far as I can see, that wishes him to stay at the Admiralty." According to her, Winston's private naval secretary had advised the prime minister "that on no account ought Churchill to be allowed to remain at the Admiralty — he was most dangerous there." Even Asquith, whose punishment Winston was taking, joined the posse. Churchill, he complained, "is impulsive & borne along on the flood of his all too copious tongue," and, further, "it is a pity that Winston has not got a better sense of proportion. I am really fond of him, but I regard his future with many misgivings. I do not think he will ever get to the top in English politics with all his wonderful gifts." In war, losers, even more than winners, need to create martyrs. Churchill was England's Armenian.[129]

He suffered. His Black Dog had never been so bad; he was in the pit of the worst depression of his life. After he had said his goodbyes at the Admiralty on Saturday and sent a farewell telegram to the Royal Naval Division, Eddie Marsh wrote Violet Asquith: "I am miserably sorry for Winston. You can imagine what a horrible wound and mutilation it is for him to be torn away from his work there . . . it's like Beethoven deaf." Sir George Riddell called on him and wrote in his *War Diary:* "He looked very worn out and harassed. He greeted me . . . and said, 'I am the victim of a political intrigue. I am finished!' " Lloyd George later said that it was "the brutality of the fall" that "stunned" Winston, and Churchill himself wrote afterward: "Like a sea-beast fished up from the depths, or a diver too suddenly hoisted, my veins threatened to burst from the fall in pressure. . . . At a moment when every fibre of my being was inflamed to action, I was forced to remain a spectator of the tragedy, placed cruelly in a front seat." Clementine later told Martin Gilbert: "The Dardanelles haunted him for the rest of his life. He always believed in it. When he left the Admiralty he thought he was finished. . . . I thought he would never get over the Dardanelles; I thought he would die of grief."[130]

At the time she, too, was distraught. After calling at Admiralty House, Edwin Montagu wrote Venetia, now his fiancée: "I went by request to see poor Mrs Winston. She was so sweet but so miserable and crying all the time. I was very inarticulate, but how I feel for her and him." Back in his Treasury office he wrote Clementine that "Winston is far too great to be more than pulled up for a period. . . . Have no misgivings as to the future; I have none, I'm sure he has none." But Winston had many, and what cut deepest were the lost chances which had gone up in the smoke rising from British ineptitude in Turkey. One of his dinner guests at this time was Ellis Ashmead-Bartlett, a war correspondent who had just returned from Gallipoli. Unlike young Churchill in India, the Sudan, and South Africa, journalists covering this campaign had been heavily censored — a full month had passed before the *Illustrated London News* had been permitted to publish photographs of the fighting — and an uninformed public, susceptible to rumor, had contributed to Churchill's ruin. Ashmead-Bartlett wanted to talk to him about that. But his host wouldn't listen to anyone. Ashmead-Bartlett noted in his diary: "I am much surprised at the change in Winston Churchill. He looks years older, his face is pale, he seems very depressed and to feel keenly his retirement from the Admiralty. . . . At dinner the conversation was more or less general, nothing was said about the Dardanelles, and Winston was very quiet. It was only towards the very end that he suddenly burst forth into a tremendous discourse on the Expedition and what might have been, addressed directly across the table in the form of a lecture to his mother, who listened most attentively. Winston seemed unconscious of the limited number of his audience, and continued quite heedless of those around him. He insisted over and over again that the battle of March 18th had never been fought to a finish, and, had it been, the Fleet must have got through the Narrows. This is the great obsession of his mind, and will ever remain so." Jennie wrote Leonie: "If they had made the Dardanelles policy a certainty, Constantinople would have been in our hands ages ago. *In confidence*, it is astounding how Winston foresaw it all."[131]

His obsession with what might have been kept him in civilian clothes for six months. Asquith promised him a seat on the War Council, now renamed the Dardanelles Committee, if he would accept the lowest of cabinet posts, chancellor of the duchy of Lancaster. "Where is Lancaster?" jeered the *Bystander*. "And what is a Duchy?" The position was a sinecure, which, as Lloyd George put it, was "generally reserved either for beginners in the Cabinet or for distinguished politicians who had reached the final stages of unmistakable decrepitude." The chancellor's only duty was to appoint county magistrates. In false cheeriness Winston wrote Jack Seely: "The Duchy of Lancaster has been mobilized. A strong flotilla of magistrates for the 1915 programme will shortly be laid down." His salary was immediately cut from £4,500 to £2,000 a year. Asquith offered to let the Churchills stay on in Admiralty House, but Clementine refused to accept charity from the man who, as she saw it, had sacrificed her husband to save his own office. Ivor Guest gave his cousin the temporary use of his house at 21 Arlington Street, behind the Ritz; then they would move in with Goonie in Jack Churchill's South Kensington house at 41 Cromwell Road, opposite the Natural History Museum. On May 23, eight days after the crisis over Fisher's resignation had erupted, Winston turned the Admiralty over to Balfour. One of the new first lord's first decisions was to scrap the tank project. According to Captain D'Eyncourt's memoirs, *A Shipbuilder's Yarn,* the new first lord called him in and asked: "Have not you and your department enough to do looking after the design and construction of ships without concerning yourself about material for the Army?" Appropriations already in the pipeline produced a small number of tanks in 1916. To Churchill's dismay, Lloyd George told him that the army planned to use them immediately. Winston went to Asquith, pleading against untimely use of the trench weapon which, he believed, could be decisive. He was ignored. On September 15 a handful of tanks went into action on the Somme. The British infantry was unprepared to consolidate their quick gains, and the element of surprise was squandered. "My poor 'land battleships,'" Churchill wrote, "have been let off prematurely and on a petty scale. In that idea resided one real victory." Here he, too, was premature. The tank's time would come again, and yet again.[132]

In the weeks after he cleared out his Admiralty desk his depression deepened. "It is odious to me," he wrote Seely, "to remain here watching sloth and folly with full knowledge & no occupation." To Jack on Gallipoli he wrote: "The war is terrible: the carnage grows apace, & the certainty that no result will be reached this year fills my mind with melancholy thoughts. The youth of Europe — almost a whole generation — will be shorn away. I find it vy painful to be deprived of any direct means of action." Beginning in late May, he took his and his brother's families to a rental property in Surrey each weekend. "I am off to Hoe Farm," he wrote Jack on June 19. "How I wish you cd be there. It really is a delightful valley and the garden gleams with summer jewelry. We live vy simply — but with all the essentials of life well understood & provided for — hot baths, cold champagne, new peas, & old brandy." Yet even here he drew apart from the others and paced endlessly between the garden and a small wooden summerhouse. He tried golf again and again and hated it; it was, he said, "like chasing a quinine pill around a cow pasture." Then, in a flash of inspiration, his sister-in-law introduced him to painting. Goonie painted herself; she set up her easel in the garden one Sunday, and when she noticed Winston watching her with interest, she suggested he try it, using some of the children's watercolors. There was plenty to paint, she pointed out: the garden, the woods, the house, a nearby pond. He tried, liked it, and did it well. He had a natural visual eye, and knew it; during the Boer War he had supplemented his dispatches with sketches drawn in the field; touched up by newspaper illustrators, they had been published. Obviously, he could be good if he applied himself. It struck him that in this dark hour of life the "Muse of Painting" might have come to his rescue — "out of charity and out of chivalry, because after all she had nothing to do with me — and said, 'Are these toys any good to you? They amuse some people.' "[133]

But watercolors would not do. Being Churchill, whatever he did had to be done for the ages. He told Clementine: *"La peinture à l'huile est bien difficile, mais c'est beaucoup plus beau que la peinture à l'eau."* She needed only that hint; she was off and running, and when she returned she brought a palette, canvases, an easel, a smock, and tubes. Unfortunately she had neglected to bring turpentine, and that aborted his first venture. Finally he was ready. Later he described his sensations on the threshold of that first attempt. With everything assembled, "the next step was to *begin.* But what a step to take! The palette gleamed with beads of colour; fair and white rose the canvas; the empty brush hung poised, heavy with destiny, irresolute in the air. My hand seemed arrested by a silent veto. But after all the sky on this occasion was unquestionably blue, and a pale blue at that. There could be no doubt that blue paint mixed with white should be put on the top of the canvas. One really does not need to have had an artist's training to see that. It is a starting-point open to all. So very gingerly I mixed a little blue paint on the palette with a very small brush, and then with infinite precaution made a mark about as big as a pea upon the affronted snow-white shield. It was a challenge, a deliberate challenge; but so subdued, so halting, indeed so cataleptic, that it deserved no response."[134]

At that most appropriate moment an automobile was heard in the drive, and out stepped Hazel Lavery, a neighbor, the wife of an artist, and a gifted painter herself. Her appearance was not a coincidence. Clementine was making up for the turpentine. Hazel strode up and said: "What are you hesitating about? Let me have a brush — the big one." She splashed it into turpentine, socked it into the blue and white, thrashed it about on the palette, and delivered several huge, savage strokes on what Winston called "the absolutely cowering canvas." Anyone could see, he wrote, "that it could not hit back. No evil fate avenged the jaunty violence. The canvas grinned in helplessness before me. The spell was broken." He was delighted. This was his style; this was how he lived. It was inevitable that he should become an audacious painter, and a gaudy one; nothing that he ever touched was done by halves. "I cannot pretend to be impartial about the colours," he wrote. "I rejoice with the brilliant ones, and am genuinely sorry for the poor browns." When he reached heaven he would "require a still gayer palette than I get here below. I expect orange and vermilion will be the darkest, dullest colours upon it, and beyond them there will be a whole range of wonderful new colours which will delight the celestial eye."[135]

Eddie Marsh, who watched his first efforts, thought that "the new enthusiasm . . . was a distraction and a sedative that brought a measure of ease to his frustrated spirit." In fact, it would be a solace to him for the next fifty years. He had, he believed, discovered the solution to anxiety and tension. Exercise, travel, retreat, solitude, forced gaiety — he had tried these and none had worked. "Change," he now wrote, "is the master key. A man can wear out a particular part of his mind by continually using it and tiring it . . . the tired parts of the mind can be rested and strengthened, not merely by rest, but by using other parts. . . . It is only when new cells are called into activity, when new stars become lords of the ascendant, that relief, repose, refreshment are afforded."[136]

He painted landscapes and still lifes; never people. For one of his studies of bottles he coined a word: *bottlescape.* The dazzling hues were always there, a kind of signature. He knew desperation, but never a gray day. Once, painting in a drab, monochrome countryside, he introduced a dramatic range of mountains which were not there. A puzzled companion asked if he had seen a mirage. No, said Churchill; he just "couldn't leave it quite as dull as that." In time he became very good. An art critic scrutinized his work at a Royal Academy exhibition and wrote: "I was bound to recognize that their creator is a real artist. His canvases bear the mark of the spontaneity of a sincere and exuberant, but undisciplined vocation. His landscapes are vigorous and sometimes sensitive. His use of colour is often happy. . . . I think his fame as a statesman has prejudiced his reputation as an artist."[137]

At Hoe Farm he also rejoiced in the company of small children. Sarah was still an infant, but Diana was six and Randolph four, and his two nephews, Johnny and Peregrine, were also there. Long afterward Johnny would recall how, when he and his brother were given a box of Meccano — a kind of Erector Set — they started building a cantilever crane in the farmhouse dining room. Their uncle appeared, puffing on a cigar. He watched thoughtfully for a while, and then murmured: "Hm. A bascule bridge would be better, you know." Johnny explained that they hadn't enough pieces. Churchill waved his hand impatiently, summoned a servant, and sent her out to buy several Meccano boxes. Then, Johnny remembers, he "took off his coat and began preparing the largest model bascule bridge ever. . . . The final construction was a gigantic piece of engineering some fifteen feet long and eight feet high, with a roadway which could be lifted by means of wheels, pulleys and yards of string." It was so big that the dining room became unusable. The family had to eat elsewhere.[138]

He also played "gorilla" with the children. Donning his oldest clothes, he would lurk behind shrubbery, waiting for one of them to appear. When one did, he would leap out roaring "Grr! Grr!" and advance menacingly, his arms swinging limply at his sides. "The realism was alarming," Johnny recalls, "but we squealed with delight and enjoyed this exclusive performance hugely. Few people can say that they have seen an ex–First Lord of the Admiralty crouching in the branches of an oak, baring his teeth and pounding his chest with his fists." Winston's son remembered that when his father dropped from a limb, "we would all scatter in various directions. He would pursue us and the one he caught would be the loser."[139]

In the Dardanelles Committee the ex–first lord was less effective, but he had lost none of his persuasive powers, and in the beginning most of his recommendations were adopted. On June 1 he circulated a paper among the other members, arguing that while a decision in France had proved impossible, a relatively small expansion of Hamilton's army could bring victory. "It seems most urgent," he wrote, "to try to obtain a decision here and wind up the enterprise in a satisfactory manner as soon as possible." Bonar Law and Sir Edward Carson, another old Churchill adversary, disagreed, but the committee voted to send five more divisions to Gallipoli. In France, Sir Henry Wilson raged: "That makes 9 there and 22 here, and not a single Boche facing the 9. How they will laugh in Berlin." In any event there was no doubt that Britain was betting heavily on Gallipoli. Hamilton's army now numbered 120,000 troops. Surely he could break through.[140]

He didn't. An old military maxim runs: "Never reinforce failure." That is how Hamilton used his fresh troops. Churchill telegraphed him, urging a landing on the Bulair Isthmus. Hamilton, obsessed with logistics and matériel, replied that he doubted his troops were capable of the effort, or that it could succeed under the best of conditions. His troops, bogged down, fought, not only Turks, but also summer flies. Discipline grew lax; the men grumbled that they were victims of "the politicians." Hamilton wired the War Office that he needed ninety-five thousand more men to provide "the necessary superiority."[141] Kitchener told him that Gallipoli had had its chance, and the Dardanelles Committee, to Winston's alarm, began to consider evacuating the peninsula. Whatever the problems in the east, Churchill said, the west was not the answer. In September the first troops of Kitchener's army went over the top in France to capture the village of Loos and the high ground a mile beyond. After two days fifteen thousand English and Scottish soldiers had been killed and the German wire was intact. Churchill searched the map again, and, the following month, when Bulgaria entered the war as a German ally, drew up a four-point plan of attack to open a broad Balkan front from the Aegean, offering opportunities for movement and thrusts.

It was rejected. Churchill's theories of war, Aitken concluded, were "so hare-brained that it would be humorous if the lives of men were things to joke about, or, I might add, to trifle with." Even Violet Asquith, who defended him passionately, rated him "a guided gambler." In fact, his military thought was on a plane so extraordinary that others simply could not grasp it. In his multivolume history of the Great War he dwelt upon the significance of maneuver, which, he wrote, may assume many forms, "in time, in diplomacy, in mechanics, in psychology." Only when military and political thought were joined could leaders discover "easier ways, other than sheer slaughter, of achieving the main purpose." As he conceived of it, the "distinction between politics and strategy diminishes as the point of view is raised. At the summit true politics and strategy are one."[142] Thus the internal political complexes of the Balkan states, in his mind, were linked to events on all European battlefields. Because these states were politically weak, the opportunities were there and should be seized. Others, lacking his imaginative grasp, dismissed him as superficial. Actually, he was plumbing depths whose very existence was unsuspected by them.

And so the achievements his genius might have wrought were irrevocably lost. His credibility had shrunk as Hamilton's prospects for victory faded. Once more he was being blamed for a plan that had not been his. Accustomed to respect and even deference, he now had to endure slights which, less than a year ago, would have been unthinkable. Balfour recalled Fisher from Scotland and appointed him chairman of the Admiralty's Committee on Inventions and Research. Churchill angrily wrote Asquith: "Fisher resigned his office without warning or parley. . . . You ordered Fisher to return to his post in the name of the King. He paid no attention to yr order. You declared that he had deserted his post in time of war; & the facts are not open to any other construction. For ten days or more the country was without a First Sea Lord as Fisher did not even do his duty till his successor was appointed." To Balfour he added: "All this must be viewed in relation to a very old man." He decided not to send the letter, but made his views known to the prime minister through a mutual friend. It didn't matter. His protest was ignored. The next week Kitchener suggested that he make an official trip to the Dardanelles and Gallipoli. Winston was delighted. Since all British positions on the peninsula were within range of Turkish artillery, he took out a new insurance policy, giving him £10,300 coverage. In addition he held £1,000 in Witbank Collieries stock. He explained all this in a letter to Clementine, to be delivered in the event of his death, and told her where she could find the "complete" Admiralty papers documenting his record. "There is no hurry," he wrote, "but some day I shd like the truth to be known. Randolph will carry on the lamp. Do not grieve for me too much. I am a spirit confident of my rights. Death is only an incident, & not the most important wh happens to us in this state of being. On the whole, especially since I met you my darling one I have been happy, & you have taught me how noble a woman's heart can be. If there is anywhere else I shall be on the look out for you. Meanwhile, look forward, feel free, rejoice in life, cherish the children, guard my memory. God bless you. Good bye. W."[143]

Kitchener suggested that Hankey accompany him, and it was agreed. The King sent word to him that he was "glad to hear" of his mission. A warm note arrived from Grey. Winston spent a final Sunday with the family at Hoe Farm. Then, after the cabinet meeting had broken up Monday morning, Asquith, Kitchener, and Grey gathered around to wish him a fond farewell. At that point a Tory minister unexpectedly returned and asked where Churchill was going. Told, he made a beeline for Bonar Law. The upshot was that the Conservatives opposed the trip. Asquith again caved in rather than, as he told Churchill, face "any serious division of opinion." Lord Curzon, one of the Tories who had protested, wrote Winston that "we shared a doubt as to the reception that public opinion might give to such an act, for which the Govt would be held collectively responsible." The unkindest cut came from Kitchener. The reason he had asked Hankey to go along, he said, was that he thought someone should watch Churchill. After discussing the Tory veto with K of K, Lord Esher wrote in his diary: "He laughed over it a good deal and admitted that he would not have been sorry to get rid of Winston for a while." News of this reached Churchill. The message to him was clear. He wasn't wanted. He wasn't even trusted.[144]

If others had doubts about forcing the Narrows, British submarine commanders didn't. They slipped in and out, roaming the Sea of Marmara and the Black Sea and sinking Turkish ships within sight of Constantinople. Because of them, enemy troops were chronically short of ammunition. Nevertheless, the British learned from prisoners, aerial reconnaissance, and agents in Constantinople that Turkish reinforcements were pouring into Gallipoli. Hamilton wrung his hands. On October 16 he was sacked and General Sir Charles Monro, who had been fighting in France, replaced him. One of Monro's first duties, the War Office told him, would be to determine whether or not the peninsula should be abandoned. Since he was an ardent Westerner, scornful of this theater, there could be little doubt about his decision. Churchill later called him "an officer of quick decision. He came, he saw, he capitulated." Before he could take over, however, Roger Keyes made a last plea for a naval assault on the Narrows. He arrived in London on October 28 and converted Balfour and the sea lords. Churchill saw a sparkle of hope. "I believe," he wrote, "we have been all these months in the position of the Spanish prisoner who languished for twenty years in a dungeon until one morning the idea struck him to push the door which had been open all the time."[145]

When Kitchener joined his proselytes, Keyes seemed to have won. Asquith, Balfour, and Kitchener gathered to plan "an abrupt naval coup de main upon the Straits." But Balfour, hedging his bet, said the navy would act only if the army also attacked — which would require Monro's approval — and Law threatened to resign unless the whole Turkish theater was shut down. After a communications breakdown between London and the Aegean, Kitchener personally visited the peninsula. He met Keyes aboard the *Dartmouth.* "Well, I have seen the place," he said. "It is an awful place, and you will never get through." Keyes asked what had changed his mind. K of K was vague, but it is a fair guess that Monro had decided him. Hamilton's successor was on the scene now, spreading defeatism. Kitchener wired London that the Suvla and Anzac beachheads should be evacuated. Cape Helles would be held "for the time being."[146]

On November 6 the Dardanelles Committee was renamed the War

Cabinet and Winston was excluded from it. It was time for him to go; past time. He had known it for weeks. Early in September he had asked Asquith for a field command, suggesting that a major general's commission and the command of an army corps would be appropriate for someone with his knowledge and experience. The prime minister approached Kitchener, who said that he "would like to get rid of Churchill, but could not offend the Army." Winston then proposed that he be appointed "Governor-General and Military Commander-in-Chief of British East Africa." He felt sure he could raise an army of Africans. Balfour told Hankey and James Masterton-Smith, a veteran civil servant at the Admiralty, a version of this. Hankey entered it in his diary. Churchill, according to Balfour, had given Asquith "a scheme for attacking the Germans" in their African colonies "with armoured cars." He added that perhaps if he succeeded in this, the "military objections to his [assuming] a high post of command would disappear. All this tickled Mr. Balfour so much that he positively pirouetted on one foot, looking very odd in his long frock coat, so that Masterton-Smith and I fairly roared with laughter."[147]

The laughingstock of the cabinet submitted his resignation on November 11. Asquith accepted it the next day. Not many mourned his departure. The *Manchester Guardian* was one; an editorial described it as "a great national loss, for in our opinion — though we dare say there are few who now share it — he had the best strategic sense in the Government. . . . There have been two opportunities of winning the war. One was last October before the fall of Antwerp, the other was this spring when a great effort by land and sea would have won through to Constantinople and saved us all of our troubles in the East now. Mr Churchill saw them both at the time and though his ideas were adopted, neither in Flanders nor in the East did they have anything like a fair chance."[148]

Churchill was without political office for the first time in ten years, and as was customary when ministers stepped down, he made a personal statement in the House of Commons — a privilege which had been withheld from him when he left the Admiralty. Later he expanded his remarks before the commission investigating the Turkish campaign. He denied that he had "foisted" a civilian plan upon "reluctant officers and experts." He said: "You may condemn the men who tried to force the Dardanelles, but your children will keep their condemnation for those who did not rally to their aid." In his peroration he cried: "Undertake no operation in the West which is more costly to us in life than to the enemy. In the East, take Constantinople. Take it by ships if you can. Take it by soldiers if you must. Take it by whichever plan, military or naval, commends itself to your military experts. But take it; take it soon; take it while time remains." Asquith rose from the Treasury Bench to acknowledge his departure briefly. He praised him as "a wise counsellor, a brilliant colleague, and a faithful friend," but did not mention his own role in the Dardanelles decisions. His daughter, who had watched from the gallery, wrote Winston "one line to say I thought your speech *quite* flawless — I have seldom been more moved. . . . Is there anything you *haven't* got for the Front? Compass? Luminous wristwatch? Muffler & Tinderlighter? If there is any lacuna in your equipment let me fill it."[149]

There was one, but she could do nothing about it. He needed a command. At the very least, he thought, he should be given a brigade, preferably in a division fighting Turks. He didn't get one. It was fashionable that fall, in Parliament and the War Office, to deride him as an attitudinarian who had been a "mere subaltern." In fact, his military qualifications were more substantial than that. He was a reserve major who had commanded the defense of Antwerp. As a young officer he had seen fighting in Cuba, India, the Sudan, and South Africa. Twice he had witnessed German war maneuvers, an advantage no one on the general staff shared. He had made a thorough study of the arts of war and had published five books on military subjects. His years as first lord ought to have counted for a great deal. "Instead," as Max Aitken wrote afterward, "he was extruded from the centre of action by men of lesser ability and initiative, and his knowledge and his inventiveness of mind — all were wasted."[150] Asquith and Kitchener ignored his every appeal. In the end he had only his commission in the Queen's Own Oxfordshire Hussars — that and his acquaintances among the redtabs in France, which, because of his genteel birth and public career, were several. He decided to join his regiment in France. There, at least, he would be among friends. He would see what else he could manage along the way.

On Tuesday, November 16, he held a farewell luncheon at 41 Cromwell Road, inviting Goonie, Nellie Hozier, Eddie Marsh, and Margot and Violet Asquith. Violet would later remember that "Clemmie was admirably calm and brave, the rest of us trying to 'play up' and hide our leaden hearts. Winston alone was at his gayest and his best and he and Margot held the table between them. They had always been an uneasy combination, as neither of them really enjoyed the other's society and she could not forbear from rubbing in the evils which had followed in the wake of the coalition and reminding him that he had always wanted one. He made his stock reply, that we should have sought one, not in our hour of weakness but at a time of strength." For the rest of the group, Violet thought, the lunch "was a kind of wake."[151]

Wednesday, Aitken arrived, bursting with energy, as always, and found "the whole household was upside down while the soldier-statesman was buckling on his sword." He was also supervising the packing of cigars, port, vermouth, whiskey, camping equipment, and assorted creature comforts. "Downstairs," Aitken saw, "Mr 'Eddie' Marsh, his faithful secretary, was in tears. . . . Upstairs, Lady Randolph was in a state of despair at the idea of her brilliant son being relegated to the trenches. Mrs Churchill seemed to be the only person who remained calm, collected and efficient." On Thursday, Major Churchill crossed the Channel aboard a regular steamer to Boulogne, where, to his surprise, a car had been sent by Sir John French to meet him. After reporting to his regiment, he joined the BEF's commander in chief for dinner at Saint-Omer "in a fine château," he wrote home, "with hot baths, beds, champagne & all the conveniences." French received him warmly; his own position had become highly precarious, and he could empathize with the fallen Churchill. More generous than Asquith or the War Office, he offered him a choice between serving here as an ADC or commanding a brigade. "The brigade," Winston instantly replied. It was settled that he would first spend a training period with the Grenadier Guards. He wrote home: "Midnight. My dearest soul — (this is what the gt d of Marlborough used to write from the low countries to his cat) All is vy well arranged . . . but as I do not know to wh battalion I am to be sent, I cannot tell the rota in wh we shall go into the trenches."[152]

Approaching the front in that war was a shocking experience. Winston hadn't been in the field in fifteen years, and he had never seen anything like this. He was a middle-aged man, accustomed to indulgence, whose skin felt unchafed only when caressed by silk. There would be none of that here. On Saturday he lunched at La Gorgue and learned that he had been attached to the grenadiers' Second Battalion, commanded by Lieutenant Colonel George "Ma" Jeffreys, the only surviving officer of the original battalion which had gone into action here in 1914. They would be reentering the line that night in front of Merville, near Neuve Chappelle, one of the many villages, like Ypres, Bullecourt, and Messines, whose very names had become symbols for the suffering here. He was driven part of the way toward the thundering artillery and then proceeded on foot with Jeffreys's sweating, heavy-laden, sleepy-eyed headquarters staff. "It was a dull November afternoon," he would write in the March 1924 issue of *Nash's Pall Mall.* "An icy drizzle fell over the darkening plain. As we approached the line, the red flashes of the guns stabbed the sombre landscape on either side of the road, to the sound of an intermittent cannonade." After nearly four hours they reached battal-

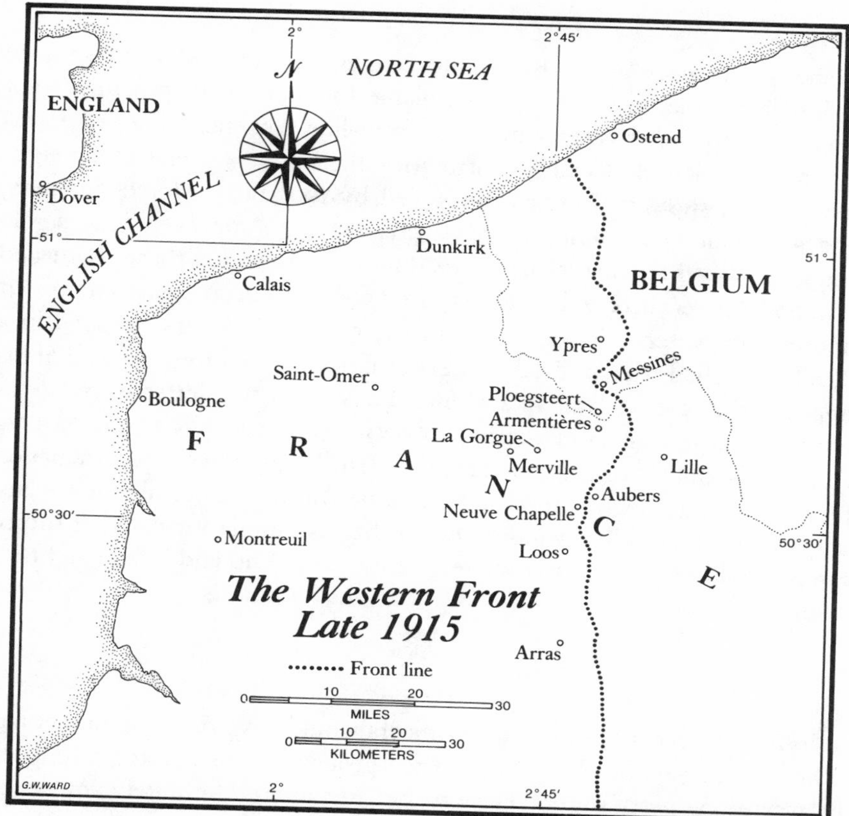

ion headquarters, "a pulverized ruin called Ebenezer Farm," where they were provided with rations and "strong tea with condensed milk" — not his idea of liquid refreshment.[153]

Jeffreys greeted him coldly: "I think I ought to tell you that we were not at all consulted in the matter of your coming to us." Winston respectfully replied that the decision had not been his; he ventured to say it would work; in any case they must make the best of it. After a long, hostile silence, the adjutant said: "I am afraid we have had to cut down your kit rather, Major. There are no communication trenches here. We are doing all our reliefs over the top. The men have little more than what they stand up in. We have found a servant for you, who is carrying a spare pair of socks and your shaving gear. We have had to leave the rest behind." Churchill said that was "quite all right"; he was sure he would be "very comfortable."[154]

No one spoke to him again as they moved up. He felt, he said afterward, "like a new boy at school in charge of the Headmaster, the monitors, and the senior scholars." He knew why; every British soldier in

France was bitter about the reinforcements which had been sent to Gallipoli, and he, of course, was to blame for that. At length they leapt over a parapet and rushed into the front-line trenches. There he was given his choice of sleeping quarters for the night, a signal office eight feet square, stiflingly hot, and occupied by four busy Morse signalers, and a dugout two hundred yards away. Having "surveyed" the signal room, he asked for directions to the dugout and was led there. It turned out, he later recalled, to be "a sort of pit four feet deep containing about one foot of water." It was there, in the mud of Flanders, trapped in a deadlock he had tried so hard to break, that he learned the outcome of his hopes in the east. It came in a scrawled postscript to a letter from Clementine: "Large posters just out: — TROOPS WITHDRAWN FROM DARDANELLES — OFFICIAL." After 213,980 British casualties, the evacuation of Gallipoli had begun. It would continue through December into January. Not a man fell in winding down the operation. Virtually all future losses would be here on the western front, where no end was in sight.[155]

So frosty a reception by fellow officers would have daunted almost any other newcomer, but Winston was too proud, and his ego too strong, to be scarred by petty slights. He was, he later wrote, "infinitely amused at the elaborate pains they took to put me in my place and to make me realize that nothing counted at the front except military rank and behaviour." Here they were wrong. He expected special treatment and he got it. Soldiers' mail was notoriously slow; letters to and from Cromwell Road, carried by a King's messenger from the Admiralty, were delivered overnight. No other fighting man could speak to his wife over a telephone. Churchill did; he rode back to French's GHQ and heard her over a special Admiralty line. After hanging up he wrote Clementine that because another officer had been in the room, "I cd not say much & even feared you might think I was abrupt." She wrote that the conversation had been "very tantalising, as there is so much I want to say to you which cannot be shouted into an unsympathetic receiver!" But millions of husbands and wives would have given much to be so constrained, and so tantalized.[156]

August visitors traipsed up to the trenches to see him: Lord Curzon, General Seely, and F. E. Smith, now attorney general, who, to his fury, was arrested by a sentry for want of a proper pass. At Saint-Omer, Winston had encountered another acquaintance, Edward Louis Spiers. They had met before the war in the home of Venetia Stanley's sister Sylvia.

Spiers, now a young cavalry captain, was serving as a liaison officer between the BEF and Joffre's staff. He invited Winston to join him in a tour of the French lines. Churchill was confident that he was immune to AWOL charges — he was right — and off they went. A French general insisted on being photographed with Winston. Churchill wrote home: "I was received with much attention, more so in fact than when I went as 1st Lord." As a parting gift he was crowned with a poilu's steel helmet, "wh I am going to wear," he told Clementine, "as it looks so nice & will perhaps protect my valuable cranium."[157]

The battalion adjutant could not limit him to spare socks and a razor. He was entitled to his kit; he got it, and more. If he had to live in such conditions, he intended to be properly equipped. His wife sent him a pillow. That was a start. Somehow he acquired a tin bathtub, a pocket Shakespeare, then brandy — Jeffreys kept a "dry" mess — and a stock of fine cigars. Clementine wrote: "I wake up in the night & think of you shivering in the trenches; it makes me so miserable (You know how warm the Kat has to be before she can sleep)." Like Violet Asquith, she wanted to know if she could send him anything to make his life more endurable. As a matter of fact, he replied, she could. He wanted a leather waistcoat, a pair of wading boots ("water proof canvas tops coming right up to the thigh"), a periscope ("most important"), a sheepskin sleeping bag, two pairs of khaki trousers, a pair of brown buttoned boots, and three small face towels. *"Voilà tout!"* he wrote at the end. "Your little pillow is a boon & a pet."[158]

How did the other officers feel about this? Astonishingly, they not only tolerated him; he became genuinely popular. He invited them to share his brandy, cigars, tub, and the groaning hampers of food from Cromwell Road. "I never saw such dainties & such profusion," he wrote Clementine of one which arrived when the battalion was in a rear area. "We shall eat them sparingly keeping the best for the trenches." He volunteered to join Jeffreys on his daily rounds of the lines, and thereafter, as he put it, he and the colonel "slid or splashed or plodded together through snow or mud . . . for two or three hours at a time each day and night; and bit by bit he forgot that I was a 'politician' and that he 'had not been consulted in the matter of my coming to his battalion.' " Presently the second in command went on leave; Winston was asked to take his place. He accepted, solemnly declaring this "one of the greatest honours I have ever received." Then he startled Jeffreys by suggesting that he could learn more about trench warfare if he lived, not in the comparative comfort of battalion headquarters, but up with one of the line companies, on the edge of no-man's-land.[159]

Lieutenant Colonel Churchill, 1916

Amazingly, he learned to like it. "It is," he admitted, "a vy curious life to live." But after the humble, fettered duchy of Lancaster, after being blamed for what went wrong when he lacked the power to make it right, he felt free. "I do not feel any prick of conscience at being out here," he wrote Curzon. "I was and am sure that for the time being my usefulness was exhausted and that I could only recover it by a definite and perhaps a prolonged withdrawal. . . . I do not know when I have passed a more joyous three weeks: . . . I share the fortunes of a company of Grenadiers. It is a jolly life with nice people; and one does not mind the cold and wet and general discomfort." The "indomitable good temper" and "inflexible discipline" of the grenadiers impressed him. He in turn charmed them by referring to himself as "the escaped scapegoat" and saying: "Perhaps it is better to be irresponsible and right than responsible and wrong." Major General the Lord Cavan, the commander of the Guards Division, proposed that he wait at brigade headquarters, away from the slime of the front, until a suitable command could be found for him. He declined, writing Clementine: "I said I wouldn't miss a day of it. Nor did I." He wrote again: "I am vy happy here. I did not know what release from care meant. It is a blessed peace. How I ever cd have wasted so many months in impotent misery, wh I might have spent in war, I cannot tell."[160]

He won the affection of the men by his easy manner with them. He wrote: "I keep watch during part of the night so that others may sleep. Last night I found a sentry asleep on his post. I frightened him dreadfully but did not charge him with the crime. He was only a lad, & I am not an officer of the regiment. The penalty is death or at least 2 years." The troops also delighted in his treatment of visiting officers from Saint-Omer; he insisted they join him in an inspection of the front line, where their highly polished boots became spattered with mud and their elegant whipcord breeches torn on the barbed wire. One pompous brigadier, arriving after the battalion's position had been damaged by a heavy barrage, told him that *this really would not do,* that the place must be made *safe:* "You know, it's dangerous — positively *dangerous.*" Churchill replied: "Yes, sir. But this is a very dangerous war." No major British offensives were launched during his six months in Flanders, but it was a wretched existence, and why he should have looked forward to his spells on the brink of no-man's-land so eagerly is difficult to grasp. As he later wrote, "cannonade and fusillade were unceasing" and "no one was ever dry or warm." Part of the reason lay in his remarkable gift for romanticizing squalor. In a letter to his wife he wrote: "Last night . . . after dinner, I had a splendid walk with Archie [Archibald Sinclair, his second in command and later a political colleague] all over the top of the ground. We left the trenches altogether and made a thorough examination of all the fields, tracks, ruins etc immediately behind our line. You cannot show yourself here by day, but in the bright moonlight it is possible to move about without danger (except from random bullets) & to gain a vy clear impression. Archie was a vy good guide. We also went in front of our parapet into the No man's land & prowled about looking at our wire & visiting our listening posts. This is always exciting." On November 30 the Germans celebrated his forty-first birthday by shelling him for three hours — which is how he, the ultimate egoist, regarded it. Then the battalion left the line for a rest, and he exulted in telling Clementine how they marched "while the men sang 'Tipperary' and the 'Farmer's Boy' and the guns boomed applause. It is like getting to a jolly good tavern after a long day's hunting, wet & cold & hungry, but not without having had sport." He was, he confessed, dazzled by "the bright eyes of danger."[161]

Undoubtedly he enjoyed isolation from the abuse and intrigues of London. But the essence of his Flanders mood — finding profound satisfaction where others saw only horror — lay deeper. It derived from a hard, medieval streak, a capacity for viewing bestiality and senseless brutality with a clear, untroubled gaze, responding in kind, even glorying in it. He was fascinated by scenes which revolted others. Few men, whatever their peacetime pursuits, could bear the sight of bloated rats feeding on corpses. In one stretch of earthworks abandoned by the Germans, Edward Spiers later recalled, the rodents "were appalling things; they were huge. . . . Had you fallen in a trench you would never have gotten out alive. They would have devoured you. One heard them at night running about in the barbed wire." Churchill thought them immensely interesting. "Winston," Spiers remembered, "pointed out that they played a very useful role in eating human bodies." In a letter to Clementine, he described a patrol of Tommies returning from no-man's-land with a captured German: "Such men you never saw. The scene in the little dugout when the prisoner was brought in surrounded by these terrific warriors, in jerkins & steel helmets with their bloody clubs in hand — looking pictures of ruthless war — was one to stay in the memory. *C'est très bon.*"[162]

And yet . . .

The mind-set of the warrior is rigid, inflexible, fiercely intolerant. He cannot think kindly of the enemy; cannot, usually, regard him as human. And any suggestion that his own view of war may be even slightly flawed is both provocative and profoundly resented. Churchill did not fit that mold at all. He was, in fact, its obverse. In World War II he would shock Britain by praising the generalship of Erwin Rommel. In this war he became captivated by the poetry of England's most eloquent pacifist, an officer spared by a court-martial solely because of his valiant combat record. One of Winston's acquaintances wrote a friend: "By the way, *who* is Siegfried Sassoon? . . . Winston knows his last volume of poems by heart, and rolls them out on every possible occasion." A lieutenant, recalling such a recitation, wrote: "I had never heard of Sassoon or his poems and we were soon told something of his history. . . . We quickly realized that the main theme of the poems was anti-war, the futility of war and the misery war brought. We heard that the Generals were seriously worried at the damage to morale these poems might inflict on the troops." An officer said to Churchill: "I should leave that man alone if I were you. He might start writing a poem about *you.*" Churchill instantly replied: "I am not a bit afraid of Siegfried Sassoon. That man can think. I am afraid only of people who cannot think."[163]

Later in the war, when Winston was back in London, Eddie Marsh introduced the two men. Sassoon's recollection of the meeting survives. He found Winston "leisurely, informal, and friendly. Almost at once I began to feel a liking for him. . . . He broached — in a good-humoured way — the subject of my attitude to the War, about which — to my surprise — he seemed interested to hear my point of view." Churchill, Sassoon recalled, "was making me feel that I should like to have him as my company commander." There came a point, however, when the conversation developed into a monologue: "Pacing the room, with a big cigar in the corner of his mouth, he gave me an emphatic vindication of militarism as an instrument of policy and stimulator of glorious individual achievements. . . . Transfixed and submissive in my chair, I realized that what had begun as a persuasive confutation of my anti-war convictions was now addressed, in pauseful and perorating prose, to no one in particular." As the dazed poet left, Winston offered him a civilian appointment. "Had he," Sassoon wondered, "been entirely serious . . . when he said that 'war is the normal occupation of man'? He had indeed qualified the statement by adding 'war — and gardening.' But it had been unmistakable that for him war was the finest activity on earth."[164]

Certainly it stimulated *him.* On December 28, 1915, *The Times* carried an interview with a corporal, an Orangeman, who was quoted as saying of Churchill, "A cooler and braver officer never wore the King's uniform. . . . During the Ulster business before the war there was no man more detested in Belfast, but after what we have seen of him here we are willing to let bygones be bygones — and that is a big concession for Ulstermen to make. . . . His coolness is the subject of much discussion among us, and everybody admires him." Repeatedly, when he was elsewhere on the line, his frail sandbagged shelter was demolished by direct hits. Like Douglas MacArthur, who also defied enemy fire here two years later, he felt shielded by mysterious intervention, believing that "Chance, Fortune, Luck, Destiny, Fate, Providence seem to me only different ways of expressing the same thing, to wit, that a man's own contribution to his life story is continually dominated by an external superior power." One experience, as he saw it, seemed to confirm him. At the end of his first week at the front he received word that the corps commander wanted to see him in Merville; a car would meet him at the Rouge Croix crossroads. It was a muddy, three-mile hike, under German observation most of the time; he would write afterward that "the shriek of [enemy] shells" was constant, but he and his batman "toiled and sweated on," until, on arrival, they were dumbfounded to learn that the general had changed his mind. What, Churchill asked a staff officer, was the point of the rendezvous? "Oh, it was nothing in particular," the staff officer replied. "He thought as he was coming up this way he would like to have a talk with you." Winston was furious. He began "another long, sliding, slippery, splashing waddle back to the trenches. . . . The sedentary life of a Cabinet Minister, which I had quitted scarcely a month before, had not left me much opportunity to keep fit." Back with the grenadiers, someone shouted to him: "You're in luck today." Five minutes after he had left, his dugout had been blown up. The officer with whom he shared it had been annihilated. "Suddenly," Churchill wrote afterward, "I felt my irritation against General ——— pass completely from my mind. All sense of grievance departed in a flash. . . . How thoughtful it had been of him to wish to see me again, and to show courtesy to a subordinate. . . . And then upon these quaint reflections there came the strong sensation that a hand had been stretched out to move me in the nick of time from a fatal spot."[165]

His mother begged him to "be sensible" and "take the trenches in small doses" — as though he could manage that. Jennie felt close to him now; like his father at about the same age, he had quit the cabinet in disgrace. But Winston was unresponsive to her; his daily missives went to Clementine. In a typical letter from a rear area he began: "I sit in a battered wicker chair within this shell scarred dwelling by the glowing coals of a brazier in the light of an acetyline lamp." The grenadiers had been "hunted by shells during these last two days in 'rest billets.' " His bedroom had been pierced by shells three times; a nearby church steeple, which had withstood sixteen months of fighting, had been obliterated. "One lives calmly on the brink of the abyss," he wrote. He had come to understand how the unremitting strain transformed men, their first ebullience fading and leaving only "dull resentment." The infantrymen he had spoken to during his trench tours sensed the "utter inability to take a decision on the part of the Government. . . . Some urge me to return and try to break them up. I reply no — I will not go back unless I am wounded; or unless I have effective control." Clementine was the one constant, indispensable figure in his squalid trench life. He endorsed virtually all of her political judgments; she was his "vy wise & sagacious pussy cat." Once several days passed with no mail from Cromwell Road; he signed himself "your vilely neglected pig." His letters to her often read like those of a child writing home from camp, and like a camper he made many small demands: "I want 2 more pairs of thick Jaeger draws [sic] vests & socks (soft), 2 more pairs of brown leather gloves (warm) 1 more pair of field boots (like those I had from Fortnum & Mason) only from the fourth hole from the bottom instead of holes there shd be good strong tags for lacing quicker. One size larger than the last. Also one more pair of Fortnum & M's ankle boots. . . . With these continual wettings and no means of drying one must have plenty of spares. . . . Also send me a big bath towel. I now have to wipe myself all over with things that resemble pocket handkerchiefs."[166]

She eagerly complied. Her need was as great as his, her worry greater.

When he wrote her of his aborted rendezvous with the corps commander, she replied in anguish: "It is horrible to sit here in warmth & luxury while danger & suffering are so close to you. That dreadful walk across the fields there & back among falling shells was on Nov. 24th & now it is 10 days later & Heaven knows what narrow escapes you may have had since." One of Winston's cousins — his aunt Clara's daughter Clare, who, like Venetia Stanley, had been a bridesmaid at their wedding — had just learned that her husband had been killed in France. Clementine wrote: "My darling, I don't know how one bears such things. I feel I could not weather such a blow. She has a beautiful little son 8 weeks old, but now her poor 'black puss' sleeps in Flanders. You *must* come back to me my dear one." She prayed that he wore "a steel helmet always & not the Glengarry." She had "ceased to have ambitions for you. Just come back to me alive that's all." She loved him "very much more even than I thought I did — for Seven years you have filled my whole life & now I feel more than half my life has vanished across the channel." She wondered: "If I came to Dieppe could you get 2 days' leave? I'm very very lonely." Dieppe proved impossible, but later he slipped home from time to time. Like all wartime couples they desperately sought privacy during their brief hours together, once in Dover Pier's dreary Lord Walden Hotel and once in Cromwell Road, after which they had to cut it rather fine at Victoria Station. In her note to him that evening one recognizes the powerful tug between the shadow of death and the light of desire: "I could not tell you how much I wanted you at the station. I was so out of breath with running for the train."[167]

Love letters should not be taken literally. Their very language is hyperbole. Winston did not really mean that he was determined to stay at the front until either wounded or recalled to high office. Nor had Clementine forsaken her hopes for his career. Both saw future greatness for him on a far shore; the problem was to navigate the bewildering currents between here and there. Sir John French's promise of a brigade — four thousand men — might provide a way. A brilliant stroke in the field could bring acclaim, a reversal of his political fortunes, and, conceivably, a chance to change the direction of the war. "The hour of Asquith's punishment and K's exposure draws nearer," he wrote his wife. These "wretched men," he went on, "have nearly wrecked our chances. It may fall to me to strike the blow. I shall do it without compunction."[168]

"I long for you to have a Brigade," she wrote back. But she had misgivings. The leap from major to brigadier general was a mighty one. Lord Cavan counseled caution. Lead a battalion first, he advised Winston; get the feel of handling troops and then take on the greater responsibility. Clementine thought that wise: "I am absolutely certain that whoever is C. in C., you will rise to high commands. . . . But everyone who *really* loves you & has your interest at heart wants you to go step by step whereas I notice the Downing Street tone is 'of course Winston will have a brigade in a fortnight.' Thus do they hope to ease their conscience from the wrong they have done you, and then hope to hear no more of you. . . . Do get a battalion *now* & a brigade later."[169]

Upon reflection, he agreed. The field marshal, however, wouldn't hear of it. Churchill wrote: "I proposed to French that I shd take a battalion; but he rejected it, & said 'no a brigade at once' & that he wd settle it quickly in case any accident shd happen to him. I have acquiesced." One doubts he had been hard to persuade. He was dreaming of glory on the battlefield. On December 2 Edward Grigg, a grenadier officer, wrote his mother: "Winston was attached to the Company again for all the last period in the firing line. It was very cold and very wet — first a bitter frost, and then rain, sleet and thaw, which puts us up to the calf in mud and slime. That part of the line is in bad order, too, and we had nothing but a small dug-out about 2 ft 6 high with a wet mud floor to live and sleep in, and we all got kinks in our spines getting in and out of the beastly thing. But Winston accepted the situation with great cheerfulness and we had quite a good time. He has forgotten his political legacy from Lord Randolph, and thinks much more, I am sure, of the military instincts which have descended to him from the great Duke of Marlborough."[170]

Later in the month he was summoned to GHQ. French was in England, he was told, but his appointment as brigadier general was definite. He would command the Fifty-sixth Brigade in the Nineteenth Division, which, he wrote home, "is a regular Division in the second new army, & the Bde I shall command comprises 4 Lancashire Battalions. . . . Altogether it is a vy satisfactory arrangement." He anticipated some "criticism & carping" at home, but no more than if he had taken a battalion for a few weeks, in which case it would have been said that he had used it "merely as a stepping stone etc." He was "satisfied this is the right thing to do in the circumstances, & for the rest my attention will concentrate upon the Germans." Spiers would be his brigade major; Eddie Marsh, he hoped, would be brought over in one capacity or another. He asked Clementine to order a new tunic bearing a brigadier's insignia. She, for her part, forgot her qualms, and wrote back that she was "thrilled."[171]

Not everyone in London was thrilled. Over lunch, in the crowded grillroom of the Berkeley Hotel in Piccadilly, Lord Esher, just back from Saint-Omer, told her: "Of course you know Winston is taking a Brigade & as a personal friend of his I am very sorry about it; as I think he is making a great mistake. Of course it's not his fault, Sir John forced it upon him." She put all this in a letter to her husband, adding: "He then launched forth again, saying that you had been in the greatest danger, in more than was necessary etc & that French had determined to give you this Brigade as he was convinced you wd otherwise be killed. After this I crawled home quite stunned & heart-broken." Churchill himself was unsurprised; he had begun to appreciate the unpopularity of the appointment. At GHQ Sir Henry Wilson wrote in his diary: "Winston came up this morning to my room & had a long talk. I advised him *not* to take a Brigade as it would be bad for Sir John, Winston and the Brigade, but I did not convince him."[172]

Sir Henry was dissembling — a complex man, he couldn't even be candid in his diary — for by then he surely knew that Sir John was beyond help or harm. At that moment the commander in chief was facing the music in Downing Street, the victim of bad strategy, worse tactics, an impossible war, and, to some extent, the disloyal intrigues of his senior subordinate, Sir Douglas Haig. Asquith wrote that he "had for some time felt past fears and growing doubts as to Sir John French's capacity to stand the strain of his task with its ever-increasing and unforseeable responsiblities." So he dismissed him. Before they parted, French mentioned that he had given Churchill a brigade, and, according to him, "Asquith said he was delighted." But the prime minister was also a political weather vane, and he shortly learned that rumors of Churchill's promotion had already aroused hostility in Parliament. Sir Charles Hunter, a Tory MP with a military background, rose at Question Time to ask "if Major Winston Churchill has been promised the command of an Infantry brigade; if this officer has ever commanded a battalion of Infantry; and for how many weeks he has served at the front as an Infantry Officer." After an interval the under secretary of state for war deftly replied: "I have no knowledge myself, and have not been able to obtain any, of a promise of command of an Infantry brigade having been made to my right hon[orable] and gallant Friend referred to in the question." Having "consulted books of reference and other authentic sources of information," he had found that his gallant Friend had never commanded a battalion. As to the time he had been in combat, "the answer to the last part of the question would be about four weeks." The House laughed. Hunter then demanded to know if Churchill had been assured of a battalion command. Several of Winston's friends cried, "Why not?" Sir Charles Robertson, a former India army officer and an admirer of Churchill's, inquired sarcastically: "Is not the question absurd on the face of it, Major Winston Churchill being under sixty years of age?" But another Tory MP, Evelyn Cecil, ended the exchange on a venomous note, asking: "Is the right hon[orable] Gentleman aware that if this appointment were made it would be thought by very many persons both inside and outside this House a grave scandal?"[173]

Aitken had the impression that this "apparently frightened The Block." He also heard that Bonar Law had expressed "unswerving antagonism to Churchill," arguing that "to give Churchill an influence on the conduct of affairs in France would be a disaster," and that Lloyd George "would not give any countenance to projects for Churchill's preferment." If true — Aitken was a prodigious gossip — this is puzzling, for when Law and George visited Haig at GHQ a month later, they told the new commander in chief that if he saw fit to give Winston a brigade there would be "no difficulty at home." Whatever the pressures, Asquith swiftly buckled. He sent a note to French, who had not yet been formally relieved, saying that on reflection, far from being delighted, he feared that "with regard to our conversation about our friend — the appointment might cause some criticism" and was therefore inadvisable. "Perhaps," he added, "you might give him a battalion." Dismayed and embarrassed, French phoned Churchill at GHQ. "I have something extremely unpleasant to say," he began, and then he read the prime minister's veto. Winston was astonished. If he had wanted a battalion, he could have had it long ago; six months earlier, when the Dardanelles was winding down, he had been offered one in the QOOH. Churchill had just finished a letter to Clementine when the field marshal's call had been put through. He unsealed the envelope and added on a slip marked "later": "I reopen my letter to say that French has telephoned from London that the P.M. has written to him that I am not to have a Brigade but a Battalion. I hope however to secure one that is going into the line. You will cancel the order for the tunic! Do not allow the P.M. to discuss my affairs with you. Be vy cool & detached and avoid any sign of acquiescence in anything he may say." She instantly replied: "My Dear — your letter has just come telling me that your hopes of a Brigade have vanished. I do trust that Haig will give you one later. If he does it may be all for the best — but if not it is cruel that the change at G.H.Q. came before all was fixed. . . . My own Darling I feel such absolute confidence in your future — it is your present which causes me agony — I feel as if I had a tight band of pain round my heart."[174]

Winston's resentment deepened. "I am awfully bitter and so is French," he wrote F. E. Smith; "what ill-fortune." Brooding, he wrote Clementine: "To measure Asquith's performance one has to remember that on my leaving the Admiralty he offered me a Brigade: & that when I told him three months ago of the offers French had made to me if I came out to the front, he advised me to go and assured me that any advancement wh was thought fitting by the C in C would have his hearty concurrence. One has to remember all the rest too of a long story of my work & connexion with him. Altogether I am inclined to think that his conduct reaches the limit of meanness & ungenerousness. Sentiments of friendship expressed in extravagant terms; coupled with a resolve not to incur the slightest criticism or encounter the smallest opposition — even from the most unworthy quarter. Personally I feel that every link is severed: & while I do not wish to decide in a hurry — my feeling is that all relationship should cease." Clementine loved and honored her husband, but she did not always obey him. "You know I'm not good at pretending," she wrote him, "but I am going to put my pride in my pocket and reconnoitre Downing Street." Nothing came of it. Winston was unsurprised. The prime minister was a "weak and disloyal chief," he said; "Asquith will throw anyone to the wolves to keep himself in office." During a winter thaw, she accepted an invitation to join the Asquiths at Walmer Castle and wrote Winston of how they could "distinctly hear the rumble of heavy guns" across the Channel. She played golf with "the Prime who was feeling very pleasant & mellow . . . at one moment [I] thought I was going to give the boy a good beating (which I shd have relished) but Alas! I fell off towards the end & he won by a short length." Winston reproached her mildly for going and asked what Asquith had said. She replied: "You know what the P.M. is — He loathes talking about the War or work of any sort — He asked anxiously if you were happy."[175]

The Block could be left to the mercies of Lloyd George, who now began his intricate campaign to dethrone the prime minister and then replace him. Churchill, meanwhile, had to deal with a new commander in chief. His wife wrote him: "Do you know Sir Douglas Haig? Did he agree to your appointment or was it finally settled before he supervened? He looks a superior man, but his expression is cold and prejudiced, & I fear he is narrow." Actually, he and Winston had been acquainted in the early Edwardian years, when he was a major and Winston a young MP, but that had been long ago, and Haig, a dour Scot, was elusive even to those who were close to him. At Oxford he had been regarded as "headstrong, bad-tempered, and intractable." In the army he had learned to control his temper, and he brought valuable qualities to Saint-Omer: a remarkable grasp of detail, tranquillity under pressure, and absolute self-confidence. He was blindly loyal to military tradition, however. "The role of the Cavalry on the battlefield," he wrote, "will always go on increasing"; bullets, he believed, had "little stopping power against a horse." One has the distinct feeling that to him, machine guns, tanks, and aircraft were, if not contemptible, at least bad form. His greatest assets in his rise had been his powerful social connections. His wife had been a member of the royal household, and he knew the King well enough to write him that French, his immediate superior, "is quite unfit for his command at a time of crisis in our nation's history."[176]

The way to break through the German trench line, Haig thought, was to use horses in "mass tactics" — a theory which, as Leon Wolff points out, had been abandoned by even the most ardent cavalry officers. The official British history of the war would tactfully conclude that he was "not swift of thought." Bernard Shaw, who visited GHQ shortly after Haig took over, wrote: "He was, I should say, a man of chivalrous and scrupulous character. He made me feel that the war would last thirty years, and that he would carry on irreproachably until he was superannuated." Haig and Sir William ("Wully") Robertson, the new chief of the Imperial General Staff, were exponents of attrition. Churchill, attrition's heretic, could expect little from them. No compromise was possible between his concept of war and theirs. After reading a Churchill memorandum on the use of tanks and mortars, Leo Amery wrote in his diary: "Whatever his defects may be, there is all the difference in the world between the tackling of a big problem like this by a man of real brain and imagination, and its handling by good second-rate men like Robertson and Haig, who still live in the intellectual trench in which they have been fighting." On arriving in France, Winston had headed straight for the front to see for himself what it was like. In the whole course of the war, Haig never visited the trenches. Scenes of carnage, he said, might influence his judgment. Afterward Churchill etched him in acid. Haig, he wrote, reminded him of "a great surgeon before the days of anesthetic, versed in every detail of such science as was known to him: sure of himself, steady of poise, knife in hand, intent upon the operation; entirely removed in his professional capacity from the agony of the patient, the anguish of relations, or the doctrines of rival schools, the devices of quacks, or the first-fruits of new learning. He would operate without excitement, or he would depart without being affronted; and if the patient died, he would not reproach himself."[177]

This judgment lay in the future on December 18, 1915, Sir John French's last day as commander in chief, when, after picnicking in the countryside with Winston, French returned to GHQ and approached Haig on what he called "a delicate personal matter." He explained the broken promise to Churchill — broken by Asquith — and then, according to Haig's diary, said he was "anxious that Winston should have a Battalion. I replied that I had no objection because Winston had done good work in the trenches, and we were short of Battalion CO's." The new commander in chief then sent for Churchill, who wrote Clementine that evening: "He treated me with the utmost kindness & consideration, assured me that nothing wd give him greater pleasure than to give me a Brigade, that his only wish was that able men shd come to the front, & that I might count on his sympathy in every way." Beaming, Winston asked whether Haig would like to read "Variants of the Offensive," a memorandum on trench warfare he had written while the grenadiers were in the rear area. He wrote home that Haig replied that "he wd be 'honoured' — ! So I am back on my perch again with my feathers stroked down." Spiers wrote: "WC has Douglas Haig to heel. DH is ready to do anything for him."[178]

He was ready to do nothing of the sort. It is doubtful that Haig read "Variants of the Offensive." If he had, he probably wouldn't have understood it. And had he understood it, he would certainly have felt affronted. Churchill proposed flamethrowers, improvised infantry shields, wire-cutting torches fueled by gas cylinders, and massive tunneling operations. And he looked beyond the siege warfare in France and Belgium to fluid movements in other theaters of action. "He was probably the only member of Asquith's Cabinet," Clement Attlee would later write, "who had a grasp of strategy." Certainly he seemed to be the only British officer in Flanders who grasped the desperate need for innovations. Civilization was bleeding to death. "The chaos of the first explosions," he wrote, "has given place to the slow fire of trench warfare: the wild turbulence of the incalculable, the terrible sense of adventure have passed. . . . A sombre mood prevails in Britain. The faculty of wonder has been dulled; emotion and enthusiasm have been given place to endurance; excitement is bankrupt, death is familiar, and sorrow numbs. The world is in twilight; and from beyond the dim flickering horizons comes tirelessly the thudding of the guns."[179]

On New Year's Day, 1916, Haig appointed Churchill a lieutenant colonel and gave him an infantry battalion, the Sixth Royal Scots Fusiliers, consisting largely of Lowland Scots, many of them miners from the Ayrshire coalfields. Winston wrote home that he would be glad to see the last of Saint-Omer, "a desert" since French had left. He was now responsible for thirty officers and seven hundred men, and that evening he dined with the divisional commander at his headquarters in Merris. The grenadier colonel's welcome had been cold, but here, he wrote, "they evidently will like vy much to have me. The general — Furse — is extremely well thought of here and is a thoroughly frank & broadminded man. . . . Most of the staff had met me soldiering somewhere or other, & we had a pleasant evening."[180]

His assurance was premature. Cheery greetings from the general and his staff were one thing; the battalion was another. The Sixth Royal Scots had been badly mauled at Loos and were deeply attached to their commanding officer, whom Churchill was replacing. The switch was therefore unpopular with them. Hakewill Smith, the battalion's only regular officer, later recalled that he heard of it with "horror." "When the news spread," wrote Andrew Gibb, the young adjutant, "a mutinous spirit grew. . . . Why could not Churchill have gone to the Argylls if he must have a Scottish regiment! We should all have been greatly interested to see him in a kilt. . . . Indeed, any position at all in the Expeditionary Force seemed not too exalted for Winston if only he had left us our own CO and refrained from disturbing the peace of the pastures of Moolenacker." Winston arrived there mounted, at the head of a cavalcade bearing his luggage, bathtub, and a boiler for heating the bath water. Moolenacker Farm, the battalion's reserve billet, consisted, in his words, of "squalid little French farms rising from a sea of soppy field and muddy lanes." The farm wives were awed. They whispered: *"Monsieur le Ministre! Monsieur le Colonel!" "Ah, c'est lui?" "C'est votre Ministre?"* The soldiers were less impressed. His first parade, after lunch, was a farce. The men were standing at slope arms when their new CO rode up on a black charger and cried: "Royal Scots Fusiliers! Fix bayonets!" As a cavalryman he did not know that this order could not be carried out from the slope. A few men put their rifles on the ground and yanked their bayonets from their scabbards; the rest stood immobile, baffled. Gibb whispered to him that "Order arms" must intervene, and Churchill growled the command. He inspected his troops and then barked another cavalry order: "Sections right!" This meant nothing to the Jocks. They didn't budge. Gibb had to rescue him again.[181]

But he was determined to learn. He got the drill down, enrolled in nearby machine-gun and bomb-throwing schools, and patrolled the battalion area each night with Archie Sinclair. His batman found warm, dry quarters for him in one of the farmhouses, where, he wrote home, "the guns boom away in the distance, & at night the sky to the Northward blinks & flickers with the wicked lights of war." It never entered his mind that he was not entitled to every available comfort; nor, in that day, before the rise of the egalitarian passion, did it occur to his men. But he was not an insensitive officer. To boost morale, he organized a concert and games. He wrote: "Poor fellows — nothing like this has been done for them before. They do not get much to brighten their lives — short though they might be." He decided to brighten each of their days with a lecture from their CO. One day he struck a dogged pose and announced sonorously: "War is declared, gentlemen — on lice!" There followed, in Gibb's words, "such a discourse on *pulex Europaeua,* its origin, growth, and nature, its habit and its importance as a factor in wars ancient and modern, as left one agape at the force of its author." And then the Sixth Royal Scots Fusiliers were thoroughly deloused.[182]

Sometimes he was preposterous. The outline of one speech he made to his junior officers survives. He sensibly began: "Keep a special pair of boots to sleep in & only get them muddy in a real emergency. Use alcohol in moderation but don't have a great parade of bottles in yr dugouts. Live well but do not flaunt it." Then he said: "Laugh a little, & teach your men to laugh — gt good humour under fire — war is a game that is played with a smile. If you can't smile grin. If you can't grin keep out of the way till you can." In Churchill, G. A. Henty still lived. On the other hand, he was a source of invaluable advice on master masonry and the handling of sandbags, all of which would be immensely useful when they moved up on the line. He devised clever plans for shelters, scarps, counterscarps, half-moon dugouts, and ravelins. These might save their lives; they appreciated that. But when he announced that batmen must serve as bodyguards, sacrificing their lives, if necessary, for their officers, laughter drowned him out. Some of his schemes, said Gibb, were "too recherchés, too subtle to stand the practical test of everyday fighting." If a parapet was hit during the day, he ordered, it must not be repaired until nightfall; that way, the Germans would not know what damage they had done. Later, under fire, bullets passed through the gaps and men were hit. The order was quietly countermanded.[183]

On January 24 they were ready. At eight o'clock that morning, with

Churchill riding on his horse at the head of the column, they marched from Moolenacker Farm into the Belgian village of Ploegsteert, or "Plug Street," as the Tommies called it — the jump-off point for a maze of paths and shallow communications trenches which led soldiers eastward to and from the front — taking casualties from the German shellfire along the way. Churchill lodged that night in a battered convent (the "Hospice," he called it) belonging to the Sisters of Charity. It was the twenty-first anniversary of Lord Randolph's death. He wrote his mother: "I thought of my father on Jan 24 & wondered what he would think of it all. I am sure I am doing right." To his wife he wrote: "I am extremely well-lodged here — with a fine bedroom looking out across the fields to the German lines 3,000 yards away. Two nuns remain here and keep up the little chapel which is part of the building. . . . On the right & left the guns are booming; & behind us a British field piece barks like a spaniel at frequent intervals." He contrasted the view from his Admiralty office, from which he had been able to see the Horse Guards Parade and the windows of the Cabinet Room at No. 10, to the prospect here: "2 bright red pigs rooting about among the shellholes."[184]

In the darkness the battalion moved up to the front-line trenches. Churchill established his headquarters in a shattered building known as Lawrence Farm — he called it his "Conning Tower" — about five hundred yards behind no-man's-land. He was responsible for a thousand yards of trenches. Following deep, winding, sandbagged gullies, he could move up to the British wire and then check the entire position. "It takes nearly 2 hours to traverse this labyrinth of mud," he wrote. "On the average," wrote Gibb, "he went around three times a day, which was no mean task in itself, as he had plenty of other work to do. At least one of these visits was after dark, usually about 1 A.M. In wet weather he would appear in a complete outfit of waterproof stuff, including trousers and overalls, and with his French light-blue helmet he presented a remarkable and unusual figure." Lieutenant Jock McDavid saw him "stand on the fire step in broad daylight, to encourage the Jocks, and to prove . . . how little danger there was of being hit." He was undismayed when, from time to time, his experiments demonstrated that the danger was very great indeed. Once he and his adjutant were in an advance trench when Winston suggested they peer over the parapet, to get a better look at the German fortifications. They drew small-arms fire, and then shellfire. "Do you like war?" Churchill asked dreamily. "At that moment," Gibb wrote, "I profoundly hated war. But at that and every moment I believe Winston Churchill revelled in it."[185]

On February 3, he and Archie were lunching with several other officers at Lawrence Farm when, he wrote Clementine, "there was a tremendous crash, dust & splinters came flying through the room, plates were smashed, chairs broken. Everyone was covered with debris and the Adjutant (he is only 18) hit on the finger. A shell had struck the roof and burst in the next room — mine & Archie's. . . . The wonderful good luck is that the shell (a 4.2) did not — & cd not have — burst properly. Otherwise we shd have had the wall thrown in on us — & some wd surely have been hurt." Probably it disturbed her more than him. "I slept peacefully in my tiny war-scarred room last night," he added, "after a prolonged tour of the trenches." He even found time to acquire an easel and oils and paint shell holes. She wrote frantically: "*Please* leave that wretched farm and find a safer place." She wanted to join him: "It wd be so easy & I cd live with the poor French women in a ruined cottage & hoe turnips." The sensible course for him would have been to omit such alarming accounts from his letters, but Churchill was never sensible about taking risks, or thoughtful about the impact his vivid details would have on those who loved him. Since peril never upset him, it may never have occurred to him that it might distress others. "It is one long holiday for me," he wrote her, ". . . like my African journey."[186]

By now all distrust of the new CO had vanished. "I am firmly convinced," wrote Gibb, "that no more popular officer ever commanded troops. As a soldier he was hard-working, persevering and tough. . . . He lived soldiering: it lay near his heart and I think he could have been a very great soldier." Winston was touched and pleased to find that the battalion's junior officers "put up my photograph in the trenches, & I am sure they would make an effort if I asked them and some big test came upon us." He was asking a lot of them as it was. McDavid later remembered Winston's first venture into no-man's-land: "Clad in his long trench waterproof, shining knee-high trench boots and blue steel helmet, with his revolver and powerful flash-lamp attached to his web-belt, he preceded me on the journey through the wire. All went well until we were within a few yards of the first post. Then enemy machine-gun fire swept the sphere of operations." They dove into a shell crater. Abruptly a blinding ray of light appeared in the hole. Churchill roared: "Put out that bloody light!" It was his own flashlight. As he crouched he had pressed the switch. "Corrective action," McDavid recalled, "swiftly followed." Thereafter, according to Hakewill Smith, he "would often go into no-man's-land. It was a nerve-racking experience to go with him. He would call out in his loud, gruff voice — far too loud it seemed to us — 'You go that way, I will go this. . . . Come here, I have found a gap in the German wire. Come over here at once!' " By now he "never fell when a shell went off; he never ducked when a bullet went past with its loud crack." Lieutenant Francis Napier Clavering was with him when Winston decided that they should climb over the top of the parapet and walk along the entire thousand-yard length of the Royal Scots' line. "Up went a Verey [sic] light," he recalled. "Churchill was on his knees at the time, measuring the depth of the earth" with a yardstick. Under the flare they were clearly visible to the enemy. "The Hun machine guns opened up, belly high. Why the hell we weren't killed I just don't understand. I didn't want to die. . . . 'For God's sake keep still, Sir,' I hissed. But he didn't take the slightest notice. He was a man who had no physical fear of dying."[187]

He abandoned Lawrence Farm, as Clementine had asked, only to establish himself in what he called his "Advance Headquarters," a hundred yards closer to the wire. Here, as in India nearly twenty years earlier, he hoped to win recognition, mention in dispatches, possibly a medal or two — some distinction which would attract attention in London. Back in reserve at the convent for two days he wrote Clementine: "If I come through all right my strength will be greater than it ever was. I wd much rather go back to the trenches tonight, than go home in any position of mediocre authority. But I *shd* like to see my beloved pussy cat." Actually, the time was approaching when he would prefer even mediocre authority to Flanders, not because of the discomfort and jeopardy at the front, but because in Parliament he could at least hope to exert greater influence on the conduct of the war. His disclaimer to his mother — "All I hear confirms me in my satisfaction to be freed from my share in the present [parliamentary] proceedings" — cannot be taken seriously. In the same letter he urged her to "keep in good touch with all my friends." But here again, it was his wife who was his real eyes and ears — and tongue. There was talk of creating a minister for air. She invited Curzon to lunch and suggested that Winston would be ideal for the job. "Oh my darling I long so for it to happen, & feel that it would except for the competition for the post inside the Cabinet," she wrote. Nothing came of it. In early February she and Goonie lunched with Curzon at his mansion, and he raised the possibility that Churchill would "be made a Brigadier almost at once" — he even gave Clementine three bottles of brandy as a token of congratulation — yet this, too, was vain.[188]

Lloyd George lunched in Cromwell Road, but this was a great strain on his hostess. He said all the right things, expressing "great distress at you not being in the Government," she wrote, and saying repeatedly, "We must get Winston back." She didn't believe him. In her view he, not Asquith, was her husband's nemesis. "I don't trust him one bit," she wrote, characterizing him as "fair of speech, shifty of eye, treacherous of heart." Again: "I get on so well with him & I know he likes me, but he is a sneak. . . . He is a barometer, but not a really useful one as he is always measuring his own temperature [sic] not yours!" And again: "Before taking LlG's [hand] I would have to safeguard myself with charms, touch-woods, exorcisms & by crossing myself. I can always get along with him & yesterday I had a good talk, but you can't hold his eyes, they shift away." She thought her husband had been too hard on the prime minister: "I think my Darling you will have to be very patient — Do not burn any boats — The P.M. has not treated you worse than Ll. G has done. . . . I feel sure that if the choice were equal you would prefer to work with the P.M. than with Ll. G." She lunched with Asquith in Downing Street. "He talked a great deal about you and asked a great many questions. I was perfectly natural (except perhaps that I was a little too buoyant) & he tried to be natural too, but it was an effort." She said she would take *his* hand, "tho' I would give it a nasty twist." Winston replied that while Lloyd George was "no doubt all you say," he had been opposed to the Dardanelles and not, like the prime minister, a "co-adventurer" who had destroyed the plan by his own incompetence. Still, Churchill wanted to know more about her hour with Asquith: "I shd like a *verbatim* report of the Kat's conversation with the old ruffian." Unfortunately, there was little to tell. Most of the talk at No. 10 had been trivial. "The chief topic of social gossip," she told him, "is who is going to India as Viceroy. . . . It seems incredible."[189]

All this was very hard on her. Clementine did not carry her husband's weight. She was admired and respected, but there could be no substitute for Churchill's presence. And she found it disagreeable to pass along his messages to political allies and confidants, particularly those she distrusted. She wrote: "Oh Winston I do not like all these letters I have to forward — I prefer Charlotte Corday — Shall I do it for you?" The unavoidable fact was that he could not be an effective parliamentary force while prowling near the enemy wire in Flanders. Nor was the army always considerate toward officers who were also MPs, particularly when they lacked political muscle. Learning of a secret session of the House of Commons, Churchill applied for leave to attend it. Permission was granted with the understanding that he would return the moment debate ended. When an open session followed, and he asked for an extension of his leave, the appeal was denied in a War Office telegram informing him that no exception could be made "while you are commanding R Scots Fus and your battalion is in trenches." Clementine was furious. He could have altered policy during the session, she wrote him afterward when he was back on the front, "if only you had been here and spoken." She could not blame this on Lloyd George. Asquith was responsible, and she acknowledged it. "The Government," she wrote, "are in a shameful position."[190]

Actually, he would have been wise to have stayed in Flanders that spring. It was while in Parliament on another leave that he delivered one of the most unfortunate speeches of his life. Late in the afternoon on Tuesday, March 7, 1916, he rose from the front Opposition bench to offer a closely reasoned critique of governmental blunders in the prosecution of the war. "I shall have to strike a jarring note," he began. He indicted Balfour's tenure at the Admiralty in the strongest language the House had heard since the outbreak of the war, charging "slackness, indifference, want of push and drive." The U-boat challenge was not being met, he said; there was strong evidence that German shipyards were outbuilding Britain's. The zeppelins were getting through; mismanagement of the navy could lead to defeat. It was an exceptionally impressive speech. He had the complete attention of every man there. And then, at the very end, he destroyed his message, and dealt a savage blow to his credibility, in a single sentence: "I urge the First Lord of the Admiralty without delay to fortify himself, to vitalise and animate his Board of Admiralty by recalling Lord Fisher to his post as First Sea Lord."[191]

It was unbelievable. He was actually advocating a return to power of the old man who had ruined his Dardanelles strategy and evicted him from the Admiralty. The House sat stunned. Asquith confessed that he was "speechless at the time"; afterward, he called Winston's bombshell "suicidal" and "a piece of the grossest effrontery." In the Strangers' Gallery, Eddie Marsh wept. Clementine, aghast, concluded that her husband had demolished his last parliamentary support. Lloyd George simply gasped: "A great error!" The only congratulatory note came from a predictable source, the last man with any right to expect praise from Churchill. Fisher wrote him: "SPLENDID!!! You'll have your Reward! All I entreat you now is to entrench yourself as Leader of the Opposition! and wait for the Big thing to come to you! . . . Your attitude so excellent — a helpful (*not a hostile*) critic. *Anyhow my heart is very full!* I feel the good old times are back!"[192]

Churchill left Parliament unaware of the ridicule about to envelop him. Violet Asquith, finding him in his mother's house, asked: "What possessed you? *Why* did you do it?" All London was asking the same question, but she was the first to be answered. He said he had conceived his proposal, she wrote, "as a great gesture of magnanimity — the forgiveness of the wrongs Fisher had done to him, for the sake of a greater aim, our naval supremacy." Gently she dissolved his illusion. It would not be so interpreted, she said; rather, others would see it "as a clumsy gambler's throw for his own ends." By noon Wednesday he, too, saw this. The question now was whether to stay in London and carry on the debate, or take the next boat back to Flanders. Wednesday morning Fisher appeared gaily in Cromwell Road, insisting that Churchill speak again, pressing on; other MPs, the old admiral was confident, would rally around him. Clementine vehemently disagreed. After some hesitation Winston went to the House that afternoon, thereby exposing himself to the full force of Balfour's withering reply.[193]

Balfour ignored Churchill's closely reasoned arguments, even though he knew them to be unimpeachable — knew, for example, that the German submarine campaign would soon threaten England with starvation. Instead, he humiliated him. He did not imagine "that there was a single person who heard my right hon[orable] Friend's speech who did not listen to the latter part of it with profound stupefaction." Churchill had "never made the smallest concealment, either in public or in private, of what he thought of Lord Fisher." What, AJB asked, had Winston said in delivering his "farewell speech" the previous autumn, "when he exchanged a political for a military career? He told us that the First Sea Lord, Lord Fisher, did not give him, when he was serving in the same Admiralty with him, either the clear guidance before the event or the firm support after it which he was entitled to expect." The essence of the matter was "that the right hon[orable] Gentleman, who could not get along with Lord Fisher — I will not say that, but with whom Lord Fisher could not get on — says that Lord Fisher, who according to my right hon[orable] Friend neither supported him nor guided him, is nevertheless the man who ought to be given as a supporter and a guide to anybody who happens to hold at this moment the responsible position of First Lord of the Admiralty. It is a paradox of the wildest and most extravagant kind." It was more — "the most amazing proposition that has ever been laid before the House of Commons." In a final turn of the knife, Balfour said slowly: "I should regard myself as contemptible beyond the power of expression if I were to yield an inch to a demand of such a kind, made in such a way."[194]

Stung, Churchill replied that Balfour, "a master of parliamentary sword play and every dialectical art," had mocked a member "who is so much younger than himself" — this was absurd, and unworthy of Winston — to evade "a note of warning" which "should be sounded, and sounded in time." As to Fisher: "The real fact is that if we could associate in some way or another the driving power and energy of Lord Fisher, with the carrying out of Lord Fisher's programme at the highest possible speed, there is no reason to believe that great public advantage would not result from that." It was a weak defense of what would have been a strong case, had he left the old admiral out of it the day before. No one's mind was changed. All those who had been bruised by his invective in the past, who had distrusted his interlocking brilliance and instability, the inevitable handmaidens of genius, were now after him in full cry. Once more the growing frustration over the insatiable war left a residue of bitterness. Considering who they were, their breeding and their gentility, the backlashes of some were startling. Margot Asquith wrote Balfour: "I hope & believe that Winston will never be forgiven for his yesterday's speech. Henry & I were thunderstruck at the *meanness* & the gigantic folly of it. I've never varied in my opinion of Winston I am glad to say." (This was flagrantly untrue.) "He is a hound of the lowest sense of political honour, a fool of the lowest judgement & contemptible. . . . Henry & I thought you admirable and if H had not had a deputation he said he wd have given Winston 10 of the nastiest minutes of his life he was so *disgusted.*"[195]

Violet Asquith, who took the other side, nevertheless wrote that "whatever his motive, he realized that he had hopelessly failed to accomplish what he had set out to do." Back in Cromwell Road he pondered his next move. Fisher wanted him to quit the army and lead a full-fledged attack on the government: "Write at once and resign! *I beg you to do this!* . . . I assure you that I am not so much thinking of your personal interests (*immense as they are! because you have the Prime Ministership in your grasp!*) but of saving the country! *Now now now* is the time to save the country NOT 3 months ahead!" Had Winston's stock stood at its prewar level, this might have been sensible. With each passing day it became clearer that Asquith's war policy was a failure. He could not remain at No. 10 much longer. Tempted, Churchill secured a written promise from Asquith on Saturday that "if hereafter you should find your sense of public duty called upon you to return to political life here, no obstacle will be put in your way, and your relief will be arranged for, as soon as it can be effected without detriment to the Service." Monday, on the train to Dover, Winston argued the point with his wife. At the port he wrote Asquith holding him to his word, scribbled a press release announcing his return to civilian life, and left it in Clementine's hands.[196]

Late that afternoon, back in Belgium, he changed his mind and dispatched telegrams from Ploegsteert withdrawing the letter and the release. But then he switched back, and for good. He was preoccupied now, not with the Germans on the other side of no-man's-land, but with his former colleagues who had taunted him from the Treasury Bench. Ten days after his return to his battalion he wrote Clementine that he had resolved to leave the army at the first opportunity. He had served in the trenches since November, "almost always in the front line, certainly without discredit." Over the past fifteen years he had built a strong political reputation, "enabling me to command the attention . . . of my fellow countrymen in a manner not exceeded by 3 or 4 living men." England's fate was at stake, "and almost every question both affecting war & peace conditions, with wh I have always been formostly [sic] connected, is now raised." To remain in Flanders would be irresponsible. "Surely," he wrote, "these facts may stand by themselves in answer to sneers & cavillings. At any rate I feel I can rest upon them with a sure & easy conscience. Do not my darling one underrate the contribution I have made to the public cause, or the solidarity of a political position acquired by so many years of work & power."[197]

Clementine was unconvinced. The misjudgment, she knew, was his; he simply did not understand the transformation of his reputation wrought by the Dardanelles, or the depth of his self-inflicted wound in the exchange with Balfour. His reasons were "weighty & well expressed," she tactfully replied, "but it would be better if they were stated by others than yourself." Actually, he had put her in a ghastly position. In Flanders he risked death. In London he would risk political ruin. She wrote him: "My Darling own Dear Winston I am so torn and lacerated over you. If I say 'stay where you are' a wicked bullet may find you which you might but for me escape," but if he left his troops the consequences might be "a lifelong rankling regret which you might never admit even to yourself & on which you would brood & spend much time in arguing to yourself that it *was* the right thing to do — And you would rehearse all the past events over & over again & gradually live in the past instead of in the present and in the great future." Six days later she wrote: "The present Government may not be strong enough to beat the Germans, but I think they are powerful enough to do you in & I pray to God you do not give the heartless brutes the chance —."[198]

Nevertheless, the yeast of revolt continued to work in him. He knew he was not needed here, nor even particularly wanted. Haig had summoned him to Saint-Omer. Back at Lawrence Farm, Winston told Hakewill Smith that the BEF commander in chief had offered him a brigade but suggested that he could be more useful by returning to London and guiding a conscription bill through the House. At the same time, GHQ informed him that his battalion would be merged with another, the Seventh Royal Scots Fusiliers, and the CO of the Seventh, being senior to Churchill, would assume command of the hybrid. Thus, as he happily put it, "I am not leaving my battalion; my battalion is leaving me." Ignoring Asquith this time, he sent his resignation to Kitchener, who accepted it with the proviso that he not reapply for active service for the duration of the war. The *London Gazette* reported that he was relinquishing his lieutenant colonelcy. On April 28 he led his troops into the front line for the last time. Clementine, reconciled, wrote him from Blenheim: "Let me hear that you are coming home for *good* to take up your *real* work." He sent her his last letter from Lawrence Farm on May 2. He intended to relax before plunging into politics again: "Wd it not be vy nice to go to Blenheim for the Sunday. If you arrange this, please get me 3 large tubes of *thin* White (not stiff) from Robersons: also 3 more canvasses: and a bottle of that poisonous solution wh cleans the paint off old canvasses. . . . The Germans have just fired 30 shells at our farm hitting it 4 times: but no one has been hurt. This is I trust a parting salute."[199]

The next morning he and his troops left Ploegsteert for reassignment, and three days later, in Armentières, he entertained his officers at a farewell luncheon. In toasting them he said he had learned that the young Scot "is a formidable fighting animal." Gibb remembered afterward: "I believe every man in the room felt Winston Churchill's leaving us a real personal loss." The following day Winston received a highly political note from General W. T. Furse: "It seems to me peculiarly up to you and to Lloyd George to concentrate all your efforts on breaking such a futile Govt — and that, immediately. How can anyone suppose that the same men in the same flat bottomed tub can do any better in the future than they have done in the past?" Churchill optimistically wrote his wife: "The Government is moribund. I only trust they will not die too soon." It was characteristic of him that he regarded himself as the obvious alternative to Asquith. Clementine had warned him that such optimism was unrealistic, but he had not believed her. Now he would learn the lesson from other, harsher critics.[200]

Churchill was never a complete outcast. During each of the several political exiles in his life his solitude was tempered by friends willing to compromise their own futures for his sake, or allies who found common cause with him. Three MPs now invited him to join them in a patriotic Opposition: Arthur Markham, George Lambert, and — Ireland forgotten — Sir Edward Carson. The *Manchester Guardian* rejoiced that

Winston was back; the *Observer* wanted to see him in a ministry. F. E. Smith was a source (though his only source) of goings-on in the cabinet. Lloyd George, though bland, was at least willing to be seen with him. The unfilial Violet reported events in the Asquith household. And although Winston's popularity with the people was greatly diminished, he retained a national constituency. Max Aitken later recalled accompanying him into a railway station and passing a train crowded with British tars returning from leave. As Winston "walked up the platform," Aitken wrote, "the bluejackets gave him an immense reception, cheering him with enthusiasm. Churchill was deeply moved and declared that he was encouraged to believe that he was not after all the Forgotten Man."[201]

He would never be forgotten; he was unforgettable. But he could be ignored, mortified, and taunted, and all these would be his miserable lot throughout the year ahead. In Parliament, Bonar Law, now colonial secretary, baited him mercilessly. He was told that resignation of his command proved that he was a cheap opportunist. He learned that the Conservative Lord Derby, writing to Lloyd George, had vowed that, whatever the truce between the parties, "Winston could not possibly be in it. Our party will not work with him and as far as I am concerned personally nothing would induce me to support any Government of which he is a member. . . . He is absolutely untrustworthy as was his father before him, and he has got to learn that just as his father had to disappear from politics so must he, or at all events from official life."[202] The patriotic Opposition grew shaky when Lord Milner, a prospective member of it, refused to be reconciled with Churchill. It then collapsed after Asquith deprived it of its chief issue, conscription, by accepting compulsory military service. Inductions began on May 25, 1916. During the previous twenty-two months two and one-half million Britons had voluntarily joined the colors — a testament to the extraordinary patriotism of their generation.

Winston tried to reopen parliamentary discussion of diversionary attacks in the Baltic and the Middle East. His speeches were followed by studied silence. The U-boat threat, he said, could be met by convoys. The Admiralty said, and did, nothing. (When at his insistence convoys were introduced the following year, the monthly loss of merchant ship tonnage dropped from 874,576 to 351,105.) Kitchener's appeal for men, he pointed out, had attracted volunteers from key jobs in shipyards, mines, and munitions factories. They should be discharged from the army and put back to work: "We hear a great deal . . . about 'comb this industry,' or 'comb that,' but I say to the War Office, 'Physician, comb thyself.' " Nothing was done. His experience in the trenches led him to make practical suggestions about the front. A network of light railways behind the lines would improve logistics. British trench lights, inferior to the enemy's, should be improved immediately. The supply of steel helmets was inadequate. Staff officers safely beyond the range of the German artillery were pinning medals on one another, and that was outrageous: "It is the privates, the non-commissioned officers, and the regimental officers whose case requires the sympathetic attention of the House and of the Secretary of State. Honour should go where death and danger go." Logistics, trench lights, the helmet shortage, and the pernicious decorations policy went unchanged.[203]

He felt that the troops comfortably stationed in England and the safe ports of the Empire should be rotated in combat. At the front, he told inattentive MPs, he had witnessed "one of the clearest and grimmest class distinctions in the world — the distinction between the trench and the non-trench population." Under the present system, "the trench population lives almost continuously under the fire of the enemy. It returns again and again, after being wounded twice and sometimes three times, and it is continually subject, without respite, to the hardest tests that men have ever been called upon to bear, while all the time the non-trench population scarcely suffers at all. . . . I wish to point out to the House this afternoon that the part of the army that really counts for ending the war is this killing, fighting, suffering part." He described red-tabbed officers in warm, safe châteaux confidently moving pins on maps, forgetting that each pin represented a multitude of human beings whose outlook was very different from their own. "The hopes of decisive victory" grew "with every step away from the front line," reaching "absolute conviction in the Intelligence Department." The result — doomed offensives — troubled him more than any other aspect of the government's war policy. Victory would not be gained, he wrote in the *Sunday Pictorial*, "simply by throwing in masses of men on the western front." In the days after his return from Flanders he was particularly worried about Haig's attack, now imminent, north of the Somme River. He begged for restraint. But the cabinet agreed that as an "amateur" he could hardly match the army's expertise. Indeed, no minister deigned to reply to him. Instead, Harold Tennant, an under secretary at the War Office, rose and followed Balfour's example by saying contemptuously: "There is one thing which I envy my right hon[orable] and gallant Friend, and that is the time he had in order to prepare his carefully thought-out speeches. I wish I had the same opportunity."[204]

On July 1, 1916, after a prolonged bombardment, the British infantry went over the top, and by nightfall eighty thousand Englishmen had

fallen, twenty thousand of them dead. The Ulster Volunteer Force, brave beyond belief, had been cut to pieces in the swampy valley of the Ancre. It was the bloodiest day in the history of combat. Yet Haig refused to break off the Somme action. Churchill prepared a memorandum marshaling the arguments for disengagement. "So long as an army possesses a strong offensive power," he wrote, "it rivets its adversary's attention. But when the kick is out of it, when the long-saved-up effort has been expended, the enemy's anxiety is relieved, and he recovers his freedom of movement. This is the danger into which we are now drifting. We are using up division after division — not only those originally concentrated for the attack, but many taken from all parts of the line." It would take months, he pointed out, for "these shattered divisions" to recover. In the interval the Germans could withdraw troops from this front and send them against Russia.[205]

F. E. Smith wrote an introduction to this analysis and had it printed for the cabinet. Everyone else discounted it. Even before it had gone to press Hankey wrote in his diary that Sir William Robertson had "told me that F. E. Smith was writing a paper to show that the big offensive in France had failed. I suspect that Ll George & Winston Churchill are at the back of it. Personally I think it is true but it is a mistake to admit it yet." A copy of the memo reached Saint-Omer. To Lord Northcliffe, who was visiting him there, Haig insisted that the drive must continue, and Northcliffe, convinced, wrote the editor of *The Times:* "Let me once more say and urge that what is taking place on the Somme must not be measured in metres. It is the first time we have had a proper scientific attack. There are no complaints of bad Staff work. . . . If we wrote communiqués as well as the Germans, we would lay much more stress on the German losses, which are *known* to be immense." In fact, the campaign, when it finally petered out, had cost the British 481,842 men to the enemy's 236,194 — and the only gain was a few square miles of worthless mud. *The Times,* however, never mentioned Churchill's warning.[206]

The *Daily Mail* accused him of conspiring against Haig and Robertson, and therefore against England. "The country," it reported when the Somme bloodletting was at its height, had "seen a Cabinet minister who had just enough intelligence to know that Antwerp and Constantinople were places of importance and yet was mad enough to embark on adventures in both places. . . . In the Dardanelles affair in particular a megalomaniac politician risked the fate of our Army in France and sacrificed thousands of lives to no purpose." He had dragged "too pliant officers" with him "into these reckless and hopeless 'gambles' " at a time when his sole duty "was simply to supply the Navy with men and material." Tragedy would have been averted if the admirals had been "men of the stamp of Sir Douglas Haig and Sir William Robertson." The lesson was: *"Ministerial meddling means military muddling."* Churchill was put on notice: "No politician who remembers the contemptible fiasco of Antwerp and the ghastly blunder of Gallipoli need expect either patience or forgiveness from the British public if he interferes with the soldiers in charge of our operations." H. A. Gwynne of the *Morning Post* wrote Asquith of "a sort of plot whose ramifications I am not altogether able to trace"; its purpose was "to get rid of DH," and its ringleader, he believed, was the former first lord. The *Spectator* accused Churchill of playing "the part of a political adventurer . . . with a want of scruple and want of consideration for public interests, and with a reckless selfishness, to which our political history affords no parallel."[207]

After reading this Lloyd George told Sir George Riddell that it was "on the whole part true." He and Asquith had become convinced, in the words of Martin Gilbert, that "the imaginative, constructive, hard-working colleague of prewar years was being eaten up by personal ambition, and that his judgment had been impaired." Winston learned of this and thought it incomprehensible. It was one thing to be slandered by Balfour, Bonar Law, and Lord Derby. That was politics. The Tories were only giving as good as they had got from him. But to be distrusted, suspected, and even condemned by men who had long been friends as well as colleagues was beyond his understanding. It was not, however, beyond Clementine's. Others fawned on him and then cut him behind his back. She told him, and wrote him, that he was sometimes curt, insensitive, and inconsiderate; that he was too given to extravagant overstatement; that his manner was dictatorial and often insulting. It was not enough to be right. His assumption that he alone should stand at the center of events, she said, offended men whose own achievements entitled them to share the stage and disagree. He lacked patience and tolerance. He was often strident and scornful, and because this had alienated first-rate men, he was driven to seek the company of others, who, as she saw it, could do him no good and might bring harm. When they had left Admiralty House, Clementine thought she had seen the last of Lord Fisher. To her horror, Winston continued to correspond with him, sent him birthday greetings, and even invited him to Cromwell Road as an honored guest. There she could not contain herself. F. E. Smith heard her tell the old admiral: "Keep your hands off my husband. You have all but ruined him once. Leave him alone now." Sometimes Churchill himself realized that he had fallen among companions who were, if not evil, at least unworthy. At one function he approached a fellow guest and said shakily: "Get me a stiff whisky and soda, and get it quick. I have just done something I hoped I would never have to do. I have shaken hands with de Robeck."[208]

Max Aitken, who remained constant, later wrote of Churchill in this dark time: "He cared for the Empire profoundly, and he was honestly convinced that only by his advice and methods could it be saved. His ambition was in essence disinterested. He suffered tortures when he thought that lesser men were mismanaging the business." Another friend described him as "a character depressed beyond the limits of description. . . . When the Government was deprived of his guidance he could see no hope anywhere." He told Riddell: "I am finished. I am banished from the scene of action." On July 5 he wrote Archie Sinclair: "I do not want office, but only war direction. . . . I am profoundly unsettled: & cannot use my gift. Of that last I have no doubts. I do not feel that my judgments have been falsified, or that the determined pursuance of my policy through all the necessary risks was wrong. I wd do it all again if the circumstances were repeated. But I am faced with the problem of living through days of 24 hours each: & averting my mind from the intricate business I had in hand — wh was my life." In his anguish he sent his brother a long, tormented letter on July 15. "Is it not damnable," he asked, "that I should be denied all real scope to serve this country, in this tremendous hour?" Asquith, he wrote, "reigns supine, sodden and supreme." Then: "Tho' my life is full of comfort, pleasure and prosperity I writhe hourly not to be able to get my teeth effectively into the Boche. But to plunge as a battalion commander unless ordered — into this mistaken welter — when a turn of the wheel may enable me to do 10,000 times as much would not be the path of patriotism or of sense. . . . Jack my dear I am learning to hate."[209]

The western front haunted him — both its futility and the thought that there, at least, he might be contributing something, if only a mite, to the war effort. "I look back a gt deal to our Plugstreet days," he wrote Sinclair later in the year, "& wish I cd have cut myself more adrift from London & its whirlpools and been more content with the simple animal life (& death) wh the trenches offered." Forgetting his pledge to Kitchener, he declared: "When I am *absolutely* sure there is no prospect of regaining control or part of it here, I shall return again to that resort & refuge." He was struck by a bitter irony. Volunteering to fight had been "a costly excursion" for him; in doing so he had sacrificed the power he now craved. "If I had stayed Chancellor of the Duchy and shut my mouth & drawn my salary, I shd today be one of the principal personages in direction of affairs. . . . Under a fair pretence of fine words, there is a gt *déconsideration* of all who wear uniform. Not one of these gallant MPs who has fought through the Somme at the head of their battalions, stands a chance agst less clever men who have stopped & chattered at home. This to me is the most curious phenomenon of all. It is quite inexplicable to me."[210]

He seldom addressed the House now. C. P. Scott of the *Guardian,* calling on him in South Kensington, urged him to keep his flag flying in Parliament. Eventually, he predicted, recruits would rally to him. Winston shook his head. Except in Scott's paper, his remarks were unreported. Indeed, they were largely unheard; few members came in to hear him — "what a contrast with the old days, when my rising was the signal for the House to fill!"[211] He preferred to reach his public through the *Sunday Pictorial.* Writing an article took no longer than preparing a speech; every word was printed, and he was paid £250, about five shillings a word, for each piece. That was important. He needed every penny he could make. His brother, now fighting under Haig, had only his officer's salary. Jennie, who had let her own house and moved into 41 Cromwell Road while Winston was in the trenches, contributed £40 a month, but with three adults, and five children in the nursery under a nanny, they had to run a tight ship. The Christmas holidays were another matter. Sunny invited them all to Blenheim — his political quarrels with Winston and Clementine had been long forgotten — and they welcomed the new year with an enormous bonfire. Winston tossed an effigy of the kaiser on the flames. Across the Channel, at the stroke of midnight, the Germans filled the sky with brilliant green flares. A British battery fired ten shells, paused, and fired seven more. It was 1917.

Clementine had seen the way to sever his knot of agony nearly a year earlier, while he was still in Flanders. Once the facts about the Dardanelles were made public, she believed, her husband would be absolved of all blame, for both the failure to force the strait and the subsequent tragedy on the peninsula. On January 11 she had written Winston: "If you ask the P.M. to publish the Dardanelles papers let me know what happens. If he refuses or delays I beg you not to do anything without telling me first & giving me time to give you my valuable (!) opinion on it. . . . If he dissents I fear you will have to wait. If you insisted on publication against his wish you would have against you all the forces of cohesion & stability including every member of the Cabinet. On the other hand when the papers are eventually published his refusal to do so earlier will have a very bad effect for him. . . . I am very anxious that you should not blunt this precious weapon prematurely."[212]

That same day, Churchill had read in *The Times,* Carson had said in the House that the expedition against Turkey had been "admirably conceived." From Lawrence Farm, Winston had written his wife: "Gradually people will see what I saw so vividly this time last year, but alas too late forever." It was never too late to correct the record, she replied, and when he returned to Parliament as a civilian he found that in this case it was imperative. During a debate over conscription Asquith had proposed that Ireland be exempt. The Easter rebellion in Dublin the previous

April had been followed by executions; feeling ran high there. Winston, disagreeing with the exclusion, said: "This is a time for trying to overcome difficulties and not for being discouraged or too readily deterred by them." An Irish Nationalist shouted: "What about the Dardanelles?" It was a cry he was to hear again and again, in the House, in meeting halls, and on the streets. Clementine had been right. He had to clear his name. And only the truth — in the documents — would do it.[213]

On June 1, 1916, in what was surely one of the most ill-advised political decisions of his life, the prime minister agreed. The decision was reported in the next day's *Times.* Bonar Law, speaking for Asquith, told the House that all papers relevant to the campaign would be assembled and laid before the country. Churchill wrote the prime minister the next morning, offering to help sort them out. Ian Hamilton's reputation was also at stake, and although his hopes for exoneration were less realistic than Winston's, he nonetheless cherished them. Three days later he and Churchill dined at the general's home in Hyde Park Gardens. Afterward they reviewed Hamilton's copies of twenty telegrams he had sent to the War Office from Gallipoli. Not one of them, Churchill realized, had been laid before the cabinet. This was powerful evidence of negligence on Kitchener's part. There seemed to be no way he could explain it away. While they talked, a voice became audible on the street outside. Someone was shouting K of K's name. As Hamilton told it in his memoirs: "We jumped up and Winston threw the window open. As he did so an apparition passed beneath us. I can use no other word to describe the strange looks of this newsvendor of wild and uncouth aspect. He had his bundle of newspaper under his arm and as we opened the window was crying out 'Kitchener drowned! No survivors!' " The war minister, on a mission to Saint Petersburg, had been aboard H.M.S. *Hampshire* when she hit a mine. Hamilton wrote: "The fact that he should have vanished at the very moment Winston and I were making out an unanswerable case against him was one of those *coups* with which his career was crowded — he was not going to answer!"[214]

Kitchener having joined the Glorious Dead, the K of K myth was strengthened tenfold. Blaming him was impolitic now; the number of those who shared the Dardanelles guilt had been diminished by one. Asquith then had second thoughts about a full disclosure of the documents. Two weeks later Hankey wrote Churchill that the prime minister had resolved not to open the minutes of the War Council on the ground that ministers, fearing that their remarks might be "liable to publication," would be hesitant to speak out in future meetings, and that "it would be very difficult to resist a pressure to publish proceedings in regard to other aspects of the war which might not be in the public interest." Winston protested to Asquith that only the council's archive could show, among other things, "the strong support of the naval project given by you, Grey, Kitchener & A. Balfour" and his own "disclaimer of responsibility if a military disaster occurred through inadequate troops not being sent in time," which "was not an ordinary incident of discussion, but that I asked formally & at that time that my dissent shd be placed on record." It was inconceivable to him that the prime minister could not appreciate "that this fact is vy important for a true judgement on the event." Asquith, replying, repeated the argument that "the public interest" might suffer. To Lloyd George, who had succeeded Kitchener at the War Office, Winston bitterly remonstrated that the promise to release the minutes had been given to the House "after prolonged consideration & with full knowledge both of the facts and of the suitability of the documents for publication at this juncture." Surely the country had a right to know the role played by the prime minister, "who alone cd have co-ordinated the naval and military action & given to the war-policy of the country the necessary guidance & leadership." That, of course, was precisely what the prime minister did not want the country to know. His ruling stood. Winston wrote his brother: "The Govt have decided to repudiate their pledge to publish the D'lles papers. My dossier was more than they could face. There will be a row, but there are many good arguments in the public interest against publishing: and many more good arguments in the Government interest!"[215]

But Parliament was not so easily gulled. There was a tremendous row in the middle of July, when Asquith informed the House that "the presentation of these papers must be postponed," that his commitment to release them "cannot for the moment . . . be fulfilled" because it would entail "omissions so numerous and so important that the papers actually presented would be incomplete and misleading." Carson led the attack on this position, and he had great support; Bonar Law's assurance had been given, not to Churchill, but to the entire House, and the MPs' curiosity was immense. Lloyd George proposed that a secret committee of MPs investigate the Turkish campaign. Asquith accepted the compromise. He announced the appointment of a select commission, comprising eight distinguished Englishmen headed by Lord Cromer, "to inquire into the conduct of the Dardanelles operations." This Royal Commission of Inquiry into the Dardanelles did not satisfy Churchill. He told the House that it was a poor substitute for opening the books, "as was originally intended and promised by the Prime Minister, in the name of the Government." But at least it would not be a whitewash. Cromer couldn't be

Churchill in the summer of 1916

bought. And Winston would be allowed to testify and submit evidence.[216]

The commission's hearings opened on August 17. Winston devoted five months to his defense. "I am hopeful that the truth may be published," he wrote Seely. "But failure & tragedy are all that are left to divide." It was hard to reconstruct the past, key evidence was unavailable to him, he had to skirt the issue of Kitchener's incompetence, and since the commissioners included a field marshal, an admiral, and a captain, it was difficult to criticize the conduct of officers in the strait and on Gallipoli. In one of his appearances, on September 28, he declared that the facts proved five points: there had been full authority for the assault, a reasonable chance of success, "all possible care and forethought exercised" in preparing for the attacks, "vigour and determination" in the execution, and no compromise of military interests elsewhere. "Everything I hear about the D'lles Commission encourages me," he wrote Sinclair at the end of November. "The interim report cannot now be long delayed and I have good hopes that there will be a fair judgement. I sh'd like to have it out as soon as possible. But the days slip away."[217]

They were slipping away from Asquith, too. Less than a week later he was maneuvered into resigning, undone by Lloyd George and widespread Tory dissatisfaction with his conduct of affairs. George had finally made it. On December 7, 1916, he "set out," in Winston's words, "upon his march as High Constable of the British Empire," with Balfour moving from the Admiralty to the Foreign Office and Bonar Law becoming chancellor of the Exchequer, leader of the House, and the government's second in command. Since most of the Liberal ministers, offended by George's coup, had resigned with Asquith, the old Welsh radical's government was dominated by Conservatives. There was no place in it for Churchill. He had assumed there would be. But he was still widely regarded as a discredited adventurer. The *World,* a weekly journal which carried a popular column on politics, had commented on November 14: "Mr Churchill, in his frantic effort to reinstate himself in public esteem, is enlisting the support of some powerful newspaper interest. . . . But if a serious attempt is being made to foist Winston once more on the British public the matter would assume a different aspect. . . . Winston Churchill is responsible for the *opéra bouffe* Antwerp expedition which made the British nation ridiculous in the eyes of the world. . . . He was responsible for the disastrous Dardanelles expedition which ranks with Walcheren as one of the greatest military disasters of our time."* There was still a spark of defiance in Lloyd George. He toyed with the idea of appointing Churchill and then bent to the storm. In his memoirs he recalled asking Bonar Law, "Is he more dangerous *for* you than when he is *against* you?" Law answered: "I would rather have him against us every time." A colleague had drawn up a list of possible ministers. Churchill was not on it. George wrote in the margin: "? Air Winston." But there was still no air ministry and he did not create one. The last blow to Churchill's chances of office came on December 7, when four members of the new cabinet — Lord Curzon, Lord Robert Cecil, Austen Chamberlain, and Walter Long — told Lloyd George that they would serve only on the condition that Churchill be excluded.[218]

The Lloyd George Winston had once known would have bridled at a Tory veto. He didn't now, but at the time Churchill knew of neither the challenge nor the submission to it. Discussing the political future with Scott of the *Guardian*, he had said, according to Scott's account, that "Lloyd George, 'with all his faults,' was the only possible alternative Prime Minister. I asked if in case George formed a ministry he could count on being included. He said he thought so — that George would desire it and that it would be in his interest." In fact, he believed he would be offered a choice of posts. All things considered, he rather pre-

* Walcheren was the scene of an attempt, conceived by the second Earl of Chatham in 1809 during the Napoleonic Wars, to capture Antwerp. It was a catastrophe.

ferred a return to the Admiralty. The brutal fact that he would have nothing was revealed to him after a dinner in F. E. Smith's Belgravia house. The new prime minister was there; the purpose of the meeting was to discuss the makeup of the new government. Incredibly, Lloyd George had suggested that Churchill be invited. Winston naturally took this to mean that he would be offered a seat on the Treasury Bench. Early in the conversation the guest of honor was summoned to Buckingham Palace. He asked Max Aitken to join him for the taxi ride. In the cab, George said that there would be no office for Winston and, Aitken later wrote, "asked me to convey a hint of this on my return to the party. . . . He thought Churchill too confident of high office in the new regime. It would be better if Churchill were dashed a bit at first." Back at the table Aitken found the unsuspecting Winston in a jovial mood. Choosing his words carefully, Aitken said: "The new Government will be very well disposed towards you. All your friends will be there. You will have a great field of common action with them." Aitken's account continues: "Something in the very restraint of my language carried conviction to Churchill's mind. He suddenly felt he had been duped by his invitation to the dinner, and he blazed: 'Smith, this man knows that I am not to be included in the new Government.' " According to Aitken, an "almost ludicrous" scene followed: "Churchill changed from complete optimism to violent anger and depression. He abused me most violently, and when I got tired of it and replied in kind he picked up his hat and coat and, without even putting them on, dashed into the street. Smith ran out after him and tried to calm him, but in vain." In the morning Winston telephoned to apologize. "It was really quite unnecessary on his part," Aitken wrote. "It is impossible to feel hurt at anything Churchill says in this vein, for he is always so willing to take as good as he gives, and makes no complaint about the counter-blow." Aitken himself was feeling resentful, but for another reason. He, too, had hoped for office. Instead, the new prime minister offered him a peerage. He reluctantly agreed. Thus he became — and spent the rest of his life regretting it — Lord Beaverbrook.[219]

Reconciled, Churchill wrote Sinclair: "It will be odd now on the direct opposition Bench with all the furious ex Ministers arriving. I expect they will be vy anxious to be civil to me. But I intend to sit in the corner seat in a kind of isolation." He seemed puzzled at being passed over. Clementine's shrewd eye saw the transformation in Lloyd George, however. "At one time he abused the Dukes to please the working-men," she wrote. "Now he has abused the working-men to please the soldiers." He had deposed Asquith by insisting that he would prosecute the war more vigorously, providing the generals with everything they needed. This tactic had been effective because the politicians and the press, to keep civilian morale at fever pitch, had glorified the military hierarchy, endowing it with an almost ecclesiastical aura. After the appalling Somme and Verdun casualty lists, the sensible move for the Allies would have been the pursuit of a negotiated peace. Lord Lansdowne recommended just that. A meaningful victory, he suggested in a cabinet memorandum, was clearly impossible. He asked: "Can we afford to go on paying the same sort of price for the same sort of gains?" Haig, responding, assessed the outlook for 1917 as "excellent." Robertson wrote: "Quite frankly, and at the same time respectfully, I can only say that I am surprised that the question should be asked. The idea had not before entered my head that any member of His Majesty's Government has a doubt on the matter." Lloyd George called Lansdowne's letter "a terrible paper."*[220]

What made this gifted statesman climb into bed with Douglas Haig and Wully Robertson? There is only one possible explanation. He had been twisted by his yearning for power. He profoundly disagreed with Robertson's western strategy, but he had been unable to change it because of the ennoblement of the general staff by an adoring country. Privately he said that the War Office kept "three sets of figures, one to mislead the public, another to mislead the Cabinet, and the third to mislead itself." He also said: "If people really knew, the war would be stopped tomorrow, but of course they don't — and can't know. The correspondents don't write and the censorship wouldn't pass the truth. The thing is horrible, and beyond human nature to bear, and I feel I can't go on any longer with the bloody business." But of course he did go on, as men in high office always have, justifying themselves to themselves, by making little adjustments in their reasoning. Haig held him in contempt. When he heard that Lloyd George had asked Foch's opinion of British strategy, he said tightly: "I could not have believed that a British minister could have been so ungentlemanly." Later, when 1917 had become even madder than 1916, he wrote in his diary: "L.G. is feeling that his position as P.M. is shaky and means to try and vindicate his conduct of the war" — as though it had been Lloyd George's, not Haig's and Robertson's — "in the eyes of the public and try to put the people against the soldiers." He added a patronizing note: "Quite a nice little man when one had him

* Churchill also disapproved of it. He did not believe that the main effort should be made on the western front, but the only solution acceptable to him was a German surrender. Commenting on Lansdowne's proposal, he asked: "What is the contrary view? It is in a sentence that *this war has got to be won & that it is not won yet.*" He added, in a phrase which would become familiar to Americans when President Truman dismissed General MacArthur in 1951: "Let us not delude ourselves by thinking that there is any substitute for victory."

alone, but I should think most unreliable." Robertson agreed. He wrote of George: "I can't believe that a man such as he is can remain for long head of any government. Surely *some* honesty and truth are required."[221]

Churchill, who could have been invaluable to his old colleague when the 1917 campaign was being planned, remained in purgatory. But the end of his personal martyrdom was in sight. In January the Royal Commission of Inquiry issued an interim report. Its only criticism of Churchill was that he had been "carried away by his sanguine temperament and his firm belief in the success of the operation which he had advocated." The heavy losers were Asquith and Kitchener. Asquith was faulted for failing to keep his colleagues informed and for "the atmosphere of vagueness and want of precision which seem to have characterized the proceedings of the War Council." Kitchener's failure to consult his general staff, the commissioners concluded, had created "confusion and want of efficiency," and his delays in sending troops — delays Winston had protested at the time — had been ruinous. Three months later the commission's final report disposed of all accusations against Churchill. He had always acted with the full support of his naval advisers, it found, and had been blameless of any "incorrect" behavior. In the commissioners' view his plans had been right; others had been responsible for the flaws of execution. Asquith was again condemned, even more severely. Winston was not completely satisfied — the findings, he said, omitted "proof that when we stopped the naval operations the Turks had only three rounds of ammunition" — but he thought they were "at any rate an instalment of fair play" and he told the House that the commissioners had "swept away directly, or by implication, many serious and reckless charges which have passed . . . throughout the land during the long months of the last two years." By telling their "long, tangled, complicated story," they had relieved him of the burdens "which have been thrown on me and under which I have greatly suffered." Now "the current of public opinion and the weight of popular displeasure" which had been "directed upon me" could recede.[222]

They didn't; not yet. He had been cleared in the House, but acquittal in the public's view was another matter. Hatred of Churchill, like the later hatred of Franklin Roosevelt, satisfied the emotional needs of too many people. As a politician Lloyd George had to reckon with their feelings. He thought he understood one reason for their distrust of Winston. "Here is the explanation," he later wrote. Churchill's "mind was a powerful machine, but there lay hidden in its material or make-up some obscure defect which prevented it from always running true. They could not tell what it was. When the mechanism went wrong, its very power made the action disastrous, not only to himself but to the causes in which he was engaged and the men with whom he was co-operating. . . . He had in their opinion revealed some tragic flaw in the metal." Such people ignored the commission's report, or discounted it, or found him objectionable for other reasons. No. 10 extended no invitation to him through the remainder of April and May. It was June 18 before Lloyd George summoned him, and then it was to say that he would "try" to get him back the duchy of Lancaster. Winston felt insulted. He declined it on the spot. Frances Stevenson, a reliable guide to George's moods, described Winston as "very sulky" when the two men met at a Guildhall function, and noted in her diary that everyone "remarked how surly he was looking."[223]

But the prime minister could no longer dismiss him from his thoughts. Churchill cut a different figure in the House now. Vindicated in the eyes of Parliament, he was once again heard with respect, and, Bonar Law's views to the contrary, Churchill against you was formidable. The *Nation,* which refused to join in the press choir deifying the military hierarchy, had prepared a series of articles demonstrating how the British had been outmaneuvered by an enemy tactical withdrawal. The first piece had already appeared in London and was being widely reprinted in Germany. The general staff demanded that the rest of the series be suppressed. Lloyd George did it, defended the action in a highly emotional speech, and then left the floor as Winston rose to reply — an exit Winston noted with biting wit. The *Nation*'s disclosures were "absolutely immaterial and innocent," Churchill said; they made "mild reading compared with the Dardanelles Report from the point of view of public confidence." Gagging editors would only bring "a universal harmonious chorus of adulation from morning to night about whatever was done, until some frightful disaster took place." The prime minister's move demonstrated "an undue love of the assertion of arbitrary power." In George's absence, Winston asked Bonar Law to consider the uneasiness of the House. Law interrupted to say that that would be reflected in parliamentary votes — the weakest of replies. Churchill sprang: "Do not look for quarrels, do not make them; make it easy for every party, every force in this country, to give you its aid and support, and remove barriers and obstructions and misunderstandings that tend to be superficial and apparent divergence among men whose aim is all directed to our common object of victory, on which all our futures depend." It was the government's duty to treat Opposition concern "fairly and justly" — not to answer with "the kind of rhetoric or argument which might do very well on public platforms but is entirely unsuitable to the cool discussion in the House of Commons."[224]

This was the kind of appeal which could rally Liberal, Labour, and Irish Nationalist MPs behind him, and if they united, Lloyd George could be unseated. But Churchill saw a looming issue far greater than the silencing of the press. The United States had just declared war on Germany. Churchill suspected that Haig wanted to win the war before U.S. soldiers could reach France in strength. (He was right; on June 10 Haig wrote in his diary: "There must be no thought of staying our hand until America puts an Army in the field next year.") Winston asked his cousin Freddie, the government's chief whip, to propose a secret session of the House. Lloyd George scheduled it for May 10. Asquith's seniority permitted him to speak first, but he was unprepared; so was everyone else in the Opposition except Churchill, who began by asking: "Is it not obvious that we ought not to squander the remaining armies of France and Britain in precipitate offensives before the American power begins to be felt on the battlefields?" The logic, to him, was inescapable: "We have not got the numerical superiority necessary for a successful offensive. We have no marked artillery preponderance over the enemy. We have not got the numbers of tanks which we need. We have not established superiority in the air. We have discovered neither the mechanical nor the tactical methods of piercing an indefinite succession of fortified lines defended by German troops." The exigent question, therefore, was: "Shall we then in such circumstances cast away our remaining manpower in desperate efforts on the Western Front before large American forces are marshalled in France? Let the House implore the Prime Minister to use the authority which he wields, and all his personal weight, to prevent the French and British High Commands from dragging each other into fresh bloody and disastrous adventures. Master the U-boat attack. Bring over the American millions, so as to economize French and British lives, and so as to train, increase and perfect our armies and our methods for a decisive effort in a later year." George's reply, when he appeared, was evasive — he was already committed to a new attack in Flanders — but Churchill had preyed on doubts already in the prime minister's mind. As the session ended, the two met fortuitously behind the Speaker's chair. Churchill later recalled: "In his satisfaction at the course the Debate had taken, he assured me of his determination to have me at his side. From that day, although holding no office, I became to a large extent his colleague. He repeatedly discussed with me every aspect of the war and many of his secret hopes and fears."[225]

How deep, Lloyd George asked Beaverbrook in June, did the Tory animosity toward Winston really go? It was still there, Beaverbrook replied, but he thought it could be defied. Office therefore came to Churchill once more on July 17, 1917, when the prime minister appointed him minister of munitions. "Not allowed to make the plans," he later wrote wryly, "I was set to make the weapons." The prime minister had confided in no one; everyone, including his closest colleagues, learned of his decision from the newspapers. The reaction was sharp. The secretary for war threatened to resign. The colonial secretary wrote No. 10 that the prospect of facing Winston across the cabinet table made it "extremely difficult for many of my friends to continue their support." Leo Amery wrote in his diary that bringing Churchill "into the Government has shaken its prestige and reputation seriously," and Lloyd George agreed; the antagonism, he said in his memoirs, "swelled to the dimensions of a grave ministerial crisis which threatened the life of the Government." It peaked when forty Tory MPs sailed into Bonar Law's office to protest. Law, though angry himself, told them that the issue was not strong enough to topple the coalition. Thereafter the danger receded, though resentment remained. Nothing in recent memory had created "such widespread bitterness," said the *Morning Post,* which, as usual, led the Fleet Street pack, commenting that the appointment "proves that although we have not yet invented the unsinkable ship, we have discovered the unsinkable politician." The Dardanelles was exhumed, as though the commission had never existed. That debacle, said the *Post,* was "managed more or less personally by Mr Churchill, whose overwhelming conceit led him to imagine he was a Nelson at sea and a Napoleon on land." More calamities would ensue, the paper predicted: "We confidently anticipate that he will continue to make colossal blunders at the cost of the nation." The Tory minister Walter Long wrote on July 29, 1917: "The real effect has been to destroy all confidence in Ll. G. It is widely held that for purposes of his own quite apart from the war he has deceived and jockeyed us. The complaints come from our very best supporters, quiet, steady staunch men, and W. C. has made matters worse by stating at Dundee that the opposition comes from his political opponents."[226]

It is hard to conceive of where else it could have come from; Churchill, as a new minister, was fighting a by-election in Dundee. But if the uproar in London startled him, as it must have, he showed no scars. C. à C. Repington, the military writer, described him as "looking a different man . . . I never saw anyone so changed, and to such an advantage, in so short a time." The return to office was largely responsible for this, but since the spring he had also presided over a happier family. The lease on 33

Eccleston Square having expired, they moved back there. They had also acquired a second home. Clementine had always dreamed of living in "a little country basket," and Winston had bought a gray-stone cottage in Lullenden, near East Grinstead in Kent, for £6,000, cashing in £5,000 of Pennsylvania Railroad stock and a £1,000 Exchequer war bond. The property had many attractions: a large barn nearby where the children could play, a pony and light carriage for transportation when Churchill had the car in London, landscapes he could paint, and a large high room downstairs where Clementine, pregnant for the fourth time, could nap on lazy summer afternoons and still be within earshot of the nanny. At first they only went down for weekends, but after German air raids on the capital increased, they were there all the time. Winston loved Kent — the coastal country from which the sea retreats in southeastern England — and during his first summer as proprietor he was often in Lullenden, leaving it to campaign fitfully in Dundee. On July 29 he was reelected with a majority 5,266 votes. Two days later he took his seat on the front bench and was greeted, according to *The Times*, "with some cheers." It was twenty months since he had held office. During the interval 340,973 British soldiers had been killed in action and 804,457 wounded. The missing, mutilated beyond recognition, would be remembered in annual memorial ceremonies as the "unknown."[227]

The Ministry of Munitions, a small empire employing over twelve thousand civil servants divided into fifty departments, was directed from the fashionable Hotel Metropole in Northumberland Avenue, abutting on Trafalgar Square. Churchill had convened its staff before the votes had been counted in Dundee, and one member, Harold Bellman, later described the meeting in his memoirs. Like everyone else in England, Bellman's colleagues had decided views about Churchill. They were nervous, they were worried, and many were hostile. "Those who attended from the secretariat," Bellman wrote, "fully expected a stormy scene." Winston, he said, "was received rather coldly, and opened by saying that he had perceived that 'he started at scratch in the popularity stakes.' He went on boldly to indicate his policy and to outline his proposals for an even swifter production of munitions. As he elaborated his plans the atmosphere changed perceptibly. This was not an apology. It was a challenge. Those who came to curse remained to cheer. The courage and eloquence of the new minister dispelled disaffection and the minister took up his task with a willing staff. It was a personal triumph at a critical juncture."[228]

His responsibilities were not limited to guns and ammunition. They included the railroads, airplanes, and tanks. Nor was the mandate confined to British needs. The Americans were building a "bridge of ships" across the Atlantic to transport six U.S. armies — forty-eight divisions — to France. They would need, among other weapons, 12,000 artillery pieces. Churchill quickly established contact with his American counterpart, Bernard Baruch, the chairman of the U.S. War Industries Board, who, when they met later at the peace conference, would become his lifelong friend. Winston signed a £100,000,000 contract and entered into a gentleman's agreement with Baruch under which Britain agreed to make no profit and the United States promised to make good any loss. In the ministry itself, Winston undertook a massive reorganization. The fifty departments were reduced to twelve, and in conversation and correspondence he referred to each by a letter: finance became "F," design "D," projectiles "P," explosives "X," and so on. British businessmen were recruited and then governed by what he called a " 'Clamping' committee." He surveyed his new realm with pride. "Instead of struggling through the jungle on foot," he later wrote, "I rode comfortably on an elephant, whose trunk could pick up a pin or uproot a tree with equal ease, and from whose back a wide scene lay open."[229]

In a speech at Bedford he identified his primary objective: the production of "masses of guns, mountains of shells, clouds of airplanes." Always the total warrior, he was indignant when told that the International Red Cross had proposed outlawing poison gas and that the French were sympathetic. He sharply pointed out that it was after all the Germans who had introduced gas to the battlefield, at Ypres in April 1915. To Louis Loucheur, France's under secretary of state for munitions, he wrote: "Apparently France is strongly in favour of our offering to give up this form of warfare, or at any rate of accepting a German offer. I do not believe this is to our advantage. . . . Anyhow I would not trust the German word." He predicted that the enemy would let the Allies "fall into desuetude" and then break the agreement. Far from banning it, he favored "the greatest possible development of gas-warfare, and of the fullest utilisation of the winds, which favour us so much more than the enemy." His view prevailed, and he doubled the British output of gas shells; by 1918 one out of every three shells fired by Haig's artillerymen contained gas. The Red Cross protested that it was inhumane. So, Winston replied, was the rest of the war. No principle was exempt from sacrifice. The Allied Aeroplane Works was strikebound. Churchill simply took over its factories in the name of the government and ignored *The Times*'s comment that there was "no precedent for such a measure." Munitions workers walked out in Coventry, Manchester, and Birmingham. Lloyd George temporized. Christopher Addison, the previous munitions minister, was among those who breakfasted with Winston to discuss the crisis, and he noted in his diary that Churchill came "out hotfoot against the strikers, his prescription being a simple one, viz., that their exemptions should be withdrawn and that they should be called up for military service. There was considerable demur, with which I agreed, to using the Military Service Act as an agent in an industrial dispute." But when 300,000 munitions workers threatened to strike in Leeds, Winston persuaded the prime minister to threaten them with conscription. The warning worked, though British labor, which has a long memory and had not forgotten Tonypandy, put another black mark against his name.[230]

It was Churchill's energy, efficiency, and imagination which had brought him back to office, and with Eddie Marsh at his elbow, he invigorated a ministry which until now had been grim and dull. Presently countless new projects were flourishing under his direction, and he kept himself informed about all of them by ordering that all reports submitted to him must be "on a single sheet of paper." During his first eight months in the Metropole he visited France four times, questioning generals on their munitions needs. Often he slept in his office. This, he wrote a friend, "has many conveniences from the point of view of getting work done. It enables me to work up to dinner, and to begin with shorthand assistance as early as I choose in the morning." He invested his tasks with drama and color. He was, he boasted, "the Nitrate King." Writing in the *Sunday Pictorial* while still a back-bencher, he had argued that technological innovations could be used as "a substitute for men." Now he ordered a thousand warplanes, assigned a task force of engineers to improve trench mortars, and, in his spare time, sketched extraordinary Leonardesque machines of war. Most were absurd. Two weren't: prototypes of the amphibious landing craft and man-made "Mulberry" moorings of World War II. As the father of the tank he gave it priority.* This, he said, was the surest way to "beat the trench," to "augment the power of the human hand and shield the sacred chalice of human life." Its present

* After the war a royal commission investigating the claims of inventors reported that it was "due to the receptivity, courage, and driving force of the Rt. Hon. Winston Spencer-Churchill that the general idea of the use of such an instrument of war as the tank was converted into practical shape, but Mr Churchill has very properly taken the view that all his thought and time belonged to the State and that he was not entitled to make any claim for an award, even if he had liked to do so. But it seems proper that the above view should be recorded by way of tribute to Mr Winston Churchill."

role was "miniature and experimental," he wrote, but "the resources are available, the knowledge is available, the result is certain: nothing is lacking except the will." On the afternoon of January 3, 1916, one of his darker days at Ploegsteert, he had been summoned to Haig's GHQ, told that the Operations Division of the War Office wanted to explore his concept of a "caterpillar," and asked "who to apply to in England about them." Churchill, furious, had written Clementine that evening: "This after 9 months of actual manufacture and committees unending. God, for a month of power & a good shorthand writer." He had the authority and the staff now, and he set two goals: 4,459 tanks by the spring of 1919 and twice that by the following September. Not everyone approved. The military hierarchy was skeptical. Haig in particular took a jaundiced view of Churchill's emphasis on armor. "This is done," he complained in his diary, "without any consideration of the manpower situation and the crews likely to be available to put into them." But the grumbling in GHQ was predictable. The relationship between the commander in chief and the munitions minister had become dissonant even before Churchill took office, borne only because neither could survive without the other. Even Haig could not ignore Winston's accomplishments. In another diary entry he wrote warily: "For the time being he is most friendly and is doing all he can to help the Army. He has certainly improved the output of the munitions factories very greatly, and is full of energy in trying to release men for the Army, and replace them by substitutes." The key phrase, however, is "for the time being." In the long run, Haig knew, he could expect nothing but trouble from Winston. The new minister had, in fact, become his savage critic.[231]

Churchill had joined the cabinet too late, and with too small a power base, to influence Haig's Flanders offensive of 1917. He had known it was coming. On May 10, still a political outcast, he had begged the House, in secret session, not to permit "fresh, bloody and disastrous adventures" on the western front. Parliament was unresponsive. Thus the stage was set for the terrible, heartbreaking struggle known to historians as the third battle of Ypres and to the men who fought there as the battle of Passchendaele, Passchendaele being the Belgian crossroads village which the BEF hoped to reach in its first lunge. By any name it was Haig's masterpiece and should never be forgotten. He was convinced that he could break through the German wire, take the ridges overlooking the British position, and then recapture the vital Channel ports of Ostend, Zeebrugge, and Antwerp. On May 1 he wrote in his diary: "Success seems reasonably possible. It will give valuable results on land and sea. If full measure of success is not gained, we shall be attacking the

Sir Douglas Haig

enemy on a front where he cannot refuse to fight, and our purpose of wearing him down will be given effect to."[232]

"Our purpose of wearing him down will be given effect to." That syntactical atrocity sums up the scripture of attrition. Its high priest was Haig's chief of staff, Lieutenant General Launcelot Kiggell, a tall, morose professional soldier who had been commandant of the Staff College in 1914. J. F. C. Fuller, who later became a tank commander, was one of his students there. Fuller recalled afterward that "the only thing I distinctly remember his saying was, 'In the next war we must be prepared for very heavy casualties.' His theory of war was to mass every available man, horse, and gun on a single battlefield, and . . . wear down the enemy until his last reserves were exhausted, and then annihilate him." In one of those small collapses of prewar integrity which increased as the desperate war wore on, Jellicoe was persuaded to lie to Lloyd George, solemnly predicting: "If the Army cannot get the Belgian ports, the Navy cannot hold the channel and the war is as good as lost." Brigadier General John Charteris, Haig's chief of intelligence and a co-conspirator, later wrote: "No one really believed this amazing view, but it had sufficient weight to make the Cabinet agree to our attack."[233]

The balloon went up, as they said then, on July 31. Nine days earlier

Churchill, newly appointed and still facing his by-election in Dundee, had written the prime minister of his apprehensions over any "renewed offensive in the west" and begged him to "limit the consequences" of any drive which had already been approved. This merely justified the Tories' fears. They saw it as proof that he had no intention of confining himself to his ministry. Hankey, who came to tea at Lullenden, noted in his diary: "Lloyd George had given him [Churchill] my War Policy report & he was already well up in the whole situation and knew exactly what our military plans were, which I thought quite wrong." Soon Winston was taking an active interest in the Admiralty and the War Office, transferring some of Haig's howitzers to the Russian front, advocating antisubmarine techniques, and urging that heavy battleship guns be moved ashore. The secretary for war protested and the first lord threatened to resign. Lloyd George soothed their ruffled feelings and reminded Winston that he was not a member of the War Cabinet. Churchill, unchastened, crossed to Flanders for a firsthand look at such tiny villages as Bullecourt and Messines, where so much British blood had been spilled. One of Haig's generals barred him from the trenches. Haig himself was more cordial — "quite genial and cracked several jokes," Marsh wrote — but inflexible about his objectives. That evening the commander in chief observed in his diary that Churchill "means to do his utmost to provide the army with all it requires, but at the same time he can hardly stop meddling in the larger questions of strategy and tactics; for the solution of the latter he has no real training, and his agile mind only makes him a danger because he can persuade Lloyd George to adopt and carry out the most idiotic policy."[234]

George later wished that had been true. Actually, the prime minister had been among those gulled by the high command. Marsh had noted that "the tone of GHQ is tremendously optimistic." The servile press served as GHQ's megaphone. *Punch* was running cartoons of cringing Germans whimpering "*Kamerad!*" to insouciant Tommies. The *Spectator* reported: "Our Staff work in the field seems to be irreproachable. . . . The infantry, whose losses are said to be comparatively light, march behind the moving curtain of shells and bless the gunners as they go." German newspapers were carrying accurate accounts of the fighting, but *The Times* headlined a summary of them ENEMY LIES EXPOSED: *What the Germans Are Told — Falsification of Battle News — The Lie as a Buttress of Morale.* Communiqués from across the Channel reported that the enemy was "visibly cracking," that patrols found enemy troops "preparing for emergencies," and that there were signs which could be interpreted as being "preliminary to withdrawal." The War Cabinet questioned none of this. "It naturally pleased Haig," Lloyd George would bitterly recall, "to have carefully chosen and nicely cooked little tidbits of 'intelligence' about broken German divisions, heavy German casualties, and diminishing German morale served up to him. . . . He beamed satisfaction and confidence. His great plan was prospering. The whole atmosphere of this secluded little community reeked of that sycophantic optimism which is the curse of autocratic power. . . . As for General Kiggell, the Chief of Staff, he had the air of a silent craftsman, whose plans, worked out by his art in the seclusion of his workshop, were turning out well and proceeding inexorably without a hitch to the destined end."[235]

The reality was horrible beyond imagining. Here, as on every front in the war, including Gallipoli, defensive strengths had spiked the attackers' guns, sheathed their bayonets, broken their swords, and left the once proud war-horse to forage behind the lines, entangling communications. The British infantry never had a chance. Haig's long preliminary bombardment had deprived them of surprise and, at the same time, destroyed the Flemish drainage system. The water, having nowhere else to go, flooded the trenches, and to make the field soggier, the rains were among the worst in thirty years. After three and a half months in this dismal sinkhole, the British army had barely taken Passchendaele village. The filthy, bleeding, battered men were exhausted. Many, burdened by their heavy packs, fell into brimming shell holes and drowned. In London the ambulance trains unloaded at night, smuggling casualties home out of consideration for civilian morale. Siegfried Sassoon wrote of those who fought on: "Shoulder by aching shoulder, side by side / They trudged away from life's broad wealds of light."

British casualties were 448,614. In Flanders fields the poppies grew between the crosses, row on uncompromising row, that marked more than 150,000 fresh British graves. The offensive had gained less than six miles of wasteland. Yet the red-tabbed generals of the high command were exultant. Against all evidence, Charteris reported that the German losses had been enormous. They congratulated one another, pinned new decorations on one another's tunics, and agreed that it would all have been over long ago if only the politicians had left the fighting to the professionals. Robertson, whose job it was to deal with the government, actually held it in contempt. He wrote Haig that Lloyd George "is a real bad 'un. The other members of the War Cabinet seem afraid of him. Milner is a tired, dyspeptic old man. Curzon is a gas-bag. Bonar Law equals Bonar Law." Churchill, not being a member of the War Cabinet, wasn't even mentioned. Yet he was the one public figure who saw precisely what was happening. Gaining access to the casualty lists, he asked:

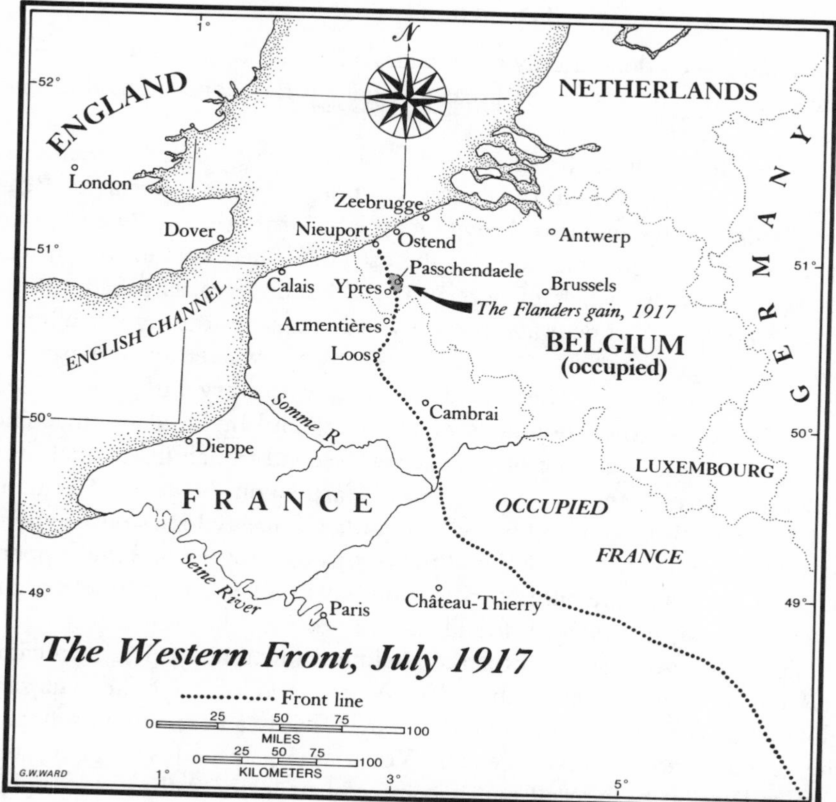

The Western Front, July 1917

"If we lose three or four times as many officers and nearly twice as many men in our attack as the enemy in his defense, how are we wearing him down?" Haig insisted that, whatever the result, he had saved the French army by distracting the enemy. This, as Churchill later pointed out, was mythical: "The French Army was no doubt saving its strength as much as possible, but the casualty tables show that during 1917 they inflicted nearly as many losses on the Germans as did our own troops." He continued: "Accusing as I do without exception all the great ally offensives of 1915, 1916, and 1917, as needless and wrongly conceived operations of infinite cost, I am bound to reply to the question, What else could be done? And I answer it, pointing to the Battle of Cambrai, '*This* could have been done.' " At Cambrai, launched as the Passchendaele drive petered out, 381 of Churchill's tanks, lurching forward without an artillery bombardment, broke through the enemy defenses on a six-mile front, gained over forty-two square miles, and captured ten thousand Germans at a cost of fifteen hundred British soldiers. "This in many variants, this in larger and better forms," he wrote, "ought to have been done, and would have been done if only the Generals had not been content to fight machine-gun bullets with the breasts of gallant men, and think that that was waging war."[236]

To see for himself, he crossed the Channel and visited a sector in which, after a tank thrust, the enemy position had been overrun by British infantry. In his report to Lloyd George he wrote that he "went on up to the extreme high watermark of the attack." The German trench was deep, defended by a belt of wire nearly a hundred yards broad. "This wire was practically uncut and had only little passages through it, all presumably swept by machine guns. Yet the troops walked over these terrific obstacles, without the wire being cut, with very little loss, killed many Germans, took thousands of prisoners and hundreds of machine guns." The same was true of the enemy's second trench line, which was "almost as strong and more deceptive." Farther on, however, Germans in "just a few little pits and holes" had inflicted heavy losses on the British infantry. Here, he concluded, "the troops had got beyond the support of the Tanks, and the bare open ground gave no shelter." He felt vindicated. He had, he believed, found the way to beat the trench.[237]

Lloyd George was uncomforted. He knew now that the Flanders campaign had been a criminal blunder. At the end of 1916 he had said gloomily: "We are going to lose this war." Nearly a year had passed, and the prospect now was far bleaker. Yet it was part of his tragedy, and England's, that he himself had become a strut in the web of deceit. He wrote: "The people are not ready to pay any heed to good counsel. They still cherish illusions of a complete victory." And he encouraged them. He felt that the mood of the country left him no alternative. Here, again, British journalists bore much of the blame. In October, when Haig lost nearly twenty-six thousand men in taking an insignificant ridge, Lloyd George had bitterly called it "still another smashing triumph a few hundred yards ahead." But the *Times* correspondent had described it as "the most important British victory of the war" and applauded the commander in chief's "calm, unhurried persistence" which compelled "the admiration of the world" because "with each successive stride the arrangements grow more exact, the results more certain, the losses lighter." Philip Gibbs of the *Daily Chronicle* interviewed a German prisoner, "a professor," who told him: "It will not be long before Germany makes a great bid for peace by offering to give up Belgium. By mid-winter she will yield Alsace-Lorraine; Russia will remain as before the war, except for an autonomous Poland; Italy will have what she has captured; and Germany will get back some of her colonies." In the climate of public opinion created by such dispatches, Lloyd George did not dare break openly with his high command. Instead, he promoted Haig to field marshal and doggedly said, in an impromptu speech at Birkenhead: "We shall just win." The irrepressible *Nation* inquired: "Win What?"[238]

After the Germans' titanic attempt to take Verdun in 1916, this had become a quiet theater for the kaiser's assault troops. Their communiqués routinely reported *"Im Westen nichts Neues"* — "All quiet on the western front." Elsewhere their fighting men had provided plenty of news, however, nearly all of it good for them. Blessed with interior lines, they could strike anywhere by rescheduling trains, and as the deadlock continued in the west they crushed a weak eastern ally each autumn, thus releasing more troops for Belgium and France. In 1914 they mauled the Russians in East Prussia at Tannenberg and the Masurian Lakes, where Paul von Hindenburg and Erich Ludendorff made their reputations. In 1915, after de Robeck's failure to force the Dardanelles, Bulgaria joined them to knock Serbia out of the war. In 1916 Rumania, encouraged by temporary Russian gains and hungry for land, threw in its lot with the Allies. The result was a fiasco. Rumania had doubled its army over the preceding two years, but was strategically isolated, and its officer corps danced in Bucharest while spies blew up a dump of nine million shells outside the city and a dozen enemy divisions, drawn from the western front, swarmed up the Carpathians. Just before winter snows sealed the passes the Germans broke through and Rumania quit. In 1917, with a succession of revolutionary governments sidestepping to the left in Russia, it was Italy's turn. Germany sent a phalanx of picked divisions, with young Lieutenant Erwin Rommel among them, to reinforce Austria's Caporetto sector in Italy. On October 24, two weeks before Passchendaele fell, they attacked out of the Julian Alps in a thick fog. In twelve hours General Luigi Cardona's defenders were on the run. By November terrified Venetians were hiding the bronze horses of Saint Mark's and preparing to flee.

Churchill was at Lullenden, playing with his children, when Lloyd George telephoned from Riddell's country home at Walden Heath, where he was staying, and asked him to drive there at once. Arriving, Winston was shown the shocking telegrams from Rome. The prime minister was badly shaken. An attack on Caporetto had been expected, but Haig had assured them only a few days earlier that Italy would "be able to hold her ground unaided." Asked on October 27 if he could send two British divisions there, the field marshal now replied that the best way to help England's embattled ally was to keep "Ludendorff busy" in Flanders. That evening Haig meticulously wrote in his diary: "If the Italian Army is demoralized we cannot spare enough troops to fight their battles for them." But this time he stood alone. Even Robertson understood the need to reinforce Italy. Sir Henry Wilson, after a talk with Churchill, also began to see the light. "We may lose this war yet if we try," his diary entry began that evening. He compared "the different strategies — ours and the Boches': 1, We take Bullecourt, they take Rumania; 2, we take Messines, they take Russia; 3, we don't take Passchendaele, they take Italy." To Haig's indignation, the War Cabinet ordered five BEF divisions out of the trenches and through the tunnels under the Alps to rally the Italians on the Piave. Cardona was fired. He had lost 800,000 men. Italy, unmanned, was unable to mount a counterattack.[239]

Nor was that the worst. Russia, cut off from its allies since the sealing of the Dardanelles, was collapsing within. On November 6, in the middle of the Caporetto rout, Bolshevik mobs, soldiers of the Petrograd garrison, sailors from Kronstadt, and the workers' Red Guards stormed the czar's Winter Palace. Chaos followed, but all parties reached agreement on one point. Nine million Russian soldiers had been lost in the war, and every leftist politician wanted peace — at any price. Trotsky accepted the kaiser's brutal terms at Brest-Litovsk, a railroad junction on the Bug River. The implications for Britain, France, and the United States were vast. Russia was no longer an ally. Overnight it was a new war. The Central Powers were now confident of victory, and with good reason. Brest-Litovsk freed three thousand German guns and a million men — enough to give Ludendorff the whip hand on the western front provided he struck before America's waxing strength eclipsed his edge. The German strategist had designed a brilliant new assault technique, stressing stealth, surprise bombardment, gas, and infiltration, and encoded his coming operation in the west *Kaiserschlacht* (kaiser's battle). This entailed a complex of thrusts in France. By April 1, Hindenburg promised the kaiser, they would be in Paris. The Allies dug in and waited numbly. They couldn't tell where or when or how the enemy was coming, but they knew the storm was imminent. And there was almost nothing they could do about it. They were spent. Even Haig yearned for U.S. troops now. Robertson said, "Our only hope lies in American reserves," and France's Pétain said, *"J'attends les américains et les tanks."* Publicly and privately Churchill had anticipated them by several months. In Paris the previous September 17, Eddie Marsh had written in his diary: "Winston very eloquent on the necessity of bringing every possible American soldier over to France as soon as possible, and training them here or in England instead of in America — so as not to waste transport during the time of training." His tanks would not be available in significant numbers for another year, but he could, and did, stockpile other munitions. Convinced that the Germans would bag enormous quantities of equipment in their first drive, he redoubled his efforts at the Metropole, often working through the night. He expected the enemy's great offensive to open in the third week of February. Actually, it came a month later, on March 21, 1918. And he was there when it started.[240]

Although he was not in the War Cabinet, Lloyd George sought his advice with increasing frequency. He respected Churchill's judgment, valued his experience in the trenches, and wanted him to serve as his eyes and ears at the front. On Monday, March 18, at the prime minister's request, Churchill crossed the Channel and was driven to Saint-Omer. Unlike George, he believed that Haig would be the right man in the coming crisis. He wasn't very good at advancing, but he would be a poor retreater, too. The very stubbornness and lack of imagination which had handicapped him on the offensive would steady him when the waves of *feldgrau* came rolling across no-man's-land. Haig had many complaints that Monday, mostly about the French, yet Churchill felt he anticipated the approaching struggle "with an anxious but resolute eye." Together they studied the map. The immediate threat was not in Flanders but south of the Ypres salient, on a fifty-mile stretch of front which the War Cabinet, at the insistence of Premier Georges Clemenceau, had just taken over from the French. Here, north of the Oise River, 57 British divisions were confronted by 110 German divisions — over five times the German strength when they had attacked Verdun two years earlier. Haig, Winston reported, was "daily expecting an attack of the first magnitude."[241] He was far more vulnerable than the French and the newly arrived Americans, both of whom, at the moment, outnumbered the enemy concentrations facing them. Part of Haig's problem was that Lloyd George, after Passchendaele, had deliberately kept him short of troops to prevent him from renewing his attack. The enemy was aware of this weakness. It was logical to anticipate the first German attack of 1918 on the British front in the sector between Arras and Fère-en-Tardenois. And Ludendorff was logical.

Leaving Haig at three o'clock in the afternoon, Churchill decided to visit the Ninth Division, commanded by Major General Henry Tudor, who had been a fellow subaltern in India. Tudor's headquarters were in the ruined village of Nurlu. "When do you think it will come?" Winston asked him. Tudor replied: "Perhaps tomorrow morning, perhaps the day after, perhaps the week after." The next day they toured the trenches together, and Churchill was still in Nurlu Wednesday night. As they turned in, Tudor said: "It's certainly coming now. Trench raids this evening have identified no less than eight enemy battalions on a single half-mile of front." Churchill woke at four o'clock Thursday morning and lay awake for thirty minutes, listening in the quiet. The silence ended at 4:40 A.M., when he heard several explosions in the distance. They were enemy mines, sapped beneath British positions. "And then," Churchill later wrote, "exactly as a pianist runs his hands across the keyboard from treble to bass, there rose in less than one minute the most tremendous cannonade I shall ever hear." In a matter of minutes all British communications were destroyed. Gas was spreading over artillery parks and machine-gun nests. "The flame of the bombardment," he wrote, "lit like flickering firelight my tiny cabin." He found Tudor on the duckboards outside. The general said: "This is *it.* I have ordered all our batteries to open fire. You will hear them in a minute." Churchill didn't: "The crash of the German shells bursting on our trench lines eight thousand yards away was so overpowering that the accession to the tumult of nearly two hundred guns firing from much nearer could not be even distinguished." A few minutes after six o'clock over 500,000 Germans, outnumbering the defenders three or four to one, loomed out of a dense fog. Winston left "with mingled emotions" and "motored without misadventure to Peronne." The road to Peronne was cut behind him. By dusk he was in Saint-Omer. The British were reeling backward. Ludendorff had hoped to split the weak seam between the British and the French at Amiens, but although Amiens didn't fall on Friday, when the Germans advanced ten miles, all contact between the two allies was broken.[242]

Churchill reached London on Saturday. At No. 10 he reviewed the situation with Lloyd George and Sir Henry Wilson, who, having outwitted all his rivals, had succeeded Robertson as chief of the Imperial General Staff. Then the prime minister took Winston aside and asked how, with its intricate trench system destroyed and troops falling back, the BEF could remain intact. Churchill answered that "every offensive loses its force as it proceeds. It is like throwing a bucket of water over the floor. It first rushes forward, then soaks forward, and finally stops altogether until another bucket can be brought. After thirty or forty miles there will certainly come a considerable breathing space, when the front can be reconstituted if every effort is made." Lloyd George invited him to meet with the War Cabinet at 4:00 P.M. They broke up after two hours, and Hankey recorded the dismal conclusion: "Our casualties are going to be huge." Lloyd George and Hankey dined with the Churchills at Eccleston

Square on Sunday. The news was all bad; the fury of the enemy drive was unabated. Monday evening Winston was one of several ministers who gathered at Downing Street. Hankey wrote: "Balfour & Churchill whom I found in company with the PM were ridiculously optimistic." Sir John French, now Viscount French, arrived and said bitterly that Haig had "badly let down the army in shattering it in the hopeless Flanders offensive."[243]

During the next three days the reports from France grew blacker and blacker. Lloyd George, badly frightened, wondered how much the poor bloody infantry could stand. On Thursday he asked Churchill whether he could "get away for a few days to France." The day before, Foch had become generalissimo of all forces fighting the Germans, "charged by the British and French Governments to co-ordinate the action of the Allied Armies on the Western Front." To relieve the pressure on the faltering British, the prime minister wanted Winston to request a "vigorous" French attack on Ludendorff's southern flank. Churchill would take with him the Duke of Westminster ("Bender"), an old foxhunting friend and the brother-in-law of Jennie's second husband. Meanwhile, Bonar Law and Sir Henry Wilson were conspiring to thwart him. His task, they felt, was an affront to Lord Milner, the new war minister. They were actually planning to prevent Churchill from reaching the French leaders when Lloyd George got wind of their intrigue and broke it up. He wired that after calling on Haig, Churchill should "go straight to Clemenceau" in Paris. Reaching the new BEF headquarters in Montreuil, Winston and Bender were astonished to learn that the British field marshal was off taking his afternoon horseback ride. Certainly this was no weather for riding; the rain, Churchill later recalled, "streamed down in torrents in the silent, empty streets of this peaceful little old-world town." Nor did this seem a propitious time for Haig to be unavailable. Telephones were ringing constantly with news of troop movements. His new chief of staff told his visitors that the fighting was "devouring" their reserves, that the enemy was still "pouring through the gap," and that during the past week the BEF had lost 1,000 guns and 100,000 men. The need for a French diversion was desperate.[244]

Driving through Amiens, which was already being shelled by the Germans, Churchill and the duke arrived in Paris and headed for what Winston called "the luxuries of an almost empty Ritz." Leo Amery found him there and wrote: "We had a good talk while he wallowed in a hot bath and then went to bed. (Winston is in extraordinary shape and wears a long nightgown!). . . . His only preoccupation was whether the French were only counter-attacking piecemeal or were getting everything together for a really big stroke." He sent word of his mission to the premier through the head of the British military mission at 37, rue Faubourg-Saint-Honoré. Clemenceau grandly replied: "Not only shall Mr Winston Churchill see everything, but I will myself take him tomorrow to the battle and we will visit all the Commanders of Corps and Armies engaged." The seventy-six-year-old "Tiger" — he really looked like a tiger — was quite serious. Churchill thought the premier ought to stay away from the battlefield. Clemenceau said: *"C'est mon grand plaisir."* He pointed out that danger was everywhere now; even the capital wasn't safe. It was quite true. Shells had been landing in Paris since Saturday, fired from Krupp's remarkable *Pariskanone,* whose range was eighty-one miles. In a striking example of Teutonic *Schrecklichkeit,* one shell had crashed through the roof of Saint-Gervais-l'Eglise on Good Friday and exploded in the transept during Mass, killing ninety-one worshipers. London newspapers had carried accounts of this, and Clementine wrote Winston: "I do hope that when the long range guns start firing you take cover."* [245]

Their motorcade set out at ten o'clock in the morning. At Beauvais they mounted a stone staircase, passed through double doors which were opened at their approach, and were welcomed by the diminutive, mustachioed Foch. He led them into a huge, elegant conference room. Pinned to a wall before him was an enormous map of the front. "General Foch seized a pencil," Churchill recalled in the *Strand Magazine* of December 1930, "as if it were a weapon, and without the slightest preliminary advanced upon the map and proceeded to describe the situation." Everything about his method of delivery impressed Winston: "his animation, his gestures, his habit of using his whole body to emphasize and illustrate as far as possible the action which he was describing or the argument which he was evolving, his vivid descriptiveness, his violence and vehemence of utterance." Most of the time he spoke in French, and his tongue was so quick that Churchill missed phrases and sometimes whole sentences, but the generalissimo's meaning was quite clear. He pointed to the German gains on the offensive's first day and cried: "Oh! Oh! Oh! How big!" Then his pencil sketched the second stage of the drive, also huge: *"Deuxième journée d'invasion. Ah! Ah!"* The third lunge, again enormous: *"Troisième journée. Aie! Aie!"* But as he progressed it became clear that each day's conquests grew steadily smaller. It was Churchill's

* Most people, including Churchill, called (and still call) this weapon "Big Bertha." *Die dicke Bertha,* literally "fat Bertha" — named for a member of the Krupp family — was actually a huge howitzer which flung a projectile weighing a ton nine miles. These guns had been used in the siege of Liège and, later, at Verdun.

water-bucket metaphor translated into geography. Finally he said: *"Hier, dernière journée d'invasion,"* and "his whole attitude and manner," wrote Winston, "flowed out in pity for this poor, weak, miserable little zone of invasion which was all that had been achieved by the enemy on the last day. . . . The hostile effort was exhausted. The mighty onset was coming to a standstill. The impulse which had sustained it was dying away. The worst was over." Abruptly Foch cried: "Stabilization. Sure, certain, soon. And afterwards. Ah, afterwards. That is my affair." There was a silence. Then the premier moved toward him, murmuring: *"Alors, Général, il faut que je vous embrasse."*[246]

It was spectacular, but it did not, of course, answer the question Churchill had brought from London. When were the French going to lance the German canker? Leaving Foch, the motorcade proceeded to the closest British headquarters, in Drury, twelve miles south of Amiens. It was rough driving. The road was rutted with new shell holes. Obviously Ludendorff was close. At their destination, as in Montreuil, telephones never stopped ringing. Haig was there. One by one his officers described their emergency. The BEF had been stumbling backward for ten days. Churchill asked one British general if his men could regroup and form a new line. "No one can tell," the general said. "We have hardly anything between us and the enemy except utterly exhausted, disorganized troops . . . dead from want of sleep and rest." The presentation ended. It was, all agreed, the worst show any of them had seen — perhaps the worst in history. Finally Clemenceau, who had been feasting on chicken and sandwiches as he heard them out, sat back contented and raised his voice above the phones. He said in English: "Very well, then, it is all right. . . . Never mind what has been arranged before. If your men are tired, and we have fresh men, our men shall come up at once and help you." But instead of attacking the German flank, poilus would be fed into the line where the British were weakest.[247]

Churchill relayed Clemenceau's decision to Lloyd George over one of the telephones. The French premier then rose from his lunch and said: "I claim my reward. I wish to pass the river and see the battle." The British remonstrated, but the Tiger waved them off. He pointed to his military aide and said: "A few shells will do [him] good." Back at the cars he said: "Mr. Winston Churchill, we are in the British lines. Will you take charge of us? We will do what you say." Winston, delighted, asked: "Where do you want to go?" The premier replied: "As far as is possible. But you shall judge." Winston sat beside the driver in the lead car, map in hand, and off they went, across the bridge and toward the battlefield. He saw streams of Tommies, many of whom "walked as if they were in a

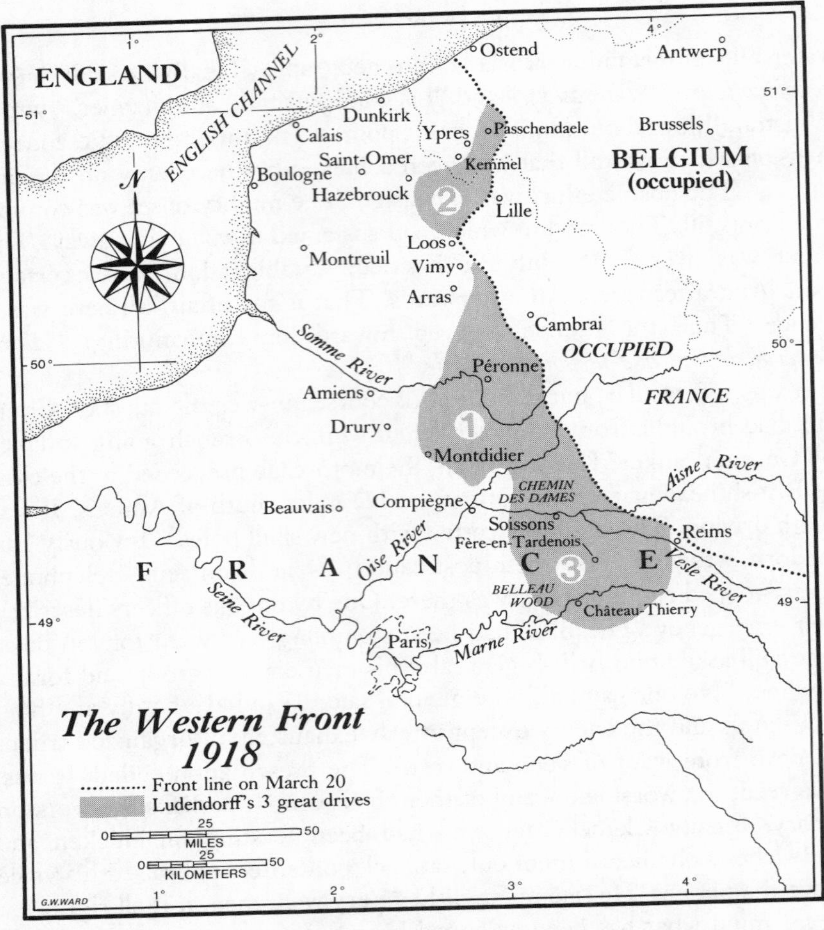

dream, and gave no notice of our file of brightly flagged cars. Others again, recognizing me, gave me a wave or a grin, as they would no doubt have done to George Robey or Harry Lauder" — music hall stars — "or any other well known figure which carried their minds back to vanished England and the dear days of peace and party politics." Presently they heard shells moaning and rumbling overhead. Some burst in the fields on either side of the road. Next small-arms fire became audible. A heavy rain was falling, and mists of evening began to gather. If they followed the map much farther, they would encounter Germans. "On our left towards the enemy," Churchill wrote, "was a low ridge crowned with trees about three hundred yards away. Among these trees a few dark figures moved about. . . . I thought on the whole that we had gone about far enough."[248]

Another guide would have turned back, but if the Tiger found danger beguiling, so did Winston. The two of them left the motorcade and proceeded on foot among stragglers and bursts of shrapnel. They stood together on a small rise, surveying the disorderly scene. Several weary British officers recognized them, saluted them, and came over. Clemenceau and Churchill gave them the contents of their cigar cases. As they were leaving, a shell burst among a group of horses. One, wounded and riderless, "came in a staggering trot towards us. The poor animal was streaming with blood." The old premier advanced toward it and quickly seized its bridle, bringing it to a halt. His aide hurried up and said they really must leave *tout de suite.* "Clemenceau," Churchill wrote, "turned reluctantly towards his car. As he did so, he gave me a sidelong glance and observed in an undertone, *'Quel moment délicieux!'* "[249]

After calling on General Henri Pétain, the commander of all French ground troops and therefore Haig's counterpart, and dining with him in what Winston called his "travelling military palace," they returned to Paris. At the Ritz in the small hours of the next morning Churchill wrote Clementine that it had been 1:00 A.M. when "Clemenceau, alert and fresh as when we started, dismissed me. The old man is vy gracious to me & talks in the most confidential way. He is younger even than I am!" Then Winston wired Lloyd George a full account of the day. The British divisions, he reported, were "in many cases only skeletons," but French reinforcements would soon be arriving "as fast as they can come up. . . . Nothing more can be done than what they are doing." At 4:00 A.M. his report went to London in cipher; it was decoded at the War Office and delivered to No. 10 at 8:30. Churchill saw the premier again at noon, and together they drafted an appeal to Woodrow Wilson for the speedy arrival of heavy American contingents. Winston telegraphed a copy of this to Lloyd George and, after lunching at the Ritz with Bender and Amery, set out alone for another tour of the front. Everything he saw convinced him that the war was approaching its climax. He wondered if this was appreciated at No. 10. Clemenceau could hardly have been more courteous, and Winston was never one to underrate his own importance, but premiers, he felt, should talk to premiers. Back at the Ritz he wired this to Lloyd George, adding: "It is considered certain here that the Germans will pursue this struggle to a final decision all through the summer and their resources are at present larger than ours. . . . Every effort must be made if we are to escape destruction."[250]

The prime minister was handed this message when he awoke the next morning in Downing Street. He told his valet to start packing. Sir Henry Wilson joined him, and Churchill met their destroyer at Boulogne. Winston accompanied them as far as Montreuil, but the general staff insisted that he be excluded from the military talks. The council of war, held in Beauvais, included Clemenceau, Foch, Spiers (who acted as interpreter), and two American generals: John "Black Jack" Pershing and Tasker Bliss. The meeting formally endorsed the understanding Churchill had reached with the premier. In addition, Pershing brought President Wilson's reply to the plea from Clemenceau and Churchill: 480,000 doughboys were on their way.

Lloyd George's party, including Churchill, was back in London at 2:30 the following morning. Winston went straight to his desk at the Metropole. By the weekend the situation in France was reasonably clear. Montreuil had fallen, and one of the railways between Amiens and the capital had been cut. At that point, however, Teutonic discipline had collapsed. The starved German troops — starved by the Admiralty blockade Churchill had organized in 1914 — had turned to pillage. By the time they re-formed, the hollow-eyed Tommies, their ranks thickened by French reserves from the south, had turned, anchored their lines, and were grimly holding on. Ludendorff had driven them back thirty-five miles, inflicted over 300,000 casualties, and created a huge bulge in the middle of the Allied line, but he hadn't broken through. The first crisis was over. Churchill wrote on April 6: "I have been able to replace everything in the munitions sphere without difficulty. Guns, tanks, aeroplanes will all be ahead of personnel. We have succeeded in pulling the gun position round so completely since last summer that we can deliver 2000 guns as fast as they can be shipped. It has been touch & go on the front. We stood for some days within an ace of destruction."[251]

As he sealed the envelope the second crisis was rising 136 miles to the east of him, in Flanders.

By early April Ludendorff had moved his "battering ram" (*Sturmbock*) opposite the old Ypres salient. A few minutes after midnight on Sunday, April 7, some twenty-five hundred muzzles roared in unison, sending the first of what would be thirty thousand shells toward Armentières and fouling the air with mustard gas. The German storm troops had fog again, and just before dawn Monday morning they buckled on their coal-scuttle helmets, climbed over their parapets, and lurched across no-man's-land. Once again they ruptured the British trench line, this time on a thirty-mile front along the river Lys. Everything Haig had won in his Passchendaele drive was lost in a few days. By Wednesday evening Armentières had fallen; the loss of Ploegsteert, which Churchill had fortified as a battalion commander, swiftly followed. Spiers wrote in his diary: "Situation very critical. . . . British foresee severance with French & German objective gained."[252]

On April 18, with the outlook obscure, Winston sent the prime minister an analysis of their strategic choices. If worst came to worst, there would be only two: "whether we should let go our left hand or our right: abandon the Channel ports, or abandon all contact with the French front line." Loss of the ports would mean German dominance in the Strait of Dover, bottling up the Port of London, the shutdown of England's key naval bases, and bombardment of "a large part of Kent and Sussex." But the Allied line would be intact, with "the whole of France open for dilatory retirement or manoeuvre." The alternative was worse. They could "wire in" and wait. Ludendorff would undoubtedly pivot southward toward the French. But after the Germans had crushed the poilus, "the British army would be at their disposal. They could deal with it at their convenience." This, clearly, was the line Ludendorff hoped Britain would take. He appeared to be following an elementary principle: "Divide your enemy's forces into two parts: hold off the weaker part while you beat the stronger: the weaker is then at your mercy."[253]

A week later Churchill told the House that the Ministry of Munitions was in a position to deliver "a fairly good report." Since the opening of the first German offensive five weeks earlier the BEF had lost about a thousand artillery pieces and some five thousand machine guns. Yet the troops now had "more serviceable guns as a whole, and more of practically every calibre, than there were when the battle began." He crossed the Channel three days later to talk to Haig about shell supplies. Most of his time was now spent meeting the needs of the arriving Americans. Ludendorff, meanwhile, was battering his way toward the sea. On April 25 he took Mount Kemmel — a "mountain," on the flat Flanders plain, being a peak 350 feet high — as his men, toiling up the slope, sang the gunners' fighting song: *"Wenn einer wüsste, Wie einem ist!"* In the House, Churchill paid tribute to the British spirit: "No demand is too novel or too sudden to be met. No need is too unexpected to be supplied. No strain is too prolonged for the patience of our people. No suffering or peril daunts their hearts."[254]

The enemy was now within five miles of Hazebrouck, a vital railway junction and Ludendorff's chief objective. If it fell the British would face Churchill's alternatives. In London the general staff had already reached his conclusion: they must not allow the enemy to drive a wedge between them and the French. But if Hazebrouck fell, Haig would have to withdraw his entire left wing, abandoning Dunkirk and putting the Channel at risk. Haig, stepping entirely out of character, was stirred to eloquence. He issued an "order of the day" to all ranks: "There is no other course open to us but to fight it out! Every position must be held to the last man: there must be no retirement. With our backs to the wall, and believing in the justice of our cause, each one of us must fight on to the end. The safety of our homes and the freedom of mankind alike depend on the conduct of each one of us at this critical moment." The situation was not really as bad as it seemed. The German divisions accustomed to fighting Russians were finding the British unexpectedly tough. And at this crucial point Ludendorff also behaved uncharacteristically. He hesitated. He couldn't decide which way to attack, and by the time he had made up his mind the obstinate Tommies had dug in. Foch studied his situation map and told Haig: "*La bataille d'Hazebrouck est finie.*" Ludendorff had driven in another huge bulge. Yet he still faced an unbroken Allied front. He had again achieved a tactical victory but a strategic defeat. Afterward German military historians agreed that the battle had been a *Misserfolg* — a failure.[255]

As the spring wore on, Churchill's trips to France increased. He had established munitions plants on the Continent, and he needed proximity to military headquarters for coordinating the demands of all Allied forces. Haig therefore provided him with quarters of his own, the Château Verchocq. There, Winston wrote Clementine, he was "very comfortable. . . . I have a charming room filled with the sort of ancient woodcarved furniture that you admire and which seems to me to be very fine and old. The grounds contain avenues of the most beautiful trees, beech and pine, grown to an enormous height and making broad walks like the aisles of cathedrals. One of these must be nearly half a mile long."[256] He was here, going over reports, when Ludendorff's third blow fell. Despite his two failures, none of the Allied leaders doubted that the kaiser's military prodigy would strike again. He had the men and he was fighting the calendar; the blockade was crippling his homeland and the American menace grew daily. Foch, ever alert, called for a "foot-by-foot" defense of the Allied ground, and in Chaumont, General John Pershing, who had been reluctant to commit his troops piecemeal, now put all doughboys at the generalissimo's disposal. Foch and Haig had agreed that Ludendorff would pounce upon the British again. In the larger view, they were right. His ultimate objective was, not seizure of the Channel ports or splitting the Allies, but the complete destruction of the British army. First, however, there would be a massive feint, an intermezzo, in the south. He meant to maul the French so savagely that they would be incapable of supporting their ally to the north.

Pétain's troops were weaker than they appeared. They, too, had bled needlessly in 1917. Their Passchendaele had been the Nivelle campaign, named for General Georges Nivelle, who had replaced the bovine Joffre and whose star had seemed ascendant in the spring of that year. His answer to the trench had been "the unlimited offensive." Nivelle was handsome, swashbuckling, and popular. Even the English liked him (his mother had been British), and in the châteaux far behind the lines where staff officers moved pins on maps, Allied generals had thrilled to his battle cry: "One and a half million Frenchmen cannot fail!"[257] Unfortunately the excitement, the cry, and even the plan of attack had reached Ludendorff. The drive had been predicted in French newspapers and in orders circulated as low as company level, which meant that the Germans picked up prisoners carrying them. Nivelle had known this. He had also known that the enemy, as a result, were riposting with a strategic withdrawal called *Alberich* (after the evil dwarf in the Nibelungenlied), poisoning wells and sowing booby traps as they went. Nivelle had insisted that this hadn't changed a thing. In fact, it had changed everything. The new Hindenburg line was a defender's dream. It had turned Nivelle's drive into a welter of slaughter. He had made no real gains, and the moment he stopped, revolt had spread among French troops. At the height of their mutiny, fourteen out of sixteen divisions on the Champagne front had been disabled. Even troops who didn't rebel had marched into the trenches bleating in unison, demonstrating that they regarded themselves as sheep being led to the slaughter. Had the enemy known all this, Germany could have won the war with a single bold stroke. As it was, France's army had been severely crippled. The French had lost nearly 300,000 men in 1914 and now, with Nivelle's losses, they lacked the time and the resources to build a new striking force. The poilus had huddled sullenly in their trenches, and to redress their grievances the government had replaced Nivelle with Pétain, who was known to be cautious and receptive to demands from resentful troops. Even so, Clemenceau was worried about the possibility of a civilian uprising against the war. Although Churchill didn't know it, at the time of their tour of the front the premier was keeping four crack divisions in the interior of France to deal with any insurrection. The threat was real. The dissidents weren't called Bolsheviks, but France had subversive firebrands, too.

Curiously, it was the Americans, the newcomers, who picked the spot where the third German onslaught would come. The Chemin des Dames ridge, north of the Aisne, was so formidable a natural stronghold that the French had manned it with four divisions of their least reliable troops and three exhausted British divisions sent south for a rest. It happened that this was the sector closest to Paris. Ludendorff's plan was to hit it so hard that every French reserve would be committed to the defense of the capital, and when that happened he was going to wheel and drive Haig into the sea. His preparations were superb. The American prediction that a great assault on the ridge was imminent was dismissed by Foch because there wasn't a trace of activity in the German lines in that sector. Observation posts reported nothing, aerial photographs were a blank. Apparently there weren't even any enemy batteries. Actually, there were nearly four thousand heavy Krupp guns there. You just couldn't see them. Moving at night and hiding in woods during the day, with horses' hooves wrapped in rags and the sounds of creaking gun carriages masked by cages of croaking frogs, Ludendorff had massed forty-one crack divisions in a wild weald of giant trees opposite the ridge and entrusted the command to Crown Prince Rupprecht. At one o'clock in the morning of Thursday, April 25, the war's heaviest bombardment opened up and continued for nearly three hours. Before it ended, at 3:40 A.M., some of the defenders were raving, literally out of their minds. Pétain's local commander had erred in stationing his men too far forward, where they were naked to the artillery cannonade, and in failing to establish defenses in depth. The Germans swarming up the slope behind a tornado of gas and shrapnel found that the Allied forces had virtually disintegrated. And there appeared to be nothing behind them but open country. The Germans were stupefied. The Allied center was a void. Nothing like this had been seen in four years of trench warfare. Ludendorff, receiving their almost incredible report, sensed that what he had meant to be a feint could lead to swift victory. He shifted his gaze from Flanders to Paris.

The Allied reserve in this part of the line comprised seven French and two other tired British divisions. It was pitifully inadequate. The Germans, with their vast superiority in numbers and morale, overran them. To the further astonishment of the attackers, the bridges over the Aisne were intact. On their flank, near Soissons, some French resistance was developing, but the center continued to gape wide open. By dusk that Thursday they had advanced ten miles and were on the Vesle. The French capital was eighty miles away. In the morning they crossed the Vesle, whose fine bridges were also undamaged, and surged onward, hobnail boots thumping and *feldgrau* trousers swishing weirdly in the sunshine. By May 30, when Soissons fell, they had overrun five French lines. On June 3 they were back on the Marne for the first time in nearly four years, the tip of their salient at a place called Château-Thierry. Churchill wrote Clementine: "The fate of the capital hangs in the balance — only 45 miles away."[258]

At this point, writes Cyril Falls, the British military historian, "something astonishing happened. Up the Marne came marching new men. They were two divisions only, but they strode proudly through the flotsam and jetsam always present on the fringe of a stricken battlefield. . . . They were fine-looking men and even the rawest had a soldierly air." The first Americans had arrived. Their vanguard was a brigade of U.S. Marines, an odd mix of tough professionals and Ivy League students who, like their Oxford and Cambridge counterparts of 1914 — most of whom were now dead or maimed — had enlisted the week after their country entered the war. As they formed their line of battle an elderly French peasant shouted at them: *"La guerre est finie!" "Pas finie!"* a Harvard undergraduate shouted back, giving the sector its name.[259] For five days the marines held five miles of Pas Finie against the gray enemy columns which came hurtling across the wheat field. Then they counterattacked, driving five divisions of Germans back through a boulder-strewn, gully-laced forest called Belleau Wood. Only one in four survived unscratched. More than a hundred were decorated for heroism. The French renamed the wood for them. Six days later doughboys recaptured the village of Vaux, on the other side of Château-Thierry. The crown prince ordered a halt and then a general withdrawal.

Thus ended the last of Ludendorff's sledgehammer blows. Early in July he launched a *Friedensturm,* or peace offensive, sending fifty-six divisions in a pincer movement around Reims. But Foch had developed new defensive tactics, posting thinly held forward positions to confuse the enemy and then decimating the advancing German infantry with precise artillery strikes. Moreover, ten thousand American soldiers were now disembarking every day. They reached Reims in strength, and the Germans, after initial successes, were thrown back. Returning from the front, Churchill told an audience at the Central Hall, Westminster: "When I have seen during the past few weeks the splendour of American manhood striding forward on all the roads of France and Flanders, I have experienced emotions which words cannot describe." Britain would claim no fruits of victory, he said, no "territorial or commercial advantage," only the "supreme reconciliation" of Englishmen and Americans. "That is the reward of Britain," he said. "That is the lion's share." He wrote

Sinclair the following week: "If all goes well, England and U.S. may act permanently together. We are living 50 years in one at this rate."[260]

His American mother chose this extraordinary moment to remarry. Her fiancé was Montagu Porch, a member of the Colonial Service who was three years younger than Winston. Jennie was sixty-four but she continued to be interested in men and they in her. "I can still remember the first time I saw her," Porch told a reporter from the *Daily Express.* It had been just before the war; "she was sitting with some friends. She wore a green dress. Was it long or short? Don't remember. But she was very beautiful." He had asked her to dance, and she had replied with a smile: "I think you'd better go and dance with some of the younger girls." He thought otherwise, and their remarkable courtship began. Porch was slender, he wore an elegant mustache, and his hair was prematurely white. Jennie had been dyeing her hair black; now she stopped. Porch was stationed in Nigeria, and after the war broke out he was commissioned in the Cameroons Expeditionary Force. Home on leave, he visited Jennie. Later he said he didn't remember proposing, but somehow, by the time he departed, he had the definite impression that they were engaged. On May 31, at the height of the Chemin des Dames crisis, Repington wrote in his diary: "Lady R charming about her future. Mr Porch quite good-looking and intelligent. They get married tomorrow and go to Windsor for the weekend. Winston says he hopes marriage won't become the vogue among ladies of his mother's age."[261]

The ceremony was held in the Harrow Road Register Office. On its eve, Porch wrote Winston from the Connaught Hotel, thanking him in advance for attending the wedding and adding discreetly: "I have carefully considered the position from every point of view — your Mother's financial affairs are understood." Jennie was, in fact, finally in the money. Under these improbable circumstances, in the autumn of her life, she became the bride of a man of means. The Porch wealth came from Australian sheep and was substantial. Although she told the press that she would continue to be known as Lady Randolph Churchill, she was clearly in love with her new husband. When his leave expired and he returned to Africa, she assumed that she would accompany him. It seemed incredible to her that, after so many men, she should be deprived of her legal lover. Yet that was the case. "She took steps to get a passport to Nigeria," the newspaper *West Africa* later reported, "but Downing Street refused because of the submarine peril. . . . She pleaded over and over again, but permission was withheld." To her sister Clara she wrote: "Poor Porchey is very lonely." So was poor Jennie. But peace seemed near, and she was confident that the marriage would work. "He has a future and I have a past," she told Lady Essex, "so we should be all right." Meanwhile, she sought amusement in the frantic parties of the time, learning to dance the turkey trot, patronizing the new nightclubs which had mushroomed in the West End, and finding solace in wine. Lady Diana Cooper remembers the evening a home in her neighborhood was hit in a zeppelin raid; the wounded were being treated in her basement and the kitchen maids screaming when there "arrived Jennie Churchill and Maud Cunard, both a little tipsy, dancing and talking wildly. They had been walking and got scared, and had stopped for a drink." Now they planned to attend the opera, explaining, "It being a raid night, the public required example."[262]

Churchill's own homelife was erratic that year, chiefly because of his frequent and prolonged absences, but also because they had to move again. Income from leasing the Eccleston Square house was indispensable, so they found a tenant and moved into Winston's aunt Cornelia's house at 3 Tenterden Street, just off Hanover Square. Here Clementine gave birth to another redheaded daughter, Marigold, who promptly became "the Duckadilly." Except during her confinement Clementine was busy with war work, running canteens, though she made sure she was always home when Winston could be there. And wherever he was, she was always in his thoughts. Writing from the Ritz when the crown prince was advancing on Paris, he told her: "Weather permitting & the rest of it I propose to fly to Kenley Aerodrome Wed or Thursday. I will send you notice. Try to be at Lullenden so that we can be together." The zeppelins over England worried him far more than the Krupp shells bursting near him: "This vy clear weather & the state of the moon will certainly expose you to danger," he wrote, urging her to stay in the country. "I do not like to think of you & the kittens in London." On June 3, the day after he had introduced a regular, scheduled air service between England and France, he wrote her of the maiden flight: "My darling, I had a touching vision of you & yr kittens growing rapidly smaller and the aerodrome & its sheds dwindling into distant perspective as I whirled away."[263]

The love letters of statesmen rarely stand the test of time. They tend to be mawkish, fatuous, and distorted by the egocentricity which usually fuels great political achievement. Lloyd George was a man of intellect and vision. The war diminished him, as it attenuated the leaders of all belligerent powers, but what remained was still impressive. His mistress was a charming, cultivated Irishwoman. His missives to her ought to be moving. They aren't. Typically he wrote her, in that summer of 1918: "When I woke up at 6 my first thought was of the loving little face engraved on my heart & I had a fierce thought to go there & then to cover it with kisses. But darling I am jealous once more. I know your thoughts are on roast mutton & partridge & chicken & potatoes & that you are longing to pass them through the lips which are mine & to bite them with luscious joy with the dazzling white teeth that I love to press. I know that today I am a little out of it & that your heart is throbbing for other thrills. . . . Your very jealous old Lover." Frances had told him she was hungry, and that had inspired this.[264]

Churchill, who in public had far less control over his emotions than Lloyd George, sent Clementine notes that are stirring even now. This year marked their tenth wedding anniversary. "Ten years ago my beautiful white pussy cat you came to me," he wrote her from the Château Verchocq. "They have certainly been the happiest years of my life, & never at any moment did I feel more profoundly & eternally attached to you. I do hope & pray that looking back you will not feel regrets. If you do it [is] my fault & the fault of those that made me. I am grateful beyond words to you for all you have given me. My sweet darling I love you vy dearly." Then, in a second letter: "I reproach myself vy much for not having been more to you. But at any rate in these ten years the sun has never yet gone down on our wrath. Never once have we closed our eyes in slumber with an unappeased difference. My dearest sweet I hope & pray that future years may bring you serene & smiling days, & full & fruitful occupation. I think that you will find real scope in the new world opening out to women, & find interests wh will enrich yr life. And always at yr side in true & tender friendship as long as he breathes will be your ever devoted, if only partially satisfactory, W."[265]

He was, as he acknowledged, an imperfect husband, less considerate of her than the tone of his letters to her suggests. To abide by his wishes constantly, as she did, was a sign of strength and forbearance not found in all wives. In following his star he sometimes hurt her deeply. She shared his mortification when he was in political eclipse. That could not be helped. But he could have spared her much. When he needlessly courted death she writhed in her bed, dreaming him dead. He could have commuted to France by sea. Instead, he flew at every opportunity. She shouldn't worry, he told her: "It gives me a feeling of tremendous conquest over space, & I know you wd love it yourself."[266] If he really believed he was not taking risks, he was deceiving himself. Her anxiety was fully justified. In the aircraft of 1918 eventual mishaps were inevitable. He was defying the law of averages, flying to the front every morning and returning to work at the Metropole through the evening. Once his plane caught fire over the Channel. Another of his planes somersaulted after takeoff; the pilot made a forced landing. Later, when he was piloting himself in a dual-control aircraft over Croydon airfield, the guiding stick failed. Their speed was about sixty miles per hour and they were seventy or eighty feet above the ground. The plane nose-dived and crashed. Winston's copilot was badly injured; he himself was bleeding and badly bruised. Nevertheless, he insisted on driving off and delivering a speech. Those who urged him to see a doctor were curtly dismissed.

He did not like to be told what to do. He was climbing into a cockpit, puffing on a cigar, when his flier reminded him that when they became airborne the cigar would be extremely dangerous. He scrambled down, flung the butt on the airstrip, and stamped on it. One evening in France he and Eddie Marsh were driving to his château in a Rolls-Royce. It was a trying journey, as Marsh described it in his diary: "First a tyre burst with one of those loud bursts which make one think one has been assassinated — and then . . . Winston gave a wrong direction, left instead of right, at a crossroad." The chauffeur protested, Churchill abruptly put him in his place, "and on we went in the dark, on and on literally for kilometres between the close hedges of the roadside, it must be the original 'long lane that has no turning.' It's impossible to imagine anything more comical and provoking." Eventually they turned around and got on the right road. Churchill accepted none of the blame. Eddie wrote: "The climax of Winston's cursing was, 'Well, it's the most absolutely f——ing thing in the whole of my bloody life.'"[267]

He expected to live as he pleased, doing exactly what he wanted to do when he wanted to do it, assuming that others would alter their plans to suit his. He couldn't get away with it when dealing with, say, Lloyd George or Clemenceau, but that was only because their authority exceeded his. When he was top man, which was most of the time, he exercised his prerogatives. On another automobile trip, this time near the front, Marsh wrote: "Winston was attracted by the sight of shells bursting in the distance — irresistible! Out we got, put on our steel helmets, hung our gas-masks round our necks, and walked for half-an-hour towards the firing. There was a great deal of noise, shells whistling over our heads, and some fine bursts in the distance — but we seemed to get no nearer, and the firing died down, so we went back after another hour's delay. Winston's disregard of time, when there's anything he wants to do, is sublime — he firmly believes that it waits for him."[268]

Visiting him after the uproar over his return to the cabinet, Hankey had noted in his diary: "On the whole he was in a chastened mood. He admitted to me that he had been 'a bit above himself' at the Admiralty, and surprised me by saying that he had no idea of the depth of public opinion against his return to public life, until the appointment was made." But humility was foreign to him, and it didn't last. In the spring of 1918 he made a naked attempt to widen his domain. At present, he wrote Lloyd George, "the War Cabinet alone have the power of decision & the right of regular & continuous consultation." Moreover, most of the great offices "are filled by Tories." He proposed that the prime minister "fortify" himself by appointing "a proper Cabinet of responsible Ministers," independent of the War Cabinet, to determine policy. He wrote: "I do not seek this power." But that is precisely what he *was* seeking. He declared: "Certainly I will never accept political responsibility without recognized regular power." He was not only accepting it, but seizing it, at every opportunity. He sent Lloyd George several memoranda appealing for responsibilities and prerogatives which would have increased his authority. The prime minister didn't even reply.[269]

Despite his small significance and slight influence at the Ministry of Munitions, at least one of his fellow ministers regarded him as "a dangerously ambitious man." Everyone recognized his enormous potential. Like Krakatau, he was capable of erupting at any moment. But he was also curiously inconsistent. More than any other man he had recognized the folly of the trench deadlock on the western front. His proposed solutions, the Dardanelles and then the tank, had revealed an imaginative genius unique among the belligerent parties on both sides. He sensed that the terrible slaughter of the rising generation could destroy Europe's world hegemony and undo the bonds of the British Empire. Yet he still believed in military glory, still thrilled to the sound of bugles and drums. In the summer of 1918 he could tell a meeting of the Anglo-Saxon Fellowship in London: "I am persuaded that the finest and worthiest moment in the history of Britain was reached on that August night, now nearly four years ago, when we declared war on Germany."[270]

John Squire of the *New Statesman*, a friend of Marsh's, wanted to meet him, and Eddie introduced them in the lounge of the Savoy. Later Squire set down his impressions of Churchill: "He has enormous qualities, especially the primary quality of courage; one defect — the defect of romanticism — or rather, since romanticism may be good, of *sentimentalism.* You don't sum up Russia by calling Lenin a traitor, or by calling munitions workers well-fed malcontents. That is melodrama." Yet, he added, "I have met many politicians; this is the first one who was alive." Squire, a poet and literary critic, had missed the one source of Churchill's political strength which, one feels, he should have identified immediately. It wasn't courage; bravery is common. What distinguished Winston was his remarkable mastery of the language. As he used it, the English tongue was a weapon and a benediction. It fascinated him; he adored it, and could spend hours musing over its charms and the ways to employ it with maximum effect. Gilbert Hall, one of Winston's young pilots, later recalled a dinner at his château: "One could never predict what Mr Churchill would come up with next. During a lull he suddenly, without any warning, uttered the word 'stunt.' 'Stunt,' " he repeated. " 'That's a remarkable word, and it has come to stay.' " He asked each of his guests to define it while he rolled his cigar across the top of his coffee cup. "The cigar," Hall remembered, "was held between the first finger and thumb of each hand and he practiced this untiringly and I think unconsciously for long periods, meanwhile commenting on our efforts to define this wonderful new word 'stunt' that had come over to us from America."[271]

Ludendorff had not abandoned his Flanders dream. He was maneuvering for position, hoping for a *Siegessturm,* a stroke of victory, while Foch, on the other side of no-man's-land, was planning a general offensive. Haig, resentful of being subordinate to a French generalissimo, schemed alone. His relationship with Churchill had improved. Winston's conduct during Ludendorff's March offensive had, in Haig's opinion, proved that he was "a real gun in a crisis." The general intended to use 456 of Churchill's newly arrived tanks east of Amiens on Thursday, August 8, and Winston decided to go over and watch. "We had a very pleasant fly over," he wrote Clementine, "and passed fairly close to Lullenden. I could follow the road through Croyden and Caterham quite easily."[272]

Thick morning mist veiled the tanks, and the British advanced six miles, a spectacular achievement. But the infantry and cavalry — Haig had insisted on sending in horsemen — couldn't keep up with the machines. Here, as on the Somme in 1916 and at Cambrai in 1917, German resistance to the clanking new weapon stiffened and the line re-formed. Churchill, however, was elated. He wrote Lloyd George that the assault had been "a very great success which may well be the precursor of further extremely important events. . . . It seems to me that this is the greatest British victory that has been won in the whole war, and the worst defeat that the German army has yet sustained." He thought Haig should be congratulated. The prime minister disagreed. George believed that the general had lost a golden opportunity: "Had Haig flung his army into the gap created and pursued the broken and demoralised Germans without respite, an even greater victory was within his grasp. When the enemy was scattered and unnerved, and their reserves were not yet up, Haig did not press forward with relentless drive and the Germans were given time to recover and reform their lines."[273]

Both Lloyd George and Churchill were right. Haig had bungled; he wasn't prepared for a breakthrough. Nevertheless, the significance of the tanks' brief breakthrough was profound. "It is a commonplace in military history," writes Isaac Deutscher, Trotsky's biographer, "that there exists a continuity between the closing phase of one war and the opening phase of the next: the weapons and the ideas invented or formed toward the end of one armed conflict dominate the first stage of the next conflict." And the tank attack of August 8, 1918, we now know, was the turning point in the war's last convulsion. Ludendorff later called it "the black day of the German army." It meant that the sacred Hindenburg line had been breached — only briefly, to be sure, but what had happened once could happen again. When the news was brought to Ludendorff's headquarters (situated, ironically, in the Hôtel Britannique), he leapt to his feet and began cursing, not the Allies, but the kaiser, the Reichstag, the German navy, and the civilians on the home front. A. J. P. Taylor notes that the tank assault that Thursday deprived the German strategist of nothing "vital from a strategical point of view." His position was intact, some useless salients had been abandoned, the new trench complex was stronger, and Allied casualties had, as usual, been heavier than those of the defenders. "The real effect," Taylor writes, "was psychological. It shattered the faith in victory which, until that moment, carried the Germans forward. The German soldiers had been told that they were fighting the decisive battle. Now they realized that the decision had gone against them. They no longer wanted to win. They wanted only to end the war." In their great 1918 offensives the Germans had lost 688,000 men. "They were worn down," Churchill said later, "not by Joffre, Nivelle and Haig, but by Ludendorff."[274]

Thus the momentum shifted to the Allies. Slowly their line crept forward. By August 26 the British forces on the Somme had regained all the ground lost in the spring and were back where they had been in Flanders. Churchill, after two weeks in London, flew back to follow the Allied armies. In Ploegsteert, he wrote Clementine, "all my old farms are mere heaps of brick & mouldering sandbags. . . . I missed Ploegsteert's church. We ran past the place where it had stood without recognizing it! My strong dugout however wh I built at Lawrence farm has stood out the whole two years of battering, & is still in use. . . . Otherwise utter ruin." In early September he drove from the Château Verchocq to Paris. "I was alone," he wrote her, "& took the road by Montdidier in order to see the ruin the war has brought on this unlucky town." He drove for an hour "through devastated, shell pitted facias — scraggy shreds of woods — along the road where Clemenceau & I had stood on that melancholy April day when the whole front was quivering & buckling back. Montdidier is a heap of ruins. But bad as it is, it does not reach the utter destruction of Bailleul & Meteren in the North. There the British artillery has been at work — regardless of expense — & nothing but red smears of brickbats mark the site of what was [sic] in the spring thriving townships."[275]

Foch was charting an "arpeggio" of drives against the Hindenburg line. "Everyone is to attack as soon as they can, as strong as they can, for as long as they can," he said, and: *"L'Edifice commence à craquer. Tout le monde à la bataille!"* Actually, it was better organized than that. There was a master plan, and the American army was its fulcrum. Pershing's troops now held ninety-four miles on the extreme right of the Allied line. In the center were the French, with the British to their left and King Albert of Belgium on the sea, leading a combined group which included two American divisions. The main American force, 1.2 million doughboys, would join in the tattoo of attacks, advancing through the deeply fortified Forêt d'Argonne, but their chief strategic task would be to crack the whip, with the Belgians swinging free on the other end. Six weeks of rain, fog, and heavy fighting followed. Then, abruptly, the weather cleared, revealing the trees in their autumnal splendor — coppery, golden, purplish, deep scarlet. The Allies surged forward. "There is no hope," Ludendorff concluded. "All is lost." On the first day of November, the enemy's last scribbly ditches caved in, and four days later the Germans had no front at all. Their rear guard, Sergeant Alexander Woollcott wrote in the *Stars and Stripes,* resembled an escaping man who "twitches down a chair behind him for his pursuers to stumble over."[276] Apart from the stolid German machine gunners, who kept their murderous barrels hot to the end, the Second Reich's soldiers had become a disorderly mob of refugees. Reports from their fatherland were appalling. Ludendorff had been sacked, there was revolution in the streets, and the fleet had mutinied when ordered off on a death-or-glory ride against the

British. Each chill dawn the doughboys, Tommies, and poilus went over the top in fighting kit, driving the frail wraiths in *feldgrau* up against the hills of Belgium and Luxembourg.

Bulgaria had surrendered on September 28 and Turkey on October 21. Austria was next. "A drizzle of empires," Churchill said, was "falling through the air." On October 28 he had been invited to review British soldiers parading in Lille's Grande Place — among the party in the reviewing stand was one Lieutenant Colonel Bernard Law Montgomery, the Forty-second London Division's chief of staff — and he was at his desk in the Metropole on November 10, when Hindenburg advised Berlin that he could no longer guarantee the loyalty of the army and the kaiser fled into Holland. The Eiffel Tower in Paris beamed directions to the enemy's peace envoys, telling them which trenches to approach and where to pick up their guides. That evening Lloyd George invited Churchill to join a special cabinet which would study the implications of the peace. At five o'clock the next morning the German envoys signed Foch's dictated terms in his railroad car at Compiègne. All firing was to cease six hours later. Churchill would recall that full moment: "It was a few minutes before the eleventh hour of the eleventh day of the eleventh month. I stood at the window of my room looking up Northumberland Avenue towards Trafalgar Square, waiting for Big Ben to tell that the War was over." It struck, and he could hear the baying of the crowds outside, but he felt no jubilation. "Scarcely anything which I was taught to believe had lasted," he wrote. "And everything I was taught to believe impossible had happened." Since 1914 Britain had lost 908,371 dead, 2,090,212 wounded, and 191,652 missing. Victory had indeed been "bought so dear as to be indistinguishable from defeat." Then Clementine arrived and proposed that they go to Downing Street and congratulate Lloyd George. Twenty excited revelers, cheering wildly, jumped on their car as it moved slowly through the rejoicing mass. F. E. Smith and Sir Henry Wilson were already with the prime minister. Others joined them. They discussed the advantage of calling an election now, whether or not to intervene in the civil war raging between Red and White Russians, and what peace terms should be presented to Germany. The "fallen foe," Churchill pointed out, was close to starvation. He proposed rushing "a dozen great ships crammed with provisions" to Hamburg. His colleagues eyed him coldly. (That evening Wilson would write in his diary: "LG wants to shoot the Kaiser. Winston does not.")* Out-

* To assure German compliance with the peace terms, the Allied blockade was not lifted until April 1919. Thus Germans continued to starve for five months after Armistice Day.

side, the rapturous demonstrations continued through the afternoon, frolickers romping over the Mall, throwing firecrackers and confetti. Suddenly the weather took an ominous turn. The sky darkened. Rain began to fall, hard. Some Londoners sought refuge in the lap of Queen Victoria's statue, but after huddling there a few minutes they climbed down. They had found little shelter there, and less comfort. The arms were stone cold.[277]

In a Pomeranian military hospital a twice-decorated German noncommissioned dispatch runner, who had been temporarily blinded during a heavy gas attack on the night of October 13, learned of the capitulation from a sobbing pastor. The invalided noncom was still ready to fight, still throbbing with patriotic fervor, but now there would be no more fighting. Six years later the future Führer of the Third Reich set down a description of his reaction in November 1918. Night after night he lay awake, blazing with hatred for those whom he believed responsible for what he considered a betrayal:

Ich wusste, dass alles verloren war. Auf die Gnade des Feindes zu hoffen, konnten höchstens Narren fertigbringen — oder Lügner und Verbrecher. In diesen Nächten wuchs mir der Hass, der Hass gegen die Urheber dieser Tat. . . . Elende und verkommene Verbrecher! Je mehr ich mir in dieser Stunde über das ungeheuer Ereignis klarzuwerden versuchte, um so mehr brannte mir die Scham der Empörung und der Schande in der Stirn. Was war der ganze Schmerz [*meiner*] *Augen gegen diesen Jammer? Was in den Tagen darauf wurde mir auch mein Schicksal bewusst. . . . Ich aber beschloss, Politiker zu werden.*

[I knew that all was lost. Only fools, liars, and criminals could hope for mercy from the enemy. In these nights hatred grew in me, hatred for those responsible for this deed. . . . Miserable and degenerate criminals! The more I tried to achieve clarity on the monstrous event in this hour, the more the shame of indignation and disgrace burned my brow. What was all the pain in my eyes compared to this misery? In the days that followed, my own fate became known to me. . . . I resolved to go into politics.][278]

FIVE

Oxbow

1918–1932

It was with feelings which do not lend themselves to words," Churchill recalled afterward, "that I heard the cheers of the brave people who had borne so much and given all, who had never wavered, who had never lost faith in their country or its destiny, and who could be indulgent to the faults of their servants when the hour of deliverance had come." One simple cheer, a curious eight-word antiphon now locked in the memory of history, was heard that Monday night and throughout the following day wherever London crowds gathered, in Mayfair and Whitechapel, Leicester Square and Regent's Park, Streatham and Harrow-on-the-Hill. It echoed and reechoed, repeated by beaming, tearful, proud, grieving, exultant Britons who rejoiced in the irrefutable evidence that their sacrifices had been redeemed and the Glorious Dead had not, after all, died in vain. Someone in a throng would chant, "Who won the war?" and the rest would roar back, "*We* won the war!" Then once more: "Who won the war?" Again a thundering: "*WE* won the war!" And so it went. Eventually they grew hoarse, and the tedium of it drove them away one by one, until at last all had fallen silent. Nevertheless, every one of them believed it. They actually thought that Britain had won the war.[1]

At dawn's first light on November 21, ten days after the Armistice, the light cruiser H.M.S. *Cardiff* steamed out of Scottish waters flying an enormous blue ensign. Twenty miles out, as prearranged, she rendezvoused with the German High Seas Fleet — the kaiser's titanic armada, most of whose guns hadn't even been fired since 1914: 179 battleships, cruisers, destroyers, submarines, and other vessels, now commanded by Admiral Ludwig von Reuter, who was, that day, the most wretched seaman in Europe. Von Reuter had prayed for cloudy skies to mask his shame, but this was *Kaiserwetter,* clear, if blustery, and very bright. *Car-*

diff led the humiliated enemy vessels back to May Island, in the mouth of the Firth of Forth, where Admiral Sir David Beatty, nineteen subordinate admirals, and 90,000 bluejackets awaited them on the decks of England's Grand Fleet, the greatest concentration of sea power in history. Beatty presided over 370 warships, all of whose crews were at battle stations, their guns trained on their recent foe, their battle flags snapping angrily in the rising wind. The British warships formed two parallel lines, the classic Spithead formation. Thirteen squadrons of capital ships (among them the *Queen Elizabeth,* her role in the Dardanelles forgotten) escorted the defeated fleet into the firth and then ordered it to anchor. "The German flag," Beatty signaled von Reuter, "will be hauled down at sunset today, Thursday, and will not be hoisted again without permission."[2] By dusk swarms of English pleasure boats were festively cruising around the wretched ships of the vanquished *hohe Herr,* hooting and beating buckets with bilge pumps.

Of all the belligerents who had lunged at one another's throats four years earlier, only Britain, it seemed, had emerged strengthened. France's loveliest provinces were a wasteland of denuded earth, barbed wire, and rotting corpses. The Austro-Hungarian dual monarchy was disintegrating. Czarist Russia had ceased to exist. The fallen Second Reich, founded by Bismarck, was racked by strife and a proliferation of *Femen,* or political assassins — Hans Kohn called this frightening new phenomenon "the sudden brutalization of German political life" — and for the next quarter century its menace would darken all Europe.[3] England's enormous prewar wealth was gone, but its factories were intact, its armed forces had never been mightier, and although England owed the United States five billion dollars in war debts, its continental allies were indebted to it for far more than that. At the Versailles peace conference Britain could, in effect, cast six votes because Canada, South Africa, Australia, New Zealand, and India, all separately represented, supported the Mother Country on most issues. Woodrow Wilson's resistance to territorial acquisitions, and his insistence upon self-determination, was ingeniously met by the creation of the League of Nations mandates. Allied flags flew over these possessions, but, diplomats told the President with straight faces, they were not really annexations because ultimately — no one knew just when — they would become independent. Thus the Empire emerged from the Hall of Mirrors swollen by 988,000 square miles of new territory, inhabited by 13,000,000 people, many of whom had not even known a war was being fought. The Union Jack now flew over German New Guinea, South-West Africa, Tanganyika, parts of Togoland and Cameroon, more than a hundred German islands wrenched from the kaiser, and the Middle Eastern lands which later became Iraq, Iran, Jordan, and Israel. Rhodes's dream of a Cape-to-Cairo corridor had been achieved at last.

Best of all, for those who cherished old customs, the King-Emperor's expansion could be attributed to his Royal Navy, which, as the "Senior Service," had been England's original instrument of imperial growth. The army had done the dying, but even before the Versailles treaty (or *Diktat,* as the resentful Germans called it) Britons knew that trench warfare had been futile. It was the Grand Fleet which had blockaded the enemy, starving them into surrender. So tradition had triumphed after all. Englishmen liked that. They were proud of their eccentricities, even the dowdiness of their women's fashions and the odd customs of taking long hikes in the wet, bathing in cold water, flinging open windows in winter, deferring to bowler-hatted retired officers with bristling white mustaches, and driving on what was, for most of the world's motorists, the wrong side of the street. As R. H. Tawney put it, " 'Back to 1914' became a common cry." Some wanted to go even farther back. On the eve of the war sophisticated Englishmen had felt uneasy about Britain's hegemony. But as Churchill's Harrow schoolmate Leo Amery told Lloyd George after Armistice Day, if the Empire grew mightier after the valor of its youth, "Who has the right to complain?"[4]

The Empire had flourished on certitude and myth. "It is the virtue of the Englishman," Goldsworthy Lowes Dickinson had written in 1913, "that he never doubts. That is what the system does for him." Englishmen treasured chivalric legends. In 1912 London children, and many who were no longer children, had packed the Savoy Theatre to see *Where the Rainbow Ends,* an improbable play about two innocents, brother and sister. They are threatened by a Dragon King. Enter Saint George. He seems inadequate: silver-haired and obscured by a billowing cloak. Then the girl says tremulously: "I am an English maiden in danger, and I ask for your aid." Instantly, the cloak disappears and we behold a knight in dazzling armor, a great red cross on his breastplate and his hand on the hilt of a glittering Excalibur. The Dragon King boasts of degrading the British ("I flung my gold dust in the people's eyes and lulled them into false security"), but Saint George reminds Britons of their duty to "fight aggression and foul tyranny." As the end of the last act approaches he cries to the playgoers: "Rise, Youth of England, let your voices ring / For God, for Britain, and for Britain's King!" They then stand and join the cast in singing "God Save the King."[5]

The pull of such lore retained its power, on the home front at least, while the men in the trenches were fighting a very different struggle. At Mons, it was said, an angel had led lost Tommies to safety. The *Evening News* of September 29, 1914, had carried a poem by Arthur Machen, "The Bowmen." In it an embattled British soldier about to be overwhelmed by waves of enemy infantry remembers and repeats Saint George's motto: *Adsit Anglis Sanctus Georgius,* which he once saw on a plate in a London restaurant. Suddenly he hears "a great voice" calling: "St. George! St. George! . . . St. George for Merrie England!" Simultaneously, the attacking "grey men" begin "falling by thousands." They have been shot by Agincourt bowmen in the sky. No sooner had Machen's poem appeared than dispatches from France and Belgium began reporting dead Germans slain by arrows. As late as 1917, when, one would think, the truth about the war ought to have been evident to everyone, Henry Newbolt ("Play up! Play up! and play the game!") published his *Book of the Happy Warrior,* full of chivalric fables about the events across the Channel, and E. B. Osborn brought out *The Muse in Arms,* in which he explained the gaiety of British soldiers going into action: "The Germans, and even our Allies, cannot understand why this stout old nation persists in thinking of war as sport; they do not know that sportsmanship is our new homely name, derived from a racial predilection for comparing great things with small, for the *chevaleries* of the Middle Ages." Today this sounds inane, but it had some basis in fact. In at least two offensives British soldiers went over the top dribbling soccer balls across no-man's-land. One occurred on July 11, 1916, when Captain W. P. Nevill and his company of the East Surrey Regiment booted a ball back and forth as they advanced along the Somme. Nevill and most of his men were killed in less than an hour. Ineluctably they inspired a poem:[6]

On through the heat of slaughter
Where gallant comrades fall
Where blood is poured like water
They drive the trickling ball
The fear of death before them
Is but an empty name
True to the land that bore them
The Surreys play the game.

It is outrageous, it is preposterous, and to a later generation it is completely baffling. What *game,* in the name of God, were the Surreys playing? Ah, but they knew, and that was enough for them. Being mythical, that knowledge was imperishable, and its vitality was still strong on that sunlit morning when Beatty received the surrender of von Reuter's fleet. As the German warships approached the Firth of Forth, the British crew on the battleship *Royal Oak* heard a mysterious drumbeat coming from the lower decks. It was audible on the bridge. Twice officers dispatched bluejackets to investigate. They found nothing, but the drum continued to roll until the enemy's anchor chains ran out. The next day's newspapers carried Newbolt's old poem *Drake's Drum:*

Take my drum to England, hang et by the shore,
Strike et when your powder's runnin' low;
If the Dons sight Devon, I'll quit the port o' Heaven,
And drum them up the Channel as we drummed them long ago.

Seven months later, on a prearranged signal from Admiral von Reuter, German crews pulled the sea cocks of his 10 battleships, 9 armored cruisers, 8 large cruisers, 50 torpedo boats, and 102 submarines, sending them to the bottom while the horrified, helpless British officers and ratings looked on. Among those witnessing this extraordinary event was a party of schoolchildren on an excursion from Stromness in the Orkneys. Being children, they thought the show was for them. It was. It was for everybody — a defiant gesture declaring that Germany had surrendered but had not quit. In Berlin, Ludendorff, dining with Major General Sir Neill Malcolm, the chief of Britain's military mission in Berlin, explained in his tumescent, inarticulate way that his home front had let him down. "Do you mean," asked Malcolm, "that you were stabbed in the back?" Ludendorff pounced. "Stabbed in the back?" he repeated. "Yes, that's exactly it. We were stabbed in the back [*Dolchstoss in den Rücken*]." Hindenburg heard the phrase from him and testified before a political committee of inquiry: "As an English general has very truly said, the German Army was stabbed in the back." Stabbed by whom? Presently an answer emerged: the hilt of the dagger had been held by the Jews.[7]

The British were very cross with von Reuter. His conduct, they felt, had been most unsportsmanlike, and doubtless there were those who expected retribution from the angel of Mons, Saint George, the Agincourt bowmen, or the footballers of the Somme. If they felt chagrined, so, for very different reasons, did His Majesty's diplomats in Versailles, the following week, when the peace treaty was signed. They were satisfied with their spoils of war but departed feeling somehow diminished in the eyes of the civilized world. Lloyd George, they had assumed, would dominate the conference. In the words of a contemporary, he was regarded as the "one statesman in England who counted." And Winston was almost as familiar to the British public as his chief. Robert Rhodes James has left us a vivid portrait of Churchill at this time: "Much of the early aggressiveness has been softened by age and experience. In manner he remains alert, thrusting, eager, or in sharp contrast fitting his mood, somber, portentous, and scowling with leaden responsibility. . . . His dedication to his career is total, even obsessive. Experience has not dimmed the originality of his mind, nor the intensity of his emotions, nor the volubility of his conversation."[8]

Churchill saw Versailles as "grimly polished and trellised with live wires" over which the British prime minister repeatedly tripped. He tried, but failed, to dilute Clemenceau's draconian demands upon the Germans. Lloyd George's support of President Wilson's proposal for a League of Nations was — to Churchill's deep disappointment — uncharacteristically tepid. The fact is that George was jealous of Wilson. The austere President was upstaging him. A weary Europe found the American's earnest idealism fresh and stirring. The center of Sir William Orpen's painting of the signing ceremony features Lloyd George, surrounded by an Australian, a Canadian, an Afrikaner, a turbaned Indian, Balfour, Curzon, and Milner. "But somehow the eye strays," wrote James Morris, to "the stiff ascetic person of President Wilson: for he is looking directly, deliberately, at the artist, with an almost accusatory expression, as though he is staring hard into the future, and willing it his way." Lloyd George distrusted the President, and with good reason, for the Wilsonian doctrine of self-determination — the right of a people to decide their own political status — was a threat to the very survival of imperialism. Indeed, the Empire delegations, led by Australia's mercurial Prime Minister W. M. Hughes, narrowly defeated a clause in the League Covenant, proposed by Japan, which would have declared that all races were inherently equal. Hughes, a fellow Welshman, was Lloyd George's natural ally. Besides, Australia had its eye on German archipelagoes in the Pacific. Wilson, offended, asked Hughes if he really meant to defy world opinion by a naked grab for colonies. The feisty Australian replied: "That's about the size of it, Mr. President." Thus the emergence of the Third World debuted on the international stage as a moral issue. It would be crowded into the wings again and again, only to reappear cast in ever larger roles, to the exasperation and dismay of, among others, Winston Churchill.[9]

Almost unnoticed among the miles of Union Jacks in the Firth of Forth on the day of von Reuter's surrender had been a little squadron of six warships flying the Stars and Stripes. When the Admiralty signaled Beatty that morning, affirming that the enemy's capitulation "will remain for all time the example of the wonderful silence and sureness with which sea power attains its end," it meant *British* sea power.[10] The Royal Navy's treatment of its American cousins had been patronizing and at times even rude, but one of the first signs that England's *belle époque* was ending appeared in a naval agreement, reached in Washington after the Versailles signing, which would have been unthinkable before the war. At the turn of the century England had been spending almost twice as much on its navy as any other country. Its policy, followed by both parties, had kept its fleet strength at a level greater than that of any other two nations combined. Now England consented to observe the ratio of 5 (Great Britain), 5 (United States), 3 (Japan), 1.75 (France), and 1.75 (Italy). Imperial warship designs were discarded; the agreement stipulated the size and type of every vessel. There would never be another *Queen Elizabeth.* After the pact, the Royal Navy was required to scrap 657 ships, including dreadnoughts, battleships, and cruisers — much of the Grand Fleet's backbone. The Admiralty pledged itself never to build a naval base at Hong Kong. England's absolute command of the seas, so vital to the Empire, was over. Britannia no longer ruled the waves, not because world opinion objected, but because, having spent £5,000,000 a day during the war, it simply couldn't afford to.

It is impossible to pinpoint the beginning of imperial decline. In a sense eventual freedom became inevitable the moment a British possession was conquered, because Britain selectively extended its institutions into its colonies with the establishment of legislative councils, later to become parliaments. In the beginning this happened only in colonies dominated by white settlers. Canada became a self-governing federation in 1867 and imposed a tariff on British imports the following year. Gladstone's cabinet was outraged, but the GOM pointed out that if you grant people rights, you must expect them to flex their new muscles, however disagreeable the consequences. Self-government then came to Australia in 1901, to New Zealand in 1907, and, in 1910, to South Africa.

As early as the 1880s, farsighted members of England's ruling class, seeing where all this would lead, expressed alarm that Free Trade and self-government would end in the "dismemberment" of the Empire. To stop it, they founded the Imperial Federation League in 1884. Rhodes, Milner, Rosebery, and Joseph Chamberlain gave the league their heartiest support. Chamberlain, who had admired Bismarck's skill in uniting the former German states for commercial and military ends without sacrificing the autonomy of the Second Reich, proposed a British imperial defense league, patterned on the Reich's Kriegsverein, and a customs union along the lines of Bismarck's Zollverein. However, the Empire's self-governing colonies — now coming to be called Dominions — were not interested. They came to London for imperial conferences and loyally knelt before the throne, but when they declared war on the Central Powers in 1914, each of their prime ministers was careful to point out that his government was making its own decision, not following London's instructions, whatever constitutional theorists might say. After the war, thoughtful men in Whitehall realized that the United States and the USSR would eventually dominate *Weltpolitik*. They tried to press the cause of imperial federation, in the hope that all countries flying the Union Jack might combine to form a third superpower.

Gradually, however, they realized that they were playing upon a losing wicket. The Washington treaty was but one of several omens. India having supported the war effort, India's politicians now demanded a quid pro quo. Their leaders, some of them educated in English public schools, infuriated the British establishment by quoting Burke and Macaulay in support of the demands for immediate parliamentary self-government. They didn't get it, but their contribution of a million men and £500,000,000 to the war effort could not go unrecognized. A resolution introduced by Lloyd George in 1917, and then passed by Parliament in 1919, proved to be the first step toward Indian independence. Before 1914 both the resolution and the Washington naval treaty would have meant the fall of the government. Now press and public seemed indifferent. H. G. Wells estimated that 95 percent of England's population was as ignorant of the Empire as of the Italian Renaissance. Both the Colonial Office and the Indian Civil Service marked a sharp drop in the number and quality of their applicants. In large measure this was a consequence of the recent slaughter. The war had left 160,000 young English widows and 300,000 fatherless children. The flower of England's youth, its university students and recent graduates, had joined Kitchener's armies and crossed to France, most of them as infantry lieutenants. The number of those who fell is incalculable, but some figures are suggestive. In his mindless Passchendaele offensive, Haig lost 22,316 junior officers, compared to only 6,913 Germans of similar rank. We shall never know how many potential prime ministers, cabinet ministers, poets, scientists, physicians, lawyers, professors, and distinguished civil servants perished in the mud of France and Belgium, but the conclusion is inescapable: an entire generation had lost most of its ablest men. Those who survived, like Anthony Eden, of the King's Royal Rifle Corps, gassed on the Somme, and thrice-wounded Harold Macmillan of the Grenadier Guards, who had studied Horace by candlelight in his dugout, emerged with a weltanschauung which was incomprehensible to their fathers.

Part of the loss of brio may be attributed to the lack of heroes. Chivalric myth required heroic leaders. The reading public now had to settle for the thin fictional gruel of Bulldog Drummond and Richard Hanney. The war had produced no Marlboroughs, Wellingtons, Nelsons, or Gordons.

Kitchener was a tarnished legend. Only the young archaeologist T. E. Lawrence, whose achievements as a colonel in the Middle East were genuine, had a postwar following. Victory had eluded Jellicoe at Jutland, the war's only major naval engagement, because, out of excessive caution, he had evaded three crucial decisions. All the British generals had been discredited, with consequences which reached far beyond the British Isles. Before the war, the Empire's overseas subjects had regarded England with affection and respect. Young Mahatma Gandhi, who had struggled up Spion Kop as a stretcher-bearer that night when Churchill was frantically rushing from colonel to colonel, trying to save the hill from the Boers — Gandhi had been decorated for his bravery afterward — later wrote of his anglophilia then: "Hardly ever have I known anyone to cherish such loyalty as I did to the British Constitution. . . . I vied with Englishmen in loyalty to the throne." In 1914, James Morris wrote, "the white colonials had gone to war trustingly, innocently almost, satisfied for the most part to be loyal assistants to the Mother Country. They had been inexperienced still, as soldiers and as statesmen, and they were as indoctrinated as the British at home in their ingenuous respect for British traditions and achievements. Though they often made fun of the British, their toffs, their drawls and their domesticity, they still looked up to the Old Country, and believed as the British did themselves in the value of its systems and the skill of its leaders."[11]

At the time of the Somme, when the fate of civilization seemed to hang in the balance, Australian boys at Melbourne's Scotch College wept when they sang the stanzas of "Bugles of England." The legend of Saint George was as revered in Durban and Ottawa as in London. Proud of their membership in the Empire, the colonials assumed that the graduates of Sandhurst were the finest officers in the world. In the trenches they learned otherwise. The Australians learned to despise both Major General Alexander Godley, who at Gallipoli had led them ashore, not to a beach, but to the base of a cliff, and Ian Hamilton, who, when they asked to be evacuated, had replied: "You have got through the difficult business, now you have only to dig, dig, dig, until you are safe." In self-mockery the survivors called themselves "diggers" and made ribald jokes about British redtabs. Godley, they said, "couldn't find the balls on a bull." Some of the wittiest wartime scatology ever written was inspired by Louisa Godley, the general's wife, who visited wounded New Zealanders in an Egyptian hospital and complained that they had insulted her by not lying at attention.[12]

The Canadians were also disillusioned. On Easter Sunday, 1917, on Vimy Ridge, they had won the reputation of being the finest soldiers on the western front. Haig wasted them, of course; his lethal hand struck down everything it touched. But he also slighted them. He described a delegation of visiting Canadians, including their minister of war, as a "well-meaning but second-rate sort of people." Indeed, he let it be known that in his judgment all "colonial generals" were "ignorant and conceited." Australians and New Zealanders, he said, were likely to desert at the first opportunity. He made it a point to keep them separated from British divisions, explaining to his staff that they would exert "a bad influence." It was probably impossible to deepen the contempt of Irish Catholics for the British, but Kitchener had a try at it, issuing orders that under no circumstances would Catholics be permitted to fight under their own officers.[13]

By Armistice Day the image of the Mother Country in its greatest possessions had been irretrievably altered, although there was little understanding of this in London. Someone in the royal household — it is impossible to trace the source — thought it a splendid idea for the King's four sons to reign over the four Dominions. The question was raised in Ottawa, Canberra, Wellington, and Cape Town; then quietly shelved. The Empire's five additional votes at Versailles had been misunderstood. They were a sign, not of imperial unity, but of the Dominions' independence. As early as 1917 their four prime ministers, meeting in London, had resolved that when the fighting ended they must have an "adequate voice in [imperial] foreign policy and in foreign relations." Jan Christiaan Smuts, South Africa's next premier, even called them "autonomous nations." British omniscience had been exposed as a fraud. They were less willing to accept decisions made in Whitehall and Westminster, though the tug was still strong; when the first summons came, they wavered, awed by the momentous decision to defy parental authority. The test came shortly over an incident in Turkey, and here, as so often in the making of British history during his life, Churchill, then at the Colonial Office, was right in the middle of it. He sent an "inquiry" to the Dominions, asking whether they were prepared, if the need arose, to send troops to the troubled area. *The Times* was offended. This, said its editorial, was a typical example of Winston's lack of good judgment; imperial possessions weren't asked, they were *told*. "Although the Dominions may speak with many voices for themselves as individuals," its leader declared, "they speak as one when the time comes to speak for the Empire." But they didn't. They spoke as many. Only New Zealand and Newfoundland meekly complied. The Australians agreed under protest. The South Africans refused. "Very important questions of policy would be involved as far as the Union is concerned," Smuts cabled, "by any decision of the

Union Government to take part in military operations in Eastern Europe and it is felt by the Union Government that such a step should not be taken without calling Parliament together." The Canadian prime minister, Mackenzie King, took the same stand. King fully understood the implications of his response, but in his diary he wrote: "If membership in the British Empire means participation by the Dominions in any and every war in which Great Britain becomes involved, I can see no hope for an enduring relationship."[14]

As it turned out, the men weren't needed, but the precedent had been set. The King's statesmen brooded. Most of his British subjects, however, gave the issue neither first nor second thought. Imperialism, so thrilling a creed only a few years earlier, had lost its charisma. They simply didn't care. The young in particular were more concerned with finding a home and a steady job. Labour, now the most exciting of the parties, was either indifferent toward the Empire or downright hostile. Newspapers found that events in England's far-flung possessions bored their readers. "Back to 1914"? They wanted no part of it. The chairman of the Empire Day Committee acknowledged that Britons were simply incurious about the "many dark corners where the rays of our Empire sun have not been able to penetrate." Philip Guedalla discovered that in the early 1920s the doctrine of Imperialism attracted merely "a dim interest [among] research students."[15] Intellectuals jeered at values *fin de siècle* Britain had held sacred. Lytton Strachey's sardonic, sniggering *Eminent Victorians* was an immediate success when it appeared in 1918. His next book, *Queen Victoria,* which presented its subject as a trivial, quirky woman, became required reading in universities between the wars. And the generals, who had seemed mighty only yesterday, were left to the merciless pens of cartoonists.

Sometimes a social event, wholly divorced from political considerations and affairs of state, can illumine the mood of a time. In this sense, the British Empire Exhibition at Wembley is immensely instructive about the temper of postwar England. Assembled at the terminus of the London underground railway at a cost of £4,000,000, it dwarfed Britain's last great fair, the Crystal Palace. Pavilions celebrated the genius of the imperial peoples, the fair managers enlisted Kipling to acclaim imperial glory, and Edward Elgar provided the music, which largely comprised various renditions of his "Land of Hope and Glory." Tibetan trumpeters blew bugle calls. The tomb of Tutankhamen was reconstructed, he being, as W. S. Gilbert would have put it, a sort of British ancestor by purchase. Visitors traveling on the exhibition's Never-Stop Railway passed beneath thousands of massed Union Jacks, and Lord Milner expressed the conviction that Wembley would prove a "powerful bulwark" against subversives who would undermine the Empire. The King himself went on the radio to hawk its attractions. ("This great achievement reveals to us the whole Empire in little. . . .") The exhibition, solemnly conceived, should have reaffirmed Britain's confidence in its imperial destiny.[16]

It didn't. It became a joke. The most popular feature had been lifted from an American carnival. "I've brought you here to see the wonders of the Empire," a Noel Coward character told his children, "and all you want to do is go to the Dodgems." P. G. Wodehouse's Bertie Wooster drawled: "I mean to say, millions of people, no doubt, are so constituted that they scream with joy and excitement at the spectacle of a stuffed porcupine fish or a glass jar of seeds from Western Australia — but not Bertram. . . . By the time we had tottered out of the Gold Coast Village and were looking towards the Palace of Machinery, everything pointed to my shortly executing a quiet sneak in the direction of that rather jolly Planters' Bar in the West Indies section." The intellectuals of Bloomsbury and Hampstead, solidly anti-imperialist, organized a group called the WGTW, the Won't Go To Wembleys. Mayfair's Bright Young Things, soon to find their minstrel in Evelyn Waugh, treated it, James Morris wrote, "as a spree." They performed naughty acts in the Nigerian Handicrafts Exhibition — "Did you Wemble?" they slyly asked one another, and if you nodded it meant you had performed a lewd act under the eyes of the wogs — after which the bobbies usually released them, because the boys bore patrician names and so many of the naked girls turned out to be widows of the Glorious Dead. "A great empire and little minds," Edmund Burke had said in 1775, "go ill together." Now T. S. Eliot wrote: "I had not thought death had undone so many."[17]

Churchill watched all this and grieved. In the notes for a speech to his constituents he wrote: "What a disappointment the twentieth century has been. How terrible & how melancholy is long series of disastrous events wh have darkened its first 20 years. We have seen in ev country a dissolution, a weakening of those bonds, a challenge to those principles, a decay of faith, an abridgement of hope on wh structure & ultimate existence of civilized society depends. . . . Can you doubt, my faithful friends, as you survey this sombre panorama, that mankind is passing through a period marked not only by an enormous destruction & abridgement of human species, not only by a vast impoverishment & reduction in means of existence but also that destructive tendencies have not yet run their course?'"[18]

Honor, as he understood it, seemed dead in England, and gone with it were innocence, rationalism, optimism, and the very concept of an ordered society. He asked almost pathetically: "Why should war be the only purpose capable of uniting us? All for war — nothing is too good for war. Why cannot we have some of it for peace?" An age, the age he had adored, appeared to have reached journey's end, and journeys no longer ended in lovers meeting. The government seemed to need, not diplomats, but economists, of whom he knew almost nothing. The disposition of the British public was a backlash against everything he cherished, and he found that hard to bear. "I was," he wrote, "a child of the Victorian era, when the structure of our country seemed firmly set, when its position in trade and on the seas was unrivalled, and when the realisation of the greatness of our Empire and of our duty to preserve it was growing ever stronger." Now that was threatened, and threatened from within. He reflected that the "shadow of victory is disillusion. The reaction from extreme effort is prostration. The aftermath even of successful war is long and bitter." These, he realized, would be years of "turbulence and depression." But he would soldier on. Surely the great imperial strengths, tradition and continuity, could not be long denied. Eventually the tide would turn. He was certain of it. It never crossed his mind that the ebb might be permanent — that he and all he cherished would, in the end, be stranded forever.[19]

He continued to think of the Empire as an "old lion, with her lion cubs by her side," and while he could shrug off the Stracheys and the Wodehouses and the WGTW as temporary abhorrences — he could never have accepted the Wembley circus as a metaphor for imperial majesty anyhow — he was deeply angered by any retreat from the distant frontiers of what he regarded as Britain's rightful realms. When Curzon supported Milner's recommendations for Egyptian sovereignty, Winston passed him a note: "It leaves me absolutely baffled why you shd be on this side, or why you shd have insisted on keeping Egyptian affairs in yr hands" — Curzon had been an able imperial administrator as viceroy of India (1898–1905) and foreign secretary (1919–1921) — "only to lead to this melancholy conclusion. It grieves me profoundly to see what is unfolding." In a City of London speech on November 4, 1920, he sounded paranoid, hinting at a sinister "world-wide conspiracy against our country, designed to deprive us of our place in the world and rob us of victory." He did not see how, in the long run, such a plot could succeed: "Having beaten the most powerful military empire in the world, having emerged triumphantly from the fearful struggle of Armageddon, we should not allow ourselves to be pulled down and have our Empire disrupted by a malevolent and subversive force, the rascals and rapscallions of mankind . . . now on the move against us. Whether it be the Irish murder gang, or the arch-traitors we had at home, they should feel the weight of the British arm. It was strong enough to break the Hindenburg line; it will be strong enough to defend the main interests of the British people."[20]

Confronted by foes, he was always like this: galloping, mud-spattered, high in oath. But once a foe was down, he sprang from his saddle and extended a helping hand. Had Arthur reappeared in modern Britain, Churchill would have been his Galahad. It is not without significance that he loved round tables and always had at least one in each of his several homes. His faith in gallantry ran deep. Years later he told his physician how, at the end of an engagement on the western front, when one of his tank crews had to surrender to the enemy, the Germans saluted them and complimented them on their valiant fight. He smiled. He said: "That is how I like war to be conducted." Even in the last weeks of 1918, when the popular slogans were "Hang the Kaiser!" and "Squeeze them till the pips squeak!" he repeated his watchwords: "In victory, magnanimity; in peace, goodwill." He agreed with the Germans that the Versailles terms had been dictated by the victors; he would have preferred a negotiated settlement. "I was all for war," he told Bernard Baruch when they met. "Now I'm all for peace." In a long memorandum to himself he concluded that both sides had been guilty of atrocities unprecedented in war between civilized states. Germany had been "in the van," but had been "followed step by step" by Britain, France, and their allies. "Every outrage against humanity or international law," he wrote, "was repaid by reprisals — often of a greater scale and of longer duration" than Germany's. "No truce or parley mitigated the strife of the armies. The wounded died between the lines: the dead mouldered into the soil. Merchant ships and neutral ships and hospital ships were sunk on the seas and all on board left to their fate, or killed as they swam. Every effort was made to starve whole nations into submission without regard to age or sex. Cities and monuments were smashed by artillery. Bombs from the air were cast down indiscriminately. Poison gas in many forms stifled or seared the soldiers. Liquid fire was projected upon their bodies. Men fell from the air in flames, or were smothered often slowly in the dark recesses of the sea. The fighting strength of armies was limited only by the manhood of their countries. . . . Torture and Cannibalism were the only two expedients that the civilised scientific Christian States had been able to deny themselves: and these were of doubtful utility." Nor had the Armistice ended it. Relief for the prostrate nations was wholly inadequate. All they were accomplishing, he told a friend, was the return of victims "again and again to the shambles. Nothing is wasted that can contribute to the process of waste."[21]

It is a sign of Churchill's stature as a politician that what he wrote in private, and said to friends, he repeated from the platform when campaigning for office. Immediately after the Armistice, Lloyd George called England's second khaki election of the century. Winston told his constituents that the Germans must be clothed, sheltered, and fed, that the triumphant Allies ought not "to be drawn into extravagances by the fullness of their victory." He particularly deplored staggering reparations. Immediately James K. Foggie, a leading Dundee Liberal, wrote him: "I think the great card to play & one which will give you a huge victory, is that you declare, 'that Germany must pay this country & the other allied Nations, all expenses caused by the War.' Germany started the War, & has been defeated, therefore it stands to reason she must pay. Had Germany beaten our Empire she certainly without doubt, would have made us pay all expenses. Dundee will stand for nothing else. Dundee has given over 30,000 soldiers. Almost 20% . . . have been killed." Doubtless Foggie spoke for an overwhelming majority of the Dundee electorate, but Churchill wouldn't budge. As it happened, it didn't matter. Lloyd George's timing had been precise. The coalition was swept back into office — though the Tories had outpolled the Liberals for the first time in thirteen years, and Labour strength was growing.[22]

Winston had been reelected by what his bitterest adversary in the constituency, the Tory Dundee *Advertiser,* called the "immense majority" of 15,365. Clearly he was entitled to a more prestigious cabinet post. His stubborn courage in adversity since Gallipoli, his capacity for taxing work, his brilliance and force — all argued strongly against extending his exclusion from the government's highest councils. He wanted to return to the Admiralty but realized that was impolitic. The War Office was available, however; Milner was moving to the Colonial Office. Winston's critics trembled at the prospect of entrusting military decisions to him again. Leo Amery wrote the prime minister: "Don't put Churchill in the War Office. I hear from all sorts of quarters that the Army are terrified at the idea." The *Daily Mail* and *Morning Post* echoed Amery's warning, but nothing could have given Lloyd George greater pleasure than dismaying the men responsible for the Somme and Passchendaele. On January 9, 1919, he relieved his minister of munitions, whose desk at the

Metropole had long been cleared anyway, and invested him with twin portfolios. Churchill was now secretary of state for war and air.[23]

He inherited an army crisis. The vast mass of the troops were civilians who had signed up for the duration. They wanted their discharges as soon as possible. Of the 3.5 million men under arms, fewer than a third would be needed for armies of occupation in Germany and the Middle East. A majority, therefore, were eligible to return home as soon as transport could be arranged. The difficulty lay in deciding who should go first. Senior officers, whose temporary rank depended upon the size of their commands, were in no hurry to expedite the process. Milner had established a system under which priority was assigned to "key men" in industry. But these blue-collar workers, by the very fact of their indispensability, had been among the last to be called up; many had not been drafted until the manpower crisis of the previous March. Now they were being released from the service while volunteers who had fought in the trenches for four years remained there. In the week before Churchill moved into Whitehall, soldiers had rioted in Dover and Folkestone, demanding immediate demobilization. Two days later Milner had issued new regulations under which only men with job offers could be discharged. This left three million Tommies with no prospect of an early return to civilian life, and their mood was ugly. On Winston's first day in his new office he was handed a telegram from Haig, reporting a rapid deterioration of army morale under the latest rules. Proof of it lay in London, within earshot of the War Office. A mob of insubordinate Tommies had gathered on the Horse Guards Parade, waving seditious signs. Had they but known it, that was the last way to win concessions from Churchill. He called in a group of anxious officers and asked them: "How many troops have we got to deal with them?" A battalion of guards, he was told, and three squadrons of the Household Cavalry. "Are they loyal?" he inquired. The officers replied that they hoped so. He asked: "Can you arrest the mutineers?" They were uncertain but had no other suggestions. He said: "Then arrest the mutineers." He watched from his window while the demonstrators, deflated, permitted the guards to surround them and then lead them away.[24]

By now reports of barracks disturbances were arriving from commanding officers in France, Flanders, Mesopotamia, Palestine, Greece, and Italy. Haig warned that unless the stampede was stopped, "the Germans will be in a position to negotiate another kind of peace." Churchill was more worried about the impact upon the Bolsheviks, in Moscow and Saint Petersburg, who were calling for uprisings by soldiers all over the world. There were Communist agitators in Britain, too, particularly around military and air bases. Sir Henry Wilson noted in his diary that the new war minister directed him to bring home "all reliable troops, i.e. Household & other Cavalry, Yeomanry, Home County Rgts: etc." At the same time Winston decided that no men would be mustered out who had fought less than two years in France; eligibility for discharge would be determined by age, length of service, and wounds. But young conscripts would still be needed to police the new territories being absorbed by the Empire. No one liked compulsory service — until three years earlier the country had never known any form of conscription, even in wartime — but there was no alternative. Since Lloyd George was at Versailles, the cabinet had to act in his absence. After consulting Austen Chamberlain, the new chancellor of the Exchequer, Churchill drew up plans for an army to garrison the British Zone in occupied Germany. The War Cabinet approved and advised George of its action. An announcement was prepared. By the time it was released to the press, Wilson wrote in his diary, "the great adventure of 'compulsing' a million men in time of peace to serve abroad will have begun." In his view it came in the nick of time, because "all our power over the Army is slipping away."[25]

Britons accustomed to wartime regimentation accepted the extension of conscription, partly because the new demobilization scheme seemed fair. In the meantime, however, Milner's old regulations had kindled a major revolt in Calais, where five thousand Tommies, newly arrived from England, demanded that they be returned home immediately. Haig reported to Winston that their attitude was "threatening, insubordinate, and mutinous." At his direction, he said, General Henry G. Sandilands sent a brigade with fixed bayonets into their camp and arrested the three ringleaders. He wanted them executed; otherwise, he believed, "the discipline of the whole Army will suffer, both immediately & for many years to come." Churchill disagreed. Execution, Winston wrote, "should be used only under what may be called life and death conditions, and public opinion will only support it when other men's lives are endangered by criminal or cowardly conduct." The field marshal spared the three men, but he was incensed by what he regarded as civilian meddling. He noted in his diary that he had the "power by Warrant" to put men before firing squads without consulting the War Office. His days of wielding such power were numbered, however. Parliament awarded him £100,000 and made him an earl, but the historians were beginning to catch up with Douglas Haig. Lesser generals were appointed to lofty civilian roles: governor-general of Canada, high commissioner for Egypt, high commissioner for Palestine, governor of Malta, offices in the Indian Empire. London never summoned Haig from his retirement in Scotland. Forgotten and ignored, he died of a heart attack in 1928.[26]

By the end of January, 1919, some 980,000 soldiers had been repatriated, and eight months after assuming office, Churchill had reduced Britain's military expenditures by nearly 70 percent. Britain's army, he said, had "melted away." The demobilization had been a triumph of organization, but it left him uneasy. England, he believed, now needed a large standing army. Postwar Europe had become dangerous. In the spring some 70,000 of Ludendorff's former troops, marching under the banner of the Rote Soldatenbund (Red Soldiers' League), had seized a cache of arms in Bochum, defeated a right-wing *Freikorps* in a pitched battle, and occupied six Ruhr cities, proclaiming workers' republics in each. Under Versailles the Ruhr was out-of-bounds to German and Allied troops, but Berlin sent in troops of the Reichswehr, the Weimar Republic's army, and suppressed the revolt; rebels were tried before *Freikorpskämpfer* military courts and shot. Britain, Italy, and the United States approved the Reichswehr action, but the French, infuriated by this invasion of the "neutral" Ruhr, countered by occupying four German towns. In Paris, Winston discussed the incident with André Lefevre, the French minister of war. He told him that France had "committed a grave error in tactics and had lost far more in prestige and authority than they had gained." The present threat to Western civilization, he said, was not German militarism; it was bolshevism. By now the Ruhr was quiet. The Rote Soldatenbund having been shattered, both Berlin and Paris withdrew their troops. Churchill's anxiety over the spread of communism did not fade, however. Years later Bernard Baruch wrote him recalling one day in Paris, when the Versailles talks were in progress and the two of them "were walking through the Bois de Boulogne, talking of the problems which burdened a world exhausted by war and groping for peace." A wind had risen; the sky was darkening; Baruch expressed concern about the weather. His letter continued: "Suddenly you broke your brisk stride, paused and, lifting your walking stick, pointed to the East. Your voice rumbled ominously: 'Russia! Russia! That's where the weather is coming from!' "[27]

In the spring of 1918, when Ludendorff was plunging his bloody fists into the Allied line in France and Belgium, the Bolsheviks in central

Russia stood naked to invasion. And no regime, not even Napoleon's, had ever been threatened by more formidable enemies. Led by the czar's professional officers, over 300,000 "White" Russians, loyal to the Romanovs, were forming armies on the Reds' five-thousand-mile front — over ten times the length of the western front. On December 30, 1917, Japan had become the first foreign country to intervene in Russia's internal struggle, landing troops at Vladivostok in Siberia. Two battalions of Tommies from Hong Kong occupied Murmansk next, and, six weeks later, with Frenchmen at their side, Archangel. American doughboys joined them. Meanwhile, British soldiers from Salonika and Persia seized the Baku-Batum railroad while British warships blockaded Russia's Black Sea and Baltic ports. National motives varied. All felt vindictive toward an ally who, as they saw it, had betrayed them by signing a separate peace, and they were determined to recover vast stores of munitions they had shipped to Russia — arms which the Germans, in that last crisis of the war, were bent on capturing. Japan also wanted to annex Russian territory. The Americans were determined to prevent that and, at the same time, to free beleaguered Czechoslovaks.

The Allies were united in their resolve to crush bolshevism, though in those months it appeared to be disintegrating without their help. The Ukraine had proclaimed its independence on January 28. In April and May similar declarations followed in the Caucasian states of Georgia, Armenia, and Azerbaijan. Lenin had agreed to the Germans' terms at Brest-Litovsk in order to gain some "breathing space," but every day the Bolsheviks had less space in which to breathe. By signing the treaty they had yielded Poland, the Baltic provinces, and Finland. Now the Whites and the Allies vowed to take the rest. The Red Army was in a pitiful state. Some troops were approaching starvation. Few had coats; half of them lacked boots and underwear. Rifles were in short supply. So was ammunition. Weapons rusted because oil was unavailable. Horses died; there was no fodder. The logistical situation was appalling. Coal mines had been flooded. Factories had been demolished. The sources of fuel, steel, and iron were in White hands. Lenin had spoken grandly of riding to triumph on a wildly careening "locomotive of history," but on Russia's railroad tracks his trains labored forward at a speed of one mile an hour. His only two military assets were interior lines and the ingenuity of his commissar of war, Leib Davydovich Bronstein, who had taken the name of Leon Trotsky and who, over the next two years, was to prove himself a commander of genius.[28]

Even with Trotsky the Reds would have been doomed had they been forced to fight during the first winter of their revolution. But the White counterrevolutionaries were still gathering their forces, and the Allies were pinned down by the Germans. It was typical of this confused, tumultuous war that the first shots were fired by soldiers who were neither Reds, Whites, nor Allies. Before the overthrow of the czar, his officers had organized a Czechoslovakian legion comprising seventy thousand prisoners of war eager to fight the Austrians. These were the men who concerned Woodrow Wilson. Brest-Litovsk had stipulated they be disarmed by the Bolsheviks, but it wasn't done, and the Allies had been unable to spare the shipping to evacuate them. They were being marched and countermarched aimlessly across the Urals and Siberia when they learned that the Reds were planning to disarm them. In June 1918 they revolted and seized a section of the Trans-Siberian Railway. That feat attracted the attention of the counterrevolutionary Admiral Aleksandr Kolchak. He recruited them under his banner and opened the civil war's first great offensive, capturing Omsk, Ekaterinburg, and, against negligible opposition, most of the country between the Volga and the Pacific. In Omsk the Siberians announced that they were now an autonomous nation — another territorial loss for the Bolsheviks. Among the casualties during this drive had been the czar, his family, their doctor, and three servants. They had been imprisoned in Ekaterinburg; when Czech troops approached in July, their guards shot them. They would have been killed anyway. The Reds had read Marat: "Woe to the revolution which has not enough courage to behead the symbol of the ancien régime." But Trotsky was disappointed. He had looked forward to prosecuting Nicholas in a public trial, and had designated himself as public prosecutor.

By the summer of 1918 it seemed likely that Trotsky himself would stand in the dock, with Kolchak as his hanging judge. On August 6 the Red Army broke and fled from Kazan on the east bank of the upper Volga, over four hundred miles west of Ekaterinburg and the last important strongpoint between the Whites and central Russia. If Kolchak and his Czechs crossed the river there, they could pour across the open plain — that muddy okra-sown countryside grazed by brown, low-slung cows — and take undefended Moscow, which had become the seat of the new government in March. Nothing could stop them; the villages were completely indefensible. The Central Executive of the Soviets declared the regime to be in danger. Trotsky ordered conscription and left for the front aboard a train which would serve as his mobile headquarters for the better part of three years. Arriving in Svyazhsk, a village on the west bank of the Volga, opposite Kazan, he rallied his panicked soldiers with fiery eloquence and led them back to the front. There he boarded a rusty boat and summoned the sailors of Kronstadt to swell his ranks. Leaders who had joined their men in the rout were brought before him and sentenced to death. He issued a proclamation: "If any detachment retreats without orders, the first to be shot will be the commissar, the next the commander. . . . Cowards, scoundrels, and traitors will not escape the bullet — for this I vouch before the whole Red Army."[29] Heavy fighting continued throughout that month and into the next, until, on September 10, the Bolsheviks recaptured Kazan. By the end of the month the entire Volga basin was back in their hands. Moscow had been saved. Trotsky celebrated the victory by executing hostages and launching his first Red Terror against civilians who had not actively supported his troops.

Meanwhile, the White general Anton Denikin was planning an attack with thirty thousand counterrevolutionaries from his base on the Don while a third counterrevolutionary army, under General Nickolay Yudenich, was bearing down on Petrograd, whose Red defenders were led by the Ossetian Joseph Stalin. It was at this point, in mid-1918, that Churchill's participation in the Russian struggle began to be felt. He was still a junior minister then, and his role was severely limited, but he was the revolution's most vehement British foe. He had been the first to grasp the strategic significance of the Czechs. At his urging, the cabinet voted to remain in Murmansk and Archangel, recognize the Omsk regime, send munitions to Denikin and the rebels in the Baltic states, occupy the Baku-Batum railway in the Caucasus, and establish a strong British expeditionary force in Siberia.

Winston then set out to warn the British public against what he called the "poison peril" in the East. In Dundee, he said: "Russia is being rapidly reduced by the Bolsheviks to an animal form of barbarism. . . . The Bolsheviks maintain themselves by bloody and wholesale butcheries and murders. . . . Civilisation is being completely extinguished over gigantic areas, while Bolsheviks hop and caper like troops of ferocious baboons amid the ruins of cities and the corpses of their victims." In a memorandum he wrote: "Nobody wants to intervene in Russian affairs. Russia is a vy large country, a vy old country, a vy disagreeable country inhabited by immense numbers of ignorant people largely possessed of lethal weapons & in a state of extreme disorder. Also Russia is a long way off." He understood England's yearning for peace. "Unhappily," he continued, "events are driving in a different direction, and nowadays events are vy powerful things. There never was a time when events were so much stronger than human beings. We may abandon Russia: but Russia will not abandon us. We shall retire & she will follow. The bear is padding on bloody paws across the snows to the Peace Conference."[30]

He conferred with the War Cabinet again on December 31 to discuss the government's Russian policy, but Lloyd George was becoming critical of his hawkish stand. George told Riddell: "Winston . . . wants to conduct a war against the Bolsheviks. That *would* cause a revolution!" The prime minister toyed with the idea of opening talks with the Reds. Churchill, hearing of it, rushed to Downing Street and, according to the diary of Mary Borden, Edward Spiers's wife, "Winston told LG one might as well legalize sodomy as recognize the Bolsheviks." Nevertheless, on the eve of Churchill's appointment to the War Office, the cabinet, supporting the prime minister, voted against any attempt to topple the Reds by force; British troops already in Russia would be eventually withdrawn. When the *Daily Express* reported "ominous signs" of a "gigantic campaign" against Russia — and commented that the "frozen plains of Eastern Europe are not worth the bones of a single British grenadier" — it misread the government's mood. Backing the counterrevolutionaries in other ways was still possible, however, and the new war minister meant to do it, ignoring, if necessary, the views of his colleagues.[31]

The immensity of Russia determined the strategy of the civil war. As a theater of military operations it was the antipode of the western front: deep White thrusts into the interior would be followed by Red thrusts, equally deep, toward the country's outer fringes. Where Haig had measured gains and losses in yards, Trotsky and his enemies thought in terms of hundreds of miles. The conflict was fought out in three theaters bearing the names of their counterrevolutionary commanders, Kolchak, Denikin, and Yudenich, and was followed by a Polish invasion, which must be considered separately. As of New Year's Day, 1919, the Whites were being supported by over 180,000 troops from Britain, France, Italy, Greece, Serbia, Japan, the United States, and the Czechoslovaks. Germany's capitulation had left them with no excuse for intervention, but bolshevism was not a Russian movement; Lenin said again and again that his objective was a world revolution. Moreover, the Reds were committing acts which, even after the horrors of the war just ended, were regarded as unprecedented atrocities. Photographs had been smuggled out; the victims were of both sexes and all ages, and the evidence of extraordinary torture and obscene mutilation was unmistakable. The Red Cross wanted to bring food to the afflicted. Lenin approved. Trotsky refused. "Fools and charlatans" would misunderstand his tactics, he said; he wanted no outsiders to witness what they described as "the burning and scorching" of the "bourgeois."[32] Churchill had acquired copies of the pictures and was trying, without success, to get them published in England.

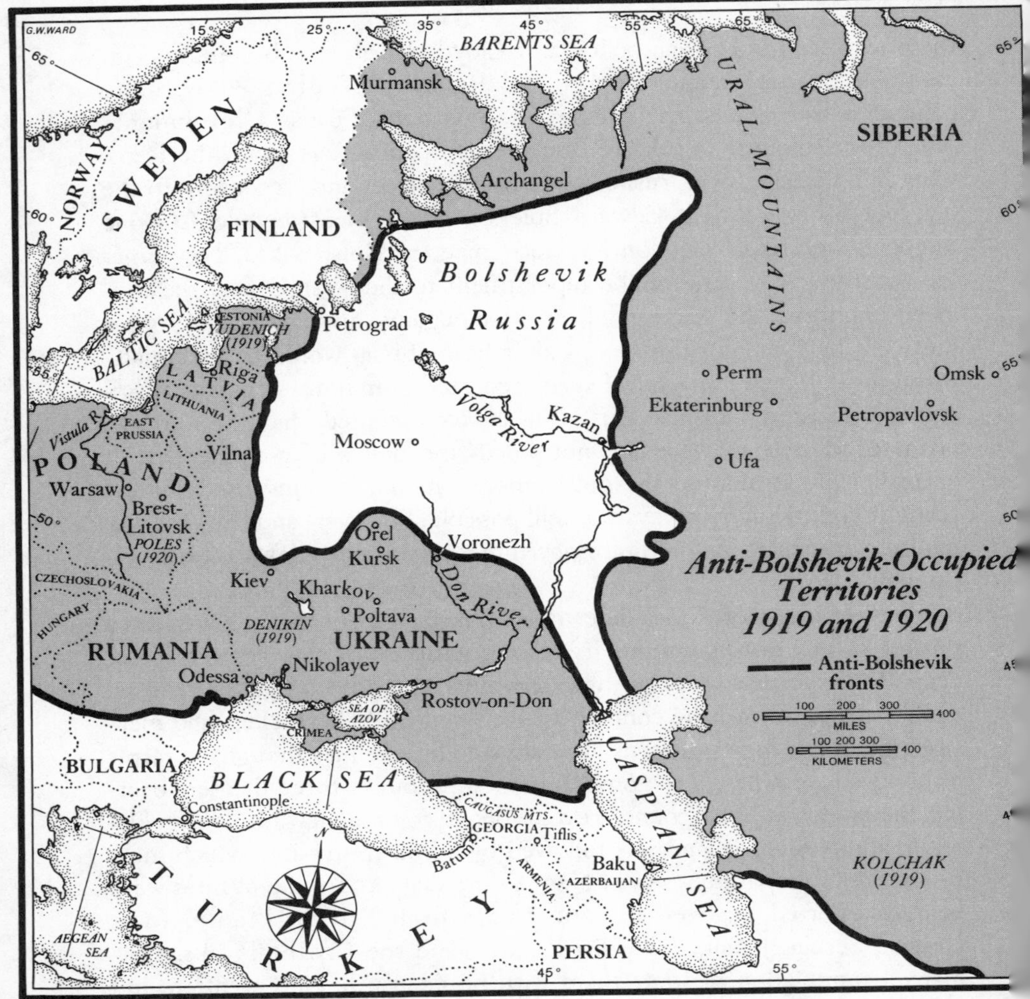

The defeat of the Germans and Austro-Hungarians also meant the withdrawal of their armies westward. That left a vast vacuum in central Europe. Trotsky wanted to fill it with the Red Army, but the defense of the homeland came first. His troops were tied down by Kolchak in the Urals and Denikin in the south. Petrograd was Stalin's problem; Trotsky was in no hurry to solve it for him. Lenin could not be ignored, however. Now that Kolchak had been stopped in his tracks, Lenin wanted to clear the Don and the northern Caucasus of the enemy. Trotsky thought the Ukraine more tempting; he believed new foreign expeditions would soon land on the Black Sea beaches. The debate became academic when Kolchak, reinforced by peasant farmers who revered the czar's memory, broke through the Red defenses and captured Ufa and Perm. This was a crisis; a linkup of Kolchak and Denikin on the Volga seemed imminent. Red counterattacks flung Kolchak back. Then twelve thousand French poilus — Clemenceau's antibolshevism was far more ardent than Lloyd George's or President Wilson's — arrived from the Black Sea, as Trotsky had feared, and took Odessa and Nikolayev. Unfortunately Clemenceau had forgotten the Nivelle disaster and its impact on the morale of French soldiers. The poilus resented their mission. Bolshevik agitators infiltrated their ranks and found them receptive. They rebelled, and the entire French expeditionary force had to be evacuated. Simultaneously, Bolshevik guerrillas and the Red Guards in the Ukraine, who had been scorned by Lenin and Trotsky, surprised them by seizing Kharkov, in the eastern Ukraine, on February 3. Everything had happened and nothing had happened. Neither side was strong enough to subdue the other. But leaders on both sides were discouraged. Clemenceau and Foch began assembling a new force of French infantry. And in Whitehall, Winston Churchill had moved into the War Office with the authority and determination to deal the Bolsheviks savage blows.

Churchill did not rejoin the inner cabinet until November 1919, but as secretary of state for war and air he frequently appeared before it, and there, six weeks after the Armistice, he first raised the Bolshevik issue with the government's highest council. England had two options, he said; it could either permit Russians "to murder each other without let or hindrance" or intervene "thoroughly with large forces, abundantly supplied with mechanical appliances." He proposed to reinforce the troops already there with as many as thirty divisions. The prime minister wanted no part of it. Sir Henry Wilson wrote in his diary: "Winston all against Bolshevism and therefore, in this, against Lloyd George." A week later the two clashed again. Churchill urged the dispatch of an Allied army "to restore the situation and set up a democratic government"; the Reds, he believed, "represent a mere fraction of the population, and would be exposed and swept away by a General Election held under Allied auspices." George vehemently disagreed; he was "definitely opposed to military intervention." Yet he was equally reluctant to abandon Kolchak, Denikin, and Yudenich. He said he thought it best that the Russians settle their differences among themselves, but he agreed to keep the British battalions in Murmansk and Archangel until the dust had settled. The fact is that the old champion of social reform had never felt comfortable with foreign affairs. He was vacillating, always an alarming symptom in a national leader and one which, in this case, threatened the very survival of the Liberal party. The coalition still ruled, but Tories dominated it. They were siding with Churchill. Balfour told Winston: "I admire the exaggerated way you tell the truth." When Churchill attacked Lenin and Trotsky in the House, the loudest cheers came from the Conservative benches.[33]

Squaring off against his party's prime minister was not, however, good politics. Neither was it wise. He was repeating his mistakes of 1914 and 1915. He had been right about Antwerp and the Dardanelles, but wrong in trying to direct the campaigns from the Admiralty. Only the man at No. 10 Downing Street could make policy. Churchill had lacked the power to override doubters then, and he lacked it now. And now, as then, his high profile guaranteed that, should the attempt to destroy the new masters of the Kremlin fail, he would be blamed. Nevertheless, he persevered. The emergence of Communists as leaders of a great nation aroused his powerful aggressive instincts. Not until Hitler showed his fist would Winston again be so vehement. As a monarchist he had been shocked by the brutal murder of the Romanovs; Lloyd George said that "his ducal blood revolted against the wholesale elimination of Grand Dukes." Yet he never advocated a restoration of the Russian monarchy. Instead, he proposed a social democratic regime in Moscow. It was the Red dictatorship which outraged him. Its atrocities and pogroms were, he believed, the inevitable consequence of Marxism in action. To him they represented a new barbarism. As a conservative in the purest sense — a defender of freedom, justice, and the great achievements of the past — he saw civilization gravely endangered. Bolshevism, he said, was "a ghoul descending from a pile of skulls." He told the House: "It is not a policy; it is a disease. It is not a creed; it is a pestilence." The Red Executive Committee was "subhuman." Lenin "was sent into Russia by the Germans in the same way that you might send a phial containing a culture of typhoid or of cholera to be poured into the water supply of a great city, and it worked with amazing accuracy."*[34]

* Later, in *The World Crisis: The Aftermath*, he rephrased this: "They transported Lenin in a sealed truck like a plague bacillus from Switzerland into Russia." If this rhetoric sounds extravagant, it should be remembered that the Bolshevik holocaust — five years of fighting, pestilence, and famine — cost fifteen million lives.

When President Wilson proposed a Russian armistice and the withdrawal of all Allied forces, Churchill replied that this would mean "the destruction of all non-Bolshevik armies in Russia" and "an interminable vista of violence and misery." He said: "The theories of Lenin and Trotsky . . . have driven man from the civilization of the twentieth century into a condition of barbarism worse than the Stone Age and left him the most awful and pitiable spectacle in human experience, devoured by vermin, racked by pestilence, and deprived of hope." Allied intervention was only temporary, he said: "There are now good reasons for believing that the tyranny will soon be overthrown by the Russian nation. We have steadfastly adhered to our principles that Russia must be saved by Russian manhood." No conscripts would be sent to Murmansk and Archangel, he assured the House, and the families of British soldiers killed there would be told "what purpose these men are serving," but the effort must be made. If Lloyd George recognized the Soviet regime, he hinted, he would resign. The repatriation of Russian prisoners of war from German camps angered him; instead of being returned to Moscow, he said, they should have been recruited by the counterrevolutionary armies. "Of all tyrannies in history," he declared in April 1919, "the Bolshevik tyranny is the worst, the most destructive, and the most degrading." In his view it was far viler than the kaiser's Second Reich. His nightmare was a military alliance between a hostile Russia and a vengeful Germany. Instead, he suggested the Germans be encouraged to invade Russia — or, as he put it to Violet Asquith, to "Kill the Bolshie and Kiss the Hun." Exceeding his authority, he sent howitzers to Kolchak and Denikin and appealed to British volunteers who would join a "Slavo-British Legion," serving as a rear guard when Murmansk and Archangel were evacuated. A whole generation of Englishmen knew nothing but fighting, and over eight thousand actually enlisted.[35]

"Churchill's eloquence, enthusiasm, and personality," Hankey noted, produced "an electrical effect." They also triggered a reaction. Even in the War Cabinet his supporters were a minority. Sir Henry Wilson wrote in his diary that "neither LG nor the Cabinet would throw their hearts into beating the Bolsheviks. . . . I am all in favour of declaring war on the Bolsheviks, but the others, except Winston, won't." Curzon, the foreign secretary, described the White Russian situation as one of "complete failure." Austen Chamberlain at the Exchequer was doubtful of "any good results" because the Whites were "completely untrustworthy," the British forces were "very tired," and even the Czechs were "less willing to fight." All in all, he concluded, the intervention was "hopeless." Lloyd

George came down on one side, then the other. He observed enigmatically that although England was "at war" with the Bolsheviks, the country had decided "not to make war." Then he strengthened the naval blockade of Petrograd. Swinging back again, he complained that the first six months of intervention had cost the government £73,000,000 "for our military forces alone, including transport," and if naval expenditures were included the figure would be twice that — for what, he said, "were after all very insignificant operations." Next he raised the figure to £100,000,000 but wrote Churchill: "If Russia were anxious to overthrow Bolshevik rule, the help we have given her would have provided her with a full opportunity. We have discharged faithfully our honourable obligations to Denikin and to Kolchak. We have never entered into any with Yudenitch and I hope we shall not do so. The British public will not tolerate the throwing away of more millions on foolish military enterprises. . . . Let us therefore attend to our own business and leave Russia to look after hers." The prime minister's thinking, Winston observed, stopped "short of a definite character on which a policy, or even a provisional policy," could be based.[36]

Readers of British newspapers had the impression that Churchill was acting alone. The press headlined the fighting in Russia as "Mr Churchill's Private War." The *Daily Express* declared: "The country is absolutely unwilling to make a great war in Russia. . . . Let us have done with the megalomania of Mr Winston Churchill, the military gamester. Let us bring our men back — if we can." The strongest opposition, however, came from the Labour party, which in these months was quietly making converts of thousands of Liberals disillusioned with Lloyd George's postwar drifting, and thereby reshaping Britain's political future. Lenin and Trotsky had assumed that the Russian revolution would be followed by a "German October," a "French October," and an "English October." Although they were to be disappointed, the war had thickened socialist ranks everywhere, and the new left did not share Churchill's hatred of the Soviet Union. Sir David Shackleton, a civil servant, warned the government that British socialists deeply resented the intervention in Siberia. In June 1919 a Labour party conference at Southport unanimously passed a resolution condemning "the war in the interests of financial capitalism" and calling for "the unreserved use . . . of political and industrial power" to end all British opposition to the Communists "whether by force of arms, by supply of munitions, by financial subsidies, or by commercial blockade." At the London docks longshoremen refused to load munitions on the *Jolly George* when they learned that the cargo was destined for White enemies of the Bolsheviks. Ramsay MacDonald, the Labour party leader, wrote in the *Socialist Review:* "Churchill pursues his mad adventure as though he were Emperor of these Isles . . . delighting his militarists and capitalists." MacDonald predicted "new offensives, new bogus governments, new military captains as allies." In the Albert Hall one Colonel C. J. L'Estrange Malone, a disillusioned officer, spoke glowingly of the Red achievements and urged his audience to overthrow Parliament. "What are a few Churchills and Curzons on lamp posts," he asked, "compared to the massacre of thousands of human beings?"[37]

Malone was sentenced to six months in prison for inciting revolt. The British left regarded him as a martyr. Churchill, speaking to his Dundee constituents, said of the Bolsheviks, "I know they have got a few friends here, but it is very lucky for those people that the great mass of the British nation is sensible, solid, and sound, because when it comes to revolutions the revolutionaries are the first to suffer, and when the revolution has come to an end all the most excitable people have been put out of the way, and you have got a great period of reaction, with probably a military dictator at the head of the state." Replying to MacDonald in the *Weekly Review* of June 22 he wrote: "Bolshevism means in every country a civil war of the most merciless kind between the discontented, criminal, and mutinous classes on one hand and the contented or law-abiding on the other. . . . Bolshevism, wherever it manifests itself openly and in concrete form, means war of the most ruthless character, the slaughter of men, women, and children, the burning of homes, and the inviting in of tyranny, pestilence, and famine." He then wrote a provocative piece for the London *Evening News* urging Germany and Poland to build a dike against bolshevism. A Labour spokesman called him "sinister and dangerous," and added: "We repudiate him and his works." The leftist Robert Smillie sardonically thanked "our comrade Winston Churchill for uniting the British democracy. We could not do it: the people would not believe us. But Winston and his friends have done it." Ernest Bevin declared that Winston had damaged himself by "appealing to the old enemy — with whom we were never going to speak or trade — to rise to the occasion and defeat Soviet Russia." Churchill replied that Labour was "quite unfitted for the responsibility of Government." The spread of bolshevism, he solemnly warned the House, might threaten Britain's imperial possessions, including India. This was greeted with laughter, but it wasn't as farfetched as it seemed; Trotsky, according to Isaac Deutscher, had suggested that "the Red Army might find the road to India much shorter and easier than the road to Soviet Hungary. . . . The revolution's road to Paris and London might lead through Kabal, Calcutta, and Bombay."[38]

Nothing came of it, because Lenin recognized Trotsky's proposal for what it was: a cry of anguish, an attempt to sound a note of hope at a time when Communist fortunes were at one of their low points. On the battlefronts the seesaw continued. In the spring of 1919 Kolchak renewed his broad advance toward the Volga, and Moscow once more held its breath. Trotsky now had 500,000 men under arms, but his most reliable troops were fighting elsewhere. Then, in late April, one of his officers, a former colonel on the czar's general staff, outflanked Kolchak, cut his supply lines, and sent him reeling back toward the Urals. Before the Red Army could celebrate its victory, however, Denikin lunged back into the Ukraine. He met negligible resistance. The peasants greeted his troops as heroes; bolshevism was unpopular here, and it grew more so when bands of defeated Reds crisscrossed the countryside looting, raping, and pillaging. On May 29 Churchill told the House that Denikin "has advanced his whole front, in some places, to a distance of eighty miles, and in this he has been aided by rebellions which have broken out among the people."[39] In Siberia, Kolchak dug in after a 180-mile retreat and threw back Red Army attacks. Meanwhile, the French had evacuated Odessa, the American and Italian expeditionary forces sailed away, and soviets were proclaimed in Hungary and Bavaria. The spring campaigns, in short, were indecisive.

So was Lloyd George. On this issue he had lost control of his ministers. British warships, he suggested, should be withdrawn from Petrograd waters, and Curzon, supporting him, urged his colleagues to "proceed with caution" because there was "a strong element in the House of Commons that is opposed to intervention." Nevertheless, the War Cabinet, after hearing Churchill, resolved that "a state of war" existed "between Great Britain and the Bolshevik Government of Russia" and, therefore, that "our Naval forces in Russian waters should be authorized to engage enemy forces by land and sea, when necessary." Winston wanted supplies and munitions rushed to Denikin. He even proposed building a railroad for him. Yet his support was far from blind. He demanded that the White general adopt a land-reform program, establish "a constituent assembly on a democratic franchise to decide the future form of Russian Government," and recognize the independence of Poland, Finland, and the Baltic states. Later he also asked for a written promise to suppress anti-Semitism. Six million Jews lived in Russia. Reports of Ukrainian pogroms had reached London, and British Jews were furious. But Denikin, confident of imminent triumph, ignored all of Churchill's conditions.[40]

Events in the early fall of 1919 seemed to confirm Denikin. Kiev, the capital city of the Ukraine, had fallen to him on the last day of August. He swiftly retook Kharkov, took Odessa and Rostov-on-Don, and was pressing the Reds' weak center, toward Kursk and Voronezh, along the shortest line to Moscow. Simultaneously, Yudenich, armed by Churchill and supported by the Royal Navy, fought his way into the outskirts of Petrograd. Lenin, telegraphing that "the fate of the entire Revolution is in question," ordered that positions be defended "to the last drop of blood." Trotsky retorted that weapons and ammunition which he had been promised had not arrived, and attempts to suppress White marauders roaming behind Red Army lines had "up to now yielded almost no result." Lenin proposed abandonment of the city and withdrawal of all Red Army units from all fronts for a circle-the-wagons defense of Moscow. If that were lost, he said, they would retreat to the Urals. Trotsky protested. Petrograd, he told the Politburo, was "the cradle of the Revolution."[41] Stalin agreed; the loss of Russia's two great cities, he said, could not be borne. Boarding a train to take personal command of Petrograd's defenses, Trotsky was handed a copy of a Churchill statement claiming that troops from fourteen nations would soon join in an anti-Soviet crusade. He dismissed it with a scornful laugh and said he would defend the beleaguered city house by house and, if necessary, room by room. Bad news awaited him on arrival. Yudenich had seized Krasnoe Selo, the last strongpoint between him and the center of the city. His drive was spearheaded by British tanks, newly arrived from Churchill. Their appearance had panicked the defenders.

This was Trotsky's hour. Improvising armored cars in Petrograd factories, he inspired the Red troops, and, in a week, threw the Whites back. Lenin wired him: "It is damnably important to us to finish off Yudenich. . . . If the offensive is to be launched, cannot a further 20 thousand or so Petrograd workers be mobilized, plus 10 thousand or so of the bourgeoisie, machine guns to be posted to the rear of them, a few hundred shot and a real mass assault on Yudenich assured?" His commissar of war had anticipated him; it had been done. Trotsky then turned to the southern theater. Believing the Whites there were overextended, he ordered a counterattack, and Denikin fell back in confusion on Kiev, Poltava, and Kharkov. Then Kolchak's army was crushed in Siberia. The three great counterrevolutionary armies had been defeated in just three weeks — this time for good. By December the Red Army was back in Petropavlovsk and Omsk. Denikin had been beaten back to Kursk, eighty miles south of Orel. Yudenich was retreating toward the Estonian border. Kolchak's headquarters were in remote Irkutsk, fifteen hundred miles east of Omsk. The British expedition had been evacuated. Sir Henry Wilson wrote in his diary: "So ends in practical disaster another of Winston's military attempts. Antwerp, Dardanelles, Denikin. His judgment is always at fault, & he is hopeless when in power." Churchill himself wrote: "There seems to be very little doubt of the complete victory of the Bolsheviks in the near future. The Japanese will no doubt hold up to Lake Baikal. . . . Everywhere else we must look for a complete smash up." Lloyd George's vacillation was over. On the day Kharkov fell, he and Clemenceau met at No. 10 and agreed not to "enter into any further commitments as to furnishing assistance to the anti-Bolshevik elements in Russia, whether in the form of troops, war material or financial aid." They added that "a strong Poland" was "in the interests of the Entente powers."[42]

The blunt truth is that a strong Poland was in the interests of Poland and no one else. Since the split of its ancient kingdom in 1138 the country had been partitioned and repartitioned by Russia, Prussia, and Austria-Hungary, and between 1795 and the proclamation of a Polish republic by General Józef Pilsudski in 1918, it could be found on no map. Pilsudski was the archetypal Polish patriot. He had been exiled to Siberia by the czar and jailed by the Germans, and he had fought with the Austrians between 1914 and 1916, when he had left the field to nurse his dream of an independent nation. Now that dream had been realized, but, like most of his countrymen, he was less interested in peace than in acquiring adjacent territories occupied by Russians. In September 1919 Ignace Paderewski, the republic's premier, asked the Allies to finance a drive toward the Soviet capital by 500,000 Poles. Churchill disapproved, as did Wilson, and for the same reason: "I quite agree with you that it would be madness for us to advise Paderewski, and to support him in any attempt to occupy Moscow. If anything could combine all Russia into a whole, it would be a march of the Poles on Moscow. I can almost conceive Denikin and Lenin joining hands to defeat such an object."[43]

Pilsudski struck in the first week of March, seized Kiev and Vilna, and occupied most of the Ukraine. But his triumph was a brief, doomed flicker. As Churchill and Wilson had foretold, the invasion of Mother Russia deeply stirred her masses. To followers of the Greek Orthodox faith this was a struggle with Roman Catholic heretics, and to men who still cherished loyalty to the Romanovs, a fight with a hereditary enemy — "a truly Russian war," as Deutscher put it, "even though waged by Bolshevik internationalists." Aleksei Brusilov, the late czar's commander in chief, put his sword at Trotsky's disposal. Ukrainians found the Poles even more lawless than the Reds and Whites and expelled them. On June 12 Kiev was retaken. By August 14 the Red Army, now five million strong, had reached the outskirts of Warsaw. "Nothing can save Poland now," Churchill wrote gloomily and left London to play polo at Rugby.[44] Curzon offered to mediate the dispute; Lloyd George gave both sides ultimata, but the days were past when British statesmen could settle foreign quarrels by fiat. Salvation reached Warsaw in the form of General Maxime Weygand and a French military mission. The Poles and the poilus rallied on the Vistula. The Reds retreated; Pilsudski, unchastened by his rout, marched on the Caucasus. A provisional peace was signed on October 12 at Riga, though fighting between Russians and Poles, supported by Rumanian allies, continued until late in the 1920s.

Disaster having been averted, Winston, relieved, wrote: "Poland has saved herself by her exertions & will I trust save Europe by her example." Yet in some obscure way the Polish adventure had damaged him. The British press depicted the Bolsheviks as victims of aggression — worse, aggression that failed — and Churchill was England's most vigorous anti-Bolshevik. Every Red victory was a blow to his prestige, and, now that the tide had turned, the pins representing counterrevolutionary forces on the War Office's map of Russia were being plucked out one by one. By February 7 Kolchak had been captured and executed by Bolsheviks in Irkutsk. Yudenich had fled to England. On March 27 Denikin, abandoning hope, turned his command over to Baron Pëtr von Wrangel and sailed for France. Because the Red Army was busy fighting Poles, Wrangel, driving north from his base on the Sea of Azov, overran much of southern Russia, but after Riga the Reds wheeled and hurled him back into the Crimea. Churchill begged the inner cabinet to support Wrangel. Their response was icy. One minister wrote in his diary: "At the Cabinet this morning the PM gave Winston a dressing down about Russia. Winston had been complaining that we have no policy. This the PM described as ridiculous. Our policy was to try to escape the results of the evil policy which Winston had persuaded the Cabinet to adopt." Another diarist wrote: "Churchill bumbles on about Russia." On November 1 Wrangel evacuated his army to Constantinople. Two weeks later the Bolsheviks were in Constantinople, and tens of thousands of White refugees boarded French ships and vanished into permanent exile.[45]

Churchill wouldn't quit. His defiance in defeat, which would thrill England twenty years later, embarrassed his colleagues now. British officers in Berlin informed London that Ludendorff wanted to confer with Churchill about the Bolshevik menace. To the astonishment of his fellow cabinet members, Winston expressed interest. H. A. L. Fisher, minister for education, wrote Lloyd George that he was "alarmed." He was convinced that Ludendorff's goals were sinister. Churchill didn't see it that way. "In my view," he wrote in a minute, "the objective wh we shd pursue at the present time is the building up of a strong but peaceful Germany wh will not attack our French allies, but will at the same time act as a moral bulwark against the Bolshevism of Russia." He added that "the advice of the WO throughout the last 15 months has constantly tended to that recovery, stability, & tranquilisation of Europe, wh wd enable Britain to enjoy the fruits of victory. It is a pity it has fallen on deaf ears."[46]

Certainly the cabinet was deaf to his proposals that he confer with the Second Reich's discredited warlord, and after reflection he dropped the idea. Thus the Russian epic was played out without further British intrusions. The Bolsheviks still faced obstacles. Japanese troops remained in Vladivostok after all the other Allies had left, drove off a Soviet attack, inflicting heavy losses, and did not leave Russian soil until the autumn of 1922. The Baltic states of Estonia, Latvia, and Lithuania retained their freedom until 1940. Extending Red control over the Caucasus was a slow, exasperating business. Long after Wrangel had left, Georgia continued to be ruled by Mensheviks. Trotsky had agreed to leave the Georgians alone, but in 1921, while he was absent on an inspection tour of the Urals, the Red Army invaded the republic and, after severe fighting, seized Tiflis, its capital. The man who had done this, sabotaging Trotsky's promise to Georgia, was himself a native Georgian. He hated Trotsky even more than he hated Churchill for intervening, and he was Joseph Stalin.

Winston had one arrow left in his anti-Bolshevik quiver. Lloyd George had been a radical young parliamentarian, but now, like all British prime ministers, he was dedicated to expansion of British trade, and when a Soviet trade mission arrived in London after the counterrevolutionaries had been overwhelmed, the prime minister saw to it that they were provided with every comfort. There was no alternative to peaceful coexistence with them, George told the House; it had become "perfectly clear now to every unprejudiced observer that you cannot crush Bolshevism by force of arms." But Churchill was not an unprejudiced observer. He refused to "grasp the hairy paw of the baboon." Commercial ties with England would strengthen Lenin's regime, he said, and "as long as any portion of this nest of vipers is left intact, it will continue to breed and swarm." Besides, he asked Lloyd George, how would the Reds pay for British goods?

The answer outraged him. The Russians planned to barter with gold and precious stones taken from the czarist nobility. "This treasure does not belong to the Russian Bolshevik Government," he said at a cabinet meeting. "It has been forcibly seized by these usurpers. . . . The jewels have been stolen from their owners in Russia and in many cases from their corpses." The gold was similarly "bloodstained." England would be giving the Reds "a special title to this plundered gold in order that with it they may make purchases in the British market. It seems to me that this is a very serious step to take."[47]

Nevertheless, the government took it a few minutes later. Winston almost resigned on the spot. He was "so upset by the decision," Hankey noted in his diary, "that he declared himself unequal to discussing other items on the Agenda affecting the army. He was quite pale and did not speak again during the meeting." As it broke up he glowered at the prime minister and inquired heavily whether any minister would now be "fettered" if he wished to deliver anti-Communist speeches. Assured that he was free to say what he pleased, he drove to Oxford that evening and addressed the Oxford Union. Flaying the Lenin government, he said he believed "that all the harm and misery in Russia has arisen out of the wickedness and folly of the Bolshevists and that there will be no recovery of any kind in Russia or in Eastern Europe while these wicked men, this vile group of cosmopolitan fanatics, hold the Russian nation by the hair of its head and tyrannize over its great population. . . . The policy I will always advocate is the overthrow and destruction of that criminal regime."[48]

He had been candid, he had been prophetic, and he paid a price. Men who had forgotten the Dardanelles remembered it now and felt their earlier assessment of him confirmed. A new rift had opened between him and Lloyd George. The growing delegation of Labour MPs marked him as their chief enemy. In some instances their enmity did him honor; it was later found, for example, that the *Daily Herald,* a Labour newspaper, was subsidized by Russian money. But his bitterness and his isolation from old friends were curiously at variance with his usual generosity of spirit. H. G. Wells, returning from Russia, declared that Red excesses had been necessary to "establish a new social order" and that the British naval blockade had been partly responsible for Russian starvation. Churchill, replying in the *Sunday Express,* wrote: "We see the Bolshevik cancer eating into the flesh of the wretched being; we see the monstrous growth swelling and thriving upon the emaciated body of his victim. And now Mr Wells, that philosophical romancer, comes forward with the proposition that the cancer is the only thing that can pull the body round; that we must feed and cultivate that. After all, it is another form of life. It is 'a new social order.' Why be so narrow-minded as to draw the line between health and disease, still less between right and wrong? Adopt an impartial attitude. Put your money on the disease if you think it is going to win." Wells struck back with asperity. He had known Churchill for years, he wrote in the next week's *Sunday Express.* He liked him and admired him. "But," he said, "I will confess that it distresses me that he should hold any public office at this time. . . . I want to see him out of any position of public responsibility whatever." Winston's retirement and his return to private life, he suggested, would not "be a tragic fall. . . . Mr Churchill has many resources. He would, for instance, be a brilliant painter."[49]

On Lloyd George's fifty-seventh birthday, Churchill lunched with the prime minister, and Frances Stevenson noted that he "waxed very eloquent on the old world & the new, taking up arms in defence of the former." He was, she wrote, "simply *raving*" about "trading with Russia" which "absolutely & finally ruins his hopes of a possible war in the East." When another guest chided him, she wrote, "Winston glared at him, & almost shouted 'You are trying to make mischief!' " That evening Lloyd George, Frances, and Churchill dined at Ciro's. Winston, she noted, was still "ragging D[avid] about the New World. 'Don't you make any mistake,' he said to D. 'You're not going to get your new world. The old world is a good enough place for me, & there's life in the old dog yet. It's going to sit up & wag its tail.' " The prime minister remarked that Winston was "the only remaining specimen of a real Tory." That, too, was prophetic.[50]

It is a striking fact that Churchill, the acmic warrior, left a colorless record at the Ministry of War and Air, and not only because his Russian policy was a complete failure. The postwar demobilization was his only real accomplishment at the War Office. Otherwise, his military policies were cautious and stingy. Wherever he found fat he cut it, but he cut a great deal that was lean, too. He preserved the separate identity of the Royal Air Force yet left it little but its name. On Armistice Day, Britain had been the world's greatest air power; two years later England was reduced to three home squadrons, as against France's forty-seven. And three months after that, when Churchill resigned from the ministry to become colonial secretary, *The Times* observed: "He leaves the body of

British flying well nigh at that last gasp when a military funeral would be all that would be left for it." His management of the army had been equally disappointing. Young career officers, appreciative of his role in tank development, expected that he would refashion their services along modern lines. Unaware of his sentimental yearning for his golden days with the Fourth Hussars and the Twenty-first Lancers, they were stunned when he sided with the red-tabbed diehards and shared their yearning for a return to 1914. His most shortsighted policy was his acceptance of Lloyd George's guiding principle, endorsed by the War Cabinet in August 1919, that "the British Empire will not be engaged in any great war during the next ten years and that no Expeditionary Force will be required." At times Winston even echoed the litany of the Little Englanders. On June 18, 1920, he told the cabinet that "the military forces at the disposal of Great Britain" were "insufficient to meet the requirements of the policies now being pursued in the various theatres." One would have expected Churchill, the tribune of Empire, to call for an increase in those forces. Instead, he argued that a cutback in imperial commitments was "indispensable if grave risk of disaster is not to be incurred." Otherwise, he said, "the possibility of disaster occurring in any or all of these theatres must be faced, and the likelihood of this will increase every day."[51]

He was always readier to defy public opinion than most public men, but here he was trimming his sails to meet the prevailing political winds. After the survivors of the western front came home, Britons wanted nothing more to do with war; most of them hoped never again to lay their eyes on an Englishman in uniform, and they were losing their taste for Empire. Privately he worried about that. A bellicose war minister and a pacifistic electorate would not work comfortably in harness, however, and though he would later reconcile himself to such an incompatibility, in those early postwar years he did not feel the risk justifiable. As Liddell Hart wrote, Churchill "was eager to make a fresh mark in current political affairs, and the best chance lay in the postwar retrenchment of expenditure."[52] It was expedient to cut taxes and he did it ruthlessly. His objectives, however, were unchanged. He freely entered into agreements in which the eventual use of force, or threat of it, was implicit, confident that if he had to show the flag, Englishmen would support him.

By now it was clear that he was too strong and too able to be confined to a single ministry. As home secretary he had often appeared at the Treasury; at the Admiralty he had led Irish policy; as lowly minister of munitions he had managed to influence the conduct of the war. Now he freely crossed ministerial lines of authority and assumed responsibilities which rightfully belonged in the India Office, the Colonial Office, and the Foreign Office. Naturally, his colleagues resented this, but the offended minister almost always found himself a minority of one. The others recognized Churchill's gifts. Even the prime minister, who frequently discovered himself at loggerheads with him now, tolerated what, in another man, would have been called meddling and might even have merited dismissal. Churchill had become the most powerful speaker in Parliament. No one, not even the gifted Lloyd George, could hold the House as Winston did. Indeed, on one memorable occasion he accomplished a rare feat. Eloquence, wit, and charm have not been uncommon in that body, but seldom in its six centuries has a speech actually changed the opinion of the majority, transforming imminent defeat into triumph. Churchill did it on July 8, 1920, thereby vindicating England's honor.

The origins of that day's controversy lay in a shocking episode. A few months after the war an Englishwoman, a missionary, had reported that she had been molested on a street in the Punjab city of Amritsar. The Raj's local commander, Brigadier General Reginald Dyer, had issued an order requiring all Indians using that street to crawl its length on their hands and knees. He had also authorized the indiscriminate, public whipping of natives who came within lathi length of British policemen. On April 13, 1919, a multitude of Punjabis had gathered in Amritsar's Jallianwallah Bagh to protest these extraordinary measures. The throng, penned in a narrow space smaller than Trafalgar Square, had been peacefully listening to the testimony of victims when Dyer appeared at the head of a contingent of British troops. Without warning, he ordered his machine gunners to open fire. The Indians, in Churchill's words, were "packed together so that one bullet would drive through three or four bodies"; the people "ran madly this way and the other. When the fire was directed upon the centre, they ran to the sides. The fire was then directed upon the sides. Many threw themselves down on the ground, and the fire was then directed on the ground. This was continued for eight or ten minutes, and it stopped only when the ammunition had reached the point of exhaustion." Dyer then marched away, leaving 379 dead and over 1,500 wounded. Back in his headquarters, he reported to his superiors that he had been "confronted by a revolutionary army," and had been obliged "to teach a moral lesson to the Punjab." In the storm of outrage which followed, the brigadier was promoted to major general, retired, and placed on the inactive list. This, incredibly, made him a martyr to millions of Englishmen. Senior British officers applauded his suppression of "another Indian Mutiny." The Guardians of the Golden Temple enrolled him in the Brotherhood of Sikhs. The House of Lords passed a measure commending him. Readers of the Tory *Morning Post*, Churchill's old scourge, subscribed £2,500 for a testimonial. Leading Conservative MPs took up his cause, and Lloyd George reluctantly agreed to a full-dress debate. Venetia Montagu's husband, Edwin, now the secretary of state for India, would open for the government, with Churchill scheduled at the end.[53]

Montagu's speech was a calamity. He was a Jew and there were anti-Semites in the House. He had been warned to be quiet and judicial. Instead, he was sarcastic; he called Dyer a terrorist; he worried about foreign opinion; he "thoroughly roused most of the latent passions of the stodgy Tories," as one MP noted, and "got excited . . . and became more racial and more Yiddish in screaming tone and gesture," with the consequence that "a strong anti-Jewish sentiment was shown by shouts. . . . Altogether it was a very astonishing exhibition of anti-Jewish feeling." The Ulster MPs had decided to vote against Dyer. After Montagu's speech they conferred and reversed themselves. Sir Edward Carson rose to praise the general — who was watching from the Strangers' Gallery — as "a gallant officer of thirty-four years service . . . without a blemish on his record" who had "no right to be broken on the *ipse dixit* of any Commission or Committee, however great, unless he has been fairly tried — and he has not been tried." Carson ended: "I say, to break a man under the circumstances of this case is un-English." "Un-English," in the context of the time, was anti-Semitic — roughly the equivalent of "kike." MPs roared their approval. The government was in trouble. Lloyd George being absent, Bonar Law, the leader of the House, asked Churchill to speak immediately.[54]

Churchill's approach was entirely unlike Montagu's. He called for "a calm spirit, avoiding passion and avoiding attempts to excite prejudice." Dyer, he said, had not been dismissed in disgrace; "he had simply been informed that there was no further employment for him under the Government of India." But the incident in Jallianwallah Bagh was "an extraordinary event, a monstrous event, an event which stands in singular and sinister isolation." He quietly observed that the number of Indians killed was almost identical with the number of MPs now sitting within range of his voice. An officer in such a situation as Dyer's, he said, should ask himself whether the crowd is either armed or about to mount an attack. "Men who take up arms against the State must expect at any moment to be fired upon. . . . At Amritsar the crowd was neither armed nor attacking." Thus the general had not, as he claimed, faced a "revolutionary army." Another useful military guide, Churchill continued, was the maxim that "no more force should be used than is necessary to secure compliance with the law." In the Great War, he and many other members of the House had seen British soldiers "exerting themselves to show pity and to help, even at their own peril, the wounded." Dyer had failed to follow their example; after the massacre, his troops had simply swung around and marched away. Churchill knew, and many members of Parliament knew, of many instances in which officers, in "infinitely more trying" situations than the one in the Bagh, had, unlike the general, displayed an ability to arrive "at the right decision." Then, as if with a stiletto, Churchill knifed Dyer: "Frightfulness is not a remedy known to the British pharmacopoeia."[55]

He twisted the blade. Dyer's most vocal champions agreed with Churchill's stand in Russia. It was compassion and its absence, he said, which marked the difference between Englishmen and Bolsheviks. His own hatred of Lenin's regime was "not founded on their silly system of economics, or their absurd doctrine of an impossible equality." It arose from "the bloody and devastating terrorism which they practise . . . and by which alone their criminal regime can be maintained." It was intolerable in Russia; it was intolerable in Amritsar. "I do not think," he said, "that it is in the interests of the British Empire or of the British Army for us to take a load of that sort for all time upon our backs. We have to make it absolutely clear, some way or another, that this is not the British way of doing business." He quoted Macaulay: "The most frightful of all spectacles [is] the strength of civilisation without its mercy." England's "reign in India, or anywhere else," Churchill continued, "has never stood on the basis of physical force alone, and it would be fatal to the British Empire if we were to try to base ourselves only upon it. The British way of doing things . . . has always meant and implied close and effectual cooperation with the people. In every part of the British Empire that has been our aim." As for Dyer, Churchill himself would have preferred to see the general disciplined. Instead, he had been allowed to resign with no plan for further punishment, "and to those moderate and considered conclusions we confidently invite the assent of the House."[56]

He sat and they rose crying, "Hear, hear." After five more hours of debate they voted for the government, 247 to 37. Carson's motion for mild approval of Dyer was defeated 230 to 129. The Archbishop of Canterbury wrote Curzon that Churchill's speech had been "unanswerable." *The Times* called it "amazingly skilful" and declared that it had "turned the House (or so it seemed) completely round. . . . It was not only a brilliant speech, but one that persuaded and made the result certain." Winston, the editorial concluded, had "never been heard to greater advantage."[57]

Late in 1920 Churchill told Lloyd George that he wanted to move to another cabinet post — the Foreign Office, the Colonial Office, or, preferably, the Exchequer. He was tired of wringing half crowns from frugal military budgets, presiding over troop withdrawals, and trying to suppress terrorism in southern Ireland with responsibility for order but no power to negotiate a political solution. Moreover, the prime minister shared few of his views about the army and the RAF. On January 23 of the new year Winston told Sir Henry Wilson that he could not last "much longer in the W.O. owing to differences with L.G." He bluntly wrote George: "I am vy sorry to see how far we are drifting apart. . . . When one has reached the summit of power & surmounted so many obstacles, there is danger of becoming convinced that one can do anything one likes, & that any strong personal view is necessarily acceptable to the nation & can be enforced upon one's subordinates." He understood that. "No doubt I in my time of important affairs was led astray like this. I suddenly found a vy different world around me: though of course all my fortunes were on a petty scale compared with yours. . . . But is yr policy going to be successful? I fear it is going wrong." Churchill thought it a mistake to negotiate with the new Russian leaders, thought George underestimated the returning popularity of the Conservative party, and believed that "one of the main causes of trouble throughout the Middle East is *your* quarrel with the remnants of Turkey. . . . All the soldiers continually say they disapprove of the policy against Turkey. . . . This soaks in." On February 14, 1921, the prime minister, unwilling to lose the most talented member of his cabinet, appointed him colonial secretary. That evening Churchill received his new seals from George V. He wrote Clementine that his room at the Colonial Office "is very fine and sedate . . . at least twice as big as the old one — an enormous square, but well warmed. It is like working in the saloon at Blenheim."[58]

His immediate concerns were Ireland and the Middle East, which was in chaos. Because Turkey had been on the losing side in the war, the old Ottoman Empire had disintegrated. In the peace settlements Turkey had been reduced to a shadow of its former self, a small Asiatic state in the Anatolian uplands around Ankara. During the fighting in the desert against the Turks, France's and England's most powerful ally had been the army of Husein ibn-Ali, sharif of Mecca and ruler of the ancient kingdom of Hejaz (now part of Saudi Arabia). In October 1918 forces led by the sharif's son Faisal had entered Damascus in triumph. Faisal had appeared at Versailles, registered at the Hotel Metropole, and emerged dressed in immaculate Hashemite robes and attended by two enormous Nubians carrying glittering swords. But when he had appealed for Arabian self-determination, speaking as the emissary of "my father, who, by request of Britain and France, led the Arab rebellion against the Turks" and asking that "the Arabic-speaking peoples of Asia . . . be recognized as independent sovereign peoples, under the guarantee of the League of Nations," he was ignored.[59] Afterward diplomats from Whitehall and the Quai d'Orsay met quietly in San Remo, Italy, and divided up the Middle East in a muffled version of their nineteenth-century scramble for African possessions. Husein remained as sovereign of Hejaz, but France got Syria and Lebanon; Persia (Iran) was under British protection; and Mesopotamia (Iraq) and Palestine came within Britain's sphere of influence, providing the Empire with a direct overland route between imperial troops in Egypt and the Persian Gulf.

But Arabs were not docile Punjabis. Back in Damascus, Faisal was proclaimed king of Syria. Neither France nor England would recognize him; indeed, French troops arrived, dethroned him, and forced him to flee. Then his brother Abdullah recruited a private army in Mecca, capital of Hejaz, and announced that he would march on Damascus and drive the poilus into the sea. Next the Iraqis rose and besieged several British garrisons. Arabs rioted in Jerusalem, and, most ominous of all, Bolshevik forces were reported crossing into Iran. A British infantry division, transferred from India to Baghdad by Churchill, pacified Iraq. Persian cossacks drove the Bolsheviks across the border. Then as now, however, the knottiest problem of all lay in Palestine. The Balfour declaration, promulgated in 1917 when Arthur Balfour was the coalition's foreign secretary and Jewish political power was at its zenith in London, had proclaimed that the British government favored "the establishment of a national home for the Jewish people and will use their best endeavours to facilitate the achievement of that object, it being clearly understood that nothing shall be done which may prejudice the civil and religious rights of existing non-Jewish communities in Palestine."[60]

When Churchill took over at the Colonial Office, this declaration was part of his legacy. His feelings about Balfour's largess appear to have been mixed. Of Zionism he had written in 1908: "Jerusalem must be the only ultimate goal. When it will be achieved it is vain to prophesy; but that it will some day be achieved is one of the few certainties of the future." But after the declaration he peevishly wrote that the Jews "take it for granted that the local population will be cleared out to suit [their] convenience." Later, in the *Illustrated Sunday Herald,* he hailed Chaim Weizmann's "inspiring movement" to build a new nation "by the banks of the Jordan" as a "simpler, a truer, and a far more attainable goal" than the "absolutely destructive" Bolshevik conspiracy to establish "a world wide communistic state under Jewish domination." This backhanded endorsement carried a sour tang of anti-Semitism, and it surfaced again in 1920, when, opposing economic aid to Russia, he said he saw "the gravest objections to giving all this help to the tyrannic Government of these Jew commissars." That same year he expressed fresh reservations about the creation of a Zionist state, writing Lloyd George on June 13, 1920, that "Palestine is costing us 6 millions a year to hold. The Zionist movement will cause continued friction with the Arabs. The French ensconced in Syria with 4 divisions (paid for by not paying us what they owe us) are opposed to the Zionist movement & will try to cushion the Arabs off on us as the real enemy. The Palestine venture is the most difficult to withdraw from & one wh certainly will never yield any profit of a material kind."[61]

Nevertheless, by the time he entered the Colonial Office he was committed to it. The more he pondered the issue, the more his enthusiasm for a Jewish homeland grew, and he reaffirmed the declaration at a time when a majority of the British officials in the Middle East were urging that it be repudiated. Lieutenant General Sir Walter Congreve, commander in chief of His Majesty's forces in the Middle East, typically predicted that the Arabs would not return to tranquillity until their "aspirations are attended to," which "means Zionist aspirations being greatly curbed." He continued: "As long as we persist in our Zionist policy we have got to maintain our present forces in Palestine to enforce a policy hateful to the great majority — a majority which means to fight & to continue to fight and has right on its side." Walter Smart, a senior civil servant in Egypt, wrote bitterly of "Anglo-French bargaining about other peoples' property, the deliberate bribing of international Jewry at the expense of the Arabs who were already our allies in the field, the immature political juggleries of amateur Oriental experts, the stultification of Arab independence and unity . . . all the immorality and incompetence inevitable in the stress of a great war."[62]

Churchill decided to sail out to the eastern Mediterranean on the French steamship *Sphinx* and see for himself, taking with him Colonel T. E. Lawrence, Air Marshal Sir Hugh Trenchard, and Archie Sinclair, now Winston's private secretary. The Arabs could not have chosen a more passionate spokesman than Lawrence — "Lawrence of Arabia," who spoke fluent Arabic, had led them against the Turks, had suffered several grave wounds, and, after surviving capture and torture, had emerged as a shining figure. His shyness was legendary. Privately Winston wondered about that. Lawrence, he said wryly, "has a way of backing into the limelight." But including him in the delegation was a brilliant political stroke. Outraged by the betrayal at San Remo, he had begun writing his great *Seven Pillars of Wisdom,* the leitmotiv of which would be British shame. When George V had received him at a royal audience and attempted to award him the DSO and a Companionship in the Order of the Bath, Lawrence had politely refused the decorations, leaving the shocked monarch, in the King's own words, "holding the box in my hand." If this man of honor supported a Middle Eastern settlement, the shiekhs of Araby would hesitate to reject it.[63]

The *Sphinx* would stop at Marseilles to pick up Clementine, who had been visiting friends in France. From the Hotel Bristol in Beaulieu she wrote Winston: "I am thrilled by the idea & so so longing to see you." Replying, he told her to pack the proper clothing for sight-seeing trips and tennis — "Do not forget your racquet." In a second letter he wrote: "We shall have a beautiful cabin together. If only it is not rough — then I shall hide in any old dog hole far from yr sight. . . . If it is fine, it will be lovely & I shall write & paint & we will talk over all our affairs." His mother, now living in Berkeley Square, dropped him "a line to wish you bon voyage — & a speedy return — Give my love to Clemmie. . . . I will look after the children & give you news of them. They are great darlings & do you both great credit!"[64]

Meanwhile, Weizmann had told the Political Committee of the Zionist Organization that he was worried about Churchill's mission. The new colonial secretary was "of a highly impressionable temperament," he said, and he expected the Arabs to "organize an agitation to greet him on his arrival in the East." On March 1, Winston's last day in London before the six-day voyage, Weizmann sent him a long letter, demanding that the Jewish state's eastern boundary be extended east of the Jordan River to include all of Transjordan (now Jordan). Transjordan, he wrote, "has from the earliest time been an integral and vital part of Palestine." Here the tribes of Manasseh, Gad, and Reuben "first pitched their tents and pastured their flocks." The climate was "invigorating," the soil "rich," irrigation would be "easy," and the hills were "covered with forests." There "Jewish settlement could proceed on a large scale without friction with the local population." How friction with the Arab inhabitants could

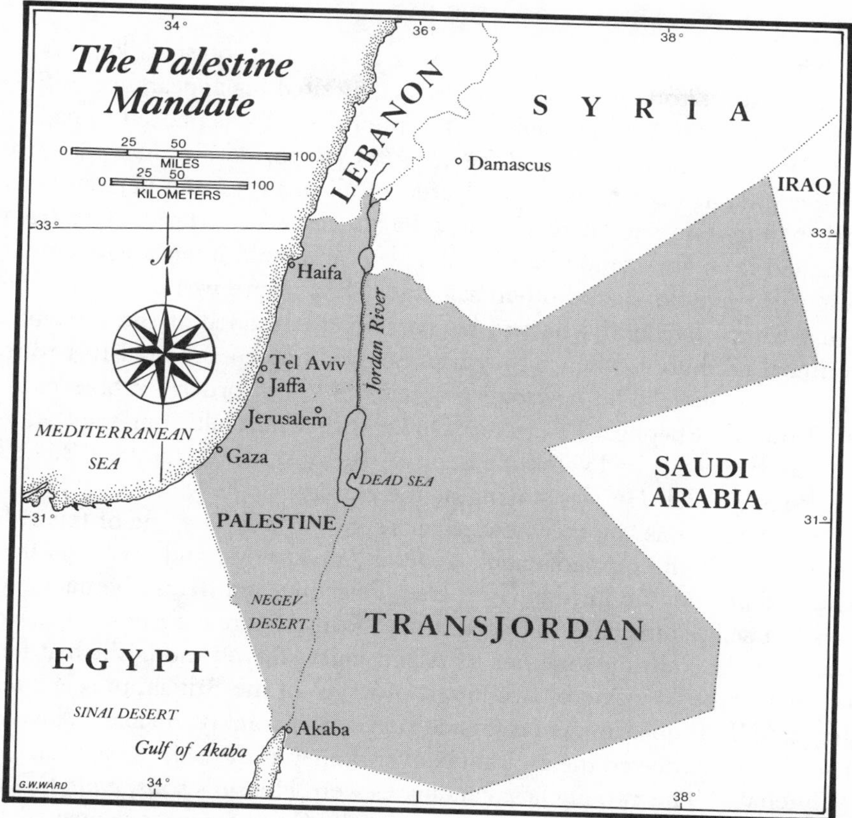

be avoided he did not say. Nor was that all. Weizmann also wanted Palestine's southern frontier pushed southward. Churchill was noncommittal. He favored including the triangular wedge of the Negev Desert in the Palestine Mandate, but not the east bank of the Jordan. Two days later, when the ship paused at Marseilles, a newspaperman came aboard and asked him the purpose of his trip. He replied disingenuously: "I am endeavouring to realise French and British unity in the East. My journey to Egypt and Asia Minor is proof of this. We must at any price coordinate our actions to the extent of uniting them. It is by those means only that we shall be able to arrive at lasting quiet, and diminish the enormous expenditure we are both making." Privately he was more entertaining. He told his party: "What the horn is to the rhinoceros, what the sting is to the wasp, the Mohammedan faith is to the Arabs — a faculty of offense or defense."[65]

As Weizmann had predicted, Churchill's arrival in Cairo was a tumultuous event. A few weeks earlier he had publicly described Egypt as part of the British Empire, and newspapers here had carried the story. El

Azhar University students were staging a one-day protest strike. Thousands of spectators, many carrying rocks, awaited his appearance in Station Square. The bridge leading into Shubra Road was packed to capacity. "Various notables," the *Palestine Weekly* reported, "waited patiently in the station, which had been cleared of all unauthorised persons, and Bristol Fighters and huge Handley Pages circled overhead. The train steamed in to the station half an hour late and amid intense excitement disgorged five boxes and other baggage." But where was Churchill, the great Satan? Prudently, he and his party had detrained at the suburban terminal of Shubra, whence they had motored unseen and undisturbed to their destination. The newspaper noted that "a disorderly rabble gathered outside Shepheard's crying 'Down with Churchill!' but they were dispersed speedily and without casualty." Being students, they had picked the wrong hotel. He was staying at the Semiramis.[66]

The Semiramis, another newspaper reported, was "a scene of feverish bustle," as high commissioners, generals, governors, and civil servants checked in from the Persian Gulf, Iraq, Palestine, and British Somaliland. His Marseilles interview to the contrary, Winston's real purpose in Cairo was, not the knitting together of Allied unity, frayed though it had become, but the choosing of two kings, protégés of the British, to rule over Iraq and Transjordan. As Lawrence later wrote frankly, he and Winston had already reviewed the aspirants "over dinner at the Ship Restaurant in Whitehall." The two likeliest candidates were Husein's sons, *amīr* Faisal and *amīr* Abdullah. On March 12, 1921, the Cairo conference opened at the Mena House. "Practically all the experts and authorities on the Middle East were summoned," Churchill wrote afterward, a singular description of a meeting at which, of the thirty-eight participants, thirty-six were British. Lawrence suggested that Faisal be crowned head of Iraq, "not only," the minutes read, "because of his personal knowledge and friendship for the individual, but also on the ground that in order to counteract the claims of rival candidates and to pull together the scattered elements of a backward and half-civilized country, it was essential that the first ruler should be an active and inspiring personality." His motion, with Churchill's approval, carried without dissent. Abdullah, in Lawrence's opinion, was "lazy and by no means dominating," but though unfit to rule Iraq he would be permitted to reign over Transjordan under the watchful eye of a British high commissioner. Churchill announced his intention to appoint Abdullah in Palestine, and in later years he would say: "The Emir Abdullah is in Transjordania, where I put him one Sunday afternoon in Jerusalem." Zionism's hopes were honored; Sir Herbert Samuel, the Empire's high commissioner in Palestine, was instructed to foster a Jewish homeland. It was all very insular — Faisal and Abdullah would send their sons to public schools in England — and it was also rather medieval. Churchill enjoyed this feudal role immensely. And Lawrence was delighted. He continued to hold other politicians in contempt, but in the *Seven Pillars* he would write enthusiastically of Winston's accomplishments, concluding that, as a result of them, "I must put on record my conviction that England is out of the Arab affair with clean hands." When at long last the book was published he sent an inscribed copy to "Winston Churchill, who made a happy ending to this show. . . . And eleven years after we set our hands to making an honest settlement, all our work still stands; the countries have gone forward, our interests having been saved, and nobody having been killed, either on one side or the other. To have planned for eleven years is statesmanship. I ought to have given you two copies of this work!" James Morris wrote: "The routes to India were safe as never before, the oil wells of Iran and the Persian Gulf, the Abadan refinery, all were securely in British possession."[67]

Other matters lay before the conference, notably the occupation of Iraq by British troops. Churchill decided to withdraw them, and, in a grand if absurd gesture, declared that the entire country — 116,600 square miles — would be defended by the emaciated RAF, thereby saving the Exchequer £25,000,000 a year. Then he left the details to subordinates in Mena House and departed to enjoy leisure outside. The Egyptian climate is at its most pleasant in March, and he sprawled happily beneath its sun. He knew he was unpopular with the Egyptians — many vehicles carried stickers reading *"à bas Churchill"* — "but," as Jessie Crosland, the wife of a civil servant, recalled a half-century later, "he didn't care. He took his easel out and sat in the road painting — he also talked so loudly in the street that the generals got quite nervous." Cordons of police held back furious mobs who had come to stone him. Carried to and fro in an armored car, he painted the Sphinx and the Pyramids while Clementine admired them, and he even held a one-man show of his canvases. On an expedition in the desert he was careening forward on a loping camel when his saddle slipped, dashing him off. Several colorfully dressed bedouins galloped up and offered one of their horses, but he rose, dusted himself off, and growled: "I started on a camel and I shall finish on a camel." An Englishwoman who attended the conference remembers: "When things were boring in the hotel everyone would cheer up when Winston came in, followed by an Arab carrying a pail and a bottle of wine." On their last day in Egypt, Winston and Clementine were driven to a Nile dam, which he painted. Returning, they crashed

Churchill and a friend in Egypt with T. E. Lawrence (right)

into another car. Churchill, a journalist observed, was "far more concerned about the safety of his painting than about himself." According to the *Egyptian Gazette*, no one was hurt. Indeed, at a farewell ball given by Lord Allenby, the country's high commissioner, Clemmie was reported to have danced until "close on midnight."[68]

Her husband had left the dance floor earlier in the evening, when Sir Herbert Samuel arrived from Jerusalem. The *Palestine Weekly* noted that "Mr Churchill at once went upstairs with him and was seen no more." The discussion of the river Jordan, its banks, and its people, had begun. At midnight on March 23, Winston, Clementine, Sir Herbert, and Lawrence boarded a train in Cairo Station for their first Palestinian stop, Gaza. There, early the following morning, they confronted a mob of 150,000 Arabs, whose "chief cry," according to a British officer, "over which they waxed quite frenzied, was: 'Down with the Jews! Cut their throats!' " This, incredibly, was unexpected. Winston's Arabists had assured him that there was no incongruity in England's separate pledges to the Jews and to the Arabs. Even Lawrence had believed that Palestinian hostility to Zionism had been overrated and could easily be contained; he had endorsed Abdullah, despite his reservations about him, because he thought Abdullah could persuade his people to accept a Jewish homeland. But when he heard the shouting crowds at Gaza and successive stops, he realized his error. Churchill, misunderstanding their fervor, thought they were acclaiming him and waved back cheerfully. Lawrence then translated their chants, and Winston muttered that he was at least grateful they weren't stoning him. Actually, they were plotting violence, but against the Jews, not him. Abdullah's appeals for calm were ignored. So was a government ban on all demonstrations during Churchill's tour. In Haifa ten Jews and five policemen were wounded by missiles and knives, and two innocent bystanders, a young boy and a Moslem woman, were killed. The Executive Committee of the Haifa Congress of Palestinian Arabs, calling on Winston, handed him a twelve-thousand-word statement denouncing the Balfour declaration and the concept of Palestine as a Jewish homeland. Jews, they said, had been scattered over the earth for thousands of years, "and have become nationals of the various nations amongst whom they settled. They have no separate political or lingual existence. . . . Hebrew is a dead language." If there was such a thing as Jewish power and a Jewish nation, what was the status "of those high

Jewish officials who are serving England to-day? Are they Jewish nationals or English nationals? . . . It is obvious they cannot be both at the same time."[69]

This was debatable, but reasonable — very different from the throngs that screamed "Palestine for the Arabs! Down with the Zionists!" — and Churchill was attentive. But then they made a mistake. They threatened him. "If England does not take up the cause of the Arabs," they declared, "other Powers will. . . . If she does not listen, then perhaps Russia will take up their call some day, or perhaps even Germany." Now his temper rose. As Lawrence wrote a friend, "The man's as brave as six, as good-humored, shrewd, self-confident & considerate as a statesman can be: & several times I've seen him chuck the statesmanlike course & do the honest thing instead." The political response to such an overture would be equivocation. Winston bluntly told them that it had been Englishmen, not Palestinian Arabs, who had overthrown their Turkish oppressors: "The position of Great Britain in Palestine is one of trust, but it is also one of right." Nearby, he reminded them, more than two thousand British soldiers were buried, "and there are many other graveyards, some even larger, scattered about in this land." To fulfill that trust, "and for the high purposes we have in view, supreme sacrifices were made by all these soldiers of the British Empire, who gave up their lives and blood."[70]

Whatever his previous doubts about the justice of creating a Zionist state, they were gone now. He knew that it would be expensive. He said: "In Africa the population is docile and the country fruitful; in Mesopotamia the country is arid and the population ferocious. A little money goes a long way in Africa and a lot of money goes a very little way in Arabia." But he believed the price must be paid. At the same time, however, he urged the Jews to be realistic. After trying to speak at the Mosque of Omar, where he was shouted down by Arabs, he visited the Hebrew University, still under construction, to plant a symbolic tree. "Personally," he told his audience, "my heart is full of sympathy for Zionism." He believed "that the establishment of a Jewish National Home in Palestine will be a blessing to . . . Great Britain." Then he reminded them that when the British promised to support Zionism, they also "assured the non-Jewish inhabitants that they should not suffer in consequence. Every step you take should therefore be also for the moral and material benefit of all Palestinians." He said: "I am now going to plant a tree, and I hope that in its shadow peace and prosperity may return once more to Palestine."[71]

It will surprise no one who has lived in the Middle East that the tree broke as it was handed to him, that there was no backup, and that they had to settle for a scrawny palm which wouldn't even grow in that soil. Harry Sacher, an English Zionist who was practicing law in Palestine, wrote a friend that "Churchill spoke very plainly in reaffirming the Balfour Declaration, both to the Jews and the Arabs. But he also told the Jews that they must do their bit, and he enlarged upon the pressures on the [British] taxpayer, and the anti-Zionist critics in Parliament. The Arabs are angry, and there was a bit of trouble in Haifa, where a crowd was dispersed by force, perhaps too much force. I am not happy about the Arab position." He wondered "whether the British Government may not finish by dropping the whole thing and clearing out — for financial reasons. I really don't know whether England today can afford such a luxury as a foreign policy, with or without mandates."[72]

Back in England the House discovered that Winston's commitment to the Palestine problem was absolute. At times it seemed a thankless task. Some English Zionists regarded the creation of Transjordan as a betrayal of Balfour's pledge; one of them, Richard Meinertzhagen, wrote a friend that he had confronted Winston and "told him it was grossly unfair to the Jews, that it was another promise broken and that it was a most dishonest act, that the Balfour Declaration was being torn up by degrees and that the official policy of H.M.G. to establish a Home for the Jews in Biblical Palestine was being sabotaged; that I found the Middle East Department whose business it was to implement the Mandate almost one hundred per cent hebraphobe and could not the duration of Abdullah's Emirate in Transjordan be of a temporary nature, say for seven years. . . . Churchill listened and said he saw the force of my argument and would consider the question. He thought it was too late to alter but a time limit to Abdullah's Emirate in Transjordan might work."[73] It wouldn't have worked, and he must have known that, but on this very delicate issue he had to listen to all sides and, however great the strain, exercise an uncharacteristic restraint.

On May 31, 1921, he reported to the cabinet that the "pronounced suspicion of Zionism" among Palestinian Arabs was unjustified. There was no validity in "current accounts of the inferior quality of recent Jewish immigrants." Indeed, they had "created a standard of living far superior to that of the indigenous Arabs." But they would need protection. The rioting in Haifa had spread to Jaffa; Jews were dying. "Zionist battalions," he believed, were not the solution. He recommended "a strong local gendarmerie." Nor did he favor elections; the Arab majority "would undoubtedly prohibit further immigration of Jews." But how many Jews? At present Palestine was inhabited by over 500,000 Moslems and fewer than 80,000 Jews. Two weeks later he assured the House that Arab fears that "in the next few years they are going to be swamped by scores of thousands of immigrants from Central Europe, who will push them off the land," were "illusory." Jewish immigration would be "a very slow process, and the rights of the existing non-Jewish population would be strictly preserved." Here he was dissembling. His private papers show that he anticipated a Zionist state of between three and four million — Israel's population today.[74]

Arab violence in Palestine was growing. On the fourth anniversary of the Balfour declaration Samuel cabled Churchill that a gang of "roughs" had invaded Jerusalem's Jewish quarter; gunfire had been exchanged and policemen had found four corpses, three of them Jews. Meanwhile, Winston had delivered a major speech in the House on Middle Eastern developments. Arabs had fought with the Allies during the war, he reminded them, and Allied "pledges were given that the Turkish rule should not be reintroduced in these regions." At the same time, a promise "of a very important character" had been given to the Jews — that Britain would do its best "to establish a Jewish national home in Palestine." England was "at this moment in possession of these countries," providing "the only form of Government existing there." To redeem these assurances he had created Iraq and Transjordan, which had given "satisfaction to Arab nationality." Now he promised to move toward a political solution in Palestine. If the Arabs were provided with a democratic form of government, they would "veto any further Jewish immigration," and this would violate England's pledge, which would mean "that the word of Britain no longer counts throughout the East and the Middle East." He believed the riddle could be solved. He could not guarantee "complete success, but I do believe that the measures which we are taking are well calculated to that end." He had "great confidence in the experts and high authorities" working on the problem, and he asked Parliament to give them "support in the difficult and delicate process of reduction and conciliation which lies before us, and on which we are already embarking."[75]

Applause was prolonged. "Winston has had a great success," Austen Chamberlain wrote Lloyd George, "both as to his speech & his policy, & has changed the whole atmosphere of the House on the Middle East question." But many were unconvinced. Churchill was not the only English politician to believe that there was a predominance of Jews in Red Moscow, and hebraphobia, as Meinertzhagen called it, was still quite respectable then. Lord Winterton warned Winston that "once you begin to buy land for the purpose of settling Jewish cultivators you will find yourself up against the hereditary antipathy, which exists all over the world, to the Jewish race." The Zionists were alarmed, but Churchill, undiscouraged, proceeded to draft a Palestinian constitution which would prevent the Arab majority from barring Jewish investment and immigration. He assured the nervous Zionist leaders that "His Majesty's Government have no intention of repudiating the obligations into which they have entered toward the Jewish people." A House referendum on the declaration and the constitution was scheduled for June, and anti-Zionists in both the Commons and the Lords began to hold strategy meetings. In the upper house they were a heavy majority; despite an appeal from Balfour, a newly created earl, the peers voted down his declaration, 60 to 29. Churchill told the House that it couldn't be renounced, that it was "an integral part of the whole mandatory system, as inaugurated by agreement between the victorious Powers and by the Treaty of Versailles." To those who argued that the Arabs could develop Palestine's economic wealth by themselves, he said: "Who is going to believe that? Left to themselves, the Arabs of Palestine would not in a thousand years have taken effective steps towards the irrigation and electrification of Palestine. They would have been quite content to dwell — a handful of philosophic people — in the wasted sun-drenched plains, letting the waters of the Jordan continue to flow unbridled and unharnessed into the Dead Sea." An Arab delegation called at the Colonial Office. He told them bluntly: "The British Government mean to carry out the Balfour Declaration. I have told you so again and again. I told you so at Jerusalem. I told you so at the House of Commons the other day." The House backed him, 292 to 35, rendering the Lords' vote meaningless. On July 22 the League of Nations approved. All legal hurdles for the birth of Israel had been cleared.[76]

Yet it remained in gestation for another quarter century. British Arabists remained militant. On August 19, 1922, Lord Sydenham wrote *The Times* that in Palestine the British had adopted "a policy of forcing by British bayonets a horde of aliens, some of them eminently undesirable, upon the original owners of the country." Later that year, when Churchill was all but immersed in the bogs of Ireland, the government issued a White Paper affirming the declaration but adding that this did not mean "the imposition of a Jewish nationality upon the inhabitants of Palestine as a whole." This bland concession to the Arabs infuriated Weizmann without placating the Arabs. The only alternative seemed to be a continuance of British rule. In 1928 the Zionists, with British encouragement, established the Jewish Agency for Palestine to manage their interests there. The immediate response of the Arabs was a pogrom. A succession of British commissions studied the Palestine dilemma in 1929, 1936, 1938, and 1939. Some suggested restrictions on Jewish immigration; one proposed partition. The Arabs struck back with violence, terrorism, and boycotts of British goods. With the outbreak of World War II, England once more needed the Arabs as allies, and nothing was done until the postwar years, when Jewish terrorists took matters into their own hands. Robert Rhodes James, who is perhaps Churchill's most astute critic, believes that his failure "to produce a workable solution in the area cannot be held against him. It was a task beyond his capacities, but it is probably true to say that it was beyond the capacities of any individual to accomplish. At the time it seemed as though he had skillfully reconciled the conflicting wartime assurances made by the British to the Arabs and the Jews." His successors in the Colonial Office were either lacking his determination, intimidated by the Arabs, or infected by racial prejudice. Poring over the old documents, one has the feeling that they themselves did not know.[77]

In his speech of June 14, 1921, Churchill had told the House that any successful Middle Eastern policy would eventually depend upon "a peaceful and lasting settlement with Turkey."[78] That was precisely what Britain lacked, and it is a supreme irony that the most damaging blow to Winston's prestige during his two years as colonial secretary came from — of all places — the Dardanelles. Moreover, the man who dealt it was the victor of Gallipoli, General Mustapha Kemal, now Kemal Atatürk ("the Great Turk"), who had become an enlightened dictator consecrated to the transformation of his homeland into a modern state. At San Remo and in the Treaty of Sèvres, imposed on the weak sultan by the Allies, Turkey had been stripped, not only of its Arab possessions, but of many lands inhabited by Turkish people. The Bosporus and the Dardanelles were internationalized and the shores of both straits demilitarized. Moreover, Greece, Turkey's ancient enemy, had been awarded Smyrna, Thrace, and the sultan's Aegean islands.

Lloyd George was responsible for this. A passionate philhellenist, under the spell of Premier Venizelos, he believed the Greeks were completely justified in their determination to regain what they regarded as their lost territories in Asia Minor, including areas not awarded them at Sèvres. Churchill vehemently disagreed. For eight months he urged Lloyd George to negotiate with Kemal. The prime minister replied that

Kemal was a rebel and an outcast. At a cabinet meeting in the first week of 1920, Winston recommended that British troops be withdrawn from Constantinople. George said they would leave only when Greek soldiers were ready to replace them. Curzon, the foreign secretary, agreed with Winston; so did the foreign ministers of France and Italy. Churchill pointed out that since England was not prepared to field an army against the Turks, its support of Greece's adventurism was dangerous. Championing Kemal's revolution as vigorously as he opposed Lenin's, he wrote George that an attempt to force new terms on him "wd require great & powerful armies & long costly operations. On this world so torn with strife I dread to see you let loose the Greek armies." He received no reply. He sent feelers to the Turks and learned that "Mustapha Kemal is willing to negotiate." Again he wrote the prime minister: "No doubt my opinions seem a vy unimportant thing. But are you sure that about Turkey the line wh you are forcing us to pursue wd commend itself to the present H. of C.?" In a war, he predicted, the Turks would defeat the Greeks, and "to let the Greeks collapse at Smyrna will leave us confronted with a Turkish triumph and the Turks will have got back Smyrna by their own efforts instead of as the result of a bargain with us." To Lord Derby he wrote: "I think we should use Kemal and a reconciled Turkey as a barrier against the Bolsheviks and to smooth down our affairs in the Middle East and in India."[79]

To Lloyd George's embarrassment, the Venizelos government fell. George still wouldn't budge, however. Greek friendship, he told the House, was essential for England, and he was unwilling "to purchase a way out of our difficulties by betraying others." He also reported that his ministers were in "unanimous agreement" that Smyrna should not be returned to Turkey. That was untrue, and Churchill angrily reminded Hankey, who had drafted the minutes of the meeting, that he had expressed his conviction that "the restoration of Turkish sovereignty or suzerainty over the Smyrna Province is an indispensable step to the pacification of the Middle East." It was also his impression that these views had been shared by the lord privy seal, the chancellor of the Exchequer, and the secretary of state for India.[80]

As Lloyd George climbed farther and farther out on his limb, Kemal completed his ruthless suppression of his Turkish rivals and united the country behind him. The caliphate had been abolished, ending fourteen centuries of Islamic rule. Elected president and appointed commander in chief of the armed forces, Kemal vowed to reconquer all Turkish territories occupied by foreign forces. In defiance of the Allies, he had kept the sultan's army intact, and his *askari,* with their preference for the bayonet and their fearsome war cry — *"Uhra, Uhra!"* ("Kill, Kill!") — routed the Armenians and Georgians in the east and then the French in the south. While he was preoccupied with these theaters, the Greek army invaded Turkey. At first their advance was virtually unopposed. Riddell wrote in his diary: "L.G. is still very pro-Greek and much elated at the Greek military successes. He said we always regarded the Turk as a first-class fighting man but even here he had broken down. L.G. told me he believes the Greeks will capture Constantinople, and he evidently hopes they will." Frances Stevenson wrote: "D. very interested in the Greek advance. He has had a great fight in the Cabinet to back the Greeks (not only in the field but morally) & he & Balfour are the only pro-Greeks there. All the others have done their best to obstruct & the W.O. have behaved abominably. However D. has got his way, but he is much afraid lest the Greek attack should be a failure, & he should be proved to have been wrong. He says his political reputation depends a great deal on what happens in Asia Minor." He kept such doubts from his colleagues, jubilantly telling the House: "Turkey is no more!"[81]

He was wrong. In the summer of 1921, when the Greek invaders were within thirty miles of Angora (now Ankara), Kemal turned and defeated them on the Sakarya River. The Allies, alarmed, tried appeasing him by forbidding the Greeks to approach Constantinople and offering unspecified revisions of the Sèvres treaty. Kemal, who had already denounced its provisions, ignored them. Mounting a counteroffensive, he crushed the Greeks in the battles of Afyon Karahisar and Bursa. They broke and fled in confusion across the Dumlu Pinar plateau, toward the coast. In the second week of August he was within a day's march of Smyrna. By now he had become a terrible myth — *"le mangeur d'homme,"* the French called him — and his frantic enemies, unable to stand against him, turned on the civilian population. Every Turkish village in the path of their flight was burned to the ground. Inside Smyrna, Turkish women and children were put to the sword. But Smyrna was home to thousands of Armenians and Greeks, too. When the Greek soldiers escaped by sea, and Armenians unwisely resisted the onrushing *askari,* the Turks ran amok. Moving systematically from street to street, they dragged all civilians who weren't Turks from their hiding places and butchered them on their own thresholds. Those who sought refuge in Smyrna's wooden churches faced an even ghastlier fate. The church walls were drenched with benzine and then fired. Refugees who attempted escape from cremation were bayoneted as they leapt out. The flames spread. Kemal's men sealed off the Turkish quarter, encircled the rest of the city, and cheered as it was reduced to ashes. The few civilians still alive were then massacred. Except for the homes of the Turkish natives and a few buildings near the Kassambra railroad station, Smyrna was destroyed.

These appalling events were unknown to the outside world for several weeks. Royal Marines had evacuated British subjects from Smyrna before the atrocities began. It was the consensus of European statesmen — with the exception of Lloyd George, who stubbornly doubted the Greeks had suffered "a complete debacle" — that the invaders had asked for it. Paris urged Athens to sue for an armistice, and Sir Horace Rumbold, the British high commissioner in Constantinople, agreed, cabling Curzon that any such truce must be followed by "the immediate and orderly evacuation of Asia Minor by Greeks."[82] But by now the situation was beyond the control of anyone except Kemal, whose momentum kept growing. Soon the straits and even the Gallipoli peninsula were in danger. Here the Turks faced, not Greeks, but British, French, and Italian soldiers. At Sèvres the Allies had established "neutral zones," including the Dardanelles, the Sea of Marmara, and the Bosporus, which were proclaimed international waters to be guarded by Allied infantry. Kemal, however, recognized no neutrals in his struggle. On Turkish soil anyone not for him was against him, and putting Smyrna behind him, he wheeled toward the Sea of Marmara, on whose shores a force of demoralized Greek soldiers had taken refuge. But they were not his main objective. The horrified maritime powers — chiefly England — realized that he meant to close the straits.

Now, as in 1915, the key position there was Chanak, the Dardanelles' port of entry, a seedy waterfront town of crooked streets and high walls still pocked and pitted from de Robeck's shelling. Once it became clear that Kemal had designs upon it, the French and Italian contingents stationed there withdrew, leaving a few thousand British troops to confront fifty-two thousand Turks. Churchill suggested that the Tommies be boated across to the European shore, thereby yielding everything on the Asian side to Kemal. If this were done, the first lord of the Admiralty assured the cabinet, the Royal Navy could still keep the channel open. The War Office forwarded the proposal to General Sir Charles Harington, the commander of the occupation force in Constantinople, but Harington insisted that his men remain in the town as a rear guard. Lloyd George was against Winston's idea anyway. He said that if they were to "scuttle" from the threat, "our credit would entirely disappear."[83] Colonel Digby Shuttleworth, a tactful officer, was dispatched to Chanak. At his request, the Admiralty sent the battleships *Ajax, Iron*

Duke, and *Marlborough* and the seaplane carrier *Pegasus* to anchor between Chanak and Gallipoli and train their guns on the approaches to the town.

Churchill had a sickening feeling of déjà vu. The ghosts of de Robeck, Fisher, and Kitchener rose before him. He told the cabinet that he felt "very uncomfortable" about the weakness of Shuttleworth's position and recommended that not only Chanak but also Constantinople be abandoned, drawing "the whole of the British forces" into Gallipoli. This, he said, would involve "no serious risk," and had "the very great merit that it would mystify, confuse, and hold up the enemy." Lloyd George shook his head. To take that line, he said, "would be the greatest loss of prestige which could possibly be inflicted on the British Empire." Churchill withdrew his motion and switched course. "The line of deep water separating Asia from Europe," he said, was "a line of great significance, and we must make that line very secure by every means within our power. If the Turks take the Gallipoli Peninsula . . . we shall have lost the whole fruits of our victory, and another Balkan war would be inevitable." He then joined Lloyd George, Balfour, Sir Laming Worthington-Evans, and F. E. Smith — who had become Lord Birkenhead in 1919 — in a hard-line bloc. "We made common cause," Winston later wrote. "The Government might break up, and we might be relieved of our burden. The nation might not support us; they could find others to advise them. The Press might howl; the Allies might bolt. We intended to force the Turk to a negotiated peace before he set foot in Europe."[84]

On September 15, 1922, they sent Kemal an ultimatum. He was told that he remained in the neutral zones at his peril: "It is the intention of His Majesty's Government to reinforce immediately . . . the troops at the disposal of Sir Charles Harington, the Allied Commander-in-Chief at Constantinople, and orders have been given to the British Fleet in the Mediterranean to oppose by every means any infraction of the neutral zones by the Turks or any attempt by them to cross the European shores." But where were Harington's reinforcements coming from? Not from Italy or France; their men were gone. Raymond Poincaré had announced in Paris that the French "would not consider themselves bound by any responsibility for any development that might result from the action which General Harington had been authorized to take." And not from the Empire, either; it was on this occasion that Churchill, on instructions from Lloyd George, asked the Dominions for troops and was turned down by all except New Zealand and Newfoundland. Winston was dining at Sir Philip Sassoon's Park Lane home on September 25 when word arrived that Kemal had finally responded to the British note.

He had rejected it. Churchill was furious. Hankey, a fellow guest, wrote in his diary: "We talked late into the night. Winston, hitherto a strong Turko-phile, had swung round at the threat to his beloved Dardanelles and become violently Turko-phobe and even Phil-Hellene."[85]

Actually, the crisis had come and gone four days earlier, after some two hundred *askari* had occupied the village of Eren Keui, less than ten miles from Chanak, and moved toward the British outposts. Told to retire, they halted but stood their ground. Then eight hundred Turkish horsemen rode closer. The British retreated toward prepared positions. The horsemen, to their relief, did not pursue them. Shuttleworth wired Harington: "Peaceful penetration by armed men who did not wish to fight, and yet refused either to withdraw or to halt, had not been foreseen." Harington cautioned him to avoid any "unnecessary" exchanges of fire.[86] The tension continued for two weeks, and at one point Harington seriously considered ordering an attempt to drive the Turks off, but early in October they marched away on Kemal's orders. After reflection Atatürk announced that he would respect the neutral zones; the Greek soldiers on the Sea of Marmara were permitted to retire unmolested into Thrace. An armistice was signed, and the following year, in the Treaty of Lausanne, the straits, Eastern Thrace, and Constantinople — which Kemal renamed Istanbul in 1930 — were peaceably awarded to Turkey.

In his biography of Curzon, Harold Nicolson writes: "To Mr Lloyd George, and above all to Mr Churchill, is due our gratitude for having at this juncture defied not the whole world merely, but the full hysterical force of British public opinion." Yet they paid a price, George deservedly, Winston less so. No one outside the cabinet knew of Churchill's wise counsel during the months before the highly charged name of Chanak suddenly reappeared on front pages, reminding readers of his earlier misfortune there. The *Daily Mail* then screamed "STOP THIS NEW WAR!" and cried that not a single British soldier should fall "in order that Mr Winston Churchill may make a new Gallipoli." To some extent, however, he was responsible for his loss in stature. He had been genuinely affronted by what he regarded as Kemal's insolence in defying a British demand. And then he learned of the destruction of Smyrna, described in a belated report to Curzon from Sir Harry Lamb, the British consul general in the ruined city. The sack of the city outraged Winston even as Bolshevik savagery had. It was an account of "pillage, rape and massacre," he wrote. "Sir Harry Lamb counted 20 corpses in 50 yards during the infernal orgy" which found "few parallels in the history of crime." His reaction to barbarism would always be unrestrained, and often misunderstood. Mrs. Keppel wrote that Winston was "longing to drop the paint brush for the sword," and Hankey noted in his diary: "I walked across the Park with Churchill one evening towards the end of the crisis and he quite frankly regretted that the Turks had not attacked us at Chanak, as he felt that the surrender of Eastern Thrace to them was humiliating, and that the return of the Turks to Europe meant an infinity of troubles."[87]

The British, alternately baffled and amused by the incompatibility of Arabs and Jews, never saw the parallel between the running canker in the Middle East and their own ancient quarrel with the Irish. Yet the two were not unlike, and the second, among people presumed to be more civilized, is the more perplexing. It is a source of endless wonder that these two islands, lying side by side off the coast of Europe, should have been the fount of so much anguish, each for the other. One spawned the mightiest empire in history, and its arrogant overlords were loathed by their repressed neighbors across the Irish Sea. The other, small, poor, with virtually no valuable natural resources, supported a people conspicuously lacking in political gifts and afflicted with an extraordinary incidence of alcoholism ("It is a very moist climate," Churchill once observed), yet endowed with immense charm, romantic vision, and remarkable genius — it was the homeland of Swift, Shaw, Yeats, Joyce, Millington Synge, O'Casey, O'Faolain, and Dublin's Abbey Theatre.[88]

Ireland's impact on British public life ought to have been slight. In fact, it had been enormous. The Irish question had been a primordial parliamentary issue for generations. It had driven Pitt from office, defeated Gladstone at the height of his powers, toppled the Tories in 1885, and held the balance in the House between 1910 and 1914. When the issue of Home Rule made its periodic appearances, London newspaper accounts of it were so dense you could hardly find the non sequiturs; Churchill told his Dundee constituents: "*The Times* is speechless, and takes three columns to express its speechlessness."[89] On the eve of the Great War, the British cabinet had been absorbed in drawing a temporary border between Ulster and Eire, narrowing it down first to the counties of Fermanagh and Tyrone, next to parishes and groups of parishes inside Fermanagh and Tyrone — and even then was unable to reach a solution which would satisfy either side. Irish hearts and English hearts beat to a different rhythm. The Irish hated the English, and Englishmen who did not return the hatred were fascinated by the Irish. Nietzsche had warned against staring too long into an abyss because eventually, he said, it would stare back. Ireland was England's abyss and it never blinked.

Like many British politicians, Winston had personal ties to Ireland. Dublin's Sackville Street, since renamed O'Connell Street, had been familiar to his grandfather, his father, and, in his childhood, to Winston himself. Yet although he could never conceive of its secession from the United Kingdom, he had never been, and never would be, accused of publicly taking sides in its draining religious feud. To him it was "the Empire's ailing child," which he also compared to a forest in which friends were indistinguishable from foes. "My views," he said once, when asked how he stood on the question, "are a harmonious process, which keeps them in relation to the current movement of events." He never broke completely with North or South. History's verdict, he then believed, would be clear: "Ireland will be revealed to have been strong only in her grievance, and England weak only in the assertion of her power in interior Irish affairs." Since Ireland, unlike the Dominions, lacked self-government, its problems had become part of his responsibilities when he entered the Colonial Office. In the opinion of the British public it was, indeed, the largest part. As Alan Moorehead observes, "in the early 1920s it seemed at times that this issue eclipsed every other and that there could be no solution of it." Churchill himself saw "the dreary steeples of Fermanagh and Tyrone emerging once again."[90]

Actually, they had been there all the time. Though he and the rest of England had been looking eastward toward the Continent between 1914 and 1918, the abyss had continued to stare at their backs. Frustrated by the prewar failures of John Redmond's Irish Nationalists, the people of southern Ireland, or Eire, as we now know it, turned increasingly, during the war years, to the leaders of the Sinn Féin. The Sinn Féiners were unwilling to settle for a parliament in Dublin. They wanted a republic like the United States, independent of England. The Easter rebellion of the Irish Republican Brotherhood (IRB) in 1916, planned in conjunction with German agents, was doomed before the first shot was fired, but the British execution of Patrick Pearse and several other rebel leaders — Eamon de Valera was spared because he had been born in America — invested them with martyrdom, an attribute highly valued in a country which cherishes the maxim that "grass soon grows over a battlefield but never over a scaffold." In the summer of the following year most of the survivors were belatedly amnestied, De Valera being released on July 11. Early in 1918 Redmond died, and the British then delivered two further blows to Anglo-Irish friendship. They rearrested De Valera and the rest of the Sinn Féin leadership for subversion. And then they attempted to induct Eire's men into the British army. This was a fiasco. Inducted, the men immediately deserted en masse. "Irish conscription," Churchill said, "was handled in such a fashion . . . that we had the worst of both worlds, all the resentment against compulsion and in the end no law and no men."[91] Meanwhile, Orangemen had been fighting gallantly on the western front — Kitchener had asked them for a brigade of volunteers, and they had given him a complete division — assuring Ulster status as a privileged Protestant sanctuary when Home Rule came.

Ulster excepted, Sinn Féin candidates swept Ireland in the parliamentary elections of 1918. Like Churchill in the Boer War, they had successfully exploited imprisonment as a political asset. But instead of crossing to London and taking the House of Commons' oath to a King they scorned, they met in Dublin, adopted the Easter rebellion program, formed a Dáil Eireann ("Irish Assembly"), and elected De Valera president of it. The Dáil (pronounced "Doyle") was suppressed by the British. De Valera went back behind bars, but in February 1919 he was rescued from Lincoln Jail — and smuggled, disguised, into New York — by the daring Michael Collins, a veteran of the Easter Rising, adjutant general of the Irish Republican Army, and leader of the IRA guerrilla warfare which now began. The British put a price of £5,000 on Collins's head, but like the rest of the desperate measures adopted that year it accomplished nothing. Except in the northeastern Protestant counties civil order was disintegrating. The IRA held Eire in a thralldom of loyalty or, where that was lacking, of terror. The British authorities in Dublin Castle were under virtual siege.

In August 1919, when the Dáil was proclaimed an illegal organization, Churchill, then still minister of war, told the cabinet that the time was not propitious for an Irish solution. Yet something had to be done. Violence had become the official policy of Eire's real leaders. The relationship between their "Irish Republic" and Great Britain amounted to a state of war. In the United States — where he had raised over five million dollars from Irish Americans — De Valera, describing negotiations between Dublin and London, said that "the hand of Irishmen held out in good faith was spurned and spat upon." Eire's hands now held grenades or revolvers. That year the IRA was responsible for eighteen murders of Englishmen, seventy-seven armed attacks, and an attempt to ambush the viceroy. In 1920 it grew worse. On March 26 the resident magistrate in Dublin was dragged from a streetcar and slain on the spot. Clementine wrote Winston: "This new Irish murder is very terrible." He replied that Irish terrorism was "really getting very serious. . . . What a diabolical streak they have in their character! I expect it is that treacherous, assassinating, conspiring trait which has done them in in bygone ages of history and prevented them from being a great responsible nation with stability and prosperity. It is shocking that we have not been able to bring the murderers to justice." By April, British constables were being shot down daily, five of them in one burst of gunfire in county Galway. Four British staff officers were killed in broad daylight aboard a train between Cork and Bandon. Sir Henry Wilson, now chief of the Imperial General Staff, wrote in his diary: "Tonight Winston insinuated that the murdered officers were careless, useless fellows & ought to have taken precautions. This fairly roused me & I let fly about the Cabinet being cowards and not governing Ireland." Winston felt the torment of frustration. So did the cabinet. Exasperated during a parliamentary inquiry, Churchill asked the attorney general for Ireland: "Why not make life intolerable in a particular area?" This had already been tried, he was told: "We made ten thousand raids in six months. We did not get hold of the revolvers. They bury them in bogs."[92]

Not all Eire patriots were killers. Terence McSwiney, lord mayor of Cork, went on a hunger strike and died two months later. And some terrorists favored abduction. Scotland Yard reported: "At a Sinn Féin meeting in a private house in Glasgow last Saturday night it was decided that the best form of reprisals against the British Government would be the kidnapping of any of the following Ministers: — the Prime Minister, Mr Bonar Law, Lord French, Mr Winston Churchill, Sir Hamar Greenwood." Six members of the Sinn Féin executive had been appointed to this mission and provided with £250 to carry it out. The Yard warned cabinet members to avoid Scotland "for the next few days or weeks." Detective Sergeant W. H. Thompson was assigned to Churchill as a bodyguard; he would be at Churchill's side, off and on, for the rest of Winston's political life. Churchill, characteristically, overreacted to challenge. His early responses to the Irish crisis were unrealistic. He proposed rewards for the capture of Sinn Féiners, blind to the bloody fate which would await any Irish informer. In Dundee he opposed consideration of Home Rule while "the murder gang in Ireland" went unpunished. No settlement could be reached by "surrender to treacherous murder, but only on the basis of justice and generosity," he said, unaware that it was the lack of justice and generosity which had sown the seeds of terrorism. In the *Illustrated Sunday Herald* he wrote inaccurately: "No nation has ever established its title-deeds by a campaign of assassination. The British nation, having come grimly through the slaughter of Armageddon, are certainly not going to be scared by the squalid scenes of sporadic warfare which are being enacted across the Irish Channel." Clementine, troubled, cautioned him: "Do my darling use your influence now for some sort of moderation or at any rate justice in Ireland. Put yourself in the place of the Irish. If you were ever leader you would not be cowed by severity & certainly not by reprisals which fall like rain from Heaven upon the Just & upon the Unjust. . . . It always makes me unhappy & disappointed when I see you inclined to take for granted that the rough, iron-fisted, 'Hunnish' way will prevail."[93]

But he was determined that the ironfisted way should be tried first. The impulse to fight fire with fire, always plausible and always barren, was too strong to be suppressed. From the outset it raised problems, however, among them the question of who should provide the retaliatory fire. Greenwood, the new chief secretary for Ireland, told a committee of ministers: "The Dublin police cannot be relied upon, nor the Post Office, nor the Civil Service." Churchill observed: "It is monstrous that we have some two hundred murders and no one hung." Turning to the prime minister, he reminded him that "you agreed six or seven months ago that there should be hanging." Lloyd George confirmed it and asked Denis Henry, the attorney general: "I feel certain you must hang. Can you get convictions from Catholics?" Henry replied: "Substantially, no." The possibility of martial law was raised. Churchill wrote Sir Henry Wilson, as chief of the general staff, asking him how many men he could spare. The answer was discouraging. Of England's forty-six peacetime battalions, ten were of the guards needed for defense of the homeland and eight more were unsuitable because they were Irish. That left only twenty-eight. "If 8 were sent to Ireland," Wilson wrote, "we should have very little for our own internal troubles & nothing for India, Egypt, C-ople, etc." Sir Nevil Macready, chief commissioner of Scotland Yard, had crossed to embattled Dublin Castle with broad powers and reported that the Royal Irish Constabulary was inadequate for the job. Churchill felt it imperative to snuff out the uprising before "flames of orange and green flashed out of the Irish furnace." Unfortunately the extinguisher he chose contained gasoline. He proposed the establishment of a temporary RIC branch, to be called the "Special Emergency Gendarmerie." The cabinet approved it on May 11, stipulating that the force be raised, paid, and "administered" by Churchill's ministry. Eight thousand recruits were to be sought in England, chiefly among former soldiers. In addition, another thousand ex-officers would serve in an "Auxiliary Division" of the RIC. The "Auxis," as they came to be known, received a pound a day. Members of the Gendarmerie, who were paid ten shillings a day, were issued army surplus khaki uniforms and the black belts of the RIC. They became infamous as the "Black and Tans," or, more simply, the "Tans."[94]

All over Europe the hardened dregs of disbanded armies were distorting postwar politics — in Germany the former Corporal Hitler was organizing veterans into *Ordnertruppe,* or strong-arm squads — and eight thousand British survivors of the trenches were now set loose in Eire. In his diary Wilson called this "a panic measure," predicting that "raising 8000 scallawags" would "give us no military value but great anxieties." But he did not know the worst. He assumed that they, like the RIC, would serve as policemen. Instead, they were trained to use IRA methods against the IRA, which, in practice, meant against the people of southern Ireland. Churchill wrote Lloyd George: "I am prepared to support and to defend in Parliament a policy of reprisals within strict limits and under strict control in certain districts in which it should be declared that conditions approximating a state of war exist. I believe that such a policy would be less discreditable and more effective than what is going on." He went farther. The Tans, he argued, should not be disciplined for excesses: "I cannot feel it right to punish the troops when, goaded in the most brutal manner and finding no redress, they take action on their own account." It was becoming increasingly difficult to pin George down on the Irish question — one day he would speak of the need to "hunt down" the killers and the next of hopes for "lasting reconciliation" — but he supported Winston's Tans publicly, declaring: "We have murder by the throat . . . we had to reorganize the police, and when the Government was ready we struck the terrorists and now the terrorists are complaining of terror."[95]

But others were complaining, too. Greenwood, the Westmoreland of his day, told the press that the countryside was being pacified by the Tans, and that they were innocent of atrocities. That was untrue. The extent of their guilt is unclear; self-serving claims were made by both sides. Robert Rhodes James writes that "no doubt their record has been excessively besmirched," yet adds: "After every allowance has been made, theirs is a record of squalor that was, unhappily, not without precedent, but which increasingly nauseated civilized opinion in Britain and abroad." One notorious incident was the razing of Cork on December 11, 1920. Greenwood denied that the Tans had started the fire. Nevertheless, the cabinet authorized an investigation and then suppressed the subsequent report on the ground that "the effects of publishing" it "would be disastrous to the Government's whole policy in Ireland." In 1974 Henry Pelling wrote that the savagery of the fighting between the Sinn Féin and the Tans "is still a bitter memory."[96]

After Cork critics arose on all sides. The Labour party's Commission on Ireland charged: "Things are being done in the name of Britain which make her name stink in the nostrils of the world." Sir Henry Wilson noted: "I told Winston that I thought this a scandal & Winston was very angry. He said these 'Black & Tans' were honourable & gallant officers, etc., etc. & talked much nonsense. . . . It is an amazing & scandalous thing." Later he wrote: "At Balbriggan, Thurles & Galway yesterday the local police marked down certain SFs as in their opinion actual murderers or instigators & then coolly went & shot them without question or trial. Winston saw very little harm in this but it horrifies me." Austen Chamberlain asked for reassurance that the law-enforcement officers were not proceeding "without control." Greenwood was instructed "to endeavour to limit reprisals," but a majority of the cabinet approved a resolution "that it would be a mistake for the Government to take the initiative in any suspension of military activities in Ireland, and that the present policy in that country should be pursued." In public, Churchill weakly argued that the Tans merely enjoyed "the same freedom as the Chicago or New York police in dealing with armed gangs." After martial law had been declared in the counties of Kilkenny, Limerick, Kerry, and Cork he wrote an archbishop who had protested, that the government had had no choice because "no body is in corporate and continuous existence which has the power or even the constitutional right to speak for Ireland," that both "well-meaning individuals" and "the Irish people" were "paralysed by the terroristic action of a violent and desperate body of men," and, the ultimate reason: "Britain will never consent, while life and strength remain, to the destruction of the integrity of the British Empire. Was it not [Thomas Colley] Grattan who said 'The Channel forbids union; the ocean forbids separation'?"[97]

Privately, however, his view was changing. The Tans had been given a free hand and nothing had been accomplished. England and Eire were farther apart than ever. Churchill the warrior was being transformed into Churchill the peacemaker. On November 3, 1920, he told the cabinet: "I do not consider that the present Government attitude on reprisals can be maintained much longer. It is not fair on the troops, it is not fair on the officers who command them." In a subsequent meeting the question of an armistice was raised. Thomas Jones, first assistant secretary (later deputy secretary) to the cabinet, noted: "All through the recent discussions of the Irish problem the most irreconcilable Minister has been Balfour. Churchill has frankly acknowledged the failure of force." Strongly supported by Churchill, Lloyd George approved of a truce offer, and the Sinn Féin accepted a respite in the killing. The quixotic Sir Henry Wilson was indignant. He had changed course 180 degrees. In his diary he wrote: "So the murderers have won & the coward L.G. has gone down on his knees, & all his miserable Cabinet on their hunkers behind him."[98]

Churchill had transferred his faith to a new Home Rule bill which he and Birkenhead had steered through Parliament. On December 23, 1920, the Government of Ireland Act became law, dividing Ireland into two states, the twenty-six counties of Eire and the six counties of Ulster, each of which would elect its own legislature. Eire's powers were to be greater than those provided in the 1914 bill, but defense, foreign affairs, and customs would remain in British hands. Winston, ever striving to unify the House, acclaimed the act as a "gift," not of one English political party, but "the achievement of a coalition." He considered it a turning point. So did the Orangemen. Eire did not. Southern Ireland went to the polls in May 1921, and of the 128 legislative candidates elected, 124 belonged to the Sinn Féin. They met in June, swore never to accept partition of Ireland, took a republican oath, elected De Valera president, and then voted themselves out of office. At this point a deus ex machina appeared in the form of George V. Opening Belfast's new parliament on June 22, the King appealed for an end to fratricidal strife. His sovereign's initiative forced Lloyd George to send De Valera a message via courier, suggesting negotiations. The leader of the Sinn Féin replied that they could meet only if it were agreed in advance that he, as a "President," was senior to Lloyd George, who was only a "Prime Minister." George indignantly refused, thereby dropping into De Valera's trap. The truce broke down and the killing resumed. Eire's people were weary, however. Even IRA members demanded an end to the bloodshed. The Tans had thinned the ranks of their battalions, and the survivors begged for at least a glimmer of relief. When Lloyd George offered again in October to negotiate, therefore, De Valera yielded slightly. The message had invited him to discuss how "the British Empire can be best reconciled with Irish National aspirations." He answered: "The Irish Republic would be glad to discuss this question with the Community of Nations known as the British Empire." Himself would never go to London, but he agreed to send his two most trusted lieutenants, Arthur Griffith, founder of the Sinn Féin, and Michael Collins, until then known in England only as a notorious IRA gunman.[99]

Eamon de Valera and Arthur Griffith, July 1921

Churchill also yielded a little. Speaking in Dundee on September 24, he said that the establishment of "a separate foreign Republic in Ireland" was out of the question; it would bring "certain war — real war, not mere bushranging" between Eire and England, which would mean that "every Irishman in the British Empire would become an alien enemy, and would be in exactly the same position as the unfortunate Germans who were in this country during the Great War." The threat of Armageddon was his stick. His carrot was something Eire had never been offered before: partial dominion status, putting Eire almost on a par with Canada, Australia, New Zealand, and South Africa. Britain, he said, could do no more. The Irish delegates must realize that. "Squander this conference," he said, "and peace is bankrupt." *The Times* commented: "The country will be grateful to MR CHURCHILL for the breadth and lucidity of his speech . . . whether men agree with him or not, MR CHURCHILL's able and calm review of the situation helps to restore confidence."[100]

On the morning of October 11, Collins and Griffith were cordially welcomed at No. 10 and introduced to the cabinet across an unusually wide table — Lloyd George had anticipated that some of his ministers

Michael Collins, 1922

would refuse to shake hands with men they regarded as murderers. Churchill did not share that view. He knew the Irish delegates were brave men, and to him courage was admirable in itself. Collins in particular attracted him. He and Winston were, in fact, alike in many ways: fearless, charismatic, fiercely patriotic, ready to sacrifice everything for principle. Both had cherubic features but bulldog expressions, and they shared a ready wit. "Winston and Michael Collins appear to fascinate each other and are bosom friends," wrote the amazed Stanley Salvidge. Their friendship grew; after a day of exhausting deliberations, Winston would take his recent enemy home and sit up late, talking, arguing, drinking, even singing. Later he recalled one evening when Lloyd George and Griffith were also there. "It was at a crisis," he wrote, "and the negotiations seemed to hang only by a thread. Griffith went upstairs to parley with Mr Lloyd George alone. Lord Birkinhead and I were left with Michael Collins meanwhile. He was in his most difficult mood, full of reproaches and defiances, and it was very easy for everyone to lose his temper. 'You hunted me day and night!' he exclaimed. 'You put a price on my head!' 'Wait a minute,' I said. 'You are not the only one.' And I took from my wall the framed copy of the reward offered for my recapture by the Boers. 'At any rate it was a good price — £5,000. Look at me — £25 dead or alive. How would you like that?' " Another time he slyly produced a thumbnail appraisal of himself which Collins had written: "Will sacrifice all for political gain. . . . Inclined to be bombastic. Full of ex-officer jingo or similar outlook. Don't actually trust him."[101] There was a moment of silence; then both men burst into laughter.

Collins trusted him now, but it was Churchillian charm which kept them together, for Winston had no intention of giving much more ground. He still believed that eventually "Ulster will join herself with Southern Ireland . . . the national unity of Ireland within the British Empire will be attained," and he would make no concession which might jeopardize that dream, although, of course, he could not repeal the 1920 act. England, he insisted, must keep its two naval bases in the south, at Queenstown and Berehaven. Eire would be permitted no navy. Neither could it remain neutral in any future war: "The position of absolute neutrality would have been a great difficulty to Britain in the late war. We could not have used your ports as bases from which to defend ourselves against submarine attack." All men elected to Eire's parliament must take an oath to the King. He told Collins, and then the House: "We do not recognize the Irish Republic." Instead, southern Ireland would be known as the Irish Free State, or, in Gaelic, Saorstát Eireann. The Crown would be represented by an officer "to be appointed in like manner as the Governor General of Canada," and the Free State would assume responsibility for a share of Britain's national debt. Collins and Griffith won some points — Eire could raise an army and arm vessels to protect Irish fishermen — but they were few. Nevertheless, the Irishmen signed the treaty in the first week of December. Churchill had warned them that if they didn't, England would invade Eire, and Lloyd George had backed him up. Both sides were taking risks. As he put down his pen, Birkenhead said: "I may have signed my political death warrant tonight." But for once F.E. did not have the last word. Collins said softly: "I may have signed my actual death warrant." There was a long moment of silence. They realized that he had meant it. To ease Collins's reception in Dublin, Churchill raised a sensitive issue with the cabinet the following morning. He pointed out that several Sinn Féiners had been convicted of murder and sentenced to hang. "Winston," Jones noted, "suggested that the Irish should be informed privately that the extreme sentence will not be carried out." It was approved; officials were instructed to quietly assure "prisoners now lying under sentence of death that the death penalty will not be enforced."[102]

None of this reconciled De Valera, who immediately repudiated the pact, or die-hard Tories, particularly the Orangemen, to whom the Free State was anathema. Ulster's Unionists were furious at the government for even holding conversations with the men from Eire. Carson charged that Northern Ireland had been used as a "puppet" in a "political game." He denounced each of the ministers in turn, coming down particularly hard on Curzon, who, he felt, had betrayed him. Churchill rose the following day to defend the treaty. He pointed to "a remarkable phenomenon." Yesterday Curzon, who had signed it, had been damned by Carson "with brilliant and corrosive invective" as a traitor to Britain. In Dublin, at that hour, De Valera had been excoriating Collins "for a similar offence." Churchill asked: "Are we not getting a little tired of all this? These absolutely sincere, consistent, unswerving gentlemen, faithful in all circumstances to their implacable quarrels, seek to mount their respective national war horses, in person or by proxy, and to drive at full tilt at one another, shattering and splintering down the lists, to the indescribable misery of the common people and to the utter confusion of our Imperial affairs." The rest of the United Kingdom was ready, if they were not, to close the door on the "grim, grave, and in many cases, shocking realities" of the past. "Ireland," he said, "is not a daughter State. She is a parent nation. The Irish are an ancient race. Intermingled with the whole life of the Empire," they were needed to sustain it, particularly in its new acquisitions. The time had come, indeed it was past time, to resolve the island's internal quarrel: "If we can free ourselves from it, if we can to some extent reconcile the spirit of the Irish nation to the British Empire in the same way that Scotland and Wales have been reconciled, then indeed we shall have secured advantages which may well repay the trouble and the uncertainties of the present time."[103]

The House, convinced, swiftly ratified the agreement. Across St. George's Channel, however, De Valera remained intractable. Dominion status and, particularly, taking the hated oath were unacceptable to him. He would settle for nothing less than a republic. The Sinn Féin split on the issue — a schism mirrored today in Eire's two major parties, the Fianna Fáil and the Fine Gael — but the men elected to the Dáil took their seats. Griffith and Collins persuaded a majority that these were the best terms they could get, and on January 9, 1922, they approved the Free State treaty by a slim margin, 64 to 57. De Valera resigned, sought reelection, and lost by an even thinner margin, 60 to 58. Griffith replaced him, with Collins elected chairman of a provisional government which would serve until the next general election, to be held as soon as possible. "So Ireland has decided!" a friend in Cairo wrote Churchill. "Now I hope we shall not leave a soldier or penny there & we shall see some pretty doings!" Winston could not be so gay. At Lloyd George's request, he now moved to stage center, guiding legislation transferring powers to Dublin through the House, and becoming "a principal," in his words, "in British-Irish affairs." During the interim he would be responsible to three constituencies, in Parliament Square, O'Connell Street, and Ulster Hall. He assured the House: "We have not given complete Dominion Home Rule. There are special reservations in this Treaty." The situation across St. George's Channel was even more delicate. At Christmas he had said: "Should the Dáil ratify, the first step should be to get an Irish delegation . . . over here at the earliest moment." But priorities had shifted. The overriding question now was the survival of the Griffith-Collins government. De Valera had gone underground again and plunged the Free State into civil war. Homes were again being burned, trucks hijacked, warehouses emptied, trains destroyed, and bridges and viaducts blown up. "Traitors to the republic" were being "executed" by IRA veterans whom De Valera had christened his "Irregulars." On the last day of March, when the Free State bill became law, a column of Irregulars swept through Dublin, killing a Protestant policeman and four Catholics and wounding three Catholic children. De Valera declared that both the Dublin and Belfast governments were illegitimate. Thugs prevented Collins from addressing a crowd in county Mayo. Sir Henry Wilson wrote on April 3: "Valera is daily strengthening, & Collins daily weakening. Collins at Castlebar was ordered to stop speaking and obeyed! We are coming near the Republic."[104]

In the House, Wilson, who was retiring as chief of the general staff to become Northern Ireland's chief defense adviser, had become the new spokesman of Ulster's MPs. He and Churchill dueled hotly. Wilson ridiculed the very idea of self-government in southern Ireland. Winston said: "It is, I think, too soon to mock or jeer. Two months ago it was too soon to rejoice. It is still too soon to lament." Macready wrote from Dublin Castle: "The optimistic imagination of Mr Winston Churchill, that the acceptance of the treaty would result in cessation of disturbance and a loyal interpretation of its terms, is by no means shared by the Crown forces in Ireland." Actually, Winston's private thoughts were far from optimistic. He told Clementine: "The Irish position seems very dark and troubled." He wrote Collins and Griffith, complimenting them on "the spirit and personal courage which you have constantly shown in confronting the enemies of free speech and fair play," and he began shipping guns and ammunition to Free State forces in Clare, Sligo, Athlone, and Dublin. Collins, crossing to London, submitted grievances about troublemakers entering the Free State from Ulster. Churchill was already negotiating countless questions of border demarcation with Belfast, trying, as he told the House, to free England "from the terrible curse of this long internal Irish quarrel." In a confidential note to Alfred Cope, the assistant under secretary for Ireland, he asked: "Do you think there is any fighting quality in the Free State Government? Will anybody die for it or kill for it?" In dealing with Irish politicians, he had learned, tact was a prerequisite. His customary broadsword would not do. The cabinet instructed him to send Collins a formal note expressing its concern over the confusion in Eire. "Instead of this," he wrote Collins, knowing that formality would strike the wrong note, "I write to you man to man." Again and again Wilson and his followers tried to shake his confidence in the Irish signers of the treaty. In the House one of them asked him "whether the British authorities in Ireland have evidence of some forty-one orders for assassination which were signed by Mr Michael Collins." Winston snapped: "No sir, and I regret that the hon[orable] Gentleman should have placed such a question." Trust in Collins and Griffith was an absolute necessity; it was that or land a British army, which at the moment did not exist, on Free State soil. Winston knew his political situation was shaky. The Conservatives, out of power for sixteen years, had become reckless and irresponsible. Liberals and Labour MPs, as he wrote in *The Aftermath,* "watched with tender solicitude" while he fought for implementing legislation, trying to "nurse into being" a strong Belfast government.[105]

He pushed Collins as hard as he could. Learning that IRA men of all convictions were planning to meet, and that they would consider renunciation of the treaty, he put him on notice: "An adverse decision by the convention of the Irish Republican Army (so-called) would . . . be a very grave event at the present juncture. I presume that you are quite sure there is no danger of this." In reality Collins could be quite sure of very little. A band of Irregulars had occupied Dublin's Four Courts — its law buildings — and he hadn't ordered them evicted because he wasn't certain he would be obeyed. On May 20 startling news reached the Colonial Office from one of Winston's friends in Dublin. Collins and De Valera had met on neutral ground and signed a pact, agreeing that Free State men would have sixty-four seats in the new Dáil and the Irregulars fifty-seven, thus preserving the existing ratio, and that after the election Eire would be governed by a coalition of five Free Staters and four Irregulars. "The Irish masses," Churchill tartly wrote afterward, "just like the Russians two or three years before, were not to be allowed a voice in their fate." Churchill's informant had told him that Collins was beginning to have doubts about the agreement, however, and a confrontation might "make him break down." Winston wrote Collins: "I had better let you know at once . . . that as far as we are concerned in this country, we should certainly not be able to regard any such arrangement as a basis on which we could build."[106] Half abashed and half mutinous, Collins arrived in London with Griffith and William Cosgrave, another Free State leader, and tried to explain the inexplicable: that in Ireland's present chaos, any measure, however makeshift, was preferable to ravagement and slaughter. But Churchill had no time for them just then. He was rushing to the House to battle their real English adversaries. At No. 10 the three Irishmen were given tickets to the Strangers' Gallery, and they watched his fight from there.

Hardly had he reached the Treasury Bench when Sir Henry Wilson challenged him. What, he asked angrily, were the British troops in Dublin doing? "They are not there to keep order," he answered himself, "because they are not allowed to keep order." Winston tried to speak, but Wilson overrode him, shouting another question: Were not the colonial secretary's reports to the House "from end to end an admission that every single development of the Irish problem has been miscalculated?" In replying, Churchill reassumed a fighting stance. His militant moves to suppress the Curragh mutiny eight years earlier were, he knew, remembered by almost all the MPs present. Now he had to convince them that he could be as stern with Eire as he had been with Ulster then. He said: "We shall not under any circumstances agree to deviate from the Treaty either in the strict letter or the honest spirit." Should an Irish coalition attempt to destroy it "by setting up a Republic, it would be the intention of the Government to hold Dublin as one of the preliminary and essential steps in military operations." He was confident he could mobilize enough veterans of the trenches to hold the city. Shipments of munitions to the provisional government had been stopped, he said, to avoid the possibility that they might be used later against Englishmen. The outcome of the election, now scheduled for June 16, would go far toward clarifying the situation. Wilson, unreassured, lashed back: "The Colonial Secretary says we can wait. Can we? All this time murders are going on at the rate of . . . six or seven a day." Winston demurred: "I think there were only three or four murders in southern Ireland in the last ten days. The number has been larger in Northern Ireland." Wilson pressed him again: "My point is, can you wait while men are murdered like that?"[107]

It was not only men, of course. After the House rose Collins showed Winston a photograph of an entire family of Catholics, the McMahons, who had just been massacred in Ulster. According to Frank O'Connor,

Collins's biographer, "Churchill wept." The Troubles were worsening. The Free State's provisional government was losing control of the country. Collins acknowledged it, and said he understood Churchill's threat to draw England's sword. De Valera was defiant: "Mr. Churchill's threats do not affect us. We deny the right of any English authority to prescribe what an Irishman shall or shall not do." But Churchill wrote Clementine: "Our position is a vy strong one, so long as we adhere to the Treaty. And Ulster's position is a vy strong one so long as she respects the law. I have made it clear I will defend or conceal no irregularities of any kind. I will expose them coldly to Parliament whoever is guilty. We must not get back into that hideous bog of reprisals, from which we have saved ourselves."[108]

All through that spring the horrors of internecine strife clotted in suffering Eire. Hemorrhaging within as IRA Irregulars fought the Free State, its battered people faced the growing possibility of intervention by Britons and Orangemen. The frontier disputes loomed ever larger. Lloyd George wrote Churchill that he had conducted the negotiations with "skill and patience," but he was "profoundly disquieted by the developments on the Ulster border. We are not merely being rushed into a conflict, but we are gradually being manoeuvered into giving battle on the very worst grounds which could possibly be chosen for the struggle. I cannot say whether Henry Wilson and de Valera are behind this but if they are their strategy is very skillful." He suspected the Orangemen of planning to incite violence and warned against encouraging them to believe they might be reinforced by Englishmen: "We have surely done everything that Ulster can possibly expect to ensure its security." Churchill agreed, but he pointed out that Belfast's fears were not entirely unjustified. He could not discount the danger that the factions in southern Ireland might unite to invade the smaller state in the north. During one of Collins's calls at the Colonial Office, Winston told him that "if any part of the Irish Republican Army, either pro-Treaty or anti-Treaty, invaded Northern soil, we would throw them out." In point of fact he contemplated the use, not of troops, but of warships. In a memorandum he wrote: "The effect of a blockade would not starve the Irish people, but it would at a stroke ruin their prosperity. Out of 205 millions exported from Ireland last year, 203 were purchased by Great Britain. This fact alone is decisive."[109]

Once more he was captivated by the possibilities of force: deep within him lurked the imaginative child who had played with toy soldiers in his Mayfair nursery. If he meant to stiffen Collins's spine, however, it was unnecessary. The man was a paradigm of valor. And in the end Winston knew it, knew that Collins was not only the best but the only alternative to De Valera, who, in Winston's words, had "come to personify not a cause but a catastrophe." Reversing the policy he had presented to the House, he instructed Cope to resume consignments of weapons to Dublin, drawing "arms from the British Government, which has a large surplus." He added: "I am quite ready to continue the steady flow of arms to trustworthy Free State troops." Collins was constantly commuting between Ireland and England, sleeping in deck chairs, electioneering at home and drawing up Eire's constitution with Churchill and Colonial Office advisers. Confirming Winston's faith in him, he agreed to constitutional changes which could only sharpen the conviction of IRA hardliners that he had turned his coat. The King would be invested with the formalities of executive power in the Free State; judges would be nominated by the governor-general; any constitutional amendment conflicting with the treaty would be void. These provisions would not, however, be published until the early hours of election day. Shaking Churchill's hand as he left London, Collins said, "I shall not last long. My life's forfeit, but I'll do my best. After I'm gone it will be easier for the others. You'll find they will be able to do more than I can do." It was his valediction. Winston, profoundly moved, stammered a quotation from Johannes Brand, a pro-British Boer who had helped him hammer out the terms of peace in South Africa: *"Alles zal regt kom"* — "All will come right." Collins said he doubted it. He was right.[110]

But on Friday, June 16, he won a great victory. That morning De Valera, fulminating against the constitution's final draft, told reporters: "As it stands it will exclude from public service, and practically disenfranchise, every honest Republican. Its test code is as comprehensive against Republicans as the test acts of the Clarendon and Shaftesbury code against Catholics and dissenters in the reign of Charles II." But most of southern Ireland's voters had never heard of Clarendon or Shaftesbury, and, more important, Irish republicanism, in the eyes of many, had been discredited by the crimes of the Irish Republican Army. When the ballots were counted that evening they showed that the people of Eire had elected 93 candidates committed to the treaty and only 35 Irregulars. The *New York Times* called the results "a triumph for imperial methods of pacification." De Valera, whose terrorism had nullified his pact with Collins, described it to a *Times* correspondent as a victory of "outrage, murder, and massacre" and said ominously, "England's gain is for the moment only." Once his people discovered that they had chosen lackeys of "Churchill's hate," who dared "blacken forever the fair name of this fair nation," he said, Ireland would "rise up and fling them from the positions they have usurped and dishonoured."[111] One of his gunmen, Reginald Dunne, a member of the IRA's London branch, received orders to wreak vengeance for the lost election by striking at the heart of the British establishment. On Thursday, June 22, six days after the Free Staters had gone to the polls, Sir Henry Wilson donned his field marshal's uniform and unveiled a memorial to Britain's war dead in London's Liverpool Street Station. Returning to his Eaton Place home by the tube and then by taxi, he was mounting his steps when Dunne and another IRA man opened fire from behind a nearby hedge. Sir Henry's hand instinctively flew to his sword hilt, but they emptied their pistols into his chest and left him sprawled on the pavement, dying.

The killers were caught before they could escape Belgravia. Within an hour Churchill was standing beside Lloyd George at No. 10, staring down dumbly at the two pistols which, in his words, had "drunk this loyal man's blood." Scotland Yard collared an IRA Irregular carrying a list of prominent Englishmen marked for death. Churchill's name led it. All were assigned bodyguards and the public gallery in the House was closed. As young Randolph recalled later, he and his sister Diana returned from roller-skating in Holland Park that Thursday afternoon and "found the house surrounded by policemen. Indoors all sorts of tough-looking men were running up and down the stairs, looking in cupboards, attics and cellars." That night Winston told Clementine he would sleep in the attic. Erecting a metal shield between himself and the attic door, he waited till dawn, gripping a Colt revolver. After breakfast he ordered an armchair reinforced with steel, and for months he slept in it, the pistol in his lap. He was, he told his wife, ready to "fight it out." Norman Harding, a real-estate agent with whom he had made an appointment to see country properties, afterward recalled joining him in the backseat of his automobile and remarking that it was "the darkest car I have ever been in." Churchill explained: "Well, you see, it is armoured, and the windows are bullet resisting, and I have a loaded revolver." Detective Thompson sat in the front seat. Introducing him, Winston said, "he also has a revolver." He then turned around, the agent later remembered, and "slid back a small shutter and asked, 'You see that car behind us?' Harding did, and counted three men in it. Churchill said, 'That car will accompany us ten miles out of town, and, on our return, will pick us up again and escort us back to the Colonial Office or to my home. I have had a number of threatening letters each week, some telling me the actual time and method of my death, and I don't like it."[112]

After the assassination of Sir Henry a wave of rage against the Irish swept England. It scalded Churchill; Lady Wilson let it be known

Churchill and Sir Henry Wilson, February 1919

that no one who had negotiated the Free State treaty would be welcome at her husband's funeral. Bonar Law demanded that the government act. Churchill had to respond. On the Monday after the crime he stood in the well of the House and observed that IRA Irregulars, calling their post "Headquarters of the Republican Executive," still held out in Dublin's Four Courts. "Their presence is a gross breach of the Treaty," he said. "If it does not come to an end . . . then it is my duty to say, in behalf of His Majesty's Government, that we shall regard the Treaty as having been formally violated, that we shall take no further steps to carry out or legalize its further stages, and that we shall resume full liberty of action in any direction that may seem proper and to any extent that may be necessary to defend the interests and the rights that are entrusted to our care." In that gentler time this was the strongest diplomatic language he could use to goad the provisional government into action. Collins realized it. During the early hours of Wednesday morning he ordered the law buildings shelled. De Valera protested that "soldiers of the Army of the Republic have been attacked by forces of the Provisional Government at the instigation of English politicians . . . in order to avert from themselves political consequences which they feared," and Rory O'Connor, the leader of the embattled Irregulars inside the buildings, sent out a statement to the press charging that "the enemy is the old enemy, England. . . . Mr Churchill cracked the whip in his speech . . . when he ordered the Provisional Government to attack the Four Courts." English soldiers, he said, were preparing to rush his position. Collins and Griffith scoffed at this: "Statements that British troops are cooperating . . . are false and malicious. None but Irish forces, with the cooperation of citizens, who are loyally and enthusiastically supporting the Government, are engaged in putting down the disorderly element who attempt to tyrannize over the people and defy their will." In London, Churchill announced: "The Provisional Government is solely responsible for the operations. . . . They have declined assistance except so far as equipment is concerned."[113]

The operative sentence was the last one, and it gave the lie to the rest. Macready had secretly lent Collins a battery of fieldpieces and ammunition for them. Griffith later acknowledged that he and Collins had taken their cue from Winston; they knew he would move if they did not, and so "finally we went on." But the real significance of the cannonade, and the subsequent storming of the position by Collins's volunteers, was much larger than that. It was an answer to Winston's earlier question. Men *were* ready to fight for the Free State. On Friday they captured a corner of the Four Courts. The defenders, abandoning hope, set the buildings ablaze and then surrendered. O'Connor subsequently became the first of seventy-seven IRA men to be executed by Free State firing squads. Churchill cheered the Free Staters' militancy, their uncompromising justice, and the implications of their readiness to raze the law buildings: "They have not even hesitated, in order to stamp out the armed resistance to the Treaty, to invade by force of arms, and to destroy as a result of their assault, even their own property." Privately he wrote Collins that he understood that this had been a "terrible ordeal for you and your colleagues" but believed it "indispensable if Ireland is to be saved from anarchy and the Treaty from destruction. We had reached the end of our tether over here at the same time as you had in Ireland. I could not have sustained another debate in the House of Commons on the old lines without fatal consequences to . . . the Treaty. . . . Now all is changed. Ireland will be mistress in her own house, and we over here in a position to safeguard your Treaty rights and further your legitimate interests effectually."[114]

Yet it was far from over. Indeed, the Irish tragedy was approaching another crisis. On August 12 the quiet Griffith, exhausted by the accumulated strain of the past two years and privately appalled by Collins's belligerence, dropped dead of a heart attack. "How sad for Ireland,"

Clementine wrote Winston, "is Arthur Griffith's death." IRA Irregulars captured Dundalk that same day, but before the week was out they had been driven back. The Free State, backed by the population, was winning everywhere now. Then, at 7:30 P.M. on August 22, a band of De Valera's gunmen ambushed Collins and his convoy on a back road in county Cork, in a gulley called Bealnamblath, between Macroos and Bandon, and Collins was slain. He was thirty years old. Almost his last words were: "Tell Winston we could never have done it without him." The martyred hero was wrapped in the green flag for which he had sacrificed his life, and his keening mourners sang, to the tune of the "Londonderry Air," that most haunting of Irish songs, now, for him, a dirge:

Oh, darlin' boy, the pipes, the pipes are calling
From glen to glen, and down the mountain side,
The summer's gone and all the roses falling,
It's you, it's you must go and I must bide.

But come ye back when summer's in the meadow,
Or when the valley's hushed and white with snow,
It's I'll be here in sunshine and in shadow,
Oh, darlin' boy, I love you, love you so!

Churchill wrote: "The presentiment of death had been strong upon him for some days, and he only narrowly escaped several murderous traps. . . . His funeral was dignified by the solemn ritual of the Roman Catholic Church and every manifestation of public sorrow. Then Silence. But his work was done. Successor to a sinister inheritance, reared among fierce conditions and moving through ferocious times, he supplied those qualities of action and personality without which the foundation of Irish nationhood would not have been reestablished." Cosgrave became president, with Kevin O'Higgins as his field commander. Ireland, said O'Higgins, presented "the spectacle of a country bleeding to death, of a country steering straight for anarchy, futility, and chaos." Then O'Higgins, too, was trapped and slain by IRA gunmen.[115]

It was a scowling year in Eire's history, but the Irish have a genius for transforming squalor into nobility. Early in the treaty negotiations Churchill had come to know, and dislike, Erskine Childers, a fervent nationalist now remembered for his classic suspense story *The Riddle of the Sands.* Childers threw in his lot with De Valera's Irregulars and became a killer of Free Staters. When he was caught and sentenced to die, Winston, in a rare moment of vindictiveness, publicly expressed satisfaction over the

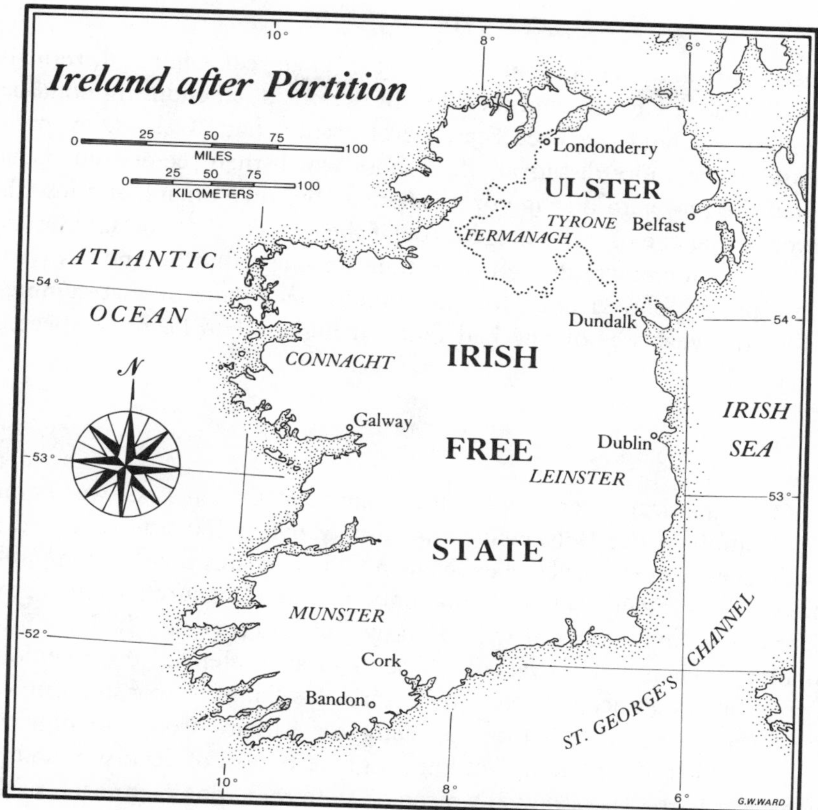

fate of this "mischiefmaking, murderous renegade and malicious hater." On the eve of his death Childers wrote, "I feel what Churchill said about my 'hatred' and 'malice' against England is untrue. . . . I die loving England, and praying that she may change completely, and finally toward Ireland." Learning later that Childers had fought gallantly against the Germans in the Cuxhaven raid of New Year's Day, 1915, Winston issued a retraction, calling him a man of "distinction, ability, and courage" who had died "with the utmost composure."[116]

In October the Dáil adopted the constitution, as drafted by Collins, Griffith, and Churchill. The Free State was then admitted to the League of Nations. After protracted deliberations, the boundary with Ulster was settled. The IRA was outlawed by the men who had served in it. De Valera was captured, imprisoned, freed; agreed to take the oath, lost election after election, and finally, ten years after Collins's murder, striking a deal with Labour deputies, became president. Ultimately his pitiless will prevailed; seeing his chance when the Empire was transformed into the Commonwealth, he proclaimed the Free State's sovereignty, the penultimate step toward republicanism, in 1937. That year Churchill, remembering Collins, Griffith, and their bright dreams of an enduring bond between Britain and the Free State, wrote sadly that "Ireland, by paths eventually far more disastrous than those which then seemed open, has gained the power to manage or mismanage her own affairs, and lost the power to manage or mismanage those of the Empire."[117] In 1922 he had dared hope for more, though even then he knew that he and his party would pay a political price for the tumultuous events of that summer. Before the year was out he had found it higher than he had expected.

Other political reverses were the collapse of Britain's postwar boom, the triumph of the Bolsheviks, and dismay over what was regarded as recklessness in the Dardanelles. Martin Gilbert writes that "in the public mind it was widely believed, not only that both Churchill and Lloyd George had hoped for war with Turkey, but also that they had been disappointed when it was averted." They had also offended the coalition's Tories, who had been shocked by Churchill's failure to consult Curzon, the foreign secretary, before appealing for Empire troops to fight for Chanak. This slight had in fact been a grave breach of decorum, and for many it was the last straw. Two senior statesmen, one from each of the two major parties, came out of retirement to register their disapproval. Asquith complained of slipshod diplomacy by "amateurs in Downing Street." Then Bonar Law denounced the entire Turkish affair in a letter to *The Times.* It was wrong, he wrote, "to show any hostility or unfairness" toward the leading Moslem power, and irresponsible to do so without French support. "We cannot act alone," he said, "as the policeman of the world." In those ten words Law wrote an epitaph for the Empire's golden era, and it says much about the 1920s that no one saw it as such.[118]

In the opinion of many, Lloyd George and his cabinet had won the war but lost the peace. It was remarked upon that the prime minister's role at Versailles had been lackluster, and he was blamed for the fact that the membership of the League of Nations, in which so much hope had been invested, did not include the United States, Germany, and Russia. A few Conservative ministers — notably Birkenhead and Austen Chamberlain — remained loyal to George. The others were restless. Critics of the prime minister were appearing on all sides, partly because he had unwisely abandoned the custom of consulting Parliament before taking action. Harold Laski wrote: "He seems determined to sacrifice upon the altar of his private ambition the whole spirit of our public life." *The Times* declared that the word of England had "lost currency throughout the greater part of the world as the word of an upright land." Francis Williams observed that the coalition had "produced at the centre an atmosphere more like an oriental court at which favourites struggled unceasingly for position than anything seen in Britain for a century or more." It moved Sir Edward Grey "to indignation and despair such as I have never felt about any other British Government." After a weekend with Lloyd George, Austen Chamberlain, and Birkenhead, Arnold Bennett noted: "I never heard principles or the welfare of the country mentioned." Leo Amery later recalled that Conservatives "felt that they no longer had any policy of their own, but were being dragged along in the wake of an erratic Prime Minister whom they once again profoundly distrusted, by a little group of their own leaders who had lost, not only their principles, but their heads."[119]

It was Churchill's fellow Harrovian Amery, then parliamentary and financial secretary to the Admiralty, who organized what came to be known as the "Revolt of the Under Secretaries," inviting all Tory MPs to meet at the Carlton Club on October 19, 1922. The annual National Union of Conservative Associations was just a month away, and Tory back-benchers felt their seats were in jeopardy. Austen Chamberlain, then regarded as the party's emerging leader, thought it wrong to appease them; he said he intended "to tell them bluntly that they must either follow our advice or do without us, in which case they must find their own Chief, and form a Government *at once.* They would be in a d——d fix." He and Birkenhead counted heavily on the results, to be announced that day, of a by-election in Newport. The Tory candidate, running against the coalition, was expected to come in last. Bonar Law, opening the meeting, was contemptuous of Lloyd George's record. His old colleagues nodded in agreement, though only one cabinet minister rose to echo him. This was the shrewd, stolid, pipe-smoking Stanley Baldwin, president of the Board of Trade, who, at that time, was largely unknown to the general public. Baldwin introduced a resolution which would dissolve the coalition. His biographer writes that he had discovered "a new eloquence; direct, conversational, monosyllabic: rising and falling without strain or effort between the homeliest humour and the most moving appeal." It was the voice of the new England: uncomfortable with greatness, wary of excellence, indifferent to challenges abroad. Baldwin argued that although Lloyd George was a dynamic force, "a dynamic force is a very terrible thing" — an appropriate debut for this evangelist of political mediocrity.[120] Then the stunning tally from Newport was announced. The Tory had won by 2,090 votes; the coalition's man had come in a bad third. Upon learning this, the MPs in the Carlton Club voted, and to everyone's surprise the result was lopsided: 87 for the coalition, 187 against. They then rejected Austen Chamberlain and picked Bonar Law to lead them. Informed of the result, Lloyd George submitted his resignation at Buckingham Palace that same afternoon. Law formed a government and a general election was scheduled for November 15, 1922.

Churchill was flat on his back in a Dorset Square nursing home, undergoing an emergency appendectomy. He was widely blamed for the coalition's fall, and not only because of his controversial policies. His loyalty to Lloyd George was suspect. Seven months earlier George had received several letters suggesting that Winston was conspiring against him. Charles McCurdy, the coalition whip, wrote him that "Liberals are commencing to canvass the situation that would arise" if Churchill defected to the Tories. Another correspondent told him that Winston was plotting the formation of a new coalition, to be headed by Austen Chamberlain, with himself at the Exchequer. Max Beaverbrook warned him that Winston's "tendency is all to the Right, and his principles are becoming more Tory. I am sure he would not fancy being shut up in a coop with you even for a short time because such collocation within a narrow circle would cloud his own brilliance in the light of your superiority." If this sounds strange coming from one of Winston's friends, it can only be added that Beaverbrook was always a strange friend. His virtue was that when Winston was in desperate trouble, he rallied to his aid. He was a fair-weather adversary, a foul-weather ally.[121]

Winston's relationship with Lloyd George was more complicated, and had changed often. In their early days together, as radical reformers they had worked splendidly in tandem. After Winston's eviction from the Admiralty in 1915 he believed that George had betrayed him; on June 9 that year he had written Archie Sinclair that between him and George "*tout est fini.*" When George moved into No. 10, Winston had fumed because no place had been found for him in the coalition cabinet; and in the spring of 1917 he had assailed the prime minister for his "undue love of the assertion of arbitrary power" — an odd charge from one whose own thirst for authority was unslakable. Installed as minister of munitions, he had put this enmity behind him. By 1921 he believed that George would make him the next chancellor of the Exchequer. Then, during his absence in Palestine, George had bypassed him. Austen Chamberlain had written his sister: "Winston has come back from the Middle

East as cross as a bear with a sore head & thinks that all the world is out of joint since he is not C/E." Beaverbrook believed he had "just grounds for his hostility." The editor of the *Daily Mail* reported to Lord Northcliffe: "Winston is fed up with Lloyd George. He wanted to be Chancellor but Ll. G. refused to give him the job. Winston holds it is not compatible with his seniority . . . when he wants a little money." Frances Stevenson noted that Churchill now wrote to her lover as " 'Dear Prime Minister' whereas it used to be 'Dear LlG,' or 'My dear David.' " Winston himself thought George's attitude toward him revealed "a certain vein of amiable malice," and he was infuriated when, in a November 1921 cabinet meeting, the prime minister taunted him about Gallipoli. Nevertheless, the old Welsh spellbinder could still work feats of magic on him. Lord Boothby recalls waiting in a hall while the two men were closeted for about an hour. Afterward he asked Winston: "How did it go?" Churchill said slowly: "Within five minutes the old relationship between us was completely re-established. The relationship between Master and Servant. And I was the Servant." He wrote George: "My interests as well as inclinations march with yours, & in addition there is our long friendship wh I so greatly value. . . . I wd gladly at your side face political misfortune."[122]

Churchill faced it now, though he was slow to grasp his peril. He proudly wrote that "the session of 1922 was the most prosperous I have ever had as a Minister in the House of Commons." And others agreed. Clement Attlee later recalled: "I learned in that Parliament of 1922 what a master he was in the art of answering Parliamentary Questions. He could deliver a knock-out blow or give the retort courteous with equal facility. . . . One never could anticipate just what line he would take, except that it would generally be effective." After the Irish debate of May 31, Austen Chamberlain had written the King of "Mr Churchill's great and growing parliamentary qualities," commending "to Your Majesty's particular attention a speech faultless in manner and wording, profoundly impressive in its delivery and of the first consequence as a statement of policy. It gripped the attention of the House from the opening sentences and held it, breathlessly intent, to the end." On February 8 Winston had decided to address the House extemporaneously about Iraq — he had not tried speaking without notes in eighteen years — and afterward he wrote Clementine: "It was really a great success: no worry, nor work, but quite an agreeable experience. . . . I think I have really got my full freedom now in debate, and I propose to make far less use of notes than ever before." He had learned to be savage in the attack and, in the next moment, completely disarming. When the teetotal, American-born Lady

Astor became the House's first woman MP, he paused in his address to refresh himself, saying, "I think it is a great pleasure for the noble lady, the member of the Sutton division of Plymouth, to see me drinking water." Afterward in the smoking room he said: "Nancy, when you first entered the House, I felt you had come upon me in my bath and I had nothing to protect me but my sponge."[123]

But wit and oratorical pyrotechnics, though dazzling in Parliament, could not be readily translated into votes in a general election. Preoccupied with imperial and foreign issues, he had lost touch with the new, growing forces on the left. Churchill had not entirely lost his reforming zeal; he had wanted to see social legislation introduced. So had Lloyd George. But they had been thwarted by the Tory dominance in the coalition. As a consequence, the Liberal party was being devoured by Labour, which, lacking membership in the coalition, had become its most effective opposition. British socialism brought out the worst in Churchill. When he saw red at public meetings — literally saw it, for hecklers waved red flags and drowned him out by stridently singing "The Red Flag" — his instincts overcame his good judgment. In his view, the Labour party was a sinister strand in a Bolshevik rope braided to lynch England's political and social institutions. Therefore he stalked it, declaring that "the enthronement in office of a Socialist Government would be a serious national misfortune such as has usually befallen great states on the morrow of their defeat in war." It would, he predicted, turn all Britain into a "bear garden." He thought Labour's proposal to lend the Russians money confirmed him. Socialism, he said, would bring "Government of the duds, by the duds, for the duds." If England survived its misrule Labour would vanish "unwept, unhonored, unsung and unhung." Behind its movement "crouched the shadow of Communist folly and Bolshevik crime."[124]

This was superb as obloquy. It was an effective antidote for his Black Dog. And it is arguable that he foresaw socialist egalitarianism — from the few who are rich to the many who are poor — as the decisive blow to leadership by a talented, privileged elite. Yet he recruited only a handful of converts. Even his wife urged him to take "a less hostile and negative attitude" toward the socialists. When he insisted that they were mounting "a great vehement, deliberate attack upon the foundations of society," Baldwin replied that he simply didn't believe it. Asquith thought the socialist leaders should be given posts of responsibility, that excluding their party from power would only embitter them. Winston told Violet Asquith that he passionately disagreed. As a consequence, he became the bogeyman of the British left. Emmanuel Shinwell, a Labour MP, recalls:

"The mention of his name at Labour gatherings was the signal for derisive cheers; when a Labour speaker found himself short of arguments, he had only to say, 'Down with Winston Churchill.' This never failed to draw thunderous applause. Undoubtedly, he was our most valuable propaganda asset." They distributed pamphlets describing "Winston's Black Record." Considered the chief obstacle to Labour's ambitions, he was, Shinwell recalls, "the target for every epithet in the English language." A Labour spokesman charged: "Mr Churchill did all he could to maintain militarism in Europe and to march armies against Russia." The *Daily Herald* denounced him for sending "munitions which cost us over twenty million pounds sterling to produce" to Russian counterrevolutionaries, "all of which has gone down the drain." In another issue, the *Herald* declared that "Churchill cannot see that the revolt in far-off costly and reactionary adventures grows into 'turbulence' at home," that he was "utterly out of touch with public opinion, here as everywhere else."[125]

It was true, and it was especially true in Dundee. Now, as in 1908 — when he had jubilantly claimed it as his "life seat" — Dundee was a two-member, working-class constituency of shipbuilding craftsmen, linen weavers, jute sackers, marmalade bottlers, and commercial bakers. But he had changed since then, and so had they. After four years of disillusionment and Labour blandishments the voters saw their most illustrious MP in a new light. Unemployment was high; they were concerned with bread-and-butter issues. Winston knew that. Earlier in the year he had advised the National Liberal Council that the party must back "better social and industrial conditions for the people." Workers, he said, "must know that earnest effort will reap its own reward, that the cost of living will fall." In a statement to the Dundee electorate, written in the nursing home bed where he was convalescing from his appendectomy, he vowed to provide improved public services, increases in unemployment compensation, and better housing. The Tories, he said, represented the antithesis of this: "Mr Bonar Law has described his policy as one of negation. Such a message . . . will strike despair in the heart of every striver after social justice. It cannot be accepted by any generous-hearted man or woman. . . . Over the portals of 10 Downing Street the new Prime Minister has inscribed his words: 'Abandon hope ye who enter here.' "[126]

Yet he had to temper his attacks on Tories. He had asked Dundee's Conservatives to support him as "a Free Trader," writing them that "the formidable socialist attack which is gathering" demonstrated "the need for patriotic men and women of sincere goodwill to stand together." He singled out his leftist opponents: "A predatory and confiscatory programme fatal to the reviving prosperity of the country, inspired by class jealousy and the doctrines of envy, hatred and malice, is appropriately championed in Dundee by two candidates both of whom had to be shut up during the late war to prevent them from hampering the national defence." The Labour vote, he warned those around him, "will be a very heavy one." The local Tories agreed to put up no candidate against him, and he ran on the coalition's record, charging that the Carlton Club rebellion was attributable to "the fury of the Die-Hards at the Irish Treaty," a settlement which nevertheless would "live and prosper." The Chanak crisis had been admirably resolved; "I regard my association with it as one of the greatest honours in my long official life." He supported Lloyd George, though his praise was oddly phrased: "I am sure that among the broad masses of faithful, valiant, toiling, Britain-loving men and women whom he led to victory, there will still be found a few to wish him well." But he turned again and again to his radical adversaries, Georges Morel-de-Ville, who had been endorsed by Labour, and William Gallacher, a Communist. Each had been a wartime pacifist; both were meat for Churchill. Morel-de-Ville, he declared, was a member of "that band of degenerate international intellectuals who regard the greatness of Britain and the stability and prosperity of the British Empire as a fatal obstacle to their subversive sickness." Of Gallacher, who had organized strikes in defense industries when Winston was minister of munitions, he said that he would be remembered for his "crazy and ferocious outpourings" and "long record of malignant if ineffectual blows" at the integrity and safety of England, though on the whole the "crudity" of his speeches "renders them less pernicious and certainly less harmful than the more slimy and insidious propaganda of his companion and comrade Mr Morel," by which, of course, he meant that Morel was more popular in Dundee and therefore a greater threat at the polls.[127]

This was vintage Churchill, but though the words were the words of Winston, the voice was the voice of a party representative in Dundee. The incumbent was still confined to his bed in Dorset Square. His being hors de combat, a supporter wrote him, "has really been a disaster . . . in these critical days." The press, here and throughout the country, was hostile to the coalition. Beaverbrook, an admirer of Bonar Law, was bankrolling Tory candidates in many constituencies where Lloyd George men were unopposed, thus splitting the anti-Labour vote and boosting the socialists' chances. In Dundee the two local newspapers, owned by

D. C. Thompson, had come out against Churchill. Moreover, he was not the only Liberal candidate. Ever since Lloyd George's eviction of Asquith in 1916 the party had been divided into Asquithians and Georgians, and Asquith was fielding his own national slate. To Churchill's dismay and indignation, his old ally C. P. Scott of the *Manchester Guardian* supported Asquith's man in Dundee. Winston wrote Scott, protesting "wrecking and splitting candidatures between Liberals" and "the pursuance of personal vendettas," adding: "I expect you are pretty well ashamed in your heart of hearts at the line your caucus is taking in its bitter malevolence." But the *Guardian* continued to trumpet the virtues of the "Independent Liberal," although it became increasingly clear that he had no chance of winning.[128]

Winston asked his wife to stump the district for him during the last ten days of the campaign, and off she went, carrying her last baby — an "unbaptized infant" as the Dundee *Courier* maliciously put it. Among the Churchill friends who had come to do their part was the former Edward Spiers, now Spears; he had changed the spelling of his surname in 1918. Spears watched women spit on Clementine and wrote: "Clemmie's bearing was magnificent — like an aristocrat going to the guillotine in a tumbril." Her first meeting was bedlam. In an unusual dirty trick, rival partisans filled the hall with sneezing powder, and both speaker and audience were convulsed. "The meeting," the delighted *Courier* reported, "was in a state of uproar almost from the beginning to end." Outside, as Clementine fled, a taunting mob waved red flags and green IRA banners. Putting a bright face on it, she wrote Winston, "Every rowdy meeting rouses sympathy & brings votes & will especially as you have been so ill. Even in the rowdiest foulest place all of the people tho' abusive were really good-natured." The newspapers, she said, were *"vile."* He was being called a warmonger, "but I am exhibiting you as a Cherub Peace Maker with little fluffy wings round your chubby face." She thought "Smash the Socialists" was the wrong line to take. The Labour line was very convincing in Dundee, especially among the destitute, who were many: "My darling, the misery here is appalling. Some of the people look absolutely starving. Morel's Election address just out *very moderate* & in favor of only constitutional methods. So one cannot compare him with Gallacher." She felt "the minute you arrive the atmosphere will change & the people will be roused. . . . I am longing to see you & so is Dundee — I shall be heartbroken if you don't get in." Clemmie gamely remounted the stump, was hissed, heard her husband described as the head of England's "Fascisti party" — Mussolini had seized power in Rome the week before — and left, head high, a reporter wrote, when a meeting "broke up in disorder." Birkenhead arrived to help. She wished he hadn't. He assailed Morel on the peculiar ground that he was French. "France is a very great country," he said, "and, on the whole, I like a man to stick to the country, particularly if it is a great one, in which he was born." Clementine commented tartly: "He was no use at all. He was drunk."[129]

A very shaky Churchill arrived four days before the election and checked into Dundee's Royal Hotel. Sitting in a padded chair, he spoke that evening at the Caird Hall, defending the coalition, the Irish Free State, and Britain's "unshaken and unshakable" position in the world. At the end he rose painfully and asked the voters to send "a message which will resound far beyond the limits of this small island and carry its good cheer to the suffering, struggling, baffled humanity the wide world o'er." This, according to one journalist, was followed by "loud cheers." But the Caird Hall audience was friendly; it had been carefully picked. Two days later his reception was very different. "As I was carried through the yelling crowd of Socialists at the Drill Hall to the platform," he later wrote, "I was struck by the looks of passionate hatred on the faces of some of the younger men and women. Indeed, but for my helpless condition I am sure they would have attacked me." They booed, hissed, and refused to let him speak. He managed to say: "The electors will know how to deal with a party whose only weapon is idiotic clamour"; then, according to the *Courier,* "pandemonium broke out anew." His voice rose in brief snatches: ". . . if about a hundred young men and women in the audience choose to spoil the meeting — if about a hundred of these young reptiles. . . . We will not submit to the bullying of the featherheads, we will not be ruled by a mob. . . ." But in the end he did submit, telling the appalled platform party: "I am finished." Detective Thompson slept by his hotel door that night, pistol in hand. A champagne party was in progress across the hall. Spears later remembered that each time a cork popped, "We thought it was Winston being shot."[130]

In the morning Churchill was grim. Only a desperate candidate attacks the press, and it is a measure of his plight that he lashed out at the Dundee publisher, holding him up "here in the district where he lives to the reprobation of his fellow citizens." D. C. Thompson, he said, had subjected him to "ceaseless detraction, spiteful, malicious detraction" and was "narrow, bitter, unreasonable, eaten up with his own conceit, consumed with his own petty arrogance." The poll was held on November 15, 1922. That morning Thompson managed, as publishers always do, to have the last word. His editorial described Winston as a man "in a vile temper. He takes no pains to conceal the fact. Like the disappointed man on the station platform he kicks out at anybody who happens to be near him. He has sprayed Labour with invective, has sprinkled many doses of it upon his fellow candidates . . . and now he has turned the full blast of his vituperation upon the Dundee newspapers. Whose turn it will be to-morrow God only knows."[131]

Dundee elected Morel-de-Ville and a Prohibitionist. Of 151,701 votes cast, Churchill received 20,466 — less than 14 percent of the total. For the first time in twenty-two years, nearly thirteen of which had been spent in the cabinet, he was out of Parliament. He left Dundee at once, explaining that he "was far from well." In London he found himself, as he put it, "without an office, without a seat, without a party, and without an appendix." Replying to Stamfordham, who conveyed the King's regrets, he wrote: "It was very trying, having to do three days of electioneering with a wound so newly healed. It was quite impossible for me to defend myself in so short a time. I have always held Dundee by speeches and argument and at least three weeks are required to deal with such a large number of electors." T. E. Lawrence wrote Eddie Marsh: "I'm more sorry about Winston than I can say." Lord Esher wrote Sir Philip Sassoon: "The women put Winston out. When he loses his temper, he looks so damned ugly." A fellow guest at a dinner party, Lloyd George's former private secretary, noted that "Winston was so down in the dumps he could scarcely speak the whole evening. He thought his world had come to an end — at least his political world. I thought his career was over." The *Daily Mail* crowed: "Mr Churchill has had as many lives as the proverbial cat, but the indictment against him is a long one." The *Daily Telegraph,* although never his admirer, had a more charitable word: "The House of Commons loses, for a time, its most brilliant and dazzling speaker. . . . His is perhaps the most sensational defeat of the whole election."[132]

That was saying a great deal. Nationally, the repudiation of the coalition had been overwhelming; 81 percent of the electorate had gone to the polls, most of them to register disapproval of the government. The Tories had swept the country, winning 345 seats. Labour, with 142, was now the principal Opposition party. Lloyd George's "National" Liberals had carried only 62; Asquith's Liberals, a mere 54. Neither man would ever hold office again. Asquith wrote Venetia Montagu that he was "inclined to gloat over the corpses on the battlefield," but five-sixths of his candidates had gone down to defeat. Churchill was far from through; on the morrow after the returns he was offered a dozen seats, among them that of Spears, who had just been elected member for Loughborough. Winston replied that he was "greatly touched by the extreme kindness of yr offer & the willing sacrifice that it involves. It is a splendid proof of yr friendship. I cd not accept it from you. I want you to enjoy yr seat in Parliament & I shall like to feel I have one or two friends there. . . . The Whips will find me a seat if I want one; but what I want now is a rest." Margot Asquith advised him to "lie low" for a while, to "do nothing in politics, go on writing all the time & painting; do not join yr former colleagues who are making prodigious asses of themselves in every possible manner: Keep friends in every port — lose *no* one. . . . If you have the patience of Disraeli with your fine temper glowing mind & real kind unvindictive nature you cd still command a great future." It was sensible advice, and Churchill took it. He decided to recuperate on the Riviera, renting a villa, Le Rêve d'Or, near Cannes, for the winter. The whole family joined him there for Christmas and New Year's. He worked on his Admiralty memoirs. Paul Maze, the painter, encountered him on a beach and said: "Well, Winston, I'm painting hard, trying to forget all about the war. What are you doing?" Churchill said he was writing a book on the war. Maze said that was "like digging up a cemetery." Winston replied: "Yes, but with a resurrection."[133]

His political resurrection was to be delayed again and again. But Margot had been right: this was a good time to be publicly invisible. Two years later he would write in the *Weekly Dispatch* that when the coalition government was dismembered "it was already perfectly clear to many of us that a period of political chaos would ensue. To the best of my ability, I warned the public of what was in store. But nobody would listen. Everyone was delighted to get back to party politics. Dear to the hearts of all the small politicians were the party flags, the party platforms, the party catchwords. How gleefully they clapped their hands and sang aloud for joy that the good pre-war days of faction had returned!" He was glad to be out of it. In February 1923 he wrote: "The weather here has been indifferent, but I am getting much better in myself." His friends in the House missed him. One advised him the following month: "Don't lie low too long. Things are in the 'melting pot.' L.G. is playing what *looks* like a good game but it isn't. Nobody trusts him. . . . There can only be *two* parties. That is the line of country to ride. There are hundreds of thousands who won't vote at all at present. They have *no* party. But they are anti-labour. . . . The passivity of the present Govt is beyond belief. They *settle* nothing."[134]

Bonar Law, who had waited so long for power, was proving inept at No. 10. He had become prime minister, Philip Guedalla wrote caustically, "for the simple and satisfying reason that he was not Mr. Lloyd George. At an open competition in the somewhat negative exercise of not being Lloyd George that was held in November 1922, Mr. Law was found to be more indubitably not Mr. Lloyd George than any of the other competitors; and in consequence, by the mysterious operation of the British Constitution, he reigned in his stead." Ill, he resigned after less than six months in office. After the fall of Austen Chamberlain, Curzon had been the favorite to succeed Law, but Baldwin, who was emerging as a master of intrigue, outmaneuvered Curzon's supporters and moved into Downing Street in May 1923. The country's chief domestic problem was a million jobless Englishmen. The solution, Baldwin believed, was Joe Chamberlain's old nostrum — high tariffs. Law, however, had campaigned against them; his pledge could not be dishonored. Therefore Baldwin dissolved Parliament and went to the country again in November. Free Trade was the one issue which could reconcile the two wings of the Liberal party. It also brought Churchill back into public life. *The Times* had observed that he "has latterly become more conservative, less from conviction than from a hardening of his political arteries. His early Liberal velleities have dried up, the generous impulses of youth throb more slowly, and apart from some intellectual gristle his only connections with Liberalism are personal." That was close to the mark, but for Churchill a call for Free Trade was a summons to the colors, to the blazing idealism of his early years in the House. In a statement to the press he called it "vital to the British people and indispensable to the recovery of their prosperity." The future of a reunited party, he said, would know "no limits." On November 19 he accepted an invitation from the West Leicester Liberal Association to run as their candidate. The National Liberal Club removed his portrait from its cellar, dusted it off, and restored it to its place of prominence upstairs.[135]

West Leicester, east of Birmingham, was known for its manufacture of hosiery, boots, and shoes, and his Labour opponent, F. W. Pethick-Lawrence, was formidable. Pethick-Lawrence had proposed a "Capital Levy," a surtax on all Britons worth more than £5,000. Workmen thought it an excellent idea. Clementine was anxious; Winston had been offered several safe seats and — unwisely, she thought — had turned them down. Equally unwise, in her opinion, was any affiliation with Lloyd George. Churchill had accepted an invitation to dine with George at Beaverbrook's home. On the morning of the dinner she left a note on his dresser: "I want to appeal to you again before you go to Max's this evening. Ll. G. is not in the same position as you — He is in not out & he shares or practically shares the throne with Asquith." Word might get around, she wrote, that Winston was working toward a new coalition. She also wished he weren't running against a Labour aspirant. It would be much better, in her view, "to be beaten by a Tory (which would rouse Liberal sympathy) than by a Socialist. My Darling it is important — I shall say *nothing* if you go, but consider the imprudence of losing the offer of a good Wee Free Seat (as opposed to extinct Nat[ional] Liberal) for the sake of a pleasant evening." He went. Also, to his subsequent sorrow, he lunched with Beaverbrook at London's Embassy Club, where he wagered that Labour would not reach power within a year and that Asquith would move back into No. 10. The club menu survives, with their handwriting: "I bet £5 against Winston's £4 that Labour forms a government in 1924. M.B." and "I bet £15 against Winston's £5 that Asquith is NOT P.M. in 1924. W. Churchill. M.B."[136]

In West Leicester, Churchill again faced a hostile press and wild, disorderly meetings. At one of them, the *Leicester Mail* reported, Winston and Clementine were "greeted by groans and hoots, not a single cheer being heard in the building." A gang of hecklers accompanied him wherever he went; he christened them the "Socialist travelling circus." One of Churchill's recent acquaintances, young, redheaded Brendan Bracken, scouted halls in advance and told him what to expect. The expectations were almost always the same — more trouble. Cecil Roberts, the prolific writer, afterward remembered how "hatred of him [Churchill] was aflame. No insults were too gross to hurl at him. One, of course, the Dardanelles fiasco, regarded as his particular crime, was always brought up." Toward the end of a frustrating evening he shouted back: "What do you know about that? The Dardanelles might have saved millions of lives. Don't imagine I am running away from the Dardanelles. I glory in it." Douglas Jerrold, the official historian of the Royal Naval Division, arrived in Leicester on his own initiative to confirm him. Jerrold told a mocking mob: "I venture to say that had the campaign been prosecuted as it should have been, with enthusiasm, courage, and energy, in the same spirit in which it was begun by Mr Churchill, the war would have ended in 1917." Few listened; fewer believed him. It seemed Winston would wear that albatross around his neck for the rest of his life. An American publicist wrote that it was "doubtful if even Great Britain could survive another world war and another Churchill," and an English critic declared: "The ghosts of the Gallipoli dead will always rise up to damn him anew in time of national emergency. Neither official historians, nor military hack writers, will explain away or wipe out the memories of the Dardanelles."[137]

New bullyraggers appeared when he spoke in London. As he left one rally, a newspaperman reported, a "vast crowd closed round the car hooting and jeering. Despite the vigilance of the police, one man broke through and smashed one of the windows of Mr Churchill's car. The police took him into custody. When this fact became known more booing ensued, and many people spat upon the car as it drove away." At another meeting, in Walthamstow, "What about the Dardanelles?" was joined by "What about Antwerp?" A youth eluded mounted police and threw a brick at Winston. Others stood shaking their fists in impotent rage. Winston told an *Evening News* reporter that the Walthamstow mob was "the worst crowd I have ever seen in twenty-five years of public life. They were more like Russian wolves than British workmen — howling, foaming and spitting, and generally behaving in a way absolutely foreign to the British working classes." Meanwhile, Clementine, keeping the flame alight in West Leicester, answered a pest who shouted that her husband was unqualified to represent workmen. Except for Lloyd George, she said, Churchill had done more "for the benefit of the working classes than any other statesman," and she cited his Shop Hours Act, Coal Mines Regulation Act, Unemployment Insurance Act, and Sweated Industries Act. She added for good measure: "A great many people think he is essentially a military man, but I know him very well, and I know he is not like that at all. In fact one of his greatest talents is the talent of peacemaking."[138]

In his final Leicester speech he damned tariffs and the capital levy. Churchill, never comfortable on the defensive, kept trying to make the issue, not himself, but Tory protectionism and Baldwin's claim that he had called this election to avoid breaking Bonar Law's election promise. Winston cried: "Who is Mr Baldwin to acclaim himself such a singularly honest man? He is a man whom we only know in the last few months through the eulogies of the newspapers. He has no achievements to his record. He is an unknown man." Unfortunately Labour, too, was against tariffs. And Labour now had a firm grip on this constituency. Pethick-Lawrence trounced Churchill, 13,634 to 9,236; the Tory, running third, polled 7,696. In Parliament the balance had shifted once more; Baldwin's Conservative strength had been reduced by 87 seats. The Tories now held 258, as against Labour's 191 and the Liberals' 158. Lloyd George deferred to Asquith, who declared that under no circumstances would he unite with the Tories to exclude Ramsay MacDonald, Labour's leader, from office. Alarmed, Churchill wrote Violet Asquith that her father's position meant that there was "no possibility of averting the great misfortune of a Socialist Government being formed." On January 17, 1924, he issued a statement predicting that "strife and tumults, deepening and darkening, will be the only consequence of minority Socialist rule."[139] That was hardly fair, since Labour's chief objective at the time, the defense of Free Trade, was also his. His warning was unheeded anyhow; four days later, when Baldwin lost a motion of confidence, Asquith threw his support to MacDonald, who thereby rode off to the palace to become Labour's first prime minister. Beaverbrook had been right. The alliance was too unstable to last, but Winston felt betrayed by his party. Resuming his rightward march, he resigned from it, and the National Liberal Club put his portrait back in its basement.

Less than five weeks after MacDonald moved into No. 10, Churchill dined with Beaverbrook and Rothermere, Britain's two greatest press lords. They offered him, as he wrote Clementine the following day, their "full support" should he contest an imminent by-election in the Abbey division of Westminster. Westminster, the Conservatives' choicest preserve, included the Houses of Parliament, Buckingham Palace, the homes of at least a hundred MPs, the greatest concentration of celebrities in England, and, as he reminded her, Pall Mall, the Victoria Palace, "Drury Lane theatre & Covent Garden!" There was a distinct possibility that the Conservative Association might endorse him. His wife, again wary, wrote back: "Do not . . . let the Tories get you too cheap. They have treated you so badly in the past & they ought to be made to pay." It seemed unlikely. After his Leicester defeat Austen Chamberlain had written him: "I am very sorry you are still out of Parl," but welcoming him back into the Conservative party was another matter; according to Beaverbrook, Austen was now "very frigid and said he would not support Churchill for Westminster until he repented in sackcloth and ashes for his Liberal past, and joined the Tories openly as a penitent convert." That, of course, was even unlikelier. In the end the association backed Captain Otho Nicholson, a nephew of the previous member. The *Evening Standard* found strong sentiment in the district for Winston to run as an independent, however, and on March 4 he announced that he would do just that, though he expanded his label to "independent Anti-Socialist." Significantly, he declared: "My candidature is in no way hostile to the Conservative Party and its leaders. On the contrary, I recognize that the party must now become the main rallying ground for opponents of the Socialist Party." Sir Philip Sassoon wrote him: "I am so glad you are standing. You are BOUND to get in." Others were less pleased.

Leo Amery declared: "The menace of Socialism is not to be fought by negatives, however brilliantly phrased." And Labour could not be counted out, even here. Its candidate charged that as war minister "Mr Churchill did all he could to maintain militarism in Europe and to march armies against Russia. He wasted £100,000,000 of the taxpayers' money of this country — money sorely needed to deal with unemployment, housing etc — in mad, stupid, wicked and suicidal adventures."[140]

A wealthy friend, James Rankin, converted his London home into Churchill's headquarters, and presently eminent canvassers were seen hurrying in and out: Sir Philip, Lord Darling, Sir Eric Geddes, Lord Rothermere's sole surviving son — the other two had been killed in France — and Winston's cousin the duke. Sunny went into Westminster's shabbier neighborhoods, unselfconsciously tapping on dilapidated doors with his gold-headed stick. Bracken solicited support in nightclubs and brokers' offices, and even recruited campaigners among the girls at the Gaiety. Presently, as Churchill recalled afterward, "I began to receive all kinds of support. Dukes, jockeys, prize-fighters, courtiers, actors and businessmen, all developed a keen partisanship. The chorus girls of Daly's Theatre sat up all night addressing the envelopes and despatching the election address." Arthur Balfour told Baldwin (who remained sphinxlike throughout the campaign) that he thought Amery's intervention had been unsportsmanlike. Balfour himself was seriously considering an endorsement of Churchill. H. A. Gwynne of the *Morning Post,* still Winston's sworn enemy, heard of this and rushed to Baldwin, urging him to forbid support of Churchill by ex-ministers — to be "strong and ruthless, if necessary." That enraged Balfour, who promptly wrote Winston an open letter expressing his "strong desire" to see him win and use his "brilliant gifts" in Parliament. "Your absence from the House of Commons," he concluded, "is greatly to be deplored." Two dozen other Tories then declared for Winston. Inevitably, all this drew fire from the socialists, with the odd result that the Tory favorite in a Tory district was largely ignored. Fenner Brockway, the Labour aspirant, concentrated all his fire on Churchill, who, he said, had "previously charged Labour with setting class against class. It is he who is now the chief exponent of a class war. He raised the bogy of Socialism, and seeks to combine all the selfish and vested interests who fear the onward march of Labour. . . . Of all the politicians Mr Churchill has shown himself most unfit for the responsibility of government. His forte is to be a disturber of the peace, whether at home or abroad. He is a political adventurer, with a genius for acts of mischievous irresponsibility. He is militant to his finger-tips. . . . Mr Churchill's record shows him to be a public danger and a menace to the peace of the world." But as a polemicist Brockway was no match for Winston, who scorned Ramsay MacDonald's indifference toward the Dominions, particularly his proposal to abandon Singapore, which Australia and New Zealand regarded as essential to their defense, while dealing generously with the Russians. Churchill cried: "Our bread for the Bolshevik serpent; our aid for foreigners of every country; our favours for Socialists all over the world who have no country; but for our own daughter States across the oceans, on whom the future of the British island and nation depends, only the cold stones of indifference, aversion, and neglect. That is the policy with which the Socialist Government confronts us, and against that policy we will strive to marshal the unconquerable might of Britain."[141]

Churchill's public appearances were marked by the usual commotion. Winifred Holtby, a critical observer who had never seen him before, wrote a friend of how he dealt with it. His solution was confrontation: "He really and truly points an accusatory finger at the crowd, and cries in sepulchral tones, 'I say that if another war is fought, civilization will perish.' (Laughter. A sweeping gesture.) 'A man laughs,' (out goes the finger). 'That man dares to laugh. He dares to think the destruction of civilization a matter for humour!' Indeed, he is such a preposterous little fellow, with his folded arms and tufted forelock and his Lyceum Theatre voice, that if one did not detest him one might love him from sheer perversity." Set speeches, however, were a greater problem. Here, as when he had been challenged by prewar suffragettes, he was vulnerable. During his final address, in Victoria Palace, *The Times* reported that "the candidate was subjected to much interruption, the main burden of which consisted of remarks on Gallipoli and taunts by women about 'murder in Ireland.' "[142]

Churchill closed on an elegiac note, describing how the British Empire, "so powerful and splendid but a few years ago," was now, under a Labour government, "almost ready to apologize for our very existence, ready to lay down our burden in any one of the great Oriental countries if a stick be shaken by any irresponsible chatterbox." The constituency voted the following day, March 10. After the first hurried tally someone shouted to Winston: "You're in by a hundred." His followers cheered. But the shouter was premature. The official results gave him 8,114 against Nicholson's 8,187 — a difference of exactly 73 — with Brockway a close third. The Labour candidate was watching Churchill at this moment of chagrin. "He began to tramp the length of the hall," Brockway later wrote in *Inside the Left,* "head down, body lurching, like a despairing animal."[143]

In writing of Jellicoe's three lost opportunities to destroy the German fleet at Jutland, Churchill said: "Three times is a lot." That is equally true of three lost elections. At *The Times,* Geoffrey Dawson, later to become an archpriest of appeasement, sourly wrote of Winston's Westminster checkmate: "The features of his late campaign that attracted legitimate criticism were his ill-timed insistence on sheer anti-Socialism as the paramount claim on the electors at this moment, and the impulse that drove him, holding these views, to jeopardize a seat which without him was at least anti-Socialist. It is no new thing, after all, to discover that judgment is not the most conspicuous of Mr Churchill's remarkable gifts." House wags talked of organizing a dinner for the MPs who had beaten him at the polls. He had lacked a seat for nearly a year and a half now. His principal achievement had been the alienation of the socialists, in whose eyes, according to Shinwell, his "crowning sin was the fatuous declaration that Labour was unfit to govern, an accusation that gave the greatest offense to members of the Labour party."[144]

Churchill's refusal to accept the socialists as legitimate heirs to the fading Liberals was undoubtedly crippling; so was his scorn for the second-rate politicians, led by Baldwin, who had seized the leadership of the Conservative party. Yet in neither case could he have done otherwise and remained true to himself. He had always despised socialism, supporting welfare legislation which would deprive Labour candidates of social issues, and he would do so again. On a more profound level, as the tribune of excellence he was baffled by the hostility to brilliance which was, perhaps, the most striking feature of Britain's public life between the two world wars. How, he wondered, could the House endure year after year of what he called Baldwin's "very mediocre intellect"? He could not grasp how lesser men were mollified, comforted, and flattered by Baldwin's bland manner and tolerance of conduct which any other prime minister would have regarded as inexcusable. If you voted for Baldwin's legislation, nothing else you did would offend him. After an MP had delivered an unforgivable personal attack on him, Amery later wrote, "S.B. would meet him presently in the Lobby and would greet him genially with, 'Well, old chap, I expect you feel better after that.' " Beaverbrook observed that Churchill "resents an assault on his public policy as much as Lloyd George does an attack on his private life." Baldwin, a political placebo, resented neither. He was content to squat on the Treasury Bench as a benign abacist, counting votes and beaming at the results.[145]

Yet Churchill, for whom no accommodation with Labour was possible, slowly came to realize that he would have to come to terms with this in-

Austen Chamberlain, Stanley Baldwin, and Churchill in 1924

sipid man. Winston's position was stronger than it seemed. At the time, his setback in Westminster was generally regarded as a blunder, another example of his impetuosity. Actually, for reasons he could not have anticipated, it advanced his prospects. Had he routed the Tories' candidate, they would have found it hard to forgive him. As it was, his impressive showing as an independent, with neither a local organization nor a following in the district, was a remarkable demonstration of his personal appeal and skill as a campaigner. After the vote, Monteith Erskin, an influential Conservative, wrote Baldwin: "My conviction was and is that Winston Churchill would have done more to strengthen the Conservative Party than would his opponent. It seems a pity that the best interests of the country should often be at the mercy of a local Association divided in its own Councils. . . . The 25 or 30 MPs who came out in the open for Winston in no way measure the actual feeling in the House. Any number told me they wanted him to win & were quietly working for his return." The following day Lord Londonderry, a Churchill cousin who had been among his campaigners in Westminster, urged him to rejoin the Tories, writing: "Please Winston reflect — a half way house is no use to anyone, least of all to you." Sunny advised caution: "I personally think you are wise to preserve a detached position from the Tory party — till you can command your terms, and get hold of the title deeds." Eight days later, however, Churchill received a "unanimous invitation" from the Liverpool Conservatives, asking him to address their annual convention early in the following month. Now he had to decide. He hesitated. Once before he had switched parties, and he still bore scars of the wounds inflicted then. Abuse would be unavoidable. He wondered if he could survive with his credibility intact. "Anyone can rat," he told a friend, "but it takes a certain amount of ingenuity to re-rat."[146]

In the autumn of that year Churchill turned fifty, and he looked it: portly, bald, stooped, his face lined with wrinkles accumulated during countless crises, any one of which would have aged most men overnight. Yet the overall effect was pleasant. He had begun to resemble the cartoonist's conception of John Bull, hearty and prosperous, with an ovoid torso and a low center of gravity, good-humored if you let him have his way but stubborn and even refractory if you didn't. His height was just under five feet, seven inches, which would have surprised those who knew him only through newspaper photographs, because his massive shoulders led one to expect a taller man. His manner was always forthright, never devious; no one ever called him enigmatic. As unsubtle as the rare roast beef he (and John Bull) loved, his expression invariably reflected his mood. He beamed, looked puckish, frowned, wept, or brooded, but of the thousands of Churchill photographs, none shows him bored. When with him it was impossible to forget one was in the presence of a great original. By now his props — the cigar, the blue polka-dot bow tie, the elegant malacca gold-topped walking stick he had inherited when Clementine's brother Bill committed suicide in a Paris hotel room — were familiar throughout England. Controversy accompanied him everywhere. Had George Gallup been conducting his polls then, and had Britons been asked their judgment of Churchill, there would have been very few No Opinions. Nearly everyone had decided views about him, which he relished, though he was ever alert to the possibilities of slander and libel. On December 10, 1923, he appeared in the Old Bailey to testify against Lord Alfred Douglas, Oscar Wilde's faithless lover. This noisome peer had distributed 30,000 pamphlets accusing Churchill of having accepted a £40,000 bribe to issue a false communiqué about the battle of Jutland, thereby enabling "a group of Jewish financiers" to manipulate the stock market.* Had he chosen to take civil action, Winston would have won a large reward, but he believed scandalmongers belonged behind bars. He put this one there; a jury took just eight minutes to find Douglas guilty of criminal libel, and he was sentenced to six months in prison. Douglas's performance was inexcusable, but it is barely possible that he had been confused by the fact that Winston did pick up sums in the City from time to time when out of office; in 1923 he earned £5,000 as a lobbyist for Royal Dutch Shell and the Burmah Oil Company.

Though no longer in Parliament, he was always busy, always doing *something*. He had abandoned a second attempt to master flying after a postwar crash at Croydon — dusting himself off, he presided at a dinner honoring General Pershing two hours later, although, Lord Riddell noted in his diary, "Winston's forehead was scratched and his legs were black and blue" — and he was seen less often on polo fields, particularly after two bad falls, the first at Eaton Hall, the Duke of Westminster's home near Chester, and the second at Hurlingham, where he broke his collarbone. He was reluctant to give up the game altogether, however. "I do dumbbells every day," he had written the Prince of Wales, "trying to get my elbow right for next year: not many more polo years at 47!" In fact, he was the star of a game between the House of Commons and the House of Lords. (The Commons won.) As a private citizen he followed public affairs as closely as he had in the cabinet, and was in the public eye almost as often, rebuking the French for their occupation of the Ruhr, criticizing the Harding administration ("so many hard things are said about us over there and . . . they are wringing the last penny out of their unfortunate allies"), and unveiling statues of wartime leaders, two of whom, Jellicoe and Beatty, had been appointed to their commands by him. Alone, he wrote, corrected galleys, carried on an enormous correspondence, and painted. Anything from his pen commanded an instant audience. The slightest of his articles is worth rereading today. In the early 1920s he wrote: "May there not be methods of using exploding energy incomparably more intense than anything heretofore discovered? Might not a bomb no bigger than an orange be found to possess a secret power to destroy a whole block of buildings — nay, to concentrate a force of a thousand tons of cordite and blast a township at a stroke?"[147]

* After the Battle of Jutland on May 31, 1916, Churchill had drafted a communiqué on the action at Balfour's request, to bolster public confidence. It had merely served to identify him with public frustration over Jutland's inconclusive results.

Churchill playing polo with the Prince of Wales, 1924

Of all his roles, the warmest, and most endearing, was that of paterfamilias. Winston adored children, and saw to it that his own would never suffer the starvation for parental affection which had made his childhood, even now, a painful memory. He built them hideouts in the woods; played "Bear," "Gorilla," charades, and other games; read to them, spun them yarns at the fireside, gave them new nicknames. In 1921 Diana, "the gold-cream kitten," was twelve; Randolph, "the Rabbit," was ten ("He looks such a thin shrimp in trousers and Eton collar!" Clementine wrote Winston); and Sarah, "the Bumblebee," seven. Marigold, a two-year-old, would never be three. Her birth had been difficult for her mother, but by the time she could talk she was a treasure, one of those irresistible little heartbreakers of fey charm and manic energy whose very presence in a room endows everyone there with a fresh joy. Her father called her "the Duckadilly." She would race pell-mell around the dining room table while her parents entertained guests at lunch; her mother, afraid she might crack her head on one of the table's sharp corners, padded them. The Duckadilly had "a sweet, true little voice," as one member of the family later recalled, and her signature tune was the 1921 hit:[148]

I'm forever blowing bubbles,
Pretty bubbles in the air.
They fly so high, nearly reach the sky,
Then like my dreams they fade and die.
Oh, fortune's always hiding,
I've looked everywhere.
I'm forever blowing bubbles,
Pretty bubbles in the air.

It had been a hard winter of hacking coughs and sore throats; Marigold had fallen ill twice, and once it had become necessary to summon a physician. The family rented a seaside cottage at Broadstairs for that summer of 1921. Clementine, leaving there, and Winston, boarding a train in London, would travel by separate routes to the remote Scotland estate of the Duke of Westminster. The elder children would later entrain to join them, Marigold being left at Broadstairs with a young French governess. The Duckadilly's sickness returned. Before leaving the shore, Randolph wrote his mother on August 2: "Marigold has been rather ill, but is ever so much better today." The improvement was only temporary. Alone with the young governess, after her brother and sisters had departed, she sickened again. Her throat grew worse; by August 14 she had contracted septicemia. The governess was slow to call the doctor and slower to telegraph Clementine. By the time her mother reached her bedside, the Duckadilly's condition was grave. Clementine telegraphed Winston, who arrived on the next train from London. On Monday, August 22, he wrote Curzon: "The child is a little better than she was, but we are still dreadfully anxious about her." On Wednesday evening she began to sink. Clementine was sitting beside her. Suddenly the little girl asked: "Sing me 'Bubbles.'" Her mother tried. She struggled. She tried again. Marigold put out her hand. She whispered: "Not tonight . . . finish it tomorrow." But Clementine never finished it. On Thursday the child died. She was two years and nine months old. Her mother and father were at her bedside when life fled from her, and long afterward Winston told Mary, now grown, that Clementine shrieked in agony, "like an animal in mortal pain." He could not speak of his own agony. On Saturday they buried Marigold in London's Kensal Green cemetery. Press photographers arrived, but Winston appealed to them to leave, and they did. He wrote Lord Crewe the following week: "We have suffered a vy heavy & painful loss. It also seems so pitiful that this little life sh'd have been extinguished just when it was so beautiful & so happy — just when it was beginning." The governess was dismissed, but dismissing the grief was impossible. "Alas," he wrote Clementine when he was next separated from her, "I keep on feeling the hurt of the Duckadilly." She wrote back: "I took the children on Sunday to Marigold's grave and as we knelt round it — would you believe that a little white butterfly . . . fluttered down & settled on the flowers which are now growing on it. We took some little bunches. The children were very silent all the way home." And seven months later, on April 4, 1922, he wrote her: "I pass through again those sad scenes of last year when we lost our dear Duckadilly. Poor lamb — it is a gaping wound, whenever one touches it & removes the bandages & plasters of daily life." To the end of her life Clementine could never speak of her lost child. Mary, the last of the Churchills' children, was born that autumn. She grew up puzzled by the identity of the little girl whose framed picture stood on her mother's dressing table, wondering who she could be.[149]

Marigold's death was one of three to sadden the family that year, though the other two, coming after fruitful lives, were easier to bear. The Countess of Airlie, Clementine's austere grandmother, expired at the age of ninety, and Winston's mother died of complications after an accident caused, appropriately, by a pair of fashionable but impractical Italian shoes. At sixty-seven Jennie was a Bright Old Thing, the grayest flapper in postwar Mayfair. She was still on the watch for new experiences. Meeting a jovial, monocled RAF officer at a party, she persuaded him to take her up, sitting in the wickerwork of his little passenger cockpit and soaring over Kent at ninety miles an hour. "An extraordinary experience," she told her friends. "Right above the clouds in a little coupe." She played a part in a film. She was forty years older than the rest of the cast, but one of the other actresses said, "She was just one of us." She scorned a Philadelphia clergyman who denounced short skirts, saying that people, not clothes, were moral or immoral. Long dresses, said she, speaking with the voice of experience, were no insurance against sexual license.[150]

Returning from a lively trip to Rome, Jennie was on her way to a tea party, hurrying down a staircase in her new shoes when, three steps from a landing, she tripped, fell, and broke her left leg. It was a simple fracture; the bone was quickly set. She was convalescing in her new home in Westbourne Street, just around the corner from Sussex Square, when, two weeks after the fall, gangrene set in. Winston, informed, sent for a surgeon. Immediate amputation was necessary. Jennie calmly said she would learn "to put my best foot forward" and added: "Be sure you cut high enough." The cut was above the knee. Over the next two weeks she appeared to be healing. Suddenly, after a hearty breakfast, the femoral artery in her left thigh hemorrhaged; she passed into a coma, and was dead before noon. Winston had hurried over in his pajamas; he was with her at the end. DEATH OF LADY RANDOLPH, said the news posters; LADY RANDY GONE. Asquith told a reporter, "She lived every inch of her life up to the edge," and Churchill wrote a family friend: "She suffers no more pain; nor will she ever know old age, decrepitude, loneliness. . . . I wish you could have seen her as she lay at rest — after all the sunshine & storm of life was over. Very beautiful & splendid she looked. Since the morning with its pangs, thirty years have fallen from her brow. She recalled to me the countenance I had admired as a child when she was in her heyday and the old brilliant world of the eighties & nineties seemed to come back." Her last husband was hurrying home from Nigeria, but before he could reach England she had been buried in Bladon churchyard beside Lord Randolph. Shane Leslie wrote: "The feeling shewn was very considerable." After the others had left, Winston stood alone by the open grave. He wept; and threw in a spray of crimson roses. But he was mourning his own lost youth, and the imperial glory of those years, as much as his mother. To Lord Crewe he wrote that the England "in wh you met her is a long way off now, & we do not see its like today. I feel a vy great sense of deprivation."[151]

Jennie herself had never given him a sense of fulfillment. There had been a time when he had needed her help, or rather the help of her powerful admirers, but that had long since passed. Since 1908 the overarching figure in his life had been his wife, and none of his other relationships, not even his love for his children, held him as closely as the matrimonial bond. It was not seamless. An oddity of the triumphant Churchill marriage, and possibly one reason for its success, is that Winston and Clementine usually took separate vacations. In 1919 they toured occupied Germany, and she accompanied him to the Cairo conference, but those were official occasions, offering no moments of intimacy. It was not until 1921 that they left England for their first joint holiday since before the war. Even then they shared their Nice beach with Sir Ernest Cassel and his granddaughter Edwina, the future Lady Mountbatten, and they had hardly settled in when Winston was recalled to London. He wrote Clementine that he hoped she would continue to enjoy the sunshine in his absence "& preen yr poor feathers in it," adding, in another letter, when she was competing in an Eaton racket tournament: "I hope you are having fun & tennis & *above all* recharging yr accumulators." In 1925 and 1927 they would visit Venice together, but usually one of them remained in London while the other relaxed in this spa or that lodge. In most instances the vacationer was Winston. Clementine stayed at Saint-Jean-

Cap-Ferrat in February 1921, participated in a tennis tournament later in the year, and spent subsequent summers at Frinton-on-Sea, Cromer, or Broadstairs with the children, but that was the extent of her recreation in the early 1920s. Winston was always urging her to cut loose: "I strongly recommend yr going to the Ritz & pigging it there while passing thro London." She never did. Her Spartan sense of duty kept her home.[152]

That was one reason. She had another reason. Their taste in playgrounds was, literally, miles apart. Clementine, unlike her husband, had been raised in a thrifty home and taught to distrust the voluptuous. If abroad, she instinctively sought to justify the trip by improving her mind. She enjoyed brisk sight-seeing when she did cross the Channel, preferred British seaside resorts if she needed relaxation, and disliked the exotic Riviera. Winston detested galleries and museums. He liked to hunt, play polo, and, eager for lush surroundings and colorful scenes he might paint, sought, to use his word, "paintatious" locales bathed in bright, continual sunshine. Each tried to convert the other. Neither succeeded. If wealthy friends lured them to villas on the Mediterranean, she would decline or make only a brief *acte de présence.* Winston would reluctantly appear at a cottage she had rented on an English beach, play with the children for a day or two, and depart muttering excuses.

Occasionally she resented his absences. Early in 1922, when he was staying in southern France, first with Lady Essex and then with Beaverbrook, she had been nursing Diana, Randolph, and a maid through bouts of flu. Winston wasn't there to catch it, and she was glad for that, but she sent him a long letter describing her "deep misery & depression." She wished "I were with you basking in the sun." The only letter she had received from him had been typed, which was "piling Pelium on Ossa coming after one of the most dreary & haunted weeks I have ever lived through" with "all the sad events of last year, culminating in Marigold, passing & repassing . . . thro my sad heart." After posting it, she wired him, asking him to destroy it unread. He wrote: "My darling, I cd not bear not opening yr letter in the cream coloured envelope, in spite of yr telegram. In law it was my property once it was delivered to me, & any letter from you is better than none at all. My poor sweet. . . . I am so sorry you had such a churlish message. I do so love & value yr being pleased to hear from me, & even the shadow cast by that pleasure when disappointed is dear to me." He had, in fact, written her at length, in his own hand. The letter had been delayed in the mail, which perhaps was just as well, for it bore alarming news: "I must confess to you that I have lost some money here; though nothing like as much as last year. It excites me so much to play — foolish moth." Clementine always worried

The Duke of Sutherland rescues a sunburned Churchill at Deauville

about his gambling, but once it brought her a pleasant surprise. On one of those rare occasions when she accompanied him to Monte Carlo, she left the tables early, finding the play and the players tiresome, and retired to bed. He stayed with the green baize and hit a lucky streak. When she awoke next morning she found every inch of her bedspread covered with bank notes.[153]

Despite her anxiety and periodic threats of mutiny, she approved of his trips, pleased that he had "Painting for your leisure and Polo for excitement," and he kept her fully informed of all his activities. September of that year found him at Dunrobin, the Duke of Sutherland's castle in Scotland, writing: "In the afternoon I went out and painted a beautiful river in the afternoon light with crimson and golden hills in the background." That same year he reported from the Riviera: "Yesterday Monday & today I have painted or am about to paint at Consuelo's villa. I have done a beautiful picture of Eze which I know you will want, but wh I cannot give you because Consuelo & Balzan praised it so much I gave it to them. Now I am doing one of the workmen building their house — all in shimmering sunshine & violet shades. . . . A big beastly gt cloud has just come over the mountains & threatens to spoil my sunshine. Isn't it cruel! And these tiresome stupid inhabitants actually say: they *want* rain. It is too much." Ever alert for choice gossip or the misbehavior of the eminent, he added a postscript to one letter describing Asquith's arrival at a party given by Sir Philip Sassoon: "The old boy turned up at Philip's party vy heavily loaded. The P.M. accompanied him up the stairs & was chivalrous enough to cede him the banister. It was a wounding sight. He kissed a great many people affectionately. I presume they were all relations."[154]

"No gambling — I lost only 500 francs & was frankly bored by it," he wrote cheerfully from Deauville a few months later. Thence he proceeded to Paris, took the night sleeper to Bordeaux, crossed to Mimizan by boat, and continued on to Biarritz by train. The Duke of Westminster's stables excited him: "24 magnificent steeds & any number of hounds. I am going to ride every morning to try to get myself fit." Clementine was expecting Mary then, and he added: "I think a gt deal about the coming kitten & about you my sweet pet. I feel it will enrich yr life and brighten our home to have the nursery started again. I pray God to watch over us all." She replied from Frinton: "I love to think of you resting & painting and riding in that lovely forest." She was "getting very stationary & crawl even to the beach with difficulty. I long for it to be over. It has seemed a very long nine months." Later he wrote: "Your own adventure is vy near now & I look forward so much to seeing you safe & well with a new darling kitten to cherish." Late in August he joined the family at Frinton, where he promptly organized the children, their nanny, and his bodyguard — this was only two months after the assassination of Sir Henry Wilson — to join in the construction of a gigantic sand fortress, which then made a brave if hopeless stand against the rising tide. In September they were back in London for Clementine's last confinement. The sorrow of the lost Duckadilly would never fade completely, but "Mary the Mouse" was doubly cherished for the void left by the sister she would never know.[155]

Churchill was not dawdling abroad while Clementine raised the family at home. He swam, he rode, he painted, he gambled, he cruised on Beaverbrook's yacht. But he also worked furiously on manuscripts, and no one knew better than his wife that this toil was absolutely necessary for their financial survival. After acknowledging a gambling loss he noted:

Winston having fun at the beach

"But I have earned many times what I have lost by the work I have done here on my book." Usually he worked in bed from breakfast until noon, but writing from Mimizan he described an altered regimen: "I ride from 7:30 to 9, work at my book till lunch, 12:30." Unless the skies were overcast — in which case he kept writing — afternoons were spent at his easel. After dinner he resumed work, continuing until the early hours of the following morning. Clementine prayed that the manuscripts would sell. The children were unaware, as Mary recalls, of "how fragile was the raft which supported our seemingly so solid way of life." From time to time they were told, "Papa and Mummie are economizing," were lectured about the need to turn off lights and reprimanded for long telephone conversations, yet, in Mary's words, the manner of the life her parents led "belied the insecurity and fragility of their financial situation. They lived and entertained elegantly; they traveled; they brought up and educated their four surviving children handsomely. But had Winston's diligence, health, or genius failed, the whole fabric of their life would have crashed, for they literally lived from book to book, and from one article to the next."[156]

Like most writers he derived his income from various sources: newspaper and magazine sales, publishers' advances, royalties from books sold in England and other countries, and the sale of first serial rights — selec-

Churchill with Mary, aged two, at Chartwell

tions from books which appear in periodicals before publication date. And, like every other ink-stained wretch, he could never be certain of future income. During his two years out of Parliament he supported his life-style by writing, apart from books and edited collections of his speeches, thirty-three articles for the *Empire Review*, *Pearson's Magazine*, the *Daily Chronicle*, the *Strand Magazine*, *Nash's Pall Mall*, *English Life*, the *Sunday Chronicle*, *John Bull*, the *Weekly Dispatch*, the *Daily Mail*, and, in the United States, *Cosmopolitan*. His earnings from these alone were about £13,200, or, with the pound pegged at $4.86, about $64,152, the equivalent of $200,000 today. It made him unique among upper-class British politicians, most of whom had private incomes or lived on parliamentary salaries, and Clementine worried about that. She recognized the absolute necessity of his free-lancing, but was afraid it might be considered beneath his dignity and therefore an obstacle to high office. Her eye was on No. 10. Eventually, she believed, Winston's moment would come. She thought it might arrive in the near future. Once returned to the House, his gifts would carry him straight into the cabinet, where his chief rival — Stanley Baldwin not yet having consolidated his strength — would be Curzon, or, as she called him, the "All Highest."

She wrote Winston: "I have a sort of feeling that the 'All Highest' rejoices every time you write an Article & thinks it brings *him* nearer the Premiership, tho' I think that a man who had had to bolster himself up with two rich wives to keep himself going is not so likely to keep the Empire going as you who for 12 years have been a Cabinet Minister & have besides kept a fortuneless Cat & four hungry Kittens."[157]

At that time he was considering a piece on his painting. She thought it a bad idea; to her it smacked of hackwork. What, she asked him, was he going to write about? "Art in general? I expect the professionals would be vexed & say you do not yet know enough about Art. . . . Your own pictures in particular? The danger there seems to me that it may be thought naif or conceited." The *Strand* had offered him £1,000 for two articles, to be illustrated by four-color and monochrome reproductions of his landscapes. She was "as anxious as you are to snooker that £1,000 & as proud as you can be that you have had the offer; but just now I do not think it would be wise to do anything which would cause you to be discussed trivially, as it were." Nevertheless, he went ahead. The result was his charming essay "Painting as a Pastime," which was later republished in *Thoughts and Adventures,* a collection of his pieces, and, later still, combined with an article on "Hobbies" he had written for *Pall Mall,* was issued as a slender volume which sold 5,000 copies in Great Britain, was published in the United States, translated into French, German, Finnish, and Japanese, and ultimately appeared as a Penguin paperback. Among the pieces he ground out during his exile from Parliament between 1922 and 1924 were "Who Rules Britain?," "The Case for Singapore," "Plugstreet," "Socialism and Sham," "The Danger Ahead in Europe," "Should Strategists Veto the Channel Tunnel?," "My Dramatic Days with the Kaiser," "If We Could Look into the Future," "My Own True Spy Story," "When I Risked Court Martial in Search of War," "A Hand-to-Hand Fight with Desert Fanatics," and profiles of Kitchener, MacDonald, Birkenhead, and Lloyd George. It occurred neither to him nor to Clementine that a time would come when, once more in political Coventry and with the survival of England at stake, he would arouse the nation with powerful articles in the press. During the 1920s he wrote for newspapers and magazines with money as his chief object. In a typical note to his wife on August 14, 1923, he reported: "I have 8 articles to write as soon as the book is finished: £500, £400, & £200. We shall not starve."[158]

"The book" was not to be completed for eight more years; it would run to five thick volumes, 2,517 pages, and would never be described as a potboiler. As originally conceived, it was to be a two-volume memoir of his years at the Admiralty. During the war he had carefully filed memoranda, documents, and letters, explaining, in a letter to Clementine on July 17, 1915, "Someday I shd like the truth to be known," and in March 1920 Sir Frederick Macmillan, at his request, set these in type so they would be readily usable. He began organizing them when Lord Esher published a distorted account of the Antwerp operation in *The Tragedy of Lord Kitchener*, charging that Churchill had "slipped away" to Belgium on his own while Kitchener was "in bed asleep." By October, Winston was hard at work, singling out quotations from other men's memoirs, pasting the passages Macmillan had set on large sheets of blank paper, writing commentary in the margins, and drafting transitions. Admiral Jackson checked his facts; Eddie Marsh, his grammar, punctuation, and style. An exchange between Eddie and Winston survives:

CHURCHILL TO MARSH: Eddie. You are very free with your commas. I always reduce them to a minimum: and use "and" or an "or" as a substitute not as an addition. Let us argue it out. W.

MARSH TO CHURCHILL: I look on myself as a bitter enemy of superfluous commas, and I think I could make a good case for any I have put in — but I won't do it any more! E.

CHURCHILL TO MARSH: No do continue. I am adopting provisionally. But I want to argue with you. W.[159]

Soon the news that Winston was writing about the war was all over London. It was unnerving for some and exciting for others, if only because of the money involved. Late in November, Thornton Butterworth, working through Winston's agent, Curtis Brown, advanced him £9,000; Scribner's paid £5,000 as an advance for American publication. The magazine *Metropolitan* had offered nearly £8,000 for first serial rights, but he chose *The Times* instead. His deadline for both volumes was December 31, 1922, which subjected him to an unremitting pressure, but he liked it that way. On January 1, 1921, he attended another Sassoon party, at Lympne, in Kent. Riddell, a fellow guest, noted in his diary: "I had a long talk with Winston about his book. He says he has written a great part of the first volume. He proposed to dictate 300,000 words, and then cut down the matter and polish it up. He added that it was very exhilarating to feel that one was writing for half a crown a word! He went upstairs to put in two or three hours' work on the book. When he came down, I said to L.G., with whom I had been talking, 'It is a horrible thought that while we have been frittering away our time, Winston has been piling up words at a half a crown each.' This much amused L.G."[160]

It did not amuse Bonar Law, who said that if Churchill was quoting government documents, which he was, he was violating his privy councillor's oath. The problem of copyright torments every writer who uses contemporary sources, and Winston was no exception. He pointed out that Fisher, Jellicoe, and one of Kitchener's biographers had used confidential material. Hankey told Law that Churchill's point was a good one, but the matter was raised again and again as the several volumes appeared. Later, when he himself was back in the cabinet, Churchill learned that Birkenhead was working on a book about Woodrow Wilson. Dismayed that it might come out before the appearance of Winston's next volume and provoke an embargo on ministers publishing while still in office, he unreasonably begged F.E. to drop the idea. It was a false alarm; the issue was never raised. Most of his former colleagues had nothing to fear from an accurate account of the past, but all were immensely curious. They wondered, among other things, about the title. So did the author. In the last throes of the first volume, on January 30, 1922, he wrote Clementine, "I am so busy that I hardly ever leave the Ritz except for meals," adding that Dawson of *The Times* had called "and suggested himself the title 'The Great Amphibian,' but I cannot get either Butterworth or Scribner . . . to fancy it. They want 'The World Crisis' or possibly 'Sea Power and the World Crisis.' We have to settle tomorrow for certain."[161]

They settled on *The World Crisis.* "Winston has written an enormous book about himself," a colleague remarked, "and called it *The World Crisis.*" Balfour said he was reading Churchill's "autobiography disguised as a history of the universe." A volume appeared in 1927, *The World Crisis: A Criticism,* comprising essays quarreling with some of his statistics and minor points of strategy and tactics. They didn't amount to much. Beaverbrook was offended by the treatment of Law, whose friend he was, and the *Times* reviewer observed: "Serious students will not need, and others will not heed, the warning that an apologia may be first-class material for history but cannot be history itself."[162] The reviewer was absolutely wrong. It is indeed the precise strength of the work — which covers events from the prewar "Vials of Wrath" to the aftershocks of 1922 — that the historian was either in the thick of events or had special access to many who were. He was a cabinet minister before the war, during the early and latter parts of it, and after the Armistice. In this regard *The World Crisis* is perhaps unique. Many statesmen have published memoirs; few have attempted a comprehensive account of their times. Caesar's *De Bello Gallico* and *De Bello Civili* are dry and unimaginative; Frederick the Great had a first-class mind, but his *Histoire de mon temps* was written in a language he had not mastered; Talleyrand's *Mémoires* is largely based on letters he himself did not write; Metternich is characteristically vain and obscure; Bismarck's three-volume *Gedanken und Erinnerungen* is insular, confusing, and inchoate. Thucydides' *History of the Peloponnesian War,* Clarendon's *History of the Rebellion and Civil Wars in England,* and the memoirs of Grant and Henry Kissinger, though immensely valuable, lack the breadth of *The World Crisis.* Churchill's perspective is amazingly broad. Even in describing the activities of Lenin and Trotsky, whom he loathed, he is scrupulous of facts and objective in examining the social matrix which made their rise possible.

But his achievement is greater than that. T. E. Lawrence described the second volume as "far and away the best war-book I've yet read in any language." John Maynard Keynes, finishing the fourth, wrote in the *Nation:* "With what feelings does one lay down Mr Churchill's two-thousandth page? Gratitude to one who can write with so much eloquence and feeling of things which are part of the lives of all of us of the war generation, but which he saw and knew much closer and clearer. Admiration for his energies of mind and his intense absorption of intellectual interest and elemental emotion on what is for the moment the matter in hand — which is his best quality. A little envy, perhaps, for his undoubting conviction that frontiers, races, patriotisms, even wars if need be, are ultimate verities for mankind, which lends for him a kind of dignity and even nobility to events, which for others are only a nightmare interlude, something to be permanently avoided." Keynes had touched on the work's deepest theme: its re-creation of the past, the illusion of immediacy created by the author's powerful presence. Keynes had also identified the reasons for Bloomsbury's reservations about it: the author's certitude and his lack of curiosity about subconscious motivation. Malcolm Muggeridge points out that Churchill, as a historian and biographer, "remained obstinately Victorian and pre–Lytton Strachey" — interested in public events, that is, not in private lives. Writers like Strachey, literary beneficiaries of a decade in which irony and understatement were fashionable, dismissed Churchill's style as outmoded. In reality its essence is timeless; it found its greatest audience in 1940, when it moved an entire nation, but it lives today in allusion and everyday speech.[163]

Here he writes about the eve of Britain's 1916 offensive:

> A sense of the inevitable broods over the battlefields of the Somme. The British armies were so ardent, their leaders so confident, the need and appeals of our Allies so clamant, and decisive results seemingly so near, that no human power

could have prevented the attempt. All the spring the French had been battling and dying at Verdun, immolating their manhood upon that anvil-altar; and every chivalrous instinct in the new British armies called them to the succour of France, and inspired them with sacrifice and daring. . . . The British Generals . . . were quite sure they were going to break their enemy and rupture his invading lines in France. They trusted to the devotion of their troops, which they knew was boundless; they trusted to masses of artillery and shells never before accumulated in war; and they launched their attack in the highest sense of duty and the strongest conviction of success.

And after the Somme:

A young army, but the finest we have ever marshalled; improvised at the sound of the cannonade, every man a volunteer, inspired not only by love of country but by a widespread conviction that human freedom was challenged by military and Imperial tyranny, they grudged no sacrifice however unfruitful and shrank from no ordeal however destructive. Struggling forward through the mire and filth of the trenches, across the corpse-strewn crater fields, amid the flaring, crashing, blasting barrages and murderous machine-gun fire, conscious of their race, proud of their cause, they seized the most formidable soldiery in Europe by the throat, slew them and hurled them unceasingly backward. If two lives or ten lives were required by their commanders to kill one German, no word of complaint ever rose from the fighting troops. No attack however forlorn, however fatal, found them without ardour. No slaughter however desolating prevented them from returning to the charge. No physical conditions however severe deprived their commanders of their obedience and loyalty. Martyrs not less than soldiers, they fulfilled the high purpose of duty with which they were imbued. The battlefields of the Somme were the graveyards of Kitchener's Army. The flower of that generous manhood which quitted peaceful civilian life in every kind of workaday occupation, which came at the call of Britain, and as we may still hope, at the call of humanity, and came from the most remote parts of her Empire, was shorn away for ever in 1916. Unconquerable except by death, which they had conquered, they have set up a monument of native virtue which will command the wonder, the reverence and the gratitude of our island people as long as we endure as a nation among men.[164]

Churchill had received the first payment of his American advance, a check for £3,000, in July 1921, and on August 19 he paid £2,550 for a new Rolls-Royce. It was a token of his faith in the work's popularity, and it was more than justified. The British editions alone sold 80,551 copies. Since his British royalties ranged between 30 and 33 percent, this brought him £58,846, or $285,996. Moreover, *The Times* serialized four of the five volumes. Further excerpts appeared in the *Sunday Chronicle*. An indefatigable worker, he produced the last three volumes of *The World Crisis* when serving as the cabinet's busiest minister. Considered in their entirety, his achievements as an author in that decade were prodigious, though he was not the most successful political author of those years. Five days before Christmas, 1924, when he was writing his version of the Somme, a former German soldier who had been wounded in that battle left Landsberg Prison in southern Bavaria, where he had been serving time for attempting to overthrow the government, with the rough draft of a very different account under his arm. Like Churchill, Adolf Hitler had a problem with his title. He wanted to call it *Viereinhalb Jahre Kampf gegen Lüge, Dummheit und Feigheit* ("Four and a Half Years of Struggle against Lies, Stupidity and Cowardice"), but his publisher persuaded him to settle for *Mein Kampf* ("My Struggle"). Within a few years, when its writer came to power, *Mein Kampf*'s presence would be almost obligatory in the homes of respectable burghers, and it led the list of his country's most popular graduation and wedding gifts through the 1930s. How many actually read it — plowing through those desperate Teutonic sentences to find the verb at the end — is unknown, but its sales eventually exceeded six million copies, making it Germany's number-one best-seller and bringing Hitler $1.8 million in royalties. Unlike Churchill, he paid no taxes on this income after 1933, having declared himself exempt from them. His prose, however, has not borne the test of time.

Late in 1919, pressed for cash and not yet a wealthy writer, Churchill had sold his Lullenden estate to Ian Hamilton and moved his family in with the Freddie Guests, sharing expenses with his cousin while Clementine hunted for a new London home. A tall, handsome house at 2 Sussex Square, a block from Hyde Park's Victoria Gate and adjoined by a mews which would serve as Winston's studio, proved highly suitable, but he still yearned for a country home. Early in 1922 this became possible. On January 26 his first cousin once removed, Lord Herbert Vane-Tempest, died in a train accident. Lord Herbert had been a bachelor; Winston, as his heir, came into several thousand pounds. Clementine felt "like a cork bobbing on a sunny sea," while her husband sought out real-estate agents. He looked at several properties and found the one he wanted near Westerham, in Kent, some twenty-five miles from London and just a mile north of Lullenden. The house itself was ugly. Built of pleasant red brick during the reign of Henry VII, the original structure

Chartwell

had been charming, but during the nineteenth century its owners had added ponderous bays and oriels, two ungainly wings, stifling clots of ivy, and heavy flora: rhododendrons, laurels, and conifers. Its view, however, was magnificent. Sited on eighty acres above a combe, it overlooked the great Kentish Weald, with its smooth meadows, suave green slopes, and sheltering woods of oak, beech, and chestnut, watered here by a clear spring, the Chart Well, which gave the manor its name. Years later, looking down on it, Churchill said: "I bought Chartwell for that view." At the time, however, he wondered if he could afford it. Clementine was in Scotland then, so he drove Diana, Randolph, and Sarah there, telling them he wanted to show them an estate he might buy. They adored it. Sarah recalled: "We did a complete tour of the house and grounds, my father asking anxiously — it is still clear in my mind — 'Do you like it?' Did we like it? We were delirious. 'Oh, do buy it! Do buy it!' we exclaimed." The asking price was £5,500. On September 15 Winston offered £4,800, explaining: "The house will have to be very largely rebuilt, and the presence of dry rot in the northern wing is I am advised a very serious adverse factor." Norman Harding, the agent, told him his offer was unacceptable. "He strode up and down," Harding recalled afterward, "using every argument he could think of. . . . Eventually, with very bad grace, he gave way." They compromised on £5,000.[165]

Chartwell

Churchill had been right; the rot was advanced, and the mansion had to be reconstructed from the ground up. An architect was engaged, a friend of his aunt Leonie's who had just finished a country place at Churt for Lloyd George. The ivy and Victorian trimmings were stripped away, high crowstepped gables were added, and also a new wing for a drawing room, dining room, and Clementine's bedroom. The job took more than two years. Winston grew impatient. Clementine didn't. Her husband had committed a grave error. He had made the purchase without consulting her. And when she saw it, she disliked it. "At first," she told Martin Gilbert, "I did not want to go to Chartwell at all. But Winston had his heart set on it." Mary remembers that her mother "tried very hard to love the place which so enthralled Winston. She worked like a Trojan to make it the home and haven for us all that he dreamed of. But it never acquired for her the nature of a venture shared; rather, it was an extra duty, gallantly undertaken, and doggedly carried through." Among other things, she was concerned about the expense. The cost of rebuilding the house rose to £13,000, then £15,000, and finally £18,000. Winston wrote her: "My beloved, I do beg you not to worry about money, or to feel insecure. On the contrary the policy we are pursuing aims above all at *stability* (like Bonar Law!). Chartwell is to be our *home*. It will have cost us £20,000 and will be worth at least £15,000 apart from a fancy price.

We must endeavour to live there for many years & hand it on to Randolph afterwards. We must make it in every way possible economically self contained. It will be cheaper than London." He contemplated selling the house in Sussex Square: "Then with the motor we shall be well equipped for business or pleasure. If we go into office we will live in Downing Street!"[166]

During the reconstruction of "Cosy Pig," as he called it, he leased Hosey Rigg, a nearby house where, he was delighted to learn, Lewis Carroll had written *Alice in Wonderland*. On weekends he would prowl around his new property, the children tagging along. He wrote his wife: "I am going to amuse them on Saturday and Sunday by making them an aerial house in the lime tree. You may be sure I will take the greatest precautions to guard against their tumbling down." Sarah would remember the tree house as "a two-storeyed affair; it was a good twenty feet high, and was reached by first shinning up a rope and then climbing on carefully placed struts between the four stems of the elm." During the Easter holiday of 1924 he and the children began sleeping at the manor in what Mary calls "camping" style. To Clementine, who was laid up, he wrote: "This is the first letter I have ever written from this place, & it is right that it shd be to you. I am in bed in your bedroom (wh I have annexed temporarily) & wh is sparsely but comfortably furnished with the pick of yr two van loads. . . . You cannot imagine the size of these rooms till you put furniture in them. This bedroom of yours is a magnificent aerial bower. Come as soon as you feel well enough to share it." The children, he said, had "worked like blacks." He added a couplet: "Only one thing lack these banks of green — / The Pussy Cat who is their queen."[167]

Under his supervision — and his straining muscles — the grounds began to take shape. To Cosy Pig's natural setting he added three hundred asparagus plants, two hundred strawberry runners, and a large consignment of fruit trees: apple, pear, plum, damson, and quince. For Clementine he created a water garden, and, beyond it, a fragrant azalea glade. White foxglove was planted, then blue anchusa. Carp swam in a warm pond. Black swans, a gift from the Australian government, cruised across a large, pleasant lake which a previous owner had created by damming the spring. "Why only one dam?" Winston asked. He wanted a place to swim. Another site was excavated and water diverted into it. Sir Samuel Hoare, in the neighborhood, wrote Beaverbrook: "I had never seen Winston in the role of landed proprietor," and described him as engaged in "engineering works" which "consist of making a series of ponds in the valley." He added: "Winston appeared to be a great deal more interested in them than in anything else in the world." But both lakes, Churchill decided, were too weedy and muddy for swimming, so he decided to abandon one to wildfowl, drain the other, scoop out a third, waterproof its bottom, and build another dike, hiring a crew of workmen and pressing Detective Thompson into service. Thomas Jones arrived and found Churchill "attired in dungarees and high Wellington boots superintending the building of a dam by a dozen navvies. This is the third lake, and the children are wondering what their father will do next year, as there is room for no more lakes." Writing Clementine on August 19 of his first Chartwell summer, Winston mentioned — fleetingly, almost impatiently — that Conservatives in the Epping constituency, "one of the safest seats in the country," were actively courting him, and then hurried on to what was, for him, more exciting news: "Work on the dam is progressing. . . . The water has been rising steadily. We have this evening seven feet. It will be finished by next Tuesday, or eight weeks from its initiation. I am at it all day and every day." A foot of mud remained in the old lake, and he was clearing it out: "Thompson and I have been wallowing in the most filthy black mud you ever saw, with the vilest odour, getting the beastly stuff to drain away. The moor hens and dab chicks have migrated in a body to the new lake and taken up their quarters in the bushes at the upper end." Thompson recalls pulling on rubber waders each morning before going out to "the dig" with Winston, shoveling, patching, lining the bottom of the new excavation with bitumen, "thick slimy mud everywhere," and one occasion of rare mirth when "I dropped a dollop of mud on his pate."[168]

It was all in vain. The bitumen leaked, and the new dam, though built of cement, threatened to slide down the hill. Undaunted, Churchill built a circular pool by the house, fed by the Chart Well, whose waters came purling down through fern-fringed channels and rocks fetched by train from Cumberland. The spring was supplemented by an electric pump, which sent water to and from the ponds "rather like a stage army," in Sarah's phrase, or, in Winston's, "filtered to limpidity." It was a heated pool, then a novelty; a visiting engineer assured him that the boilers were big enough to heat the Ritz. The uselessness of the dams was frustrating, but erecting them had not been a complete waste; the lakes were comely, and the work, like his landscaping and gardening, had been a diversion from politics. Thompson believes it was good for Churchill "to get close to the ground and the fine smell of it, and to work it and plant it and make it bloom and yield." After the voters of Westminster had rejected him Winston wrote a friend: "I am content for the first time in my life to look after my own affairs, build my house and cultivate my garden."

Once the mansion was completely finished and the family had spent two strenuous days moving in, he continued to toil outside, devising rookeries, miniature waterfalls in the water garden, elaborate waterworks for the golden carp, and planting bamboo, wisteria, and acers on the banks of the carps' pool. Then, after putting up a garden wall of Kentish ragstone, he decided to become a bricklayer. Returning from London one evening, he paused in Westerham to visit Quebec House, General James Wolfe's birthplace. After examining the wall, with its dentils surmounted by a sloping top, he said: "That's what I want." Shortly thereafter James Scrymgeour-Wedderburn, an early Chartwell guest, scribbled in his diary: "Winston is building with his own hands a house for his butler, and also a garden wall!"[169]

He built much more than that. Altogether he finished two cottages, several walls, and a playhouse for Mary. Scrymgeour-Wedderburn wrote: "He works at bricklaying for hours a day, and lays 90 bricks an hour, which is a very high output." He himself never claimed more than one a minute, but his craftsmanship was admirable; the sturdy results stand today. He wrote Baldwin: "I have had a delightful month building a cottage and dictating a book: 200 bricks and 2,000 words a day." Stories about his skill reached James F. Lane, an official of the Amalgamated Union of Building Trade Workers. Lane wrote Winston, proposing that he join the union. Winston replied: "Would you mind letting me know whether there is any rule regulating the number of bricks which a man may lay in a day; also, is there any rule that a trade unionist may not work with one who is not a trade unionist; and what are the restrictions on overtime? I may say that I shall be very pleased to join the union if that would not be unwelcome to your members." As it turned out, he was unwelcome. Lane sent him a union card and a certificate of membership, and addressed him as "Brother Churchill," but a Manchester local protested that his recruitment invited "public contempt and ridicule." The executive committee voted that Churchill was ineligible. He kept the certificate, however, and framed it.[170]

Like many another country gentleman, admiring his new estate, Winston decided to "live off the land" — to make Cosy Pig pay. The consequences were uniformly disappointing. Poultry, sheep, cattle, and pigs arrived healthy and then languished. He kept hoping for success; in the summer of 1924 he wrote Clementine: "The 9 elder swine are sold for £31. They have eaten less than £1 a week for 18 weeks of life — so there is a profit of £13. Not bad on so small a capital." But he really knew nothing of livestock, and his wife regarded the creatures with great apprehension. He liked them; he remarked: "The world would be better

Churchill building a wall at Chartwell, 1928

off if it were inhabited only by animals." Yet he resisted modern techniques of scientific farming, and was indignant when a prosperous breeder suggested artificial insemination. Churchill growled: "The beasts will not be deprived — not while I'm alive!" The fact is that he couldn't bear to think of livestock exploited and then slaughtered. To him they were all pets, to be cherished and pampered: the golden orfe, a marmalade cat, Carolina ducks, chickens, sheldrakes, the swans, polo ponies, Canada geese, cygnets, assorted dogs, and bottle-fed lambs. One day Sarah and Mary came to him in tears. Mary's pug, they cried, was desperately ill. Their father, almost as upset as they were, dashed off an incantation to be chanted whenever the dog fell sick:[171]

Oh, what is the matter with poor puggy-wug?
Pet him and kiss him and give him a hug.
Run and fetch him a suitable drug,
Wrap him up tenderly all in a rug,
That is the way to cure Puggy-wug.

Once he had said good morning to it, almost any creature at Chartwell was safe. An exception was a goose; his wife had it cooked for dinner. At the table he picked up the knife, hesitated, and handed it to Clementine. "You carve him, Clemmie," he said. "He was a friend of mine." The only animal to fall from grace was a ram named Charmayne. Winston had nursed Charmayne as a lamb, but when it grew up it turned vicious and butted everyone. A veterinarian was summoned. He performed an operation. If anything, the beast grew worse. The children were afraid of it; Clementine begged Winston to get rid of it. He scoffed at the idea. "How ridiculous. You don't have to be frightened. It is very nice and knows me." However, one day, to the secret delight of the children, Charmayne got behind Churchill, charged, butted the back of his knees, and knocked him flat. Before the sun set, the ram had vanished. How he had disposed of it he would not say, but Clementine hoped it had been sold, and for a good price; she wanted to see something at Chartwell pay for itself.[172]

Clementine was frequently absent from her husband's Cosy Pig in those early years. The children always missed her terribly. "DARLING, DARLING Mummy," Sarah wrote. "Don't forget to come home sometime. Papa is miserable and frightfully naughty without you!" But she had other obligations. Lady Blanche was dying in Dieppe and needed her daughter by her side. Churchill, ever anxious if Clementine was unhappy, wrote her: "Yr mother is a gt woman: & her life has been a noble life. When I think of all the courage & tenacity & self denial that she showed . . . I feel what a true mother & grand woman she proved herself, & I am more glad & proud to think her blood flows in the veins of our children. My darling I grieve for you." Back in London after the funeral, shopping in the Brompton Road, Clementine was hit by a bus, and although she took a taxi home without assistance, her doctor prescribed six weeks of rest in Venice. She wanted Winston to join her, but he declined to leave Kent. "Every day away from Chartwell," he said, "is a day wasted." He told her that "every minute of my day here passes delightfully. There are an enormous amount of things I want to do — and there is of course also the expense to consider." Clementine was well aware of their expenses. It was one of her worries about Chartwell. The payroll alone was staggering: a cook, a farmhand, a groom for the ponies, three gardeners, a nanny, a nursery maid, an "odd-man" (dustbins, boilers, boots), two housemaids, two kitchen maids, two more in the pantry, Clementine's lady's maid, who also did the family sewing, and Winston's two secretaries.[173]

Occasionally Churchill himself became alarmed. He sent his wife one long memorandum on economy covering fourteen points. Trips were to be curtailed, their only winter visits to Chartwell would be "picnics with hampers," all livestock except two polo ponies would be sold, few guests would be invited "other than Jack and Goonie," and "Item 14," headed "BILLS," was a detailed analysis of savings to be made in the consumption of cigars and wines, the number of dress shirts he should wear for dinner each week, and even a reduction in the boot-polish inventory. He also considered renting Chartwell for the following summer for eighty guineas a week, though he wasn't really serious, and quickly backed off when Clementine took him up on it. She suggested they "establish the children in a comfortable but economical hotel near Dinard, go there ourselves for part of the time & travel about painting for you, sight seeing for me, or we could go to Tours & do the 'Chateaux' again — and we could go to Florence & Venice." Churchill had an alternative. He thought he could put them in the black by "going into milk." Dismayed, she sent him a seven-page letter pointing out that all his adventures in husbandry had been disastrous: "You will remember that the chickens and chicken houses got full of red mite and vermin; and you will also remember that one sow was covered with lice."[174]

Invariably he became bored with issues of thrift and airily dismissed them. His wife couldn't. She had to deal with the thickening backlog of unpaid bills and the local tradesmen who called for their money. It was mortifying and, at times, infuriating. Clementine aroused was formidable, and not just within the family. Their guests crossed her at their peril. Afterward Winston, rueful but proud of her, would say, "Clemmie gave poor Smith a most fearful mauling," or "She dropped on him like a jaguar out of a tree!" Yet she was never a match for her own husband. He was too verbal, too skillful in debate, so she usually wrote him, even when they were in the same room. Occasionally, however, she lashed out at him in exasperation; Mary recalls that "on one occasion she became so enraged that she hurled a dish of spinach at Winston's head. She missed, and the dish hit the wall, leaving a telltale mark."[175] But that was unlike her. She usually pursued her objectives quietly, letting servants go and cutting household costs in ways Winston would not notice until it was too late to undo what she had done. In time she left her own imprint on their country home, if only because she couldn't afford an interior decorator. Chartwell today reflects her simple, excellent taste: the clean colors — pale cream, pale blue, cerulean blue — bright moire on her four-poster bed, chintzes with bold floral designs, rush carpets, unstained oak chairs and tables, and other graceful furniture, inherited or picked up at auctions.

Hospitality was a constant source of joy to Churchill. He loved to show Chartwell off. Cyril Connolly wrote: "A man with a will to power can

Churchill building a snowman

have no friends." Winston was an exception. No man yearned for dominion more than Cosy Pig's owner, and few have had more friends. They came to Kent in a constant stream: Lloyd George, Bernard Baruch, the Birkenheads, the Duff Coopers, Eddie Marsh, Bob Boothby, the Archie Sinclairs, Brendan Bracken, the Bonham Carters, cabinet members, publishers, writers — men and women who often shared but one trait: they were gifted, and therefore worthy foils for their host. Brendan Bracken, with his quaint spectacles and carrot-red hair flaming in a tousled mop, was particularly striking. Churchill had been amused when he heard that Bracken was rumored to be his illegitimate son; even more amused when he learned that Bracken wouldn't deny it; and delighted when Bracken took to addressing him as "Father." At Chartwell, Margot Asquith wrote, "every ploy became 'a matter of pith and moment.' " Lord Rawlinson would come to discuss hunting and painting. Beaverbrook arrived with an enormous gift for Churchill's fifty-first birthday, a refrigerator, so Winston could drink champagne without ice. T. E. Lawrence descended the stairs to dinner wearing — to the enchantment of the children — the robes of a prince of Arabia. Professor F. A. Lindemann, "the Prof," looked dull in his bowler hat, but in his way he was more wonderful than Lawrence. In 1916 RAF pilots were dying daily in nose dives. At the Royal Aircraft Establishment in Farnborough, Lindemann had worked out, with mathematical precision, a maneuver which, he said, would bring any aircraft out of a tailspin. The pilots said it wouldn't work. The Prof taught himself to fly, took off without a parachute, deliberately sent the aircraft down in a spin, and brought it out so successfully that mastering his solution became required of every beginning flier. One evening at Chartwell, Winston said: "Prof, tell us in words of one syllable, and in no longer than five minutes, what is the Quantum Theory." He produced his gold watch. Lindemann did it — and at the end the entire family burst into applause. But the children's greatest thrill was provided by Charlie Chaplin. On first meeting Chaplin, Winston had written Clementine: "You cd not help liking him. . . . He is a marvellous comedian — bolshy in politics & delightful in conversation." His evening at Chartwell began badly. He wanted to discuss the gold standard. Churchill lapsed into a moody silence. Suddenly his guest snatched up two rolls of bread, thrust two forks in them, and did the famous dance from his 1925 film *The Gold Rush.* "Immediately the atmosphere relaxed," recalls Boothby, who was there, "and thereafter we spent a happy evening, with both Churchill and Chaplin at the top of their form."[176]

Of these years Churchill would later write: "I never had a dull or idle moment from morning till midnight." Even today one senses the Churchillian presence at Chartwell, in the vast study, by the dining room's round table, in the solid brick walls, the seat by the fishpond where he liked to meditate, and the studio in which his stunning paintings stand row on row, awaiting eventual public display. Perhaps, as Mary says, his painting, writing, and manual labor "were sovereign antidotes to the depressive element in his nature." If so, never was depression so thoroughly routed by activity and wit. One can almost hear the merry rumble of his voice when, introduced to a young man on the eve of his twenty-fifth birthday, Winston said: "Napoleon took Toulon before his twenty-fifth birthday," and, whipping out the gold watch, cried: "Quick, quick! You have just time to take Toulon before you are twenty-five — go and take Toulon!"[177]

In fantasy one envisages long-ago summer afternoons here, with young voices calling scores from the tennis court, the middle-aged basking by the pool, and couples discussing imperial issues over tea and strawberries in the loggia. But if those who knew the Churchills could choose one moment of the year to relive, it would be Christmas. For them, in a nostalgic chamber of the mind, it will always be that magical eve when the entire family has gathered here, including Jack and Goonie and their young, with Randolph home from Eton, the girls rehearsing an amateur theatrical, Clementine helping the servants build a snowman, and Churchill upstairs writing one of his extraordinary love letters to her. ("The most precious thing in my life is yr love for me. I reproach myself for many shortcomings. You are a rock & I depend on you & rest on you.") Presents, hidden all week in an out-of-bounds closet, the "Genii's cupboard," are about to appear. Fires crackle; the house is hung with holly, ivy, laurel, and yew; the Christ child gazes down lovingly from a large Della Robbia plaque. Now the double doors between the library and the drawing room are flung open and the Christmas tree is revealed in all its splendor, a hundred white wax candles gleaming, the scent of pine and wax like a breath of rapture, and Churchill, the benign sovereign in this absolutely English castle, leads the way across the threshold toward his annual festival of joy "with my happy family around me," as he would later write, "at peace within my habitation."[178]

The prickly marriage of convenience between Asquith's Liberals and Ramsay MacDonald's Labour government lasted less than a year. In the suit for divorce, bolshevism was named as correspondent. MacDonald

COPYRIGHT BY PHILIPPE HALSMAN

Churchill in the garden at Chartwell

had recognized Lenin's regime, lent it money, and dropped charges against a Communist editor who had incited mutiny among British troops. Asquith thereupon withdrew his support, and Labour lost a vote of confidence, 364 to 198. The campaign which followed became known as the "Red Letter Election" because a few days before the polling the Foreign Office published a letter allegedly written by Grigori Zinoviev, president of the Third International, calling on British socialists to organize an armed rebellion. Labour bitterly renounced it as a fake. Churchill shed crocodile tears. Many Labour MPs, he said, were politicians "of high reputation" who "stood by their country in the war" but whose position now was "pathetic. They have been unable to keep their feet upon the slippery slopes on which they have tried to stand." Down they slid, the way greased by the Red Letter; in October 1924 the Conservatives won 419 seats, Labour 151, and the fading Liberals a mere 40.[179]

Among the triumphant candidates was Churchill, who became the member for Epping, a seat he was to hold for the rest of his public life, although in 1945 the constituency boundary was changed and it became the Woodford constituency. He was once more a supporter of Tory policies. In May, accompanied by Clementine, he had entrained to Liverpool and, for the first time in twenty years, addressed a Conservative party rally. Afterward he introduced his wife to their hosts. She was somewhat subdued, and he said: "She's a Liberal, and always has been. It's all very strange for her. But to me, of course, it's just like coming home." Presently the party's chief parliamentary whip sent him congratulations "upon your brilliant speech." He had spoken to a public meeting in Epping, coming down hard on MacDonald's friendly overtures to Russia, "unquestionably one of the worst and meanest tyrannies in the history of the world." Nominally he was a "Constitutionalist," but the local Conservatives had adopted him as their nominee, and he won by nearly ten thousand, polling almost 60 percent of the votes cast, whereupon he accepted the Tory label. The *Sunday Times* reported that in Trafalgar Square "the great cheer of the day was reserved for Mr Winston Churchill's victory at Epping." T. E. Lawrence wrote him, "This isn't congratulations, it's just the hiss of excess delight rushing out," and Ivor Guest, now Lord Wimborne, wrote: "I hope to goodness the Tories have the good sense to offer you high office. It will be reassuring to think of a progressive mind among their counsels, as a majority such as theirs is hardly conducive to a programme of social reforms." But Churchill doubted there would be a ministry for him: "I think it very likely that I shall not be invited to join the Government, as owing to the size of its majority it will probably be composed only of impeccable conservatives."[180]

He was wrong. Baldwin, a shrewder politician than Churchill, very much wanted him in the cabinet. Despite the size of his party's majority, he was afraid that Churchill and Lloyd George might form a center party and persuade Birkenhead to back them in the Lords, thus pitting the prime minister against Parliament's three most eloquent speakers. Therefore he decided to separate Winston and George. Opportunity unexpectedly presented itself when Austen Chamberlain's half brother Neville, who had only recently entered politics at the age of forty-nine but shared old Joe's political legacy, declined the chancellorship of the Exchequer. Tory indifference to tariff reform had soured him; he preferred the Ministry of Health. Actually, it was Neville who suggested that Winston run the Treasury. Baldwin replied that the party would "howl." Neville said that the howl would be louder if Churchill were returned to the Admiralty. Upon reflection the prime minister agreed; summoning the Epping turncoat he asked him if he would serve as "Chancellor." Winston asked: "Of the Duchy?" "No," said Baldwin, "of the Exchequer." Churchill later wrote that he had been tempted to ask: "Will the bloody duck swim?" Instead, he replied: "This fulfills my ambition. I still have my father's robes as Chancellor. I shall be proud to serve you in this splendid office." He also pledged his loyalty to Baldwin and said: "You have done more for me than Lloyd George ever did."[181]

When Winston told Clementine, he wrote afterward, he had "the greatest difficulty in convincing my wife that I was not merely teasing her." Convinced, she made him vow he would keep it from the press, letting the announcement come from No. 10. That was asking too much, however — it was like his pledge to keep their engagement a secret. That evening Winston dined at Beaverbrook's home with Freddie Guest and Birkenhead, who had been appointed secretary of state for India. They all asked Churchill: "Are you in?" He said he was, but when pressed to name the ministry, he said: "I am sorry, but I would prefer not to disclose that just now." He was obviously bursting to tell them, and they were indignant that he wouldn't, but he didn't want Beaverbrook to turn it into headlines. Finally he cried: "I am Chancellor of the Exchequer!" The phone rang; another source confirmed him; Beaverbrook decided to break the story. Birkenhead thought Winston had behaved badly by not sharing the tidings at once. According to Beaverbrook: "Suddenly a kind of flash of intuition came to me and I made a wild but shrewd guess. 'I don't believe Churchill is really to blame. He promised somebody he wouldn't tell me before he came — yes — he promised his wife.' Churchill said, 'You are right. She drove me to the door of your house.' "[182]

The howl Baldwin had predicted followed. The *Morning Post* sourly observed that "the idea of scrapping the Conservative Party in order to make a home for lost Liberals and returning prodigals does not appear to us to promise success." *The Times* agreed. At the Admiralty Sir William Bridgeman, the new first lord, wrote his wife: "I am afraid that turbulent pushing busybody Winston is going to split the party. I can't understand how anybody can want him or put any faith in a man who changes sides, just when he thinks it is to his own personal advantage to do so." Austen Chamberlain, unaware of Neville's role, wrote his wife: "Beloved: S.B. is mad! . . . I feel that this particular appointment will be a great shock to the party." Sir John Simon told an amused audience: "There is a new piece of jazz music now being played which has been called 'the Winston Constitution.' You take a step forward, two steps backward, a side step to the right, and then reverse. You can see that the piece is well named." His faithful old Liberal ally, the *Guardian,* commented mournfully: "Mr Churchill for the second time has — shall we say? — quitted the sinking ship and for the second time the reward of this fine instinct has been not safety only but high promotion."[183]

The Exchequer was the highest gift a prime minister could bestow.

Keeping the Sussex Square house was no longer an issue; it was sold, and the family moved into No. 11 Downing Street, sharing the garden behind it with the Baldwins at No. 10. Gladstone's famous red dispatch case was entrusted to Winston. Lord Randolph's Exchequer robes, put away in tissue paper and camphor by Winston's mother on Christmas Day, 1886, were aired and donned by him for his first official function, the "Pricking [selection] of the Sheriffs" on November 13, 1924. Afterward he lunched with Reginald McKenna, who wrote Beaverbrook: "He tells me he means to master the intricacies of finance and I think he will succeed, though he will find it more difficult than he imagines." Actually, he appears to have had no concept of the challenge. Lord Boothby recalls that Churchill "soon discovered that the Treasury was not congenial to him, and that he was basically uninterested in the problems of high finance." After a meeting with Treasury officials, economists, and bankers, Winston told Boothby: "I wish they were admirals or generals. I speak their language, and can beat them. But after a while these fellows start talking Persian. And then I am sunk." As an MP, Boothby became Winston's parliamentary private secretary. After it had become clear that Churchill was having difficulties in his new office, Boothby asked P. J. Grigg, a senior civil servant at the Exchequer, why that should be. Grigg replied: "There is only one man who has ever made the Treasury do what it didn't want to do. That was Lloyd George. There will never be another."[184]

Certainly Winston wasn't one. Late in life he remarked: "Everyone said I was the worst Chancellor of the Exchequer that ever was, and now I am inclined to agree with them." But that was going too far. To be sure, he had no economic convictions apart from his blind faith in Free Trade, and it was disconcerting to hear the seigneur of British finance say loftily: "The higher mind has no need to concern itself with the meticulous regimentation of figures." He was far from being the worst chancellor, however, or even one of the worst; unlike his father, he knew what "those damned dots" meant, and he had a vision, a revival of the social strategy he and Lloyd George had conceived in the first decade of the century. Welfare legislation was very much on his mind. He envied Neville Chamberlain at the Ministry of Health, telling him: "You are in the van. You can raise a monument. You can leave a name in history." Drafting his first budget at Chartwell, he wrote Clementine: "I have been working all day (Sunday) at pensions & am vy tired." In a Treasury minute two days later he wrote: "It is when misfortune comes upon the household, when prolonged unemployment, or old age, or sickness, or the death of the breadwinner comes upon this household, that you see how narrow was the margin on which it was apparently living so prosperously, and in a few months the result of the thrift of years may be swept away, and the house broken up." Addressing a skeptical audience — the British Bankers' Association — he said that economic aid for "every class and every section . . . is our aim: the appeasement of class bitterness, the promotion of a spirit of cooperation, the stabilisation of our national life, the building of the financial and social plans upon a three or four years' basis instead of a few months' basis, an earnest effort to give the country some period of recuperation after the vicissitudes to which it has been subjected."*[185]

It was Churchill's misfortune, and Britain's, that he came to the Treasury with the right ideas at the wrong time. The country's economists were torn between, on the one hand, those who regarded the classical law of supply and demand as an article of absolute faith and, on the other hand, the followers, still few in numbers, of John Maynard Keynes's concept of a managed economy. A heavy parliamentary majority believed that the budget must be balanced, whatever the cost. Given the plight of the Treasury in the mid-1920s, this was wildly unrealistic. England's great prewar assets were gone, spent, like the blood of its youth, in the trenches and no-man's-land across the Channel. After the brief boom in the years immediately following the Armistice, management's prewar troubles with organized labor returned, redoubled by a huge hard core of jobless men, refugees from giant industries — coal, cotton, shipbuilding, and steel and iron — which had once thrived on exports and could no longer find markets abroad. The miners' union, exasperated with the coalfields' shortsighted, reactionary, incompetent proprietors, turned to the government. An official inquiry recommended nationalization of the mines, but nothing was done. In 1921 a mine lockout was followed by competition from the revived German coal industry, which led to wage cuts in the British coalfields. Unrest was growing there.

Another of Winston's unwelcome legacies was the servicing of England's war debt to America. Great Britain owed the United States the preposterous sum of $4,933,701,642. Interest on this exceeded £35,000,000 a year. Again and again Churchill explained to England's former ally, now its creditor, that Britain couldn't repay the principal until France had paid Britain *its* war debt. Sometimes he thought he was succeeding. On January 10, 1925, he wrote Clementine: "I have had tremendous battles with the Yanks, & have beaten them down inch by inch

* Ironically, Churchill may have been the first public figure to use *appeasement* in a modern political context. As a foreign policy proposal it first appeared on May 9, 1934, in a letter to *The Times* from Lord Lothian, who suggested "a limitation of armaments by political appeasement."

to a reasonable figure. In the end we are fighting over tripe like £100,000!" But agreement after agreement collapsed, President Coolidge saying inanely: "They hired the money, didn't they?" A Chartwell guest noted in his diary: "Winston talked very freely about the U.S.A. He thinks they are arrogant, fundamentally hostile to us, and that they want to dominate world politics."[186]

In the House of Commons annual calendar, Budget Day belongs to the chancellor of the Exchequer. Churchill's first such occasion was April 28, 1925. A large crowd awaited him outside No. 11 as he emerged smiling, the dispatch case in his hand. "Let me take the box, sir," said Detective Thompson, and Winston recoiled in horror, saying: "No, no! There's but one person to guard this box and it's me!" The spectators tagged along as he proceeded down Parliament Street and into the crowded House, where Clementine, Diana, and Randolph were seated in the Strangers' Gallery. His two-and-a-half-hour speech was lucid and witty; at one point he produced a pint of whiskey, poured some in a glass, and said: "It is imperative that I should fortify the revenue and I shall now, with the permission of the Commons, proceed to do so." Everyone cheered as he sipped except Lady Astor, who had urged Britain to follow America's example and adopt Prohibition. Bowing to her, he noted that she was "noble" but added: "I do not think we are likely to learn much from the liquor legislation of the United States."[187]

Like all budgets, this one required careful scrutiny, and those who studied it line by line realized that in many ways it was an abrupt departure from the traditional Tory approach to ways and means. Churchill believed that the key to fiscal health was productivity, that the leisure class was "but the glittering scum on the deep river of production." He wanted to lower taxes on the poor and raise them on unearned income: "The process of the creation of new wealth is beneficial to the whole community. The process of squatting on old wealth though valuable is a far less lively agent." At the same time, the Treasury must assume responsibility for the victims of industrial distress. His proposals included a reduction in the pensionable age from seventy to sixty-five, immediate payment of benefits to over 200,000 widows and 350,000 orphans, and abolition of what he called "restrictions, inquisitions and means tests" for welfare applicants — "it would be nobody's business what they had or how they employed their time." He believed that "by giving a far greater measure of security to the mass of wage-earners, their wives and children, it may promote contentment and stability, and make our Island more truly a home for all these people." Funds would be set aside to provide health insurance for thirty million Britons; it was here, he argued, that "the State, with its long and stable finance, can march in and fill the immense gap." A special sense of urgency, he felt, should spur the government's obligation to help those rendered helpless by circumstances over which they had had no control, adding passionately: "It is the stragglers, the exhausted, the weak, the wounded, the veterans, the widows and orphans to whom the ambulances of State aid should be directed."[188]

Winston had stolen Neville Chamberlain's thunder, and Chamberlain resented it. The chancellor's mandate did not include the needy. But rustling was an old Churchillian habit, and few Tories would object if he could find the funds and balance the budget without raising taxes. He could and did. He had searched the files and minds of the Treasury's senior civil servants, and had reached two momentous decisions. The first was a return to the gold standard, of which more presently; the second, a £10,000,000 cut in the service estimates, with the Admiralty as the heavy loser. Only the RAF had emerged unshorn. His reasons were various. One, perhaps, was a tribute to his father's failed crusade. But others were stronger. If he were to win pensions, health insurance, and help for the helpless, he had to wield his scalpel somewhere, and the public mood would support drastic reductions in expensive armaments. Clementine spoke for millions of Britons when she wrote urging him to "stand up to the Admiralty. . . . don't be fascinated or flattered or cajoled by Beatty." Now that the kaiser's fleet lay on the bottom of the Firth of Forth, Winston reasoned, Britain was secure at sea. The only foreign fleets of any size were those of the United States, which was hardly likely to declare war on England, even over debts, and Japan, whose military establishment, despite its successes against the Bolsheviks, was considered laughable. Churchill assumed that the Germans would keep their word and refrain from building another fleet to challenge British sea power, though later he described this supposition as "the acme of gullibility."[189]

The Royal Navy felt betrayed. Here was a former first lord, whose memory was still cherished in wardrooms, "committed," as Admiral Sir William James puts it, "to fight the Admiralty inch by inch for every penny of their estimates." His chief adversary, the first sea lord, was David Beatty, a Churchill friend since Omdurman. Winston argued that battleships had been obsolescent for some time and were now obsolete. They had been torpedoed at the Yalu River in 1894, at Port Arthur in 1904, and, repeatedly, in the Great War; the American air power evangelist Billy Mitchell had just proved that they could be sunk by Martin MB-2 twin-engined bombers. At the height of the controversy Beatty wrote his wife: "Yesterday I was vigorously engaged with Winston and I think on the whole got the better of him. I must say, although I had to say some pretty strong things, he never bears any malice and was good-humoured through the engagement." Later he joined those who thought Winston had lost his sense of proportion, writing her heatedly: "That extraordinary fellow Winston has gone mad. Economically mad, and no sacrifice is too great to achieve what in his shortsightedness is the panacea for all evils — to take 1 S off the Income Tax. Nobody outside a lunatic asylum expects a shilling off the Income Tax this Budget. . . . As we at the Admiralty are the principal Spending Department, he attacks us with virulence." And again: "I have to tackle Winston and had 2½ hours with him this evening. It takes a good deal out of me when dealing with a man of his calibre with a very quick brain. A false step, remark, or even gesture is immediately fastened upon, so I have to keep my wits about me. We of course arrived at nothing. . . . We are working up a case for the Prime Minister to adjudicate on the differences which exist between us."[190]

Baldwin, with his great skill at compromise, restored some of the Admiralty estimates, but Churchill won in the long run; during each of his five years as chancellor, every service except the RAF saw its appropriations dwindle. Even so, the public temper was such that he was frequently attacked as a military spendthrift; the *Economist* faulted him on the ground that 3 percent of the national income was being allocated to defense, compared with 2 percent in the later years of Victoria's reign. Perhaps any other chancellor would have done the same. But one expects more from Churchill, and the saddest page in this record is his repeated insistence that the ten-year rule adopted in August 1919 be extended from year to year.* He convinced the Committee of Imperial Defence that it was sound policy, though there was one demurrer. The minutes of the committee's two hundred thirty-sixth meeting record that: "LORD BALFOUR was of the opinion that nobody could say that from any one moment war was an impossibility for the next ten years and that we could not rest in a state of unpreparedness on such an assumption by anybody. To suggest that we could be 9½ years away from preparedness would be a most dangerous suggestion."[191]

Churchill was to oppose rearmament as late as 1929, when B. H. Liddell Hart wrote in the *Daily Telegraph* that "every important foreign Power has made startling, indeed ominous, increases of expenditure on its army. . . . Our Government, which has to keep watch for storm signals, would be false to its duty to this nation if it reduced our slender military strength more drastically until other nations imitate the lead which

* It remained in effect until 1932, "by which time," Telford Taylor dryly observes, "it was a very bad forecast indeed" (in *Munich: The Price of Peace* [New Yoık, 1979], page 201).

we have so repeatedly given." In one instance Churchill was false to himself. He had inveighed against MacDonald for suggesting that the naval base at Singapore be abandoned. Now he argued that Singapore, like Iraq, could be defended by the RAF. He objected to "measuring our naval strength" against a "fancied" threat from Dai Nippon, commenting that the Admiralty was "unduly stressing the Japanese danger." Indeed, he had been in No. 11 less than a month when he asked the Foreign Office to declare that war with Nippon would be impossible for the next twenty years. Austen Chamberlain hesitated, but the decision was made. Early in 1924 the Admiralty recommended the establishment of a submarine base at Hong Kong and the installation "as fast as possible" of new naval guns at Singapore. "For what?" asked Winston, who only a few months earlier had been Singapore's staunchest champion. "A war with Japan! But why should there be a war with Japan? I do not believe there is the slightest chance of it in our lifetime." He was convinced that "war with Japan is not a possibility any reasonable government need take into account." Beatty thought otherwise. Later, with an eye on history, Winston claimed that he had been at a disadvantage because Beatty had not told him of secret telegrams bearing evidence of Japan's aggressive designs. Still, one feels that this was not Churchill's finest hour.[192]

The most sensational moment in Churchill's first budget was his dramatic disclosure that Britain, which had left the gold standard during the war, was back on it. *The Times* reported that this announcement was greeted with "tremendous cheers." After the applause had died down he said: "No responsible authority has advocated any other policy. It has always been a matter of course that we should return to it." This was simply untrue. Beaverbrook had been against it; on the evening of Budget Day he wrote Bracken: "My opinion of Winston has not altered. I knew from the beginning that he would give in to the bankers on the Gold Standard, which, I think, is the biggest sin in this budget." Half a century later Boothby, looking back on a long public life, said of the return to gold that "with the exception of the unilateral guarantee to Poland without Russian support, this was the most fatal step taken by the country."[193]

Beaverbrook and Boothby were among the few Jeremiahs on the issue then; others, and they were almost the only others, were Winston's old colleague Reginald McKenna, a former chancellor; John Maynard

Keynes; and Vincent Vickers, who protested the move by resigning from the board of the Bank of England. Churchill has been blamed for it, and rightly so, because as chancellor he made the decision. The step was not taken lightly, however, or without learned advice. Responsibility was collective and bipartisan. In 1918 the step had been recommended by a standing committee of experts appointed by Lloyd George; a majority of Conservatives, Liberals, and Labourites had then endorsed it. Churchill regarded that endorsement as binding. According to Grigg, the new chancellor invited gold's advocates and adversaries to dinner. Sir Otto Niemeyer of the Bank of England stated the case for gold; McKenna and Keynes argued against it. Winston thought some of the points made by McKenna and Keynes were valid. "But," he added, staying off gold "isn't entirely an economic matter; it [would be] a political decision, for it involves proclaiming that we cannot, for the time being at any rate, complete the undertaking which we all acclaimed was necessary in 1918, and introducing legislation accordingly."[194]

The roster of men who supported it on economic grounds alone was formidable; they included Austen Chamberlain, another ex-chancellor; Montague Norman, the governor of the Bank of England; and Labour's Philip Snowden, Churchill's immediate predecessor at No. 11, who had intended to put Britain back on gold himself had he remained chancellor. After yielding his seals of office Snowden had eloquently set forth the case for gold in the *Observer*. One Labour MP, Hugh Dalton, a Keynes disciple, challenged Winston's decision: "We on these benches will hold the Chancellor of the Exchequer strictly to account, and strictly responsible, if, as we fear, there should be a further aggravation of unemployment and of the present trade depression as a result of his action, and should it work out that men who are employed lose their jobs as a result of this deflation. Should that be so we will explain who is to blame." But Dalton was almost alone in his own party. Labour's leaders didn't even put the issue to a vote. Indeed, years passed before they grasped what had happened. In 1946 Ernest Bevin told the House that Churchill had acted impulsively and "like a bolt from the blue we were suddenly met with the complete upset of the wage structure in this country." Bevin neglected to mention that in 1929, four years after Winston had brought England back to the prewar parity of gold, Ramsay MacDonald became Labour's prime minister for the second time while vowing to "save the pound" — to keep the British economy belted in its twenty-four-karat straitjacket.[195]

Why did they do it, and what did it mean? British financiers, in the Treasury and in the City, were convinced that England's future prosperity could be assured only if London were reestablished as the financial center of the globe. This, they held, would be impossible until "the pound can look the dollar in the face." Churchill told the House: "We have entered a period on both sides of the Atlantic when political and economic stability seems to be more assured than it has for some years. If this opportunity were missed, it might not recur soon, and the whole finance of the country would be clouded over for an indefinite period by the fact of uncertainty. 'Now is the appointed time.' " Niemeyer asked doubters: "How are we, a great exporting and importing country, to live with an exchange fluctuating with gold, when the United States of America, Germany, Austria, Sweden, Holland, Switzerland, the Dominions . . . and Japan have a stable gold exchange?"[196] To bankers, reestablishing the credit of the pound was worth any risk. In reality, any precious metal or even a flourishing economy can serve as well as gold, and many do today. The Niemeyers, Normans, and Snowdens were living in the past, when Britannia ruled the waves and the pound was regarded with respect and awe in all the world's money markets. They assumed that the restoration of the pound's parity with the American dollar would reestablish Britain's prewar prosperity. None seemed to realize that England had squandered its wealth between Sarajevo and Versailles, or that the country's shrunken export trade could no longer provide the surplus needed to reestablish London's fiscal ascendancy over the rest of the world.

Keynes now emerged. In the *Nation,* the *Evening Standard,* and finally in a pamphlet, "The Economic Consequences of Mr Churchill," he went for Winston's jugular, declaring that the chancellor had acted "partly, perhaps, because he has no instinctive judgment to prevent him from making mistakes; partly, because, lacking this instinctive judgment, he was defeated by the clamorous voice of conventional finance; and most of all, because he was gravely misled by the experts." The return to gold, Keynes said, "shackled" and "enslaved" the country. "The whole object is to link *rigidly* the City and Wall Street," and this alarmed him because America, with its rapidly expanding economy, "lives in a vast and unceasing crescendo. Wide fluctuations, which spell unemployment and misery for us, are swamped for them in the general upward movement." The United States could afford "temporary maladjustments" because its productivity was growing "by several per cent per annum." Once, when Victoria reigned, that had been true of Britain. "This, however, is not our state now. Our rate of progress is slow at best," and flaws which could have been dismissed in the nineteenth century "are now fatal. The slump of 1921 was even more violent in the United States than here, but by the end of 1922 recovery was practically complete. We still, in 1925, drag on with a million unemployed."[197]

The effect of going back to gold, said Beaverbrook, was "making yet more difficult the selling of British goods abroad and so aggravating unemployment at home." Events soon proved Keynes and Beaverbrook right. English goods which had been priced at eighteen shillings in foreign markets now cost twenty — a full pound. This handicapped all British exporters; some became hopelessly crippled. The owners of British collieries could not compete with German and American coal if they charged higher rates. Their only alternative was to cut their miners' wages. That was ominous. Coal mining, Britain's basic industry, was also the most highly organized and politicized; Keir Hardie, the founder of the Labour party, had been a Scottish miner. The miners' union protested the drop in pay. The Trade Union Congress, or TUC, the English equivalent of America's AFL–CIO, promised to back the miners all the way, and Labour MPs declared their solidarity with them. In July 1925, two days before the cuts were to go into effect, Baldwin temporized. The Treasury, he said, would subsidize the mine owners while a commission headed by Sir Herbert Samuel investigated the situation. The prime minister bought nine months of labor peace, but the cost — first estimated at £10,000,000 but ultimately £23,000,000 — was exorbitant. Churchill had agreed to the stopgap, but he protested, with the rest of the cabinet, when the prime minister proposed to extend it. Keynes was in the thick of things. He asked: "Why should coal miners suffer a lower standard of life than other classes of labour? They may be lazy, good-for-nothing fellows who do not work so hard or so long as they ought to. But is there any evidence that they are more lazy or more good-for-nothing than other people?" They were, he said, "victims of the economic juggernaut," pawns being sacrificed to bridge the gap, required by the return to gold, between $4.40 and $4.86. "The plight of coal miners," he concluded, "is the first — but not, unless we are very lucky, the last — of the Economic Consequences of Mr Churchill."[198]

Winston retorted angrily: "I have never heard of any argument more strange and so ill-founded, as that the Gold Standard is responsible for the condition of affairs in the coal industry. The Gold Standard is no more responsible than is the Gulf Stream."[199] But evidence to the contrary was accumulating; week by week the tension in the mines grew. On March 1, 1926, the Samuel Report was released. It was a thoughtful, practical document, the result of profound research, and its conclusions were an indictment of the coal owners. Over the years, Samuel and his colleagues found, the proprietors had reaped enormous profits while bleeding the industry, refusing to replace obsolete equipment. As a consequence, theirs had become a losing business. Unless the government continued its subsidy, or nationalized the collieries, the miners would have to accept lower wages now. Later, after modern equipment had been installed, their pay would rise. No one could tell when that would be. The report gave the owners and the union six weeks to reach an agreement.

At this point the prime minister should have taken a strong stand. That is what leaders are for. The owners, with their accumulated wealth, could have been pressed to a settlement. But Baldwin had recently compromised himself, declaring publicly: "All the workers of this country have got to take reductions in wages in order to help put industry on its feet." So he temporized again. The commission's findings, he said, were disappointing, but if both parties could live with them, the government would not object. This encouraged extremists on each side; they shredded the report with technical arguments and then rejected it outright. Up to this point, Churchill's sympathies had been with the miners. Labour didn't appreciate that; when the coal subsidy forced him to cut health and unemployment insurance appropriations, there were cries of "Robber!" from the Opposition benches, to which he replied that for one who had frequently been called a "murderer," this was "a sort of promotion." Unknown to them, he had sent young Harold Macmillan to Newcastle, asking him to report on the situation there, and on April 10 Macmillan — who felt it "a great honour to be taken into your confidence" — wrote describing "the appalling conditions in this area." He thought that "the patience and the endurance of the workers as a whole is really remarkable. Certainly adversity brings out greater virtues than prosperity in all classes, but peculiarly so among the working people." Churchill was optimistic; he felt certain that a way to reward these virtues would be found. After all, those on both sides were Englishmen. Speaking to the Belfast Chamber of Commerce he said that he did not share the opinion, so widespread abroad, particularly in the United States, "that Britain is down and out, that the foundations of our commerce and industrial greatness have been sapped; that the stamina of our people is impaired; that the workmen are lazy; that our employers are indolent; that our Empire is falling to pieces. I have never been able to take that view." He assured his audience that the justifiable grievances of "our much-abused coal miners" would be peacefully resolved.[200]

They weren't. Strife was now inevitable, and before it ended the conflict would cost over £800,000,000. The crisis began on May Day, 1926. That Saturday morning miners who had assembled for the day's first seven-hour shift were notified that their future pay envelopes would be thinner. They protested and the owners locked them out. At noon the TUC General Council, meeting in London, unanimously agreed that unless wage levels were restored at once, a nationwide general strike would begin Monday at one minute before midnight. The general strike is labor's ultimate weapon. If prolonged, it can destroy society. English legal scholars then and since have agreed that to call one, or even threaten one, is a violation of the British constitution. The prospect made the entire country tremble. Yet grave as the situation was, the TUC decision was followed by forty-eight hours of chaos more appropriate in a Marx Brothers film than in the British establishment. The General Council, after alerting affiliates to its decision, sent the prime minister a letter, formally setting the deadline and offering to negotiate. Baldwin asked for two weeks' grace, "confident that a settlement can be reached on the basis of the Samuel Report." Since that implied a temporary acceptance of the wage cut, and since the miners had developed the slogan "Not a penny off the pay, not a minute on the day," the TUC replied that its membership must be consulted. It was then discovered that the miners had left London and gone home. Telegrams were dispatched recalling them, but it was late Sunday before a TUC delegation was ready to approach the government. That evening the union men called at No. 10. Nobody was home. The cabinet was meeting next door in Churchill's house. After a long, confused delay, while the delegates waited on the pavement, Baldwin emerged with Birkenhead and said: "Gentlemen, I am sorry to say that our efforts for peace are unavailing. Something has happened at the *Daily Mail* and the Cabinet has empowered me to hand you this letter." They shook hands and he said: "Goodbye; this is the end." Gathering under a Downing Street lamp, they opened the envelope and learned that compositors at Lord Rothermere's *Daily Mail*, members of the National Society of Operative Printers and Assistants, had refused to set type for a vehemently antilabor editorial titled "For King and Country." Printers at the *Express* and other papers had indicated that they were prepared to do the same.[201]

It has become part of Labour myth that Churchill exploited this incident to force a showdown with the unions. Ernest Bevin repeated the accusation again and again; the cabinet was within "five minutes" of reaching terms for a settlement, he said, when Winston learned what was happening at the *Daily Mail*, "dashed up to Downing Street, ordered a meeting of the Cabinet, rushed Baldwin off his feet . . . and in a few minutes the ultimatum was given to us." Stories that Churchill was hostile toward organized labor had, of course, been in circulation since Tonypandy in 1909. The misunderstanding had grown, in part, because of his diatribes on socialism, which, under Labour's banner, had become the political voice of the working class. But he himself drew a distinction. "When all is said and done," he wrote, "there are very few well-informed persons in Great Britain, and not many employers of labour on a large scale, who would not sooner have to deal with the British trade unions as we know them, than with the wide vagaries of communist-agitated and totally disorganized discontent." As he had written James Lane of the bricklayers: "I take a high view of the dignity both of craftsmanship and manual labour." Bevin's account is absurd anyhow. Since the cabinet had gathered in Churchill's Downing Street home, he would hardly have "dashed up Downing Street" to reach it. The conference had already begun when Baldwin and his ministers learned of the *Mail* wildcatters. And the news came, not from Winston, but by telephone.[202]

After the *Mail* bombshell, Churchill was among the most vehement ministers — the others were Amery, Neville Chamberlain, and "Jix" Joynson-Hicks, the home secretary — in vowing not to capitulate. But there were no dissenters. The vote to break off talks was unanimous. Baldwin later told the House that the cabinet interpreted the phone call as a sign that "the first overt move in the General Strike was being actually made, by trying to suppress the press. We felt that in those circumstances the whole situation was changed." One wonders why. It would have been easy to learn the truth by placing a few more calls. The fact was that the printers' action had been impulsive and in no way reflected a larger strategy. The TUC leaders had been unaware of it and disowned it the moment they read Baldwin's letter. The attempt to intimidate a free press outraged as many Labour MPs as Tories; more, perhaps, because some Tory back-benchers had been praying for a casus belli. Nevertheless, at 1:00 A.M. Monday reporters in Downing Street were given a brief announcement that negotiations had been discontinued. A few hours later a TUC delegation arrived at No. 10, bearing a written repudiation of the *Mail* printers. Ramsay MacDonald told the House "they found the door locked and the whole place in darkness."[203] That was inexcusable, but so was the TUC's action Saturday in raising the specter of a general strike — for which the unions were completely unprepared — and the cloudy understanding between the miners and the TUC. The miners had authorized the unions' national leadership to negotiate for them, but not to bargain. Thus, though sporadic attempts to resume talks continued through Monday, the TUC's inability to compromise without the miners' sanction hardened the cabinet's position. And as the evening wore on Churchill, facing the imminent rupture of

British order, grew increasingly defiant. He would be the most visible leader on one side; Bevin, on the other.

Bevin at that time was general secretary of the Transport and General Workers' Union, a merger of twenty-two unions, and at 11:59 P.M., as commander in chief of the general strike, he pushed the button. Six million Britons were thereby committed to walking off the job. Iron and steel foundries closed down. Bus drivers abandoned their buses. Newspapers ceased publication. No trains moved, no trucks; the tubes were silent. Building-trade workers, dockworkers, workers in the chemical industry, stayed home. Gas, sanitary, health, and food services deemed "essential" were supposed to be spared, but many gas and electricity works came to a standstill. The government was not unprepared, however. In 1920 Churchill had devised a plan against just such a contingency. The country was divided into nine areas, each with a central controller and staff. Troops would be dispatched to convoy vehicles carrying food and fuel. The police were fully mobilized; Hyde Park became a military post; the Welsh Guards were billeted on the Victoria Embankment. Joynson-Hicks appealed for volunteers, and thousands of Englishmen and Englishwomen of the upper and middle classes drove trucks, trams, taxis, and even locomotives. Some members of the House of Lords served as railway porters. It was a peculiarly British emergency; there was little or no violence, and in many places volunteers, strikers, and policemen mingled with civility and even gaiety. Churchill, however, was not among the skylarkers. He felt grim. The miners' strike had been legitimate, even admirable, he said, "but that is an entirely different thing from the concerted, deliberate organized menace of a General Strike in order to compel Parliament to do something which otherwise it would not do." He wanted to intimidate the strikers with a show of force; at his suggestion, territorials were encouraged to enlist as civil constabulary reserves, and only after a long argument did his colleagues persuade him that the recruits should wear, not military uniforms, but mufti with armbands, and their weapons be limited to truncheons. Some ministers worried about costs. Churchill rumbled: "The Exchequer will pay! If we start arguing about petty details, we'll have a tired-out police force, a dissipated army and bloody revolution." He was embattled, and wondered why the country didn't share his mood. He said: "One of the great difficulties of the situation is that large numbers of working people feel quite detached from the conflict; and they are waiting, as if they were spectators at a football match, to see whether the Government or the Trade Union is the stronger." His provocative comments, friends warned him, were deepening labor's resentment of him. He replied that he rejoiced in their hostility: "People who are not prepared to do unpopular things and to defy clamour are not fit to be Ministers in times of stress."[204]

That would have ruled out the prime minister. "Baldwin," in the words of one British historian, now "adopted a policy of masterly inactivity." Churchill's delight in battle puzzled him; essentially gentle, he himself shrank from discord almost as a matter of principle. Yet he snorted when told that Beaverbrook had remarked: "Churchill is the real power in the Government." He knew this to be quite untrue. Beyond casting his vote, Winston had played no role in the severance of negotiations after the *Mail* episode. Later, Baldwin had excluded him from the select cabinet council which met daily to discuss supervising strikebreaking tactics. But Winston kept trying to intervene, and his combative stance loomed ever larger in the public view. Baldwin didn't want to offend him — Churchill was now next in line for the prime ministership, and his militancy was winning grudging converts among some Tory diehards — but he did want him out of his hair. Then a solution presented itself. H. A. Gwynne of the *Morning Post* approached John Davidson, a senior civil servant. If his premises were protected, he said, he would put his presses at the disposal of the government. The Tories could have their own newspaper. In a week, he predicted, he could build a circulation as high as 400,000 copies. Sir Samuel Hoare, told of the offer, proposed publishing a government paper to be called the *British Gazette*. The prime minister agreed but did not want Gwynne as its director. Instead, he appointed Churchill editor in chief. It was, Baldwin later said, "the cleverest thing I ever did."[205]

He may have been right. In his long career Baldwin did few clever things, and this decision prevented the chancellor from playing a major role in determining the outcome of the strike. Winston himself savored a delicious irony. For twenty years Gwynne had been his most savage press critic, and now the *Morning Post*'s perennial target would be running the *Post*'s shop. He announced that the paper would be written, edited, and published by volunteers. Printers were a problem. On instructions from their union, Gwynne's compositors stayed out. Beaverbrook said he could send a printer's foreman at once. Given time, he could find other willing hands among his idle *Daily Express* employees, and the *Daily Mail* thought some of their men might pitch in. Winston wouldn't wait. Beric Holt, who had agreed to serve as one of the *Gazette*'s editorial assistants, recalls joining a small procession of men who, in the early hours of Tuesday, May 4, "filed up the narrow back stairs of the *Morning Post* building just off the Strand." In the composing room Sydney Long, night superintendent of the *Daily Express,* was already sitting at a Linotype machine, setting copy. Irish Guards and bobbies restrained an angry crowd of strikers on the street below. Churchill, in shirt sleeves, was peering down at large enamel mugs on the floor. He asked their purpose. Holt, who had been there before, replied: "Beer, sir." "Have they got enough?" asked Winston. A man answered: "Oh yes, sir, plenty." "Nonsense!" boomed Churchill, producing a pound note. "There is no such thing! Send out for some more."[206]

The presses ran all night, and by 6:00 A.M. they had printed 232,000 copies, all of which were sold within an hour. The entire issue had been set single-handedly by Long. The lead article, unsigned but written by Churchill, set the tone: "This great nation, on the whole the strongest community which civilisation can show, is for the moment reduced in this respect to the level of African natives dependent only on the rumours which are carried from place to place. In a few days if this were allowed to continue, rumours would poison the air, raise panics and disorders, inflame fears and passions together, and carry us all to the depths which no sane man of any party or class would care even to contemplate." On the second day the circulation rose to 507,000. A week later, on the last day of the general strike, it soared to 2,209,000. The cabinet had been under the impression that the *Gazette*'s contents would be limited to public notices, official statements, and indispensable information. Winston had assured British newspaper publishers: "I do not contemplate violent partisanship, but fair, strong encouragement to the great mass of loyal people." No one who knew him believed that — Beaverbrook had burst into laughter when told of it — for he was incapable of impartiality. When push came to shove, as it now had in England, he believed that the standards of traditional journalism were anemic. "The field of battle," he now wrote grandly, "is no longer transport but news." Then: "The State cannot be impartial between itself and that section of subjects with whom it is contending." And, most memorably, when reproached in the House for his ringing editorial denunciations of the strike: "I decline utterly to be impartial between the fire brigade and the fire."[207]

That was defensible. The paper's pretense of objectivity in its news columns was not. Under the heading FALSE NEWS appeared the notice: "Many false rumours are current. Believe nothing until you see it in an authoritative journal like the *British Gazette.*" Yet readers of the *Gazette* were led to believe that the country was in the grip, not of an industrial dispute, but of incipient revolution. The strike was described as "a direct challenge to ordered government." Strikers were "the enemy." A specious claim from a French paper that Bolsheviks were behind the TUC was reprinted in full. *Gazette* accounts of House debates were outrageously distorted, one Labour MP being described as "a wild Socialist, passionate and shouting." An MP's conviction that a settlement was at hand was denied by an unidentified "Cabinet Minister." Heavy coverage was given to Sir John Simon's irresponsible statement that each TUC leader could be successfully sued to "the utmost farthing of his personal possessions." At a time when the walkout had virtually paralyzed Britain a headline reported that the strike was NOT SO COMPLETE AS HOPED BY ITS PROMOTERS. All Englishmen were "calm and confident" that it would fail — the six million strikers, apparently, were no longer regarded as English. Strikebreakers were reassured: "No man who does his duty loyally to the country in the present crisis will be left unprotected by the State from subsequent reprisals" — a pledge, involving forces of the Crown, to which the King took strong exception. Patriotic poetry appeared frequently: Kipling, and, in three issues, Tennyson's "Soul of England." While Baldwin's speeches and statements were bland, offensive to no one, the *Gazette* repeatedly blared that until the TUC surrendered unconditionally, "there can be no question of compromise of any kind."[208]

The *Gazette*'s belligerence troubled many of Churchill's old friends and allies. Lloyd George disapproved of the strike, but, as he told the House, "I know a great many of the people responsible. They are as little revolutionaries as any men in this House. They have fought the rebellious ones in their own Party." He accused Winston of sabotaging a TUC attempt to reach an agreement and called his paper "a first-class indiscretion, clothed in the tawdry garb of third-rate journalism." Churchill replied: "It is not the duty of the *British Gazette* to publish a lot of defeatist trash." Gwynne, of course, was sharply critical. Thomas Jones noted in his diary that the *Morning Post* editor "has sent several messages begging that Winston should be kept away from that office where the 'British Gazette' is being printed. He butts in at the busiest hours and insists on changing commas and full stops until the staff is furious." But the heaviest protests naturally came from the strike leaders. They countered with a paper of their own, the *British Worker*. Winston was its chief target; the idea of calling an industrial dispute a revolutionary movement, the *Worker* declared, "was mainly Mr Churchill's. It is a melodramatic 'stunt' on Sydney [sic] Street lines. . . . The nation has kept its head in spite of the alarming tricks played upon it. Mr Churchill has failed again, and everybody knows . . . that 'revolution' exists nowhere save in Mr Churchill's heated and disorderly imagination." The following day the *Worker* observed that "day by day in the Cabinet's newspaper, Mr Churchill, acting as its super-editor, publishes articles by prominent men. These are suspiciously like one another. . . . The reference to the Strike being directed by a 'relatively small body of extremists' again betrays Mr Churchill's hand. It is mere violent, headlong, foolish propaganda — foolish because no sensible person will believe it." They only wished that were true. Winston's articles *were* believed; his flaming prose was being read in millions of upper- and middle-class homes, which was why the unions, too, had turned to journalism. They failed. Their editorials were dense and dull. Their greatest circulation was 713,000 for a single edition. In desperation, one firebrand slipped into the *Post* building and threw a steel bar into a press. Holt recalls: "Suddenly there was a horrible shattering jar. Power was turned off." Workers at the Hoe Company, makers of the machine, refused to repair it. Churchill called the Chatham Dockyard, and Royal Navy ratings arrived in an impressive convoy, departed, and returned with mended parts wrapped in a Union Jack. Winston then issued each member of the staff a mauve pass. Nobody could enter the building without one.[209]

Not all *Gazette* critics lay outside the Establishment. The British Broadcasting Company was struggling to keep its news reports impartial, but Winston, according to John Reith, then its managing director, tried to treat the BBC as "an offshoot of the *British Gazette.*" Reith appealed to Davidson, Joynson-Hicks, and Baldwin, and when Churchill asked the cabinet to let him run the BBC he was turned down. Reith did permit him to address the radio audience, however, and Beatrice Webb, perhaps the first to appreciate his mastery of this medium, described the talk as "a vividly rhetorical representation of his own case. . . . Except that his voice is harsh, he is a first rate broadcaster." He vexed London's press lords that week, though not over a matter of principle. As the *Gazette*'s popularity rocketed, he began commandeering all the newsprint in London. Dawson remonstrated, then Rothermere, and finally Beaverbrook wrote him that the two hundred tons of paper at the *Daily Express* would be needed the moment the strike ended. Impossible, Winston replied: "We are expecting to publish over three millions tonight, and we shall probably have to requisition every scrap of newsprint which is available and suitable." They met. Beaverbrook liked to tell friends that Winston had two moods, "Winston Up" and "Winston Down." Down, facing defeat, he was magnificent, but "in a position of uncontrolled power and authority," as he was at this point, he could be frightening. Of the newsprint confrontation Beaverbrook later recalled: "If any other man living had used such outrageous language to me as he did on that occasion I should never have forgiven him. Churchill on top of the wave has in him the stuff of which tyrants are made."[210]

This "terrible scene," as Beaverbrook thereafter called it, turned out to be unnecessary. Early the following morning — Wednesday, May 12, the ninth day of the crisis — the unions capitulated. Their treasury was empty, the government's attrition policy was working, and public opinion, fired by the *Gazette,* was hostile. Arthur Pugh, the TUC chairman, called at No. 10 to surrender. Accompanying him was the TUC's general secretary, who wrote in his diary that evening: "While we were talking, Churchill, Baldwin, and Sir Arthur Steel-Maitland [minister of labor] were pacing rapidly up and down the garden, talking animatedly. There was no sign of jubilation amongst them, and Pugh muttered to me: 'I saw Churchill a few minutes ago, and he said, "Thank God it's over, Mr Pugh." ' " That afternoon Winston announced that the next issue of the *Gazette* would be the last. Its final headline was unfortunate. It gloated: SURRENDER RECEIVED BY PREMIER IN DOWNING STREET. In an envoi Churchill told his readers: "The *British Gazette* may have had a short life, but it has fulfilled the purpose of living. It becomes a memory; but it remains a monument." That evening he took a large party to see Adele and Fred Astaire in *Lady Be Good,* then playing at the old Empire Theatre. As he entered, the audience rose and gave him a standing ovation.[211]

Labor's intellectuals now singled him out for attack. Kingsley Martin, a young leftist writer, studied the columns of the *Gazette,* noted its incendiary style, found certain striking omissions — Churchill had suppressed an appeal from the church which had blamed both sides — and concluded that Winston had been "discredited." The *New Statesman,* then as now a journal of eccentric opinion, perpetrated a fraud. On the night of May 10, it reported, Churchill had led a "war party" of ministers who threatened to resign at once unless talks with the union leaders were broken off. The Churchill faction, it continued, had been "in favour of war at all costs." This piece of outright fiction declared: "Mr Churchill was the villain of the piece. He is reported to have remarked that he thought 'a little blood-letting' would be all to the good." Winston considered pressing charges of criminal libel against the editors. Sir Douglas Hogg, the government's attorney general, advised against it. He would certainly win, Hogg said, but in court the defendants could discuss cabinet deliberations "in detail," which would offend Baldwin Tories. Winston reluctantly let the matter drop, though it was already clear to him that run-of-the-mill Conservatives viewed him with little more favor than the Labourites. Dawson of the *Times*, in a widely read account of the strike, concluded that "Winston seems to have been the only minister who rather lost his head. He was excitable, provocative, and a great trial to his colleagues. They tried to divert his energies at an early stage to the editing of the *British Gazette*, an official propagandist organ, in which he became a similar trial to us."[212]

Curiously, one journalist who commended Churchill's editorial performance was the irascible Gwynne. He wrote him: "May I lay at your feet my tribute of admiration at your wonderful energy and your marvellous powers of seeing things through?" In time Winston recalled his *Gazette* experience with nostalgia. On June 10, 1927, he wrote Gwynne: "I shall always look back to that extraordinary ten days. They form one of the most vivid experiences of my somewhat variegated life, and were utterly different from every other episode. I am glad to think they have left behind them a better understanding between us." He even exploited the episode in one of his quick turns of parliamentary wit. In a tense debate he faced the Opposition and said solemnly: "I have no wish to make threats or use language which would disturb the House and cause bad blood. But this I must say: make your minds perfectly clear that if ever you loose upon us again a General Strike, we will loose upon you" — angry shouts were on Labour lips — "another *British Gazette.*" The expected storm, Baldwin wrote the King, "gave way to an outburst of unrestrained laughter in which the House was convulsed."[213]

In a long public life clouded with misunderstandings, none was more tragic than the inexpiable enmity between Churchill and Labour. He had been a progressive home secretary; he was a humane chancellor. His record on liberal issues in many ways resembles that of Bismarck, another farsighted conservative. It was far more impressive than that of, say, Ramsay MacDonald, who waffled again and again when in power. But Winston's visceral reaction against socialism — he was always mistaking pink for red — led him into one rhetorical excess after another. It was Churchillian bombast which had touched off the Labourites' antagonism toward him. They took him at his word, despite the fact that his word, however prickly, was often conspicuously at odds with his deeds. The Dawsons of the Conservative party distrusted him for an altogether different reason. When the strikers had unsheathed their sword, he had lunged for his; he could never back away from a challenge. But at heart he still believed that the miners were right and the mineowners wrong. When the TUC collapsed he had written Baldwin: "To-night surrender. Tomorrow magnanimity." He had been moved to pity by Macmillan's descriptions of the hovels in which the miners lived, their brutish working conditions, and their sickly children. Now that members of the other unions had gone back to work, ending the threat to domestic tranquillity, he was eager to settle the grievances in the coalfields, which were still idle. To his dismay, the strike there dragged on for more than five months, and he and Amery were the only members of the cabinet who urged action. "I'm all on the miners' side now," he told Boothby after closing down the *Gazette.* Baldwin, departing for an extended holiday at Aix-les-Bains, left the matter in Winston's hands.[214]

It was a delicate, heartbreaking — and, in the end, doomed — task. The Tory ministers' hostility toward the coal strikers was unabated. By the sheer force of will, intellect, and volubility, Winston preserved the workers' right to picket peacefully; he throttled legislation to outlaw strikes when, in his words, "a majority of those affected are in favour of it"; he used Treasury funds, not to subsidize the mines' proprietors, but to build miners' homes and fund "training schemes and other forms of assistance for displaced miners"; and he saved the workers' right to the secret ballot — the owners argued that this would increase the number of strikes — because he was "convinced that the majority of working men would adopt sound and sensible attitudes," and because private polling, in his view, restricted the influence of the unions' "extremist members."[215]

MacDonald, he knew, was close to Herbert Smith, the president of the miners' union. On Winston's initiative, Churchill and MacDonald held two long, secret meetings, first at Chartwell and then in Sir Abe Bailey's London home on Bryanston Square, near Marble Arch. Smith had authorized MacDonald to speak for him, and the two men forged an agreement. Winston then drew up an ultimatum to be delivered to the colliery proprietors, omitting the strikers' most extravagant demands but including those terms which were minimal for them and the Labour party. Keeping Baldwin informed, he laid this compromise before the cabinet: "Do not, I beg you, throw this chance upon the rubbish heap of so many others." His colleagues disapproved of this proposal — they thought it gave the workers too much — but, as one said afterward, "We couldn't repudiate Winston." The real question, as he had told MacDonald, was whether the coal barons would bow to the ultimatum. It was "quite likely," he had said, that they "might refuse to come, or, if they did come, might take a line that would make progress impossible." In that event, the government "would make no secret of their opinion that they were in the wrong," but "the powers of actual coercion that the Government possesses are very limited." The miners now believed that Churchill was their best hope; the *Evening Standard* reported that both they and the TUC, asked to choose between Winston and any other member of the government, had expressed "a marked preference for Mr Churchill as mediator."[216]

It proved an impossible task. The owners, speaking through Evan Williams, the president of the Mining Association of Great Britain, refused to make any concession whatever. They knew the men were desperate, growing hungrier every day, with winter dead ahead. Thomas Jones described one meeting between Williams and Churchill as "acute and at times acrimonious," but Williams wouldn't budge. He fought every attempt at reconciliation. They met again at No. 10; Jones called it "a ding-dong debate" which accomplished nothing. Winston's anger at the owners grew. He poured it out in letters to Clementine. She replied: "I fear you are having a very anxious and difficult time"; the proprietors' position, she said, seemed "hard and cruel." He wrote her that the talks were leading toward a "serious collision." She hoped he wasn't shouldering the other ministers aside and thus alienating them: "You are having an anxious but a thrilling and engrossing time with power & scope which is what the Pig likes — I suppose Steel-Maitland and George Lane-Fox [secretary for mines] are not often allowed near the trough? If the cat were Minister of Labour or Mines she would not give up her place there without a few 'miaows.' "[217]

But Steel-Maitland and Lane-Fox would cede the miners nothing. And Baldwin, when he returned to London, agreed with them. Churchill proposed statutory intervention. Other wealthy contributors to Tory coffers had taken an interest in the talks, however, and when Winston wrote Baldwin, "I do hope that a little employers' agitation will not prevent H.M.G. from advancing with courage & conviction against . . . detractors of the public interest," he found that the agitation of Williams's clients had done just that. The most the prime minister would promise was a toothless appeal tribunal. After Churchill scorned "the greedy appetites of the coal trade," two of his closest friends, Birkenhead and Lord Londonderry, reproached him. Londonderry, a mineowner and one of Winston's cousins, argued that the owners were fighting bolshevism. Winston replied: "With those parts of your letter which deal with the necessity for combating Bolshevism I am in entire accord. But there could be no worse way of combating Bolshevism than to identify the

Conservative Party and His Majesty's Government with the employers, and particularly with a body of employers like those headed by Mr Evan Williams. . . . The duty of the Government is to occupy an impartial position in the interests of the State and of the whole community. . . . You say that the Owners are fighting Socialism. It is not the business of Coal Owners as Coal Owners to fight Socialism. If they declare it their duty, how can they blame the Miners' Federation for pursuing political ends? The business of the Coal Owners is to manage their industry successfully, to insist upon sound economic conditions as regards hours and wages, and to fight Socialism as citizens and not as owners of a particular class of property."[218]

It was hopeless. He wanted to warn the owners that if they continued to be "unreasonable," the government would appoint arbitrators and fix a national minimum wage. It seemed clear to him that a few rich Englishmen, and they alone, were blocking a settlement. When they refused even to participate in tripartite talks with the government and the union, he told the cabinet that their position was "wholly wrong and unreasonable, an attitude without precedent in recent times," and charged that they had even influenced Tory whips in the House, who had "been at some of the Ministers, urging them to do nothing." Certainly the cabinet's reluctance to subject the owners to any pressure whatever is singular; the impasse, after all, was eroding the national economy. Harold Laski, after accompanying miner delegates to one meeting, wrote a friend that he thought Baldwin "quite tragic . . . hard and a little cynical and impatient of all criticism. . . . Churchill who was there was bigger and more skillful in every way — he knew how to negotiate. Baldwin merely blundering uncouthly." Of the 1,250,000 union members, 100,000 demoralized men had returned to work by early October. Boothby, like Macmillan, went into the coalfields to talk to strikers. On October 9 he wrote Churchill from the Carlton Club: "It is the impression, growing every day, that the Government has now divested itself of all responsibility for the conduct of our national industries . . . that despite the promise of the first months it has become . . . a Government of reaction." It would, he continued, "be difficult to exaggerate the effect of your vigorous intervention in the mining dispute last month" or "the disappointment which attended the failure of your efforts." In the end the owners' obduracy was triumphant. As Leo Amery wrote later: "The miners straggled back to the pits on the owners' terms, including longer hours, a beaten and resentful army."[219]

Worse followed. In the wake of the broken strike, the parliamentary

Conservatives passed a wave of antilabor legislation. All the gains Churchill had achieved for the unions were abolished. Picketing was outlawed; no worker could be disciplined for refusing to join a strike deemed "illegal"; the attorney general was authorized to seize union funds; the Trades Dispute Act of 1906, which exempted unions from legal suit, was repealed. In a blow at the Labour party, unions were prohibited from collecting money from their members for political purposes unless they had secured their written consent. For Churchill, the low point came when a delegation of miners arrived at the Treasury and charged him with betraying them. Jones wrote in his diary that this was grossly unfair; that Winston had tried "to go to great lengths in the way of legislation on hours, wages and conditions — which terrified his colleagues." But all the workmen knew was that he had failed them. Smith, their leader, stood before Winston, trembling with rage. Gaunt and pale, he was a symbol of their deprivation; born in a Lancashire workhouse, the posthumous son of a miner killed in a mine accident, he himself had begun working in the pits on his tenth birthday. Later he would write of this meeting: "We said to Churchill: 'We understand you were a man of courage, but you have broken down at the first fence. You have dismounted. Have you been doing wrong while the masters have been away; and got reprimanded?' He did not like it."[220]

He hated it, and could not reply; he understood their bitterness, for he shared it. In less than two years he would grasp the magnitude of his error in putting England back on the gold standard. Writing Grigg on July 2, 1928, he dealt savagely with the financial experts who had urged him to do it: "They have caused an immense amount of misery and impoverishment by their rough and pedantic handling of the problem. In ruined homes, in demoralised workmen, in discouraged industry, in embarrassed finances, in inflated debt and cruel taxation we have paid the price." Eleven years after the tumult of 1926 he wrote that industrial strife "has introduced a narrowing element into our public life. It has been a keenly felt impediment to our productive and competitive power. It has become the main foundation of a socialist political party which has ruled the State greatly to its disadvantage, and will assuredly do so again."[221] Churchill was not the only statesman to be baffled by twentieth-century economics. He was, however, among the very few British Conservatives who had seen the justice of the workers' cause. It is not the least of the ironies in his career that within twenty years, when he was at the peak of his achievements, their resentment would coalesce to drive him from office.

Today's Europeans and Americans who reached the age of awareness after mid-century, when the communications revolution led to expectations of instantaneity, are exasperated by the slow toils of history. They assume that the lightning of cause will be swiftly followed by the thunderclap of effect. Great political sea changes move at a testudinal pace, however. Change is preceded by reappraisals, false starts, and frequent setbacks. William Lloyd Garrison founded the *Liberator* in 1831, yet over thirty years passed before Lincoln freed the slaves. The big Swede christened Joseph Hagglund and remembered as Joe Hill was executed by a firing squad on November 19, 1915. It would be another generation before organized labor was ready to test its strength. Alexander Fleming discovered penicillin at St. Mary's Hospital, London, in 1928. Not until the later stages of World War II would it become available to physicians, and then in limited supply. The American Equal Rights Association was founded by New York feminists on May 10, 1866, but their great-great-granddaughters are still struggling to realize their dream. Even so cataclysmic an event as the First World War did not reach its maximum impact until more than ten years after the Armistice, when Remarque's *All Quiet on the Western Front,* Hemingway's *Farewell to Arms,* Graves's *Goodbye to All That,* and Sassoon's *Memoirs of an Infantry Officer* reached audiences ready, at last, to believe what, until then, had been thought unbelievable.

So it was with the general strike of 1926 and the career of Winston Churchill. During the three years which followed, he rode a crest of acclaim in the middle and upper classes, unbruised by the grievances of those at both ends of the political spectrum who had been angered by his performance during the nine days and the long aftermath. The strike had been broken, the government had won, the miners were back in the pits, and he had been the cabinet's most colorful cheerleader. His mistakes were unobserved; hardly anyone understood economics anyway. But he certainly sounded as though *he* did. Each budget speech was more brilliant than the last. Altogether he presided over five Budget Days, a record matched only by Walpole, Pitt, Peel, and Gladstone, each of whom became prime minister. Bets were made on when Churchill would move into No. 10. His only rival was the rising star Neville Chamberlain, and even Chamberlain wrote of him in 1928: "One doesn't often come across a real man of genius or, perhaps, appreciate him when one does.

Winston is such a man." It was generally agreed that Churchill was mellowing. Lord Winterton wrote: "The remarkable thing about him is the way he has suddenly acquired, quite late in Parliamentary life, an immense fund of tact, patience, good humor and banter on almost all occasions; no one used to 'suffer fools ungladly' more fully than Winston; now he is friendly and accessible to everyone, both in the House, and in the lobbies, with the result that he has become what he never was before the war, very popular in the House generally — a great accretion to his already formidable Parliamentary power."[222]

His wit could still wound — "Politics are very much like war," he said; "we even use poison gas at times" — and once he devastated a hostile woman MP who berated him during a dinner party, ending her diatribe by observing with scorn: "Mr. Churchill, you are drunk." "And you, madam," Churchill replied, "are ugly. But I shall be sober tomorrow." Yet his humor now was often gentle, even self-deprecating. After a small dinner at Pratt's Club in London, F.E. proposed that Lord Melchett, the richest man in the party, should pay the bill. Winston demurred: "My dear Freddie, surely you would not deprive me of the pride and pleasure of giving a crust to Croesus?" After he had switched parties and Baldwin had made him chancellor, Churchill said: "You know, the family motto of the House of Marlborough from which I descend is 'Faithful but Unfortunate.' " A gushing woman asked him: "Doesn't it thrill you, Mr. Churchill, to know that every time you speak the hall is packed to overflowing?" Winston said: "It is quite flattering, but whenever I feel this way I always remember that, if instead of making a political speech, I was being hanged, the crowd would be twice as big."[223]

Baldwin was dazzled by him, and during these years, when there was no threat to it, their relationship approached genuine friendship. On the evening of each Budget Day the prime minister sent the King an appraisal of the chancellor's presentation. Each was giddier than the last. In one he wrote that Churchill "has a power of attraction which nobody in the House of Commons can excel." Another spoke of Churchill's "masterpiece of cleverness and ingenuity." In a third, reporting on a speech which had lasted three and a half hours, he wrote: "The House became intensely interested in watching a master in the art of oratory and tantalizing the imagination unfold his ideas in a speech packed with ideas, yet so simple and clear that there could be no possible misunderstanding." Then he sent Winston himself a note: "I hate to use the word 'brilliant': it has been worked to death and is too suggestive of brilliantine: but, if I may use it in its pristine virginity, so to speak, it is the right one. I congratulate you with both hands." Some veteran MPs across the aisle were also impressed. Lloyd George called him "the merriest tax collector since the days of Robin Hood." And the press, for once, was on his side. Cartoonists depicted him as the "Smiling Chancellor," and "Winsome Winston." The *Times of India* commented: "In appearance Mr Churchill is almost jovial; one can imagine him, dressed in a cowl, the incarnation of the jolly monks and friars of centuries ago."[224]

Of course, there were those who saw him very differently. Ardent Labour MPs attacked him relentlessly, Snowden crying after one budget speech: "There is not one penny of relief for the wage-earning classes. Shorn of all the glamour of the Right Honourable Gentleman's eloquence, this is his Budget. No more of a rich man's Budget has ever been presented. It will not take long for the glamour to disappear, and then the great toiling masses will realize the true character of this Budget, and will realize, too, that the Tory Party is still more than ever what Lord George Hamilton declared many years ago: 'A party that looks after its own friends, whether it be in office or out of office.' " On Churchill's own side of the House, Conservative back-benchers had not forgotten his stands on Home Rule and Free Trade, and their wrath was rekindled in 1928, when, led by Leo Amery, they made a fresh attempt to follow the American example and introduce protective tariffs, arguing that they would put a million Englishmen back to work. Churchill blocked them; Baldwin supported him. Amery wrote angrily in his diary of "the whole attitude of the Cabinet under Winston's influence, and the PM's decision not to do anything"; Lane-Fox noted that the protectionists were "now very angry and a lot is going on. It is the first sign of a real party fissure that I have yet seen." The storm was small and it passed quickly. Winston wrote Clementine: "Really I feel vy independent of them all."[225]

That was precisely his problem. His independence had become a point of political vulnerability. Of all the major prewar public men, he alone had survived; as A. G. Gardiner put it, "Like the camomile, the more he is trodden on, the more he flourishes." Yet after nearly three decades in public life he still floated free of any power base. Epping was a mere convenience. Unlike most senior members of the House, he had no national following, controlled no political hierarchy. Party discipline has always been taken more seriously in Britain than in the United States, and Churchill had been a disciplinary problem all his life. Beaverbrook noted that he "neither tied the Liberals to him nor conciliated the Tories." Gardiner wrote in 1926: "If he changes parties with the facility of partners at a dance, he has always been true to the only Party he really believes in — that which is assembled under the hat of Mr. Winston Churchill." Gwynne's *Morning Post,* now more generous in tone, observed:

"Mr Churchill is still his own Party, and the chief of the partisans. He still sees himself as the only digit in the sum of things, all other men as mere cyphers, whose function it is to follow after and multiply his personal value a million-fold." Harold Nicolson saw him as "the most interesting man in London. He is more than interesting: he is a phenomenon, an enigma. How can a man so versatile and so brilliant avoid being considered volatile and unsound?" Arthur Ponsonby, who had switched allegiance from the Liberals to Labour, wrote Eddie Marsh that Winston was "far and away the most talented man in political life. . . . But that does not prevent me from feeling politically he is a great danger, largely because of his love of crises and faulty judgment. He once said to me years ago, 'I like things to happen, and if they don't happen I like to make them happen.' "[226]

The Conservative party's rank and file didn't want anything to happen, ever. They could identify with Neville Chamberlain, not with Churchill. Winston could have won their loyalty at the Treasury had he pursued traditional Conservative fiscal policies. Instead, he had alienated them by introducing welfare legislation. In Parliament he was not Scottish, Welsh, or a representative of the Midlands; he was known only as a Londoner who had been elected by none of London's constituencies. That was a grave weakness in a man who hoped to become No. 10's next occupant. He seemed completely unaware of the danger inherent in an eminence acquired solely by ministerial talents, parliamentary skills, and Baldwin's fosterage. The *Weekly Dispatch* of July 10, 1927, reported that during the past week the chancellor had filled more pages in *Hansard* than any other six MPs put together; that he, not Baldwin, was leading the party, and doing it adroitly; and that he "also has a way of dealing with the Socialists which, while it never lacks anything in force or directness, yet appeals to their sense of fair play and good humour. 'Winston is up!' empties the smoking room quicker than any other announcement." The piece ended: "Yet with all his talents and his force of character, the main body of conservatives would never follow him as Prime Minister." Even Baldwin doubted that the Tories would choose Churchill as his successor. "Our people like him," he wrote a friend in September 1927. "They love listening to him in the House, look on him as a star turn, and settle down in the stalls with anticipatory grins. But for leadership, they would turn him down every time."[227]

The real complaint about Churchill's years at the Exchequer is that for the only time in his life he ignored his instincts. Intuition had warned him to shun the goldmongers, but, uncharacteristically unsure of himself, he learned the rules of fiscal orthodoxy and, for the most part, followed them. His policies were not wholly unimaginative; he established a reparations pool, whereby the Treasury would be enriched by German goods sold in Britain, and — over the strong objections of Neville Chamberlain — he introduced the rating apportionment bill of 1928 (actually young Harold Macmillan's idea), under which industry and agriculture were provided with local tax relief, the gap in income being plugged by cuts in defense and a gasoline tax which brought in £15,000,000 a year. Because England's economy had been crippled by the general strike, he had little room for maneuver in the two budgets following it. The deficits were met by a temporary tax on rubber tires and increased levies on wines, matches, and tobacco; by taking £12,000,000 from the Road Fund; by reducing the brewers' credit period by a month; and by rescheduling property taxes. But it was all legerdemain — "jugglery and deceit," as Snowden called it. Winston himself acknowledged that he had drawn on his "adventitious resources." Grigg pointed out that "in spite of all the Keynesian gibes, his main object was always the reduction of unemployment." Tinkering wouldn't do the job, however, and Churchill shied away from the deficits and bold governmental intervention Roosevelt would introduce within a few years in the depressed United States. Amery summed up Winston's financial program in a letter to Baldwin: "A few hand-to-mouth dodges for picking up odd windfalls, a hope that better trade and a few millions saved by cheese-paring here and there may ride matters over the next year: that is the beginning and end of it."[228]

It was certainly the end of it. Churchill's last budget, presented on April 15, 1929, after the Tories had lost nine safe seats in by-elections over the past two months, offered little to calm their growing anxieties. His delivery, as always, was masterly. Taxpayers were to be allowed deductions for each child ("Another example of our general policy of helping the producer"). Labour's demand for deficit spending was "the policy of buying a biscuit early in the morning and walking about all day looking for a dog to give it to." The *Sunday Times* called his performance "the most brilliantly entertaining of modern Budget speeches," and Harold Macmillan would write of the Churchillian style in his *Winds of Change* that none of the new generation of MPs "had ever heard anything of the kind . . . such mastery of language, such careful deployment of the arguments, such dexterous covering of any weak point." But as political nourishment it was poor fare. He abolished taxes on tea, gambling, and railway passage; reduced taxes on motorcycles and bicycles; raised them on telephone service; and introduced new duties on tobacco, beer, and liquor. It was a swan song in falsetto. Grigg thought it not inappropriate.

As chancellor, he said, Winston had "tended to overestimate revenue and underestimate expenditure," had "convinced himself that there was a good deal to be said at that time for respectability . . . in economic affairs," was "apt to spoil a brilliant project by not assuring himself in advance of sufficient resources to carry it through to the end," and was "therefore reduced to all sorts of shifts and expedients in order to avoid having to go back on the policies on which he had perhaps too confidently embarked."[229] Yet it's fair to add that during Churchill's Exchequer tenure state benefits had been extended to 344,800 children, 236,800 widows, 450,000 Britons over sixty-five years old, and 227,000 over seventy. He may have been no better at handling Britain's finances than his family's, but here, as at home, he had established the right priorities.

In retrospect there is an air of foreboding about the English upper classes' late 1920s, a feeling that everyone of consequence is wearing tennis whites, gabbling manically, and emptying magnums of Dom Perignon in a Rolls-Royce racing headlong toward the edge of a towering precipice. It is illusion, of course, a vision of hindsight. At the time these years seemed fruitful and teeming with hope. One pictures a typical country weekend, with the Duke of York striding off the eighteenth green, Sir Samuel Hoare immaculate and not even perspiring after winning three straight sets six–love, Rex Whistler absorbed in his painting, Balfour dozing in a leather armchair, Osbert Sitwell laughing his infectious laugh as the Prof describes his recent trip to India, and Churchill and Bernard Shaw arguing over teacups about Shaw's newly published *Intelligent Woman's Guide to Socialism and Capitalism.* In other homes Sir Jacob Epstein is sculpturing his *Madonna and Child;* Virginia Woolf is writing *To the Lighthouse;* D. H. Lawrence, *Lady Chatterley's Lover;* Trevelyan, his *History of England;* Evelyn Waugh, *Decline and Fall;* and A. A. Milne, to the delight of a much larger if less discriminating audience, *Winnie-the-Pooh.* In Washington, Andrew W. Mellon, "the best Secretary of the Treasury since Hamilton," is spreading his gospel, an echo of Sackville-West, that ostentatious consumption by the rich is a source of great pleasure for the poor. At No. 11 Downing Street a buoyant chancellor of the Exchequer is supplementing his ministerial salary by writing "The United States of Europe" for the *Saturday Evening Post,* and, for the *Daily Telegraph,* a series of articles exposing welfare cheats called "The Abuse of the 'Dole.' " T. S. Eliot has become a British citizen. England is preparing to launch an experimental public television service. Bernard Shaw has concluded that in the absence of a world government, the British Empire is best qualified to rule the world. That world is at peace; Britain still dominates world politics. A disarmament conference, with the United States participating, is convening in Geneva. Germany has been admitted to the League of Nations. The Kellogg-Briand Pact, sponsored by the U.S. secretary of state, has outlawed war and provided for a pacific settlement of disputes. Italy has just signed a twenty-year friendship treaty with Ethiopia.

Among those gulled by the Italian dictator, now in his fifth year of power, was Winston Churchill. Once the coal strike had ended he had plunged into his third *Crisis* volume and accepted an invitation from Roger Keyes, now an admiral, to join a week-long cruise on the Mediterranean. "On leaving you," he wrote the admiral, "I am going to stay in Rome for a few days to see Mussolini (while he lasts), and I am taking with me my brother Jack, whom you know, and my boy Randolph." After Christmas at Chartwell they departed aboard the *Esperia*. On January 4, 1927, he wrote Clementine from Genoa that he was greatly taken by the Fascist society: "This country gives the impression of discipline, order, smiling faces. A happy strict school — no talking among the pupils. Great changes have taken place since you & I disembarked [here] nearly 6 years ago." The local Fascists and the employees at his hotel were particularly attentive: "They have been saluting in their impressive manner all over the place, & . . . gave us a most cordial welcome."[230]

Correcting proofs until 2:30 A.M. in his hotel room, he sent them off to his publisher "under threats of vengeance from Mussolini if anything goes wrong." In Rome he saw the Duce twice and then held what can only be described as an unfortunate press conference. It was perfectly clear, he said, that his host "thought of nothing but the lasting good, as he understands it, of the Italian people." Indeed: "If I had been an Italian, I am sure I should have been whole-heartedly with you from the start to finish in your triumphant struggle against the bestial appetites and passions of Leninism." Englishmen had "not yet had to face this danger in the same deadly form," but when the time came "we shall succeed in grappling with Communism and choking the life out of it — of that I am absolutely sure." In his opinion the Duce had "provided the necessary antidote to the Russian poison. Here after, no great nation will be unprovided with an ultimate means of protection against cancerous growths, and every responsible labour leader in the country ought to feel his feet

Work: In London

more firmly planted in resisting levelling and reckless doctrines." As a consequence, "Externally, your movement has rendered a service to the whole world."[231]

The text of these remarks was published in *The Times* of January 21, 1927. Liberals and Labourites were choleric. The *New Leader* stormed: "We have always suspected that Mr Winston Churchill was a Fascist at heart. Now he has openly avowed it." C. P. Scott of the *Manchester Guardian* was so incensed that he all but lay down and drummed his heels on the floor. Clementine wrote Winston: "Scott is I see vexed over your partiality to 'Pussolini.' " Her husband was unruffled. He took the classic view of British foreign policy: England should support any continental regime which was hostile to England's greatest enemy — in this case, at that time, Soviet Russia. Later, when the Duce became a piratical adventurer, Churchill would scorn him as "Mussolini the swine," and "Mussolini the jackal."[232]

Vesuvius obligingly erupted when Winston, Jack, and young Randolph visited Naples. Churchill played his last polo game on Malta ("It is dreadful giving it up for ever," he wrote), reported to Clementine on their son ("The Rabbit is a very good travelling companion," he disclosed, adding with relish: "We have played a great deal of chess in

Play: At Chartwell

which I give him either a Queen or two castles, or even castle, bishop and knight — and still wallop him"), and, with Randolph, was received by Pope Pius XI. The audience was preceded by much wrangling over protocol. As an important minister serving under a Protestant monarch, Winston absolutely refused to kneel. They compromised on three bows as he entered the pontiff's reception hall. Randolph later wrote in his memoirs: "The early part of the conversation was a little sticky. Then my father and the Pope got on to the subject of the Bolsheviks and had a jolly half hour saying what they thought of them." After stops at Athens, Paris, Dieppe, and Consuelo's villa at Eze, Churchill and his party arrived at Newhaven aboard the night ferry on January 29. A box of Treasury papers from Grigg awaited him in his car; he studied them on the way to Chartwell.[233]

Between the Exchequer and his publishers' deadlines, nearly all his holidays were working holidays. He meant to take most of the summer of 1927 off, painting at Chartwell, entertaining friends there, and sweating over walls, dams, and ponds, but then he decided to start writing an account of his youth. It is his most delightful book. Subsequently serialized in the *News Chronicle* and published by Thornton Butterworth as *My Early Life,* it sold 13,753 copies in Britain, was issued by Scribner's in the United States under the title *A Roving Commission,* appeared, condensed, in the *Reader's Digest,* and was translated into thirteen languages and Braille. Not all his conceptions reached full term. He planned a book on socialism with the working title *The Creed of Failure* but abandoned it after outlining the first five chapters. Then T. E. Lawrence, now 338171 Aircraftman Shaw, suggested Churchill's major biographical work, writing him from his RAF base: "If the Gods give you a rest, some day, won't you write a life of the great Duke of Marlborough? About our only international general . . . and so few people seem to see it."[234]

Winston's immense output — he was still writing regularly for magazines and newspapers — was possible because of his extraordinary methods of work. Like Dr. Johnson producing his dictionary, he assembled a committee of researchers and secretaries and guided them as they tackled one topic after another. Asked about the thread of narrative, he said, "Oh, I have all that in my head." And he continued to work all hours. However late his Chartwell guests had retired, he would pace his study, dictating; one visitor recalls wakening to hear "the sounds of footfalls on the boards and his familiar voice clearly audible." In one month, he told Clementine, he had banked the equivalent of $72,414: a £6,000 advance for the Marlborough, £5,200 in stock dividends, £1,700 in *World Crisis* royalties, and nearly £2,000 from magazines — "a small fortune," he wrote, of which he was "trying to keep 2,000 fluid for investment & speculation with Vickers & McGowan. This 'mass of manoeuvre' is of the utmost importance & must not be frittered away." It seemed sound. But most of his investments were in the New York stock market. And the year was 1929.[235]

A few months earlier, during a finance bill debate, he had been stricken by influenza, and his slow recovery suggested a weakened constitution. Those around him were worried; they were afraid he was driving himself toward a nervous collapse. The only way to divert him from public or private work was to put him on a ship or a hunt, in front of an easel, or in the midst of a crowd. Beaverbrook persuaded him to spend five days sailing to Amsterdam and back on his private yacht; the Duke of Westminster induced him to fish and hunt stags in Scotland; by royal command he hunted grouse with George V at Balmoral and painted the Highland scene from his window there. (The painting was subsequently auctioned for £120.) He wrote a friend: "I had a particularly pleasant luncheon with the King when we went out deer-driving, and a very good talk about all sorts of things. I am very glad that he did not disapprove of my using the Ministerial room as a studio, and I took particular care to leave no spots on the Victorian tartans."[236] Especially sweet was a return trip to Belfast, where, on his last visit, he and Clementine had narrowly escaped a lynch mob. This time Queen's University awarded him an honorary degree, and cheering students, after presenting him with a shillelagh and a "paddy hat," rode him around on their shoulders.

The older Churchill children were in boarding school now, with only Mary at home, but Chartwell was never lonely. As a host he was as affable as ever. Convoys of friends arrived, some as early as Thursday, for long weekends. He greeted them eagerly and was genuinely sorry to see them leave. One guest wrote in his diary: "He was in a marvellous mood and just would not let us go. I played the piano and we talked on cricket, on music and politics." The toys of war still fascinated him. James Lees-Milne, a friend of young Randolph's, told Martin Gilbert of one evening when "we remained at that round table till after midnight. The table cloth had long ago been removed. Mr. Churchill spent a blissful two hours demonstrating with decanters and wine glasses how the Battle of Jutland was fought. . . . He got all worked up like a schoolboy, making barking noises in imitation of gunfire and blowing cigar smoke across the battle scene in imitation of gun smoke."[237]

His closest friend was still Birkenhead — F.E. — with the Prof a close second. He and Beaverbrook became somewhat less intimate. The publisher wanted Winston filmed by the American Telephone and Telegraph Company, which was gathering a celluloid history of the period using what he called "the new process of talking pictures." The cameramen had already shot reels of Coolidge, Mussolini, and Poincaré. Churchill declined on the ground that "I am in a far humbler class than the individuals you mention, and have no right to such prominence." This humility is suspicious, and, in fact, he had another motive. In 1928 Beaverbrook had asked permission to print the letter Winston had sent Bonar Law in 1915, begging Law not to dismiss him from the Admiralty. As one who often earned his living by quoting the correspondence of others, Churchill could hardly refuse, but his reply was curt: "You make me tear open old wounds and their sting returns. Certainly publish the letter as you propose, not as a thing thrust into publicity by me but on your own responsibility."[238] In addition, the flag of Free Trade was under fire again, and Beaverbrook was sponsoring the United Empire League, a lobby for tariffs. Now in 1929 the Conservatives had been in office for five years; Baldwin had to call for a general election. United Empire candidates were running well in by-elections. Free Trade had lost its great popularity, and the prime minister committed himself to tariff reform. It was the first of several issues which were to estrange Baldwin and Churchill. England's political climate had changed, and once again, as in 1915 and 1922, Winston felt the chill of isolation gathering round, found that MPs of all parties were beginning to avoid him.

Any party in power tries to take the public's pulse from time to time, and on September 2, 1928, Churchill had written the prime minister at Aix-les-Bains: "I cannot feel that there is any decisive drift agst us. But Labour will have a heavy class vote; & the Liberals will queer the pitch — (what else *can* they do?)." They could continue to join Labour in droves, and that is what they were doing. That winter the Tory sky darkened; of nine by-elections in what had been considered safe Conservative constituencies, Labour had won three and the Liberals two, and the four surviving Tories had narrowly escaped defeat. Party morale was deteriorating, the cabinet was apathetic, the number of jobless growing. Beaverbrook thought that "unemployment will be the one and only issue which counts." Churchill, with whom he conferred, though their manner toward one another had become distant, disagreed with him, arguing that it was "confined to certain areas which will go against the Government anyhow." Yet within a week Winston's optimism had evaporated. He now despaired; the Conservatives were vulnerable on too many other issues. "He accepts electoral defeat in advance," wrote Beaverbrook, though he added that "his judgement on such matters is worse than any prominent man I know."[239]

In January, five months before the country went to the polls, Churchill told Baldwin that the voters should be warned that they faced a choice between socialism, which had been responsible for the general strike, and "modern" conservatism. The trend in all countries, he said, was toward cooperation between nations and a continuum of national policy; "women can feel these tide movements by instinct." A graver, more delicate matter was dissension within the cabinet. Baldwin's successor would be either Winston or Neville Chamberlain, minister of health, and several ministers shared Lord Derby's view: "I believe in Winston's capability if only he were a bit more steady. But you never know what kite he is going to fly next." The first step for Chamberlain's supporters was to get Churchill out of the Exchequer. Amery wrote the prime minister in March: "The essential thing is to move Winston. . . . In spite of all his brilliancy and verbal originality, he is entirely lacking in constructive thought and imagination. . . . He has been, in every direction, a paralysing negative influence, and the Party knows it and would breathe a profound sigh of relief if he were shifted." The force behind the maneuvering was the man who stood to benefit from it. Chamberlain, who had suggested Winston's appointment as chancellor, had resolved to evict the Churchills from No. 11. Baldwin, susceptible to pressure, contemplated appointing Churchill secretary of state for India, even though the viceroy thought Winston unsuitable because he was "out of sympathy" with Indian political aspirations and was even "rather disposed to despise" them. The prime minister made the offer anyway and Churchill flatly turned it down. Birkenhead was doing a good job at the India Office, he said, and he shared F.E.'s "deep misgivings about that vast sub-continent." Nevertheless, determined to avoid friction with Chamberlain if possible, he wrote Baldwin that he wanted to "associate Neville" with major Treasury decisions. Neville declined. His objective hadn't changed; he was turning to intrigue. Anticipating the possibility that the coming election might leave the Liberals holding the balance of power between the Tories and Labour, as in 1924, Churchill sounded out Lloyd George on his terms for a Conservative-Liberal alliance. This, Chamberlain told Baldwin, was disloyal. Baldwin disagreed, though he said that if the voting ended in a stalemate, he couldn't possibly share responsibility with Lloyd George. Neville wrote in his diary: "S.B. said the King's government must be carried on, but that he personally would not serve with L.G. I said I was in the same position; and S.B. said in that case he supposed the leadership would go to Winston." Yet by spring it was obvious that Chamberlain had become Baldwin's favorite minister. Churchill realized that making common cause with his Tory critics was impossible. He wrote Clementine: "I have made up my mind that if N. Ch. is made leader of the CP or anyone else of that kind, I clear out of politics & see if I cannot make you & the kittens a little more comfortable before I die. Only one goal still attracts me, & if that were barred I shd quit the dreary field for pastures new."[240]

Polling was set for May 30. As a national figure Churchill was expected to stump for all Conservative candidates, but he faced a strong Liberal challenger in Epping, so while he was speaking elsewhere, Clementine took soundings among the voters there. "Darling," she hastily scrawled, "I do hope you enjoy your Scotch Meetings — I wish I were coming with you. But I think it is wise for me to be here & start the ball rolling." She rented an Epping cottage — "I think you will find this house a snug retreat," she wrote him, "from which to sally forth on the constituency" — and, because there were no large halls in the town, ordered the erection of two huge tents in which Winston might address his constituents. Speaking in one of them he suggested that state insurance might be available, not just to wage earners, but to all Britons. It was his one positive note in an otherwise deplorable campaign. In Liverpool he denounced Ramsay MacDonald's wartime pacifism: "I do not forget that, nor ought it to be forgotten." The scientist Sir John Boyd-Orr had a surer sense of the country's mood: "A ruling class living on dividends, masses of the people on the dole, and a Government trying to maintain an uneasy *status quo* is a picture which fills thinking people with despair." Churchill meanwhile was calling for a vote of confidence in Baldwin's "capable, sedate Government." If MacDonald were returned to office, he predicted, Labour would "bring back the Russian Bolsheviks, who will immediately get busy in the mines and factories, as well as among the armed forces, planning another general strike." On April 30, 1929, he addressed the nation by radio. Conservatives, he said, had given England peace abroad, stable government at home, honest administration, goodwill, public and private thrift, and relief from "the burden of galling rates." He said: "Avoid chops and changes of policy; avoid thimble-riggers and three-card trick men; avoid all needless borrowing; and above all avoid, as you would the smallpox, class warfare and violent political strife." The message wasn't much, but the delivery was remarkable, and this time Beatrice Webb wasn't the only one to remark on it. The next morning's *Daily Express* commented on its effectiveness. Churchill's performance, the editorial said, "knocked the six preceding broadcasts into a cocked hat . . . as an exhibition of polemical oratory it was superb. His voice was edged alternately with sarcasm and warning. There was a note in it of extraordinary intimacy with his audience. He began with statistics . . . and ended high on the pinnacle of perfervid patriotism."[241]

It is singular how the brightest of politicians can convince themselves, against all evidence, that they are going to win. On May 28 Winston told his constituents: "Victory is in the air." It wasn't. Two evenings later he joined Baldwin at No. 10 to follow the returns. Thomas Jones recalls that at one desk "sat the PM with narrow slips of paper on which he inscribed the . . . lists as they arrived." At another "sat Winston doing similar lists in red ink, sipping whisky and soda, getting redder and redder, rising and going out often to glare at the machine himself, hunching his shoulders, bowing his head like a bull about to charge. As Labour gain after Labour gain was announced, Winston became more and more flushed with anger, left his seat and confronted the machine in the passage; with his shoulders hunched he glared at the figures, tore the sheets and behaved as though if any more Labour gains came he would smash the whole apparatus. His ejaculations to the surrounding staff were quite unprintable."[242]

By the following afternoon the final results were in: Labour, 288 seats; Conservatives, 260; Liberals, 59. Churchill himself had been reelected, but with only 48 percent of the vote. Among the losers were two of his young protégés, Macmillan and Alfred Duff Cooper. The Liberals once more held the balance of power. Churchill and Austen Chamberlain urged the prime minister to strike a bargain with Lloyd George. That was easy for them to say; they were old friends of George's. But Baldwin, who had been the architect of George's ruin in 1922, had decided that such an alliance was out of the question. After spending a weekend at Chequers thinking it over, he informed the cabinet he was going to resign. Ramsay MacDonald could take over again. All the Tory ministers then donned frock coats and boarded the Windsor train to hand the King their seals of office. Being a civil servant, Eddie Marsh could not continue as Churchill's secretary; they parted tearfully. T. E. Lawrence wrote Eddie: "The General election means that Winston goes out, I suppose. For himself I'm glad. He's a good fighter, and will do better out than in, and will come back in a stronger position than before. I want him to be PM somehow." That view was not shared by the man now moving out of No. 10. According to Beaverbrook, Winston visited Baldwin in the prime minister's House office — "the PM's room" — and told him of a strong movement to oust William Henry Davison, the party manager. Davison, said Winston, had become a focus of unpopularity. "Baldwin told Churchill," Beaverbrook wrote, "that there was nobody more unpopular than himself. The difficulty of carrying Churchill, said Baldwin, was one of the main reasons for losing the election." If true, this was the first real break between the two men.[243]

Evicted from No. 11, the Churchills rented the London home of Venetia Montagu, Asquith's old inamorata. Winston was planning a trip through Canada and the United States, to promote his books and line up editors and publishers for future writing assignments, and he left the details to Clementine. As a member of the Conservative Business Committee, or shadow cabinet, he expected to be an active Tory strategist and policymaker. "Do not hesitate to engage one or two extra servants," he wrote her. "Now that we are in opposition we must gather colleagues & M.P.s together a little at lunch & dinner. Also I have now a few business people who are of importance. We ought to be able to have lunches of 8–10 often, & dinners of the same size about twice a week. You should have a staff equal to this." But his assumption that he would be in the thick of things was unjustified. Baldwin had been right; many senior members of the party held him responsible for their defeat. This was revealed to him when Ramsay MacDonald had been in power less than a week. The new prime minister announced his intention to evacuate all British troops from Egypt except those in the canal zone. Winston objected vehemently, but "when I rose in my place on the Front Opposition Bench to interrogate the Government," he wrote in a note long afterward, Baldwin "sat silent and disapproving. I immediately perceived that the . . . honoured leader did not think this was a good point to press. Murmurs and even cries of dissent from the Conservative benches were added to the hostile Government interruptions, and it was evident that I was almost alone in the House."[244]

On August 3, 1929, the *Empress of Australia* steamed out of Southampton, bound for Quebec. Among its first-class passengers were Churchill; his brother, Jack; Randolph, now eighteen; and Jack's young son Johnny. Winston spent most of the voyage working or attending to his personal exchequer. He wrote two pieces, "Will the British Empire Survive?" for *Answers,* and a profile of a peer for *Nash's Pall Mall. John Bull* had already paid him for a piece on the election, "Why We Lost." The *Daily Telegraph* had agreed to pay him £2,500 for ten articles on this trip. In addition, £1,000 in *World Crisis* royalties had arrived before he left London, and a sale of utility shares had brought him another £2,000. He invested every shilling he could spare in the New York stock market. Financial security, he wrote Clementine from the ship, was "a wonderful thing."[245]

The warmth of his Canadian welcome was also wonderful. "The workmen in the streets," he wrote her, "the girls who work the lifts, the ex-service men, the farmers, up to the highest functionaries have shewn such unaffected pleasure to see me & shake hands that I am profoundly touched." The Canadian Pacific had put a stenographer-typist at his disposal for the journey across the continent, and Bernard Baruch had persuaded Charles Schwab to lend Churchill his private railway car, with double beds, private bathrooms, a parlor, a dining room (which Winston converted into an office), a kitchen, servants' quarters, a refrigerator, fans, and a radio. The radio, he wrote Clementine, was especially useful: "The wireless is a great boon, and we hear regularly from [Horace] Vickers [his broker] about the stock markets. His news has, so far, been entirely satisfactory." The passing scenery fascinated him. He wrote that he wanted "to see the country at close quarters, and nibble the grass and champ the branches." To Randolph he said, "Fancy cutting down all those beautiful trees to make pulp for those bloody newspapers and calling it civilization."[246]

Along the way he paused to open exhibitions, dedicate memorials, consult with officials, and deliver speeches, in one of which he deplored proposals to reduce France's army, reminding his audience that Germany had twice as many youths of military age as France, which had been invaded by Germans twice within living memory. After driving across the Rockies, which he painted, a sombrero shielding him from the sun, they visited Vancouver and took the ferry to Victoria, their last Canadian stop. The next day Randolph wrote in his diary: "We are now on the ship bound to Seattle, American soil and Prohibition. But we are well-equipped. My big flask is full of whisky and the little one contains brandy. I have reserves of both in medicine bottles. It is almost certain that we shall have no trouble. Still if we do, Papa pays the fine and I get the publicity." Papa would have been hit by both; *he* had a case of brandy in stone hot-water bottles. In San Francisco the British consul general met their train and drove them southward through the redwoods. Winston wrote his wife that the greater part of their six-hundred-mile journey "lay through the woods with these enormous trees. They are really astonishing. One we saw, the biggest, 380 foot high, was three thousand or four thousand or even five thousand years old and it took fourteen of us to join our arms around its stem."[247]

The high point of their California trip was a four-day visit with their chief California host, William Randolph Hearst, a fervent anglophobe who nevertheless wanted Churchill's by-line in his papers. Winston was willing, though he drove a hard bargain: £40,000 for twenty-two pieces. He was dumbfounded by San Simeon, Hearst's thirty-million-dollar castle. Blenheim pales beside San Simeon, a composite of all the European palaces and cathedrals the owner had admired, with tapestries, sarcophagi, stained glass, corbels, choir stalls, Gothic rooms, carved staircases, fretwork-ornamented towers, stables, swimming pools, and tennis courts. The entire property was surrounded by a transplanted forest. The man of the house dwelt in a third-floor "Celestial Suite," from which he descended in an elevator whose walls were hung with priceless paintings. Winston was charmed by Hearst's mistress, Marion Davies, formerly an MGM star, and enchanted when they all went off on a picnic accompanied by sixteen pack mules loaded with caviar, champagne, and a hillbilly band. Of Hearst himself, Churchill wrote home that he was "most interesting to meet, & I got to like him — a grave simple child — with no doubt a nasty temper — playing with the most costly toys. A vast income always overspent: ceaseless building & collecting not vy discriminatingly works of art: two magnificent establishments, two charming wives [Mrs. Hearst and Marion]; complete indifference to public opinion, a strong liberal and democratic outlook, a 15 million daily circulation, oriental hospitalities, extreme personal courtesy (to us at any rate) & the appearance of a Quaker elder — or perhaps better Mormon elder." One afternoon the householder was conferring with his attorney when a maid rushed in. "Mr Churchill is fainting!" she cried. "He wants some turpentine!" Hearst rushed out to a terrace, where he found Winston painting, not fainting, awaiting a thinner for his oils and placidly puffing a fat cigar.[248]

Churchill and his party moved on to Santa Barbara and then, for five nights, to the Biltmore in Los Angeles — their hotel bills, Winston wrote, were paid by "a hearty Banker" — where they toured the Hollywood studios and were Hearst's guests once again, at the Montmartre Club. That evening they dined with sixty guests, including Charlie Chaplin. Winston wrote his wife that Chaplin had "acted his new film for us in a wonderful way. It is to be his gt attempt to prove that the silent drama or pantomime is superior to the new talkies."* Randolph noted in his diary: "Papa wants him to act the young Napoleon and has promised to write the Scenario." Instead, said Chaplin, he intended to play Jesus Christ. Churchill thought a moment and then asked: "Have you cleared the rights?"[249]

After a fishing expedition off Catalina Island (Winston caught a 188-pound swordfish in twenty minutes), his party proceeded eastward, again in Schwab's private car, across the Mojave Desert, by the Grand Canyon, to Chicago. Baruch met him at the station there and introduced him to the Commercial Club. Asked about Ramsay MacDonald, who was also in the United States at the time, negotiating naval disarmament, Churchill replied that England was fortunate to be represented "by so experienced a statesman and so distinguished a man" — and then called for more British *and* American warships. On the Atlantic coast he paid a courtesy call on Herbert Hoover; toured Civil War battlefields, to pick up material for a series of *Collier's* pieces; and was in New York, staying at the Savoy-Plaza Hotel, when the market crashed. Still shaky on economics, he was slow to grasp what was happening. On the evening of "Black Tuesday," when the stock market, honeycombed with credit, collapsed of its own weight, sixteen million shares changing hands, he dined at Bernard Baruch's Fifth Avenue mansion. The other guests were bankers and financiers. When one rose to toast their British visitor, he addressed the company as "friends and former millionaires."[250]

* *City Lights* (1931).

Churchill visits Charlie Chaplin at his Hollywood studio

The next morning Churchill heard shouts below the Savoy-Plaza apartment and looked out, he wrote, to find that "under my window a gentleman [had] cast himself down fifteen storeys and was dashed to pieces, causing a wild commotion and the arrival of the fire brigade." Ever the curious journalist, he made his way to Wall Street. There, recognized by a stranger, he was invited inside the Stock Exchange. "I had expected to see pandemonium," he wrote, "but the spectacle that met my eyes was one of calm and orderliness." No wonder; apparently he hadn't been told that brokers are forbidden to run on the floor of the exchange, and the big sellout was over anyhow, stocks now being offered for a fraction of their value. Churchill concluded: "No one who has gazed on such a scene could doubt that this financial disaster, huge as it is, cruel as it is to thousands, is only a passing episode in the march of a valiant and serviceable people who by fierce experiment are hewing new paths for man, and showing to all nations much that they should attempt and much that they should avoid."[251]

He still hadn't made the connection, still didn't grasp that since September 3, when he had left Vancouver, Wall Street investors had lost over thirty billion dollars, almost as much as the United States had spent on World War I. Later he would realize that this "Economical Blizzard," as he came to call it, was responsible for turning all England into "one vast soup kitchen," driving the country back off the gold standard, doubling the number of British unemployed, and radicalizing politics throughout Europe, especially in Germany. In California, coming under the spell of a local stockbroker, he had been persuaded to speculate heavily. The Wall Street fever of that autumn had afflicted him; he had written his wife: "Since my last letter from Santa Barbara I have made another £1,000 by speculating in a stock called Simmons. It is a domestic furniture business. They say, 'You can't go wrong on a Simmons mattress.' There is a stock exchange [ticker] in every big hotel. You go & watch the figures being marked up on slates every few minutes. Mr Van Antwerp advises me. He is a stockbroker & one of the leading firms. I think he is a vy good man. This powerful firm watch my small interests like a cat a mouse." William Van Antwerp was a member of E. F. Hutton, a reliable company, but the most stable brokers were impotent in the panic selling of Winston's last week in New York. Though he had not been wiped out, his financial independence had disappeared in the reams of ticker tape. Throughout the coming decade he would have to write furiously to keep his family and style of living afloat. This bleak dawn was just beginning to break upon him when he sailed from New York on October 30. But when he reached Southampton he momentarily forgot it. A more immediate threat hung over the world he loved. Lord Irwin,* the new viceroy in New Delhi, had recommended "the attainment of Dominion status" as Britain's goal for its Indian Empire, Labour had endorsed Irwin's proposal, and so, without consulting other leaders of the Conservative party, had Stanley Baldwin.[252]

Describing his new Hollywood acquaintances to Clementine, Winston had written that he had entertained "the leading men I like best, mostly British born, & all keenly pro-England." Among the English expatriates there was a craggy-faced, forty-six-year-old ex-soldier named Victor McLaglen who had served three years in the Life Guards, commanded a company of the Irish Fusiliers in the Middle East during the war, and, during the months which followed the Armistice, policed Baghdad as provost marshal. After touring the Empire as a boxer, wrestler, and vaudeville stunt man, McLaglen had arrived in Hollywood and found employment on the Fox lot, where he was now rehearsing *The Black*

* In 1934 he would become Lord Halifax, and is best remembered by that title.

Watch under the direction of John Ford. A few blocks away, MGM was shooting two other motion pictures: *Trader Horn,* with W. S. Van Dyne, Harry Carey, and C. Aubrey Smith, and, simultaneously, *Son of India,* starring Smith. These three were the first in a series of films which, for the next several years, would provide millions of moviegoers with images of the glory, legends, and myths of the British Empire. They included *The Lost Patrol* (McLaglen, Gary Cooper, Boris Karloff), *Lives of a Bengal Lancer* (Cooper, Franchot Tone), *Clive of India* (Ronald Colman and Loretta Young), *Rhodes of Africa* (Walter Huston), *The Charge of the Light Brigade* (Errol Flynn), *Gunga Din* (Douglas Fairbanks, Jr., Sam Jaffe, Joan Fontaine, Cary Grant, McLaglen), *Wee Willie Winkie* (Shirley Temple, McLaglen, Smith), and *Stanley and Livingstone,* which tugged at many a heart when Spencer Tracy, courteously removing his hat, approached Sir Cedric Hardwicke and said: "Dr. Livingstone, I presume?"[253]

It was great entertainment, if poor history — Colman and Huston were not in the least like the ruthless Clive and Rhodes — and the lush California countryside was far more romantic than the stark Khyber and the African bush. But it was presented as history, something over and done with, and therein lies its real significance. No one outside England, not even Hollywood's dream merchants, could pretend that the Empire was still like that. Inside England was another matter. Opinion was divided there. Imperial destiny still had its rapt congregations in Britain, even in the Labour party; they believed that Britain's position in the world, even its self-confidence, depended upon its far-flung realms. The faithful joined the Victoria League, the United Empire League, the British Empire Union, the League of Britons Overseas, and the Empire Day movement, whose only achievement was securing a half-holiday once a year for England's schoolchildren. The Tory press, notably the *Daily Express,* remained fiercely chauvinistic. Boy Scouts, then at the height of their popularity, wore the broad-brimmed hats of the Boer War and shared their motto "Be Prepared" with the South African police. British soldiers continued to fight colonial wars in Iraq, Afghanistan, Yemen, and Palestine, battling first the Mad Mullah of Somaliland and then a Burmese monk whose followers believed he could fly if he chose, though to their disappointment he never so chose. Indeed, imperial possessions were still being acquired; the Empire reached its territorial peak in 1933 with the conquest of the Hadhramaut, a remote (and worthless) tract in southern Arabia. When a battle cruiser bearing the Prince of Wales passed through the Suez Canal and sailed down the Red Sea, with RAF biplanes forming a ceremonial umbrella overhead, native troops on both banks cheered, and in Aden the prince was greeted by massed Union Jacks and an enormous streamer: TELL DADDY WE ARE VERY HAPPY UNDER BRITISH RULE. In Buckingham Palace, Daddy addressed all his global subjects by radio every Christmas. Imperial conferences, determining policies vital to the Dominions, were still held regularly in London. So enlightened a parliamentarian as Boothby, visiting Jamaica, was reassured to see four Royal Navy battle cruisers anchored off Kingston, "one of them waving the flag of the Commander-in-Chief, West Indies Station. . . . The British Empire still existed." At No. 10 Stanley Baldwin proclaimed: "The British Empire stands firm as a great force for good. It stands in the sweep of every wind, by the wash of every sea." No public event in England was complete without a passionate chorus of "Land of Hope and Glory" or "Soldiers of the Queen," with its affirmation that "England is master" and:[254]

We're not forgetting it
We're not letting it
Fade away and gradually die

Yet Baldwin was now preparing to let the Indian Raj do just that. He wasn't moved by principle. If Churchill's symbol is the hand forming a *V* for victory, Baldwin's was the wetted forefinger held up to test the wind. He did it very well. In England, he knew, ardent imperialists were a minority. Labourites were at best indifferent to the Empire; the billion pounds invested in India wasn't theirs. The passion of the new age was egalitarian. Even among the aristocracy one found young patricians who felt guilty about their membership in a privileged class. For most postwar Britons, it seemed, imperial songs and slogans had become empty rituals; in their hearts they didn't much care. "The British were losing interest in their Empire," James Morris wrote, "and there was a falling-off of recruitment for the Indian services." By the early 1930s the Indian Civil Service had shrunk to five hundred men. In England news from remote colonies interested the older generation; their children, including Oxbridge graduates, found it rather tiresome. As late as February 9, 1933, with Hitler in power, the Oxford Union debated the resolution "that this House will in no circumstances fight for its King and Country" — and then approved it, 275 to 153. The King himself, still Emperor of India and the British Dominions beyond the Seas, wrote somberly, if awkwardly: "I cannot look into the future without feeling no little anxiety about the continued unity of the Empire." Walter Lippmann, echoing Burke while pondering the indifference or even hostility of young aristocrats to imperial strength, reminded them that no empire in history has long survived without a devoted, steadfast ruling class.[255]

The fashionable — and fashionable Englishmen have far greater influence than their counterparts in, say, the United States — rejected every symbol of the Victorian era, from oratorios and organs to antimacassars. Kipling was mocked. The Prince of Wales was popular because he himself was rebelling against the Establishment he soon would lead, it was then assumed, for the rest of his life. When abroad he flirted with unsuitable young colonial women, fox-trotted until long after midnight, and rode bucking broncos. He didn't even dress properly. Tieless, in trousers too short to cover his ankles, his cap on the back of his head, he looked far more like one of Mayfair's Bright Young Things than the royal family's heir apparent. This was not only conduct unbecoming to England's future sovereign; it was downright "un-British." His critics didn't actually mean he seemed Jewish. The term had been expanded during the 1920s. In the past, English dignity had been stiffened by the intangible concept of British national character. Even Ireland had been awed by it. The Dominions and Crown Colonies were expected, not only to admire it, but to imitate it. As the 1920s were succeeded by the 1930s it became evident that they were letting the side down, were becoming un-British. Canadians were aping the Americans; Toronto was indistinguishable from Buffalo. The Australians talked like cockneys, and loud cockneys at that. English settlers in South Africa, it was said, had become effete, unlike the robust Afrikaners. Worst of all, for those loyal to the Empire, was the mockery of imperial solemnity at home — the braying, irreverent laughter of their own intellectuals. The image of the traditional, fatherly British colonel, once exemplified by men like C. Aubrey Smith, was being replaced by David Low's Colonel Blimp, who told tedious barracks tales to obese chums in a Turkish bath. P. G. Wodehouse depicted sons of the aristocracy as weak, incompetent, dipsomaniacal clowns, and J. B. Morton — a Harrovian and an Oxonian who had led troops in France — ran mocking little pieces in the *Daily Express:* "ADVERTISEMENT CORNER: Will the gentleman who threw an onion at the Union Jack and repeatedly and noisily tore cloth during the singing of 'Land of Hope and Glory' at the Orphans' Outing on Thursday, write to Colonel Sir George Jarvis Delamaine Spooner, late of Poona, telling him what right he has to the Old Cartbusian braces which burst when he was arrested?"[256]

The Raj was the chief target of the English literati. Aldous Huxley, grandson of the great Thomas Henry, was another traitor to his class; India, he wrote, reminded him of the old man of Thermopylae, who never did anything right. "All over India," wrote George Orwell, "there are Englishmen who secretly loathe the system of which they are part." E. M. Forster's *Passage to India,* perhaps the finest English novel of the 1920s, written by a Bloomsbury author who had been private secretary to a maharaja, was a devastating, though perhaps unjust, portrayal of Indian Civil Service racism. In the eyes of such men all imperial achievements were dross. Burma was part of the Indian Empire; Orwell had served there as a policeman, and he dismissed the sum of British efforts there as "second-rate." Bombay was, in Huxley's opinion, "one of the most appalling cities in either hemisphere." The architecture of rebuilt Kuala Lumpur, the capital of British Malaya, was similarly derided, and so was New Delhi, the work of Edwin Lutyens and Sir Herbert Baker, though here the critics may have had a point. The only city expressly designed to intimidate a people, New Delhi was begun in 1911, when George V traveled there during the Coronation Durbar to lay the foundation stone, and it was finished just in time for the British to move out, an ambiguity vaguely preserved in its disconcerting Secretariat. But what dismayed traditionalists most was the intellectuals' total renunciation of every value, every standard, every icon which had been cherished in the imperial past. Nothing was sacred, not even the Crown. When George V died his last words were: "How is the Empire?" The story got around London drawing rooms and the common rooms in Oxford and Cambridge that he had actually said: "What's on at the Empire?"[257]

All this was threatening to the defenders of a rich national legacy, and it was a new experience for them. Their fathers had snorted and had ignored the Ruskins and Paters and Wildes because British supremacy, in those days, had been unquestioned. No more; since the Armistice, England had steadily lost ground to competitors abroad in virtually every field of endeavor. Yet Englishmen could not rid themselves of the old complacency. Cunarders, they told one another, were the world's finest ocean liners, and R.M.S. *Queen Mary,* now about to be launched, would set a standard none could surpass.* They were right, but steamships, like locomotives, in the construction of which the Victorians had also excelled, were not the transport of the future. Britannia had ruled the waves and the railway tracks, but was far from indomitable on highways and in the air — especially the air. Imperial Airways, Morris wrote, "enjoyed semi-official privileges," yet its management was inefficient and its schedules ridiculous; a person flying from London to Cape Town had to

* Originally she was to have been christened the *Queen Victoria.* A Cunard executive told George V that the company wanted to name her after "the greatest of all English queens." The King was delighted. "Oh," he said, "my wife *will* be pleased."

change planes six times.[258] Seasoned British travelers preferred KLM. But Britain's greatest aerial fiasco was the maiden voyage of the R 101, the costliest airship ever built in England, a few months after Churchill's return from the United States. Great hopes were reposed in the R 101. A pet project of Ramsay MacDonald's, it was expected to demonstrate Britain's enduring dominance in technology and provide mail and passenger service between Canada, South Africa, Australia, and India. This superzeppelin, powered by diesel engines, took off from Cardington in Bedfordshire on October 4, 1930, bound for Karachi, 3,652 miles away. It had traveled 300 miles when it struck a low hill on the outskirts of Beauvais, northwest of Paris, and collapsed in flames. The Empire's prime ministers, assembled in London to draft the Statute of Westminster, observed a minute of silent prayer. It should have been longer. They were mourning the passing of something far more momentous than a dirigible.

But the Dominion leaders had much to celebrate, too. In 1926 England and its white possessions had become "autonomous communities within the British Empire, equal in status, in no way subordinate to each other in any aspect of their domestic or foreign affairs, though united by a common allegiance to the Crown, and freely associated as members of the British Commonwealth of Nations." Now came the Statute of Westminster, which was just beginning its two-year progress through the parliamentary process. It was a historic measure, international in its implications, perhaps the vastest piece of legislation ever to pass through this or any other legislative body. Arthur Balfour called it "the most novel and greatest experiment in Empire-building the world has ever seen."[259] Jan Christiaan Smuts, its author, knew better. The statute was in fact a blueprint for the dismantling of the Empire. Under its terms, the Mother Country relinquished all authority over the white Dominions; laws passed by the House of Commons were inapplicable in them, and the House could not overrule acts of Dominion parliaments, which, indeed, were granted veto power over the succession to the British throne.

The Statute of Westminster was not only flexible; it was equivocal. Its language might be interpreted any way you liked. *Civis Britannicus Sum* could be translated to mean everything or nothing. A New Zealand lawyer could cite a precedent in Britain's elaborate imperial judicial system; the New Zealand judge could defer to the precedent or laugh it out of court. Ireland could and did quote the statute as justifying its complete secession from the Commonwealth, converting itself into "a sovereign, independent and democratic State."[260] While the imperial conference was deliberating over the phrasing of the statute, and the R 101 was disappearing in a bellying sheet of flame, taking forty-eight British lives with it, Mohandas Gandhi was observing his sixty-first birthday in a Poona jail. Since the statute in this early draft excluded possessions inhabited by men with pigmented skin, Gandhi and his cause, it would seem, gained nothing from it. But the language of Lord Irwin's presentation defined the Commonwealth as color-blind — if it hadn't, the pressure of twentieth-century history would have made the discrimination indefensible anyhow. Even as Victor McLaglen, Ronald Colman, and C. Aubrey Smith held audiences enthralled, the Empire they were celebrating was fading with the credits.

In every age there are certain articles of faith which society accepts unquestioningly, with or without evidence; often, indeed, in the face of inconvenient facts. The faith may be religious, moral, or political. During the last quarter of the twentieth century it has become political. Creeds, like streams, gather strength as they narrow, thriving on bigotry — at present, liberal bigotry. In our time the institution of European colonialism is condemned as an abomination. No defense of it is admissible. The transformation of former colonies into emerging nations is regarded as inherently benign, one of the few great achievements in a troubled century. Africa, we are told, is free. Certainly it is free of foreign administration, but the question of whether the people of Libya, Uganda, Angola, or Katanga enjoy political freedom — not to mention the four freedoms, from fear and want and of religion and speech, proclaimed by Churchill and Roosevelt in 1941 — is so provocative that raising it is bad taste. Yet despite the hopes raised by Gandhi and his gifted successor, Jawaharlal Nehru, the results of their statecraft are rather different from those they anticipated. The old Indian Empire is now split into five nations. In all of them the beneficence which was expected to replace the departed Raj is, if present, extremely well camouflaged. This is not an argument against the rise of national pride in what we have come to call the Third World. To disapprove of what Macmillan called "the winds of change" would be like passing judgment on the decline of Rome, the Reformation, the Renaissance, or the Industrial Revolution. History can never be put in the dock. But before examining it, one should clear the mind of cant.

In 1885 a clique of upper-class Indians established, as an annual custom, a three-day Christmas-week picnic. They called it the Indian National Congress. Except in 1906, when its members approved a mild resolution favoring some form of Indian self-government in domestic affairs, the congress had no political overtones until 1920. Nevertheless, the damage to imperial authority had been done long before that. It is obvious now that the ultimate failure of the Raj was social, not political. Lord Willingdon told Boothby he once invited a distinguished Indian prince, a friend of his, to lunch at Bombay's Yacht Club. When they were ordering drinks, a porter came over and told Willingdon: "I am sorry, your Excellency, but the secretary has asked me to tell you that niggers are not allowed in this club." Boothby himself agreed with Clemenceau's observation that Englishmen and Indians in the Raj "do not mingle at all." Had the picnickers of 1885 included English families, the congress might have remained a frolic. Like Gandhi, who conceived of England as "a land of philosophers and poets, the very centre of civilization," the original congressmen were fervent anglophiles.[261] But this, from the British point of view, was less a blessing than it seemed. The most sophisticated of them spent several years in the Mother Country — Gandhi was admitted to the Inner Temple, one of London's four law colleges ("inns of court") — or sent their sons there: Jawaharlal Nehru, like Churchill, attended Harrow. Inspired by the liberal idealism of their English teachers, they returned home with a new sense of purpose, which grew, after the Armistice, when they followed the events in Ireland with intense interest. Under Gandhi's guidance the congress became a mass movement, with Indian freedom as its objective. Motilal Nehru, Jawaharlal's father, became co-founder of the Swarajya party. *Hind Swaraj* is a subtle Hindi phrase; under Motilal it was translated as "Indian home rule," or the achievement of dominion status; later, when his son rose to power, it came to mean independence — a socialist republic.

In either case, the task confronting the congress was almost beyond imagining. Ireland was difficult, but in India the problems of nationhood were increased a thousandfold. The Raj wasn't even entirely British; France ruled five small colonies there and Portugal three. The subcontinent's vast population, which increased by some thirty-four million each decade, was divided into four dominant ethnic strains: Caucasoid, Mongoloid, Australoid, and Negroid. They spoke 225 main languages; each of the most popular 12 was the native tongue for at least ten million Indians. The illiteracy rate in the Indian Empire was 88 percent; the average diet, between six and seven hundred calories a day. Idols, and there were thousands of them, were worshiped by Hindus, Moslems, Jains, Buddhists, Sikhs, and Zoroastrians, and the possibilities for religious conflict were limitless. Moslems regarded swine as unclean. To Hindus,

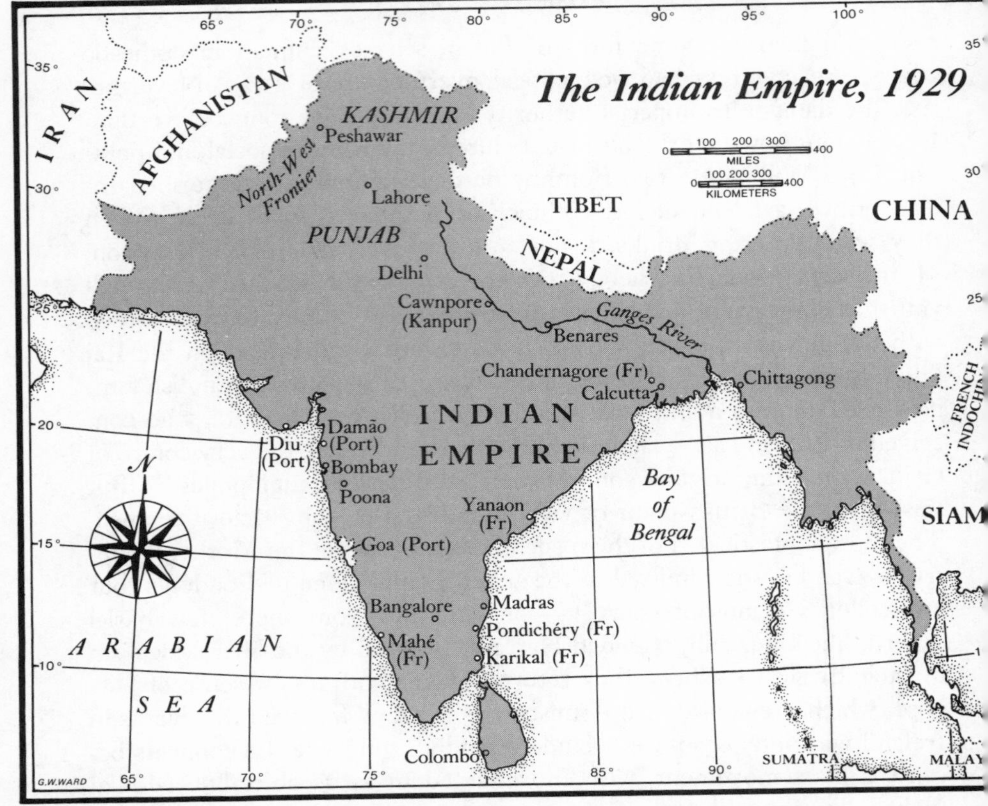

cows, monkeys, and the waters of the Ganges were sacred. Assam headhunters knelt before the skulls of their victims and chewed their fathers' bones, regarding the marrow as an aphrodisiac. To offer a Sikh a cigarette, or to light up near one of his shrines, could be suicidal. Hindus and Moslems were forever stalking one another with daggers, swords, spears, and torches. The followers of these warring faiths did not live apart; they mingled daily. Segregating them, even roughly, would require the relocation of between fourteen and sixteen million people. Moreover, native rulers and their subjects often prayed at different altars. The nawab of Junadagh was a Moslem; 81 percent of his people were Hindus. The maharaja of Kashmir was a Hindu; of his four million Kashmiris, 80 percent were Moslems. "India is an abstraction," Churchill said. "India is a geographical term. It is no more a united nation than the Equator."[262]

Two out of every three Indians were Hindus. Because of their beliefs, seven hundred million cattle roamed unharmed in a country which always teetered on the brink of starvation and sometimes plunged into famine. Hinduism is an exquisite maze of twistings and circlings and doublings-back, of poetry and philosophy and taboos, of hauntingly lovely corridors and frightening tunnels into the darker places in the human mind, and many pilgrims from the West, having studied it, have emerged the better for the journey. One of them, Frank Lloyd Wright, once told a group of fellow architects that Hindu thought takes a longer route on its way to reach a conclusion and "gathers more richness along the way." In an illustration which would almost certainly have baffled Churchill, Wright drew a diagram:[263]

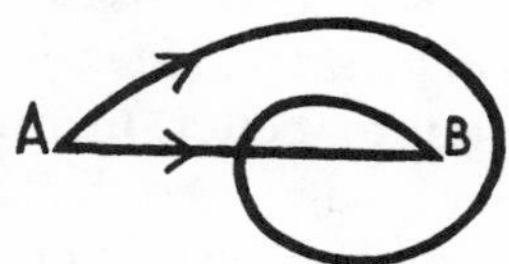

To those who have not mastered it, the reasoning in the Bhagavad-Gita or the more complex Upanishads can be immensely frustrating. A single idea sets off a series of cerebral reactions so complex that one may become quickly, and hopelessly, entangled — as in the Dharma Chakra, or Wheel of Asoka, now displayed on the Indian flag. The wheel dates from 228 B.C., and its hub, rim, and spokes blend concepts of light, truth, simplicity, compassion, renunciation, humility, faith, strength, fellowship, and interdependence, all entwined in an image which links, reinforces, and merges them. You do not have to understand it to feel its conceptual power, but the learned Hindu will pity you for your ignorance. He will also feel superior to you in other ways. High Brahmins, for example, seem to their Western friends to bathe incessantly. They are probably the cleanest people in the world. To them, Englishmen and Americans are coarse and crude, with unspeakable personal habits.

But the social expression of Hinduism is the doctrine, or, more accurately, the practice, of caste, and though its scholars find the subject distasteful, the historical origins of this pernicious system lie in a racism starker than any bigotry found in the veld of South Africa or the red clay of northern Georgia. Over a thousand years before the birth of Christ, Aryans of uncertain origins conquered the black Dravidian and Munda natives and imposed a hierarchical structure on the entire subcontinent. Brahmanism and its major gods — Siva, Vishnu, Krishna, Rama, and the creator Brahma — evolved through successive generations, but the basic principle, or lack of it, endured: the lighter your skin, the higher your caste. Historically, the four great castes are the Brahmins, scholars and priests; Kshatriyas, soldiers and administrators; Vaishyas, merchants; and Sudras, servants and manual laborers. Gandhi was a Vaishya; Nehru, a

Kashmiri Brahmin. But there are countless subcastes, including one for prostitution: if a girl is born into it, she spends her life as a whore; if the child is a boy, he will be a pimp until, having raised another generation of whores and pimps, he dies. You can see his sisters and daughters today, locked in the Cages of Bombay.* One caste makes beds, another washes dishes, a third dries them — which is why every British household in the Raj required swarms of servants. Any member of any caste would perish before moving his own garbage, which is the duty of those who have no caste at all — the Untouchables. There were between sixty and seventy million Untouchables in Gandhi's day. He called them *harijans* ("beloved of God") and worked hard to better their lot, but even Mahatma ("great-souled") Gandhi never suggested the abolition of caste, a reform which, Churchill held, would be absolutely necessary before India could be considered civilized.

Vaishyaism was not the only theological influence in Gandhi's childhood home. Jainism was also esteemed there, and his respect for it was to shape the destiny of the subcontinent. Jains believe in tolerance, vegetarianism, fasting for self-purification, and ahimsa, the doctrine of the sanctity of every living creature. A devout Jain will not even swat a mosquito. Gandhi never went that far, but his belief in nonviolence was absolute. That was why he had become a stretcher-bearer, not a soldier, in the Boer War, and *satyāgraha,* Hindi for "nonviolence," was to be his most effective tactic in the struggle for Indian independence; among its subsequent converts were American civil rights workers, who adopted it in the 1960s. Punishing a man who keeps turning the other cheek is frustrating and, eventually, pointless. Beginning in the 1920s, Raj policemen arrested thousands of the Mahatma's *satyāgrahis,* who cheerfully lined up outside prisons, waiting to be escorted to their cells. Unfortunately, the tension between Hindus and Moslems mounted as their enthusiasm for the movement grew; and the possibilities of violence multiplied. The Mahatma sought to overcome it by calling for national unity, coining the slogan *"Hindu-Moslim ek hai!"* ("Hindu and Moslem are one!") Few accepted it, however, and after a series of sinister ritualistic murders a congress mob stormed a police station in the United Provinces and slew the constables. Gandhi called off his campaign. His people, he said, had failed to grasp his message. But the British, who had been itching to get their hands on him, arrested him just the same, and on March 18, 1922, he was tried for sedition in what the docket called "Case No 45 of the Ah-

* The cages are for display purposes. They are there, not to lock the girls *in,* but to lock the customers *out* — until rupees have changed hands.

medabad Sessions, *Rex Imperator v Gandhi.*" The evidence was a series of articles he had written in his political journal, *Young India.* He pleaded guilty and asked for penal servitude: "To preach disaffection towards the existing system of Government has become almost a passion with me . . . I am here therefore to submit to the highest penalty that can be inflicted upon me, for what in law is a deliberate crime, and what appears to me to be the highest duty of a citizen." The puzzled young English magistrate paid tribute to his sincerity and sentenced him to six years, adding: "I should like to say in doing so that if the course of events in India should make it possible to reduce the period and release you, no one would be better pleased than I."[264]

Gandhi was out in two years. He found his movement was in disarray. It had split into two factions over whether or not to accept a British invitation to join local legislatures. More depressing, the enmity between Hindu and Moslem members was deepening. Gandhi fasted for three weeks; it solved nothing. In London, Birkenhead, adamantly against any concessions to congress demands, was winning every skirmish. Immediately after the war Parliament had authorized an investigation of the Indian political scene by a royal commission. Appointing the members was F.E.'s job. In 1927, after a long series of delaying actions, he named a panel of undistinguished British back-benchers — not a single Indian — under the chairmanship of Sir John Simon, of whom Birkenhead said patronizingly: "How much better in life and how much more paying it is to be blameless rather than brilliant."[265] By the fall of 1929 Simon and his colleagues (who included the still unknown Clement Attlee) were completing a ponderous document which, when published the following year, would omit any mention of dominion status, the key issue in India. Then Lord Irwin surprised everyone by facing the issue squarely. He asked Labour's William Wedgwood Benn, father of the future Tony Benn and later Birkenhead's successor in the India Office, to summon a conference which would include, not only Britons, but also members of the congress and representatives of the maharajas ruling India's princely states. Wedgwood Benn was delighted. Depressed by the stodgy Simon Commission, Labour had been searching for some way to mollify the Indian nationalists. Here, clearly, was a superb opportunity. Notice of the conference was published in the *Indian Gazette* of October 31, 1929. The same issue carried Irwin's declaration that granting dominionhood was implicit in the humane, enlightened tradition of the Raj, and Baldwin's endorsement of this position.

Uproar followed. Birkenhead furiously attacked Irwin in the House of Lords. Lord Reading, following him, said flatly: "It is frankly inconceivable that India will ever be fit for Dominion self-government." In the House of Commons, Baldwin was facing a revolt. Tories were questioning, not only his wisdom, but also his integrity. On October 23, when Winston was visiting the War Museum in Richmond, examining a tattered Confederate flag, the Conservative leader had informed the shadow cabinet of Irwin's coming statement and added that he approved of it. Churchill would disagree, of course, and so would the City, with its massive investments in the subcontinent, but Baldwin believed that the voters, weary of India, would be glad to shuck off the burden. With the exception of Sir Samuel Hoare, the prime minister's senior colleagues had told him they thought it would be a mistake to support the viceroy. They thought they had convinced him. And now he had done it anyway. Three of them threatened to resign. Faced with the possibility of a party split, he offered lame excuses. He had acted in his "personal capacity," he said, not as leader. They weren't having any of that. Then he told them he had been under the impression that Irwin had spoken out at the urging of the Simon Commission. But the commission hadn't completed its inquiries, and friends of its members knew the report would be weak. The shadow cabinet meeting broke up in confusion. To make sure his views were understood, the fourth Marquess of Salisbury, son of the great prime minister, wrote Baldwin: "*I need not say what a shock* it was to learn that the declaration was to be made before anything had been laid before the country, though we had appointed a Commission for this very purpose." He felt mortified: "What a dislocation! Poor Conservative Party!" Salisbury regarded Indian self-government as an "extreme absurdity" and hoped "you will be able to stop it, to convince the Gvt and to convince Edward Irwin that the Party will be shaken to its centre" if this line were not abandoned. He ended: "We must resist it." George Lane-Fox sent Irwin word that the Tories were "not very comfortable" with his position. Geoffrey Dawson, who thought the viceroy was right, nevertheless wrote him: "The tide here is running pretty strongly against your ideas, and you cannot hope to carry them out by depending on the Labour Party alone."[266]

Baldwin refused to budge. As leader of the Conservatives and a superb politician, he had resources stronger than his party critics', even though they constituted, at that time, a majority. The whips belonged to him, and also the party machine, including the constituency committees and associations. He could count on the support of *The Times* and of Reith at the BBC. Most of his MPs were indebted to him in one way or another. He called in these IOUs and had just about suppressed the rebellion when, on Tuesday, November 5, Winston Churchill returned from the United States.

Earlier, Irwin had urged Churchill to update his views on India by talking to some members of the congress. Winston had replied: "I am quite satisfied with my views on India, and I don't want them disturbed by any bloody Indians." Since leaving Bangalore in 1899 he had taken little interest in the subcontinent. He seems to have been unaware that the Simon Commission and all that followed were the consequences of a pledge made by Lloyd George in 1917, defining England's aim in India as "the granting of self-governing institutions with a view to the progressive realisation of responsible Government in India as an integral part of the British Empire." But although Winston had seldom thought of the Raj, his feelings about it were strong. No Englishman was more persuaded of Queen Victoria's wisdom in saying, "I think it very unwise to give up what we hold." Indeed, that summed up his attitude toward the entire Empire. He considered it, among other things, a matter of national self-interest. To Churchill, Amery observed, "England is still the starting point and the ultimate object of policy." The Empire gave Britain its prestige; it made Britain the world's most powerful nation. Without its imperial possessions the country would be merely an obscure island lying off the European continent. England deprived of its imperial possessions would, for him, be like Samson shorn of his hair or Antaeus without his feet on earth. Moreover, his vision of India, in particular, was crowned by a romantic nimbus. It was the magic land he had known as an impressionable young cavalry officer, a realm of rajas' palaces, the Taj, shikar, bazaars, fakirs, temples, shrines, and howdahs, a symbol of imperial splendor and proud glory, Britian's most priceless possession. To yield it, he said, would be "a hideous act of self-mutilation."[267]

Many, including some who were close to him, concluded that he lived in the past, a "mid-Victorian," as Amery called him in August 1929, "steeped in the politics of his father's period, and unable ever to get the modern view." Certainly Churchill often quoted pronouncements about the subcontinent made long ago by men now deep in their graves. One of them, indeed, was Lord Randolph: "Our rule in India is, as it were, a sheet of oil spread out over and keeping free from storms a vast and profound ocean of humanity." Another was Lord Morley: "There is a school of thought who say that we might wisely walk out of India and that the Indians could manage their own affairs better than we can. Anybody who pictures to himself the anarchy, the bloody chaos that would follow from any such deplorable step might shrink from that sinister decision." And, from J. R. Seeley's *Expansion of England,* published in 1883, when Winston was an Ascot schoolboy, he remembered the judgment that British withdrawal from the subcontinent would be "the most inexcusable of all conceivable crimes and might possibly cause the most stupendous of all conceivable calamities."[268]

There was another side to this, and it should be examined thoughtfully. As a boy at the Crystal Palace Winston had described the ruffian who accosted Count Kinsky as a "sort of Kaffir" and a "Mulatto." In Cuba, fresh out of Sandhurst, he had distrusted "the negro element among the insurgents." He never outgrew this prejudice. Late in life he was asked if he had seen the film *Carmen Jones.* He had walked out on it, he replied, because he didn't like "blackamoors." His physician was present, and Winston asked what happened when blacks got measles. Could the rash be spotted? The doctor replied that blacks suffered a high mortality rate from measles. Churchill said lightly, "Well, there are plenty left. They've got a high rate of production."[269] He could greet Louis Botha and Michael Collins as equals, but his relationship with any Indian, even an accomplished barrister like Gandhi or a fellow Harrovian like Nehru, could never be as between compeers. It followed, therefore, that their country must remain a vassal state. This was the underside of his position in the great debates over India's future which began in 1929. Today it would be called an expression of racism, and he, as its exponent, a racist. But neither word had been coined then; they would not appear in the Oxford English dictionary or Webster's for another generation. Until recently — beginning in the late 1940s — racial intolerance was not only acceptable in polite society; it was fashionable, even assumed.

The popularity of prejudice when Parliament was pondering the India question is demonstrated by the extraordinary success of Katherine Mayo's *Mother India,* which went through forty printings in the 1920s. Churchill read it in 1927, as two notes by Chartwell visitors attest. On August 10 Victor Cazalet reported that his host "admires the book *Mother India* very much," and on September 27 Lord Lloyd wrote: "I was staying a weekend recently with Winston who was immediately struck with Mother India — Miss Mayo's book. It's all true." Viewed from the 1980s, her work seems almost comparable to the *Protocols of Zion.* Vile in its insinuations, wildly inaccurate, and above all hypocritical, this single volume by an elderly prig poisoned the minds of millions who might otherwise have reflected thoughtfully on Gandhi's movement. Her case against the Hindu custom of child marriage is indisputable, but she did not stop there. Hindu mothers, she said, taught their sons and daughters to masturbate. Citing "highest medical authority," she charged that every child practicing onanism "bears on its body the signs of this habit," and that "when constantly practiced during mature life," which she declared was the case in India, "its devastation of body and nerves will scarcely be questioned." This chapter ends: "Given men who enter the world physical bankrupts out of bankrupt stock, rear them through childhood in influences and practices that devour their vitality; launch them at the dawn of maturity on an unrestrained outpouring of their whole provision of creative energy in one single direction; find them, at an age when the Anglo-Saxon is just coming into full glory of manhood, broken-nerved, low-spirited, petulant ancients; and need you, while this remains unchanged, seek for other reasons why they are poor and sick and dying and why their hands are too weak, too fluttering, to seize the reins of Government?" "Miss Mayo has dropped a brick," Irwin wrote Neville Chamberlain. "It will make the Hindus of course see red." Winston Churchill, being a larger figure than Katherine Mayo, dropped a bigger brick by sanctioning it. The same can be said of liberal men and women on both sides of the Atlantic who accepted her vicious fantasy without demur. The *Spectator* observed that "the evils which Miss Mayo attacks are widespread and deep-rooted," and that until they had been expunged, "India can hardly take the place that she ought to occupy in the family of nations." *Survey*'s reviewer called the book "challenging, prickly with facts and neglected angles of approach. . . . I confess I learned more from this book on the inner Indian and why the East is East than I ever knew before." The leftist *New Statesman* described it as "the most important and truthful book that has been written about India for a good deal more than a generation." Across the Atlantic, the *New Republic* welcomed it. *Outlook* found it "free from sentimentalism, artisanship, and preconceived notions. It is a straight-forward account." *Catholic World* commented: "There is no gainsaying her statements." To the *New York Herald Tribune, Mother India* was "calm, hard-headed — though not hard-hearted." The *New York Times* reported: "Her detachment is obvious. If she quotes, she gives her authority. If she describes, it is an eyewitness. The facts that she states are not likely to be disputed."[270]

Churchill, however, always had second and third thoughts, and they usually improved as he went along. It was part of his pattern of response to any political issue that while his early reactions were often emotional, and even unworthy of him, they were usually succeeded by reason and generosity. Given time, he could devise imaginative solutions. Russia had been more than he could handle — though it should be remembered that he would have been content to see a socialist regime there provided it renounced wholesale slaughter — but his record had been impressive in South Africa, the Middle East, and Ireland. He was prepared to accept provincial self-government in India provided Britain retained certain rights of "paramountcy," including control of foreign affairs, communications, and defense. What he could not overlook was that India, Gandhian *satyāgraha* notwithstanding, was a land of violence. Even as Churchill was binding up his loins to confront Baldwin in the House, Indian terrorists tried to assassinate Irwin, of all people, as the viceregal train entered Delhi. (Churchill cabled Irwin congratulations on his escape; the viceroy, who himself was not untainted by racial condescension, replied that, luckily for him, Indians "seem to be less efficient in their execution than in their design.") Bengalis then raided an arsenal in Chittagong, killing eight British guards. An uprising in Peshawar left thirty dead. After a terrorist had been executed in Cawnpore (now Kanpur), Hindus rioted and murdered over three hundred Moslems. Churchill said: "Wednesday's massacres at Cawnpore, a name of evil import" — in June 1857 the British community there had been wiped out by mutineers who, legend has it, threw their corpses down a well — "are a portent. Because it is believed that we are about to leave the country, the struggle for power is now beginning between the Moslems and Hindus. . . . The British troops are now pacifying and calming the terrified and infuriated populace. But the feud is only at its beginning." His dire warning outraged leaders of the congress, and was discounted by Wedgwood Benn and Baldwin. Today it is discredited; in 1967 Professor Arno J. Mayer of Princeton wrote that the freeing of India "never produced any of the dire consequences predicted by Churchill." But it did. Eighteen years after his warning, when the Raj ended and the last British soldiers sailed from Bombay, over two million Hindus and Moslems were slain during six months of savagery. Like Turkey's slaughter of the Armenians, the Russian civil war, and the destruction of the European Jews in the early 1940s, it was a great human disaster; in a word, a holocaust.[271]

Back in England with Hearst and Wall Street behind him, Churchill took the boat train from Southampton, reaching Venetia Montagu's house on the evening of Tuesday, November 5. Clementine had told him that a half-dozen worried Tories awaited him in the drawing room. They thought Baldwin wrong about India but were concerned about party reprisals. Not to worry, Winston told them cheerfully; he would stand alone, if necessary, and speak for all of them. As it happened, he had company. Lloyd George, though his powers were waning, was still effective and beyond Baldwin's reach. The debate on the Irwin declaration opened on Friday. MacDonald spoke for it; Baldwin announced that the Conservatives supported him. George then rose to reply. Davidson wrote that Churchill had "sat through S.B.'s speech glowering and unhappy" but he leaned "forward during the 'Goat's' speech cheering every mischievous passage in it." Davidson estimated that at least a third of the Tory MPs would vote against the declaration. They had listened glumly to their leader; their applause for him had been perfunctory. Dawson wrote Irwin: "The naked truth is that his speech, to which I listened, was heard in almost icy silence by the House." Hoare wrote: "It is certainly true that scarcely anyone in the party liked it. The diehards were much upset and . . . Austen, FE, Winston and Worthy [Sir Laming Worthington-Evans] were violently opposed to it." Hoare thought he himself had been "the only supporter of Stanley's attitude." It was his impression that "Winston was almost demented with fury." Lane-Fox observed that "there were several people such as Winston and Worthy whom I saw and heard crying 'No.' " Had there been a vote, he thought, half the Tory MPs would have defected, but he felt confident that "since they have had time to think, the vast majority of the Conservatives have returned to their loyalty to SB."[272]

Churchill's first attack on the declaration came, not on the floor of the House, but in the columns of the *Daily Mail*. It appeared on November 16, establishing a position on the issue from which he never wavered. Britain's "rescue of India from ages of barbarism, internecine war, and tyranny," he wrote, "and its slow but ceaseless forward march to civilisation" constituted "upon the whole the finest achievement of our history." Now it was "the duty of public men and women to make it plain without delay that the extension of Dominion Status to India is not practicable at the present time and that any attempt to secure it will encounter the earnest resistance of the British nation." Self-government was unthinkable for a community which "treats sixty millions of its members, toiling at their side, as 'Untouchables,' whose approach is an affront and whose very presence is a pollution," and it was absurd to contemplate it "while India is a prey to fierce racial and religious dissensions and when the withdrawal of British protection would mean the immediate resumption of medieval ways." If the viceregal proposal were adopted the British Raj would be replaced by a "Gandhi Raj" because "the political classes in India represent only an insignificant fraction of the three hundred and fifty millions for whose welfare we are responsible." England could not, and indeed should not, "close the long avenues of the future." But the idea that "Home Rule for India or Dominion Status or full responsible status for India can emerge from anything that is now being done is not only fantastic in itself but criminally mischievous in its effects."[273]

The struggle over Indian self-government mounted throughout 1930 and was fought against a background of tumultuous events. The Cawnpore riots resumed and the death toll passed one thousand, Afridi tribesmen emerged from the hills and attacked a strong British garrison in Peshawar, and Gandhi delivered his most brilliant political stroke, his Salt March to the Indian Ocean. He had been searching for some way to make his movement comprehensible to the masses. The Raj held a monopoly on the production and sale of salt. But salt should be free, said the Mahatma; the seas alone held enough to satisfy the world's population a thousand times over. So he began his trek on March 12, scooping a spoonful of salt from brackish earth along the way. He never reached the seaside. While sleeping by a river, he was arrested by nervous British policemen; they had arrived stealthily in the middle of night to avoid a riot. But the Salt March continued without him. His original spoonful was sold for sixteen hundred rupees. Professors led their students to the shore. The Raj banned newspapers congratulating them. Indian youths raided a Raj salt depot. The British police responded with brutality and mass arrests; by the end of May, 100,000 Gandhi followers were behind bars, Nehru among them. He wrote his leader, who was cheerfully spinning cotton in another prison: "May I congratulate you on the new India you have created by your magic touch?"[274]

Churchill's response to all this was that the viceroy had asked for it. His declaration had displayed weakness; enemies of the Raj were exploiting it. The Afridis had stormed Peshawar because they had been encouraged to believe that "Lord Irwin's Government was clearing out of India, and that rich spoils lay open to their raids." During his service on the frontier, before the turn of the century, the fathers of these tribesmen had hidden in the hills. To hunt them had been "like going into the water to fight a shark." Now they were witnessing "the shark coming out to the beach." To Boothby he wrote that it would be "easy . . . to crush Gandhi and the Congress." The party should be broken up and its leaders exiled to another British possession. The difficulty, as he saw it, was the indecisiveness of MacDonald's government and the lack of leadership on either side of the House. "When eagles are silent," he said, "the parrots begin to jabber." On September 28 he distributed a brief statement to the press declaring that he would remain in public life until the India issue was settled. Lord Burnham, owner of the *Daily Telegraph* and a Tory ally, wrote him that "the scales are most unfairly weighted against such of us as believe that our betrayal of India would be a crime against civilisation. . . . The real tragedy is that India is crying out to be governed and we refuse to govern." Burnham added: "F. E.'s illness is a great blow."[275]

F.E.'s death, which swiftly followed, was a far greater blow. He was relatively young — still in his fifties — and to Churchill he had almost been a member of the family. On October 1 Clementine wrote Margaret Smith, Lady Birkenhead: "Last night Winston wept for his friend. He said several times 'I feel so lonely.' " F.E., secure in the House of Lords, had confidently led the defenders of the Raj; now they turned to Winston. Churchill's position in the Commons, very different from his lost friend's, was growing more difficult every week. Yet he could see no alternative. He wrote: "When I think of the way in which we poured out blood and money to take Contalmaison or to hold Ypres, I cannot understand why it is that we should now throw away our conquests and our inheritance with both hands, through helplessness and pusillanimity." On September 24 he had written Baldwin: "What times we live in! The most serious of all our problems is India. I am now receiving, in consequence of my speeches, streams of letters from our people in India and the feeling of anxiety that we are being let down. . . . I do earnestly hope that you will not allow your friendship with Irwin to affect your judgement or the action of your party upon what, since the War, is probably the greatest question Englishmen have had to settle. Very strong currents of feeling and even passion are moving under the stagnant surface of our affairs, and I must confess myself to care more about this business than anything else in public life."[276]

Baldwin was unmoved. He had already confided to a friend that if he formed another government, Churchill would not be part of it. Winston's incapacity for teamwork, he said, far outweighed his talents. Clementine saw what was coming. Politics, she wrote their son, "have taken an orientation not favourable to Papa." India was the main issue, but Baldwin, strongly supported by the shadow cabinet in this instance, endorsed high tariffs. Churchill protested. On October 14 the two men held a long private talk and agreed that there was a definite breach between them. That evening Baldwin wrote Churchill of his "profound regret that there is a real parting of the ways and a friendship towards you which has grown up through six years of loyal and strenuous work together." He insisted that he continued to "cherish the hope that you may yet see your way to stay with us," but by his actions he was sabotaging that hope, if indeed it existed. The Tory tariff policy remained unchanged, and Winston contemplated resignation from the shadow cabinet. He was nudged again when Lord Lloyd, the strong British high commissioner in Cairo, was recalled with Baldwin's approval as the first step in the evacuation of all British troops, except those in the canal zone, from Egypt. "During the last forty years," a furious Churchill told the House, "everything has turned upon the British garrison in Cairo. With its departure the once glorious episode of England in Egypt comes to an end. It is not without a bitter pang that I contemplate this." He observed that "there is a sombre philosophy nowadays which I hear in some quarters about Egypt and India. It is said: 'Give them all they ask for! Clear out and let things go to smash, and then there will be a case for us to come back again!' " Such a doctrine, he said, "is no foundation for the continuance of British fame and power. Once we lose our confidence in our mission in the East . . . it will be a presence which cannot long endure."[277]

Baldwin wrote a friend that Churchill wanted "to go back to pre-war and govern with a strong hand. He has become once more the subaltern of hussars of '96." But Winston was far from alone. The very die-hard members of the party to whom he had once been anathema founded the Indian Empire Society and invited him to address their first meeting. It was held in London's Cannon Street Hotel, hard by St. Paul's, on December 12, 1930. They wanted powerful political medicine, and he believed he knew the prescription. In Lahore, Kipling's beloved citadel in the Punjab, members of the congress had burned the Union Jack. Their meeting, said Winston, should have been "broken up and its leaders deported." Gandhi had been treated far too leniently in the beginning; he should have been arrested and tried "as soon as he broke the law." Even now, firm measures, demonstrating Parliament's resolve "to govern and guide the destinies of the Indian people in faithful loyalty to Indian interest," could, perhaps within a few months, "bring this period of tantalized turmoil to an end." Each Indian province should be given "more real, more intimate, more representative organs of self-government," leaving the central authority in the hands of the Raj. But there could be no compromise with "the forces of sedition and outrage," because "the truth is that Gandhi-ism and all it stands for will, sooner or later, have to be grappled with and finally crushed. It is no use trying to satisfy a tiger by feeding him with cat's meat. The sooner this is realised, the less trouble and misfortune will there be for all concerned."[278]

"What a monstrous speech Winston has just made," Irwin wrote Geoffrey Dawson at *The Times*. Dawson, agreeing, ran an editorial declaring that Churchill was "no more representative of the Conservative Party" than "the assassins of Calcutta" were of the Indian Congress, and his speech would "have just as little influence." Dawson and his fellow lords of the British media were doing something about this last. Churchill wanted to address the nation on the issue. He offered Sir John Reith £100 for ten minutes on the BBC. Reith, like any trapped civil servant, scurried to higher authority, in this case Wedgwood Benn, who replied that he felt "most apprehensive" at the prospect of Winston on the air; he was afraid the consequence would do "immense harm to India." Reith thereupon rejected Churchill's proposal, explaining that he opposed "American" broadcasting methods. This, Winston said, was an "oppressive decision." He thought "the American plan would be better than the present British methods of debarring public men from access to a public who wish to hear"; when "an Imperial issue like the discharge of our mission in India is being debated, it seems to me that at least an equal solicitude for impartiality is required from you." The Establishment was closing ranks against him. News accounts of his speeches in Parliament shrank and appeared deeper and deeper in newspapers' inside pages. He protested to Rothermere of the *Daily Mail* that they were "the only weapon I have for fighting this battle." If the *Mail* buried its accounts of them, "Baldwin with the Times at his back is master of the fate of India." Gagged, he struggled on, addressing the Indian Empire Society twice more, always assailing Gandhi, whose cause and dedication were incomprehensible to him. In his view the Mahatma was "a malignant and subversive fanatic," a cynical manipulator of "Brahmins who mouth and patter principles of Western Liberalism and pose as philosophic and democratic politicians." And all the time he continued to attend meetings of the shadow cabinet. If his colleagues felt awkward, he was not in the least embarrassed. As he saw it he was true to the widow's uniform he had once worn:[279]

Dear-bought and clear, a thousand year,
Our fathers' title runs.
Make we likewise their sacrifice,
Defrauding not our sons.

As the rift grew between Baldwin and Churchill, Conservative MPs were faced with the nightmare of every workaday politician: the obligation to choose sides in an intramural quarrel. Some found it relatively easy. Lord Weir thought Britain needed "inspiration" and Winston could provide it. Lord Knutsford wrote him: "Some day you must lead the whole country. I look for this." But others were more vulnerable. Neville Chamberlain privately wrote a young MP on November 29: "I, myself, would very much prefer to go more slowly in the matter of Indian reform, and try a series of cautious experiments, which might perhaps last for fifty years or more, before culminating in a complete system of Central and Provincial self-government." Publicly, however, Chamberlain was among Baldwin's most enthusiastic backers. Lane-Fox wrote Irwin that the party was "not very comfortable" with his declaration, and in another letter told him: "The average Conservative was of course rather shocked by the way in which Gandhi was originally allowed to break the law in the matter of his salt campaign and march to the sea." A clear majority of the Tory MPs thought Churchill right, but most of them had too much to lose to say so. Despite their convictions, men like Chamberlain persuaded themselves that they were bound by a higher loyalty to oppose, in his words, those who were "either hostile" to their leaders "or disposed to join cliques led by men whose motives are much more complicated." This last referred to the possibility that Winston was planning a revolt, deliberately dividing the party, as his father had, hoping to reach No. 10 through a coup. Davidson put it bluntly in a letter to Irwin: "Winston's game, of course, has been obvious, as it always is. He is not the son of Randolph for nothing." Beaverbrook thought Churchill's stand revealed "a defect of character" and a willingness "to take up anything as long as it leads to power"; that he had changed "party, political friends and political dogmas so often" that his credibility was "nearly gone." At present, said Beaverbrook, he was "trying to make a corner for himself in Indian affairs. He is now taking up the stand of a veritable die-hard. But," he concluded, "he does not carry conviction. . . . His voice lacks that note of sincerity for which the country looks." Irwin disagreed. To him, Churchill presented a real threat. Irwin noted that at least twenty times between March and December Winston had challenged the leadership's position on India, and, on each occasion, Baldwin had barely mustered a majority of Tories.[280]

Clearly a break between Churchill and him was imminent. Yet where could Winston go? In 1904 he had crossed to the Liberals; in 1924, back to the Conservatives. But Labour was now the Opposition, and he and they glared at one another from opposite ends of the parliamentary spectrum. Therefore his only choice was what political journalists call "the wilderness" — the cold, bleak, barren limbo of discredited or incompetent MPs whom no party wants. Nevertheless, no one can doubt that he was moved by a genuine conviction. That cannot be said of those with whom he was parting company. The Tory leaders were uninspired by Indian nationalism. One searches in vain for ringing affirmations of freedom or admiration for Gandhian saintliness in their speeches, letters, and diaries. What comes through, like the pounding on a wall of a man who wants the party in the next apartment to quiet down so he can sleep, is a determination to avoid discord, unpleasantness, or any rude interruption of long serene weekends in the country. England's ruling class, or those of them in power, had lost their fathers' inflexible determination. A. G. Gardiner had described the English patrician as "a personality that is entirely fearless," belonging to "a caste that never doubts itself." A. L. Rowse, fellow of All Souls College, Oxford, quotes Gardiner and then adds: "Never till 1931, we may say; for in that year the caste lost confidence in itself and, undermined by fear, it lost not only confidence but conscience. Confused in mind about everything, except the main chance — its own preservation — it survived from year to year, from month to month, from day to day, by blurring the clarity of all issues, even the most dangerous — that of the nation's safety; it maintained its enormous majority by electoral trickery, it spoke and perhaps thought in the language of humbug, it hoped to stave off conflict . . . by offering appeasement."[281]

By January 8, 1931, Churchill had made his decision. He foresaw MacDonald's fall and the formation of a new government, but, he wrote his son, "I have no desire to join such an administration and be saddled with all the burden of whole-hog Protection, plus unlimited doses of Irwinism for India. I shall be much more able to help the country from outside." The "breaking-point in my relation with Mr Baldwin," as he later called it, came less than three weeks later. Irwin wanted to lay the foundations for his "round-table" conference with the congress leaders, to be held in London. To clear the air he planned to release Gandhi from jail, and on January 23 he cabled Baldwin: "My immediate fear is lest, in the forthcoming debate in Parliament, Winston should make mischief. Do, if you can, get some helpful and cordial speeches made from our side to discount possible bad effect of what he may say. Best of all, speak yourself and send him to Epping for the day."[282]

Gandhi was freed forty-eight hours later. Outraged Raj officials in India and Conservative associations throughout England were speechless. Churchill, of course, was not. On the evening of Monday, January

26, he rose in the House and — his other remarks on India having been delivered elsewhere, "out of doors," in the parliamentary expression, and therefore being forgivable — took his first fateful step into the wilderness. "I must of course first of all make it clear," he said at the outset, "that I do not speak for the official Opposition nor for my right hon[orable] friend the Leader of the Opposition." He spoke, he said, "solely as a Member of Parliament, of some service in this House," whose views ought not to go "unrepresented in this discussion." He then laced into the viceroy's declaration, deplored the tabling of the Simon Report, and criticized the government's decision to bar Simon and his fellow commissioners from the round table. "Our trusted friends and lawful, formal authoritative advisers are set aside," he charged, "in order to placate those who are the bitterest opponents of British rule in India." The promise of dominion status was to be laid before "the gleaming eyes of excitable millions" while sixty thousand Indian agitators were locked up, a situation virtually without precedent, at least since the Mutiny. To imagine that these resentful men would emerge docile was, he thought, absurd. Britons should not permit themselves "to be edged, pushed, talked and cozened out of India." After two hundred years of fidelity and achievement, and thousands of British soldiers' lives sacrificed "on a hundred fields," Englishmen had earned "rights of our own in India." Public opinion in the United Kingdom would not tolerate the spectacle of British women and children "in hourly peril amidst the Indian multitudes," yet this was the future to which, "step by step and day by day, we are being remorselessly and fatuously conducted."[283]

By custom, either MacDonald or Wedgwood Benn should have replied to him. Baldwin did it instead. His decision was unwise; he answered Winston's rolling, cadenced rhetoric with a meandering, legalistic defense of the round table. Lane-Fox reported to Irwin that "while S.B. was vigorously cheered by the Socialists, there was an ominous silence on our benches. And I am afraid this represents the position in our party on many things." Nevertheless, it was Churchill who had sinned, and now he must pay the forfeit for flagrant disobedience of his party's leader. Tuesday morning Lord Hailes approached him, like a summons server, with the formal request for his resignation from the shadow cabinet. Afterward Hailes set down Winston's reaction. "Face reddened then went white. Pouted furiously. Walked to a corner of the room, picked up his silver knobbed cane, came back and brought the cane down full force on the table. As he looked at me, I imagined that I might be the next victim. Then his face suddenly puckered into a smile. 'So the Conservative P. wants to get rid of me, does it? All right, I'll go quietly now.' " He scrawled a paragraph to Baldwin: "Now that our divergences of view upon India policy have become public" — persisting in the quaint conceit that nothing in British politics becomes public until uttered in the House — "I feel that I ought not any longer to attend the meetings of your 'Business Committee' to which you have hitherto so kindly invited me." Baldwin replied on Wednesday: "I am grateful to you for your kind letter of yesterday and much as I regret your decision not to attend the meetings of your old colleagues, I am convinced that your decision is correct in the circumstances."[284]

Churchill's departure left the shadow chancellorship vacant. To fill the void, Baldwin appointed Neville Chamberlain.

Churchill's parliamentary career had come to resemble the Greek legend of Sisyphus, who was condemned to toil up a steep hill pushing a huge stone which, just before he reached the top, always rolled back to the bottom. Twice he had been regarded as England's next prime minister, first as a Liberal, then as a Conservative. Now he was once more cut off from all inner political councils. But during those first months in the wilderness he felt unfettered, exhilarated, free to loose verbal thunderbolts whenever so moved. Young MPs who thought they had heard Churchillian philippics at their most venomous now learned otherwise. When Gandhi arrived in Delhi to meet Irwin, Winston thundered: "It is alarming and also nauseating to see Mr Gandhi, a seditious Middle Temple lawyer, now posing as a fakir of a type well-known in the East, striding half-naked up the steps of the Vice-regal palace, while he is still organising and conducting a defiant campaign of civil disobedience, to parley on equal terms with the representative of the King-Emperor." And even as die-hard back-benchers howled with appreciative laughter, they were shocked at the cruel attack on MacDonald, the titular prime minister, who was permitting Baldwin to run his government. Winston told the House: "I spoke the other day, after he had been defeated in an important division, about his wonderful skill in falling without hurting himself. He falls, but he comes up again smiling, a little dishevelled but still smiling." Then, staring at MacDonald across the well, he continued: "I remember when I was a child being taken to the celebrated Barnum's Circus which contained an exhibition of freaks and monstrosities, but the exhibit on the programme which I most desired to see was the one described as 'The Boneless Wonder.' My parents judged that the spectacle would be too revolting and demoralizing for my youthful eyes, and I have waited fifty years to see the Boneless Wonder sitting on the Treasury Bench."[285]

Epping staunchly supported its member. His constituents, he wrote Clementine, were "loving, ardent, and unanimous." Indeed, he believed there was "no doubt that the whole spirit of the Conservative party is with me, and that much of their dissatisfaction with S.B. turns itself into favour with me." This was no illusion; that same week the party's principal agent wrote Neville Chamberlain: "Many of our supporters are worried about the question of India. They lean much more towards the views of Mr Churchill than to those expressed by Mr Baldwin in the House of Commons." Nevertheless, when a Gandhi-Irwin pact was signed in early March — the Mahatma agreed to call off all *satyāgraha* and attend the round-table conference in London to discuss India's future — Baldwin endorsed it. He opened the House debate on March 12 and was followed by Wedgwood Benn, who accused Winston of advocating a policy of "the lathi, the bayonet, the machine-gun and artillery." Churchill reminded the House of his speech in the Dyer debate and his repeated opposition to "brutal force in India," and pointed out that most of the Indians who had died over the past year had been killed, not by British troops, but in "religious fights" between Moslems and Hindus. It was all true. Yet the feeling persisted that he was scheming for power. Leo Amery wrote in his diary that upon leaving Parliament he had "heard Winston haranguing a press correspondent in the Lobby to the effect that he was not going to let India be betrayed without telling England all about it. I am afraid we are in for some difficulties over the India business. Winston has chosen his moment and his excuse for separating with the Party very adroitly."[286]

He enjoyed frequent successes. At his urging Lord Lloyd agreed to challenge Baldwin in the party's India Committee, and at one point Lloyd mustered a majority of diehards against the round table. "Winston has done a good deal to corrupt them," Dawson wrote Irwin. Churchill's eloquent plea for the Untouchables was particularly effective. ("A multitude as big as a nation, men, women and children deprived of hope and of the status of humanity. Their plight is worse than that of slaves, because they have been taught to consent not only to a physical but to a psychic servitude and prostration.") The *Daily Mail* and the *Daily Express* provided him with such full coverage that Baldwin, like virtually all leaders stung by a free press, protested. "What the proprietorship of the papers is aiming at," he charged, "is power and power without responsibility — the prerogative of the harlot." At the Albert Hall, Tory back-benchers heard Churchill describe how dissent was being suppressed by the alliance of political chieftains now sharing the same nest. Baldwin had "decided that we are to work with the Socialists, and that we must make our action conform with theirs. We therefore have against us at the present time the official machinery of all the three great parties in the State. We meet under a ban. Every Member of Parliament or Peer who comes here must face the displeasure of the party Whips." In the House, despite jeers, hostile interruptions, and outbursts, he roared until he was heard: "By your actions you have produced misery such as India has not seen for half a century. You have poisoned relations between the Mohammedans and the Hindus." Then he flourished photographs of Indian corpses mutilated in the communal killings, pictures taken on the spot which were, he cried, "so revolting that no paper would be able to publish them." All spring and throughout the summer he kept up his drumfire, and in the *Daily Mail* of September 7, when Gandhi was on his way to London — no other Indian politician accompanied him; he alone would speak for India's 350 million — Churchill warned that the round table would lead to "nothing but further surrenders of British authority." Without the "guidance and control" of the Raj, he wrote, such "pure savagery" as the Cawnpore killings would be repeated all over the subcontinent, an inevitable consequence of unchecked Hinduism and its "whole apparatus," as represented at Benares on the Ganges, "with its palaces and temples, its shrines and its burning ghats, its priests and ascetics, its mysterious practices and multiform ritual . . . unchanged through the centuries, untouched by the West."[287]

This was Churchill at his most effective. His prose soared. His commitment was total. At that time, on that issue, he was speaking for most Englishmen. And yet . . .

It was all as sounding brass or a tinkling cymbal. The public was distracted by the growing financial crisis. The House had wearied of India. Lloyd George had to enter the hospital for a major operation; Churchill, ostracized, left for Chartwell. Britain therefore was deprived of the two authentic geniuses in its public life; "as we have said several times in the last few days," Hoare wrote Neville Chamberlain on August 31, "we have had some great good luck in the absence of Winston and L.G." Thus Baldwin and MacDonald were free to pursue their separate grails: business as usual for Baldwin; disarmament for MacDonald. Winston returned and spent six months trying to pry them apart, but Baldwin ignored him, attending the round-table talks and accepting Labour's lead in the conferences with Gandhi, while MacDonald — who never forgave him for the Boneless Wonder gibe — lost his poise but once. Baited by

Brendan Bracken, who was quoting Churchill, the prime minister glared at Bracken and shouted, "You swine!" — an indiscretion which, Dawson being away for the time, appeared in *The Times,* to Winston's delight. Some senior Tories worried about their restless back-benchers. Sir Malcolm Hailey wrote of the round-table discussion that he was "beginning to feel" that Baldwin "may not have been quite correct in believing that he could carry the whole of the Conservative Party in any decision at which he might arrive." He concluded, however, that "the general block" of Tory MPs were likelier to follow the leader than be "swayed by the very extreme views of Winston Churchill." Seeing Winston isolated, others were reluctant to join him in Coventry. Churchill, their elders told them, was a rogue elephant, an opportunist; his pleas for Indian minorities, his support of Indian self-government on the local level, and his prediction of a bloodbath should the Raj leave were dismissed as wily diversions or hyperbole. He wrote Boothby: "Politics are very interesting. My late colleagues are more interested in doing me in than in any trifling questions connected with India or tariffs."[288]

They were careful not to accost him in the House, where he was at his most dangerous. After one of his most effective speeches, Wedgwood Benn completely ignored his arguments and evasively replied that although Winston had "entered the Irish Conference with a dripping sword, he emerged with a dripping pen, and I am not without hope that even here, as he did in the Irish case, he will come in this matter to a better judgment." Baldwin blunted his thrusts with sweeping generalizations. Ignoring the issue of Indian independence, he said that it was England's aim to introduce "self-governing institutions" to the subcontinent "with a view to the progressive realisation of responsible Government in India as an integral part of the British Empire" — an Empire which, although he did not say so, the Statute of Westminster, not to mention future events, would eventually dismantle. He said: "We have impregnated India ourselves with Western ideas, and, for good or ill, we are reaping the fruits of our own work." But only a fraction of the subcontinent's population had been exposed to Western thought, and it was this elite which would rule India when the Raj pulled out.* Baldwin thought the House should agree "to keep India out of party politics." It had been in party politics for three centuries; if Parliament couldn't determine the future of the Raj, who should? He was "firmly convinced"

* During the early 1950s, when this writer was living in Delhi as a foreign correspondent, social scientists began a comprehensive poll of Indian villages to determine how many natives knew British rule had ended in 1947. The survey was aborted when it was discovered that a majority didn't know the British had even arrived. England's East India Company was chartered in 1600.

Churchill entering the political wilderness over the India issue

that such articles as Churchill's pieces in the *Daily Mail* "will do more to lose India for the British Empire, will do more to cause a revolutionary spirit, than anything that can be done in any way by anyone else." Even though "the rank and file refuse to face facts," he said, "the leader has to look at them, and he has to warn his people." It was "the supreme duty of a political figure to tell the people of the country the truth, because truth is greater than tactics." The question which stumped Pontius Pilate held no mysteries for Stanley Baldwin, and in his gentlest, most civil manner he advised his colleagues to keep their opinions in this matter to themselves and leave all decisions to him, the prime minister, and the secretary of state for India.[289]

But Churchill had the bone in his teeth, and wouldn't yield it until events wrenched it from him. Intricate efforts to resolve the Indian question continued on what he called their "downward slurge," ending in the Government of India Act of 1935, the longest single piece of legislation ever to emerge from the House of Commons — "a gigantic split," said Churchill, "of jumbled crochet work." He had fought it for three years in what was probably the most brilliant parliamentary performance of his life. He lost, but so did everyone else; the act's ultimate objective, an all-India federation which would weave together all the provinces and states on the subcontinent, was rejected by the congress, the Moslems, and the Indian princes. Nevertheless, it was a long step toward dissolution of the Raj. British India was destined to vanish in Winston's own lifetime. A harbinger was the welcome England extended to Gandhi when he arrived in the fall of 1931, clad only in his homespun shawl and swaddling dhoti, a long loincloth worn by Indian men at home but never, until now, seen in Britain. Had the phrase Radical Chic existed then, it would have described the Mahatma's reception. He planted trees, gave unsolicited advice on a thousand topics, was extolled by Anglican clergymen, entered the goat which supplied his milk in an English dairy show and was awarded first place, had lunch with Lady Astor, and was invited to tea with the King and Queen. Everyone of consequence clamored to meet Gandhi, with one exception. Churchill refused to see him. Winston was roundly criticized for this, though he had company outside Britain. On December 13 the Mahatma called at the Vatican for an audience with the pope and was turned away. The reason, he was told, was his "inadequate clothing."[290]

The Crash of '29, like the Blizzard of '88, is identified with a specific year. Even more is it associated with an American city and a particular street. But it wasn't confined to Wall Street — the first European quake had come in Vienna, when the Credit-Anstalt, Austria's largest bank, closed its doors — and the repercussions were international. Wall Street's significance derived from the new role of the American financial community as successor to London's City. It was the linchpin of the world's economic system, and when it snapped the whole structure came tumbling down. The New York Stock Exchange, more familiarly known as the Big Board, was the trading center for Churchill's securities, and he was among those who discovered to their dismay that the Crash was only the beginning; price levels sank lower and lower throughout 1930, and by the summer of 1931 they made the ticker readings of the '29 panic look lofty. Britain, in trouble since the return to gold, was mired in its worst fiscal crisis since the bursting of the South Sea Bubble in 1720. Indeed, this was worse. South Sea stock had plunged to 13.5 percent of its highest quotation, but then it had rallied; the company had continued to do business for eighty years and paid dividends. By the end of 1931, however, the average securities in New York and London were worth 11 percent of their pre-Crash value. Investors in the Big Board had lost seventy-four billion dollars. The panic was spinning in vicious circles. Retail sales ebbed, so costs were cut by laying off workers. The workers laid off could not buy the goods of other industries. Therefore sales dropped further, leading to more layoffs and a general shrinkage of purchasing power, until farmers were pauperized by the poverty of industrial workers. In forming his second government, Ramsay MacDonald had hoped to break this cycle. Instead, the lines of jobless Britons grew longer. The TUC declared that it would accept no cuts in unemployment benefits. England having left the gold standard, the pound dropped from $4.86 to $3.49. The King called MacDonald to Buckingham Palace and asked him to remain in power as head of an all-party national government. Two Labour ministers, Snowden and J. H. Thomas, agreed to serve with him; the rest of the Labour party called them traitors and withdrew their support. Baldwin went along, however, and with Lloyd George still ill, Simon and Sir Herbert Samuel committed the Liberals.

Churchill was the last man in Parliament entitled to criticize any government's Treasury policy, but, never conspicuous for lack of gall, he did so anyhow, describing Snowden's management of the Exchequer as "incompetent." He agreed that all parties should "come to the rescue of a Socialist Government reduced to impotence." At the same time, he warned that he would remember his "grievous complaints" against those he held responsible for the plight of the economy. The dole was reduced despite the unions, and after £25,000,000 had been withdrawn from the Bank of England in a single day — a record — the Old Lady of Threadneedle Street was saved from bankruptcy by credits from Washington. But so many makeshift decisions trembled in the balance that the House required a national referendum. Before the general election, Hoare wrote that he was "very nervous" about the outcome. He needn't have been. The results were an astonishing triumph for the national government, which won 554 of the 615 seats in the House. It was a landslide, but there was more to it than that; the largest part of the avalanche was a historic Tory sweep. The Conservative party was now represented by 473 MPs, over three-fourths of the House, while Labour had dropped from 236 to 52 — the bitter fruit of MacDonald's split with mainstream Labourites. So huge was the Conservative majority that Baldwin was expected to form a new government. He declined; they had campaigned as a coalition, he said, and should so rule. He knew he could oust MacDonald whenever he chose, but this was not the moment. Instead, he installed himself as lord president of the council and picked the new cabinet: eleven Tories, including Hoare at the India Office; five National Liberals; and four National Labourites. Under any other circumstances, Churchill, with his seniority and achievements, would have received a major ministry. His own reelection had been spectacular. Although MacDonald had disparaged him on the stump, and one government minister, Samuel, had actually appeared in Epping to call for his defeat, Winston's margin of victory had exceeded twenty thousand votes, nearly two out of every three. He nursed a faint hope that a summons might arrive from No. 10. None did. His popularity in the country remained high, but his cause had been repudiated; only twenty candidates endorsed by the Indian Empire Society had been elected, and even before the polling Baldwin and MacDonald had agreed that there would be no place for Churchill. "Like many others," he wryly wrote afterward, "I had felt the need of a national concentration. But I was neither surprised nor unhappy when I was left out of it. . . . What I should have done if I had been asked to join I cannot tell. It is superfluous to discuss doubtful temptations that have never existed." Snowden was elevated to the peerage and Neville Chamberlain robed as chancellor of the Exchequer. To Winston, England's political future seemed hopeless. MacDonald, Baldwin, Chamberlain — the reign of mediocrities stretched over the horizon and beyond. In all Parliament he could count on the absolute support of just two MPs, Boothby and Bracken. His isolation was virtually complete. "Now, truly," writes Kenneth Young, Beaverbrook's biographer, "Churchill was out in the cold."[291]

He accepted it, "defiant," by his maxim, "in defeat." In the House he sat on the front bench, on the government's side, just below the aisle. "What a gap there is," wrote Guy Eden, "what a vast, terrific chasm, between the Treasury Bench, seat of power, and that seat just two feet, six inches away, below the gangway!" Clement Attlee later recalled: "Here he was well placed to fire on both parties. I remember describing him as a heavily armed tank cruising in No Man's Land." What intrigued Eden "above all else was the manner of his treatment by the Tory members. I have watched him, accompanied by a sole companion, walking broodingly through the corridors of the House or conversing in the Smoking Room with a few admirers like Brendan Bracken and Robert Boothby. But generally, Tory members gave him a wide berth." In opposition he adopted a technique of maintaining constant streams of objections, some audible and to the point, others quite unintelligible. One afternoon a minister in the middle of a speech was distracted by Churchill. Winston was making movements of disagreement. The irritated minister said: "I see my right honourable friend shakes his head, but I am only expressing my own opinion." "And I," said Winston, without looking up, "am only shaking my own head."[292]

That was clever and gentle, but his tongue had a much rougher side, and many who had been slashed by it, inside the House and out, now descended upon him like vultures homing in on carrion, believing, as Beaverbrook did, that he had "finally shot his bolt." Churchill had accused all MPs who favored dominion status for India, whatever their party allegiance, of defeatism and inadequate patriotism. Samuel now flung this back at him: "If indeed the truest patriot is a man who breathes hatred, who lays the seeds of war, and stirs up the greatest number of enemies against his country, then Mr Churchill is a great patriot." Now that he was down, many MPs, hitherto silent, reached the conclusion that Churchill was obsessed by a relentless *besoin de faire* which had expressed itself in such adventures as Gallipoli, the Russian civil war, and the breaking of the general strike. Publicists wrote of him as an outcast, as untouchable as the *harijans* he had championed. "The tragedy of Mr Churchill," one commented in 1931, "is that whilst in reality he had nothing to *offer* the genuine Labour man, he fails to command the confidence of the Conservative. For the ghosts of Gallipoli will always rise up to damn him anew. . . . What sensible man is going to place confidence in Mr Churchill in any situation which needs cool-headedness, moderation, or tact?"[293]

In the rooms and halls of Parliament he was humiliated and subjected to sneers, snubs, patronizing nudging, and indifferent shruggings from those who saw him coming and turned their backs. Detective Thompson, still assigned to him — Winston had told the Yard he no longer needed a bodyguard, but the Yard, intercepting threats on his life from Indian nationalists, decided otherwise — was angry and puzzled. A rough, brusque man, unintimidated by rank, Thompson questioned some who had slighted Churchill. "He's like a weather-vane," explained one. Another said: "His life is one long speech. He does not talk. He orates. . . . He does not want to hear your views. He does not want to disturb the beautiful clarity of his thoughts by the tiresome reminders of the other side." Baldwin told friends and even casual acquaintances how pleasant it was to attend meetings without Winston there to ignore the agenda and introduce "some extremely clever memorandum submitted by him on the work of some department other than his own." Churchill's critics called him rash, impetuous, tactless, contentious, inconsistent, unsound, an amusing parliamentary celebrity who was forever out of step. "We just don't know what to make of him," a troubled Tory MP told Lady Astor. She asked brightly: "How about a nice rug?"[294]

He was hurt and baffled. Long afterward a legend arose that he had endured these slights philosophically. "In the midst of so many outward upheavals," Alan Moorehead wrote, Churchill was "the least displaced person one could possibly imagine." He himself lent credence to the myth. "There was much mocking in the press about my exclusion," he said later, "but now one can see how lucky I was. Over me beat the invisible wings." At the time they were both invisible and inaudible. Guy Eden has recalled: "He clearly hated it and a bitterness crept into his speeches which had not been there before and which has not been there since. . . . Political life is a merciless affair, and the man who has been at the top of the tree is most ruthlessly 'clawed' — to use one of Churchill's own favorite words — when he falls, or even slips." Bewildered, Winston said: "I have never joined in an intrigue. Everything I have got I have fought for. And yet I am more hated than anybody." In a rare moment of self-pity he told a friend: "Here I am, after almost thirty years in the House of Commons, after holding many of the highest offices of state. Here I am, discarded, cast away, marooned, rejected, and disliked." There seemed no way out. He saw little to choose between Baldwin and MacDonald — "two nurses," he called them, "fit to keep silence in a darkened room."[295]

He missed Birkenhead terribly and found solace in one of F.E.'s old speeches: "The world still has its glittering prizes for those who have stout hearts and sharp swords." But this, he realized, was not the time for either. No glittering prizes awaited Britons like him in 1931 or for long thereafter; stout hearts were suspect in the early 1930s, and sharp swords scorned, even by those whose lives would depend upon them in a crisis. It was time to hibernate. He let the lease on Venetia Montagu's house lapse and made Chartwell his family's year-round residence. The Churchills had no London home now. Winston kept a pied-à-terre in Morpeth Mansions, near Parliament, but the House seldom saw him. He was toiling on Chartwell's outside grounds, driving his Black Dog away by hard manual labor and, inside, writing his way out of debt. If he were to survive his political wilderness, he would need much more than the £500 stipend of a back-bencher. He intended to make a new fortune and invest it wisely, relying on Baruch's advice, avoiding speculation, and turning away from all the fiscal totems he had deified at the Treasury. "I have gone whole hog against gold," he wrote Boothby. "To hell with it! It has been used as a vile trap to destroy us. I would pay the rest of the American debt in gold as long as the gold lasted, and then say — 'Henceforward, we will only pay in goods. Pray specify what goods you desire.' "[296]

Less than two weeks after surrendering his chancellor's seals at Windsor he had begun research on his Marlborough biography, working in

Blenheim's archives with two assistants: Maurice Ashley, a young scholar whom he hired at £300 a year, and Colonel Charles Holdern, at £500. His literary approach, he wrote Ashley, "will probably not be to 'defend' or 'vindicate' my subject, but to tell the tale with close adherence to chronology in such a way and in such proportions and with such emphasis as will produce upon the mind of the reader the impersonation I wish to give. I have first of all to visualize this extraordinary personality. This I can only do gradually as my knowledge increases." He was one of those authors — this writer is another — who believe that the past should not be judged by the standards of the present. He wrote: "One has got to find out what the rules of the age were — there certainly were rules. Murder plots, for instance, were treated quite differently from treason even in its grossest form." To the proprietor of the *Daily Telegraph,* who was dickering for the Marlborough serial rights, he wrote: "I have no doubt that I shall be able to tell this famous tale from a modern point of view that will rivet attention."[297]

At Chartwell several pots were always boiling on his stove; while researching Marlborough he was finishing *My Early Life,* correcting galleys for an additional *World Crisis* volume, on the war's eastern front, and pouring out a flood of magazine articles. At one point he was contracting to write twelve pieces for a British magazine, contributing regularly to *Collier's* and the Hearst Syndicate, and denouncing abuse of wealth in the *Daily Mail.* Editors were bombarded with his suggestions for topics: "*Women and the future.* To what heights will the ascendancy of women go? Will there be a woman prime minister? *Women and finance.* A world controlled by women? *If they had lived long ago.* Take a number of the world's most prominent men and imagine their careers in past eras. Henry Ford in Cromwellian days. . . . Mussolini with Henry VIII, Ramsay MacDonald in the French Revolution, Bernard Shaw with the ancient Greeks, and so on." In a note to his son he wrote: "I have got a good crop of articles for 1931, and indeed am quite weighed down with work. But that is much better than being unemployed." And while absent on a research trip he sent Clementine a hasty scrawl: "Am vy remiss writing. Much pressed business. Everything continues satisfactory. Arranged twenty-two new articles in weeklies, all maturing before June and usual terms, monthly in advance, all involving heavy work in return."[298] During the two years between his eviction from No. 11 and the end of 1931 he published 104 pieces, including excerpts from his books, in, among other periodicals, *Scribner's, The Times,* the *Strand,* the *Saturday Review,* the *Sunday John Bull, Nash's Pall Mall,* the *News Chronicle,* and the *Daily Telegraph.* His topics ranged from "Government of the / by the / for the Dole-Drawers" to (from him, of all people) "Back to the Spartan Life in Our Public Schools." He dashed off twelve profiles of famous public figures — MacDonald, Nancy Astor, Bernard Shaw, Baden-Powell, Lloyd George, and Arthur Balfour among them — for which the *Sunday Pictorial* paid him £200 each. Then he published these sketches in a volume, *Great Contemporaries.* Another collection of pieces appeared in book form as *Thoughts and Adventures* in Britain, and in the United States as *Amid These Storms.* In addition, eight collections of his speeches appeared in the bookstores, including one volume dealing with India and the Raj. Few professional writers, who devote their working lives to their trade, produce as much over entire lifetimes as he turned out during this brief span.

In protesting the slack press coverage of his parliamentary speeches on India, he had written Rothermere that each of them required "an effort which is equal to that which would enable me to earn £3/400 by writing one of the numerous articles I have or my books."[299] This was no exaggeration. Churchill wrote superb copy, and eager editors on both sides of the Atlantic knew it. As a consequence, he was one of the world's most highly paid writers. In America his *World Crisis* volumes had earned him, after Curtis Brown's commissions, $20,633.10. In one month book royalties, publishers' advances, and magazine checks brought in £3,750. The *Sunday Pictorial* paid £2,400 for a series of character studies. A single piece in the *Daily Mail* sold for £600, and a series for the *Mail* brought £7,800. George Harrap, the publisher, advanced him £10,000 for the Marlborough; Scribner's paid £5,000 for the American rights. And his impressions of the United States, set down in twenty-two articles and widely reprinted abroad, eventually earned £40,000. By the end of 1931 his writing income for that year had reached £33,500, and his peak years lay ahead; in less than five years his magazine sales in the United States alone, after commissions, would bring him $35,379.78.

At fifty-seven he was a skillful literary craftsman, knew it, and rejoiced in his mastery of the language. "I have been reading a good deal on 'Marlborough,'" he wrote Clementine. "It is a wonderful thing to have all these contracts satisfactorily settled, and to feel that two or three years agreeable work is mapped out and, if completed, will certainly be rewarded. In order to make sure of completing the task within three years instead of leaving it to drag on indefinitely, I am going to spend money with some freedom upon expert assistance." Ashley, who was providing some of that assistance — though £300 a year does not suggest that his employer's expenditures for expertise were particularly free — had found, as had others, that Winston's method of composition was beguiling and unorthodox. He remembers how Churchill "would walk up and down the room (and when I worked for him it was usually his bedroom), puffing a cigar while a secretary took it down as best she could in Pitman. Occasionally he would say 'Scrub that and start again.' At times he would stop . . . at others he would be entirely swept on by the stimulus of his imagination."[300]

Like a battlefield veteran who avoids any mention of combat, Winston seldom mentioned politics during his early days in the wilderness. Lloyd George and Bracken were fellow guests at a country weekend in Coombe. So was Harold Nicolson, who wrote in his diary: "LlG begins at once: 'Now, what about this National Government? We here must form a National Opposition.' " George was "throwing out little sparks of compliments to right and left, drawing Winston in," Nicolson noted. "The impression was that of a master-at-drawing sketching in a fig leaf, not in outline, but by means of shadows around it." Nevertheless, Churchill, who had always found talk of political maneuvering irresistible, refused to be drawn. He was vivacious, but on other topics. Nicolson concluded: "Winston is very brilliant and amusing but not constructive."[301] However, he continued to follow developing situations at home and abroad. Each morning he and Clementine carefully read newspapers and sent notes to each other, via servants, on significant items. One consequence of this was that Churchill became the first statesman in England to discover that, for the second time in a generation, a strange light had appeared and was growing upon the map of Europe.

Germany's Nationalsozialistische Deutsche Arbeiterpartei (National Socialist Workers' party), which became famous and then infamous as the Nazi party, began in Munich as one of hundreds of splinter movements spawned in the wake of Versailles. Adolf Hitler, then a police spy, attended a meeting — since only two dozen people were present, it could hardly be called a rally — in September 1919. Hitler came to observe, but, seeing possibilities invisible to almost everyone else, he enrolled as the workers' party's seventh member. After the country's inflationary panic of 1923, he thought he saw his chance to lunge for power, but his attempted coup that November, which turned into a fiasco, was ridiculed throughout the Republic of Germany as the *"Bürgerbräu-Putsch"* ("Beer Hall Riot") and his storm troopers' public tantrums were dismissed as an example of postwar Germany's black humor. The Nazis were to have the last, mad laugh, but not then; the 1920s were desperate years for Hitler and his movement. Prosperity means thin gruel for revolutionaries, and as long as the boom lasted, life in the Weimar Republic was, on the whole, calm, pleasant, and amusing. American bankers had lent the country seven billion dollars, on terms so generous as to make it almost a gift. Fueled by these loans, Weimar's economy seemed stable. German business was good; unemployment dropped to 650,000, an irreducible figure which meant that just about everyone in the country who wanted a job had one.

The Nazis' hopes had risen at the end of 1924, when their leader was released from Landsberg. Ludendorff had repudiated them, and Göring was in exile, but they believed Hitler's gifts as a spellbinder would put things right. They forgot that he was only on parole. The judge had warned him against disruptive activities, which was like King Canute instructing the tides. In his first public appearance after leaving prison, the parolee told a crowd that Weimar, like Marxists and Jews, was Germany's "enemy." He cried: "In this struggle of ours there are only two possible outcomes — either the enemy passes over our bodies or we pass over theirs." He was confident the Nazis would win because they would not shrink from wielding "weapons of spiritual and physical terror [*geistigen und körperlichen terrors*]." The judge decided he had violated his parole and enjoined him from public speaking for the next two years.[302]

But Hitler was more than an orator. He was also an excellent administrator. At that time there were fewer than 27,000 Nazis in the country. His recruiting drives slowly lengthened the rolls: 49,000 in 1923; 72,000 in 1927; 108,000 in 1928. Subgroups were organized: the Deutsches Jungvolk for children, the Bund Deutscher Mädel for girls, the N.S. Frauenschaften for women, and the Kulturbund for intellectuals. The most visible Nazis were the brawling brownshirts of the Sturmabteilung (SA), but while their leader spoke affectionately of these "*alten Kämpfern*" ("old fighters"), he relied more heavily on his Schutzstaffel (SS), who swore personal loyalty to him, wore black uniforms in frank imitation of the Italian Fascisti, and were led by a deceptively mild-mannered Waldtrudering chicken farmer, Heinrich Himmler. Hermann Göring (already known throughout Germany as the Fat One) was soliciting contributions from his family's wealthy friends. And a crippled, twenty-eight-year-old Rhinelander with journalistic aspirations, whose applications for a reporter's job had been repeatedly rejected by the *Berliner Tageblatt,* joined the small staff of the party's fortnightly newsletter, the *N.S. Briefe.* This was Joseph Goebbels, who would become the Nazi megaphone. As chief of this tightly knit political conspiracy, Hitler invested himself with the title *Partei- und Oberster-Sturmabteilung, Führer Vorsitzender der Nationalsozialistische Deutsche Arbeiter Kerband.* One word survived: *Führer.* It means "leader." History would remember him by it. Later the mere mention of the German Führer would terrify Europe and countries beyond the seas, but during those lean years the Nazis were only impressing one another. In the national election of May 20, 1928, they polled some 810,000 votes — 2.6 percent of the 31,000,000 cast. Hitler, now in his fortieth year, found diversion from defeat that summer by falling in love with his blond, beautiful, twenty-year-old niece, Geli Raubal, the daughter of his widowed half sister. Royalties from sales of *Mein Kampf* — the book had already earned 59,058 reichsmarks — permitted him to keep Geli, Geli's mother, and Geli's sister in the Villa Wachenfelt, on the Obersalzberg, overlooking Berchtesgaden. All three women acquiesced in the establishment of this strange household. His niece's feelings seem to have been ambivalent. She admired her powerful uncle and was flattered by his attentions. Yet she slowly came to resent his tyrannical manner toward her, and she was, and was to remain, sexually passive. Hitler's infatuation, on the other hand, was absolute. The following year he sent the mother and the sister packing and moved his niece into his nine-room luxury flat on Munich's Prinzregentenstrasse. There was talk. Several party members suggested to him that this was unwise; the party might pay a heavy political price for it. Infuriated, he forbade them even to mention her name in his presence. His intentions were probably honorable; he gave every sign of preparing for marriage. In retrospect his love for Geli seems to have been the one humane emotion in his life, though it was, of course, incestuous.

Nazi political prospects brightened after the Crash. The Republic of Germany was a victim of the Crash — the principal victim. No other country was hit so hard. All sources of American largess dried up; every scheduled loan was canceled. Lacking markets for Germany's export trade, Weimar could not afford imports; not even essentials, including food. The republic's most prestigious financial institution was the Darmstäder und Nationalbank. When it failed, all other Berlin banks closed, too. Thousands of businesses went bankrupt. The world's longest breadline stretched down the Kurfürstendamm. Hitler, rejoicing in the *Völkischer Beobachter,* the Nazi newspaper, wrote: "Never in my life have I been so well disposed and inwardly contented as in these days, for hard reality has opened the eyes of millions of Germans to the unprecedented swindles, lies and betrayals of the Marxist deceivers of the people."[303] Demoralization in the Reichstag led to legislative paralysis, which was succeeded, in turn, by new elections on September 14, 1930.

Hitler furiously crisscrossed the country, promising jobs and bread for all, exposure of bureaucratic corruption, the rebuilding of a strong Germany, ruthless punishment of the Jewish financiers who had precipitated this crisis, and repudiation of the Versailles *Diktat*.

The election returns startled everyone, including Hitler. All extremist parties had gained. The Communist vote had risen 25 percent. But 6,409,600 Germans had cast their ballots for Nazi candidates — a gain of over 690 percent. In twenty-eight months, they had vaulted from the smallest party in the Reichstag to the second-largest, second only to the Social Democrats. Until now their leader had been regarded as a wild-eyed, seedy man in a dirty trench coat, consigned to the lunatic fringe of Weimar politics, constantly in trouble with the tax authorities, too humble to enter the halls of the great and powerful. Now he was courting industrialists and senior generals of the Reichswehr, and all of them were listening very carefully. In one of those flashes which demonstrated his political genius, he decided to testify at the trial of three Leipzig lieutenants who, in defiance of a standing order, had smuggled copies of the *Völkischer Beobachter* into their barracks. Those who expected him to defend the young officers did not yet know their Führer. In the witness box he disowned them and recommended that they be punished. Spectators gasped; they didn't realize that he was wooing the defendants' superiors. Using the trial as a forum, he promised that Nazis would "see to it, when we come to power, that out of the present Reichswehr a great Army of the German people shall arise." The judge asked if the Nazis would reach power through constitutional means. Hitler affirmed it; knowing how the German mind worked, he had abandoned any thought of a coup and meant, instead, to become head of state by legal means, with a formal mandate from the Reichstag. But he was also aware of the Teutonic love for inflammatory phrases. Shifting in his chair, he added: "I can assure you that when the National Socialist movement is victorious in this struggle, there will be a National Socialist Court of Justice, too. Then the November 1918 revolution will be avenged and heads will roll [*Köpfe rollen*]!"[304]

Köpfe rollen! A delicious shudder passed through Germany. Here was the imperious voice they had missed since the kaiser had fled. By now the entire country was familiar with the Nazis' symbol, their *Hakenkreuz*, or swastika — a black crooked cross imprinted on a white circle against a red background — and their party anthem, "Die Fahne Hoch" ("Raise the Banner"), written by Horst Wessel, a clergyman's son who had abandoned his family and university classrooms to live in a slum with a retired prostitute, work for the party, and roam Berlin's streets fighting

Adolf Hitler

Communists. In February 1931 the Communists murdered Wessel, making him an instant martyr. Over 100,000 men were now enrolled in the SA and SS, forming a private army larger than Weimar's Reichswehr, whose senior officers, studying the transcript of the Leipzig trial, decided that they had found their man. Soldiers were no longer disciplined for reading the *Völkischer Beobachter*. The country's millionaires conferred with Hitler, Göring, and the financial wizard Hjalmar Schacht, a recent Nazi convert. A majority of them decided that although the Nazi leader was a vulgar demagogue, he had an extraordinary gift for rousing latent patriotism in the people and might be able to suppress Weimar's weak democracy, stubborn trade unions, and the Socialists and Communists. Contributions from big business, which had been distributed among other conservative parties in the past, were channeled into the Nazi coffers. Gustav Krupp, the munitions tycoon, became, in the word of a fellow industrialist, *"ein Obernazi"* — "a super Nazi." As 1931 approached its end, Germany seemed sickened by a disease without a cure. Over five million men were out of work. Crippled veterans of the war were begging on street corners. Farmers' mortgages were being foreclosed. Inflation had all but wiped out the middle classes. The Reichstag foundered in confusion; its 107 Nazi deputies were using fists and clubs to break up debates and drown out parliamentary motions. President Hindenburg, now eighty-four, was withdrawing into the stupor of senility. Gregor Strasser, who had led the party while Hitler was in prison, told a reporter: "*Alles, was dazu dient, die Katastrophe zu beschleunigen . . . ist gut, sehr gut, für uns und unsere deutsche Revolution* [All that serves to precipitate the catastrophe . . . is good, very good for us and our German revolution]."[305]

At this historic moment Hitler was struck by a personal tragedy. Before their affair Geli had been taking voice lessons in Vienna, which she adored; now she wanted to return and resume them. Her uncle absolutely refused to consider it. They quarreled bitterly. On the morning of September 17, after he had descended the stairs from their apartment and was entering his car, she thrust her head out a window. Neighbors heard her cry: "Then you won't let me go to Vienna?" He shouted back, "No!" and drove off.[306] The next morning her body was found in the flat. She had shot herself through the heart. Hitler was incoherent with grief. In death she achieved what he had denied her in life; she was buried in the family's Viennese plot. Hitler could not attend the funeral. Six years earlier, to avoid deportation while paroled, he had renounced his Austrian citizenship. Since his application for German citizenship had not been approved, he was *staatenlos,* stateless — a man without a country. Under these circumstances foreigners, who could not fathom his growing mystique in central Europe, found it difficult to take him seriously.

Churchill took him seriously. Germany had worried Winston since the Armistice. On September 24, 1924, when Hitler was still in Landsberg, dictating his book to Rudolf Hess, Winston had warned that "the soul of Germany smoulders with dreams of a War of Liberation or Revenge." It could not, he wrote, "be kept in permanent subjugation." He read *Mein Kampf* in its entirety as soon as E. J. Dugdale's translation became available, but long before that he had studied translated excerpts, and, perhaps because of his own aggressive instincts, he grasped Hitler's message. The book's "main thesis," he wrote, "is simple. Man is a fighting animal; therefore the nation, being a community of fighters, is a fighting unit." It was Hitler's argument that the ferocity "of a race depends on its purity. Hence the need for ridding it of foreign defilements. The Jewish race, owing to its universality, is of necessity pacifist and internationalist." Hitler believed that only "brute force" could assure Germany's survival. As Churchill understood it, *Mein Kampf* proposed a sweeping Teutonic political strategy, proposing that "the new Reich . . . gather within its fold all the scattered German elements in Europe. A race which has suffered defeat can be rescued by restoring its self-confidence. Above all things the Army must be taught to believe in its own invincibility."[307]

Charisma and patriotism were qualities Churchill greatly admired. They had formed his first impression of Mussolini, and he did not, at first, find Hitler completely beyond the pale. He respected him, Guy Eden writes, "as a man of vision, even if it was distorted vision, and drive, even if it was a drive to evil." Hitler's early life had been a catalogue of failures, Churchill observed, but "these misfortunes did not lead him into Communist ranks. By an honourable inversion he cherished all the more an abnormal sense of racial loyalty and fervent and mystic admiration for Germany and the German people." Afterward, when Hitler had become Führer of the entire nation, a prophet of outrageous dogmas, Winston said that while he despised Nazism, he hoped that, should England ever lose a war, it would "find a champion as indomitable to restore our courage and lead us back to our place among the nations." Nevertheless, he had realized, while Hitler was still in his own wilderness, that sooner or later the man must be destroyed. It is arguable that Churchill was one of the first to comprehend Hitler's menace because each man was a mirror image of the other. Hitler, with his own remarkable instincts, seems to have sensed that Churchill, though a political outcast then, would ultimately be his archenemy. He told a British diplomat in Berlin that he regarded Churchill as a *"Deutschenfresser"* — a "devourer of Germans." "I naturally cannot prevent the possibility of this *Herr* entering the Government in a couple of years," he said, adding that he foresaw difficulties "if Churchill comes to power in Great Britain instead of Chamberlain."[308]

Long before his countrymen understood the Nazi challenge, Winston realized that Hitler was the very embodiment of evil, but even when they were locked in the most desperate war Europe had ever known, Churchill referred to him as "this monstrous product of former wrongs and shame." He meant Versailles. He agreed with Hitler; the treaty had, he believed, been a humiliating *Diktat.* This was not entirely reasonable. The Allied terms had been far less harsh than those Germany had imposed on Russia at Brest-Litovsk in 1918. German pride had been mortified at Versailles, however; the subsequent resentment was not rational but emotional, and Winston, emotional himself, grasped it because, had their roles been reversed, he, too, would have been enraged. That rage was a political reality, and, he believed, ugly consequences were inevita-

Europe, 1931
0 100 200 300 400 500
MILES
0 100 200 300 400 500
KILOMETERS
NORTH SEA
NORWAY
SWEDEN
FINLAND
ESTONIA
LATVIA
LITHUANIA
EAST PRUSSIA
DANZIG
BALTIC SEA
SCOTLAND
ULSTER
IRISH FREE STATE
GREAT BRITAIN
WALES
ENGLAND
DENMARK
NETH.
BELGIUM
LUX.
GERMANY
POLAND
RUSSIA
ATLANTIC OCEAN
FRANCE
SWITZERLAND
AUSTRIA
CZECHOSLOVAKIA
HUNGARY
RUMANIA
YUGOSLAVIA
BULGARIA
ALBANIA
GREECE
AEGEAN SEA
BLACK SEA
TURKEY
SYRIA
ITALY
ADRIATIC SEA
CORSICA
SARDINIA
SICILY
SEA
PORTUGAL
SPAIN
BALEARIC IS
MEDITERRANEAN
AFRICA
55°
50°
45°
40°
35°
15°
5°
15°
25°
35°
45°

ble. In 1925 he wrote that "from one end of Germany to the other an intense hatred of France unifies the whole population," and he suggested the establishment of neutral zones on German frontiers. He also urged "a substantial rectification" of Weimar's eastern border, consistent with ethnic realities. Sooner or later, he warned, "Germany will be rearmed"; steps should be taken to prevent "aggression against Poland," which could draw both France and England into another European conflict. He saw them preparing to do it again and felt premonitions of "future catastrophe." By 1928 he realized that the ten-year rule had been "a grievous error." The United States was urging Britain and France to reduce their defense establishments and reduce German reparations payments. Churchill disagreed. Writing a friend about "these stupid disarmament manoeuvres," he commented that "personally I deprecate all these premature agreements on disarmament." In a cabinet meeting he opposed any reparations cuts as long as Washington remained adamant on the issue of Britain's war debts; "we have given everything, and paid everything," he argued, "and we cannot make any new sacrifice." A strong French army, he maintained, would shield England from the "most probable danger" of being drawn into another conflict on the Continent.[309]

Few were convinced, or even interested. His stand on India was popular among die-hard Tory back-benchers, but even they turned away when he raised the question of another war. The last one had been so ghastly that any resumption of it was unthinkable. And men in public life dreaded the charge of "warmonger," with its attendant possibility that one day they might be held answerable for mass slaughter. H. G. Wells had warned them: "We must put ourselves and our rulers and our fellow men on trial. We must ask: 'What have you done, and what are you doing, to help or hinder the peace and order of mankind?' A time will come when a politician who has willfully made war and promoted international dissention will be as sure of the dock and much surer of the noose than a private homicide. It is not reasonable that those who gamble with men's lives should not stake their own." Throughout 1930 Churchill fought almost alone, and always unsuccessfully, against the Labour government's decision to accept a reduction of naval power below the Admiralty's specifications of Britain's minimal requirements. He rose in the House to warn against emasculation of the navy, and for the first time found support in the *Morning Post.* "I think this naval business is going to carry us a long way," he wrote H. A. Gwynne in response. "It may become part of a definite movement to a strong assertion of the life-strength of the British Empire." It didn't; Baldwin supported Labour, and Tory MPs refused to sign Winston's petition of protest. Walter

Lippmann wrote: "The people are tired, tired of noise, tired of inconvenience, tired of greatness and longing for a place where the world is quiet and where all trouble seems dead leaves, and spent waves riot in doubtful dreams of dreams." Churchill himself thought England had entered a "period of exhaustion which has been described as Peace."[310]

By June of 1931 even MacDonald felt that disarmament had gone "pretty near the limit of example." Churchill believed the limit had been passed, and called for rearmament. "England's hour of weakness is Europe's hour of danger," he told the House. Britain was now "extremely vulnerable," he said; its army, "cut to the bone," was little more than a "glorified police force," and the RAF's strength was an eighth of that of France's air arm. On August 10 he wrote in the Hearst papers: "German youth mounting in its broad swelling flood will never accept the conditions and implications of the Treaty of Versailles." Germany and Austria announced the creation of a customs union, and he was alarmed. "Beneath the Customs Union," he wrote, "lurks the 'Anschluss' or union between the German mass and the remains of Austria." The consequence of such a combination would be a "solid German block of seventy millions" threatening two nations: France, with its dwindling population, and Czechoslovakia. The Czechs had "three million five hundred" Austrian-Germans in their midst. "These unwilling subjects are a care. But the *Anschluss* means that Czechoslovakia will not only have the indigestible morsel in its interior, but will be surrounded on three sides by other Germans. They will become almost a Bohemian island in a boisterous fierce-lapping ocean of Teutonic manhood and efficiency."[311]

The French and the Italians, after reading his speech, objected to the customs union — on economic, not military, grounds — and Weimar, ever unsure of itself, dissolved it, demonstrating that even out of office Churchill was still a force in European politics. Prince Otto von Bismarck-Schönhausen, grandson of the great chancellor and himself a diplomat posted to Germany's London embassy, had sought an interview with him the year before. The two men had met on Saturday, October 18, 1930. In a secret memorandum Bismarck had reported to Berlin that Churchill had been following newspaper accounts of German political developments "in detail," and had spoken of the Nazis in "cutting terms." Hitler, he had held, had "contributed towards a considerable deterioration of Germany's external position." The Nazi leader was now insisting that he would never wage aggressive war, but Winston didn't believe him. By his own admission, the man was untrustworthy; Churchill quoted *Mein Kampf:* "The great masses of the people . . . will more easily fall victims to a great lie than to a small one." He was "convinced," Bismarck wrote, "that Hitler or his followers will seize the first available opportunity to resort to armed force." In their discussion Bismarck had referred to the "unsuitability" of the Polish Corridor — a strip of territory which gave Poland, otherwise landlocked, access to the free port of Danzig and the Baltic. Winston had replied that "Poland must have an outlet to the sea." He pointed out that German freight and railroad traffic passed through the corridor every day to enter East Prussia. Bismarck delivered his report to Albrecht Bernstorff, the embassy's senior counselor. Bernstorff, in turn, forwarded it to the Wilhelmstrasse. In a covering note he commented: "Although one should always bear in mind Winston Churchill's very temperamental personality when considering his remarks, they nevertheless deserve particular attention," on the ground that "as far as can be humanly foreseen he will play an influential role in any Conservative government in years to come — however difficult his personal position may be in the Conservative party, where he is mistrusted as an erstwhile Liberal and free-trader."[312]

It was at this point that Churchill decided to monitor Britain's preparedness. He asked the prime minister for access to figures on the strength of the country's armed forces. MacDonald found military matters tiresome, even trivial. He casually approved his request, and then, apparently, forgot about it. The consequence of this exchange of notes was one of those bureaucratic decisions which are self-perpetuating, remaining in effect unless or until withdrawn. Future prime ministers, unaware of it, would brood over the source of Churchill's detailed information about service developments. The answer lay, undiscovered, in their own files at No. 10.

Geli Raubal had lain long in her grave when the Austrian government finally approved Hitler's request to cross the border. He spent an entire evening in the cemetery, on his knees, weeping over her tombstone.

That same week Charles de Gaulle, a French major recently returned from a military mission in the Middle East, was working quietly at his desk in his home at 110, boulevard Raspail, in the sixth arrondissement of Paris, writing *Le Fil de l'épée* (The Edge of the Sword), a short book on the essence of leadership. Francisco Franco was also in Paris; having defeated Abd-el Krim's Riff army in Morocco and sworn allegiance to the new Spanish republic, he was studying at l'Ecole Militaire, France still being considered proficient in military science.

On the other side of the world, Hideki Tojo was serving on the staff of Japan's Kwangtung army, which, using the Mukden incident of September 19 as an excuse, had invaded Manchuria and was now investing the Chinese city of Harbin. Chiang Kai-shek, the new generalissimo of the Chinese Nationalist forces, the Kuomintang, was prevented from launching a counteroffensive by a Yangtze flood and flank skirmishes with Mao Tse-tung's Chinese Communist guerrillas.

Benito Mussolini had survived an assassination attempt the week before only to be thrown by his horse, forcing him to cancel plans for a Berlin visit. His pride had been restored by a *New York Times* feature article describing the tremendous "force of his personality" and a statement from Boston's William Cardinal O'Connell calling him "a genius given to Italy by God."[313]

In Moscow a Kremlin spokesman informed foreign correspondents that Joseph Stalin, general secretary of the Central Committee of the Communist party, was writing a book "dealing with Soviet challenges."[314] Actually, Stalin was no writer and not much of a reader. He usually spent his evenings reading junk fiction; his favorite novel was a translation of Edgar Rice Burroughs's *Tarzan of the Apes,* and he was looking forward to an early screening of MGM's film *Tarzan, the Ape Man,* starring Johnny Weissmuller, Maureen O'Sullivan, and C. Aubrey Smith. Stalin had just expelled an American woman, Mrs. E. G. Grady, for telling a joke about his crudity. He was extremely sensitive about his image, and though he cultivated the myth that he enjoyed anonymity, he was constantly in the news, congratulating factory workers who had met their quota of tractor production, for example, and demonstrating the success of his agricultural collectivization policy by exporting grain. This was specious. Because of his agricultural policy, ten million peasants were starving to death. Stalin's wife, Nadezhda Alliluyeva, begged him to relent; having failed to persuade him, she, like Hitler's Geli, would take her own life within a year.

The most interesting politician in the United States was Governor Franklin D. Roosevelt of New York. Reelected by a thundering plurality of 725,000 votes, he had persuaded his legislature, a few weeks earlier, to establish the state's Temporary Emergency Relief Administration, thus making his the first state to assume responsibility for victims of the Depression. In Albany his wife was packing for Warm Springs, the date of their departure depending on his mother's health.

None of these men knew any of the others, but Franklin Roosevelt and Winston Churchill passed within hailing distance of each other on the evening of Saturday, December 12, 1931. The governor was in his Manhattan town house at 49 East Sixty-fifth Street, conferring with J. H. McCooey, a Tammany politician, and Winston was in a taxi between the Waldorf-Astoria and Bernard Baruch's mansion at 1055 Fifth Avenue. Churchill, accompanied by Clementine and Diana, was in New York on business. Early in November he had signed a contract which would bring him £10,000 for forty lectures in the United States. In addition, Esmond Harmsworth of the *Daily Mail* had agreed to pay him £8,000 for a series of pieces on America's situation, prospects, and mood.

The Churchills had planned to leave England earlier, but parliamentary matters had detained him. The House was rewording the final clauses of the Statute of Westminster, which meant another debate on India. Kay Halle, an American journalist and an early flame of Randolph's, was staying at Chartwell the evening before he spoke, and she remembers him "rehearsing that speech all night." The statute, he told the House the following evening, set forth the Raj's new permissiveness in "cold legal language." Indian agitators would be emboldened by the limitations on British power now inherent in dominion status. He was troubled by the transfer of defense, finance, and police powers to native leaders, and the lack of safeguards for minorities. The front bench was tense; Hoare had written Irwin that he was "very nervous" about the new House — needlessly, it turned out, for when Churchill introduced an amendment rephrasing the statute, Sir John Simon, Sir Austen Chamberlain, and Baldwin spoke against it, and it was defeated overwhelmingly, 369 to 43. Having affronted the Conservatives, Winston then gratuitously offended Labour by saying that MacDonald had performed an "inestimable service" for Britain: "He has destroyed the Socialist Party as a Parliamentary force."[315] With that, he was off. Everything he did was contentious now. The morning of his departure from Southampton, newspapers ran editorials castigating him on another issue. They had been promoting a "Buy Britain" campaign. Churchill, the staunch Free Trader, had ignored the Cunard line and booked passage on the German steamship *Europa*.

His first lecture, in Worcester, Massachusetts, on December 11, was an appeal for Anglo-American unity: "We shall travel more securely if we do it like good companions." Most of the next day was spent in his Waldorf Tower apartment, 39 A, preparing future lectures and writing for the *Daily Mail.* Baruch had invited him to dine that evening with mutual friends, but after climbing into the taxi Winston discovered that he could not remember the address of the mansion. The driver was of little help; he was new to Manhattan. They cruised around for an hour, Winston growing increasingly exasperated with the traffic lights, which were new to him; they had not yet been introduced in England. Finally he told the driver to let him out on the Central Park side of Fifth Avenue. He believed he could recognize the house from the sidewalk. Turning to cross the street, he made two mistakes. The light was against him, and he had forgotten that Americans drive on the right. He glanced in the other direction, saw nothing coming, and stepped off the curb. Immediately he was hit by a car driving over thirty miles an hour. Mauled, he was dragged several yards by the car, and then flung into the street. He later wrote: "There was a moment of a world aglare, of a man aghast . . . I do not understand why I was not broken like an eggshell, or squashed like a gooseberry." In fact, he was gravely injured, bleeding heavily from his head and both thighs. A small crowd gathered. The driver, an unemployed mechanic named Mario Constasino, was distraught. Though in shock and great pain, Winston wiped the streaming blood from his face and assured the mechanic that he had been blameless. The fault was entirely his own; he had looked the wrong way. Churchill was cold; the temperature was in the low forties, and a wind was rising. Another taxi stopped, and he was helped into it. At Lenox Hill Hospital he was moved into a wheelchair. He thought he had reached sanctuary, but inside he learned that even hospitals have bureaucrats. A receptionist asked him to identify himself. "I am Winston Churchill," he said, "a British statesman." He added: "I do not wish to be hurt any more. Give me chloroform or something." It wasn't that easy. How was he going to pay for this? Lenox Hill was a private hospital, and these were hard times. He had only a few dollars in his pocket. He asked them to call the Waldorf, and after what seemed an eternity, Clementine and Detective Thompson hurried in. Churchill said faintly, "They almost got me that time, Thompson." Clementine having produced the cash, chloroform was administered. "A few breaths," he wrote afterward, "and one has no longer the power to speak to the world."[316]

Otto C. Pickardt was the physician who examined him. Clementine cabled Pickardt's findings to Randolph: "Temperature 100.6 Pulse normal. Head scalp wound severe." (It had, in fact, been cut to the bone.) "Two cracked ribs. Simple slight pleural irritation of right side. Generally much bruised. Progress satisfactory." If the hospital had any doubts about the eminence of its new patient, they were resolved when King George telephoned to inquire about his condition. In the beginning Winston's recovery was swift. He quickly made friends with Pickardt, and then with Constasino, who appeared during visitors' hours to apologize again. Churchill cabled Lindemann, asking him to calculate the shock, to a stationary body weighing two hundred pounds, of a car weighing twenty-four hundred pounds and traveling between thirty and thirty-five miles an hour, bearing in mind that he had been "carried forward on the cowcatcher until brakes eventually stopped car, when I dropped off" and that "brakes did not operate till car hit me." He needed the information as quickly as possible, he said, adding: "Think it must be impressive. Kindly cable weekend letter at my expense." The Prof replied: "Collision equivalent falling thirty feet on pavement. Equal six thousand foot pounds energy. Equivalent stopping ten-pound brick dropped six hundred feet or two charges buckshot point-blank range. Rate inversely proportional thickness cushion surrounding skeleton and give of frame. If assume average one inch your body transferred during impact at rate eight thousand horsepower. Congratulations on preparing suitable cushion and skill in bump."[317]

Churchill wanted the figures for a piece he was scribbling, propped up in bed, on "My New York Adventures." In it he wrote: "I certainly suffered every pang, physical and mental, that a street accident or, I suppose, a shell wound can produce. None is unendurable. There is neither the time nor the strength for self-pity. There is no room for remorse or fears. If at any moment in the long series of sensations a grey veil deepening into blackness had descended upon the sanctum I should have felt or feared nothing additional. Nature is merciful and does not try her children, man or beast, beyond their compass. It is only where the cruelty of man intervenes that hellish torments appear. For the rest — live dangerously; take things as they come, dread naught; all will be well." He telegraphed this to the *Daily Mail* three days after Christmas with a note to the editor: "Am now able to crawl around fairly well. . . . Good wishes for New Year and love to your pets Ramsay and Baldwin." Harmsworth cabled back £600.[318]

Pickardt prescribed a rest, and back at the Waldorf, Clementine packed for Nassau. On their return he would need a secretary, and she hired Phyllis Moir, a young Englishwoman who had worked in the British Foreign Office. Thompson met Miss Moir at the door of Apartment 39 A and said softly: "You'll find him pretty weak and tired. That accident gave him a nasty jolt and he only came out of the hospital a few days ago." She recalls that her first impression of Churchill was of "a humpty-dumpty sort of figure reading a letter." He was wearing a brown pin-striped suit, a matching polka-dot bow tie, and "black buttoned boots with odd-looking cloth tops." She was particularly impressed by "his small, delicate, beautifully shaped hands — the hands of an artist." He was smoking "a huge cigar," which he laid aside to say, rather distantly: "I understand you are willing to accompany me in my peregrinations." Miss Moir confirmed it, and when the Churchills sailed for the Bahamas on New Year's Eve, she set about converting a maid's room in the apartment into an office for herself. It had been her impression that he would soon be fit and ready to work. That had been his, too, and his American lecture agent urged him to be back by January 15, 1932, pointing out that every week's delay meant the loss of engagements and thousands of dollars.[319]

It proved impossible. In Nassau he suffered from severe aftershock and depression. "Vitality only returning slowly," he wired the agent on January 3. Five days later a nervous reaction struck. He wrote Pickardt that he had experienced "a great and sudden lack of power of concentration, and a strong sense of being unequal to the task which lay so soon ahead of me." Clementine and the physician dealt with the agent while Winston, attended by a night nurse, fought insomnia with nightly sedation, and forced himself to exercise a few minutes each day. His easel was there, but did not attract him. He wrote his son: "I have not felt like opening the paint box, although the seas around these islands are luminous with the most lovely tints of blue and green and purple." Clementine wrote Randolph: "Last night he was very sad & said that he had now in the last 2 years had 3 very heavy blows. First the loss of all that money in the crash, then the loss of his political position in the Conservative Party and now this terrible injury — He said he did not think he would ever recover completely from the three events."[320]

On January 15 his spirits began to return. He outlined two lectures: another call for closer ties between Washington and London and an analysis of the Depression's impact on Europe. But he warned his agent that he was still "astonishingly feeble" and that "you will find me, I am afraid, a much weaker man than the one you welcomed on December 11. I walk about five hundred yards every day and swim perhaps one hundred and fifty. But I tire so quickly and have very little reserve." A few days later, reporting that he was "steadily improving and gaining strength," he agreed to a formidable schedule: fourteen lectures, moving to a different city almost every day. Pickardt had rescued him from the hardship of Prohibition with a note on his stationery: "This is to certify that the

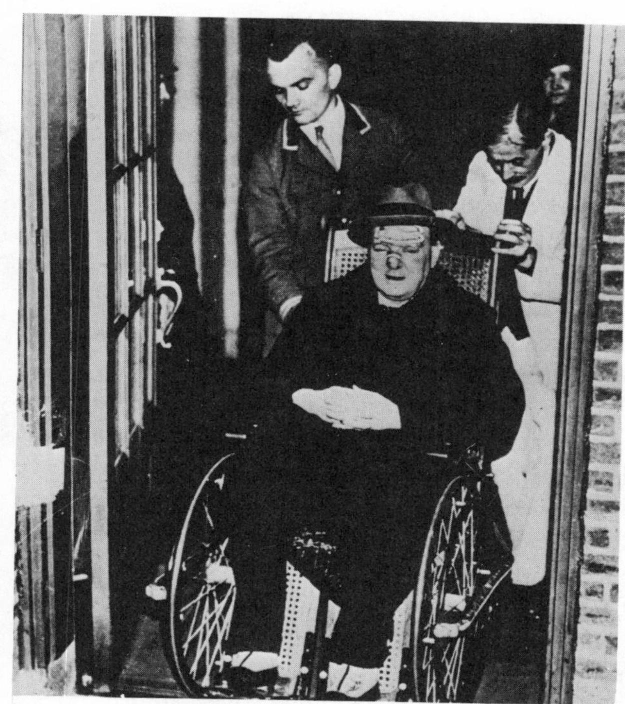

Churchill leaving Lenox Hill Hospital

post-accident convalescence of the Hon. Winston S. Churchill necessitates the use of alcoholic spirits especially at meal times. The quantity is naturally indefinite but the minimum requirements would be 250 cubic centimeters [slightly over eight ounces]."[321]

Thus fortified, and accompanied by Miss Moir, to whom he dictated a constant stream of notes and observations — she had yet to master his lisp, and was disconcerted by "his curious habit of whispering each phrase to himself before he said it aloud" — he spoke to two thousand people in the Brooklyn Academy of Music on January 28, picking up momentum as the evening progressed. They were enthusiastic, and so was Churchill. He was all business now, granting interviews, writing Boothby to suggest that they both attend the American political conventions in the summer, and visiting Washington for long talks with key senators and a short one with Hoover. In the capital he stayed with the British ambassador, Sir Ronald Lindsay. Miss Moir remembers that "these two made the oddest contrast, the immensely dignified diplomat standing ill at ease at the foot of the old-fashioned four-poster and the Peter Pan of British politics sitting up in bed, a cigar in his mouth, his tufts of red hair as yet uncombed scanning the morning newspapers." Diana used the embassy for a party, inviting all her young American acquaintances. One morning Winston approached his new secretary, grinning mischievously. "I've done something really dreadful, Miss Moir. I've just asked the Washington exchange operator for a glass of sherry, thinking I was speaking on the house telephone. I'm afraid I gave her rather a shock."[322]

His lecture tour was a success; the *Daily Telegraph* called it "a triumphal progress." He liked Americans, and they sensed it. As a foreign politician he could not support any presidential candidate, but his admiration for Roosevelt was obvious, and that, too, was popular that year. During a radio interview the announcer told his audience that, next to the King, Churchill was "probably the best-liked man under the Union Jack." Winston solemnly told them: "War, today, is bare — bare of profit and stripped of all its glamour. The old pomp and circumstance are gone. War now is nothing but toil, blood, death, and lying propaganda." Peace would be assured, he continued, provided France kept a strong army and England and the United States remained masters of the seas. The interviewer asked: "I take it that you haven't a high opinion of these disarmament conferences?" Churchill said vehemently: "No, I have not! I think that since the Great War they have done more harm than good."[323]

Before sailing home on the *Majestic* — he had Bought British after all — Winston conferred with Charles Scribner over future books, planned an investment program with Baruch, and visited the *Collier's* office to discuss further ideas for magazine pieces. Outwardly he seemed to have recovered from his accident. It was an illusion. His euphoric spells alternated with periods of weakness and gloom. The trip was "drawing wearily" to a close, he wrote Randolph, and he had missed his *Daily Mail* deadlines. "I have been terribly remiss in my articles," he wrote Harmsworth, "but, although I have got several very good ones in my head, I have not had the margin of life and strength to do them while travelling and speaking so many nights in succession." To Thornton Butterworth, his British publisher, he wrote: "I am much better, but I feel I need to rest and not to have to drive myself as hard. You have no idea what I have been through." His friends realized he had suffered an ordeal, however. While he was still in Nassau, Brendan Bracken had approached them, suggesting that they show their affection by buying him a new car. Among the contributors were Harold Macmillan, John Maynard Keynes, Lindemann, Lord Lloyd, Austen Chamberlain, Charlie Chaplin, Beaverbrook, Rothermere, the architect Sir Edwin Lutyens, the painter Sir John Lavery, and the Prince of Wales, whose romantic involvement would presently become interwoven, and then knotted, with Churchill's political future. The gift — a £2,000 Daimler — awaited him at Paddington Station. Several of the donors were there, and they sang: "For he's a Jolly Good Fellow." Winston tried to smile, then bowed his head and wept.[324]

At Chartwell he toiled on the grounds, roughed out articles, and slowly worked his way back into the Marlborough material with the help of F. W. D. Deakin, a young don from Christ Church, Oxford. Like all Chartwell guests, Bill Deakin was expected to work with his hands from time to time. One day, in the middle of building a wall, Churchill looked up and gloomily asked him: "Do you suppose that in five hundred years these bricks will be excavated as a relic of Stanley Baldwin's England?"[325]

His life, Virginia Cowles wrote, had "apparently ended in a quagmire from which there seemed to be no rescue." Reith of the BBC, believing his fangs drawn, at least on fiscal issues, permitted him to discuss monetary policy in his first radio broadcast to the United States. "Believe me," Winston told the Americans, "no one country, however powerful, can combat this evil alone." The audience listening at their Philcos and Atwater Kents was estimated at thirty million, but in Britain the event passed almost unnoticed. In Moscow, Stalin was receiving a British delegation led by Lady Astor. He inquired about politicians in England. "Chamberlain," she said, "is the coming man." Stalin asked: "What about Churchill?" Her eyes widened. *"Churchill?"* she said. She gave a scornful little laugh and replied, "Oh, he's *finished.*"[326]

ACKNOWLEDGMENTS

David (now Sir David) Pitblado introduced me to Winston Churchill (himself still unknighted) in the Verandah Grill of the *Queen Mary,* that greatest of Cunarders, on January 24, 1953. The prime minister, or "P.M.," as his entourage called him, was returning home with his family after a holiday and a series of meetings in Washington. As a young foreign correspondent on my way to the Middle East and India, I was delighted to discover that my cabin, M 101, was adjacent to Churchill's suite. Even better, Pitblado, then the prime minister's principal private secretary, had read the British edition of my first book and thought it commendable. He graciously arranged for me to see the P.M. from time to time during our five-day voyage to Southampton. It would be inaccurate to say that Churchill and I conversed. Alone with him I was mute, having, in fact, nothing to say. He had everything to say, and like Gladstone speaking to Victoria, he addressed me as though I were a one-man House of Commons. It was superb. I was enthralled, and eagerly accepted an invitation to tour the rooms of No. 10 Downing Street, with a Scotland Yard inspector as my guide, during my layover in London.

Thus began my accumulating debt to British hospitality. It is now immense. While researching this work I took a flat in Mayfair, but I seldom dined there alone. The "Churchillians," as Sir John Colville calls them, entertained me in their homes, answered all my questions, suggested other sources, and provided me with valuable introductions. Lady Soames, DBE (Mary Churchill), packed a picnic lunch and drove me to Chartwell, where we spent the day wandering through the mansion and its grounds and examining scores of her father's canvases. It was in the flat of Jane Williams, who is triply qualified as an observer of the English patriciate — she worked with Churchill and is the niece of both Lord Butler ("Rab") and Lord Portal of the RAF — that I first found myself at a table with "Jock" Colville, Churchill's assistant private secretary during most of World War II and joint principal private secretary during the P.M.'s second premiership in the early 1950s. Butler himself received me in his country home shortly before his death. So did Lord Head at Throope Manor; General Sir Ian Jacob, military assistant secretary to the War Cabinet from 1939 to 1945, at Woodridge; and Harold Macmillan at Birch Grove House in Sussex. It was typical of Macmillan's gallantry that although he felt too ill to eat, he had laid out a champagne lunch for me.

Such graciousness can lead to pleasant embarrassment. When my London hack drew up outside the Oxford studio of Oscar Nemon, sculptor of Churchill, Nemon raced out of the house, his smock flying behind him, and insisted, to the point of physical pummeling, on paying the cabby. At No. 1 Eaton Square, Lord Boothby broke out a shining bottle of prime bourbon although it was only 2:00 P.M. Sir John Martin in Watlingham, Martin Gilbert on Oxford's Harcourt Hill, and R. L. James on Oxford's Blenheim Drive clearly assumed that I would arrive with an enormous appetite. Sir William Hawthorne, Master of Churchill College, Cambridge, expected me to be both omnivorous and omnibibulous; when we rose from his high table and left the room I felt sheathed in an alcoholic mist. But as it cleared, I met two meticulous Churchill scholars: Captain Stephen Roskill, RN, and Correlli Barnett, keeper of the Churchill Archives. Remarkable shortcuts were disclosed in social situations. Over biscuits in Twisden Road, for instance, A. J. P. Taylor guided me toward Lloyd George, Bonar Law, and Beaverbrook papers. Churchill himself was never a clubman, but in exploring the web of his friendships I found those last bastions of male chauvinism invaluable. Holding honorary membership in three London clubs, I could entertain and then interview, sotto voce, men who would have been reticent in other surroundings. But here, once again, I was guest more often than host — of Sir David Hunt at the Athenaeum, for example, and Sir William Deakin at the Oxford and Cambridge, and George Malcolm Thompson at the Garrick. It was from the Reform Club that Graham Norton and I sallied forth one glistening evening for a nightlong exploration of Victorian London's architectural relics, winding up near Covent Garden.

Others who welcomed me or visited me for taped sessions were Cecily "Chips" Gemmell, Lord Soames, Lady Diana Cooper, Lord Selkirk, Lord Hailsham, John Griggs, Malcolm MacDonald (son of Ramsay and himself an MP), Lord Strauss, Sir Fitzroy MacLean, Mark Bonham Carter, Mrs. Kathleen Hill, Grace Hamlin, A. A. Montague Browne, Richard Hill, Velma Salmon, Lady Avon, Noel Mander, Lord Geoffrey Lloyd, Julian Amery, Denis Kelly, Sir Charles Martin, Lord Southborough, and, in his delightful Sussex cottage outside Robertsbridge, Malcolm Muggeridge. Not all my respondents were British. Virginia Cowles is undeniably American, though in her Belgravia home she evokes the presence of Mrs. Miniver. Averell Harriman is a triumph of the English-Speaking Union; he seems at home in either London or New York, provided the background is expensive and in exquisite taste. His wife, Pamela, though active in U.S. politics, will never pass as American. She was born a Digby in Dorset, Thomas Hardy country, and you know it from her every gesture. Her first husband was Randolph Churchill; their son, born during the Battle of Britain, is the second Winston Spencer Churchill, MP, who was my thoughtful host at lunch in the House of Commons.

Documents of contemporary history are less accessible in the United Kingdom than in the United States. Britain has no Freedom of Information Act. All

Churchill papers in the Royal Archives are reserved for the official biography. The seal cannot be broken on other sensitive government documents — cabinet, War Office, Foreign Office, Admiralty, Colonial Office, and Air Ministry — until fifty years after the event. Moreover, the papers of prominent public men are more scattered than those in U.S. presidential libraries. By far the largest single source of evidence for this volume is in the Churchill College Archives Centre at Cambridge University, the repository of 215 collections of private papers, including those of McKenna, Bridgeman, P. J. Grigg, Bevin, Bracken, Carson, de Robeck, Fisher, Crewe, Keyes, Rawlinson, Shane Leslie, E. L. Spears (partial), Beatty (partial), and Hankey (partial).

Documents left by other public men are frequently found beneath different roofs. Balfour's papers are in Scotland's National Register of Archives, the Public Record Office, the Reference Division of the British Library (formerly the British Museum Library), and in the private collection of Lord Rayleigh. Asquith's are in Oxford's Bodleian Library ("Bodley"), in the Smuts Archive, and in the collection of Mark Bonham Carter. Halifax's are filed in the India Office Library, the Public Record Office, and the estate of his heir. Some of Lord Esher's are in the Bodleian and some at Churchill College. Northcliffe's are dispersed among the *Times* Archive, the British Library, and the Bodleian. T. E. Lawrence's may be found in the Bodleian, the British Library, the Houghton Library at Harvard University, and the University of Texas Library. One would expect all of Beaverbrook's to be in the Beaverbrook Library, but no; some are there and some in the House of Lords Record Office. Because Lloyd George decided to take a peerage in the last weeks of World War II, some of his papers are in the House of Lords. (At about the same time he married his mistress, who became the Countess Lloyd George of Dwyfor; *her* extraordinary diaries, covering the years 1912 to 1949, are in the Beaverbrook Library.) Other valuable Lloyd George material is on the shelves of the Lloyd George Archive in Great Missenden, Buckinghamshire; the National Library of Wales; and the Beaverbrook Library. Bonar Law's papers are in the Bodleian, the Beaverbrook Library, and the Lords. Hankey's war diary (1912–1938) is in the Public Record Office, the diaries of Prince Louis of Battenberg in the Milford Haven Collection. Samuel's papers are in the Lords, as are Churchill documents on the founding of Iraq and his anti-Bolshevik years after Versailles. The Cecil, Jellicoe, and C. P. Scott papers are in the British Library. Milner's and H. A. L. Fisher's are housed in the Bodleian; Haldane's, Rosebery's, Haig's, and Margot Asquith's in the National Library of Scotland, Edinburgh; Hamilton's and Robertson's at King's College, London; Cockran's and some of Marsh's in the New York Public Library; Joseph and Austen Chamberlain's in the Birmingham University Library; most of Sir Henry Wilson's, including his microfilmed diaries, in the Imperial War Museum; those of Mottistone and Cherwell ("the Prof") in the Library of Nuffield College, Oxford; Curzon's in the India Office Library; Derby's at Liverpool University; and Baldwin's in the

Cambridge University Library. Amery's, some of Spears's, Philip Sassoon's, some of Marsh's, Ponsonby's, and Asquith's letters to Venetia Stanley Montagu — probably the most valuable single source for the government's prosecution of the war between 1914 and 1916 — remain in private possession. The cabinet and War Council minutes, the Dardanelles Commission evidence, and imperial conference minutes are filed in the Public Record Office. Verbatim accounts of all proceedings in the House of Commons and the House of Lords between 1881 and 1932 may be found in the *Parliamentary Debates* (*Hansard*).

Tracing all these would have been impossible without the original research, generosity, and encouragement of Martin Gilbert. As he wrote me, "our work goes in tandem." My gratitude toward him is profound.

On my own behalf and that of my archival research assistant in England, Deborah Baker, whose task it was to sift and sort out documents, I should like to thank D. G. Vaisey (Department of Western Manuscripts, the Bodleian Library), Diana Grimwood Jones and Gillian Grant (Middle East Centre, St. Anthony's College, Oxford), Mrs. P. Piper and N. A. M. Rodger (Public Record Office, Kew, Richmond, Surrey), G. J. Slater (Public Record Office of Northern Ireland), Marion Stewart (Churchill College, Cambridge), H. S. Cobb and F. Johnson (Record Office, House of Lords), A.N.E.D. Schofield and D. H. Bourke (British Library), D. M. Smith and C. C. Webb (Borthwick Institute of Historical Research, University of York), Wing Commander R. Martin Sparkes (Annexe), Wayne Furman (New York Public Library), A. E. Cormack and R. F. Barker (Royal Air Force Museum, Hendon), Gordon Phillips (*Times* Archive), Patricia Methven (Liddell Hart Centre for Military Archives, King's College, University of London), D. A. Clarke and G. E. A. Raspin (British Library of Political and Economic Science), R. A. W. Suddaby (Imperial War Museum), B. C. Bloomfield (India Office Library and Records), J. K. Bates (National Register of Archives, Scotland), Dr. B. S. Benedikz (Special Collections, University of Birmingham), Henry James Scrymgeour-Wedderburn (Dundee Archives), E. P. Scott (Hove Area Library, East Sussex), Kay Chapman and R. J. B. Knight (National Maritime Museum), Christine Kennedy (Nuffield College Library, Oxford), Peter McNiven (University of Manchester), Ralph Malbon and W. Wilcox (City Library of Liverpool), D. M. Griffiths and R. Geraint Gruffydd (National Library of Wales, Aberystwyth, Dyfed), L. R. Day (Science Museum Library, South Kensington), V. E. Knight (Library of the University of Liverpool), E. C. Blayney (Foreign and Commonwealth Office), A. D. Maclean, Mrs. Diane Nuting, the second Viscount Trenchard, and John Spencer-Churchill, eleventh Duke of Marlborough, who gave me the freedom of Blenheim Palace.

Once again I express my deep appreciation to the staff of Wesleyan University's Olin Library, in particular to J. Robert Adams, Caleb T. Winchester Librarian; and to Joan Jurale, head reference librarian; Edmund A. Rubacha and Susanne Javorski, reference librarians; Margaret Halstead, reference secretary; Erhard F. Konerding, documents librarian; Steven Lebergott, chief of interlibrary loans; and Alice Henry, circulation assistant. Other members of the staff who were especially helpful were Suzanne Fall; Ann Frances Wakefield; Dale Lee; and Alan Nathanson, bibliographer.

I am immensely indebted to Dr. Robert Byck, professor of psychiatry at Yale Medical School, for his observations on depression, Carl Jung, and Dr. Anthony Storr's analysis of Churchill's "Black Dog"; and to my friend and colleague Jeffrey Butler, professor of history at Wesleyan, for his meticulous review of the completed manuscript in the interests of historical accuracy, a vital service which was also provided — and provided superbly — by two British readers, Peter Day and Nigel Viney.

I am most appreciative of assistance furnished by Adoreen M. McCormick and Marilyn Dekker of the Library of Congress, who were helpful in verifying the lyrics of popular songs quoted in the text; Perry Knowlton, Adam Deixel, and Iam Gonzalez at the Curtis Brown literary agency, who provided access to Churchill's American royalty statements; and Mrs. J. A. Openshaw of North Kingston, R.I., for generously sharing the recollections and memorabilia of her father, William J. Harvest, who, as a lance corporal in the Fourth Hussars, served under Lieutenant Winston Churchill in Bangalore between 1896 and 1899.

My inestimable assistant, Margaret Kennedy Rider, has, as always, proved to be understanding, perceptive, loyal, and tireless. Deborah Baker was as reliable as the sturdiest English oak. Virginia Creeden and Diana Scott were invaluable in securing permission to quote from letters, diaries, documents, and published works, as was Ellen Panarese in the matter of photo research. Finally, I once more offer deepest thanks to Don Congdon, my literary agent; Roger Donald, my editor; and Melissa Clemence, my tireless, gifted copy editor — three dedicated professionals without whose patience and counsel the publication of this work would have been literally impossible.

W.M.

Wesleyan University
February 1983

SOURCE NOTES

In these notes on sources of quoted material, works have generally been cited by author's last name only, or, in the case of an author of multiple works, by author's name and brief title; for full listings, see the bibliography.

Works by Churchill, which include collections of his writings or remarks compiled by others, are cited by abbreviated title only, but are also listed in full in the bibliography. Please note the following forms of citation:

Aftermath = *The World Crisis: The Aftermath*
Crisis I–V = *The World Crisis,* Volumes I to V
RC = *A Roving Commission*
Wars = *Young Winston's Wars*

The Official Biography of Winston Spencer Churchill and its companion volumes are cited as follows:

WSC I–V = The five biographical volumes
CV I/1–V/2 = The companion volumes, from Volume I, Part 1, to Volume V, Part 2

Complete listings of this work appear at the beginning of the bibliography.

In addition, the following forms of citation are used:

NYT = *New York Times*
Times = *The Times* (London)
WM = Author's interviews

A discussion of the author's interview subjects and of various document collections may be found in the author's acknowledgments.

Preamble: The Lion at Bay

1. *Hansard* 5/28/40
2. Berlin 15
3. WM / Lady Soames 10/27/80; Laurence Thompson 96
4. *Irrepressible* 218; Laurence Thompson 148, 169
5. Moran 833; Laurence Thompson 133; *Hansard* 5/13/40; Herbert in Marchant 105; *Hansard* 6/4/40
6. Berlin 5; *Churchill Years* 102; WM / Pamela Harriman 8/22/80; Berlin 6; Longford *Churchill* 127; Nel 53, 54

7. *NYT* 5/30/40; Moran 655
8. CV I/2 1004; Harriman 205
9. *Wars* 112; CV I/2 974; Sarah Churchill 71; *RC* 65
10. *Wars* xxvi; Stevenson 38; WSC III 31; CV II/3 1989; Gardner 254, 285
11. *RC* 64; *Irrepressible* 286; McGowan 47; *Irrepressible* 300; Moran 674, 595; WSC V 837–838
12. WM / Jane Williams 10/7/80; McGowan 163; Howells 70; *Irrepressible* 224, 222, 318, 160; Moran 722
13. *Churchill Years* 22; Moran 717; *Irrepressible* 167
14. *Irrepressible* 225; Attlee in Stansky 197
15. Boothby *Rebel* 63
16. *RC* 10; WM / Sir John Martin 10/23/80; Martin in Wheeler-Bennett 143; WM / Richard Hill 11/7/80
17. Attlee in Stansky 189
18. *Observer* 12/20/51; *Hansard* 6/18/40, 6/4/40; Berlin 8
19. *RC* 5, 73
20. Storr in A. J. P. Taylor et al. 237
21. CV I/1 414; *Irrepressible* 265
22. Storr in A. J. P. Taylor et al. 238–239; Bryant 12–13; Moran 57; H. H. Asquith *Letters* 267
23. *Times* 1/21/27; *Step by Step* 57, 170; Moran 835
24. Liddell Hart in Stansky 95; *Irrepressible* 234; Moran 834
25. Moran 835; Rhodes James *Failure* 349; W. H. Thompson 87; Bonham Carter 9; Moran 776; Gardiner in Stansky 52; W. H. Thompson 44
26. *Churchill Years* 21; CV II/1 104; *Churchill Years* 237
27. *RC* 330–331; *Hansard* 11/12/40
28. CV I/1 584; *Savrola* 31–32, 234; Sarah Churchill 17
29. Beaverbrook *War* I 128; Moran 179; Storr in A. J. P. Taylor et al. 262
30. Storr in A. J. P. Taylor et al. 262; Riddell *War Diary* 49; Nel 139; CV I/2 862; Storr in A. J. P. Taylor et al. 270; Moran 796
31. Storr in A. J. P. Taylor et al. 259
32. Attlee in Stansky 198; Moran 827; Moir 203; Howells 61; *Irrepressible* 263, 6; *Wit* 45–46
33. *Wit* 65; Cowles *Churchill* 93
34. *Irrepressible* 263; Moran 460; Storr in A. J. P. Taylor et al. 254; Cowles *Churchill* 10
35. Moran 576; Hunt 65
36. *River War* II 110; Stansky xi
37. WSC V 1106
38. Moran 453; Hunt 67, 68
39. Berlin 2; *Great Contemporaries* 342, 372; Bonham Carter 119
40. Bonham Carter 4; Moran 457, 511; McGowan 161; Herbert in Marchant 110; *Irrepressible* 154
41. Coote in Eade 181; Chandos 166; *Irrepressible* 69, 159
42. *Amid These Storms* 300; Moran 746; *Irrepressible* 166; Chandos 184; Brooks in Eade 363
43. Moran 456; Eden in Eade 84; McGowan 24; *Irrepressible* 122
44. Rhodes James *Failure* 27; WM / Jane Williams 10/7/80; Hunt 70; Nel 50
45. Cowles *Churchill* 5; *Churchill Years* 206
46. *Irrepressible* 195, 204–205; McGowan 145; *Irrepressible* 340
47. *Irrepressible* 85, 325, 255, 272, 181; WM / Sir David Pitblado 10/21/80
48. Attlee in Stansky 206; Shaw in Eade 463
49. *Irrepressible* 63
50. *Irrepressible* 203; Howells 110; McGowan 93; Gardner 169
51. Moran 472; *Churchill Years* 14; Cowles *Churchill* 336; McGowan 39; Martin in Wheeler-Bennett 141
52. Howells 85; WM / Viscount Head 11/17/80
53. Howells 85; *Irrepressible* 186
54. Mary Soames to Virgil Johnston 6/13/72; Hunt 65

Prologue: Land of Hope and Glory

1. WM / Lord Boothby 10/16/80
2. Cross 143; Morris *Pax* 177; *Wars* 139–140
3. Morris *Pax* 109
4. Edmund Taylor 22; WM / Virginia Cowles 10/25/80
5. Morris in Perry and Mason 153
6. Collier 94–95; Morris *Pax* 133; Morris in Perry and Mason 146
7. Morris *Pax* 51
8. Morris *Pax* 132, 137
9. Moorehead *Nile* 290
10. Morris *Pax* 465
11. Morris *Pax* 187; Nicholson in Perry and Mason 207, 209; Morris *Pax* 188
12. Cross 89
13. Morris *Pax* 119
14. CV I/2 690, 684

15. CV I/2 688
16. Henry James 1–6
17. Coleman in Perry and Mason 60
18. McGregor in Perry and Mason 180, 181
19. Bailey 44
20. Davis *Cousins* 149–150
21. Norton 105
22. Best 75–76
23. Norton in Perry and Mason 171, 172; G. M. Young *England* 24
24. Phillips 197
25. Phillips 87
26. Best 75, 74, 117, 119
27. G. M. Young *England* 2; Phillips 62; G. M. Young *England* 7
28. Best 233, 212
29. Konig "Eleventh Edition"
30. Best 281; McGregor in Perry and Mason 178
31. Frost and Jay 39; Oxford English Dictionary definition of *weekend*
32. Edmund Taylor 31; Martin I 40; Collier 96, 104–105; Phillips 42; Martin I 164, 54
33. *Crisis* I 199; Gardner 31n; Best 243–244
34. Frost and Jay 39
35. Best 240; *Little Dorrit* ch. 34
36. Best 230; Cowles *Churchill* 71–72
37. *Times* 7/20/1863
38. Reader 20, 22; Best 165
39. Cross 32; *Last Chronicle of Barset* ch. 83
40. *Blenheim* 2
41. *Lord Randolph* I 1
42. Longford *Wellington* 399
43. McGregor in Perry and Mason 178; Martin I 278; WM / Graham Norton 10/8/80; Martin II 140
44. Martin II 360; Edmund Taylor 24
45. McGregor in Perry and Mason 178; WM / Pamela Harriman 8/22/80; Tuchman *Proud* 20
46. Martin I 44–45
47. Sackville-West 17
48. WM / Graham Norton 10/8/80
49. WSC I 6, 7
50. WSC I 13–14
51. WSC I 15
52. Blake *Disraeli* 692
53. Harris 485–486, 483
54. Harris 483
55. CV I/1 8; Howard 77
56. Howard 77
57. Eliot *Heiresses* 63; Moran 636; Eliot *Heiresses* 62
58. Moran 636–637
59. Martin I 99
60. Martin I 50, 52
61. CV I/1 8–9, 14
62. Martin I 53; CV I/1 11; *Lord Randolph* I 41, 42
63. CV I/1 12
64. CV I/1 15, 19, 21
65. CV I/1, 20; Martin I 91; *Blenheim* 2
66. CV I/1 1–2; Martin I 107
67. CV I/1 2
68. Martin I 108; Pelling 19; *Blenheim* 16

Part One: Headwaters, 1874–1895

1. Longford *Churchill* 17; CV I/1 6
2. *RC* 5; Bonham Carter 12; Eliot *Heiresses* 67–68; *Lord Randolph* I 72–73
3. Eliot *Heiresses* 69–70
4. *Lord Randolph* I 74
5. CV I/1 26–27, 28
6. CV I/1 29; WSC I 29; CV I/1 31, 57, 39; *Lord Randolph* I 74
7. WSC I 31; *RC* 8; CV I/1 48
8. *RC* 4
9. WSC I 35–36; Margot Asquith *Autobiography* I 64
10. *RC* 5, 111; *Savrola* 33
11. Storr in A. J. P. Taylor et al. 248; WSC I 43; *RC* 4, 8; Martin I 138; *Wit* 32
12. *RC* 1, 2
13. *Lord Randolph* I 92; WSC I 39; CV I/1 77
14. *Great Contemporaries* 55
15. Goertzel and Goertzel 262; *RC* 8
16. CV I/1 79; *RC* 3
17. *RC* 10, 11
18. *RC* 12; CV I/1 82, 88, 84, 83
19. CV I/1 84, 83, 86, 89, 87, 88, 83n
20. CV I/1 86; *RC* 13
21. WSC I 51
22. WSC I 48, 47; CV I/1 92, 93, 94, 95, 96
23. CV I/1 98; Cowles *Churchill* 30; CV I/1 154
24. CV I/1 98, 99, 125, 136, 143, 146, 149, 115; *RC* 13
25. CV I/1 131, 108; Cowles *Churchill* 31
26. CV I/1 152, 135, 136
27. CV I/1 111; Cowles *Churchill* 32; *RC* 19
28. *RC* 112
29. CV I/1 150, 151
30. CV I/1 152

31. CV I/1 160, 116, 117, 118, 119
32. CV I/1 120
33. *RC* 13; CV I/1 120, 121
34. Eliot *Heiresses* 72
35. CV I/1 111, 101, 142, 133, 103, 126, 227, 128
36. CV I/1 105, 127, 113
37. Harris 485
38. Pelling 28
39. Martin I 249, 250, 277, 299, 177
40. Martin I 227, 176, 319
41. Martin II 9
42. CV I/1 256; *Savrola* 157
43. Cowles *Churchill* 33; CV I/1 106
44. *RC* 46; Cowles *Churchill* 33
45. CV I/1 100, 304, 305, 143–144
46. CV I/1 100, 103
47. CV I/1 103, 122, 125, 133
48. Margot Asquith *Autobiography* II 65; Harris 472, 478
49. *Lord Randolph* I 283–284
50. *RC* 8; *Lord Randolph* I 120, 121, 209–210
51. CV I/1 88, 89; *Lord Randolph* I 295; Harris 474
52. WSC I 65
53. *Lord Randolph* II 65
54. WSC I 73; Harris 478; Margot Asquith *Autobiography* I 140
55. Rhodes James *Lord Randolph* 203; Martin I 219
56. Harris 478
57. Harris 660; WSC I 74; Harris 480; WSC I 79
58. *RC* 47; WSC I 81
59. Rhodes James *Lord Randolph* 295; Martin I 230; Harris 479
60. Eliot *Heiresses* 72; Martin I 230; Harris 481
61. CV I/1 144, 108, 137, 143
62. CV I/1 102; *RC* 15
63. CV I/1 156, 157, 158; *RC* 15
64. CV I/1 157, 158
65. CV I/1 162; *RC* 16
66. Tomlin in Chaplin 30
67. WSC I 108; Chaplin 84–87
68. CV I/1 161; Wollaston in Eade 20; *RC* 39; Tomlin in Chaplin 28
69. Wollaston in Eade 19; Siddons in Chaplin 18; Cowles *Churchill* 36; Wollaston in Eade 21
70. *RC* 30, 34–35; Bromage 3
71. *RC* 31; Tomlin in Chaplin 28; Martin I 217, 255
72. CV I/1 161; Mottistone in Chaplin 33, 34; Amery in Chaplin 21, 22
73. CV I/1 311; Cowles *Churchill* 36
74. *RC* 27, 22
75. CV I/1 192, 193–194
76. CV I/1 168–169
77. Siddons in Chaplin 11–12
78. CV I/1 204, 205; *RC* 25
79. *RC* 16–17
80. CV I/1 152, 159, 162; Chaplin 87–88
81. Mottistone in Chaplin 34
82. Siddons in Chaplin 17; Chaplin 57
83. WSC I 115, CV I/1 176, 177, 178
84. CV I/1 179, 180, 185, 186, 292, 300, 198
85. CV I/1 275–276, 292
86. CV I/1 292, 218
87. *Spectator* 7/25/91; *Review of Reviews* 4/1892
88. CV I/1 204, 182, 187, 185, 274, 275, 254
89. CV I/1 254, 247
90. CV I/1 250–251, 253
91. CV I/1 256
92. CV I/1 257–258, 256
93. CV I/1 256, 257
94. CV I/1 257
95. CV I/1 257
96. CV I/1 204, 323, 268, 256
97. CV I/1 284, 287, 259, 290
98. CV I/1 291–292
99. CV I/1 293, 294, 295, 296
100. CV I/1 297, 299, 301, 304, 303
101. CV I/1 301, 299, 300, 303
102. CV I/1 299, 301, 302, 304, 306
103. CV I/1 301, 305–306
104. CV I/1 306–307, 295; Rhodes James *Failure* 10
105. CV I/1 197; *RC* 19; CV I/1 222, 223; WSC I 130
106. CV I/1 259; *RC* 27, 113–114; McGowan 96; WSC I 151
107. CV I/1 337; *RC* 110, 111; CV I/1 338, 347–348
108. CV I/1 339, 325, 326; WSC I 171
109. Farwell *Kipling* 144; CV I/1 353, 359
110. Goertzel and Goertzel 273; *RC* 30; CV I/1 365
111. *RC* 28, 29
112. *RC* 26–27; CV I/1 371
113. CV I/1 376
114. CV I/1 380, 387
115. CV I/1 388
116. CV I/1 390–391
117. CV I/1 397, 393, 394
118. *RC* 37; CV I/1 402, 404
119. CV I/1 414
120. CV I/1 386, 413, 414
121. *RC* 31, 32
122. CV I/1 378; *RC* 33
123. *Spectator* 8/5/93
124. *RC* 33, 46
125. CV I/1 386

126. CV I/1 423; Cowles *Churchill* 33; *RC* 38–39; Bonham Carter 15; McGowan 44; *RC* 31, 32
127. Bonham Carter 14; Harris 471; Martin I 312; *River War* I 37; WSC I 232
128. CV I/1 468, 469
129. CV I/1 470, 471, 478
130. CV I/1 419
131. CV I/1 424, 425
132. *RC* 59, 38, 43, 44
133. *RC* 43, 44
134. "The Royal Military College"
135. "The Royal Military College"; *RC* 45
136. Farwell *Kipling* 145
137. CV I/1 439, 433n; *RC* 59
138. *RC* 60
139. Farwell *Kipling* 68
140. *RC* 52, 54
141. *RC* 55; Martin I 334; Cowles *Churchill* 40
142. CV I/1 532, 530, 528, 527; *Irrepressible* 24
143. WM / R. A. Butler 11/5/80
144. CV I/1 540
145. *RC* 61–62
146. CV I/1 478, 433; *RC* 59–60
147. Foster 217
148. Foster 378; WSC I 226
149. Blunt *Diaries* I 142; Harris 487, 488
150. Harris 489, 490, 491
151. WSC I 226; Martin I 326, 327; *Harper's Weekly* 1/5/95; Harris 491
152. CV I/1 535
153. CV I/1 540
154. CV I/1 531
155. CV I/1 533; *Lord Randolph* II 484; *RC* 49, 62
156. *Review of Reviews* 3/1895; *Outlook* 2/2/95; Martin I 228; *Harper's Weekly* 1/5/95; CV I/1 545
157. Marchant 20; *RC* 62, 74
158. *RC* 62; CV I/1 557
159. CV I/1 555–556; *RC* 63; CV I/1 559
160. CV I/1 562, 565, 567
161. CV I/1 635, 625
162. CV I/1 627, 626
163. Farwell *Kipling* 68; CV I/1 556, 559, 562
164. *RC* 65, 66
165. *RC* 64; CV I/1 577; *RC* 89, 90
166. *RC* 72
167. CV I/1 566
168. *RC* 73
169. CV I/1 579; WSC I 246; CV I/1 578

Part Two: Stream, 1895–1901

1. Farwell *Kipling* 49; Norton in Perry and Mason 132; Farwell *Kipling* 70, 72
2. Norton in Perry and Mason 131, 132
3. Farwell *Kipling* 62, 110
4. Bond "Why the Thin Red Line Was So Thin"
5. Farwell *Kipling* 116, 119
6. *RC* 75
7. CV I/1 590, 592, 593
8. CV I/1 595
9. CV I/1 596, 597
10. CV I/1 599, 598, 600, 597
11. CV I/1 597; Martin II 68, 69; *Amid These Storms* 52
12. *RC* 77; CV I/1 604
13. CV I/1 606
14. CV I/1 606
15. CV I/1 604, 611–612
16. CV I/1 612; *RC* 80; CV I/1 613; *Wit* 64
17. CV I/1 614, 615
18. WSC I 266; CV I/1 620
19. CV I/1 621, 622
20. WSC I 267; CV I/1 666; WSC I 269
21. *RC* 99–100; CV I/2 723–724; WSC I 270
22. *RC* 89; Martin II 61; CV I/1 579; *RC* 93, 94
23. *RC* 89; CV I/1 672
24. CV I/2 743, 747, 922
25. CV I/2 742; CV I/1 673, 674
26. CV I/1 676
27. CV I/2 680, 682–683
28. Wollaston in Perry and Mason 67
29. *RC* 101–102
30. *RC* 102, 101, 103, 104; Lockhart in Stansky 12
31. CV I/2 688
32. *RC* 107
33. WSC I 314; *RC* 103, 105–106
34. CV I/2 697, 684, 702, 753–754, 705, 722
35. *Churchill Years* 70
36. CV I/2 685, 686–687, 692
37. *RC* 109, 110
38. *RC* 111; CV I/2 724, 742, 726, 730
39. CV I/2 746, 730
40. CV I/2 767, 768, 765
41. *RC* 115–116, 117
42. CV I/2 746, 779
43. CV I/2 779, 702, 716, 704, 731, 729
44. CV I/2 734, 748, 750

45. CV I/2 754, 755, 756; Martin II 105; CV I/2 768
46. *RC* 120–121
47. CV I/2 770, 771
48. CV I/2 772, 773, 774
49. CV I/2 807n
50. CV I/2 775; *RC* 123
51. *RC* 124
52. *RC* 126–127; CV I/2 781, 784
53. *Wars* 19
54. CV I/2 787–788, 797; *RC* 132; CV I/2 797
55. CV I/2 792, 793, 796–797, 800
56. CV I/2 788; *RC* 132; CV I/2 792; *RC* 137
57. *Wars* 22; *RC* 137, 139
58. *RC* 140, 141, 142; CV I/2 799
59. CV I/2 799; *RC* 142, 143
60. CV I/2 799; *RC* 147
61. WSC I 349; CV I/2 830; *Wars* 60; Cowles *Churchill* 50
62. CV I/2 804, 805, 809, 811, 814
63. CV I/2 808, 839, 835
64. Moorehead *Churchill Trial* 10; Cowles *Churchill* 49; CV I/2 883, 806; *RC* 158–159
65. CV I/2 922, 869, 912, 889; *RC* 211; *Wit* 45; CV I/2 839, 840
66. CV I/2 841, 913, 895
67. *Athenaeum* 3/16/98; *RC* 154–155
68. CV I/2 930, 931; *RC* 155; CV I/2 855, 813, 856
69. *Crisis* I 251; *RC* 151–152; CV I/2 949, 948, 837, 882, 883; Martin II 129
70. *RC* 164
71. WSC I 378, 379
72. CV I/2 951; *RC* 167, 170; CV I/2 964
73. CV I/2 949–950
74. CV I/2 952; *RC* 167; CV I/2 956; *Wars* 71; *RC* 168; *Wars* 75
75. *Wars* 122, 123
76. *River War* II 40, 59; *Wars* 89
77. *Wars* 96; CV I/2 969; *RC* 169; CV I/2 971; *River War* II 73
78. *Wars* 85, 86, 87, 88
79. *RC* 173; *Wars* 99; *RC* 174
80. *Wars* 100, 101
81. *RC* 174, 175, 177
82. *RC* 178, 180
83. *RC* 183; CV I/2 977, 972; *RC* 184, 185; *River War* II 112, 111
84. *River War* II 130, 132
85. *RC* 188; CV I/2 978
86. CV I/2 978
87. CV I/2 978; *RC* 192, 191
88. CV I/2 973; *RC* 192; CV I/2 978; *RC* 193, 102
89. *RC* 193
90. CV I/2 979, 973; *Wars* 133
91. *Wars* 131–132, 133
92. *Wars* 122; CV I/2 979; *River War* II 44; *Wars* 123; *RC* 196
93. Girouard "When Chivalry Died"
94. *River War* II 212
95. CV I/2 1004; *River War* II 195; CV I/2 979, 999, 984
96. *Wars* 130; CV I/2 974, 995
97. *RC* 197, 198
98. *River War* II 128; *Wars* 111, 113
99. *Wars* 126, 128
100. CV I/2 984
101. WSC I 408, 409; CV I/2 990
102. CV I/2 697, 989
103. CV I/2 1003; *RC* 201, 199; CV I/2 1015
104. WSC I 295; CV I/2 1011
105. WSC I 422; *RC* 211; CV I/2 996
106. Steevens in Eade 64, 65–66
107. CV I/2 1016–1017, 1020
108. CV I/2 1023; *RC* 228
109. CV I/2 1028, 1033, 1035, 1036
110. *RC* 224, 226
111. Martin II 183; *Manchester Courier* 7/7/99; *RC* 225–226
112. CV I/2 1038; *RC* 227
113. CV I/2 1051; Pakenham 171
114. *RC* 231
115. *Irrepressible* 36
116. Pakenham 32, 7; WSC I 435; Pakenham 113
117. Pakenham 110; Margot Asquith *Autobiography* II 85
118. *RC* 234; *London to Ladysmith* 3; CV I/2 1055–1056; WSC I 441; *RC* 236
119. *RC* 237; *London to Ladysmith* 16; CV I/2 1058
120. *RC* 234, 241
121. *London to Ladysmith* 42; *Wars* 158
122. WSC I 447
123. Pakenham 177; *Wars* 158; *RC* 244; *Wars* 172
124. *RC* 245
125. *Wars* 172; *RC* 248; *Wars* 169; WSC I 450, 452
126. *RC* 250, 252
127. WSC I 460; *RC* 253; *Wars* 269
128. *RC* 258
129. *RC* 259
130. CV I/2 1077–1078, 1063–1064, 1075, 1074, 1084
131. CV I/2 1086
132. CV I/2 1102
133. CV I/2 1085, 1085n
134. Cowles *Churchill* 64
135. *Wars* 183, 184
136. *Wars* 185
137. *RC* 281, 282

138. *RC* 282, 283, 284
139. *RC* 285, 283
140. CV I/2 1090; WSC I 481
141. *RC* 290, 299; CV I/2 1091; WSC I 481
142. *RC* 290
143. WSC I 489; *Johannesburg Star* 12/22/23; *RC* 295
144. *RC* 296; CV I/2 1131; Martin II 210; CV I/2 1093
145. *RC* 303, 301; CV I/2 1093; *RC* 304
146. *RC* 304, 305
147. *London to Ladysmith* 364; CV I/2 1144; *Wars* 231
148. Pakenham 307
149. Pakenham 308, 310
150. *London to Ladysmith* 307; CV I/2 1147, 1146
151. *London to Ladysmith* 309, 310, 311; *Wars* xxi
152. Eliot *Heiresses* 74
153. WSC I 495; CV I/2 1151, 1149–1150
154. *RC* 325–326; *Wars* 265
155. CV I/2 1167; *Irrepressible* 3; CV I/2 1164; *RC* 329; CV I/2 1161
156. CV I/2 1143, 1151, 1144, 1147
157. *RC* 327; *London to Ladysmith* 345, 346; CV I/2 1168
158. CV I/2 1172
159. CV I/2 1145; *Wars* 290, 291–292
160. *Wars* 292
161. *Ian Hamilton's March* 262; Moran 203
162. *RC* 349
163. *RC* 350; WSC I 512
164. WSC I 513; *Wars* 288
165. CV I/2 1178
166. CV I/2 1199
167. Cowles *Churchill* 67; *RC* 355
168. CV I/2 1201; *RC* 355; Pakenham 492; *Daily Mail* 9/27/1900; WSC to Oldham Conservative Club 9/29/1900; Oldham Conservative Club to WSC 9/30/1900
169. CV I/2 1196; *RC* 357; Bonham Carter 53; *RC* 356; CV I/2 1206
170. WSC I 282; Bonham Carter 56
171. *RC* 360; CV I/2 1222n, 1222; *Irrepressible* 42
172. CV I/2 1225, 1224
173. *RC* 361; CV I/2 1225
174. CV I/2 1231
175. Steevens in Eade 66

Part Three: River, 1901–1914

1. *NYT* 2/15/01
2. *NYT* 2/15/01
3. WSC II 6
4. *RC* 362, 363; *Hansard* 2/18/01; *RC* 364
5. *Hansard* 2/18/01; *RC* 364
6. *RC* 364, 365; *Daily Chronicle* 2/19/01; *Daily Express* 2/19/01; *Daily Telegraph* 2/19/01; *Morning Post* 2/19/01; *Daily News* 2/19/01; *RC* 366, 367
7. *Daily Mail* 6/7/01; Moir 205–206; *Irrepressible* 50, 49
8. Webb *Partnership* 269; Rhodes James *Failure* 16, 15, 20; Blunt *Diaries* II 74–75
9. *Daily Mail* 6/7/01; *Punch* 6/8/04; *RC* 366; *Amid These Storms* 55; WSC II 17
10. *Hansard* 5/13/01
11. Cowles *Churchill* 87; WSC II 20; Cowles *Churchill* 88; Bonham Carter 72
12. *RC* 367; CV II/1 49; Coote in Marchant 39; *Wit* 29; Cowles *Churchill* 92, 94
13. Bonham Carter 5, 6; Rhodes James *Failure* 29
14. CV II/1 62, 64; *Hansard* 3/18/03
15. Cowles *Churchill* 94; *RC* 369
16. *RC* 369–370
17. Cowles *Churchill* 95; Bonham Carter 81
18. *Hansard* 7/31/02; CV II/1 162; Bonham Carter 77; CV II/1 174
19. WSC II 54; *Hansard* 5/28/03; *Review of Reviews* 10/1903
20. WSC II 58; CV II/1 185
21. Coote in Marchant 38; Cowles *Churchill* 96
22. *Times* 3/7/05
23. *RC* 367; CV II/1 188; Bonham Carter 93
24. Cowles *Churchill* 89–90; CV I/2 751; CV II/1 239
25. *Irrepressible* 51; WSC II 63; CV II/1 218; Cowles *Churchill* 98
26. CV II/1 225, 243, 244
27. CV II/1 266; Cowles *Churchill* 98; CV II/1 269, 288, 289
28. *Daily Mail* 3/30/04; *Monthly Review* 11/1903; *Irrepressible* 52; *Hansard* 3/28/05; Rhodes James *Failure* 23; *Hansard* 7/24/05; WSC II 63; *Hansard* 3/24/04
29. *Hansard* 7/24/05, 7/27/05
30. CV II/1 225; WSC II 72; Rhodes James *Failure* 32; Brooks in Eade 359; Winterton in Eade 86–87; *Irrepressible* 50

31. Cowles *Churchill* 99; Brooks in Eade 359; Marchant 47; *Punch* 6/8/04; Moorehead *Churchill Trial* 25; Bonham Carter 85
32. *Daily Mail* 3/30/04; WSC II 76; *Pall Mall Gazette* 3/31/04
33. *Daily Mail* 4/23/04; WSC II 77; Bonham Carter 88
34. Cowles *Churchill* 102; *Hansard* 5/16/04; Bonham Carter 89
35. *Punch* 6/8/04; Cowles *Churchill* 103
36. WSC II 79; *Punch* 6/8/04
37. Margot Asquith *Autobiography* II 134; *Sunday Times* 5/27/24; *Wit* 24
38. Cowles *Churchill* 99; WSC II 71
39. Pelling 87; WSC I 527; CV I/2 1229
40. WSC II 244; CV II/1 587
41. Boothby *Rebel* 24; *Wit* 84; Moir 79
42. Soames 118; Longford *Churchill* 37; WSC II 241; Bonham Carter 3–4
43. Bonham Carter 117–118; CV II/2 800; CV I/2 1232
44. Paul Thompson 71, 72
45. Sackville-West 86, 52
46. Martin II 275; Sackville-West 193–194
47. Martin II 276
48. Tuchman *Proud* 20
49. WSC II 89, 88
50. Anita Leslie *Lady Randolph* 308; WSC II 120
51. Rhodes James *Failure* 16; *Harper's Weekly* 8/6/04
52. Blunt *Diaries* II 74; Hore-Belisha in Eade 393, 394; Bonham Carter 6–7; Anita Leslie *Lady Randolph* 303; *Wit* 43; *Great Contemporaries* 176; *Wit* 42
53. Rhodes James *Failure* 17
54. Cowles *Churchill* 91
55. CV II/1 164–165, 587
56. Bonham Carter 172–173; Marsh 166
57. CV II/2 798; Rhodes James *Failure* 60
58. *Crisis* I 199
59. *Crisis* I 199
60. Ensor 551
61. *Irrepressible* 116
62. Cowles *Churchill* 104; *Punch* 3/22/05; Cowles *Churchill* 103
63. Moorehead *Churchill Trial* 26; Samuel in Marchant 49
64. Bonham Carter 120; Marsh 149
65. CV II/1 421; Marsh 152, 153; Martin II 304
66. WSC II 111; *Churchill Years* 36; WSC II 427; Bonham Carter 101–102; WSC II 120
67. *Daily Mail* 1/5/06; *Manchester Guardian* 1/11/06
68. Bonham Carter 102; WSC II 119–120
69. *Amid These Storms* 207–208
70. *Hansard* 2/27/06
71. *Hansard* 2/28/06, 3/14/06, 3/21/06
72. Margot Asquith *Autobiography* II 86; Marsh 151; Hyam in Stansky 30; CV II/1 534; WSC II 180
73. Marsh 150; CV II/2 797; Hyam in Stansky 22; Pelling 98, 99; Hyam in Stansky 23, 30
74. Hyam in Stansky 24
75. Hyam in Stansky 24–25, 29
76. *Wit* 37; Memorandum of 2/8/07 concerning Aliens Act, Home Office Papers
77. CV II/1 530; Hyam in Stansky 34; *Hansard* 6/30/06; Bonham Carter 110; *Daily Mail* 7/1/06
78. *Liberalism* 98; CV II/2 684
79. WSC II 221; CV II/2 692, 693
80. CV II/2 693, 732; *Outlook* 5/2/08
81. CV II/2 765; Cowles *Churchill* 115; Marsh 163; McGowan 153; Eden in Eade 110
82. *Amid These Storms* 208–209; WSC II 254–255; *Times* 4/24/08
83. WSC II 250; *Morning Post* 4/25/08; CV II/2 789, 787
84. Bonham Carter 171
85. *Irrepressible* 62; WSC II 242
86. Soames 50; CV II/2 781; Soames 54–55
87. CV II/2 798, 800–801; Soames 55
88. *Irrepressible* 17
89. CV II/2 801, 803
90. Soames 67; Blunt *Diaries* II 214
91. *RC* 370; CV II/2 820; Bonham Carter 173
92. McGowan 39; Blunt *Diaries* II 271; Soames 71
93. WSC II 284–285, 339; Soames 91
94. *Irrepressible* 264; CV II/2 918
95. *Savrola* 57; Soames 127, 128
96. Pelling 174; *Great Contemporaries* 174; WSC II 339–340; Soames 110
97. CV II/2 765; Soames 117
98. WSC II 386; CV II/3 1715; Soames 79
99. Cowles *Churchill* 122; *Nation* 3/7/08; WSC II 267; *Liberalism* 81
100. Webb *Partnership* 417; Moorehead *Churchill Trial* 31; Bonham Carter 107
101. Cowles *Churchill* 106
102. Cowles *Churchill* 107
103. WSC II 272, 273
104. WSC II 499; CV II/2 938; Cowles *Churchill* 126; *Crisis* I 33
105. WSC II 299
106. WSC II 305–306, 311
107. CV II/2 887; Soames 73; *Hansard* 4/29/09; Cowles *Churchill* 128; Bonham Carter 146

108. *Hansard* 6/25/07
109. Cowles *Churchill* 129; *Daily Express* 9/6/09; *Times* 9/6/09
110. *Daily Express* 9/6/09; Cowles *Churchill* 132; WSC II 315; Soames 109
111. Pelling 109; CV II/2 967; *Irrepressible* 64; WSC II 316, 315, 320
112. CV II/2 909, 968; WSC II 321
113. Margot Asquith *Autobiography* II 138; Soames 129; Tuchman *August* 1
114. WSC III 87
115. WSC II 347; Cowles *Churchill* 127; WSC II 442, 463
116. Moran 472; WSC II 352, 351, 349
117. *Wit* 29
118. Bonham Carter 151, 174
119. CV II/2 1141; Memorandum "Imprisonment for Debt" 8/23/10, Home Office Papers; WSC II 375, 373; *Yale Review* 2/1911
120. *Times* 7/23/10; WSC II 377; CV II/2 1034, 1094
121. WSC II 329; WSC III 179; Rhodes James *Failure* 42, 60; Bonham Carter 107; Rhodes James *Failure* 39; Webb *Partnership* 404
122. WSC II 419–420
123. Cowles *Churchill* 144
124. Cowles *Churchill* 143n; *Hansard* 11/24/10; *Daily Mail* 2/9/50; Cowles *Churchill* 144
125. *Times* 11/9/10; *Daily Express* 11/9/10; CV II/2 1207
126. *Amid These Storms* 68
127. *Amid These Storms* 69–70
128. WSC II 394; *Daily News* 1/4/11
129. WSC II 395; *Amid These Storms* 72; Rhodes James *Failure* 43; Pelling 138
130. WSC II 365; CV II/2 1274
131. WSC II 370; CV II/2 1282
132. CV II/2 1285; WSC II 371; CV II/2 1290
133. Rhodes James *Failure* 43, 44; *Hansard* 8/22/11; Isaacs in Eade 371
134. *Wit* 28
135. *Great Contemporaries* 37; CV II/1 582; WSC II 191
136. CV II/2 723, 903, 911, 913, 910
137. CV II/2 911–912
138. CV II/2 1079
139. Cowles *Churchill* 153; *Crisis* I 44
140. CV II/2 1105, 1116
141. *Crisis* I 49
142. *Crisis* I 60–61; Cowles *Churchill* 154
143. Soames 97, 98
144. Cowles *Churchill* 157; Bonham Carter 188
145. *Crisis* I 68
146. Soames 99; *Crisis* I 122; Soames 124, 121
147. Soames 126, 101
148. Soames 84; CV II/3 1723; Soames 123; Bonham Carter 190
149. Pelling 147; *Crisis* I 71; WSC II 558
150. *Crisis* I 123–124
151. Cowles *Churchill* 157; CV II/3 1595, 1504, 1597
152. Tuchman *August* 50; *Crisis* I 101, 102
153. *Crisis* I 103; *Daily News* 2/10/12; Bonham Carter 197; WSC II 546
154. Tuchman *August* 53, 326
155. Tuchman *August* 326, 330
156. CV II/3 1517, 1518
157. CV II/2 1316; Tuchman *August* 195, 203; *Crisis* I 81
158. Cowles *Churchill* 158; *Crisis* I 72
159. WSC II 527–528
160. *Crisis* I 76; Bacon *Fisher* II 138
161. *Crisis* I 90, 146–147; Marder II 416
162. Marder II 430; *Crisis* I 78; Bacon *Fisher* II 148; WSC II 565; Marder II 459, 461; WSC II 566
163. Bonham Carter 202–203; Marder II 467
164. *Crisis* I 123; *Irrepressible* 71
165. *Fleet* 10/1912; Pelling 149; *Wit* 57
166. Tuchman *August* 422; Manchester "Great War" 110; *Crisis* I 338; Low in Eade 444
167. Tuchman *August* 239; CV II/3 1874; Wrench in Eade 291; *Crisis* I 337
168. Joubert in Eade 160; CV II/3 1883–1884; Soames 130
169. WSC II 681, 682
170. WSC II 682; Joubert in Eade 161; Pelling 168
171. CV II/3 1889, 1890; Soames 131
172. CV II/3 1893; Cowles *Churchill* 7; Soames 131; CV II/3 1920
173. Soames 132, 133, 134
174. CV II/3 1921–1922
175. *Crisis* I 111; WSC II 552; Churchill to Viscount Grey 1/20/12, quoting letter from Berlin, Grey Papers; CV II/3 1492; Churchill to Grey 10/24/13, Grey Papers
176. WSC II 636–637
177. Tuchman *August* 91
178. *Daily Chronicle* 1/3/14; Pelling 153; WSC II 662; CV II/3 1872
179. WSC II 663
180. *Great Contemporaries* 345; Blunt *Diaries* II 289; Eden in Eade 110; *Lord Randolph* II 59
181. Morris *Trumpets* 222; *Great Contemporaries* 82; WSC II 444; *Review of Reviews* 3/1912

182. Bonham Carter 228; *Times* 2/7/12
183. Bonham Carter 228; *Times* 2/9/12; Soames 104
184. Bonham Carter 228; Bromage 21–22
185. Bonham Carter 230; *Irrepressible* 70; WSC II 484
186. WSC II 484; Cowles *Churchill* 168; WSC II 456; Bromage 31–32, 30
187. *Great Contemporaries* 347; Bromage 37, 31
188. WSC II 454; Bromage 35; Pelling 158; *Times* 10/9/13; Bonham Carter 236
189. WSC II 463–464
190. Morris *Trumpets* 225; Bromage 39, 36, 31; Bonham Carter 230
191. Cowles *Churchill* 169
192. Morris *Trumpets* 227
193. Bromage 43
194. Bonham Carter 237; *Times* 3/15/14; Bromage 42; WSC II 474
195. CV II/3 1414
196. Bromage 47
197. Cowles *Churchill* 170; Bonham Carter 239; Rhodes James *Failure* 54
198. *Hansard* 4/28/14; *Crisis* I 195
199. *Hansard* 4/28/14; Bonham Carter 243; CV II/3 1418
200. Bromage 38; WSC II 488
201. *Crisis* I 205
202. *Crisis* I 201, 210; CV II/3 1421; WSC III 3
203. CV II/3 1987–1988
204. WSC III 4; CV II/3 1987; Tuchman *August* 71; *Crisis* I 209
205. WSC III 6
206. WSC III 8; Soames 137; CV II/3 1988
207. Tuchman *August* 93; *Crisis* I 225; *Great Contemporaries* 148; *Crisis* I 226
208. WSC III 5; CV II/3 1989
209. Tuchman *August* 96; H. H. Asquith *Letters* 138; WSC III 22; CV II/3 1991, 1995–1996
210. *Crisis* I 236, 238
211. CV II/3 1993–1994
212. *Crisis* I 524; CV II/3 1992; Tuchman *August* 140; *Crisis* I 37
213. Tuchman *August* 72, 95, 90; H. H. Asquith *Memories* II 10
214. Martin II 365; Rhodes James *Failure* 65–66; H. H. Asquith *Memories* II 11; Tuchman *August* 96
215. Tuchman *August* 96, 92; WSC II 24, 23
216. Beaverbrook *War* I 22, 23
217. Kenneth Young 34; *Crisis* I 231; CV II/3 1997–1998
218. Kenneth Young 34; H. H. Asquith *Letters* 146
219. Tuchman *August* 143; *Crisis* I 239; Tuchman *August* 94, 118; *Crisis* I 235; Edel 200, 202; Tuchman *August* 122
220. Soames 140; *Crisis* I 239; H. H. Asquith *Letters* 150–151
221. Tuchman *August* 323; CV II/3 1999
222. Margot Asquith *Autobiography* II 196

Part Four: Cataract, 1914–1918

1. WSC III 44; Soames 145; CV III/1 28
2. WSC III 83
3. H. H. Asquith *Letters* 334; Pelling 188
4. *Crisis* I 306, 305; WSC III 50, 43; Rhodes James *Failure* 45; Martin II 370
5. WSC III 35; *Crisis* I 252; *Crisis* II 391
6. CV III/1 28, 31; Soames 144
7. CV III/1 28; Soames 143
8. WSC III 59, 84; *Crisis* I 432
9. *Morning Post* 10/21/14; WSC III 86; Bonham Carter 280; *Crisis* I 432
10. Stevenson 10; CV III/1 250, 128
11. CV III/1 70, 66; Bonham Carter 280; CV III/1 173; H. H. Asquith *Letters* 287, 290
12. CV III/1 220, 221, 225–226
13. CV III/1 203; Bonham Carter 280; CV III/1 118–119; *Crisis* I 436–437; Bonham Carter 281
14. WSC III 187; Beaverbrook *War* I 105; Rhodes James *Failure* 68; CV III/1 221, 224–225; H. H. Asquith *Letters* 305; CV III/1 232
15. WSC III 153; CV III/1 243; WSC III 154
16. *Crisis* I 441; *Great Contemporaries* 339; WSC III 262
17. *Crisis* I 289; WSC III 35
18. Tuchman *August* 387, 388; *Times* 8/30/14
19. Tuchman *August* 33, 34
20. Tuchman *August* 190
21. Tuchman *August* 235, 243
22. Tuchman *August* 224, 319
23. Tuchman *August* 52; CV III/1 97
24. H. H. Asquith *Letters* 227–228; WSC III 73–74; CV III/1 135; *Irrepressible* 75
25. *Crisis* I 303; Soames 141; CV III/1 141
26. CV III/1 96, 97; WSC III 101

27. WSC III 101; H. H. Asquith *Letters* 258, 259
28. *Crisis* I 367; CV III/1 157; H. H. Asquith *Letters* 260
29. Rhodes James *Failure* 71; CV III/1 161; WSC III 109, 108
30. WSC III 48; H. H. Asquith *Letters* 262; Bonham Carter 276–277
31. CV III/1 163
32. CV III/1 167–168; H. H. Asquith *Letters* 262, 263
33. CV III/1 167, 170; WSC III 115
34. CV III/1 172, 173
35. CV III/1 173; WSC III 119; H. H. Asquith *Letters* 275
36. CV III/1 177, 173, 178
37. Bonham Carter 277; H. H. Asquith *Letters* 268
38. WSC III 110; *Morning Post* 10/13/14; CV III/1 195; *Daily Mail* 10/14/14
39. CV III/1 174, 175; WSC III 133–134, 132; CV III/1 191; Stevenson 6; WSC III 329, 330
40. WSC III 129; H. H. Asquith *Letters* 271, 296; Bonham Carter 278–279; WSC III 125
41. Rhodes James *Failure* 71–72; CV III/1 26
42. H. H. Asquith *Letters* 266–267
43. Manchester "Great War" 111
44. Blunden *Mind's Eye* 38
45. CV III/1 272–273, 274
46. H. H. Asquith *Letters* 346; CV III/1 350, 351; *Crisis* II 2; CV III/2 1306; *Crisis* II 79
47. CV III/1 132, 377–378
48. WSC III 536
49. WSC III 536, 537; *Churchill Years* 62
50. Higgins 144
51. Margot Asquith *Autobiography* II 203; CV III/1 75, 76; WSC III 205; CV III/1 95
52. CV III/1 236
53. CV III/1 278, 279; Higgins 75; CV III/1 297
54. Moorehead *Gallipoli* 37; WSC III 220n; CV III/1 326, 367; H. H. Asquith *Letters* 345; CV III/1 344; WSC III 236–237; H. H. Asquith *Letters* 357–358
55. WSC III 232; CV III/1 391
56. CV III/1 393
57. Higgins 1
58. Moorehead *Gallipoli* 73
59. WSC III 219; Bonham Carter 296
60. WSC III 220; CV III/1 367
61. CV III/1 380; WSC III 248, 250; CV III/1 381, 406
62. CV III/1 406–407; Moorehead *Gallipoli* 40; CV III/1 409, 410; WSC III 252; CV III/1 411
63. Higgins 117; *Crisis* I 438; Bonham Carter 290
64. WSC III 313; Higgins 65
65. Cowles *Churchill* 214; Moorehead *Churchill Trial* 48; CV III/1 410; Higgins 174–175
66. Higgins 224
67. Higgins 117; Wolff 190
68. CV III/1 411, 410
69. CV III/1 414, 429–430; H. H. Asquith *Letters* 387
70. CV III/1 436, 453, 454
71. CV III/1 460
72. CV III/1 463; *Crisis* II 164; CV III/1 464
73. H. H. Asquith *Letters* 405; WSC III 273, 274; CV III/1 469
74. Rhodes James *Failure* 85; Higgins 136; Liddell Hart *Fog of War* 288
75. Higgins 49; Rowse in Eade 495
76. H. H. Asquith *Letters* 429; CV III/1 513; WSC III 287
77. CV III/1 516
78. CV III/1 517–518, 525; H. H. Asquith *Letters* 436
79. CV III/1 557, 569, 558
80. CV III/1 573–574, 580
81. CV III/1 554–555
82. WSC III 305–306
83. *Times* 4/26/15
84. Moorehead *Gallipoli* 56
85. CV III/1 584; H. H. Asquith *Letters* 456; Bonham Carter 302
86. CV III/1 605–606, 680, 690, 617–618
87. CV III/1 634
88. *Crisis* I 274; CV III/1 645
89. Moorehead *Gallipoli* 57
90. Moorehead *Gallipoli* 58
91. CV III/1 677–678, 687–688
92. WSC III 337; CV III/1 706
93. Moorehead *Gallipoli* 69
94. Moorehead *Churchill Trial* 45; Moorehead *Gallipoli* 74; *World's Work* 12/1929
95. CV III/1 636, 730; WSC III 357, 358; CV III/1 712
96. Moorehead *Gallipoli* 79; CV III/1 698, 677
97. Rhodes James *Failure* 87
98. CV III/1 559
99. CV III/1 560, 664; Moorehead *Gallipoli* 80, 83
100. H. H. Asquith *Letters* 257; CV III/1 629
101. WSC III 358; Moorehead *Gallipoli* 86; WSC III 363; CV III/1 711, 718–719

102. Moorehead *Gallipoli* 86, 87, 88
103. CV III/1 723–724
104. Moorehead *Gallipoli* 91; WSC III 364–365; Rhodes James *Failure* 84
105. CV III/1 732, 729; *Morning Post* 3/25/15; Higgins 171
106. CV III/1 752, 753
107. CV III/1 753; WSC III 411
108. Moorehead *Gallipoli* 143
109. Moorehead *Gallipoli* 257
110. CV III/2 852, 855; Moorehead *Gallipoli* 165
111. CV III/1 770; WSC III 411–412; Bonham Carter 310; WSC III 419
112. Moorehead *Gallipoli* 166
113. *Crisis* II 364; Moorehead *Gallipoli* 168; *Crisis* II 361; CV III/2 884–885
114. WSC III 345; CV III/2 885
115. *Crisis* II 373–374; Bacon *Fisher* II 256; CV III/2 888; Moorehead *Gallipoli* 170; WSC III 439
116. *Crisis* II 377; CV III/2 892; WSC III 442
117. CV III/2 906, 907, 911
118. WSC III 430; CV III/2 880; *Times* 5/14/15; Moorehead *Gallipoli* 157; WSC III 555
119. Rhodes James *Failure* 88; *Times* 5/18/15; WSC III 424, 425; Stevenson 50
120. H. H. Asquith *Letters* 585, 586, 596; WSC III 447
121. *Crisis* II 385; WSC III 488–489
122. WSC III 414; *Crisis* II 381; CV III/2 940; WSC III 448; CV III/2 898
123. WSC III 455; CV III/2 908
124. Stevenson 52, 74; Cowles *Churchill* 201; WSC III 476; Moorehead *Gallipoli* 171
125. CV III/2 914, 915, 920, 922, 923–924
126. CV III/2 925, 926, 921
127. CV III/2 932; Kenneth Young 37; CV III/2 924, 926, 927, 932; WSC III 466
128. Bonham Carter 330; Moorehead *Gallipoli* 118
129. CV III/2 894; Dundee *Advertiser* 5/23/15; WSC III 399; *Times* 5/22/15; Stevenson 52, 53; H. H. Asquith *Letters* 546, 508
130. Pelling 204–205; WSC III 457; Rhodes James *Failure* 91; *Amid These Storms* 307; WSC III 473
131. CV III/2 948, 955; Moorehead *Gallipoli* 172; Martin II 372
132. CV III/2 1017; WSC III 537; CV III/2 1559
133. CV III/2 1180, 1042; *Irrepressible* 77; *Amid These Storms* 307
134. *Amid These Storms* 307–308
135. *Amid These Storms* 308, 313–314
136. Marsh 248–249; *Amid These Storms* 297
137. *Wit* 50; Rothenstein in Marchant 150; Holliday and Pernes 18
138. J. G. S. Churchill 34
139. J. G. S. Churchill 32
140. CV III/2 982
141. Moorehead *Gallipoli* 236
142. Kenneth Young 36; Longford *Churchill* 61; *Crisis* II 6
143. CV III/2 1081, 1084, 1098
144. CV III/2 1100, 1101, 1103
145. *Crisis* II 516; Moorehead *Gallipoli* 318–319
146. Higgins 228; Moorehead *Gallipoli* 324, 326
147. CV III/2 1183; Pelling 208; WSC III 563
148. *Manchester Guardian* 11/13/15
149. *Hansard* 11/15/15; Bonham Carter 351; CV III/2 1272
150. Beaverbrook *Power* 118
151. Bonham Carter 352, 353
152. Beaverbrook *War* II 74; CV III/2 1276; WSC III 572; CV III/2 1277
153. *Amid These Storms* 101, 102
154. *Amid These Storms* 101
155. *Amid These Storms* 101, 103; Soames 196
156. *Amid These Storms* 103; CV III/2 1324; Soames 186
157. CV III/2 1314, 1318
158. Soames 173; CV III/2 1283, 1284
159. CV III/2 1370; *Amid These Storms* 103, 104
160. CV III/2 1320; *Amid These Storms* 105; CV III/2 1315; *Irrepressible* 76; CV III/2 1300, 1278
161. CV III/2 1289; Bonham Carter 364; *Amid These Storms* 105; CV III/2 1425, 1290; Bonham Carter 365
162. WSC III 625; CV III/2 1331
163. CV IV/1 373; WSC IV 140
164. Sassoon *Journey* 116–119
165. *Amid These Storms* 106, 108, 109, 110
166. CV III/2 1293, 1423, 1432, 1433, 1309–1310; WSC IV 135; CV III/2 1291, 1311
167. Soames 182; WSC III 595; Soames 211, 193, 173, 207, 197
168. CV III/2 1331
169. WSC III 583; Soames 184–185
170. CV III/2 1311, 1302–1303
171. CV III/2 1322; Soames 189
172. Soames 192, 193; CV III/2 1325
173. H. H. Asquith *Memories* 136; CV III/2 1333; *Hansard* 12/16/15
174. Beaverbrook *War* II 75, 76; WSC III 697; Soames 190; WSC III 611; CV III/2 1332; Soames 193–194

175. WSC III 615; CV III/2 1333; Soames 200; CV III/2 1352; WSC III 666; Soames 219, 220
176. Soames 192; Wolff 32, 35
177. Wolff 35, 36; WSC IV 51; *Great Contemporaries* 227
178. WSC III 614; CV III/2 1334, 1335, 1336
179. Attlee in Stansky 199; "Four Crises in the Great War" 7/30/16
180. CV III/2 1351
181. WSC III 629, 630; CV III/2 1361; WSC III 632
182. CV III/2 1365, 1377; WSC III 639
183. CV III/2 1399; Cowles *Churchill* 211
184. CV III/2 1405, 1396, 1398
185. CV III/2 1399; Cowles *Churchill* 211; WSC III 657
186. CV III/2 1412; WSC III 661; CV III/2 1410
187. Pelling 217; CV III/2 1482; WSC III 657, 658, 672
188. CV III/2 1405; WSC III 604; Soames 218
189. WSC III 622, 698; Soames 209, 200, 199, 202; CV III/2 1352, 1363, 1369–1370; WSC III 683
190. Soames 238; WSC III 758
191. *Hansard* 3/7/16
192. Bonham Carter 369; WSC III 725; CV III/2 1443
193. Bonham Carter 371
194. *Hansard* 3/8/16
195. *Hansard* 3/8/16; CV III/2 1443, 1444
196. Bonham Carter 371; CV III/2 1444, 1450
197. CV III/2 1460, 1461
198. Soames 234, 236, 238
199. Pelling 216; WSC III 759; CV III/2 1498
200. WSC III 760; CV III/2 1501, 1498
201. Kenneth Young 41
202. CV III/2 1545
203. *Hansard* 5/23/16, 7/24/16
204. *Hansard* 5/23/16; WSC IV 14; Pelling 222; WSC III 774
205. CV III/2 1538
206. CV III/2 1534
207. *Daily Mail* 10/13/16; WSC III 811; *Spectator* 3/11/16
208. Pelling 216; WSC III 825; Bonham Carter 368–369; Boothby *Rebel* 50
209. Cowles *Churchill* 214; CV IV/1 5; CV III/2 1530, 1531
210. CV IV/1 37–38
211. WSC III 816
212. Soames 204
213. WSC III 685; CV III/2 1372; WSC III 762
214. WSC III 780
215. CV III/2 1518, 1520, 1529, 1530
216. WSC III 789, 790
217. CV III/2 1533, 1570; CV IV/1 34
218. Boothby *Rebel* 19; WSC III 822
219. CV III/2 1584; Kenneth Young 44–45
220. CV IV/1 36; WSC III 681; Wolff 28
221. Wolff 25, 271, 157, 48
222. *New Republic* 6/14/17; WSC IV 9; *Hansard* 3/20/17
223. Cowles *Churchill* 221; WSC IV 26; Stevenson 157
224. *Hansard* 4/17/17
225. Wolff 205; WSC IV 17; *Crisis* III 262
226. *Crisis* IV 2; CV IV/1 102, 103; Pelling 229; *Morning Post* 7/19/17; WSC IV 29; CV IV/1 118
227. Pelling 230; Soames 220; WSC IV 35
228. WSC IV 32
229. *Crisis* IV 7, 9
230. WSC IV 61; CV IV/1 300, 301; *Times* 7/11/18; WSC IV 127–128
231. WSC IV 38; *Crisis* IV 199; WSC IV 72; CV III/2 1354
232. WSC IV 17; Wolff 72
233. Wolff x
234. WSC IV 33; CV IV/1 108; WSC IV 47
235. WSC IV 47; Wolff 155–157; *Times* 8/18/17
236. Wolff 157, 263; *Crisis* IV 43, 61
237. CV IV/1 390–391
238. Wolff 24, 204, 162
239. Wolff 240, 241
240. Manchester "Great War" 114; WSC IV 48
241. *Crisis* IV 128
242. *Crisis* IV 129, 130, 131
243. *Crisis* IV 144; WSC IV 81; CV IV/1 278, 279
244. *Amid These Storms* 165; WSC IV 85; CV IV/1 282; *Amid These Storms* 166, 167
245. *Amid These Storms* 168; CV IV/1 282; WSC IV 89; *Amid These Storms* 177; CV IV/1 288
246. *Amid These Storms* 170, 171
247. WSC IV 95; *Amid These Storms* 173
248. *Amid These Storms* 173, 174, 175
249. *Amid These Storms* 176
250. *Amid These Storms* 177; CV IV/1 291, 288, 289, 294
251. CV IV/1 300
252. WSC IV 106
253. WSC IV 107, 108
254. *Hansard* 4/25/18
255. Toland 156; Falls 345
256. CV IV/1 368
257. Manchester *Krupp* 300

258. CV IV/1 324
259. Falls 345; Manchester "Great War" 121
260. WSC IV 122; CV IV/1 343
261. Martin II 364; WSC IV 115
262. WSC IV 115; Martin II 390, 389, 385; WM / Lady Diana Cooper 10/20/80
263. CV IV/1 324, 249, 323
264. Toland 374
265. CV IV/1 393, 395
266. CV IV/1 387
267. WSC IV 154
268. WSC IV 48
269. CV IV/1 108, 309, 315, 302, 310
270. WSC III 23; WSC IV 123
271. WSC IV 149–150, 139
272. *Churchill Years* 64; CV IV/1 368
273. CV IV/1 370
274. Deutscher 476; *Crisis* IV 231–232; A. J. P. Taylor *First World War* 152; Wolff 271
275. CV IV/1 251, 394
276. Manchester "Great War" 123, 127
277. WSC IV 158; *Crisis* IV 273; Moir 215; WSC IV 166
278. Shirer 48

Part Five: Oxbow, 1918–1932

1. *Crisis* IV 275; *NYT* 11/17/18
2. Morris *Trumpets* 206
3. Kohn 308
4. Rhodes James *Failure* 109; Morris *Trumpets* 205
5. Girouard *Camelot* 2
6. Girouard *Camelot* 284–285; Osborn viii–ix
7. Shirer 51n–52n
8. Cowles *Churchill* 229; Rhodes James *Failure* 106
9. *Wit* 24; Morris *Trumpets* 211, 209n
10. Morris *Trumpets* 206
11. Gandhi 212; Morris *Trumpets* 212
12. Moorehead *Gallipoli* 155
13. Morris *Trumpets* 213
14. Morris *Trumpets* 212, 215; CV IV/3 2029
15. Morris *Trumpets* 304
16. Morris *Trumpets* 300–301
17. Morris *Trumpets* 302
18. WSC IV 915
19. WSC IV 171; *RC* vii
20. CV IV/3 1736; *Daily Telegraph* 11/5/20
21. Moran 443; Soames 247; WSC IV 913–914
22. CV IV/1 422–423
23. Dundee *Advertiser* 12/29/18; CV IV/1 448
24. *Crisis* V 63
25. WSC IV 182; CV IV/1 451, 479
26. CV IV/1 501, 502; WSC IV 193
27. WSC IV 196; CV IV/2 1069; Baruch in Marchant 164
28. Deutscher 388
29. Deutscher 421
30. *Evening News* 7/28/20; *Times* 11/27/18; WSC IV 228
31. WSC IV 229; Riddell *Intimate* 21; WSC IV 235; *Daily Express* 1/3/19
32. Deutscher 421
33. Rhodes James *Failure* 117–118; CV IV/1 471; WSC IV 356
34. Lloyd George *Treaties* 325; *Irrepressible* 78, 80, 79
35. Rhodes James *Failure* 122; WSC IV 365, 244; *Times* 4/12/19; WSC IV 278
36. Hankey *Control* 70; CV IV/1 525; WSC IV 240; Rhodes James *Failure* 125; WSC IV 324–325; Beaverbrook *Power* 406
37. WSC IV 349; *Daily Express* 1/3/19; "The Red Fever"; Rhodes James *Failure* 134; WSC IV 305; Rhodes James *Failure* 136; WSC IV 433–434
38. WSC IV 290; *Weekly Review* 6/22/19; WSC IV 365–366; Deutscher 457
39. *Hansard* 5/29/19
40. CV IV/2 729; CV IV/1 660
41. WSC IV 325; Deutscher 442
42. WSC IV 352; CV IV/2 1059, 987; WSC IV 362
43. WSC IV 329
44. Deutscher 460; CV IV/2 1190
45. CV IV/2 1190n, 1035
46. CV IV/2 1048, 1049
47. *Hansard* 2/10/20; CV IV/2 1111, 1238
48. CV IV/2 1246; WSC IV 440
49. WSC IV 441; *Sunday Express* 12/5/20, 12/12/20
50. Stevenson 196–197
51. Liddell Hart "Churchill in War"; Rhodes James *Failure* 139; CV IV/2 1123
52. Liddell Hart "Churchill in War"
53. *Hansard* 7/8/20
54. CV IV/2 1140, 1141; *Hansard* 7/8/20
55. *Hansard* 7/8/20
56. *Hansard* 7/8/20

57. WSC IV 411; *Times* 7/9/20
58. CV IV/2 1319, 1260–1261, 1262, 1354–1355
59. Morris *Trumpets* 257–258
60. Pelling 261–262
61. WSC IV 484; "Zionism vs. Bolshevism"; CV IV/2 1120
62. WSC IV 615; Morris *Trumpets* 258
63. Sarah Churchill 35
64. Soames 259; CV IV/2 1368, 1380, 1384
65. WSC IV 540, 541, 543; *Irrepressible* 44
66. WSC IV 544
67. *Times* 3/4/21; Morris *Trumpets* 260, 259; WSC IV 545; *Irrepressible* 132; *Great Contemporaries* 163
68. WSC IV 557; W. H. Thompson 33; *Egyptian Gazette* 3/24/21
69. WSC IV 552, 558, 563
70. WSC IV 562, 895, 565
71. *Times* 6/8/21, 3/31/21
72. CV IV/2 1423
73. WSC IV 583
74. CV IV/3 1484; WSC IV 597; "Zionism vs. Bolshevism"
75. WSC IV 637, 594, 596, 597, 598
76. CV IV/3 1505; WSC IV 599; *Hansard* 7/4/22; WSC IV 628
77. Rhodes James *Failure* 149
78. *Hansard* 6/14/21
79. CV IV/2 1054–1055, 1260, 1268, 1272
80. *Hansard* 12/22/20; CV IV/2 1264
81. WSC IV 611; Stevenson 230; *Hansard* 7/21/20
82. CV IV/3 1980; WSC IV 820
83. CV IV/3 2043
84. CV IV/3 2040, 1241, 2043, 1980; *Aftermath* 449
85. CV IV/3 1995, 2057; WSC IV 841
86. WSC IV 835
87. Cowles *Churchill* 239; *Daily Mail* 9/18/21; *Aftermath* 464–465; WSC IV 862
88. WSC IV 467
89. *Irrepressible* 61
90. *NYT* 12/12/18; Coote in Marchant 40; Moorehead *Churchill Trial* 60–61; *Aftermath* 335–336
91. *Aftermath* 294
92. Bromage 62; WSC IV 449; CV IV/2 1062, 1248; WSC IV 453
93. CV IV/2 1232; *Aftermath* 303; "The Murder Campaign in Ireland"; Soames 270
94. WSC IV 452, 453; CV IV/2 1090; *Hansard* 2/23/20; *Aftermath* 287
95. WSC IV 451, 463–464; Rhodes James *Failure* 143
96. Rhodes James *Failure* 141, 142; Pelling 268
97. Rhodes James *Failure* 144; CV IV/2 1195, 1214; WSC IV 466; Rhodes James *Failure* 142; *Hansard* 2/23/20; CV IV/2 1274, 1275
98. Rhodes James *Failure* 142; *Aftermath* 301–302; WSC IV 666
99. Bromage 63; WSC IV 667, 668
100. Dundee *Advertiser* 9/24/21; WSC IV 669
101. Bromage 66; *Crisis* V 305
102. *Hansard* 12/15/21; Bromage 69; *Hansard* 2/16/22; *Gathering Storm* 276; WSC IV 677
103. Bromage 71; *Hansard* 12/15/21
104. *Aftermath* 324–325; *Hansard* 3/2/22; *Aftermath* 329; WSC IV 703
105. WSC IV 707; Bromage 75–76; WSC IV 688, 711; *Aftermath* 355, 338; WSC IV 708; *Hansard* 2/16/22; *Aftermath* 328
106. *Aftermath* 340, 349, 348
107. Bromage 83; *Hansard* 5/31/22
108. O'Connor 251; *NYT* 6/2/22; CV IV/3 1768
109. Macardle 966; *Aftermath* 355; CV IV/3 1849–1850
110. *Aftermath* 342; CV IV/3 1881; *Aftermath* 355
111. *NYT* 6/22/22, 6/18/22; *Aftermath* 359–360
112. *Crisis* IV 111; Soames 312; WSC IV 739
113. *Hansard* 6/26/22; *NYT* 7/7/22, 6/29/22; *Aftermath* 364
114. Bromage 91; Macardle 757; *Aftermath* 367
115. WSC IV 745; *Aftermath* 369, 370
116. *Times* 11/13/22; Bromage 96–97; *Aftermath* 370
117. *Great Contemporaries* 322
118. WSC IV 861; *Times* 10/7/22
119. *Nation* 10–11/1919; Rhodes James *Failure* 154, 155
120. WSC IV 864; G. M. Young *Baldwin* 40
121. WSC IV 773; Kenneth Young 60
122. WSC IV 907, 581; Stevenson 210; Boothby *Rebel* 52; CV IV/2 1055, 1054
123. *Amid These Storms* 213; Attlee in Marchant 74; WSC IV 901; CV IV/3 1766; *Irrepressible* 243, 85
124. CV IV/1 94; WSC IV 883; *Wit* 68; WSC IV 774
125. Shinwell in Eade 122, 121; *Daily Herald* 6/7/19, 8/1/19
126. *Times* 11/7/22
127. *Times* 10/28/22; WSC IV 874

128. CV IV/3 2097, 2116–2117
129. WSC IV 878; Dundee *Courier* 11/7/22; Soames 272, 273; WSC IV 879, 878, 880
130. Dundee *Courier* 11/12/22; *Amid These Storms* 212; Dundee *Courier* 11/14/22; WSC IV 885
131. WSC IV 886; Dundee *Courier* 11/15/22
132. WSC IV 887; *Amid These Storms* 213; CV IV/3 2128, 2125, 2126; WSC IV 892, 888; *Daily Telegraph* 11/17/22
133. CV V/1 3, 47; *Irrepressible* 93
134. "The Future of Mr Lloyd George"; CV V/1 29, 41
135. Rhodes James *Failure* 164; *Times* 11/15/20; WSC V 15
136. WSC V 18; Kenneth Young 67
137. WSC V 19, 19n; *Review of Reviews* 1/1924; Rhodes James *Failure* 98
138. WSC V 20; Rhodes James *Failure* 166; Cowles *Churchill* 251
139. WSC V 20; CV V/1 92–93, 96
140. CV V/1 112, 113; Soames 274; CV V/1 83; Cowles *Churchill* 253; CV V/1 116; WSC V 35, 34
141. *Amid These Storms* 214–215; Rhodes James *Memoirs* 194–195; WSC V 35; Rhodes James *Failure* 169
142. Rhodes James *Failure* 169–170; *Times* 3/19/24
143. WSC V 36, 37; Pelling 291
144. *Times* 3/21/24; Shinwell in Eade 121
145. Telford Taylor 551; Beaverbrook *Press* 108
146. CV V/1 132, 133, 40; *Wit* 70
147. WSC IV 210; CV IV/3 1710; CV IV/2 1353; *Gathering Storm* 41
148. WSC IV 387; Soames 255
149. Soames 263; CV IV/3 1618; Soames 264; CV IV/3 1623, 1957
150. Martin II 394
151. *London Evening News* 6/18/21; Martin II 398, 399, 401; CV IV/3 1532; WSC IV 604; CV IV/3 1536
152. Soames 253; CV IV/3 1934
153. WSC IV 763; Soames 266; CV IV/3 1713
154. Soames 284; WSC IV 613; CV IV/3 1712, 1933
155. CV IV/3 1952, 1956; WSC III 791; CV IV/3 1958
156. CV IV/3 1713, 1957; Soames 306, 305
157. Soames 257–258
158. Soames 257; CV V/1 55
159. CV III/2 1098; WSC IV 757, 758–759
160. WSC IV 752
161. WSC V 4
162. Cowles *Churchill* 246; *Times* 4/10/23
163. CV V/1 86; *Nation* 3/9/29; Muggeridge in Eade 347
164. *Crisis* III 170, 197
165. Soames 257; Fedden 14; Sarah Churchill 22; WSC IV 793, 794
166. WSC IV 11; Soames 287–288; CV V/1 58
167. CV V/1 56; Sarah Churchill 29–30; Soames 292; CV V/1 144, 145
168. Sarah Churchill 25; CV V/1 655, 746, 179, 178; W. H. Thompson 123
169. Sarah Churchill 25, 24; W. H. Thompson 88; Fedden 21; CV V/1 1340
170. CV V/1 1340, 1333, 1347–1348; Pelling 316; CV V/1 1348n
171. CV V/1 179; *Irrepressible* 261, 262; Sarah Churchill 28
172. Cowles *Churchill* 274; Sarah Churchill 27
173. Soames 347; WSC V 107; WM / Lady Soames 10/9/80; CV V/1 1055
174. Soames 296, 297
175. Soames 303; WM / Lady Soames 10/9/80
176. Rhodes James *Failure* 336; WM / Lady Soames 10/27/80; Longford *Churchill* 79; CV V/2 97; Boothby *Rebel* 51
177. Rhodes James *Failure* 337–338; WM / Lady Soames 10/27/80; WSC V 302
178. Soames 306; Fedden 9
179. CV V/1 215
180. Pelling 292; CV V/1 152; WSC V 53; *Sunday Times* 10/31/24; CV V/1 226, 232, 233
181. WSC V 59, 60
182. WSC V 60; Kenneth Young 71, 72, 73
183. Rhodes James *Failure* 170; WSC V 60; *Times* 12/9/24; *Manchester Guardian* 10/7/24
184. WSC V 62; Boothby *Rebel* 46
185. *Wit* 69; *Irrepressible* 98; CV V/1 264, 445, 448–449; *Current Opinion* 2/1925
186. CV V/1 337, 1342
187. W. H. Thompson 70; *Irrepressible* 99; W. H. Thompson 71
188. *Hansard* 4/28/25
189. Soames 277; James in Eade 149
190. James in Eade 148; WSC V 78; CV V/1 356, 376
191. Rhodes James *Failure* 184
192. Rhodes James *Failure* 185; CV V/1 306, 307
193. *Times* 4/29/25; *Hansard* 4/28/25; Kenneth Young 74; Boothby *Rebel* 39
194. WSC V 100
195. *Hansard* 5/4/25, 2/13/46
196. Rhodes James *Failure* 176; WSC V 97
197. Cowles *Churchill* 260; *Nation* 2/21/25

198. *Sunday Express* 7/12/25; Keynes 23
199. *Times* 7/13/25
200. *Hansard* 5/5/26, 4/22/26; WSC V 147–148, 146
201. Cowles *Churchill* 264; *Hansard* 5/5/26; Cowles *Churchill* 265
202. *Hansard* 2/13/46; *Great Contemporaries* 375; WSC V 300n
203. *Hansard* 5/5/26
204. *Hansard* 5/3/26; WSC V 164, 165; *Churchill Years* 79
205. Rhodes James *Failure* 191, 188
206. Holt in Eade 187, 189
207. WSC V 158; Liddell Hart *Memoirs* II 144; Holt in Eade 191; Pelling 314
208. Rhodes James *Failure* 189, 190
209. *Hansard* 5/3/26; CV V/1 713; Rhodes James *Failure* 192; WSC V 168; Holt in Eade 189
210. Webb *Diaries* 166; CV V/1 718; Kenneth Young 71, 84
211. Kenneth Young 84; CV V/1 721; WSC V 172
212. Pelling 315; *New Statesman* 5/22/26; CV V/1 727; *Times* 6/8/26
213. WSC V 172; CV V/1 1014; *Hansard* 7/7/26; CV V/1 740
214. CV V/1 717; Boothby *Rebel* 44
215. CV V/1 728, 730, 733
216. WSC V 212, 189; CV V/1 765; *Evening Standard* 10/19/26
217. CV V/1 807; WSC V 193; CV V/1 820, 823, 824
218. WSC V 202; CV V/1 866
219. CV V/1 760; WSC V 208, 219; CV V/1 851, 852; Rhodes James *Failure* 193
220. WM / Harold Macmillan 11/4/80; WM / Lord Boothby 10/16/80
221. CV V/1 1307; *Great Contemporaries* 375
222. CV V/1 1328, 1006
223. *Wit* 23, 13; *Irrepressible* 104, 6; McGowan 138
224. CV V/1 985, 1272, 1464; *Hansard* 4/11/27; WSC V 235; *Times of India* 4/11/27
225. *Hansard* 4/29/25; WSC V 292; CV V/1 1316, 1326
226. Rhodes James *Failure* 207, 206, 205; CV V/1 1443–1444
227. CV V/1 1050
228. *Hansard* 4/11/27; CV V/1 984
229. WSC V 324; Macmillan 176; Rhodes James *Failure* 196
230. CV V/1 878, 908, 907
231. CV V/1 908; *Times* 1/21/27
232. *New Leader* 1/28/27; WSC V 226
233. CV V/1 909
234. CV V/1 1448
235. CV V/2 87
236. CV V/1 1052
237. WSC V 265
238. Kenneth Young 100; CV V/1 1052, 1236
239. CV V/1 1332; Kenneth Young 104; CV V/1 1375; Kenneth Young 105
240. CV V/1 1412; Rhodes James *Failure* 205; CV V/1 1444; Gilbert *Churchill Wilderness* 18, 19; WSC V 317; CV V/2 61
241. WSC V 327, 328; Rhodes James *Failure* 201; WSC V 313, 325; *Daily Express* 5/1/29
242. WSC V 328
243. CV V/1 1474; Kenneth Young 118n
244. CV V/2 85–86; WSC V 337
245. CV V/2 40
246. CV V/2 61, 40; WSC V 340; CV V/2 42
247. WSC V 345; CV V/2 82
248. CV V/2 96–97; Swanberg 494
249. CV V/2 97; WSC V 348; Sarah Churchill 35
250. WSC V 349, 350
251. WSC V 350; *Gathering Storm,* 34; "The American Mind and Ours"
252. *Irrepressible* 106; CV V/2 95; WSC V 353
253. CV V/2 98; Smith and Cawkwell 173, 318–438 passim
254. Morris *Trumpets* 334; Boothby *Rebel* 37; Morris *Trumpets* 311
255. Morris *Trumpets* 278; Telford Taylor 197–199; Morris *Trumpets* 335
256. Morris *Trumpets* 305
257. Morris *Trumpets* 307, 364, 337n
258. Morris *Trumpets* 357
259. Morris *Trumpets* 335, 337
260. Morris *Trumpets* 337
261. Boothby *Rebel* 54; Gandhi 278–279
262. *Wit* 27
263. Day 65
264. Morris *Trumpets* 283–285
265. Rhodes James *Failure* 216
266. Rhodes James *Failure* 215; CV V/2 107, 108; WSC V 367
267. Morris *Trumpets* 298; Rhodes James *Failure* 221, 222
268. Rhodes James *Failure* 206, 222
269. Moran 692
270. CV V/1 1042, 1054; Mayo 26, 32; WSC V 243n; *Spectator* 7/16/27; *Survey* 8/1/27; *New Statesman* 7/16/27; *Catholic World* 10/27/27; *New York Herald Tribune* 6/12/27; *NYT* 6/5/27
271. CV V/2 126; WSC V 401–402; Mayer in Stansky 183

272. WSC V 354–355; CV V/2 111
273. *Daily Mail* 11/16/29
274. Morris *Trumpets* 290
275. WSC V 368; Boothby *Rebel* 53; *Wit* 29; WSC V 370
276. Soames 331; CV V/2 186
277. CV V/2 226, 193; WSC V 338; Rhodes James *Failure* 218
278. CV V/2 222; WSC V 376, 377
279. WSC V 377; *Times* 12/13/30; WSC V 358; CV V/2 287; WSC V 359; CV V/2 258; Rhodes James *Failure* 219
280. WSC V 373, 375n2, 367; CV V/2 290, 293; Kenneth Young 116
281. Rowse in Eade 499
282. CV V/2 243; *Gathering Storm* 33; CV V/2 250
283. *Hansard* 1/26/31
284. CV V/2 252, 250–251
285. *India* 94; Moorehead *Churchill Trial* 74
286. CV V/2 280, 279; *Hansard* 3/12/31; CV V/2 265
287. CV V/2 291; WSC V 400, 398; *Hansard* 5/13/31; *Daily Mail* 9/7/31
288. Boothby *Rebel* 83; WSC V 377; Boothby *Rebel* 54
289. WSC V 404–405; *Hansard* 3/12/31
290. Morris *Trumpets* 297; *NYT* 12/14/31
291. *Hansard* 9/8/31; Gilbert *Churchill Wilderness* 39; Kenneth Young 118
292. Eden in Eade 107; Attlee in Marchant 74–75; Shinwell in Eade 124; W. H. Thompson 71
293. Gardner 2, 1
294. *Daily Telegraph* 11/15/40; WM/Lord Butler 11/5/80
295. Moorehead *Churchill Trial* 71; Longford *Churchill* 84; Eden in Eade 106, 107; Rhodes James *Failure* 205; *Irrepressible* 6, 117
296. Birkenhead *Professor* 135; CV V/2 399
297. CV V/2 18, 26–27
298. Birkenhead *Professor* 133; CV V/2 244, 105
299. CV V/2 258
300. CV V/2 38; Pelling 414
301. CV V/2 334
302. Payne 212; Shirer 119
303. Shirer 136
304. *Frankfurter Zeitung* 9/26/30
305. Shirer 149
306. Shirer 132
307. "Shall We All Commit Suicide?"; *Gathering Storm* 55–56
308. Eden in Eade 116; *Step by Step* 144; WM / Lord Butler 11/5/80; Hitler in Eade 210
309. *Amid These Storms* 249; WSC V 123; CV V/1 1335; WSC V 304–305
310. Rhodes James *Failure* 241n
311. *Hansard* 6/29/31; *New York American* 8/10/31; *New York Journal* 3/31/31
312. WSC V 406, 407
313. *NYT* 1/25/31
314. *NYT* 6/11/31
315. WM / Kay Halle 8/6/80; WSC V 418, 417
316. *Worcester Telegram* 12/13/31; "My New York Adventures"; W. H. Thompson 108
317. CV V/2 382; Birkenhead *Professor* 134–135
318. "My New York Adventures"; CV V/2 386
319. Moir 30, 31, 32
320. CV V/2 396, 393
321. Gilbert *Churchill Wilderness* 43–44
322. Moir 36, 82–83
323. WSC V 426; Gilbert *Churchill Wilderness* 45
324. CV V/2 406, 410; Gilbert *Churchill Wilderness* 46
325. *Wit* 83
326. Cowles *Churchill* 285; WSC V 431; Moran 65

SELECT BIBLIOGRAPHY

In most books it is impossible for a scholar to single out one source which towers above all others. In this case, however, it is not only possible; it is essential. The Official Biography of Winston Spencer Churchill, which has been in preparation, under the supervision of the Chartwell Trust, for eighteen years, is the definitive work on his life. Indeed, some documents, including those in the Royal Archives, Windsor Castle, are closed to other researchers until the official biography is complete.

Thus far the work — which has reached the year 1939 — comprises eighteen volumes totaling 20,827 pages. And World War II is yet to come. At this writing, Martin Gilbert, the official biographer, has just completed a manuscript covering the years 1939 to 1941. It is, he says, as long as this volume of mine. In its entirety, the official work is grouped into five biographical volumes and thirteen companion volumes. The biographical works have been issued under five major headings:

Volume I: *Youth, 1874–1900,* by Randolph S. Churchill. Boston, 1966.

Volume II: *Young Statesman, 1901–1914,* by Randolph S. Churchill. Boston, 1967.

Volume III: *The Challenge of War, 1914–1916,* by Martin Gilbert. Boston, 1971.

Volume IV: *The Stricken World, 1916–1922,* by Martin Gilbert. Boston, 1975.

Volume V: *The Prophet of Truth, 1922–1939,* by Martin Gilbert. Boston, 1977.

The companion volumes, 16,359 pages, are similarly grouped and consist of reproduced documents:

Companion Volume I, Part 1, 1874–1896, edited by Randolph S. Churchill. Boston, 1967.

Companion Volume I, Part 2, 1896–1900, edited by Randolph S. Churchill. Boston, 1967.

Companion Volume II, Part 1, 1901–1907, edited by Randolph S. Churchill. Boston, 1969.

Companion Volume II, Part 2, 1907–1911, edited by Randolph S. Churchill. Boston, 1969.

Companion Volume II, Part 3, 1911–1914, edited by Randolph S. Churchill. Boston, 1969.

Companion Volume III, Part 1, July 1914–April 1915, edited by Martin Gilbert. Boston, 1973.

Companion Volume III, Part 2, May 1915–December 1916, edited by Martin Gilbert. Boston, 1973.

Companion Volume IV, Part 1, January 1917–June 1919, edited by Martin Gilbert. Boston, 1978.

Companion Volume IV, Part 2, July 1919–March 1921, edited by Martin Gilbert. Boston, 1978.

Companion Volume IV, Part 3, April 1921–November 1922, edited by Martin Gilbert. Boston, 1978.

Companion Volume V, Part 1, The Exchequer Years, 1922–1929, edited by Martin Gilbert. Boston, 1981.

Companion Volume V, Part 2, The Wilderness Years, 1929–1935, edited by Martin Gilbert. Boston, 1981.

Companion Volume V, Part 3, 1936–1939, edited by Martin Gilbert. Forthcoming.

The liveliest biographer of Winston Churchill is Winston Churchill. He led a fascinating life, he knew it, and he exploited it. Like most journalists, he told his choicest stories over and over. He wrote no fewer than nine versions of his dramatic escape from the Boer prisoner-of-war camp in 1899. One, "How I Escaped from the Boers," was published in the Johannesburg *Standard and Diggers' News* on December 23, 1899. Three others appeared in the *Morning Post*, on December 27 and 28, 1899, and January 24, 1900. Later came "How I Escaped from Pretoria" (*War Pictures*, March 3, 1900), "My Escape from the Boers" (*Strand*, December 1923 and January 1924), "My Escape from Pretoria" (*News of the World*, February 10, 1935), "How I Escaped" (*Sunday Chronicle*, January 2, 1938), and the version in chapters 21 and 22 of his book *A Roving Commission*. This last account has appeared in several anthologies, and Churchill lectured on this feat innumerable times. There are no significant discrepancies among the many versions. He told this tale, and others, over and over simply because he had a family — and an expensive life-style — to support.

I. By Winston Spencer Churchill

1. BOOKS

Amid These Storms: Thoughts and Adventures. New York, 1932. (Published in the United Kingdom as *Thoughts and Adventures;* London, 1932.)

The Gathering Storm. Vol. I of *The Second World War.* Boston, 1948.

Great Contemporaries. London, 1937.

Ian Hamilton's March. London, New York, and Bombay, 1900.

Immortal Jester: A Treasury of the Great Good Humor of Sir Winston Churchill. Compiled by Lester Frewen. London, 1973.

India. Speeches and introduction. London, 1931.

Irish Home Rule: A Speech . . . at Belfast on February 8th, 1912. London, 1912.

Irrepressible Churchill: A Treasury of Winston Churchill's Wit. Selected and compiled with historical commentary by Kay Halle. New York, 1966.
Liberalism and the Social Problem. London, 1909.
London to Ladysmith: Via Pretoria. London, New York, and Bombay, 1900.
Lord Randolph Churchill. 2 vols. London and New York, 1906.
Maxims and Reflections. Selected by Colin Coote and Denzil Batchelor. London, 1947.
My African Journey. London, 1908.
On Naval Armaments: From a Speech on the Naval Estimate in the House of Commons, March 26, 1913. London, 1913.
Painting as a Pastime. London, 1948.
The River War: An Historical Account of the Reconquest of the Soudan. 2 vols. London, New York, and Bombay, 1899.
A Roving Commission: My Early Life. New York, 1930. (Published in the United Kingdom as *My Early Life;* London, 1930.)
Savrola: A Tale of the Revolution in Laurania. Reprinted New York, 1956.
Step by Step: 1936–1939. Articles. London, 1939.
The Story of the Malakand Field Force: An Episode of Frontier War. London, New York, and Bombay, 1898.
The Wit of Sir Winston. Edited by Adam Sykes and Icia Sproat. London, 1965.
The World Crisis, Vol. I (1911–1914). New York, 1923.
The World Crisis, Vol. II (1915). New York, 1923.
The World Crisis, Vol. III (1916–1918, part 1). New York, 1927.
The World Crisis, Vol. IV (1916–1918, part 2). New York, 1927.
The World Crisis: The Aftermath (1918–1928). New York, 1929.
The World Crisis, Vol. V: *The Eastern Front.* New York, 1931.
Young Winston's Wars: The Original Despatches of Winston S. Churchill, War Correspondent, 1897–1900. Edited by Frederick Woods. New York, 1972.

2. ARTICLES

"The Abuse of the 'Dole.'" *Daily Telegraph,* March 26 and 27, 1930.
"The American Mind and Ours." *Strand,* August 1931.
"Antwerp: The Story of Its Siege and Fall." *Sunday Pictorial,* November 9, 1916.
"Arthur James Balfour." *Strand,* April 1931.
"Asquith." *News of the World,* February 16, 1936.
"Astor and G. Bernard Shaw." *Sunday Pictorial,* August 16, 1931.
"Back to the Spartan Life in Our Public Schools." *Daily Mail,* December 1, 1931.
"Back to the Wild Tumult of Peace." *News of the World,* March 24, 1935.
"Balfour." *News of the World,* March 22, 1936.
"Battle of Sidney Street." *Pall Mall,* February 1924.
"Birkenhead." *News of the World,* March 1, 1936.
"The Blunder That Beat Germany." *Sunday Chronicle,* January 9, 1938.
The Boer War: sixty-six telegrams and thirty-five letters to the *Morning Post,* dated November 16, 1899, to July 25, 1900.
"B.-P." *Sunday Pictorial,* August 30, 1931.
"British Cavalry." *Anglo-Saxon Review,* March 1901.
"The British Officer." *Pall Mall Magazine,* January 1901.
"Cartoons and Cartoonists." *Strand,* June 1931.
"The Case for Singapore." *Sunday Chronicle,* March 30, 1924.
"Chamberlain." *News of the World,* March 29, 1936.
"Chamberlain." *Pall Mall,* February 1930.
"Changing the Political Camp." *News of the World,* February 24, 1935.
"Charge!" *Sunday Chronicle,* December 19, 1937.
"Charge of the Twenty-first Lancers." *News of the World,* January 27, 1935.
"Clemenceau." *News of the World,* March 15, 1936.
"Clemenceau: The Man and the Tiger." *Strand,* December 1930.
"Consistency in Politics." *Pall Mall,* July 1927.
"Could Labour Govern the Country?" *Illustrated Sunday Herald,* November 16, 1919.
"Crucial Events in the Great War." Thirteen essays in the *Daily Telegraph,* May 5 to July 15, 1930.

The Cuban Insurrection: five dispatches to the *Daily Graphic* published in December 1895 and January 1896, and three essays in the *Saturday Review,* dated February 15, March 7, and August 29, 1896.
"Curzon." *News of the World,* March 8, 1936.
"The Dangers Ahead in Europe." *Weekly Dispatch,* June 15, 1924.
"The Dardanelles Held the Key to Peace." *News of the World,* March 17, 1935.
"A Day with Clemenceau." *Strand,* December 1930.
"The Decisive Factor in the Allied Victory." *News of the World,* June 13, 1937.
"A Difference with Kitchener." *Cosmopolitan,* November 1924.
"Douglas Haig." *Pall Mall,* November 1928.
"The Dover Barrage." *Daily Telegraph,* November 30, 1931.
"Dreadnoughts at Bay." *Collier's,* July 5, 1930.
"The Dream." *Sunday Telegraph,* January 31, 1966.
"The Election." *Daily Chronicle,* November 6, 1922.
"Election Memories." *Strand,* September 1931.
"The Ethics of Foreign Policy." *United Services Magazine,* August 1898.
"False Security." *Sunday Chronicle,* February 17, 1924.
"Fashoda Incident." *North American Review,* December 1898.
"Fifty Years Hence." *Strand,* December 1931.
"Fisher." *News of the World,* January 19, 1936.
"Foch the Indomitable." *Pall Mall,* July 1929.
"Four Crises in the Great War." *Sunday Pictorial,* July 9, July 16, July 23, and July 30, 1916.
"French." *News of the World,* February 2, 1936.
"Frontier Days in India." *News of the World,* January 20, 1935.
"The Future of Mr Lloyd George." *Weekly Dispatch,* June 29, 1924.
"The Gentle Art of Losing." *The Times,* April 4, 1930.
"George Curzon." *Pall Mall,* January 1929.
"The German Splendour." *Cosmopolitan,* August 1924.
"Government of the / by the / for the Dole-Drawers." *Daily Mail,* June 18, 1931.
"Great Events." Articles in *News of the World,* May 30 to July 4, 1937, and October 10 to November 21, 1937.
"Great Men of the Times." Twelve sketches in *News of the World,* January 12 to April 5, 1936.
"The Great War by Land and Sea." Six installments in *London Magazine,* October 1916 to March 1917.
"Haig." *News of the World,* February 9, 1936.
"Haig . . . the Man They Trusted." *Daily Mail,* October 3, 1935.
"A Hand-to-Hand Fight with Desert Fanatics." *Cosmopolitan,* December 1924.
"Have We Done with Germany?" *Illustrated Sunday Herald,* November 23, 1919.
"Herbert Henry Asquith." *Pall Mall,* August 1928.
"Hindenburg in War and Peace." *Daily Mail,* August 2, 1934.
"Hobbies." *Pall Mall,* December 1925.
"Homage to Kipling." *John O'London's,* November 26, 1937.
"The House of Commons and Its Business." *World,* July 13, 1909.
"How Antwerp Saved the Channel Ports." *Sunday Pictorial,* November 26, 1916.
"How I Escaped." *Sunday Chronicle,* January 2, 1938.
"How I Escaped from Pretoria." *War Pictures,* March 3, 1900.
"How I Escaped from the Boers." *Standard and Diggers' News* (Johannesburg), December 23, 1899.
"How I Placated Lord Roberts." *Pall Mall,* October 1927.
"How the Grand Fleet Went to War." *News of the World,* March 10, 1935.
"How We Made the Irish Treaty." *Pictorial Weekly,* January 20, 1934.
"If I Were a Boer, I Hope I Should Be Fighting in the Field." *Westminster Gazette,* March 18, 1901.
"In an Indian Valley." *Pall Mall,* September 1927.
"India: The Coming Clash." *Daily Mail,* October 14, 1933.
"India and Dominion Status." *The Times,* November 25, 1931.
"The India Bill." *The Times,* March 5, 1935.
"India in 1917." *The Times,* February 14, 1935.

"India Insistent." *Daily Mail,* September 7, 1931.
"The Influenza." A poem written in 1890 and published for the first time in the *Harrovian* of December 10, 1940.
"In the Air." *Pall Mall,* June 1924.
"The Irish Treaty." *Pall Mall,* January 1924.
"Is Parliament Played Out?" *Illustrated Sunday Herald,* May 30, 1920.
"I Was a Prisoner of War." *Sunday Chronicle,* December 26, 1937.
"I Was Conscious Through It All." *Daily Mail,* January 5, 1932.
"Jellicoe." *Sunday Chronicle,* October 24, 1937.
"Joseph Chamberlain." *Daily Mail,* December 1, 1932.
"Kitchener." *News of the World,* January 12, 1936.
"Kitchener." *Sunday Chronicle,* October 31, 1937.
"Lawrence of Arabia's Name Will Live!" *News of the World,* May 26, 1935.
Letter to the Editor concerning the School Display and Gymnasium, signed "Junius Junior." *Harrovian,* March 17, 1892.
"Liberalism." *English Life,* January 1924.
"Lloyd George." *News of the World,* February 16, 1936.
"Lloyd George." *Sunday Pictorial,* September 6, 1931.
"Lloyd George's Memoirs." *Daily Mail,* September 7, 1933.
"Lord Birkenhead: The Man and His Career." *Weekly Dispatch,* August 31, 1924.
"Lord Kitchener." *The Times,* October 16, 1923.
"Lord Oxford as I Knew Him." *Daily Mail,* October 18, 1932.
"Lord Roberts." *World's Work,* June 1901; reprinted in *Windsor Magazine,* July 1901.
"Lord Rosebery." *Pall Mall,* October 1929.
"Lord Ypres." *Pall Mall,* January 1930.
"Ludendorff at Tannenberg." *Collier's,* May 17, 1930.
"Ludendorff's 'All or Nothing.' " *Daily Telegraph,* July 14, 1930.
"Ludendorff's Last Card." *Collier's,* July 12, 1930.
"Man Overboard." A short story. *Harmsworth Magazine,* January 1899.
"Man Power Problem: Wanted — a Policy." *Sunday Pictorial,* April 8, 1917.
"The Man Who Saved Paris." *Collier's,* May 31, 1930.
"Mass Effects in Modern Life." *Strand,* May 1931.
"The Meaning of Verdun." *Collier's,* November 18, 1916.
"Memoirs of the House of Commons." *Pearson's Magazine,* December 1923–January 1924.
"Men Who Have Influenced or Impressed Me." *Strand,* February 1931.
"Mesopotamia and the New Government." *Empire Review,* July 1923.
"Methods of Barbarism." *The Times,* June 28, 1901.
"Mobilization in 1914." *The Times,* April 9, 1936.
"Monarchy vs. Autocracy." *Illustrated Sunday Herald,* February 1, 1920.
"Moses." *Sunday Chronicle,* November 11, 1931.
"Mr Asquith and Lord Kitchener." *The Times,* November 1, 1923.
"Mr H. G. Wells and the British Empire." *Empire Review,* November 1923.
"Mr Snowden's Horoscope." *Weekly Dispatch,* August 10, 1924.
"Mr Wells and Bolshevism: A Reply." *Sunday Express,* December 5, 1920.
"The Murder Campaign in Ireland." *Illustrated Sunday Herald,* June 13, 1920.
"My African Journey." *Strand,* March to November 1908.
"My Budget Forecast." *Sunday Pictorial,* April 19, 1931.
"My Dramatic Days with the Kaiser." *Cosmopolitan,* August 1924.
"My Entry into Politics." *News of the World,* February 17, 1935.
"My Escape from Pretoria." *News of the World,* February 10, 1935.
"My Escape from the Boers." *Strand,* December 1923 and January 1924.
"My Happy Days in the West Indies." *Daily Mail,* March 23, 1932.
"My New York Adventures." *Daily Mail,* January 4, 1932.
"My Spy Story." *Cosmopolitan,* September 1934.
"The Mystery of the Marne." *Collier's,* June 14, 1930.
"The 1921 Speech: Meaning of Dominion Status." *The Times,* February 16, 1935.
The Northwest Frontier: five telegrams to the Allahabad *Pioneer Mail* dated September 9 to December 15, 1897; five letters to the *Pioneer Mail* dated September 24 to November 5, 1897; and fifteen dispatches to the London *Daily Telegraph,* dated October 6 to December 6, 1897.

"Observations of the United States." Twelve letters to the *Daily Telegraph,* November 18, 1929, to February 3, 1930.
"Officers and Gentlemen." *Saturday Evening Post,* December 29, 1900.
"On the Flank of the Army." A short story. *Youth's Companion,* December 18, 1902.
"Our Task for Peace in Palestine." *Glasgow Evening News,* February 28, 1930.
"Painting as a Pastime." *Strand,* December 1921 and January 1922.
"The Palestine Crisis." *Sunday Times,* September 22, 1929.
"Panic in the East." *Collier's,* May 3, 1930.
"The 'Panther' Affair." *Saturday Review,* October 3, 1931.
"Partition Perils in Palestine." *Evening Standard,* July 23, 1937.
"The Peril in India." *Daily Mail,* November 16, 1929.
"Personal Contacts." *Strand,* February 1931.
"Philip Snowden." *Sunday Pictorial,* August 2, 1931.
"Plugstreet." *Pall Mall,* March 1924.
"The Poison Peril from the East." *Evening News,* July 28, 1920.
"The Profound Abyss." *Evening News,* March 19, 1920.
"Proposal for a New Political Party." *Living Age,* September 13, 1919.
"Ramsay MacDonald." *Sunday Pictorial,* July 26, 1931.
"Ramsay MacDonald: The Man and the Politician." *Weekly Dispatch,* May 25, 1924.
"The Real Kitchener." *Illustrated Sunday Herald,* April 25, 1920.
"The Real Need of the British Navy." *Sunday Pictorial,* June 24, 1917.
"The Red Fever." *Illustrated Sunday Herald,* January 25, 1920.
"The Red Plot — and After." *Weekly Dispatch,* November 2, 1924.
"Reflections on the Strategy of the Allies." *Century,* May 1917.
"A Review of T. E. Lawrence's *Seven Pillars of Wisdom.*" *Daily Mail,* July 29, 1935.
"The Right to Strike." *Illustrated Sunday Herald,* December 7, 1919.
"Rise and Fall of Parties and Politicians." *News of the World,* March 31, 1935.
"The Royal Military College, Sandhurst." *Pall Mall Magazine,* December 1896.
"Russia: Is It the Turning Point?" *Sunday Pictorial,* July 8, 1917.
"Savrola: A Military and Political Romance." Serialization of Churchill's novel in *Macmillan's Magazine,* May to December 1899.
"Shall We All Commit Suicide?" *Pall Mall,* September 1924.
"Ships Could Have Forced the Dardanelles." *Daily Mail,* October 2, 1934.
"Should Strategists Veto the Channel Tunnel?" *Weekly Dispatch,* July 27, 1924.
"Sidney Street and 'Peter the Painter.'" *News of the World,* March 3, 1935.
"Singapore: Key to the Pacific." *Pictorial Weekly,* March 24, 1934.
"Sir Edward Marsh's Death: Mr Churchill's Tribute." *The Times,* January 14, 1953.
"Sir Herbert Samuel." *Sunday Pictorial,* November 15, 1931.
"Sir John Simon." *Sunday Pictorial,* November 8, 1931.
"Sketches of Twelve Key Figures." *Sunday Pictorial,* July 26 to November 15, 1931.
"A Smooth Way with the Peers." *Nation,* March 9, 1907.
"Socialism and Sham." *Sunday Chronicle,* April 6, 1924.
"Socialist Quackery." *Daily Mail,* May 8, 1929.
"Some Impressions of the War in South Africa." *Journal of the Royal United Services Institution,* July 1901.
"Stark Truths about India." *Daily Mail,* December 12, 1930.
"State Insurance." *People's Journal* (Dundee), June 19, 1909.
"Taken Prisoner by the Boers." *News of the World,* February 3, 1935.
"The Three Cruisers." *The Times,* February 26, 1923.
"Three-Party Confusion." *Sunday Chronicle,* March 2, 1924.
"Tragedy of the Torpedoed *Lusitania.*" *News of the World,* June 6, 1937.
"A Trapped Armored Train." *Cosmopolitan,* January 1925.
"Tribute to Lord Birkenhead." *The Times,* October 1, 1930.
"Tribute to Rupert Brooke." *The Times,* April 26, 1915.
"Trotsky: The Ogre of Europe." *Pall Mall,* December 1929.
"The True Story of the Tank." *Sunday Chronicle,* January 16, 1938.
"The Truth about 'Jix.'" *Sunday Pictorial,* August 9, 1931.
"The Truth about the Navy." *Illustrated Sunday Herald,* November 9, 1919.
"The Truth about War Debts." *Answers,* March 17, 1934.

"Twenty-one Years Ago Today: The Inside Story of the War." *Sunday Chronicle*, August 4, 1935.
"The U-Boat War." *Daily Telegraph*, November 1931.
"Under Fire." *Sunday Chronicle*, December 12, 1937.
"The United States of Europe." *Saturday Evening Post*, February 15, 1930.
"The Victim of Sarajevo." *Saturday Review*, September 26, 1931.
"The War by Land and Sea." *Collier's Weekly*, September 30, 1916.
"The War on the Nile." Thirteen letters to the London *Morning Post*, dated August 31 to October 13, 1898.
"What I Heard and Saw In America." *Daily Telegraph*, November 18, 1929, to February 1930.
"When Britain Nearly Starved." *Sunday Chronicle*, January 23, 1938.
"When I Risked Court Martial in Search of War." *Cosmopolitan*, October 1924.
"When I Was Young." *Strand*, December 1924.
"When the Crash Came to the United States." *News of the World*, June 20, 1937.
"Who Rules Britain?" *John Bull*, March 22, 1924.
"Why I Gave Up Flying." *Pall Mall*, July 1924.
"Why More Taxes?" *John Bull*, April 12, 1930.
"Why We Lost." *John Bull*, June 15, 1929.
"Will America Fail Us?" *Illustrated Sunday Herald*, November 30, 1919.
"Will the British Empire Last?" *Answers*, October 26, 1929.
"With Buller to the Cape." *Pall Mall*, November 1927.
"Zionism vs. Bolshevism." *Illustrated Sunday Herald*, February 8, 1920.

II. About Winston Spencer Churchill

1. BOOKS

Ashley, M. *Churchill as Historian.* London, 1968.
Bardens, Dennis. *Churchill in Parliament.* London, 1967.
Bonham Carter, Violet. *Winston Churchill: An Intimate Portrait.* New York, 1965.
Cawthorne, Graham, ed. *The Churchill Legend: An Anthology.* London, 1965.
Chaplin, E. D. W., ed. *Winston Churchill and Harrow.* London, 1941.
Churchill, Randolph, and Helmut Gernsheim, eds. *Churchill: His Life in Photographs.* New York, 1955.
Churchill, Sarah. *A Thread in the Tapestry.* New York, 1967.
The Churchill Years: 1874–1965. By the editors of the Viking Press, text by *The Times* of London, with a foreword by Lord Butler of Saffron Walden. New York, 1965.
Coombs, D. *Churchill: His Paintings.* Cleveland, 1967.
Cowles, Virginia. *Winston Churchill: The Era and the Man.* New York, 1953.
D'Abernon, Viscount. *Portraits and Appreciations.* London, 1930.
Dawson, R. MacGregor. *Winston Churchill at the Admiralty, 1911–1915.* Toronto, 1940.
Eade, Charles, ed. *Churchill by His Contemporaries.* London, 1953.
Eden, Guy. *Portrait of Churchill.* New York, 1945.
Fedden, Robin. *Churchill and Chartwell.* Westerham, Kent, 1968.
Gardner, Brian. *Churchill in Power: As Seen by His Contemporaries.* Boston, 1970.
Gibb, Captain A. D. *With Winston Churchill at the Front.* Glasgow, 1924.
Gilbert, Martin. *Churchill's Political Philosophy.* Oxford, 1981.
———. *Winston Churchill: The Wilderness Years.* London, 1981.
Gilbert, Martin, ed. *Churchill.* Englewood Cliffs, N.J., 1967.
———. *Churchill: A Photographic Portrait.* Boston, 1974.
Graubard, Stephen Richards. *Burke, Disraeli, and Churchill: The Policies of Perseverance.* Cambridge, 1961.
Gretton, Admiral Sir Peter. *Former Naval Person: Winston Churchill and the Royal Navy.* London, 1968.
Guedalla, Philip. *Mr Churchill: A Portrait.* London, 1941.
Holliday, Frank F., and P. Sousa Pernes. *The Statesman and the Writer.* London, 1957.
Howells, R. *Simply Churchill.* New York, 1965.
Kraus, René. *Winston Churchill in the Mirror: His Life in Pictures and Story.* New York, 1944.
Longford, Elizabeth. *Winston Churchill.* Chicago, 1974.
McGowan, Norman. *My Years with Churchill.* New York, 1958.

Marchant, J., ed. *Winston Spencer Churchill: Servant of Crown and Commonwealth.* London, 1954.
Moir, Phyllis. *I Was Winston Churchill's Private Secretary.* New York, 1941.
Moorehead, Alan. *Churchill: A Pictorial Biography.* London, 1960.
———. *Winston Churchill in Trial and Triumph.* Boston, 1955.
Moran, Lord. *Churchill, Taken from the Diaries of Lord Moran: The Struggle for Survival, 1940–1965.* Boston, 1966.
Nel, Elizabeth. *Mr. Churchill's Secretary.* New York, 1958.
Nott, Stanley. *The Young Churchill: A Biography.* New York, 1941.
Observer, ed. *Churchill by His Contemporaries: An Observer Appreciation.* London, 1965.
Paterson, Tony. *A Seat for Life.* Dundee, 1980.
Pelling, Henry. *Winston Churchill.* New York, 1974.
Reid, Percy G. *Churchill: Townsman of Westerham.* London, 1969.
Rhodes James, Robert. *Churchill: A Study in Failure, 1900–1939.* New York, 1970.
Scott, Alexander MacCallum. *Winston Churchill in Peace and War.* London, 1916.
———. *Winston Spencer Churchill.* London, 1905.
Sencourt, R., ed. *Winston Churchill.* London, 1940.
Snow, C. P. *Variety of Men.* New York, 1967.
Stansky, Peter, ed. *Churchill: A Profile.* New York, 1973.
Taylor, A. J. P. *Churchill: Four Faces and the Man.* London, 1969.
Taylor, A. J. P., et al. *Churchill Revised: A Critical Assessment.* New York, 1969.
Thompson, Malcolm. *The Life and Times of Winston Churchill.* London, 1945.
Thompson, Walter Henry. *Assignment: Churchill.* New York, 1955.
Urquhart, Fred, ed. *WSC: A Cartoon Biography.* London, 1955.
Wheeler-Bennett, Sir John, ed. *Action This Day: Working with Churchill.* New York, 1969.
Young, Kenneth. *Churchill and Beaverbrook: A Study in Friendship and Politics.* New York, 1966.

2. ARTICLES

Attlee, Clement. "Churchill on Balance," in *Churchill by His Contemporaries: An Observer Appreciation.* London, 1965.
Bacon, R. H. "Tragedy of the Dardanelles: Conflicting Views of Winston Churchill and Lord Fisher." *World's Work,* December 1929.
"Balfour and Churchill." *Commonweal,* February 18, 1931.
Beaverbrook, Lord. "Political Battles of the World War: The Fisher-Churchill Row and the Fall of Asquith." *World's Work,* September 1928.
Berlin, Sir Isaiah. "Winston Churchill in 1940," in *Personal Impressions.* London, 1980.
"Bravery of Winston Churchill." *Current Literature,* March 1900.
"Britain's Big Trio: Asquith, Lloyd-George, and Winston Churchill." *Current Literature,* November 1912.
Buell, R. L. "Winston Churchill's Criticism of President Hoover." *Current History,* June 1929.
"Chamberlain and Churchill." *Outlook,* November 19, 1924.
"Churchill in Parliament." *Independent,* September 22, 1904.
"Churchill's Queer Position." *Living Age,* January 24, 1914.
Colvin, Ian. "Great Mr. Churchill." *Atlantic,* January 3, 17, 24, and February 27, 1925.
Commager, H. S. "Winston Churchill: An Appreciation." *American Mercury,* August 1945.
Corbett, James. "Winston Churchill and the Future." *Fortnightly Review,* November 1926.
Dedijer, Vladimir. "Participants as Historians." *Times Literary Supplement,* May 30, 1968.
Ehrman, John. "Lloyd George and Churchill as War Ministers," in *Transactions of the Royal Historical Society.* London, 1961.
"England's Proposal to Germany for a Naval Holiday." *Independent,* October 30, 1913.
Gardiner, A. G. "Churchill and Federalism." *Fortnightly Review,* November 1912.
———. "Genius without Judgment: Churchill at Fifty," in *Portraits and Portents.* New York, 1926.
Hirst, F. W. "Churchillian Finance: The Fifth Budget." *Contemporary Review,* June 1929.
Liddell Hart, B. H. "Churchill in War." *Encounter,* April 1966.
Lucy, Sir Henry. "Arthur Balfour and Winston Churchill: A Parliamentary Duel." *Nation,* March 30, 1916.
———. "Lord Haldane and Winston Churchill." *Nation,* December 9, 1915.
———. "Mr Churchill's Resignation." *Nation,* December 2, 1915.

———. "Winston Churchill." *Nation*, July 22, 1915.
———. "Winston Churchill at the Admiralty." *Nation*, November 19, 1914.
Marshall, D. J. "Winston Churchill: England's Political Bad Boy." *Living Age*, April 8, 1929.
Mayer, Arno J. "The Power Politician and Counterrevolutionary," in *The Critical Spirit*, edited by Kurt H. Wolff and Barrington Moore, Jr. Boston, 1967.
"Men Who Control the Destiny of Europe: Winston Spencer Churchill." *World's Work*, September 1914.
"Mr Churchill's Failure to Stop Naval Rivalry." *Literary Digest*, November 15, 1913.
Muggeridge, Malcolm. "The Totemization of Sir Winston Churchill," in *Smiling Through the Apocalypse*. New York, 1960.
Repington, C. à Court. "Churchillian Strategy." *Blackwood's*, November 1923.
Rowse, A. L. "Churchill Considered Historically." *Encounter*, January 1966.
Rusticus Expectans. "Mr Winston Churchill and Democracy." *Westminster Review*, January 1906.
Sidebotham, H. "Expert or Strategist: Mr Churchill and the Dardanelles Report." *New Republic*, May 5, 1916.
"Signal Defeat." *Outlook*, May 2, 1908.
Stead, W. T. "On the Eve of the Irish Home Rule Bill." *Review of Reviews*, March 1912.
———. "Winston Churchill's Offer." *Independent*, April 11, 1912.
Strachey, J. St. Loe. "Churchill's Chance: The British Chancellor and Opportunism." *Independent*, June 27, 1925.
Sydenham of Combe. "Mr Churchill as Historian." *Quarterly Review*, July 1927.
Weerd, H. A. De. "Winston Churchill: A British War Lord." *Current History*, January 1929.
Whittemore, Reed. "Churchill and the Limitations of Myth." *Yale Review*, December 1954.
"Winston Churchill, MP, as a Man of Letters." *Bookman*, July 1908.
"Winston Churchill and Irish Home Rule." *Outlook*, October 26, 1912.
"Winston Churchill's Approval of Fascism." *Literary Digest*, February 26, 1927.
"Winston Churchill's Versatility." *Blackwood's*, September 1912.
"Winston Churchill's War on the War Leaders." *Literary Digest*, February 26, 1927.

III. About the Churchills

I. BOOKS

Balsan, Consuelo Vanderbilt. *The Glitter and the Gold.* New York, 1925.
Blenheim Palace. Woodstock, Oxfordshire, 1979.
Churchill, J. G. S. *A Churchill Canvas.* Boston, 1961.
Churchill, Peregrine, and Julian Mitchell. *Jennie, Lady Randolph Churchill: A Portrait with Letters.* London, 1974.
Churchill, Lady Randolph. *Small Talks on Big Subjects.* London, 1916.
Churchill, Randolph S. *Twenty-one Years.* London, 1965.
Cornwallis-West, Mrs. George. *The Reminiscences of Lady Randolph Churchill.* London, 1908.
Eliot, Elizabeth. *Heiresses and Coronets.* New York, 1959.
———. *They All Married Well.* London, 1960.
Escott, Thomas H. S. *Randolph Spencer-Churchill as a Product of His Age: Being a Personal and Political Monography.* London, 1895.
Fishman, Jack. *My Darling Clementine.* New York, 1963.
Fleming, Kate. *The Churchills.* London, 1975.
Foster, R. F. *Lord Randolph Churchill: A Political Life.* Oxford, 1981.
Gorst, Harold. *The Fourth Party.* London, 1906.
Jennings, L. J., ed. *Speeches of the Right Honourable Lord Randolph Churchill.* London, 1889.
Leslie, Anita. *Lady Randolph Churchill: The Story of Jennie Jerome.* New York, 1969.
———. *The Remarkable Mr. Jerome.* New York, 1954.
Martin, Ralph G. *Jennie: The Life of Lady Randolph Churchill.* 2 vols. New York, 1969, 1971.
Peacock, Virginia. *Famous American Belles of the Nineteenth Century.* Philadelphia, 1901.
Rhodes James, Robert. *Lord Randolph Churchill: Winston Churchill's Father.* New York, 1960.
Roberts, Brian. *Churchills in Africa.* New York, 1970.
Rosebery, Lord. *Lord Randolph Churchill.* London, 1906.
Rowse, A. L. *The Churchills: From the Death of Marlborough to the Present.* New York, 1958.

———. *The Early Churchills.* New York, 1958.
———. *The Later Churchills.* London, 1958.
Soames, Mary. *Clementine Churchill: The Biography of a Marriage.* Boston, 1979.

2. ARTICLES

Cornwallis-West, Mrs. George. "The Reminiscences of Lady Randolph Churchill: English Social Traits — Life at Blenheim." *Century,* December 1907.
Escott, T. H. S. "Lord Randolph Churchill." *Fortnightly Review,* March 1895.
"Lady Randolph Churchill and Her Friends." *Bookman,* December 1908.
"Lord Randolph Churchill." *Harper's Weekly,* January 5, 1895.
"Lord Randolph Churchill." *Review of Reviews,* March 11, 1895.
"Lord Randolph Churchill." *Spectator,* August 5, 1893.
"Lord Randolph Churchill on the Descent of Woman." *Spectator,* July 25, 1891.
"Lord Randolph's Pose." *Spectator,* March 15, 1890.
Lucy, Henry W. "Lord Randolph as I Knew Him." *Blackwood's,* May–June 1907; *Putnam's,* May 1907.
Mann, J. S. "Love Story of a Famous Statesman." *Current Literature,* April 1906.
Maxwell, Sir Herbert. "Lord Randolph Churchill." *Living Age,* April 6, 1895.
Quinault, R. E. "The Fourth Party and the Conservative Opposition to Bradlaugh." *English Historical Review,* April 1976.
———. "Lord Randolph Churchill and Tory Democracy." *History* (London), April 1979.
"Reminiscences," a review of Lady Randolph Churchill's book. *Bookman,* December 1908.
"Rosebery on Statesmanship." *Living Age,* November 10, 1906.
"Statesmanship and Politics." *Blackwood's,* February 1906.

IV. General Works

1. BOOKS

Adams, James Truslow. *Empire on the Seven Seas.* New York, 1940.
Amery, Julian. *Joseph Chamberlain and the Tariff Reform Campaign,* Vols. V and VI. London, 1969.
Amery, L. S. *My Political Life.* 3 vols. London, 1953.
Amery, L. S., ed. *The Times History of the War in South Africa.* 3 vols. London, 1900–1905.
Antwerp expedition: a summary of facts in the official *Military Operations: France and Belgium, 1914,* Vol. II. London, 1926.
Arnot, R. Page. *The Miners: A History of the Miners' Federation of Great Britain.* London, 1949.
Ashmead-Bartlett, E. *The Uncensored Dardanelles.* London, 1928.
Askwith, G. R. *Industrial Problems and Disputes.* London, 1920.
Aspinall-Oglander, C. F. *Roger Keyes.* London, 1951.
Asquith, Lady Cynthia. *Diaries, 1915–1918.* New York, 1969.
Asquith, H. H. *Fifty Years of Parliament.* 2 vols. London, 1926.
———. *Letters to Venetia Stanley.* Edited by Michael and Eleanor Brock. Oxford, 1982.
———. *Memories and Reflections, 1852–1927.* 2 vols. Boston, 1928.
Asquith, Margot. *The Autobiography of Margot Asquith.* 2 vols. London, 1920.
———. *More Memories.* 2 vols. London, 1922.
Atkins, J. B. *Incidents and Reflections.* London, 1947.
Bacon, Admiral Sir R. H. *The Life of Lord Fisher of Kilverstone.* 2 vols. New York, 1929.
Bagehot, Walter. *The English Constitution.* Garden City, N.Y., 1961.
Bailey, J. M. *England from a Back-Window.* Boston, 1878.
Baldwin, A. W. *My Father: The True Story.* London, 1955.
Balfour, A. J. *Chapters of Autobiography.* Edited by B. Dugdale. London, 1930.
Banks, Olive. *Prosperity and Parenthood: A Study of Family Planning among the Victorian Middle-Classes.* London, 1954.
Barnes, J. *The Great War Trek, with the British Army on the Veldt.* New York, 1901.
Barnett, Correlli. *Britain and Her Army.* New York, 1970.
———. *The Collapse of the British Power.* New York, 1972.
Barrymore, Ethel. *Memories.* New York, 1955.
Beaverbrook, Lord. *The Decline and Fall of Lloyd George.* London, 1963.
———. *Men and Power.* London, 1956.
———. *Politicians and the Press.* London, 1925.

———. *Politicians and the War: 1914–1916.* 2 vols. New York, 1928.
Begbie, Harold. *The Mirrors of Downing Street.* London, 1920.
Best, Geoffrey. *Mid-Victorian Britain, 1851–1875.* New York, 1972.
Birkenhead, Second Earl of. *"F.E."* London, 1960.
———. *Halifax.* London, 1965.
———. *The Professor and the Prime Minister: The Official Life of Professor F. A. Lindemann, Viscount Cherwell.* Boston, 1962.
Blake, Robert. *Disraeli.* New York, 1967.
Blake, Robert, ed. *Private Papers of Douglas Haig, 1914–1919.* London, 1952.
Blunden, Edmund. *Mind's Eye.* London, 1934.
———. *Undertones of War.* New York, 1929.
Blunt, W. S. *Gordon at Khartoum.* London, 1911.
———. *My Diaries: Being a Personal Narrative of Events, 1888–1914.* 2 vols. New York, 1921.
Bond, Maurice. *The Houses of Parliament: The Palace of Westminster.* London, 1973.
Boothby, Lord. *I Fight to Live.* London, 1947.
———. *Recollections of a Rebel.* London, 1978.
Boraston, J. H. *Haig's Despatches, 1915–1919.* London, 1919.
Bott, Alan, and Irene Clephane. *Our Mothers.* London, 1932.
Bowle, John. *The Imperial Achievement.* London, 1974.
———. *Viscount Samuel: A Biography.* London, 1959.
Boyle, Andrew. *Poor Dear Brendan.* London, 1974.
Brett, M. V., ed. *Journals and Letters of Reginald Viscount Esher.* London, 1934.
Briggs, A. *The Birth of Broadcasting.* London, 1961.
Brockway, A. F. *Inside the Left.* London, 1947.
Bromage, Mary C. *Churchill and Ireland.* South Bend, Ind., 1964.
Brownrigg, Sir Douglas E. R. *Indiscretions of the Naval Censor.* New York, 1920.
Bryant, Sir Arthur. *Turn of the Tide: 1939–1943.* London, 1957.
Buckley, Jerome Hamilton. *The Victorian Temper: A Study in Literary Culture.* Harvard, 1951.
Bullough, Vern and Bonnie. *Sin, Sickness, and Sanity: A History of Sexual Attitudes.* New York, 1977.
Burn, W. L. *The Age of Equipoise.* London and New York, 1964.
Butler, Jeffrey. *The Liberal Party and the Jameson Raid.* Oxford, 1968.
Butler, Colonel Lewis. *Sir Redvers Buller.* London, 1909.
Callwell, Charles E. *Field-Marshal Sir Henry Wilson.* 2 vols. London, 1927.
Campion, Lord. *Parliament: A Survey.* London, 1952.
Chalmers, Rear Admiral W. S. *The Life and Letters of David, Earl Beatty.* London, 1951.
Chamberlain, Sir Austen. *Politics from Inside: An Epistolary Chronicle, 1906–1914.* New Haven, 1937.
Chandos, Viscount. *Memoirs.* London, 1962.
Charques, Richard. *The Twilight of Imperial Russia.* London, 1958.
Charteris, Brigadier General John. *At GHQ.* London, 1931.
———. *Field-Marshal Earl Haig.* New York, 1929.
Clark, G. N., ed. *The Oxford History of England.* Oxford, 1936.
Cleugh, J. *Secret Enemy: The History of a Disease.* London, 1954.
Coffey, Thomas M. *Agony at Easter.* New York, 1969.
Cole, Margaret, ed. *Beatrice Webb's Diaries, 1924–1932.* London, 1932.
Collier, Robert Laird. *British Home Life.* Boston, 1886.
Colville, Sir John. *The Churchillians.* London, 1981.
———. *Footprints in Time.* London, 1976.
Cook, Olive. *The English Country House: An Art and a Way of Life.* London, 1974.
Cooper, Lady Diana. *The Rainbow Comes and Goes.* Boston, 1958.
Cornwallis-West, George. *Edwardian Hey-Days.* New York: 1930.
Cowles, Virginia. *Edward VII and His Circle.* London, 1956.
Cowling, Maurice. *The Impact of Labour, 1920–1924.* Cambridge, 1971.
Cross, Colin. *The Fall of the British Empire.* New York and London, 1968.
Cruttwell, C.R.M.F. *History of the Great War.* Oxford, 1934.
D'Abernon, Viscount. *An Ambassador of Peace.* 3 vols. London, 1929–1930.
Dardanelles Commission. *Final Report.* London, 1919.
———. *First Report.* London, 1917.

Davis, Richard Harding. *Our English Cousins.* New York, 1894.
———. *Real Soldiers of Fortune.* New York, 1906.
Dawson, Robert M. *The Development of Dominion Status, 1906–1936.* London, 1937.
Day, Price. *Experiment in Freedom.* Baltimore, 1948.
De Gaulle, Charles. *Lettres, Notes et Carnets, 1919–Juin 1940.* Paris, 1980.
Dennie, C. C. *A History of Syphilis.* Springfield, Ill., 1962.
Deutscher, Isaac. *The Prophet Armed: Trotsky, 1879–1921.* London, 1954.
Dickinson, F. A. *Lake Victoria to Khartoum.* London, 1910.
Dilke, Charles. *Greater Britain.* London, 1968.
Divine, A. D. *D.S.M. Dunkirk.* New York, 1948.
Drake, Emma. *What a Young Wife Ought to Know.* Philadelphia, 1901.
Driberg, Tom. *Beaverbrook: A Study in Power and Frustration.* London, 1956.
Duff-Cooper, Alfred. *Haig.* New York, 1936.
Dugdale, B. E. C. *Arthur James Balfour, KG, OM, FRS.* 2 vols. London, 1930.
Edel, Leon. *Bloomsbury: A House of Lions.* New York, 1979.
Edmonds, J. E. *British Official History of the War.* London, 1948.
Edwards, Michael. *British India, 1772–1947.* London, 1967.
———. *High Noon of Empire.* London, 1965.
Eireann, Dáil. *Official Report: Debate on the Treaty between Great Britain and Ireland, December 1921–January 1922.* Dublin, n.d.
Elibank, Viscount. *A Man's Life.* London, 1934.
Ensor, R. C. K. *England, 1870–1914.* London, 1936.
Escott, Thomas H. S. *Great Victorians.* London, 1916.
———. *Social Transformations in the Victorian Age.* London, 1897.
———. *Society in the Country House.* London, n.d.
Esher, Viscount Reginald. *Journals and Letters.* 4 vols. London, 1934–1938.
Evans, Hilary and Mary. *The Party That Lasted 100 Days: The Late Victorian Season.* London, 1976.
Evans, Dr. Joan. *The Victorians.* Cambridge, 1966.
Falls, Cyril. *The Great War.* New York, 1959.
Farwell, Byron. *Mr. Kipling's Army.* New York, 1981.
———. *Queen Victoria's Little Wars.* New York, 1972.
Feiling, Sir Keith. *The Life of Neville Chamberlain.* London, 1946.
Fisher, Admiral of the Fleet Lord. *Memories.* London, 1919.
Fitzroy, Sir Almeric. *Memoirs.* 2 vols. London, 1926.
Florinsky, Michael F. *The End of the Russian Empire.* New Haven, 1931.
Fortesque, Granville. *Russia, the Balkans and the Dardanelles.* Melrose, 1915.
Fraser, P. *Joseph Chamberlain.* London, 1966.
Frost, David, and Antony Jay. *The English.* New York, 1969.
Fussell, Paul. *The Great War and Modern Memory.* New York and London, 1975.
Gandhi, M. K. *Gandhi's Autobiography.* Washington, 1954.
Gardiner, A. G. *Certain People of Importance.* London, 1926.
———. *Prophets, Priests and Kings.* London, 1908.
Garnett, David, ed. *Letters of T. E. Lawrence.* New York, 1939.
Gathorne-Hardy, Jonathan. *The Rise and Fall of the British Nanny.* London, 1972.
General Sir Ian Hamilton's Dispatches. May 20, August 26, December 11, 1915. London, 1915.
Gilbert, B. B. *The Evolution of National Insurance in Great Britain.* London, 1966.
Gilbert, Martin. *Churchill and Zionism.* London, 1974.
Girouard, Mark. *The Return to Camelot: Chivalry and the English Gentleman.* New Haven, 1981.
Goertzel, Victor, and Mildred George Goertzel. *Cradles of Eminence.* Boston, 1962.
Graubard, S. R. *British Labour and the Russian Revolution.* Boston, 1956.
Green, Martin. *Children of the Sun: A Narrative of "Decadence" in England after 1918.* New York, 1927.
Grenville, J. A. S. *Lord Salisbury and Foreign Policy: The Close of the Nineteenth Century.* Oxford, 1964.
Grey of Fallodon, Viscount. *Twenty-Five Years, 1892–1916.* London, 1925.
Grierson, J. M. *The British Army.* London, 1899.
Grigg, P. J. *Prejudice and Judgment.* London, 1948.

Haig, Douglas. *Private Papers of Douglas Haig, 1914–1919.* Edited by Robert Blake. London, 1952.
Haldane, Sir James Aylmer L. *How We Escaped from Pretoria.* London, 1901.
———. *A Soldier's Saga.* Edinburgh, 1948.
Haldane, Viscount Richard B. *An Autobiography.* New York, 1929.
———. *Before the War.* New York, 1920.
Halifax, The Earl of. *Fullness of Days.* London, 1957.
Hamer, W. S. *The British Army: Civil-Military Relations, 1885–1905.* Oxford, 1970.
Hamilton, General Sir Ian. *Gallipoli Diary.* 2 vols. London, 1920.
———. *Listening for the Drums.* London, 1944.
Hamilton, W. G. *Parliamentary Reminiscences and Reflections, 1868–1885.* London, 1917.
A Handbook for Travellers in India and Pakistan, Burma and Ceylon: Including the Portuguese and French Possessions and the Indian States, 16th ed. London, 1949.
Hankey, Lord. *The Supreme Command, 1914–1918.* London, 1961.
———. *The Supreme Control at the Paris Peace Conference, 1919.* London, 1963.
Harriman, W. Averell, and Elie Abel. *Special Envoy to Churchill and Stalin, 1941–1946.* New York, 1975.
Harris, Frank. *My Life and Loves.* New York, 1963.
Hassall, Christopher. *Edward Marsh: Marsh's Letters Quoted.* London, 1959.
Healy, T. M. *Letters and Leaders of My Day.* New York, 1929.
Herbertson, A. J., and O. J. R. Howarth, eds. *The Oxford Survey of the British Empire.* Oxford, 1914.
Higgins, Trumbull. *Winston Churchill and the Dardanelles.* New York, 1963.
Hitler, Adolf. *Mein Kampf.* Munich, 1932.
Hobson, J. A. *Imperialism: A Study.* London, 1902.
———. *Problems of Poverty.* London, 1891.
Houghton, Walter. *The Victorian Frame of Mind, 1830–1870.* London, 1957.
Howard, Michael. *The Franco-Prussian War.* London, 1961.
Hübner, Baron von. *Through the British Empire.* London, 1886.
Hunt, Sir David. *On the Spot: An Ambassador Remembers.* London, 1975.
Hurst, M. *Joseph Chamberlain and Liberal Reunion: The Round Table Conference of 1887.* London, 1967.
Hyde, M. M. *Carson.* London, 1953.
India Defence League. *Prominent Supporters of the I.D.L.,* 3rd ed. London, 1934.
Jackson, Holdbrook. *The Eighteen Nineties.* London, 1939.
James, Henry. *English Hours.* New York, 1960.
Jenkins, Roy. *Asquith.* London, 1964.
———. *Mr Balfour's Poodle.* London, 1954.
Jog, Narayan Gopal. *Churchill's Blind Spot: India.* Bombay, 1944.
Jones, Ralph E. *Fighting Tanks since 1916.* Harrisburg, Pa., 1933.
Jones, Thomas. *A Diary with Letters.* Oxford, 1954.
———. *Lloyd George.* Cambridge, Mass., 1951.
———. *Whitehall Diary.* 3 vols. Edited by K. Middlemas. London and New York, 1969–1971.
Kee, Robert. *Ireland: A History.* Boston, 1982.
Kennedy, A. L. *Salisbury.* London, 1953.
Kerr, M. *Prince Louis of Battenberg.* London, 1934.
Keyes, Admiral Sir Roger. *Naval Memoirs.* London, 1934.
Keynes, J. M. *Economic Consequences of Mr Churchill.* London, 1925.
Kincaid, Dennis. *British Social Life in India.* London, 1938.
Knightley, Philip, and Colin Simpson. *The Secret Lives of Lawrence of Arabia.* London, 1969.
Kohn, Hans. *The Mind of Germany.* New York, 1960.
Kruger, Rayne. *Goodbye Dolly Gray.* London, 1949.
Laver, James. *Victorian Vista.* London, 1954.
Lavery, J. *The Life of a Painter.* London, 1940.
Lawrence, A. W., ed. *T. E. Lawrence by His Friends.* London, 1937.
Lawrence, T. E. *Seven Pillars of Wisdom.* London, 1973.
Lee, Sir Sidney. *King Edward VII,* Vol II. New York and London, 1925.

Lehmann, Joseph H. *All Sir Garnet.* London, 1964.
Leslie, Anita. *Edwardians in Love.* London, 1972.
Leslie, Sir Shane. *Men Are Different.* London, 1937.
The Letters of Queen Victoria. London, 1926.
Liddell Hart, Sir Basil H. *A History of the First World War.* Boston, 1964.
———. *Memoirs.* 2 vols. London, 1965, 1966.
———. *Reputations Ten Years After.* Boston, 1928.
———. *Through the Fog of War.* New York, 1938.
———. *The War in Outline.* New York, 1936.
Limon von Sanders, Otto. *Five Years in Turkey.* Annapolis, Md., 1927.
Lloyd, T. E. *Empire to Welfare State.* New York, 1970.
Lloyd George, David. *The Truth about the Peace Treaties.* London, 1938.
———. *War Memoirs.* Boston, 1934.
Longford, Elizabeth. *Queen Victoria: Born to Succeed.* New York, 1965.
———. *The Suffragette Movement.* London, 1931.
———. *Wellington: The Years of the Sword.* New York, 1969.
Lucy, H. W. *The Balfourian Parliament, 1900–1905.* London, 1906.
———. *Memories of Eight Parliaments.* London, 1908.
Ludwig, Emil. *The Nile: The Life-Story of a River.* New York, 1937.
Lunt, W. E. *History of England.* New York, 1928.
Macardle, Dorothy. *The Irish Republic.* Dublin, 1953.
Macaulay, T. B. *Critical and Historical Essays.* London, 1907.
McElwee, William. *Britain's Locust Years, 1918–1940.* London, 1962.
McGurrin, James, and Bourke Cockran. *A Free Lance in American Politics.* New York, 1948.
Mackay, Ruddock R. *Fisher of Kilverstone.* Oxford, 1973.
McKee, Alexander. *Vimy Ridge.* London, 1966.
Mackenzie, Sir Compton. *Gallipoli Memories.* London and Toronto, 1929.
McKenzie, R. T., and Allan Silver. *Angels in Marble: Working-Class Conservatives in Urban England.* London, 1968.
Macleod, Iain. *Neville Chamberlain.* London, 1961.
Macmillan, Harold. *Winds of Change.* London, 1966.
Macready, General Sir Nevil. *Annals of an Active Life.* New York, 1925.
MacVeagh, Jeremiah. *Home Rule in a Nutshell: A Pocket Book for Speakers and Electors,* 4th ed. With an introduction by Right Hon. Winston S. Churchill, MP. London, 1912.
Manchester, William. *The Arms of Krupp, 1587–1968.* Boston, 1968.
Mansfield, Peter. *The British in Egypt.* New York, 1972.
Marder, Arthur J., ed. *Fear God and Dread Nought.* 3 vols. London, 1952–1959.
Margetson, Stella. *Victorian High Society.* London, 1980.
Marlowe, John. *Milner.* London, 1976.
Marsh, Sir Edward Howard. *A Number of People: A Book of Reminiscences.* New York and London, 1939.
Massingham, H. J., and Hugh Massingham. *The Great Victorians.* New York, 1932.
Maurice, Sir F. *Haldane, 1856–1915.* 2 vols. London, 1937.
Mayo, Katherine. *Mother India.* London, 1930.
Meijer, Jan M., ed. *The Trotsky Papers, 1917–1922.* 2 vols. The Hague, 1964, 1971.
Meinertzhagen, Colonel Richard. *Middle East Diary, 1917–1956.* New York, 1959.
Melchett, A. M. M., First Baron. *The Jewish National Home and Its Critics: The Oxford Speeches, by Sir Alfred Mond and Dr. Chaim Weizmann.* London, 1922.
Middlemas, Robert Keith, and J. Barnes. *Stanley Baldwin.* London, 1969.
Milne, Admiral Sir Archibald Berkeley. *The Flight of the Goeben and the Breslau.* London, 1921.
Milner, Alfred, Viscount. *The Nation and the Empire.* London, 1913.
Moggridge, D. E. *The Return to Gold, 1925.* Cambridge, Mass., 1971.
Monroe, Elizabeth. *Britain's Moment in the Middle East.* Baltimore, 1963.
Moorehead, Alan. *Gallipoli.* New York, 1956.
———. *The Russian Revolution.* New York, 1958.
———. *The White Nile.* New York, 1960.
Morgenthau, Henry. *Secrets of the Bosphorus.* London, 1918.
Morley, Lord. *Memorandum on Resignation, August, 1914.* London, 1928.

Morris, James. *Farewell the Trumpets: An Imperial Retreat.* New York, 1978.
———. *Pax Britannica: The Climax of an Empire.* New York, 1968.
Nevill, Lady Dorothy. *Leaves from the Notebooks of Lady Dorothy Nevill.* Edited by Ralph Nevill. London, 1907.
Nevinson, Henry W. *The Dardanelles Campaign.* New York, 1918.
Nicolson, Harold. *Curzon: The Last Phase.* London, 1934.
———. *Some People.* Boston, 1926.
Nicolson, Nigel, ed. *Harold Nicolson: Diaries and Letters, 1930–1939.* London, 1966.
Norton, Graham. *Victorian London.* London, n.d.
O'Connor, Frank. *Death in Dublin: Michael Collins and the Irish Revolution.* Garden City, N.Y., 1937.
O'Hegarty, P. S. *The Victory of Sinn Fein.* Dublin, 1924.
Osborn, E. B., ed. *The Muse in Arms.* London, 1917.
Owen, Frank. *Tempestuous Journey: Lloyd George, His Life and Times.* London, 1954.
Pakenham, Thomas. *The Boer War.* New York, 1979.
Pankhurst, Sylvia. *The Home Front.* London, 1933.
Payne, Robert. *Life and Death of Adolf Hitler.* New York, 1973.
Pease, A. *Elections and Recollections.* London, 1932.
Peel, Mrs. C. S. *How We Lived Then: 1914–1918.* London, 1929.
Perry, George, and Nicholas Mason, eds. *The Victorians: A World Built to Last.* New York, 1974.
Peruginia, Mark Edward. *Victorian Days and Ways.* London, 1936.
Petrie, Sir Charles. *Life and Letters of the Right Honourable Sir Austen Chamberlain, 1939–1940.* 2 vols. London, 1940.
———. *The Victorians.* London, 1960.
Phillips, Janet and Peter. *Victorians at Home and Away.* London, 1978.
Ponsonby, Sir Frederick. *Recollections of Three Reigns.* London, 1951.
Pound, R. *The Strand Magazine, 1891–1950.* London, 1966.
Priestley, J. B. *The Edwardians.* New York, 1970.
Quennell, Peter. *Victorian Panorama.* London, 1937.
Rabinowicz, Oskar K. *Winston Churchill on Jewish Problems: A Half-Century Survey.* London, 1950.
Raymond, E. T. *Mr Lloyd George: A Biography.* London, 1922.
———. *Uncensored Celebrities.* London, 1918.
Reader, W. J. *Life in Victorian England.* New York, 1964.
Recollections of Dublin Castle and of Dublin Society by a Native. London, 1902.
Redesdale, Lord. *Memories.* London, 1915.
Redmayne, R. A. S. *Men, Mines and Memories.* London, 1942.
Reith, J. C. W. *Into the Wind.* London, 1949.
Repington, Lieutenant Colonel Charles à Court. *A Diary.* Boston and New York, 1922.
———. *The First World War, 1914–1918,* Vol. I. London, 1920.
Rhodes James, Robert. *Memoirs.* New York, 1970.
Richards, J. Brinsley. *Seven Years at Eton.* London, 1883.
Riddell, Lord. *Intimate Diary of the Peace Conference and After.* London, 1933.
———. *More Pages from My Diary, 1908–1914.* London, 1934.
———. *War Diary, 1914–1918.* London, 1933.
Robb, Janet Henderson. *The Primrose League, 1883–1906.* New York, 1942.
Roberts, Cecil. *The Bright Twenties. London,* 1970.
Robinson, Ronald, and John Gallagher, with Alice Denny. *Africa and the Victorians.* London, 1965.
Roskill, S. W. *Hankey.* 3 vols. London, 1973.
———. *Naval Policy between the Wars, 1919–1929,* Vol. I. London, 1968.
Rowse, A. L. *The English Spirit.* London, 1944.
Rumblelow, Donald. *The Siege of Sidney Street.* New York, 1973.
Ryan, A. P. *Mutiny at the Curragh.* London, 1956.
Sackville-West, V. *The Edwardians.* New York, 1930.
Samuel, Lord. *Memoirs.* London, 1948.
Sassoon, Siegfried. *Memoirs of an Infantry Officer.* New York, 1930.
———. *The Poems of Siegfried Sassoon.* London, 1938.

———. *Siegfried's Journey, 1916–1920.* New York, 1946.
Seal, A. *The Emergence of Indian Nationalism: Competition and Collaboration in the Later Nineteenth Century.* Cambridge, 1971.
Searight, Sarah. *The British in the Middle East.* New York, 1970.
Seeley, J. R. *The Expansion of England.* London, 1883.
Seely, Major General the Right Honourable J. E. B. *Adventure.* London, 1930.
Sheridan, Clare. *Nuda Veritas.* New York, 1928.
Shirer, William. *The Rise and Fall of the Third Reich.* New York, 1960.
Slatin, R. C. *Fire and Sword in the Sudan.* London and New York, 1896.
"S.L.S." [John St. Loe Strachey]. *The Great Bread Riots, Or What Became of Fair Trade.* London, 1883.
Smalley, George. *Anglo-American Memories.* New York and London, 1911.
Smith, John M., and Tim Cawkwell. *World Encyclopedia of Film.* New York, 1972.
Somervell, D. C. *British Politics since 1900.* London, 1933.
Spears, Brigadier General Edward L. *Liaison, 1914: A Narrative of the Great Retreat.* New York, 1931.
———. *Prelude to Victory.* London, 1939.
Spender, J. A. *The Life of the Right Honourable Sir Henry Campbell-Bannerman.* 2 vols. London, 1923.
Spiers, Edward M. *The Army and Society, 1815–1914.* London, 1980.
———. *Haldane: An Army Reformer.* Edinburgh, 1980.
The Spion Kop Despatches. London, 1902.
Steevens, G. W. *Egypt in 1898.* Edinburgh, 1898.
———. *From Cape Town to Ladysmith.* Edinburgh and New York, 1900.
———. *In India.* Edinburgh, 1899.
———. *With Kitchener to Khartoum.* New York, 1898.
Stern, A. *Tanks, 1914–1918.* London, 1919.
Stevenson, Frances. *Lloyd George: A Diary by Frances Stevenson.* Edited by A. J. P. Taylor. New York, 1971.
Strike Nights in Printing House Square. London, 1926.
Sueter, M. *Evolution of the Tank.* London, 1937.
Swanberg, W. A. *Citizen Hearst.* New York, 1963.
Sydenham of Combe et al. *The World Crisis: A Criticism.* London, 1977.
Taylor, A. J. P. *A History of the First World War.* New York, 1966.
Taylor, A. J. P., ed. *Lloyd George: A Diary by Frances Stevenson.* London, 1971.
———. *My Darling Pussy: The Letters of Lloyd George and Frances Stevenson.* London, 1975.
Taylor, Edmund. *The Fall of the Dynasties.* New York, 1963.
Taylor, Rex. *Michael Collins.* London, 1958.
Taylor, Telford. *Munich: The Price of Peace.* New York, 1979.
Thompson, Laurence. *1940.* New York, 1966.
Thompson, Paul. *The Edwardians: The Remaking of British Society.* Bloomington and London, 1975.
Thornton, A. P. *The Imperial Idea and Its Enemies.* London, 1959.
Tillett, Ben. *History of the London Transport Workers' Strike, 1911.* Published from the offices of the National Transport Workers' Federation, West India Dock Road. London, 1911.
Toland, John. *No Man's Land: 1918, the Last Year of the Great War.* Garden City, N.Y., 1980.
Trevelyan, George Macaulay. *British History in the Nineteenth Century and After (1782–1919).* London, 1937.
———. *History of England.* New York, 1926.
Trotsky, Leon. *The Russian Revolution.* New York, 1936.
Tuchman, Barbara W. *The Guns of August.* New York, 1962.
———. *The Proud Tower: A Portrait of the World before the War, 1890–1914.* New York, 1966.
Ullman, R. H. *Britain and the Russian Civil War.* Princeton, 1968.
———. *Intervention and the War: Anglo-Soviet Relations, 1917–1921.* Princeton, 1961.
Walder, David. *The Chanak Affair.* London, 1969.
Warwick, Frances, Countess of. *Discretions.* New York, 1931.
Webb, Beatrice. *Diaries, 1924–1932.* London, 1956.
———. *Our Partnership.* London, 1948.
Wemyss, V. M. A. Wester. *Life and Letters of Lord Wester Wemyss.* London, 1935.

Williams-Ellis, Clough. *The Tank Corps.* New York, 1919.
Wilson, T. *Downfall of the Liberal Party.* London, 1966.
Wilson, T., ed. *Political Diaries of C. P. Scott, 1911–1918.* London, 1970.
Winterton, Earl. *Orders of the Day.* London, 1953.
Wolff, Leon. *In Flanders Fields: The 1917 Campaign.* New York, 1958.
Woodcock, George. *Who Killed the British Empire?* London, 1974.
Woodham-Smith, Cecil. *The Great Hunger.* New York, 1962.
———. *Queen Victoria: Her Life and Times.* London, 1972.
Woodruff, Philip. *The Men Who Ruled India.* 2 vols. London, 1953, 1954.
Wrench, Evelyn. *Alfred, Lord Milner.* London, 1958.
Wrench, J. E. *Geoffrey Dawson and Our Times.* London, 1955.
Wright, Peter E. *Portraits and Criticisms.* London, 1925.
Young, G. M. *Stanley Baldwin.* London, 1951.
———. *Victorian England: Portrait of an Age.* London, 1936.

2. ARTICLES

"Ambassador Morgenthau's Story." *World's Work,* August 1918.
Asquith, Herbert H. "The Genesis of the War." *Saturday Evening Post,* July 21, 1923.
"A Belfast Riot That Evaporated." *Literary Digest,* February 24, 1912.
Bond, Brian. "Why the Thin Red Line Was So Thin." *Times Literary Supplement,* August 22, 1980.
"Britain's Meteoric and Versatile Chancellor of the Exchequer." *Current Opinion,* February 1925.
British Officer. "A Social Life of the British Army." *Pall Mall Magazine,* January 1901.
"The British Sovereign Back from the War." *Literary Digest,* May 9, 1925.
"British Statesmen Debate the London Treaty." *Congressional Digest,* June 1930.
Gardiner, A. "Who Will Succeed Lloyd George?" *Century,* October 1921.
Girouard, Mark. "When Chivalry Died." *New Republic,* September 30, 1981.
Guedalla, Philip. "Portrait of a Buccaneer." *Harper's,* June 1927.
Kennan, George F. "Toward August 1914." *New Republic,* November 3, 1979.
Konig, Hans. "The Eleventh Edition." *New Yorker,* March 2, 1981.
Laski, Harold. "More Political Portraits." *Living Age,* May 1931.
Liddell Hart, Sir Basil H. "World War," in *Encyclopaedia Britannica,* 14th ed., Vol. XXIII. London, 1929.
Littlefield, Walter. "Great Britain's Literary Government." *Critic,* May 1906.
Manchester, William. "The Great War," in *Controversy and Other Essays in Journalism.* Boston, 1976.
Masterman, Lucy. "Churchill: The Liberal Phase." *History Today,* November and December 1964.
Panter-Downes, Mollie. "Books." *New Yorker,* August 31, 1981.
Rosenstone, Robert A. "The Generation of 1914." *New Republic,* November 3, 1979.
Taylor, A. J. P. "How a World War Began." *Observer,* November 1958.

COPYRIGHT ACKNOWLEDGMENTS

The author is grateful to the following publishers, individuals, and companies for permission to reprint excerpts from selected material as noted below.

Quotations from H. H. Asquith's letters to Venetia Stanley are made by kind permission of the Hon. Mark Bonham Carter and are published in *H. H. Asquith: Letters to Venetia Stanley,* edited by Michael and Eleanor Brock (Oxford University Press, Oxford and New York, 1982).

Lord Beaverbrook from *Politicians and the War: 1914–1916.* Copyright 1928 by Doubleday & Company, Inc; copyright renewed 1956 by Lord Beaverbrook. Reprinted by permission of Methuen.

Wilfrid Scawen Blunt from *My Diaries: Being a Personal Narrative of Events, 1888–1914.* Copyright 1921 by Wilfrid Scawen Blunt. Reprinted by permission of Alfred A. Knopf, Inc., and Martin Secker & Warburg Limited.

Violet Bonham Carter from *Winston Churchill: An Intimate Portrait.* Copyright © 1965 by Violet Bonham Carter. Reprinted by permission of Harcourt Brace Jovanovich, Inc., and Eyre & Spottiswoode (Publishers) Ltd.

Mary Bromage from *Churchill and Ireland.* Copyright © 1964 by the University of Notre Dame Press. Reprinted by permission of University of Notre Dame Press.

"Peace" and "The Soldier" by Rupert Brooke from *The Collected Poems of Rupert Brooke.* Reprinted by permission of Dodd, Mead and Company.

Winston S. Churchill from *Amid These Storms: Thoughts and Adventures.* Copyright 1932 by Charles Scribner's Sons; copyright renewed 1960 Winston S. Churchill. Reprinted by permission of Charles Scribner's Sons and the Hamlyn Publishing Group Limited. Originally published by Odhams Press Ltd.

Winston S. Churchill from *My Early Life: A Roving Commission.* Copyright 1930 by Charles Scribner's Sons; copyright renewed 1958 Winston S. Churchill. Reprinted by permission of Charles Scribner's Sons and the Hamlyn Publishing Group Limited. Originally published by Odhams Press Ltd.

Winston S. Churchill from *The World Crisis,* 1911–1914, and *The World Crisis,* 1915, copyright 1923 by Charles Scribner's Sons, copyright renewed 1951 Winston S. Churchill; from *The World Crisis,* 1916–1918 (2 vols.), copyright 1927 by Charles Scribner's Sons, copyright renewed 1955 Winston S. Churchill; from *The Aftermath,* 1918–1928, copyright 1929 by Charles Scribner's Sons, copyright renewed 1957 Winston S. Churchill. Reprinted by permission of Charles Scribner's Sons and the Hamlyn Publishing Group Limited. Originally published by Odhams Press Ltd.

Winston S. Churchill's dispatches from *Young Winston's Wars: Original Despatches of Winston Churchill, War Correspondent, 1897–1900,* edited by Frederick Woods. Reprinted by permission of Seeley, Service & Cooper.

Winston S. Churchill; Volume I, *Youth, 1874–1900*, by Randolph S. Churchill. Copyright © 1966 by C & T Publications, Ltd. *Companion Volume I, Part 1, 1874–1896.* Copyright © 1967 by C & T Publications, Ltd. *Companion Volume I, Part 2, 1896–1900.* Copyright © 1967 by C & T Publications, Ltd. Reprinted by permission of Houghton Mifflin Company and William Heinemann Ltd.

Winston S. Churchill; Volume II, *Young Statesman, 1901–1914,* by Randolph S. Churchill. Copyright © 1967 by C & T Publications, Ltd. *Companion Volume II, Part 1, 1901–1907.* Copyright © 1969 by C & T Publications, Ltd. *Companion Volume II, Part 2, 1907–1911.* Copyright © 1969 by C & T Publications, Ltd. *Companion Volume II, Part 3, 1911–1914.* Copyright ©

1969 by C & T Publications, Ltd. Reprinted by permission of Houghton Mifflin Company and William Heinemann Ltd.

Winston S. Churchill; Volume III, *The Challenge of War, 1914–1916,* by Martin Gilbert. Copyright © 1971 by C & T Publications, Ltd. *Companion Volume III, Part 1, July 1914–April 1915.* Copyright © 1973 by C & T Publications, Ltd. *Companion Volume III, Part 2, May 1915–December 1916.* Copyright © 1973 by C & T Publications, Ltd. Reprinted by permission of Houghton Mifflin Company and William Heinemann Ltd.

Winston S. Churchill; Volume IV, *The Stricken World, 1916–1922,* by Martin Gilbert. Copyright © 1975 by C & T Publications, Ltd. *Companion Volume IV, Part 1, January 1917–June 1919.* Copyright © 1977 by C & T Publications, Ltd. *Companion Volume IV, Part 2, July 1919–March 1921.* Copyright © 1977 by C & T Publications, Ltd. *Companion Volume IV, Part 3, April 1921–November 1922.* Copyright © 1977 by C & T Publications, Ltd. Reprinted by permission of Houghton Mifflin Company and William Heinemann Ltd.

Winston S. Churchill; Volume V, *The Prophet of Truth, 1922–1939,* by Martin Gilbert. Copyright © 1976 by C & T Publications, Ltd. *Companion Volume V, Part 1, The Exchequer Years, 1922–1929.* Copyright © 1980 by C & T Publications, Ltd. *Companion Volume V, Part 2, The Wilderness Years, 1929–1935.* Copyright © 1981 by C & T Publications, Ltd. Reprinted by permission of Houghton Mifflin Company and William Heinemann Ltd.

Virginia Cowles from *Winston Churchill: The Era and the Man.* Copyright 1953 by Virginia Cowles; copyright renewed © 1981 by Virginia Cowles. Reprinted by permission of Harper & Row, Publishers, Inc.

Charles Eade, editor, from *Churchill by His Contemporaries.* Copyright © 1953 by Hutchinson & Co. Publisher, Ltd; copyright renewed © 1982 by Christine Eade. Reprinted by permission of Simon & Schuster.

Kay Halle from *The Irrepressible Churchill.* Copyright © 1966 by Kay Halle. Reprinted by permission of the author.

Lord Hankey from his book *The Supreme Command.* Reprinted by permission of David Higham Associates Limited and George Allen & Unwin (Publishers) Ltd.

Frank Harris from *My Life and Loves.* Copyright 1925 by Frank Harris; copyright renewed © 1963 by Nellie Harris. Copyright © 1963 by Arthur Leonard Ross, Executor of the Estate of Frank Harris. Reprinted by permission of Grove Press, and Ralph Ross and Edgar M. Ross.

Edward Marsh from *A Number of People.* Copyright 1939 by Edward Marsh. Reprinted by permission of Harper & Row, Publishers, Inc., and Hamish Hamilton Ltd.

Lord Moran from *Churchill: Taken from the Diaries of Lord Moran.* Copyright © 1966 by The Trustees of Lord Moran. Reprinted by permission of Houghton Mifflin Company and William Heinemann Ltd.

James Morris from *Farewell the Trumpets.* Reprinted by permission of Harcourt Brace Jovanovich, Inc., and Faber & Faber, Ltd. Copyright © 1978 by Jan Morris.

Robert Rhodes James from *Churchill: A Study in Failure.* Copyright © 1970 by Robert Rhodes James. Reprinted with the permission of George Weidenfeld & Nicolson, Ltd.

Material from the Royal Archives reproduced with the permission of the Controller of Her Majesty's Stationery Office.

Mary Soames from *Clementine Churchill: The Biography of a Marriage.* Copyright © 1979 by Thompson Newspapers Limited. Reprinted by permission of Houghton Mifflin Company, Curtis Brown (London) Ltd., and General Publishing Co. Limited.

Frances Stevenson from *Lloyd George: A Diary by Frances Stevenson,* edited by A. J. P. Taylor. Copyright © 1971 by The First Beaverbrook Foundation. Reprinted by permission of Harold Ober Associates Incorporated and David Higham Associates Limited.

Quotations from Henry Wilson's diaries at the Imperial War Museum appear through the courtesy of the Trustees of the Imperial War Museum and Major C. J. Wilson.

Lyrics to "Bubbles" by Jean Kenbrovin reprinted by permission of Warner Bros. Inc. Copyright 1919 (renewed) Warner Bros. Inc. All rights reserved.

Lyrics to "Danny Boy" by F. E. Weatherly, which appear in a slightly altered form on page 734, copyright 1913 by Boosey & Co., Ltd; renewed copyright 1941.

Photographs on the pages indicated were supplied or reproduced by kind permission of the following:

Associated Newspapers Limited, page 732
BBC Hulton Picture Library, pages 96, 109, 159, 264, 337, 365, 425, 429, 491, 722, 723, 857
The Bettmann Archive, Inc., page 97
Brown Brothers, pages 272, 442
C & T Publications, page 305
The Trustees of the Churchill Archives Settlement; The Master and Fellows of Churchill College; The National Trust, Chartwell, pages 98, 103, 121, 122, 311, 881
The Trustees of the Churchill Archives Settlement; The Master and Fellows of Churchill College; Mr. Winston Churchill, MP, pages 100, 118, 206, 217, 224, 253, 287, 290, 302, 313, 482, 578, 702, 762, 765, 780
Culver Pictures, page 446
European Picture Services, page 405
Philippe Halsman, page 783
Imperial War Museum, pages x, 545, 622, 869
Keystone Press Agency, pages 106, 754, 777
The National Trust Photographic Library, London, pages 772, 773
The Press Association Limited, pages 413, 477, 610, 653, 816
The Mary Soames Collection, page 396
Sport & General Press Agency, page 764
Time Inc. Picture Collection, pages 345, 405, 439
United Press International Photo, pages 1, 9, 117, 354, 355, 511, 757, 827

INDEX

CHRONOLOGY

1874	WSC born November 30 at Blenheim
1886	His father becomes chancellor of the Exchequer
	His mother is now a great Victorian courtesan
1888	WSC enters Harrow; gets lowest marks in school
1893	Admitted to Sandhurst on third try
1894	Commissioned cavalry subaltern, Fourth Hussars
1895	His father dies
	WSC covers the guerrilla warfare in Cuba
1896	Educates himself in India; discovers Macaulay and Gibbon
	Writes first book
1897	Sees heavy fighting in Khyber Pass
1898	Omdurman: WSC in the last cavalry charge
1899	WSC runs for Parliament; loses
	Captured in the Boer War
	His sensational escape
1900	Recommended for VC
	Elected to Parliament
	Tours United States, Canada
1901	Queen Victoria dies
	WSC's maiden speech
1904	Quits Tories for Liberals
1905	Becomes colonial under secretary
1907	Tours East Africa
1908	Promoted to cabinet
	Marries Clementine Hozier
	His alliance with Lloyd George
	They declare war on House of Lords
1910	WSC becomes home secretary
	His welfare-state programs
1911	Battle of Sidney Street
	WSC becomes first lord of the Admiralty
	Father of the tank
1912–14	Irish Home Rule crisis